May 19–22, 2012
New York, New York, USA

Association for
Computing Machinery

Advancing Computing as a Science & Profession

STOC'12

Proceedings of the 2012 ACM
Symposium on Theory of Computing

Sponsored by:

ACM SIGACT

Supported by:

Microsoft, Google, IBM, & NEC

Volume 1

Association for
Computing Machinery

Advancing Computing as a Science & Profession

The Association for Computing Machinery
2 Penn Plaza, Suite 701
New York, New York 10121-0701

Notice to Past Authors of ACM-Published Articles
ACM intends to create a complete electronic archive of all articles and/or other material previously published by ACM. If you have written a work that has been previously published by ACM in any journal or conference proceedings prior to 1978, or any SIG Newsletter at any time, and you do NOT want this work to appear in the ACM Digital Library, please inform permissions@acm.org, stating the title of the work, the author(s), and where and when published.

ISBN: 978-1-4503-1658-3 (Digital)

ISBN: 978-1-4503-1942-3 (Print Vol. 1)

Additional copies may be ordered prepaid from:

ACM Order Department
PO Box 30777
New York, NY 10087-0777, USA

Phone: 1-800-342-6626 (USA and Canada)
+1-212-626-0500 (Global)
Fax: +1-212-944-1318
E-mail: acmhelp@acm.org
Hours of Operation: 8:30 am – 4:30 pm ET

Printed in the USA

Foreword

The papers in this volume were presented at the 44th Annual ACM Symposium on Theory of Computing (STOC 2012), held in New York, NY, May 20–22, 2012. The Symposium was sponsored by the ACM Special Interest Group on Algorithms and Computation Theory (SIGACT).

The program committee met on January 27-28, 2012 in Toronto, Ontario, Canada, and selected 90 papers from 303 detailed abstracts submitted. One pair of papers was merged into a single talk, and one paper was withdrawn, resulting in a total of 88 talks presented at the conference, and 89 papers in this proceedings. The submissions were not formally refereed, and many of them represent reports of continuing research. It is expected that most of them will appear in a more polished and complete form in scientific journals.

In addition to the regular program, there were several other avenues for research presentations. The program committee invited Michael Kearns to present a tutorial in the morning of May 19, 2012, before the main conference, on the topic of Algorithmic Trading and Computational Finance. In the afternoon of May 19, 2012, STOC hosted four workshops, in the areas of: Computational Sustainability, Algorithms for Distributed and Streaming Data, Algorithms for Memory-Sensitive Computing, and the Unique Games Conjecture and Related Advances. Lastly, many additional papers were presented during a poster session held on the evening of May 20, 2012.

From the many outstanding candidates, the STOC program committee selected the following two papers as recipients of the Best Paper Award: "Linear vs. Semidefinite Extended Formulations: Exponential Separation and Strong Lower Bounds" by Samuel Fiorini, Serge Massar, Sebastian Pokutta, Hans Raj and Ronald de Wolf, and "The Cell Probe Complexity of Dynamic Range Counting," by Kasper Green Larsen. The latter of these two papers is also the recipient of the Danny Lewin Best Student Paper Award.

I would like to thank first and foremost the program committee for their excellent reviews, wisdom, and extremely hard work and dedication. I would also like to thank the external reviewers who provided expert opinions and assessments on many of the papers. Their names are listed separately; I regret if, despite our best efforts, a few names are omitted from this list.

I would like to gratefully acknowledge the International Association of Cryptologic Researchers (IACR) for hosting the submission server. I am especially grateful to Shai Halevi for his excellent software that handled the electronic submission and review process, for his patience and time answering my endless emails, and for making the process run smoothly. I would also like to thank the Local Arrangements Chair, Yevgeniy Dodis; the General Chair, Howard Karloff; and SIGACT Chair, Lance Fortnow, for providing useful advice and for dealing with the logistics of the conference. I gratefully acknowledge Lynda Barnes, Joseph Raghubar, Wah-Ming Wong, and especially Wu Yu for help with the program committee meeting in Toronto.

I am indebted to Paul Beame, Salil Vadhan, Avi Wigderson, and Richard Zemel for providing essential advice on many occasions. Lastly, I would like to thank the authors of all submitted papers for their contribution in keeping STOC an excellent conference.

Toniann Pitassi
University of Toronto
STOC 2012 Program Chair

Table of Contents

Session 8A

Session 8B

Session 9A

Session 9B

Session 10

Session 11A

Session 11B

Session 12A

Session 12B

Session 13A

Session 13B

STOC 2012 Conference Organization

SIGACT Chair: Lance Fortnow *(Northwestern University)*

General Chair: Howard Karloff *(AT&T Labs–Research)*

Local Arrangements Chair: Yevgeniy Dodis *(New York University)*

Program Chair: Toniann Pitassi *(University of Toronto)*

Program Committee:
Richard Cleve *(University of Waterloo)*
Parikshit Gopalan *(Microsoft Research SVC)*
Jason Hartline *(Northwestern University)*
Tom Hayes *(University of New Mexico)*
Anna Karlin *(University of Washington)*
Sanjeev Khanna *(University of Pennsylvania)*
Andrew McGregor *(University of Massachusetts)*
Rina Panigrahy *(Microsoft Research SVC)*
Toniann Pitassi *(University of Toronto,* ***chair****)*
Ran Raz *(Weizmann Institute)*
Charles Rackoff *(University of Toronto)*
Satish Rao *(University of California, Berkeley)*
Oded Regev *(Tel-Aviv University and ENS Paris)*
Dana Ron *(Tel-Aviv University)*
Guy Rothblum *(Princeton and Microsoft Research SVC)*
Amin Saberi *(Stanford University)*
Rahul Santhanam *(University of Edinburgh)*
Shubhangi Saraf *(Institute for Advanced Study)*
Daniel Spielman *(Yale University)*
Madhur Tulsiani *(Toyota Technological Institute, Chicago)*
Suresh Venkatasubramanian *(University of Utah)*
Avi Wigderson *(Institute for Advanced Study)*
David Williamson *(Cornell University)*

SIGACT Extended Executive Committee:
Lance Fortnow, chair *(Northwestern University)*
Michael Mitzenmacher, vice-chair *(Harvard University)*
Anna Lysyanskaya, secretary-treasurer *(Brown University)*
Cynthia Dwork, member-at-large *(Microsoft Research)*
Mike Saks, member-at-large *(Rutgers University)*
Amit Chakrabarti, publicity chair *(Dartmouth College)*
Wolfgang Bein, TheoryNet moderator *(University of Nevada, Las Vegas)*
David Shmoys, awards coordinator *(Cornell University)*
Brendan Mumey, editor *(Montana State University)*
Richard Ladner, past chair *(University of Washington)*
Burkhard Monien, EATCS president liaison *(Universität Paderborn)*
Paul Beame, TCMFCS Chair *(University of Washington)*

Sponsor: SIGACT

STOC '12 Additional Reviewers

Scott Aaronson
Amirali Abdullah
Ittai Abraham
Dimitris Achlioptas
Gagan Aggarwal
Saeed Alaei
Noga Alon
Andris Ambainis
Matthew Anderson
Alex Andoni
Matthew Andrews
Elliot Anshelevich
Benny Applebaum
Per Austrin
Yossi Azar
Moshe Babaioff
Boaz Barak
Leonid Barenboim
Mohammad Hossein Bateni
Tugkan Batu
Paul Beame
Michael Bender
Michael Ben-Or
Eli Ben-Sasson
Anand Bhalgat
Arnab Bhattacharyya
Kshipra Bhawalkar
Andrej Bogdanov
Benedikt Bollig
Allan Borodin
Glencora Borradaile
Niv Buchbinder
Andrei Bulatov
Harry Buhrman
Sam Buss
Ran Canetti
Amit Chakrabarti
Deepranab Chakrabarty
Sourav Chakraborty
Erin Wolf Chambers
Siu On Chan
Steven Chaplick
Arkadev Chattopadhyay
Shuchi Chawla
Chandra Chekuri
Ho-Lin Chen
Ning Chen
Xi Chen
Steve Chien
Eden Chlamtac
Julia Chuzhoy
Josef Cibulka
Andrea Clementi
Paolo Codenotti
Gil Cohen
Amin Coja-Oghlan
Seshadhri Comandur
Steve Cook
Derek G. Corneil
Michael Crouch
Pranav Dandekar
Varsha Dani
Sanjoy Dasgupta
Sandy Davie
Anindya De
Eric Demaine
Amit Deshpande
Nikhil Devanur
Tamal Dey
Ilias Diakonikolas
Shahar Dobzinski
Dave Doty
Andrew Drucker
Shaddin Dughmi
Zeev Dvir
Zdenek Dvorak
Cynthia Dwork
Martin Dyer
Michelle Effros
Klim Efremenko
Michael Elkin
Edith Elkind
Faith Ellen
Amr Elmasry
Matthias Englert
David Eppstein
Jeff Erickson
Kousha Etessami
Amos Fiat
Lisa Fleischer
Michael Forbes
Lance Fortnow
Pierre Fraigniaud
Dmitry Gavinsky
Craig Gentry
Wesley George
Shayan Oveis Gharan
George Giakkoupis
Anna Gilbert
Seth Gilbert
Ashish Goel
Gagan Goel
Leslie Ann Goldberg
Oded Goldreich
Vipul Goyal
Nick Gravin
Martin Grohe
Jonathan Gross
Sudipto Guha
Anupam Gupta
Venkatesan Guruswami
Iftach Haitner
Mohammad Taghi Hajiaghayi
Shai Halevi
Sean Hallgren
Moritz Hardt
Sariel Har-Peled
Prahladh Harsha
Nick Harvey
Avinatan Hassidim
Elad Hazan
Martin Hoefer
Pavel Hrubes
Zhiyi Huang
John Iacono
Nicole Immorlica
Piotr Indyk
Sandy Irani
Michael Janes
Maurice Jansen
Mark Jerrum
Hossein Jowhari
Brendan Juba
Ali Juma
Satyen Kale

Sampath Kannan
Michael Kapralov
Jonathan Katz
Tali Kaufman
Neeraj Kayal
Michael Kearns
Jonathan Kelner
Rohit Khandekar
Subhash Khot
Samir Khuller
Robert Kleinberg
Adam Klivans
Robert Koenig
Leszsek Kolodziejczyk
Swastik Kopparty
Paris Koutris
Robert Krauthgamer
Andrei Krokhin
Fabian Kuhn
Amit Kumar
Gabor Kun
Orna Kupferman
Gadi Landau
Michael Langberg
Silvio Lattanzi
James R. Lee
Asaf Levin
Moshe Lewenstein
Katrina Ligget
Huijia (Rachel) Lin
Yehuda Lindell
Daniel Lokshtanov
Shachar Lovett
Aleksander Madry
Mohammad Mahmoody
Michael Mahoney
Konstantin Makarychev
Yuri Makarychev
David Malec
Azarakhsh Malekian
Tal Malkin
Elitza Maneva
Rajsekar Manokaran
Yishay Mansour
Daniel Marx
Kevin Matulef
Pierre McKenzie
Silvio Micali
Vahab Mirrokni
John Moeller
Ankur Moitra
Mike Molloy
Andrea Montanari
Cristopher Moore
Haiko Muller
Assaf Naor
Hariharan Narayanan
Deanna Needell
Jelani Nelson
Thanh Nguyen
Kobbi Nissim
Ryan O'Donnell
Krzysztof Onak
James Orlin
Joel Ouaknine
Ozgur Ozcan
Rasmus Pagh
Martin Pal
Omer Paneth
Debmalya Panigrahi
Rafael Pass
Matthew Patitz
Mihai Patrascu
Boaz Patt-Shamir
Christopher Peikert
David Peleg
Seth Pettie
Jeff Phillips
Reinhard Pichler
Preyas Popat
Ely Porat
Manoj Prabhakaran
Kirk Pruhs
Yuval Rabani
Prasad Raghavendra
Rajmohan Rajaraman
Sofya Raskhodnikova
Renato Renner
Leonid Reyzin
Liam Rodity
Benjamin Rossman
Gunter Rote
Aaron Roth
Thomas Rothvoss
Tim Roughgarden
Atri Rudra
Jared Saia
Michael Saks
Mohammad Reza Salavatipour
Louis Salvail
Saket Saurabh
Michael Schapira
Grant Schoenebeck
Berry Schoenmakers
Gil Segev
Rocco Servedio
C. Seshadri
Dana Shapira
Nir Shavit
Abhi Shelat
Bruce Shepherd
David Shmoys
Igor Shparlinski
Amir Shpilka
Anastasios Sidiropoulos
Hans-Ulrich Simon
Alistair Sinclair
Yaron Singer
Mohit Singh
Ramesh Sitaraman
Sebastian Skritek
Alex Slivkins
Rann Smorodinsky
Christian Sohler
David Soloveichik
Christian Sommer
Alex Sprintson
Srikanth Srinivasan
Nikhil Srivastava
Isabelle Stanton
Aaron Sterling
David Steurer
Leen Stougie
Martin Strauss
Madhu Sudan
Subhash Suri
Mario Szegedy
Kunal Talwar
Cheewei Tan
Tony Tan
Kavitha Telikepalli
Shang-Hua Teng
Pascal Tesson
Prasad Tetali

Justin Thaler
Robin Thomas
Mikkel Thorup
Marc Thurley
Amitabh Trehan
Gilad Tsur
Jonathan Ullman
Chris Umans
Alper Ungor
Alasdair Urquhart
Salil Vadhan
Yevgeniy Vahlis
Vinod Vaikuntanathan
Wim van Dam
Kasturi Varadarajan
Sergei Vassilvitskii
Vijay Vazirani
Laci Vegh
Mikael Vejdemo-Johansson
Santosh Vempala
Muthu Venkitasubramaniam
Adrian Vetta
Aravindan Vijayaraghavan
Emanuele Viola
Rakesh Vohra
Ilya Volkovich
Jan Vondrak
Bei Wang
Hoeteck Wee
Dror Weitz
Tom Wexler
Daniel Wichs
Udi Wieder
Ryan Williams
Andreas Winter
Christian Wulff-Nilsen
David Xiao
Qiqi Yan
Mihalis Yannakakis
Jon Yard
Amir Yehudayoff
Sergey Yekhanin
Neal Young
Lenka Zdeborova
Li Zhang
Aviv Zohar
David Zuckerman

STOC 2012 Corporate Supporters

SIGACT and ACM gratefully acknowledge the financial support of

Microsoft

at the Platinum level;

Google

for helping to cover student participation in the conference;

IBM

at the Friends level; and

NEC

at the Friends level as well.

Faster Approximate Multicommodity Flow Using Quadratically Coupled Flows *

Jonathan A. Kelner †
MIT
kelner@mit.edu

Gary L. Miller
CMU
glmiller@cs.cmu.edu

Richard Peng ‡
CMU §
yangp@cs.cmu.edu

ABSTRACT

The maximum multicommodity flow problem is a natural generalization of the maximum flow problem to route multiple distinct flows. Obtaining a $1-\epsilon$ approximation to the multicommodity flow problem on graphs is a well-studied problem. In this paper we present an adaptation of recent advances in single-commodity flow algorithms to this problem. As the underlying linear systems in the electrical problems of multicommodity flow problems are no longer Laplacians, our approach is tailored to generate specialized systems which can be preconditioned and solved efficiently using Laplacians. Given an undirected graph with m edges and k commodities, we give algorithms that find $1-\epsilon$ approximate solutions to the maximum concurrent flow problem and maximum weighted multicommodity flow problem in time $\tilde{O}(m^{4/3}\mathbf{poly}(k,\epsilon^{-1}))$.

Categories and Subject Descriptors

F.2 [**Theory of Computation**]: Analysis of Algorithms and Problem Complexity

Keywords

Laplacian linear systems, Multicommodity flow problems, Multiplicative weights update method.

1. INTRODUCTION

The multicommodity flow problem is a natural extension of the maximum flow problem. One of its variations, maximum concurrent multicommodity flow, asks to route multiple demands simultaneously in a network subject to capacity constraints. In this setting we're given an undirected, capacitated graph $G=(V,E,\mathbf{u})$ where $\mathbf{u}: E \to \Re^+$, and k source-sink pairs $(s_1,t_1)\dots(s_k,t_k)$. The goal is to find the maximum λ such that there exist k flows $\mathbf{f}_1\dots\mathbf{f}_k$ where $\mathbf{f}_i$ routes λ units of flow between s_i and t_i, and the total flow along each edge obey the following capacity constraint:

$$\sum_i |\mathbf{f}_i(e)| \leq \mathbf{u}(e) \qquad \forall e \in E$$

1.1 Related Work

The simplest version of the problem is with two commodities in an undirected graph. In this case the problem was shown to be reducible to two single commodity maximum flow problems [15]. When there are 3 or more commodities though, this connection no longer holds and all of the (almost) exact algorithms for multicommodity flow problems involve solving a linear programming formulation. For these linear programs, the method with the best asymptotic behavior is the interior point algorithm, which requires solving $O(m^{1/2})$ linear systems. By tracking inverses of these systems and making low rank updates, Vaidya showed an algorithm with running time $\tilde{O}(k^{5/2}m^{3/2}n)$ [19]. This is not very far from the natural barrier of $\tilde{\Omega}(k^{1/2}m^{1/2}n^2)$ for this type of approach, which arises from the need to compute a dense matrix-vector product involving the inverse in each iteration.

Subsequent work on multicommodity flow focused on obtaining $1+\epsilon$ approximate solutions in faster time. This work initially focused on the case of small k, and the algorithms are based on solving multiple minimum cost flow problems [13]. When combined with the minimum cost flow algorithm from [7], these algorithms gave a running time of $\tilde{O}(m^{1.5}\mathbf{poly}(k,\epsilon^{-1}))$.

More recent approaches have favored using a less expensive inner loop to obtain better bounds when k is large. Specifically multiplicative weights update method using single source shortest path routines as oracles [9, 8]. The most recent among these approaches obtained a running time of $\tilde{O}(nm/\epsilon^2)$ using dynamic graph data structures[14]. These methods give better performance the case where k is large. However, when applied to instances with a smaller value of k these approaches encounter similar issues to those encountered by path based single-commodity flow algorithms: the

*Partially supported by the National Science Foundation under grant number CCF-1018463.

†Partially supported by NFS Awards 0843915 and 1111109

‡Supported by a Microsoft Fellowship

§Part of this work was done while at Microsoft Research New England flow decomposition barrier at $\Omega(nm)$. This barrier stems from the fact that if we decompose a flow into a list of paths of paths, the total size of these paths can be $\Omega(nm)$.

An alternate approach to solving linear systems, has led to a possible way to circumvent both the dense inverse and flow decomposition barrier. The graph-like nature of the underlying linear system, graph Laplacians, allows one to find sparse approximations of it, which, when used to precondition iterative solvers, led to speedups in solving such systems [20]. This approach using graph Laplacians has been extended greatly in subsequent works, leading to algorithms with nearly-linear running times [17]. Graph Laplacians are closely connected with problems involving a single flow, such as maximum flow, minimum cost flows and shortest path. To the best of our knowledge this connection was first observed in [7], leading to, among others, a faster algorithm for minimum cost flow. This algorithm is used as a subroutine in the $\tilde{O}(m^{1.5}\mathbf{poly}(k, \epsilon^{-1}))$ algorithm mentioned earlier.

1.2 Our Work

Recently, the running time for approximate maximum flow in undirected graphs has been improved to $\tilde{O}(m^{4/3})$ [5]. A natural question arising from this is whether this algorithm can also be extended to multicommodity flow. Even though in the 2-commodity setting their algorithm can be invoked in a black-box manner [15], a more general examination of this setting is helpful for understanding the main components of our extensions.

In order to further simplify the 2-commodity case, we assume that each edge have unit capacity. That is, we want to find two flows $\mathbf{f}_1$ and $\mathbf{f}_2$ that meet their respective demands, and satisfy the following capacity constraint on each edge e.

$$|\mathbf{f}_1(e)| + |\mathbf{f}_2(e)| \leq 1$$

One way to visualize this constraint is by considering each flow assignment as a coordinate in the 2-D plane. Then a point $(\mathbf{f}_1(e), \mathbf{f}_2(e))$ obeys this constraint if it's inside the unit L_1 ball, as shown in Figure 1. The Christiano et al. algorithm [5] produces a flow that approximately satisfies edge capacities by solving a series of electrical problems. To form such electrical problems, they assign one resistor per edge, leading to a quadratic term of the form $\mathbf{f}(e)^2$. Since $\mathbf{f}(e) \leq 1$ is equivalent to $\mathbf{f}(e)^2 \leq 1$, they're able to bound the energy of each of these terms by 1. A natural generalization to two commodities would be to bound the sum of the squares of the two flows, leading to an instance of what we define as **Quadratically Capacitated Flows**. Specifically we would like the following to hold along each edge:

$$\mathbf{f}_1(e)^2 + \mathbf{f}_2(e)^2 \leq 1$$

Note that the flow $(\mathbf{f}_1(e), \mathbf{f}_2(e)) = (1, 0)$ has energy 1, so the RHS value of 1 is tight. This corresponds to allowing any $(\mathbf{f}_1(e), \mathbf{f}_2(e))$ that's within the unit L_2 ball, and as shown in Figure 1. However, in the 2-commodity case it's possible for flow settings that over-congest the edge to still satisfy this energy constraint. In other words, it's possible for a point to be in the unit L_2 ball but outside the unit L_1 ball. For example, the flow $(\mathbf{f}_1(e) = \sqrt{2}/2, , \mathbf{f}_2(e) = \sqrt{2}/2)$ also meets this energy constraint despite having a congestion $\sqrt{2}$.

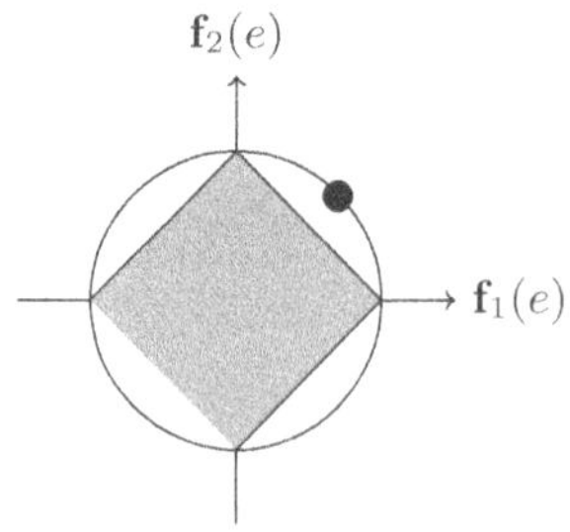

Figure 1: Unit l_1 ball representing region of feasible flows (gray), with unit l_2 ball being the quadratic capacity constraint. The point $(\mathbf{f}_1(e) = \sqrt{2}/2, \mathbf{f}_2(e) = \sqrt{2}/2)$ obeys this constraint, but exceeds the edge's capacity

One possible remedy to this problem is to introduce more intricate quadratic coupling between the two commodities. However, we still need to set the constraint so that any flow whose total congestion is below the capacity falls within this ellipse. This is equivalent to the ellipse containing the unit L_1 ball, which along with the fact that ellipses have smooth boundaries means we must allow some extra points. For example, the modified ellipse in Figure 2 once again allows the returned solution to have large congestion. In general, computing a single quadratically capacitated flow can lead to the edge being over-congested by a factor of $\sqrt{k}$, giving a $\sqrt{k}$ approximation.

As a result, instead of computing a single quadratically capacitated flow, we compute a sequence of them and **average** the result. Note that although both $(\mathbf{f}_1(e) = \sqrt{2}/2, , \mathbf{f}_2(e) = \sqrt{2}/2)$ and $(\mathbf{f}_1(e) = \sqrt{2}/2, , \mathbf{f}_2(e) = -\sqrt{2}/2)$ have congestion of $\sqrt{2}$, if we average them we're left with a flow with congestion only $\sqrt{2}/2$. If we're only concerned with keeping the average congestion small, the flows computed in previous iterations can give us some 'slack' in certain directions. As it turns out, if we compute the coupling matrix based on the flows returned so far, it's possible to move the average gradually get closer to the unit L_1 ball. For example, the average of the two flows returned in Figure 2 is inside the unit L_1 ball despite both falling outside of it.

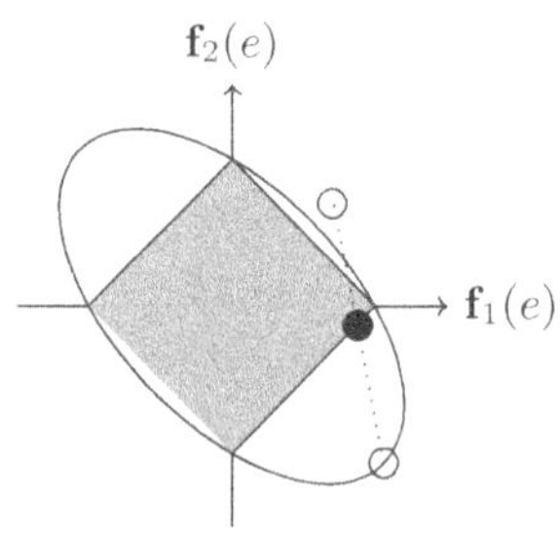

Figure 2: Modified energy constraint after a flow of $(\sqrt{2}/2, \sqrt{2}/2)$ has been added. Note that the point returned is still outside of the unit l_1 ball, but the average is within it.

The problem now becomes finding feasible quadratically

capacitated flows. The Christiano et al. algorithm [5] can be adapted naturally to this problem, providing that we can find flows that minimizes a weighted sum of the energy terms. We define this generalization of electrical flows as **quadratically coupled flows**. Just like their single commodity version, the minimum energy quadratic coupled flows can also be computed by solving linear systems.

The remaining difficulty of the problem is now with solving these linear systems. Most of the combinatorial preconditioning framework relies on the system being decomposable into 2-by-2 blocks corresponding to single edges. For quadratically coupled flows, the resulting systems are only decomposable into $2k$-by-$2k$ blocks. These systems are also encountered in stiffness matrices of finite element systems [4], and k-dimensional trusses [6, 2]. To date a nearly-linear time solver that can handle all such systems remains elusive.

Instead of solving these systems directly, we show, by more careful analysis of our algorithm that generates the quadratically capacitated flow problems, that it suffices to consider a more friendly subset of them. It can be shown that the $\sqrt{k}$ factor deviation that occurs in the uncoupled electrical problem is also the extent of our loss if we try to approximate these more friendly quadratically coupled flows with uncoupled ones. However, in the quadratic case such losses are fixable using preconditioned iterative methods, allowing us to solve the systems arising from quadratically coupled flows by solving a number of graph Laplacians instead. This leads us our main result, which can be stated as:

THEOREM 1.1. *Given an undirected, capacitated graph $G = (V, E, \mathbf{u})$ with m edges, along with k commodities and their demands $\mathbf{d}_1 \dots \mathbf{d}_i$. There is an algorithm that computes an $1-\epsilon$ approximate maximum concurrent flow in time:*

$$\tilde{O}(m^{4/3}\boldsymbol{poly}(k, \epsilon^{-1}))$$

An overview of the main steps of the algorithm is shown in Section 3. Our approach also extends to maximum weighted multicommodity flow, which we show in Appendix B.

2. PRELIMINARIES

The maximum concurrent multicommodity problem concerns the simultaneous routing of various commodities in a capacitated network. For our purposes, the graph is an undirected, capacitated graph $G = (V, E, \mathbf{u})$ where $\mathbf{u} : E \to R^+$ is the capacity of each edge. If we assign an arbitrary orientation to the edges, we can denote the edge-vertex incidence matrix $\mathbf{B} \in \Re^{m\times n}$ as:

$$\mathbf{B}(e, u) = \begin{cases} 1 & \text{if u is the head of e} \\ -1 & \text{if u is the tail of e} \\ 0 & \text{otherwise} \end{cases} \quad (2.1)$$

Then, for a (single commodity) flow $\mathbf{f}$, the excess of the flow at each vertex is given by the length n vector $\mathbf{B}^T\mathbf{f}$.

Throughout the paper we let k be the number of commodities routed. It can be shown that it suffices to solve the k-commodity flow problem for fixed vertex demands $\mathbf{d}_1, \mathbf{d}_2 \dots \mathbf{d}_k$ one for each commodity. The goal of finding a flow that concurrently routes these demands in turn becomes finding $\mathbf{f}_i$ for each commodity such that:

$$\mathbf{B}^T\mathbf{f}_i = \mathbf{d}_i \quad (2.2)$$

The other requirement for a valid flow is that the flows cannot exceed the capacity of an edge. Specifically we need the following constraint for each edge e:

$$\sum_{1\le i\le k} |\mathbf{f}_i(e)| \le \mathbf{u}(e) \quad (2.3)$$

2.1 Notations for k-Commodity Flow and Vertex Potentials

The extension of a single variable indicating flow/vertex potential on an edge/vertex to k variables creates several notational issues. We use a length km vector $\mathbf{f} \in \Re^{km}$ to denote a k-commodity flow, and allow for two ways to index into it based on commodity/edge respectively. Specifically, for a commodity i, we use $\mathbf{f}_i$ to denote the length m vector with the flows of commodity i along all edges and for an edge e, we use $\mathbf{f}(e)$ to denote the length k vector containing the flows of all k commodities along this edge.

This definition extends naturally to vectors over all (vertex, commodity) pairs as well. We let $\mathbf{d} \in \Re^{nk}$ be the column vector obtained by concatenating the length k demand vector over all n vertices. If the edges are labeled $e_1 \dots e_m$ and the vertices $v_1 \dots v_n$, then $\mathbf{f}$ and $\mathbf{d}$ can be written as:

$$\mathbf{f}^T = \left[\mathbf{f}(e_1)^T, \mathbf{f}(e_2)^T, \dots, \mathbf{f}(e_m)^T\right] \quad (2.4)$$

$$\mathbf{d}^T = \left[\mathbf{d}(v_1)^T, \mathbf{f}(v_2)^T, \dots, \mathbf{d}(v_n)^T\right] \quad (2.5)$$

We can also define larger matrices that allows us to express these conditions across all k commodities, and their interactions more clearly. The edge-vertex incidence matrix that maps between $\mathbf{d}$ and $\mathbf{f}$ is the Kronecker product between $\mathbf{B}$ and the $k \times k$ identity matrix $\mathbf{I}_k$.

$$\Gamma = \mathbf{B} \otimes \mathbf{I}_k \quad (2.6)$$

and $\mathbf{f}$ meeting the demands can be written as:

$$\Gamma^T \mathbf{f} = \mathbf{d} \quad (2.7)$$

Note that flows of two commodities passing in opposite directions through the edge do not cancel each other out.

By obtaining crude bounds on the flow value using bottle neck shortest paths and binary searching in the same way as in [5], the maximum concurrent multicommodity flow problem can be reduced to $O(\log n)$ iterations of checking whether there is a k-commodity flow $\mathbf{f}$ that satisfies the following:

$$||\mathbf{f}(e)||_1 = \sum_{i=1}^{k} |\mathbf{f}_i(e)| \le u(e) \qquad \forall e \in E$$

$$\Gamma \mathbf{f} = \mathbf{d}$$

2.2 Quadratic Generalizations

We define two generalizations of electrical flows to multiple commodities. Our main goal is to capture situations where the amount of flows of one type allowed on an edge depends inversely on the amount of another flow, so the flows are "coupled." To do so, we introduce a positive-definite, block-diagonal matrix $\mathbf{P} \in \Re^{km \times km}$ such that $\mathbf{P} = \sum_e \mathbf{P}(e)$ and each $\mathbf{P}(e)$ is a $k \times k$ positive definite matrix defined over the k entries corresponding to the flow values on edge e.

For each edge the k flows along an edge e, $\mathbf{f}(e)$ we get a natural quadratic penalty or energy dissipation term:

$$\mathcal{E}_{\mathbf{f}}(\mathbf{P}, e) = \mathbf{f}(e)^T \mathbf{P}(e)\mathbf{f}(e) \tag{2.8}$$

Summing these gives the total energy dissipation of a set of flows, denoted using $\mathcal{E}$.

$$\begin{aligned}\mathcal{E}_{\mathbf{f}}(\mathbf{P}) =& \sum_e \mathcal{E}_{\mathbf{f}}(\mathbf{P}, e) \\ =& \mathbf{f}^T \mathbf{P} \mathbf{f}\end{aligned} \tag{2.9}$$

In the **Quadratically Coupled Flow** problem, we aim to find a flow $\mathbf{f}$ that satisfies all of the demand constraints and minimizes the total energy dissipation, namely:

$$\begin{aligned}\min \quad & \mathcal{E}_{\mathbf{f}}(\mathbf{P}) & (2.10)\\ \text{subject to:} \quad & \Gamma^T \mathbf{f} = \mathbf{d} & (2.11)\end{aligned}$$

The minimum is denoted by $\mathcal{E}(\mathbf{P})$. We can define the related potential assignment problem, where the goal is to assign potentials to the vertices to separate the demands. Note that due to there being k commodities, a potential can be assigned to each (flow, vertex) pair, creating $\phi \in \Re^{kn}$. This vector can also be viewed as being composed of n length k vectors, with the vector at vertex u being $\phi(u)$. Given an edge $e = (u, v)$ whose end points connects vertices with potentials $\phi(u)$ and $\phi(v)$, the difference between its end points is $\phi(u) - \phi(v)$. In order to map this length nk vector into the same support as the k-commodity flows along edges, we need to multiply it by Γ, and we denote the resulting vector as $\mathbf{y}$:

$$\mathbf{y} = \Gamma \phi \tag{2.12}$$

The energy dissipation of an edge with respect to ϕ can in turn be defined as:

$$\mathcal{E}_{\phi}(\mathbf{P}, e) = \mathbf{y}\mathbf{P}(e)^{-1}\mathbf{y} \tag{2.13}$$

Note that this definition relies on $\mathbf{P}(e)$ being positive definite and therefore invertible on the support corresponding to edge e. This can in turn be extended analogously to the energy dissipation of a set of potentials as:

$$\begin{aligned}\mathcal{E}_{\phi}(\mathbf{P}) =& \sum_e \mathcal{E}_{\phi}(\mathbf{P}, e) \\ =& \phi^T \Gamma^T \mathbf{P}^{-1} \Gamma \phi\end{aligned} \tag{2.14}$$

We further generalize the definition of a Laplacian to k commodities:

$$\mathcal{L} = \Gamma^T \mathbf{P}^{-1} \Gamma \tag{2.15}$$

Thus, the energy dissipation of a set of potentials also equals to $\phi^T \mathcal{L} \phi$. Which leads to the following maximization problem, which is the dual of the quadratically coupled flow problem.

$$\begin{aligned}\max \quad & (\mathbf{d}^T \phi)^2 & (2.16)\\ \text{subject to:} \quad & \mathcal{E}_{\phi}(\mathbf{P}) \leq 1 & (2.17)\end{aligned}$$

We denote the optimum of this value using $\mathcal{C}_{eff}(\mathbf{P})$ and will show in Section 4.1 that $\mathcal{C}_{eff}(\mathbf{P}) = \mathcal{E}(\mathbf{P})$.

Another coupled flow problem that's closer to the maximum concurrent flow problem is one where we also bound the **saturation** of them w.r.t. $\mathbf{P}$, where **saturation** is the square root of the energy dissipation.

$$\mathbf{saturation}_{\mathbf{f}}(\mathbf{P}, e) = \sqrt{\mathbf{f}(e)^T \mathbf{P}(e) \mathbf{f}(e)} \tag{2.18}$$

Finding a flow with bounded saturation per edge will be then called the **Quadratically Capacitated Flow** problem.

3. OVERVIEW OF OUR APPROACH

A commonality of the algorithms for flow with Laplacian solves as an inner loop [7, 5] is that they make repeated computations of an optimum electrical flow in a graph with adjusted edge weights. The main problem with extending these methods to k-commodity flow is that the Laplacian for k-commodity electrical flow $\mathcal{L}$ is no longer symmetrically diagonally dominant. Our key observation in resolving this issue is that when the energy matrices $\mathbf{P}(e)$ are well-conditioned, we can precondition $\mathbf{P}$ with a diagonal matrix. Then using techniques similar to those in [1], we can solve systems involving $\mathcal{L}$ using a small number of Laplacian linear system solves. Our algorithm for k-commodity flow has the following layers with a description in Figure 3 as well.

1. We adapt the algorithm from [13] to use flows with electrical capacity constraints associated with the k commodities instead of minimum cost flow as its oracle call. At the outermost level, the approximately multi-commodity flow algorithm, repeatedly computes a positive definite matrix $\mathbf{P}(e)$ for each edge based on the flows on it so far on that edge, and boost their diagonal entries to keep their condition number at most $\mathbf{poly}(k)$. The outermost level then calls an algorithm that computes quadratically capacitated flow that is:

$$\mathbf{saturation}_{\tilde{\mathbf{f}}}(\mathbf{P}, e) \leq \max_{\mathbf{f}, ||\mathbf{f}(e)||_1 \leq \mathbf{u}(e)} \mathbf{saturation}_{\mathbf{f}}(\mathbf{P}, e) \tag{3.19}$$

   After repeating this process $\mathbf{poly}(k)$ times, averaging these flows gives one where $||\tilde{\mathbf{f}}(e)||_1 \leq (1 + \epsilon)\mathbf{u}(e)$ on all edges. We give two methods for computing $\mathbf{P}$ in Sections 6 and 7.

2. We use an algorithm that's a direct extension of the electrical flow based maximum flow algorithm from [5] to minimize the maximum saturation of an edge. This stage of the algorithm in turn solves $\tilde{O}(m^{1/3})$ quadratically coupled flows where the energy coupling on an

MaxConcurrentFlow
Constraint on desired flow: For each e, total flow $|f_e| \leq 1$.
Repeatedly updates energy matrices using matrix multiplicative weights. Makes poly(k) oracle calls to:

> QuadraticCapacitatedFlow
> **Constraint on desired flow:** For each e, $\mathbf{saturation}_{\mathbf{f}}(\mathbf{P}, e) = \sqrt{\mathbf{f}(e)^T \mathbf{P}(e) \mathbf{f}(e)} \leq 1$.
> Repeatedly updates energy matrices using (scalar) multiplicative weights. Makes $\tilde{O}(m^{1/3})$ oracle calls to:
>
> > QuadraticCoupledFlow
> > **Constraint on desired flow:** Minimize total dissipated energy $\mathcal{E}_{\mathbf{f}}(\mathbf{P}) = \sum_e \mathbf{f}(e)^T \mathbf{P}(e) \mathbf{f}(e)$. Solves 1 linear system using:
> >
> > > PreconCheby
> > > Solves non-Laplacian system by preconditioning with k $n \times n$ Laplacians. Solves these using k calls to nearly-linear time Laplacian solvers.

Figure 3: The high-level structure of the algorithm and the approximate number of calls made to each routine (for fixed ϵ).

edge is $\tilde{\mathbf{P}}(e) = \mathbf{w}_e \mathbf{P}(e)$. Note that since $\mathbf{P}(e)$ was chosen to be well conditioned and $\mathbf{w}_e$ is a scalar, the $\tilde{\mathbf{P}}(e)$s that we pass onto the next layer on remains well-conditioned. This is presented in Section 5.

3. In turn the Quadratically Capacitated Flow Algorithm makes calls to an algorithm that computes a quadratically coupled flow. The almost-optimal quadratically coupled flow is obtained by linear solves involving $\mathcal{L}$. Specifically, we show that preconditioning each $P(e)$ with a diagonal matrix allows us to decouple the k-flows, at the cost of a mild condition number set in the outermost layer. Then using preconditioned Chebyshev iteration, we obtain an almost optimal quadratically coupled flow using $\mathbf{poly}(k, \epsilon^{-1})$ Laplacian solves on a matrix with m non-zero entries. Properties of the k-commodity electrical flow, as well as bounds on the error and convergence of the solves are shown in Section 4.

4. APPROXIMATE COMPUTATION OF QUADRATICALLY COUPLED FLOWS

4.1 Relation Between Quadratically Coupled Flow and Effective Resistances

Let $\bar{\mathbf{x}}$ be the vector such that $\mathcal{L}\bar{\mathbf{x}} = \mathbf{d}$. It can be shown that $\mathcal{E}(\mathbf{P}, \phi)$ is maximized when ϕ is a multiple of $\bar{\mathbf{x}}$. Then the scaling quantity $\bar{\lambda}$ as well as the optimum set of potential $\bar{\phi}$ are:

$$\bar{\lambda} = \sqrt{\mathbf{d}^T \mathcal{L}^+ \mathbf{d}} \tag{4.20}$$

$$\begin{aligned}\bar{\phi} &= \frac{1}{\bar{\lambda}} \bar{\mathbf{x}} \\ &= \frac{1}{\bar{\lambda}} \mathcal{L}^+ \mathbf{d}\end{aligned} \tag{4.21}$$

Note that $\mathbf{d}$ satisfies $\mathbf{1}_i^T \mathbf{d} = 0$ for all $1 \leq i \leq k$. Also, since $\mathbf{P}$ is positive-semidefinite, the null space of $\mathcal{L}$ is precisely the space spanned by the k vectors $\mathbf{1}_i$. Therefore $\mathbf{d}$ lies completely within the column space of $\mathcal{L}$ and we have $\mathcal{L}\mathcal{L}^+ \mathbf{d} = \mathbf{d}$. The value of $\mathbf{d}^T \bar{\phi}$ is then:

$$\begin{aligned}\mathbf{d}^T \bar{\phi} &= \mathbf{d}^T \frac{1}{\bar{\lambda}} \mathcal{L}^+ \mathbf{d} \\ &= \bar{\lambda}\end{aligned} \tag{4.22}$$

The optimal quadratically coupled flow can be obtained from the optimal vertex potentials as follows:

$$\begin{aligned}\bar{\mathbf{f}} &= \mathbf{P}^{-1} \Gamma \bar{\mathbf{x}} \\ &= \bar{\lambda} \mathbf{P}^{-1} \Gamma \bar{\phi}\end{aligned} \tag{4.23}$$

We can prove the following generalizations of standard facts about electrical flow/effective resistance for multicommodity electrical flows.

Fact 4.1. *1. $\bar{\boldsymbol{f}}$ satisfies the demands, that is $\Gamma^T \bar{\boldsymbol{f}} = \boldsymbol{d}$.*

2. $\mathcal{E}(\boldsymbol{P}, \bar{\boldsymbol{f}}) = \boldsymbol{d}^T \mathcal{L}^+ \boldsymbol{d}$

3. For any other flow $\boldsymbol{f}$ that satisfies the demands, $\mathcal{E}(\boldsymbol{P}, \boldsymbol{f}) \geq \mathcal{E}(\boldsymbol{P}, \bar{\boldsymbol{f}})$.

Proof
Part 1

$$\begin{aligned}\Gamma^T \bar{\mathbf{f}} &= \bar{\lambda} \Gamma^T \mathbf{P} \Gamma \bar{\phi} \\ &= \bar{\lambda} \mathcal{L} \frac{1}{\bar{\lambda}} \mathcal{L}^+ \mathbf{d} \\ &= \mathbf{d}\end{aligned} \tag{4.24}$$

Part 2

$$\begin{aligned}\mathcal{E}(\mathbf{P}, \bar{\mathbf{f}}) &= \bar{\mathbf{f}}^T \mathbf{P} \bar{\mathbf{f}} \\ &= \mathbf{d}^T \mathcal{L}^+ \mathbf{d} (\mathbf{P}^{-1} \Gamma \bar{\phi})^T \mathbf{P} (\mathbf{P}^{-1} \Gamma \bar{\phi}) \\ &= \mathbf{d}^T \mathcal{L}^+ \mathbf{d} \bar{\phi}^T \Gamma^T \mathbf{P}^{-1} \mathbf{P} \mathbf{P}^{-1} \Gamma \bar{\phi} \\ &= \mathbf{d}^T \mathcal{L}^+ \mathbf{d} \bar{\phi}^T \mathcal{L} \bar{\phi} \\ &= \mathbf{d}^T \mathcal{L}^+ \mathbf{d} \quad \text{Since } \bar{\phi}^T \mathcal{L} \bar{\phi} = 1\end{aligned} \tag{4.25}$$

Part 3
Let $\mathbf{f}$ be any flow satisfying $\Gamma^T \mathbf{f} = \mathbf{d}$. Then we have:

$$\begin{aligned}\mathcal{E}(\mathbf{P}, \mathbf{f}) &\geq (\mathbf{f}^T \mathbf{P} \mathbf{f})(\bar{\phi}^T \Gamma^T \mathbf{P}^{-1} \Gamma \bar{\phi}) && \text{Since } \bar{\phi}^T \mathcal{L} \bar{\phi} = 1 \\ &= \|\mathbf{P}^{1/2} \mathbf{f}\|_2^2 \|\mathbf{P}^{-1/2} \Gamma \bar{\phi}\|_2^2 \\ &\geq (\mathbf{f}^T \Gamma \bar{\phi})^2 && \text{By Cauchy-Schwartz inequality} \\ &= (\mathbf{d}^T \bar{\phi})^2 && \text{Since } \mathbf{f} \text{ satisfies the demands} \\ &= \mathcal{E}(\mathbf{P}, \bar{\mathbf{f}}) && \text{By Part 2}\end{aligned} \tag{4.26}$$

■

4.2 Find Almost Optimal Vertex Potentials

The main part of computing an almost optimal set of vertex potentials from 4.21 is the computation of $\mathcal{L}^+\mathbf{d}$. Since $\mathbf{P}$ is no longer a diagonal, the matrix $\mathcal{L}$ is no longer a Laplacian matrix. However, in certain more restrictive cases that still suffice for our purposes we can use lemma 2.1 of [4]:

LEMMA 4.2. *For any matrices V, G, H, if $H \preceq G \preceq \kappa H$, then $VHV^T \preceq G \preceq \kappa VHV^T$.*

Proof Consider any vector x, we have:

$$x^T VHV^T x = (V^T x)^T H(V^T x) \preceq (V^T x)^T G(V^T x) = x^T VGV^T x \quad (4.27)$$

and

$$x^T VGV^T x = (V^T x)^T G(V^T x) \preceq \kappa (V^T x)^T H(V^T x) = \kappa x^T VHV^T x \quad (4.28)$$

■

This lemma allows us to precondition $\mathbf{P}$ when each of $\mathbf{P}(e)$ is well-conditioned, specifically:

LEMMA 4.3. *If there exist a constant κ such that for all e, $\kappa\lambda_{\min}(\boldsymbol{P}(e)) \geq \lambda_{\max}(\boldsymbol{P}(e))$, then we can find a Laplacian matrix $\tilde{\mathcal{L}}$ such that $\tilde{\mathcal{L}} \preceq \mathcal{L} \preceq \kappa\tilde{\mathcal{L}}$.*

Proof Consider replacing $\mathbf{P}(e)$ with $\tilde{\mathbf{P}}(e) = \lambda_{min}(\mathbf{P}(e))\mathbf{I}(e)$ where $\mathbf{I}(e)$ is the k - by - k identity matrix.

Then since $\mathbf{P}(e) \preceq \lambda_{max}\mathbf{I}(e)$ as well, we have:

$$\tilde{\mathbf{P}}(e) \preceq \mathbf{P}(e) \preceq \lambda_{max}(\mathbf{P}(e))\mathbf{I}(e) = \frac{\lambda_{max}(\mathbf{P}(e))}{\lambda_{\min}(\mathbf{P}(e))}\tilde{\mathbf{P}}(e) \quad (4.29)$$

Then applying Lemma 4.2 with $V = \Gamma^T$, $G = \mathbf{P}$ and $H = \tilde{\mathbf{P}}$ gives:

$$\tilde{\mathcal{L}} \preceq \mathcal{L} \preceq \kappa\tilde{\mathcal{L}} \quad (4.30)$$

■

The following fact then allows us to solve linear equations on $\mathcal{L}$ by solving linear systems on $\tilde{\mathcal{L}}$ instead:

LEMMA 4.4. *(preconditioned Chebyshev) [16, 3] Given matrix A, vector b, linear operator B and a constant κ such that $B \preceq A^+ \preceq \kappa B$ and a desired error tolerance θ. We can compute a vector x such that $||x - A^+b||_A \leq \theta||A^+b||_A$ using $O(\sqrt{\kappa}\log 1/\theta)$ evaluations of the linear operators A and B.*

Note that due to Γ being k copies of the edge-vertex incidence matrix, the matrix $\tilde{L}$ is actually k Laplacians arranged in block-diagonal form. This allows us to apply SDD linear system solves to apply an operator that is close to the pseudo-inverse of $\tilde{\mathcal{L}}$, which we in turn use to solve systems involving $\mathcal{L}$ using Lemma 4.4.

LEMMA 4.5. *[17, 11, 12] Given a Laplacian matrix of the form $\boldsymbol{L} = \boldsymbol{B}^T W \boldsymbol{B}$ for some diagonal matrix $W \geq 0$, there is a linear operator A such that*

$$A \preceq L^+ \preceq 2A$$

And for any vector $\boldsymbol{x}$, $A\boldsymbol{x}$ can be evaluated in time $\tilde{O}(m)$ where m is the number of non-zero entries in $\boldsymbol{L}$.

We can now prove the main result about solving systems involving $\mathcal{L}$.

LEMMA 4.6. *Given any set of energy matrices on edges $\boldsymbol{P}$ such that $\lambda_{max}(\boldsymbol{P}(e)) \leq \kappa\lambda_{min}(\boldsymbol{P}(e))$, a vector $\mathbf{d}$ and error parameter δ. We can find an almost optimal set of vertex potentials $\tilde{\boldsymbol{x}}$ such that:*

$$||\tilde{\boldsymbol{x}} - \bar{\boldsymbol{x}}||_{\mathcal{L}} \leq \delta||\bar{\boldsymbol{x}}||_{\mathcal{L}} \quad (4.31)$$

In time $\tilde{O}(mk^2\sqrt{\kappa}\boldsymbol{poly}(\epsilon^{-1}))$.

Proof Applying Lemma 4.5 to each of the Laplacians that make up $\tilde{\mathcal{L}}$, we can obtain a linear operator A such that:

$$\tilde{\mathcal{L}}^+ \preceq A \preceq 2\tilde{\mathcal{L}}^+ \quad (4.32)$$

Such that $A\mathbf{x}$ can be evaluated in time $\tilde{O}(mk)$.

Combining these bounds then gives:

$$A \preceq 2\tilde{\mathcal{L}}^+ \preceq 2\kappa A \quad (4.33)$$

Then the running time follows from Lemma 4.4, which requires an extra κ iterations, and the fact that a forward multiply involving $\mathbf{P}$ costs $O(mk^2)$. ■

Using this extension to the solver we can prove our main theorem about solving quadratically coupled flows, which we prove in Appendix A.

THEOREM 4.7. *There is an algorithm* QUADRATICCOUPLEDFLOW *such that for any $\delta > 0$ and $F > 0$, any set of energy matrices $\boldsymbol{P}(e)$ such that $I \preceq \boldsymbol{P}(e) \preceq UI$ for a parameter U and $\kappa\lambda_{\min}(\boldsymbol{P}(e)) \geq \lambda_{\max}(\boldsymbol{P}(e))$, and any demand vector $\mathbf{d}$ such that the corresponding minimum energy flow is $\bar{\boldsymbol{f}}$, computes in time $\tilde{O}((\sqrt{\kappa}k^2 + k^{\omega})m\log(U/\delta))$ a vector of vertex potentials $\tilde{\phi}$ and a flow $\tilde{\boldsymbol{f}}$ such that*

1. *$\tilde{\boldsymbol{f}}$ satisfies the demands in all the commodities $\Gamma^T\tilde{\boldsymbol{f}} = \mathbf{d}$*
2. *$\mathcal{E}_{\tilde{f}}(\boldsymbol{P}) \leq (1+\delta)\mathcal{E}_{\bar{f}}(\boldsymbol{P})$*
3. *for every edge e, $|\mathcal{E}_{\tilde{f}}(\boldsymbol{P}, e) - \mathcal{E}_{\bar{f}}(\boldsymbol{P}, e)| \leq \delta\mathcal{E}_{\bar{f}}(\boldsymbol{P})$*
4. *The energy given by the potentials $\mathcal{E}(\boldsymbol{P}, \tilde{\phi})$ is at most 1. and its objective, $\mathbf{d}^T\tilde{\phi}$ is at least $(1-\delta)\mathcal{C}_{eff}(\boldsymbol{P})$.*

5. APPROXIMATELY SOLVING QUADRATICALLY CAPACITATED FLOWS

We now show that we can repeatedly solve quadratically coupled flows inside a multiplicative weights routine to minimize the maximum saturation of an edge. Pseudocode of our algorithm is shown in Algorithm 1.

The guarantees of this algorithm can be formalized as follows:

THEOREM 5.1. *Given a graph $G = (V, E)$ and energy matrices $\boldsymbol{P}(e)$ on each of the edges such that $\kappa\lambda_{min}\boldsymbol{P}(e) > \lambda_{max}\boldsymbol{P}(e)$ and a parameter ϵ,* QUADRATICCAPACITATEDFLOW *returns one of the following in $\tilde{O}(mk^2\kappa\epsilon^{-8/3})$ time:*

Algorithm 1 Multiplicative weights update routine for approximately solving quadratic capacitated flows

QUADRATICCAPACITATEDFLOW

Input: Weighted graph $G = (V, E, w)$, energy matrix $\mathbf{P}(e)$ for each edge e, demands $\mathbf{d}_1 \dots \mathbf{d}_k$ for each commodity. Error bound ϵ.

Output: Either a collection of flows $\mathbf{f}$ such that $\mathbf{saturation}_{\mathbf{f}}(\mathbf{P}, e) \leq 1 + \epsilon$, or FAIL indicating that there does not exist a solution $\mathbf{f}$ where $\mathbf{saturation}_{\mathbf{f}}(\mathbf{P}, e) \leq 1 - 2\epsilon$.

1: $\rho \leftarrow 10m^{1/3}\epsilon^{-2/3}$
2: $N \leftarrow 20\rho \ln m\epsilon^{-2} = 200m^{1/3} \ln m\epsilon^{-8/3}$
3: Initialize $\mathbf{w}^{(0)}(e) = 1$ for all $e \in E$
4: $\mathbf{f} \leftarrow \mathbf{0}$
5: $N_1 \leftarrow 0$
6: **for** $t = 1 \dots N$ **do**
7: Compute $\mu^{(t-1)} = \sum_e \mathbf{w}^{(t-1)}(e)$
8: Compute reweighed energy matrices, $\mathbf{P}^{(t-1)}(e) = \left(w^{(t-1)}(e) + \frac{\epsilon}{m}\mu^{(t-1)}\right)\mathbf{P}(e)$
9: Query QUADRATICCOUPLEDFLOW with energy matrices $\mathbf{P}^{(t-1)}(e)$ and error bound $\delta = \frac{\epsilon}{m}$, let the flow returned be $\tilde{\mathbf{f}}^{(t)}$
10: **if** $\mathcal{E}_{\tilde{\mathbf{f}}^{(t)}}(\mathbf{P}^{(t-1)}) > \mu^{(t-1)}$ **then**
11: **return fail**
12: **else**
13: **if** $\mathbf{saturation}_{\tilde{\mathbf{f}}^{(t)}}(\mathbf{P}^{(t-1)}, e) \leq \rho$ for all e **then**
14: $\mathbf{f} \leftarrow \mathbf{f} + \tilde{\mathbf{f}}^{(t)}$
15: $N_1 \leftarrow N_1 + 1$
16: **end if**
17: **for** $e \in E$ **do**
18: $\mathbf{w}^{(t)}(e) \leftarrow \mathbf{w}^{(t-1)}(e)\left(1 + \frac{\epsilon}{\rho}\mathbf{saturation}_{\tilde{\mathbf{f}}^{(t)}}(\mathbf{P}^{(t-1)}, e)\right)$
19: **end for**
20: **end if**
21: **end for**
22: **return** $\frac{1}{N_1}\mathbf{f}$

- *A k-commodity flow $\tilde{\boldsymbol{f}}$ such that:*

$$\boldsymbol{saturation}_{\boldsymbol{f}}(\boldsymbol{P}, e) \leq 1 + 10\epsilon$$

for all edges e and

$$\Gamma \boldsymbol{f} = \boldsymbol{d}$$

- ***fail** indicating that there does not exist a k-commodity flow **f** that satisfies all demands and have*

$$\boldsymbol{saturation}_{\boldsymbol{f}}(\boldsymbol{P}, e) \leq 1 - \epsilon$$

on all edges.

We first state the following bounds regarding the overall sum of potentials $\mu^{(t)}$, the weight of a single edge $\mathbf{w}^{(t)}(e)$ and the effective conductance given by the reweighed energy matrices at each iteration, $\mathcal{E}(\mathbf{P}^{(t)})$.

LEMMA 5.2. *The following holds when $\tilde{\boldsymbol{f}}$ satisfies*

$$\sum_e \boldsymbol{saturation}_{\tilde{\boldsymbol{f}}}(\boldsymbol{P}^{(t-1)}, e) \leq \mu^{(t-1)}$$

1.

$$\mu^{(t)} \leq \exp\left(\frac{\epsilon}{\rho}\right)\mu^{(t-1)} \tag{5.34}$$

2. $\boldsymbol{w}^{(t)}(e)$ is non-decreasing in all iterations, and if

$$\boldsymbol{saturation}_{\tilde{\boldsymbol{f}}^{(t)}}(\boldsymbol{P}^{(t)}, e) \leq \rho$$

, we have:

$$\boldsymbol{w}^{(t)}(e) \geq \exp\left(\frac{\epsilon}{\rho}\boldsymbol{saturation}_{\tilde{\boldsymbol{f}}^{(t)}}(\boldsymbol{P}^{(t)}, e)\right)\boldsymbol{w}^{(t-1)}(e) \tag{5.35}$$

3. If for some edge e we have $\boldsymbol{saturation}_{\tilde{\boldsymbol{f}}^{(t)}}(\boldsymbol{P}, e) \geq \rho$, then $\mathcal{C}_{eff}(\boldsymbol{P}^{(t)}) \geq \mathcal{C}_{eff}(\boldsymbol{P}^{(t-1)})\exp\left(\frac{\epsilon^2\rho^2}{5m}\right)$

The proof of Lemma 5.2 relies on the following facts about $\exp(x)$ when x is close to 1:

FACT 5.3. *1. If $x \geq 0$, $1 + x \leq \exp(x)$.*

2. If $0 \leq x \leq \epsilon$, then $1 + x \geq \exp((1-\epsilon)x)$.

Proof of Part 1:

$$\begin{aligned}
&\mu^{(t)} \\
=&\sum_e \mathbf{w}^{(t)}(e) \\
=&\sum_e \mathbf{w}^{(t-1)}(e)(1 + \frac{\epsilon}{\rho}\mathbf{saturation}_{\tilde{\mathbf{f}}^{(t)}}(\mathbf{P}, e)) \\
&\text{By the update rule} \\
=&\left(\sum_e \mathbf{w}^{(t-1)}(e)\right) + \frac{\epsilon}{\rho}\left(\sum_e \mathbf{w}^{(t-1)}(e)\mathbf{saturation}_{\tilde{\mathbf{f}}^{(t)}}(\mathbf{P}, e)\right) \\
\leq&\mu^{(t-1)} + \frac{\epsilon}{\rho}\mu^{(t-1)} \\
&\text{By definition of } \mu^{(t-1)} \text{ and total weighted saturation} \\
=&(1 + \frac{\epsilon}{\rho})\mu^{(t-1)} \leq \exp(\frac{\epsilon}{\rho})\mu^{(t-1)} \\
&\text{By Fact 5.3.1}
\end{aligned} \tag{5.36}$$

■(Part 1)

Proof of Part 2:

If $\mathbf{saturation}_{\tilde{\mathbf{f}}^{(t)}}(\mathbf{P}^{(t)}, e) \leq \rho$, then $\frac{\epsilon}{\rho}\mathbf{saturation}_{\tilde{\mathbf{f}}^{(t)}}(\mathbf{P}^{(t)}, e) \leq \epsilon$ and:

$$\begin{aligned}
&\mathbf{w}^{(t)}(e) \\
=&\mathbf{w}^{(t-1)}(e)\left(1 + \frac{\epsilon}{\rho}\mathbf{saturation}_{\tilde{\mathbf{f}}^{(t)}}(\mathbf{P}^{(t)}, e)\right) \\
\leq&\mathbf{w}^{(t-1)}(e)\exp\left(\frac{\epsilon(1-\epsilon)}{\rho}\mathbf{saturation}_{\tilde{\mathbf{f}}}(\mathbf{P}, e)\right) \\
&\text{By Fact 5.3.2}
\end{aligned} \tag{5.37}$$

■(Part 2)

Proof of Part 3:

Let e be the edge where $\mathbf{saturation}_{\tilde{\mathbf{f}}}(\mathbf{P}, e) \geq \rho$, then since $\mathbf{P}^{(t-1)}(e) \succeq \frac{\epsilon}{m}\mu I$ by line 8, we have:

$$\begin{aligned}&\mathbf{saturation}_{\tilde{\mathbf{f}}}(\mathbf{P}^{(t-1)}, e)^2\\ \geq&\frac{\epsilon}{3m}\mu^{(t-1)}\rho^2\\ \geq&\frac{\epsilon\rho^2}{3m}\mathcal{E}(\mathbf{P}^{(t-1)}, \tilde{\mathbf{f}})\end{aligned}$$

By assumption of the energy of the flow returned (5.38)

Invoking the guarantees proven in Theorem 4.7, we have:

$$\begin{aligned}&\mathbf{saturation}_{\bar{\mathbf{f}}}(\mathbf{P}^{(t-1)}, e)^2\\ \geq&\mathbf{saturation}_{\tilde{\mathbf{f}}}(\mathbf{P}^{(t-1)}, e)^2 - |\mathbf{saturation}_{\tilde{\mathbf{f}}}(\mathbf{P}^{(t-1)}, e)^2\\ &- \mathbf{saturation}_{\bar{\mathbf{f}}}(\mathbf{P}^{(t-1)}, e)^2\\ \geq&\mathbf{saturation}_{\tilde{\mathbf{f}}}(\mathbf{P}^{(t-1)}, e)^2 - \delta\mathcal{E}(\mathbf{P}^{(t-1)})\\ &\text{By Part 3}\\ \geq&\frac{\epsilon\rho^2}{3m}\mathcal{E}_{\tilde{\mathbf{f}}^{(t)}}(\mathbf{P}^{(t-1)})) - \delta\mathcal{E}(\mathbf{P}^{(t-1)})\\ &\text{By Equation 5.38}\\ \geq&\frac{\epsilon\rho^2}{3(1+\delta)m}\mathcal{E}(\mathbf{P}^{(t-1)}) - \delta\mathcal{E}(\mathbf{P}^{(t-1)})\\ &\text{By Part 2}\\ \geq&\frac{\epsilon\rho^2}{4m}\mathcal{E}(\mathbf{P}^{(t-1)}) \qquad (5.39)\end{aligned}$$

Then by the relation between $\bar{\phi}$ and $\bar{\mathbf{f}}$, we have that

$$\mathcal{E}_{\bar{\phi}^{(t-1)}}(\mathbf{P}^{(t-1)}(e)) \geq \frac{\epsilon\rho^2}{4m}\mathcal{E}_{\bar{\phi}^{(t-1)}}(\mathbf{P}^{(t-1)}) \qquad (5.40)$$

Then since $\mathbf{w}^{(t)}(e) \geq (1+\epsilon)\mathbf{w}^{(t-1)}(e)$, using the current set of optimal potential gives:

$$\mathcal{E}_{\bar{\phi}^{(t-1)}}(\mathbf{P}^{(t)}) \leq (1 - \frac{\epsilon^2\rho^2}{4m})\mathcal{E}(\mathbf{P}^{(t-1)}, \bar{\phi}) \qquad (5.41)$$

Which means that when $\epsilon < 0.01$, $\sqrt{1 + \frac{\epsilon^2\rho^2}{5m}}\bar{\phi}^{(t-1)}$ is a valid set of potentials for $\mathbf{P}^{(t)}$ and therefore:

$$\begin{aligned}&\mathcal{C}_{eff}(\mathbf{P}^{(t)})\\ \geq&(\mathbf{d}^T\sqrt{1+\frac{\epsilon^2\rho^2}{5m}}\bar{\phi}^{(t-1)})^2\\ \geq&\exp\left(\frac{\epsilon^2\rho^2}{5m}\right)(\mathbf{d}^T\bar{\phi}^{(t-1)})^2\\ =&\exp\left(\frac{\epsilon^2\rho^2}{5m}\right)\mathcal{C}_{eff}(\mathbf{P}^{(t-1)}) \qquad (5.42)\end{aligned}$$

■(Part 3)

Proof of Theorem 5.1:

Since $\sum_e(w^{(t-1)}(e) + \frac{\epsilon}{m}\mu^{(t-1)}) = (1+\epsilon)\mu^{(t-1)}$, if there exist a flow $\mathbf{f}$ such that $\mathbf{saturation}_{\mathbf{f}}(\mathbf{P}, e) \leq 1 - 2\epsilon$ for all e, we have that $\mathcal{E}_{\tilde{\mathbf{f}}^{(t)}}(\tilde{\mathbf{P}}) \leq (1-\epsilon)\mu^{(t-1)}$. Then if the algorithm does not return **fail**, Theorem 4.7 means that $\tilde{\mathbf{f}}^{(t)}$ satisfies:

$$\begin{aligned}\mathcal{E}_{\tilde{\mathbf{f}}^{(t)}} \leq&(1+\delta)(1-\epsilon)\mu^{(t-1)}\\ \leq&\mu^{(t-1)} \qquad (5.43)\end{aligned}$$

$$\sum_e \mathbf{w}^{(t-1)}(e)\mathbf{saturation}_{\tilde{\mathbf{f}}^{(t)}}(\mathbf{P}^{(t-1)}, e)^2 \leq \sum_e \mathbf{w}^{(t-1)}(e) \qquad (5.44)$$

Multiplying both sides by $\mu^{(t-1)}$ and applying the Cauchy-Schwarz inequality gives:

$$\begin{aligned}&\left(\sum_e \mathbf{w}^{(t-1)}(e)\right)^2 \qquad (5.45)\\ \geq&\left(\sum_e \mathbf{w}^{(t-1)}(e)\right)\left(\sum_e \mathbf{w}^{(t-1)}(e)\mathbf{saturation}_{\tilde{\mathbf{f}}^{(t)}}(\mathbf{P}^{(t-1)}, e)^2\right)\\ \geq&\left(\sum_e \mathbf{w}^{(t-1)}(e)\mathbf{saturation}_{\tilde{\mathbf{f}}^{(t)}}(\mathbf{P}^{(t-1)}, e)\right) \qquad (5.46)\end{aligned}$$

Taking the square root of both sides gives:

$$\sum_e \mathbf{w}^{(t-1)}(e)\mathbf{saturation}_{\tilde{\mathbf{f}}^{(t)}}(\mathbf{P}^{(t-1)}, e) \leq \mu^{(t-1)} \qquad (5.47)$$

Therefore inductively applying Lemma 5.2 Part 1, we have:

$$\begin{aligned}\mu^{(N)} \leq&\mu^{(0)}\cdot\left(\exp(\frac{\epsilon}{\rho})\right)^N\\ =&\exp\left(\frac{\epsilon N}{\rho}\right)m\\ \leq&\exp\left(\frac{21\ln m}{\epsilon}\right) \qquad (5.48)\end{aligned}$$

We now bound N', the number of iterations t where there is an edge with $\mathbf{saturation}_{\tilde{\mathbf{f}}^{(t)}}(\mathbf{P}^{(t-1)}, e) \geq \rho$. Suppose $\mathcal{C}_{eff}(\mathbf{P}^{(0)}) \leq 1/2$, then in the flow returned, no edge e has $\mathbf{saturation}_{\tilde{\mathbf{f}}^{(0)}}(\mathbf{P}^{(0)}, e) \geq 1$, which means that the algorithm can already return that flow.

Then by the monotonicity of $\mathcal{C}_{eff}(\mathbf{P}^{(t)})$ and Lemma 5.2 Part 3, we have:

$$\mathcal{C}_{eff}(\mathbf{P}^{(N)}) \geq 1/2\cdot\exp\left(\frac{\epsilon^2\rho^2 N'}{5m}\right) \qquad (5.49)$$

Combining this with

$$\mathcal{C}_{eff}(\mathbf{P}^{(t)}) \leq \mu^{(N)} \qquad (5.50)$$

gives:

$$\begin{aligned}\frac{\epsilon^2\rho^2 N'}{5m} \leq&\frac{21\ln m}{\epsilon}\\ N' \leq&\frac{105m\ln m}{\rho^2\epsilon^3}\\ \leq&\epsilon N \qquad (5.51)\end{aligned}$$

Then in all the $N - N' \geq (1-\epsilon)N$ iterations, we have $\mathbf{saturation}_{\tilde{\mathbf{f}}^{(t)}}(\mathbf{P}^{(t-1)}, e) \leq \rho$ for all edges e. Then we have:

$$\begin{aligned}
&\textbf{saturation}_{\sum_t \tilde{\mathbf{f}}^{(t)}}(\mathbf{P}, e) & (5.52)\\
&\leq \sum_t \textbf{saturation}_{\tilde{\mathbf{f}}^{(t)}}(\mathbf{P}, e)\\
&\qquad \text{Since } \mathbf{P}(e) \text{ defines a norm}\\
&\leq \log(\mu^{(t)})/(\frac{\epsilon}{\rho})\\
&\qquad \text{By Lemma 5.2 Part 2}\\
&= \frac{1}{1-\epsilon} T' \leq (1+2\epsilon) T' & (5.53)
\end{aligned}$$

■

6. ALGORITHM FOR MAXIMUM CONCURRENT MULTICOMMODITY FLOW

One of the main difficulties in directly applying the flow algorithm from [5] is that single commodity congestion constraints of the form $||\mathbf{f}(e)||_1 \leq u_e$ are 'sharper' than the L_2 energy functions due to the sign changes when each of the commodities are around 0.

As a result, we use the primal Primal-Dual SDP algorithm from [1] to generate the energy matrix. Pseudocode of the outermost layer of our algorithm for maximum concurrent flow is shown in Algorithm 2.

Where the update routine, UPDATE is shown in Algorithm 3. Note that χ_i indicates the matrix that's 1 in entry (i,i) and 0 everywhere else, and $\bar{\mathbf{M}}^{(t)}$ is used to store the sum of $\mathbf{M}^{(r)}$ over $1 \leq r \leq t$ to we do not need to pass all of them to each invocation of UPDATE.

We start off by bounding the condition number of $\mathbf{P}^{(t)}(e)$.

LEMMA 6.1.

$$\lambda_{max}(\boldsymbol{P}^{(t)}(e)) \leq 2k\epsilon^{-1}\lambda_{min}(\boldsymbol{P}^{(t)}(e))$$

Proof Since $\mathbf{W}(e)$ is positive semi definite, we have $\mathbf{P}^{(t)}(e) \succeq \epsilon\mathbf{I}$. Also, by definition of $i^{(t)}(e)$, we have that the maximum diagonal entry of $\mathbf{W}^{(t-1)}(e)/||\mathbf{W}^{(t-1)}(e)||_\infty$ is 1. Therefore $\mathbf{tr}(\mathbf{P}^{(t)}(e)) \leq k + \mathbf{tr}(\epsilon\mathbf{I}) \leq 2k$. This in turn implies $\lambda_{max}(\mathbf{P}^{(t)}(e)) \leq 2k$, which gives the required result. ■

We first show that when a flow exist, QUADRATICCAPACITATEDFLOW returns a flow $\tilde{\mathbf{f}}^{(t)}(e)$ with low energy on each edge.

LEMMA 6.2. *If there is $\bar{\boldsymbol{f}}$ such that $|\bar{\boldsymbol{f}}(e)|_1 \leq 1$, then at each iteration t we have $\mathcal{E}_{\tilde{\boldsymbol{f}}^{(t)}}(\boldsymbol{P}^{(t-1)}, e) \leq 1 + 2\epsilon$.*

Proof

Algorithm 2 Algorithm for minimizing L_1 congestion

MAXCONCURRENTFLOW

Input: Capacitated graph $G = (V, E, \mathbf{u})$ and demands $\mathbf{d}$. Algorithm for computing energy matrices based on a list of k flows, ENERGY and for minimizing the maximum energy along an edge. Iteration count N and error tolerance ϵ.

Output: Either a flow $\mathbf{f}$ that meets the demands and $||\mathbf{f}(e)||_1 \leq (1+10\epsilon)\mu(e)$ on all edges, or **fail** indicating that there does not exist a flow $\mathbf{f}$ that meets the demands and satisfy $||\mathbf{f}(e)||_1 \leq \mu(e)$ on all edges.

$\rho \leftarrow \sqrt{k\epsilon^{-1}}$
$\epsilon_1 \leftarrow \frac{\epsilon}{k\rho} = \frac{\epsilon^{1/2}}{k^{3/2}}$
$\epsilon_1' \leftarrow -\ln(1-\epsilon_1)$
$N \leftarrow \rho\epsilon_1'^{-2}\log k = k^{7/2}\epsilon^{-3/2}\log k$
Initialize $\bar{\mathbf{M}}^0(e) = \mathbf{0}$, $\mathbf{W}^0(e) = \mathbf{I}$
for $t = 1 \ldots N$ **do**
  for $e \in E$ **do**
    $\mathbf{P}^{(t-1)}(e) = \frac{1}{\mathbf{u}^2}\left(\mathbf{W}^{(t-1)}(e)/||\mathbf{W}^{(t-1)}||_\infty + \epsilon\mathbf{I}\right)$
  end for
  Query QUADRATICCAPACITATEDFLOW with matrix $\mathbf{P}^{(t-1)}$
  if QUADRATICCAPACITATEDFLOW returns **fail then**
    return fail
  else
    Let the flow returned be $\tilde{\mathbf{f}}^{(t)}$
    for $e \in E$ **do**
      $(\bar{\mathbf{M}}^{(t)}(e), \mathbf{W}^{(t)}(e)) \leftarrow$
        UPDATE$(\bar{\mathbf{M}}^{(t-1)}(e), \mathbf{W}^{(t-1)}(e), \tilde{\mathbf{f}}^{(t)})$
    end for
  end if
end for
return $\frac{1}{N}\sum_{t=1}^{N}\tilde{\mathbf{f}}^{(t)}$

$$\begin{aligned}
&\mathcal{E}_{\bar{\mathbf{f}}(e)}(\mathbf{W}^{(t-1)}(e))\\
&= \bar{\mathbf{f}}(e)^T \mathbf{W}^{(t-1)(e)} \bar{\mathbf{f}}\\
&= \sum_{ij} \bar{\mathbf{f}}_i(e)\bar{\mathbf{f}}_j(e)\mathbf{W}_{ij}^{(t-1)}(e)\\
&\leq \sum_{ij} |\bar{\mathbf{f}}_i(e)||\bar{\mathbf{f}}_j(e)||\mathbf{W}_{ij}^{(t-1)}(e)|\\
&\leq ||\mathbf{W}^{(t-1)}||_\infty (\sum_{ij} |\bar{\mathbf{f}}_i(e)||\bar{\mathbf{f}}_j(e)|)\\
&= ||\mathbf{W}^{(t-1)}||_\infty \left(\sum_i |\bar{\mathbf{f}}_i(e)|\right)^2\\
&\leq ||\mathbf{W}^{(t-1)}(e)||_\infty \mathbf{u}(e)^2 & (6.54)
\end{aligned}$$

Therefore we have:

$$\begin{aligned}
&\mathcal{E}_{\tilde{\mathbf{f}}^{(t)}}(\mathbf{P}^{(t-1)}, e)\\
&\leq \frac{1}{\mathbf{u}(e)^2}\left(\frac{1}{||\mathbf{W}^{(t-1)}(e)||_\infty}\mathcal{E}_{\bar{\mathbf{f}}(e)}(\mathbf{W}^{(t-1)(e)}) + \mathcal{E}_{\bar{\mathbf{f}}(e)}(\epsilon\mathbf{I})\right)\\
&\leq 1 + 2\epsilon & (6.55)
\end{aligned}$$

Algorithm 3 Matrix exponential based algorithm for generating energy matrix

UPDATE

Input: $\bar{\mathbf{M}}^{(t-1)}(e), \mathbf{W}^{(t-1)}(e)$ from previous iterations, flow from iteration t, $\tilde{\mathbf{f}}^{(t)}(e)$, Capacity $\mathbf{u}(e)$, Parameter ϵ_1'.

Output: Sum matrix from current iteration S, Energy matrix X.

1: Find $i^{(t-1)}(e) = \arg\max_i \mathbf{W}_{ii}^{(t-1)}(e)$

2: $\mathbf{M}^{(t)}(e) \leftarrow \frac{1}{2\rho}\left((1+2\epsilon)\chi_{i^{(t-1)}(e)} - \frac{1}{\mathbf{u}(e)^2}\mathbf{f}^{(t)}(e)(\mathbf{f}^{(t)}(e))^T + \rho\mathbf{I}\right)$

Where χ_i has 1 in (i,i) and 0 everywhere else

3: $\bar{\mathbf{M}}^{(t)}(e) \leftarrow \bar{\mathbf{M}}^{(t-1)}(e) + \mathbf{M}^{(t)}(e)$

4: $\mathbf{W}^{(t)}(e) = \exp(-\epsilon_1'\bar{\mathbf{M}}^{(t)}(e))$

5: **return** $(\bar{\mathbf{M}}^{(t)}(e), \mathbf{W}^{(t)}(e))$

Since $\mathcal{E}_{\bar{\mathbf{f}}(e)}(\epsilon\mathbf{I})) = \epsilon||\bar{\mathbf{f}}(e)||_2^2 \leq \epsilon||\bar{\mathbf{f}}(e)||_1^2 \leq \mathbf{u}(e)^2$.

And the properties of $\mathbf{f}^{(t)}(e)$ follows from the guarantees of Theorem 5.1. ■

Using this width bound, we can now adapt the analysis in [1] to show that the sum of flows can be bounded in the matrix sense.

LEMMA 6.3. *If in all iterations the flows returned satisfy $\boldsymbol{f}^{(t)}(e)(\boldsymbol{f}^{(t)}(e))^T \preceq \rho\boldsymbol{u}^2 I$, then we have the following by the end of N iterations:*

$$\left(\sum_{t=1}^{N}\frac{1}{\boldsymbol{u}(e)^2}\boldsymbol{f}^{(t)}(e)(\boldsymbol{f}^{(t)}(e))^T\right) \preceq (1+2\epsilon)\boldsymbol{u}^2\sum_{t=0}^{N-1}\chi_{i^{(t)}} + \frac{\epsilon N}{k}\boldsymbol{I}$$

Proof

The proof is similar to the proofs of Theorems 10 and 1 in Section 6 of [1]. We have:

$$\begin{aligned}
&\mathbf{tr}\left(\mathbf{W}^{(t)}(e)\right)\\
=&\mathbf{tr}\left(\exp(-\epsilon_1'\sum_{r=0}^{t}\mathbf{M}^{(r)}(e))\right)\\
\leq&\mathbf{tr}\left(\exp(-\epsilon_1'\sum_{r=0}^{(t-1)}\mathbf{M}^{(r)}(e))\exp(-\epsilon_1'\mathbf{M}^{(t)}(e))\right)\\
&\quad\text{By the Golden-Thompson inequality}\\
=&\mathbf{tr}\left(\mathbf{W}^{(t-1)}(e)\exp(-\epsilon_1'\mathbf{M}^{(t)}(e))\right)\\
\leq&\mathbf{tr}\left(\mathbf{W}^{(t-1)}(e)(\mathbf{I}-\epsilon_1\mathbf{M}^{(t)}(e))\right)\\
&\quad\text{Since }\exp(-\epsilon_1'\mathbf{A}) \preceq (\mathbf{I}-\epsilon_1'\mathbf{A})\text{ when }0\preceq A\preceq\mathbf{I}\\
=&\mathbf{tr}(\mathbf{W}^{(t-1)}(e)) - \epsilon_1\,\mathbf{tr}(\mathbf{W}^{(t-1)}(e)\mathbf{M}^{(t)}) \qquad (6.56)
\end{aligned}$$

The construction of $\mathbf{W}(e)$ from line 4 of UPDATE means that $\mathbf{W}(e)$ is positive semi-definite. This in turn implies that $||\mathbf{W}(e)||_\infty \leq \max_i \mathbf{W}_{ii}$. Substituting gives:

$$\begin{aligned}
&\mathbf{tr}\left(\mathbf{W}^{(t-1)}(e)\mathbf{M}^{(t)}(e)\right)\\
=&\mathbf{tr}\left(\mathbf{W}^{(t-1)(e)}\cdot\left((1+2\epsilon)\chi_{i^{(t-1)}} - \mathbf{f}^{(t)(e)}(\mathbf{f}^{(t)}(e))^T + \rho\mathbf{I}\right)/2\rho\right)\\
=&\frac{1}{2\rho}\left((1+2\epsilon)||\mathbf{W}^{(t-1)}(e)||_\infty - \frac{1}{\mathbf{u}(e)^2}(\mathbf{f}^{(t)}(e))^T\mathbf{W}^{(t-1)}(e)\mathbf{f}^{(t)}(e)\right)\\
&+\frac{1}{2}\mathbf{tr}(\mathbf{W}^{(t-1)}(e))\\
\leq&\frac{1}{2\rho}\left((1+2\epsilon)||\mathbf{W}^{(t-1)}(e)||_\infty\right.\\
&\left.-||\mathbf{W}^{(t-1)}(e)||_\infty(\mathbf{f}^{(t)}(e))^T\mathbf{P}^{(t-1)}(e)\mathbf{f}^{(t)}(e)\right) + \frac{1}{2}\mathbf{tr}(\mathbf{W}^{(t-1)}(e))\\
&\quad\text{Since }\frac{\mathbf{W}^{(t-1)}(e)}{\mathbf{u}(e)^2||\mathbf{W}^{(t-1)}(e)||_\infty} \preceq \mathbf{P}^{(t-1)}(e)\\
\geq&\frac{1}{2}\mathbf{tr}(\mathbf{W}^{(t-1)}(e)) \qquad \text{By Lemma 6.2} \qquad (6.57)
\end{aligned}$$

Combining these two gives:

$$\begin{aligned}
&\mathbf{tr}\left(\exp(-\epsilon_1'\bar{\mathbf{M}}^{(N)}(e))\right)\\
=&\mathbf{tr}\left(\mathbf{W}^N(e)\right)\\
\leq&k\left(1-\frac{\epsilon_1}{2}\right)^N\\
\leq&k\exp\left(-\frac{\epsilon_1}{2}N\right)\\
\leq&\exp\left(-\frac{(1-\epsilon_1)\epsilon_1}{2}N\right)\\
&\quad\text{Since }N = 10\rho\epsilon_1'^{-2}\log k \qquad (6.58)
\end{aligned}$$

Using the fact that $\exp(-\lambda_{\max}(\mathbf{A})) \leq \mathbf{tr}(-\exp(\mathbf{A}))$, we get:

$$\begin{aligned}
&\frac{(1-\epsilon_1)\epsilon_1}{2}N\mathbf{I}\\
\preceq&\epsilon_1'\sum_{t=0}^{N}\mathbf{M}^{(t)}(e)\\
=&\epsilon_1'\sum_{t=0}^{N}\left((1+2\epsilon)\chi_{i^{(t)}} - \frac{1}{\mathbf{u}^2}\mathbf{f}^{(t)}(e)(\mathbf{f}^{(t)}(e))^T + \rho\mathbf{I}\right)/2\rho \qquad (6.59)\\
&-\epsilon_1'\rho N\mathbf{I}\\
\preceq&\sum_{t=0}^{N}\left((1+2\epsilon)\chi_{i^{(t)}} - \frac{1}{\mathbf{u}^2}\mathbf{f}^{(t)}(e)(\mathbf{f}^{(t)}(e))^T\right) \qquad (6.60)\\
&\frac{1}{\mathbf{u}^2}\left(\sum_{t=1}^{N}\mathbf{f}^{(t)}(e)(\mathbf{f}^{(t)}(e))^T\right)\\
\preceq&(1+2\epsilon)\sum_{t=0}^{N-1}\chi_{i^{(t)}} + \epsilon_1'\rho N\mathbf{I} \qquad (6.61)
\end{aligned}$$

Substituting in the setting of $\epsilon_1 = \frac{\epsilon}{k\rho}$ gives the desired result.

■

This in turns lets us bound the L_1 congestion of the flow returned after T iterations.

THEOREM 6.4. *After $N = \tilde{O}(k^{7/2}\epsilon^{-5/2}\log k)$ iterations,* MAXCONCURRENTFLOW *returns a flow* $\boldsymbol{f}$ *where for each edge* e*, we have:*

$$\left|\left|\frac{1}{N}\sum_{t=1}^{N} \boldsymbol{f}^{(t)}\right|\right|_1 \leq (1+3\epsilon)\boldsymbol{u}$$

Proof

We first bound the width of each update step. Note that by construction we have:

$$\frac{\epsilon}{\mathbf{u}^2 k}(\mathbf{f}^{(t)}(e))^T \mathbf{I}\mathbf{f}^{(t)}(e) \leq (1+\epsilon) \quad (6.62)$$

$$\frac{1}{\mathbf{u}^2}(\mathbf{f}^{(t)}(e))^T \mathbf{I}\mathbf{f}^{(t)}(e) \leq 2k\epsilon^{-1} \quad (6.63)$$

Then by the Cauchy-Schwarz inequality we have:

$$\begin{aligned}\left|\left|\frac{\mathbf{f}^{(t)}(e)}{\mathbf{u}(e)}\right|\right|_1^2 \leq & k\left|\left|\frac{\mathbf{f}^{(t)}(e)}{\mathbf{u}(e)}\right|\right|_2^2 \\ = & 2k\epsilon^{-1} \end{aligned} \quad (6.64)$$

Which gives that $\rho = \sqrt{2k\epsilon^{-1}}$ suffices as width parameter.

Let $\mathbf{s}$ be the vector corresponding to the signs of the entries of $\sum_{t=1}^{N}\mathbf{f}^{(t)}(e)$, aka. $\mathbf{s}^T\sum_{t=1}^{N}\mathbf{f}^{(t)}(e) = ||\sum_{t=1}^{N}\mathbf{f}^{(t)}(e)||_1$. Then:

$$\begin{aligned} & \left|\left|\frac{1}{\mathbf{u}N}\sum_{1\leq t\leq N}\mathbf{f}^{(t)}(e)\right|\right|_1^2 \\ = & \left(\mathbf{s}^T\frac{1}{N}\sum_{t=1}^{N}\mathbf{f}^{(t)}(e)\right)^2 \\ = & \frac{1}{\mathbf{u}^2N^2}\left(\mathbf{s}^T\sum_{t=1}^{N}\mathbf{f}^{(t)}(e)\right)^2 \\ \leq & \frac{1}{N}\sum_{t=1}^{N}\left(\mathbf{s}^T\mathbf{f}^{(t)}(e)\right)^2 \\ & \text{By the Cauchy-Schwarz inequality} \\ = & \frac{1}{N}\mathbf{s}^T\left(\sum_{t=1}^{N}\frac{1}{\mathbf{u}^2}\mathbf{f}^{(t)}(e)(\mathbf{f}^{(t)}(e))^T\right)\mathbf{s} \\ \leq & \frac{1}{N}\mathbf{s}^T\left(\sum_{t=1}^{N}(1+2\epsilon)\chi_{i(t)} + \frac{\epsilon N}{k}\mathbf{I}\right)\mathbf{s} \\ & \text{By Lemma 6.3} \\ = & 1+3\epsilon \quad \text{Since } \mathbf{s}_i = \pm 1 \text{ and } \mathbf{s}^T\mathbf{s} = k \end{aligned} \quad (6.65)$$

■

The running time of the algorithm can then be bounded as follows:

LEMMA 6.5. *Each iteration of the* MAXCONCURRENTFLOW *runs in* $\tilde{O}(m^{4/3}k^{5/2}\epsilon^{-19/6} + mk^{\omega})$ *time, giving an overall running time of* $\tilde{O}(m^{4/3}k^{6}\epsilon^{-17/3} + mk^{7/2+\omega}\epsilon^{-5/2})$*, where* ω *is the matrix multiplication exponent.*

Proof The first term follows from the running time of QUADRATICCAPACITATEDFLOW proven in Theorem 5.1 and $\kappa(\mathbf{P}(e)) \leq O(\sqrt{k\epsilon^{-1}})$ from Lemma 6.1. For the second term, the bottleneck is the computation of matrix exponentials. This can be done in **poly**$(\log k)$ matrix multiplies using [21], giving the $\tilde{O}(k^{\omega})$ bound in the each of the iterations. ■

7. ALTERNATIVE OUTER ALGORITHM

We show a modified formulation of the capacity bounds as 2^k constraints per edge that brings us back to minimizing the maximum congestion. This gives a more combinatorial approach to minimizing the maximum L_1 congestion, although the algorithm is slightly more intricate. As the computation of energy matrices only rely on the sum of flows so far (aka. history independent), we describe its computation in a separate routine ENERGY and first state the overall algorithm in Algorithm 4.

Algorithm 4 Alternate Algorithm for Maximum Concurrent Multicommodity Flow

---

MAXCONCURRENTFLOW1

Input: Capacitated graph $G = (V, E, \mathbf{u})$ and demands $\mathbf{d}$.
Algorithm for computing energy matrices based on a list of k flows, ENERGY and for minimizing the maximum energy along an edge, QUADRATICALLYCAPACITATEDFLOW. Width parameter ρ, iteration count N and error tolerance ϵ.

Output: Either a flow $\tilde{\mathbf{f}}$ that meets the demands and $||\tilde{\mathbf{f}}(e)||_1 \leq (1+10\epsilon)\mu(e)$ on all edges, or **fail** indicating that there does not exist a flow $\mathbf{f}$ that meets the demands and satisfy $||\mathbf{f}(e)||_1 \leq \mu(e)$ on all edges.

```
for t = 1...N do
    for e ∈ E do
        P^(t)(e) = ENERGY(∑_{1≤r<t} f^(r)(e))
    end for
    Query QUADRATICCAPACITATEDFLOW with matrix P^(t)
    if QUADRATICCAPACITATEDFLOW returns fail then
        return fail
    end if
end for
return (1/N) ∑_{t=1}^{N} f^(N)
```

We start with the following observation that the maximum among the sums given by all 2^k choices of signs to $\boldsymbol{f}_i(e)$ equals congestion.

OBSERVATION 7.1.

$$\sum_{i=1}^{k}|\boldsymbol{f}_i(e)| = \max_{s_1,s_2\ldots s_k\in\{-1,1\}^k}\sum_i s_i\boldsymbol{f}_i(e)$$

We let $\mathcal{S}$ to denote the set of all 2^k settings of signs. This allows us to reformulate the constraint of $||\mathbf{f}(e)||_1 \leq \mathbf{u}(e)$ as:

$$\mathbf{s}^T\mathbf{f}(e) \leq \mathbf{u}(e) \qquad \forall \mathbf{s} \in \mathcal{S} \quad (7.66)$$

This reduces the problem back to minimizing the maximum among all $|\mathcal{S}| = 2^k$ dot products with $\mathbf{f}(e)$. To solve this problem we can once again apply the multiplicative weights framework. We state the convergence result in a more general form:

THEOREM 7.2. *If for all flows $\boldsymbol{f}(e)$,* ENERGY($\boldsymbol{f}(e)$) *returns a matrix*

$$\boldsymbol{P}(e) = \frac{1}{\sum_{s \in \mathcal{S}} \tilde{\boldsymbol{w}}(\boldsymbol{s})} \sum_{s \in \mathcal{S}} \frac{\tilde{\boldsymbol{w}}(e)}{\boldsymbol{u}(e)^2} \boldsymbol{s}\boldsymbol{s}^T + \frac{\epsilon}{\boldsymbol{u}(e)^2} \boldsymbol{I} \quad (7.67)$$

Where $\tilde{\boldsymbol{w}}(\boldsymbol{s})$ satisfies

$$\exp\left(\frac{\epsilon \boldsymbol{s}^T \boldsymbol{f}(e)}{\rho \boldsymbol{u}(e)}\right) \leq \tilde{\boldsymbol{w}}(\boldsymbol{s}) \leq (1+\epsilon) \exp\left(\frac{\epsilon \boldsymbol{s}^T \boldsymbol{f}(e)}{\rho \boldsymbol{u}(e)}\right) \quad (7.68)$$

Then:

1. $\lambda_{max}(\boldsymbol{P}(e)) \leq 2k\epsilon^{-1}\lambda_{min}(\boldsymbol{P}(e))$.
2. *If there exist a flow $\bar{\boldsymbol{f}}$ that meets all the demands and have $||\bar{\boldsymbol{f}}(e)||_1 \leq (1-3\epsilon)\boldsymbol{u}(e)$,* MAXCONCURRENTFLOW *with $\rho = k$ and $N = \rho k \epsilon^{-2}$ returns a flow $\tilde{\boldsymbol{f}}$ that meets the demands and satisfy $||\tilde{\boldsymbol{f}}(e)||_1 \leq (1+3\epsilon)\boldsymbol{u}(e)$ over all edges.*

Proof of Part 1:

For $\lambda_{min}(\mathbf{P}(e))$, we have $\mathbf{P}(e) \succeq \frac{\epsilon}{\mathbf{u}(e)^2} I$ and the condition number bound follows from $\lambda_{min}(I) = 1$.

We can bound the maximum eigenvalue with the trance. Note that $\mathbf{tr}(\mathbf{s}\mathbf{s}^T) = k$ since the diagonal of $\mathbf{s}\mathbf{s}^T$ is all 1. This gives:

$$\begin{aligned}
\lambda_{max}(\mathbf{P}(e)) \leq& \mathbf{tr}(\mathbf{P}(e)) \\
=& \frac{1}{\sum_{\mathbf{s} \in \mathcal{S}} \tilde{\mathbf{w}}(\mathbf{s})} \sum_{\mathbf{s} \in \mathcal{S}} \frac{\tilde{\mathbf{w}}(e)}{\mathbf{u}(e)^2} \mathbf{tr}\, \mathbf{s}\mathbf{s}^T + \frac{\epsilon}{\mathbf{u}(e)^2} \mathbf{tr}\, \mathbf{I} \\
=& \frac{1+\epsilon}{\mathbf{u}(e)^2} k \quad (7.69)
\end{aligned}$$

Therefore we get:

$$\begin{aligned}
\frac{\lambda_{\max}(\mathbf{P}(e))}{\lambda_{\min}(\mathbf{P}(e))} \leq& \frac{1+\epsilon}{\mathbf{u}(e)^2} k\epsilon^{-1} \\
\leq& 2k\epsilon^{-1} \quad (7.70)
\end{aligned}$$

■

Proof of Part 2:

We define the exact set of weights that $\tilde{\mathbf{w}}(\mathbf{s})$ are trying to approximate:

$$\mathbf{w}(\mathbf{s})^{(t)} = \exp\left(\frac{\epsilon}{\rho} \frac{\mathbf{s}^T \mathbf{f}^{(t)}}{\mathbf{u}(e)}\right) \quad (7.71)$$

We also let $\bar{\mathbf{w}}^{(t)} = \sum_{\mathbf{s} \in \mathcal{S}} \mathbf{w}(\mathbf{s})^{(t)}$.

We have that at any iteration:

$$\begin{aligned}
\bar{\mathbf{w}}^{(t)} \geq& \max_{\mathbf{s}} \mathbf{w}(\mathbf{s})^{(t)} \\
=& \exp(\max_{\mathbf{s}} \mathbf{f}^{(t)}) \quad (7.72) \\
=& \exp(||\mathbf{f}^{(t)}||_1) \quad (7.73)
\end{aligned}$$

Therefore it suffices to upper bound the value of $\mu^{(t)}$. First note that if there is a flow $\bar{\mathbf{f}}$ such that $||\bar{\mathbf{f}}(e)||_1 \leq (1-3\epsilon)\mathbf{u}(e)$, then we have $\mathbf{s}^T\bar{\mathbf{f}}(e) \leq ||\bar{\mathbf{f}}(e)||_1 \leq \mathbf{u}(e)$ for any $\mathbf{s}$ Squaring this and taking sum over all $\mathbf{s} \in \mathcal{S}$ gives:

$$\begin{aligned}
&\bar{\mathbf{f}}(e)^T \mathbf{P}(e)^{(t-1)} \bar{\mathbf{f}}(e) \\
=&\bar{\mathbf{f}}(e) \left(\frac{1}{\sum_{\mathbf{s} \in \mathcal{S}} \tilde{\mathbf{w}}(\mathbf{s})^{(t-1)}} \sum_{\mathbf{s} \in \mathcal{S}} \frac{\tilde{\mathbf{w}}(e)^{(t-1)}}{\mathbf{u}(e)^2} \mathbf{s}\mathbf{s}^T + \frac{\epsilon}{k\mathbf{u}(e)^2} \mathbf{I} \right) \bar{\mathbf{f}}(e) \\
=& \frac{1}{\sum_{\mathbf{s} \in \mathcal{S}} \tilde{\mathbf{w}}(\mathbf{s})^{(t-1)}} \sum_{\mathbf{s} \in \mathcal{S}} \tilde{\mathbf{w}}(\mathbf{s})^{(t-1)} \left|\left| \frac{\mathbf{s}^T \bar{\mathbf{f}}(e)}{\mathbf{u}(e)} \right|\right|^2 + \epsilon \left|\left| \frac{\bar{\mathbf{f}}(e)}{\mathbf{u}(e)} \right|\right|_2^2 \\
\leq& \frac{1}{\sum_{\mathbf{s} \in \mathcal{S}} \tilde{\mathbf{w}}(\mathbf{s})^{(t-1)}} (1-3\epsilon)^2 \sum_{\mathbf{s} \in \mathcal{S}} \tilde{\mathbf{w}}(\mathbf{s})^{(t-1)} + \epsilon \\
\leq& (1-2\epsilon)^2 \quad (7.74)
\end{aligned}$$

This means that there exist a flow $\mathbf{f}$ such that:

$$\mathbf{saturation}_{\bar{\mathbf{f}}}(\mathbf{P}^{(t-1)}, e) \leq 1 - 2\epsilon$$

Therefore by Theorem 5.1, we have that for all edges e:

$$\mathbf{saturation}_{\tilde{\mathbf{f}}^{(t)}}(\mathbf{P}^{(t-1)}, e) \leq 1 - \epsilon$$

This has two consequences:

1. $$\frac{\epsilon}{\mathbf{u}(e)^2} (\tilde{\mathbf{f}}^{(t)})^T \mathbf{I} \tilde{\mathbf{f}}^{(t)} \leq 1 - \epsilon \qquad \text{Since } \mathbf{P}(e) \succeq \frac{\epsilon}{\mathbf{u}(e)^2}\mathbf{I}$$

   $$\left|\left| \frac{\tilde{\mathbf{f}}^{(t)}}{\mathbf{u}(e)} \right|\right|_1^2 \leq k \left|\left| \frac{\tilde{\mathbf{f}}^{(t)}}{\mathbf{u}(e)} \right|\right|_2^2 = \frac{k}{\epsilon} \quad (7.75)$$

   By Cauchy-Schwarz inequality

   Squaring both sides gives that $\frac{||\tilde{\mathbf{f}}^{(t)}||_1}{\mathbf{u}(e)} \leq \sqrt{k}\epsilon^{-1/2}$, which allows us to bound the width of the multiplicative updates.

2. Expanding out the first term in the formulation of $\mathbf{P}(e)$ gives:

   $$\sum_{\mathbf{s} \in \mathcal{S}} \tilde{\mathbf{w}}(\mathbf{s})^{(t-1)} \left(\frac{\mathbf{s}^T \tilde{\mathbf{w}}(e)}{\mathbf{u}(e)} \right)^2 \leq (1-\epsilon) \sum_{\mathbf{s} \in \mathcal{S}} \tilde{\mathbf{w}}(\mathbf{s})^{(t-1)} \quad (7.76)$$

   Multiplying both sides by $\sum_{\mathbf{s} \in \mathcal{S}} \tilde{\mathbf{w}}(\mathbf{s})^{(t-1)}$ and applying Cauchy-Schwarz inequality gives:

   $$\sum_{\mathbf{s} \in \mathcal{S}} \tilde{\mathbf{w}}(\mathbf{s})^{(t-1)} \left| \frac{\mathbf{s}^T \tilde{\mathbf{w}}(e)}{\mathbf{u}(e)} \right| \leq \sum_{\mathbf{s} \in \mathcal{S}} \tilde{\mathbf{w}}(\mathbf{s})^{(t-1)} \quad (7.77)$$

   Combining with the fact that $\mathbf{w} \leq \tilde{\mathbf{w}} \leq (1+\epsilon)\mathbf{w}$ gives:

   $$\sum_{\mathbf{s} \in \mathcal{S}} \mathbf{w}(\mathbf{s})^{(t-1)} \left| \frac{\mathbf{s}^T \tilde{\mathbf{w}}(e)}{\mathbf{u}(e)} \right| \leq (1+\epsilon) \sum_{\mathbf{s} \in \mathcal{S}} \mathbf{w}(\mathbf{s})^{(t-1)} \quad (7.78)$$

Using Fact 5.3 we have:

$$\begin{aligned}
&\bar{\mathbf{w}}^{(t-1)} \\
&= \sum_{\mathbf{s}\in\mathcal{S}} \mathbf{w}(\mathbf{s})^{(t-1)} \exp\left(\frac{\epsilon}{\rho}\frac{\mathbf{s}^T\tilde{\mathbf{w}}(e)}{\mathbf{u}(e)}\right) \\
&\leq \sum_{\mathbf{s}\in\mathcal{S}} \mathbf{w}(\mathbf{s})^{(t-1)} \exp\left(\frac{\epsilon}{\rho}\left|\frac{\mathbf{s}^T\tilde{\mathbf{w}}(e)}{\mathbf{u}(e)}\right|\right) \\
&\quad \text{Since } \exp(x) \text{ is monotonic and } x \leq |x| \\
&\leq \sum_{\mathbf{s}\in\mathcal{S}} \mathbf{w}(\mathbf{s})^{(t-1)} \frac{(1+2\epsilon)\epsilon}{\rho}\left|\frac{\mathbf{s}^T\tilde{\mathbf{w}}(e)}{\mathbf{u}(e)}\right| \\
&\quad \text{By Fact 5.3 Part 2 and } \left|\frac{\mathbf{s}^T\tilde{\mathbf{w}}(e)}{\mathbf{u}(e)}\right| \leq \rho \\
&\leq \frac{\epsilon}{\rho}(1+2\epsilon)(1+\epsilon)\sum_{\mathbf{s}\in\mathcal{S}} \mathbf{w}(\mathbf{s})^{(t-1)} \\
&\leq \frac{\epsilon(1+4\epsilon)}{\rho}\bar{\mathbf{w}}^{(t-1)} \\
&\leq \exp\left(\frac{\epsilon(1+4\epsilon)}{\rho}\right)\bar{\mathbf{w}}^{(t-1)} \\
&\quad \text{By Fact 5.3 Part 1}
\end{aligned} \tag{7.79}$$

Applying this inductively along with the fact that $\bar{\mathbf{w}}^{(0)} = 2^k$ gives:

$$\begin{aligned}
\bar{\mathbf{w}}^{(t)} &\leq 2^k \exp\left(\frac{\epsilon(1+4\epsilon)}{\rho}\right)^t \\
&= \exp\left(\frac{\epsilon(1+4\epsilon)t}{\rho} + k\right)
\end{aligned} \tag{7.80}$$

Substituting in $N = \frac{\rho k}{\epsilon^2}$ gives:

$$\begin{aligned}
\bar{\mathbf{w}}^N &\leq \exp\left(\frac{\epsilon(1+4\epsilon)\rho k}{\rho\epsilon^2} + k\right) \\
&= \exp\left(\frac{(1+5\epsilon)k}{\epsilon}\right) \\
&= \exp\left(\frac{\epsilon}{\rho}(1+5\epsilon\right)N)
\end{aligned} \tag{7.81}$$

Which gives $\frac{1}{N}|\mathbf{f}^{(N)}(e)|_1 \leq (1+\epsilon)\mathbf{u}(e)$. ∎

7.1 Efficient Estimation of the Energy Matrix

The algorithm as stated has an iteration complexity that's $O(k^{3/2}\epsilon^{-5/2})$, which is small enough for our purposes.

However, a direct implementation of the generation of the energy matrix $\mathbf{P}(e)$ requires looping through each of the 2^k sign vectors $\mathbf{s} \in \mathcal{S}$ and computing $\mathbf{s}^T\mathbf{f}$, which takes time exponential in k.

To alleviate this problem, note that the requirement of Theorem 7.2 allows us to compute the matrix for some set of weights $\tilde{\mathbf{w}}$ where $\mathbf{w}(\mathbf{s}) \leq \tilde{\mathbf{w}} \leq (1+\epsilon)\mathbf{w}(\mathbf{s})$. Specifically we show the following:

THEOREM 7.3. *Given a flow $\boldsymbol{f}$ such that $||\boldsymbol{f}||_1 \leq \rho'\boldsymbol{u}$, there is an algorithm* ENERGY *that computes a matrix $\boldsymbol{P}$ where*

$$P = \sum_s \tilde{w} s s^T \tag{7.82}$$

$$\exp\left(\frac{s^T f}{u}\right) \leq \tilde{w} \leq (1+\epsilon)\exp\left(\frac{s^T f}{u}\right) \tag{7.83}$$

In $\tilde{O}(k^4\rho'\epsilon^{-1})$ time.

Since we have the signs of each of the $\mathbf{f}_i$, we can easily find the value $\mathbf{s}$ that maximizes $\mathbf{s}^T\mathbf{f}$. We let this set of signs be $\bar{\mathbf{s}}$, then we have for all $\mathbf{s} \in \mathcal{S}$:

$$\exp\left(\frac{\mathbf{s}^T\mathbf{f}}{\mathbf{u}}\right) = \exp\left(\frac{\bar{\mathbf{s}}^T\mathbf{f}}{\mathbf{u}}\right)\exp\left(-\frac{(\bar{\mathbf{s}}-\mathbf{s})^T\mathbf{f}}{\mathbf{u}}\right) \tag{7.84}$$

The first term is a constant, therefore it suffices to get good approximations for the second term. To do so we round each entry of $\mathbf{f}$ to the lowest integral multiple of $\frac{\epsilon}{k}$ and bound the error as follows:

LEMMA 7.4. *Let $\tilde{\boldsymbol{f}}$ be $\boldsymbol{f}$ with each entry rounded towards 0 to the nearest multiple of $\frac{\epsilon}{3k}\boldsymbol{u}$. Then we have:*

$$\begin{aligned}
\exp\left(-\frac{(\bar{s}-s)^T f}{u}\right) &\leq \exp\left(-\frac{(\bar{s}-s)^T\tilde{f}}{u}\right) \\
&\leq (1+\epsilon)\exp\left(-\frac{(\bar{s}-s)^T f}{u}\right)
\end{aligned} \tag{7.85}$$

Also, $||\tilde{\boldsymbol{f}}||_1 \leq \rho'\boldsymbol{u}$ as well.

Proof of Theorem 7.3: Note that by the choice of $\bar{\mathbf{s}}$, $\bar{\mathbf{s}}_i\mathbf{f}_i \geq 0$ in each of commodity i. Therefore $(\bar{\mathbf{s}}-\mathbf{s})_i\mathbf{f}_i$ is either 0 or $2\mathbf{f}_i$. By the rounding rule we have:

$$|\mathbf{f}_i| - \frac{\epsilon}{3k}\mathbf{u} \leq |\tilde{\mathbf{f}}_i| \leq |\mathbf{f}_i| \tag{7.86}$$

Which gives us the bound on $||\tilde{\mathbf{f}}||_1$. When combined with the fact that $\tilde{\mathbf{f}}_i$ having the same sign as $\mathbf{f}_i$ gives:

$$(\bar{\mathbf{s}}-\mathbf{s})_i\mathbf{f}_i - \frac{2\epsilon}{3k}\mathbf{u} \leq (\bar{\mathbf{s}}-\mathbf{s})_i\tilde{\mathbf{f}}_i \leq (\bar{\mathbf{s}}-\mathbf{s})_i\mathbf{f}_i \tag{7.87}$$

Summing this over the k commodities gives:

$$(\bar{\mathbf{s}}-\mathbf{s})^T\mathbf{f} - \frac{2\epsilon}{3}\mathbf{u} \leq (\bar{\mathbf{s}}-\mathbf{s})^T\tilde{\mathbf{f}} \leq (\bar{\mathbf{s}}-\mathbf{s})^T\mathbf{f} \tag{7.88}$$

Exponentiating both sides of Fact 5.3 Part 2 gives $\exp(\frac{2\epsilon}{3}) \leq (1+\epsilon)$, from which the result follows. ∎

After this rounding, the values of $\mathbf{s}^T\tilde{\mathbf{f}}$ can only be multiples of $\frac{\epsilon}{k}\mathbf{u}$ between $[-\rho'\mathbf{u}, \rho'\mathbf{u}]$. This allows us to narrow down the number of possible values of $\exp(\frac{\mathbf{s}^T\tilde{\mathbf{f}}}{\mathbf{u}})$ to one of $O(\rho' k\epsilon{-}1)$ values. Further more, notice that to calculate $\mathbf{P}_{ij}$ it suffices to find the list of values of $\frac{\mathbf{s}^T\tilde{\mathbf{f}}}{\mathbf{u}}$ among all $\mathbf{s}$ such that $\mathbf{s}_i = \mathbf{s}_j$ and the list where $\mathbf{s}_i \neq \mathbf{s}_j$. Each of these calculations can be done in $\tilde{O}(\rho' k^2\epsilon^{-1})$ time using the following lemma:

LEMMA 7.5. *Given a list of positive integer values $a_1, a_2, \ldots a_k$ such that $\sum_i a_i = N$, there is an algorithm* CONVOLVEALL *that computes in $\tilde{O}(Nk\log^2 N)$ time for each $j \in [1, N]$ the number of subsets $S \subseteq \{1, 2, \ldots k\}$ such that $\sum_{i\in S} a_i = j$.*

Proof Since the ordering is irrelevant, we may assume that $a_1 \leq a_2 \leq \ldots a_k$. Then there exist an index i such that $\sum_{1 \leq j \leq i} a_j$ and $\sum_{i+1 \leq j \leq k-1} a_j$ are both at most $N/2$. Suppose we have two lists containing the number of sums for each value between 0 and $N/2$, then taking their convolution can be done in $O(N \log N)$ multiplications involving k bit numbers. The last entry of a_k can be dealt with similarly. Let the time required to compute the answer when the total sum is N be $T(N)$, then this gives the following recurrence:

$$T(N) \leq 2T(N/2) + O(Nk \log N) \tag{7.89}$$

Solving gives $T(N) = O(Nk \log^2 N)$. ■

Algorithm 5 Algorithm for computing approximate energy matrix

ENERGY

Input: A k commodity flow $\mathbf{f}$. Capacity $\mathbf{u}$, parameter ρ' such that $||\mathbf{f}||_1 \leq \rho' \mathbf{u}$. Error bound ϵ.

Output: Approximate energy matrix satisfying the guarantees of Theorem 7.3

```
Compute the set of signs that maximizes s^T f, s̄
for i = 1...k do
   if f_i ≥ 0 then
      f̃_i = u (ε/k) ⌊(f_i/k) ε^{-1}⌋
   else
      f̃_i = −u (ε/k) ⌊−(f_i/k) ε^{-1}⌋
   end if
end for
for i = 1...k do
   for j = 1...k do
      for Each setting of s_i, s_j do
         for Each l ≠ i, j do
            Create a_l = 2 (f̃_l/u) k ε^{-1}
         end for
         b ← CONVOLVEALL(a)
         for −ρ' k ε^{-1} ≤ l ≤ ρ' k ε^{-1} do
            P_ij ← P_ij + b_l · s_i · s_j · exp((ε/ρ) (s̄^T f / u) − l)
         end for
      end for
   end for
end for
return P
```

The overall pseudocode for computing this energy matrix is shown in Algorithm 5. Summing over all $O(k^2)$ entries gives the total running time. It's worth noting that because the matrix entries consists of differences of weights, the matrix that we obtain can have some entries that are very different than what we would obtain if we use the exact values of $\mathbf{w}(\mathbf{s})$. Their similarity is obtained through the similarity of $\tilde{w}$ and $\hat{w}$ as they are weights on positive semi-definite outer products.

We can now bound the overall running time of the algorithm:

COROLLARY 7.6. MAXCONCURRENTFLOW1 *runs in* $\tilde{O}(k^{3/2}\epsilon^{-5/2})$ *iterations, where each iteration takes time* $\tilde{O}(m^{4/3}k^{5/2}\epsilon^{-19/6} + mk^5\epsilon^{-3/2})$, *for a total running time of* $\tilde{O}(m^{4/3}k^4\epsilon^{-17/3} + mk^{13/2}\epsilon^{-4})$.

Proof The iteration count from 7.2 completes the proof. The first term follows from Theorem 5.1 and $\kappa(\mathbf{P}(e)) \leq \sqrt{k}\epsilon^{-1/2}$, Theorem 7.2 Part 2 gives that $||\mathbf{f}^{(t)}||_1 \leq O(N)$, which gives $||\frac{\epsilon}{\rho}\mathbf{f}^{(t)}||_1 \leq \frac{\epsilon N}{\rho} = \tilde{O}(k)$. Letting $\rho' = \tilde{O}(k)$ in Theorem 7.3 then gives the second term in the bound. ■

8. COMMENTS/EXTENSIONS

We have shown an approach of dealing with the coupling of the k commodities by associating an energy matrix with them. This allows us to approximate multicommodity flows in time $\tilde{O}(m^{4/3}\mathbf{poly}(k, \epsilon^{-1}))$. We believe that our approach is quite general and extends naturally to other couplings between sets of k flows/vertex labels, with the most natural generalization being Markov random fields [10, 18]. Since reductions from multicommodity flow to $\tilde{O}(k\epsilon^{-2})$ calls of minimum cost flows are known [13]. A stronger result would be an approximation of minimum cost flow that runs in $\tilde{O}(m^{4/3}\mathbf{poly}(k, \epsilon^{-1})$ time. This problem is significantly harder due to it incorporating both L_∞ and L_1 constraints. Therefore, it's likely that a more intricate set of energy matrices is needed to proceed in this direction.

When viewed from the perspective of combinatorial preconditioning, we were able to solve multicommodity electrical flows by adding ϵ slack to the edges, thus 'fixing' the condition number. For the purpose of obtaining $1 \pm \epsilon$ approximations to combinatorial problems, this does not modify the solution by too much. However, it is unlikely to be applicable inside algorithms whose dependency on ϵ is $O(\log(1/\epsilon))$, as very little slack can be added onto the edges. As a result, we believe that obtaining fast solvers for the class of matrices that arise from quadratically coupled flows is an interesting direction for future work.

9. REFERENCES

[1] S. Arora and S. Kale. A combinatorial, primal-dual approach to semidefinite programs. In *STOC*, pages 227–236, 2007. 6, 6, 6

[2] H. Avron and S. Toledo. Effective stiffness: Generalizing effective resistance sampling to finite element matrices. *CoRR*, abs/cs/1110.4437, 2011. 1.2

[3] O. Axelsson. *Iterative Solution Methods*. Cambridge University Press, New York, NY, 1994. 4.1

[4] E. G. Boman, B. Hendrickson, and S. A. Vavasis. Solving elliptic finite element systems in near-linear time with support preconditioners. *CoRR*, cs.NA/0407022, 2004. 1.2, 3, 4.2

[5] P. Christiano, J. A. Kelner, A. Mądry, D. Spielman, and S.-H. Teng. Electrical Flows, Laplacian Systems, and Faster Approximation of Maximum Flow in Undirected Graphs. In *Proceedings of the 43rd ACM Symposium on Theory of Computing (STOC)*, 2011. 1.2, 1.2, 2.1, 3, 2, 6, A

[6] S. I. Daitch and D. A. Spielman. Support-graph preconditioners for 2-dimensional trusses. *CoRR*, abs/cs/0703119, 2007. 1.2

[7] S. I. Daitch and D. A. Spielman. Faster approximate lossy generalized flow via interior point algorithms. *CoRR*, abs/0803.0988, 2008. 1.1, 3

[8] L. K. Fleischer. Approximating fractional multicommodity flow independent of the number of commodities. *SIAM Journal on Discrete Mathematics*, 13:505–520, 2000. 1.1

[9] N. Garg and J. Könemann. Faster and simpler algorithms for multicommodity flow and other fractional packing problems. In *In Proceedings of the 39th Annual Symposium on Foundations of Computer Science*, pages 300–309, 1998. 1.1

[10] R. Kindermann and J. L. Snell. *Markov random fields and their applications*. American Mathematical Society, Providence, R.I., 1980, 1980. 8

[11] I. Koutis, G. L. Miller, and R. Peng. Approaching optimality for solving SDD systems. *CoRR*, abs/1003.2958, 2010. 4.5

[12] I. Koutis, G. L. Miller, and R. Peng. Solving sdd linear systems in time $\tilde{O}(m \log n \log(1/\epsilon))$. *CoRR*, abs/1102.4842, 2011. 4.5

Algorithm 6 Algorithm for computing near-optimal electrical potential/flow pair

QuadraticCoupledFlow

Input: Graph $G = (V, E)$ with corresponding edge-vertex incidence matrix $\mathbf{B}$. Demand vector $\mathbf{d}$ Energy matrices for the edges $\mathbf{P}$ along with bounds U, κ such that $I \preceq \mathbf{P} \preceq U \cdot I$ and $\lambda_{\max}(\mathbf{P}(e)) \preceq \kappa\lambda_{\min}(\mathbf{P}(e))$. Error bound δ.

Output: Approximate vertex potentials $\tilde{\phi}$ and flow $\tilde{\mathbf{f}}$ that satisfies the constraints of Theorem

Let $\mathcal{L}$ be an implicit representation of the matrix $\Gamma\mathbf{P}\Gamma$
Use PreconCheby to find $\tilde{\mathbf{x}} = \mathcal{L}^{+}\mathbf{d}$ with error of $\epsilon = \frac{\delta}{5m^6k^2U^4}$
$\tilde{\lambda} \leftarrow \sqrt{\tilde{\mathbf{x}}^T\mathcal{L}\tilde{\mathbf{x}}}$
$\tilde{\phi} = \frac{1}{\tilde{\lambda}}\tilde{\mathbf{x}}$
Compute ohmic flow $\hat{\mathbf{f}} = \mathbf{P}^{-1}\Gamma\tilde{\mathbf{x}}$
for $i = 1 \dots k$ **do**
  $\tilde{\mathbf{f}}_i \leftarrow$ MakeKirchhoff$(G, \mathbf{d}_i, \hat{\mathbf{f}}_i)$
end for
return $\tilde{\phi}, \tilde{\mathbf{f}}$

[13] T. Leighton, F. Makedon, S. Plotkin, C. Stein, E. Tardos, and S. Tragoudas. Fast approximation algorithms for multicommodity flow problems. In *JOURNAL OF COMPUTER AND SYSTEM SCIENCES*, pages 487–496, 1991. 1.1, 1, 8

[14] A. Madry. Faster approximation schemes for fractional multicommodity flow problems via dynamic graph algorithms. In *STOC '10: Proceedings of the 42nd ACM symposium on Theory of computing*, pages 121–130, New York, NY, USA, 2010. ACM. 1.1

[15] B. Rothschild and A. Whinston. Feasibility of two commodity network flows. *Operations Research*, 14(6):pp. 1121–1129, 1966. 1.1, 1.2

[16] Y. Saad. *Iterative Methods for Sparse Linear Systems*. http://www-users.cs.umn.edu/~saad/books.html, 1996. 4.4

[17] D. A. Spielman and S.-H. Teng. Nearly-linear time algorithms for preconditioning and solving symmetric, diagonally dominant linear systems. *CoRR*, abs/cs/0607105, 2006. 1.1, 4.5

[18] R. Szeliski, R. Zabih, D. Scharstein, O. Veksler, V. Kolmogorov, A. Agarwala, M. Tappen, and C. Rother. A comparative study of energy minimization methods for markov random fields with smoothness-based priors. *IEEE Transactions on Pattern Analysis and Machine Intelligence*, 30:1068–1080, 2008. 8

[19] P. M. Vaidya. Speeding-up linear programming using fast matrix multiplication. In *Proceedings of the 30th Annual Symposium on Foundations of Computer Science*, pages 332–337, Washington, DC, USA, 1989. IEEE Computer Society. 1.1

[20] P. M. Vaidya. Solving linear equations with symmetric diagonally dominant matrices by constructing good preconditioners. A talk based on this manuscript was presented at the IMA Workshop on Graph Theory and Sparse Matrix Computation, October 1991. 1.1

[21] S.-T. Yau and Y. Y. Lu. Reducing the symmetric matrix eigenvalue problem to matrix multiplications. *SIAM J. Sci. Comput.*, 14:121–136, January 1993. 6

APPENDIX

A. OBTAINING ALMOST OPTIMAL ELECTRICAL FLOW FROM POTENTIALS

This approximate solve then allows us to compute electrical flows in a way analogous to theorem 2.3 of [5]. Pseudocode of the algorithm is shown in Algorithm 6.

The algorithm makes calls to MakeKirchoff, which converts a flow $\hat{\mathbf{f}}$ that doesn't satisfy conservation of flow at vertices in W to one that does without too much increase in congestion. Its properties are proven in Lemma A.1.

Algorithm 7 Algorithm for making an arbitrary flow Kirchhoff

MakeKirchhoff

Input: Graph $G = (W \subseteq V, E)$ with demands $\mathbf{d}$. A Ohmic flow $\mathbf{f}$.

Output: A flow that satisfies conservation of flow at all vertices in W

$\tilde{\mathbf{f}} \leftarrow \mathbf{f}$
Pick any vertex r
compute a spanning tree, T
for each vertex $u \neq r$ **do**
  route $\mathbf{d}_u - (\Gamma\tilde{\mathbf{f}})_u$ units of flow from u to r along T
end for
return $\tilde{\mathbf{f}}$

We start by bounding the errors incurred by MakeKirchhoff

Lemma A.1. *Given a capacitated graph $G = (V, E, \boldsymbol{u})$, a set of demands $\boldsymbol{d}$ a flow $\hat{\boldsymbol{f}}$ such that $||\Gamma^T\hat{\boldsymbol{f}}||_\infty \leq \gamma$.* MakeKirchhoff$(G, \boldsymbol{d}, \hat{\boldsymbol{f}})$ *returns a flow $\tilde{\boldsymbol{f}}$ such that:*

1. $\Gamma^T\tilde{\boldsymbol{f}} = \boldsymbol{d}$.

2. For all edges $e \in E$, $||\hat{\boldsymbol{f}}_e - \tilde{\boldsymbol{f}}_e||_\infty \leq m\gamma$.

Proof Part 1 follows from the construction for each vertex $u \neq r$ and $\mathbf{1}^T\mathbf{d} = 0$. To bound the extra congestion, note that each edge in the tree is used in at most $n < m$ paths that route at most γ units of flow each. This gives an extra congestion of at most $m\gamma$ and therefore Part 2. ■

Proof of Theorem 4.7:

We start off by showing that $\tilde{\lambda}$ does not differ by much from $\bar{\lambda} = \sqrt{\bar{\phi}^T\mathcal{L}\bar{\phi}}$:

Lemma A.2.

$$|\tilde{\lambda} - \bar{\lambda}| \leq \epsilon\bar{\lambda}$$

Proof

$$\begin{aligned} |\tilde{\lambda} - \bar{\lambda}| &= |||\tilde{\mathbf{x}}||_{\mathcal{L}} - ||\bar{\mathbf{x}}||_{\mathcal{L}}| \\ &\leq ||\tilde{\mathbf{x}} - \bar{\mathbf{x}}||_{\mathcal{L}} \quad \text{Since } ||\cdot||_{\mathcal{L}} \text{ is a norm} \\ &\leq \epsilon||\bar{\mathbf{x}}||_{\mathcal{L}} = \epsilon\bar{\lambda} \end{aligned} \tag{1.90}$$

■(Lemma A.2)

Algebraic manipulations of this give:

Corollary A.3.

$$(1-\epsilon)\bar{\lambda} \leq \tilde{\lambda} \leq (1+\epsilon)\bar{\lambda} \tag{1.91}$$

$$(1-2\epsilon)\frac{1}{\bar{\lambda}} \leq \frac{1}{\tilde{\lambda}} \leq (1+2\epsilon)\frac{1}{\bar{\lambda}} \tag{1.92}$$

This allows us to show that $\tilde{\mathbf{f}} = \tilde{\lambda}\mathbf{P}^{-1}\Gamma\tilde{\mathbf{x}}$ does not differ from $\bar{\mathbf{f}} = \bar{\lambda}\mathbf{P}^{-1}\Gamma\bar{\mathbf{x}}$ by too much:

LEMMA A.4.

$$\begin{aligned}||\hat{f}-\bar{f}||_P \leq & \sqrt{(\tilde{f}-\bar{f})^T P(\tilde{f}-\bar{f})} \\ \leq & 4\epsilon\bar{\lambda}^2 \\ = & 4\epsilon\mathcal{E}_{\tilde{f}}(P)\end{aligned} \quad (1.93)$$

Proof

$$\begin{aligned}||\hat{\mathbf{f}}-\bar{\mathbf{f}}||_{\mathbf{P}} = & ||\mathbf{P}^{-1}\Gamma\tilde{\mathbf{x}}-\mathbf{P}^{-1}\Gamma\bar{\mathbf{x}}||_{\mathbf{P}} \\ = & ||\tilde{\mathbf{x}}-\bar{\mathbf{x}}||_{\mathcal{L}} \qquad \text{By definition of } \mathcal{L} \\ \leq & \epsilon||\bar{\mathbf{x}}||_{\mathcal{L}}\end{aligned} \quad (1.94)$$

■(Lemma A.4)

This in turn gives bounds on the maximum entry-difference of $\hat{\mathbf{f}}$ and $\bar{\mathbf{f}}$:

COROLLARY A.5.

$$||\tilde{f}-\bar{f}||_\infty \leq \epsilon\bar{\lambda}$$

Proof Follows from $\mathbf{P} \succeq \mathbf{I}$ and $||\mathbf{v}||_\infty \leq ||\mathbf{v}||_2$ for any vector $\mathbf{v}$. ■(Corollary A.5)

Since $\hat{\mathbf{f}}$ meets the demands at each vertex, the amount that $\hat{\mathbf{f}}$ does not meet the demand by is at most $\epsilon m k\bar{\lambda}$. Lemma A.1 gives that the difference along each edge after running MAKEKIRCHHOFF is at most $\epsilon m^2k^2\bar{\lambda}$. The following two bounds are immediate consequences of this:

1.

$$\begin{aligned}||\tilde{\mathbf{f}}-\bar{\mathbf{f}}||_{\mathbf{P}} \leq & ||\tilde{\mathbf{f}}-\hat{\mathbf{f}}||_{\mathbf{P}} + ||\hat{\mathbf{f}}-\bar{\mathbf{f}}||_{\mathbf{P}} \\ \leq & \epsilon U m^2k^2\bar{\lambda}+\epsilon\bar{\lambda} \qquad \text{Since } \mathbf{P} \preceq U\mathbf{I} \\ \leq & 2\epsilon U^2m^2k^2\bar{\lambda}\end{aligned} \quad (1.95)$$

2.

$$\begin{aligned}|\sqrt{\mathcal{E}_{\tilde{\mathbf{f}}}(\mathbf{P})}-\sqrt{\mathcal{E}_{\bar{\mathbf{f}}}(\mathbf{P})}| = & |||\tilde{\mathbf{f}}||_{\mathbf{P}}-||\bar{\mathbf{f}}||_{\mathbf{P}}| \\ \leq & ||\tilde{\mathbf{f}}-\bar{\mathbf{f}}||_{\mathbf{P}} \leq 2\epsilon U^2m^2k^2\bar{\lambda}\end{aligned} \quad (1.96)$$

Which in turn implies that

$$\sqrt{\mathcal{E}_{\tilde{\mathbf{f}}}(\mathbf{P})} \leq (1+5\epsilon U^2m^2k^2)\sqrt{\mathcal{E}_{\bar{\mathbf{f}}}(\mathbf{P})}$$

When $\epsilon U^2m^2k^2 < 0.01$.

This enables us to derive the overall bound for the L_2 energy difference of the two flows. We first need one more identity about the pointwise difference $|\mathcal{E}_{\tilde{\mathbf{f}}}(\mathbf{P},e)-\mathcal{E}_{\bar{\mathbf{f}}}(\mathbf{P},e)|$. Since $\mathbf{P}(e)$ is positive definite, we may write it as $\mathbf{Q}(e)^T\mathbf{Q}(e)$. Then the difference in energy can be written as:

$$\begin{aligned}&|\mathcal{E}_{\tilde{\mathbf{f}}}(\mathbf{P},e)-\mathcal{E}_{\bar{\mathbf{f}}}(\mathbf{P},e)| \\ =&|||\mathbf{Q}(e)\tilde{\mathbf{f}}(e)||_2^2-||\mathbf{Q}(e)\bar{\mathbf{f}}(e)||_2^2| \\ =&|(\mathbf{Q}(e)\tilde{\mathbf{f}}(e)+\mathbf{Q}(e)\bar{\mathbf{f}}(e))^T(\mathbf{Q}(e)\tilde{\mathbf{f}}(e)-\mathbf{Q}(e)\bar{\mathbf{f}}(e))| \\ &\quad \text{By applying } a^2-b^2=(a+b)(a-b) \text{ entry-wise} \\ \leq&||\mathbf{Q}(e)\tilde{\mathbf{f}}(e)+\mathbf{Q}(e)\bar{\mathbf{f}}(e)||_2||\mathbf{Q}(e)\tilde{\mathbf{f}}(e)-\mathbf{Q}(e)\bar{\mathbf{f}}(e)||_2 \\ &\quad \text{by the Cauchy-Schwarz inequality} \\ =&||\tilde{\mathbf{f}}(e)+\bar{\mathbf{f}}(e)||_{\mathbf{P}(e)}||\tilde{\mathbf{f}}(e)-\bar{\mathbf{f}}(e)||_{\mathbf{P}(e)}\end{aligned} \quad (1.97)$$

Since $\mathbf{P}$ is a block diagonal matrix divided by the edges, we have $||\mathbf{v}||_{\mathbf{P}} = \sum_e ||\mathbf{v}(e)||_{\mathbf{P}(e)}$ for any vector $\mathbf{v}$. Therefore:

$$\begin{aligned}&||\tilde{\mathbf{f}}(e)+\bar{\mathbf{f}}(e)||_{\mathbf{P}(e)} \\ \leq&||\tilde{\mathbf{f}}+\bar{\mathbf{f}}||_{\mathbf{P}}\end{aligned} \quad (1.98)$$

$$\begin{aligned}\leq&\sqrt{4\mathcal{E}_{\tilde{\mathbf{f}}}(\mathbf{P})} \\ &\quad \text{since } (a+b)^2 \leq 2(a^2+b^2) \text{ and } \mathcal{E}_{\bar{\mathbf{f}}}(\mathbf{P}) \leq \mathcal{E}_{\tilde{\mathbf{f}}}(\mathbf{P})\end{aligned} \quad (1.99)$$

$$\begin{aligned}&||\tilde{\mathbf{f}}(e)-\bar{\mathbf{f}}(e)||_{\mathbf{P}(e)} \\ \leq&||\tilde{\mathbf{f}}-\bar{\mathbf{f}}||_{\mathbf{P}} \\ \leq&(1+5\epsilon U^2m^2k^2)\bar{\lambda}\end{aligned} \quad (1.100)$$

Combining them gives:

$$\begin{aligned}&|\mathcal{E}_{\tilde{\mathbf{f}}}(\mathbf{P},e)-\mathcal{E}_{\bar{\mathbf{f}}}(\mathbf{P},e)| \\ \leq&\left(5\epsilon U^2m^2k^2\bar{\lambda}\right)\left((1+5\epsilon U^2m^2k^2)\bar{\lambda}\right) \\ \leq&10\epsilon U^2m^2k^2\mathcal{E}_{\tilde{\mathbf{f}}}(\mathbf{P}) \\ &\quad \text{When } 5\epsilon U^2m^2k^2 < 1\end{aligned} \quad (1.101)$$

It can be checked that when $\delta < 0.1$, setting $\epsilon = \frac{\delta}{2m^2k^2U}$ satisfies the condition for the last inequality, as well as bounding the last term by δ. For this setting, we have $\log(1/\epsilon) \leq O(\log(Umk/\delta))$.

■(Theorem 4.7)

B. MAXIMUM WEIGHTED MULTICOMMODITY FLOW

The maximum weighted multicommodity flow problem is a related problem that maximizes $\sum_i \lambda_i\mathcal{F}_i$ for a series of weights $\lambda \in \Re_+^k$, where $\mathcal{F}_i$ is the amount of flow of commodity i that's routed between the demand pairs. In this section we give an overview of how to extend our algorithm to this problem. However, due to space limitations we omit the analysis of errors incurred by the solver.

In our notation, the problem can be formulated as finding flows $\mathbf{f}_1\dots\mathbf{f}_k$ such that $\mathbf{B}\mathbf{f}_i = \mathcal{F}_i\mathbf{d}_i$ and maximizing $\sum_i \lambda_i\mathcal{F}_i$. Furthermore it can be reduced to the decision problem of finding $\mathbf{f}_i$, $\mathcal{F}_i$ such that $\sum_i \mathcal{F}_i = 1$. Note that due to the undirected nature of the flow, we can allow $\mathcal{F}_i$ to be negative since $\lambda_i \geq 0$ means negating the flow of the ith commodity can only improve the overall objective. Once we introduce the k additional variables $\mathcal{F}_1\dots\mathcal{F}_k$, the maximum weighted multicommodity flow problem can be formulated as:

$$\begin{aligned}\text{maximize:} \quad & \sum_i \mathcal{F}_i \\ \text{subject to:} \quad & \sum_{i=1}^k |\mathbf{f}_i(e)| \leq u(e) && \forall e \in E \\ & \mathbf{B}^T\mathbf{f}_i = \mathcal{F}_i\mathbf{d}_i && \forall 1 \leq i \leq k\end{aligned}$$

By binary search and appropriate scaling of $\mathbf{d}_i$, it suffices to check whether there is a solution $(\mathbf{f}, \mathcal{F})$ where $\mathbf{1}^T\mathcal{F} = 1$. Furthermore we can use $\mathbf{D}$ to denote the $kn \times k$ matrix with column i being $\mathbf{d}_i$ extended to all kn vertex/commodity pairs. Then if we let $\mathcal{F}$ denote the vector containing all the flow values, the corresponding quadratically coupled flow problem becomes:

$$\begin{aligned} \text{minimize: } & \mathcal{E}(\mathbf{P}, \mathbf{f}) \\ \text{subject to: } & \Gamma^T \mathbf{f} = \mathbf{D}\mathcal{F} \\ & \mathbf{1}^T \mathcal{F} = 1 \end{aligned}$$

As before, we let $\mathcal{L} = \Gamma^T \mathbf{P} \Gamma$. We now compute the following quantities:

$$\lambda = \frac{1}{\mathbf{1}^T(\mathbf{D}\mathcal{L}^+\mathbf{D})^+\mathbf{1}} \quad (2.102)$$

$$\bar{\mathcal{F}} = \lambda(\mathbf{D}\mathcal{L}^+\mathbf{D})^+\mathbf{1} \quad (2.103)$$

$$\bar{\phi} = \mathcal{L}^+\mathbf{D}\bar{\mathcal{F}} \quad (2.104)$$

$$\bar{\mathbf{f}} = \mathbf{P}^{-1}\Gamma\bar{\phi} \quad (2.105)$$

Note that the matrix $\mathbf{D}\mathcal{L}^+\mathbf{D}$ can be explicitly computed using k^2 solves, and the resulting k-by-k matrix can be inverted using direct methods in $O(k^\omega)$ time. The following lemmas similar to the ones about quadratically coupled flows shown in Section 4 can be checked in an analogous way.

LEMMA B.1.

$$\Gamma^T \bar{\boldsymbol{f}} = \boldsymbol{D}\bar{\mathcal{F}}$$

Proof

$$\begin{aligned} \Gamma^T \bar{\mathbf{f}} &= \Gamma^T \mathbf{P}^{-1} \Gamma \bar{\phi} \\ &= \mathcal{L}\bar{\phi} \\ &= \mathcal{L}\mathcal{L}^+\mathbf{D}\bar{\mathcal{F}} && (2.106) \\ &= \mathbf{D}\bar{\mathcal{F}} && (2.107) \end{aligned}$$

■

LEMMA B.2.

$$\mathcal{E}(\boldsymbol{P}, \bar{\boldsymbol{f}}) = \mathcal{E}(\bar{\phi}) = \lambda$$

Proof

$$\begin{aligned} \mathcal{E}(\mathbf{P}, \bar{\mathbf{f}}) &= \bar{\mathbf{f}}^T \mathbf{P} \bar{\mathbf{f}} \\ &= \bar{\phi}^T \Gamma^T \mathbf{P}^{-1} \mathbf{P} \mathbf{P}^{-1} \Gamma \bar{\phi} \\ &= \bar{\phi}^T \mathcal{L} \bar{\phi} \\ &= \bar{\mathcal{F}} \mathbf{D}^T \mathcal{L}^+ \mathcal{L} \mathcal{L}^+ \mathbf{D} \bar{\mathcal{F}} \\ &= \bar{\mathcal{F}} \mathbf{D}^T \mathcal{L} \mathbf{D} \bar{\mathcal{F}} \\ &= \lambda^2 \mathbf{1}^T (\mathbf{D}\mathcal{L}^+\mathbf{D})^+ (\mathbf{D}^T \mathcal{L} \mathbf{D}) (\mathbf{D}\mathcal{L}^+\mathbf{D})^+ \mathbf{1} \\ &= \lambda^2 \frac{1}{\lambda} = \lambda && (2.108) \end{aligned}$$

■

LEMMA B.3. *For any* $(\boldsymbol{f}, \mathcal{F})$ *pair that satisfies* $\Gamma^T \boldsymbol{f} = \boldsymbol{D}\mathcal{F}$ *and* $\boldsymbol{1}^T \mathcal{F} = 1$, *we have:*

$$\mathcal{E}(\boldsymbol{P}, \boldsymbol{f}) \geq \lambda$$

Proof Since $\mathcal{E}(\bar{\phi}) = \lambda$ by Lemma B.2, it suffices to show $\mathcal{E}(\mathbf{P}, \mathbf{f})\mathcal{E}(\bar{\phi}) \geq \lambda^2$.

$$\begin{aligned} \mathcal{E}(\mathbf{P}, \mathbf{f})\mathcal{E}(\bar{\phi}) &= (\mathbf{f}^T \mathbf{P} \mathbf{f})((\Gamma\bar{\phi})^T \mathbf{P}^{-1} (\Gamma\bar{\phi})) \\ & \qquad \text{By definition of } \mathbf{f} \text{ in Equation 2.105} \\ &\geq (\mathbf{f}^T \Gamma \bar{\phi})^2 \\ & \qquad \text{By Cauchy-Schwarz inequality} \\ &= (\mathcal{F}^T \mathbf{D}^T \bar{\phi})^2 \\ & \qquad \text{Since } \Gamma^T \mathbf{f} = \mathbf{D}\mathcal{F} \\ &= (\mathcal{F}^T \mathbf{D}^T \mathcal{L}^+ \mathbf{D} \bar{\mathcal{F}})^2 \\ & \qquad \text{By definition of } \bar{\phi} \text{ in Equation 2.104} \\ &= (\mathcal{F}^T (\lambda \mathbf{1}))^2 \\ & \qquad \text{By definition of } \bar{\mathcal{F}} \text{ in Equation 2.103} \\ &= \lambda^2 \qquad \text{Since } \mathbf{1}^T \mathcal{F} = 1 && (2.109) \end{aligned}$$

■

It's worth noting that the proof of Lemma 5.2, Part 3, which is crucial for showing an increase in the minimum energy of the quadratically coupled flow, still holds. Specifically, Equations 5.40 and 5.41 adapts readily with the ϕ.

Thus we obtain an analogous result for approximating the maximum weighted multicommodity flow problem:

THEOREM B.4. *Given an instance of the maximum weighted multicommodity flow problem with* k *commodities on a graph with* m *edges and an error parameter* $\epsilon > 0$. *A solution with weight at least* $(1 - \epsilon)$ *of the maximum can be produced in* $\tilde{O}(m^{4/3}\boldsymbol{poly}(k, \epsilon^{-1}))$ *time.*

When the Cut Condition is Enough: A Complete Characterization for Multiflow Problems in Series-Parallel Networks*

Amit Chakrabarti† Lisa Fleischer† Christophe Weibel†‡

ABSTRACT

Let $G = (V, E)$ be a supply graph and $H = (V, F)$ a demand graph defined on the same set of vertices. An assignment of capacities to the edges of G and demands to the edges of H is said to satisfy the *cut condition* if for any cut in the graph, the total demand crossing the cut is no more than the total capacity crossing it. The pair (G, H) is called *cut-sufficient* if for any assignment of capacities and demands that satisfy the cut condition, there is a multiflow routing the demands defined on H within the network with capacities defined on G.

We prove a previous conjecture, which states that when the supply graph G is series-parallel, the pair (G, H) is cut-sufficient if and only if (G, H) does not contain an *odd spindle* as a minor; that is, if it is impossible to contract edges of G and delete edges of G and H so that G becomes the complete bipartite graph $K_{2,p}$, with $p \geq 3$ odd, and H is composed of a cycle connecting the p vertices of degree 2, and an edge connecting the two vertices of degree p. We further prove that if the instance is *Eulerian* — that is, the demands and capacities are integers and the total of demands and capacities incident to each vertex is even — then the multiflow problem has an integral solution. We provide a polynomial-time algorithm to find an integral solution in this case.

In order to prove these results, we formulate properties of tight cuts (cuts for which the cut condition inequality is tight) in cut-sufficient pairs. We believe these properties might be useful in extending our results to planar graphs.

Categories and Subject Descriptors

F.2.2 [**Theory of Computation**]: Analysis of algorithms and problem complexity—*Nonnumerical Algorithms and Problems*

*This work is supported in part by NSF grants CCF-0728869, CCF-1016778, and IIS-0916565. A full version of the article is available at http://arxiv.org/abs/1203.4041.

†Dartmouth College, Computer Science, Hanover NH. {ac,lkf}_AT_cs.dartmouth.edu, christophe.weibel_AT_gmail.com.

‡Now affiliated with Google, Inc.

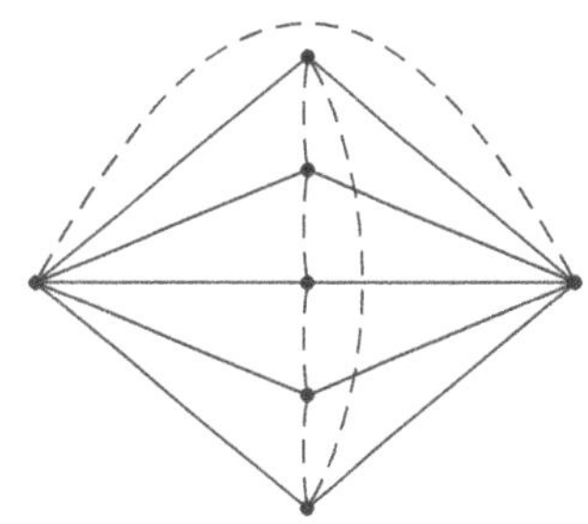

Figure 1: A 5-spindle. Supply edges are solid and demand edges are dashed.

General Terms

Algorithms, Theory

Keywords

Network flows, Series-parallel graphs

1. INTRODUCTION

When does a network admit a flow that satisfies a given collection of point-to-point demands? This broad question has led to a number of important results over the last several decades. The most fundamental of these considers the case of a *single* demand, from a source vertex to a sink vertex. In this case, the network is able to satisfy the demand if and only if for every cut separating the source from the sink, the total capacity of network edges crossing the cut is no less than the demand: this holds regardless of the topology of the network. This is the famous max-flow min-cut theorem, celebrated both for its elegance and its very wide applicability across computer science, graph theory, and operations research.

Things get much more interesting, and intricate, when we generalize to the multicommodity case. It is easy to see that in order to have a flow satisfying all demands, it is necessary that for all cuts the total capacity crossing the cut is no less than the total demand crossing it. This is called the *cut condition*. Unlike in the single-commodity case, this is no longer a sufficient condition in general [14]. This has led to two kinds of generalizations: (1) finding conditions on the topology of the network and/or the structure of the demands that make the cut condition sufficient, and (2) understanding how "far" from sufficient the cut condition can be. We shall discuss both categories of results below, after the necessary basic definitions. The work presented in this paper falls into the first category.

The simplest example demonstrating that the cut condition does not suffice is the network $K_{2,3}$, with unit capacities and unit demand between each pair of non-adjacent vertices. This example has a natural generalization to the network $K_{2,p}$ for odd $p \geq 3$, as suggested by Figure 1. Our main theorem says that for the important class of series-parallel networks, these examples — which we call *odd spindles* — are (in a sense) the *only* ones where the cut condition does not suffice.

The single-commodity flow problem has another nice property that does not extend to the multicommodity case: if the demand and the capacities are integers and the network can satisfy the demand, then it can do so with an *integral* flow. In our work, we show that integral multicommodity flow instances on series-parallel networks that satisfy the cut condition and avoid the above odd spindles admit *half-integral* flows satisfying the demands (in fact, we show a stronger result which implies this; see below). Moreover, for such instances, we give a polynomial time algorithm to compute such a flow.

Basic Definitions and Background.

Given an undirected graph $G = (V, E)$, with capacities c_e on the edges $e \in E$, let $\mathcal{P}$ be the set of simple paths in G. A *multiflow* is an assignment $f : \mathcal{P} \to \mathbb{R}_+$. It is said to be *feasible* if, for each $e \in E$, we have $\sum_{P \in \mathcal{P}(e)} f_P \leq c_e$, where $\mathcal{P}(e)$ is the set of paths in G that contain the edge e. Let $H = (V, F)$ be another graph on the same set of vertices, with demands D_i on the edges $i \in F$. The multiflow f is said to *satisfy* H if for each $i \in F$, we have $\sum_{P \in \mathcal{P}[i]} f_P \geq D_i$, where $\mathcal{P}[i]$ is the set of paths in G between the endpoints of i. The tuple (G, H, c, D) forms an instance of the multiflow (or multicommodity flow) problem, which asks whether there exists a feasible multiflow in G satisfying H; if so, the instance is *routable*. We call G and H the *supply graph* and *demand graph* (respectively) of the instance.

For each set $C \subseteq V$, the *cut* $\delta_G(C)$ generated by C in G is defined to be the set of edges in G with exactly one endpoint in C. We define $\delta_H(C)$ similarly. The *surplus* $\sigma(C)$ of C is the total capacity crossing C minus the total demand crossing it: $\sigma(C) = \sum_{e \in \delta_G(C)} c_e - \sum_{i \in \delta_H(C)} D_i$. The cut condition is then the statement that every cut has nonnegative surplus: $\sigma(C) \geq 0$ for all $C \subseteq V$. As noted above, an instance (G, H, c, D) must satisfy the cut condition in order to be routable. Our goal is to understand when this condition is sufficient.

The graph pair (G, H) is *cut-sufficient* if for all assignments of capacities c and demands D that satisfy the cut condition, the instance (G, H, c, D) is routable. One of the earliest cut-sufficiency theorems is due to Hu [7] and states that (G, H) is cut-sufficient if H is the union of two stars, i.e., if all of its edges can be covered by two vertices. Notice that this theorem applies to a general G, but it greatly restricts H. Network flow literature abounds with other cut-sufficiency theorems [7, 11, 13, 14, 16, 18, 19]. Many of these impose conditions on both G and H; a well-known example is the Okamura-Seymour Theorem, which states that a pair (G, H) is cut-sufficient if G is planar and all edges of H have their endpoints on a single face of G [14]. Schrijver [17, Chapter 70] surveys several cut-sufficiency theorems and many related concepts and topics.

Our Contributions.

We give a sharp characterization of cut-sufficient graph pairs where the supply graph is *series-parallel*. Further, for integral multiflow instances on such cut-sufficient pairs, we show that the cut condition together with a natural "Eulerian" condition imply that a feasible integral solution exists; we also give a polynomial time algorithm to find an integral solution. Finally, our work here suggests to us a conjecture that would characterize cut-sufficiency in *planar* graphs. The details follow.

We define a *p-spindle* to be a pair of graphs (G, H) such that the supply graph G is $K_{2,p}$, with $p \geq 3$, and the demand graph H consists of a cycle connecting the p vertices of degree 2 in G, and an additional demand edge between the two remaining vertices. An *odd spindle* is a p-spindle with p odd.

THEOREM 1.1 (FRACTIONAL ROUTING; CUT-SUFFICIENCY). *If the supply graph G is series-parallel, then the pair (G, H) is cut-sufficient if and only if the pair (G, H) cannot be reduced to an odd spindle by contraction of edges of G and deletion of edges of G and H.*

Schrijver [17, Section 70.11] gives a number of sufficient conditions for cut-sufficiency; our characterization above is sharper than all of these when G is series-parallel. The above result was conjectured in Chekuri et al. [3, Conjecture 3.5]. To prove it, we first revisit the connection between multiflow problems and metric embeddings via linear programming duality. Unlike previous works that used this approach, we exploit *complementary slackness* to derive some LP-based conditions for cut-sufficiency, in Section 3. These conditions do not refer to the structure of G, and so could be useful in extending our results from series-parallel graphs to more general classes. The proof of Theorem 1.1 itself appears in Section 4.

We say that an instance (G, H, c, D) is *Eulerian* if all capacities c_e and demands D_i are integers and $\sigma(C)$ is even for all $C \subseteq V$; recall that σ depends on c and D.

THEOREM 1.2 (INTEGRAL ROUTING). *If G is series-parallel, (G, H) is cut-sufficient, and the multiflow instance (G, H, c, D) satisfies the cut condition and is Eulerian, then the problem has an integral solution. Moreover, under these conditions, an integral solution can be computed in polynomial time.*

This implies that under the same assumptions except for the Eulerian condition, the multiflow problem has a half-integral solution. Similar uses of the Eulerian condition are ubiquitous in the literature [13, 14, 16]. We prove the above result in Section 5. The algorithm is described in Section 5.1.

Planar supply graphs allow one other obstruction to cut-sufficiency, beside the odd spindles. We conjecture, in Section 6, that there are no further examples: this would extend our results to planar G.

Other Related Work.

A different approach to the relation between multiflows and cuts was pioneered by Leighton and Rao [9], who asked how "far" from sufficient the cut condition could be. To be precise, let the *minimum congestion* of a multiflow instance (G, H, c, D) be the smallest $\alpha \geq 1$ such that $(G, H, \alpha c, D)$ is routable. For a pair of graphs (G, H), the *flow-cut gap* is the maximum, over all choices of demands and capacities that satisfy the cut condition, of the minimum congestion. The larger this gap the further the pair (G, H) is from cut-sufficiency. Clearly, a pair is cut-sufficient if and only if its flow-cut gap is 1.

There has been intense research on finding the flow-cut gaps for various classes of graphs, a line of work originally motivated by the problem of approximating sparsest cuts [1, 2, 5, 6, 10]. The class of series-parallel instances is notable, as it is one of the very few classes for which there are precise bounds on the flow-cut gap: Chakrabarti et al. [2] show that the gap cannot be more than 2, whereas Lee and Raghavendra [8] show that it can be as close to 2 as desired. Chekuri et al. [4] show that series-parallel instances have *integral multiflows* that do not use more than 5 times the capacity of the supply graph. A special case of the integer multiflow problem is the *disjoint paths problem*, where $D_i = 1$ for all i and

$c_e = 1$ for all e. In general, the disjoint paths problem is NP-complete even when restricted to series-parallel graphs [12].

The seminal work of Linial et al. [10] connected flow-cut gaps to metric embeddings via LP duality: we now briefly explain this connection, which we also use in our work. Every positive length function l on the edges of a graph determines a *shortest-path metric*, which is a distance function d on the vertices of the graph, such that $d(u,v) = \min_{P \in \mathcal{P}[u,v]} \sum_{e \in P} l_e$; here $\mathcal{P}[u,v]$ denotes the set of paths between the vertices u and v. Every assignment of non-negative real values x_C to subsets C of vertices of a graph determines a *cut-cone metric*, which is a distance function d on the vertices of the graph defined by $d(u,v) = \sum_{C:|\{u,v\} \cap C|=1} x_C$. For any two distance functions d and d' defined on the vertices of a graph such that $d \geq d'$, the *distortion* from d to d' is defined to be $\max_{u \neq v} d(u,v)/d'(u,v)$. For a distance function d and a family of metrics $\mathcal{M}$, the minimum distortion embedding of d into $\mathcal{M}$ is a distance function d' in $\mathcal{M}$ that minimizes the distortion from d to d'. Linial et al. [10] show that the maximum congestion required for a particular supply graph G equals the maximum distortion required to embed any possible shortest-path metric on G into the family of cut-cone metrics.[1] We shall call this the *congestion-distortion equivalence* theorem.

Organization.

We give all major steps of our proofs in this extended abstract, omitting proofs of technical lemmas. A stand-alone full version of the paper that spells out all details appears as an appendix.

2. DEFINITIONS AND PRELIMINARIES

A subset of vertices $C \subseteq V$ and the corresponding cut $\delta_G(C)$ are called *central* if both C and $V \setminus C$ are connected in G. It is well-known and easy to prove that if the surplus σ is nonnegative for all central cuts, then the cut condition is satisfied [17, Theorem 70.4]. A subset C and the cut $\delta_G(C)$ are *tight* if $\sigma(C) = 0$.

We assume that the supply graph G is biconnected (otherwise the multiflow problem can be solved separately on its biconnected components). A biconnected graph is *series-parallel* if and only if it does not contain K_4 as a minor. A pair of graphs (G,H) is series-parallel if the supply graph G is series-parallel.

We use an extension of graph minors to pairs (G,H) of supply and demand graph, as proposed in [4]. Let (G,H) and (G',H') be two pairs of graphs. Then (G',H') is a *minor* of (G,H) if we can obtain (G',H') from (G,H) by contracting and deleting edges of G, and deleting edges of H. Here, *deleting* an edge means removing it, and *contracting* an edge means removing it and merging its endpoints.

For disjoint subsets $X, Y \subseteq V$, let $\delta_G(X,Y)$ and $\delta_H(X,Y)$ be the set of edges in G, respectively H, with one endpoint in X and one in Y, and let $\sigma(X,Y) := \sum_{e \in \delta_G(X,Y)} c_e - \sum_{e \in \delta_H(X,Y)} D_i$. In particular, $\sigma(X, V \setminus X) = \sigma(X)$. The surplus function σ satisfies the following useful identities (proofs appear in Section B, in the appendix).

LEMMA 2.1. *Let A and B be two subsets of V. Then*
(a) If $B_1, \ldots, B_k$ is a partition of B, then $\sigma(A,B) = \sigma(A,B_1) + \cdots + \sigma(A,B_k)$.
(b) In particular, if $B = V \setminus A$, then $\sigma(A) = \sigma(A,B_1) + \cdots + \sigma(A,B_k)$.
(c) $\sigma(A \cup B) + \sigma(A \cap B) = \sigma(A) + \sigma(B) - 2\sigma(A \setminus B, B \setminus A)$.
(d) $\sigma(A \setminus B) + \sigma(B \setminus A) = \sigma(A) + \sigma(B) - 2\sigma(A \cap B, V \setminus (A \cup B))$.
(e) In particular, if A and B are disjoint, then $\sigma(A \cup B) = \sigma(A) + \sigma(B) - 2\sigma(A,B)$.

[1] It is a simple exercise to show that the family of cut-cone metrics coincides with that of ℓ_1-embeddable metrics.

3. PROOF OF CONGESTION-DISTORTION EQUIVALENCE VIA LP DUALITY AND CONSEQUENCES

We now give our new proof of the congestion-distortion equivalence theorem (see Section 1), using only basic notions of linear programming duality. Our proof will reveal several additional relations between LP variables that are useful later: in particular, they give us cut-sufficiency conditions based on certain LP variables. The starting point of the proof is a well-known fact: multiflows are tightly related to metrics, because the dual of the LP expressing a multiflow problem can be interpreted as the problem of finding a certain graph metric.

The proof via LP duality.

Fix a "supply graph" $G = (V,E)$ and a "demand graph" $H = (V,F)$. The crux of the proof is to identify a certain nonlinear maximization problem (+) in variables $c = \{c_e\}_{e \in E}$, $D = \{D_i\}_{i \in F}$, $l = \{l_e\}_{e \in E}$, and $d = \{d_i\}_{i \in F}$ that has the following two properties. First, for each setting of c and D satisfying the cut condition, the program (+) reduces to a maximization LP whose dual is the problem of finding the minimum congestion for the multiflow problem (G,H,c,D). Second, for each setting of l and d satisfying certain metric inequalities, the program (+) reduces to a different maximization LP whose dual is the problem of finding the minimum distortion embedding, into the family of cut-cone metrics, of the metric given by l and d. It follows that the maximum possible congestion over all capacity/demand settings equals the maximum possible distortion over all length settings. We now give the details.

For each $i \in F$, let $\{P^i_1, P^i_2, \ldots\}$ be a listing of $\mathcal{P}[i]$, the set of simple paths in G connecting the endpoints of the demand i. The minimum congestion for the multiflow instance (G,H,c,D) can be written as an LP, presented below with it dual. *In this section, all boldface characters represent non-negative variables.*

$$\begin{array}{llcll} \min & \alpha & & & \\ s.t. & \sum_j \mathbf{f^i_j} & \geq & D_i & \forall i \in F \\ & \sum_{i,j:\, e \in P^i_j} \mathbf{f^i_j} & \leq & c_e \alpha & \forall e \in E \end{array} \qquad \text{(P)}$$

$$\begin{array}{llcll} \max & \sum_i D_i \mathbf{d_i} & & & \\ s.t. & \sum_e c_e \mathbf{l_e} & = & 1 & \\ & \mathbf{d_i} & \leq & \sum_{e \in P^i_j} \mathbf{l_e} & \forall i,j \end{array} \qquad \text{(D)}$$

Here, $\mathbf{f^i_j}$ is the variable indicating the amount routed on path P^i_j, $\mathbf{l_e}$ can be thought of as the *length* of edge e in G, and $\mathbf{d_i}$ as the *distance* between the endpoints of i. The second set of constraints in (D) are *metric inequalities*, which ensure that $\mathbf{d_i}$ is no more than the shortest-path distance between the endpoints of i induced by the lengths $\mathbf{l_e}$. Let $z(c,D)$ be the optimal value to (P) and (D).

In order to find the flow-cut gap of a pair (G,H), we need to find the maximum value to (P) (and (D)) over all choices of capacities c and demands D that satisfy the cut condition, which can be expressed as

$$\max z(\mathbf{c},\mathbf{D}) \quad s.t. \quad \sum_{i \in \delta_H(C)} \mathbf{D_i} \leq \sum_{e \in \delta_G(C)} \mathbf{c_e} \quad \forall C \subseteq V \qquad (1)$$

Since the linear program (D) is a maximization problem, we can write the problem of finding the flow-cut gap as a single maximization problem on variables $\mathbf{c}$, $\mathbf{D}$, $\mathbf{l}$ and $\mathbf{d}$:

$$\begin{array}{lrcll} \max \sum_i \mathbf{D_i}\mathbf{d_i} \quad s.t. & \sum_e \mathbf{c_e}\mathbf{l_e} & = & 1 & \\ & \mathbf{d_i} & \leq & \sum_{e \in P^i_j} \mathbf{l_e} & \forall i,j \\ & \sum_{i \in \delta_H(C)} \mathbf{D_i} & \leq & \sum_{e \in \delta_G(C)} \mathbf{c_e} & \forall C \subseteq V \end{array} \qquad (+)$$

This is not a linear program, since some of the variables multiply each other. However, there are two ways we can transform it into a linear program by setting some variables to be parameters. If we fix $\mathbf{c_e}$ for all e and $\mathbf{D_i}$ for all i to be parameters that satisfy the cut condition, we obtain the linear program (D). But if we fix $\mathbf{l_e}$ for all e and $\mathbf{d_i}$ for all i to be parameters that satisfy the metric inequalities, we find a different linear program in variables $\mathbf{c_e}$ and $\mathbf{D_i}$, presented in (D′), with its dual below in (P′):

$$\begin{array}{llcll} \max & \sum_i d_i \mathbf{D_i} & & & \\ s.t. & \sum_e l_e \mathbf{c_e} & = & 1 & \\ & \sum_{i\in\delta_H(C)} \mathbf{D_i} & \leq & \sum_{e\in\delta_G(C)} \mathbf{c_e} & \forall C \subseteq V \end{array} \quad (\mathrm{D}')$$

$$\begin{array}{llcll} \min & \gamma & & & \\ s.t. & \sum_{C:i\in\delta_H(C)} \mathbf{x_C} & \geq & d_i & \forall i \in F \\ & \sum_{C:e\in\delta_G(C)} \mathbf{x_C} & \leq & l_e\gamma & \forall e \in E, \end{array} \quad (\mathrm{P}')$$

Let $w(l,d)$ be the optimal value to (P′) and (D′). The flow-cut gap problem (1) and (+) is then equal to

$$\max w(\mathbf{l},\mathbf{d}) \quad s.t. \quad \mathbf{d_i} \leq \sum_{e\in P^i_j} \mathbf{l_e} \quad \forall i,j \qquad (2)$$

The system (P′) has a variable $\mathbf{x_C}$ for each subset $C \subsetneq V$. The values of these variables define a cut-cone metric; call it d'. The first constraint says that the d'-length of an edge e is at most γ times its "true" length l_e. The second constraint says that the d'-distance between the endpoints of a demand i is at least d_i, which, for l and d achieving the maximum in (2), equals the "true" distance given by l. Thus, (P′) can be seen as approximating (at least between endpoints of demands) the shortest-path metric induced by l by a cut-cone metric, within an approximation factor γ as small as possible.

As a clean special case, when H is a complete graph on V, then $d_e = l_e$ for each edge e, and thus the two constraints in (P′) say (respectively) that $d \geq d'/\gamma$ and that the distortion from d to d'/γ is at most γ. Thus, d embeds into the family of cut-cone metrics with distortion at most γ. The equivalence of (1), (+), and (2) means that the flow-cut gap of (G,H) is equal to the minimum distortion required to embed an arbitrary shortest-path metric defined on G into the family of cut-cone metrics. This completes the proof of the congestion-distortion equivalence, entirely through basic notions of linear programming.

Implications of the new proof.

Suppose that, for some pair of graphs (G,H), with $G = (V,E)$, $H = (V,F)$, we have an optimal solution (c^*, D^*, l^*, d^*) to the non-linear program (+). By the properties of linear programming duality, there are solutions f^* and x^* to the flow problem (P) and the cut metric problem (P′) that satisfy complementary slackness. We call $(c^*, D^*, l^*, d^*, f^*, x^*)$ a *general solution* to the pair (G,H).

LEMMA 3.1. *A general solution satisfies the following properties.*
$\langle a\rangle$ *If* $x^*_C > 0$, *then* $\sum_{i\in\delta_H(C)} D^*_i = \sum_{e\in\delta_G(C)} c^*_e$. *Thus, only tight cuts have positive x-value in (P′).*
$\langle b\rangle$ *If* $f^{i*}_j > 0$ *then* $d^*_i = \sum_{e\in P^i_j} l^*_e$; *and for each i with* $D^*_i > 0$, *there is a path* P^i_{j*} *for which this is true.*

LEMMA 3.2. *There is a solution* x^* *to the problem* (P′) *such that only central cuts have a positive x-value.*

We assume from now on that in a general solution, if $x^*_C > 0$ then C is central. We define a *simple pair* to be a pair (G,H) that has a general solution such that $c^*_e > 0$ and $l^*_e > 0$ for each e, and $D^*_i > 0$ for each i.

LEMMA 3.3. *For each pair* (G,H), *there is a simple pair with the same flow-cut gap.*

LEMMA 3.4. *Let* (G,H) *be a simple pair with general solution* $(c^*, D^*, l^*, d^*, f^*, x^*)$. *Then*

$$\forall\, i \in F\ \forall\, P \in \mathcal{P}[i] \ :\ \sum_{C:i\in\delta_H(C)} x^*_C = d^*_i \leq \sum_{e\in P} l^*_e = \frac{1}{\gamma^*}\sum_{e\in P}\sum_{C:e\in\delta_G(C)} x^*_C, \qquad (3)$$

with equality if P is a shortest path for the shortest-path metric defined by l^*.

By Lemma 3.1$\langle b\rangle$, in the metric defined by x^*, for each path P^i_j with $f^{i*}_j > 0$, the ratio between the sum of lengths of edges in the path and the distance between endpoints of the path is equal to the flow-cut gap.

THEOREM 3.5. *Let* (G,H) *be a simple pair with general solution* $(c^*, D^*, l^*, d^*, f^*, x^*)$. *Suppose there exist* $i \in F$ *and* $P \in \mathcal{P}[i]$ *such that P crosses each tight cut at most once. Then* (G,H) *is cut-sufficient.*

PROOF. Pick a tight set $C \subsetneq V$. If $i \notin \delta_H(C)$, then P must not cross C; otherwise P must cross C exactly once. By Lemma 3.1$\langle a\rangle$, only tight cuts may have non-zero x^*-values. This implies that $\sum_{C:i\in\delta_H(C)} x^*_C = \sum_{e\in P}\sum_{C:e\in\delta_G(C)} x^*_C$. In view of Lemma 3.4, this means that

$$\gamma \sum_{C:i\in\delta_H(C)} x^*_C \leq \sum_{e\in P}\sum_{C:e\in\delta_G(C)} x^*_C = \sum_{C:i\in\delta_H(C)} x^*_C.$$

Since the pair (G,H) is simple, each l^*_e is non-zero and thus, so is $\sum_{C:i\in\delta_H(C)} x^*_C$. It follows that $\gamma = 1$ and the flow-cut gap is one, as claimed. ☐

4. PROOF OF THE FRACTIONAL ROUTING THEOREM

In this section, we prove Theorem 1.1. Namely, for series-parallel graphs G, we show that the pair (G,H) is cut-sufficient if and only if it does not contain an odd spindle as a minor. The following special case of this theorem was proven earlier in Chekuri et al. [3], and we use it in our proof.

THEOREM 4.1 ([3, SECTION 3.3]). *Suppose G is* $K_{2,m}$, *with possibly one more supply edge between the two vertices not of degree 2. Then* (G,H) *is cut-sufficient iff it does not contain an odd spindle as a minor.*

The "only if" direction of Theorem 1.1 is easy, and is proven in Section 3.3 of [3] and in our full paper. We now prove the "if" direction. Suppose the pair (G,H) has flow-cut gap more than 1. By Lemma 3.3, we may assume that (G,H) is simple. For a demand (u,v), a *bubble* for (u,v) is a central set defining a tight cut, but containing neither u nor v. The set $\mathcal{P}[u,v]$ (of paths in G between u and v) is *covered by bubbles* if every path in it crosses a bubble at least once. From Theorem 3.5, and a parity argument, we get the following:

OBSERVATION 4.2. *If* $P \in \mathcal{P}[u,v]$ *does not cross any bubble, then P crosses some tight cut* $t > 1$ *times, where t is odd.* ☐

To prove Theorem 1.1, we first prove that if there is a demand (u,v) such that $\mathcal{P}[u,v]$ is covered by bubbles, then the instance must contain an odd spindle as a minor (Lemma 4.3). We then prove that there must be such a demand (Lemma 4.7).

LEMMA 4.3. *If there is a demand* (u,v) *such that* $\mathcal{P}[u,v]$ *is covered by bubbles, then the instance must contain an odd spindle as a minor.*

Proof. Let $F_{u,v}$ be a minimal family of bubbles covering all simple paths from u to v. If $F_{u,v} = \{B\}$ for a bubble B, then the vertices u and v are in different connected components of $V \setminus B$. This contradicts the fact that B is central. Therefore, we have the following two cases: $|F_{u,v}| \geq 3$, or $|F_{u,v}| = 2$. The proof proceeds using a sequence of claims.

Claim 4.4. *If $|F_{u,v}| \geq 3$, then the bubbles in $F_{u,v}$ are disjoint, with no supply edges between them.*

Proof. For each bubble in $F_{u,v}$, there is a path crossing it that does not cross any other bubble in $F_{u,v}$ (otherwise we could remove that bubble and $F_{u,v}$ would not be minimal). Suppose bubbles A and B intersect. Let P_A, P_B be the paths through A and B respectively. Consider $p \in A \cap B$. Since A and B are both connected, there is a path in A from a node in $P_A \cap A$ to p and a path in B from $P_B \cap B$ to p. This creates a K_4 minor with any third path from u to v, which exists since $|F_{u,v}| \geq 3$, contradicting the series-parallelness of G; and so A and B do not intersect. If there is an edge connecting the bubbles A and B, there is again a path in $A \cup B$ connecting P_A to P_B, which again creates a K_4 minor. ☐

We contract every edge that does not cross a cut defined by a bubble in $F_{u,v}$. We get a vertex f_i for each bubble, a vertex u' for the part of G reachable from u without crossing the bubbles, and a vertex v' for the part reachable from v without crossing the bubbles. The contracted supply graph is a $K_{2,m}$. Each degree-2 vertex f_i, being a contraction of a tight set, defines a tight cut. So in any fractional solution to the contracted instance, the two supply edges leaving f_i have just enough capacity to route the demands incident to f_i, and no flow can go from u' to v' through f_i. Since there is a demand from u' to v', this means that the instance has no solution, and therefore, by Theorem 4.1, it contains an odd spindle as a minor.

This finishes the case $|F_{u,v}| \geq 3$. We are left with the case $F_{u,v} = \{A, B\}$, for distinct bubbles A, B.

Claim 4.5. *If $F_{u,v} = \{A, B\}$, for distinct bubbles A, B, then A and B intersect.*

Proof. Let R be the connected component of $V \setminus (A \cup B)$ containing v. Let $X = A \cup R$ and $Y = B \cup R$. Suppose A and B are disjoint. Then $X \cap Y = R$.

Now $\sigma(X \setminus Y) = \sigma(A) = 0$, and $\sigma(Y \setminus X) = \sigma(B) = 0$. By Lemma 2.1$\langle d \rangle$, we have $\sigma(X) + \sigma(Y) = \sigma(X \setminus Y) + \sigma(Y \setminus X) + 2\sigma(X \cap Y, V \setminus (X \cup Y)) < 0$, because $\sigma(X \cap Y, V \setminus (X \cup Y))$ includes the demand (u, v) and $X \cap Y = R$ which is disconnected from the rest of the graph by A and B. However, by the cut condition, $\sigma(X) \geq 0$ and $\sigma(Y) \geq 0$, a contradiction. Therefore A and B intersect. ☐

Claim 4.6. *If we contract every edge of G that is neither in $\delta_G(A)$, nor in $\delta_G(B)$, and merge parallel edges, we get a $K_{2,m}$, with possibly one extra supply edge connecting the two vertices not of degree 2.*

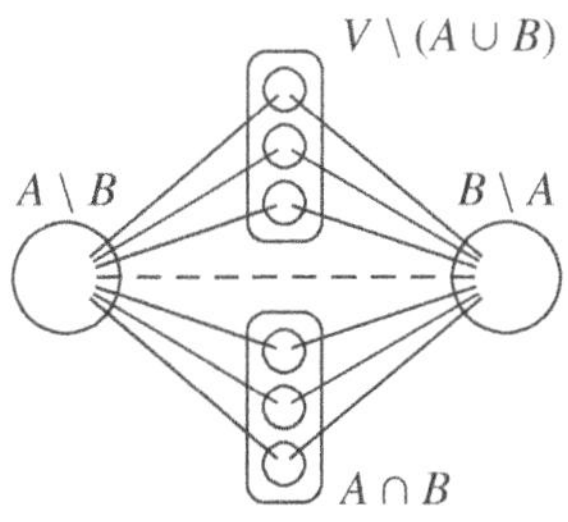

Proof. It is possible to prove that $A \setminus B$ and $B \setminus A$ are connected. The rest of the graph is composed of $A \cap B$, which has at least one connected component by Claim 4.5, and $V \setminus (A \cup B)$, which has at least two connected components containing u and v respectively. There is an edge connecting $A \setminus B$ to each connected component of $A \cap B$ (because both are in A, which is central), and there is an edge connecting $A \setminus B$ to each connected component of $V \setminus (A \cup B)$ (because neither is in B, which is central). Similarly, there is an edge connecting $B \setminus A$ to each connected component of $A \cap B$ and $V \setminus (A \cup B)$. This implies that for each connected component of $A \cap B$ and $V \setminus (A \cup B)$, there is a path connecting $A \setminus B$ to $B \setminus A$ through that component. As a consequence, there is never an edge going from a connected component of $A \cap B$ to a connected component of $V \setminus (A \cup B)$, because this would create a K_4 with $A \setminus B$ and $B \setminus A$, which are also connected through at least another connected component of $V \setminus (A \cup B)$. ☐

Let us perform the contraction described in Claim 4.6. The demand edge (u, v) remains, and its endpoints are still separated by tight sets A and B. So the contracted instance is not routable, even though it satisfies the cut condition; i.e., it is not cut-sufficient. But since the contracted supply graph is a $K_{2,m}$, Theorem 4.1 implies that the contracted pair contains an odd spindle as a minor. Therefore, so does the original pair (G, H). We are now done with the case $|F_{u,v}| = 2$. *This completes the proof of Lemma 4.3.*

The next lemma states that the conditions of Lemma 4.3 are satisfied. In order to prove this, we need to introduce some terminology (more details in Section B.2). In a biconnected series-parallel graph G, a pair of vertices (s, t) is a *split pair* if the graph G remains series-parallel after adding an edge from s to t, and if (s, t) is a split pair, there is a unique way to *orient* the edges of G so that any simple path from s to t is oriented from s to t. For any orientation of G defined by a split pair (s, t), a pair (u, v) is *non-compliant* if there is no oriented path from u to v. If (u, v) is non-compliant, then there is a unique pair (w, z) of *terminals of* (u, v) such that any cycle containing u and v is composed of two oriented paths from w to z. For any orientation of G defined by a split pair (s, t), a pair of vertices (w, z) is said to *bracket* another pair (u, v) if there is an oriented path from w to z containing u and v. If (w, z) brackets (u, v) but $w \neq u$ or $z \neq v$, then (w, z) *strictly brackets* (u, v). Since the orientation is acyclic, the bracketing relation defines a partial order.

Lemma 4.7. *If a simple pair (G, H) has flow-cut gap greater than 1, then there is a demand (u, v) such that $\mathcal{P}[u, v]$ is covered by bubbles.*

Proof. We choose an arbitrary split pair in graph G, and orient G accordingly. By Theorem 3.1 of [4], there must exist a non-compliant demand. Let (u, v) be a non-compliant demand such that its pair of terminals does not strictly bracket the pair of terminals of any other non-compliant demand. This is always possible, since in the set of pairs of terminals, the bracket relation is a partial order and must have a minimal pair. Suppose $\mathcal{P}[u, v]$ is *not* covered by bubbles. We shall demonstrate a contradiction with our choice of (u, v).

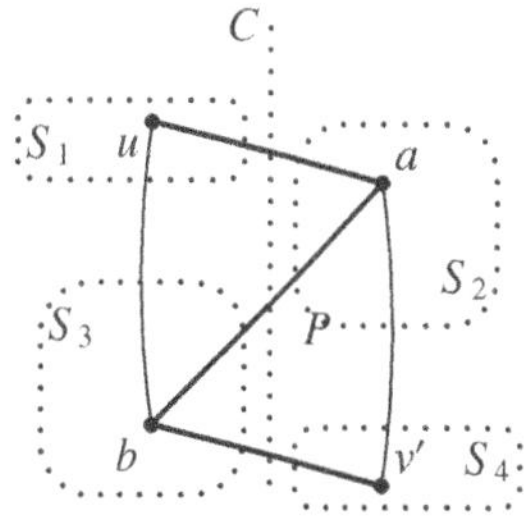

Let $P_1, \ldots, P_k$ be the paths in $\mathcal{P}[u, v]$ not covered by any bubble. For each $j \in \{1, \ldots, k\}$, let C_j be the set of tight cuts that P_j crosses an odd number of times, three or more, and let m_j be the sum over all cuts $C' \in C_j$ of the number of times that P_j crosses C'. By Observation 4.2, each C_j is nonempty. We choose a path $P = P_j$ such that m_j is minimal. Let C be a cut in C_j (therefore P crosses C at least three times), and let S_1, S_2, S_3 and S_4 be the first four connected components in order of $P \setminus \delta_G(C)$, with $S_1, S_3 \subseteq C$ (see figure). Since C is central, S_1 and S_3 are connected by a path P_{13} inside of C, and S_2 and S_4 are connected by a path P_{24} outside of C. Let a be the endpoint of P_{24} in S_2, let b be the endpoint of P_{13} in S_3, and let v' be the endpoint of P_{24} in S_4. Note that there are three vertex-disjoint paths from a to b, and so (a, b) is a 2-vertex-cut separating u from v', for otherwise G would have a K_4 minor.

The proof proceeds using a sequence of claims. The following arguments use C, u and b, but apply symmetrically to $V \setminus C$, v' and a.

Claim 4.8. *Any path from u to b inside C must cross some tight cut at least twice.*

Recall that (a, b) is a 2-vertex-cut separating u from v'. Let S_u and S_v be the connected components of $V \setminus \{a, b\}$ containing u and v'. Let $S_u^* = S_u \cup \{a, b\}$ and $S_v^* = S_v \cup \{a, b\}$. For $S, C \subseteq V$ and vertices $u, b \in C$, we say that S *separates u from b inside C* if u and b are in two different connected components of $C \setminus S$.

Claim 4.9. *There is a 2-vertex-cut (x, y) in S_u^*, with $|\{x, y\} \cap \{a, b\}| \leq 1$, with two vertex-disjoint paths Q_1, Q_2 from x to y, with $a, b \notin (Q_1 \cup Q_2) \setminus \{x, y\}$, and a demand i from $Q_1 \setminus \{x, y\}$ to $Q_2 \setminus \{x, y\}$.*

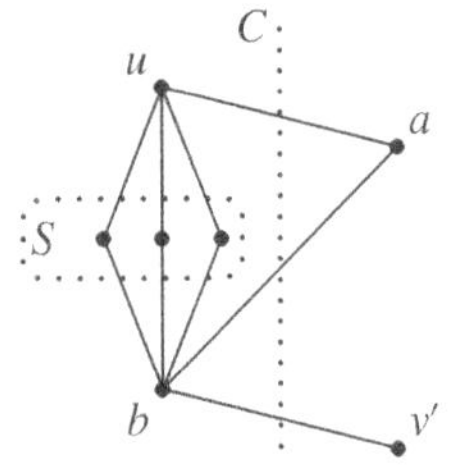

Proof. We present an outline of the proof. Since C is central, u and b are connected inside C, and by Claim 4.8, any path from u to b crosses some tight cut at least twice more than P. Either there is a single tight cut crossed by all such paths, or there is not. We leave the first case to the appendix, and prove the second one. For every path connecting u to b inside C, we choose a tight cut crossed twice, and we contract all edges of the path that do not cross that tight cut. Each of the paths now has two edges. Let S denote the set of vertices in the middle of these paths. There are no supply edges from a vertex in S to any vertex except u or b because that would create a K_4 minor. Since every path from u to b crosses some central tight cut twice, every vertex in S defines a bubble separating u from b inside C. The supply graph induced by u, b and vertices in S is a $K_{2,m}$. By assumption, there is no single tight cut crossed twice by all paths, so $\sigma(S) > 0$, even though every vertex in S defines a tight cut. And so, by Lemma 2.1$\langle e \rangle$, there must exist demands between vertices of S. ☐

Note that Claim 4.9 also applies to S_v^*, and so there is in S_v^* a 2-cut (x', y'), with two vertex-disjoint paths from x' to y', and a demand i' connecting these two paths (see Figure 2). Recall that (s, t) is a split pair. Since (a, b) is a 2-vertex-cut connected by three disjoint paths, s and t cannot be in different connected components of $V \setminus \{a, b\}$, because otherwise an (s, t) edge would create a K_4. So at least one of S_u or S_v contains neither s nor t.

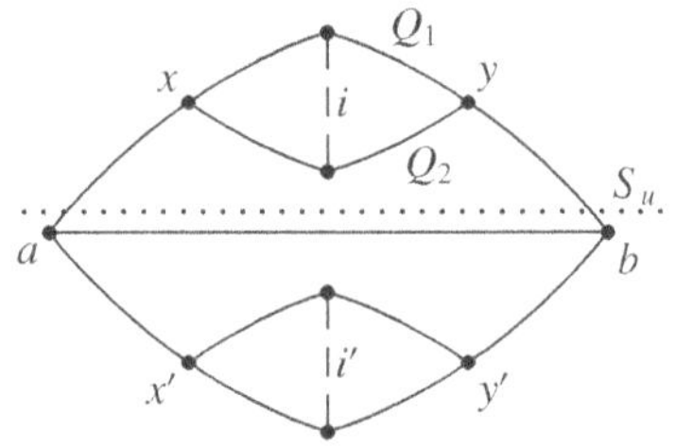

Figure 2: Subgraph of relations of the 2-vertex-cut (a, b), (x, y) and (x', y'). One of x or y (x' or y') may be a or b, but not both. The demands i and i' are dashed.

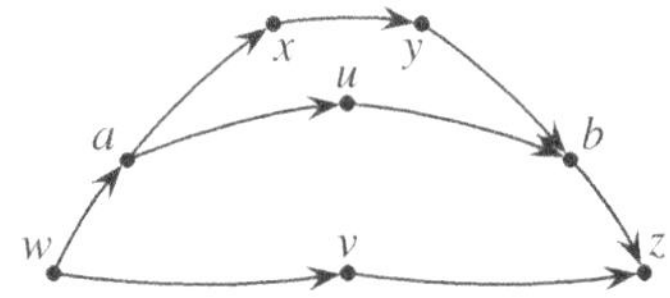

Figure 3: Relative positions of w, z, a, b, x, y, u and v. Possibly, $w = a$ or $z = b$. Vertex u may (but needn't) be on the a–b path containing x and y.

Claim 4.10. *Suppose S_u contains neither s nor t. Then i is non-compliant; the pair (x, y) which separates its endpoints is its pair of terminals, and this pair of terminals is strictly bracketed by the pair (w, z) of terminals of (u, v).*

Proof. Recall that G is biconnected. It follows that for any $v' \in S_u$, there is a simple path from s to t containing v', so there is a simple path from s to t that goes through S_u, and so contains a and b. Without loss of generality, assume that the path meets a before b on the way from s to t. Since the orientation is acyclic, there is no simple s-to-t path that meets b before a. Each edge in G is oriented in the direction it appears on any simple s-to-t path, so each edge in S_u^* is oriented in the direction it appears on any simple a-to-b path. So a is the unique source in S_u^*, and b the unique sink. Any simple path from a to b through an endpoint of i contains x and y, and does not contain the other endpoint of i. So i is a non-compliant demand, and (x, y) is its pair of terminals, which is bracketed by (a, b). Note that (x, y) is not the same as (a, b).

We prove that (a, b) is bracketed by the pair (w, z) of terminals of (u, v), which means that (x, y) is bracketed by (w, z). By the properies of biconnected series-parallel graphs, any cycle C containing u and v also contains the terminals w and z of the demand (u, v), and is composed of two oriented paths from one terminal to the other, say from w to z, and w is the unique source of C and z its unique sink. The cycle C must contain a and b since (a, b) is a 2-vertex-cut separating u from v. Since any simple path from a to b in S_u^* is oriented from a to b, the part of C in S_u^* is oriented from a to b. So neither w nor z is in S_u, because then they would not be source or sink of C. So C contains a path Q from w to z through u, and Q contains a and b; so (a, b) is bracketed by (w, z). So (x, y) is bracketed by (w, z). ☐

Since at least one of S_u and S_v contains neither s nor t, at least one of (x, y) and (x', y') is bracketed by (w, z), contradicting our choice of (u, v). *This completes the proof of Lemma 4.7.*

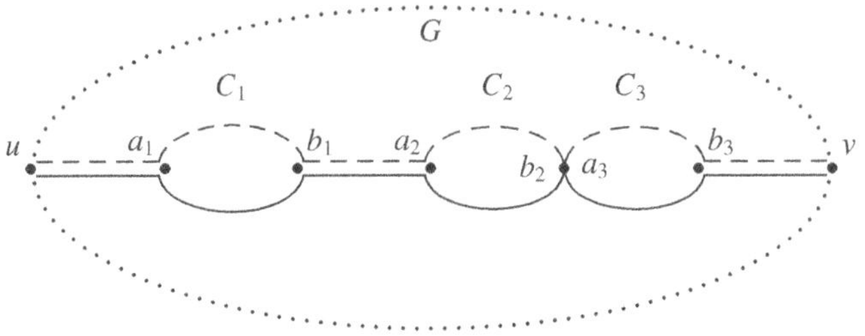

Figure 4: Illustration of the planar embedding with u and v on the outside face. The dotted cycle represents the outside face of G, the paths P_1 is in solid, and the path P_k in dashed.

5. INTEGRALLY ROUTABLE SERIES-PARALLEL INSTANCES

In this section, we prove Theorem 1.2. Since an instance that does not satisfy the cut condition cannot have a solution, integral or otherwise, we only need to prove the other direction.

For any demand $d = (u, v)$ and vertex w in a multiflow instance, *pushing a unit of d to w* consists of removing one unit of demand d, and creating two demand edges of unit demand from u to w and w to v. This can be seen as taking the decision of routing at least one unit of the demand d through w.

For any demand d whose endpoints are connected by a path P, *routing a unit of d along P* consists of removing one unit of capacity along each edge of P, and removing one unit of demand from d. Supply edges whose capacity falls to zero are removed from G, and demand edges whose demand falls to zero are removed from H. For each $S \subsetneq V$, define $n_S = |\delta_G(S) \cap P|$. The operation reduces the surplus $\sigma(S)$ by $2\lfloor n_S/2 \rfloor$: it reduces the total of capacities crossing $\delta_G(S)$ by n_S; and if n_S is odd, then $d \in \delta_H(S)$ and it reduces the total demand crossing $\delta_H(S)$ by 1. Thus, the surplus of any cut is reduced by an even number.

Suppose we are given a series-parallel instance that is cut-sufficient, Eulerian, and satisfies the cut condition, with a demand $d = (u, v)$. We prove that (A) there is a sequence of push operations to move a unit of demand d to a path Q of unit demands from u to v without breaking the cut condition; and (B) the unit demands in Q can all be routed without breaking the cut condition. Thus, the demands in Q fall to zero, and are removed. The two operations are equivalent to routing one unit of d; thus, we get a smaller instance which has the same properties. We can therefore recursively build a solution to the whole problem.

We embed G in the plane such that the endpoints u and v are on the outside face (Lemma B.8). Any path P from u to v thus partitions $G \setminus P$ into two sides, one to the left and one to the right of P. Two paths P and P' *cross* if P' contains vertices on both sides of P. We decompose the flow of the fractional solution routing the demand d into paths in the series-parallel supply graph such that no two paths cross. This gives an ordering of the paths $P_1, \ldots, P_k$ such that if P_1 and P_k have a common vertex, then all paths P_j, $j = 1, \ldots, k$ go through that vertex. We examine the subgraph $P_1 \cup P_k$. Since u and v are on the outside face of G, the graph $P_1 \cup P_k$ is composed of a family of cycles (whenever P_1 and P_k are disjoint) connected by paths (whenever P_1 and P_k coincide). Let $C_1, \ldots, C_j$ be the cycles in $P_1 \cup P_k$, and for any cycle C_i, let a_i and b_i be the two vertices of C_i in both P_1 and P_k. See Figure 4.

Lemma 5.1. *In any instance of the multiflow problem satisfying the cut condition, if there is a fractional solution such that all paths $P_1, \ldots, P_k$ routing demand $d = (u, v)$ go through the same vertex w, then it is possible to push a unit of the demand d to the vertex w without breaking the cut condition.*

We push the demand d to every vertex in $P_1 \cap P_k$. By Lemma 5.1, we can do this without breaking the cut condition, since all paths routing d in the fractional solution go through these vertices. This creates a path Q of unit demands from u to v, where vertices of Q are those in both P_1 and P_k. This proves part (A).

We next argue that we can route the demands in Q. We need to identify paths in G to do this. The path Q has a unit demand parallel to every edge in the paths connecting the cycles $C_1, \ldots, C_j$, and a unit demand from a_i to b_i for every cycle C_i, $i = 1, \ldots, j$. We will route demands in Q along the paths connecting the cycles, and then along one side of each cycle. The side we pick is guided by the next two lemmas.

For any cycle C_i not containing v, we say a vertex $w \in C_i$ is *linked to v* if there is a path in G from w to v disjoint from C_i.

Lemma 5.2. *Any cycle C_i not containing v contains at most one vertex apart from b_i that is linked to v.*

Proof. Contract the connected component of $G \setminus C_i$ containing v. The resulting vertex is connected by an edge to any vertex of C_i that is linked to v. If there are three, this forms a K_4. □

We define the path P from u to v by choosing for each cycle C_i the side of C_i from a_i to b_i that does not contain a vertex linked to v. This is always possible by Lemma 5.2.

If $\delta_G(S)$ is a central cut, by Lemma B.3 it crosses a cycle C_i either twice, or not at all. For any u-to-v path P' in $P_1 \cup P_k$ obtained by choosing for each cycle C_i either $C_i \cap P_1$ or $C_i \cap P_k$, the cut $\delta_G(S)$ crosses $P' \cap C_i$ zero, once, or twice for every $i = 1, \ldots, j$. Our choice of P given above is special:

Lemma 5.3. *For any central cut $\delta_G(S)$, there is at most one cycle C_i such that $\delta_G(S)$ crosses $P \cap C_i$ twice.*

Lemma 5.4. *We can route the unit demands in Q along the path P without breaking the cut condition.*

Proof. The path P goes through both extremities of every demand we created by pushing d. Routing any demand parallel to a supply edge consists of removing one unit of capacity from the supply edge and removing the unit demand. The surplus of any cut crossing such a demand is not affected by this. Routing a demand across a cycle C_i, from a_i to b_i, consists of removing one unit of capacity of each supply edge in $P \cap C_i$, and removing the unit demand. If a central cut $\delta_G(S)$ separates a_i from b_i, it crosses $P \cap C_i$ exactly once, and so its surplus $\sigma(S)$ is not affected by this. If a central cut $\delta_G(S)$ does not separate a_i from b_i, then its surplus is reduced by two or unchanged, depending on whether it crosses $P \cap C_i$ twice or not at all. For any central cut $\delta_G(S)$, there is at most one cycle C_i such that $\delta_G(S)$ crosses $P \cap C_i$ twice, by Lemma 5.3. So the surplus of any cut is reduced at most by two. As there is a positive flow routing demand d along path P in the fractional solution, no cut that crosses P more than once is tight: because in any solution to the multiflow problem, the supply edges crossing a tight cut have their capacity completely used to route the demands that also cross it. As the instance is Eulerian, any cut that is not tight has a surplus of at least two. And so routing one unit along P does not break the cut condition. □

The flow routing all the demands created by pushing d is also a way of routing one unit of $d = (u, v)$ in the original problem; so we have found a path P from u to v such that routing one unit of d along this path does not break the cut condition. After doing this, the reduced instance still does not have any odd spindle as a minor, since no demand edges were introduced; is still Eulerian, and still satisfies the cut condition. By induction, we can find an integral routing for the instance.

5.1 Polynomial-Time Algorithm

The method described in the proof of Theorem 1.2 routes one unit of flow at a time. We show that each unit can be routed in polynomial-time. This gives us a pseudo-polynomial-time algorithm for an instance (G, H, c, D); the algorithm is polynomial in the size of G, H and the bit-size of c, but only polynomial in D, instead of the *bit-size* of D. So first, in polynomial time, we reduce the original instance to another one in which D is polynomial in the size of G and H.

To reduce D, we find a fractional solution in polynomial time by solving by a polynomial-sized linear program using edge-flow variables (e.g. Section 70.6 of [17]) via interior point methods. For each demand $i \in F$, we do a path decomposition of the flow routing i. This yields $k \leq m := |E|$ paths $P^i_1, \ldots, P^i_k$ per demand i. For each path P routing a quantity f^i_P of flow between endpoints of i, we send $\lfloor f^i_P \rfloor$ units of flow on P. After this, each path P routes an amount of flow smaller than 1, and since there are no more than m paths routing each demand, we are left with at most $m|F|$ units of demand to route. These are routed one unit at a time as follows.

First, solve the LP with the reduced demands. Next, embed the planar graph G' into the plane, in time linear in the number of vertices [15]. Next, decompose the flow of the fractional solution routing a demand into paths $P_1, \ldots, P_k$, with $k \leq m$ in $O(km)$ time. Finally, for each of the $\leq m$ cycles in $P_1 \cup P_k$, find the side without the vertex linked to v. This can be done by an exploration algorithm in $O(m)$ time, which makes $O(m^2)$ time in total. The operation of routing a unit through the path P is done in $O(m)$ time.

6. DISCUSSION

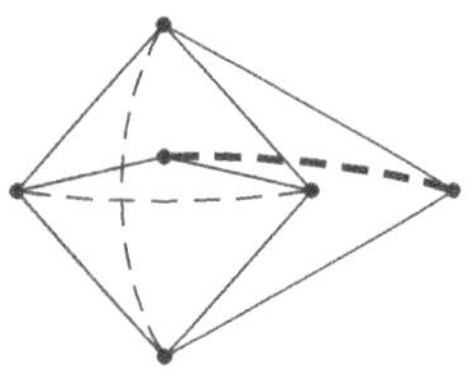

A natural extension of our results is to planar pairs, i.e., pairs where the supply graph is planar. There are planar pairs that are not cut-sufficient, yet do not have an odd spindle as a minor. A *bad-K_4-pair* is the example above, attributed by [17] to Papernov, which is of particular interest. Apart from odd spindles, it is the only pair we know that is not cut-sufficient but has only cut-sufficient pairs as minor. Supply edges are solid, and demands are dashed.

Conjecture 6.1. *A planar pair is cut-sufficient if and only if it does not contain an odd spindle or the bad-K_4-pair as a minor.*

Acknowledgments.

The third author gratefully thanks Bruce Shepherd for many discussions.

7. REFERENCES

[1] Y. Aumann and Y. Rabani. An $O(\log k)$ approximate min-cut max-flow theorem and approximation algorithm. *SIAM J. Comput*, 27:291–301, 1998.

[2] A. Chakrabarti, A. Jaffe, J. Lee, and J. Vincent. Embeddings of topological graphs: Lossy invariants, linearization, and 2-sums. In *Foundations of Computer Science, 2008. FOCS '08. IEEE 49th Annual IEEE Symposium on*, pages 761 –770, October 2008.

[3] C. Chekuri, B. Shepherd, and C. Weibel. Flow-cut gaps for integer and fractional multiflows. Submitted to the *Journal of Computational Theory Series B*; available at arXiv:1008.2136v1, July 2010.

[4] C. Chekuri, B. Shepherd, and C. Weibel. Flow-cut gaps for integer and fractional multiflows. In *Proceedings of the 21st Annual ACM-SIAM Symposium on Discrete Algorithm (SoDA 2010)*, pages 1198–1208, January 2010.

[5] O. Günlük. A new min-cut max-flow ratio for multicommodity flows. *SIAM J. Discret. Math.*, 21(1):1–15, 2007.

[6] A. Gupta, I. Newman, Y. Rabinovich, and A. Sinclair. Cuts, trees and ℓ_1-embeddings of graphs. *Combinatorica*, 24(2):233–269, 2004.

[7] T. C. Hu. Multi-commodity network flows. *Operations Research*, 11(3):344–360, 1963.

[8] J. R. Lee and P. Raghavendra. Coarse differentiation and multi-flows in planar graphs. In *APPROX '07/RANDOM '07: Proceedings of the 10th International Workshop on Approximation and the 11th International Workshop on Randomization, and Combinatorial Optimization. Algorithms and Techniques*, pages 228–241, Berlin, Heidelberg, 2007. Springer-Verlag.

[9] T. Leighton and S. Rao. Multicommodity max-flow min-cut theorems and their use in designing approximation algorithms. *J. ACM*, 46(6):787–832, 1999.

[10] N. Linial, E. London, and Y. Rabinovich. The geometry of graphs and some of its algorithmic applications. *Combinatorica*, 15:577–591, 1994.

[11] Lomonosov. Combinatorial approaches to multiflow problems. *Discrete Applied Mathematics*, 11(1):1 – 93, 1985.

[12] T. Nishizeki, J. Vygen, and X. Zhou. The edge-disjoint paths problem is NP-complete for series-parallel graphs. *Discrete Applied Mathematics*, 115(1-3):177–186, 2001.

[13] H. Okamura. Multicommodity flows in graphs. *Discrete Applied Mathematics*, 6(1):55 – 62, 1983.

[14] H. Okamura and P. Seymour. Multicommodity flows in planar graphs. *Journal of Combinatorial Theory, Series B*, 31(1):75 – 81, 1981.

[15] W. Schnyder. Embedding planar graphs on the grid. In *Proceedings of the first annual ACM-SIAM symposium on Discrete algorithms (SoDA 1990)*, SODA '90, pages 138–148, Philadelphia, PA, USA, 1990. Society for Industrial and Applied Mathematics.

[16] A. Schrijver. The Klein bottle and multicommodity flows. *Combinatorica*, 9:375–384, 1989. 10.1007/BF02125349.

[17] A. Schrijver. *Combinatorial Optimization: Polyhedra and Efficieny*, volume 24 of *Algorithms and Combinatorics*. Springer-Verlag, New York, 2003.

[18] P. Seymour. Matroids and multicommodity flows. *European Journal of Combinatorics*, 2:257–290, 1981.

[19] P. Seymour. On odd cuts and plane multicommodity flows. *Proceedings of the London Mathematical Society*, 3(1):178, 1981.

Strongly Polynomial Algorithm for a Class of Minimum-Cost Flow Problems with Separable Convex Objectives

László A. Végh*
College of Computing
Georgia Institute of Technology
Atlanta, GA
veghal@cs.elte.hu

ABSTRACT

A well-studied nonlinear extension of the minimum-cost flow problem is to minimize the objective $\sum_{ij\in E} C_{ij}(f_{ij})$ over feasible flows f, where on every arc ij of the network, C_{ij} is a convex function. We give a strongly polynomial algorithm for finding an exact optimal solution for a broad class of such problems. The key characteristic of this class is that an optimal solution can be computed exactly provided its support.

This includes separable convex quadratic objectives and also certain market equilibria problems: Fisher's market with linear and with spending constraint utilities. We thereby give the first strongly polynomial algorithms for separable quadratic minimum-cost flows and for Fisher's market with spending constraint utilities, settling open questions posed e.g. in [15] and in [35], respectively. The running time is $O(m^4 \log m)$ for quadratic costs, $O(n^4+n^2(m+n\log n)\log n)$ for Fisher's markets with linear utilities and $O(mn^3+m^2(m+n\log n)\log m)$ for spending constraint utilities.

Categories and Subject Descriptors

G.2.1 [**Combinatorics**]: [Combinatorial algorithms]; F.2 [**Analysis of Algorithms and Problem Complexity**]: [General]

General Terms

Theory, Algorithms, Economics

Keywords

network flow algorithms, convex optimization, strongly polynomial algorithms, market equilibrium

*Supported by NSF Grant CCF-0914732.

1. INTRODUCTION

The flow polyhedron is defined on a directed network $G=(V,E)$ by arc capacity and node demand constraints. For feasible solutions f, we aim to minimize $\sum_{ij\in E} C_{ij}(f_{ij})$, where on each arc $ij\in E$, C_{ij} is a differentiable convex function. Assume that each C_{ij} can be described by some numerical parameters (for example, if $C_{ij}(\alpha)=c_{ij}\alpha^2+d_{ij}\alpha$, then it is described by the values c_{ij}, d_{ij}). By a strongly polynomial algorithm for such a problem, we mean the following: (i) the algorithm uses only elementary arithmetic operations and comparisons; (ii) the number of these operations is bounded as a polynomial of the number of nodes (n) and arcs of the network (m); (iii) if the input consists of rational numbers, then the size of all numbers during the computations is polynomially bounded in n, m, and the size of the input numbers.

Flows with separable convex objectives are natural convex extensions of minimum-cost flows with several applications as matrix balancing or traffic networks, see [1, Chapter 14] for further references. Polynomial-time combinatorial algorithms were given by Minoux [25] in 1986, by Hochbaum and Shantikumar [17] in 1990, and by Karzanov and McCormick [21] in 1997. The latter two approaches are able to solve even more general problems of minimizing a separable (not necessarily differentiable) convex objective over a polytope given by a matrix with a bound on its largest subdeterminant. Both approaches give polynomial, yet not strongly polynomial algorithms.

In contrast, for the same problems with linear objectives, Tardos [33, 34] gave strongly polynomial algorithms. One might wonder whether this could also be extended to the convex setting. This seems impossible for arbitrary convex objectives by the very nature of the problem: the optimal solution might be irrational, and thus the exact optimum cannot be achieved.

Beyond irrationality, the result of Hochbaum [15] shows that it is impossible to find an ε-approximate solution in strongly polynomial time even for a network consisting of parallel arcs between a source and a sink node and the C_{ij}'s being polynomials of degree at least three. This is based on Renegar's [30] result showing the impossibility of finding ε-approximate roots of polynomials in strongly polynomial time.

The remaining class of polynomial objectives with hope of strongly polynomial algorithms is convex quadratic. For these functions, the existence of a rational optimal solution is always guaranteed. Granot and Skorin-Kapov [12] extended Tardos's method [34] to solving separable convex quadratic optimization problems where the running time depends only on the entries of the constraint matrix and the coefficients of the quadratic terms in the objective. However, in a strongly polynomial algorithm, the running time should only depend on the matrix.

The existence of a strongly polynomial algorithm for the quadratic flow problem thus remained an important open question (mentioned e.g. in [15, 4, 16, 12, 32]). The survey paper [16] gives an overview of special cases solvable in strongly polynomial time. This includes fixed number of suppliers (Cosares and Hochbaum, [4]), and series-parallel graphs (Tamir [32]). We resolve this question affirmatively, providing a strongly polynomial algorithm for the general problem in time $O(m^4 \log m)$.

There is an analogous situation for convex closure sets: [15] shows that no strongly polynomial algorithm may exist in general, but for quadratic cost functions, Hochbaum and Queyranne gave a strongly polynomial algorithm [14].

An entirely different motivation of our study comes from the field of market equilibrium algorithms. Devanur et al. [5] developed a polynomial time combinatorial algorithm for a classical problem in economics, Fisher's market with linear utilities. This motivated a line of research to develop combinatorial algorithms for other market equilibrium problems. For a survey, see [27, Chapter 5] or [36]. All these problems are described by rational convex programs. For the linear Fisher market problem, a strongly polynomial algorithm was given by Orlin [29].

To the extent of the author's knowledge, this field has been considered so far as an entirely new domain in combinatorial optimization. An explicit connection to classical flow problems was pointed out in the recent paper [37]. It turns out that the linear Fisher market, along with several other problems, is captured by a concave extension of the classical generalized flow problem, solvable by a polynomial time combinatorial algorithm.

The paper [37] uses the convex programming formulation of linear Fisher markets by Eisenberg and Gale [7]. An alternative convex program for the same problem was given by Shmyrev [31]. This formulation turns out to be a convex separable minimum-cost flow problem. Consequently, equilibrium for linear Fisher market can be computed by the general algorithms [17] or [21] (with a final transformation of a close enough approximate solution to the exact optimal one).

The class of convex flow problems solved in this paper also contains the formulation of Shmyrev, yielding an alternative strongly polynomial algorithm for linear Fisher market. This formulation can be extended to spending constraint utilities, a market defined by Vazirani [35]. For this problem, we obtain the first strongly polynomial algorithm. Our running time bounds are $O(n^4 + n^2(m + n\log n)\log n)$ for linear and $O(mn^3 + m^2(m+n\log n)\log m)$ for spending constraint utilities, with m being the number of segments in the latter problem. Orlin [29] used the assumption $m = O(n^2)$ and achieved running time $O(n^4 \log n)$, the same as ours under this assumption. So far, no extensions of [29] are known for other market settings. Using the general framework enables a simpler treatment as in [29].

1.1 Prior work

For linear minimum-cost flows, the first polynomial time algorithm was the scaling method of Edmonds and Karp [6]. The current most efficient strongly polynomial algorithm, given by Orlin [28], is also based on this framework. On the other hand, the algorithm of [6] has also been extended to the convex minimum-cost flow problem, first by Minoux [24] to convex quadratic flows, later to general convex objectives (Minoux [25], Hochbaum and Shantikumar [17]). Our algorithm is an enhanced version of these later algorithms, in the spirit of Orlin's technique [28]. However, there are important differences that make the nonlinear setting significantly harder. Let us remark that Orlin's strongly polynomial algorithm for linear Fisher market [29] is also based on the ideas of [28]. To get an overview on linear and nonlinear minimum-cost flow algorithms, we refer the reader to [1].

The algorithm of Edmonds and Karp consists of Δ-phases, and the scaling factor Δ decreases at least by a factor of two for the next phase. The elementary step of the Δ-phase transports Δ units of flow from a node with excess at least Δ to another with demand at least Δ. This is done on a shortest path in the Δ-residual network, the graph of residual arcs with capacity at least Δ. An invariant property maintained in the Δ-phase is that the Δ-residual network does not contain any negative cost cycles. When moving to the next phase, the flow on the arcs has to be slightly modified to restore the invariant property.

Orlin's algorithm [28] works on a problem instance with no upper capacities on the arcs (every minimum-cost flow problem can be easily transformed to this form). The basic idea is that once an arc ij has flow at least $4n\Delta$ in the Δ-phase, then the flow on ij must be positive in some optimal solution. Such an arc is called *abundant*. Using primal-dual slackness, this means that ij must be tight for an arbitrary dual optimal solution. It can be shown that within $O(\log n)$ scaling phases, an abundant arc ij appears.

Based on this observation, one can obtain the following simple algorithm. Let us contract ij, and restart the Edmonds-Karp algorithm in the smaller graph. Iterating this method, we can find an optimal dual solution, which easily enables to compute an optimal primal solution. Instead of explicitly contracting and restarting, [28] (see also [1, Chapter 10.7]) continues the scaling method after finding an abundant arc, and maintains the forest F of such arcs. A new arc enters F in $O(\log n)$ phases, and the running time can be bounded by $O(m \log n(m+n\log n))$, so far the most efficient minimum-cost flow algorithm known.

Let us now turn to the nonlinear setting. The Edmonds-Karp algorithm naturally extends here (see [24, 25, 17]). In the Δ-phase, the invariant is that the Δ-residual graph contains no negative cycle for the linearization of the cost function into Δ-chunks. That is, the cost of the arc ij is defined as $(C_{ij}(f_{ij}+\Delta) - C_{ij}(f_{ij}))/\Delta$. When transporting Δ-units of flow on a shortest path with respect to this cost function, the invariant is maintained. A key observation is that when moving to the $\Delta/2$-phase, the invariant can be restored by changing the flow on each arc by at most $\Delta/2$. As Δ approaches 0, the cost of ij converges to the derivative $C'_{ij}(f_{ij})$. By the KKT conditions, a flow f is optimal if and only if the residual graph contains no negative cycles for the derivatives. A variant of this algorithm is outlined in Section 3.

1.2 Our results

The class of problems where we give a strongly polynomial algorithm is defined by four assumptions. We need to have an oracle access to the derivatives of the C_{ij}'s by Assumption 1. The technical Assumption 2 restricts the problem instances where each cost functions is either strictly convex or linear.

Two main ingredients of the algorithm are black box subroutines provided by Assumptions 3 and 4. The first subroutine returns a solution that satisfies optimally the KKT-conditions on a subset of edges. In particular, it returns an optimal solution if the input is the support of an optimal solution. For quadratic cost functions and for the Fisher markets, this can be implemented by solving simple systems of equations. The second is a technical subroutine measuring the quality of a candidate solution, returning its distance from optimality in a certain metric. This subroutine appears to be the bottleneck in complexity: for quadratic costs, it needs a minimum cost-to-time ratio cycle computation (also known as the tramp steamer problem). For the Fisher markets, an all pairs shortest paths computation is performed. The main result of the paper is the following.

THEOREM 1.1. *Let Assumptions 1-4 hold for the problem of minimizing $\sum_{ij \in E} C_{ij}(f_{ij})$ over feasible flows f in a network on n nodes and m arcs, m_N among them having nonlinear cost functions. Let $\rho_T(n,m)$ and $\rho_E(n,m)$ denote the running time of the subroutines defined in Assumptions 3 and 4, and let $\rho_S(n,m)$ be the running time needed for a single shortest path computation. Then an exact optimal solution can be found in $O((n+m_N)(\rho_T(n,m)+\rho_E(n,m)) + (n+m_N)^2\rho_S(n,m)\log m)$ time.*

This gives an $O(m^4 \log m)$ algorithm for quadratic convex objectives. For Fisher markets, we obtain $O(n^4 + n^2(m + n\log n)\log n)$ running time for linear and $O(mn^3 + m^2(m + n\log n)\log m)$ for spending constraint utilities.

We shall now outline the basic ideas of our strongly polynomial algorithm. The problem is first transformed to an instance with no upper bounds on the arcs. All cost functions C_{ij} are assumed to be differentiable. From a complexity perspective, cost functions are provided via oracles (Assumption 1), as in [17] and [21].

For simplicity of presentation, let us now assume that there exists a unique optimal solution f^*. We shall assume that f^* can be computed exactly (in particular, it is rational). Let F^* denote the set of arcs ij with $f^*_{ij} > 0$. By the KKT conditions, $\pi_j - \pi_i = C'_{ij}(f^*_{ij})$ for each $ij \in F^*$ and for the Lagrangian multipliers π. Assumption 3 guarantees that if we can somehow guess the set F^*, then we can obtain the optimal f^* by solving the above equality system.

Our starting point is the nonlinear scaling scheme as described above, with the only difference that the linearized cost function is replaced by $C'_{ij}(f_{ij} + \Delta)$. This has similar properties but is easier to handle. As in [28], we can identify an abundant arc ij in $O(\log n)$ steps, which must be contained in F^*. However, contraction does not work. The reason is that the KKT-conditions give $\pi_j - \pi_i = C'_{ij}(f^*_{ij})$, a condition containing both primal and dual (more precisely, Lagrangian) variables simultaneously.

In each phase of the algorithm, we shall maintain a set $F \subseteq F^*$ of arcs, called *revealed* arcs. F will be extended by a new arc in every $O(\log n)$ phases; thus we find F^* in $O(m \log n)$ steps. We change the terminology from abundant as they will not necessarily carry a huge amount of flow. Indeed, for revealed arcs, we delete the lower capacity and even allow the flow value to become negative. Accordingly, we keep both ij and ji for $ij \in F$ in the set of residual arcs.

The second important difference is that in contrast to Orlin's algorithm, we cannot assume that F is acyclic: there are simple quadratic instances with the support of an optimal solution containing cycles. In Orlin's algorithm, progress is always made by connecting two components of F. This will also be an important event in our algorithm, but sometimes F must also be extended with arcs inside a component.

At the end of each phase when F is extended, we compute the discrepancy of F, the maximum absolute value of the sum of node demands in a component of F. If this value is large, then it can be shown that F will be extended within $O(\log n)$ phases as in Orlin's algorithm.

If the discrepancy is small, the procedure TRIAL-AND-ERROR is performed. We pretend that $F = F^*$ and try to compute an optimal solution $\hat{f}$ under this hypothesis, which can be done by a subroutine guaranteed by Assumption 3. If $F \subsetneq F^*$, then $\hat{f}$ is not optimal. Another subroutine, described in Assumption 4, enables us to compute the smallest $\hat{\Delta}$ value for which $\hat{f}$ is $\hat{\Delta}$-feasible (that is, it satisfies the necessary conditions for a $\hat{\Delta}$-phase). If $\hat{\Delta} < \Delta/2$, then we set $\hat{\Delta}$ as our next scaling value and $f = \hat{f}$ as the next pseudoflow. Otherwise, the usual transition to phase $\Delta/2$ is done with keeping the same flow f. The analysis shows that a new arc shall be revealed in every $O(\log n)$ phases. The key lemma is a proximity result between f and $\hat{f}$, which implies that TRIAL-AND-ERROR cannot return the same $\hat{f}$ if performed again after $O(\log n)$ phases, implying that the set F cannot be the same.

The paper is organized as follows. Section 2 contains the basic definitions and notation. Section 3 presents the simple adaptation of the Edmonds-Karp algorithm for convex cost functions, following Minoux [25]. Our algorithm in Section 4 is built on this algorithm with the addition of the subroutine TRIAL-AND-ERROR, that guarantees strongly polynomial running time. Analysis is given in Section 5. Section 6 adapts the general algorithm for quadratic utilities, and for Fisher's market with linear and with spending constraint utilities. Section 7 contains a final discussion of the results and some open questions.

2. PROBLEM DEFINITIONS

Let $G = (V, E)$ be a directed graph possibly containing parallel arcs. Let $n = |V|$, $m = |E|$. We are given lower and upper capacities $\ell, u : E \to \mathbb{R} \cup \{\infty\}$ on the arcs, and node demands $b : V \to \mathbb{R}$ with $\sum_{i \in V} b_i = 0$. On each arc $ij \in E$, $C_{ij} : (-\infty, \infty) \to \mathbb{R} \cup \{\infty\}$ is a convex function. Either it is differentiable everywhere, or it is ∞ on $(-\infty, \ell_{ij})$ and is differentiable on (ℓ_{ij}, ∞). The minimum-cost flow problem with separable convex objective is defined as follows.

$$\min \sum_{ij \in E} C_{ij}(x_{ij})$$

$$\sum_{j:ji \in E} f_{ji} - \sum_{j:ij \in E} f_{ij} = b_i \qquad \forall i \in V \qquad \text{(P)}$$

$$\ell_{ij} \le f_{ij} \le u_{ij} \qquad \forall ij \in E$$

Throughout the paper, we shall work with the uncapacitated version, that is, $\ell \equiv 0$ and $u \equiv \infty$. With a standard method, every problem can be transformed to an equivalent uncapacitated form. Indeed, let us replace each arc $ij \in E$ by a path ikj of length 3, by introducing a new node k. Let us set $b_k = u_{ij} - \ell_{ij}$, $C_{ik}(\alpha) = C_{ij}(\alpha + \ell_{ij})$, $C_{kj} \equiv 0$. Furthermore, let us increase b_i by ℓ_{ij} and decrease b_j by u_{ij}. It is easy to see that this gives an equivalent optimization problem, and if the original graph had n' nodes and m' arcs, the transformed instance has $n = n' + m'$ nodes and $m = 2m'$ arcs.

By a *pseudoflow* we mean a function $f : E \to \mathbb{R}$ satisfying the capacity constraints. For the uncapacitated problem, it simply means $f \geq 0$. Let

$$\rho_f(i) := \sum_{j:ji \in E} f_{ji} - \sum_{j:ij \in E} f_{ij},$$

and let $Ex(f) = Ex_b(f) = \sum_{i \in V} \max\{\rho_f(i) - b_i, 0\}$ denote the total positive excess. For an arc set F, let $\overleftarrow{F}$ denote the set of backward arcs and let $\overleftrightarrow{F} = F \cup \overleftarrow{F}$. We shall use the vector norms $||x||_\infty = \max |x_i|$ and $||x||_1 = \sum |x_i|$.

Following [17] and [21], we do not require the functions C_{ij} to be given explicitly, but assume oracle access only.

ASSUMPTION 1. *For each arc ij, we are given a differential oracle that returns the value $C'_{ij}(\alpha)$ in $O(1)$ time for any $\alpha \in \mathbb{R}$.*

Note that we do not assume an evaluation oracle returning $C_{ij}(\alpha)$. The main algorithm needs only access to a differential oracle; however, the subroutines described in Assumptions 4 and 3 may need stronger oracles. For quadratic objectives, the derivatives are linear functions, however, for the market applications, we will have logarithmic derivatives. As we shall argue in Section 6.2, in those settings, access is provided to the exact values $e^{C'_{ij}(\alpha)}$, which is also sufficient for all applications of the oracle, most importantly, shortest path computations. Assumptions 2, 3, and 4 shall be given in Section 4.

Given a pseudoflow f, let us define the residual graph E_f by $ij \in E_f$ if $ij \in E$, or $ji \in E$ and $f_{ji} > 0$. Arcs of the first type are called *forward*, those of the latter type *backward arcs*. We use the convention that on a backward arc ji, $f_{ji} = -f_{ij}$, $C_{ji}(\alpha) = C_{ij}(-\alpha)$, also convex and differentiable. The *residual capacity* is ∞ on forward arcs and f_{ij} on the backward arc ji.

The Karush-Kuhn-Tucker conditions assert that the solution f to (P) is optimal if and only if there exists $\pi : V \to \mathbb{R}$ such that

$$\pi_j - \pi_i \leq C'_{ij}(f_{ij}) \quad \forall ij \in E_f. \tag{1}$$

For a value $\Delta > 0$, let $E_f(\Delta)$ denote the subset of arcs in E_f that have residual capacity at least Δ (in particular, it contains E). We say that the pseudoflow f is Δ-feasible, if $E_f(\Delta)$ contains no negative cycles with respect to the cost function $C'_{ij}(f_{ij} + \Delta)$. This is equivalent to the existence of a potential $\pi : V \to \mathbb{R}$ so that

$$\pi_j - \pi_i \leq C'_{ij}(f_{ij} + \Delta) \quad \forall ij \in E_f(\Delta). \tag{2}$$

If ji is a reverse arc, then this condition gives $C'_{ij}(f_{ij} - \Delta) \leq \pi_j - \pi_i$. This is different (and weaker) than the condition in [25] and [17], where $(C_{ij}(f_{ij} + \Delta) - C_{ij}(f_{ij}))/\Delta$ is used in the place of $C'_{ij}(f_{ij} + \Delta)$.

The following lemma shows that a 2Δ-feasible pseudoflow can be transformed to a Δ-feasible pseudoflow by small changes on the arcs.

LEMMA 2.1. *If the pseudoflow $\bar{f}$ is 2Δ-feasible, then there exists a Δ-feasible pseudoflow f with $\bar{f}_{ij} - f_{ij} \in \{0, \pm\Delta\}$ on each $ij \in E$. Consequently, $Ex(f) \leq Ex(\bar{f}) + m\Delta$.*

PROOF. Consider a potential π satisfying (2) with $\bar{f}$ and 2Δ. We want to prove that modifying $\bar{f}$ on each arc by $\pm\Delta$ or 0 will give a solution f satisfying (2) with Δ and the same π.

Let $ij \in E$ be a forward arc. If the condition is violated on ij, then $C'_{ij}(\bar{f}_{ij} + \Delta) < \pi_j - \pi_i$. However, by 2Δ-feasibility we know $\pi_j - \pi_i \leq C'_{ij}(\bar{f}_{ij} + 2\Delta)$. These show that setting $f_{ij} = \bar{f}_{ij} + \Delta$ satisfies (2) for both ij and ji, using that $C'_{ij}(f_{ij} - \Delta) \leq C'_{ij}(\bar{f}_{ij}) = C'_{ij}(\bar{f}_{ij} + \Delta) < \pi_j - \pi_i$.

In the sequel, assume that (2) holds for $ij \in E$. If $ji \notin E_{\bar{f}}(\Delta)$ or (2) holds for ji, then we set $f_{ij} = \bar{f}_{ij}$. Assume now $ji \in E_{\bar{f}}(\Delta)$ but (2) is violated for ji, meaning $\pi_j - \pi_i < C'_{ij}(\bar{f}_{ij} - \Delta)$. Let us set $f_{ij} = \bar{f}_{ij} - \Delta$. ij satisfies (2) by $\pi_j - \pi_i < C'_{ij}(\bar{f}_{ij} - \Delta) \leq C'_{ij}(f_{ij}) = C'_{ij}(f_{ij} + \Delta)$.

If $ji \in E_{\bar{f}}(2\Delta)$, then we have $C'_{ij}(f_{ij} - \Delta) = C'_{ij}(\bar{f}_{ij} - 2\Delta) \leq \pi_j - \pi_i$, and thus (2) also holds for ji. Finally, if $ji \in E_{\bar{f}}(\Delta) - E_{\bar{f}}(2\Delta)$, then $ji \notin E_f(\Delta)$. $\square$

The subroutine ADJUST(Δ) performs the simple steps of the proof.

Finally, we may assume without loss of generality that $G = (V, E)$ is strongly connected. Indeed, we can add a new node t with edges vt, tv for any $v \in V$, with extremely high (possibly linear) cost functions on the edges. This guarantees that an optimal solution shall not use such edges, whenever the problem is feasible. We will also assume $n \leq m$.

3. THE BASIC ALGORITHM

Let us now outline the (weakly) polynomial algorithm by Minoux [25], a simple extension of the Edmonds-Karp algorithm.

We start with the Δ_0-feasible solution $f^0 \equiv \mathbf{0}$ with $Ex(f^0) \leq (2n+m)\Delta_0$. The algorithm consists of Δ-phases, starting with $\Delta = \Delta_0$, with Δ decreasing by exactly a factor of two between two phases.

Each Δ-phase consists of a preprocessing part and a main part. In the first, Δ_0-phase, no preprocessing is needed. In each later phase, we start with a 2Δ-feasible pseudoflow f'. We perform ADJUST(Δ) to obtain a Δ-feasible pseudoflow f.

In the main part of phase Δ, let $S(\Delta) = \{i \in V : \rho_f(i) - b_i \geq \Delta\}$ and $T(\Delta) = \{i \in V : \rho_f(i) - b_i \leq -\Delta\}$. As long as $S(\Delta) \neq \emptyset$, $T(\Delta) \neq \emptyset$, send Δ units of flow from a node $s \in S(\Delta)$ to a node $t \in T(\Delta)$ on a shortest path in $E_f^F(\Delta)$ with respect to the cost function $C'_{ij}(f_{ij} + \Delta)$. If $S(\Delta) = \emptyset$ or $T(\Delta) = \emptyset$, we proceed to the next phase with scaling factor $\Delta/2$.

3.1 Analysis

We omit the proof of the following two simple lemmas; their analogous counterparts for the enhanced algorithm will be proved in Section 5.

LEMMA 3.1. *(i) In the Δ-phase, the pseudoflow is an integer multiple of Δ on each arc, and consequently, $E_f^F(\Delta) = E_f^F$.*

(ii) Δ-feasibility is maintained when augmenting on a shortest path.

(iii) At the beginning of the main part, $Ex(f) \le (2n+m)\Delta$, and at the end, $Ex(f) \le n\Delta$.

(iv) The main part consists of at most $2n+m$ flow augmentation steps.

LEMMA 3.2. *Let f be the pseudoflow at the end of the Δ-phase and f' in an arbitrary later phase. Then $\|f - f'\|_\infty \le (2n+m+1)\Delta$. If $f_{ij} > (2n+m+1)\Delta$ at the end of the Δ-phase, then this property is maintained in all later phases, and there exists an optimal solution f^* with $f_{ij}^* > 0$.*

4. THE ENHANCED ALGORITHM

4.1 Revealed arc sets

We investigate a slightly restricted class of functions C_{ij}.

ASSUMPTION 2. *Each cost function $C_{ij}(\alpha)$ is either linear or strictly convex, that is, $C'_{ij}(\alpha)$ is either constant or strictly monotone increasing.*

Arcs with $C_{ij}(\alpha)$ linear are called *linear arcs*, the rest is called *nonlinear arcs*. Let m_L and m_N denote their numbers, respectively. We use the terms linear and nonlinear for the reverse arcs as well.

Let F^* denote the set of arcs that are tight in every optimal solution. Formally, $ij \in F^*$ if for all pairs (f,π) satisfying (1), $\pi_j - \pi_i = C'_{ij}(f_{ij})$ holds. The next lemma shows that F^* contains the support of every optimal solution.

LEMMA 4.1. *Let f be an arbitrary optimal solution to (P), and $f_{ij} > 0$ for some $ij \in E$. Then $ij \in F^*$.*

The proof needs the following notion, also used later. Let $x, y : E \to \mathbb{R}$ be two vectors. Let us define the *difference graph* $D_{x,y} = (V, E_{x,y})$ with $ij \in E_{x,y}$ if $x_{ij} > y_{ij}$ or if $x_{ji} < y_{ji}$.

PROOF OF LEMMA 4.1. Let f^* be a different optimal solution, and consider potentials π and π^* with both (f,π) and (f^*,π^*) satisfying (1). If $f_{ij}^* > 0$, then $ji \in E_{f^*}$ and thus $\pi_j^* - \pi_i^* = C'_{ij}(f_{ij}^*)$ must hold.

Assume now $f_{ij}^* = 0$. Consider the difference graph D_{f,f^*}. Since $f_{ij} > f_{ij}^*$, it follows that $ij \in E_{f,f^*}$. Because of $\rho_{f^*} \equiv \rho_f$, E_{f,f^*} must contain a cycle C containing ij. For every arc $ab \in C$, $f_{ab} > f_{ab}^*$ and thus $ab \in E_{f^*}$ and $ba \in E_f$. By (1),

$$0 = \sum_{ab\in C} \pi_b^* - \pi_a^* \quad \le \sum_{ab\in C} C'_{ab}(f_{ab}^*) \text{ and}$$

$$0 = \sum_{ab\in C} \pi_a - \pi_b \quad \le \sum_{ab\in C} C'_{ba}(f_{ba}) = -\sum_{ab\in C} C'_{ab}(f_{ab}).$$

Since each function C_{ab} is convex, $f_{ab} > f_{ab}^*$ gives $C'_{ab}(f_{ab}) \ge C'_{ab}(f_{ab}^*)$. In the above inequalities, equality must hold everywhere, implying $\pi_j^* - \pi_i^* = C'_{ij}(f_{ij}^*)$ as desired. $\square$

We shall see that under Assumption 3, finding the set F^* enables us to compute an optimal solution. In the basic algorithm, $F = \{ij \in E : f_{ij} > (2n+m+1)\Delta\}$ is always a subset of F^* by Lemma 3.2. Furthermore, once an edge enters F, it stays there in all later phases. Yet there is no guarantee (and it is in fact not true) that in the basic algorithm, F is extended in some number of steps polynomially bounded in n and m. We shall modify the algorithm in order to guarantee that within $O(\log n)$ phases, a new arc is guaranteed to enter F.

In each step of the enhanced algorithm, there will be an arc set F, called the *revealed arc set*, which is guaranteed to be a subset of F^*. We remove the lower capacity 0 from arcs in F and allow also negative values here.

Formally, a vector $f : E \to \mathbb{R}$ is an *F-pseudoflow*, if $f_{ij} \ge 0$ for $ij \in E - F$ (but it is allowed to be negative on F). For such an f, let us define $E_f^F = E_f \cup \overleftarrow{F}$. If $ij \in F$, then the residual capacity of ji is ∞. We shall maintain an F-pseudoflow when $F \subseteq F^*$ is the set of revealed arcs in some phase of the algorithm.

We say that $f : E \to \mathbb{R}$ is *F-optimal*, if it is an F-pseudoflow with $Ex_b(f) = 0$ and there exists $\pi : V \to \mathbb{R}$ with

$$\pi_j - \pi_i \le C'_{ij}(f_{ij}) \quad \forall ij \in E_f^F. \tag{3}$$

The definition of F^* implies that any optimal f^* is also F-optimal if $F \subseteq F^*$. We shall prove that given an F-optimal solution, we can easily find an optimal solution as well.

LEMMA 4.2. *Assume that for a subset $F \subseteq F^*$, an F-optimal solution f is provided. Then an optimal solution to (P) can be found by a maximum flow computation. Further, $ij \in F^*$ whenever $f_{ij} > 0$.*

PROOF. Assume (f,π) and $(\bar{f},\bar{\pi})$ both satisfy (3). We prove that *(i)* $f_{ij} = \bar{f}_{ij}$ whenever ij is a nonlinear arc; and *(ii)* if ij is a linear arc with $f_{ij} \ne \bar{f}_{ij}$, then $\pi_j - \pi_i = C'_{ij}(f_{ij}) = C'_{ij}(\bar{f}_{ij}) = \bar{\pi}_j - \bar{\pi}_i$.

(ii) immediately implies the second half of the claim as it can be applied for an arbitrary optimal f^*. The proof uses the same argument as for Lemma 4.1.

W.l.o.g. assume $f_{ij} > \bar{f}_{ij}$ for an arc ij, and consider the difference graph $D_{f,\bar{f}}$. Since $f_{ij} > \bar{f}_{ij}$, ij must be contained on a cycle $C \subseteq E_{f,\bar{f}}$. For every arc $ab \in C$, $ab \in E_{\bar{f}}^F$ and $ba \in E_f^F$ follows (using $\overleftrightarrow{F} \subseteq E_{\bar{f}}^F \cap E_f^F$). By (3),

$$0 = \sum_{ab\in C} \bar{\pi}_b - \bar{\pi}_a \quad \le \sum_{ab\in C} C'_{ab}(\bar{f}_{ab}) \text{ and}$$

$$0 = \sum_{ab\in C} \pi_a - \pi_b \quad \le \sum_{ab\in C} C'_{ba}(f_{ba}) = -\sum_{ab\in C} C_{ab}(f_{ab}).$$

Now convexity yields $C'_{ab}(f_{ab}) = C'_{ab}(\bar{f}_{ab})$ for all $ab \in C$. Assumption 2 implies that all arcs in C are linear, in particular, ij. This immediately proofs *(i)*. To verify *(ii)*, observe that all above inequalities must hold with equality.

This suggests the following simple method to transform an F-optimal solution f to an optimal f^*. For every nonlinear arc ij, we must have $f_{ij}^* = f_{ij}$. On the set of linear arcs satisfying $\pi_j - \pi_i = C'_{ij}(f_{ij})$, we can solve a feasible circulation problem with node demands being the same as the $\rho_f(i)$ values, lower capacities 0 and upper capacities ∞. The feasible solutions are precisely the optimal solutions. Indeed, if f^* is an optimal solution, then (3) and *(ii)* imply $\pi_j - \pi_i = C'_{ij}(f_{ij})$ for all ij with $f_{ij}^* > 0$. $\square$

Let F be the set of revealed arcs in the Δ-phase. We maintain an F-pseudoflow f, but instead of Δ-feasibility, we require the following slightly stronger property. Let $E_f^F(\Delta)$

denote the set of arcs in E_f^F with residual capacity at least Δ. We say that the F-pseudoflow F is *(Δ, F)-feasible*, if $E_f^F(\Delta)$ contains no negative cycle with respect to the cost function $C'_{ij}(f_{ij}+\Delta)$. Equivalently, there exists a potential $\pi : V \to \mathbb{R}$ so that

$$\pi_j - \pi_i \le C'_{ij}(f_{ij}+\Delta) \quad \forall ij \in E_f^F(\Delta). \tag{4}$$

We shall also maintain that the set of revealed arcs, F is *linear acylic*, meaning that F does not contain any cycle of linear arcs.

4.2 Subroutine assumptions

Given the set $F \subseteq F^*$ of revealed arcs, we will try to find out whether F already contains the support of an optimal solution. This motivates the following definition. We say that the (not necessarily nonnegative) vector $x : E \to \mathbb{R}$ is *F-tight*, if $x_{ij} = 0$ whenever $ij \notin F$ and there exists a potential $\pi : V \to \mathbb{R}$ with

$$\pi_j - \pi_i = C'_{ij}(x_{ij}) \quad \forall ij \in F. \tag{5}$$

For example, any optimal solution is F^*-tight by Lemma 4.1. Notice that an F-tight vector f is not necessarily F-optimal as (3) might be violated for edges in $E - F$ and also since $Ex_b(f) > 0$ is allowed. On the other hand, an F-optimal set is not necessarily F-tight as it can be nonzero on $E - F$.

Given F and some node demands $\hat{b} : V \to \mathbb{R}$, we would like to find an F-tight x with $Ex_{\hat{b}}(x) = 0$. Let us define the *discrepancy* $D_{\hat{b}}(F)$ of F as the maximum of $|\sum_{i \in K} \hat{b}_i|$ over undirected connected components K of F. A trivial necessary condition for solvability is $D_{\hat{b}}(F) = 0$.

ASSUMPTION 3. *Assume we have a subroutine* TRIAL$(F, \hat{b})$ *so that for any linear acyclic $F \subseteq E$ and any vector $\hat{b} : V \to \mathbb{R}$ satisfying $D_{\hat{b}}(F) = 0$, it delivers an F-tight solution x with $Ex_{\hat{b}}(x) = 0$ in running time $\rho_T(n, m)$.*

For quadratic cost functions and also for Fisher markets, this subroutine can be implemented by solving simple systems of equations.

Consider now an F-tight f, and let

$$err_F(f) = \inf\{\Delta : f \text{ is } (\Delta, F)\text{-feasible}\}.$$

Because of continuity, this infimum is actually a minimum whenever the set is nonempty. If f is not (Δ, F)-feasible for any Δ, then let $err_F(f) = \infty$. f is F-optimal if and only if f is a feasible flow (that is, $Ex_b(f) = 0$) and $err_F(f) = 0$. As f is assumed to be F-tight, $E_f^F(\Delta) = E \cup \overleftarrow{F}$, the same arc set in (4) for any value of Δ.

ASSUMPTION 4. *Assume a subroutine* ERROR(f, F) *is provided, that returns $err_F(f)$ for any F-tight pseudoflow f in running time $\rho_E(n, m)$. Further, if $err_\emptyset(\mathbf{0}) = \infty$, then (P) is unbounded.*

This subroutine seems significantly harder to implement for the applications: we need to solve a minimum cost-to-time ratio cycle problem for quadratic costs and all pairs shortest paths for the Fisher markets.

4.3 Description of the enhanced algorithm

The algorithm starts with the $(\Delta_0, \emptyset)$-feasible solution $\mathbf{0}$ with $Ex(\mathbf{0}) \le (2n + m_N)\Delta_0$. The appropriate value can be chosen as $\Delta_0 = \max\{err_\emptyset(\mathbf{0}), Ex_b(\mathbf{0})/(2n + m_N)\}$. By the second part of Assumption 4, $err_\emptyset(\mathbf{0})$ must be finite or the problem is unbounded. We initialize the revealed arc set $F = \emptyset$.

The algorithm consists of Δ-phases, starting with $\Delta = \Delta_0$. In the Δ-phase, we shall maintain a linear acyclic revealed arc set $F \subseteq F^*$, and a (Δ, F)-feasible F-pseudoflow f. Besides preprocessing and main part, the phases have a third part, TRIAL-AND-ERROR, where the next value of Δ is also determined.

No preprocessing is done in the Δ_0-phase. In a later phase, either we have a Δ-feasible pseudoflow from the previous phase, or the scaling factor in the previous phase was 2Δ, and thus we have a 2Δ-feasible f. In the latter case, ADJUST(Δ) provides a Δ-feasible pseudoflow.

The main part of the Δ-phase is the same as in the basic algorithm. Let $S(\Delta) = \{i \in V : \rho_f(i) - b_i \ge \Delta\}$ and $T(\Delta) = \{i \in V : \rho_f(i) - b_i \le -\Delta\}$. As long as $S(\Delta) \ne \emptyset$, $T(\Delta) \ne \emptyset$, send Δ units of flow from a node $s \in S(\Delta)$ to a node $t \in T(\Delta)$ on a shortest path in $E_f^F(\Delta)$ with respect to the cost function $C'_{ij}(f_{ij} + \Delta)$.

After the main part is finished, EXTEND(F, f, Δ) adds some arcs $ij \in E - F$ with $f_{ij} > (2n+m+1)\Delta$ to F. We add all nonlinear such ij's to F, and keep adding linear arcs as long as the linear acyclic property is maintained. Consider a linear arc ij, which is not admitted to F because there exists a path $P \subseteq \overleftrightarrow{F}$ between i and j. Then we reroute the entire amount f_{ij} of flow from ij to P.

If no new arc enters F, then we move to the next scaling phase with the same f and set the scaling factor to $\Delta/2$. This is done also if F is extended, but it still has a high discrepancy: $D_b(F) > \Delta$.

Otherwise, the subroutine TRIAL-AND-ERROR(F, f, Δ) determines the next f and Δ. Based on the arc set F, we find a new F-pseudoflow f and scaling factor at most $\Delta/2$. The subroutine may also terminate with an F-optimal solution, which enables us to find an optimal solution to (P) by a maximum flow computation due to Lemma 4.2.

Algorithm ENHANCED CONVEX FLOW
$f \leftarrow \mathbf{0}$; $\Delta \leftarrow \max\{err_\emptyset(f), Ex_b(f)/(2n + m_N)\}$;
$F \leftarrow \emptyset$;
repeat //Δ-phase
  if f is not Δ-feasible **then** ADJUST(Δ);
  do //main part
    $S(\Delta) \leftarrow \{i \in V : \rho_f(i) - b_i \ge \Delta\}$;
    $T(\Delta) \leftarrow \{i \in V : \rho_f(i) - b_i \le -\Delta\}$;
    $P \leftarrow$ shortest $s - t$ path in E_f^F
      with $s \in S(\Delta)$, $t \in T(\Delta)$;
    send Δ units on P from s to t;
  while $S(\Delta), T(\Delta) \ne \emptyset$;
  EXTEND(F, f, Δ);
  if F was extended *and* $(D_b(F) \le \Delta)$
    then TRIAL-AND-ERROR(F, f, Δ)
    else $\Delta \leftarrow \Delta/2$;

The Trial-and-Error subroutine

The subroutine assumes that the discrepancy of F is small: $D_b(F) \le \Delta$.

Step 1. First, modify b to $\hat{b}$: in each (undirected) component K of F, pick a node $j \in K$ and change b_j by $-\sum_{i\in K} b_i$; leave all other b_i values unchanged. Thus we get a $\hat{b}$ with $D_{\hat{b}}(F) = 0$. TRIAL$(F, \hat{b})$ returns an F-tight vector $\hat{f}$.

Step 2. Call the subroutine ERROR$(\hat{f}, F)$. If $b = \hat{b}$ and $err_F(\hat{f}) = 0$, then $\hat{f}$ is F-optimal. By Lemma 4.2, an optimal solution to (P) can be found by a single maximum flow computation. In this case, the algorithm terminates. If $err_F(\hat{f}) \ge \Delta/2$, then keep the original f, and go to the next scaling phase with scaling factor $\Delta/2$. Otherwise, set $f = \hat{f}$ and define the next scaling factor as

$$\Delta_{next} = \max\{err_F(\hat{f}), Ex_b(\hat{f})/(2n + m_N)\}.$$

5. ANALYSIS

TRIAL-AND-ERROR replaces f by $\hat{f}$ if $err_F(\hat{f}) \le \Delta/2$ and keeps the same f otherwise. The first case will be called a *successful* trial, the latter is *unsuccessful*. The following is (an almost identical) counterpart of Lemma 3.1.

LEMMA 5.1. *(i) In the Δ-phase, the F-pseudoflow f is an integer multiple of Δ on each arc $ij \in E - F$, and consequently, $E_f^F(\Delta) = E_f^F$.*

(ii) (Δ, F)-feasibility is maintained in the main part and in subroutine EXTEND(F, f, Δ).

(iii) At the beginning of the main part, $Ex(f) \le (2n + m_N)\Delta$, and at the end, $Ex(f) \le n\Delta$.

(iv) The main part consists of at most $2n + m_N$ flow augmentation steps.

PROOF. For *(i)*, f is zero everywhere in $E - F$ at the beginning of the algorithm and after every successful trial. In every other case, the previous phase had scaling factor 2Δ, and thus by induction, the flow is an integer multiple of 2Δ at the beginning of the Δ-phase. This is maintained in the preprocessing, as ADJUST may only modify by Δ. The shortest path augmentations also change the flow by Δ. This implies $E_f^F(\Delta) = E_f^F$.

For *(ii)*, P is a shortest path if there exists potentials π verifying (4) with $\pi_j - \pi_i = C'_{ij}(f_{ij} + \Delta)$ on each arc $ij \in P$. We show that when augmenting on the shortest path P, (4) is maintained with the same π. If neither of ij, ji is in P, then it is trivial as the flow is not changed on ij. If $ij \in P$, then the new flow value will be $f_{ij} + \Delta$, hence we need $\pi_j - \pi_i \le C'_{ij}(f_{ij} + 2\Delta)$, obvious as C'_{ij} is monotonely increasing. Finally, if $ji \in P$, then the new flow is $f_{ij} - \Delta$, and thus we need $\pi_j - \pi_i \le C'_{ij}(f_{ij})$. By $ji \in P$ we had $\pi_i - \pi_j = C'_{ji}(f_{ji} + \Delta)$, which is equivalent to $\pi_j - \pi_i = C'_{ij}(f_{ij} - \Delta)$, implying again the claim.

In subroutine EXTEND, we reroute the flow f_{ij} from a linear arc ij if $\overleftrightarrow{F}$ contains a directed path P from i to j. This cannot affect feasibility since the C'_{ij}'s are constant on linear arcs. Also note that arcs in $\overleftrightarrow{F}$ have infinite residual capacities.

For *(iii)*, $Ex(f) \le n\Delta$ as the main part terminates with either $S(\Delta) = \emptyset$ or $T(\Delta) = \emptyset$. If the original flow f is kept and the next scaling factor is $\Delta/2$, then $Ex(f) \le 2n(\Delta/2)$ at the beginning of the next phase. ADJUST$(\Delta/2)$ increases the excess by at most $\Delta/2$ on each nonlinear arc, and it does not change values on linear arcs. If a successful trial replaced Δ by Δ_{next}, then by definition, the new excess is at most $(2n+m_N)\Delta_{next}$, and ADJUST(Δ_{next}) does not change anything as the flow is already Δ_{next}-feasible. *(iii)* immediately implies *(iv)*, as each flow augmentation decreases $Ex(f)$ by Δ. □

LEMMA 5.2. *$F \subseteq F^*$ holds in each step of the algorithm.*

PROOF. The proof is by induction. A new arc ij may enter F if $f_{ij} > (2n + m + 1)\Delta$ for a (Δ, F)-feasible f. We shall prove that $f_{ij} > 0$ for some F-optimal solution, and thus Lemma 4.2 gives $ij \in F^*$.

After the phase when ij entered, let us continue with running the basic algorithm in all later phases: we do not extend F and do not perform TRIAL-AND-ERROR in any of the later phases, and always choose the next scaling factor as $\Delta/2$. In a Δ'-phase, the flow is modified by at most Δ' on ij during preprocessing and $(2n+m_N)\Delta'$ during the main part by Lemma 5.1(v). Consequently, in all phases after Δ, the total modification is bounded by $(2n+m+1)(\Delta/2+\Delta/4+...) \le (2n + m + 1)$.

If we leave the algorithm running forever, it converges to the F-optimal solution f^*. By the above observation, $f^*_{ij} > 0$. □

The next lemma is of key importance.

LEMMA 5.3. *In* TRIAL-AND-ERROR(F, f, Δ), $err_F(\hat{f}) \le 2(2n + m + 4)m\Delta$.

Before proving the lemma, we show how it provides the strongly polynomial bound.

THEOREM 5.4. *The enhanced algorithm terminates in at most $O((n + m_N)\log m)$ scaling phases.*

PROOF. The set of revealed arcs can be extended at most m_N+n-1 times, since there can be at most $(n-1)$ linear arcs because of the linear acyclic property. We shall show that after any Δ-phase, a new arc is revealed within $2\lceil \log_2 T\rceil$ phases, for $T = 8(2n+m+4)m$. As Δ decreases by at least a factor of two between two phases, after $\lceil \log_2 T\rceil$ steps we have $\Delta_T \le \Delta/T$. Assume that in the Δ_T phase, we still have the same revealed arc set F as in the Δ-phase.

Assume first $D_b(F) > \Delta$. At the end of the main part of the Δ_T-phase, $D_b(F) > (2n + m + 2)m\Delta_T$. Thus there is a connected component K of F with $|\sum_{i\in K} b_i| > (2n + m + 2)m\Delta_T$. We have

$$|\rho_f(K)| = \left|\sum_{i\in K} \rho_f(i)\right| \ge \left|\sum_{i\in K} b_i\right| - Ex_b(f) >$$
$$> (2n + m + 2)m\Delta_T - n\Delta_T \ge (2n + m + 1)m\Delta_T.$$

There must be an arc ij entering or leaving K with $f_{ij} > 2n+m+1$, a contradiction as at least one such arc must be added to F in EXTEND(F, f, Δ_T).

Assume next $D_b(F) \le \Delta$. We may assume that either we are at the very beginning of the algorithm with $F = \emptyset$, or in a phase when F just has been extended; otherwise, we could consider an earlier phase with this property. We can interpret the initial solution **0** and Δ_0 as the output of TRIAL-AND-ERROR(**0**).

If $D_b(F) > \Delta_T$, the above argument shows that within the next $\lceil \log_2 T\rceil$ steps, F shall be extended. Otherwise, we can apply the analysis of the TRIAL-AND-ERROR subroutine for the Δ_T-phase. (Even if the subroutine is not actually performed, its analysis is valid provided that $D_b(F) \le \Delta_T$.)

Let $\hat{f}$ be the arc set found by TRIAL$(F, \hat{b})$. This is the same in the Δ and the Δ_T-phase (we may assume that b is modified to $\hat{b}$ always the same way for the same F). In the event of an unsuccessful trial in the Δ-phase, $\Delta/2 < err_F(\hat{f})$. Using Lemma 5.3 for the Δ_T-phase,

$$err_F(\hat{f}) \le 2(2n+m+4)m\Delta_T \le \Delta/4 < err_F(\hat{f})/2,$$

a contradiction. On the other hand, if we had a successful trial in the Δ-phase, then $\Delta_T \le 2\Delta_{next}/T$. Also, $Ex_b(\hat{f}) \le nD_b(F) \le n\Delta_T$. Thus

$$\Delta_{next} = \max\{err_F(\hat{f}), Ex_b(\hat{f})/(2n+m_N)\} \le$$
$$\le 2(2n+m+4)m\Delta_T \le \Delta_{next}/2,$$

a contradiction again. □

Some preparation is needed to prove Lemma 5.3.

LEMMA 5.5. *For a linear acylic arc set $F \subseteq E$, let x and y be two F-tight vectors. Then $||x-y||_\infty \le ||\rho_x - \rho_y||_1$ holds.*

PROOF. First, we claim that the difference graph $D_{x,y} = (V, E_{x,y})$ is acyclic. Indeed, if there existed a cycle $C \subseteq E_{x,y}$, then we get $0 = \sum_{ab\in C} C'_{ab}(x_{ab}) = \sum_{ab\in C} C'_{ab}(y_{ab})$. As $x_{ab} > y_{ab}$ for every $ab \in C$, this is only possible if all arcs of C are linear, contradicting the linear acyclic property of F. (Note that $E_{x,y} \subseteq \overleftrightarrow{F}$).

Define the function g by $g_{ij} = x_{ij} - y_{ij} > 0$ for $ij \in E_{x,y}$ (again with the convention $x_{ji} = -x_{ij}, y_{ji} = -y_{ij}$ if $ij \in E$). $\rho_g \equiv \rho_x - \rho_y$, therefore we have to prove $g_{ij} \le ||\rho_g||_1$ for $ij \in E_{x,y}$. This property indeed holds for every positive g with acyclic support.

Consider a reverse topological ordering $v_1, \dots, v_n$ of V, where $v_p v_q \in E_{x,y}$ implies $p > q$. For the arc $ij \in E_{x,y}$, let $i = v_{t'}$ and $j = v_t$ $(t' > t)$. Let $V_t = \{v_1, \dots, v_t\}$. V_t is a directed cut in $E_{x,y}$, thus

$$\sum_{p>t\ge q} g_{v_p v_q} = \sum_{p\le t} \rho_g(v_p).$$

As g is positive on all arcs, this implies $g_{v_a v_b} \le \sum_{p\le t} \rho_g(v_p) \le ||\rho_g||_1$ for all such arcs, in particular, for ij. □

CLAIM 5.6. *If f and $\hat{f}$ are F-pseudoflows with $\hat{f}_{ij} = 0$ for $ij \in E - F$, and f is (Δ, F)-feasible, then $\hat{f}$ is $\Delta + ||f - \hat{f}||_\infty$ feasible.*

PROOF. There is a potential π so that f and π satisfy (4), that is, $\pi_j - \pi_i \le C'_{ij}(f_{ij} + \Delta)$ if $ij \in E_f^F(\Delta)$. For $\alpha = ||f - \hat{f}||_\infty$, we have $f_{ij} + \Delta \le \hat{f}_{ij} + \Delta + \alpha$. Consequently, (4) is satisfied for $\hat{f}_{ij}$, π and $\Delta + \alpha$ for every arc in $E_f^F(\Delta)$.

By the assumption that $\hat{f}$ is zero outside F, we have $E_{\hat{f}}^F(\Delta + \alpha) = E \cup \overleftarrow{F} \subseteq E_f^F(\Delta)$ and thus the claim follows. □

PROOF OF LEMMA 5.3. f is (Δ, F)-feasible with some potential π. We claim that there is an F-tight $\bar{f}$ so that $|\bar{f}_{ij} - f_{ij}| \le \Delta$ for every $ij \in F$, and $Ex_b(f) \le (2n+m+2)m\Delta$.

Indeed, (Δ, F)-feasibility gives

$$C'_{ij}(f_{ij} - \Delta) \le \pi_j - \pi_i \le C'_{ij}(f_{ij} + \Delta) \quad \forall ij \in F.$$

As C'_{ij} is continuous, there must be a value $f_{ij} - \Delta \le \beta \le f_{ij} + \Delta$ with $C'_{ij}(\beta) = \pi_j - \pi_i$. Let us set $\bar{f}_{ij} = \beta$. This increases $Ex_b(f)$ by at most $|F|\Delta$.

Let us set $\bar{f}_{ij} = 0$ for $ij \in E - F$. Using that $f_{ij} \le (2n+m+1)\Delta$ if $ij \notin F$ and $Ex_b(f) \le n\Delta$, we obtain an F-tight $\bar{f}$ with

$$Ex_b(\bar{f}) \le n\Delta + |F|\Delta + (2n+m+1)(m - |F|)\Delta$$
$$\le (2n+m+2)m\Delta.$$

On the other hand, $Ex_b(\hat{f}) \le nD_b(F) \le n\Delta$. Consequently,

$$||\rho_{\bar{f}} - \rho_{\hat{f}}||_1 \le ||\rho_{\bar{f}} - b||_1 + ||\rho_{\hat{f}} - b||_1 =$$
$$= 2Ex_b(\bar{f}) + 2Ex_b(\hat{f}) \le 2(2n+m+3)m\Delta.$$

Applying Lemma 5.5 for $x = \bar{f}$ and $y = \hat{f}$ gives $||\bar{f} - \hat{f}||_\infty \le 2(2n+m+3)m\Delta$. Now $\bar{f}$ is $2(2n+m+4)m\Delta$-feasible by Claim 5.6. □

THEOREM 5.7. *Let $\rho_S(n,m)$ be the running time needed for one shortest path computation. Then the running time of the algorithm is bounded by*

$$O((n+m_N)(\rho_T(n,m)+\rho_E(n,m))+(n+m_N)^2\rho_S(n,m)\log m).$$

PROOF. By Theorem 5.4, there are at most $(n+m_N)\log m$ scaling phases, each dominated by $O(n+m_N)$ shortest path computations. The subroutine TRIAL-AND-ERROR is performed only when F is extended, that is, at most $n + m_N$ times, and performs the subroutines TRIAL and ERROR. □

We may not use $O(\log n) = O(\log m)$ as the graph is allowed to contain parallel arcs.

REMARK 5.8. *A shortest path computation can be performed in time $\rho_S(n,m) = O(m + n\log n)$, see [9]. Recall that the original problem instance was on n' nodes and m' arcs, and it was transformed to an uncapacitated instance on $n = n' + m'$ nodes and $m = 2m'$ arcs. However, as in Orlin's [28] algorithm, we can use the bound $O(m' + n'\log n')$ instead of $O(m' + m'\log n')$ because shortest path computations can be essentially performed on the original network.*

6. APPLICATIONS

6.1 Quadratic convex costs

Assume that $C_{ij}(\alpha) = c_{ij}\alpha^2 + d_{ij}\alpha$ for each $ij \in E$, with $c_{ij} \ge 0$. This clearly satisfies Assumption 1 since $C'_{ij}(\alpha) = 2c_{ij}\alpha + d_{ij}$. Also, Assumption 2 is satisfied.

The subroutine TRIAL(F, b) can be implemented by solving a system of linear equations.

$$\pi_j - \pi_i = 2c_{ij}x_{ij} + d_{ij} \qquad \forall ij \in F \qquad (6)$$
$$\sum_{j:ji\in F} x_{ji} - \sum_{j:ij\in F} x_{ij} = b_i \qquad \forall i \in V$$

To verify Assumption 3, we show that this system is solvable if F is linear acyclic and $D_b(F) = 0$. Clearly, we can solve the system separately on different connected components of F. In the sequel, let us focus on a connected component K.

Consider first the case when all arcs are linear. Then we can solve the equalities corresponding to edges and nodes separately. As F is assumed to be linear acyclic, it forms a tree. If we fix one π_j value arbitrarily, it determines all other π_i values by moving along the edges in the tree. The x_{ij}'s can be found by solving a flow problem on the same tree with the demands b_i. Both tasks can be performed in linear time.

Assume next both linear and nonlinear arcs are present, and let T be a connected component of linear arcs. As above, all $\pi_j - \pi_i$ values for $i, j \in T$ are uniquely determined. If there is a nonlinear arc $ij \in F$ with $i, j \in T$, then $x_{ij} = \alpha$ is also uniquely determined. We can remove this edge by replacing b_i by $b_i + \alpha$ and b_j by $b_j - \alpha$. Hence we may assume that the components of linear edges span no nonlinear edges.

Next, we can contract each such component T to a single node t by setting $b_t = \sum_{i \in T} b_i$ and modifying the d_{ij} values on incident arcs appropriately. A solution to the contracted problem can be extended to the original instance.

For the rest, we can assume all arcs are nonlinear, that is, $c_{ij} > 0$ for all $ij \in F$. Let A be the node-arc incidence matrix of F on component K: $A_{i,ij} = -1$, $A_{i,ji} = 1$ for all $ij \in F$, and all other entries are 0. Let C be the $|F| \times |F|$ diagonal matrix with $C_{ij,ij} = -2c_{ij}$. (6) can be written in the form

$$\begin{pmatrix} A^T & C \\ 0 & A \end{pmatrix} (\pi, x) = \begin{pmatrix} d \\ b \end{pmatrix}.$$

This can be transformed into

$$\begin{pmatrix} A^T & C \\ L & 0 \end{pmatrix} (\pi, x) = \begin{pmatrix} d \\ b' \end{pmatrix},$$

where L is the weighted $|K| \times |K|$ Laplacian matrix with $L_{ii} = \sum_{j: ij \in \overleftrightarrow{F}} \frac{1}{2c_{ij}}$, $L_{ij} = L_{ji} = -\frac{1}{2c_{ij}}$ if $ij \in F$ and $L_{ij} = 0$ otherwise, and b' is an appropriate vector with $\sum_{i \in K} b'_i = 0$.

The main task is to solve the system $L\pi = b'$. It is well-know that in the component K of F, L has rank $|K| - 1$ and the system is always solvable whenever $\sum_{i \in K} b'_i = 0$. A solution can be found in $O(n^{2.37})$ time [3]. All previously described operations can be done in $O(m)$ time, hence we obtain $\rho_E(n, m) = O(n^{2.37})$.

To implement ERROR(f, F), we have to find the minimum Δ-value such that there exists a π potential with

$$\pi_j - \pi_i \le (2c_{ij}x_{ij} + d_{ij}) + 2c_{ij}\Delta \quad \forall ij \in E \cup \overleftarrow{F}. \qquad (7)$$

We show that this can be reduced to the minimum-cost-to-time ratio cycle problem (see [1, Chapter 5.7]). In a directed graph, there is a cost function p_{ij} and a time $\tau_{ij} \ge 0$ associated with each arc. The aim is to find a cycle C minimizing $(\sum_{ij \in C} p_{ij}) / (\sum_{ij \in C} \tau_{ij})$. A strongly polynomial algorithm was given by Megiddo [22, 23] that solves the problem in $\min\{O(n^3 \log^2 n), O(n \log n(n^2 + m \log\log n))\}$ time. The problem can be equivalently formulated as

$$\min \mu \text{ s. t. there are no negative cycles for the cost function } p_{ij} - \mu\tau_{ij}. \qquad (8)$$

Our problem fits into this framework with $p_{ij} = 2c_{ij}x_{ij} + d_{ij}$ and $\tau_{ij} = 2c_{ij}$. In (8), the optimal μ value is $-\Delta$. However, [22] defines the minimum ratio cycle problem with $\tau_{ij} > 0$ for every $ij \in E$. This property is not essential for Megiddo's algorithm, which uses a parametric search method for μ to solve (8) under the only (implicit) restriction that the problem is feasible.

In our setting $\tau_{ij} > 0$ holds for nonlinear arcs, but $\tau_{ij} = 0$ for linear arcs. Also, there can be cycles C with $\sum_{ij \in C} \tau_{ij} = 0$. (This can happen even if F is linear acyclic, as C can be any cycle in $E \cup \overleftarrow{F}$.) If we have such a cycle C with $\sum_{ij \in C} p_{ij} < 0$, then (8) is infeasible. In every other case, the problem is feasible and thus Megiddo's algorithm can be applied.

For this reason, we first check whether there is a negative cycle with respect to the p_{ij}'s in the set of linear arcs in $E \cup \overleftarrow{F}$. If there exists one, then (7) is infeasible, thus $\Delta = \infty$, and (P) is unbounded as we can send arbitrary flow around this cycle. Otherwise, we have $\sum_{ij \in C} \tau_{ij} > 0$ for any cycle with $\sum_{ij \in C} p_{ij} < 0$, and consequently, there exists a finite Δ satisfying (7).

Consequently, $\rho_T(n, m) = \min\{O(n^3 \log^2 n), O(n \log n(n^2 + m \log\log n))\}$. Theorem 5.7 gives the following running time bound.

THEOREM 6.1. *For convex quadratic objectives on an uncapacitated instance on n nodes and m arcs, the algorithm finds an optimal solution in $O(m(n^3 \log^2 n + m \log m(m + n \log n)))$. For a capacitated instance, the running time can be bounded by $O(m^4 \log m)$.*

The bottleneck is clearly the m minimum-cost-to-time computations. As in Remark 5.8, it is likely that one can get the same running time $O(m(n^3 \log^2 n + m \log m(m + n \log n)))$ for capacitated instances as well analyzing Megiddo's algorithm.

6.2 Fisher's market with linear utilities

In the *linear Fisher market model*, we are given a set B of buyers and a set G of goods. Buyer i has a budget m_i, and there is one divisible unit of each good to be sold. For each buyer $i \in B$ and good $j \in G$, $U_{ij} \ge 0$ is the utility accrued by buyer i for one unit of good j. Let $n = |B| + |G|$; let E be the set of pairs (i, j) with $U_{ij} > 0$ and let $m = |E|$. We assume that there is at least one edge incident to each i and to each j.

An equilibrium solution consist of prices p_i on the goods and an allocation x_{ij}, so that *(i)* all goods are sold, *(ii)* all money of the buyers is spent, and *(iii)* each buyer i buys a best bundle of goods, that is, goods j maximizing U_{ij}/p_j.

The classical convex programming relaxation of this problem was given by Eisenberg and Gale [7] in 1959. Recently, Shmyrev [31] gave the following alternative relaxation. The variable f_{ij} represents the money payed by buyer i for product j.

$$\begin{aligned} \min \sum_{i \in G} p_j(\log p_j - 1) - \sum_{ij \in E} f_{ij} \log U_{ij} & \\ \sum_{j \in G} f_{ij} = m_i & \qquad \forall i \in B \\ \sum_{i \in B} f_{ij} = p_j & \qquad \forall j \in G \\ f_{ij} \ge 0 & \qquad \forall ij \in E \end{aligned}$$

Let us construct a network on node set $B \cup G \cup \{t\}$ as follows. Add an arc ij for every $i \in B$, $j \in G$ with $U_{ij} > 0$, and an arc jt for every $j \in G$. Set $b_i = -m_i$ for $i \in B$, $b_j = 0$ for $j \in G$ and $b_t = \sum_{i \in B} m_i$. Let all lower arc capacities be 0 and upper arc capacities ∞. With p_j representing the flow on arc jt, the above formulation is a minimum-cost flow problem with separable convex objective. In this section, the convention $p_j = f_{jt}$ shall be used for some pseudoflow f in the above problem.

Let us justify that an optimal solution gives a market equilibrium. Let f be an optimal solution that satisfies (1) with $\pi : B \cup G \cup \{t\} \to \mathbb{R}$. We may assume $\pi_t = 0$. $C'_{jt}(\alpha) = \log \alpha$ implies $\pi_j = -\log p_j$. On each $ij \in E$ we have $\pi_j - \pi_i \le -\log U_{ij}$ with equality if $f_{ij} > 0$. With $\beta_i = e^{\pi_i}$, this is equivalent to $U_{ij}/p_j \le \beta_i$, verifying that every buyer buys a best bundle of goods.

Assumption 2 is clearly satisfied, however, Assumption 1 needs oracle access to the derivatives. On the arcs ij between buyers and goods, this is $-\log U_{ij}$, while on an arc jt it is $\log f_{jt}$, hence we cannot determine the exact values.

The derivative oracle is used in two parts of the algorithm: for computing shortest paths between $S(\Delta)$ and $T(\Delta)$ in the main part, and for the subroutine ADJUST(Δ) in the preprocessing part. We can solve both these problems provided the rational values $e^{C'_{ij}(\alpha)}$. For shortest path computations, we use a multiplicative version of Dijkstra's algorithm, computing products instead of sums on the arcs. For ADJUST(Δ), we need a potential π verifying that f is (Δ, F)-feasible. Instead of the π_j values we can use the e^{π_j} values, that can be chosen as rational numbers.

Let us turn to Assumption 3. When the subroutine TRIAL is called, we transform b to $\hat{b}$ by changing the value at one node of each component K of F. For simplicity, let us always modify b_t if $t \in K$. We shall verify Assumption 3 only for such $\hat{b}$'s; the argument can easily be extended to arbitrary $\hat{b}$ (although it is not necessary for the algorithm). Let us call the component K containing t the *large component*.

In TRIAL(F), we want to find a potential $\pi : B \cup G \cup \{t\} \to \mathbb{R} \cup \{\infty\}$, money allocations f_{ij} for $ij \in F$, $i \in B$, $j \in G$, and prices $p_j = f_{jt}$ for $jt \in F$ such that

$$\begin{aligned} \pi_j - \pi_i &= -\log U_{ij} && \forall ij \in F, i \in B, j \in G \\ \pi_t - \pi_j &= \log p_j && \forall jt \in F \\ p_j &= \sum_{i \in B, ij \in F} f_{ij} && \forall jt \in F \end{aligned}$$

We may again assume $\pi_t = 0$. Let $P_j = e^{-\pi_j}$ for $j \in G$ and $R_i = e^{\pi_i}$ for $i \in B$. With this notation, $U_{ij}/P_j = R_i$ for $ij \in F$. If $jt \in F$, then $P_j = p_j$.

Finding f and π can be done independently on the different components of F. For any component different from the large one, all edges are linear. Therefore we only need to find a feasible flow on a tree, and independently, P_j and R_i values satisfying $U_{ij}/P_j = R_i$ on arcs ij in the component. Both of these can be performed in linear time in the number of edges in the tree. Note that multiplying each P_j by a constant $\alpha > 0$ and dividing each R_i by the same α yields another feasible solution.

Let $T_1, \ldots, T_k$ be the components of the large component after deleting t. If T_ℓ contains a single good j, then we shall set $p_j = P_j = 0$ ($\pi_j = 0$). If T_ℓ is nonsingular, then F restricted to T_ℓ forms a spanning tree. The equalities $U_{ij}/P_j = R_i$ uniquely define the ratio $P_j/P_{j'}$ for any $j, j' \in G \cap T_\ell$. Using that $p_j = P_j$ and $\sum_{i \in B \cap T_\ell} m_i = \sum_{j \in G \cap T_\ell} p_j$, this uniquely determines the prices in the component. Then the edges in F simply provide the allocations f_{ij}. All these computations can be performed in $\rho_T(n, m) = O(m)$ time.

For Assumption 4, we show that ERROR(f, F) can be implemented based on the Floyd-Warshall algorithm. Let π be the potential witnessing that f is (Δ, F)-feasible. Assuming $\pi_t = 0$, and using again the notation $P_j = e^{-\pi_j}$ for $j \in G$ and $R_i = e^{\pi_i}$ for $i \in B$, we get $U_{ij}/P_j \le R_i$ if $i \in B$, $j \in G$, $ij \in E$, with equality if $ji \in E_f^F$. Furthermore, we have $p_j - \Delta \le P_j \le p_j + \Delta$ if $p_j > 0$ and $P_j \le \Delta$ if $p_j = 0$.

Let us now define $\beta : G \times G \to \mathbb{R}$ as

$$\beta_{jj'} = \max \left\{ \frac{U_{ij'}}{U_{ij}} : i \in B, ji, ij' \in E_f^F \right\}.$$

If no such i exists, define $\beta_{jj'} = 0$; let $\beta_{jj} = 1$ for every $j \in G$.

Clearly, $P_{j'} \ge P_j \beta_{jj'}$ must hold to guarantee that edges ij with $ji \in E_f^F$ have the best bang-per-buck values. Conversely, if the prices P_j satisfy this property, then we can set the R_i values as best bang-per-buck ratios, thus satisfying the necessary inequalities on all edges.

If there is a directed cycle C with $\Pi_{ab \in C} \beta_{ab} > 1$, then f cannot be (Δ, F)-feasible for any Δ. Otherwise, we may compute $\tilde{\beta}_{jj'}$ as the maximum of $\Pi_{ab \in P} \beta_{ab}$ over all directed paths P from j to j' (setting the value 0 again if no such path exists). This can be done by the multiplicative version of the Floyd-Warshall algorithm in $O(n^3)$ time (note that this is equivalent to finding all-pair shortest paths for $-\log \beta_{ab}$).

For (Δ, F)-feasibility, we clearly need to satisfy

$$(p_j - \Delta)\tilde{\beta}_{jj'} \le P_j \tilde{\beta}_{jj'} \le P_{j'} \le p_{j'} + \Delta.$$

Let us define Δ as the smallest value satisfying all these inequalities, that is,

$$\Delta = \max \left\{ 0, \max_{j, j' \in G} \frac{p_j \tilde{\beta}_{jj'} - p_{j'}}{\tilde{\beta}_{jj'} + 1} \right\}. \tag{9}$$

We claim that f is (Δ, F)-feasible with the above choice. For each $j \in G$, let $P_j = \max_{h \in G} \tilde{\beta}_{hj}(p_h - \Delta)$. It is easy to verify that these P values satisfy $P_{j'} \ge P_j \beta_{jj'}$, and $p_j - \Delta \le P_j \le p_j + \Delta$.

The complexity of ERROR(f, F) is dominated by the Floyd-Warshall algorithm, $O(n^3)$ [8]. The problem is defined on an uncapacitated network, with the number of nonlinear arcs $m_N = |G| < n$. Thus Theorem 5.7 gives the following.

THEOREM 6.2. *For Fisher's market with linear utilities, the algorithm finds an optimal solution in $O(n^4 + n^2(m + n \log n) \log n)$.*

The algorithm by Orlin [29] runs in $O(n^4 \log n)$ time, assuming $m = O(n^2)$. Under this assumption, we get the same running time bound.

6.3 Fisher's market with spending constraint utilities

The *spending constraint utility* extension of linear Fisher markets was defined by Vazirani [35]. In this model, the utility of a buyer decreases as the function of the money spent on the good. Formally, for each pair i and j there is a sequence $U_{ij}^1 > U_{ij}^2 > \ldots > U_{ij}^{\ell_{ij}} > 0$ of utilities with numbers $L_{ij}^1, \ldots, L_{ij}^{\ell_j} > 0$. Buyer i accrues utility U_{ij}^1 for every unit of j he purchased by spending the first L_{ij}^1 dollars on good j, U_{ij}^2 for spending the next L_{ij}^2 dollars, etc. These ℓ_{ij} intervals corresponding to the pair ij are called *segments*. $\ell_{ij} = 0$ is allowed, but altogether at least one segment is required to be incident to each good i and to each buyer j. Let $n = |B| + |G|$ denote the total number of buyers and goods, and m denote the total number of segments. Note that $m > n^2$ is also possible.

No extension of the Eisenberg-Gale convex program is known to capture this problem. The existence of a convex programming formulation is left as an open question in [35]. This was settled by Devanur et al. [2], showing that Shmyrev's formulation naturally extends here. Let f_{ij}^k represent the money payed by buyer i for the k'th segment of product j, $1 \le k \le \ell_{ij}$.

$$\min \sum_{i \in G} p_j(\log p_j - 1) - \sum_{i \in B, j \in G, 1 \le k \le \ell_{ij}} f_{ij}^k \log U_{ij}^k$$

$$\sum_{j \in G, 1 \le k \le \ell_{ij}} f_{ij}^k = m_i \quad \forall i \in B$$

$$\sum_{i \in B, 1 \le k \le \ell_{ij}} f_{ij}^k = p_j \quad \forall j \in G$$

$$0 \le f_{ij}^k \le L_{ij}^k \quad \forall ij \in E.$$

This gives a convex cost flow problem again on the node set $B \cup G \cup \{t\}$, by adding ℓ_{ij} parallel arcs from $i \in B$ to $j \in G$, and arcs jt for each $j \in G$. The upper capacity on the k'th segment for the pair ij is L_{ij}^k. To apply our method, we first need to transform it to an equivalent problem without upper capacities. This is done by replacing the arc representing the k'th segment of ij by a new node (ij, k) and two arcs $i(ij, k)$ and $j(ij, k)$. The node demand on the new node is set to L_{ij}^k, while on the good j, we replace the demand 0 by $-\sum_{i,k} L_{ij}^k$, the negative of the sum of capacities of all incident segments. The cost function on $i(ij, k)$ is $-\log U_{ij}^k \alpha$, while the cost of $j(ij, k)$ is 0. Let S denote the set of the new (ij, k) nodes. This modified graph has $n' = n + m + 1$ nodes and $m' = 2m + |G|$ arcs.

Assumptions 1 and 2 are satisfied the same way as for linear Fisher markets, using an oracle for the $e^{C'_{ij}(\alpha)}$ values.

In TRIAL(F), we want to find an F-tight flow f' on the extended network, witnessed by the potential $\pi : B \cup S \cup G \cup \{t\} \to \mathbb{R}$. We may assume $\pi_t = 0$. Let $P_j = e^{-\pi_j}$ for $j \in G$ and $R_i = e^{\pi_i}$ for $i \in B$ and $S_{ij}^k = e^{-\pi(ij,k)}$. For the k'th segment of ij, $U_{ij}^k / S_{ij}^k \le R_i$ and $S_{ij}^k \ge P_j$. If $i(ij, k) \in F$ then $U_{ij}^k / P_j \ge R_i$ and if $j(ij, k) \in F$ then $U_{ij}^k / P_j \le R_i$.

As for linear Fisher markets, if a component of F does not contain t, we can simply compute all potentials and flows as F is a spanning tree of linear edges in this component.

For the component K with $t \in K$, let T_ℓ be a component of $K - t$. F is a spanning tree of linear edges in T_ℓ as well, therefore the ratio $P_j / P_{j'}$ is uniquely defined for any $j, j' \in G \cap T_\ell$. On the other hand, we must have $P_j = p_j$, and we know that $\sum_{j \in G \cap T_\ell} p_j = -\sum_{v \in T_\ell} b_v$ by flow conservation. These determine the $P_j = p_j$ values, and thus all other R_i and S_{ij}^k values in the component as well. The support of the flow f_{ij} is a tree and hence it can also easily computed. The running time of TRIAL is again linear, $\rho_T(n', m') = O(m') = O(m)$.

ERROR(f, F) can be implemented the same way as for the linear Fisher market. We shall define the values $\beta : G \times G \to \mathbb{R}$ so that $P_{j'} \ge P_j \beta_{jj'}$ must hold, and conversely, given P_j prices satisfying these conditions, we can define the R_i and S_{ij}^k values feasibly. Let

$$\beta_{jj'} = \max\Big\{ \frac{U_{ij'}^{k'}}{U_{ij}^k} : i \in B, \\ j(ij, k), (ij, k)i, i(ij', k'), (ij', k')j' \in E_f^F \Big\}.$$

Given these $\beta_{jj'}$ values, the $\tilde{\beta}_{jj'}$ values can be computed by the Floyd-Warshall algorithm and the optimal Δ obtained by (9) as for the linear case.

Finding the $\beta_{jj'}$ values can be done in $O(m')$ time, and the Floyd-Warshall algorithm runs in $O(|G|^3)$. This gives $\rho_E(n', m') = O(m' + |G|^3) = O(m + n^3)$. From Theorem 5.7, together with Remark 5.8, we obtain:

THEOREM 6.3. *For an instance of Fisher's market with spending constraint utilities with $n = |B| + |G|$ and m segments, the running time can be bounded by $O(mn^3 + m^2(m + n \log n) \log m)$.*

7. DISCUSSION

We have given strongly polynomial algorithms for a class of minimum-cost flow problems with separable convex objectives. This gives the first strongly polynomial algorithms for quadratic convex cost functions and for Fisher's market with spending constraint utilities. For Fisher's market with linear utilities, we get the same complexity as Orlin [29].

The bottleneck in complexity of all applications is the subroutine TRIAL. However, the exact value of $err_F(f)$ is not needed: a constant approximation would also yield the same complexity bounds. Unfortunately, no such algorithm is known for the minimum cost-to-time ratio cycle problem that would have significantly better, strongly polynomial running time. Finding such an algorithm would immediately improve the running time for quadratic costs.

A natural future direction could be to develop strongly polynomial algorithms for quadratic objectives and constraint matrices with bounded subdeterminants. This would be a counterpart of Tardos' [34] for linear programs. Such an extension could be possible by extending our techniques to the setting of Hochbaum and Shantikumar [17].

The recent paper [37] shows that linear Fisher market, along with several extension, can be captured by a concave extension of the generalized flow model. A natural question is if there is any direct connection between the concave generalized flow model and the convex minimum cost flow model studied in this paper. Despite certain similarities, no reduction is known in any direction. Indeed, no such reduction is known even between the linear special cases, that is, generalized flows and minimum-cost flows. The perfect price discrimination model by Goel and Vazirani [11], and the Arrow-Debreu Nash-bargaining problem by Vazirani [36], are instances of the concave generalized flow model, but they are not known to be reducible to convex cost flows. On the other hand, the spending constraint utility model investigated in this paper is not known to be reducible to concave generalized flows.

The algorithm in [37] is not strongly polynomial. Moreover, no strongly polynomial algorithm is known for linear generalized flows, despite the huge literature on polynomial time algorithms. Developing a strongly polynomial algorithm for generalized flows is a fundamental open question. Resolving it could lead to strongly polynomial algorithms for the market problems that fit into the concave generalized flow model.

A related problem is finding a strongly polynomial algorithm for minimizing a separable convex objective over a submodular polyhedron. Fujishige [10] showed that for separable convex quadratic costs, this is essentially equivalent to submodular function minimization. Submodular utility allocation markets by Jain and Vazirani [20] also fall into this class, and are solvable in strongly polynomial time; see also Nagano [26]. Other strongly polynomially solvable special cases are given by Hochbaum and Hong [13].

A common generalization of this problem and ours is minimizing a separable convex objective over a submodular flow polyhedron. Weakly polynomial algorithms were given by Iwata [18] and by Iwata, McCormick and Shigeno [19]. One might try to develop strongly polynomial algorithms for some class of separable convex objectives; in particular, for separable convex quadratic functions.

8. REFERENCES

[1] R. K. Ahuja, T. L. Magnanti, and J. B. Orlin. *Network Flows: Theory, Algorithms, and Applications.* Prentice-Hall, Inc., Feb. 1993.

[2] B. Birnbaum, N. R. Devanur, and L. Xiao. Distributed algorithms via gradient descent for Fisher markets. In *Proceedings of ACM EC*, pages 127–136, 2011.

[3] D. Coppersmith and S. Winograd. Matrix multiplication via arithmetic progressions. *Journal of Symbolic Computation*, 9(3):251–280, 1990.

[4] S. Cosares and D. S. Hochbaum. Strongly polynomial algorithms for the quadratic transportation problem with a fixed number of sources. *Mathematics of Operations Research*, pages 94–111, 1994.

[5] N. R. Devanur, C. H. Papadimitriou, A. Saberi, and V. V. Vazirani. Market equilibrium via a primal–dual algorithm for a convex program. *Journal of the ACM (JACM)*, 55(5):22, 2008.

[6] J. Edmonds and R. M. Karp. Theoretical improvements in algorithmic efficiency for network flow problems. *Journal of the ACM (JACM)*, 19(2):248–264, 1972.

[7] E. Eisenberg and D. Gale. Consensus of subjective probabilities: The pari-mutuel method. *The Annals of Mathematical Statistics*, 30(1):165–168, 1959.

[8] R. Floyd. Algorithm 97: shortest path. *Communications of the ACM*, 5(6):345, 1962.

[9] M. L. Fredman and R. E. Tarjan. Fibonacci heaps and their uses in improved network optimization algorithms. *Journal of the ACM (JACM)*, 34(3):596–615, 1987.

[10] S. Fujishige. Submodular systems and related topics. *Mathematical Programming at Oberwolfach II*, pages 113–131, 1984.

[11] G. Goel and V. V. Vazirani. A perfect price discrimination market model with production, and a (rational) convex program for it. *Mathematics of Operations Research*, 36:762–782, 2011.

[12] F. Granot and J. Skorin-Kapov. Towards a strongly polynomial algorithm for strictly convex quadratic programs: An extension of Tardos' algorithm. *Mathematical Programming*, 46(1):225–236, 1990.

[13] D. Hochbaum and S. Hong. About strongly polynomial time algorithms for quadratic optimization over submodular constraints. *Mathematical programming*, 69(1):269–309, 1995.

[14] D. Hochbaum and M. Queyranne. Minimizing a convex cost closure set. *SIAM Journal on Discrete Mathematics*, 16:192, 2003.

[15] D. S. Hochbaum. Lower and upper bounds for the allocation problem and other nonlinear optimization problems. *Mathematics of Operations Research*, 19(2):390–409, 1994.

[16] D. S. Hochbaum. Complexity and algorithms for nonlinear optimization problems. *Annals of Operations Research*, 153(1):257–296, 2007.

[17] D. S. Hochbaum and J. G. Shanthikumar. Convex separable optimization is not much harder than linear optimization. *Journal of the ACM (JACM)*, 37(4):843–862, 1990.

[18] S. Iwata. A capacity scaling algorithm for convex cost submodular flows. *Mathematical Programming*, 76(2):299–308, 1997.

[19] S. Iwata, S. Mccormick, and M. Shigeno. Fast cycle canceling algorithms for minimum cost submodular flow. *Combinatorica*, 23(3):503–525, 2003.

[20] K. Jain and V. V. Vazirani. Eisenberg-Gale markets: Algorithms and game-theoretic properties. *Games and Economic Behavior*, 70(1):84–106, 2010.

[21] A. V. Karzanov and S. T. McCormick. Polynomial methods for separable convex optimization in unimodular linear spaces with applications. *SIAM J. Comput.*, 26(4):1245–1275, 1997.

[22] N. Megiddo. Combinatorial optimization with rational objective functions. *Mathematics of Operations Research*, 4(4):414–424, 1979.

[23] N. Megiddo. Applying parallel computation algorithms in the design of serial algorithms. *Journal of the ACM (JACM)*, 30(4):852–865, 1983.

[24] M. Minoux. A polynomial algorithm for minimum quadratic cost flow problems. *European Journal of Operational Research*, 18(3):377–387, 1984.

[25] M. Minoux. Solving integer minimum cost flows with separable convex cost objective polynomially. *Mathematical Programming Study*, 25:237, 1985.

[26] K. Nagano. On convex minimization over base polytopes. *Integer Programming and Combinatorial Optimization*, pages 252–266, 2007.

[27] N. Nisan, T. Roughgarden, E. Tardos, and V. Vazirani. *Algorithmic Game Theory.* Cambridge University Press New York, NY, USA, 2007.

[28] J. B. Orlin. A faster strongly polynomial minimum cost flow algorithm. *Operations Research*, 41(2):338–350, 1993.

[29] J. B. Orlin. Improved algorithms for computing Fisher's market clearing prices. In *Proceedings of the 42nd ACM Symposium on Theory of Computing (STOC)*, pages 291–300. ACM, 2010.

[30] J. Renegar. On the worst-case arithmetic complexity of approximating zeros of polynomials. *Journal of Complexity*, 3(2):90–113, 1987.

[31] V. I. Shmyrev. An algorithm for finding equilibrium in the linear exchange model with fixed budgets. *Journal of Applied and Industrial Mathematics*, 3(4):505–518, 2009.

[32] A. Tamir. A strongly polynomial algorithm for minimum convex separable quadratic cost flow problems on series-parallel networks. *Mathematical Programming*, 59:117–132, 1993.

[33] É. Tardos. A strongly polynomial minimum cost

circulation algorithm. *Combinatorica*, 5(3):247–255, 1985.

[34] É. Tardos. A strongly polynomial algorithm to solve combinatorial linear programs. *Operations Research*, 34(2):250–256, 1986.

[35] V. V. Vazirani. Spending constraint utilities with applications to the adwords market. *Mathematics of Operations Research*, 35(2):458–478, 2010.

[36] V. V. Vazirani. The notion of a rational convex program, and an algorithm for the Arrow-Debreu Nash bargaining game. *Journal of ACM (JACM)*, 59(2), 2012.

[37] L. A. Végh. Concave generalized flows with applications to market equilibria. *Arxiv preprint arXiv:1109.3893*, 2011.

Quantum Money from Hidden Subspaces*

Scott Aaronson[†] Paul Christiano[‡]

ABSTRACT

Forty years ago, Wiesner pointed out that quantum mechanics raises the striking possibility of money that cannot be counterfeited according to the laws of physics. We propose the first quantum money scheme that is

(1) *public-key*—meaning that anyone can verify a banknote as genuine, not only the bank that printed it, and

(2) *cryptographically secure*, under a "classical" hardness assumption that has nothing to do with quantum money.

Our scheme is based on *hidden subspaces*, encoded as the zero-sets of random multivariate polynomials. A main technical advance is to show that the "black-box" version of our scheme, where the polynomials are replaced by classical oracles, is *unconditionally* secure. Previously, such a result had only been known relative to a *quantum* oracle (and even there, the proof was never published).

Even in Wiesner's original setting—quantum money that can only be verified by the bank—we are able to use our techniques to patch a major security hole in Wiesner's scheme. We give the first private-key quantum money scheme that allows unlimited verifications and that remains unconditionally secure, even if the counterfeiter can interact adaptively with the bank.

Our money scheme is simpler than previous public-key quantum money schemes, including a knot-based scheme of Farhi et al. The verifier needs to perform only two tests, one in the standard basis and one in the Hadamard basis—matching the original intuition for quantum money, based on the existence of complementary observables.

Our security proofs use a new variant of Ambainis's quantum adversary method, and several other tools that might be of independent interest.

*Extended abstract. For the full version, see www.scottaaronson.com/papers/money.pdf

[†]MIT. Email: aaronson@csail.mit.edu. This material is based upon work supported by the National Science Foundation under Grant No. 0844626. Also supported by a DARPA YFA grant, an NSF STC grant, a TIBCO Chair, and a Sloan Fellowship.

[‡]MIT. Email: paulfchristiano@gmail.com.

STOC'12, May 19–22, 2012, New York, New York, USA.

Categories and Subject Descriptors

F.1.2 [**Theory of Computation**]: Computation by Abstract Devices—*Modes of Computation*; E.3 [**Data**]: Data Encryption

General Terms

Theory, Security

1. INTRODUCTION

"Information wants to be free"—this slogan expresses the idea that classical bits, unlike traditional economic goods, can be copied an unlimited number of times. The copyability of classical information is one of the foundations of the digital economy, but it is also a nuisance to governments, publishers, software companies, and others who wish to prevent copying. Today, essentially all electronic commerce involves a trusted third party, such as a credit card company, to mediate transactions. Without such a third party entering at *some* stage, it is impossible to prevent electronic cash from being counterfeited, regardless of what cryptographic assumptions one makes.[1]

Famously, though, quantum bits do *not* "want to be free" in the same sense that classical bits do: in many respects, they behave more like gold, oil, or other traditional economic goods. Indeed, the *No-Cloning Theorem*, which is an immediate consequence of the linearity of quantum mechanics, says that there is no physical procedure that takes as input an unknown[2] quantum pure state $|\psi\rangle$, and that produces as output two unentangled copies of $|\psi\rangle$, or even a close approximation thereof. The No-Cloning Theorem is closely related to the *uncertainty principle*, which says that there exist "complementary" properties of a quantum state (for example, its position and momentum) that cannot both be measured to unlimited accuracy.[3]

[1]The recent Bitcoin system is an interesting illustration of this principle: it gets rid of the centralized third party, but still uses a "third party" distributed over the community of Bitcoin users.

[2]The adjective "unknown" is needed because, if we knew a classical description of a procedure to *prepare* $|\psi\rangle$, then of course we could run that procedure multiple times to prepare multiple copies.

[3]Indeed, if we could copy $|\psi\rangle$, then we could violate the uncertainty principle by measuring one observable (such as

1.1 The History of Quantum Money

But can one actually *exploit* the No-Cloning Theorem to achieve classically-impossible cryptographic tasks? This question was first asked by Wiesner [39], in a remarkable paper written around 1970 (but only published in 1983) that arguably founded quantum information science. In that paper, Wiesner proposed a scheme for *quantum money* that would be physically impossible to clone. In Wiesner's scheme, each "banknote" would consist of a classical serial number s, together with a quantum state $|\psi_s\rangle$ consisting of n unentangled qubits, each one $|0\rangle$, $|1\rangle$, $\frac{|0\rangle+|1\rangle}{\sqrt{2}}$, or $\frac{|0\rangle-|1\rangle}{\sqrt{2}}$ with equal probability. The issuing bank would maintain a giant database, which stored a classical description of $|\psi_s\rangle$ for each serial number s. Whenever someone wanted to *verify* a banknote, he or she would take it back to the bank—whereupon the bank would use its knowledge of how $|\psi_s\rangle$ was prepared to measure each qubit in the appropriate basis, and check that it got the correct outcomes. On the other hand, it can be proved [31] that someone who did *not* know the appropriate bases could copy the banknote with success probability at most $(3/4)^n$.

Though historically revolutionary, Wiesner's money scheme suffered at least three drawbacks:

(1) **The "Verifiability Problem":** The only entity that can verify a banknote is the bank that printed it.

(2) **The "Online Attack Problem":** A counterfeiter able to submit banknotes for verification, and get them back afterward, can easily break Wiesner's scheme ([28, 3]; see also Section 7).

(3) **The "Giant Database Problem":** The bank needs to maintain a database with an entry for every banknote in circulation.

In followup work in 1982, Bennett, Brassard, Breidbart, and Wiesner [14] (henceforth BBBW) at least showed how to eliminate the giant database problem: namely, by generating the state $|\psi_s\rangle = |\psi_{f_k(s)}\rangle$ using a *pseudorandom function* f_k, with key k known only by the bank. Unlike Wiesner's original scheme, the BBBW scheme is no longer *information-theoretically* secure: a counterfeiter can recover k given exponential computation time. On the other hand, a counterfeiter cannot break the scheme in polynomial time, unless it can *also* distinguish f_k from a random function.

These early ideas about quantum money inspired the field of *quantum cryptography* [13]. But strangely, the subject of quantum money itself lay dormant for more than two decades, even as interest in quantum computing exploded. However, the past few years have witnessed a "quantum money renaissance." Some recent work has offered partial solutions to the verifiability problem: for example, Mosca and Stebila [32] suggested that the bank use a *blind quantum computing* protocol to offload the verification of banknotes to local merchants, while Gavinsky [23] proposed a variant of Wiesner's scheme that requires only *classical* communication between the merchant and bank.

position) on some copies, and a complementary observable (such as momentum) on other copies. Conversely, if we could measure all the properties of $|\psi\rangle$ to unlimited accuracy, then we could use the measurement results to create additional copies of $|\psi\rangle$.

However, most of the focus today is on a more ambitious goal: namely, creating what Aaronson [3] called *public-key quantum money*, or quantum money that *anyone* could authenticate, not just the bank that printed it. As with public-key cryptography in the 1970s, it is far from obvious *a priori* whether public-key quantum money is possible at all. Can a bank publish a description of a quantum circuit that lets people feasibly *recognize* a state $|\psi\rangle$, but does not let them feasibly prepare or even copy $|\psi\rangle$?

Aaronson [3] gave the first formal treatment of public-key quantum money, as well as related notions such as copy-protected quantum software. He proved that there exists a *quantum oracle* relative to which secure public-key quantum money is possible. Unfortunately, that result, though already involved, did not lead in any obvious way to an explicit (or "real-world") quantum money scheme.[4] He raised as an open problem whether secure public-key quantum money is possible relative to a *classical* oracle. In the same paper, Aaronson also proposed an explicit scheme, based on random stabilizer states, but could not offer any evidence for its security. And indeed, the scheme was broken about a year afterward by Lutomirski et al. [30], using an algorithm for finding planted cliques in random graphs due to Alon, Krivelevich, and Sudakov [7].

Recently, Farhi et al. [22] took a completely different approach to public-key quantum money. They proposed a quantum money scheme based on *knot theory*, where each banknote is a superposition over exponentially-many oriented link diagrams. Within a given banknote, all the link diagrams L have the same Alexander polynomial $p(L)$ (a certain knot invariant).[5] This $p(L)$, together with a digital signature of $p(L)$, serves as the banknote's "classical serial number." Besides the unusual mathematics employed, the work of Farhi et al. [22] (building on [30]) also developed an idea that will play a major role in our work. That idea is to construct public-key quantum money schemes by composing two "simpler" ingredients: first, objects that we call *mini-schemes*; and second, classical digital signature schemes.

The main disadvantage of the knot-based scheme, which it shares with every previous scheme, is that no one can say much about its security—other than that it has not yet been broken, and that various known counterfeiting strategies fail. Indeed, even characterizing *which quantum states Farhi et al.'s verification procedure accepts* remains a difficult open problem, on which progress seems likely to require major advances in knot theory! In other words, there might be states that look completely different from "legitimate banknotes," but are still accepted with high probability.

In followup work, Lutomirski [29] proposed an "abstract" version of the knot scheme, which gets rid of the link diagrams and Alexander polynomials, and simply uses a classical oracle to achieve the same purposes. Lutomirski raised the challenge of proving that this *oracle* scheme is secure—in which case, it would have yielded the first public-key

[4] Also, the proof of Aaronson's result never appeared—an inexcusable debt that this paper finally repays, with interest.

[5] Instead of knots, Farhi et al. [22] could also have used, say, superpositions over n-vertex *graphs* having the same eigenvalue spectrum. But in that case, their scheme would have been breakable, the reason being that the *graph isomorphism problem* is easy for random graphs. By contrast, it is not known how to solve *knot isomorphism* efficiently, even with a quantum computer and even for random knots.

quantum money scheme that was proven secure relative to a classical oracle. Unfortunately, proving the security of Lutomirski's scheme remains open, and seems hard.[6]

As alluded to earlier, there is already some research on ways to *break* quantum money schemes. Besides the papers by Lutomirski [28] and Lutomirski et al. [30] mentioned before, let us mention the beautiful work of Farhi et al. on *quantum state restoration* [21]. As we discuss in Section 7, quantum state restoration can be used to break many public-key quantum money schemes: roughly speaking, any scheme where the banknotes contain only limited entanglement, and where verification consists of a rank-1 projective measurement. This fact explains why our scheme, like the knot-based scheme of Farhi et al. [22], will require highly-entangled banknotes.

1.2 The Challenge

Work over the past few years has revealed a surprising richness in the quantum money problem—both in the ideas that have been used to construct public-key quantum money schemes, *and* in the ideas that have been used to break them. Of course, this record also underscores the need for caution! To whatever extent we can, we ought to hold quantum money schemes to modern cryptographic standards, and not be satisfied with "we tried to break it and failed."

It is easy to see that, if public-key quantum money is possible, then it must rely on *some* computational assumption, in addition to the No-Cloning Theorem.[7] The best case would be to show that secure, public-key quantum money is possible, *if* (for example) there exist one-way functions resistant to quantum attack. Unfortunately, we seem a long way from showing anything of the kind. The basic problem is that *uncloneability* is a novel cryptographic requirement: something that would not even make sense in a classical context. Indeed, work by Farhi et al. [21] and Aaronson [3] has shown that it is sometimes possible to copy quantum banknotes, via attacks that do not even *measure* the banknotes in an attempt to learn a classical secret! Rather, these attacks simply perform some unitary transformation on a legitimate banknote $|\$\rangle$ together with an ancilla $|0\rangle$, the end result of which is to produce $|\$\rangle^{\otimes 2}$. Given such a strange attack, how can one deduce the failure of any "standard" cryptographic assumption?

Yet despite the novelty of the quantum money problem—or perhaps because of it—it seems reasonable to want *some* non-tautological evidence that a public-key quantum money scheme is secure. A minimal wish-list might include:

(1) Security under *some* plausible assumption, of a sort cryptographers know how to evaluate. Such an assumption should talk only about computing a classical output from a classical input; it should have nothing to do with cloning of quantum states.

(2) A proof that the money scheme is secure against *black-box counterfeiters*: those that do not exploit the structure of some cryptographic function f used in verifying the banknotes.

(3) A "simple" verification process, which accepts all valid banknotes $|\$\rangle$ with probability 1, and rejects all banknotes that are far from $|\$\rangle$.

1.3 Our Results

Our main contribution is a new public-key quantum money scheme, which achieves all three items in the wish-list above, and which is the first to achieve (1) or (2). Regardless of whether our particular scheme stands or falls, we introduce at least four techniques that should be useful for the design and analysis of *any* public-key quantum money scheme. These are:

- The "inner-product adversary method," a new variant of Ambainis's quantum adversary method [8] that can be used to rule out black-box counterfeiting strategies.
- A notion of *mini-schemes*, and a proof that (together with standard cryptographic assumptions) these objects imply full-fledged quantum money schemes.
- A method to *amplify* weak counterfeiters into strong ones, so that one only needs to rule out the latter to show security.
- A new connection between the security of quantum money schemes and *direct-product assumptions* in cryptography.

A second contribution is to construct the first *private-key* quantum money schemes that remain *unconditionally* secure, even if the counterfeiter can interact adaptively with the bank. This gives the first solution to the "online attack problem," a major security hole in the Wiesner [39] and BBBW [14] schemes pointed out by Lutomirski [28] and Aaronson [3]. These private-key schemes are direct adaptations of our public-key scheme.

In more detail, our quantum money scheme is based on *hidden subspaces* of the vector space $\mathbb{F}_2^n$. Each of our money states is a uniform superposition of the vectors in a random $n/2$-dimensional subspace $A \leq \mathbb{F}_2^n$. We denote this superposition by $|A\rangle$. Crucially, we can recognize the state $|A\rangle$ using only membership oracles for A and for its dual subspace $A^{\perp}$. To do so, we apply the membership oracle for A, then a Fourier transform, then the membership oracle for $A^{\perp}$, and then a second Fourier transform to restore the original state. We prove that this operation computes a rank-1 projection onto $|A\rangle$.

Underlying the security of our money schemes is the assertion that the states $|A\rangle$ are difficult to clone, even given membership oracles for A and $A^{\perp}$. Or more concretely: *any quantum algorithm that maps $|A\rangle$ to $|A\rangle^{\otimes 2}$ must make $2^{\Omega(n)}$ queries to the $A, A^{\perp}$ oracles.*

In order to prove this statement, we introduce a new method for proving lower bounds on quantum query complexity, which we call the *inner-product adversary method.* This technique considers a single counterfeiting algorithm

[6] One way to understand the difficulty is that any security proof for Lutomirski's scheme would need to contain Aaronson's quantum lower bound for the *collision problem* [1] as a (tiny) special case. The lower bound for the collision problem is proved using the polynomial method of Beals et al. [11]. In this work, by contrast, we will only manage to prove the security of *our* oracle scheme using a specially-designed variant of Ambainis's quantum adversary method [8]. Despite great progress in quantum lower bounds over the past decade, it is still not known (except implicitly) how to prove the collision lower bound using an adversary argument.

[7] This is because a counterfeiter with unlimited time could simply search for a state $|\psi\rangle$ that the (publicly-known) verification procedure accepted.

being run in parallel to clone two distinct states $|A\rangle$ and $|A'\rangle$, with each having access to the membership oracles for $A, A^\perp$ or $A', A'^\perp$, as appropriate. To measure how much progress the algorithm has made, we consider the inner product between the states produced by the parallel executions: because $\langle A|^{\otimes 2} |A'\rangle^{\otimes 2} < \langle A|A'\rangle$ for many pairs of subspaces A, A', in order to succeed a counterfeiter will have to reduce this inner product substantially. We prove that when averaged over a suitable distribution of pairs A, A', the *expected inner product* between the two states produced by the counterfeiter cannot decrease too much with a single query to the membership oracles. We conclude that in order to produce $|A\rangle^{\otimes 2}$ given $|A\rangle$ and membership oracles for $A, A^\perp$, a counterfeiter must use exponentially many queries.

Having ruled out the possibility of nearly perfect cloning, we introduce a new amplification protocol, which allows us to transform a counterfeiter who succeeds with $\Omega(1/\operatorname{poly}(n))$ success probability into a counterfeiter who succeeds with probability arbitrarily close to 1. This technique is based on combining standard Grover search with a monotonic state amplification protocol of Tulsi, Grover, and Patel [38], to obtain monotonic convergence with the quadratic speedup of Grover search.[8] Combining this amplification with the inner-product adversary method, and applying a random linear transformation to convert the counterfeiter's worst case to its average case, we conclude that no counterfeiting algorithm can succeed with any non-negligible probability on a non-negligible fraction of states $|A\rangle$.

Using these results, how do we produce a secure quantum money scheme? We now need to step back, and discuss some general constructions of this paper that have nothing to do with hidden subspaces in particular. Before constructing a quantum money scheme, we first introduce the notion of a *quantum money mini-scheme*, a formalization of the setting in which the bank issues only a single money state and maintains no secret information. Formally, a mini-scheme is a protocol Bank for outputting pairs (s, ρ_s) and a verification procedure Ver_s for identifying ρ_s. We say a mini-scheme is *complete* if the state ρ_s passes the verification Ver_s with high probability, and we say the scheme is *secure* if furthermore no counterfeiter can take a single state ρ_s, and produce two (possibly-entangled) states ρ_1 and ρ_2 which simultaneously pass the verification procedure with non-negligible probability.

In the case of hidden subspace money, for example, we can use our uncloneability result to produce a secure mini-scheme relative to a classical oracle. The algorithm Bank queries the classical oracle to obtain a serial number s and the description of a subspace A. Using this description it prepares $|A\rangle$, and publishes $(s, |A\rangle)$. The verification procedure uses the serial number s as an index into another classical oracle, which allows it to test membership in A and $A^\perp$. We prove that the uncloneability of the states $|A\rangle$ implies that this mini-scheme is secure.

Crucially, we also give a general reduction from quantum money schemes to mini-schemes, based on combining a mini-scheme with a secure signature scheme. The bank maintains a secret key for the signature scheme, and to issue a banknote, it runs Bank to produce a pair (s, ρ_s), then digitally signs the serial number s. Special cases of this reduction appeared in [22, 30], but we provide the first rigorous security proof.

By combining this reduction with our mini-scheme, we are able to obtain a "black-box" public key quantum money scheme relative to a classical oracle, which is unconditionally secure:

Theorem (Security of Hidden Subspace Money)**.** *Relative to some (classical) oracle A, there exists a secure public-key quantum money scheme.*

More precisely, there is an algorithm KeyGen^A *which outputs pairs* $(k_{\text{private}}, k_{\text{public}})$*, an algorithm* $\mathsf{Bank}^A(k_{\text{private}})$ *which generates a "quantum banknote"* $|\$\rangle$*, and a verification algorithm* $\mathsf{Ver}^A(k_{\text{public}}, |\$\rangle)$ *which tests the authenticity of a purported banknote. These algorithms have the following properties:*

Completeness: *If* $(k_{\text{private}}, k_{\text{public}})$ *is produced by* KeyGen^A*, then* $\mathsf{Ver}^A(k_{\text{public}}, \mathsf{Bank}^A(k_{\text{private}}))$ *accepts with certainty.*

Soundness: *Suppose a would-be counterfeiter with access to A and k_{public} is given q valid banknotes. If this counterfeiter outputs any number of (possibly-entangled) quantum states, there is at most an exponentially-small probability that* Ver^A *will accept more than q of them.*

By adapting these ideas to the private-key setting, we are also able to provide the first *private*-key quantum money scheme that is unconditionally secure, even if the counterfeiter is able to interact adaptively with the bank. This patches a security hole in Wiesner's original scheme which was observed in [28, 3], but which has not previously been addressed in a provably-secure way.

Finally, we provide a candidate cryptographic protocol for obfuscating the indicator functions of subspaces $A \leq \mathbb{F}_2^n$. In order to obfuscate a membership oracle for A, we provide a random system of polynomials $p_1, \ldots, p_m$ that vanish on A. Membership in A can be tested by evaluating the p_i's, but given only the p_i's, we conjecture that it is difficult to recover A. Combining this protocol with the black-box money scheme, we obtain an *explicit* quantum money scheme. This scheme is also the first public-key quantum money scheme whose security can be based on a plausible "classical" cryptographic assumption. Here is the assumption:

Conjecture (*)**.** *Suppose A is a uniformly-random $n/2$-dimensional subspace of $\mathbb{F}_2^n$, and that $\{p_i\}_{1\leq i\leq 2n}, \{q_i\}_{1\leq i\leq 2n}$ are systems of degree-d polynomials from $\mathbb{F}_2^n$ to $\mathbb{F}_2$, which vanish on A and $A^\perp$ respectively but are otherwise uniformly-random. Then for large enough constant d, there is no polynomial-time quantum algorithm that takes as input descriptions of the p_i's and q_i's, and that outputs a basis for A with success probability $\Omega\left(2^{-n/2}\right)$.*

Note that we can trivially guess a *single* nonzero A element with success probability $2^{-n/2}$, but guessing a whole *basis* for A would succeed with probability only $2^{-\Omega(n^2)}$. Conjecture (*) asserts that it is harder to find many elements of A than to find just one element.

The following theorem says that, *if* a counterfeiter could break our quantum money scheme, then with nontrivial success probability, it could *also* recover a description of A from the p_i's and q_i's alone—even without having access to a bank that provides a valid money state $|A\rangle$.

Theorem. *Assuming Conjecture (*), there exists a public-key quantum money scheme with perfect completeness and*

[8] Although the "quadratic speedup" part is not strictly necessary for us, it improves our lower bound on the number of queries the counterfeiter needs to make—to the tight one, in fact—and might be of independent interest.

exponentially-small soundness error. That is, the verifier always accepts valid banknotes, and a would-be counterfeiter succeeds only with exponentially-small probability.[9]

The problem of recovering a subspace A, given a system of equations that vanish on A, is closely related to *algebraic cryptanalysis*, and in particular to the so-called *polynomial isomorphism problem*. In the latter problem, we are given as input two polynomials $p, q : \mathbb{F}^n \to \mathbb{F}$ related by an unknown linear change of basis L; the challenge is to find L. When $\deg(p) = \deg(q) = 3$, the best known algorithms for the polynomial isomorphism problem require exponential time [35, 24, 17]. An attacker *might* be able to use known techniques to effectively reduce the degree of the polynomials in our scheme by 1, at the expense of an exponentially reduced success probability [17]. Provided the degree is at least 4, however, recovering A seems to be well beyond existing techniques.

1.4 Motivation

Unlike the closely-related task of *quantum key distribution* [13] (which is already practical), quantum money currently seems to be a long way off. The basic difficulty is how to maintain the *coherence* of a quantum money state for an appreciable length of time. *All* money eventually loses its value unless it is spent, but money that decohered on a scale of microseconds would be an extreme example!

So one might wonder: why develop rigorous foundations for a cryptographic functionality that seems so far from being practical? One answer is that, just as quantum key distribution uses many of the same ideas as private-key quantum money, but without requiring long-lasting coherence, so it is not hard to imagine protocols that would use many of the same ideas as *public*-key quantum money without requiring long-lasting coherence. Indeed, depending on the problem, rapid decoherence might be a *feature* rather than a bug!

As one example, public-key quantum money that decohered quickly could be used to create **non-interactive uncloneable signatures**. These are n-qubit quantum states $|\psi\rangle$ that an agent can efficiently prepare using a private key, then freely hand out to passersby. By feeding $|\psi\rangle$, together with the agent's *public* key, into suitable measuring equipment, anyone can verify on the spot that the agent is who she says she is and not an impostor. Compared with *classical* identification protocols, the novel feature here is that the agent does not need to respond to a *challenge*—for example, digitally signing a random string—but can instead just hand out a fixed $|\psi\rangle$ non-interactively. Furthermore, because $|\psi\rangle$ decoheres in a matter of seconds, and recovering a classical *description* of $|\psi\rangle$ from measurements on it is computationally intractable, someone who is given $|\psi\rangle$ cannot use it later to impersonate the agent.

Of course, if an attacker managed to solve the technological problem of keeping $|\psi\rangle$ coherent for very long times, then he could break this system, by collecting one or more copies of $|\psi\rangle$ that an agent had handed out, and using them to impersonate the agent. But in that case, whatever method the attacker was using to keep the states coherent could *also*—once discovered—be used to create a secure public-key quantum money scheme!

However, we believe the "real" reason to study quantum money is basically the same as the "real" reason to study quantum computing as a whole—or for that matter, to study the many interesting aspects of *classical* cryptography that are equally far from application. As theoretical computer scientists, we are in the business of mapping out the inherent capabilities and limits of information processing.

In our case, what quantum money provides is a near-ideal playground for understanding the implications of the uncertainty principle and the No-Cloning Theorem. In the early days of quantum mechanics, Bohr [15] and others argued that the uncertainty principle requires us to change our conception of science itself—their basic argument being that, in physics, predictions are only ever as good as our knowledge of a system's initial state $|\psi\rangle$, but the uncertainty principle might mean that the initial state is unknowable even with arbitrarily-precise measurements.

But does this argument have any "teeth"? In other words: among the properties of a quantum state $|\psi\rangle$ that make the state impossible to learn precisely or to duplicate, can any of those properties ever *matter empirically*? To us, quantum money is interesting precisely because it gives one of the clearest examples where the answer to that question is yes.

2. PRELIMINARIES

To begin, we fix some notation. Let $[N] = \{1, \ldots, N\}$. Given a subspace S of a vector space V, let $S^{\perp}$ be the orthogonal complement of S (that is, the set of $y \in V$ such that $x \cdot y = 0$ for all $x \in S$). We call a function $\delta(n)$ *negligible* if $\delta(n) = o(1/p(n))$ for every polynomial p.

By a *classical oracle*, we will mean a unitary transformation of the form $|x\rangle \to (-1)^{f(x)} |x\rangle$, for some Boolean function $f : \{0,1\}^* \to \{0,1\}$. Note that, unless specified otherwise, even a classical oracle can be queried in quantum superposition. A *quantum oracle*, by contrast, is an arbitrary n-qubit unitary transformation U (or rather, a collection of such U's, one for each n) that a quantum algorithm can apply in a black-box fashion. Quantum oracles were defined and studied by Aaronson and Kuperberg [5].

2.1 Cryptography

Before we construct quantum money schemes, it will be helpful to have some "conventional" cryptographic primitives in our toolbox. Foremost among these is a *digital signature scheme secure against quantum chosen-message attacks.* We now define digital signature schemes—both for completeness, and to fix the quantum attack model that is relevant for us.

Definition 1 (Digital Signature Schemes). *A (classical, public-key)* ***digital signature scheme*** *$\mathcal{D}$ consists of three probabilistic polynomial-time classical algorithms:*

- KeyGen, *which takes as input a security parameter 0^n, and generates a* ***key pair*** $(k_{\text{private}}, k_{\text{public}})$.
- Sign, *which takes as input k_{private} and a message x, and generates a* ***signature*** $\mathsf{Sign}(k_{\text{private}}, x)$.[10]

[9]This theorem remains true even if the statement of Conjecture (*) is weakened by adding random noise to the p_i's and q_i's, so that only a constant fraction of them vanish on A or $A^{\perp}$. The presence of noise interferes substantially with known techniques for solving systems of equations, though an attacker who was able to recover A from a *single* polynomial would of course not be hindered by such noise.

[10]We indulge in slight abuse of notation, since if Sign is ran-

- Ver, *which takes as input* k_{public}, *a message* x, *and a claimed signature* w, *and either accepts or rejects.*

We say $\mathcal{D}$ *has* ***completeness error*** ε *if*

$$\mathsf{Ver}\left(k_{\text{public}}, x, \mathsf{Sign}\left(x, k_{\text{private}}\right)\right)$$

accepts with probability at least $1-\varepsilon$ *for all messages* x *and key pairs* $(k_{\text{private}}, k_{\text{public}})$. *Here the probability is over the behavior of* Ver *and* Sign.

Let C *(the* ***counterfeiter****) be a quantum circuit of size* $\text{poly}(n)$ *that takes* k_{public} *as input and does the following:*

(1) *Probabilistically generates a classical list of messages* $x_1, \ldots, x_m$, *and submits them to a* ***signing oracle*** $\mathcal{O}$.

(2) *Gets back independently-generated signatures* $w_1, \ldots, w_m$, *where* $w_i := \mathsf{Sign}(k_{\text{private}}, x_i)$.

(3) *Outputs a pair* (x, w).

We say C ***succeeds*** *if* $x \notin \{x_1, \ldots, x_m\}$ *and* $\mathsf{Ver}(k_{\text{public}}, x, w)$ *accepts. We say* $\mathcal{D}$ *has* ***soundness error*** δ *if every counterfeiter* C *succeeds with probability at most* δ. *Here the probability is over the key pair* $(k_{\text{private}}, k_{\text{public}})$ *and the behavior of* C, Sign, *and* Ver.

We call $\mathcal{D}$ ***secure against nonadaptive quantum chosen-message attacks*** *if it has completeness error* $\leq 1/3$ *and negligible soundness error.*

Intuitively, we call a signature scheme "secure" if no *quantum* counterfeiter with *nonadaptive, classical* access to a signing oracle $\mathcal{O}$ can forge a signature for any message that it did not submit to $\mathcal{O}$. Depending on the application, one might want to change Definition 1 in various ways: for example, by giving the counterfeiter *adaptive* or *quantum* access to $\mathcal{O}$, or by letting KeyGen, Sign, and Ver be quantum algorithms themselves. For this paper, however, Definition 1 provides all we need.

Do signature schemes secure against quantum attack exist? Naturally, signature schemes based on RSA or other number-theoretic problems can all be broken by a quantum computer. However, building on earlier work by Naor and Yung [33] (among many others), Rompel [37] showed that a secure public-key signature scheme can be constructed from *any* one-way function—not necessarily a trapdoor function. Furthermore, Rompel's security reduction, from breaking the signature scheme to inverting the one-way function, is *black-box*: in particular, nothing in it depends on the assumption that the adversary is classical rather than quantum. We therefore get the following consequence:

Theorem 2 (Quantum-Secure Signature Schemes [37]). *If there exists a (classical) one-way function* f *secure against quantum attack, then there also exists a digital signature scheme secure against quantum chosen-message attacks.*

Recently, Boneh et al. [16] proved several results similar to Theorem 2, and they needed nontrivial work to do so. However, a crucial difference is that Boneh et al. were (justifiably) concerned with quantum adversaries who can make *quantum* queries to the signing oracle $\mathcal{O}$. By contrast, as mentioned earlier, for our application it suffices to consider adversaries who query $\mathcal{O}$ *classically*—and in that case, the standard security reductions go through essentially without change.

Let us state another consequence of Theorem 2, which will be useful for our oracle construction in Section 5.

Theorem 3 (Relativized Quantum-Secure Signatures). *Relative to a suitable oracle* A, *there exists a digital signature scheme secure against quantum chosen-message attacks.*

PROOF SKETCH. It is easy to give an oracle $A : \{0,1\}^* \rightarrow \{0,1\}$ relative to which there exists a one-way function $f_n : \{0,1\}^n \rightarrow \{0,1\}^{p(n)}$ secure against quantum adversaries. Now, the security reduction of Rompel [37] is not only black-box but *relativizing*: that is, it goes through if all legitimate and malicious parties have access to the same oracle A. So by Theorem 2, starting from $\{f_n\}$ one can construct a digital signature scheme relative to the same oracle A, which is secure against quantum chosen-message attacks. Further details are given in the full version. ■

2.2 Quantum Information

Let us collect a few facts about quantum pure and mixed states that are used in the paper. We assume basic familiarity with the formalism of bras, kets, density matrices, etc.; see Nielsen and Chuang [34] for a good overview.

Given two mixed states ρ and σ, their *trace distance* is defined as $D(\rho,\sigma) := \frac{1}{2}\sum_{i=1}^{N} |\lambda_i|$, where $\lambda_1, \ldots, \lambda_N$ are the eigenvalues of $\rho - \sigma$. Trace distance is a metric and satisfies $0 \leq D(\rho,\sigma) \leq 1$. Also, the *fidelity* $0 \leq F(\rho,\sigma) \leq 1$ is defined, in this paper, as the maximum of $|\langle\psi|\varphi\rangle|$ over all purifications $|\psi\rangle$ of ρ and $|\varphi\rangle$ of σ.[11] By extension, given a subspace S, we let $F(\rho, S)$ be the maximum of $|\langle\psi|\varphi\rangle|$ over all purifications $|\psi\rangle$ of ρ and all unit vectors $|\varphi\rangle \in S$. While fidelity is *not* a metric, it does satisfy the following inequality, which will be helpful in Section 5.

Lemma 4 ("Triangle Inequality" for Fidelity). *Suppose*

$$\min\left\{\langle\psi|\rho|\psi\rangle, \langle\varphi|\sigma|\varphi\rangle\right\} \geq 1-\varepsilon.$$

Then $F(\rho,\sigma) \leq |\langle\psi|\varphi\rangle| + 2\varepsilon^{1/4}$.

PROOF. Deferred to the full version. ■

Finally, the following lemma of Aaronson [2] will imply that, as long as a quantum money scheme has small *completeness error* (i.e., small probability of rejecting a valid banknote), the banknotes can be reused many times.

Lemma 5 ("Almost As Good As New Lemma" [2]). *Suppose a measurement on a mixed state* ρ *yields a particular outcome with probability* $1-\varepsilon$. *Then after the measurement, one can recover a state* $\widetilde{\rho}$ *such that* $\|\widetilde{\rho}-\rho\|_{\text{tr}} \leq \sqrt{\varepsilon}$.

2.3 Quantum Search

In our security proof for quantum money, a crucial step will be to *amplify* a counterfeiter who copies a banknote \$ with any non-negligible fidelity to a counterfeiter who copies \$ almost perfectly. Taking the contrapositive, this will imply that to rule out the former sort of counterfeiter, it suffices to rule out the latter.

In this section, we first review two variants of Grover's search algorithm [25] that are useful for amplifying the fidelity of quantum states. We then introduce a new variant that combines the advantages of both.

domized then the signature need not be a function of k_{private} and x.

[11] Some authors instead define "fidelity" as the maximum of $|\langle\psi|\varphi\rangle|^2$.

Throughout, assume we are given a pure initial state $|\text{Init}\rangle$, in some Hilbert space $\mathcal{H}$. Our goal is to map $|\text{Init}\rangle$ to a final state $|\Psi\rangle$ that lies in (or close to) a "good subspace" $G \leq \mathcal{H}$. We have oracle access to two unitary transformations:

- U_{Init}, which maps $|\text{Init}\rangle$ to $-|\text{Init}\rangle$, and acts as the identity on all $|v\rangle$ orthogonal to $|\text{Init}\rangle$.
- U_G, which maps $|v\rangle$ to $-|v\rangle$ for all $|v\rangle \in G$, and acts as the identity on all $|v\rangle$ orthogonal to G.

We are promised that $F(|\text{Init}\rangle, G) = \max_{|\psi\rangle \in G} \langle \text{Init}|\psi\rangle$, the fidelity of the initial state with G, is at least some $\varepsilon > 0$. In this scenario, *provided* $F(|\text{Init}\rangle, G)$ *is known*, the amplitude amplification framework of Brassard, Høyer, Mosca, and Tapp [18] lets us prepare a state close to G using $\Theta(1/\varepsilon)$ iterations:

Lemma 6 (Amplitude Amplification [18]). *Write* $|\text{Init}\rangle$ *as* $\sin\theta\,|\text{Good}\rangle + \cos\theta\,|\text{Bad}\rangle$, *where* $|\text{Good}\rangle$ *is the unit vector in* G *closest to* $|\text{Init}\rangle$ *and* $|\text{Bad}\rangle$ *is orthogonal to* $|\text{Good}\rangle$. *Then by using* $O(T)$ *oracle calls to* U_{Init} *and* U_G, *we can prepare the state*

$$|\Phi_T\rangle := \sin[(2T+1)\theta]\,|\text{Good}\rangle + \cos[(2T+1)\theta]\,|\text{Bad}\rangle$$

Note that Grover's algorithm is simply a special case of Lemma 6, where $|\text{Init}\rangle$ is the uniform superposition over N basis states $|1\rangle, \ldots, |N\rangle$, and G is the subspace spanned by "marked" states.

However, Lemma 6 has an annoying drawback, which it shares with ordinary Grover search. Namely, the algorithm does *not* converge monotonically toward the target subspace G, but could instead "wildly overshoot it," cycling around the 2-dimensional subspace spanned by $|\text{Bad}\rangle$ and $|\text{Good}\rangle$. If we know the fidelity $F(|\text{Init}\rangle, G)$ in advance (rather than just a lower bound on the fidelity), *or* if we can prepare new copies of $|\text{Init}\rangle$ "free of charge" in case of failure, then this overshooting is not a serious problem. Alas, neither of those conditions will hold in our application.

Fortunately, for independent reasons, in 2005 Tulsi, Grover, and Patel [38] introduced a new quantum search algorithm that *does* guarantee monotonic convergence toward G, by alternating unitary transformations with measurements. (Their algorithm was later simplified and improved by Chakraborty, Radhakrishnan, and Raghunathan [19].)

Lemma 7 (Fixed-Point Quantum Search [38, 19]). *By using* T *oracle calls to* U_{Init} *and* U_G, *we can prepare a state* $|\Psi\rangle$ *such that* $F(|\Psi\rangle, G) \geq 1 - \exp(-T\varepsilon^2)$.

Rearranging, Lemma 7 lets us prepare a state $|\Psi\rangle$ such that $F(|\Psi\rangle, G) \geq 1 - \delta$ using $T = O\left(\frac{1}{\varepsilon^2}\ln\frac{1}{\delta}\right)$ iterations. On the positive side, the dependence on $1/\delta$ in this bound is logarithmic: we get not only monotonic convergence toward G, but *exponentially-fast* convergence. On the negative side, notice that the dependence on ε has worsened from $1/\varepsilon$ to $1/\varepsilon^2$—negating the quadratic speedup that was the original point of quantum search!

Thus, in the full version, we give a "hybrid" quantum search algorithm that *combines* the advantages of Lemmas 6 and 7—i.e., it converges monotonically toward the target subspace G (rather than "overshooting" G), but *also* achieves a quadratic speedup. In the context of our security proof for quantum money, the hybrid algorithm leads to a quadratically-better lower bound on the number of queries that a counterfeiter needs to make, compared to what we would get from using Lemma 7 by itself. While this quadratic improvement is perhaps only of moderate interest, we hope it might find other applications.

Theorem 8 (Faster Fixed-Point Search). *Let* $\delta \geq 2\varepsilon$. *Then by using* $O\left(\frac{\log 1/\delta}{\varepsilon\delta^2}\right)$ *oracle calls to* U_{Init} *and* U_G, *we can prepare a state* ρ *such that* $F(\rho, G) \geq 1 - \delta$.

PROOF. Deferred to the full version. ∎

Note that Theorem 8 loses the *exponentially-fast* convergence toward the target subspace G, but that property will not be important for us anyway. We leave as an open problem whether there exists a hybrid algorithm with exponentially-fast convergence.

3. FORMALIZING QUANTUM MONEY

In this section, we first give a formal cryptographic definition of *public-key quantum money schemes*. Our definition is similar to that of Aaronson [3]. However, departing from [3], we next define the new notion of a *quantum money mini-scheme*, which is easier to construct and analyze than a full-blown quantum money scheme. A mini-scheme is basically a quantum money scheme where only *one* banknote ever needs to printed, not many banknotes; and where the procedure for verifying that banknote is treated as given (rather than something that *itself* needs to be authenticated using the bank's public key). We then prove two basic results: the amplification of weak counterfeiters into strong ones (Theorem 13), and the construction of full-blown quantum money schemes from mini-schemes together with quantumly-secure digital signature schemes (Theorem 14).

3.1 Quantum Money Schemes

Intuitively, a *public-key quantum money scheme* is a scheme by which

(1) a trusted "bank" can feasibly generate an unlimited number of quantum banknotes,

(2) anyone can feasibly verify a valid banknote as having come from the bank, but

(3) no one besides the bank can feasibly map $q = \text{poly}(n)$ banknotes to $r > q$ banknotes with any non-negligible success probability.[12]

We now make the notion more formal.

Definition 9 (Quantum Money Schemes). *A* ***public-key quantum money scheme*** $\mathcal{S}$ *consists of three polynomial-time quantum algorithms:*

- KeyGen, *which takes as input a security parameter* 0^n, *and probabilistically generates a key pair* $(k_{\text{private}}, k_{\text{public}})$.
- Bank, *which takes as input* k_{private}, *and probabilistically generates a quantum state* \$ *called a* ***banknote***. *(Usually* \$ *will be an ordered pair* (s, ρ_s), *consisting of a classical* ***serial number*** s *and a* ***quantum money state*** ρ_s, *but this is not strictly necessary.)*

[12]Previously, Aaronson [3] required only that no polynomial-time counterfeiter could increase its *expected* number of valid banknotes. However, the stronger condition required here is both achievable, and seemingly more natural from the standpoint of security proofs.

- Ver, *which takes as input* k_{public} *and an alleged banknote* $\cent$, *and either accepts or rejects.*

We say $\mathcal{S}$ *has* ***completeness error*** ε *if* Ver $(k_{\text{public}}, \$)$ *accepts with probability at least* $1-\varepsilon$ *for all public keys* k_{public} *and valid banknotes* \$. *If* $\varepsilon = 0$ *then* $\mathcal{S}$ *has* ***perfect completeness***.

Let Count *(the* ***money counter****) take as input* k_{public} *as well as a collection of (possibly-entangled) alleged banknotes* $\cent_1, \ldots, \cent_r$, *and output the number of indices* $i \in [r]$ *such that* Ver $(k_{\text{public}}, \cent_i)$ *accepts. Then we say* $\mathcal{S}$ *has* ***soundness error*** δ *if, given any quantum circuit* $C(k_{\text{public}}, \$_1, \ldots, \$_q)$ *of size* $\text{poly}(n)$ *(called the* ***counterfeiter****), which maps* $q = \text{poly}(n)$ *valid banknotes* $\$_1, \ldots, \$_q$ *to* $r = \text{poly}(n)$ *(possibly-entangled) alleged banknotes* $\cent_1, \ldots, \cent_r$,

$$\Pr[\text{Count}(k_{\text{public}}, C(k_{\text{public}}, \$_1, \ldots, \$_q)) > q] \leq \delta.$$

Here the probability is over the key pair $(k_{\text{private}}, k_{\text{public}})$, *valid banknotes* $\$_1, \ldots, \$_q$ *generated by* Bank (k_{private}), *and the behavior of* Count *and* C.

We call $\mathcal{S}$ ***secure*** *if it has completeness error* $\leq 1/3$ *and negligible soundness error.*

In the full version, we show that the completeness error in any quantum money scheme can be amplified to $1/2^{\text{poly}(n)}$, at the cost of only a small increase in the soundness error. Note that, by Lemma 5 (the "Almost As Good As New Lemma"), once we make the completeness error exponentially small, we can also give our scheme the property that *any banknote* \$ *can be verified exponentially many times*, before \$ gets "worn out" by repeated measurements. This observation is part of what justifies our use of the term "money."[13]

In this paper, we will often consider **relativized** quantum money schemes, which simply means that the three procedures KeyGen, Bank, Ver—as well as the counterfeiter C—all get access to exactly the same oracle $A : \{0,1\}^* \rightarrow \{0,1\}$. We will also consider relativized digital signature schemes, etc., which are defined analogously.

A **private-key quantum money scheme** is the same as a public-key scheme, except that the counterfeiter C no longer gets access to k_{public}. (Thus, we might as well set $k := k_{\text{public}} = k_{\text{private}}$, since the public and private keys no longer play separate roles.) We call a private-key scheme **query-secure**—a notion "intermediate" between private-key and public-key—if the counterfeiter C is allowed to interact repeatedly with the bank. Given any alleged banknote σ, the bank runs the verification procedure Ver (k, σ), then returns to C both the classical result (i.e., accept or reject) *and* the post-measurement quantum state $\widetilde{\sigma}$.

3.2 Mini-Schemes

While Definition 9 captures our intuitive requirements for a public-key quantum money scheme, experience has shown that it is cumbersome to work with in practice. So in this section, we introduce a simpler primitive called *mini-schemes*, which require only *one* uncopyable banknote. We also prove an amplification theorem for a large class of mini-schemes. Then, in Section 3.3, we will show how mini-schemes can be generically combined with conventional digital signature schemes to create full public-key quantum money schemes.

Definition 10 (Mini-Schemes). *A (public-key)* ***mini-scheme*** $\mathcal{M}$ *consists of two polynomial-time quantum algorithms:*

- Bank, *which takes as input a security parameter* 0^n, *and probabilistically generates a banknote* $\$ = (s, \rho_s)$, *where* s *is a classical* ***serial number****, and* ρ_s *is a quantum money state.*
- Ver, *which takes as input an alleged banknote* $\cent$, *and either accepts or rejects.*

We say $\mathcal{M}$ *has* ***completeness error*** ε *if* Ver (\$) *accepts with probability at least* $1-\varepsilon$ *for all valid banknotes* \$. *If* $\varepsilon = 0$ *then* $\mathcal{M}$ *has perfect completeness. If, furthermore,* $\rho_s = |\psi_s\rangle\langle\psi_s|$ *is always a pure state, and* Ver *simply consists of a projective measurement onto the rank-1 subspace spanned by* $|\psi_s\rangle$, *then we say* $\mathcal{M}$ *is* ***projective***.[14]

Let Ver_2 *(the* ***double verifier****) take as input a single serial number* s *as well as two (possibly-entangled) states* σ_1 *and* σ_2, *and accept if and only* Ver (s, σ_1) *and* Ver (s, σ_2) *both accept. We say* $\mathcal{M}$ *has* ***soundness error*** δ *if, given any quantum circuit* C *of size* $\text{poly}(n)$ *(the* ***counterfeiter****),* $\text{Ver}_2(s, C(\$))$ *accepts with probability at most* δ. *Here the probability is over the banknote* \$ *output by* Bank (0^n), *as well as the behavior of* Ver_2 *and* C.

We call $\mathcal{M}$ ***secure*** *if it has completeness error* $\leq 1/3$ *and negligible soundness error.*

We observe a simple relationship between Definitions 9 and 10:

Proposition 11. *If there exists a secure public-key money scheme* $\mathcal{S} = (\text{KeyGen}_{\mathcal{S}}, \text{Bank}_{\mathcal{S}}, \text{Ver}_{\mathcal{S}})$, *then there also exists a secure mini-scheme* $\mathcal{M} = (\text{Bank}_{\mathcal{M}}, \text{Ver}_{\mathcal{M}})$.

Proof. Each banknote output by $\text{Bank}_{\mathcal{M}}(0^n)$ will have the form $(k_{\text{public}}, \text{Bank}_{\mathcal{S}}(k_{\text{private}}))$, where $(k_{\text{private}}, k_{\text{public}})$ is a key pair output by $\text{KeyGen}_{\mathcal{S}}(0^n)$. Then $\text{Ver}_{\mathcal{M}}(s, \rho_s)$ will accept if and only if $\text{Ver}_{\mathcal{S}}(s, \rho_s)$ does. Any counterfeiter $C_{\mathcal{M}}$ against $\mathcal{M}$ can be converted directly into a counterfeiter $C_{\mathcal{S}}$ against $\mathcal{S}$. ■

Call a mini-scheme $\mathcal{M}$ = (Bank, Ver) **secret-based** if Bank works by first generating a uniformly-random classical string r, and then generating a banknote $\$_r := (s_r, \rho_r)$. Intuitively, in a secret-based scheme, the bank can generate many identical banknotes by simply reusing r, while in a non-secret-based scheme, *not even the bank* might be able to generate two identical banknotes. Here is an interesting observation:

Proposition 12. *If there exists a secure, secret-based mini-scheme, then there also exists a one-way function secure against quantum attack.*

Proof. The desired OWF is $\text{SerialNum}(r) := s_r$. If there existed a polynomial-time quantum algorithm to recover r given s_r, then we could use that algorithm to produce an unlimited number of additional banknotes $\$_r$. ■

All of the mini-schemes developed in this paper will be secret-based. By contrast, the earlier schemes of Lutomirski

[13] By contrast, BBBW [14] introduced the term "subway tokens" for quantum money states that get destroyed immediately upon verification.

[14] We similarly call a full quantum money scheme projective, if Ver (\$) consists of a measurement on one part of \$ in the computational basis, followed by a rank-1 projective measurement on the remaining part.

et al. [30] and Farhi et al. [22] are non-secret-based, since the serial number s is only obtained as the outcome of a quantum measurement.

The following result is one of the most useful in the paper. Intuitively, it says that in projective mini-schemes, a counterfeiter that copies a banknote with *any* non-negligible fidelity can be "amplified" to a counterfeiter that copies the banknote almost *perfectly*—or conversely, that to rule out the former sort of counterfeiter, it suffices to rule out the latter. The proof makes essential use of the amplitude amplification results from Section 2.3.

Theorem 13 (Amplification of Counterfeiters). *Let $\mathcal{M} = (\mathsf{Bank}, \mathsf{Ver})$ be a projective mini-scheme, and let $\$ = (s, \rho)$ be a valid banknote in $\mathcal{M}$. Suppose there exists a counterfeiter C that copies $\$$ with probability $\varepsilon > 0$: that is,*

$$\Pr\left[\mathsf{Ver}_2\left(s, C\left(\$\right)\right) \text{ accepts}\right] \geq \varepsilon.$$

Then for all $\delta > 0$, there is also a modified counterfeiter C' (depending only on ε and δ, not $\$$), which makes

$$O\left(\frac{\log 1/\delta}{\sqrt{\varepsilon}\left(\sqrt{\varepsilon} + \delta^2\right)}\right)$$

queries to C, C^{-1}, and Ver and which satisfies

$$\Pr\left[\mathsf{Ver}_2\left(s, C'\left(\$\right)\right) \text{ accepts}\right] \geq 1 - \delta.$$

PROOF. Write $\$$ as a mixture of pure states:

$$\$ = \sum p_i \left|\psi_i\right\rangle\left\langle\psi_i\right|.$$

By linearity, clearly it suffices to show that

$$\Pr\left[\mathsf{Ver}_2\left(s, C'\left(\left|\psi_i\right\rangle\right)\right) \text{ accepts}\right] \geq 1 - \delta$$

for all i such that $p_i > 0$. We focus on $\left|\psi\right\rangle := \left|\psi_1\right\rangle$ without loss of generality.

By assumption, there exists a subspace S such that

$$\Pr\left[\mathsf{Ver}\left(\rho\right) \text{ accepts}\right] = F\left(\rho, S\right)$$

for all ρ. Then $F\left(\$, S\right) = F\left(\left|\psi\right\rangle, S\right) = 1$.

Now, just as Ver is simply a projector onto S, so Ver_2 is a projector onto $S^{\otimes 2}$. Thus

$$F\left(C\left(\left|\psi\right\rangle\right), S^{\otimes 2}\right) \geq \sqrt{\varepsilon}.$$

So consider performing a fixed-point Grover search, with $C\left(\left|\psi\right\rangle\right)$ as the initial state and $S^{\otimes 2}$ as the target subspace. By Lemma 7, this will produce a state ρ such that $F\left(\rho, S^{\otimes 2}\right) \geq 1 - \delta$ using $O\left(\frac{1}{\varepsilon}\log\frac{1}{\delta}\right)$ Grover iterations. Each iteration requires a reflection about $C\left(\left|\psi\right\rangle\right)$ and a reflection about $S^{\otimes 2}$, which can be implemented using $O\left(1\right)$ queries to C, C^{-1} and Ver respectively. Therefore the number of queries to C, C^{-1} and Ver is $O\left(\frac{1}{\varepsilon}\log\frac{1}{\delta}\right)$ as well.

If δ is large compared to ε, then we can instead use Theorem 8, which produces a state ρ such that $F\left(\rho, S^{\otimes 2}\right) \geq 1 - \delta$ using $O\left(\frac{1}{\sqrt{\varepsilon}\delta^2}\log\frac{1}{\delta}\right)$ iterations. Taking the minimum of the two bounds gives us the claimed bound on query complexity. ■

Theorem 13 is unlikely to hold for *arbitrary* (non-projective) mini-schemes, for the simple reason that we can always create a mini-scheme where Ver accepts *any* state with some small nonzero probability ε. We leave it as an open problem to find the largest class of mini-schemes for which Theorem 13 holds.

3.3 The Standard Construction

We are now ready to define the "standard construction" of public-key quantum money schemes from mini-schemes and digital signature schemes, and to prove this construction's security.

Theorem 14 (Standard Construction of Public-Key Quantum Money). *Let $\mathcal{M}$ be any secure mini-scheme, and let $\mathcal{D}$ be any digital signature scheme secure against quantum chosen-message attacks. By combining $\mathcal{M}$ and $\mathcal{D}$, we can create a secure public-key quantum money scheme $\mathcal{S}$.*

PROOF. Given

$$\mathcal{M} = \left(\mathsf{Bank}_{\mathcal{M}}, \mathsf{Ver}_{\mathcal{M}}\right),$$
$$\mathcal{D} = \left(\mathsf{KeyGen}_{\mathcal{D}}, \mathsf{Sign}_{\mathcal{D}}, \mathsf{Ver}_{\mathcal{D}}\right),$$

our quantum money scheme $\mathcal{S} = \left(\mathsf{KeyGen}_{\mathcal{S}}, \mathsf{Bank}_{\mathcal{S}}, \mathsf{Ver}_{\mathcal{S}}\right)$ is defined as follows:

$\mathsf{KeyGen}_{\mathcal{S}}$ is simply $\mathsf{KeyGen}_{\mathcal{D}}$ from the digital signature scheme.

$\mathsf{Bank}_{\mathcal{S}}$ first calls $\mathsf{Bank}_{\mathcal{M}}$ from the mini-scheme to obtain a banknote (s, ρ). It then outputs (s, ρ) together with a digital signature of the serial number s:

$$\mathsf{Bank}_{\mathcal{S}}\left(k_{\text{private}}\right) := \left(s, \mathsf{Sign}_{\mathcal{D}}\left(k_{\text{private}}, s\right), \rho\right).$$

$\mathsf{Ver}_{\mathcal{S}}$ accepts an alleged banknote (s, w, σ), if and only if $\mathsf{Ver}_{\mathcal{M}}\left(s, \sigma\right)$ and $\mathsf{Ver}_{\mathcal{D}}\left(k_{\text{public}}, s, w\right)$ both accept.

Now, suppose there exists a counterfeiter $C_{\mathcal{S}}$ against $\mathcal{S}$: that is, a polynomial-time quantum algorithm such that

$$\Pr\left[\mathsf{Count}\left(k_{\text{public}}, C_{\mathcal{S}}\left(k_{\text{public}}, \$_1, \ldots, \$_q\right)\right) > q\right] \geq \frac{1}{p(n)}.$$

Here $\$_i := (s_i, w_i, \rho_i)$ is a valid banknote, Count is the money counter from Definition 9, and p is some polynomial. Also, the probability is over the key pair $\left(k_{\text{private}}, k_{\text{public}}\right)$, the valid banknotes $\$_1, \ldots, \$_q$, and the behavior of Count and $C_{\mathcal{S}}$. Suppose further that $\mathcal{D}$ is secure. Then it suffices to show that, by using $C_{\mathcal{S}}$, we can construct a counterfeiter $C_{\mathcal{M}}$ against the underlying mini-scheme $\mathcal{M}$. Let $\mathsf{New}\left(k_{\text{public}}, \$_1, \ldots, \$_q\right)$ be an algorithm that does the following:

(1) Records the serial numbers $s_1, \ldots, s_q$ of $\$_1, \ldots, \$_q$, and lets $U := \{s_1, \ldots, s_q\}$.

(2) Runs $C_{\mathcal{S}}\left(k_{\text{public}}, \$_1, \ldots, \$_q\right)$, and examines the output states $\cent_1, \ldots, \cent_r$.

(3) Returns the number of $i \in [r]$ such that $\mathsf{Ver}_{\mathcal{S}}\left(\cent_i\right)$ accepts, *and* $\cent_i$'s serial number s'_i does not belong to U.

Then we claim that $\Pr\left[\mathsf{New}\left(k_{\text{public}}, \$_1, \ldots, \$_q\right) > 0\right]$ is negligibly small, where the probability is over the same variables as before. The proof is simply that, if this were not so, then we could easily create a counterfeiter $C_{\mathcal{D}}$ against the digital signature scheme $\mathcal{D}$. With non-negligible probability, $C_{\mathcal{D}}$ would generate a valid signature $\mathsf{Sign}_{\mathcal{D}}\left(k_{\text{private}}, s'_i\right)$, for a message s'_i for which $C_{\mathcal{D}}$ had never before seen a valid signature, by running $C_{\mathcal{S}}\left(k_{\text{public}}, \$_1, \ldots, \$_q\right)$, then measuring $\cent_i = (s'_i, w'_i, \rho'_i)$ for a uniformly random $i \in [r]$. (Note that $C_{\mathcal{D}}$ can generate q money states $\$_1, \ldots, \$_q$, without knowledge of k_{private}, by generating the s_i's and ρ_i's on its own, then calling the signing oracle $\mathcal{O}$ to get the w_i's.)

But now we can define a counterfeiter $C_{\mathcal{M}}$ against the mini-scheme $\mathcal{M}$, which works as follows. First, $C_{\mathcal{M}}$ runs

$\mathsf{KeyGen}_{\mathcal{D}}(0^n)$ to generate a *new* key pair $(k'_{\text{private}}, k'_{\text{public}})$. Next, it labels the banknote to copied (s_ℓ, ρ_ℓ), for some $\ell \in [q]$ chosen uniformly at random. It repeatedly calls $\mathsf{Bank}_{\mathcal{M}}(0^n)$ to generate $q-1$ serial numbers and quantum money states, labeled (s_i, ρ_i) for all $i \in [q] \setminus \{\ell\}$. Let $U := \{s_1, \ldots, s_q\}$. Then $C_{\mathcal{M}}$ generates a digital signature $w_i := \mathsf{Sign}_{\mathcal{D}}(k'_{\text{private}}, s_i)$ for each $i \in [q]$. Let $\$_i := (s_i, w_i, \rho_i)$. Next, $C_{\mathcal{M}}$ runs the counterfeiter $C_{\mathcal{S}}(k_{\text{public}}, \$_1, \ldots, \$_q)$, to obtain $r > q$ alleged banknotes $¢_1, \ldots, ¢_r$ where $¢_j = (s'_j, w'_j, \rho'_j)$. Finally, $C_{\mathcal{M}}$ chooses $j, k \in [r]$ uniformly at random without replacement, and output (ρ'_j, ρ'_k) as a candidate for two copies of ρ_ℓ.

Suppose that $\mathsf{Count} > q$, as happens with probability at least $\frac{1}{p(n)}$. Also suppose that $\mathsf{New} = 0$, as happens all but a negligible fraction of the time. Then by the pigeonhole principle, there must exist indices $j \neq k$ such that $s'_j = s'_k$. With probability at least $1/\binom{r}{2}$, the counterfeiter $C_{\mathcal{M}}$ will find such a (j,k) pair. Therefore it succeeds with overall probability $\Omega(1/\operatorname{poly}(n))$. ∎

Theorem 14 reduces the construction of a public-key quantum money scheme to two "smaller" problems: constructing a mini-scheme, and constructing a signature scheme secure against quantum attacks.

In practice, however, the situation is even better, since in this paper, all of our constructions of mini-schemes will *also* yield signature schemes "free of charge"! The following proposition explains why:

Proposition 15. *If there exists a secure, secret-based mini-scheme $\mathcal{M}$, then there also exists a secure public-key quantum money scheme $\mathcal{S}$.*

Proof. Starting from $\mathcal{M}$, we can get a one-way function secure against quantum attack from Proposition 12, and hence a digital signature scheme $\mathcal{D}$ secure against quantum chosen-message attack from Theorem 2. Combining $\mathcal{M}$ and $\mathcal{D}$ now yields $\mathcal{S}$ by Theorem 14. ∎

Finally, let us make explicit what Theorem 14 means for oracle construction.

Corollary 16. *Suppose there exists a mini-scheme $\mathcal{M}$ that is provably secure relative to some oracle $A_{\mathcal{M}}$ (i.e., any counterfeiter $C_{\mathcal{M}}$ against $\mathcal{M}$ must make superpolynomially many queries to $A_{\mathcal{M}}$). Then there exists a public-key quantum money scheme $\mathcal{S}$ that is provably secure relative to some other oracle $A_{\mathcal{S}}$.*

Proof. By Theorem 3, relative to a suitable oracle $A_{\mathcal{D}}$ (in fact, a *random* oracle suffices), there exists a signature scheme $\mathcal{D}$, such that any quantum chosen-message attack against $\mathcal{D}$ must make superpolynomially many queries to $A_{\mathcal{D}}$.

The oracle $A_{\mathcal{S}}$ will simply be a concatenation of $A_{\mathcal{M}}$ with $A_{\mathcal{D}}$. Relative to $A_{\mathcal{S}}$, we claim that the mini-scheme $\mathcal{M}$ and signature scheme $\mathcal{D}$ are *both* secure—and therefore, by Theorem 14, we can construct a secure public-key quantum money scheme $\mathcal{S}$.

The only worry is that a counterfeiter $C_{\mathcal{M}}$ against $\mathcal{M}$ might gain some advantage by querying $A_{\mathcal{D}}$; or conversely, a counterfeiter $C_{\mathcal{D}}$ against $\mathcal{D}$ might gain some advantage by querying $A_{\mathcal{M}}$. However, this worry is illusory, for the simple reason that the oracles $A_{\mathcal{D}}$ and $A_{\mathcal{M}}$ are generated independently. Thus, if $C_{\mathcal{M}}$ can break $\mathcal{M}$ by querying $A_{\mathcal{D}}$, then it can *also* break $\mathcal{M}$ by querying a randomly-generated "mock-up" $A'_{\mathcal{D}}$ of $A_{\mathcal{D}}$; and conversely, if $C_{\mathcal{D}}$ can break $\mathcal{D}$ by querying $A_{\mathcal{M}}$, then it can also break $\mathcal{D}$ by querying a randomly-generated mock-up $A'_{\mathcal{M}}$ of $A_{\mathcal{M}}$. Regardless of the *computational* cost of generating these mock-ups, they give us a break against $\mathcal{D}$ or $\mathcal{M}$ that makes only $\operatorname{poly}(n)$ oracle queries, thereby giving the desired contradiction. ∎

4. INNER-PRODUCT ADVERSARY METHOD

At least in the black-box setting, our goal is to create quantum money (mini-)schemes that we can *prove* are secure—by showing that any counterfeiter would need to make exponentially many queries to some oracle. Proving security results of this kind turns out to require interesting quantum lower bound machinery. In this section, we introduce the *inner-product adversary method*, a new variant of Ambainis's quantum adversary method [8] that is well-adapted to proving the security of quantum money schemes, and that seems likely to find other applications.

Let us explain the difficulty we need to overcome. In a public-key quantum money scheme, a counterfeiter C has *two* powerful resources available:

(1) One or more copies of a "legitimate" quantum money state $|\psi\rangle$.

(2) Access to a *verification procedure* V, which accepts $|\psi\rangle$ and rejects every state orthogonal to $|\psi\rangle$.

Indeed, for us, the situation is even better for C (i.e., worse for us!), since C can query not only the verification procedure V itself, but also an underlying *classical* oracle U that the legitimate buyers and sellers use to implement V. But let us ignore that issue for now.

As a first step, of course, we should understand how to rule out counterfeiting given (1) or (2) separately. If C has a copy of $|\psi\rangle$, but no oracle access to V, then the impossibility of preparing $|\psi\rangle|\psi\rangle$ essentially amounts to the No-Cloning Theorem. Conversely, if C has oracle access to V, but no copy of $|\psi\rangle$, then given unlimited time, C *can* prepare as many copies of $|\psi\rangle$ as it wants, by using Grover's algorithm to search for a quantum state that V accepts. The problem is "merely" that, if $|\psi\rangle$ has n qubits, then Grover's algorithm requires $\Theta\left(2^{n/2}\right)$ iterations, and the BBBV hybrid argument [12] shows that Grover's algorithm is optimal.

What we need, then, is a theorem showing that any counterfeiter needs exponentially many queries to V to prepare $|\psi\rangle|\psi\rangle$, *even if* the counterfeiter has a copy of $|\psi\rangle$ to start with. Such a theorem would contain both the No-Cloning Theorem and the BBBV hybrid argument as special cases. Aaronson [3] called the desired generalization the *Complexity-Theoretic No-Cloning Theorem*, and sketched a proof of it using Ambainis's adversary method. Based on that result, Aaronson also argued that there exists a *quantum oracle* (i.e., a black-box unitary transformation V) relative to which secure public-key quantum money is possible. However, the details were never published.

In this section, we prove a result—Theorem 18—that is much more general than Aaronson's previous Complexity-Theoretic No-Cloning Theorem [3]. Then, in Section 5, we apply Theorem 18 to prove the security of public-key quantum money relative to a *classical* oracle. In the full version, we also apply Theorem 18 to prove the "original" Complexity-Theoretic No-Cloning Theorem [3], which involves Haar-random n-qubit states $|\psi\rangle$, rather than superpositions $|A\rangle$ over subspaces $A \leq \mathbb{F}_2^n$.[15]

4.1 Idea of Method

So, what *is* the inner-product adversary method? In Ambainis's adversary method [8]—like in the BBBV hybrid argument [12] from which it evolved—the basic idea is to upper-bound how much "progress" a quantum algorithm Q can make at distinguishing pairs of oracles, as the result of a single query. Let $|\Psi_t^U\rangle$ be Q's state after t queries, assuming that the oracle is U. Then *normally*, before any queries have been made, we can assume that $|\Psi_0^U\rangle = |\Psi_0^V\rangle$ for all oracles U and V. By contrast, after the final query T, for all oracle pairs (U, V) that Q is trying to distinguish, we must have (say) $|\langle\Psi_T^U|\Psi_T^V\rangle| \leq 1/2$. Thus, *if* we can show that the inner product $|\langle\Psi_t^U|\Psi_t^V\rangle|$ can decrease by at most ε as the result of a single query, then it follows that Q must make $\Omega(1/\varepsilon)$ queries.

But when we try to apply the above framework to quantum money, we run into serious difficulties. Most obviously, it is no longer true that $|\Psi_0^U\rangle = |\Psi_0^V\rangle$ for all oracles U, V. Indeed, before Q makes even a *single* query to its oracle V, it already has a great deal of information about V, in the form of a legitimate money state $|\psi\rangle$ that V accepts. The task is "merely" to prepare a second copy of a state that Q already has! Worse yet, once we fix two oracles U and V, we find that Q generally *can* exploit the "head start" provided by its initial state to decrease the inner product $|\langle\Psi_t^U|\Psi_t^V\rangle|$ by a constant amount, by making just a single query to U or V respectively.

Our solution is as follows. We first carefully choose a distribution $\mathcal{D}$ over oracle pairs (U, V). We then analyze how much the *expected* inner product

$$\mathop{\mathrm{E}}_{(U,V)\sim\mathcal{D}}\left[\left|\left\langle\Psi_t^U|\Psi_t^V\right\rangle\right|\right]$$

can decrease as the result of a single query to U or V. We will find that, even if Q can substantially increase the angle between $|\Psi_t^U\rangle$ and $|\Psi_t^V\rangle$ for *some* (U, V) pairs by making a single query, it cannot do so for *most* pairs.

To illustrate, let $|\psi\rangle$ and $|\varphi\rangle$ be two possible quantum money states, which satisfy (say) $\langle\psi|\varphi\rangle = 1/2$. Then if a counterfeiting algorithm succeeds perfectly, it must map $|\psi\rangle$ to $|\psi\rangle^{\otimes 2}$, and $|\varphi\rangle$ to $|\varphi\rangle^{\otimes 2}$. Since

$$\langle\psi|^{\otimes 2}|\varphi\rangle^{\otimes 2} = (\langle\psi|\varphi\rangle)^2 = \frac{1}{4},$$

this means that the counterfeiter must *decrease the corresponding inner product* by at least $1/4$. However, we will show that the *average* inner product can decrease by at most $1/\exp(n)$ as the result of a single query. From this it will follow that the counterfeiter needs to make $2^{\Omega(n)}$ queries.

Let us mention that today, there are several "sophisticated" versions of the quantum adversary method [9, 27], which *can* yield lower bounds for quantum state generation tasks not unlike the ones we consider. However, a drawback of these methods is that they are extremely hard to apply to concrete problems: doing so typically requires eigenvalue bounds, and often the use of representation theory. For this reason, even if one of the "sophisticated" adversary methods (or a variant thereof) could be applied to the quantum money problem, our approach might still be preferable.

[15]For whatever it is worth, we get a lower bound of $\Omega\left(2^{n/2}\right)$ on the number of queries needed to copy a Haar-random state, which is quadratically better than the $\Omega\left(2^{n/4}\right)$ that we get for subspace states.

4.2 The Method

We now introduce the inner-product adversary method. Let $\mathcal{O}$ be a set of quantum oracles acting on n qubits each. For each $U \in \mathcal{O}$, assume there exists a subspace $S_U \leq \mathbb{C}^{2^n}$ such that

(i) $U|\psi\rangle = -|\psi\rangle$ for all $|\psi\rangle \in S_U$, and

(ii) $U|\eta\rangle = |\eta\rangle$ for all $|\eta\rangle \in S_U^\perp$.

Let $R \subset \mathcal{O}\times\mathcal{O}$ be a symmetric binary relation on $\mathcal{O}$, with the properties that

(i) $(U, U) \notin R$ for all $U \in \mathcal{O}$, and

(ii) for every $U \in \mathcal{O}$ there exists a $V \in \mathcal{O}$ such that $(U, V) \in R$.

Suppose that for all $U \in \mathcal{O}$ and all $|\eta\rangle \in S_U^\perp$, we have

$$\mathop{\mathrm{E}}_{V\,:\,(U,V)\in R}\left[F(|\eta\rangle, S_V)^2\right] \leq \varepsilon,$$

where $F(|\eta\rangle, S_V) = \max_{|\psi\rangle\in S_V}|\langle\eta|\psi\rangle|$ is the fidelity between $|\eta\rangle$ and S_V. Let Q be a quantum oracle algorithm, and let Q^U denote Q run with the oracle $U \in \mathcal{O}$. Suppose Q^U begins in the state $|\Psi_0^U\rangle$ (possibly already dependent on U). Let $|\Psi_t^U\rangle$ denote the state of Q^U immediately after the tth query. Also, define a *progress measure* p_t by

$$p_t := \mathop{\mathrm{E}}_{U,V\,:\,(U,V)\in R}\left[\left|\left\langle\Psi_t^U|\Psi_t^V\right\rangle\right|\right].$$

The following lemma bounds how much p_t can decrease as the result of a single query.

Lemma 17 (Bound on Progress Rate)**.**

$$p_t \geq p_{t-1} - 4\sqrt{\varepsilon}.$$

PROOF. Let $|\Phi_t^U\rangle$ denote the state of Q^U immediately *before* the tth query. Then for all t, it is clear that $\langle\Phi_t^U|\Phi_t^V\rangle = \langle\Psi_{t-1}^U|\Psi_{t-1}^V\rangle$: in other words, the unitary transformations that Q performs in between query steps have no effect on the inner products. So to prove the lemma, it suffices to show the following inequality:

$$\mathop{\mathrm{E}}_{U,V\,:\,(U,V)\in R}\left[\left|\left\langle\Phi_t^U|\Phi_t^V\right\rangle\right|\right] - \mathop{\mathrm{E}}_{U,V\,:\,(U,V)\in R}\left[\left|\left\langle\Psi_t^U|\Psi_t^V\right\rangle\right|\right] \leq 4\sqrt{\varepsilon}. \quad (*)$$

Let $\{|i\rangle\}_{i\in[B]}$ be an arbitrary orthonormal basis for Q's workspace register. Then we can write

$$\begin{aligned}\left|\Phi_t^U\right\rangle &= \sum_{i\in[B]}\alpha_{t,i}^U|i\rangle\left|\Phi_{t,i}^U\right\rangle \\ &= \sum_{i\in[B]}|i\rangle\left(\beta_{t,i}^U\left|\eta_{t,i}^U\right\rangle + \gamma_{t,i}^U\left|\psi_{t,i}^U\right\rangle\right),\end{aligned}$$

where $|\eta_{t,i}^U\rangle \in S_U^\perp$ and $|\psi_{t,i}^U\rangle \in S_U$. (By normalization, $|\beta_{t,i}^U|^2 + |\gamma_{t,i}^U|^2 = |\alpha_{t,i}^U|^2$.) A query transforms the above state to

$$\left|\Psi_t^U\right\rangle = \sum_{i\in[B]}|i\rangle\left(\beta_{t,i}^U\left|\eta_{t,i}^U\right\rangle - \gamma_{t,i}^U\left|\psi_{t,i}^U\right\rangle\right).$$

So for all $U, V \in \mathcal{O}$,

$$\begin{aligned}&\left\langle \Phi_t^U | \Phi_t^V \right\rangle - \left\langle \Psi_t^U | \Psi_t^V \right\rangle \\ &= \sum_{i\in[B]} \left(\overline{\beta}_{t,i}^U \left\langle \eta_{t,i}^U\right| + \overline{\gamma}_{t,i}^U \left\langle \psi_{t,i}^U\right|\right) \left(\beta_{t,i}^V \left|\eta_{t,i}^V\right\rangle + \gamma_{t,i}^V \left|\psi_{t,i}^V\right\rangle\right) \\ &\quad - \sum_{i\in[B]} \left(\overline{\beta}_{t,i}^U \left\langle \eta_{t,i}^U\right| - \overline{\gamma}_{t,i}^U \left\langle \psi_{t,i}^U\right|\right) \left(\beta_{t,i}^V \left|\eta_{t,i}^V\right\rangle - \gamma_{t,i}^V \left|\psi_{t,i}^V\right\rangle\right) \\ &= 2\sum_{i\in[B]} \left(\overline{\beta}_{t,i}^U \gamma_{t,i}^V \left\langle \eta_{t,i}^U | \psi_{t,i}^V\right\rangle + \overline{\gamma}_{t,i}^U \beta_{t,i}^V \left\langle \psi_{t,i}^U | \eta_{t,i}^V\right\rangle\right).\end{aligned}$$

By Cauchy-Schwarz, the above implies that

$$\begin{aligned}\left|\left\langle \Phi_t^U | \Phi_t^V \right\rangle\right| - \left|\left\langle \Psi_t^U | \Psi_t^V \right\rangle\right| &\leq 2 \max_{i\in[B]} \left|\left\langle \eta_{t,i}^U | \psi_{t,i}^V\right\rangle\right| \\ &\quad + 2 \max_{i\in[B]} \left|\left\langle \psi_{t,i}^U | \eta_{t,i}^V\right\rangle\right|.\end{aligned}$$

Now fix $U \in \mathcal{O}$ and $i \in [B]$. Then again applying Cauchy-Schwarz,

$$\begin{aligned}\mathop{\mathrm{E}}_{V\,:\,(U,V)\in R}\left[\left|\left\langle \eta_{t,i}^U | \psi_{t,i}^V\right\rangle\right|\right] &\leq \sqrt{\mathop{\mathrm{E}}_{V\,:\,(U,V)\in R}\left[\left|\left\langle \eta_{t,i}^U | \psi_{t,i}^V\right\rangle\right|^2\right]} \\ &\leq \sqrt{\mathop{\mathrm{E}}_{V\,:\,(U,V)\in R}\left[\max_{|\psi\rangle\in S_V} \left|\left\langle \eta_{t,i}^U | \psi\right\rangle\right|^2\right]} \\ &\leq \sqrt{\varepsilon}.\end{aligned}$$

Hence

$$\mathop{\mathrm{E}}_{U,V\,:\,(U,V)\in R}\left[\left|\left\langle \eta_{t,i}^U | \psi_{t,i}^V\right\rangle\right|\right] \leq \sqrt{\varepsilon}$$

as well, and likewise

$$\mathop{\mathrm{E}}_{U,V\,:\,(U,V)\in R}\left[\left|\left\langle \psi_{t,i}^U | \eta_{t,i}^V\right\rangle\right|\right] \leq \sqrt{\varepsilon}$$

by symmetry. Putting everything together,

$$\begin{aligned}p_{t-1} - p_t &= \mathop{\mathrm{E}}_{U,V\,:\,(U,V)\in R}\left[\left|\left\langle \Phi_t^U | \Phi_t^V \right\rangle\right| - \left|\left\langle \Psi_t^U | \Psi_t^V \right\rangle\right|\right] \\ &\leq 2 \mathop{\mathrm{E}}_{U,V\,:\,(U,V)\in R}\left[\max_{i\in[B]} \left|\left\langle \eta_{t,i}^U | \psi_{t,i}^V\right\rangle\right|\right] \\ &\quad + 2 \mathop{\mathrm{E}}_{U,V\,:\,(U,V)\in R}\left[\max_{i\in[B]} \left|\left\langle \psi_{t,i}^U | \eta_{t,i}^V\right\rangle\right|\right] \\ &\leq 4\sqrt{\varepsilon}.\end{aligned}$$

This proves inequality (*) and hence the lemma. ■

From Lemma 17 we immediately deduce the following.

Theorem 18 (Inner-Product Adversary Method). *Suppose that initially* $\left|\left\langle \Psi_0^U | \Psi_0^V \right\rangle\right| \geq c$ *for all* $(U, V) \in R$, *whereas by the end we need* $\left|\left\langle \Psi_T^U | \Psi_T^V \right\rangle\right| \leq d$ *for all* $(U, V) \in R$. *Then* Q *must make* $T = \Omega\left(\frac{c-d}{\sqrt{\varepsilon}}\right)$ *oracle queries.*

5. CLASSICAL ORACLE SCHEME

In this section, we construct a mini-scheme, called the *Hidden Subspace Mini-Scheme*, that requires only a classical oracle. We then use the inner-product adversary method from Section 4 to show that our mini-scheme is secure—indeed, that any counterfeiter must make $\Omega\left(2^{n/4}\right)$ queries to copy a banknote. By the results of Sections 3.3 and 2.1, our mini-scheme will automatically imply a full-blown public-key quantum money scheme, which requires only a classical oracle and is unconditionally secure.

5.1 The Hidden Subspace Mini-Scheme

We identify n-bit strings $x \in \{0, 1\}^n$ with elements of the vector space $\mathbb{F}_2^n$ in the standard way. Then in our mini-scheme, each n-qubit money state will have the form

$$|A\rangle := \frac{1}{\sqrt{|A|}} \sum_{x\in A} |x\rangle,$$

where A is some randomly-chosen subspace of $\mathbb{F}_2^n$ (i.e., a set of codewords of a linear code), with $\dim A = n/2$. Let $A^\perp$ be the orthogonal complement of A, so that $\dim A^\perp = n/2$ as well. Notice that we can transform $|A\rangle$ to $|A^\perp\rangle$ and vice versa by simply applying $H_2^{\otimes n}$: a Hadamard gate on each of the n qubits, or equivalently a quantum Fourier transform over $\mathbb{F}_2^n$.

The basic idea of the mini-scheme is as follows: the bank can easily prepare the quantum money state $|A\rangle$, starting from a classical description $\langle A\rangle$ of A (e.g., a list of $n/2$ generators). The bank distributes the state $|A\rangle$, but keeps the classical description $\langle A\rangle$ secret. Along with $|A\rangle$ itself, the bank also publishes details of how to *verify* $|A\rangle$ by querying two classical oracles, U_A and $U_{A^\perp}$. The first oracle, U_A, decides membership in A: for all n-qubit basis states $|x\rangle$,

$$U_A |x\rangle = \begin{cases} -|x\rangle & \text{if } x \in A \\ |x\rangle & \text{otherwise} \end{cases}$$

The second oracle, $U_{A^\perp}$, decides membership in $A^\perp$ in the same way.

Using U_A, it is easy to implement a projector $\mathbb{P}_A$ onto the set of basis states in A. To do so, simply initialize a control qubit to $|+\rangle = \frac{|0\rangle+|1\rangle}{\sqrt{2}}$, then apply U_A conditioned on the control qubit being in state $|1\rangle$, then measure the control qubit in the $\{|+\rangle, |-\rangle\}$ basis, and postselect on getting the outcome $|-\rangle$. Likewise, using $U_{A^\perp}$, it is easy to implement a projector $\mathbb{P}_{A^\perp}$ onto the set of basis states in $A^\perp$. Then V_A, the public verification algorithm for the money state $|A\rangle$, will simply consist of $\mathbb{P}_A$, then a Fourier transform, then $\mathbb{P}_{A^\perp}$, and finally a second Fourier transform to return the legitimate money state back to $|A\rangle$:

$$V_A := H_2^{\otimes n} \mathbb{P}_{A^\perp} H_2^{\otimes n} \mathbb{P}_A.$$

We show in Lemma 19 that $V_A = |A\rangle\langle A|$ is just a projector onto $|A\rangle$. This means, in particular, that $V_A |A\rangle = |A\rangle$, and that V_A accepts an arbitrary state $|\psi\rangle$ with probability $|\langle\psi|A\rangle|^2$. Thus, our mini-scheme is *projective* and has *perfect completeness.*

But what about security? Intuitively, a counterfeiter could query U_A or $U_{A^\perp}$ to find a generating set for A or $A^\perp$—but that would require an exponentially-long Grover search, since $|A| = |A^\perp| = 2^{n/2} \ll 2^n$. Alternatively, the counterfeiter could measure $|A\rangle$ in the standard or Hadamard bases—but that would reveal just *one* random element of A or $A^\perp$. Neither ability seems useful for *copying* $|A\rangle$, let alone recovering a full classical description of A.[16]

[16]Obviously, if the counterfeiter had $\Omega(n)$ copies of $|A\rangle$, then it *could* recover a generating set for A, by simply measuring each copy independently in the standard basis. That is why, in our full quantum money scheme, the counterfeiter will *not* have $\Omega(n)$ copies of $|A\rangle$. Instead, each banknote will involve a completely different subspace $A_s \leq \mathbb{F}_2^n$ (parameterized by its unique serial number s), so that measuring one banknote reveals nothing about the others.

And indeed, using the inner-product adversary method plus some other tools, we will prove the following tight lower bound (Theorem 23): even if given a single copy of $|A\rangle$, as well as oracle access to U_A and $U_{A^\perp}$, a counterfeiter still needs $\Omega\left(\epsilon 2^{n/4}\right)$ queries to prepare a state that has fidelity ϵ with $|A\rangle^{\otimes 2}$. This will imply that our mini-scheme has *exponentially-small soundness error.*

5.2 Formal Specification

We are not quite done, since we never explained how the bank provides access to U_A and $U_{A^\perp}$. Thus, in our "final" mini-scheme $\mathcal{M} = (\mathsf{Bank}_{\mathcal{M}}, \mathsf{Ver}_{\mathcal{M}})$, the bank, verifier, and counterfeiter will all have access to a *single* classical oracle U, which consists of four components:

A **banknote generator** $\mathcal{G}(r)$, which takes as input a random string $r \in \{0,1\}^n$, and outputs a set of linearly independent generators $\langle A_r\rangle = \{x_1, \dots, x_{n/2}\}$ for a subspace $A_r \le \mathbb{F}_2^n$, as well as a unique $3n$-bit *serial number* $s_r \in \{0,1\}^{3n}$. The function $\mathcal{G}$ is chosen uniformly at random, subject to the constraint that the serial numbers are all distinct.[17]

A **serial number checker** $\mathcal{H}(s)$, which outputs 1 if $s = s_r$ is a valid serial number for some $\langle A_r\rangle$, and 0 otherwise.

A **primal subspace tester** $\mathcal{T}_{\text{primal}}$, which takes an input of the form $|s\rangle |x\rangle$, applies U_{A_r} to $|x\rangle$ if $s = s_r$ is a valid serial number for some $\langle A_r\rangle$, and does nothing otherwise.

A **dual subspace tester** $\mathcal{T}_{\text{dual}}$, identical to $\mathcal{T}_{\text{primal}}$ except that it applies $U_{A_r^\perp}$ instead of U_{A_r}.

Then $\mathcal{M} = (\mathsf{Bank}_{\mathcal{M}}, \mathsf{Ver}_{\mathcal{M}})$ is defined as follows:

- $\mathsf{Bank}_{\mathcal{M}}(0^n)$ chooses $r \in \{0,1\}^n$ uniformly at random. It then looks up $\mathcal{G}(r) = (s_r, \langle A_r\rangle)$, and outputs the banknote $|\$_r\rangle = |s_r\rangle |A_r\rangle$.
- $\mathsf{Ver}_{\mathcal{M}}(¢)$ first uses $\mathcal{H}$ to check that $¢$ has the form (s, ρ), where $s = s_r$ is a valid serial number. If so, then it uses $\mathcal{T}_{\text{primal}}$ and $\mathcal{T}_{\text{dual}}$ to apply $V_{A_r} = H_2^{\otimes n}\mathbb{P}_{A_r^\perp} H_2^{\otimes n}\mathbb{P}_{A_r}$, and accepts if and only if $V_{A_r}(\rho)$ accepts.

5.3 Analysis

We now analyze the mini-scheme defined in Sections 5.1 and 5.2. For convenience, we assume for most of the proof that the subspace $A \le \mathbb{F}_2^n$ is *fixed*, and that the counterfeiter (who does not know A) only has access to the oracles U_A and $U_{A^\perp}$. Then, at the end, we will explain how to generalize the conclusions to the "final" mini-scheme $\mathcal{M}$.

It will be convenient to consider the subset $A^* \subset \{0,1\}^{n+1}$, defined by $A^* := (0, A) \cup (1, A^\perp)$. Let S_{A^*} be the subspace of $\mathbb{C}^{2^{n+1}}$ that is spanned by basis states $|x\rangle$ such that $x \in A^*$. Then we can think of the pair of oracles $(U_A, U_{A^\perp})$ as being a *single* oracle U_{A^*}, which satisfies $U_{A^*}|\psi\rangle = -|\psi\rangle$ for all $|\psi\rangle \in S_{A^*}$, and $U_{A^*}|\eta\rangle = |\eta\rangle$ for all $|\eta\rangle \in S_{A^*}^\perp$.

Recall the definition of the verifier V_A:

$$V_A := H_2^{\otimes n}\mathbb{P}_{A^\perp} H_2^{\otimes n}\mathbb{P}_A,$$

where $\mathbb{P}_A$ and $\mathbb{P}_{A^\perp}$ denote projective measurements that accept a basis state $|x\rangle$ if and only if x belongs to A or $A^\perp$ respectively. The following lemma shows that V_A "works," and indeed that it gives us a projective mini-scheme.

[17]Note that one can implement $\mathcal{G}$ using an ordinary random oracle. In that case, the requirement that the serial numbers are distinct will be satisfied with probability $1 - O(2^{-n})$.

Lemma 19. *$V_A = |A\rangle\langle A|$ is simply a projector onto $|A\rangle$. So in particular,* $\Pr[V_A(|\psi\rangle) \text{ accepts}] = |\langle\psi|A\rangle|^2$.

PROOF. It suffices to show that $V_A|A\rangle = |A\rangle$ and that $V_A|\psi\rangle = 0$ for all $|\psi\rangle$ orthogonal to $|A\rangle$. First,

$$\begin{aligned} V_A|A\rangle &= H_2^{\otimes n}\mathbb{P}_{A^\perp} H_2^{\otimes n}\mathbb{P}_A|A\rangle \\ &= H_2^{\otimes n}\mathbb{P}_{A^\perp} H_2^{\otimes n}|A\rangle \\ &= H_2^{\otimes n}\mathbb{P}_{A^\perp}|A^\perp\rangle \\ &= H_2^{\otimes n}|A^\perp\rangle \\ &= |A\rangle. \end{aligned}$$

Second, if $\langle\psi|A\rangle = 0$ then we can write

$$|\psi\rangle = \sum_{x\in 2^n} c_x|x\rangle$$

where $\sum_{x\in A} c_x = 0$. Then

$$\begin{aligned} V_A|\psi\rangle &= H_2^{\otimes n}\mathbb{P}_{A^\perp} H_2^{\otimes n}\mathbb{P}_A \sum_{x\in 2^n} c_x|x\rangle \\ &= H_2^{\otimes n}\mathbb{P}_{A^\perp} H_2^{\otimes n}\sum_{x\in A} c_x|x\rangle \\ &= \frac{1}{\sqrt{2^n}} H_2^{\otimes n}\mathbb{P}_{A^\perp}\sum_{x\in A} c_x \sum_{y\perp x}|y\rangle \\ &= \frac{1}{\sqrt{2^n}} H_2^{\otimes n}\sum_{y\in A^\perp}|y\rangle\sum_{x\in A} c_x \\ &= 0. \end{aligned}$$

■

We now show that perfect counterfeiting requires exponentially many queries to U_{A^*}.

Theorem 20 (Lower Bound for Perfect Counterfeiting). *Given one copy of $|A\rangle$, as well as oracle access to U_{A^*}, a counterfeiter needs $\Omega\left(2^{n/4}\right)$ queries to prepare $|A\rangle^{\otimes 2}$ with certainty (for a worst-case $|A\rangle$).*

PROOF. We will apply Theorem 18. Let the set $\mathcal{O}$ contain U_{A^*} for every possible subspace $A \le \mathbb{F}_2^n$ with $\dim A = n/2$. Also, put $(U_{A^*}, U_{B^*}) \in R$ if and only if $\dim(A\cap B) = n/2 - 1$. Then given $U_{A^*} \in \mathcal{O}$ and $|\eta\rangle \in S_{A^*}^\perp$, let

$$|\eta\rangle = \sum_{x\in\{0,1\}^{n+1}\setminus A^*} \alpha_x|x\rangle.$$

We have

$$\begin{aligned} &\mathop{\mathrm{E}}_{U_{B^*}\,:\,(U_{A^*},U_{B^*})\in R}\left[F(|\eta\rangle, S_{B^*})^2\right] \\ &= \mathop{\mathrm{E}}_{B\,:\,\dim(B)=n/2,\dim(A\cap B)=n/2-1}\left[\sum_{x\in B^*\setminus A^*}|\alpha_x|^2\right] \\ &\le \max_{x\in\{0,1\}^{n+1}\setminus A^*}\left(\Pr_{B\,:\,\dim(B)=n/2,\dim(A\cap B)=n/2-1}[x\in B^*]\right) \\ &= \max_{x\in\{0,1\}^{n}\setminus A}\left(\Pr_{B\,:\,\dim(B)=n/2,\dim(A\cap B)=n/2-1}[x\in B]\right) \\ &= \frac{|B\setminus A|}{|\{0,1\}^n\setminus A|} \quad (\text{for } \dim(B) = n/2,\ \dim(A\cap B) = n/2-1) \\ &= \frac{2^{n/2-1}}{2^n - 2^{n/2}} \\ &\le \frac{1}{2^{n/2}}. \end{aligned}$$

Here the first line uses the definition of fidelity, the second line uses the easy direction of the minimax theorem, the third line uses the symmetry between A and $A^{\perp}$, and the fourth line uses the symmetry among all $2^n - 2^{n/2}$ strings $x \in \{0,1\}^n \backslash A$. The conclusion is that we can set $\varepsilon := 2^{-n/2}$.

Fix $(U_{A^*}, U_{B^*}) \in R$. Then $|\langle A|B\rangle| = 1/2$. On the other hand, if the counterfeiter succeeds, it must map $|A\rangle$ to some state $|f_A\rangle := |A\rangle|A\rangle|\text{garbage}_A\rangle$, and $|B\rangle$ to some state $|f_B\rangle := |B\rangle|B\rangle|\text{garbage}_B\rangle$. Therefore $|\langle f_A|f_B\rangle| \leq 1/4$. So setting $c = 1/2$ and $d = 1/4$, Theorem 18 tells us that the counterfeiter must make

$$\Omega\left(\frac{c-d}{\sqrt{\varepsilon}}\right) = \Omega\left(2^{n/4}\right)$$

queries to U_{A^*}. ■

A simple modification to the proof of Theorem 20 shows that even to counterfeit money *almost* perfectly, one still needs exponentially many queries to U_{A^*}.

Corollary 21 (Lower Bound for Small-Error Counterfeiting). *Given one copy of $|A\rangle$, as well as oracle access to U_{A^*}, a counterfeiter needs $\Omega\left(2^{n/4}\right)$ queries to prepare a state ρ such that $\langle A|^{\otimes 2} \rho |A\rangle^{\otimes 2} \geq 0.9999$ (for a worst-case $|A\rangle$).*

PROOF. Let $|\langle A|B\rangle| = c$, and let $\epsilon = 0.00001$. If the counterfeiter succeeds, it must map $|A\rangle$ to some state ρ_A, and $|B\rangle$ to some state ρ_B, such that $\langle A|^{\otimes 2} \rho_A |A\rangle^{\otimes 2}$ and $\langle B|^{\otimes 2} \rho_B |B\rangle^{\otimes 2}$ are both at least $1-\epsilon$. So letting $|f_A\rangle$ and $|f_B\rangle$ be purifications of ρ_A and ρ_B respectively, we have

$$\begin{aligned} |\langle f_A|f_B\rangle| &\leq F(\rho_A, \rho_B) \\ &\leq \left|\langle A|^{\otimes 2} |B\rangle^{\otimes 2}\right| + 2\epsilon^{1/4} \\ &= c^2 + 2\epsilon^{1/4} \end{aligned}$$

where the second line follows from Lemma 4. So setting $d := c^2 + 2\epsilon^{1/4}$, Theorem 18 tells us that the counterfeiter must make

$$\Omega\left(\frac{c - c^2 - 2\epsilon^{1/4}}{\sqrt{2^{-n/2}}}\right)$$

queries to U_{A^*}. Fixing $c := 1/2$, the above is $\Omega\left(2^{n/4}\right)$. ■

Since the verifier V_A is projective, we can now combine Corollary 21 with Theorem 13 to obtain the following "amplified" lower bound.

Corollary 22 (Lower Bound for High-Error Counterfeiting). *Let $1/\varepsilon = o\left(2^{n/2}\right)$. Given one copy of $|A\rangle$, as well as oracle access to U_{A^*}, a counterfeiter needs $\Omega\left(\sqrt{\varepsilon}2^{n/4}\right)$ queries to prepare a state ρ such that $\langle A|^{\otimes 2} \rho |A\rangle^{\otimes 2} \geq \varepsilon$ (for a worst-case $|A\rangle$).*

PROOF. Suppose we have a counterfeiter C that makes $o\left(\sqrt{\varepsilon}2^{n/4}\right)$ queries to U_{A^*}, and prepares a state σ such that $\langle A|^{\otimes 2} \sigma |A\rangle^{\otimes 2} \geq \varepsilon$. Let $\delta := 0.00001$. Then by Theorem 13, there exists an amplified counterfeiter C' that makes

$$O\left(\frac{\log 1/\delta}{\sqrt{\varepsilon}\left(\sqrt{\varepsilon} + \delta^2\right)}\right) = O\left(\frac{1}{\sqrt{\varepsilon}}\right)$$

calls to C and V_A, and that prepares a state ρ such that $\langle A|^{\otimes 2} \rho |A\rangle^{\otimes 2} \geq 1-\delta$. Now, counting the $o\left(\sqrt{\varepsilon}2^{n/4}\right)$ queries from each C invocation and $O(1)$ queries from each V_A invocation, the total number of queries that C' makes to U_{A^*} is

$$\left[o\left(\sqrt{\varepsilon}2^{n/4}\right) + O(1)\right] \cdot O\left(\frac{1}{\sqrt{\varepsilon}}\right) = o\left(2^{n/4}\right).$$

But this contradicts Corollary 21. ■

So far, we have only made statements about the *worst* case for a would-be counterfeiter. But such guarantees are clearly not enough: it could be that *most* money states $|A\rangle$ are easy to duplicate, without contradicting any of the results we have seen so far.

We will show that the problem faced by a counterfeiter is *random self-reducible*: if a counterfeiter could duplicate a uniformly-random money state $|A\rangle$, then it could duplicate *any* $|A\rangle$. Thus the bank can ensure security by creating uniformly-random money states.

In what follows, let $\mathcal{S}$ be the set of all subspaces $A \leq \mathbb{F}_2^n$ such that $\dim A = n/2$. Also, let $V_A^{\otimes 2} = (|A\rangle\langle A|)^{\otimes 2}$ be the projector onto $|A\rangle^{\otimes 2}$.

Theorem 23 (Lower Bound for Average-Case Counterfeiting). *Let $A \leq \mathbb{F}_2^n$ be a uniformly-random element of $\mathcal{S}$. Then given one copy of $|A\rangle$, as well as oracle access to U_{A^*}, a counterfeiter C needs $\Omega\left(\sqrt{\varepsilon}2^{n/4}\right)$ queries to prepare a $2n$-qubit state ρ that $V_A^{\otimes 2}$ accepts with probability at least ε, for all $1/\varepsilon = o\left(2^{n/2}\right)$. Here the probability is taken over the choice of $A \in \mathcal{S}$, as well as the behavior of C and $V_A^{\otimes 2}$.*

PROOF. Suppose we had a counterfeiter C that violated the above. Using C as a black box, we will show how to construct a new counterfeiter C' that violates Corollary 22.

Given a (deterministically-chosen) money state $|A\rangle$ and oracle access to U_{A^*}, first choose an invertible linear map $f : \mathbb{F}_2^n \to \mathbb{F}_2^n$ uniformly at random. Then $f(A)$, the image of A under f, is a uniformly-random element of $\mathcal{S}$. Furthermore, the state $|A\rangle$ can be transformed into $|f(A)\rangle$ straightforwardly, and the oracle $U_{f(A)^*}$ can be simulated by composing f with U_{A^*}. So by using the counterfeiter C for uniformly-random states, we can produce a state ρ_f that $V_{f(A)}^{\otimes 2}$ accepts with probability at least ε. By applying f^{-1} to both registers of ρ_f, we can then obtain a state ρ that $V_A^{\otimes 2}$ accepts with probability at least ε, thereby contradicting Corollary 22. ■

We are now ready to prove security for the "final" mini-scheme $\mathcal{M}$ defined in Section 5.2.

Theorem 24 (Security of Mini-Scheme). *The mini-scheme $\mathcal{M} = (\mathsf{Bank}_{\mathcal{M}}, \mathsf{Ver}_{\mathcal{M}})$, which is defined relative to the classical oracle U, has perfect completeness and exponentially-small soundness error.*

PROOF SKETCH. That $\mathcal{M}$ has perfect completeness follows from its definition and from Lemma 19. That $\mathcal{M}$ has exponentially-small soundness error *essentially* follows from Theorem 23. We only need to show that, given a banknote of the form $|\$_r\rangle = |s_r\rangle|A_r\rangle$, a polynomial-time counterfeiter C can gain no additional advantage by querying the "full" oracles $\mathcal{G}, \mathcal{H}, \mathcal{T}_{\text{primal}}, \mathcal{T}_{\text{dual}}$, beyond what it gains from querying $U_{A_r^*} = \left(U_{A_r}, U_{A_r^{\perp}}\right)$. This follows from some simple observations: first, let $r \in \{0,1\}^n$ be the random string chosen by the bank, so that $\mathcal{G}(r) = (s_r, \langle A_r\rangle)$. Then assuming C does not know r, the BBBV hybrid argument [12] tells us that C can gain nothing by querying $\mathcal{G}$: indeed, if we randomly *change* the value of $\mathcal{G}(r)$, it will affect C's output by at most an exponentially small amount. However, once we make that change, an adversary trying to counterfeit $|A\rangle$ given U_A and $U_{A^\perp}$ can easily "mock up" a serial number s, as well as the oracles $\mathcal{G}, \mathcal{H}, \mathcal{T}_{\text{primal}}$ and $\mathcal{T}_{\text{dual}}$, for itself. Just like in Corollary 16, since our security guarantees are query complexity bounds, we do not care about the *computational* complexity of creating the mock-ups. By using the mock-ups, one can convert any successful attack on $\mathcal{M}$ into successful counterfeiting of $|A\rangle$, given oracle access to U_A and $U_{A^\perp}$ only. But the latter contradicts Theorem 23. Further details of the argument are deferred to the full version. ■

Finally, using Theorem 24 together with Corollary 16, we can obtain a secure public-key quantum money scheme, relative to a classical oracle.

Theorem 25 (Security of Hidden Subspace Money). *By combining the mini-scheme $\mathcal{M}$ with a digital signature scheme, it is possible to construct a public-key quantum money scheme $\mathcal{S} = (\mathsf{KeyGen}_{\mathcal{S}}, \mathsf{Bank}_{\mathcal{S}}, \mathsf{Ver}_{\mathcal{S}})$, defined relative to some classical oracle U', which has perfect completeness and exponentially-small soundness error.*

6. EXPLICIT QUANTUM MONEY SCHEME

We have shown how to construct a provably-secure public-key quantum money scheme, when an appropriate classical oracle is available. In this section, we propose a way to obtain the same functionality without an oracle. The key challenge is this:

> *Given a subspace $A \leq \mathbb{F}_2^n$, how can a bank distribute an "obfuscated program" P_A, which legitimate buyers and sellers can use to decide membership in both A and $A^\perp$, but which does not reveal anything else about A that might facilitate counterfeiting?*

Note that, aside from the detail that we need security against quantum adversaries, the above challenge is purely "classical"; it and its variants seem interesting even apart from our quantum money application.

We will suggest a candidate protocol to achieve the challenge, based on *multivariate polynomial cryptography*. Given a collection $p_1, \ldots, p_m : \mathbb{F}_2^n \to \mathbb{F}_2$ of multivariate polynomials over $\mathbb{F}_2$, it is generally hard to find a point $v \in \mathbb{F}_2^n$ on which all of the p_i's vanish. On the other hand, it is easy to check whether a *particular* point v has that property. To "hide" a subspace A, we will provide uniformly-random low-degree polynomials $p_1, \ldots, p_m$ that vanish on each point of A. This information is sufficient to decide membership in A. On the other hand, there is no known efficient algorithm to *find* A given the polynomials, and current techniques seem unlikely to yield even a quantum algorithm.

We can also introduce a constant fraction of *noise* into our scheme without interfering with its completeness. In other words, if only $(1-\epsilon)m$ of the polynomials $p_1, \ldots, p_m$ are chosen to vanish on A, and the remaining ϵm are random, then counting the number of p_i's that vanish at a point v still suffices to determine whether $v \in A$. Although we know of no attack even against our noise-free scheme, adding noise in this way might improve security.

Crucially, we will state a "classical" conjecture about the security of multivariate polynomial cryptography, and show that the conjecture *implies* the security of our explicit money scheme. For the benefit of cryptographers, let us now state an "abstract" version of our conjecture, which implies what we need, and which might hold even if our concrete conjecture about multivariate polynomials fails.

Conjecture 26 (Subspace-Hiding Conjecture, Sufficient for Quantum Money). *There exists a polynomial-time algorithm that takes as input a description of a uniformly-random subspace $A \leq \mathbb{F}_2^n$ with $\dim(A) = n/2$, and that outputs circuits C_A and $C_{A^\perp}$, such that the following holds.*

(i) $C_A(v)$ decides whether $v \in A$, and $C_{A^\perp}(v)$ decides whether $v \in A^\perp$, for all $v \in \mathbb{F}_2^n$.

(ii) Given descriptions of C_A and $C_{A^\perp}$, no polynomial-time quantum algorithm can find a generating set for A with success probability $\Omega\left(2^{-n/2}\right)$.

Later, Conjecture 32 will specialize Conjecture 26 to the setting of multivariate polynomials.

6.1 Useful Facts About Polynomials

By viewing elements of $\mathbb{F}_2^n$ as n-tuples $(x_1, \ldots, x_n)$, we can evaluate a polynomial $p(x_1, \ldots, x_n)$ on points of $\mathbb{F}_2^n$.

Given a subspace $A \leq \mathbb{F}_2^n$ and a positive integer d, let $\mathcal{I}_{d,A}$ be the set of degree-d polynomials (not necessarily homogeneous) that vanish on A. Since we are working over $\mathbb{F}_2$, note that $x_i^2 = x_i$, so it suffices to consider *multilinear* polynomials (in which no x_i is ever raised to a higher power than 1).

Before presenting our scheme, we need to establish some basic properties of polynomials over $\mathbb{F}_2^n$. First, we observe that the set of polynomials does not depend on the choice of basis.

Proposition 27. *Let L be any invertible linear transformation on $\mathbb{F}_2^n$. Then the map $p(v) \mapsto p(Lv)$ defines a permutation on the set of degree-d polynomials, which maps $\mathcal{I}_{d,A}$ to $\mathcal{I}_{d,L^{-1}A}$.*

Implementing our scheme will require sampling uniformly from $\mathcal{I}_{d,A}$, which the next lemma shows is possible.

Lemma 28. *It is possible to sample a uniformly-random element of $\mathcal{I}_{d,A}$ in time $O(n^d)$.*

PROOF. By Proposition 27, we can instead sample from the space of polynomials which vanish on $\operatorname{span}(x_1, \ldots, x_{n/2})$, and then apply an appropriate change of basis to obtain a sample from $\mathcal{I}_{d,A}$. So assume without loss of generality that $A = \operatorname{span}(x_1, \ldots, x_{n/2})$.

We claim that a polynomial p vanishes on A if and only if every monomial of p intersects $\{x_{n/2+1}, \ldots, x_n\}$. This will immediately give an $O(n^d)$-time sampling algorithm, because we can consider each of the $O(n^d)$ degree-d monomials in turn, and include each one independently with probability $1/2$ if it intersects $\{x_{n/2+1}, \ldots, x_n\}$.

To prove the claim: first, if every monomial intersects $\{x_{n/2+1}, \ldots, x_n\}$, then clearly p vanishes on A. Otherwise, let m be a minimal monomial that does *not* intersect $\{x_{n/2+1}, \ldots, x_n\}$. Consider the vector $v = (v_1, \ldots, v_n)$ with $v_i = 1$ if and only if $x_i \in m$. Since m does not intersect $\{x_{n/2+1}, \ldots, x_n\}$, clearly $v \in A$. Also, since m is minimal, every other monomial must evaluate to 0 on v. Thus $p(v) = m(v) = 1$, so p is not identically zero on A. ■

In addition to sampling polynomials that vanish on A, we would like to guarantee that a sufficiently large system of such polynomials uniquely determines the space A, so that such a system can be effectively used as a membership oracle.

Lemma 29. *Fix $A \leq \mathbb{F}_2^n$ and $\beta > 1$, and choose βn polynomials $p_1, \ldots, p_{\beta n}$ uniformly and independently from $\mathcal{I}_{d,A}$. Let Z be the set of $v \in \mathbb{F}_2^n$ such that $p_i(v) = 0$ for all $i \in [\beta n]$. Then $A \subseteq Z$, and $\Pr[A = Z] = 1 - 2^{-\Omega(n)}$.*

PROOF. $A \subseteq Z$ is clear. For the second part, for each $v \notin A$, there must be some $w \in A^{\perp}$ such that $w \cdot v = 1$. Then the map $p(v) \mapsto p(v) + w \cdot v$ defines an involution of $\mathcal{I}_{d,A}$, such that exactly one of $p(v)$ and $p(v) + w \cdot v$ is zero. This means that exactly half of the polynomials in $\mathcal{I}_{d,A}$ vanish at v. Hence $\Pr[p_1(v) = \cdots = p_{\beta n}(v) = 0] = 2^{-\beta n}$. By the union bound, the probability that there are *any* shared zeroes $v \notin A$ is therefore at most $2^n 2^{-\beta n} = 2^{-\Theta(n)}$. ■

As mentioned earlier, we would also like to allow sampling from *noisy* systems of equations, defined as follows: let $\mathcal{R}_{d,A,m,\epsilon}$ be the probability distribution over m-tuples $(p_1, \ldots, p_m)$ that sets exactly $(1-\epsilon)m$ of the polynomials p_i (chosen uniformly at random) to be uniformly-random samples from $\mathcal{I}_{d,A}$, and that sets the remaining ϵm of the polynomials p_i to be uniformly-random samples from $\mathcal{I}_{d,A'}$, for a uniformly-random subspace $A' \leq \mathbb{F}_2^n$ of dimension $\dim(A)$. (Note that a *different* A' is chosen for every such p_i.) Then using a Chernoff bound, it is not hard to show that, provided m is large enough compared to n, a sample from $\mathcal{R}_{d,A,m,\epsilon}$ *also* uniquely defines the subspace A with overwhelming probability.

Lemma 30. *Fix $A \leq \mathbb{F}_2^n$ and $\epsilon < 1/2$, let $\beta \geq \frac{3}{(1-2\epsilon)^2}$, and choose polynomials $p_1, \ldots, p_{\beta n}$ from $\mathcal{R}_{d,A,\beta n,\epsilon}$. Let $w(v) := \sum_{i=1}^{\beta n} p_i(v)$, and let Z be the set of $v \in \mathbb{F}_2^n$ such that $w(v) \leq \epsilon \beta n$. Then $A \subseteq Z$, and $\Pr[A = Z] = 1 - 2^{-\Omega(n)}$.*

PROOF. Deferred to the full version. ■

6.2 Explicit Hidden-Subspace Mini-Scheme

In our explicit mini-scheme, the bank chooses a subspace A randomly and publishes sets of polynomials drawn from $\mathcal{R}_{d,A,\beta n,\epsilon}$ and $\mathcal{R}_{d,A^{\perp},\beta n,\epsilon}$, along with the quantum money state $|A\rangle$. By Lemma 30, a user can use these polynomials to test membership in A and $A^{\perp}$, and can therefore implement the oracle mini-scheme in Section 5.1.

Formally, the mini-scheme $\mathcal{E}$ is defined as follows. Parameters $\epsilon \in [0, 1/2)$, $\beta \geq \frac{3}{(1-2\epsilon)^2}$, and $d \geq 4$ are fixed. The complexity of the verification procedure will grow like $O(\beta n^{d+1})$, but security might also improve for larger ϵ and d. Then:

- $\mathsf{Bank}(0^n)$ selects an $n/2$-dimensional subspace $A \leq \mathbb{F}_2^n$ uniformly at random, say by selecting $n/2$ random linearly-independent generators. It then sets $s := (s_A, s_{A^{\perp}})$, where s_A and $s_{A^{\perp}}$ are lists of polynomials drawn from $\mathcal{R}_{d,A,\beta n,\epsilon}$ and $\mathcal{R}_{d,A^{\perp},\beta n,\epsilon}$ respectively. It prepares the money state $|A\rangle$ and outputs the banknote $|\$_s\rangle := |s\rangle |A\rangle$.
- $\mathsf{Ver}(¢)$ first checks that $¢$ has the form $(s_A, s_{A^{\perp}}, \rho)$ where $s_A = (p_1, \ldots, p_{\beta n})$ and $s_{A^{\perp}} = (q_1, \ldots, q_{\beta n})$ are lists of βn polynomials over $\mathbb{F}_2^n$. If not, it rejects. If so, then it lets Z and $Z^{\perp}$ be the sets of points $v \in \mathbb{F}_2^n$ such that $\sum_{i=1}^{\beta n} p_i(v) \leq \epsilon \beta n$ and $\sum_{i=1}^{\beta n} q_i(v) \leq \epsilon \beta n$ respectively. (Recall that with overwhelming probability, $Z = A$ and $Z^{\perp} = A^{\perp}$.) It then applies the operation $V_Z := H_2^{\otimes n} \mathbb{P}_{Z^{\perp}} H_2^{\otimes n} \mathbb{P}_Z$ to ρ, and accepts $¢$ if and only if $V_Z(\rho)$ accepts.

6.3 Analysis

We first observe that the mini-scheme $\mathcal{E}$ has perfect completeness.

Theorem 31. *$\mathcal{E}$ has perfect completeness.*

PROOF. This follows from Lemmas 29 and 30, and particularly from the fact that $A \subseteq Z$ and $A^{\perp} \subseteq Z^{\perp}$ with certainty. From this it follows that $V_Z := H_2^{\otimes n} \mathbb{P}_{Z^{\perp}} H_2^{\otimes n} \mathbb{P}_Z$ accepts the state $|A\rangle$ with probability 1. ■

Let us remark that, if the fraction ϵ of bad polynomials is in $[1/2, 1)$, one can still define a variant of our scheme—for example, where Ver guesses that $v \in A$ if $\sum_{i=1}^{\beta n} p_i(v) \leq \frac{1}{4}(1+\epsilon)\beta n$, and that $v \notin A$ otherwise. The only disadvantage is that we now lose the property of perfect completeness, and can only guarantee a completeness error that is exponentially small.

We now wish to argue about $\mathcal{E}$'s soundness. Naturally, we can only hope to prove soundness assuming some computational hardness conjecture. What is nice, though, is that we can base $\mathcal{E}$'s soundness on a conjecture that talks only about the hardness of a "classical" cryptographic problem (i.e., a problem with classical inputs and outputs). Let us now state that conjecture, which is simply the abstract Conjecture 26 specialized to the setting of multivariate polynomials.

Conjecture 32 (Direct Product for Finding Subspace Elements). *Let $\epsilon < 1/2$ and $\beta := \frac{3}{(1-2\epsilon)^2}$. Given samples from $\mathcal{R}_{d,A,\beta n,\epsilon}$ and $\mathcal{R}_{d,A^{\perp},\beta n,\epsilon}$, no polynomial-time quantum algorithm can find a complete list of generators for A with success probability $\Omega\left(2^{-n/2}\right)$.*

Note that it is easy to find *one* nonzero element of A with success probability $2^{-n/2}$, by choosing $x \in \mathbb{F}_2^n$ randomly. Conjecture 32 asserts both that it is impossible to do too much better using $\mathcal{R}_{d,A,\beta n,\epsilon}$ and $\mathcal{R}_{d,A^{\perp},\beta n,\epsilon}$, and that finding multiple elements of A is significantly harder than finding one element.

The security of mini-scheme $\mathcal{E}$ follows easily from Conjecture 32, *despite* the fact that a would-be counterfeiter has access to a valid quantum banknote, whereas Conjecture 32 involves no such assumption.

Theorem 33 (Security Reduction for Explicit Mini-Scheme). *If Conjecture 32 holds, then $\mathcal{E}$ is secure.*

PROOF. Let $C_{\mathcal{E}}$ be a counterfeiter against $\mathcal{E}$. Then we need to show that, using $C_{\mathcal{E}}$, we can find a complete list of generators for A with $\Omega\left(2^{-n/2}\right)$ success probability.

Given $A \leq \mathbb{F}_2^n$ with $\dim(A) = n/2$, let $s := (s_A, s_{A^{\perp}})$ where s_A and $s_{A^{\perp}}$ are samples from $\mathcal{R}_{d,A,\beta n,\epsilon}$ and $\mathcal{R}_{d,A^{\perp},\beta n,\epsilon}$ respectively. Recall from Lemma 30 that $\Pr[A = Z] = 1 - 2^{-\Omega(n)}$ and $\Pr[A^{\perp} = Z^{\perp}] = 1 - 2^{-\Omega(n)}$. Provided both of these events occur, we can use s to decide membership in A, and can therefore apply the projective measurement $\mathbb{P}_A$. So let us prepare the uniform superposition over all 2^n elements of $\mathbb{F}_2^n$, and then apply $\mathbb{P}_A$ to it. With probability $2^{-n/2}$, this produces the state $|A\rangle$.

Once we have s and $|A\rangle$, we can then form the banknote $|\$\rangle := |s\rangle |A\rangle$, and provide this banknote to the counterfeiter $C_{\mathcal{E}}$. By hypothesis, $C_{\mathcal{E}}$ outputs a (possibly-entangled) state ρ on two registers, such that $\langle A|^{\otimes 2} \rho |A\rangle^{\otimes 2} \geq \Delta$ for some $\Delta = \Omega(1/\operatorname{poly}(n))$. But now, because the mini-scheme $\mathcal{E}$ is projective, Theorem 13 applies, and we can *amplify* ρ to increase its fidelity with $|A\rangle^{\otimes 2}$. After $O\left(\frac{1}{\Delta^2}\log n\right)$ calls to $C_{\mathcal{E}}$, this gives us a state σ such that

$$\langle A|^{\otimes 2} \sigma |A\rangle^{\otimes 2} \geq 1 - \frac{1}{n^2}.$$

More generally, by alternating counterfeiting steps and amplification steps, we can produce as many registers as we like that each have large overlap with $|A\rangle$. In particular, we can produce a state ξ such that

$$\langle A|^{\otimes n} \xi |A\rangle^{\otimes n} \geq 1 - o(1).$$

If we now run Ver on each of the registers of ξ, the probability that every invocation accepts is $1 - o(1)$. Furthermore, supposing that happens, the state we are left with is simply $|A\rangle^{\otimes n}$. Finally, we measure each register of $|A\rangle^{\otimes n}$ in the standard basis. This gives us n elements $x_1, \ldots, x_n \in A$, which are independent and uniformly random. So by standard estimates, the probability that $x_1, \ldots, x_n$ do *not* contain a complete generating set for A is $1/\exp(n)$.

Overall, the procedure above succeeded with probability $2^{-n/2}(1 - o(1))$, thereby giving us the desired contradiction with Conjecture 32. ■

Using the standard construction of quantum money schemes, we can now produce a complete explicit money scheme, whose security follows from Conjecture 32.

Theorem 34 (Security Reduction for Explicit Scheme). *Assuming Conjecture 32, there exists a public-key quantum money scheme with perfect completeness and soundness error $2^{-\Omega(n)}$.*

PROOF. We apply the standard construction of Theorem 14 with the mini-scheme $\mathcal{E}$, whose completeness and soundness follow from Theorems 31 and 33 respectively, assuming Conjecture 32. ■

6.4 Justifying Our Hardness Assumption

Though our hardness assumption is new, it is closely related to standard assumptions in *multivariate polynomial cryptography*. Given a system of multivariate quadratics over $\mathbb{F}_2$, finding a common zero is known to be NP-hard; moreover, it is strongly believed that the problem remains hard even for *random* systems of multivariate polynomials, and cryptosystems based on this hardness assumption are considered promising candidates for post-quantum cryptography [20]. Therefore, if Conjecture 32 fails, it will almost certainly be because some additional structure in this problem facilitates a new attack.

There are several ways in which Conjecture 32 is stronger than the assumption that solving random systems of multivariate polynomials is hard. First, our systems have large, well-structured solution spaces A and $A^{\perp}$. Systems with many solutions are not normally considered in the literature, and while there seem to be no known attacks that exploit this structure, the possibility is not ruled out. Second, we provide two related systems, one with zeroes in A and one with zeroes in $A^{\perp}$. Again, this is a very specific structural property which has not been considered, and there might be unexpected attacks exploiting it. Third, Conjecture 32 asserts that no adversary can succeed with probability $2^{-n/2}$, which seems significantly easier than succeeding with non-negligible probability.

On the other hand, Conjecture 32 is *weaker* than typical assumptions in multivariate polynomial cryptography in at least one respect: a would-be counterfeiter needs to solve a system of polynomial equations with a constant fraction of noise. Solving noisy systems of *linear* equations over $\mathbb{F}_2$ is called the *learning parity with noise* problem, and is generally believed to be hard even for quantum computers [36]. If true, this suggests that Gaussian elimination is fundamentally hard to adapt to the presence of noise. But computing a Gröbner basis is a strict generalization of Gaussian elimination to higher degree, and involves a nearly identical process of elimination. It therefore seems unlikely that these approaches can be efficiently adapted to the setting with noise. The problem of solving polynomials with noise has been studied recently, and the best-known approaches involve performing an exponential time search to determine which equations are noisy [6].

But if solving linear systems with noise is already hard, why do we even use higher-degree polynomials in our scheme? The reason is that, alas, the "dual" structure of our money scheme facilitates a simple attack in the case $d = 1$.

Claim 35. *For all $\epsilon < 1$, there exists a β such that one can recover A efficiently given samples from $\mathcal{R}_{d,A,\beta n,\epsilon}$ and $\mathcal{R}_{d,A^{\perp},\beta n,\epsilon}$.*

PROOF. Let $p_1, \ldots, p_m$ and $q_1, \ldots, q_m$ be homogeneous linear polynomials, of which a $1 - \epsilon$ fraction vanish on A and $A^{\perp}$ respectively. Then the key observation is that each p_i vanishes on A if and only if it has the form $p_i(v) = u_i \cdot v$ for some $u_i \in A^{\perp}$, while each q_i vanishes on $A^{\perp}$ if and only if it has the form $q_i(v) = w_i \cdot v$ for some $w_i \in A$. But by Lemma 30, if $\beta > \frac{3}{(1-2\epsilon)^2}$, then for each $i \in [m]$, we can efficiently *decide* whether $u_i \in A^{\perp}$ by counting the number of j's for which $q_j(u_i) = 0$, and can likewise decide whether $w_i \in A$ by counting the number of j's for which $p_j(w_i) = 0$.[18] Thus we can learn $\Theta(n)$ random elements of A or $A^{\perp}$, and thereby recover a basis for A. ■

There *might* be a more sophisticated attack for higher degrees, but this is suggested only weakly by the existence of an attack in the linear case. Indeed, the relation between the complementary linear subspaces A and $A^{\perp}$ is precisely the sort of structure that should be preserved by linear maps, but *not* by higher-degree polynomials!

For degree-2 polynomials, it is possible to obtain a similar attack which recovers A from only a *single* sample. This attack relies on the observation that quadratics have an easily-computed canonical form [17], from which a basis for A can be extracted in polynomial time. The essential problem is that quadratic polynomials are very closely related to bilinear forms, and that powerful methods from linear algebra can therefore be applied to them.

Fortunately, the linear structure seems to be computationally obscured when $d \geq 3$. This phenomenon is related to the sharp discontinuity in the difficulty of tensor problems

[18] If $\epsilon \geq 1/2$, then we can use a variant of Lemma 30 (not stated in this extended abstract), for which it suffices to take $\beta \geq \frac{12}{(1-\epsilon)^2}$. We lose perfect completeness, but that is not important here.

with order 3 and higher. More concretely, the coefficients of a degree-d polynomial can be viewed as the entries of an order-d tensor, and the existence of an attack in the degree $d = 2$ case corresponds to the possibility of efficient operations on order-2 tensors. Basic operations on order-3 tensors are NP-hard [26], however, and this suggests that analogous attacks might not exist against degree-3 polynomials.

This state of affairs is reflected in existing attacks on a standard cryptographic assumption called *polynomial isomorphism with one secret*. Here we are given two polynomials p, q which are related by an unknown linear change of coordinates L, and the task is to find such an L. For degree-2 polynomials, this problem can be easily solved in polynomial time [17], but already for degree-3 polynomials the best known attacks take exponential time [35, 24, 17]. However, if an attacker is given n bits of partial information about the linear transformation, then even in the $d = 3$ case, it becomes possible to find the linear transformation that relates the polynomials [17]. This does *not* directly facilitate an attack on our assumption, but it suggests that a similar attack *might* be possible when $d = 3$, since an attacker is only required to succeed with $2^{-n/2}$ probability. Fortunately, this attack seems to rely on the particular structure of degree 2 and 3 polynomials. Of course it is possible that similar algorithms may be discovered for higher-degree polynomials, but this would represent an advance in algebraic cryptanalysis.

7. PRIVATE-KEY QUANTUM MONEY

Recall that a *private-key* quantum money scheme is one where only the bank itself is able to verify banknotes, using an n-bit key $k = k_{\text{private}} = k_{\text{public}}$ that it keeps a closely-guarded secret. Compensating for this disadvantage, private-key schemes are known with much stronger security guarantees than seem possible for public-key schemes.

In particular, as mentioned in Section 1.1, already forty years ago Wiesner [39] described how to create private-key quantum money that is *information-theoretically secure*. In Wiesner's scheme, each banknote consists of n unentangled qubits together with a classical serial number s. Wiesner's scheme also requires a giant database of serial numbers maintained by the bank, or in our setting, access to a random oracle R. But in followup work, BBBW [14] pointed out that we can simply replace R by any *pseudorandom function family* $\{f_k\}_k$, to obtain a private-key quantum money scheme that is computationally secure, *unless* a polynomial-time counterfeiter can distinguish the f_k's from random functions.

Strangely, we are unaware of any rigorous proof of the security of Wiesner's scheme until recently. However, answering a question by one of us,[19] Molina, Vidick and Watrous [31] have now supplied the key ingredient for a security proof. Specifically they show that, if a counterfeiter tries to copy an n-qubit banknote $|\$\rangle$ in Wiesner's scheme, then the output can have squared fidelity at most $(3/4)^n$ with $|\$\rangle^{\otimes 2}$. (They also show that this is tight: there *exists* a non-obvious counterfeiting strategy that succeeds with $(3/4)^n$ probability.)

To complete the security proof, one needs to show that, even given q banknotes $|\$_1\rangle, \ldots, |\$_q\rangle$, a counterfeiter cannot prepare an additional banknote with non-negligible probability (even with a new serial number). In a forthcoming paper [4], we will show how to adapt the methods of Section 3 to prove that claim. Briefly, one can first define a notion of *private-key mini-schemes*, in close analogy to public-key mini-schemes. The work of Molina et al. [31] then directly implies the security of what we call the "Wiesner mini-scheme." Next, one can give a general reduction, showing how to construct a full-blown private-key quantum money scheme $\mathcal{S}$ starting from

(1) any private-key *mini*-scheme $\mathcal{M}$, and

(2) any random or pseudorandom function family R.

Though the details turn out to be more complicated in the private-key case, the proof of correctness for this reduction is conceptually similar to the proof of Theorem 14. Namely, one shows that any counterfeiter would yield *either* a break of the underlying mini-scheme $\mathcal{M}$, or *else* a way to distinguish R from a random function. Notice that the analysis is completely unified: if R is a "true" random oracle, then we get information-theoretic security (as in Wiesner's scheme), while if R is pseudorandom, then we get computational security (as in the BBBW scheme).

Unfortunately, as pointed out by Lutomirski [28] and Aaronson [3], the Wiesner and BBBW schemes both have a serious security hole. Namely, suppose a counterfeiter C can repeatedly submit alleged banknotes to a "naïve and trusting bank" for verification. Given a quantum state σ, such a bank not only tells C whether the verification procedure accepted or rejected, but also, in either case, *gives the post-measurement state* $\widetilde{\sigma}$ *back to* C. Then starting from a single valid banknote $|\$\rangle$, we claim that C can recover a complete classical description of $|\$\rangle$, using $O(n \log n)$ queries to the bank. Once it has such a description, C can of course prepare as many copies of $|\$\rangle$ as it likes.

The attack is simple: let $|\$\rangle = |\theta_1\rangle \cdots |\theta_n\rangle$ (we omit the classical serial number s, since it plays no role here). Then for each $i \in [n]$, the counterfeiter tries "swapping out" the ith qubit $|\theta_i\rangle$ and replacing it with $|b\rangle$, for each of the four possibilities $|b\rangle \in \{|0\rangle, |1\rangle, |+\rangle, |-\rangle\}$. It then uses $O(\log n)$ queries to the bank, to estimate the probability that the state $|\theta_1\rangle \cdots |\theta_{i-1}\rangle |b\rangle |\theta_{i+1}\rangle \cdots |\theta_n\rangle$ passes the verification test. By doing so, C can learn a correct value of $|\theta_i\rangle$ with success probability $1 - o(1/n)$. The crucial point is that none of these queries damage the qubits *not* being investigated ($|\theta_j\rangle$ for $j \neq i$), since the bank measures those qubits in the correct bases. Therefore C can reuse the same banknote for each query.

More generally, recall from Section 3.1 that we call a private-key quantum money scheme *query-secure*, if it remains secure even assuming the counterfeiter C can make adaptive queries to $\mathsf{Ver}(k, \cdot)$. Then we saw that the Wiesner and BBBW schemes are *not* query-secure. Recently, Farhi et al. [21] proved a much more general "no-go" theorem—which says intuitively that, if we want query-secure quantum money, then the banknotes *must* hide information in the "global correlations" between large numbers of qubits.

On the positive side, any *public-key* quantum money scheme—for example, our multivariate polynomial scheme from Section 6—immediately yields a query-secure scheme with the same security guarantee. This is because a counterfeiter who knows the code of Ver can easily simulate oracle access

[19] See http://theoreticalphysics.stackexchange.com/questions/370/rigorous-security-proof-for-wiesners-quantum-money

to Ver. But can we do any better than that, and construct a query-secure money scheme whose security is *unconditional* (as in Wiesner's scheme), or else based on a pseudorandom function (as in the BBBW scheme)?

In the forthcoming paper [4], we will answer this question in the affirmative, by *directly* adapting the hidden subspace scheme from Section 5 (i.e., the scheme based on a classical oracle). Since the idea is an extremely simple one, let us sketch it here.

Theorem 36 (Query-Secure Variant of Wiesner's Scheme). *Relative to a random oracle R,[20] there exists a private-key quantum money scheme, with perfect completeness and $2^{-\Omega(n)}$ soundness error, that is information-theoretically query-secure. One can also replace the random oracle R by a pseudorandom function family $\{f_k\}_k$, to obtain a private-key quantum money scheme, with no oracle, that is query-secure assuming that the f_k's cannot be distinguished from random in quantum polynomial time.*

PROOF SKETCH. For each key k and a serial number s, we will think of the random oracle R as encoding a classical description $R(k,s)$ of a subspace $A_{k,s} \leq \mathbb{F}_2^n$, which is uniformly random subject to $\dim(A_{k,s}) = n/2$. Let $|A_{k,s}\rangle$ be a uniform superposition over $A_{k,s}$. Then the private-key money scheme $\mathcal{S} = (\mathsf{KeyGen}, \mathsf{Bank}, \mathsf{Ver})$ is defined as follows:

- $\mathsf{KeyGen}(0^n)$ generates an n-bit key k uniformly at random.
- $\mathsf{Bank}(k)$ outputs a banknote $|\$_s\rangle := |s\rangle |A_{k,s}\rangle$, for a random serial number $s \in \{0,1\}^n$.
- $\mathsf{Ver}(k,(s,\rho))$ applies a projective measurement that accepts ρ with probability $\langle A_{k,s}|\rho|A_{k,s}\rangle$.

Now, suppose it were possible to break $\mathcal{S}$ (i.e., to counterfeit $|A_{k,s}\rangle$), using $\mathrm{poly}(n)$ adaptive queries to $\mathsf{Ver}(k,\cdot)$. Then we claim that it would *also* be possible to break our *public-key* scheme from Section 5, and thereby contradict the unconditional security proof for the latter! The reason is simply that any query to Ver, of the form $\mathsf{Ver}(k,(s,\rho))$, can easily be simulated using queries to $U_{A_{k,s}}$ and $U_{A_{k,s}^{\perp}}$, the membership oracles for $A_{k,s}$ and $A_{k,s}^{\perp}$ respectively that are available to a counterfeiter against the public-key scheme.

Finally, suppose we replace $R(k,s)$ by a pseudorandom function $f_k(s)$. Then just like with the original BBBW scheme [14], we can argue as follows. Since we already showed that $\mathcal{S}$ is information-theoretically secure when instantiated with a "true" random function, any break of $\mathcal{S}$ in the pseudorandom case would thereby distinguish the function f_k from random. ∎

8. OPEN PROBLEMS

The "obvious" problem is to better understand the security of our explicit scheme based on polynomials. Are there nontrivial attacks, for example using Gröbner-basis algorithms? Can we base the security of our scheme—or a related scheme—on some cryptographic assumption that does *not* involve exponentially-small success probabilities? What happens as we change the field size or polynomial degree? Does "hiding" a subspace $A \leq \mathbb{F}_2^n$ in the way we suggest, as the set of common zeroes of multivariate polynomials $p_1,\ldots,p_m : \mathbb{F}_2^n \to \mathbb{F}_2$, have other cryptographic applications, for example to *program obfuscation* [10]?

Of course, there is also tremendous scope for inventing new schemes, which might be based on different assumptions and have different strengths and weaknesses.

Let us move on to some general questions about public-key quantum money. First, is there an unconditionally-secure public-key quantum money scheme relative to a *random* oracle R? (Recall that Wiesner's original scheme [39] was unconditionally-secure and used only a random oracle, but was private-key. Meanwhile, our scheme from Section 5 is unconditionally-secure and public-key, but requires a nonrandom oracle.) Second, is there a public-key quantum money scheme where the banknotes consist of *single, unentangled qubits*, as in Wiesner's scheme? Note that the results of Farhi et al. [21] imply that, if such a scheme exists, then it cannot be projective. Third, is there a general way to amplify soundness error in quantum money schemes?[21] (We show how to amplify *completeness* error in the full version.)

8.1 Quantum Copy-Protection and More

Quantum money is just *one* novel cryptographic use for the No-Cloning Theorem. Given essentially *any* object of cryptographic interest, one can ask whether quantum mechanics lets us make the object uncloneable. Section 1.4 already discussed one example—*uncloneable signatures*—but there are many others, such as commitments and proofs.[22]

Along those lines, Aaronson [3] proposed a task that, if achievable, would arguably be an even more dramatic application of the No-Cloning Theorem than quantum money: namely, *quantum software copy-protection*. He gave explicit schemes—which have not yet been broken—for copy-protecting a restricted class of functions, namely the *point functions*. In these schemes, given a "password" $s \in \{0,1\}^n$, a software vendor can prepare a quantum state $|\psi_s\rangle$, which allows its holder to *recognize* s: in other words, to decide whether $x = s$ given $x \in \{0,1\}^n$ as input. On the other hand, given $|\psi_s\rangle$, it seems intractable not only to *find* s for oneself, but even to prepare a *second* quantum state with which s can be recognized.

Admittedly, recognizing passwords is an extremely restricted functionality. However, relative to a quantum oracle, Aaronson [3] also described a scheme to quantumly copy-protect *arbitrary* programs, just as well as if the software vendor were able to hand out uncloneable black boxes.[23] In the spirit of this paper, we can now ask: is there likewise a way to quantumly copy-protect arbitrary programs relative to a *classical* oracle? We conjecture that the answer is yes, and in fact we have plausible candidate constructions, which are directly related to the hidden-subspace money scheme of Section 5. However, the security of those constructions seems to hinge on the following conjecture.

Conjecture 37 (Direct Product for Finding Black-Box Subspace Elements). *Let A be a uniformly-random subspace of*

[20] Or alternatively, assuming the bank has access to a giant random number table, as in Wiesner's original setup [39].

[21] Theorem 13 gives *some* soundness amplification for projective schemes: namely, from constant to $1/\mathrm{poly}(n)$. Here we are asking whether one can do anything better.

[22] Even within complexity theory, it would be interesting to study the class QMA (Quantum Merlin-Arthur) subject to the constraint that witnesses must be hard to clone—or alternatively, that witnesses must be *easy* to clone!

[23] As usual, full details have not yet appeared yet.

$\mathbb{F}_2^n$ *satisfying* $\dim(A) = n/2$. *Then given membership oracles for both A and* $A^{\perp}$, *any quantum algorithm needs* $2^{\Omega(n)}$ *queries to find two distinct nonzero elements* $x, y \in A$, *with success probability* $\Omega\left(2^{-n/2}\right)$.

Besides its applications for copy-protection, a proof of Conjecture 37 would be an important piece of formal evidence for Conjecture 32, on which we based the security of our explicit money scheme.

9. ACKNOWLEDGMENTS

We thank Andris Ambainis, Boaz Barak, Dmitry Gavinsky, Daniel Gottesman, Aram Harrow, Yuval Ishai, Shaunak Kishore, Greg Kuperberg, Andy Lutomirski, Abel Molina, Rafi Ostrovsky, Amit Sahai, Peter Shor, and John Watrous for helpful discussions and correspondence; and the anonymous reviewers for their comments.

10. REFERENCES

[1] S. Aaronson. Quantum lower bound for the collision problem. *STOC*, p. 635–642, 2002. quant-ph/0111102.

[2] S. Aaronson. Limitations of quantum advice and one-way communication. *Theory of Computing*, 1:1–28, 2005. quant-ph/0402095.

[3] S. Aaronson. Quantum copy-protection and quantum money. *IEEE Complexity*, p. 229–242, 2009.

[4] S. Aaronson. On the security of private-key quantum money, 2011. In preparation.

[5] S. Aaronson and G. Kuperberg. Quantum versus classical proofs and advice. *Theory of Computing*, 3(7):129–157, 2007. quant-ph/0604056.

[6] M. Albrecht and C. Cid. Cold boot key recovery by solving polynomial systems with noise. In J. Lopez and G. Tsudik, ed., *Applied Cryptography and Network Security 2011*, LNCS vol. 6715, p. 57–72, 2011.

[7] N. Alon, M. Krivelevich, and B. Sudakov. Finding a large hidden clique in a random graph. *SODA*, p. 594–598, 1998.

[8] A. Ambainis. Quantum lower bounds by quantum arguments. *JCSS*, 64:750–767, 2002. quant-ph/0002066.

[9] A. Ambainis, L. Magnin, M. Roetteler, and J. Roland. Symmetry-assisted adversaries for quantum state generation. *IEEE Complexity*, p. 167–177, 2011. arXiv:1012.2112.

[10] B. Barak, O. Goldreich, R. Impagliazzo, S. Rudich, A. Sahai, S. Vadhan, and K. Yang. On the (im)possibility of obfuscating programs. *CRYPTO*, p. 1–18, 2001. ECCC TR01-057.

[11] R. Beals, H. Buhrman, R. Cleve, M. Mosca, and R. de Wolf. Quantum lower bounds by polynomials. *J. ACM*, 48(4):778–797, 2001. quant-ph/9802049.

[12] C. Bennett, E. Bernstein, G. Brassard, and U. Vazirani. Strengths and weaknesses of quantum computing. *SIAM J. Comput.*, 26(5):1510–1523, 1997. quant-ph/9701001.

[13] C. H. Bennett and G. Brassard. Quantum cryptography: public key distribution and coin tossing. *Proc. IEEE Int. Conf. on Computers Systems and Signal Proc.*, p. 175–179, 1984.

[14] C. H. Bennett, G. Brassard, S. Breidbart, and S. Wiesner. Quantum cryptography, or unforgeable subway tokens. *CRYPTO*, p. 267–275, 1982.

[15] N. Bohr. *Atomic Physics and Human Knowledge*. Dover, 2010. First published 1961.

[16] D. Boneh, Ö. Dagdelen, M. Fischlin, A. Lehmann, C. Schaffner, and M. Zhandry. Random oracles in a quantum world. *ASIACRYPT*, p. 41–69, 2011. arXiv:1008.0931.

[17] C. Bouillaguet, J.-C. Faugère, P.-A. Fouque, and L. Perret. Practical cryptanalysis of the identification scheme based on the isomorphism of polynomial with one secret problem. *Public Key Cryptography*, p. 473–493, 2011.

[18] G. Brassard, P. Høyer, M. Mosca, and A. Tapp. Quantum amplitude amplification and estimation. In S. J. Lomonaco and H. E. Brandt, ed., *Quantum Computation and Information*, AMS, 2002. quant-ph/0005055.

[19] S. Chakraborty, J. Radhakrishnan, and N. Raghunathan. Bounds for error reduction with few quantum queries. *APPROX-RANDOM*, p. 245–256, 2005.

[20] J. Ding and B.-Y. Yang. Multivariate public key cryptography. In D. J. Bernstein, J. Buchmann, and E. Dahmén, ed., *Post-Quantum Cryptography*, p. 198–242, Springer-Verlag, 2009.

[21] E. Farhi, D. Gosset, A. Hassidim, A. Lutomirski, D. Nagaj, and P. Shor. Quantum state restoration and single-copy tomography. *Phys. Rev. Lett.*, 105(190503), 2010. arXiv:0912.3823.

[22] E. Farhi, D. Gosset, A. Hassidim, A. Lutomirski, and P. Shor. Quantum money from knots. *ITCS*, p. 276–289, 2012. arXiv:1004.5127.

[23] D. Gavinsky. Quantum money with classical verification. arXiv:1109.0372, 2011.

[24] W. Geiselmann, W. Meier, and R. Steinwandt. An attack on the isomorphisms of polynomials problem with one secret. *Int. J. Inf. Sec*, 2(1):59–64, 2003.

[25] L. K. Grover. A fast quantum mechanical algorithm for database search. *STOC*, p. 212–219, 1996. quant-ph/9605043.

[26] C. Hillar and L.-H. Lim. Most tensor problems are NP hard, 2009. arXiv:0911.1393.

[27] T. Lee, R. Mittal, B. W. Reichardt, R. Špalek, and M. Szegedy. Quantum query complexity of state conversion. *FOCS*, p. 344–353, 2011. arXiv:1011.3020.

[28] A. Lutomirski. An online attack against Wiesner's quantum money. arXiv:1010.0256, 2010.

[29] A. Lutomirski. Component mixers and a hardness result for counterfeiting quantum money. arXiv:1107.0321, 2011.

[30] A. Lutomirski, S. Aaronson, E. Farhi, D. Gosset, A. Hassidim, J. Kelner, and P. Shor. Breaking and making quantum money: toward a new quantum cryptographic protocol. *ITCS*, p. 20–31, 2010. arXiv:0912.3825.

[31] A. Molina, T. Vidick, and J. Watrous. Optimal counterfeiting attacks and generalizations for Wiesner's quantum money. arXiv:1202.4010, 2012.

[32] M. Mosca and D. Stebila. Quantum coins. In *Error-Correcting Codes, Finite Geometries and Cryptography*, vol. 523, p. 35–47, AMS, 2010. arXiv:0911.1295.

[33] M. Naor and M. Yung. Universal one-way hash functions and their cryptographic applications. *STOC*, p. 33–43, 1989.

[34] M. Nielsen and I. Chuang. *Quantum Computation and Quantum Information*. Cambridge, 2000.

[35] J. Patarin, L. Goubin, and N. Courtois. Improved algorithms for isomorphisms of polynomials. *EUROCRYPT*, p. 184–200, 1998.

[36] O. Regev. On lattices, learning with errors, random linear codes, and cryptography. *STOC*, p. 84–93, 2005.

[37] J. Rompel. One-way functions are necessary and sufficient for secure signatures. *STOC*, p. 387–394, 1990.

[38] T. Tulsi, L. Grover, and A. Patel. A new algorithm for fixed point quantum search. *Quantum Inf. and Comput.*, 6(6):483–494, 2006. quant-ph/0505007.

[39] S. Wiesner. Conjugate coding. *SIGACT News*, 15(1):78–88, 1983. Original manuscript written circa 1970.

Certifiable Quantum Dice

Or, True Random Number Generation Secure Against Quantum Adversaries

[Extended Abstract]

Umesh Vazirani[*]
Computer Science division
UC Berkeley, USA
vazirani@eecs.berkeley.edu

Thomas Vidick[†]
Computer Science and Artificial Intelligence Laboratory
Massachusetts Institute of Technology, USA
vidick@csail.mit.edu

ABSTRACT

We introduce a protocol through which a pair of quantum mechanical devices may be used to generate n bits that are ε-close in statistical distance from n uniformly distributed bits, starting from a seed of $O(\log n \log 1/\varepsilon)$ uniform bits. The bits generated are certifiably random based only on a simple statistical test that can be performed by the user, and on the assumption that the devices do not communicate in the middle of each phase of the protocol. No other assumptions are placed on the devices' inner workings. A modified protocol uses a seed of $O(\log^3 n)$ uniformly random bits to generate n bits that are $\text{poly}^{-1}(n)$-indistinguishable from uniform even from the point of view of a quantum adversary who may have had prior access to the devices, and may be entangled with them.

Categories and Subject Descriptors

G.3 [**Probability and Statistics**]: Random number generation—*complexity measures, performance measures*
; F.1.2 [**Computation by Abstract Devices**]: Modes of Computation—*Probabilistic Computation*

General Terms

Theory

Keywords

Certifiable Randomness, Quantum Computing, Entanglement, Random Number Generator

[*]Supported by NIST award No. 60NANB10D262, ARO Grant W911NF-09-1-0440 and NSF Grant CCF-0905626
[†]Supported by NSF Grant 0844626. Part of this work was completed while at UC Berkeley, supported by ARO Grant W911NF-09-1-0440 and NSF Grant CCF-0905626.

STOC'12, May 19–22, 2012, New York, New York, USA.

1. INTRODUCTION

A source of independent random bits is a basic resource in many modern-day computational tasks, such as cryptography, game theoretic protocols, algorithms and physical simulations. However, constructing a physical source of randomness is an unexpectedly tricky task [1] — one that touches on fundamental questions about the nature of randomness. What makes this task particularly challenging is this: how can one even test whether one has succeeded? In other words, suppose someone was to claim that a given box outputs uniformly random bits; is there a practical test to verify that claim?

The root of the difficulty in carrying out such a test is the following: a uniform random generator must output every n-bit sequence with equal probability $1/2^n$, and there seems to be no basis on which to reject any particular output in favor of any other. On the face of it, testing the output of the box amounts to classifying a *single* n-bit string x (or a very small sample of the exponentially many n-bit strings) as being random or not random.

Starting in the mid-80's, computer scientists explored a different approach to the question of designing a uniform random number generator: they assumed that they already had access to a physical device that was guaranteed to output random strings, except that the randomness was of "low quality". They modeled such devices as adversarially controlled sources of randomness, starting with the semi-random source [24], and weak random sources [31]. This sequence of papers has culminated in sophisticated algorithms called randomness extractors that are guaranteed to output a sequence that is arbitrarily close to truly random bits from physical sources of low-quality randomness (see [25] for a survey). It was clear, in a classical World, that these results were the best one could hope for — since it was necessary to assume that randomness in some form was output by the device in the first place, the only progress could be in minimizing the assumptions placed on the quality of that randomness.

[1]The quest for good hardware number generators goes as far back as the first commercially available computer, the Ferranti Mark I, and continues through Intel's recently announcement of the first *digital* such generator, as part of its new "Ivy bridge" microprocessor [28].

Quantum nonlocality and a test for randomness.

Unlike classical physics, where randomness is implicitly an assertion about our lack of knowledge or computational ability, quantum mechanics offers a source of intrinsic randomness, ensconced in the Born rule, one of the fundamental axioms of the theory. So in principle, it is very simple to design a quantum device that outputs a sequence of independent unbiased bits: simply pass a sequence of qubits in state $|0\rangle$ through a Hadamard gate and measure. This brings us back to the main question addressed in this paper: is it possible to certify that the output of a randomness generating device (based on quantum mechanics) is "really random" even though the user does not trust the experimental skills of the manufacturer, the calibration of the device, the manufacturer's motivations (particularly in cryptographic settings), or even the correctness of quantum mechanics? We describe the construction of a specific kind of quantum random number generator for which the answer to these questions is affirmative. This construction builds upon a proposal of Colbeck [6] and follow up work by Pironio et al. [21] that provides a link between randomness certification and quantum non-locality. Before we can describe the actual construction, we must introduce some basic ideas behind quantum non-locality.

Non-locality is one of the most interesting features of quantum mechanics, and was famously explored in the work of Einstein, Podolski and Rosen [11], and later in the work of Bell [2, 3]. We focus here on a concrete realization of an experiment inspired by Bell's work, that is best phrased as a game, the CHSH game (illustrated in Figure 1), named after its inventors Clauser, Horne, Shimony and Holt [5]. In this game two *non-communicating* parties, represented by spatially separated boxes A, B, are given inputs $x, y \in \{0,1\}$ respectively. Their task is to produce outputs $a, b \in \{0,1\}$ such that the *CHSH condition* $a \oplus b = x \wedge y$ holds. Let p_{CHSH} be the probability that a certain pair of boxes produces outputs satisfying this condition, when the inputs x, y are chosen uniformly at random.

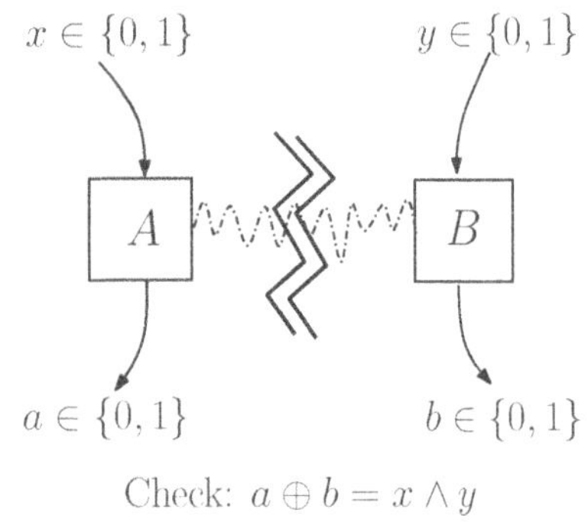

Figure 1: The CHSH game. Any pair of boxes A, B is characterized by a distribution $p(a, b|x, y)$ which is required to be *no-signaling*: the marginal distribution of b is independent of x, and that of a is independent of y.

While classical players can achieve a success probability at most $p_{\text{CHSH}} \leq 3/4$ in this game, there is a simple quantum strategy that succeeds with $p_{\text{CHSH}} = \cos^2 \pi/8 \approx 0.85$. Hence we may define a *quantum regime* corresponding to success probability $3/4 < p_{\text{CHSH}} \leq \cos^2 \pi/8 \approx 0.85$. For any value in that range there is a simple quantum-mechanical pair of boxes, still obeying the condition of no communication, which achieves that success probability.

These well-known facts have a striking consequence: any boxes producing correlations that fall in the quantum regime *must be randomized*! Indeed, deterministic boxes are inherently classical, so that their success probability must fall in the classical regime $p_{\text{CHSH}} \leq 3/4$. Hence a simple *statistical test* guaranteeing the presence of randomness, under a single assumption on the process that produced the bits: that it obeys the no-communication condition.[2] This powerful observation was first made in Colbeck's Ph.D. thesis [6] (see also [7] for an expanded version). The idea was then developed in [21], in which the authors showed that Colbeck's idea could be used to device a procedure that expands an initial seed of $\sqrt{n}$ bits into n bits that are guaranteed to contain a linear amount of min-entropy.[3] (An extractor could then be applied to produce linearly many near-uniform bits.) Pironio et al. even reported an experimental realization of their scheme, demonstrating the generation of 42 new random numbers, in addition to the randomness used to execute the protocol.

Our results.

Let n be an integer, and $\varepsilon > 0$ a parameter such that ε is at least an inverse polynomial in n. We introduce a very simple protocol which uses a random seed of length $O(\log^3 n)$ to generate an n-bit string that is ε-close to uniformly random in statistical distance. This exponentially improves upon the quadratic expansion of [21]. Moreover, the procedure comes with a test which guarantees that the bits produced are ε-close to being indistinguishable from uniform bits even from the point of view of an arbitrary quantum adversary. Establishing such a strong security guarantee was an important open question left open in previous works.

The protocol to achieve this prescribes the interaction of a trusted user with an *untrusted physical device* which we assume is made of two separate boxes, $\mathcal{A}$ and $\mathcal{B}$. The boxes may have been tampered with by the adversary, who could for instance have decided to initialize them in an entangled quantum state that extends into her own laboratory.

The protocol consists of $m = \text{poly}(n)$ phases. Each phase lasts for $k = O(\log n + \log 1/\varepsilon)$ rounds, during each of which the user inputs a single bit to each box and collects a single bit as output. This sequence of mk interactions is non-adaptive: the user can generate the $2mk$ input bits in advance from his $O(\text{poly}\log(n, 1/\varepsilon))$-bit random seed before the interaction. It is of critical importance that he reveals the input bits of phase $i+1$ to the boxes only after the completion of phase i. In each phase the user also performs a very simple statistical test (which simply checks that a large fraction of rounds satisfy a CHSH-like condition). If the test is passed in all phases, then the output of box $\mathcal{B}$, say, is efficiently (and classically) post-processed to produce the final output, an-n bit string. If the test is failed in any phase, then the user outputs a special "fail" symbol.

[2]By this we mean that the probability distribution $p(a, b|x, y)$ describing the distribution of the boxes' outputs, as a function of their inputs, should be *no-signaling*: the marginal distribution of either box's outputs should be independent from inputs to the other.

[3]The paper [21] contained an error that was later fixed in work of Fehr et. al. [12].

We show that, however the adversary may have prepared the physical boxes, provided the bits they produce in the protocol are accepted in the user's test, the maximum success probability with which the adversary can guess the n bits output at the end of the protocol is exponentially small in n. This condition is stronger than the mere fact that the bits produced contain a linear amount of min-entropy: it implies that no outside adversary can have gained any information about them, and in particular they may be securely used in subsequent post-quantum cryptographic primitives.[4] This conclusion is guaranteed to hold provided the following conditions are met:

1. The user's private random bits are uniformly random.
2. The simple statistical test is passed in all m phases of the protocol.
3. Boxes $\mathcal{A}$ and $\mathcal{B}$ are arbitrary, but their functioning must admit a description consistent with quantum mechanics. In addition, *there must not be any communication between $\mathcal{A}$ and $\mathcal{B}$* throughout the duration of any given phase of the protocol. Formally, this last requirement states the following: for each phase i, the marginal distribution of outputs produced by $\mathcal{A}$ (resp. $\mathcal{B}$) during phase i is independent of all inputs to $\mathcal{B}$ (resp. $\mathcal{A}$) in phase i.

As we shall see, it is possible to implement using very simple quantum mechanics a pair of boxes $\mathcal{A}$ and $\mathcal{B}$ that pass the statistical tests in all m phases with high probability. However, the key point established by our results is that by using such a device as prescribed by the protocol, its outputs can be trusted based only on a belief in the correctness of quantum mechanics (and even that assumption will be relaxed in our second result) and in the fact that there is no communication between the devices — it is not required to, say, believe that the device's manufacturer is trustworthy, experimentally skilled, or that the device is always well calibrated.

We state informally our main result, referring to Section 5 for a precise statement.

THEOREM 1 (INFORMAL). *Let n be an integer, and $\varepsilon = n^{-\alpha}$ for some $\alpha > 0$. Let $(\mathcal{A},\mathcal{B})$ be an arbitrary pair of boxes, and assume that the physical behavior of $\mathcal{A}$ and $\mathcal{B}$ can be described by two isolated but possibly entangled quantum-mechanical systems (and in particular there is no possibility for communication in-between the boxes). Suppose Protocol B, as described in Figure 3, is executed with $\mathcal{A}$ and $\mathcal{B}$. This execution requires the use of $\tilde{O}(\log^2 n \log 1/\varepsilon)$ random bits, and results in an output string B of* poly(n) *bits. Let* CHSH *be the event that the boxes' outputs pass the test performed by the user at the end of an execution of Protocol B, as described in Figure 3, and suppose that* $\Pr(\text{CHSH}) \geq \varepsilon$.

Then no adversary can guess B with success probability greater than 2^{-n}. More precisely, if $\mathbf{E}$ denotes an arbitrary quantum system, possibly entangled with $\mathcal{A}$ and $\mathcal{B}$ (but such that no communication occurs between $\mathcal{A},\mathcal{B}$ and $\mathbf{E}$ during the execution of the protocol), then

$$H_\infty^\varepsilon(B|\mathbf{E}) \geq n,$$

where H_∞^ε is the smooth *quantum conditional min entropy.*

We note that the assumption $\Pr(\text{CHSH}) \geq \varepsilon$ is necessary, as there is always an unavoidable chance that the boxes successfully guess their whole inputs, and deterministically produce matching outputs. While the theorem as stated only guarantees that the bits output by the device have large (smooth) min-entropy, one can obtain bits that are (close to) uniformly random by applying an extractor. In order to preserve the security against quantum adversaries, one should use a construction that is also secure against quantum adversaries. Such constructions exist: for instance an efficient classical extractor due to Trevisan [29], which only requires an additional $O(\log^2 n)$ bits of seed, has been shown secure even against quantum adversaries [27, 9].

In case one is not concerned with the possibility of quantum adversaries, but solely with the production of high-entropy bits, we introduce a simplified protocol that generates n bits that are ε-close to being uniformly random (after application of an efficient extractor, such as the one in [14]), starting from a seed of only $O(\log n \log 1/\varepsilon)$ uniformly random bits. The protocol consists of $m = O(n)$ phases, each lasting for $k = O(\log n + \log 1/\varepsilon)$ rounds. Moreover, the output sequence of n bits is ε-close to uniformly random provided there is no communication between $\mathcal{A}$ and $\mathcal{B}$ in the middle of any phase (a condition enforced, say, by the speed of light limit imposed by special relativity). For the conclusion to hold, it is unnecessary to assume that the boxes are described by quantum mechanics.[5]

We note that a dependence of the initial seed on $\log(1/\varepsilon)$ is clearly necessary to guarantee that the output is ε-close to uniform in statistical distance. This is because a malicious device could attempt to guess the user's private random bits, and behave accordingly. If the user only uses $\log 1/\varepsilon$ random bits, the device's guess will be successful with probability ε, and in that case it can deterministically satisfy all the user's requirements (since they are known in advance). One can also argue (perhaps a little less emphatically) that $\log n$ bits may be necessary, since at best the device acts like a weak random source, and a random seed of $\log n$ bits is necessary to extract that randomness.

THEOREM 2 (INFORMAL). *Let $\varepsilon > 0$ be given, and n an integer. Let $(\mathcal{A},\mathcal{B})$ be an arbitrary pair of non-communicating boxes. Suppose Protocol A, described in Figure 2, is executed with $\mathcal{A}$ and $\mathcal{B}$. This execution requires the use of $\tilde{O}(\log n \log(1/\varepsilon))$ random bits, and results in an output string B of $O(n)$ bits. Let* CHSH *be the event that the boxes' outputs are accepted in the final test described in the protocol, and suppose that* $\Pr(\text{CHSH}) \geq \varepsilon$. *Then*

$$H_\infty^\varepsilon(B|\text{CHSH}) \geq n.$$

In the simplified setting of Theorem 2 we are able to explicitly work through the constants involved in our bounds,

[4]It may also be worth emphasizing that the bits eventually produced, after application of an extractor, will be guaranteed to be *statistically* indistinguishable from uniform, a much stronger condition that the computational indistinguishability that is the criterion for cryptographic pseudo-random generators [26, 4, 30].

[5]One might say that the randomness is "Einstein certifiable", in the sense that the tests should convince even a quantum skeptic — viz, Einstein's famous quote from his 1926 letter to Max Born expressing his unhappiness with quantum mechanics as "God does not play dice with the Universe".

and obtain actual estimates for the amount of randomness produced. For example, if one sets an error tolerance parameter $\varepsilon = 10^{-5}$, 15Kb of seed are necessary to produce roughly 15Kb of min-entropy: a shorter seed will only produce less entropy than it contained. Once that threshold is passed, however, the exponential expansion kicks in very quickly, and 30Kb of seed are already sufficient to generate one Terabyte of min-entropy!

Techniques.

The proofs of both our results proceed by contradiction. Suppose given a pair of boxes $(\mathcal{A}, \mathcal{B})$ that violate either theorem's conclusions: when subjected to an interaction as prescribed by Protocol A or Protocol B, the boxes produce bits that pass the user's test with good probability, but still contain little min-entropy. Our goal is to show that such boxes must violate the theorems' assumptions: they must be signaling.

In order to demonstrate this we introduce two ingredients. The first is a decomposition of the protocol into *phases*, which are consecutive sequences of a fixed number $k = O(\log n + \log 1/\varepsilon)$ of rounds of interaction between the user and the boxes. Each box always receives identical inputs throughout all rounds in a given phase. The purpose of the decomposition into phases is to enable the user to perform a robust verification of the CHSH condition: his final test will enforce that in *every* phase, a significantly larger than $3/4$ fraction of pairs of outputs satisfy the CHSH condition (with respect to the corresponding pair of outputs). This lets us argue about the *Hamming distance* between Alice and Bob's k-bit outputs in any phase: if the CHSH constraint was of the form $a \oplus b = 0$ then the outputs should be close in Hamming distance, whereas if it had the form $a \oplus b = 1$ then they should be far apart.

The second ingredient builds upon the first. Consider the following simple *guessing game*: two players, Alice and Bob, each get a uniformly random bit as input. They win the game if Alice outputs a bit that equals Bob's input. Clearly, any strategy with success probability larger than $1/2$ must involve communication between Alice and Bob. Ignoring quantum adversaries for now, suppose given a pair of boxes violating the conclusion of Theorem 2. Then such boxes can be used to devise a successful strategy in the guessing game: a contradiction of the no-signaling assumption. The main point is that if box $\mathcal{B}$'s output is not random enough, then in a certain block of the protocol it is likely to output a particular k-bit string almost deterministically. In that case, by using the CHSH condition Alice, given access to $\mathcal{A}$, can guess $\mathcal{B}$'s input $y \in \{0, 1\}$ based on whether $\mathcal{A}$'s k-bit output in that block is "close" or "far" in Hamming distance from that particular string. This provides a way for Alice to guess $\mathcal{B}$'s input with probability greater than $1/2$, violating the no-signaling condition placed on the boxes. This style of reasoning can be used to establish that $\mathcal{B}$'s output must have high min-entropy, thus yielding Theorem 6.

Proving security in the presence of a quantum adversary involves additional challenges. Indeed, indication that dealing with such adversaries may present substantial new difficulties may already be found in the area of strong extractor constructions: there are examples of such constructions, secure against classical adversaries, that dramatically fail in the presence of quantum adversaries with even smaller prior information [13]. We need to rule out the following catastrophic scenario: the adversary Eve inserted an undetectable "back-door" by entangling $\mathcal{A}$ and $\mathcal{B}$ together with her own, private, laboratory. Eve knows how the protocol proceeds, and how the boxes will behave (her only unknown are the poly $\log n$ random bits of seed used by the user). Based on this she repeatedly makes a specific measurement on her system, which reliably produces the same output bits as $\mathcal{A}$ and $\mathcal{B}$: while $\mathcal{B}$'s outputs may appear random in isolation, they are totally insecure![6]

Interestingly, the proof of Theorem 1 makes crucial use of the properties of a specific construction of a quantum-proof extractor, based on Trevisan's construction and the t-XOR code, that was first outlined in [10]. This construction is used to prove a key information-theoretic lemma, which we state informally below. The lemma gives an operational interpretation to a random variable having small smooth min-entropy conditioned on a quantum system, and may be of independent interest.

LEMMA 3 (INFORMAL). *Let X be a random variable distributed over m-bit strings, and for every $x \in \{0,1\}^m$, ρ_x a quantum state. Let $\varepsilon = \Omega(\text{poly}^{-1}(m))$, and suppose that the smooth min-entropy of X, given ρ_X, is $K = H_\infty^\varepsilon(X|\rho_X)$. Then there exists a collection of $O(K \log m)$ subsets of $O(\log m)$ positions of X each, and a measurement on ρ_X, depending on the parities of the bits of X in each of those subsets, that produces a string Y such that with inverse-polynomial probability, Y agrees with X in a fraction at least $1 - \frac{1}{\log m}$ of positions.*

Lemma 3 formalizes the intuition that if $H_\infty^\varepsilon(X|\rho_X) = K$, then given access to ρ_X one is only "missing" roughly K bits of information about X: there exists specific "advice bits" (the parities of the bits of X in each of the $O(K \log m)$ subsets) such that, given these advice bits, one can measure ρ_X and recover most of X with inverse-polynomial success probability.[7] The proof of Lemma 3 is based directly on the proof of security of Trevisan's extractor against quantum adversaries presented in [9]. Since however it does not follow as a black-box, we give a detailed outline of the proof of the lemma in Appendix A.

Finally, note that while the *proof* of Lemma 3 requires the use of a specific construction of an extractor secure against quantum adversaries, as a result we can show that the bits output in Protocol B contain a large amount of conditional min-entropy — and hence *any* good quantum-proof extractor can be applied to those bits in order to obtain near-uniform bits.

Related work.

Two concurrent and independent papers, the first by Fehr, Gelles and Schaffner [12] and the second by Pironio and Massar [22], consider the problem of randomness expansion in the presence of *classical* adversaries. Both papers give a

[6]This is so even after the application of the extractor by the user, as if Eve knows the whole input to the extractor, but not the seed, she still has about $n - O(\text{poly} \log n)$ bits of information on the n output bits.

[7]Note that in the range of large K (at least inverse-polynomial in m), an inverse-polynomial success is much higher than the inverse-exponential probability of guessing correctly the whole of X that one would get by measuring ρ_X directly, without using any "advice" bits.

more rigorous proof of the results originally presented in [21], in particular concluding that the protocol introduced in that paper is composable, provided the adversary only possesses classical side information. Using this they are able to obtain a protocol with exponential randomness expansion; however their protocol requires the use of at least two pairs of boxes that are not entangled (in contrast, our protocol requires a single pair of boxes, and is secure even in the presence of arbitrary entanglement between them and any potential adversary).

Recent work by Colbeck and Renner [8] studies a related question, that of improving the quality of a given source of weak randomness. Specifically, they show that if one is given access to a so-called Santha-Vazirani source then one can produce bits that are guaranteed to be statistically close to uniform by using the violation of a specific Bell inequality by a pair of untrusted no-signaling devices.

Organization of the paper.

We begin with some preliminaries in Section 2. In Section 3 we introduce the *guessing game*, an important conceptual tool in the proofs of both Theorem 6 and Theorem 8. In Section 4 we prove Theorem 6, while Theorem 8 is proven in Section 5. The proof of Lemma 3 mostly follows from known results, and is given in Appendix A.

2. PRELIMINARIES

Notation.

Given two n-bit strings x, y we let $d_H(x,y) = \frac{1}{n}\sum_{i=1}^n |x_i - y_i|$ denote their relative Hamming distance. For $i \in [n]$, we let x_i be the i-th bit of x, and $x_{<i}$ its $(i-1)$-bit prefix.

Classical random variables.

Given a random variable $X \in \{0,1\}^n$, its min-entropy is

$$H_\infty(X) = -\log \max_x \Pr(X = x).$$

For two distributions p, q on a domain D, their statistical distance is

$$\|p - q\|_1 := (1/2)\sum_{x \in D} |p(x) - q(x)|_1.$$

This notion of distance can be extended to random variables with the same range in the natural way. Given $\varepsilon > 0$, the smooth min-entropy of a random variable X is

$$H_\infty^\varepsilon(X) = \sup_{Y,\, \|Y - X\|_1 \leq \varepsilon} H_\infty(Y).$$

The following simple and well-known claim will be useful.

CLAIM 4. *Let $\alpha, \varepsilon > 0$ and X a random variable such that $H_\infty^\varepsilon(X) \leq \alpha$. Then there exists a set B such that $\Pr(X \in B) \geq \varepsilon$ and for every $x \in B$, it holds that $\Pr(X = x) \geq 2^{-\alpha}$.*

PROOF. Let B be the set of x such that $\Pr(X = x) \geq 2^{-\alpha}$, and suppose $\Pr(X \in B) < \varepsilon$. Define Y so that $\Pr(Y = x) = \Pr(X = x)$ for every $x \notin B$, $\Pr(Y = x) = 0$ for every $x \in B$. In order to normalize Y, introduce new values z such that $\Pr(X = z) = 0$, and extend Y by defining $\Pr(Y = z) = 2^{-\alpha-1}$ until it is properly normalized. Then $\|Y - X\|_1 < \varepsilon$ and $H_\infty(Y) > \alpha$, contradicting the assumption on the smooth min-entropy of X. □

Quantum states.

Let X be a register containing a classical random variable, which we also call X, and E a register containing a quantum state, possibly correlated to X. Then the whole system can be described using the cq-state (cq stands for classical-quantum) $\rho_{XE} = \sum_x p_X(x)|x\rangle\langle x| \otimes \rho_x$, where for every x ρ_x is a density matrix, i.e. a positive matrix with trace 1. Given such a state, the guessing entropy $p_{guess}(X|E)$ is the maximum probability with which one can predict X, given access to E. Formally, it is defined as

$$p_{guess}(X|E)_\rho = \sup_{\{M_x\}} \sum_x p_X(x)\mathrm{Tr}\big(M_x \rho_x\big),$$

where the supremum is taken over all projective operator-valued measurements (POVMs) on E.[8] The conditional min-entropy can be defined through the guessing entropy as $H_\infty(X|E)_\rho = -\log p_{guess}(X|E)_\rho$ [18]. We will often omit the subscript ρ, when the underlying state is clear. The appropriate distance measure on quantum states is the trace distance, which derives from the trace norm $\|A\|_{tr} = \mathrm{Tr}(\sqrt{A^\dagger A})$. This lets us define a notion of smooth conditional min-entropy:

$$H_\infty^\varepsilon(X|E)_\rho = \sup_{\sigma_{XE},\, \|\sigma_{XE} - \rho_{XE}\|_{tr} \leq \varepsilon} H_\infty(X|E)_\sigma,$$

where here the supremum is taken over all sub-normalized cq-state σ_{XE}. As in the purely classical setting, it is known that this measure of conditional min-entropy is the appropriate one from the point of view of extracting uniform bits [23]: if $H_\infty^\varepsilon(X|E) = K$ then $K - O(\log 1/\varepsilon)$ bits can be extracted from X that are ε-close to uniform, even from the point of view of E.

The CHSH game.

The following game was originally introduced by Clause, Horne, Shimony and Holt [5] to demonstrate the non-locality of quantum mechanics. Two collaborating but non communicating parties, Alice and Bob, are each given a bit $x, y \in \{0,1\}$ distributed uniformly at random. Their goal is to produce bits a, b respectively such that $a \oplus b = x \wedge y$. It is not hard to see that classical parties (possibly using shared randomness) have a maximum success probability of 3/4 in this game. In contrast, quantum mechanics predicts that the following strategy, which we will sometimes refer to as the "honest" strategy, achieves a success probability of $\cos^2(\pi/8) \approx 0.85$. Alice and Bob share an EPR pair $|\Psi\rangle = \frac{1}{\sqrt{2}}|00\rangle + \frac{1}{\sqrt{2}}|11\rangle$. Upon receiving her input, Alice measures either in the computational ($x = 0$) or the Hadamard ($x = 1$) basis. Bob measures in the computational basis rotated by either $\pi/8$ ($y = 0$) or $3\pi/8$ ($y = 1$). One can verify that for every pair of inputs (x, y) this strategy produces correct outputs with probability exactly $\cos^2(\pi/8)$.

3. THE GUESSING GAME

Consider the following simple guessing game. In this game, there are two cooperating players, Alice and Bob. At the start of the game Bob receives a single bit $y \in \{0,1\}$ chosen uniformly at random. The players are then allowed to

[8] A POVM $\{M_x\}$ is given by a set of positive matrices which sum to identity. We refer the reader to the standard textbook [20] for more details on the basics of quantum information theory.

perform arbitrary computations, but are not allowed to communicate. At the end of the game Alice outputs a bit a, and the players win if $a = y$.

Clearly, any strategy with success probability larger than $\frac{1}{2}$ indicates a violation of the no-communication assumption between Alice and Bob. At the heart of the proofs of both Theorem 6 and Theorem 8 is a reduction to the guessing game. Assuming there existed a pair of boxes violating the conclusions of either theorem, we will show how these boxes may be used to devise a successful strategy in the guessing game, contradicting the no-signaling assumption placed on the boxes.

To illustrate the main features of the strategies we will design later, consider the following simplified setting. Let $\mathcal{A}, \mathcal{B}$ be a given pair of boxes taking inputs $X, Y \in \{0,1\}$ and producing outputs $A, B \in \{0,1\}^k$ respectively, where k is a parameter. Assume the following two properties hold. First, if the input to $\mathcal{B}$ is $Y = 0$ then its output B is essentially deterministic, in the sense that $B = b_0$ with high probability. Second, whatever their inputs, the boxes' outputs satisfy the CHSH constraint on average with a slightly higher probability than could any classical boxes: there is a fixed $\delta > 0$ such that a fraction at least $3/4 + \delta$ of $i \in [k]$ are such that $A_i \oplus B_i = X \wedge Y$. Then we claim that there is a strategy for Alice and Bob in the guessing game, using $\mathcal{A}$ and $\mathcal{B}$, that succeeds with probability strictly larger than 1/2.

Alice and Bob's strategy is the following. Alice is given access to $\mathcal{A}$ and Bob to $\mathcal{B}$. Upon receiving his secret bit y, Bob inputs it to $\mathcal{B}$, collecting outputs $b \in \{0,1\}^k$. Alice chooses an $x \in \{0,1\}$ uniformly at random, and inputs it to $\mathcal{A}$, collecting outputs $a \in \{0,1\}^k$. Let b_0 be the k-bit string with the highest probability of being output by $\mathcal{B}$, conditioned on $y = 0$. Alice makes a decision as follows: she computes the relative Hamming distance $d = d_H(a, b_0)$. If $d < 1/4$ she claims "Bob's input was 0". Otherwise, she claims "Bob's input was 1".

By assumption, if Bob's secret bit was $y = 0$, then his output is almost certainly b_0. By the CHSH constraint, independently of her input Alice's output a lies in a Hamming ball of radius $1/4 - \delta$ around b_0. So in this case she correctly claims "Bob's input was 0".

In the case that Bob's secret bit was $y = 1$, the analysis is more interesting. Let b be the actual output of $\mathcal{B}$. Let a_0 and a_1 be $\mathcal{A}$'s output in the two cases $x = 0$ and $x = 1$ respectively. We claim that the Hamming distance $d_H(a_0, a_1) \geq 1/2 + 2\delta$. This is because by the CHSH constraint, $d_H(a_0, b) \leq 1/4 - \delta$, while $d_H(a_1, b) \geq 3/4 + \delta$. Applying the triangle inequality

$$d_H(a_0, a_1) \geq \left|d_H(a_1, b) - d_H(a_0, b)\right| \geq 1/2 + 2\delta,$$

as claimed. Hence both a_0 and a_1 cannot lie in the Hamming ball of radius 1/4 around the fixed string b_0 (observe that this argument makes no use of the actual location of b!). Thus in the case $y = 1$, Alice correctly claims "Bob's input was 1" with probability at least 1/2.

Overall Alice and Bob succeed in the guessing game with probability at least 3/4, implying the boxes $\mathcal{A}$, $\mathcal{B}$ allowed them to communicate, and hence do not satisfy the no-signaling condition.

Clearly there is a lot of slack in the above reasoning, since for contradiction it suffices to succeed in the guessing game with any probability strictly greater than 1/2. By being more careful it is possible to allow Bob's output on $y = 0$ to not be fully deterministic, as well as allow for a small probability that the boxes' outputs may not satisfy the CHSH constraint:

Lemma 5. *Let $\beta, \gamma > 0$ be such that $\gamma/2 + 3\beta < 1/4$, and k an integer. Suppose given a pair of boxes $\mathcal{A}, \mathcal{B}$, taking inputs $X, Y \in \{0,1\}$ and producing outputs $A, B \in \{0,1\}^k$ each. Suppose the following conditions hold:*

1. *When given input 0, the distribution of outputs of $\mathcal{B}$ has low min-entropy: there exists a $b_0 \in \{0,1\}^k$ such that $\Pr(B = b_0|Y = 0) \geq 1 - \gamma$,*
2. *The boxes' outputs fall in the "quantum regime" of the CHSH inequality: there exists a constant $\delta > 0$ such that*

$$\Pr\left(d_H(A \oplus B, (X \wedge Y, \ldots, X \wedge Y)) > 1/4 - \delta\right) \leq \beta,$$

where the probability is taken over the choice of uniformly random X, Y, and the boxes' internal randomness.

Then there is a strategy for Alice and Bob, using $\mathcal{A}$ and $\mathcal{B}$, which gives them success probability strictly greater than 1/2 in the guessing game.

Proof. Alice and Bob's strategy in the guessing game is as described above. Let b_0 be the k-bit string that is most likely to be output by $\mathcal{B}$, conditioned on $y = 0$.

We first show that, if Bob's input was $y = 0$, then Alice claims that Bob had a 0 with probability at least $1 - \gamma - 2\beta$. By the first condition in the lemma, Bob obtains the output b_0 with probability at least $1 - \gamma$. Moreover, by the second condition the CHSH constraint will be satisfied with probability at least $1 - 2\beta$ on average over Alice's choice of input, given that Bob's input was $y = 0$. Given $y = 0$, whatever the input to $\mathcal{A}$ the CHSH constraint implies that $d_H(a, b) < 1/4$. Hence by a union bound Alice will obtain an output string a at relative Hamming distance at most 1/4 from b_0 with probability at least $1 - \gamma - 2\beta$.

Next we show that, in case Bob's input in the guessing game is $y = 1$, Alice claims that Bob had a 1 with probability at least $\frac{1}{2}(1 - 8\beta)$. The second condition in the lemma implies that for any of the two possible choices for Alice's input $X = x \in \{0,1\}$, it holds that

$$\Pr_{ABY}\left(d_H(A \oplus B, (X \wedge Y), \ldots, X \wedge Y)) > \frac{1}{4} - \delta \,|X = x\right) \leq 2\beta. \quad (1)$$

Let b' be Bob's output, and suppose that b' is such that for every $x \in \{0,1\}$, (1) holds conditioned on $B = b'$, with the 2β replaced by a 4β. It follows from (1) and Markov's inequality that this condition holds with probability at least $1 - 4\beta$ over b'.

If Alice chooses $x = 0$ then the CHSH constraint indicates that the corresponding a_0 should be such that $d_H(a_0, b') < 1/4 - \delta$, while in case she chooses $x = 1$ her output a_1 should satisfy $d_H(a_1, b') > 3/4 + \delta$. By the triangle inequality,

$$d_H(a_0, a_1) \geq \left|d_H(a_1, b') - d_H(a_0, b')\right| > 1/2 + 2\delta,$$

so that whatever the value of b', at most one of a_0 or a_1 can be at distance less than 1/4 from b_0. Since Alice's input is chosen uniformly at random, taking into account the choice of b' we have shown that with probability at least $(1-8\beta)/2$ Alice will choose an input that will make her correctly claim that Bob had a 1.

The two bounds proven above together show that Alice's probability of correctly guessing Bob's input in the guessing game is at least

$$p_{succ} \geq \frac{1}{2}(1-\gamma-2\beta)+\frac{1}{2}\frac{1-8\beta}{2} = \frac{1}{2}+\Big(\frac{1}{4}-3\beta-\frac{\gamma}{2}\Big),$$

which is greater than $1/2$ whenever $3\beta+\gamma/2 < 1/4$, proving Lemma 5. □

4. A PROTOCOL WITH EXPONENTIAL RANDOMNESS EXPANSION

In this section we prove Theorem 2, which can be stated formally as follows.

THEOREM 6. *Let $\varepsilon > 0$ be given, and n an integer. Let $(\mathcal{A}, \mathcal{B})$ be an arbitrary pair of no-signaling boxes used to execute Protocol A, as described in Figure 2, B the random variable describing the bits output by $\mathcal{B}$, and CHSH the event that the boxes' outputs are accepted in the final test described in the protocol. Then for all large enough n at least one of the following holds :*

- *Either $H_\infty^\varepsilon(B|\text{CHSH}) \geq n$,*
- *Or $\Pr(\text{CHSH}) \leq \varepsilon$.*

Moreover, inputs in Protocol A can be generated using $\tilde{O}(\log n \log(1/\varepsilon))$ uniformly random bits, and it makes $O(n(\log n + \log(1/\varepsilon)))$ uses of the boxes.

Protocol A is described in Figure 2. It uses two main ideas in order to save on the randomness used by the user to select inputs to the boxes. The first idea is to restrict the inputs to $(0,0)$ most of the time.[9] Only a few randomly placed checks (the Bell blocks) are performed in order to verify that the boxes are generating their inputs honestly. There are about $O(\log 1/\varepsilon)$ such blocks. Note that the boxes usually do not know when they are being checked: for instant, if the input is $(0,1)$ then even though box $\mathcal{B}$ knows that it is in a Bell round, box $\mathcal{A}$ by itself cannot differentiate that particular round from one in which both inputs are 0. This implies in particular that the strategy it uses to determine its output cannot be different from what it would have been had the inputs been the more frequent $(0,0)$.

The second main idea, as already explained in the introduction, consists in decomposing the protocol into *phases* (we also use *blocks* when specifically referring to the sequence of inputs or outputs in a given phase), which are consecutive sequences of a fixed number $k = O(\log n + \log 1/\varepsilon)$ of rounds of interaction between the user and the boxes, and whose purpose of the decomposition in phases is to enable the user to perform a robust verification of the CHSH condition.

Altogether, Protocol A only requires the use of random bits in order to select the position of the Bell blocks, as well as to select inputs in these blocks. The $O(\log 1/\varepsilon)$ Bell blocks can be chosen among the $O(n)$ rounds using

[9]This idea was already used in [21], and led to their protocol with quadratic $\sqrt{n \log 1/\varepsilon} \to n$ expansion of randomness.

Protocol A

1. Let n, ε be parameters given as input. Set $m = 500n$, $\Delta = 200\lceil\ln(1/\varepsilon)\rceil$, $\ell = m/\Delta$ and $k = 100\lceil\log n + \log 1/\varepsilon\rceil$.
2. Choose $T \subseteq [m]$ uniformly at random by selecting each position independently with probability $1/\ell$.
3. Repeat, for $i = 1, \ldots, m$:
   - 3.1 If $i \notin T$, then
     - 3.1.1 Set $x = y = 0$ and choose x, y as inputs for k consecutive steps. Collect outputs $a, b \in \{0,1\}^k$.
     - 3.1.2 If $a \oplus b$ has more than $\lceil 0.2k \rceil$ 1's then reject and abort the protocol. Otherwise, continue.
   - 3.2 If $i \in T$,
     - 3.2.1 Pick $x, y \in \{0,1\}$ uniformly at random, and set x, y as inputs for k consecutive steps. Collect outputs $a, b \in \{0,1\}^k$.
     - 3.2.2 If $a \oplus b$ differs from $x \wedge y$ in more than $\lceil 0.2k \rceil$ positions then reject and abort the protocol. Otherwise, continue.
4. If all steps accepted, then accept.

Figure 2: Protocol A uses $O(\log n \log 1/\varepsilon)$ bits of randomness and makes $O(n(\log n + \log 1/\varepsilon))$ uses of the boxes. Theorem 6 (in Section 4) shows that n bits of randomness are produced with confidence $1-\varepsilon$. The threshold $0.2k$ in steps 3.1.2 and 3.2.2 is arbitrary, and any value strictly lower than $k/4$ would work.

$\tilde{O}(\log n \log 1/\varepsilon)$ random bits (see e.g. [17]), and corresponding uniformly distributed inputs may be generated using an additional $O(\log 1/\varepsilon)$ random bits.

Before proceeding, we should verify that "honest" boxes, which play the optimal quantum strategy for the CHSH game independently in every round, are accepted by the user with high probability. Indeed, we have seen that such boxes will satisfy the CHSH constraint independently with probability $\cos^2 \pi/8$ in each round. Hence when one considers a block of k successive rounds, the probability that the CHSH constraint is *not* satisfied in more than 20% of those rounds will be exponentially small in k. Precisely, a simple Chernoff bound shows that the probability that the honest strategy satisfies the CHSH condition in less than 80% of any k successive rounds is at most $\exp\big(-(\cos^2 \pi/8 - 0.80)^2 k/2\big)$. Given our choice of $k = 100\lceil \log n + \log 1/\varepsilon \rceil$, it can be verified that for large enough n this expression is smaller than ε/m, where $m = 500n$ is the total number of blocks in the protocol. By a union bound, such boxes will fail to produce correlations satisfying the user in even just one of these blocks with probability at most ε.

Modeling events in the protocol.

Let $x = (x_i), y = (y_i), a = (a_i), b = (b_i) \in \big(\{0,1\}^k\big)^m$ denote the boxes' respective input and output strings in an execution of Protocol A, as described in Figure 2. Let X, Y, A, B be the corresponding random variables. The boxes' behavior is characterized by a probability distribution $p_{AB|XY}(a,b|x,y)$. The iterative structure of the protocol implies that $p_{AB|XY}$ can be factored as follows:

$$p_{AB|XY}(a,b|x,y) = \prod_{i=1}^{mk} p_{A_iB_i|X_iY_iH_i}(a_i, b_i|x_i, y_i, h_i),$$

where for any $i \in [mk]$, $H_i = (A_{<i}, B_{<i}, X_{<i}, Y_{<i})$ and $h_i = (a_{<i}, b_{<i}, x_{<i}, y_{<i})$. We impose a single additional condition on $p_{AB|XY}$: that it obeys the no-signaling condition in every block, that is for every k-round block $S_i \subseteq \{0,1\}^{mk}$, where $i \in [m]$, $a_{S_i}, x_{S_i}, y_{S_i}, y'_{S_i}$ and h_{S_i}, it holds that

$$\sum_{b_{S_i} \in \{0,1\}^k} p_{A_{S_i}B_{S_i}|Z_i}(a_{S_i}, b_{S_i}|z_i) = \sum_{b_{S_i} \in \{0,1\}^k} p_{A_{S_i}B_{S_i}|Z_i}(a_{S_i}, b_{S_i}|z'_i),$$

where we used $Z_i = X_{(k-1)i+1}Y_{(k-1)i+1}H_{(k-1)i+1}$ and $z_i = x_{(k-1)i+1}, y_{(k-1)i+1}, h_{(k-1)i+1}$ and $z'_i = x_{(k-1)i+1}, y'_{(k-1)i+1}, h_{(k-1)i+1}$ as shorthands, and a symmetric condition holds when marginalizing over a_{S_i}. For $i \in [m]$, let CHSH_i be the event that $d_H(A_{S_i} \oplus B_{S_i}, X_{S_i} \wedge Y_{S_i}) \leq 0.2$, and $\mathrm{CHSH} = \bigwedge_i \mathrm{CHSH}_i$. We will also use the shorthand $\mathrm{CHSH}_{<i} = \bigwedge_{j<i} \mathrm{CHSH}_j$. Finally, we let $T_j \in [m]$ be a random variable denoting the j-th Bell block, i.e. the j-th element of the set T chosen by the user in step 2. of Protocol A.

Claim 7. *Let n be an integer, and $2^{-n/10} < \varepsilon < 1/100$. Suppose that both conditions (i) $H^\varepsilon_\infty(B|CHSH) \leq n$, and (ii) $\Pr(\mathrm{CHSH}) \geq \varepsilon$ hold. Then for all large enough n there exists an index j_0 and a subset G of output strings satisfying $\Pr(B \in G) \geq \varepsilon^3$ such that the following hold.*

- *Conditioned on $\mathcal{B}$'s input in the j_0-th Bell block T_{j_0} being 0, its output in that block is essentially deterministic: $\forall b \in G$,*

$$\Pr(B_{T_{j_0}} = b_{T_{j_0}}|\mathrm{CHSH}_{<T_{j_0}}, B_{<T_{j_0}} = b_{<T_{j_0}}, Y_{T_{j_0}} = 0) \geq 0.92, \qquad (2)$$

- *The CHSH condition is satisfied with high probability in the j_0-th Bell block T_{j_0}: $\forall b \in G$,*

$$\Pr(\mathrm{CHSH}_{T_{j_0}}|\mathrm{CHSH}_{<T_{j_0}}, B_{<T_{j_0}} = b_{<T_{j_0}}) \geq 0.95. \qquad (3)$$

Proof. As in Protocol A, set $m = 500n$, $\ell = m/\Delta$ and $\Delta = 200\lceil \ln(1/\varepsilon)\rceil$. Let BAD be the set of strings $b \in \big(\{0,1\}^k\big)^m$ such that $\Pr(B = b|\mathrm{CHSH}) > 2^{-n}$. Assumption (i) together with Claim 4 show that $\Pr(\mathrm{BAD}|\mathrm{CHSH}) \geq \varepsilon$. Using (ii) and Baye's rule we get that for every $b = (b_1, \ldots, b_m) \in \mathrm{BAD}$,

$$\begin{aligned}\Pr(B = b, \mathrm{CHSH}) &= \prod_{i=1}^{m} \Pr(B_i = b_i, \mathrm{CHSH}_i|\mathrm{CHSH}_{<i}, B_{<i} = b_{<i}) \\ &> 2^{-n}\varepsilon.\end{aligned}$$

Taking logarithms on both sides,

$$\begin{aligned}\sum_{i=1}^{m} -\log \Pr(B_i = b_i, \mathrm{CHSH}_i|\mathrm{CHSH}_{<i}, B_{<i} = b_{<i}) &< n + \log(1/\varepsilon) \\ &\leq (1 + 1/10)n,\end{aligned}$$

assuming as in the statement of the claim that ε is not too small. By an averaging argument at least 9/10 of all $i \in [m]$ are such that a fraction at least 6/10 (in probability) of all $b \in \mathrm{BAD}$ are such that

$$\begin{aligned}\Pr(B_i = b_i|\mathrm{CHSH}_{<i}, B_{<i} = b_{<i}) &\geq 2^{-(100/4)(1+1/10)(n/m)} \\ &\geq 2^{-28/500} \geq 0.96. \qquad (4)\end{aligned}$$

Since in the protocol Bob's input is a 0 with probability at least 1/2 irrespective of the type of block, we may ensure that (4) holds (with a slightly smaller probability) conditioned on $Y_i = 0$, an event that is independent from both $\mathrm{CHSH}_{<i}$ and $B_{<i} = b_{<i}$ (for any $b_{<}i$):

$$\Pr(B_i = b_i|\mathrm{CHSH}_{<i}, B_{<i} = b_{<i}, Y_i = 0) \geq 0.92. \qquad (5)$$

Let S be the set of $i \in [m]$ such that (5) holds for a fraction at least 6/10 of $b \in \mathrm{BAD}$. S is a random variable of size $|S| \geq 9m/10$.

We apply the same reasoning once more, focusing on the CHSH constraint being satisfied in a Bell block. Let T be a random variable containing the indices of the blocks that have been designated as Bell blocks in the protocol. Let $N = |T \cap S|$. We may write N as the sum of Boolean random variables N_j, where $N_j = 1$ if and only if the j-th element of S falls in T. Since for every i the i-th block is chosen to be a Bell block independently with probability $1/\ell$ (independently of past events such as $\mathrm{CHSH}_{<i}$ and $B_{<i} = b_{<i}$), the random variables N_j, for $j \leq |S|$, are independent.

Recall that $|S| \geq 9m/10$, and by a Chernoff bound

$$\Pr\left(N_1 + \cdots + N_{9m/10} \geq 9m/10 \cdot 1/(2\ell)\right) \geq 1 - e^{-(9m/10\ell)(1/2)^2/2} \geq 1 - e^{-\Delta/10} \geq 1 - \varepsilon^3,$$

given that $m/\ell = \Delta$. Let K denote the event that this bound holds: $\Pr(K) \geq 1 - \varepsilon^3$, and conditioned on K it holds that $N = |S \cap T| \geq 9m/(20\ell) \geq 9\Delta/20$. Starting from $\Pr(\text{CHSH}|\text{BAD}) \geq \varepsilon^2$, further conditioning on K gives

$$\Pr(\text{CHSH}|\text{BAD}, K) = \frac{\Pr(\text{CHSH}, K|\text{BAD})}{\Pr(K|\text{BAD})} \geq \varepsilon^2 - \varepsilon^3 \geq \varepsilon^2/2.$$

Using Baye's rule as before we then obtain

$$\sum_{i \in T \cap S} -\log \Pr(\text{CHSH}_i|\text{CHSH}_{<i}, \text{BAD}_{<i}, K) \leq 2\log(2/\varepsilon).$$

Using the lower bound on N this implies that there exists an $i \in T \cap S$ such that

$$\Pr(\text{CHSH}_i|\text{CHSH}_{<i}, \text{BAD}_{<i}, K) \geq 2^{-2\log(2/\varepsilon)/N} \geq 0.978, \qquad (6)$$

given the choice of Δ made in the claim. Given our assumption on ε, removing the conditioning on K in this equation at most decreases the lower bound to 0.975. Let $i \in T \cap S$ be a Bell block for which (6) holds. By Markov's inequality, for a fraction at least 1/2 of $b \in \text{BAD}$ it holds that

$$\Pr(\text{CHSH}_i|\text{CHSH}_{<i}, B_{<i} = b_{<i}) \geq 0.95. \qquad (7)$$

By the union bound, at iteration i (7) will hold simultaneously with (5) for a subset G of BAD of size at least

$$\Pr(G) = \Pr(G|\text{BAD})\Pr(\text{BAD}) \geq (6/10 - 1/2)\varepsilon^2 \geq \varepsilon^3,$$

given our choice of parameters. Eq. (7) implies (3) in the claim, and (5) implies (2). □

In order to conclude the proof of Theorem 6 it remains to show how the special block identified in Claim 7 can lead to a successful strategy in the guessing game.

Consider the following strategy for Alice and Bob in the guessing game. In a preparatory phase (before Bob receives his secret bit y), Alice and Bob run the protocol with the boxes $\mathcal{A}$ and $\mathcal{B}$, up to the T_{j_0}-th block (excluded). Bob communicates $\mathcal{B}$'s outputs up till that block to Alice. Together they check that the CHSH constraint is satisfied in all blocks preceding the T_{j_0}-th; if not they abort. They also verify that Bob's outputs are the prefix of a string $b \in G$; if not they abort. The guessing game can now start: Alice and Bob are separated and Bob is given his secret input y.

Given the conditioning that Alice and Bob have performed, once they are ready to start the game boxes $\mathcal{A}$ and $\mathcal{B}$ satisfy both conditions of Lemma 5. Condition 1. in Lemma 5 holds with $\gamma = 0.08$ as a consequence of item 1 in Claim 7 and condition 2 in Lemma 5 follows from item 2 in Claim 7 with $\beta = 0.05$. Since $\gamma/2 + 3\beta = 0.19 < 1/4$, Lemma 5 lets us conclude that the boxes $\mathcal{A}$ and $\mathcal{B}$ must be signaling in the T_{j_0}-th block, a contradiction. This finishes the proof of Theorem 6.

5. SECURITY IN THE PRESENCE OF A QUANTUM ADVERSARY

In this section we prove our main theorem, which can be formally stated as follows.

THEOREM 8. *Let n and $\alpha > 0$ be given, and set $\varepsilon = n^{-\alpha}$. Let $(\mathcal{A}, \mathcal{B})$ be an arbitrary pair of no-signaling boxes used to execute Protocol B, described in Figure 3, and assume that $\mathcal{A}$ and $\mathcal{B}$ can be described by two isolated but possibly entangled quantum-mechanical systems. Let* CHSH *be the event that the boxes' outputs are accepted in the protocol, and B' the random variable describing the bits output by $\mathcal{B}$, conditioned on* CHSH. *Let* **E** *denote an arbitrary quantum system, possibly entangled with $\mathcal{A}$ and $\mathcal{B}$, but such that no communication occurs between $\mathcal{A}, \mathcal{B}$ and* **E** *once the protocol starts. Then for all large enough n at least one of the following holds:*

- *Either $H_\infty^\varepsilon(B'|\mathbf{E}) \geq n$,*
- *Or $\Pr(\text{CHSH}) \leq \varepsilon$.*

Moreover, inputs in Protocol B may be generated using only $\tilde{O}(\log^3 n)$ bits of randomness.

We first give an overview of the proof, describing the main steps, in the next section. The formal proof is given in Section 5.3.

5.1 The protocol

Theorem 8 is based on Protocol B, a variant of Protocol A which replaces the use of the CHSH game by the following "extended" variant. In this game each box may receive one of four possible inputs, which we label as $(A,0), (A,1), (B,0), (B,1)$. An input such as "$(A,1)$" to either box means: "perform the measurement that $\mathcal{A}$ would have performed in the honest CHSH strategy, in case its input had been a 1". The advantage of working with this game is that there exists an optimal strategy (the one directly derived from the honest CHSH strategy) in which both players always output identical answers when their inputs are equal.

Protocol B follows the same structure as Protocol A. Inputs are divided into groups of $k = O(\log^2 n)$ identical inputs. There are $m = O(n^{10+8\alpha}\log^2 n)$ successive blocks. Each round of the protocol selects inputs to the boxes coming from the "extended CHSH" game. That game has four questions per party: $(A,0), (A,1), (B,0), (B,1)$. We expect honest boxes to apply the following strategy. They share a single EPR pair, and perform the same measurement if provided the same input. On input $(A,0)$ the measurement is in the computational basis $\{|0\rangle, |1\rangle\}$, and on input $(A,1)$ it is in the Hadamard basis $\{|+\rangle, |-\rangle\}$, with the outcome $|+\rangle$ being associated with the output '0'. On input $(B,0)$ the measurement is in the basis $\{\cos^2(\pi/8)|0\rangle + \sin^2(\pi/8)|1\rangle, \sin^2(\pi/8)|0\rangle - \cos^2(\pi/8)|1\rangle\}$, with the first vector being associated with the outcome '0'.

5.2 Proof overview

As in the proof of Theorem 6 we prove Theorem 8 by contradiction, through a reduction to the guessing game. In the non-adversarial case the crux of the reduction consisted in identifying a special block $j_0 \in [m]$ in which $\mathcal{B}$'s output B was essentially deterministic, conditioned on past outputs. In the adversarial setting, however, B may be perfectly uniform, and such a block may not exist. Instead, we start by assuming for contradiction that the min-entropy of Bob's output conditioned on Eve's information is small: $H^{\varepsilon}_{\infty}(B|\mathbf{E}) \leq n$.

Previously in the guessing game Alice tried to guess Bob's secret input $y \in \{0,1\}$. She did so by using her prediction for $\mathcal{B}$'s outputs, together with the CHSH constraint and her own box $\mathcal{A}$'s outputs. Here we team up Alice and Eve. Alice will provide Eve with some information she obtained in previous blocks of the protocol, and based on that information Eve will attempt to make an accurate prediction for $\mathcal{B}$'s outputs in the special block. Alice will then use that prediction to guess y, using as before the CHSH constraint and her own box $\mathcal{A}$'s outputs.

Protocol B

1. Let n and $\alpha > 0$ be given as input. Set $\ell = n^{10+8\alpha}$, $k = 100\lceil \log \ell + \log 1/\varepsilon \rceil$ and $m = \lceil C\ell \log^2 \ell \rceil$, where $C > 0$ is a large constant.
2. Choose $T \subseteq [m]$ uniformly at random by selecting each position independently with probability $1/\ell$.
3. Repeat, for $i = 1, \ldots, m$:
   - 3.1 If $i \notin T$, then
     - 3.1.1 Set $x = y = (A, 0)$ and choose x, y as inputs for k consecutive steps. Collect outputs $a, b \in \{0,1\}^k$.
     - 3.1.2 If $a \neq b$ then reject and abort the protocol. Otherwise, continue.
   - 3.2 If $i \in T$,
     - 3.2.1 Pick $x \in \{(A,0),(A,1)\}$ and $y \in \{(A,0),(B,0)\}$ uniformly at random, and set x, y as inputs for k consecutive steps. Collect outputs $a, b \in \{0,1\}^k$.
     - 3.2.2 If either $a = b$ and $x = y$, or $d_H(a,b) \leq 0.16$ and $y = (B,0)$, or $d_H(a,b) \in [0.49, 0.51]$ and $x = (A,1)$ and $y = (A,0)$ then continue. Otherwise reject and abort the protocol.
4. If all steps accepted, then accept.

Figure 3: Protocol B uses $\tilde{O}(\log^3 n)$ bits of randomness and makes $\mathrm{poly}(n)$ uses of the boxes. Theorem 8 shows that n bits of randomness are produced, with confidence $\varepsilon = n^{-\alpha}$.

The reconstruction paradigm.

We would like to show that, under our assumption on $H^{\varepsilon}_{\infty}(B|\mathbf{E})$, Eve can perform the following task: accurately predict (part of) B, given auxiliary information provided by Alice. We accomplish this by using the "reconstruction" property of certain extractor constructions originally introduced by Trevisan [29]. Recall that an extractor is a function which maps a string B with large min-entropy (conditioned on side information contained in the quantum register $\mathbf{E}$) to a (shorter) string Z that is statistically close to uniform even from the point of view of an adversary holding $\mathbf{E}$. The reconstruction proof technique proceeds as follows: Suppose an adversary breaks the extractor. Then there exists another adversary who, given a small subset of the bits of the extractor's input as "advice", can reconstruct the *whole* input. Hence the input's entropy must have been at most the number of advice bits given.

For the purposes of constructing extractors, one would then take the contrapositive to conclude that, provided the input has large enough entropy, the extractor's output must be indistinguishable from uniform, thereby proving security. Here we work *directly* with the reconstruction procedure. Suppose that B has low min-entropy, conditioned on Eve's side information. If we were to apply an extractor to B in order to extract *more* bits than its conditional min-entropy, then certainly the output would not be secure: Eve would be able to distinguish it from a uniformly random string. The reconstruction paradigm states that, as a consequence, there is a strategy for Eve that successfully predicts the *entire* string B, given a subset of its bits as advice — exactly what is needed from Eve to facilitate Alice's task in the guessing game.

The t-XOR extractor.

At this stage we are faced with two difficulties. The first is that the reconstruction paradigm was developed in the context of classical adversaries, who can repeat predictive measurements at will. Quantum information is more delicate, and may be modified by the act of measuring. The second has to do with the role of the advice bits: since they come from $\mathcal{B}$'s output B we need to ensure that, in the guessing game, Alice can indeed provide this auxiliary information to Eve, *without* communicating with Bob.

In order to solve both problems we focus on a specific extractor construction, the t-XOR extractor E_t (here t is an integer such that $t = O(\log^2 n)$). For our purposes it will suffice to think of E_t as mapping the mk-bit string B to a string of $r \ll n$ bits, each of which is the parity of a certain subset of t out of B's mk bits. Which parities is dictated by an extra argument to the extractor, its seed, based on the use of combinatorial designs. Formally,

$$E_t : \{0,1\}^{mk} \times \{0,1\}^s \to \{0,1\}^r$$
$$(b,y) \mapsto \big(C_t^1(b,y), \ldots, C_t^r(b,y)\big),$$

where $C_t^i(b,y)$ is the parity of a specific subset of t bits of x, depending on both i and y.

Suppose that Eve can distinguish the output of the extractor $Z = E_t(B,Y)$ from a uniformly random string with success probability ε. In the first step of the reconstruction proof, a hybrid argument is used to show that Eve can predict the parity of t bits of B chosen at random with success ε/r, given access to the parities of $O(r)$ other subsets of t bits of B as advice. This step uses specific properties of the combinatorial designs.

The next step is the most critical. One would like to argue that, since Eve can predict the parity of a random subset of t of B's bits, she can recover a string that agrees with *most* of the t-XORs of B. One could then appeal to the approximate list-decoding properties of the t-XOR code in order to conclude that Eve may deduce a list of guesses for the string B itself. Since, however, Eve is quantum, the fact that she has a measurement predicting *any* t-XOR does not imply she has one predicting *every* t-XOR: measurements are destructive and distinct measurements need not be compatible. This is a fundamental difficulty, which arises e.g. in the analysis of random access codes [1]. To overcome it one has to appeal to a subtle argument due to Koenig and Terhal [19]. They show that without loss of generality one may assume that Eve's measurement has a specific form, called the *pretty-good measurement*. One can then argue that this specific measurement may be refined into one that predicts a guess for the whole list of t-XORs of B, from which a guess for B can be deduced by list-decoding the t-XOR code.

The security of the t-XOR extractor against quantum adversaries was first shown by Ta-Shma [27], and later improved in [10, 9]. As such, the argument above is not new. Rather, our contribution is to observe that it proves *more* than just the extractor's security. Indeed, summarizing the discussion so far we have shown that, if $H_\infty^\varepsilon(B|\mathbf{E}) \leq n$, then there is a measurement on $\mathbf{E}$ which, given a small amount of information about B as advice, reconstructs a good approximation to the *whole* string B with success probability $\mathrm{poly}(\varepsilon/r)$. This fact is what we already described in Lemma 3 in the introduction, and it can be formally stated as follows.

Lemma 9. *Let ρ_{XE} be a state such that X is a classical random variable distributed over m-bit strings, and E is an arbitrarily correlated quantum system. Let $\varepsilon = \Omega(m^{-c})$, where $c > 0$ is an arbitrary constant, and $K = H_\infty^\varepsilon(X|E)$. Then there exists a subset $V \subseteq [m]$ of size $v = |V| = O(K \log^2 m)$, and for every v-bit string z a measurement M_z on E such that, with probability at least $\Omega(\varepsilon^6/m^6)$, M_{X_V} produces a string Y that agrees with X in a fraction at least $1 - \frac{1}{\log m}$ of positions.*

The lemma is proved in Appendix A. Crucially, the bits of information required as advice are localized to a small subset of bits of B, of the order of the number of bits of information Eve initially has about that string. This property holds thanks to the specific extractor we are using, which is *local*: every bit of the output only depends on few bits of the input.

Completing the reduction to the guessing game.

In the guessing game it is Alice who needs to hand the advice bits to Eve. Indeed, if Bob, holding box $\mathcal{B}$, was to hand them over, they could leak information about his secret input y: some of the advice bits may fall in blocks of the protocol that occur *after* the special block j_0 in which Bob is planning to use his secret y as input. This leak of information defeats the purpose of the guessing game, which is to demonstrate signaling between $\mathcal{A}$ and $\mathcal{B}$.

Hence the "extended" variant of the CHSH game introduced in Protocol B: since in most blocks the inputs to both $\mathcal{A}$ and $\mathcal{B}$ are identical, by the extended CHSH constraint enforced in the protocol their outputs should be identical. The relatively few advice bits needed by Eve occupy a fixed set of positions, and with good probability all Bell blocks will fall outside of these positions, in which case Alice can obtain the advice bits required by Eve directly from $\mathcal{A}$'s outputs.

The proof of Theorem 8 is now almost complete, and one may argue as in Lemma 5 that Alice and Eve together will be able to successfully predict Bob's secret input in the guessing game, contradicting the no-signaling assumption placed on $\mathcal{A}$ and $\mathcal{B}$. A more detailed proof of the theorem is given in the next section.

5.3 Proof of Theorem 8

We proceed to formally prove Theorem 8, performing a reduction to the guessing game through the use of Lemma 9. Let n and $\alpha > 0$ be given, $\varepsilon = n^{-\alpha}$, and ℓ, m, k as specified in Protocol B (described in Figure 3.)

Modeling.

Let $x = (x_i), y = (y_i), a = (a_i), b = (b_i) \in \big(\{0,1\}^k\big)^m$ denote the boxes' respective input and output strings in Protocol B, and denote the corresponding random variables by $X = (X_i), Y = (Y_i), A = (A_i), B = (B_i) \in \big(\{0,1\}^k\big)^m$. In contrast to Section 4, here we require the behavior of the boxes $\mathcal{A}, \mathcal{B}$ to follow the laws of quantum mechanics. Let $\rho_{\mathbf{ABE}}$ denote the state of the system at the start of the protocol. Here $\mathbf{A}, \mathbf{B}$ denote registers held by $\mathcal{A}, \mathcal{B}$ respectively, while $\mathbf{E}$ denotes a register held by the environment (the potential eavesdropper Eve). We could take $\rho_{\mathbf{ABE}}$ to be pure, but this will not be necessary.

At every step $i \in [km]$ of the protocol, Alice and Bob each make a binary-outcome measurement $\{A_{i,x}^0, A_{i,x}^1\}$ and $\{B_{i,y}^0, B_{i,y}^1\}$ respectively. In general their measurement may also depend on past inputs and outputs, but without loss of generality we may assume that those are recorded in the post-measurement state $\rho_{\mathbf{ABE}}^{h_i}$ resulting from $\mathcal{A}$ and $\mathcal{B}$'s measurements in previous rounds (here, as in Section 4, $h_i = (a_{<i}, b_{<i}, x_{<i}, y_{<i})$ denotes the protocol history). For every $i \in [km]$ we may then write

$$p_{A_i B_i | X_i Y_i H_i}(a_i, b_i | x_i, y_i, h_i) = \mathrm{Tr}\big((A_{i,x_i}^{a_i} \otimes B_{i,y_i}^{b_i} \otimes \mathbb{I}_{\mathbf{E}})\, \rho_{\mathbf{ABE}}^{h_i}\big). \quad (8)$$

Assuming the conditions of Lemma 9 are met, let V be the fixed subset of $\{0,1\}^{mk}$, of size v, whose existence is guaranteed in its conclusion. For every v-bit string z let $\{M_v^e\}_{e \in \{0,1\}^{mk}}$ be the measurement on register $\mathbf{E}$ whose existence is also guaranteed in the lemma. V and M depend on the state $\rho_{\mathbf{XYE}}$ and the measurements performed by $\mathcal{A}$ and $\mathcal{B}$, but not on the specific execution of the protocol performed by the user: as long as $\mathcal{A}$ and $\mathcal{B}$ are fixed they are, too. We introduce two new random variables to model the outcomes obtained from performing the measurement $\{M^e_z\}$ on register $\mathbf{E}$, for different choices of z. We use $E^A = (E^A_i) \in (\{0,1\}^k)^m$ to denote the outcome when the string z is the string a_V taken from $\mathcal{A}$'s outputs, and $E^B = (E^B_i) \in (\{0,1\}^k)^m$ to denote its outcome when it is the string b_V taken from $\mathcal{B}$'s output.

Let G^A be the event that $d_H(E^A, B) < f_e$, and G^B the event that $d_H(E^B, B) < f_e$, where $f_e > 0$ is a parameter to be specified later. Let $j \in T$ be an index that runs over the blocks that have been designated as Bell blocks in Step 2. of the protocol (T itself is a random variable). Given a Bell block j, let G^A_j be a boolean random variable such that $G^A_j = 1$ if and only if either $d_H(E^A_j, B) < 0.01$ and $Y_j = (A,0)$, or $d_H(E^A_j, B) < 0.17$ and $Y_j = (B,0)$. Define G^B_j symmetrically with respect to E^B instead of E^A.

Finally, for $i \in [m]$, let CHSH_i be the following event:

$$\mathrm{CHSH}_i = \begin{cases} A_i = B_i & \text{if } X_i = Y_i, \\ d_H(A_i, B_i) \le 0.16 & \text{if } Y_i = (B,0), \\ d_H(A_i, B_i) \in [0.49, 0.51] & \text{if } X_i = (A,1) \\ & \text{and } Y_i = (A,0). \end{cases}$$

Honest CHSH boxes as described above satisfy CHSH_i with probability $1 - 2^{-\Omega(k)}$. Let $\mathrm{CHSH} = \bigwedge_i \mathrm{CHSH}_i$.

We prove Theorem 8 by contradiction. Assume that the theorem's conclusions are violated, so that (i) $H^\varepsilon_\infty(B'|\mathbf{E}) \ge n$, where B' is a random variable describing the distribution of $\mathcal{B}$'s outputs conditioned on CHSH, and $\Pr(\mathrm{CHSH}) \le \varepsilon$. Here $\varepsilon = n^{-\alpha}$, where $\alpha > 0$ is a parameter.

The first step is to apply Lemma 9 with $X = B'$. The conclusion of the lemma is that there exists a subset $V \subseteq [km]$ of size $|V| = O(n \log^2 n)$ such that, letting $f_e = 1/(\log mk)$, we have $p_s := \Pr(G^B|\mathrm{CHSH}) = \Omega(\varepsilon^7/n^6) = \Omega(n^{-6-7\alpha})$, where G^B denotes the event that Eve correctly predicts B on a fraction at least $1 - f_e$ of positions. Since in Protocol B the Bell blocks form only a very small fraction of the total, a priori it could still be that Eve's prediction is systematically wrong on all Bell blocks, preventing us from successfully using them in the guessing game.

The following claim shows Eve's errors cannot be concentrated in the Bell blocks. The intuition is the following. If $\mathcal{B}$'s input in a Bell block is $(A,0)$ then nothing distinguishes this block from most others, so that Eve's prediction has no reason of being less correct than average. However, blocks in which its input is $(B,0)$ are distinguished. We rule out the possibility that Eve's errors are concentrated in such blocks by appealing to the no-signaling condition between Eve and $\mathcal{A}$. Indeed, about half of Bell blocks in which $\mathcal{B}$'s input is $(B,0)$ are such that $\mathcal{A}$'s input for the same block is $(A,0)$: looking only at $\mathcal{A}$'s inputs they are indistinguishable from most other blocks. We will argue that, as long as the CHSH constraint is satisfied, Eve might as well have been given the advice bits by Alice, in which case there is no reason for her to make more errors than average in those blocks.

CLAIM 10. *Let T be the set of Bell blocks selected in Protocol B. Then there exists a constant $c_e < 10^{-3}$ such that the following holds.*

$$\Pr\Big(\mathrm{E}_{j\in T}\big[\,G^A_j\,\big] > 1 - \frac{c_e}{\log n}, \mathrm{CHSH}\Big) = \Omega(p_s\varepsilon) = \Omega\big(n^{-6-8\alpha}\big).$$

PROOF. By definition, $\Pr(G^B) \ge p_s \Pr(\mathrm{CHSH}) \ge p_s\varepsilon$. Conditioned on G^B, by Markov's inequality it must be that $d_H(E^B, B) < 0.01$ on a fraction at least $1 - 100 f_e$ of blocks in which the input to B was $(A,0)$. Let $f'_e = 100 f_e$. Let $\eta = 2^{-10^{-5} f'_e |T|/(2\cdot 100^2)}$, and assume C chosen large enough so that $\eta \le p_s\varepsilon/6 = \Omega(n^{-6-8\alpha})$. This is possible since $|T|$ is sharply concentrated around $C \log^2 \ell$ and $f'_e = \Omega(1/\log \ell)$.

Among the blocks in which Eve's prediction is correct, nothing distinguishes those Bell blocks in which $\mathcal{B}$'s input is $(A,0)$: indeed, we may think of those only being designated as Bell blocks *after* Eve has made her prediction. By a Chernoff bound the probability that more than a fraction $2f'_e$ of such blocks fall into those for which G^B_j does not hold is upper-bounded by η. Hence the following holds

$$\Pr\big(\mathrm{E}_{j\in T: Y_j=(A,0)}\, G^B_j > 1 - 2f'_e | G^B\big) \ge 1 - \eta. \quad (9)$$

Since V is a fixed subset of $[km]$ of size $|V| = O(n \log^2 m)$, the probability that any of the randomly chosen $O(\log^2 \ell)$ Bell blocks intersects it is at most $O(n^{2-(10+8\alpha)} \log^4 n)$ for large enough n. This quantity is much smaller than (our upper bound on) η, and for the remainder of the proof we will neglect the chance of this happening.

Conditioning further on CHSH can only blow-up the error by a factor $1/\Pr(\mathrm{CHSH}|G^B) \le 1/(p_s\varepsilon)$. In that case $G^A = G^B$ (Eve's prediction only depends on the advice bits she is given, and these bits are the same when taken from either $\mathcal{A}$ and $\mathcal{B}$'s outputs whenever the CHSH condition holds), so we obtain:

$$\begin{aligned} &\frac{\Pr\big(\mathrm{E}_{j\in T: Y_j=(A,0)}\, G^A_j > 1 - 2f'_e, \mathrm{CHSH}|G^A\big)}{\Pr\big(\mathrm{CHSH}|G^A\big)} \\ &= \Pr\big(\mathrm{E}_{j\in T: Y_j=(A,0)}\, G^A_j > 1 - 2f'_e | G^A, \mathrm{CHSH}\big) \\ &\ge 1 - \eta/(p_s\varepsilon). \end{aligned} \quad (10)$$

Suppose Eve makes more than a fraction $5f'_e$ of errors in predicting $\mathcal{A}$'s output on those Bell blocks in which its input is $(A,0)$. By a Chernoff bound with probability at least $1 - \eta$ the input to $\mathcal{B}$ will also be $(A,0)$ in at least 40% of those blocks. Indeed, since Eve now receives her advice bits from $\mathcal{A}$'s outputs, by the no-signaling condition we may think of the choice of $\mathcal{B}$'s inputs as being made *after* both Alice and Eve have completed their measurements. Whenever this condition holds, Eve's prediction will be wrong on a total fraction more than $2f'_e$ of $\mathcal{B}$'s $(A,0)$-input Bell blocks, contradicting (10). Indeed, whenever CHSH holds, if the input to both boxes is $(A,0)$ then Eve being correct in predicting $\mathcal{B}$'s output is equivalent to her being correct in predicting $\mathcal{A}$'s output. Hence the following holds:

$$\begin{aligned} &\Pr\big(\mathrm{E}_{j\in T: X_j=(A,0)}\, G^A_j > 1 - 5f'_e, \mathrm{CHSH}|G^A\big) \\ &\ge \Pr\big(\mathrm{E}_{j\in T: Y_j=(A,0)}\, G^A_j > 1 - 2f'_e, \mathrm{CHSH}|G^A\big) - \eta \\ &\ge (1 - \eta/(p_s\varepsilon)) \Pr\big(\mathrm{CHSH}|G^A\big) - \eta \\ &\ge (1 - 2\eta/(p_s\varepsilon)) \Pr\big(\mathrm{CHSH}|G^A\big), \end{aligned} \quad (11)$$

where the second inequality follows from(10) and the last uses $\Pr(\mathrm{CHSH}|G^A) \ge p_s\varepsilon$. As previously, since $G^A \wedge \mathrm{CHSH} = G^B \wedge \mathrm{CHSH}$, (11) implies the following:

$$\begin{aligned} &\Pr\big(\mathrm{E}_{j\in T: X_j=(A,0)}\, G^B_j > 1 - 5f'_e | G^B, \mathrm{CHSH}\big) \\ &\ge 1 - 2\eta/(p_s\varepsilon). \end{aligned} \quad (12)$$

Next, suppose Eve makes a prediction that is wrong on a fraction at least $14f'_e$ of the Bell blocks, irrespective of Bob's inputs. Then again with high probability at least 40% of the inputs to $\mathcal{A}$ in those blocks will be $(A,0)$, implying that Eve is wrong on more than a fraction $5f'_e$ of $\mathcal{A}$'s $(A,0)$ inputs, contradicting (12). Hence the following is proven just as (11) was:

$$\Pr\left(\mathrm{E}_{j\in T}\, G_j^B > 1-14f'_e | G^B, \mathrm{CHSH}\right) \geq 1-3\eta/(p_s\varepsilon). \quad (13)$$

Hence

$$\Pr\left(\mathrm{E}_{j\in T}\, G_j^A > 1-14f'_e | G^A, \mathrm{CHSH}\right) \geq 1-3\eta/(p_s\varepsilon),$$

which is greater than $1/2$ given our choice of η. Removing all conditioning, whenever Eve is given advice bits by Alice, it holds that

$$\Pr\left(\mathrm{E}_{j\in T}\, G_j^A > 1-14f'_e, \mathrm{CHSH}\right) \geq \Omega(p_s\varepsilon).$$

□

Based on Claim 10 we can show an analogue of Claim 7 which will let us complete the reduction to the guessing game. Claim 10 shows that with probability $\Omega(p_s\varepsilon)$ Eve's prediction will be correct on a fraction at least $1-c_e/\log n$ of Bell blocks. Since there are $O(\log^2 n)$ such blocks in Protocol B, with the same probability Eve only makes errors on a total number $w_e = O(\log n)$ of Bell blocks. Group the Bell blocks in groups of $20w_e$ successive blocks, and let k be an index that runs over such groups; there are $O(\log n)$ of them. Let G_k^A be the event that Eve's prediction is correct in at least 99% of the Bell blocks in group k: $G_k^A = 1$ if and only if $\mathrm{E}_{j\sim k} G_j^A \geq 0.99$, where the average is taken over the Bell blocks comprising group k. By Markov's inequality, it follows from Claim 10 that $\Pr(\wedge_k G_k^A, \mathrm{CHSH}) = \Omega(p_s\varepsilon)$.

CLAIM 11. *For all large enough n there exists a Bell block $j_0 \in T$ such that, in that block, it is highly likely that both Eve's prediction (when given advice bits from $\mathcal{A}$'s output) is correct and the CHSH constraint is satisfied, conditioned on this being so in past iterations:*

$$\Pr(G_{j_0}^A, CHSH_{j_0} | CHSH_{j<j_0}, G_{k<k_0}^A) \geq 0.98, \qquad (14)$$

where k_0 is the index of the group containing the j_0-th Bell block.

PROOF. By the chain rule, since there are $O(\log n)$ groups there will exist a group k_0 in which Eve's prediction is correct, and the CHSH condition is satisfied, with probability at least 0.99, when conditioned on the same holding of all previous groups. Since by definition Eve being correct in the group means that she is correct in 99% of that group's blocks, there is a specific block j_0 in which she is correct with probability at least 0.98. □

The reduction to the guessing game should now be clear, and follows along the same lines as the proof of Theorem 6 given in Section 4. Alice and Bob run protocol B, including the selection of all Bell blocks T, with the boxes $\mathcal{A}$ and $\mathcal{B}$, up to the j_0-th Bell block (excluded). Bob communicates $\mathcal{B}$'s outputs up till that block to Alice. They check that the CHSH constraint is satisfied in all blocks previous to the j_0-th; if not they abort. The guessing game can now start: Alice and Bob are separated and Bob is given his secret input y. If $y = 0$ then he chooses $(A,0)$ as input to $\mathcal{B}$ in the j_0-th block; otherwise he chooses $(B,0)$. He then completes the protocol honestly. Alice chooses an input $x \in \{(A,0),(A,1)\}$ at random for the j_0-th block, and then completes the protocol honestly.

In order to help her guess Bob's input, Alice has access to the eavesdropper Eve. Alice gives the bits a_V taken from $\mathcal{A}$'s output string a as advice bits to Eve. Eve makes a prediction e for Bob's output. Alice checks that the event $G_{<k_0}^A$ is satisfied. If not she aborts. If so, by Claim 11 we know that both CHSH_{j_0} and $G_{j_0}^A$ are satisfied with probability at least 0.98, so this must be so with probability at least 0.92 for each of the four possible pair of inputs (x,y) given to $\mathcal{A}$ and $\mathcal{B}$ in the j_0-th block.

Alice makes her prediction as follows: if either $\mathcal{A}$'s input was $(A,0)$ and its output agrees with Eve's prediction on at least a 0.99 fraction of positions (in the j_0-th block), or $\mathcal{A}$'s input was $(A,1)$ and its output agrees with Eve's prediction on a fraction of positions that is between 0.48 and 0.52 she claims "Bod had a 0". Otherwise she claims "Bob had a 1".

Clearly if Bob is using $(A,0)$ as his input then Alice will predict correctly with probability at least 0.92, since in that case $G_{j_0}^A$ implies that Eve predicts $\mathcal{B}$'s output with at most 1% of error. If he is using $(B,1)$ then $G_{j_0}^A$ implies that Eve's prediction will be within 0.17 relative Hamming distance of $\mathcal{B}$'s output in block j_0. By the CHSH constraint $\mathcal{A}$'s output must also be within 0.16 of $\mathcal{B}$'s output, whatever input Alice chooses. Hence $\mathcal{A}$'s output is always within $0.43 < 0.49$ of $\mathcal{B}$'s, meaning Alice will correctly claim Bob had a 1 whenever her input is $(A,1)$. Hence in that case she correctly predicts Bob's input with probability at least $0.92/2$.

Overall, conditioned on Alice not aborting her prediction is correct with probability at least 0.69 over the choice of a random input for Bob, indicating a violation of the no-signaling assumption on the boxes and proving Theorem 8.

Acknowledgments.

We thank Matthew Coudron for useful comments on a preliminary draft of this paper.

6. REFERENCES

[1] A. Ambainis, A. Nayak, A. Ta-Shma, and U. Vazirani. Dense quantum coding and quantum finite automata. *Journal of the ACM*, 49(4):496–511, 2002.

[2] J. S. Bell. On the Einstein-Podolsky-Rosen paradox. *Physics*, 1:195–200, 1964.

[3] J. S. Bell. On the problem of hidden variables in quantum theory. *Rev. Mod. Phys.*, 38:447–452, 1966.

[4] M. Blum and S. Micali. How to generate cryptographically strong sequences of pseudo-random bits. *SIAM J. Comput.*, 13:850–864, November 1984.

[5] J. F. Clauser, M. A. Horne, A. Shimony, and R. A. Holt. Proposed experiment to test local hidden-variable theories. *Phys. Rev. Lett.*, 23:880–884, 1969.

[6] R. Colbeck. *Quantum And Relativistic Protocols For Secure Multi-Party Computation.* PhD thesis, Trinity College, University of Cambridge, Nov. 2009.

[7] R. Colbeck and A. Kent. Private randomness expansion with untrusted devices. *Journal of Physics A: Mathematical and Theoretical*, 44(9):095305, 2011.

[8] R. Colbeck and R. Renner. Free randomness amplification. arXiv:1105.3195, 2011.

[9] A. De, C. Portmann, R. Renner, and T. Vidick. Trevisan's extractor in the presence of quantum side information. *CoRR*, abs/0912.5, 2009.
[10] A. De and T. Vidick. Near-optimal extractors against quantum storage. In *Proceedings of the 42nd ACM symposium on Theory of computing*, STOC '10, pages 161–170, New York, NY, USA, 2010. ACM.
[11] A. Einstein, P. Podolsky, and N. Rosen. Can quantum-mechanical description of physical reality be considered complete? *Phys. Rev.*, 47:777–780, 1935.
[12] S. Fehr, R. Gelles, and C. Schaffner. Security and composability of randomness expansion from Bell inequalities. Technical report arXiv:1111.6052, 2011.
[13] D. Gavinsky, J. Kempe, I. Kerenidis, R. Raz, and R. de Wolf. Exponential separation for one-way quantum communication complexity, with applications to cryptography. *SIAM Journal of Computing*, 38(5):1695–1708, 2008. Preliminary version in *Proc. of STOC 2007*.
[14] V. Guruswami, C. Umans, and S. Vadhan. Unbalanced expanders and randomness extractors from parvaresh-vardy codes. In *Proceedings of the Twenty-Second Annual IEEE Conference on Computational Complexity, CCC '07*, pages 96–108, Washington, DC, USA, 2007. IEEE Computer Society.
[15] T. Hartman and R. Raz. On the distribution of the number of roots of polynomials and explicit weak designs. *Random Structures and Algorithms*, 23(3):235–263, 2003.
[16] R. Impagliazzo, R. Jaiswal, and V. Kabanets. Approximately list-decoding direct product codes and uniform hardness amplification. In *Foundations of Computer Science, 2006. FOCS '06. 47th Annual IEEE Symposium on*, pages 187 –196, oct. 2006.
[17] A. Knuth, D. Yao. *Algorithms and Complexity: New Directions and Recent Results*, Chapter *The complexity of nonuniform random number generation.* Academic Press, 1976.
[18] R. König, R. Renner, and C. Schaffner. The operational meaning of min- and max-entropy. *IEEE Transactions on Information Theory*, 55(9):4337–4347, 2009.
[19] R. König and B. Terhal. The bounded storage model in presence of a quantum adversary. *IEEE Transactions on Information Theory*, 54(2):749–762, 2008.
[20] M. Nielsen and I. Chuang. *Quantum Computation and Quantum Information.* Cambridge University Press, 2000.
[21] S. Pironio, A. Acin, S. Massar, A. B. De La Giroday, D. N. Matsukevich, P. Maunz, S. Olmschenk, D. Hayes, L. Luo, T. A. Manning, and et al. Random numbers certified by Bell's theorem. *Nature*, 464(7291):10, 2009.
[22] S. Pironio and S. Massar. Security of practical private randomness generation. Technical report arXiv:1111.6056, 2011.
[23] R. Renner. *Security of Quantum Key Distribution.* PhD thesis, Swiss Federal Institute of Technology Zurich, Sept. 2005.
[24] M. Santha and U. V. Vazirani. Generating quasi-random sequences from slightly-random sources. In *Proceedings of the 25th Annual Symposium on Foundations of Computer Science*, pages 434–440, Washington, DC, USA, 1984. IEEE Computer Society.
[25] R. Shaltiel. Recent developments in explicit constructions of extractors. *Bulletin of the European Association for Theoretical Computer Science*, 77:67–95, June 2002.
[26] A. Shamir. On the generation of cryptographically strong pseudorandom sequences. *ACM Trans. Comput. Syst.*, 1:38–44, February 1983.
[27] A. Ta-Shma. Short seed extractors against quantum storage. In *Proceedings of the 41st annual ACM symposium on Theory of computing, STOC '09*, pages 401–408, New York, NY, USA, 2009. ACM.
[28] G. Taylor and G. Cox. Behind intel's new random-number generator. *IEEE Spectrum*, September 2011.
[29] L. Trevisan. Extractors and pseudorandom generators. *J. ACM*, 48:860–879, July 2001.
[30] A. C. Yao. Theory and application of trapdoor functions. In *Proceedings of the 23rd IEEE Annual Symposium on Foundations of Computer Science (FOCS)*, SFCS '82, pages 80–91, Washington, DC, USA, 1982.
[31] D. Zuckerman. General weak random sources. In *Proceedings of the 31st Annual Symposium on Foundations of Computer Science*, pages 534–543. IEEE Comput. Soc. Press, 1990.

APPENDIX

A. PROOF OF LEMMA 9

In this appendix we give the proof of Lemma 9. The proof crucially uses properties of a specific extractor construction based on Trevisan's construction paradigm [29]. A specific construction based on this paradigm was first shown to be secure in the presence of quantum bounded-storage adversaries in [27]. The construction we use here was shown secure in the more general setting of quantum bounded-information adversaries in [9]. We first describe the extractor.

A.1 The t-XOR extractor

The t-XOR extractor E_t, parametrized by an integer t, follows Trevisan's general construction paradigm [29]. It is based on two main ingredients, the t-XOR code and a combinatorial design construction due to Hartman and Raz [15]. For us, only the details of the t-XOR code will be important.

The t-XOR code.

Given integers m and $t \leq m$, let $C_t : \{0,1\}^m \to \{0,1\}^{\binom{m}{t}}$ map an m-bit string to the string of parities of all subsets of t out of its m bits. Two properties of this encoding will be relevant for us. The first is that it is locally computable: each bit of the codeword only depends on t bits of the input. The second is that it is approximately list-decodable (see Lemma 16 below).

Combinatorial designs.

Given integers s, m, r and $\rho > 0$, a collection of subsets $S_1, \ldots, S_r \subseteq [s]$ is called a (s, m, r, ρ) weak design if for all $i \in [r]$, $|S_i| = m$ and for all j, $\sum_{i<j} 2^{|S_i \cap S_j|} \leq \rho(r-1)$. For our purposes it will suffice to note that Hartman and

Raz [15] proved the existence of a $(s, m, r, 1+\gamma)$ design for every m, $0 < \gamma < 1/2$, $s = O(m^2 \log 1/\gamma)$ and $r > s^{\Omega(\log s)}$.

The t-XOR extractor.

We define the extractor that we will use in the proof of Lemma 9.

DEFINITION 12. *Let m, r, t, s be given integers such that $t = O(\log m)$ and $s = O(\log^4 n)$. Then $E_t : \{0,1\}^m \times \{0,1\}^s \to \{0,1\}^r$ maps $(x, y) \in \{0,1\}^m \times \{0,1\}^s$ to $C_t(x)_{y_{S_1}}, \dots, C_t(x)_{y_{S_r}}$, where $(S_1, \dots, S_r)$ is a $(s, t\log m, r, 5/4)$ design and y_{S_i} designates the bits of y indexed by S_i, interpreted as a t-element subset of $[m]$.*

While, as shown in Corollary 5.11 in [9], E_t is a strong extractor with good parameters, we will not use this fact directly. Rather, we will use specific properties that arise from the "reconstruction paradigm"-based *proof* that it is an extractor secure against quantum adversaries. Indeed, one may argue that Lemma 9 is implicit in the proof of security of E_t given in [9]. Since it does not follow directly from the mere statement that E_t is an extractor, we give more details here. We will show the following lemma, which is more general than Lemma 9.

LEMMA 13. *Let m, r, t be integers, $\varepsilon > 0$, and suppose that $t = O(\log^2 m)$. Let ρ_{XE} be a cq-state such that X is a random variable distributed over m-bit strings. Let U_r be uniformly distributed over r-bit strings, and suppose that*

$$\left\|\rho_{Ext(X,Y)E} - \rho_{U_r} \otimes \rho_E\right\|_{tr} > \varepsilon, \tag{15}$$

i.e. an adversary Eve holding register E can distinguish the output of the extractor from a uniformly random r-bit string. Then there exists a fixed subset $V \subseteq [m]$ of size $|V| = O(tr)$ such that, given the string X_V as advice, with probability at least $\Omega(\varepsilon^2/r^2)$ over the choice of $x \sim p_X$ and her own randomness Eve can output a list of $\ell = O(r^4/\varepsilon^4)$ strings $\tilde{x}^1, \dots, \tilde{x}^\ell$ such that there is an $i \in [\ell]$, $d_H(\tilde{x}^i, x) \le (2/t)\ln(4r/\varepsilon)$.

It is not hard to see why Lemma 13 implies Lemma 9. First note that if r is chosen in Lemma 13 so that $r > 2H_\infty^\varepsilon(X|E)$ then the assumption (15) is automatically satisfied as a consequence of the data processing inequality.[10] The conclusion of Lemma 9 then follows from that of Lemma 13 by having Eve output a random string out of her ℓ predictions, and choosing $t = \Omega(\log^2 m)$ to ensure that the bound $(2/t)\ln(4r/\varepsilon) \le 1/\log m$ holds.

In the remainder of this section we sketch the proof of Lemma 13. The first step, explained in Section A.2, consists in using a hybrid argument to show that, given (15), Eve can predict a random t-XOR of X's bits with reasonable success probability, given sufficiently many "advice bits" about X. In the second step, detailed in Section A.3, we show using an argument due to Koenig and Terhal [19] that this implies the adversary can in fact recover most t-XORs of X, simultaneously. Finally, in Section A.4 we use the list-decoding properties of the XOR code to show that as a consequence the adversary can with good probability produce a string that agrees with X on a large fraction of coordinates.

[10]The extra randomness coming from the seed of the extractor will be small, as its size can be taken to be $s = O(\log^4 m)$.

A.2 The hybrid argument

Suppose that (15) holds. Proposition 4.4 from [9] shows that a standard hybrid argument, together with properties of Trevisan's extractor (specifically the use of the seed through combinatorial designs), can be used to show the following claim.

CLAIM 14. *There exists a subset $V \subseteq [m]$ of size $|V| = O(tr)$ such that, given the bits X_V, Eve can predict a random t-XOR of the bits of X with advantage ε/r. Formally,*

$$\left\|\rho_{C_t(X)_Y YVE} - \rho_{U_1} \otimes \rho_Y \otimes \rho_{VE}\right\|_{tr} > \frac{\varepsilon}{r}, \tag{16}$$

where Y is a random variable uniformly distributed over $\left[\binom{m}{t}\right]$ and V is a register containing the bits of X indexed by V.

A.3 Recovering all t-XORs.

The next step in the proof of Lemma 13 is to argue that Eq. (16) implies that an adversary given access to $E' = VE$ can predict not only a random XOR of X, but a string Z of length $\binom{m}{t}$ such that Z agrees with the string $C_t(X)$ of all t-XOR's of X in a significant fraction of positions. Classically this is trivial, as one can just repeat the single-bit prediction procedure guaranteed by (16) for all possible choices Y of the t bits whose parity one is trying to compute. In the quantum setting it is more subtle. We will follow an argument from [19] showing that (16) implies that there is a single measurement, independent of Y, that one can perform on E and using the (classical) result of which one can predict the bits $C_t(X)_Y$ with good success on average (over the measurement's outcome and the choice of Y).

CLAIM 15. *Suppose (16) holds. Then there exists a measurement $\mathcal{F}$, with outcomes in $\{0,1\}^m$, such that*

$$\Pr_{x \sim p_X,\, y \sim U_{t\log m}}\big(C_t(x)_Y = C_t(\mathcal{F}(VE))_y\big) \ge \frac{1}{2} + \frac{\varepsilon^2}{4r^2}, \tag{17}$$

where $\mathcal{F}(VE)$ denotes the outcome of $\mathcal{F}$ when performed on the cq-state ρ_{VE}.

PROOF. Our argument closely follows the proof of Theorem III.1 from [19]. Given an arbitrary cq-state ρ_{ZQ}, define the non-uniformity of Z given Q as

$$d(Z \leftarrow Q) := \left\|\rho_{ZQ} - \rho_{U_z} \otimes \rho_Q\right\|_{tr}.$$

Let ρ_x denote the state contained in registers VE, conditioned on $X = x$. For a fixed string y, define two states

$$\rho_0^y := \sum_{x:\, C_t(x)_y = 0} p_X(x)\,\rho_x,$$

$$\rho_1^y := \sum_{x:\, C_t(x)_y = 1} p_X(x)\,\rho_x.$$

Then, by definition $d\big(C_t(X)_y \leftarrow VE\big) = \left\|\rho_0^y - \rho_1^y\right\|_{tr}$ is the adversary's maximum success probability in distinguishing those states ρ_x which correspond to an XOR of 0 from those which correspond to an XOR of 1. Let $\mathcal{E}_y = \{E_y^0, E_y^1\}$ be the pretty good measurement corresponding to the pair of states $\{\rho_0^y, \rho_1^y\}$:

$$E_y^0 = \rho_{VE}^{-1/2}\rho_0^y\rho_{VE}^{-1/2} \quad \text{and} \quad E_y^1 = \rho_{VE}^{-1/2}\rho_1^y\rho_{VE}^{-1/2},$$

where $\rho_{VE} = \sum_x P_X(x)\rho_x$. Lemma 2 from [19] (more precisely, Eq. (19)), shows that the following holds as a consequence of (16):

$$\sqrt{\mathrm{E}_y\big[\,2\,d\big(C_t(X)_y \leftarrow \mathcal{E}^y(VE)\big)\big]} + d(C_t(X)_Y \leftarrow Y) > \frac{\varepsilon}{r}, \tag{18}$$

where $\mathcal{E}^y(VE)$ is the result of the POVM $\mathcal{E}^y$ applied on ρ_{VE}, and $d(C_t(X)_Y \leftarrow Y)$ is the distance from uniform of the one-bit extractor's output, in the absence of the adversary. We may as well assume this term to be small: indeed, if it is more than $\varepsilon/(2r)$ then (17) is proved without even having to resort to the quantum system E. Hence (18) implies

$$\mathrm{E}_y\left[\,d\big(C_t(X)_y \leftarrow \mathcal{E}^y_{pgm}(VE)\big)\,\right] > \frac{\varepsilon^2}{2r^2},$$

which can be equivalently re-written as

$$\mathrm{E}_y\left[\,\mathrm{Tr}\big(E_y^0\,\rho_y^0\big) + \mathrm{Tr}\big(E_y^1\,\rho_y^1\big)\,\right] > \frac{1}{2} + \frac{\varepsilon^2}{4r^2}. \tag{19}$$

Following the argument in [19], we define a new measurement $\mathcal{F}$ with outcomes in $\{0,1\}^m$ and POVM elements $F^x = P_X(x)\rho_{VE}^{-1/2}\rho_x\,\rho_{VE}^{-1/2}$. The important point to notice is that for $z \in \{0,1\}$ we have $E_y^z = \sum_{x:\,C_t(x)_y=z} F^x$, hence (19) can be re-written as

$$\mathrm{E}_y\Bigg[\sum_{b:\,C_t(b)_y=0}\mathrm{Tr}\big(F^x\,\rho_y^0\big) + \sum_{b:\,C_t(b)_y=1}\mathrm{Tr}\big(F^x\,\rho_y^1\big)\Bigg] > \frac{1}{2} + \frac{\varepsilon^2}{4r^2},$$

which is exactly (17). □

A.4 List-decoding the XOR code.

The following lemma (for a reference, see [16], Lemma 42) states the list-decoding properties of the t-XOR code C_t that are important for us.

LEMMA 16. *For every $\eta > 2t^2/2^m$ and $z \in (\{0,1\}^m)^t$, there is a list of $\ell \leq 4/\eta^2$ elements $x^1, \ldots, x^\ell \in \{0,1\}^m$ such that the following holds: for every $z' \in \{0,1\}^m$ which satisfies*

$$\Pr_{\{y_1,\ldots,y_t\}\in\binom{m}{t}}\big[z_{(y_1,\ldots,y_t)} = \oplus_{i=1}^t z'_{y_i}\big] \geq \frac{1}{2} + \eta,$$

there is an $i \in [\ell]$ such that

$$\Pr_{y\sim\mathcal{U}_N}\big[x^i_y = z'_y\big] \geq 1 - \delta,$$

with $\delta = (1/t)\ln(2/\eta)$.

Claim 15 implies that, with probability at least $\varepsilon^2/(8r^2)$ over the choice of x and over Eve's own randomness, when measuring her system with $\mathcal{F}$ she will obtain a string $\tilde{z}$ whose t-XORs agree with those of x with probability at least $1/2 + \varepsilon^2/(8r^2)$. Lemma 16 shows that in that case she can recover a list of at most $2^8 r^4/\varepsilon^4$ "candidate" strings $\tilde{z}^i$ such that there exists at least one of these strings which agrees with x at a (possibly adversarial) fraction $1-\delta$ of positions, where $\delta = (2/t)\ln(4r/\varepsilon)$ given our choice of parameters. Hence Lemma 13 is proved.

Span Programs for Functions with Constant-Sized 1-certificates

[Extended Abstract]

Aleksandrs Belovs
University of Latvia
Raina bulv. 19
Riga, Latvia, LV-1586
stiboh@gmail.com

ABSTRACT

Besides the Hidden Subgroup Problem, the second large class of quantum speed-ups is for functions with constant-sized 1-certificates. This includes the OR function, solvable by the Grover algorithm, the element distinctness, the triangle and other problems. The usual way to solve them is by quantum walk on the Johnson graph.

We propose a solution for the same problems using span programs. The span program is a computational model equivalent to the quantum query algorithm in its strength, and yet very different in its outfit.

We prove the power of our approach by designing a quantum algorithm for the triangle problem with query complexity $O(n^{35/27})$ that is better than $O(n^{13/10})$ of the best previously known algorithm by Magniez *et al.*

Categories and Subject Descriptors

H.2.4 [**Database Management**]: Systems—*Query processing*; F.2.2 [**Analysis of Algorithms and Problem Complexity**]: Nonnumerical Algorithms and Problems—*Computations on discrete structures*; G.2.2 [**Discrete Mathematics**]: Graph Theory—*Graph Algorithms*

General Terms

Algorithms

Keywords

Quantum Algorithms

1. INTRODUCTION

In this paper we are interested in quantum query complexity of functions with 1-certificate complexity bounded by a constant. Research on quantum algorithms for such functions was launched shortly after the beginnings of quantum computation. The first example is Grover search [10] for the OR function. The element distinctness and the triangle problems also belong to this class.

One can distinguish two main design paradigms for quantum algorithms for such functions. The first one includes application of the Grover search and its close relative—quantum amplitude amplification. This paradigm resulted in the algorithm for the collision problem with complexity $O(n^{1/3})$ by Brassard *et al.* [7], the $O(n^{3/4})$-algorithm for the element distinctness problem by Buhrman *et al.* [9], the $O(n^{10/7})$-algorithm for the triangle problem by Magniez *et al.* [13], and others.

The second paradigm is based on quantum walks on the Johnson graph. It was pioneered by Ambainis with his $O(n^{2/3})$-algorithm for the element distinctness problem [3]. The triangle-finding algorithm with complexity $O(n^{13/10})$ by Magniez *et al.* [13] also belongs to this class.

In this paper, we develop an alternative approach to these problems using the computational model of a *learning graph*. We build a reduction from learning graphs to quantum query algorithms using span programs. The span program is a computational model proven by Reichardt to be equivalent to the quantum query algorithm [15, 16]. Despite this equivalence, the actual applications of this model have been limited, mostly, to formulae evaluation [17].

We show that span programs are useful for other well-studied problems in quantum computation. We build analogues of the algorithms for the OR function and the element distinctness problem with optimal complexity. We demonstrate the power of our approach by designing an algorithm for the triangle problem with complexity $O(n^{35/27})$, that is better than $O(n^{13/10})$ of the algorithm by Magniez *et al.*

The paper is organized as follows. In Section 2, we review the notions of certificate complexity, span programs, and define the problems being solved. In Section 3, we define learning graphs as our approach to functions with small 1-certificate complexity. In Section 4, we introduce the concept of stages that is illustrated by an example of a learning graph for the element distinctness problem. In Section 5, we discuss how symmetry of the problem can be used in the design of learning graphs, and finally, in Section 6, we give our algorithm for the triangle problem.

2. PRELIMINARIES

For the basic concepts of quantum algorithms, the reader may refer to [14]. We are interested in the query complexity of quantum algorithms, i.e., we measure the complexity of a problem by the number of queries to the input the best algorithm should make. Clearly, the query complexity provides a lower bound on the time complexity. For many algorithms, the query complexity can be analyzed easier than the time complexity. For the definition of query complexity and its basic properties, as well as the properties of certificate complexity, a good reference is [8].

Consider a multivariable function $f : \mathcal{D} \to \{0,1\}$, with domain $\mathcal{D} \subseteq [m]^n$. With use $[m]$ to denote $\{1,2,\dots,m\}$. We identify the set of input variables with $[n]$. An *assignment* is a function $\sigma : S \to [m]$ with $S \subseteq [n]$. One should think of this function as fixing values for input variables in S. We say an input $x = (x_i)_{i\in[n]}$ *agrees* with assignment σ if $\sigma(i) = x_i$ for all $i \in S$. By x_S we denote the only assignment with domain S agreeing with x. The *size* of the assignment is the size of its domain S.

An assignment σ is called a *b-certificate* for f, if any input from $\mathcal{D}$ consistent with σ is mapped to b by f. The *certificate complexity* $C_x(f)$ of function f on input x is defined as the minimal size of a certificate for f that agrees with x. The b-certificate complexity $C^{(b)}(f)$ is defined as $\max_{x\in f^{-1}(b)} C_x(f)$.

As it has been said, we are interested in algorithms for families of functions such that $C^{(1)}(f)$ remains bounded by a constant. Many quantum algorithms have been constructed for functions from this class. We mostly work with the following two functions:

Element Distinctness Problem.

The *element distinctness* function $f\colon [m]^n \to \{0,1\}$ is defined as follows. The function $f(x_1,\dots,x_n)$ equals 1 iff there are equal elements among $\{x_1,\dots,x_n\}$, i.e., $i \neq j$ such that $x_i = x_j$; otherwise, it's 0. It has 1-certificate complexity 2.

The first quantum algorithm for the element distinctness problem had complexity $O(n^{3/4})$ and was due to Buhrman *et al.* [9]. This was later improved to $O(n^{2/3})$ by Ambainis [3]. This is the first natural problem solved by an algorithm based on a *quantum walk*. This algorithm is optimal due to the results by Aaronson and Shi [1] and Ambainis [2].

Triangle Problem.

Consider a complete graph on n vertices. The input variables of the function are in correspondence to the edges of the graph. Denote by x_{ij}, where $1 \le i < j \le n$, the input variable corresponding to the edge $\widetilde{ij}$. The task is to detect whether there is a triangle with all edges marked by 1, i.e., whether there are indices $i < j < k$ such that $x_{ij} = x_{ik} = x_{jk} = 1$. The 1-certificate complexity of the triangle problem is 3.

The best previously known quantum query algorithm for this problem is due to Magniez *et al.* [13] and has complexity $O(n^{13/10})$. We describe this algorithm in Section 6. In the same section, we improve the complexity to $O(n^{35/27})$. The best known lower bound is just $\Omega(n)$ by a simple reduction from the OR function [9].

2.1 Span Programs

In this section, we define span programs following [15].

Definition 1. A span program $\mathcal{P}$ is specified by a non-zero *target vector* $t \in \mathbb{R}^d$ and sets $V_{1,0}, V_{1,1}, \dots, V_{n,0}, V_{n,1}, V_{\rm free}$ of *input vectors* from $\mathbb{R}^d$.

We use the same notation $V_{i,n}$ and $V_{\rm free}$ to denote matrices having the vectors from the corresponding sets as columns. We say that the input vectors in $V_{i,b}$ are *labeled* by the value b of the ith input variable x_i. The vectors from $V_{\rm free}$ are called *free input vectors*.

Define the following matrix consisting of all input vectors

$$V = \begin{pmatrix} V_{1,0} & V_{1,1} & \cdots & V_{n,0} & V_{n,1} & V_{\rm free}\end{pmatrix}.$$

Also, for an input $x = (x_i) \in \{0,1\}^n$, define the following matrix

$$V(x) = \begin{pmatrix} V_{1,x_1} & V_{2,x_2} & \cdots & V_{n,x_n} & V_{\rm free}\end{pmatrix}.$$

The columns of $V(x)$ are called the *available input vectors*. The other input vectors are called the *false input vectors*.

The span program $\mathcal{P}$ computes a Boolean function $f_{\mathcal{P}} : \{0,1\}^n \to \{0,1\}$ defined as follows: $f_{\mathcal{P}}(x) = 1$ if and only if t lies in the column space of $V(x)$. We say $\mathcal{P}$ *computes* a partial Boolean function f, if f agrees with $f_{\mathcal{P}}$ on its domain.

A useful notion of span program complexity is the *witness size*.

- If $\mathcal{P}$ evaluates to 1 on input x, a *witness* for this input is a pair of vectors w and $w_{\rm free}$ such that $t = V_{\rm free}w_{\rm free} + V(x)w$. Its witness size is defined as $\|w\|^2$.
- If $f_{\mathcal{P}}(x) = 0$ then a witness for x is any vector $w' \in \mathbb{R}^d$ such that $\langle w', t\rangle = 1$ and w' is orthogonal to all available input vectors. Since t is not in the column space of $V(x)$, such a vector exists. The witness size of w' is defined as $\|V^T w'\|^2$. This equals the sum of the squares of the inner products of w' with all false input vectors.

The witness size $\mathrm{wsize}(\mathcal{P}, x)$ of span program $\mathcal{P}$ on input x is defined as the minimal size among all witnesses for x. For $\mathcal{D} \subseteq \{0,1\}^n$ and $b \in \{0,1\}$, let

$$\mathrm{wsize}_b(\mathcal{P},\mathcal{D}) = \max_{x\in\mathcal{D}: f_{\mathcal{P}}(x)=b} \mathrm{wsize}(\mathcal{P},x) . \qquad (1)$$

Then the witness size of $\mathcal{P}$ on domain $\mathcal{D}$ is defined as

$$\mathrm{wsize}(\mathcal{P},\mathcal{D}) = \sqrt{\mathrm{wsize}_0(\mathcal{P},\mathcal{D})\,\mathrm{wsize}_1(\mathcal{P},\mathcal{D})} . \qquad (2)$$

This is equivalent to the standard definition; see Eq. (2.8) in [15].

The following important theorem is a combination of results from [16] and [15] and it shows why span programs are important for quantum computation:

THEOREM 1. *For any partial Boolean function $f\colon \mathcal{D} \to \{0,1\}$ with $\mathcal{D} \subseteq \{0,1\}^n$ and for any span program $\mathcal{P}$ computing f, there exists a 2-sided bounded error quantum algorithm calculating f in $O(\mathrm{wsize}(\mathcal{P},\mathcal{D}))$ queries.*

Conversely, if f can be evaluated by a bounded-error quantum algorithm in Q queries then there is a span program for f with $O(Q)$ witness size [15]. Thus, a search for a good quantum query algorithm is essentially equivalent to a search for a span program with small witness size.

3. LEARNING GRAPHS

Our main model of computation is *learning graph*. In this section we define it, and prove that any learning graph may be reduced to a span program with almost the same complexity. In Section 4, we will describe a special case of learning graphs we use throughout the paper.

Definition 2. A *learning graph* $\mathcal{G}$ is a directed acyclic connected graph with vertices labeled by subsets of $[n]$, the input indices. It has arcs connecting vertices S and $S \cup \{j\}$ only, where $S \subseteq [n]$ and $j \in [n] \setminus S$. The root of $\mathcal{G}$ is the vertex labeled by $\emptyset$. Each arc e is assigned positive real *weight* w_e.

A learning graph can be thought of as modeling the development of one's knowledge about the input during a query algorithm. Initially, nothing is known, and this is represented by the root labeled by $\emptyset$. When at a vertex labeled by $S \subseteq [n]$, the values of the variables in S have been learned. Following an arc e connecting S to $S \cup \{j\}$ can be interpreted as querying the value of variable x_j. We say the arc *loads* element j. When talking about vertex S, we call S the set of *loaded elements.*

The graph $\mathcal{G}$ itself has a very loose connection to the function being calculated. The following notion is the essence of our construction.

Definition 3. Let $\mathcal{G}$ be a learning graph on n input variables, and $f : \mathcal{D} \to \{0, 1\}$ be a function with domain $\mathcal{D} \subseteq [m]^n$. A *flow* on $\mathcal{G}$ is a real-valued function $p_e(x)$ where e in an arc of $\mathcal{G}$ and $x \in f^{-1}(1)$. For a fixed input x, the flow $p_e = p_e(x)$ has to satisfy the following properties:

- vertex $\emptyset$ is the only source of the flow, and it has intensity 1. In other words, the sum of p_e over all e's leaving $\emptyset$ is 1;
- vertex S is a sink iff it contains a 1-certificate for f on input x. Such vertices are called *accepting.* Thus, if $S \neq \emptyset$ and S is not accepting then, for vertex S, the sum of p_e over all in-coming arcs equals the sum of p_e over all out-going arcs.

We always assume a learning graph $\mathcal{G}$ is occupied with a function f and a flow p that satisfy the constraints of Definition 3. Define the *negative complexity* of $\mathcal{G}$ as $\mathcal{C}^0(\mathcal{G}) = \sum_{e \in E} w_e$ where E is the set of arcs of $\mathcal{G}$. The *positive complexity for input* $x \in f^{-1}(1)$ is defined as $\mathcal{C}^1(\mathcal{G}, x) = \sum_{e \in E} p_e(x)^2 / w_e$. The *positive complexity* $\mathcal{C}^1(\mathcal{G})$ of $\mathcal{G}$ is the maximum of $\mathcal{C}^1(\mathcal{G}, x)$ over all $x \in f^{-1}(1)$. Finally, the *(total) complexity* of $\mathcal{G}$ is defined as $\mathcal{C}(\mathcal{G}) = \sqrt{\mathcal{C}^0(\mathcal{G})\mathcal{C}^1(\mathcal{G})}$. The following theorem links learning graphs and quantum query algorithms:

THEOREM 2. *Assume there exists a learning graph for a function $f : \mathcal{D} \to \{0, 1\}$ with $\mathcal{D} \subseteq [m]^n$ having complexity C. Then there exits a bounded error quantum query algorithm for the same function with complexity $O(C \log m)$.*

PROOF. We prove Theorem 2 using the span program technique from Section 2.1. In [4], an alternative proof of the theorem is given that uses the dual of the Adversary Bound. This technique is better suited for large alphabet sizes, for instance, it allows to prove the complexity upper bound without the $\log m$ factor.

The current proof also is of interest, because we believe both techniques have their merits. In particular, span programs in [5] may be considered as a generalization of the span program in the proof of Theorem 2.

Thus, we aim to apply Theorem 1, i.e., to build a span program and estimate its witness size. Let us start with the Boolean case $m = 2$.

Description of the Span Program.

Let us describe the vector space of the span program. Each vertex S of the learning graph is represented by $2^{|S|}$ vectors $\{t_\sigma\}$ where σ is an element of $\{0, 1\}^S$. We assume all these vectors are orthonormal. One may think of t_σ as representing the values learned while querying elements of S, while vertex S represents the sole fact the variables have been queried. Vector $t_\emptyset$, that corresponds to vertex $\emptyset$, is the target of the span program. If $\sigma : S \to \{0, 1\}$ is a 1-certificate for f, t_σ is a free input vector.

Consider an arc e from S to $S \cup \{j\}$ with weight w_e. For each vector t_σ such that σ has domain S, we add two input vectors

$$\sqrt{w_e}\left(t_\sigma - t_{\sigma \cup \{j \mapsto b\}}\right), \qquad b = 0, 1. \tag{3}$$

Here $\sigma \cup \{j \mapsto b\}$ is the assignment with domain $S \cup \{j\}$ that maps i to $\sigma(i)$ for $i \in S$ and maps j to b. Each of these two vectors is labeled by value b of variable x_j.

Negative Witness Size.

Let us describe the negative witness w' of the span program. Fix an input $x \in f^{-1}(0)$. For each t_σ, we let $\langle w', t_\sigma \rangle = 1$ if σ agrees with the input. Otherwise, we let $\langle w', t_\sigma \rangle = 0$.

Consider a free input vector of the form t_σ. Since $f(x) = 0$, and σ is a 1-certificate, σ does not agree with the input. By the construction, t_σ is orthogonal to the witness.

Consider an available input vector of the form (3). There are two cases

- Inner product $\langle w', t_\sigma \rangle$ equals 0. In this case σ does not agree with the input, and, *a fortiori*, none of $\sigma \cup \{j \mapsto 0\}$ and $\sigma \cup \{j \mapsto 1\}$ does. Hence, both vectors of (3) are orthogonal to the witness.
- Inner product $\langle w', t_\sigma \rangle$ equals 1. In this case, the available input vector is the one with $b = x_j$. Note that $\sigma \cup \{j \mapsto x_j\}$ agrees with the input. Hence, the available input vector is orthogonal to the witness.

This proves that w' is a negative witness. Let us calculate the size of w'. Let e be an arc from S to $S \cup \{j\}$. We claim there is exactly one input vector that arises from e and isn't orthogonal to the witness. Let σ have domain S. By the first point above, if σ does not agree with the input, both input vectors of (3) are orthogonal to w'. If $\sigma = x_S$, the inner product of the false input vector from (3) and w' is $\sqrt{w_e}$. By summation over all arcs, the size of w' equals to $\sum_e w_e$, i.e., to the negative complexity of the learning graph.

Positive Witness Size.

Now, let us calculate the positive witness size. Fix an input x such that $f(x) = 1$, and let $p_e = p_e(x)$ be the corresponding flow. We give a linear combination of the available input vectors that equals $t_\emptyset$.

Let e be an arc from S to $S \cup \{j\}$ with weight w_e. Let $\sigma = x_S$ and take the available input vector from (3) with coefficient $p_e / \sqrt{w_e}$. Multiplied by the coefficient, the vector equals $p_e(t_{x_S} - t_{x_{S \cup \{j\}}})$.

Suppose vector S is a sink. Then, t_{x_S} is a free input vector. Take it with the coefficient equal to the difference of the in-flow to S and the out-flow of S.

By the properties of the flow, the sum of all these vectors equals the target $t_\emptyset$. The witness size is $\sum_e p_e^2 / w_e$, i.e., the positive complexity of the learning graph. This proves the theorem for the Boolean case.

Non-Boolean Case.

Now consider the case $m > 2$. Fix a representation of elements of $[m]$ using $k = \lceil \log m \rceil$ bits. For $j \in [n]$, construct a set B_j of k Boolean variables representing x_j. Consider the Boolean function $f' : \{0,1\}^{\cup_j B_j} \to \{0,1\}$ obtained from f by encoding the inputs variables. Construct a learning graph $\mathcal{G}'$ for f' from the learning graph $\mathcal{G}$ for f in the following way. Replace each vertex S by $S' = \cup_{j\in S} B_j$. For an arc from S to $S \cup \{j\}$ with weight w_e, fix an arbitrary order $y_1, \dots, y_k$ of elements in B_j and represent the arc as path $S', S' \cup \{y_1\}, \dots, S' \cup \{y_1, \dots, y_k\}$ in $\mathcal{G}'$ of k arcs, each of weight w_e.

Clearly, the negative complexity of $\mathcal{G}'$ is k times the negative complexity of $\mathcal{G}$. Accepting vertices of $\mathcal{G}$ are transformed into accepting vertices of $\mathcal{G}'$, and each flow through $\mathcal{G}$ can be transformed into a flow through $\mathcal{G}'$ in an obvious way. This increases the positive complexity k times. Hence, the complexity of $\mathcal{G}'$ is at most k times the complexity of $\mathcal{G}$, and, for $\mathcal{G}'$, we can apply the construction from the first part of the proof. □

Remark 1. Under a reasonable assumption $p_e \geq 0$, one can consider the flow as a random walk, i.e., a path from the source to a sink such that the probability an arc e is used in the path is exactly p_e. In contrary to random walks used previously to build quantum walks, this is rather a random walk *through* the graph than *on* it. We utilize this probabilistic language in Section 6.

For a fixed learning graph, the minimal positive complexity on input x equals the energy of the electrical current of value 1 from the source to the sinks, where the conductance of an edge equals its weight [6]. But we go in the opposite direction: at first designing the flow, and then coming up with the weights of the arcs minimizing the total complexity.

Remark 2. In Section 4, we will use learning graphs with more than one vertex labeled by the same subset $S \subseteq [n]$. We denote them by (S, a) where S is a subset of $[n]$ and a is some additional label used to distinguish vertices with the same subset. The proof of Theorem 2 goes through for such learning graphs as well.

By analyzing the proof of Theorem 2, one can see that the weight of an arc from S to $S\cup\{j\}$ may depend on the value of the variables inside S. We call such learning graphs *adaptive*, and the one defined in Definition 2 *non-adaptive*. Adaptive learning graphs are strictly stronger than non-adaptive ones. In particular, it is possible to prove the following result due to Kothari and Mittal [11].

THEOREM 3. *For any non-adaptive learning graph $\mathcal{G}$ for a function f, its complexity is at least the 1-certificate complexity of f.*

This justifies why we are interested in functions with small 1-certificate complexity. For adaptive learning graphs, we don't know of any lower bound of such simple form, but we believe they have asymptotically larger complexity than span programs for some class of functions. All learning graphs considered in this paper are non-adaptive ones. For an example of an application of adaptive learning graphs, refer to [4].

4. ELEMENT DISTINCTNESS PROBLEM: LEARNING BY STAGES

In the remaining part of the paper we use learning graph of quite specific form. We describe it in this section using the element distinctness problem as an illustrative example. The learning graph for this problem doesn't beat the complexity of Ambainis' algorithm [3]. Prior to this paper, however, no explicit optimal span program for this problem was known, although, it had been known to exist.

Definition 4. A *reduced learning graph* is defined as follows. Let $V_0 = \{\emptyset\}, V_1, \dots, V_k$ be sets of L-vertices. Any two $S \in V_{i-1}$ and $S' \in V_i$, where $S \subseteq S'$, may be connected by a *transition* e. Each transition is weighted by a positive real number w_e. The set of all transitions from V_{i-1} to V_i is called the *i-th stage*.

The reduced learning graph is transformed into a learning graph as follows. Let e be a transition from S to S'. Fix an arbitrary ordering of elements of $S' \setminus S = \{s_1, \dots, s_\ell\}$. Represent e by the path

$$S, (S \cup \{s_1\}, e), (S \cup \{s_1, s_2\}, e), \dots, (S' \setminus \{s_\ell\}, e), S' \quad (4)$$

in the learning graph. Here the additional labels e in the internal vertices are like in Remark 2: thus we assure that the paths corresponding to the transitions do not intersect, except at the ends. All arcs in the path are assigned weight w_e. We define the *length* $\ell(e)$ of the transition as $|S' \setminus S|$. Note the similarity of this construction to the non-Boolean case in the proof of Theorem 2. All learning graphs in the paper will have this structure, and we will usually omit the adjective "reduced".

For example, for the element distinctness problem, the learning graph has 3 stages where V_1, V_2 and V_3 consist of all subsets of $[n]$ of sizes r, $r+1$ and $r+2$, respectively, where $r = o(n)$ is some parameter. We add all possible transitions from a subset to a superset (see Figure 1).

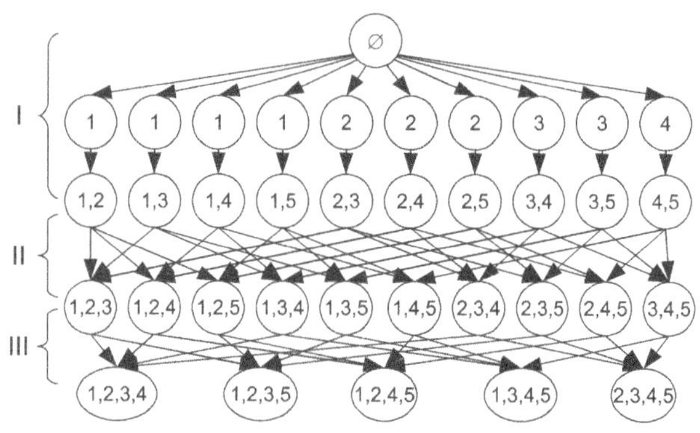

Figure 1: The learning graph for the element distinctness problem in case $n = 5$ and $r = 2$. Stages I, II and III shown.

We define a flow through a reduced learning graph as in Definition 3 with arcs replaced by transitions. The expression for the complexity is modified to include lengths of transitions as described below. We are going to analyze the complexity of the learning graph stage-wise. This motivates the following definitions. Let E_i be the set of all transitions of the i-th stage. The *negative* and the *positive complexities*

I.	Load r items different from a and b.
II.	Load a.
III.	Load b.

Table 1: Stages for the element distinctness problem.

of stage i are defined as

$$\mathcal{C}_i^0(\mathcal{G}) = \sum_{e\in E_i} \ell(e)w_e, \quad \mathcal{C}_i^1(\mathcal{G}) = \max_{x\in f^{-1}(1)} \sum_{e\in E_i} \frac{\ell(e)p_e(x)^2}{w_e}.$$

The *total complexity of stage i* is defined as

$$\mathcal{C}_i(\mathcal{G}) = \sqrt{\mathcal{C}_i^0(\mathcal{G})\mathcal{C}_i^1(\mathcal{G})}$$

PROPOSITION 1. *Assume a reduced learning graph $\mathcal{G}$ for function f has $k = O(1)$ stages. Then one can build a learning graph for the same function with complexity $O(\mathcal{C}_1(\mathcal{G}) + \cdots + \mathcal{C}_k(\mathcal{G}))$.*

PROOF. Transform the reduced learning graph $\mathcal{G}$ into a learning graph $\mathcal{G}'$ as described above. Divide the weights of arcs on stage i by $\mathcal{C}_i^0(\mathcal{G})$. The negative complexity of the whole learning graph becomes $k = O(1)$. The total complexity of the learning graph becomes

$$O\left(\sqrt{\sum_{i=1}^k \mathcal{C}_i^0(\mathcal{G})\mathcal{C}_i^1(\mathcal{G})}\right) = O\left(\sqrt{\sum_{i=1}^k \mathcal{C}_i(\mathcal{G})^2}\right),$$

that is $O(\mathcal{C}_1(\mathcal{G}) + \cdots + \mathcal{C}_k(\mathcal{G}))$. □

Let us define a flow for the element distinctness problem. Consider any positive input x. Let a and b be two equal elements, i.e., $x_a = x_b$. On stage I, we let flow $\binom{n-2}{r}^{-1}$ along any transition ending in a vertex with both a and b not loaded. Denote such a vertex by S. After that we forward the flow along the transitions to $S \cup \{a\}$ and then to $S \cup \{a, b\}$ on stages II and III, respectively. The last vertex is a sink, so we may stop.

The description of this flow is given in Table 1. The table describes the transitions used by the flow, assuming the flow is divided uniformly among all out-going transitions satisfying the conditions. The set of transitions of the learning graph is the union of these transitions over all positive inputs. For a fixed positive input, we call the transitions used by the flow *valid*.

Assume all transitions have weight 1. Stage I has $\binom{n}{r}$ transitions. The length of each transition is r. There are $\binom{n-2}{r}$ transitions used by the flow. Thus, the complexity of the first stage is

$$\mathcal{C}_1(\mathcal{G}) = \sqrt{\left(\binom{n}{r}r\right)\left(\binom{n}{r-2}r\binom{n}{r-2}^{-2}\right)} = O(r).$$

Similarly, the complexity of the second stage is

$$\sqrt{\left((n-r)\binom{n}{r}\right)\left(\binom{n}{r-2}\binom{n}{r-2}^{-2}\right)} = O(\sqrt{n}),$$

and that of the third stage is

$$\sqrt{\left((n-r-1)\binom{n}{r+1}\right)\binom{n}{r-2}\binom{n}{r-2}^{-2}} = O\left(\frac{n}{\sqrt{r}}\right).$$

Hence, the total complexity, by Proposition 1, is

$$O(r + \sqrt{n} + n/\sqrt{r}),$$

that attains its optimal value $O(n^{2/3})$ when $r = n^{2/3}$. Note that in the learning graph attaining this optimum, arcs will have different weights because of the re-weighting in the proof of Proposition 1.

5. USING SYMMETRY

The *symmetry group* Σ of a function $f : \mathcal{D} \to \{0, 1\}$ with $\mathcal{D} \subseteq [m]^n$ is the group of permutations σ on $[n]$ such that $f(x_{\sigma 1}, \ldots, x_{\sigma n}) = f(x_1, \ldots, x_n)$ for all $x \in \mathcal{D}$.

Many natural problems are symmetric. For instance, the OR and the element distinctness problems remain invariant under the action of the full symmetric group. The triangle problem is invariant under permuting vertices of the graph.

We will identify transitions of the learning graph that are *equivalent*, and, hence, should have the same weight. If not specified otherwise, we call transitions e from S to T and e' from S' to T' equivalent, if one can be transformed into another by an element of Σ, i.e., if there exists $\sigma \in \Sigma$ such that $\sigma(S) = S'$ and $\sigma(T) = T'$. According to this definition, for the element distinctness problem, all transitions in one stage are equivalent.

Symmetries usually help in constructing algorithms. For learning graphs, we capture this by the following notion.

Definition 5. We say the flow $p_e(x)$ on a learning graph is *symmetric* on stage i if, for each equivalence class of stage i, the following two conditions hold:

- the flow through transitions of the class takes two values only, one of which is 0, and the other one is some p, where p depends neither on the arc nor the input (but may depend on the equivalence class);
- the number of valid (with non-zero flow) transitions in the class is the same for all inputs.

We define *speciality* $\tau(e)$ of transition e as the ratio of the size of the equivalence class containing e to the number of valid transitions in it. For the usual definition of equivalence, it equals the inverse of the probability of obtaining a valid transition when a random permutation from Σ is applied to e. Define the *average length* L_i of stage i as $\sum_{e\in E_i} p_e(x)\ell(e)$. If the flow is symmetric, these two quantities do not depend on the input. Finally, let T_i denote the maximal speciality of a transition on stage i.

THEOREM 4. *Assume the flow is symmetric on stage i. Then one can assign weights to transitions on stage i so that the complexity of the stage becomes at most $L_i\sqrt{T_i}$.*

PROOF. Consider $e \in E_i$ and let $p'(e)$ be the flow through a valid transition equivalent to e. By the above assumptions, $p'(e)$ does not depend on the input. Hence, it is possible to define the weight of transition e equal to $p'(e)$. Then the complexity of the stage is

$$\sqrt{\left(\sum_{e\in E_i} \ell(e)p'(e)\right)\left(\sum_{e\in E_i} \frac{\ell(e)p_e(x)^2}{p'(e)}\right)}$$

$$= \sqrt{\left(\sum_{e\in E_i} \ell(e)\tau(e)p_e(x)\right)\left(\sum_{e\in E_i} \ell(e)p_e(x)\right)} \le L_i\sqrt{T_i}.$$

Stage	I	II	III
Length	r	1	1
Speciality	1	n	n^2/r

Table 2: Parameters (up to a constant factor) of the stages of the learning graph for the element distinctness problem of Table 1.

I.	Load a complete subgraph on $r = o(n)$ vertices that does not contain vertices a, b and c.
II.	Load all edges connecting a to the subgraph.
III.	Load all edges connecting b to the subgraph (including a). This results in a complete subgraph on $r+2$ vertices with a and b inside, but c outside.
IV.	Load $\ell = o(r)$ edges that connect c to ℓ vertices of the subgraph other than a and b.
V.	Load edge $\widetilde{ac}$.
VI.	Load edge $\widetilde{bc}$.

Table 3: Stages for the triangle problem according to the algorithm of [13].

□

It is easy to verify that the flow for the element distinctness problem in Table 1 satisfies conditions of Theorem 4 and to check Table 2, where each entry is given up to a constant factor. For example, consider the speciality of stage III. If we take a transition on stage III and apply a random permutation, it is mapped to a valid transition iff the element being loaded is mapped to b and one of the elements of the origin of the transition is mapped to a. The first event happens with probability $1/n$, and the second one—with probability $\Omega(r/n)$. Thus, the speciality is $O(n^2/r)$. We say element a is *hidden* among $r + 1$ elements of the vertex.

6. TRIANGLE PROBLEM

We start with a brief description of a learning graph for the triangle problem that is a direct analog to the algorithm from [13]. For a positive input, denote the vertices of some triangle by a, b and c. Stages of the learning graph are described in Table 3.

It is not hard to check that the flow is symmetric. The parameters of the stages are in Table 4. We don't give more detail here, because Theorem 5 describes in detail a more general learning graph. By Theorem 4, the complexity of the learning graph is

$$O\left(r^2 + r\sqrt{n} + n\sqrt{r} + n^{3/2}\ell/r + n^{3/2}/\sqrt{r} + n^{3/2}/\sqrt{\ell}\right).$$

It is optimized when $r = n^{3/5}$ and $\ell = n^{2/5}$. The optimum is $O(n^{13/10})$.

Let us analyze Table 4. The point of the learning graph is to minimize the speciality of stage VI using the previous stages. Also, the complexities of stages II and V are majorized by the complexities of stages III and VI, respectively. Thus, we should concentrate on stages I, III, IV and VI. Their complexities are $n^{12/10}$, $n^{13/10}$, $n^{13/10}$ and $n^{13/10}$, respectively. It looks like resources of stage I are not used to the full extent. The problem is in stage III: it is too long. The main idea behind our construction is to reduce the length of stage III.

Stage	I	II	III	IV	V	VI
Length	r^2	r	r	ℓ	1	1
Speciality	1	n	n^2/r	n^3/r^2	n^3/r	n^3/ℓ

Table 4: Parameters (up to a constant factor) of the stages of the learning graph of Table 3

I.	Load a random subgraph on $r = o(n)$ vertices that does not contain vertices a, b and c.
II.	Load edges connecting a to the vertices of the subgraph, independently at random, each with probability s.
III.	Load edges connecting b to the subgraph (including a), independently at random, each with probability s.
IIIa.	Select those L-vertices that do not contain edge $\widetilde{ab}$ and contain at least $sr^2/4$ edges.
IIIb.	Load edge $\widetilde{ab}$.
IV.	Load $\ell = o(r)$ edges connecting c to vertices of the subgraph other than a and b.
V.	Load edge $\widetilde{ac}$.
VI.	Load edge $\widetilde{bc}$.

Table 5: Stages for the triangle problem.

THEOREM 5. *There exists a quantum algorithm solving the triangle problem with bounded error in $O(n^{35/27})$ queries.*

Note that $35/27 \approx 1.2963 < 1.3$ of the previous algorithm.

PROOF. First, let us agree that for the vertices of the learning graph we use term L-vertex in order to distinguish them from the vertices of the input graph. In the learning graph we have transitions, whereas in the input graph we have edges.

We use a symmetric approach based on stages as in Section 5. The symmetry group consists of all permutations of vertices. Unlike the learning graphs in Tables 1 and 3, where all transitions of the same stage are equivalent, this time each stage will have many equivalence classes. Thus, we will not only describe the valid transitions, but also specify the value of the flow through them, because different equivalence classes may (and will) have different non-zero flows even in a symmetric flow.

To specify the flow, we use the probabilistic language of Remark 1. Before we do that, let us clarify our usage of the term "random subgraph on k vertices". By this we understand a subgraph of the complete graph on n vertices constructed in the following way. Take a subset U of k vertices uniformly at random. Then, for each edge with both ends in U, add it to the subgraph with some prescribed probability s, independently at random. The description of the random subgraph contains both the vertex set U and the selected edges. We add the vertex set to the description, as it might happen some of the vertices inside U end up with degree 0.

The stages of the algorithm are in Table 5. We will describe each stage in more detail later, but let us say now that stage IIIa is different from the others. It is not a stage in the previous definition, it is a modifier for the flow before it. The reason behind its inclusion is that we want the flow to satisfy conditions of IIIa, but we don't want to give an explicit construction of a flow that achieves this. Instead of that, we construct flow p' on stages I to III that is easy to analyze, and prove that the actual flow has at most by a constant larger complexity than p'.

It is straightforward to check that the flow is symmetric on stages I to III. For example, the flow through a valid transition on stage III that originates in a subgraph having m edges and loads k edges is

$$\binom{n-3}{r}^{-1} s^{m+k}(1-s)^{\binom{r+2}{2}-m-k}.$$

The specialities of transitions on stages I, II and III are $O(1)$, $O(n)$ and $O(n^2/r)$, respectively, by the same argument as for the element distinctness problem. The average length of a transition on stage I is $O(sr^2)$ by a standard probabilistic argument. Similarly, conditioned on leaving a fixed valid L-vertex, the average length of a transition on stages II and III is $O(sr)$. Hence, it coincides with the (unconditioned) average length of a transition on stages II and III.

Now, we switch to stage IIIa. The set of L-vertices after the stage is the subset of L-vertices before it having at least $sr^2/4$ edges. The stage uses no transitions. What it does, it modifies the flow on stages I to III constructed so far. Consider L-vertices after stage III. Additionally to the condition to contain a and b and to not contain c, that is stated for stage III, we require the subgraph to not contain edge $\widetilde{ab}$ and to have at least $sr^2/4$ edges.

It's easy to see that the number of edges in the L-vertex after stage III in the random walk follows the binomial distribution $B\left(\binom{r+2}{2}, s\right)$. Denote the probability of the L-vertex after stage III to satisfy the constraints in IIIa by p. By an easy probabilistic argument, under reasonable assumptions $s = o(1)$ and $sr^2 = \omega(1)$, the probability is $1-o(1)$. Assume the instance is large enough, so that $p \geq 1/2$. Then, we scale the flow prior stage IIIa $1/p$ times, and remove all the flow going to the L-vertices that don't satisfy the constraint. After that the value of the flow is 1 again, and the flow on each transition has increased at most $1/p \leq 2$ times. Hence, this operation changes the complexity of stages I-III by at most a factor of 2, and thus, we can ignore it in our calculations.

Now consider stage IIIb. In the learning graph, an L-vertex after stage IIIa is connected to all possible L-vertices where an edge connecting two vertices of the underlying vertex set is added. The transition is used by the flow iff the edge added is $\widetilde{ab}$. For each equivalence class, the probability a random permutation of vertices identifies the edge being added with $\widetilde{ab}$ is exactly $\frac{2}{n(n-1)}$. Moreover, provided that this happens, the probability that c is not used in the vertex set of the subgraph is $\Omega(1)$. Hence, the speciality is $O(n^2)$. The length of the stage is 1.

Stages IV-VI are conceptually similar to the element distinctness learning graph on the edge set joining c to the vertices in U. We call two transitions of the same stage equivalent iff the number of edges loaded in their heads is equal. Note that this is a looser notion than the one in Section 5. We use it because it simplifies the analysis and makes the maximal speciality smaller.

With this definition, the flow is symmetric. The first condition of the symmetric flow is satisfied because the nonzero flow after stage IIIb is equal for L-vertices with the same number of edges. The second condition is also easy to check. Let's calculate the speciality.

Stage	I	II	III	IIIb	IV	V	VI
Length	sr^2	sr	sr	1	ℓ	1	1
Speciality	1	n	n^2/r	n^2	n^3/sr^2	n^3/sr	$n^3/s\ell$

Table 6: Parameters (up to a constant factor) of the stages of the learning graph of Table 5

To get a random representative of an equivalence class with m edges in the random subgraph, act as follows. Take a random $(r+2)$-subset U of the vertex set, a vertex v outside it, and a subset of edges joining v to U that depends on the stage. On stage IV, it is a subset of ℓ edges; on stage V, a subset of ℓ edges plus a new edge; on stage VI, a subset of $\ell+1$ edges plus a new edge. After that add a random subset of m edges in U. To get a valid transition, the following should hold:

- v should be equal to c. Probability of this is $1/n$;
- a and b should be joined by an edge. Provided they both are in U, the probability of this is $\Omega(s)$, because $m \geq sr^2/4$;
- on stage IV, a and b should be in U but not connected to v. Assuming $\ell < r/2$, the probability is $\Theta(r^2/n^2)$;
- on stage V, a should be connected by the new edge to v, and b should be in U but not connected to v. With the same assumption, the probability of this is $\Theta(r/n^2)$;
- finally, on stage VI, b should be connected by the new edge to v, and a should be among $\ell+1$ vertices joined to v by an edge. The probablity is $\Theta(\ell/n^2)$.

Multiplying all this, the specialities of stages IV, V and VI are $O(n^3/sr^2)$, $O(n^3/sr)$ and $O(n^3/s\ell)$, respectively. Our estimates are summarized in Table 6. Stage II is majorized by stage III, and V by VI. Adding everything else up, the complexity of the learning graph is

$$O\left(sr^2 + sr\frac{n}{\sqrt{r}} + n + \ell\sqrt{\frac{n^3}{sr^2}} + \sqrt{\frac{n^3}{s\ell}}\right).$$

This is optimized when $r = n^{2/3}$, $\ell = n^{4/9}$, and $s = n^{-1/27}$. The optimum equals $O(n^{35/27})$. Note that complexities of stages I, III, IV and VI are equal this time. □

7. SUMMARY AND SUBSEQUENT DEVELOPMENTS

An approach towards quantum algorithms for functions with small 1-certificate complexity using span programs has been proposed in the paper. It seems to be at least as powerful as the previous approach of quantum walk on the Johnson graph. The analysis of the algorithm contains no spectral analysis. It uses an optimization of a quadratic function over the set of flows.

A nice property of the new approach is that is has build-in tools for amortization. If some computational paths in the program take less queries than the others, the complexity of the program is calculated using the average rather than the maximal cost, as it is in the previous approaches.

We mention some subsequent developments. Zhu [18] and Lee, Magniez and Santha [12] extended algorithm from Theorem 5 for the containment of arbitrary subgraphs. Belovs and Lee [4] developed, using the concept of the learning graph, an algorithm for the k-distinctness problem that beats the $O(n^{k/(k+1)})$-query algorithm by Ambainis [3], given some prior information about the input. Belovs and Reichardt [5] use a more general learning graph than in the proof of Theorem 2 to obtain an optimal algorithm for finding paths and claws of arbitrary length in a graph. Also, they address time-efficient implementation of such span programs.

8. ACKNOWLEDGEMENTS

I would like to thank Andris Ambainis for his suggestion to research on abilities concealed in the span programs as well as many useful discussions; Ben Reichardt and others for pointing out the connection between electrical circuits and learning graphs; Robin Kothari and Rajat Mittal for sharing their proof of Theorem 3 and other valuable comments; and anonymous reviewers for valuable comments.

This work has been supported by the European Social Fund within the project "Support for Doctoral Studies at University of Latvia" and FP7 FET-Open project QCS.

9. REFERENCES

[1] S. Aaronson and Y. Shi. Quantum lower bounds for the collision and the element distinctness problems. *Journal of the ACM*, 51(4):595–605, 2004.

[2] A. Ambainis. Quantum lower bounds for collision and element distinctness with small range. *Theory of Computing*, 1:37–46, 2005.

[3] A. Ambainis. Quantum walk algorithm for element distinctness. *SIAM Journal on Computing*, 37:210–239, 2007.

[4] A. Belovs and T. Lee. Quantum algorithm for k-distinctness with prior knowledge on the input. Technical Report 1108.3022, arXiv, 2011.

[5] A. Belovs and B. Reichardt. Span programs and quantum algorithms for st-connectivity and claw detection. Technical Report 1203.2603, arXiv, 2012.

[6] B. Bollobás. *Modern Graph Theory*. Springer, 1998.

[7] G. Brassard, P. H. yer, and A. Tapp. Quantum algorithm for the collision problem. In *Proc. 3rd LATIN*, pages 163—169, 1998.

[8] H. Buhrman and R. de Wolf. Complexity measures and decision tree complexity: a survey. *Theoretical Computer Science*, 288.

[9] H. Buhrman, C. Dürr, M. Heiligman, P. Høyer, F. Magniez, M. Santha, and R. de Wolf. Quantum algorithms for element distinctness. *SIAM Journal on Computing*, 34(6):1324–1330.

[10] L. K. Grover. A fast quantum mechanical algorithm for database search. In *Proc. 28th ACM STOC*, pages 212–219.

[11] R. Kothari and R. Mittal. Personal communication, 2011.

[12] T. Lee, F. Magniez, and M. Santha. A learning graph based quantum query algorithm for finding constant-size subgraphs. Technical Report 1109.5135, arXiv, 2011.

[13] F. Magniez, M. Santha, and M. Szegedy. Quantum algorithms for the triangle problem. *SIAM Journal on Computing*, 37(2):413–424.

[14] M. Nielsen and I. Chuang. *Quantum Computation and Quantum Information*. Cambridge University Press, Cambridge, 2000.

[15] B. Reichardt. Span programs and quantum query complexity: The general adversary bound is nearly tight for every boolean function. Technical Report 0904.2759, arXiv, 2009.

[16] B. Reichardt. Reflections for quantum query algorithms. In *Proc. 22nd ACM-SIAM SODA*, pages 560–569, 2011.

[17] B. Reichardt and R. Špalek. Span-program-based quantum algorithm for evaluating formulas. In *Proc. 40th ACM STOC*, pages 103—112.

[18] Y. Zhu. Quantum query complexity of subgraph containment with constant-sized certificates. Technical Report 1109.4165, arXiv, 2011.

The Cell Probe Complexity of Dynamic Range Counting

Kasper Green Larsen*
MADALGO[†] Department of Computer Science
Aarhus University
Aarhus, Denmark
larsen@cs.au.dk

ABSTRACT

In this paper we develop a new technique for proving lower bounds on the update time and query time of dynamic data structures in the cell probe model. With this technique, we prove the highest lower bound to date for any explicit problem, namely a lower bound of $t_q = \Omega((\lg n/\lg(wt_u))^2)$. Here n is the number of update operations, w the cell size, t_q the query time and t_u the update time. In the most natural setting of cell size $w = \Theta(\lg n)$, this gives a lower bound of $t_q = \Omega((\lg n/\lg\lg n)^2)$ for any polylogarithmic update time. This bound is almost a quadratic improvement over the highest previous lower bound of $\Omega(\lg n)$, due to Pătraşcu and Demaine [SICOMP'06].

We prove our lower bound for the fundamental problem of weighted orthogonal range counting. In this problem, we are to support insertions of two-dimensional points, each assigned a $\Theta(\lg n)$-bit integer weight. A query to this problem is specified by a point $q = (x, y)$, and the goal is to report the sum of the weights assigned to the points dominated by q, where a point (x', y') is dominated by q if $x' \leq x$ and $y' \leq y$. In addition to being the highest cell probe lower bound to date, our lower bound is also tight for data structures with update time $t_u = \Omega(\lg^{2+\varepsilon} n)$, where $\varepsilon > 0$ is an arbitrarily small constant.

Categories and Subject Descriptors

E.1 [**Data**]: Data Structures

Keywords

Data Structures, Cell Probe, Lower Bounds, Range Searching, Computational Geometry

*Kasper Green Larsen is a recipient of the Google Europe Fellowship in Search and Information Retrieval, and this research is also supported in part by this Google Fellowship.
†Center for Massive Data Algorithmics, a Center of the Danish National Research Foundation.

STOC'12, May 19–22, 2012, New York, New York, USA.

1. INTRODUCTION

Proving lower bounds on the operational time of data structures has been an active line of research for decades. During these years, numerous models of computation have been proposed, including the cell probe model of Yao [12]. The cell probe model is one of the least restrictive lower bound models, thus lower bounds proved in the cell probe model apply to essentially every imaginable data structure, including those developed in the popular upper bound model, the word RAM. Unfortunately this generality comes at a cost: The highest lower bound that has been proved for any explicit data structure problem is $\Omega(\lg n)$, both for static and even dynamic data structures[1].

In this paper, we break this barrier by introducing a new technique for proving dynamic cell probe lower bounds. Using our technique, we obtain a query time lower bound of $\Omega((\lg n/\lg\lg n)^2)$ for any polylogarithmic update time. We prove the bound for the fundamental problem of dynamic *weighted orthogonal range counting* in two-dimensional space. In dynamic weighted orthogonal range counting (in 2-d), the goal is to maintain a set of (2-d) points under insertions, where each point is assigned an integer weight. In addition to supporting insertions, a data structure must support answering queries. A query is specified by a query point $q = (x, y)$, and the data structure must return the sum of the weights assigned to the points *dominated* by q. Here we say that a point (x', y') is dominated by q if $x' \leq x$ and $y' \leq y$.

1.1 The Cell Probe Model

A dynamic data structure in the cell probe model consists of a set of memory cells, each storing w bits. Each cell of the data structure is identified by an integer address, which is assumed to fit in w bits, i.e. each address is amongst $[2^w] = \{0, \ldots, 2^w - 1\}$. We will make the additional standard assumption that a cell also has enough bits to address any update operation performed on it, i.e. we assume $w = \Omega(\lg n)$ when analysing a data structures performance on a sequence of n updates.

When presented with an update operation, a data structure reads and updates a number of the stored cells to reflect the changes. We refer to the reading or writing of a cell as probing the cell, hence the name cell probe model. The update time of a data structure is the number of cells probed when processing an update operation.

To answer a query, a data structure similarly probes a

[1]This is true under the most natural assumption of cell size $\Theta(\lg n)$.

number of cells from the data structure, and from the contents of the probed cells, the data structure must return the correct answer to the query. We similarly define the query time of a data structure as the number of cells probed when answering a query.

Previous Results.

In the following, we give a brief overview of the most important techniques that have been introduced for proving cell probe lower bounds for dynamic data structures. We also review the previous cell probe lower bounds obtained for orthogonal range counting and related problems. In Section 2 we then give a more thorough review of the previous techniques most relevant to our work, followed by a description of the key ideas in our new technique.

In their seminal paper [2], Fredman and Saks introduced the celebrated chronogram technique. They applied their technique to the *partial sums* problem and obtained a lower bound stating that $t_q = \Omega(\lg n / \lg(wt_u))$, where t_q is the query time and t_u the update time. In the partial sums problem, we are to maintain an array of n $O(w)$-bit integers under updates of the entries. A query to the problem consists of two indices i and j, and the goal is to compute the sum of the integers in the subarray from index i to j. The lower bound of Fredman and Saks holds even when the data structure is allowed amortization and randomization.

The bounds of Fredman and Saks remained the highest achieved until the breakthrough results of Pătraşcu and Demaine [9]. In their paper, they extended upon the ideas of Fredman and Saks to give a tight lower bound for the partial sums problem. Their results state that $t_q \lg(t_u/t_q) = \Omega(\lg n)$ and $t_u \lg(t_q/t_u) = \Omega(\lg n)$ when the integers have $\Omega(w)$ bits, which in particular implies $\max\{t_q, t_u\} = \Omega(\lg n)$. We note that they also obtain tight lower bounds in the regime of smaller integers. Again, the bounds hold even when allowed amortization and randomization. For the most natural cell size of $w = \Theta(\lg n)$, this remains until today the highest achieved lower bound.

The two above techniques both lead to smooth tradeoff curves between update time and query time. While this behaviour is correct for the partial sums problem, there are many examples where this is certainly not the case. Pătraşcu and Thorup [10] recently presented a new extension of the chronogram technique, which can prove strong threshold lower bounds. In particular they showed that any data structure for maintaining the connectivity of a graph under edge insertions and deletions, must either have amortized update time $\Omega(\lg n)$ or the query time explodes to $n^{1-o(1)}$.

In the search for super-logarithmic lower bounds, Pătraşcu introduced a dynamic set-disjointness problem named the multiphase problem [8]. Based on a widely believed conjecture about the hardness of 3-SUM, Pătraşcu first reduced 3-SUM to the multiphase problem and then gave a series of reductions to different dynamic data structure problems, implying polynomial lower bounds under the 3-SUM conjecture.

Finally, we mention that Pătraşcu [6] presented a technique capable of proving a query time lower bound of $t_q = \Omega((\lg n/\lg(wt_u))^2)$ for dynamic weighted orthogonal range counting, but only when the weights are $\lg^{2+\Omega(1)} n$-bit integers. Thus the magnitude of the lower bound compared to the number of bits, δ, needed to describe an update operation or a query, remains below $\Omega(\delta)$. This bound holds when t_u is the worst case update time and t_q the expected average[2] query time of a data structure.

The particular problem of orthogonal range counting has received much attention from a lower bound perspective. In the static case, Pătraşcu [6] first proved a lower bound of $t = \Omega(\lg n / \lg(Sw/n))$ where t is the expected average query time and S the space of the data structure in number of cells. This lower bound holds for regular counting (without weights), and even when just the parity of the number of points in the range is to be returned. In [7] he reproved this bound using an elegant reduction from the communication game known as lop-sided set disjointness. Subsequently Jørgensen and Larsen [3] proved a matching bound for the strongly related problems of range selection and range median. Finally, as mentioned earlier, Pătraşcu [6] proved a $t_q = \Omega((\lg n/\lg(wt_u))^2)$ lower bound for dynamic weighted orthogonal range counting when the weights are $\lg^{2+\Omega(1)} n$-bit integers. In the concluding remarks of that paper, he posed it as an interesting open problem to prove the same lower bound for regular counting.

Our Results.

In this paper we introduce a new technique for proving dynamic cell probe lower bounds. Using this technique, we obtain a lower bound of $t_q = \Omega((\lg n/\lg(wt_u))^2)$, where t_u is the worst case update time and t_q is the expected average query time of the data structure. Our lower bound holds for any cell size $w = \Omega(\lg n)$, and is the highest achieved to date in the most natural setting of cell size $w = \Theta(\lg n)$. For polylogarithmic t_u and logarithmic cell size, this bound is $t_q = \Omega((\lg n/\lg\lg n)^2)$, i.e. almost a quadratic improvement over the highest previous lower bound of Pătraşcu and Demaine.

We prove our lower bound for dynamic weighted orthogonal range counting in two-dimensional space, where the weights are $\Theta(\lg n)$-bit integers. This gives a partial answer to the open problem posed by Pătraşcu by reducing the requirement of the magnitude of weights from $\lg^{2+\Omega(1)} n$ to just logarithmic. Finally, our lower bound is also tight for update time $t_u = \lg^{2+\Omega(1)} n$, hence deepening our understanding of one of the most fundamental range searching problems.

Overview.

In Section 2 we discuss the two previous techniques most related to ours, i.e. that of Fredman and Saks [2] and of Pătraşcu [6]. Following this discussion we give a description of the key ideas behind our new technique. Having introduced our technique, we proceed to the lower bound proof in Section 3 and finally we conclude in Section 5 with a discussion of the limitations of our technique and the intriguing open problems these limitations pose.

2. TECHNIQUES

In this section, we first review the two previous techniques most important to our work, and then present our new technique.

[2] i.e. for any data structure with a possibly randomized query algorithm, there exists a sequence of updates U, such that the expected cost of answering a uniform random query after the updates U is t_q.

Fredman and Saks [2].

This technique is known as the chronogram technique. The basic idea is to consider batches, or *epochs*, of updates to a data structure problem. More formally, one defines an epoch i for each $i = 1, \ldots, \lg_\beta n$, where $\beta > 1$ is a parameter. The i'th epoch consists of performing β^i carefully chosen updates to a data structure. The epochs occur in time from largest to smallest epoch, and at the end of epoch 1, every cell of the constructed data structure is associated to the epoch in which it was last updated. The goal is to argue that to answer a query after epoch 1, the query algorithm has to probe one cell associated to each epoch. Since a cell is only associated to one epoch, this gives a total query time lower bound of $\Omega(\lg_\beta n)$.

Arguing that the query algorithm must probe one cell associated to each epoch is typically done by setting β somewhat larger than the worst case update time t_u. Since cells associated to an epoch j cannot contain useful information about an epoch $i < j$ (the updates of epoch j where performed before knowing what the updates of epoch i was), one can ignore cells associated to previous epochs when analysing the probes to an epoch i. Similarly, since all epochs following epoch i (future updates) writes a total of $O(\beta^{i-1}t_u) = o(\beta^i)$ cells, these cells do not contain enough information about the β^i updates of epoch i to be of any use. Thus if the answer to a query depends on an update of epoch i, then the query algorithm must probe a cell associated to epoch i to answer the query.

We note that Fredman and Saks also defined the notion of epochs over a sequence of intermixed updates and queries. Here the epochs are defined relative to each query, and from this approach they obtain their amortized bounds.

Pătraşcu [6].

This technique uses the same setup as the chronogram technique, i.e. one considers epochs $i = 1, \ldots, \lg_\beta n$ of updates, followed by one query. The idea is to use a static $\Omega(\lg_\beta n)$ lower bound proof to argue that the query algorithm must probe $\Omega(\lg_\beta n)$ cells from each epoch, and not just one. Summing over all epochs, this gives a lower bound of $\Omega(\lg_\beta^2 n)$. In the following, we give a coarse overview of the general framework for doing so.

One first proves a lower bound on the amount of communication in the following (static) communication game (for every epoch i): Bob receives all epochs of updates to the dynamic data structure problem and Alice receives a set of queries and all updates of the epochs preceding epoch i. The goal for them is to compute the answer to Alice's queries after all the epochs of updates.

When such a lower bound has been established, one considers each epoch i in turn and uses the dynamic data structure to obtain an efficient protocol for the above communication game between Alice and Bob. The key idea is to let Alice simulate the query algorithm of the dynamic data structure on each of her queries, and whenever a cell associated to epoch i is requested, she asks Bob for the contents. Bob replies and she continues the simulation. Clearly the amount of communication is proportional to the number of probes to cells associated to epoch i, and thus a lower bound follows from the communication game lower bound. The main difficulty in implementing this protocol is that Alice must somehow recover the contents of the cells not associated to epoch i without asking Bob for it. This is accomplished by first letting Bob send all cells associated to epochs $j < i$ to Alice. For sufficiently large β, this does not break the communication lower bound. Now Alice can execute the updates of the epochs preceding epoch i (epochs $j > i$) herself, and she knows the cells associated to epochs $j < i$, thus all she needs to realize the protocol is a way to recognize whether a cell requested belongs to epoch i or not. If not, she has the contents herself, and if it does, she asks Bob for the contents. This last step is solved by changing to a non-deterministic communication game and letting an all-powerful prover send a Bloom filter to Alice, specifying the cells that Alice will probe from epoch i. This last step is expensive, costing at least one bit for each of the t_q cells probed by each of Alice's queries. This is the reason why the lower bound of Pătraşcu requires large weights assigned to the input points (by having larger weights, the lower bound on the communication game increases since knowing the answer to a query reveals more information).

Our Technique.

Our new technique elegantly circumvents the limitations of Pătraşcu's technique by exploiting recent ideas by Panigrahy et al. [5] for proving static lower bounds. The basic setup is the same, i.e. we consider epochs $i = 1, \ldots, \lg_\beta n$, where the i'th epoch consists of β^i updates. As with the two previous techniques, we associate a cell to the epoch in which it was last updates. Lower bounds now follow by showing that any data structure must probe $\Omega(\lg_\beta n)$ cells associated to each epoch i when answering a query at the end of epoch 1. Summing over all $\lg_\beta n$ epochs, this gives us a lower bound of $\Omega(\lg_\beta^2 n)$.

To show that $\Omega(\lg_\beta n)$ probes to cells associated to an epoch i are required, we assume for contradiction that a data structure probing $o(\lg_\beta n)$ cells associated to epoch i exists. Using this data structure, we then consider a game between an encoder and a decoder. The encoder receives as input the updates of all epochs, and must from this send a message to the decoder. The decoder then sees this message and all updates preceding epoch i and must from this uniquely recover the updates of epoch i. If the message is smaller than the entropy of the updates of epoch i (conditioned on preceding epochs), this gives an information theoretic contradiction. The trick is to find a way for the encoder to exploit the small number of probed cells to send a short message.

As mentioned, we use the ideas in [5] to exploit the small number of probes. In [5] it was observed that if S is a set of cells, and if the query algorithm of a data structure probes $o(\lg_\beta n)$ cells from S on average over all queries (for large enough β), then there is a subset of cells $S' \subseteq S$ which *resolves* a large number of queries. Here we say that a subset of cells $S' \subseteq S$ resolves a query, if the query algorithm probes no cells in $S \setminus S'$ when answering that query. What this observation gives us compared to the approach of Pătraşcu, is that we can find a large set of queries that are all resolved by the same small subset of cells associated to an epoch i. Thus when amortizing over all the queries resolved by the set S', we no longer have to use t_q bits per query just to specify the cells it probes.

With this observation in mind, the encoder proceeds as follows: First he executes all the updates of all epochs on the claimed data structure. He then sends all cells associated to epochs $j < i$. For large enough β, this message is smaller than the entropy of the β^i updates of epoch i. Letting S_i denote the cells associated to epoch i, the decoder then finds a subset of cells $S_i' \subseteq S_i$, such that a large number of queries are resolved by S_i'. He then sends a description of those cells and proceeds by finding a subset Q of the queries resolved by S_i', such that knowing the answer to all queries in Q reduces the entropy of the updates of epoch i by more than the number of bits needed to describe S_i', Q and the cells associated to epochs $j < i$. He then sends a description of Q followed by an encoding of the updates of epoch i, conditioned on the answers to queries in Q. Since the entropy of the updates of epoch i is reduced by more bits than was already send, this gives our contradiction (if the decoder can recover the updates from the above messages).

To recover the updates of epoch i, the decoder first executes the updates preceding epoch i. His goal is to simulate the query algorithm for every query in Q to recover all the answers. He achieves this in the following way: For each cell c requested when answering a query $q \in Q$, he examines the cells associated to epochs $j < i$ (those cells were send by the encoder), and if c is contained in one of those he immediately recovers the contents. If not, he proceeds by examining the set S_i'. If c is included in this set, he has again recovered the contents and can continue the simulation. Finally, if c is not in S_i', then c must be associated to an epoch preceding epoch i (since queries in Q probe no cells in $S_i \setminus S_i'$), thus the decoder recovers the contents of c from the updates that he executed initially. In this manner, the decoder can recover the answer to every query in Q, and from the last part of the message he recovers the updates of epoch i.

The main technical challenge in using our technique lies in arguing that if $o(\lg_\beta n)$ cells are probed amongst the cells associated to epoch i, then the claimed cell set S_i' and query set Q exists. In the next section, we demonstrate the technique on a concrete problem by proving our lower bound for dynamic weighted orthogonal range counting.

3. DYNAMIC LOWER BOUND

In this section we prove our main result, which we have formulated in the following theorem:

THEOREM 1. *Any data structure for dynamic weighted orthogonal range counting in the cell probe model, must satisfy $t_q = \Omega((\lg n / \lg(wt_u))^2)$. Here t_q is the expected average query time and t_u the worst case update time. This lower bound holds when the weights of the inserted points are $\Theta(\lg n)$-bit integers.*

We prove Theorem 1 by devising a hard distribution over updates, followed by one uniform random query. We then lower bound the expected cost (over the distribution) of answering the query for any *deterministic* data structure with worst case update time t_u. By Yao's principle [11], this translates into a lower bound on the expected average query time of a possibly randomized data structure. In our proof we assume the weights are $4 \lg n$-bit integers and note that our lower bound applies to any $\varepsilon \lg n$-bit weights, where $\varepsilon > 0$ is an arbitrarily small constant, simply because a data structure for $\varepsilon \lg n$-bit integer weights can be used to solve the problem for any $O(\lg n)$-bit integer weights with a constant factor overhead by dividing the bits of the weights into $\lceil \delta / (\varepsilon \lg n) \rceil = O(1)$ chunks and maintaining a data structure for each chunk. We begin our proof by presenting our hard distribution over updates and queries.

Hard Distribution.

Our updates arrive in batches, or *epochs*, of exponentially decreasing size. For $i = 1, \dots, \lg_\beta n$ we define epoch i as a sequence of β^i updates, for a parameter $\beta > 1$ to be fixed later. The epochs occur in time from biggest to smallest epoch, and at the end of epoch 1 we execute a uniform random query in $[n] \times [n]$.

What remains is to specify which updates are performed in each epoch i. The updates of epoch i are chosen to mimic the hard input distribution for static orthogonal range counting on a set of β^i points. We first define the following point set known as the Fibonacci lattice:

DEFINITION 1 ([4]). *The Fibonacci lattice F_m is the set of m two-dimensional points defined by $F_m = \{(i, if_{k-1} \bmod m) \mid i = 0, \dots, m-1\}$, where $m = f_k$ is the k'th Fibonacci number.*

The β^i updates of epoch i now consists of inserting each point of the Fibonacci lattice F_{β^i}, but scaled to fit the input region $[n] \times [n]$, i.e. the j'th update of epoch i inserts the point with coordinates $(n/\beta^i \cdot j, n/\beta^i \cdot (jf_{k_i - 1} \bmod \beta^i))$, for $j = 0, \dots, \beta^i$. The weight of each inserted point is a uniform random integer amongst $[\Delta]$, where Δ is the largest prime number smaller than $2^{4 \lg n} = n^4$. This concludes the description of our hard distribution.

The Fibonacci lattice has the desirable property that it is very uniform. This plays an important role in our lower bound proof, and we have formulated this property in the following lemma:

LEMMA 1 ([1]). *For the Fibonacci lattice F_{β^i}, where the coordinates of each point have been multiplied by n/β^i, and for $\alpha > 0$, any axis-aligned rectangle in $[0, n - n/\beta^i] \times [0, n - n/\beta^i]$ with area $\alpha n^2 / \beta^i$ contains between $\lfloor \alpha / a_1 \rfloor$ and $\lceil \alpha / a_2 \rceil$ points, where $a_1 \approx 1.9$ and $a_2 \approx 0.45$.*

Note that we assume each β^i to be a Fibonacci number (denoted f_{k_i}), and that each β^i divides n. These assumptions can easily be removed by fiddling with the constants, but this would only clutter the exposition.

For the remainder of the paper, we let $\mathbf{U}_i$ denote the random variable giving the sequence of updates in epoch i, and we let $\mathbf{U} = \mathbf{U}_{\lg_\beta n} \cdots \mathbf{U}_1$ denote the random variable giving all updates of all $\lg_\beta n$ epochs. Finally, we let $\mathbf{q}$ be the random variable giving the query.

A Chronogram Approach.

Having defined our hard distribution over updates and queries, we now give a high-level proof of our lower bound. Assume a deterministic data structure solution exists with worst case update time t_u. From this data structure and a sequence of updates $U = U_{\lg_\beta n}, \dots, U_1$, where each U_j is a possible outcome of $\mathbf{U}_j$, we define $S(U)$ to be the set of cells stored in the data structure after executing the updates U. Now associate each cell in $S(U)$ to the last epoch in which its contents were updated, and let $S_i(U)$ denote the subset of $S(U)$ associated to epoch i for $i = 1, \dots, \lg_\beta n$. Also let $t_i(U, q)$ denote the number of cells in $S_i(U)$ probed by the query algorithm of the data structure when answering the query $q \in [n] \times [n]$ after the sequence of updates U. Finally, let $t_i(U)$ denote the average cost of answering a query $q \in [n] \times [n]$ after the sequence of updates U, i.e. let $t_i(U) = \sum_{q \in [n] \times [n]} t_i(U, q) / n^2$. Then the following holds:

LEMMA 2. *If* $\beta = (wt_u)^9$, *then* $\mathbb{E}[t_i(\boldsymbol{U}, \mathbf{q})] = \Omega(\lg_\beta n)$ *for all* $i \geq \frac{15}{16} \lg_\beta n$.

Before giving the proof of Lemma 2, we show that it implies Theorem 1: Let β be as in Lemma 2. Since the cell sets $S_{\lg_\beta n}(\mathbf{U}), \ldots, S_1(\mathbf{U})$ are disjoint, we get that the number of cells probed when answering the query $\mathbf{q}$ is $\sum_i t_i(\mathbf{U}, \mathbf{q})$. It now follows immediately from linearity of expectation that the expected number of cells probed when answering $\mathbf{q}$ is $\Omega(\lg_\beta n \cdot \lg_\beta n) = \Omega((\lg n / \lg(wt_u))^2)$, which completes the proof of Theorem 1.

The hard part thus lies in proving Lemma 2, i.e. in showing that the random query must probe a lot of cells associated to each of the epochs $i = \frac{15}{16} \lg_\beta n, \ldots, \lg_\beta n$. This will be the focus of the next section.

3.1 Bounding the Probes to Epoch i

As also pointed out in Section 2, we prove Lemma 2 using an encoding argument. Assume for contradiction that there exists a data structure solution such that under our hard distribution, with $\beta = (wt_u)^9$, there exists an epoch $i^* \geq \frac{15}{16} \lg_\beta n$, such that the claimed data structure satisfies $\mathbb{E}[t_{i^*}(\mathbf{U}, \mathbf{q})] = o(\lg_\beta n)$.

First observe that $\mathbf{U}_{i^*}$ is independent of $\mathbf{U}_{\lg_\beta n} \cdots \mathbf{U}_{i^*+1}$, i.e. $H(\mathbf{U}_{i^*} \mid \mathbf{U}_{\lg_\beta n} \cdots \mathbf{U}_{i^*+1}) = H(\mathbf{U}_{i^*})$, where $H(\cdot)$ denotes binary entropy. Furthermore, we have $H(\mathbf{U}_{i^*}) = \beta^{i^*} \lg \Delta$, since the updates of epoch i^* consists of inserting β^{i^*} fixed points, each with a uniform random weight amongst the integers $[\Delta]$. Our goal is to show that, conditioned on $\mathbf{U}_{\lg_\beta n} \cdots \mathbf{U}_{i^*+1}$, we can use the claimed data structure solution to encode $\mathbf{U}_{i^*}$ in less than $H(\mathbf{U}_{i^*})$ bits in expectation, i.e. a contradiction. We view this encoding step as a game between an encoder and a decoder. The encoder receives as input the sequence of updates $\mathbf{U} = \mathbf{U}_{\lg_\beta n}, \ldots, \mathbf{U}_1$. The encoder now examines these updates and from them sends a message to the decoder (an encoding). The decoder now sees this message, as well as $\mathbf{U}_{\lg_\beta n}, \ldots, \mathbf{U}_{i^*+1}$ (we conditioned on these variables), and must from this uniquely recover $\mathbf{U}_{i^*}$. If we can design a procedure for constructing and decoding the encoder's message, such that the expected size of the message is less than $H(\mathbf{U}_{i^*}) = \beta^{i^*} \lg \Delta$ bits, then we have reached our contradiction.

Before presenting our encoding and decoding procedures, we show exactly what breaks down if the claimed data structure probes too few cells from epoch i^*. For this, we first introduce some terminology. For a query point $q = (x, y) \in [n] \times [n]$, we define for every epoch $i = 1, \ldots, \lg_\beta n$ the *incidence vector* $\chi_i(q)$, as a vector in $\{0,1\}^{\beta^i}$. The j'th coordinate of $\chi_i(q)$ is 1 if the j'th point inserted in epoch i is dominated by q, and 0 otherwise. More formally, for a query $q = (x, y)$, the j'th coordinate $\chi_i(q)_j$ is given by:

$$\chi_i(q)_j = \begin{cases} 1 & \text{if } jn/\beta^i \leq x \wedge (jf_{k_i - 1} \bmod \beta^i)n/\beta^i \leq y \\ 0 & \text{otherwise} \end{cases}$$

Similarly, we define for a fixed sequence of updates U_i, where U_i is a possible outcome of $\mathbf{U}_i$, the β^i-dimensional vector u_i for which the j'th coordinate equals the weight assigned to the j'th inserted point in U_i. We note that U_i and u_i uniquely specify each other, since all possible outcomes of $\mathbf{U}_i$ inserts the same fixed points, only the weights vary.

Finally observe that the answer to a query q after a fixed sequence of updates $U_{\lg_\beta n}, \ldots, U_1$ is $\sum_{i=1}^{\lg_\beta n} \langle \chi_i(q), u_i \rangle$, where $\langle \cdot, \cdot \rangle$ denotes the standard inner product. With these definitions, we now present the main result forcing a data structure to probe many cells from each epoch:

LEMMA 3. *Let* $i \geq \frac{15}{16} \lg_\beta n$ *be an epoch, and let* $U = U_{\lg_\beta n}, \ldots, U_1$ *be a fixed sequence of updates, where each* U_j *is a possible outcome of* $\mathbf{U}_j$. *If* $t_i(U) = o(\lg_\beta n)$, *then there exists a subset of cells* $C_i \subseteq S_i(U)$ *and a set of query points* $Q \subseteq [n] \times [n]$ *such that:*

1. $|C_i| = O(\beta^{i-1} w)$.
2. $|Q| = \Omega(\beta^{i-3/4})$.
3. *The set of incidence vectors* $\chi_i(Q) = \{\chi_i(q) \mid q \in Q\}$ *is a linearly independent set of vectors in* $[\Delta]^{\beta^i}$.
4. *The query algorithm of the data structure solution probes no cells in* $S_i(U) \setminus C_i$ *when answering a query* $q \in Q$ *after the sequence of updates* U.

The contradiction that this lemma intuitively gives us, is that the queries in Q reveal more information about U_i than the bits in C_i can describe. We note that Lemma 3 essentially is a generalization of the results proved in the static range counting papers [6, 3], simply phrased in terms of cell subsets answering many queries instead of communication complexity. Since the proof contains only few new ideas, we have deferred it to Section 4 and instead move on to show how we use this lemma in our encoding and decoding procedures.

Encoding.

Let $U = U_{\lg_\beta n}, \ldots, U_1$ be a fixed sequence of updates given as input to the encoder, where each U_j is a possible outcome of $\mathbf{U}_j$. Also let $i^* \geq \frac{15}{16} \lg_\beta n$ be the epoch for which $\mathbb{E}[t_{i^*}(\mathbf{U}, \mathbf{q})] = o(\lg_\beta n)$. We construct the message of the encoder by the following procedure:

1. First the encoder executes the sequence of updates U on the claimed data structure, and from this obtains the sets $S_{\lg_\beta n}(U), \ldots, S_1(U)$. He then simulates the query algorithm on the data structure for every query $q \in [n] \times [n]$. From this, the encoder computes $t_{i^*}(U)$ (just the average number of cells in $S_{i^*}(U)$ that are probed).
2. If $t_{i^*}(U) > 2\mathbb{E}[t_{i^*}(\mathbf{U}, \mathbf{q})]$, then the encoder writes a 1-bit, followed by $\lceil \beta^{i^*} \lg \Delta \rceil = H(\mathbf{U}_{i^*}) + O(1)$ bits, simply specifying each weight assigned to a point in U_{i^*} (this can be done in the claimed amount of bits by interpreting the weights as one big integer in $[\Delta^{\beta^{i^*}}]$). This is the complete message send to the decoder when $t_{i^*}(U) > 2\mathbb{E}[t_{i^*}(\mathbf{U}, \mathbf{q})]$.
3. If $t_{i^*}(U) \leq 2\mathbb{E}[t_{i^*}(\mathbf{U}, \mathbf{q})]$, then the encoder first writes a 0-bit. Now since $t_{i^*}(U) \leq 2\mathbb{E}[t_{i^*}(\mathbf{U}, \mathbf{q})] = o(\lg_\beta n)$, we get from Lemma 3 that there must exist a set of cells $C_{i^*} \subseteq S_{i^*}(U)$ and a set of queries $Q \subseteq [n] \times [n]$ satisfying 1-4 in Lemma 3. The encoder finds such sets C_{i^*} and Q simply by trying all possible sets in some arbitrary but fixed order (given two candidate sets C'_{i^*} and Q' it is straight forward to verify whether they satisfy properties 1-4 of Lemma 3). The encoder now writes down these two sets, including addresses

and contents of the cells in C_{i^*}, for a total of at most $O(w) + 2|C_{i^*}|w + \lg \binom{n^2}{|Q|}$ bits (the $O(w)$ bits specifies $|C_{i^*}|$ and $|Q|$).

4. The encoder now constructs a set X, such that $X = \chi_{i^*}(Q)$ initially. Then he iterates through all vectors in $\{0,1\}^{\beta^{i^*}}$, in some arbitrary but fixed order, and for each such vector x, checks whether x is in span(X). If not, the encoder adds x to X. This process continues until dim(span(X)) $= \beta^{i^*}$, at which point the encoder computes and writes down $(\langle x, u_{i^*}\rangle \mod \Delta)$ for each x that was added to X. Since dim(span($\chi_{i^*}(Q)$)) $= |Q|$ (by point 3 in Lemma 3), this adds a total of $\lceil(\beta^{i^*} - |Q|)\lg \Delta\rceil$ bits to the message (by interpreting the values as one big integer in $[\Delta^{\beta^{i^*}-|Q|}]$).

5. Finally, the encoder writes down all of the cell sets $S_{i^*-1}(U), \dots, S_1(U)$, including addresses and contents, plus all of the vectors $u_{i^*-1}, \dots, u_1$. This takes at most $\sum_{j=1}^{i^*-1}(2|S_j(U)|w + \beta^j \lg \Delta + O(w))$ bits. When this is done, the encoder sends the constructed message to the decoder.

Before analysing the expected size of the encoding, we present the decoding procedure.

Decoding.

In the following, we describe our decoding procedure. The decoder receives as input the updates $U_{\lg_\beta n}, \dots, U_{i^*+1}$ and the message from the encoder. The decoder now recovers U_{i^*} by the following procedure:

1. The decoder examines the first bit of the message. If this bit is 1, then the decoder immediately recovers U_{i^*} from the encoding (step 2 in the encoding procedure). If not, the decoder instead executes the updates $U_{\lg_\beta n} \cdots U_{i^*+1}$ on the claimed data structure solution and obtains the cells sets $S^{i^*+1}_{\lg_\beta n}(U), \dots, S^{i^*+1}_{i^*+1}(U)$ where $S^{i^*+1}_j(U)$ contains the cells that were last updated during epoch j when executing updates $U_{\lg_\beta n}, \dots, U_{i^*+1}$ (and not the entire sequence of updates $U_{\lg_\beta n}, \dots, U_1$).

2. The decoder now recovers $Q, C_{i^*}, S_{i^*-1}(U), \dots, S_1(U)$ and $u_{i^*-1}, \dots, u_1$ from the encoding. For each query $q \in Q$, the decoder then computes the answer to q as if all updates $U_{\lg_\beta n}, \dots, U_1$ had been performed. The decoder accomplishes this by simulating the query algorithm on q, and for each cell requested, the decoder recovers the contents of that cell as it would have been if all updates $U_{\lg_\beta n}, \dots, U_1$ had been performed. This is done in the following way: When the query algorithm requests a cell c, the decoder first determines whether c is in one of the sets $S_{i^*-1}(U), \dots, S_1(U)$. If so, the correct contents of c (the contents after the updates $U = U_{\lg_\beta n}, \dots, U_1$) is directly recovered. If c is not amongst these cells, the decoder checks whether c is in C_{i^*}. If so, we have again recovered the contents. Finally, if c is not in C_{i^*}, then from point 4 of Lemma 3, we get that c is not in $S_{i^*}(U)$. Since c is not in any of $S_{i^*}(U), \dots, S_1(U)$, this means that the contents of c has not changed during the updates $U_{i^*}, \dots, U_1$, and thus the decoder finally recovers the contents of c from $S^{i^*+1}_{\lg_\beta n}(U), \dots, S^{i^*+1}_{i^*+1}(U)$. The decoder can therefore recover the answer to each query q in Q if it had been executed after the sequence of updates $U_{\lg_\beta n}, \dots, U_1$, i.e. for all $q \in Q$, he knows $\sum_{i=1}^{\lg_\beta n}\langle \chi_i(q), u_i\rangle$.

3. The next decoding step consists of computing for each query q in Q, the value $\langle \chi_{i^*}(q), u_{i^*}\rangle$. For each $q \in Q$, the decoder already knows the value $\sum_{i=1}^{\lg_\beta n}\langle \chi_i(q), u_i\rangle$ from the above. From the encoding of $u_{i^*-1}, \dots, u_1$, the decoder can compute the value $\sum_{i=1}^{i^*-1}\langle \chi_i(q), u_i\rangle$ and finally from $U_{\lg_\beta n}, \dots, U_{i^*+1}$ the decoder computes $\sum_{i=i^*+1}^{\lg_\beta n}\langle \chi_i(q), u_i\rangle$. The decoder can now recover the value $\langle \chi_{i^*}(q), u_{i^*}\rangle$ simply by observing that $\langle \chi_{i^*}(q), u_{i^*}\rangle = \sum_{i=1}^{\lg_\beta n}\langle \chi_i(q), u_i\rangle - \sum_{i\neq i^*}\langle \chi_i(q), u_i\rangle$.

4. Now from the query set Q, the decoder construct the set of vectors $X = \chi_{i^*}(Q)$, and then iterates through all vectors in $\{0,1\}^{\beta^{i^*}}$, in the same fixed order as the encoder. For each such vector x, the decoder again verifies whether x is in span(X), and if not, adds x to X and recovers $\langle x, u_{i^*}\rangle \mod \Delta$ from the encoding. The decoder now constructs the $\beta^{i^*} \times \beta^{i^*}$ matrix A, having the vectors in X as rows. Similarly, he construct the vector $\mathbf{z}$ having one coordinate for each row of A. The coordinate of $\mathbf{z}$ corresponding to a row vector x, has the value $\langle x, u_{i^*}\rangle \mod \Delta$. Note that this value is already known to the decoder, regardless of whether x is also in $\chi_{i^*}(Q)$ (simply taking modulo Δ on the value $\langle \chi_{i^*}(x), u_{i^*}\rangle$ computed above for each vector in $\chi_{i^*}(Q)$), or was added later. Since A has full rank, and since the set $[\Delta]$ endowed with integer addition and multiplication modulo Δ is a finite field, it follows that the system of equations $A \otimes \mathbf{y} = \mathbf{z}$ has a unique solution $\mathbf{y} \in [\Delta]^{\beta^{i^*}}$ (here $\otimes$ denotes matrix-vector multiplication modulo Δ). But $u_{i^*} \in [\Delta]^{\beta^{i^*}}$ and $A \otimes u_{i^*} = \mathbf{z}$, thus the decoder now solves the linear system of equations $A \otimes \mathbf{y} = \mathbf{z}$ and uniquely recovers u_{i^*}, and therefore also U_{i^*}. This completes the decoding procedure.

Analysis.

We now analyse the expected size of the encoding of $\mathbf{U}_{i^*}$. We first analyse the size of the encoding when $t_{i^*}(\mathbf{U}) \leq 2\mathbb{E}[t_{i^*}(\mathbf{U}, \mathbf{q})]$. In this case, the encoder sends a message of

$$2|C_{i^*}|w + \lg \binom{n^2}{|Q|} + (\beta^{i^*} - |Q|)\lg \Delta$$

$$+O(w \lg_\beta n) + \sum_{j=1}^{i^*-1}(2|S_j(\mathbf{U})|w + \beta^j \lg \Delta)$$

bits. Since $\beta^{i^*} \lg \Delta = H(\mathbf{U}_{i^*})$ and $|C_{i^*}|w = o(|Q|)$, the above is upper bounded by

$$H(\mathbf{U}_{i^*}) - |Q|\lg(\Delta/n^2) + o(|Q|) + \sum_{j=1}^{i^*-1}(2|S_j(\mathbf{U})|w + \beta^j \lg \Delta).$$

Since $\beta \geq 2$, we also have $\sum_{j=1}^{i^*-1}\beta^j \lg \Delta < 2\beta^{i^*-1}\lg \Delta = o(|Q|\lg \Delta)$. Similarly, we have $|S_j(\mathbf{U})| \leq \beta^j t_u$, which gives us $\sum_{j=1}^{i^*-1} 2|S_j(\mathbf{U})|w < 4\beta^{i^*-1}wt_u = o(|Q|)$. From standard results on prime numbers, we have that the largest prime number smaller than n^4 is at least n^3 for infinitely many n, i.e. we can assume $\lg(\Delta/n^2) = \Omega(\lg \Delta)$. Therefore, the above is again upper bounded by

$$H(\mathbf{U}_{i^*}) - \Omega(|Q| \lg \Delta) = H(\mathbf{U}_{i^*}) - \Omega(\beta^{i^*-3/4} \lg \Delta).$$

This part thus contributes at most

$$\Pr[t_{i^*}(\mathbf{U}) \leq 2\mathbb{E}[t_{i^*}(\mathbf{U}, \mathbf{q})]] \cdot (H(\mathbf{U}_{i^*}) - \Omega(\beta^{i^*-3/4} \lg \Delta))$$

bits to the expected size of the encoding. The case where $t_{i^*}(\mathbf{U}) > 2\mathbb{E}[t_{i^*}(\mathbf{U}, \mathbf{q})]$ similarly contributes $\Pr[t_{i^*}(\mathbf{U}) > 2\mathbb{E}[t_{i^*}(\mathbf{U}, \mathbf{q})]] \cdot (H(\mathbf{U}_{i^*}) + O(1))$ bits to the expected size of the encoding. Now since $\mathbf{q}$ is uniform, we have $\mathbb{E}[t_{i^*}(\mathbf{U})] = \mathbb{E}[t_{i^*}(\mathbf{U}, \mathbf{q})]$, we therefore get from Markov's inequality that $\Pr[t_{i^*}(\mathbf{U}) > 2\mathbb{E}[t_{i^*}(\mathbf{U}, \mathbf{q})]] < \frac{1}{2}$. Therefore the expected size of our encoding is upper bounded by $O(1) + \frac{1}{2}H(\mathbf{U}_{i^*}) + \frac{1}{2}(H(\mathbf{U}_{i^*}) - \Omega(\beta^{i^*-3/4} \lg \Delta)) < H(\mathbf{U}_{i^*})$ finally leading to our contradiction and completing the proof of Lemma 2.

4. THE STATIC SETUP

Finally, in this section we prove Lemma 3, the last piece in our lower bound proof. As already mentioned, we prove the lemma by extending on previous ideas for proving lower bounds on static range counting. We note that we have chosen a more geometric (and we believe more intuitive) approach to the proof than the previous papers.

For the remainder of the section, we let $U = U_{\lg_\beta n}, \ldots, U_1$ be a fixed sequence of updates, where each U_j is a possible outcome of $\mathbf{U}_j$, and $i \geq \frac{15}{16} \lg_\beta n$ an epoch. Furthermore, we assume that the claimed data structure satisfies $t_i(U) = o(\lg_\beta n)$, and our task is to show that the claimed cell set C_i and query set Q exists.

Our first step is to find a geometric property of a set of queries Q, such that $\chi_i(Q)$ is a linearly independent set of vectors. One property that ensures this, is that the queries in Q are sufficiently *well spread*. To make this more formal, we introduce the following terminology:

A *grid* G with *width* $\mu \geq 1$ and *height* $\gamma \geq 1$, is the collection of *grid cells* $[j\mu, (j+1)\mu) \times [h\gamma, (h+1)\gamma)$ such that $0 \leq j < n/\mu$ and $0 \leq h < n/\gamma$. We say that a query point $q = (x, y) \in [n] \times [n]$ *hits* a grid cell $[j\mu, (j+1)\mu) \times [h\gamma, (h+1)\gamma)$ of G, if the point (x, y) lies within that grid cell, i.e. if $j\mu \leq x < (j+1)\mu$ and $h\gamma \leq y < (h+1)\gamma$. Finally, we define the *hitting number* of a set of queries Q' on a grid G, as the number of distinct grid cells in G that is hit by a query in Q'.

With this terminology, we have the following lemma:

LEMMA 4. *Let Q' be a set of queries and G a grid with width μ and height $n^2/\beta^i\mu$ for some parameter $n/\beta^i \leq \mu \leq n$. Let h denote the hitting number of Q' on G. Then there is a subset of queries $Q \subseteq Q'$, such that $|Q| = \Omega(h - 6n/\mu - 6\mu\beta^i/n)$ and $\chi_i(Q)$ is a linearly independent set of vectors in $[\Delta]^{\beta^i}$.*

We defer the proof of Lemma 4 to Section 4.1, and instead continue our proof of Lemma 3.

In light of Lemma 4, we set out to find a set of cells $C_i \subseteq S_i(U)$ and a grid G, such that the set of queries Q_{C_i} that probe no cells in $S_i(U) \setminus C_i$, hit a large number of grid cells in G. For this, first define the grids $G_2, \ldots, G_{2i-2}$ where G_j has width $n/\beta^{i-j/2}$ and height $n/\beta^{j/2}$. The existence of C_i is guaranteed by the following lemma:

LEMMA 5. *Let $i \geq \frac{15}{16} \lg_\beta n$ be an epoch and $U_{\lg_\beta n}, \ldots, U_1$ a fixed sequence of updates, where each U_j is a possible outcome of $\mathbf{U}_j$. Assume furthermore that the claimed data structure satisfies $t_i(U) = o(\lg_\beta n)$. Then there exists a set of cells $C_i \subseteq S_i(U)$ and an index $j \in \{2, \ldots, 2i-2\}$, such that $|C_i| = O(\beta^{i-1}w)$ and Q_{C_i} has hitting number $\Omega(\beta^{i-3/4})$ on the grid G_j.*

To not remove focus from our proof of Lemma 3 we have moved the proof of this lemma to Section 4.2. We thus move on to show that Lemma 4 and Lemma 5 implies Lemma 3. By assumption we have $t_i(U) = o(\lg_\beta n)$. Combining this with Lemma 5, we get that there exists a set of cells $C_i \subseteq S_i(U)$ and an index $j \in \{2, \ldots, 2i-2\}$, such that $|C_i| = O(\beta^{i-1}w)$ and the set of queries Q_{C_i} has hitting number $\Omega(\beta^{i-3/4})$ on the grid G_j. Furthermore, we have that grid G_j is a grid of the form required by Lemma 4, with $\mu = n/\beta^{i-j/2}$. Thus by Lemma 4 there is a subset $Q \subseteq Q_{C_i}$ such that $|Q| = \Omega(\beta^{i-3/4} - 12\beta^{i-1}) = \Omega(\beta^{i-3/4})$ and $\chi_i(Q)$ is a linearly independent set of vectors in $[\Delta]^{\beta^i}$. This completes the proof of Lemma 3.

4.1 Proof of Lemma 4

We prove the lemma by giving an explicit construction of the set Q.

First initialize Q to contain one query point from Q' from each cell of G that is hit by Q'. We will now repeatedly eliminate queries from Q until the remaining set is linearly independent. We do this by *crossing out* rows and columns of G. By crossing out a row (column) of G, we mean deleting all queries in Q that hits a cell in that row (column). Our procedure for crossing out rows and columns is as follows:

First cross out the bottom two rows and leftmost two columns. Amongst the remaining columns, cross out either the even or odd columns, whichever of the two contains the fewest remaining points in Q. Repeat this once again for the columns, with even and odd redefined over the remaining columns. Finally, do the same for the rows. We claim that the remaining set of queries are linearly independent. To see this, order the remaining queries in increasing order of column index (leftmost column has lowest index), and secondarily in increasing order of row index (bottom row has lowest index). Let $q_1, \ldots, q_{|Q|}$ denote the resulting sequence of queries. For this sequence, it holds that for every query q_j, there exists a coordinate $\chi_i(q_j)_h$, such that $\chi_i(q_j)_h = 1$, and at the same time $\chi_i(q_k)_h = 0$ for all $k < j$. Clearly this implies linear independence. To prove that the remaining vectors have this property, we must show that for each query q_j, there is some point in the scaled Fibonacci lattice F_{β^i} that is dominated by q_j, but not by any of $q_1, \ldots, q_{j-1}$: Associate each remaining query q_j to the two-by-two crossed out grid cells to the bottom-left of the grid cell hit by q_j. These four grid cells have area $4n^2/\beta^i$ and are contained within the rectangle $[0, n - n/\beta^i] \times [0, n - n/\beta^i]$, thus from Lemma 1 it follows that at least one point of the scaled Fibonacci lattice F_{β^i} is contained therein, and thus dominated by q_j. But all q_k, where $k < j$, either hit a grid cell in a column with index at least three less than that hit by q_j (we crossed out the two columns preceding that hit by q_j), or they hit a grid cell in the same column as q_j but with a row index that is at least three lower than that hit by q_j (we crossed out the two rows preceding that hit by q_j). In either case, such a query cannot dominate the point inside the cells associated to q_j.

What remains is to bound the size of Q. Initially, we have $|Q| = h$. The bottom two rows have a total area of $2n^3/\beta^i\mu$, thus by Lemma 1 they contain at most $6n/\mu$ points. The leftmost two columns have area $2n\mu$ and thus contain at most $6\mu\beta^i/n$ points. After crossing out these rows and column we are therefore left with $|Q| \geq h - 6n/\mu - 6\mu\beta^i/n$. Finally, when crossing out even or odd rows we always choose the one eliminating fewest points, thus the remaining steps at most reduce the size of Q by a factor 16. This completes the proof of Lemma 4.

4.2 Proof of Lemma 5

We prove the lemma using another encoding argument. However, this time we do not encode the update sequence, but instead we define a distribution over query sets, such that if Lemma 5 is not true, then we can encode such a query set in too few bits.

Let $U = U_{\lg_\beta n}, \dots, U_1$ be a fixed sequence of updates, where each U_j is a possible outcome of $\mathbf{U}_j$. Furthermore, assume for contradiction that the claimed data structure satisfies both $t_i(U) = o(\lg_\beta n)$ and for all cell sets $C \subseteq S_i(U)$ of size $|C| = O(\beta^{i-1}w)$ and every index $j \in \{2, \dots, 2i-2\}$, it holds that the hitting number of Q_C on grid G_j is $o(\beta^{i-3/4})$. Here Q_C denotes the set of all queries q in $[n] \times [n]$ such that the query algorithm of the claimed data structure probes no cells in $S_i(U) \setminus C$ when answering q after the sequence of updates U. Under these assumptions we will construct an impossible encoder. As mentioned, we will encode a set of queries:

Hard Distribution.

Let $\mathbf{Q}$ denote a random set of queries, constructed by drawing one uniform random query (with integer coordinates) from each of the β^{i-1} vertical slabs of the form

$$[hn/\beta^{i-1}, (h+1)n/\beta^{i-1}) \times [0, n),$$

where $h \in [\beta^{i-1}]$. Our goal is to encode $\mathbf{Q}$ in less than $H(\mathbf{Q}) = \beta^{i-1}\lg(n^2/\beta^{i-1})$ bits in expectation. Before giving our encoding and decoding procedures, we prove some simple properties of $\mathbf{Q}$:

Define a query q in a query set Q' to be *well-separated* if for all other queries $q' \in Q'$, where $q \neq q'$, q and q' do not lie within an axis-aligned rectangle of area $n^2/\beta^{i-1/2}$. Finally, define a query set Q' to be *well-separated* if at least $\frac{1}{2}|Q'|$ queries in Q' are well-separated. We then have:

LEMMA 6. *The query set $\mathbf{Q}$ is well-separated with probability at least 3/4.*

PROOF. Let $\mathbf{q}_h$ denote the random query in $\mathbf{Q}$ lying in the h'th vertical slab. The probability that $\mathbf{q}_h$ lies within a distance of at most $n/\beta^{i-3/4}$ from the x-border of the h'th slab is precisely $(2n/\beta^{i-3/4})/(n/\beta^{i-1}) = 2/\beta^{1/4}$. If this is not the case, then for another query $\mathbf{q}_k$ in $\mathbf{Q}$, we know that the x-coordinates of $\mathbf{q}_h$ and $\mathbf{q}_k$ differ by at least $(|k-h|-1)n/\beta^{i-1} + n/\beta^{i-3/4}$. This implies that $\mathbf{q}_h$ and $\mathbf{q}_k$ can only be within an axis-aligned rectangle of area $n^2/\beta^{i-1/2}$ if their y-coordinates differ by at most $n/((|k-h|-1)\beta^{1/2} + \beta^{1/4})$. This happens with probability at most $2/((|k-h|-1)\beta^{1/2} + \beta^{1/4})$. The probability that a query $\mathbf{q}_h$ in $\mathbf{Q}$ is not well-separated is therefore bounded by

$$\frac{2}{\beta^{1/4}} + (1 - \frac{2}{\beta^{1/4}}) \sum_{k \neq j} \frac{2}{(|k-h|-1)\beta^{1/2} + \beta^{1/4}}$$

$$\leq \frac{10}{\beta^{1/4}} + \sum_{k \neq j} \frac{2}{|k-h|\beta^{1/2}} = O\left(\frac{1}{\beta^{1/4}} + \frac{\lg n}{\beta^{1/2}}\right).$$

Since $\beta = (wt_u)^9 = \omega(\lg^2 n)$ this probability is $o(1)$, and the result now follows from linearity of expectation and Markov's inequality. □

Now let $S_i(Q, U) \subseteq S_i(U)$ denote the subset of cells in $S_i(U)$ probed by the query algorithm of the claimed data structure when answering all queries in a set of queries Q after the sequence of updates U (i.e. the union of the cells probed for each query in Q). Since a uniform random query from $\mathbf{Q}$ is uniform in $[n] \times [n]$, we get by linearity of expectation that $\mathbb{E}[|S_i(\mathbf{Q}, U)|] = \beta^{i-1}t_i(U)$. From this, Lemma 6, Markov's inequality and a union bound, we conclude

LEMMA 7. *The query set $\mathbf{Q}$ is both well-separated and $|S_i(\mathbf{Q}, U)| \leq 4\beta^{i-1}t_i(U)$ with probability at least 1/2.*

With this established, we are now ready to give our impossible encoding of $\mathbf{Q}$.

Encoding.

In the following we describe the encoding procedure. The encoder receives as input a set of queries Q, where Q is a possible outcome of $\mathbf{Q}$. He then executes the below procedure to encode Q:

1. The encoder first executes the fixed sequence of updates U on the claimed data structure, and from this obtains the sets $S_{\lg_\beta n}(U), \dots, S_1(U)$. He then runs the query algorithm for every query $q \in Q$ and collects the set $S_i(Q, U)$.
2. If Q is not well-separated or if $|S_i(Q, U)| > 4\beta^{i-1}t_i(U)$, then the encoder sends a 1-bit followed by a straight forward encoding of Q using $H(\mathbf{Q}) + O(1)$ bits in total. This is the complete encoding procedure when either Q is not well-separated or $|S_i(Q, U)| > 4\beta^{i-1}t_i(U)$.
3. If Q is both well-separated and $|S_i(Q, U)| \leq 4\beta^{i-1}t_i(U)$, then the encoder first writes a 0-bit and then executes the remaining four steps.
4. The encoder examines Q and finds the at most $\frac{1}{2}|Q|$ queries that are not well-separated. Denote this set Q'. The encoder now writes down Q' by first specifying $|Q'|$, then which vertical slabs contain the queries in Q' and finally what the coordinates of each query in Q' is within its slab. This takes $O(w) + \lg\binom{|Q|}{|Q'|} + |Q'|\lg(n^2/\beta^{i-1}) = O(w) + O(\beta^{i-1}) + |Q'|\lg(n^2/\beta^{i-1})$ bits.
5. The encoder now writes down the cell set $S_i(Q, U)$, including **only** the addresses and **not** the contents. This takes $o(H(\mathbf{Q}))$ bits since

$$\lg\binom{|S_i(U)|}{|S_i(Q, U)|} = O(\beta^{i-1}t_i(U)\lg(\beta t_u)) = o(\beta^{i-1}\lg(n^2/\beta^{i-1})),$$

where in the first line we used that $|S_i(U)| \le \beta^i t_u$ and $|S_i(Q,U)| \le 4\beta^{i-1}t_i(U)$. The second line follows from the fact that $t_i(U) = o(\lg_\beta n) = o(\lg(n^2/\beta^{i-1})/\lg(\beta t_u))$ since $\beta = \omega(t_u)$.

6. Next we encode the x-coordinates of the well-separated queries in Q. Since we have already encoded which vertical slabs contain well-separated queries (we really encoded the slabs containing queries that are not well-separated, but this is equivalent), we do this by specifying only the offset within each slab. This takes $(|Q|-|Q'|)\lg(n/\beta^{i-1})+O(1)$ bits. Following that, the encoder considers the last grid G_{2i-2}, and for each well-separated query q, he writes down the y-offset of q within the grid cell of G_{2i-2} hit by q. Since the grid cells of G_{2i-2} have height n/β^{i-1}, this takes $(|Q|-|Q'|)\lg(n/\beta^{i-1})+O(1)$ bits. Combined with the encoding of the x-coordinates, this step adds a total of $(|Q|-|Q'|)\lg(n^2/\beta^{2i-2})+O(1)$ bits to the size of the encoding.

7. In the last step of the encoding procedure, the encoder simulates the query algorithm for every query in $[n]\times[n]$ and from this obtains the set $Q_{S_i(Q,U)}$, i.e. the set of all those queries that probe no cells in $S_i(U) \setminus S_i(Q,U)$. Observe that $Q \subseteq Q_{S_i(Q,U)}$. The encoder now considers each of the grids G_j, for $j = 2,\ldots,2i-2$, and determines both the set of grid cells $G_j^{Q_{S_i(Q,U)}} \subseteq G_j$ hit by a query in $Q_{S_i(Q,U)}$, and the set of grid cells $G_j^Q \subseteq G_j^{Q_{S_i(Q,U)}} \subseteq G_j$ hit by a well-separated query in Q. The last step of the encoding consists of specifying G_j^Q. This is done by encoding which subset of $G_j^{Q_{S_i(Q,U)}}$ corresponds to G_j^Q. This takes $\lg\binom{|G_j^{Q_{S_i(Q,U)}}|}{|G_j^Q|}$ bits for each $j = 2,\ldots,2i-2$.

   Since $|S_i(Q,U)| = o(\beta^{i-1}\lg_\beta n) = o(\beta^{i-1}w)$ we get from our contradictory assumption that the hitting number of $Q_{S_i(Q,U)}$ on each grid G_j is $o(\beta^{i-3/4})$, thus $|G_j^{Q_{S_i(Q,U)}}| = o(\beta^{i-3/4})$. Therefore the above amount of bits is at most

$$\begin{aligned}(|Q|-|Q'|)\lg(\beta^{i-3/4}e/(|Q|-|Q'|))(2i-3) &\le \\ (|Q|-|Q'|)\lg(\beta^{1/4})2i + O(\beta^{i-1}i) &\le \\ (|Q|-|Q'|)\tfrac{1}{4}\lg(\beta)2\lg_\beta n + O(\beta^{i-1}\lg_\beta n) &\le \\ (|Q|-|Q'|)\tfrac{1}{2}\lg n + o(H(\mathbf{Q}))&\end{aligned}$$

   This completes the encoding procedure, and the encoder finishes by sending the constructed message to the decoder.

Before analysing the size of the encoding, we show that the decoder can recover Q from the encoding.

Decoding.

In this paragraph we describe the decoding procedure. The decoder only knows the fixed sequence $U = U_{\lg_\beta n},\ldots,U_1$ and the message received from the encoder. The goal is to recover Q, which is done by the following steps:

1. The decoder examines the first bit of the message. If this is a 1-bit, the decoder immediately recovers Q from the remaining part of the encoding.

2. If the first bit is 0, the decoder proceeds with this step and all of the below steps. The decoder executes the updates U on the claimed data structure and obtains the sets $S_{\lg_\beta n}(U),\ldots,S_1(U)$. From step 4 of the encoding procedure, the decoder also recovers Q'.

3. From step 5 of the encoding procedure, the decoder now recovers the addresses of the cells in $S_i(Q,U)$. Since the decoder has the data structure, he already knows the contents. Following this, the decoder now simulates every query in $[n]\times[n]$, and from this and $S_i(Q,U)$ recovers the set $Q_{S_i(Q,U)}$.

4. From step 6 of the encoding procedure, the decoder now recovers the x-coordinates of every well-separated query in Q (the offsets are enough since the decoder knows which vertical slabs contain queries in Q', and thus also those that contain well-separated queries). Following that, the decoder also recovers the y-offset of each well-separated query $q \in Q$ within the grid cell of G_{2i-2} hit by q (note that the decoder does not know what grid cell it is, he only knows the offset).

5. From the set $Q_{S_i(Q,U)}$ the decoder now recovers the set $G_j^{Q_{S_i(Q,U)}}$ for each $j = 2,\ldots,2i-2$. This information is immediate from the set $Q_{S_i(Q,U)}$. From $G_j^{Q_{S_i(Q,U)}}$ and step 7 of the encoding procedure, the decoder now recovers G_j^Q for each j. In grid G_2, we know that Q has only one query in every column, thus the decoder can determine uniquely from G_2^Q which grid cell of G_2 is hit by each well-separated query in Q. Now observe that the axis-aligned rectangle enclosing all $\beta^{1/2}$ grid cells in G_{j+1} that intersects a fixed grid cell in G_j has area $n^2/\beta^{i-1/2}$. Since we are considering well-separated queries, i.e. queries where no two lie within an axis-aligned rectangle of area $n^2/\beta^{i-1/2}$, this means that G_{j+1}^Q contains at most one grid cell in such a group of $\beta^{1/2}$ grid cells. Thus if q is a well-separated query in Q, we can determine uniquely which grid cell of G_{j+1} that is hit by q, directly from G_{j+1}^Q and the grid cell in G_j hit by q. But we already know this information for grid G_2, thus we can recover this information for grid $G_3, G_4,\ldots,G_{2i-2}$. Thus we know for each well-separated query in Q which grid cell of G_{2i-2} it hits. From the encoding of the x-coordinates and the y-offsets, the decoder have thus recovered Q.

Analysis.

Finally we analyse the size of the encoding. First consider the case where $\mathbf{Q}$ is both well-separated and $|S_i(\mathbf{Q},U)| \le 4\beta^{i-1}t_i(U)$. In this setting, the size of the message is bounded by

$$|\mathbf{Q}'|\lg(n^2/\beta^{i-1})+(|\mathbf{Q}|-|\mathbf{Q}'|)(\lg(n^2/\beta^{2i-2})+\tfrac{1}{2}\lg n)+o(H(\mathbf{Q}))$$

bits. This equals

$$|\mathbf{Q}|\lg(n^{2+1/2}/\beta^{2i-2}) + |\mathbf{Q}'|\lg(\beta^{i-1}/n^{1/2}) + o(H(\mathbf{Q}))$$

bits. Since we are considering an epoch $i \ge \frac{15}{16}\lg_\beta n$, we have $\lg(n^{2+1/2}/\beta^{2i-2}) \le \lg(n^{5/8}\beta^2)$, thus the above amount of bits is upper bounded by

$$|\mathbf{Q}|\lg(n^{5/8}\beta^2) + |\mathbf{Q}'|\lg(n^{1/2}) + o(H(\mathbf{Q})).$$

Since $|\mathbf{Q}'| \leq \frac{1}{2}|\mathbf{Q}|$, this is again bounded by

$$|\mathbf{Q}| \lg(n^{7/8}\beta^2) + o(H(\mathbf{Q}))$$

bits. But $H(\mathbf{Q}) = |\mathbf{Q}| \lg(n^2/\beta^i) \geq |\mathbf{Q}| \lg n$, i.e. our encoding uses less than $\frac{15}{16}H(\mathbf{Q})$ bits.

Finally, let E denote the event that $\mathbf{Q}$ is well-separated and at the same time $|S_i(\mathbf{Q}, U)| \leq 4\beta^{i-1}t_i(U)$, then the expected number of bits used by the entire encoding is bounded by

$$O(1) + \Pr[E](1 - \Omega(1))H(\mathbf{Q}) + (1 - \Pr[E])H(\mathbf{Q})$$

The contradiction is now reached by invoking Lemma 7 to conclude that $\Pr[E] \geq 1/2$.

5. CONCLUDING REMARKS

In this paper we presented a new technique for proving dynamic cell probe lower bounds. With this technique we proved the highest dynamic cell probe lower bound to date under the most natural setting of cell size $w = \Theta(\lg n)$, namely a lower bound of $t_q = \Omega((\lg n/\lg(wt_u))^2)$.

While our results have taken the field of cell probe lower bounds one step further, there is still a long way to go. Amongst the results that seems within grasp, we find it a very intriguing open problem to prove an $\omega(\lg n)$ lower bound for a problem where the queries have a one bit output. Our technique crucially relies on the output having more bits than it takes to describe a query, since otherwise the encoder cannot afford to tell the decoder which queries to simulate. Since many interesting data structure problems have a one bit output size, finding a technique for handling this case would allow us to attack many more fundamental data structure problems.

Applying our technique to other problems is also an important task, however such problems must again have a logarithmic number of bits in the output of queries.

6. ACKNOWLEDGMENT

The author wishes to thank Peter Bro Miltersen for much useful discussion on both the results and writing of this paper.

7. REFERENCES

[1] A. Fiat and A. Shamir. How to find a battleship. *Networks*, 19:361–371, 1989.

[2] M. Fredman and M. Saks. The cell probe complexity of dynamic data structures. In *Proc. 21st ACM Symposium on Theory of Computation*, pages 345–354, 1989.

[3] A. G. Jørgensen and K. G. Larsen. Range selection and median: Tight cell probe lower bounds and adaptive data structures. In *Proc. 22nd ACM/SIAM Symposium on Discrete Algorithms*, pages 805–813, 2011.

[4] J. Matoušek. *Geometric Discrepancy.* Springer, 1999.

[5] R. Panigrahy, K. Talwar, and U. Wieder. Lower bounds on near neighbor search via metric expansion. In *Proc. 51st IEEE Symposium on Foundations of Computer Science*, pages 805–814, 2010.

[6] M. Pătraşcu. Lower bounds for 2-dimensional range counting. In *Proc. 39th ACM Symposium on Theory of Computation*, pages 40–46, 2007.

[7] M. Pătraşcu. Unifying the landscape of cell-probe lower bounds. In *Proc. 49th IEEE Symposium on Foundations of Computer Science*, pages 434–443, 2008.

[8] M. Pătraşcu. Towards polynomial lower bounds for dynamic problems. In *Proc. 42nd ACM Symposium on Theory of Computation*, pages 603–610, 2010.

[9] M. Pătraşcu and E. D. Demaine. Logarithmic lower bounds in the cell-probe model. *SIAM Journal on Computing*, 35:932–963, April 2006.

[10] M. Pătraşcu and M. Thorup. Don't rush into a union: Take time to find your roots. In *Proc. 43rd ACM Symposium on Theory of Computation*, 2011. To appear. See also arXiv:1102.1783.

[11] A. C.-C. Yao. Probabilistic computations: Toward a unified measure of complexity. In *Proc. 18th IEEE Symposium on Foundations of Computer Science*, pages 222–227, 1977.

[12] A. C. C. Yao. Should tables be sorted? *Journal of the ACM*, 28(3):615–628, 1981.

Linear vs. Semidefinite Extended Formulations: Exponential Separation and Strong Lower Bounds

Samuel Fiorini[*]
Université libre de Bruxelles,
Brussels, Belgium
sfiorini@ulb.ac.be

Serge Massar[†]
Université libre de Bruxelles,
Brussels, Belgium
smassar@ulb.ac.be

Sebastian Pokutta
Friedrich-Alexander-Universität,
Erlangen-Nürnberg, Germany
sebastian.pokutta@math.uni-erlangen.de

Hans Raj Tiwary[‡]
Université libre de Bruxelles,
Brussels, Belgium
htiwary@ulb.ac.be

Ronald de Wolf[§]
CWI and University of Amsterdam
Amsterdam, The Netherlands.
rdewolf@cwi.nl

ABSTRACT

We solve a 20-year old problem posed by Yannakakis and prove that there exists no polynomial-size linear program (LP) whose associated polytope projects to the traveling salesman polytope, even if the LP is not required to be symmetric. Moreover, we prove that this holds also for the cut polytope and the stable set polytope. These results were discovered through a new connection that we make between one-way quantum communication protocols and semidefinite programming reformulations of LPs.

Categories and Subject Descriptors

F.2.2 [**Analysis of Algorithms and Problem Complexity**]: Nonnumerical Algorithms and Problems; G.2.0 [**Discrete Mathematics**]: General

General Terms

Theory

[*]Partially supported by the *Actions de Recherche Concertées* (ARC) fund of the French community of Belgium.

[†]Partially supported by the European Commission under the project QCS (Grant No. 255961).

[‡]Postdoctoral Researcher of the *Fonds National de la Recherche Scientifique* (F.R.S.–FNRS).

[§]Partially supported by a Vidi grant from the Netherlands Organization for Scientific Research (NWO), and by the European Commission under the project QCS (Grant No. 255961)

Keywords

Combinatorial optimization, linear programming, communication complexity, semidefinite programming, quantum communication complexity

1. INTRODUCTION

In 1986–1987 there were attempts [42] to prove P = NP by giving a polynomial-size LP that would solve the traveling salesman problem (TSP). Due to the large size and complicated structure of the proposed LP for the TSP, it was difficult to show directly that the LP was erroneous. In a groundbreaking effort to refute all such attempts, Yannakakis [47] proved that every symmetric LP for the TSP has exponential size (see [48] for the journal version). Here, an LP is called *symmetric* if every permutation of the cities can be extended to a permutation of all the variables of the LP that preserves the constraints of the LP. Because the proposed LP for the TSP was symmetric, it could not possibly be correct.

In his paper, Yannakakis left as a main open problem the question of proving that the TSP admits no polynomial-size LP, *symmetric or not.* We solve this question by proving a super-polynomial lower bound on the number of inequalities in *every* LP for the TSP. We also prove such unconditional super-polynomial lower bounds for the maximum cut and maximum stable set problems. Therefore, it is impossible to prove P = NP by means of a polynomial-size LP that expresses any of these problems. Our approach is inspired by a close connection between semidefinite programming reformulations of LPs and one-way quantum communication protocols that we introduce here.

1.1 State of the Art

Solving a Problem Through an LP.

A combinatorial optimization problem such as the TSP comes with a natural set of binary variables. When we say that an LP solves the problem, we mean that there exists an LP over this set of variables plus extra variables that returns the correct objective function value for all instances over the same set of natural variables, that is, for *all* choices of weights for the natural variables.

From Problems to Polytopes.

When encoded as 0/1-points in $\mathbb{R}^d$, the feasible solutions of a combinatorial optimization problem yield a polytope that is the convex hull of the resulting points (see Appendix A for background on polytopes). Solving an instance of the problem then amounts to optimizing a linear objective function over this polytope.

For example, the *TSP polytope* TSP(n) is the convex hull of all points $x \in \{0,1\}^{\binom{n}{2}}$ that correspond to a Hamiltonian cycle in the complete n-vertex graph K_n. If we want to solve a TSP instance with edge-weights w_{ij}, the goal would be to minimize $\sum_{i<j} w_{ij}x_{ij}$ for $x \in \text{TSP}(n)$. This minimum is attained at a vertex of the polytope, i.e., at an $x \in \{0,1\}^{\binom{n}{2}}$ that corresponds to a Hamiltonian cycle.

The idea of representing the set of feasible solutions of a problem by a polytope forms the basis of a standard and powerful methodology in combinatorial optimization, see, e.g., [39].

Extended Formulations and Extensions.

Even for polynomially solvable problems, the associated polytope may have an exponential number of facets. By working in an extended space, it is often possible to decrease the number of constraints. In some cases, a polynomial increase in dimension can be traded for an exponential decrease in the number of constraints. This is the idea underlying extended formulations.

Formally, an *extended formulation* (EF) of a polytope $P \subseteq \mathbb{R}^d$ is a linear system

$$E^{\leqslant}x + F^{\leqslant}y \leqslant g^{\leqslant},\ E^{=}x + F^{=}y = g^{=} \tag{1}$$

in variables $(x,y) \in \mathbb{R}^{d+k}$ such that $x \in P$ if and only if there exists y such that (1) holds. The *size* of an EF is defined as its number of *inequalities* in the system.[1] Optimizing any objective function $f(x)$ over all $x \in P$ amounts to optimizing $f(x)$ over all $(x,y) \in \mathbb{R}^{d+k}$ satisfying (1), provided (1) defines an EF of P.

An *extension* of the polytope P is another polytope[2] $Q \subseteq \mathbb{R}^e$ such that P is the image of Q under a linear map. We define the *size* of an extension Q as the number of facets of Q. If P has an extension of size r, then it has an EF of size r. Conversely, it is known that if P has an EF of size r, then it has an extension of size at most r (see Theorem 3 below). In this sense, the concepts of EF and extension are essentially equivalent.

The Impact of Extended Formulations.

EFs have pervaded the areas of discrete optimization and approximation algorithms for a long time. For instance, Balas' disjunctive programming [5], the Sherali-Adams hierarchy [41], the Lovász-Schrijver closures [32], lift-and-project [6], and configuration LPs are all based on the idea of working in an extended space. Recent surveys on EFs in the context of combinatorial optimization and integer programming are [11, 43, 23, 46].

Symmetry Matters.

Yannakakis [48] proved a $2^{\Omega(n)}$ lower bound on the size of any *symmetric* EF of the TSP polytope TSP(n) (defined above and in Section 3.4). Although he remarked that he did "not think that asymmetry helps much", it was recently shown by Kaibel *et al.* [24] (see also [35]) that symmetry is a restriction in the sense that there exist polytopes that have polynomial-size EFs but no polynomial-size symmetric EF. This revived Yannakakis's tantalizing question about unconditional lower bounds. That is, bounds which apply to the *extension complexity* of a polytope P, defined as the minimum size of an EF of P.

0/1-Polytopes with Large Extension Complexity.

The strongest unconditional lower bounds so far were obtained by Rothvoß [37]. By an elegant counting argument inspired by Shannon's theorem [40], it was proved that there exist 0/1-polytopes in $\mathbb{R}^d$ whose extension complexity is at least $2^{d/2-o(d)}$. However, Rothvoß's technique does not provide *explicit* 0/1-polytopes with an exponential extension complexity.

The Factorization Theorem.

Yannakakis [48] discovered that the extension complexity of a polytope P is determined by certain factorizations of an associated matrix, called the *slack matrix* of P, that records for each pair (F, v) of a facet F and vertex v, the algebraic distance of v to a hyperplane supporting F. Defining the *nonnegative rank* of a matrix M as the smallest natural number r such that M can be expressed as $M = TU$ where T and U are nonnegative matrices (i.e., matrices whose elements are all nonnegative) with r columns (in case of T) and r rows (in case of U), respectively, it turns out that the extension complexity of every polytope P is exactly the nonnegative rank of its slack matrix.

This *factorization theorem* led Yannakakis to explore connections between EFs and communication complexity. Let S denote the slack matrix of the polytope P. He proved that: (i) every deterministic communication protocol of complexity k computing S gives rise to an EF of P of size at most 2^k, provided S is a 0/1-matrix; (ii) the nondeterministic communication complexity of the *support matrix* of S (i.e., the binary matrix that has 0-entries exactly where S is 0) yields a lower bound on the extension complexity of P, or more generally, the nondeterministic communication complexity of the support matrix of every nonnegative matrix M yields a lower bound on the nonnegative rank of M.[3]

[1] Another possible definition of size is the sum of the number of variables and total number of constraints (equalities plus inequalities) defining the EF. This makes little difference because if $P \subseteq \mathbb{R}^d$ has an EF with r inequalities, then it has an EF with $d+r$ variables, r inequalities and at most $d+r$ equalities (see the proof of Theorem 3 below).

[2] We could allow unbounded polyhedra here, but it again makes little difference because it can be shown that every extension of a polytope with a minimum number of facets is also a polytope.

[3] The classical nondeterministic communication complexity of a binary communication matrix is defined as $\lceil \log B \rceil$, where B is the minimum number of monochromatic 1-rectangles that cover the matrix, see [26]. This last quantity is also known as the *rectangle covering bound*. It is easy to see that the rectangle covering bound of the support matrix of any matrix M lower bounds the nonnegative rank of M (see Theorem 4 below).

Tighter Communication Complexity Connection.
Faenza *et al.* [15] proved that the base-2 logarithm of the nonnegative rank of a matrix equals, up to a small additive constant, the minimum complexity of a randomized communication protocol *with nonnegative outputs* that computes the matrix *in expectation*. In particular, every EF of size r can be regarded as such a protocol of complexity $\log r + O(1)$ bits that computes a slack matrix in expectation.

The Clique vs. Stable Set Problem.
When P is the stable set polytope $\mathrm{STAB}(G)$ of a graph G (see Section 3.3), the slack matrix of P contains an interesting row-induced 0/1-submatrix that is the communication matrix of the *clique vs. stable set problem* (also known as the *clique vs. independent set problem*): its rows correspond to the cliques and its columns to the stable sets (or independent sets) of graph G. The entry for a clique K and stable set S equals $1 - |K \cap S|$. Yannakakis [48] gave an $O(\log^2 n)$ deterministic protocol for the clique vs. stable set problem, where n denotes the number of vertices of G. This gives a $2^{O(\log^2 n)} = n^{O(\log n)}$ size EF for $\mathrm{STAB}(G)$ whenever the whole slack matrix is 0/1, that is, whenever G is a perfect graph.

A notoriously hard open question is to determine the communication complexity (in the deterministic or nondeterministic sense) of the clique vs. stable set problem. (For recent results that explain why this question is hard, see [27, 28].) The best lower bound to this day is due to Huang and Sudakov [22]: they obtained a $\frac{6}{5}\log n - O(1)$ lower bound.[4] Furthermore, they state a graph-theoretical conjecture that, if true, would imply a $\Omega(\log^2 n)$ lower bound, and hence settle the communication complexity of the clique vs. stable set problem. Moreover it would give a worst-case $n^{\Omega(\log n)}$ lower bound on the extension complexity of stable set polytopes. However, a solution to the Huang-Sudakov conjecture seems only a distant possibility.

1.2 Contribution

Our contribution in this paper is three-fold.

- First, inspired by earlier work [45], we define a $2^n \times 2^n$ matrix $M = M(n)$ and show that the nonnegative rank of M is $2^{\Omega(n)}$ because the nondeterministic communication complexity of its support matrix is $\Omega(n)$. The latter was proved in [45] using the well-known disjointness lower bound of Razborov [36]. We use the matrix M to prove a $2^{\Omega(n)}$ lower bound on the extension complexity of the cut polytope $\mathrm{CUT}(n)$ (Section 3.2). That is, we prove that *every* EF of the cut polytope has an exponential number of inequalities. Via reductions, we infer from this: (i) an infinite family of graphs G such that the extension complexity of the corresponding stable set polytope $\mathrm{STAB}(G)$ is $2^{\Omega(n^{1/2})}$, where n denotes the number of vertices of G (Section 3.3); (ii) that the extension complexity of the TSP polytope $\mathrm{TSP}(n)$ is $2^{\Omega(n^{1/4})}$ (Section 3.4).

  In addition to settling simultaneously the above-mentioned open problems of Yannakakis [48] and Rothvoß [37], our results provide a lower bound on the extension complexity of stable set polytopes that goes beyond what is implied by the Huang-Sudakov conjecture (thanks to the fact that we consider a different part of the slack matrix). Although our lower bounds are strong, unconditional and apply to explicit polytopes that are well-known in combinatorial optimization, they have very accessible proofs.

- Second, we generalize the factorization theorem to *conic* EFs, that is, reformulations of an LP through a conic program. In particular, this implies a factorization theorem for *semidefinite* EFs: the *semidefinite extension complexity* of a polytope equals the *positive semidefinite rank* (*PSD rank*) of its slack matrix.

- Third, we generalize the tight connection between linear[5] EFs and classical communication complexity found by Faenza *et al.* [15] to a tight connection between semidefinite EFs and quantum communication complexity. We show that any *rank-r PSD factorization* of a (nonnegative) matrix M gives rise to a one-way quantum protocol computing M in expectation that uses $\log r + O(1)$ qubits and, *vice versa*, that any one-way quantum protocol computing M in expectation that uses q qubits results in a PSD factorization of M of rank 2^q. Via the semidefinite factorization theorem, this yields a characterization of the semidefinite extension complexity of a polytope in terms of the minimum complexity of quantum protocols that compute the corresponding slack matrix in expectation.

  Then, we give a complexity $\log r + O(1)$ quantum protocol for computing a nonnegative matrix M in expectation, whenever there exists a rank-r matrix N such that M is the entry-wise square of N. This implies in particular that every d-dimensional polytope with 0/1 slacks has a semidefinite EF of size $O(d)$.

  Finally, we obtain an exponential separation between classical and quantum protocols that compute our specific matrix $M = M(n)$ in expectation. On the one hand, our quantum protocol gives a rank-$O(n)$ PSD factorization of M. On the other hand, the nonnegative rank of M is $2^{\Omega(n)}$ because the nondeterministic communication complexity of the support matrix of M is $\Omega(n)$. Thus we obtain an exponential separation between nonnegative rank and PSD rank.

We would like to point out that some of our results in the two last sections were also obtained by Gouveia, Parillo and Thomas. This applies to Theorem 13, Corollary 15, Theorem 18 and Corollary 19. We were aware of the fact that they had obtained Theorem 13 and Corollary 15 prior to writing this paper. However, their proofs were not yet publicly available at that time. Theorem 18 and Corollary 19 were obtained independently, and in a different context. All their results are now publicly available, see [21].

1.3 Related Work

Yannakakis's paper has deeply influenced the TCS community. In addition to the works cited above, it has inspired a whole series of papers on the quality of restricted *approximate* EFs, such as those defined by the Sherali-Adams hi-

[4] All logarithms in this paper are computed in base 2.

[5] In this paragraph, and later in Sections 4 and 5, an EF (in the sense of the previous section) is called a *linear* EF. The use of adjectives such as "linear", "semidefinite" or "conic" will help distinguishing the different types of EFs.

erarchies and Lovász-Schrijver closures starting with [3] ([4] for the journal version), see, e.g., [9, 38, 16, 10, 19, 18, 7].

We would also like to point out that the lower bounds on the extension complexity of polytopes established in Section 3 were obtained by first finding an efficient PSD factorization or, equivalently, an efficient one-way quantum communication protocol for the matrix $M = M(n)$. In this sense our classical lower bounds stem from quantum considerations somewhat similar in style to [25, 1, 2]. See [14] for a survey of this line of work.

1.4 Organization

The discovery of our lower bounds on extension complexity crucially relied on finding the right matrix M and the right polytope whose slack matrix contains M. In our case, we found these through a connection with quantum communication. However, these quantum aspects are not strictly necessary for the resulting lower bound proof itself. Hence, in order to make the main results more accessible to those without background or interest in quantum computing, we start by giving a purely classical presentation of those lower bounds.

In Section 2 we define our matrix M and lower bound the nondeterministic communication complexity of its support matrix. In Section 3 we embed M in the slack matrix of the cut polytope in order to lower bound its extension complexity; further reductions then give lower bounds on the extension complexities of the stable set, and TSP polytopes. In Section 4 we state and prove the factorization theorem for arbitrary closed convex cones. In Section 5 we establish the equivalence of PSD factorizations of a (nonnegative) matrix M and one-way quantum protocols that compute M in expectation, and give an efficient quantum protocol in the case where some entry-wise square root of M has small rank. This is then used to provide an exponential separation between quantum and classical protocols for computing a matrix in expectation (equivalently, an exponential separation between nonnegative rank and PSD rank). Concluding remarks are given in Section 6.

2. A SIMPLE MATRIX WITH LARGE RECTANGLE COVERING BOUND

In this section we consider the following $2^n \times 2^n$ matrix $M = M(n)$ with rows and columns indexed by n-bit strings a and b, and real nonnegative entries:

$$M_{ab} := (1 - a^{\intercal}b)^2.$$

Note for later reference that M_{ab} can also be written as

$$M_{ab} = 1 - \langle 2\operatorname{diag}(a) - aa^{\intercal}, bb^{\intercal}\rangle, \qquad (2)$$

where $\langle \cdot, \cdot \rangle$ denotes Frobenius inner product[6] and $\operatorname{diag}(a)$ is the $n \times n$ diagonal matrix with the entries of a on its diagonal. Let us verify this identity, using $a, b \in \{0,1\}^n$:

$$\begin{aligned}1 - &\langle 2\operatorname{diag}(a) - aa^{\intercal}, bb^{\intercal}\rangle \\ &= 1 - 2\langle \operatorname{diag}(a), bb^{\intercal}\rangle + \langle aa^{\intercal}, bb^{\intercal}\rangle \\ &= 1 - 2a^{\intercal}b + (a^{\intercal}b)^2 = (1 - a^{\intercal}b)^2.\end{aligned}$$

[6]The *Frobenius inner product* is the component-wise inner product of two matrices. For matrices X and Y of the same dimensions, this equals $Tr[X^{\intercal}Y]$. When X is symmetric this can also be written $Tr[XY]$.

Let $\operatorname{suppmat}(M)$ be the binary support matrix of M, so

$$\operatorname{suppmat}(M)_{ab} = \begin{cases} 1 & \text{if } M_{ab} \neq 0, \\ 0 & \text{otherwise.} \end{cases}$$

De Wolf [45] proved that an exponential number of (monochromatic) rectangles are needed to cover all the 1-entries of the support matrix of M. Equivalently, the corresponding function $f : \{0,1\}^n \times \{0,1\}^n \to \{0,1\}$ has nondeterministic communication complexity of $\Omega(n)$ bits. For the sake of completeness we repeat the proof here:

THEOREM 1 ([45]). *Every 1-monochromatic rectangle cover of* $\operatorname{suppmat}(M)$ *has size* $2^{\Omega(n)}$.

PROOF. Let $R_1, \dots, R_k$ be a 1-cover for f, i.e., a set of (possibly overlapping) 1-monochromatic rectangles in the matrix $\operatorname{suppmat}(M)$ that together cover all 1-entries in $\operatorname{suppmat}(M)$.

We use the following result from [26, Example 3.22 and Section 4.6], which is essentially due to Razborov [36]:

> There exist sets $A, B \subseteq \{0,1\}^n \times \{0,1\}^n$ and probability distribution μ on $\{0,1\}^n \times \{0,1\}^n$ such that all $(a,b) \in A$ have $a^{\intercal}b = 0$, all $(a,b) \in B$ have $a^{\intercal}b = 1$, $\mu(A) = 3/4$, and there are constants $\alpha, \delta > 0$ (independent of n) such that for all rectangles R,
>
> $$\mu(R \cap B) \geqslant \alpha \cdot \mu(R \cap A) - 2^{-\delta n}.$$
>
> (For sufficiently large n, $\alpha = 1/135$ and $\delta = 0.017$ will do.)

Since the R_i are 1-rectangles, they cannot contain elements from B. Hence $\mu(R_i \cap B) = 0$ and $\mu(R_i \cap A) \leqslant 2^{-\delta n}/\alpha$. However, since all elements of A are covered by the R_i, we have

$$\frac{3}{4} = \mu(A) = \mu\left(\bigcup_{i=1}^{k}(R_i \cap A)\right) \leqslant \sum_{i=1}^{k}\mu(R_i \cap A) \leqslant k \cdot \frac{2^{-\delta n}}{\alpha}.$$

Hence $k \geqslant 2^{\Omega(n)}$. □

3. STRONG LOWER BOUNDS ON EXTENSION COMPLEXITY

Here we use the matrix $M = M(n)$ defined in the previous section to prove that the (linear) extension complexity of the cut polytope of the n-vertex complete graph is $2^{\Omega(n)}$, i.e., every (linear) EF of this polytope has an exponential number of inequalities. Then, via reductions, we prove superpolynomial lower bounds for the stable set polytopes and the TSP polytopes. To start, let us define more precisely the slack matrix of a polytope. For a matrix A, let A_i denote the ith row of A and A^j to denote the jth column of A.

DEFINITION 2. *Let* $P = \{x \in \mathbb{R}^d \mid Ax \leqslant b\} = \operatorname{conv}(V)$ *be a polytope, with* $A \in \mathbb{R}^{m \times d}$, $b \in \mathbb{R}^m$ *and* $V \subseteq \mathbb{R}^d$, $V = \{v_1, \dots, v_n\}$. *Then* $S \in \mathbb{R}_+^{m \times n}$ *defined as* $S_{ij} := b_i - A_i v_j$ *with* $i \in [m] := \{1, \dots, m\}$ *and* $j \in [n] := \{1, \dots, n\}$ *is the* slack matrix *of* P *w.r.t.* $Ax \leqslant b$ *and* V. *We sometimes refer to the submatrix of the slack matrix induced by rows corresponding to facets and columns corresponding to vertices simply as the* slack matrix *of* P, *denoted by* $S(P)$.

Let $P \subseteq \mathbb{R}^d$ be a polytope. Recall that:

1. an EF of P is a linear system in variables (x, y) such that $x \in P$ if and only if there exists y satisfying the system;
2. an extension of P is a polytope $Q \subseteq \mathbb{R}^e$ such that there is a linear map $\pi : \mathbb{R}^e \to \mathbb{R}^d$ with $\pi(Q) = P$;
3. the extension complexity of P is the minimum size (i.e., number of inequalities) of an EF of P.

We denote the extension complexity of P by $\mathrm{xc}(P)$.

3.1 The Factorization Theorem

A *rank-r nonnegative factorization* of a (nonnegative) matrix M is a factorization $M = TU$ where T and U are nonnegative matrices with r columns (in case of T) and r rows (in case of U), respectively. The nonnegative rank of M (denoted by: $\mathrm{rank}_+(M)$) is thus simply the minimum rank of a nonnegative factorization of M. Note that $\mathrm{rank}_+(M)$ is also the minimum r such that M is the sum of r nonnegative rank-1 matrices. In particular, the nonnegative rank of a matrix M is at least the nonnegative rank of any submatrix of M.

The following factorization theorem was proved by Yannakakis (see also [17]). It can be stated succinctly as: $\mathrm{xc}(P) = \mathrm{rank}_+(S)$ whenever P is a polytope and S a slack matrix of P. We include a sketch of the proof for completeness.

THEOREM 3 ([48]). *Let $P = \{x \in \mathbb{R}^d \mid Ax \leqslant b\} = \mathrm{conv}(V)$ be a polytope with $\dim(P) \geqslant 1$, and let S denote the slack matrix of P w.r.t. $Ax \leqslant b$ and V. Then the following are equivalent for all positive integers r:*

(i) S has nonnegative rank at most r;

(ii) P has an extension of size at most r;

(iii) P has an EF of size at most r.

PROOF (SKETCH). It should be clear that (ii) implies (iii). We prove that (i) implies (ii), and then that (iii) implies (i).

First, consider a rank-r nonnegative factorization $S = TU$ of the slack matrix of P. Notice that we may assume that no column of T is zero, because otherwise r can be decreased. We claim that P is the image of

$$Q := \{(x, y) \in \mathbb{R}^{d+r} \mid Ax + Ty = b,\ y \geqslant \mathbf{0}\}$$

under the projection π_x onto the x-space. We see immediately that $\pi_x(Q) \subseteq P$ since $Ty \geqslant \mathbf{0}$. To prove the inclusion $P \subseteq \pi_x(Q)$, it suffices to remark that for each point $v_j \in V$ the point (v_j, U^j) is in Q since

$$Av_j + TU^j = Av_j + b - Av_j = b \text{ and } U^j \geqslant \mathbf{0}.$$

Since no column of T is zero, Q is a polytope. Moreover, Q has at most r facets, and is thus an extension of P of size at most r. This proves that (i) implies (ii).

Second, suppose that the system

$$E^{\leqslant}x + F^{\leqslant}y \leqslant g^{\leqslant},\ E^{=}x + F^{=}y = g^{=}$$

with $(x, y) \in \mathbb{R}^{d+k}$ defines an EF of P with r inequalities. Let $Q \subseteq \mathbb{R}^{d+k}$ denote the set of solutions to this system. Thus Q is a (nonnecessarily bounded) *polyhedron*. For each point $v_j \in V$, pick $w_j \in \mathbb{R}^k$ such that $(v_j, w_j) \in Q$. Because

$$Ax \leqslant b \iff \exists y : E^{\leqslant}x + F^{\leqslant}y \leqslant g^{\leqslant},\ E^{=}x + F^{=}y = g^{=},$$

each inequality in $Ax \leqslant b$ is valid for all points of Q. Let S_Q be the nonnegative matrix that records the slacks of the points (v_j, w_j) with respect to the inequalities of $E^{\leqslant}x + F^{\leqslant}y \leqslant g^{\leqslant}$, and then of $Ax \leqslant b$. By construction, the submatrix obtained from S_Q by deleting the r first rows is exactly S, thus $\mathrm{rank}_+(S) \leqslant \mathrm{rank}_+(S_Q)$. Furthermore, it follows from Farkas's lemma (here we use $\dim(P) \geqslant 1$) that every row of S_Q is a nonnegative combination of the first r rows of S_Q. Thus, $\mathrm{rank}_+(S_Q) \leqslant r$. Therefore, $\mathrm{rank}_+(S) \leqslant r$. Hence (iii) implies (i). □

We will prove a generalization of Theorem 3 for arbitrary closed convex cones in Section 4, but for now this special case is all we need.

We would like to emphasize that we will not restrict the slack matrix to have rows corresponding only to the facet-defining inequalities. This is not an issue since appending rows corresponding to redundant[7] inequalities does not change the nonnegative rank of the slack matrix. This fact was already used in the second part of the previous proof (see also Lemma 14 below).

Theorem 3 shows in particular that we can lower bound the extension complexity of P by lower bounding the nonnegative rank of its slack matrix S; in fact it suffices to lower bound the nonnegative rank of any submatrix of the slack matrix S corresponding to an implied system of inequalities. To that end, Yannakakis made the following connection with nondeterministic communication complexity. Again, we include the (easy) proof for completeness.

THEOREM 4 ([48]). *Let M be any matrix with nonnegative real entries and $\mathrm{suppmat}(M)$ its support matrix. Then $\mathrm{rank}_+(M)$ is lower bounded by the rectangle covering bound for $\mathrm{suppmat}(M)$.*

PROOF. If $M = TU$ is a rank-r nonnegative factorization of M, then S can be written as the sum of r nonnegative rank-1 matrices:

$$S = \sum_{k=1}^{r} T^k U_k.$$

Taking the support on each side, we find

$$\begin{aligned}\mathrm{supp}(S) &= \bigcup_{k=1}^{r} \mathrm{supp}(T^k U_k) \\ &= \bigcup_{k=1}^{r} \mathrm{supp}(T^k) \times \mathrm{supp}(U_k).\end{aligned}$$

Therefore, $\mathrm{suppmat}(M)$ has a 1-monochromatic rectangle cover with r rectangles. □

3.2 Cut Polytopes

Let $K_n = (V_n, E_n)$ denote the n-vertex complete graph. For a set X of vertices of K_n, we let $\delta(X)$ denote the set of edges of K_n with one endpoint in X and the other in its

[7] An inequality of a linear system is called *redundant* if removing the inequality from the system does not change the set of solutions.

complement $\bar{X}$. This set $\delta(X)$ is known as the *cut* defined by X. For a subset F of edges of K_n, we let $\chi^F \in \mathbb{R}^{E_n}$ denote the *characteristic vector* of F, with $\chi^F_e = 1$ if $e \in F$ and $\chi^F_e = 0$ otherwise. The *cut polytope* $\mathrm{CUT}(n)$ is defined as the convex hull of the characteristic vectors of all cuts in the complete graph $K_n = (V_n, E_n)$. That is,

$$\mathrm{CUT}(n) := \mathrm{conv}\{\chi^{\delta(X)} \in \mathbb{R}^{E_n} \mid X \subseteq V_n\}.$$

We will not deal with the cut polytopes directly, but rather with 0/1-polytopes that are linearly isomorphic to them. The *correlation polytope* (or *boolean quadric polytope*) $\mathrm{COR}(n)$ is defined as the convex hull of all the rank-1 binary symmetric matrices of size $n \times n$. In other words,

$$\mathrm{COR}(n) := \mathrm{conv}\{bb^\intercal \in \mathbb{R}^{n \times n} \mid b \in \{0,1\}^n\}.$$

We use the following known result:

THEOREM 5 ([12]). *For all n, $\mathrm{COR}(n)$ is linearly isomorphic to $\mathrm{CUT}(n+1)$.*

Because M is nonnegative, Eq. (2) gives us a linear inequality that is satisfied by all vertices $bb^\intercal$ of $\mathrm{COR}(n)$, and hence (by convexity) is satisfied by all points of $\mathrm{COR}(n)$:

LEMMA 6. *For all $a \in \{0,1\}^n$, the inequality*

$$\langle 2\,\mathrm{diag}(a) - aa^\intercal, x\rangle \leqslant 1 \tag{3}$$

is valid for $\mathrm{COR}(n)$. Moreover, the slack of vertex $x = bb^\intercal$ with respect to (3) is precisely M_{ab}.

We remark that (3) is weaker than the *hypermetric inequality* [13] $\langle \mathrm{diag}(a) - aa^\intercal, x\rangle \leqslant 0$, in the sense that the face defined by the former is strictly contained in the face defined by the latter. Nevertheless, we persist in using (3). Now, we prove the main result of this section.

THEOREM 7. *There exists some constant $C > 0$ such that, for all n,*

$$\mathrm{xc}(\mathrm{CUT}(n+1)) = \mathrm{xc}(\mathrm{COR}(n)) \geqslant 2^{Cn}.$$

In particular, the extension complexity of $\mathrm{CUT}(n)$ is $2^{\Omega(n)}$.

PROOF. The equality is implied by Theorem 5. Now, consider any system of linear inequalities describing $\mathrm{COR}(n)$ starting with the 2^n inequalities (3), and a slack matrix S w.r.t. this system and $\{bb^\intercal \mid b \in \{0,1\}^n\}$. Next delete from this slack matrix all rows except the 2^n first rows. By Lemma 6, the resulting $2^n \times 2^n$ matrix is M. Using Theorems 3, 4, and 1, and the fact that the nonnegative rank of a matrix is at least the nonnegative rank of any of its submatrices, we have

$$\begin{aligned}\mathrm{xc}(\mathrm{COR}(n)) &= \mathrm{rank}_+(S)\\ &\geqslant \mathrm{rank}_+(M)\\ &\geqslant 2^{Cn}\end{aligned}$$

for some positive constant C. □

3.3 Stable Set Polytopes

A *stable set* S (also called an *independent set*) of a graph $G = (V, E)$ is a subset $S \subseteq V$ of the vertices such that no two of them are adjacent. For a subset $S \subseteq V$, we let $\chi^S \in \mathbb{R}^V$ denote the *characteristic vector* of S, with $\chi^S_v = 1$ if $v \in S$ and $\chi^S_v = 0$ otherwise. The *stable set polytope*, denoted $\mathrm{STAB}(G)$, is the convex hull of the characteristic vectors of all stable sets in G, i.e.,

$$\mathrm{STAB}(G) := \mathrm{conv}\{\chi^S \in \mathbb{R}^V \mid S \text{ stable set of } G\}.$$

Recall that a polytope Q is an extension of a polytope P if P is the image of Q under a linear projection.

LEMMA 8. *For each n, there exists a graph H_n with $O(n^2)$ vertices such that $\mathrm{STAB}(H_n)$ contains a face that is an extension of $\mathrm{COR}(n) \cong \mathrm{CUT}(n+1)$.*

PROOF. Consider the complete graph K_n with vertex set $V_n := [n]$. For each vertex i of K_n we create two vertices labeled $ii, \overline{ii}$ in H_n and an edge between them. For each edge ij of K_n, we add to H_n four vertices labeled $ij, \overline{ij}, \underline{ij}, \underline{\overline{ij}}$ and all possible six edges between them. We further add the following eight edges to H_n:

$$\{ij, \overline{ii}\}, \{ij, \overline{jj}\}, \{\overline{ij}, ii\}, \{\overline{ij}, \overline{jj}\},$$
$$\{\underline{ij}, \overline{ii}\}, \{\underline{ij}, jj\}, \{\underline{\overline{ij}}, ii\}, \{\underline{\overline{ij}}, jj\}.$$

See Fig. 1 for an illustration. The number of vertices in H_n is $2n + 4\binom{n}{2}$.

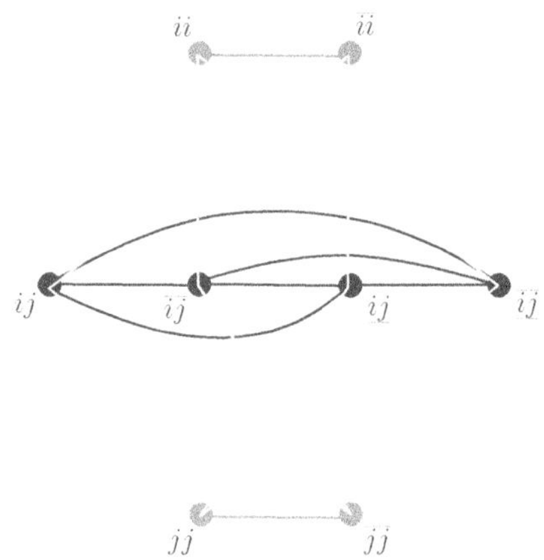

Figure 1: The edges and vertices of H_n corresponding to vertices i, j and edge ij of K_n.

Thus the vertices and edges of K_n are represented by cliques of size 2 and 4 respectively in H_n. We will refer to these as *vertex-cliques* and *edge-cliques* respectively. Consider the face $F = F(n)$ of $\mathrm{STAB}(H_n)$ whose vertices correspond to the stable sets containing exactly one vertex in each vertex-clique and each edge-clique. (The vertices in this face correspond exactly to stable sets of H_n with maximum cardinality.)

Consider the linear map $\pi : \mathbb{R}^{V(H_n)} \to \mathbb{R}^{n \times n}$ mapping a point $x \in \mathbb{R}^{V(H_n)}$ to the point $y \in \mathbb{R}^{n \times n}$ such that $y_{ij} = y_{ji} = x_{ij}$ for $i \leqslant j$. In this equation, the subscripts in y_{ij} and y_{ji} refer to an ordered pair of elements in $[n]$, while the subscript in x_{ij} refers to a vertex of H_n that corresponds either to a vertex of K_n (if $i = j$) or to an edge of K_n (if $i \neq j$).

We claim that the image of F under π is $\mathrm{COR}(n)$, hence F is an extension of $\mathrm{COR}(n)$. Indeed, pick an arbitrary stable set S of H_n such that $x := \chi^S$ is on face F. Then define $b \in \{0,1\}^n$ by letting $b_i := 1$ if $ii \in S$ and $b_i := 0$ otherwise (i.e., $\overline{ii} \in S$). Notice that for the edge ij of K_n we have $ij \in S$ if and only if both vertices ii and jj belong to S. Hence, $\pi(x) = y = bb^\intercal$ is a vertex of $\mathrm{COR}(n)$. This proves $\pi(F) \subseteq \mathrm{COR}(n)$. Now pick a vertex $y := bb^\intercal$ of $\mathrm{COR}(n)$ and consider the unique maximum stable set S that contains vertex ii if $b_i = 1$ and vertex $\overline{ii}$ if $b_i = 0$. Then $x := \chi^S$ is a vertex of F with $\pi(x) = y$. Hence, $\pi(F) \supseteq \mathrm{COR}(n)$. Thus $\pi(F) = \mathrm{COR}(n)$. This concludes the proof. □

Our next lemma establishes simple monotonicity properties of the extension complexity used in our reduction.

LEMMA 9. *Let P, Q and F be polytopes. Then the following hold:*

(i) if F is an extension of P, then $\mathrm{xc}(F) \geqslant \mathrm{xc}(P)$;

(ii) if F is a face of Q, then $\mathrm{xc}(Q) \geqslant \mathrm{xc}(F)$.

PROOF. The first part is obvious because every extension of F is in particular an extension of P. For the second part, notice that a slack matrix of F can be obtained from the (facet-vs-vertex) slack matrix of Q by deleting columns corresponding to vertices not in F. □

Using previous results, we can prove the following result about the worst-case extension complexity of the stable set polytope.

THEOREM 10. *For all n, one can construct a graph G_n with n vertices such that the extension complexity of the stable set polytope $\mathrm{STAB}(G_n)$ is $2^{\Omega(n^{1/2})}$.*

PROOF. W.l.o.g., we may assume $n \geqslant 18$. For an integer $p \geqslant 3$, let $f(p) := |V(H_p)| = 2p + 4\binom{p}{2}$. Given $n \geqslant 18$, we define p as the largest integer with $f(p) \leqslant n$. Now let G_n be obtained from H_p by adding $n - f(p)$ isolated vertices. Then $\mathrm{STAB}(H_p)$ is linearly isomorphic to a face of $\mathrm{STAB}(G_n)$. Using Theorem 7 in combination with Lemmas 8 and 9, we find that

$$\begin{aligned} \mathrm{xc}(\mathrm{STAB}(G_n)) &\geqslant \mathrm{xc}(\mathrm{STAB}(H_p)) \\ &\geqslant \mathrm{xc}(\mathrm{COR}(p)) \\ &= 2^{\Omega(p)} \\ &= 2^{\Omega(n^{1/2})}. \end{aligned}$$

□

3.4 TSP Polytopes

Recall that $\mathrm{TSP}(n)$, the *traveling salesman polytope* or *TSP polytope* of $K_n = (V_n, E_n)$, is defined as the convex hull of the characteristic vectors of all subsets $F \subseteq E_n$ that define a tour of K_n. That is,

$$\mathrm{TSP}(n) := \mathrm{conv}\{\chi^F \in \mathbb{R}^{E_n} \mid F \subseteq E_n \text{ is a tour of } K_n\}.$$

It is known that for every p-vertex graph G, $\mathrm{STAB}(G)$ is the linear projection of a face of $\mathrm{TSP}(n)$ with $n = O(p^2)$, see [48, Theorem 6]. Combining with Theorem 10 gives:

THEOREM 11. *The extension complexity of the TSP polytope $\mathrm{TSP}(n)$ is $2^{\Omega(n^{1/4})}$.*

4. CONIC AND SEMIDEFINITE EFs

In this section we extend Yannakakis's factorization theorem (Theorem 3) to arbitrary closed convex cones. The proof of that theorem shows that, in the linear case, any EF can be brought in the form $Ex + Fy = g$, $y \geqslant \mathbf{0}$ without increasing its size. This form is the basis of our generalization: we replace the nonnegativity constraint $y \geqslant \mathbf{0}$ by a general conic constraint $y \in C$.

Let $Q = \{(x, y) \in \mathbb{R}^{d+k} \mid Ex + Fy = g,\ y \in C\}$ for an arbitrary closed convex cone $C \subseteq \mathbb{R}^k$, where $E \in \mathbb{R}^{p \times d}, F \in \mathbb{R}^{p \times k}$, and $g \in \mathbb{R}^p$. Let $C^* := \{z \in \mathbb{R}^k \mid z^\intercal y \geqslant 0, \forall y \in C\}$ denote the *dual cone* of C. We define the *projection cone of* Q as

$$C_Q := \{\mu \in \mathbb{R}^p \mid F^\intercal \mu \in C^*\}$$

and

$$\mathrm{proj}_x(Q) := \{x \in \mathbb{R}^d \mid \mu^\intercal E x \leqslant \mu^\intercal g, \forall \mu \in C_Q\}.$$

In a first step we show that $\mathrm{proj}_x(Q)$ equals

$$\pi_x(Q) := \{x \in \mathbb{R}^d \mid \exists y \in \mathbb{R}^k : (x, y) \in Q\},$$

the projection of Q to the x-space.

LEMMA 12. *With the above notation, we have $\pi_x(Q) = \mathrm{proj}_x(Q)$.*

PROOF. Let $\alpha \in \pi_x(Q)$. Then there exists $y \in C$ with $E\alpha + Fy = g$. Pick any $\mu \in C_Q$. Then, $\mu^\intercal E\alpha + \mu^\intercal F y = \mu^\intercal g$ holds. Since $F^\intercal \mu \in C^*$ and $y \in C$ we have that $(F^\intercal \mu)^\intercal y = \mu^\intercal F y \geqslant 0$. Therefore $\mu^\intercal E \alpha \leqslant \mu^\intercal g$ holds for all $\mu \in C_Q$. We conclude $\alpha \in \mathrm{proj}_x(Q)$ and as α was arbitrary $\pi_x(Q) \subseteq \mathrm{proj}_x(Q)$ follows.

Now suppose $\pi_x(Q) \neq \mathrm{proj}_x(Q)$. Then there exists α such that $\alpha \in \mathrm{proj}_x(Q)$ but $\alpha \notin \pi_x(Q)$. In other words there is no $y \in C$ such that $Fy = g - E\alpha$ or, equivalently, the convex cone $F(C) := \{Fy \mid y \in C\}$ does not contain the point $g - E\alpha$. Since C is a closed cone, so is $F(C)$. Therefore, by the Strong Separation Theorem there exists $\mu \in \mathbb{R}^p$ such that $\mu^\intercal z \geqslant 0$ is valid for $F(C)$ but $\mu^\intercal(g - E\alpha) < 0$. Then $\mu^\intercal z = \mu^\intercal(Fy) = (\mu^\intercal F)y \geqslant 0$ is valid for C, i.e., $(\mu^\intercal F)y \geqslant 0$ holds for all $y \in C$, implying $F^\intercal \mu \in C^*$. Because $\mu^\intercal(g - E\alpha) < 0$ we have $\mu^\intercal E\alpha > \mu^\intercal g$. On the other hand we have $F^\intercal \mu \in C^*$ so that $\mu \in C_Q$ implying $\mu^\intercal E\alpha \leqslant \mu^\intercal g$; a contradiction. Hence, $\pi_x(Q) = \mathrm{proj}_x(Q)$ follows. □

Let $P = \{x \in \mathbb{R}^d \mid Ax \leqslant b\} = \mathrm{conv}(V)$ be a polytope, with $A \in \mathbb{R}^{m \times d}$, $b \in \mathbb{R}^m$ and $V = \{v_1, \dots, v_n\} \subseteq \mathbb{R}^d$. Then $Ex + Fy = g$, $y \in C$ is a *conic EF* of P whenever $x \in P$ if and only if there exists $y \in C$ such that $Ex + Fy = g$. The set $Q = \{(x, y) \in \mathbb{R}^{d+k} \mid Ex + Fy = g,\ y \in C\}$ is then called a *conic extension* of P w.r.t. C.

We now prove a factorization theorem for the slack matrix of polytopes that generalizes Yannakakis's factorization theorem in the linear case. Yannakakis's result can be obtained as a corollary of our result by taking $C = \mathbb{R}^k_+$, and using Theorem 13 together with the fact that $(\mathbb{R}^k_+)^* = \mathbb{R}^k_+$.

THEOREM 13. *Let $P = \{x \in \mathbb{R}^d \mid Ax \leqslant b\} = \mathrm{conv}(V)$ be a polytope with $\dim(P) \geqslant 1$ defined by m inequalities and n points respectively, and let S be the slack matrix of P w.r.t. $Ax \leqslant b$ and V. Also, let $C \subseteq \mathbb{R}^k$ be a closed convex cone. Then, the following are equivalent:*

(i) There exist T, U such that (the transpose of) each row of T is in C^*, each column of U is in C, and $S = TU$.

(ii) There exists a conic extension $Q = \{(x, y) \in \mathbb{R}^{d+k} \mid Ex + Fy = g,\ y \in C\}$ with $P = \pi_x(Q)$.

Before proving the theorem, we prove a lemma which will allow us to get rid of rows of a slack matrix that correspond to redundant inequalities. Below, we call a factorization as in (i) a factorization of S *w.r.t.* C.

LEMMA 14. *Let $P \subseteq \mathbb{R}^d$ be a polytope with $\dim(P) \geqslant 1$, let S and S' be two slack matrices of P, and let $C \subseteq \mathbb{R}^k$ be a closed convex cone. Then S has a factorization w.r.t. C iff S' has a factorization w.r.t. C.*

PROOF. It suffices to prove the theorem when S' is the submatrix of S induced by the rows corresponding to facet-defining inequalities and the columns corresponding to vertices, that is, when $S' = S(P)$. One implication is clear: if S has a factorization w.r.t. C, then S' also because S' is a submatrix of S.

For the other implication, consider a system $Ax \leqslant b$ of m inequalities and a set $V = \{v_1, \ldots, v_n\}$ of n points such that $P = \{x \in \mathbb{R}^d \mid Ax \leqslant b\} = \text{conv}(V)$. Assume that the f first inequalities of $Ax \leqslant b$ are facet-defining, while the remaining $m - f$ are not, and that the v first points of V are vertices, while the remaining $n - v$ are not.

Consider an inequality $A_i x \leqslant b_i$ with $i > f$. Suppose first that the inequality is redundant. By Farkas's lemma (using $\dim(P) \geqslant 1$), there exist nonnegative coefficients $\mu_{i,k}$ ($k \in [f]$) such that $A_i = \sum_{k \in [f]} \mu_{i,k} A_k$ and $b_i = \sum_{k \in [f]} \mu_{i,k} b_k$ as P is a polytope. If the inequality is not redundant, since it is not facet-defining, it is satisfied with equality by all points of P. In this case, we let $\mu_{i,k} := 0$ for all $k \in [f]$. Finally, for $i \leqslant f$ we let $\mu_{i,k} := 1$ if $i = k$ and $\mu_{i,k} := 0$ otherwise.

Next, consider a point v_j with $j > v$. Because v_j is in P, it can be expressed as a convex combination of the vertices of P: $v_j = \sum_{\ell \in [v]} \lambda_{j,\ell} v_\ell$, where $\lambda_{j,\ell}$ ($\ell \in [v]$) are nonnegative coefficients that sum up to 1. Similarly as above, for $j \leqslant v$ we let $\lambda_{j,\ell} := 1$ if $j = \ell$ and $\mu_{j,\ell} := 0$ otherwise.

Now, let $S' = TU$ be a factorization of S' w.r.t. C. That is, we have row vectors $T_1, \ldots, T_f$ with $(T_k)^\intercal \in C^*$ (for $k \in [f]$) and column vectors $U^1, \ldots, U^v$ with $U^\ell \in C$ (for $\ell \in [v]$) such that $b_k - A_k v_\ell = S'_{k\ell} = T_k U^\ell$ for $k \in [f], \ell \in [v]$.

We extend the factorization of S' into a factorization of S by letting $T_i := \sum_{k \in [f]} \mu_{i,k} T_k$ and $U^j := \sum_{\ell \in [v]} \lambda_{j,\ell} U^\ell$ for $i > f$ and $j > v$. Given our choice of coefficients, these equations also hold for $i \leqslant f$ and $j \leqslant v$. Clearly, each T_i (transposed) is in C^* and each U^j is in C. A straightforward computation then shows $T_i U^j = S_{ij}$ for all $i \in [m], j \in [n]$. Therefore, T_i ($i \in [m]$) and U^j ($j \in [n]$) define a factorization of S w.r.t. C. □

PROOF OF THEOREM 13. We first show that a factorization induces a conic extension. Suppose there exist matrices T, U as above. We claim that Q with $E := A$, $F := T$ and $g := b$ has the desired properties. Let $v_j \in V$, then $S^j = TU^j = b - Av_j$ and so it follows that $(v_j, U^j) \in Q$ and $v_j \in \pi_x(Q)$. Now let $x \in \pi_x(Q)$. Then, there exists $y \in C$ such that $Ax + Ty = b$. Since $T_i y \geqslant 0$ for all $i \in [m]$, we have that $x \in P$. This proves the first implication.

For the converse, suppose $P = \pi_x(Q)$ with Q being a conic extension of P. By Lemma 12, $\pi_x(Q) = \{x \in \mathbb{R}^d \mid \mu^\intercal Ex \leqslant \mu^\intercal g, \forall \mu \in C_Q\}$, where $C_Q = \{\mu \in \mathbb{R}^p \mid F^\intercal \mu \in C^*\}$. By Lemma 14, it suffices to prove that the submatrix of S induced by the rows corresponding to the inequalities of $Ax \leqslant b$ that define facets of P admits a factorization w.r.t. C. Thus, we assume for the rest of the proof that all rows of S correspond to facets of P. Then, for any facet-defining inequality $A_i x \leqslant b_i$ of P there exists $\mu_i \in C_Q$ such that $\mu_i^\intercal Ex \leqslant \mu_i^\intercal y$ defines the same facet as $A_i x \leqslant b_i$. (This follows from the fact that C_Q is closed; see also [29, Theorem 4.3.4].) Scaling μ_i if necessary, this means that $\mu_i^\intercal E = A_i + c^\intercal$ and $\mu_i^\intercal g = b_i + \delta$, where $c^\intercal x = \delta$ is satisfied for *all* points of P. We define $T_i := \mu_i^\intercal F$ for all i; in particular $(T_i)^\intercal \in C^*$ as $\mu_i \in C_Q$. Now let $v_j \in V$. Since $P = \pi_x(Q)$, there exists a $y_j \in C$ such that $Ev_j + Fy_j = g$ and so $\mu_i^\intercal Ev_j + \mu_i^\intercal Fy_j = \mu_i^\intercal g$. With the above we have $A_i v_j + c^\intercal v_j + T_i y_j = b_i + \delta$, hence $A_i v_j + T_i y_j = b_i$ and as $v_j \in \pi_x(Q)$ we deduce $T_i y_j \geqslant 0$. The slack of v_j w.r.t. $A_i x \leqslant b_i$ is $b_i - A_i v_j = \mu_i^\intercal g - \mu_i^\intercal Ev_j = \mu_i^\intercal Fy_j = T_i y_j$. This implies the factorization $S = TU$ with $T_i = \mu_i^\intercal F$ and $U^j = y_j$. □

For a positive integer r, we let $\mathbb{S}_+^r$ denote the cone of $r \times r$ symmetric positive semidefinite matrices embedded in $\mathbb{R}^{r(r+1)/2}$ in such a way that, for all $y, z \in \mathbb{S}_+^r$, the scalar product $z^\intercal y$ is the Frobenius product of the corresponding matrices. A *semidefinite EF (resp. extension) of size* r is simply a conic EF (resp. extension) w.r.t. $C = \mathbb{S}_+^r$. The *semidefinite extension complexity* of polytope P, denoted by $\text{xc}_{SDP}(P)$, is the minimum r such that P has a semidefinite EF of size r. Observe that $(\mathbb{S}_+^r)^* = \mathbb{S}_+^r$. Hence, taking $C := \mathbb{S}_+^k$ and $k := r(r+1)/2$ in Theorem 13, we obtain the following factorization theorem for semidefinite EFs.

COROLLARY 15. *Let $P = \{x \in \mathbb{R}^d \mid Ax \leqslant b\} = \text{conv}(V)$ be a polytope. Then the slack matrix S of P w.r.t. $Ax \leqslant b$ and V has a factorization $S = TU$ so that $(T_i)^\intercal, U^j \in \mathbb{S}_+^r$ if and only if there exists a semidefinite extension $Q = \{(x, y) \in \mathbb{R}^{d+r(r+1)/2} \mid Ex + Fy = g,\ y \in \mathbb{S}_+^r\}$ with $P = \pi_x(Q)$.*

Analogous to nonnegative factorizations and nonnegative rank, we can define PSD factorizations and PSD rank. A *rank-r PSD factorization* of an $m \times n$ matrix M is a collection of $r \times r$ symmetric positive semidefinite matrices $T_1, \ldots, T_m$ and $U^1, \ldots, U^n$ such that the Frobenius product $\langle T_i, U^j \rangle = Tr\left[(T_i)^\intercal U^j\right] = Tr\left[T_i U^j\right]$ equals M_{ij} for all $i \in [m], j \in [n]$. The *PSD rank* of M is the minimum r such that M has a rank-r PSD factorization. We denote this $\text{rank}_{PSD}(M)$. By Corollary 15 (and also Lemma 14), the semidefinite extension complexity of a polytope P is equal to the PSD rank of any slack matrix of P: $\text{xc}_{SDP}(P) = \text{rank}_{PSD}(S)$ whenever S is a slack matrix of P. In the next section we will show that $\text{rank}_{PSD}(M)$ can be expressed in terms of the amount of communication needed by a one-way quantum communication protocol for computing M in expectation (Corollary 17).

5. QUANTUM COMMUNICATION AND PSD FACTORIZATIONS

In this section we explain the connection with quantum communication. This yields results that are interesting in their own right, and also clarifies where the matrix M of Section 2 came from.

For a general introduction to quantum computation we refer to [34, 33], and for quantum communication complexity we refer to [44, 8]. For our purposes, an r-dimensional *quantum state* ρ is an $r \times r$ PSD matrix of trace 1.[8] A *k-qubit state*

[8]For simplicity we restrict to real rather than complex entries, which doesn't significantly affect the results.

is a state in dimension $r = 2^k$. If ρ has rank 1, it can be written as an outer product $|\phi\rangle\langle\phi|$ for some unit vector $|\phi\rangle$, which is sometimes called a *pure state*. We use $|i\rangle$ to denote the pure state vector that has 1 at position i and 0s elsewhere. A quantum measurement (POVM) is described by a set of PSD matrices $\{E_\theta\}_{\theta\in\Theta}$, each labeled by a real number θ, and summing to the r-dimensional identity: $\sum_{\theta\in\Theta} E_\theta = I$. When measuring state ρ with this measurement, the probability of outcome θ equals $Tr[E_\theta \rho]$. Note that if we define the PSD matrix $E := \sum_{\theta\in\Theta}\theta E_\theta$, then the *expected value* of the measurement outcome is $\sum_{\theta\in\Theta}\theta Tr[E_\theta\rho] = Tr[E\rho]$.

5.1 Quantum Protocols

A *one-way quantum protocol with r-dimensional messages* can be described as follows. On input i, Alice sends Bob an r-dimensional state ρ_i. On input j, Bob measures the state he receives with a POVM $\{E^j_\theta\}$ for some *nonnegative* values θ, and outputs the result. We say that such a protocol *computes a matrix M in expectation*, if the expected value of the output on respective inputs i and j, equals the matrix entry M_{ij}. Analogous to the equivalence between classical protocols and nonnegative factorizations of M established by Faenza *et al.* [15], such quantum protocols are essentially equivalent to PSD factorizations of S:

THEOREM 16. *Let $M \in \mathbb{R}^{m\times n}_+$ be a matrix. Then the following holds:*

(i) A one-way quantum protocol with r-dimensional messages that computes M in expectation, gives a rank-r PSD factorization of M.

(ii) A rank-r PSD factorization of M gives a one-way quantum protocol with $(r+1)$-dimensional messages that computes M in expectation.

PROOF. The first part is straightforward. Given a quantum protocol as above, define $E^j := \sum_{\theta\in\Theta}\theta E^j_\theta$. Clearly, on inputs i and j the expected value of the output is $Tr\left[\rho_i E^j\right] = M_{ij}$.

For the second part, suppose we are given a PSD factorization of a matrix M, so we are given PSD matrices $T_1,\dots,T_m$ and $U^1,\dots,U^n$ satisfying $Tr\left[T_i U^j\right] = M_{ij}$ for all i,j. In order to turn this into a quantum protocol, define $\tau = \max_i Tr[T_i]$. Let ρ_i be the $(r+1)$-dimensional quantum state obtained by adding a $(r+1)$st row and column to T_i/τ, with $1 - Tr[T_i]/\tau$ as $(r+1)$st diagonal entry, and 0s elsewhere. Note that ρ_i is indeed a PSD matrix of trace 1, so it is a well-defined quantum state. For input j, derive Bob's $(r+1)$-dimensional POVM from the PSD matrix U^j as follows. Let λ be the largest eigenvalue of U^j, and define $E^j_{\tau\lambda}$ to be U^j/λ, extended with a $(d+1)$st row and column of 0s. Let $E^j_0 = I - E^j_{\tau\lambda}$. These two operators together form a well-defined POVM. The expected outcome (on inputs i,j) of the protocol induced by the states and POVMs that we just defined, is

$$\tau\lambda Tr\left[E^j_{\tau\lambda}\rho_i\right] = Tr\left[T_i U^j\right] = M_{ij},$$

so the protocol indeed computes M in expectation. □

We obtain the following corollary which summarizes the characterization of semidefinite EFs:

COROLLARY 17. *For a polytope P with slack matrix S, the following are equivalent:*

(i) P has a semidefinite extension $Q = \{(x,y) \in \mathbb{R}^{d+r(r+1)/2} \mid Ex + Fy = g, y \in \mathbb{S}^r_+\}$;

(ii) the slack matrix S has a rank-r PSD factorization;

(iii) there exists a one-way quantum communication protocol with $(r+1)$-dimensional messages (i.e., using $\lceil\log(r+1)\rceil$ qubits) that computes S in expectation (for the converse we consider r-dimensional messages).

5.2 A General Upper Bound on Quantum Communication

Now, we provide a quantum protocol that efficiently computes a nonnegative matrix M in expectation, whenever there exists a low rank matrix N whose entry-wise square is M. The quantum protocol is inspired by [45, Section 3.3].

THEOREM 18. *Let M be a matrix with nonnegative real entries, N be a rank-r matrix of the same dimensions such that $M_{ij} = N^2_{ij}$. Then there exists a one-way quantum protocol using $(r+1)$-dimensional pure-state messages that computes M in expectation.*

PROOF. Let $N^\intercal = U\Sigma V$ be the singular value decomposition of the transpose of N; so U and V are unitary, Σ is a matrix whose first r diagonal entries are nonzero while its other entries are 0, and $\langle j|U\Sigma V|i\rangle = N_{ij}$. Define $|\phi_i\rangle = \Sigma V|i\rangle$. Since only its first r entries can be nonzero, we will view $|\phi_i\rangle$ as an r-dimensional vector. Let $\Delta_i = \||\phi_i\rangle\|$ and $\Delta = \max_i \Delta_i$. Add one additional dimension and define the normalized $(r+1)$-dimensional pure quantum states $|\psi_i\rangle = (|\phi_i\rangle/\Delta, \sqrt{1-\Delta_i^2/\Delta^2})$. Given input i, Alice sends $|\psi_i\rangle$ to Bob. Given input j, Bob applies a 2-outcome POVM $\{E^j_{\Delta^2}, E^j_0 = I - E^j_{\Delta^2}\}$ where $E^j_{\Delta^2}$ is the projector on the pure state $U^*|j\rangle$ (which has no support in the last dimension of $|\psi_i\rangle$). If the outcome of the measurement is $E^j_{\Delta^2}$ then Bob outputs Δ^2, otherwise he outputs 0. Accordingly, the expected output of this protocol on input (i,j) is

$$\Delta^2 \Pr[\text{outcome } E^j_{\Delta^2}] = \Delta^2\langle\psi_i|E^j_{\Delta^2}|\psi_i\rangle = \langle\phi_i|E^j_{\Delta^2}|\phi_i\rangle$$
$$= |\langle j|U|\phi_i\rangle|^2 = |\langle j|U\Sigma V|i\rangle|^2 = N^2_{ij} = M_{ij}.$$

The protocol only has two possible outputs: 0 and Δ^2, both nonnegative. Hence it computes M in expectation with an $(r+1)$-dimensional quantum message. □

Note that if M is a 0/1-matrix then we may take $N = M$, hence any low-rank 0/1-matrix can be computed in expectation by an efficient quantum protocol. We obtain the following corollary (implicit in Theorem 4.2 of [20]) which also implies a compact (i.e., polynomial size) semidefinite EF for the stable set polytope of perfect graphs, reproving the previously known result by [30, 31]. We point out that the result still holds when $\dim(P)+2$ is replaced by $\dim(P)+1$, see [21]. (This difference is due to normalization.)

COROLLARY 19. *Let P be a polytope such that S(P) is a 0/1 matrix. Then $\mathrm{xc}_{SDP}(P) \leqslant \dim(P) + 2$.*

5.3 Quantum vs Classical Communication, and PSD vs Nonnegative Factorizations

We now give an example of an exponential separation between quantum and classical communication in expectation, based on the matrix M of Section 2. This result actually preceded and inspired the results in Section 3.

THEOREM 20. *For each n, there exists a nonnegative matrix $M \in \mathbb{R}^{2^n \times 2^n}$ that can be computed in expectation by a quantum protocol using $\log n + O(1)$ qubits, while any classical randomized protocol needs $\Omega(n)$ bits to compute M in expectation.*

PROOF. Consider the matrix $N \in \mathbb{R}^{2^n \times 2^n}$ whose rows and columns are indexed by n-bit strings a and b, respectively, and whose entries are defined as $N_{ab} = 1 - a^\intercal b$. Define $M \in \mathbb{R}_+^{2^n \times 2^n}$ by $M_{ab} = N_{ab}^2$. This M is the matrix from Section 2. Note that N has rank $r \leqslant n + 1$ because it can be written as the sum of $n + 1$ rank-1 matrices. Hence Theorem 18 immediately implies a quantum protocol with $(n + 2)$-dimensional messages that computes M in expectation.

For the classical lower bound, note that a protocol that computes M in expectation has positive probability of giving a nonzero output on input a, b iff $M_{ab} > 0$. With a message m in this protocol we can associate a rectangle $R_m = A \times B$ where A consists of all inputs a for which Alice has positive probability of sending m, and B consists of all inputs b for which Bob, when he receives message m, has positive probability of giving a nonzero output. Together these rectangles will cover exactly the nonzero entries of M. Accordingly, a c-bit protocol that computes M in expectation induces a rectangle cover for the support matrix of M of size 2^c. Theorem 1 lower bounds the size of such a cover by $2^{\Omega(n)}$, hence $c = \Omega(n)$. □

Together with Theorem 16 and the equivalence of randomized communication complexity (in expectation) and nonnegative rank established in [15], we immediately obtain an exponential separation between the nonnegative rank and the PSD rank.

COROLLARY 21. *For each n, there exists $M \in \mathbb{R}_+^{2^n \times 2^n}$, with $\text{rank}_+(M) = 2^{\Omega(n)}$ and $\text{rank}_{PSD}(M) = O(n)$.*

In fact a simple rank-$(n + 1)$ PSD factorization of M is the following: let $T_a := \binom{1}{-a}\binom{1}{-a}^\intercal$ and $U^b := \binom{1}{b}\binom{1}{b}^\intercal$, then $\text{Tr}[(T_a)^\intercal U^b] = (1 - a^\intercal b)^2 = M_{ab}$.

6. CONCLUDING REMARKS

In addition to proving the first unconditional super-polynomial lower bounds on the size of linear EFs for the cut polytope, stable set polytope and TSP polytope, we demonstrate that the rectangle covering bound can prove strong results in the context of EFs. In particular, it can be super-polynomial in the dimension and the logarithm of the number of vertices of the polytope, settling an open problem of Fiorini *et al.* [17].

The exponential separation between nonnegative rank and PSD rank that we prove here (Theorem 20) actually implies more than a super-polynomial lower bound on the extension complexity of the cut polytope. As noted in Theorem 5, the polytopes $\text{CUT}(n)$ and $\text{COR}(n-1)$ are affinely isomorphic. Let $Q(n)$ denote the polyhedron isomorphic (under the same affine map) to the polyhedron defined by (3) for $a \in \{0,1\}^n$. Then (i) *every* polytope (or polyhedron) that contains $\text{CUT}(n)$ and is contained in $Q(n)$ has exponential extension complexity; (ii) there exists a low complexity spectrahedron that contains $\text{CUT}(n)$ and is contained in $Q(n)$. (A *spectrahedron* is an intersection of the positive semidefinite cone with an affine subspace, or any projection of such convex set.)

An important problem also left open in [48] is whether the perfect matching polytope has a polynomial-size linear EF. Yannakakis proved that every *symmetric* EF of this polytope has exponential size, a striking result given the fact that the perfect matching problem is solvable in polynomial time. He conjectured that asymmetry also does not help in the case of the perfect matching polytope. Because it is based on the rectangle covering bound, our argument would not yield a super-polynomial lower bound on the extension complexity of the perfect matching polytope. Even though a polynomial-size linear EF of the matching polytope would not prove anything as surprising as P=NP, the existence of a polynomial-size EF or an unconditional super-polynomial lower bound for it remains open.

We hope that the new connections developed here will inspire more research, in particular about approximate EFs. Here are two concrete questions left open for future work: (i) find a *slack matrix* that has an exponential gap between nonnegative rank and PSD rank; (ii) prove that the cut polytope has no polynomial-size *semidefinite* EF (that would rule out SDP-based algorithms for optimizing over the cut polytope, in the same way that this paper ruled out LP-based algorithms).

Acknowledgements

We thank Giannicola Scarpa for useful discussions. We also thank Monique Laurent for information about hypermetric inequalities. Finally, we thank the three anonymous referees for suggesting improvements to the text.

7. REFERENCES

[1] S. Aaronson. Lower bounds for local search by quantum arguments. In *Proc. STOC 2004*, pages 465–474, 2004.

[2] D. Aharonov and O. Regev. Lattice problems in NP ∩ coNP. In *Proc. FOCS 2004*, pages 362–371, 2004.

[3] S. Arora, B. Bollobás, and L. Lovász. Proving integrality gaps without knowing the linear program. In *Proc. FOCS 2002*, pages 313–322, 2002.

[4] S. Arora, B. Bollobás, L. Lovász, and I. Tourlakis. Proving integrality gaps without knowing the linear program. *Theory Comput.*, 2:19–51, 2006.

[5] E. Balas. Disjunctive programming and a hierarchy of relaxations for discrete optimization problems. *SIAM J. Algebraic Discrete Methods*, 6:466–486, 1985.

[6] E. Balas, S. Ceria, and G. Cornuéjols. A lift-and-project algorithm for mixed 0-1 programs. *Math. Programming*, 58:295–324, 1993.

[7] S. Benabbas and A. Magen. Extending SDP integrality gaps to Sherali-Adams with applications to quadratic programming and MaxCutGain. In *Proc. IPCO 2010*, pages 299–312, 2010.

[8] H. Buhrman, R. Cleve, S. Massar, and R. de Wolf. Nonlocality and communication complexity. *Rev. Modern Phys.*, 82:665, 2010.

[9] J. Buresh-Oppenheim, N. Galesi, S. Hoory, A. Magen, and T. Pitassi. Rank bounds and integrality gaps for cutting planes procedures. *Theory Comput.*, 2:65–90, 2006.

[10] M. Charikar, K. Makarychev, and Y. Makarychev. Integrality gaps for Sherali-Adams relaxations. In *Proc. STOC 2009*, pages 283–292, 2009.

[11] M. Conforti, G. Cornuéjols, and G. Zambelli. Extended formulations in combinatorial optimization. *4OR*, 8:1–48, 2010.

[12] C. De Simone. The cut polytope and the Boolean quadric polytope. *Discrete Math.*, 79:71–75, 1989/90.

[13] M.M. Deza and M. Laurent. *Geometry of cuts and metrics*, volume 15 of *Algorithms and Combinatorics*. Springer-Verlag, 1997.

[14] A. Drucker and R. de Wolf. Quantum proofs for classical theorems. *Theory Comput., Graduate Surveys*, 2, 2011.

[15] Y. Faenza, S. Fiorini, R. Grappe, and H. R. Tiwary. Extended formulations, non-negative factorizations and randomized communication protocols. arXiv:1105.4127, 2011.

[16] W. Fernandez de la Vega and C. Mathieu. Linear programming relaxation of Maxcut. In *Proc. SODA 2007*, pages 53–61, 2007.

[17] S. Fiorini, V. Kaibel, K. Pashkovich, and D. O. Theis. Combinatorial bounds on nonnegative rank and extended formulations. arXiv:1111.0444, 2011.

[18] K. Georgiou, A. Magen, T. Pitassi, and I. Tourlakis. Integrality gaps of $2 - o(1)$ for vertex cover SDPs in the Lovász-Schrijver hierarchy. *SIAM J. Comput.*, 39:3553–3570, 2010.

[19] K. Georgiou, A. Magen, and M. Tulsiani. Optimal Sherali-Adams gaps from pairwise independence. In *Proc. APPROX-RANDOM 2009*, pages 125–139, 2009.

[20] J. Gouveia, P.A. Parrilo, and R. Thomas. Theta bodies for polynomial ideals. *SIAM J. Optim.*, 20:2097–2118, 2010.

[21] J. Gouveia, P.A. Parrilo, and R. Thomas. Lifts of convex sets and cone factorizations. arXiv:1111.3164, 2011.

[22] H. Huang and B. Sudakov. A counterexample to the alon-saks-seymour conjecture and related problems. arXiv:1002.4687, 2010.

[23] V. Kaibel. Extended formulations in combinatorial optimization. *Optima*, 85:2–7, 2011.

[24] V. Kaibel, K. Pashkovich, and D.O. Theis. Symmetry matters for the sizes of extended formulations. In *Proc. IPCO 2010*, pages 135–148, 2010.

[25] I. Kerenidis and R. de Wolf. Exponential lower bound for 2-query locally decodable codes via a quantum argument. In *Proc. STOC 2003*, pages 106–115, 2003.

[26] E. Kushilevitz and N. Nisan. *Communication complexity*. Cambridge University Press, 1997.

[27] E. Kushilevitz and E. Weinreb. The communication complexity of set-disjointness with small sets and 0-1 intersection. In *Proc. FOCS 2009*, pages 63–72, 2009.

[28] E. Kushilevitz and E. Weinreb. On the complexity of communication complexity. In *Proc. STOC 2009*, pages 465–474, 2009.

[29] C. Lemaréchal and J.B. Hiriart-Urruty. *Convex analysis and minimization algorithms I*. Springer, 1996.

[30] L. Lovász. On the Shannon capacity of a graph. *IEEE Trans. Inform. Theory*, 25:1–7, 1979.

[31] L. Lovász. Semidefinite programs and combinatorial optimization. In *Recent advances in algorithms and combinatorics*, volume 11 of *CMS Books Math./Ouvrages Math. SMC*, pages 137–194. Springer, 2003.

[32] L. Lovász and A. Schrijver. Cones of matrices and set-functions and 0-1 optimization. *SIAM J. Optim.*, 1:166–190, 1991.

[33] N.D. Mermin. *Quantum computer science: an introduction*. Cambridge University Press, 2007.

[34] M. A. Nielsen and I. L. Chuang. *Quantum computation and quantum information*. Cambridge University Press, 2000.

[35] K. Pashkovich. Symmetry in extended formulations of the permutahedron. arXiv:0912.3446, 2009.

[36] A. A. Razborov. On the distributional complexity of disjointness. *Theoret. Comput. Sci.*, 106(2):385–390, 1992.

[37] T. Rothvoß. Some 0/1 polytopes need exponential size extended formulations. arXiv:1105.0036, 2011.

[38] G. Schoenebeck, L. Trevisan, and M. Tulsiani. Tight integrality gaps for Lovasz-Schrijver LP relaxations of vertex cover and max cut. In *Proc. STOC 2007*, pages 302–310, 2007.

[39] A. Schrijver. *Combinatorial optimization. Polyhedra and efficiency*. Springer-Verlag, 2003.

[40] C. E. Shannon. The synthesis of two-terminal switching circuits. *Bell System Tech. J.*, 25:59–98, 1949.

[41] H. D. Sherali and W. P. Adams. A hierarchy of relaxations between the continuous and convex hull representations for zero-one programming problems. *SIAM J. Discrete Math.*, 3:411–430, 1990.

[42] E. R. Swart. P = NP. Technical report, University of Guelph, 1986; revision 1987.

[43] F. Vanderbeck and L. A. Wolsey. Reformulation and decomposition of integer programs. In M. Jünger et al., editor, *50 Years of Integer Programming 1958-2008*, pages 431–502. Springer, 2010.

[44] R. de Wolf. Quantum communication and complexity. *Theoret. Comput. Sci.*, 287:337–353, 2002.

[45] R. de Wolf. Nondeterministic quantum query and communication complexities. *SIAM J. Comput.*, 32:681–699, 2003.

[46] L. A. Wolsey. Using extended formulations in practice. *Optima*, 85:7–9, 2011.

[47] M. Yannakakis. Expressing combinatorial optimization problems by linear programs (extended abstract). In *Proc. STOC 1988*, pages 223–228, 1988.

[48] M. Yannakakis. Expressing combinatorial optimization problems by linear programs. *J. Comput. System Sci.*, 43(3):441–466, 1991.

[49] G. M. Ziegler. *Lectures on Polytopes*, volume 152 of *Graduate Texts in Mathematics*. Springer-Verlag, 1995.

APPENDIX

A. BACKGROUND ON POLYTOPES

A *(convex) polytope* is a set $P \subseteq \mathbb{R}^d$ that is the convex hull $\text{conv}(V)$ of a finite set of points V. Equivalently, P is a polytope if and only if P is bounded and the intersection of a finite collection of closed halfspaces. This is equivalent to saying that P is bounded and the set of solutions of a finite system of linear inequalities and possibly equalities (each of which can be represented by a pair of inequalities).

Let $P \subseteq \mathbb{R}^d$ be a polytope. A closed halfspace H^+ that contains P is said to be *valid* for P. In this case the hyperplane H that bounds H^+ is also said to be *valid* for P. A *face* of P is either P itself or the intersection of P with a valid hyperplane. Every face of a polytope is again a polytope. A face is called *proper* if it is not the polytope itself. A *vertex* is a minimal nonempty face. A *facet* is a maximal proper face. An inequality $c^\mathsf{T} x \leqslant \delta$ is said to be *valid* for P if it is satisfied by all points of P. The face it defines is $F := \{x \in P \mid c^\mathsf{T} x = \delta\}$. The inequality is called *facet-defining* if F is a facet. The *dimension* of a polytope P is the dimension of its affine hull $\mathrm{aff}(P)$.

Every (finite or infinite) set V such that $P = \mathrm{conv}(V)$ contains all the vertices of P. Conversely, letting $\mathrm{vert}(P)$ denote the vertex set of P, we have $P = \mathrm{conv}(\mathrm{vert}(P))$. Suppose now that P is *full-dimensional*, i.e., $\dim(P) = d$. Then, every (finite) system $Ax \leqslant b$ such that $P = \{x \in \mathbb{R}^d \mid Ax \leqslant b\}$ contains all the facet-defining inequalities of P, up to scaling by positive numbers. Conversely, P is described by its facet-defining inequalities.

If P is not full-dimensional, these statements have to be adapted as follows. Every (finite) system describing P contains all the facet-defining inequalities of P, up to scaling by positive numbers and adding an inequality that is satisfied with equality by *all* points of P. Conversely, a linear description of P can be obtained by picking one inequality per facet and adding a system of equalities describing $\mathrm{aff}(P)$.

A $0/1$-*polytope* in $\mathbb{R}^d$ is simply the convex hull of a subset of $\{0,1\}^d$.

A (convex) *polyhedron* is a set $P \subseteq \mathbb{R}^d$ that is the intersection of a finite collection of closed halfspaces. A polyhedron P is a polytope if and only if it is bounded.

For more background on polytopes and polyhedra, see the standard reference [49].

Polyhedral Clinching Auctions and the Adwords Polytope

Gagan Goel
Google Research, NYC
gagangoel@google.com

Vahab Mirrokni
Google Research, NYC
mirrokni@google.com

Renato Paes Leme*
Cornell University
renatoppl@cs.cornell.edu

ABSTRACT

A central issue in applying auction theory in practice is the problem of dealing with budget-constrained agents. A desirable goal in practice is to design incentive compatible, individually rational, and Pareto optimal auctions while respecting the budget constraints. Achieving this goal is particularly challenging in the presence of nontrivial combinatorial constraints over the set of feasible allocations.

Toward this goal and motivated by AdWords auctions, we present an auction for *polymatroidal* environments satisfying the above properties. Our auction employs a novel clinching technique with a clean geometric description and only needs an oracle access to the submodular function defining the polymatroid. As a result, this auction not only simplifies and generalizes all previous results, it applies to several new applications including AdWords Auctions, bandwidth markets, and video on demand. In particular, our characterization of the AdWords auction as polymatroidal constraints might be of independent interest. This allows us to design the first mechanism for Ad Auctions taking into account simultaneously budgets, multiple keywords and multiple slots.

We show that it is impossible to extend this result to generic polyhedral constraints. This also implies an impossibility result for multi-unit auctions with decreasing marginal utilities in the presence of budget constraints.

Categories and Subject Descriptors

J.4 [**Social and Behavioral Sciences**]: Economics
; F.2.0 [**Theory of Computation**]: Analysis of Algorithms and Problem Complexity

Keywords

Clinching Auctions, Budgets, Polymatroids, AdWords

*This work was done while this author was an intern at Google Inc. During the academic year, he is supported by a Microsoft Research Fellowship.

STOC'12, May 19–22, 2012, New York, New York, USA.

1. INTRODUCTION

A large part of auction theory deals with the problem of designing truthful mechanisms for quasi-linear settings. For these settings, the VCG mechanism, or variants of it like affine-maximizers, can be applied to get optimal or near-optimal auctions. However, when we deviate from the quasi-linear model, very little is known. One of the most natural and practically important feature missing from the quasi-linear model is the presence of *budget constraints*. Budgets play a major role in several real-world auctions where the magnitude of the transactions involved naturally put a financial constraint on the bidders. Examples of such auctions include those used for the privatization of public assets in eastern Europe, or those for the distribution of radio spectra in the US (for a discussion on this, see Benoit and Krishna [6]). Another important example is that of Ad Auctions where advertisers explicitly declare budget constraints. In such settings, respecting the declared budget constraints is a necessary property any mechanism must satisfy. There is much discussion on the source of budget constraints (we refer to Che and Gale [11] for a detailed discussion on this topic).

Satisfying budget constraints while keeping incentive compatibility and efficiency is a challenging problem, and it becomes even harder in the presence of complex combinatorial constraints over the set of feasible allocations. In the presence of budgets, individual rationality and truthfulness cannot be satisfied at the same time as maximizing social welfare [14], and thus the goal of maximizing efficiency can be achieved mainly through *Pareto-optimal* auctions [1]. Therefore, a desirable goal under budget constraints is to design incentive-compatible (IC) and individually-rational (IR) auctions while producing Pareto-optimal outcomes. The first successful example of such mechanisms was developed in the seminal paper of Dobzinski, Lavi and Nisan [14], where the authors adapt the clinching auction framework of Ausubel [5] to give a truthful mechanism that achieves Pareto-optimality. Their setting, however, captures only a simple allocation constraint: there is a limited supply of k items and each player has a value of v_i for each item (and hence value of $v_i \cdot t$ for getting t items) and budget B_i.

As for more general allocation constraints, there have been

[1]An auction is Pareto-optimal if it outputs an allocation and payments such that no alternative set of allocation and payments improves the utility of at least one agent and keeps the other agents at least as happy as before. Here agents include bidders and the auctioneer where the auctioneer's utility is its revenue

a couple of subsequent work capturing special families of allocation constraints, e.g., unit demands [2], or multi-unit demands with matching constraints [18]. Although these results are mainly based on Ausubel's clinching auction, each of them need to develop independent techniques to deal with their specific environment - for example, Fiat, Leonardi, Saia, and Sankowski [18] define a complex clinching procedure based on trading paths in a bipartite graph and computing *S-avoid matchings*. Our goal in this paper is to extend these results to a much more general class of polyhedral constraints. In particular, we would like to understand for what polyhedral environments one can design such auctions, and also identify simple environments for which designing such auctions is not possible.

Our Results and Techniques. Firstly, inspired by an application in Sponsored Search Ad Auctions and several other applications, we study *polymatroid* constraints over feasible allocations and give an auction that achieves all the desired properties, i.e., it satisfies IC, IR, and produces Pareto-optimal outcomes while satisfying the budget constraints. We assume that the budgets are public - which was shown in [14] to be a necessary assumption[2]. While following Ausubel's framework to design this auction, we need to invent the main component of the mechanism, i.e., the *clinching step* that copes with the polyhedral allocation constraints. Our clinching step uses submodular minimization as a subroutine and only needs a value oracle access to the submodular function corresponding to the polymatroid. As a result, our mechanism has a clean geometric description that abstracts away the combinatorial complications of previous designs. This leaves the auctioneer free to focus on modeling the environment, and then use our mechanism as a black-box. This general technique not only generalizes (and simplifies) the previously known results like multi-unit auctions with matching constraints [14, 18], but also extend clinching auctions to many other applications like the AdWords Auction and settings like spanning tree auctions and video on demand [8]. Our main application is in sponsored search auctions where we model the AdWords Auction with multiple keywords and multiple position slots per keyword as a polymatroid called the *AdWords polytope* (See Section 4.1 for details).

In order to extend this result to more general polyhedral constraints, we turn our attention to 2-player auctions with budget constraints and prove several structural properties of Pareto-optimal truthful auctions for polyhedral environments In particular, we present a characterization of such auctions that results in various impossibility results and one positive result. On the positive side, we present a truthful individually rational Pareto-optimal auction for any environment if only one player is budget-constrained. On the other hand, if more than one player is budget-constrained, we illustrate simple polytope constraints for which it is impossible to achieve a truthful Pareto-optimal auction even for two players. Moreover, as a byproduct of this characterization, we get an impossibility result for multi-unit auctions with decreasing marginal utilities. This impossibility result disproves an implied conjecture by Ausubel [5] which has been reinforced by follow-up papers [14, 21]. In fact, this conjecture was reinforced by the fact that getting such an auction is possible whenever the marginals are flat. In appendix D we provide an explicit counter-example for this case.

Applications to Sponsored Search. Online advertisement is a growing business that was worth 25 billion dollars in 2010. It also has become a central piece in the current internet landscape, since it is the primary way internet companies monetize their services. Large part of this revenue comes from the search advertisement, hence it is not surprising that is has been extensively studied in the literature. The basic model of sponsored search ad auctions was proposed simultaneously by Edelman, Ostrovky and Schwarz [16] and Varian [31]. The authors model the current auction as a non-truthful mechanism and analyze its equilibrium properties. The social welfare of such equilibria were studied in [28, 22, 10] and its revenue properties in [23].

In search advertising, there are usually multiple keywords and each keyword has multiple slots associated with it. Most of the previous work treat auctions for different keywords as being independent, and therefore focus on a single keyword. A recent paper by Dhangwatnotai [13] approaches the problem of analyzing keyword auctions for multiple keywords, but it is restricted to a special case of one slot per page. Similarly, the work of Fiat et al [18] can be seen as an auction for multiple keywords with only one slot per page.

To the best of our knowledge, our work is the first work to combine multiple slots per page and multiple keywords. We do so by giving a non-trivial characterization of the set of all feasible allocations of clicks: we call it the *AdWords Polytope*. We show it has the structure of a polymatroid and therefore we can use our result to generate a truthful Pareto-optimal auction for this setting.

Other Related Work. There are two streams of related work. The first, like ours, is on designing truthful mechanisms when players have budget constraints with the goal of achieving Pareto-optimal outcomes; for example, [14], and [18]. Bhattacharya et al [7] show a budget-monotonicity property for the clinching auction of [14], therefore arguing that no player can improve his utility by under-reporting his budget. For the case of unit-demand players, Aggrawal et al [2] design auctions for unit-demand players with budget constraints.

On the question of maximizing revenue, Borgs et al [9] gave a truthful auction whose revenue is asymptotically within a constant factor of the optimal revenue. These results were improved by Abrams [1]. Subsequently, Hafalir, Ravi and Sayedi [20] relax the truthfulness requirement, moving to ex-post Nash equilibrium as a solution concept, and give an auction that, in equilibrium, has good efficiency and revenue properties. More recently, Pai and Vohra [29] gave a revenue-optimal auction for the Bayesian version of the problem. We would like to highlight that the above work focused on the multi-unit setting only.

Our auction also generalizes the ascending auction of Bikhchandani et al [8]. The authors consider environments where the set of allocations is defined by a polymatroid, but don't consider budget constraints.

The second line of related work relates to the practical problem of designing mechanisms for Ad Auctions. The work of Feldman et al [17] design an auction for the envi-

[2]Dobzinski et. al. [14] showed that with private budgets, truthfulness and Pareto-optimality cannot be achieved using deterministic mechanisms - not even for multi-unit auctions

ronment with one keyword and multiple slots. Their model is, however, different from the standard utilitarian utility model. Instead of being profit maximizers, the players are clicks maximizers, i.e., the players want to get as many clicks as possible without exhausting their budget and without paying more per click than their value, which is a simpler setting than ours. In order to design their auction, they describe the structure of the set of possible randomized allocations of players to slots. We note that the structure they identify is in fact a polymatroid and use this fact to apply our auction to this setting. We further extend this characterization to the setting with multiple keywords.

Also for one keyword and multiple slots, Ashlagi et al [4] design an auction for the usual utility model but relax the truthfulness requirement and get an auction that is Pareto-optimal for all ex-post Nash equilibria. The main weakness in the setting of [4] is that the agents are allowed to be allocated only to one slot position for all the different queries of the given keyword. However, in reality, agents can be allocated to different slot positions for different queries of a given keyword. In the restricted setting of [4], the Pareto-optimality requirement becomes easier to satisfy.

Independently of our work, Colini-Baldeschi et al [12] also study the problem of designing incentive compatible, individually rational, budget feasible and Pareto-optimal auctions for sponsored search. The authors present two auctions satisfying those properties: one for the case with a single keyword but multiple slots with different click-through-rates and one for the case of multiple keywords and multiple slots with homogeneous click-through-rates (i.e. all slots are identical).

Impossibility results. The impossibility of a Pareto-optimal auction for heterogeneous goods in the budgeted setting was given in [18]. It remained an open problem whether an auction was possible if goods where identical, i.e., utilities depended only on the number items acquired and not on which items they were. A very recent result by Lavi and May [21] shows an impossibility result for the case where the valuation can be an arbitrary function of the number of items - i.e. players are allowed to express complementarities. Since their setting is more expressive, an impossibility result is easier. Our impossibility result for multi-unit auctions can be seen as a stronger version of their result, since we allow players only to express valuations with diminishing marginals. This came as a surprise to us, since it was generally believed that such a positive result could be achieved using a variation of [14].

2. AUCTIONS FOR POLYHEDRAL ENVIRONMENTS

Consider n players, where player i has a positive value v_i per unit of some good g and a budget of B_i. We assume that the valuations are private information of the players, whereas the budgets are public. We are also given a subset $X \subseteq \mathbb{R}^n_+$ that defines all the possible ways to allocate the good g. We assume that the subset X is a convex set that is bounded and downward closed[3]. We will call this set X an *environment*. Note that if player i receives x_i amount of good g and pays p_i, her utility u_i is equal to $v_i x_i - p_i$ if $p_i \leq B_i$ and $-\infty$ otherwise. However, since we will require the mechanism to never charge more than the budgets, we won't have to deal with the latter case. Our goal is to design an auction mechanism that elicits valuations v from the players and outputs a feasible allocation $x(v) \in X$ and a feasible payment vector $p(v) \leq B$ that satisfies the following three properties:

- *Individual Rationality* (a.k.a. voluntary participation): Each player has net non-negative utility from participating in the auction, i.e., $u_i \geq 0$.
- *Incentive compatibility* (a.k.a. truthfulness) : It is a dominant strategy for each player to participate in the auction and report their true value, i.e.,

  $$v_i x_i(v_i, v_{-i}) - p_i(v_i, v_{-i}) \geq v_i x_i(v_i', v_{-i}) - p_i(v_i', v_{-i}).$$

  The characterization of single-parameter truthful mechanisms in [25, 3] states that this is equivalent to x_i being a non-decreasing function of v_i (for a fixed v_{-i}) and payments being calculated by

  $$p_i(v_i, v_{-i}) = v_i x_i(v_i, v_{-i}) - \int_0^{v_i} x_i(u, v_{-i}) du.$$
- *Pareto-optimality*: An allocation $x(v) \in X$ and payments $p(v) \leq B$ is Pareto-optimal if and only if there is no alternative allocation and payments where all players' utilities and the revenue of the auctioneer do not decrease, and at least one of them increases. In other words, there is no alternative (x', p') such that $v_i x_i' - p_i' \geq v_i x_i(v) - p_i(v)$, $\sum_i p_i' \geq \sum_i p_i(v)$ and at least one of those inequalities is strict.

Next we prove a useful lemma about the structure of Pareto-optimal outcomes.

Lemma 2.1 *A feasible outcome (x, p), i.e. $x \in X$ and $p \leq B$, is Pareto-optimal iff there is no $d \in \mathbb{R}^n$ in a dominated direction at x (i.e. $x + d \in X^0 := \{x' \in X; \exists \hat{x} \in X \setminus x', \hat{x} \geq x'\}$) such that $d^t v \geq 0$ and $d_i \leq 0$ for all i that have $p_i = B_i$.*

PROOF. In order to show the $\Rightarrow$ direction, assume there is a dominated direction d such that $d^t v \geq 0$ and $d_i \leq 0$ for all i that have $p_i = B_i$. Then define $x_i' = x_i + d_i$ and $p_i' = p_i + v_i d_i$ and we obtain same utilities and the total payment didn't decrease, since $\sum_i p_i' - \sum_i p_i = d^t v \geq 0$. Now, since $x + d$ is not in the boundary of the polytope, we can give some more of good g to some players without charging extra payments and increase their utility. Therefore (x, p) is not Pareto-optimal.

For the $\Leftarrow$ direction, suppose (x', p') is a Pareto improvement. Define $d = x' - x$. First we claim that $d^t v > 0$. By the definition of Pareto optimality, $v_i x_i - p_i \leq v_i x_i' - p_i'$, $\sum_i p_i \leq \sum_i p_i'$ and at least one inequality is strict. Summing them all, we get that $\sum_i v_i x_i < \sum_i v_i x_i'$, which implies that $d^t v > 0$. Now, consider two cases:

If $x_i' \leq x_i$ for all i with $p_i = B_i$, then $d_i \leq 0$ for all such i. Simply pick some i for which $d_i > 0$ and decrease d_i slightly. The result will be a dominated direction d' (since $x + d' \leq x + d$ and $x + d' \neq x + d$) with $d'^t v > 0$ and $d_i' \leq 0$ for all i with $p_i = B_i$.

If $x_i' > x_i$ for some i with $p_i = B_i$. Then define d' such that $d_i' = d_i$ if $p_i < B_i$ and $d_i' = \min\{0, d_i\}$ if $p_i = B_i$.

[3]This is without loss of genearality if one is allowed to randomize between outcomes, and can allocate lesser amount of the good g to any player.

Now, consider $x'' = x + d'$ and $p'' = p'$. Clearly d' is a dominated direction (since $x+d' \leq x+d$ and $x+d' \neq x+d$) and $d'_i \leq 0$ for $p_i = B_i$ by definition. Now, we will show that $d''^t v \geq 0$. Notice that $\sum_i p''_i = \sum_i p'_i \geq \sum_i p_i$. Also, except for i with $x'_i > x_i$ and $p_i = B_i$ we have: $v_i x''_i - p''_i = v_i x'_i - p'_i \geq v_i x_i - p_i$. For theremaining i, one has: $v_i x''_i - p''_i = v_i x_i - p'_i \geq v_i x_i - p_i$. Summing all those inequalities, we get $\sum_i v_i x''_i \geq \sum_i v_i x_i$, implying that $d''^t v \geq 0$. ■

Another simple observation is that if (x, p) is a Pareto-optimal outcome in which no budget is fully exhausted, then $x = \text{argmax}_{x \in X} v^t x$. For small valuations, any Pareto-optimal mechanism that satisfies individually rationality cannot exhaust budgets, so it must behave like VCG.

2.1 Polymatroidal environments

Our most interesting applications correspond to settings where the environment is a packing polytope $P = \{x \in \mathbb{R}^n_+; Ax \leq b\}$ for some $m \times n$ matrix with $A_{ij} \geq 0$ and $b \in \mathbb{R}^m_+$. We call such environments a polyhedral environment. Examples of polyhedral environments are ubiquitous in game theory (see [26, 27] for many examples).

A rich subclass of packing polytopes is the class of polymatroids, which are polytopes that can be written as $P = \{x \in \mathbb{R}^n_+; \sum_{i \in S} x_i \leq f(S)\}$ where $f : 2^{[n]} \to \mathbb{R}_+$ is a monotone submodular function, i.e., a function satisfying:

$$f(S \cup T) + f(S \cap T) \leq f(S) + f(T), \forall S, T \subseteq [n]$$

$$f(S) \leq f(T), \forall S \subseteq T \subseteq [n]$$

Such polymatroidal environments generalize matroid environments. It is easy to see that all previously studied settings are instances of a these environments: Dobzinski et al's result [14] corresponds to the *uniform matroid* and Fiat et al's result [18] corresponds to the *transversal matroid.* Bikhchandani et al [8] give many examples of polymatroid environments including scheduling with due dates, network planning, pairwise kidney exchange, spatial markets, bandwidth markets and multi-class queueing systems [8]. In section 4 we discuss some of those applications in more depth and present a novel application of polymatroids to sponsored search auctions.

3. CLINCHING AUCTION FOR POLYMATROIDS

In this section, we describe our main positive result, i.e., an auction with all the desirable properties for polymatroidal environments. This auction is based on the clinching auctions framework of Ausubel [5]. Before we study more complicated constraints, let's recall the clinching auction [5, 14] for the multi-unit setting, i.e., $P = \{x; \sum_i x_i \leq s_0\}$. We begin by setting the supply $s = s_0$ and B_i the budget available to each agent. We maintain a price clock p that begins at zero and gradually ascends. For each price p, the agents are asked how much of the good they demand at the current price. Their demand will be $d_i = \frac{B_i}{p}$ (how much they can afford with their remaining budget) if $p \leq v_i$, and zero otherwise (the case where the price exceeds their marginal value). Then agent i is able to *clinch* an amount $\delta_i = [s - \sum_{j \neq i} d_j]^+$, which is the minimum amount we can give to player i while we are still able to meet the aggregate demands of the other players. *Clinching* means that player i gets δ_i amounts of the good, and $\delta_i p$ is subtracted from his budget. The price increases and we repeat the process until the supply is completely sold.

The heart of the mechanism is the clinching step and generalizing it for more complicated environments involves various challenges: how does one define the notion of supply and aggregate demand (it is not a single number anymore, since there are constraints restraining the possible allocation)? Finally, we need to make sure the clinching step doesn't violate feasibility.

Clinching Framework. First, in Algorithm 1, we consider a slightly modified version of the clinching framework: we maintain a price vector $p \in \mathbb{R}^n_+$ and increase the prices one player at a time. The vector $\rho \in \mathbb{R}^n_+$ contains the promised allocations in each step and its final value is the final allocation of the mechanism. The payment of each agent is the total amount that was deducted from their budget during the execution [4].

Algorithm 1 Polyhedral Clinching Auction

Input: P, v_i, B_i
$p_i = 0$, $\rho_i = 0$, $\hat{i} = 1$
do
  $d_i = B_i/p_i$ if $p_i < v_i$ and $d_i = 0$ otherwise,
  $\delta = \textbf{clinch}(P, \rho, d)$,
  $\rho_i = \rho_i + \delta_i$, $B_i = B_i - p_i\delta_i$,
  $d_i = B_i/p_i$ if $p_i < v_i$ and $d_i = 0$ otherwise,
  $p_{\hat{i}} = p_{\hat{i}} + \epsilon$, $\hat{i} = \hat{i} + 1 \mod n$
while $d \neq 0$

For each price, we calculate the demand d_i of each player, which is the amount of the good they would like to get for price p. Then we invoke a procedure called **clinch** which decides the amount to grant to each player at that price. We update the promises, remaining budget and adjust demands[5]. Then we increase the price.

In order to define clinching, we need to define analogues of the remnant supply and to demands for the case where the the environment is a generic polytope. Instead of being a single number as in the multi-unit auctions case, the remnant supply and aggregate demands will be polytopes:

Definition 3.1 (aggregate demands) *Given P, a vector of promised allocation $\rho \in P$, the remnant supply is described by the polytope $P_\rho = \{x \geq 0; \rho + x \in P\}$. If $d \in \mathbb{R}^n_+$ is the demand vector, the aggregate demand is defined by $P_{\rho,d} = \{x \geq 0; \rho + x \in P, x \leq d\}$.*

In the multi-unit auctions case, the amount player i clinched was the maximum amount we could give him while still being able to meet the demands of the other players. We generalize this notion to polyhedral environments (the concepts are depicted in Figure 1):

Definition 3.2 (polyhedral clinching) *The* demand set *of players $[n] \setminus i$ if one allocates x_i to player i is represented by the polytope $P^i_{\rho,d}(x_i) = \{x_{-i} \in \mathbb{R}^{[n]\setminus i}_+; (x_i, x_{-i}) \in P_{\rho,d}\}$.*

[4] Note that the details of the main procedure **clinch** is not described in this algorithm.

[5] Clearly updating demands is not necessary at this point, but we do in order to make the analysis cleaner.

Since P is a packing polytope, clearly $P^i_{\rho,d}(x_i) \supseteq P^i_{\rho,d}(x'_i)$ if $x_i \leq x'_i$. The amount player i is able to ***clinch*** *is the maximum amount we can give him without making any allocation for the other players infeasible. More formally, $\delta_i = \sup\{x_i \geq 0; P^i_{\rho,d}(x_i) = P^i_{\rho,d}(0)\}$.*

We need to ensure that the clinching step is well-defined, i.e., that after clinching is performed, the vector of promised allocations is still feasible. This is done by the following lemma:

Lemma 3.3 *For each step of the auction above, if $\rho \in P$, then $\rho + \delta \in P$.*

Proof. Let χ^i be the i-th coordinate vector. Note that $\delta_1\chi^1 \in P_{\rho,d}$ by definition of δ. Now, notice that $\delta_1\chi^1 \in P^2_{\rho,d}(0) = P^2_{\rho,d}(\delta_2)$, so: $\delta^1\chi_1 + \delta_2\chi^2 \in P_{\rho,d}$. By induction, we can show that $\sum_{i=1}^{j} \delta_i\chi^i \in P_{\rho,d}$. The induction is easy: $\sum_{i=1}^{j} \delta_i\chi^i \in P^{j+1}_{\rho,d}(0) = P^{j+1}_{\rho,d}(\delta_{j+1})$, so $\sum_{i=1}^{j+1} \delta_i\chi^i \in P^{j+1}_{\rho,d}$. ■

This auction is clearly truthful, since each player i reports only v_i, and she can stop her participation earlier (which she doesn't want, since she will potentially miss items she are interested in) or later (which will potentially give her items for a price higher than her valuation). It is also individually rational, since players only get items for prices below their valuation and respect budgets by the definition. Notice that those facts are true regardless of the trajectory of the price vector: any process that increases prices (in a potentially non-uniform way) has this property.

Lemma 3.4 *The auction in Algorithm 1 along with the clinching step described in Definition 3.2 is truthful, individually-rational and budget-feasible.*

Clinching for polymatroids. Notice that we haven't used anything from polymatroids yet, so Lemma 3.4 holds for any polytope P. However, two things are left to be shown: (i) that amount clinched can be computed efficiently and (ii) that the outcome is Pareto optimal. To show both of these properties, we use the fact that P is a polymatroid.

Lemma 3.5 *If the environment is a polymatroid P defined by a submodular function f, then the amount player i clinches in Algorithm 1 is given by:*

$$\delta_i = (\max_{x \in P_{\rho,d}} \mathbb{1}^t x) - (\max_{x \in P_{\rho,d}} \mathbb{1}^t_{-i} x_{-i}).$$

Moreover, this can be calculated efficiently using submodular minimization.

The main ingredients of the proof are the following two facts about polymatroids:

Fact 3.6 (Schrijver [30], sections 44.1 and 44.4) *If P is a polymatroid defined by the submodular function f, then $P_{\rho,d}$ is also a polymatroid defined by the following submodular function:*

$$\hat{f}(S) = \min_{T \subseteq S}\{f(T) - \rho(T) + d(S \setminus T)\}.$$

Notice that $\hat{f}(\cdot)$ might not be monotone. However,

$$\bar{f}(S) = \min_{S' \supseteq S} \hat{f}(S')$$

is a monotone submodular function that defines the same polymatroid.

Fact 3.7 *Given two monotone submodular functions $f, \tilde{f}$, then the polymatroids $P, \tilde{P}$ defined by them are equal iff the functions are equal. The ($\Leftarrow$) direction is trivial. For the other direction, notice that if $f(S) < \tilde{f}(S)$ say for $S = \{1, \ldots, i\}$, notice that the point x such that $x_j = \tilde{f}(\{1..j\}) - \tilde{f}(\{1..j-1\})$ for $j \leq i$ and zero otherwise is such that $x \in \tilde{P} \setminus P$.*

Proof of Lemma 3.5 : Using the fact 3.6, we know that $P^i_{\rho,d}(x_i)$ is also a polymatroid defined over $[n] \setminus i$ by the function $\tilde{f}(S) = \min\{\bar{f}(S), \bar{f}(S \cup i) - x_i\}$. Now, we use Fact 3.7 to see that $P^i_{\rho,d}(x_i) = P^i_{\rho,d}(0)$ iff $\bar{f}(S) \leq \bar{f}(S \cup i) - x_i, \forall S \subseteq [n] \setminus i$. So, $\delta_i = \min_{S \subseteq [n] \setminus i} \bar{f}(S \cup i) - \bar{f}(S)$. Since $\bar{f}$ is submodular, the smallest marginal can only be

$$\bar{f}([n]) - \bar{f}([n] \setminus i) = \max\{0, \hat{f}([n]) - \hat{f}([n] \setminus i)\}$$

which is exactly the expression in the statement of the lemma. Now, one can easily see that evaluating $\hat{f}$ is a submodular minimization problem. ■

Now we prove that the outcomes are Pareto-optimal in two steps. The first step is to characterize Pareto-optimal allocations for polymatroids. This characterization is stronger than that of Lemma 2.1, since it explores the structure of polymatroids. Afterwards, we show that the outcomes of the chinching auction defined in Algorithm 1 satisfy the two conditions in the characterization lemma.

In the following, for a vector $x \in \mathbb{R}^n$ and $S \subseteq [n]$ we denote $x(S) = \sum_{i \in S} x_i$.

Lemma 3.8 *For a polymatroidal environment P defined by a submodular function f, an allocation (x, p) is Pareto optimal iff:*

1. *All items are sold, i.e., $x([n]) = f([n])$, and*
2. *Given a player i with $p_i < B_i$ and player j with $v_j < v_i$, then there exists a set S such that $x(S) = f(S)$, $i \in S$ and $j \notin S$*

The following elementary facts about submodular functions will be useful in the proof of the Lemma 3.8:

Fact 3.9 *Given a vector $x \in P$, if two sets S, T are tight (i.e. $x(S) = f(S)$ and $x(T) = f(T)$), then $S \cap T$ and $S \cup T$ are also tight. The proof is quite elementary: $x(S \cup T) = x(S) + x(T) - x(S \cap T) \geq f(S) + f(T) - f(S \cap T) \geq f(S \cup T)$. So, all the inequalities must be tight and therefore $x(S \cup T) = f(S \cup T)$ and $x(S \cap T) = f(S \cap T)$.*

Fact 3.10 *If $x([n]) < f([n])$ then there is one component x_i that we can increase by $\delta > 0$ such that x is still in P. It follows from the previous fact: if all players i were contained in a tight set, one could take the union of those and $[n]$ would be tight. Then there is some element i which is in no tight set.*

Proof of Lemma 3.8 : The ($\Rightarrow$) direction is easy. If $x([n]) < f([n])$ then we can increase some x_i (Fact 3.10) and still get point P generating a Pareto improvement. Also, if

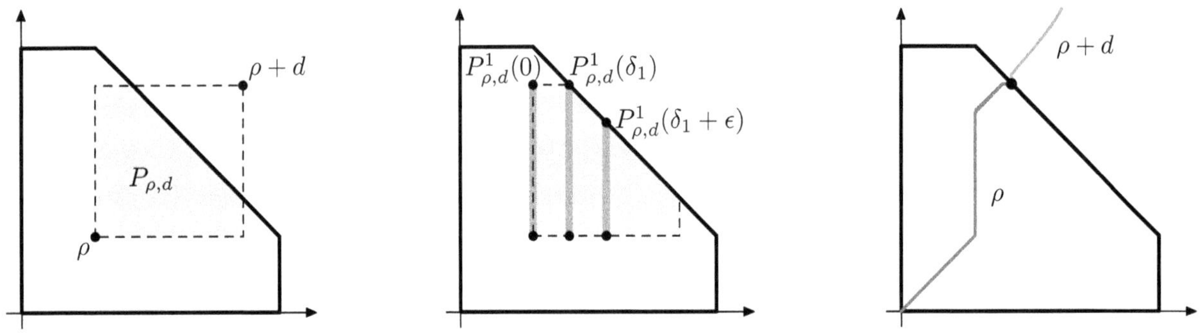

Figure 1: Illustration of polyhedral clinching: the first two figures depict the polytopes defined in Definitions 3.1 and 3.2. The third depicts the mechanism running on polytope P: during the execution, the vector ρ walks inside the polytope (blue line) and the vector $\rho + d$ walks outside it (red line), until they meet at the boundary. The point they meet corresponds to the final allocation.

there is $p_i < B_i$ and $v_j < v_i$ and no tight set separating them, then we can consider another outcome where we increase x_i by some $\delta > 0$, decrease x_j by some $\delta < 0$ and still get a feasible point improving $x^t v$. Now, this would not be Pareto optimal by Lemma 2.1.

For the ($\Leftarrow$) direction, let (x, p) be an outcome satisfying properties 1 and 2 and suppose (x', p') is a Pareto-improvement. This means that $v_i x'_i - p'_i \geq v_i x_i - p_i$ and $\sum_i p'_i \geq \sum_i p_i$.

Let $\{i_1, \ldots, i_k\} = \{n\} \cup \{i; p_i < B_i\}$, sorted in non-increasing order of v_i. Using property 2 (notice it holds for player n trivially) together with fact 3.9, we define the following family of tight sets $S_1 \subseteq S_2 \subseteq \ldots \subseteq S_k = [n]$, tight in the sense that $x(S_i) = f(S_i)$. For all $v_t < v_{i_1}$ there is a tight set S_{1t} that has i_1 but not t. Let S_1 be the intersection of such sets. Now, given $S_1 \subseteq \ldots \subseteq S_{j-1}$, we define S_j in the following way: If $i_j \in S_{j-1}$, take $S_j = S_{j-1}$ (notice can only happen if $v_{i_j} = v_{i_{j-1}}$). If not, for each $v_t < v_{i_j}$ there is a tight set S_{jt} that has i_j but not t. Now, define S_j as the union of S_{j-1} and the intersection of the S_{jt} sets.

By eliminating duplicates and its corresponding elements from $\{i_1 \ldots i_k\}$, we get a family $S_1 \subset \ldots \subset S_k$. Define $T_j = S_j \setminus S_{j-1}$ and it is clear the family obtained has the following properties:

- all $t \in S_j$ have $v_t \geq v_{i_j}$
- $i_j \in T_j$
- for all $i \in T_j$ either $v_i = v_{i_j}$ or $p_i = B_i$.

Let $T'_j = \{i \in T_j; v_i \neq v_{i_j}\}$ and $T''_j = \{i \in T_j; v_i = v_{i_j}\}$. Since the players in T'_j have exhausted their budget, $p_i \geq p'_i$. Using that and Pareto-optimality, we get:

$$\begin{aligned} &\sum_{i \in T'_j} p_i - p'_i \geq \\ &\quad \geq \sum_{i \in T'_j, x_i \geq x'_i} p_i - p'_i \geq \sum_{i \in T'_j, x_i \geq x'_i} v_i(x_i - x'_i) \overset{*}{\geq} \\ &\quad \geq \sum_{i \in T'_j, x_i \geq x'_i} v_{i_j}(x_i - x'_i) \overset{**}{\geq} \sum_{i \in T'_j} v_{i_j}(x_i - x'_i) \end{aligned} \quad (1)$$

Now, we can add the inequality $p_i - p'_i \geq v_{i_j}(x_i - x'_i)$ for $i \in T''_j$ and obtain:

$$\sum_{i \in T_j} p_i - p'_i \geq \sum_{i \in T_j} v_{i_j}(x_i - x'_i) \quad (2)$$

Summing those for all j and get:

$$\begin{aligned} \sum_i p_i - p'_i &\geq \sum_j \sum_{i \in T_j} v_{i_j}(x_i - x'_i) = \\ &= \sum_j (v_{i_j} - v_{i_{j+1}}) \sum_{i \in S_j} (x_i - x'_i) \geq 0 \end{aligned}$$

since $x(S_j) = f(S_j) \geq x'(S_j)$. Therefore $\sum_i p_i \geq \sum_i p'_i$ and therefore equal. This means in particular all of the inequalities in (1) and (2) must be tight. Therefore for all $i \in T'_j$ we need to have $x_i = x'_i$, since if $x_i > x'_i$ then inequality $*$ in (1) would be strict. If $x_i < x'_i$, then inequality $**$ would be strict. We use this fact to show that $\sum_{i \in S_j} v_i(x_i - x'_i) \geq 0$ by induction on j. If we show that, we can take $j = k$ and then we are done, since this will imply that $\sum_i v_i x_i \geq \sum_i v_i x'_i$ and therefore (x', p') cannot be a Pareto-improvement.

For $j = 1$, this is trivial, since we can write:

$$\sum_{i \in S_1, v_i \neq v_{i_1}} v_i(x_i - x'_i) \geq \sum_{i \in S_1, v_i \neq v_{i_1}} v_{i_1}(x_i - x'_i)$$

since both terms are zero, and then sum $v_i(x_i - x'_i)$ for the rest of the elements in S_1 and use the fact that S_1 is tight. For other j, we use that:

$$\begin{aligned} &\sum_{i \in S_j} v_i(x_i - x'_i) \geq \\ &\quad \geq v_{i_{j-1}} \sum_{i \in S_{j-1}} (x_i - x'_i) + \sum_{i \in T'_j} v_i(x_i - x'_i) \\ &\quad + \sum_{i \in T''_j} v_{i_j}(x_i - x'_i) \geq \\ &\quad \geq v_{i_j} \sum_{i \in S_j} (x_i - x'_i) = v_{i_j}(x(S_j) - x'(S_j)) \geq 0, \end{aligned}$$

by the fact that S_j is tight. ∎

Now, we argue that, for sufficiently small ϵ, the outcome satisfied the two properties in Lemma 3.8 and hence is Pareto-optimal. We prove this fact using the following sequence of lemmas:

Lemma 3.11 *After the clinching step is executed, and before updating prices, $\hat{f}([n]) \leq \hat{f}([n] \setminus j), \forall j \in [n]$.*

PROOF. In the clinching step, given an initial $\hat{f}_0$, we define $\delta_i = \max\{0, \hat{f}_0([n]) - \hat{f}_0([n] \setminus i)\}$. After we update ρ, B, d, $\hat{f}$ is updated to $\hat{f}_1(S) = \hat{f}_0(S) - \delta(S)$. Now, it is easy to check that:

$$\hat{f}_1([n]) = \hat{f}_0([n]) - \sum_i \delta_i = \hat{f}_0([n]) - \delta_j - \sum_{i \neq j} \delta_i \leq$$

$$\leq \hat{f}_0([n] \setminus j) - \sum_{i \neq j} \delta_i = \hat{f}_1([n] \setminus j)$$

■

Lemma 3.12 *The outcome (x, p) of the clinching auction is such that $x([n]) = f([n])$.*

PROOF. We show the following invariant: if we define $\hat{f}$ as in Fact 3.6, updating it each round as ρ, d changes, we claim that the value of $\mathbb{1}^t \rho + \hat{f}([n])$ remains constant.

To do so, we consider the events that can cause it to drop:

1. clinching: just after clinching occurs (i.e. ρ_i increases by δ_i, budgets decrease by $p\delta_i$, demands are adjusted, but before the price increases), the amount $\mathbb{1}^t \rho + \hat{f}([n])$ remains the same since $\rho^t \mathbb{1}$ increases by $\delta^t \mathbb{1}$ and for all S, $\hat{f}(S)$ decreases by $\delta(S)$, because to each i, ρ increases by δ_i and d_i decreases by δ_i.

2. price p_i increases and d_i decreases by $\theta, 0 \leq \theta \leq d_i$. If $\mathbb{1}^t \rho + \hat{f}([n])$ decreased then there was some $T, i \notin T$ such that:

   $$\hat{f}([n] \setminus i) + d_i - \theta \leq f(T) - \rho(T) + d([n] \setminus T) - \theta < \hat{f}([n])$$

   Using Lemma 3.11, we know that $\hat{f}([n]) \leq \hat{f}([n] \setminus i)$, so $d_i < \theta$ which is not true.

■

The proofs of the previous two lemmas intuitively establishes the maximality of the clinching procedure. Lemma 3.11 can be interpreted as saying that if we apply the clinching procedure twice, without updating prices, then the second time will have no effect. The proof of Lemma 3.12 identifies an invariant that is maintained during the execution of the mechanism.

Lemma 3.13 *If $\epsilon < \min_{v_i \neq v_j} |v_i - v_j|$, then property 2 of Lemma 3.8 is satisfied.*

PROOF. Suppose not and for the final outcome there are $v_j < v_i$, $p_i < B_i$ and all sets S such that $i \in S$, $j \notin S$ are not tight. First, clearly $x_j \neq 0$, otherwise $[n] \setminus j$ would be tight by Lemma 3.12. Then consider $\tilde{x}$ where $\tilde{x}_i = x_i + \theta$, $\tilde{x}_j = x_j - \theta$ and $\tilde{x}_k = x_k$ for all $k \neq i, j$. It is feasible for some small θ.

Now, consider the promised allocation ρ and demands d just before the last time player j clinched an amount $\delta_j > 0$. If necessary decrease θ so that it becomes smaller than this last amount clinched, i.e., $\theta < \delta_j$. At this point $\rho \leq x \leq \rho + d$. By the definition of clinching: $P^j_{\rho,d}(\delta_j) = P^j_{\rho,d}(\theta) = P^j_{\rho,d}(0)$.

At this point, $\rho \leq x$ and $\rho_j + \theta < \rho_j + \delta_j = x_j$. Therefore $\tilde{x} \geq \rho$. Also, we have that $x - \rho \leq d$ and $x_i - \rho_i < d_i$, since agent i hasn't dropped his demand to zero yet and his demand never increases and won't be met while $v_i < p_i$. Here we are strongly using that $\epsilon < \min_{v_i \neq v_j} |v_i - v_j|$ to ensure that for the last time player j clinches, player i demand is not zero yet. This implies that $\tilde{x} - \rho \in P_{\rho,d}$ so $(\tilde{x} - \rho)_{-j} \in P^j_{\rho,d}(0)$. Now, the fact that $P^j_{\rho,d}(0) = P^j_{\rho,d}(\delta_i)$ implies that $\hat{x} = (x_j, \tilde{x}_{-j}) \in P$. But $\hat{x}([n]) = x([n]) + \theta = f([n]) + \theta > f([n])$, which is an absurd. ■

We can summarize the results as:

Theorem 3.14 *For a polymatroidal environment, the auction in Algorithm 1 along with the clinching step described in Definition 3.2 has all the desirable properties.*

Extensions and limitations of the clinching framework: The clinching framework described in Algorithm 1 and Definition 3.2 is quite flexible: one can change the way clinching is done or the way prices ascend and obtain an auction that is still truthful, individually rational, and respects budgets. Pareto-optimality, however, is a delicate property to achieve. A natural question is for which environments Pareto-optimality is still achievable? In appendix A, we show we can extend this framework a little further (to scaled polymatroids), but not further than that.

Faster clinching: We showed in this section that for a generic polymatroid, we can calculate the clinched amount using submodular minimization as a sub-routine. For each individual environment, however, one can usually find much faster clinching subroutines. We illustrate this in appendix B for the single-keyword AdWords polytope.

4. THE ADWORDS POLYTOPE AND OTHER APPLICATIONS

We begin by discussing some interesting applications of the auction presented in section 3. Then we introduce a novel application of polymatroidal constraints to sponsored search auctions that generalizes the classical models of Edelman et al [16] and Varian [31].

- *Multi-unit auctions [14]:* corresponds to the polymatroids associated with constant submodular functions, i.e., $f(S) = Q, \forall S$.
- *Combinatorial auctions with matching constraints [18]:* there is a bipartite graph $([m], [n], E)$ between items $[m]$ and bidders $[n]$ and each buyer i has additive value 1 for each item j such that $(i, j) \in E$ and value 0 for each item not connected to him. We can represent this setting by a polymatroid where $f(S)$ is the number of items connected to some player in S. This is called the *transversal matroid.*
- *Video on demand [8]:* Consider company that provides video on demand that is located on a node s of a direct network with capacities on the edges $G = (V, E, c)$. Each buyer corresponds to a node in the network. An allocation x is feasible if it is possible to transmit at rate x_i for each player i simultaneously. This is possible if for each subset $S \subseteq [n]$ of players, $\sum_{i \in S} x_i$ is smaller then the min-cut from s to S. Using the submodularity of the cut-function, it is easy to see that the environment is a polymatroid.

- *Spanning tree auctions:* Consider the abstract setting where the agents are edges of a graph G and the auctioneer is allowed to allocate goods to a set only if it has no cycles. This corresponds to the graphical matroid of graph G. A more practical setting is when a telecommunication company owns a network that contains cycles and decides to auction their redundant edges. This setting corresponds to the dual-graphical matroid of G.

4.1 AdWords Polytope

Consider n advertisers and m keywords. Each advertiser i is interested in a subset of the keywords $\Gamma(i) \subseteq [m]$. For a keyword k, we denote by $\Gamma(k)$, the set of advertisers interested in this keyword. With each keyword k, we associate $|\Gamma(k)|$ positions. Position j for keyword k has click-through-rate α_j^k (possibly zero) such that $\alpha_1^k \geq \alpha_2^k \geq \ldots \geq \alpha_{|\Gamma(k)|}^k$ for each k.

Assuming that each keyword gets a large amount of queries, we see α_j^k as the sum of number of clicks that the j-th position of keyword k gets across all queries that it matches. For now, let's assume that the number of clicks a player gets in slot j of keyword k depends only on j, k and not on the identity of the player. One is able to relax this assumption, as we see later.

Let $\mathcal{A}_k = \{\pi_k : \Gamma(k) \hookrightarrow [|\Gamma(k)|]\}$ be the set of all allocations (one-to-one maps) from players to slots for keyword k. Also, let $\Delta(\mathcal{A}_k)$ be the distributions of such allocations. Given that, we can define the AdWords polytope in the following way: an allocation of clicks x is feasible if there is a distribution over allocations of players to slots for each keyword such that player i gets x_i clicks in expectation. More formally:

Definition 4.1 (AdWords Polytope) *The* AdWords polytope *is the set of feasible allocations* [6] *of clicks $x = (x_1, \ldots, x_n)$ such that there are distributions $\mathcal{D}_k \in \Delta(\mathcal{A}_k)$ for each keyword, and*

$$x_i \leq \sum_{k \in \Gamma(i)} \mathbb{E}_{\pi_k \sim \mathcal{D}_k}[\alpha^k_{\pi_k(i)}]$$

Our main result in this Section is that:

Theorem 4.2 *The AdWords polytope is a polymatroid.*

In order to prove the theorem, we first consider the setting with a single keyword and all advertisers interested in it. Let the click-through-rates be $\alpha_1 \geq \ldots \geq \alpha_n$. Feldman et al [17] relate the problem of deciding if a vector x is feasible to a classical problem in machine scheduling, i.e., scheduling in related machines with preemptions ($Q|pmtn|C_{\max}$ [19]). What follows is a re-statement of their characterization in a format that makes it clear it is a polymatroidal environment.

Lemma 4.3 (Feldman et al [17]) *An allocation vector x is feasible iff for each S, $x(S) \leq \sum_{j=1}^{|S|} \alpha_j$, where $x(S) = \sum_{i \in S} x_i$ for each set $S \subseteq [n]$.*

[6]Since the number of clicks is typically very large we treat them as divisible goods and consider also fractional allocations.

Notice that $f_k(S) = \sum_{j=1}^{|S|} \alpha_j^k$ is a submodular function, so the set of feasible allocations for the single-keyword setting is a polymatroid.

For the multiple-keyword setting, we say that an allocation vector x is feasible if we can write $x_i = \sum_{k \in \Gamma(i)} x_i^k$ in such a way that the vector $(x_i^k)_{i \in \Gamma(k)}$ is feasible for keyword k, i.e., $x^k(S) \leq f_k(S)$ for every $S \subseteq \Gamma(k)$.

The fact that this allocation set is a polymatroid is a direct consequence of the following theorem, which is a polymatroidal version of Rado's Theorem due to McDiarmid [24].

Theorem 4.4 (McDiarmid [24]) *Given a bipartite graph $([n] \cup [m], E)$, its neighborhood map $\Gamma(\cdot)$, m submodular functions $f_1, \ldots, f_m$ and their respective polymatroids $P_1, \ldots, P_m$, then the set:*

$$P^* = \{x \in \mathbb{R}^n_+; x_i = \sum_{k \in \Gamma(i)} x_i^k \text{ and } x^k \in P_k\}$$

is a polymatroid defined by the function

$$f^*(S) = \sum_k f_k(S \cap \Gamma(k))$$

.

Quality factors: So far, we assumed that the click-through-rate of player i allocated to slot j of keyword k depends solely on k and j. More generally, we would like to consider the click-through-rate of a slot depending also on the player allocated in that slot. Let $\alpha_{j,i}^k$ be the click-through-rate of position j of keyword j when player i is placed there. Traditionally, we consider the click-through-rates in a product form, i.e., $\alpha_{j,i}^k = \alpha_j^k \cdot \gamma_i^k$ where γ_i^k is called *quality factor*. Assuming quality factors are public information, one can, in a similar way, define a polytope of feasible allocations. In general it will not be a polymatroid.

If the quality factors are uniform among all queries, i.e., $\gamma_i^k = \gamma_i$, the the set of feasible allocations is given by $P^*_\gamma = \{x; (\frac{x_i}{\gamma_i})_i \in P^*\}$ where P^* is the AdWords polytope defined as a function of α_j^k. It is a scaled polymatroid, for which a variant of the auction in section 3 satisfies all desirable properties (see appendix A).

5. LIMITATIONS OF AUCTIONS FOR BUDGET-CONSTRAINED AGENTS

Previously, we argued why simple modifications to the clinching auction would not work for polyhedral environments beyond (scaled) polymatroids. Here, we explore the possibility of designing an auction of a different format achieving those properties and show that this is not possible even for two players. We do so through a general characterization of Pareto-optimal auctions with desirable properties. Before stating the characterization, we study the case with one budget-constrained player and prove some lemmas that are useful in proving the general characterization result later.

5.1 One budget-constrained player

For ease of exposition, we first focus on 2 players and assume that the feasible set of allocations P has a smooth and strictly-concave boundary, in the sense that for each $v \in \mathbb{R}^2_+$ there is a single point $x^*(v) \in P$ maximizing $v^t x$ such that $x^*(v)$ is a $\mathcal{C}^\infty$-function. In fact, one can approximate any polytope by such a set using the technique of Dolev et al [15]. Using compactness arguments, it is possible to get an auction for the original environment by taking the limit of the auctions obtained for its $\mathcal{C}^\infty$-approximations.

Assume that player 1 is not budget constrained and player 2 has budget B_2 and let (x^*, p^*) be the VCG mechanism for this setting. Now, we can define the function:

$$\xi(v_1) = \min\{v_2; p_2^*(v_1, v_2) \geq B_2\}$$

Theorem 5.1 *The allocation rule*

$$x(v_1, v_2) = x^*(v_1, \min\{v_2, \xi(v_1)\})$$

is monotone. Moreover, when coupled with the appropriate payment rule, it generates a Pareto-optimal and budget feasible mechanism

PROOF. The main part of the proof is to show that the allocation is monotone. If we show that, it is clearly budget feasible for player 2, since we use the VCG-payment rule until the point the budget of player 2 gets exhausted and from that point on, the allocation is constant. When the budgets of the players are not exhausted, the allocation is efficient (since it mimics VCG) and therefore is Pareto-optimal. The allocation when the budget of player 2 is exhausted is equivalent to the VCG allocation of a pair (v_1, v_2') with $v_2' \leq v_2$, so player 1 is getting $x_1^*(v_1, v_2') \geq x_1^*(v_1, v_2)$ by monotonicity of VCG. This implies Pareto-optimality as a consequence of Lemma 2.1.

Monotonicity: The allocation rule is clearly monotone for player 2. We need to show it is monotone for player 1, i.e. that the function $t \mapsto x_1(v_1 + t, v_2)$ is monotone non-decreasing. It is clearly so for intervals where $\xi(v_1+t) \geq v_2$, so let's assume that for $t \in (-\epsilon, +\epsilon)$ we have $\xi(v_1 + t) < v_2$. Our goal is to show that: $\frac{d}{dt}x_1^*(v_1+t, \xi(v_1+t)) \geq 0$. Since the VCG-allocation lies in the boundary of P, this is the same as showing that $\frac{d}{dt}x_2^*(v_1 + t, \xi(v_1 + t)) \leq 0$. The crucial observation is that the VCG-payment for player 2 on the curve $(v_1 + t, \xi(v_1 + t))$ is constant, i.e.:

$$B_2 \equiv p_2^*(v_1 + t, \xi(v_1 + t)) =$$

$$= \xi(v_1 + t)x_2^*(v_1 + t, \xi(v_1 + t)) - \int_0^{\xi(v_1+t)} x_2^*(v_1 + t, u)du$$

Now, we can simply derivate it with respect to t. We use the notation $\partial_i f(\cdot)$ for the derivative of f with respect to the i-th variable. We also define $x_2^*(t) = x_2^*(v_1 + t, \xi(v_1 + t))$. Now,

$$0 = \xi'(v_1 + t)x_2^*(t) + \xi(v_1 + t)\frac{d}{dt}x_2^*(t) -$$

$$- \xi'(v_1 + t)x_2^*(t) - \int_0^{\xi(v_1+t)} \partial_1 x_2^*(v_1 + t, u)du$$

$$\xi(v_1 + t)\frac{d}{dt}x_2^*(t) = \int_0^{\xi(v_1+t)} \partial_1 x_2^*(v_1 + t, u)du \leq 0$$

since $x_2^*(v_1, v_2)$ decreases with v_1 by the definition of the VCG allocation. ■

A variant of the proof can be used to show the following result for 2 budget constrained players. This is useful for our general characterization.

Corollary 5.2 *If the functions $\xi_1(v_2), \xi_2(v_1)$ are such that the regions $\{v; v_2 \geq \xi_2(v_1)\}$ and $\{v; v_1 \geq \xi_1(v_2)\}$ are disjoint, then one can define*

$$x(v_1, v_2) = x^*(\min\{v_1, \xi_1(v_2)\}, \min\{v_2, \xi_2(v_1)\})$$

$$p_i(v) = v_i x_i(v) - \int_0^{v_i} x_i(u, v_{-i})du.$$

If $p_2(v_1, \xi_2(v_1)) \equiv B_2$ and $p_1(\xi_1(v_2), v_2) \equiv B_1$, then (x, p) is a mechanism with the desirable properties.

The above corollary has a strong fixed-point flavour and it is tempting to believe one could get the existence of such a mechanism from this theorem. This is however not true, as shown in the next section. However, this result remains useful as a tool for searching for such mechanisms whenever they exist. For example, one can extend the above theorem to prove the existence of the mechanisms for polyhedral environments when B_1 is much larger then B_2.

5.2 Characterization and impossibility

Now we discuss our main negative result: which states an impossibility of extending the auction for polymatroids to general polyhedral environments.

Theorem 5.3 (Impossibility) *There is no general auction for every polyhedral environment and every pair of budgets that satisfies the desirable properties.*

We prove it in two steps: first we prove a sequence of lemmas characterizing 2-player auctions for polyhedral environments satisfying all the desirable properties. Then we fix a specific polyhedral environment and argue that no mechanism can possibly satisfy this characterization.

First, we begin by understanding the format of an auction with the desirable properties where the environment is a packing polytope $P \subseteq \mathbb{R}_+^2$. We start by defining a family of VCG auctions.

VCG-family: We say that a mechanism is in the *VCG-family* if its allocation $x(v) \in P$ is such that

$$x(v) \in X^*(v) := \text{argmax}_{x\in P} v^t x.$$

Notice that there might be more than one such mechanism: if v is normal to an edge of the polytope, then the entire edge is in the argmax. Nevertheless, $x(v_1+, v_2) = \lim_{v_1' \downarrow v_1} x(v_1', v_2)$ and $x(v_1, v_2+) = \lim_{v_2' \downarrow v_2} x(v_1, v_2')$ are common for the entire family, as we see in the following lemma. A consequence of this fact is that the payment function might not be unique, but $p(v_1+, v_2)$ and $p(v_1, v_2+)$ are unique.

Lemma 5.4 *Given a convex set $P \subseteq \mathbb{R}_+^2$ and two allocation rules $x(v), \tilde{x}(v) \in X^*(v) := argmax_{x\in P} v^t x$, then $x(v_1+, v_2) = \tilde{x}(v_1+, v_2)$, where $x(v_1+, v_2) = \lim_{v_1' \downarrow v_1} x(v_1', v_2)$.*

The proof is elementary and can be found in Appendix C. To illustrate this fact, consider the simple case of $P = \{x \in \mathbb{R}_+^2; x_1 + x_2 \leq 1\}$. Then the VCG mechanism is well-defined for $x_1 \neq x_2$, which is, simply to allocate to the player with the highest value the entire amount. But notice that completing this mechanism with any allocation in the points (v, v) generates a truthful mechanism. The payments of different mechanisms of the VCG family differ on (v, v), for example $p_i(v, v) = vx_i(v)$, but notice that the payments everywhere else are well-defined.

Pareto-optimal mechanisms: Now we turn our attention back to Pareto-optimal mechanisms for two budget-constrained players. Let (x, p) be such mechanism. As a direct consequence of the characterization of Pareto optimal outcomes (Lemma 2.1), we know the following:

- if $p_i(v) < B_i$ then $x_i(v) \geq \min\{x_i; x \in X^*(v)\}$
- if $p_1(v) < B_1, p_2(v) < B_2$ then $x(v) \in X^*(v)$

And a simple consequence of truthfulness:

- if $p_i(v) = B_i$ then for all $v_i' \geq v_i$, $x(v_i', v_{-i}) = x(v_i, v_{-i})$.

Now, we are ready to start proving the characterization theorem. We will characterize the mechanism in terms of the regions in the space of valuations where the budgets get exhausted. For formally, we are interested in understanding the sets:

$$E_i = \{v \in \mathbb{R}^2_+; p_i(v) = B_i\}$$

Lemma 5.5 *If mechanism (x, p) has the desirable properties, then either $E_1 \cap E_2 = \emptyset$ or there exists some $a \in \mathbb{R}^2_+$ such that $\{v; v > a\} \subseteq E_1 \cap E_2 \subseteq \{v; v \geq a\}$.*

PROOF. Assume that $E_1 \cap E_2$ is not empty. Then we will prove the lemma in two parts. For the first part we will prove two statements: (i) if that if $v^0 \in E_1 \cap E_2$ and $v \geq v^0$ then $x(v) = x(v^0)$ and (ii) if $v, v' \in E_1 \cap E_2$ and $v_i^* = \min\{v_i, v_i'\}$ then $x(v^*) = x(v) = x(v')$. Then for the second part, we show that this whole region that has constant allocation has budget exhausted for the two players. See figure 2 for an illustration of the proof.

For (i), let $v^1 = (v_1, v_2^0)$ and $v^2 = (v_1^0, v_2)$ and notice that $x(v^0) = x(v^1) = x(v^2)$, since budgets are exhausted so the allocation can't increase. By monotonicity, $x_2(v) \geq x_2(v^1) = x_2(v^0)$ and $x_1(v) \geq x_1(v^2) = x_1(v^0)$. Since all allocations lie in the boundary of the polytope, we must have $x(v) = x(v^0)$.

The proof of (ii) is very similar, define $v_i^0 = \max\{v_i, v_i'\}$. Then by (i), $x(v) = x(v^0) = x(v')$ now, by the exact same argument as above we show that $x(v^*) = x(v^0)$.

Now, if $a_i = \inf\{v_i; v \in E_1 \cap E_2\}$, let us show that for $v > a$, $v \in E_1 \cap E_2$. Let us show that $v \in E_2$ and then E_1 is analogous. By definition, there is some $v' \in E_1 \cap E_2$ with $v_1' < v_1$. Then $(v_1', v_2) \in E_2$ since the allocation is constant, for $v > a$, the budget of 2 is exhausted in (v_1', v_2) iff it is exhausted in (v_1', v_2'). Now, note that by monotonicity $x_1(v_1', u) \leq x_1(v_1, u)$ and since allocation is in the boundary of the polytope $x_2(v_1', u) \geq x_2(v_1, u)$. By the payment formula, $p_2(v) = v_2 x_2(v) - \int_0^{v_2} x_2(v_1, u)du$ and by the fact that $x_2(v) = x_2(v_1', v_2)$, we have that $B_2 \geq p_2(v) \geq p_2(v_1', v_2) = B_2$, so $v \in E_2$. ∎

The next lemma further describes the regions E_1 and E_2:

Lemma 5.6 *If P is a packing polytope, there is a finite set of vectors $\{u^1, u^2, \ldots, u^k\}$ such that for $v \neq tu^i$ for some $t \geq 0$, the VCG family is uniquely defined. Moreover, if (x, p) is a mechanism with the desirable properties and $E_1 \cap E_2 \subseteq \{v; v \geq a\}$ then if $\xi_i(v_{-i}) = \inf\{v_i; p_i(v_i, v_{-i}) = B_i\}$ and $v_{-i} < a_{-i}$, then $(\xi_i(v_{-i}), v_{-i}) = tu^i$ for some t, i.*

PROOF. The set of vectors $\{u^1, u^2, \ldots, u^k\}$ is simply the set of normals of the edges of the polytope as depicted in the first part of Figure 3. If v is not an edge in the polytope, then the point in P maximizing $v^t x$ is a vertex and therefore uniquely defined. If we draw the lines $u^i \cdot t$ for $t > 0$ we divide the space of all possible valuations in regions (see second part of the figure): the regions correspond to the vertices and the lines to edges of the polytope.

Now, given a certain mechanism (x, p), suppose that $v_1 < a_1$ the vector $(v_1, \xi_2(v_1))$ is not normal to any edge of P. Then clearly $x^*(v_1, \xi_2(v_1))$ is well-defined and moreover, for some $\delta > 0$ and $v_2' \in [\xi_2(v_1) - \delta, \xi_2(v_1) + \delta]$, $x^*(v_1, v_2')$ is well-defined and constant in the v_2'-range. Also $(v_1, v_2') \notin E_1 \cap E_2$, since $v_1 < a_1$. For such $v_2' > \xi_2(v_1)$, we know that $(v_1, v_2') \in E_2$, thus it is not in E_1 and therefore $x_2(v_1, v_2') = x_2(v_1, \xi_2(v_1)) \leq x_2^*(v_1, \xi_2(v_1))$. For $v_2' < \xi_2(v_1)$, $(v_1, v_2') \notin E_2$ so $x_2(v_1, v_2') \geq x_2^*(v_1, v_2')$. Using that $x_2(v_1, v_2')$ is constant in v_2' in this range and taking $v_2' \uparrow \xi_2(v_1)$, we get: $x_2(v_1, v_2') \geq x_2^*(v_1, \xi_2(v_1))$.

Now, by monotonicity, we have $x_2(v_1, v_2') = x_2^*(v_1, \xi_2(v_1))$ for all v_2' in the interval $(\xi_2(v_1) - \delta, \xi_2(v_1) + \delta)$. Therefore the budget of player 2 could not have been exhausted on $\xi_2(v_1)$. ∎

The third part of Figure 3 illustrates how the region E_2 typically looks like. If $u^1, u^2, \ldots, u^k$ are sorted such that u^1 corresponds to the edge that is higher to the left and u^k corresponds to the edge that is lower to the right, then we can divide $[0, a_1)$ in segments $[0, r_1), [r_1, r_2), \ldots, [r_k, a_1)$ such that for $v_1 \in [0, r_1)$, $\xi_2(v_1) = \infty$, and for $v_1 \in [r_i, r_{i+1})$, $(v_1, \xi_2(v_1))$ is in the line $\{t \cdot u^i; t \geq 0\}$. To see why this is true, consider $v_1 < v_1'$ and assume that $(v_1, \xi_2(v_1))$ is in the line $\{t \cdot u^i; t \geq 0\}$. Then $(v_1', \xi_2(v_1'))$ cannot be strictly above this line, by a similar argument used in Lemma 5.5: look at the allocation curves $x_2(v_1, v_2) \geq x_2(v_1', v_2)$ and the payment formula – then player 2 must be paying just above the $\{t \cdot u^i; t \geq 0\}$ for v_1' line at least as much as he was paying above this line for v_1 and hence his budgets must be exhausted.

5.3 Proof of the Impossibility Theorem

Now, we are ready to prove Theorem 5.3, which states that there is no general auction with all the desirable properties for all polyhedral environments P. We fix the following setting: a set of feasible allocations

$$P = \{x \in \mathbb{R}^2_+; 2x_1 + x_2 \leq 6, x_1 + 2x_2 \leq 6\}$$

and budgets $B_1 = B_2 = 1$. Assume that (x, p) is a mechanism with the desirable properties for this setting. We will use the characterization lemmas in Section 5.2 to find a contradiction. We illustrate the flow of the proof in Figure 4 (a brief summary of the proof is given in the caption of the figure).

Fact 5.7 *In the region $[0, \frac{2}{3}) \times [0, \frac{2}{3})$, the mechanism (x, p) produces an efficient allocation (i.e., it is equal to some mechanism of the VCG family).*

PROOF. First notice that no mechanism in the VCG-family for P exhausts the budget in $[0, \frac{2}{3}) \times [0, \frac{2}{3})$. Now, we turn our attention to the mechanism (x, p), which is a mechanism with the desirable properties for this setting.

In $[0, \frac{1}{3}) \times [0, \frac{2}{3})$, player 1 cannot exhaust his budget, since $x_1 \leq 3$ and $v_1 < \frac{1}{3}$. We claim that in this area the mechanism needs to behave like VCG. If there is a point in this

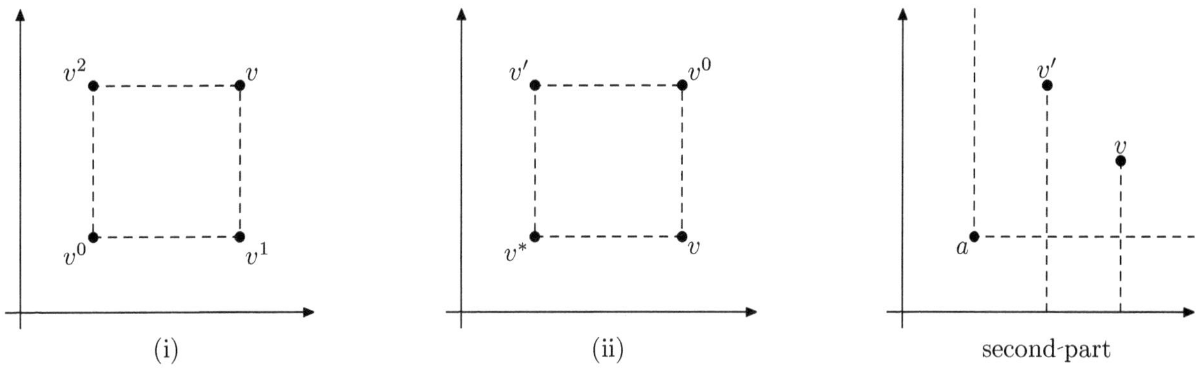

Figure 2: Illustration of the proof of Lemma 5.5

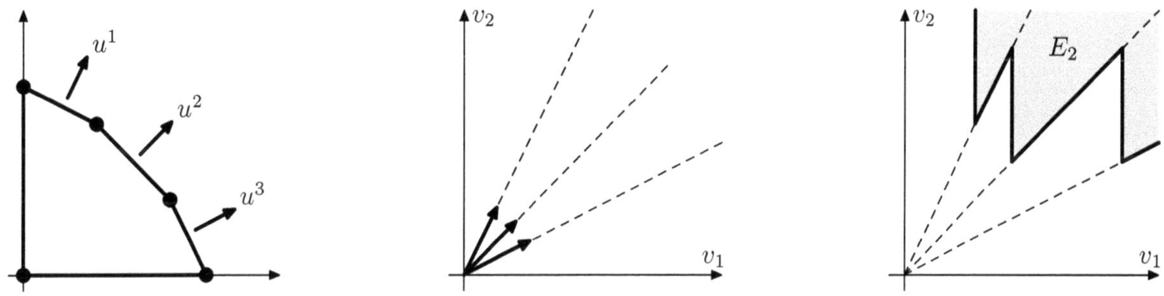

Figure 3: Illustration of the proof of Lemma 5.6

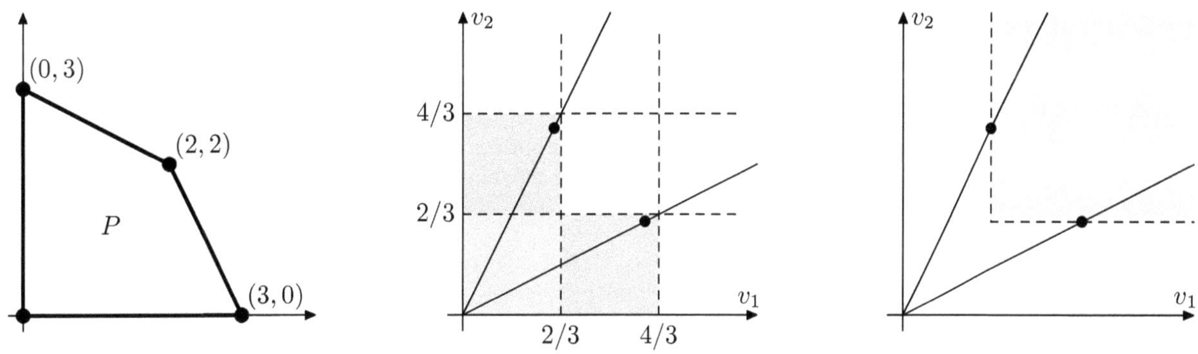

Figure 4: Illustration of the proof of the impossibility theorem: in the first part we represent the polytope P, in the second we represent the first main steps: we show that any auction must resemble VCG in the red region (Fact 5.7) and extend the definition of the auction to the blue region (Facts 5.8 and 5.9), showing that the budget of player 1 must get exhausted at the point $(\frac{1.2381}{2}, 1.2381)$ and the budget of player 2 must get exhausted at the point $(1.2381, \frac{1.2381}{2})$. We use this fact to show that the allocation must be constant in the green region (Fact 5.10), contradicting Pareto-optimality for allocation of the form (v_1, v_2) where $\frac{1.2381}{2} < v_1 < \frac{2}{3}$ as $v_2 \to \infty$.

region where $x(v)$ doesn't maximize $v^t x$ for $x \in P$, then the budget of player 2 must be exhausted. So, there is some (v_1, v_2) such that for $v_2' > v_2$, $p_2(v_1, v_2') = B_2$ and for $v_2' < v_2$, $x(v_1, v_2')$ is in the VCG family. Now, notice that the allocation for $v_2' > v_2$ must be $x_2(v_2', v_1) \leq x_2^*(v_2', v_1)$. This contradicts the fact that the budget is exhausted for $v_2' \downarrow v_2$. So, this shows that (x, p) must allocate efficiently on $[0, \frac{1}{3}) \times [0, \frac{2}{3})$. Now, for $[0, \frac{2}{3}) \times [0, \frac{1}{3})$, we can do the same argument. Now, what remains are the points in $[\frac{1}{3}, \frac{2}{3}) \times [\frac{1}{3}, \frac{2}{3})$. Let v be such a point. Notice that for $(\frac{1}{3} - \epsilon, v_2)$ and $(v_1, \frac{1}{3} - \epsilon)$, the allocation must be $(2, 2)$ because of the previous argument. By monotonicity, $x(v) = (2, 2)$ which is the efficient allocation. ■

Now, we know how any mechanism (x, p) with the desirable properties should look like in the red region of Figure 4. Next, we try to understand how it should look in the blue region. In order to do so, we need some definitions. From Lemma 5.5 we know that there is $a \in \mathbb{R}_+^2 \cup \{(\infty, \infty)\})$ such that: $\{v; v > a\} \subseteq E_1 \cap E_2 \subseteq \{v; v \geq a\}$. We also define:

$$\tilde{v}_2 = \min\{v_2; p_1(\frac{v_2}{2}+, v_2) = 1\}$$

$$\tilde{v}_1 = \min\{v_1; p_2(v_1, \frac{v_1}{2}+) = 1\}$$

And we focus on the region R, which we define as the interior of the rectangle between $(0, 0)$ and $(\tilde{v}_2/2, \tilde{v}_2)$.

Fact 5.8 *The budget of player* 1 *does not get exhausted in* R. *Also,* $\frac{2}{3} < \tilde{v}_2 \leq 1.2381$

PROOF. First, assume $\tilde{v}_2 < 4/3$. Then by Fact 5.7, the budget of player 1 does not get exhausted in $[0, \frac{2}{3}) \times [0, \frac{2}{3})$ and by the definition of $\tilde{v}_2$ and lemma 5.6 it cannot be exhausted for $[0, \frac{\tilde{v}_2}{2}) \times (\frac{1}{3}, \tilde{v}_2)$. Notice that a cannot be in this region, because it would also contradict the definition of $\tilde{v}_2$.

Given this fact, let us analyze how the mechanism should be in this setting. We do so, by fixing v_1 and looking at $x_2(v_1, v_2)$. We can use the same argument as in the previous fact to argue that $x(v_1, v_2)$ must be the efficient allocation for $v_2 < 2v_1$ in R and also for all $v_1 \leq \frac{1}{3}$. For $v_1 > \frac{1}{3}$ and $v_2 > 2v_1$, if we allocate as in VCG, we exceed the budget. So, the allocation for those points must exactly match the budget of player 2. So, the only possible value must be such that:

$$2 \cdot \frac{1}{2} v_1 + (x_2(v) - 2) 2 v_1 = 1$$

and therefore the allocation must be

$$x(v) = \left(3 - \frac{1}{v_1}, 2 + \frac{1 - v_1}{2v_1}\right).$$

Now, this determines the payment of player 1 in the rectangle. We know that for $\delta \downarrow 0$, $p_1(\frac{\tilde{v}_2}{2} - \delta, \tilde{v}_2 - 3\delta) < 1$, which we can write as:

$$\lim_{\delta \downarrow 0} p_1(\frac{\tilde{v}_2}{2} - \delta, \tilde{v}_2 - 3\delta) = 2 \cdot \frac{\tilde{v}_2}{2} - \int_{1/3}^{\tilde{v}_2/2} 3 - \frac{1}{z} dz =$$

$$= 1 - \frac{\tilde{v}_2}{2} + \log\left(\frac{3}{2}\tilde{v}_2\right) \leq 1$$

This implies that $\tilde{v}_2 \leq 1.2381$. Notice that this excludes the fact that $\tilde{v}_2 > 4/3$, otherwise we could have done the same analysis on $[0, \frac{2}{3}] \times [0, \tilde{v}_2]$ and arrived in the same conclusion that $\tilde{v}_2 \leq 1.2381$. ■

Fact 5.9 $\tilde{v}_2 = 1.2381$ *and* $x(\frac{\tilde{v}_2}{2}+, \tilde{v}_2) = (2, 2)$.

PROOF. Since $\frac{2}{3} < \tilde{v}_2 \leq 1.2381$, we know that $x_2(\frac{\tilde{v}_2}{2}+, \tilde{v}_2) \geq 2$ by using that $x_2(\frac{\tilde{v}_2}{2}+, \frac{1}{3}) = 2$ (Fact 5.7) and monotonicity. Therefore, $x_1(\frac{\tilde{v}_2}{2}+, \tilde{v}_2) \leq 2$. Writing the payment for player 1 at this point we get:

$$1 = p_1(\frac{\tilde{v}_2}{2}+, \tilde{v}_2) = x_1(\frac{\tilde{v}_2}{2}+, \tilde{v}_2) \cdot \frac{\tilde{v}_2}{2} - \int_{1/3}^{\tilde{v}_2/2} 3 - \frac{1}{z} dz \leq$$

$$\leq 1 - \frac{\tilde{v}_2}{2} + \log\left(\frac{3}{2}\tilde{v}_2\right)$$

which implies that $\tilde{v}_2 = 1.2381$ and $x(\frac{\tilde{v}_2}{2}+, \tilde{v}_2) = (2, 2)$, since all inequalities must be tight. ■

Fact 5.10 $\tilde{v}_1 = \tilde{v}_2 = 1.2381$ *and* $x(v) = (2, 2)$ *for all valuation profiles* $v > (\frac{\tilde{v}_1}{2}, \frac{\tilde{v}_2}{2})$.

PROOF. We can apply the same argument exchanging 1 and 2 and conclude that $\tilde{v}_1 = \tilde{v}_2$. Now, to see that for $v_1', v_2' > \frac{\tilde{v}_i}{2}$ we have $x(v_1', \tilde{v}_2) = x(\tilde{v}_1, v_2') = (2, 2)$, we analyze four regions. If $v \in (\tilde{v}_i/2, \tilde{v}_i] \times (\tilde{v}_i/2, \tilde{v}_i]$ or $v \in [\tilde{v}_i, \infty) \times [\tilde{v}_i, \infty)$ we can use the standard monotonicity argument to show that $x(v) = (2, 2)$.

For the regions $[\tilde{v}_1, \infty) \times (\frac{\tilde{v}_1}{2}, \tilde{v}_1)$ and $(\frac{\tilde{v}_2}{2}, \tilde{v}_2) \times [\tilde{v}_2, \infty)$ is a little trickier. We do the analysis for the first one. The second is analogous.

Clearly $p_2(\tilde{v}_1, \tilde{v}_2) = 1$. Now, for $v_1' > \tilde{v}_1$, $x(v_1', \tilde{v}_2) = x(\tilde{v}_1, \tilde{v}_2) = (2, 2)$. And for all v_2 we have $x_1(v_1', v_2) \geq x_1(\tilde{v}_1, v_2)$ and therefore $x_2(v_1', v_2) \leq x_2(\tilde{v}_i, v_2)$. Now, since $p_2(v_1, v_2) = v_2 x_2(v) - \int_0^{v_2} x_2(v_1, u) du$ clearly $p_2(v_1', \tilde{v}_2) \geq p_2(\tilde{v}_1, \tilde{v}_2) = 1$. Therefore $p_2(v_1', \tilde{v}_2) = 1$, since the mechanism respects budgets. Notice that the only way it can be true is that if $x_2(v_1', v_2) = x_2(\tilde{v}_i, v_2)$, so we must have $x_2(v_1', v_2) = (2, 2)$ for $v_1' \in [\tilde{v}_i, \infty)$.

We can use the exact same argument for region: $(\frac{\tilde{v}_i}{2}, \tilde{v}_i) \times [\tilde{v}_i, \infty)$. ■

Now we are ready to prove Theorem 5.3:

Proof of Theorem 5.3 : Now, by putting Fact 5.10 and Fact 5.7 together, we get a contradiction with the Pareto-optimality: consider $\frac{\tilde{v}_i}{2} < v_1 < \frac{2}{3}$ then by facts 5.10 and 5.7 combined, we know that $x_2(v_1, v_2) = 0$ for $v_2 < \frac{v_1}{2}$ and $x_2(v_1, v_2) = 2$ for $v_2 > \frac{v_1}{2}$, so the budget of player 2 never gets exhausted even for $v_2 \to \infty$. This contradicts Pareto-optimality for $v_2 > 2v_1$, since if his budget is not exhausted, he should get allocated at least as much as he gets in VCG. ■

5.4 Multi-unit auctions with decreasing marginals

As a by-product of Theorem 5.3, we can answer in a negative way the question of the existence of truthful Pareto-optimal auctions for multi-unit auctions with decreasing marginals. Consider the following setting:

Setting: Consider a supply of s of a certain divisible good and two players in such a way that the feasible allocations are (x_1, x_2) such that $x_1 + x_2 \leq s$. Player i has a public budget B_i and a private valuation which is a increasing concave function $V_i : [0, s] \to \mathbb{R}_+$. Upon getting x_i units of the good and paying p_i, player i has utility $u_i = V_i(x_i) - p_i$.

It is tempting to believe that one could adapt the clinching framework in Algorithm 1 to deal with this setting, by simply redefining the demand function as something like:

$$d_i = \min\left\{\frac{B_i}{p}, \max\{x_i; \partial V_i(\rho_i + x_i) \le p\}\right\}$$

where $\partial V_i(x_i)$ is the marginal valuation at x_i. Indeed, if $V_i(x_i) = v_i \cdot x_i$, this recovers the original way of calculating demands. In appendix D we give a counter-example showing that the clinching framework with this new demand function results in a non-truthful mechanism. The intuition behind the counter example is that some player can increase his declared value on items he won't get anyway in order to increase the payment of his opponent, exhausting his budget earlier. This way, he is able to get items for cheaper in the end.

In the following theorem, we show that no auction mechanism can satisfy all the desirable properties for this setting:

Theorem 5.11 *There is no truthful, Pareto-optimal and budget-feasible auction for this setting.*

PROOF. Suppose that $(\hat{x}(V_1, V_2), \hat{p}(V_1, V_2))$ is a mechanism satisfying all the desirable properties for multi-unit auctions with decreasing marginals. Then we can use it as a black-box to construct a mechanism for a general polyhedral environment, contradicting Theorem 5.3. Given a certain polyhedral environment, we can describe

$$P = \{x \in [0, \alpha] \times [0, \beta]; x_2 \le h(x_1)\}$$

where $h : [0, \alpha] \to [0, \beta]$ is a monotone non-increasing concave function, $h(0) = \beta$ and $h(\alpha) = 0$. Now, using $(\hat{x}, \hat{p})$ for $s = 1$, build the following mechanism: if players report valuations v_1, v_2 build the following concave functions: $V_1(x_1) = v_1 \cdot \alpha x_1$ and $V_2(x_2) = v_2 \cdot h(\alpha - \alpha x_2)$.

Now, simply define

$$x(v_1, v_2) = (\alpha \hat{x}_1, h(\alpha \hat{x}_1))$$
$$p(v_1, v_2) = \hat{p}(V_1, V_2).$$

The mechanism is clearly truthful, individually rational and budget-feasible. It is also easy to see that sets of allocation can me mapped 1-1 between those two settings, preserving Pareto-optimality. ■

6. REFERENCES

[1] Z. Abrams. Revenue maximization when bidders have budgets. In *SODA*, pages 1074–1082, 2006.

[2] G. Aggarwal, S. Muthukrishnan, D. Pál, and M. Pál. General auction mechanism for search advertising. In *WWW*, pages 241–250, 2009.

[3] A. Archer and É. Tardos. Truthful mechanisms for one-parameter agents. In *FOCS*, pages 482–491, 2001.

[4] I. Ashlagi, M. Braverman, A. Hassidim, R. Lavi, and M. Tennenholt. Position auctions with budgets: Existence and uniqueness. In *B.E. journal of Theoretical Economics âĂŞ Advances, forthcoming*, 2011.

[5] L. M. Ausubel. An efficient ascending-bid auction for multiple objects. *American Economic Review*, 94, 1997.

[6] J.-P. Benoit and V. Krishna. Multiple-object auctions with budget constrained bidders. *Review of Economic Studies*, 68(1):155–79, January 2001.

[7] S. Bhattacharya, V. Conitzer, K. Munagala, and L. Xia. Incentive compatible budget elicitation in multi-unit auctions. In *SODA*, pages 554–572, 2010.

[8] S. Bikhchandani, S. de Vries, J. Schummer, and R. V. Vohra. An ascending vickrey auction for selling bases of a matroid. *Operations Research*, 59(2):400–413, 2011.

[9] C. Borgs, J. T. Chayes, N. Immorlica, M. Mahdian, and A. Saberi. Multi-unit auctions with budget-constrained bidders. In *ACM Conference on Electronic Commerce*, pages 44–51, 2005.

[10] I. Caragiannis, P. Kanellopoulos, C. Kaklamanis, and M. Kyropoulou. On the efficiency of equilibria in generalized second price auctions. In *EC'11*, 2011.

[11] Y.-K. Che and I. Gale. Standard auctions with financially constrained bidders. *Review of Economic Studies*, 65(1):1–21, January 1998.

[12] R. Colini-Baldeschi, M. Henzinger, S. Leonardi, and M. Starnberger. On multiple round sponsored search auctions with budgets. *CoRR*, abs/1112.6361, 2011.

[13] P. Dhangwatnotai. Multi-keyword sponsored search. In *ACM Conference on Electronic Commerce*, pages 91–100, 2011.

[14] S. Dobzinski, R. Lavi, and N. Nisan. Multi-unit auctions with budget limits. In *FOCS*, pages 260–269, 2008.

[15] D. Dolev, D. G. Feitelson, J. Y. Halpern, R. Kupferman, and N. Linial. No justified complaints: on fair sharing of multiple resources. In *ICTS*, pages 68–75, 2012.

[16] B. Edelman, M. Ostrovsky, and M. Schwarz. Internet advertising and the generalized second-price auction: Selling billions of dollars worth of keywords. *The American Economic Review*, 97(1):242–259, March 2007.

[17] J. Feldman, S. Muthukrishnan, E. Nikolova, and M. Pál. A truthful mechanism for offline ad slot scheduling. In *SAGT*, pages 182–193, 2008.

[18] A. Fiat, S. Leonardi, J. Saia, and P. Sankowski. Single valued combinatorial auctions with budgets. In *ACM Conference on Electronic Commerce*, pages 223–232, 2011.

[19] R. L. Graham, E. L. Lawler, J. K. Lenstra, and A. H. G. R. Kan. Optimization and approximation in deterministic sequencing and scheduling: a survey. *Ann. Discrete Math.*, 4:287–326, 1979.

[20] I. Hafalir, R. Ravi, and A. Sayedi. Sort-cut: A pareto optimal and semi-truthful mechanism for multi-unit auctions with budget-constrained bidders. *Ad Auctions Workshop*.

[21] R. Lavi and M. May. A note on the incompatibility of strategy-proofness and pareto-optimality in quasi-linear settings with public budgets. *WINE*.

[22] B. Lucier and R. Paes Leme. Gsp auctions with correlated types. In *EC'11*, 2011.

[23] B. Lucier, R. Paes Leme, and Éva Tardos. On revenue in the generalized second price auction. In *Ad Auctions Workshop*, 2011.

[24] C. J. H. McDiarmid. Rado's theorem for polymatroids. *Mathematical Proceedings of the Cambridge Philosophical Society*, 78(02):263–281, 1975.

[25] R. Myerson. Optimal auction design. *Mathematics of Operations Research*, 6(1):58–73, 1981.
[26] T. Nguyen and É. Tardos. Approximately maximizing efficiency and revenue in polyhedral environments. In *ACM Conference on Electronic Commerce*, pages 11–19, 2007.
[27] T. Nguyen and M. Vojnovic. The weighted proportional sharing mechanisms. In *SIGMETRICS*, 2011.
[28] R. Paes Leme and E. Tardos. Pure and bayes-nash price of anarchy for generalized second price auctions. In *FOCS10: 51st Annual IEEE Symposium on Foundations of Computer Science*, 2010.
[29] M. M. Pai and R. Vohra. Optimal auctions with financially constrained bidders. Discussion papers, Northwestern University, Center for Mathematical Studies in Economics and Management Science, Aug 2008.
[30] A. Schrijver. *Combinatorial Optimization - Polyhedra and Efficiency*. Springer, 2003.
[31] H. R. Varian. Position auctions. *International Journal of Industrial Organization*, 2006.

APPENDIX

A. EXTENSIONS AND LIMITATIONS OF THE CLINCHING FRAMEWORK

Scaled polymatroids: If $P \subseteq \mathbb{R}_+^n$ is a polymatroid, $\gamma \in \mathbb{R}_+^n$, then we call $P_\gamma = \{x; (\frac{x_i}{\gamma_i})_i \in P\}$ a scaled polymatroid. If the environment is P_γ, it is easy to see that a truthful, individually-rational, Pareto-optimal and budget-feasible auction is obtained by running the polymatroid clinching auction on P with inputs $\gamma_i v_i$ instead of v_i. It is simple to see that this is equivalent to a standard clinching auction with input values v_i but price clocks advancing on a different speed for each player. Scaled polymatroids are important since they correspond to the setting of AdWords with Quality Factors discussed at the end of section 4.1).

Beyond scaled polymatroids: one could change the way clinching is done and one could change the price trajectories, maybe in a more sophisticated way then the one we did for the scaled polymatroids. If the trajectory is such that it only depends on P and budgets (not on values) and p_i never decreases, the auction retains truthfulness and budget feasibility. Here we argue that none of such changes would generate a Pareto-optimal auction when P is not a scaled polymatroid. Assume $n = 2$ for simplicity and imagine that there is trajectory for the price vector p and a clinching procedure. Also assumes valuations are much smaller than budgets in such a way that the mechanism cannott exhaust budgets and therefore the auction must allocate like VCG. Any such mechanism must decide on the whole allocation the first time $p_i = v_i$ for some component, having only the information that $v_j \geq p_j$ for the other component, since at this point he needs to allocate to the second player. So, the environment must be such that there is a price trajectory $p(t)$, where the optimal allocation is constant for all points (p_1, v_2) for all $v_2 > p_2$. And also, it should be constant for all (v_1, p_2) for all $v_1 > p_1$. Notice that scaled polymatroids are exactly those environments.

B. FASTER CLINCHING SUB-ROUTINES

In Lemma 3.5 we showed that for any generic polymatroidal environment P we can perform the clinching step in polynomial time if we have oracle access to the submodular function defining the polymatroid. In order to do so, we solve a submodular minimization problem. For most practical applications, however, one can design much simpler and faster algorithms for clinching. Clinching involves solving the following problem: given an environment P, $\rho \in P$ and $d \in \mathbb{R}_+^n$ we want to compute:

$$\max\{\mathbb{1}^t x; x + \rho \in P, 0 \leq x \leq d\} \qquad (3)$$

We illustrate how to solve this problem efficiently for the single-keyword AdWords polytope: given $\alpha_1 \geq \alpha_2 \geq \ldots \geq \alpha_n$, consider the environment:

$$P = \{x \in \mathbb{R}_+^n; x(S) \leq \textstyle\sum_{j=1}^{|S|} \alpha_j, \forall S \subseteq [n]\}$$

Lemma B.1 *For the single-keyword AdWords polytope, the optimization problem defined in equation (3) can be solved using the following greedy algorithm: we can assume wlog that the components are sorted such that $\rho_1 + d_1 \geq \rho_2 + d_2 \geq \ldots \geq \rho_n + d_n$. Now, define inductively*

$$z_i = \min\{\rho_i + d_i, \textstyle\sum_{j=1}^{i} \alpha_j - \sum_{j=1}^{i-1} z_j\}.$$

Then $\sum_i z_i - \rho_i$ is the solution to the problem.

PROOF. If we drop the restriction that $x \geq 0$ in (3), then it is easy to see that $x = z - \rho$ is an optimal solution to this problem using, for example, a local exchange argument. Now, we show that we can fix this problem, by modifying z such that $z \geq \rho$.

In order to fix that, consider the smaller i such that $z_i < \rho_i$. By the definition of z_i, it must be the case that $z_i = \sum_{j=1}^{i} \alpha_j - \sum_{j=1}^{i-1} z_j$, so $\sum_{j=1}^{i} z_j = \sum_{j=1}^{i} \alpha_j$. Then there must be some $k < i$ such that $z_k > \rho_k$, otherwise we would have $\sum_{j=1}^{i} \rho_j > \sum_{j=1}^{i} \alpha_j$ contradicting the fact that $\rho \in P$. Notice we can increase z_i by some small δ and decrease z_k by a small δ. And obtain another vector z which is also such that $z \in P, z \leq \rho + d$ and has the same $\mathbb{1}^t z$ value (the fact that $z \in P$ after this transformation is due to the nature of the constraints). We can repeat this process until we get $z \geq \rho$. ■

C. MISSING PROOFS IN SECTION 5

Proof of Lemma 5.4 : Suppose that $x(v_1+, v_2) \neq \tilde{x}(v_1+, v_2)$, then say that $x_1(v_1+, v_2) > \tilde{x}_1(v_1+, v_2)$. Since both are in the boundary of the polytope, it means that for all (v_1', v_2) with $v_1' > v_1$, $\tilde{x}_1(v_1', v_2) \geq x_1(v_1+, v_2)$, since the points to the right of $x(v_1+, v_2)$ are clearly better then the ones to the left of it. So $\tilde{x}_1(v_1', v_2)$ can't converge to $\tilde{x}_1(v_1+, v_2) < x_1(v_1, x_2)$. ■

D. COUNTER-EXAMPLE TO CLINCHING WITH DECREASING MARGINALS

Consider the setting of multi-unit auctions with decreasing marginals described in section 5.4, and the variant of the clinching auction in Algorithm 1 where demands are calculated by:

$$d_i = \min\left\{\frac{B_i}{p}, \max\{x_i; \partial V_i(\rho_i + x_i) \leq p\}\right\}$$

Our main claim here is that this auction is not truthful. We show that by providing an example: consider an initial supply of $s = 2$ budgets $B_1 = \infty, B_2 = 4$ and valuations:

$$V_1(x) = \begin{cases} 4x, & x \in [0,1] \\ 4 + x, & x \in [1,2] \end{cases} \qquad V_2(x) = 3x, \quad x \in [0,2]$$

The outcome of that is $x_1 = 1, x_2 = 1$ and $p_1 = 3, p_2 = 1$ since budgets never get exhausted. Now, we show that player 1 has a profitable deviation. He could report the following valuation instead:

$$\tilde{V}_1(x) = \begin{cases} 4x, & x \in [0,1] \\ 4 + 2x, & x \in [1,2] \end{cases}$$

The the price clock increases up to 2 without any clinching. For 2+, the demand of player 1 drops and player 2 is able to clinch one unit by the price of 2, remaining with budget 2. Now, as price goes up, player 2's demand keeps decreasing, since his leftover budget is only 2 and the price is greater than 2. As a result, player 1 will be able to start clinching at price $p = 2+$ and therefore will have $\tilde{x}_1 = 1$, $\tilde{p}_1 < 3$, which is a strict improvement over the truth-telling strategy.

Matroid Prophet Inequalities

Robert Kleinberg*
Department of Computer Science
Cornell University, Ithaca NY 14853
rdk@cs.cornell.edu

S. Matthew Weinberg†
Department of Electrical Engineering
and Computer Science
MIT, Cambridge, MA 02139
smweinberg@csail.mit.edu

ABSTRACT

Consider a gambler who observes a sequence of independent, non-negative random numbers and is allowed to stop the sequence at any time, claiming a reward equal to the most recent observation. The famous prophet inequality of Krengel, Sucheston, and Garling asserts that a gambler who knows the distribution of each random variable can achieve at least half as much reward, in expectation, as a "prophet" who knows the sampled values of each random variable and can choose the largest one. We generalize this result to the setting in which the gambler and the prophet are allowed to make more than one selection, subject to a matroid constraint. We show that the gambler can still achieve at least half as much reward as the prophet; this result is the best possible, since it is known that the ratio cannot be improved even in the original prophet inequality, which corresponds to the special case of rank-one matroids. Generalizing the result still further, we show that under an intersection of p matroid constraints, the prophet's reward exceeds the gambler's by a factor of at most $O(p)$, and this factor is also tight.

Beyond their interest as theorems about pure online algoritms or optimal stopping rules, these results also have applications to mechanism design. Our results imply improved bounds on the ability of sequential posted-price mechanisms to approximate optimal mechanisms in single-parameter and multi-parameter Bayesian settings. In particular, our results imply the first efficiently computable constant-factor approximations to the Bayesian optimal revenue in certain multi-parameter settings.

*Supported in part by NSF awards CCF-0643934, IIS-0905467, and AF-0910940, AFOSR grant FA9550-09-1-0100, an Alfred P. Sloan Foundation Fellowship, a Microsoft Research New Faculty Fellowship, and a Google Research Grant.

†Supported by a NSF Graduate Research Fellowship and a NPSC Graduate Fellowship.

STOC'12, May 19–22, 2012, New York, New York, USA.

Categories and Subject Descriptors

F.2.2 [**Theory of Computation**]: Analysis of Algorithms and Problem Complexity—*Nonnumerical Algorithms and Problems*; G.3 [**Mathematics of Computing**]: Probability and Statistics—*Probabilistic algorithms*

General Terms

Algorithms, Theory, Economics

Keywords

Online Optimization, Matroids, Prophet Inequalities, Optimal Stopping, Bayesian Mechanism Design

1. INTRODUCTION

In 1978, Krengel, Sucheston and Garling [18] proved a surprising and fundamental result about the relative power of online and offline algorithms in Bayesian settings. They showed that if $X_1, X_2, \ldots, X_n$ is a sequence of independent, non-negative, real-valued random variables satisfying $\mathbb{E}[\max_i X_i] < \infty$, then there exists a stopping rule τ such that

$$2 \cdot \mathbb{E}[X_\tau] \geq \mathbb{E}\left[\max_i X_i\right]. \qquad (1)$$

In other words, if we consider a game in which a player observes the sequence $X_1, X_2, \ldots, X_n$ and is allowed to terminate the game at any time, collecting the most recently observed reward, then a prophet who can foretell the entire sequence and stop at its maximum value can gain at most twice as much payoff as a player who must choose the stopping time based only on the current and past observations. The inequality (1) became the first[1] of many "prophet inequalities" in optimal stopping theory. Expressed in computer science terms, these inequalities compare the performance of online algorithms versus the offline optimum for problems that involve selecting one or more elements from a random sequence, in a Bayesian setting where the algorithm knows the distribution from which the sequence will be sampled whereas the offline optimum knows the values of the samples themselves and chooses among them optimally. Not surprisingly, these inequalities have important applications in the design and analysis of algorithms, especially in algorithmic mechanism design, a connection that we discuss further below.

[1]More precisely, it was the second prophet inequality. The same inequality with a factor of 4, instead of 2, was discovered a year earlier by Krengel and Sucheston [17].

In this paper, we prove a prophet inequality for matroids, generalizing the original inequality (1) which corresponds to the special case of rank-one matroids. More specifically, we analyze the following online selection problem. One is given a matroid whose elements have random weights sampled independently from (not necessarily identical) probability distributions on $\mathbb{R}_+$. An online algorithm, initialized with knowledge of the matroid structure and of the distribution of each element's weight, must select an independent subset of the matroid by observing the sampled value of each element (in a fixed, prespecified order) and making an immediate decision whether or not to select it before observing the next element. The algorithm's payoff is defined to be the sum of the weights of the selected elements. We prove in this paper that for every matroid, there is an online algorithm whose expected payoff is least half of the expected weight of the maximum-weight basis. It is well known that the factor 2 in Krengel, Sucheston, and Garling's inequality (1) cannot be improved (see Section 5 for a lower bound example) and therefore our result for matroids is the best possible, even in the rank-one case.

Our algorithm is quite simple. At its heart lies a new algorithm for achieving the optimal factor 2 in rank-one matroids: compute a threshold value $T = \mathbb{E}[\max_i X_i]/2$ and accept the first element whose weight exceeds this threshold. This is very similar to the algorithm of Samuel-Cahn [20], which uses a threshold T such that $\Pr(\max_i X_i > T) = \frac{1}{2}$ but is otherwise the same, and which also achieves the optimal factor 2. It is hard to surpass the elegance of Samuel-Cahn's proof, and indeed our proof, though short and simple, is not as elegant. On the other hand, our algorithm for rank-one matroids has a crucial advantage over Samuel-Cahn's: it generalizes to arbitrary matroids without weakening its approximation factor. The generalization is as follows. After having selected some set A and considering adding the next element x_i, the algorithm asks, "How much reward would a prophet expect if he were forced to start with the set A (not counting the weight of A)? And how much would this decrease if he were forced to start with $A \cup \{x_i\}$ instead (not counting the weight of A and x_i)?" If the weight of x_i exceeds half this expected decrease, then we accept it. Otherwise we reject. Note that this algorithm, specialized to rank-one matroids, is precisely the one proposed at the start of this paragraph: the expected value of a prophet who accepts nothing is exactly $\mathbb{E}[\max_i X_i]$, and the expected value of a prophet who is forced to start already having accepted an element is 0.

We next extend our algorithm to the case in which the feasibility constraint is given by a matroid intersection rather than a single matroid. For intersections of p matroids, we present an online algorithm whose expected payoff is at least $\frac{1}{4p-2}$ times the expected maximum weight of a feasible set. The algorithm is a natural extension of the one described earlier, but slightly more complex to account for the change in setting. Having already accepted A and considering x_i, the algorithm again considers the expected reward of a prophet forced to start with A versus one forced to start with $A \cup \{x_i\}$. With matroid intersections, the expected reward of a prophet doesn't behave as nicely as with a single matroid, so we make two modifications. First, we further restrict the prophet so that the set he accepts is not only feasible when combined with A, but is also a subset of the true max-weight feasible set. This restriction is vacuous with a single matroid, as the prophet will always choose such a subset anyway. Second, rather than using the correct feasibility constraints, we pretend that one matroid will be chosen uniformly at random and the constraints from the remaining ones will be ignored. Again, this is vacuous with a single matroid as it will always be chosen. After these modifications to the "prophet," the algorithm is the same: if the weight of x_i exceeds half the expected decrease in the prophet's reward, we accept it.

In Section 5 we show that our result for matroid intersections is almost tight: we present a lower bound demonstrating that the ratio $4p-2$ cannot be improved by more than a constant factor.

As mentioned earlier, Bayesian optimal mechanism design problems provide a compelling application of prophet inequalities in computer science and economics. In Bayesian optimal mechanism design, one has a collection of n agents with independent private types sampled from known distributions, and the goal is to design a mechanism for allocating resources and charging prices to the agents, given their reported types, so as to maximize the seller's expected revenue in equilibrium. Chawla et al. [5] pioneered the study of approximation guarantees for *sequential posted pricings* (SPMs), a very simple class of mechanisms in which the seller makes a sequence of take-it-or-leave-it offers to the agents, with each offer specifying an item and a price that the agent must pay in order to win the item. Despite their simplicity, sequential posted pricings were shown in [5] to approximate the optimal revenue in many different settings. Prophet inequalities constitute a key technique underlying these results; instead of directly analyzing the revenue of the SPM, one analyzes the so-called *virtual values* of the winning bids, proving via prophet inequalities that the combined expected virtual value accumulated by the SPM approximates the offline optimum. Translating this virtual-value approximation guarantee into a revenue guarantee is an application of standard Bayesian mechanism design techniques introduced by Roger Myerson [19]. In the course of developing these results, Chawla et al. prove a type of prophet inequality for matroids that is of considerable interest in its own right: they show that if the algorithm is allowed to specify the order in which the matroid elements are observed, then it can guarantee an expected payoff at least half as large as the prophet's. Our result can be seen as a strengthening of theirs, achieving the same approximation bound without allowing the algorithm to reorder the elements. Unlike our setting, in which the factor 2 is known to be tight, the best known lower bound for algorithms that may reorder the elements is $\sqrt{\pi/2} \cong 1.25$.

In order to extend the aforementioned results from single-parameter to multi-parameter domains, Chawla et al. define in [5] a general class of multi-parameter mechanism design problems called Bayesian multi-parameter unit-demand (BMUMD). SPMs in this setting are not truthful but can be modified to yield mechanisms that approximate the Bayesian optimal revenue with respect to a weaker solution concept: implementation in undominated strategies. A narrower class of mechanisms called *oblivious posted pricings* (OPMs) yields truthful mechanisms, but typically with weaker approximation guarantees; for example, it is not known whether OPMs can yield constant-factor approximations to the Bayesian optimal revenue in matroid settings, except for special cases such as graphic matroids. Without resolving this question, our results lead to an equally strong positive result for the BMUMD: truthful mechanisms that 2-approximate the optimal Bayesian revenue in matroid settings and $(4p-2)$-approximate it in settings defined by an intersection of p matroid constraints.

1.1 Related work

The genesis of prophet inequalities in the work of Krengel, Sucheston, and Garling [17, 18] was discussed earlier. It would be impossible in this amount of space to do justice to the extensive literature on prophet inequalities. Of particular relevance to our work are the so-called *multiple-choice prophet inequalities* in which either the gambler, the prophet, or both are given the power to choose more than one element. While several papers have been written on this topic, e.g. [13, 14, 15], the near-optimal solution of the most natural case, in which both the gambler and the prophet have $k > 1$ choices, was not completed until the work of Alaei [1], who gave a factor-$(1 - 1/\sqrt{k+3})^{-1}$ prophet inequality for k-choice optimal stopping; a nearly-matching lower bound of $1 + \Omega(k^{-1/2})$ was already known from prior work.

Research investigating the relationship between algorithmic mechanism design and prophet inequalities was initiated by Hajiaghayi, Kleinberg, and Sandholm [12], who observed that algorithms used in the derivation of prophet inequalities, owing to their monotonicity properties, could be interpreted as truthful online auction mechanisms and that the prophet inequality in turn could be interpreted as the mechanism's approximation guarantee. Chawla et al. [5] discovered a much subtler relation between the two subjects: questions about the approximability of offline Bayesian optimal mechanisms by sequential posted-price mechanisms could be translated into questions about prophet inequalities, via the use of virtual valuation functions. A fuller discussion of their contributions appears earlier in this section. Recent work by Alaei [1] deepens still further the connections between these two research areas, obtaining a near-optimal k-choice prophet inequality and applying it to a much more general Bayesian combinatorial auction framework than that studied in [5].

While not directly related to our work, the matroid secretary problem [3] also concerns relations between optimal stopping and matroids, this time under the assumption of a randomly ordered input, rather than independent random numbers in a fixed order. In fact, the "hard examples" for many natural examples in the matroid-secretary setting also translate into hard examples for the prophet inequality setting. In light of this relation, it is intriguing that our work solves the matroid prophet inequality problem whereas the matroid secretary problem remains unsolved, despite intriguing progress on special cases [7, 16], general matroids [4], and relaxed versions of the problem [22].

Finally, the Bayesian online selection problem that we consider here can be formulated as an exponential-sized Markov decision process, whose state reflects the entire set of decisions made prior to a specified point during the algorithm's execution. Thus, our paper can be interpreted as a contribution to the growing CS literature on approximate solutions of exponential-sized Markov decision processes, e.g. [6, 10, 11]. Most of these papers use LP-based techniques. Combinatorial algorithms based on simple thresholding rules, such as ours, are comparatively rare although there are some other examples in the literature on such problems, for example [9].

2. PRELIMINARIES

Bayesian online selection problems.

An instance of the Bayesian online selection problem (abbreviated BOSP) is specified by a ground set $\mathcal{U}$, a downward-closed set system $\mathcal{I} \subseteq 2^{\mathcal{U}}$, and for each $x \in \mathcal{U}$ a probability distribution F_x supported on the set $\mathbb{R}_+$ of non-negative real numbers. These data determine a probability distribution over functions $w : \mathcal{U} \to \mathbb{R}_+$, in which the random variables $\{w(x) \mid x \in \mathcal{U}\}$ are independent and $w(x)$ has distribution F_x. We refer to $w(x)$ as the *weight of* x, and we extend w to an additive set function defined on $2^{\mathcal{U}}$ by $w(A) = \sum_{x \in A} w(x)$. Elements of $\mathcal{I}$ are called *feasible sets.* For a given assignment of weights, w, we let $\mathsf{MAX}(w)$ denote the maximum-weight feasible set and $\mathsf{OPT}(w)$ denotes its weight; we will abbreviate these to MAX and OPT when the weights w are clear from context.

An *input sequence* is a sequence σ of ordered pairs (x_i, w_i) $i = 1, \dots, n$, each belonging to $\mathcal{U} \times \mathbb{R}_+$, such that every element of $\mathcal{U}$ occurs exactly once in the sequence $x_1, \dots, x_n$. A *deterministic online selection algorithm* is a function A mapping every input sequence σ to a set $A(\sigma) \in \mathcal{I}$ such that for any two input sequences σ, σ' that match on the first i pairs $(x_1, w_1), \dots, (x_i, w_i)$, the sets $A_i(\sigma) = A(\sigma) \cap \{1, \dots, i\}$ and $A_i(\sigma') = A(\sigma') \cap \{1, \dots, i\}$ are identical. A *randomized online selection algorithm* is a probability distribution over deterministic ones. The algorithm's choices define *decision variables* $b_i(\sigma)$ which are indicator functions of the events $x_i \in A(\sigma)$. An algorithm is *monotone* if increasing the value of w_i (while leaving the rest of σ unchanged) cannot decrease the value of $\mathbb{E}[b_i(\sigma)]$, where the expectation is over the algorithm's internal randomness but not the randomness of σ (if any). A monotone deterministic online selection algorithm can be completely described by a sequence of thresholds $T_1(\sigma), \dots, T_n(\sigma)$, where $T_i(\sigma) \in \mathbb{R}_+ \cup \{\infty\}$ is the infimum of the set of weights w such that $i \in A(\sigma')$ when σ' is obtained from σ by modifying w_i to w. Conversely, for any sequence of threshold functions $T_1, \dots, T_n$ such that $T_i(\sigma)$ depends only on the first $i-1$ elements of σ and $T_i(\sigma) = \infty$ whenever $A_{i-1}(\sigma) \cup \{i\} \notin \mathcal{I}$, there is a corresponding monotone deterministic online selection algorithm that selects x_i whenever $w_i \geq T_i(\sigma)$.

Notice that an algorithm as defined above is agnostic to the order in which the matroid elements will be presented, i.e. it has a well-defined behavior no matter what order the elements appear in the input sequence. One could also consider *order-aware* algorithms that know the entire sequence $x_1, \dots, x_n$ in advance (but not the weights $w_1, \dots, w_n$). In the matroid setting, our factor-2 prophet inequality for order-agnostic algorithms reveals that order-aware algorithms have no advantage over order-agnostic ones in the worst case; it is an interesting open question whether the same lack of advantage holds more generally.

One can similarly distinguish between adversaries with respect to their power to choose the ordering of the sequence. The original BOSP treated in previous work [17, 18] considers a *fixed-order* adversary. That is, the adversary chooses an ordering (or distribution over orderings) for revealing the elements of $\mathcal{U}$ *without knowing any of the weights* $w(x)$. Our main result is an algorithm that achieves $\frac{1}{2}\mathsf{OPT}$ (or

$\frac{1}{4p-2}$OPT) against a fixed-order adversary. This result combined with the techniques of [5] immediately yields OPMs for single-parameter mechanism design. To extend our results to BMUMD, we must consider a stronger type of adversary. There are many ways that an adversary could adapt to the sampled weights and/or the algorithm's decisions, some more powerful than others. The type of adaptivity that is relevant to our paper will be called an *online weight-adaptive* adversary. An online weight-adaptive adversary chooses the next element of $\mathcal{U}$ to reveal one at a time. After choosing $x_1, \ldots, x_{i-1}$ and learning $w(x_1), \ldots, w(x_{i-1})$, the online weight-adaptive adversary chooses the next x_i to reveal *without knowing the weight* $w(x_i)$ (or any weights besides $w(x_1)$ through $w(x_{i-1})$). Fortunately, the same exact proof shows that our algorithm, without any modification, also achieves $\frac{1}{2}$OPT (or $\frac{1}{4p-2}$OPT) against an online weight-adaptive adversary. The connection between BMUMD and online weight-adaptive adversaries is not trivial, and is explained in Section 6.

Matroids.

A *matroid* $\mathcal{M}$ consists of a ground set $\mathcal{U}$ and a non-empty downward-closed set system $\mathcal{I} \subseteq 2^{\mathcal{U}}$ satisfying the *matroid exchange axiom*: for all pairs of sets $I, J \in \mathcal{I}$ such that $|I| < |J|$, there exists an element $x \in J$ such that $I \cup \{x\} \in \mathcal{I}$. Elements of $\mathcal{I}$ are called *independent sets* when $(\mathcal{U}, \mathcal{I})$ is a matroid. A maximal independent set is called a *basis*. If A is a subset of $\mathcal{U}$, its *rank*, denoted by rank(A), is the maximum cardinality of an independent subset of A. Its *closure* or *span*, denoted by cl(A), is the set of all $x \in \mathcal{U}$ such that $\text{rank}(A \cup \{x\}) = \text{rank}(A)$. It is well known that the following greedy algorithm selects a maximum-weight basis of a matroid: number the elements of $\mathcal{U}$ as $x_1, \ldots, x_n$ in decreasing order of weight, and select the set of all x_i such that $x_i \notin \text{cl}(\{x_1, \ldots, x_{i-1}\})$.

3. ALGORITHMS FOR MATROIDS

In this section we prove our main theorem, asserting the existence of algorithms whose expected reward is at least $\frac{1}{2}$OPT when playing against any online weight-adaptive adversary. Here is some intuition as to the considerations guiding the design of our algorithm. Imagine a prophet that is forced to start by accepting the set A, and let the *remainder* of A (denoted $R(A)$, defined formally in the following section) denote the subset that the restricted prophet adds to A. Let the *cost* of A (denoted $C(A)$, defined formally in the following section) denote the subset that the unrestricted prophet selected in place of A. Then the restricted prophet makes $w(A) + \mathbb{E}[w(R(A))]$ in expectation, while the unrestricted prophet makes $\mathbb{E}[w(C(A))] + \mathbb{E}[w(R(A))]$. So if A satisfies $w(A) \geq \frac{1}{\alpha}\mathbb{E}[w(C(A))]$ for a small constant α, it is not so bad to get stuck holding set A. However, just because A is not a bad set to start with does not mean we shouldn't accept anything that comes later. After all, the empty set is not a bad set to start with. If we can choose A in a way such that for any V we reject with $A \cup V \in \mathcal{I}$, $w(V) \leq \frac{1}{\alpha}\mathbb{E}[w(R(A))]$, then A is not a bad set to finish with. Simply put, we want to choose thresholds that are large enough to guarantee that $w(A)$ compares well to $\mathbb{E}[w(C(A))]$, but small enough to guarantee that everything we reject is not too heavy. Indeed, the first step in our analysis is to define this property formally and show that an algorithm with this property obtains a $\frac{1}{\alpha}$-approximation.

3.1 Detour: The rank-one case

To introduce the ideas underlying our algorithm and its analysis, we start with a very simple analysis of the case of rank-one matroids. This is the special case of the problem in which the algorithm is only allowed to make one selection, i.e. the same setting as the original prophet inequality (1). Thus, the algorithm given in this section can be regarded as providing a new and simple proof of that inequality.

Let the random weights of the elements by denoted by $X_1, \ldots, X_n$, and let $T = \mathbb{E}[\max_i X_i]/2$. We will show that an algorithm that stops at the first time τ such that $X_\tau \geq T$ makes at least T in expectation. Let $p = \Pr[\max_i X_i \geq T]$. Then we get the following inequality, for any $x > T$:

$$\Pr[X_\tau > x] \geq (1-p) \sum_{i=1}^{n} \Pr[X_i > x]$$

This is true because with probability $1-p$ the algorithm accepts nothing, so with probability at least $(1-p)$ it has accepted nothing by the time it processes X_i. So the probability that the algorithm accepts X_i and that $X_i > x$ is at least $(1-p)\Pr[X_i > x]$. It is also clear, by the union bound, that

$$\sum_{i=1}^{n} \Pr[X_i > x] \geq \Pr[\max_i X_i > x]$$

and therefore, for all $x > T$,

$$\Pr[X_\tau > x] \geq (1-p)\Pr[\max_i X_i > x].$$

Now, observe that $\mathbb{E}[\max_i X_i] = \int_0^T \Pr[\max_i X_i > x]\,dx + \int_T^\infty \Pr[\max_i X_i > x]\,dx = 2T$. As the first term is clearly at most T, the second term must be at least T. So finally, we write:

$$\begin{aligned}\mathbb{E}[X_\tau] &= \int_0^T \Pr[X_\tau > x]\,dx + \int_T^\infty \Pr[X_\tau > x]\,dx \\ &\geq pT + (1-p)\int_T^\infty \Pr[\max_i X_i > x]\,dx \\ &\geq pT + (1-p)T = T = \frac{1}{2}\mathbb{E}\left[\max_i X_i\right]\end{aligned}$$

which completes the proof of (1).

3.2 Defining α-balanced thresholds

To design and analyze algorithms for general matroids, we begin by defining a property of a deterministic monotone algorithm that we refer to as *α-balanced thresholds.* In this section we prove that the expected reward of any such algorithm is at least $\frac{1}{\alpha}$OPT. In the following section we construct an algorithm with 2-balanced thresholds, completing the proof of the main theorem.

To define α-balanced thresholds, we must first define some notation. Let $w, w' : \mathcal{U} \to \mathbb{R}_+$ denote two assignments of weights to $\mathcal{U}$, both sampled indepedently from the given distribution. We consider running the algorithm on an input sequence $\sigma = (x_1, w(x_1)), \ldots, (x_n, w(x_n))$ and comparing the value of its selected set, $A = A(\sigma)$, with that of the basis B that maximizes $w'(B)$. The matroid exchange axiom ensures that there is at least one way to partition B into disjoint subsets C, R such that $A \cup R$ is also a basis of $\mathcal{M}$.

(Consider adding elements of B one-by-one to A, preserving membership in $\mathcal{I}$, until the two sets have equal cardinality, and let R be the set of elements added to A.) Among all such partitions, let $C(A), R(A)$ denote the one that maximizes $w'(R)$.

Definition 1. *For a parameter $\alpha > 1$, a deterministic monotone algorithm has* α-balanced thresholds *if it has the following property. For every input sequence σ, if $A = A(\sigma)$ and V is a set disjoint from A such that $A \cup V \in \mathcal{I}$, then*

$$\sum_{x_i \in A} T_i(\sigma) \geq \left(\frac{1}{\alpha}\right) \cdot \mathbb{E}\left[w'(C(A))\right] \tag{2}$$

$$\sum_{x_i \in V} T_i(\sigma) \leq \left(1 - \frac{1}{\alpha}\right) \cdot \mathbb{E}\left[w'(R(A))\right], \tag{3}$$

where the expectation is over the random choice of w'.

Intuitively, Equation 2 guarantees that the set we accept is not too bad. The idea is that by selecting A, we have stopped the prophet from accepting $C(A)$, so we should make sure that $w(A)$ is comparable to $\mathbb{E}\left[w'(C(A))\right]$. Equation 3 guarantees that any set we reject is not too heavy. A prophet expects reward equal to $\mathbb{E}\left[w'(R(A))\right]$ when adding elements to A, so if there is no way for the gambler to make even $(1 - \frac{1}{\alpha})\mathbb{E}\left[w'(R(A))\right]$, he is not missing out on much by rejecting everything. Proposition 1 below states formally that this intuition holds.

Proposition 1. *If a monotone algorithm has α-balanced thresholds, then it satisfies the following approximation guarantee against online weight-adaptive adversaries:*

$$\mathbb{E}\left[w(A)\right] \geq \frac{1}{\alpha}\mathsf{OPT}. \tag{4}$$

Proof. We have

$$\mathsf{OPT} = \mathbb{E}\left[w'(C(A)) + w'(R(A))\right] \tag{5}$$

because $C(A) \cup R(A)$ is a maximum-weight basis with respect to w', and w' has the same distribution as w. For any real number z, we will use the notation $(z)^+$ to denote $\max\{z, 0\}$. The proof will consist of deriving the following three inequalities, in which w_i stands for $w(x_i)$.

$$\mathbb{E}\left[\sum_{x_i \in A} T_i\right] \geq \frac{1}{\alpha}\mathbb{E}\left[w'(C(A))\right] \tag{6}$$

$$\mathbb{E}\left[\sum_{x_i \in A} (w_i - T_i)^+\right] \geq \mathbb{E}\left[\sum_{x_i \in R(A)} (w'(x_i) - T_i)^+\right] \tag{7}$$

$$\mathbb{E}\left[\sum_{x_i \in R(A)} (w'(x_i) - T_i)^+\right] \geq \frac{1}{\alpha}\mathbb{E}\left[w'(R(A))\right]. \tag{8}$$

Summing (6)-(8) and using the fact that $T_i + (w_i - T_i)^+ = w_i$ for all $x_i \in A$, we obtain

$$\mathbb{E}\left[w(A)\right] \geq \frac{1}{\alpha}\mathbb{E}\left[w'(C(A))\right] + \frac{1}{\alpha}\mathbb{E}\left[w'(R(A))\right].$$

Inequality (6) is a restatement of the definition of α-balanced thresholds. Inequality (7) is deduced from the following observations. First, the algorithm selects every i such that $w_i > T_i$, so $\sum_{x_i \in A}(w_i - T_i)^+ = \sum_{i=1}^n (w_i - T_i)^+$. Second, the online property of the algorithm and the fact that weight-adaptive adversaries do not learn w_i before choosing to reveal x_i imply that T_i can depend on the revealed pairs $(x_1, w_1), \ldots, (x_{i-1}, w_{i-1})$ and that the random variables $w(x_i), w'(x_i), T_i$ are independent. As $w_i = w(x_i)$ and $w'(x_i)$ are identically distributed, it follows that

$$\mathbb{E}\left[\sum_{i=1}^n (w_i - T_i)^+\right] = \mathbb{E}\left[\sum_{i=1}^n (w'(x_i) - T_i)^+\right] \geq \mathbb{E}\left[\sum_{x_i \in R(A)} (w'(x_i) - T_i)^+\right],$$

and (7) is established. Finally, we apply Property (3) of α-balanced thresholds, using the set $V = R(A)$, to deduce that

$$\begin{aligned}
&\mathbb{E}\left[\sum_{x_i \in R(A)} w'(x_i)\right] \\
&\leq \mathbb{E}\left[\sum_{x_i \in R(A)} T_i\right] + \mathbb{E}\left[\sum_{x_i \in R(A)} (w'(x_i) - T_i)^+\right] \\
&\leq \left(1 - \frac{1}{\alpha}\right)\mathbb{E}\left[\sum_{x_i \in R(A)} w'(x_i)\right] \\
&+ \mathbb{E}\left[\sum_{x_i \in R(A)} (w'(x_i) - T_i)^+\right] \\
\Rightarrow &\frac{1}{\alpha}\mathbb{E}\left[\sum_{x_i \in R(A)} w'(x_i)\right] \leq \mathbb{E}\left[\sum_{x_i \in R(A)} (w'(x_i) - T_i)^+\right]
\end{aligned}$$

Consequently (8) holds, which concludes the proof. □

3.3 Achieving 2-balanced thresholds

This section presents an algorithm with 2-balanced thresholds. The algorithm is quite simple. In step i, having already selected the (possibly empty) set A_{i-1}, we set threshold $T_i = \infty$ if $A_{i-1} \cup \{x_i\} \notin \mathcal{I}$. Otherwise, imagine that a prophet resamples the sequence and starts over having already accepted A_{i-1}. Such a prophet would obtain expected reward exactly equal to $\mathbb{E}\left[w'(R(A_{i-1}))\right]$. Imagine also a prophet resampling and starting over having already accepted $A_{i-1} \cup \{x_i\}$. Such a prophet obtains expected reward exactly equal to $\mathbb{E}\left[w'(R(A_{i-1} \cup \{x_i\}))\right]$. We set T_i equal to exactly half of what a prophet would lose in expectation by accepting $\{x_i\}$, or formally:

$$\begin{aligned}
T_i &= \tfrac{1}{2}\mathbb{E}\left[w'(R(A_{i-1})) - w'(R(A_{i-1} \cup \{x_i\}))\right] &(9)\\
&= \tfrac{1}{2}\mathbb{E}\left[w'(C(A_{i-1} \cup \{x_i\})) - w'(C(A_{i-1}))\right] &(10)
\end{aligned}$$

The algorithm selects element x_i if and only if $w_i \geq T_i$. The fact that both (9) and (10) define the same value of T_i is easy to verify. Let B denote the maximum weight basis of $\mathcal{M}$ with weights w'.

$$\begin{aligned}
w'(C(A_{i-1})) + w'(R(A_{i-1})) &= w'(B) \\
&= w'(C(A_{i-1} \cup \{x_i\})) + w'(R(A_{i-1} \cup \{x_i\})) \\
w'(R(A_{i-1})) - w'(R(A_{i-1} \cup \{x_i\})) & \\
&= w'(C(A_{i-1} \cup \{x_i\})) - w'(C(A_{i-1}))
\end{aligned}$$

Property (2) in the definition of α-balanced thresholds follows from a telescoping sum.

$$\begin{aligned}\sum_{x_i \in A} T_i &= \tfrac{1}{2} \sum_{x_i \in A} \mathbb{E}\left[w'(C(A_{i-1} \cup \{x_i\})) - w'(C(A_{i-1}))\right] \\ &= \tfrac{1}{2} \sum_{x_i \in A} \mathbb{E}\left[w'(C(A_i)) - w'(C(A_{i-1}))\right] \\ &= \tfrac{1}{2}\mathbb{E}\left[w'(C(A_n)) - w'(C(A_0))\right] \\ &= \tfrac{1}{2}\mathbb{E}\left[w'(C(A))\right].\end{aligned}$$

The remainder of this section is devoted to proving Property (3) in the definition of α-balanced thresholds. In the present context, with $\alpha = 2$ and thresholds T_i defined by (9), the property simply asserts that for every pair of disjoint sets A, V such that $A \cup V \in \mathcal{I}$,

$$\mathbb{E}\left[\sum_{x_i \in V} w'(R(A_{i-1})) - w'(R(A_{i-1} \cup \{x_i\}))\right] = 2 \sum_{x_i \in V} T_i(\sigma) \leq \mathbb{E}\left[w'(R(A))\right]$$

We will show, in fact, that this inequality holds for every non-negative weight assignment w' and not merely in expectation. The proof appears in Proposition 2 below. To establish it, we will need some basic properties of matroids.

DEFINITION 2 ([21], SECTION 39.3). *If $\mathcal{M}$ is a matroid and S is a subset of its ground set, the* deletion $\mathcal{M} - S$ *and the* contraction $\mathcal{M}/S$ *are two matroids with ground set $\mathcal{U} - S$. A set T is independent in $\mathcal{M} - S$ if T is independent in $\mathcal{M}$, whereas T is independent in $\mathcal{M}/S$ if $T \cup S_0$ is independent in $\mathcal{M}$, where S_0 is any maximal independent subset of S.*

LEMMA 1. *Suppose $\mathcal{M} = (\mathcal{U}, \mathcal{I})$ is a matroid and $V, R \in \mathcal{I}$ are two independent sets of equal cardinality.*

1. *There is a bijection $\phi : V \to R$ such that for every $v \in V$, $(R - \{\phi(v)\}) \cup \{v\}$ is an independent set.*
2. *For a weight function $w' : \mathcal{U} \to \mathbb{R}$, suppose that R has the maximum weight of all $|R|$-element independent subsets of $V \cup R$. Then the bijection ϕ in part 1 also satisfies $w'(\phi(v)) \geq w'(v)$.*

PROOF. Part 1 is Corollary 39.12a in [21]. To prove part 2, simply observe that the weight of $(R - \{\phi(v)\}) \cup \{v\}$ cannot be greater than the weight of R, by our assumptions on R and ϕ. □

The next two lemmas establish basic properties of the function $S \mapsto R(S)$.

LEMMA 2. *For any independent set A, the set $R(A)$ is equal to the maximum weight basis of $\mathcal{M}/A$.*

PROOF. Let B be the maximum-weight basis of $\mathcal{M}$. Over all bases of $\mathcal{M}/A$ that are contained in B, the set $R(A)$ is, by definition, the one of maximum weight. Therefore, if it is not the maximum-weight basis of $\mathcal{M}/A$, the only reason can be that there is another basis of $\mathcal{M}/A$, not contained in B, having strictly greater weight. But we know that the maximum-weight basis of $\mathcal{M}/A$ is selected by the greedy algorithm, which iterates through the list $y_1, \ldots, y_k$ of elements of $\mathcal{U} - A$ sorted in order of decreasing weight, and picks each element y_i that is not contained in $\text{cl}(A \cup \{y_1, \ldots, y_{i-1}\})$. In particular, every y_i chosen by the greedy algorithm on $\mathcal{M}/A$ satisfies $y_i \notin \text{cl}(\{y_1, \ldots, y_{i-1}\})$ and therefore belongs to B. Thus the maximum-weight basis of $\mathcal{M}/A$ is contained in B and must equal $R(A)$. □

LEMMA 3. *For any independent set J, $f(S) = w'(R(S))$ is a submodular set function on subsets of J.*

PROOF. For notational convenience, in this proof we will denote the union of two sets by '+' rather than '∪'. Also, we will not distinguish between an element x and the singleton set $\{x\}$.

To prove submodularity it suffices to consider an independent set $S+x+y$ and to prove that $f(S) - f(S+x) \leq f(S+y) - f(S+x+y)$. Replacing $\mathcal{M}$ by $\mathcal{M}/S$, we can reduce to the case that $S = \emptyset$ and prove that $f(\emptyset) - f(x) \leq f(y) - f(x+y)$ whenever $\{x, y\}$ is a two-element independent set.

What is the interpretation of $f(\emptyset) - f(x)$? Recall that $f(\emptyset) = w'(R(\emptyset))$ is the weight of the maximum-weight basis B of $\mathcal{M}$. Similarly, $f(x)$ is the weight of the maximum-weight basis B_x of $\mathcal{M}/\{x\}$. Let $b_1, b_2, \ldots, b_r$ denote the elements of B in decreasing order of weight. Consider running two executions of the greedy algorithm to select B and B_x in parallel. The only step in which the algorithms make differing decisions is the first step i in which $\{b_1, \ldots, b_i\} \cup \{x\}$ contains a circuit. In this step, b_i is included in B but excluded from B_x. Similarly, when we run two executions of the greedy algorithm to select B_y and B_{xy} — the maximum-weight bases of $\mathcal{M}/\{y\}$ and $\mathcal{M}/\{x, y\}$, respectively — the only step in which differing decisions are made is the earliest step j in which $\{b_1, \ldots, b_j\} \cup \{x, y\}$ contains a circuit. But j certainly cannot be later than i, since $\{b_1, \ldots, b_i\} \cup \{x, y\}$ is a superset of $\{b_1, \ldots, b_i\} \cup \{x\}$ and hence contains a circuit. We may conclude that

$$f(\emptyset) - f(x) = b_i \leq b_j = f(y) - f(x+y),$$

and hence f is submodular as claimed. □

PROPOSITION 2. *For any disjoint sets A, V such that $A \cup V \in \mathcal{I}$,*

$$\sum_{x_i \in V} w'(R(A_{i-1})) - w'(R(A_{i-1} \cup \{x_i\})) \leq w'(R(A)).$$

PROOF. The function $f(S) = w'(R(S))$ is submodular on subsets $S \subseteq A \cup V$, by Lemma 3. Hence

$$\sum_{x_i \in V} w'(R(A_{i-1})) - w'(R(A_{i-1} \cup \{x_i\})) \tag{11}$$

$$\leq \sum_{x \in V} w'(R(A)) - w'(R(A \cup \{x\})). \tag{12}$$

Apply Lemma 1 to the independent sets $V, R(A)$ in $\mathcal{M}/A$ to obtain a bijection ϕ such that $w'(\phi(x)) \geq w'(x)$ and $A \cup (R(A) - \phi(x)) \cup \{x\} \in \mathcal{I}$ for all $x \in V$. By definition of $R(\cdot)$, we know that $A \cup \{x\} \cup R(A \cup \{x\})$ is the maximum weight independent subset of $A \cup \{x\} \cup B$ that contains $A \cup \{x\}$.

One such set is $A \cup (R(A) - \phi(x)) \cup \{x\}$, so

$$w'(A) + w'(R(A)) - w'(\phi(x)) + w'(x) \leq w'(A) + w'(R(A \cup \{x\})) + w'(x) \quad (13)$$

$$w'(R(A)) - w'(R(A \cup \{x\})) \leq w'(\phi(x)) \quad (14)$$

$$\sum_{x \in V} w'(R(A)) - w'(R(A \cup \{x\})) \leq \sum_{x \in V} w'(\phi(x)) = w'(R). \quad (15)$$

The proposition follows by combining (11) and (15). □

One might notice that our choice of thresholds involves computing the expectation of a random variable. In practice, computing our thresholds exactly may be unrealistic. However, it is not hard to see that the work in this section also provides a proof of the following proposition:

PROPOSITION 3. *Let T_i denote the thresholds used by our algorithm to obtain 2-balanced thresholds, and let T'_i denote thresholds used by some other monotone algorithm. Then if $T'_i \leq T_i \leq (1+\epsilon)T'_i$ for all i, the thresholds T'_i are $2(1+\epsilon)$-balanced thresholds.*

Proposition 3 can be deduced by observing that decreasing the thresholds cannot possibly hurt the ratio of Property (3), but it might hurt the ratio of Property (2). We proved Property (2) by simply observing a telescoping sum. It is clear that lower bounding the telescoping sum instead of computing it exactly provides the bound $\sum_{x_i \in A} T_i(\sigma) \geq \frac{1}{\alpha(1+\epsilon)} \mathbb{E}\left[w'(C(A))\right]$.

4. MATROID INTERSECTIONS

Our algorithm and proof for matroid intersections is quite similar. We need to modify some definitions and extend some proofs, but the spirit is the same.

4.1 Generalizing α-balanced thresholds

We first have to extend our notation a bit. Denote the independent sets for the p matroids as $\mathcal{I}_1, \ldots, \mathcal{I}_p$. Denote the "truly independent" sets as $\mathcal{I} = \cap_j \mathcal{I}_j$. Still let $w, w' : \mathcal{U} \to \mathbb{R}_+$ denote two assignments of weights to $\mathcal{U}$, both sampled indepedently from the given distribution. We consider running the algorithm on an input sequence σ, where $\sigma = (x_1, w(x_1)), \ldots, (x_n, w(x_n))$ and comparing the value of its selected set, $A = A(\sigma)$, with that of the $B \in \mathcal{I}$ that maximizes $w'(B)$. For all j, the matroid exchange axiom ensures that there is at least one way to partition B into disjoint subsets C_j, R_j such that $A \cup R_j \in \mathcal{I}_j$, and $B \subseteq \mathrm{cl}_j(A \cup R_j)$. Among all such partitions, let $C_j(A), R_j(A)$ denote the one that maximizes $w'(R_j)$ (greedily add elements from B to R_j unless it creates a dependency in $\mathcal{I}_j$). We denote by $R(A) = \cap_j R_j(A)$ and $C(A) = \cup_j C_j(A)$.

DEFINITION 3. *For a parameter $\alpha > 0$, a deterministic monotone algorithm has* α-balanced thresholds *if it has the following property. For every input sequence σ, if $A = A(\sigma)$ and V is a set disjoint from A such that $A \cup V \in \mathcal{I}$, then*

$$\sum_{x_i \in A} T_i(\sigma) \geq \left(\frac{1}{\alpha}\right) \cdot \mathbb{E}\left[\sum_j w'(C_j(A))\right] \quad (16)$$

$$\sum_{x_i \in V} T_i(\sigma) \leq \left(\frac{1}{\alpha}\right) \cdot \mathbb{E}\left[\sum_j w'(R_j(A))\right], \quad (17)$$

where the expectation is over the random choice of w'.

PROPOSITION 4. *If a monotone algorithm has α-balanced thresholds for $\alpha \geq 2$, then it satisfies the following approximation guarantee against weight-adaptive adversaries when $\mathcal{I}$ is the intersection of p matroids:*

$$\mathbb{E}\left[w(A)\right] \geq \frac{\alpha - p}{\alpha(\alpha - 1)} \mathsf{OPT}. \quad (18)$$

The proof closely parallels the proof of Proposition 1, and is given in the appendix.

4.2 Obtaining α-balanced thresholds

This section presents an algorithm obtaining α-balanced thresholds for any $\alpha > 1$. One can take a derivative to see that the optimal choice of α for the intersection of p matroids is $\alpha_p = p + \sqrt{p(p-1)}$. For simplicity, we will instead just use $\alpha = 2p$, as this is nearly optimal and always at least 2. When $\alpha = 2p$, the approximation guarantee from Proposition 4 is $\frac{1}{4p-2}$. We now define our thresholds:

$$T(A, i, j) = \frac{1}{\alpha} \mathbb{E}\left[w'(R_j(A)) - w'(R_j(A \cup \{x_i\}))\right]$$
$$= \frac{1}{\alpha} \mathbb{E}\left[w'(C_j(A \cup \{x_i\})) - w'(C_j(A))\right]$$
$$T(A, i) = \sum_j T(A, i, j).$$

In step i, having already selected the (possibly empty) set A_{i-1}, we set threshold $T_i = \infty$ if $A_{i-1} \cup \{i\} \notin \mathcal{I}$, and $T_i = T(A_{i-1}, i)$ otherwise. In other words, each $T(A, i, j)$ is basically the same as the threshold used for the single matroid algorithm if $\mathcal{I}_j$ was the only matroid constraint. It is not exactly the same, because $R(A)$ when $\mathcal{I}_j$ is the only matroid is not the same as $R_j(A)$ in the presence of other matroid constraints. $T(A, i)$ just sums $T(A, i, j)$ over all matroids.

The proof of Equation (16) follows exactly the proof of Equation (2).

The proof of Equation (17) follows from Proposition 2, although perhaps not obviously. As $A \cup V \in \mathcal{I}$, we clearly have $A \cup V \in \mathcal{I}_j$ for all j. So the hypotheses of Proposition 2 are satisfied for all j. Summing the bound we get in Proposition 2 over all j gives us Equation (17).

Similar to our thresholds for matroids, our thresholds for matroid intersections are robust to small errors in computation. The same reasoning provides us with the following proposition:

PROPOSITION 5. *Let T_i denote the thresholds used by our algorithm to obtain α-balanced thresholds, and let T'_i denote thresholds used by some other monotone algorithm. Then if $T'_i \leq T_i \leq (1+\epsilon)T'_i$ for all i, the T'_i are $\alpha(1+\epsilon)$-balanced thresholds.*

5. LOWER BOUNDS

Here we provide two examples. The first is the well-known example of [17] showing that the factor of 2 is tight for matroids. We present their construction here for completeness. The second shows that the ratio $O(p)$ is tight for the intersection of p matroids.

We start with the well-known example of [17]. Consider the 1-uniform matroid over 2 elements. We have $w(1) = 1$ with probability 1, $w(2) = n$ with probability $1/n$ and 0 otherwise. Then the prophet obtains $2 - 1/n$ in expectation, but the gambler obtains at most 1, as his optimal strategy is just to take the first element always.

The example for the intersection of p matroids has appeared in other forms in [3, 5]. Let q be a prime between $p/2$ and p. Then let $\mathcal{U} = \{(i,j) \mid 0 \le i \le q^q - 1, 0 \le j \le q-1\}$. Then let $\mathcal{I}$ contain all sets of the form $\{(i,j_1), \ldots, (i,j_x)\}$. Now let $w(i,j) = 1$ with probability $1/q$, and $w(i,j) = 0$ otherwise, for all i,j. Reveal the elements in any order. No matter what strategy the gambler uses to pick the first element, his optimal strategy from that point on is to just accept every remaining element with the same first coordinate. However the gambler winds up with his first element, he makes at most $1 - 1/q$ in expectation from the remaining elements he is allowed to pick (as there are at most $q-1$ remaining elements, and each has $\mathbb{E}[w(i,j)] = 1/q$). Therefore, the expected payoff to the gambler is less than 2. However, with probability at least $(1-1/e)$, there exists an i such that $w(i,j) = 1$ for all j (as the probability that this occurs for a fixed i is $1/q^q$ and there are q^q different i's). So the expected payoff to the prophet is $\Theta(q)$.

Finally, we just have to show that $\mathcal{I}$ can be written as the intersection of q matroids. Let $\mathcal{I}_x$ be the partition matroid that partitions $\mathcal{U}$ into $\sqcup_j S_j = \sqcup_j \cup_i \{(i, xi + j \pmod{q})\}$, and requires that only one element of each S_j be chosen. Then clearly, $\mathcal{I} \subseteq \cap_{x \in \mathbb{Z}_q} \mathcal{I}_x$ as any two elements with the same first coordinate lie in different partitions in each of the $\mathcal{I}_x$. In addition, $\cap_{x \in \mathbb{Z}_q} \mathcal{I}_x \subseteq \mathcal{I}$. Consider any (i,j) and (i',j') with $i \neq i'$. Then when $(j - j') \pmod{q} = x(i - i') \pmod{q}$, (i,j) and (i',j') are in the same partition of $\mathcal{I}_x$. As q is prime, this equation always has a solution. Therefore, we have shown that $\mathcal{I} = \cap_{x \in \mathbb{Z}_q} \mathcal{I}_x$, and $\mathcal{I}$ can be written as the intersection of $q \le p$ matroids. As the prophet obtains $\Theta(p)$ in expectation, and the gambler obtains less than 2 in expectation, no algorithm can achieve an approximation factor better than $O(p)$.

6. INTERPRETATION AS OPM'S

Here, we describe how to use our algorithm to design OPMs for unit-demand multi-parameter bidders under matroid and matroid intersection feasibility constraints. We begin by recalling the definition of Bayesian multi-parameter unit-demand mechanism design (BMUMD) from [5]. In any such mechanism design problem, there is a set of services, $\mathcal{U}$, partitioned into disjoint subsets $J_1, \ldots, J_n$, one for each bidder. The mechanism must allocate a set of services, subject to downward-closed feasibility constraints given by a collection $\mathcal{I}$ of feasible subsets. We assume that the feasibility constraints guarantee that no bidder receives more than a single service, i.e. that the intersection of any feasible set with one of the sets J_i contains no more than one element. (If this property is not already implied by the given feasibility constraints, it can be ensured by intersecting the given constraints with one additional partition matroid constraint.)

As in the work of Chawla et al. [5], we assume that each bidder i's values for the services in set J_i are independent random variables, and we analyze BMUMD mechanisms for any such distribution by exploring a closely-related single-parameter domain that we denote by $\mathcal{I}^{\text{copies}}$. In $\mathcal{I}^{\text{copies}}$ there are $|\mathcal{U}|$ bidders, each of whom wants just a single service x and has a value v_x for receiving that service. The feasibility constraints are the same in both domains — the mechanism may select any set of services that belongs to $\mathcal{I}$ — and the joint distribution of the values v_x ($x \in \mathcal{I}$) is the same as well; the only difference between the two domains is that an individual bidder i in the BMUMD problem becomes a set of competing bidders (corresponding to the elements of J_i) in the domain $\mathcal{I}^{\text{copies}}$. As might be expected, the increase in competition between bidders results in an increase in revenue for the optimal mechanism; indeed, the following lemma from [5] will be a key step in our analysis.

LEMMA 4. *Let $\mathcal{A}$ be any individually rational, truthful deterministic mechanism for instance $\mathcal{I}$ of BMUMD. Then the expected revenue of $\mathcal{A}$ is no more than the expected revenue of the optimal mechanism for $\mathcal{I}^{\text{copies}}$.*

A second technique that we will borrow from [5] (and, ultimately, from Myerson's original paper on optimal mechanism design [19]), is the technique of analyzing the expected revenue of mechanisms indirectly via their virtual surplus. We begin by reviewing the definitions of virtual valuations and virtual surplus. Assume that v_x, the value of bidder i for item $x \in J_i$, has cumulative distribution function F_x whose density f_x is well-defined and positive on the interval on which v_x is supported. Then the virtual valuation function ϕ_x is defined by

$$\phi_x(v) = v - \frac{1 - F_x(v)}{f_x(v)},$$

and the *virtual surplus* of an allocation $A \in \mathcal{I}$ is defined to be the sum $\sum_{x \in A} \phi_x(v_x)$. Myerson [19] proved the following:

LEMMA 5. *In all single-parameter domains where bidders have independent valuations with monotone increasing virtual valuation functions, the expected revenue of any mechanism in Bayes-Nash equilibrium is equal to its expected virtual surplus.*

The distribution of v_x is said to be *regular* when the virtual valuation function ϕ_x is monotonically increasing. We will assume throughout the rest of this section that bidders' values have regular distributions, in order to apply Lemma 5. To deal with non-regular distributions, it is necessary to use a technique known as *ironing*, also due to Myerson [19], which in our context translates into randomized pricing via a recipe described in Lemma 2 of [5].

Our plan is now to design truthful mechanisms $\mathcal{M}$ and $\mathcal{M}^{\text{copies}}$ for the BMUMD domain $\mathcal{I}$ and the associated single-parameter domain $\mathcal{I}^{\text{copies}}$, respectively, and to relate them to the optimal mechanisms for those domains via the following chain of inequalities. Below, $R(\cdot)$ and $\Phi(\cdot)$ denote the expected revenue and expected virtual surplus of a mechanism, respectively, and α denotes the approximation guarantee of a prophet inequality algorithm embedded in our mechanism. Thus, $\alpha = 2$ when $\mathcal{I}$ is a matroid, and more

Algorithm 1: Mechanism $\mathcal{M}$ for unit-demand multi-dimensional bidders

```
Initialize A = ∅.
for i = 1, 2, ..., n do
  for all x ∈ J_i do
    Set p_x = { φ_x^{-1}(T(A, x))   if A ∪ {x} ∈ I
              { ∞                   otherwise.
  end for
  Post price vector (p_x)_{x∈J_i}.
  Bidder i chooses an element x ∈ J_i, or possibly
  nothing at these posted prices.
  if x is chosen then
    Allocate x to bidder i and charge price p_x.
    A ← A ∪ {x}
  else
    Allocate nothing to bidder i and charge price 0.
  end if
end for
```

generally $\alpha = 4p - 2$ when $\mathcal{I}$ is given by an intersection of p matroid constraints.

$$\begin{aligned} R(\mathcal{M}) &\geq R(\mathcal{M}^{\text{copies}}) \\ R(\mathcal{M}^{\text{copies}}) &= \Phi(\mathcal{M}^{\text{copies}}) \\ \Phi(\mathcal{M}^{\text{copies}}) &\geq \frac{1}{\alpha}\Phi(\mathsf{OPT}^{\text{copies}}) \\ \frac{1}{\alpha}\Phi(\mathsf{OPT}^{\text{copies}}) &= \frac{1}{\alpha}R(\mathsf{OPT}^{\text{copies}}) \\ \frac{1}{\alpha}R(\mathsf{OPT}^{\text{copies}}) &\geq \frac{1}{\alpha}R(\mathsf{OPT}). \end{aligned} \tag{19}$$

Most of the steps in line (19) are already justified by the lemmas from prior work discussed above. The relation $R = \Phi$ for mechanisms $\mathcal{M}^{\text{copies}}$ and $\mathsf{OPT}^{\text{copies}}$ is a consequence of Lemma 5, while Lemma 4 provides $R(\mathsf{OPT}^{\text{copies}}) \geq R(\mathsf{OPT})$. We will derive the relation $\Phi(\mathcal{M}^{\text{copies}}) \geq \frac{1}{\alpha}\Phi(\mathsf{OPT}^{\text{copies}})$ as a natural consequence of the prophet inequality. To do so, it suffices to define mechanism $\mathcal{M}^{\text{copies}}$ such that its allocation decisions result from running the prophet inequality algorithm on an input sequence consisting of the virtual valuations $\phi_x(v_x)$, presented in an order determined by an online weight-adaptive adversary. The crux of our proof will consist of designing said adversary to ensure that the relation $R(\mathcal{M}) \geq R(\mathcal{M}^{\text{copies}})$ also holds.

Given these preliminaries, we now describe the mechanisms $\mathcal{M}$ and $\mathcal{M}^{\text{copies}}$. Central to both mechanisms is a pricing scheme using thresholds $T(A, x)$, defined as the threshold T_s that our online algorithm would use at step s when $x_s = x$ and the algorithm has accepted the set A so far. (Contrary to previous sections of the paper in which steps of the online algorithm's execution were denoted by i, here we reserve the variable i to refer to bidders in the mechanism, using s instead to denote a step of the online algorithm. Note that the thresholds assigned by our algorithm depend only on A and x, not on s, hence the notation $T(A, x)$ is justified.) Mechanism $\mathcal{M}$, described by the pseudocode in Algorithm 1, simply makes posted-price offers to bidders $1, 2, \ldots, n$ in that order, defining the posted price for each item by applying its inverse-virtual-valuation function to the threshold that the prophet inequality algorithm sets for that item.

To define mechanism $\mathcal{M}^{\text{copies}}$, we first define an online weight-adaptive adversary and then run the prophet inequality algorithm on the input sequence presented by this adversary, using its thresholds to define posted prices exactly as in mechanism $\mathcal{M}$ above. The adversary is designed to minimize the mechanism's revenue, subject to the constraint that the elements are presented in an order that runs through all of the elements of J_1, then the elements of J_2, and so on. In fact, it is easy to compute this worst-case ordering by backward induction, which yields a dynamic program presented in pseudocode as Algorithm 2. The dynamic programming table consists of entries $V(A, i)$ denoting the expected revenue that $\mathcal{M}^{\text{copies}}$ will gain from selling elements of the set $J_{i+1} \cup \cdots \cup J_n$, given that it has already allocated the elements of A. Computing and storing these values requires exponential time and space, but we are not concerned with making $\mathcal{M}^{\text{copies}}$ into a computationally efficient mechanism because its role in this paper is merely to provide an intermediate step in the analysis of mechanism $\mathcal{M}$.

The formula for $V(A, i)$ is guided by the following considerations. Since $\mathcal{M}^{\text{copies}}$ will post prices $p_x = \phi_x^{-1}(T(A, x))$ for all $x \in J_{i+1}$ given that it has already allocated A, it will not allocate any element of J_{i+1} if $v_x < p_x$ for all $x \in J_{i+1}$, and otherwise it will allocate some element $x \in J_{i+1}$. In the former case, its expected revenue from the remaining elements will be $V(A, i+1)$. In the latter case, it extracts revenue p_x from bidder $i+1$ and expected revenue $V(A \cup \{x\}, i+1)$ from the remaining bidders. Thus, an adversary who wishes the minimize the revenue obtained by the mechanism will order the elements $x \in J_{i+1}$ in increasing order of $p_x + V(A \cup \{x\}, i+1)$. Denoting the elements of J_{i+1} in this order by $x_1, x_2, \ldots, x_k$, we obtain the formula

$$\begin{aligned} V(A, i) &= \left(\prod_{j=1}^{k} F_{x_j}(p_{x_j})\right) \cdot V(A, i+1) \\ &\quad + \sum_{\ell=1}^{k} P_1(\ell) \cdot P_2(\ell) \cdot P_3(\ell) \qquad (20) \\ P_1(\ell) &= \prod_{j=1}^{\ell-1} F_{x_j}(p_{x_j}) \\ P_2(\ell) &= 1 - F_{x_\ell}(p_{x_\ell}) \\ P_3(\ell) &= p_{x_\ell} + V(A \cup \{x_\ell\},\, i+1). \end{aligned}$$

The first term on the right side accounts for the possibility that bidder $i+1$ buys nothing, while the sum accounts for the possibility that bidder $i+1$ buys x_ℓ, for each $\ell = 1, \ldots, k$: $P_1(\ell)$ is the probability that bidder $i+1$ did not buy any of $\{x_1, \ldots, x_\ell\}$, $P_2(\ell)$ is the probability that bidder $i+1$ is willing to purchase x_ℓ, and $P_3(\ell)$ is the expected value of $V(A, i)$ given that bidder $i+1$ purchases x_ℓ.

Mechanism $\mathcal{M}^{\text{copies}}$ has already been described above, and is specified by pseudocode in Algorithm 3. We note that $\mathcal{M}^{\text{copies}}$ does not satisfy the definition of an OPM in [5], since the price p_x for $x \in J_i$ may depend on the bids b_y for $y \in J_1 \cup \cdots \cup J_{i-1}$. However, it retains a key property of OPMs that make them suitable for analyzing multi-parameter mechanisms: the prices of elements of J_i are pre-determined before any of the bids in J_i are revealed.

THEOREM 1. *Mechanism $\mathcal{M}$ for BMUMD settings with independent regular valuations obtains a 2-approximation to*

Algorithm 2: Online weight-adaptive adversary for $\mathcal{I}^{\text{copies}}$

```
for i = n, n − 1, ..., 1 do
  // Preprocessing loop: fill in DP table
  for all feasible sets A ⊆ J_1 ∪ ··· ∪ J_i do
    if i = n then
      V(A, i) = 0
    else
      p_x = φ_x^{-1}(T(A, x)) for all x ∈ J_{i+1}.
      Sort J_{i+1} in order of increasing
        p_x + V(A ∪ {x}, i + 1).
      Denote this sorted list by x_1, ..., x_k.
      Compute V(A, i) using formula (20).
    end if
  end for
end for
  // Main loop: choose the ordering of each set J_i
Initialize A = ∅.
for i = 1, ..., n do
  p_x = φ_x^{-1}(T(A, x)) for all x ∈ J_i.
  Sort the elements of J_i in order of increasing
    p_x + V(A ∪ {x}, i − 1).
  Present the elements of J_i to the online algorithm
    in this order.
  if ∃x ∈ J_i s.t. v_x ≥ p_x then
    Find the first such x in the ordering of J_i, and
      insert x into A.
  end if
end for
```

the revenue of the optimal deterministic mechanism for matroid feasibility constraints, and a $(4p-2)$-approximation to the revenue of the optimal deterministic mechanism for feasibility constraints that are the intersection of p matroids.

PROOF. Both $\mathcal{M}$ and $\mathcal{M}^{\text{copies}}$ are posted-price (hence, truthful) mechanisms that always output a feasible allocation. To prove that the allocation is always feasible, one can argue by contradiction: if not, there must be a step in which the set A becomes infeasible through adding an element x. However, in both $\mathcal{M}$ and $\mathcal{M}^{\text{copies}}$, we can see that the price p_x is infinite in that case, while bid b_x is greater than or equal to p_x, a contradiction.

The proof of the approximate revenue guarantee follows the outline given by equation (19) above. As explained earlier, the only two steps in that equation that do not follow from prior work are the relations

$$R(\mathcal{M}) \geq R(\mathcal{M}^{\text{copies}}) \tag{21}$$

$$\Phi(\mathcal{M}^{\text{copies}}) \geq \frac{1}{\alpha}\Phi(\mathsf{OPT}^{\text{copies}}). \tag{22}$$

To justify the second line, observe that the "adversary" (Algorithm 2) that computes the ordering of the bids is an online weight-adaptive adversary. This is because the adversary does not need to observe the values $v_x\,(x \in J_i)$ in order to sort the elements of J_i in order of increasing $p_x + V(A \cup \{x\}, i-1)$. Thus, the prophet inequality algorithm running on the input sequence specified by the adversary achieves an expected virtual surplus that is at least $\frac{1}{\alpha}\Phi(\mathsf{OPT}^{\text{copies}})$. Furthermore, the set of elements selected by $\mathcal{M}^{\text{copies}}$ is exactly the same as the set of elements se-

Algorithm 3: Mechanism $\mathcal{M}^{\text{copies}}$ for single-parameter domain $\mathcal{I}^{\text{copies}}$.

```
  // Set prices using adversary and with BOSP
Obtain bids b_x for all bidders x ∈ U.
Run Algorithm 2, using v_x = b_x for all x, to obtain
  an ordering of U.
Set w(x) = φ_x(b_x) for all x ∈ U.
Present the pairs (x, w(x)) to the prophet inequality
  algorithm, in the order computed above.
Obtain thresholds T(A, x) from the prophet inequality
  algorithm.
Set price p_x = φ_x^{-1}(T(A, x)) for all x ∈ U.
  // Determine allocation and payments
Initialize A = ∅
for i = 1, ..., n do
  for all x ∈ J_i do
    if b_x ≥ p_x and b_y < p_y for all y ∈ J_i that precede
      x in the ordering then
      Add x to the set A.
      Charge price p_x to bidder x.
    end if
  end for
end for
```

lected by the prophet inequality algorithm — the criterion $b_x \geq p_x$ is equivalent to the criterion $w(x) \geq T(A, x)$ because $w(x) = \phi_x(b_x)$, $T(A, x) = \phi_x(p_x)$, and ϕ is monotone increasing. This completes the proof of (22).

To prove (21) we use an argument that, in effect, justifies our claim that Algorithm 2 is a worst-case adversary for mechanism $\mathcal{M}^{\text{copies}}$. Specifically, for each $i = 0, \ldots, n$ and each feasible set $A \subseteq J_1 \cup \cdots \cup J_i$, let $R(\mathcal{M}, A, i)$ and $R(\mathcal{M}^{\text{copies}}, A, i)$ denote the expected revenue that $\mathcal{M}$ (respectively, $\mathcal{M}^{\text{copies}}$) obtains from selling items in $J_{i+1} \cup \cdots J_n$ conditional on having allocated set A while processing the bids in $J_1 \cup \cdots \cup J_i$. (In evaluating the expected revenue of the two mechanisms, we assume that the bidders are presented to $\mathcal{M}$ in the order $i = 1, \ldots, n$, and that they are presented to $\mathcal{M}^{\text{copies}}$ in the order determined by the adversary, Algorithm 2.) We will prove, by downward induction on i, that

$$\forall i, A \quad R(\mathcal{M}, A, i) \geq R(\mathcal{M}^{\text{copies}}, A, i) = V(A, i)$$

and then (21) follows by specializing to $i = 0, A = \emptyset$. When $i = n$, we have $R(\mathcal{M}, A, i) = R(\mathcal{M}^{\text{copies}}, A, i) = V(A, i) = 0$ so the base case of the induction is trivial. The relation $R(\mathcal{M}^{\text{copies}}, A, i) = V(A, i)$ for $i < n$ is justified by the discussion preceding equation (20). To prove $R(\mathcal{M}, A, i) \geq R(\mathcal{M}^{\text{copies}}, A, i)$, suppose that both mechanisms have allocated set A while processing the bids in $J_1 \cup \cdots \cup J_i$. Conditional on the set of $x \in J_{i+1}$ such that $v_x \geq p_x$ being equal to any specified set K, we will prove that $\mathcal{M}$ obtains at least as much expected revenue as $\mathcal{M}^{\text{copies}}$ from selling the elements of $J_{i+1} \cup \cdots \cup J_n$. If K is empty, then the two mechanisms will obtain expected revenue $R(\mathcal{M}, A, i+1)$ and $R(\mathcal{M}^{\text{copies}}, A, i+1)$, respectively, from elements of $J_{i+1} \cup \cdots \cup J_n$, and the claim follows from the induction hypothesis. Otherwise, $\mathcal{M}^{\text{copies}}$ obtains expected revenue $\min\{p_x + V(A \cup \{x\}, i+1) \mid x \in K\}$ while $\mathcal{M}$ obtains expected revenue $p_y + R(\mathcal{M}, A \cup \{y\}, i+1)$ where $y \in K$ is the element of K chosen by bidder $i+1$ when presented with the menu of posted prices for the elements of J_{i+1}. The induction hypothesis implies

$$\begin{aligned} p_y &+ R(\mathcal{M}, A \cup \{y\}, i+1) \\ &\geq p_y + V(A \cup \{y\}, i+1) \\ &\geq \min\{p_x + V(A \cup \{x\}, i+1) \mid x \in K\}, \end{aligned}$$

and this completes the proof. □

7. REFERENCES

[1] Saeed Alaei. Bayesian combinatorial auctions: Expanding single buyer mechanisms to many buyers. In *Proc. 52nd IEEE Symp. on Foundations of Computer Science*, pages 512–521, 2011.

[2] Susanne Albers, Alberto Marchetti-Spaccamela, Yossi Matias, Sotiris E. Nikoletseas, and Wolfgang Thomas, editors. *Automata, Languages and Programming, 36th Internatilonal Collogquium, ICALP 2009, Rhodes, greece, July 5-12, 2009, Proceedings, Part II*, volume 5556 of *Lecture Notes in Computer Science*. Springer, 2009.

[3] Moshe Babaioff, Nicole Immorlica, and Robert Kleinberg. Matroids, secretary problems, and online mechanisms. In *Proc. 18th ACM Symp. on Discrete Algorithms*, pages 434–443, 2007.

[4] Sourav Chakraborty and Oded Lachish. Improved competitive ratio for the matroid secretary problem. In *SODA12*. to appear.

[5] Shuchi Chawla, Jason D. Hartline, David L. Malec, and Balasubramanian Sivan. Multi-parameter mechanism design and sequential posted pricing. In *Proc. 41st ACM Symp. on Theory of Computing*, pages 311–320, 2010.

[6] Brian C. Dean, Michel X. Goemans, and Jan Vondrák. Approximating the stochastic knapsack problem: The benefit of adaptivity. In *FOCS*, pages 208–217. IEEE Computer Society, 2004.

[7] Nedialko B. Dimitrov and C. Greg Plaxton. Competitive weighted matching in transversal matroids. In Luca Aceto, Ivan Damgård, Leslie Ann Goldberg, Magnús M. Halldórsson, Anna Ingólfsdóttir, and Igor Walukiewicz, editors, *ICALP (1)*, volume 5125 of *Lecture Notes in Computer Science*, pages 397–408. Springer, 2008.

[8] Shayan Oveis Gharan and Jan Vondrak. On variants of the matroid secretary problem. In *Proc. 19th Annual European Symposium on Algorithms*, pages 225–346, 2011.

[9] Ashish Goel, Sanjeev Khanna, and Brad Null. The ratio index for budgeted learning, with applications. In Claire Mathieu, editor, *SODA*, pages 18–27. SIAM, 2009.

[10] Sudipto Guha and Kames h Munagala. Multi-armed bandits with metric switching costs. In Albers et al. [2], pages 496–507.

[11] Sudipto Guha, K amesh Munagala, and Peng Shi. Approximation algorithms for restless bandit problems. *J. ACM*, 58(1):3, 2010.

[12] MohammadTaghi Hajiaghayi, Robert Kleinberg, and Tuomas W. Sandholm. Automated mechanism design and prophet inequalities. In *Proc. 22nd AAAI Conference on Artificial Intelligence*, pages 58–65, 2007.

[13] D. P. Kennedy. Optimal stopping of independent random variables and maximization prophets. *Ann. Prob.*, 13:566–571, 1985.

[14] D. P. Kennedy. Prophet-type inequalities for multi-choice optimal stopping. *Stoch. Proc. Appl.*, 24:77–88, 1987.

[15] R. P. Kertz. Comparison of optimal value and constrained maxima expectations for independent random variables. *Adv. Appl. Prob.*, 18:311–340, 1986.

[16] Nitish Korula and Martin Pál. Algorithms for secretary problems on graphs and hypergraphs. In Albers et al. [2], pages 508–520.

[17] Ulrich Krengel and Louis Sucheston. Semiamarts and finite values. *Bull. Amer. Math. Soc.*, 83:745–747, 1977.

[18] Ulrich Krengel and Louis Sucheston. On semiamarts, amarts, and processes with finite value. *Adv. in Prob. Related Topics*, 4:197–266, 1978.

[19] Roger B. Myerson. Optimal Auction Design. *Mathematics of Operations Research*, 6:58–73, 1981.

[20] Ester Samuel-Cahn. Comparison of threshold stop rules and maximum for independent nonnegative random variables. *Annals of Probability*, 12(4):1213–1216, 1984.

[21] Alexander Schrijver. *Combinatorial Optimization*, volume B. Springer, 2003.

[22] José A. Soto. Matroid secretary problem in the random assignment model. In *SODA11*, pages 1275–1284, 2011.

APPENDIX

A. PROOF OF PROPOSITION 4

PROOF. We have

$$\mathsf{OPT} = \mathbb{E}\left[w'(C_j(A)) + w'(R_j(A))\right] \ \forall j \tag{23}$$

$$\mathsf{OPT} = \mathbb{E}\left[w'(C(A)) + w'(R(A))\right] \tag{24}$$

because $C_j(A) \cup R_j(A)$ is a maximum-weight independent set with respect to w' for all j, as is $C(A) \cup R(A)$, and w' has the same distribution as w. The proof will again consist of deriving the following three inequalities.

$$\mathbb{E}\left[\sum_{x_i \in A} T_i\right] \geq \frac{1}{\alpha}\mathbb{E}\left[\sum_j w'(C_j(A))\right] \tag{25}$$

$$\mathbb{E}\left[\sum_{x_i \in A} (w_i - T_i)^+\right] \geq \mathbb{E}\left[\sum_{x_i \in R(A)} (w'(x_i) - T_i)^+\right] \tag{26}$$

$$\mathbb{E}\left[\sum_{x_i \in R(A)} (w'(x_i) - T_i)^+\right] \geq \mathbb{E}\left[w'(R(A))\right] - \frac{1}{\alpha}\mathbb{E}\left[\sum_j w'(R_j(A))\right]. \tag{27}$$

Summing (25) + (26) + $\frac{1}{\alpha-1}$(27) and using the fact that $T_i + (w_i - T_i)^+ = w_i$ for all $x_i \in A$, we obtain

$$\begin{aligned}\mathbb{E}\left[w(A)\right] \geq &\left(\frac{1}{\alpha-1} - \frac{1}{\alpha(\alpha-1)}\right)\mathbb{E}\left[\sum_j w'(C_j(A))\right] \\ &+ \frac{\alpha-2}{\alpha-1}\mathbb{E}\left[\sum_{x_i \in R(A)} (w'(x_i) - T_i)^+\right] \\ &+ \frac{1}{\alpha-1}\mathbb{E}\left[w'(R(A))\right] \\ &- \frac{1}{\alpha(\alpha-1)}\mathbb{E}\left[\sum_j w'(R_j(A))\right].\end{aligned}$$

Subsituting in Equations (23) and (24) (and observing that $\frac{\alpha-2}{\alpha-1} \geq 0$ whenever $\alpha \geq 2$), we get:

$$\mathbb{E}\left[w(A)\right] \geq \frac{1}{\alpha-1}\mathsf{OPT} - \frac{p}{\alpha(\alpha-1)}\mathsf{OPT} = \frac{\alpha-p}{\alpha(\alpha-1)}\mathsf{OPT}$$

It remains to show that Equations (25) - (27) hold for any α-balanced thresholds. Equation (25) is again a restatement of the definition of α-balanced thresholds. Inequality (26) is deduced from the same observations as Equation (7). Finally, as in Proposition 1, we apply Property (17) of α-balanced thresholds, using the set $V = R(A)$, to deduce

$$\begin{aligned}\mathbb{E}\left[\sum_{x_i \in R(A)} w'(x_i)\right] &\leq \mathbb{E}\left[\sum_{x_i \in R(A)} T_i\right] \\ &+ \mathbb{E}\left[\sum_{x_i \in R(A)} (w'(x_i) - T_i)^+\right] \\ &\leq \frac{1}{\alpha}\mathbb{E}\left[\sum_j w'(R_j(A))\right] \\ &+ \mathbb{E}\left[\sum_{x_i \in R(A)} (w'(x_i) - T_i)^+\right] \\ \Rightarrow \mathbb{E}\left[w'(R(A))\right] - \frac{1}{\alpha}\mathbb{E}\left[\sum_j w'(R_j(A))\right] &\leq \mathbb{E}\left[\sum_{x_i \in R(A)} (w'(x_i) - T_i)^+\right]\end{aligned}$$

Consequently (27) holds, which concludes the proof.

□

B. SIMPLE THRESHOLDING RULES

Most existing prophet inequalities for the rank-one case (including ours) are based on especially simple algorthms: they compute a single threshold T, and accept any element whose weight exceeds T. We'll call such an algorithm a *simple thresholding rule*. In this section, we show that the algorithm of [8] for the matroid secretary problem implies the existence of a constant-competitive simple thresholding rule for the BOSP when $\mathcal{M}$ is uniformly dense [2] and each F_x is identical. However, we also show that even if we restrict $\mathcal{M}$ to be uniformly dense, that no simple thresholding rule can achieve a constant competitive ratio when the F_x are non-identical. It is worth noting the algorithm of [8] combined with the reduction of [22] also implies a constant competitive algorithm for all matroids when each F_x is identical, although it is no longer a simple thresholding rule.

The problem solved in [8] is called the AO-RA-MK version of the matroid secretary problem. That is, a matroid $\mathcal{M} = (\mathcal{U}, \mathcal{I})$ is given as input. An adversary chooses a fixed ordering of the elements of $\mathcal{U}$, $x_1, \ldots, x_n$ and n non-negative weights. Then, the weights are randomly permuted into $w_1, \ldots, w_n$. One at a time, the pair (x_i, w_i) is revealed to the algorithm, which must decide to accept or reject x_i, and must maintain that the set of accepted elements is always in $\mathcal{I}$. Like in the BOSP, the goal is to have the expected weight of the accepted set be large relative to the weight of the maximum weight basis. The following theorem is shown in [8]:

THEOREM 2. *([8]) A 40-competitive solution to the AO-RA-MK version of the matroid secretary problem exists when $\mathcal{M}$ is uniformly dense. The algorithm observes the first half of the revealed weights without accepting anything, sets a single threshold T equal to the $(\lfloor \mathrm{rank}(\mathcal{M})/4 \rfloor + 1)^{st}$ largest observed weight, and accepts every remaining element whose weight exceeds T (without creating a dependency in $\mathcal{M}$).*

[2] A matroid is uniformly dense if $\mathcal{U} \in \mathrm{argmax}_{S \subseteq \mathcal{U}} \frac{|S|}{\mathrm{rank}(S)}$.

COROLLARY 1. *A 20-competitive simple thresholding rule exists for the BOSP when each F_x is identical, and $\mathcal{M}$ is uniformly dense.*

PROOF. We claim that the following simple thresholding rule gets a competitive ratio of 20 for the BOSP: Take n independent samples from F_x (which is the same for all x) and call them $w'_1, \ldots, w'_n$. Let T denote the $(\lfloor \text{rank}(\mathcal{M})/4 \rfloor + 1)^{st}$ largest weight and use threshold T. Clearly, if this method for choosing T achieves a competitive ratio of 20, then there exists a deterministic choice of T that achieves a competitive ratio of 20 as well.

Because each F_x is identical, we may sample each w_i and w'_i in the following manner: First, take $2n$ independent samples from F_x and call the collection of weights $\vec{w}$. Then, pick a permutation uniformly at random and permute the weights accordingly (i.e. weights may be swapped between the samples used to set T as well as the online samples). Fixing any collection of weights $\vec{w}$ and taking expectations with respect to the random permutation of the weights, if $V_P(\vec{w})$ denotes the expected value of the prophet and $V_G(\vec{w})$ denotes the expected value of the gambler using the simple thresholding rule, we will show that $V_G(\vec{w}) \geq V_P(\vec{w})/20$. We will prove this by showing that this is exactly an execution of the algorithm from [8] when the weights are $\vec{w}$.

Let $\mathcal{M}'$ be a copy of $\mathcal{M}$ on a disjoint ground set $\mathcal{U}'$, and let $\mathcal{M}''$ be the direct sum $\mathcal{M} \cup \mathcal{M}'$. Then because $\mathcal{M}$ is uniformly dense, so is $\mathcal{M}''$. Consider any fixed ordering that reveals every element of $\mathcal{U}'$ before revealing any element of $\mathcal{U}$. If we run the algorithm of [8], it is clear that we will only accept elements of $\mathcal{U}$, as their algorithm does not accept anything in the first half of the input. It is also clear that their algorithm will choose T in the same manner as our simple thresholding rule. Therefore, the expected weight achieved by their algorithm in this setting is exactly $V_G(\vec{w})$. Finally, it is clear that the expected weight of the maximum-weight basis of $\mathcal{M}''$ is exactly $2V_P(\vec{w})$. Because their algorithm achieves a competitive ratio of 40, we must have $V_G(\vec{w}) \geq V_P(\vec{w})/20$. □

PROPOSITION 6. *There is no constant-competitive simple thresholding rule for the BOSP if the F_x are non-identical, even if $\mathcal{M}$ is uniformly dense.*

PROOF. Let $\mathcal{M}$ be the rank-one matroid on two elements, and let $\mathcal{M}'$ be the partition matroid with $n = \sum_{i=1}^{k} k^{i-1}$ disjoint copies of $\mathcal{M}$. Then $\mathcal{M}'$ is uniformly dense. For $i = 0, \ldots, k$, define F_i to be the distribution that samples k^i with probability 1. For all $1 \leq i \leq k$, pick k^{k-i} copies of $\mathcal{M}$ and let the distribution for one element be F_{i-1}, and the other be F_i. Order the elements in increasing order of weight.

It is clear that the prophet can obtain $\sum_i k^{k-i}k^i = k^{k+1}$ by accepting the heavier element from every partition. It is also clear that whenever we have $k^i \leq T < k^{i+1}$ that the value obtained by the gambler using threshold T is $k^k + \sum_{j>i} k^{k-j}k^{j-1} \leq 2k^k$. So no simple thresholding rule can obtain a competitive ratio better than $k/2$. □

Online Matching with Concave Returns

[Extended Abstract]

Nikhil R. Devanur
Microsoft Research
1 Microsoft Way
Redmond, WA 98052.
nikdev@microsoft.com

Kamal Jain*
Ebay Research
2065 Hamilton Avenue
San Jose, California 95125
kamaljain@gmail.com

ABSTRACT

We consider a *significant* generalization of the Adwords problem by *allowing arbitrary concave returns, and we characterize the optimal competitive ratio achievable*. The problem considers a sequence of items arriving online that have to be allocated to agents, with different agents bidding different amounts. The objective function is the sum, over each agent i, of a monotonically non-decreasing concave function $M_i : \mathbf{R}_+ \rightarrow \mathbf{R}_+$ of the total amount allocated to i. All variants of online matching problems (including the Adwords problem) studied in the literature consider the special case of budgeted linear functions, that is, functions of the form $M_i(u_i) = \min\{u_i, B_i\}$ for some constant B_i. The distinguishing feature of this paper is in allowing arbitrary concave returns. The main result of this paper is that for each concave function M, there exists a constant $F(M) \leq 1$ such that

- there exists an algorithm with competitive ratio of $\min_i\{F(M_i)\}$, independent of the sequence of items.
- No algorithm has a competitive ratio larger than $F(M)$ over all instances with $M_i = M$ for all i.

Our algorithm is based on the primal-dual paradigm and makes use of convex programming duality. The upper bounds are obtained by formulating the task of finding the right counterexample as an optimization problem. This path takes us through the calculus of variations which deals with optimizing over continuous functions. The algorithm and the upper bound are related to each other via a set of differential equations, which points to a certain kind of duality between them.

Categories and Subject Descriptors

F.1.2 [**Modes of Computation**]: Online computation

General Terms

Algorithms, Theory

*Part of the work done while the author was at Microsoft Research.

Keywords

Adwords, Online, Bipartite Matching, Concave returns

1. INTRODUCTION

In recent years, variants of the online bipartite matching problem (most notably the *Adwords* problem) have been the subject of intense investigation. These problems are motivated by their application to online advertising. They are also considered fundamental problems in the theory of online algorithms. In this paper we consider a *significant* generalization of the Adwords problem by *allowing arbitrary concave returns, and we characterize the optimal competitive ratio achievable.*

Consider the following problem, the *online matching problem with concave returns*. An instance of the problem is given by

- a set of agents, L. For each agent i, a monotonically non-decreasing concave function $M_i : \mathbf{R}_+ \rightarrow \mathbf{R}_+$.
- A *sequence* of items. For each item j the bid of each agent i, given by b_{ij}. R denotes the set of all items.

An algorithm for the problem allocates items to agents. Fractional allocations are allowed. Let x_{ij} be the fraction of item j allocated to agent i, with $\sum_i x_{ij} \leq 1$. The allocation of item j can only depend on the items earlier in the sequence,[1] making this an "online" problem. The goal of the algorithm is to maximize its revenue, denoted by ALG.

$$\text{ALG} = \sum_i M_i\left(\sum_j b_{ij}x_{ij}\right).$$

The performance of an algorithm is measured by *competitive analysis*. ALG is compared with the offline optimum revenue, OPT, which is the optimal revenue taken over all valid allocations, given the entire set of items. An algorithm is *F-competitive*, or equivalently, has a *competitive ratio* of F if for all instances, ALG/OPT $\geq F$. The competitive ratio may also be defined on subsets of instances, such as by restricting the M_i's to belong to a particular family of concave functions.

This problem generalizes the Adwords problem. In the Adwords problem the returns are given by *budgeted linear functions*, that is, functions of the form $M_i(u_i) = \min\{u_i, B_i\}$ for some constant B_i, the *budget* of i. All variants of online matching problems studied in the literature (as briefly summarized in Section 4) consider budgeted linear functions, and the distinguishing feature of this paper is in allowing arbitrary concave returns. The motivation for considering concave returns is discussed in Section 1.1.

[1]and, of course, the functions M_i

For the Adwords problem it is known that the optimal competitive ratio is $1 - 1/e$ [16].[2] That is, there is an algorithm that has a competitive ratio of $1 - 1/e$ and no algorithm has a better competitive ratio. We generalize this result to our problem. The main result of this paper is that for each concave function M, there exists a constant $F(M) \leq 1$ such that

- there exists an algorithm with competitive ratio of $\min_i\{F(M_i)\}$, independent of the sequence of items.
- No algorithm has a competitive ratio larger than $F(M)$ over all instances with $M_i = M$ for all i.

All budgeted linear functions have $F = 1 - 1/e$, so our result does generalize the Adwords result. In fact, $F(M) \geq 1 - 1/e$ for all concave functions, and could be much larger. For instance for $M(x) = x^\delta$ for any $\delta \in [0, 1]$, $F(M) = \delta^\delta$. For $\delta = 0.5, \delta^\delta \simeq 0.7 > 1 - 1/e \simeq 0.63$. In general, $F(M)$ does not have a closed form (in fact, M itself is arbitrary, so that is not surprising).

In order to understand the difficulty in proving something like the above, let us look at how it is proven for the Adwords problem. An algorithm is designed and an analysis shows that the competitive ratio is $1 - 1/e$. A family of instances is designed and analyzed to argue that no algorithm has a competitive ratio better than $1 - 1/e$. However there is no insight into why we got the same number in both cases, except that it seems like a lucky coincidence. How do we get lucky when this number is not a nice number such as $1 - 1/e$ or even something we can explicitly calculate? Our analysis peels off a layer of mystery shrouding this coincidence: *we show that these two numbers are the same because they correspond to solutions of the same differential equations.* The coincidence is removed from being "the same number" to being "the same differential equations". Why this is so is still a bit of a mystery and we leave this as an open problem.

We overcome several technical hurdles in proving the results. Our algorithm is based on the primal-dual paradigm and makes use of convex programming duality. The standard form of convex programming duality that uses conjugate functions is somewhat complicated and unwieldy. We give a significantly simpler form that is easy to understand and is a better fit for our algorithm. Another important feature of our algorithm is that once you adopt certain basic principles of primal-dual algorithm design, the rest of the algorithm follows naturally with no *non-deterministic* choices. This "organic" approach leads to certain differential equations that govern the competitive ratio of the algorithm.

The bigger difficulty lies in showing matching upper bounds on the competitive ratio. It is not natural, in fact it is not at all clear how the upper bound would be related to the differential equations from the algorithm. Once again, looking to the Adwords problem for inspiration, the upper bound for the Adwords problem comes from what is known as the *upper triangular graph*. The intuition about why this graph is hard for the Adwords problem carries over for any concave function, so it is natural to use the same graph for the more general case. Unfortunately there are concave functions for which this graph does not give a matching upper bound.[3] One breakthrough was the realization that we can create a family of instances by parametrizing the upper triangular graph by a certain "supply function", and this can give better upper bounds on the competitive ratio. One could try to *guess* the right supply function to get the desired bounds, but this too is quite messy, even for simple concave functions. It turns out that the correct way is to formulate the task of finding the right supply function as an optimization problem. What happens then is that the optimality conditions can be shown to be equivalent to the differential equations from the algorithm, finally giving the sought after connection. This path takes us through the calculus of variations which deals with optimizing over continuous functions (rather than optimizing over a finite set of variables). This connection points to a certain kind of duality between the algorithm and these instances used in the upper bound; this duality warrants further exploration.

[2] with the assumption that bid $\ll$ budget

[3] At this point it was very tempting to conjecture that there is a better algorithm.

1.1 Motivations for concave returns

Concave returns are actually very natural in the setting of online matching. They capture the commonly occurring "diminishing returns" property. We present here some specific examples where concave returns come up.

Display ads: A popular form of selling display ads is via "guaranteed delivery", where the publisher promises to deliver a certain number of impressions to an advertiser. On not delivering on such a promise, the publisher pays an *under-delivery penalty* which is a convex function of the under-delivered amount. When translated into returns as a function of the number of allocated impressions, this becomes a concave function.

Pay-per-click advertisements: In pay-per-click advertisements, the publisher allocates *impressions* to advertisers, but gets paid only for *clicks*. It has been empirically observed that the number of clicks is a concave function of the number of impressions.

Soft budgets: Budget constraints are treated as hard constraints in the Adwords problem, but often in practice there is some leeway. If getting more items is still profitable, an agent could borrow money (and pay an interest rate on it) to pay beyond his budget. This translates to a concave profit function.

Proportional fairness One may want to optimize objectives other than revenue, especially some measure that incorporates fairness of allocation. One such measure, popular in the networking community, is *Proportional fairness*, introduced by Kelly [13]. Proportional fairness maximizes a weighted sum of logs, a concave function.

Organization: The rest of the paper is organized as follows: Section 2 has the description and analysis of the algorithm. Section 3 gives the matching upper bounds. In Section 4 we discuss flexibility of our algorithmic approach, related work, and open problems and directions for future research.

2. THE ALGORITHM

For the rest of the paper we make the assumption that the M_i's have continuous second derivatives. Our approach can actually handle non-smooth functions, but this involves sub-gradients, etc. We make this assumption to keep the exposition simple.

The algorithm is based on an extension of the primal-dual paradigm to convex programs. OPT is the optimum value of a convex program, called the *Primal* program (the one on the left below). The first step is to define a dual program to the Primal convex program. We present a simple and direct construction of the dual program and a proof of (weak) duality. These are based on the simple geometric fact that a concave function is upper bounded by any of its tangents. Let $Y_i(v_i) := M_i(v_i) - v_i M_i'(v_i)$. This is the y-intercept of the tangent to $M_i()$ at v_i, that is, if you draw a tangent to $M_i()$

at v_i then $(0, Y_i(v_i))$ is the point of intersection of the tangent with the y-axis. The *Dual* program, with v_i's and β_j's as variables is stated below on the right.

$$\begin{array}{ll} \text{maximize} \sum_i M_i(u_i) \text{ s.t.} & \text{minimize} \sum_i Y_i(v_i) + \sum_j \beta_j \text{ s.t.} \\ \forall\, i, u_i = \sum_j b_{ij} x_{ij}. & \forall\, i, j, \beta_j \geq b_{ij} M_i'(v_i). \\ \forall\, j, \sum_i x_{ij} \leq 1. & \forall\, i, j, v_i, \beta_j \geq 0. \\ \forall\, i, j, x_{ij} \geq 0. & \end{array}$$

LEMMA 1. *(Weak duality) The optimum value of the Dual program $\geq$ OPT.*

PROOF. Since M_i is concave, a tangent to M_i at any point v_i (in the domain of M_i) is an upper bound on M_i.

$$\forall\, i, \forall\, v_i \geq 0, M_i(u_i) \leq M_i(v_i) + (u_i - v_i) M_i'(v_i)$$
$$= M_i'(v_i) u_i + Y_i(v_i).$$

Suppose we fix v_i for all i, and replace M_i by the upper bound in the inequality above, thus linearizing the objective function of the Primal program. Let $D(\boldsymbol{v})$ be the value of the following linear program (on the left). The dual of this LP is on the right, the optimum value of which is also $D(\boldsymbol{v})$ by strong LP duality. ($\boldsymbol{v}$ is the vector of v_i's.)

$$\begin{array}{ll} \text{maximize} \sum_i M_i'(v_i) u_i \text{ s.t.} & \text{minimize} \sum_j \beta_j \text{ s.t.} \\ \forall\, i, u_i = \sum_j b_{ij} x_{ij}. & \forall\, i, j, \beta_j \geq b_{ij} M_i'(v_i). \\ \forall\, j, \sum_i x_{ij} \leq 1. & \forall\, j, \beta_j \geq 0. \\ \forall\, i, j, x_{ij} \geq 0. & \end{array}$$

For every choice of $\boldsymbol{v}$ we get an upper bound on OPT.

$$\forall\, \boldsymbol{v}, \text{OPT} \leq D(\boldsymbol{v}) + \sum_i Y_i(v_i).$$

In the above LPs (in particular, the dual LP), v_i's are considered as constants. We can instead think of them as variables and obtain a single mathematical program with v_i's and β_j's as variables. This is exactly what the Dual program is, $\min_{\boldsymbol{v}} \{D(\boldsymbol{v}) + \sum_i Y_i(v_i)\}$. The lemma follows. □

The primal-dual paradigm as applied to online algorithms is to maintain a set of dual variables that guide the primal solution. The evolution of the primal solution in turn determines how the dual variables are updated. The part of dual variables guiding the primal solution usually follows very naturally from the complementary slackness conditions (or with the duals being interpreted as costs, etc). The non-trivial part is how the dual variables are updated. This requires that

- the dual variables remain feasible and that
- the ratio of the values of the primal and the dual solutions remains within desirable bounds.

The algorithm design principle we espouse in this paper is that *once we determine that the dual variables satisfy the above conditions, their dependence on the primal solution can be "reverse-engineered"*. The above conditions often take the form of a differential equation which can be solved (either in a closed form or numerically) to give the dual update method.

We now describe the algorithm. Recall that the algorithm has to determine the allocation x_{ij} in an online manner. The algorithm also constructs a solution to the Dual program. The algorithm maintains for each i, the variable $u_i = \sum_j b_{ij} x_{ij}$. The dual variable v_i is set as a (smooth) function of u_i, such that v_i is monotonically non-decreasing. The exact dependence of v_i on u_i is left unspecified for now. The dual variables guide the primal allocation via complementary slackness conditions. For instance, one complementary slackness condition says that $x_{ij} > 0$ implies $\beta_j = b_{ij} M_i'(v_i)$. This means we must allocate j to $\arg\max_i \{b_{ij} M_i'(v_i)\}$. However the arg max may change as a *result* of the allocation, since allocating j to i increases u_i, which increases v_i, which decreases $M_i'(v_i)$. If the arg max is unique and does not change even after allocating j completely to i, then j is allocated completely to i (that is $x_{ij} = 1$). If either the arg max is not unique or it changes when we allocate j to i, we need to allocate fractionally. The allocation is best described as a continuous process. As you start allocating j to i, u_i increases, which changes v_i which in turn could change the arg max. To describe the process, let t denote time and we specify x_{ij} as a function of t. In turn, u_i and v_i are also functions of t. In fact the allocations change smoothly over time and we only specify $\frac{dx_{ij}}{dt}$. We set $\frac{dx_{ij}}{dt} = 0$ if $i \notin \arg\max_i \{b_{ij} M_i'(v_i)\}$. Otherwise $\frac{dx_{ij}}{dt} > 0$ is such that $b_{ij} \frac{dM_i'(v_i(t))}{dt}$ is the same for all the agents in the arg max. Note that this only specifies $\frac{dx_{ij}}{dt}$ upto a constant factor. This does not matter since the "speed of time" is immaterial to the algorithm. Allocation stops when $\sum_j x_{ij} = 1$. The dual variable β_j is set as follows.

$$\beta_j = \int \sum_i \{b_{ij} M_i'(v_i)\} \frac{dx_{ij}}{dt} dt. \tag{1}$$

β_j is only needed for the analysis of the algorithm and does not affect the run of the algorithm itself.

The description of the algorithm is completed by specifying the dependence of v_i on u_i. As mentioned before these are reverse-engineered from the properties we want the dual solution to satisfy (Lemmas 2 and 3 here). These take on the form of a solution to a first order differential equation, which we present below. Let $F > 0$ be some constant. A solution to the following differential equation gives v as a function of u.

$$M'(u)/F = Y'(v)\frac{dv}{du} + M'(v). \tag{2}$$

$$\frac{dv}{du} \geq 0.$$

Boundary conditions: when $u = 0, Y(v) = 0$. $u, v \geq 0$.

Suppose that for some constant F, for all agents i, (2) has a solution with $M = M_i$. Let the dependence of v_i on u_i in the algorithm be given by such a solution. The algorithm is summarized below.

The analysis of the algorithm is by bounding the ratio of the primal and dual solutions constructed. Let P and D be respectively the values of the primal and the dual solutions created by the algorithm throughout its run.

Algorithm 1: Algorithm for the online matching problem with concave returns.

Input: functions M_i for all i.

Let F be a constant such that for all agents i, (2) has a solution with $M = M_i$;

Throughout the algorithm, maintain the following invariants

for *each* i **do**

  $u_i = \sum_j b_{ij} x_{ij}$;

  v_i is a function of u_i that satisfies (2);

for *each* j *when* j *arrives* **do**

  allocate j to $\arg\max_i\{b_{ij} M_i'(v_i)\}$ in a continuous fashion ;

  set β_j as in (1);

LEMMA 2. *The following is an invariant throughout the algorithm.*

$$\frac{dP}{dD} = F.$$

PROOF. The differential equation (2) has already been defined to make this lemma go through. Suppose dx of j is allocated to i. Then

$$dP = M_i'(u_i) b_{ij} dx = M_i'(u_i) du_i.$$

$$dD = Y_i'(v_i) dv_i + b_{ij} M_i'(v_i) dx = Y_i'(v_i) dv_i + M_i'(v_i) du_i.$$

Lemma now follows from (2). □

LEMMA 3. *The variables v_i and β_j constructed by the algorithm form a feasible solution to the Dual program.*

PROOF. This is easy to see since we allocate j only to $\arg\max_i\{b_{ij} M_i'(v_i)\}$, and the fact that $M_i'(v_i)$ is monotonically non-increasing throughout the algorithm. □

THEOREM 4. *The algorithm has a competitive ratio of F.*

PROOF. The theorem follows immediately from Lemmas 1, 2 and 3, and the fact that when $P = 0$, $D = 0$. □

Note: It is easy to see for instance, that the greedy algorithm has a competitive ratio of $\frac{1}{2}$. The greedy algorithm corresponds to the solution $v = u$. In this case, consider the integral form of (2) with $F = \frac{1}{2}$ and note that the left hand side is $2M(u)$ and the right hand side is $Y(u) + M(u)$. Since $M(u) \geq Y(u)$, the conclusion follows. This also shows that $F(M) \geq \frac{1}{2}$ for all M. In fact it can be shown that $F(M) \geq 1 - 1/e$ for all M, via an indirect argument which we will not go into here.

Note that this completes the first part of the main result. For a given concave function M define $F(M)$ to be the largest constant such that (2) has a solution. Then the algorithm has a competitive ratio of $\min_i\{F(M_i)\}$.

3. THE UPPER BOUND

In this secion we prove the second part of our main result, by showing a matching upper bound on the competitive ratio of any algorithm. Such an upper bound is proven by constructing instances and arguing that no algorithm can perform well on all the instances. We begin by some simplifying observations.

In order to prove an upper bound on the competitive ratio, we need to consider randomized algorithms as well. In case of randomized algorithms, we consider the expected revenue of the algorithm. However for this problem, randomization does not help. To see this, for any randomized algorithm, consider the deterministic algorithm whose allocation is equal to the expected allocation of the given randomized algorithm. The revenue of the deterministic algorithm is no lower than the expected revenue of the randomized algorithm due to the concavity of the M_i's. Thus we can restrict ourselves to deterministic algorithms only.

We show that for a certain family of instances we can characterize the optimal algorithm, the one with the largest competitive ratio. This enables us to prove the upper bound by simply bounding the competitive ratio of the optimal algorithm. Consider a bipartite graph $\mathcal{G} = (L, R, E)$, with vertex sets $L = R = \{1, 2, \ldots, n\}$ and edges $(i, j) \in E$ iff $i \geq j$. This graph is commonly called the "upper triangular" graph, since its adjacency matrix is upper triangular. Fix a concave function M. Consider instances of the problem with the set of agents being isomorphic to L, modulo the identity of agents. That is, we have n agents and consider all possible bijections of agents to L. $M_i = M$ for all i. The items are the vertices in R, arriving in the increasing order. $b_{ij} = 1$ if $(i, j) \in E$ and 0 otherwise. The first item is adjacent to all the agents. Every subsequent item is adjacent to all the agents the previous item was adjacent to, except one. The algorithm has to make its allocation without knowing which agent will be "left out" for the next item.

We claim that the algorithm that divides the items equally among all its neighbors is the optimal algorithm for these instances. That is, this algorithm has the largest competitive ratio taken over all these instances. If an algorithm has an inequitable allocation then an adversary picking the instance can take advantage of this by picking the agent with the lowest allocation to be left out for the next item. This results in a lower objective function than the equitable allocation because of concavity of returns. Thus, it is sufficient to show an upper bound on the competitive ratio of the equitable algorithm. That is, if we show that for this algorithm ALG/OPT $\leq F$ then no algorithm can have a competitive ratio better than F on these instances, and in turn on all instances with $M_i = M$ for all i.

In fact, we extend the above to instances where the items could have an arbitrary "supply". Suppose item j has supply f_j, then the supply constraint is that $\sum_i x_{ij} \leq f_j$. It is easy to see that the assertion about the equitable algorithm being optimal still holds.

With these simplifying observations, the aim is to construct for any M, a supply function f_j such that ALG/OPT for that instance is arbitrarily close to $F(M)$, the largest constant such that (2) has a solution. A direct way to show that would be to consider any constant larger than $F(M)$ and construct an f so that ALG/OPT is equal to that constant. Alas we don't know of any such direct construction; the difficulty is in relating this to (2). It turns out that the relation of (2) with this family of instances is somewhat indirect. *We show that if you formulate the task of finding the f that minimizes ALG/OPT as an optimization problem, then the conditions that characterize the optimal choice are equivalent to (2)!!* From this it follows that for the optimal choice of f we have that ALG/OPT $= F(M)$, giving the result we were after.

In fact, to follow the plan as outlined above, we consider a continuous version of the upper triangular graph. We define a bipartite graph $\mathcal{G} = (L, R, E)$, with the vertex sets $L = R = [0, 1]$. $(x, y) \in E$ iff $x \geq y$. Many of the concepts in the discrete version are based on summations, but they break down since we cannot take summations in the continuous version. We now specify how to extend all the concepts to their continuous counterparts. The "supply" of items is given by a function $f : R \to \mathbf{R}_+$. An allocation is given by a function $A(x, y)$. The supply constraint translates to

$$\forall y \in R, \int_y^1 A(x, y)dx = f(y).$$

The amount allocated to x, say $u(x)$ is given by

$$u(x) = \int_0^x A(x, y)dy.$$

The revenue of the algorithm is

$$\text{ALG} = \int_0^1 M(u(x))dx.$$

The optimal algorithm has the allocation

$$A(x, y) = \frac{f(y)}{1-y} \; \forall x \geq y.$$

$$\text{Thus } u(x) = \int_0^x \frac{f(y)}{1-y}dy.$$

The offline optimal allocation is

$$A(x, y) = f(y)\delta_y(x)$$

where $\delta_y(x)$ is the dirac-delta function with peak at y. With this allocation the amount allocated to x is $f(x)$. Thus

$$\text{OPT} = \int_0^1 M(f(x))dx.$$

3.1 Calculus of variations

As mentioned before, the key to the upper bound proof is to formulate the task of finding an f that minimizes the ratio ALG/OPT as an optimization problem. A quantity that is a function of a function, such as ALG/OPT, is called a *functional* (and is denoted ALG/OPT$[f]$). The subject of finding extremal functions, that is functions that optimize a functional is called the *calculus of variations*. The calculus of variations is used for instance to find geodesics on surfaces, or in physics to apply the "principle of least action". It will be used here crucially.

We will consider functions from $\mathcal{C}$, the class of all real valued functions defined on the domain $[0, 1]$, that are *right-continuous*. The dot product of two functions is defined as

$$f \cdot g := \int_0^1 f(x)g(x)dx.$$

The gradient of a functional H (at some f_0) is another function ∇H such that for any other function η, the rate of change of H in the direction of η starting from f is $\nabla H \cdot \eta$. That is,

$$\frac{dH[f_0 + \epsilon\eta]}{d\epsilon}\Big|_{\epsilon=0} = \nabla H \cdot \eta.$$

It is easy to compute the gradient of OPT:

$$\nabla\text{OPT}(x) = M'(f(x)).$$

It is a little harder to compute the gradient of ALG.

LEMMA 5.

$$\nabla ALG(x) = \frac{1}{1-x}\int_x^1 M'(u(t))dt.$$

PROOF. Recall that

$$\text{ALG}[f] = \int_0^1 M(u(x))dx, \text{ where}$$

$$u(x) = \int_0^x \frac{f(y)}{1-y}dy.$$

Let $f = f_0 + \epsilon\eta$.

$$\frac{d\text{ALG}[f]}{d\epsilon} = \int_0^1 \frac{dM(u(x))}{d\epsilon}dx = \int_0^1 M'(u(x))\frac{du(x)}{d\epsilon}dx.$$

$$\frac{du(x)}{d\epsilon} = \int_0^x \frac{d}{d\epsilon}\frac{f(y)}{1-y}dy = \int_0^x \frac{\eta(y)}{1-y}dy.$$

Putting the two together and changing the order of integration gives

$$\frac{d\text{ALG}[f]}{d\epsilon} = \int_0^1 M'(u(x))\int_0^x \frac{\eta(y)}{1-y}dydx$$

$$= \int_0^1 \frac{\eta(y)}{1-y}\int_y^1 M'(u(x))dxdy$$

$$= \int_0^1 \frac{\eta(x)}{1-x}\int_x^1 M'(u(t))dtdx.$$

The last equality is a result of change of integration variables. □

For a given $L > 0$, let $\mathcal{C}_L$ be the class of all real-valued functions f defined on the domain $[0, 1]$ that are right-continuous, with $f(0) = 0$ and bounded above by L.[4] From now on, let H denote the functional ALG/OPT. For every L, and $f \in \mathcal{C}_L$, we get an upper bound of $H[f]$ on the competitive ratio of any algorithm. We are interested in the least upper bound we can obtain this way. We define the following quantities for ease of notation.

$$\inf_{f \in \mathcal{C}_L} H[f] =: \lambda_L^*, \text{and}$$

$$\inf_L \lambda_L^* =: \lambda^*.$$

We first establish the existence of a minimizer of H in the class $\mathcal{C}_L$.

THEOREM 6. *$\exists f^* \in \mathcal{C}_L$ such that $H[f^*] = \lambda_L^*$.*

The proof of the above theorem is broken down into Lemmas 7–9. To begin with, the definition of λ_L^* implies there exists a sequence of functions $f_1, f_2, \ldots, f_n, \ldots \in \mathcal{C}_L$ such that

$$\lim_{n\to\infty} H[f_n] = \lambda_L^*.$$

LEMMA 7. *We may assume without loss of generality that the functions f_n are monotonically non-decreasing.*

PROOF. Suppose f_n is not monotonically non-decreasing. Suppose for simplicity that there is only one interval where f_n is decreasing. Let $\hat{f}_n$ be the "ironed"[5] version of f_n. The function $\hat{f}_n$ is monotonically non-decreasing, f_n and $\hat{f}_n$ agree except on an interval $[a, b]$ and $\int_a^b f_n dx = \int_a^b \hat{f}_n dx$. Let $\eta = \hat{f}_n - f_n$. We will argue that $\nabla\text{ALG} \cdot \eta \leq 0$ and $\nabla\text{OPT} \cdot \eta \geq 0$, which implies that $\nabla H \cdot \eta \leq 0$. Therefore $H[\hat{f}_n] \leq H[f_n]$ and f_n can be replaced by $\hat{f}_n$ in the sequence.

Further subdivide the interval $[a, b]$ as $[a, c]$ and $[c, b]$ such that $\eta \leq 0$ in $[a, c]$ and $\eta \geq 0$ in $[c, b]$. For $x \in [a, c]$, $f(x) \geq f(c)$, therefore $M'(f(x)) \leq M'(f(c))$. Further, since $\eta(x) \leq 0$, $\eta(x)M'(f(x)) \geq \eta(x)M'(f(c))$. Vice versa, for $x \in [c, b]$,

[4]Strictly speaking we want to let $f(0) = \sup\{v : Y(v) = 0\}$, but we will ignore this for the sake of ease of notation.

[5]This is the same as Myerson's ironing [17] used in Bayesian mechanism design.

$f(x) \leq f(c)$, therefore $M'(f(x)) \geq M'(f(c))$. Here $\eta(x) \geq 0$, so once again $\eta(x)M'(f(x)) \geq \eta(x)M'(f(c))$. Therefore

$$\nabla \text{OPT} \cdot \eta = \int_a^b \eta(x)M'(f(x))dx$$

$$\geq M'(f(c)) \int_a^b \eta(x) = 0.$$

Similarly, it is easy to check that ∇ALG is a non-increasing function of x and hence for $x \in [a, c]$, $\nabla \text{ALG}(x) \geq \nabla \text{ALG}(c)$, and for $x \in [c, b]$, $\nabla \text{ALG}(x) \leq \nabla \text{ALG}(c)$. Using an argument that is similar to the one above, we get that $\nabla \text{ALG} \cdot \eta \leq 0$. □

LEMMA 8. *(Hally-Bray. See also [19], Section 17.5.) Given a sequence of non-decreasing functions (f_n) in $\mathcal{C}_L$, there exists a convergent subsequence $(f_{n_i} : i \in \mathbb{N}) \to f^*$ with pointwise convergence. $f^* \in \mathcal{C}_L$ is non-decreasing, but may not be continuous.*

LEMMA 9. *H is continuous. That is, if a sequence $(f_n : n \in \mathbb{N}) \to f$ pointwise, then $(H[f_n]) \to H[f]$.*

PROOF. It is easy to see that ALG and OPT are continuous. Also H is always in $[\frac{1}{2}, 1]$. Hence H is continuous. □

Theorem 6 now follows since

$$\lim_{i \to \infty} H[f_{n_i}] = H[f^*] = \lambda_L^*.$$

Now we show several properties of f^* with the goal of relating f^* to (2). Let $l := \inf\{x : f^*(x) = L\}$. By right continuity of f^*, it follows that $f^*(l) = L$.

THEOREM 10. *([18])*

$$\nabla H[f^*](x) = 0 \, \forall \, x \in [0, l].$$

PROOF. The above theorem is the standard theorem in the calculus of variations, giving necessary conditions for extremal functions. The exact form stated here is obtained by considering all variations η such that $\eta(0) = 0 = \eta(x)$ for all $x \in [l, 1]$. □

LEMMA 11.

$$\nabla ALG[f^*] = \lambda_L^* \nabla OPT[f^*] \, \forall \, x \in [0, l].$$

PROOF. The lemma follows essentially from the quotient rule for differentiation along with Theorem 10. □

We next show that in fact f^* is a differentiable function.

LEMMA 12. *f^* is differentiable in $[0, 1)$ (and is therefore continuous).*

PROOF. Note that $\nabla \text{ALG}[f^*]$ is differentiable in $[0, 1)$. From Lemma 11 so is $\nabla \text{OPT}[f^*]$. However, $\nabla \text{OPT}[f^*] = M'(f^*)$, and M' is differentiable. Therefore it follows that f^* is differentiable. □

We have established that for every L, the minimizer f^* of H in $\mathcal{C}_L$ exists, is non-decreasing, and is also differentiable in $[0, 1)$. We are now ready to relate f^* to the primal differential equation. We define a relaxation of (2) by requiring the conditions to hold only for $v \leq L$. To be precise consider the system of equations,

$$M'(u)/F = Y'(v)\frac{dv}{du} + M'(v), \tag{3}$$

for all u such that $v(u) \leq L$.

$$\frac{dv}{du} \geq 0.$$

Boundary conditions: when $u = 0, Y(v) = 0$. $u, v \geq 0$.

Let F_L^* be the supremum of all F such that (3) has a solution. Clearly $F_L^* \geq F(M)$ since a solution to (2) also satisfies (3). It is also easy to see that

$$\inf_L F_L^* = F(M).$$

We now state a lemma that shows that f^* can be used to construct a solution to (3).

LEMMA 13.

$$\forall \, L, \lambda_L^* \leq F_L^*.$$

PROOF. Recall that a solution to (3) is to contruct v as a function of u. Note that $\frac{du}{dx} > 0$ for $u > 0$ and hence one can invert the function $u(x)$ and think of x as a function of u. Define $v(u) = f^*(x(u))$. We now show that this solution satisfies (3) with $F = \lambda_L^*$. The lemma then follows from the definition of F_L^*.

We start with the conclusion of Lemma 11: for all $x \in [0, l]$,

$$\nabla \text{ALG}[f^*] = \lambda_L^* \nabla \text{OPT}[f^*].$$

$$\frac{1}{1-x} \int_x^\infty M'(u(t))dt = \lambda_L^* M'(f^*(x)).$$

$$\frac{1}{\lambda_L^*} \int_x^\infty M'(u(t))dt = (1 - x)M'(f^*(x)).$$

Differentiating both sides w.r.t. x,

$$\frac{-1}{\lambda_L^*} M'(u(x)) = -M'(f^*(x)) + (1 - x)M''(f^*(x))\frac{df^*}{dx}.$$

Use the fact that $\frac{df^*}{dx} = \frac{df^*}{du}\frac{du}{dx}$ and $\frac{du}{dx} = \frac{f^*}{1-x}$.

$$\frac{1}{\lambda_L^*} M'(u(x)) = M'(f^*(x)) - f^* M''(f^*(x))\frac{df^*}{du}.$$

Substitute $v = f^*$ and use $Y'(v) = -vM''(v)$.

$$\frac{1}{\lambda_L^*} M'(u) = M'(v) + Y'(v)\frac{dv}{du},$$

for all u such that $v(u) \leq L$. □

The main theorem of this section now follows from Lemma 13 easily, by taking infimums.

THEOREM 14. $\lambda^* = F(M)$.

4. DISCUSSIONS AND CONCLUSION

Flexibility of our approach

Another strength of our algorithmic approach is its flexibility: suppose that even for budgeted linear functions, the algorithm designer knows (based on historic data, for instance) that an agent is guaranteed to get a certain number of items. Our algorithm can be tuned to take advantage of this, by appropriately changing the boundary conditions in the differential equations. This leads to a better competitive ratio. In general this approach opens up the possibility of incorporating other kinds of beliefs about the instance and get the optimal algorithm based on these beliefs.

Related work

The Adwords problem was introduced by [16], who gave a $1 - 1/e$ competitive algorithm, based on a factor revealing LP, with the assumption that bid $\ll$ budget. They also showed that this is the best competitive ratio achievable. [4] gave a primal-dual analysis of the same result. Our algorithm is a generalization of the primal-dual approach of [4]. [12] considered the online bipartite matching problem and gave a $1 - 1/e$ competitive randomized algorithm. This is a special case of Adwords with bids = 0 or 1 and budgets = 1, but this does not satisfy the bid $\ll$ budget assumption. [10] gave a $1 - 1/e$ competitive algorithm for the b-matching problem with large b, a special case of Adwords with budgets = b and bids = 0 or 1. The Adwords problem without the bid $\ll$ budget assumption is open, with the best known algorithm being $1/2$-competitive. A $1 - 1/e$ competitive algorithm is also known for another special case of Adwords without the bid $\ll$ budget assumption, which is the vertex-weighted version of online matching [1].

Most of the papers lately consider *stochastic* variants of online matching, with the dominant theme of "beating" the $1 - 1/e$ bound. These make some distributional assumptions about the sequence of items and analyze the performance of the algorithm in expectation over the distribution. A partial list of papers is as follows: [9, 5, 2, 7, 6, 8, 15, 3, 11, 14].

Open problems and directions

One open problem is to dig deeper into the coincidence of differential equations. This seems to point to a different kind of duality between the algorithm and the counterexample. Understanding this duality would lead to greater insights into what looks like a fundamental issue in the design of online algorithms. Another open problem is to use this approach to get optimal competitive ratios for other online problems. In fact, an ambitious goal is to be able to reverse engineer: can hard instances (believed to be worst case instances) of problems be used to design the algorithms?

5. ACKNOWLEDGMENTS

We would like to thank Yuval Peres, Alexander Holroyd, Mark Braverman, David Levin and Oded Schramm for useful discussions and pointers to references.

6. REFERENCES

[1] G. Aggarwal, G. Goel, C. Karande, and A. Mehta. Online vertex-weighted bipartite matching and single-bid budgeted allocations. In *SODA*, pages 1253–1264, 2011.

[2] S. Agrawal, Z. Wang, and Y. Ye. A dynamic near-optimal algorithm for online linear programming. arXiv:0911.2974v1, 2009.

[3] B. Bahmani and M. Kapralov. Improved bounds for online stochastic matching. In *ESA*, pages 170–181, 2010.

[4] N. Buchbinder, K. Jain, and J. S. Naor. Online primal-dual algorithms for maximizing ad-auctions revenue. In *ESA'07: Proceedings of the 15th annual European conference on Algorithms*, pages 253–264, Berlin, Heidelberg, 2007. Springer-Verlag.

[5] N. R. Devanur and T. P. Hayes. The adwords problem: online keyword matching with budgeted bidders under random permutations. In J. Chuang, L. Fortnow, and P. Pu, editors, *ACM Conference on Electronic Commerce*, pages 71–78. ACM, 2009.

[6] N. R. Devanur, K. Jain, B. Sivan, and C. A. Wilkens. Near optimal online algorithms and fast approximation algorithms for resource allocation problems. In Y. Shoham, Y. Chen, and T. Roughgarden, editors, *ACM Conference on Electronic Commerce*, pages 29–38. ACM, 2011.

[7] J. Feldman, M. Henzinger, N. Korula, V. S. Mirrokni, and C. Stein. Online stochastic packing applied to display ad allocation. In *ESA*, pages 182–194, 2010.

[8] J. Feldman, A. Mehta, V. Mirrokni, and S. Muthukrishnan. Online stochastic matching: Beating 1-1/e. In *FOCS '09: Proceedings of the 2009 50th Annual IEEE Symposium on Foundations of Computer Science*, pages 117–126, Washington, DC, USA, 2009. IEEE Computer Society.

[9] G. Goel and A. Mehta. Online budgeted matching in random input models with applications to adwords. In *SODA '08: Proceedings of the nineteenth annual ACM-SIAM symposium on Discrete algorithms*, pages 982–991, Philadelphia, PA, USA, 2008. Society for Industrial and Applied Mathematics.

[10] B. Kalyanasundaram and K. R. Pruhs. An optimal deterministic algorithm for online b-matching. *Theor. Comput. Sci.*, 233(1-2):319–325, 2000.

[11] C. Karande, A. Mehta, and P. Tripathi. Online bipartite matching with unknown distributions. In *STOC*, pages 587–596, 2011.

[12] R. M. Karp, U. V. Vazirani, and V. V. Vazirani. An optimal algorithm for on-line bipartite matching. In *STOC '90: Proceedings of the twenty-second annual ACM symposium on Theory of computing*, pages 352–358, 1990.

[13] F. P. Kelly. Charging and rate control for elastic traffic. *European Transactions on Telecommunications*, 8:33–37, 1997.

[14] M. Mahdian and Q. Yan. Online bipartite matching with random arrivals: an approach based on strongly factor-revealing lps. In *STOC*, pages 597–606, 2011.

[15] V. H. Manshadi, S. O. Gharan, and A. Saberi. Online stochastic matching: Online actions based on offline statistics. In *SODA*, pages 1285–1294, 2011.

[16] A. Mehta, A. Saberi, U. Vazirani, and V. Vazirani. Adwords and generalized on-line matching. In *In FOCS âĂŹ05: Proceedings of the 46th Annual IEEE Symposium on Foundations of Computer Science*, pages 264–273. IEEE Computer Society, 2005.

[17] R. Myerson. Optimal auction design. *Mathematics of Operations Research*, 6(1):58–73, 1981.

[18] H. Sagan. *Introduction to the Calculus of Variations*. Dover Publications Inc., 1969.

[19] D. WIlliams. *Probability with Martingales*. Cambridge University Press, 1991.

Computing a Nonnegative Matrix Factorization – Provably

Sanjeev Arora * Rong Ge † Ravi Kannan ‡ Ankur Moitra §

ABSTRACT

The Nonnegative Matrix Factorization (NMF) problem has a rich history spanning quantum mechanics, probability theory, data analysis, polyhedral combinatorics, communication complexity, demography, chemometrics, etc. In the past decade NMF has become enormously popular in machine learning, where the factorization is computed using a variety of local search heuristics. Vavasis recently proved that this problem is NP-complete.

We initiate a study of when this problem is solvable in polynomial time. Consider a nonnegative $m \times n$ matrix M and a target inner-dimension r. Our results are the following:

1. We give a polynomial-time algorithm for exact and approximate NMF for every constant r. Indeed NMF is most interesting in applications precisely when r is small.

2. We complement this with a hardness result, that if exact NMF can be solved in time $(nm)^{o(r)}$, 3-SAT has a sub-exponential time algorithm. Hence, substantial improvements to the above algorithm are unlikely.

3. We give an algorithm that runs in time polynomial in n, m and r under the *separablity* condition identified by Donoho and Stodden in 2003. The algorithm may be practical since it is simple and noise tolerant (under benign assumptions). Separability is believed to hold in many practical settings.

To the best of our knowledge, this last result is the first polynomial-time algorithm that provably works under a non-trivial condition on the input matrix and we believe that this will be an interesting and important direction for future work.

*Princeton University, Computer Science Department and Center for Computational Intractability. Email: arora@cs.princeton.edu. This work is supported by the NSF grants CCF-0832797 and CCF-1117309.

†Princeton University, Computer Science Department and Center for Computational Intractability. Email: rongge@cs.princeton.edu. This work is supported by the NSF grants CCF-0832797 and CCF-1117309.

‡Microsoft Research labs., India. Email: kannan@microsoft.com

§Institute for Advanced Study, School of Mathematics. Email: moitra@ias.edu. Research supported in part by NSF grant No. DMS-0835373 and by an NSF Computing and Innovation Fellowship.

STOC'12, May 19–22, 2012, New York, New York, USA.

Categories and Subject Descriptors

F.2.1 [**Analysis of Algorithms and Problem Complexity**]: Numerical Algorithms and Problems—*Computations on matrices*; G.3 [**Probability and Statistics**]: Multivariate statistics

General Terms

Theory, Algorithms

Keywords

nonnegative matrix factorization, semi-algebric sets, data analysis

1. INTRODUCTION

In the *Nonnegative Matrix Factorization* (NMF) problem we are given an $n \times m$ matrix M with nonnegative real entries (such a matrix will be henceforth called "nonnegative") and an integer $r > 0$. Our goal is to express M as AW where A and W are nonnegative matrices of size $n \times r$ and $r \times m$ respectively. We refer to r as the *inner-dimension* of the factorization and the smallest value of r for which there is such a factorization as the *nonnegative rank* of M. An equivalent formulation is that our goal is to write M as the sum of r nonnegative rank-one matrices.[1] We note that r must be at least the rank of M in order for such a factorization to exist. In some applications, it makes sense to instead ask for AW to be a good approximation to M in some suitable matrix norm. We refer to the problem of finding a nonnegative A and W of inner-dimension r that (approximately) minimizes $\|M - AW\|_F$ as *Approximate NMF*, where $\|\|_F$ denotes the Frobenius norm. Without the restriction that A and W be nonnegative, both the exact and approximate problems can be solved exactly via singular value decomposition [12].

[1]It is a common misconception that since the real rank is the maximum number of linearly independent columns, the non-

NMF is a fundamental problem that has been independently introduced in a number of different contexts and applications. Many interesting heuristics and local search algorithms (including the familiar Expectation Maximization or EM) have been proposed to find such factorizations. One compelling family of applications is data analysis, where a nonnegative factorization is computed in order to extract certain latent relationships in the data and has been applied to image segmentation [24], [25] information retrieval [16] and document clustering [35]. NMF also has applications in fields such as chemometrics [23] (where the problem has a long history of study under the name *self modeling curve resolution*) and biology (e.g. in vision research [7]): in some cases, the underlying physical model for a system has natural restrictions that manifest themselves as nonnegativity constraints on A and W. In demography (see e.g., [15]), NMF is used to model the dynamics of marriage through a mechanism similar to the chemical laws of mass action.

In combinatorial optimization, Yannakakis [37] characterized the number of extra variables needed to succinctly describe a given polytope as the nonnegative rank of an appropriate matrix (called the "slack matrix"). In communication complexity, Aho et al [1] showed that the log of the nonnegative rank of a Boolean matrix is polynomially related to its deterministic communication complexity - and hence the famous Log-Rank Conjecture of Lovasz and Saks [26] is equivalent to showing a quasi-polynomial relationship between real rank and nonnegative rank for Boolean matrices. In complexity theory, Nisan used nonnegative rank to prove lower bounds for non-commutative models of computation [28]. Additionally, the 1993 paper of Cohen and Rothblum [8] gives a long list of other applications in statistics and quantum mechanics. That paper also gives an exact algorithm that runs in exponential time.

QUESTION 1. *Can a nonnegative matrix factorization be computed efficiently when the inner-dimension, r, is small?*

Vavasis recently proved that the NMF problem is NP-hard when r is large [36], but this only rules out an algorithm whose running time is polynomial in all of the parameters (n, m and r). Arguably, in most significant applications, r is small. Usually the algorithm designer posits a two-level generative model for the data and uses NMF to compute "hidden" variables that explain the data. This explanation is interesting precisely when the number of hidden variables (r) is much smaller than the number of examples (m) or the number of observations per example (n).

In information retrieval, one often chooses M to be a "term-by-document" matrix where the $(i, j)^{th}$ entry in M is the frequency of occurrence of the ith term in the jth document in the database. In this context, a NMF computes r "topics" which are each a distribution on words (corresponding to the r columns of A) and each document (a column in M) can be expressed as a distribution on topics given by the corresponding column of W [16]. This example will be a useful metaphor for thinking about nonnegative factorization. In particular it justifies the assertion r should be small – the number of topics should be much smaller than the total number of documents in order for this representation to be meaningful. See Section A for more details.

Focusing on applications, and the overwhelming empirical evidence that heuristic algorithms do find good-enough factorizations in practice, motivates our next question.

QUESTION 2. *Can we design very efficient algorithms for NMF if we make reasonable assumptions about M?*

1.1 Our Results

We resolve the complexity of NMF when the target inner-dimension r is small (Question 1) . We give both an exact algorithm that runs in polynomial time for any constant value of r and we complement this with an intractability result that an exact algorithm that runs in time $(nm)^{o(r)}$ would yield a sub-exponential time algorithm for 3-SAT. Hence, under the Exponential Time Hypothesis [20] NMF cannot be solved exactly in time $(nm)^{o(r)}$.

THEOREM 1.1. *There is an exact algorithm for the NMF problem (where r is the target inner-dimension) that runs in time $O((nm)^{r^2 2^r})$.*

This result is based on algorithms for deciding the first order theory of the reals - roughly the goal is to express the decision question of whether or not the matrix M has nonnegative rank at most r as a system of polynomial equations and then to apply algorithms in algebraic geometry to determine if this semi-algebraic set is non-empty. The complexity of these procedures is dominated by the number of distinct variables occurring in the system of polynomial equations. In fact, the number of distinct variables plays an analogous role to VC-dimension, in a sense and the running time of algorithms for determining if a semi-algebraic set is non-empty depend exponentially on this quantity but depend only polynomially on the number of constraints and the maximum degree. Additionally these algorithms can compute successive approximations to a point in the set at the cost of an additional factor in the run time that is polynomial in the number of bits in the input and output.

The naive formulation of the NMF decision problem as a non-emptiness problem is to use $nr + mr$ variables, one for each entry in A or W [8]. This would be unacceptable, since even for constant values of r, the associated algorithm would run in time exponential in n and m. So at the heart of our algorithm is a method to reduce the number of variables needed to define the associated semi-algebraic set. We are able to express the decision problem for NMF (of inner-dimension at most r) using $r^2 2^r$ distinct variables. Thus we obtain the algorithm quoted in the above theorem. Prior to our work (even for $r = 3$), the best known exact algorithms ran in exponential time and ours runs in polynomial time for any $r = O(1)$.

A natural requirement on A is that its columns be linearly independent. In most applications, NMF is used to express a large number of observed variables using a small number of hidden variables. If the columns of A are not linearly independent then Radon's Lemma implies that this expression can be far from unique. In the example from information retrieval, this translates to: there are candidate documents that can be expressed as a convex combination of one set of topics, or could alternatively be expressed as a convex combination of an entirely disjoint set of topics

negative rank must be the size of the largest set of columns in which no column can be written as a nonnegative combination of the rest. This is false, and has been the source of many incorrect proofs demonstrating a gap between rank and nonnegative rank. A correct proof finally follows from the results of Fiorini et al [11].

(see Section 2.1). When we add the requirement that the columns of A be linearly independent and that $rank(M) = r$ (again, see Section 2.1), we refer to the associated problem as the *Simplicial Factorization* (SF) problem. In this case the doubly-exponential dependence on r in the previous theorem can be improved to singly-exponential. Our algorithm is again based on the first order theory of the reals, but here the system of equations is much smaller so in practice one may be able to use heuristic approaches to solve this system.

THEOREM 1.2. *There is an exact algorithm for the SF problem (where r is the target inner-dimension) that runs in time* $O((nm)^{r^2})$.

We complement these algorithms with a fixed parameter intractability result. We make use of a recent result of Patrascu and Williams [30] (and engineer low-dimensional gadgets inspired by the gadgets of Vavasis [36]) to show that under the Exponential Time Hypothesis [20], there is no exact algorithm for NMF that runs in time $(nm)^{o(r)}$. This intractability result holds also for the SF problem.

THEOREM 1.3. *If there is an exact algorithm for the Simplicial Factorization problem (or for the NMF problem) that runs in time* $O((nm)^{o(r)})$ *then 3-SAT can be solved in* $2^{o(n)}$ *time on instances with n variables.*

Now we turn to Question 2. We consider the nonnegative matrix factorization problem under the "separability" assumption introduced by Donoho and Stodden [10] in the context of image segmentation. Roughly, this assumption asserts that there are r rows of A that can be permuted to form the identity matrix. If we knew the names of these rows, then computing a nonnegative factorization would be easy. The challenge in this context, is to avoid brute-force search (which runs in time n^r) and to find these rows in time polynomial in n, m *and* r. To the best of our knowledge the following is the first example of a polynomial-time algorithm that provably works under a non-trivial condition on the input matrix. It is elementary and may be practical.

THEOREM 1.4. *There is an exact algorithm that can compute a separable, nonnegative factorization* $M = AW$ *(where r is the inner-dimension) in time polynomial in n, m and r if such a factorization exists.*

Donoho and Stodden [10] argue that the separability condition is naturally met in the context of image segmentation. Additionally, Donoho and Stodden prove that separability in conjunction with some other conditions guarantee that the solution to the NMF problem is unique. Our theorem above is an algorithmic counterpart to their results, but requires only separability. Our algorithm can also be made noise tolerant, and hence works even when the separability condition only holds in an approximate sense. Indeed, an approximate separability condition is regarded as a fairly benign assumption and is believed to hold in many practical contexts in machine learning. For instance it is usually satisfied by derived parameters fitted to various generative models (e.g. LDA [5] in information retrieval) [4].

Lastly, we consider the case in which the given matrix M does not have an exact low-rank NMF but rather can be approximated by a nonnegative factorization with small inner-dimension.

THEOREM 1.5. *There is a* $2^{\mathrm{poly}(r \log(1/\epsilon))}\mathrm{poly}(n, m)$*-time algorithm that, given M for which there is a nonnegative factorization AW of inner-dimension r which is an* ϵ*- approximation to M in Frobenius norm, computes nonnegative* A' *and* W' *satisfying*

$$\|M - A'W'\|_F \le O(\epsilon^{1/2} r^{1/4}) \|M\|_F .$$

The rest of the paper is organized as follows: In Section 2 we give an exact algorithm for the SF problem and in Section 3 we give an exact algorithm for the general NMF problem. In Section 4 we prove a fixed parameter intractability result for the SF problem. And in Section 5 and Section 6 we give algorithms for the separable and noisy NMF problems. Throughout this paper, we will use the notation that M_i and M^j are the ith column and j^{th} row of M respectively.

2. SIMPLICIAL FACTORIZATION

Here we consider the simplicial factorization problem which is a restriction of the general NMF problem to the case in which the target inner-dimension r is equal to the rank of M. Hence in any factorization $M = AW$ (where r is the inner-dimension), A must have full column rank and W must have full row rank.

2.1 Rationale

Here we argue that the extra restriction imposed in simplicial factorization is natural in many contexts: we can assume through a re-scaling (see Section 5 for more details), that the columns of M, A and W all have unit ℓ_1 norm. The factorization $M = AW$ can be interpreted probabilistically: each column of M can be expressed as a convex combination (given by the corresponding column of W) of columns in A. In the example in the introduction, columns of M represent documents and the columns of A represent "topics". Hence a nonnegative factorization is an "explanation" of many observed variables by a small number of latent variables : each document can be expressed as a convex combination of the topics.

But if A does not have full column rank then this explanation is seriously deficient. This follows from a restatement of Radon's Lemma. Let $conv(A_U)$ be the convex hull of the columns A_i for $i \in U$.

OBSERVATION 1. *If A is an* $n \times r$ *(with* $n \ge r$*) matrix and* $rank(A) < r$*, then there are two disjoint sets of columns* $U, V \subset [r]$ *so that* $conv(A_U) \cap conv(A_V) \ne \emptyset$.

The observation implies that there is some candidate document x that can be expressed as a convex combination of topics (in U), or instead can be expressed as a convex combination of an entirely disjoint set (V) of topics. The end goal of NMF is often to use the representation of documents as distributions on topics to perform various tasks, such as clustering or information retrieval. But if (even given the set of topics in a database) it is this ambiguous to determine how we should represent a given document as a convex combination of topics, then the topics we have extracted cannot be very useful for clustering! In fact, it seems unnatural to not require the columns of A to be linearly independent!

We note that it is also natural to assume that the rank of M is r since any reasonable probabilistic process that generates columns of M from the columns of A would almost surely result in a matrix M whose rank equals the rank of A.

Hence, we arrive at a restriction to the general NMF problem that we call the *Simplicial Factorization* (SF) problem.

2.2 Algorithm for Simplicial Factorization

In this section we give an exact algorithm that solves the simplicial factorization problem in $(nm)^{O(r^2)}$ time. Let L be the maximum bit complexity of any coefficient in the input.

THEOREM 2.1. *There is an $O((nm)^{O(r^2)})$ time algorithm for deciding if the simplicial factorization problem has a solution of inner-dimension at most r. Furthermore, we can compute a rational approximation to the solution up to accuracy δ in time*

$$\text{poly}(L, (nm)^{O(r^2)}, \log 1/\delta).$$

In fact, we reduce the problem of finding a simplicial factorization to finding a point inside a semi-algebraic set with $poly(n)$ constraints and $2r^2$ real-valued variables (or deciding that this set is empty). This decision problem can in turn be solved using the well-known algorithm of Basu et. al.[3] in $n^{O(r^2)}$ time. We can instead use the algorithm of Renegar [32] (and a bound of $\text{poly}(L, (nm)^{O(r^2)})$ on the bit complexity of the coefficients in the solution due to Grigor'ev and Vorobjov [13]) to compute a rational approximation to the solution up to accuracy δ in time polynomial in $L, (nm)^{O(r^2)}$ and $\log 1/\delta$.

This reduction uses the fact that since A, W have full rank each has a "pseudo-inverse" A^+, W^+ which are dimension $r \times n$ and $n \times r$ matrices respectively and satisfy $A^+A = WW^+ = I_{r\times r}$. Thus $A^+M_i = A^+AW_i = W_i$ and similarly $M^jW^+ = A^j$.

DEFINITION 2.2. *Let $C = \{u_1, u_2, ..u_r\}$ be a basis for the columns of M in $\mathbb{R}^n$, and let $R = \{v_1, v_2, ...v_r\}$ be a basis for the rows of M in $\mathbb{R}^m$. Let M_C (a size $r \times m$ matrix) denote the columns of M expressed in the basis $\mathcal{C}$, and similarly let M_R (a size $n \times r$ matrix) denote the rows of M expressed in the basis $\mathcal{R}$.*

LEMMA 2.3. (Structure Lemma) *M has a simplicial factorization of inner-dimension r if and only if for every basis C for the columns and basis R for the rows of M, there are $r \times r$ matrices T_C, T_R such that:*

- *T_CM_C and M_RT_R are nonnegative matrices*
- *$M_RT_RT_CM_C = M$*

Proof: ("if") Suppose the conditions in the theorem are met. Then set $A = M_RT_R$ and $W = T_CM_C$. These matrices are nonnegative and have size $n \times r$ and $r \times m$ respectively, and furthermore are a factorization for M. Since $rank(M) = r$, A and W are a simplicial factorization.

("only if") Conversely suppose that there is a simplicial factorization $M = AW$. Let $\mathcal{C} = \{,,..\}$ and $\mathcal{R} = \{,,...\}$ be *arbitrary* bases for the columns and rows of M respectively. Let U and V be the corresponding $n \times r$ and $m \times r$ matrices. Let M_C and M_R be $r \times m$ and $n \times r$ representations in this basis for the columns and rows of M - i.e. $UM_C = M$ and $M_RV^T = M$.

Define $r \times r$ matrices $T_C = A^+U$ and $T_R = V^TW^+$ where A^+ and W^+ are the respective pseudoinverses of A, W. Let us check that this choice of T_C and T_R satisfies the conditions in the theorem.

We can re-write $T_CM_C = A^+UM_C = A^+M = W$ and hence the first condition in the theorem is satisfied. Similarly $M_RT_R = M_RV^TW^+ = MW^+ = A$ and hence the second and third condition are also satisfied. ■

3. GENERAL NMF

Here we consider the NMF problem where the factor matrices A, W need not have full rank.

THEOREM 3.1. *There is a $O((nm)^{cr^2 2^r})$ time deterministic algorithm that given an $n \times m$ nonnegative matrix M outputs a factorization AW of inner dimension r if such a factorization exists.*

As in the Simplicial case the main idea will again be a reduction to an existence question for a semi-algebraic set, but this reduction is significantly more complicated than Lemma 2.3.

3.1 General Structure Theorem I

Our goal is to re-cast nonnegative matrix factorization (for constant r) as a system of polynomial inequalities where the number of variables is constant, the maximum degree is constant and the number of constraints is polynomially bounded in n and m. The main obstacle is that A and W are *large* - we cannot afford to introduce a new variable to represent each entry in these matrices. We will demonstrate there is always a "minimal" choice for A and W so that:

- There is a collection of linear transformations
$$T_1, T_2, \ldots T_{f(r)}$$
from the column-span of M to $\mathbb{R}^r$ and a choice function $\sigma_W : [m] \to [f(r)]$
- And there is a collection of linear transformations
$$S_1, S_2, \ldots S_{g(r)}$$
from the row-span of M to $\mathbb{R}^r$ and a choice function $\sigma_A : [n] \to [g(r)]$

And these linear transformations and choice functions satisfy the conditions:

- For each $i \in [n]$, $W_i = T_{\sigma_W(i)}M_i$.
- And for each $j \in [m]$, $A^j = M^jS_{\sigma_A(j)}$.

Furthermore, the number of possible choice functions σ_W is at most $m^{cr^2 f(r)}$ and the number of possible choice functions for σ_A is at most $n^{cr^2 g(r)}$.

These choice functions are based on the notion of a simplicial partition, which we introduce later. We then give an algorithm for enumerating all simplicial partitions (this is the primary bottleneck in the algorithm). Fixing the choice functions σ_W and σ_A, the question of finding linear transformations $T_1, T_2, ...T_{g(r)}$ and $S_1, S_2, ...S_{g(r)}$ that satisfy the above constraints (and the constraint that $M = AW$, and A and W are nonnegative) is exactly a system of polynomial inequalities with $O(r^2g(r))$ variables (each matrix T_i or S_j is $r \times r$), degree at most four and furthermore there are at most $O(mn)$ polynomial constraints.

In this subsection, we will give a procedure (which given A and W) generates a "minimal" choice for A and W (call this minimal choice A' and W'), and we will later establish that this "minimal" choice satisfies the structural property stated informally above.

DEFINITION 3.2. *Let $\mathcal{C}(A) \subset 2^{[r]}$ denote the subsets of $[r]$ corresponding to maximal independent sets of columns (of A). Similarly let $\mathcal{R}(W) \subset 2^{[r]}$ denote the subsets of $[r]$ corresponding to maximal independent sets of rows (of W).*

A basic fact from linear algebra is that all maximal independent sets of columns of A have exactly $rank(A)$ elements and all maximal independent sets of rows of W similarly have exactly $rank(W)$ elements.

DEFINITION 3.3. *Let $\succ_s$ be the total ordering on subsets of $[r]$ of size s so that if U and V are both subsets of $[r]$ of size s, $U \prec_s V$ iff U is lexicographically before V.*

DEFINITION 3.4. *Given a column M_i, we will call a subset $U \in \mathcal{C}(A)$ a minimal basis for M_i (with respect to A) if $M_i \in cone(A_U)$ and for all $V \in \mathcal{C}(A)$ such that $M_i \in cone(A_V)$ we must have $U \prec_s V$.*

CLAIM 3.5. *If $M_i \in cone(A)$, then there is some $U \in \mathcal{C}(A)$ such that $M_i \in cone(A_U)$.*

DEFINITION 3.6. *A proper chain (A, W, A', W') is a set of nonnegative matrices for which $M = AW$, $M = AW'$ and $M = A'W'$ (the inner dimension of these factorizations is r) and functions $\sigma_{W'} : [m] \to \mathcal{C}(A)$ and $\sigma_{A'} : [n] \to \mathcal{R}(W')$ such that*

1. *For all $i \in [m]$, $AW'_i = M_i$, $supp(W'_i) \subset \sigma_{W'}(i)$ and $\sigma_{W'}(i)$ is a minimal basis with respect to A for M_i.*
2. *For all $j \in [n]$, $A'_j W' = M^j$, $supp(A^j) \subset \sigma_{A'}(j)$ and $\sigma_{A'}(j)$ is a minimal basis with respect to W' for M^j.*

Note that the extra conditions on W' (i.e. the minimal basis constraint) is with respect to A and the extra conditions on A' are with respect to W'. This simplifies the proof that there is always some proper chain, since we can compute a W' that satisfies the above conditions with respect to A and then find an A' that satisfies the conditions with respect to W'.

LEMMA 3.7. *If there is a nonnegative factorization $M = AW$ (of inner-dimension r), then there is a choice of nonnegative A', W' of inner-dimension r and functions $\sigma_{W'} : [m] \to \mathcal{C}(A)$ and $\sigma_{A'} : [n] \to \mathcal{R}(W')$ such that (A, W, A', W') and $\sigma_{W'}, \sigma_{A'}$ form a proper chain.*

Proof: The condition that there is some nonnegative W for which $M = AW$ is just the condition that for all $i \in [m]$, $M_i \in cone(A)$. Hence, for each vector M_i, we can choose a minimal basis $U \in \mathcal{C}(A)$ using Claim 3.5. Then $M_i \in cone(A_U)$ so there is some nonnegative vector W'_i supported on U such $AW'_i = M_i$ and we can set $\sigma_{W'}(i) = U$. Repeating this procedure for each column M_i, results in a nonnegative matrix W' that satisfies the condition $M = AW'$ and for each $i \in [m]$, by design $supp(W'_i) \subset \sigma_{W'}(i)$ and $\sigma_{W'}(i)$ is a minimal basis with respect to A for M_i.

We can re-use this argument above, setting $M^T = (W'^T)A^T$ and this interchanges the role of A and W. Hence we obtain a nonnegative matrix A' which satisfies $M = A'W'$ and for each $j \in [n]$, again by design we have that $supp(A^j) \subset \sigma_{A'}(j)$ and $\sigma_{A'}(j)$ is a minimal basis with respect to W for M^j. ■

DEFINITION 3.8. *Let $\Pi(A, U)$ (for $U \in \mathcal{C}(A)$) denote the $r \times n$ linear transformation that is zero on all rows not in U (i.e. $\Pi(A, U)^j = \vec{0}$ for $j \notin U$) and restricted to U is $\Pi(A, U)^U = (A_U)^+$ (where the $+$ operation denotes the Moore-Penrose pseudoinverse).*

LEMMA 3.9. *Let (A, W, A', W') and $\sigma_{W'}$ and $\sigma_{A'}$ form a proper chain. For any index $i \in [m]$, let $U_i = \sigma_{W'}(i)$ and for any index $j \in [n]$ let $V_j = \sigma_{A'}(j)$. Then $W'_i = \Pi(A, U_i)M_i$ and $A'^j = M^j \Pi(W'^T, V_j)^T$.*

Notice that in the above lemma, the linear transformation that recovers the columns of W' is based on column subsets of A, while the linear transformation to recover the rows of A' is based on the row subsets of W' (not W).

Proof: Since (A, W, A', W') and $\sigma_{W'}$ and $\sigma_{A'}$ form a proper chain we have that $AW' = M$. Also $supp(W'_i) \subset U_i = \sigma_{W'}(i)$. Consider the quantity $\Pi(A, U_i)M_i$. For any $j \notin U_i$, $(\Pi(A, U_i)M_i)_j = 0$. So consider

$$(\Pi(A, U_i)M_i)_{U_i} = (A_{U_i})^+ AW'_i = (A_{U_i})^+ A_{U_i}(W'_i)_{U_i}$$

where the last equality follows from the condition $supp(W'_i) \subset U_i$. Since $U_i \in \mathcal{C}(A)$ we have that $(A_{U_i})^+ A_{U_i}$ is the $|U_i| \times |U_i|$ identity matrix. Hence $W'_i = \Pi(A, U_i)M_i$. An identical argument with W' replaced with A' and with A replaced by W'^T (and i and U_i replaced with j and V_j) respectively implies that $A'^j = M^j \Pi(W'^T, V_j)^T$ too. ■

Note that there are at most $|\mathcal{C}(A)| \leq 2^r$ linear trasformations of the form $\Pi(A, U_i)$ and hence the columns of W' can be recovered by a constant number of linear transformations of the column span of M, and similarly the rows of A' can also be recovered.

The remaining technical issue is we need to demonstrate that there are not too many (only polynomially many, for constant r) choice functions $\sigma_{W'}$ and $\sigma_{A'}$ and that we can enumerate over this set efficiently. In principle, even if say $\mathcal{C}(A)$ is just two sets, there are exponentially many choices of which (of the two) linear transformation to use for each column of M. However, when we use lexicographic ordering to tie break (as in the definition of a minimal basis), the number of choice functions is polynomially bounded. We will demonstrate that the choice function $\sigma_{W'} : [m] \to \mathcal{C}(A)$ arising in the definition of a proper chain can be embedded in a restricted type of geometric partitioning of M which we call a simplicial partition.

3.2 General Structure Theorem II

Here, we establish that the choice functions $\sigma_{W'}$ and $\sigma_{A'}$ in a proper chain are combinatorially simple. The choice function $\sigma_{W'}$ can be regarded as a partition of the columns of M into $|\mathcal{C}(A)|$ sets, and similarly the choice function $\sigma_{A'}$ is a partition of the rows of M into $|\mathcal{R}(W')|$ sets. Here we define a geometric type of partitioning scheme which we call a simplicial partition, which has the property that there are not too many simplicial partitions (by virtue of this class having small VC-dimension), and we show that the partition functions $\sigma_{W'}$ and $\sigma_{A'}$ arising in the definition of a proper chain are realizable as (small) simplicial partitions.

DEFINITION 3.10. *A (k,s)-simplicial partition of the columns of M is generated by a collection of k sets of s hyperplanes*

$$\mathcal{H}^1 = \{h_1^1, h_2^1, ...h_s^1\},$$

$$\mathcal{H}^2 = \{h_1^2, h_2^2, ...h_s^2\}, ...\mathcal{H}^k = \{h_1^k, h_2^k, ...h_s^k\}.$$

Let $Q_i = \{i' \text{ s.t. for all } j \in [s], h_j^i \cdot M_{i'} \geq 0\}$. Then this collection of sets of hyperplanes results in the partition

- $P_1 = Q_1$
- $P_2 = Q_2 - P_1$
- $P_k = Q_k - P_1 - P_2 ... - P_{k-1}$
- $P_{k+1} = [m] - P_1 - P_2 ... - P_k$

If $rank(A) = s$, we will be interested in a $(\binom{r}{s}, s)$-simplicial partition.

LEMMA 3.11. *Let (A, W, A', W') and $\sigma_{W'}$ and $\sigma_{A'}$ form a proper chain. Then the partitions corresponding to $\sigma_{W'}$ and to $\sigma_{A'}$ (of columns and rows of M respectively) are a $(\binom{r}{s}, s)$-simplicial partition and a $(\binom{r}{t}, t)$-simplicial partition respectively, where $rank(A) = s$ and $rank(W') = t$.*

Proof: Order the sets in $\mathcal{C}(A)$ according to the lexicographic ordering $\succ_s$, so that $V_1 \prec_s V_2 \prec_s ...V_k$ for $k = |\mathcal{C}(A)|$. Then for each j, let $\mathcal{H}^j$ be the rows of the matrix $(A_{V_j})^+$. Note that there are exactly $rank(A) = s$ rows, hence this defines a (k, s)-simplicial partition.

CLAIM 3.12. *$\sigma_{W'}(i) = j$ if and only if $M_i \in P_j$ in the (k, s)-simplicial partition generated by $\mathcal{H}^1, \mathcal{H}^2, ...\mathcal{H}^k$.*

Proof: Since (A, W, A', W') and $\sigma_{W'}$ and $\sigma_{A'}$ forms a proper chain, we have that $M = AW'$. Consider a column i and the corresponding set $V_i = \sigma_{W'}(i)$. Recall that V_j is the jth set in $\mathcal{C}(A)$ according to the lexicographic ordering $\succ_s$. Also from the definition of a proper chain V_i is a minimal basis for M_i with respect to A. Consider any set $V_{j'} \in \mathcal{C}(A)$ with $j' < j$. Then from the definition of a minimal basis we must have that $M_i \notin cone(A_{V_{j'}})$. Since $V_{j'} \in \mathcal{C}(A)$, we have that the transformation $(A_{V_{j'}})(A_{V_{j'}})^+$ is a projection onto $span(A)$ which contains $span(M)$. Hence $(A_{V_{j'}})(A_{V_{j'}})^+ M_i = M_i$, but $M_i \notin cone(A_{V_{j'}})$ so $(A_{V_{j'}})^+ M_i$ cannot be a nonnegative vector. Hence M_i is not in $P_{j'}$ for any $j' < j$. Furthermore, M_i is in Q_j: using Lemma 3.9 we have $\Pi(A, V_j)M_i = \Pi(A, V_j)AW_i' = W_i' \geq \vec{0}$ and so $(A_{V_j})^+ M_i = (\Pi(A, V_j)M_i)_{V_j} \geq \vec{0}$. ∎

We can repeat the above replacing A with W'^T and W' with A', and this implies the lemma. ∎

3.3 Enumerating Simplicial Partitions

Here we give an algorithm for enumerating all (k, s)- simplicial partitions (of, say, the columns of M) that runs in time $O(m^{ks(r+1)})$. An important observation is that the problem of enumerating all simplicial partitions can be reduced to enumerating all partitions that arise from a single hyperplane. Indeed, we can over-specify a simplicial partition by specifying the partition (of the columns of M) that results from each hyperplane in the set of ks total hyperplanes that generates the simplicial partition. From this set of partitions, we can recover exactly the simplicial partition.

A number of results are known in this domain, but surprisingly we are not aware of any algorithm that enumerates all partitions of the columns of M (by a single hyperplane) that runs in polynomial time (for $dim(M) \leq r$ and r is constant) without some assumption on M. For example, the VC-dimension of a hyperplane in r dimensions is $r + 1$ and hence the Sauer-Shelah lemma implies that there are at most $O(m^{r+1})$ distinct partitions of the columns of M by a hyperplane. In fact, a classic result of Harding (1967) gives a tight upper bound of $O(m^r)$. Yet these bounds do not yield an algorithm for efficiently enumerating this structured set of partitions without checking *all* partitions of the data.

A recent result of Hwang and Rothblum [18] comes close to our intended application. A separable partition into p parts is a partition of the columns of M into p sets so that the convex hulls of these sets are disjoint. Setting $p = 2$, the number of separable partitions is exactly the number of distinct hyperplane partitions. Under the condition that M is in general position (i.e. there are no t columns of M lying on a dimension $t - 2$ subspace where $t = rank(M) - 1$), Hwang and Rothblum give an algorithm for efficiently enumerating all distinct hyperplane partitions [18].

Here we give an improvement on this line of work, by removing any conditions on M (although our algorithm will be slightly slower). The idea is to encode each hyperplane partition by a choice of not too many data points. To do this, we will define a slight generalization of a hyperplane partition that we will call a hyperplane separation:

DEFINITION 3.13. *A hyperplane h defines a mapping (which we call a hyperplane separation) from columns of M to $\{-1, 0, 1\}$ depending on the sign of $h \cdot M_i$ (where the sign function is 1 for positive values, -1 for negative values and 0 for zero).*

A hyperplane partition can be regarded as a mapping from columns of M to $\{-1, 1\}$ where we adopt the convention that M_i such that $h \circ M_i$ is mapped to 1.

DEFINITION 3.14. *A hyperplane partition (defined by h) is an extension of a hyperplane separation (defined by g) if for all i, $g(M_i) \neq 0 \Rightarrow g(M_i) = h(M_i)$.*

LEMMA 3.15. *Let $rank(M) = s$, then for any hyperplane partition (defined by h), there is a hyperplane g that contains s affinely independent columns of M and for which h (as a partition) is an extension of g (as a separation).*

Proof: After an appropriate linear transformation (of the columns of M and the hyperplanes), we can assume that M is full rank. If the h already contains s affinely independent columns of M, then we can choose $g = h$. If not we can perturb h in some direction so that for any column with $h(M_i) = 0$, we maintain the invariant that M_i is contained on the perturbed hyperplane h'. Since $rank(M) = s$ this perturbation has non-zero inner product with some column in M and so this hyperplane h' will eventually contain a new column from M (without changing the sign of $h(M_i)$ for any other column). We can continue this argument until the hyperplane contains s affinely independent columns of M and by design on all remaining columns agrees in sign with h. ∎

LEMMA 3.16. *Let $rank(M) = s$. For any hyperplane h (which defines a partition), there is a collection of $k \leq s$ sets* *of (at most s) columns of M, $S_1, S_2, ..S_k$ so that any hyperplanes $g_1, g_2, ..g_k$ which contain $S_1, S_2, ...S_k$ respectively satisfy: For all i, $h(M_i)$ (as a partition) is equal to the value of $g_j(M_i)$, where j is the smallest index for which $g_j(M_i) \neq 0$. Furthermore these subsets are nested: $S_1 \supset S_2 \supset ... \supset S_k$.*

Proof: We can apply Lemma 3.15 repeatedly. When we initially apply the lemma, we obtain a hyperplane g_1 that can be extended (as a separation) to the partition corresponding to h. In the above function (defined implicitly in the lemma) this fixes the partition of the columns except those contained in g_1. So we can then choose M' to be the columns of M that are contained in g_1, and recurse. If S_2 is the largest set of columns output from the recursive call, we can add columns of M contained in g_1 to this set until we obtain a set of $s+1$ affinely independent columns contained in g_1, and we can output this set (as S_1). ■

THEOREM 3.17. *Let $rank(M) = s$. There is an algorithm that runs in time $O(m^s(s+2)^s)$ time to enumerate all hyperplane partitions of the columns of M.*

Proof: We can apply Lemma 3.16 and instead enumerate the sets of points $S_1, S_2, ...S_s$. Since these sets are nested, we can enumerate all choices as follows:

- choose at most s columns corresponding to S_1
- initialize an active set $T = S_1$
- until T is empty either
  - choose a column to be removed from the active set
  - or indicate that the current active set represents the next set S_i and choose the sign of the corresponding hyperplane

There are at most $O(m^s(s+2)^s)$ such choices, and for each choice we can then run a linear program to determine if there is a corresponding hyperplane partition. (In fact, all partitions that result from the above procedure will indeed correspond to a hyperplane partition). The correctness of this algorithm follows from Lemma 3.16. ■

This immediately implies:

COROLLARY 3.18. *There is an algorithm that runs in time $O(m^{ks^2})$ that enumerates a set of partitions of the columns of M that contains the set of all (k, s)-simplicial partitions (of the columns of M).*

3.4 Systems of Polynomial Inequalities

The results of Basu et al [3] give an algorithm for finding a point in a semi-algebraic set defined by $O(mn)$ constraints on polynomials of total degree at most d, and $f(r)$ variables in time $O((mnd)^{cf(r)})$. Using our structure theorem for nonnegative matrix factorization, we will re-cast the decision problem of whether a nonnegative matrix M has nonnegative rank r as an existence question for a semi-algebraic set.

THEOREM 3.19. *There is an algorithm for deciding if a $n \times m$ nonnegative matrix M has nonnegative rank r that runs in time $O((nm)^{O(r^2 2^r)})$. Furthermore, we can compute a rational approximation to the solution up to accuracy δ in time $\text{poly}(L, (nm)^{O(r^2 2^r)}, \log 1/\delta)$.*

We first prove the first part of this theorem using the algorithm of Basu et al [3], and we instead use the algorithm of Renegar [32] to compute a rational approximation to the solution up to accuracy δ in time $\text{poly}(L, (nm)^{O(r^2 2^r)}, \log 1/\delta)$.

Proof: Suppose there is such a factorization. By Lemma 3.7, there is also a proper chain. We can apply Lemma 3.11 and using the algorithm in Theorem 3.17 we can enumerate over a superset of simplicial partitions. Hence, at least one of those partitions will result in the choice functions $\sigma_{W'}$ and $\sigma_{A'}$ in the proper chain decomposition for $M = AW$.

Using Lemma 3.9 there is a set of at most 2^r linear transformations $T_1, T_2, ...T_{2^r}$ which recover columns of W' given columns of M, and similarly there is a set of at most 2^r linear transformations $S_1, S_2, ...S_{2^r}$ which recover the rows of A' given rows of M. Note that these linear transformations are from the column-span and row-span of M respectively, and hence are from subspaces of dimension at most r. So apply a linear transformation to columns of M and one to rows of M to to recover matrices M_C and M_R respectively (which are no longer necessarily nonnegative) but which are dimension $r \times m$ and $n \times r$ respectively. There will still be a collection of at most 2^r linear transformations from columns of M_C to columns of W', and similarly for M_R and A'.

We will choose r^2 variables for each linear transformation, so there are $2 \times r^2 \times 2^r$ variables in total. Then we can write a set of m linear constraints to enforce that for each column of $(M_C)_i$, the transformation corresponding to $\sigma_{W'}(i)$ recovers a nonnegative vector. Similarly we can define a set of n constraints based on rows in M_R.

Lastly we can define a set of constraints that enforce that we do recover a factorization for M: For all $i \in [m], j \in [n]$, let $i' = \sigma_{W'}(i)$ and $j' = \sigma_{A'}(j)$. Then we write the constraint $(M_C)^j S_{j'} T_{i'} (M_R)_i = M_i^j$. This constraint has degree at two in the variables corresponding to the linear transformations. Lemma 3.7 implies that there is some choice of these transformations that will satisfy these constraints (when we formulate these constraints using the correct choice functions in the proper chain decomposition). Furthermore, any set of transformations that satisfies these constraints does define a nonnegative matrix factorization of inner dimension r for M.

And of course, if there is no inner dimension r nonnegative factorization, then all calls to the algorithm of Basu et al [3] will fail and we can return that there is no such factorization. ■

The result in Basu et. al. [3] is a quantifier elimination algorithm in the Blum, Shub and Smale (BSS) model of computation [6]. The BSS model is a model for real number computation and it is natural to ask what is the bit complexity of finding a rational approximation of the solutions. There has been a long line of research on the decision problem for first order theory of reals: given a quantified predicate over polynomial inequalities of reals, determine whether it is true or false. What we need for our algorithm is actually a special case of this problem: given a set of polynomial inequalities over real variables, determine whether there exists a set of values for the variables so that all polynomial inequalities are satisfied. In particular, all variables in our problem are quantified by existential quantifier and there are no alternations. For this kind of problem Grigor'ev and Vorobjov [13] first gave a singly-exponential time algorithm that runs in $(nd)^{O(f(r)^2)}$ where n is the number of polynomial inequalities, d is the maximum degree of the polynomials and $f(r)$ is the number of variables. The bit complexity of the algorithm is poly$(L, (nd)^{O(f(r)^2)})$ where L is the maximum length of the coefficients in the input. Moreover, their algorithm also gives an upperbound of poly$(L, (nd)^{O(f(r))})$ on the number of bits required to represent the solutions. Renegar[32] gave a better algorithm that for the special case we are interested in takes time $(nd)^{O(f(r))}$. Using his algorithm with binary search (with search range bounded by Grigor'ev et.al.[13]), we can find rational approximations to the solutions with accuracy up to δ in time poly$(L, (nm)^{O(f(r))}, \log 1/\delta)$.

We note that our results on the SF problem are actually a special case of the theorem above (because our structural lemma for simplicial factorization is a special case of our general structure theorem):

COROLLARY 3.20. *There is an algorithm for determining whether the positive rank of a nonnegative $n \times m$ matrix M equals the rank and this algorithm runs in time $O((nm)^{cr^2})$.*

Proof: If $rank(M) = r$, then we know that both A and W must be full rank. Hence $\mathcal{C}(A)$ and $\mathcal{R}(W)$ are both just the set $\{1, 2, ...r\}$. Hence we can circumvent the simplicial partition machinery, and set up a system of polynomial constraints in at most $2r^2$ variables. ■

4. STRONG INTRACTABILITY

Here we show that exact simplicial factorization (of target inner-dimension r) cannot be solved in $(nm)^{o(r)}$ time unless 3-SAT can be solved in $2^{o(n)}$ time. Surprisingly, even the NP-hardness of the problem for general r was only proved quite recently by Vavasis [36] and our gadgets are inspired by those in [36]. Our reduction is based on the d-SUM Problem.

DEFINITION 4.1 (d-SUM). *In the d-SUM problem we are given a set of N values $\{s_1, s_2, ...s_N\}$ each in the range $[0, 1]$, and the goal is to determine if there is a set of d numbers (not necessarily distinct) that sum to exactly $d/2$.*

This definition for the d-SUM Problem is slightly unconventional in that here we allow repetition (i.e. the choice of d numbers need not be distinct). Patrascu and Williams [30] recently proved that if d-SUM can be solved in $N^{o(d)}$ time then 3-SAT has a sub-exponential time algorithm. In fact, in the instances constructed in [30] we can allow repetition of numbers without affecting the reduction since in these instances choosing any number more than once will never result in a sum that is exactly $d/2$. Hence we can re-state the results in [30] for our (slightly unconventional definition for) d-SUM.

THEOREM 4.2. *If $d < N^{0.99}$ and if d-SUM instances of N distinct numbers each of $O(d \log N)$ bits can be solved in $N^{o(d)}$ time then 3-SAT on n variables can be solved in time $2^{o(n)}$.*

Given an instance of the d-SUM, we will reduce to an instance of the Intermediate Simplex problem defined in [36].

DEFINITION 4.3 (INTERMEDIATE SIMPLEX). *Given a polyhedron $P = \{x \in \mathbb{R}^{r-1} : Hx \geq b\}$ where H is an $n \times (r-1)$ size matrix and $b \in \mathbb{R}^n$ such that the matrix $[H, b]$ has rank r and a set S of m points in $\mathbb{R}^{r-1}$, the goal of the Intermediate Simplex Problem is to find a set of points T that form a simplex (i.e. T is a set of r affinely independent points) each in P such that the convex hull of T contains the points in S.*

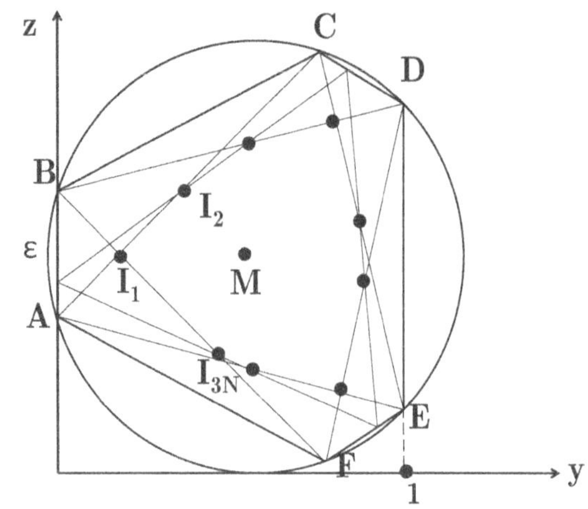

Figure 1: The Gadget

Vavasis [36] proved that Intermediate Simplex is equivalent to the Simplicial Factorization problem.

THEOREM 4.4 (VAVASIS, 2009 [36]). *There is a polynomial time reduction from Intermediate Simplex problem to Simplicial Factorization problem and vice versa and furthermore both reductions preserve the value of r.*

Interestingly, an immediate consequence of this theorem is that Simplicial Factorization is easy in the case in which $rank(M) = 2$ because mapping these instances to instances of intermediate simplex results in a one dimensional problem - i.e. the polyhedron P is an interval.

4.1 The Gadget

Given the universe $U = \{s_1, s_2, \ldots, s_N\}$ for the d-SUM problem, we construct a two dimensional Intermediate Simplex instance as shown in Figure 1. We will show that the Intermediate Simplex instance has exactly N solutions, each representing a choice of s_i. Later in the reduction we use d such gadgets to represent the choice of d numbers in the set U.

Recall for a two dimensional Intermediate Simplex problem, the input consists of a polygon $\mathcal{P}$ (which is the hexagon $ABCDEF$ in Figure 1) and a set of points $S = \{I_1, I_2, \ldots, I_3$ inside $\mathcal{P}$ (which are the dots, except for M). A solution to this two dimensional Intermediate Simplex instance will be a triangle inside $\mathcal{P}$ such that all the points in S are contained in the triangle (in Figure 1 ACE is a valid solution).

We first specify the polygon $\mathcal{P}$ for the Intermediate Simplex instance. The polygon $\mathcal{P}$ is just the hexagon $ABCDEF$ inscribed in a circle with center M. All angles in the hexagon are $2\pi/3$, the edges $AB = CD = EF = \epsilon$ where ϵ is a small constant depending on N, d that we determine later. The other 3 edges also have equal lengths $BC = DE = FA$.

We use $y(A)$ and $z(A)$ to denote the y and z coordinates for the point A (and similarly for all other points in the gadget). The hexagon is placed so that $y(A) = y(B) = 0$, $y(D) = y(E) = 1$.

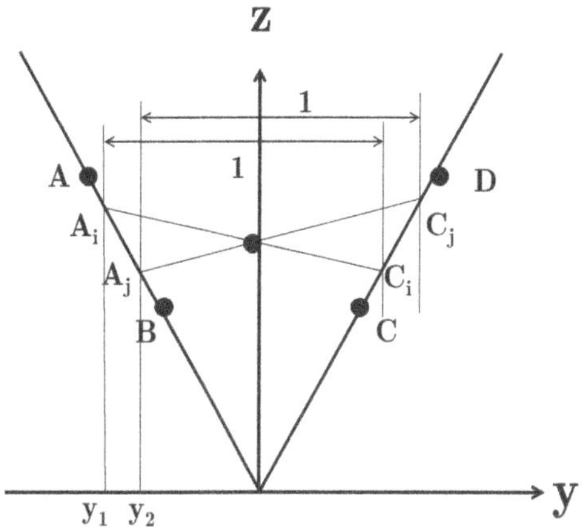

Figure 2: Proof of Lemma 4.5

Now we specify the set S of $3N$ points for the Intermediate Simplex instance. To get these points first take N points in each of the 3 segements AB, CD, EF. On AB these N points are called A_1, A_2, ..., A_N, and $|AA_i| = \epsilon s_i$. Similarly we have points C_i's on CD and E_i's on EF, $|CC_i| = |EE_i| = \epsilon s_i$. Now we have N triangles $A_iC_iE_i$ (the thin lines in Figure 1). We claim (see Lemma 4.5 below) that the intersection of these triangles is a polygon with $3N$ vertices. The points in S are just the vertices of this intersection.

LEMMA 4.5. *When $\epsilon < 1/50$, the points $\{A_i\}$, $\{C_i\}$, $\{E_i\}$ are on AB, CD, EF respectively and $AA_i = CC_i = EE_i = \epsilon s_i$, the intersection of the N triangles $\{A_iC_iE_i\}$ is a polygon with $3N$ vertices.*

Proof: Since the intersection of N triangles $A_iC_iE_i$ is the intersection of $3N$ halfplanes, it has at most $3N$ vertices. Therefore we only need to prove every edge in the triangles has a segment remaining in the intersection. Notice that the gadget is symmetric with respect to rotations of $2\pi/3$ around the center M. By symmetry we only need to look at edges A_iC_i. The situation here is illustrated in Figure 2.

Since all the halfplanes that come from triangles $A_iC_iE_i$ contain the center M, later when talking about halfplanes we will only specify the boundary line. For example, the halfplane with boundary A_iC_i and contains E_i (as well as M) is called halfplane A_iC_i.

The two thick lines in Figure 2 are extensions of AB and CD, now they are rotated so that they are $z = \pm\sqrt{3}y$. The two thin lines are two possible lines A_iC_i and A_jC_j. The differences between y coordinates of A_i and C_i are the same for all i (here normalized to 1) by the construction of the points A_i's and C_i's. Assume the coordinates for A_i, A_j are $(y_i, -\sqrt{3}y_i)$ and $(y_j, -\sqrt{3}y_j)$ respectively. Then the coordinates for the intersection is $(y_i+y_j+1, \sqrt{3}(1+y_i+y_j+2y_iy_j))$. This means if we have N segments with $y_1 < y_2 < \ldots < y_N$, segment i will be the highest one when y is in range $(y_{i-1}+y_i+1, y_i+y_{i+1}+1)$ (indeed, the lines with $j > i$ have higher slope and will win when $y > y_i+y_j+1 \geq y_i+y_{i+1}+1$; the lines with $j < i$ have lower slope and will win when $y < y_i + y_j + 1 \leq y_i + y_{i-1} + 1$).

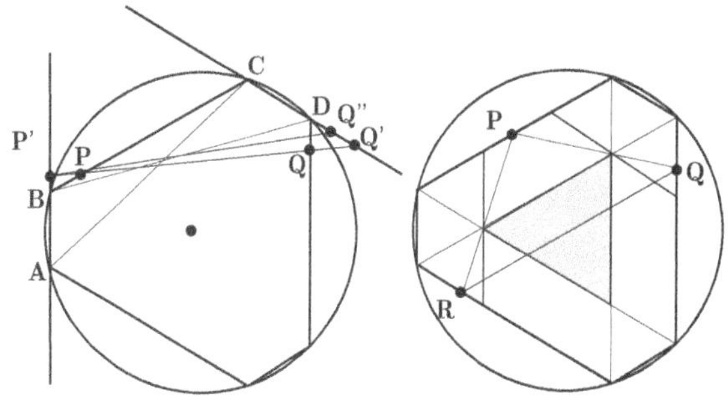

Figure 3: Proof of Lemma 4.6

We also want to make sure that all these intersection points are inside the halfplanes C_iE_i's and E_iA_i's. Since $\epsilon < 1/50$, all the y_i's are within $[-1/2 - 1/20, -1/2 + 1/20]$. Hence the intersection point is always close to the point $(0, \sqrt{3}/2)$, the distance is at most $1/5$. At the same time, since ϵ is small, the distances of this point $(0, \sqrt{3}/2)$ to all the C_iE_i's and E_iA_i's are all larger than $1/4$. Therefore all the intersection points are inside the other $2N$ halfplanes and the segments will indeed remain in the intersection. The intersection has $3N$ edges and $3N$ vertices. ■

The Intermediate Simplex instance has N obvious solutions: the triangles $A_iC_iE_i$, each one corresponds to a value s_i for the d-SUM problem. In the following Lemma we show that these are the only possible solutions.

LEMMA 4.6. *When $\epsilon < 1/1000$, if the solution of the Intermediate Simplex problem is PQR, then PQR must be one of the $A_iC_iE_i$'s.*

Proof: Suppose PQR is a solution of the Intermediate Simplex problem, since M is in the convex hull of $\{I_1, I_2, \ldots, I_{3N}\}$, it must be in PQR. Thus one of the angles $\angle PMQ$, $\angle QMR$, $\angle RMP$ must be at least $2\pi/3$ (their sum is 2π). Without loss of generality we assume this angle is $\angle PMQ$ and by symmetry assume P is either on AB or BC. We shall show in either of the two cases, when P is not one of the A_i's, there will be some I_k that is not in the halfplane PQ (recall the halfplanes we are interested in always contain M so we don't specify the direction).

When P is on AB, since $\angle PMQ \geq 2\pi/3$, we have $CQ \geq AP$ (by symmetry when $CQ = AP$ the angle is exactly $2\pi/3$). This means we can move Q to Q' such that $CQ' = AP$. The intersection of halfplane PQ' and the hexagon $ABCDEF$ is at least as large as the intersection of halfplane PQ and the hexagon. However, if P is not any of the points $\{A_i\}$ (that is, $|PQ'|/\epsilon \notin \{s_1, s_2, ..., s_N\}$), then PQ' can be viewed as $A_{N+1}C_{N+1}$ if we add $s_{N+1} = |AP|/\epsilon$ to the set U. By Lemma 4.5 introducing PQ' must increase the number of vertices. One of the original vertices I_k is not in the hyperplane PQ', and hence not in PQR. Therefore when P is on AB it must coincide with one of the A_i's, by symmetry PQR must be one of $A_iC_iE_i$'s.

When P is on BC, there are two cases as shown in Figure 3.

First observe that if we take $U' = U \cup \{1-s_1, 1-s_2, \ldots, 1-s_N\}$, and generate the set $S = \{I_1, I_2, \ldots, I_{6N}\}$ according to U', then the gadget is further symmetric with respect to flipping along the perpendicular bisector of BC. Now without loss of generality $BP \leq BC/2$. Since every I_k is now in the intersection of $2N$ triangles, in particular they are also in the intersection of the original N triangles, it suffices to show one of I_k ($k \in [6N]$) is outside halfplane PQ.

The first case (left part of Figure 3) is when $BP < \epsilon$. In this case we extend PQ to get intersection on AB (P') and intersection on CD (Q'). Again since $\angle PMQ \geq 2\pi/3$, we have $DQ \geq BP$. At the same time we know $\angle DQQ' \geq \angle P'PB$, so $DQ' > BP'$. Similar to the previous case, we take Q'' so that $CQ'' = AP'$. The intersection of hyperplane $P'Q''$ and the hexagon $ABCDEF$ is at least as large as the intersection of halfplane PQ and the hexagon. When $\epsilon < 1/1000$, we can check $AP' < 2\epsilon \ll 1/50$, therefore we can still view $P'Q''$ as some $A_{2N+1}C_{2N+1}$ for $s_{2N+1} < 2$. Now Lemma 4.5 shows there is some vertex I_k not in halfplane $P'Q''$ (and hence not in halfplane PQ).

The final case (right part of Figure 3) is when $BP \geq \epsilon$. In this case we notice the triangle with 3 edges AD, BE, CF (the shaded triangle in the figure) is contained in every $A_iC_iE_i$, thus it must also be in PQR. However, since $BC/2 \geq BP \geq \epsilon$, we know $AR \leq \epsilon$ and $DQ \leq \epsilon$. In this case PQR does not even contain the center M. ■

4.2 The Reduction

Suppose we are given an instance of the d-SUM Problem with N values $\{s_1, s_2, ...s_N\}$. We will give a reduction to an instance of Intermediate Simplex in dimension $r-1 = 3d+1$.

To encode the choice of d numbers in the set $\{s_1, s_2, ..., s_N\}$, we use d gadgets defined in Section 4.1. The final solution of the Intermediate Simplex instance we constructed will include solutions to each gadget. As the solution of a gadget always corresponds to a number in $\{s_1, s_2, ..., s_N\}$ (Lemma 4.6) we can decode the solution and get d numbers, and we use an extra dimension w that "computes" the sum of these numbers and ensures the sum is equal to $d/2$.

We use three variables $\{x_i, y_i, z_i\}$ for the ith gadget.

VARIABLES 1. *We will use* $3d+1$ *variables: sets* $\{x_i, y_i, z_i\}$ *for* $i \in [d]$ *and* w.

CONSTRAINTS 1 (BOX). *For all* $i \in [d]$, $x_i, y_i \in [0,1]$, $z_i \in [0,2]$ *and also* $w \in [0,1]$.

DEFINITION 4.7. *Let* $G \subset \mathbb{R}^2$ *be the hexagon* $ABCDEF$ *in the two-dimensional gadget given in the Section 4.1.Let* $H \subset \mathbb{R}^3$ *be the set* $conv(\{(x_i, y_i, z_i) \in \mathbb{R}^3 | (y_i, z_i) \in G, x_i = 1\}, \vec{0})$.

H is a tilted-cone that has a hexagonal base G and has an apex at the origin.

DEFINITION 4.8. *Let* R *be a* 7×3 *matrix and* $b \in \mathbb{R}^7$ *so that* $\{x | Rx \geq b\} = H$.

We will use these gadgets to define (some of the) constraints on the polyhedron P in an instance of intermediate simplex:

CONSTRAINTS 2 (GADGET). *For each* $i \in [d]$:

$$R(x_i, y_i, z_i) \geq b$$

Hence when restricted to dimensions x_i, y_i, z_i the ith gadget G is on the plane $x_i = 1$.

We hope that in a gadget, if we choose three points corresponding to the triangle for some value s_i, that of these three points only the point on the AB line will have a non-zero value for w and that this value will be s_i. The points on the lines CD or EF will hopefully have a value close to zero. We add constraints to enforce these conditions:

CONSTRAINTS 3 (CE). *For all* $i \in [d]$:

$$w \leq 1 - y_i + (1 - x_i)$$

These constraints make sure that points on CD or EF cannot have large w value.

Recall that we use $z(A)$ to denote the z coordinate of A in the gadget in Section 4.1.

CONSTRAINTS 4 (AB). *For all* $i \in [d]$:

$$w \in \Big[\frac{(z_i - z(A)x_i)}{\epsilon} \pm (\frac{10}{\epsilon} y_i + (1 - x_i))\Big]$$

These constraints make sure that each point A_i has the corresponding value s_i.

The AB and CE constraints all have the property that when $x_i < 1$ (i.e. the corresponding point is off of the gadget on the plane $x_i = 1$) then these constraints gradually become relaxed.

To make sure the gadget still works, we don't want the extra constraints on w to rule out some possible values for x_i, y_i, z_i's. Indeed we show the following claim.

CLAIM 4.9. *For all points in* $(x_i, y_i, z_i) \in H$, *there is some choice of* $w \in [0,1]$ *so that* x_i, y_i, z_i *and* w *satisfy the* CE *and* AB *Constraints.*

The proof is by observing that Constraints AB have almost no effect when $y > 0$ and Constraints CE have no effect when $y = 0$.

Constraints 1 to 4 define a polyhedron P in $3d+1$- dimensional space and furthermore the set of constraints that define P have full rank (in fact even the inequalities in the Box Constraints have full rank). Thus this polyhedron is a valid polyhedron for the Intermediate Simplex problem.

Next we specify the points in S for the Intermediate Simplex problem(each of which will be contained in the polyhedron P). Let I_k (for $k \in [3N]$) be the set S in the gadget in Section 4.1. As before, let $z(I_k)$ and $y(I_k)$ be the z and y coordinates of I_k respectively.

DEFINITION 4.10 (w-max(I_k)). *Let* w-max(I_k) *be the maximum possible* w*-value of any point* I *with* $x_i = 1$, $y_i = y(I_k)$, $z_i = z(I_k)$ *and* $x_j, y_j, z_j = 0$ *for all* $j \neq i$ *so that* I *is still contained in* P.

DEFINITION 4.11 (O, W, I_k^i, Q). *The set* S *of points for the Intermediate Simplex problem is*

O point: *For all* $i \in [d]$, $x_i, y_i, z_i = 0$ *and* $w = 0$

W point: *For all* $i \in [d]$, $x_i, y_i, z_i = 0$ *and* $w = 1$

I_k^i points: *For each* $i \in [d]$, *for each* $k \in [3N]$ *set* $x_i = 1/4$, $y_i = 1/4y(I_k)$, $z_i = 1/4z(I_k)$ *and for* $j \neq i$ *set* $x_j, y_j, z_j = 0$. *Also set* w *to be the* $1/4 \times w$-max(I_k).

Q point: *For each* $i \in [d]$, $x_i = 1/d$, $y_i = y(M)/d$, $z_i = z(M)/d$ *and* $w = 1/6$

This completes the reduction of 3-SUM to intermediate simplex, and next we establish the COMPLETENESS and SOUNDNESS of this reduction.

4.3 Completeness and Soundness

The completeness part is straight forward: for i^{th} gadget we just select the triangle that corresponds to s_{k_i}.

LEMMA 4.12. *If there is a set $\{s_{k_1}, s_{k_2}, ... s_{k_d}\}$ of d values (not necessarily distinct) such that $\sum_{i\in[d]} s_{k_i} = d/2$ then there is a solution to the corresponding Intermediate Simplex Problem.*

Proof: We will choose a set of $3d + 2$ points T: We will include the O and W points, and for each s_{k_i}, we will choose the triangle corresponding to the value s_{k_i} in the ith gadget. Recall the triangle is $A_{k_i}C_{k_i}E_{k_i}$ in the gadget defined in Section 4.1. The points we choose have $x_i = 1$ and y_i, z_i equal to the corresponding point in the gadget. We will set w to be s_{k_i} for the point on the line AB and we will set w to be zero for the other two points not contained in the line AB. The rest of the dimensions are all set to 0.

Next we prove that the convex hull of this set of points T contains all the points in S: The points O and W are clearly contained in the convex hull of T (and are in fact in T!). Next consider some point I_k^i in S corresponding to some intersection point I_k in the gadget G. Since I_k is in the convex hull of the triangle corresponding to s_{k_i} in the gadget G, there is a convex combination of the these three points $A_{k_i}, C_{k_i}, E_{k_i}$ in T (which we call J) so that $1/4J$ matches I_k^i on all coordinates except possibly the w-coordinate. Furthermore the point J has some value in the coordinate corresponding to w and this must be at most the corresponding value in I_k^i (because we chose the w-value in I_k^i to be $1/4 \times w\text{-max}(I_k)$). Hence we can distribute the remaining 3/4 weight among the O and W points to recover I_k^i exactly on all coordinates.

Lastly, we observe that if we equally weight all points in T (except O and W) we recover the point Q. In particular, the w coordinate of Q should be $\frac{1}{3d}\sum_{i=1}^{d} s_{k_i} = 1/6$. ■

Next we prove SOUNDNESS for our reduction. Suppose the solution is T, which is a set of $3d + 2$ points in the polyhedron P and the convex hull of points in T contains all the O, W, I_k^i, Q points (in Definition 4.11).

CLAIM 4.13. *The points O and W must be in the set T.*

Proof: The points O and W are vertices of the polyhedron P and hence cannot be expressed as a convex combination of any other set of points in P. ■

Now we want to prove the rest of the $3d$ points in set T is partitioned into d triples, each triple belongs to one gadget. Set $T' = T - \{O\} - \{W\}$.

DEFINITION 4.14. *For $i \in [d]$, let*

$$T_i' = \{Z \in T' \left| \begin{array}{l} j \neq i \Rightarrow x_j(Z), y_j(Z), z_j(Z) = 0, \\ \text{one of } x_i(Z), y_i(Z), z_i(Z) \neq 0 \end{array} \right. \}$$

CLAIM 4.15. *The sets T_i' partition T' and each contain exactly 3 nodes.*

Proof: The sets T_i' are disjoint, and additionally each set T_i' must contain at least 3 nodes (otherwise the convex hull of T_i' even restricted to x_i, y_i, z_i cannot contain the points I_k^i). This implies the Claim. ■

Recall the gadget in Section 4.1 is a two dimensional object, but it is represented as a three dimensional cone in our construction. We would like to apply Lemma 4.6 to points on the plane $x_i = 1$ (in this plane the coordinates y_i,z_i act the same as y, z in the gadget).

DEFINITION 4.16. *For each point $Z \in T_i'$, let $ext(Z) \in \mathbb{R}^3$ be the intersection of the line connecting the origin and $(x_i(Z), y_i(Z), z_i(Z))$ with the $x_i = 1$ base of the set $\{(x_i, y_i, z_i) | R(x_i, y_i, z_i) \geq b\}$. Let $ext(T_i')$ be the point-wise ext operation applied to each point in T_i'.*

Since the points I_k^i are in the affine hull of T_i' when restricted to x_i, y_i, z_i , we know $ext(I_k^i)$ must be in the convex hull of $ext(T_i')$. Using Lemma 4.6 in Section 4.1, we get:

COROLLARY 4.17. *$ext(T_i')$ must correspond to some triangle $A_{k_i}C_{k_i}E_{k_i}$ for some value s_{k_i}.*

Now we know how to decode the solution T and get the numbers s_{k_i}. We will abuse notation and call the 3 points in T_i' A_{k_i}, C_{k_i}, E_{k_i} (they were used to denote the corresponding points in the 2-d gadget in Section 4.1).We still want to make sure the w coordinate correctly "computes" the sum of these numbers. As a first step we want to show that the x_i of all points in T_i' must be 1 (we need this because the Constraints AB and CE are only strict when $x_i = 1$).

LEMMA 4.18. *For each point $Z \in T_i'$, $x_i(Z) = 1$*

Proof: Suppose, for the sake of contradiction, that $x_i(Z) < 1$ (for $Z \in T_i'$). Then consider the point Q. Since $\sum_{i\in[d]} x_i(Q) = 1$, and for any point in T $\sum_{i\in[d]} x_i \leq 1$, there is no convex combination of points in T that places non-zero weight on Z and equals Q.

Let T_i'' be $T_i' \backslash \{Z\}$, we observe that the points in T_i'' are the only points in T that have any contribution to (x_i, y_i, z_i) when we want to represent Q (using a convex combination). For now we restrict our attention to these three dimensions.When trying to represent Q we must have $1/d$ weight in the set T_i'' (because of the contribution in x_i coordinate). The y_i, z_i coordinates of Q are $y(M)/d$, $z(M)/d$ respectively. This means if we take projection to y_i, z_i plane M must be in the convex hull of T_i''. However that is impossible because no two points in $A_kC_kE_k$ contain M in their convex hull. This contradiction implies the Lemma. ■

LEMMA 4.19. *Any convex combination of points in T that equals the point Q must place equal weight on all points in T'.*

Proof: Using Lemma 4.18, we conclude that the total weight on points in T_i' is exactly $1/d$, and there is a unique convex combination of the points T_i' (restricted to y_i, z_i) that recover the point M which is the $1/3, 1/3, 1/3$ combination. This implies the Lemma. ■

Now we are ready to compute the w value of the point Q and show the sum of s_{k_i} is indeed $d/2$.

LEMMA 4.20 (SOUNDNESS). *When $\epsilon < N^{-Cd}$ for some large enough constant C, if there is a solution to the Intermediate Simplex instance, then there is a choice of d values that sum up to exactly $d/2$.*

Proof: As we showed in previous Lemmas, the solution to the Intermediate Simplex problem must contain O, W, and for each gadget i the solution has 3 points T_i' that correspond to one of the solutions of the gadget. Suppose for gadget i the triangle we choose is $A_{k_i}C_{k_i}E_{k_i}$. By Constraints AB we know $w(A_{k_i}) = s_{k_i}$, by Constraints CE we know $w(C_{k_i}) \leq \epsilon$ and $w(E_{k_i}) \leq \epsilon$.

By Lemma 4.19 there is only one way to represent Q, and $w(Q) = \frac{1}{3d}\sum_{i=1}^{d}[w(A_{k_i}) + w(C_{k_i}) + w(E_{k_i})] = 1/6$.

$$\sum_{i=1}^{d} s_{k_i} = \sum_{i=1}^{d} w(A_{k_i}) = \frac{d}{2} - \sum_{i=1}^{d}[w(C_{k_i}) + w(E_{k_i})]. \quad (1)$$

Since $w(C_{k_i})$ and $w(E_{k_i})$'s are small, we have

$$\sum_{i=1}^{d} s_{k_i} \in [d/2 - 2d\epsilon, d/2].$$

However the numbers only have $O(d \log N)$ bits and ϵ is so small, the only valid value in the range is $d/2$. Hence the sum $\sum_{i=1}^{d} s_{k_i}$ must be equal to $d/2$. ■

5. FULLY-EFFICIENT FACTORIZATION UNDER SEPARABILITY

Earlier, we gave algorithms for NMF that run in time exponential in r, and demonstrated that an $(nm)^{o(r)}$ time algorithm would yield a sub-exponential time algorithm for 3-SAT, and hence is unlikely. Here we consider conditions on the input that allow the factorization to be found even faster – in time polynomial in all of the parameters of the problem.

We consider the condition of *separability* (defined later) – in the context of topic models, this corresponds to assuming that for each topic there is some word that (when it occurs in a document) is a perfect indicator of the topic. This condition is usually satisfied [4] by model parameters fitted to various generative models (e.g. LDA [5] in information retrieval) and seems to be quite a natural condition.

Under the condition of separability, we give an algorithm that runs in time polynomial in n, m, and r and computes a nonnegative matrix factorization (if one exists). To the best of our knowledge this is the first example of an algorithm that runs in polynomial time in all of the parameters and provably works under a non-trivial condition (separability) on the input matrix. In Section 5.1, we give a noise-tolerant version of this algorithm.

We note that this condition first appeared in the work of Donoho and Stodden [10], who identified sufficient conditions for an NMF to be unique (motivated by applications of NMF to a database of images), but gave no algorithm for this task. Our algorithm provably works and assumes only one of their conditions is met.

Definition 5.1 (Separability). *A nonnegative factorization $M = AW$ is called* separable *if for each i there is some row $f(i)$ of A that has a single nonzero entry and this entry is in the ith column.*

Let us consider this condition in the context of topic models (see also the Introduction): Recall that each a column of M corresponds to a document. Each column of A represents a topic and its entries specify the probability that a word occurs in that topic. The NMF thus "explains" the ith document as AW_i where the column vector W_i has (nonnegative) coordinates summing to one—in other words, W_i represents a convex combination of topics. In practice, the total number of words n may number in the thousands or tens of thousands, and the number of topics in the dozens. Thus it is not unusual to find factorizations in which each topic is flagged by a word that appears only in that topic and not in the other topics [4]. The separability condition asserts that this happens for every topic[1].

For simplicity we assume without loss of generality that the rows of M are normalized to have unit ℓ_1-norm. After normalizing M, we can still normalize W (while preserving the factorization) by re-writing the factorization as $M = AW = (AD)(D^{-1}W)$ for some $r \times r$ nonnegative diagonal matrix D. By setting $D_{i,i} = \|W^i\|_1$ the rows of $D^{-1}W$ will all have l_1 norm 1. When rows of M and W are all normalized the rows of A must also have unit ℓ_1-norm because

$$\begin{aligned} 1 &= \left\|M^i\right\|_1 = \left\|\sum_{j=1}^{r} A_{i,j} W^j\right\|_1 = \sum_{j=1}^{r} A_{i,j} \left\|W^j\right\|_1 \\ &= \sum_{j=1}^{r} A_{i,j}. \end{aligned}$$

The third equality uses the nonnegativity of W. Notice that after this normalization, if a row of A has a unique nonzero entry (the rows in separability), that particular entry must be one.

We introduce the following definition:

Definition 5.2 (simplicial matrix). *A nonnegative matrix W is* simplicial *if no row in W can be represented in the convex hull of the remaining rows in W.*

The next lemma shows that without loss of generality we may assume W is simplicial.

Lemma 5.3. *If a nonnegative matrix M has a separable factorization AW of inner-dimension at most r then there is one in which W is simplicial.*

Proof: Suppose W is not simplicial, and let the jth row W^j be in the convex hull of the remaining rows. Then we can represent $W^j = \vec{u}^T W$ where $\vec{u}$ is a nonnegative vector with $|\vec{u}|_1 = 1$ and the jth coordinate is 0.

Now modify A as follows. For each row $A^{j'}$ in A that has a non-zero j^{th} coordinate, we zero out the jth coordinate and add $A^{j'}_j \vec{u}$ to the row $A^{j'}$. At the end the matrix is still nonnegative but whose j^{th} column is all zeros. So delete the jth column and let the resulting $n \times (r-1)$ matrix be A'. Let W' be the matrix obtained by deleting the jth row of W. Then by construction we have $M = A'W'$. Now we claim A' is separable.

Since A was originally separable, for each column index i there is some row, say the $f(i)^{th}$ row, that has a non-zero entry in the ith column and zeros everywhere else. If $i \neq j$ then by definition the above operation does not change the $f(i)^{th}$ row of A. If $i = j$ the jth index is deleted at the end. In either case the final matrix A' satisfies the separability condition.

Repeating the above operation for all violations of the simplicial condition we end with a separable factorization of M (again with inner-dimension at most r) where W is simplicial. ■

[1]More realistically, the word may appear in other topics only with negligible property instead of zero probability. This is allowed in our noise-tolerant algorithm later.

THEOREM 5.4. *There is an algorithm that runs in time polynomial in n, m and r and given a matrix M outputs a separable factorization with inner-dimension at most r (if one exists).*

Proof: We can apply Lemma 5.3 and assume without loss of generality that there is a factorization $M = AW$ where A is separable and W is simplicial. The separability condition implies that every row of W appears among the rows of M. Thus W is hiding in plain sight in M; we now show how to find it.

Say a row M^j is a *loner* if (ignoring other rows that are copies of M^j) it is not in the convex hull of the remaining rows. The simplicial condition implies that the rows of M that correspond to rows of W are loners.

CLAIM 5.5. *A row M^j is a loner iff M^j is equal to some row W^i*

Proof: Suppose (for contradiction) that a row in M^j is not a loner and but it is equal to some row W^i. Then there is a set S of rows of M so that M^j is in their convex hull and furthermore for all $j' \in S$, $M^{j'}$ is not equal to M^j. Thus there is a nonnegative vector $u \in \mathbb{R}^n$ that is 0 at the jth coordinate and positive on indices in S such that $u^T M = M^j$.

Hence $u^T AW = M^j = W^i$, but $u^T A$ must have unit ℓ_1-norm (because $\|u\|_1 = 1$, all rows of A have unit ℓ_1-norm and are all nonnegative), also $u^T A$ is non-zero at position j'. Consequently W^i is in the convex hull of the other rows of W, which yields a contradiction.

Conversely if a row M^j is not equal to any row in W, we conclude that M^j is in the convex hull of the rows of W. Each row of W appears as a row of A (due to the separability condition). Hence M^j is not a loner because M^j is in the convex hull of rows of M that are not equivalent to M^j itself. ∎

Using linear programming, we can determine which rows M^j are loners. Due to separability there will be exactly r different loner rows, each corresponds to one of the W^i. Thus we are able to recover W' that is equal to W after permutation over rows.We can compute a nonnegative A' such that $A'W' = M$, and such solution A' is necessarily separable (since it is just equal to A after permutation over columns). ∎

5.1 Adding Noise

In any practical setting, the data matrix M will not have an exact NMF of low inner-dimension since its entries are invariably subject to noise. Here we consider how to extend our separability-based algorithm to work in presence of noise.

We assume that the input matrix M' is obtained by perturbing each row of M by adding a vector of ℓ_1-norm at most ϵ, where M has a separable factorization of inner-dimension r. Alternatively, $\|M'^i - M^i\|_1 \le \epsilon$ for all i. Notice that the case in which the separability condition is only approximately satisfied is a subcase of this: If for each column there is some row in which the entry in that column is at least $1-\epsilon$ and the sum of the remaining row entries is less than ϵ then necessarily the matrix M' will satisfy the condition stated above. (Note that M, A, W have been scaled as discussed above.)

Depending on the level of noise (the value of ϵ) that we want to overcome, we will need to make a corresponding assumption about the matrix W: we require the unknown matrix W to be "robustly" simplicial instead of just simplicial.

DEFINITION 5.6 (α-ROBUST SIMPLICIAL). *We call W α-robust simplicial if no row in W has ℓ_1 distance smaller than α to the convex hull of the remaining rows in W. (Here all rows have unit ℓ_1-norm.)*

Recall from Lemma 5.3 that the simplicial condition can be assumed without loss of generality under separability. In general α-robust simplicial condition does not follow from separability. However, any reasonable generative model would surely posit that the matrix W —whose columns after all represents distributions—satisfies the condition above. For instance, if columns of W are picked randomly from the unit ℓ_1 ball then after normalization α is more than $1/10$. Regardless of whether or not one self-identifies as a Bayesianist, it seems reasonable that any suitably generic model to pick column vectors would tend to satisfy the α-robust-simplicial property.

THEOREM 5.7. *Suppose $M = AW$ where A is separable and W is α-robust simplicial. Let ϵ satisfy $20\epsilon/\alpha + 13\epsilon < \alpha$. Then there is a polynomial time algorithm that given M' such that for all rows $\|M'^i - M^i\|_1 < \epsilon$, finds a nonnegative matrix factorization $A'W'$ of the same inner dimension such that the ℓ_1 norm of each row of $M' - A'W'$ is at most $10\epsilon/\alpha + 7\epsilon$.*

Proof: Separability implies that for any column index i there is a row $f(i)$ in A whose only nonzero entry is in the ith column. Then $M^{f(i)} = W^i$ and consequently $\left\|M'^{f(i)} - W^i\right\|_1 < \epsilon$. Let us call these rows $M'^{f(i)}$ for all i the *canonical rows*. From the above description the following claim is clear since the rows of M can be expressed as a convex combination of W^i's.

CLAIM 5.8. *Every row M'^j has ℓ_1-distance at most 2ϵ to the convex hull of canonical rows.*

Proof: We have:

$$\left\|M'^j - \sum_{k=1}^{r} A_{j,k} M'^{f(k)}\right\|_1 \le \left\|M'^j - M^j\right\|_1 + \left\|M^j - \sum_{k=1}^{r} A_{j,k} M^{f(k)}\right\|_1 + \left\|\sum_{k=1}^{r} A_{j,k}(M^{f(k)} - M'^{f(k)})\right\|_1$$

and we can bound the right hand side by 2ϵ. ∎

Next, we show how to find the canonical rows. For a row M'^j, we call it a *robust-loner* if upon ignoring rows whose ℓ_1 distance to M'^j is less than $d = 5\epsilon/\alpha + 2\epsilon$, the ℓ_1-distance of M'^j to the convex hull of the remaining rows is more than 2ϵ. Note that we can identify robust-loner rows using linear programming.

The following two claims establish that a row of M'^j is a robust-loner if and only if it is close to some row W^i.

CLAIM 5.9. *If M'^j has distance more than $d+\epsilon$ to all of the W^i's, then it cannot be a robust loner.*

Proof: Such an M'^j has distance at least d to each of the canonical rows. The previous claim shows M'^j is close to the convex hull of the canonical rows and thus by definition it cannot be a robust-loner. ■

CLAIM 5.10. *All canonical rows are robust-loners.*

Proof: Since $\left\|M'^{f(i)} - W^i\right\|_1 \le \epsilon$, when we check if $M'^{f(i)}$ is a robust-loner (using linear programming), we leave out of consideration all rows that have ℓ_1-distance at most $5\epsilon/\alpha+\epsilon$ to W^i. In particular, this omits any row M'^j such that $M^j = \sum_{k=1}^r A_{j,k}W^k$ and $A_{j,i} \ge 1 - 5\epsilon/\alpha$. All remaining rows have $A_{j,i} \le 1 - 5\epsilon/\alpha$, and hence the ℓ_1 distance of W^i to $conv(W\backslash W^i)$ is at least α (by the α-robust simplicial property), we conclude that the distance between W^i and the convex hull of remaining M^j's must be at least $5\epsilon/\alpha*\alpha = 5\epsilon$. Since M' is close to M the ℓ_1-distance between $M'^{f(i)}$ and the convex hull of remaining rows M'^j's must be at least $5\epsilon - 2\epsilon = 3\epsilon$. Therefore $M'^{f(i)}$ is a robust-loner. ■

The previous claim implies that each robust-loner row is within ℓ_1-distance $d+\epsilon$ to some W^i and conversely, for every W^i there is at least one robust-loner row that is close to it. Since the ℓ_1-distances between W^i's are at least $4(d+\epsilon)$, we can apply distance based clustering on the robust-loner rows: place two robust-loner rows into the same cluster if and only if these rows are within ℓ_1-distance at most $2(d+\epsilon)$. Clearly we will obtain r clusters, one corresponding to each of the W^i's. Choose one row from each of the cluster, and using similar argument as Claim 5.8 we deduce that every row of M' is within $2(d+\epsilon)+\epsilon = 10\epsilon/\alpha+7\epsilon$ to the convex hull of the rows we selected. Therefore these rows form a nonnegative W' and we can find A' so that $\left\|M'^j - (A'W')^j\right\|_1 \le 10\epsilon/\alpha + 7\epsilon$ for all j. ■

6. APPROXIMATE NONNEGATIVE MATRIX FACTORIZATION

Here we consider the case in which the given matrix does not have an exact low-rank NMF but rather can be approximated by a nonnegative factorization with small inner-dimension. Unlike the algorithm in Theorem 5.7, the algorithm here works with general nonnegative matrix factorization: we do not make any assumptions on matrices A and W. Throughout this section we will use $\|\|_F$ to denote the Froebenius norm, $\|\|_2$ to denote the spectral norm and $\|\|$ applied to a vector will denote the standard Euclidean norm.

THEOREM 6.1. *Let M be an $n \times m$ nonnegative matrix such that there is a factorization AW satisfying $\|M - AW\|_F \le \epsilon \|M\|_F$, where A and W are nonnegative and have inner-dimension r. There is an algorithm that computes A' and W' satisfying*

$$\|M - A'W'\|_F \le O(\epsilon^{1/2}r^{1/4})\|M\|_F$$

in time $2^{\text{poly}(r\log(1/\epsilon))}\text{poly}(n, m)$.

Note that the matrix M need not have low rank, but we will be able to assume M has rank at most r without loss of generality: Let M' be the best rank at most r approximation (in terms of Frobenius norm) to M. This can be computed using a truncated singular value decomposition (see e.g. [12]). Since A and W have inner-dimension r, we get:

CLAIM 6.2. $\|M' - M\|_F \le \|M - AW\|_F$

Throughout this section, we will assume that the input matrix M has rank at most r - since otherwise we can compute M' and solve the problem for M'. Then using the triangle inequality, any good approximation to M' will also be a good approximation to M.

Throughout this section, we will use the notation A_t to denote the tth column of A and W^t to denote the tth row of W. Note that W^t is a row vector so we will frequently use A_tW^t to denote an outer-product. Next, we apply a simple re-normalization that will allow us to state the main steps in our algorithm in a more friendly notation.

LEMMA 6.3. *We can assume without loss of generality that for all t:*

- $\|W^t\| = 1$
- $\|A_t\| \le (1+\epsilon)\|M\|_F$
- *and* $\|A\|_F \le (1+\epsilon)\|M\|_F$.

Proof: We can write $AW = \sum_{t=1}^r A_tW^t$. So we may scale A_t, W^t to ensure that $\|W^t\| = 1$. Next, since A and W are nonnegative we have $\|AW\|_F \ge \|A_tW^t\|_F = \|A_t\|\|W^t\|$ and $\|AW\|_F \le (1+\epsilon)\|M\|_F$ and this implies the first condition in the lemma.

Next we observe

$$\|AW\|_F^2 = \sum_{i=1}^n\sum_{j=1}^m\Big[\sum_{t=1}^r (A_tW^t)_{i,j}\Big]^2 \ge \sum_{t=1}^r\sum_{i=1}^n\sum_{j=1}^m [A_tW^t]_{i,j}^2 = \|A\|_F^2,$$

where the inequality follows because all entries in A and W are nonnegative, and the last equality follows because $\|W^t\| = 1$. ■

Note that this lemma immediately implies that $\|W\|_F$ is at most $\sqrt{r}$.

The intuition behind our algorithm is to decompose the unknown matrix W as the sum of two parts: $W = W_0 + W_1$. The first part W_0 is responsible for how good AW is as an approximation to M (i.e., $\|M - AW_0\|_F$ is small) but could be negative; the second part W_1 has little effect on the approximation but is important in ensuring the sum W_0+W_1 is nonnegative. The algorithm will find good approximations to W_0, W_1.

What are W_0, W_1? Since removing W_1 has little effect on how good AW is as an approximation to M, this matrix should be roughly the projection of W onto the "less significant" singular vectors of A. Namely, let the singular value decomposition of A be

$$A = \sum_{t=1}^r \sigma_t u_t v_t^T. \quad (2)$$

and suppose that $\sigma_1 \ge \sigma_2 .... \ge \sigma_r$. Let t_0 be the largest t for which $|\sigma_t| \ge \delta\|M\|_F$ (where δ is a constant that is polynomially related to r and ϵ and will be specified later). Then set

$$W_0 = \sum_{t=1}^{t_0} (v_t v_t^T) W; \qquad W_1 = \sum_{t=t_0+1}^{r} (v_t v_t^T) W. \quad (3)$$

LEMMA 6.4. $\|M - AW_0\|_F \le \epsilon \|M\|_F + \delta\sqrt{r}\|M\|_F$

Proof:
By the triangle inequality

$$\|M - AW_0\|_F \le \|M - AW\|_F + \|AW_1\|_F.$$

Also

$$AW_1 = \sum_{t=t_0+1}^{r} \sigma_t (u_t v_t^T) W,$$

so we have

$$\begin{aligned}\|AW_1\|_F &= \left\| \sum_{t=t_0+1}^{r} \sigma_t (u_t v_t^T) W \right\|_F \\ &\le \left\| \sum_{t=t_0+1}^{r} \sigma_t (u_t v_t^T) \right\|_2 \|W\|_F \\ &\le \delta \|M\|_F \sqrt{r},\end{aligned}$$

where the last inequality follows because $\|W\|_F \le \sqrt{r}$ and the spectral norm of the matrix $\sum_{t=t_0+1}^{r}(u_t v_t^T)$ is at most $|\sigma_t| \le \delta \|M\|_F$. ■

Next, we establish a lemma that shows how W_0 is closely related to the matrix M. This will be useful when searching for (an approximation to) W_0:

LEMMA 6.5. *There is an $r \times m$ matrix W_0' whose rows are in the span of the rows of M and which satisfies $\|W_0' - W_0\|_F \le 2\epsilon/\delta$.*

Proof: Consider the matrix $A^+ = \sum_{t=1}^{t_0} \frac{1}{\sigma_t} v_t u_t^T$[2]. Thus A^+ is a pseudo-inverse of the truncated SVD of A. Note that $W_0 = A^+AW$ and the spectral norm $\|A^+\|_2$ is $\sigma_{t_0}^{-1} \le 1/(\delta\|M\|_F)$. Then we can choose $W_0' = A^+M$. Clearly, each row of W_0' is in the span of the rows of M. Furthermore, we have

$$\begin{aligned}\|W_0' - W_0\|_F &= \|A^+(M - AW)\|_F \\ &\le \|A^+\|_2 \|M - AW\|_F \\ &\le \frac{1}{\delta\|M\|_F} \cdot 2\epsilon \|M\|_F \\ &\le \frac{2\epsilon}{\delta}.\end{aligned}$$

and this completes the proof. ■

LEMMA 6.6. *There is an algorithm that runs in time*

$$2^{\text{poly}(r\log(1/\epsilon))}\text{poly}(n, m)$$

and finds W_0'', W_1' and A' such that $W_0'' + W_1' \ge 0$, $A' \ge 0$ and $\|M - A'(W_0'' + W_1')\|_F$ is at most

$$O(\frac{\epsilon}{\delta}\|A\|_F + \epsilon\|M\|_F + \delta\sqrt{r}\|M\|_F).$$

[2]Usually A^+ is the pseudo-inverse of A, here we abuse notation and use it for pseudo-inverse of the truncated version of A

Proof: The main idea is to use exhaustive enumeration to find a close approximation to the matrix W_0' of Lemma 6.5, and then use convex programming to find W_1', A':

The exhaustive enumeration is simple because the ϵ-net in d dimensions for radius t ball contains only $(tr/\epsilon)^{O(d)}$ points: try all vectors that lie in some ϵ_1-net in the span of the rows of M, where $\epsilon_1 = \epsilon/\delta$. Such an ϵ_1-net is easily enumerated in the provided time since the row vectors are smaller than $\|W\|_F = \sqrt{r}$ and their span is r-dimensional. Contained in this net there must be an W_0'' such that $\|A^+M - W_0''\|_F \le \epsilon_1$. Using Lemma 6.5, $\|W_0 - W_0'\|_2 \le 2\epsilon/\delta$, so the triangle inequality implies $\|W_0 - W_0''\|_F \le 2\epsilon/\delta + \epsilon_1 \le 4\epsilon/\delta$.

Next, we give a method to find suitable substitutes W_1', A' for W_1, A respectively so that $W_0' + W_1' \ge 0$ and $A'(W_0' + W_1')$ is a good approximation to M.

Let us assume we know the vectors v_i appearing in the SVD expression (2) and $\|A\|_F$. This is easy to guarantee since we can enumerate over all choices of the v_i's (which are unit vectors in $\mathbb{R}^r$) using a suitable ϵ_2-net where $\epsilon_2 = \min\{\frac{\epsilon}{\delta r}, 0.1\}$. Also, $\|A\|_F$ is a scalar value that can be easily guessed within multiplicative factor 1.01.

Let $W_1' = Z$ be the optimal solution to the following convex program:

$$\begin{aligned}\min \quad & \|A\|_F^2 \sum_{t=1}^{t_0} \left\|v_i^T Z\right\|^2 + \delta^2 \|M\|_F^2 \sum_{t=t_0+1}^{r} \left\|v_i^T Z\right\|^2 \\ s.t. \quad & W_0'' + Z \ge 0.\end{aligned}$$

This optimization problem is convex since the constraints are linear and the objective function is quadratic but convex. (In fact this optimization problem can be separated into m smaller convex programs because the constraints between different columns of W_1' are independent).

When the vectors we enumerated (denoted as $\{v_i'\}$) are close enough to the true values $\{v_i\}$, that is, when

$$\sum_{i=1}^{r} \left\|v_i' - v_i\right\|^2 \le \min\{\frac{\epsilon^2}{\delta^2 r}, 0.01\},$$

the value of the objective function after substituting v by v' can only change by at most $O(\frac{\epsilon^2}{\delta^2}\|A\|_F^2 + r\delta^2\|M\|_F^2)$. From now on we work with the true values of $\{v_i\}$. The claim below and arguments after will still be true although the vectors are not exact.

CLAIM 6.7. *The optimal value of this convex program is at most $O(\frac{\epsilon^2}{\delta^2}\|A\|_F^2 + r\delta^2\|M\|_F^2)$.*

Proof: We prove that $W_1' = W - W_0'' = (W_0 - W_0'') + W_1$ is a feasible solution and that the objective value of this solution is the value claimed in the lemma.

Since $W_1 = \sum_{t=t_0+1}^{r}(v_t v_t^T)W$ only contributes to the second term of the objective function in, we can upper bound the objective as

$$\|W_0 - W_0''\|_F^2 \|A\|_F^2 + (\|W_0 - W_0''\|_F + \|W_1\|_F)^2 \delta^2 \|M\|_F^2.$$

The proof is completed because $\|W_0 - W_0''\|_F = O(\frac{\epsilon}{\delta})$ and $\|W_1\|_F \le \|W\|_F = \sqrt{r}$. ■

After solving the convex program, we obtain a candidate W_1'. Let $W' = W_0'' + W_1'$. To get the right A' (since W' is fixed) we can find the A' that minimizes $\|M - A'W'\|_F^2$ by solving a least-squares problem. Clearly such an A' satisfies

$$\|M - A'(W_0'' + W_1')\|_F \leq \|M - A(W_0'' + W_1')\|_F$$

and the latter quantity is bounded by

$$\|M - AW_0\|_F + \|A(W_0 - W_0'')\|_F + \|AW_1'\|_F.$$

Lemma 6.4 bounds the first term and Lemma 6.5 bounds the second term. The square of the last term is bounded by the objective function of the convex program. ■

Finally, we choose $\delta = \frac{\sqrt{\epsilon}}{r^{1/4}}$ and we obtain A' and $W' = W_0'' + W_1'$ such that

$$\|M - A'W'\|_F \leq O(\epsilon^{1/2} r^{1/4}) \|M\|_F.$$

7. CONCLUDING REMARKS

Here, we initiated a rigorous study of nonnegative matrix factorization. Our hardness result rules out significant improvements over our worst-case results for fixed inner-dimension r. We believe that our poly(m, n, r)-time algorithm for finding separable factorizations may point the way for future work. What other plausible conditions can one impose on the factors in real-life applications? We also hope our work promotes further theoretical study of nonnegative rank.

This work is part of a broader agenda of bringing greater rigor to the analysis of algorithms used in machine learning. Currently, heuristic approaches are popular because the solution concepts are believed to be intractable. Our results, for example our algorithm for NMF under the separability condition, raise hope that sometimes the solution concepts may not be intractable after all.

Acknowledgements

We thank David Blei and Saugata Basu for useful discussions. We also thank participants in the summer reading group at Princeton, whose comments were helpful at early stages of this work.

8. REFERENCES

[1] A. Aho, J. Ullman and M. Yannakakis. On notions of information transfer in VLSI circuits. *STOC*, pp. 133–139, 1983.

[2] N. Alon and S. Onn. Separable partitions. *Discrete Applied Math.*, pp. 39–51, 1999.

[3] S. Basu, R. Pollack and M. Roy. On the combinatorial and algebraic complexity of quantifier elimination. *Journal of the ACM*, pp. 1002–1045, 1996. Preliminary version in *FOCS* 1994.

[4] D. Blei. Personal communication.

[5] D. Blei, A. Ng and M. Jordan. Latent Dirichlet allocation. *Journal of Machine Learning Research*, pp. 993–1022, 2003. Preliminary version in *NIPS* 2001.

[6] L. Blum, F. Cucker, M. Shub and S. Smale. *Complexity of Real Computations.* Springer Verlag, 1998.

[7] G. Buchsbaum and O. Bloch. Color categories revealed by non-negative matrix factorization of Munsell color spectra. *Vision Research*, pp. 559-563, 2002.

[8] J. Cohen and U. Rothblum. Nonnegative ranks, decompositions and factorizations of nonnegative matices. *Linear Algebra and its Applications*, pp. 149–168, 1993.

[9] S. Deerwester, S. Dumais, T. Landauer, G. Furnas and R. Harshman. Indexing by latent semantic analysis. *JASIS*, pp. 391–407, 1990.

[10] D. Donoho and V. Stodden. When does non-negative matrix factorization give the correct decomposition into parts? *NIPS*, 2003.

[11] S. Fiorini, T. Rothvoß and H. Tiwary. Extended formulations for polygons. Arxiv, 2011.

[12] G. Golub and C. van Loan. *Matrix Computations* The Johns Hopkins University Press, 1996.

[13] D. Yu. Grigor'ev and N.N. Vorobjov Jr. Solving systems of polynomial inequalities in subexponential time, Journal of Symbolic Computation, Volume 5, Issues 1-2, February-April 1988, pp. 37-64

[14] E. Harding. The number of partitions of a set of N points in k dimensions induced by hyperplanes. *Edinburgh Math. Society*, pp. 285–289, 1967.

[15] L. Henry. Schémas de nuptialité: déséquilibre des sexes et célibat. *Population* 24:457-486, 1969.

[16] T. Hofmann. Probabilistic latent semantic analysis. *UAI*, pp. 289–296, 1999.

[17] P. Hoyer. Non-negative matrix factorization with sparseness constraints. *Journal of Machine Learning Research*, pp. 1457–1469, 2004.

[18] F. Hwang and U. Rothblum. On the number of separable partitions. *Journal of Combinatorial Optimization*, pp. 423–433, 2011.

[19] A. Hyvärinen, J. Karhunen and E. Oja. *Independent Component Analysis.* Wiley Interscience, 2001.

[20] R. Impagliazzo and R. Paturi. On the complexity of k-SAT. *J. Computer and System Sciences* 62(2):pp. 367–375, 2001.

[21] J. Kleinberg and M. Sandler. Using mixture models for collaborative filtering. JCSS, pp. 49–69, 2008. Preliminary version in *STOC* 2004.

[22] R. Kumar, P. Raghavan, S. Rajagopalan and A. Tomkins. Recommendation systems: a probabilistic analysis. *JCSS*, pp. 42–61, 2001. Preliminary version in *FOCS* 1998.

[23] W. Lawton and E. Sylvestre. Self modeling curve resolution. *Technometrics*, pp. 617– 633, 1971.

[24] D. Lee and H. Seung. Learning the parts of objects by non-negative matrix factorization. *Nature*, pp. 788-791, 1999.

[25] D. Lee and H. Seung. Algorithms for non-negative matrix factorization. *NIPS*, pp. 556–562, 2000.

[26] L. Lovász and M. Saks. Communication complexity and combinatorial lattice theory. *JCSS*, pp. 322–349, 1993. Preliminary version in *FOCS* 1988.

[27] J. Matousek. *Lectures on Discrete Geometry.* Springer, 2002.

[28] N. Nisan. Lower bounds for non-commutative computation (extended abstract). *STOC*, pp. 410–418, 1991.

[29] P. Paatero and U. Tapper. Positive matrix factorization: a non-negative factor model with optimal utilization of error estimates of data values. *Environmetrics*, pp. 111-126, 1994.

[30] M. Patrascu and R. Williams. On the possibility of faster SAT algorithms. *SODA*, pp. 1065–1075, 2010.

[31] C. Papadimitriou, P. Raghavan, H. Tamaki and S.

Vempala. Latent semantic indexing: a probabilistic analysis. *JCSS*, pp. 217–235, 2000. Preliminary version in *PODS* 1998.

[32] J. Renegar. On the Computational Complexity and Geometry of the First-Order Theory of the Reals. Journal of Symbolic Computation, Volume 13, Issue 3, March 1992, pp. 255-352.

[33] A. Seidenberg. A new decision method for elementary algebra. *Annals of Math*, pp. 365–374, 1954.

[34] A. Tarski. A decision method for elementary algebra and geometry. *University of California Press*, 1951.

[35] W. Xu and X. Liu and Y. Gong. Document clustering based on non-negative matrix factorization. *SIGIR*, pp. 267–273, 2003.

[36] S. Vavasis. On the complexity of nonnegative matrix factorization. *SIAM Journal on Optimization*, pp. 1364-1377, 2009.

[37] M. Yannakakis. Expressing combinatorial optimization problems by linear programs. *JCSS*, pp. 441–466, 1991. Preliminary version in *STOC* 1988.

APPENDIX

A. EXTENDED DISCUSSION

Here we explain an application of NMF in detail. Perhaps the best approach is to contrast the NMF problem with a more well-known matrix factorization, the singular value decomposition (SVD): A $n \times m$ matrix M can be written as $M = \sum_i \sigma_i u_i v_i^T$ where the set $\{u_i\}_i$ and the set $\{v_i\}_i$ are orthonormal and $\sigma_1 \geq \sigma_2 .... \geq \sigma_r > 0$ (see e.g. [12]). In a number of applications, we imagine that the columns of M represent examples and the rows of M represent observed variables. In the context of information retrieval one often forms M as a "term-by-document" matrix where the $(i,j)^{th}$ entry in M is the frequency of occurrence of the ith term in the jth document in the database. The SVD of M (e.g. in Latent Semantic Indexing (LSI) [9]) is often interpreted as a method to extract "topics" in the database: The set of vectors $\{u_i\}_i$ (in a truncated SVD) is the subspace that contains the maximum variance of the documents, and projecting columns of M (i.e. documents) onto this basis is interpreted as a decomposition of each document into constituent topics. Documents can then be compared based on an inner-product in this space.

In some sense, the decomposition into "topics" generated via SVD is inconsistent with our intuitive notion of what a topic is. The vectors $\{u_i\}_i$ have both positive and negative values – these vectors are orthogonal. For example, imagine some documents are about cars and some others are about the weather. These "topics" would both be negatively correlated with mentioning the word "elephant" – i.e. documents about either topic are unlikely to use this word. What this means is that when we compute the similarity of a pair of documents, the documents will be judged to be more similar if both omit the word "elephant". But this is not consistent with our intuitive model, and would lead to spurious latent relationships. We would expect similarity to be based on positive occurrences only.

Hofman introduced a related approach (Probabilistic Latent Semantic Indexing [16]) in which each document is normalized to be a distribution on words, and the goal is to compute a small set of r topics (which are each distributions on words) and represent each document as a distribution on topics. This is equivalent (after an appropriate renormalization) to computing a nonnegative factorization of the term-by-document matrix M into AW, where the columns of A represent a set of r topics and each column of W expresses the corresponding document as a distribution on topics. The advantage of requiring this factorization to be nonnegative is that in Hofman's PLSI documents are judged to be similar based on words that they both contain. In LSI, documents can also be judged to be similar based on words they both omit. Arguably, Hofman's model is more consistent with our intuition and maybe this helps explain why (computational issues aside) a nonnegative factorization is, in many cases, preferred over an unrestricted one.

On Identity Testing of Tensors, Low-rank Recovery and Compressed Sensing

[Extended Abstract] *

Michael A. Forbes†
MIT CSAIL
Cambridge, USA
miforbes@mit.edu

Amir Shpilka‡
Faculty of Computer Science
Technion — Israel Institute of Technology
Haifa, Israel
shpilka@cs.technion.ac.il

ABSTRACT

We study the problem of obtaining efficient, deterministic, *black-box polynomial identity testing algorithms* for depth-3 set-multilinear circuits (over arbitrary fields). This class of circuits has an efficient, deterministic, white-box polynomial identity testing algorithm (due to Raz and Shpilka [ ]), but has no known such black-box algorithm. We recast this problem as a question of finding a low-dimensional subspace $\mathcal{H}$, spanned by rank 1 tensors, such that any non-zero tensor in the dual space $\ker(\mathcal{H})$ has high rank. We obtain explicit constructions of essentially optimal-size hitting sets for tensors of degree 2 (matrices), and obtain the first quasi-polynomial sized hitting sets for arbitrary tensors.

We also show connections to the task of performing *low-rank recovery* of matrices, which is studied in the field of compressed sensing. Low-rank recovery asks (say, over $\mathbb{R}$) to recover a matrix M from few measurements, under the promise that M is rank $\leq r$. In this work, we restrict our attention to recovering matrices that are exactly rank $\leq r$ using deterministic, non-adaptive, linear measurements, that are free from noise. Over $\mathbb{R}$, we provide a set (of size $4nr$) of such measurements, from which M can be recovered in $\mathcal{O}(rn^2 + r^3n)$ field operations, and the number of measurements is essentially optimal. Further, the measurements can be taken to be all rank-1 matrices, or all sparse matrices. To the best of our knowledge no explicit constructions with those properties were known prior to this work.

We also give a more formal connection between low-rank recovery and the task of *sparse (vector) recovery*: any sparse-recovery algorithm that exactly recovers vectors of length n and sparsity $2r$, using m non-adaptive measurements, yields a low-rank recovery scheme for exactly recovering $n \times n$ matrices of rank $\leq r$, making $2nm$ non-adaptive measurements. Furthermore, if the sparse-recovery algorithm runs in time τ, then the low-rank recovery algorithm runs in time $\mathcal{O}(rn^2 + n\tau)$. We obtain this reduction using linear-algebraic techniques, and not using convex optimization, which is more commonly seen in compressed sensing algorithms.

Finally, we also make a connection to *rank-metric codes*, as studied in coding theory. These are codes with codewords consisting of matrices (or tensors) where the distance of matrices M and N is $\text{rank}(M - N)$, as opposed to the usual hamming metric. We obtain essentially optimal-rate codes over matrices, and provide an efficient decoding algorithm. We obtain codes over tensors as well, with poorer rate, but still with efficient decoding.

Categories and Subject Descriptors

F.2.1 [**Analysis of Algorithms and Problem Complexity**]: Numerical Algorithms and Problems; E.4 [**Data**]: Coding and Information Theory

General Terms

Theory

Keywords

Polynomial Identity Testing, Low-rank Recovery, Sparse Recovery, Tensor Rank, Derandomization

1. INTRODUCTION

We start with a motivating example. Let $\mathbf{x}$ and $\mathbf{y}$ be vectors of n variables each. Let M be an $n \times n$ matrix (over some field, say $\mathbb{R}$), and define the quadratic form

$$f_M(\mathbf{x}, \mathbf{y}) \stackrel{\text{def}}{=} \mathbf{x}^\dagger M \mathbf{y} .$$

Suppose now that we are given an oracle to f_M, that can evaluate f_M on inputs $(\mathbf{x}, \mathbf{y})$ that we supply. The type of question we consider is: how many (deterministically chosen) evaluations of f_M must we make in order to determine whether M is non-zero?

It is not hard to show that n^2 evaluations to f_M are necessary and sufficient to determine whether M is non-zero. The

9*A full version of this paper is available at http://arxiv.org/abs/1111.0663

†Supported by NSF grant 6919791, MIT CSAIL and a Siebel Scholarship.

‡The research leading to these results has received funding from the European Community's Seventh Framework Programme (FP7/2007-2013) under grant agreement number 257575.

question becomes more interesting when we are promised that $\text{rank}(M) \leq r$. That is, given that $\text{rank}(M) \leq r$, can we (deterministically) determine whether $M = 0$ using $\ll n^2$ evaluations of f_M? It is not hard to show that there (non-explicitly) *exist* $\approx 2nr$ evaluations to determine whether $M = 0$, and one of the new results in this paper is to give an *explicit* construction of $2nr$ such evaluations (over $\mathbb{R}$).

We also consider various generalizations of this problem. The first generalization is to move from matrices (which are in a sense 2 dimensional) to the more general notion of *tensors* (which are in a sense d-dimensional). That is, a tensor is a map $T : [n]^d \to \mathbb{F}$ and like a matrix we can define a polynomial

$$f_T(x_{1,1}, \ldots, x_{1,n}, \ldots, x_{d,1}, \ldots, x_{d,n}) \stackrel{\text{def}}{=} \sum_{i_1,\ldots,i_d \in [n]} T(i_1, \ldots, i_d) \prod_{j=1}^{d} x_{j,i_j} .$$

As with matrices, tensors have a notion of rank (defined later), and we can ask: given that $\text{rank}(T) \leq r$ how many (deterministically chosen) evaluations of f_T are needed to determine whether $T = 0$. As $T = 0$ iff $f_T = 0$, we see that this problem is an instance of *polynomial identity testing*, which asks: given oracle access to a polynomial f that is somehow "simple", how many (deterministically chosen) queries to f are needed to determine whether $f = 0$?

The above questions ask whether a certain matrix or tensor is zero. However, we can also ask for more, and seek to reconstruct this matrix/tensor fully. That is, how many (deterministically chosen) evaluations to f_M are needed to determine M? This question can be seen to be related to compressed sensing and sparse recovery, where the goal is to reconstruct a "simple" object from "few" measurements. In this case, "simple" refers to the matrix being low-rank, as opposed to a vector being sparse. As above, it is not hard to show that there *exist* $\approx 4nr$ evaluations that determine M, and this paper gives an *explicit* construction of $4nr$ such evaluations, as well as an efficient algorithm to reconstruct M from these evaluations.

We will now place this work in a broader context by providing background on polynomial identity testing, compressed sensing and low-rank recovery and the theory of rank-metric codes.

1.1 Polynomial Identity Testing

Polynomial identity testing (PIT) is the problem of deciding whether a polynomial (specified by an arithmetic circuit) computes the identically zero polynomial. The obvious deterministic algorithm that completely expands the polynomial unfortunately takes exponential time. This is in contrast to the fact that there are several (quite simple) randomized algorithms that solve this problem quite efficiently. Further, some of these randomized algorithms treat the polynomial as a *black-box*, so that they only use the arithmetic circuit to evaluate the polynomial on chosen points, as opposed to a *white-box* algorithm which can examine the internal structure of the circuit. Even in the white-box model, no efficient deterministic algorithms are known for general circuits.

Understanding the deterministic complexity of PIT has come to be an important problem in theoretical computer science. Starting with the work of Kabanets and Impagliazzo [ ], it has been shown that the existence of efficient deterministic (white-box) algorithms for PIT has a tight connection with the existence of explicit functions with large circuit complexity. As proving lower bounds on circuit complexity is one of the major goals of theoretical computer science, this has led to much research into PIT.

Stronger connections are known when the deterministic algorithms are black-box. For, any such algorithm corresponds to a *hitting set*, which is a set of evaluation points such that any small arithmetic circuit computing a non-zero polynomial must evaluate to non-zero on at least one point in the set. Heintz and Schnorr [ ], as well as Agrawal [ ], showed that any deterministic black-box PIT algorithm very easily yields explicit polynomials that have large arithmetic circuit complexity. Moreover, Agrawal and Vinay [ ] showed that a deterministic construction of a polynomial size hitting set for arithmetic circuits of depth-4 gives rise to a quasi-polynomial sized hitting set for general arithmetic circuits. Thus, the black-box deterministic complexity of PIT becomes interesting even for constant-depth circuits. However, currently no polynomial size hitting sets are known for general depth-3 circuits. Much of recent work on black-box deterministic PIT has identified certain subclasses of circuits for which small hitting sets can be constructed, and this work fits into that paradigm. See [ ] for a survey of recent results on PIT.

One subclass of depth-3 circuits is the model of *set multilinear* depth-3 circuits, first introduced by Nisan and Wigderson [ ]. Raz and Shpilka [ ] gave a polynomial-time white-box PIT algorithm for non-commutative arithmetic formulas, which contains set-multilinear depth-3 circuits as a subclass. However, no polynomial-time black-box deterministic PIT algorithm is known for set-multilinear depth-3 circuits. The best known black-box PIT results for the class of set-multilinear circuits, with top fan-in $\leq r$ and degree d, are hitting sets of size $\min(n^d, \mathsf{poly}((nd)^r))$, where the first part of bound comes from a simple brute-force argument, and the second part of the bound ignores that we have set-multilinear polynomials, and simply uses the best known hitting sets for so-called $\Sigma\Pi\Sigma(k)$ circuits as established by Saxena and Seshadhri [ ]. For non-constant d and r, these bounds are super-polynomial. Improving the size of these hitting sets is the primary motivation for this work.

To connect PIT for set-multilinear depth-3 circuits with the above questions on matrices and tensors, we now note that any such circuit of top fan-in $\leq r$, degree d, on dn variables (and thus size $\leq dnr$), computes a polynomial f_T, where T is an $[n]^d$ tensor of rank $\leq r$. Conversely, any such f_T can be computed by such a circuit. Thus, constructing better hitting sets for this class of circuits is exactly the question of finding smaller sets of (deterministically chosen) evaluations to f_T to determine whether $T = 0$.

1.2 Low-Rank Recovery and Compressed Sensing

Low-rank Recovery (LRR) asks (for matrices) to recover an $n \times n$ matrix M from few *measurements* of M. Here, a measurement is some inner product $\langle M, H \rangle$, where H is an $n \times n$ matrix and the inner product $\langle \cdot, \cdot \rangle$ is the natural inner product on n^2 long vectors. This can be seen as the natural generalization of the *sparse recovery* problem, which asks to recover sparse vectors from few linear measurements. For, over matrices, our notion of sparsity is simply that of being low-rank.

Sparse recovery and compressed sensing are active areas of research, see for example [ ]. Much of this area focuses on constructing distributions of measurements such that the unknown sparse vector can be recovered efficiently, with high probability. Also, it is often assumed that the sequence of measurements will not depend on any of the measurement results, and this is known as *non-adaptive sparse recovery*. We note that Indyk, Price and Woodruff [ ] showed that *adaptive sparse recovery* can outperform non-adaptive measurements in certain regimes, but, in general, adaptivity cannot give much improvement [ ]. Much of the existing work also focuses on efficiency concerns, and various algorithms coming from convex programming have been used. As such, these algorithms tend to be stable under noise, and can recover approximations to the sparse vector (and can even do so only if the original vector was approximately sparse). One of the initial achievements in this field is an efficient algorithm for recovery of a k-sparse[1] approximation of n-entry vector in $\mathcal{O}(k \log(n/k))$ measurements [ ].

Analogous questions for low-rank recovery have also been explored (for example, see [ ] and references there in). Initial work (such as [,]) asked the question of low-rank *matrix completion*, where entries of a low-rank matrix M are revealed individually (as opposed measuring linear combinations of matrix entries). It was shown in these works that for an $n \times n$ rank $\le r$ matrix, $\mathcal{O}(nr\mathsf{polylog}n)$ noisy samples suffice for *nuclear-norm minimization* to complete the matrix efficiently. Further works (such as [ ] and [ ] for higher dimensional tensors) prove that a randomly chosen set of measurements (with appropriate parameters) gives enough information for low-rank recovery, other works (such as [,]) giving explicit conditions on the measurements that guarantee that the nuclear norm minimization algorithm works, and finally other works seek alternative algorithms for certain ensembles of measurements (such as[2] [ ]). As in the sparse recovery case, most of these work seek stable algorithms that can deal with noisy measurements as well as matrices that are only approximately low-rank. Finally, we note that some applications (such as quantum state tomography) have additional requirements for their measurements (for example, they should be easy to prepare as quantum states) and some work has gone into this as well [,].

We now make a crucial observation which shows that black-box PIT for the quadratic form f_M is actually very closely related to low-rank recovery of M. Note that

$$f_M(\mathbf{x}, \mathbf{y}) = \mathbf{x}^\dagger M \mathbf{y} = \langle M, \mathbf{x}^\dagger \mathbf{y} \rangle \ .$$

That is, an evaluation of f_M corresponds to a measurement of M, and in particular this measurement is realized as a rank-1 matrix. Thus, we see that any low-rank-recovery algorithm that only uses rank-1 measurement can also determine if M is non-zero, and thus also performs PIT for quadratic forms. Conversely, suppose we have a black-box PIT algorithm for rank $\le 2r$ quadratic forms. Note then that for any M, N with rank $\le r$, $M - N$ has rank $\le 2r$. Thus, if $M \neq N$ then f_{M-N} will evaluate to non-zero on some point in the hitting set. As $f_{M-N} = f_M - f_N$, it follows that a hitting set for rank $\le 2r$ matrices will distinguish M and N. In particular, this shows that information-theoretically any hitting set for rank $\le 2r$ matrices is also an LRR set. Thus, in addition to constructing hitting sets for the quadratic forms f_M, this paper will also use those hitting sets as LRR sets and also give efficient LRR algorithms for these constructions.

1.3 Rank-Metric Codes

Most existing work on LRR has focused on random measurements, whereas the interesting aspect of PIT is to develop deterministic evaluations of polynomials. As the main motivation for this paper is to develop new PIT algorithms, we will seek deterministic LRR schemes. Further, we will want results that are field independent, and so this work will focus on noiseless measurements (and matrices that are exactly of rank $\le r$). In such a setting, LRR constructions are very related to *rank-metric codes*. These codes (related to *array codes*), are error-correcting codes where the messages are matrices (or tensors) and the normal notion of distance (the Hamming metric) is replaced by the rank metric (that is, the distance of matrices M and N is $\mathrm{rank}(M - N)$). Over matrices, these codes were originally introduced independently by Gabidulin, Delsarte and Roth [, , , ,]. They showed, using ideas from BCH codes, how to get optimal (that is, meeting an analogue of the Singleton bound) rank-metric codes over matrices, as well as how to decode these codes efficiently. A later result by Meshulam [ ] constructed rank-metric codes where every codeword is a Hankel matrix. Roth [ ] also showed how to construct rank-metric codes from *any* hamming-metric code, but did not provide a decoding algorithm. Later, Roth [ ] considered rank-metric codes over tensors and gave decoding algorithms for a constant number of errors. Roth also discussed analogues to the Gilbert-Varshamov and Singleton bounds in this regime. This alternate metric is motivated by *crisscross errors* in data storage scenarios, where corruption can occur in bursts along a row or column of a matrix (and are thus rank-1 errors).

We now explain how rank-metric codes are related to LRR. Suppose we have a set of matrices $\mathcal{H}$ which form a set of (non-adaptive, deterministically chosen) LRR measurements that can recover rank $\le r$ matrices. Define the code $\mathcal{C}$ as the set of matrices orthogonal to each matrix in $\mathcal{H}$. Thus, $\mathcal{C}$ is a linear code. Further, given some $M \in \mathcal{C}$ and E such that $\mathrm{rank}(E) \le r$, it follows that $\mathcal{H}(M + E) = \mathcal{H}E$ (where we abuse notation and treat M and E as n^2-long vectors, and $\mathcal{H}$ as an $|\mathcal{H}| \times n^2$ matrix). That $\mathcal{H}$ is an LRR set means that E can be recovered from the measurements $\mathcal{H}E$. Thus the code $\mathcal{C}$ can correct r errors (and has minimum distance $\ge 2r + 1$, by a standard coding theory argument). Similarly, given a rank-metric code $\mathcal{C}$ that can correct up to rank $\le r$ errors, the parity checks of this code define an LRR scheme. Thus, a small LRR set is equivalent to a rank-metric code with good rate.

The previous subsection showed the tight connection between LRR and PIT. Via the above paragraph, we see that hitting sets for quadratic forms are equivalent to rank-metric codes, when the parity check constraints are restricted to be rank 1 matrices.

9[1] A vector is k-sparse if it has at most k non-zero entries.

9[2] Interestingly, [ ] use what they call *subspace expanders* a notion that was studied before in a different context in theoretical computer science and mathematics under the name of *dimension expanders* [,].

1.4 Reconstruction of Arithmetic Circuits

Even more general than the PIT and LRR problems, we can consider the problem of reconstruction of general arithmetic circuits only given oracle access to the evaluation of that circuit. This is the arithmetic analog of the problem of learning a function using membership queries. For more background on reconstruction of arithmetic circuits we refer the reader to [ ]. Just as with the PIT and LRR connection, PIT for a specific circuit class gives information-theoretic reconstruction for that circuit class. As we consider the PIT question for tensors, we can also consider the reconstruction problem.

The general reconstruction problem for tensors of degree d and rank r was considered before in the literature [, ,] where learning algorithms were given for any value of r. However, those algorithms are inherently randomized. Also of note is that the algorithms of [,] output a *multiplicity automata*, which in the context of arithmetic circuits can be thought of as an *arithmetic branching program*. In contrast, the most natural form of the reconstruction question would be to output a degree d tensor.

1.5 Our Results

In this subsection we informally summarize our results. We again stress that our results handle matrices of exactly rank $\leq r$, and we consider non-adaptive, deterministic measurements. We have two main results. The first gives a quasi-polynomially sized hitting sets for set-multilinear depth-3 circuits. Our second main result is the connection showing that low-rank recovery reduces to performing sparse-recovery, and that we can use dual Reed-Solomon codes to instantiate the sparse-recovery oracle to achieve a low-rank recovery set that only requires rank-1 (or even sparse) measurements. We find the fact that we can transform an algorithm for a combinatorial property (recovering sparse signals) to an algorithm for an algebraic property (recovering low-rank matrices) quite interesting.

Hitting Sets for Matrices and Tensors.

We begin with constructions of hitting sets for matrices, so as to get black box PIT for quadratic forms. By improving a construction of rank-preserving matrices from Gabizon-Raz [ ], we are able to show the following result, which we can then leverage to construct hitting sets.

THEOREM 1.1. *Let $n \geq r \geq 1$. Let $\mathbb{F}$ be a "large" field, and let $\omega \in \mathbb{F}$ have "large" multiplicative order. Let M be an $n \times n$ matrix of rank $\leq r$ over $\mathbb{F}$. Let $\hat{f}_M(x, y) = \mathbf{x}^\dagger M\mathbf{y}$ be the bivariate polynomial defined by the vectors $\mathbf{x} \in \mathbb{F}^n$ and $\mathbf{y} \in \mathbb{F}^n$ such that[3] $(\mathbf{x})_i = x^i$ and $(\mathbf{y})_i = y^i$.*

Then M is non-zero iff one of the univariate polynomials $\hat{f}_M(x, x), \hat{f}_M(x, \omega x), \ldots, \hat{f}_M(x, \omega^{r-1}x)$ is non-zero.

Intuitively this says that we can test if the quadratic form f_M is zero by testing whether each of r univariate polynomials are zero. As these univariate polynomials are of degree $< 2n$, it follows that we can interpolate them fully using $2n$ evaluations. As such a univariate polynomial is zero iff all of these evaluations are zero, this yields a $2nr$ sized hitting set. While this only works for "large" fields, we can combine this with results on simulation of large fields to derive results over any field with some loss. This is encapsulated in the next results for black-box PIT, where the log factors are unnecessary over large fields.

THEOREM 1.2. *Let $n \geq r \geq 1$. Let $\mathbb{F}$ be any field, then there is a $\mathsf{poly}(n)$-explicit[4] hitting set for $n \times n$ matrices of rank $\leq r$, of size $\mathcal{O}(nr \lg^2 n)$.*

For tensors of higher degree we prove the following theorem.

THEOREM 1.3. *Let $n, r \geq 1$ and $d \geq 2$. Let $n, r \geq 1$, $d \geq 2$. Over any field $\mathbb{F}$, there is an $\mathsf{poly}(n, d, r)^{\mathcal{O}(\lg d)} \cdot \mathcal{O}(\lg(dnr))^d$-explicit hitting set for $[\![n]\!]^d$-tensors of rank $\leq r$, of size $dn \cdot \mathcal{O}(dr^2 \ln(nd))^{\mathcal{O}(\lg d)} \cdot \mathcal{O}(\lg(dnr))^d$. If $|\mathbb{F}| \geq \mathsf{poly}(n, d, r)$, then there is an $\mathsf{poly}(n, d, r)^{\mathcal{O}(\lg d)}$-explicit hitting set for $[\![n]\!]^d$-tensors of rank $\leq r$, of size $dn \cdot \mathcal{O}(dr^2 \ln(nd))^{\mathcal{O}(\lg d)}$.*

Thus, if we are allowed access to a field extension to the base field (which is a common assumption in black-box polynomial identity testing), then this yields the first quasi-polynomial sized hitting set for tensors, improving on the $\min(n^d, \mathsf{poly}((nd)^r))$ sized hitting set achievable by invoking the best known results for $\Sigma\Pi\Sigma(k)$ circuits [ ]. We note that this result improves on the two obvious hitting sets. The first gives n^d tensors in the hitting set and is $\mathsf{polylog}(n, d, r)$-explicit while the second gives a set of size $\approx dnr$ while not being explicit at all. The above result non-trivially interpolates between these two results.

We also remark here that the actual construction claimed in the above result on tensors has qualitative similarities to a conjectured hitting set of Agrawal [ ]. One of the main differences is that our hitting set is on $\lg d$ variables (which we brute-force interpolate), but Agrawal conjectures that a single variable is sufficient.

Low-Rank Recovery.

As mentioned in the previous section, black-box PIT results imply LRR constructions in an information theoretic sense. Thus, the above hitting sets imply LRR constructions but the algorithm for recovery is not implied by the above result. To yield algorithmic results, we actually establish a stronger claim. That is, we first show that the above hitting sets embed a natural sparse-recovery set arising from the dual Reed-Solomon code. Then we develop an algorithm that shows that *any* sparse-recovery set gives rise to a low-rank-recovery set, and that recovery can be performed efficiently given an oracle for sparse recovery. This connection (in the context that any error-correcting code in the hamming metric yields an error-correcting code in the rank-metric) was independently made by Roth [ ] (see Theorem 3), who did not give a recovery procedure for the resulting LRR scheme. The next theorem, which is the main result of the paper, shows this connection is also efficient with respect to recovery.

THEOREM 1.4. *Let $n \geq r \geq 1$. Let $\mathcal{V}$ be a t-explicit set of (non-adaptive) measurements for $2r$-sparse-recovery for n-long vectors. Then there is a $\mathsf{poly}(n, t)$-explicit set $\mathcal{H}$, which*

[3]In this paper, vectors and matrices are indexed from zero, so $\mathbf{x} = (1, x, x^2, \ldots, x^{n-1})^\dagger$.

[4]A $n \times n$ matrix is t-explicit if each entry can be (deterministically) computed in t steps, where field operations are considered unit cost.

is a (non-adaptive) rank $\leq r$ low-rank-recovery set for $n \times n$ matrices, with a recovery algorithm running in time $\mathcal{O}(rn^2 + n\tau)$, where τ is the amount of time needed to do sparse-recovery from $\mathcal{V}$. Further, $|\mathcal{H}| = 2n|\mathcal{V}|$, and each matrix in $\mathcal{H}$ is n-sparse.

This result shows that sparse-recovery and low-rank recovery (at least in the exact case) are very closely connected. Interestingly, this shows that sparse-recovery (which can be regarded as a combinatorial property) and low-rank recovery (which can be regarded as an algebraic property) are tightly connected. Many fruitful connections have taken this form, such as in spectral graph theory, and perhaps the connection presented here will yield yet further results.

Also, the algorithm used in the above result is purely linear-algebraic, in contrast to the convex optimization approaches that many compressed sensing works use. However, we do not know if the above result is stable to noise, and regard this issue as an important question left open by this work.

When the above result is combined with our hitting set results, we achieve the following LRR scheme for matrices (as well as an LRR scheme for tensors, with parameters similar to the hitting set results mentioned above).

THEOREM 1.5. *Let $n \geq r \geq 1$. Over any field $\mathbb{F}$, there is an $\mathsf{poly}(n)$-explicit set $\mathcal{H}$, of $\mathcal{O}(rn \lg^2 n)$ size, such that measurements against $\mathcal{H}$ allow recovery of $n \times n$ matrices of rank $\leq r$ in time $\mathsf{poly}(n)$. Further, the matrices in $\mathcal{H}$ can be chosen to be all rank 1, or all n-sparse.*

We note again that over large fields these logarithmic factors are seen to be unneeded.

Some prior work [, , , ,] on LRR focused on finite fields, and as such based their results on BCH codes. The above result is based on (dual) Reed-Solomon codes, and as such works over any field (when combined with results allowing simulation of large fields by small fields). Other prior work [ ] on exact LRR permitted randomized measurements, while we achieve deterministic measurements.

Further, we are able to do LRR with measurements that are either all n-sparse, or all rank-1. As Roth [ ] independently observed, the n-sparse LRR measurements can arise from any (hamming-metric) error-correcting code (but he did not provide decoding). Tan, Balzano and Draper [ ] showed that random $(n \lg n)$-sparse measurements provide essentially the same low-rank recovery properties as random measurements. Thus, our results essentially achieve this deterministically.

We further observe that a specific code (the dual Reed-Solomon code) allows a change of basis for the measurements, and in this new basis the measurements are all rank 1. Recht et al. [ ] asked whether low-rank recovery was possible when the measurements were rank 1 (or "factored"), as such measurements could be more practical as they are simpler to generate and store in memory. Thus, our construction answers this question in the positive direction, at least for exact LRR.

Rank-Metric Codes.

Appealing to the connection between LRR and rank-metric codes, we achieve the following constructions of rank-metric codes.

THEOREM 1.6. *Let $\mathbb{F}$ be any field, $n \geq 1$ and $1 \leq r \leq n/2$. Then there are $\mathsf{poly}(n)$-explicit rank-metric codes with $\mathsf{poly}(n)$-time decoding for up to r errors, with parameters $[[n]^2, n^2 - 4(n-r)r \cdot \mathcal{O}(\lg^2 n), 2r+1]_{\mathbb{F}}$, and the parity checks on this code can be chosen to be all rank-1 matrices, or all n-sparse matrices.*

Earlier work on rank-metric codes over finite fields [, , , ,] achieved $[[n]^2, n(n-2r), 2r+1]_{\mathbb{F}_q}$ rank-metric codes, with efficient decoding algorithms. These are optimal (meeting the analogue of the Singleton bound for rank-metric codes). However, these constructions only work over finite fields. While our code achieves a worse rate, its construction works over any field, and over infinite fields the $\mathcal{O}(\lg^2 n)$ term is unneeded. Further, Roth [ ] observed that the resulting $[[n]^2, (n-2r)^2, 2r+1]$ code is optimal (see discussion of his Theorem 3) over algebraically closed fields (which are infinite).

We are also able to give rank-metric codes over tensors, which can correct errors up to rank $\approx n^{d/\lg d}$ (out of a maximum n^{d-1}), while still achieving constant rate. The rank-metric code arising from the naive low-rank recovery never achieves constant rate, and prior work by Roth [ ] only gave decoding against a constant number of errors.

THEOREM 1.7. *Let $\mathbb{F}$ be any field, $n, r \geq 1$ and $d \geq 2$. Then there are $\mathsf{poly}((nd)^d, r^{\lg d})$-explicit rank-metric codes with $\mathsf{poly}((nd)^d, r^{\lg d})$-time decoding for up to r errors, with parameters $[[n]^d, n^d - \mathcal{O}(d^2 n r^{\lg d} \lg(dn)), 2r+1]_{\mathbb{F}}$.*

We note here that our decoding algorithm will return the *entire* tensor, which is of size n^d. Trivially, any algorithm returning the entire tensor must take at least n^d time. In this case, the level of explicitness of the code we achieve is reasonable. However, a more desirable result would be for the algorithm to return a rank $\leq r$ representation of the tensor, and thus the n^d lower bound would not apply so that one could hope for faster decoding algorithms. Unfortunately, even for $d = 3$ an efficient algorithm to do so would imply P = NP. That is, if an algorithm (even one which is not a rank-metric decoding or low-rank recovery algorithm) could produce a rank $\leq r$ decomposition for any rank $\leq r$ tensor, then one could compute tensor-rank as it is the minimum r such that the resulting rank $\leq r$ decomposition actually computes the desired tensor (this can be checked in $\mathsf{poly}(n^d)$ time). However, Håstad [ ] showed that tensor-rank (over finite fields) is NP-hard for any fixed $d \geq 3$. It follows that for any (fixed) $d \geq 3$, if one could recover (even in $\mathsf{poly}(n^d)$-time) a rank $\leq r$ tensor into its rank $\leq r$ decomposition, then P = NP. While it is conceivable to instead output a rank $\leq r'$ decomposition, for some r' based on r, we do not explore this idea. We only discuss recovery of a tensor by reproducing its entire list of entries, as opposed to its more concise representation.

Finally, we remark that in [ ] Roth discussed the question of decoding rank-metric codes of degree $d = 3$, gave decoding algorithms for errors of rank 1 and 2, and wrote that "Since computing tensor rank is an intractable problem, it is unlikely that we will have an efficient decoding algorithm ... otherwise, we could use the decoder to compute the rank of any tensor. Hence, if there is any efficient decoding algorithm, then we expect such an algorithm to recover the error tensor without necessarily obtaining its rank. Such an algorithm, that can handle any prescribed number of errors, is not yet known." Thus, our work gives the first such algorithm for tensors of degree $d > 2$.

1.6 Proof Overview

In this section we give proof outlines of the results mentioned so far.

Hitting Sets for Matrices.

The main idea for our hitting set construction is to reduce the question of hitting (non-zero) $n \times n$ matrices to a question of hitting (non-zero) $r \times r$ matrices. Once this reduction is performed, we can then run the naive hitting set, which queries all r^2 entries. This can loosely be seen in analogy with the kernelization process in fixed-parameter tractability, where a problem depending on the input size, n, and some parameter, k, can be solved by first reducing to an instance of size $f(k)$, and then brute-forcing this instance.

To perform this kernelization, we first note that any $n \times n$ matrix M of rank exactly r can be written as $M = PQ^\dagger$, where P and Q are $n \times r$ matrices of rank exactly r. To reduce M to an $r \times r$ matrix, it thus suffices to reduce P and Q each to $r \times r$ matrices, denoted P' and Q'. As this reduction must preserve the fact that M is non-zero, we need that $P'Q' \neq 0$. We enforce this requirement by insisting that P' and Q' are also rank exactly r, so that $M' = P'Q'$ is also non-zero.

To achieve this rank-preservation, we turn to a lemma of Gabizon-Raz [ ] (we note that this lemma has been used before for black-box PIT [,]). They gave an explicit family of $\mathcal{O}(nr^2)$-many $r \times n$-matrices $\{A_\ell\}_\ell$, such that for any P and Q of rank exactly r, at least one matrix A_ℓ from the family is such that $\mathrm{rank}(A_\ell P) = \mathrm{rank}(A_\ell Q) = r$. Translating this result into our problem, it follows that one of the $r \times r$ matrices $A_\ell M A_\ell^\dagger$ is full-rank. The (i, j)-th entry of $A_\ell M A_\ell^\dagger$ is $\langle M, (A_\ell)_i (A_\ell)_j^\dagger \rangle$, where $(A_\ell)_i$ is the i-th row of A_ℓ. It follows that querying each entry in these $r \times r$ matrices corresponds to a rank 1 measurement of M, and thus make up a hitting set. As there were $\mathcal{O}(nr^2)$ choices of ℓ and r^2 choices of (i, j), this gives a $\mathcal{O}(nr^4)$-sized hitting set.

To achieve a smaller hitting set, we use the following sequence of ideas. First, we observe that in the above, we can always assume $i = 0$. Loosely, this is because when $A_\ell M A_\ell^\dagger$ is full-rank, none of its rows are all zero. Thus, only the first row of $A_\ell M A_\ell^\dagger$ needs to be queried to determine this. Second, we improve upon the Gabizon-Raz lemma, and provide an explicit family of rank-preserving matrices with size $\mathcal{O}(nr)$. This follows from modifying their construction so the degree of a certain determinant is smaller. To ensure that the determinant is a non-zero polynomial, we show that it has a unique monomial that achieves maximal degree, and that the term achieving maximal degree has a non-zero coefficient as a Vandermonde determinant (formed from powers of an element ω, which has large multiplicative order) is non-zero. Finally, we observe that the hitting set constraints can be viewed as constraints regarding polynomial interpolation. This view shows that some of the constraints are linearly-dependent, and thus can be removed. Each of the above observations saves a factor of r in the size of the hitting set, and thus produces an $\mathcal{O}(nr)$-sized hitting set.

Low-Rank Recovery.

Having constructed hitting sets, a standard argument implies that the same construction yields low-rank-recovery sets. As this lemma does not provide a recovery algorithm, we provide one. To do so, we must first change the basis of our hitting set. That is, the hitting set $\mathcal{B}$ yields a set of constraints on a matrix M, and we are free to choose another basis for these constraints, which we call $\mathcal{D}$. The virtue of this new basis is that each constraint is non-zero only on some k-diagonal (the entries (i, j) such that $i + j = k$). It turns out that these constraints are the parity checks of a dual Reed-Solomon code with distance $\Theta(r)$. This code can be decoded efficiently using standard BCH decoding techniques, such Berlekamp-Massey [,] or Gorenstein-Peterson-Zierler (which is also known as Prony's method [ ], which was developed in 1795). In the full version of this work, we give an exposition of the Gorenstein-Peterson-Zierler method, where we show how to syndrome-decode this code up to half its minimum distance, counting erasures as half-errors. Thus, given a $\Theta(r)$-sparse vector (which can be thought of as errors from the vector $\mathbf{0}$) these parity checks impose constraints from which the sparse vector can be recovered. Put another way, our low-rank-recovery set naturally embeds a sparse-recovery set along each k-diagonal.

Thus, in designing a recovery algorithm for our low-rank recovery set, we do more and show how to recover from any set of measurements which embed a sparse-recovery set along each k-diagonal. In terms of error-correcting codes, this shows that any hamming-metric code yields a rank-metric code over matrices, and that decoding the rank-metric code efficiently reduces to decoding the hamming-metric code.

To perform recovery, we introduce the notion of a matrix being in $(< k)$-upper-echelon form. Loosely, this says that $M^{(<k)}$, the entries (i, j) of the matrix with $i + j < k$, are in row-reduced echelon form. We then show that for any matrix M in $(< k)$-upper-echelon form, the k-diagonal is $2\,\mathrm{rank}(M)$-sparse. As an example, suppose $M^{(<k)}$ was entirely zero. It follows then that M is in $(< k)$-upper-echelon form. Further, the rows that have non-zero entries on the k-diagonal of M are then linearly-independent, as they form a triangular system. It follows that the k-diagonal can only have $\mathrm{rank}(M)$ non-zero entries. The more general case is slightly more complicated technically, but not conceptually. Thus, this echelon-form translates the notion of low-rank into the notion of sparsity.

The algorithm then follows naturally. We induct on k, first putting $M^{(<k)}$ into $(< k)$-upper-echelon form (using row-reduction), and then invoking a sparse-recovery oracle on the k-diagonal of M to recover it. This then yields $M^{(\leq k)}$, and we increment k. However, as described so far, the use of the sparse-recovery oracle is adaptive. We show that the row-reduction procedure can be understood such that the adaptive use of the sparse-recovery oracle can be simulated using non-adaptive calls to the oracle. More specifically, we will apply the measurements of the sparse-recovery oracle on each k-diagonal of M (which may not be sparse), and show how to compute the measurements of the adaptive algorithm (where the k-diagonals are sparse) from the measurements made. Putting these steps together, this shows that exact non-adaptive low-rank-recovery reduces to exact non-adaptive sparse-recovery. Instantiating this claim with our hitting sets from above gives a concrete low-rank-recovery set, with accompanied recovery algorithm.

Hitting Sets and Low-Rank Recovery for Tensors.

The results for matrices naturally generalize to tensors in the sense that an $[\![n]\!]^{2d}$ tensor can be viewed as an $[\![n^d]\!]^2$ matrix. However, we can do better. Specifically, the hitting set results were done via *variable reduction*, which shows that a rank $\le r$ bivariate polynomial

$$f_M(x, y) = (1, x, x^2, \ldots, x^{n-1})M(1, y, y^2, \ldots, y^{n-1})^\dagger$$

is zero iff a set of r univariate polynomials are all zero. Further, the degrees of these polynomials is only twice the original degree. As each univariate polynomial can be interpolated using $\mathcal{O}(n)$ measurements, this yields $\mathcal{O}(nr)$ measurements total. This motivates the more general idea of treating a degree d tensor as a d-variate polynomial, and showing that we can test whether this polynomial is zero by testing if a collection of d'-variate polynomials are zero, for $d' < d$. Recursing on this procedure then reduces the d-variate case to the univariate case, and the univariate case is brute-force interpolated.

The recursion scheme we develop for this is to show that a d-variate polynomial is zero iff r $d/2$-variate polynomials are zero, and this naturally leads to an $\mathcal{O}(dnr^{\lg d})$-sized hitting set. To prove its correctness, we show that the bivariate case (corresponding to matrices) applied to two groups of variables allows us to reduce to a single group of variables (with an increase in the number of polynomials to test). Finally, since we saw how to do low-rank recovery for matrices, and the tensor-case essentially only uses the matrix case, we can also turn this hitting set procedure into a low-rank recovery algorithm.

However, the above scheme will require elements of order $\approx n^d$, which makes the scheme not very explicit. Improving upon an earlier version of this paper, we show how techniques from Klivans and Spielman [ ] can be used to reduce the need for an element of large order. This allows the hitting set to be both quasi-polynomial sized and constructible in quasi-polynomial time.

Simulation of Large Fields by Small Fields.

Most all of the results mentioned require a field of size $\approx \mathsf{poly}(n, d, r)$. When getting results over small fields, we show that, with some loss, we can simulate such large fields inside the hitting sets. We break-up each tensor H in the original hitting set into new tensors $\tilde{H}_i$ such that for any $\mathbb{F}$-tensor T, $\langle T, H\rangle$ can be reconstructed from the set of values $\{\langle T, \tilde{H}_i\rangle\}_i$. To do so, we use the well-known representation of a extension field $\mathbb{K}$ of $\mathbb{F}$ as a field of matrices over $\mathbb{F}$. As the entries of a rank-1 tensor are multiplications of d elements of $\mathbb{K}$, we can expand these multiplications out as iterated matrix multiplications, which yields $(\dim_{\mathbb{F}} \mathbb{K})^{d+1}$ terms to consider, each of which corresponds to some $\tilde{H}_i$.

Note that if we did not insist on generating rank-1 matrices over the small field, then we could achieve this with a loss of only one log factor, by simply expanding each tensor to $\log(\mathsf{poly}(n, d, r)) = \mathcal{O}(\log(ndr))$ tensors, where the ith tensor consists of the ith bit of each of the entries of the original tensor.

Rank-Metric Codes.

The above techniques give the existence of low-rank recovery sets (and corresponding algorithms) for tensors, over any field. Via the connections presented in Section 1.3, this readily yields rank-metric codes with corresponding parameters.

2. DISCUSSION

We briefly discuss some directions for further research.

Reducing Noisy Low-Rank Recovery to Noisy Sparse Recovery.

We show that low-rank-recovery of matrices can be done using any sparse-recovery oracle. This reduction was for non-adaptive measurements, and was done in the presence of no noise. As much of the compressed sensing community is interested in the noisy case (so M is only close to rank $\le r$) the main open question of this work is whether the reduction extends to the noisy case.

Smaller Hitting Sets.

While the observations of Roth [ ] show that our hitting set for matrices is optimal over algebraically closed fields, our results over tensors with $d > 2$ are much larger than the existential bounds. Can these hitting sets be improved to size $\mathcal{O}(\mathsf{poly}(d)n^{o(d)}r^k)$ for $k = \mathcal{O}(1)$? As mentioned in the preliminaries section in the full version, any such hitting set with $k < 2$ would yield improved tensor-rank lower bounds. However, as the best tensor-rank lower bounds for $d = 3$ are $\Theta(n)$ and our hitting set (over infinite fields) yields this bound (with a smaller constant), even improving our hitting set for $d = 3$ by constant factors could yield interesting new results. Specifically, for $d = 3$ can one construct (say over infinite fields) a hitting set of size $\le nr^2/10$ for $[\![n]\!]^3$ tensors of rank $\le r$?

Large Field Simulation.

Our results show that hitting sets (and low-rank recovery sets) that involve tensors over an extension field imply hitting sets (and LRR sets) over the base field. While we show that we can preserve the rank-1 property of these tensors while doing so, it introduces an $\exp(d)$ factor in the size of the hitting set. Can this be improved?

Connection to rigidity.

In [ ] Valiant defined the notion of an (r, k)-rigid matrix and proved that if a matrix M is $(n/\log\log(n), n^\epsilon)$-rigid then the function $f(x) = M \cdot x$ cannot be computed by a linear sized logarithmic depth linear circuit. A matrix M is (r, k)-rigid if one cannot have $M = A+B$ where $\text{rank}(A) \le r$ and each row in B has at most k nonzero elements (we call such B a k-row sparse matrix). Note that any k-row sparse B defines a sparse bilinear form $B(x, y) = x^t By$. Namely, a bilinear form that has only nk nonzero monomials. Imagine that we could find a hitting set $\mathcal{H}$ for the class of all matrices that can be written as a sum of rank $\le r$ matrix and a k-row sparse matrix. Then, as before, any nonzero matrix in the dual of $\mathcal{H}$ will be (r, k)-rigid. In this work we constructed optimal hitting sets for rank $\le r$ matrices and in earlier works PIT algorithms for sparse polynomials were given (see e.g. the survey [ ]). If we could find a way to combine the two hitting sets then we will be able to find an explicit rigid matrix, which is a major open problem in circuit complexity.

Acknowledgements

We would like to thank Olgica Milenkovic for pointing us to the low-rank recovery problem, and Madhu Sudan for some helpful comments regarding decoding dual Reed-Solomon codes. We thank Zeev Dvir for pointing out the connection of our work to the problem of constructing rigid matrices.

Part of this work was done while the first author was visiting Stanford University, as well as when the second author was visiting the Bernoulli center at EPFL.

3. REFERENCES

[1] http://dsp.rice.edu/cs.

[2] http://perception.csl.uiuc.edu/matrix-rank/.

[3] M. Agrawal. Proving lower bounds via pseudo-random generators. In *Proceedings of the 25th FSTTCS*, volume 3821 of *LNCS*, pages 92–105, 2005.

[4] M. Agrawal and V. Vinay. Arithmetic circuits: A chasm at depth four. In *Proceedings of the 49th Annual FOCS*, pages 67–75, 2008.

[5] E. Arias-Castro, E. J. Candes, and M. Davenport. On the fundamental limits of adaptive sensing. *arXiv:1111.4646*, 2011.

[6] A. Beimel, F. Bergadano, N. H. Bshouty, E. Kushilevitz, and S. Varricchio. Learning functions represented as multiplicity automata. *J. ACM*, 47(3):506–530, 2000.

[7] F. Bergadano, N. H. Bshouty, and S. Varricchio. Learning multivariate polynomials from substitution and equivalence queries. *ECCC*, 3(8), 1996.

[8] E. R. Berlekamp. *Algebraic coding theory*. McGraw-Hill Book Co., New York, 1968.

[9] E. Candes, J. Romberg, and T. Tao. Stable Signal Recovery from Incomplete and Inaccurate Measurements. *arXiv:math/0503066*, Mar. 2005.

[10] E. J. Candes and Y. Plan. Matrix Completion With Noise. *ArXiv e-prints*, Mar. 2009.

[11] E. J. Candés and Y. Plan. Tight oracle inequalities for low-rank matrix recovery from a minimal number of noisy random measurements. *IEEE Trans. Inform. Theory*, 57(4):2342–2359, 2011.

[12] E. J. Candes and T. Tao. The Power of Convex Relaxation: Near-Optimal Matrix Completion. *ArXiv e-prints*, Mar. 2009.

[13] G. C. F. M. R. de Prony. Essai éxperimental et analytique: sur les lois de la dilatabilité de fluides élastique et sur celles de la force expansive de la vapeur de l'alkool, à différentes températures. *Journal de l'école Polytechnique*, 1:24–76, 1795.

[14] P. Delsarte. Bilinear forms over a finite field, with applications to coding theory. *J. Combin. Theory Ser. A*, 25(3):226–241, 1978.

[15] Z. Dvir and A. Shpilka. Towards dimension expanders over finite fields. In *Proceedings of the 23rd Annual IEEE Conference on Computational Complexity (CCC)*, pages 304–310, 2008.

[16] Y. C. Eldar, D. Needell, and Y. Plan. Unicity conditions for low-rank matrix recovery. *arXiv:1103.5479*, 2011.

[17] A. Emad and O. Milenkovic. Information theoretic bounds for tensor rank minimization over finite fields. *arXiv:1103.4435*, 2011.

[18] E. M. Gabidulin. Optimal array error-correcting codes. *Probl. Peredach. Inform.*, 21(2):102–106, 1985.

[19] E. M. Gabidulin. Theory of codes with maximum rank distance. *Probl. Inform. Transm.*, 21(1):1–12, 1985.

[20] E. M. Gabidulin and V. I. Korzhik. Codes correcting lattice-pattern errors. *Zzvestiya VUZ. Radioelektronika*, 1972.

[21] A. Gabizon and R. Raz. Deterministic extractors for affine sources over large fields. *Combinatorica*, 28(4):415–440, 2008.

[22] D. Gross. Recovering low-rank matrices from few coefficients in any basis. *ArXiv e-prints*, Oct. 2009.

[23] D. Gross, Y.-K. Liu, S. T. Flammia, S. Becker, and J. Eisert. Quantum state tomography via compressed sensing. *Phys. Rev. Lett.*, 105:150401, Oct 2010.

[24] J. Håstad. Tensor rank is NP-complete. *J. Algorithms*, 11(4):644–654, 1990.

[25] J. Heintz and C. P. Schnorr. Testing polynomials which are easy to compute (extended abstract). In *Proceedings of the 12th annual STOC*, pages 262–272, 1980.

[26] P. Indyk, E. Price, and D. P. Woodruff. On the Power of Adaptivity in Sparse Recovery. *Foundations of Computer Science*, Oct. 2011.

[27] V. Kabanets and R. Impagliazzo. Derandomizing polynomial identity tests means proving circuit lower bounds. *Computational Complexity*, 13(1-2):1–46, 2004.

[28] Z. S. Karnin and A. Shpilka. Deterministic black box polynomial identity testing of depth-3 arithmetic circuits with bounded top fan-in. In *Proceedings of the 23rd Annual CCC*, pages 280–291, 2008.

[29] A. Khajehnejad, S. Oymak, and B. Hassibi. Subspace expanders and matrix rank minimization. *arXiv:1102.3947v1*, 2011.

[30] A. Klivans and A. Shpilka. Learning restricted models of arithmetic circuits. *Theory of computing*, 2(10):185–206, 2006.

[31] A. Klivans and D. Spielman. Randomness efficient identity testing of multivariate polynomials. In *Proceedings of the 33rd Annual STOC*, pages 216–223, 2001.

[32] A. Lubotzky and Y. Zelmanov. Dimension expanders. *J. Algebra*, 319(2):730–738, 2008.

[33] J. L. Massey. Shift-register synthesis and BCH decoding. *IEEE Trans. Information Theory*, IT-15:122–127, 1969.

[34] R. Meshulam. Spaces of Hankel matrices over finite fields. *Linear Algebra Appl.*, 218:73–76, 1995.

[35] N. Nisan and A. Wigderson. Lower bound on arithmetic circuits via partial derivatives. *Computational Complexity*, 6:217–234, 1996.

[36] R. Raz and A. Shpilka. Deterministic polynomial identity testing in non commutative models. *Computational Complexity*, 14(1):1–19, 2005.

[37] B. Recht, M. Fazel, and P. Parrilo. Guaranteed minimum-rank solutions of linear matrix equations via nuclear norm minimization. *SIAM Review*, 52(3):471–501, 2010.

[38] R. M. Roth. Maximum-rank array codes and their application to crisscross error correction. *IEEE*

Transactions on Information Theory, 37(2):328–336, 1991.

[39] R. M. Roth. Tensor codes for the rank metric. *IEEE Transactions on Information Theory*, 42(6):2146–2157, 1996.

[40] N. Saxena and C. Seshadhri. Blackbox identity testing for bounded top fanin depth-3 circuits: the field doesn't matter. In *Proceedings of the 43rd Annual STOC*, pages 431–440, 2011.

[41] A. Shpilka and A. Yehudayoff. Arithmetic circuits: A survey of recent results and open questions. *Foundations and Trends in Theoretical Computer Science*, 5(3-4):207–388, 2010.

[42] V. Y. F. Tan, L. Balzano, and S. C. Draper. Rank minimization over finite fields: Fundamental limits and coding-theoretic interpretations. *arXiv:1104.4302v2*, 2011.

[43] L. G. Valiant. Graph-theoretic arguments in low-level complexity. In *Lecture notes in Computer Science*, volume 53, pages 162–176. Springer, 1977.

Structure Theorem and Isomorphism Test for Graphs with Excluded Topological Subgraphs

Martin Grohe
Institut für Informatik
Humboldt-Universität zu Berlin
Berlin, Germany
grohe@informatik.hu-berlin.de

Dániel Marx*
Computer and Automation Research Institute,
Hungarian Academy of Sciences (MTA SZTAKI)
Budapest, Hungary
dmarx@informatik.hu-berlin.de

ABSTRACT

We generalize the structure theorem of Robertson and Seymour for graphs excluding a fixed graph H as a minor to graphs excluding H as a topological subgraph. We prove that for a fixed H, every graph excluding H as a topological subgraph has a tree decomposition where each part is either "almost embeddable" to a fixed surface or has bounded degree with the exception of a bounded number of vertices. Furthermore, such a decomposition is computable by an algorithm that is fixed-parameter tractable with parameter $|H|$.

We present two algorithmic applications of our structure theorem. To illustrate the mechanics of a "typical" application of the structure theorem, we show that on graphs excluding H as a topological subgraph, PARTIAL DOMINATING SET (find k vertices whose closed neighborhood has maximum size) can be solved in time $f(H,k) \cdot n^{O(1)}$ time. More significantly, we show that on graphs excluding H as a topological subgraph, GRAPH ISOMORPHISM can be solved in time $n^{f(H)}$. This result unifies and generalizes two previously known important polynomial-time solvable cases of GRAPH ISOMORPHISM: bounded-degree graphs [18] and H-minor free graphs [22]. The proof of this result needs a generalization of our structure theorem to the context of invariant treelike decomposition.

Categories and Subject Descriptors

F.2 [**Theory of Computing**]: Analysis of Algorithms and Problem Complexity; G.2.2 [**Mathematics of Computing**]: Discrete Mathematics—*Graph Theory*

General Terms

Algorithms

*Research supported by the European Research Council (ERC) grant 280152.

Keywords

topological minors, fixed-parameter tractability, graph isomorphism

1. INTRODUCTION

We say that a graph H is a *minor* of G if H can be obtained from G by deleting vertices, deleting edges, and contracting edges. A graph G is H*-minor free* if H is not a minor of G. Robertson and Seymour [25] proved a structure theorem for the class of H-minor graphs: roughly speaking, every H-minor free graph can be decomposed in a way such that each part is "almost embeddable" into a fixed surface. This structure theorem has important algorithmic consequences: many natural computational problems become easier when restricted to H-minor free graphs [4, 13, 6, 15, 14, 5, 10]. These algorithmic results can be thought of as far-reaching generalizations of algorithms on planar graphs and bounded-genus surfaces.

A more general way of defining restricted classes of graphs is to exclude topological subgraphs instead of minors. A graph H is a *topological subgraph* (or *topological minor*) of graph G if a subdivision of H is a subgraph of G. It is easy to see that if H is a topological subgraph of G, then H is also a minor of G. Thus the class of graphs excluding H as a topological subgraph is a more general class than H-minor free graphs.

One can ask if graphs excluding H as a topological subgraph admit a similar structure theorem as H-minor free graphs. However, graphs excluding a topological subgraph can be much more general. For example, no 3-regular graph can contain a subdivision of K_5 (as K_5 is 4-regular). Therefore, the class of graphs excluding K_5 as a topological subgraph includes in particular every 3-regular graph. This suggests that it is unlikely that this class can be also characterized by (almost) embeddability into surfaces.

Nevertheless, our first result is a structure theorem for graphs excluding a graph H as a topological subgraph. We prove that, in some sense, only the bounded-degree graphs make this class more general than H-minor free graphs. More precisely, we prove a structure theorem that decomposes graphs excluding H as a topological subgraph into almost bounded-degree parts and into H'-minor free parts (for some other graph H'). The H'-minor free parts can be further refined into almost-embeddable parts using the structure theorem of Robertson and Seymour [25], to obtain our main structural result (see Corollary 4.4 for the precise statement):

THEOREM 1.1 (INFORMAL). *For every fixed graph H, every graph excluding H as a topological subgraph has a tree decomposition where every torso*

(i) either has bounded degree with the exception of a bounded number of vertices, or
(ii) almost embeddable into a surface of bounded genus.

Furthermore, such a decomposition can be computed in time $f(H) \cdot |V(G)|^{O(1)}$ for some computable function f.

Our structure theorem allows us to lift problems that are tractable on both bounded-degree graphs and on H-minor free graphs to the class of graphs excluding H as a topological subgraph. We demonstrate this principle on the PARTIAL DOMINATING SET problem (find k vertices whose closed neighborhood is maximum). Following a bottom-up dynamic programming approach, we solve the problem in each bag of the tree decomposition (using the fact that the problem can be solved in linear-time on both bounded-degree and on almost-embeddable graphs).

THEOREM 1.2. PARTIAL DOMINATING SET *can be solved in time $f(k, H) \cdot n^{O(1)}$ when restricted to graphs excluding H as a topological subgraph.*

One could prove similar results for other basic problems such as INDEPENDENT SET or DOMINATING SET. However, a result of Dvorak et al. [7] shows that problems expressible in first-order logic can be solved in linear time on classes of graphs having bounded expansion, and therefore on graphs excluding H as a topological subgraph. The problems INDEPENDENT SET and DOMINATING SET (for a fixed k) can be expressed in first-order logic, thus the analogs of Theorem 1.2 for these problems follow from [7]. On the other hand, PARTIAL DOMINATING SET is not expressible in first-order logic, hence the techniques of Dvorak et al. [7] do not apply to this problem.

The main algorithmic result of the paper concerns the GRAPH ISOMORPHISM problem (given graphs G_1 and G_2, decide if they are isomorphic). GRAPH ISOMORPHISM is known to be polynomial-time solvable for bounded-degree graphs [18, 2] and for H-minor free graphs [22, 9]. In fact, for these classes of graphs, even the more general canonization problem can be solved in polynomial time: there is an algorithm labeling the vertices of the graph with positive integers such that isomorphic graphs get isomorphic labelings. It is tempting to expect that our structure theorem together with a bottom-up strategy give a canonization algorithm for graphs excluding H as a topological subgraph: in each bag, we use the canonization algorithm either for bounded-degree graphs or H-minor free graphs (after encoding somehow the canonized versions of the child bags, which seems to be a technical problem only). However, this approach is inherently doomed to failure: there is no guarantee that our decomposition algorithm produces isomorphic decompositions for isomorphic graphs. Therefore, even if two graphs are isomorphic, the bottom-up canonization algorithm could be working on two completely different decompositions and therefore could obtain different results on the two graphs.

We overcome this difficulty by generalizing our structure theorem to the context of treelike decompositions introduced by the first author in [11, 9]. A treelike decomposition is similar to a tree decomposition, but it is defined over a directed acyclic graph instead of a rooted tree, and therefore it contains several tree decompositions. The Invariant Decomposition Theorem (Section 8) generalizes the structure theorem by giving an algorithm that computes a treelike decomposition in a way that the decompositions obtained for isomorphic graphs are isomorphic. Then the Lifting Lemma (Section 9) formalizes the bottom-up strategy informally described in the previous paragraph: if we can compute treelike decompositions for a class of graphs in an invariant way and we have a canonization algorithm for the bags, then we have a canonization algorithm for this class of graphs. Although the idea is simple, in order to encode the child bags, we have to state this algorithmic result in a more general form: instead of graphs, we have to work with weighted relational structures. This makes the statement and proof of the Lifting Lemma more technical. Putting together these results, we obtain:

THEOREM 1.3. *For every fixed graph H,* GRAPH ISOMORPHISM *can be solved in polynomial-time restricted to graphs excluding H as a topological subgraph.*

Let us quickly remark that it is unlikely that Theorem 1.3 could be generalized to all classes of graphs with bounded expansion, as the isomorphism problem on such a class can be as hard as on general graphs. To see this, consider two graphs G_1 and G_2 on n-vertices and let us obtain G'_1 and G'_2 by subdividing each edge with n new vertices. Now G'_1 and G'_2 have bounded expansion and they are isomorphic if and only if G_1 and G_2 are.

Actually, we not only obtain a polynomial time isomorphism test, but also a polynomial time canonisation algorithm. Our theorem generalizes and unifies the results of Babai and Luks [18, 2] on bounded-degree graphs and of Ponomarenko [22] on H-minor free graphs. Let us remark that Ponomarenko's result implies that there is a polynomial time isomorphism test for all classes of graphs of bounded genus, which has been proved earlier by Filotti and Mayer [8] and Miller [21], and for all classes of graphs of bounded tree width, which was also proved later (independently) by Bodlaender [3]. Miller [20] gave a common generalization of the bounded degree and bounded genus classes to classes that he called k-contractible. These classes do not seem to have a simple graph-theoretic characterization; they are defined in terms of properties of the automorphism groups needed for the algorithm. Excluding topological subgraphs, on the other hand, is a natural graph theoretic restriction that generalizes both bounding the degree and excluding minors and hence bounding the genus.

For the convenience of the reader, let us summarize how the different results in the present paper depend on previous results in the literature:

- The proof of the existence of the decomposition into H-minor free and almost bounded-degree parts is self-contained. The algorithm computing such a decomposition needs the minor testing algorithm of [24] or [16].
- The proof of the existence of the more refined decomposition into almost-embeddable and almost bounded-degree parts needs the graph structure theorem of Robertson and Seymour [25]. The algorithm computing such a decomposition needs the algorithmic version of the structure theorem [5]; to achieve $f(H) \cdot n^{O(1)}$ running time, a more recent stronger algorithmic result is needed [17].

- The algorithm for Partial Dominating Set needs the more refined decomposition, hence it relies on [24, 17]. Additionally, it needs the fact proved in [10] that almost-embeddable graphs have bounded local treewidth.
- The result on Graph Isomorphism needs the minor testing algorithm of [24] or [16] to compute the treelike decomposition. Additionally, the canonization algorithms for bounded-degree graphs [2] and for H-minor free graphs ([22] or [9]) are needed.

Note that none of the results rely on the topological subgraph testing algorithm of [12] or need any substantial result from the monograph [9].

The paper is organized as follows. Sections 2–3 introduce the notation used in the paper. Section 4 states the structure theorem and shows how it can be proved by appropriate local decomposition lemmas. Section 5 introduces the notion of tangles, which is an important tool in the proofs of the local decomposition lemmas in Section 6. Section 7 uses the structure theorem in an algorithm for Partial Dominating Set. Section 8 introduces treelike decomposition and proves the Invariant Decomposition Theorem. Section 9 proves the Lifting Lemma for canonizations, completing the proof of Theorem 1.3.

2. PRELIMINARIES

$\mathbb{Z}$ and $\mathbb{N}$ denote the sets of integers and nonnegative integers, respectively. For $m, n \in \mathbb{Z}$, we let $[m, n] := \{\ell \in \mathbb{Z} \mid m \leq \ell \leq n\}$ and $[n] := [1, n]$. The power set of a set S is denoted by 2^S, and the set of all k-element subsets of S by $\binom{S}{k}$. For a mapping f defined on S, we let $f(S) := \{f(s) \mid s \in S\}$. The cardinality of a set S is denoted by $|S|$.

Let G be a graph. The *order* of a graph G is $|G| := |V(G)|$. The set of all neighbors of a vertex $v \in V(G)$, called the *open neighborhood of* v, is denoted by $N^G(v)$. The *closed neighborhood* of v is the set $N^G[v] := \{v\} \cup N^G(v)$. The *closed* and *open neighborhood* of a subset $W \subseteq V(G)$ are the sets $N^G[W] := \bigcup_{w \in W} N^G[w]$ and $N^G(W) := N^G[W] \setminus W$, respectively, and the *closed* and *open neighborhood* of a subgraph $H \subseteq G$ are the sets $N^G[H] := N^G[V(H)]$ and $N^G(H) := N^G(V(H))$, respectively. We omit the index ^{G} if G is clear from the context, and we do the same for similar notations introduced later. We let $\partial^G(W) = |N^G(W)|$.

For every set V, we let $K[V]$ be the complete graph with vertex set V, and for every $n \in \mathbb{N}$, we let $K_n := K\big[[n]\big]$.

Let G be a graph. A graph H is a *minor* of G (denoted by $H \preceq G$) if H can be obtained from G by deleting vertices, deleting edges, and contracting edges. Equivalently, we can define $H \preceq G$ the following way. Two sets $S, T \subseteq V(G)$ *touch* if either $S \cap T = \emptyset$ or there is an edge $vw \in V(G)$ such that $v \in S$ and $w \in T$. It can be shown that $H \preceq G$ if and only if there is a family $(I_w)_{w \in V(H)}$ of pairwise disjoint connected subsets of $V(G)$ such that for every $u, v \in V(H)$ that are adjacent in H, the sets I_u and I_v touch in G. We call this family I an *image* of H in G and the sets I_w are the *branch sets* of the image.

Theorem 2.1 ([24, 16]). *There is an $f(H) \cdot |V(G)|^3$ time algorithm (for some computable f) that finds a H-minor image in G, if exists.*

A *subdivision* H' of a graph H is obtained by replacing each edge of H by a path of length at least 1. We say that H is a *topological subgraph* (or *topological minor* of G) and denote it by $H \preceq_T G$ if a subdivision of H is a subgraph of G. Equivalently, H is a topological subgraph of G if H can be obtained from G by deleting edges, deleting vertices, and dissolving degree 2 vertices (which means deleting the vertex and making its two neighbors adjacent). For fixed H, it can be decided in cubic time whether a graph G contains a subdivision of H (although we do not need this result in the current paper):

Theorem 2.2 ([12]). *There is an $f(H) \cdot |V(G)|^3$ time algorithm (for some computable f) that finds a subdivision of H in G, if exists.*

Let D be digraph. For every $t \in V(D)$, we let $N^D(t) := \{u \in V(D) \mid tu \in E(D)\}$. We call vertices of in-degree 0 *roots* and vertices of out-degree 0 *leaves* of D. The *height* of an acyclic digraph D is the length of the longest path in D.

It will be convenient for us to view trees as being directed, unless we explicitly call them undirected. Hence for us, a *tree* is an acyclic digraph T that has a unique node (the *root*) such that for every node t there is a exactly one path from $r(T)$ to t.

For two graphs A and B, the graph $A \cup B$ is defined by $V(A \cup B) = V(A) \cup V(B)$ and $E(A \cup B) = E(A) \cup E(B)$. Let G be a graph. A *separation* of G is a pair (A, B) of subgraphs of G such that $A \cup B = G$ and $E(A \cap B) = \emptyset$. The *order* of a separation (A, B) is $|V(A) \cap V(B)|$.

3. TREE DECOMPOSITIONS

A *tree decomposition* of a graph is a pair (T, β), where T is a rooted tree and $\beta : V(T) \to 2^{V(G)}$, such that for all nodes $v \in V(G)$ the set $\{t \in V(G) \mid v \in \beta(t)\}$ is nonempty and connected in the undirected tree underlying T, and for all edges $e \in E(G)$ there is a $t \in V(T)$ such that $e \subseteq \beta(t)$. Most readers will be familiar with this definition, but it will be convenient for us to view tree decompositions from a different perspective here.

If (T, β) is a tree decomposition of a graph G, then we define mappings $\sigma, \gamma, \alpha : V(T) \to 2^{V(G)}$ by letting for all $t \in V(T)$

$$\sigma(t) := \begin{cases} \emptyset & \text{if } t \text{ is the root of } T, \\ \beta(t) \cap \beta(s) & \text{if } s \text{ is the parent of } t \text{ in } T, \end{cases} \tag{3.1}$$

$$\gamma(t) := \bigcup_{u \text{ is a descendant of } t} \beta(u), \tag{3.2}$$

$$\alpha(t) := \gamma(t) \setminus \sigma(t). \tag{3.3}$$

We call $\beta(t), \sigma(t), \gamma(t), \alpha(t)$ the *bag* at t, *separator* at t, *cone* at t, *component* at t, respectively. It is easy to verify that the following conditions hold:

(TD.1) T is a tree.

(TD.2) For all $t \in V(D)$ it holds that $\alpha(t) \cap \sigma(t) = \emptyset$ and $N^G(\alpha(t)) \subseteq \sigma(t)$.

(TD.3) For all $t \in V(D)$ and $u \in N^D(t)$ it holds that $\alpha(u) \subseteq \alpha(t)$ and $\gamma(u) \subseteq \gamma(t)$.

(TD.4) For all $t \in V(D)$ and all distinct $u_1, u_2 \in N^D(t)$ it holds that $\gamma(u_1) \cap \gamma(u_2) = \sigma(u_1) \cap \sigma(u_2)$.

(TD.5) For the root r of T it holds that $\sigma(r) = \emptyset$ and $\alpha(r) = V(G)$.

Conversely, consider a triple (T, σ, α), where T is a digraph and $\sigma, \alpha : V(T) \to 2^{V(G)}$. We define $\gamma, \beta : V(T) \to 2^{V(G)}$ by

$$\gamma(t) := \sigma(t) \cup \alpha(t), \tag{3.4}$$

$$\beta(t) := \gamma(t) \setminus \bigcup_{u \in N^T(t)} \alpha(u) \tag{3.5}$$

for all $t \in V(T)$. Then it is easy to prove that if (TD.1)–(TD.5) are satisfied, then (T, β) is a tree decomposition (see [9] for a proof). Thus we may also view triples (T, σ, α) satisfying (TD.1)–(TD.5) as tree decompositions. We jump back and forth between both versions of tree decompositions, whichever is more convenient. The treelike decompositions introduced in Section 8 need to be defined as triples (T, σ, α), thus looking at tree decompositions also this way in the first part of the paper makes the transition between the two concepts smoother.

Let (T, β) be a tree decomposition of a graph G. The *width* of (T, β) is $\max\{|\beta(t)| - 1 \mid t \in V(T)\}$, and the *adhesion* of (T, β) is $\max\{|\sigma(t)| \mid t \in V(T)\}$. The *tree width* of a graph is the minimum possible width of a tree decomposition of G. However, in the current paper, rather than minimizing tree width (i.e., minimizing the size of the bags), we are mostly interested in decompositions where the graph induced by each bag (plus some additional edges) is "nice" in a certain sense. For every node $t \in V(T)$, the *torso* at t is the graph

$$\tau(t) := G[\beta(t)] \cup K[\sigma(t)] \cup \bigcup_{u \in N^D(t)} K[\sigma(u)]. \tag{3.6}$$

That is, we take the graph induced by bag $\beta(t)$, turn $\sigma(t)$ into a clique, and make vertices x, y adjacent if they appear together in the separator (or equivalently, the cone) of some child u of t. For a class $\mathcal{A}$ of graphs, (T, β) is a tree decomposition *over* $\mathcal{A}$ if all its torsos are in $\mathcal{A}$.

A related notion is the *torso* of G with respect to a set $C \subseteq V(G)$, denoted by torso(G, C), which is defined as graph on C where $u, v \in V(G)$ are adjacent if there is a path P in G with endpoints u and v such that the internal vertices of P are disjoint from C. In other words,

$$\text{torso}(G, C) := G[C] \cup \bigcup_{X \text{ is a component of } G \setminus C} K[N^G(X)].$$

It is easy to see that $\tau(G, \beta(t)) \subseteq \tau(t)$. Equality is not true in general: $G[\alpha(u)]$ for some $u \in N^D(t)$ is not necessarily connected, thus it is not necessarily true that $\sigma(u)$ is $N^G(X)$ for some component X of $G \setminus \beta(t)$.

4. LOCAL AND GLOBAL STRUCTURE THEOREMS

The main structural result of the paper is a decomposition theorem for graphs excluding a topological subgraph:

THEOREM 4.1 (GLOBAL STRUCTURE THEOREM). *For every $k \in \mathbb{N}$, there exists constants $a(k)$, $b(k)$, $c(k)$, $d(k)$, $e(k)$, such that the following holds. Let H be a graph on k vertices. Then for every graph G with $H \not\preceq_T G$ there is a tree decomposition (T, β) of adhesion at most $a(k)$ such that for all $t \in V(T)$ one of the following three conditions is satisfied:*

(i) $|\beta(t)| \le b(k)$.
(ii) $\tau(t)$ has at most $c(k)$ vertices of degree larger than $d(k)$.
(iii) $K_{e(k)} \not\preceq \tau(t)$.

Furthermore, there is an algorithm that, given graphs G, H of sizes n, k, respectively, in time $f(k) \cdot n^{O(1)}$ for some computable function f, computes either such a decomposition (T, β) or a subdivision of H in G.

The reader could find it convenient to refer to the constants a, b, c, d, e as the bounds on the adhesion, bag size, number of apices, maximum degree, and excluded clique. We remark that all the constants are polynomially large. Note that (i) is redundant: by choosing $d(k)$ or $e(k)$ sufficiently large, a bag satisfying (i) trivially satisfies (ii) and (iii). We state the result this way, because it shows the high-level structure of the proof, which involves three decomposition results corresponding to the three cases.

The proof of the Global Structure Theorem 4.1 builds a tree decomposition step by step, iteratively decomposing the graph locally in each step. The Local Structure Theorem describes the "local" structure of a graph, as seen from a single node of a tree decomposition. We describe this local structure in terms of star decompositions, to be defined next. A *star* is a tree of height 1. We usually call the root of a star its *center* and the leaves of a star its *tips*. A *star decomposition* of a graph G is a tree decomposition (T, β) where T is a star. Note that if (T, β) is a star decomposition, then for every tip t of the star T it holds that $\beta(t) = \gamma(t)$.

THEOREM 4.2 (LOCAL STRUCTURE THEOREM). *For every $k \in \mathbb{N}$, there exists constants $a(k)$, $b(k)$, $c(k)$, $d(k)$, $e(k)$ such that the following holds. There is an $f(k) \cdot |V(G)|^{O(1)}$ time algorithm that, given a graph G, a set S of size $\le a(k)$, and an integer k,*

(1) either returns a subdivision of K_k in G,
(2) or computes a star decomposition $\Sigma_S = (T_S, \alpha_S, \sigma_S)$ of $G \cup K[S]$ of adhesion $\le a(k)$ such that $S \subseteq \beta_S(s)$ for the center s, $\alpha(t) \subset \alpha(s)$ for every tip t, and one of the following three conditions is satisfied:
   (a) $|\beta_S(s)| \le b(k)$.
   (b) $\tau_S(s)$ does not contain a $K_{e(k)}$-minor.
   (c) At most $c(k)$ vertices of $\tau_S(s)$ have degree more than $d(k)$ in $\tau(s)$.

The condition that $\alpha(t)$ is a proper subset of $\alpha(s)$ makes sure that we make progress and compute a tree decomposition after a finite number of applications of Theorem 4.2. Note the technical detail that Σ_S in (2) is a decomposition of $G \cup K[S]$ instead of G. As $G \cup K[S]$ has more edges than G, this makes the statement slightly stronger (because it makes harder to satisfy the requirements on $\tau_S(s)$). The proof of the Global Structure Theorem 4.1 needs this extra condition, since the set S will connect the graph to the part of the tree decomposition already computed. In (1), however, the K_k-subdivision is found in G (which is a slightly stronger statement than finding it in $G \cup K[S]$).

The proof of the Global Structure Theorem 4.1 follows from the Local Structure Theorem by a fairly simple induction (see below). In Section 4.2, we show that Local Structure Theorem 4.2 can be proved by putting together three decomposition lemmas. We prove these lemmas in Sections 5–6. Let us remark the Global Structure Theorem can be seen as an instance of a general theorem due to Robertson and Seymour [23, (11.3)], explaining how to construct a tree decomposition whose torsos have a "nice structure" in graphs with a "nice local structure", where the local structure is described with respect to a tangle (see Section 5). Our proof follows the ideas of Robertson and Seymour's construction, but as Robertson and Seymour's theorem is not algorithmic, and since there would be a large notational overhead, we see no benefit in appealing to Robertson and Seymour's theorem here and instead carry out our own version of the construction, which is not very difficult anyway.

PROOF (OF THE GLOBAL STRUCTURE THEOREM 4.1). Let $a(k)$, $b(k)$, $c(k)$, $d(k)$, $e(k)$ as in the Local Structure Theorem 4.2. Let G be a graph. We shall describe the construction of a tree decomposition (T, β) of G satisfying all conditions asserted in the lemma. The construction may fail, but in that case it yields a subdivision of H in G.

We will built the tree T inductively starting from the root. For every node t we will define the set $N^T(t)$ of its children and sets $\sigma(t), \alpha(t)$ such that $|\sigma(t)| \le a(k)$ and $N^G(\alpha(t)) \subseteq \sigma(t)$. As usual, we define $\gamma(t)$, $\beta(t)$, and $\tau(t)$ as in (3.4), (3.5), and (3.6). In each step, we will prove that $\tau(t)$ satisfies one of (i), (ii), or (iii).

We start with a root r of T and let $\sigma(r) := \varnothing$ and $\alpha(r) := V(G)$. For the inductive step, let t be a node for which $\sigma(t)$ and $\alpha(t)$ are defined, but $N^D(t)$ is not yet defined. We let $G_t := G[\gamma(t)]$. Let us run the algorithm of Theorem 4.2 on G_t (as G), $\sigma(t)$ (as S), and k. If it returns a subdivision of K_k in G_t, then we can clearly return a subdivision of H in G and we are done. Otherwise, it returns a star decomposition $\Sigma_t := (T_t, \sigma_t, \alpha_t)$ of $G \cup K[\sigma(t)]$ having adhesion at most $a(k)$; let s_t be the center of T_t. We let $N^T(t) := V(T_t) \setminus \{s_t\}$ be the set of tips of T_t, where without loss of generality we assume that this set is disjoint from the tree T constructed so far. For every $u \in N^T(t)$ we let $\sigma(u) := \sigma_t(u)$ and $\alpha(u) := \alpha_t(u)$. Observe that we have $\beta(t) = \gamma(t) \setminus \bigcup_{u \in N^T(t)} \alpha(u) = \beta_t(s_t)$. Furthermore, since Σ_t is a decomposition of $G \cup K[\sigma(t)]$ and $\sigma(t)$ induces a clique in $G \cup K[\sigma(t)]$, we have that $\tau(t) = \tau_t(s_t)$. Thus one of the three cases of Theorem 4.2 holds for the bag $\beta(t)$ as well.

To see that (T, β) is a tree decomposition, it is easiest to verify it satisfies (TD.2)–(TD.4): it follows from the fact that the star decomposition Σ_t used in each step of the construction does satisfy these conditions. Condition (TD.1) is obvious and (TD.5) follows because we start the construction with a node t having $\alpha(t) = V(G)$ and $\sigma(t) = \varnothing$. Note that the bound $a(k)$ on the adhesion of Σ_t implies the same bound on the adhesion of (T, β).

To see that the construction terminates, note that for all $t \in V(T)$, Theorem 4.2 states that $\alpha_t(u) \subset \alpha_t(s_t)$ for every tip u of T_t. This means that that $\alpha(u) \subset \alpha(t)$ holds for every $u \in N^T(t)$ and hence the height of the tree is at most $|V(G)|$. Moreover, $\alpha(u_1)$ and $\alpha(u_2)$ are disjoint for two distinct children of node t and it follows that the total number of leaves can be bounded by $|V(G)|$. Thus the algorithm, excluding the calls to Theorem 4.2, runs in polynomial time. The claim on the running time follows from Theorem 4.2. □

4.1 Almost Embeddable Graphs and a Refined Structure Theorem

In this section, we combine our structure theorem with Robertson and Seymour's structure theorem for graphs with excluded minors [25], which says that for graph H, all graphs excluding H as a minor have a tree decomposition into torsos that are almost embeddable into some surface.

We start by reviewing Robertson and Seymour's structure theorem. We need first the definition of (p, q, r, s)-almost embeddable graphs (for the current paper, the exact definition will not be important, thus the reader can safely skip the details). We assume that the reader is familiar with the basics of surface topology and graph embeddings. A *path decomposition* is a tree decomposition (P, β) where P is a path. For every $n \in \mathbb{N}$, by P^n we denote the path with vertex set $[n]$ and edges $i(i+1)$ for all $i \in [n-1]$. A *p-ring* is a tuple $(R, v_1, \dots, v_n)$, where R is a graph and $v_1, \dots, v_n \in V(R)$ such that there is a path decomposition (P^n, β) of R of width p with $v_i \in \beta(i)$ for all $i \in [n]$. A graph G is *(p, q)-almost embedded* in a surface $\mathbf{S}$ if there are graphs $G_0, G_1, \dots, G_q$ and mutually disjoint closed disks $\mathbf{D}_1, \dots, \mathbf{D}_q \subseteq \mathbf{S}$ such that:

(i) $G = \bigcup_{i=0}^{q} G_i$.
(ii) G_0 is embedded in $\mathbf{S}$ and has a nonempty intersection with the interiors of the disks $\mathbf{D}_1, \dots, \mathbf{D}_q$.
(iii) The graphs $G_1, \dots, G_q$ are mutually disjoint.
(iv) For all $i \in [q]$ we have $E(G_0 \cap G_i) = \varnothing$, and there are $n_i \in \mathbb{N}$ and $v_1^i, \dots, v_{n_i}^i \in V(G)$ such that $V(G_0 \cap G_i) = \{v_1^i, \dots, v_{n_i}^i\}$, and the vertices $v_1^i, \dots, v_{n_i}^i$ appear in cyclic order on the boundary of the disk $\mathbf{D}_i$.
(v) For all $i \in [q]$ the tuple $(G_i, v_1^i, \dots, v_{n_i}^i)$ is a p-ring.

A graph G is *(p, q, r, s)-almost embeddable* if there is an *apex set* $X \subseteq V(G)$ of size $|X| \le s$ such that $G \setminus X$ is isomorphic to a graph that is (p, q)-almost embedded in a surface of Euler genus r.

THEOREM 4.3 ([25, 17]). *For every graph H there are constants $p, q, r, s \in \mathbb{N}$ such that every graph G with $H \not\preceq G$ has a tree decomposition (T, β) such that for all $t \in V(T)$ the torso $\tau(t)$ is (p, q, r, s)-almost embeddable.*

Furthermore, there is an algorithm that, given G and H, in time $f(|H|) \cdot n^3$ for some computable function f, either finds a H-minor image in G, or computes such a tree decomposition and moreover, computes an apex set Z_t of size at most s for every $t \in V(T)$.

As a corollary of this theorem and our structure theorem we get:

COROLLARY 4.4. *For every graph H there are constants $c, d, p, q, r, s \in \mathbb{N}$ such that every graph G with $H \not\preceq_T G$ has a tree decomposition (T, β) such that for all $t \in V(T)$,*

(i) either $\tau(t)$ is (p, q, r, s)-almost embeddable,
(ii) or at most c vertices of $\tau(t)$ have degree greater than d.

Furthermore, there is an algorithm that, given G and H, in time $f(|H|) \cdot n^{O(1)}$ for some computable function f, either finds a subdivision of H in G, or computes such a tree decomposition, and moreover computes an apex set Z_t of size at most s for every bag of the first type.

4.2 The Three Local Decomposition Lemmas

We prove the Local Structure Theorem 4.2 by stacking three decomposition lemmas on top of each other (see Figure 4.1). Each lemma provides either a star decomposition corresponding to one of the three cases (i)–(iii) or an "obstruction" which can be feeded into the next lemma as input.

The first decomposition lemma either finds a star decomposition where the center bag has bounded size or finds a "highly connected" set in the following sense:

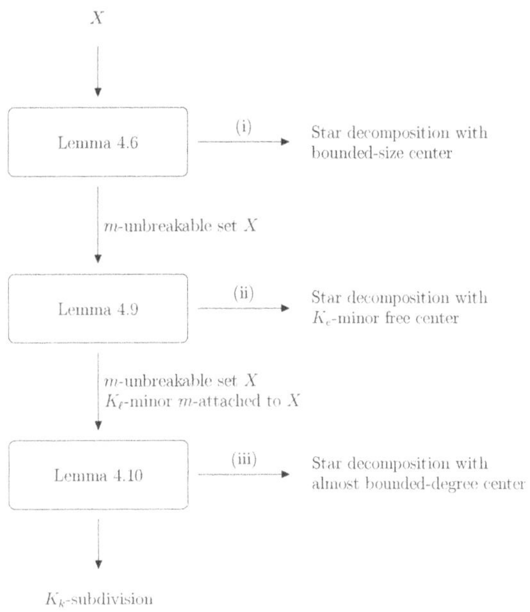

Figure 4.1: The three decomposition lemmas in the proof of Local Structure Theorem 4.2.

DEFINITION 4.5. *Let G be a graph and $X \subseteq V(G)$. A separation (A, B) of G* breaks *X if $|(V(A) \cap X) \cup V(A \cap B)| < |X|$ and $|(V(B) \cap X) \cup V(A \cap B)| < |X|$.*

The set X is m-unbreakable *if there is no separation (A, B) of G of order $< m$ that breaks X.*

There is a simple way of detecting if a set X is m-unbreakable by considering all possible ways of breaking X. Note that the running time of the following algorithm is exponential in the size of the set, but we will use it only on unbreakable sets of bounded size.

LEMMA 4.6. *There is an algorithm that, given a graph G and a set $X \subseteq V(G)$ and a $m \in \mathbb{N}$, either computes a separation of G of order $< m$ that breaks X or correctly decides that $|X|$ is m-unbreakable in time $3^{|X|} n^{O(1)}$.*

It is not difficult to see that a large unbreakable set is an obstruction for having small treewidth, that is, for having a tree decomposition where every bag has small size. Therefore, it is not surprising that the proof of the first local decomposition lemma is very similar to algorithms finding tree decompositions.

LEMMA 4.7 (BOUNDED-SIZE STAR DECOMPOSITION). *For every $m \in \mathbb{N}$, there is a constant $b^*(m)$ such that the following holds. There is an $f(m) \cdot |V(G)|^{O(1)}$ time algorithm that, given a graph G, an integer m, a set X of size $\le 3m - 2$, and an integer k,*

(1) either finds an m-unbreakable set $X' \supseteq X$ of size $3m-2$.
(2) or computes a star decomposition $\Sigma_X = (T_X, \alpha_X, \sigma_X)$ of $G \cup K[X]$ having adhesion $< 3m - 2$ such that $X \subseteq \beta_X(s)$ and $|\beta_X(s)| \le b^*(m)$ for the center s of T_X.

PROOF. Let $b^*(m) = 4m - 3$. If $|V(G)| < 3m - 2$, then we can return a star decomposition consisting of a single center node s with $\alpha(s) = V(G)$ and $\sigma(s) = \emptyset$. Otherwise, let X' be an arbitrary superset of X having size $3m - 2$. Let us use the algorithm of Lemma 4.6 to test if X' is m-unbreakable; if so, then we can return X' and we are done. Otherwise, there is a separation (A, B) of G having order $< m$ such that $|(X' \cap V(A)) \cup Q|, |(X' \cap V(B)) \cup Q| < |X'| = 3m - 2$ for $Q = V(A) \cap V(B)$. Let us construct a star decomposition $\Sigma_X = (T_X, \alpha_X, \sigma_X)$ with center s and a tips t_A, t_B. First, let $\alpha(s) = V(G)$ and $\sigma(s) = \emptyset$. Let $\alpha(t_A) = V(A) \setminus (Q \cup X')$ and $\sigma(t_A) = |(X' \cap V(A)) \cup Q|$; it is clear that $|\sigma(t_A)| < 3m - 2$. Similarly, let $\alpha(t_B) = V(B) \setminus (Q \cup X')$ and $\sigma(t_B) = |(X' \cap V(B)) \cup Q|$. It is straightforward to verify that this is indeed a star decomposition of $G \cup K[X]$ with adhesion $< 3m - 2$. Furthermore, $|\beta(s)| = |Q \cup X'| \le m - 1 + 3m - 2 = b^*(m)$. □

The second local decomposition lemma takes an unbreakable set X of appropriate size, and either finds a star decomposition where the torso of the center node excludes some minor or finds a large clique minor. Furthermore, this clique minor has the additional property that it is close to the unbreakable set X in the following sense:

DEFINITION 4.8. *Let I be an H-minor image in G and let X be a set of vertices. We say that I is* m-attached *to X if there is no separation (A, B) of order $< m$ such that $I(v) \subseteq V(A) \setminus V(B)$ for some $v \in V(H)$ and $|(V(B) \cap X) \cup V(A \cap B)| \ge |X|$.*

In particular, if X is an m-unbreakable set and I is m-attached to X, then whenever $I(v) \subseteq V(A) \setminus V(B)$ for some $v \in V(H)$ and separation (A, B) of order $< m$, then we know that $|(V(A) \cap X) \cup V(A \cap B)| \ge |X|$. Thus in every every separation, I is on the same side as the larger part of X.

LEMMA 4.9 (EXCLUDED-MINOR STAR DECOMPOSITION). *For every $\ell, m \in \mathbb{N}$, there is a constant $e^*(\ell, m)$ such that the following holds. There is an $f(\ell, m) \cdot |V(G)|^{O(1)}$ time algorithm that, given a graph G, integers ℓ, m, and an m-unbreakable set X of size $3m - 2$*

(1) either finds a K_ℓ-minor image I in G that is m-attached to X,
(2) or computes a star decomposition $\Sigma_X = (T_X, \alpha_X, \sigma_X)$ of $G \cup K[X]$ having adhesion $< |X|$ such that $X \subseteq \beta_X(s)$ and $\tau_X(s)$ does not contain a $K_{e^*(\ell,m)}$-minor for the center s of T_X.

Furthermore, suppose that the algorithm computes Σ_X on input (G, X) and let (G', X') be a pair such that there is an isomorphism f from G to G' with $f(X) = X'$. Then the algorithm computes a star decomposition $\Sigma'_{X'}$ on input (G', X') and there exists an isomorphism g from T_X to $T_{X'}$ such that for all $t \in V(T_X)$ we have $\sigma_{X'}(g(t)) = f(\sigma_X(t))$ and $\alpha_{X'}(g(t)) = f(\alpha_X(t))$.

Lemma 4.9 states an invariance condition saying that for isomorphic input the decomposition is isomorphic. This condition is not required for the proof of the Global Structure Theorem 4.1, but will be essential for the proof of the Invariant Decomposition Theorem 8.3 in Section 8. Note that Lemma 4.7 does not state such an invariance condition and in fact there does not seem to be an obvious way of ensuring invariance (for example, already the selection of X' in the first step of the proof is completely arbitrary and hence cannot be done in an invariant way). This is precisely the reason why we need to use the more general treelike decompositions in Sections 8–9 if we want the construction to be invariant.

The proof of Lemma 4.9 is deferred to Section 6.1. The algorithm repeatedly finds K_ℓ-minor images and tests if they are m-attached to S. If so, it returns it, otherwise there is a separator that we can use to decrease the bag of the center in such a way that this particular image is no longer in the torso of the center. Note that when we exclude some vertices from the bag, then new cliques can appear in the torso. The main technical challenge is to ensure that no new clique minor images are created when decreasing the size of the bag.

The third and final decomposition lemma takes a clique minor image I attached to an unbreakable set S and finds either a star decomposition where the torso of the center has "almost bounded degree" (that is, bounded degree with the exception of a bounded number of vertices) or a subdivision of a clique.

LEMMA 4.10 (BOUNDED-DEGREE STAR DECOMPOSITION). *For every $k \in \mathbb{N}$, there exist constants $c^*(k)$, $d^*(k)$, $m^*(k)$, $\ell^*(k)$ such that the following holds. There is an $f(k)|V(G)|^{O(1)}$ time algorithm that given a graph G, integer k, an m-unbreakable set X of size $3m-2$ (for $m := m^*(k)$) and an image I of K_ℓ that is m-attached to X (for $\ell := \ell^*(k)$),*

(1) either finds a subdivision of K_k in G,
(2) or computes a star decomposition $\Sigma_X = (T_X, \sigma_X, \alpha_X)$ of $G \cup K[X]$ having adhesion $< |X|$ such that $X \subseteq \beta(s)$ and at most $c^*(k)$ vertices of $\tau(s)$ have degree greater than $d^*(k)$ in $\tau(s)$, where s is the center of T_X.

Furthermore, suppose that the algorithm computes Σ_X on input (G, X) and let (G', X') be a pair such that there is an isomorphism f from G to G' with $f(X) = X'$. Then the algorithm computes a star decomposition $\Sigma'_{X'}$ on input (G', X') and there exists an isomorphism g from T_X to $T_{X'}$ such that for all $t \in V(T_X)$ we have $\sigma_{X'}(g(t)) = f(\sigma_X(t))$ and $\alpha_{X'}(g(t)) = f(\alpha_X(t))$.

The proof of Lemma 4.10 is deferred to Section 6.2. The main idea is that we are trying to remove every high-degree vertex from the bag of the center using appropriate separations. If there are at least k high-degree vertices that cannot be removed this way, then these vertices are close to the clique minor image I, and we can use this fact to construct a subdivision of a clique.

With the three local decomposition algorithms of Lemmas 4.7–4.10 at hand, we are ready to prove Local Structure Theorem 4.2:

PROOF PROOF OF LOCAL STRUCTURE THEOREM 4.2. Let $c(k) = c^*(k)$, $d(k) = d^*(k)$, $\ell = \ell(k) = \ell^*(k)$, $m = m(k) = m^*(k)$ using the functions c^*, d^*, ℓ^*, m^* in Lemma 4.10. Let $e(k) = e^*(\ell, m)$ for the function e^* in Lemma 4.9. Let $b(k) = b^*(m)$ for the function $b^*(k)$ in Lemma 4.7. Let $a(k) = 3m-3$. Note that $b^*(m) \geq 3m-3$ in Lemma 4.7: otherwise, neither (1) nor (2) would be possible if $X = V(G)$ and $|X| = 3m-3$. Thus we can assume $b(k) \geq a(k)$.

If $S = V(G)$, then we can return a star decomposition consisting of a single center node s with $\alpha(s) = V(G)$ and $\sigma(s) = \varnothing$ (here we use that $b(k) \geq a(k) \geq |S|$). Let $X := S \cup \{v\}$ for an arbitrary vertex $v \notin S$. Let us call the algorithm of Lemma 4.7 on G, X, and m. If it returns a star decomposition $\Sigma_X = (T_X, \alpha_X, \sigma_X)$, then we return it and we are done. Note that in this case $v \in X \subseteq \beta_X(s)$ for the root s of T_X, thus $v \notin \alpha_X(t)$ for any tip t of T_X, which means that the requirement $\alpha_X(t) \subset \alpha_X(s)$ indeed holds. Otherwise, let X' be the m-unbreakable superset of X returned by the algorithm. Let us call the algorithm of Lemma 4.9 with G, ℓ, m, and X'. Again, if it returns a star decomposition, we are done. Otherwise, it returns a K_ℓ-minor image I that is m-attached to I. Let us call the algorithm of Lemma 4.10 with G, k, X', and I. It returns either a K_k-subdivision or a star decomposition; we are done in both cases. □

5. TANGLES

In the proofs of the local decomposition lemmas (Section 6), we need to deal with separations that separate some set from (the larger part of) an unbreakable set. Robertson and Seymour [23] defined the abstract notion of *tangles*, which is a convenient tool for describing such separations. While in principle our results could be described without introducing tangles (in particular, we are not using any previous results about tangles), we feel that they provide a convenient notation for our purposes, and they make our results slightly more general.

Let $m \in \mathbb{N} \setminus \{0\}$. A *tangle of order m* in a graph G is a set $\mathfrak{T}$ of separations of G of order $< m$ such that the following axioms are satisfied:

(TA.1) For every separation (A, B) of G of order $< m$, either $(A, B) \in \mathfrak{T}$ or $(B, A) \in \mathfrak{T}$.

(TA.2) For all $(A_1, B_1), (A_2, B_2), (A_3, B_3) \in \mathfrak{T}$ it holds that $A_1 \cup A_2 \cup A_3 \neq G$.

(TA.3) For all $(A, B) \in \mathfrak{T}$ it holds that $V(A) \neq V(G)$.

Intuitively, one can think of each separation (A, B) in the tangle $\mathfrak{T}$ as having a "small side" A and "big side" B. Axiom (TA.2) states that the "small side" is so small that not even three of them can cover the whole graph.

In this paper, we only consider tangles of a special form. These tangles are defined by unbreakable sets (in the sense of Definition 4.5).

LEMMA 5.1. *Let X be an m-unbreakable set of size at least $(3m-2)$ in graph G. Let $\mathfrak{T}$ contain every separation of order $< m$ such that $|(X \cap V(B)) \cup V(A \cap B)| \geq |X|$. Then $\mathfrak{T}$ is a tangle of order m in G (and we call it the tangle of order m defined by the set X). Furthermore, for every separation $(A, B) \in \mathfrak{T}$ it holds that $|V(A) \cap X| \leq |V(A \cap B)| < m$.*

The size of a tangle (even of small order) can be exponential in the size of the graph. Observe that specifying the vertex set $V(A) \cap V(B)$ is not sufficient for describing the separation (A, B). For example, a star with n leaves have at least 2^n separations of order 1. Therefore, when stating algorithmic results that take a graph and a tangle as input, we have to state how the tangle is represented. To obtain maximum generality of the results, we assume that the tangle is given by an oracle. We define two type of oracles. The first type simply answers if a separation (A, B) is a member of the tangle. However, in applications we often need to find a separation of small order in the tangle that separates two given sets S and T. The min-cut oracle answers queries of this type. Note that there are more than one natural way of defining such oracles, in particular, we might want to allow or forbid the separator $V(A) \cap V(B)$ to intersect S and/or T. We define the min-cut oracle in a way that includes all these possibilities: the query contains a set F of forbidden vertices and we require the separator to be disjoint from F.

DEFINITION 5.2. *Let $\mathfrak{T}$ be a tangle of order k in a graph G.*

(1) An oracle *for $\mathfrak{T}$ answers in constant time whether a given separation (A,B) is in $\mathfrak{T}$.*
(2) Given sets $S,T,F \subseteq V(G)$ and an integer $\lambda < k$, a min cut oracle *for $\mathfrak{T}$ returns in constant time either a separation $(A,B) \in \mathfrak{T}$ of order at most λ such that $S \subseteq V(A)$, $T \subseteq V(B)$, and $V(A) \cap V(B) \cap F = \emptyset$, or "no" if no such separation exists.*

For tangles defined by unbreakable sets it is easy to implement both type of oracles:

LEMMA 5.3. *Let X be an m-unbreakable set of size at least $3m-2$ in a graph G and let $\mathfrak{T}$ be the tangle of order m defined by X.*

(1) The oracle for $\mathfrak{T}$ can be implemented in polynomial time.
(2) The min cut oracle for $\mathfrak{T}$ can be implemented in time $2^{|X|} \cdot |V(G)|^{O(1)}$.

5.1 Boundaries and separations

In this section, we summarize some useful properties of boundaries of sets and their relations to tangles. These facts will be used extensively in Section 6.

Recall that $\partial^G(X) = |N^G(X)|$. The following lemma states that the function ∂ satisfies the submodular inequality and a variant of the posimodular inequality:

LEMMA 5.4. *Let G be a graph and $X,Y \subseteq V(G)$.*

(1) $\partial(X) + \partial(Y) \geq \partial(X \cap Y) + \partial(X \cup Y)$.
(2) $\partial(X) + \partial(Y) \geq \partial(X \setminus N^G[Y]) + \partial(Y \setminus N^G[X])$.

We often work with separations that separate a subset of vertices from the rest of the graph:

DEFINITION 5.5. *Let G be a graph and $X \subseteq V(G)$. Then we define the separation $S_G(X) = (A,B)$ by $A = G[N^G[X]]$, $V(B) = V(G) \setminus X$, $E(B) = E(G) \setminus E(A)$.*

Note that the order of $S_G(X)$ is exactly $\partial^G(X)$.

The following observation, together with Lemma 5.4, will allow us to use uncrossing arguments in Section 6:

LEMMA 5.6. *Let $\mathfrak{T}$ be a tangle of order m in graph G and let $X,Y \subseteq V(G)$ be sets such that $S_G(X), S_G(Y) \in \mathfrak{T}$.*

(1) For every $X' \subseteq X$, if $S_G(X')$ is of order $< m$, then $S_G(X') \in \mathfrak{T}$.
(2) If $S_G(X \cap Y)$ is of order $< m$, then $S_G(X \cap Y) \in \mathfrak{T}$.
(3) If $S_G(X \cup Y)$ is of order $< m$, then $S_G(X \cup Y) \in \mathfrak{T}$.

We say that a separation *removes* a set $X \subseteq V(G)$ if $X \subseteq V(A) \setminus V(B)$. Note that $S_G(W)$ removes X if and only if $X \subseteq W$. It follows from Lemmas 5.4 and 5.6 that for every set X, there is a unique "closest minimum cut" of the tangle that removes X:

LEMMA 5.7. *Let $\mathfrak{T}$ be a tangle of order m in a graph G. Suppose that $X \subseteq V(G)$ is a set such that there is a $W \subseteq V(G)$ with $X \subseteq W$ and $S_G(W) \in \mathfrak{T}$. Then there is a unique $W(X) \subseteq V(G)$ such that*

(1) $X \subseteq W(X)$,
(2) $S_G(W(X)) \in \mathfrak{T}$,
(3) the order of $S_G(W(X))$ is minimum possible, and
(4) among such sets, $|W(X)|$ is minimum possible.

Furthermore, given a min cut oracle for $\mathfrak{T}$, this unique minimal set can be found in polynomial time.

PROOF. Let $m_0 < m$ be the minimum possible order of a separation $S_G(W) \in \mathfrak{T}$ over all W containing X. To prove the uniqueness of $W(X)$, we show a stronger statement: there is such a $W(X)$ with the property that $W(X) \subseteq W$ for every $W \supseteq X$ with $S_G(W) \in \mathfrak{T}$ and $\partial(W) = m_0$. To prove this statement, suppose that $W_1, W_2 \supseteq X$ are sets such that $S_G(W_1), S_G(W_2) \in \mathfrak{T}$ both have order m_0. By Lemma 5.4(1),

$$2m_0 = \partial(W_1) + \partial(W_2) \geq \partial(W_1 \cap W_2) + \partial(W_1 \cup W_2).$$

Observe that $W_1 \cap W_2$ and $W_1 \cup W_2$ both contain X. If $\partial(W_1 \cup W_2) < m_0$, then $S_G(W_1 \cup W_2) \in \mathfrak{T}$ by Lemma 5.6(3), contradicting the minimality of the order of $S_G(W_1)$ and $S_G(W_2)$. If $\partial(W_1 \cup W_2) \geq m_0$, then $\partial(W_1 \cap W_2) \leq m_0$. By Lemma 5.6(2), $S_G(W_1 \cap W_2) \in \mathfrak{T}$, and its order is not larger than the order of $S_G(W_1)$ and $S_G(W_2)$. Thus the intersection of the two sets is also a set satisfying the requirements. It follows that the common intersection of every $W_i \supseteq X$ such that $\partial(W_i) = m_0$ and $S_G(W_i) \in \mathfrak{T}$ is the required minimal set $W(I)$.

To find this unique set $W(X)$, we let $S := X$, initially define $T = \emptyset$, and use the min cut oracle to check if there is a separation (A,B) of order at most λ with $X \subseteq V(A)$, $T \subseteq V(B)$, and $V(A) \cap V(B)$ disjoint from $F := X$. Let us fix the smallest λ for which the answer is yes: then the min cut oracle returns a separation $(A,B) \in \mathfrak{T}$, such that $W := V(A) \setminus V(B)$ satisfies the first three properties above. To ensure that the last property holds as well, we pick a vertex $v \in W$, and call the min cut oracle to check if there is a separation $(A',B') \in \mathfrak{T}$ of order λ such that $X \subseteq V(A')$, $T \cup \{v\} \subseteq V(B')$, and $V(A') \cap V(B')$ disjoint from X. If there is such a separation, then we include v in T, and repeat this process with the new separation (A',B'). As the size of T strictly increases, eventually we arrive at a set W such that including any vertex $v \in W$ into T increases the minimum cut size to above λ. We have seen that this set W contains the unique minimal set $W(X)$ defined above. Furthermore, $W = W(X)$ has to hold: otherwise, including a vertex $v \in W \setminus W(X)$ into T would not increase the minimum cut size. □

The following observation is immediate:

PROPOSITION 5.8. *If $G[X]$ is connected, then $G[W(X)]$ is connected.*

6. PROOFS OF THE LOCAL DECOMPOSITION LEMMAS

This section completes the proof of Global Structure Theorem 4.1 by proving Lemmas 4.9 and 4.10 (Sections 6.1 and 6.2). Note that the proofs in this section contain somewhat more work than what is strictly necessary for the proof of the Global Structure Theorem 4.1: the proof of the invariance conditions in Lemmas 4.9 and 4.10 require extra arguments. These invariance conditions are not needed for the Global Structure Theorem, but they will be crucial for the invariance of the treelike decompositions in Section 8 and therefore for the results of Section 9 on isomorphism and canonization.

We prove variants of Lemmas 4.9 and 4.10 stated in terms of tangles instead of unbreakable sets (Lemmas 6.9 and 6.11, respectively); the proofs of Lemmas 4.9 and 4.10 follows easily from these variants. The statements involving tangles need the following definitions:

DEFINITION 6.1. *Let $\mathfrak{T}, \mathfrak{T}'$ be tangles in graphs G, G', respectively. An* isomorphism *from $(G, \mathfrak{T})$ to $(G', \mathfrak{T}')$ is an isomorphism f from G to G' such that for all $(A, B) \in \mathfrak{T}$ we have $(f(A), f(B)) \in \mathfrak{T}'$.*

DEFINITION 6.2. *Let $\Sigma = (T, \beta)$ be a star decomposition of graph G and let $\mathfrak{T}$ be a tangle of G. We say that Σ* respects *$\mathfrak{T}$ if for every tip t of T the separation (A, B) with $A = G[\gamma(t)]$ and $V(B) = V(G) \setminus \alpha(t)$ is in $\mathfrak{T}$. In particular, this implies $S_G(\alpha(t)) \in \mathfrak{T}$ and $|\sigma(t)|$ is less than the order of $\mathfrak{T}$.*

A key tool in our proofs is the following lemma, which follows from [24, (5.3)]:

LEMMA 6.3 ([24]). *For every $r \in \mathbb{N}$, there is a constant $t(r) = O(r^2)$ such that the following holds. Let G be a graph and $R \subseteq V(G)$ with $|R| = r$. Let $t \geq t(r)$ and let $(B_i)_{i\in[t]}$ be an image of a K_t-minor in G. Suppose that there is no separation (G_1, G_2) of G of order $< |R|$ with $R \subseteq V(G_1)$ and $B_b \cap V(G_1) = \emptyset$ for some $b \in [t]$. Then there is a $K_{|R|}$-minor image in G such that every branch set contains exactly one vertex of R and such an image can be found in polynomial time.*

6.1 Star decomposition with clique-minor free center

We prove Lemma 4.9 in this section. First we prove a variant of the lemma stated in terms of tangles (Lemma 6.9) and then deduce Lemma 4.9 it at the end of the section.

Recall that a separation (A, B) removes a set X if $X \subseteq V(A) \setminus V(B)$. We say that a separation (A, B) *removes* the H-minor image $I = (I_w)_{w\in V(H)}$ if it removes one of the branch sets, that is, $I_w \subseteq V(A) \setminus V(B)$ for some $w \in V(H)$. A tangle $\mathfrak{T}$ in G *removes an H-minor image I* if I is removed by some $(A, B) \in \mathfrak{T}$ with order $< |H|$. The following lemma is analogous to Lemma 5.7: for every clique minor, there is a unique "closest minimum separation" that removes it.

LEMMA 6.4. *Let $\mathfrak{T}$ be a tangle of order m in a graph G and let $e > 2m$. For every image I of K_e in G removed by $\mathfrak{T}$, there is a unique $W(I) \subseteq V(G)$ such that*

(1) $S_G(W(I))$ removes I,
(2) $S_G(W(I)) \in \mathfrak{T}$,
(3) the order of $S_G(W(I))$ is minimum possible, and
(4) among such sets, $|W(I)|$ is minimum possible.

Furthermore, $G[W(I)]$ is connected and there is a polynomial-time algorithm that, given G, m, I, and a min cut oracle for $\mathfrak{T}$, either finds $W(I)$ or concludes that $\mathfrak{T}$ does not remove I.

PROOF. As $\mathfrak{T}$ removes I, there has to be at least one separation $(A, B) \in \mathfrak{T}$ that removes I. Thus the set $W = V(A) \setminus V(B)$ is one such set. To prove the uniqueness, suppose that there are two distinct minimal sets X and Y. By Lemma 5.4(1), either $\partial(X \cap Y) \leq \partial(X)$ or $\partial(X \cup Y) < \partial(Y)$.

Suppose first that $\partial(X \cap Y) \leq \partial(X) < m$. By Lemma 5.6(2), $S_G(X \cap Y) \in \mathfrak{T}$. We claim that $S_G(X \cap Y)$ removes I. As both $S_G(X)$ and $S_G(Y)$ remove I, there are vertices $x, y \in V(K_e)$ such that $V(I_x) \subseteq X$ and $V(I_y) \subseteq Y$. Since $\partial(X), \partial(Y) < m$ and $e > 2m$, there is a vertex $z \in K_e$ such that $V(I_z)$ is disjoint from $N^G(X) \cup N^G(Y)$. As K_e is a clique, a vertex of $V(I_z)$ has to be adjacent to $V(I_x) \subseteq X$, which is only possible if this vertex is also in X (since it cannot be in $N^G(X)$). It follows that $V(I_z)$ is fully contained in X. A symmetrical argument shows that $V(I_z) \subseteq Y$. Thus $V(I_z) \subseteq X \cap Y$, i.e., $S_G(X \cap Y)$ removes I. Therefore, $X \cap Y \subset X$ and $\partial(X \cap Y) \leq \partial(X)$ contradicts the minimality of X.

Suppose now that $\partial(X \cup Y) < \partial(Y) < m$. By Lemma 5.6(3), $S_G(X \cup Y) \in \mathfrak{T}$. Clearly, $S_G(X \cup Y)$ removes I (as any branch set contained in X or Y is also contained in $X \cup Y$). Therefore, $X \cup Y$ contradicts the minimality of Y.

To check if an image I is removed by $\mathfrak{T}$, we use the algorithm of Lemma 5.7 to compute the set $W(I_v)$ for every $v \in V(K_e)$ (if such a set exists). If $\mathfrak{T}$ removes I, then at least one of these sets should exist. Furthermore, if $\mathfrak{T}$ removes I, then it should be clear that $W(I)$ is equal to one of these sets $W(I_v)$: if $W(I)$ contains I_v, then it cannot be different from $W(I_v)$ (as it would contradict the minimality and uniqueness of either $W(I)$ or $W(I_v)$). As $W(I_v)$ is connected by Prop. 5.8, it follows that $W(I)$ is connected as well. □

A simple uncrossing argument shows that the minimum separations defined in Lemma 6.4 cannot properly intersect each other:

LEMMA 6.5. *Let $\mathfrak{T}$ be a tangle of order m in a graph G and let $e > 2m$. Let I^x and I^y be two K_e-minor images removed by $\mathfrak{T}$. Then either*

(1) $W(I^x) \subseteq W(I^y)$,
(2) $W(I^x) \supseteq W(I^y)$, or
(3) $W(I^x)$ and $W(I^y)$ are disjoint and do not touch.

PROOF. Let $X := W(I^x)$ and $Y := W(I^y)$ and suppose that none of the three possibilities hold. Assume first that I^x has a branch set fully contained in $X \cap Y \subset X$. If $\partial(X \cap Y) \leq \partial(X) < m$, then $S_G(X \cap Y) \in \mathfrak{T}$ by Lemma 5.6(2) and $S_G(X \cap Y)$ removes I^x, contradicting the minimality of $W(I^x)$. Thus we can assume that $\partial(X \cap Y) > \partial(X)$. By Lemma 5.4, it follows that $\partial(X \cup Y) < \partial(Y) < m$. Therefore, $S_G(X \cup Y)$ is in $\mathfrak{T}$ by Lemma 5.6(3) and it clearly removes I^y (since $S_G(Y)$ already does), contradicting the minimality of $Y = W(I^y)$.

We have proved that I^x has no branch set fully contained in $X \cap Y$, and a symmetrical argument shows that I^y has no such branch set either. By Lemma 5.4(2), either $\partial(X) \geq \partial(X \setminus N[Y])$ or $\partial(Y) \geq \partial(Y \setminus N[X])$. Assume without loss of generality the first case. Consider a branch set I_1^x of I^x fully contained in X (such a set exists, as $S_G(X)$ removes I^x) and a branch set I_2^x disjoint from $N^G(X) \cup N^G(Y)$ (since $e > 2m$, there has to be such a set). The branch set I_2^x has a vertex adjacent to $I_1^x \subseteq X$. Since I_2^x is disjoint from $N^G(X)$, this is only possible if I_2^x is fully contained in X. Moreover, we assumed that I_2^x is disjoint from $N^G(Y)$ and it is not fully contained in $X \cap Y$, thus I_2^x is fully contained in $X \setminus N^G[Y]$, that is, the separation $S_G(X \setminus N^G[Y])$ removes I^x. Note that $X \setminus N^G[Y]$ is a proper subset of X, otherwise X and Y are disjoint and do not touch. Lemma 5.6(1) implies that $S_G(X \setminus N[Y]) \in \mathfrak{T}$, and therefore $X \setminus N[Y] \subset X$ violates the minimality of $X = W(I^x)$. □

Another useful property of the definition of minimum separation in Lemma 6.4 is that if $S_G(W(I)) = (A, B)$, then the clique minor I allows us to connect vertices of $V(A) \cap V(B)$

with each other using paths in A in an arbitrary way. We use the following definition to state this property:

DEFINITION 6.6. *We say that a separation (A,B) of order m is* generic *if there is a K_m-minor image in A such that each branch set contains exactly one vertex of $V(A)\cap V(B)$. Such an image is called a* witness.

LEMMA 6.7. *Let $\mathfrak{T}$ be a tangle of order m in a graph G and let $e > t(m)+m$ for the function t of Lemma 6.3. For every image I of K_e in G removed by $\mathfrak{T}$, the separation $S_G(W(I))$ is generic. Furthermore, given I and a min cut oracle for $\mathfrak{T}$, a witness can be found in polynomial time.*

PROOF. Let $S_G(W(I)) = (A,B)$ and $R = V(A)\cap V(B)$. By definition, (A,B) removes I, thus at least one branch set of I is contained in $V(A)\setminus V(B)$ and at most $|R| < m$ branch sets intersect R. Thus at least $t(m)$ branch sets are fully contained in $V(A)\setminus V(B)$. Therefore, A contains a $K_{t(m)}$-minor image I'. We verify that the conditions of Lemma 6.3 hold for graph A and set R. Suppose that there is a separation (G_1,G_2) of order $< |R|$ with $R \subseteq G_1$ and $I'_w \subseteq V(G_2)\setminus V(G_1)$ for some branch set I'_w of I' (which is also a branch set of I). Let $X' = V(G_2)\setminus V(G_1) \subset V(A)\setminus V(B) = W(I)$. It follows that $S_G(X')$ has order $< |R|$ (which is the order of (A,B)) and is in $\mathfrak{T}$ by Lemma 5.6(1). However, $S_G(X')$ also removes I, contradicting the minimality of $W(I)$. We can conclude that A and R satisfy the conditions of Lemma 6.3, and the existence of the required $K_{|R|}$-minor image follows. □

It follows from Lemma 6.7 that if $W(I) = (A,B)$, then removing $V(A)\setminus V(B)$ and replacing $V(A)\cap V(B)$ with the clique $K[V(A)\cap V(B)]$ does not create any new clique minor images in B (because the edges in the clique $K[V(A)\cap V(B)]$ can be simulated by connections in A in the original graph). Repeated application of this observation shows that after removing all the clique minor images, we get a bag whose torso does not contain clique minors of the given size.

LEMMA 6.8. *Let $\mathfrak{T}$ be a tangle of order m in a graph G and let $e > t(m)+m$ for the function t of Lemma 6.3. Let $I^1, \dots, I^p$ be K_e-minor images removed by $\mathfrak{T}$. Let $W = \bigcup_{i=1}^p W(I^i)$ and let $G' = \mathrm{torso}(G, V(G)\setminus W)$. The graph G' has a K_e-minor I' if and only if G has a K_e-minor image I not removed by any $S_G(W(I^i))$. Furthermore, given a min cut oracle for $\mathfrak{T}$ and such a K_e-minor image I, one can compute a K_e-minor image I' in G' in polynomial time and vice versa.*

PROOF. We can assume that the sets $W(I^1),\dots,W(I^m)$ are pairwise incomparable (because if $W(I^i)\subseteq W(I^j)$, then omitting I^i from this collection does not change W), thus by Lemma 6.5, we can assume that these sets are pairwise disjoint and do not touch. This means that $R_i = N^G(W(I^i))$ is a subset of $V(G)\setminus W$ and induces a clique in G'. By Lemma 6.4, each $G[W(I^i)]$ is connected. Thus $G' = \mathrm{torso}(G, V(G)\setminus W)$ is exactly the union of $G\setminus W$ with a clique on each R_i.

Let I' be the image of a K_e-minor in G'. Note that this is not necessarily a K_e-minor image in $G\setminus W$ as G' has edges that $G\setminus W$ do not have. However, we can use the subgraph inside $G[W(I^i)]$ to simulate these edges. By Lemma 6.7, every $S_G(W(I^i))$ is generic and we can obtain the corresponding clique minor images. This means that for each R_i, there is a set of r pairwise disjoint and touching connected subgraphs in $G[N^G[W(I^i)]]$. Using these connected sets, we can extend each I'_w of G' into a connected set I_w of G and obtain a K_e-minor image I in G.

For the reverse direction, let I be a K_e-minor image in G not removed by any $S_G(W(I^i))$. Let I' be defined by $I'_w = G'[V(I_w)\setminus W]$ for every $w \in V(K_e)$. Note that $V(I'_w) \neq \emptyset$: this would be only possible if $V(I_w) \subseteq W(I^i)$ for some $1 \le i \le p$, which would imply that $S_G(W(I^i))$ removes I. We claim that I' is a K_e-minor image. The connectedness of I'_w is easy to see: any path with internal vertices in $W(I^i)$ can be replaced by an edge in R_i (as R_i induces a clique in G'). To see that I'_w and I'_u touch for every $w,u \in V(K_e)$, consider an edge e between I_w and I_u in G. If both endpoints of e are in $W(I^i)\cup R_i$, then I'_w and I'_u both intersect R_i, hence they touch. Otherwise, e is an edge of $G\setminus W$, implying that it is also an edge of G'. □

Now we state and prove a version of Lemma 4.9 in terms of tangles:

LEMMA 6.9. *For every $\ell, m \in \mathbb{N}$, there is a constant $e'(\ell,m)$ such that the following holds. There is an $f(\ell,m)\cdot|V(G)|^{O(1)}$ time algorithm that, given a graph G, ℓ, m, a min cut oracle for a tangle $\mathfrak{T}$ of order m, either*

(1) finds a K_ℓ-minor image I not removed by $\mathfrak{T}$, or
(2) computes a $\mathfrak{T}$-respecting star decomposition $\Sigma_{\mathfrak{T}} = (T_{\mathfrak{T}}, \alpha_{\mathfrak{T}}, \sigma_{\mathfrak{T}})$ with center s such that $\tau_{\mathfrak{T}}(s)$ does not contain a $K_{e'(\ell,m)}$-minor.

Furthermore, if the algorithm returns $\Sigma_{\mathfrak{T}}$ for $(G,\mathfrak{T})$ and $\mathfrak{T}'$ is another tangle of order m in a graph G', and f is an isomorphism from $(G,\mathfrak{T})$ to $(G',\mathfrak{T}')$, then the algorithm returns a star decomposition $\Sigma_{\mathfrak{T}'}$ for $(G',\mathfrak{T}')$ such that there is an isomorphism g from $T_{\mathfrak{T}}$ to $T_{\mathfrak{T}'}$ such that for all $t\in V(T_{\mathfrak{T}})$ we have $\sigma_{\mathfrak{T}'}(g(t)) = f(\sigma_{\mathfrak{T}}(t))$ and $\alpha_{\mathfrak{T}'}(g(t)) = f(\alpha_{\mathfrak{T}}(t))$.

PROOF. Let $e = e'(\ell,m) = \max(\ell, t(m)+m+1)$ for the function t in Lemma 6.3. We show first that if $\mathfrak{T}$ removes every K_ℓ-minor image (and therefore every K_e-minor image as $e \ge \ell$), then there exists a star decomposition satisfying the requirements. Suppose that $\mathfrak{T}$ removes every K_ℓ-minor image, implying that $W(I)$ is defined for every K_e-minor image I. Let $I^1, \dots, I^p$ be the list of all K_e-minor images for which $W(I^i)$ is inclusionwise maximal. By Lemma 6.5, $W(I^i)$ and $W(I^j)$ are disjoint and do not touch for $i \neq j$. Let $W = \bigcup_{i=1}^p W(I^i)$. We construct a star decomposition $\Sigma_{\mathfrak{T}} = (T_{\mathfrak{T}}, \sigma_{\mathfrak{T}}, \alpha_{\mathfrak{T}})$ with center s and p tips t_i $(1 \le i \le p)$. We set $\alpha_{\mathfrak{T}}(s) = V(G)$, $\sigma_{\mathfrak{T}}(s) = \emptyset$, $\alpha_{\mathfrak{T}}(t_i) = W(I^i)$, and $\sigma_{\mathfrak{T}}(t_i) = N^G(W(I^i))$.

It easy easy to verify that Δ is a tree decomposition:

Claim 1. Δ satisfies properties (TD.1)–(TD.5).

The definition of $W(I^i)$ implies that $S_G(W(I^i)) \in \mathfrak{T}$ for every $1 \le i \le p$. Therefore,

Claim 2. Δ respects $\mathfrak{T}$.

Claim 3. $G' = \tau(s) = \mathrm{torso}(G, V(G)\setminus W)$ does not contain a K_e.

Proof. If G' contains a K_e-minor, then Lemma 6.8 implies that there is a K_e-minor image I in G not removed by any of the separations $S_G(W(I^i))$. However, this contradicts the assumption that $I^i, \dots, I^p$ is the list of all images for which $W(I^i)$ is inclusionwise maximal. ⌟

Algorithmically, we can find the set W defined above as follows. We construct collections $\mathcal{I}^{(0)} \subset \mathcal{I}^{(1)} \subset \dots$ of K_e-minor images, each of which is removed by $\mathfrak{T}$. We start with $\mathcal{I}^{(0)} = \emptyset$. Given $\mathcal{I}^{(j)}$, we construct $\mathcal{I}^{(j+1)}$ as follows. Let $W^{(j)} = \bigcup_{I \in \mathcal{I}^{(j)}} W(I)$ and $G^{(j)} = \text{torso}(G, V(G) \setminus W^{(j)})$. We test if $G^{(j)}$ has a K_e-minor (using the algorithm of Theorem 2.1). By Lemma 6.8, if there is a K_e-minor model I' in $G^{(j)}$, then there is a corresponding K_e-minor model $I^{(j)}$ of G which is not removed by $S_G(W(I))$ for any $I \in \mathcal{I}^{(j)}$. Let us use the algorithm of Lemma 6.4 to compute the set $W(I^{(j)})$. If the algorithm returns that $W(I^{(j)})$ is not defined, that is, $I^{(j)}$ is not removed by $\mathfrak{T}$, then we can stop and return $I^{(j)}$ (or more precisely, as $e \geq \ell$, a restriction of $I^{(j)}$ to a K_ℓ-minor) and we are done. Otherwise, let us obtain $\mathcal{I}^{(j+1)}$ from $\mathcal{I}^{(j)}$ by inserting $I^{(j)}$. Let us observe that $W(I^{(j)}) \notin W^{(j)}$: by Lemma 6.5, $W(I^{(j)}) \subseteq W^{(j)}$ is only possible if $W(I^{(j)}) \subseteq W(I)$ for some $I \in \mathcal{I}^{(j)}$, but this means that $S_G(W(I))$ already removes $I^{(j)}$, a contradiction. It follows that $W^{(j)} \subset W^{(j+1)}$. After including $I^{(j)}$ into $\mathcal{I}^{(j+1)}$, we repeat this procedure until we arrive to a j such that $G^{(j)}$ has no K_e-minor.

As the size of $W^{(j)}$ strictly increases in each step, the process described above stops in at most $|V(G)|$ steps with a $G^{(j)}$ that does not contain a K_e-minor.

Claim 4. $W^{(j)} = W$.

Proof. Suppose that $W^{(j)} \neq W$, i.e., there is an image I^* such that $W(I^*) \notin W^{(j)}$. Since $G^{(j)}$ has no K_e-minor, by Lemma 6.8, there is an $I \in \mathcal{I}^{(j)}$ such that $S_G(W(I))$ removes I^*. As $S_G(W(I))$ and $S_G(W(I^*))$ both remove I^*, the sets $W(I)$ and $W(I^*)$ both contain a branch set of I^*, hence it is not possible that the two sets are disjoint and do not touch. Therefore, by Lemma 6.5, one of the two sets is contained in the other. From $W(I^*) \notin W^{(j)}$, we know that $W(I^*) \subseteq W(I)$ is not possible, hence we have $W(I) \subset W(I^*)$, implying that $S_G(W(I^*))$ removes I as well. Now $\partial(W(I^*)) < \partial(W(I))$ would contradict the minimality of $W(I)$ and $\partial(W(I^*)) \leq \partial(W(I))$ would contradict the minimality of $W(I^*)$ (as $|W(I)| < |W(I^*)|$). Thus we have proved that $W^{(j)}$ obtained by this procedure is indeed the set W defined at the beginning of the proof. ⌟

What remains to be proven is the invariance condition. Suppose that $\mathfrak{T}'$ is another tangle of order m in a graph G'. Let f be an isomorphism from $(G, \mathfrak{T})$ to $(G', \mathfrak{T}')$. Let $I = (I_v)_{v \in V(K_\ell)}$ be a K_e-minor image in G and let $I' = (f(I_v))_{v \in V(K_e)}$ be the corresponding K_e-minor image in G'. Let $W(I)$ and $W'(I')$ be the set given by Lemma 6.4 on I and I', respectively.

Claim 5. $W'(I') = f(W(I))$.

Proof. The definition of the set $W(I)$ depends only on the branch sets of I, the tangle $\mathfrak{T}$ and the graph-theoretical properties of G (size of the boundaries of certain sets etc.) and all these properties are preserved by f. ⌟

Therefore, if $\{W(I^1), \dots, W(I^p)\}$ is the collection of inclusionwise maximal sets appearing in the definition of W for $(G, \mathfrak{T})$, then exactly $\{f(W(I^1)), \dots, f(W(I^p))\}$ is the collection of sets appearing in the definition of W'. If follows that for every t_i, there is a $g(t_i)$ such that $\alpha_{\mathfrak{T}}(t_i) = W(I^i)$ and $\alpha_{\mathfrak{T}'}(g(t_i)) = f(W(I^i))$. Moreover, $\sigma_{\mathfrak{T}}(t_i) = N^G(W(I^i))$ and $\sigma_{\mathfrak{T}'}(g(t_i)) = N^{G'}(f(W(I^i))) = f(N^G(W(I^i)))$ follows, as required. Setting $g(s) = s'$ (where s' is the center of the decomposition of G') completes the definition of g. □

Finally, we can prove Lemma 4.9 by invoking Lemma 6.9 on the tangle defined by the unbreakable set X:

Proof (of Lemma 4.9). Let $e^*(\ell, m) = e'(\ell, m) + 3m - 2$ for the function x' in Lemma 6.9. Let $\mathfrak{T}$ be the tangle of order m defined by the m-unbreakable set X; Lemma 5.1 provides an implementation of the min-cut oracle for $\mathfrak{T}$. Let us call the algorithm of Lemma 6.9 with G, $\mathfrak{T}$, ℓ, and m. If it returns a K_ℓ-minor image I not removed by $\mathfrak{T}$, then this is equivalent to saying that I is m-attached to X. Thus we can return I and we are done. Otherwise, the algorithm of Lemma 6.9 returns a $\mathfrak{T}$-respecting star decomposition $\Sigma_{\mathfrak{T}} = (T_{\mathfrak{T}}, \alpha_{\mathfrak{T}}, \sigma_{\mathfrak{T}})$ of G. We construct a star decomposition $\Sigma_X = (T_X, \alpha_X, \sigma_X)$ as follows. First, let $T_X = T_{\mathfrak{T}}$ and for the center s of T_X, let $\alpha_X(s) = V(G)$ and $\sigma_X(s) = \emptyset$. For every tip t of T_X, we let $\alpha_X(t) = \alpha_{\mathfrak{T}}(t) \setminus X$ and $\sigma_X(t) = \sigma_{\mathfrak{T}}(t) \cup (X \cap \alpha_{\mathfrak{T}}(t))$. It is straightforward to verify that Σ_X is also a star decomposition of G, and in fact it is star decomposition even for the supergraph $G \cup K[X]$ (since $X \subseteq \beta_X(s)$). Note that $\tau_{\mathfrak{T}}(s) \setminus X = \tau_X(s) \setminus X$ (because the two bags differ only in the vertices of X and all the extra edges of $G \cup K[X]$ are incident to X). As $\tau_{\mathfrak{T}}(s)$ has no $K_{e'(\ell,m)}$-minor, this means that $\tau_X(s)$ cannot have a clique minor of order $e'(\ell, m) + |X| = e^*(\ell, m)$, as required. Furthermore, as $\Sigma_{\mathfrak{T}}$ is $\mathfrak{T}$-respecting, it follows that $|\sigma_{\mathfrak{T}}(t)| < m$ and $S_G(\alpha_{\mathfrak{T}}(t)) \in \mathfrak{T}$ for every tip t. By Lemma 5.1, this also means that $|\alpha_{\mathfrak{T}}(t) \cap X| \leq m - 1$ and therefore $|\sigma_X(t)| \leq m - 1 + m - 1 < |X|$. Thus the adhesion of Σ_X is less than $|X|$, as required.[1] The invariance condition follows easily from the invariance condition of Lemma 6.9: if f is an isomorphism from G to G' with $f(X) = X'$ and $\mathfrak{T}$ and $\mathfrak{T}'$ are the tangles defined by the unbreakable sets X and X', respectively, then f is an isomorphism from $(G, \mathfrak{T})$ to $(G', \mathfrak{T}')$. □

6.2 Star decomposition with a bounded-degree center

The proof of Lemma 4.10 has the same high-level strategy as the proof of Lemma 4.9 in Section 6.1: we identify those parts of the graph that we want to exclude from the bag of the center (this time, the high-degree vertices) and we use an uncrossing argument to show that all of them can be removed more or less independently from each other. The uncrossing argument is somewhat more involved due to the technicality that a high-degree vertex can be part of the separator removing some other high-degree vertex.

First we need the following lemma, which shows that all but at most k high-degree vertices can be removed by separations in the tangle, or we can find a K_k-subdivision.

[1] This is the point (and the analogous argument in the proof of Lemma 4.10) where it becomes motived why we used the tangle $\mathfrak{T}$ defined by the unbreakable set X. If we have no bound on $|\alpha_{\mathfrak{T}}(t) \cap X|$, then moving X to the center can increase the adhesion by up to $|X| = 3m - 2$, which means that the bound on the adhesion would be larger than $|X|$. Therefore, the repeated application of this lemma in the proof of Global Structure Theorem 4.1 would increase the adhesion in each step. In all the arguments in the section, we were careful enough to use only separations that are in $\mathfrak{T}$, and therefore we have the bound that the component of each child of t contains at most $m - 1$ vertices of X.

LEMMA 6.10. *For every $k \in \mathbb{N}$, there is a constant $\ell'(k)$ such that the following holds. For a graph G, integer $k \in \mathbb{N}$, tangle $\mathfrak{T}$ of order at least $k(k-1)$, and an image I of $K_{\ell'(k)}$ not removed by $\mathfrak{T}$, let Z contain a vertex $v \in V(G)$ if v has degree at least k and either $W(\{v\})$ is undefined or $\partial(W(\{v\})) \geq k(k-1)$. If $|Z| \geq k$, then given G, k, a min-cut oracle for $\mathfrak{T}$, and I, a subdivision of K_k in G can be found in polynomial time.*

PROOF. Let $\ell'(k) = t(k(k-1))$ for the function t appearing in Lemma 6.3. We show that if $|Z| \geq k$, then we can find a subdivision of K_k in G. Let Z_0 be a subset of Z of size exactly k. Let G' be the graph obtained from G by extending each vertex $z \in Z_0$ into a clique K_z of $k-1$ vertices: for every $z \in Z_0$, we introduce $k-2$ new vertices that are adjacent to each other, to vertex z, and to every neighbor of z. The clique K_z contains z and these $k-2$ new vertices. Let $R := \bigcup_{z \in Z_0} K_z$.

Let $I_1, \ldots, I_\ell$ be the branch sets in the K_ℓ minor image I. Let us show first that the conditions of Lemma 6.3 hold for R in G'. Suppose for contradiction that (A', B') is a separation of G' of order less than $|R| = k(k-1)$ with $R \subseteq V(A')$ and $I_b \subseteq V(B') \setminus V(A')$ for some $b \in [\ell]$. Let $Q' := V(A') \cap V(B')$ be the separator. Without loss of generality, we may assume that for all $z \in Z_0$, either $K_z \cap Q' = \emptyset$ or $K_z \subseteq Q'$. Let $A := A' \setminus (R \setminus Z_0)$ and $B := B' \setminus (R \setminus Z_0)$ (i.e., we remove from Q' the extra vertices that were introduced in the definition of G'). Then (A, B) is a separation of G; let $Q = V(A) \cap V(B)$ be the separator. Now it is clear that $|Q| \leq |Q'| < k(k-1)$. Furthermore, there has to be a vertex $z \in Z_0$ which is not in Q: otherwise, $Z_0 \subseteq Q$ implies that the size of Q' in G' is at least $k(k-1)$. Therefore, (A, B) is a separation of order $< k(k-1)$ with $z \in V(A) \setminus V(B)$. This separation is in $\mathfrak{T}$: otherwise, $(B, A) \in \mathfrak{T}$ by (TA.1) (here we use that the order of $\mathfrak{T}$ is at least $k(k-1)$) and $I_b \subseteq V(B)$ means that $\mathfrak{T}$ removes I, contradicting our assumption on I. It follows that $(A, B) \in \mathfrak{T}$ is a separation of order $< k(k-1)$ with $z \in V(A) \setminus V(B)$, contradicting $z \in Z$ and the definition of Z. Thus we can conclude that there is no such separation (G'_1, G'_2) of G', and the conditions of Lemma 6.3 hold for Z and G'.

Lemma 6.3 gives us a $K_{k(k-1)}$-minor image, that is, for every $q \in R$, a connected set I_q such that these sets are pairwise disjoint and touch. Consider a partition of R into $\binom{k}{2}$ classes, each of size 2, such that for every pair $z_1, z_2 \in Z_0$ of distinct vertices, there is a class of the partition containing a vertex of $\hat{z}_1 \in K_{z_1}$ and a vertex of $\hat{z}_2 \in K_{z_2}$. (As the size of each K_z is exactly $k-1$, such a partition is possible.) We define a path $P'_{\{z_1,z_2\}} \subseteq I_{\hat{z}_1} \cup I_{\hat{z}_2}$ connecting $\hat{z}_1$ and $\hat{z}_2$; let $\mathcal{P}'$ be the collection of these $\binom{k}{2}$ paths. For each such path $P'_{\{z_1,z_2\}} \in \mathcal{P}'$ of G', there is a corresponding path $P_{\{z_1,z_2\}}$ in G: whenever $P'_{\{z_1,z_2\}}$ contains a vertex of some K_z, then we replace it by z. Let $\mathcal{P}$ be the collection of these $\binom{k}{2}$ paths in G. As the paths $\mathcal{P}'$ are pairwise disjoint, the corresponding paths in $\mathcal{P}$ can intersect only in Z_0. Therefore, we have k vertices Z_0 and a collection of $\binom{k}{2}$ internally pairwise disjoint paths that connect every pair of vertices in Z_0. In other words, we have formed a K_k topological minor image in G, which we can return. □

The following lemma is a version of Lemma 4.10 stated in terms of tangles:

LEMMA 6.11. *For every integer $k \in \mathbb{N}$, there are constants $d'(k), m'(k), \ell'(k)$ such that the following holds. There is a polynomial-time algorithm that, given a graph G, an integer k, min cut oracle for a tangle $\mathfrak{T}$ of order $m'(k)$, and an image I of $K_{\ell'(k)}$ not removed by $\mathfrak{T}$, either*

(1) finds a subdivision of K_k in G, or
(2) computes a $\mathfrak{T}$-respecting star decomposition $\Sigma_{\mathfrak{T}} = (T_{\mathfrak{T}}, \sigma_{\mathfrak{T}}, \alpha_{\mathfrak{T}})$ of G with center s such that at most k vertices of $\tau_{\mathfrak{T}}(s)$ have degree more than $d'(k)$.

Furthermore, if the algorithm returns $\Sigma_{\mathfrak{T}}$ for $(G, \mathfrak{T})$ and $\mathfrak{T}'$ is another tangle of order m in a graph G', and f is an isomorphism from $(G, \mathfrak{T})$ to $(G', \mathfrak{T}')$, then the algorithm returns a star decomposition $\Sigma_{\mathfrak{T}'}$ for $(G', \mathfrak{T}')$ such that there is an isomorphism g from $T_{\mathfrak{T}}$ to $T_{\mathfrak{T}'}$ such that for all $t \in V(T_{\mathfrak{T}})$ we have $\sigma_{\mathfrak{T}'}(g(t)) = f(\sigma_{\mathfrak{T}}(t))$ and $\alpha_{\mathfrak{T}'}(g(t)) = f(\alpha_{\mathfrak{T}}(t))$.

PROOF. Let $\ell'(k)$ be as in Lemma 6.10. We will define later (in Claim 4) a constant a depending on k; let $m'(k) = \max\{k(k-1), a+1\}$. Let Z contain a vertex $v \in V(G)$ if v has degree at least k and $\partial(W(\{v\})) \geq k(k-1)$. If $|Z| \geq k$, then we can use the algorithm of Lemma 6.10 to return a subdivision of K_k in G, and we are done.

Otherwise, let $L \subseteq V(G)$ be the set of vertices not in Z having degree at least k. For every $v \in L$, let us use the algorithm of Lemma 5.7 to compute the unique minimal set $W_v = W(\{v\})$ (as $v \notin Z$, such a set exists). By Prop. 5.8, $G[W_v]$ is connected.

Let $\mathcal{W}$ contain the inclusionwise-maximal sets in $\{W_v \mid v \in L\}$; i.e., $W_v \in \mathcal{W}$ if and only if there is no $u \in L$ with $W_v \subset W_u$. Note that we define $\mathcal{W}$ such that it does not contain duplicate sets.

Claim 1. Every $b \in V(G)$ appears in $O(k^2)$ members of $\mathcal{W}$.

Proof. For every $W \in \mathcal{W}$, let us choose a representative $v \in L$ with $W = W_v$; let $M \subseteq L$ be the set of selected representatives. We define a directed graph $\vec{H}$ on M where $\vec{vu} \in E(\vec{H})$ if and only if $u \in N^G(W_v)$. Note that $|N^G(W_v)| < k(k-1)$ implies that the outdegree of v is at most $k(k-1)-1$. This further implies that the maximum clique size in the undirected graph H underlying $\vec{H}$ is at most $2k(k-1)-1$: the average degree of every subgraph of H is at most $2k(k-1)-2$.

We show that the representatives of the sets in $\mathcal{W}$ containing b form a clique in H, thus by the argument in the previous paragraph, there can be at most $2k(k-1)-1$ sets in $\mathcal{W}$ containing b. Consider two distinct vertices $u, v \in M$ with $b \in W_u$ and $b \in W_v$. We claim that u and v are adjacent in the undirected graph H. Otherwise, $u \notin N^G(W_v)$ and $v \notin N^G(W_u)$. We consider the following cases:

Case 1: $u \in W_u \cap W_v$. By Lemma 5.4(1), we have two possibilities:

(1) $\partial(W_u \cup W_v) < \partial(W_v)$. In this case $W_u \cup W_v$ contradicts the minimality of W_v (note that by Lemma 5.6(3), $S_G(W_u \cup W_v) \in \mathfrak{T}$).
(2) $\partial(W_u \cup W_v) \geq \partial(W_v)$ and $\partial(W_u \cap W_v) \leq \partial(W_u)$. In this case, $W_u \cap W_v$ contradicts the minimality of W_u (by Lemma 5.6(2), $S_G(W_u \cap W_v) \in \mathfrak{T}$).

Case 2: $v \in W_u \cap W_v$. Similar to case 1.

Case 3: $u \in W_u \setminus W_v$ and $v \in W_v \setminus W_u$. Let $W'_u := W_u \setminus N^G[W_v]$ and $W'_v := W_v \setminus N^G[W_u]$. Note that $b \in W_u \cap W_v$ implies that $W'_u \subset W_u$ and $W'_v \subset W_v$. Furthermore, the assumptions $u \in W_u \setminus W_v$ and $u \notin N^G(W_v)$ imply that $u \in W'_u$, and we have $v \in W'_v$ in a similar way. By Lemma 5.4(2), either $\partial(W'_u) \leq \partial(W_u)$ or $\partial(W'_v) \leq$

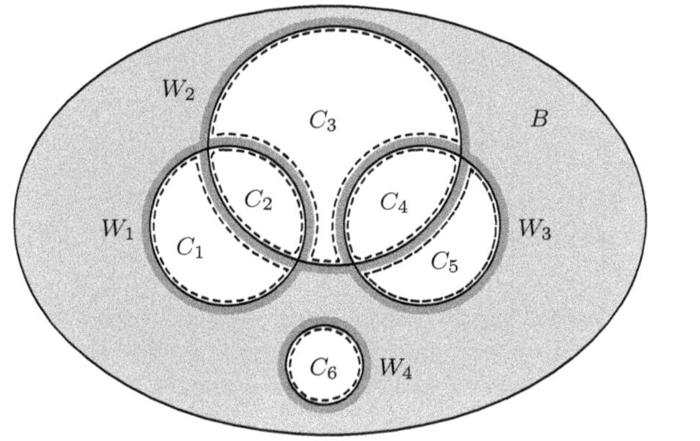

Figure 6.1: Definition of the set B in Lemma 6.11. The four solid circles represent the sets W_1, W_2, W_3, W_4 contained in $\mathcal{W}$. The dark gray area contains the boundaries of these sets. Set B (light and dark gray area) is defined to be the union of these boundaries and the area outside these sets. The six regions C_1, ..., C_6 with dashed outline are the components of $G \setminus B$.

$\partial(W_v)$. If, say, $\partial(W'_u) \leq \partial(W_u)$, then $S_G(W'_u) \in \mathfrak{T}$ follows by Lemma 5.6(1), contradicting the minimality of W_u.

Therefore, the vertices u of M for which $b \in W_u$ form a clique in H, thus there are less than $2k(k-1)$ such vertices. ⌟

We define

$$B := (V(G) \setminus \bigcup_{W \in \mathcal{W}} W) \cup \bigcup_{W \in \mathcal{W}} N^G(W)$$

(see Figure 6.1).

Claim 2. For every $W \in \mathcal{W}$, $|N^G[W] \cap B| = O(k^6)$.

Proof. Let us fix a $W \in \mathcal{W}$. We bound first the number of sets $Y \in \mathcal{W}$ such that $N^G(Y)$ intersects W. As $G[Y]$ is connected and Y is not contained in W (by the definition of $\mathcal{W}$), Y has to contain a vertex $b \in N^G(W)$. By Claim 1, there are at most $O(k^2)$ sets in $\mathcal{W}$ containing a particular $b \in N^G(W)$. Together with $|N^G(W)| < k(k-1)$, this gives a total bound of $O(k^4)$ on the number of sets $Y \in \mathcal{W}$ for which $N^G(Y)$ intersects W. As $|N^G(Y)| < k(k-1)$ for every $Y \in \mathcal{W}$, this means that W contains at most $O(k^6)$ vertices of B. Additionally, $N^G(W)$ can contain at most $|N^G(W)| < k(k-1)$ vertices of B, and the claim follows. ⌟

Let C_1, ..., C_m be the connected components of $G \setminus B$. We construct a star decomposition $\Sigma_{\mathfrak{T}} = (T_{\mathfrak{T}}, \sigma_{\mathfrak{T}}, \alpha_{\mathfrak{T}})$ with center s and p tips t_i $(1 \leq i \leq p)$. We set $\alpha_{\mathfrak{T}}(s) = V(G)$, $\sigma_{\mathfrak{T}}(s) = \emptyset$, $\alpha_{\mathfrak{T}}(t_i) = C_i$, and $\sigma_{\mathfrak{T}}(t_i) = N^G(C_i)$.

It easy easy to verify that Δ is a tree decomposition:

Claim 3. Δ satisfies properties (TD.1)–(TD.5).

The following claim implies a bound on the adhesion of Δ:

Claim 4. There is a constant $a = O(k^6)$ such that $|\sigma_{\mathfrak{T}}(t_i)| \leq a$ for every $1 \leq i \leq p$.

Proof. The definition of B implies that for every $t \notin B$, there is a $W \in \mathcal{W}$ with $t \in W$. As $N^G(W) \subseteq B$, we have that $\alpha_{\mathfrak{T}}(t_i) \subseteq W_v$ and therefore $\sigma_{\mathfrak{T}}(t_i) \subseteq N^G[W_v] \cap B$. By Claim 2, $|N^G[W_v] \cap B| = O(k^6)$, and we have the required bound on $|\sigma_{\mathfrak{T}}(t)|$. ⌟

Using the bound on the adhesion, it is easy to show that Δ respects $\mathfrak{T}$:

Claim 5. $S_G(\alpha_{\mathfrak{T}}(t_i)) \in \mathfrak{T}$ for every $1 \leq i \leq p$.

Proof. Recall that $\alpha_{\mathfrak{T}}(t_i)$ is disjoint from B and therefore it has to be fully contained in W_v for some $v \in M$: vertices outside every W_v are in B and $N^G(W_v) \subseteq B$. The order of $S_G(\alpha_{\mathfrak{T}}(t_i))$ is exactly $|\sigma_{\mathfrak{T}}(t)|$, which is at most a by Claim 4. As the order of $\mathfrak{T}$ is $m'(k) > a$ and $\alpha_{\mathfrak{T}}(t) \subseteq W_v$, $S_G(W_v) \in \mathfrak{T}$ hold, Lemma 5.6(1) implies that $S_G(\alpha_{\mathfrak{T}}(t_i)) \in \mathfrak{T}$ holds as well. ⌟

The following claim proves the bound on the maximum degree:

Claim 6. There is a constant $d'(k) = O(k^7)$ such that every vertex $v \notin Z$ has degree at most $d'(k)$ in $\tau(s)$,

Proof. Let us observe first that for every $W \in \mathcal{W}$, the graph $\tau(s)$ has no edge between $W \cap B$ and $B \setminus N^G[W]$. To see this, recall that, for every $1 \leq i \leq p$, $\sigma(t_i) = N^G(\alpha_{\mathfrak{T}}(t_i))$, $G[\alpha_{\mathfrak{T}}(t')]$ is connected, and $\alpha_{\mathfrak{T}}(t_i) \cap B = \emptyset$. As $N^G(W) \subseteq B$, it follows that $\alpha_{\mathfrak{T}}(t_i)$ cannot have a neighbor both inside W and outside $N^G[W]$. Therefore, $\sigma(t_i)$ is either a subset $N^G[W]$ or disjoint from W. This means that in the definition of $\tau(s)$, there is no clique that introduces an edge between a vertex in W and a vertex outside $N^G[W]$.

Consider a $u \in B \setminus Z$.

Case 1: $u \in W$ for some $W \in \mathcal{W}$. By our observation above, every neighbor of u in $\tau(t) \setminus Z$ is contained in $N^G[W]$. Therefore, Claim 2 gives a bound of $O(k^6)$ on the degree of u in $\tau(t)$.

Case 2: $u \notin W$ for any $W \in \mathcal{W}$. As $u \notin Z$, this is only possible if the degree of u is at most k in G. Therefore, u is adjacent to at most k components of $G \setminus B$. Each new clique in $\tau(t)$ corresponds to the neighborhood of such a component. Thus u is part of at most k cliques introduced in the definition of $\tau(t)$. The size of each clique can be bounded by the adhesion of Δ, which is at most a by Claim 4. Therefore, k receives at most $k \cdot O(k^6)$ new edges. ⌟

What remains to be proven is the invariance condition. Suppose that $\mathfrak{T}'$ is another tangle of order k in a graph G'. Let f be an isomorphism from $(G, \mathfrak{T})$ to $(G', \mathfrak{T}')$. Let B and B' be the sets computed by the algorithm on $(G, \mathfrak{T})$ and $(G', \mathfrak{T}')$, respectively.

Claim 7. $B' = f(B)$.

Proof. Let $\mathcal{W}$ and $\mathcal{W}'$ be the two collection of sets constructed by the algorithm on $(G, \mathfrak{T})$ and $(G', \mathfrak{T}')$, respectively. Let us observe that $W \in \mathcal{W}$ if and only if $f(W) \in \mathcal{W}'$: the definition of $\mathcal{W}$ depends only on the definition of the sets W_v, which depends only on the tangle $\mathfrak{T}$ and the graph-theoretic properties of G, all of which are preserved by the isomorphism f. Taking into account that the definition of B depends only on the sets in $\mathcal{W}$ and their neighborhoods in G, we can deduce $B' = f(B)$. ⌟

As $B' = f(B)$, for every component of $G \setminus B$, there is a corresponding component of $G' \setminus B'$. Let C'_1, ..., C'_p be the components of G', as enumerated by running the algorithm on $(G', \mathfrak{T}')$, and let s', $t'_1, \ldots, t'_p$ be the nodes of the constructed star decomposition. Let us define $g(s) = s'$ and let $g(t_i) = t'_j$ such that $f(C_i) = C'_j$.

Claim 8. For all $t \in V(T_{\mathfrak{T}})$ we have $\sigma_{\mathfrak{T}'}(g(t)) = f(\sigma_{\mathfrak{T}}(t))$ and $\alpha_{\mathfrak{T}'}(g(t)) = f(\alpha_{\mathfrak{T}}(t))$.

Proof. The statement immediately follows from the fact that $\alpha_{\mathfrak{T}}(t_i) = C_i$ and $\alpha_{\mathfrak{T}'}(g(t_i)) = f(C_i)$ by definition of G, and hence $\sigma_{\mathfrak{T}}(t_i) = N^G(C_i)$ and $\sigma_{\mathfrak{T}'}(g(t_i)) = N^{G'}(f(C_i)) = f(N^G(C_i))$. ⌟

□

Finally, we can prove Lemma 4.10 by invoking Lemma 6.11 on the tangle defined by the unbreakable set X:

PROOF (OF LEMMA 4.10). Let $c^*(k) = k+3m-2$, $d^*(k) = d'(k)+3m-2$, $\ell^*(k) = \ell'(k)$, $m^*(k) = m'(k)$ for the functions d', ℓ', m' in Lemma 6.11. Let $\mathfrak{T}$ be the tangle of order m defined by the m-unbreakable set X; Lemma 5.1 provides an implementation of the min-cut oracle for $\mathfrak{T}$. Let us call the algorithm of Lemma 6.11 with G, $\mathfrak{T}$, k, ℓ, and m. If it returns a subdivision of K_k in G, then we are done. Otherwise, the algorithm of Lemma 6.11 returns a $\mathfrak{T}$-respecting star decomposition $\Sigma_{\mathfrak{T}} = (T_{\mathfrak{T}}, \alpha_{\mathfrak{T}}, \sigma_{\mathfrak{T}})$ of G. We construct a star decomposition $\Sigma_X = (T_X, \alpha_X, \sigma_X)$ as follows. First, let $T_X = T_{\mathfrak{T}}$ and for the center s of T_X, let $\alpha_X(s) = V(G)$ and $\sigma_X(s) = \emptyset$. For every tip t of T_X, we let $\alpha_X(t) = \alpha_{\mathfrak{T}}(t) \setminus X$ and $\sigma_X(t) = \sigma_{\mathfrak{T}}(t) \cup (X \cap \alpha_{\mathfrak{T}}(t))$. It is straightforward to verify that Σ_X is also a star decomposition of G, and in fact it is star decomposition even for the supergraph $G \cup K[X]$ (since $X \subseteq \beta_X(s)$). As $\tau_{\mathfrak{T}}(s) \setminus X = \tau_X(s) \setminus X$, and $\tau_{\mathfrak{T}}(s)$ contains at most k vertices of degree higher than $d^*(k)$, we have that $\tau_X(s)$ contains at most $k + |X| = c^*(k)$ vertices of degree higher than $d^*(k)$. The bound $< |X|$ on the adhesion and the invariance requirement can be proved the same way as in Lemma 4.9. □

7. PARTIAL DOMINATING SET

The goal of this section is to prove that PARTIAL DOMINATING SET (find k vertices whose closed neighborhood has maximum size) can be solved in time $f(H,k) \cdot n^{O(1)}$ on graphs excluding H as a topological subgraph. We intend this result as a demonstration of the algorithmic use of the Global Structure Theorem 4.1: it shows that by combining the techniques that work on almost-embeddable and on bounded-degree graphs, we can solve problems on graphs excluding a topological subgraph. We would like to emphasize that all the algorithmic techniques in this section are standard: it is the new structure theorem that allows us to use these standard techniques on a larger class of graphs. We remark that an $f(k) \cdot n^{f(H)}$ algorithm was known for PARTIAL DOMINATING SET on H-minor free graphs [1], but instead of extending this algorithm, we give here a self-contained presentation of the result on graphs excluding H as a topological subgraph.

We begin by defining a generalization of PARTIAL DOMINATING SET, which will be convenient for computations on tree decompositions. We extend the problem by introducing a *cost function* $\kappa : V(G) \to \{0,1\}$ and *value function* $\nu : V(G) \to \{0,1\}$; now the goal is to find a set $Z \subseteq V(G)$ with $\kappa(Z) \le k$ such that $\nu(N^G[Z])$ is maximizied. (As usual, κ and ν are extended to sets by $\nu(Z) = \sum_{v \in Z} \nu(v)$ and $\kappa(Z) = \sum_{v \in Z} \kappa(v)$.) That is, the vertices with $\kappa(v) = 0$ can be used for "free" and the domination of a vertex with $\nu(v) = 0$ does not increase the objective function.

DEFINITION 7.1. *Let G be a graph and $S \subseteq V(G)$ a set of vertices. The k-profile of G with respect to S is a function $\pi(z, \kappa, \nu)$, which, for every integer $0 \le z \le k$ and functions $\kappa, \nu : V(G) \to \{0,1\}$ that have value 1 on $V(G) \setminus S$, gives the maximum of $\nu(N^G[Z])$ taken over every $Z \subseteq V(G)$ with $\kappa(Z) \le z$.*

That is, the k-profile with respect to S is described by $(k+1) \cdot 2^{|S|} \cdot 2^{|S}$ integers. Observe that if the k-profile with respect to S is known, then it is easy to deterimine the k-profile with respect to some $S' \subseteq S$.

First we show that the k-profile can be computed in a bottom-up manner on a tree decomposition if every bag is small, that is, the decomposition has bounded width. Then we use a standard layering argument to compute the k-profile on almost-embeddable torsos by reducing it to the bounded-treewidth case. For this reduction, we need the fact that almost-embeddable graphs have bounded *local treewidth:*

THEOREM 7.2 ([10]). *For every $p, q, r \in \mathbb{N}$, there is a constant $\lambda > 0$ such that the following holds. Let G be a minor of a $(p,q,r,0)$-almost embeddable graph, let $x \in V(G)$, and let $N_d(\{x\}) \subseteq V(G)$ be the set of vertices at distance at most d from x. Then $G[N_d(\{x\})]$ has treewidth at most $\lambda \cdot d$ for every $d \ge 0$.*

Finally, we compute the k-profile on almost bounded-degree torsos by using a standard random coloring technique.

LEMMA 7.3. *Let (T, σ, α) be a tree decomposition of a graph G and t a node of T. Suppose that, for every child t' of t, the k-profile of $G[\gamma(t')]$ with respect to $\sigma(t')$ is known. Then the k-profile of $G[\gamma(t)]$ with respect to $\sigma(t)$ can be computed*

(1) in time $f(s) \cdot n^{O(1)}$ if $|\beta(t)| \le s$ and $|N^T(t)| \le 2$.
(2) in time $f(w) \cdot n^{O(1)}$ if a tree decomposition of $\tau(t)$ having width w is given.
(3) in time $f(k,p,q,r,s,a) \cdot n^{O(1)}$ if $|\sigma(t)| \le a$ and a set P of size at most s is given such that $\tau(t) \setminus P$ is almost $(p,q,r,0)$-embeddable.
(4) in time $f(k,c,d,a) \cdot n^{O(1)}$ if $|\sigma(t)| \le a$ and all but at most c vertices have degree at most d in $\tau(t)$.

Theorem 1.2 follows immediately by putting together Corollary 4.4 and Lemma 7.3(3–4): in a bottom-up order, for every node t of the decomposition given by Corollary 4.4, we can compute the k-profile of $G[\gamma(t)]$ with respect to $\sigma(t)$, which gives us the value of the optimum solution of PARTIAL DOMINATING SET.

Recall that a graph is *d-degenerate* if every subgraph has a vertex of degree at most d. A classical result of Mader [19] shows that every graph excluding H as a topological subgraph is d_H-degenerate for some constant d_H depending on H, thus it is a natural question whether Theorem 1.2 can be generalized to the more general class of d-degenerate graphs. However, PARTIAL DOMINATING SET is W[1]-hard parameterized by k and d on d-degenerate graphs. To see this, note that MAXIMUM INDEPENDENT SET, parameterized by the size k of the solution, is W[1]-hard even on regular graphs. Let G be an r-regular graph ($r \ge 3$) and let us subdivide every edge by a new vertex. It is not difficult to see that G

has an independent set of size k if and only if the new graph G' has a set of k vertices whose closed neighborhood has size $(r+1)k$. As G' is 2-degenerate, an $f(k,d)\cdot n^{O(1)}$ time algorithm for PARTIAL DOMINATING SET on d-degenerate graphs would imply an $f(k)\cdot n^{O(1)}$ time algorithm for MAXIMUM INDEPENDENT SET. Thus the fixed-parameter tractability of PARTIAL INDEPENDENT SET on graph excluding H as a topological subgraph is not simply a consequence of the sparsity/degeneracy of such graphs, but essentially depends on the structural properties of this class of graphs.

8. COMPUTING INVARIANT TREELIKE DECOMPOSITIONS

In this section, we relax the notion of tree decomposition to the more liberal notion of treelike decomposition. The reason is that we want to make our decompositions invariant under automorphisms of the underlying graph, and this is not possible for tree decompositions. Treelike decompositions are based on the axiomatisation of tree decompositions by (TD.1)–(TD.5). From now on, a *decomposition* of a graph is a triple $\Delta = (D,\sigma,\alpha)$, where D is a digraph and $\sigma,\alpha : V(D) \mapsto 2^{V(G)}$. For every $t \in V(D)$, we define sets $\gamma(t),\beta(t) \subseteq V(G)$ and a graph $\tau(t)$ as in (3.4), (3.5), and (3.6). The *width* and *adhesion* of a decomposition are defined, as for tree decompositions, to be the maximum size of the bags minus one and the maximum size of the separators, respectively. Two nodes $t,u \in V(D)$ are Δ*-equivalent* (we write $t \approx u$) if $\sigma(t) = \sigma(u)$ and $\alpha(t) = \alpha(u)$. Note that $t \approx u$ implies $\gamma(t) = \gamma(u)$, but not $\beta(t) = \beta(u)$ or $\tau(t) = \tau(u)$. We will occasionally work with several decompositions at the same time, and in such situations may use an index $^{\Delta}$, as for example in $\sigma^{\Delta}(t)$ or $t \approx^{\Delta} u$, to indicate which decomposition we are referring to. However, we usually prefer implicit naming conventions such as the following: If we have a decomposition $\Delta' = (D',\sigma',\alpha')$, then we will denote $\gamma^{\Delta'}(t)$ by $\gamma'(t)$, $\beta^{\Delta'}(t)$ by $\beta'(t)$, et cetera.

DEFINITION 8.1. *A* treelike decomposition *of a graph G is a decomposition $\Delta = (D,\sigma,\alpha)$ of G that satisfies the following axioms:*

(TL.1) *D is acyclic.*

(TL.2) *For all $t \in V(D)$ it holds that $\alpha(t) \cap \sigma(t) = \varnothing$ and $N^G(\alpha(t)) \subseteq \sigma(t)$.*

(TL.3) *For all $t \in V(D)$ and $u \in N^D(t)$ it holds that $\alpha(u) \subseteq \alpha(t)$ and $\gamma(u) \subseteq \gamma(t)$.*

(TL.4) *For all $t \in V(D)$ and $u_1,u_2 \in N^D(t)$, either $u_1 \approx u_2$ or $\gamma(u_1) \cap \gamma(u_2) = \sigma(u_1) \cap \sigma(u_2)$.*

(TL.5) *For every connected component A of G there is a $t \in V(D)$ with $\sigma(t) = \varnothing$ and $\alpha(t) = V(A)$.*

Note that (TD.2) coincides with (TL.2) and (TD.3) coincides with (TL.3). Moreover, (TD.1) implies (TL.1) and (TD.4) implies (TL.4). For connected graphs G, (TD.5) coincides with (TL.5), and thus every tree decomposition of a connected graph is a treelike decomposition. For disconnected graphs, this is not necessarily the case, but it can be shown that from every treelike decomposition one can construct a tree decomposition with the same torsos. (See [9] for details.)

Figure 8.1(a) shows the cycle C_5. Figure 8.1(b) shows a tree decomposition (T,β) of C_5 of width 2. Note that this tree decomposition is not invariant under automorphisms of C_5, in the sense that there is an automorphism f of C_5 for which we cannot find an automorphism g of T such that for all $t \in V(T)$ we have $f(\beta(t)) = \beta(g(t))$. It is easy to see that there is no tree decomposition of C_5 of width 2 that is invariant under automorphisms.

Figure 8.1(b) shows a treelike decomposition (D',σ',α') of C_5 of width 2. Actually, the sets displayed in the nodes are the bags, but we can easily compute the separators and components using (3.1) and (3.3). For instance, for the grey node t with bag $\beta'(t) = \{1,3,5\}$ we have $\sigma'(t) = \{1,3\}$ and $\alpha'(t) = \{4,5\}$. For the sake of completeness, we observe that $\gamma'(t) = \{1,3,4,5\}$ and $\tau'(t) = K[\{1,3,5\}]$.

Note that the "subdecomposition" induced by the four grey nodes is precisely the tree decomposition shown in Figure 8.1(b). The treelike decomposition contains many other tree decompositions of C_5; actually, it contains all images of the decomposition shown in Figure 8.1(b) under automorphisms of C_5. And indeed, the treelike decomposition is invariant under automorphisms.

This example illustrates how treelike decompositions can be made "invariant." However, the automorphism invariance of the example is not sufficient for our purposes, we need a more general notion of invariance that involves decompositions of more than one graph.

DEFINITION 8.2. *A* decomposition mapping *for a class $\mathcal{C}$ of graphs is a mapping Δ that associates with each $G \in \mathcal{C}$ a decomposition $\Delta_G = (D_G,\sigma_G,\alpha_G)$ of G.*

Δ is invariant *if for all isomorphic graphs $G,G' \in \mathcal{C}$ and all isomorphisms f from G to G' there is an isomorphism g from D_G to $D_{G'}$ such that for all $t \in V(D_G)$ we have $\sigma_{G'}(g(t)) = f(\sigma_G(t))$ and $\alpha_{G'}(g(t)) = f(\alpha_G(t))$.*

We need some additional terminology about decomposition mappings: We say that a decomposition mapping Δ for a class $\mathcal{C}$ is *treelike* if for all $G \in \mathcal{C}$ the decomposition Δ_G is treelike, and it has *adhesion at most a* if for all $G \in \mathcal{C}$ the adhesion of Δ_G is at most a. We say that a class $\mathcal{C}$ *admits polynomial time computable invariant treelike decompositions over $\mathcal{A}$ (of adhesion at most a)* if there is a polynomial time computable invariant treelike decomposition mapping for $\mathcal{C}$ over $\mathcal{A}$ (of adhesion a). Let us remark that the decomposition schemes of [9] yield polynomial time computable invariant decomposition mappings.

The main result of the section is the following:

THEOREM 8.3 (INVARIANT DECOMPOSITION THEOREM). *For every graph H there are constants $a,b,c,d,e \in \mathbb{N}$ and a polynomial time computable invariant treelike decomposition mapping Δ of adhesion at most a for the class of graphs G with $H \not\preceq_T G$ such that for every G with $\Delta_G = (D,\sigma,\alpha)$ and every $t \in V(D)$ one of the following three conditions is satisfied:*

(i) $|\beta(s)| \le b$

(ii) At most c vertices of $\tau(t)$ have degree greater than d.

(iii) $K_e \not\preceq \tau(t)$.

PROOF. We let $k := |H|$. We choose $c = c^*(k)$, $d = d^*(k)$, $\ell = \ell^*(k)$, and $m = m^*(k)$ according to Lemma 4.10 and $e = e^*(\ell,m)$ according to Lemma 4.9. We let $a := 3m-3$ and $b := 4m-3$..

Let G be a graph with $H \not\preceq_T G$. We shall define a decomposition $\Delta_G = (D,\sigma,\alpha)$ of G of adhesion at most a such that every node t satisfies one of (i)–(iii). Then we will argue that

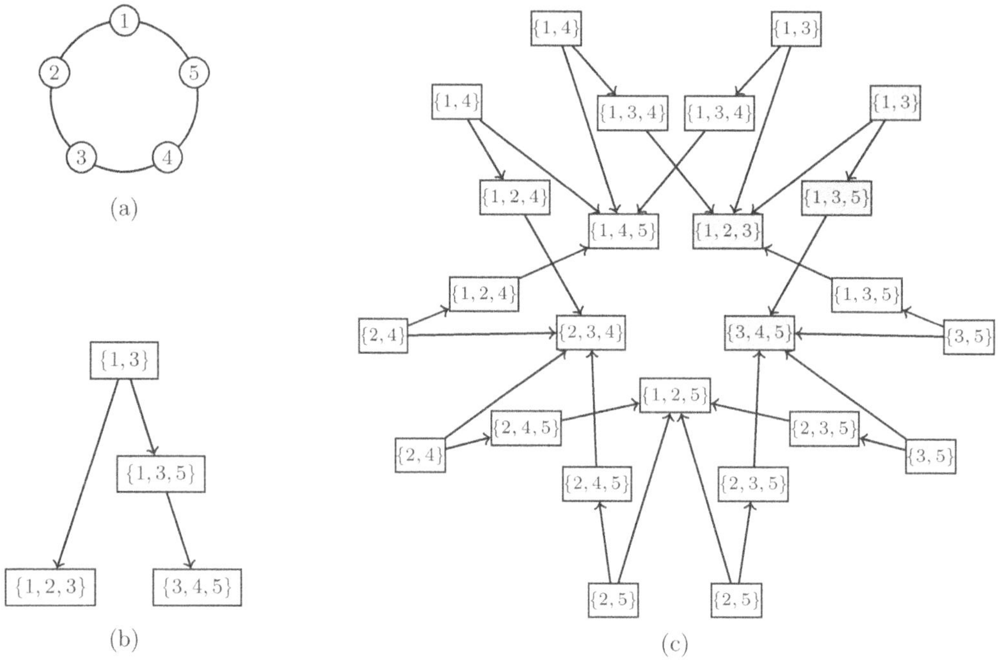

Figure 8.1: (a) The cycle C_5 with (b) a tree decomposition and (c) an automorphism-invariant treelike decomposition

the decomposition $G \mapsto \Delta_G$ is polynomial time computable and invariant.

There will be three kinds of nodes in $V(D)$: b-nodes ("bounded nodes"), d-nodes ("bounded degree nodes"), and e-nodes ("excluded minor nodes"). All nodes are triples $t = (A_t, X_t, Y_t)$ satisfying the following conditions:

(A) A_t is a connected induced subgraph of G with $|N^G(A_t)| \le a$. To simplify the notation, in the following we let $C_t := G[N^G[A_t]]$.

(B) $X_t \subseteq V(C_t)$ such that $N^G(A_t) \subset X_t$ and $|X_t| = \min\{a+1, |C_t|\}$.

(C) $Y_t \subseteq V(C_t)$ such that $|Y_t| < m$. (Actually, Y_t will be empty for d-nodes and e-nodes.)

Let us call such triples "nodes" and let U be the set of all nodes (the actual nodes of D will form a subset of U). For every node $t \in U$ we let $\alpha(t) := V(A_t)$, $\sigma(A_t) := N^G(A_t)$, and $\gamma(t) := V(C_t)$.

(D) A *b-node* is a node $t \in U$ such that for every connected component A of $C_t \setminus Y_t$ it holds that $|(V(A) \cap X_t) \cup Y_t| < |X_t|$.

Let V_b be the set of all b-nodes. Let U_b be the set of all nodes $t \in U$ for which there exists a $Y \subseteq V(C_t)$ of size $|Y| < m$ such that for every connected component of A of $C_t \setminus Y$ it holds that $|(V(A) \cap X_t) \cup Y| < |X_t|$. Note that $V_b \subseteq U_b$ and that that for every $t \in U \setminus U_b$ the set X_t is m-unbreakable in C_t.

(E) An *e-node* is a node $t \in U \setminus U_b$ such that $Y_t = \emptyset$ and the algorithm of Lemma 4.9 on C_t, ℓ, m, and X_t returns star decomposition $\Sigma_t := \Sigma_{X_t}$ of $C_t \cup K[X_t]$.

(F) A *d-node* is a node $t \in U \setminus U_b$ such that $Y_t = \emptyset$ and the algorithm of Lemma 4.9 on C_t, ℓ, m, and X_t returns an image I of K_ℓ in C_t that is m-attached to X_t. In this case, the algorithm of Lemma 4.10 applied to C_t, k, the set X_t, and the image I computes a star decomposition $\Sigma_t := \Sigma_{X_t}$ of $C_t \cup K[X_t]$ (since $K_k \not\preceq_T C_t$ by assumption).

Let V_d and V_e be the sets of d-nodes and e-nodes, respectively. Note that the three sets V_b, V_d, V_e are mutually disjoint. We let $V(D) := V_b \cup V_d \cup V_e$.

Claim 1. Let A be a (nonempty) connected induced subgraph of G with $|N^G(A)| \le a$. Then there is a node $t \in V(D)$ such that $A_t = A$.

Proof. Let $C := G[N^G[A]]$, and choose an arbitrary $X \subseteq V(C)$ such that $N^G(A) \subset X$ and $|X| = \min\{a+1, |C|\}$. Clearly, such a set X exists, because $A \neq \emptyset$ and $|N^G(A)| \le a$.

If there is a set $Y \subseteq V(G)$ such that $|Y| < m$ and for every connected component A' of $C \setminus Y$ it holds that $|(V(A') \cap X) \cup Y| < |X|$, then $(A, X, Y) \in V_b$.

Suppose there is no such set Y. Then $(A, X, \emptyset) \notin U_b$ and thus $(A, X, \emptyset) \in V_e \cup V_d$. ⌟

By (E) and (F), for all $t \in V_e \cup V_d$ we have a star decomposition $\Sigma_t =: (T_t, \sigma_t, \alpha_t)$. Let s_t be the center of T_t. To define the edge relation $E(D)$, for every node $t \in V(D)$ we define the set $N^D(t)$ of its children in D.

(G) For $t \in V_b$, we let $N^D(t)$ be the set of all $u \in V(D)$ such that A_u is a connected component of $C_t \setminus (X_t \cup Y_t)$.

(H) For $t \in V_d \cup V_e$, we let $N^D(t)$ be the set of all $u \in V(D)$ such that A_u is a connected component of $C_t \setminus \beta_t(s_t)$.

This completes the definition of the decomposition $\Delta_G = (D, \sigma, \alpha)$.

Claim 2. Δ_G is a treelike decomposition of G.

Proof. It follows immediately from the definitions of σ and α that Δ_G satisfies (TL.2).

To verify (TL.3), let $tu \in E(D)$. We have $X_t \subseteq \beta_t(s_t)$ (either by (G) or by the statements of Lemmas 4.9 and 4.10). Therefore, by (G) and (H) we have

$$\alpha(u) = V(A_u) \subseteq V(C_t) \setminus \beta_t(s_t) \subseteq V(C_t) \setminus X_t \subset V(C_t) \setminus N^G(A_t) = \alpha(t). \tag{8.1}$$

Moreover, if $t \in V_b$, then we have $N^{C_t}(A_u) \subseteq X_t \cup Y_t$. Since every vertex of C_t with a neighbor outside C_t is in $N^G(A_t) \subseteq X_t$ and we have $V(A_u) \cap X_t = \emptyset$, this implies $N^G(A_u) \subseteq X_t \cup Y_t$. Hence $\gamma(u) = V(A_u) \cup N^G(A_u) \subseteq V(C_t) = \gamma(t)$. If $t \in V_e \cup V_b$ then we have $N^{C_t}(A_u) \subseteq \beta_t(s_t)$. Again, every vertex of C_t with a neighbor outside C_t is in $N^G(A_t) \subseteq X_t \subseteq \beta_t(s_t)$ and $V(A_u) \cap \beta_t(s_t) = \emptyset$. Hence $\gamma(u) = V(A_u) \cup N^G(A_u) \subseteq V(C_t) = \gamma(t)$.

Note that in (8.1) we proved that for all edges $tu \in E(D)$ the inclusion $\alpha(u) \subset \alpha(t)$ is strict. This implies that D is acyclic, that is, (TL.1).

To verify (TL.4), let $t \in V(D)$ and $u_1, u_2 \in N^D(t)$. For $i = 1, 2$, we let $C_i := C_{u_i}$ and $X_i := X_{u_i}$ and $A_i := A^t_{u_i}$.

Case 1: $t \in V_b$.
Then by (G), both A_1 and A_2 are connected components of $C_t \setminus (X_t \cup Y_t)$. Hence either $A_1 = A_2$ or $A_1 \cap A_2 = \emptyset$. If $A_1 = A_2$ then $\alpha(u_1) = V(A_1) = V(A_2) = \alpha(u_2)$ and $\sigma(u_1) = N^G(A_1) = N^G(A_2) = \sigma(u_2)$ and thus $u_1 \approx u_2$. Suppose that $A_1 \cap A_2 = \emptyset$. Note that we also have $V(A_1) \cap N^G(A_2) \subseteq A_1 \cap (X_t \cup Y_t) = \emptyset$ and, symmetrically, $V(A_2) \cap N^G(A_1) = \emptyset$. This implies $\gamma(u_1) \cap \gamma(u_2) = V(C_1) \cap V(C_2) = N^G(A_1) \cap N^G(A_2) = \sigma(u_1) \cap \sigma(u_2)$.

Case 2: $t \in V_e \cup V_d$.
Then both A_1 and A_2 are connected components of $C_t \setminus \beta_t(s_t)$, and we can argue as in Case 1.

To verify (TL.5), let A be a connected component of G. Then $N^G(A) = \emptyset$, and by Claim 1 there is a $t \in V(D)$ such that $C_t = A$. For each such t, we have $\sigma(t) = N^G(A) = \emptyset$ and $\alpha(t) = V(A)$. ⌟

Claim 3. Let $t \in V(D)$.

(1) If $t \in V_b$ then $\beta(t) = X_t \cup Y_t$.
(2) If $t \in V_e \cup V_d$ then $\beta(t) = \beta_t(s_t)$ and $\tau(t) \subseteq \tau_t(s_t)$.

Proof. Recall that $\beta(t) = \gamma(t) \setminus \bigcup_{u \in N^D(t)} \alpha(u) = V(C_t) \setminus \bigcup_{u \in N^D(t)} V(A_u)$.

To prove (1), suppose that $t \in V_b$. It follows from (G) that for all $u \in N^D(t)$ we have $V(A_u) \subseteq V(C_t) \setminus (X_t \cup Y_t)$. Hence $(X_t \cup Y_t) \subseteq \beta(t)$. To prove the converse inclusion, we shall prove that for every connected component A of $C_t \setminus (X_t \cup Y_t)$ there is a $u \in N^D(t)$ with $A_u = A$. By (G) and Claim 1, it suffices to prove that $|N^G(A)| \leq a$. But this follows from the definition of b-nodes in (D) (we used a similar argument in the proof of Claim 1).

To prove (2), let $t \in V_e \cup V_d$. By (H), for all $u \in N^D(t)$ we have $V(A_u) \subseteq V(C_t) \setminus \beta_t(s_t)$. Hence $\beta_t(s_t) \subseteq \beta(t)$. For the converse inclusion, let A be a connected component of $C_t \setminus \beta_t(s_t)$. Then there is a tip x of T_t such that A is a connected component of $C_t[\alpha_t(x)] = G[\alpha_t(x)]$. We have $N^G(A) \subseteq \sigma_t(x)$, and as the adhesion of Σ_t is $< |X_t|$, we have $|N^G(A)| \leq |\sigma_t(x)| < |X_t| = a + 1$. Thus by Claim 1 and (H), there is a $u \in N^D(t)$ with $A_u = A$.

It remains to prove that $\tau(t) \subseteq \tau_t(s_t)$. First, note that for all $u \in N^D(t)$ there is an $x \in N^{T_t}(s_t)$ such that $\sigma(u) \subseteq \sigma_t(x)$. Furthermore, Σ_t is a decomposition of $C_t \cup K[X_t]$, thus $\sigma(t) \subseteq X_t$ is a clique in $\tau_t(s_t)$. Let us remark that $\tau_t(s_t) \subseteq \tau(t)$ is not necessarily true: X_t is a proper superset of $\sigma(t)$, thus X_t is a clique $\tau_t(s_t)$, but it is not necessarily a clique in $\tau(t)$. ⌟

It follows from (A) that the adhesion of Δ_G is at most a. By Claim 3(1), every $t \in V_b$ satisfies (i). By Claim 3(2) and Lemmas 4.10 and 4.9, every $t \in V_d$ satisfies (ii) and every $t \in V_e$ satisfies (iii).

It it easy to see that the decomposition mapping Δ is polynomial time computable. Indeed, note first that the set U has size $O(n^{a+1+3m-2+m-1})$ (here we use n^{a+1} as an upper bound for the number of connected induced subgraphs A of G with $N^G(A)| \leq a$) and that the set is polynomial time computable. Remember that the parameters a, m et cetera are all treated as constants depending only on H. The subset U_b is also polynomial time computable, because to decide whether $t \in U_b$ we can go through all subsets $Y \subseteq V(C_t)$ of size less than m and see if the condition is satisfied. Now it follows from Lemmas 4.9 and 4.10 that the sets V_e and V_d are polynomial time computable. Hence $V(D)$ is polynomial time computable. Since for nodes $t \in V_e \cup V_d$ the star decomposition Σ_t is polynomial time computable (again by Lemmas 4.9 and 4.10), the edge relation $E(D)$ is polynomial time computable as well. Since the mappings σ and α are almost trivially polynomial time computable, this shows that Δ is polynomial time computable.

It remains to prove that Δ is invariant. To prove this, we take isomorphic graphs G, G' with $H \not\preceq G, G'$ and let f be an isomorphism from G to G'. Let $\Delta_G = (D, \sigma, \alpha)$ and $\Delta_{G'} = (D', \sigma', \alpha')$. We define the sets U, U_b, V_b, V_e, V_d for G as above and let $U', U'_b, V'_b, V'_e, V'_d$ be the corresponding sets for G'. We denote the constituents of a node $t' \in U'$ by $(A'_{t'}, X'_{t'}, Y'_{t'})$ and let $C'_{t'} := G'[N^{G'}[A'_t]]$. For $t' \in V_e \cup V_d$ we denote the star decomposition of $C'_{t'}$ (obtained as above) by $\Sigma'_{t'}$. The isomorphism f has a natural extension of subsets of $V(G)$, tuples of subsets, and similar objects defined in terms of $V(G)$. We denote this extension by f^*. As f is an isomorphism, we obviously have $f^*(U) = U'$, $f^*(U_b) = U'_b$, and $f^*(V_b) = V'_b$. Moreover, for every $t \in U$ we have $f^*(A_t) = A'_{f^*(t)}$, $f^*(C_t) = C'_{f^*(t)}$, et cetera. It follows from the invariance conditions of Lemmas 4.9 and 4.10 that $f^*(V_e) = V'_e$ and $f^*(V_d) = V'_d$ and that for every $t \in V_e \cup V_d$ there is an isomorphism g_t from T_t to T'_t such that $f^*(\sigma_t(x)) = \sigma_{f^*(t)}(g_t(x))$ and $f^*(\alpha_t(x)) = \alpha_{f^*(t)}(g_t(x))$ for all $x \in V(T_t)$. But this implies that $N^D(f^*(t)) = \{f^*(u) \mid u \in N^D(t)\}$. As $f^*(C_t) = C'_{f^*(t)}$ and $f^*(X_t) = X'_{f^*(t)}$ and $f^*(Y_t) = Y'_{f^*(t)}$, we also have $N^D(f^*(t)) = \{f^*(u) \mid u \in N^D(t)\}$ for all $t \in V_b$. Hence the restriction of f^* to $V(D)$ is an isomorphism from D to D'. As $f^*(A_t) = A'_{f^*(t)}$ for all $t \in V(D)$, we have $f(\alpha(t)) = \alpha'(f^*(t))$ and thus $f(\sigma(t)) = f(N^G(\alpha(t))) = N^{G'}(f(\alpha(t))) = N^{G'}(\alpha'(f^*(t))) = \sigma'(f^*(t))$. This proves that Δ is invariant. □

9. CANONIZATION

A *canonisation mapping* $\mathfrak{c}$ for a class $\mathcal{C}$ of graphs is a mapping that associates with each graph $G \in \mathcal{C}$ a graph $\mathfrak{c}(G) \cong G$ such that for all $G, H \in \mathcal{C}$ we have $G \cong H \iff \mathfrak{c}(G) = \mathfrak{c}(H)$. That is, $\mathfrak{c}(G)$ and $\mathfrak{c}(H)$ are not only isomorphic, but they are actually the same graph on the same set of vertices. Thus the isomorphism of G and H can be tested simply by comparing $\mathfrak{c}(G)$ and $\mathfrak{c}(H)$. A *canonisation algorithm* computes a canonisation mapping. Without loss of generality we may always assume a canonisation mapping $\mathfrak{c}$ to map graphs G to graphs $\mathfrak{c}(G)$ with vertex set $V(\mathfrak{c}(G)) = [n]$, where $n := |G|$. We say that a class $\mathcal{C}$ of graphs *admits polynomial time canonisation* if there is a polynomial time algorithm that computes a canonisation mapping for $\mathcal{C}$.

FACT 9.1 (BABAI AND LUKS [2]). *For every $d \in \mathbb{N}$ the class of all graphs of maximum degree at most d admits polynomial time canonisation.*

FACT 9.2 (PONOMARENKO [22]). *For every graph H the class of all graphs excluding H as a minor admits polynomial time canonisation.*

Our goal in this section is to prove a "Lifting Lemma" that allows us to lift a canonisation from the torsos of a treelike decomposition of a graph to the whole graph. To be able to prove such a lemma, we need to work with more general structures than graphs and a stronger notion of canonisation.

We often denote tuples $(v_1, \dots, v_k)$ by $\vec{v}$. For $\vec{v} = (v_1, \dots, v_k)$, by $\tilde{v}$ we denote the set $\{v_1, \dots, v_k\}$. A *vocabulary* is a finite set of relation symbols, each of which has a prescribed arity in $\mathbb{N}$. (Note that we admit 0-ary relation symbols. For every set S the set S^0 just consists of the empty tuple.) Let λ be a vocabulary. A *weighted λ-structure* A consists of a *universe* (or *vertex set*) $V(A)$ and for each k-ary relation symbol $R \in \lambda$ a mapping $R^A : V(A)^k \to \mathbb{N}$. A (plain) λ-structure is a weighted λ-structure A with range$(R^A) \subseteq \{0, 1\}$ for all $R \in \lambda$. We usually identify a function $R^A : V(A)^k \to \{0, 1\}$ with the relation $R(A) := \{\vec{v} \in V(A)^k \mid R^A(\vec{v}) = 1\}$ and view a plain structure as a finite set (the universe) together with a collection of relations on this universe. For example, graphs and digraphs may be viewed as plain $\{E\}$-structures, where E is a binary relation symbol. Graphs with multiple edges may be viewed as weighted $\{E\}$-structures.

Let λ, μ be vocabularies with $\lambda \subseteq \mu$, and let A be a weighted λ-structure and B a weighted μ-structure. Then A is the *λ-restriction* of B if $V(A) = V(B)$ and $R^A = R^B$ for all symbols $R \in \lambda$. Conversely, B is a *μ-expansion* of A if A is the λ-restriction of B. For every $W \subseteq V(A)$, we define the *induced substructure* $A[W]$ to be the weighted λ-structure with universe $V(A[W]) := W$, relations $R^{A[W]} := R^A \upharpoonright_{W^k}$ for all k-ary $R \in \lambda$. We let $A \setminus W := A[V(A) \setminus W]$. If f is a mapping with domain $V(A)$, we let $f(A)$ be the weighted λ-structure with universe $V(f(A)) := f(V(A))$ and mappings $R^{f(A)}$ defined by $R^{f(A)}(f(\vec{a})) := R^A(\vec{a})$. If A and B are weighted λ-structures such that for all k-ary $R \in \lambda$ and all $\vec{v} \in V(A)^k \cap V(B)^k$ we have $R^A(\vec{v}) = R^B(\vec{v})$, then we define the union $A \cup B$ to be the weighted λ-structure with $V(A \cup B) := V(A) \cup V(B)$ and

$$R^{A \cup B}(\vec{a}) := \begin{cases} R^A(\vec{a}) & \text{if } \vec{a} \in V(A)^k, \\ R^B(\vec{a}) & \text{if } \vec{a} \in V(B)^k, \\ 0 & \text{otherwise.} \end{cases}$$

for all k-ary relation symbols $R \in \lambda$ and $\vec{a} \in V(A \cup B)^k$.

The *Gaifman graph* of a weighted λ-structure A is the graph G_A with vertex set $V(G_A) := V(A)$ and edge set

$$E(G_A) := \Big\{ vw \in \binom{V(A)}{2} \;\Big|\; \exists k\text{-ary } R \in \lambda, \vec{v} \in V(A)^k \text{ with } R^A(\vec{v}) > 0 \text{ and } v, w \in \tilde{v} \Big\}.$$

An *isomorphism* from a weighted λ-structure A to a weighted λ-structure B is a bijective mapping $f : V(A) \to V(B)$ such that for all k-ary $R \in \lambda$ and all $\vec{v} \in V(A)^k$ we have $R^A(\vec{v}) = R^B(f(\vec{v}))$. Canonisation mappings and algorithms for weighted structures are defined in the obvious way. We say that a class $\mathcal{C}$ of graphs *admits polynomial time strong canonisation* if for every vocabulary λ there is a polynomial time computable canonisation mapping for the class of all weighted λ-structures with Gaifman graph in $\mathcal{C}$. The following statements can be derived from Facts 9.1 and 9.2 by a simple gadget construction.

LEMMA 9.3. *For all $d \in \mathbb{N}$ the class of all graphs of maximum degree at most d admits polynomial time strong canonisation.*

LEMMA 9.4. *For every graph H, the class of graphs G with $H \npreceq G$ admits polynomial time strong canonisation.*

COROLLARY 9.5. *For all $c, d \in \mathbb{N}$ the class of all graphs G such that at most c vertices of G have degree greater than d admits polynomial time strong canonisation and $k \in \mathbb{N}$.*

The main result of the section is the following lemma:

LEMMA 9.6 (LIFTING LEMMA). *Let $\mathcal{A}, \mathcal{C}$ be a classes of graphs and $a \in \mathbb{N}$. Suppose that $\mathcal{A}$ admits polynomial time strong canonisation and that $\mathcal{C}$ admits polynomial time computable invariant treelike decompositions over $\mathcal{A}$ of adhesion a.*

Then $\mathcal{C}$ admits polynomial time strong canonisation.

Before we prove the lemma, we define the *lexicographical order* $\leq^\lambda_{\text{lex}}$ on weighted λ-structures A with $V(A) \subseteq \mathbb{N}$. Let $\lambda = \{R_1, \dots, R_m\}$, where R_i is k_i-ary. The order $\leq^\lambda_{\text{lex}}$ actually not only depends on the set λ, but on the order in which the relations are listed. Hence we fix this order. We first review the lexicographical order on tuples and sets of integers:

- For tuples $\vec{x} = (x_1, \dots, x_k) \in \mathbb{N}^k$, $\vec{y} = (y_1, \dots, y_\ell) \in \mathbb{N}^\ell$ we let $\vec{x} <_{\text{lex}} \vec{y}$ if and only if either there exists an $i \leq \min\{k, \ell\}$ such that $x_i < y_i$ and $x_j = y_j$ for $1 \leq j < i$ or $k < \ell$ and $x_i = y_i$ for all $i \leq k$.
- For sets $X, Y \subseteq \mathbb{N}$ we let $X <_{\text{lex}} Y$ if and only if there exists an $i \in Y \setminus X$ such that for all $j < i$ it holds that $j \in X \iff j \in Y$.

Now let A, B be weighted λ-structures with $V(A), V(B) \subseteq \mathbb{N}$. Then we let $A <^\lambda_{\text{lex}} B$ if one of the following conditions is satisfied:

- $V(A) <_{\text{lex}} V(B)$. Note that if both $V(A)$ and $V(B)$ are initial segments of the positive integers then this just means $|A| < |B|$.
- $V(A) = V(B) =: V$ and there is an $i \in [m]$ and a tuple $\vec{a} \in V^{k_i}$ such that $R^A_j = R^B_j$ for $1 \leq j < i$, and $R^A_i(\vec{a}) < R^B_i(\vec{a})$, and $R^A_i(\vec{b}) = R^B_i(\vec{b})$ for all $\vec{b} \in V^{k_i}$ with $\vec{b} <_{\text{lex}} \vec{a}$.

We let $A \leq^\lambda_{\text{lex}} B$ if $A <^\lambda_{\text{lex}} B$ or $A = B$. Note that $\leq^\lambda_{\text{lex}}$ is indeed a linear order on the class of weighted λ-structures whose universe is a set of natural numbers and that given A, B, it can be decided in polynomial time whether $A \leq^\lambda_{\text{lex}} B$.

As another small piece of terminology, we say that an *enumeration* of a finite set S is a tuple $(x_1, \dots, x_k)$ such that $k = |S|$ and $S = \{x_1, \dots, x_k\}$.

PROOF (OF THE LIFTING LEMMA 9.6). We shall describe a polynomial time computable a canonisation mapping $\mathfrak{c}$ for the class of all weighted λ-structures with Gaifman graph in $\mathcal{C}$.

Let $P_1, \ldots, P_a, Q_1, \ldots, Q_a \notin \lambda$ be fresh relation symbols, where P_i and Q_i are i-ary for all $i \in [a]$. Let $\mu := \lambda \cup \{P_1, \ldots, P_a, Q_1, \ldots, Q_a\}$. Let $\mathfrak{a}$ be a polynomial time computable canonisation mapping on the class of all weighted μ-structures whose Gaifman graph is in $\mathcal{A}$. Such a mapping $\mathfrak{a}$ exists by the assumption that $\mathcal{A}$ admits polynomial time strong canonisation. Let Δ be a polynomial time computable invariant treelike decomposition mapping for $\mathcal{C}$ over $\mathcal{A}$ of adhesion at most a.

To explain our canonisation mapping $\mathfrak{c}$, let us fix a λ-structure C with Gaifman graph $G_C \in \mathcal{C}$. Without loss of generality we may assume that G_C is connected. Let $\Delta_{G_C} = (D, \sigma, \alpha)$. For every $t \in V(D)$ we let $C_t := C[\gamma(t)]$ and $s_t := |\sigma(t)|$. Note that $0 \le s_t \le a$. By induction on D, starting from the leaves, for every node $t \in V(D)$ and every enumeration $\vec{x}$ of $\sigma(t)$ we define a copy $C^*_{t,\vec{x}}$ of C_t and a mapping $g_{t,\vec{x}} : \sigma(t) \to V(C^*_{t,\vec{x}})$ with the following properties:

(A) $V(C^*_{t,\vec{x}})$ is an initial segment of the positive integers.
(B) There is an isomorphism f from C_t to $C^*_{t,\vec{x}}$ such that $g_{t,\vec{x}} \subseteq f$.

Let $t \in V(D)$, and let $\vec{x} = (x_1, \ldots, x_{s_t})$ be an enumeration of $\sigma(t)$. Let $u_1, \ldots, u_m$ be the children of t in D. For every $i \in [m]$, let $C_i := C_{u_i}$ and $n_i := |\alpha(u_i)|$ and $s_i := s_{u_i}$. Note that $|C_i| = n_i + s_i$. For all $i, j \in [m]$, let $i \simeq j :\Leftrightarrow u_i \simeq^{\Delta_{G_C}} u_j$. For every $i \in [m]$ and every tuple $\vec{y}$ that enumerates $\sigma(u_i)$, let $C^*_{i,\vec{y}} := C^*_{u_i,\vec{y}}$ and $g_{i,\vec{y}} := g_{u_i,\vec{y}}$. Then $C^*_{i,\vec{y}}$ and $g_{i,\vec{y}}$ satisfy (A) and (B).

Let $\mathcal{Y}$ be the set of all $\vec{y} \in \beta(t)^{\le a}$ that enumerate $\sigma(u_i)$ for some $i \in [m]$. For each $\vec{y} \in \mathcal{Y}$, let $M_{\vec{y}}$ be the set of all $i \in [m]$ with $\sigma(u_i) = \tilde{y}$. Let $\le_{\vec{y}}$ be a linear order on $M_{\vec{y}}$ such that for all $i, j \in M_{\vec{y}}$:

(C) If $C^*_{i,\vec{y}} <^{\lambda}_{\text{lex}} C^*_{j,\vec{y}}$ then $i <_{\vec{y}} j$.
(D) If $C^*_{i,\vec{y}} = C^*_{j,\vec{y}}$ and $g_{i,\vec{y}}(\vec{y}) <_{\text{lex}} g_{j,\vec{y}}(\vec{y})$ then $i <_{\vec{y}} j$.

Note that conditions (C) and (D) do not determine a linear order on $M_{\vec{y}}$, since there may be distinct $i, j \in M_{\vec{y}}$ such that $C^*_{i,\vec{y}} = C^*_{j,\vec{y}}$ and $g_{i,\vec{y}}(\vec{y}) = g_{j,\vec{y}}(\vec{y})$. If this is the case, decide arbitrarily whether $i <_{\vec{y}} j$ or $j <_{\vec{y}} i$. No matter how we decide, the resulting structure $C_{t,\vec{x}}$ and mapping $g_{t,\vec{x}}$ will be the same.

Note that for every $\simeq$-equivalence class K, either $K \cap M_{\vec{y}} = \emptyset$ or $K \subseteq M_{\vec{y}}$. Let $N_{\vec{y}}$ be the system of representatives for the $\simeq$-equivalence classes in $M_{\vec{y}}$ that contains the $\le_{\vec{y}}$-smallest element of each class. Let i_0 be the minimal element of $N_{\vec{y}}$. We define $D^*_{\vec{y}}$ to be the structure obtained in the following three steps:

(E) For each $i \in N_{\vec{y}}$, we take a copy $C^{**}_{i,\vec{y}}$ of $C^*_{i,\vec{y}}$ and shift the universes of these copies in such a way that they are disjoint intervals of nonnegative integers arranged in the order given by $\le_{\vec{y}}$.
(F) We take the union of all the $C^{**}_{i,\vec{y}}$. Then for each $i \in N_{\vec{y}}$ we identify the tuple $g_{i,\vec{y}}(\vec{y})$ with the tuple $g_{i_0,\vec{y}}(\vec{y})$.
(G) We shrink the universe so that it becomes an initial segment of the positive integers.

Then $D^*_{\vec{y}}$ is an isomorphic copy of the union $D_{\vec{y}}$ of all structures $C_{i,\vec{y}}$ for $i \in N_{\vec{y}}$. Let $\vec{y}^* := g_{i_0,\vec{y}}(\vec{y})$. Observe that $D^*_{\vec{y}}$ and $\vec{y}^*$ indeed do not depend on the order $\le_{\vec{y}}$, as long as it satisfies (C) and (D).

Let ρ be the unique mapping from $\mathcal{Y}$ to an initial segment of the positive integers such that $\rho(\vec{y}) \le \rho(\vec{z})$ if and only if one of the following two conditions is satisfied:

(H) $D^*_{\vec{y}} <^{\lambda}_{\text{lex}} D^*_{\vec{z}}$.
(I) $D^*_{\vec{y}} = D^*_{\vec{z}}$ and $\vec{y}^* \le_{\text{lex}} \vec{z}^*$.

Then $\rho(\vec{y}) = \rho(\vec{z})$ if and only if $D^*_{\vec{y}} = D^*_{\vec{z}}$ and $\vec{y}^* = \vec{z}^*$. Let $r := \max\{\rho(\vec{y}) \mid \vec{y} \in \mathcal{Y}\}$.

We let $A_{t,\vec{x}}$ be the μ-expansion of $C[\beta(t)]$ defined as follows:

(J) For all $i \in [a]$ we define $P_i(A_{t,\vec{x}})$ by
$$P_i^{A_{t,\vec{x}}}(\vec{y}) := \begin{cases} 1 & \text{if } i = s_t \text{ and } \vec{y} = \vec{x}, \\ 0 & \text{otherwise,} \end{cases}$$
for all $\vec{y} \in \beta(t)^i$.
(K) For all $i \in [a]$ we define $Q_i(A_{t,\vec{x}})$ by
$$Q_i^{A_{t,\vec{x}}}(\vec{y}) := \begin{cases} \rho(\vec{y}) & \text{if } \vec{y} \in \mathcal{Y}, \\ 0 & \text{otherwise,} \end{cases}$$
for all $\vec{y} \in \beta(t)^i$.

Observe that the Gaifman graph of $A_{t,\vec{x}}$ is $\tau(t)$, because the sets $\tilde{x} = \sigma(t)$ and $\tilde{y} = \sigma(u_i)$ for all $\vec{y} \in \mathcal{Y}$ are cliques in $\tau(t)$. Hence the canonisation mapping $\mathfrak{a}$ is applicable to $A_{t,\vec{x}}$. Let $A^*_{t,\vec{x}} := \mathfrak{a}(A_{t,\vec{x}})$.

We define the structure $C^*_{t,\vec{x}}$ as follows: We take the disjoint union of $A^*_{t,\vec{x}}$ with copies of the structures $D^*_{\vec{y}}$ for $\vec{y} \in \mathcal{Y}$. These copies are chosen such that their universes are consecutive intervals of positive integers and such that $D^*_{\vec{y}}$ comes before $D^*_{\vec{z}}$ if $\rho(\vec{y}) < \rho(\vec{z})$. Let C^1 be the resulting structure. Then for each tuple $\vec{z} \in V(A^*_{t,\vec{x}})$ with $q := Q_{|\vec{z}|}^{A^*_{t,\vec{x}}}(\vec{z}) \in [1, r]$ we choose a tuple $\vec{y} \in \mathcal{Y}$ with $\rho(\vec{y}) = q$ and identify the copy of $\vec{y}^*$ in the copy of $D^*_{\vec{y}}$ in C^1 with $\vec{z}$. Of course there may be several $\vec{z}$ with $Q_{|\vec{z}|}^{A^*_{t,\vec{x}}}(\vec{z}) = q$, say, $\vec{z}_1 <_{\text{lex}} \vec{z}_2 <_{\text{lex}} \ldots <_{\text{lex}} \vec{z}_\ell$. Then there are $\vec{y}_1, \ldots, \vec{y}_\ell \in \mathcal{Y}$ with $\rho(\vec{y}_j) = q$. For all these, the structures $D^*_{\vec{y}_j}$ are isomorphic and their copies appear consecutively in C^1. We identify $\vec{z}_j$ with the copy of $\vec{y}_j^*$ in the copy of $D^*_{\vec{y}_j}$. After doing all these identifications, we shrink the universe of the structure so that it is an initial segment of the positive integers. Let C^2 be the resulting μ-structure, and let $C^*_{t,\vec{x}}$ be the λ-restriction of C^2. If $s_t = 0$ (and thus $\vec{x}$ is the empty tuple) we let $g_{t,\vec{x}}$ be the empty mapping. Otherwise, there is a unique tuple $\vec{x}^* = (x_1^*, \ldots, x_{s_t}^*) \in P_{s_t}(A^*_{t,\vec{x}})$. We define $g_{t,\vec{x}}$ by letting $g_{t,\vec{x}}(x_i) := x_i^*$ for all all $i \in [s_t]$.

To define the canonical copy $\mathfrak{c}(C)$ of C, we let $M \subseteq V(D)$ be the set of all nodes t with $\sigma(t) = \emptyset$ and $\gamma(t) = V(C)$. Such nodes exist by (TL.5), because G_C is connected. We look at the set $\mathcal{M}$ of all structures C^*_t for nodes $t \in T$. (Here we write C^*_t instead of $C^*_{t,()}$, omitting the empty tuple enumerating $\sigma(t) = \emptyset$.) By (B), all structures in $\mathcal{M}$ are isomorphic to C. We let $\mathfrak{c}(C)$ be the $\le^{\lambda}_{\text{lex}}$-minimal structure in $\mathcal{M}$.

It is important to note that our construction is "invariant", that is, completely determined by the structure C and the decomposition Δ_{G_C}. The only freedom we have during the construction is in the exact order of the children $u_1, \ldots, u_m$ of t, but we have already noted that conditions (C) and (D) restrict the choices we can make in such a way that they do no longer matter because the resulting structures will be isomorphic. The invariance of Δ implies that if f is an isomorphism from C to a λ-structure C' then, letting

$\Delta_{G'_C} = (D', \sigma', \alpha')$, there is an isomorphism g from D to D' such that for all $t \in V(D)$ and all enumerations $\vec{x}$ of $\sigma(t)$ the restriction of f to $\gamma(t)$ is an isomorphism from $C_{t,\vec{x}}$ to $C_{g(t),f(\vec{x})}$. By the invariance of our construction, it follows that $C^*_{t,\vec{x}} = {C'}^*_{g(t),f(\vec{x})}$ and $g_{t,\vec{x}}(\vec{x}) = g_{g(t),f(\vec{x})}(f(\vec{x}))$. This implies that $\mathcal{M} = \mathcal{M}'$, where $\mathcal{M}'$ is defined from C' and $\Delta_{G'_C}$ in the same way as $\mathcal{M}$ is defined from C and Δ_{G_C}, and thus $\mathfrak{c}(C) = \mathfrak{c}(C')$.

As the decomposition mapping Δ is polynomial time computable, the canonization mapping $\mathfrak{c}$ is polynomial time computable as well. □

Now we are ready to prove the main algorithmic result of the paper (which proves Theorem 1.3 in the introduction):

THEOREM 9.7. *For every graph H, the class of graphs excluding H as topological subgraph admits polynomial time strong canonisation.*

PROOF. Choose the constants a, b, c, d, e as in the Invariant Decomposition Theorem 8.3. Let $\mathcal{A}_1$ be the class of all graphs G with $|V(G)| \leq b$, and let $\mathcal{A}_2$ be the class of all graphs G with $K_x \not\preceq G$, and let $\mathcal{A}_3$ be the class of all graphs G such that at most c vertices of G have degree higher than d. The class $\mathcal{A}_1$ trivially admits polynomial time strong canonisation. The class $\mathcal{A}_2$ admits polynomial time strong canonisation by Lemma 9.4. The class $\mathcal{A}_3$ admits polynomial time strong canonisation by Corollary 9.5. As $\mathcal{A}_1$ and $\mathcal{A}_3$ are polynomial time decidable ($\mathcal{A}_2$ is as well, but we do not need this), it follows that the class $\mathcal{A} := \mathcal{A}_1 \cup \mathcal{A}_2 \cup \mathcal{A}_2$ admits polynomial time strong canonisation as well. That is, the canonization algorithm for $\mathcal{A}$ uses the algorithm for $\mathcal{A}_1$ if $|V(G)| \leq b$; otherwise it uses the algorithm for $\mathcal{A}_3$ if there are at most c vertices having degree higher than d; otherwise it uses the algorithm for $\mathcal{A}_2$.

By the Invariant Decomposition Theorem 8.3 the class of H-topological subgraph free graphs admits polynomial time invariant treelike decompositions over $\mathcal{A}$ of adhesion a. Hence by the Lifting Lemma 9.6, the class of graphs excluding H as topological subgraph admits polynomial time strong canonisation. □

10. REFERENCES

[1] O. Amini, F. V. Fomin, and S. Saurabh. Implicit branching and parameterized partial cover problems. *J. Comput. Syst. Sci.*, 77(6):1159–1171, 2011.

[2] L. Babai and E. Luks. Canonical labeling of graphs. In *STOC*, pages 171–183, 1983.

[3] H. Bodlaender. Polynomial algorithms for graph isomorphism and chromatic index on partial k-trees. *Journal of Algorithms*, 11:631–643, 1990.

[4] E. D. Demaine, M. Hajiaghayi, and K. Kawarabayashi. Contraction decomposition in H-minor-free graphs and algorithmic applications. In *STOC*, pages 441–450, 2011.

[5] E. D. Demaine, M. T. Hajiaghayi, and K. Kawarabayashi. Algorithmic graph minor theory: Decomposition, approximation, and coloring. In *FOCS*, pages 637–646, 2005.

[6] F. Dorn, F. V. Fomin, and D. M. Thilikos. Catalan structures and dynamic programming in H-minor-free graphs. In *SODA*, pages 631–640, 2008.

[7] Z. Dvorak, D. Král, and R. Thomas. Deciding first-order properties for sparse graphs. In *FOCS*, pages 133–142, 2010.

[8] I. S. Filotti and J. N. Mayer. A polynomial-time algorithm for determining the isomorphism of graphs of fixed genus. In *STOC*, pages 236–243, 1980.

[9] M. Grohe. Descriptive complexity, canonisation, and definable graph structure theory. Manuscript. `http://www2.informatik.hu-berlin.de/~grohe/cap`.

[10] M. Grohe. Local tree-width, excluded minors, and approximation algorithms. *Combinatorica*, 23(4):613–632, 2003.

[11] M. Grohe. Definable tree decompositions. In *LICS*, pages 406–417, 2008.

[12] M. Grohe, K. Kawarabayashi, D. Marx, and P. Wollan. Finding topological subgraphs is fixed-parameter tractable. In *STOC*, pages 479–488, 2011.

[13] K. Kawarabayashi, E. D. Demaine, and M. Hajiaghayi. Additive approximation algorithms for list-coloring minor-closed class of graphs. In *SODA*, pages 1166–1175, 2009.

[14] K. Kawarabayashi and B. Mohar. Approximating the list-chromatic number and the chromatic number in minor-closed and odd-minor-closed classes of graphs. In *STOC*, pages 401–416, 2006.

[15] K. Kawarabayashi and B. Mohar. Some recent progress and applications in graph minor theory. *Graphs and Combinatorics*, 23(1):1–46, 2007.

[16] K. Kawarabayashi and P. Wollan. A shorter proof of the graph minor algorithm: the unique linkage theorem. In *STOC*, pages 687–694, 2010.

[17] K. Kawarabayashi and P. Wollan. A simpler algorithm and shorter proof for the graph minor decomposition. In *STOC*, pages 451–458, 2011.

[18] E. Luks. Isomorphism of graphs of bounded valance can be tested in polynomial time. *J. Comput. Syst. Sci.*, 25:42–65, 1982.

[19] W. Mader. Homomorphieeigenschaften und mittlere Kantendichte von Graphen. *Math. Ann.*, 174:265–268, 1967.

[20] G. Miller. Isomorphism of k-contractible graphs. A generalization of bounded valence and bounded genus. *Information and Control*, 56:1–20, 1983.

[21] G. L. Miller. Isomorphism testing for graphs of bounded genus. In *STOC*, pages 225–235, 1980.

[22] I. N. Ponomarenko. The isomorphism problem for classes of graphs that are invariant with respect to contraction. *Zap. Nauchn. Sem. Leningrad. Otdel. Mat. Inst. Steklov. (LOMI)*, 174(Teor. Slozhn. Vychisl. 3):147–177, 182, 1988. In Russian.

[23] N. Robertson and P. Seymour. Graph minors X. Obstructions to tree-decomposition. *Journal of Combinatorial Theory, Series B*, 52:153–190, 1991.

[24] N. Robertson and P. Seymour. Graph minors XIII. The disjoint paths problem. *Journal of Combinatorial Theory, Series B*, 63:65–110, 1995.

[25] N. Robertson and P. Seymour. Graph minors XVI. Excluding a non-planar graph. *Journal of Combinatorial Theory, Series B*, 77:1–27, 1999.

Short Proofs for the Determinant Identities

Pavel Hrubeš
Department of Computer Science
University of Calgary
Alberta, Canada
pahrubes@gmail.com

Iddo Tzameret*
Institute for Theoretical Computer Science at IIIS
Tsinghua University
Beijing 100084, China
tzameret@tsinghua.edu.cn

ABSTRACT

We study arithmetic proof systems $\mathbb{P}_c(\mathbb{F})$ and $\mathbb{P}_f(\mathbb{F})$ operating with arithmetic circuits and arithmetic formulas, respectively, that prove polynomial identities over a field $\mathbb{F}$. We establish a series of structural theorems about these proof systems, the main one stating that $\mathbb{P}_c(\mathbb{F})$ proofs can be balanced: if a polynomial identity of syntactic degree d and depth k has a $\mathbb{P}_c(\mathbb{F})$ proof of size s, then it also has a $\mathbb{P}_c(\mathbb{F})$ proof of size $\text{poly}(s, d)$ and depth $O(k + \log^2 d + \log d \cdot \log s)$. As a corollary, we obtain a quasipolynomial simulation of $\mathbb{P}_c(\mathbb{F})$ by $\mathbb{P}_f(\mathbb{F})$, for identities of a polynomial syntactic degree.

Using these results we obtain the following: consider the identities

$$\det(XY) = \det(X) \cdot \det(Y) \quad \text{and} \quad \det(Z) = z_{11} \cdots z_{nn},$$

where X, Y and Z are $n \times n$ square matrices and Z is a triangular matrix with $z_{11}, \ldots, z_{nn}$ on the diagonal (and det is the determinant polynomial). Then we can construct a polynomial-size arithmetic circuit det such that the above identities have $\mathbb{P}_c(\mathbb{F})$ proofs of polynomial-size and $O(\log^2 n)$ depth. Moreover, there exists an arithmetic formula det of size $n^{O(\log n)}$ such that the above identities have $\mathbb{P}_f(\mathbb{F})$ proofs of size $n^{O(\log n)}$.

This yields a solution to a basic open problem in propositional proof complexity, namely, whether there are polynomial-size $\mathbf{NC}^2$-Frege proofs for the determinant identities and the *hard matrix identities*, as considered, e.g. in Soltys and Cook [14] (cf., Beame and Pitassi [1]). We show that matrix identities like $AB = I \rightarrow BA = I$ (for matrices over the two element field) as well as basic properties of the determinant have polynomial-size $\mathbf{NC}^2$-Frege proofs, and quasipolynomial-size Frege proofs.

*Supported in part by the National Basic Research Program of China Grant 2011CBA00300, 2011CBA00301, the National Natural Science Foundation of China Grant 61033001, 61061130540, 61073174.

STOC'12, May 19–22, 2012, New York, New York, USA.

Categories and Subject Descriptors

F.2.2 [**Analysis of Algorithms and Problem Complexity**]: Nonnumerical Algorithms and Problems—*Complexity of proof procedures*

General Terms

Theory

Keywords

Proof complexity, algebraic complexity, Frege systems, linear algebra, determinant

1. INTRODUCTION

The field of proof complexity is dominated by the question of how hard is it to prove propositional tautologies. For weak proof systems, such as resolution, many hardness results are known (cf., [10] for a recent technical survey), but for strong propositional proof systems like Frege or extended Frege the question remains completely open. In this paper we continue to investigate a different but related problem: how hard is it to prove polynomial identities? For this purpose, various systems for proving polynomial identities were introduced in [4]. The main feature of these systems is that they manipulate arithmetic equations of the form $F = G$, where F, G are arithmetic formulas over a given field. Such equations are manipulated by means of simple syntactic rules, in such a way that $F = G$ has a proof if and only if F and G compute the same polynomial. The central question in this framework is the following:

> What is the *length* of such proofs, namely, does every true polynomial equation have a short proof, or are there hard equations that require extremely long proofs?

In this paper, we focus on two arithmetic equational proof systems (arithmetic proofs systems, for short) for proving polynomial identities: $\mathbb{P}_f$ and $\mathbb{P}_c$. The former system was introduced in [4] and the latter is an extension of it. The difference between the two systems is that $\mathbb{P}_f$ operates with *arithmetic formulas*, whereas $\mathbb{P}_c$ operates with *arithmetic circuits*—this is analogous to the distinction between Frege and extended Frege proof systems (Frege and extended Frege proofs are propositional proof systems establishing propositional tautologies, essentially operating with boolean formulas and circuits, respectively).

The study of proofs of polynomial identities is motivated by at least two reasons. First, as a study of the Polynomial Identity Testing (PIT) problem. As a decision problem, polynomial identity testing can be solved by an efficient randomized algorithm [9, 19], but no efficient deterministic algorithm is known. In fact, it is not even known whether there is a polynomial time non-deterministic algorithm or, equivalently, whether PIT is in **NP**. A proof system such as $\mathbb{P}_c$ can be interpreted as a specific non-deterministic algorithm for PIT: in order to verify that an arithmetic formula F computes the zero polynomial, it is sufficient to guess a proof of $F = 0$ in $\mathbb{P}_c$. Hence, if every true equality has a polynomial-size proof then PIT is in **NP**. Conversely, $\mathbb{P}_f$ and $\mathbb{P}_c$ systems capture the common syntactic procedures used to establish equality of algebraic expressions. Thus, showing the existence of identities that require superpolynomial arithmetic proofs would imply that those syntactic procedures are not enough to solve PIT efficiently.

The second motivation comes from propositional proof complexity. The systems $\mathbb{P}_f$ and $\mathbb{P}_c$ are in fact *restricted* versions of their propositional counterparts, Frege and extended Frege, respectively (when operating over $GF(2)$). One may hope that the study of the former would help to understand the latter. Arithmetic proof systems have the advantage that they work with arithmetic circuits. The structure of arithmetic circuits is perhaps better understood than the structure of their Boolean counterparts, or is at least different, suggesting different techniques and fresh perspectives.

In order to understand the strength of the systems $\mathbb{P}_f$ and $\mathbb{P}_c$, as well as their relative strength, we investigate quite a specific question, namely, how hard is it to prove basic properties of the determinant? In other words, we investigate lengths of proofs of identities such as $\det(AB) = \det(A)\cdot\det(B)$, or the cofactor expansion of the determinant. We show that such identities have polynomial-size $\mathbb{P}_c$ proofs of depth $O(\log^2 n)$ and quasipolynomial size $\mathbb{P}_f$ proofs (both results hold over any field).[1]

The determinant polynomial has a central role in both linear algebra and arithmetic circuit complexity. Therefore, an immediate motivation for our inquiry is to understand whether arithmetic proof systems are strong enough to reason efficiently about the determinant. More importantly, we take the determinant question as a pretext to present several structural properties of $\mathbb{P}_c$ and $\mathbb{P}_f$. A large part of this work is not concerned with the determinant at all, but is rather a series of general theorems showing how classical results in arithmetic circuit complexity can be translated to the setting of arithmetic proofs. We thus show how to capture efficiently the following results: (i) homogenization of arithmetic circuits (implicit in [16]); (ii) Strassen's technique for eliminating division gates over large enough fields (also in [16]); (iii) eliminating division gates over small fields—this is done by simulating large fields in small ones; and (iv) balancing arithmetic circuits (Valiant et al. [18]; see also [5]). Most notably, the latter result gives a collapse of polynomial-size $\mathbb{P}_c$ proofs to polynomial-size $O(\log^2 n)$-depth $\mathbb{P}_c$ proofs (for proving identities of polynomial syntactic degrees) and a quasipolynomial simulation of $\mathbb{P}_c$ by $\mathbb{P}_f$. This is one important point where the arithmetic systems differ from Frege and extended Frege, for which no non-trivial simulation is known.

Furthermore, the proof complexity of linear algebra attracted a lot of attention in the past. This was motivated, in part, by the goal of separating the propositional proof systems Frege and extended Frege. A classical example, originally proposed by Cook and Rackoff (cf., [1, 14, 15, 12, 13]), is the so called *inversion principle* asserting that $AB = I \rightarrow BA = I$. When A, B are $n \times n$ matrices over $GF(2)$, the inversion principle is a collection of propositional tautologies. Soltys and Cook [14, 12] showed that the principle has polynomial size extended Frege proofs. On the other hand, no feasible Frege proof is known, and hence the inversion principle is a candidate for separating the two proof systems. Other candidates, including several based on linear algebra, were presented by Buss et al. [3]. The inversion principle is one of the "hard matrix identities" explored in [14]. Inside Frege, the hard matrix identities have feasible proofs from one another, and they have short proofs from the aforementioned determinant identities. This connection between the hard matrix identities and the determinant identities serves as an evidence for the conjecture that hard matrix identities require superpolynomial Frege proofs: it seems that every Frege proof must in some sense construct the determinant, which is believed to require a superpolynomial-size formula.

A related question is whether the hard matrix identities and the determinant identities have polynomial-size $\mathbf{NC}^2$-Frege proofs[2]. This was conjectured in, e.g., [3], based on the intuition that the determinant is $\mathbf{NC}^2$ computable, and so by the analogy between circuit classes and proofs, it is natural to assume that the determinant properties are efficiently provable in $\mathbf{NC}^2$-Frege. Again, a polynomial-size extended Frege proofs of the determinant identities have been constructed in [14]. Whether these identities have polynomial-size $\mathbf{NC}^2$-Frege proofs (and hence, quasipolynomial-size Frege proofs) remained open. In this paper, we positively answer this question: we show that over $GF(2)$, the hard hard matrix identities and the determinant identities have polynomial-size $\mathbf{NC}^2$-Frege proofs. This is a simple corollary of the results on arithmetic proof systems. Over the two element field, an $O(\log^2 n)$-depth $\mathbb{P}_c$ proof is formally also $\mathbf{NC}^2$-Frege proof[3]. Thus, if determinant identities like $\det(AB) = \det(A) \cdot \det(B)$ have polynomial-size $\mathbb{P}_c(GF(2))$ proofs with depth $O(\log^2 n)$, then the corresponding propositional tautologies have polynomial-size $\mathbf{NC}^2$-Frege proofs.

Let us remark that one can also consider propositional translations of the determinant identities (and the hard matrix identities) over different finite fields or even the rationals. We do not explicitly study these translations, but there is no apparent obstacle to extending the result to these cases.

To understand our construction of short arithmetic proofs for the determinant identities, let us consider the following example. In [2], Berkowitz constructed a quasipolynomial size arithmetic formula for the determinant. He used a clever combinatorial argument designed *specifically* for the determinant function. However, one can build such a formula in a completely oblivious way: first compute the determinant by, say, Gaussian elimination algorithm. This gives an

[1]The parameter n is the dimension of the matrices A, B, and quasipolynomial size means size $n^{O(\log n)}$.

[2]That is, polynomial size proofs using circuits of $O(\log^2 n)$-depth

[3]When $+$ and $\cdot$ modulo 2 are interpreted as Boolean connectives and $=$ is interpreted as logical equivalence.

arithmetic circuit with division gates. Second, show that any circuit with division gates computing a polynomial can be efficiently simulated by a division-free circuit [16], and finally, show that any arithmetic circuit of a polynomial degree can be transformed to an $O(\log^2 n)$-depth circuit computing the same polynomial, with only a polynomial increase in size [18] (or to a formula with at most a quasipolynomial increase in size [5]). This paper follows a similar strategy, but in the proof-theoretic framework.

It should be stressed that in full generality, the structural theorems about $\mathbb{P}_c$ and $\mathbb{P}_f$ *cannot* be reproduced for propositional Frege and extended Frege systems. As already mentioned, no non-trivial simulation between Frege and extended Frege is known, and the other theorems are difficult to even formulate in the Boolean context. This also illustrates one final point: in order to construct a Frege proof of a tautology T, it may be useful to interpret T as a polynomial identity and prove it in some of the—weaker but better structured—arithmetic proof systems.

1.1 Arithmetic proofs with circuits and formulas

Before presenting and explaining the main results of this paper (in Section 2), we need to introduce our basic arithmetic proof systems.

Arithmetic circuits and formulas.

Let $\mathbb{F}$ be a field. *An arithmetic circuit* F is a finite directed acyclic graph as follows. Nodes (or gates) of in-degree zero are labeled by either a variable or a field element in $\mathbb{F}$. All the other nodes have in-degree two and they are labeled by either $+$ or $\times$. Unless stated otherwise, we assume that F has exactly one node of out-degree zero, called the *output node*, and that moreover the two edges going into a gate v labeled by $\times$ or $+$ are labeled by *left* and *right*. This is to determine the order of addition and multiplication[4]. An arithmetic circuit is called a *formula*, if the out-degree of each node in it is one (and so the underlying graph is a directed tree). The *size* of a circuit is the number of nodes in it, and the *depth* of a circuit is the length of the longest directed path in it. Arithmetic circuits and formulas will be referred to simply as *circuits* and *formulas*.

For a circuit F and a node u in F, F_u denotes the subcircuit of F with output node u. If F, G are circuits then

$$F \oplus G \text{ and } F \otimes G$$

abbreviate any circuit H whose output node is $u+v$ and $u \cdot v$, respectively, where $H_u = F$ and $H_v = G$. Furthermore,

$$F + G \text{ and } F \cdot G$$

denote the unique circuit of the form $F' \oplus G'$ and $F' \otimes G'$, respectively, where F', G' are disjoint copies of F and G. In particular, if F and G are formulas then so are $F + G$ and $F \cdot G$.

A circuit F computes a polynomial $\widehat{F}$ with coefficients from $\mathbb{F}$ in the obvious manner. That is, if F consists of a single node labeled with z, a variable or an element of $\mathbb{F}$, we have $\widehat{F} := z$. Otherwise, F is either of the form $G \oplus H$ or $G \otimes H$, and we let $\widehat{F} := \widehat{G} + \widehat{H}$ or $\widehat{F} := \widehat{G} \cdot \widehat{H}$, respectively.

[4]Although ultimately, addition and multiplication are commutative.

Substitution is understood in the following sense. Let $F = F(z)$ be a circuit and z a variable. For a circuit G, the circuit $F(G)$ is defined as follows: let $z_1, \ldots, z_k$ be the nodes in F labeled by z. Introduce k disjoint copies $G_1, \ldots, G_k$ of G, and let $F(G)$ be the union of $F, G_1, \ldots, G_k$ where we replace the node z_i by the output node of G_i. Specifically, if F and G are formulas then so is $F(G)$. $F(G)$ will also be written as $F(z/G)$.

The system $\mathbb{P}_f(\mathbb{F})$

We now define two proof systems for deriving polynomial identities. The systems manipulate *arithmetic equations*, that is, expressions of the form $F = G$. In the case of $\mathbb{P}_f(\mathbb{F})$, F, G are formulas, and in the case of $\mathbb{P}_c(\mathbb{F})$, F, G are circuits (see [4] for similar proof systems).

Let $\mathbb{F}$ be a field. The system $\mathbb{P}_f(\mathbb{F})$ proves equations of the form $F = G$, where F, G are *formulas* over $\mathbb{F}$. The inference rules are:

R1 $$\frac{F = G}{G = F}$$

R2 $$\frac{F = G \quad G = H}{F = H}$$

R3 $$\frac{F_1 = G_1 \quad F_2 = G_2}{F_1 + F_2 = G_1 + G_2}$$

R4 $$\frac{F_1 = G_1 \quad F_2 = G_2}{F_1 \cdot F_2 = G_1 \cdot G_2}.$$

The axioms are equations of the following form, with F, G, H formulas:

A1 $F = F$

A2 $F + G = G + F$

A3 $F + (G + H) = (F + G) + H$

A4 $F \cdot G = G \cdot F$

A5 $F \cdot (G \cdot H) = (F \cdot G) \cdot H$

A6 $F \cdot (G + H) = F \cdot G + F \cdot H$

A7 $F + 0 = F$

A8 $F \cdot 0 = 0$

A9 $a = b + c, a' = b' \cdot c'$, if $a, b, c, a', b', c' \in \mathbb{F}$, are such that the equations hold in $\mathbb{F}$.

The rules and axioms can be divided into two groups. The rules R1-R4 and axiom A1 determine the logical properties of equality "=", and axioms A2-A9 assert that polynomials form a commutative ring over $\mathbb{F}$.

A proof S in $\mathbb{P}_f(\mathbb{F})$ is a sequence of equations $F_1 = G_1, F_2 = G_2, \ldots, F_k = G_k$, with F_i, G_i formulas, such that every equation is either an axiom A1-A9, or was obtained from previous equations by one of the rules R1-R4. An equation $F_i = G_i$ appearing in a proof is also called a *proof line*. We consider two measures of complexity for S: the *size of S* is the sum of the sizes of F_i and G_i, $i \in [k]$, and the *number of proof lines in S* is k. (Throughout the paper, $[k]$ stands for $\{1, \ldots, k\}$.)

The system $\mathbb{P}_c(\mathbb{F})$

The system $\mathbb{P}_c(\mathbb{F})$ differs from $\mathbb{P}_f(\mathbb{F})$ in that it manipulates equations with *circuits*. $\mathbb{P}_c(\mathbb{F})$ has the same rules R1-R4 and axioms A1-A9 as $\mathbb{P}_f(\mathbb{F})$, but with $F, G, H, F_1, F_2, G_1, G_2$

ranging over circuits, augmented with the following two axioms:

C1 $\quad F_1 \oplus F_2 = F_1 + F_2 \qquad$ C2 $\quad F_1 \otimes F_2 = F_1 \cdot F_2$.

A *proof in* $\mathbb{P}_c(\mathbb{F})$ is a sequence of equations $F_1 = G_1, \dots, F_k = G_k$, where F_i, G_i are circuits, and every equation is either an axiom or was derived by one of the rules. As for $\mathbb{P}_f(\mathbb{F})$, the *size* of a proof is the sum of the sizes of all the circuits F_i and G_i, $i \in [k]$, and the *number of proof lines* of the proof is k. The *depth* of a $\mathbb{P}_c(\mathbb{F})$ proof is the maximal depth of a circuit appearing in the proof.

The main property of the two proof systems $\mathbb{P}_c(\mathbb{F})$ and $\mathbb{P}_f(\mathbb{F})$ is that they are sound and complete with respect to polynomial identities. The systems prove an equation $F = G$ if and only if F, G compute the same polynomial:

PROPOSITION 1. *Let $\mathbb{F}$ be a field.*

(i) For any pair F, G of arithmetic **formulas**, *$\mathbb{P}_f(\mathbb{F})$ proves $F = G$ iff $\widehat{F} = \widehat{G}$.*

(ii) For any pair F, G of arithmetic circuits, $\mathbb{P}_c(\mathbb{F})$ proves $F = G$ iff $\widehat{F} = \widehat{G}$.

Part i was shown in [4], part ii is almost identical. Soundness can be easily proved by induction on the number of lines and completeness by rewriting F and G as a sum of monomials.

It should be noted that $\mathbb{P}_f$ and $\mathbb{P}_c$ proofs are closed under substitution. If $F_1 = G_1, \dots, F_k = G_k$ is a $\mathbb{P}_c$ proof, z a variable and H a circuit then $F_1(z/H) = G_1(z/H), \dots, F_k(z/H) = G_k(z/H)$ is also a $\mathbb{P}_c$ proof (similarly for $\mathbb{P}_f$ and a formula H). This means that from a general proof, one can obtain the proof of its instance.

For simplicity, we often suppress the explicit dependence on the field $\mathbb{F}$ in $\mathbb{P}_c$ and $\mathbb{P}_f$, if the relevant statement holds over any field.

Comments on the proof systems.

The system $\mathbb{P}_c$ is an algebraic analogue of the propositional proof system *circuit Frege* (CF). Circuit Frege is polynomially equivalent to the more well-known *extended Frege* system (EF) (see [7, 6]). Following this analogy, one can define an *extended* $\mathbb{P}_f$ proof system, $\mathrm{E}\mathbb{P}_f$, as follows: an $\mathrm{E}\mathbb{P}_f$ proof is a $\mathbb{P}_f$ proof in which we are allowed to introduce new "extension" variables $z_1, z_2, \dots$ via the axiom $z_i = F_i$, where we require that (i) the variable z_i appears in neither F_i nor in any previous proof-line; and (ii) the last equation in the proof contains none of the extension variables $z_1, z_2, \dots$.

The following is completely analogous to the propositional case (see [7, 6]):

PROPOSITION 2.

(i) The systems $\mathbb{P}_c$ and $\mathrm{E}\mathbb{P}_f$ polynomially simulate each other. More exactly, there is a polynomial p such that for every pair of formulas F, G, if $F = G$ has a $\mathbb{P}_c$ proof of size s then it has an $\mathrm{E}\mathbb{P}_f$ proof of size $p(s)$, and if $F = G$ has an $\mathrm{E}\mathbb{P}_f$ proof of size s then it has a $\mathbb{P}_c$ proof of size $p(s)$.

(ii) If F and G are circuits of size s and $F = G$ has a $\mathbb{P}_c$ proof with k proof lines then $F = G$ has a $\mathbb{P}_c$ proof of size poly(s, k).

The second part of this statement is especially useful, because it is often easier to estimate the number of lines in a proof rather than its size.

REMARK 3. *An alternative, polynomially equivalent, definition for $\mathbb{P}_c$ can be given as follows. For a circuit F, define $F^\bullet$ as the unfolding of F into a* formula. *That is, $F^\bullet := F$, if F is a leaf, and $(G \oplus H)^\bullet := G^\bullet + H^\bullet$, $(G \otimes H)^\bullet := G^\bullet \cdot H^\bullet$. We say that F and G are* similar circuits, *if $F^\bullet$ is the same formula as $G^\bullet$. Then A1, C1, C2 could be replaced by the following single axiom:*

A1' $\qquad F = G, \qquad$ whenever F and G are similar.

The axiom A1' can be proved from A1, C1, C2 by a polynomial-size proof, and vice versa.

Notation for matrices inside proofs.

In this paper, matrices are understood as matrices whose entries are circuits and operations on matrices are operations on circuits. We illustrate this for square matrices. Let $F = \{F_{ij}\}_{i,j \in [n]}$ be an $n \times n$ matrix whose entries are circuits F_{ij}; and similarly $G = \{G_{ij}\}_{i,j \in [n]}$. Addition and multiplication is defined in the obvious way, namely

$$F + G = \{F_{ij} + G_{ij}\}_{i,j \in [n]}, \quad F \cdot G = \{\sum_{p=1}^{n} F_{ip} \cdot G_{pj}\}_{i,j \in [n]},$$

where $+$ and $\cdot$ on the right-hand side is addition and multiplication on circuits. If a is a single circuit, $a \cdot F$ is the matrix $\{a \cdot F_{ij}\}_{i,j \in [n]}$. An equation $F = G$ denotes the set of equations $F_{ij} = G_{ij}$, $i, j \in [n]$.

2. OVERVIEW OF RESULTS AND TECHNIQUES

2.1 Main theorem

It is well known that the determinant can be uniquely characterized as the function that satisfies the following two identities for any pair of $n \times n$ matrices X, Y and any (upper or lower) triangular matrix Z with $z_{11}, \dots, z_{nn}$ on the diagonal:

$$\det(X \cdot Y) = \det(X) \cdot \det(Y), \quad (1)$$

$$\det(Z) = z_{11} \cdots z_{nn}. \quad (2)$$

Moreover, other properties of the determinant, such as the cofactor expansion, easily follow from (1) and (2).

The main goal of this paper is to prove the following theorem:

THEOREM 4 (MAIN THEOREM). *For any field $\mathbb{F}$:*

(i) There exists a circuit det *such that (1) and (2) have polynomial-size $\mathbb{P}_c(\mathbb{F})$ proofs. Moreover, every[5] circuit in the proof has depth at most $O(\log^2(n))$.*

(ii) There exists a formula det *such that (1) and (2) have $\mathbb{P}_f(\mathbb{F})$ proofs of size $n^{O(\log n)}$.*

As mentioned before, a large part of the construction is not related directly to the determinant. It is rather a series of structural theorems about the systems $\mathbb{P}_f$ and $\mathbb{P}_c$. These are obtained by reproducing classical results in arithmetic circuit complexity in the setting of arithmetic proofs (for a recent survey on arithmetic circuit complexity see [11]). The

[5]We assume that the product $z_{11} \cdots z_{nn}$ in (2) is written as a formula of depth $O(\log n)$.

most important of those results is showing that $\mathbb{P}_c$ proofs can be balanced, in the sense that $\mathbb{P}_c$ proofs of size s (of polynomially bounded syntactic degree equations) can be polynomially simulated by $\mathbb{P}_c$ proofs in which each circuit has depth $O(\log^2 s)$.

We do not know whether it is possible to prove Theorem 4 directly, perhaps by formalizing the elegant algorithm of Berkowitz [2]. One advantage of the algorithm is that, being division-free, it would dispense of Theorem 9 and allow to generalize Theorem 4 to an arbitrary commutative ring (as opposed to a field). We also admit that working with circuits and proofs with divisions turned out to be quite tedious. However, our construction is intended to emphasize general properties of arithmetic proof systems, and the structural theorems are in fact our main contribution.

2.2 Balancing $\mathbb{P}_c$ proofs and simulating $\mathbb{P}_c$ by $\mathbb{P}_f$

In the seminal paper [18], Valiant et al. showed that if a polynomial f of degree d can be computed by an arithmetic circuit of size s, then f can be computed by a circuit of size poly(s,d) and depth $O(\log s \log d + \log^2 d)$. This is a strengthening of an earlier result by Hyafil [5], showing that f can be computed by a formula of size $(s(d+1))^{O(\log d)}$. We will show that those results can be efficiently simulated within the framework of arithmetic proofs.

Instead of the degree of a polynomial, we focus on the syntactic degree of a circuit. Let F be an arithmetic circuit. *The syntactic degree* of F, $\deg F$, is defined as follows:

(i) If F is a field element or a variable, then $\deg F = 0$ and $\deg F = 1$, respectively;

(ii) $\deg(F \oplus G) = \max(\deg F, \deg G)$, and $\deg(F \otimes G) = \deg F + \deg G$.

The *syntactic degree of an equation* $F = G$ is $\max(\deg F, \deg G)$, and the *syntactic degree of a proof* S is the maximum of the syntactic degrees of equations in S. If F is a circuit and u is a node in F we also write $\deg(v)$ to denote $\deg F_v$.

In accordance with [18], we will construct a map $[\cdot]$ that maps any given circuit F of size s and syntactic degree d to a circuit $[F]$ computing the same polynomial, such that $[F]$ has size poly(s,d) and depth $O(\log s \log d + \log^2 d)$. We will show the following:

THEOREM 5. *Let F, G be circuits of syntactic degree at most d such that $F = G$ has a $\mathbb{P}_c$ proof of size s. Then:*

(i) The equation $[F] = [G]$ has a $\mathbb{P}_c$ proof of size poly(s,d) and depth $O(\log s \cdot \log d + \log^2 d)$.

(ii) If F, G have depth at most k then $F = G$ has a $\mathbb{P}_c$ proof of size poly(s,d) and depth $O(k + \log s \cdot \log d + \log^2 d)$.

We also obtain the following simulation of $\mathbb{P}_c$ by $\mathbb{P}_f$:

THEOREM 6. *Assume that F, G are formulas of syntactic degree $\leq d$ such that $F = G$ has a $\mathbb{P}_c$ proof of size s. Then $F = G$ has a $\mathbb{P}_f$ proof of size $(s(d+1))^{O(\log d)} \leq s^{O(\log s)}$.*

This simulation is polynomial if F and G have a constant syntactic degree. Let us emphasize that the syntactic degree of a formula of size s is at most s, and hence the simulation is at most *quasipolynomial*.

Homogenization and degree bound in arithmetic proofs.

One ingredient of Theorems 5 and 6 is to show that using circuits of high syntactic degree cannot significantly shorten $\mathbb{P}_c$ proofs. That is, if we want to prove an equation of syntactic degree d, we can without loss of generality use only circuits of syntactic degree at most d. This result is the proof-theoretic analog of a result by Strassen, who showed how to separate arithmetic circuits into their homogeneous parts (implicit in [16]).

We say that a circuit F is *syntactically homogeneous*, if for every sum-gate $u_1 + u_2$ in F we have $\deg(u_1) = \deg(u_2)$. For a circuit F and a number k, we introduce a circuit $F^{(k)}$ which computes the syntactically k-homogeneous part of F (see Section 3 for the definition). The *syntactic degree of a $\mathbb{P}_c$ proof* is the maximal syntactic degree of a circuit appearing in it. We show the following:

PROPOSITION 7. *Assume that $F = G$ has a $\mathbb{P}_c$ proof of size s. Then*

(i) $F^{(k)} = G^{(k)}$ has a $\mathbb{P}_c$ proof of size $s \cdot$ poly(k) and a syntactic degree at most k, for any k.

(ii) If $\deg F, \deg G \leq d$ then $F = G$ has a $\mathbb{P}_c$ proof of syntactic degree at most d and size $s \cdot$ poly(d).

2.3 Circuits and proofs with division

We denote by $\mathbb{F}(X)$ the field of formal rational functions in the variables X over the field $\mathbb{F}$. It is convenient to extend the notion of a circuit so that it computes rational functions in $\mathbb{F}(X)$. This is done in the following way: *a circuit with division F* is a circuit which may contain an additional type of gate with fan-in 1, called an *inverse* or a *division* gate, denoted $(\cdot)^{-1}$. If a node v computes the rational function f, then v^{-1} computes the rational function $1/f$. Moreover, we require that for every division node v^{-1} in F, v does not compute the zero rational function. If no division gate computes the zero rational function we say that F *is defined*, and otherwise, we say that F is *undefined*. One should note, for instance, that the circuit $(x^2 + x)^{-1}$ over $GF(2)$ is defined, since $x^2 + x$ is *not* the zero rational function (although it vanishes as a function over $GF(2)$).

We define the system $\mathbb{P}_c^{-1}(\mathbb{F})$, operating with equations $F = G$ for F and G circuits with division computing rational functions in $\mathbb{F}(X)$. First, we extend the axioms of $\mathbb{P}_c(\mathbb{F})$ to apply to circuits with division. Second, we add the following axiom:

$$\text{D} \qquad F \cdot F^{-1} = 1\,,$$

provided that F^{-1} is defined.

REMARK 8. *The system $\mathbb{P}_c^{-1}(\mathbb{F})$ polynomially simulates the rule*

$$\frac{F = G}{F^{-1} = G^{-1}}\,.$$

Moreover, the identities $(F^{-1})^{-1} = F$ and $(F \cdot G)^{-1} = G^{-1} \cdot F^{-1}$ have linear size proofs in $\mathbb{P}_c^{-1}(\mathbb{F})$.

As before, we sometimes suppress the explicit dependence on the field in $\mathbb{P}_c^{-1}(\mathbb{F})$ if the relevant statement is field independent.

Strassen [16] showed that division gates can be eliminated from arithmetic circuits computing polynomials over large enough fields, with only a polynomial increase in size. We will show the proof-theoretic analog of Strassen's result over *arbitrary* fields, namely that $\mathbb{P}_c(\mathbb{F})$ polynomially simulates $\mathbb{P}_c^{-1}(\mathbb{F})$ for any field $\mathbb{F}$:

THEOREM 9. *Let $\mathbb{F}$ be any field and assume that F and G are circuits without division gates such that $\deg F, \deg G \leq d$. Suppose that $F = G$ has a $\mathbb{P}_c^{-1}(\mathbb{F})$ proof of size s. Then $F = G$ has a $\mathbb{P}_c(\mathbb{F})$ proof of size $s \cdot poly(d)$.*

A corollary of Theorem 9 is that $\mathbb{P}_c(\mathbb{F})$ polynomially simulates the rule

$$\frac{F \cdot G = 0}{F = 0}, \quad \text{if } \widehat{G} \neq 0$$

(provided the syntactic degree of G is polynomially bounded).

To prove Theorem 9, we first assume that the underlying field $\mathbb{F}$ has an exponential size. Under this assumption, we cannot eliminate division gates in $GF(2)$ which is, from the Boolean proof complexity viewpoint, the most interesting field. To deal with small fields and specifically $GF(2)$ we have to show how to simulate large fields in small ones, as we explain in what follows.

Simulating large fields in small fields.

The idea behind simulating large fields in small ones is to treat the elements of $GF(p^n)$ as $n \times n$ matrices over $GF(p)$. This enables one to simulate computations and proofs over $GF(p^n)$ by those over $GF(p)$. We prove the following:

THEOREM 10. *Let p be a prime power and n a natural number and let F, G be circuits over $GF(p)$. Assume that $F = G$ has a $\mathbb{P}_c(GF(p^n))$ proof of size s. Then $F = G$ has a $\mathbb{P}_c(GF(p))$ proof of size $s \cdot poly(n)$.*

2.4 The determinant as a rational function and as a polynomial

To prove the main theorem (Theorem 4) one needs to construct a circuit (and a formula) computing the determinant polynomial which can be used efficiently inside arithmetic proofs. We first compute the determinant as a *rational function*, using a circuit with divisions denoted $\mathrm{DET}(X)$, and show that $\mathbb{P}_c^{-1}$ admits short proofs of the properties of $\mathrm{DET}(X)$. This is achieved by defining $\mathrm{DET}(X)$ in terms of the matrix inverse X^{-1} and inferring properties of DET from the identities $X \cdot X^{-1} = X^{-1}X = I$, which are shown to have polynomial-size $\mathbb{P}_c^{-1}$ proofs. The argument is basically a Gaussian elimination.

However, we cannot yet conclude Theorem 4 which speaks about (division-free) $\mathbb{P}_c$ proofs (it is worth mentioning that we also cannot **yet** conclude the short $\mathbf{NC}^2$-Frege proofs for the determinant identities, because $\mathbb{P}_c^{-1}$ proofs do not immediately correspond to propositional Frege proofs). Theorem 9 cannot be directly applied because it allows to eliminate division gates in $\mathbb{P}_c^{-1}$ proofs only if the equations proved are themselves division-free. We therefore proceed to construct a division-free circuit $\det(X)$, computing the determinant as a *polynomial*. Assuming we can prove efficiently in $\mathbb{P}_c^{-1}$ that $\det(X) = \mathrm{DET}(X)$, we are done, since we can now eliminate division gates from $\mathbb{P}_c^{-1}$ proofs of division-free equations, using Theorem 9. To this end, we define the $\det(X)$ polynomial as the nth term of the Taylor expansion of $\mathrm{DET}(I+zX)$ at $z = 0$. This enables us to demonstrate short proofs of $\det(X) = \mathrm{DET}(X)$ and conclude the argument.

2.5 Applications

Equipped with feasible proofs of the determinant identities, short proofs of several related identities follow. Cofactor expansion of the determinant will be given in Section 9. Another example is the formula completeness of the determinant. In [17], Valiant showed that every formula of size s can be written as a projection of a determinant of a matrix of a linear dimension. We can conclude that this holds feasibly already in $\mathbb{P}_c$:

PROPOSITION 11. *Let F be a formula of size s. Then there exists a matrix M of dimension $2s \times 2s$ whose entries are variables or elements of $\mathbb{F}$ such that the identity*

$$F = \det(M)$$

has a polynomial-size $O(\log^2 s)$-depth $\mathbb{P}_c(\mathbb{F})$ proof (and hence also a quasipolynomial-size $\mathbb{P}_f(\mathbb{F})$ proof), where det *is the circuit (resp. the formula) from Theorem 4.*

In this paper we are mainly interested in proofs with *no* assumptions other than the axioms A1-A9. Nevertheless, we can introduce the notion of a *proof from assumptions* as follows: let S be a set of equations. Then *a $\mathbb{P}_c$ proof from the assumptions S* is a proof that can use equations in S as additional axioms (and similarly for $\mathbb{P}_f$ proofs from assumptions). Proofs from assumptions are far less well-behaved than **standard arithmetic proofs**. For instance, neither Theorem 6 nor Theorem 9 hold for proofs from a general nonempty set S of assumptions. We now give an important example of a proof from assumptions.

Given a pair of $n \times n$ matrices X, Y, recall that the expressions $XY = I$ and $YX = I$, are abbreviations for the list of n^2 equalities between the appropriate entries.

PROPOSITION 12. *Let $\mathbb{F}$ be any field. The equations $YX = I_n$ have polynomial-size and $O(\log^2 n)$-depth $\mathbb{P}_c(\mathbb{F})$ proofs from the equations $XY = I_n$. In the case of $\mathbb{P}_f(\mathbb{F})$, the proof has a quasipolynomial-size.*

Determinant identities in $\mathbf{NC}^2$-Frege and Frege systems.

When considering the field $\mathbb{F}$ to be $GF(2)$, there is a close connection between our proof systems and the standard propositional proof systems. Consider the propositional proof systems Frege (F), extended Frege (EF) and circuit Frege (CF). For the definitions of Frege and extended Frege see [7] and for the definition of circuit Frege see [6], where it is also shown that CF and EF are polynomially equivalent.

For simplicity, we shall assume that F, EF and CF are all in the Boolean basis $+, \cdot, 0, 1$ (addition and multiplication modulo 2, logical equivalence, and the two Boolean constants)[6]. Then every arithmetic circuit *is automatically also a Boolean circuit*, and an equality like $G = H$ can be interpreted as the logical equivalence $G \equiv H$, written as $(G + H) + 1$. Hence $\mathbb{P}_f(GF(2))$ and $\mathbb{P}_c(GF(2))$ can be considered as *fragments* of F and CF, respectively: the finite

[6]Note that by Reckhow's result, as stated in [7], the particular choice of basis is immaterial. We could also have $\equiv$ as a primitive.

set of (schematic) axioms and rules of $\mathbb{P}_f(GF(2))$ now serve as Frege axioms and rules, and similarly for $\mathbb{P}_c(GF(2))$. Note that $x^2 = x$ is a propositional tautology but not a polynomial identity, and hence F and CF are (expressively) stronger than their arithmetic counterparts. In fact, one can polynomially simulate the full F or CF systems by adding the following new axiom

$$G^2 = G$$

to $\mathbb{P}_f(GF(2))$ or $\mathbb{P}_c(GF(2))$, where G is any formula or a circuit, respectively. To see this, it is sufficient to show that the augmented systems are complete with respect to propositional tautologies: they prove $F = 1$ whenever F evaluates to 1 on every $0,1$-input.

This means that upper bounds in $\mathbb{P}_f(GF(2))$ and $\mathbb{P}_c(GF(2))$ are in fact upper bounds in F and CF (and hence also in EF), respectively.

In what follows $XY = I_n$, and similarly $YX = I_n$, denote the conjunction of n^2 formulas of the form $(x_{i,1} \cdot y_{1,j} + \cdots + x_{i,n} \cdot y_{n,j}) \equiv \delta_{ij}$, where $+, \cdot$ are addition and multiplication modulo 2, respectively, $\equiv$ is the logical equivalence, and $\delta_{ij} \in \{0,1\}$ is given by $\delta_{ij} = 1$ iff $i = j$. We have the following:

THEOREM 13.

(i). The properties of the determinant as in Theorem 4 (interpreted as Boolean tautologies over $GF(2)$) have polynomial-size circuit Frege proofs, with every circuit of depth at most $O(\log^2 n)$. In the case of Frege, the proofs have quasipolynomial-size.

(ii). The implication $(XY = I_n) \to (YX = I_n)$ has a polynomial-size circuit Frege proof, with every circuit of depth at most $O(\log^2 n)$, and a quasipolynomial-size Frege proof.

PROOF. Part (i) is a direct consequence of Theorem 4 and (ii) of Proposition 12, both using the fact that proofs in $\mathbb{P}_c(GF(2))$ and $\mathbb{P}_f(GF(2))$ can be interpreted as proofs in circuit Frege and Frege, respectively. QED

A family of polynomial-size CF proofs in which every proof-line G is of depth $O(\log^2 |G|)$, is also called an $\mathbf{NC}^2$-Frege proof. Hence, Theorem 13 states that $\mathbf{NC}^2$-Frege has polynomial-size proofs of the propositional tautologies $(XY = I) \to (YX = I)$.

Theorem 13 thus settles an important open problem in proof complexity and feasible mathematics, namely, whether basic properties of the determinant like $\det(A) \cdot \det(B) = \det(AB)$ and the cofactor expansion (see Proposition 44), as well as the hard matrix identities, have polynomial-size proofs in a proof system which corresponds to the circuit class $\mathbf{NC}^2$.

REMARK 14. *We believe that Theorem 13 can be extended to any finite field or the field of rationals (after encoding field elements as Boolean strings). For finite fields, this is rather straightforward. In the rational case, one would have to show that the $\mathbb{P}_c(\mathbb{Q})$ proofs constructed in Theorem 4 involve only constants whose Boolean representation is polynomial.*

3. HOMOGENIZATION AND BOUNDING THE DEGREE IN $\mathbb{P}_c(\mathbb{F})$ PROOFS

In this section we wish to construct the circuits $F^{(k)}$ computing the k-homogeneous part of F and prove Proposition 7. First, let us say that a circuit F is *non-redundant*, if either F is the constant 0, or F does not contain the constant 0 at all. Any circuit F can be transformed to a non-redundant circuit $F^\sharp$ as follows: successively replace all nodes of the form $u + 0$, $0 + u$ by u and $u \cdot 0$, $0 \cdot u$ by 0, until no such replacement is possible.

Let k be a natural number. We define $F^{(k)}$ as follows. For every node u in F, introduce $k+1$ new nodes $u^{(0)}, \ldots, u^{(k)}$.

(i). Assume u is a leaf. Then, $u^{(0)} := u$, in case u is a field element, and $u^{(1)} := u$ in case u is a variable, and $u^{(i)} := 0$ otherwise.

(ii). If $u = u_1 + u_2$, let $u^{(i)} := u_1^{(i)} + u_2^{(i)}$, for every $i = 0, \ldots, k$.

(iii). If $u = u_1 \cdot u_2$, let $u^{(i)} := \sum_{j=0}^{i} u_1^{(j)} \cdot u_2^{(i-j)}$.

Finally, we define $F^{(k)}$ as the circuit $G^\sharp$, where G is the circuit with the output node $w^{(k)}$ and w is the output node of F.

Note the following:

(1) $F^{(k)}$ has size $O(s(k+1)^2))$, where s is the size of F.

(2) $F^{(k)}$ is a syntactically homogeneous non-redundant circuit. Its syntactic degree is either k, or F is the constant 0.

Notation: We allow circuits and formulas to use only sum gates with fan-in two. An expression $\sum_{i=1}^{k} x_i$ is an abbreviation for a formula of size $O(k)$ and depth $O(\log k)$ with binary sum gates. For example, define $\sum_{i=1}^{k} x_i := \sum_{i=1}^{\lfloor k/2 \rfloor} x_i + \sum_{i=\lceil k/2 \rceil}^{k} x_i$. One can see that basic identities such as

$$\sum_{i=1}^{k} x_i = \sum_{i=1}^{m} x_i + \sum_{i=m+1}^{k} x_i, \quad \text{or} \quad y \cdot \sum_{i=1}^{k} x_i = \sum_{i=1}^{k} y x_i$$

have $\mathbb{P}_f$ proofs of size $O(k^2)$ and depth $O(\log k)$.

LEMMA 15. *Let F_1, F_2 be circuits of size $\leq s$ and k a natural number. The following have proofs of size $s \cdot poly(k)$ and syntactic degree $\leq k$.*

(i). $(F_1 \oplus F_2)^{(k)} = F_1^{(k)} + F_2^{(k)}$,

(ii). $(F_1 \otimes F_2)^{(k)} = \sum_{i=0}^{k} F_1^{(i)} \cdot F_2^{(k-i)}$.

PROOF. It is easy to see that for any circuit H of size s, $H = H^\sharp$ has a proof of size $O(s)$. This, and the definition of $F^{(k)}$, gives $(F_1 \oplus F_2)^{(k)} = F_1^{(k)} \oplus F_2^{(k)}$. Hence $(F_1 \oplus F_2)^{(k)} = F_1^{(k)} + F_2^{(k)}$ by axiom C1. Since $F_1^{(k)}, F_2^{(k)}, (F_1 \oplus F_2)^{(k)}$ have size $O(s(k+1))^2$, we obtain (i). Part (ii) is similar. QED

LEMMA 16. *If F is a circuit with syntactic degree $\leq d$ and size s then*

$$F = \sum_{k=0}^{d} F^{(k)}$$

has a $\mathbb{P}_c(\mathbb{F})$ proof of syntactic degree $\leq d$ and size $s \cdot poly(d)$.

PROOF. For every node u in F, construct a proof of $F_u = \sum_{k=0}^{\deg(u)} F_u^{(k)}$. This is done by induction on depth of u. If u is a leaf, this stems from the definition of $F_u^{(k)}$, and if $u = u_1 + u_2$ or $u = u_1 \cdot u_2$, it is an application of the previous lemma. QED

Proof of Proposition 7. Part (ii) follows from (i) by Lemma 16, hence it is sufficient to prove part (i). Let us first show that if $F = G$ is an axiom of $\mathbb{P}_c(\mathbb{F})$ of size s then $F^{(k)} = G^{(k)}$ has a proof of size $s \cdot \mathrm{poly}(k)$ and syntactic degree $\leq k$. This is an application of Lemma 15. Let c be the constant such that equations (i) and (ii) in Lemma 15 have proofs of size $O(s \cdot (k+1)^c)$.

The lemma gives a proof $(F_1 \oplus F_2)^{(k)} = (F_1 + F_2)^{(k)}$ and $(F_1 \otimes F_2)^{(k)} = (F_1 \cdot F_2)^{(k)}$, as required for the axioms C1 and C2.

A1 and A9 are immediate. For the other axioms, consider for example the axiom $F_1 \cdot (F_2 \cdot F_3) = (F_1 \cdot F_2) \cdot F_3$, where the circuits have size $\leq s$. We have to construct a proof of

$$(F_1 \cdot (F_2 \cdot F_3))^{(k)} = ((F_1 \cdot F_2) \cdot F_3)^{(k)} . \quad (3)$$

By part (ii) of Lemma 15 the equations

$$(F_1 \cdot (F_2 \cdot F_3))^{(k)} = \sum_{i=0}^{k} F_1^{(i)} \left(\sum_{j=0}^{k-i} F_2^j F_3^{k-i-j} \right) \quad (4)$$

$$((F_1 \cdot F_2) \cdot F_3)^{(k)} = \sum_{i=0}^{k} \left(\sum_{j=0}^{i} F_1^j F_2^{i-j} \right) \cdot F_3^{(k-i)}, \quad (5)$$

can be proved by proofs with size roughly $s \cdot (k+1)^c \cdot (k+1)$. In $\mathbb{P}_c(\mathbb{F})$, the right hand sides of both (4) and (5) can be written as $\sum_{i+j+l=k} F_1^{(i)} F_2^{(j)} F_3^{(l)}$, by a proof of size roughly $s(k+1)^4$. This gives the proof of (3) of size $s \cdot \mathrm{poly}(k)$.

Next, assume that $F = G$ is derived from the equations $F_1 = G_1, F_2 = G_2$ by means of the rules R1-R4, and we need to construct the proof of $F^{(k)} = G^{(k)}$ from the set of equations $F_1^{(i)} = G_1^{(i)}, F_2^{(i)} = G_2^{(i)}, i = 0, \ldots k$. The hardest case is the rule

$$\frac{F_1 = G_1 \qquad F_2 = G_2}{F_1 \cdot F_2 = G_1 \cdot G_2} .$$

We have to prove $(F_1 \cdot F_2)^{(k)} = (G_1 \cdot G_2)^{(k)}$. By Lemma 15, we have proofs of $(F_1 \cdot F_2)^{(k)} = \sum_{i=0,\ldots k} F_1^{(i)} F_2^{(k-i)}$ and $(G_1 \cdot G_2)^{(k)} = \sum_{i=0,\ldots k} G_1^{(i)} G_2^{(k-i)}$. Hence $(F_1 \cdot F_2)^{(k)} = (G_1 \cdot G_2)^{(k)}$ can be proved from the assumptions $F_1^{(i)} = G_1^{(i)}, F_2^{(i)} = G_2^{(i)}, i = 0, \ldots k$. The proof has size roughly $s \cdot (k+1)^c (k+1)$. QED

4. BALANCING $\mathbb{P}_c$ PROOFS

In this section we prove Theorem 5 which is a proof-theoretic analog of the following result:

THEOREM 17 (VALIANT ET AL. [18]). *Let F be an arithmetic circuit of size s computing a polynomial f of degree d. Then there exists an arithmetic circuit $[F]$ computing f with depth $O(\log^2 d + \log s \cdot \log d)$ and size poly(d, s).*

We first give an outline of the construction of $[F]$, which closely follows that in [18] (we also refer the reader to [8] for an especially clear exposition). We emphasize that in our case, the relevant parameter is the *syntactic* degree of F: $[F]$ will have size poly(s, d) and depth $O(\log^2 d + \log s \cdot \log d)$, where d is the syntactic degree of F.

We write $u \in F$ to mean that u is a node in the circuit F. The following definition is important for the construction of balanced circuits: let w, v be two nodes in F. We define the *polynomial* $\partial w F_v$ as follows:

$$\partial w F_v := \begin{cases} 0, & \text{if } w \notin F_v, \\ 1, & \text{if } w = v \text{ , and otherwise:} \\ \partial w F_{v_1} + \partial w F_{v_2}, & v = v_1 + v_2; \\ (\partial w F_{v_1}) \cdot F_{v_2}, & \text{if either } v = v_1 \cdot v_2 \text{ and} \\ & \quad \deg(v_1) \geq \deg(v_2), \\ & \text{or } v = v_2 \cdot v_1 \text{ and} \\ & \quad \deg(v_1) > \deg(v_2). \end{cases}$$

The idea behind this definition is the following: let w, v be two nodes in F such that $2\deg(w) > \deg(v)$. Then for any product node $v_1 \cdot v_2 \in F_v$, w can be a node in at most one of F_{v_1}, F_{v_2}, namely the one of a higher syntactic degree. If we replace the node w in F_v by a new variable z, F_v then computes a polynomial $g(z, x_1, \ldots, x_n)$ which is linear in z, and $\partial w F_v$ is the usual partial derivative $\partial z g$.

It is not hard to show the following:

CLAIM 18. *Let w, v be two nodes in a circuit F. Then the polynomial $\partial w F_v$ has degree at most* $\deg(v) - \deg(w)$.

In order to construct $[F]$, we can assume without loss of generality that F itself is a syntactic homogenous circuit of size $s' = O(d^2 \cdot s)$. This is because a circuit of size s and syntactic degree d can be written as a sum of $d+1$ syntactically homogeneous circuits of size at most s' and syntactic degree at most d. Now the construction proceeds by induction on $i = 0, \ldots, \lceil \log d \rceil$. In each step $i = 0, \ldots, \lceil \log d \rceil$ we construct:

(i). Circuits computing $\widehat{F}_v$, for all nodes v in F with $2^{i-1} < \deg(v) \leq 2^i$;

(ii). Circuits computing $\partial w F_v$, for all nodes w, v in F with $2^{i-1} < \deg(v) - \deg(w) \leq 2^i$ and $\deg(v) < 2\deg(w)$.

Each step adds depth $O(\log s')$, which at the end amounts to a depth $O(\log^2 d + \log d \cdot \log s)$ circuit. Furthermore, each node v in F adds $O(s')$ nodes in the new circuit and each pair of nodes v, w in F adds also $O(s')$ nodes in the new circuit. This finally amounts to a circuit of size $O(s'^3) = O(d^6 \cdot s^3)$.

Let us now give the formal definition of $[F]$. First, for a circuit G and a natural number m, let

$$\mathcal{B}_m(G) := \{t \in G \, : \, t = t_1 \cdot t_2, \deg(t) > m \text{ and } \deg(t_1), \deg(t_2) \leq m\}.$$

Definition of $[F]$.

Let F be an arithmetic circuit of syntactic degree d.

If F is not syntactic homogenous, let

$$[F] := [F^{(0)}] + \ldots + [F^{(d)}] .$$

Otherwise, assume that F is a syntactically homogenous circuit of degree d. For any *node* $v \in F$ we introduce the corresponding *node* $[F_v]$ in $[F]$ (intended to compute the polynomial $\widehat{F}_v$); and for any pair of nodes $v, w \in F$ such that $2\deg(w) > \deg(v)$, we introduce the node $[\partial w F_v]$ in $[F]$ (intended to compute the polynomial $\partial w F_v$).

The construction is defined by induction on $i = 0, \ldots, \lceil \log d \rceil$, as follows:

Part (I).

Let $v \in F$:

Case 1: Assume that **deg(v)** ≤ 1, then F_v computes a linear polynomial $a_1x_1 + \ldots + a_nx_n + b$ (where, by homogeneity of F, $b \neq 0$ **implies that** all a_i's equal 0). Define

$$[F_v] := a_1x_1 + \ldots + a_nx_n + b.$$

Case 2: Assume that for some $0 \leq i \leq \lceil \log(d) \rceil$:

$$2^i < \deg(v) \leq 2^{i+1}.$$

Put $m = 2^i$, and define

$$[F_v] := \sum_{t \in \mathcal{B}_m(F_v)} [\partial t F_v] \cdot [F_{t_1}] \cdot [F_{t_2}],$$

where t_1, t_2 **are nodes such that** $t = t_1 \cdot t_2$. (Note that here $[\partial w F_v], [F_{t_1}]$ and $[F_{t_2}]$ are *nodes*.)

Part (II).

Let w, v be a pair of nodes in F with $2\deg(w) > \deg(v)$:

Case 1: Assume w is not a node in F_v. Define

$$[\partial w F_v] := 0.$$

Case 2: Assume that w is in F_v and $0 \leq \deg(v) - \deg(w) \leq 1$. Thus, by Claim 18, the polynomial $\partial w f_v$ is a linear polynomial $a_1x_1 + \ldots + a_nx_n + b$. Define

$$[\partial w F_v] := a_1x_1 + \ldots + a_nx_n + b.$$

Case 3: Assume that w is in F_v and that for some $0 \leq i \leq \lceil \log(d) \rceil$:

$$2^i < \deg(v) - \deg(w) \leq 2^{i+1}.$$

Put $m = 2^i + \deg(w)$. Define:

$$[\partial w F_v] := \sum_{t \in \mathcal{B}_m(F_v)} [\partial t F_v] \cdot [\partial w F_{t_1}] \cdot [F_{t_2}],$$

where t_1, t_2 **are nodes such that** $t = t_1 \cdot t_2$ **and** $\deg(t_1) \geq \deg(t_2)$, **or** $t = t_2 \cdot t_1$ **and** $\deg(t_2) > \deg(t_1)$. Finally, define $[F]$ as the circuit with the output node $[F_u]$, where u is the output node of F.

One should make sure that the definition of $[F]$ is well defined, and that it has the correct depth and size:

Lemma 19. *Let F be a circuit of size s and syntactic degree d. Then $[F]$ is a circuit computing $\widehat{F}$, $[F]$ is of size poly(s,d) and depth $O(\log^2 d + \log s \log d)$. Moreover, every node $[\partial w F_v]$ in $[F]$ computes the polynomial $\partial w F_v$.*

Proof. The proof is as in [18] (see also [8]). We shall give a partial sketch of the proof here, for the benefit of the reader.

First, assume that F is syntactic homogeneous of degree d. We need to verify that $[F]$ is well-defined. That is, at stage $i = 0, \ldots, \lceil \log d \rceil$, we compute all $[F_v]$ and $[\partial_w F_u]$ for all nodes $v, u, w \in F$ such that $2^i < \deg(v) \leq 2^{i+1}$ and $2^i < \deg(v) - \deg(u) \leq 2^{i+1}$, and we want to show that the computation uses only nodes computed in previous stages.

Take, for example, Case 2 in Part (I). For any $t \in \mathcal{B}_m(F_v)$, $m < \deg(t) \leq \deg(v) \leq 2m$. This implies that $\deg(v) - \deg(t) \leq m = 2^i$ and $\deg(t) < 2\deg(v)$. Hence, we have already computed $[\partial t F_v]$. We have also already constructed $[F_{t_1}], [F_{t_2}]$, since $\deg(t_1), \deg(t_2) < m = 2^i$.

Inspecting the construction, $[F]$ has size poly(s) and depth $O(\log s \cdot \log d)$, given that F is syntactically homogeneous of size s and degree d. If F is not syntactically homogeneous, the definition $[F] = \left[F^{(0)}\right] + \ldots \left[F^{(d)}\right]$ gives a circuit of size poly(s,d) and depth $O(\log^2 d + \log s \cdot \log d)$, since every $F^{(k)}$ has size $O(s \cdot k^2)$. QED

We need to show that properties of $[F]$ can be proved inside the system $\mathbb{P}_c$. The key ingredient is given by the following Lemma.

Lemma 20 (Main simulation lemma). *Let F_1, F_2 be circuits of syntactic degree at most d and size at most s. Then there exist $\mathbb{P}_c$ proofs of:*

$$[F_1 \oplus F_2] = [F_1] + [F_2], \quad (6)$$

$$[F_1 \otimes F_2] = [F_1] \cdot [F_2], \quad (7)$$

such that the proofs have size poly(s,d) and depth $O(\log^2 d + \log d \cdot \log s)$.

The proof of Lemma 20 is deferred to the end of this section. We now use Lemma 20 to prove Theorems 5 and 6.

Theorem 21 (Theorem 5 restated). *Let F, G be circuits of syntactic degrees at most d such that $F = G$ has a $\mathbb{P}_c$ proof of size s. Then*

(i). $[F] = [G]$ has a $\mathbb{P}_c$ proof of size poly(s,d) and depth $O(\log s \cdot \log d + \log^2 d)$.

(ii). If F, G have depth at most t then $F = G$ has a $\mathbb{P}_c$ proof of size poly(s,d) and depth at most $O(t + \log s \cdot \log d + \log^2 d)$.

Proof. Part (i). Assume that $F = G$ has syntactic degree d and a $\mathbb{P}_c$ proof of size s. By Proposition 7, $F = G$ has a $\mathbb{P}_c$ proof of syntactic degree d and size $s' = s \cdot \text{poly}(d)$. So let us consider such a proof S. By induction on the number of lines in S, construct a $\mathbb{P}_c$ proof of $[F_1] = [F_2]$, where $F_1 = F_2$ is a line in S.

Let m_0 and k_0 be such that (6) and (7) have $\mathbb{P}_c$ proofs of size at most m_0 and depth k_0, whenever $F_1 \oplus F_2$, respectively, $F_1 \otimes F_2$ have size at most s' and syntactic degree at most d. By Lemma 20, we can choose $m_0 = \text{poly}(s', d)$ and $k_0 = O(\log s' \cdot \log d + \log^2 d)$.

First, show that if a line $F = H$ in S is a $\mathbb{P}_c$ *axiom* then $[F] = [H]$ has a $\mathbb{P}_c$ proof of size $c_1 m_0$ and depth $c_2 k_0$, where c_1, c_2 are some constants independent of s', d. The axiom A1 is immediate and the axiom A9 follows from the fact that $[F] = \widehat{F}$, if $\deg(F) = 0$. The rest of the axiom are an application of Lemma 20, as follows. Axioms C1 and C2 are already the statement of Lemma 20. For the other axioms, take, for example,

$$F_1 \cdot (G_1 + G_2) = F_1 \cdot G_1 + F_1 \cdot G_2 .$$

We are supposed to give a proof of

$$[F_1 \cdot (G_1 + G_2)] = [F_1 \cdot G_1 + F \cdot G_2] ,$$

with a small size and depth. By Lemma 20 we have a $\mathbb{P}_c$ proof

$$[F_1 \cdot (G_1 + G_2)] = [F_1] \cdot [G_1 + G_2]$$
$$= [F_1] \cdot [G_1] + [F_1] \cdot [G_2] = [F_1] \cdot ([G_1] + [G_2]) .$$

Lemma 20 gives again

$$[F_1]\cdot([G_1]+[G_2]) = [F_1]\cdot[G_1+G_2] = [F_1\cdot(G_1+G_2)]\ .$$

Here we applied Lemma 20 to circuits of size at most s', and the proof of $[F_1\cdot(G_1+G_2)] = [F_1\cdot G_1 + F\cdot G_2]$ has size at most, say, $100m_0$ and depth at most $10k_0$.

An application of rules R1, R2 translates to an application of R1, R2. For the rules R3 and R4, it is sufficient to show the following: if S uses the rule

$$\frac{F_1=F_2 \qquad G_1=G_2}{F_1\circ G_1 = F_2\circ G_2},\ \circ\in\{\cdot,+\},$$

then there is a proof of $[F_1\circ G_1 = F_2\circ G_2]$, of size c_1m_0 and depth c_2k_0, from the equations $[F_1]=[G_1]$ and $[F_2]=[G_2]$. This is again an application of Lemma 20.

Altogether, we obtain a proof of $[F]=[G]$ of size at most $c_1s'm_0$ and depth c_2k_0.

Part (ii). Using (i), it is sufficient to prove the following:

CLAIM 22. *If F is a circuit with depth t, syntactic degree d and size s, then $F=[F]$ has a $\mathbb{P}_c$ proof of size poly(s,d) and depth at most $O(t+\log s\cdot\log d+\log^2 d)$.*

Using Lemma 20, this claim can be easily proved by induction on s. QED

THEOREM 23 (THEOREM 6 RESTATED). *Assume that F,G are formulas of syntactic degree at most d such that $F=G$ has a $\mathbb{P}_c$ proof of size s. Then $F=G$ has a $\mathbb{P}_f$ proof of size $(s(d+1))^{O(\log d)}$.*

PROOF. Recall the definition of the formula $F^\bullet$ from Remark 3. It is not hard to show the following:

CLAIM 24. *If $H_1=H_2$ has a $\mathbb{P}_c$ proof with p proof lines and depth k, then $H_1^\bullet = H_2^\bullet$ has a $\mathbb{P}_f$ proof of size $O(p2^k)$.*

Let F and G be as in the assumption. The previous theorem and Claim 24 give a $\mathbb{P}_f$ proof of

$$[F]^\bullet = [G]^\bullet$$

of size $s\cdot 2^{O(\log s\cdot\log d+\log^2 d)} = (s(d+1))^{O(\log d)}$.

To complete the proof, it is sufficient to show that:

CLAIM 25. *If H is a formula of size s and syntactic degree d, then $[H]^\bullet = H$ has a $\mathbb{P}_f$ proof of size $(s(d+1))^{O(\log d)}$.*

This is proved by induction on s using Lemma 20. QED

Proof of Lemma 20

It is sufficient to prove the statement under the assumption that $F_1\oplus F_2$ and $F_1\otimes F_2$ are syntactically homogeneous. This is because of the following: assume that the lemma holds for syntactically homogeneous circuits. First, note that for any circuit of syntactic degree d,

$$[F] = \left[F^{(0)}\right] + \left[F^{(1)}\right] + \cdots + \left[F^{(d)}\right]$$

has a proof of size poly(s,d) and depth $O(\log d\cdot\log s+\log^2 d)$: if F is not syntactically homogeneous, then this stems from the definition of $[F]$; otherwise, F is syntactically homogeneous, and so $[F^{(k)}]$ is the circuit 0 whenever $k<d$ and it is sufficient to construct the proof of $[F]=[F^{(d)}]$, which can be done by induction on the size of F. Second, if for example $F_1\oplus F_2$ is not syntactically homogenous, then by definition of $[\cdot]$, we have

$$[F_1\oplus F_2] = \sum_{k=0}^{d}\left[(F_1\oplus F_2)^{(k)}\right],$$

where $d = \deg(F_1\oplus F_2)$. By the definition of $F^{(k)}$, $(F_1\oplus F_2)^{(k)}$ is a syntactically homogeneous circuit which is either of the form $F_1^{(k)}\oplus F_2^{(k)}$, or it is of the form $F_e^{(k)}$, if $F_{e'}^{(k)}=0$, $\{e,e'\}=\{1,2\}$. In both cases we obtain a proof of $[(F_1+F_2)^{(k)}] = [F_1^{(k)}]+[F_2^{(k)}]$, of small size and depth. This gives a $\mathbb{P}_c$ proof of

$$\sum_{k=0}^{d}\left[(F_1\oplus F_2)^{(k)}\right] = \sum_{k=0}^{d}\left[(F_1)^{(k)}\right]+\left[(F_2)^{(k)}\right] = \sum_{k=0}^{d}\left[(F_1)^{(k)}\right]+\sum_{k=0}^{d}\left[(F_2)^{(k)}\right].$$

We thus consider the syntactically homogeneous case. Let $m(s,d)$ and $r(s,d)$ be functions such that for any circuit F of syntactic degree d and size s, $[F]$ has depth at most $r(s,d)$ and size at most $m(s,d)$. By Lemma 19, we can choose

$$m(s,d)=\text{poly}(s,d) \quad\text{and}\quad r(s,d)=O(\log^2 d+\log d\cdot\log s).$$

Notation: In the following, $[F_v]$ and $[\partial wF_v]$ will denote *circuits*: $[F_v]$ and $[\partial wF_v]$ are the subcircuits of $[F]$ with output nodes $[F_v]$ and $[\partial wF_v]$, respectively; the defining relations between the nodes of $[F]$ (see the definition of $[F]$ above) translate to equalities between the corresponding circuits. For example, if v and m are as in Case 2, part (I) of the definition of $[F]$, then, using just the axioms C1 and C2, we can prove

$$[F_v] = \sum_{t\in\mathcal{B}_m(F_v)} [\partial tF_v]\cdot[F_{t_1}]\cdot[F_{t_2}]\ . \tag{8}$$

Here, the left hand side is understood as the circuit $[F_v]$ in which $[\partial tF_v], [F_{t_1}], [F_{t_2}]$ appear as *subcircuits*, and so can share common nodes, while on the right hand side the circuits have *disjoint nodes*. Also, note that if F has size s and degree d, the proof of (8) has size $O(s^2m(s,d))$ and has depth $O(r(s,d))$. We shall use these kind of identities in the current proof.

The following statement suffices to conclude the lemma. The recurrence (9) implies $\lambda(s,d)=\text{poly}(s,d)$ and it is enough to take F in the statement as either $F_1\oplus F_2$ or $F_1\otimes F_2$, and v as the root of F.

Statement.

Let F be a syntactically homogenous circuit of syntactic degree d and size s, and let $i=0,\ldots,\lceil\log d\rceil$. There exists a function $\lambda(s,i)$ not depending on F with

$$\lambda(s,0)=O(s^4) \quad\text{and}\quad \lambda(s,i)\le O(s^4\cdot m(s,d))+\lambda(s,i-1), \tag{9}$$

and a $\mathbb{P}_c$ proof-sequence Ψ_i of size at most $\lambda(s,i)$ and depth at most $O(r(s,d))$, such that the following hold:

Part (I): For every node $v \in F$ with

$$\deg(v) \leq 2^i, \tag{10}$$

Ψ_i contains the following equations:

$$[F_v] = [F_{v_1}] + [F_{v_2}], \quad \text{in case } v = v_1 + v_2, \quad \text{and} \tag{11}$$
$$[F_v] = [F_{v_1}] \cdot [F_{v_2}], \quad \text{in case } v = v_1 \cdot v_2. \tag{12}$$

Part (II): For every pair of nodes $w \neq v \in F$, where $w \in F_v$, and with

$$\deg(v) - deg(w) \leq 2^i \quad \text{and} \tag{13}$$
$$2\deg(w) > \deg(v), \tag{14}$$

Ψ_i contains the following equations:

$$[\partial w F_v] = [\partial w F_{v_1}] + [\partial w F_{v_2}], \quad \text{in case } v = v_1 + v_2; \tag{15}$$
$$[\partial w F_v] = [\partial w F_{v_1}] \cdot [F_{v_2}], \tag{16}$$
$$\text{in case } v = v_1 \cdot v_2 \text{ and } \deg(v_1) \geq \deg(v_2)$$
$$\text{or } v = v_2 \cdot v_1 \text{ and } \deg(v_1) > \deg(v_2).$$

We proceed to construct the sequence Ψ_i by induction on i.

Base case: $i = 0$. We need to devise the proof sequence Ψ_0.

Part (I).

Let $\deg(v) \leq 2^0$. By definition, $[F_v] = \sum_{i=1}^n a_i x_i + b$, where a_i's and b are field elements. If $v = v_1 + v_2$, we have also $[F_{v_e}] = \sum_{i=1}^n a_i^{(e)} x_i + b^{(e)}$, for $e = 1, 2$. Hence the equation $[F_v] = [F_{v_1}] + [F_{v_2}]$ is the (true) identity:

$$\sum_{i=1}^n a_i x_i + b = \sum_{i=1}^n a_i^{(1)} x_i + b^{(1)} + \sum_{i=1}^n a_i^{(2)} x_i + b^{(2)},$$

which has a proof of size $O(s^2)$ and depth $O(\log s)$ (we assume without loss of generality that $n \leq s$).

In case $v = v_1 \cdot v_2$, either $\deg(v_1) = 0$ or $\deg(v_2) = 0$ and the proof of $[F_v] = [F_{v_1}] \cdot [F_{v_2}]$ is similar.

Part (II).

Since $\deg(v) - \deg(w) \leq 1$, we have $[\partial w F_v] = \sum_{i=1}^n a_i x_i + b$, for some field elements a_i's and b.

In case $v = v_1 + v_2$, we have $\deg(v_e) - \deg(w) \leq 1$ and so $[\partial w F_{v_e}] = \sum_{i=1}^n a_i^{(e)} x_i + b^{(e)}$, where $e = 1, 2$. The assumption $w \neq v$ and Lemma 19, guarantee that $[\partial w F_v] = [\partial w F_{v_1}] + [\partial w F_{v_2}]$ is a correct identity, and we can thus proceed as the base case of Part (I) above.

In case $v = v_1 \cdot v_2$, assume without loss of generality that $\deg(v_1) \geq \deg(v_2)$. Again, we have $[\partial w F_{v_1}] = \sum_{i=1}^n a_i^{(1)} x_i + b^{(1)}$. From the assumptions, we have that $w \in F_{v_1}$, which implies $\deg(v_1) \geq \deg(w)$ and so $\deg(v_2) \leq 1$. Hence $[F_{v_2}] = \sum_{i=1}^n a_i^{(2)} x_i + b^{(2)}$. (One can note that at least one of $[\partial w F_{v_1}]$ or $[F_{v_2}]$ is constant). Thus we can prove the (correct, by virtue of the assumption $w \neq v$) identity $[\partial w F_v] = [\partial w F_{v_1}] \cdot [F_{v_2}]$ with a $\mathbb{P}_c(\mathbb{F})$ proof of size $O(s^2)$ and depth $O(\log s)$.

Overall, Ψ_0 will be the union of all the above proofs, so that Ψ_0 contains all equations (11), (12) (for all nodes v satisfying (10)), and all equations (15) and (16) (for all nodes v, w satisfying (13) and (14)). The proof sequence Ψ_0 has size $\lambda(s, 0) = O(s^4)$ and is and depth $O(\log s)$.

Induction step: We wish to construct the proof-sequence Ψ_{i+1}.

Part (I).

Let v be any node in F such that

$$2^i < \deg(v) \leq 2^{i+1}.$$

Case 1: Assume that $v = v_1 + v_2$. We show how to construct the proof of $[F_v] = [F_{v_1}] + [F_{v_2}]$. Let $m = 2^i$. From the definition of $[\cdot]$ we have:

$$[F_v] = [F_{v_1+v_2}] = \sum_{t \in \mathcal{B}_m(F_v)} [F_{t_1}] \cdot [F_{t_2}] \cdot [\partial t(F_{v_1+v_2})]. \tag{17}$$

Since $\deg(v_1) = \deg(v_2) = \deg(v)$, we also have

$$[F_{v_e}] = \sum_{t \in \mathcal{B}_m(F_{v_e})} [F_{t_1}] \cdot [F_{t_2}] \cdot [\partial t(F_{v_e})], \quad \text{for } e \in \{0, 1\}. \tag{18}$$

If $t \in \mathcal{B}_m(F_v)$ then $\deg(t) > m = 2^i$. Therefore, for any $t \in \mathcal{B}_m(F_v)$, since $\deg(v) \leq 2^{i+1}$, we have $\deg(v) - \deg(t) < 2^i$ and $2\deg(t) > \deg(v)$ and $t \neq v$ (since t is a product gate). Thus, by induction hypothesis, the proof-sequence Ψ_i contains, for any $t \in \mathcal{B}_m(F_v)$, the equations

$$[\partial t(F_{v_1+v_2})] = [\partial t F_{v_1}] + [\partial t F_{v_2}].$$

Therefore, having Ψ_i as a premise, we can prove that (17) equals:

$$\sum_{t \in \mathcal{B}_m(F_v)} [F_{t_1}] \cdot [F_{t_2}] \cdot ([\partial t F_{v_1}] + [\partial t F_{v_2}])$$
$$= \sum_{t \in \mathcal{B}_m(F_v)} [F_{t_1}] \cdot [F_{t_2}] \cdot [\partial t F_{v_1}] + \sum_{t \in \mathcal{B}_m(F_v)} [F_{t_1}] \cdot [F_{t_2}] \cdot [\partial t F_{v_2}]. \tag{19}$$

If $t \in \mathcal{B}_m(F_v)$ and $t \notin F_{v_1}$ then $[\partial t F_{v_1}] = 0$. Similarly, if $t \in \mathcal{B}_m(F_v)$ and $t \notin F_{v_2}$ then $[\partial t F_{v_2}] = 0$. Hence we can prove

$$\sum_{t \in \mathcal{B}_m(F_v)} [\partial t F_{v_e}] = \sum_{t \in \mathcal{B}_m(F_{v_e})} [\partial t F_{v_e}], \quad \text{for } e = 1, 2. \tag{20}$$

Thus, using (18) we have that (19) equals:

$$\sum_{t \in \mathcal{B}_m(F_{v_1})} [F_{t_1}] \cdot [F_{t_2}] \cdot [\partial t F_{v_1}] + \sum_{t \in \mathcal{B}_m(F_{v_2})} [F_{t_1}] \cdot [F_{t_2}] \cdot [\partial t F_{v_2}]$$
$$= [F_{v_1}] + [F_{v_2}]. \tag{21}$$

The above proof of (21) from Ψ_i has size $O(s^2 \cdot m(s, d))$ and depth $O(r(s, d))$.

Case 2: Assume that $v = v_1 \cdot v_2$. We wish to prove $[F_v] = [F_{v_1}] \cdot [F_{v_2}]$. Let $m = 2^i$. We assume without loss of generality that $\deg(v_1) \geq \deg(v_2)$. By the definition of $[\cdot]$, we have:

$$[F_v] = [F_{v_1 \cdot v_2}] = \sum_{t \in \mathcal{B}_m(F_v)} [F_{t_1}] \cdot [F_{t_2}] \cdot [\partial t F_v].$$

If $v \in \mathcal{B}_m(F_v)$, then $\mathcal{B}_m = \{v\}$ and we have $[F_v] = [F_{v_1}] \cdot [F_{v_2}] \cdot [\partial_v F_v]$. Since $[\partial_v F_v] = 1$, this gives $[F_v] = [F_{v_1}] \cdot [F_{v_2}]$, and we are done.

Otherwise, assume $v \notin \mathcal{B}_m(F_v)$. Then $m = 2^i < \deg(v_1)$ (since, if $\deg(v_1) \leq m$, then also $\deg(v_2) \leq m$ and so by definition $v \in \mathcal{B}_m(F_v)$). Because, moreover, $\deg(v_1) \leq 2^{i+1}$, we have

$$[F_{v_1}] = \sum_{t \in \mathcal{B}_m(F_{v_1})} [F_{t_1}] \cdot [F_{t_2}] \cdot [\partial t F_{v_1}]. \tag{22}$$

Since $\deg(v) \leq 2^{i+1}$ and $\deg(t) > m = 2^i$, for any $t \in \mathcal{B}_m(F_v)$, we have

$$\deg(v) - \deg(t) \leq 2^i \quad \text{and} \quad 2\deg(t) > \deg(v).$$

Since $v \neq t$, by induction hypothesis, Ψ_i contains, for any $t \in \mathcal{B}_m(F_v)$, the equation:

$$[\partial t(F_{v_1 \cdot v_2})] = [\partial t F_{v_1}] \cdot [F_{v_2}]. \tag{23}$$

Using (23) for all $t \in \mathcal{B}_m(F_v)$, we can prove the following with a $\mathbb{P}_c(\mathbb{F})$ proof of size $O(s^2 \cdot m(s,d))$ and depth $O(r(s,d))$:

$$\begin{aligned}\sum_{t\in\mathcal{B}_m(F_v)} [F_{t_1}]\cdot[F_{t_2}]\cdot[\partial t F_v] &= \sum_{t\in\mathcal{B}_m(F_v)} [F_{t_1}]\cdot[F_{t_2}]\cdot[\partial t(F_{v_1\cdot v_2})] \\ &= \sum_{t\in\mathcal{B}_m(F_v)} [F_{t_1}]\cdot[F_{t_2}]\cdot([\partial t F_{v_1}]\cdot[F_{v_2}]) \\ &= [F_{v_2}]\cdot \sum_{t\in\mathcal{B}_m(F_v)} [F_{t_1}]\cdot[F_{t_2}]\cdot[\partial t F_{v_1}].\end{aligned} \tag{24}$$

Since $\mathcal{B}_m(F_{v_1}) \subseteq \mathcal{B}_m(F_v)$, we can conclude as in (20) that

$$\sum_{t\in\mathcal{B}_m(F_v)} [F_{t_1}]\cdot[F_{t_2}]\cdot[\partial t F_{v_1}] = \sum_{t\in\mathcal{B}_m(F_{v_1})} [F_{t_1}]\cdot[F_{t_2}]\cdot[\partial t F_{v_1}].$$

Using (22), (24) equals $[F_{v_2}] \cdot [F_{v_1}]$. The above proof-sequence (using Ψ_i as a premise) has size $O(s^2 \cdot m(s,d))$ and depth $O(r(s,d))$.

We now append Ψ_i with all proof-sequences of $[F_v] = [F_{v_1}] + [F_{v_2}]$ for every v from Case 1, and all proof-sequences of $[F_v] = [F_{v_1}] \cdot [F_{v_2}]$ for every v from Case 2. We obtain a proof-sequence Ψ'_{i+1} of size

$$\lambda(s, i+1) \leq O(s^3 \cdot m(s,d)) + \lambda(s,i),$$

and depth $O(r(s,d))$.

In Part (II), we extend Ψ'_{i+1} with more proof-sequences to obtain the final Ψ_{i+1}.

Part (II).

Let $v \neq w$ be a pair of nodes in F such that $w \in F_v$ and assume that

$$2^i < \deg(v) - \deg(w) \leq 2^{i+1} \quad \text{and} \quad 2\deg(w) > \deg(v).$$

Let

$$m = 2^i + \deg(w).$$

Case 1: Suppose that $v = v_1 + v_2$. We need to prove

$$[\partial w F_v] = [\partial w F_{v_1}] + [\partial w F_{v_2}] \tag{25}$$

based on Ψ_i as a premise. By construction of $[\partial w F_v]$,

$$\begin{aligned}[\partial w F_v] &= \sum_{t\in\mathcal{B}_m(F_v)} [\partial t F_v]\cdot[\partial w F_{t_1}]\cdot[F_{t_2}] \\ &= \sum_{t\in\mathcal{B}_m(F_v)} [\partial t(F_{v_1+v_2})]\cdot[\partial w F_{t_1}]\cdot[F_{t_2}].\end{aligned} \tag{26}$$

Since $\deg(v_1) = \deg(v_2) = \deg(v)$, we also have

$$[\partial w F_{v_e}] = \sum_{t\in\mathcal{B}_m(F_{v_e})} [\partial t F_{v_e}]\cdot[\partial w F_{t_1}]\cdot[F_{t_2}], \quad \text{for } e = 1, 2. \tag{27}$$

Since $m = 2^i + \deg(w)$, we have $\deg(t) > 2^i + \deg(w)$, for any $t \in \mathcal{B}_m(F_v)$. Thus, by $\deg(v) - \deg(w) \leq 2^{i+1}$, we get that for any $t \in \mathcal{B}_m(F_v)$:

$$\deg(v) - \deg(t) \leq 2^i \quad \text{and} \quad 2\deg(t) > \deg(v), \quad \text{and} \\ t \neq v \text{ (since } t \text{ is a product gate).}$$

Therefore, by induction hypothesis, for any $t \in \mathcal{B}_m(F_v)$, Ψ_i contains the equation

$$[\partial t(F_{v_1+v_2})] = [\partial t F_{v_1}] + [\partial t F_{v_2}].$$

Thus, based on Ψ_i, we can prove that (26) equals:

$$\begin{aligned}&\sum_{t\in\mathcal{B}_m(F_v)} ([\partial t F_{v_1}] + [\partial t F_{v_2}])[\partial w F_{t_1}][F_{t_2}] \\ &= \sum_{t\in\mathcal{B}_m(F_v)} [\partial t F_{v_1}][\partial w F_{t_1}][F_{t_2}] + \sum_{t\in\mathcal{B}_m(F_v)} [\partial t F_{v_2}][\partial w F_{t_1}][F_{t_2}].\end{aligned} \tag{28}$$

As in (20), using (27) we can derive the following from (28):

$$\sum_{t\in\mathcal{B}_m(F_{v_1})} [\partial t F_{v_1}][\partial w F_{t_1}][F_{t_2}] + \sum_{t\in\mathcal{B}_m(F_{v_2})} [\partial t F_{v_2}][\partial w F_{t_1}][F_{t_2}] \\ = [\partial w F_{v_1}] + [\partial w F_{v_2}].$$

The proof of (25) from Ψ_i shown above has size $O(s^2 \cdot m(s,d))$ and depth $O(r(s,d))$.

Case 2: Suppose that $v = v_1 \cdot v_2$. We assume without loss of generality that $\deg(v_1) \geq \deg(v_2)$ and show how to prove

$$[\partial w F_v] = [\partial w F_{v_1}] \cdot [F_{v_2}]. \tag{29}$$

By construction of $[\partial w F_v]$:

$$\begin{aligned}[\partial w F_v] &= \sum_{t\in\mathcal{B}_m(F_v)} [\partial t F_v]\cdot[\partial w F_{t_1}]\cdot[F_{t_2}] \\ &= \sum_{t\in\mathcal{B}_m(F_v)} [\partial t(F_{v_1\cdot v_2})]\cdot[\partial w F_{t_1}]\cdot[F_{t_2}].\end{aligned} \tag{30}$$

Similar to the previous case, for any $t \in \mathcal{B}_m(F_v)$ we have

$$\deg(v) - \deg(t) < 2^i \quad \text{and} \quad 2\deg(t) > \deg(v).$$

If $v \in \mathcal{B}_m(F_v)$ then $\mathcal{B}_m(F_v) = \{v\}$ and so (30) is simply $\partial v F_v \cdot [\partial w F_{v_1}] \cdot [F_{v_2}] = [\partial w F_{v_1}] \cdot [F_{v_2}]$ as required. Otherwise, assume that $v \notin \mathcal{B}_m(F_v)$. By induction hypothesis, Ψ_i contains the following equation, for any $t \in \mathcal{B}_m(F_v)$:

$$[\partial t(F_{v_1\cdot v_2})] = [\partial t F_{v_1}] \cdot [F_{v_2}].$$

Using Ψ_i as a premise, we can then prove that (30) equals:

$$\begin{aligned}&\sum_{t\in\mathcal{B}_m(F_v)} ([\partial t F_{v_1}]\cdot[F_{v_2}])\cdot[\partial w F_{t_1}]\cdot[F_{t_2}] = \\ &\left(\sum\nolimits_{t\in\mathcal{B}_m(F_v)} [\partial t F_{v_1}]\cdot[\partial w F_{t_1}]\cdot[F_{t_2}]\right)\cdot[F_{v_2}].\end{aligned} \tag{31}$$

As in (20), we have $\sum_{t\in\mathcal{B}_m(F_v)} [\partial t F_{v_1}] \cdot [\partial w F_{t_1}] \cdot [F_{t_2}] = \sum_{t\in\mathcal{B}_m(F_{v_1})} [\partial t F_{v_1}] \cdot [\partial w F_{t_1}] \cdot [F_{t_2}]$. Also, since $v_1 \cdot v_2 = v \notin \mathcal{B}_m(F_v)$, we have $\deg(v_1) > m = 2^i + \deg(w)$, and so

$$[\partial w F_{v_1}] = \sum_{t\in\mathcal{B}_m(F_{v_1})} [\partial t F_{v_1}]\cdot[\partial w F_{t_1}]\cdot[F_{t_2}]. \tag{32}$$

Hence by (32), (31) equals $[\partial_w F_{v_1}] \cdot [F_{v_2}]$.

The above proof of (29) from Ψ_i has size $O(s^2 \cdot m(s,d))$ and depth $O(r(s,d))$.

We now append Ψ_i' from Part (I) (which also contains Ψ_i) with all proof-sequences of $[\partial w F_v] = [\partial w F_{v_1}] + [\partial w F_{v_2}]$ in Case 1 and all proof sequences $[\partial w F_v] = [\partial w F_{v_1}] \cdot [F_{v_2}]$ in Case 2, above. We obtain the proof-sequence Ψ_{i+1} of size

$$\lambda(s, i+1) \le O(s^4 \cdot m(s,d)) + \lambda(s,i),$$

and depth $O(r(s,d))$, as required.

5. PROOFS WITH DIVISION

In this section, we investigate proofs with divisions (as defined in Section 2.3), and prove Theorem 9.

Let us first turn the reader's attention to some peculiarities of the system $\mathbb{P}_c^{-1}$:

- We must be careful not to divide by zero in $\mathbb{P}_c^{-1}$. Hence $\mathbb{P}_c^{-1}$ proofs are *not closed under substitution*. It may happen that $F(z) = G(z)$ has a $\mathbb{P}_c^{-1}$ proof S, $F(0) = G(0)$ is defined, but substituting z by 0 throughout S is not a correct proof.
- Whereas $\mathbb{P}_c^{-1}$ is sound with respect to polynomial identities, it behaves erratically if one considers *proofs from assumptions*. For example, $\mathbb{P}_c^{-1}$ augmented with the axiom $x^2 - x = 0$ proves that $1 = 0$.
- Prima facie, it is not clear whether a $\mathbb{P}_c^{-1}$ proof of equation $F = G$ can be transformed to a proof of $F = G$ which contains only the variables contained in F and G. See Remark 29.

In the sequel, we will consider substitution instances of equations we prove in $\mathbb{P}_c^{-1}$. For instance, we will need to substitute 0 for some variables in the matrix X, when proving equations involving the circuit DET(X), and we have to guarantee that our proofs remain correct after such a substitution.

There are two *general* ways how to securely handle substitutions in $\mathbb{P}_c^{-1}$ proofs. The first one is to substitute only *algebraically independent elements*: replacing variables $z_1, \dots, z_k$ with circuits $H_1, \dots, H_k$ can never produce an undefined proof, if the circuits compute algebraically independent rational functions. The second way is offered in Corollary 33. This corollary allows one to construct a new proof of $F(0) = G(0)$ from the proof of $F(z) = G(z)$. Note, however, that in Corollary 33 the new proof will be polynomial only if the syntactic degree of F and G is polynomial.

Since the determinant circuit DET has an exponential syntactic degree (see Section 7), the second approach to substitution is not suitable for the DET identities. The first approach, which substitutes algebraically independent elements, often cannot cannot be used either, because we need to substitute variables by field elements. Therefore we must sometimes simply make sure that the specific substitutions used do not make the proofs undefined. To this end, we use the following terminology: let $\overline{x} = (x_1, \dots, x_k)$ be a list of variables and $U = (U_1, \dots, U_k)$ a list of circuits with divisions. We say that a circuit $F(\overline{x})$ with divisions is *defined* for $\overline{x} = U$, if no divisions by zero occur in $F(U)$; likewise, we say that a $\mathbb{P}_c^{-1}$ proof S is defined for $\overline{x} = U$ (or simply defined, if the context is clear), if every circuit in S is defined for $\overline{x} = U$.

5.1 Eliminating division gates over large enough fields

We first prove Theorem 9 under the assumption that the underlying field $\mathbb{F}$ is large. To eliminate division gates from proofs, we follow the construction of Strassen [16], in which an inverse gate is replaced by a truncated power series. In order to eliminate division gates over small fields, additional work will be needed (see Section 6).

Let F be a circuit with divisions. We say that F is a circuit *with simple divisions*, if for every inverse gate v^{-1} in F the circuit F_v does not contain inverse gates. A size s circuit with division F can be converted to a size $O(s)$ circuit of the form $F_1 \cdot F_2^{-1}$, where F_1, F_2 do not contain inverse gates, as follows.

For every node v introduce two nodes Den(v) and Num(v) which will compute the numerator and denominator of the rational function computed by v, respectively, as follows:

(i) If v is an input node of F, let $\mathrm{Num}(v) := v$ and $\mathrm{Den}(v) = 1$.

(ii) If $v = u^{-1}$, let $\mathrm{Num}(v) := \mathrm{Den}(u)$ and $\mathrm{Den}(v) := \mathrm{Num}(u)$.

(iii) If $v = u_1 \cdot u_2$, let $\mathrm{Num}(v) := \mathrm{Num}(v_1) \cdot \mathrm{Num}(v_2)$ and $\mathrm{Den}(v) := \mathrm{Den}(v_1) \cdot \mathrm{Den}(v_2)$.

(iv) If $v = u_1 + u_2$, let $\mathrm{Num}(v) := \mathrm{Num}(u_1) \cdot \mathrm{Den}(u_2) + \mathrm{Num}(u_2) \cdot \mathrm{Den}(u_1)$ and $\mathrm{Den}(v) := \mathrm{Den}(u_1) \cdot \mathrm{Den}(u_2)$.

Let Num(F) and Den(F) be the circuits with the output node Num(w) and Den(w), respectively, where w is the output node of F. The following lemma will be used in Proposition 28:

LEMMA 26. *Let $\mathbb{F}$ be any field.*

(i). If F is a size s circuit with division, then

$$F = \mathit{Num}(F) \cdot \mathit{Den}(F)^{-1}$$

has a $\mathbb{P}_c^{-1}(\mathbb{F})$ proof of size $O(s)$. The proof is defined whenever F is defined.

(ii). Let F, G be circuits with division. Assume that $F = G$ has a $\mathbb{P}_c^{-1}(\mathbb{F})$ proof of size s. Then $\mathit{Num}(F) \cdot \mathit{Den}(F)^{-1} = \mathit{Num}(G) \cdot \mathit{Den}(G)^{-1}$ has a $\mathbb{P}_c^{-1}(\mathbb{F})$ proof of size $O(s)$ such that every circuit in the proof is a circuit with simple divisions.

PROOF. Part (i) is proved by straightforward induction on the size of F and part (ii) by induction on the number of proof lines. We omit the details. QED

Let k be a fixed natural number and define $\mathrm{pow}_k(1-z)$ to be the circuit

$$\mathrm{pow}_k(1-z) := 1 + z + \cdots + z^k .$$

In other words, $\mathrm{pow}_k(1-z)$ is the first $k+1$ terms of the power series expansion of $1/(1-z)$ at $z = 0$.

Let F be a division-free circuit and let $a := \widehat{F(0)}$. Assume that $a \neq 0$, that is, the polynomial computed by F has a nonzero constant term, and let $\mathrm{Inv}_k(F)$ denote the circuit

$$\mathrm{Inv}_k(F) := a^{-1} \cdot \mathrm{pow}_k(a^{-1}F)$$
$$= a^{-1} \cdot \left(1 + (1-a^{-1}F) + (1-a^{-1}F)^2 + \ldots + (1-a^{-1}F)^k\right) .$$

Note that a^{-1} is a field element and hence $\mathrm{Inv}_k(F)$ is a circuit *without division*. The following lemma shows that $\mathrm{Inv}_k(F)$ can *provably* serve as the inverse polynomial of F "up to the k power":

LEMMA 27. *Let $\mathbb{F}$ be any field and let F be a size s circuit without division such that $\widehat{F^{(0)}} \neq 0$. Then the following have $\mathbb{P}_c(\mathbb{F})$ proofs of size $s \cdot poly(k)$:*

$$(F \cdot Inv_k F)^{(0)} = 1 \quad (33)$$

$$(F \cdot Inv_k F)^{(i)} = 0, \text{ for } 1 \leq i \leq k. \quad (34)$$

PROOF. Let z abbreviate the circuit $1 - a^{-1}F$. Then $F = a(1-z)$ and $\mathrm{Inv}_k(F) = a^{-1}(1 + z + z^2 + \cdots + z^k)$. By elementary rearrangement, we can prove

$$F \cdot \mathrm{Inv}_k(F) = (1-z)(1 + z + z^2 + \ldots z^k) = 1 - z^{k+1}.$$

By Lemma 15, $(F \cdot \mathrm{Inv}_k(F))^{(0)} = 1 - (z^{k+1})^{(0)}$ and $(F \cdot \mathrm{Inv}_k(F))^{(i)} = (z^{k+1})^{(i)}$, for $i > 0$. It is therefore sufficient to prove for every $i \leq k$, $(z^{k+1})^{(i)} = 0$. This follows by induction using Lemma 15 and the fact that $z^{(0)} = 0$. QED

The dependency on the field comes from the following fact, which follows from the Schwartz-Zippel lemma [9, 19]:

FACT 1. *Let $f_1, \ldots, f_s \in \mathbb{F}[X]$ be non-zero polynomials of degree $\leq d$, where $X = \{x_1, \ldots x_n\}$. Assume that $|\mathbb{F}| > sd$. Then there exists $\bar{a} \in \mathbb{F}^n$ such that $f_i(\bar{a}) \neq 0$ for every $i \in \{1, \ldots, s\}$.*

PROPOSITION 28. *There exists a polynomial p such that the following holds. Let F, G be circuits without division of syntactic degree at most d. Assume that $F = G$ has a $\mathbb{P}_c^{-1}(\mathbb{F})$ proof with divisions of size at most s and suppose that $|\mathbb{F}| > 2^{\Omega(s)}$. Then $F = G$ has a $\mathbb{P}_c(\mathbb{F})$ proof of size $s \cdot p(d)$.*

PROOF. Let S be a $\mathbb{P}_c^{-1}(\mathbb{F})$ proof of $F = G$ of size s. By Lemma 26, we can assume that the proof contains only simple divisions. Let $\mathcal{C}$ be the set of circuits H such that S contains a circuit with a node u^{-1} such that u computes H. Then $|\mathcal{C}| \leq s$ and $\deg H \leq 2^{\Omega(s)}$ for every $H \in \mathcal{C}$, since H has size at most s. By the Fact above, there exists a point $b \in \mathbb{F}^n$ such that $\widehat{H}(b) \neq 0$ for every $H \in \mathcal{C}$, where n is the number of variables in S.

Without loss of generality, we can assume that $b = \langle 0, \ldots, 0 \rangle$. Let S' be the sequence of equations obtained by replacing every circuit $(H)^{-1}$ in S by $\mathrm{Inv}_k(H)$. The sequence S' does not contain divisions, but is not yet a correct proof, since the translation $F \cdot \mathrm{Inv}_k(F) = 1$ of the axiom D is not satisfied. However, we claim that for every equation $F_1 = F_2$ in S' and every $k \leq d$, $F_1^{(k)} = G_1^{(k)}$ has a $\mathbb{P}_c$ proof of size $s \cdot p(d)$ for a suitable polynomial p. The proof is constructed by induction on the length of S', as in Proposition 7. The case of the axiom D follows from Lemma 27: $(F \cdot \mathrm{Inv}_k(F))^{(0)} = 1 = 1^{(0)}$ and $(F \cdot \mathrm{Inv}_k(F))^{(j)} = 0 = 1^{(j)}$, if $j > 0$. Consequently, we obtain proofs of $F^{(k)} = G^{(k)}$, for every $k \leq d$. By Lemma 16, we have $\mathbb{P}_c(\mathbb{F})$ proofs of $F = \sum_{k \leq d} F^{(k)}$, $G = \sum_{k \leq d} G^{(k)}$. This gives $\mathbb{P}_c(\mathbb{F})$ proofs of $F = G$ with the correct size. QED

Another application of Schwartz-Zippel lemma is the following:

REMARK 29. *Let $\mathbb{F}$ be an arbitrary field and assume that $F = G$ has a $\mathbb{P}_c^{-1}(\mathbb{F})$ proof of size s. Then there exists a $\mathbb{P}_c^{-1}(\mathbb{F})$ proof of $F = G$ of size $O(s^2)$ which contains only the variables appearing in F or G.*

PROOF. Let S be a proof of $F = G$ of size s which contains variables $z_1, \ldots, z_m$ not appearing in F or G. Assume that F or G actually contain at least one variable x, otherwise the statement is clear. It is sufficient to find a substitution $z_1 = H_1, \ldots, z_m = H_m$ for which the proof S is defined and $H_1, \ldots, H_m$ are circuits of size $O(s)$ in the variable x only. We will choose the substitution from the set $M = \{x^1, x^2, x^3 \ldots, x^{2^{cs}}\}$, where c is a sufficiently large constant. Note that x^p can be computed by a circuit of size $\log_2 p + 2$, and so every circuit in M has size $O(s)$. That such a substitution exists can be shown as in Proposition 28, when we consider M as a subset of the field of rational functions. QED

5.2 Taylor series

For a later application, we need to introduce the basic notion of a power series. Let $F = F(\overline{x}, z)$ be a circuit with division. We will define $\Delta_{z^k}(F)$ as a circuit in the variables $\overline{x}$, computing the coefficient of z^k in F, when F is written as a power series at $z = 0$. This is done as follows:

Case 1: Assume first that no division gates in F contain the variable z. Then we define $\Delta_{z^k}(F)$ by the following rules (the definition is similar to that of $F^{(k)}$ in Section 3, and so we will be less formal here):

(i) $\Delta_z(z) := 1$ and $\Delta_{z^k}(z) := 0$, if $k > 1$.

(ii) If F does not contain z, then $\Delta_{z^0}(F) := F$ and $\Delta_{z^k}(F) := 0$, if $k > 0$.

(iii) $\Delta_{z^k}(F + G) = \Delta_{z^k}(F) + \Delta_{z^k}(G)$.

(iv) $\Delta_{z^k}(F \cdot G) = \sum_{i=0}^{k} \Delta_{z^i}(F) \cdot \Delta_{z^{k-i}}(G)$.

Case 2: Assume now that some division gate in F contains z. We let:

$$F_0 := ((\mathrm{Den}(F))(z/0)^\sharp,$$

where, given a circuit G, $G^\sharp$ is the non-redundant version of G (see definition in Section 3) and $G(z/0)$ is obtained by substituting in G all occurrences of z by the constant 0.

In case $\widehat{F_0} \neq 0$, we define:

$$\Delta_{z^k}(F) := F_0^{-1} \cdot \Delta_{z^k}\left(\mathrm{Num}(F) \cdot \mathrm{pow}_k\left(F_0^{-1} \cdot \mathrm{Den}(F)\right)\right).$$

Note that z does not occur in any division gate inside $\mathrm{Num}(F) \cdot \mathrm{pow}_k\left(F_0^{-1} \cdot \mathrm{Den}(F)\right)$, and so $\Delta_{z^k} F$ is well-defined.

We summarize the main properties of Δ_{z^k} as follows:

PROPOSITION 30. *(i). If F is a circuit without divisions of syntactic degree $\leq d$ and size s then $F = \sum_{i=0}^{d} \Delta_{z^i}(F) \cdot z^i$ has a $\mathbb{P}_c$ proof of size $s \cdot poly(d)$.*

(ii). If $F_0, \ldots, F_k$ are circuits with divisions not containing the variable z, then $\Delta_{z^j}(\sum_{i=0}^{k} F_i z^i) = F_j$ has a polynomial size $\mathbb{P}_c^{-1}$ proof, for every $j \leq k$.

(iii). Assume that F, G are circuits with divisions such that $F = G$ has a $\mathbb{P}_c^{-1}$ proof of size s which is defined for $z = 0$. Then

$$\Delta_{z^k}(F) = \Delta_{z^k}(G)$$

has a $\mathbb{P}_c^{-1}$ proof of size $s \cdot poly(k)$.

The proofs are almost identical to those of Proposition 7 and Proposition 28. We omit the details.

6. SIMULATING LARGE FIELDS IN SMALL ONES

Recall the notation on matrices given in Section 1.1. Mainly, matrices are understood as matrices whose entries are circuits and operations on matrices are operations on circuits.

LEMMA 31. *Let X, Y, Z be $n \times n$ matrices of distinct variables and I_n the identity matrix. Then the following identities have polynomial-size $\mathbb{P}_c(\mathbb{F})$ proofs:*

$$X + Y = Y + X \qquad X + (Y + Z) = (X + Y) + Z$$
$$X \cdot (Y + Z) = X \cdot Y + X \cdot Z \qquad (Y + Z) \cdot X = Y \cdot X + Z \cdot X$$
$$X \cdot (Y \cdot Z) = (X \cdot Y) \cdot Z \qquad X \cdot I_n = I_n \cdot X = X.$$

Similarly for non-square matrices of appropriate dimension.

PROOF. Each of the equalities is a set of n^2 correct equations with degree ≤ 3 and size $O(n)$. Every such equation has a $\mathbb{P}_c$-proof of size $O(n^3)$. QED

Let $\mathbb{F}_1 = GF(p)$ and $\mathbb{F}_2 = GF(p^n)$, where p is a prime power. We will show how to simulate proofs in $\mathbb{P}_c(\mathbb{F}_2)$ by proofs in $\mathbb{P}_c(\mathbb{F}_1)$. Recall that $\mathbb{F}_2$ can be represented by $n \times n$ matrices with elements from $\mathbb{F}_1$, that is, there is an isomorphism θ between $\mathbb{F}_2$ and a subset of $GL_n(\mathbb{F}_1)$. We can also assume that $\theta(a) = aI_n$ if $a \in \mathbb{F}_1 \subseteq \mathbb{F}_2$. This allows one to treat a polynomial f over $\mathbb{F}_2$ as a matrix of n^2 polynomials over $\mathbb{F}_1$. Similarly, we can define a translation of circuits: let F be a circuit with coefficients from $\mathbb{F}_2$. Let $\overline{F}$ be an $n \times n$ matrix of circuits $\{\overline{F}_{ij}\}$, $i, j \in [n]$ with coefficients from $\mathbb{F}_1$, defined as follows: for every gate u in F, introduce n^2 gates $\bar{u} = \{\bar{u}_{ij}\}_{i,j\in[n]}$, and let:

(i). If $u \in \mathbb{F}_2$ is a constant, let $\bar{u} := \theta(u)$.

(ii). If u is a variable, let $\bar{u} := u \cdot I_n$.

(iii). If $u = v + w$, let $\bar{u} := \bar{v} + \bar{w}$, and if $u = v \cdot w$, let $\bar{u} := \bar{v} \cdot \bar{w}$

Then $\overline{F}$ is the matrix computed by $\bar{w}$ where w is the output of F.

Here, $\bar{v} + \bar{w}$, $(\bar{v} \cdot \bar{w})$ and $u \cdot I_n$ are understood as the corresponding matrix operations on circuit nodes.

LEMMA 32. *Let F, G be circuits of size $\leq s$ with coefficients from $\mathbb{F}_2$. Then*

$$\overline{F \oplus G} = \overline{F} + \overline{G}, \quad \overline{F \otimes G} = \overline{F} \cdot \overline{G}, \quad (35)$$
$$\overline{F} \cdot \overline{G} = \overline{G} \cdot \overline{F} \quad (36)$$

have $\mathbb{P}_c(\mathbb{F}_1)$ proofs of size $s \cdot poly(n)$

PROOF. Identities (35) follow from the definition of $\overline{F}$ by means of axioms C1, C2.

Identity (36) follows by induction on the circuit sizes of F and G. We first need to construct the proof of

$$\overline{z_1} \cdot \overline{z_2} = \overline{z_2} \cdot \overline{z_1},$$

where each z_1, z_2 is either a variable or an element of $\mathbb{F}_2$. So assume that z_1 is a variable. Then $\overline{z_1} = z_1 \cdot I_n$. This gives $\overline{z_1} \cdot \overline{z_2} = z_1 \cdot \overline{z_2}$. But $\overline{z_2}$ is a matrix for which each entry commutes with z_1, which gives a proof of $z_1 \cdot \overline{z_2} = \overline{z_2} \cdot z_1 = \overline{z_2} \cdot \overline{z_1}$. The case of z_2 being a variable is similar. If both $z_1, z_2 \in \mathbb{F}_2$, we are supposed to prove $\theta(z_1) \cdot \theta(z_2) = \theta(z_2) \cdot \theta(z_1)$. But this is a set of n^2 true equations of size $O(n)$ which contain only elements of $\mathbb{F}_1$, and hence it has a proof of size $O(n^3)$. In the inductive step, use (35) and Lemma 31 to construct proofs of $(\overline{F_1} + \overline{F_2}) \cdot \overline{G} = \overline{G}(\overline{F_1} + \overline{F_2})$ and of $(\overline{F_1} \cdot \overline{F_2}) \cdot \overline{G} = \overline{G}(\overline{F_1} \cdot \overline{F_2})$ from the proofs of $\overline{F_1} \cdot \overline{G} = \overline{G} \cdot \overline{F_1}$ and $\overline{F_2} \cdot \overline{G} = \overline{G} \cdot \overline{F_2}$. QED

PROOF PROOF OF THEOREM 10. Let F, G be circuits with coefficients from $\mathbb{F}_2$ such that $F = G$ has a $\mathbb{P}_c(\mathbb{F}_2)$ proof of size s. We wish to show that $\overline{F} = \overline{G}$ have proofs of size $s \cdot \text{poly}(n)$ in $\mathbb{P}_c(\mathbb{F}_1)$. This implies Theorem 10, for if F, G contain only coefficients from $\mathbb{F}_1$ then $\overline{F}_{11} = F$ and $\overline{G}_{11} = G$.

The proof is constructed by induction on the number of lines. Axioms C1, C2 follow from equations (35) in Lemma 32, and A4 from equation (36). A9 is a set of n^2 true constant equations. The rest of the axioms are application of Lemma 31. The rules R1, R2 are immediate, and R3, R4 are given by Lemma 32. QED

PROOF OF THEOREM 9. Theorem 9 follows from Theorem 10 and Proposition 28. QED

For a circuit with division F, define its syntactic degree by

$$\deg F := \deg(\text{Num}F) + \deg(\text{Den}F).$$

COROLLARY 33. *Let $\mathbb{F}$ be any field and let F, G, H be circuits with divisions. Assume that $\deg(F)$ and $\deg(G)$ is at most d and that H has size s_1. Suppose that $F = G$ has a $\mathbb{P}_c^{-1}(\mathbb{F})$ proof of size s_2 and that $F(z/H)$, $G(z/H)$ are defined. Then $F(z/H) = G(z/H)$ has a $\mathbb{P}_c^{-1}(\mathbb{F})$ proof of size $s_1 s_2 \cdot poly(d)$.*

PROOF. We aim to construct a proof of $F = G$ of size $s_2 \cdot \text{poly}(d)$ such that the proof is defined for $z = H$. We can then substitute H for z throughout the proof to obtain a proof of $F(z/H) = G(z/H)$ of the required size. By Lemma 26, we have proofs of

$$F = \text{Num}(F) \cdot \text{Den}(F)^{-1} \qquad G = \text{Num}(G) \cdot \text{Den}(G)^{-1}. \quad (37)$$

This and $F = G$ gives a $\mathbb{P}_c^{-1}(\mathbb{F})$ proof of

$$\text{Num}(F) \cdot \text{Den}(G) = \text{Num}(G) \cdot Den(F),$$

of size $O(s_2)$. The last equation does not contain division gates, and so it has a $\mathbb{P}_c(\mathbb{F})$ proof of size $s_2 \cdot \text{poly}(d)$ by Theorem 9. This proof is defined for $z = H$ because it does not contain division gates. By Lemma 26, the proofs of (37) are defined for $z = H$ (because $F(z/H)$ and $G(z/H)$ are defined by assumption). In particular, both $\text{Den}(F)(z/H)$ and $\text{Den}(G)(z/H)$ are nonzero, and we have a proof of

$$\text{Num}(F) \cdot \text{Den}(F)^{-1} = \text{Num}(G) \cdot \text{Den}(G)^{-1}$$

which is defined for $z = H$. Using (37) we obtain a proof of $F = G$ of size $s_2 \cdot \text{poly}(d)$ which is defined for $z = H$. QED

7. COMPUTING THE DETERMINANT

We are now done proving the structural properties of $\mathbb{P}_c$ and $\mathbb{P}_f$ and we proceed to construct proofs of the properties of the determinant. We first compute the determinant as a rational function.

7.1 The determinant as a rational function

The definition of X^{-1} *and* DET(X)

Let $X = \{x_{ij}\}_{i,j\in[n]}$ be a matrix consisting of n^2 distinct variables. Recursively, we define $n \times n$ matrix X^{-1} whose entries are circuits with divisions.

(i). If $n = 1$, let $X^{-1} := (x_{11}^{-1})$.

(ii). If $n > 1$, partition X as

$$X = \begin{pmatrix} X_1 & v_1^t \\ v_2 & x_{nn} \end{pmatrix}, \tag{38}$$

where $X_1 = \{x_{ij}\}_{i,j\in[n-1]}$, $v_1 = (x_{1n}, \ldots, x_{(n-1)(n-1)})$ and $v_2 = (x_{n1}, \ldots, x_{n(n-1)})$. Assuming we have constructed X_1^{-1}, let

$$\delta(X) := x_{nn} - v_2 X_1^{-1} v_1^t\,. \tag{39}$$

$\delta(X)$ computes a single non-zero rational function and so $\delta(X)^{-1}$ is defined. Finally, let

$$X^{-1} := \tag{40}$$

$$\begin{pmatrix} X_1^{-1}(I_{n-1}+\delta(X)^{-1}v_1^t v_2 X_1^{-1}) & -\delta(X)^{-1}X_1^{-1}v_1^t \\ -\delta(X)^{-1}v_2X_1^{-1} & \delta(X)^{-1} \end{pmatrix}.$$

DET(X) is defined is follows.

(i). If $n = 1$, let DET$(X) := x_{11}$.

(ii). If $n > 1$, partition X as in (38) and let $\delta(X)$ be as in (39). Let

$$\text{DET}(X) := \text{DET}(X_1)\cdot\delta(X) = \text{DET}(X_1)(x_{nn} - v_2X_1^{-1}v_1^t).$$

The definition in (40) should be understood as a circuit with n^2 outputs which takes $X_1^{-1}, v_1, v_2, x_{nn}$ as inputs and moreover, such that the inputs from X_1^{-1} occur exactly once (so we slightly deviate from earlier notation). Altogether, we obtain polynomial size circuits for X^{-1} and DET(X). The fact that DET(X) indeed computes the determinant (as a rational function) is a consequence Proposition 38 below, where we show that $\mathbb{P}_c^{-1}$ can prove the two identities which characterize the determinant. That X^{-1} computes the matrix inverse is proved in Proposition 34.

It should be emphasized that both X^{-1} and DET(X) are circuits with divisions and hence not always defined when substituting for X. Let $A := \{a_{ij}\}_{i,j\in[n]}$ be an $n \times n$ matrix whose entries are circuits with division. We will say that A is *invertible* if the circuit A^{-1} is defined—that is, when we substitute the entries of A into X^{-1}, the circuit does not use divisions by zero. Note that A^{-1} may be undefined even if A has inverse "in the real world". For example, if

$$A = \begin{pmatrix} 0 & 1 \\ 1 & 0 \end{pmatrix}$$

then both A^{-1} and DET(A) are undefined, and so A is not invertible in our sense. Moreover, note that DET(X) has an *exponential* syntactic degree which, in view of Corollary 33, further obscures substitution in $\mathbb{P}_c^{-1}$ proofs.

On the other hand, let us state the basic cases when the determinant and matrix inverse are defined.

(i). If A is invertible (meaning the circuit A^{-1} is defined) then DET(A) is defined.

(ii). If the entries of A compute algebraically independent rational functions then A^{-1} is defined.

(iii). If A is a triangular matrix with $a_{11}, \ldots, a_{nn}$ on the diagonal such that $a_{11}^{-1}, \ldots, a_{nn}^{-1}$ are defined then A is invertible.

(iv). Setting $A[k] := \{a_{ij}\}_{i,j\in[k]}$, the matrix A is invertible if and only if $A[1], \ldots, A[n-1]$ are invertible and $\delta(A)^{-1}$ is defined.

Properties of matrix inverse

PROPOSITION 34. *Let $X = \{x_{ij}\}_{i,j\in[n]}$ be a matrix with n^2 distinct variables. Then both*

$$X \cdot X^{-1} = I_n \quad \textit{and} \quad X^{-1}\cdot X = I_n$$

have a polynomial-size $\mathbb{P}_c^{-1}$ proof. The proof is defined for $X = A$, whenever A is invertible.

PROOF. Let us construct the proofs of $X \cdot X^{-1} = I_n$ and $X^{-1}\cdot X = I_n$ by induction on n. If $n = 1$, we have $x_{11}\cdot x_{11}^{-1} = x_{11}^{-1}\cdot x_{11} = 1$ which is a $\mathbb{P}_c^{-1}$ axiom. Otherwise let $n > 1$ and X be as in (38). We want to construct a polynomial size proof of $X\cdot X^{-1} = I_n$ from the assumption $X_1X_1^{-1} = I_{n-1}$. This implies that $X\cdot X^{-1} = I_n$ has a polynomial size proof.

For brevity, let $a := \delta(X)$. Using some rearrangements, and the definition of a, we have:

$$X\cdot X^{-1} =$$

$$\begin{pmatrix} X_1 & v_1^t \\ v_2 & x_{nn}\end{pmatrix}\cdot\begin{pmatrix} X_1^{-1}(I_{n-1}+a^{-1}v_1^tv_2X_1^{-1}) & -a^{-1}X_1^{-1}v_1^t \\ -a^{-1}v_2X_1^{-1} & a^{-1}\end{pmatrix}$$

$$= \begin{pmatrix} I_{n-1} + a^{-1}v_1^tv_2X_1^{-1} - a^{-1}v_1^tv_2X_1^{-1} & -a^{-1}v_1^t + a^{-1}v_1^t \\ v_2X_1^{-1} + a^{-1}(v_2X_1^{-1}v_1^t - x_{nn})v_2X_1^{-1} & a^{-1}(-v_2X_1^{-1}v_1^t + x_{nn}) \end{pmatrix}$$

$$= \begin{pmatrix} I_{n-1} & 0 \\ v_2X_1^{-1} - a^{-1}av_2X_1^{-1} & a^{-1}a \end{pmatrix}$$

$$= \begin{pmatrix} I_{n-1} & 0 \\ 0 & 1\end{pmatrix}.$$

Here we use the fact that basic properties of matrix addition and multiplication have feasible proofs (see Lemma 31).

The proof of $X^{-1}\cdot X = I_n$ is constructed in a similar fashion (where we use the assumption $X_1^{-1}X_1 = I_{n-1}$ instead). Moreover, if A is an $n\times n$ matrix such that A^{-1} is defined, the proofs of $A\cdot A^{-1} = A^{-1}\cdot A = I_n$ are defined. (This is because they employ only the inverse gates appearing already in the definition of X^{-1}.) QED

COROLLARY 35. *The identity $(XY)^{-1} = Y^{-1}X^{-1}$ has a polynomial-size proof in $\mathbb{P}_c^{-1}$. The proof is defined for $X = A, Y = B$ whenever A, B and AB are invertible.*

Beware that invertibility of A and B does not guarantee invertibility of AB.

PROOF. Let $Z := (XY)^{-1}$. Then $(Z(XY))Y^{-1}X^{-1} = Y^{-1}X^{-1}$. On the other hand, $(Z(XY))Y^{-1}X^{-1} = Z(X(YY^{-1})X^{-1} = Z$ and so $Z = Y^{-1}X^{-1}$. QED

An application of the Corollary is the following technical observation. Let X be as in (38) and similarly $Y = \begin{pmatrix} Y_1 & u_1^t \\ u_2 & y_{nn}\end{pmatrix}$. Comparing the entries in the bottom right corners of $(XY)^{-1}$ and $Y^{-1}X^{-1}$, we obtain that

$$\delta(Y)\delta(X) = \delta(XY)(1 + u_2Y_1^{-1}X_1^{-1}v_1^t)\,, \tag{41}$$

has a polynomial size $\mathbb{P}_c^{-1}$ proof (the proof is defined for $X, Y = A, B$ whenever A, B and AB are invertible).

It is often easier to argue about triangular matrices. We summarize their useful properties in the following:

PROPOSITION 36. *(i). Let A, L, U be $n\times n$ matrices with L lower triangular and U upper triangular. If A, L, U are invertible then so are LA and AU.*

(ii). Let X be a $n \times n$ matrix of distinct variables. Then there exists a lower triangular matrix $L(X)$ and an upper triangular matrix $U(X)$ such that $X = L(X) \cdot U(X)$ has a polynomial size $\mathbb{P}_c^{-1}$ proof. The proof is defined for $X = A$ whenever A is invertible, and then also $L(A), U(A)$ are invertible.

PROOF. Part (i) follows from the fact that $(LA)[k] = L[k]A[k]$ and $\delta((LA)[k]) = \delta(L[k])\delta(A[k])$ for every $k \in \{1, \ldots, n\}$ (where $A[k]$ is defined as $\{a_{ij}\}_{i,j\in[k]}$.)

In part (ii), the matrices $L(X), U(X)$, as well as the $\mathbb{P}_c^{-1}$ proof, are constructed by induction on n. If $n = 1$, let $L(x_{11}) = x_{11}$ and $U(x_{11}) = 1$. If $n > 1$, write X as in (38). Assuming we have $X_1 = L(X_1)U(X_1)$, we have

$$\begin{pmatrix} X_1 & v_1^t \\ v_2 & x_{nn} \end{pmatrix} =$$
$$\begin{pmatrix} L(X_1) & 0 \\ v_2U(X_1)^{-1} & x_{nn} - v_2X_1^{-1}v_1^t \end{pmatrix} \cdot \begin{pmatrix} U(X_1) & L(X_1)^{-1}v_1^t \\ 0 & 1 \end{pmatrix}.$$

Verifying that the proof is defined for an invertible A, and that $L(A), U(A)$ are invertible, is straightforward. QED

Properties of DET

We now want to prove Proposition 38 which is a $\mathbb{P}_c^{-1}$ analogy of Theorem 4. We first prove the following lemma.

LEMMA 37. *Let A be an invertible $n \times n$ matrix and let v_1, v_2 be $n \times 1$ vectors such that $A + v_1^tv_2$ is invertible. Then*

$$DET(A + v_1^tv_2) = DET(A)(1 + v_2A^{-1}v_1^t) \qquad (42)$$

has a polynomial size $\mathbb{P}_c^{-1}$ proof.

PROOF. The proof is constructed by induction on n. If $n = 1$, the identity is immediate. If $n > 1$, partition A and $A + v_1^tv_2$ as in (38), i.e.,

$$A = \begin{pmatrix} A_1 & w_1^t \\ w_2 & a_{nn} \end{pmatrix} \quad \text{and}$$
$$A + v_1^tv_2 = \begin{pmatrix} A_1 + u_1^tu_2 & w_1^t + c_2u_1^t \\ w_2 + c_1u_2 & a_{nn} + c_1c_2 \end{pmatrix},$$

where $v_1 = (u_1, c_1)$ and $v_2 = (u_2, c_2)$. We want to construct a polynomial size proof of (42) from the assumption $\mathrm{DET}(A_1 + u_1^tu_2) = \mathrm{DET}(A_1)(1 + u_2A_1^{-1}u_1^t)$. This implies that (42) has a polynomial size proof.

By the definition of DET, we have

$$\mathrm{DET}(A) = \mathrm{DET}(A_1)\delta(A), \quad \text{and}$$
$$\mathrm{DET}(A + v_1^tv_2) = \mathrm{DET}(A_1 + u_1^tu_2)\delta(A + v_1^tv_2).$$

By the assumption, $\mathrm{DET}(A_1 + u_1^tu_2) = \mathrm{DET}(A_1)(1 + u_2A_1^{-1}u_1^t)$ and so (42) is equivalent to

$$\mathrm{DET}(A_1)(1 + u_2A_1^{-1}u_1^t)\delta(A + v_1^tv_2)$$
$$= \mathrm{DET}(A_1)\delta(A)(1 + v_2A^{-1}v_1^t).$$

Hence in order to prove (42), it is sufficient to prove

$$(1 + u_2A_1^{-1}u_1^t)\delta(A + v_1^tv_2) = \delta(A)(1 + v_2A^{-1}v_1^t). \qquad (43)$$

In order to prove (43), we first prove its special case

$$(1 + \bar{u}_2\bar{u}_1^t)\delta(I_n + \bar{v}_1^t\bar{v}_2) = (1 + \bar{v}_2\bar{v}_1^t). \qquad (44)$$

where $\bar{v}_1 = (\bar{u}_1, \bar{c}_1)$ and $\bar{v}_2 = (\bar{u}_2, \bar{c}_2)$ are vectors such that $I_n + \bar{v}_1^t\bar{v}_2$ is invertible. Let $\alpha := \bar{u}_2\bar{u}_1^t$. By the definition of δ

$$\delta(I_n + \bar{v}_1^t\bar{v}_2) = (1 + \bar{c}_1\bar{c}_2 - \bar{c}_1\bar{c}_2\bar{u}_2(I_{n-1} + \bar{u}_1^t\bar{u}_2)^{-1}\bar{u}_1^t)$$

and it is easy to verify that

$$(I_{n-1} + \bar{u}_1^t\bar{u}_2)^{-1} = I_{n-1} - (1 + \alpha)^{-1}\bar{u}_1^t\bar{u}_2.$$

Hence we obtain

$$\begin{aligned}
&(1 + \bar{u}_2\bar{u}_1^t)\delta(I_n + \bar{v}_1^t\bar{v}_2) \\
&= (1 + \alpha)(1 + \bar{c}_1\bar{c}_2 - \bar{c}_1\bar{c}_2\bar{u}_2(I_{n-1} - (1 + \alpha)^{-1}\bar{u}_1^t\bar{u}_2)\bar{u}_1^t \\
&= (1 + \alpha)(1 + \bar{c}_1\bar{c}_2 - \bar{c}_1\bar{c}_2\bar{u}_2\bar{u}_1^t - \bar{c}_1\bar{c}_2(1 + \alpha)^{-1}(\bar{u}_2\bar{u}_1^t)^2) \\
&= (1 + \alpha)(1 + \bar{c}_1\bar{c}_2 - \bar{c}_1\bar{c}_2\alpha - \bar{c}_1c_2(1 + \alpha)^{-1}\alpha^2) \\
&= 1 + \bar{c}_1\bar{c}_2 + \alpha = 1 + \bar{v}_2\bar{v}_1^t
\end{aligned}$$

which proves (44).

In order to conclude (43), let $L := L(A)$ and $U := U(A)$ be the matrices from Proposition 36. That is, L and U is an invertible lower resp. upper triangular matrix so that $A = LU$, and hence also $A^{-1} = U^{-1}L^{-1}$, has a polynomial size proof. Let

$$\bar{v}_1^t := L^{-1}v_1^t \text{ and } \bar{v}_2 := v_2U^{-1}.$$

The definition guarantees that

$$\bar{u}_2\bar{u}_1^t = u_2A_1^{-1}u_1^t, \; \bar{v}_2\bar{v}_1^t = v_2A^{-1}v_1^t \qquad (45)$$

have polynomial size proof. Moreover, $A + v_1^tv_2 = L(I_n + \bar{v}_1^t\bar{v}_2)U$, which also shows that $I_n + \bar{v}_1^t\bar{v}_2$ is invertible. (41) implies that $\delta(LB) = \delta(L)\delta(B)$ and $\delta(BU) = \delta(B)\delta(U)$ has a polynomial proof (for any invertible B). Hence

$$\delta(A + v_1^tv_2) = \delta(L)\delta(U)\delta(I_n + \bar{v}_1^t\bar{v}_2) = \delta(A)\delta(I_n + \bar{v}_1^t\bar{v}_2).$$

This and (45) gives (43) from (44). QED

PROPOSITION 38. *(i). Let U be an (upper or lower) triangular matrix with $u_1, \ldots u_n$ on the diagonal. If $u_1^{-1}, \ldots, u_n^{-1}$ are defined then*

$$DET(U) = u_1 \cdots u_n$$

has a polynomial-size $\mathbb{P}_c^{-1}$ proof.

(ii). Let X and Y be $n \times n$ matrices, each consisting of pairwise distinct variables. Then

$$DET(X \cdot Y) = DET(X) \cdot DET(Y) \qquad (46)$$

has a polynomial-size $\mathbb{P}_c^{-1}$ proof. The proof is defined for $X = A, Y = B$ provided[7] *$A[k], B[k]$ and $A[k]B[k]$ are invertible for every $k \in \{1, \ldots, n\}$.*

PROOF. Part (i) readily follows from the definition of DET.

Part (ii) is proved by induction on n. If $n = 1$, it is immediate. Assume that $n > 1$. Let

$$X = \begin{pmatrix} X_1 & v_1^t \\ v_2 & x_{nn} \end{pmatrix}, \; Y = \begin{pmatrix} Y_1 & u_1^t \\ u_2 & y_{nn} \end{pmatrix}.$$

[7] $A[k]$ is defined as $\{a_{ij}\}_{i,j\in[k]}$.

We want to construct a polynomial size proof of $\mathrm{DET}(XY) = \mathrm{DET}(X)\mathrm{DET}(Y)$ from the assumption $\mathrm{DET}(X_1Y_1) = \mathrm{DET}(X_1)\mathrm{DET}(Y_1)$. This implies that $\mathrm{DET}(XY) = \mathrm{DET}(X)\mathrm{DET}(Y)$ has a polynomial size proof.

By the definition of DET, we have

$$\mathrm{DET}(X) = \mathrm{DET}(X_1)\delta(X)\,,\ \mathrm{DET}(Y) = \mathrm{DET}(Y_1)\delta(Y)$$

and $\mathrm{DET}(XY) = \mathrm{DET}(X_1Y_1 + v_1^t u_2)\delta(XY)$, and we are supposed to prove:

$$\mathrm{DET}(X_1Y_1+v_1^tu_2)\delta(XY) = \mathrm{DET}(X_1)\delta(X)\cdot\mathrm{DET}(Y_1)\delta(Y)\,. \tag{47}$$

By the previous lemma, we have $\mathrm{DET}(X_1Y_1 + v_1^tu_2) = \mathrm{DET}(X_1Y_1)(1 + u_2(X_1Y_1)^{-1}v_1^t)$. By the assumption $\mathrm{DET}(X_1Y_1) = \mathrm{DET}(X_1)\mathrm{DET}(Y_1)$, this yields

$$\mathrm{DET}(X_1Y_1+v_1^tu_2) = \mathrm{DET}(X_1)\mathrm{DET}(Y_1)(1+u_2Y_1^{-1}X_1^{-1}v_1^t)\,.$$

Hence in order to prove (47), it is sufficient to prove

$$(1 + u_2Y_1^{-1}X_1^{-1}v_1^t)\delta(XY) = \delta(X)\delta(Y)\,.$$

But this follows from (41).

On the inductive step, we have assumed invertibility of X, Y, XY, X_1, Y_1 and X_1Y_1, as well as invertibility of $X_1Y_1 + v_1^tu_2$. The latter follows from invertibility of XY since $(X_1Y_1 + v_1^tu_2)^{-1}$ is used to define XY^{-1}. Since $X_1 = X[n-1]$, $Y_1 = Y[n-1]$, the proof altogether assumes invertibility of $X[k], Y[k]$ and $X[k]Y[k]$ for every $k \in \{1,\dots,n\}$. QED

Let us explicitly state the important cases when the proof of $\mathrm{DET}(AB) = \mathrm{DET}(A)\mathrm{DET}(B)$ is defined. This is so, if A and B are invertible and if

(i). the entries of A, B compute algebraically independent rational functions, or

(ii). A is lower triangular or B is upper triangular, or

(iii). the entries of A are field elements and the entries of B are algebraically independent, or vice versa.

The following lemma shows that elementary Gaussian operations are well-behaved with respect to DET.

LEMMA 39. *Let $X = \{x_{ij}\}_{i,j\in[n]}$ be an $n \times n$ matrix of distinct variables. Then the following have polynomial-size $\mathbb{P}_c^{-1}$ proofs:*

(i). $DET(X) = -DET(X')$, where X' is a matrix obtained from X by interchanging two rows or columns.

(ii). $DET(X'') = uDET(X)$, where X'' is obtained by multiplying a row in X by u, such that u^{-1} is defined (and similarly for a column).

(iii). $DET(X) = DET(X''')$, where X''' is obtained by adding a row to a different row in X (and similarly for columns).

(iv). $DET(X) = x_{nn}DET(X_1 - x_{nn}^{-1}v_1^tv_2)$, where X_1, v_1 and v_2 are from the decomposition (38).

PROOF. Items (ii) and (iii) follow from Proposition 38 and the fact that $X'' = AX$ and $X''' = A'X$, where A, A' are suitable triangular matrices. We cannot infer (i) directly from Proposition 38, since $X' = TX$ implies only that T is a transposition matrix and hence not invertible in our sense. However, we can write $T = A_1A_2$, where A_1, A_2 are invertible with $\mathrm{DET}(A_1)\mathrm{DET}(A_2) = -1$: note that $\begin{pmatrix} 0 & 1 \\ 1 & 0 \end{pmatrix} = \begin{pmatrix} 1 & 1 \\ 1 & 0 \end{pmatrix}\begin{pmatrix} 1 & 0 \\ -1 & 1 \end{pmatrix}$. Since X is a matrix of distinct variables, the following is defined:

$$\begin{aligned}\mathrm{DET}(A_1A_2X) &= \mathrm{DET}(A_1)\mathrm{DET}(A_2X)\\ &= \mathrm{DET}(A_1)\mathrm{DET}(A_2)\mathrm{DET}(X)\,.\end{aligned}$$

Part (iv) follows from Lemma 37. QED

7.2 The determinant as a polynomial

Note that we cannot yet apply Theorem 9 to obtain Theorem 4, because DET itself contains division gates. For our purpose it will suffice to compute the determinant by a circuit without division, denoted $\det(X)$, and construct a proof of $\det(X) = \mathrm{DET}(X)$ in $\mathbb{P}_c^{-1}$. In order to do that, we will define $\det(X)$ as the nth term of the Taylor expansion of $\mathrm{DET}(I + zX)$ at $z = 0$, as follows: using notation from Section 5.2, let

$$\det(X) := \Delta_{z^n}\left(\mathrm{DET}(I + zX)\right). \tag{48}$$

Let us note that

(i). $\det(X)$ indeed computes the determinant of X,

(ii). $\det(X)$ is a circuit without divisions of syntactic degree n.

This is because every variable from X in the circuit $\mathrm{DET}(I+zX)$ occurs in a product with z. Hence $\Delta_{z^n}(\mathrm{DET}(I + zX))$ is the n-th homogeneous part of the determinant of $I + X$ - the determinant of X. By the definition of Δ_{z^n}, $\Delta_{z^n}(\mathrm{DET}(I + zX))$ contains exactly one inverse gate, namely the inverse of $\mathrm{Den}(\mathrm{DET}(I+zX))$ at the point $z = 0$. But $a := (\mathrm{Den}(\mathrm{DET}(I + zX)))(z/0)^\sharp$ is a constant circuit computing a non-zero field element, and we can identify a^{-1} with the field constant it computes.

LEMMA 40. *Let X be an $n \times n$ matrix of distinct variables. There exist circuits with divisions $P_0, \dots, P_{n-1}$ not containing the variable z, such that*

$$DET(zI_n + X) = z^n + P_{n-1}z^{n-1} + \cdots + P_0$$

has a polynomial-size $\mathbb{P}_c^{-1}(\mathbb{F})$ proof. Moreover, this proof is defined for $z = 0$.

PROOF. Let F be a circuit in which z does not occur in the scope of any inverse gate. Then, we define the *z-degree of F* as the syntactic-degree of F considered as a circuit computing a univariate polynomial in z (so that all other variables are treated as constants).

By induction, we will construct matrices $A_1, \dots, A_n$ with the following properties:

1. $A_1 = X + zI_n$,

2. Every A_k is an $(n-k+1) \times (n-k+1)$ matrix of the form

$$\begin{pmatrix} z^k + f & w \\ v^t & zI_{n-k} + Q \end{pmatrix}$$

where all the entries are circuits with division in which z does not occur in the scope of any division gate, v, w are $1 \times (n-k)$ vectors and moreover: f as well as every entry of w have z-degree less than k and v, Q do not contain the variable z.

3. The identity $\mathrm{DET}(A_k) = \mathrm{DET}(A_{k+1})$ has a polynomial-size proof.

4. The entries of A_k are algebraically independent (this is to guarantee that divisions are defined).

Assume that A_k is given, and let us partition it as

$$A_k = \begin{pmatrix} z^k + f_1 & w & f_2 \\ u_1^t & zI_m + Q & u_2^t \\ a_1 & v & z + a_2 \end{pmatrix}$$

where $m = (n - k - 1)$ and we allow the alternative that $m = 0$. Only f_1, w, f_2 can depend on z and have z-degree $< k$. By Lemma 39 part (iv), we can switch the first and last column to obtain a $\mathbb{P}_c^{-1}$ proof of

$$\mathrm{DET}(A_k) = -\mathrm{DET}\begin{pmatrix} f_2 & w & z^k + f_1 \\ u_2^t & zI_m + Q & u_1^t \\ z + a_2 & v & a_1 \end{pmatrix}.$$

By Lemma 39 part (iv), we have

$$\mathrm{DET}(A_k) =$$

$$-a_1\mathrm{DET}\begin{pmatrix} f_2 - a_1^{-1}(z^k + f_1)(z + a_2) & w - a_1^{-1}(z^k + f_1)v \\ u_2^t - a_1^{-1}u_1^t(z + a_2) & zI_m + Q - a_1^{-1}u_1^t v \end{pmatrix}$$

$$= \mathrm{DET}\begin{pmatrix} (z^k + f_1)(z + a_2) - a_1 f_2 & a_1 w - (z^k + f_1)v \\ u_2^t - a_1^{-1}u_1^t(z + a_2) & zI_m + Q - a_1^{-1}u_1^t v \end{pmatrix}.$$

We can write $(z^k + f)(z + a_2) = z^{k+1} + (fz + a_2 z^k + fa_2)$, where the z-degree of $(fz + a_2 z^k + fa_2)$ as well as of every entry of $a_1 w - (z^k + f_1)v$ is at most k. Hence the matrix is of the right form, apart from the occurrence of zu_1^t in the first column. This can be remedied by multiplying by $\begin{pmatrix} 1 & 0 \\ a_1^{-1}u_1^t & I_m \end{pmatrix}$ from the right to obtain A_{k+1} of the required form.

This indicates that, given a circuit computing A_k, we can compute A_{k+1} using polynomially many additional gates. Altogether, every A_k has a polynomial size circuit. The proof of $\mathrm{DET}(A_k) = \mathrm{DET}(A_{k+1})$ has a polynomial number of lines and, as it involves polynomial size circuits, also polynomial size.

Finally, we obtain a polynomial size proof of $\mathrm{DET}(A_n) = \mathrm{DET}(A_1) = z^n + f$, where f is a circuit with z-degree $< n$ in which z is not in the scope of any division gate. Writing f as $\sum_{i=0}^{n-1} P_i z^i$ concludes the lemma. QED

PROPOSITION 41. *(i). If U is a triangular matrix with $u_1, \ldots, u_n$ on the diagonal then $\det(U) = u_1 \cdots u_n$ has a polynomial size $\mathbb{P}_c^{-1}$ proof.*

(ii). Let X be an $n \times n$ matrix of distinct variables. Then $\mathrm{DET}(X) = \det(X)$ has a polynomial-size $\mathbb{P}_c^{-1}$ proof.

PROOF. Part (i) follows from Proposition 38. For we have $\mathrm{DET}(I_n + zU) = (1 + zu_1) \cdots (1 + zu_n)$, and the proof is defined for $z = 0$. By Proposition 30, $\det(U) = \Delta_{z^n}((1 + zu_1) \cdots (1 + zu_n)) = u_1 \cdots u_n$ has a polynomial size $\mathbb{P}_c^{-1}$ proof.

(ii) follows from the previous lemma. We obtain polynomial-size $\mathbb{P}_c^{-1}$ proof of the following substitution instance:

$$\mathrm{DET}(zI_n + X^{-1}) = z^n + Q_{n-1}z^{n-1} + \cdots + Q_0, \quad (49)$$

where the Q_i's are circuits with divisions which do not contain the variable z and the proof is defined for $z = 0$.

By Proposition 38 we have a polynomial-size $\mathbb{P}_c^{-1}$ proof of

$$\mathrm{DET}(I_n + zX) = \mathrm{DET}(zI_n + X^{-1}) \cdot \mathrm{DET}(X).$$

The proof is defined for $z = 0$ (as is witnessed by letting $X := I_n$). From equation (49) we get a polynomial-size proof of

$$\mathrm{DET}(I_n + zX) = z^n\mathrm{DET}(X) + z^{n-1}Q'_{n-1} + \cdots + Q'_0,$$

where $Q'_{n-1}, \ldots, Q'_0$ do not contain z. The proof is defined for $z = 0$ and so Proposition 30gives a polynomial-size $\mathbb{P}_c^{-1}$ proof of

$$\Delta_{z^n}(\mathrm{DET}(I_n + zX)) =$$
$$\Delta_{z^n}(z^n\mathrm{DET}(X) + z^{n-1}Q'_{n-1} + \cdots + Q'_0).$$

But by the definition of $\det(X)$, $\Delta_{z^n}(\mathrm{DET}(I + zX))$ is $\det(X)$ and by the definition of Δ_{z^n}, $\Delta_{z^n}(z^n\mathrm{DET}(X) + z^{n-1}Q'_{n-1} + \cdots + Q'_0)$ is $\mathrm{DET}(X)$, and we are done. QED

8. CONCLUDING THE MAIN THEOREM

We can now finally prove Theorem 4 (Main Theorem), which we rephrase as follows:

PROPOSITION 42 (THEOREM 4, REPHRASED). *Let X, Y, Z be $n \times n$ matrices such that X, Y consist of different variables and Z is a triangular matrix with $z_{11}, \ldots, z_{nn}$ on the diagonal. Then there exist an arithmetic circuit $\det_c$ and a formula $\det_f$ such that:*

(i). The identity $\det_c(XY) = \det_c(X) \cdot \det_c(Y)$ and $\det_c(Z) = z_{11} \cdots z_{nn}$ have polynomial-size $O(\log^2 n)$ depth proofs in $\mathbb{P}_c$.

(ii). The identity $\det_f(XY) = \det_f(X) \cdot \det_f(Y)$ and $\det_f(Z) = z_{11} \cdots z_{nn}$ have $\mathbb{P}_f$ proofs of size $n^{O(\log n)}$.

PROOF. Let $\det(X) = \Delta_{z^n}\mathrm{DET}(I + zX)$ be the circuit defined in (48). Lemma 41 part (ii) and Proposition 38 imply that the equations

$$\det(XY) = \det(X) \cdot \det(Y) \quad \text{and} \quad \det(Z) = z_{11} \cdots z_{nn} \quad (50)$$

have polynomial-size $\mathbb{P}_c^{-1}$ proofs. By definition, the syntactic degree of $\det(X)$ is at most n. Hence, by Theorem 9 the identities in (50) have polynomial-size $\mathbb{P}_c$ proofs. This almost concludes part (i), except for the bound on the depth. To bound the depth, let

$$\det_c(X) := [\det(X)],$$

where $[F]$ is the balancing operator as defined in Section 4. Thus, Theorem 5 implies that $[\det(XY)] = [\det(X) \cdot \det(Y)]$ and $[\det(Z)] = [z_{11} \cdots z_{nn}]$ have $\mathbb{P}_c$ proofs of polynomial-size and depth $O(\log^2 n)$. By means of Lemma 20, we have such proofs also for

$$[\det(X) \cdot \det(Y)] = [\det(X)] \cdot [\det(Y)] = \det_c(X) \cdot \det_c(Y)$$

and $[\det(Z)] = z_{11} \cdots z_{nn}$. Hence it is sufficient to construct (polynomial-size and $O(\log^2 n)$ depth proofs) of

$$[\det(XY)] = \det_c(XY) \quad \text{and} \quad [\det(Z)] = \det_c(Z)$$

(note that defining $\det_c(X)$ as $[\det(X)]$ does not imply that $[\det(XY)] = \det_c(XY)$). This follows from the following more general claim:

Claim 43. *Let $F(x_1/g_1, \ldots, x_n/g_n)$ be a circuit of size s and syntactic degree d. Then*

$$[F(x_1/g_1, \ldots, x_n/g_n)] = [F(x_1, \ldots, x_n)] (x_1/[g_1], \ldots, x_n/[g_n])$$

has a $\mathbb{P}_c$ proof of size poly(n,d) and depth $O(\log d \log s + \log^2 d)$.

Proof. This follows by induction using Lemma 20. We omit the details. QED

To prove part (ii), recall the definition of $F^\bullet$ from Remark 3. Let $\det_f(X) := (\det_c(X))^\bullet$. Then the statement follows from part (i) and Claim 24 of the proof of Theorem 23. QED

We should note that in the $\mathbb{P}_c$-proof of the equation $\det(XY) = \det(X) \cdot \det(Y)$ no divisions occur and so it is defined for any substitution. In particular,

$$\det(AX) = \det(A) \cdot \det(X) = a \det(X)$$

has a short $\mathbb{P}_c$ proof for any matrix A of field elements whose determinant is $a \in \mathbb{F}$. Similarly, the elementary Gaussian operations stated in Lemma 39 carry over to polynomial-size $\mathbb{P}_c$ proofs of the corresponding properties of det.

9. APPLICATIONS

In this section, we prove Propositions 11 and 12. First, one should show that the cofactor expansion of the determinant has short proofs. For an $n \times n$ matrix X and $i, j \in [n]$, let $X_{i,j}$ denote the $(n-1) \times (n-1)$-matrix obtained by removing the ith row and jth column from X. Let Adj(X) be the $n \times n$ matrix whose (i,j)-th entry is $(-1)^{i+j}\det_c(X_{j,i})$ (where $\det_c$ is the circuit from Proposition 42).

Proposition 44 (Cofactor expansion). *Let $X = \{x_{ij}\}_{i,j \in [n]}$ be an $n \times n$ matrix. Then the following identities have polynomial-size $O(\log^2 n)$-depth $\mathbb{P}_c$ proofs:*

(i) $\det_c(X) = \sum_{j=1}^{n} (-1)^{i+j} x_{ij} \det_c(X_{i,j})$, for any $i \in [n]$;

(ii) $X \cdot Adj(X) = Adj(X) \cdot X = \det_c(X) \cdot I$.

The proof of this proposition appears in the full version of this article.

Proposition 45 (Proposition 12 restated). *The identities $YX = I_n$ have polynomial-size and $O(\log^2 n)$-depth $\mathbb{P}_c$ proofs from the equations $XY = I_n$. In the case of $\mathbb{P}_f$, the proofs have quasipolynomial-size.*

Proof. Note that we are dealing with a $\mathbb{P}_c$ proof from assumptions, and hence we are not allowed to use division gates. The proof is constructed as follows. Assume $XY = I_n$. By Proposition 42, this gives $\det_c(X)\det_c(Y) = 1$. By Proposition 44, we can multiply from left both sides of $XY = I_n$ by Adj(X), to obtain $\det_c(X)Y = $ Adj(X). Hence,

$$\det_c(X) Y X = \text{Adj}(X) X = \det_c(X) I_n,$$

and so

$$\det_c(Y)\det_c(X) Y X = \det_c(Y)\det_c(X) I_n,$$

which, using $\det_c(X)\det_c(Y) = 1$ gives $YX = I_n$. The $\mathbb{P}_f$ proof is identical, except that the steps involving the determinant require a quasipolynomial size. QED

Proof of Proposition 11. The proof proceeds via a simulation of the construction in [17]. Due to lack of space, we refer the reader to the full version of this article for more details. QED

10. REFERENCES

[1] Paul Beame and Toniann Pitassi. Propositional proof complexity: past, present, and future. *Bull. Eur. Assoc. Theor. Comput. Sci. EATCS*, (65):66–89, 1998.

[2] Stuart J. Berkowitz. On computing the determinant in small parallel time using a small number of processors. *Inf. Process. Lett.*, 18:147–150, 1984.

[3] Maria Luisa Bonet, Samuel R. Buss, and Toniann Pitassi. Are there hard examples for Frege systems? In *Feasible mathematics, II*, volume 13 of *Progr. Comput. Sci. Appl. Logic*, pages 30–56. Birkhäuser, 1995.

[4] Pavel Hrubeš and Iddo Tzameret. The proof complexity of polynomial identities. In *Proceedings of the 24th IEEE Conference on Computational Complexity*, pages 41–51, 2009.

[5] Laurent Hyafil. On the parallel evaluation of multivariate polynomials. *SIAM J. Comput.*, 8(2):120–123, 1979.

[6] Emil Jeřábek. Dual weak pigeonhole principle, Boolean complexity, and derandomization. *Ann. Pure Appl. Logic*, 129(1-3):1–37, 2004.

[7] Jan Krajíček. *Bounded arithmetic, propositional logic, and complexity theory*, volume 60 of *Encyclopedia of Mathematics and its Applications*. Cambridge, 1995.

[8] Ran Raz and Amir Yehudayoff. Balancing syntactically multilinear arithmetic circuits. *Comput. Complexity*, 17:515–535, 2008.

[9] Jacob T. Schwartz. Fast probabilistic algorithms for verification of polynomial identities. *Journal of the ACM*, 27(4):701–717, 1980.

[10] Nathan Segerlind. The complexity of propositional proofs. *Bull. Symbolic Logic*, 13(4):417–481, 2007.

[11] Amir Shpilka and Amir Yehudayoff. Arithmetic circuits: A survey of recent results and open questions. *Foundations and Trends in Theoretical Computer Science*, 5(3-4):207–388, 2010.

[12] Michael Soltys. *The complexity of derivations of matrix identities*. PhD thesis, University of Toronto, 2001.

[13] Michael Soltys. Feasible proofs of matrix properties with csanky's algorithm. In *19th International Workshop on Comp. Sci. Log.*, pages 493–508, 2005.

[14] Michael Soltys and Stephen Cook. The proof complexity of linear algebra. *Ann. Pure Appl. Logic*, 130(1-3):277–323, 2004.

[15] Michael Soltys and Alasdair Urquhart. Matrix identities and the pigeonhole principle. *Arch. Math. Logic*, 43(3):351–357, 2004.

[16] Volker Strassen. Vermeidung von divisionen. *J. Reine Angew. Math.*, 264:182–202, 1973. (in German).

[17] Leslie G. Valiant. Completeness classes in algebra. In *Proceedings of the 11th Annual ACM Symposium on the Theory of Computing*, pages 249–261. ACM, 1979.

[18] Leslie G. Valiant, Sven Skyum, S. Berkowitz, and Charles Rackoff. Fast parallel computation of polynomials using few processors. *SIAM J. Comput.*, 12(4):641–644, 1983.

[19] Richard Zippel. Probabilistic algorithms for sparse polynomials. In *Proceedings of the International Symposiumon on Symbolic and Algebraic Computation*, pages 216–226. Springer-Verlag, 1979.

Time-Space Tradeoffs in Resolution: Superpolynomial Lower Bounds for Superlinear Space

Paul Beame*
University of Washington
Seattle, WA 98195
beame@cs.washington.edu

Chris Beck†
Princeton University
Princeton, NJ 08544
cbeck@princeton.edu

Russell Impagliazzo‡
Institute for Advanced Study
Princeton, NJ 08540
and the University of California
San Diego, CA 92093
russell@cs.ucsd.edu

ABSTRACT

We give the first time-space tradeoff lower bounds for Resolution proofs that apply to superlinear space. In particular, we show that there are formulas of size N that have Resolution refutations of space and size each roughly $N^{\log_2 N}$ (and like all formulas have Resolution refutations of space N) for which any Resolution refutation using space S and length T requires $T \geq (N^{0.58 \log_2 N}/S)^{\Omega(\log \log N/ \log \log \log N)}$. By downward translation, a similar tradeoff applies to all smaller space bounds.

We also show somewhat stronger time-space tradeoff lower bounds for Regular Resolution, which are also the first to apply to superlinear space. Namely, for any space bound S at most $2^{o(N^{1/4})}$ there are formulas of size N, having clauses of width 4, that have Regular Resolution proofs of space S and slightly larger size $T = O(NS)$, but for which any Regular Resolution proof of space $S^{1-\epsilon}$ requires length $T^{\Omega(\log \log N/ \log \log \log N)}$.

Categories and Subject Descriptors

F.0 [**Theory of Computation**]: General; F.2.3 [**Analysis of Algorithms and Problem Complexity**]: Tradeoffs between Complexity Measures

General Terms

Theory

Keywords

Proof Complexity, Time-Space Tradeoffs

*Research supported by NSF grants CCF-0830626, DMS-0835373, and by the Ellentuck Fund. Much of this research was done at the Institute for Advanced Study, Princeton.

†Research supported by NSF grant CCF-0832797.

‡Research supported by NSF grants DMS-0835373, CCF-0832797, and The Oswald Veblen Fund.

STOC'12, May 19–22, 2012, New York, New York, USA.

1. INTRODUCTION

For many modern SAT solvers, memory use is as much a bottleneck as time. Earlier DPLL-based SAT-solvers used very little memory, just needing to keep track of the stack in recursion. However, a major reason for the improved performance of recent SAT solvers is the inclusion of clause learning [18], which adds a large number of derived clauses to the input clauses. Clause learning uses considerable extra space corresponding to the number (and size) of derived clauses that are active at any one time. This creates opportunities for finding smaller refutations of unsatisfiable formulas, but at the cost of potentially requiring huge amounts of memory. Balancing these two factors is an art that determines the success of the SAT-solver. (See e.g, [29] for a discussion of how one successful SAT-solver handles this.)

This raises the question of whether such tradeoffs between total time and memory is an inherrent limitation, or just an artifact of the known algorithms. To make this question precise while also being general enough to handle the wide variety of SAT-solving algorithms, we can use the well-known correspondence between these algorithms and the Resolution proof system. All of the DPLL-based SAT solvers, when run on unsatisfiable formulas, implicitly or explicitly find resolution refutations of the input formulas. Thus, the minimum size of such a refutation is a lower bound on the time taken by any such algorithm. This observation has been part of the motivation for proof complexity studies of resolution for many years. More recently, an analogous measure of the *space* of a resolution proof has been introduced, which lower bound the number of derived clauses that must be remembered throughout the algorithm, and hence bounds the memory requirements of resolution-based SAT solvers.

If we use a pure backtracking approach to SAT-solving, like many of the earlier generation of SAT-solvers did, the proofs generated have at most linear space. Thus, we cannot hope to prove a super-linear space lower bound in isolation. Our goal is instead to show that the small space of these proofs come at the expense of being substantially larger than proofs using more space, i.e., to give time-space tradeoffs for proof complexity. There has been substantial work devoted to understanding space in proof complexity, proving almost linear lower bounds on the space required, and giving sharp time-space tradeoffs for refutations. However, previous work always hit a barrier at linear space. Until this current paper, no known time-space trade-off lower bound for proof complexity was meaningful when the space allowed was greater than that of the input formula. Since SAT solvers have ample memory to hold the input formulas, this meant that such work was not of direct benefit to understanding time-memory trade-offs for SAT-solvers. Ben-Sasson (see [22, 21]) posed the question of whether such trade-offs existed as follows: do all CNF formulas have resolution proofs of linear space that are at most polynomially larger than the resolution proof length possible when space is unrestricted?

We give a strong negative answer to this question. We give explicit CNF tautologies of size N that have proofs of size $T_{UB} \leq N^{O(\log_2 N)}$ (and hence space at most T_{UB}), but when space is restricted to $S_{LB} \leq T_{UB}^{1/2}$, any resolution proof requires size $T_{LB} \geq (T_{UB})^{\Omega(\log\log N/\log\log\log N)}$. In other words, restricting memory to any polynomial in the input formula size has a super-polynomial cost in terms of time the SAT-solver will take. Our formulas are Tseitin graph tautologies for complete bipartite graphs connected along a path and so are totally explicit, as are the proofs in the upper bound on T_{UB}. In fact, [2] has shown that proofs of such tautologies are derivable by standard SAT-solving techniques in time proportional to T_{UB}, so the trade-off applies to actual SAT-solvers, not just the theoretical optimal SAT-solver.

We obtain an even stronger tradeoff for Regular Resolution, a subclass of Resolution proofs that includes most natural Resolution proofs. Using Tseitin formulas on a family of grid graphs, we show that for any integer m, there is a size $N = O(m^4)$ formula with unbounded space regular resolution proof size at most $T_{UB} = poly(m)2^m$ so that any space $S_{LB} \leq 2^{m(1-\Omega(1))}$ proof requires size $T_{LB} \geq (T_{UB})^{\Omega(\log\log m/\log\log\log m)}$. This is an improvement over the previous result in that space restrictions provably cost in terms of size even for (weak) exponential amounts of space. Furthermore, the lower bound holds for space almost equal to the upper bound on total size. Finally, the tautologies where we prove this lower bound are constant width.

These results show that restricting space can increase size by more than a polynomial amount. It seems possible that space restrictions could have an exponential cost; however, that would require a different kind of tautology than the ones we consider. The quasipolynomial time-space tradeoff lower bound we achieve for Resolution proofs of these Tseitin tautologies is qualitatively not far from optimal. In particular, the Tseitin tautologies to which our bounds apply have Regular Resolution refutations of space $O(\log T_{UB} \log n)$ and size $T_{UB}^{O(\log n)}$. A recent result [12] shows a general purpose resolution based SAT algorithm which finds this proof as well, answering a question of [2]; see also [4]. [12] also gives an algorithm for high space which finds a refutation matching our high space refutation – this is also achieved by the algorithm of [2].

1.1 History and Related Work

Much initial work on proof space concentrated on the space required by Resolution proofs as a parameter on its own. Early work [13] showed that every unsatisfiable formula has a Resolution refutation in which the total space required is at most the number of variables (plus one), and the focus moved to finding matching space lower bounds. Atserias and Dalmau [3] showed that Resolution space is at least Resolution *width*, the length of the longest clause in any Resolution proof, for which $\Omega(n)$ lower bounds were already known for many formulas because width lower bounds are the most widely used method for proving Resolution proof size lower bounds [10]. (Despite its utility, Resolution width alone can be far from characterizing Resolution space [19].)

Lately, there has been great theoretical interest in understanding the interplay between the resources of Resolution proof length (time) and space [22, 7], and in showing tradeoffs between them [8]. For example, Nordström [20] shows that there are formulas with linear size proofs but for which reducing the total space used by a constant increases the length required to exponential[1]. At higher space levels, Ben-Sasson and Nordström [8] recently showed the existence of families of formulae that have linear size (and hence linear space) proofs, but which require exponentially large proofs when the space is constrained to be $O(n/\log n)$.

1.2 Overview of our techniques

Many of the earlier papers on bounds for sub-linear space proofs modified arguments taken from time-space tradeoffs for pebbling games. We also use arguments based on time-space tradeoffs for straight-line programs such as [27, 23]. In such a bound, one typically defines a notion of "progress", and divides up the program into intervals called "epochs". Then one shows that, starting from any given point in the program, on a random input, one is unlikely to make significant progress in a short amount of time. The conclusion is that either there are many values that are in memory at those points, or the length of epochs is large, giving a time-space trade-off.

We follow a similar strategy, combined with a "bottleneck counting" argument as introduced in [15]. We consider the time steps to be the derived clauses in order, and divide these into equal sized intervals, or *epochs*. We consider the sets of clauses in memory at the start and end of epochs. We use a simple measure of the complexity of clauses, akin to those in [15, 10], the number of vertices of the graph G associated with the input clauses of the Tseitin formula that are required to derive them. The input clauses have complexity 1, the final contradiction has complexity $|V(G)|$, and each resolution step can at most double the complexity. Thus, clauses of each approximate (to within factors of 2) complexity between 1 and $|V(G)|$ must occur in the proof. The current complexities of clauses in memory is our measure of progress.

We show that clauses of intermediate complexities involve many variables and are hence intuitively are "unlikely" to be false, and we show that the likelihoods of very different clauses are in some sense independent. Because of the small space, the clauses in memory at the frontiers of epochs are "bottlenecks" ; it is unlikely that clauses of many distinct complexities are in memory at these times. If this does not happen, we must make a great deal of progress during some epoch, in that the largest complexity of a clause in memory has increased substantially. We then apply the argument recursively to that epoch.

While this intuitive picture is the same for the two lower bounds, the techniques used to formalize them are quite different. For general resolution, we formalize "likelihood" by looking at the proof after a random restriction. We show that if we apply a restriction to a Tseitin formula on a suit-

[1] This was claimed in [16] which used a more complicated approach, but this has been retracted as has the claim that determining the minimum space required for Resolution refutations is PSPACE-hard.

able graph G, then the probability that a clause has medium complexity after the restriction is quite small, and the probability that k clauses simultaneously have different intermediate complexities is a $\Theta(k)$-th power of this small probability. We use this to show that, with high probability, there are not many distinct complexities in memory at the frontiers of epochs after the restriction. Thus, after the restriction, there is one epoch that contains clauses of many approximate complexities within a large interval. We then use a recursive version of the same argument to show that this is also unlikely.

In the case of regular resolution, we define a probabilistic process that works its way backwards from the contradiction to one of the input clauses. It always visits clauses of each approximate complexity. "Likelihood" is then the probability of being visited in this process. We show that this probability is small for intermediate complexity clauses, and, with a few exceptions, uncorrelated for clauses of very different complexities. A bottleneck counting argument then shows that it is unlikely that this process visits many different clauses of distinct complexities that are each in memory at the frontiers of epochs, and thus must almost always visit a large interval of complexities within some epoch. The argument is repeated recursively within the chosen epoch.

2. BASIC DEFINITIONS AND NOTATION

We consider Boolean formulas over a set of variables $X = \{x_1, ..x_n\}$. As usual, a literal is a Boolean variable or its negation, a clause is a disjunction of literals, and a CNF is a conjunction of clauses. We think of clauses as being specified by their sets of literals, and CNFs as specified by their sets of clauses. For a clause C, we write $vars(C)$ to be the set of variables appearing in C. The *width* $w(C)$ of a clause C is $|vars(C)|$ and the width of a set or sequence of clauses F, is the maximum width of clauses in F. The *size* of a CNF formula F is the total number of literal occurrences in the formula, i.e., $\sum_{C \in F} w(C)$.

One of the simplest and most widely studied propositional proof systems is resolution which operates with clauses and has one rule of inference, the resolution rule: $\frac{A \vee x \qquad B \vee \overline{x}}{A \vee B}$. We say that the variable x is *resolved* in this instance of the resolution rule. A *resolution refutation* of a CNF formula (a set of clauses) is a sequence of clauses ending in the unsatisfiable empty clause $\perp$, each of which is either a clause of from the formula (an "axiom") or follows from two previous clauses via the resolution rule. (The term *resolution proof* is used more generally to refer to any inference of this sort that may not necessarily result in $\perp$.) Every resolution proof naturally corresponds to a directed acyclic graph (DAG), known as the proof DAG, in which every clause derived via the resolution inference rule has a directed edge "backwards" from a derived clause to each of its antecedents. (Note that, formally, a resolution proof corresponds to one of possibly many topological sorts of its proof DAG.)

A resolution proof is *regular* if along each path in the proof DAG, each variable is resolved at most once. (Regular) resolution is *sound and complete* in that every CNF formula is unsatisfiable if and only if it has a regular resolution refutation.

The *size* or *length* of a resolution proof is the total number of clauses in the proof. The usual definition of the *space* (*clause space*) used by a resolution proof is the maximum number of clauses which need to be held in memory at any one time when carrying out the proof. Say that a clause is active at time step t if it has been derived before t but is still needed for an inference step to be made at time t or later. Then the clause space is the maximum number of clauses active at any time step. In the most straightforward model, the initial clauses are made available at $t = 0$. To consider sublinear space, this model is modified, and the input clauses become available only as needed, accessed by "axiom download" steps, and may be cleared from local memory and derived again later, in analogy with the usual off-line definition of Turing machine space. In our results, we will be considering superlinear space and hence it is unnecessary to treat the input clauses this way. Doing so does not increase the space bound by even a constant factor. We allow clauses to be derived multiple times in a proof, since that may allow fewer clauses to be active at any one time.

A *restriction* is a mapping $\rho : X \to \{0, 1, \star\}$. Restrictions on X can be identified with partial assignments on V by viewing unassigned inputs as being mapped to $\star$ and vice versa. We will use the two terms interchangeably, depending on the context. Given two partial assignment π and ρ that are *compatible*, i.e., they agree on $\mathrm{dom}(\pi) \cap \mathrm{dom}(\rho)$, we use $\rho \cup \pi$ to denote the partial assignment that applies both assignments. The restriction of a clause C by ρ, denoted by $C|_\rho$ is the clause obtained from C by setting the value of each $x \in \rho^{-1}(\{0,1\})$ to $\rho(x)$, and leaving each $x \in \rho^{-1}(\star)$ as a variable. The restriction of a set of clauses is defined by restricting each one.

2.1 Tseitin Tautologies

Following [28] we use the following formula to represent the principle that every undirected graph has even total degree.

DEFINITION 2.1. *Let $G = (V, E)$ be an undirected graph, and $\chi : V \to \{0,1\}$ an* odd charge function, *i.e. one such that $\bigoplus_{v \in V} \chi(v)$ is odd. For each edge $e \in E$, we have a variable x_e. For $v \in V, \epsilon \in \{0,1\}$, let*

$$PARITY_{v,\epsilon} := \bigwedge \{ \bigvee_{e \sim v} x_e^{a(e)} | \bigoplus_{e} (a(e) \oplus 1) \not\equiv \epsilon \}$$

be the CNF representation of the parity constraint $\bigoplus_{e \sim v} x_e \equiv \epsilon$. The Tseitin tautology *on (G, χ) is defined by the conjunction*

$$\tau(G, \chi) := \bigwedge_v PARITY_{v,\chi(v)} \ .$$

Also, independent of whether or not G is connected and χ has odd charge, the resulting formula is known as a Tseitin formula. Frequently we will suppress reference to χ, since when G is connected, any two odd charge functions χ give essentially equivalent formulae.

By a simple counting argument, if charge function χ is odd, then the parity constraints cannot all be satisfied – this would correspond to an undirected graph such that the sum of its degrees is odd.

OBSERVATION 2.2. *When χ is odd, $\tau(G, \chi)$ is unsatisfiable.*

When the degree of the graph is d, each constraint can be written as a CNF formula of $O(2^d)$ clauses of width d. It is easy to see that the formula $\tau(G)$ has size $O(2^d|V|)$.

DEFINITION 2.3. *Let $G = (V, E)$ be a graph. For $E' \subset E$ let $G|E'$ denote the graph $G = (V, E - E')$. When π is a partial assignment to E, we overload the notation $G|\pi$ to mean $G|dom(\pi)$. (Alternatively, if ρ is a restriction then $G|\rho$ denotes $G|\rho^{-1}(\{0,1\})$.)*

DEFINITION 2.4. *If χ is a charge function on a graph $G = (V, E)$ and π is a partial assignment to E then let $\chi \oplus \pi$ denote the new charge function χ' on V given by $\chi'(v) = \chi(v) \oplus \bigoplus_{v \in e \in dom(\pi)} \pi(e)$.*

The following formalizes how restrictions affect Tseitin formulas.

PROPOSITION 2.5. *If $\tau(G, \chi)$ is a Tseitin formula and ρ is a restriction on the edges of G, then $\tau(G, \chi)|_\rho$ is $\tau(G|\rho, \chi \oplus \rho)$, and the parity of χ and $\chi \oplus \rho$ are the same.*

2.2 Resolution refutations of Tseitin formulas

For the graphs we will consider, some generic resolution refutations of odd charged Tseitin formulas follow from bounds on their *cut width.* We give two such refutations. One uses large space and implies that our lower bound results yield tradeoffs of the form that restricting the space does increase the minimum proof length required. The other uses a very small amount of space (indeed, exponentially less) and shows that there is a quasi-polynomial upper limit on the kind of tradeoff one can prove for the formulas we consider.

DEFINITION 2.6. *The* cut width *of a graph G is the smallest W such that there is a linear ordering of the vertices $v_1, \ldots, v_n$ such that, for every $1 \le t \le n$, there are no more than W edges crossing the cut $(\{v_1, \ldots, v_t\}, \{v_{t+1}, \ldots, v_n\})$.*

LEMMA 2.7. *Let G be a graph with n vertices, maximum degree d, and cut width W. Then there is a regular resolution refutation of a Tseitin tautology on G using $\le n \cdot 2^d \cdot 2^{(W-1)}$ resolution steps, and space $\le 2 \cdot 2^{(W-1)} + d$, plus space for the initial axioms.*

Note that the number of resolution steps is within a constant factor of the proof size.

This refutation described by this lemma works by maintaining clauses corresponding to parities of the edges in the cuts and slowly moving those cuts from one end to the other end of the graph. It mirrors a refutation for similar formulas given in [11]. A detailed proof is given in the appendix.

The following lemma shows that for the graphs we consider here, even radically restricted space can only increase the size required for Tseitin tautologies with small cut width by an $O(\log n)$ power.

LEMMA 2.8. *Under the same conditions as Lemma 2.7, the Tseitin tautology on $\tau(G)$ has a tree-like Resolution refutation using space $W\lceil \log n \rceil$ and $2^{W\lceil \log n \rceil}$ resolution steps.*

The refutation in this case involves simulating a binary search for a charge violation over the vertex ordering that achieves the cut width. At each cut in the search, the proof maintains all the clauses in the parities of the edges crossing that cut. A detailed proof is given in the appendix.

Though the graphs we consider all have small cutwidth, there are versions of both these upper bounds that can be expressed in terms of a smaller and more precise parameter, *carving width.* Moreover, some of these refutations can also be found algorithmically with similar complexity. Details are in the appendix.

2.3 A measure of complexity of clauses

First we need some preliminary definitions.

DEFINITION 2.9. *Consider assignments to the variables of a Tseitin formula τ. A* critical assignment *is a total assignment that violates exactly one clause of τ. The vertex associated with that constraint is said to be its* bad vertex. *For any partial assignment π, we denote by $Crit(\pi)$ the set of critical assignments extending π.*

DEFINITION 2.10. *Given a partial assignment π to a Tseitin formula τ over graph G, we say that a vertex v is a* critical vertex for π *iff v is bad for some critical assignment to the edges of G consistent with π. We define $crit_\tau(\pi)$ to be the set of critical vertices for π. We drop the subscript τ when it is understood from the context. We also define critical vertices for clauses by letting $crit(C)$ be the set of critical vertices of the partial assignment associated with $\neg C$.*

Fortunately, for Tseitin tautologies, the set $crit(\pi)$ has a nice, well-known characterization:

PROPOSITION 2.11. *$crit(\pi)$ is non-empty if and only if $G|\pi$ has exactly one component of odd charge, in which case $crit(\pi)$ is equal to that component.*

Let S be a subset of nodes. We write $\delta(S)$ for the edges on the boundary of set S.

COROLLARY 2.12. *If π is a partial assignment with $crit(\pi) = S$, then every edge on the boundary of S is assigned by π.*

Finally, we note how partial assignments impact critical sets.

PROPOSITION 2.13. *Let $\tau(G, \chi)$ be a Tseitin formula and ρ be a restriction (partial assignment) on the edges of G. Then for any partial assignment π compatible with ρ, $crit_{\tau(G,\chi)^\rho}(\pi) = crit_{\tau(G,\chi)}(\pi \cup \rho)$.*

PROOF. This follows immediately from the fact that the set of critical assignments for $\tau(G, \chi)$ that are consistent with ρ is precisely the set of critical assignments for $\tau(G, \chi)^\rho$ with assignment ρ appended. □

We use $|crit(C)|$ as a measure of the complexity of clause C.

PROPOSITION 2.14. *Fix any odd-charged Tseitin formula τ over a connected graph G.*

(a) $|crit_\tau(\bot)| = |V(G)|$ where $\bot$ is the empty clause.

(b) For any clause C of τ, $|crit_\tau(C)| = 1$.

(c) If clause C follows from clauses C_1, C_2 by resolution then $|crit_\tau(C)| \le |crit_\tau(C_1)| + |crit_\tau(C_2)|$.

PROOF. Part (a) and (b) follow immediately from Proposition 2.11. Part (c) follows from the soundness of resolution since any critical assignment that falsifies C must falsify either C_1 or C_2, hence $Crit(C) \subseteq Crit(C_1) \cup Crit(C_2)$. □

Subadditivity of $|crit(C)|$ from Proposition 2.14(c), immediately implies the following.

COROLLARY 2.15. *For any t, any resolution derivation of a clause D with $|crit(D)| > 2t$ from a collection of clauses C having $|crit(C)| \leq t$, must contain a clause C' such that $t < |crit(C')| \leq 2t$.*

PROOF. If not, then at the first point where such a D is derived, it must be derived from two clauses with complexity $\leq t$, contradicting subadditivity. □

3. TIME-SPACE TRADEOFF FOR GENERAL RESOLUTION

To show lower bounds in General Resolution, we consider Tseitin tautologies on a graph $G = (V, E)$ that is a path of length ℓ of complete bipartite graphs $K_{n,n}$, where the left side of one is the right side of the next. Equivalently, this is the tensor product of the complete graph K_n with the path graph P_ℓ. For $c > 0$ an absolute constant, our results hold for any $2^{cn} > \ell > n^4$, but are most impressive for larger ℓ. We picture the vertices of this graph as lying in an $n \times \ell$ grid, with each column corresponding to a vertex of P_ℓ. We let V_i denote the set of vertices in the i-th column, and E_i denote the edges between the i-th column and the $(i+1)$-st column.

PROPOSITION 3.1. *Any Tseitin tautology over $G = K_n \otimes P_\ell$ has (regular) resolution size at most $O(2^{n^2+2n}n\ell)$.*

PROOF. It is easy to see that G has cut width n^2 so this is immediate from Lemma 2.7. □

The main result of this section is the following time-space tradeoff lower bound for general resolution.

THEOREM 3.2. *If n is sufficiently large and $2n^4 \leq \ell < (4n)^{-1}\left(\frac{9}{8}\right)^n$ for any resolution refutation of a Tseitin tautology on the graph $G = K_n \otimes P_\ell$ of size T and space S*

$$T \geq \left(\frac{2^{0.58n^2}}{S}\right)^{\frac{\log_2 L}{\log_2\log_2 L}}$$

where $L = \log_2(\ell/(2n^3))$.

COROLLARY 3.3. *There is a $c > 0$ such that for sufficiently large N and any S satisfying $N \leq S \leq N^{\frac{1}{9}\log_2 N}$, there is a CNF formula of size N that has a resolution refutation of size at most $T_{UB} \leq N \cdot S$ and space at most S such that any resolution refutation using space $S^{1/2}$ requires size $T_{LB} \geq T_{UB}^{c\log_2\log_2 N/\log_2\log_2\log_2 N}$.*

PROOF. Choose the largest n such that $2^{n^2} \leq S$. Since $N \leq S \leq N^{\frac{1}{9}\log_2 N}$, we must have $2^{3n} \leq N \leq 2^{n^2}$ and hence $log_2 \log_2 N$ is $\Theta(\log n)$. Set $\ell = 2^{n/8} < (9/8)^n/(4n)$. With this value of ℓ, L is at least $n/9$ for N sufficiently large and hence $\log_2 L/\log_2\log_2 L$ is $\Theta(\log\log N/\log\log\log N)$. Since the Tseitin formula for $K_n \otimes P_\ell$ has size at most $\ell n 2^{2n} < N$. We can pad this formula by dummy clauses until it has N clauses. Applying the above theorem to this formula with space $S^{1/2}$ instead of S yields the claimed lower bound. □

We use the "progress argument" sketched in the introduction, together with a bottleneck counting based on random restrictions. One subtle point is that, although our argument is applied recursively, we only apply the random restriction once, not after each step of the recursion.

We use the complexity measure on clauses defined in the previous section, which is 1 for the input clauses, is $|V(G)|$ for the final contradiction $\perp$, and grows slowly throughout a resolution proof (possibly not monotonically). We define many different medium complexity levels of clauses.

DEFINITION 3.4. *Let $t_0 = n^4$. Define $\mathcal{L}_i = \{C \in \Pi : 2^i t_0 < |crit(C)| \leq 2^{i+1}t_0\}$ for $0 \leq i < \log_2(\ell n/t_0) - 1$. Each $\mathcal{L}_i$ represents a different* complexity level. *We say that a clause of* Π *has* medium complexity *if it is in one of the $\mathcal{L}_i$.*

We will use the fact that the restriction of a proof of a Tseitin tautology is itself a proof of a Tseitin tautology on a subgraph of the original graph; hence the proof for a graph G contains proofs of Tseitin tautologies for all of the subgraphs of G. We choose such a restriction randomly from a suitable distribution that is overwhelmingly likely to keep the complexity of the final contradiction high.

Following standard notation, let $\mathcal{R}_{1/3}$ be the probability distribution on restrictions $\rho : E \to \{0, 1, *\}$ such that for each e independently, $\Pr_{\rho\sim R_{1/3}}[\rho(e) = 0] = \Pr_{\rho\sim R_{1/3}}[\rho(e) = 1] = \Pr_{\rho\sim R_{1/3}}[\rho(e) = *] = 1/3$.

After we apply a random $\rho \sim R_{1/3}$ to a refutation of $\tau(G, \chi)$, we get a refutation of the Tseitin formula on the smaller graph $G|\rho$ with properties as in Proposition 2.5. We will measure the progress of the proof using the medium complexity levels of its clauses. We therefore will compute bounds on the probability that a clause becomes a medium complexity clause for the Tseitin tautology on the graph $G|\rho$ after such a restriction; we will do the same for the probability that a set of clauses have different medium complexity levels after restriction.

The graph $G|\rho$ and the charge $\chi \oplus \rho$ that results from applying the restriction ρ to $\tau(G, \chi)$ is not fixed. Therefore, it is easier to analyze the critical sets and complexity of the restricted clauses using Proposition 2.13 which says that for any partial assignment π compatible with ρ, $crit_{\tau(G,\chi)^\rho}(\pi) = crit_{\tau(G,\chi)}(\pi \cup \rho)$. For any clause C over G, this means that

$$crit_{\tau(G,\chi)^\rho}(C|_\rho) = crit_{\tau(G,\chi)}(C \vee \overline{\rho})$$

where $\overline{\rho}$ is the clause that is falsified precisely on those assignments consistent with ρ. This allows us simply to work with clauses $C \vee \overline{\rho}$ defined over the original graph G, so for the remainder of this section we write $crit$ for $crit_{\tau(G,\chi)}$.

Now, we view a refutation of total size T and space S as ordered into epochs and sub-epochs as follows: Let L be the number of different medium complexity levels, $L = \log_2((n\ell)/(2t_0)) \geq \log_2 n$. Let $k = \lfloor\log_2 L\rfloor - 1$ and $h = \lfloor\log_2 L/\log_2\log_2 L\rfloor < (k+2)/\log_2 k$. With these values we have $(k+1)k^{h-1} < L$. Now choose

$$m \leq \left\lfloor \frac{(3/2)^{n^2}\ell^{-1}L^{-1}2^{-4n}}{S} \right\rfloor^{1-3/\log_2 k}.$$

One can easily verify that $m \geq \max(8, 2^{0.58n^2}/S)$ for sufficiently large n.

The theorem follows immediately if $T \geq m^h$ so assume, by contradiction, that $T < m^h$. An *epoch at the leaf level* is an interval of m consecutive clauses in the proof, beginning at a time step that is a multiple of m. We consider all clauses in the leaf level epoch to be *frontier* clauses. An *epoch at level* $2 \leq i \leq k$ is an interval of m^i consecutive clauses in the proof, beginning at a time step that is a multiple of m^i.

Its sub-epochs are the epochs of level $i-1$ within the epoch, and the *frontier* clauses for the epoch are the ones that are active at the end of any of its sub-epochs. Thus, leaf level epochs have m frontier clauses and higher level epochs have at most mS frontier clauses, since at most S clauses are active at each of the m times when a sub-epoch ends.

LEMMA 3.5. *For any refutation of a Tseitin tautology on a connected graph with $n\ell$ nodes, at least one epoch has k frontier clauses of distinct medium complexity levels.*

PROOF. Assume that no such epoch exists, at any level of epochs. We will inductively find an epoch E_j at level $k-j$ and medium complexity levels i_{min} and $i_{max} \geq i_{min} + L/k^j$ so that all active clauses at the start of E have complexity at most that of medium complexity level i_{min} and some clause at the end of E has complexity at least that of complexity level i_{max}.

At the start, we can choose E_0 to be the entire proof, since at the beginning, we have only clauses of complexity 1 (input clauses) and at the end, we have only the empty clause, $\perp$, of complexity $n\ell$.

Assume that we have E_j, i_{min} and i_{max} as above. Consider the partition of E_j into m sub-epochs at level $k-j-1$. Because there are at most $k-1$ distinct complexities among E_j's frontier clauses, there must be a sub-interval i'_{min} to i'_{max} of length at least $(i_{max} - i_{min})/k \geq L/k^{j+1}$ where no frontier clause is of medium complexity level between i'_{min} and i'_{max}. Consider the first sub-epoch of E_j that ends with an active clause of medium complexity level at least i'_{max}; since E_j ends with a clause of medium complexity level $i_{max} \geq i'_{max}$, such a sub-epoch must exist. Since no clause of medium complexity level at least i'_{max} was active at the start of this sub-epoch, and no clause of medium complexity level between i'_{min} and i'_{max} is active at the start of any sub-epoch, we can choose this first sub-epoch as E_{j+1}.

Inductively, we get a leaf-level epoch E_{h-1} and an interval i_{min} to i_{max} of length at least $L/k^{h-1} \geq k+1$ so that all active clauses at its start have complexity at most that of medium complexity level i_{min} and at least one clause has medium complexity level i_{max} or greater at the end. Then clauses of all k medium complexity levels between i_{min} and i_{max} appear in the leaf-level epoch. Since all lines in a leaf-level epoch are frontier clauses, this is a contradiction. $\square$

To use the above to get a contradiction, we show that, for $G = K_n \otimes P_\ell$s, the graph is very likely to stay connected after a random restriction, and any small set of clauses is very unlikely to contain many different medium complexity levels of clauses after the restriction. We then apply the above lemma to the restricted proof.

The following lemmas, proved in the next section, summarize our bounds on these probabilities.

DEFINITION 3.6. *Let $CONN(\rho)$ denote the event that each bipartite graph $(V_i, V_{i+1}, E_i \setminus dom(\rho))$ is connected.*

PROPOSITION 3.7. $\Pr_\rho[\neg CONN(\rho)] \leq \ell \cdot 2(n-1)(8/9)^n$.

LEMMA 3.8. *For $k \leq 1/3L$, any k clauses $C_1 \dots C_k$, and any k medium complexity levels $\ell_1, \dots, \ell_k$ with $\ell_{i+1} \geq \ell_i + 3$ for $1 \leq i \leq k-1$,*

$$\Pr_{\rho \sim \mathcal{R}_{1/3}}[CONN(\rho) \wedge \forall i, (C_i \vee \overline{\rho}) \in \mathcal{L}_{\ell_i}] \leq \left(\ell \cdot 2^{4n} \cdot (2/3)^{n^2 \cdot}\right)^k$$

COROLLARY 3.9. *Let $\mathcal{C}$ be a collection of $\leq M$ clauses. The probability that $\mathcal{C}|_\rho$ contains k clauses of distinct medium complexity levels is at most $\left(ML(2/3)^{n^2}\ell 2^{4n}\right)^{\lceil k/3 \rceil}$.*

PROOF. If there are k distinct medium complexity levels, a subset of $\lceil k/3 \rceil$ of them are mutually separated by 3. There are at most $L^{\lceil k/3 \rceil}$ choices for this subset of medimum complexity levels $\ell_1, .., \ell_{\lceil k/3 \rceil}$, and for each element of the subset, at most M choices for a clause $C_i \in \mathcal{C}$ to become this complexity. Since the complexity of $C_i|_\rho$ is the same as that of $C_i \vee \overline{\rho}$ we can apply the previous lemma with a union bound to get the probability bound in the corollary. $\square$

PROOF OF THEOREM 3.2. Assume that m, k, and h are defined as above and that there is a refutation of the Tseitin tautology on $K_n \otimes P_\ell$ of space S and size $T < m^h$. Under any restriction ρ, either $G|\rho$ is disconnected, or after the restriction ρ some epoch in the proof contains frontier clauses of k distinct medium complexity levels. By proposition 3.7, the first probability is $< 1/2$. There are fewer than $2m^{h-1}$ epochs in all, and each has a frontier set of size at most $M = mS$. Thus, from the above corollary, the probability that there is an epoch that has k distinct medium complexity levels among the restriction of its frontier clauses is at most

$$\begin{aligned}
&2m^{h-1}\left(mSL(2/3)^{n^2}\ell 2^{4n}\right)^{\lceil k/3 \rceil} \\
&< \frac{1}{2}\left(m^{1+3/\log_2 k}SL(2/3)^{n^2}\ell 2^{4n}\right)^{\lceil k/3 \rceil} \\
&\qquad\qquad \text{since } m \geq 8 \text{ and } h < (k+2)/\log_2 k \\
&\leq \frac{1}{2}\left[\left(\frac{(3/2)^{n^2}\ell^{-1}L^{-1}2^{-4n}}{S}\right)^{1-9/\log_2^2 k} SL(2/3)^{n^2}\ell 2^{4n}\right]^{\lceil k/3 \rceil} \\
&\leq \frac{1}{2}.
\end{aligned}$$

This is a contradiction to Lemma 3.5 and the theorem follows. $\square$

3.1 Medium complexity clauses and random restrictions

In this section, we prove the lemmas about the effect of random restrictions on Tseitin tautology clauses. We begin with the proof of Proposition 3.7 that the graph remains connected after a random restriction is applied.

PROOF OF PROPOSITION 3.7. We apply a union bound over the columns and compute an explicit bound for the well-known connectivity properties of random bipartite graphs $G(n, n, \frac{1}{3})$.

Consider the left side of $G(n, n, 1/3)$. For any two vertices here, the probability that they are not connected with a two-step path in $G(n, n, 1/3)$ is at most $(8/9)^n$, since there are n possible disjoint two-step paths. By a union bound, the left side and right side are both connected to themselves except with probability $2(n-1)(8/9)^n$. Since these imply that an edge exists, the $G(n, n, 1/3)$ is connected except with this probability. $\square$

Note that the condition $\ell < (4n)^{-1}(9/8)^n$ implies that $\Pr_\rho[\neg CONN(\rho)] < 1/2$.

LEMMA 3.10. *For every clause C and every fixed set of edges $E' \subseteq E$, the probability over $\rho \sim \mathcal{R}_{1/3}$ that $C \vee \overline{\rho}$ is non-trivial and $E' \subseteq vars(C \vee \overline{\rho})$ is at most $(2/3)^{|E'|}$.*

PROOF. For $C \vee \overline{\rho}$ to be non-trivial, ρ must not set any edge to falsify C. In particular, this applies to each edge in E' that appears in $vars(C)$. In order for $E' \subseteq vars(C \vee \overline{\rho})$, each edge in E' not in $vars(C)$ must be set by ρ. For each edge in E', these successes happen with probability 2/3 and the probabilities are independent, so the total probability that $E' \subseteq \delta(crit(C \vee \overline{\rho}))$ is at most $(2/3)^{|E'|}$. □

To prove a non-trivial tradeoff lower bound using our outline above, we need a stronger lower bound than the upper bound for unrestricted space of roughly 2^{n^2} given in Proposition 3.1. Therefore, we need to be able to argue that after such a restriction the probability that a clause will become a medium complexity clause is exponentially small in n^2.

Intuitively, a set of vertices S of size at least n^2 and less than $\ell n/2$ will have a boundary of size at least n^2 for the following reasons. If it has as many as n "partial columns" in which it contains some, but not all, of the vertices, then each such column will contribute at least n boundary edges. If it has fewer than n partial columns, it must contain a full column and an empty column, and its not hard to see that deleting the elements in the partial columns cannot decrease the size of the boundary, so this configuration has a boundary of at least n^2 as well.

By Corollary 2.12, for every clause C, $crit(C \vee \overline{\rho}) = S \subset V$ only if $\delta(S) \subseteq vars(C \vee \overline{\rho})$. Therefore, by Lemma 3.10, $\Pr_{\rho \sim \mathcal{R}_{1/3}}[crit(C \vee \overline{\rho}) = S] \leq (2/3)^{n^2}$ for any C and any S of size between n^2 and $\ell n/2$. Though the bound for a single S is of the form we want, the number of such S is huge, so a simple union bound over all choices of S is insufficient to derive the bound we need. Nonetheless, we can show a bound very close to this one for the probability that $crit(C \vee \overline{\rho})$ is *any* medium sized set. We also generalize it to show bounds on the probability that, after applying ρ, k clauses appear from k different $\mathcal{L}_i$

DEFINITION 3.11. *Let S denote a connected subset of the vertices V. Define $S_i := S \cap V_i$ and $s_i := |S_i|/|V_i|$. We say that*

- *i is a* full column *of S if $s_i = 1$, an* empty column *if $s_i = 0$, and a* partial column *otherwise;*
- *i is a* transition point *of S if $i-1, i, i+1, i+2 \in \{1, \ldots, \ell\}$ are columns, and either both $s_i \geq 1/2$ and $s_{i+1} \leq 1/2$, or both $s_i \leq 1/2$ and $s_{i+1} \geq 1/2$;*
- *S has a transition point with signature (i, A_0, A_1, A_2, A_3) if i is a transition point of S, $S_{i-1} = A_0$, $S_i = A_1$, $S_{i+1} = A_2$, and $S_{i+2} = A_3$.*

The transition point concept is useful because of the following lemma which says that the existence of a transition point for a set S implies that S has a large boundary.

LEMMA 3.12 (TRANSITION POINT LEMMA). *If i is a transition point of S, then $|\delta(S)| \geq n^2$. Moreover, for any signature (i, A_0, A_1, A_2, A_3), there exists a set of at least n^2 edges, $E^* \subseteq E_{i-1} \cup E_i \cup E_{i+1}$, depending only on (i, A_0, A_1, A_2, A_3), such that if S has a transition point with signature (i, A_0, A_1, A_2, A_3) then $E^* \subseteq \delta(S)$.*

There are only $\ell \cdot 2^{O(n)}$ possible signatures, but, by this lemma, the probability that $crit(C \vee \overline{\rho})$ has a transition point with a specific signature is at most $2^{-\Omega(n^2)}$ for any particular C, so this will allow us to obtain a very strong upper bound on the probability that C has any transition point at all.

PROOF OF TRANSITION POINT LEMMA. Let S be a connected set of vertices and have a transition point with signature (i, A, B, C, D). We would like to find, from this information only, a set of E^* edges on the boundary of S. We write $a = |A|/n$, $b = |B|/n$, $c = |C|/n$ and $d = |D|/n$. Without loss of generality we can assume that $b \geq 1/2, c \leq 1/2$.

We will find a set of n^2 edges in the columns E^{i-1}, E^i, E^{i+1} on the boundary of any S with this signature. Since the signature determines exactly which edges in these columns are boundary edges, and the graph between each pair of layers is the complete bipartite graph, only the numbers (a, b, c, d) matter. The number of boundary edges may be computed exactly as

$$n^2(a(1-b)+b(1-a)+b(1-c)+c(1-b)+c(1-d)+d(1-c)) .$$

However,

$$\begin{aligned} a(1-b) + b(1-a) &= a(1-2b) + b \\ &= 1 - b + (2b-1)(1-a) \\ &\geq 1 - b \qquad \text{since } b \geq 1/2 \end{aligned}$$

and

$$\begin{aligned} c(1-d) + d(1-c) &= c + d(1-2c) \\ &\geq c \qquad \text{since } c \leq 1/2. \end{aligned}$$

So, the expression above is at least

$$\begin{aligned} n^2(1-b+b(1-c)+c(1-b)+c) &= n^2(1+2c-2bc) \\ &= n^2 + n^2 2c(1-b) \\ &\geq n^2 \end{aligned}$$

as claimed. □

In the informal argument that medium sized sets of vertices have at least n^2 edges on their boundaries, we identified two cases to handle – those with many partial columns and those with few. If the set is in the right size range and has few partial columns, it can be shown to have both a full column and an empty column, and it is easy to see that such sets must have a transition point somewhere between the full and empty column. We handle the other case, with many partial columns, by showing that it holds conditioned on the graph being connected.

LEMMA 3.13. *For any clause C and restriction ρ, if $CONN(\rho)$ holds then $|C|$ is at least the number of partial columns in $crit(C \vee \overline{\rho})$.*

PROOF. Let $S = crit(C \vee \overline{\rho})$. If i is a partial column of S, then both $S_i \cup S_{i+1}$ and its complement in $V_i \cup V_{i+1}$ are nonempty. If $CONN(\rho)$ holds, then these two sets of vertices are adjacent, and in fact there is an edge between them that is not assigned by ρ. By Corollary 2.12, all edges on the boundary of the critical set must be assigned, so C must assign some edge in E_i. Thus C contains at least one edge for each partial column of S. □

Now we will show our bound for the probability that multiple clauses come to occupy many separated medium complexity levels. We will use the separation in complexity levels to argue that there must be many transition points for these clauses rather than just one. This will be based on bounding the number of distinct endpoints of sets of intervals of increasing size on a line or circle for which we will use the following lemma proved in Section 4.

LEMMA 3.14. *Suppose that we have k points of the n point circle $a_i \in Z_n$, and k natural numbers $d_i \leq n/2$, determining k intervals on the circle $(a_i, b_i = a_i + d_i)$ each of length d_i. Let U denote the set of endpoints of these intervals; i.e., $U := \bigcup_i \{a_i, b_i\}$. It follows that*

1. *if $\forall i,\ d_{i+1} \geq 2d_i$, and $1 \leq d_1, d_k \leq n/2$ then $|U| \geq k+1$.*
2. *Further, if for some a, $k \cdot a < d_1$, then there exists a subset U' of U such that $|U'| \geq k+1$ and any two points of U' are at distance greater than a from each other.*

The same argument we give can also be used to prove a more general statement, but we limit ourselves to the following for simplicity.

PROOF OF LEMMA 3.8. If any C_i is as large as kn^2, it has probability at most $(2/3)^{kn^2}$ to survive the restriction and we are done, so suppose that this is not the case. Using Lemma 3.13, we can restrict attention to candidate critical sets S^i that have fewer than $kn^2 \leq n^3/3$ partial columns, containing fewer than $n^4/3$ vertices. Because $t_0 = n^4$, for each S^i there must be many full columns. There are also many empty columns since the largest critical sets in medium complexity levels have size at most $\ell n/2$.

So, we can already see that each S^i has a transition point. What we would like to see is that there must be at least k transition points among all of them, and that these transition points are all far apart from each other. We use Lemma 3.14 for this.

For each S^i, let a_i denote the first column from the left so that $|S^i_{a_i}| \geq n/2$, and let b_i similarly denote the first such column from the right. So long as b_i is not one of $\{1, 2, \ell-1, \ell\}$, it is a transition point, and the same is true for $a_i - 1$. So, it suffices to prove that $\left|\bigcup_i \{a_i - 1, b_i\} \setminus \{1, 2, \ell-1, \ell\}\right| \geq k$. In fact it suffices to meet the requirements for the strong form of Lemma 3.14 with $a \geq 3$, since then at most one point of U' is in the set $\{1, 2, \ell-1, \ell\}$.

Let d_i denote the difference $b_i - (a_i - 1)$. Since C_i has medium complexity level ℓ_i, d_i is at least the number of full columns, i.e., $d_i \geq 2^{\ell_i} t_0/n - n^3/3$. We can also upper bound the total number of full and partial columns as $2^{\ell_i+1} t_0/n + n^3/3$, which is an upper bound on d_i, since S^i is connected. Since $\ell_{i+1} \geq \ell + 3$ and $t_0 \geq n^3$, we have $2^{\ell_{i+1}} \geq 4 \cdot 2^{\ell_i + 1}$ and

$$\frac{d_{i+1}}{d_i} \geq \frac{4 - \frac{1}{3}}{1 + \frac{1}{3}} > 2\,.$$

Further, $d_k \leq \ell n/4 + n^3/3 < \ell n/2$, as required, and $d_1 \geq \frac{2}{3}n^3$, while $k < n/3$ implies $3k+1 < n+1 << d_1$. Therefore, Lemma 3.14 may be applied to say that there are k distinct transition points that are far apart.

If we fix a particular sequence of signatures for these transition points then the Transition Point Lemma implies that there is a fixed set E' of kn^2 edges, which depends only on the signatures, contained in $\bigcup_{i=1}^{k} \delta(C_i \vee \overline{\rho})$, consisting of the union of the k disjoint sets of edges for each transition point. As in the proof of Lemma 3.10, any such edge must either be set by ρ, or appear in some C_i and hence cannot be set by ρ to violate that C_i. Each such event occurs with probability at most $2/3$ and therefore, by the independence over edges, the total probability is at most $(2/3)^{kn^2}$. The number of sequences of k signatures is at most $(\ell \cdot 2^{4n})^k$ and the bound follows. □

4. ENDPOINTS OF INTERVALS

This section is devoted to the proof of Lemma 3.14.

Suppose that we have a collection of k intervals on the line. How many distinct endpoints are there? If nothing else is known about the intervals, there can be as few as $\mathbf{O}(\sqrt{k})$ endpoints. However, if each interval is at least twice as long as the interval before it, then intuitively the intervals cannot be packed together so nicely; we will see that under this assumption there are at least $k+1$ distinct endpoints.

Although we only care about the line, in Lemma 3.14 it is more convenient to analyze the case of the circle.

PROOF OF LEMMA 3.14. Suppose that we have k points of the n point circle $a_i \in Z_n$, and k natural numbers $d_i \leq n/2$, determining k intervals on the circle $(a_i, b_i = a_i + d_i)$ each of length d_i. Let U denote the set of endpoints

$$U := \bigcup_i \{a_i, b_i\}\,.$$

Suppose that $d_{i+1} \geq 2d_i$ for all i and $1 \leq d_1, d_k \leq n/2$. Let us define a graph G on vertex set is U, and for each i, an edge from a_i to b_i. Thus there are k total edges. For the first claim, the strategy is to show that this graph is a forest, and hence has at least $k+1$ vertices. To show the second claim, we will show a process which constructs an acceptable set of $k+1$ vertices.

We will still use the terms "distance" and "displacement" to refer to distances in the circle.

Consider any walk in G which does not use any edges more than once. (Note that this is not the same as a path, as it may include cycles.) The total displacement as we move along from vertex to vertex can be written

$$\sum_{i \in S} \pm d_i$$

where S is the set of indices corresponding to edges appearing on the walk.

By induction on $|S|$, we see that for any nonempty S

$$\sum_{i \in S, i < \max S} d_i \leq d_{\max S} - d_1.$$

The base case is trivial, and if the claim holds for S, we may add $d_{\max S}$ to both sides, and we can apply the assumption $2d_{\max S} \leq d_{\max S+1} \leq d_{s'}$ for any $s' > \max S$, and so deduce the claim for $S \cup \{s'\}$, thus the inductive hypothesis also holds.

Suppose S is nonempty. By the triangle inequality,

$$d_1 \leq \left|\sum_{i \in S} \pm d_i\right| \leq 2d_{\max S} - d_1 \leq n - d_1\,,$$

using the $d_k \leq n/2$ assumption.

Now we can deduce the first claim. Suppose the graph contains a cycle. Then there is a walk in G as before which starts and ends at the same vertex, thus the total displacement is 0 $\mod n$. But since the $1 \le d_1$, the above inequality contradicts this. Thus G contains no cycles and hence is a forest with k edges – this implies there are at least $k+1$ vertices, or $|U| \ge k+1$ as desired.

To see the second claim, we will show a greedy algorithm to find U'.

1. Begin with $U' := \emptyset$. We will process the components of the graph in some order. The first one we can just add entirely to U'.
2. While a component we have not yet processed contains some vertex v within a of anything in U', choose such a v and add every other vertex in that component C_v to U'.
3. If all of the remaining components have every vertex at distance greater than a from U', call the algorithm recursively on the remaining unprocessed components.

Our first observation is that the algorithm omits at most one vertex from any component from U', and for at least one component omits none. Since a forest on k edges and c components has at least $k+c$ vertices, U' will always contain at least $k+c-(c-1) = k+1$ vertices at the end.

It suffices to show the algorithm never adds any two vertices at distance less than a to U'. Call such a pair of vertices an "unsafe pair". The idea is that when $d_1 > k \cdot a$, the argument before that G is cycle-free will hold even if we add as many as k unsafe pairs as edges to the graph G, since these new edges can only change the sum above by at most $k \cdot a$, and d_1 is large enough that we can tolerate that. Our strategy is to view the $(k-1)$ unsafe pairs identified in step 2 as edges which we add to G. For any vertices of U' which become connected by this, we will argue that the path connecting them contains at least one original edge of G and so the previous calculation shows their distance is at least a. For any vertices which were not connected by this, we will see that they could not have formed an unsafe pair – this can only happen when step 3 occurs, and we will handle this scenario as follows.

It suffices to assume that step (3) never happens. When step 3 happens, there are no unsafe pairs between the remaining components and the U' obtained from the components processed already. If the algorithm didn't add any unsafe pairs when run just on the first group of components, and also doesn't add any unsafe pairs when just run on the second group of components, it will succeed when run on all of the components, so we may break up the current instance of the problem into two subinstances and restrict attention to these subinstances. Appealing to this argument sufficiently many times, it suffices to show correctness in cases where step (3) never occurs. (To make this completely precise, one could remove the arbitrary choice in the definition of the algorithm by assigning a priority to each component, and specify that the algorithm deterministically chooses to process the highest priority component with an unsafe pair to U'. Then, when we split an instance on which step (3) occurs into two subinstances, the subinstances inherit a priority ordering, and the U' returned by the algorithm on the initial instance will be exactly the union of the U''s returned by the algorithm on the two subinstances, so correctness indeed follows from correctness of the runs on the two subinstances.)

Therefore without loss, step 1 occurs once and then step 2 occurs $k-1$ times. When step 2 occurs, by definition there is some vertex $u \in U'$ and some vertex v which is chosen so that uv is an unsafe pair, and component C_v is the next processed component. Let G' be the graph G, plus an edge for each such uv. The edge uv connects the component C_v to the previously processed components. When we start, G is a forest, and at the end, every component has been processed, so G' is a tree.

Now consider a walk in G' which does not use any edge more than once. As long as it contains at least one edge of G, by the triangle inequality the total displacement is between $d_1 - (k-1) \cdot a$ and $n - (d_1 - (k-1) \cdot a)$, so since $d_1 > k \cdot a$, the start and end point of such a walk do not form an unsafe pair.

The tree G' contains a path connecting every $u, u' \in U'$, so it suffices to see that this path contains at least one edge of G. What vertices are connected using only the edges of G' that don't appear in G? By construction this set of edges forms a collection of stars with vertices of U' at the centers, since for each unsafe pair found in step 2, the vertex v corresponds to a distinct component, and v may not be chosen as u at some later step since it is not added to U'. Thus for no two distinct points of U' does the unique path in G' consist only of unsafe pair edges – each such pair has a path in G' with at least one edge of G, so they do not form an unsafe pair. □

5. TIME-SPACE TRADEOFF FOR REGULAR RESOLUTION

For regular resolution, it is possible to use a fairly different argument to get super-polynomial size lower bounds for space that is polynomially large for Tseitin formulas on a family of constant-degree graphs (and hence constant clause size) in contrast to the large degree of the graphs we used in the general case. Though not qualitatively different, the tradeoffs themselves are slightly sharper than in the general case and also apply in the case of substantially larger space bounds (up to sub-exponential space rather than up to quasipolynomial space).

To achieve this, the random restriction argument from the case of general resolution is replaced with a random adversary argument and the analysis now takes a top-down flavor. This gives much more freedom in the choice of hard graphs since we no require connectivity under random restrictions that we needed in the general resolution case. We still must use graphs that are "long and skinny" as before. For simplicity and for applicability to a wider range of space bounds than for the graphs we used previously, we will choose the $n \times \ell$ grid graph, $G_{n,\ell}$ of n rows and ℓ columns.

We first note that the Tseitin tautologies over grid graphs have short regular resolution refutations.

PROPOSITION 5.1. *Any Tseitin tautology over $G_{n,\ell}$ has a regular resolution refutation size at most $32\ell n \cdot 2^n$ and space at most $2^{n+1} + 5 + |\{axioms\}|$, and $|\{axioms\}| \le 8\ell n$.*

PROOF. $G_{n,\ell}$ has cut width $n+1$ and maximum degree 4 so this follows from Lemma 2.7. The number of axioms is easily counted as $\le 2^{d-1}|V|$. □

By contrast, the main result that we will prove in this section is that if the space allowed is reduced significantly below 2^n, and ℓ is not too large then such a formula requires regular resolution refutations of superpolynomial size.

THEOREM 5.2. *For any ℓ such that $n^3 \le \ell < 2^n$, any size T and space S regular resolution refutation of the Tseitin tautology on a n by ℓ grid must satisfy*

$$T \geq \left(\frac{2^{(1-o(1))n}}{S}\right)^{\frac{\log_2 L}{2\log_2\log_2 L}}$$

where $L = \log_2(\ell/(4n^2))$.

To prove Theorem 5.2, we will begin with a regular resolution refutation Π, and repeatedly subdivide Π into polynomially many epochs, at each point choosing an epoch in which enough "progress" happens that we may continue subdividing the epoch. The process peters out after $\mathbf{O}\left(\frac{\log L}{\log\log L}\right)$ subdivisions.

In the next three subsections we develop the main technical tools that allow us to derive this lower bound. In section 5.1 we modify the complexity measure for clauses from general resolution to a complexity measure specific to regular resolution. This measure has the advantage of growing monotonically with the inferences in the proof, which makes it a much more precise tool. We use this measure to define the complexity levels that are the indicators for progress through the proof. In section 5.2 we describe a probabilistic adversary that follows the inferences in the proof. One can think of this adversary as observing the progress of the proof. We show that the probability that adversary reaches a clause (or set of clauses) can be analyzed in terms of a potential function Φ applied to a set of edges associated with that clause (or set of clauses). Φ turns out to be the rank function of a certain matroid and we characterize several properties of Φ that we need in the overall argument. In section 5.3, we give fairly straightforward proofs that the potential Φ will be large for sets that correspond to clauses of many different medium complexity levels.

In section 5.4, we put the pieces together and give the inductive argument that yields Theorem 5.2. The base case shows simply that any sub-epoch in the proof in which the adversary has a reasonable probability of visiting clauses of many different complexity levels must have length exponential in the width n of the grid graph. The inductive step shows that if one divides an epoch of the proof through which the adversary passes into sub-epochs then either the adversary visits clauses of many different complexity levels at the boundaries between sub-epochs or the adversary sees a large fraction of the overall progress in complexity levels within a single sub-epoch. If the space is small then the first case is very unlikely; if the second case holds then we can subdivide that sub-epoch and apply the argument recursively.

5.1 Read-once branching programs and common information

It is well known (cf. [17]) that a resolution refutation yields a branching program for the "clause search problem" and this branching program is read-once if and only if the resolution refutation is regular. In this construction, we start with the proof DAG and labeled the edges by the following rule: If $C \vee D$ is derived by resolving $C \vee x$ with $D \vee \neg x$, then the node for clause $C \vee D$ is also labeled by a query to x, the edge directed from $C \vee D$ to $C \vee x$ is labeled $x = 0$, and the edge from $C \vee D$ to $D \vee \neg x$ is labeled $x = 1$. Like the proof DAG, the single-source, or root, of the branching program is the contradiction $\perp$ and the sinks, or leaves, are the input clauses or axioms. Note that paths p in this branching program correspond to partial assignments. We identify a regular resolution proof with both its DAG and its associated branching program. The following is immediate from the definition.

PROPOSITION 5.3. *Every node reached by an assignment starting at the root of the branching program for any regular resolution proof Π is labeled by a clause that is falsified by that assignment.*

For purposes of a top-down analysis, more relevant than the literals appearing in a clause (node) in a proof is a closely related concept we call its *common information*. A similar definition has appeared previously, e.g. in [24].

DEFINITION 5.4. *For C a clause in a regular resolution refutation Π, define the* (common) information *at C in Π to be a partial assignment $I_{C,\Pi}$ in terms of the proof Π as follows:*

If every directed path in Π from the contradiction $\perp$ to C contains the label $x = 1$, then $I_{C,\Pi}$ assigns $x = 1$; if every such path contains the label $x = 0$, then $I_{C,\Pi}$ assigns $x = 0$; Otherwise $I_{C,\Pi}$ does not assign x.

Note that, by definition, $I_{C,\Pi}$ assigns C to false since every literal in C must be made false on any path between C and $\perp$. The regularity assumption permits us to prove the following crucial consistency lemma.

LEMMA 5.5. *Let τ be a Tseitin tautology on graph G with regular resolution refutation Π. If a clause C is reachable from the root $\perp$ by a path p in Π consistent with a critical assignment, then $crit_\tau(I_{C,\Pi}) = crit_\tau(p)$, and p and $I_{C,\Pi}$ assign all edges incident to this critical set identically.*

PROOF. Let p be such a path from $\perp$ to C, consistent with a critical assignment σ with bad vertex b. Let e be any edge incident to b, and p' be any other path in Π from $\perp$ to C. Then we claim that p, p' assign e identically.

The assignment σ corresponds to a root-to-leaf path in Π extending p. Let q denote the portion of this path which occurs after it reaches C, so that pq is the entire root-to-leaf path. By the regularity assumption, $p'q$ is also consistent with some assignment, and by correctness of the proof, $p'q$ violates the axiom labeling the leaf that $p'q$ and pq both reach, which is also violated by pq. e is a variable of this axiom, so $p'q(e) = pq(e)$, and both do assign e. If p assigns e, then q does not assign e, so p' must assign e, and in the same way as p does. If p does not assign e, then q must, so p' cannot, by the regularity assumption.

By definition of $I_{C,\Pi}$, we conclude that $I_{C,\Pi}$ and p assign all edges incident to $crit_\tau(p)$ identically, and so $crit_\tau(I_{C,\Pi}) \subseteq crit_\tau(p)$ since $I_{C,\Pi}$ and p assign the boundary of $crit_\tau(p)$ in the same way and with the same parity. But since p also extends $I_{C,\Pi}$ then $crit_\tau(p) \subseteq crit_\tau(I_{C,\Pi})$, and so they are equal. □

For the rest of this section we will drop the subscript τ because there will be one fixed τ for our arguments. For regular resolution, our measure of complexity for a clause C will be $|crit(I_{\Pi,C})|$.

DEFINITION 5.6. *Let* $\mathcal{L}_i^* = \{C \in \Pi : 2^i n^3 < |crit(I_{\Pi,C})| \leq 2^{i+1}n^3\}$ *for* $0 \leq i \leq \log_2(\ell/(4n^2)) - 1$. *Each* $\mathcal{L}_i^*$ *represents a different complexity level. We say that a clause of* Π *has* medium complexity *if it is in one of the* $\mathcal{L}_i^*$.

The following is a key property that makes regular resolution refutations much each easier for us to analyze than general resolution ones, namely that the complexity of clauses decreases monotonically throughout the proof, insofar as the critical assignments are concerned.

LEMMA 5.7. *Let* Π *be a regular resolution refutation of a Tseitin tautology. If there is a path consistent with a critical assignment from the root to clause* C *to* D *in* Π *then* $crit(I_{D,\Pi}) \subseteq crit(I_{C,\Pi})$

PROOF. By Lemma 5.5, $crit(I_{C,\Pi}) = crit(p)$ for any path p from the root to C consistent with a critical assignment. Let q be any path from C to D in Π. Again, $crit(I_{D,\Pi}) = crit(pq)$, and the result follows immediately from the fact that by definition $crit$ is monotonically decreasing over partial assignments and that pq extends p. □

5.2 A probabilistic adversary

For this section we fix a connected graph $G = (V, E)$, a Tseitin tautology τ over G, and a regular resolution refutation Π of τ. Rather than fix a distribution over partial assignments or total assignments depending only on G as we did for general resolution, for regular resolution we can use a probabilistic adversary which navigates Π to define a distribution on assignments that depends on Π itself.

DEFINITION 5.8. *The* probabilistic adversary A_Π *responds to the queries in the proof* Π *in the following way. Let* σ *be the assignment that the adversary has given to the queries already asked, and suppose that* Π *queries edge* e *at the proof node reached by following the path labeled* σ,

- *If* e *is not a cut edge of* $G|\sigma$, *then the adversary responds randomly.*
- *If* e *is a cut edge of* $G|\sigma$, *then the adversary responds so as to maximize the size of the critical vertex set, breaking ties arbitrarily. More precisely, letting* σ_0 *and* σ_1 *denote the extensions of* σ *that assign 0 or 1 to* e, *respectively, the adversary answers according to the larger of* $|crit(\sigma_0)|$ *and* $|crit(\sigma_1)|$.

It is notable that our adversary strategy is very similar to one used in studying Prover-Delayer games and lower bounds for tree-like resolution as in [6, 26, 25].

The sizes of the critical sets associated with the clauses visited by the adversary satisfy some basic properties analogous to ones shown in Proposition 2.14 and Lemma 2.15 for general resolution, as well as an extra monotonicity property.

PROPOSITION 5.9. *Let* p *be any root-leaf path in* Π *in the support of the distribution induced by* A_Π *and let* $C_0 = \bot, C_1, \ldots, C_r$ *be the clauses labeling the nodes of* p *in order.*

1. $crit(I_{\bot,\Pi}) = V$.
2. $|crit(I_{C_r,\Pi})| = 1$.
3. $|crit(I_{C_{i+1},\Pi})| \leq |crit(I_{C_i,\Pi})|$ *for every* i *with* $0 \leq i < r$.
4. $|crit(I_{C_{i+1},\Pi})| \geq |crit(I_{C_i,\Pi})|/2 > 0$ *for every* i *with* $0 \leq i < r$.

PROOF. Let p_i be the partial assignment given by the length i prefix of path p. Observe that $crit(I_{C_i,\Pi}) = crit(p_i)$. The first two are immediate, the third follows immediately because by definition $crit$ is monotone decreasing over partial assignments and the fourth follows from sub-additivity of $crit$ and the maximizing choice of the adversary. □

COROLLARY 5.10. *For any* t *with* $1 \leq t \leq |V|/2$, *the path taken by adversary* A_π *must pass through a clause* C *with* $t < |crit(I_{C,\Pi})| \leq 2t$. *In particular, the path taken by* A_π *must pass through a clause from every* $\mathcal{L}_i^*$.

To make use of the probability distribution given by the adversary, we will need to understand the probability that the adversary reaches a given in Π, as well as the conditional probability of reaching a clause given that the adversary has already followed some partial path Π. The following measure will allow us to bound these probabilities.

DEFINITION 5.11. *Let* $\#(H)$ *denote the number of connected components of a subgraph* H *of* G. *Define a function* Φ *on (pairs of) subsets of the edges* E *of* G *by*

- $\Phi(A|B) = |A\backslash B| - \#(G|(A \cup B)) + \#(G|B)$, *for* A, $B \subseteq E$, *and*
- $\Phi(A) = \Phi(A|\emptyset)$ *for* $A \subseteq E$.

For ρ, σ, *both partial assignments to the edges of* G, *we write* $\Phi(\rho|\sigma)$ *for* $\Phi(dom(\rho)|dom(\sigma))$.

The following gives some simple intuition about Φ.

PROPOSITION 5.12. *Let* $A \subseteq E$. *For any edge set* A *and edge* $e \notin A$,

$$\Phi(A \cup \{e\}) - \Phi(A) = \begin{cases} 0 & \text{if } e \text{ cuts } G|A \\ 1 & \text{if not.} \end{cases}$$

PROOF. By definition,

$$\begin{aligned} &\Phi(A \cup \{e\}) - \Phi(A) \\ &= |A \cup \{e\}| - |A| - \#(G|A \cup \{e\}) + \#(G|A) \\ &= 1 - \#(G|A \cup \{e\}) + \#(G|A). \end{aligned}$$

and the result follows immediately. □

DEFINITION 5.13. *We call a set of edges in* G independent *if and only if their removal from* G *does not increase the number of connected components of* G.

COROLLARY 5.14. $\Phi(A)$ *is the maximum size of an independent set* $A' \subseteq A$.

PROOF. Apply the Proposition 5.12 inductively starting with $\Phi(\emptyset)$ and adding the edges in A one at a time beginning with the edges in A'. □

REMARK 5.15. $\Phi(A)$ *is the rank of edge set* A *in the* cut matroid *(also known as on the* bond matroid*) of the graph* G. *This is the dual of the more well-known cycle matroid of* G. *The independent sets of the cut matroid are those sets of edges that do not separate any component of the graph, as in our definition. The rank of a set of edges* A *in the cut matroid is the the cardinality of the largest independent* $A' \subseteq A$. *In the literature,* $\Phi(\cdot|\cdot)$ *is called the* conditional rank *of the cut matroid.*

Our reason for using this definition is the following lemma, which is the key to understanding the distribution on assignments given by our probabilistic adversary arguments. Though the formulation looks fairly different from the arguments based on the sizes of boundaries of critical sets that we used in the case of general resolution, it deals with a similar property. In particular, in the case of a connected set of vertices S (such as a critical set) whose complement also happens to be connected, it is easy to check that $\Phi(\delta(S)) = |\delta(S)| - 1$.

LEMMA 5.16. *[Main Adversary Lemma] Let Π be a regular resolution refutation of a Tseitin tautology. For any clause C in Π of with information $I_{C,\Pi} = \rho$, the probability that adversary A_Π reaches C conditioned on following a path labeled σ is at most $2^{-\Phi(\rho|\sigma)}$. In particular, the probability that the adversary A_Π reaches a clause C with information $I_{C,\Pi} = \rho$ is at most $2^{-\Phi(\rho)}$.*

PROOF. For a fixed ρ, we prove the bound by induction on the length of σ, with large σ as the base case.

If the assignment given by σ contains ρ, the result holds trivially, since the bounding expression is 1. Similarly, for σ not consistent with ρ the probability of the event is 0, so the bound holds.

Suppose inductively that the result is true for every assignment strictly larger than σ. If the adversary has followed the path labeled σ in Π, at which point edge e is resolved on, then, by the induction hypothesis, the bound holds for $\sigma_0 = \sigma \cup \{e = 0\}$ and $\sigma_1 = \sigma \cup \{e = 1\}$. We always have $\Phi(\rho|\sigma_0) = \Phi(\rho|\sigma_1)$ since σ_0 and σ_1 make assignments to the same set of edges.

Suppose that $\Phi(\rho|\sigma) \le \Phi(\rho|\sigma_0)$. Since σ is not as large as ρ, the probability that the adversary reaches C after following σ is a weighted average of the probabilities that the adversary reaches C after following σ_0 and σ_1, respectively. Therefore, by induction, the conditional probability of reaching C after following σ is at most $2^{-\Phi(\rho|\sigma_0)} \le 2^{-\Phi(\rho|\sigma)}$ as required.

Suppose now that $\Phi(\rho|\sigma_0) < \Phi(\rho|\sigma)$. There are two subcases, depending on whether e is assigned by ρ. Consider first the subcase that e is assigned by ρ. Then $\mathrm{dom}(\rho) \cup \mathrm{dom}(\sigma) = \mathrm{dom}(\rho) \cup \mathrm{dom}(\sigma_0)$. Therefore, since $\Phi(\rho|\sigma_0) < \Phi(\rho|\sigma)$, we have

$$\begin{aligned} 0 &< \Phi(\rho|\sigma) - \Phi(\rho|\sigma_0) \\ &= |\mathrm{dom}(\rho)\backslash\mathrm{dom}(\sigma)| - |\mathrm{dom}(\rho)\backslash\mathrm{dom}(\sigma_0)| \\ &\quad -[\#(G|(\rho\cup\sigma)) - \#(G|(\rho\cup\sigma_0))] \\ &\quad +\#(G|\sigma) - \#(G|\sigma_0) \\ &= 1 + \#(G|\sigma) - \#(G|\sigma_0). \end{aligned} \tag{1}$$

Hence $\#(G|\sigma) - \#(G|\sigma_0) > -1$. Therefore, since $\#(G|\sigma) \le \#(G|\sigma_0)$ we must have $\#(G|\sigma) = \#(G|\sigma_0)$, which means that e is not a cut edge of $G|\sigma$. Moreover, (1) implies that $\Phi(\rho|\sigma_0) = \Phi(\rho|\sigma) - 1$. By the definition of the adversary, the value the adversary assigns to e is chosen randomly in this case. However, one of σ_0 and σ_1 is inconsistent with ρ because ρ assigns some particular value to e. So, without loss of generality,

$$\Pr_{adv}[\rho|\sigma] = \frac{1}{2}\Pr_{adv}[\rho|\sigma_0] \le 2^{-\Phi(\rho|\sigma)},$$

as desired. Now consider the subcase that e is not assigned by ρ. In this case we follow the definitions of $\Phi(\rho|\sigma_0)$ and $\Phi(\rho|\sigma)$ and observe that $|\mathrm{dom}(\rho)\backslash\mathrm{dom}(\sigma_0)| = |\mathrm{dom}(\rho)\backslash\mathrm{dom}(\sigma)|$. Since $\Phi(\rho|\sigma_0) < \Phi(\rho|\sigma)$ we must have

$$\begin{aligned} 0 &< \Phi(\rho|\sigma) - \Phi(\rho|\sigma_0) \\ &= -[\#(G|(\rho\cup\sigma)) - \#(G|(\rho\cup\sigma_0))] + \#(G|\sigma) - \#(G|\sigma_0) \end{aligned} \tag{2}$$

and hence

$$\#(G|(\rho\cup\sigma_0)) - \#(G|(\rho\cup\sigma)) > \#(G|\sigma_0) - \#(G|\sigma).$$

The left hand side is equal to 1 or 0 indicating whether e cuts $G|(\rho\cup\sigma)$, and the right hand side indicates whether e cuts $G|\sigma$. The inequality implies the former is one and the latter is zero, hence e is not a cut edge of $G|\sigma$ but it is a cut edge of $G|(\rho\cup\sigma)$. Plugging these facts back in (2), we see that the potential drop is exactly one; that is, $\Phi(\rho|\sigma_0) = \Phi(\rho|\sigma) - 1$. Again, by the definition of the adversary, e is assigned randomly here.

CLAIM 5.17. *Only one of σ_0, σ_1 can permit the adversary to reach ρ.*

Suppose to the contrary that π_0 and π_1 extend σ_0 and σ_1 respectively, each corresponding to paths that can be travelled by the adversary and that meet at the target clause C with information ρ. Then, $crit(\pi_0) = crit(\pi_1) \neq \emptyset$, by Lemma 5.5 and Proposition 5.9 (4). But, by the definition of common information, π_0 and π_1 extend $\sigma_0 \cup \rho$ and $\sigma_1 \cup \rho$ respectively, and by Proposition 2.11 these two assignments have disjoint critical sets since e cuts $G|(\rho\cup\sigma)$. Since by definition $crit$ is monotone decreasing over partial assignments, $crit(\pi_0)$ and $crit(\pi_1)$ are also disjoint, a contradiction.

The claim now implies the bound we need exactly as before, and thus completes the proof. □

If C is a clause and p is a path from the root of Π, it is most convenient to abbreviate the conclusion of the lemma as

$$\Pr_{adv}[C|p] \le 2^{-\Phi(I_{C,\Pi}|p)}.$$

For our superpolynomial bounds we need to use the following properties of Φ, all of which are consequences of Φ being a matroid rank function. While these can be proved easily using matroid theory, we sketch simple proofs for our specific case without relying on matroids.

PROPOSITION 5.18. *For all non-empty sets of edges A, B, and C in G,*

(a) $\Phi(\cdot)$ is non-negative and monotone increasing.

(b) $\Phi(A|B) = \Phi(A\cup B) - \Phi(B)$.

(c) (Non-negativity and Monotonicity) $\Phi(\cdot|\cdot)$ is non-negative, increasing in its first argument, and decreasing in its second argument.

(d) (Chain Rule) $\Phi(A) \le \Phi(A|B) + \Phi(B)$. More generally, $\Phi(A|C) \le \Phi(A|B) + \Phi(B|C)$ when $B \supseteq C$.

(e) (Subadditivity) $\Phi(A\cup B|C) \le \Phi(A|C) + \Phi(B|C)$.

PROOF. Part (a) is immediate from Corollary 5.14. By definition,

$$\begin{aligned} &\Phi(A\cup B) - \Phi(B) \\ &= |A\cup B| - |B| - \#(G|(A\cup B)) + \#(G|B) \\ &= |A\backslash B| - \#(G|(A\cup B)) + \#(G|B) \end{aligned}$$

so part (b) follows. The nonnegativity and monotonicity in the first argument given in (c) follow from (b) and the monotonicity from (a). The monotonicity in the second argument given in (c) follows from (b), Proposition 5.12, and the fact that if e is not a cut edge with respect to $B \supseteq B'$ then e is not a cut edge with respect to B' either. For part (d), since $C \subseteq B$, we have $B \cup C = B$ and $\Phi(A \cup C) \leq \Phi(A \cup B)$ by the monotonicity of Φ. Therefore by (b),

$$\begin{aligned}\Phi(A|C) &= \Phi(A \cup C) - \Phi(C) \\ &\leq \Phi(A \cup B) - \Phi(B) + \Phi(B \cup C) - \Phi(C) \\ &= \Phi(A|B) + \Phi(B|C)\end{aligned}$$

which yields the chain rule. By the chain rule,

$$\Phi(A \cup B|C) \leq \Phi(A \cup B|B \cup C) + \Phi(B \cup C|C) ,$$

but by definition $\Phi(B \cup C|C) = \Phi(B|C)$, and also $\Phi(A \cup B|B \cup C) = \Phi(A|B \cup C)$ which, by monotonicity, is bounded above by $\Phi(A|C)$. Hence subadditivity (e) follows. □

We will also need this fact, specific to cut matroids.

LEMMA 5.19. *[Matroid Cut Argument] Suppose that S is a set of vertices of G, and that $\delta(S) \subseteq B$. Then for any A,*

$$\Phi(A|B) = \Phi(A \sqcap S|B \sqcap S) + \Phi(A \sqcap \overline{S}|B \sqcap \overline{S}) ,$$

where $E' \sqcap V' := \{e \in E' : e \text{ is incident to } V'\}$, for E' a set of edges and V' a set of vertices.

PROOF. We can easily prove this by induction on $|A|$. Suppose that $e \notin A$. We would like to show that when e is added to A, the equality still holds. If $e \in B$, then none of $\Phi(A|B)$, $\Phi(A \sqcap S|B \sqcap S)$, or $\Phi(A \sqcap \overline{S}|B \sqcap \overline{S})$ can change; so, without loss of generality $e \notin B$. This implies that $e \notin \delta(S)$ as well. Without loss of generality, e is adjacent to S but not $\overline{S}$, so the only terms that can change are $\Phi(A|B)$ and $\Phi(A \sqcap S|B \sqcap S)$. It is enough to show that these terms must change in the same way when e is added; so, in fact, it is enough to see that $\Phi(A \cup B)$ changes the same way as $\Phi((A \cup B) \sqcap S)$ does when e is added. In light of Proposition 5.12, this holds because an edge e is a cut edge in a graph G if and only if it is a cut edge in the component containing it. □

5.3 Isoperimetric inequality for grid graphs

In light of Lemma 5.16, for regular resolution we replace the "isoperimetric inequality" used for general resolution which showed that medium sized sets S have have many edges on their boundaries (large $\delta(S)$) by one showing that such sets have large $\Phi(\delta(S))$, i.e. large independent subsets in $\delta(S)$.

For every medium size set of vertices S of $G_{n,\ell}$, we will show that $\delta(S)$ has large rank ($\Phi(\delta(S))$ is large) rather than large cardinality. Moreover, we show that for several medium-sized sets of vertices $S_1 \ldots S_k$ of sufficiently separated cardinalities, the rank of $\bigcup_i \delta(S_i)$ grows linearly with k. We will be able to prove a tight lower bound on these ranks without much more difficulty, and without giving up much compared to cardinality.

The following is an analog of the properties we proved in the case of general resolution using transition points and Lemma 4 about endpoints of intervals of increasing sizes. The proof here uses the same lemma on intervals but directly uses common information rather than transition points.

LEMMA 5.20. *Let $S_1 \ldots S_k$ be sets of vertices in $G_{n,\ell}$. If $2kn^2 \leq |S_1|$, for each $i \in [k-1]$, $4|S_i| \leq |S_{i+1}|$, and $|S_k| \leq n\ell/4$, then $\Phi(\bigcup_i \delta(S_i)) \geq k(n-1)$.*

PROOF. If any S_i contains $k(n-1)$ partial columns, then each such column contributes a vertical edge to $\bigcup_i \delta(S_i)$, and these vertical edges together form an independent set of the necessary size, so we are done.

If no S_i contains $k(n-1)$ partial columns, then by the size bounds on S_i, each contains a full column, and an empty column. In particular, each S_i contains a horizontal edge in every row. We will show that each row contains at least k edges of $\bigcup_i \delta(S_i)$. Choosing any $n-1$ rows and the k edges from each such row give an independent set of size $k(n-1)$, so this will finish the proof.

Fix a row r. Let a_i be the column number of the leftmost vertex in S_i and in the r-th row, let b_i be the column number of the rightmost such vertex. Then S_i has boundary edges with left endpoints in columns $a_i - 1$ and b_i, provided that these are not 0 or ℓ. Thus all we need to show is that

$$\left|\bigcup_i \{a_i - 1, b_i\} \setminus \{0, \ell\}\right| \geq k .$$

Since 0 and ℓ are the same modulo ℓ, it suffices to show that these intervals meet the conditions for the first part of Lemma 3.14.

Since S_i has fewer then $k(n-1)$ partial columns, $b_i - (a_i - 1) > |S_i|/n - k(n-1)$. On the other hand, the number of full columns in S_i is at most $|S_i|/n$, so $b_i - (a_i - 1) < |S_i|/n + k(n-1)$. Thus the ratio of successive differences is at least

$$\begin{aligned}\frac{b_{i+1} - (a_{i+1} - 1)}{b_i - (a_i - 1)} &> \frac{|S_{i+1}| - kn(n-1)}{|S_i| + kn(n-1)} \\ &\geq \frac{4|S_i| - kn(n-1)}{|S_i| + kn(n-1)} .\end{aligned}$$

Since $|S_i| \geq |S_1| \geq 2kn^2$, the ratio is at least $\frac{7}{3} > 2$ and we can apply Lemma 3.14 as desired. □

It is convenient to have a lower bound on $|S_1|$ that does not depend on k. To do this we need to upper bound ℓ.

COROLLARY 5.21. *Suppose that $\ell \leq 2^n$. Let $S_1 \ldots S_k$ be sets of vertices in $G_{n,\ell}$. If $n^3 \leq |S_1|$, $4|S_i| \leq |S_{i+1}|$ for each i, and $|S_k| \leq n\ell/4$, then $\Phi(\bigcup_i \delta(S_i)) \geq k(n-1)$.*

PROOF. Since $\ell \leq 2^n$, and $|S_1| \geq n^3$, we have $k \leq 1 + \log_4(|S_k|/|S_1|) \leq \log_2 n/2 \leq n/2$ and Lemma 5.20 applies. □

5.4 Regular resolution time-space tradeoff for grid graphs

To prove Theorem 5.2, we will begin with a regular resolution refutation Π, and repeatedly subdivide Π into polynomially many epochs, at each point choosing an epoch in which enough progress happens that we may continue subdividing it. The process peters out after $\mathbf{O}\left(\frac{\log L}{\log \log L}\right)$ steps.

By Corollary 5.10, the adversary path will pass through clauses of every medium complexity level. In this analysis, an epoch in the refutation is viewed as representing a lot of progress if there is a path p to a clause appearing in that epoch such that, conditioned on having followed p, the adversary *probably* reaches a *much smaller* complexity clause by the end of that epoch than it began with. The major technical step is to show how to divide an epoch that represents a significant amount of progress into much smaller epochs, one of which does a comparable amount of work.

LEMMA 5.22. *Let $0 < \epsilon < 1$ and Π be a regular resolution refutation of a Tseitin tautology on the grid graph $G_{n,\ell}$ for $\ell \leq 2^n$. Suppose that p is a path in Π from the root to some clause C. Let $0 \leq \ell_1 < \cdots < \ell_k$ satisfy $\ell_{i+1} \geq \ell_i + 3$ for each $i \in [k]$. If for each $i \in [k]$ there is some $C_i \in \mathcal{L}^*_{\ell_j}$ appearing in Π with $\Pr_{adv}[C_i|p] \geq 2^{-(1-\epsilon)(n-1)}$ then $\Phi(I_{C,\Pi}) \geq k\epsilon(n-1)$.*

PROOF. Fix the choices of ℓ_i and the associated clauses C_i. In order to make it relatively likely to reach each of the C_i from C as in the hypothesis, we show that the extra information at C_i over that at C cannot be too large. On the other hand we can show, using the isoperimetric properties of the grid graph, that the clauses C_i in total have a large amount of information and hence C must also. We start with the latter.

Let $S_i = crit(I_{C_i,\Pi})$ for $i = 1, \ldots, k$ and $S = crit(p)$. Since $\ell_{i+1} \geq \ell_i + 3$ we have $|crit(I_{C_{i+1},\Pi})| \geq 4|crit(I_{C_i,\Pi})|$ and Corollary 5.21 implies that

$$\Phi(\bigcup_i \delta(S_i)) \geq k(n-1) \tag{3}$$

On the other hand, by Lemma 5.16, the hypothesis that $\Pr_{adv}[C_i|p] \geq 2^{-(1-\epsilon)(n-1)}$ implies that $\Phi(I_{C_i,\Pi}|p) \leq (1-\epsilon)(n-1)$ where, as usual, we have identified p with the partial assignment labeling it. Moreover, since $\Pr_{adv}[C_i|p] > 0$, there is some path q_i from C to C_i in Π. Therefore,

$$S_i = crit(I_{C_i,\Pi}) = crit(pq_i) \subseteq crit(p) = S,$$

where the third equality follows from Lemma 5.5 and the containment follows since by definition *crit* is monotone decreasing over partial assignments. Note that Lemma 5.5 also implies that $p \sqcap S = I_{C,\Pi} \sqcap S$ and Corollary 2.12 implies that $\delta(S) \subseteq \mathrm{dom}(p)$. Therefore, we may apply Proposition 5.19 with $B = \mathrm{dom}(p)$ to obtain

$$\begin{aligned}
\Phi(I_{C_i,\Pi}|p) &\geq \Phi(\delta(S_i)|p) && \text{by monotonicity} \\
&= \Phi(\delta(S_i) \sqcap S|p \sqcap S) + \Phi(\delta(S_i) \sqcap \overline{S}|p \sqcap \overline{S}) && \text{by Lemma 5.19} \\
&\geq \Phi(\delta(S_i) \sqcap S|p \sqcap S) && \text{by nonnegativity} \\
&= \Phi(\delta(S_i)|p \sqcap S) && \text{since } S_i \subseteq S \\
&= \Phi(\delta(S_i)|I_{C,\Pi} \sqcap S) && \text{by Lemma 5.5} \\
&\geq \Phi(\delta(S_i)|I_{C,\Pi}) && \text{by monotonicity.}
\end{aligned}$$

It follows that $\Phi(\delta(S_i)|I_{C,\Pi}) \leq (1-\epsilon)(n-1)$ for each $i \in [k]$. Hence, by the subadditivity of Φ given in Proposition 5.18 we have

$$\Phi(\bigcup_i \delta(S_i)|I_{C,\Pi}) \leq (1-\epsilon)k(n-1).$$

On the other hand, by the chain rule of Proposition 5.18 and (3) above, we have

$$\begin{aligned}
\Phi(I_{C,\Pi}) &\geq \Phi(\bigcup_i \delta(S_i)) - \Phi(\bigcup_i \delta(S_i)|I_{C,\Pi}) \\
&\geq k(n-1) - (1-\epsilon)k(n-1) = \epsilon k(n-1)
\end{aligned}$$

which is what we needed to prove. □

The real value of Lemma 5.22 is in its contrapositive. If the proof is small, then by Lemma 5.16, the vast majority of the time the adversary path will only reach clauses C with $\Phi(I_{C,\Pi})$ small. Moreover, there can only be a few medium complexity levels of clauses that the adversary is now relatively likely to visit. For most of the levels, the adversary on visiting C has essentially no greater chance to reach any clauses of that complexity level than the chance when the adversary began at the $\perp$ clause.

With this lemma in hand we can now try to implement the overall plan for the proof of Theorem 5.2. Based on some parameters that we will set later, we first specify a property of clauses, which, by Lemma 5.16 and a union bound, are rarely encountered by an adversary in any refutation that is not too large.

DEFINITION 5.23. *Let $0 < \epsilon < 1$ and m be parameters, which we will fix later. We say that a clause C has* high potential *if $\Phi(I_C) \geq \epsilon m(n-1)$.*

Recall that a refutation is a *sequence* of clauses ending in $\perp$, and that the adversary walks down the proof DAG starting at $\perp$, which involves moving backwards through this sequence, possibly jumping over intermediate clauses. The ordering on the sequence of clauses gives a sequence of *time steps.* Write $time(C)$ for the time step in the proof sequence in which clause C appears. Recall that every arc in the proof DAG that crosses from one time step to an earlier one corresponds to a clause that must be in memory during all intervening time steps. Moreover, by Corollary 5.10, the adversary path must pass through clauses in every $\mathcal{L}^*_i$ starting from large values of i and ending with $i = 0$. For a medium complexity clause C we write $level(C)$ to denote the i such that $C \in \mathcal{L}^*_i$. These properties motivate us to define a way to measure the progress of a portion of the proof.

DEFINITION 5.24. *Let C be a medium complexity clause in Π. Say that a path p in Π from the root to clause C is a (T, gap, δ)-path in Π if, conditioned on following p, with probability at least $1-\delta$, the adversary A_Π*

- *does not reach any high potential clauses, and*
- *reaches a clause C' with $level(C') \leq level(C) - gap$ such that $time(C') \geq time(C) - T$.*

LEMMA 5.25 (INDUCTIVE STEP). *Let Π be a space S regular resolution refutation of a Tseitin tautology on $G_{n,\ell}$ for $n^3 \leq \ell \leq 2^n$. Suppose that p is a (T, gap, δ)-path in Π, $gap \geq 1$, and B is any natural number. Then there exists a (T', gap', δ')-path p' in Π extending p such that*

- *$T' = \lceil T/B \rceil$,*
- *$gap' = \lfloor \frac{gap}{3m} \rfloor$, and*
- *$\delta' = \delta + B \cdot S \cdot 2^{-(1-\epsilon)(n-1)}$.*

PROOF. If $\delta \geq 1$ then the claim is vacuous, so assume that $\delta < 1$. Let C be the clause reached by p. By hypothesis, $level(C) \geq gap$ and C must not have high potential.

Therefore, by the contrapositive of Lemma 5.22 with $k = m$, there do not exist m complexity levels $\ell_1 < \ldots < \ell_m$ with $\ell_{i+1} \geq \ell_i + 3$ such that there is a clause $D_i \in \mathcal{L}^*_{\ell_i}$ with $\Pr_{adv}[C_i|p] \geq 2^{-(1-\epsilon)(n-1)}$. In particular, this means that there do not exist $3m$ distinct complexity levels of clauses $\mathcal{L}_j^*$ such that there is a clause $D \in \mathcal{L}_j^*$ with $\Pr_{adv}[D|p] \geq 2^{-(1-\epsilon)(n-1)}$.

It follows that there exists a sequence of at least $gap' = \lfloor \frac{gap}{3m} \rfloor$ *consecutive* complexity levels between $level(C)$ and $level(C) - gap$, such that for any D in one of these levels, $\Pr[D|p] \leq 2^{-(1-\epsilon)(n-1)}$. Let i' be the largest level in this sequence, and $i' - gap' + 1$ be the smallest.

Divide the T time steps between $time(C)$ and $time(C) - T$, into B epochs of length at most $T' = \lceil T/B \rceil$, and let $\mathcal{M}$ denote the union over the B breakpoints between these epochs (including the start of the first epoch), of the sets of clauses in memory that are of complexity level between i' and $i' - gap' + 1$. By a union bound,

$$\Pr[\text{adversary reaches some } C'' \in \mathcal{M}] \leq B \cdot S \cdot 2^{-(1-\epsilon)(n-1)}.$$

Thus, except with probability at most δ', the adversary A_Π, conditioned on following p,

1. does not hit any high potential clauses,
2. reaches a clause C' with $level(C') \leq level(C) - gap$ and $time(C') \geq time(C) - T$, and
3. does not hit any clause in $\mathcal{M}$.

By averaging, there must exist a path p' extending p and reaching a clause $C' \in \mathcal{L}_{i'}^*$ such that this also holds, except with probability at most δ'.

Then, we claim that p' is a (T', gap', δ')-path. Let C' denote the clause reached by p'. C' falls in some epoch of length at most T'. If no clause in $\mathcal{M}$ is reached and the adversary has followed p', then by the beginning of the epoch containing C', the complexity level of the clause reached by the adversary must be less than or equal to $i' - gap'$. Thus, by construction, p' is indeed a (T', gap', Δ')-path in Π. □

Additionally, whenever we have a (T, gap, δ)-path p in Π with nontrivial gap and δ parameters, we can show that T is nontrivial.

LEMMA 5.26 (BASE CASE). *Let Π be a regular resolution refutation of a Tseitin tautology on $G_{n,\ell}$ for $n^3 \leq \ell \leq 2^n$. If p is a (T, gap, δ)-path in Π with $gap > 3m$, then $T \geq (1-\delta)2^{(1-\epsilon)(n-1)}$.*

PROOF. If $\delta \geq 1$, the claim is trivial. Suppose that $\delta < 1$. Let C be the clause reached by p and consider the clauses in the epoch between time steps $time(C) - T$ and $time(C)$ in Π.

By Lemma 5.22, there exists some complexity level $\mathcal{L}_i^*$ with $i > level(C) - gap$ such that, conditioned on following p, the adversary A_Π

- reaches a clause $C' \in \mathcal{L}_i^*$, with $time(C') \geq step(C) - T$ with probability at least $(1-\delta)$, and
- does not reach any fixed clause D in $\mathcal{L}_i^*$, except with probability at most $2^{-(1-\epsilon)(n-1)}$.

By a union bound over the clauses in this epoch, we conclude that $T \geq (1-\delta)2^{(1-\epsilon)(n-1)}$. □

We now have the ingredients needed to complete the proof of our time-space tradeoff for regular resolution.

PROOF OF THEOREM 5.2. We begin with a regular resolution proof Π of length T that uses space S and refutes a Tseitin tautology on $G_{n,\ell}$. There are $L = \log_2(\ell/(4n^2))$ distinct medium complexity levels of clauses with respect to T. By Corollary 5.10, the path followed by adversary A_Π must pass through clauses with each of these complexity levels.

The outline of the remainder of the proof is as follows:

- First we show, via a union bound over the number of steps in the proof, that there is a (T, L, δ_0)-path in Π for some suitably small δ_0. This step only involves calculating the probability that the adversary passes through some high potential clause. This calculation will require that $\epsilon \cdot m$ not be small compared to $\frac{\log_2 T}{\log_2 n}$.
- Next we choose an appropriate value for B and continually apply the inductive step from Lemma 5.25, until either the accumulated error δ becomes too large, or the gap becomes too small. (We use the same value of B at each step.)
- Finally, some number r of rounds, just before gap has become too small after r rounds, we apply the base case Lemma 5.26 to deduce that the T' at the last step is reasonably large, and that $T \geq B^r \cdot T'$.

Let r denote the number of rounds that we will apply the inductive step and let gap_i denote the value of gap after each round and δ_i denote the value of δ after each round. We will set $gap_0 = L = \log_2(\ell/(4n^2))$. By Lemma 5.16, the probability that A_Π reaches a high potential clause is at most $2^{-\epsilon m(n-1)}$. Therefore if

$$T \cdot 2^{-\epsilon m(n-1)} \leq \delta_0 \tag{4}$$

the adversary must reach some clause of complexity L. Fix any path to such a clause. We obtain that this path is a (T, L, δ_0)-path,

We will choose B so that gap, rather than the error δ, is the limiting resource, so we take

$$r = \frac{\log_2 L}{\log_2(3m)} - 1 \tag{5}$$

Observe that by Lemma 5.25, $\delta_r = \delta_0 + r \cdot B \cdot S \cdot 2^{-(1-\epsilon)(n-1)}$. and applying Lemma 5.26 after the r-th round point yields $T' \geq (1-\delta_r)2^{(1-\epsilon)(n-1)}$. By choosing

$$\delta_0 = \frac{1}{3} \text{ and } B = \frac{1}{3} \cdot \frac{2^{(1-\epsilon)(n-1)}}{S \cdot r},$$

we obtain that $\delta_r = 2/3$ and hence

$$T \geq \frac{1}{3} 2^{(1-\epsilon)(n-1)} \cdot \left(\frac{2^{(1-\epsilon)(n-1)}}{3 \cdot S \cdot r} \right)^r. \tag{6}$$

Together with the $n^3 \leq \ell \leq 2^n$ and the values of δ_0, L, and r, inequalities (4) and (6) provide the only constraints on our parameters. It remains to choose m and ϵ to optimize them and derive a convenient tradeoff lower bound. It is convenient to choose $m = \log_2 L$ so that $r = \log_2 L / \log_2(3m) - 1$ is between $\frac{1}{2} \log_2 L / \log_2 \log_2 L$ and $\log_2 L / \log_2 \log_2 L$. For convenience we also choose ϵ to be $2/\log_2 m = 2/\log_2 \log_2 L$. With these choices, the constraint (4) is satisfied whenever T is at most $\frac{1}{3} 2^{\frac{2 \log_2 L}{\log_2 \log_2 L}(n-1)}$ and this upper bound is strictly larger than the lower bound from (6). On the other hand, since $r \leq \log_2 L / \log_2 \log_2 L$ and $L \leq n$, the $3^{r+1} r^r$ in the denominator of the expression in (6) is at most $2^{(1-\epsilon)(n-1)}$. Hence

$$T \geq \left(\frac{2^{(1-\frac{2}{\log_2 \log_2 L})(n-1)}}{S} \right)^{\frac{\log_2 L}{2 \log_2 \log_2 L}}.$$

Since L is grows at least logarithmically with n, the statement of the theorem follows. □

6. CONCLUSION

We have shown superpolynomial size-space tradeoff lower bounds for resolution proofs which are the first to apply for superlinear space. The two different methods for deriving these bounds are based on a similar recursive decomposition of proofs into epochs. Our results suggest a number of open questions: Can this decomposition framework be applied to show size-space tradeoffs for stronger proof systems? With very small space, resolution size upper bounds for the Tseitin formulas we consider are $\log_2 n$ powers of their size for unlimited space. Is this tight? Can we increase the exponent in our lower bound from $\Theta(\log\log n/\log\log\log n)$ to $\Theta(\log n)$? More generally, is it true that for every k and every formula of size n with a proof of size n^k, there exists a proof in space $O(n)$ with size $n^{O(\log n)}$? with size 2^{n^ϵ} for any $\epsilon > 0$? Finally, our tradeoff lower bound can be viewed as a separation between two search paradigms: dynamic programming vs. divide and conquer. Can we find other settings in which these paradigms may be separated?

7. REFERENCES

[1] M. Alekhnovich, J. Johannsen, T. Pitassi, and A. Urquhart. An exponential separation between regular and general resolution. Technical Report TR01-56, Electronic Colloquium in Computation Complexity, `http://www.eccc.uni-trier.de/eccc/`, 2001.

[2] M. Alekhnovich and A. A. Razborov. Satisfiability, branch-width and tseitin tautologies. In *Proceedings 43nd Annual Symposium on Foundations of Computer Science*, pages 593–603, Vancouver, BC, November 2002. IEEE.

[3] A. Atserias and V. Dalmau. A combinatorial characterization of resolution width. In *Proceedings Eighteenth Annual IEEE Conference on Computational Complexity*, pages 239–247, Aarhus, Denmark, July 2003.

[4] Fahiem Bacchus, Shannon Dalmao, and Toniann Pitassi. Solving #sat and Bayesian inference with backtracking search. *jair*, 34:391–442, 2009.

[5] P. Beame and T. Pitassi. Simplified and improved resolution lower bounds. In *Proceedings 37th Annual Symposium on Foundations of Computer Science*, pages 274–282, Burlington, VT, October 1996. IEEE.

[6] E. Ben-Sasson, R. Impagliazzo, and A. Wigderson. Near-optimal separation of treelike and general resolution. *Combinatorica*, 24(4):585–603, 2004.

[7] E. Ben-Sasson and J. Nordström. Short proofs may be spacious: An optimal separation of space and length in resolution. In *Proceedings 49th Annual Symposium on Foundations of Computer Science*, pages 709–718, Philadelphia,PA, October 2008. IEEE.

[8] E. Ben-Sasson and J. Nordström. Understanding space in resolution: Optimal lower bounds and exponential tradeoffs. Technical Report TR09-034, Electronic Colloquium in Computation Complexity, `http://www.eccc.uni-trier.de/eccc/`, 2009.

[9] E. Ben-Sasson and J. Nordström. Understanding space in proof complexity: Separations and trade-offs via substitutions. Technical Report arXiv:1008.1789, arxiv, 2010.

[10] E. Ben-Sasson and A. Wigderson. Short proofs are narrow – resolution made simple. In *Proceedings of the Thirty-First Annual ACM Symposium on Theory of Computing*, pages 517–526, Atlanta, GA, May 1999.

[11] S. R. Buss. Polynomial-size Frege and resolution proofs of *st*-connectivity and Hex tautologies. *Theoretical Computer Science*, 357(1–3):35–52, 2006.

[12] S. Chen, T. Lou, P. Papakonstantinou, and B. Tang. Width-parameterized SAT: Time-space tradeoffs. Technical Report arXiv:1108.2385, CoRR, 2011.

[13] J. L. Esteban and J. Toran. Space bounds for resolution. In *(STACS) 99: 16th Annual Symposium on Theoretical Aspects of Computer Science*, volume 1563 of *Lecture Notes in Computer Science*, pages 530–539, Trier, Germany, March 1999. Springer-Verlag.

[14] Z. Galil. On the complexity of regular resolution and the Davis-Putnam procedure. *Theoretical Computer Science*, 4:23–46, 1977.

[15] A. Haken. The intractability of resolution. *Theoretical Computer Science*, 39:297–305, 1985.

[16] P. Hertel and T. Pitassi. Exponential time/space speedups for resolution and the pspace-completeness of black-white pebbling. In *Proceedings 48th Annual Symposium on Foundations of Computer Science*, pages 137–149, Berkeley, CA, October 2007. IEEE.

[17] J. Krajíček. *Bounded Arithmetic, Propositional Logic and Complexity Theory*. Cambridge University Press, 1996.

[18] João P. Marques-Silva and Karem A. Sakallah. Grasp – a new search algorithm for satisfiability. In *Proceedings of the International Conference on Computer-Aided Design*, pages 220–227, San Jose, CA, November 1996. ACM/IEEE.

[19] J. Nordström. Narrow proofs may be spacious: Separating space and width in resolution. *SIAM Journal on Computing*, 39(1):59–121, 2009.

[20] J. Nordström. A simplified way of proving trade-off results for resolution. *Information Processing Letters*, 109(18):1030–1035, 2009.

[21] J. Nordström. Pebble games, proof complexity, and time-space trade-offs. *Logical Methods in Computer Science*, 2011. To appear.

[22] J. Nordström and J. Håstad. Towards an optimal separation of space and length in resolution. In *Proceedings of the Fortieth Annual ACM Symposium on Theory of Computing*, pages 701–710, Victoria, BC, May 2008.

[23] Wolfgang J. Paul and Robert E. Tarjan. Time-space trade-offs in a pebble game. *Acta Informatica*, 10:111–115, 1978.

[24] T. Pitassi and R. Raz. Lower bounds for regular

resolution proofs of the weak pigeonhole principle. In *Proceedings of the Thirty-Third Annual ACM Symposium on Theory of Computing*, pages 347–355, Hersonissos, Crete, Greece, July 2001.

[25] Pavel Pudlák. Proofs as games. *American Math. Monthly*, June-July:541–500, 2000.

[26] Pavel Pudlák and Russell Impagliazzo. A lower bound for DLL algorithms for k-SAT. In *Proceedings of the Eleventh Annual ACM-SIAM Symposium on Discrete Algorithms*, pages 128–136, 2000.

[27] Martin Tompa. Time-space tradeoffs for computing functions, using connectivity properties of their circuits. *Journal of Computer and System Sciences*, 20:118–132, April 1980.

[28] G. S. Tseitin. On the complexity of derivation in the propositional calculus. In A. O. Slisenko, editor, *Studies in Constructive Mathematics and Mathematical Logic, Part II*. 1968.

[29] Lintao Zhang, Conor F. Madigan, Matthew H. Moskewicz, and Sharad Malik. Efficient conflict driven learning in a boolean satisfiability solver. In *Proceedings of the International Conference on Computer-Aided Design*, pages 279–285, San Jose, CA, November 2001. ACM/IEEE.

APPENDIX

A. SOME UPPER BOUNDS

For the graphs we will consider, some generic upper bounds follow from bounds on their *cut width*. The first will form the high space upper bound in our time space trade-off result, and the second is a low space upper bound we use to argue about the tightness of the lower bound we get for low space.

DEFINITION A.1. *The* cut width *of a graph G is the smallest W such that there is a linear ordering of the vertices $v_1, \ldots, v_n$ such that, for every $1 \leq t \leq n$, there are no more than W edges crossing the cut $(\{v_1, \ldots, v_t\}, \{v_{t+1}, \ldots, v_n\})$.*

Throughout this section we will use the following well-known fact which we prove for completeness:

The *rank* of a resolution proof is the height of its proof DAG.

OBSERVATION A.2. *Any tree-like proof of rank r has size at most 2^{r+1} and clause space at most $r+1$.*

PROOF. The first is an elementary fact about binary trees of height r. The second, we prove by induction. In the base case, suppose that a proof has rank 1. Then the proof consists of one step and so we need 2 units of space to hold both resolvents. Now suppose the inductive hypothesis holds for rank r, and that we have a proof of rank $r+1$. Suppose C is the last clause of the proof, and A, B are its children. Then the derivations leading up to A, B are rank r. We then derive C as follows – run the derivation of A using r clause space, then A is the only remaining active clause by the tree-like assumption, so clear all of this space and store only A. Then, derive B using r clause space. When we have B, resolve it with A to finish the derivation of C. We only needed $r+1$ space in total, as desired. □

LEMMA A.3 (LEMMA 2.7). *Let G be a graph with n vertices, maximum degree d, and cut width W. Then there is a resolution refutation of a Tseitin tautology on G using $\leq n \cdot 2^{d+W}$ resolution steps, and space $\leq \cdot 2^W + d + 1$, plus space for the initial axioms.*

PROOF. We will specify a sequence of $n+1$ collections $\mathcal{C}_i$ of clauses, such that

1. $\mathcal{C}_1$ is a subset of the axioms .
2. $|\mathcal{C}_i| \leq 2^{W-1}$ for all i .
3. $\mathcal{C}_n = \{\bot\}$.
4. Given a configuration with $\mathcal{C}_i$ and the axioms in memory, we derive any clause in $\mathcal{C}_{i+1}$ using at most 2^{d+1} proof steps and $d+1$ extra work cells.

This construction mirrors a construction in [11]. For each $1 \leq i < n$, let E_i be the collection of at most W edges crossing the cut $(\{v_1 \ldots v_i\}, \{v_{i+1}, \ldots, v_n\})$ as described in the assumption. Let $\mathcal{C}_i$ be the collection of $2^{|E_i|-1}$ clauses whose conjunction is semantically equivalent to the parity constraint $\bigoplus_{e \in E_i} x_e \equiv \bigoplus_{1 \leq j \leq i} \chi(j)$.

We've defined everything so that (1), (2) and (3) hold immediately. Now we will show that item (4) holds for $i < n-1$.

The symmetric difference of E_i and E_{i+1} is, by definition, the edges incident tohas v_{i+1}. Let A_{i+1} denote the axioms associated with vertex v_{i+1}. By definition A_{i+1} is logically equivalent to the constraint $\bigoplus_{e \sim v_{i+1}} x_e \equiv \chi(i+1)$. If we think of parity constraints as $\mathcal{GF}(2)$-linear equations, and we add the two equations associated with A_{i+1} and $\mathcal{C}_i$, we obtain the equation associated with $\mathcal{C}_{i+1}$, so we conclude that

$$A_{i+1}, \mathcal{C}_i \models \mathcal{C}_{i+1} \ .$$

This move from $\mathcal{C}_i$ to $\mathcal{C}_{i+1}$ thus corresponds to adding two linear equations together and deleting one of them from memory.

Since resolution is implicationally complete, it is clear that it is possible to complete this move. We would like to now say that with at most 2^{d+1} size and $d+1$ space, we can derive any particular clause of $\mathcal{C}_{i+1}$, so that we can complete the move using $|\mathcal{C}_{i+1}| \cdot 2^{d+1}$ size and $d+1$ work space in addition to the space needed just to hold $\mathcal{C}_i, \mathcal{C}_{i+1}$ and the axioms.

Let C be an arbitrary clause in $\mathcal{C}_{i+1}$. It is well known that we may convert any derivation

$$A_{i+1}|_{\neg C} \ , \ \mathcal{C}_i|_{\neg C} \ \vdash \bot$$

into a derivation

$$A_{i+1}, \mathcal{C}_i \ \vdash C \ ,$$

using exactly the same proof DAG and possibly with some weakening steps added. It should be clear that weakening steps can be eliminated at the end of our construction without increasing the space or size used.

Since $\mathcal{C}_{i+1}$ is logically equivalent to a parity constraint, every $C \in \mathcal{C}_{i+1}$ assigns every variable E_{i+1}. Thus the only variables remaining in any of the $\mathcal{C}_i$ after the restriction $\neg C$ is applied correspond to edges incident to v_{i+1}. Thus there are at most d variables in any such derivation, and this derivation may be carried out trivially in a tree-like fashion using only 2^{d+1} size and $d+1$ space.

So, by completing a sequence of 2^{W-1} derivations each of length 2^{d+1}, reusing the $d+1$ space for each, we may fill 2^{W-1} new cells with the clauses in $\mathcal{C}_{i+1}$. We may then safely delete the cells used to hold $\mathcal{C}_i$, so that we never need more than $2 \cdot 2^{W-1} + d + 1$ space, plus the space for the axioms.

Finally we will see (4) holds for $i = n$, that is, from $\mathcal{C}_{n-1}$ and the axioms, we may derive a contradiction using 2^{d+1} size and $d+1$ space.

Since E_{n-1} is just the set of neighbors of v_n, $\mathcal{C}_{n-1}$ is logically equivalent to $\bigoplus_{e \sim v_n} x_e \equiv \bigoplus_{1 \le j \le n-1} \chi(j)$. But A_n is logically equivalent to $\bigoplus_{e \sim v_n} x_e \equiv \chi(n)$, which by assumption that χ is odd-charged, is of different parity. So $\mathcal{C}_{n-1}$ and A_n are contradictory sets of clauses, and on at most d variables. Thus a contradiction can be derived in tree-like fashion as claimed.

In total we carried out n phases, each with $2^{W-1}2^{d+1} = 2^{d+W}$ steps, and each using $2 \cdot 2^{W-1} + d + 1$ workspace in addition to the axioms. If we include the axioms in the space budget we will need additional space for $n2^{d-1}$ clauses. □

A little thought shows that this proof may be carried out in regular resolution, since within each phase, the derivation is tree-like, and the phases can be seen to operate on disjoint sets of variables.

We will appeal to this lemma to establish upper bounds for large space, against which we will prove size-space tradeoffs. The following lemma shows that for Tseitin graphs satisfying the conditions of Lemma 2.7, which include the ones that we consider here, even radically restricted space can only increase the size required by a $O(\log n)$ power.

LEMMA A.4 (LEMMA 2.8). *Under the same conditions as Lemma 2.7, the Tseitin tautology on $\tau(G)$ has a tree-like Resolution refutation using space $W\lceil \log n \rceil + 1$ and $\le 2^{W\lceil \log n \rceil + 1}$ resolution steps.*

PROOF. We prove that when n is a power of two, $\tau(G)$ has a tree-like refutation of rank $W \log n$, which implies the claim. Suppose that G is such a graph of size n. Suppose inductively that the claim holds on graphs of size $n/2$. As before let $E_{n/2}$ denote the edges crossing the cut

$$(\{v_1, \ldots, v_{n/2}\}, \{v_{n/2+1}, \ldots, v_n\}) .$$

Let C be any clause containing every variable in $E_{n/2}$. Then $\tau(G)|_{\neg C}$ can be written as a pair of disjoint Tseitin formulae, one from each side of the cut, one of which is odd and therefore unsatisfiable. The induced subgraphs on either side of have cut width at most W, therefore $\tau(G)|_{\neg C}$ has a tree-like resolution refutation of rank at most $W(\log n - 1)$, which can be lifted to a tree-like derivation of C from the axioms $\tau(G)$ in the same rank.

It is easy to see that there is a tree-like refutation of rank $|E_{n/2}| \le W$ using the set of all such C as axioms. By replacing the appearances of these axioms in that refutation with their $W(\log n - 1)$ rank tree-like refutations from the $\tau(G)$ axioms, we obtain a $W \log n$ rank tree-like refutation of $\tau(G)$. □

Generalizations

These ideas can be generalized to the stronger notion of carving width, yielding both a high space version and a low space version for any graph. For the high space version, we essentially just restate part of the main result of Aleknovich and Razborov [2]:

DEFINITION A.5. *A* carving *of a graph G is a rooted binary tree $\mathcal{T}$ whose leaves are in bijection with the vertices of G. For t a node of $\mathcal{T}$, we let $v(t)$ denote the vertices corresponding to leaves which are under t, and $Cut(t)$ denote the edges on the boundary of $v(t)$. The size of the largest $Cut(t)$ is the* width *of a particular carving, and the* carving width *of a graph G is the width of the narrowest carving of G.*

OBSERVATION A.6. *The carving width is always less than the cut width – given any linear ordering of the vertices yielding cut width W, we can obtain a carving of width W by taking a maximally unbalanced binary tree, and assigning vertices to leaves as dictated by the linear ordering. The cuts corresponding to internal nodes then correspond exactly to the cuts occurring in the definition of cut width.*

COROLLARY A.7. *[2] For every n vertex graph G of carving width W, the corresponding Tseitin tautology has a regular resolution refutation of size $poly(n) \cdot 2^{O(W)}$, and uses comparable space.*

PROOF SKETCH:. There is a natural way to convert a carving into a refutation – for each node t, we will have an associated set of clauses on the variables $Cut(t)$:

For t a leaf corresponding to vertex v, we will simply take all the axioms associated to vertex v.

For t an internal node, we will take the clauses associated to its children t_1, t_2, which are on variables $Cut(t_1)$ or $Cut(t_2)$, and make all derivations possible which yield clauses on $Cut(t)$ and only which resolve on variables from $Cut(t_1) \cup Cut(t_2) \setminus Cut(t)$.

To analyze this, we observe there are at most $3^{|Cut(t)|}$ clauses derived for any node, and each one can be derived from clauses at the children by resolving on at most $2W$ variables, hence in 2^{2W} time. There are only $2n$ nodes in total since there are n leaves, and so there is $poly(n) \cdot exp(O(W))$ total work, and at most $poly(n) \cdot exp(O(W))$ active clauses at any point. We omit the proof that this actually does result in deriving a contradiction at the end – Aleknovich and Razborov refer to (Krajicek 1992, Theorem 4.2.1). It is straightforward to see this when considering only Tseitin tautologies, since then the clauses associated to t will always correspond to a parity constraint on the variables $Cut(t)$, and the derivation of t from t_1, t_2 corresponds to addition of linear equations; Aleknovich and Razborov in fact establish this claim for any tautology. □

LEMMA A.8. *For every graph G on n nodes with carving width W, the corresponding Tseitin tautology has a tree-like refutation of rank at most $W \log_{\frac{3}{2}} n$. In particular, it has a refutation with size $n^{W \log \frac{3}{2}}$, using at most $W \log_{\frac{3}{2}} n + 1$ clause space.*

PROOF. Given an optimal carving T of G, we use the classic $\frac{1}{3}, \frac{2}{3}$ lemma for binary trees to find an edge which represents a balanced cut in T. Suppose that t is the lower vertex of this edge. (More explicitly: observe that if we define a function f on nodes of the tree s.t. $f(t) = |v(t)|$, then f is a subadditive function on the tree, that is $f(t) \le f(t_1) + f(t_2)$, where t_1, t_2 are the children of t. f of each leaf is 1, and f of the root is n, therefore there exists t such that $\frac{n}{3} \le f(t) \le \frac{2n}{3}$.)

First observe that the induced subgraph on $v(t)$, and the induced subgraph on $V \setminus v(t)$, both have carving width at most W, and at most $\frac{2}{3}n$ vertices by assumption. Therefore by induction hypothesis, Tseitin tautologies on these graphs have refutations of rank at most $W(\log_{\frac{3}{2}} n-1)$. This implies that every clause containing exactly the variables of $Cut(t)$ has a tree-like derivation of rank at most $W(\log_{\frac{3}{2}} n-1)$, since any such clause falsifies at least one component of $G \setminus Cut(t)$.

If we may start with all clauses on exactly $Cut(t)$, it is easy to see that there is a tree-like refutation of rank $|Cut(t)| \leq W$, by branching on each variable of $Cut(t)$ in succession. By replacing the leaves in this refutation with corresponding small rank tree-like derivations of these clauses, we get a tree-like refutation of rank at most $W \log_{\frac{3}{2}} n$ as desired. □

It is worth pointing out that while this lemma shows that small space proofs exist, it generally does not yield a small space method for finding them. The results of [2] show that it is possible to find a good carving or branch decomposition in small space; however, they left open the question of how to exploit this to solve small width SAT instances efficiently in small space. Important progress has been made by [4], [12].

Some algorithmic upper bounds from the literature

While we have described two different resolution *proofs* for Tseitin tautologies, it remains to be seen whether these upper bounds really correspond to the executions of actual algorithms. There has been a series of SAT algorithms [2, 4, 12] based on branch width or tree width that achieve this.

CLAIM A.9. *The branch-width based algorithm of Aleknovich and Razborov [2] gives an efficient implementation of Lemma 2.7, matching the space and time usage up to constants in the exponent. A recent algorithm of [12] achieves this as well.*

CLAIM A.10. *The small space variation of [12] achieves a runtime matching the size of the proof in Lemma 2.8, up to constants in the exponent, and achieving memory usage which is polynomial in $n = |G|$. The branch width-based algorithm [4] achieves memory usage which is near linear in $|G|$, after a near optimal branch decomposition has been computed. Both results essentially appeal to the branch decomposition routine of [2] to achieve their results.*

A further contribution of [12] is to provide a smooth interpolation between the high space parameters and the low space parameters. Their results are phrased in terms of tree-width parameterized SAT, and they show that time T and space S are feasible when

$$\alpha\left(\log T/TW(\phi)\log|\phi|\right) + \beta \log S \geq TW(\phi) + \gamma \log|\phi|,$$

for appropriate constants α, β, and γ. They conjecture that this essentially cannot be improved. Specifically, they conjecture that any SAT algorithm that runs in time T with $\log T = o(TW(\phi)\log(|\phi|))$ requires space exponential in $TW(\phi)$.

We note that one way to prove that this is true, at least for backtracking algorithms, would be to improve the lower bound result given in Lemma 3.2 for Tseitin tautologies, by improving the exponent to match the small space upper bounds.

On the Virtue of Succinct Proofs: Amplifying Communication Complexity Hardness to Time-Space Trade-offs in Proof Complexity

[Extended Abstract]

Trinh Huynh
Swiss Federal Institute of Technology (ETH)
8092 Zurich, Switzerland
trinh@inf.ethz.ch

Jakob Nordström
KTH Royal Institute of Technology
100 44 Stockholm, Sweden
jakobn@kth.se

ABSTRACT

An active line of research in proof complexity over the last decade has been the study of proof space and trade-offs between size and space. Such questions were originally motivated by practical SAT solving, but have also led to the development of new theoretical concepts in proof complexity of intrinsic interest and to results establishing nontrivial relations between space and other proof complexity measures.

By now, the resolution proof system is fairly well understood in this regard, as witnessed by a sequence of papers leading up to [Ben-Sasson and Nordström 2008, 2011] and [Beame, Beck, and Impagliazzo 2012]. However, for other relevant proof systems in the context of SAT solving, such as polynomial calculus (PC) and cutting planes (CP), very little has been known.

Inspired by [BN08, BN11], we consider CNF encodings of so-called pebble games played on graphs and the approach of making such pebbling formulas harder by simple syntactic modifications. We use this paradigm of hardness amplification to make progress on the relatively longstanding open question of proving time-space trade-offs for PC and CP. Namely, we exhibit a family of modified pebbling formulas $\{F_n\}_{n=1}^{\infty}$ such that:

- The formulas F_n have size $\Theta(n)$ and width $O(1)$.
- They have proofs in length $O(n)$ in resolution, which generalize to both PC and CP.
- Any refutation in CP or PCR (a generalization of PC) in length L and space s must satisfy $s \log L \gtrsim \sqrt[4]{n}$.

A crucial technical ingredient in these results is a new two-player communication complexity lower bound for composed search problems in terms of block sensitivity, a contribution that we believe to be of independent interest.

Categories and Subject Descriptors: F.2.3[Analysis of Algorithms and Problem Complexity]: Tradeoffs among Complexity Measures; F.1.3[Computation by Abstract Devices]: Complexity Measures and Classes —*Relations among complexity measures*; I.2.3[Artificial Intelligence]: Deduction and Theorem Proving; F.4.1[Mathematical Logic and Formal Languages]: Mathematical Logic —*computational logic*

General Terms: Theory

Keywords: Proof complexity, resolution, polynomial calculus, PCR, cutting planes, size, length, space, trade-offs

1. INTRODUCTION

Ever since Cook's landmark paper [29], the question of how hard it is to prove formulas in propositional logic has been a flagship problem in theoretical computer science. While this problem is generally believed to be intractable in the worst case, impressive algorithmic developments in the last ten to fifteen years have led to so-called SAT solvers that can deal with real-world problem instances with millions of variables. A somewhat surprising aspect of this is that at the core, state-of-the-art SAT solvers today are still based on the fairly simple Davis-Putnam-Logemann-Loveland (DPLL) procedure [34, 35] from the early 1960s augmented with clause learning [6, 48]; these programs are also known as conflict-driven clause learning (CDCL) solvers. Despite the fact that such solvers in effect search for proofs in the relatively weak *resolution proof system*, for which numerous exponential lower bounds are known, they have dominated the international SAT competition [61] in recent years.

The field of proof complexity, initiated by Cook and Reckhow [30], also considers the hardness of proving propositional logic formulas, but from the slightly different (nonconstructive) angle of asking how succinct such proofs can be, regardless of how hard or easy it is to find them. In its most general form, a proof system for a language L is defined as a predicate $P(x, \pi)$, computable in time polynomial in $|x|$ and $|\pi|$, such that for all $x \in L$ there is a string π (a *proof*) such that P accepts the input (x, π), whereas for any $x \notin L$ it holds for all π that P rejects (x, π). A proof system is said to be polynomially bounded if for every $x \in L$ there is a proof π_x of size at most polynomial in $|x|$. A *propositional proof system* is a proof system for the language of tautologies in propositional logic.

One important motivation for the study of proof complexity is the problem of P vs. NP, in that [30] showed that one way of establishing co-NP $\neq$ NP, and hence P $\neq$ NP, would be to prove that there are no polynomially bounded propositional proof systems. This goal remains very distant, however, and it is probably fair to say that most current work in proof complexity is primarily driven by other concerns.

One such concern is the connection to the SAT problem and practical SAT solving. By studying proof systems that are, or could potentially be, used by SAT solvers, one can hope to gain a better understanding of the potential and limitations of such solvers. There is a growing literature of such papers, with [4, 15, 55] being a very subjective pick of just three recent interesting examples.

The subject matter of the current paper, namely time-space trade-offs in proof complexity, should be understood as being mainly motivated by this latter reason. The two main bottlenecks for modern SAT solvers are running time and memory usage. By studying proof size/length, proof space, and trade-offs between these two measures in different proof systems, we want to understand how the important resources of time and space are connected to one another and whether they can be optimized simultaneously or have to be traded for one another in SAT solvers using these proof systems.[1]

Concluding this brief general discussion, let us mention that some good starting points for a further study of proof complexity in general are [8, 62], while the upcoming survey [53] by the second author focuses specifically on time-space trade-offs and related questions. Also, a recent, very compehensive, reference on the SAT problem in practice is [19].

1.1 Previous Work

Any formula in propositional logic can be converted to a CNF formula that is only linearly larger and is unsatisfiable if and only if the original formula is a tautology. Therefore, any sound and complete system for refuting unsatisfiable CNF formulas can be considered as a general propositional proof system. All proof systems considered in this paper are of this type.

The *resolution* proof system already mentioned above was introduced in [20] and began to be investigated in connection with automated theorem proving in the 1960s [34, 35, 60]. In resolution, one derives new disjunctive clauses from the clauses of the original CNF formula until a contradiction is reached. For this proof system, it is most straightforward to prove bounds on the *length* of refutations, i.e., the number of clauses, rather than on the total size (the two measures are easily seen to be polynomially related). One of the early break-throughs in proof complexity was the result by Haken [39] that CNF formulas encoding the pigeonhole principle (PHP formulas) require proofs of exponential length. There have been a sequence of follow-up papers establishing quantitatively stronger bounds for other formula families in, for instance, [11, 18, 27, 64].

Motivated by the fact that memory usage is a major concern in applied SAT solving, and by the question of whether proof complexity could say anything interesting about this, the study of proof space in resolution was initiated by Esteban and Torán in [37] and was later extended to a more general setting by Alekhnovich et al. in [1]. Intuitively, the (clause) space of a resolution refutation is the maximal number of clauses one needs to keep in memory while verifying the refutation. Perhaps somewhat surprisingly, it turns out that one need never use more than linear clause space, and a sequence of papers [1, 14, 37] have proven matching linear lower bounds.

Another sequence of papers [50, 54, 16] involving the second author clarified the relation between length and space, showing that hardness with respect to space is "maximally uncorrelated" with hardness with respect to length. More formally, while it follows from [3] that small space complexity implies the existence of short resolution refutations, it was established in [16] that there exist explicit formulas that are maximally easy with respect to length, having refutations in length $O(n)$, but which are hard for space in that their clause space complexity is $\Omega(n/\log n)$ (and this separation is optimal).

Regarding trade-offs between length and space, some results in restricted settings were presented in [13, 51] and strong trade-offs for full, unrestricted resolution were finally obtained in [17] and even more recently in [9] for a different range of parameters. In this context it should also be mentioned that for the more general k-DNF resolution proof systems [43], there have also been shown strong lower bounds on length and space as well as length-space trade-offs in, for instance, [17, 36, 63].

In *polynomial calculus (PC)* [28], clauses are interpreted as multilinear polynomial equations over some field, which in this paper we always take to be finite, and an unsatisfiable CNF formula is refuted by showing that there is no common root for the polynomials corresponding to the clauses. The minimal refutation size of a formula in this proof system turns out to be closely related to the total degree of the polynomials appearing in the refutation [41], and a number of strong lower bounds on proof size have been obtained by proving degree lower bounds in, for instance, [2, 41, 59].

The treatment of negated and unnegated literals in PC is asymmetric and means that wide clauses with literals of the wrong sign can blow up to polynomial equations of exponential size. To get a cleaner, more symmetric theoretical treatment of space, [1] introduced *polynomial calculus resolution (PCR)* as a common extension of polynomial calculus and resolution. Briefly, in PCR one adds an extra set of parallel formal variables $x', y', z', \ldots$ as well as axioms specifing that x and x' must always take opposite signs. In this way, negated and unnegated literals can both be represented in a space-efficient fashion. In this stronger system, [1] established nontrivial lower bounds on space measured as the number of monomials, but only for formulas of unbounded width (namely, PHP formulas). It was only very recently that [38] showed space lower bounds for formulas of constant width, and there is still quite a large gap between the best known worst-case lower and upper bounds even for PC. To the best of our knowledge, there have not been any trade-off results shown for PC or PCR.

Initially, there was quite some excitement about polynomial calculus since this proof system seemed to hold out the promise of better SAT solvers than those based on resolution. This promise has failed to materialize so far, however. There are PC-based solvers such as PolyBoRi [24], but in general they seem to be an order of magnitude slower than state-of-the-art CDCL solvers (although [25] reports that PolyBoRi can be faster on certain industrial instances).

[1]And this should not necessarily be considered to be just wishful thinking—as a case in point, experimental work reported in [42] seems to indicate that theoretical space complexity in resolution is correlated with practical hardness for CDCL solvers.

The *cutting planes* proof system, or *CP* for short, was introduced in [32]. In a CP-refutation clauses of a formula are translated to linear inequalities, or hyperplanes, and the formula is refuted by showing that the polytope defined by these hyperplanes does not have any zero-one integer points (corresponding to satisfying assignments). Cutting planes is an intriguing proof system in that we only know of one superpolynomial lower bound on length [57] (improving on a bound [21] in a somewhat restricted setting). It is natural to define the *line space* of a CP-refutation to be the maximal number of linear inequalities that need to be kept in memory simultaneously during the refutation. Just as for monomial space in PCR, line space in CP is easily seen to be a generalization of clause space in resolution and is hence upper bounded by the clause space complexity. As far as we are aware, no space lower bounds are known for cutting planes.

Cutting planes is known to be exponentially stronger than resolution, and so it would be very interesting if efficient CP-based SAT solvers could be built. But although there do exist some SAT solvers that use cutting planes (see, for instance, [45, 46] and references therein) again it seems they have a hard time competing with resolution-based solvers.

1.2 Our Results

As discussed above, there is a wealth of results on space lower bounds and time-space trade-offs for resolution and even k-DNF resolution, and it is probably fair to say that these are by now reasonably well understood proof systems. When it comes to polynomial calculus, polynomial calculus resolution, and cutting planes, the situation is very different. As far as we are aware no trade-offs have been known. Also, for cutting planes there seem to exist no space lower bounds whatsoever, and for polynomial calculus/PCR the current state of knowledge regarding space lower bounds is quite limited as well.

In this paper, we report length-space trade-off results that apply for both polynomial calculus resolution and cutting planes (and that concern formulas of bounded width).

THEOREM 1. *There are k-CNF formulas $\{F_n\}_{n=1}^{\infty}$ of size $\Theta(n)$ that can be refuted in length $\mathrm{O}(n)$ in resolution, polynomial calculus (and hence also PCR) and Cutting Planes, but for which the following holds:*

- *Any PCR-refutation of F_n in length L and monomial space s must satisfy $s \log L = \Omega(\sqrt[8]{n})$.*
- *Any CP-refutation of F_n in length L and line space s must satisfy $s \log L \log(s \log L) = \Omega\left(\sqrt[4]{n} / \log^2 n\right)$.*

The formulas used in Theorem 1 are a particular flavour of so-called pebbling contradictions, which is a well-studied family of CNF formulas in proof complexity. A nice technical feature of the results that is worth pointing out is that the bounds are actually slightly stronger than stated above—they hold also for *semantic* versions of the proof systems (as defined in [1]), where anything that is implied by the current memory configuration can be derived immediately in one step regardless of the syntactic rules (which makes the systems exponentially stronger with respect to length).

The trade-offs in Theorem 1 are obtained by studying the concept of *critical block sensitivity* of search problems, which is a new notion generalizing the well-studied block sensitivity of (Boolean) functions and which will be formally defined in Section 4. We prove that lower bounds on the critical block sensitivity of the search problem associated with a CNF formula—i.e., given an assignment, finding a clause falsified by it—can be amplified to lower bounds on length-space trade-offs in PCR and CP (and also to lower bound on tree-like length in CP). Our techniques are inspired by the joint work of the first author with Beame and Pitassi [10], but also crucially use a new result in communication complexity that we believe should merit independent interest. Namely, we obtain the first strong randomized communication complexity lower bounds for *lifts of search problems* in terms of critical block sensitivity. We refer to Section 3, where we define lifting of search problems and *consistent* randomized communication protocols, for a more precise statement of the next theorem. Informally, however, let us just say for now that the communication problem of solving the *lift* of a given search problem on m input bits is defined by giving Alice an array of $n > m$ bits and Bob an m-subset of $\{1, \ldots, n\}$ and asking them to solve the search problem in question on m particular bits of Alice's input as selected by Bob's index set.

THEOREM 2 (INFORMAL). *If $S \subseteq \{0,1\}^m \times Q$ is a search problem over input domain $\{0,1\}^m$ and output range Q and the* critical block sensitivity *of S is at least s, then any* consistent *randomized (and hence also any deterministic) two-party protocol solving $G = \mathit{Lift}(S)$ requires $\Omega(s)$ bits of communication.*

Returning to our proof complexity trade-offs in Theorem 1, we want to mention that interestingly, and intriguingly, it is not quite clear whether this theorem provides trade-offs in a strict sense. The issue is that to be able to speak about a "true" trade-off between length and space, we would also like the formulas to have space complexity smaller than the lower bound on the right-hand side of the inequalitites in Theorem 1. However, it is not known how to refute these formulas in space less than $\mathrm{O}(\sqrt{n})$. And in fact, given the structure of the formulas it is also hard to see why there should be a trade-off at all in the sense that larger proof length would somehow help to bring down the proof space.

Even more intriguingly, the bounds in Theorem 1 closely parallel the result obtained for resolution in 2002 by Ben-Sasson (journal version in [13]), where it was shown for a similar family of formulas that a trade-off on the form $s \log L = \Omega(n / \log n)$ must hold for any resolution refutation in length L and clause space s. Six years later, the factor $\log L$ was shown to be an artifact of the proof technique and was removed in a joint paper by Ben-Sasson and the second author [16] to obtain an unconditional space lower bound $\Omega(n/\log n)$ as mentioned above.

It is very tempting to conjecture that the situation should be the same for polynomial calculus resolution and cutting planes, so that Theorem 1 should be understood as providing "conditional space lower bounds" from which we should strive to remove the $\log L$ factor. If this could be done, it would imply that the combinatorics of pebbling on graphs is very robust, in that the properties of a concrete problem instance survives even the transformation of being (a) encoded as a CNF formula, (b) then translated from CNF into polynomial equations or linear inequalities, and (c) finally subjected to general-purpose propositional proof systems for reasoning in terms of such polynomial equations or linear equalities. The implication would be that no matter how polynomial calculus or cutting planes would try to work with these syntactic objects, which are very distinct from the graphs in terms of which they were generated, there would be no way to use less space than the lower bounds applying for pebbling strategies for the original graphs. And this would in turn open up the possibility of obtaining strong trade-off results for PCR and CP from pebbling time-space trade-offs along the lines of [17].

Before obtaining the results in this paper, we considered it very much unclear whether anything along those lines should have been expected to hold, but Theorem 1 does seem to provide fairly strong circumstantial evidence supporting such hypotheses. We are currently not able to prove this, however, but neither do we know of any formal obstacles to carrying out such a program.

1.3 Outline of This Paper

The rest of this paper is organized as follows. We start by presenting some standard proof complexity preliminaries in Section 2. In Section 3, we then give a more detailed overview of our proof complexity trade-off results, and describe the key concepts used in the proofs. In the end, this boils down to proving communication complexity lower bounds, and we discuss this separately in Section 4 and give an outline of that part of the argument. For the full proof of the communication complexity result, however, we refer the reader to the full-length version of this paper. Finally, in Section 5, we make some concluding remarks and mention a few of the many fascinating problems in this area that remain open.

2. SOME PROOF COMPLEXITY PRELIMINARIES

For x a Boolean variable, a *literal over* x is either the variable x itself, called a *positive literal over* x, or its negation, denoted $\neg x$ or $\overline{x}$ and called a *negative literal over* x. A *clause* $C = a_1 \vee \cdots \vee a_k$ is a disjunction of literals, and a *term* $T = a_1 \wedge \cdots \wedge a_k$ is a conjunction of literals. Below we will think of clauses and terms as sets, so that the ordering of the literals is inconsequential and that, in particular, no literals are repeated. A clause (term) containing at most k literals is called a *k-clause* (*k-term*). A *CNF formula* $F = C_1 \wedge \cdots \wedge C_m$ is a conjunction of clauses, and a *DNF formula* is a disjunction of terms. We will think of CNF and DNF formulas as sets of clauses and terms, respectively. A *k-CNF formula* is a CNF formula consisting of k-clauses, and a *k-DNF formula* consists of k-terms.

The *variable set* of a clause C, denoted $Vars(C)$, is the set of Boolean variables over which there are literals in C, and we write $Lit(C)$ to denote the set of literals in C. The variable and literal sets of a term are similarly defined and these definitions are extended to CNF and DNF formulas by taking unions. If V is a set of Boolean variables and $Vars(C) \subseteq V$ we say C is a clause *over* V and similarly define terms, CNF formulas, and DNF formulas over V.

We write α, β to denote truth value assignments. Truth value assignments are functions to $\{0, 1\}$, where we identify 0 with false and 1 with true. We have the usual semantics that a clause is true under α, or *satisfied* by α, if at least one literal in it is true, and a term is true if all literals evaluate to true. We write $\perp$ to denote the empty clause without literals that is false under all truth value assignments. A CNF formula is satisfied if all clauses in it are satisfied, and for a DNF formula we require that some term should be satisfied. In general, we will not distinguish between a formula and the Boolean function computed by it.

If $\mathbb{C}$ is a set of Boolean functions we say that an assignment satisfies $\mathbb{C}$ if and only if it satisfies every function in $\mathbb{C}$. For $\mathbb{D}, \mathbb{C}$ two sets of Boolean functions over a set of variables V, we say that $\mathbb{D}$ *implies* $\mathbb{C}$, denoted $\mathbb{D} \vDash \mathbb{C}$, if and only if every assignment $\alpha : V \mapsto \{0, 1\}$ that satisfies $\mathbb{D}$ also satisfies $\mathbb{C}$. In particular, $\mathbb{D} \vDash \perp$ if and only if $\mathbb{D}$ is *unsatisfiable* or *contradictory*, i.e., if no assignment satisfies $\mathbb{D}$. If a CNF formula F is unsatisfiable but for any clause $C \in F$ it holds that the clause set $F \setminus \{C\}$ is satisfiable, we say that F is *minimally unsatisfiable*.

We say that a proof system is *sequential* if a proof π in the system is a *sequence* of lines $\pi = \{L_1, \ldots, L_\tau\}$ of some prescribed syntactic form depending on the proof system in question, where each line is derived from previous lines by one of a finite set of allowed *inference rules*. Following the exposition in [37], we view a proof as similar to a non-deterministic Turing machine computation, with a special read-only input tape from which the clauses of the CNF formula F being refuted (the *axioms*) can be downloaded and a working memory where all derivation steps are made. Then the length of a proof is essentially the time of the computation and space measures memory consumption. The following definition is a straightforward generalization of [1].

DEFINITION 3 (REFUTATION). *For a sequential propositional proof system $\mathcal{P}$, a $\mathcal{P}$-*configuration *$\mathbb{D}$ is a set of lines L of the syntactic form prescribed by $\mathcal{P}$. A sequence of configurations $\{\mathbb{D}_0, \ldots, \mathbb{D}_\tau\}$ is a $\mathcal{P}$-*derivation *from a CNF formula F if $\mathbb{D} = \emptyset$ and for all $t \in [\tau]$, the set $\mathbb{D}_t$ is obtained from $\mathbb{D}_{t-1}$ by one of the following* derivation steps*:*

Axiom Download $\mathbb{D}_t = \mathbb{D}_{t-1} \cup \{L_C\}$, *where L_C is the encoding of a clause $C \in F$ in the syntactic form prescribed by the proof system (an* axiom*).*

Inference $\mathbb{D}_t = \mathbb{D}_{t-1} \cup \{L\}$ *for some L inferred by one of the inference rules for $\mathcal{P}$ from a set of assumptions $L_1, \ldots, L_m \in \mathbb{D}_{t-1}$.*

Erasure $\mathbb{D}_t = \mathbb{D}_{t-1} \setminus \{L\}$ *for some $L \in \mathbb{D}_{t-1}$.*

A $\mathcal{P}$-refutation $\pi : F \vdash \perp$ of a CNF formula F is a derivation $\pi = \{\mathbb{D}_0, \ldots, \mathbb{D}_\tau\}$ such that $\mathbb{D}_0 = \emptyset$ and $\perp \in \mathbb{D}_\tau$, where $\perp$ is the representation of contradiction (e.g. for resolution and $\mathcal{R}(k)$-systems the empty clause without literals).

If every line L in a derivation is used at most once before being erased (though it can possibly be rederived later), we say that the derivation is tree-like*. This corresponds to changing the inference rule so that $L_1, \ldots, L_d$ must all be erased after they have been used to derive L.*

To every refutation π we can associate a DAG G_π, with the lines in π labelling the vertices and with edges from the assumptions to the consequence for each application of an inference rule. There might be several different derivations of a line L during the course of the refutation π, but if so we can label each occurrence of L with a time-stamp when it was derived and keep track of which copy of L is used where. Using this representation, a refutation π can be seen to be tree-like if G_π is a tree.

DEFINITION 4 (SIZE, LENGTH AND SPACE). *For a given measure of size $S(L)$ for lines L in $\mathcal{P}$-derivations (which we usually think of as the number of symbols in L, but other definitions can also be appropriate depending on the context), the* size *of a $\mathcal{P}$-derivation π is the sum of the sizes of all lines in a derivation, where lines that appear multiple times are counted with repetitions (once for every vertex in G_π). The* length *of a $\mathcal{P}$-derivation π is the number of axiom downloads and inference steps in it, i.e., the number of vertices in G_π.*[2] *For a space measure $Sp_{\mathcal{P}}(\mathbb{D})$ defined for $\mathcal{P}$-configurations, the* space *of a derivation π is defined as the maximal space of a configuration in π.*

If π is a refutation of a formula F in size S and space s, then we say that F can be refuted in size S and space s simultaneously. *Similarly, F can be refuted in length L and space s simultaneously if there is a $\mathcal{P}$-refutation $\mathcal{P}$ with $L(\pi) = L$ and $Sp(\pi) = s$.*

*We define the $\mathcal{P}$-*refutation size *of a formula F, denoted $S_{\mathcal{P}}(F \vdash \bot)$, to be the minimum size of any $\mathcal{P}$-refutation of it. The $\mathcal{P}$-*refutation length *$L_{\mathcal{P}}(F \vdash \bot)$ and $\mathcal{P}$-*refutation space *$Sp_{\mathcal{P}}(F \vdash \bot)$ of F are analogously defined by taking the minimum with respect to length or space, respectively, over all $\mathcal{P}$-refutations of F.*

When the proof system in question is clear from context, we will drop the subindex in the proof complexity measures.

Let us next give formal definitions of the proof systems that will be of interest in this paper. Below, the notation $\dfrac{G_1 \quad \cdots \quad G_m}{H}$ means that if $G_1, \ldots, G_m$ have been derived previously in the proof (and are currently in memory), then we can infer H.

DEFINITION 5 (k-DNF RESOLUTION). *The k-*DNF resolution *proof systems are a family of sequential proof systems $\mathcal{R}(k)$ parameterized by $k \in \mathbb{N}^+$. Lines in a k-DNF-resolution refutation are k-DNF formulas and we have the following inference rules (where G, H denote k-DNF formulas, T, T' denote k-terms, and $a_1, \ldots, a_k$ denote literals):*

$$k\text{-}\textbf{cut} \quad \frac{(a_1 \wedge \cdots \wedge a_{k'}) \vee G \qquad \overline{a}_1 \vee \cdots \vee \overline{a}_{k'} \vee H}{G \vee H}, \; k' \leq k.$$

$$\wedge\text{-}\textbf{introduction} \quad \frac{G \vee T \qquad G \vee T'}{G \vee (T \wedge T')}, \; |T \cup T'| \leq k.$$

$$\wedge\text{-}\textbf{elimination} \quad \frac{G \vee T}{G \vee T'} \text{ for any } T' \subseteq T.$$

$$\textbf{Weakening} \quad \frac{G}{G \vee H} \text{ for any } k\text{-DNF formula } H.$$

For standard resolution, i.e., $\mathcal{R}(1)$, the k-cut rule simplifies to the *resolution rule*

$$\frac{B \vee x \qquad C \vee \overline{x}}{B \vee C} \tag{2.1}$$

for clauses B and C. We refer to (2.1) as *resolution on the variable* x and to $B \vee C$ as the *resolvent* of $B \vee x$ and $C \vee \overline{x}$ on x. Clearly, in resolution the $\wedge$-introduction and $\wedge$-elimination rules do not apply. It can also be shown that the weakening rule never needs to be used in resolution refutations, but it can be convenient to allow it to simplify some technical arguments in proofs.

[2]The reader who so prefers can instead define the length of a derivation $\pi = \{\mathbb{D}_0, \ldots, \mathbb{D}_\tau\}$ as the number of steps τ in it, since the difference is at most a factor of 2. We have chosen the definition above for consistency with previous papers defining length as the number of lines in a listing of the derivation.

For $\mathcal{R}(k)$-systems, the length measure is as defined in Definition 4, and for space we get the two measures *formula space* and *total space* depending on whether we consider the number of k-DNF formulas in a configuration or all literals in it, counted with repetitions. For standard resolution there are two more space-related measures that will be relevant, namely *width* and *variable space*. For clarity, let us give an explicit definition of all space-related measures for resolution that will be of interest.

DEFINITION 6 (RESOLUTION WIDTH AND SPACE). *The* width *$W(C)$ of a clause C is the number of literals in it, and the width of a CNF formula or clause configuration is the size of a widest clause in it. The* clause space *(as the formula space measure is known in resolution) $Sp(\mathbb{C})$ of a clause configuration $\mathbb{C}$ is $|\mathbb{C}|$, i.e., the number of clauses in $\mathbb{C}$, the* variable space *$VarSp(\mathbb{C})$ is $|\,Vars(C)|$, i.e., the number of distinct variables mentioned in $\mathbb{C}$, and the* total space *$TotSp(\mathbb{C})$ is $\sum_{C \in \mathbb{C}} |C|$, i.e., the total number of literals in $\mathbb{C}$ counted with repetitions.*

The width or space of a refutation π is the maximum that the corresponding measures attain over any clause configuration $\mathbb{C} \in \pi$, and taking the minimum over all resolution refutations of a CNF formula F, we can define the width $W_{\mathcal{R}}(F \vdash \bot) = \min_{\pi : F \vdash 0}\{W(\pi)\}$ of refuting F, and analogously the clause space $Sp_{\mathcal{R}}(F \vdash \bot) = \min_{\pi : F \vdash 0}\{Sp(\pi)\}$, variable space $VarSp_{\mathcal{R}}(F \vdash \bot) = \min_{\pi : F \vdash 0}\{VarSp(\pi)\}$, and total space $TotSp_{\mathcal{R}}(F \vdash \bot) = \min_{\pi : F \vdash 0}\{TotSp(\pi)\}$ of refuting F.

When studying and comparing the complexity measures for resolution in Definition 6, as was noted in [1] it is preferable to prove the results for k-CNF formulas, i.e., formulas where all clauses have size upper-bounded by some constant. This is so since the width and space measures can "misbehave" rather artificially for formula families of unbounded width (see [51, Section 5] for a discussion of this). Since every CNF formula can be rewritten as an equivalent formula of bounded width by using auxiliary variables, it therefore seems natural to insist that the formulas under study should have width bounded by some constant.

The *cutting planes* proof system, or *CP* for short, was introduced in [32]. Here, clauses are translated to linear inequalities—for instance, $x \vee y \vee \overline{z}$ gets translated to $x + y + (1 - z) \geq 1$, i.e., $x + y - z \geq 0$—and these linear inequalities are then manipulated to derive a contradiction.

DEFINITION 7 (CUTTING PLANES). *Lines in a cutting planes proof are linear inequalities with integer coefficients. The derivation rules are as follows:*

$$\textbf{Variable axioms} \quad \frac{}{x \geq 0} \text{ and } \frac{}{-x \geq -1} \text{ for all } x.$$

$$\textbf{Addition} \quad \frac{\sum a_i x_i \geq A \qquad \sum b_i x_i \geq B}{\sum (a_i + b_i) x_i \geq A + B}$$

$$\textbf{Multiplication} \quad \frac{\sum a_i x_i \geq A}{\sum c a_i x_i \geq cA} \text{ for a positive integer } c.$$

$$\textbf{Division} \quad \frac{\sum c a_i x_i \geq A}{\sum a_i x_i \geq \lceil A/c \rceil} \text{ for a positive integer } c.$$

A CP-refutation ends when the inequality $0 \geq 1$ has been derived. The cutting planes measures we will focus on in this paper are the length measure and the line space *measure, the latter of which is the number of linear inequalities that are kept simultaneously on the blackboard during the refutation.*

Line space in cutting planes is easily seen to be a generalization of clause space in resolution, and since cutting planes can simulate resolution proofs it follows that the line space complexity of a formula in cutting planes is upper-bounded by its clause space complexity in resolution.

The k-DNF resolution proof systems are *logic-based* systems in the sense that they manipulate logic formulas, and cutting planes is an example of a *geometric* proof systems where clauses are treated as geometric objects. We will also be interested in two *algebraic* proof systems in this paper. The first of these is *polynomial calculus (PC)*, which was introduced in [28] under the name of "Gröbner proof system." In a PC-refutation, clauses are interpreted as multilinear polynomials. For instance, the requirement that the clause $x \vee y \vee \overline{z}$ should be satisfied gets translated to the equation $(1-x)(1-y)z = 0$ or $xyz - xz - yz + z = 0$, and we derive contradiction by showing that there is no common root for the polynomial equations corresponding to all the clauses.[3]

Definition 8 (Polynomial calculus). *In a polynomial calculus proof, lines are multivariate polynomial equations $p = 0$, where $p \in \mathbb{F}[x, y, z, \ldots]$ for some (fixed) field $\mathbb{F}$. It is customary to omit "$= 0$" and only write p. The derivation rules are as follows, where $\alpha, \beta \in \mathbb{F}$, $p, q \in \mathbb{F}[x, y, z, \ldots]$, and x is any variable:*

Boolean axioms $\dfrac{}{x^2 - x}$ *(forcing 0/1-solutions).*

Linear combination $\dfrac{p \quad q}{\alpha p + \beta q}$

Multiplication $\dfrac{p}{xp}$

A PC-refutation ends when 1 has been derived (i.e., $1 = 0$). The size *of a PC-refutation is defined as the total number of monomials in the refutation, the* length *of a refutation is the number of polynomial equations, and the* (monomial) space *is the maximal number of monomials in any configuration (counted with repetitions). Another important measure is the* degree *of a refutation, which is the maximal (total) degree of any monomial.*

The representation of a clause $\bigvee_{i=1}^{n} x_i$ as a PC-polynomial is $\prod_{i=1}^{n}(1 - x_i)$, which means that the number of monomials is exponential in the clause width. This problem arises only for positive literals, however—a large clause with only negative literals is translated to a single monomial. This is a weakness of monomial space in polynomial calculus when compared to clause space in resolution. In order to obtain a cleaner, more symmetric treatment of proof space, in [1] the proof system *polynomial calculus resolution (PCR)* was introduced as a common extension of polynomial calculus and resolution. The idea is to add an extra set of parallell formal variables $x', y', z', \ldots$ so that positive and negative literals can both be represented in a space-efficient fashion.

Definition 9 (Polynomial calculus resolution). *The lines in a PCR-derivation are polynomials over the ring $\mathbb{F}[x, x', y, y', z, z', \ldots]$, where as before $\mathbb{F}$ is some field. We have all the axioms and rules of PC plus the following axioms:*

Complementarity $\dfrac{}{x + x' - 1}$ *for all pairs (x, x').*

Size, length, and degree are defined as for polynomial calculus, and the (monomial) space of a PCR-refutation is again the maximal number of monomials in any PCR-configuration counted with repetitions.[4]

The point of the complementarity rule is to force x and x' to have opposite values in $\{0, 1\}$, so that they encode complementary literals. This means one can potentially avoid an exponential blow-up in size measured in the number of monomials (and thus also for space). Our running example clause $x \vee y \vee \overline{z}$ is rendered as $x'y'z$ in PCR. In PCR, monomial space is a natural generalization of clause space since every clause translates into a monomial as just explained.

In general, the admissible inferences in a proof system according to Definition 3 are defined by a set of syntactic inference rules. In what follows, we will also be interested in a strengthened version of this concept, which was made explicit in [1].

Definition 10 (Syntactic and semantic proofs). *We refer to proofs according to Definition 3, where each new line L has to be inferred by one of the inference rules for $\mathcal{P}$, as* syntactic *proofs. If instead* any line L *that is semantically implied by the current configuration can be derived in one atomic step, we talk about a* semantic *proof.*

Clearly, semantic proofs are at least as strong as syntactic ones, and they are easily seen to be superpolynomially stronger with respect to length for any proof system where superpolynomial lower bounds are known. This is so since a semantic proof system can download all axioms in the formula one by one, and then deduce contradiction in one step since the formula is unsatisfiable. Therefore, semantic versions of proof systems are mainly interesting when we want to reason about space or the relationship between space and length. But if we can prove lower bounds not just for syntactic but even semantic versions of proof systems, this of course makes these bounds much stronger.

Let us finally remark that although the measure of total space, considering the total number of symbols in memory, is perhaps a priori the most natural one, most papers on proof space have focused on space measured as the number of lines in memory (e.g., clauses, k-DNF formulas, or inequalities). However, as observed in [1], for strong enough proof systems, this "line space" measure is no longer interesting since just one unit of memory can contain a big AND of all formulas derived so far. The "line space" measure makes perfect sense for resolution and k-DNF resolution, and seems to do so also for cutting planes. For PC/PCR, however, measuring just

[3]In fact, from a mathematical point of view it seems more natural to think of 0 as true and 1 as false in polynomial calculus, so that the unit clause x gets translated to $x = 0$. For simplicity and consistency in this paper, however, we stick to thinking about $x = 1$ as meaning that x is true and $x = 0$ as meaning that x is false.

[4]We remark that in [1] space was defined as the number of *distinct* monomials (i.e., not counted with repetitions), but we find this restriction to be somewhat arbitrary.

the number of polynomial equations is not very meaningful, since every equation can be of exponential size and encode very much information. Instead, the natural generalization of clause space is monomial space.

3. OVERVIEW OF PROOF COMPLEXITY TRADE-OFFS

In this section, we describe which ingredients go into our results stated in Section 1.2 and how these results are proven. Our goal is to give an accessible high-level outline of the proofs, but still make clear what the main technical points in the arguments are and how they fit together. Briefly, the structure of our argument is as follows (where italicized words are concepts that we will make precise below):

1. We construct a family of CNF formulas of constant width by *lifting* so-called *pebbling contradictions* defined over *pyramid graphs*.

2. We then show that efficient refutations of these formulas, i.e., refutations in short length and small space, in polynomial calculus resolution or cutting planes give rise to efficient protocols for a certain *two-party communication complexity problem*. Although this is a fairly straightforward argument, we are not aware of this line of reasoning having been used before to prove time-space trade-offs in proof complexity.

3. Finally, we prove that *this communication complexity problem is hard*, so there cannot exist too good protocols. This is where essentially all of the work in this paper is, and where Theorem 2 comes into the picture.

Putting all of this together, Theorem 1 follows. The proof of this theorem is given in Section 3.4.

3.1 Lifting

The idea behind *lifting* (a term coined in [33]) is that we can take a base function f over some domain and extend it to a function over tuples from the same domain by combining it with a *selector* function that determines on which coordinates from the tuples f should be evaluated. The formal definition unfortunately turns out to be slightly involved, but it is absolutely crucial for our argument and so we start by making this definition precise.

Given a function $f : \{0,1\}^m \mapsto Q$ for some range Q and an integer $\ell > 0$, the *lift of length ℓ of f* is defined to be the function $Lift_\ell(f) : \{0,1\}^{m\times\ell} \times [\ell]^m \mapsto Q$ such that for any bit-vector $\{x_{i,j}\}_{i\in[m],j\in[\ell]}$ and any $y \in [\ell]^m$, the function evaluated on these arguments is

$$Lift_\ell(f)(x,y) = f(x_{1,y_1}, x_{2,y_2}, \ldots, x_{m,y_m}) \quad (3.1)$$

(in words, the vector y selects which coordinates of the x-vector should be fed to f).

Let S be any *search problem* defined as a subset of $A \times Q$ for some input domain A and output range Q; that is, on any input $a \in A$, the problem is to find some $q \in Q$ such that $(a,q) \in S$. If $A = \{0,1\}^m$ and $\ell > 0$ is any integer, we define the *lift of length ℓ of S* to be a new search problem $Lift_\ell(S) \subseteq \{0,1\}^{m\times\ell} \times [\ell]^m \times Q$ with input domain $\{0,1\}^{m\times\ell} \times [\ell]^m$ and output range Q such that for any bit-vector $\{x_{i,j}\}_{i\in[m],j\in[\ell]}$, any $y \in [\ell]^m$ and any $q \in Q$, it holds that

$$(x,y,q) \in Lift_\ell(S) \text{ if and only if } ((x_{1,y_1}, x_{2,y_2}, \ldots, x_{m,y_m}), q) \in S \ . \quad (3.2)$$

Lifted CNF formulas, as first introduced in [10], are constructed in the following way.

Definition 11 (Lift of CNF formula [10]). *Given any CNF formula F consisting of clauses $C_1, \ldots, C_m$ over variables $u_1, \ldots, u_n$, and any integer $\ell > 0$, the* lift of length ℓ of F *is a CNF formula $Lift_\ell(F)$ over $2\ell n$ variables denoted by $\{x_{i,j}\}_{i\in[n],j\in[\ell]}$ (*main variables*) and $\{y_{i,j}\}_{i\in[n],j\in[\ell]}$ (*selector variables*), consisting of the following clauses:*

- *For every $i \in [n]$, an* auxiliary clause

$$y_{i,1} \lor y_{i,1} \lor \cdots \lor y_{i,\ell} \ . \quad (3.3)$$

- *For every clause $C_i \in F$, where $C_i = u_{i_1} \lor \cdots \lor u_{i_s} \lor \overline{u}_{i_{s+1}} \lor \cdots \lor \overline{u}_{i_{s+t}}$ for some $i_1, \ldots, i_{s+t} \in [n]$, and for every tuple $(j_1, \ldots, j_{s+t}) \in [\ell]^{s+t}$, a* main clause

$$\overline{y}_{i_1,j_1} \lor x_{i_1,j_1} \lor \cdots \lor \overline{y}_{i_s,j_s} \lor x_{i_s,j_s} \lor \overline{y}_{i_{s+1},j_{s+1}} \lor \overline{x}_{i_{s+1},j_{s+1}} \lor \cdots \lor \overline{y}_{i_{s+t},j_{s+t}} \lor \overline{x}_{i_{s+t},j_{s+t}} \ . \quad (3.4)$$

Let us elaborate on what Definition 11 means. The purpose of the auxiliary clauses in (3.3) is to make sure that in every block of variables $\{y_{i,j} \mid 1 \le j \le \ell\}$ at least one of the selector y-variables is true. Noting that every pair $\overline{y}_{i,j} \lor x_{i,j}$ in a main clause (3.4) is equivalent to an implication $y_{i,j} \rightarrow x_{i,j}$, we can rewrite (3.4) as

$$(y_{i_1,j_1} \rightarrow x_{i_1,j_1}) \lor \cdots \lor (y_{i_{s+t},j_{s+t}} \rightarrow \overline{x}_{i_{s+t},j_{s+t}}) \ . \quad (3.5)$$

What this boils down to is that for every clause C_i, the auxiliary clauses encode that there is at least one choice of selector variables $y_{i,j}$ which are all true, and for this choice of selector variables the $x_{i,j}$-variables will play the role of the u_i-variables, giving us back the original clause C_i. It is easily verified that F is unsatisfiable if and only if $G = Lift_\ell(F)$ is unsatisfiable, and if F is a k-CNF formula with m clauses, then G is a $\max(2k,\ell)$-CNF formula with at most $m\ell^k + n$ clauses.

3.2 Pebbling Contradictions and Pyramids

Pebbling is a tool for studying time-space relationships by means of a game played on directed acyclic graphs. This game models computations where the execution is independent of the input and can be performed by straight-line programs. Pebble games were originally devised for studying programming languages and compiler construction, but have later found a broad range of applications in computational complexity theory. In the last decade, there has been renewed study of pebbling in the context of proof complexity. An excellent survey of pebbling up to ca 1980 is [56], and some more recent developments are covered in the second author's upcoming survey [52].

The way pebbling results have been used in proof complexity has mainly been by studying so-called *pebbling contradictions* as defined in [18]. These are CNF formulas encoding the pebble game played on a DAG G by postulating the sources to be true and the sink to be false, and specifying that truth propagates through the graph according to the pebbling rules.

DEFINITION 12 (PEBBLING CONTRADICTION). *Let G be a DAG with sources S and a unique sink z. Identify every vertex $v \in V(G)$ with a propositional logic variable v. The* pebbling contradiction *over G, denoted Peb_G, is the conjunction of the following clauses:*

- *for all $s \in S$, a unit clause s (*source axioms*),*
- *For all non-sources v with predecessors $pred(v)$, the clause $\bigvee_{u \in pred(v)} \overline{u} \vee v$ (*pebbling axioms*),*
- *for the sink z, the unit clause $\overline{z}$ (*sink axiom*).*

If the DAG G has n vertices and maximal indegree d, the formula Peb_G is a minimally unsatisfiable $(1+d)$-CNF formula with $n + 1$ clauses over n variables.

In this paper, we will focus on pebbling contradictions over *pyramid graphs*. For an example of such a pebbling contradiction, see the CNF formula in Figure 1(b) defined in terms of the graph in Figure 1(a). For completeness, the formal definition of a pyramid graph is as follows.

DEFINITION 13 (PYRAMID). *The* pyramid graph Π_h *of height h is a layered DAG with $h + 1$ levels, where there is one vertex on the highest level (the sink z), two vertices on the next level et cetera down to $h + 1$ vertices at the lowest level 0. The ith vertex at level L has incoming edges from the ith and $(i + 1)$st vertices at level $L - 1$.*

To make the connection back to Definition 11, in Figure 2 we present the lift of length 2 of the CNF formula in Figure 1(b), with the auxiliary clauses at the top of the left column followed by the main clauses one by one, listed for all tuples of selector indices (with the only difference that since the variables in this formula are u, v, w, x, y, z rather than $u_1, \ldots, u_n$, we denote the main variables by $x_{u,j_1}, x_{v,j_2}, x_{w,j_3}$, et cetera, rather than $x_{i_1,j_1}, x_{i_2,j_2}, \ldots$). We will refer to the main clauses in Figure 1(b) as source axioms, pebbling axioms, and sink axioms, respectively, when they have been obtained by lifting of the corresponding axioms in the pebbling contradiction.

We remark that the process of lifting formulas is similar to, but different from, the substitution used in [17], where some (fixed) function $f(x_1, \ldots, x_\ell)$ is substituted for every variable x and the resulting formula is expanded out to CNF again using De Morgan's laws. Although we believe that lifted pebbling formulas should share many of the properties of substitution pebbling formulas, the proofs in [17] would require modifications to work for lifted formulas, and we have not studied in any detail if and how such modifications could be made.

3.3 Two-Player Communication Complexity

The basic two-player model of communication complexity suffices for our purposes in this paper. We briefly review this model below and refer to [44] for further details and formal definitions.

For any function $f : X \times Y \mapsto Q$, where X and Y are some domains and Q is some range, in the communication problem of computing f Alice is given an input $x \in X$, Bob is given an input $y \in Y$, and they are required to compute $f(x, y)$ minimizing the communication between them. Similarly, for any search problem $S \subseteq X \times Y \times Q$, where X and Y are some input domains and Q is some output range, the communication problem solving S is one in which Alice is given $x \in X$, Bob is given $y \in Y$, and they are required to communicate to find some q such that $(x, y, q) \in S$. The cost of a communication protocol is the maximum number of bits communicated on any input. The *deterministic communication complexity* of a function f (or a search problem S) is the minimum cost of any communication protocol solving f (or S, respectively).

We are also concerned with randomized communication, in which each player has access to a private infinite source of random bits[5] and the messages can depend on both the input and the random bits. We say that a randomized communication protocol solves a function f (or a search problem S) with error ϵ if on any input, the protocol outputs a correct answer with probability at least $1 - \epsilon$ over the random choices. Note that in a search problem, an input may have more than one correct output, and the protocol is allowed to output different correct outputs depending on the random choices. The *randomized communication complexity* with error ϵ of a function f (or a search problem S) is the minimum cost of any randomized protocol with error ϵ solving f (or S, respectively).

A key notion for this paper is that a randomized communication protocol is said to solve a search problem *consistently* if on any input assignment, the protocol outputs a *unique* correct output with probability at least 3/4 over its random choices.

Probabilistic errors in randomized protocols can be reduced by a small blow-up in communication cost as stated next.

PROPOSITION 14. *For any $0 < \epsilon' < \epsilon < 1/2$, if there exists a randomized protocol Π with communication cost c and error ϵ to compute a function f, then there exists a randomized protocol Π' with cost $O(c \cdot \log_\epsilon \epsilon')$ and error ϵ' to compute f.*

The proof is standard and we omit the details. The idea is to repeat the protocol Π $O(\log_\epsilon \epsilon')$ times and take a majority vote. The analysis uses Chernoff bounds.

3.4 Leveraging Communication Complexity to Obtain Proof Complexity Trade-offs

Let us now provide formal lemmas implementing the steps in the argument outlined at the beginning of this section.

Given any CNF formula G, the *(falsified clause) search problem* for G is the problem of finding, given any truth value assignment α, a clause $C \in G$ falsified by α. We denote this problem by G^{search}. The next lemma says that if a CNF formula G has a polynomial calculus resolution refutation (or cutting planes refutation, respectively) in simultaneous short length and small space, then there is a small deterministic (or randomized, respectively) two-player protocol that solves G^{search} for any truth assignment and any partition of the variables between Alice and Bob. We remark that this lemma holds also for the stronger *semantic* versions of these proof systems in the sense of Definition 10.

LEMMA 15. *Let G be any CNF formula over n variables, and suppose that each of these variables is given to either one of Alice and Bob. Then the followings holds:*

[5]Here "private" means that one player cannot see the random bits of the other. There is also a public-coin randomized communication model [44], but it is not our concern in this paper.

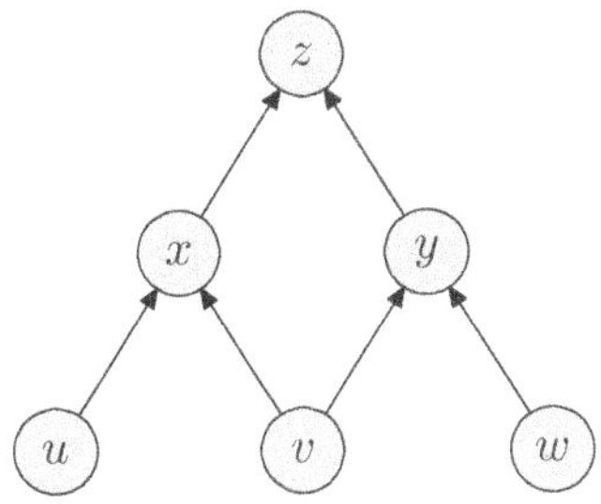

(a) Pyramid graph Π_2 of height 2.

$$
\begin{aligned}
& u \\
\wedge\ & v \\
\wedge\ & w \\
\wedge\ & (\overline{u} \vee \overline{v} \vee x) \\
\wedge\ & (\overline{v} \vee \overline{w} \vee y) \\
\wedge\ & (\overline{x} \vee \overline{y} \vee z) \\
\wedge\ & \overline{z}
\end{aligned}
$$

(b) Pebbling contradiction Peb_{Π_2}.

Figure 1: Pebbling contradiction for the pyramid graph Π_2.

$$
\begin{aligned}
& (y_{u,1} \vee y_{u,2}) \\
\wedge\ & (y_{v,1} \vee y_{v,2}) \\
\wedge\ & (y_{w,1} \vee y_{w,2}) \\
\wedge\ & (y_{x,1} \vee y_{x,2}) \\
\wedge\ & (y_{y,1} \vee y_{y,2}) \\
\wedge\ & (y_{z,1} \vee y_{z,2}) \\
\wedge\ & (\overline{y}_{u,1} \vee x_{u,1}) \\
\wedge\ & (\overline{y}_{u,2} \vee x_{u,2}) \\
\wedge\ & (\overline{y}_{v,1} \vee x_{v,1}) \\
\wedge\ & (\overline{y}_{v,2} \vee x_{v,2}) \\
\wedge\ & (\overline{y}_{w,1} \vee x_{w,1}) \\
\wedge\ & (\overline{y}_{w,2} \vee x_{w,2}) \\
\wedge\ & (\overline{y}_{u,1} \vee \overline{x}_{u,1} \vee \overline{y}_{v,1} \vee \overline{x}_{v,1} \vee \overline{y}_{x,1} \vee x_{x,1}) \\
\wedge\ & (\overline{y}_{u,1} \vee \overline{x}_{u,1} \vee \overline{y}_{v,1} \vee \overline{x}_{v,1} \vee \overline{y}_{x,2} \vee x_{x,2}) \\
\wedge\ & (\overline{y}_{u,1} \vee \overline{x}_{u,1} \vee \overline{y}_{v,2} \vee \overline{x}_{v,2} \vee \overline{y}_{x,1} \vee x_{x,1}) \\
\wedge\ & (\overline{y}_{u,1} \vee \overline{x}_{u,1} \vee \overline{y}_{v,2} \vee \overline{x}_{v,2} \vee \overline{y}_{x,2} \vee x_{x,2}) \\
\wedge\ & (\overline{y}_{u,2} \vee \overline{x}_{u,2} \vee \overline{y}_{v,1} \vee \overline{x}_{v,1} \vee \overline{y}_{x,1} \vee x_{x,1}) \\
\wedge\ & (\overline{y}_{u,2} \vee \overline{x}_{u,2} \vee \overline{y}_{v,1} \vee \overline{x}_{v,1} \vee \overline{y}_{x,2} \vee x_{x,2}) \\
\wedge\ & (\overline{y}_{u,2} \vee \overline{x}_{u,2} \vee \overline{y}_{v,2} \vee \overline{x}_{v,2} \vee \overline{y}_{x,1} \vee x_{x,1}) \\
\wedge\ & (\overline{y}_{u,2} \vee \overline{x}_{u,2} \vee \overline{y}_{v,2} \vee \overline{x}_{v,2} \vee \overline{y}_{x,2} \vee x_{x,2})
\end{aligned}
$$

$$
\begin{aligned}
\wedge\ & (\overline{y}_{v,1} \vee \overline{x}_{v,1} \vee \overline{y}_{w,1} \vee \overline{x}_{w,1} \vee \overline{y}_{y,1} \vee x_{y,1}) \\
\wedge\ & (\overline{y}_{v,1} \vee \overline{x}_{v,1} \vee \overline{y}_{w,1} \vee \overline{x}_{w,1} \vee \overline{y}_{y,2} \vee x_{y,2}) \\
\wedge\ & (\overline{y}_{v,1} \vee \overline{x}_{v,1} \vee \overline{y}_{w,2} \vee \overline{x}_{w,2} \vee \overline{y}_{y,1} \vee x_{y,1}) \\
\wedge\ & (\overline{y}_{v,1} \vee \overline{x}_{v,1} \vee \overline{y}_{w,2} \vee \overline{x}_{w,2} \vee \overline{y}_{y,2} \vee x_{y,2}) \\
\wedge\ & (\overline{y}_{v,2} \vee \overline{x}_{v,2} \vee \overline{y}_{w,1} \vee \overline{x}_{w,1} \vee \overline{y}_{y,1} \vee x_{y,1}) \\
\wedge\ & (\overline{y}_{v,2} \vee \overline{x}_{v,2} \vee \overline{y}_{w,1} \vee \overline{x}_{w,1} \vee \overline{y}_{y,2} \vee x_{y,2}) \\
\wedge\ & (\overline{y}_{v,2} \vee \overline{x}_{v,2} \vee \overline{y}_{w,2} \vee \overline{x}_{w,2} \vee \overline{y}_{y,1} \vee x_{y,1}) \\
\wedge\ & (\overline{y}_{v,2} \vee \overline{x}_{v,2} \vee \overline{y}_{w,2} \vee \overline{x}_{w,2} \vee \overline{y}_{y,2} \vee x_{y,2}) \\
\wedge\ & (\overline{y}_{x,1} \vee \overline{x}_{x,1} \vee \overline{y}_{y,1} \vee \overline{x}_{y,1} \vee \overline{y}_{z,1} \vee x_{z,1}) \\
\wedge\ & (\overline{y}_{x,1} \vee \overline{x}_{x,1} \vee \overline{y}_{y,1} \vee \overline{x}_{y,1} \vee \overline{y}_{z,2} \vee x_{z,2}) \\
\wedge\ & (\overline{y}_{x,1} \vee \overline{x}_{x,1} \vee \overline{y}_{y,2} \vee \overline{x}_{y,2} \vee \overline{y}_{z,1} \vee x_{z,1}) \\
\wedge\ & (\overline{y}_{x,1} \vee \overline{x}_{x,1} \vee \overline{y}_{y,2} \vee \overline{x}_{y,2} \vee \overline{y}_{z,2} \vee x_{z,2}) \\
\wedge\ & (\overline{y}_{x,2} \vee \overline{x}_{x,2} \vee \overline{y}_{y,1} \vee \overline{x}_{y,1} \vee \overline{y}_{z,1} \vee x_{z,1}) \\
\wedge\ & (\overline{y}_{x,2} \vee \overline{x}_{x,2} \vee \overline{y}_{y,1} \vee \overline{x}_{y,1} \vee \overline{y}_{z,2} \vee x_{z,2}) \\
\wedge\ & (\overline{y}_{x,2} \vee \overline{x}_{x,2} \vee \overline{y}_{y,2} \vee \overline{x}_{y,2} \vee \overline{y}_{z,1} \vee x_{z,1}) \\
\wedge\ & (\overline{y}_{x,2} \vee \overline{x}_{x,2} \vee \overline{y}_{y,2} \vee \overline{x}_{y,2} \vee \overline{y}_{z,2} \vee x_{z,2}) \\
\wedge\ & (\overline{y}_{z,1} \vee \overline{x}_{z,1}) \\
\wedge\ & (\overline{y}_{z,2} \vee \overline{x}_{z,2})
\end{aligned}
$$

Figure 2: Lifted formula $Lift_2(Peb_{\Pi_2})$ of length 2 obtained from the pebbling contradiction over Π_2.

- *If G has a (semantic) PCR-refutation in monomial space s and length L, then there is a deterministic protocol of cost $\mathrm{O}(s \log L)$ bits for G^{search}.*
- *If G has a (semantic) CP-refutation in line space s and length L, then there is a* consistent *randomized protocol of cost $\mathrm{O}(s \log L \log^2 n \log(s \log L))$ bits with error $1/4$ for G^{search}.*

PROOF. In one line, the proof is that Alice and Bob will use the refutation of G to do binary search for a falsified clause.

In a little bit more detail, suppose Alice and Bob are given their two parts of an assignment α. Fix a refutation $\pi = \{\mathbb{D}_0, \mathbb{D}_1, \ldots, \mathbb{D}_L\}$ as in the statement of the lemma, where as before $\mathbb{D}_0 = \emptyset$ and $\bot \in \mathbb{D}_L$. For ease of notation, suppose the length L of the refutation is actually the total number of derivation steps including erasures, as discussed in the footnote in Definition 4 (which is a very minor technicality).

Alice and Bob consider the configuration $\mathbb{D}_{L/2}$ in the refutation at time $L/2$ and with joint efforts (involving some communication, which we will discuss shortly) evaluate the truth value of $\mathbb{D}_{L/2}$ under the assignment α. If $\mathbb{D}_{L/2}$ is true under α, they continue their search in the subderivation $\{\mathbb{D}_{L/2}, \mathbb{D}_1, \ldots, \mathbb{D}_L\}$. If $\mathbb{D}_{L/2}$ is false, the search continues in the first half of the refutation $\{\mathbb{D}_0, \mathbb{D}_1, \ldots, \mathbb{D}_{L/2}\}$ Note that $\mathbb{D}_0 = \emptyset$ evaluates to true by default, and since $\bot \in \mathbb{D}_L$ this configuration evaluates to false, and the binary search is carried out so as to maintain that the first configuration in the current subderivation under consideration evaluates to true and the last one evaluates to false. Hence, after $\log L$ steps Alice and Bob find a $t \in [L]$ such that $\mathbb{D}_{t-1}$ is true under α but $\mathbb{D}_t$ is false. Since the proof system is sound, the derivation step to get from $\mathbb{D}_{t-1}$ to $\mathbb{D}_t$ cannot have been an inference or erasure, but must be a download of some axiom clause $C \in G$. This clause C must be false under α, and so Alice and Bob give C as their answer.

Now all that remains is to discuss how much communication is needed to evaluate a configuration in the refutation. For PCR, Alice and Bob can just look at all the monomials in the the current configuration $\mathbb{D}$, say $m_1, m_2, \ldots, m_{s'}$ for $s' \leq s$. For each monomial m_i, Alice evaluates the part m_i^A containing her variables and Bob the part m_i^B containing his, they communicate the values with a constant number of bits (since the field is finite), and multiply to get $m_i = m_i^A \cdot m_i^B$. There are at most s monomials, so the total communication for the configuration is $\mathrm{O}(s)$, and then they both know the truth value of the configuration. Note also that the communication clearly is deterministic.

For cutting planes, the same argument applies, except that to check the truth of each line, we have to do a randomized protocol. Fortunately, this can be achieved with communication cost $O(\log^2 n)$ with constant error as shown in Lemma 5 in [40] (also in [12]). Applying a standard reduction of randomized error by a small blow-up in communication cost as in Proposition 14, we can make the error sufficiently small, say $\frac{1}{4s \log L}$, with communication cost $\mathrm{O}\big(\log^2 n \log(s \log L)\big)$ for each line check. Thus, by a union bound, except with probability $1/4$, all $s \log L$ line checks in the protocol are done correctly, and hence the protocol outputs a unique answer. In this way we obtain a consistent randomized protocol. The lemma follows. □

Given Lemma 15, in order to prove Theorem 1, we need to find a family of CNF formulas whose search problem has large communication complexity. This is achieved by the following lemma.

LEMMA 16. *Let $\{Peb_{\Pi_h}\}_{h=1}^{\infty}$ denote the family of pebbling contradictions over pyramid graphs of height h, and let $G_h = Lift_3(Peb_{\Pi_h})$. Then any consistent randomized (and hence also any deterministic) two-party protocol solving the search problem associated with G_h requires $\Omega(\sqrt{h})$ bits of communication, where Alice receives the x-variables and Bob receives the y-variables in G_h.*

We remind the reader that for purposes of illustration, a lift *of length* 2 of a pyramid pebbling contradiction can be found in Figure 2.

To prove Lemma 16, we first need to establish the communication complexity lower bound stated in Theorem 2. We discuss in more detail in Section 4 how to prove this theorem, but the reader is referred to the full-length version for a complete proof. Taking Lemma 16 on faith for the time being, however, we can now prove our main proof complexity result.

THEOREM 1 (RESTATED). *There is a family of k-CNF formulas $\{F_n\}_{n=1}^{\infty}$ of size $\Theta(n)$ that can be refuted in length $\mathrm{O}(n)$ in resolution, polynomial calculus (and hence also polynomial calculus resolution) and cutting planes, but for which the following holds:*

- *For any PCR-refutation of the formula F_n in simultaneous length L and monomial space s it must hold that $s \log L = \Omega(\sqrt[4]{n})$.*
- *For any CP-refutation of the formula F_n in simultaneous length L and line space s it must hold that $s \log L \log(s \log L) = \Omega\left(\sqrt[4]{n} / \log^2 n\right)$.*

PROOF. We set $F_n = Lift_3(Peb_{\Pi_h})$ for $h = \Theta(\sqrt{n})$, since pebbling contradictions over pyramids have size quadratic in the pyramid height. The lower bounds follow by looking at the communication protocols constructed from purported refutations of F_n in Lemma 15 and applying the lower bound in Lemma 16.

It remains to prove the upper bound. This is fairly standard, and we will not go into too much details. The proof closely follows similar proofs in, e.g., [17]. The idea is that we look at a black pebbling strategy for pyramid graphs (or for any DAG over which we have defined a pebbling contradiction). For pyramids, there are black pebbling strategies in linear time and space $\Theta(h)$. Then we build a resolution proof that simulates this pebbling strategy step by step to refute a lifted pyramid pebbling contradiction of length length ℓ for any $\ell = \mathrm{O}(1)$ (in particular, for $\ell = 3$).

We maintain the invariant that when a vertex v is pebbled, we derive $\overline{y}_{v,i} \vee x_{v,i}$ for all $i \in [\ell]$. In this way, when we get to the sink z, the clauses $\overline{y}_{z,i} \vee x_{z,i}$ together with the auxiliary clause $y_{z,1} \vee \cdots \vee y_{z,\ell}$ and the sink axioms $\overline{y}_{z,i} \vee \overline{x}_{z,i}$ for all $i \in [\ell]$ immediately yield a contradiction. The base case for the inductive argument are the source vertices, for which these clauses are just the source axioms. Consider a non-source vertex w and suppose for concreteness that it has exactly two immediate predecessors u and v. When a black pebble is placed on w, the vertices u and v must also have black pebbles on them by the rules of the pebble game, and so by induction we have the clauses $\overline{y}_{u,i} \vee x_{u,i}$ and $\overline{y}_{v,i} \vee x_{v,i}$ in memory for all $i \in [\ell]$. Download the pebbling axioms

$\overline{y}_{u,h} \vee \overline{x}_{u,h} \vee \overline{y}_{v,i} \vee \overline{x}_{v,i} \vee \overline{y}_{w,j} \vee x_{w,j}$ for all $h, i, j \in [\ell]$, as well as the auxiliary clauses $y_{u,1} \vee \cdots \vee y_{u,\ell}$ and $y_{v,1} \vee \cdots \vee y_{v,\ell}$. Then it is not hard to verify that all of these clauses together imply $\overline{y}_{w,j} \vee x_{w,j}$ for all $j \in [\ell]$, and by the implicational compleness of resolution there must then exist a derivation of these clauses. Since the number of variables involved is constant, this derivation has constant length, width, and space (and it is possible to do much better than the trivial upper bounds one gets from this argument, but we are not interested in optimizing constants here).

Thus, every step in the pebbling can be simulated in constant length and with constant extra clause space, so simulating the whole pebbling yields a resolution refutation in length $O(n)$ and clause space $O(\sqrt{n})$. Since this resolution refutation also has width $O(1)$, it can be simulated in CP and PC (and hence also PCR) with at most a constant factor blow-up in length and space. □

We remark that for the same family of formulas $\{F_n\}_{n=1}^{\infty}$ in Theorem 1, we can show that any tree-like *semantic* CP refutation of this formula must have length L such that $L \log L = \exp(\Omega(\sqrt[4]{n}/\log^2 n))$. This is shown by the same proof as for Theorem 1, except that we use the reduction from small tree-like semantic CP proof to small consistent randomized communication protocol for search problems as presented in [10] (and which can also be found implicitly in [12, 40]). To our knowledge, this is the first result showing that *semantic* tree-like CP cannot polynomially simulate resolution. A separation between *syntactic* tree-like CP and resolution was shown in [22] using the so-called interpolation method, which is not known to be applicable to semantic CP.

4. OBTAINING COMMUNICATION COMPLEXITY LOWER BOUNDS

In order to prove Lemma 16, we show a new communication complexity lower bound for the falsified clause search problems of CNF formulas. More generally, we show that if S is a search problem with a certain property, then the communication complexity of another search problem which is obtained by lifting S (using length $\ell \geq 3$) is large. This is stated in Theorem 2 and is our main technical contribution, and we consider this to be an interesting new result in communication complexity in its own right.

Before going into a more detailed discussion of Theorem 2, we need to define formally the concepts that we will use. Let us start by recalling the well-known notion of block sensitivity of (usually Boolean) functions as introduced by Nisan [49], and then generalize this notion for search problems. Let $f : \{0,1\}^m \mapsto Q$ be any function to some range Q. For an input $\alpha \in \{0,1\}^m$ and a subset $B \subseteq [m]$, we say that f is *sensitive to* B *on* α if $f(\alpha) \neq f(\alpha^B)$, where α^B is obtained from α by flipping all bits in B. The *block sensitivity of* f *on* α, denoted $bs(f, \alpha)$, is the maximum number s of pairwise disjoint blocks $B_1, \ldots B_s \subseteq [m]$ such that f is sensitive to each B_i on α. For any subset of assignments $A' \subseteq \{0,1\}^m$, we define the *block sensitivity over* A' *of* f, denoted $bs(f, A')$, as

$$bs(f, A') = \max_{\alpha \in A'} bs(f, \alpha) \ . \tag{4.1}$$

Thus, the well-known notion of block sensitivity of f is the block sensitivity of f over the full set of assignments $\{0,1\}^m$.

Let $S \subseteq A \times Q$ be any search problem with input domain A and output range Q. If $A = \{0,1\}^m$, we say that a function $f : \{0,1\}^m \mapsto Q$ *solves* or *satisfies* the search problem S if on any input $\alpha \in \{0,1\}^m$ it holds that $(\alpha, f(\alpha)) \in S$. A *critical input* α for a search problem $S \subseteq \{0,1\}^m \times Q$ is one with a *unique* $q \in Q$ such that $(\alpha, q) \in S$. This brings us to the concept of *critical block sensitivity of search problems*, which plays a key role in this paper and which we therefore highlight in a formal definition.

DEFINITION 17. *The* block sensitivity of a search problem $S \subseteq \{0,1\}^m \times Q$ *over* $A' \subseteq \{0,1\}^m$*, is defined as*

$$bs(S, A') = \min\{bs(f, A') \mid f : \{0,1\}^m \mapsto Q \text{ solves } S\}$$

(or in words, $bs(S, A')$ *is the minimum block sensitivity over* A' *of any function* f *satisfying* S*). If* $A' = \{0,1\}^m$*, we simply write* $bs(S) = bs(S, A')$*. We will be mostly interested in the set of all critical inputs of* $S \subseteq \{0,1\}^m \times Q$*, which we denote* A_c*, and we define* $bs_{crit}(S) = bs(S, A_c)$ *to be the* critical block sensitivity *of* S*.*

Note that if S is a function, then $bs_{crit}(S)$ reduces to the usual notion of block sensitivity of functions. We are now ready to give a more precis formal statement of Theorem 2.

THEOREM 18 (FORMAL VERSION OF THEOREM 2). *Let* $S \subseteq \{0,1\}^m \times Q$ *be any search problem over input domain* $\{0,1\}^m$ *and range* Q*. Then it holds for any* $\ell \geq 3$ *that any consistent randomized (and hence also any deterministic) two-party protocol solving* $G = Lift_\ell(S)$ *requires* $\Omega(bs_{crit}(S))$ *bits of communication, where Alice receives the* x*-variables and Bob receives the* y*-variables in* G*.*

We remark that for any search problem S, there is a simple deterministic two-player protocol solving $G = Lift_3(S)$ with communication cost $O(D(S))$, where $D(S)$ is the *deterministic decision tree complexity* of S. This protocol works by simply simulating the decision tree. It can also be proven that $bs(S) = \Omega(D(S)^{1/3}/\log_2|Q|)$ by a simple extension of an analogous inequality for Boolean functions [7]. Thus, if we could replace $\Omega(bs_{crit}(S))$ in the lower bound in Theorem 18 by $\Omega(bs(S))$, that would yield a stronger lower bound, which would be within a polynomial of the simple upper bound mentioned above. We are not able to prove nor disprove such a bound, however, so this remains an interesting open question.

One can observe, however, that it is often the case in the literature (e.g., in the case of the lower bounds for resolution proven in [23, 39]) that lower bounds are obtained by studying only critical assignments. In such cases, if the decision tree complexity of solving a search problem S restricted to critical inputs is large, then this can be taken to suggest that $bs_{crit}(S)$ should also be large. And indeed, the second key ingredient that we use together with Theorem 18 in our proof of Lemma 16 is the following lemma, saying that the search problem for pyramid pebbling contradictions (which can easily be shown to have large decision tree complexity even when restricted to critical inputs) has large critical block sensitivity.

LEMMA 19. *Let* $\{Peb_{\Pi_h}\}_{h=1}^{\infty}$ *be the family of pebbling contradictions over pyramid graphs of height* h*. Then the critical block sensitivity of the search problem for the formula* Peb_{Π_h} *is* $\Omega(\sqrt{h})$*.*

We refer to the full-length version of the paper for the proofs of Theorem 18 and Lemma 19. Let us just mention here, however, that the proof of Theorem 18 is a new application of the information-theoretic approach in two-player communication complexity as presented in [5, 26]. To the best of our knowledge, this is the first time such an approach has been used to derive strong, general communication lower bounds for a search problem.

To conclude this section, let us discuss some previous work related to Theorem 18 and in this way give some background and motivation for our new result. Although Theorem 18 is certainly not the first in the literature that shows strong communication lower bounds for search problems related to CNF formulas, previous results do not suffice for our purposes in this paper. One such result was proved by Raz and McKenzie [58] and improved by Bonet et al. [22], who showed that for a certain broad class of search problems $S \subseteq \{0,1\}^m \times Q$ (in particular, the search problem S for any CNF formula F), the deterministic[6] communication complexity of $\mathit{Lift}_\ell(S)$ is essentially $D(S)$ provided that $\ell \geq m^{14}$. Although this lower bound is tight, it requires polynomially large length ℓ. Thus, the lifted CNF formula $\mathit{Lift}_\ell(F)$ does not have bounded width, and may not be refutable in polynomial length in resolution. Moreover, deterministic communication complexity lower bounds do not suffice for us to derive length-space tradeoffs for CP.

Strong (and non-consistent) randomized communication complexity for the search problems of some families of CNF formulas were also known previously. In [40], Impagliazzo et al. proved one such two-player lower bound for a specific family of CNF formulas. However, this formula family have clauses of polynomially large width. In [12], Beame et al. proved a strong multiparty randomized communication lower bounds in the so-called *number-on-the-forehead* model for a search problem of another family of formulas (namely, Tseitin formulas over certain expander graphs with a non-trivial modification). Similarly to the last result, this family of formulas also have unbounded (logarithmic) width. Furthermore, the formulas in both of these results are known to require exponential refutation length in resolution, and no polynomial-size refutations are known for them in PCR or CP. Since the formulas in these results must be carefully chosen for the techniques to be applicable, it is not known whether previous techniques yield lower bounds for any formulas that do not suffer from the aforementioned drawbacks.

Therefore, although on the face of it it might look straightforward to apply Lemma 15 with previously known communication complexity results to obtain strong length-space trade-offs for PCR and/or CP, such trade-offs would have several shortcomings. In particular, the formulas would all have unbounded width, and also we would not know any upper bounds showing that these formulas actually have polynomial-size refutations. But in Theorem 18, for the first time[7] we are able to give a consistent[8] randomized two-player communication lower bound for search problems in terms of their general characteristics (critical block sensitivity) and apply this lower bound to the search problem of a family of CNF formulas which have constant width and are refutable in polynomial length in resolution.

[6]Bonet et al. [22] actually proved the result for the model of *real* communication complexity which is stronger than deterministic communication complexity. However this model is nothing we are concerned with in this paper.

[7]We remark that an easier and more direct way to obtain our results in Theorem 1 would have been to apply the ideas in [10] (in particular, Theorem 3.6 in that paper). However, we have recently found a serious problem in the key Lemma 3.5 in [10], and therefore we cannot use this approach.

[8]We want to pointout that it is necessary to restrict our attention to *consistent* randomized protocols in order to get strong lower bounds in Theorem 18 (i.e., polynomially related to the deterministic decision tree complexity of the search problem). This is because for some search problems, exponential separations are known between deterministic and (non-consistent) randomized decision tree complexity [47].

5. CONCLUDING REMARKS

In this paper, we report the first time-space trade-offs for polynomial calculus, polynomial calculus resolution, and cutting planes. We want to point out that the results are in a sense slightly more general in that the only property of the proof systems that we use to show our trade-off results is that the correctness of each inferred line in a refutation can be checked by a small two-player communication protocol, and so our results also hold for any other proof system with this property. We interpret our results to suggest that lifted pebbling formulas should inherit time-space trade-offs properties from the graphs in terms of which they are defined, which if true would mean that the black-white pebble game in [31] could be used to obtain strong(er) trade-offs in these proof systems (as was done for resolution and k-DNF resolution in [17]).

Despite the amount of research focused on the space measure in proof complexity over the last decade, it seems fair to argue that space is still not a very well understood concept, and many fascinating (and basic) questions remain open. We highlight some such questions below.

Proving optimal lower bounds on the monomial space of refuting (preferably bounded-width) CNF formulas in PCR, or at least in polynomial calculus, is a problem that has been open for a while but might be more accessible now given recent advances in [38]. Establishing lower bounds on line space in cutting planes seems harder, since here nothing is known. However, as we have already mentioned, we believe that our results suggest that appropriate flavours of pebbling formulas should be hard with respect to space in all of these proof systems. If this could be proven, the next step would be to see if pebbling time-space trade-offs also carry over to PCR and/or cutting planes, analogously to what happens for resolution and k-DNF resolution.

It seems natural to expect that PCR and cutting planes should both be stronger than resolution with respect to space, but as far as we are aware this is open. Thus, it would be interesting to separate PCR from resolution with respect to space by finding a k-CNF formula that has low monomial space complexity in PCR but large clause space complexity in resolution, and similarly for CP with respect to resolution.

Another fairly longstanding open question, as mentioned in [1, 14] and other papers, is to prove superlinear lower bounds on total space (measured in the size of the formula) for resolution refutations of some family of k-CNF formulas (or even CNF formulas of unbounded width).

Concluding our discussion of open questions in proof complexity related to the current paper, it is hard to avoid mentioning the well-known problem of proving lower bound on proof size for cutting planes. This proof system remains very poorly understood, and it seems like a very interesting, but possibly also very challenging, open problem to prove that, for instance, random k-CNF formulas or Tseitin formulas require CP-proofs of exponential size.

Finally, let us also discuss some interesting questions in communication complexity that arise from our work on Theorem 2. An obvious open question is to improve the lower bound in that theorem. In particular, a lower bound in terms of the (non-critical) block sensitivity of the search problem would not only give a lower bound that is polynomial related to the simple upper bound in terms of decision tree complexity, but would also produce a general "black-box" hardness amplification result in proof complexity based on our approach, in the sense that lower bounds on the rank (also known as depth) in resolution for any CNF formula F would turn into into space-length tradeoffs in PCR and CP for the formula $Lift(F)$.

Another related problem is to gain more understanding of the critical block sensitivity of search problems. For instance, is the critical block sensitivity always polynomially related to the block sensitivity for any search problem? If this were true, it would imply the same hardness amplification result as mentioned above.

Acknowledgements

The first author performed part of this work while visiting KTH Royal Institute of Technology supported by the foundations *Johan och Jakob Söderbergs stiftelse*, *Stiftelsen Längmanska kulturfonden*, and *Helge Ax:son Johnsons stiftelse*. The research of the second author was supported by Swedish Research Council grant 621-2010-4797 and by the European Research Council under the European Union's Seventh Framework Programme (FP7/2007–2013) / ERC grant agreement no 279611.

The authors would like to thank Arkadev Chattopadhyay for several enjoyable (and above all *illuminating*) discussions during the weeks spent jointly at KTH Royal Institute of Technology. We are also grateful to the anonymous referees for several comments that helped to improve the presentation of this paper.

6. REFERENCES

[1] M. Alekhnovich, E. Ben-Sasson, A. A. Razborov, and A. Wigderson. Space complexity in propositional calculus. *SIAM Journal on Computing*, 31(4):1184–1211, 2002. Preliminary version appeared in *STOC '00*.

[2] M. Alekhnovich and A. A. Razborov. Lower bounds for polynomial calculus: Non-binomial case. *Proceedings of the Steklov Institute of Mathematics*, 242:18–35, 2003. Available at `http://people.cs.uchicago.edu/~razborov/files/misha.pdf`. Preliminary version appeared in *FOCS '01*.

[3] A. Atserias and V. Dalmau. A combinatorial characterization of resolution width. *Journal of Computer and System Sciences*, 74(3):323–334, May 2008. Preliminary version appeared in *CCC '03*.

[4] A. Atserias, J. K. Fichte, and M. Thurley. Clause-learning algorithms with many restarts and bounded-width resolution. *Journal of Artificial Intelligence Research*, 40:353–373, Jan. 2011. Preliminary version appeared in *SAT '09*.

[5] Z. Bar-Yossef, T. Jayram, R. Kumar, and D. Sivakumar. An information statistics approach to data stream and communication complexity. *Journal of Computer and System Sciences*, 68(4):702–732, June 2004. Preliminary version appeared in *FOCS '02*.

[6] R. J. Bayardo Jr. and R. Schrag. Using CSP look-back techniques to solve real-world SAT instances. In *Proceedings of the 14th National Conference on Artificial Intelligence (AAAI '97)*, pages 203–208, July 1997.

[7] R. Beals, H. Buhrman, R. Cleve, M. Mosca, and R. de Wolf. Quantum lower bounds by polynomials. *Journal of the ACM*, 48(4):778–797, 2001.

[8] P. Beame. Proof complexity. In S. Rudich and A. Wigderson, editors, *Computational Complexity Theory*, volume 10 of *IAS/Park City Mathematics Series*, pages 199–246. American Mathematical Society, 2004.

[9] P. Beame, C. Beck, and R. Impagliazzo. Time-space tradeoffs in resolution: Superpolynomial lower bounds for superlinear space. In *Proceedings of the 44th Annual ACM Symposium on Theory of Computing (STOC '12)*, May 2012. To appear.

[10] P. Beame, T. Huynh, and T. Pitassi. Hardness amplification in proof complexity. In *Proceedings of the 42nd Annual ACM Symposium on Theory of Computing (STOC '10)*, pages 87–96, June 2010.

[11] P. Beame, R. Karp, T. Pitassi, and M. Saks. The efficiency of resolution and Davis-Putnam procedures. *SIAM Journal on Computing*, 31(4):1048–1075, 2002. Preliminary versions of these results appeared in *FOCS '96* and *STOC '98*.

[12] P. Beame, T. Pitassi, and N. Segerlind. Lower bounds for Lovász–Schrijver systems and beyond follow from multiparty communication complexity. *SIAM Journal on Computing*, 37(3):845–869, 2007. Preliminary version appeared in *ICALP '05*.

[13] E. Ben-Sasson. Size space tradeoffs for resolution. *SIAM Journal on Computing*, 38(6):2511–2525, May 2009. Preliminary version appeared in *STOC '02*.

[14] E. Ben-Sasson and N. Galesi. Space complexity of random formulae in resolution. *Random Structures and Algorithms*, 23(1):92–109, Aug. 2003. Preliminary version appeared in *CCC '01*.

[15] E. Ben-Sasson and J. Johannsen. Lower bounds for width-restricted clause learning on small width formulas. In *Proceedings of the 13th International Conference on Theory and Applications of Satisfiability Testing (SAT '10)*, volume 6175 of *Lecture Notes in Computer Science*, pages 16–29. Springer, July 2010.

[16] E. Ben-Sasson and J. Nordström. Short proofs may be spacious: An optimal separation of space and length in resolution. In *Proceedings of the 49th Annual IEEE Symposium on Foundations of Computer Science (FOCS '08)*, pages 709–718, Oct. 2008.

[17] E. Ben-Sasson and J. Nordström. Understanding space in proof complexity: Separations and trade-offs via substitutions. In *Proceedings of the 2nd Symposium on Innovations in Computer Science (ICS '11)*, pages

401–416, Jan. 2011. Full-length version available at `http://eccc.hpi-web.de/report/2010/125/`.

[18] E. Ben-Sasson and A. Wigderson. Short proofs are narrow—resolution made simple. *Journal of the ACM*, 48(2):149–169, Mar. 2001. Preliminary version appeared in *STOC '99*.

[19] A. Biere, M. J. H. Heule, H. van Maaren, and T. Walsh, editors. *Handbook of Satisfiability*, volume 185 of *Frontiers in Artificial Intelligence and Applications*. IOS Press, Feb. 2009.

[20] A. Blake. *Canonical Expressions in Boolean Algebra*. PhD thesis, University of Chicago, 1937.

[21] M. Bonet, T. Pitassi, and R. Raz. Lower bounds for cutting planes proofs with small coefficients. In *Proceedings of the 27th Annual ACM Symposium on Theory of Computing (STOC '95)*, pages 575–584, May 1995.

[22] M. L. Bonet, J. L. Esteban, N. Galesi, and J. Johannsen. On the relative complexity of resolution refinements and cutting planes proof systems. *SIAM Journal on Computing*, 30(5):1462–1484, 2000. Preliminary version appeared in *FOCS '98*.

[23] M. L. Bonet and N. Galesi. Optimality of size-width tradeoffs for resolution. *Computational Complexity*, 10(4):261–276, Dec. 2001. Preliminary version appeared in *FOCS '99*.

[24] M. Brickenstein and A. Dreyer. PolyBoRi: A framework for Gröbner-basis computations with Boolean polynomials. *Journal of Symbolic Computation*, 44(9):1326–1345, Sept. 2009.

[25] M. Brickenstein, A. Dreyer, G.-M. Greuel, M. Wedler, and O. Wienand. New developments in the theory of Gröbner bases and applications to formal verification. *Journal of Pure and Applied Algebra*, 213(8):1612–1635, Aug. 2009.

[26] A. Chakrabarti, Y. Shi, A. Wirth, and A. C.-C. Yao. Informational complexity and the direct sum problem for simultaneous message complexity. In *Proceedings of the 42nd Annual IEEE Symposium on Foundations of Computer Science (FOCS '01)*, pages 270–278, Oct. 2001.

[27] V. Chvátal and E. Szemerédi. Many hard examples for resolution. *Journal of the ACM*, 35(4):759–768, Oct. 1988.

[28] M. Clegg, J. Edmonds, and R. Impagliazzo. Using the Groebner basis algorithm to find proofs of unsatisfiability. In *Proceedings of the 28th Annual ACM Symposium on Theory of Computing (STOC '96)*, pages 174–183, May 1996.

[29] S. A. Cook. The complexity of theorem-proving procedures. In *Proceedings of the 3rd Annual ACM Symposium on Theory of Computing (STOC '71)*, pages 151–158, 1971.

[30] S. A. Cook and R. Reckhow. The relative efficiency of propositional proof systems. *Journal of Symbolic Logic*, 44(1):36–50, Mar. 1979.

[31] S. A. Cook and R. Sethi. Storage requirements for deterministic polynomial time recognizable languages. *Journal of Computer and System Sciences*, 13(1):25–37, 1976.

[32] W. Cook, C. R. Coullard, and G. Turán. On the complexity of cutting-plane proofs. *Discrete Applied Mathematics*, 18(1):25–38, Nov. 1987.

[33] M. David, T. Pitassi, and E. Viola. Improved separations between nondeterministic and randomized multiparty communication. *ACM Transactions on Computation Theory*, 1:5:1–5:20, Sept. 2009.

[34] M. Davis, G. Logemann, and D. Loveland. A machine program for theorem proving. *Communications of the ACM*, 5(7):394–397, July 1962.

[35] M. Davis and H. Putnam. A computing procedure for quantification theory. *Journal of the ACM*, 7(3):201–215, 1960.

[36] J. L. Esteban, N. Galesi, and J. Messner. On the complexity of resolution with bounded conjunctions. *Theoretical Computer Science*, 321(2-3):347–370, Aug. 2004. Preliminary version appeared in *ICALP '02*.

[37] J. L. Esteban and J. Torán. Space bounds for resolution. *Information and Computation*, 171(1):84–97, 2001. Preliminary versions of these results appeared in *STACS '99* and *CSL '99*.

[38] Y. Filmus, M. Lauria, J. Nordström, N. Thapen, and N. Zewi. Space complexity in polynomial calculus. In *Proceedings of the 27th Annual IEEE Conference on Computational Complexity (CCC '12)*, June 2012. To appear.

[39] A. Haken. The intractability of resolution. *Theoretical Computer Science*, 39(2-3):297–308, Aug. 1985.

[40] R. Impagliazzo, T. Pitassi, and A. Urquhart. Upper and lower bounds for tree-like cutting planes proofs. In *Proceedings of the 9th Annual IEEE Symposium on Logic in Computer Science (LICS '94)*, pages 220–228, July 1994.

[41] R. Impagliazzo, P. Pudlák, and J. Sgall. Lower bounds for the polynomial calculus and the Gröbner basis algorithm. *Computational Complexity*, 8(2):127–144, 1999.

[42] M. Järvisalo, A. Matsliah, J. Nordström, and S. Živný. Relating proof complexity measures and practical hardness of SAT. Submitted, 2012.

[43] J. Krajíček. On the weak pigeonhole principle. *Fundamenta Mathematicae*, 170(1-3):123–140, 2001.

[44] E. Kushilevitz and N. Nisan. *Communication complexity*. Cambridge University Press, 1997.

[45] D. Le Berre and A. Parrain. On extending SAT solvers for PB problems. In *14th RCRA workshop Experimental Evaluation of Algorithms for Solving Problems with Combinatorial Explosion (RCRA '07)*, July 2007. Available at `http://pst.istc.cnr.it/RCRA07/articoli/P14-leberre-parrain-RCRA07.pdf`.

[46] D. Le Berre, A. Parrain, and O. Roussel. The long way from conflict driven clause learning to conflict driven constraint learning. In *Guangzhou Symposium on Satisfiability and its applications*, Sept. 2004. Available at `http://www.cril.univ-artois.fr/spip/publications/kanton04.pdf`.

[47] L. Lovász, M. Naor, I. Newman, and A. Wigderson. Search problems in the decision tree model. *SIAM Journal on Discrete Mathematics*, 8(1):119–132, 1995. Preliminary version appeared in *FOCS '91*.

[48] J. P. Marques-Silva and K. A. Sakallah. GRASP—a new search algorithm for satisfiability. In *Proceedings*

of the IEEE/ACM International Conference on Computer-Aided Design (ICCAD '96), pages 220–227, Nov. 1996.

[49] N. Nisan. CREW PRAMs and decision trees. *SIAM Journal on Computing*, 20:999–1007, Dec. 1991.

[50] J. Nordström. Narrow proofs may be spacious: Separating space and width in resolution. *SIAM Journal on Computing*, 39(1):59–121, May 2009. Preliminary version appeared in *STOC '06*.

[51] J. Nordström. A simplified way of proving trade-off results for resolution. *Information Processing Letters*, 109(18):1030–1035, Aug. 2009. Preliminary version appeared in ECCC report TR07-114, 2007.

[52] J. Nordström. New wine into old wineskins: A survey of some pebbling classics with supplemental results. Manuscript in preparation. To appear in *Foundations and Trends in Theoretical Computer Science*. Current draft version available at `http://www.csc.kth.se/~jakobn/research/`, 2012.

[53] J. Nordström. Pebble games, proof complexity and time-space trade-offs. *Logical Methods in Computer Science*, 2012. To appear. Available at `http://www.csc.kth.se/~jakobn/research/`.

[54] J. Nordström and J. Håstad. Towards an optimal separation of space and length in resolution (Extended abstract). In *Proceedings of the 40th Annual ACM Symposium on Theory of Computing (STOC '08)*, pages 701–710, May 2008.

[55] K. Pipatsrisawat and A. Darwiche. On the power of clause-learning SAT solvers as resolution engines. *Artificial Intelligence*, 175:512–525, Feb. 2011. Preliminary version appeared in *CP '09*.

[56] N. Pippenger. Pebbling. Technical Report RC8258, IBM Watson Research Center, 1980. Appeared in Proceedings of the 5th IBM Symposium on Mathematical Foundations of Computer Science, Japan.

[57] P. Pudlák. Lower bounds for resolution and cutting plane proofs and monotone computations. *Journal of Symbolic Logic*, 62(3):981–998, Sept. 1997.

[58] R. Raz and P. McKenzie. Separation of the monotone NC hierarchy. *Combinatorica*, 19(3):403–435, Mar. 1999. Preliminary version appeared in *FOCS '97*.

[59] A. A. Razborov. Lower bounds for the polynomial calculus. *Computational Complexity*, 7(4):291–324, Dec. 1998.

[60] J. A. Robinson. A machine-oriented logic based on the resolution principle. *Journal of the ACM*, 12(1):23–41, Jan. 1965.

[61] The international SAT Competitions. `http://www.satcompetition.org`.

[62] N. Segerlind. The complexity of propositional proofs. *Bulletin of Symbolic Logic*, 13(4):482–537, Dec. 2007.

[63] N. Segerlind, S. R. Buss, and R. Impagliazzo. A switching lemma for small restrictions and lower bounds for k-DNF resolution. *SIAM Journal on Computing*, 33(5):1171–1200, 2004. Preliminary version appeared in *FOCS '02*.

[64] A. Urquhart. Hard examples for resolution. *Journal of the ACM*, 34(1):209–219, Jan. 1987.

Determinism versus Nondeterminism with Arithmetic Tests and Computation

[Extended Abstract]

Miklós Ajtai
IBM Almaden Research Center
650 Harry Road
San Jose, CA 95120
ajtai@almaden.ibm.com

ABSTRACT

For each natural number d we consider a finite structure $\mathbf{M}_d$ whose universe is the set of all $0,1$-sequence of length $n = 2^d$, each representing a natural number in the set $\{0, 1, ..., 2^n-1\}$ in binary form. The operations included in the structure are the four constants $0, 1, 2^n - 1, n$, multiplication and addition modulo 2^n, the unary function $\min\{2^x, 2^n - 1\}$, the binary functions $\lfloor x/y \rfloor$ (with $\lfloor x/0 \rfloor = 0$), $\max(x, y)$, $\min(x, y)$, and the boolean vector operations $\wedge, \vee, \neg$ defined on $0, 1$ sequences of length n by performing the operations on all components simultaneously. These are essentially the arithmetic operations that can be performed on a RAM, with wordlength n, by a single instruction. We show that there exists a term (that is, an algebraic expression) $F(x, y)$ built up from the mentioned operations, with the only free variables x, y, such that for all terms $G(y)$, which is also built up from the mentioned operations, the following holds. For infinitely many positive integers d, there exists an $a \in \mathbf{M}_d$ such that the following two statements are not equivalent: (i) $\mathbf{M}_d \models \exists x, F(x, a)$, (ii) $\mathbf{M}_d \models G(a) = 0$. In other words, the question whether an existential statement, depending on the parameter $a \in \mathbf{M}_d$ is true or not, cannot be decided by evaluating an algebraic expression at a.

Another way of formulating the theorem, in a slightly stronger form, is, that over the structures $\mathbf{M}_d$, quantifier elimination is not possible in the following sense. Let $\mathcal{M}$ be a first-order language with equality, containing function symbols for all of the mentioned arithmetic operations. Then there exists an existential first-order formula $\varphi(y)$ of $\mathcal{M}$, containing a single existential quantifier and the only free variable y, such that for each propositional formula $P(y)$ of $\mathcal{M}$, we have that for infinitely many positive integers d, $\varphi(y)$ and $P(y)$ are not equivalent on $\mathbf{M}_d$, that is, $\mathbf{M}_d \models \neg\forall y, \varphi(y) \leftrightarrow P(y)$.

We also show that the theorem, in both forms, remains true if the binary operation $\min\{x^y, 2^n - 1\}$ is added to the structure $\mathbf{M}_d$. A general theorem is proved as well, which describes sufficient conditions for a set of operations on a sequence of structures $\mathbf{K}_d$, $d = 1, 2, ...$ which guarantees that the analogues of the mentioned theorems holds for the structures $\mathbf{K}_d$ too.

STOC'12, May 19–22, 2012, New York, New York, USA.

Categories and Subject Descriptors

F.1.3 [**Theory of Computation**]: Computation by Abstract Devices—*Complexity Measures and Classes*; F.4.1 [**Theory of Computation**]: Mathematical Logic and Formal Languages—*Mathematical Logic*

General Terms

Theory

Keywords

nondeterministic computation, diagonalization, quantifier elimination, lower bound

1. INTRODUCTION

1.1 Motivation, historical background

One of the central questions of complexity theory is the comparison of the computational resources needed for deterministic and nondeterministic computation. Namely, assume that we want to find a $0,1$-sequence satisfying a test T. Is it true, under some natural assumptions on the test and on the algorithm searching for x, that to find x requires essentially more computation, than checking that a given x really satisfies T? In the case when both the test and the searching algorithm must be performed in polynomial time (in the length of x) by a Turing machine, this leads to the $P = NP$? question.

In this paper we consider the special case of this problem where both the test and the search consist of the evaluation of an algebraic expression as described in the abstract. First we reformulate our problem in terms of determinism versus nondeterminism for RAMs using constant time. Although, we will use the original formulation of the theorem in its proof, the RAM formulation makes it possible to compare the theorem to other already existing results of similar nature. We consider constant time computation done by a random access machine with word length n. We show that in this case nondeterministic computation is strictly sronger than deterministic computation. For each positive integer n

we define a von Neumann type machine N_n with word length n. These machines have a common finite instructions set. Each instruction has a name, which is a natural number. We consider only the machines N_n for, say, $n > 10$, where such a name fits into a memory cell. The set of these names will be denoted by $\mathcal{I}$. A program P is a sequence from the elements of $\mathcal{I}$. When we say that the machine N_n executes the program P of length k, we mean that the machine starts to work from the state where the first k memory cells contains the elements of P in their natural order and the contents of the other memory cells are 0. (The total number of memory cells is restricted only by the address space, say, it is 2^n, but this of no significance, since the constant time programs that we will consider, can be simulated in constant time on a machine which has only a constant number of memory cells.) The instruction set contains (i) arithmetic instructions: addition and multiplication modulo 2^n, the constants $0, 1, n, 2^{n-1}$, the unary function $\min\{2^x, 2^n - 1\}$, the binary functions $\lfloor x/y \rfloor$ with $\lfloor x/0 \rfloor = 0$, $\max(x, y)$, $\min(x, y)$, and the boolean vector operations $\wedge, \vee, \neg$ defined on 0, 1 sequences of length n. (ii) read, write instructions, (iii) control transfer instructions, (iv) input/output instructions, (v) halt instruction.

Assume that c, k are positive integers. A program P will be called a c-time k-ary test, if $\texttt{length}(P) \leq c$, $k \leq c$ and for all positive integers $n > 10$, and for all integers $x_1, ..., x_k \in [0, 2^n - 1]$, the program P on machine N_n, at input $x_1, ..., x_k$ produces an output $P_n(x_1, ..., x_k) \in \{0, 1\}$ in time c.

THEOREM 1. *There exists a positive integer c and a c-time binary test P, such that for all $c' > 0$, for all c'-time unary tests Q, there exist infinitely many positive integers n, such that there exists an $a \in [0, 2^n - 1]$ with the property that the following two statements are not equivalent:*
(i) $\exists x \in [0, 2^n - 1]$, $P_n(x, a) = 0$,
(ii) $Q_n(a) = 0$.

In other words, there exists a constant time test $P(x, a)$, depending on a parameter a, such that the question whether it has a solution in x or not, cannot be decided by a constant time program Q which gets a as an input, even if the time used by Q can be arbitrarily large compared to the time used by P. The theorem remains true if we add an arithmetic instruction to the instruction set of the machine N_n, which computes the function $\min\{x^y, 2^n - 1\}$.

We will prove the theorem (in an equivalent form) with Gödel type diagonalization. First we compare our results to other existing theorems where nonlinear lower bounds were given, or deterministic and nondeterministic computation were separated in general computational models. Some of these proofs were based on diagonalization arguments. In fact the high level structure of the present proof is very similar to the structures of the proofs given in [15] or [13]. The technical details however are completely different.

For multi-tape Turing machines linear time nondeterministic and deterministic computations were separated in [15] by Paul, Pippenger, Szemerédi, and Trotter in 1984. Their theorem and the present result are not comparable in the sense, that none of them follows from the other, since in the Turing model longer bitwise computations can be done than in our constant time RAM model, but the RAM model allows arithmetic operations e.g., multiplication, and division of n bit numbers, and it is not known whether these operations can be computed on a multitape Turing machine in linear time. In a similar way the present result is not comparable to the separation theorems and lower bounds where the working memory is smaller than the input, either in uniform or in nonuniform models of computation, [13], [2], [8], [9].

We can say however that the difference between these already existing lower bounds and the present one is that they are based on different properties of the computational models. Both in the case of the Turing machine model, and in the models with small working memory, a lower bound proof is possible because of the organization of the memory, which in the second case includes the input. In both cases there is some restriction on the structure/use of the memory that is the crucial property used in the proof. In contrast, our present proofs are not based on properties of the memory structure or the memory access, but on properties of the set of arithmetic instructions. Therefore Theorem 1 says something about the set of arithmetic operations multiplication, addition etc., which is used in the usual random access machines. Constant time computation in the sense of Theorem 1 frequently occurs as part of a longer computation done on a RAM. (Of course our lower bound does not imply a lower bound for the longer computation.) We will formulate the properties of the arithmetic operations, which are needed for Theorem 1, in terms of the first-order logic of the structures whose functions are the arithmetic operations of N_n. As we will show, by a counterexample, new arithmetic instructions can be added to our RAM so that the separation result does not remain valid. Our theorem however is robust enough, that it remains true, if we define addition and multiplication in some other forms, which are used in the definition of RAMs, e.g., we may define them as integer operations (and not modulo 2^n operations) which give the result only if it fits into a memory cell, and otherwise gives the value 0. We will also formulate a general theorem, Theorem 4, which gives a sufficient condition for a set of arithmetic operations for which the analogue of Theorem 1 holds, and this will imply e.g., that we may add any subset of the functions $\min(x^y, 2^n - 1)$, $\lfloor \sqrt{x} \rfloor$, $\min(\lfloor e^x \rfloor, 2^n - 1)$ to the original instruction set so that Theorem 1 remains true.

The critical property, that we will call "predictivity", of the set of the arithmetic operations used by the machines N_n, which makes our proof possible, is that each operation f, if we consider it between integers with cn bits, for a large constant c, can be defined by a first-order formula Φ_f on the structure $\mathbf{M}_d$, $d = 2^n$, of size 2^n whose functions are the arithmetic operations on n bit numbers. Of course if $c > 1$ then the cn bit numbers cannot be represented as elements of $\mathbf{M}_d$. We will represent them as binary relations on $\mathbf{M}_d$, and the formula Φ_f, using the relations representing a and b, has to define a relation representing $f(a, b)$. (We will give more rigorous definitions for this concept both in the sketch of the proof of Theorem 2, and during the formulation of Theorem 4.) The proof that the operations of N_n have this property, is not a general argument in logic, but it is a proof using the specific algebraic and analytic properties of the arithmetic operations. E.g., in the case of the operation $\lfloor x/y \rfloor$ we are using a technique which was introduced in [7] for computing $\lfloor x/y \rfloor$ by "log depth circuits".

We formulate now Theorem 1, as it was sketched already in the abstract, in a setting closer to algebra and logic. (The equivalence of the two forms can be proved easily, see section 9.) First we consider the problem for more general algebraic structures, which is also part of the motivation of the present work. Assume that S is an algebraic structure with the operations $s_1, s_2, \ldots, s_k$. For example, S can be a field or a ring and $s_1, \ldots, s_k$ can be the field/ring operations. We also assume that the structure S has a distinguished element (defined as the value of a 0-ary operation s_i for some $i = 1, \ldots, k$) that we will denote by $\mathbf{0}$. In the case of a field/ring, $\mathbf{0}$ will be always the usual zero of the field/ring. Suppose further that $F(x, y)$ is an algebraic expression built up from the operations $s_1, \ldots, s_k$. Our search problem will depend on a parameter $a \in S$. If such an $a \in S$ is fixed, then we want to find $x \in S$ such that $F(x, a) = \mathbf{0}$. That is, the test T consists of checking whether for a given x we have $F(x, a) = \mathbf{0}$. We will say that the problem has an algebraic solution, if there exists an algebraic expression $G(y)$ built up from the operations $s_1, \ldots, s_k$ such that G depends only on F, and for all $a \in S$ the following two statements are equivalent: (i) there exists an $x \in S$ with $F(x, a) = \mathbf{0}$, and (ii) $F(G(a), a) = 0$. In other words if the equation $F(x, a)$ has a solution in x then $x = G(a)$ is such a solution.

Alternately we will also consider the problem of deciding whether the equation $F(x, a)$ has a solution in S. In this case we will say that the problem can be decided by an algebraic expression if there exists an algebraic expression $G(y)$ such that for all $a \in S$, the equation $F(x, a)$ has a solution in x iff $G(a) = \mathbf{0}$.

Several classical problems of mathematics can be formulated in this framework. For example, if S is the field of real numbers and $F(x, a) = x^2 - a$ then there is no $G(y)$ built up from the field operations so that for all $a \geq 0$, $x = G(a)$ is a solution of $F(x, a) = 0$. Indeed for a rational a the value of $G(a)$ is also rational while e.g., for $a = 2$ all of the solutions, namely $\pm\sqrt{2}$, are irrational. This was proved already by Pythagoras.

A more difficult problem if S is the field of complex numbers (or any other algebraically closed field), and the operations are the field operations and taking kth roots for each positive integer k. It is a consequence of Galois theory (see [6]) that there is an equation $F(x, a) = 0$ whose solution cannot be expressed by the given operation, so there is no algebraic expression $G(y)$ with the required properties. (Actually such an F can be constructed without using the "taking k-th root" operations.) Another example of similar nature is the problem of finding the antiderivative of an elementary function. We do not describe here the structure S, we just note that the basic results, that is, the existence of an elementary function whose antiderivative is not an elementary function (see e.g., [12]), can be also expressed in the present framework.

In this paper we consider the analogue questions in finite structures which, apart from the ring operations, also contain other operations on integers which are used as instructions in random access machines. For each positive integer d we will consider a structure $\mathbf{M}_d$ whose universe is the set $\{0, 1, \ldots, 2^n - 1\}$, where $n = 2^d$. An element b of $\mathbf{M}_d$ is a natural number but sometimes we will consider it as a $0,1$-sequence of length n, defined by the binary form of b. The operations on $\mathbf{M}_d$ will be, the operations that the random access machine N_n could perform on nonnegative integers represented by n bits, where $n = 2^d$. Namely we assume that the operations of $\mathbf{M}_d$ are the following: (1) addition and multiplication modulo 2^n, (2) integer division, that is, the operation $\lfloor x/y \rfloor$ with $\lfloor x/0 \rfloor = 0$, (3) $\max(x, y), \min(x, y)$, (4) an operation $\mathbf{p}(x)$ whose value is $\min\{2^x, 2^n - 1\}$, (5) pointwise boolean negation, AND, OR, on $0,1$-sequences of length n, (6) the constants $0, 1, n, 2^n - 1$. $\mathcal{M}$ will denote a first-order language which contains for each of these operations a function symbol with the corresponding arity. Referring to this language the described operations will be called $\mathcal{M}$-operations. (The results of this paper remain valid if we include a binary operation $\bar{\mathbf{p}}(x, y)$ whose value is $\min\{x^y, 2^n - 1\}$.)

The $\mathcal{M}$-operations that we have in addition to the ring operations, make the extension of the algebraic proofs on Galois theory to the structures $\mathbf{M}_d$ impossible. In spite of that we will show in Theorem 2, that there exists an algebraic expression $F(x, y)$ (built up from $\mathcal{M}$-operations) such that for all algebraic expression $G(y)$, (also built up from $\mathcal{M}$-operations), there exist infinitely many positive integers d such that for a suitably chosen $a \in \{0, 1, \ldots, 2^{2^d} - 1\}$, we have that the following two conditions are not equivalent: (i) $F(x, a)$ has a solution $x \in \mathbf{M}_d$, and (ii) $G(a) = \mathbf{0}$ in the structure $\mathbf{M}_d$.

The proof shows only that statements (i) and (ii) are not equivalent for infinitely many positive integers d, but it seems likely, that there exists an F such that for all sufficiently large integers d and a suitably chosen $a \in \{0, 1, \ldots, 2^{2^d} - 1\}$ they are not equivalent.

The mentioned result is about deciding whether an equation $F(x, a) = \mathbf{0}$ has a solution. However it is easy to see that the result remains valid for the search problem as well.

As we have mentioned already in the abstract, our result says that quantifier elimination is not possible over the structures $\mathbf{M}_d$, that is, there exists an existential formula $\varphi(y)$ of the language $\mathcal{M}$, such that for all propositional formulas $P(y)$ of $\mathcal{M}$, there exist infinitely many positive integers d, with $\mathbf{M}_d \models \neg\forall y, \varphi(y) \leftrightarrow P(y)$. The importance of this fact is that quantifier elimination is one of the main tools of mathematical logic for giving a detailed and transparent description of a first-order structures, where this is possible at all. For example, there are algorithms for eliminating quantifiers in the cases of algebraically closed fields or real-closed fields.

Of course the set of $\mathcal{M}$-operations is somewhat arbitrary. We may want to know which other operations can be added to $\mathcal{M}$ such that the mentioned theorem remains true. We prove a general theorem, Theorem 4, about a sequence of structures $\mathbf{K}_d$, $d = 1, 2, \ldots$, with $\mathtt{universe}(\mathbf{K}_d) = \{0, 1, \ldots, 2^n - 1\}$, $n = 2^d$ which describes conditions that are sufficient for an analogue of Theorem 2.

A counterexample. We also show that our main result does not hold if we replace the operations in $\mathbf{M}_d$ with arbitrary other operations. We prove the following. Assume that a sequence of structures M_n, $n = 1, 2, \ldots$ are given with $\mathtt{universe}(M_n) = \{0, 1, \ldots, 2^n - 1\}$, where each M_n is an interpretation of a first-order language $\mathcal{L}$ with equality and with a finite number of constant and functions symbols. We show that there exists an extension $\mathcal{L}'$ of $\mathcal{L}$ with a finite number of function symbols, and for each $n = 1, 2, \ldots$ there exists an interpretation M'_n of $\mathcal{L}'$ which is an extension of M_n on the same universe, such that for all terms $F(x, y)$ of $\mathcal{L}'$, there exists a term $G(y)$ of $\mathcal{L}'$ with the property that for all sufficiently large natural number n, we have

$$M'_n \models \forall a, \Big(G(a) = \mathbf{0} \leftrightarrow \exists x, F(x, a) = \mathbf{0}\Big)$$

1.2 The formulation of the main result

Notation. 1. ω will denote the set of all natural numbers, that is $\omega = \{0, 1, 2, , \ldots\}$. The natural number n will be considered as the set of all natural numbers less than n, that is, $n = \{0, 1, \ldots, n-1\}$.

2. $\mathtt{coeff}_i(a, b)$ denotes the ith b-ary "bit" of a. More precisely, assume that $a, b \in \omega$, $b \geq 2$, and $a = \sum_{i=0}^{\infty} \alpha_i b^i$, where for all $i = \omega$, $\alpha_i \in b$. The integer α_i will be denoted by $\mathtt{coeff}_i(a, b)$.

3. The set of all functions defined on the set A with values in the set B will be denoted by $\mathtt{func}(A, B)$. The set of all k-ary functions defined on the set A with values in the set B will be denoted by $\mathtt{func}_k(A, B)$. If we say that $\varphi(x_0, \ldots, x_k)$ is a first-order formula of a language $\mathcal{L}$ then we will always assume, unless we explicitly state otherwise, that all of the free variables of the formula are among the variables $x_0, \ldots, x_k$. A first-order statement with this notation would be $\varphi()$. If we say that ψ is a first-order formula without indicating any of its variables then there is no restriction on the number of variables in ψ. We will use the same convention for indicating the free variables in terms as well.

Definition. If M is an interpretation of the first-order language $\mathcal{L}$ and X is a relation, constant or function symbol of $\mathcal{L}$, then $(X)_M$ will denote the interpretation of X in the structure M. We extend this notations for terms as well, that is, if $t(x_0, \ldots, x_{k-1})$ is a term with the free variables $x_0, \ldots, x_{k-1}$, then $(t)_M$ will denote the k-ary function which is the interpretation of this term in M.

Definition. 1. $\mathcal{M}$ will denote a first-order language with equality, which does not contain any other relation symbols, and contains the following function and constant symbols. (We consider constant symbols as 0-ary function symbols as well.)

Constant symbols: $\mathbf{0}, \mathbf{1}, \mathbf{-1}, \mathbf{n}$

Unary function symbol: $\mathcal{N}$, $\mathbf{p}$, ($\mathcal{N}$ stands for negation, $\mathbf{p}$ stands for "power").

Binary function symbols: $+$, $\times$, $\div$, max, min, $\cap$.

(The assumption that $\mathcal{M}$ is a first-order language with *equality* implies that "=" is always interpreted as the equality relation. Therefore when we define below an interpretation of a function symbol $f(x, y)$ of $\mathcal{M}$ in a structure M by $M \models z = f(x, y)$ iff a relation given $P(x, y, z)$ holds, we do not define the relation "=" on M, it is already given, we define only the value of f.)

2. Assume that $d \in \omega = \{0, 1, 2, \ldots\}$ and $n = 2^d$. $\mathbf{M}_d$ will denote the following interpretation of the language $\mathcal{M}$: $\mathtt{universe}(\mathbf{M}_d) = \{0, 1, \ldots, 2^n - 1\} = 2^n$ and for all $x, y, z \in \mathtt{universe}(\mathbf{M}_d)$,

$(\mathbf{M}_d \models +(x, y) = z)$ iff $x + y \equiv z \pmod{2^n}$,

$(\mathbf{M}_d \models \times(x, y) = z)$ iff $xy \equiv z \pmod{2^n}$,

$(\mathbf{M}_d \models \mathbf{p}(x) = z)$ iff $z = \min\{2^x, 2^n - 1\}$,

$(\mathbf{M}_d \models z = \div(x, y))$ iff $(y \neq 0 \wedge z = \lfloor x/y \rfloor) \vee (y = 0 \wedge z = 0)$

$(\mathbf{M}_d \models z = \mathbf{0})$ iff $z = 0$,

$(\mathbf{M}_d \models z = \mathbf{1})$ iff $z = 1$,

$(\mathbf{M}_d \models z = \mathbf{n})$ iff $z = n$,

$(\mathbf{M}_d \models z = \mathbf{-1})$ iff $z = 2^n - 1$,

$(\mathbf{M}_d \models z = \max(x, y))$ iff $z = \max\{x, y\}$,

$(\mathbf{M}_d \models z = \min(x, y))$ iff $z = \min\{x, y\}$,

$(\mathbf{M}_d \models z = x \cap y))$ iff "$\mathtt{coeff}_i(z, 2) = \min(\mathtt{coeff}_i(x, 2), \mathtt{coeff}_i(y, 2))$ for $i = 0, 1, \ldots, n-1$,

$(\mathbf{M}_d \models z = \mathcal{N}(x)$ iff "$\mathtt{coeff}_i(z, 2) = 1 - \mathtt{coeff}_i(x, 2)$ for $i = 0, 1, \ldots, n-1$.

We will call the interpretations $\mathbf{M}_d, d \in \omega$ of $\mathcal{M}$ the standard interpretations of $\mathcal{M}$.

3. Motivated by the definition of the standard interpretations we will use the following notation as well when we use the functions symbols of $\mathcal{M}$: $+(x, y) = x + y$, $\times(x, y) = x \times y$, $\mathbf{p}(x) = 2^x$, $\div(x, y) = x/y$. Generally we will use this notation only if it is clear from the context the we mean the function symbol interpreted in a structure $\mathbf{M}_d$, otherwise $x + y, xy, 2^x$ retain their usual meaning as operations among real numbers.

4. When we use the function symbols of $\mathcal{M}$ we will write $x - y$ for $x + (\mathbf{-1})y$ and $-y$ for $(\mathbf{-1})y$. □

Definition. 1. Assume that $\varphi(x)$, $\psi(x)$ are first-order formulas of $\mathcal{M}$ with the only free variable x. We will say that $\varphi(x)$ and $\psi(x)$ are asymptotically equivalent with respect to the sequence $\langle \mathbf{M}_d \mid d \in \omega \rangle$, iff for all sufficiently large integers d, we have $\mathbf{M}_d \models \forall x, \varphi(x) \leftrightarrow \psi(x)$.

2. Assume that $F(x, y)$ is a term of $\mathcal{M}$ with the only free variables x, y. We say that the existence of a solution of the equation $F(x, y) = 0$ in x can be decided by a term of $\mathcal{M}$ with respect to $\langle \mathbf{M}_d \mid d \in \omega \rangle$, if there exists a term $G(y)$ of $\mathcal{M}$ with the only free variable y, such that the formulas $\exists x, F(x, y) = 0$ and $G(y) = 0$ are asymptotically equivalent with respect to the sequence $\langle \mathbf{M}_d \mid d \in \omega \rangle$. □

THEOREM 2. *There exists a term $F(x, y)$ of $\mathcal{M}$ with the only free variables x, y, such that the existence of a solution of the equation $F(x, y) = 0$ in x cannot be decided by a term of $\mathcal{M}$ with respect to $\langle \mathbf{M}_d \mid d \in \omega \rangle$.*

It is an easy consequence of the definition of the structures $\mathcal{M}_d$, that for each propositional formula $P(y)$ of $\mathcal{M}$ there exists a term $G(y)$ of $\mathcal{M}$ such that for all $d \in \omega$, $\mathbf{M}_d \models \forall y, P(y) \leftrightarrow G(y) = 0$. Therefore Theorem 2 can be written in the following equivalent form, saying that quantifier elimination is not possible over the structures $\mathbf{M}_d$, $d \in \omega$.

THEOREM 3. *There exists an existential first-order formula $\varphi(y)$ of $\mathcal{M}$, containing a single existential quantifier and the only free variable y, such that for each propositional formula $P(y)$ of $\mathcal{M}$, we have that for infinitely many positive integers d, $\varphi(y)$ and $P(y)$ are not equivalent on $\mathbf{M}_d$, that is, $\mathbf{M}_d \models \neg\forall y, \varphi(y) \leftrightarrow P(y)$.*

Definition. We define another language $\bar{\mathcal{M}}$ that we get from $\mathcal{M}$ by adding to it a new binary function symbol $\bar{\mathbf{p}}$. $\bar{\mathbf{M}}_d$ will denote the interpretation of $\bar{\mathcal{M}}$ which is the extension of the interpretation $\mathbf{M}_d$ (with the same universe) defined by $(\bar{\mathbf{M}}_d \models \bar{\mathbf{p}}(x, y) = z)$ iff $z = \min\{x^y, 2^n - 1\}$, where $n = 2^d$. □

COROLLARY 1. *Theorem 2 and Theorem 3 remain true if we substitute $\bar{\mathcal{M}}$ for $\mathcal{M}$ and $\bar{\mathbf{M}}_d$ for $\mathbf{M}_d$.*

The proof of the Corollary is almost identical to the proof of Theorem 1. At a few places however we need some additional arguments in the proof of the Corollary. We will describe these these extra steps during the proof of Theorem 2.

2. A GENERALIZATION OF THEOREM 2

We formulate in this section Theorem 4 which is a generalization of Theorem 2, (and in the same way, it also have stronger form Theorem 5 which is a generalization of Theorem 3). Theorem 4 implies Theorem 2 and its proof is very similar to the proof of Theorem 2. Therefore we will give a proof only for Theorem 4 and the fact that Theorem 4 implies Theorem 2. Theorem 5 will follow the same way from Theorem 4 as Theorem 3 follows from Theorem 2. The sketch we will give for the proof of Theorem 2, will be also a sketch for the proof of Theorem 4 with minor modifications, that we will describe later. The definitions needed for the formulation of Theorem 4 will make also clearer, what are those properties of the operations in $\mathbf{M}_d$, which are used to prove Theorem 2.

Definition. We will say that $\mathbf{K}$ is a $\mathcal{K}$-sequence if the following two conditions are satisfied:

(i) $\mathcal{K}$ is a first-order language with equality, with a finite number of function symbols, and without relation symbols other than equality. (We will call the 0-ary function symbols constant symbols as well.)

(ii) $\mathbf{K} = \langle \mathbf{K}_d \mid d \in \omega \rangle$ is a sequence of interpretations of $\mathcal{K}$ with the property that for all $d \in \omega$, $\mathtt{universe}(\mathbf{K}_d) = 2^n$, where $n = 2^d$. □

Notation. 1. For the sake of brevity we will frequently write $a \in \mathbf{K}_d$ instead of $a \in \mathtt{universe}(\mathbf{K}_d)$.

2. If t is a term of $\mathcal{K}$ then we will use the notation $t^{(d)} = (t)_{\mathbf{K}_d}$.

In the following we will define several properties of a $\mathcal{K}$-sequence $\mathbf{K} = \langle \mathbf{K}_d \mid d \in \omega \rangle$ which together will imply that an analogue of Theorem 2 holds for $\mathbf{K}$. The first two properties, regularity and projectivity, ensures that each $\mathbf{K}_d$ contains enough functions so that certain elementary arguments or constructions which are available in $\mathbf{M}_d$ can be carried out in $\mathbf{K}_d$ as well.

We will say that a $\mathcal{K}$-sequence $\mathbf{K}_d$, $d \in \omega$ is regular if certain "basic" functions can be easily defined in $\mathbf{K}_d$. The expression "easily defined" means in certain cases that the functions are interpretations of suitably chosen terms of $\mathcal{K}$ while in other cases it means that the functions can be defined by first-order formulas in the structure $\mathbf{K}_d$. The mentioned functions are, roughly speaking, (i) constant functions with values 0 and 1, (ii) boolean functions of two variables, (iii) characteristic function of the equality relation, (iv) all of the functions defined on $\{0, 1, \ldots, i-1\}$ with values in the same set, provided that d is sufficiently large with respect to i, (v) a function for forming pairs, provided that d is sufficiently large compared to the elements of the pairs.

Definition. Assume that $\mathbf{K} = \langle \mathbf{K}_d \mid d \in \omega \rangle$ is a $\mathcal{K}$-sequence. We say that $\mathbf{K}$ is regular if $\mathcal{K}$ contains the constant symbols $\mathbf{0}, \mathbf{1}$ and the following conditions are satisfied:

(1). *For each sufficiently large $d \in \omega$, $(\mathbf{0})_{\mathbf{K}_d} = 0$, $(\mathbf{1})_{\mathbf{K}_d} = 1$*

(2). *For each binary function $f(x, y)$ defined on the set $\{\mathbf{0}, \mathbf{1}\}$ and with values in $\{\mathbf{0}, \mathbf{1}\}$, there exists a term $t(x, y)$ of $\mathcal{K}$, such that for all $a, b \in \{\mathbf{0}, \mathbf{1}\}$ and for all sufficiently large $d \in \omega$, we have $\mathbf{K}_d \models f(a, b) = t(a, b)$.*

(3). *There exists a term $\bar{t}(x, y)$ of $\mathcal{K}$, so that for all sufficiently large $d \in \omega$ we have $\mathbf{K}_d \models \forall x, y, (x = y \rightarrow \bar{t}(x, y) = \mathbf{0}) \wedge (x \neq y \rightarrow \bar{t}(x, y) = \mathbf{1})$.*

(4). *for each $k \in \omega$, there exists a first-order formula $\varphi(x_0, \ldots, x_{k-1}, y, z)$ of $\mathcal{K}$ such that for all $i \in \omega$ and for each k-ary function $f(x_0, \ldots, x_{k-1}) \in \mathtt{func}_k(\{0, 1, \ldots, i-1\}, \{0, 1, \ldots, i-1\})$, there exists a $j \in \omega$, such that for all sufficiently large $d \in \omega$ and for all $a_0, \ldots, a_{k-1}, b \in i$ we have that $f(a_0, \ldots, a_{k-1}) = b$ iff $\mathbf{K}_d \models \varphi(a_0, \ldots, a_{k-1}, b, j)$.*

(5). *There exists a first-order formula $\kappa(x, y, z)$ of $\mathcal{K}$ with the following property. For each $i, j \in \omega$ there exists $k \in \omega$ such that for all sufficiently large $d \in \omega$, $\mathbf{K}_d \models \forall x, y,\ \kappa(x, y, k) \leftrightarrow (x = i \wedge y = j)$.* □

We define now another property of $\mathcal{K}$-sequence a $\mathbf{K} = \langle \mathbf{K}_d \mid d \in \omega \rangle$. If $\mathbf{K}$ has this property then the elements of the direct product of 2^c copies, of $\mathbf{K}_d$, can be encoded by single elements of $\mathbf{K}_{d+c}$ so that the encoding is done by a term of $\mathcal{K}$, and the projections of the direct product to its kth component can be defined by a first-order formula Γ which contains k and c as parameters but otherwise the choice of Γ does not depend on k and c.

Definition. 1. Assume that $\mathbf{K} = \langle \mathbf{K}_d \mid d \in \omega \rangle$ is a $\mathcal{K}$-sequence. We say that $\mathbf{K}$ is projective if for all $c \in \omega$ and $k \in 2^c$, there exists a term $\pi_{c,k}$ of $\mathcal{K}$ so that the following conditions are satisfied.

(6). *for all $c \in \omega$ there exists a term τ_c of $\mathcal{K}$ such that if $d \in \omega$ is sufficiently large, and $a_0, \ldots, a_{2^c-1} \in \mathbf{K}_d$, then for all $k = 0, 1, \ldots, 2^{c-1}$, we have $\mathbf{K}_{d+c} \models \pi_{c,k}(\tau_c(a_0, \ldots, a_{2^c-1})) = a_k$.*

(7). *There exists a first-order formula $\Gamma(x, y, z, w)$ of $\mathcal{K}$ such that for all $c \in \omega$ if $d \in \omega$ is sufficiently large and $k \in 2^c$ then*

$$\mathbf{K}_{d+c} \models \forall x, y, \Gamma(x, y, c, k) \leftrightarrow \pi_{c,k}(x) = y$$

2. Assume that $\mathbf{K} = \langle \mathbf{K}_d \mid d \in \omega \rangle$ is a $\mathcal{K}$-sequence. If $\mathbf{K}$ is both regular and projective then we will say that $\mathbf{K}$ is complete. □

The following easy lemma shows that the extensions of complete structures are complete.

LEMMA 1. *Assume that $\mathbf{K}^{(i)} = \langle \mathbf{K}_d^{(i)} \mid d \in \omega \rangle$ is a $\mathcal{K}^{(i)}$ sequence for $i = 0, 1$, and $\mathcal{K}^{(0)} \subseteq \mathcal{K}^{(1)}$, that is, every symbol of $\mathcal{K}_0$ is also a symbol of $\mathcal{K}_1$. Suppose further that for all $d \in \omega$, the restriction of the model $\mathbf{K}_d^{(1)}$ of the language $\mathcal{K}^{(1)}$ to the language $\mathcal{K}^{(0)}$ is the model $\mathbf{K}_d^{(0)}$. Then we have that if the $\mathcal{K}^{(0)}$ sequence $\mathbf{K}^{(0)}$ is complete then the $\mathcal{K}^{(1)}$-sequence $\mathbf{K}^{(1)}$ is also complete.*

In the generalization of Theorem 2 we will speak about a $\mathcal{K}$ sequence $\mathbf{K} = \langle \mathbf{K}_d \mid d \in \omega \rangle$ which is complete and in addition to that it must be "retrospective" and "predictive" in the sense to be defined below. These properties establish connections between $\mathbf{K}_d$ and $\mathbf{K}_{d+c}$, where c is an arbitrary constant. Namely if we think that we construct the sequence $\mathbf{K}_0, \mathbf{K}_1, \ldots, \mathbf{K}_d, \ldots$ in this order then retrospectivity means that when we have $\mathbf{K}_d$ we are able using the functions defined in $\mathbf{K}_d$ to "look back" at $\mathbf{K}_{d-c}$ and decide the values of the functions defined in $\mathbf{K}_{d-c}$. Predictivity, in a similar way means, that using only functions defined in $\mathbf{K}_d$, we will be able to "predict", in some sense, what will be the values of the functions defined in $\mathbf{K}_{d+c}$.

The next definition describes the following property of a $\mathcal{K}$ sequence $\mathbf{K}_d$, $d \in \omega$. Assume that a g is function in $\mathbf{K}_{d-1}$ which is an interpretation of a function symbol of $\mathcal{K}$. Then, in the structure $\mathbf{K}_d$, g can be expressed by a term. If g is in $\mathbf{K}_{d-c}$, then in the structure $\mathbf{K}_d$, g can be expressed by a first-order formula containing c as a parameter.

Definition. Assume that $\mathbf{K} = \langle \mathbf{K}_d \mid d \in \omega \rangle$ is a $\mathcal{K}$-sequence. We say that $\mathbf{K}$ is retrospective if it satisfies the following two conditions:

(8). *Let $k \in \omega$ and let g be a k-ary function symbol of $\mathcal{K}$. Then there exists a term $t(x_0, \ldots, x_{k-1})$ of $\mathcal{K}$ such that if $d \in \omega$ is sufficiently large and $a_0, \ldots, a_{k-1}, b \in \mathbf{K}_{d-1}$ then $\mathbf{K}_{d-1} \models g(a_0, \ldots, a_{k-1}) = b$ iff $\mathbf{K}_d \models t(a_0, \ldots, a_{k-1}) = b$.*

(9). *Let $k \in \omega$ and let g, be a k-ary function symbol of $\mathcal{K}$. Then there exists a first-order formula $\varphi(x_0, \ldots, x_{k-1}, y, z)$ of $\mathcal{K}$ such that for all $c \in \omega$, if $d \in \omega$ is sufficiently large and $a_0, \ldots, a_{k-1}, b \in \mathbf{K}_{d-c}$ then*

$$(\mathbf{K}_{d-c} \models g(a_0, \ldots, a_{k-1}) = b) \leftrightarrow \mathbf{K}_d \models \varphi(a_0, \ldots, a_{k-1}, b, c)$$

In the next definition we will consider $\mathcal{K}$ sequences $\mathbf{K}_d$, $d \in \omega$, where in the structure $\mathbf{K}_d$ we are able to decide in a first-order way whether a function f which is defined on $\mathtt{universe}(\mathbf{K}_{d+c})$, and which is an interpretation of a function symbol of $\mathcal{K}$, takes a certain value or not. More precisely, we will consider only the case when the elements of $\mathbf{K}_{d+c}$ can be encoded by binary relations on $\mathbf{K}_d$ and the question whether the function f takes a value or not can be decided by a first-order formula over $\mathbf{K}_d$, using these relations. As we said earlier, if we consider the sequence of structures $\mathbf{K}_d$ as if they were constructed in time $d = 0, 1, \ldots$, then this property implies that at time d we will be able to predict the behavior of the functions that will be constructed at time $d + c$. (This definition differs somewhat from the one that we gave for $\mathbf{M}_d$. Each element of $\mathbf{M}_d$ was represented by a unary, relation on $\mathbf{M}_d$, while now, we are using binary relations on $\mathbf{K}_d$. This is not an essential difference. In the case of $\mathbf{M}_d$ the unary representation was the most convenient, since the binary coefficients were definable by terms, which is not necessarily true for $\mathbf{K}_d$. Now we state the existence of a representation as part of the definition, that is, as an axiom, and it is simpler to formulate it for binary relations.)

Definition. Assume that $\mathbf{K} = \langle \mathbf{K}_d \mid d \in \omega \rangle$ is a $\mathcal{K}$-sequence. We say that $\mathbf{K}$ is predictive if the following condition is satisfied

(10). *There exists a function assigning to each function symbol $f(x_0, \ldots, x_{k-1})$ of $\mathcal{K}$, (including the constant symbols for $k = 0$), a first-order formula $\Phi_f(x, y, z, Y_0, \ldots, Y_{k-1})$ of $\mathcal{K}$, where x, y, z are free individual variables and $Y_0, \ldots, Y_{k-1}$ are free binary relation variables, such that the following holds. For all $c \in \omega$ if $d \in \omega$ is sufficiently large then there exists a map $\eta_{d,c}$ of $\mathtt{universe}(\mathbf{K}_{d+c})$ into the set of binary relations on $\mathtt{universe}(\mathbf{K}_d)$ with the following properties:*

(i) For each $a, u, v \in \mathbf{K}_d$, we have $(\eta_{d,c}(a))(u, v)$ iff "$u = 0$ and $v = a$".

(ii) Suppose that $f(x_0, \ldots, x_{k-1})$ is a k-ary function symbol of $\mathcal{K}$, for some $k = 0, 1, \ldots$ (including the constant symbols for $k = 0$) and $a_0, \ldots, a_{k-1} \in \mathbf{K}_{d+c}$. Then for all $u, v \in \mathbf{K}_d$, $(\eta_{d,c}(f^{(d+c)}(a_0, \ldots, a_{k-1}))(u, v)$ iff $\mathbf{K}_d \models \Phi_f(u, v, c, \eta_{d,c}(a_0), \ldots, \eta_{d,c}(a_{k-1}))$, where $f^{(d+c)} = (f)_{\mathbf{K}_{d+c}}$. □

Predictivity is the most important nontrivial property of the sequence $\langle \mathbf{M}_d \mid d \in \omega \rangle$ that is needed for the proof of Theorem 2. If we want to add new operations to $\mathbf{M}_d$ such that the theorem remains true, then usually guaranteeing the property "predictivity" for the extended structure is the critical step.

Definition. 1. Assume that $\varphi(x)$, $\psi(x)$ are first-order formulas of $\mathcal{K}$ with the only free variable x. We will say that $\varphi(x)$ and $\psi(x)$ are asymptotically equivalent with respect to the $\mathcal{K}$-sequence $\langle \mathbf{K}_d \mid d \in \omega \rangle$, iff for all sufficiently large integers d, we have $\mathbf{K}_d \models \forall x, \varphi(x) \leftrightarrow \psi(x)$.

2. Suppose that $\mathbf{K} = \langle \mathbf{K}_d, d \in \omega \rangle$ is a $\mathcal{K}$-sequence. Assume further that $F(x, y)$ is a term of $\mathcal{K}$ with the only free variables x, y. We say that the existence of a solution of the equation $F(x, y) = \mathbf{0}$, in the unknown x, can be decided by a term of $\mathcal{K}$, if there exists a term $G(y)$ of $\mathcal{K}$ with the only free variable y, such that the formulas $\exists x, F(x, y) = \mathbf{0}$ and $G(y) = \mathbf{0}$ are asymptotically equivalent with respect to $\mathbf{K}$. □

THEOREM 4. *Assume that $\mathbf{K}$ is a $\mathcal{K}$-sequence, such that $\mathbf{K}$ is complete, retrospective, and predictive. Then there exists a term $F(x, y)$ of $\mathcal{K}$ with the only free variables x, y, such that the existence of a solution of the equation $F(x, y) = \mathbf{0}$ in the unknown x, cannot be decided by a term of $\mathcal{K}$.*

It is easy to show, in the same way as in the case of Theorem 2 and Theorem 3, that this is equivalent to the following.

THEOREM 5. *Assume that $\mathbf{K}$ is a $\mathcal{K}$-sequence, such that $\mathbf{K}$ is complete, retrospective, and predictive. Then there exists an existential first-order formula $\varphi(y)$ of $\mathcal{K}$, containing a single existential quantifier and the only free variable y, such that for each propositional formula $P(y)$ of $\mathcal{K}$, we have that for infinitely many positive integers d, $\varphi(y)$ and $P(y)$ are not equivalent on $\mathbf{K}_d$, that is, $\mathbf{K}_d \models \neg\forall y, \varphi(y) \leftrightarrow P(y)$.*

3. THE COUNTEREXAMPLE

In the following theorem we state the existence of a $\mathcal{K}$-sequence $\mathbf{K}$ where the conclusion of Theorem 4 does not hold. (Naturally some of the assumptions of the theorem do not hold either.)

THEOREM 6. *Assume that $\mathcal{L}$ is a first-order language with equality, with no relation symbols other than equality, and with a finite number of constant and function symbols, among them the constant symbol $\mathbf{0}$. Then there exists an extension $\mathcal{L}'$ of $\mathcal{L}$ with a finite number of function symbols, and there exists a function which assigns to each term $F(x, y)$ of $\mathcal{L}'$ a term $G_F(x)$ of $\mathcal{L}'$ so that the following holds.*

Assume that for all $n \in \omega$, M_n is an interpretation of $\mathcal{L}$ with $\mathtt{universe}(M_n) = 2^n$ and with $(\mathbf{0})_{M_n} = 0$. Then for all $n \in \omega$, there exists an interpretation M'_n of $\mathcal{L}'$ so that $\mathtt{universe}(M'_n) = \mathtt{universe}(M_n)$, M'_n is an extension of M_n and the sequence M'_n, $n \in \omega$ has the following property. For all terms $F(x, y)$ of $\mathcal{L}'$ and for all sufficiently large $n \in \omega$, we have

$$M'_n \models \forall a, \Big(G_F(a) = \mathbf{0} \leftrightarrow \exists x, F(x, a) = \mathbf{0}\Big)$$

This theorem shows that in Theorem 2 and Theorem 3 we really need special properties of the arithmetic operations which do not hold for arbitrary functions. Moreover the properties that are simply saying that with arithmetic operations we can compute certain functions are not enough, since even if we add these functions to the functions of the structure $\mathbf{M}_d$, there is a further extension where the analogues of the mentioned theorems do not hold. Theorem 6 will be proved in section 8.

4. PROOF OF THEOREM 2, (SKETCH)

Assume that the statement of Theorem 2 is not true. We will reach a contradiction by using Gödel's method of constructing a first-order formula φ of $\mathcal{M}$ which expresses the statement that φ is false. Let $\texttt{Form}(\mathcal{M}, k)$ be the set of all first-order formulas of $\mathcal{M}$ with at most k free variables. We will show that our indirect assumption implies that the truth value of first-order formulas in $\texttt{Form}(\mathcal{M}, 1)$ can be expressed by a single first-order formula of $\mathcal{M}$ in the following sense:

CLAIM 1. *There exists a function ρ defined on the set $\texttt{Form}(\mathcal{M}, 1)$ with values in ω and there exists a first-order formula $\psi(x, y)$ of $\mathcal{M}$ with the following property: for all $\varphi \in \texttt{Form}(\mathcal{M}, 1)$ if d is sufficiently large, then $\mathbf{M}_d \models \forall x, \varphi(x) \leftrightarrow \psi(x, \rho(\varphi))$*

Note that since $\rho(\varphi)$ is a natural number, for all sufficiently large $d \in \omega$, we have $\rho(\varphi) \in \mathbf{M}_d$, and therefore the turth value of $\psi(x, \rho(\varphi))$ is defined in $\mathbf{M}_d$. Claim 1 leads to a contradiction in the following way. Let $\varphi_0(x) = \neg\psi(x, x)$. Then Claim 1 with $\varphi := \varphi_0$ implies that for all sufficiently large d we have $\mathbf{M}_d \models \forall x, \neg\psi(x, x) \leftrightarrow \psi(x, \rho(\varphi_0))$, and therefore with $x := \rho(\varphi_0)$ we get $\mathbf{M}_d \models \psi(\rho(\varphi_0), \rho(\varphi_0)) \leftrightarrow \neg\psi(\rho(\varphi_0), \rho(\varphi_0))$, which is a contradiction. Note that in this argument we did not assume anything about the computability or definability of ρ. (Otherwise $\rho(\varphi)$ plays the role of the Gödel number of the formula φ.)

Short Sketch of the proof of Claim 1. The existence of such a formula ψ will be proved in the following way. Suppose a first-order formula $\varphi(x)$ is given, and we want to express its truth value in $\mathbf{M}_d$ in a first-order way using only a numerical code $\rho(\varphi)$ as a parameter in ψ. In this short sketch we ignore the problem of the choice of ρ since it will follow easily from the other steps of the proof.

We will show that there exists a term $T(x, y)$ of $\mathcal{M}$, which does not depend on φ, such that $\mathbf{M}_d \models \varphi(b)$ is equivalent to $\mathbf{M}_{d+c_1(\rho(\varphi))} \models T(b, \rho(\varphi)) = 0$ for all $b \in \mathbf{M}_d$, where c_1 depends only on $\rho(\varphi)$ and not on d or b. Since $\mathbf{M}$ is predictive the statement $\mathbf{M}_{d+c_1(\rho(\varphi))} \models T(b, \rho(\varphi)) = 0$ can be expressed in $\mathbf{M}_d$ by a first-order formula. This formula will be ψ.

In the step described above, it was important that the term T does not depend on φ. As a first step we construct a term T' depending on φ such that for all $d \in \omega$, $b \in \mathbf{M}_d$, and for a suitably chosen c_2 depending only on φ (but not on d or b), we have "$\mathbf{M}_d \models \varphi(b)$ iff $\mathbf{M}_{d+c_2} \models T'(b) = 0$. We get such a T' by applying repeatedly the assumption that the theorem is not true for eliminating the quantifiers from φ. This cannot be done in $\mathbf{M}_d$ since the term $F(x, a)$ in the theorem contains only a single parameter a while for the elimination process a similar statement would be needed for many parameters. We resolve this problem by eliminating the quantifiers in $\mathbf{M}_{d+c_2}$ for a suitable chosen constant c_2, where the sequence of parameters in $\mathbf{M}_d$ can be encoded by a single element of $\mathbf{M}_{d+c_2}$. We do this for each quantifier in φ while gradually increasing c_2. At the end we get a constant c_2 with the property that "$\mathbf{M}_d \models \varphi(b)$ is equivalent to $\mathbf{M}_{d+c_2} \models T'(b)$ for all $b \in \mathbf{M}_d$", where c_2 and T' may depend on φ but not d or b.

To get rid of the dependence on φ in T' we do the following. T' is a term, which can be encoded by an integer in some way, say $\sigma(T')$. We show that there exists a first-order formula ξ of $\mathcal{M}$ which does not depend on anything, and an integer c_3 depending only on T', such that for all sufficiently large d, and $b \in \mathbf{M}_d$, $\mathbf{M}_d \models T'(b) = 0$ iff $\mathbf{M}_{d+c_3} \models \xi(\sigma(T'), b)$. With this we have reduced the problem of determining the truth value of an arbitrary formula φ in $\mathbf{M}_d$, to determining the truth value of a fixed formula ξ in $\mathbf{M}_{d+c_3}$. The formula φ occurs in ξ only through its parameters. Now we repeat the described quantifier elimination process with the formula ξ (instead of φ) and get the required term T. *End of Short Sketch*

To get the formula ψ and the function ρ we start with an arbitrary $\varphi(x) \in \texttt{Form}(\mathcal{M}, 1)$. First we note that we may assume that if the formula $\varphi(x)$ is in prenex form then its propositional part is of the form $t(x) = \mathbf{0}$ where t is a term. It is easy to prove this fact using that the constants $\mathbf{0}, \mathbf{1}$, the functions $\max(x, y)$, $\min(x, y)$ are in $\mathbf{M}_d$, and the function $1 - x$ as defined in $\mathbf{M}_d$ takes 0 to 1 and 1 to 0, that is, it can paly the role of negation.

In the proof we will use the following simple property of the structures $\mathbf{M}_d$, $d \in \omega$, which essentially says that an ordered pair $\langle i, j\rangle$ of natural numbers can be encoded by a single natural number k, and this encoding can be described by a first-order a single formula of $\mathcal{M}$ in all of the structures $\mathbf{M}_d$, provided that d is sufficiently large with respect to i and j.

CLAIM 2. *There exists a first-order formula $\kappa(x, y, z)$ of $\mathcal{M}$ with the following property. For each $i, j \in \omega$, there exists $k \in \omega$ such that for all sufficiently large $d \in \omega$, $\mathbf{M}_d \models \forall z, y,\ \kappa(k, y, z) \leftrightarrow (y = i \wedge z = j)$.*

For example we may construct κ using the fact that the functions $\mathcal{F}_0(x) = x - \lfloor x^{\frac{1}{2}} \rfloor^2$, $\mathcal{F}_1(x) = \lfloor x^{\frac{1}{2}} \rfloor - \mathcal{F}_0(x)$ have the property that for each $y, z \in \omega$ there is an $x \in \omega$ with $\mathcal{F}_0(x) = y$ and $\mathcal{F}_1(x) = z$. (Indeed, if $x = (y + z)^2 + y$, then $\mathcal{F}_0(x) = y$ and $\mathcal{F}_1(x) = z$.)

First, instead of expressing the truth value of $\varphi(x)$ in the structure $\mathbf{M}_d$, we express it in a larger structure $\mathbf{M}_{d+c}$ where c depends only on φ but not on d or x. More precisely we will show that:

CLAIM 3. *If Theorem 2 does not hold for $\mathbf{M}$, then there exists a term $G(x, y)$ of $\mathcal{M}$, and there exist functions $s \in \texttt{func}(\texttt{Form}(\mathcal{M}, 1), \omega)$, $h \in \texttt{func}(\omega, \omega)$ with the following property. For all natural numbers ℓ and for all first-order formulas $\varphi(x)$ of $\mathcal{M}$ with length at most ℓ, we have that for all sufficiently large $d \in \omega$, and for all $a \in \mathbf{M}_d$, $\mathbf{M}_d \models \varphi(a)$ iff $\mathbf{M}_{d+h(\ell)} \models G(a, s(\varphi, \ell)) = \mathbf{0}$*

(We will give a more general version of this statement in Lemma 5. We will sketch the proof of Claim 3 later.) In other words the truth value of $\varphi(a)$, $a \in \mathbf{M}_d$ can be decided in the larger structure $\mathbf{M}_{d+h(\ell)}$ by evaluating a term. Although we have to use the structure $\mathbf{M}_{d+h(\ell)}$ instead of the structure $\mathbf{M}_d$, but if φ is fixed and $\ell = \texttt{length}(\varphi)$ then $h(\ell)$ is a constant (while we change d and a). For a fixed φ and $\ell = \texttt{length}(\varphi)$, the parameter $s(\varphi, \ell)$ in the expression $G(a, s(\varphi, \ell))$ is also a constant. We will get the formula

$\psi(x, y)$ by describing the computation done, while evaluating the term $G(a, s(\varphi, \ell))$, in a first-order way.

Sketch of Claim 3 → Claim 1. When we perform the computation of $G(a, s(\varphi, \ell))$ in $\mathbf{M}_{d+c}$, where $c = h(\texttt{length}(\varphi))$, we start with element $a \in \mathbf{M}_d$ and the constants $\mathbf{0}, \mathbf{1}, \mathbf{n}, -\mathbf{1}$ and perform some operations of $\mathcal{M}$, interpreted in $\mathbf{M}_{d+c}$, in a constant depth. We will represent the elements of $\mathbf{M}_{d+c}$ by unary relations on $\mathbf{M}_d$ in a way that the mentioned $\mathcal{M}$-operations on the elements of $\mathbf{M}_{d+c}$ can be carried out on the corresponding unary relations over $\mathbf{M}_d$ by first-order formulas of $\mathcal{M}$. Namely, we will represent each element $b \in \mathbf{M}_{d+c}$ by its binary form with $2^{2^{d+c}}$ bits. (Note that only the first 2^{d+c} of these bits can be nonzero.) Suppose that $b = \sum_{i=0}^{2^{2^{d+c}}-1} \beta_i 2^i$ then the element b will be represented by the unary relation $\mathbf{U}_b^{(d,c)}$ on $\mathbf{M}_d$ defined by "for all $i \in \mathbf{M}_d$, $\mathbf{U}_b^{(d,c)}(i)$ holds iff $\beta_i = 1$". Since $\texttt{universe}(\mathbf{M}_{d+c}) = 2^{2^{d+c}}$, we have the upper bound $b < 2^{2^{c+d}}$ and therefore, $\mathbf{U}_b^{(d,c)}(i)$ may hold only for $i < 2^{d+c}$. Later we will use the fact that if $x \in \mathbf{M}_d$ then the unary relation $\mathbf{U}_x^{(d,c)}$ can be expressed by a propositional formula of $\mathcal{M}$, as stated in the following claim.

Claim 4. *There exists a propositional formula $\gamma(x, y) \in \mathcal{M}$ such that for all $c \in \omega$, for all sufficiently large $d \in \omega$, and all $a, i \in \mathbf{M}_d$ we have $\mathbf{U}_a^{(d,c)}(i)$ iff $\mathbf{M}_d \models \gamma(a, i)$. Moreover $\gamma(x, y) \equiv (\min(y, \mathbf{n} - \mathbf{1}) = y) \wedge (\div(2^{\mathbf{n}-y-\mathbf{1}}x, 2^{\mathbf{n}-\mathbf{1}}) = \mathbf{1})$ meet these requirements.*

We will show that the result of an $\mathcal{M}$-operation performed on the elements of $\mathbf{M}_{d+c}$ can be defined by a first-order formula of $\mathcal{M}$ using the representations $\mathbf{U}_b^{(d,c)}$ of the arguments of the operation. More precisely we will show the following. (For the sake of notational simplicity only, in the statement below we assume that all of the function symbols of $\mathcal{M}$ are binary. The function symbols which are unary or 0-ary in the original definition of $\mathcal{M}$ are simply replaced with binary symbols whose sencond argument or both arguments are not used.)

Claim 5. *Assume that $f(x, y)$ is a binary function symbol of $\mathcal{M}$. Then there exists a first-order formula $\Phi_f(x, y, X, Y)$ of $\mathcal{M}$, where x, y are free individual variables and X, Y are free unary relation variables, such that the following holds. For all $c \in \omega$, if $d \in \omega$ is sufficiently large then for all binary function symbols f of $\mathcal{M}$, for all $a, b \in \mathbf{M}_{d+c}$, and for all $u \in \mathbf{M}_d$,*

$$\mathbf{U}^{(d,c)}_{f^{(d+c)}(a,b)}(u) \quad \leftrightarrow \quad \mathbf{M}_d \models \Phi_f(u, c, \mathbf{U}_a^{(d,c)}, \mathbf{U}_b^{(d,c)})$$

where $f^{(d+c)} = (f)_{\mathbf{M}_{d+c}}$.

E.g. the formula $\Phi_{\max}(x, y, X, Y) \equiv A_1 \vee A_2$ satisfies this condition with
$A_1 \equiv X(x) \wedge \exists z, [z = 0 \vee (X(z) \wedge \neg Y(z))] \wedge \forall w \geq z, X(w) \rightarrow Y(w)$
$A_2 \equiv Y(x) \wedge \exists z, [z = 0 \vee (Y(z) \wedge \neg X(z))] \wedge \forall w \geq z, Y(w) \rightarrow X(w)$
where $w \geq z$ stands for $w = \max(w, z)$. If f is the operation "+" of $\mathcal{M}$, the statement is true because the binary bits of $a + b$ can be defined by a first-order formula in $\mathbf{M}_d$ from the bits of a and b. Here both a and b has $2^c n$ bits where $n = 2^d$. Since in $\mathbf{M}_d$ we can quantify integers in 2^n the addition of these numbers can be easily performed in a first-order way. This property of the addition in the binary numeral system was known for a long time, usually formulated in terms of addition by constant depth circuits. The multiplication that is the formula $\Phi_\times$ is a little bit more complicated, but it can be reduced to addition with cn terms, where $n = 2^d$. In the case of the operation $\lfloor x/y \rfloor$ we follow the technique used by Beame, Cook, and Hoover (see [7]) for performing integer division by small depth circuits. Namely we reduce integer division to multiplication and addition by approximating the function $\frac{1}{1-z}$ with an initial segment of its Taylor series. For the other operations f of $\mathcal{M}$ the definition of Φ_f is simple. (The definition of Φ for operation x^y, however, is somewhat more complicated.) We may easily extend the statement of Claim 5 to terms of constant depth as well as described below. The proof is an induction on the depth of the term t.

Claim 6. *Assume that $k \in \omega$ and $t(x_0, .., x_{k-1})$ is a k-ary term of $\mathcal{M}$. Then there exists a first-order formula $\Phi_t(x, y, X_0, ..., X_{k-1})$ of $\mathcal{M}$, where x, y are free individual variables and $X_0, ..., X_{k-1}$ are free unary relation variables, such that the following holds. For all $c \in \omega$, if $d \in \omega$ is sufficiently large, then for all $a_0, ..., a_{k-1} \in \mathbf{M}_{d+c}$, and for all $u \in \mathbf{M}_d$,*

$$\mathbf{U}^{(d,c)}_{t^{(d+c)}(a_0,...,a_{k-1})}(u) \leftrightarrow \mathbf{M}_d \models \Phi_t(u, c, \mathbf{U}_{a_0}^{(d,c)}, ..., \mathbf{U}_{a_{k-1}}^{(d,c)})$$

where $t^{(d+c)} = (t)_{\mathbf{M}_{d+c}}$.

Accepting the statements described in the Claims 2, 3, 4, 5, and 6 we can construct the first-order formula ψ and the function ρ required in Claim 1 in the following way. Using Claim 2, we choose $\rho(\varphi)$ in a way that for all sufficiently large d, we have $\mathbf{M}_d \models \kappa(s(\varphi, \texttt{length}(\varphi)), h(\texttt{length}(\varphi)), \rho(\varphi))$, where the function s and h are defined in Claim 3.

Now we use Claim 6 with $t(x, y) := \min(G(x, y), \mathbf{1})$, where $G(x, y)$ is the binary term whose existence was stated in Claim 3. This definition of t implies that t may take only the values 0 and 1. Using Claim 3 we get that for all $\varphi \in \texttt{Form}(\mathcal{M}, 1)$ if $c = h(\texttt{length}(\varphi))$, $c' = s(\varphi, \texttt{length}(\varphi))$ and $d \in \omega$ is sufficiently large, then for all $x \in \mathbf{M}_d$, $\mathbf{M}_d \models \varphi(x)$ iff $\neg\mathbf{U}^{(d,c)}_{t^{(d+c)}(x,c')}(0)$. Consequently, according to Claim 6, for all $x \in \mathbf{M}_d$, $\mathbf{M}_d \models \varphi(x)$ iff $\mathbf{M}_d \models \Phi_t(0, c, \mathbf{U}_x(0), \mathbf{U}_{c'}(0))$. Therefore by Claim 4 there exists a first-order formula χ of $\mathcal{M}$ such that for all $x \in \mathbf{M}_d$, $\mathbf{M}_d \models \varphi(x)$ iff $\mathbf{M}_d \models \chi(x, c, c')$. Claim 2 and the definition of $\rho(\varphi)$ implies that c and c' are definable from $\rho(\varphi)$ in a first-order way in $\mathbf{M}_d$, using the formula κ, therefore there exists a formula $\psi(x, y)$ of $\mathcal{M}$ such that in $\mathbf{M}_d \models \chi(x, c, c') \leftrightarrow \psi(x, \rho(\varphi))$ and so the conclusion of Claim 1 holds.

Sketch of the proof of Claim 3. Step 1. We show, that if Theorem 2 does not hold, then there exists a term G and a $c \in \omega$, both depending on φ, such that for all sufficiently large $d \in \omega$, we have that for all $a \in \mathbf{M}_d$, $\mathbf{M}_d \models \varphi(a)$ is equivalent to $\mathbf{M}_{d+c} \models G(a) = \mathbf{0}$.

This statement is similar to Claim 3 but it is not the same since the term G may depend on φ. In fact the length of G, will grow with the length of φ in the construction described in the proof of Step 1.

The proof of Step 1 is using the assumption that Theorem 2 is not true and therefore an existential statement of the type $\exists x, F(x, a) = \mathbf{0}$ is equivalent to a quantifier free statement of the form $G_1(a) = \mathbf{0}$. This suggests a process of quantifier elimination applied to the formula φ. To carry out the quantifier elimination we would need to eliminate quantifiers form statements of the type $\exists x, F(x, b_1, ..., b_k, a) = \mathbf{0}$

where $b_1, ..., b_k$ are fixed elements of $\mathbf{M}_d$. In other words we would need our indirect assumption for equations with more then one parameters. We do not have such an assumption, but we can reduce the case of many parameters to the case of a single parameter by considering the same statement not in $\mathbf{M}_d$ but in $\mathbf{M}_{d+c}$, where c is sufficiently large with respect to k. In this structure the $k+1$ parameters can be encoded by a single parameter, so the indirect assumption can be used. This encoding can be done by the arithmetic operations of $\mathcal{M}$. For example pair $\langle a, b\rangle \in \mathbf{M}_d$ can be encoded by the single element $a + b2^d$ in $\mathbf{M}_{d+1}$.

Step 2. After Step 1 we have a statement of the type $\mathbf{M}_d \models G(a) = \mathbf{0}$ (with $d := d + c$) where the the term G depends on φ, in particular it G can be arbitrarily large since we used the indirect assumption in its construction, which does not provide any limit on its size. In this step we show that:

Claim 7. *There exists a first-order formula $\xi(y, z)$ of $\mathcal{M}$ so that for each term $G(y)$ of $\mathcal{M}$, and for each sufficiently large $c \in \omega$, there exists an $u_{c,G} \in \omega$, with the property that for all sufficiently large $d \in \omega$, and for all $a \in \mathbf{M}_d$, $\mathbf{M}_d \models G(a) = \mathbf{0}$ is equivalent to $\mathbf{M}_{d+c} \models \xi(y, u_{c,G})$.*

(We do not need the indirect assumption for the proof of this statement.) The important point in this statement is that the formula $\xi(x, y)$ does not depend on the term G. The dependence on G is only through a parameter of ξ. Applying Step 1 and then Step 2 we get that for all sufficiently large $d \in \omega$ and for all $a \in \mathbf{M}_d$, $\mathbf{M}_d \models \varphi(a)$ is equivalent to $\mathbf{M}_{d+c_1} \models \xi(a, c_2)$, where c_1 and c_2 depend only on φ (but not on d or a).

The proof of Claim 7 is based on the observation that the evaluation of a term can be described by existentially quantifying the values of its subterms. If the integer c of Claim 7 is sufficiently large with respect to G (which is allowed) then such an existential quantification is possible in $\mathbf{M}_{d+c}$.

Step 3. If we combine the first two steps we get, that for all sufficiently large $d \in \omega$, and for all $a \in \mathbf{M}_d$, $\mathbf{M}_d \models \varphi(a)$ is equivalent to $\mathbf{M}_{d+c_1} \models \xi(a, c_2)$, where the first-order formula ξ does not depend on anything, and $c_1, c_2 \in \omega$ depend only on φ. Now we use the quantifier elimination, described in Step 1, again, and we get the term G whose existence is claimed in Claim 3. Since ξ does not depend on φ, the term G, that we gain at the end of the elimination process, will not depend on it either, the dependence on φ will be only through the parameters of G. *End of Sketch*

5. SKETCH OF THE PROOF OF THEOREM 4

The sketch that we gave for the proof of Theorem 2 can be considered also a sketch of the proof of Theorem 4 with the following modification. In the sketch of the proof of Theorem 2 we used unary relations $\mathbf{U}_a^{(d,c)}$ defined on $\mathbf{M}_d$ to encode the elements of $\mathbf{U}_{d+c}$. Now, instead of unary, we will use binary relations on $\mathbf{K}_d$ to encode the elements of $\mathbf{K}_{d+c}$. We are forced to make this change, because we cannot encode the elements of $\mathbf{K}_d$ by their binary forms, since the needed operations for such an encoding are not necessarily operations of $\mathbf{K}_d$. Each element of $a \in \mathbf{K}_d$ will be encoded by the binary relation on $\mathbf{K}_d$ which holds only on the pair $\langle 0, a\rangle$. In the case of $\mathbf{M}_d$ the two encodings can be easily defined from each other in a first-order way. We will consider this problem in detail when we show that Theorem 2 follows from Theorem 4.

6. PROOF OF THEOREM 4

Definition. Assume that $\mathbf{K} = \langle \mathbf{K}_d \mid d \in \omega\rangle$ is a $\mathcal{K}$-sequence with respect to the language $\mathcal{K}$ and $k \in \omega$. We will say that a family of k-ary functions $f^{(d)} \in \mathtt{func}_k(\mathtt{universe}(\mathbf{K}_d), \mathtt{universe}(\mathbf{K}_d))$, $d \in \omega$, is an external $\mathbf{K}$ family. The external $\mathbf{K}$ family of k-ary functions will be called a first-order $\mathbf{K}$ family of k-ary functions, if there exists a first-order formula $\varphi(x_0, \ldots, x_{k-1}, y)$ of $\mathcal{K}$, whose free variables are among $x_0, \ldots, x_{k-1}, y$, such that for all sufficiently large $d \in \omega$, and for all $a_0, \ldots, a_{k-1}, b \in \mathbf{K}_d$, we have $b = f(a_0, \ldots, a_{k-1})$ iff $\mathbf{K}_d \models \varphi(a_0, \ldots, a_{k-1}, b)$.

The external $\mathbf{K}$ family of k-ary functions will be called an internal $\mathbf{K}$ family of k-ary functions, if there exists a term $t(x_0, \ldots, x_{k-1})$ of $\mathcal{K}$ with k free variables, such that for all sufficiently large $d \in \omega$, and for all $a_0, \ldots, a_{k-1} \in \mathbf{K}_d$ we have $t^{(d)}(a_0, \ldots, a_{k-1}) = f(a_0, \ldots, a_{k-1})$, where $t^{(d)} = (t)_{\mathbf{K}_d}$. In this case the family of functions $f^{(d)}$ is called the family of functions induced by the term t. Sometimes we will say "$\mathbf{K}$ first-order-family" instead of "first-order $\mathbf{K}$ family of functions" "$\mathbf{K}$ internal-family" instead of "internal $\mathbf{K}$ family of functions", and "$\mathbf{K}$ external-family" instead of "external $\mathbf{K}$ family of functions". □

Remark. It is important in the definition of a first-order $\mathbf{K}$ family of function that in the formula $\varphi(x_0, \ldots, x_{k-1}, y)$ we do not allow any parameters. This makes the definition somewhat different from the usual definition of a first-order definable function. □

Definition. 1. The set A is a co-finite subset of the set B, or $A \subseteq B$ is co-finite, if $A \subseteq B$ and $B \backslash A$ is finite.

2. Assume $\mathbf{K} = \langle \mathbf{K}_d \mid d \in \omega\rangle$ is a $\mathcal{K}$-sequence, with respect to the language $\mathcal{K}$, $A \subseteq \omega$ is co-finite and for all $d \in A$, $R_1^{(d)}, R_2^{(d)}$ are k-ary relations on the set $\mathtt{universe}(\mathbf{K}_d)$. We will say that the family of relations $R_1 = \langle R_1^{(d)} \mid d \in A\rangle$ and $R_2 = \langle R_2^{(d)} \mid d \in A\rangle$ are asymptotically equivalent iff for all sufficiently large $d \in \omega$, we have that $\forall a_0, \ldots, a_{k-1} \in \mathbf{K}_d, R_1^{(d)}(a_0, \ldots, a_{k-1}) \leftrightarrow R_2^{(d)}(a_0, \ldots, a_{k-1})$. We will write $R_1 \sim R_2$ for "R_1 and R_2, are asymptotically equivalent".

3. Assume that $\varphi(x_0, \ldots, x_{k-1})$ is a first-order formula of $\mathcal{K}$, $j \in \omega$. For all $d \in \omega$, $\mathcal{R}_k^{(d)}[\varphi, j]$ will be the k-ary relation on $\mathtt{universe}(\mathbf{K}_d)$ defined by: "for all $a_0, \ldots, a_{k-1} \in \mathbf{K}_d$, $(\mathcal{R}_k^{(d)}[\varphi, j])(a_0, \ldots, a_{k-1})$ iff $\mathbf{K}_{d+j} \models \varphi(a_0, \ldots, a_{k-1})$". The family of relations $\langle \mathcal{R}_k^{(d)}[\varphi, j] \mid d \in \omega\rangle$ will be denoted by $\mathcal{R}_k[\varphi, j]$. The relation $\mathcal{R}_k^{(d)}[\varphi, 0]$ will be also denoted by $\mathcal{R}_k^{(d)}[\varphi]$. The corresponding family of relations will be denoted by $\mathcal{R}_k[\varphi]$.

4. If $F(x_0, \ldots, x_{k-1})$ is a term of $\mathcal{K}$ and $j \in \omega$, $n = 1, 2, \ldots$ then the relation $\mathcal{R}_k^{(d)}[F(x_0, \ldots, x_{k-1}) = \mathbf{0}, j]$ will be denoted by $\mathcal{R}_k^{(d)}[F, j]$, and for $j = 0$ by $\mathcal{R}_k^{(d)}[F]$ as well. The corresponding families of relations will be denoted by $\mathcal{R}_k[F, j]$ and $\mathcal{R}_k[F]$. □

Remark. According to these definitions the first-order formulas $\varphi(x), \psi(x)$ are asymptotically equivalent iff the family of relations $\mathcal{R}_1^{(d)}[\varphi]$, $d \in \omega$ and $\mathcal{R}_1^{(d)}[\psi]$, $d \in \omega$ are asymptotically equivalent. □

LEMMA 2. *Assume that* $\mathbf{K} = \langle \mathbf{K}_d \mid d \in \omega \rangle$ *is a regular* $\mathcal{K}$*-sequence. For each propositional formula* $P(x_1, \ldots, x_k)$ *of* $\mathcal{K}$*, there exists a term* $T(x_1, \ldots, x_k)$ *of* $\mathcal{K}$ *so that for all sufficiently large* $d \in \omega$*, we have* $\mathbf{K}_d \models \forall x_1, \ldots, x_k, P(x_1, \ldots, x_k) \leftrightarrow T(x_1, \ldots, x_k) = \mathbf{0}$ *and* $\mathbf{K}_d \models \forall x_1, \ldots, x_k, \neg P(x_1, \ldots, x_k) \leftrightarrow T(x_1, \ldots, x_n) = \mathbf{1}$*. Consequently for each propositional formula* $P(x_1 \ldots, x_k)$ *of* $\mathcal{K}$ *there exists a term* $T(x_1, \ldots, x_k)$ *of* $\mathcal{K}$ *so that the family of relations* $\mathcal{R}_k^{(d)}[P]$*,* $d \in \omega$ *and* $\mathcal{R}_k^{(d)}[F]$*,* $d \in \omega$ *are asymptotically equivalent.*

Proof. Since the only relation symbol of the language $\mathcal{K}$ is the equality, we have that each atomic formula is of the form $t_1 = t_2$ where t_1 and t_2 are terms. By condition (3) of the definition of regularity $t_1 = t_2$ is equivalent to $\bar{t}(t_1, t_2) = \mathbf{0}$ and $\neg(t_1 = t_2)$ is equivalent to $\bar{t}(t_1, t_2) = \mathbf{1}$. Therefore using condition (2) for the various logical operations $\wedge, \vee, \neg$ etc. we can transform each propositional formula of $\mathcal{K}$ into a propositional formula into an equivalent propositional formula of the form $t = \mathbf{0}$, where t is a term. *Q.E.D.*(Lemma 2)

Notation. For an expression $x_0, \ldots, x_{k-1}$ we will sometimes write $\underline{x}$ if the choice of k is clear from the context.

PROPOSITION 1. *Assume that for each* $i = 0, 1, 2$, Φ_i *is a first-order formula with* k *variables,* $u, v \in \omega$*, and we have* $\mathcal{R}_k[\Phi_0] \sim \mathcal{R}_k[\Phi_1, u]$ *and* $\mathcal{R}_k[\Phi_1] \sim \mathcal{R}_k[\Phi_2, v]$*. Then* $\mathcal{R}_k[\Phi_0] \sim \mathcal{R}_k[\Phi_2, u + v]$*.*

Proof. Assume $\underline{x} \in (\mathbf{K}_d)^k$, where d is sufficiently large. Then $\mathbf{K}_d \models \Phi_0(\underline{x})$ iff $\mathbf{K}_{d+u} \models \Phi_1(\underline{x})$ and $\mathbf{K}_{d+u} \models \Phi_1(\underline{x})$ iff $\mathbf{K}_{d+u+v} \models \Phi_2(\underline{x})$ which implies our statement. *Q.E.D.*(Proposition 1)

Remark. If $F_i(\underline{x})$ is a term, then we may apply Proposition 1 with $\Phi_i(\underline{x})$:= "$F_i(\underline{x}) = \mathbf{0}$". Therefore the proposition remains true if some of the Φ_is are not formulas but terms. □

PROPOSITION 2. *Assume that* $\mathbf{K} = \langle \mathbf{K}_d \mid d \in \omega \rangle$ *is a retrospective and projective* $\mathcal{K}$*-sequence. Then the following condition is satisfied.*

(11). Let $k \in \omega$ *and let* $g^{(d)}$*,* $d \in \omega$ *be a* k*-ary* $\mathbf{K}$ *internal-family of functions. Then there exists a* $k+1$*-ary* $\mathbf{K}$ *first-order-family of functions* $f^{(d)}$*,* $d \in \omega$ *such that for all* $c \in \omega$*, for all sufficiently large* $d \in \omega$*, and for all* $a_0, \ldots, a_{k-1} \in \mathbf{K}_d$ *we have* $g^{(d)}(a_0, \ldots, a_{k-1}) = f^{(d+c)}(a_0, \ldots, a_{k-1}, c)$*.*

Proof of Proposition 2. The statement of the proposition requires a proof since the terms involved in $g^{(d)}$ are defined in $\mathbf{K}_d$, while the first-order formula defining $f^{(d+c)}$ must be interpreted in $\mathbf{K}_{d+c}$.

The first-order formula which $\varphi(x_0, \ldots, x_{k-1}, y)$ defined the function $f^{(d+c)}$ will say that $y \in \mathbf{K}_d$ and $g^{(d)}(x_0, \ldots, x_{k-1}) = y$. By condition (6) of the definition of projectivity, $\texttt{universe}(\mathbf{K}_d)$ is the image of the map $\pi_{c,0}^{(d)}$. Therefore $b \in \mathbf{K}_d$ iff $\mathbf{K}_{d+c} \models \exists a, \Gamma(a, b, d, c, 0)$, where Γ is the first-order formula from condition (7) from the definition of projectivity. Consequently $y \in \mathbf{K}_d$ can be stated in $\mathbf{K}_{d+c}$ in a first-order way and by condition (9) by the definition of a retrospective $\mathcal{K}$-sequence, $g^{(d)}(x_0, \ldots, x_{k-1}) = y$ can be also defined in a first-order way in $\mathbf{K}_{d+c}$. (We need the first-order formula expressing $y \in \mathbf{K}_d$, since the formula guaranteed by condition (9) speaks only about the elements of $\mathbf{K}_d$ and not of $\mathbf{K}_{d+c}$.) *Q.E.D.*(Proposition 2)

PROPOSITION 3. *Assume that* $\mathbf{K} = \langle \mathbf{K}_d \mid d \in \omega \rangle$ *is a retrospective and projective* $\mathcal{K}$*-sequence. Then the following condition is satisfied.*

(12). Let $k \in \omega$ *and let* $g(x_0, \ldots, x_{k-1})$ *be a term of* $\mathcal{K}$ *with the only free variables* $x_0, \ldots, x_{k-1}$*. Then for all* $c \in \omega$ *there exists a term* $h_{g,c}(x_0, \ldots, x_{k-1})$ *of* $\mathcal{K}$ *with the only free variables* $x_0, \ldots, x_{k-1}$ *such that for all sufficiently large* $d \in \omega$*, and for all* $a_0, \ldots, a_{k-1} \in \mathbf{K}_d$ *we have* $g^{(d)}(a_0, \ldots, a_{k-1}) = h_{g,c}^{(d+c)}(a_0, \ldots, a_{k-1})$*.*

Proof. We prove the proposition by induction on c. For $c = 1$ the statement of the proposition follows from condition (8) from the definition of retrospectivity. Assume that $c > 1$ and the proposition holds for all smaller values of c. We define $h_{g,c}$ by $h_{g,c}(x_0, \ldots, x_{k-1}) = h_{h_{g,c-1},1}(x_0, \ldots, x_{k-1})$. Assume that $a_0, \ldots, a_{k-1} \in \mathbf{K}_d \subseteq \texttt{universe}(\mathbf{K}_{d+c-1})$. We have $h_{g,c}^{(d+c)}(a_0, \ldots, a_{k-1}) = h_{h_{g,c-1},1}^{(d+c)}(a_0, \ldots, a_{k-1}) = h_{g,c-1}^{(d+c-1)}(a_0, \ldots, a_{k-1}) = g^{(d)}(a_0, \ldots, a_{k-1})$ as claimed in the conclusion of proposition. *Q.E.D.*(Proposition 3)

PROPOSITION 4. *Assume that* $\mathbf{K}$ *is a projective* $\mathcal{K}$*-sequence and for all* $c \in \omega$*,* $k \in 2^c$ *let* $\pi_{c,k}$ *be the term whose existence is stated in the definition of projectivity. Then for all* $c \in \omega$ *and for all sufficiently large* $d \in \omega$*,* $\pi_{c,k}^{(d+c)}$ *is a map of* $\texttt{universe}(\mathbf{K}_{d+c})$ *onto* $\texttt{universe}(\mathbf{K}_d)$*. As a consequence, for each first-order formula* $Q_0 x_0, \ldots, Q_{k-1} x_{k-1}, P(x_0, \ldots, x_{k-1})$ *of* $\mathcal{K}$*, where* $Q_0, \ldots, Q_{k-1}$ *are quantifiers, the following two statements are equivalent*

(i) $\mathbf{K}_{d+c} \models$
$Q_0 x_0, \ldots, Q_{k-1} x_{k-1}, P(\pi_{c,0}(x_0), \ldots, \pi_{c,0}(x_{k-1}))$

(ii) $Q_0 a_0 \in \mathbf{K}_d, \ldots, Q_{k-1} a_{k-1} \in \mathbf{K}_d,$
$\mathbf{K}_{d+c} \models P(a_0, \ldots, a_{k-1})$.

Proof. Condition (6) of the definition of projectivity implies that the image of $\pi_{c,k}^{(d)}$ is $\mathbf{K}_d$. (For the conclusions given in (i) and (ii) it is enough to use, for example, the map $\pi_{c,0}^{(d+c)}$.) *Q.E.D.*(Proposition 4)

PROPOSITION 5. *Assume that* $\mathbf{K} = \langle \mathbf{K}_d \mid d \in \omega \rangle$ *is a* $\mathcal{K}$*-sequence,* $\langle f^{(d)} \mid d \in \omega \rangle$ *is a* k*-ary* $\mathbf{K}$ *internal-family of functions and for each* $j = 0, 1, \ldots, k-1$*,* $\langle g_j^{(d)} \mid d \in \omega \rangle$ *is an* l*-ary* $\mathbf{K}$ *internal-family of functions. For each* $d \in \omega$*, we define an* l*-ary function* $h^{(d)}$ *on* $\texttt{universe}(\mathbf{K}_d)$ *by*

$$h^{(d)}(a_0, \ldots, a_{l-1}) =$$
$$f^{(d)}(g_0^{(d)}(a_0, \ldots, a_{l-1}), \ldots, g_{k-1}^{(d)}(a_0, \ldots, a_{l-1}))$$

for all $a_0, \ldots, a_{k-1} \in \texttt{universe}(\mathbf{K}_d)$*. Then* $h^{(d)}$ *is an* l*-ary* $\mathbf{K}$ *internal-family of functions.*

Proof. We get the term inducing the family $h^{(d)}$, by substituting the terms inducing the families $g_j^{(d)}$ into the corresponding term for $f^{(d)}$. *Q.E.D.*(Proposition 5)

PROPOSITION 6. *Assume that* $\mathbf{K}$ *is a retrospective and projective* $\mathcal{K}$*-sequence, and for all* $c \in \omega$*,* τ_c *is the term of* $\mathcal{K}$ *whose existence was stated in condition (6) of the definition of projectivity. Suppose further that* $F(x, y_0, \ldots, y_{k-1})$ *is a term of* $\mathcal{K}$*. Then for all* $c \in \omega$ *with* $2^c \geq k$*, there exists a term* $G(x, z)$ *of* $\mathcal{K}$ *so that for all sufficiently large* $d \in \omega$ *and for all* $a, b_0, \ldots, b_{k-1} \in \mathbf{K}_d$ *the following two statements are equivalent:*

(i) $\mathbf{K}_d \models F(a, b_0, \ldots, b_{k-1}) = \mathbf{0}$,

(ii) $\mathbf{K}_{d+c} \models G(a, \tau_c(b_0, \ldots, b_{k-1}, \mathbf{0}, \ldots, \mathbf{0})) = \mathbf{0}$.

Proof. The term G is defined by $G(x,y) = h_{F,c}(x, \pi_{c,0}(y), \pi_{c,1}(y), \ldots, \pi_{c,k-1}(y))$, where the term $h_{F,c}$ is defined in Proposition 3 and the term $\pi_{c,i}$ is from condition (7) of the definition of projectivity. Proposition 3 and the definition of projectivity imply that statements (i) and (ii) are equivalent. *Q.E.D.*(Proposition 6)

As we said earlier if Theorem 4 is not true then there is a possibility for quantifier elimination. In the next lemma we show that this really can be done with a first-order formula φ interpreted in $\mathbf{K}_d$, at the price of getting the equivalent quantifier free formula not in $\mathbf{K}_d$ but in $\mathbf{K}_{d+c}$, where the equivalence is valid for all sufficiently large d, and c depends only on φ.

Definition. Assume that $\mathbf{K} = \langle \mathbf{K}_d \mid d \in \omega \rangle$ is a complete, retrospective, and predictive $\mathcal{K}$-sequence such that the conclusion of Theorem 4 does not hold for $\mathbf{K}$. Then we will say that $\mathbf{K}$ is a counterexample for Theorem 4. □

LEMMA 3. *Assume that Theorem 4 does not hold and* $\mathbf{K} = \langle \mathbf{K}_d \mid d \in \omega \rangle$ *is a counterexample for Theorem 4. Then for each first-order formula* $\varphi(x_0, \ldots, x_{k-1})$ *of* $\mathcal{K}$, *there exist a* $c = c_\varphi \in \omega$ *and a term* $G(x_0, \ldots, x_{k-1}) = G_\varphi(x_0, \ldots, x_{k-1})$ *of* $\mathcal{K}$ *such that, the family of relations* $\mathcal{R}_k[\varphi(x_0, \ldots, x_{k-1})]$ *and* $\mathcal{R}_k[G(x_0, \ldots, x_{k-1}), c]$ *are asymptotically equivalent.*

Proof. Assume that $\varphi(\underline{x})$ has the following prenex from $\varphi(x) \equiv Q_0 z_0, \ldots, Q_{l-1} z_{l-1} P(\underline{z}, \underline{x})$, where $Q_0, \ldots, Q_{l-1}$ are quantifiers and P is a propositional formula. By Lemma 2 we may assume that P is of the form $F(\underline{z}, \underline{x}) = \mathbf{0}$ for a term F of $\mathcal{K}$. We prove the lemma in this form by induction on l, and by always assuming that the inductive assumption holds for all values of k. For $l = 0$ the statement of the lemma trivially holds with $c = 0$, $G = F$. Assume now that the lemma is true for $l := l - 1$. Lemma 2 and condition (2) from the definition of a regular $\mathcal{K}$-sequence implies that the statement of the lemma is equivalent to the same statement with $\varphi := \neg\varphi$, therefore we may assume that Q_{l-1} is the quantifier $\exists$.

As we have noted earlier, Lemma 2 implies that there exists a term F_1 of $\mathcal{K}$ so that for each sufficiently large d and for each $a_0, \ldots, a_{l-2}, b_0, \ldots, b_{k-1} \in \mathbf{K}_d$, we have that $\mathbf{K}_d \models \exists z_{l-1} P(a_0, \ldots, a_{l-2}, z_{l-1}, b_0, \ldots, b_{k-1})$ is equivalent to $\mathbf{K}_d \models \Phi_1 \equiv \exists z_{l-1} F_1(a_0, \ldots, a_{l-2}, z_{l-1}, b_0, \ldots, b_{k-1}) = \mathbf{0}$. By Proposition 6, there exists a $c_1 \in \omega$, and a term $G_1(x, z)$ of $\mathcal{K}$ so that for all sufficiently large $d \in \omega$ and for all $a_0 \ldots, a_{l-2}, b_0, \ldots, b_{k-1} \in \mathbf{K}_d$, we have that $\mathbf{K}_d \models \Phi_1$ is equivalent to $\mathbf{K}_{d+c_1} \models \exists z_{l-1} G_1(z_{l-1}, \tau_{c_1}(a_0, \ldots, a_{l-2}, b_0, \ldots, b_{k-1}, \mathbf{0}, \ldots, \mathbf{0})) = \mathbf{0}$. We will denote the term $\tau_{c_1}(x_0, \ldots, x_{k+l-2}, \mathbf{0}, \ldots, \mathbf{0})$ by $\tau'_{c_1}(x_0, \ldots, x_{k+l-2})$. Using our assumption that Theorem 4 is not true with $F := G_1$, we get that there exists a term G_2, such that for all sufficiently large $d \in \omega$ and for all $a_0 \ldots, a_{l-2}, b_0, \ldots, b_{k-1} \in \mathbf{K}_d$ we have that $\mathbf{K}_{d+c_1} \models \exists z_{l-1}, G_1(z_{l-1}, \tau'_{c_1}(a_0, \ldots, a_{l-2}, b_0, \ldots, b_{k-1})) = \mathbf{0}$ is equivalent to $\mathbf{K}_{d+c_1} \models G_2(\tau'_{c_1}(a_0, \ldots, a_{l-2}, b_0, \ldots, b_{k-1})) = \mathbf{0}$.

We got that there exists a term G_2 of $\mathcal{K}$ such that for all sufficiently large d, and for all

$$a_0, \ldots, a_{l-2}, b_0, \ldots, b_{k-1} \in \mathbf{K}_d,$$

$\mathbf{K}_d \models \exists z_{l-1} P(a_0, \ldots, a_{l-2}, z_{l-1}, b_0, \ldots, b_{k-1})$ is equivalent to $\mathbf{K}_{d+c_1} \models G_2(\tau'_{c_1}(a_0, \ldots, a_{l-2}, b_0, \ldots, b_{k-1})) = \mathbf{0}$. Consequently, by using Proposition 4, we get that the statement $\mathbf{K}_d \models Q_0 z_0, \ldots, Q_{l-1} z_{l-2}, \exists z_{l-1} P(z_0, \ldots, z_{l-1}, b_0, \ldots, b_{k-1})$ is equivalent to the following statement that we define in a larger structure: $\mathbf{K}_{d+c_1} \models Q_0 z_0, \ldots, Q_{l-1} z_{l-2}$, $G_2(\tau'_{c_1}(\pi_{c_1,0}(z_0), \ldots, \pi_{c_1,0}(z_{l-2}), b_0, \ldots, b_{k-1})) = \mathbf{0})$, which can be written in the form of $\mathbf{K}_{d+c_1} \models \varphi_1(b_0, \ldots, b_{k-1})$, where φ_1 is a first-order formula of $\mathcal{K}$ containing $l - 1$ quantifiers in its prenex form. Therefore we may apply the inductive assumption with $\varphi := \varphi_1$. We get that there exists a term G of $\mathcal{K}$ so that for all sufficiently large $d \in \omega$ and for all $b_0, \ldots, b_{k-1} \in \mathbf{K}_d$ we have that

$$\mathbf{K}_{d+c_1} \models Q_0 z_0, \ldots, Q_{l-1} z_{l-2},$$
$$G_2(\tau'_{c_1}(\pi_{c_1,0}(z_0), \ldots, \pi_{c_1,0}(z_{l-2}), b_0, \ldots, b_{k-1})) = \mathbf{0})$$

is equivalent to $\mathbf{K}_{d+c_1+c_2} \models G(b_0, \ldots, b_{k-1})$, that is, $\mathbf{K}_d \models \varphi(b_0, \ldots, b_{k-1})$ iff $\mathbf{K}_{d+c_1+c_2} \models G(b_0, \ldots, b_{k-1})$. Since this is true for all choices of $b_0, \ldots, b_{k-1} \in \mathbf{K}_d$ we have that the family of relations $\mathcal{R}_k[\varphi(x_0, \ldots, x_{k-1})]$ and $\mathcal{R}_k[G(x_0, \ldots, x_{k-1}), c_1 + c_2]$ are asymptotically equivalent. *Q.E.D.*(Lemma 3)

Our next goal is to express the relation $G(y) = \mathbf{0}$ in $\mathbf{K}_d$, where G is a term of $\mathcal{K}$, with a first-order formula $\xi(y, z)$ such that the dependence of G will be attained by substituting a parameter for z which depends on G. The formula $\xi(x, z)$ in itself will not depend on G. We will be able to do this if the formula ξ is interpreted in $\mathbf{K}_{d+c}$ where c is sufficiently large with respect to G (but it does not depend on d). We will get that for a suitably chosen $u_{c,G} \in \omega$, and for all sufficiently large $d \in \omega$, $\forall y \in \mathbf{K}_d$, $\mathbf{K}_d \models G(y) = \mathbf{0}$ iff $\mathbf{K}_{d+c} \models \xi(y, u_{c,G})$, where the parameter $u_{c,G}$ depends only on c and G. The importance of this is that we replaced an arbitrarily large term G with a first-order formula ξ of fixed size. This is important since during the quantifier elimination described in Lemma 3 we have no control on the size of the term G. This is a consequence of the fact that in the proof of Lemma 3 we use the assumption that Theorem 4 is not true and this assumption implies the existence of a term but without any bound on its size.

In the following lemma the assumption "Theorem 4 does not hold" is *not* needed.

LEMMA 4. *There exists a first-order formula* $\xi(y, z)$ *of* $\mathcal{K}$ *so that if* $\mathbf{K} = \langle \mathbf{K}_d \mid d \in \omega \rangle$ *is a* $\mathcal{K}$*-sequence then for each term* $G(y)$ *of* $\mathcal{K}$ *and for each sufficiently large* $c \in \omega$ *there exists an* $u_{c,G} \in \omega$ *with the property that the family of relations* $\mathcal{R}_1[G(y)]$ *and* $\mathcal{R}_1[\xi(y, u_{c,G}), c]$ *are asymptotically equivalent.*

Proof. We may assume that all of the function symbols of the language $\mathcal{K}$ has the same arity k, since for each $l < k$, an l-ary function $f(x_0, \ldots, x_{l-1})$ can be considered as a k-ary function which does not depend on its last $k - l$ variables $x_k, \ldots, x_{k-l-1}$. We will consider the constant symbols also as k-ary function symbols. Assume that all of the function symbols of $\mathcal{K}$, including the constant symbols, are $f_0, \ldots, f_{\nu-1}$.

λ will denote the number of subterms of the term G. We claim that there exist functions $r \in \mathtt{func}(\lambda, \nu)$, $g \in \mathtt{func}(\lambda \times k, \lambda)$ so that for all sufficiently large $d \in \omega$ and for all $a \in \mathbf{K}_d$, the following two conditions are equivalent

(i) $\mathbf{K}_d \models G(a) = \mathbf{0}$

(ii) There exists $b_0, \ldots, b_{\lambda-1} \in \mathbf{K}_d$ so that $b_0 = a$, $b_{\lambda-1} = 0$, and for all $i = 1, \ldots, j$, $b_i = f^{(d)}_{r(i)}(b_{g(i,0)}, \ldots, b_{g(i,k-1)})$.

We define the functions r, g in the following way. Let $t_0, \ldots, t_{\lambda-1}$ be all of the subterms of $G(y)$, so that t_0 is the variable y, and $t_{\lambda-1}$ is the term G, and each subterm t' comes later in the sequence than any of its proper subterms. We choose the functions r and g such that

$t_i = f_{r(i)}(t_{g(i,0)}, \ldots, t_{g(i,k-1)})$ for $i = 1, \ldots, \lambda - 1$. This completes the definition of r and g. Suppose now that condition (i) holds. Then we choose $b_i \in \mathbf{K}_d$ so that $\mathbf{K}_d \models b_i = t_i(a)$. The definitions of the functions r and g imply that condition (ii) is satisfied. Conversely assume that statement (ii) holds. Again by the definitions of the functions r and g, the sequence b_i gives the values of the terms of $t_i(a)$. Since $b_{\lambda-1} = 0$ we have $\mathbf{K}_d \models G(a) = \mathbf{0}$.

Assume that $c \in \omega$ is sufficiently large. Our next task is to express condition (ii) by a first-order formula in $\mathbf{K}_{d+c}$. First we note that the regularity of the $\mathcal{K}$-sequence $\mathbf{K}$ implies that there exist first-order formulas $\eta_0, \eta_1, \eta_2, \eta_3, \eta_4$ such that for each term $G(y)$ of $\mathcal{K}$ there exists a natural number $u_{c,G}$ so that for all sufficiently large $d \in \omega$ the following requirements are met:

(a) for all $i \in \nu + 1$, $i = \nu$ iff $\mathbf{K}_d \models \eta_0(i, u_{c,G})$

(b) for all $i \in \lambda + 1$, $i = \lambda$ iff $\mathbf{K}_d \models \eta_1(i, u_{c,G})$

(c) for all $i \in \lambda, j \in \nu$, $r(i) = j$ iff $\mathbf{K}_d \models \eta_2(i, j, u_{c,G})$

(d) for all $i \in \lambda, j \in k, l \in \lambda$, $g(i,j) = l$ iff $\mathbf{K}_d \models \eta_3(i, j, l, u_{c,G})$

(e) for all $i \in c + 1$, $i = c$ iff $\mathbf{K}_d \models \eta_4(i, u_{c,G})$

These requirements say that the numbers ν, λ and the functions r, g must be definable in a first-order way from the number $u_{c,G}$, which depends only on c, G but *not* on d, by formulas, which do *not* depend on either G or d. This means that we may speak about ν, λ, r and g in the structure $\mathbf{K}_{d+c}$ by a first-order formula which does not depend on G or d if this first-order formula contains $u_{c,G}$ as a parameter.

Condition (ii), that we want to express in $\mathbf{K}_{d+1}$, states the existence of a sequence $b_0, \ldots, b_{\lambda-1} \in \mathbf{K}_d$ with certain properties. We will encode such a sequence with a single element of $\mathbf{K}_{d+c}$, so that, these properties will be expressible in a first-order way. This will make it possible to state the existence of the sequence $b_0, \ldots, b_{\lambda-1}$ by a single existential quantification in $\mathbf{K}_{d+c}$.

Since the integer c is sufficiently large with respect to G we may assume that $2^c \geq \lambda$. Each sequence $b_0, \ldots, b_{\lambda-1} \in \mathbf{K}_d$ will be represented by the element $w = \tau_c^{(d+c)}(b_0, \ldots, b_{\lambda-1}, 0, \ldots, 0) \in \mathbf{K}_{d+c}$ where τ_c is the term whose existence is stated in the definition of projectivity.

The definition projectivity imply that there exists a first-order formula η_5 of $\mathcal{K}$ so that for all $i \in \lambda$, $b \in \mathbf{K}_{d+c}$ we have $b = b_i$ iff $\mathbf{K}_{d+c} \models \eta_5(w, b, i)$.

Finally we have to describe the equations $b_i = f_{r(i)}(b_{g(i,0)}, \ldots, b_{g(i,k-1)})$ by a first-order formula in $\mathbf{K}_{d+c}$. $\mathbf{K}$ is retrospective, therefore condition (9) of the definition of a retrospective $\mathcal{K}$-sequence implies that this is possible using c as a parameter in the formula. Condition (e) of the definition of $u_{c,G}$ implies that c is definable from $u_{c,G}$ by a first-order formula. We got that there exists a first-order formula $\xi(y, z)$ of $\mathcal{K}$ such that for all $a \in \mathbf{K}_d$ condition (ii) is satisfied iff $\mathbf{K}_{d+c} \models \xi(a, u_{v,G})$. Since conditions (i) and (ii) are equivalent for each sufficiently large d this implies the statement of the lemma. *Q.E.D.*(Lemma 4)

Definition. The first-order formula ξ whose existence is stated in Lemma 4 is not unique, but we assume that a choice for ξ has been fixed. The integer $u_{c,G}$ defined in the lemma will have the properties described there with this choice of ξ. The smallest integer $c \in \omega$ which satisfies the requirements of the Lemma 4 with ξ will be denoted by $c(G)$. □

Definition. Suppose that $\mathcal{L}$ is a first-order language and $k \in \omega$. $\texttt{Form}(\mathcal{L}, k)$ will denote the set of all first-order formulas of $\mathcal{L}$ with at most k free variables. □

LEMMA 5. *Assume that Theorem 4 does not hold and $\mathbf{K} = \langle \mathbf{K}_d \mid d \in \omega \rangle$ is a counter example for Theorem 4. Then there exists a term $G(y, z)$ of $\mathcal{K}$ and functions $h \in \texttt{func}(\omega, \omega)$, $s \in \texttt{func}(\texttt{Form}(\mathcal{K}, 1) \times \omega, \omega)$ such that for all $\ell \in \omega$, and for all first-order formulas $\varphi(y)$ of $\mathcal{K}$ with $\texttt{length}(\varphi) \leq \ell$, the families of relations $\mathcal{R}_1[G(y, s(\varphi, \ell)), h(\ell)]$ and $\mathcal{R}_1[\varphi(y)]$ are asymptotically equivalent.*

Remark. This lemma states that the truth value of a first-order formula $\varphi(y)$ as a function of y, for all formulas $\varphi(y)$ of length at most ℓ, can be determined by evaluating a term $G(y, u)$ in $\mathbf{K}_{d+v}$, where G does not depend on anything, v depends only on ℓ and u depends only on ℓ and φ. Therefore, in some sense, we reduced the question of determining the truth value of a first-order formula to the evaluation of a term. On the other hand we have to do the evaluation of this term in a larger structure, than the one where the truth value of the formula is considered. □

Proof of Lemma 5. Let $\xi(y, z)$ be the first-order formula whose existence was stated in Lemma 4. The binary term $G(y, z) = G_\xi(y, z)$ with the properties guaranteed by Lemma 3 will be also the term $G(y, z)$ whose existence is stated in the present lemma. Lemma 3, with $\varphi := \xi$, states the existence of an integer $c_\xi \in \omega$ that we will use later.

We have to define the functions h and s. Recall that if G is a term then $c(G)$ denotes the smallest $c \in \omega$ with the properties in Lemma 4. Let $c'' = \max\{c_\psi + c(G_\psi) \mid \psi \in \texttt{Form}(\mathcal{K}, 2) \wedge \texttt{length}(\psi) \leq \ell\}$, $c' = c'' - c_\varphi$, $h(\ell) = c'' + c_\xi$, and $s(\varphi, \ell) = u_{c', G_\varphi}$, where the $u_{c,G}$ is the integer whose existence is guaranteed by Lemma 4.

We prove now that for all $\ell \in \omega$, for all first-order formulas $\varphi(y)$ of $\mathcal{K}$ with $\texttt{length}(\varphi) \leq \ell$, for all sufficiently large $d \in \omega$, and for all $a \in \mathbf{K}_d$ we have

$$(13).\ \mathbf{K}_d \models \varphi(a) \textit{ iff } \mathbf{K}_{d+h(\ell)} \models G(a, s(\varphi, \ell)) = \mathbf{0}.$$

According to Lemma 3, for all $a \in \mathbf{K}_d$, $\mathbf{K}_d \models \varphi(a)$ iff $\mathbf{K}_{d+c_\varphi} \models G_\varphi(a)$. The definitions of c'' and c' implies that $c' \geq c(G_\varphi)$. Therefore by Lemma 4 we have that for all $a \in \mathbf{K}_d$, $\mathbf{K}_{d+c_\varphi} \models G_\varphi(a)$ iff $\mathbf{K}_{d+c_\varphi+c'} \models \xi(a, u_{c', G_\varphi})$. Finally using Lemma 3 again with $k := 2$, $\varphi := \xi(x_0, x_1)$ we get that for all $a \in \mathbf{K}_d$, $\mathbf{K}_{d+c_\varphi+c'} \models \xi(a, u_{c', G_\varphi})$ iff $\mathbf{K}_{d+c_\varphi+c'+c_\xi} \models G(a, u_{c', G_\varphi})$. These equivalences together imply that for all $a \in \mathbf{K}_d$, $\mathbf{K}_d \models \varphi(a)$ iff $\mathbf{K}_{d+c_\varphi+c'+c_\xi} \models G(a, u_{c', G_\varphi})$, which by the definitions of h and s implies condition (13). *Q.E.D.*(Lemma 5)

Definition. A term $G(y, z)$ of $\mathcal{K}$ with the properties described in Lemma 5, will be called a universal term. We assume that for each universal term G of $\mathcal{K}$ a pair of functions, h, s is fixed with the properties given in Lemma 5. To indicate their dependency on G, we will denote these functions by h_G, s_G. □

LEMMA 6. *Assume that $\mathbf{K}$ is a predictive $\mathcal{K}$-sequence and $H(x_0, x_1)$ is a term of $\mathcal{K}$. Then there exists a first-order formula $\Psi_H(x_0, x_1, w)$ of $\mathcal{K}$ such that for all $c \in \omega$ the family of relations $\mathcal{R}_2[H(x_0, x_1), c]$ and $\mathcal{R}_2[\Psi_H(x_0, x_1, c)]$ are asymptotically equivalent.*

Proof. We will associate with each binary term $t(x_0, x_1)$ of $\mathcal{K}$ a first-order formula $\Lambda_t(u, v, w, y_0, y_1)$. We want to define Λ_t such that for each fixed $c \in \omega$, if $d \in \omega$ is sufficiently large, then

(14). *for each fixed* $a_0, a_1, p, q \in \mathbf{K}_d$, $(\eta_{d,c}(t(a_0, a_1)))(p, q)$ *iff* $\mathbf{K}_d \models \Lambda_t(p, q, c, a_0, a_1)$,

where $\eta_{d,c}$ is the map described in the definition of predictivity.

We define Λ_t by recursion of the depth (maximal number of nested function symbols) of the term $t(x_0, x_1)$.

Assume first that $t(x_0, x_1)$ is the variable x_i for some $i \in \{0, 1\}$. In this case $\Lambda_t(u, v, w, y_0, y_1)$ is the formula $u = \mathbf{0} \wedge v = y_i$. Property (10)/(i) of the definition of a predictive $\mathcal{K}$-sequence implies that condition (14) is satisfied.

Suppose now that t is an individual constant symbol. Then $\Lambda_t(u, v, w, y_0, y_1) \equiv \Phi_t(u, v, w)$, where the first-order formula Φ_t is defined in the definition of predictivity. Property (10)/(ii) of the definition of predictivity implies that Λ_t satisfies condition (14).

Let $t(x_0, x_1)$ be a term of the form $f(t_0, \ldots, t_{k-1})$, so that Λ_{t_i}, $i = 0, 1, \ldots, k-1$ has been already defined and it satisfies condition (14). Λ_t is defined by $\Lambda(u, v, w, y_0, y_1) \equiv \Phi(u, v, w, \Lambda_{t_0}(u, v, w, y_0, y_1), \ldots, \Lambda_{t_{k-1}}(u, v, w, y_0, y_1))$. Our inductive assumption implies that for all $i = 0, 1, \ldots, i-1$ condition (14) is satisfied by $t := t_i$. Therefore property (10)/(ii) of the definition of predictivity implies that Λ_t satisfies condition (14) as well.

Finally we define the first-order formula $\Psi_H(x_0, x_1, w)$ by $\Psi_H(x_0, x_1, w) \equiv \forall u, v, \Lambda_H(u, v, w, x_0, x_1) \leftrightarrow (u = \mathbf{0} \wedge v = \mathbf{0})$.

Let $\bar{H} = (H)_{\mathbf{K}_{d+c}}$. Condition (14) implies that for all $a_0, a_1 \in \mathbf{K}_d$, $\mathbf{K}_d \models \Psi_H(a_0, a_1, c)$ is equivalent to the statement that "for all $u, v \in \mathbf{K}_d$, $(\eta_{d,c}(\bar{H}(a_0, a_1)))(u, v)$ iff $(\eta_{d,c}(0))(u, v)$" and since the map $\eta_{d,c}$ is one-to-one, this is equivalent to the statement $\bar{H}(a_0, a_1) = 0$. We got that if $c \in \omega$ is fixed then for all sufficiently large $d \in \omega$ and for all for all $a_0, a_1 \in \mathbf{K}_d$, the following two statements are equivalent: $\mathbf{K}_d \models \Psi_H(a_0, a_1, c)$ and $\mathbf{K}_{d+c} \models H(a_0, a_1) = \mathbf{0}$ which is the statement of the lemma. *Q.E.D.*(Lemma 6)

Proof of Theorem 4. Let $\kappa(x, y, z)$ be the first-order formula of $\mathcal{K}$ whose existence is stated in condition (5) of the definition of a regular $\mathcal{K}$-sequence. Assume that G is a universal term. Let φ be the formula $\forall u, v, \kappa(u, v, y) \to \neg\Psi_G(u, v, y)$, where Ψ_G is the formula whose existence is stated in Lemma 6. Let $\ell = \texttt{length}(\varphi)$, $w = s_G(\varphi, \ell)$, and $c = h_G(\ell)$. By condition (5) of the definition of a regular $\mathcal{K}$-sequence there exists an $r \in \omega$ such that for all sufficiently large $d \in \omega$ we have $\mathbf{K}_d \models \forall x, y,\ \kappa(x, y, r) \leftrightarrow (x = w \wedge y = c)$. Let $d \in \omega$ be sufficiently large. Then by Lemma 5, $\mathbf{K}_d \models \varphi(r)$ iff $\mathbf{K}_{d+c} \models G(r, w) = \mathbf{0}$, where $w = s(\varphi, \ell)$. On the other hand using $\ell = \texttt{length}(\varphi) \geq \texttt{length}(\Psi_G)$ and Lemma 6 with $c := h(\ell)$ and $z := s(\varphi, \ell)$, we get the following sequence of equivalent statements: $\mathbf{K}_d \models \varphi(r)$ iff $\mathbf{K}_d \models \forall u, v, \kappa(u, v, r) \to \neg\Psi_G(u, v, r)$ iff $\mathbf{K}_d \models \neg\Psi_G(w, c, r)$ iff $\mathbf{K}_{d+c} \models \neg G(r, w) = \mathbf{0}$. Consequently $\mathbf{K}_d \models \varphi(r)$ is equivalent to both $\mathbf{K}_{d+c} \models G(r, w) = \mathbf{0}$ and $\mathbf{K}_{d+c} \models \neg G(r, w) = \mathbf{0}$, that is, we reached a contradiction. *Q.E.D.*(Theorem 4).

7. PROOF OF THEOREM 2

Proof of Theorem 2. Theorem 4 implies that it is sufficient to prove that $\mathbf{M} = \langle \mathbf{M}_d \mid d \in \omega \rangle$ is a complete, retrospective, and predictive $\mathcal{M}$-sequence.

The definition of the language $\mathcal{M}$ and $\texttt{universe}(\mathcal{M}_d) = 2^d$, $d \in \omega$, implies that $\mathbf{M} = \langle \mathbf{M}_d \mid d \in \omega \rangle$ is an $\mathcal{M}$-sequence. We show that it is complete, retrospective, and predictive. For the completeness of $\mathbf{M}$ it is sufficient to prove that it is regular and projective.

$\mathbf{M}$ *is regular.* Condition (1) describes the interpretation of the symbols $\mathbf{0}$ and $\mathbf{1}$ as described in the definition of $\mathbf{M}_d$.

Condition (2). It is sufficient to show that the condition holds for $f(x, y) = \neg x$ and $f(x, y) = x \wedge y$ if we consider 0 and 1 as boolean values. For $f(x, y) = \neg x$ we have $t(x, y) = \mathbf{1} - x$, and for $f(x, y) = x \wedge y$ we have $t(x, y) = xy$.

Condition (3). $\bar{t}(x, y) = \min(\mathbf{1}, x - y)$ meets our requirements.

Condition (4). Such a formula can be easily constructed by using the techniques of Gödel numbering, using only the function symbols $\mathbf{0}, \mathbf{1}, -\mathbf{1}, +, \times, \max, \min$. (Not all of them are needed.)

Condition (5) We use the fact that the functions $\mathcal{F}_0(x) = x - \lfloor x^{\frac{1}{2}} \rfloor^2$, $\mathcal{F}_1(x) = \lfloor x^{\frac{1}{2}} \rfloor - \mathcal{F}_0(x)$ has the property that for each $y, z \in \omega$ there is an $x \in \omega$ with $\mathcal{F}_0(x) = y$ and $\mathcal{F}_1(x) = z$. Indeed, if $x = (y + z)^2 + y$, then $\mathcal{F}_0(x) = y$ and $\mathcal{F}_1(x) = z$. Based on this observation it is easy to see that the formula
$\kappa(x, y, z) \equiv (\max(y, x) = x) \wedge (\max(z, x) = x) \wedge$
$\wedge\ \exists u, (\max(u, x) = x) \wedge (\max(u^2, x) = x) \wedge (\max((u + 1)^2, x) \neq x) \wedge (y = x - u^2) \wedge (z = u - y)$
satisfies the requirements of this condition.

$\mathbf{M}$ *is retrospective.* Conditions (8) and (9). We prove condition (9) in the strong form where the formula $\varphi(x_0, \ldots, x_{k-1}, y, z)$ is of the form $t(x_0, \ldots, x_{k-1}, z) = y$, where t is a term of $\mathcal{K}$. Clearly this gives condition (8) with the term $t(x_0, \ldots, x_{k-1}, \mathbf{1})$.

We consider separately the various possible choices for the function symbol g and in each case we describe the required term t. The term $\mathbf{p}(\div(\mathbf{n}, \mathbf{p}(2, c)))$ will be denoted by $2^{2^{-c}\mathbf{n}}$. $g = \mathbf{1}$, $t = \mathbf{1}$; $g = \mathbf{0}$, $t = \mathbf{0}$; $g = \mathbf{n}$, $t = \div(\mathbf{n}, \mathbf{p}(2, c))$; $g = -\mathbf{1}$, $t = 2^{2^{-c}\mathbf{n}} - \mathbf{1}$; $g = xy$, $t = xy - \div(xy, 2^{2^{-c}\mathbf{n}}))2^{2^{-c}\mathbf{n}}$, $g = x + y$, $t = x + y - \div(x + y, 2^{2^{-c}\mathbf{n}})2^{2^{-c}\mathbf{n}}$; $g = \mathbf{p}(y)$, $t = \min(\mathbf{p}(y), 2^{2^{-c}\mathbf{n}} - \mathbf{1})$; $g = \div(x, y)$, $t = \div(x, y)$; $g = \min(x, y)$, $t = \min(x, y)$; $g = \max(x, y)$, $t = \max(x, y)$; $g = x \cap y$, $t = x \cap y$; $g = \mathcal{N}(x)$, $t = \mathcal{N}(x)$.

In the proof of the Corollary we will have the following: $g = \bar{\mathbf{p}}(x, y)$, $t = \min(\bar{\mathbf{p}}(x, y), 2^{2^{-c}\mathbf{n}} - \mathbf{1})$

Definition. Assume that $a, m \in \omega$, $m > 0$. The least non-negative residue of a modulo m will be denoted by $\texttt{res}(a, m)$. □

PROPOSITION 7. *Assume that* $u, v, a, b, m, i \in \omega$, $b \geq 2$, $a < b^m$, $i < m$. *Then* $\texttt{res}(u, v) = u - v\lfloor \frac{u}{v} \rfloor$ *and*

$$\texttt{coeff}_i(a, b) = b^{-(m-1)}\texttt{res}\left(b^{m-1}\left\lfloor \frac{a}{b^i} \right\rfloor, b^m\right)$$

Proof. $a = a_{m-1}b^{m-1} + \ldots + a_i b^i + \ldots + a_0$, where $a_j = \texttt{coeff}_j(a, b)$ for $j = 0, 1, \ldots, m-1$. Therefore $a/b^i = a_{m-1}b^{m-1-i} + \ldots a_{i+1}b + a_i + a_{i-1}b^{-1} + \ldots + a_0 b^{-i}$ and consequently $\lfloor a/b^i \rfloor = a_{m-1}b^{m-1-i} + \ldots + a_{i+1}b + a_i$. Multiplying both sides of the last equation by b^{m-1} we get $b^{m-1}\lfloor a/b_i \rfloor = a_{m-1}b^{m-1-i+(m-1)} + \ldots + a_{i+1}b^{1+(m-1)} + a_i b^{m-1} = Mb^m + a_i b^{m-1}$, where M is an integer. The statement of the proposition is an immediate consequence of this equation. *Q.E.D.*(Proposition 7)

$\mathbf{M}$ *is projective.* We will use in this proof that $\mathbf{n}^{(d+c)} = 2^c\mathbf{n}^{(d)}$ and so $2^d = \mathbf{n}^{(d+c)} \div 2^c$. We want to define the terms τ_c and $\pi_{c,k}$ such that if $c \in \omega$, $2^c = \nu$, $k \in \{0,1,\ldots,\nu-1\}$, and $d \in \omega$, $2^d = n$ is sufficiently large then for all $a_0, a_1, \ldots, a_{\nu-1} \in \mathbf{M}_d$ we have $\tau_c^{(d)}(a_0, a_1, \ldots, a_{\nu-1}) = \sum_{k=0}^{\nu-1} a_k(2^{2^d})^k$, and for each $a \in \mathbf{M}_{d+c}$, $\pi_{c,k}^{(d+c)}(a) = \mathtt{coeff}_k(a, 2^{2^d})$. Clearly if this holds then the terms $\tau_c, \pi_{c,k}$ satisfy condition (6) of the definition of projectivity.

The definition of τ_c is simply the arithmetic expression $\sum_{k=0}^{\nu-1} a_k(2^{2^d})^k$ written with the function symbols of $\mathcal{M}$. Since τ_c may depend on c we may express c in the form $c = \mathbf{1} + \ldots + \mathbf{1}$. All of the partial results in the expression $\sum_{k=0}^{\nu-1} a_k(2^{2^d})^k$ does not exceed the bound $2^{2^{d+c}} - 1$ so the arithmetic operations occurring in it work the same way in $\mathbf{M}_{d+c}$ as among the integers.

To define the term $\pi_{c,k}$ it is sufficient to show that $\mathtt{coeff}_k(a, 2^{2^d})$ can be computed by a term in $\mathbf{M}_{d+c}$. This is however an immediate consequence of Proposition 7 with $a := a$, $b := 2^{2^d}$, $m := 2^c$. Here we used the fact that the operation $x \times y$ in $\mathbf{M}_{d+c}$ is the least nonnegative residue of xy (computed by the multiplication among integers) modulo 2^{d+c}.

The first-order formula Γ of condition (7) describes the computation of $\pi_{c,k}$ by the term defined above, but it uses c and k directly as parameters.

$\mathbf{M}$ *is predictive.* Assume that $c \in \omega$ and d is sufficiently large. First we define the map $\eta_{d,c}$ whose existence is required by the definition of predictivity. To make our notation more concise we will write $\eta_{d,c}^{(a)}$ instead of $\eta_{d,c}(a)$.

Assume that $a \in \mathbf{M}_{d+c}$, $2^d = n$, $\nu = 2^c$. Let $a_i = \mathtt{coeff}_i(a, 2^n)$ for $i = 0, 1, \ldots, \nu-1$. We define $\eta_{d,c}$ by: "for all $u, v \in \mathbf{M}_d$, $\eta_{d,c}^{(a)}(u,v)$ iff $u \in \nu$ and $v = a_u$". This definition implies that if $a \in \mathbf{M}_d$ then for all $u, v \in \mathbf{M}_d$, $\eta_{d,c}^{(a)}(u,v)$ iff $u = 0$ and $v = a$, that is, our definition satisfies condition (10)/(i) from the definition of predictivity.

We define now the first-order formula

$$\Phi_f(x, y, z, Y_0, \ldots, Y_{k-1})$$

for each function symbol f of $\mathcal{M}$.

If $f = \mathbf{c}$ is a constant symbol of $\mathcal{M}$ then $\Phi_{\mathbf{c}} \equiv x = \mathbf{0} \wedge y = \mathbf{c}$. By the definition of $\eta_{d,c}$, the formula $\Phi_{\mathbf{c}}$ satisfies condition (10)/(ii) from the definition of predictivity, for all constant symbols $\mathbf{c}$ of $\mathcal{M}$.

We will not use the relation $\eta_{d,c}^{(a)}$ directly in the definition of Φ_f, for the remaining function symbols f of $\mathcal{M}$, but we first define another binary relation $\xi_{d,c}^{(a)}$ on $\mathbf{M}_d$ and use this relation.

Definition. 1. For each positive integer k and $u = \langle u_0, \ldots, u_{k-1}\rangle \in (\mathbf{M}_d)^k$, $u l_n$ will denote the integer $u_{k-1}n^{k-1} + u_{k-2}n^{k-2} + \ldots + u_1 n + u_0$.

2. Assume that R is a k-ary relation on the set $n = \{0, 1, \ldots, n-1\}$, where $n = 2^d$. $\mathtt{integer}_k(R)$ will denote the integer $\sum\{2^{u l_n} \mid u \in \mathbf{M}_d^k \wedge R(u)\}$. Clearly $R \to \mathtt{integer}_k(R)$ is a one-to-one map from the set of all k-ary relation on n to the set of all natural numbers less then 2^{n^k}. If $a \in [0, 2^{n^k} - 1]$ is a natural number then the unique k-ary relation R on n with $\mathtt{integer}_k(R) = a$ will be denoted by $\mathtt{integer}_k^{-1}(R)$. □

Definition. 1. Suppose that R is a k-ary relation on $\mathbf{M}_d$. We will say that the relation R is n-restricted if for all $u = \langle u_0, \ldots, u_{k-1}\rangle \in \mathbf{M}_d^k$, $R(u_0, \ldots, u_{k-1})$ implies that for all $i = 0, 1, \ldots, k-1$ with $u_i \in n$.

2. Assume that d, c are positive integers and $a < 2^{n^2}$. Then $\xi_{d,c}^{(a)}$ is the unique binary relation on $\mathbf{M}_d$ which satisfies the following two conditions: (a) The relation $\xi_{d,c}^{(a)}$ is n-restricted, and (b) $\mathtt{integer}_2(\xi_{d,c}^{(a)}) = a$. □

PROPOSITION 8. *There exists a first-order formula $\varphi(x,y,z)$ of $\mathcal{M}$ such that for all $d \in \omega$ and for all $a, b \in 2^{2^d}$ and $i \in 2^d$ we have that $b = \mathtt{coeff}_i(a,2)$ iff $\mathbf{M}_d \models \varphi(a,b,i)$.*

Proof. The statement of the proposition follows from Proposition 7. *Q.E.D.*(Proposition 8)

The following Proposition states that the relations $\xi_{d,c}^{(a)}$ and $\eta_{d,c}^{(a)}$ can be defined from each other in a first-order way. It is important that for the definition of the value $\xi_{d,c}^{(a)}(u,v)$ for a fixed pair u, v we may need the values $\eta_{d,c}^{(a)}(x,y)$ for all $x, y \in \mathbf{M}_d$ and vice versa.

PROPOSITION 9. *There exist first-order formulas $\Psi_i(x,y,z,Z)$, $i = 0,1$, where x, y, z are individual variables and Z is a variable for a binary relation such that for all $c \in \omega$, for all sufficiently large $d \in \omega$, and for all $a \in \mathbf{M}_{d+c}$ the following holds: $\mathbf{M}_d \models \forall u, v, [\xi_{d,c}^{(a)}(u,v) \leftrightarrow \Psi_0(u,v,c,\eta_{d,c}^{(a)})]$ and $\mathbf{M}_d \models \forall u, v, [\eta_{d,c}^{(a)}(u,v) \leftrightarrow \Psi_1(u,v,c,\xi_{d,c}^{(a)})]$*

Proof. Assume $a \in 2^{2^{d+c}}$ and $a = \sum_{i=0}^{(\nu-1)} a_i(2^{2^d})^\nu$. The formula Ψ_1 have to express the statement $u \le \nu \wedge v \le n \wedge \mathtt{coeff}_{un+v}(a,2) = 1$. $\mathtt{coeff}_{un+v}(a,2) = 1$ is equivalent to $\mathtt{coeff}_v(a_u, 2) = 1$. Using the relation $\eta_{d,c}^{(a)}$ we can define a_u in a first-order way in $\mathbf{M}_d$, namely $x = a_u$ iff $\mathbf{M}_d \models \eta_{d,c}^{(a)}(u,x)$. If a_u is given then, by Proposition 8, $\mathtt{coeff}_v(a_u,2)$ has a first-order definition in $\mathbf{M}_d$. This completes the definition of Ψ_0. In the first-order formula Ψ_1 we have to define a_u form its binary coefficients which can be done by using again Proposition 8. *Q.E.D.*(Proposition 9)

Proposition 9 implies that it is sufficient to prove that condition (10) of the definition of predictivity holds in the following modified form. (For the sake of notational simplicity we consider here $\mathbf{p}$ and $\mathcal{N}$ as a binary function symbols whose interpretation in each $\mathbf{M}_d$ is a binary function which depends only in its first variable.)

(15). *Suppose that f is one of the function symbols $+, \times, \mathbf{p}, \div, \max, \min, \cap, \mathcal{N}$ of $\mathcal{M}$ then there exists a first-order formula $\Phi'_f(x,y,z,Y_0,Y_1)$ where x, y, z are individual variables and Y_0, Y_1 are variables for binary relations such that for all $c \in \omega$, for all sufficiently large $d \in \omega$, and for all $a, b \in \mathbf{M}_{d+c}$, and for all $u, v \in \mathbf{M}_d$, $\xi_{d,c}^{(f^{(d+c)}(a,b))}(u,v)$ is true iff $\mathbf{M}_d \models \Phi'_f(u,v,c,\xi_{d,c}(a),\xi_{d,c}(b))$, where $f^{(d+c)} = (f)_{\mathbf{M}_{d+c}}$.*

In other words given the binary bits of $a, b \in 2^{2^{d+c}}$, each by a binary relation on $\mathtt{universe}(\mathbf{M}_d)$, we have to define in $\mathbf{M}_d$ in a first-order way the binary bits of $a+b, ab, a \div b = \lfloor a/b \rfloor, 2^a, \min(a,b), \max(a,b), a \cap b$, and $\mathcal{N}(a)$ where the operations are defined in the structure $\mathbf{M}_{d+c}$. Since $a \cap b$ and $\mathcal{N}(a)$ are defined by bitwise operations this obviously can be easily accomplished for these two operations so from now on we consider only the remaining ones.

Using the function $\texttt{integer}_k^{-1}$ we can represent natural numbers from the interval $[0, 2^{n^k} - 1]$ by k-ary relations on n. Our next goal is to represent sequences of natural numbers by relation on n, (where we have a bound both on the length of the sequence and the sizes of its elements).

Definition. 1. The set of all sequences of length i, whose elements are from the set A will be denoted by, $\texttt{seq}(i, A)$. For example the set of all sequences of length n^l whose elements are integers in the interval $[0, 2^{n^k} - 1]$ is $\texttt{seq}(n^l, 2^{n^k})$.

2. Assume that $a = \langle a_0, \ldots, a_{j-1}\rangle \in \texttt{seq}(n^l, 2^{n^k})$. We will represent this sequence by a $k + l$-ary relation $R^{(a)}$ on n defined in the following way. For all $i \leq j - 1$, and for all $u_0, \ldots, u_{k-1}, v_0, \ldots, v_{l-1} \in n$,

$$R^{(a)}(u_0, \ldots, u_{k-1}, v_0, \ldots, v_{l-1})$$

iff $(\texttt{integer}_k^{(-1)}(a_t))(u_0, \ldots, u_{k-1})$, where $t = \sum_{i=0}^{l-1} v_i n^i$. Since in this representation the length of the sequence cannot be arbitrarily chosen it must be n^l, for some $l \in \omega$, we will call this representation a representation of the sequence without its length.

3. The definition above provides representation only for sequences with exactly n^l elements for some natural number l. A sequence $a = \langle a_0, \ldots, a_{j-1}\rangle$ where $j < n^l$, $a_i \in [0, 2^{n^k} - 1]$ will be represented in the following way. We attach the number j as the first element to the sequence a and attach a sequence of 0s to its end, so that the total length of the sequence $a' = \langle j, a_0, \ldots, a_{j-1}, 0, \ldots, 0\rangle$ obtained this way is n^l. The representation of the sequence a together with its length will be the same as the representation of the sequence a' without its length, as defined earlier. In the following the representation of a sequence will always mean a representation of the sequence together with its length unless we explicitly state otherwise.

4. Assume that d is a positive integer and $n = 2^d$. We will say that the set X is $\mathbf{M}_d$-representable if there exists natural numbers k, l such that either $X = \{0, 1, \ldots, 2^{n^k} - 1\}$ or $X = \texttt{seq}_n(n^l, 2^{n^k})$. If X is an $\mathbf{M}_d$ representable set and $X = \{0, 1, \ldots, 2^{n^k} - 1\}$ then we define its weight by $\texttt{weight}(X) = k$, if $X = \texttt{seq}_n(n^l, 2^{n^k})$ then we define its weight by $\texttt{weight}(X) = k + l$. If $a \in X$, where X is an $\mathbf{M}_d$ representable set, then $\texttt{relation}_{a,n}$ will denote the k-ary or $k + l$-ary relation on n representing the element a. □

We will consider now families of functions $f^{(d)}$, $d \in \omega$ so that for each $d \in \omega$, $f^{(d)} \in \texttt{func}(X^{(d)}, Y^{(d)})$ where both $X^{(d)}$ and $Y^{(d)}$ are $\mathbf{M}_d$-representable sets with weight less then w for a constant w. We are interested in the case when such a family of functions can be defined by a first-order formula in $\mathbf{M}_d$ without using any parameters. The world "strongly" that we will use in the definition below refers to mentioned the lack of parameters.

Definition. 1. Assume that $w_i \in \omega$ for $i = 0, 1$ and for all $d \in \omega$, $A_i^{(d)}$ are $\mathbf{M}_d$ representable sets of weight w_i for $i = 0, 1$, and $f^{(d)} \in \texttt{func}(A_0^{(d)}, A_1^{(d)})$. We will say that the family of functions $f^{(d)}$ is a strongly first-order definable family function or a s.f.d.-family in $\mathbf{M}$ if there exists a first-order formula $\Gamma(x_0, \ldots, x_{w_1-1}, Z)$, where x_i, $i = 0, 1, \ldots, w_1 - 1$ are individual variables and Z is a variable for k_0-ary relations such that for all sufficiently large $d \in \omega$ and for all $a \in A_0^{(d)}$, and $b \in A_1^{(d)}$ with $f(a) = b$, we have that for all $u_0, \ldots, u_{w_1-1} \in n$, $\texttt{relation}_{b,n}(u_0, \ldots, u_{w_1-1})$ iff $\mathbf{M}_d \models \Gamma(u_0, \ldots, u_{w_1-1}, \texttt{relation}_{a,n})$. □

We prove now that condition (15) is satisfied by each function symbol of $\mathcal{M}$. As we mentioned already this statement trivially holds for the function symbols $\cap$ and $\mathcal{N}$ since the corresponding pointwise boolean operation can be executed on the relations representing the elements of $\mathbf{M}_{d+c}$. For the remaining operations we show now that the corresponding families of functions are are strongly first-order definable in $\mathbf{M}$.

For $f = \min$ and $f = \max$ the statement is trivial since $a \leq b$ iff $\texttt{integer}_2^{-1}(a) \leq \texttt{integer}_2^{-1}(b)$ according to the lexicographic ordering which clearly can be defined in $\mathbf{M}_d$ in a first-order way.

The function symbol $f =$ "+". If two integers are given in binary form each with m bits then the bits of their sum can be defined by a simple well-known constant depth circuit whose size is linear in m. This circuit is defined in a uniform way which makes it possible to translate it into a first-order formula interpreted in $\mathbf{M}_d$. For later use we also consider now the case where we have to add a sequence of integers. This question has been also studied for circuits, and it is known that if we have at most $(\log m)^{c_0}$ integers with m^{c_1} binary bits then their sum can be computed by an unlimited fan-in boolean circuit with size m^{c_2} and depth c_3, where c_2, c_3 depend only on c_0 and c_1, see [1]. The construction of the circuit is uniform, in this case too, and can be translated into a first-order formulas, that we need for our present purposes, over a structure containing the arithmetic operations. First-order formulas describing addition and multiplication in this sense were used in [5]. To make the paper more self-contained we prove all the relevant facts about the first-order definability of sums of sequences of integers.

Definition. If b is a finite sequence of integers then $\mathbf{S}b$ will denote the sum of its elements. □

LEMMA 7. *Assume that $c_0, c_1 \in \omega$. Then there exists a strongly first-order definable family of functions $f^{(d)}$, $d \in \omega$, such that for all sufficiently large d if $n = 2^d$, $j \leq n^{c_0}$ and a is sequence of length j, from elements of the set 2^{n^k}, that is, $a \in \texttt{seq}(j, 2^{n^k})$, then $\mathbf{S}a = f^{(d)}(a)$.*

Proof or Lemma 7. During the proof we will use the notation $n = 2^d$, $m = 2^n$, and we will always assume that d is sufficiently large with respect to c_0, c_1. We assume that $\langle a_0, \ldots, a_{j-1}\rangle \in \texttt{seq}(j, 2^{n^{c_1}})$ and we will define the binary bits of $\mathbf{S}a$ using the bits of the integers a_i, $a = 0, 1, \ldots, j-1$. While describing this definition which goes through several steps, we will indicate the reasons why the definition can be told in $\mathbf{M}_d$ in a first-order way. We prove the lemma through a sequence of special cases. Throughout the proof when we say that something can be defined by a first-order formula in $\mathbf{M}_d$ we will always mean a first-order formula of the type which was used in the definition of a strongly first-order definable family of functions.

PROPOSITION 10. *Lemma 7 holds with the additional assumption $j = 2$.*

Proof of Proposition 10. We have $a = a_0 + a_1$ and we have to determine the binary bits of $a_0 + a_1$. Assume that $a_0 = \sum_{i=0}^{n^k-1} \alpha_i 2^i$, $a_1 = \sum_{i=0}^{n^k-1} \beta_i 2^i$, and $u+v = \sum_{i=0}^{n^k} \gamma_i 2^i$, where

$\alpha_i, \beta_i, \gamma_i \in \{0, 1\}$. Then for all $i = 0, 1, \ldots, n^k$ we define γ_i in the following way. If there exists a $t \in \{0, 1, \ldots, i-1\}$ such that $\alpha_t = \beta_t = 1$ and for all k, with $t < k < i$, $\alpha_k + \beta_k \geq 1$, then $\gamma_i = \alpha_i + \beta_i + 1$. If such a t does not exists then $\gamma_i = \alpha_i + \beta_i$.

This definition of γ_i can be stated in $\mathbf{M}_d$ in a first-order way, since it requires quantification only on the set of integers $\{0, 1, \ldots, n^{c_0}\}$, while $\texttt{universe}(\mathbf{M}_d) = 2^n - 1$. We have used the ordering of the set $\{0, 1, \ldots, n^{c_0}\}$ which is also available since the operations $\max(x, y)$, $\min(x, y)$ define the natural ordering of $\texttt{universe}(\mathbf{M}_d)$. *Q.E.D.*(Proposition AR1.1)

Proposition 11. *Lemma 7 holds in the special case when $j \leq \sqrt{n}$ and $\max_{i=0}^{j-1} a_i \leq 2^{\sqrt{n}}$, where $a = \langle a_0, \ldots, a_{j-1} \rangle$.*

Let $s_0 = 0$, $s_\nu = \sum_{i=0}^{\nu-1} a_i$, for $\nu = 1, \ldots, j$. Each s_ν has at most $\log_2(\sum_{i=0}^{\nu-1} a_i) \leq \log_2(j \max_{i=0}^{j-1} a_i) \leq n^{\frac{1}{2}} + \log_2 j \leq 2n^{\frac{1}{2}}$ bits, so the total number of bits in the sequence $s_1, \ldots, s_j$ is at most $2jn^{\frac{1}{2}} \leq 2n$. In $\mathbf{M}_d$ with a single existential quantifier we may talk about the existence of n-bits, so in $\mathbf{M}_d$ we can define the rth bit γ_r of $\mathbf{S}a$ by saying that: $\gamma_r = 1$ if there exists a sequence $s_0, \ldots, s_j$, and a $b \in 2^n$, such that $s_0 = 0, s_j = b$, for all $i = 1, \ldots, j$, $s_j = a_{j-1} + s_j$ and the rth bit of b is 1. *Q.E.D.*(Proposition 11)

Proposition 12. *Lemma 7 holds in the special case $j \leq n^{1/2}$*

Proof of Proposition 12. Assume that $a = \langle a_0, \ldots, a_{j-1} \rangle$ and for each $i = 0, \ldots, j-1$, $a_i = \sum_{s=0}^{l-1} \alpha_{s,i} 2^s$, where $l = 2n^k$. We partition the interval $[0, l-1]$ into subintervals $I_1, \ldots, I_r$ each of lengths $\frac{1}{2}n$. For $\delta = 0, 1$, let

$$J_\delta = \bigcup \{I_\nu \mid \nu \in [1, r] \wedge \nu \equiv \delta \pmod 2\}$$

For each $i = 0, 1, \ldots, j-1$ we define two integers $u_{0,i}, v_{1,i} \in [0, 2^l - 1]$ by $u_{\delta,i} = \sum\{\alpha_{s,i} 2^s \mid s \in J_\delta\}$. Proposition 11 implies that for $\nu \in [0, l-1]$ and $\delta \in \{0, 1\}$, the integer $v_\delta^{(\nu)} = \sum\{\alpha_{s,i} 2^s \mid i \in [0, l-1], \nu \in J_\delta \cap I_\nu\}$ is first-order definable in $\mathbf{M}_d$. For fixed ν, $\texttt{coeff}_s(v_\delta^{(\nu)}, 2) \neq 0$ implies that $s \in I_\nu \cup I_{\nu+1}$, therefore for a fixed δ if we add the numbers $v_\delta^{(\nu)}$, for example, for all even integers ν, there will be no "carry over" and so the binary bits of v_δ are first-order definable in $\mathbf{M}_d$. Finally by Proposition 7 the binary bits of their sum $\mathbf{S}a = v_0 + v_1$ are also first-order definable in $\mathbf{M}_d$. *Q.E.D.*(Proposition 12)

We may complete the proof of the lemma in the following way. We may use Proposition 12 iteratively first adding blocks of size $n^{\frac{1}{2}}$ in the sum $\sum_{i=0}^{j-1} a_i$, and then repeating this for the resulting shorter sum etc. *Q.E.D.*(Lemma 7)

We prove condition (15) for $f = \times$ in a more general form then needed, namely we will consider products with more than two factors. This will be useful in the proof of (15) for the function symbol $\div$ and (in the proof of the Corollary) for function symbol $\bar{\mathbf{p}}$.

Definition. Assume that $a = \langle a_0, a_1, \ldots, a_{j-1} \rangle$ is a sequence of integers. Then $\mathbf{P}a$ will denote the number $\prod_{i=0}^{j-1} a_i$. □

Definition. Assume that $\alpha(x), \beta(x)$ are functions defined on ω with real values. We will say that the pair $\langle \alpha(x), \beta(x) \rangle$ is acceptable if there exists a strongly first-order definable family of functions $f^{(d)}$, $d \in \omega$, such that for all sufficiently large integers $d \in \omega$, for all nonnegative integers $j \leq \alpha(d)$, and for all $a \in \texttt{seq}(j, 2^{\beta(d)})$, we have $\mathbf{P}a = f^{(d)}(a)$. □

Lemma 8. *For each fixed $c > 0, \varepsilon > 0$ the pair $\alpha(x) = x^c$, $\beta(x) = 2^{x + x^{1-\varepsilon}}$ is acceptable.*

We prove the lemma by showing how can we create acceptable pairs of functions, possibly by using other acceptable pairs. These constructions are described in the following propositions. In the remaining of the paper if we say that a family of functions is first-order definable we will mean that it is strongly first-order definable.

Proposition 13. *Assume that $\langle \alpha(x), \beta(x) \rangle$ is an acceptable pair and $\bar{\alpha}(x), \bar{\beta}(x)$ are functions defined on ω with real values so that for all sufficiently large $d \in \omega$, $\bar{\alpha}(d) \leq \alpha(d)$ and $\bar{\beta}(d) \leq \beta(d)$. Then the pair $\langle \bar{\alpha}(x), \bar{\beta}(x) \rangle$ is also acceptable*

Proof. The statement of the proposition is an immediate consequence of the definition of acceptability.

Proposition 14. *For all $c > 0$ the following pair of function is acceptable: $\alpha(x) = 2$, $\beta(x) = 2^{2^{cx}}$.*

Proof. This is a consequence of Lemma 7, since the multiplication of two l bit integers can be performed as the addition of l integers each with $2l$ bits if we follow the standard method of computing a product. *Q.E.D.*(Proposition 14)

Proposition 15. *Assume that α, β are real valued functions defined on ω, $c > 0$, and for all sufficiently large $d \in \omega$ we have $(\alpha(d))^2 \beta(d) \leq cn$, where $n = 2^d$. Then the pair $\alpha(x), \beta(x)$ is acceptable.*

Proof of Proposition 14. Assume that $a = \langle a_0, \ldots, a_{j-1} \rangle$, and for all $i = 0, 1 \ldots, j$ let $p_i = \prod_{r=1}^{i-1} a_i$. Clearly $p_0 = 1$ and $p_j = \mathbf{P}a$. The integer p_i has at most $i\beta(d) \leq j\beta(d) \leq \alpha(d)\beta(d)$ binary bits. Therefore the total number of bits in the sequence $\langle p_1, \ldots, p_j \rangle$ is at most $j\alpha(d)\beta(d) \leq (\alpha(d))^2 \beta(d) \leq cn$. This implies that we are able to speak about the existence of such a sequence $\langle p_0, \ldots, p_j \rangle$ in a first-order way. As a consequence, $\mathbf{P}a = x$ will be equivalent to the following first-order formula in $\mathbf{M}_d$: "there exists a sequence $p_0, \ldots, p_{j-1}$, such that $p_0 = 0$, and for all $i = 1, \ldots, j$, $p_i = a_{i-1} p_{i-1}$ and $p_j = x$". *Q.E.D.*Proposition 15

Proposition 16. *Assume that $\langle \alpha(x), \beta(x) \rangle$ is a pair of acceptable functions, $c > 0$ and $t(x) \in \texttt{func}(\omega, \omega)$, such that for all sufficiently large $d \in \omega$ we have $(t(d))^{\alpha(d)} \leq 2^{cd}$. Then the pair $\langle \alpha(x), t(x)\beta(x) \rangle$ is also acceptable.*

Proof. Assume that $d \in \omega$ is sufficiently large and $a = \langle a_0, a_1, \ldots, a_{j-1} \rangle \in \texttt{seq}(\alpha(d), t(d)\beta(d))$. Let $h = \lfloor \beta(d) \rfloor$. For all $i = 0, 1, \ldots, j-1$, $k = 0, 1, \ldots, t(d)$ let $b_{i,k} = \texttt{coeff}_k(a_i, 2^h)$, that is, $a_i = \sum_{k=0}^{t(d)-1} b_{i,k} 2^{kh}$. Proposition 7 implies that the coefficients $b_{i,k}$ are first-order definable in $\mathbf{M}_d$.

If we compute the product $\prod_{i=0}^{j-1} a_i$ using $a_i = \sum_{k=0}^{t(d)-1} b_{i,k} 2^{kh}$ and distributivity then we get $(t(d))^j \leq (t(d))^{\alpha(d)} \leq n^c$ terms. Each of these terms is uniquely determined by a function $\lambda \in \texttt{func}(t(d), j)$, namely the term determined by such a function is $\prod_{i=0}^{j-1} \texttt{coeff}_{\lambda(i)}(a_i, 2^h) 2^{\lambda(i)h}$.

If we separate the powers of 2 in this product we can write it in the form of $2^{h\sum_{i=0}^{j-1}\lambda(i)}\prod_{i=0}^{j-1}\mathtt{coeff}_{\lambda(i)}(a,2^h)$. We have $\mathtt{coeff}_{\lambda(i)}(a,2^h)\le 2^h\le 2^{\beta(d)}$, and $j\le\alpha(d)$, therefore the acceptability of the pair $\langle\alpha(x),\beta(x)\rangle$ implies that $\prod_{i=0}^{j-1}\mathtt{coeff}_{\lambda(i)}(a,2^h)$ is first-order definable in $\mathbf{M}_d$. By Lemma 7, $\sum_{i=0}^{j-1}\lambda(i)$ is also first-order definable in $\mathbf{M}_d$. Since the total number of choices for the function $\lambda(i)$ is at most n^c, Lemma 7 implies that the sum that is $\mathbf{P}a$ is also first-order definable in $\mathbf{M}_d$. *Q.E.D.*(Proposition 16)

PROPOSITION 17. *Assume that $\alpha(x),\beta(x),\gamma(x)$ are functions defined on ω with real values in the interval $[1,\infty)$ and the pairs $\langle\alpha(x),\beta(x)\gamma(x)\rangle$, $\langle\gamma(x),\beta(x)\rangle$ are both acceptable. Then $\langle\alpha(x)\gamma(x),\beta(x)\rangle$ is also acceptable.*

Proof. Assume that $d\in\omega$ is sufficiently large and $a=\langle a_0,\ldots,a_{j-1}\rangle\in\mathtt{seq}(\alpha(d)\gamma(d),2^{\beta(d)})$. We partition the interval $[0,j-1]$ into at most $\alpha(d)$ intervals $I_0,\ldots,I_{r-1}$ each of size at most $\gamma(d)$. The pair $\langle\gamma(x),\beta(x)\rangle$ is acceptable $\gamma(x)\ge 1$ therefore we can define the products $P_k=\prod_{i\in I_k}a_i$, $k=0,1,\ldots,r-1$ in a first-order way in $\mathbf{M}_d$. Moreover the value of each of these products will be at most $(2^{\beta(d)})^{\gamma(d)}=2^{\beta(d)\gamma(d)}$. Since the pair $\langle\alpha(x),\beta(x)\gamma(x)\rangle$ is acceptable we are also able to define $\prod_{k=0}^{r-1}P_k=\mathbf{P}a$ in a first-order way in $\mathbf{M}_d$. *Q.E.D.*(Proposition AR6)

Proof of Lemma 8. Assume that a $\tau\in(0,1)$ is given. We claim that

(16). *the pair $\langle x^\tau,2^{x-x^{1-\tau}}\rangle$ is acceptable.*

This is a consequence of Proposition 15 and of the fact that for all sufficiently large $d\in\omega$, we have $d^{2\tau}2^{d-d^{(1-\tau)}}\le 2^d$. Suppose that for some integer s the pair $(x^\tau,2^{x+sx^{(1-\tau)}})$ is acceptable. We can apply Proposition 16 with $\alpha(x):=x^\tau,\beta(x):=2^{x+sx^{1-\tau}}$, $t(x):=2^{x^{1-\tau}}$. Using the fact that $(t(d))^{\alpha(d)}=2^{d^{1-\tau}d^\tau}=2^d$, we get that the pair $\langle x^\tau,2^{x+(s+1)x^{1-\tau}}\rangle$ is also acceptable. With the help of this fact and condition (16), we can show by induction on s, starting with $s=-1$, that the following holds:

(17). *for all $\tau\in(0,1)$, and for all integers s, the pair $(x^\tau,2^{x+sx^{1-\tau}})$ is acceptable.*

We want to show that

(18). *for all $\tau\in(0,1)$ and for all $k,s\in\omega$ the pair $(x^{\tau+\frac{k}{2}},2^{x+sx^{1-\tau}})$ is acceptable.*

We prove this statement by induction on k, where the inductive assumption is that the statement holds for a fixed k, with every possible choices of τ and s. For $k=0$ this is condition (17). Assume now that the statement holds for a fixed $k\in\omega$.

We apply Proposition 17 with $\alpha(x):=x^{\tau+\frac{k}{2}}$, $\gamma(x):=x^{\frac{1}{2}}$ and $\beta(x):=2^{x+sx^{1-\tau}}$. The first assumption of Proposition 17 is that the pair $A_1=(\alpha(x),\beta(x)\gamma(x))=(x^{\tau+\frac{k}{2}},x^{\frac{1}{2}}2^{x+sx^{1-\tau}})$ is acceptable. Since $x^{\frac{1}{2}}2^{x+sx^{1-\tau}}=2^{x+sx^{1-\tau}+\frac{1}{2}\log_2 x}\le 2^{x+(s+1)x^{1-\tau}}$ the inductive assumption with $s:=s+1$ and Proposition 13 implies that the pair A_1 is acceptable.

The second assumption is that the pair $A_2=(\gamma(x),\beta(x))=(x^{\frac{1}{2}},2^{x+sx^{1-\tau}})$ is acceptable. This follows directly from condition (17). Therefore by Proposition 17 the pair $(\alpha(x)\gamma(x),\beta(x))=(x^{\tau+\frac{k+1}{2}},2^{x+sx^{1-\tau}})$ is acceptable which completes the proof of (18). This and Proposition 13 together imply the statement of the lemma. *Q.E.D.*(Lemma 8)

PROPOSITION 18. *For all $\varepsilon>0$ there exists a family of functions $f^{(d)}$, $d\in\omega$, such that, for all sufficiently large $d\in\omega$ if $a=\langle a_0,a_1\rangle\in\mathtt{seq}(2,2^{2^{d+d^{1-\varepsilon}}})$, then $a_0a_1=f^{(d)}(a)$.*

Proof. The proposition is a special case of Lemma 8.

Using Proposition 18 we can show that condition (15) is satisfied by $f=\times$. Since for each fixed $c>0$ if d is sufficiently large then $d+d^{\frac{1}{2}}>d+c$, we get that multiplication in $\mathbf{M}_{d+c}$ can be defined in $\mathbf{M}_d$ in the sense of (15). This completes the proof of (15) for $f=\times$.

PROPOSITION 19. *For all $c>1,c'>1$, there exists a strongly first-order definable family of functions $f^{(d)}$, $d\in\omega$, such that for all sufficiently large $d\in\omega$, if $a=\langle a_0,\ldots,a_{j-1}\rangle$ is a sequence of natural numbers such that $a_i\le 2^{c^i}$ for all $i=0,1,\ldots,j-1$ and $c^j\le 2^{c'd}$, then $\mathbf{P}a=f^{(d)}(a)$.*

Proof. Let $p_i=\prod_{s=0}^{i-1}a_s$. Clearly $p_0=1$ and $p_j=\mathbf{P}a$. The number of binary bits in a_i is at most c^i, therefore the total number of bits in p_i is at most $\frac{c^i-1}{c-1}$ and the total number of bits in the sequence $p_1,\ldots,p_j$ is at most $(c-1)^2c^{j+2}\le(c-1)^2c^22^{c'd}\le 2^{(c'+1)d}$. Consequently in $\mathbf{M}_d$ we may speak about the existence of a sequence $p_1,\ldots,p_j$ in a first-order way. Therefore, $\mathbf{P}a=x$ will be equivalent to the following first-order formula in $\mathbf{M}_d$: "there exists a sequence $p_0,\ldots,p_{j-1}$, such that $p_0=0$, and for all $i=1,\ldots,j$, $p_i=a_{i-1}p_{i-1}$ and $p_j=x$". *Q.E.D.*Proposition 19

Now we show that condition (15) is satisfied by $f=\mathbf{p}$ and, for the proof of the Corollary, we show that it is satisfied by $f=\bar{\mathbf{p}}$. Since the proof for $f=\bar{\mathbf{p}}$ can be easily converted into a proof for $f=\mathbf{p}$ we describe here only the $f=\bar{\mathbf{p}}$ case.

PROPOSITION 20. *There exist strongly first-order definable families $f_q^{(d)}$, $d\in\omega$, $q=0,1,2$ such that for all sufficiently large d the following holds, where $n=2^d$:*

(i) if $a<2^n$, then $f_0^{(d)}(a)$ is the sequence $u=\langle u_0,\ldots,u_{j(a)-1}\rangle$, where $u_i=a^{2^i}$, and $j(a)$ is the smallest natural number with $a^{2^{j(a)}}\ge 2^n$, and $f_1^{(d)}(a)=j(a)$.

(ii) if $a<2^n$ and $b<j(a)$, then $f_2(\langle a,b\rangle)=a^b$.

Proof. Statement (i) is an immediate consequence of Proposition 19. To prove statement (ii) assume that $d\in\omega$ is sufficiently large $a<2^n$, $b<j(a)$. We have $b=\sum_{i=0}^{j(a)}\mathtt{coeff}_i(b,2)2^i$. Proposition 7 implies that $\alpha_i=\mathtt{coeff}_i(b_2)$ is first-order definable in $\mathbf{M}_d$. We may write a^b as the product $\prod_{i=0}^{j(a)}a^{\alpha_i2^i}$. Statement (i) and Proposition 19 together imply that a^b is first-order definable in $\mathbf{M}_d$. *Q.E.D.*(Proposition 20)

The integer a^b can be written in the form of $a^b=(a^{j(a)})^ka^t$, where $t<j(a)$. Assume that $a^b\le 2^{2^{cd}}$. Then $a^{j(a)}>2^d=n$ implies that $k\le c$ therefore according to Lemma 8 and Proposition 20 $a^{j(a)}$ and a^t both can be defined in $\mathbf{M}_d$, and then again by Proposition (17) their product is also first-order definable in $\mathbf{M}_d$. This completes the proof of condition (15) for $f=\bar{\mathbf{p}}$ and $f=\mathbf{p}$.

Now we prove condition (15) for $f=\div$. Assume that $a,b\in\mathbf{M}_{cd}$ is given and we want to define $\lfloor a/b\rfloor$ in $\mathbf{M}_d$

in a first-order way. First we describe a way, using general mathematical language, to compute $\lfloor a/b \rfloor$ and then we show that it can be translated into a first-order formula of $\mathcal{M}$ over $\mathbf{M}_d$.

(i) First we note that it is sufficient to find integers t, l such that $\frac{1}{b} - t2^l < 2^{-cn-1}$. The reason for this is that in the possession of the integers t, l we can compute $\alpha = at2^l$ and $|\alpha - \lfloor a/b \rfloor| < \frac{1}{2}$ so we get $\lfloor a/b \rfloor$ by rounding.

(ii) Let k be an integer so that $1 > 2^{-k}b > 1/2$. If there exists no integer with this property then the problem is trivial, since we can get the binary bits of $\lfloor a/b \rfloor$ form the bits of a simply by shift and the erasure of a block of consecutive bits. Let $u = 2^{-k}b$. Since $1 > u > \frac{1}{2}$, we have $1 < \frac{1}{u} < 2$. We may write $\frac{1}{u}$ in the form of $v2^{-(n+2)} + R$, where $v \in [0, 2^{n+2}]$ is an integer and $0 \le R < 2^{-n-1}$. (v will be determined by the first $n+1$ bits of $\frac{1}{u}$, and R is what remains from $\frac{1}{u}$ after erasing these bits.) Let $z = v2^{-(n+2)}$. The definition of v implies that $0 \le z \le 2$.

(iii) We have $zb = 1 + Rz = 1 + r$, where $|r| < 2^{-n+1}$. We consider the series $\frac{1}{zb} = \frac{1}{1-(1-zb)} = \frac{1}{1-(-r)} = 1 - r + r^2 - r^3 + \ldots$. Let w be the sum of the first $4c$ terms of this geometric series. Clearly $w = \frac{1}{zb} + R_1$, where $|R_1| < 2^{-3n}$. Consequently $\frac{1}{b} = z\frac{1}{zb} = z(w - R_1) = zw + R_2$, where $|R_2| < 2^{-2cn}$.

Now we show the all the quantities in this computation can be defined in a first-order way in $\mathbf{M}_d$.

Stage (i). The definition of t and l will be described later. However if we have t and l Proposition 18 implies that we may define the product $at2^l$ in a first-order way in $\mathbf{M}_d$. The rounding also can be done in a first-order way.

Stage (ii). The integer v has only $n+2$ bits. In $\mathbf{M}_d$ we can quantify n bits with a single existential quantifier, therefore v with the given property is first-order definable in $\mathbf{M}_d$.

Stage (iii). Proposition 18 implies that the product zb can be defined in $\mathbf{M}_d$. Using Lemma 7 we get that r can be defined as well. Each needed terms of the geometric series can be defined in $\mathbf{M}_d$, we define the ith term as a product with i factors. Lemma 8 implies that such a product can be defined in $\mathbf{M}_d$ and by Lemma 7 the sum of the first $4c$ terms can be defined as well. Therefore we defined w and by Proposition 18 we can define zw as well. This completes the proof of the fact that condition (15) is satisfied by $f = \div$, and also the proof of predictivity of $\mathbf{M}$. *Q.E.D.*(Theorem 2)

8. THE COUNTEREXAMPLE

We prove now the Theorem 6 stated in section 3.

Proof of Theorem 6. First we describe the language $\mathcal{L}'$ and the interpretations of some of its function symbols. Then we will sketch the the main ideas of proof. Assume that $f_0, \ldots, f_{k-1}$ are function symbols of a first-order language $\mathcal{L}_1$ each with arity r. We will say that the sequence $f = \langle f_0, \ldots, f_{k-1} \rangle$ is a k-dimensional function symbol vector of $\mathcal{L}_1$ with arity r. If it does not cause any misunderstanding we will write M_n instead of $\texttt{universe}(M_n)$.

The definition of $\mathcal{L}'$. We get $\mathcal{L}'$ by extending $\mathcal{L}$ with

(i) a unary function symbol $\mathbf{a}$,

(ii) a function symbol h with arity four, and

(iii) with a four dimensional function symbol vector $g = \langle g_0, g_1, g_2, g_3 \rangle$ with arity six.

We will interpret $\mathbf{a}$ in the following way, for each n, if, $u, v \in 2^n$ and $u + 1 \equiv v \pmod{2^n}$, then $M_n \models \mathbf{a}(u) = v$. That is $(\mathbf{a})_{M_n}$ is the function adding 1 mod 2^n. For each $b \in \omega$, $\tilde{b}$ will denote the term $\mathbf{a}(\ldots\mathbf{a}(\mathbf{0}))$ containing exactly b copies of $\mathbf{a}$. Clearly if $2^n > b$ then $M_n \models \tilde{b} = b$.

Let $T_0(x, y), T_1(x, y), \ldots$ be an enumeration of all binary terms of $\mathcal{L}'$, each may contain only the free variables x, y. We assume that if $i \le j$ then $\texttt{length}(T_i) \le \texttt{length}(T_j)$.

We fix a function $\vartheta(n)$, $n \in \omega$ so that $\vartheta(n)$ tends to infinity very slowly, in the sense that in the proof we will require several times that n is sufficiently large with respect to $\vartheta(n)$. These requirements will define the needed growth rate of ϑ.

Assume that $F(x, y) = T_b(x, y)$ is a term of $\mathcal{L}'$. We define the term $G_F(z)$ in the following way. First we define a sequence of four dimensional vector terms which may contain only the free variables x, y (a vector term of dimension d is a sequence consisting of d terms). The sequence $s_0(x, y), s_1(a, b), \ldots, s_i(a, b), \ldots$ of four dimensional vector terms is defined by recursion on i. $s_0(x, y) = \langle x, x, y, y \rangle$. Assume that $s_i(x, y)$ has been already defined. Then $s_{i+1}(x, y) = g(s_i(x, y), x, y)$. (This is well-defined since g has arity six and $s_i(x, y)$ is a four dimensional vector.) We define the term $G_F(z)$ by $G_F(z) = h(s_{\vartheta(n)}(z, \tilde{b}))$.

Now we define M'_n. We have already defined $(\mathbf{a})_{M'_n}$. We define now $g^{(n)} = (g)_{M'_n}$ the interpretation of g on the structure M'_n. We define $g^{(n)}$ in the following way. For each fixed $a, b \in M_n$ we the define the function $g_{a,b}(x) = g^{(n)}(x, a, b)$, $x \in M_n^4$. The function $g_{a,b}$ mapping M_n^4 into itself is chosen with uniform distribution from the set of all permutations of M_n^4, which has exactly one cycle. Moreover these random selections of $g_{a,b}$ are mutually independent for all of the possible values of n and a, b.

For the definition of $h^{(n)} = (h)_{M'_n}$ we define another interpretation M''_n of $\mathcal{L}'$. Let $\chi^{(n)}$ be the identically 0 function on M_n^4. M''_n will be an interpretation of $\mathcal{L}'$ on 2^n such that it is an extension of M_n, and $(g)_{M''_n} = g^{(n)}$ and $(h)_{M''_n} = \chi^{(n)}$. (We reserve the notation $h^{(n)}$ for the interpretation of the function symbol h in the structure M'_n.)

$h^{(n)}(x)$, $x \in M_n^4$ is defined in the following way. If there exists exactly one pair $a, b \in M_n$ so that $b \le \vartheta(\vartheta(n))$, $M'_n \models x = s_{\vartheta(n)}(a, b)$, and for this pair a, b we have $M''_n \models \exists y, T_b(y, a) = \mathbf{0}$, then $h^{(n)}(x) = 1$. Otherwise $h^{(n)}(x) = \chi^{(n)}(x) = 0$. This completes the definition of the interpretation M'_n. (Note that the term s_i does not contain the function symbol h therefore $M'_n \models x = s_{\vartheta(n)}(a, b)$ is equivalent to $M''_n \models x = s_{\vartheta(n)}(a, b)$.)

We show that with a probability 1 for the randomizations in the definition of the sequence M'_n, $n \in \omega$, the structures M'_n, $n \in \omega$ satisfy the requirements of the lemma. For the proof of this fact we need the following.

Let $V_i(x, y)$ be the set of all four dimensional term vectors $S(x, y) = \langle S_j(x, y) \mid j = 0, 1, 2, 3 \rangle$ of the language $\mathcal{L}'$, which may contain only the free variables x, y, such that $\texttt{length}(S_j(x, y)) \le i$ for all $j = 0, 1, 2, 3$. For each $a, u \in M_n$, we define a subset $\mathcal{V}_i(a, u)$ of M_n^4 by $\mathcal{V}_i(a, u) = \{(S(a, u))_{M_{n'}} \mid S(x, y) \in V_i(x, y)\}$. Clearly $|\mathcal{V}_i(a, u)| \le c_1^i$, where $c_1 > 1$ depends only on the language $\mathcal{L}$.

PROPOSITION 21. *For each fixed $i \in \omega$ if n is sufficiently large, $a, b, u \in M_n$, $b \le \vartheta(\vartheta(n))$ then the probability of $s_{\vartheta(n)}(a, b) \in \mathcal{V}_i(a, u)$ is at most $c_2^i \vartheta(n) |M_n|^{-4}$, where $c_2 > 1$ depends only on $\mathcal{L}$.*

This proposition will guarantee that changing the value of h on $\alpha = s_{\vartheta(n)}(a, b)$ does not change the fact whether $x = u$

is a solution of the equation $F(x,a) = \mathbf{0}$ or not, since α is not among the elements which are of the form $T(a,u)$ where T is a term of length at most $i = \mathtt{length}(F)$. According to the proposition with high probability this will be true simultaneously for all $u \in M_n$.

Proof. For the determination of the set $\mathcal{V}_i(a,u)$ we do not need to know the function $(h)_{M_n}$ since it may take only the values 0 and 1 which are also the values of the terms $\mathbf{0}$ and $\mathbf{a}(\mathbf{0})$. Therefore we may exclude from the definition of the set $\mathcal{V}_i$ the function symbol h. On the other hand we have to know some values of $g^{(n)}$. We start constructing the set $\mathcal{V}_i$ by recursion on i. If we have $\mathcal{V}_i$ already, then to get $\mathcal{V}_{i+1}$ we have to apply all of the M'_n interpretations of the function symbols in $\mathcal{L}'$ (with the exception of h) to the r-tuples of $\mathcal{V}_i$, where r always takes the value of the arity of the corresponding function. Each of these functions, with the exception of $g^{(n)}$, is fixed. The function $g^{(n)}$ however had a probabilistic definition. When we need a value of $g^{(n)}$ in this process then we will randomize it. Since there are only a finite number of functions symbols in $\mathcal{L}'$, we have that $|\mathcal{V}_{i+1}| \leq c_1|\mathcal{V}_i|$ for all $i = 0, 1, \ldots$, where c_1 is a suitably chosen constant. Assume now an $i \in \omega$ is fixed and n is sufficiently large. After we have constructed $\mathcal{V}_i$ in the described way, while choosing some values of $g^{(n)}$ as well, we continue the randomization of the values of $g^{(n)}(x,a,b)$, which are needed for for getting the values of $x = s_j(a,b)$, $j = 0, 1, \ldots, \vartheta(n)$.

Since n is sufficiently large with respect to i, $\vartheta(n)$ is also sufficiently large with respect to i. $g(x,a,b)$ is a permutation of M_n^4 with one cycle, therefore there exists an $j = 1, \ldots, \vartheta(n)$ such that $s_j(a,b) \notin \mathcal{V}_j(a,u)$. Since the permutation is chosen with uniform distribution with the mentioned property, the probability that there exists a $j' \in [j+1, \vartheta(n)]$, such that $s_{j'}(a,b) \in \mathcal{V}_i(a,u))$ is at most $|\mathcal{V}_i(a,u)|^2\vartheta(n)|M_n|^{-4}$, and so $|\mathcal{V}_i(a,u)| \leq c_1^i$ implies the conclusion of the proposition. *Q.E.D.*(Proposition 21)

PROPOSITION 22. *with a probability of at least* $1 - 2^{-n}$ *with respect to the randomization of the function* $g^{(n)}$ *the following conditions are satisfied:*

(19). for each fixed $x \in M_n^4$, *there exists at most one pair* $a, b \in M_n$ *such that* $b \leq \vartheta(n)$ *and* $M'_n \models x = s_{\vartheta_n}(a,b)$

(20). for all $x \in M_n^4$, $h^{(n)}(x) \neq 0$ *implies that* $x \notin \bigcup\{\mathcal{V}_i(a,u)\}a, u \in M_n, i \in [0, \vartheta(\vartheta(n))]$.

Proof. First we show that condition (19) is satisfied. Assume that we randomize all of the values of $g^{(n)}$ involved in the computation of all of the values $s_i(a,b)$ with $0 \leq i \leq \vartheta(n)$, $0 \leq b \leq \vartheta_n$, $a \in M_n$. This is altogether no more then $(\vartheta(n))^2|M_n| = (\vartheta(n))^2 2^n$ values out of the total $|M_n^4| = 2^{4n}$. Assume that we randomize these values of $g^{(n)}$ sequentially, fixing first a, b and then we randomize the values of $g^{(n)}$ which is needed to determine $s_i(a,b)$ for $i = 0, 1, \ldots, \vartheta(b)$. At the time when we have to choose $s_{\vartheta_b}(a,b)$ and the corresponding value of $g^{(n)}$ we have already chosen at most $(\vartheta(n))^2 2^n$ values of the cyclic permutation $g_{a,b}$. Therefore the probability that we will choose a value which already occurred in the process as a value of $g^{(n)}$ is at most $(\vartheta(n))^2 2^{-3n}$. Therefore the probability that this will happen for some a, b and i with the given restrictions is at most $(\vartheta(n))^4 2^{-2n} \leq 2^{-2n}$.

Condition (20) Assume that an $x \in M_n^4$ is fixed with $h^{(n)}(x) \neq 0$. For each fixed $a, u \in M_n$, $i \in [0, \vartheta(\vartheta(n))]$ we give an upper bound on $p_{a,u,i}$, the probability of the event $x \in \bigcup\{\mathcal{V}_i(a,u)\}a, u \in M_n, i \in [0, \vartheta(\vartheta(n))]$

By the definition of $h^{(n)}$, $h^{(n)}(x) \neq 0$ implies that $x = s_{\vartheta(n)}(a,b)$ for suitably chosen a and b. Therefore Proposition 21 implies that $p_{a,u,i} \leq c_2\vartheta(n)|M_n|^{-4}$. Adding the $p_{a,u,i}$ for all possible values for a, u, i we get that the probability that (20) does not hold is at most $\vartheta(n)|M_n|^{-2} \leq |M_n|^{-1} = 2^{-n}$. *Q.E.D.*(Proposition 22).

PROPOSITION 23. *For all terms* $F(x,y)$ *of* $\mathcal{L}'$, *for all sufficiently large* $n \in \omega$, *with a probability of at least* $1 - 2^n$ *the following holds:*

(21). for all $a \in M_n$, $M'_n \models \exists x, \Phi(x,a)$ *iff* $M''_n \models \exists x, \Phi(x,a)$

Proof. Clearly it is sufficient to show that conditions (19) and (20) of Proposition 22 imply condition (21) of this proposition. Assume that $u \in M_n$. Let W be the set of all elements w of M_n such that there is a subterm t of F with $t(u,a) = w$. Since n is sufficiently large we may assume that $\vartheta(\vartheta(n)) > \mathtt{length}(F)$. Therefore condition (20) implies that $h^{(n)}(w) = 0$ for all $w \in W$, and we have by definition $(h)_{M''_n}(\mathrm{w}){=}0$, for all $w \in W$. Since for all other function symbols f of $\mathcal{L}'$, $(f)_{M'_n} = (f)_{M_{n''}}$, we can prove by induction of the depth of a subterm t of F that $(t(u,a))_{M'_n} = (t(u,a))_{M''_n}$, and therefore $(F(u,a))_{M'_n} = (F(u,a))_{M''_n}$. Since this is true for all $u \in M_n$ we get the equivalence of $M'_n \models \exists x, \Phi(x,a)$ and $M''_n \models \exists x, \Phi(x,a)$. *Q.E.D.*(Proposition 23)

We return now to the proof of Theorem 6. Let $F(x,y)$ be a term of $\mathcal{L}'$, and suppose that n is sufficiently large with respect to $\mathtt{length}(F)$. We show that with a probability of at least $p_n = 2^{-n+1}$ we have that for all $a \in M_n$,

(22). $M'_n \models G_F(a) = \mathbf{0} \leftrightarrow \exists x, F(x,a) = \mathbf{0}$

Since $\sum_{n=0}^{\infty} p_n < \infty$ this will imply that with a probability 1 condition (22) holds for each sufficiently large n, that is the conclusion of Theorem 6 holds.

Proposition 22 and Proposition 23 imply that it is sufficient to prove that if all the three conditions (19), (20), and are satisfied by the structure M'_n then condition (22) is also satisfied by M_n. Assume now that the requirements of conditions (19), (20), and are met. Condition (19) and the definition of $h^{(n)}$ implies that By definition by the definition of G_F we have $M'_n \models G_F(a) = 1 - h(s_{\vartheta(n)}(a,b))$, where $F(x,y) = T_b(x,y)$. Condition (19) and the definition of $h^{(n)}$ implies that $h(s_\vartheta(n)(a,b)) = 1$ iff $M''_n \models \exists x, F(x,a)$. By condition (21) this is equivalent to $M'_n \models \exists x, F(x,a)$ which completes the proof of condition (22). *Q.E.D.*Theorem 6

9. RANDOM ACCESS MACHINES

In this section we sketch the proof of the fact that Theorem 2 implies Theorem 1.

We will use the following fact. The truth value of a propositional formula of $\mathcal{M}$ can be computed by a term of $\mathcal{M}$ uniformly in all $\mathbf{M}_d$. For a proof the following facts are sufficient: (a) in $\mathbf{M}_d$ the term $s(x,y) = \min(\mathbf{1}, x-y)$ takes only the values 0, 1, and $x = y$ iff $s(x,y) = 0$, and (b) the boolean functions $\neg x$ and $x \wedge y$ on 0, 1 values can be computed in $\mathbf{M}_d$ by the terms $1 - x$ and $\times(x,y)$. (See also Lemma 2.)

First we note that for all positive integers c_0, k, there exists a positive integer c_1, such that for each c_0-time k-ary test P_0, there exists a program P_1 with the following property. For all sufficiently large integer n, if P_0 is working till time c_0 and P_1 is working till time c_1 and they get the same input, then their outputs are identical, and P_1 is using only the first c_1 memory cells. Such a program P_1 can be constructed in the following way. P_1 simulates P_0, but P_1, instead of actually writing in arbitrary memory cells of N_n, only maintains a table which contains all of the addresses of the memory cells which were used till that time by P_0, together with their current contents. Since the time used by P_0 is at most c_0, the space and time used by P_1 for the maintenance of the table will depend only on c_0 (and not on n). This table can be maintained in the first c_2 memory cells, where c_2 depends only on c_0. The program P_1, using this table, follows the computation done by P_0, step by step, and provides the same output as P_0, while its time requirement remains below a bound c_1 depending only on c_0, and while it is using only the first c_1 memory cells.

Now we prove Theorem 1, and during this proof, based on the fact proved above, we may assume that P is a c-time k-ary test which is using only the first c_1 memory cells of the machine N_n, where c_1 depends only on c. We will also assume that the program P maintains in a memory cell the number of inputs which were already read. (This last assumption implies, that the state of the machine at time t together with the input sequence $a_1, ..., a_k$, uniquely determine the state of the machine at time $t + 1$, for all possible values of t.) We claim that:

(23). *For all c-time k-ary tests P with the assumed properties, there exists a term* $T(x_1, ..., x_k)$ *of* $\mathcal{M}$, *such that for all sufficiently large* $d \in \omega$, *if* $n = 2^d$, *then for all* $a_1, ..., a_k$, $P_n(a_0, ..., a_k) = (T(a_1, ..., a_k))_{\mathbf{M}_d}$.

This statement clearly implies that Theorem 1 follows for Theorem 2. Statement (23) can be proved by showing that for each $i \leq c$, there are terms $t_{i,0}, ..., t_{i,c_1-1}$ of $\mathcal{M}$ such that for all sufficiently large $n = 2^d$ the content of memory cell j of the machine N_n at time i is $(t_{i,j}(a_1, ..., a_k))_{\mathbf{M}_d}$. We prove this by induction on i. For $i = 0$ this is a consequence of the fact that the names of the instructions in the program P are given independently of n, so we may express each of them by a term of $\mathcal{M}$, e.g., of the type $1 + ... + 1$. Assume now that the inductive assumption holds for $i - 1$. The definition of the instructions of the machines N_n implies that for each $r \in c_1$ there exists an $s \in \omega$ and terms $\tau_{0,r}, ..., \tau_{s-1,r}$ of $\mathcal{M}$ and propositional formulas $\mathcal{P}_{0,r}, ..., \mathcal{P}_{s-1,r}$ such that, if $n = 2^d$ is sufficiently large, and the sequence of the contents of the memory cells of N_n at time $i - 1$ is $\vec{m}(i - 1)$ then the content $C_{i,r}$ of memory cell r at time i can be defined in the following form: $\mathbf{M}_d \models \bigwedge_{h \in s} \mathcal{P}_{h,r}(\vec{m}(i-1), a_1, ..., a_k) \rightarrow C_{i,r} = \tau_{h,r}(\vec{m}(i-1), a_1, ..., a_k)$. Moreover the formulas $\mathcal{P}_{h,r}$ can be chosen in a way that there is always exactly one $h \in s$ with $\mathbf{M}_d \models \mathcal{P}_{h,r}(\vec{m}(i-1), a_1, ..., a_k)$. Since the truth values of propositional formulas can be computed by terms, this implies that there exists a term σ_r of $\mathcal{M}$ such that $\mathbf{M}_d \models C_{i,r} = \sigma_r(\vec{m}(i-1), a_1, ..., a_k)$. Indeed, if $T_{h,r}$ is a 0,1- valued term with $\mathbf{M}_d \models \mathcal{P}_{h,r} \leftrightarrow (T_{h,r} = \mathbf{1})$, then $\sigma_r = \sum_{h \in s} T_{h,r}(\vec{m}(i-1), a_1, ..., a_k)\tau(\vec{m}(i-1), a_1, ..., a_k)$.

The inductive assumption implies that each component of $\vec{m}(i-1)$ can be expressed as a term at $a_1, ..., a_k$, which completes the proof of the inductive step. This completes the sketch of the proof of Theorem 1.

10. REFERENCES

[1] A.V. Aho, J.E. Hopcroft, J.D. Ullman, *The Design and Analysis of Computer Algorithms*, Addison-Wesley, 1974.

[2] M. Ajtai, *Determinism versus Nondeterminism for Linear Time RAMs with Memory Restrictions*, Journal of Computer and Systems Science, 65(1): 2-37, (2002)

[3] M. Ajtai, *Oblivious RAMs without cryptographic assumptions*, Electronic Colloquium on Computational Complexity (ECCC), 17:28, 2010.

[4] M. Ajtai. *Oblivious RAMs without cryptographic assumptions*, Proceedings of the 42nd ACM Symposium on Theory of Computing, STOC 2010, Cambridge, Massachusetts, USA, 5-8 June 2010, pages 181–190. ACM, 2010.

[5] M. Ajtai, Y. Gurevich, *Monotone versus positive*, Journal of the ACM (JACM), Vol. 34, Issue 4, Oct. 1987, pp. 1004-1015.

[6] E. Artin. *Galois Theory*, Dover Publications, 1998. (Reprinting of second revised edition of 1944, The University of Notre Dame Press).

[7] P. Beame, S. A. Cook, and H. J. Hoover, Log Depth Circuits for Division and Related Problems, SIAM Journal on Computing, 15(4):994-1003, November 1986.

[8] P. Beame, T. S. Jayram, M. Sacks, *Time-space tradeoffs for branching programs*, Journal of Computer and Systems Science, 63(4):542-572, December 2001.

[9] P. Beame, M. Sacks, Xiadong Sun, E. Vee, *Time-space trade-off lower bounds for randomized computation of decision problems*, Journal of ACM, 50(2):154-195, 2003.

[10] M. Davis, H. Putnam and J. Robinson, *The decision problem for exponential diophantine equations*, Ann. of Math. (2) 74 (1961), 425-436. 3. J. P. Jones, Three universal representations of r.e. sets, J. Symbolic Logic 43 (1978), 335-351.

[11] W. Hesse, *Division is in Uniform* TC^0, ICALP 2001: 104-114.

[12] A. Magid, *Differential Galois theory*, Notices of the American Mathematical Society 46 (9): 1999.

[13] L. Fortnow, *Time-space tradoffs for satisfiability*, Journal of Computer and System Sciences, 60:337-353, 2000.

[14] Ju. V. Matijasevic, *Enumerable sets are diophantine*, Dokl. Akad. Nauk SSSR 191 (1970), 279-282. English transi.: Soviet Math. Doklady 11 (1970), 354-358.

[15] W. Paul, N. Pippenger, E. Szemerédi, and W. Trotter. *On determinism versus nondeterminism and related problems*, In Proceedings of the 24th IEEE Symposium on Foundations of Computer Science, pages 429-438. IEEE, New York, 1983.

[16] G. Takeuti, *Proof Theory*, North-Holland, Studies in Logic and the Foundations of Mathematics, Vol. 81, Second edition, 1987.

[17] A. Yao *Separating the polynomial time hierarchy by oracles*, Proc. 26th Annu. IEEE Symp. Found. Comp. Sci. 1-10 (1985).

Solution of the Propeller Conjecture in $\mathbb{R}^3$

Extended Abstract

Steven Heilman
Courant Institute, NYU
New York NY 10012
heilman@cims.nyu.edu

Aukosh Jagannath
Courant Institute, NYU
New York NY 10012
aukosh@cims.nyu.edu

Assaf Naor
Courant Institute, NYU
New York NY 10012
naor@cims.nyu.edu

ABSTRACT

It is shown that every measurable partition $\{A_1, \dots, A_k\}$ of $\mathbb{R}^3$ satisfies

$$\sum_{i=1}^{k} \left\| \int_{A_i} x e^{-\frac{1}{2}\|x\|_2^2} dx \right\|_2^2 \leqslant 9\pi^2. \tag{1}$$

Let $\{P_1, P_2, P_3\}$ be the partition of $\mathbb{R}^2$ into 120° sectors centered at the origin. The bound (1) is sharp, with equality holding if $A_i = P_i \times \mathbb{R}$ for $i \in \{1,2,3\}$ and $A_i = \emptyset$ for $i \in \{4, \dots, k\}$. This settles positively the 3-dimensional Propeller Conjecture of Khot and Naor (FOCS 2008). The proof of (1) reduces the problem to a finite set of numerical inequalities which are then verified with full rigor in a computer-assisted fashion. The main consequence (and motivation) of (1) is complexity-theoretic: the Unique Games hardness threshold of the Kernel Clustering problem with 4×4 centered and spherical hypothesis matrix equals $\frac{2\pi}{3}$.

Categories and Subject Descriptors

F.2.2 [**Analysis of Algorithms and Problem Complexity**]: Nonnumerical Algorithms and Problems—*Geometrical problems and computations*

General Terms

Theory

Keywords

Kernel clustering, unique games hardness, semidefinite programming, Grothendieck inequalities.

1. INTRODUCTION

For $x = (x_1, \dots, x_m), y = (y_1, \dots, y_m) \in \mathbb{R}^m$ let $\langle x, y \rangle = \sum_{i=1}^m x_i y_i$ denote the standard scalar product, and also let $\|x\|_2 = \sqrt{\langle x, x \rangle}$ denote the corresponding Euclidean norm. The cross product of $x = (x_1, x_2, x_3), y = (y_1, y_2, y_3) \in \mathbb{R}^3$ is denoted $x \times y = (x_2y_3 - x_3y_2, x_3y_1 - x_1y_3, x_1y_2 - x_2y_1)$. The Gaussian measure on $\mathbb{R}^m$, i.e., the measure whose density is $x \mapsto (2\pi)^{-m/2} e^{-\|x\|_2^2/2}$, is denoted γ_m.

The following theorem is our main result, asserting that among all measurable partitions of $\mathbb{R}^3$, the "propeller partition" as depicted in Figure 1 maximizes the sum of the squared lengths of the Gaussian moments associated to the members of the partition.

THEOREM 1.1 (MAIN THEOREM; GEOMETRIC FORM). *Let $\{A_1, \dots, A_k\}$ be a partition of $\mathbb{R}^3$ into Lebesgue measurable sets. For $i \in \{1, \dots, k\}$ let $\zeta_i = \int_{A_i} x d\gamma_3(x) \in \mathbb{R}^3$ be the Gaussian moment of the set A_i. Then*

$$\sum_{i=1}^{k} \|\zeta_i\|_2^2 \leqslant \frac{9}{8\pi}. \tag{2}$$

Let $\{P_1, P_2, P_3\}$ be the partition of $\mathbb{R}^2$ into 120° sectors centered at the origin. The bound (2) cannot be improved, with equality holding if $A_i = P_i \times \mathbb{R}$ for $i \in \{1,2,3\}$ and $A_i = \emptyset$ for $i \in \{4, \dots, k\}$.

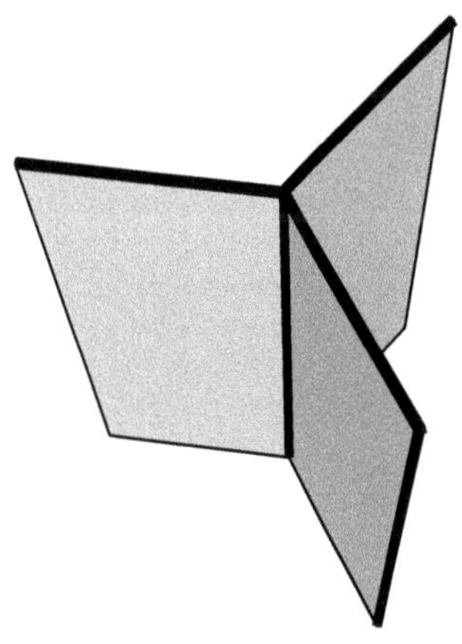

Figure 1: ***The partition of $\mathbb{R}^3$ that maximizes the sum of squared lengths of Gaussian moments is a "propeller": three planar 120° sectors multiplied by an orthogonal line, with the rest of the partition elements being empty.***

The Propeller Conjecture was posed by Khot and Naor in [22] as part of their investigation of the computational complexity of the Kernel Clustering problem from Machine

Learning. Specifically, they conjectured the validity of the bound (2) for measurable partitions of $\mathbb{R}^m$ for all $m > 2$. They proved this conjecture for $m = 2$, and for $m = 1$ they showed that the right hand side of (2) can be improved to the sharp bound $\frac{1}{\pi}$. It is also shown in [22] that, for partitions of $\mathbb{R}^3$, proving (2) when $k = 4$ implies the same conclusion for all $k \in \mathbb{N}$. Correspondingly, for partitions of $\mathbb{R}^m$ it suffices to prove this statement for $k = m + 1$.

Before explaining the complexity-theoretic consequence of Theorem 1.1, which was the motivation of [22] for posing the Propeller Conjecture, we state two equivalent formulations of it: the first probabilistic (a sharp estimate for the expected maximum of a Gaussian vector) and the second analytic (a sharp Grothendieck inequality). The equivalence of these results to Theorem 1.1 was established in [22]; for Theorem 1.2 below see [22, Lem. 3.7] and for Theorem 1.3 below see [22, Thm. 1.1].

Theorem 1.2 (Main theorem; probabilistic). *Let $(g_1, g_2, g_3, g_4) \in \mathbb{R}^4$ be a mean zero Gaussian vector (with arbitrary covariance matrix). Then*

$$\left|\mathbb{E}\left[\max_{i\in\{1,2,3,4\}} g_i\right]\right| \leqslant \frac{3}{2\sqrt{2\pi}}\sqrt{\sum_{i=1}^{4}\mathbb{E}\left[g_i^2\right]}. \tag{3}$$

The bound (3) cannot be improved, with equality holding when the covariance matrix of (g_1, g_2, g_3, g_4) equals

$$\frac{1}{2}\begin{pmatrix} 2 & -1 & -1 & 0 \\ -1 & 2 & -1 & 0 \\ -1 & -1 & 2 & 0 \\ 0 & 0 & 0 & 0 \end{pmatrix}.$$

The following analytic formulation of Theorem 1.1 is in terms of a sharp Grothendieck inequality. Grothendieck [12] pioneered in 1953 the use of inequalities of this type in functional analysis, and ever since then such inequalities have permeated many mathematical disciplines. See [22, 23, 24] for an explanation of how the result below relates to a natural extension of the Grothendieck inequality and to approximation algorithms.

Theorem 1.3 (Main theorem; analytic form). *Let (a_{ij}) be an $n \times n$ positive semidefinite matrix with $\sum_{i=1}^n \sum_{j=1}^n a_{ij} = 0$. For every $\{v_1, v_2, v_3, v_4\} \subseteq S^3$ with $\sum_{i=1}^4 v_i = 0$ we have*

$$\max_{x_1,\ldots,x_n\in S^{n-1}} \sum_{i=1}^{n}\sum_{j=1}^{n} a_{ij}\langle x_i, x_j\rangle \leqslant \frac{2\pi}{3}\max_{y_1,\ldots,y_n\in\{v_1,v_2,v_3,v_4\}} \sum_{i=1}^{n}\sum_{j=1}^{n} a_{ij}\langle y_i, y_j\rangle. \tag{4}$$

The bound (4) cannot be improved, with asymptotic equality holding when $\{v_1, v_2, v_3, v_4\}$ are the rows of the following matrix.

$$\frac{1}{2\sqrt{3}}\begin{pmatrix} 3 & -1 & -1 & -1 \\ -1 & 3 & -1 & -1 \\ -1 & -1 & 3 & -1 \\ -1 & -1 & -1 & 3 \end{pmatrix}.$$

See [23, Sec. 3.1] for a description of a family of $n\times n$ matrices (a_{ij}) for which equality in (4) is asymptotically attained (as $n \to \infty$).

Inequality (4) was proved in [22]. Our new contribution is the assertion that (4) cannot be improved, a statement that is equivalent to inequality (2) of Theorem 1.1. This is not the first time that attempts to prove sharpness of a Grothendieck inequality led to an extremal geometric partitioning question. Notably, see König's conjecture [26] as a step towards Krivine's conjecture [28] on the sharpness of his version of the classical Grothendieck inequality. Unlike the Propeller Conjecture in $\mathbb{R}^3$, these conjectures turned out to be false [8], but they do indicate the interconnection between Grothendieck inequalities and extremal geometric partitioning problems.

Remark 1.4. *An inspection of the arguments presented here, as well as the proofs of the results of [22] that we use, shows that Theorems 1.1, 1.2, 1.3 have a corresponding uniqueness statement, up to the obvious symmetries of the problem. For example, in Theorem 1.1, up to measure zero corrections, orthogonal transformations, and reordering of $\{A_1, \ldots, A_k\}$, the* only *partition at which there is equality in (2) is the propeller partition. Since this uniqueness statement is irrelevant for the complexity-theoretic motivation of the Propeller Conjecture, we do not include it here.*

The main consequence (and motivation) of Theorem 1.1 is complexity theoretic. To explain it we briefly recall Khot's Unique Games Conjecture (UGC), which asserts that for every $\varepsilon \in (0, 1)$ there exists a prime $p = p(\varepsilon) \in \mathbb{N}$ such that no polynomial time algorithm can perform the following task. The input is a system of m linear equations in n variables $x_1, \ldots, x_n$, each of which has the form $x_i - x_j \equiv c_{ij} \mod p$. The algorithm must determine whether there exists an assignment of an integer value to each variable x_i such that at least $(1-\varepsilon)m$ of the equations are satisfied, or no assignment of such values can satisfy more than εm of the equations. If neither of these possibilities occurs, then an arbitrary output of the algorithm is allowed. The UGC was introduced by Khot in [19], though the above formulation of it, which is equivalent to the original one, is due to [21]. The use of the UGC as a hardness hypothesis has become popular over the past decade; we refer to Khot's survey [20] for more information on this topic. Saying that the UGC hardness threshold of an optimization problem $\mathscr{O}$ equals $\alpha \in [1, \infty)$ means that for every $\varepsilon \in (0, 1)$ there exists a polynomial time algorithm that outputs a number that is guaranteed to be within a multiplicative factor of $\alpha + \varepsilon$ from the solution of $\mathscr{O}$, and that the existence of such an algorithm with approximation guarantee of $\alpha - \varepsilon$ would contradict the UGC.

The Kernel Clustering problem is a clustering framework for covariance matrices that originated in the work of Borgwardt, Gretton, Smola and Song [34] in the context of Machine Learning. This problem is generic in the sense that it contains well-studied optimization problems as special cases, and its versatility allows one to design a variety of algorithms tailor-made for particular applications (many of these algorithms are at present shown [34] to be successful empirically, but not rigorously). The input of the Kernel Clustering problem is an $n \times n$ symmetric positive semidefinite matrix $A = (a_{ij})$ and a $k\times k$ symmetric positive semidefinite matrix $B = (b_{ij})$ called the hypothesis matrix. Think of n as very large and k as small, the goal being to cluster the entries of A into a $k \times k$ matrix that is most correlated with the hypothesis matrix B. Formally, given a partition $\{S_1, \ldots, S_k\}$ of $\{1, \ldots, n\}$, form the associated clustered version of A by summing the entries of A over the blocks induced by the partition $\{S_1, \ldots, S_k\}$. One thus obtains a $k \times k$ matrix $C = (c_{ij})$ given by $c_{ij} = \sum_{(s,t) \in S_i \times S_j} a_{st}$. Let $\mathbf{Clust}(A|B)$ denote the maximum of $\sum_{i=1}^{k} \sum_{j=1}^{k} c_{ij} b_{ij}$ over all partitions $\{S_1, \ldots, S_k\}$ of $\{1, \ldots, n\}$. We refer to [34, 22, 23, 24] for further explanation of this clustering framework, as well as a discussion of important special cases arising from appropriate choices of the hypothesis matrix B.

In what follows, an $n \times n$ symmetric positive semidefinite matrix $A = (a_{ij})$ is called centered if $\sum_{i=1}^{n} \sum_{j=1}^{n} a_{ij} = 0$, and it is called spherical if $a_{ii} = 1$ for all $i \in \{1, \ldots, n\}$.

THEOREM 1.5 (MAIN THEOREM; COMPLEXITY FORM). *Let $\mathscr{O}$ be the following optimization problem. The input is an $n \times n$ symmetric positive semidefinite centered matrix $A = (a_{ij})$, and also a 4×4 symmetric centered and spherical positive semidefinite matrix $B = (b_{ij})$. The goal is to compute the quantity $\mathbf{Clust}(A|B)$. Then the UGC hardness threshold of $\mathscr{O}$ equals $\frac{2\pi}{3}$.*

A polynomial time algorithm with approximation ratio $\frac{2\pi}{3} + o(1)$ for the problem $\mathscr{O}$ of Theorem 1.5 was designed in [22]. The fact that Theorem 1.1 implies the matching UGC hardness result was also proved in [22]. More generally, it was shown in [22] that the validity of the m-dimensional Propeller Conjecture for some $m \geqslant 3$ would imply that the UGC hardness threshold of the variant of $\mathscr{O}$ with B being an $m \times m$ matrix equals $\frac{8\pi}{9}\left(1 - \frac{1}{m}\right)$.

This is not the first time that extremal problems in the measure space $(\mathbb{R}^m, \gamma_m)$ arose from investigations in complexity theory; see for example the Majority is Stablest Conjecture of Khot, Kindler, Mossel and O'Donnell [21], which was solved by Mossel, O'Donnell, and Oleszkiewicz [31] via a reduction to a classical isoperimetric inequality of Borell [7]. A special feature of the Propeller Conjecture is that its conclusion is quite surprising: despite allowing for partitions of $\mathbb{R}^m$ into $m+1$ sets, the optimal partition has only three nonempty sets. Note that this degeneracy property occurs for the first time when $m = 3$, since in the result of [22] for partitions of $\mathbb{R}^2$ into three sets, all three sets are indeed present in the optimal partition. Thus Theorem 1.1 is a proof of the first nonintuitive case of the Propeller Conjecture: a verification of a prediction about a clean yet unexpected geometric phenomenon that arose from an investigation in computational complexity. To the best of our knowledge this is the first time that such a development occurred in this theory.

Our proof of Theorem 1.1 proceeds as follows. First, using reductions of the Propeller Conjecture that were obtained in [22], we show that it suffices to prove an analogous partitioning problem for the sphere S^2. Namely, given a partition of S^2 into four spherical triangles, the goal is to show that the sum of the squares of lengths of the moments (with respect to the surface area measure on S^2) of these spherical triangles cannot exceed $9\pi^2/4$. Using additional geometric arguments, we further reduce the question to an optimization problem over a three dimensional search space. We thus obtain a coordinate system with three degrees of freedom, with respect to which one must solve a rather complicated nonlinear optimization problem. After proving several additional estimates that serve to further reduce the search space and give crucial modulus of continuity estimates, we show that it suffices to check that the desired estimate holds true for a finite list of spherical partitions (arising from an appropriate net of the search space). This list of inequalities that must be proved is explicit but very large, so we proceed to check it in a fully rigorous computer-assisted fashion. That is, our computation carefully accounts for all the rounding errors; equivalently the computation can be viewed as an implementation in our setting of interval arithmetic (see [16]).

The role and implications of rigorous computer-assisted proofs has been discussed at length in the literature; many such discussions appear in papers that establish striking results via a proof that has a computer-assisted component (famous examples include [1, 2, 17, 10, 14, 11]). We see no reason to include here a new treatment of this topic. Zwick's discussion in [37] is an excellent reference for a well thought out explanation of the role of computer-assisted proofs in mathematics and computer science[1]. The essence of the argument can be best conveyed by quoting Zwick directly [37, Sec. 7]:

> "A typical computer assisted proof, like ours, is essentially composed of two steps. The first step says something like: "Here is program P. If program P, when executed by an abstract computer, outputs YES, then the theorem is true, because . . . ". The second step says something like: "I ran program P and it said YES!", or more specifically: "I compiled program P using compiler A, under operating system B, and ran it on processor C, again under operating system B. It said YES!"."

Zwick then proceeds to explain that

> "The first step is a conventional mathematical proof. It simply argues that a certain program has certain properties. Such arguments are common in computer science. Anyone who objects to this step of the proof should find a flaw, or a gap, in the arguments made."

Nevertheless, Zwick explains that the second step, i.e., the claim that the compilation of the program gave the desired result, is not of the same nature:

> "The second step is more problematic. It is certainly not a proof in the conventional mathematical sense of the word. Many things can go wrong here. Program P may not have been compiled correctly by compiler A. Or, due to some bug in operating system B, the program did not run as intended. Or, processor C may suffer from a design flaw that causes an incorrect execution of the program, or perhaps the specific processor used has a short-circuit somewhere, and so on. It is possible to reduce the likelihood of such problems by compiling the program using several different compilers, and running it on different processors. But, while we may eventually be

[1]Zwick's paper [37] is another instance of a computer-assisted proof in the context of approximation algorithms. While the present article deals with an integrality gap lower bound for a semindefinite program (the left hand side of (4)), Zwick proves an integrality gap upper bound, i.e., he uses a rigorous computer-assisted argument to show that a certain algorithm performs well rather than to prove a hardness result.

able to produce mathematical correctness proofs for compilers, operating systems, and the hardware design of the processors, it seems that we would never be able to produce a mathematical proof that no hardware fault occurred during a specific computation.

What we can do, is instruct the computer executing program P to print a trace of the execution. This trace is a mathematical proof, though perhaps a not so inspiring one. Like any mathematical proof it should be checked carefully to make sure that it is correct. In many cases, however, this is not humanly possible. The main problem with computer assisted proofs, therefore, is that they are usually too long. They are also, in most cases, less insightful than conventional proofs."

The bulk of the work presented in this article consists of conventional geometric and analytic proofs, resulting in a reduction of the problem to a region where the desired inequality holds with "room to spare". This extra room allows us to complete the proof by checking a finite list of concrete inequalities (that we write explicitly) on a certain finite net. Each such inequality can be checked by hand, but the number of such checks is large, and it would be unrealistic (and probably unilluminating) to complete this final check manually. The code that we used is publicly available at the website `http://cims.nyu.edu/~aukosh/propeller/propeller.html`, which contains a command-line user interface so that interacting with the code is easy.

The code for this proof was run many times on several different computers. The technical requirements are quite modest, with the processor speed only affecting the total run time, and the total memory requirement being less than 200 Mb. One can run the code on anything from a dedicated compute server to a laptop computer (we did both). We ran the code in two different ways. The simplest way was to run it in a serial fashion. That is, we ran the program as a single instance which performed each step of the algorithm described in this paper one after the other. This took 37 hours to complete on a single processor of a compute server with 3.3 GhZ Intel Xenon processors. The second way we ran it was to parallelize the algorithm by breaking up the domain of interest into seven distinct portions and running separate instances on each. This procedure took eight hours when split between seven 3.3 GhZ Intel Xenon processors. (We also ran the program split between seven 2.4 GhZ AMD Opteron processors; this procedure took twelve hours.)

Needless to say, our proof of the Propeller Conjecture in $\mathbb{R}^3$ leaves something to be desired, since we do not have a short explanation of the validity of the computations in the final step of our proof. It is conceptually important to have a proof of this result, despite the fact that it ends in a lengthy computation, not only because it yields interesting results in mathematics and computational complexity. Importantly, since the Propeller Conjecture is a nonintuitive prediction that arose from investigations in computational complexity, knowing that the first nonintuitive case of this conjecture is indeed true puts the full Propeller Conjecture, and consequently the link between geometry and algorithms that it describes, on a stronger footing. Thus, in addition to yielding a remarkably involved UGC hardness result, our theorem will hopefully invigorate future research on this problem that might lead to a traditional mathematical proof of the Propeller Conjecture in $\mathbb{R}^3$ that can hopefully be extended to higher dimensions.

A key feature of the Propeller Conjecture is that it asserts that a natural optimization problem exhibits intermediate-dimensional symmetry breaking. There are precedents of results of this type that have been proved in the literature, mostly using Fourier-analytic methods. For this reason we are hopeful that a clean and shorter proof of the Propeller Conjecture will eventually be found. Consider for example the problem of sharp Khinchine inequalities: if $\varepsilon_1, \ldots, \varepsilon_n$ are i.i.d. symmetric random variables taking values in $\{-1, 1\}$ and $p \in [1, 2)$, the goal is to compute the minimum of $\mathbb{E}\left[\left|\sum_{i=1}^n a_i\varepsilon_i\right|^p\right]$ over all unit vectors $a = (a_1, \ldots, a_n) \in \mathbb{R}^n$. For $p = 1$ it was conjectured by Littlewood (see [15]) that this minimum occurs at $a = (1, 1, 0, \ldots, 0)/\sqrt{2}$. Littlewood's conjecture was solved affirmatively by Szarek [35] (see also [36, 29]). Haagerup [13] proved that the same two dimensional symmetry breaking occurs for $p \in [1, p_0]$, where $p_0 = 1.87...$ is the solution of the equation $2\Gamma((p+1)/2) = \sqrt{\pi}$, i.e., the unit vector that minimizes $\mathbb{E}\left[\left|\sum_{i=1}^n a_i\varepsilon_i\right|^p\right]$ equals $(1, 1, 0, \ldots, 0)/\sqrt{2}$ for $p \in [1, p_0]$ and for $p \in [p_0, 2]$ this minimum occurs at $a = (1, \ldots, 1)/\sqrt{n}$. Another famous result of this type is Ball's cube slicing theorem [3] (resolving a conjecture of Hensley [18]), asserting that the hyperplane section of $[-1, 1]^n$ with maximal $(n-1)$-dimensional volume is perpendicular to $(1, 1, 0, \ldots, 0)$; see [33] for the corresponding result for complex scalars, as well as [4, 6] for an analogous statement for projections. We refer to [32] for a unified treatment of the results of Szarek, Haagerup, and Ball. There is also a conjecture of Milman predicting a symmetry breaking phenomenon for extremal volumes of slabs in the cube $[-1, 1]^n$; see [5, 27] for partial results along these lines. We mentioned the above statements since we believe that among the literature they are most similar to the Propeller Conjecture, and perhaps (with much more work) related methods could be be used to address the Propeller Conjecture as well.

This article is organized as follows. In Section 2 we present the reduction of the Propeller Conjecture to a certain optimization problem for spherical partitions, and we explain the main ingredients of our proof, including the conventional geometric/analytic arguments and the computer-assisted component. The proofs of the geometric and analytic results leading to the final computational step are contained in Section 3 and Section 4 of the full version of this extended abstract, which is available at `http://arxiv.org/abs/1112.2993`. Section 4.1 of the full version contains a detailed explanation of how the numerical step is implemented so as to account for all possible rounding errors. We remark that our arguments extend mutatis mutandis to higher dimensions. For the sake of simplicity we present the entire argument in $\mathbb{R}^3$, since while it is conceivable that the scheme presented here can yield a computer-assisted proof of the Propeller Conjecture in higher dimensions, at some fixed dimension the computer-assisted component of the proof will become unfeasible. Now that we know that a nonintuitive case of the Propeller Conjecture is indeed correct, the next natural step is to search for a proof that extends to all dimensions, rather than attempting to prove a few more cases in low dimensions.

2. AN OVERVIEW OF THE PROOF OF THEOREM 1.1

From now on assume for the sake of eventually obtaining a contradiction that $\{A_i\}_{i=1}^4$ is a partition of $\mathbb{R}^3$ into measurable sets that violates the propeller conjecture, i.e.,

$$\sum_{i=1}^{4}\left\|\int_{A_i} x d\gamma_3(x)\right\|_2^2 > \frac{9}{8\pi}. \tag{5}$$

Assume also that the maximum of

$$\sum_{i=1}^{4}\left\|\int_{B_i} x d\gamma_3(x)\right\|_2^2$$

over all measurable partitions $\{B_i\}_{i=1}^4$ of $\mathbb{R}^3$ is attained at $\{A_i\}_{i=1}^4$. For a proof that this maximum is indeed attained, see [22, Lem. 3,1]. Using this maximality, it follows from [22, Lem. 3.3] that (up to measure zero corrections) the A_i are cones with cusp at the origin, and if we write $\zeta_i = \int_{A_i} x d\gamma_3(x)$ then $\zeta_1+\zeta_2+\zeta_3+\zeta_4 = 0$ and for each $i \in \{1,2,3,4\}$ we have

$$A_i = \left\{x \in \mathbb{R}^3 : \langle x, \zeta_i\rangle = \max_{j\in\{1,2,3,4\}} \langle x, \zeta_j\rangle\right\}. \tag{6}$$

By [22, Lem. 3.3 & Cor. 3.4] the vectors $\{\zeta_i\}_{i=1}^4$ are distinct, nonzero and not coplanar.

Since the sets in question are cones, it is beneficial to study them in terms of their intersection with the sphere S^2, i.e., define

$$T_i = A_i \cap S^2, \tag{7}$$

and letting σ denote the surface area measure on S^2 (thus $\sigma(S^2) = 4\pi$), define

$$z_i = \int_{T_i} x d\sigma(x) = \sqrt{2\pi^3}\cdot \zeta_i, \tag{8}$$

where the last equality in (8) follows from integration in polar coordinates. Being a constant multiple of the vectors $\{\zeta_i\}_{i=1}^4$, the vectors $\{z_i\}_{i=1}^4$ are also distinct, nonzero, not coplanar, and satisfy $z_1+z_2+z_3+z_4 = 0$. Moreover,

$$T_i \overset{(6)\wedge(7)\wedge(8)}{=} \left\{x \in S^2 \colon \langle x, z_i\rangle = \max_{j\in\{1,2,3,4\}} \langle x, z_j\rangle\right\}. \tag{9}$$

Consequently,

$$\forall i,j \in \{1,2,3,4\}, \quad x \in T_i \cap T_j \implies \langle z_i, x\rangle = \langle z_j, x\rangle. \tag{10}$$

Fix $\ell \in \{1,2,3,4\}$. Since $\{z_i\}_{i=1}^4$ are not coplanar there exists a unique $v_\ell \in S^2$ satisfying

$$\forall i,j \in \{1,2,3,4\} \smallsetminus \{\ell\}, \quad \langle z_i, v_\ell\rangle = \langle z_j, v_\ell\rangle > \langle z_\ell, v_\ell\rangle. \tag{11}$$

The vectors $\{v_\ell\}_{\ell=1}^4$ are the vertices of the partition $P = \{T_1,T_2,T_3,T_4\}$ of S^2. A simple argument presented in Section 3 of the full version shows that $v_i \notin \{-v_j, v_j\}$ if $i \neq j$ and each spherical triangle T_i is contained in an open hemisphere of S^2. Moreover, for distinct $i,j,\ell \in \{1,2,3,4\}$ we have $\det(v_i,v_j,v_\ell) \neq 0$, and if we define

$$\theta_{ij} = \arccos(\langle v_i, v_j\rangle),$$
$$\Theta_{ij\ell} = \arccos\left(\left\langle \frac{(v_i\times v_j)}{\|v_i\times v_j\|_2}, \frac{(v_j\times v_\ell)}{\|v_j\times v_\ell\|_2}\right\rangle\right), \tag{12}$$

then it is also argued in Section 3 of the full version that $\theta_{ij}, \Theta_{ij\ell} \in (0,\pi)$. Observe $\theta_{ij} = \theta_{ji}$, $\Theta_{ijk} = \Theta_{kji}$, and $\Theta_{ij\ell}$ is the spherical angle, at vertex v_j, of the spherical triangle with vertices $\{v_i, v_j, v_\ell\}$; the cosine of this angle is exactly the inner product of unit normals of the two planes containing $\{v_i, v_j, 0\}$ and $\{v_j, v_\ell, 0\}$ respectively. See Figure 2 for a schematic description of the notation.

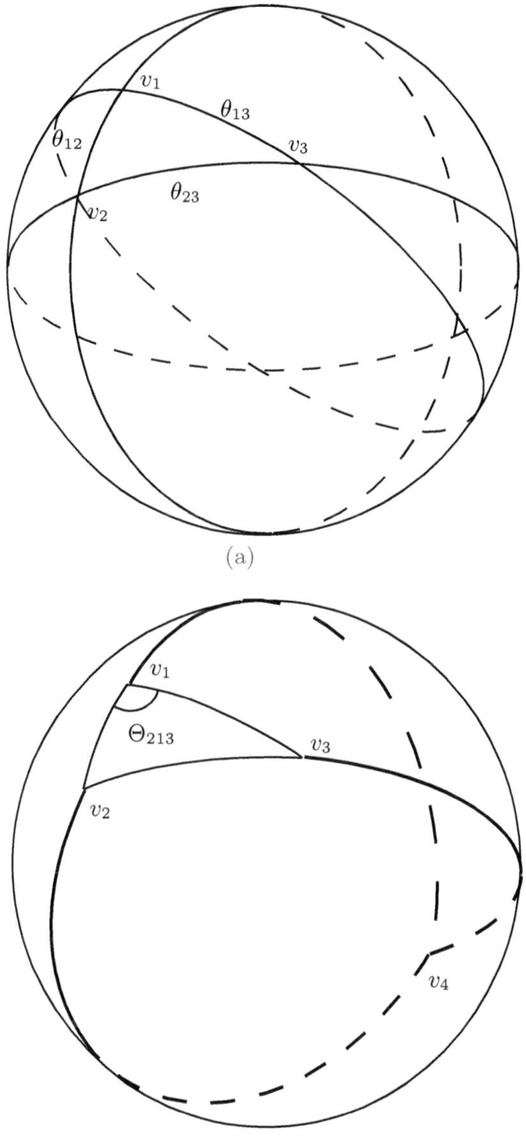

Figure 2: (a) Spherical triangle constructed with three great circles (b) Partition of the sphere into four spherical triangles.

In order to proceed we need to have a formula for the spherical moment z_4 in terms of the vertices $\{v_1,v_2,v_3\}$ of the spherical triangle T_4. In order to do so, assume that $\det(v_1,v_2,v_3) > 0$. Then

$$z_4 = \frac{1}{2}\left(\theta_{12}\frac{v_1\times v_2}{\|v_1\times v_2\|_2} + \theta_{23}\frac{v_2\times v_3}{\|v_2\times v_3\|_2} + \theta_{31}\frac{v_3\times v_1}{\|v_3\times v_1\|_2}\right) \tag{13}$$

Identity (13) was proved by Minchin in 1877; see [30, p. 259]. We also found identity (13) in [9], which is a military publication that is not publicly available (it isn't classified: we purchased access to it). Since both references for (13) are hard to find, we include a brief derivation of it in Proposition 3.2 of the full version, using the Cauchy projection formula (see [25, p. 25]).

Using (13) and geometric arguments, Lemma 3.5 of the full version shows that the vertex v_4 is determined by the vertices $\{v_1, v_2, v_3\}$ as follows; an analogous formula expresses each vertex of the partition in terms of the other three vertices.

$$v_4 = -\frac{1}{\sqrt{\lambda}}\left(\frac{\sin\theta_{23}}{\theta_{23}}v_1 + \frac{\sin\theta_{13}}{\theta_{13}}v_2 + \frac{\sin\theta_{12}}{\theta_{12}}v_3\right),$$

where

$$\begin{aligned}\lambda &= \left\|\frac{\sin\theta_{23}}{\theta_{23}}v_1 + \frac{\sin\theta_{13}}{\theta_{13}}v_2 + \frac{\sin\theta_{12}}{\theta_{12}}v_3\right\|_2^2 = \frac{\sin^2\theta_{23}}{\theta_{23}^2} \\ &+ \frac{\sin^2\theta_{13}}{\theta_{13}^2} + \frac{\sin^2\theta_{12}}{\theta_{12}^2} + 2\frac{\sin\theta_{23}\sin\theta_{13}}{\theta_{23}\theta_{13}}\cos\theta_{12} \\ &+ 2\frac{\sin\theta_{23}\sin\theta_{12}}{\theta_{23}\theta_{12}}\cos\theta_{13} + 2\frac{\sin\theta_{12}\sin\theta_{13}}{\theta_{12}\theta_{13}}\cos\theta_{23}. \quad (14)\end{aligned}$$

In Proposition 3.7 of the full version we derive the following restriction on products of opposite edges.

$$\frac{\sin\theta_{12}\sin\theta_{34}}{\theta_{12}\theta_{34}} = \frac{\sin\theta_{13}\sin\theta_{24}}{\theta_{13}\theta_{24}} = \frac{\sin\theta_{14}\sin\theta_{23}}{\theta_{14}\theta_{23}}.$$

Also, in Lemma 3.9 of the full version we obtain the following expression for the objective function at the partition $P = \{T_i\}_{i=1}^4$ as the sum of the squares of the angles between the vertices.

$$\begin{aligned}F(P) &= \|z_1\|_2^2 + \|z_2\|_2^2 + \|z_3\|_2^2 + \|z_4\|_2^2 \\ &= \theta_{12}^2 + \theta_{13}^2 + \theta_{14}^2 + \theta_{23}^2 + \theta_{24}^2 + \theta_{34}^2.\end{aligned} \quad (15)$$

Define

$$\gamma = \frac{\sin\theta_{23}}{\theta_{23}}\cos\theta_{12} + \frac{\sin\theta_{13}}{\theta_{13}} + \frac{\sin\theta_{12}}{\theta_{12}}\cos\theta_{23}. \quad (16)$$

Lemma 3.8 in the full vesrion gives the following useful restriction on a single spherical triangle appearing in the partition $\{T_1, T_2, T_3, T_4\}$.

$$\begin{aligned}&\cos\left(\sqrt{\lambda - \gamma^2}\frac{\theta_{23}\theta_{12}}{\sin\theta_{23}\sin\theta_{12}}\right) \\ &= \cos\left(\sqrt{\theta_{12}^2 + \theta_{23}^2 + 2\theta_{12}\theta_{23}\cos\Theta_{123}}\right) = -\frac{\gamma}{\sqrt{\lambda}},\end{aligned} \quad (17)$$

where λ is given in (14).

Observe that (17) is a restriction involving data from only one triangle T_4, as we see by the definitions of γ and λ. Moreover, by symmetry, every cyclic permutation of $\{\theta_{12}, \theta_{23}, \theta_{13}\}$ must also satisfy (17). And, every triangle of P must satisfy (17), with the indices of the θ_{ij} substituted appropriately. To understand the ramifications of (17) assume that $\theta_{12} = \theta_{23} = \theta_{13} =: \theta$. Then (17) simplifies to

$$\begin{aligned}&\cos\left(\sqrt{2(2\cos\theta + 1)(1 - \cos\theta)}\frac{\theta}{\sin\theta}\right) \\ &\qquad = -\frac{1}{\sqrt{3}}\sqrt{2\cos\theta + 1}. \quad (18)\end{aligned}$$

The only $\theta \in (0, 2\pi/3)$ satisfying this equation are $\theta = \arccos(-1/3) \approx 1.9106$, and $\theta \approx 1.5379684120790425$. The first solution corresponds to the partition whose vertices are those of a regular simplex inscribed in the sphere, and the second intuitively corresponds to a critical point "between" the regular partition and the propeller partition (note that $\theta = 2\pi/3$ implies $\det(v_1, v_2, v_3) = 0$, and $\theta > 2\pi/3$ cannot be achieved by a spherical triangle). The above special values of θ will play an important role in the ensuing computations.

As explained in the discussion following Lemma 3.9 of the full version, a combination of (15) and (17) can be used to express the value of our objective function at the maximizing partition P in terms of the data from a single spherical triangle in P. Specifically, we have

$$\begin{aligned}F(P) &= 3\left(\theta_{12}^2 + \theta_{23}^2 + \theta_{13}^2\right) + 2\cos(\Theta_{213})\theta_{12}\theta_{13} \\ &\quad + 2\cos(\Theta_{123})\theta_{12}\theta_{23} + 2\cos(\Theta_{231})\theta_{23}\theta_{13}.\end{aligned} \quad (19)$$

In particular, it follows that the right hand side of (19) must be the same for each set of data for all four triangles of P.

Up to now we only discussed identities that the extremal partition P must satisfy. In order to proceed we need to prove some a priori estimates on the various parameters in question. First, let $M = \max\{\theta_{12}, \theta_{13}, \theta_{23}\}$. It follows from (19) that $F(P) \leqslant 14M^2$ (using the fact that at least one Θ_{ijk} must be greater than $\frac{\pi}{3}$). Our contrapositive assumption (5) combined with (8) implies that $F(P) > \frac{9\pi^2}{4}$, so we deduce that all the triangles in P must have an edge of length greater than $\frac{3\pi}{2\sqrt{14}} > \frac{5}{4}$. Additional arguments (that are significantly more involved technically) imply that for all distinct $i, j, \ell \in \{1, 2, 3, 4\}$ we have $\theta_{ij} \leqslant \pi - \frac{1}{2}$ (Lemma 3.12 of the full version) and $\theta_{ij}, \sin\Theta_{ij\ell} > \frac{1}{10}$ (Lemma 3.16 of the full version). In Lemma 4.1 of the full version we prove that $(\theta_{12}, \theta_{13}, \theta_{23})$ must be outside the ℓ_2 ball of radius $\frac{1}{100}$ centered at (θ, θ, θ) for $\theta = \arccos\left(-\frac{1}{3}\right)$ and $\theta = 1.53796841207904$. This excludes from our search space balls centered at the two solutions of (18) that were discussed above. In Lemma 4.2 of the full version we show that, up to a relabeling of the spherical triangles T_1, T_2, T_3, T_4, we may assume that $\sqrt{\lambda} > \frac{9}{50}$.

It turns out that the above estimates suffice in order to conclude the proof of Theorem 1.1 via a search over a sufficiently fine net. To explain this endgame, note that by the spherical law of cosines we have

$$\cos\theta_{13} = \cos\theta_{12}\cos\theta_{23} + \sin\theta_{12}\sin\theta_{23}\cos\Theta_{123}.$$

It therefore follows from (14), (17), (16) that if we define $h, \lambda, \gamma : [0, \pi]^3 \to \mathbb{R}$ by

$$\begin{aligned}\lambda(x, y, z) &= \frac{\sin^2 x}{x} + \frac{\sin^2 y}{y} + \frac{\sin^2 z}{z} + 2\frac{\sin x\sin y}{xy}\cos z \\ &\quad + 2\frac{\sin x\sin z}{xz}\cos y + 2\frac{\sin y\sin z}{yz}\cos x,\end{aligned}$$

$$\gamma(x, y, z) = \frac{\sin z}{z}\cos x + \frac{\sin y}{y} + \frac{\sin x}{x}\cos z,$$

$$\begin{aligned}h(x, y, z) &= \sqrt{\lambda(x, y, z)} \\ &\cdot\cos\left(\sqrt{x^2 + z^2 + 2xz\frac{\cos y - \cos x\cos z}{\sin x\sin z}}\right) + \gamma(x, y, z),\end{aligned}$$

then $h(\theta_{12}, \theta_{13}, \theta_{23}) = 0$. This identity must hold for all cyclic permutations of the indices $\{1, 2, 3\}$, so we also have the two identities $h(\theta_{13}, \theta_{23}, \theta_{12}) = h(\theta_{23}, \theta_{12}, \theta_{13}) = 0$. It follows that if we define $H = (H_1, H_2, H_3) : [0, \pi]^3 \to \mathbb{R}^3$

by $H(x,y,z) = (h(y,z,x), h(x,y,z), h(z,x,y))$ then at the extremal partition P we have $H(\theta_{12}, \theta_{13}, \theta_{23}) = 0$.

Our strategy is therefore as follows. At every point q in the search space given by the constraints described above (specifically, see the system of equations (67) in the full version, excluding also the two balls described in Lemma 4.1 of the full version), we will show that either $H(q) \neq 0$ or $F_0(q) < 9\pi^2/4$, where F_0 is given by the right hand side of (19) (with the understanding that one expresses the quantities $\cos\Theta_{123}, \cos\Theta_{213}, \cos\Theta_{231}$ in terms of $\theta_{12}, \theta_{23}, \theta_{13}$ using the spherical law of cosines, so that F_0 is a function of $\theta_{12}, \theta_{23}, \theta_{13}$). Due to the above discussion, such an assertion will complete the proof of Theorem 1.1. Moreover, it turns out that this assertion holds "with room to spare", making a computer-assisted verification feasible.

To this end, we need to have estimates on the modulus of continuity of H and F_0. Such estimates are complicated but can be proved using elementary considerations; see Lemma 4.3 of the full version and the discussion immediately following it. Consequently, if we are given a point q in our restricted search space and $\tau \in (0,1)$ for which either $|H(q)| > \tau$ or $F_0(q) < 9\pi^2/4 - \tau$, then it would follow that for some $r > 0$ that depends on τ via our modulus of continuity estimates, in the entire ball of radius r centered at q either $H \neq 0$ or $F_0 < 9\pi^2/4$.

From this procedure we achieve a process by which we can iteratively remove from our search space macroscopically large regions of controlled size in which we are guaranteed that a counterexample to the Propeller Conjecture cannot exist. Our program proceeds to remove such balls until it eventually exhausts the entire search space, thus arriving at the conclusion that there is no counterexample to the Propeller Conjecture.

In order to make such a procedure rigorous, we carefully account for all possible rounding errors. We do this quite conservatively, i.e., while significantly overestimating the magnitude of all possible errors, as explained in detail in Section 4.1 of the full version. Note that our computer-assisted proof does not compute any computationally complicated expressions such as, say, definite integrals or implicitly defined functions: it only checks inequalities between expressions involving elementary combinations of trigonometric functions and square roots.

In summary, the validity of the Propeller Conjecture in $\mathbb{R}^3$ has mainly conceptual implications, and what remains open seems to be of a more technical nature: to perhaps find a clever transformation, e.g., as in Ball's cube slicing theorem [3], that allows one to prove the theorem analytically rather than resorting to a transversal of a net in a region where the desired inequality is actually quite weak. At present, we have a clean geometric argument which addresses directly the region where the Propeller Conjecture is most subtle, and in the remainder of the search space we do something rather crude. This has two conceptual consequences: the Propeller Conjecture as a nonintuitive link between complexity theory and geometry is correct, and moreover one has a geometric/analytic proof of this conjecture in a region where it is tightest. Nevertheless, we are lacking a technical idea that allows us to address the remaining region in a way that does not resort to "brute force". It remains a challenge to find such an idea, with the hope that it will pave the way to a proof of the Propeller Conjecture in all dimensions.

3. ACKNOWLEDGMENTS

S. H. and A. J. were supported by NSF grant CCF-0832795 and NSF Graduate Research Fellowship DGE-0813964. And A. N. was supported by NSF grant CCF-0832795, BSF grant 2006009, and the Packard Foundation. Part of this work was carried out when S. H. and A. N. were visiting the Quantitative Geometry program at MSRI.

4. REFERENCES

[1] K. Appel and W. Haken. Every planar map is four colorable. I. Discharging. *Illinois J. Math.*, 21(3):429–490, 1977.

[2] K. Appel, W. Haken, and J. Koch. Every planar map is four colorable. II. Reducibility. *Illinois J. Math.*, 21(3):491–567, 1977.

[3] K. Ball. Cube slicing in $\mathbf{R}^n$. *Proc. Amer. Math. Soc.*, 97(3):465–473, 1986.

[4] K. Ball. Mahler's conjecture and wavelets. *Discrete Comput. Geom.*, 13(3-4):271–277, 1995.

[5] F. Barthe and A. Koldobsky. Extremal slabs in the cube and the Laplace transform. *Adv. Math.*, 174(1):89–114, 2003.

[6] F. Barthe and A. Naor. Hyperplane projections of the unit ball of l_p^n. *Discrete Comput. Geom.*, 27(2):215–226, 2002.

[7] C. Borell. Geometric bounds on the Ornstein-Uhlenbeck velocity process. *Z. Wahrsch. Verw. Gebiete*, 70(1):1–13, 1985.

[8] M. Braverman, K. Makarychev, Y. Makarychev, and A. Naor. The Grothendieck constant is strictly smaller than Krivine's bound. An extended abstract will appear in 52nd Annual IEEE Symposium on Foundations of Computer Science. Preprint available at `http://arxiv.org/abs/1103.6161`, 2011.

[9] J. E. Brock. Centroid and inertia tensor of a spherical triangle. *National Technical Information Service, Naval Postgraduate School, Monterey, California*, 1974.

[10] D. Gabai, G. R. Meyerhoff, and N. Thurston. Homotopy hyperbolic 3-manifolds are hyperbolic. *Ann. of Math. (2)*, 157(2):335–431, 2003.

[11] D. Gabai, R. Meyerhoff, and P. Milley. Minimum volume cusped hyperbolic three-manifolds. *J. Amer. Math. Soc.*, 22(4):1157–1215, 2009.

[12] A. Grothendieck. Résumé de la théorie métrique des produits tensoriels topologiques. *Bol. Soc. Mat. São Paulo*, 8:1–79, 1953.

[13] U. Haagerup. The best constants in the Khintchine inequality. *Studia Math.*, 70(3):231–283 (1982), 1981.

[14] T. C. Hales. A proof of the Kepler conjecture. *Ann. of Math. (2)*, 162(3):1065–1185, 2005.

[15] R. R. Hall. On a conjecture of Littlewood. *Math. Proc. Cambridge Philos. Soc.*, 78(3):443–445, 1975.

[16] E. Hansen. *Global optimization using interval analysis*, volume 165 of *Monographs and Textbooks in Pure and Applied Mathematics*. Marcel Dekker Inc., New York, 1992.

[17] J. Hass and R. Schlafly. Double bubbles minimize. *Ann. of Math. (2)*, 151(2):459–515, 2000.

[18] D. Hensley. Slicing the cube in $\mathbf{R}^n$ and probability (bounds for the measure of a central cube slice in $\mathbf{R}^n$

by probability methods). *Proc. Amer. Math. Soc.*, 73(1):95–100, 1979.

[19] S. Khot. On the power of unique 2-prover 1-round games. In *Proceedings of the Thirty-Fourth Annual ACM Symposium on Theory of Computing*, pages 767–775 (electronic), New York, 2002. ACM.

[20] S. Khot. On the unique games conjecture (invited survey). In *Proceedings of the 25th Annual IEEE Conference on Computational Complexity*, pages 99–121, 2010.

[21] S. Khot, G. Kindler, E. Mossel, and R. O'Donnell. Optimal inapproximability results for MAX-CUT and other 2-variable CSPs? *SIAM J. Comput.*, 37(1):319–357 (electronic), 2007.

[22] S. Khot and A. Naor. Approximate kernel clustering. In *49th Annual IEEE Symposium on Foundations of Computer Science*, pages 561–570, 2008.

[23] S. Khot and A. Naor. Sharp kernel clustering algorithms and their associated grothendieck inequalities. In *Proceedings of the Twenty-First Annual ACM-SIAM Symposium on Discrete Algorithms*, pages 664–683, 2010.

[24] S. Khot and A. Naor. Grothendieck-type inequalities in combinatorial optimization. To appear in *Comm. Pure Appl. Math.*, preprint available at `http://arxiv.org/abs/1108.2464`, 2011.

[25] A. Koldobsky. *Fourier analysis in convex geometry*, volume 116 of *Mathematical Surveys and Monographs*. American Mathematical Society, Providence, RI, 2005.

[26] H. König. On an extremal problem originating in questions of unconditional convergence. In *Recent progress in multivariate approximation (Witten-Bommerholz, 2000)*, volume 137 of *Internat. Ser. Numer. Math.*, pages 185–192. Birkhäuser, Basel, 2001.

[27] H. König and A. Koldobsky. Volumes of low-dimensional slabs and sections in the cube. To appear in Advances of Appl. Math., 2011.

[28] J.-L. Krivine. Sur la constante de Grothendieck. *C. R. Acad. Sci. Paris Sér. A-B*, 284(8):A445–A446, 1977.

[29] R. Latała and K. Oleszkiewicz. On the best constant in the Khinchin-Kahane inequality. *Studia Math.*, 109(1):101–104, 1994.

[30] G. M. Minchin. *A treatise on statics, containing some of the fundamental propositions in electrostatics.* London, Longmans, Green & Co. 1877.

[31] E. Mossel, R. O'Donnell, and K. Oleszkiewicz. Noise stability of functions with low influences: Invariance and optimality. In *46th Annual Symposium on Foundations of Computer Science*, pages 21–30. IEEE Computer Society, 2005.

[32] F. L. Nazarov and A. N. Podkorytov. Ball, Haagerup, and distribution functions. In *Complex analysis, operators, and related topics*, volume 113 of *Oper. Theory Adv. Appl.*, pages 247–267. Birkhäuser, Basel, 2000.

[33] K. Oleszkiewicz and A. Pełczyński. Polydisc slicing in $\mathbf{C}^n$. *Studia Math.*, 142(3):281–294, 2000.

[34] L. Song, A. Smola, A. Gretton, and K. A. Borgwardt. A dependence maximization view of clustering. In *Proceedings of the 24th International Conference on Machine Learning*, pages 815 – 822, 2007.

[35] S. J. Szarek. On the best constants in the Khinchin inequality. *Studia Math.*, 58(2):197–208, 1976.

[36] B. Tomaszewski. A simple and elementary proof of the Kchintchine inequality with the best constant. *Bull. Sci. Math. (2)*, 111(1):103–109, 1987.

[37] U. Zwick. Computer assisted proof of optimal approximability results. In *Proceedings of the Thirteenth Annual ACM-SIAM Symposium on Discrete Algorithms*, pages 496–505, 2002.

$2^{\log^{1-\varepsilon} n}$ Hardness for the Closest Vector Problem with Preprocessing

Subhash A. Khot
New York University
New York, NY, USA.
khot@cims.nyu.edu

Preyas Popat
New York University
New York, NY, USA.
popat@cs.nyu.edu

Nisheeth K. Vishnoi
Microsoft Research
Bangalore, India
nisheeth.vishnoi@gmail.com

ABSTRACT

We prove that for an arbitrarily small constant $\varepsilon > 0$, assuming NP$\not\subseteq$DTIME($2^{\log^{O(1/\varepsilon)} n}$), the preprocessing versions of the closest vector problem and the nearest codeword problem are hard to approximate within a factor better than $2^{\log^{1-\varepsilon} n}$. This improves upon the previous hardness factor of $(\log n)^\delta$ for some $\delta > 0$ due to [AKKV05].

Categories and Subject Descriptors

F.2 [**Analysis Of Algorithms And Problem Complexity**]: Nonnumerical Algorithms and Problems

General Terms

Theory

Keywords

Lattices, Closest Vector Problem, Nearest Codeword Problem, Hardness of Approximation, PCP

1. INTRODUCTION

Given an integer lattice B and a target vector t in $\mathbb{Z}^m$, the CLOSEST VECTOR PROBLEM (CVP) asks for the vector in B nearest to t under the l_p norm. All $p \geq 1$ are interesting although, $p = 2$ case has received the most attention. An integer lattice is a set of vectors $\{\sum_{i=1}^n \alpha_i b_i \mid \alpha_i \in \mathbb{Z}\}$, where $b_1, b_2, \ldots, b_n \in \mathbb{Z}^m$ is a set of linearly independent vectors, called the *basis* of the lattice. An important variation of CVP is the pre-processing version of the problem where the lattice B is known in advance and the algorithm is allowed arbitrary pre-processing on B before the input t is revealed. This is known as the CLOSEST VECTOR PROBLEM WITH PRE-PROCESSING (CVPP). A related problem is the NEAREST CODEWORD PROBLEM (NCP) where the input is a generator matrix C of a linear code over $\mathbb{F}_2$ and a target vector t. The goal is to find the codeword nearest to t in Hamming distance. Again, if C is known in advance and arbitrary pre-computation is allowed on it, the problem is known as the NEAREST CODEWORD PROBLEM WITH PRE-PROCESSING (NCPP).

Pre-processing problems arise in cryptography and coding theory where, typically, a publicly known lattice (or a linear error-correcting code) is being used to transmit messages across a faulty channel. The decrypting or decoding of the received word is equivalent to solving an instance of CVP for the lattice being used in the protocol. The basis of the lattice being known beforehand, it becomes imperative to understand if the performance of the decoding algorithm can be improved, or if the security of the cryptographic protocol can be compromised (see [FM04, Reg04] for more details).

Potentially, this pre-computated information could make CVPP easier than CVP. Indeed, using the Korkine-Zolotarev basis, Lagarias *et al.* [LLS90] constructed an $O(n^{1.5})$ factor approximation algorithm for CVPP, which is significantly better than the best known and almost-exponential $2^{O(n \log\log n/\log n)}$ approximation factor known for CVP, see [MV10, Sch87]. This $n^{1.5}$ factor was improved to n by Regev [Reg04], and subsequently to $O(\sqrt{n/\log n})$ by Aharonov and Regev [AR05].

As for the inapproximability of CVP, it was proved by Dinur *et al.* [DKRS03] that it is NP-hard to approximate to a factor within $n^{c/\log\log n}$ for some constant $c > 0$. This improved an earlier result of [ABSS97] showing that it is quasi-NP hard to approximate to a factor within $2^{\log^{1-\varepsilon} n}$ for any constant $\varepsilon > 0$. Obtaining inapproximability results for CVPP has been a more challenging task: Feige and Micciancio [FM04] proved a $5/3 - \varepsilon$ factor NP-hardness for NCPP for any constant $\varepsilon > 0$. This was improved to $3 - \varepsilon$ by Regev [Reg04]. These authors observed that a factor C hardness for NCPP implies a factor $C^{1/p}$ hardness for CVPP under the ℓ_p norm for any $1 \leq p < \infty$.

Also, hardness results in the ℓ_∞ case can be obtained by using the norm-embedding technique due to Regev and Rosen [RR06].

The inapproximability results were improved in [AKKV05] who proved a factor C NP-hardness for CVPP and NCPP for any constant C. [AKKV05] showed how their result can be extended to a hardness of $(\log n)^\delta$ for some $\delta > 0$ under the assumption that NP $\not\subseteq$ DTIME($2^{poly(\log n)}$). They also give another reduction which achieves a hardness factor of $(\log n)^{1-\varepsilon}$ for NCPP for any $\varepsilon > 0$. This latter reduction is

STOC'12, May 19–22, 2012, New York, New York, USA.

under a certain unproved hypothesis about a pre-processing version of the PCP Theorem. [1]

1.1 Main Result and Overview

The following is the main theorem of this paper.

THEOREM 1.1 (MAIN THEOREM). *Unless* $NP \subseteq DTIME(2^{\log^{O(1/\varepsilon)} n})$, NCPP *and* CVPP *are hard to approximate to a factor within* $2^{\log^{1-\varepsilon} n}$ *for an arbitrarily small constant* $\varepsilon > 0$.

This improves on the previous hardness factor of $(\log n)^\delta$ for some $\delta > 0$ due to [AKKV05] and essentially matches the almost polynomial factor inapproximability of Dinur *et al.* [DKRS03] for CVP. We emphasize that unlike the case of CVP where the best approximation algorithm achieves a factor of $2^{n \log\log n/\log n}$, the best approximation algorithm for CVPP achieves an approximation factor of $O(\sqrt{n/\log n})$.

Overview of the proof.

We will show a hardness factor of $2^{\log^{1-\varepsilon} n}$ for the MINIMUM WEIGHT SOLUTION PROBLEM WITH PRE-PROCESSING (MWSPP). The input to this problem consists of a set of *fixed* linear forms described by $B_f \in \mathbb{F}_2^{l \times N}$, a set of *variable* linear forms $B_v \in \mathbb{F}_2^{l' \times N}$ and a target vector $t \in \mathbb{F}_2^l$. The goal is to find a solution $x \in \mathbb{F}_2^N$ to the system $B_f x = t$, which minimizes the Hamming weight of the vector $B_v x$. We allow arbitrary pre-processing on all parts of the input except the vector t. It is easy to check that MWSPP is a reformulation of NCPP. Henceforth, we focus on the MWSPP problem. See Section 3 for preliminaries and definitions and the equivalence of MWSPP with NCPP.

Our reduction builds on the second reduction of [AKKV05] to MWSPP. The authors in [AKKV05] make a certain hypothesis about the pre-processing version of the PCP Theorem. This hypothesis leads to the hardness of approximation of a pre-processing version of the LABEL COVER problem. Recall that an instance of LABEL COVER is given by a bipartite graph $G = (V, W, E, [R], [S])$ and for each edge $e = (v, w) \in V \times W$, a function $\pi_e : [R] \mapsto [S]$. A labeling to the graph consists of an assignment $A : V \mapsto [R]$, $W \mapsto [S]$. An edge $e = (v, w)$ is said to be satisfied by an assignment A if $\pi_e(A(v)) = A(w)$. The value of an instance is the maximum fraction of edges that can be satisfied by any labeling.

It is a consequence of the PCP Theorem [AS98, ALM+98] and Raz's Parallel Repetition Theorem [Raz98] that for every constant R, given an instance of LABEL COVER it is NP-hard to distinguish whether the value of the instance is 1 or at most $R^{-\gamma}$ for some absolute constant $\gamma > 0$. The authors in [AKKV05] show that a similar hardness holds for the LCPP problem under their hypothesis. In the LCPP problem, the label set $[R]$ for each vertex $v \in V$ comes with a partition, and an *allowable set* from the partition. The vertices in V are required to be assigned labels from their respective allowable sets. Pre-processing is allowed on all parts of the LCPP instance except for (the choice of) the allowable set for each vertex $v \in V$. It will be important for the reduction that the label set is equipped with a partition which admits arbitrary pre-processing and the allowable set of labels just chooses one set from the partition. In other words, it would not be useful to define the LCPP problem where the allowable set can be any arbitrary subset of the labels.

The reduction of [AKKV05] from LCPP to MWSPP uses constructions of LABEL COVER with an additional property called *smoothness*. An instance of LCPP is called δ-smooth if any two labels $i \neq i'$ of $v \in V$ map to different labels of $w \in W$ with probability at least $1 - \delta$ over the choice of neighbors w of v. The smoothness property was introduced in [Kho02] and has been used for several hardness of approximation reductions [FGRW09, GRSW10, KS11]. The hardness factor achieved by the the reduction from LCPP to MWSPP is bounded by $1/\delta$ and $1/s$ where δ is the smoothness parameter and s is the soundness of the LCPP instance. The reduction of [AKKV05] fails to give a hardness factor better than $(\log n)^{1-\varepsilon}$ for MWSPP (even assuming their hypothesis) because they use constructions of LABEL COVER which require size $n^{\Omega(1/\delta)}$ to ensure δ-smoothness. To get a better hardness factor using this reduction, we require instances of LCPP with *very good* smoothness and soundness simultaneously (relative to the size of the instance).

Our main technical contribution is to construct instances of HYPER-GRAPH LABEL COVER WITH PRE-PROCESSING (HLCPP) with *very good* soundness and smoothness. We achieve this using the low degree test [AS03, RS97], which is guaranteed to work even for very small success probability, and combine it with the sum check protocol [LFKN92], which is used to reduce the number of queries. The HLCPP problem we consider is a labeling problem similar to LCPP which differs from the latter as follows.

- The vertex set is multi-layered.
- The constraints are given by hyper-edges rather than edges. A hyper-edge contains several edges and the constraint associated with a hyper-edge is a boolean AND of constraints associated to all its edges.
- The constraints associated to edges are not *many-to-one* (projection) constraints as in LCPP but the more general *many-to-many* constraints.

We give an outline of our reduction and the analysis below.

Our reduction and analysis.

We will start with an instance of $\mathbb{F}_q$-QUADRATIC CONSTRAINT SATISFACTION PROBLEM ($\mathbb{F}_q$-QCSP) for $q = 2^r$. The instance consists of k homogeneous degree 2 polynomial equations over $\mathbb{F}_q$ with n variables, where $k = \text{poly}(n)$. Each equation is of the form $p(z_1, \ldots, z_n) = v$, and further, depends on at most 3 variables. It can be shown that deciding if there is an assignment which satisfies all the equation is NP-hard (see Theorem 3.3), even when the l.h.s. of these equations (p's) are available for pre-processing. We denote the pre-processing version by $\mathbb{F}_q$-QCSPP. Our first step is to boost soundness, i.e., to reduce the fraction of satisfied equations by any assignment, while keeping the number of variables small. This is done by combining an instance of $\mathbb{F}_q$-QCSPP with an appropriate Reed-Muller code over $\mathbb{F}_q$. We will eventually set $q = n^{\log^{O(1/\varepsilon)} n}$. This allows us to construct an $\mathbb{F}_q$-QCSPP instance where it is hard to distinguish between perfectly satisfiable instances and those where any assignment satisfies at most k/q fraction of the polynomial equations. An important feature of this reduction is that

[1]The authors claim to have a proof, but do not include it in the paper.

the variable set remains the same, so the number of variables is n, number of equations is q and the soundness is k/q (which is essentailly same as $1/q$). This quantitative setting of parameters is crucial for our result as the number of variables becomes negligible compared to the number of equations, and the reciprocal of the soundness. The details of this reduction appear in Section 3.2.

Each equation can now depend on almost all of the n variables and the next task is to deal with this. This is done by reducing checking an assignment for such a system of polynomial equations to the task to constructing a PCP which makes $O(\log n)$ queries and has soundness $1/q^e$ for some small constant $e > 0$. This is achieved by combining the low degree test and the sum check protocol and is the technical heart of the PCP construction.

First, the variables are identified with $\{0,1\}^{\log n}$ and embedded as a subcube of $\mathbb{F}_q^m$ where $m \stackrel{\text{def}}{=} \log n$. With this mapping, any assignment can be thought of as a function from $\{0,1\}^m$ to $\mathbb{F}_q$ and can be encoded as a polynomial over $\mathbb{F}_q^m$ of degree at most m. In this setting, if the equation was $\sum_{i,j\in[n]} c(i,j)z_iz_j = v = \sum_{\alpha,\beta\in\{0,1\}^m} c(\alpha,\beta)z(\alpha)z(\beta)$; z, c can be thought of as polynomials of degree at most m and $2m$ respectively. The Arora-Sudan points-vs-lines low degree test can be employed to ensure that z corresponds to a small list of degree m polynomials (assignments). This test is able to list-decode an assignment with success probability as low as $1/q^e$ for some small constant $e > 0$.

Once an assignment for the variables can be decoded, the task of verifying the polynomial equations

$$\sum_{\alpha,\beta\in\{0,1\}^m} c(\alpha,\beta)z(\alpha)z(\beta) = c$$

is equivalent to performing a weighted sum check over the sub-cube $\{0,1\}^m$. We use the sum-check protocol due to [LFKN92] to verify that the decoded assignment satisfies the equations. It can be shown that the soundness of the combined low degree test and the sum check protocol is at most $1/q^f$ for a small constant $f > 0$.

The result is a PCP with $2m+2 = O(\log n)$ layers where the first $2m$ layers correspond to the sum check protocol while the last two layers correspond to the *lines* and the *points* table respectively. Only the values to be assigned to the first table by the prover will depend on the r.h.s. of the $\mathbb{F}_q$-QCSPP instance. Further, the use of low degree polynomials in encoding the assignments implicitly gives our PCP *smoothness* properties which are used in the final reduction. While the preliminaries of the low degree test and the sum check protocol appear in Sections 3.3 and 3.4 respectively, the PCP construction appears in Section 4.1.

This view of the PCP naturally leads us to constructing an HLCPP instance which is the starting point of the reduction to MWSPP and appears in Section 4.3. Finally, the reduction from HLCPP to MWSPP is similar to the reduction of [AKKV05] from LCPP to MWSPP. This appears in Section 4. For the reduction to work, we define a notion of smoothness for HLCPP which is similar to the one for LCPP and we also need that the hyper-edges of the graph satisfy a uniformity condition which is inherited from the PCP construction.

The main differences in our reduction compared to the reduction of [AKKV05] are the following:

- As mentioned earlier, the constraints in the HLCPP graph are many-to-many constraints rather than many-to-one constraints. However, the earlier reduction to MWSPP still goes through in a relatively straightforward manner.
- We manage to construct an instance of HLCPP where the smoothness and soundness are both at most $1/q^f$ for some absolute constant $f > 0$ and the size of the instance is $q^{O(m)}$. Here $m = \log n$ where n is the number of variables in the original $\mathbb{F}_q$-QCSPP instance. It is not clear that such constructions are possible if we stick to the LCPP problem. The hardness factor can be made essentially as large as $q^{1/m}$ and we set q to be very large compared to m to get a good hardness factor relative to the size of the instance. Specifically, we set $q = n^{\log^{O(1/\varepsilon)} n}$.

2. ORGANIZATION

In Section 3 we define the problems and review some basic results which will be useful in the reduction. In Section 4 we give an outline of the proof. In Section 4.1 we describe the construction of a low query PCP using the low degree test and sum check protocol, and prove that it has low soundness in Section 4.2. In Section 4.3 we describe how the said PCP can be thought of as an instance of HLCPP. The reduction from HLCPP to MWSPP is similar to [AKKV05] and is described in Section 4.4.

3. PRELIMINARIES

In this section we state the problems we will consider and state basic results which will be useful in the construction of our PCP and the reduction.

3.1 Problem Definitions and Basic Results

We will work with various versions of pre-processing problems. The following formal definition of a pre-processing problem is taken from [AKKV11].

Pre-processing problems.

Consider a problem Π where the input is split into two components (A, B) and the length of each component is polynomial in the size parameter n. In the pre-processing version, denoted by $\Pi\mathsf{P}$ (suffix of P to Π to emphasize the pre-processing), we consider subproblems where the first component A depends only on n and is called as the *fixed* input. An algorithm which *solves* $\Pi\mathsf{P}(A,\cdot)$ *with pre-processing* is a polynomial time algorithm that solves the instance $\Pi\mathsf{P}(A,\cdot)$ given a polynomial sized advice. The advice captures arbitrary computation or pre-processing on the fixed input A and polynomial amount of stored information. The pre-processing version $\Pi\mathsf{P}(A,\cdot)$ is called NP-hard if there is a polynomial time reduction from SAT to $\Pi\mathsf{P}(A,\cdot)$ such that the fixed input A depends only on the size of the SAT instance.

We next define the quadratic CSP problem and its preprocessing version that will be a starting point of our reduction.

DEFINITION 3.1. $\mathbb{F}_q$-QUADRATIC CSP ($\mathbb{F}_q$-QCSP). *A* $\mathbb{F}_q$-QCSP *instance* $Q \stackrel{\text{def}}{=} (\{p_j\}_{j=1}^m, \{c_j\}_{j=1}^m)$ *consists of a set of polynomial constraints over variables* $\{z_1, z_2, \ldots, z_n\}$. *Each equation is of the form*

$$p_j(z_1, z_2, \ldots, z_n) = c_j,$$

where p_j is a homogeneous polynomial of degree 2, and $c_j \in \mathbb{F}_q$. The goal is to find an assignment to the variables $\{z_1, z_2, \ldots, z_n\}$ each taking a value in $\mathbb{F}_q$ which satisfies as many constraints as possible. Let $OPT(Q)$ denote the maximum, over assignments to the variables of Q, of the fraction of equations satisfied.

DEFINITION 3.2. $\mathbb{F}_q$-QUADRATIC CSP WITH PRE-PROCESSING ($\mathbb{F}_q$-QCSPP). *Given a $\mathbb{F}_q$-QCSP instance*

$$Q \stackrel{\text{def}}{=} (\{p_j\}_{j=1}^m, \{c_j\}_{j=1}^m)$$

over variables $\{z_1, z_2, \ldots, z_n\}$ taking values in $\mathbb{F}_q$, the $\mathbb{F}_q$-QCSPP problem allows arbitrary pre-processing on the polynomials $\{p_j\}_{j=1}^m$ before the inputs $\{c_j\}_{j=1}^m$ are revealed.

The following theorem can be proved in a similar manner as Theorem 4.2 in [AKKV05]. We include a proof in Section A.1.

THEOREM 3.3. $\mathbb{F}_q$-QCSPP *is NP-complete for all $q = 2^r$.*

Next we define the problem that we prove is hard to approximate and show that it is equivalent to the nearest codeword problem with pre-processing.

DEFINITION 3.4. MINIMUM WEIGHT SOLUTION PROBLEM WITH PRE-PROCESSING (MWSPP). *The input to this problem consists of a set of* fixed *linear forms described by $B_f \in \mathbb{F}_2^{l \times N}$, a set of* variable *linear forms $B_v \in \mathbb{F}_2^{l' \times N}$ and a target vector $t \in \mathbb{F}_2^l$. The goal is to find a solution $x \in \mathbb{F}_2^N$ to the system $B_f x = t$, which minimizes the Hamming weight of the vector $B_v x$. We allow arbitrary pre-processing on all parts of the input except the vector t.*

DEFINITION 3.5. NEAREST CODEWORD PROBLEM WITH AND WITHOUT PRE-PROCESSING. *An instance of* NCP *is denoted by (C, t) where $C \in \mathbb{F}_2^{n \times k}$, $t \in \mathbb{F}_2^n$. The goal is to find a solution $x \in \mathbb{F}_2^k$ which minimizes the Hamming distance between Cx and t. In the pre-processing version,* NCPP, *we allow arbitrary pre-processing on all parts of the input except the vector t.*

We note that MWSP is actually same as the NCP problem in disguise, though we find it convenient to think of it as a separate problem. To see the equivalence with NCP, let x_0 be a fixed vector such that $B_f x_0 = t$, let $w = B_v x_0$ and consider the code $C \stackrel{\text{def}}{=} \{B_v x \mid x \text{ s.t. } B_f x = 0\}$. Then

$$\begin{aligned} \min_{x: B_f x = 0} \delta(w, B_v x) &= \min_{x: B_f(x+x_0) = t} \delta(B_v x_0, B_v x) \\ &= \min_{x: B_f x = t} wt(B_v x) \end{aligned}$$

Here $\delta(\cdot,\cdot)$ measures the Hamming distance and $wt(\cdot)$ denotes the Hamming weight of a string.

Finally we note that proving the hardness for NCPP implies the hardness for CVPP.

THEOREM 3.6. *[FM04] Let $1 \leq p < \infty$. If* NCPP *(or* MWSPP*) is hard to approximate to factor f then* CVPP, *under the l_p norm, is hard to approximate to factor $f^{1/p}$.*

3.2 Boosting Soundness through Codes

The following lemma shows how to boost soundness of the $\mathbb{F}_q$-QCSPP instance although it increases the number of variables per equation. The proof of this lemma employs Reed-Muller codes and appears in Section A.2.

LEMMA 3.7. *Let Q be an instance of $\mathbb{F}_q$-QCSPP over n variables and $k = poly(n)$ equations, for any $q = 2^r$. There is a polynomial time reduction which maps Q to an instance P of $\mathbb{F}_q$-QCSPP over the same set of variables and q equations such that:*

- *If $OPT(Q) = 1$ then $OPT(P) = 1$ and*
- *if $OPT(Q) < 1$ then $OPT(P) \leq k/q$.*

In our reduction q would be $n^{\log^{O(1/\varepsilon)} n}$ and, hence, $q \gg k$.

3.3 Low Degree Test

Now we move on to developing tools necessary for keeping the number of queries in our PCP small. The first step in this is the Low Degree Test. In this section we recall the basics, the test and state the Arora-Sudan theorem which will be used.

An affine line in $\mathbb{F}_q^m$ is parametrized by $(a, b) \in (\mathbb{F}_q^m \backslash \{0\}) \times \mathbb{F}_q^m$ such that $L_{a,b} \stackrel{\text{def}}{=} \{ax + b : x \in \mathbb{F}_q\}$. Sometimes, we will drop the subscript if it is clear from the context. In what follows, if it helps, one can think of $m \stackrel{\text{def}}{=} \log n$ and $d \stackrel{\text{def}}{=} m$ as will be the case in our reduction. For a polynomial $g : \mathbb{F}_q^m \mapsto \mathbb{F}_q$ of degree d and a line $L \stackrel{\text{def}}{=} L_{a,b}$, let $g|_L$ be the restriction of g defined as $g|_L(x) \stackrel{\text{def}}{=} g(ax+b)$ for $x \in \mathbb{F}_q$. For two polynomials g, h we denote $g \equiv h$ if they are identical.

DEFINITION 3.8. LOW DEGREE TEST. *The Low Degree Test takes as input the value table of a function $f : \mathbb{F}_q^m \mapsto \mathbb{F}_q$ and for every (affine) line L of $\mathbb{F}_q^m$, the coefficients of a degree d polynomial g_L.*

The goal is to check that f is a degree d polynomial. The intention is that g_L is the restriction of f to the line L.

The test proceeds as follows:

1. *Pick a random point $x \in \mathbb{F}_q^m$ and a random line L containing x.*
2. *Test that $g_L(x) = f(x)$.*

The following theorem can be inferred from Theorem 1 and Lemma 14 in [AS03].

THEOREM 3.9. SOUNDNESS OF LOW DEGREE TEST. *There are absolute constants $0 < c_1, c_2 < 1$ such that for $\delta \stackrel{\text{def}}{=} 1/q^{c_1}$, $l \stackrel{\text{def}}{=} q^{c_2}$, if $f : \mathbb{F}_q^m \mapsto \mathbb{F}_q$ passes the Low Degree Test (Definition 3.8) with probability p, then there are l degree d polynomials $f^1, f^2, \ldots, f^l$ such that :*

$$\Pr_{L,x}\left[g_L(x) = f(x) \ \&\ \exists\, j \in \{1, 2, \ldots, l\} : g_L \equiv f^j|_L\right] \geq p - \delta.$$

In words, whenever the low degree test accepts, except with probability δ, the test picks a line L such that g_L corresponds to the restriction of one of the polynomials $f^1, f^2, \ldots, f^l$ to L.

We assume here that $d \ll q$ (in our application, $d \leq O(\log q)$).

3.4 Sum Check Protocol

We will also need the sum check protocol for our PCP. We start with some definition, state the test and the main theorem establishing the soundness of it. Think of $M = 2m$ and, hence, $\mathbb{F}_q^M = \mathbb{F}_q^m \times \mathbb{F}_q^m$ in the discussion below. Also one can think of $d = 4m$. We first need a notion of partial sums of polynomials.

DEFINITION 3.10. PARTIAL SUMS. *Let $g : \mathbb{F}_q^M \mapsto \mathbb{F}_q$ be a degree d polynomial. For every $0 \le j \le M-1$ and every $a_1, a_2, \ldots, a_j \in \mathbb{F}_q$ we define the partial sum $p_{a_1,a_2,\ldots,a_j}$ as a polynomial from $\mathbb{F}_q \mapsto \mathbb{F}_q$ as follows:*

$$p_{a_1,a_2,\ldots,a_j}(z) \stackrel{\text{def}}{=}$$

$$\sum_{b_{j+2},\ldots,b_M \in \{0,1\}} g(a_1, a_2, \ldots, a_j, z, b_{j+2}, \ldots, b_M).$$

When $j = 0$ we denote the polynomial as $p_\emptyset$. When $j = M-1$, the summation is just $g(a_1, \ldots, a_{M-1}, z)$. Note that all the polynomials so defined are of degree at most d.

DEFINITION 3.11. SUM CHECK PROTOCOL. *The Sum Check Protocol takes as input a value table for a function $g : \mathbb{F}_q^M \mapsto \mathbb{F}_q$, a target sum $c \in \mathbb{F}_q$ and for every $0 \le j \le M-1$ and every $a_1, a_2, \ldots, a_j \in \mathbb{F}_q$, the coefficients of a degree d polynomial $p_{a_1,a_2,\ldots,a_j}$. The goal is to check whether $\sum_{z \in \{0,1\}^M} g(z) = c$. The intention is that g is a degree d polynomial and $p_{a_1,a_2,\ldots,a_j}$ correspond to partial sums of g as in Definition 3.10. The test proceeds by picking $x \stackrel{\text{def}}{=} (a_1, a_2, \ldots, a_M) \in \mathbb{F}_q^M$ uniformly at random and accepts if and only if all of the following tests pass.*

1. $p_\emptyset(0) + p_\emptyset(1) = c$.
2. *For all* $1 \le j \le M-1$,
$$p_{a_1,a_2,\ldots,a_{j-1}}(a_j) = p_{a_1,a_2,\ldots,a_j}(0) + p_{a_1,a_2,\ldots,a_j}(1).$$
3. $p_{a_1,a_2,\ldots,a_{M-1}}(a_M) = g(x)$.

The following theorem will be used in our reduction. The proof appears in Section A.3.

THEOREM 3.12. SOUNDNESS OF SUM CHECK PROTOCOL. *[LFKN92] Let $g^1, g^2, \ldots, g^l : \mathbb{F}_q^M \mapsto \mathbb{F}_q$ be degree d polynomials and $g : \mathbb{F}_q^M \mapsto \mathbb{F}_q$ an arbitrary function. Suppose for every $1 \le j \le l$, $\sum_{z \in \{0,1\}^M} g^j(z) \ne c$. For $x \in \mathbb{F}_q^M$, let $\mathcal{P}(x)$ be the event that the Sum Check Protocol (Definition 3.11) accepts on inputs g, c and $p_{a_1,a_2,\ldots,a_j}$. Here x is the choice of randomness in the Sum Check Protocol.*

Then

$$\Pr_{x \in \mathbb{F}_q^M}\left[\mathcal{P}(x) \ \& \ \exists\, j \in \{1, \ldots, l\} \ : \ g(x) = g^j(x)\right] \le Mdl/q.$$

In words, the probability that the Sum Check Protocol accepts when g is consistent with one of $g^1, g^2, \ldots, g^l$ is at most Mdl/q where $g^1, g^2, \ldots, g^l$ are degree d polynomials whose sum is not the required value.

4. THE REDUCTION

The following is the main theorem about the reduction and implies Theorem 1.1 via Theorem 3.6.

THEOREM 4.1. *Unless $NP \subseteq DTIME(2^{\log^{O(1/\varepsilon)} n})$, MWSPP is hard to approximate to factor $2^{\log^{1-\varepsilon} n}$ for an arbitrary small constant $\varepsilon > 0$.*

Towards the proof of this theorem, we will give a reduction from $\mathbb{F}_q$-QCSPP to MWSPP. The reduction proceeds in three steps:

- Reduction from $\mathbb{F}_q$-QCSPP to a PCP with low query complexity (Section 4.1).
- Reformulating the PCP as an HLCPP instance (Section 4.3).
- Reduction from HLCPP to MWSPP (Section 4.4).

Finally, we will complete the proof in Section 4.5 where the choice of parameters is made.

4.1 Smooth PCP with Low Query Complexity

Note that the $\mathbb{F}_q$-QCSPP instance given by Lemma 3.7 has almost all the variables appearing in every equation. For the reduction to MWSPP we require a PCP where every query depends on a few variables. We will also crucially need a *smoothness* property from the PCP similar to the one described for LCPP in Section 1.1. To this end, we use the Low Degree Test of [AS03] and the Sum Check Protocol of [LFKN92], similarly as in [KP06].

4.1.1 Describing the PCP

Let P be the instance of $\mathbb{F}_q$-QCSPP given by Lemma 3.7 over variables $\{z_1, \ldots, z_n\}$. Let $m \stackrel{\text{def}}{=} \log n$. Here we assume that n is a power of 2. We think of the variables of P as being embedded into $\{0,1\}^m$ within $\mathbb{F}_q^m$. Henceforth, we will refer to the variables by their corresponding points in $\{0,1\}^m$. Thus, an assignment $A : \{0,1\}^m \mapsto \mathbb{F}_q$ to the variables can be extended to a degree m polynomial $f : \mathbb{F}_q^m \mapsto \mathbb{F}_q$ such that f is consistent with A on $\{0,1\}^m$.

Let the equations be $E_1, \ldots, E_q$ where each equation is of the form

$$\begin{aligned} E_i &\equiv P_i(z_1, \ldots, z_n) = C_i \\ &\equiv \textstyle\sum_{s,t \in [n]} c_i(s,t) z_s z_t = C_i \\ &\equiv \textstyle\sum_{\alpha,\beta \in \{0,1\}^m} c_i(\alpha,\beta) z_\alpha z_\beta = C_i \end{aligned}$$

For an assignment A to $\{z_\alpha\}_{\alpha \in \{0,1\}^m}$, let f_A denote the degree m polynomial encoding A. Now, checking whether an equation $E_i \in P$ is satisfied by A amounts to checking

$$\sum_{\alpha,\beta \in \{0,1\}^m} c_i(\alpha,\beta) f_A(\alpha) f_A(\beta) = C_i.$$

Note that $c_i(\alpha,\beta)$ can be thought of as a degree $2m$ polynomial over $\mathbb{F}_q^{2m}$ and is a part of the pre-processing.

The PCP we will construct expects the following tables:

1. **Points Table:** The value of a function $f : \mathbb{F}_q^m \mapsto \mathbb{F}_q$ at every point in $\mathbb{F}_q^m$. The intention is that f is a degree m polynomial which encodes a satisfying assignment to P within $\{0,1\}^m$, i.e., for a satisfying assignment A, $f(\alpha) = f_A(\alpha)$ for all $\alpha \in \{0,1\}^m$. The size of this table is q^m.

2. **Lines Table:** The coefficients of a degree m polynomial g_L for every (affine) line L of $\mathbb{F}_q^m$. The intention is that g_L is the restriction of f on L. The size of this table is at most $q^{2m} \cdot (m+1)$.

3. **Partial Sums Table:** For every equation $E_i \in P$, every $0 \leq j \leq 2m-1$ and every $a_1, a_2, \ldots, a_j \in \mathbb{F}_q$, the coefficients of a degree $4m$ polynomial $p_{i,a_1,a_2,\ldots,a_j}$. The intention is that $p_{i,a_1,a_2,\ldots,a_j}$ correspond to partial sums of g_i (Definition 3.10) where

$$g_i(\alpha, \beta) \stackrel{\text{def}}{=} c_i(\alpha, \beta) f(\alpha) f(\beta)$$

where $\alpha \stackrel{\text{def}}{=} (a_1, \ldots, a_m)$ and $\beta \stackrel{\text{def}}{=} (a_{m+1}, \ldots, a_{2m})$. Note that g_i has degree at most $4m$ and the size of the j-th partial sum table is $q \cdot q^j \cdot (4m+1)$.

The PCP Test:
Pick equation $E_i \in P$ uniformly at random. Pick $\alpha \stackrel{\text{def}}{=} (a_1, a_2, \ldots, a_m) \in \mathbb{F}_q^m$, $\beta \stackrel{\text{def}}{=} (a_{m+1}, a_{m+2}, \ldots, a_{2m}) \in \mathbb{F}_q^m$ uniformly at random. Let L be the line passing through α and β. Read the following values from the corresponding tables:

- $f(\alpha), f(\beta) \in \mathbb{F}_q$ from the Points table.
- The polynomial g_L from the Lines table.
- The polynomials $p_{i,a_1,a_2,\ldots,a_j}$ from the Partial Sums table for every $0 \leq j \leq 2m-1$.

Acceptance Criteria for the Test:
Accept if and only if all of the following tests pass.

1. $g_L(\alpha) = f(\alpha)$ and $g_L(\beta) = f(\beta)$.
2. $p_{i,\emptyset}(0) + p_{i,\emptyset}(1) = C_i$.
3. For all $1 \leq j \leq 2m-1$,
$$p_{i,a_1,a_2,\ldots,a_{j-1}}(a_j) = p_{i,a_1,a_2,\ldots,a_j}(0) + p_{i,a_1,a_2,\ldots,a_j}(1).$$
4. $p_{i,a_1,a_2,\ldots,a_{2m-1}}(a_{2m}) = c_i(\alpha, \beta) f(\alpha) f(\beta)$.

Note that we allow arbitrary pre-processing on everything except $\{C_i\}_{i=1}^m$.

4.1.2 Completeness and Soundness of the PCP

The PCP we constructed has the following guarantee:

THEOREM 4.2. LOW DEGREE AND SUM CHECK. *Let P be a $\mathbb{F}_q$-QCSPP instance. Then*

1. *If $OPT(P) = 1$, then the PCP Test succeeds with probability 1.*
2. *If $OPT(P) \leq k/q$ and $k < q^c$ for a small enough c, then the test succeeds above with probability at most $1/q^e$ for some constant $e > 0$.*

The proof of the theorem follows from the following two lemmas.

LEMMA 4.3. COMPLETENESS. *If there exists an assignment A to $\{z_1, \ldots, z_n\}$ such that $OPT(P) = 1$, i.e., $E_1, \ldots, E_q$ are all satisfied, then there is an assignment to all the tables such that the test accepts with probability 1.*

PROOF. We let $f \stackrel{\text{def}}{=} f_A$, $g_L \stackrel{\text{def}}{=} f_A|_L$ for all L, and for all $i \in [q]$, $0 \leq j \leq 2m-1$, and $a_1, \ldots, a_j \in \mathbb{F}_q$,

$$p_{i,a_1,\ldots,a_j} \stackrel{\text{def}}{=} \sum_{b_{j+2},\ldots,b_{2m} \in \{0,1\}} h_i(a_1, \ldots, a_j, z, b_{j+2}, \ldots, b_{2m}),$$

where $h_i(x, y)$ is the polynomial of degree at most $4m$ representing $c_i(x, y) f_A(x) f_A(y)$. It is clear that the test succeeds with probability 1. □

LEMMA 4.4. SOUNDNESS. *There is an absolute constant $e > 0$ such that if $OPT(P) \leq k/q$ and $k < q^c$ for a small enough c, then the PCP described above has soundness at most $1/q^e$.*

The proof of Lemma 4.4 appears in the following section.

4.2 Soundness of the PCP

Here we give the proof of Lemma 4.4. The lemma is restated for convenience.

LEMMA 4.5. SOUNDNESS. *There is an absolute constant $e > 0$ such that if $OPT(P) \leq k/q$ and $k < q^c$ for a small enough c, then the PCP described above has soundness at most $1/q^e$.*

PROOF. We first observe that Step 1 of the protocol is equivalent to running a low degree test (Definition 3.8) on L and α with input tables g_L and f respectively. This is because the choice of β is independent of α and uniform in $\mathbb{F}_q^m$. Let $0 < c_1, c_2 < 1$ be the constants given by Theorem 3.9. Let $f^1, f^2, \ldots, f^l$ be the list of $l \stackrel{\text{def}}{=} q^{c_2}$ polynomials promised by Theorem 3.9.
The following events can happen on a run of the PCP:

1. The low degree test between L and α fails. That is, $g_L(\alpha) \neq f(\alpha)$. In this case, the PCP does not accept.
2. $g_L(\beta) \neq f(\beta)$. In this case, the PCP does not accept.
3. The low degree test accepts ($g_L(\alpha) = f(\alpha)$) but there is no $1 \leq i \leq l$ such that $g_L \equiv f^i|_L$. By theorem 3.9, this happens with probability at most $\delta \stackrel{\text{def}}{=} 1/q^{c_1}$.

If none of the events listed above occur, then we have that g_L is the restriction of f_j for some $1 \leq j \leq l$. Also, since Step 1 accepts, we must have $f(\alpha) = f^j(\alpha)$ and $f(\beta) = f^j(\beta)$.
Let E_i be an equation not satisfied by any f^j for $1 \leq j \leq l$. Note that Steps 2, 3 and 4 are equivalent to running the Sum Check Protocol (Definition 3.11) on $g_i : \mathbb{F}_q^{2m} \mapsto \mathbb{F}_q$ defined as $g_i(\alpha, \beta) \stackrel{\text{def}}{=} c_i(\alpha, \beta) f(\alpha) f(\beta)$. g_i has degree at most $4m$. Let $g_i^j(\alpha, \beta) \stackrel{\text{def}}{=} c_i(\alpha, \beta) f^j(\alpha) f^j(\beta)$. Finally, for $x \in \mathbb{F}_q^{2m}$, let $\mathcal{P}_i(x)$ be the event that the Sum Check Protocol accepts.
Applying Theorem 3.12,

$$\Pr_{x \in \mathbb{F}_q^{2m}} \left[\mathcal{P}_i(x) \ \& \ \exists\, j \in \{1, \ldots, l\} : g_i(x) = g_i^j(x) \right] \leq (2m) dl/q.$$

Thus, when none of the events in the list occur, the PCP accepts with probability at most $(2m) \cdot (4m) \cdot l/q$ conditioned on choosing E_i. Note that every f^j may satisfy at most k of the q equations.
Thus, the total probability that the PCP accepts is at most $\delta + (1 - lk/q) \cdot O(m^2 l/q)$ and it is easy to check that by our choice of parameters this is smaller than $1/q^e$ for some absolute constant $e > 0$. □

4.3 PCP as Hyper-graph Label Cover

In this section, we show how the PCP can be thought of as a graph labeling problem. The labeling problem we consider is similar to the well-known LABEL COVER problem except for the following differences:

- The graph is not bipartite but consists of several layers, with edges between consecutive layers. In addition, there are hyper-edges which consist of several edges. The goal is to find a labeling which satisfies the maximum fraction of hyper-edges, where the constraint corresponding to a hyper-edge is the logical AND of the constraint corresponding to each of its edges.
- The constraints corresponding to edges are not projection constraints as in the case of LABEL COVER, but the more general *many-to-many* constraints. For an edge $e = (u, v)$, a many-to-many constraint is described by an ordered partition of the label set of u and the label set of v such that the constraint is satisfied if and only if both u and v receive labels from matching partitions. Formally, let $e = (u, v)$ be an edge and $[R_u]$, $[R_v]$ be the label sets of vertices u and v. Then the many-to-many constraint is described by a pair of maps $\pi_e : [R_u] \mapsto [R_e]$, $\sigma_e : [R_v] \mapsto [R_e]$ where $[R_e]$ is a label set associated to e. A label l to u and a label l' to v is said to satisfy edge e if $\pi_e(l) = \sigma_e(l')$.

We now formally describe the HYPER-GRAPH LABEL COVER problem. While the term HYPER-GRAPH LABEL COVER can be potentially used for a more general class of problems, in this paper we restrict our attention to a very special class of graphs useful for our reduction.

DEFINITION 4.6. HYPER-GRAPH LABEL COVER PROBLEM.

An instance

$$G(V, E, \mathcal{E}, [R_0], [R_1], \ldots, [R_{2m+1}], \{\pi_e, \sigma_e\}_{e\in E}, \{\mathcal{S}_v, S_v\}_{v\in\mathcal{L}_0})$$

of HYPER-GRAPH LABEL COVER *consists of:*

- *A graph $G(V, E)$. The vertices are partitioned into $2m + 2$ disjoint layers, $V \stackrel{\text{def}}{=} \mathcal{L}_0 \cup \mathcal{L}_1 \cup \cdots \cup \mathcal{L}_{2m+1}$. The edges in E are always between a vertex in $\mathcal{L}_i$ and a vertex in $\mathcal{L}_{i+1}$ for some i.*
- *Label sets $[R_i]$ for vertices in layer $\mathcal{L}_i$. Furthermore, for every vertex $v \in \mathcal{L}_0$, there is a partition $\mathcal{S}_v$ of $[R_0]$ and an* **allowable set** *of labels $S_v \in \mathcal{S}_v$.*
- *A many-to-many constraint for every edge. Let $e = (u, v)$ be an edge where $u \in \mathcal{L}_i$, $v \in \mathcal{L}_{i+1}$. The instance contains projections $\pi_e : [R_i] \mapsto [R_e]$, $\sigma_e : [R_{i+1}] \mapsto [R_e]$. A labeling (l, l') to (u, v) is said to satisfy e if $\pi_e(l) = \sigma_e(l')$.*
- *A set of hyper-edges $\mathcal{E}$. Every hyper-edge consists of one vertex from the first $2m+1$ layers and two vertices from the last layer, such that there is an edge between any pair of vertices in adjacent layers. A labeling to the graph satisfies a hyper-edge if all the edges contained in it are satisfied.*

The goal is to find a labeling to the vertices which satisfies the maximum fraction of hyper-edges. Vertices in $\mathcal{L}_i$ are required to receive a label from $[R_i]$. Furthermore, vertices in $\mathcal{L}_0$ are required to receive labels from their **allowable set**.

We also define a pre-processing version of the HYPER-GRAPH LABEL COVER PROBLEM similar to the LCPP problem of [AKKV05].

DEFINITION 4.7. HYPER-GRAPH LABEL COVER PROBLEM WITH PRE-PROCESSING (HLCPP).
Given an instance

$$G(V, E, \mathcal{E}, [R_0], [R_1], \ldots, [R_{2m+1}], \{\pi_e, \sigma_e\}_{e\in E}, \{\mathcal{S}_v, S_v\}_{v\in\mathcal{L}_0})$$

of HYPER-GRAPH LABEL COVER, *the* HLCPP *problem allows arbitrary pre-processing on all parts of the input except the allowable sets $\{S_v\}_{v\in\mathcal{L}_0}$.*

We will need a notion of smoothness similar to the definition of SMOOTH LABEL COVER.

DEFINITION 4.8. SMOOTHNESS. *We say that an* HLCPP *instance*

$$G(V, E, \mathcal{E}, [R_0], [R_1], \ldots, [R_{2m+1}], \{\pi_e, \sigma_e\}_{e\in E}, \{\mathcal{S}_v, S_v\}_{v\in\mathcal{L}_0})$$

is δ-smooth if for every $0 \le i \le 2m$, $u \in \mathcal{L}_i$, $l \neq l' \in [R_i]$ we have

$$\Pr_{e=(u,v)\in E}[\pi_e(l) = \pi_e(l')] \le \delta.$$

Here $v \in \mathcal{L}_{i+1}$ and (π_e, σ_e) is the many-to-many constraint associated to e.

Lastly, we will need that the hyper-edges of the graph are regular in a certain sense.

DEFINITION 4.9. UNIFORMITY. *Let* $G(V, E, \mathcal{E}, [R_0], [R_1], \ldots, [R_{2m+1}], \{\pi_e, \sigma_e\}_{e\in E}, \{\mathcal{S}_v, S_v\}_{v\in\mathcal{L}_0})$ *be an* HLCPP *instance. We say that the instance is uniform if the following conditions are satisfied:*

1. *For every $0 \le i \le 2m+1$, every vertex in layer $\mathcal{L}_i$ has the same number of hyper-edges passing through it.*
2. *For every $0 \le i \le 2m$, the following two distributions are equivalent:*
   - *Select an edge between a vertex in layer $\mathcal{L}_i$ and a vertex in layer $\mathcal{L}_{i+1}$ uniformly at random.*
   - *Select a hyper-edge $\mathcal{H} \in \mathcal{E}$ uniformly at random and then select an edge from $\mathcal{H}$ between a vertex in layer $\mathcal{L}_i$ and a vertex in layer $\mathcal{L}_{i+1}$ uniformly at random. Recall that a hyper-edge contains exactly one edge between layers $\mathcal{L}_i$ and $\mathcal{L}_{i+1}$ for $0 \le i \le 2m-1$ and two edges between layers $\mathcal{L}_{2m}$ and $\mathcal{L}_{2m+1}$.*

We next briefly describe how the PCP described in Section 4.1 can be thought of as an HLCPP instance.

- **Layers $\mathcal{L}_{2m}$ and $\mathcal{L}_{2m+1}$:** These are the Lines table and the Points table respectively. There is a vertex L in $\mathcal{L}_{2m}$ corresponding to every line in $\mathbb{F}_q^m$. There is a label to L for every possible univariate degree m polynomial over $\mathbb{F}_q$. Hence, the number of vertices in $\mathcal{L}_{2m}$ is at most q^{2m} and the size of the label set for each vertex is $R_{2m} = q^{m+1}$. There is a vertex α in $\mathcal{L}_{2m+1}$ corresponding to every $\alpha \in \mathbb{F}_q^m$. There is a label a to α for every possible $a \in \mathbb{F}_q$. Hence, the size of the vertex set in $\mathcal{L}_{2m+1}$ is q^m and size of the label set is $R_{2m+1} = q$.

There is an edge between L and α if the point α belongs to the line L. The constraint between the two vertices corresponds to Step 1 of the PCP.

- **Layers $\mathcal{L}_0$ through $\mathcal{L}_{2m}$:** These are the Partial Sums table and the Lines table respectively. For $1 \le j \le 2m-1$, there is a vertex for every $(i, a_1, a_2, \ldots, a_j)$ in $\mathcal{L}_j$ for every equation $E_i \in P$ and every $a_1, a_2, \ldots, a_j \in \mathbb{F}_q$. There is a label to $(i, a_1, a_2, \ldots, a_j)$ for every possible univariate degree $4m$ polynomial over $\mathbb{F}_q$. For $j = 0$, there is a vertex $(i, \emptyset)$ corresponding to every equation $E_i \in P$. There is a label to $(i, \emptyset)$ for every univariate degree $4m$ polynomial over $\mathbb{F}_q$. Furthermore, there is a partition of the label set into q parts, indexed by $\mathbb{F}_q$ as follows:

  $P_a \stackrel{\text{def}}{=} \{$all polynomials p of degree at most $4m$ over $\mathbb{F}_q$ such that $p(0) + p(1) = a\}$

  The **allowable set** of labels for every vertex corresponds to the part that satisfies Step 2 of the PCP. Thus, for $0 \le j \le 2m-1$, the size of $\mathcal{L}_j$ is $q \cdot q^j$ while the size the label set is $R_0 = R_1 = \cdots = R_{2m-1} = q^{4m+1}$.

  For $1 \le j \le 2m-1$, there is an edge between a vertex $(i, a_1, \ldots, a_{j-1})$ in $\mathcal{L}_{j-1}$ and a vertex $(i', a'_1, \ldots, a'_j)$ in $\mathcal{L}_j$ if $i = i'$ and $a_k = a'_k$ for $1 \le k \le j-1$. The corresponding constraints are given by Step 3 of the PCP.

  There is an edge between vertex $(i, a_1, a_2, \ldots, a_{2m-1})$ in $\mathcal{L}_{2m-1}$ and vertex L in $\mathcal{L}_{2m}$ if there is an $a_m \in \mathbb{F}_q$ such that for $\alpha \stackrel{\text{def}}{=} (a_1, \ldots, a_m)$, $\beta \stackrel{\text{def}}{=} (a_{m+1}, \ldots, a_{2m})$, the line L passes through α and β. The corresponding constraints are given by Step 4 of the PCP. Note that Step 4 requires the values of the function at points α and β both of which lie on line L. Thus, a label to L specifies the values of f at α and β.

It can be checked that the constraints so defined are many-to-many constraints.[2] Note that we allow pre-processing on everything except the **allowable set** of labels for vertices in layer $\mathcal{L}_0$ as required.

It can be seen that the HLCPP instance so constructed is $4m/q$-smooth, since no two distinct degree $4m$ polynomials over $\mathbb{F}_q$ can agree on more than $4m/q$ fraction of points in $\mathbb{F}_q$.

We record this identification of the PCP with an HLCPP instance as the following theorem.

THEOREM 4.10. *There is a reduction from an $\mathbb{F}_q$-QCSPP instance P over n variables to an HLCPP instance $L = G(V, E, \mathcal{E}, [R_0], [R_1], \ldots, [R_{2m+1}], \{\pi_e, \sigma_e\}_{e \in E}, \{\mathcal{S}_v, S_v\}_{v \in \mathcal{L}_0})$ where $m = \log n$, such that*

1. *If $OPT(P) = 1$, then $OPT(L) = 1$.*
2. *If $OPT(P) \le k/q$ and $k < q^c$ for a small enough c, then $OPT(L) \le 1/q^e$ for some constant $e > 0$.*

Furthermore, the HLCPP instance L is $(4m/q)$-smooth (Definition 4.8) and uniform (Definition 4.9).

[2]Actually, the constraint between vertices in layers $\mathcal{L}_{2m-1}$ and $\mathcal{L}_{2m}$ is not many-to-many when $c_i(\alpha, \beta) = 0$ but this happens for at most $2m/q$ fraction of vertices for every equation hence we can afford to ignore these vertices and any hyper-edges containing them.

4.4 Reduction to MWSPP

The reduction from HLCPP to MWSPP is very similar to the reduction from LCPP to MWSPP described in [AKKV05]. Let

$$G(V, E, \mathcal{E}, [R_0], [R_1], \ldots, [R_{2m+1}], \{\pi_e, \sigma_e\}_{e \in E}, \{\mathcal{S}_v, S_v\}_{v \in \mathcal{L}_0})$$

be an instance of HLCPP. For each vertex $v \in V$ and each label l to v we have a variable $w_{v,l}$. We now describe the fixed linear forms B_f of the MWSPP instance. In what follows, $\bigoplus$ denotes addition over $\mathbb{F}_2$.

Vertex constraints:

1. $\forall 1 \le j \le 2m+1$, $\forall v \in \mathcal{L}_j$, $\bigoplus_{l \in [R_j]} w_{v,l} = 1$.
2. $\forall v \in \mathcal{L}_0$, $\forall S \in \mathcal{S}_v$,

$$\bigoplus_{l \in S} w_{v,l} = 1 \text{ if } S = S_v \text{ and } 0 \text{ otherwise.} \quad (4.1)$$

Notice that only the r.h.s. depends on the input (which is S_v).

Edge constraints:

Let $e = (u, v)$ be an edge where $u \in \mathcal{L}_i$, $v \in \mathcal{L}_{i+1}$. Let $\pi_e : [R_i] \mapsto [R_e]$, $\sigma_e : [R_{i+1}] \mapsto [R_e]$ be the projections describing the many-to-many constraint associated to e. For every element $a \in [R_e]$ we add the following fixed linear form:

$$\bigoplus_{l \in [R_i] : \pi_e(l) = a} w_{u,l} = \bigoplus_{l \in [R_{i+1}] : \sigma_e(l) = a} w_{v,l}. \quad (4.2)$$

We now describe the variable forms B_v for the MWSPP instance. Let q_j be the number of vertices in layer $\mathcal{L}_j$. Let $\tilde{q} \stackrel{\text{def}}{=} \prod_{j=0}^{2m+1} q_j$. For every layer $\mathcal{L}_j$, $0 \le j \le 2m+1$, every vertex $v \in \mathcal{L}_j$ and every label l to v, we have the variable form $w^j_{v,l}$ repeated $\tilde{q}/q_j$ times. This completes the description of the MWSPP instance. It remains to prove the completeness and the soundness of this reduction which we do next.

4.4.1 *Soundness of the* MWSPP *instance*

Here we show that the MWSPP instance constructed has a large gap.

THEOREM 4.11. FROM $\mathbb{F}_q$-QCSPP TO MWSPP. *Let h be such that $1/(m^3h)^{3m} \ge 1/q^e$ for large enough m and for some fixed small constant e.*

- **Completeness:** *If P is satisfiable then the MWSPP instance constructed in Section 4.4 has a solution of weight at most $(2m+2) \cdot \tilde{q}$.*
- **Soundness:** *If P is such that $OPT(P) \le k/q$ then the MWSPP instance constructed in Section 4.4 has no solution of weight less than $h \cdot (2m+2) \cdot \tilde{q}$.*

PROOF. **Completeness.** If the $\mathbb{F}_q$-QCSPP instance P is satisfiable then the HLCPP instance has a labeling which satisfies all constraints (Theorem 4.10). For an MWSPP variable $w^j_{v,l}$ corresponding to vertex v and label l to v, we let $w^j_{v,l} = 1$ if v was assigned the label l and 0 otherwise.

It is easy to see that this satisfies all fixed linear forms and gives a solution of weight

$$\sum_{j=1}^{2m+1}\sum_{v\in\mathcal{L}_j} 1\cdot\tilde{q}/q_j = \sum_{j=1}^{2m+1} q_j\cdot\tilde{q}/q_j = (2m+2)\cdot\tilde{q}.$$

Soundness. In this case we are given that $OPT(P) \le k/q$ and, hence by Theorem 4.10, any labeling to the HLCPP instance satisfies at most $1/q^e$ fraction of the hyper-edges for some small constant e. The number of hyper-edges in the instance are $|[q]\times F_q^m \times \mathbb{F}_q^m| = q^{2m+1}$. Suppose there is a solution to the MWSPP instance of weight $h\cdot(2m+2)\cdot\tilde{q}$ which satisfies all fixed linear forms. We will give a (randomized) labeling to the HLCPP instance which in expectation satisfies more than $1/(m^3h)^{3m} \ge 1/q^e$ fraction of the hyper-edges, contradicting Theorem 4.10.

Let $\{w_{v,l}\}$ be a solution of weight at most $h\cdot(2m+2)\cdot\tilde{q}$. Call a label l for v *nonzero* if $w_{v,l} = 1$. (Note that our variables are allowed only 0/1 values.) We know from our assumption that

$$\sum_{j=0}^{2m+1}\sum_{v,l} w_{v,l}\cdot\tilde{q}/q_j = h\cdot(2m+2)\cdot\tilde{q}.$$

Let n_v^j denote the number of nonzero variables for the vertex v in the j-th layer. Then the above can be written as

$$\sum_{j=0}^{2m+1}\sum_{v} n_v^j/q_j = h\cdot(2m+2).$$

Hence, for all j, $\sum_v n_v^j/q_j \le h\cdot(2m+2)$. Hence by Markov's Inequality, for every j, the fraction of v for which $n_v^j \ge m^3h$ is atmost $h\cdot(2m+2)/(m^3\cdot h) \le 3/m^2$ for large enough m. We call a label i for a vertex v *non-zero* if $w_{v,i} = 1$. We remove all vertices from the graph which have more than $r \stackrel{\text{def}}{=} h\cdot m^3$ non-zero labels. This removes at most $3/m^2$ fraction of vertices from each layer. Next, we remove all hyper-edges containing any vertex removed in this step. To bound this number notice that our graph has this property that number of hyper-edges per vertex of layer j is at most q^{2m+1}/q_j (by Item 1 of the uniformity property: Definition 4.9). Since number of vertices removed per layer is at most $3q_j/m^2$, the number of hyper-edges removed in layer j is at most $3q^{2m+1}/q_j$. Hence, the number of hyper-edges removed overall is at most $3\cdot(2m+2)q^{2m+1}/m^2 \le 9/m\cdot q^{2m+1}$ for large enough m. Thus, the total fraction of hyper-edges removed is at most $9/m$ which is negligible. Thus, we have an HLCPP instance where every vertex has at most r non-zero labels and we wish to satisfy more than $1/q^e$ fraction of the queries.

Labeling. We define a randomized labeling for the instance of HLCPP: randomly assign a nonzero label independently for each vertex. This is possible as the sum (over $\mathbb{F}_2$) of the variables corresponding to each v is 1 and hence not all variables for a vertex can be 0.

The next claim shows that the expected fraction of hyper-edges satisfied is at least $r^{-3m} = (h\cdot m^3)^{-3m}$ which is larger than $1/q^e$ by our assumption.

Claim 4.12. *Conditioned on the hyper-edge not being removed, the expected fraction of hyper-edges satisfied by the randomized labeling defined above is at least r^{-3m} where $r = hm^3$.*

Proof of Claim. We first remove all edges e in the graph for which some pair of non-zero labels map to the same label via the constraint associated to e. Formally, let $e = (u,v)$ be an edge, $l \ne l'$ be two non-zero labels for u and (π_e, σ_e) be the maps describing the many-to-many constraint associated to e. We remove the edge e if $\pi_e(l) = \pi_e(l')$. Since the instance is $4m/q$-smooth (Definition 4.8), taking a union bound over all pairs of non-zero labels implies that the fraction of edges removed in the graph is at most $4mr^2/q$.

Next, we remove all hyper-edges containing any edge removed in the previous step. Using Item 2 of the uniformity property (Definition 4.9) and a union bound, it can be seen that the total fraction of hyper-edges removed is at most $3m\cdot 4mr^2/q \le 12m^2r^2/q$, which is negligible by our choice of parameters. Thus, we have an HLCPP instance where every vertex has at most r non-zero labels and the many-to-many constraint maps all non-zero labels to distinct labels.

For a hyper-edge to be satisfied, its vertex in $\mathcal{L}_0$ should receive a label from allowable set. By Equation (4.1), there is at least one non-zero label from this set. Thus, with probability at least $1/r$, we pick an allowed label for a hyper-edge.

For $0 \le j \le 2m$, we will show that if we have assigned label l to vertex $u \in \mathcal{L}_j$, then the probability of assigning a consistent label to any of its neighbors in $\mathcal{L}_{j+1}$ is at least $1/r$. By a consistent label we mean one which satisfies the constraint on the edge.

Suppose we have picked a label l for a vertex $u \in \mathcal{L}_j$. We claim that the left side of Equation 4.2 is 1, since there is no non-zero label l' for u such that $\pi_e(l) = \pi_e(l')$. This means that the r.h.s. is also 1 (since the fixed linear forms are satisfied). Hence there must be a non-zero label for v which satisfies the constraint associated with the edge $e = (u,v)$, and this label is assigned to v with probability at least $1/r$ (over the random choice of a labeling). Hence, the constraint between u and v is satisfied with probability at least $1/r$.

This shows that for a fixed hyper-edge, the probability (over the randomized labeling) that it is satisfied is at least $r^{-(2m+3)}$ which is the number of vertices in the hyper-edge. Thus, the expected fraction of hyper-edges satisfied is at least $r^{-(2m+3)} \ge r^{-3m}$. This completes the proof of the claim. □

Noticing that by our choice of parameters $1/q^e < r^{-3m}$, we obtain a contradiction. Hence, this completes the soundness proof and, hence, the theorem.

4.5 Choice of Parameters and the Proof of Main Theorem

Proof. (of Theorem 4.1). Let Q be the $\mathbb{F}_q$-QCSPP instance given by Theorem 3.3 over n variables and $k = poly(n)$ equations. We apply Lemma 3.7 to get an $\mathbb{F}_q$-QCSPP instance over n variables and q equations where $q \stackrel{\text{def}}{=} 2^{(\log n)^{(4/\varepsilon)}}$. We then apply the series of reductions described in Sections 4.1, 4.3 and 4.4.

Let N be the size of the MWSPP instance constructed in Section 4.4. It can be checked that $N \le q^{100m}$, where $m \stackrel{\text{def}}{=} \log n$ for large enough m. Hence, $N \le q^{\log^2 n}$ for large enough n. We need m and h to satisfy $1/r^{3m} = 1/r^{3\log n} = 1/(m^3h)^{3m} \ge 1/q^e$. This is true if $\log h \le \log q/\log^2 n$ and $\log q \gg \log n \log\log n$ and n is let to be large enough.

We set $h \stackrel{\text{def}}{=} q^{\log^{-2} n}$. For a large enough positive integer $D = 4/\varepsilon$, let q be such that $\log q \stackrel{\text{def}}{=} \log^D n$. Hence,

$\log q \gg \log n \log\log n$.
Moreover $\log N \le \log^{D+2} n$ and $\log h = \log^{D-2} n$. This implies that

$$\log^{1-\varepsilon} N = \log^{(D+2)(1-\varepsilon)} n \le \log^{D-2} n = \log h$$

Finally, $N \le q^{\log^2 n} = 2^{\log^{O(1/\varepsilon)} n}$. Summarizing, our reduction is deterministic, the hardness factor is $2^{\log^{1-\varepsilon} N}$ and takes time $2^{\log^{O(1/\varepsilon)} n}$ and, hence, holds under the hypothesis $NP \not\subseteq DTIME(n^{\log^{O(1/\varepsilon)} n})$. $\square$

5. ACKNOWLEDGEMENTS

Subhash Khot and Preyas Popat supported by NSF CAREER grant CCF-0833228, NSF Expeditions grant CCF-0832795, the Waterman Award and BSF grant 2008059.

6. REFERENCES

[ABSS97] S. Arora, L. Babai, J. Stern, and Z. Sweedyk. Hardness of approximate optima in lattices, co des, and linear systems. *Journal of Computer and System Sciences*, 54(2):317–331, 1997.

[AKKV05] Mikhail Alekhnovich, Subhash Khot, Guy Kindler, and Nisheeth K. Vishnoi. Hardness of approximating the closest vector problem with pre-processing. In *FOCS*, pages 216–225. IEEE Computer Society, 2005.

[AKKV11] Mikhail Alekhnovich, Subhash Khot, Guy Kindler, and Nisheeth K. Vishnoi. Hardness of approximating the closest vector problem with pre-processing. *Computational Complexity*, 20(4):741–753, 2011.

[ALM+98] Sanjeev Arora, Carsten Lund, Rajeev Motwani, Madhu Sudan, and Mario Szegedy. Proof verification and the hardness of approximation problems. *J. ACM*, 45(3):501–555, 1998.

[AR05] Dorit Aharonov and Oded Regev. Lattice problems in NP ∩ co-NP. *J. ACM*, 52:749–765, September 2005.

[AS98] Sanjeev Arora and Shmuel Safra. Probabilistic checking of proofs: A new characterization of np. *J. ACM*, 45(1):70–122, 1998.

[AS03] Sanjeev Arora and Madhu Sudan. Improved low-degree testing and its applications. *Combinatorica*, 23(3):365–426, 2003.

[DKRS03] Irit Dinur, Guy Kindler, Ran Raz, and Shmuel Safra. Approximating CVP to within almost-polynomial factors is NP-hard. *Combinatorica*, 23(2):205–243, 2003.

[FGRW09] V. Feldman, V. Guruswami, P. Raghavendra, and Y. Wu. Agnostic learning of monomials by halfspaces is hard. In *Proceedings of the 50th IEEE Symposium on Foundations of Computer Science*, October 2009.

[FM04] U. Feige and D. Micciancio. The inapproximability of lattice and coding problems with preprocessing. *Journal of Computer and System Sciences*, 69(1):45–67, 2004.

[GRSW10] Venkatesan Guruswami, Prasad Raghavendra, Rishi Saket, and Yi Wu. Bypassing UGC from some optimal geometric inapproximability results. *Electronic Colloquium on Computational Complexity (ECCC)*, 17:177, 2010.

[Kho02] S. Khot. Hardness results for coloring 3-colorable 3-uniform hypergraphs. In *43rd IEEE FOCS*, pages 23–32, 2002.

[KP06] Subhash Khot and Ashok Kumar Ponnuswami. Better inapproximability results for maxclique, chromatic number and min-3lin-deletion. In Michele Bugliesi, Bart Preneel, Vladimiro Sassone, and Ingo Wegener, editors, *ICALP (1)*, volume 4051 of *Lecture Notes in Computer Science*, pages 226–237. Springer, 2006.

[KS11] Subhash Khot and Rishi Saket. On the hardness of learning intersections of two halfspaces. *J. Comput. Syst. Sci.*, 77(1):129–141, 2011.

[LFKN92] Carsten Lund, Lance Fortnow, Howard J. Karloff, and Noam Nisan. Algebraic methods for interactive proof systems. *J. ACM*, 39(4):859–868, 1992.

[LLS90] J.C. Lagarias, H.W. Lenstra, and C.P. Schnorr. Korkine-Zolotarev bases and successive minima of a lattice and its reciprocal lattice. *Combinatorica*, 10:333–348, 1990.

[MV10] Daniele Micciancio and Panagiotis Voulgaris. A deterministic single exponential time algorithm for most lattice problems based on voronoi cell computations. In *STOC*, pages 351–358, 2010.

[Raz98] Ran Raz. A parallel repetition theorem. *SIAM J. Comput.*, 27(3):763–803, 1998.

[Reg04] Oded Regev. Improved inapproximability of lattice and coding problems with preprocessing. *IEEE Transactions on Information Theory*, 50(9):2031–2037, 2004.

[RR06] Oded Regev and Ricky Rosen. Lattice problems and norm embeddings. In *STOC*, pages 447–456, 2006.

[RS97] Ran Raz and Shmuel Safra. A sub-constant error-probability low-degree test, and a sub-constant error-probability pcp characterization of np. In *STOC*, pages 475–484, 1997.

[Sch87] Claus-Peter Schnorr. A hierarchy of polynomial time lattice basis reduction algorithms. *Theor. Comput. Sci.*, 53:201–224, 1987.

APPENDIX

A. OMITTED PROOFS

A.1 $\mathbb{F}_q$-QCSPP is NP-complete

THEOREM A.1. *$\mathbb{F}_q$-QCSPP is NP-complete for all $q = 2^r$.*

PROOF. We reduce 3SAT to $\mathbb{F}_q$-QCSPP . For this proof, it is convenient to view the input for 3SAT in the following form: the input is (V, E), where $V, E \in \{0,1\}^{m\times n}$ and corresponds to a 3SAT formula $\phi = C_1 \wedge \cdots \wedge C_m$ with variables $\{x_1, \ldots, x_n\}$. Each row of V corresponds to a clause C_i and V_{ij} is 1 if and only if x_j appears in C_i. Thus, each row of V

has exactly three 1's. The entry E_{ij} is 1 if and only if the variable x_j appears as a negated literal in C_i.

Since 3SAT is in NP, for every n, there is a circuit $\mathcal{C}_n$ which takes as input (V, E) and an assignment $a \in \{0,1\}^n$, such that, $\mathcal{C}_n(a, V, E) = 1$ if a is a satisfying assignment for ϕ, and 0 otherwise.

Now we present the reduction, which is exactly the same as in Theorem 4.2 of [AKKV05], except that we work over $\mathbb{F}_q$ rather than $\mathbb{F}_2$. Let (V, E) be the input corresponding to a 3SAT instance ϕ. We may assume that every gate in $\mathcal{C}_n$ has fan-in 2 and fan-out 1. For every bit in the input (a, V, E) to $\mathcal{C}_n$, there is a variable in $\mathbb{F}_q$: x_i is supposed to be assigned the i-th bit of a, x_{ij} is supposed to be assigned V_{ij}, while x'_{ij} is supposed to be assigned E_{ij}.

Associated to the output of the i-th internal gate[3] in $\mathcal{C}_n$ is a variable z_i. Further, let y_0 be the variable corresponding to the output gate which outputs whether an assignment a satisfies ϕ or not.

The computation of any gate can be written as a quadratic polynomial (over $\mathbb{F}_2$) in its inputs (call these z, z') and output (call it z''): $z'' = zz'$ for an AND gate, $z'' = 1 + (1 + z)(1 + z')$ for an OR gate, and $z'' = 1 + z$ for a NOT gate.

Note that $\mathbb{F}_2$ is a sub-field of $\mathbb{F}_q$ since $q = 2^r$ is a power of 2. Thus, each element of $\mathbb{F}_q$ can be naturally identified with a vector in $\mathbb{F}_2^r$ such that addition in $\mathbb{F}_q$ corresponds to vector addition and multiplication in $\mathbb{F}_q$ corresponds to taking dot products. In any such representation, the element $0 \in \mathbb{F}_q$ corresponds to the all 0's vector while the element $1 \in \mathbb{F}_q$ corresponds to the all 1's vector. The crucial observation is that the polynomials for the AND, OR and NOT gates described above act as co-ordinate wise AND, OR and NOT gates when the inputs and the output are elements of $\mathbb{F}_2^r$ ($\mathbb{F}_q$), when all computation is done over $\mathbb{F}_q$.

We write such an equation for every gate in $\mathcal{C}_n$. Each equation is of degree at-most 2 and has at-most 3 variables. Note that every such equation depends only on the description of $\mathcal{C}_n$. Finally, we add the additional set of equations $y_0 = 1$, $x_{ij} = V_{ij}$ and $x'_{ij} = E_{ij}$. Hence, we get a $\mathbb{F}_q$-QCSPP instance over the set of variables

$$\{x_i : i \in [n]\} \cup \{x_{ij} : i \in [m], j \in [n]\} \cup$$
$$\{x'_{ij} : i \in [m], j \in [n]\} \cup \{z_i : 1 \le i \le \text{size}(\mathcal{C}_n)\} \cup \{y_0\}.$$

Notice that $\mathcal{C}_n$ can be generated by a polynomial time algorithm which is given as input 1^n. Hence, this reduction is a polynomial time reduction.

We claim that this quadratic system has a solution (over $\mathbb{F}_q$) if and only if ϕ has a satisfying solution. The corresponding claim when all variables take values in $\mathbb{F}_2$ follows by construction. Now note that if there is a solution over $\mathbb{F}_q$ then taking the last co-ordinate of the variables (when viewed as vectors over $\mathbb{F}_2^r$) is a valid solution over $\mathbb{F}_2$, since all gates act co-ordinate wise.

The reduction described above gives constraints which are of degree at most 2, but not homogeneous. This is easy to fix by introducing an auxiliary variable z_0 and adding the constraint $z_0 z_0 = 1$. We then multiply all terms of degree less than 2 by z_0.

This completes the proof of the lemma.

□

[3]A gate is said to be internal if its output is not an output of the circuit.

A.2 Boosting Soundness through Codes

We first need some basic definitions.

DEFINITION A.2. CODES. *A matrix $C \in \mathbb{F}_q^{m \times k}$ is said to be a generator of the linear code $\{Cx : x \in \mathbb{F}_q^k\}$ with distance $1 - \delta$ if for any $x \neq y \in \mathbb{F}_q^k$, $C(x)$ and $C(y)$ agree on at most δm co-ordinates.*

FACT A.3. REED-MULLER CODES. *For any q, let $\mathbb{F}_q$ be the field over q elements. There is a family of linear codes with generator matrix $C_k \in \mathbb{F}_q^{q \times k}$ with distance $1 - k/q$. These are the so called Reed Muller codes over $\mathbb{F}_q$, where the message is thought of as the coefficients of a degree k polynomial and the codeword the evaluation of this polynomial on all the points in $\mathbb{F}_q$.*

LEMMA A.4. *Let Q be an instance of $\mathbb{F}_q$-QCSPP over n variables and $k = poly(n)$ equations, for any $q = 2^r$. There is a polynomial time reduction which maps Q to an instance P of $\mathbb{F}_q$-QCSPP over the same set of variables and q equations such that:*

- *If $OPT(Q) = 1$ then $OPT(P) = 1$ and*
- *if $OPT(Q) < 1$ then $OPT(P) \le k/q$.*

PROOF. Let $C_k \in \mathbb{F}_q^{q \times k}$ be the Reed-Muller code matrix as in Fact A.3. Let $p_1, \ldots, p_k$ be the equations of Q and let $r \in \mathbb{F}_q^k$ be a row of R. We add the constraint $\sum_{i=1}^k r_i p_i$ to P which is a $\mathbb{F}_q$-linear combination of the equations in Q. Thus, P has q equations.

It is clear that any satisfying assignment to all equations of Q is also a satisfying assignment for all equations of P. This shows that if $OPT(Q) = 1$ then $OPT(P) = 1$.

On the other hand, suppose $OPT(Q) < 1$ and fix any assignment A to the variables of Q. An equation $e_i \in Q$ is of the form $p_i(z_1, \ldots, z_n) = c_i$. Let $v^A \in \mathbb{F}_q^k$ be defined as $v_i^A \stackrel{\text{def}}{=} p_i(A(z_1), \ldots, A(z_n)) - c_i$. Since $OPT(Q) < 1$, $v^A \neq 0^k$. Thus, by the code property we have that $C_k \cdot v^A$ is zero in at most k co-ordinates. Notice that $C_k \cdot v^A$ has a 0 in a co-ordinate if and only if the corresponding equation in P is satisfied by A. Since this holds for every assignment A, the theorem follows.

□

A.3 Sum Check Protocol

THEOREM A.5. SOUNDNESS OF SUM CHECK PROTOCOL. *[LFKN92] Let $g^1, g^2, \ldots, g^l : \mathbb{F}_q^M \mapsto \mathbb{F}_q$ be degree d polynomials and $g : \mathbb{F}_q^M \mapsto \mathbb{F}_q$ an arbitrary function. Suppose for every $1 \le j \le l$, $\sum_{z \in \{0,1\}^M} g^j(z) \neq c$. For $x \in \mathbb{F}_q^M$, let $\mathcal{P}(x)$ be the event that the Sum Check Protocol (Definition 3.11) accepts on inputs g, c and $p_{a_1, a_2, \ldots, a_j}$. Here x is the choice of randomness in the Sum Check Protocol.*

Then

$$\Pr_{x \in \mathbb{F}_q^M} \left[\mathcal{P}(x) \;\&\; \exists\, j \in \{1, \ldots, l\} \;:\; g(x) = g^j(x)\right] \le Mdl/q.$$

In words, the probability that the Sum Check Protocol accepts when g is consistent with one of $g^1, g^2, \ldots, g^l$ is at most Mdl/q where $g^1, g^2, \ldots, g^l$ are degree d polynomials whose sum is not the required value.

PROOF. We will prove the theorem by induction on M.
Base Case: M=1 We consider two cases:

1. $p_\emptyset = g^j_\emptyset$ for some $1 \leq j \leq l$. In this case Step 1 fails by our assumption on g^j.
2. $p_\emptyset \neq g^j_\emptyset$ for all $1 \leq j \leq l$. In this case,

$$\begin{aligned} & \Pr_{x\in\mathbb{F}_q}\left[\mathcal{P}(x)\ \&\ \exists\, j \in \{1,\ldots,l\}\ :\ g(x) = g^j(x)\right] \\ \leq\ & \Pr_{x\in\mathbb{F}_q}\left[g(x) = p_\emptyset(x) \& \ \exists j \in \{1,\ldots,l\} : g(x) = g^j(x)\right] \\ & \text{(Since Step 3 accepts)} \\ =\ & \Pr_{x\in\mathbb{F}_q}\left[\exists\, j \in \{1,\ldots,l\}\ :\ p_\emptyset(x) = g^j(x)\right] \\ \leq\ & ld/q \end{aligned}$$

The last inequality uses the fact that any two distinct degree d polynomials can agree on at most d/q fraction of the points followed by a union bound.

Inductive Case: M = N We again consider two cases as before:

1. $p_\emptyset = g^j_\emptyset$ for some $1 \leq j \leq l$. In this case Step 1 fails by our assumption on g^j.
2. $p_\emptyset \neq g^j_\emptyset$ for all $1 \leq j \leq l$. In this case, the fraction of points $a \in \mathbb{F}_q$ such that

$$\sum_{b_2,\ldots b_N\in\{0,1\}} g^j(a, b_2, \ldots, b_N) = p_\emptyset(a) \qquad \text{(A.1)}$$

for some $1 \leq j \leq l$ is at most ld/q.

Note that for a fixed $a \in \mathbb{F}_q$, Steps 2 and 3 are equivalent to running the Sum Check Protocol for checking

$$\sum_{b_2,\ldots b_N\in\{0,1\}} g(a, b_2, \ldots, b_N) = c'$$

where $c' \stackrel{\text{def}}{=} p_\emptyset(a)$. For $x \in \mathbb{F}_q^{N-1}$, let $\mathcal{P}_a(x)$ be the event that this protocol accepts.
If Equation A.1 does not hold for any $1 \leq j \leq l$ then we can use the inductive assumption to get

$$\begin{aligned} & \Pr_{x\in\mathbb{F}_q^{N-1}}\left[\mathcal{P}_a(x)\ \&\ \exists\, j \in \{1,\ldots,l\} : g(a,x) = g^j(a,x)\right] \\ & \leq (N-1)dl/q. \end{aligned}$$

Thus, the total probability of acceptance is at most $ld/q + (N-1)dl/q \leq Ndl/q$.

□

A New Point of NP-Hardness for Unique Games

(extended abstract)

Ryan O'Donnell*, John Wright
Carnegie Mellon University
Pittsburgh, PA 15213
odonnell@cs.cmu.edu, jswright@cs.cmu.edu

ABSTRACT

We show that distinguishing $\frac{1}{2}$-satisfiable Unique-Games instances from $(\frac{3}{8}+\epsilon)$-satisfiable instances is NP-hard (for all $\epsilon > 0$). A consequence is that we match or improve the best known c vs. s NP-hardness result for Unique-Games for all values of c (except for c very close to 0). For these c, ours is the first hardness result showing that it helps to take the alphabet size larger than 2. Our NP-hardness reductions are quasilinear-size and thus show nearly full exponential time is required, assuming the ETH.

Categories and Subject Descriptors

F.2 [**Theory of Computation**]: Analysis of Algorithms and Problem Complexity

General Terms

Theory

Keywords

Unique Games Conjecture, Hardness of Approximation, NP-hardness

1. INTRODUCTION

Thanks largely to the groundbreaking work of Håstad [Hås01], we have optimal NP-hardness of approximation results for several constraint satisfaction problems (CSPs), including $3\mathsf{Lin}(Z_2)$ and 3Sat. But for many others — including most interesting CSPs with 2-variable constraints — we lack matching algorithmic and NP-hardness results. Take the $2\mathsf{Lin}(Z_2)$ problem for example, in which there are Boolean variables with constraints of the form "$x_i = x_j$" and "$x_i \neq x_j$". The largest approximation ratio known to be achievable in polynomial time is roughly .878 [GW95], whereas it is only known that achieving ratios above $\frac{11}{12} \approx .917$ is NP-hard [Hås01, TSSW00]. Which of these two results can be improved?

In the early 2000s there was some sentiment that the .878-ratio approximation algorithm could be improved [Fei99, Fei02]. However this began to change after Khot's introduction of the Unique-Games (UG) Conjecture [Kho02]. In that paper, Khot showed that $(1-\epsilon, 1-\epsilon^{1/2+o(1)})$-approximating $2\mathsf{Lin}(Z_2)$ is "UG-hard" for all $\epsilon > 0$. Assuming the UG Conjecture this would be essentially optimal because the Goemans–Williamson algorithm [GW95] efficiently $(1-\epsilon, 1-O(\epsilon^{1/2}))$-approximates $2\mathsf{Lin}(Z_2)$. Here we are using the following terminology:

DEFINITION 1.1. *A* (c, s)-approximation algorithm *for a maximization CSP is one which satisfies at least an s-fraction of the constraints on any instance where the optimal solution satisfies at least a c-fraction of the constraints.*

This was subsequently extended [KKMO07, KO09, OW08] to give matching $(c, s(c))$-approximation algorithms and UG-hardness results for $2\mathsf{Lin}(Z_2)$ for every $c \in [\frac{1}{2}, 1]$, including UG-hardness of achieving $\frac{s}{c} > .878$. In light of such sharp UG-hardness results — shown for *every* CSP by Raghavendra [Rag09] — it seemed in the late '00s that the boundary of efficient approximability had been identified.

However the pendulum swung again in 2010 with the Arora–Barak–Steurer subexponential-time algorithm for Unique-Games [ABS10] (see also the related works [Kol10, Ste10, BRS11, GS11]). For example, we now know there is a universal constant $\epsilon_0 > 0$ such that in time $2^{O(n^{.001})}$ one can both $(1-\epsilon_0, \frac{1}{2})$-approximate Unique-Games ([ABS10]) and $(\frac{1}{2}, \epsilon_0)$-approximate Unique-Games (this follows [Ste11] from [Ste10, BRS11]). There is also now speculation that approximating Max-Cut or $2\mathsf{Lin}(Z_2)$ to factor .879 may be possible in subexponential time. Yet all of these problems are predicted to NP-hard by the UG Conjecture.

This raises the question of what meaning an NP-hardness result actually has. For example, approximating Max-Clique to factor $1/n^{.999}$ is known to be NP-hard [Hås99], yet it's trivially solvable in $n^{n^{.001}+.002}$ time. Such a running time is completely practical for any plausible value of n. If one could make the above-mentioned $2^{O(n^{.001})}$-time algorithms for Unique-Games similarly practical, one might argue that this "morally" disproves the conjecture that $(1-\epsilon, \epsilon)$-approximating UG is hard for every $\epsilon > 0$. In any case, these theoretical results correspond well with the observation that "in practice",

*Supported by NSF grants CCF-0747250 and CCF-0915893, and by a Sloan fellowship. Some of this research performed while the author was a von Neumann Fellow at the Institute for Advanced Study, supported by NSF grants DMS-083537 and CCF-0832797.

decently approximating Unique-Games does not seem to be very hard. In particular, there is no known family of very "hard-seeming" instances for the UG Conjecture, as there is for, say, the 3Sat decision problem.

On the other hand, we do have evidence of extreme hardness for at least *some* gapped approximation version of Unique-Games. For example, Håstad's 1997 work [Hås97] implies that $(\frac{1}{2}, .459)$-approximating Unique-Games is NP-hard (here $.459 \approx \frac{11}{12} \cdot \frac{1}{2}$). The proof is a local gadget reduction from his result on NP-hardness of $(1-\epsilon, 1/2+\epsilon)$-approximating $3\mathsf{Lin}(Z_2)$. Furthermore, Moshkovitz and Raz [MR10] have shown that the $3\mathsf{Lin}(Z_2)$ result holds under a *quasilinear-size* reduction from 3Sat. Thus assuming the Exponential Time Hypothesis (ETH) [IP01] that deciding 3Sat requires $2^{\Omega(n)}$ time, it follows that $(\frac{1}{2}, .459)$-approximating Unique-Games is truly hard, requiring essentially full exponential time $2^{n^{1-o(1)}}$. Even if we don't assume the ETH, $(1-\epsilon, \frac{1}{2}+\epsilon)$-approximating $3\mathsf{Lin}(Z_2)$ is a problem for which we can easily generate very hard-in-practice instances (as cryptographic research on the Learning Parity with Noise problem has shown). Applying the local gadget reduction to these instances shows that the same is true of $(\frac{1}{2}, .459)$-approximating Unique-Games.

1.1 Our main result

To recap, for instances of the Unique-Games problem in which the optimal solution satisfies $\frac{1}{2}$ of the constraints, we know that satisfying a certain constant ϵ_0 fraction of the constraints is relatively "easy" (time $2^{O(n^{.001})}$), whereas satisfying the larger constant .459 fraction is "hard" (time $2^{n^{1-o(1)}}$ assuming ETH). Thus, as is often the case in the field of approximation algorithms, we are faced with the task of pinning down the truth between two constants. The main theorem of this paper is some progress on the hardness side:

THEOREM 1.2 (MAIN THEOREM). *For any constant label size q, $(\frac{1}{2}, \frac{3}{8}+\frac{1}{q^{\Theta(1)}})$-approximating Unique-Games is* NP-*hard under a quasilinear-size reduction; hence the problem requires time $2^{n^{1-o(1)}}$ under the ETH.*

(In fact, our theorem holds for $2\mathsf{Lin}(Z_q)$, $q \leq \mathrm{poly}(\log\log\log n)$.)

Although we would certainly not want to conjecture it, we have to at least raise the possibility that the optimal subexponential-time algorithm for $\frac{1}{2}$-satisfiable Unique-Games instances satisfies $\frac{3}{8}$ of the constraints.

Considerations of subexponential time vs. full exponential time aside, our result is just the second improved NP-hardness result for Unique-Games since 1997. Via trivial reductions, our Main Theorem extends to give NP-hardness of $(c, \frac{3}{4}c + o(1))$-approximating Unique-Games (for $c \leq \frac{1}{2}$) and also of $(c, 1-\frac{5}{4}(1-c)+o(1))$-approximating Unique-Games (for $c \geq \frac{1}{2}$). For all but very small $c \in (0,1)$ this subsumes or improves the best previous result, due to Håstad in 1997 [Hås97]. This best previous result involved taking $q = 2$; our result shows that hardness increases as q increases.

For $c \leq \kappa$, where κ is a small (inexplicit) positive constant, Feige–Reichman 2004 [FR04] has the best (c, s)-inapproximability result for Unique-Games. See Section 2.1 for more detailed comparison with prior work.

1.2 Our approach, and other contributions

More broadly, this paper focuses on trying to obtain unconditional NP-hardness of approximation results for 2-variable CSPs such as Unique-Games. With a few exceptions, the best such results known are derived by gadget reductions from Håstad's $(1-\epsilon, \frac{1}{2}+\epsilon)$-approximation NP-hardness for $3\mathsf{Lin}(Z_2)$. Indeed, for the well-known Boolean 2-CSPs Max-Cut, $2\mathsf{Lin}(Z_2)$, 2Sat, and 2And, the best gadgets were found via computer solution of large linear programs [TSSW00]. This state of affairs is unsatisfactory for a few reasons. First, there is almost no intuition for these computer-generated gadgets. Second, the doubly-exponential size of the linear programs involved makes it infeasible to use the computer-search approach even for 2-CSPs over a ternary domain. Third, since the $(1-\epsilon, \frac{1}{2}+\epsilon)$-hardness for $3\mathsf{Lin}(Z_2)$ is itself a (highly sophisticated) gadget reduction from Label-Cover, these kinds of results are arguably using an artificial "middleman" that could be cut out.

It makes sense then to seek direct reductions from Label-Cover to approximation of 2-CSPs. This has never been done in the "Håstad style" (Long Codes and Fourier analysis) with 2-CSPs before since it's unclear how to "get a square into the Fourier analysis". In fact we managed to reproduce the $(\frac{3}{4}, \frac{11}{16}+\epsilon)$-NP-hardness result for $2\mathsf{Lin}(Z_2)$ via a Håstad-style analysis (see the full version of the paper for details), but for the Unique-Games problem we required a more conceptual approach.

This new conceptual approach for reducing Label-Cover to 2-CSPs has three components:

1. Given a Label-Cover instance (V, E), the usual Håstad reduction methodology introduces a "prover" f_u for each vertex $u \in V$ (also known as a table, function, or collection of auxiliary variables), and replaces each constraint on $(u, v) \in E$ with a distribution on "questions" (constraints) for f_u and f_v. In our approach we also introduce a prover h_{uv} for each constraint $(u, v) \in E$.[1] From this constraint we propose generating 2-CSP questions as follows: First, generate question pairs (x, y) from a product distribution. Next, "corrupt" x to $\tilde{x}$ and y to $\tilde{y}$ in some *correlated* random way. Finally, send prover h_{uv} the pair $(\tilde{x}, \tilde{y})$, and test its answer against a random choice of $f_u(x)$ or $f_v(y)$.

2. We next develop the Invariance Principle technology [MOO-DMR09, Mos10, Rag09] to show that if the "Håstad decoding procedure" applied to f_u and f_v fails, then the analysis surrounding f_u, f_v, and h_{uv} can be performed as though the corruptions $x \to \tilde{x}$ and $y \to \tilde{y}$ were *independent*. This seems to be the first published example of using Invariance to analyze reductions from Label-Cover, as opposed to from Unique-Games or the d-to-1 Conjecture.[2]

[1] This idea is certainly not new. Indeed, for Long Code-based reductions from Label-Cover with projection constraints it is known that such provers never *need* to be introduced, though conceptually it may help to do so. Our main reduction from Label-Cover does not actually assume projection constraints, so we *do* need to add these provers.

[2] It was known to some experts [WZ10] that Invariance techniques can be used to analyze Håstad's Label-Cover to $3\mathsf{Lin}(Z_q)$ reduction, though the analysis essentially degenerates to the Håstad style used in [OWZ11].

3. Given the Invariance result, all concerns involving Fourier analysis and computational complexity are eliminated. Analyzing any proposed "test" reduces to analyzing a purely information-theoretic problem of *non-interactive correlation distillation* (NICD) type (see, e.g., [Yan07]). Such a task can still be difficult; e.g., to obtain the best known NP-hardness even for $2\mathsf{Lin}(Z_2)$ we needed to resolve a 2004 NICD conjecture of Yang [Yan04]. Still, the fact that we are reduced to information-theoretic problems makes things clean enough that we can obtain the Main Theorem for Unique-Games.

Our new approach lets us recover in a conceptual way the best known NP-hardness results [Hås97, TSSW00] for Max-Cut, $2\mathsf{Lin}(Z_2)$, 2Sat, and 2And.

2. PRELIMINARIES

We consider weighted CSPs. An instance $\mathcal{I}$ consists of a set of variables over a finite domain (of "labels"), along with a weighted list of constraints on these variables. We assume the weights are nonnegative rationals summing to 1, so we can also think of the instance as a probability distribution on constraints. We usually write n for the number of variables. The *size* of an instance is the total number of bits needed to specify the constraint relations and the weights; we will only consider instances which have size $n^{1+o(1)}$.[3] Given an assignment F to the variables we write $\mathrm{Val}_{\mathcal{I}}(F)$ for the total weight of the constraints it satisfies; we also write $\mathrm{Opt}(\mathcal{I}) = \max_F\{\mathrm{Val}_{\mathcal{I}}(F)\}$. The hardness of approximation results we prove in this paper will hold even for the problem of (c, s)-*deciding* the CSP; i.e., outputting 'YES' when $\mathrm{Opt}(\mathcal{I}) \geq c$ and outputting 'NO' when $\mathrm{Opt}(\mathcal{I}) < s$.

CSPs are distinguished by the domain of the variables and the kinds of constraints allowed. We mostly consider the case when the domain is Z_q, the additive group of integers modulo q, for some q.

DEFINITION 2.1. *Let ϕ be a predicate on Z_q^k. Then* Max-ϕ *denotes the CSP where the variables have domain Z_q and the constraints are ϕ applied to various k-tuples of variables.* Max-ϕ^+ *denotes the generalization where ϕ is applied to k-tuples of* literals*; by a literal we mean $x+c \pmod q$ where x is a variable and c is a constant. We also extend the notation to allow collections Φ of predicates.*

For $q = 2$, the familiar CSPs $2\mathsf{Lin}(Z_2)$, 2Sat, 2And, Max-Cut are equivalent to Max-$=^+$, Max-$\vee^+$, Max-$\wedge^+$, Max-$\neq$, respectively. $3\mathsf{Lin}(Z_2)$ is Max-ϕ^+ for $\phi(x, y, z) = x + y + z$. For general q, $2\mathsf{Lin}(Z_q)$ is Max-$=^+$. A related problem is $2\mathsf{Lin}(\mathbb{F}_q)$ for q a prime power, in which general 2-variable linear equations over $\mathbb{F}_q$ are allowed. The "Unique-Games" 2-CSP UG_q has variable domain Z_q, with any *bijective* constraint being allowed. We remark that $2\mathsf{Lin}(Z_q)$ is a special case of UG_q, and for $q = 2$ the problems are in fact identical. The *Unique-Games Conjecture* of Khot [Kho02] states that for all $\epsilon > 0$ there exists q such that $(1 - \epsilon, \epsilon)$-deciding UG_q is NP-hard. In [KKMO07] it is shown that the UG Conjecture implies the stronger statement that $(1 - \epsilon, q^{-\epsilon/(2-\epsilon)})$-deciding $2\mathsf{Lin}(Z_q)$ is NP-hard for all $\epsilon > 0$ and sufficiently large q.

[3]In this paper we will not concern ourselves with the bit-representation size of the rational numbers giving the weights; the reader may check that this can be accounted for without changing the statements of our theorems.

Finally, we define a (generalization) of the "Label Cover" CSP LC_{d_1K,d_2K}:

DEFINITION 2.2. *The input for LC_{d_1K,d_2K} is a biregular bipartite graph $((U, V), E)$; the vertices of U are variables with domain $[d_1K]$; the vertices of V are variables with domain $[d_2K]$. Also, for each edge $e = (u, v)$ there is given a d_1-to-1 map $\pi_{e,u} : [d_1K] \to [K]$ and a d_2-to-1 map $\pi_{e,v} : [d_2K] \to [K]$. The associated constraints (of equal weight) are that $\pi_{e,u}(u) = \pi_{e,v}(v)$.*

The more usual definition of Label Cover is the special case of $\mathsf{LC}_{K,dK}$ (i.e., $d_1 = 1$). Hardness results for $\mathsf{LC}_{K,dK}$ immediately extend to $\mathsf{LC}_{d_1K,dK}$ by duplication of labels for the U vertices.

Feige–Kilian [FK94] and Raz [Raz95] first proved that for all $\epsilon > 0$ there exists K and d such that $(1, \epsilon)$-deciding $\mathsf{LC}_{K,dK}$ is NP-hard. We will use the following strong form of this result from [MR10] (see also [DH09]):

THEOREM 2.3 (MOSHKOVITZ–RAZ THEOREM). *For any $\epsilon = \epsilon(n) \geq n^{-o(1)}$ there exists $K, d \leq 2^{\mathrm{poly}(1/\epsilon)}$ such that the problem of deciding a* 3Sat *instance of size n can be Karp-reduced in $\mathrm{poly}(n)$ time to the problem of $(1, \epsilon)$-deciding a $\mathsf{LC}_{K,dK}$ instance of size $n^{1+o(1)}$.*

For brevity, we say that $(1, \epsilon)$-deciding $\mathsf{LC}_{K,dK}$ is NP-*hard under quasilinear-size reductions.*

2.1 Comparison with prior work

To state inapproximability results for various CSPs, let us make a definition (essentially from [OW08]):

DEFINITION 2.4. *For a given CSP we say that (c, s) is a* point of NP-hardness *if $(c, s + \epsilon)$-deciding the CSP is NP-hard for all $\epsilon > 0$. We may also qualify this definition by insisting on quasilinear-size reductions.*

We now state some best known inapproximability results for Boolean 2-CSPs, from [Hås01, TSSW00]:

THEOREM 2.5. *We have the following points of NP-hardness, even under quasilinear-size reductions [MR10]: $(\frac{3}{4}, \frac{11}{16})$ for* $2\mathsf{Lin}(Z_2)$, *$(\frac{11}{12}, \frac{7}{8})$ for* 2Sat, *$(\frac{5}{12}, \frac{3}{8})$ for* 2And, *and $(\frac{17}{21}, \frac{16}{21})$ for* Max-Cut.

Chlebík and Chlebíková [CC04] have also shown that $(1 - \delta, 1 - 2.889\delta)$-deciding 2Sat (and even "Non-Mixed-2Sat") is NP-hard for all $0 < \delta < \delta_0$, where δ_0 is an unspecified positive constant. Their reduction is *not* quasilinear-size, relying as it does on the alternative PCP constructions of Dinur and Safra [DS05].

Padding.

Given a point of NP-hardness (c, s) for some CSP, one can trivially obtain some other points of NP-hardness by what we'll call "padding" (see the full version of the paper for details). Specifically, one can obtain any point (c', s') on the line segments (in $\mathbb{R}^2$) joining (c, s) to $(1, 1)$ and to (c_0, c_0). Here c_0 is a CSP-specific constant equal to the infimum of $\mathrm{Opt}(\mathcal{I})$ over all instances $\mathcal{I}$. E.g., $c_0 = \frac{1}{q}$ for $2\mathsf{Lin}(Z_q)$ because the "least satisfiable instance" (namely $\{x - y = 0, x - y = 1, \ldots, x - y = q - 1\}$) has $\mathrm{Opt} = \frac{1}{q}$. So for $2\mathsf{Lin}(Z_2)$ we obtain the points of NP-hardness $(1 - \delta, 1 - \frac{5}{4}\delta)$ for each $0 < \delta < \frac{1}{4}$ and also $(\frac{1}{2} + \frac{1}{4}\lambda, \frac{1}{2} + \frac{3}{16}\lambda)$ for each $0 < \lambda < 1$. Padding preserves quasilinearity of reduction size.

Unique-Games.

We now discuss the previous best NP-hardness of approximation for the Unique-Games problem UG_q. For $q = 2$ we have the $(\frac{3}{4}, \frac{11}{16})$ point of NP-hardness from Theorem 2.5, since $2\mathsf{Lin}(Z_2)$ and UG_2 are identical. For larger q we still have the point $(\frac{3}{4}, \frac{11}{16})$ for UG_q (at least if q is even), since $2\mathsf{Lin}(Z_2)$ can be considered a subproblem of UG_q by duplicating labels. By padding this result we get the points of NP-hardness $(1-\delta, 1-\frac{5}{4}\delta)$ for $0 < \delta < \frac{1}{4}$ and also $(\lambda \cdot \frac{3}{4} + \frac{1-\lambda}{q}, \lambda \cdot \frac{11}{16} + \frac{1-\lambda}{q}) \xrightarrow{q\to\infty} (\lambda \cdot \frac{3}{4}, \lambda \cdot \frac{11}{16})$ for $0 < \lambda < 1$. Rather surprisingly, no stronger result was previously known (except for tiny c, as we will describe shortly); in particular, the explicit hardness results in [AEH01, FR04] for $2\mathsf{Lin}(\mathbb{F}_q)$ for small q are inferior. In other words, the best known NP-hardness for UG_q involved taking $q = 2$!

We now state our Main Theorem precisely:

THEOREM 2.6 (MAIN THEOREM, PRECISE STATEMENT.). *There exists $\epsilon = \epsilon(n) = \widetilde{\Theta}(1/\log\log\log n)$ such that for each integer $2 \le q \le (\log\log\log n)^3$, there is a quasilinear-size reduction from size-n instances of 3Sat to the problem of $(\frac{1}{2} + \frac{1}{2q}, s(q) + \epsilon)$-deciding $2\mathsf{Lin}(Z_q)$, where $s(q) = \frac{3}{8} + \frac{5}{8q}$ for $q < 7$ and in general $s(q) = \frac{3}{8} + O(\frac{1}{q^{1/3}})$.*

(We believe that one can take $s(q) = \frac{3}{8} + \frac{5}{8q}$ for all q but we haven't proved this; see Section 5.) For $q = 2$ our theorem matches the previous result; we improve upon the prior work by taking $q \to \infty$, getting a point of NP-hardness for UG_q tending to $(\frac{1}{2}, \frac{3}{8})$. By padding, this extends the previous $(1-\delta, 1-\frac{5}{4}\delta)$ result and also gives the points of hardness $(\lambda \cdot \frac{1}{2}, \lambda \cdot \frac{3}{8})$ for $0 < \lambda < 1$.

As mentioned, there is one more known NP-hardness result for UG_q, due to Feige and Reichman [FR04]. For any sufficiently large prime power q they establish a point of NP-hardness for $2\mathsf{Lin}(\mathbb{F}_q)$ at $(q^{-1+\eta}, \Theta(q^{-1}))$; here $\eta > 0$ is an unspecified universal constant. The hardness holds under quasilinear-size reductions, using [MR10].

We illustrate the new state of (in)approximability for UG_q in Figure 1 (with q fixed slightly superconstant, for simplicity).

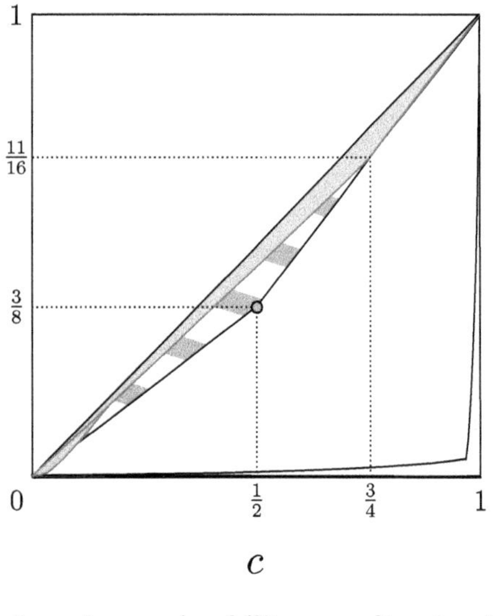

Figure 1: Approximability results for Unique-Games with label size $\omega(1) \le q \le \log\log n$

The solid pink regions in Figure 1 are the best previously known points (c, s) of NP-hardness. The triangle with vertex $(\frac{3}{4}, \frac{11}{16})$ (from [Hås01]) is drawn to scale; the bump near $c = 0$ (from [FR04]) is an "artistic impression". Our new hardness result is the red-striped region implied by the point of hardness at $(\frac{1}{2}, \frac{3}{8})$. These NP-hardness results hold under quasilinear-size reductions. In green we have illustrated (an artistic impression of) points (c, s) for which there is a subexponential-time (c, s)-time approximation algorithm for Unique-Games ([ABS10, Ste10, BRS11]). The true boundary between what is achievable in subexponential time for Unique-Games and what is not (assuming ETH) lies somewhere in the white region of the figure.

3. $2\mathsf{Lin}(Z_2)$ PROOF OUTLINE

In this section we introduce our method by showing how we can use it to recover Håstad's hardness result for $2\mathsf{Lin}(Z_2)$ [Hås01]. As a starting point, consider the hard instances of $2\mathsf{Lin}(Z_2)$ produced by Håstad: they begin by taking a d-to-1 Label Cover instance and replacing each vertex with its corresponding Long Code. Then, $3\mathsf{Lin}(Z_2)$ tests are placed between appropriately chosen Long Code vertices to produce a hard instance of the $3\mathsf{Lin}(Z_2)$ problem. Finally, the gadget from [TSSW00] is applied to the $3\mathsf{Lin}(Z_2)$ instance, resulting in a $2\mathsf{Lin}(Z_2)$ instance. The gadget works locally: given a $3\mathsf{Lin}(Z_2)$ test, it adds new vertices which are not part of any Long Code and puts in place a set of $2\mathsf{Lin}(Z_2)$ tests, each of which is performed exclusively between one vertex in the original $3\mathsf{Lin}(Z_2)$ test—a Long Code vertex—and one of the newly added vertices. We stress that the newly added vertices are unique to each $3\mathsf{Lin}(Z_2)$ test in the original $3\mathsf{Lin}(Z_2)$ instance. The result is that the final $2\mathsf{Lin}(Z_2)$ instance has groups of Long Code vertices along with clouds of vertices which sit between pairs of Long Codes and to which these Long Code pairs are compared.

Thus, it is sensible for a direct reduction from Label Cover to $2\mathsf{Lin}(Z_2)$ to take the following form: given u and v which are adjacent in the original Label Cover instance and whose Long Codes are f and g, respectively, there is a "cloud" of vertices which sits between u and v to which f and g may be compared. We think of this cloud of vertices as being labeled by some function h and indexed into by strings z from some set. A typical test will select an x for the u side, a y for the v side, and then to use the chosen x and y to select an appropriate z from the cloud. At this point, either the test $f(x) = h(z)$ is performed, or the test $g(y) = h(z)$ is performed, each with some probability. Thus, given an x and a y, the test will select a z and ask that $h(z)$ "predict" the value of $f(x)$ and $g(y)$. To help it do this, we will choose a z that contains some information about the strings x and y.

The test.

Now, we give a (mostly) complete description of our hard $2\mathsf{Lin}(Z_2)$ instance. We begin with a d-to-1 Label Cover instance over the graph $G = (U \cup V, E)$. For each $u \in U$ and each $v \in V$, introduce the Long Codes $f_u : \{-1,1\}^K \to \{-1,1\}$ and $g_v : \{-1,1\}^{dK} \to \{-1,1\}$, respectively. For each edge $(u, v) \in E$, introduce the function $h_{uv} : \{-1,1,*\}^K \times \{-1,1,*\}^{dK} \to \{-1,1\}$. We think of strings $y \in \{-1,1\}^{dK}$ as being formed of K "blocks" of size d each, so that y_1 through y_d is the first block, y_{d+1} through y_{2d} is the second block, and so forth. Denote the ith length-d block of

y by $y[i] = (y_{d(i-1)+1}, \ldots, y_{d(i-1)+d})$. Now, pick an edge $(u, v) \in E$ uniformly at random, and perform the following test on f_u, g_v, and h_{uv}:

2Lin(Z_2)-TEST

- Given functions $f : \{-1,1\}^K \to \{-1,1\}$, $g : \{-1,1\}^{dK} \to \{-1,1\}$, and $h : \{-1,1,*\}^K \times \{-1,1,*\}^{dK} \to \{-1,1\}$:
- Draw $\boldsymbol{x} \in \{-1,1\}^K$ and $\boldsymbol{y} \in \{-1,1\}^{dK}$ independently and uniformly at random.
- Form "corrupted" versions of $\boldsymbol{x}$ and $\boldsymbol{y}$ as follows: for each block $i \in [K]$, with probability 1/2 replace $\boldsymbol{x}_i$ with a $*$ and keep $\boldsymbol{y}[i]$ the same, and with probability 1/2 replace $\boldsymbol{y}[i]$ with $*^d$ and keep $\boldsymbol{x}_i$ the same. Call the corrupted versions $\widetilde{\boldsymbol{x}}$ and $\widetilde{\boldsymbol{y}}$, respectively.
- Test either $f(\boldsymbol{x}) = h(\widetilde{\boldsymbol{x}}, \widetilde{\boldsymbol{y}})$ or $g(\boldsymbol{y}) = h(\widetilde{\boldsymbol{x}}, \widetilde{\boldsymbol{y}})$, each with equal probability.

Note that this actually produces a 2Lin(Z_2) hardness instance, as equality tests are 2Lin(Z_2) tests. We think of the $*$'s as the gaps in knowledge h has about $\boldsymbol{x}$ and $\boldsymbol{y}$. The string $\widetilde{\boldsymbol{x}}$ contains about half of $\boldsymbol{x}$, and the string $\widetilde{\boldsymbol{y}}$ contains about half of $\boldsymbol{y}$. Moreover this (lack of) information is correlated: the part of $\boldsymbol{x}$ missing from $\widetilde{\boldsymbol{x}}$ is exactly the part of $\boldsymbol{y}$ *not* missing from $\widetilde{\boldsymbol{y}}$, and vice versa.

It is useful to talk about the probability that f and g pass the test without reference to h. Since in the 2Lin(Z_2) hardness instance, h_{uv} is only ever referenced when tests corresponding to the edge (u, v) are performed, we may as well assume that h_{uv} is selected to perform optimally with f_u and g_v. Thus, by "the probability that f and g pass the test" (and similar phrases) we mean the probability that f, g, and an optimal h pass the test.

Analyzing the test.

The correlation in what information is present or missing is extremely helpful in the "matching dictators" case, i.e. when $f(x) = x_i$ and $g(y) = (y[i])_j$, for $i \in [K], j \in [d]$. In this case, h is always given full information about either $f(\boldsymbol{x})$ or $g(\boldsymbol{y})$, because exactly one of $\boldsymbol{x}_i$ or $\boldsymbol{y}[i]$ is always kept when forming $\widetilde{\boldsymbol{x}}$ and $\widetilde{\boldsymbol{y}}$. As a result, h can always predict one of $f(\boldsymbol{x})$ or $g(\boldsymbol{y})$ with perfect accuracy, whereas against the other one its success is just an unbiased coin flip. Thus, f and g pass the test with $(1 + 1/2)/2 = 3/4$ probability. Interestingly, when f and g are dictators, even if h were to be given complete information about $f(\boldsymbol{x})$ and $g(\boldsymbol{y})$ (i.e., nothing was erased when forming $\widetilde{\boldsymbol{x}}$ or $\widetilde{\boldsymbol{y}}$), the test could still only be passed with probability at most 3/4. This is because f and g are balanced (+1 and -1 with equal probability), and thus are opposites of each other with probability exactly 1/2. When f and g are opposites, no matter what $h(\widetilde{\boldsymbol{x}}, \widetilde{\boldsymbol{y}})$ outputs, it will equal only one of $f(\boldsymbol{x})$ and $g(\boldsymbol{y})$. Since this happens half of the time, 1/4 of the tests must be failed, upper bounding the success probability by 3/4.

The other important case is when f and g are "nonmatching dictators", i.e. when $f(x) = x_i$ and $g(y) = (y[i'])_j$, for $i \neq i' \in [K], j \in [d]$. This case is useless when decoding to a satisfying assignment to the original Label Cover instance, and so we hope that they succeed less than 3/4 of the time. In this case, whether h receives full information of $f(\boldsymbol{x})$ is completely independent of whether it receives full information of $g(\boldsymbol{y})$, as the indices the two depend on sit in entirely different blocks. Indeed, the correlation in the erasures has no effect; the corresponding blocks of $\boldsymbol{x}$ and $\boldsymbol{y}$ could be erased with half probability *independently* of each other, and this would not help nor hinder h. A large fraction of the time (1/4, to be exact), h receives no information about either $f(\boldsymbol{x})$ or $g(\boldsymbol{y})$, as both $\boldsymbol{x}_i$ and $\boldsymbol{y}[i]$ are erased when forming $\widetilde{\boldsymbol{x}}$ and $\widetilde{\boldsymbol{y}}$ with probability 1/4. Thus, h can do nothing but guess randomly when this happens, which is again a coin flip. When this does not happen, then as argued earlier, f and g can pass the test with probability no more than 3/4 because they are balanced. The result is that the success probability in this case is $3/4 * 3/4 + 1/4 * 1/2 = 11/16$, which is less than $12/16 = 3/4$.

The intuition behind the performance of matching dictators carries over to more general functions: if f and g are functions which do not share matching "influential coordinates", then the fact that the erasures are correlated in the 2Lin(Z_2)-TEST doesn't matter. Indeed, we develop an Invariance Principle in the full version of the paper that shows that when f and g do not share matching influential coordinates, then the probability they pass the 2Lin(Z_2)-TEST is the same as the probability they pass a modified version of the test where the erasures of $\boldsymbol{x}$ and $\boldsymbol{y}$ are performed independently of each other. In fact, this Invariance Principle can be applied to *any* "function-in-the-middle" test in the above mold, meaning any test in which f and g are only every compared to an intermediary function h.

The next step is to upper bound the success probability of any pair of functions in the uncorrelated version of the 2Lin(Z_2)-TEST. This is a problem in non-interactive correlation distillation (NICD), a subject which is previewed in Section 4.1 and given full treatment in Section 6. The particular result that applies to this test is Theorem 6.6, which shows that the uncorrelated version of the test cannot be passed with probability more than 11/16. Thus, nonmatching dictators are basically optimal among functions f and g which do not share matching influential coordinates.

Encoding and decoding.

It remains to translate these results on the performance of the test to results on the hardness of the 2Lin(Z_2) instance we've generated. This part is entirely standard and follows the basic methodology of Håstad [Hås01]. We have shown above that matching dictators pass the test with probability 3/4. This means that if the starting Label Cover instance was fully satisfiable, then the 2Lin(Z_2) instance is 3/4-satisfiable. On the other hand, if on a significant fraction of the edges (u, v), the Long Codes f_u and g_v pass the 2Lin(Z_2)-TEST with probability greater than 11/16, then our Invariance Principle tells us that they must share matching influential coordinates. Thus, we can decode the Long Codes to an assignment which satisfies a constant fraction of the Label Cover edges, which concludes our soundness proof. This final part of the hardness result we present for general function-in-the-middle tests in Section 4. Therein we also show that the resulting 2Lin(Z_2) instance is of quasilinear size, implying that under the Exponential Time Hypothesis, nearly exponential time is needed to $(3/4, 11/16 + \epsilon)$-approximate 2Lin(Z_2). One question remains: why does this exactly match Håstad's hardness result? We answer this in the full version of the paper.

Hardness for other CSPs.

A general definition of a function-in-the-middle test is given in Definition 4.6. If such a test T performs its checks using predicates from the set Φ, then Theorem 4.18 automatically implies (c, s)-approximating the Max-Φ problem under quasilinear reductions, where c is the probability matching dictators pass T and s is the highest probability with which any functions can pass test T', the version of test T for which erasures are uncorrelated. The remainder of the paper constructs tests T using various sets of predicates Φ. Our main result, for $\mathsf{2Lin}(Z_q)$, is presented first in Section 5. (The description of the $\mathsf{2Lin}(Z_q)$ test is simple: take the above $\mathsf{2Lin}(Z_2)$-TEST and replace all instances of the set $\{-1, 1\}$ with Z_q.) Next, in Section 6, we analyze the $\mathsf{2Lin}(Z_2)$-TEST (an alternative analysis, using the Fourier transform method, is presented in the full version of the paper). Finally, in Section 7, we give our Max-Cut, 2And, and 2Sat tests.

Fixing the $\mathsf{2Lin}(Z_2)$-TEST.

There are a couple of technical details which we omitted in the above description of the $\mathsf{2Lin}(Z_2)$-TEST for sake of exposition. As it turns out, we can assume that the initial Label Cover instance is d-to-d rather than d-to-1, and we need not assume it is necessarily bipartite. This is the version we choose to present in full in Section 6.3. In addition, when constructing the actual hardness instance, for technical reasons we need to slightly perturb $\boldsymbol{x}$ and $\boldsymbol{y}$ after forming $\widetilde{\boldsymbol{x}}$ and $\widetilde{\boldsymbol{y}}$ and use these perturbed versions as the inputs to f and g. These noisy versions of $\boldsymbol{x}$ and $\boldsymbol{y}$ are referred to as $\dot{\boldsymbol{x}}$ and $\dot{\boldsymbol{y}}$, respectively. Details about this are presented in Section 4. Finally, we will often reverse the order the strings are selected, as the following is equivalent method of selecting $\boldsymbol{x}$, $\boldsymbol{y}$, $\widetilde{\boldsymbol{x}}$, and $\widetilde{\boldsymbol{y}}$: first select $\widetilde{\boldsymbol{x}}$ and $\widetilde{\boldsymbol{y}}$ so that they are distributed as in the $\mathsf{2Lin}(Z_2)$-TEST. Then, "fill in" their $*$'s with uniformly random elements of $\{-1, 1\}$ to form $\boldsymbol{x}$ and $\boldsymbol{y}$.

4. INAPPROXIMABILITY FROM NICD

In this section we describe our method for proving 2-CSP inapproximability results by reduction from Label Cover. It is somewhat similar the standard LC- and UG-based approaches ("Long Codes", "dictator tests", etc.) but has some twists. We prefer to think of it as reducing inapproximability to problems in *non-interactive correlation distillation* (NICD).

4.1 An example NICD problem

Before stating formal definitions, we give an example which illustrates the flavor of the NICD problems we'll encounter. Let f be a party who receives a uniformly random q-ary string $\boldsymbol{x} \in Z_q^n$. The string $\boldsymbol{x}$ is sent to a "middleman" h along an *erasure channel* which erases each symbol independently with probability 1/2; thus h receives some $\widetilde{\boldsymbol{x}} \in (Z_q \cup \{*\})^n$. Now f and h have some correlated information, but they are not allowed to interact further. Nevertheless, they would like to agree on a common symbol $\ell \in Z_q$. (This setup explains the name "non-interactive correlation distillation".) The "strategy" of f is just a function $f : Z_q^n \to Z_q$, and similarly the strategy of h is a function $h : (Z_q \cup \{*\})^n \to Z_q$. Thus the party and middleman together succeed with probability $\mathbf{Pr}_{\boldsymbol{x},\widetilde{\boldsymbol{x}}}[f(\boldsymbol{x}) = h(\widetilde{\boldsymbol{x}})]$.

The NICD problem here is to find f and h which maximize this success probability. Of course, if f and h are (matching) constant functions then the success probability is 1. However such trivial solutions are disallowed by insisting the function f be (at least) *balanced*, meaning $\mathbf{Pr}_{\boldsymbol{x}}[f(\boldsymbol{x}) = \ell] = \frac{1}{q}$ for all $\ell \in Z_q$.

This erasure-channel NICD problem was first proposed by Yang [Yan04] in the boolean ($q = 2$) case. He showed that the success probability is at most $\frac{1}{2} + \frac{1}{2\sqrt{2}} \approx .85$; he also conjectured that the best upper bound is in fact $\frac{3}{4}$, the success probability achieved when f is a *dictator* (i.e. $f(x) = x_i$ for some i) and h plays optimally for this dictator. More generally, for the binary erasure channel with erasure probability $1-\rho$, Yang bounded the success probability by $\frac{1}{2} + \frac{1}{2}\sqrt{\rho}$ but conjectured that the dictator's success probability $\frac{1}{2} + \frac{1}{2}\rho$ is optimal (at least for $\rho \leq \frac{1}{2}$). In Section 6 we prove this conjecture. Furthermore, in Section 5 we prove an analogous conjecture for the q-ary erasure channel with erasure probability $\frac{1}{2}$.

It is by designing and analyzing NICD problems of this basic flavor that we prove NP-hardness of approximability for various 2-CSPs.

4.2 NICD tests

It is natural to allow the functions in NICD problems to be "randomized". We formalize this as follows:

DEFINITION 4.1. *Let $\triangle_q$ denote the set of probability distributions over Z_q. Equivalently, $\triangle_q = \{(p_0, \ldots, p_{q-1}) \in \mathbb{R}^q_{\geq 0} \mid p_0 + \cdots + p_{q-1} = 1\}$. We often identify an element $\ell \in Z_q$ with the constant probability distribution $e_\ell = (0, \ldots, 0, 1, 0, \ldots, 0) \in \triangle_q$ (with the 1 in coordinate ℓ). We may think of a function f with range $\triangle_q$ as being a "randomized function" with range Z_q.*

We will not use the notion of a "randomized function" until Section 5, but it is convenient to point out that "non-randomized functions"–those whose range is Z_q–may be equivalently written as having domain $\triangle_q$. Such non-randomized functions only ever map to e_ℓ, for $\ell \in Z_q$. We now give the definitions which let us rule out "trivial" solutions to NICD problems:

DEFINITION 4.2. *The function $f : Z_q^m \to \triangle_q$ is* balanced *if $\mathbf{E}_{\boldsymbol{x}\sim Z_q^m}[f(\boldsymbol{x})] = (\frac{1}{q}, \ldots, \frac{1}{q})$. Here and throughout, $\boldsymbol{x} \sim Z_q^m$ means that $\boldsymbol{x}$ is uniformly distributed.*

DEFINITION 4.3. *The function $f : Z_q^m \to \triangle_q$ is* folded *(a stronger condition than being balanced) if $f(x + \ell) = \mathrm{rot}_\ell(f(x))$ for all $x \in Z_q^m$ and $\ell \in Z_q$. Here $x + \ell$ is shorthand for $x + (\ell, \ell, \ldots, \ell)$, and $\mathrm{rot}_\ell(\nu) \in \triangle_q$ is the "cyclic rotation of ν by ℓ places"; i.e., $\mathrm{rot}_\ell(\nu)_i = \nu_{(i-\ell \bmod q)}$. When $f : Z_q^m \to Z_q$ is "non-randomized", this simply means that $f(x + \ell) = f(x) + \ell$.*

We require a few more definitions:

DEFINITION 4.4. *We write $\mu^d_{q,\rho}$ for the probability distribution on $Z_q^d \cup \{*^d\}$ which is uniform on Z_q^d with probability ρ and $*^d$ with probability $1 - \rho$. If $d = 1$ or $\rho = 1$ we omit writing it. Note that $\mu^d_{q,\rho}$ is invariant under permutations of the d coordinates.*

DEFINITION 4.5. *Given a string $x \in Z_q^m$, an η*-noisy copy *is defined to be the randomly chosen string $\dot{\boldsymbol{x}}$ in which for each $i \in [m]$ independently, $\dot{\boldsymbol{x}}_i = x_i$ with probability $1 - \eta$*

and $\dot{\boldsymbol{x}}_i$ is set uniformly at random with probability η. We also define the operator T_η *on functions* $f : Z_q^m \to \triangle_q$ *by* $\mathrm{T}_\eta f(x) = \mathbf{E}_{\dot{\boldsymbol{x}}}[f(\dot{\boldsymbol{x}})]$. *We may denote this by* $\dot{\boldsymbol{x}} \sim_\rho x$.

We are now able to define the general class of NICD "tests" which will be useful for our inapproximability results. Because we are working with Label Cover our tests need to operate on "blocked" functions; i.e., functions over domains $\Sigma^{dK} \cong (\Sigma^d)^K$. Aside from this generality, we have chosen to make our definition rather narrow for the sake of simplicity. To attack inapproximability for more CSPs, one might wish to generalize this definition in several directions; however, such generalizations would require proving more complicated "Invariance" theorems.

DEFINITION 4.6. *A* 2-party, q-ary, Φ-based, (d_1, d_2)-blocked, η-noise correlated test TEST *consists of two probability distributions:*

- *A "correlated information distribution"* π *on* $(Z_q^{d_1} \cup \{*^{d_1}\}) \times (Z_q^{d_2} \cup \{*^{d_2}\})$. *Each marginal* π_j *on* $Z_q^{d_j} \cup \{*^{d_j}\}$ *(for* $j = 1, 2$*) must be equal to* μ_{q,ρ_j}^d *for some* $\rho_j \in [0, 1]$.
- *A "test distribution"* $\mathcal{T}$ *on* $\Phi \times \{1, 2\}$, *where* Φ *is a fixed collection of predicates* $\phi : Z_q \times Z_q \to \{0, 1\}$.

Given $K \in \mathbb{N}^+$, TEST *operates on blocked functions* $f : Z_q^{d_1 K} \to Z_q$, $g : Z_q^{d_2 K} \to Z_q$, *and* $h : (Z_q^{d_1} \cup \{*^{d_1}\})^K \times (Z_q^{d_2} \cup \{*^{d_2}\})^K \to Z_q$ *as follows:*

1. *A pair of strings* $(\widetilde{\boldsymbol{x}}, \widetilde{\boldsymbol{y}}) \in (Z_q^{d_1} \cup \{*^{d_1}\})^K \times (Z_q^{d_2} \cup \{*^{d_2}\})^K$ *is chosen randomly from the product distribution* $\pi^{\otimes K}$.
2. *String* $\boldsymbol{x} \in Z_q^{d_1 K}$ *is formed by randomly "filling in"* $\widetilde{\boldsymbol{x}}$*; i.e., replacing each* $*$ *by an independent uniformly random symbol from* Z_q. *Similarly* $\boldsymbol{y} \in Z_q^{d_2 K}$ *is (independently) formed by randomly filling in* $\widetilde{\boldsymbol{y}}$.
3. *String* $\dot{\boldsymbol{x}} \in Z_q^{d_1 K}$ *is set to be an* η*-noisy copy of* $\boldsymbol{x}$, *and similarly for* $\dot{\boldsymbol{y}}$.
4. *Finally,* $(\boldsymbol{\phi}, \boldsymbol{j})$ *is chosen from* $\mathcal{T}$. *If* $\boldsymbol{j} = 1$ *then one "tests"* $\boldsymbol{\phi}(f(\dot{\boldsymbol{x}}), h(\widetilde{\boldsymbol{x}}, \widetilde{\boldsymbol{y}}))$*; if* $\boldsymbol{j} = 2$ *then one "tests"* $\boldsymbol{\phi}(g(\dot{\boldsymbol{y}}), h(\widetilde{\boldsymbol{x}}, \widetilde{\boldsymbol{y}}))$.

DEFINITION 4.7. *The* success probability *or* value *of* f, g, h *on* TEST, *denoted* $\mathrm{Val}_{\mathrm{TEST}}(f, g, h)$, *is simply the probability that the test is satisfied.*

REMARK 4.8. *Given* TEST *and functions* f, g, *the optimal choice (or choices) for* h *is determined. We will often just consider varying* f *and* g, *and choosing the best* h *to go along with them. We therefore introduce the notation* $\mathrm{Val}_{\mathrm{TEST}}(f, g) = \max_h\{\mathrm{Val}_{\mathrm{TEST}}(f, g, h)\}$.

DEFINITION 4.9. *The* optimal success probability *or* optimal value *of* TEST, *denoted* Opt(TEST), *is* $\max_{f,g}\{\mathrm{Val}_{\mathrm{TEST}}(f, g)\}$. *We also define* $\mathrm{Opt}_{\mathrm{folded}}(\mathrm{TEST})$ *for when the maximization is only over folded* f *and* g, *and also* $\mathrm{Opt}_{\mathrm{balanced}}(\mathrm{TEST})$ *for when the maximization is only over balanced* f *and* g.

FACT 4.10. *Let* TEST *be a 2-party 0-noise test and let* TEST_η *be its* η*-noisy version. Then* $\mathrm{Opt}(\mathrm{TEST}) \geq \mathrm{Opt}(\mathrm{TEST}_\eta)$ *and* $\mathrm{Opt}_{\mathrm{folded}}(\mathrm{TEST}) \geq \mathrm{Opt}_{\mathrm{folded}}(\mathrm{TEST}_\eta)$.

PROOF. This is because $\mathrm{Val}_{\mathrm{TEST}_\eta}(f, g) = \mathrm{Val}_{\mathrm{TEST}}(\mathrm{T}_\eta f, \mathrm{T}_\eta g)$, and $\mathrm{T}_\eta f$, $\mathrm{T}_\eta g$ are folded if f, g are. However, we must account for the fact that $\mathrm{T}_\eta f$ and $\mathrm{T}_\eta g$ do not necessarily have the domain Z_q, even if f and g do. Consider selecting $\boldsymbol{z}$ (respectively, $\boldsymbol{w}$) from a distribution on strings in $Z_q^{d_1 K}$ (respectively, $Z_q^{d_2 K}$) for which each coordinate is independently 0 with probability η and uniform on Z_q otherwise. Then given $\boldsymbol{x}$, $\boldsymbol{x} + \boldsymbol{z}$ is distributed as $\dot{\boldsymbol{x}}$, and given $\boldsymbol{y}$, $\boldsymbol{y} + \boldsymbol{w}$ is distributed as $\dot{\boldsymbol{y}}$. Thus, in TEST_η, we may use $\boldsymbol{x} + \boldsymbol{z}$ and $\boldsymbol{y} + \boldsymbol{w}$ in place of $\dot{\boldsymbol{x}}$ and $\dot{\boldsymbol{y}}$, respectively. By the probabilistic method, there is a setting to z and w for which, conditioned on $\boldsymbol{z} = z$ and $\boldsymbol{w} = w$, the test is passed with probability at least $\mathrm{Val}_{\mathrm{TEST}_\eta}(f, g)$. Then define the functions $f' = f(\cdot + z)$ and $g' = g(\cdot + w)$. Clearly, $\mathrm{Val}_{\mathrm{TEST}}(f', g') \geq \mathrm{Val}_{\mathrm{TEST}_\eta}(f, g)$. Furthermore, f' and g' are folded if f and g are. □

4.3 Blocks, influences, Invariance, and uncorrelated tests

As mentioned, our 2-party NICD tests operate on "blocked" functions; e.g., $f : Z_q^{d_1 K} \to Z_q$, $g : Z_q^{d_2 K} \to Z_q$. In fact, for reductions from $\mathsf{LC}_{d_1 K, d_2 K}$ the "blocks" will not necessarily be contiguous. Rather, the "blocks" for f will be $\pi_u^{-1}(1), \ldots, \pi_u^{-1}(K)$ for some d_1-to-1 map $\pi_u : [d_1 K] \to [K]$, and similarly for g with a d_2-to-1 map π_v.

DEFINITION 4.11. *Given a 2-party* (d_1, d_2)*-blocked test* TEST, *we introduce the natural notion of applying it to* f, g, h under the "blocking maps" π_u and π_v. *Notice that for this to make sense, it is crucial that our definition of 2-party tests is insensitive to permutations of coordinates within blocks and also to permutations of blocks. (Briefly this is because the distributions* μ_{q,ρ_j}^d *are permutation-invariant, the test uses product distributions across the* K *blocks, and because making* η*-noisy copies acts independently on coordinates.)*

Often the optimal choice of f and g for a given 2-party NICD test is "matching dictators" (note that dictators are folded):

DEFINITION 4.12. *Suppose that* $f : Z_q^{d_1 K} \to Z_q$ *and* $g : Z_q^{d_2 K} \to Z_q$ *are* dictator functions, *meaning that* $f(x) = x_i$ *for some* $i \in [d_1 K]$ *and* $g(y) = y_j$ *for some* $j \in [d_2 K]$. *We say they are* matching dictators *(under the blocking maps* π_u, π_v*) if* $\pi_u(i) = \pi_v(j)$*; otherwise we say they are* non-matching dictators.

As is common in inapproximability, we will be concerned with functions which are "far from" being dictators in the sense of having "small noisy-influences". To make this notion precise we recall the *Hoeffding orthogonal decomposition* (or *Efron–Stein decomposition*) for functions $f : \Sigma^m \to \mathbb{R}^q$:

DEFINITION 4.13. *For* $f : \Sigma^m \to \mathbb{R}^q$ *we define* $\|f\|_2^2 = \mathbf{E}_{\boldsymbol{x} \sim \Sigma^m}[|f(\boldsymbol{x})|^2]$. *Here* $|\cdot|$ *denotes Euclidean length in* $\mathbb{R}^q$. *Note that if* $f : \Sigma^m \to \triangle_q$ *then* $\|f\|_2^2 \leq 1$.

FACT 4.14. *Every function* $f : \Sigma^m \to \mathbb{R}^q$ *can be written as* $f = \sum_{S \subseteq [m]} f^S$, *where the functions* $f^S : \Sigma^m \to \mathbb{R}^q$ *have the following properties:* $f^S(x)$ *depends only on* $(x_i)_{i \in S}$*; and,* $\mathbf{E}[\langle f^S(\boldsymbol{x}), f^{S'}(\boldsymbol{x})\rangle] = 0$ *for any* $S \neq S'$, *where* $\boldsymbol{x}$ *is uniformly distributed on* Σ^m *and* $\langle \cdot, \cdot \rangle$ *denotes the usual inner product on* $\mathbb{R}^q$. *As a consequence,*

$$\|f\|_2^2 = \sum_{S \subseteq [m]} \|f^S\|_2^2.$$

DEFINITION 4.15. *The* η-noisy influence *of* $B \subseteq [m]$ *on* $f : \Sigma^m \to \mathbb{R}^q$ *is defined to be*

$$\mathbf{Inf}_B^{(1-\eta)}[f] = \sum_{S: S \cap B \neq \emptyset} (1-\eta)^{|S|} \| f^S \|_2^2.$$

Suppose that $f : Z_q^{d_1 K} \to Z_q$ and $g : Z_q^{d_2 K} \to Z_q$ have (roughly speaking) "no influential blocks in common" (under blocks induced by π_u and π_v). For example, f and g may be non-matching dictators. In this case, we might expect that f and g cannot "take advantage" of the correlation between h's inputs $\widetilde{\boldsymbol{x}}$ and $\widetilde{\boldsymbol{y}}$ in test TEST. The key technical result we need for our hardness reduction is an "Invariance" theorem which formalizes this idea:

DEFINITION 4.16. *Given a 2-party correlated test* TEST, *its* uncorrelated version TEST' *is the same test but with the pair of strings* $(\widetilde{\boldsymbol{x}}, \widetilde{\boldsymbol{y}})$ *drawn* independently *from* π*'s marginal distributions; i.e.,* $\widetilde{\boldsymbol{x}} \sim \pi_1$ *and* $\widetilde{\boldsymbol{y}} \sim \pi_2$ *independently.*

THEOREM 4.17. *There is a function* $\kappa(\eta, \epsilon, q) > 0$ *with* $\kappa(\eta, \epsilon, q) = (\eta\epsilon/q)^{O((\log q)/\eta)}$ *such that the following holds:*

Let TEST *be a 2-party, q-ary,* (d_1, d_2)*-blocked,* η*-noise correlated test. Let* TEST' *denote its uncorrelated version. Assume we are applying these tests under the blocking maps* π_u *and* π_v*. Let* $f : Z_q^{d_1 K} \to \triangle_q$ *and* $g : Z_q^{d_2 K} \to \triangle_q$ *satisfy*

$$\min(\mathbf{Inf}^{(1-\eta)}_{\pi_u^{-1}(t)}[f], \mathbf{Inf}^{(1-\eta)}_{\pi_v^{-1}(t)}[g]) \le \kappa(\eta, \epsilon, q) \quad \forall t \in [K].$$

Then $\quad \text{Val}_{\text{TEST}}(f, g) \le \text{Opt}(\text{TEST}') + \epsilon,$

and $\quad \text{Val}_{\text{TEST}}(f, g) \le \text{Opt}_{\text{folded}}(\text{TEST}') + \epsilon,$ *if* f, g *folded.*

We prove Theorem 4.17 in the full version of the paper. Mostly, our proof follows the general outline of Mossel's Invariance theorem [Mos10], with a few differences. In the terminology of [Mos10], we have a sequence of K orthonormal ensembles, each of which corresponds to a certain block of $\widetilde{\boldsymbol{x}}$ and $\widetilde{\boldsymbol{y}}$. Mossel's Invariance theorem uses as a parameter for an application of hypercontractivity the least nonzero probability of an assignment, which in our case is $\frac{1}{2}q^{-\max\{d_1,d_2\}}$. This is too small for us. Instead, we are able to maneuver it so that we only need to worry about the hypercontractivity of Z_q.

4.4 The hardness of approximation reduction

The following theorem shows how to convert a 2-party correlation test to a hardness of approximation result. The proof is quite standard, and largely follows of Håstad's methods [Hås01] .

THEOREM 4.18.

Let TEST *be a 2-party, q-ary,* Φ*-based,* (d_1, d_2)*-blocked, 0-noise correlated test.*

Let TEST' *be its uncorrelated version.*

Suppose that matching dictators achieve success probability at least c for TEST.

Suppose also that $\text{Opt}(\text{TEST}') \le s$.

Let $\eta, \epsilon \in \mathbb{Q}^+$ *and assume* $\delta \le \epsilon \cdot \eta^2 \cdot \kappa(\eta, \epsilon, q)^2$*, where* κ *is as in Theorem 4.17.*

Then there is a reduction from $(1, \delta)$*-deciding* $\mathsf{LC}_{d_1 K, d_2 K}$ *to* $(c - \eta, s + 2\epsilon)$*-deciding* Max-$\Phi$.

If instead we assume $\text{Opt}_{\text{folded}}(\text{TEST}') \le s$ *then we get the result for* Max-Φ^+.

The reduction maps size-n instances to size-$q^{O(d_1 K + d_2 K)} n$ *instances and runs in time polynomial in the size of its output.*

PROOF. Let $((U, V), E, (\pi_{e,u}, \pi_{e,v}))$ be a given size-n instance of $\mathsf{LC}_{d_1 K, d_2 K}$. For each $u \in U$ (respectively, $v \in V$) the reduction introduces a collection of Max-Φ variables identified with $Z_q^{d_1 K}$ (respectively, $Z_q^{d_2 K}$); we think of an assignment to these variables as a function $f_u : Z_q^{d_1 K} \to Z_q$ (respectively, $g_v : Z_q^{d_2 K} \to Z_q$). Furthermore, for each edge $(u, v) \in E$ the reduction introduces a collection of Max-Φ variables identified with $(Z_q^{d_1} \cup \{*^{d_1}\})^K \times (Z_q^{d_2} \cup \{*^{d_2}\})^K$; we think of an assignment to these variables as a function h_{uv} with range Z_q.

Let TEST_η denote the η-noisy version of the test TEST (and TEST'_η its uncorrelated version). For each edge $e = (u, v) \in E$ the reduction introduces a collection of Φ-constraints on the assignments f_u, g_v, and h_{uv}. These constraints are precisely those given by applying TEST_η under the blocking maps $\pi_{e,u}$, $\pi_{e,v}$ (with weights/probabilities scaled down by a factor of $|E|$). This completes the description of the reduction.

Completeness.

Assume that $F : U \to [d_1 K], V \to [d_2 K]$ is an assignment satisfying all constraints of the $\mathsf{LC}_{d_1 K, d_2 K}$ instance. Consider the assignment to the Max-Φ instance in which for each $u \in U$ and $v \in V$ we take $f_u(x) = x_{F(u)}$, $g_v(y) = y_{F(v)}$. For $e = (u, v) \in E$, these are matching dictators with respect to $\pi_{e,u}$ and $\pi_{e,v}$, since F satisfies the constraint on e. Therefore there exists a choice for h_{uv} such that $\text{Val}_{\text{TEST}}(f_u, g_v, h_{uv}) \ge c$. Since f_u and g_v are dictators it is easy to see that $\text{Val}_{\text{TEST}_\eta}(f_u, g_v, h_{uv})$ is still at least $c - \eta$. Since this holds for each edge $(u, v) \in E$, it follows that our assignment achieves value at least $c - \eta$ on the Max-Φ instance.

Soundness.

We prove the contrapositive. Suppose there are assignments $(f_u)_{u \in U}$, $(g_v)_{v \in V}$, $(h_{uv})_{(u,v) \in E}$ for the Max-Φ which collectively achieve value exceeding $s + 2\epsilon$. Then for at least an ϵ fraction of edges $e = (u, v) \in E$ — call them "good" edges — we have $\text{Val}_{\text{TEST}_\eta}(f_u, g_v, h_{uv}) > s + \epsilon \ge \text{Opt}(\text{TEST}'_\eta) + \epsilon$, the second inequality being Fact 4.10. We may therefore apply Theorem 4.17 to deduce that for each good (u, v),

$$\exists t_{uv} \in [K] \text{ s.t. } \mathbf{Inf}^{(1-\eta)}_{\pi_{e,u}^{-1}(t_{uv})}[f_u], \mathbf{Inf}^{(1-\eta)}_{\pi_{e,v}^{-1}(t_{uv})}[g_v] \ge \kappa = \kappa(\eta, \epsilon, q). \quad (1)$$

Consider now the following randomized procedure for generating an assignment $\boldsymbol{F}$ for the LC instance. For each $u \in U$, the procedure first chooses $S \subseteq [d_1 K]$ with probability $\|f_u^S\|_2^2$. (From Definition 4.13 these numbers sum to at most 1; for any remaining probability, S can be chosen arbitrarily.) Then $\boldsymbol{F}(u)$ is set to be a uniformly random element of S (or an arbitrary label if $S = \emptyset$). An identical procedure is used to assign $\boldsymbol{F}(v)$ for $v \in V$, based on g_v. Observe that for any set $B \subseteq [d_1 K]$ and $u \in U$,

$$\begin{aligned}\mathbf{Pr}[\boldsymbol{F}(u) \in B] &\ge \sum_{S: S \cap B \neq \emptyset} \|f_u^S\|_2^2 \cdot (|S \cap B|/|S|) \\ &\ge \sum_{S: S \cap B \neq \emptyset} \|f_u^S\|_2^2 \cdot \eta(1-\eta)^{|S|/|S \cap B|} \\ &\ge \eta \sum_{S: S \cap B \neq \emptyset} \|f_u^S\|_2^2 \cdot (1-\eta)^{|S|} = \eta \mathbf{Inf}_B^{(1-\eta)}[f_u],\end{aligned} \quad (2)$$

where the second inequality follows since $r \geq \eta(1-\eta)^{1/r}$, for all $r > 0, \eta \in [0,1]$. The same holds for $v \in V$.

Now for a good edge $e = (u, v)$, let us estimate the probability (over $\boldsymbol{F}$) that $\boldsymbol{F}(u)$ and $\boldsymbol{F}(v)$ satisfy the constraint associated with e. It is

$$\begin{aligned}
&\Pr_{\boldsymbol{F}}[\pi_{e,u}(\boldsymbol{F}(u)) = \pi_{e,v}(\boldsymbol{F}(v))] \\
&\quad \geq \mathbf{Pr}[\boldsymbol{F}(u) \in \pi_{e,u}^{-1}(t_{uv}) \ \&\ \boldsymbol{F}(v) \in \pi_{e,v}^{-1}(t_{uv})] \\
&\quad = \mathbf{Pr}[\boldsymbol{F}(u) \in \pi_{e,u}^{-1}(t_{uv})] \cdot \mathbf{Pr}[\boldsymbol{F}(v) \in \pi_{e,v}^{-1}(t_{uv})] \\
&\quad \geq \eta^2 \cdot \mathbf{Inf}^{(1-\eta)}_{\pi_{e,u}^{-1}(t_{uv})}[f_u] \cdot \mathbf{Inf}^{(1-\eta)}_{\pi_{e,v}^{-1}(t_{uv})}[g_v] \geq \eta^2\kappa^2,
\end{aligned}$$

where we used (2) and then (1). It follows that expected fraction of constraints in the LC instance that $\boldsymbol{F}$ satisfies is at least $\epsilon \cdot \eta^2\kappa^2 \geq \delta$; hence the optimal value of the LC instance is at least δ.

This completes the proof except for the statement about $\mathrm{Opt}_{\mathrm{folded}}(\textsc{Test}')$ and Max-Φ^+. For this we the standard folding trick: Instead of having the reduction introduce a collection of variables corresponding to $Z_q^{d_1K}$ for each $u \in U$, we only introduce variables for $Z_q^{d_1K-1}$. We think of an assignment for these variables as the restriction of a function $f_u : Z_q^{d_1K} \to Z_q$ to inputs of the form $(0, x')$, $x' \in Z_q^{d_1K-1}$. We extend f_u to a folded function via $f_u(\ell, x') = f_u(0, x' - (\ell, \dots, \ell)) + \ell$. Is this way, any Max-$\Phi$ constraint involving $f_u(x)$ can be replaced with a Max-Φ^+ constraint involving $f_u(0, x')$. We similarly arrange for folded functions g_v. We now proceed through the above proof: for the completeness we use the fact that dictators are folded; for the soundness we use the folded versions of Fact 4.10 and Theorem 4.17. □

Corollary 4.19. *Let $2 \leq q = q(n) \leq (\log\log\log n)^3$. Assume that for all $d_2, K \in \mathbb{N}^+$ there is a $q^{O(d_2K)}$-time algorithm for generating (the description of) a (d_1, d_2)-blocked* Test *satisfying the hypotheses of Theorem 4.18, for some $d_1 \leq d_2$. Assume that $c < 1$. Then for a certain $\epsilon = \epsilon(n) = \widetilde{\Theta}(1/\log\log\log n)$, there is a quasilinear-size reduction from size-n instances of* 3Sat *to the problem of $(c, s+\epsilon)$-deciding* Max-Φ *(or* Max-Φ^+*, under the assumption* $\mathrm{Opt}_{\mathrm{folded}}(\textsc{Test}') \leq s$*).*

Proof. (Sketch.) This follows by combining the Moshkovitz–Raz Theorem with Theorem 4.18. One takes $\delta = (\log\log n)^{-c}$ for a sufficiently small constant c and $\eta = \epsilon$. With these choices the conditions of Theorem 4.18 are satisfied and the overall size of the Max-Φ instance produced is still $n^{1+o(1)}$. Using $c < 1$, we can convert the resulting $(c-\epsilon, s+2\epsilon)$-hardness into $(c, s+O(\epsilon))$-hardness using padding. □

5. A TEST FOR 2Lin(Z_Q)

In this section we state and analyze the test which yields our Main Theorem on the inapproximability of 2Lin(Z_q). We will be restricting attention to folded functions, and thus we can get a hardness result for 2Lin(Z_q) by designing a q-ary $=$-based test. In fact, our test is just the 2-party, blocked version of NICD over the q-ary $\frac{1}{2}$-erasure channel; i.e., the example NICD problem discussed at the beginning of Section 4.

2Lin(Z_q)-Test$_d$

A 2-party, q-ary, $=$-based, (d,d)-blocked, 0-noise correlated test

- The correlated information distribution π on $(Z_q^d \cup \{*^d\}) \times (Z_q^d \cup \{*^d\})$ is defined as follows:

$$(\widetilde{\boldsymbol{a}}, \widetilde{\boldsymbol{b}}) \sim \pi \text{ means } (\widetilde{\boldsymbol{a}}, \widetilde{\boldsymbol{b}}) \tag{3}$$

$$= \begin{cases} \text{uniformly random from } Z_q^d \times \{*^d\}, & \text{w/prob } \frac{1}{2}; \\ \text{uniformly random from } \{*^d\} \times Z_q^d, & \text{w/prob } \frac{1}{2}. \end{cases} \tag{4}$$

- The test distribution is: with probability $\frac{1}{2}$ test $f(\boldsymbol{x}) = h(\widetilde{\boldsymbol{x}}, \widetilde{\boldsymbol{y}})$; with probability $\frac{1}{2}$ test $g(\boldsymbol{y}) = h(\widetilde{\boldsymbol{x}}, \widetilde{\boldsymbol{y}})$.

Remark 5.1. *For this test, the block sizes are unimportant so we have chosen $d_1 = d_2 = d$ for simplicity. Thus our* NP*-hardness result for Unique-Games does not even need to reduce from Label-Cover with "projection constraints"; any* LC_{d_1K, d_2K} *would suffice.*

Notation 5.2. *For $t \in [K]$ we will write $z[t]$ for the tth block of string $z \in (Z_q^d \cup \{*^d\})^K$. We will also write simply* 2Lin(Z_q)-Test *when $d = 1$.*

Observation 5.3. *It is helpful to also think about the strings in* 2Lin(Z_q)-Test$_d$ *being generated in the opposite order, as described in Section 1.2. By this we mean the following viewpoint: First, $\boldsymbol{x}, \boldsymbol{y} \sim Z_q^{dK}$ are chosen* independently *and uniformly at random. Then $\widetilde{\boldsymbol{x}}, \widetilde{\boldsymbol{y}} \in (Z_q^d \cup \{*^d\})^K$ are formed as follows: independently for each block $t \in [K]$, exactly one of $\boldsymbol{x}[t]$, $\boldsymbol{y}[t]$ is replaced with $*^d$, with probability $\frac{1}{2}$ each. For each block t we think of h as "knowing" either $\boldsymbol{x}[t]$ or $\boldsymbol{y}[t]$, and "knowing that it doesn't know" the other one.*

For the "completeness" part of our hardness result, we compute the success probability of matching dictators:

Proposition 5.4. *Matching dictators achieve success probability $\frac{1}{2} + \frac{1}{2q}$ in* 2Lin(Z_q)-Test$_d$.

Proof. Suppose $f, g : Z_q^{dK} \to Z_q$ are of the form $f(x) = x_i$, $g(y) = y_j$, where i, j are both in the tth block (i.e., $(t-1)d < i, j \leq td$). Let $h(\widetilde{x}, \widetilde{y})$ be the following (optimal) function: if $\widetilde{x}[t] \neq *^d$ then h outputs $\widetilde{x}_i$; if $\widetilde{y}[t] \neq *^d$ then h outputs $\widetilde{y}_j$. Half of the time h is tested against the function (f or g) whose output it "knows"; then it succeeds with probability 1. The other half of the time h is tested against the function whose output it doesn't know; in this case it succeeds with probability $\mathbf{Pr}[\boldsymbol{x}_i = \boldsymbol{y}_j] = \frac{1}{q}$. Thus the overall success probability is $\frac{1}{2} + \frac{1}{2q}$. □

We are able to show that matching dictators constitute an optimal folded solution for 2Lin(Z_q)-Test$_d$. This is an immediate consequence of the following statement about the "1-party" version of the test:

Theorem 5.5. *Let q-NICD-Test denote the "1-party" version of* 2Lin(Z_q)-Test$_d$*, where we test h against f with probability 1 rather than probability $\frac{1}{2}$; in other words, the d-blocked version of the q-ary $\frac{1}{2}$-erasure NICD problem discussed in Section 4.1. Then* $\mathrm{Opt}_{\mathrm{folded}}(q\text{-NICD-Test}) \leq \frac{1}{2} + \frac{1}{2q}$.

We will prove Theorem 5.5 later in this section; we actually require it for the *soundness* part of our hardness result.

As discussed in Section 4.1, Theorem 5.5 resolves the q-ary (folded) generalization of Yang's conjecture on ρ-erasure NICD for $\rho = \frac{1}{2}$. For $q > 2$ we were unable to generalize Theorem 5.5 to any other value of $\rho \in (0, 1)$. A potentially complicating factor is the surprising fact that even for $d = 1$, there are folded functions $f : Z_q^{dK} \to Z_q$ which depend on *more* than one coordinate yet achieve $\mathrm{Val}_{q\text{-NICD-TEST}}(f) = \frac{1}{q} + \rho(1 - \frac{1}{q})$, the same value achieved by dictators. For example, the function $f : Z_3^2 \to Z_3$ defined by $f(a, a) = a$, $f(a, a-1) = a$, $f(a, a+1) = a + 1$ is folded and it is easy to check that it succeeds (using optimal h) with probability $\frac{1}{3} + \frac{2}{3}\rho$. More generally, the function $f : Z_q^2 \to Z_q$ defined by "$f(a, b) = a$ if $a - b \pmod q \in \{0, 1, \dots, \lceil q/2 \rceil - 1\}$ else $f(a, b) = b$" is folded, and it can be checked that it has value $\frac{1}{q} + \rho(1 - \frac{1}{q})$.

Let's now move on to the "soundness" part of our hardness result. For this Theorem 4.18 tells us we need to analyze the optimal success probability in the uncorrelated version of $2\mathsf{Lin}(Z_q)$-TEST_d. But before we do this, let's informally think about how well functions f and g with "no influential coordinates in common" can pass $2\mathsf{Lin}(Z_q)$-TEST_d. The usual candidates to consider are non-matching dictators and $f = g =$ Plurality. The latter case actually has very low success probability, roughly $q^{-3+2\sqrt{2}}$. As for the former case:

FACT 5.6. *Non-matching dictators achieve success probability* $\frac{3}{8} + \frac{5}{8q}$ *in* $2\mathsf{Lin}(Z_q)$-TEST_d.

PROOF. Suppose now that $f(x) = x_i$, $g(y) = y_j$ where i and j are in *different* blocks. In this case the optimal h acts as follows: If it knows *either* x_i or y_j, it outputs that value. (If it knows both, it can output either.) This happens with probability $\frac{3}{4}$, and when it happens the success probability is again $\frac{1}{2} + \frac{1}{2q}$. But when h knows neither x_i or y_j, h can only guess a label. This happens with probability $\frac{1}{4}$, and when it happens the success probability is only $\frac{1}{q}$. Thus the overall success probability is $\frac{3}{4}(\frac{1}{2} + \frac{1}{2q}) + \frac{1}{4}\frac{1}{q} = \frac{3}{8} + \frac{5}{8q}$. □

These observations "suggest" that the hardness reduction for $2\mathsf{Lin}(Z_q)$ will achieve soundness $\frac{3}{8} + \frac{5}{8q}$. Formally, we must proceed using Invariance and Theorem 4.18. To that end:

OBSERVATION 5.7. *Denote by* $2\mathsf{Lin}(Z_q)$-TEST'_d *the uncorrelated version of* $2\mathsf{Lin}(Z_q)$-TEST_d. *It works as follows: First,* $\boldsymbol{x}, \boldsymbol{y} \sim Z_q^{dK}$ *are chosen independently and uniformly at random. Then* $\widetilde{\boldsymbol{x}} \in (Z_q^d \cup \{*^d\})^K$ *is formed by replacing each block of* $\boldsymbol{x}$ *with* $*^d$ *with probability* $\frac{1}{2}$, *and* $\widetilde{\boldsymbol{y}}$ *is formed from* $\boldsymbol{y}$ *analogously. These erasures are done* independently.

The goal for the remainder of this section is to upper-bound $\mathrm{Opt}_{\mathrm{folded}}(2\mathsf{Lin}(Z_q)\text{-}\mathrm{TEST}'_d)$. We believe that matching dictators are the folded functions with highest success probability for $2\mathsf{Lin}(Z_q)$-TEST'_d. An almost identical analysis to Fact 5.8 gives:

FACT 5.8. *Matching dictators achieve success probability* $\frac{3}{8} + \frac{5}{8q}$ *in* $2\mathsf{Lin}(Z_q)$-TEST'_d.

Unfortunately, we are only able to prove that matching dictators are optimal for $q < 7$. The $q = 2$ is Theorem 6.6; the cases $3 \le q \le 6$ require computer assistance, see the full version of the paper for details. We would not be surprised if there was a short proof giving the result for all q; however for $q \ge 7$ we have only proved an upper bound of $\frac{3}{8} + O(\frac{1}{q^{1/3}})$. We now proceed to obtain this bound. The first step is to simplify matters by eliminating the "blocks" (recall that $2\mathsf{Lin}(Z_q)$-TEST denotes $2\mathsf{Lin}(Z_q)$-TEST_1):

PROPOSITION 5.9. $\mathrm{Opt}_{\mathrm{folded}}(2\mathsf{Lin}(Z_q)\text{-}\mathrm{TEST}') \ge \mathrm{Opt}_{\mathrm{folded}}(2\mathsf{Lin}(Z_q)\text{-}\mathrm{TEST}'_d)$.

PROOF. Assume $f, g : Z_q^{dK} \to Z_q$ are folded functions achieving the optimal success probability in $2\mathsf{Lin}(Z_q)$-d-to-d-Test$'$, together with function h. For $z \in Z_q^{dK}$ and $c \in (Z_q \cup \{*\})^K$, let $z + c$ denote the string in $(Z_q^d \cup \{*^d\})^K$ whose tth block equals $z[t] + (c_t, c_t, \dots, c_t)$. (In this proof we interpret $\ell + * = *$ for any $\ell \in Z_q$.) Let $\boldsymbol{x}, \boldsymbol{y}, \widetilde{\boldsymbol{x}}, \widetilde{\boldsymbol{y}}$ be chosen as in $2\mathsf{Lin}(Z_q)$-d-to-d-Test$'$. Note that we can think of $\widetilde{\boldsymbol{x}} = \boldsymbol{x} + \boldsymbol{\lambda}$, where $\boldsymbol{\lambda}$ is drawn uniformly at random from $\{0, *\}^K$; similarly we can think of $\widetilde{\boldsymbol{y}} = \boldsymbol{y} + \boldsymbol{\lambda}'$ for an independent $\boldsymbol{\lambda}' \sim \{0, *\}^K$. Finally note that for $\boldsymbol{a} \sim Z_q^K$ uniform, $\boldsymbol{x}$ and $\boldsymbol{x} + \boldsymbol{a}$ have the same distribution; similarly for $\boldsymbol{y}$ and $\boldsymbol{y} + \boldsymbol{b}$ with $\boldsymbol{b} \sim Z_q^K$ uniform. Thus

$$\begin{aligned}
&\mathrm{Opt}_{\mathrm{folded}}(2\mathsf{Lin}(Z_q)\text{-}d\text{-to-}d\text{-Test}') \\
&= \tfrac{1}{2}\,\mathbf{Pr}[f(\boldsymbol{x}) = h(\boldsymbol{x} + \boldsymbol{\lambda}, \boldsymbol{y} + \boldsymbol{\lambda})] + \tfrac{1}{2}\,\mathbf{Pr}[g(\boldsymbol{y}) = h(\boldsymbol{x} + \boldsymbol{\lambda}, \boldsymbol{y} + \boldsymbol{\lambda})] \\
&= \tfrac{1}{2}\,\mathbf{Pr}[f(\boldsymbol{x} + \boldsymbol{a}) = h(\boldsymbol{x} + \boldsymbol{a} + \boldsymbol{\lambda}, \boldsymbol{y} + \boldsymbol{b} + \boldsymbol{\lambda})] \\
&\quad + \tfrac{1}{2}\,\mathbf{Pr}[g(\boldsymbol{y} + \boldsymbol{b}) = h(\boldsymbol{x} + \boldsymbol{a} + \boldsymbol{\lambda}, \boldsymbol{y} + \boldsymbol{b} + \boldsymbol{\lambda})] \\
&= \mathop{\mathbf{E}}_{\boldsymbol{x},\boldsymbol{y}}\Big[\tfrac{1}{2}\,\mathbf{Pr}[f(\boldsymbol{x} + \boldsymbol{a}) = h(\boldsymbol{x} + \boldsymbol{a} + \boldsymbol{\lambda}, \boldsymbol{y} + \boldsymbol{b} + \boldsymbol{\lambda})] \\
&\quad + \tfrac{1}{2}\,\mathbf{Pr}[g(\boldsymbol{y} + \boldsymbol{b}) = h(\boldsymbol{x} + \boldsymbol{a} + \boldsymbol{\lambda}, \boldsymbol{y} + \boldsymbol{b} + \boldsymbol{\lambda})]\Big] \\
&\le \tfrac{1}{2}\,\mathbf{Pr}[f(x + \boldsymbol{a}) = h(x + \boldsymbol{a} + \boldsymbol{\lambda}, y + \boldsymbol{b} + \boldsymbol{\lambda})] \\
&\quad + \tfrac{1}{2}\,\mathbf{Pr}[g(y + \boldsymbol{b}) = h(x + \boldsymbol{a} + \boldsymbol{\lambda}, y + \boldsymbol{b} + \boldsymbol{\lambda})]
\end{aligned}$$

for some fixed values $x, y \in Z_q^{dK}$. But this last quantity is precisely the probability that $f(x + \cdot), g(y + \cdot) : Z_q^K \to Z_q$ pass $2\mathsf{Lin}(Z_q)$-d-to-d-Test$'$ with middleman $h(x + \cdot, y + \cdot)$. It remains to observe that $f(x + \cdot)$ and $g(y + \cdot)$ are folded since f and g are. □

Rather surprisingly, Proposition 5.9 is false if we try to replace $\mathrm{Opt}_{\mathrm{folded}}$ with $\mathrm{Opt}_{\mathrm{balanced}}$; see Section 6.2.

The second step is to prove Theorem 5.5; i.e., obtain the optimal bound for the 1-party version of $2\mathsf{Lin}(Z_q)$-TEST_d/ $2\mathsf{Lin}(Z_q)$-TEST'_d:

PROOF PROOF OF THEOREM 5.5. We may reduce bounding $\mathrm{Opt}_{\mathrm{folded}}(q\text{-NICD-TEST})$ to the case of $d = 1$ using (a simplification of) the proof of Proposition 5.9. We will now bound $\mathrm{Val}_{q\text{-NICD-TEST}}(f) \le \frac{1}{2} + \frac{1}{2q}$ for folded f, even in the case when f and h are allowed to be randomized (i.e., map into $\triangle_q$). The proof is actually somewhat simpler if we disallow randomized f and h, but we will need the generalization later.

So let $f : Z_q^K \to \triangle_q$ be folded. It's easy to see that it is optimal for $h : (Z_q \cup \{*\})^K \to \triangle_q$ to work as follows: on input $\widetilde{x}$ it computes

$$\nu = \mathbf{E}[f(\boldsymbol{x}) \mid \widetilde{\boldsymbol{x}} = \widetilde{x}] \in \triangle_q$$

and then outputs a uniformly random coordinate $\ell \in Z_q$ from among those which maximize ν_ℓ. Let us henceforth fix this optimal h, and also observe that it is "folded" in the sense that $h(\widetilde{x} + (c, \dots, c)) = \mathrm{rot}_c(h(\widetilde{x}))$ (where as before $* + c = *$).

Let us make an aside which will be useful for a future proof. Introducing the short-form notation $f(\tilde{x}) = \mathbf{E}[f(\boldsymbol{x}) \mid \tilde{\boldsymbol{x}} = \tilde{x}]$, we have that the success probability conditioned on $\tilde{\boldsymbol{x}} = \tilde{x}$ is precisely $\|f(\tilde{x})\|_\infty$. Thus

$$\mathrm{Val}_{q\text{-NICD-TEST}}(f,h) = \mathop{\mathbf{E}}_{\tilde{\boldsymbol{x}}}[\|f(\tilde{\boldsymbol{x}})\|_\infty]. \tag{5}$$

This proof shows that the above quantity is at most $\frac{1}{2} + \frac{1}{2q}$.

Let us return to the original formulation of value:

$$\mathrm{Val}_{q\text{-NICD-TEST}}(f,h) = \mathop{\mathbf{Pr}}_{\boldsymbol{x},\tilde{\boldsymbol{x}}}[f(\boldsymbol{x}) = h(\tilde{\boldsymbol{x}})] = \mathop{\mathbf{E}}_{\boldsymbol{x},\tilde{\boldsymbol{x}}}[\langle f(\boldsymbol{x}), h(\tilde{\boldsymbol{x}})],$$
$$\tag{6}$$

the latter equality because f and h are in fact randomized ($\triangle_q$-valued) functions. We now employ the following trick. Let $(\tilde{\boldsymbol{z}}, \tilde{\boldsymbol{z}}') \in (Z_q \cup \{*\})^K \times (Z_q \cup \{*\})^K$ be generated according to $\pi^{\otimes K}$, where π is defined as in (3) (with $d = 1$). I.e., for each coordinate $t \in [K]$, one of $\tilde{\boldsymbol{z}}_t, \tilde{\boldsymbol{z}}'_t$ is $*$ and the other is random from Z_q. Define the "composite string" denoted $\boldsymbol{z} = \tilde{\boldsymbol{z}} \circ \tilde{\boldsymbol{z}}' \in Z_q^K$, meaning that $\boldsymbol{z}_t$ equals the non-$*$ value among $\tilde{\boldsymbol{z}}_t, \tilde{\boldsymbol{z}}'_t$, for each $t \in [K]$. The key observation is that the pair $(\boldsymbol{z}, \tilde{\boldsymbol{z}})$ has the same distribution as $(\boldsymbol{x}, \tilde{\boldsymbol{x}})$ and that $(\boldsymbol{z}, \tilde{\boldsymbol{z}}')$ *also* has the same distribution as $(\boldsymbol{x}, \tilde{\boldsymbol{x}})$. Thus upon inserting either pair into (6) we get the same number, and hence the average of the two numbers is again the same:

$$\begin{aligned}
&\mathrm{Val}_{q\text{-NICD-TEST}}(f,h) \\
&= \mathrm{avg}\Big\{\mathop{\mathbf{E}}_{\tilde{\boldsymbol{z}},\tilde{\boldsymbol{z}}',\boldsymbol{z}}[\langle f(\boldsymbol{z}), h(\tilde{\boldsymbol{z}})\rangle], \mathop{\mathbf{E}}_{\tilde{\boldsymbol{z}},\tilde{\boldsymbol{z}}',\boldsymbol{z}}[\langle f(\boldsymbol{z}), h(\tilde{\boldsymbol{z}}')\rangle]\Big\} \\
&= \mathop{\mathbf{E}}_{\tilde{\boldsymbol{z}},\tilde{\boldsymbol{z}}',\boldsymbol{z}}[\langle f(\boldsymbol{z}), \tfrac{h(\tilde{\boldsymbol{z}})+h(\tilde{\boldsymbol{z}}')}{2}\rangle] \\
&\le \mathop{\mathbf{E}}_{\tilde{\boldsymbol{z}},\tilde{\boldsymbol{z}}'}\Big[\|\tfrac{h(\tilde{\boldsymbol{z}})+h(\tilde{\boldsymbol{z}}')}{2}\|_\infty\Big].
\end{aligned} \tag{7}$$

Here the last step uses the fact that $\langle \alpha, \beta \rangle \le \|\alpha\|_1 \|\beta\|_\infty = \|\beta\|_\infty$ for $\alpha, \beta \in \triangle_q$.

Suppose that in addition to $\tilde{\boldsymbol{z}}, \tilde{\boldsymbol{z}}'$ we also choose $\boldsymbol{\ell} \sim Z_q$ uniformly at random. Even conditioned on $\tilde{\boldsymbol{z}}'$, the distributions of $\tilde{\boldsymbol{z}}$ and $\tilde{\boldsymbol{z}} + (\boldsymbol{\ell}, \dots, \boldsymbol{\ell})$ are the same. Hence (7) equals

$$\mathop{\mathbf{E}}_{\tilde{\boldsymbol{z}},\tilde{\boldsymbol{z}}',\boldsymbol{\ell}}\Big[\|\tfrac{h(\tilde{\boldsymbol{z}}+(\boldsymbol{\ell},\dots,\boldsymbol{\ell}))+h(\tilde{\boldsymbol{z}}')}{2}\|_\infty\Big] = \mathop{\mathbf{E}}_{\tilde{\boldsymbol{z}},\tilde{\boldsymbol{z}}',\boldsymbol{\ell}}\Big[\|\tfrac{\mathrm{rot}_{\boldsymbol{\ell}}(h(\tilde{\boldsymbol{z}}))+h(\tilde{\boldsymbol{z}}')}{2}\|_\infty\Big],$$

using the foldedness of h. We will bound this by $\frac{1}{2} + \frac{1}{2q}$ for *every* pair of outcomes $h(\tilde{\boldsymbol{z}}) = \gamma$, $h(\tilde{\boldsymbol{z}}') = \gamma'$ in $\triangle_q$. The quantity to bound, $\mathbf{E}_{\boldsymbol{\ell}}[\|(\mathrm{rot}_{\boldsymbol{\ell}}(\gamma)+\gamma')/2\|_\infty]$, is a (separately) convex function of both γ and γ' (since $\|\cdot\|_\infty$ is a norm). Hence the quantity is maximized when γ and γ' are extreme points of $\triangle_q$. But for $\gamma = e_\ell$, $\gamma = e_{\ell'}$, say, one immediately calculates that $\mathbf{E}_{\boldsymbol{\ell}}[\|(\mathrm{rot}_{\boldsymbol{\ell}}(\gamma) + \gamma')/2\|_\infty] = \frac{1}{2} + \frac{1}{2q}$. This completes the proof. □

Finally, we are able to give the crucial NICD bound which will let us complete the proof of the Main Theorem:

THEOREM 5.10. $\mathrm{Opt}_{\mathrm{folded}}(2\mathsf{Lin}(Z_q)\text{-TEST}') \le \frac{3}{8} + O(\frac{1}{q^{1/3}})$.

PROOF. Again, we prove this even when f and g are allowed to be randomized. So let $f, g : Z_q^K \to \triangle_q$ be optimal folded functions for $2\mathsf{Lin}(Z_q)\text{-TEST}'$. As before it's easy to see that the optimal $h : (Z_q \cup \{*\})^K \to \triangle_q$ works as follows: on input $(\tilde{x}, \tilde{y})$ it computes

$$\nu = \tfrac{1}{2}\mathbf{E}[f(\boldsymbol{x}) \mid \tilde{\boldsymbol{x}} = \tilde{x}] + \tfrac{1}{2}\mathbf{E}[g(\boldsymbol{y}) \mid \tilde{\boldsymbol{y}} = \tilde{y}] = \tfrac{1}{2}f(\tilde{x}) + \tfrac{1}{2}g(\tilde{y})$$

and then outputs a uniformly random coordinate $\ell \in Z_q$ from among those which maximize ν_ℓ. With this h the success probability conditioned on $\tilde{\boldsymbol{x}} = \tilde{x}, \tilde{\boldsymbol{y}} = \tilde{y}$ is precisely $\|\nu\|_\infty$. Thus

$$\begin{aligned}
\mathrm{Opt}_{\mathrm{folded}}(2\mathsf{Lin}(Z_q)\text{-TEST}') &= \mathrm{Val}_{2\mathsf{Lin}(Z_q)\text{-TEST}'}(f,g) \\
&= \mathop{\mathbf{E}}_{\tilde{\boldsymbol{x}},\tilde{\boldsymbol{y}}}[\tfrac{1}{2}\|f(\tilde{\boldsymbol{x}}) + g(\tilde{\boldsymbol{y}})\|_\infty].
\end{aligned}$$

Note that $f(\tilde{\boldsymbol{x}})$ and $g(\tilde{\boldsymbol{y}})$ are independent $\triangle_q$-valued random variables. Further, by virtue of the fact that f is folded, $f(\tilde{\boldsymbol{x}})$ is "cyclically symmetric" in the sense that $\mathrm{rot}_\ell(f(\tilde{\boldsymbol{x}}))$ has the same distribution for each $\ell \in Z_q$. (The same is true of $g(\tilde{\boldsymbol{y}})$ but we won't need this.) Thus we may also write

$$\mathrm{Opt}_{\mathrm{folded}}(2\mathsf{Lin}(Z_q)\text{-TEST}') = \mathop{\mathbf{E}}_{\tilde{\boldsymbol{x}},\tilde{\boldsymbol{y}}}[\mathop{\mathrm{avg}}_{\ell \in Z_q}\{\tfrac{1}{2}\|\mathrm{rot}_\ell(f(\tilde{\boldsymbol{x}}))+g(\tilde{\boldsymbol{y}})\|_\infty\}]. \tag{8}$$

Define $m(s,t) = s+t-st$. The key to our proof is showing that

$$\mathop{\mathrm{avg}}_{\ell \in Z_q}\{\tfrac{1}{2}\|\mathrm{rot}_\ell(\sigma) + \tau\|_\infty\} \le \tfrac{1}{2}m(\|\sigma\|_\infty, \|\tau\|_\infty) + O(\tfrac{1}{q^{1/3}}) \tag{9}$$

holds for every $\sigma, \tau \in \triangle_q$. From this we can easily complete the proof: applying it to (8) gives

$$\begin{aligned}
\mathrm{Opt}_{\mathrm{folded}}(2\mathsf{Lin}(Z_q)\text{-TEST}') &\le \tfrac{1}{2}\mathop{\mathbf{E}}_{\tilde{\boldsymbol{x}},\tilde{\boldsymbol{y}}}[m(\|f(\tilde{\boldsymbol{x}})\|_\infty, \|g(\tilde{\boldsymbol{y}})\|_\infty)] + O(\tfrac{1}{q^{1/3}}) \\
&= \tfrac{1}{2}m\left(\mathop{\mathbf{E}}_{\tilde{\boldsymbol{x}}}[\|f(\tilde{\boldsymbol{x}})\|_\infty],\ \mathop{\mathbf{E}}_{\tilde{\boldsymbol{y}}}[\|g(\tilde{\boldsymbol{y}})\|_\infty]\right) \\
&\quad + O(\tfrac{1}{q^{1/3}}),
\end{aligned}$$

where we were able to pass the expectations inside the $m(\cdot,\cdot)$ using the fact that $f(\tilde{\boldsymbol{x}})$ and $g(\tilde{\boldsymbol{y}})$ are independent. But by virtue of (5) in the proof of Theorem 5.5, and by the theorem's result itself, we have $\mathbf{E}_{\tilde{\boldsymbol{x}}}[\|f(\tilde{\boldsymbol{x}})\|_\infty], \mathbf{E}_{\tilde{\boldsymbol{y}}}[\|g(\tilde{\boldsymbol{y}})\|_\infty] \le \frac{1}{2} + \frac{1}{2q}$. Since $m(s,t)$ is an increasing function of $s,t \in [0,1]$, we deduce that

$$\begin{aligned}
\mathrm{Opt}_{\mathrm{folded}}(2\mathsf{Lin}(Z_q)\text{-TEST}') &\le \tfrac{1}{2}m(\tfrac{1}{2} + \tfrac{1}{2q}, \tfrac{1}{2} + \tfrac{1}{2q}) + O(\tfrac{1}{q^{1/3}}) \\
&= \tfrac{3}{8} + O(\tfrac{1}{q^{1/3}}),
\end{aligned}$$

as needed.

It remains then to prove (9). Let $\triangle_{q,s}$ denote the convex set $\triangle_q \cap \{\sigma : \|\sigma\|_\infty \le s\}$. We will in fact show

$$\mathop{\mathrm{avg}}_{\ell \in Z_q}\{\tfrac{1}{2}\|\mathrm{rot}_\ell(\sigma) + \tau\|_\infty\} \le \tfrac{1}{2}\max(s,t) + O(\tfrac{1}{q^{1/3}}) \tag{10}$$

for all $\sigma \in \triangle_{q,s}$, $\tau \in \triangle_{q,t}$; this is stronger since $\max(s,t) \le m(s,t)$ for $s,t \in [0,1]$. Inequality (10) is obvious if either s or t is at most $\frac{1}{q^{1/3}}$; thus we need only be concerned with the case $s, t \ge \frac{1}{q^{1/3}}$.

As in the previous proof we observe that $\mathrm{avg}_{\ell \in Z_q}\{\frac{1}{2}\|\mathrm{rot}_\ell(\sigma) + \tau\|_\infty\}$ is convex in σ and in τ; hence it suffices to prove (10) when σ and τ are extreme points of $\triangle_{q,s}$ and $\triangle_{q,t}$, respectively. Note that an extreme point for $\triangle_{q,s}$ has exactly $\lceil 1/s \rceil$ nonzero coordinates, of which $\lfloor 1/s \rfloor$ equal s; similarly for $\triangle_{q,t}$. For fixed extreme σ and τ, a simple union-bound argument shows that the fraction of $\ell \in Z_q$ for which $\mathrm{rot}_\ell(\sigma)$ and τ have a nonzero coordinate in common is at most $\lceil 1/s \rceil \lceil 1/t \rceil / q$. This is at most $4/(stq) \le O(\frac{1}{q^{1/3}})$ since we are assuming $s, t \ge \frac{1}{q^{1/3}}$. On the other hand, if $\mathrm{rot}_\ell(\sigma)$ and τ do *not* have a nonzero coordinate in common, $\frac{1}{2}\|\mathrm{rot}_\ell(\sigma) + \tau\|_\infty = \frac{1}{2}\max(s,t)$. Together these facts justify (10), completing the proof. □

We may now plug our completeness result (Proposition 5.4) and our soundness result (Theorem 5.10 combined with Proposition 5.9) for $2\mathsf{Lin}(Z_q)\text{-TEST}_d$ into our hardness reduction

(Corollary 4.19) to obtain our Main Theorem on the NP-hardness of Unique-Games (in its precise form, Theorem 2.6).

6. A TEST FOR $\mathsf{2Lin}(Z_2)$

In this section, we prove our target hardness of approximation result of $\mathsf{2Lin}(Z_2)$. The analysis necessary to carry out Theorem 5.10 is complicated, and we believe it can be improved to yield the value $3/8 + 5/8q$. Theorem ?? shows this to be true when $q < 7$, but it uses a computer-assisted proof. On the other hand, when $q = 2$, we can actually prove this directly without the aid of a computer, matching the gadget-based hardness result of [Hs01, TSSW00]. Along the way to proving this, we develop an approach to solving NICD problems that will be useful not only for our $\mathsf{2Lin}(Z_2)$ result, but also for the hardness of approximation results for the remaining binary CSPs presented in Section 7. In some sense, our $\mathsf{2Lin}(Z_2)$ test and a natural 1-party version of it form the foundation of all our binary correlation tests.

6.1 Binary NICD

We begin with the model of NICD *over the erasure channel*, which considers the following test, for $0 < \rho < 1$:

NICD-TEST(ρ)

- Given functions $f : \{-1,1\}^n \to \{-1,1\}$ and $h : \{-1,1,*\}^n \to \{-1,1\}$:
- Draw $\widetilde{\boldsymbol{x}} \in \{-1,1,*\}^n$ so that each coordinate is independently a $*$ with probability $1-\rho$ and a uniformly random element of $\{-1,1\}$ otherwise.
- Form $\boldsymbol{x} \in \{-1,1\}^n$ by replacing each $*$ in $\widetilde{\boldsymbol{x}}$ with an independent uniformly random element from $\{-1,1\}$.
- Test $f(\boldsymbol{x}) = h(\widetilde{\boldsymbol{x}})$.

We call the pair (f,h) a *strategy*. This is only a 1-party test, but many of the notions we used for 2-party tests transfer over naturally. In particular, if T is a 1-party test, we may write $\mathrm{Val}_T(f,h)$ for the probability the test is satisfied, $\mathrm{Val}_T(f)$ for $\max_h\{\mathrm{Val}_T(f,h)\}$, and $\mathrm{Opt}(T)$ for $\max_f\{\mathrm{Val}_T(f)\}$.

It is easy to see that given f, an optimal h is

$$h(\widetilde{x}) = \mathrm{sign}(\mathbf{E}[f(\boldsymbol{x}) \mid \widetilde{x}]),$$

where we define $\mathrm{sign}(0) = 1$. It is also easy to see that this test can be passed always if f and h are constant; henceforth, we will only consider balanced f.

Perhaps the most obvious strategy is for f to be a dictator. In this case, the success probability of f is $1/2 + \rho/2$. Ke Yang [Yan07] conjectured that this was optimal (we assume his conjecture was for $\rho \geq 1/2$ only), and indeed our Theorem 6.1 confirms this.

THEOREM 6.1. *For $\rho \geq 1/2$, $\mathrm{Opt}_{\text{balanced}}(\text{NICD-TEST}(\rho)) = 1/2 + \rho/2$. When $\rho > 1/2$, dictators and negated dictators uniquely achieve this value.*

Which function is best for $\rho < 1/2$ is less clear, however, but what is clear is that dictators are no longer optimal. In fact, what is perhaps the only other obvious strategy for NICD—majority—outperforms dictators for these values of ρ. For n odd, we define the majority function to be

$$\mathsf{MAJ}_n(x) = \mathrm{sign}\left(\sum_{i=1}^{n} x_i\right).$$

It is clear that if f is $\mathsf{MAJ}_n(x)$, then the optimal strategy for h is

$$h(z) = \mathrm{sign}\left(\sum_{i:z_i \neq *}^{n} z_i\right),$$

which is simply the majority over the unerased bits. The exact success probability of MAJ_n for a specific n is tedious to compute and rather unilluminating, but fortunately one can compute the limiting success probability as n approaches ∞. Using the 2-dimensional Central Limit Theorem, it can be shown that the success probability is $1/2 + \arcsin(\sqrt{\rho})/\pi$ (see, for example, the analysis in [?]). For $\rho > 1/2$, this is strictly worse than the dictator strategy, but it is better for $\rho < 1/2$ and is exactly equal for $\rho = 1/2$. In fact, the case of $\rho = 1/2$ is especially nice, and the entire class of linear threshold functions succeeds here with probability exactly $3/4$.

In contrast to $\rho \geq 1/2$, what we know about NICD over the erasure channel when $\rho < 1/2$ is fairly limited. What we do know comes mainly from the following theorem of [?, Yan07] (see also [Mos10]):

THEOREM 6.2. *For $0 < \rho < 1$, $\mathrm{Opt}_{\text{balanced}}(\text{NICD-TEST}(\rho)) \leq 1/2 + \sqrt{\rho}/2$.*

The success probability of the best strategy is clearly an increasing function of ρ, so combining Theorem 6.1 with Theorem 6.2 gives the best upper bound for $\mathrm{Opt}_{\text{balanced}}(\text{NICD-TEST}(\rho))$ as $\min(3/4, 1/2 + \sqrt{\rho}/2)$, when $\rho < 1/2$. This bound is tight to within a constant as ρ approaches zero, because the success probability of majority is $1/2 + \sqrt{\rho}/\pi + \Theta(\rho^{3/2})$. Indeed, we believe that majority is the best strategy for $\rho < 1/2$ but are unable to prove it. One piece of evidence for this is the "Majority is Most Predictable" theorem of Mossel [Mos10], which states, roughly, that among "low-influence" functions, the success probability of majority is optimal. It seems reasonable that the best strategy for $\rho < 1/2$ would be a low-influence function, as any function which relies heavily on specific coordinates would be difficult to predict when the values of those coordinates are erased.

We now begin proving our results. First, we give a simple proof of Theorem 6.1 in the case where $\rho = 1/2$. The technique we use here will be reused in several of the later NICD proofs.

PROOF. Let (f,h) be a strategy where f is balanced. Consider selecting two strings $\boldsymbol{y}, \boldsymbol{y}' \in \{-1,1\}^n$ independently and uniformly at random, and forming $\widetilde{\boldsymbol{y}}$ as follows:

$$\widetilde{\boldsymbol{y}}_i = \begin{cases} \boldsymbol{y}_i & \text{if } \boldsymbol{y}_i = \boldsymbol{y}'_i, \\ * & \text{if } \boldsymbol{y}_i \neq \boldsymbol{y}'_i. \end{cases}$$

Then clearly $\widetilde{\boldsymbol{y}}$ is distributed as $\widetilde{\boldsymbol{x}}$ is in the test, and $\boldsymbol{y}$ and $\boldsymbol{y}'$ are both randomly "filled-in" versions of it. Thus,

$$\begin{aligned}\mathbf{Pr}[f(\boldsymbol{x}) = h(\widetilde{\boldsymbol{x}})] &= \mathrm{avg}\{\mathbf{Pr}[f(\boldsymbol{y}) = h(\widetilde{\boldsymbol{y}})], \mathbf{Pr}[f(\boldsymbol{y}') = h(\widetilde{\boldsymbol{y}})]\} \\ &\leq \frac{1}{2}\mathbf{E}[M(f(\boldsymbol{y}), f(\boldsymbol{y}'))],\end{aligned}$$

where M outputs the number of input bits in the majority. This is because whatever $f(\boldsymbol{y})$ and $f(\boldsymbol{y}')$ turn out to be, $h(\widetilde{\boldsymbol{y}})$ can only agree with at most $M(f(\boldsymbol{y}), f(\boldsymbol{y}'))$ of them.

Because $\boldsymbol{y}$ and $\boldsymbol{y}'$ are independent and f is balanced, $f(\boldsymbol{y})$ and $f(\boldsymbol{y}')$ are distributed as independent, uniformly-random ± 1 bits, so $M(f(\boldsymbol{y}), f(\boldsymbol{y}'))$ is either 1 or 2, each with probability 1/2. Thus, $\mathbf{E}[M(f(\boldsymbol{y}), f(\boldsymbol{y}'))] = 3/2$, and the success probability of f and h is at most 3/4. □

We will extend this proof technique to prove Theorem 6.1 in its entirety. First, we need the following well-known fact about the noise stability of balanced functions.

PROPOSITION 6.3. *For $0 < \eta < 1$ and a function $f : \{-1, 1\}^n \to \{-1, 1\}$, the* noise stability *of f at η is $\mathbb{S}_\eta(f) = \mathbf{E}_x[f(x)(T_\eta f)(x)]$. If f is balanced, then $\mathbb{S}_\eta(f) \leq \eta$. Equality holds if and only if f is a dictator or a negated dictator.*

PROOF. We assume familiarity with Fourier analysis on the Boolean hypercube. Define $\lambda \in \{-1, 1\}^n$ to be distributed so that each coordinate λ_i is independently random subject to $\mathbf{E}[\lambda_i] = \eta$. Then $y \sim_\eta x$ is identically distributed to $\lambda \cdot x$, using coordinate-wise multiplication. Thus,

$$\begin{aligned}
\mathbb{S}_\eta(f) &= \mathop{\mathbf{E}}_{x}[f(x)(T_\eta f)(x)] \\
&= \sum_{S,T \subseteq [n]} \hat{f}(S)\hat{f}(T) \mathop{\mathbf{E}}_{x, y \sim_\eta x}[\chi_S(x)\chi_T(y)] \\
&= \sum_{S,T \subseteq [n]} \hat{f}(S)\hat{f}(T) \mathop{\mathbf{E}}_{x,\lambda}[\chi_S(x)\chi_T(x \cdot \lambda)]. \qquad (11)
\end{aligned}$$

As $\chi_T(x \cdot \lambda) = \chi_T(x)\chi_T(\lambda)$, we have that

$$\mathop{\mathbf{E}}_{x,\lambda}[\chi_S(x)\chi_T(x \cdot \lambda)] = \mathop{\mathbf{E}}_{x}[\chi_S(x)\chi_T(x)] \mathop{\mathbf{E}}_{\lambda}[\chi_T(\lambda)] = \mathbf{1}_{S=T} \cdot \eta^{|T|}.$$

Substituting this into Equation (11) yields a simple formula for the noise sensitivity of f: $\mathbb{S}_\eta(f) = \sum_{S \subseteq [n]} \hat{f}(S)^2 \eta^{|S|}$. It is well-known (Parseval's theorem) that $\sum_{S \subseteq [n]} \hat{f}(S)^2 = 1$ when f is $\{-1, 1\}$-valued. Furthermore, it is easy to see that if f is balanced, then $\hat{f}(\emptyset) = 0$. Thus, for a balanced f, $\mathbb{S}_\eta(f) \leq \eta$, with equality in the case that all of f's Fourier mass is on sets of size. The only such functions are dictators and antidictators, which concludes the proof. □

We can now use this to prove Theorem 6.1.

PROOF PROOF OF THEOREM 6.1. Let (f, h) be a strategy where f is balanced. Consider selecting two strings $\boldsymbol{y}, \boldsymbol{y}' \in \{-1, 1\}^n$, where $\boldsymbol{y}$ is uniformly random and $\boldsymbol{y}'$ is a $(2\rho - 1)$-correlated copy of $\boldsymbol{y}$. Form $\widetilde{\boldsymbol{y}}$ as above:

$$\widetilde{\boldsymbol{y}}_i = \begin{cases} \boldsymbol{y}_i & \text{if } \boldsymbol{y}_i = \boldsymbol{y}'_i, \\ * & \text{if } \boldsymbol{y}_i \neq \boldsymbol{y}'_i. \end{cases}$$

Clearly, $\widetilde{\boldsymbol{y}}$ is distributed as $\widetilde{\boldsymbol{x}}$ is in the test, and $\boldsymbol{y}$ and $\boldsymbol{y}'$ are distributed like randomly "filled-in" versions of it. Thus,

$$\begin{aligned}
\mathbf{Pr}[f(\boldsymbol{x}) = h(\widetilde{\boldsymbol{x}})] &= \text{avg}\{\mathbf{Pr}[f(\boldsymbol{y}) = h(\widetilde{\boldsymbol{y}})], \mathbf{Pr}[f(\boldsymbol{y}') = h(\widetilde{\boldsymbol{y}})]\} \\
&\leq \frac{1}{2}\mathbf{E}[M(f(\boldsymbol{y}), f(\boldsymbol{y}'))],
\end{aligned}$$

where M outputs the number of input bits in the majority. This is because whatever $f(\boldsymbol{y})$ and $f(\boldsymbol{y}')$ turn out to be, $h(\widetilde{\boldsymbol{y}})$ can only agree with at most $M(f(\boldsymbol{y}), f(\boldsymbol{y}'))$ of them.

Unfortunately, $\boldsymbol{y}$ and $\boldsymbol{y}'$ are not independent, so we need a different way of analyzing the expected size of this majority.

We can write out M as $M(u_1, u_2) = 3/2 + u_1 u_2/2$. Then

$$\begin{aligned}
\frac{1}{2}\mathbf{E}[M(f(\boldsymbol{y}), f(\boldsymbol{y}'))] &= \frac{1}{2}\mathbf{E}[3/2 + f(\boldsymbol{y})f(\boldsymbol{y}')/2] \\
&= \frac{3}{4} + \frac{1}{4}\mathbf{E}[f(\boldsymbol{y})f(\boldsymbol{y}')] \\
&= \frac{3}{4} + \frac{1}{4}\mathbb{S}_{(2\rho-1)}(f). \qquad (12)
\end{aligned}$$

The final equality holds because $\boldsymbol{y}'$ is a $(2\rho - 1)$-correlated version of $\boldsymbol{y}$. By Proposition 6.3, so long as $2\rho - 1 \geq 0$, the noise stability term in equation (12) is maximized when f is a dictator, in which case its noise stability is $(2\rho - 1)$. This means that $\mathbf{Pr}[f(\boldsymbol{x}) = h(\widetilde{\boldsymbol{x}})] \leq 1/2 + \rho/2$, which is the upper bound we wanted. Furthermore, by Proposition 6.3, when $1/2 < \rho < 1$, this value is attained only by dictators and negated dictators, because they uniquely maximize the noise stability term. □

6.2 NICD with blocks

In the last section, we talked about the natural NICD test in which the functions do not have blocks. Unfortunately, due to the hardness of approximation setting, when constructing tests, we often have no choice but to ensure that the functions and strings used are blocked. This is somewhat of a pain for the analysis, and it would be nice if we could just ignore the blocks and have our results go through anyway. Indeed, Proposition 5.9 showed a method for removing blocks from tests, provided those tests involve folded functions. This leaves open the case of tests involving balanced functions, such as the NICD-TEST(ρ). Let NICD-TEST$(\rho)_d$ be the "blocked" version of NICD-TEST(ρ), in which f has domain $\{-1, 1\}^{dK}$ (and is still balanced), h has domain $\{-1, 1, *\}^{dK}$, and $\widetilde{\boldsymbol{x}} \in (Z_q \cup \{*\})^{dK}$ is drawn so that each block is independently $*^d$ with probabiltiy $(1 - \rho)$ and a uniformly random element of $\{-1, 1\}^d$ otherwise. (One could further consider the q-ary version of the test, but for our purposes the binary case is sufficient).

As in Proposition 5.9, we may show

$$\text{Opt}_{\text{folded}}(\text{NICD-TEST}(\rho)) \geq \text{Opt}_{\text{folded}}(\text{NICD-TEST}(\rho)_d):$$

crucially, when we end up with $f(x + \cdot)$, as in the proof of Proposition 5.9, we know that it is folded since f is folded. However, this fails when trying to prove a similar result for $\text{Opt}_{\text{balanced}}$, because $f(x + \cdot)$ is not necessarily balanced, even if f is. Somewhat unexpectedly, this fails for a more fundamental reason, which is that the statement $\text{Opt}_{\text{balanced}}(\text{NICD-TEST}(\rho)) \geq \text{Opt}_{\text{balanced}}(\text{NICD-TEST}(\rho)_d)$ is simply false. There are balanced protocols which pass the NICD-TEST$(\rho)_d$ test with much higher probability than even the best balanced protocol passes the q-NICD-TEST with.

The example we have of this is the "tribes" function $f : \{0, 1\}^{dK} \to \{0, 1\}$ of Ben-Or and Linial [BOL90]. For a given block size of d, let K be the nearest integer to $(\ln 2)2^d$, so that the expectation of tribes is approximately 1/2. The tribes function is defined so that $f(x)$ is 1 whenever at least one of x's blocks is all 1's, and otherwise $f(x)$ is 0. The optimal predictor $h : \{0, 1, *\}^{dK} \to \{0, 1\}$ does the same thing: on input z, if one of z's blocks is all 1's, then $f(x)$ is certainly 1, so $h(z)$ outputs 1 as well. Otherwise, it outputs 0. (Strictly speaking, the tribes function as defined here is not balanced, but it can be made so by changing its values on some $o_d(1)$ fraction of inputs; this only changes the success probability by at most $o_d(1)$.)

The analysis of the tribes protocol is relatively simple: when $f(\boldsymbol{x}) = 0$, which happens with probability $1/2$, there are no blocks of 1's for h to receive, so $h(\widetilde{\boldsymbol{x}})$ will be 0 as well, and the two will equal. On the other hand, when $f(\boldsymbol{x}) = 1$, there are some blocks in $\boldsymbol{x}$ which are all 1's, and h receives each one independently with probability ρ. When there's only 1, it outputs $h(\boldsymbol{x}) = 1$ with probability ρ, but when there are more than 1, which happens with nonzero probability, it outputs 1 with probability strictly greater than ρ. Thus, the total success probability is strictly greater than $1/2 + \rho/2$, which is the success probability of the dictator strategy, which is optimal for NICD-TEST(ρ). Indeed, it is easy to calculate the exact success probability of tribes.

PROPOSITION 6.4. *The* NICD-TEST$(\rho)_d$ *is passed by the tribes strategy with probability*

$$1 - \left(1 - \frac{\rho}{2^d}\right)^K + \left(1 - \frac{1}{2^d}\right)^K.$$

As $K \approx (\ln 2)2^d$, *the success probability of tribes in the limit as d approaches infinity is* $3/2 - 1/2^\rho$.

At $\rho = 1/2$, the success probability of tribes is about 79.3%. In contrast, dictators succeed at $\rho = 1/2$ with probability exactly 75%. It is interesting to consider whether tribes is optimal in this setting, or if there is a protocol which does better.

6.3 $\mathsf{2Lin}(Z_2)$ hardness

In this section, we give our hardness of approximation result for $\mathsf{2Lin}(Z_2)$. The test we analyze is exactly the $\mathsf{2Lin}(Z_q)$-Test when $q = 2$, except we can pin down the soundness in this special case. Let μ_d be the distribution on $\{-1,1\}^d \times \{*\}^d$ which is $*^d$ with probability 1/2 and a uniformly random element of $\{-1,1\}^d$ otherwise. Let π be as in Equation 3 in the case of $q = 2$. Then π's marginals are both μ_d, however correlated. The test is:

$\mathsf{2Lin}(Z_2)$-TEST

- Given functions $f : \{-1,1\}^{dK} \to \{-1,1\}$, $g : \{-1,1\}^{dK} \to \{-1,1\}$, and $h : \{-1,1,*\}^{dK} \times \{-1,1,*\}^{dK} \to \{-1,1\}$:
- Draw $(\widetilde{\boldsymbol{x}}, \widetilde{\boldsymbol{y}}) \sim \pi^{\otimes K}$.
- Form $\boldsymbol{x} \in \{-1,1\}^{dK}$ by replacing each $*$ of $\widetilde{\boldsymbol{x}}$ with a uniformly random element of $\{-1,1\}$. Form $\boldsymbol{y} \in \{-1,1\}^{dK}$ from $\widetilde{\boldsymbol{y}}$ similarly.
- Test either $f(\boldsymbol{x}) = h(\widetilde{\boldsymbol{x}}, \widetilde{\boldsymbol{y}})$ or $g(\boldsymbol{y}) = h(\widetilde{\boldsymbol{x}}, \widetilde{\boldsymbol{y}})$, each with equal probability.

We will be interested only in folded functions. The following fact is a special case of Proposition 5.4:

FACT 6.5. *Let f and g be matching dictators. Then* $\mathrm{Val}_{\mathsf{2Lin}(Z_2)\text{-TEST}}(f, g) = \frac{3}{4}$.

Consider $\mathsf{2Lin}(Z_2)$-TEST$'$, which is the uncorrelated version of $\mathsf{2Lin}(Z_2)$-TEST. In $\mathsf{2Lin}(Z_2)$-TEST$'$, $(\widetilde{\boldsymbol{x}}, \widetilde{\boldsymbol{y}})$ is sampled from $(\mu_d \times \mu_d)^{\otimes K}$ rather than $\pi^{\otimes K}$. If f and g are dictators, they are accepted by T' with probability $\frac{11}{16}$. Our next theorem shows that this is optimal.

THEOREM 6.6. $\mathrm{Opt}_{\mathrm{folded}}(\mathsf{2Lin}(Z_2)\text{-TEST}') = \frac{11}{16}$.

PROOF. By Proposition 5.9, it suffices to consider the case when $d = 1$. Let (f, g, h) be any strategy where f and g are folded. Consider selecting two strings $\boldsymbol{x}, \boldsymbol{x}' \in \{-1,1\}^n$ independently and uniformly at random, and forming $\widetilde{\boldsymbol{x}}$ as follows:

$$\widetilde{\boldsymbol{x}}_i = \begin{cases} \boldsymbol{x}_i & \text{if } \boldsymbol{x}_i = \boldsymbol{x}'_i, \\ * & \text{if } \boldsymbol{x}_i \neq \boldsymbol{x}'_i. \end{cases}$$

Then clearly $\widetilde{\boldsymbol{x}}$ is distributed according to $(\mu_1)^{\otimes n}$, and both $\boldsymbol{x}$ and $\boldsymbol{x}'$ are distributed as random "filled-in" versions of $\widetilde{\boldsymbol{x}}$. In addition, consider selecting two more strings $\boldsymbol{y}, \boldsymbol{y}' \in \{-1,1\}^n$ independently and uniformly at random, and forming $\widetilde{\boldsymbol{y}}$ analogously to $\widetilde{\boldsymbol{x}}$. It is also clear that $\widetilde{\boldsymbol{y}}$ is distributed according to $(\mu_1)^{\otimes n}$, and both $\boldsymbol{y}$ and $\boldsymbol{y}'$ are distributed as random "filled-in" versions of $\widetilde{\boldsymbol{w}}$. Thus,

$$\begin{aligned} &\mathrm{Val}_{\mathsf{2Lin}(Z_2)\text{-TEST}'}(f, g, h) \\ &\quad = \mathrm{avg}\{\mathbf{Pr}[f(\boldsymbol{x}) = h(\widetilde{\boldsymbol{x}}, \widetilde{\boldsymbol{y}})], \mathbf{Pr}[g(\boldsymbol{y}) = h(\widetilde{\boldsymbol{x}}, \widetilde{\boldsymbol{y}})]\} \\ &\quad = \mathrm{avg}\begin{cases} \mathbf{Pr}[f(\boldsymbol{x}) = h(\widetilde{\boldsymbol{x}}, \widetilde{\boldsymbol{y}})], \\ \mathbf{Pr}[f(\boldsymbol{x}') = h(\widetilde{\boldsymbol{x}}, \widetilde{\boldsymbol{y}})], \\ \mathbf{Pr}[g(\boldsymbol{y}) = h(\widetilde{\boldsymbol{x}}, \widetilde{\boldsymbol{y}})], \\ \mathbf{Pr}[g(\boldsymbol{y}') = h(\widetilde{\boldsymbol{x}}, \widetilde{\boldsymbol{y}})] \end{cases} \\ &\quad \leq \frac{1}{4}\mathbf{E}[M(f(\boldsymbol{x}), f(\boldsymbol{x}'), g(\boldsymbol{y}), g(\boldsymbol{y}'))], \end{aligned}$$

where M outputs the number of input bits in the majority. This is because whatever $f(\boldsymbol{x})$, $f(\boldsymbol{x}')$, $g(\boldsymbol{y})$, and $g(\boldsymbol{y}')$ turn out to be, $h(\widetilde{\boldsymbol{x}}, \widetilde{\boldsymbol{y}})$ can only agree with at most $M(f(\boldsymbol{x}), f(\boldsymbol{x}'), g(\boldsymbol{y}), g(\boldsymbol{y}'))$ of them.

By construction, $\boldsymbol{x}$, $\boldsymbol{x}'$, $\boldsymbol{y}$, and $\boldsymbol{y}'$ are all independent of each other. We require f and g to be folded, so in particular both are balanced. As a result, $f(\boldsymbol{x})$, $f(\boldsymbol{x}')$, $g(\boldsymbol{y})$, and $g(\boldsymbol{y}')$ are distributed as independent uniformly random ± 1 bits. The question remains to find the expected size of the majority of four random ± 1 bits, and it is easily verified that this is $\frac{11}{4}$. Thus, the probability that (f, g, h) passes the test is no greater than $\frac{11}{16}$. □

We invite the reader to compare this proof with the proof of Theorem 6.1 in the case of $\rho = 1/2$.

By using Fact 6.5 and Theorem 6.6 together with Corollary 4.19, we obtain the $q = 2$ case of our Main Theorem (Theorem 2.6); in other words, NP-hardness of $(\frac{3}{4}, \frac{11}{16} + \epsilon)$-deciding $\mathsf{2Lin}(Z_2)$.

7. OTHER BINARY CSPS

In this section, we design and analyze binary 2-party tests which allow us to recover the best known NP-hardness results for Max-Cut, 2Sat, and 2And.

7.1 Max-Cut hardness

Our Max-Cut-TEST is similar to our $\mathsf{2Lin}(Z_2)$-TEST, except it can no longer guarantee that the functions involved are folded. This presents a problem, as without this guarantee, f and g could both, for example, be constantly 1, in which case the $\mathsf{2Lin}(Z_2)$-TEST could be passed with probability 1. To handle this, our Max-Cut-TEST devotes a certain fraction of its tests to ensuring that f and g "look" folded. This certain fraction is chosen so that the constantly 1 protocol is no better than the dictator protocol, and it turns out that this is sufficient for making the dictator protocol optimal. Let π be as in the $\mathsf{2Lin}(Z_2)$-TEST. The test is:

Max-Cut-Test

- Given functions $f : \{-1,1\}^{dK} \to \{-1,1\}$, $g : \{-1,1\}^{dK} \to \{-1,1\}$, and $h : \{-1,1,*\}^{dK} \times \{-1,1,*\}^{dK} \to \{-1,1\}$, in which f and g are folded:
- Draw $(\widetilde{\boldsymbol{x}}, \widetilde{\boldsymbol{y}}) \sim \pi^{\otimes K}$.
- Form $\boldsymbol{x} \in \{-1,1\}^{dK}$ by replacing each $*$ of $\widetilde{\boldsymbol{x}}$ with a uniformly random element of $\{-1,1\}$. Form $\boldsymbol{y} \in \{-1,1\}^{dK}$ from $\widetilde{\boldsymbol{y}}$ similarly.
- With probability 16/21, test either $f(\boldsymbol{x}) \neq h(\widetilde{\boldsymbol{x}}, \widetilde{\boldsymbol{y}})$ or $g(\boldsymbol{y}) \neq h(\widetilde{\boldsymbol{x}}, \widetilde{\boldsymbol{y}})$, each with equal probability.
- With the remaining 5/21 probability, test either that $f(\boldsymbol{x}) \neq f(-\boldsymbol{x})$ or $g(\boldsymbol{y}) \neq g(-\boldsymbol{y})$, each with equal probability.

In other words, the Max-Cut-Test runs the 2Lin(Z_2)-Test (with inequalities) with probability 16/21, and tests folding with the remaining probability. The Max-Cut-Test doesn't fit tidily in the 2-party correlated test framework we developed in previous sections, because such tests must only test constraints which involve h. However, a natural modification to this framework, which we omit for simplicity, does cover the Max-Cut-Test. Intuitively, the "folding tests" that the Max-Cut-Test performs with probability 5/21 don't involve h or the correlated distribution π; thus, when decoupling the correlation in π, we may simply ignore these folding tests. As a result, Theorem 4.17 still holds for the Max-Cut-Test.

The following fact is easy to check:

Fact 7.1. *Let f and g be matching dictators. Then* $\mathrm{Val}_{\text{Max-Cut-Test}}(f, g) = 17/21$.

This follows from Fact 6.5: since dictators always pass the folding test, their overall success probability is $16/21 \cdot 12/16 + 5/21 \cdot 1 = 17/21$.

Consider Max-Cut-Test′, the uncorrelated version of the Max-Cut-Test. In Max-Cut-Test′, $(\widetilde{\boldsymbol{x}}, \widetilde{\boldsymbol{y}})$ is sampled from $(\mu_d \times \mu_d)^{\otimes K}$ rather than $\pi^{\otimes K}$. If f and g are dictators, they are accepted by T' with probability 16/21. Our next theorem shows that this is optimal.

Theorem 7.2. *Let* Max-Cut-Test′ *be the uncorrelated version of the* Max-Cut-Test. *Then we have* Opt(Max-Cut-Test′) = 16/21.

Proof. By an argument similar to Proposition 5.9, it suffices to consider the case when $d = 1$. Let (f, g, h) be any strategy. Say that $\theta = \mathbf{E}[f(x)]$ and $\nu = \mathbf{E}[g(y)]$. Consider selecting two strings $\boldsymbol{x}, \boldsymbol{x}' \in \{-1,1\}^n$ independently and uniformly at random, and forming $\widetilde{\boldsymbol{x}}$ as follows:

$$\widetilde{\boldsymbol{x}}_i = \begin{cases} \boldsymbol{x}_i & \text{if } \boldsymbol{x}_i = \boldsymbol{x}'_i, \\ * & \text{if } \boldsymbol{x}_i \neq \boldsymbol{x}'_i. \end{cases}$$

Then clearly $\widetilde{\boldsymbol{x}}$ is distributed according to $(\mu_1)^{\otimes n}$, and both $\boldsymbol{x}$ and $\boldsymbol{x}'$ are distributed as random "filled-in" versions of $\widetilde{\boldsymbol{x}}$. In addition, consider selecting two more strings $\boldsymbol{y}, \boldsymbol{y}' \in \{-1,1\}^n$ independently and uniformly at random, and forming $\widetilde{\boldsymbol{y}}$ analogously to $\widetilde{\boldsymbol{x}}$. It is also clear that $\widetilde{\boldsymbol{y}}$ is distributed according to $(\mu_1)^{\otimes n}$, and both $\boldsymbol{y}$ and $\boldsymbol{y}'$ are distributed as random "filled-in" versions of $\widetilde{\boldsymbol{w}}$. Thus

$$\begin{aligned}
&\mathrm{Val}_{\text{Max-Cut-Test}'}(f, g, h) \\
&= \mathrm{avg}\{\mathbf{Pr}[f(\boldsymbol{x}) \neq h(\widetilde{\boldsymbol{x}}, \widetilde{\boldsymbol{y}})], \mathbf{Pr}[g(\boldsymbol{y}) \neq h(\widetilde{\boldsymbol{x}}, \widetilde{\boldsymbol{y}})]\} \\
&= \mathrm{avg}\left\{\begin{array}{l} \mathbf{Pr}[f(\boldsymbol{x}) \neq h(\widetilde{\boldsymbol{x}}, \widetilde{\boldsymbol{y}})], \\ \mathbf{Pr}[f(\boldsymbol{x}') \neq h(\widetilde{\boldsymbol{x}}, \widetilde{\boldsymbol{y}})], \\ \mathbf{Pr}[g(\boldsymbol{y}) \neq h(\widetilde{\boldsymbol{x}}, \widetilde{\boldsymbol{y}})], \\ \mathbf{Pr}[g(\boldsymbol{y}') \neq h(\widetilde{\boldsymbol{x}}, \widetilde{\boldsymbol{y}})] \end{array}\right. \\
&\leq \frac{1}{4}\mathbf{E}[M(f(\boldsymbol{x}), f(\boldsymbol{x}'), g(\boldsymbol{y}), g(\boldsymbol{y}'))], \qquad (13)
\end{aligned}$$

where M outputs the number of input bits in the majority. This is because whatever $f(\boldsymbol{x})$, $f(\boldsymbol{x}')$, $g(\boldsymbol{y})$, and $g(\boldsymbol{y}')$ turn out to be, $h(\widetilde{\boldsymbol{x}}, \widetilde{\boldsymbol{y}})$ can only disagree with at most $M(f(\boldsymbol{x}), f(\boldsymbol{x}'), g(\boldsymbol{y}), g(\boldsymbol{y}'))$ of them.

By construction, $\boldsymbol{x}$, $\boldsymbol{x}'$, $\boldsymbol{y}$, and $\boldsymbol{y}'$ are all independent of each other. Thus, $f(\boldsymbol{x})$ and $f(\boldsymbol{x}')$ are distributed as mean-θ ± 1 bits, $g(\boldsymbol{y})$ and $g(\boldsymbol{y}')$ are distributed as mean-ν ± 1 bits, and all four are independent of each other. The function M can be written as

$$M(u, u', v, v') = \frac{11}{16} + \frac{1}{16}(uu' + uv + \ldots + u'v' + vv') - \frac{uu'vv'}{16}.$$

We can therefore calculate the expectation in Equation (13) as

$$\mathbf{E}[M(f(\boldsymbol{x}), f(\boldsymbol{x}'), g(\boldsymbol{y}), g(\boldsymbol{y}'))] = \frac{11}{16} + \frac{\theta^2}{16} + \frac{\theta\nu}{4} + \frac{\nu^2}{16} - \frac{\theta^2\nu^2}{16}.$$

The only term in this expression which depends on the signs of θ and ν is $\theta\nu/4$, and it is easy to see that it is maximized when θ has the same sign as ν. Thus, it can only improve the success probability of a protocol to assume that θ and ν have the same sign. By symmetry, we may assume that they are positive.

Given that the mean of f is θ, the highest chance it can pass the folding test is $1 - |\theta| = 1 - \theta$. Similarly, the highest chance g can pass the folding test is $1 - \nu$. The overall probability of f and g passing the entire test is therefore at most

$$\begin{aligned}
P(\theta, \nu) &:= \frac{16}{21}\left(\frac{11}{16} + \frac{\theta^2}{16} + \frac{\theta\nu}{4} + \frac{\nu^2}{16} - \frac{\theta^2\nu^2}{16}\right) + \frac{5}{21}\left(1 - \frac{\theta}{2} - \frac{\nu}{2}\right) \\
&= \frac{16}{21} - \frac{5}{42}(\theta + \nu) + \frac{\theta^2}{21} + \frac{4\theta\nu}{21} + \frac{\nu^2}{21} - \frac{\theta^2\nu^2}{21}.
\end{aligned}$$

What remains is to show that on $[0,1] \times [0,1]$, P has maximal value 16/21. As a function of θ,

$$P_\nu(\theta) := P(\theta, \nu) = \left(\frac{1}{21} - \frac{\nu^2}{21}\right) \cdot \theta^2 + \left(\frac{4\nu}{21} - \frac{5}{42}\right) \cdot \theta + \frac{\nu^2}{21} - \frac{5\nu}{42} + \frac{16}{21}.$$

The coefficient on θ^2 is always nonnegative, so $P_\nu(\theta)$ is a convex function of θ, for each fixed ν. Thus, for each fixed ν it's maximized at either $\theta = 0$ or $\theta = 1$. So it suffices to maximize $P(0, \nu)$ and $P(1, \nu)$. The latter is linear (and increasing) in ν, so $P(1, 1)$ is a possible maximizer. The former is a convex parabola, so it's maximized at $\nu = 0$ or $\nu = 1$. It remains to check the corners; indeed, $P(0, 0) = P(1, 1) = 16/21$ are the maximizers. □

Inspired by the test presented in this section, it is interesting to consider what happens in the model of NICD over the erasure channel presented in Section 6.1 if we drop the requirement that f be balanced and add a folding test to compensate. If one sets the probability of performing the original test at 4/5 and the probability of performing the folding test at 1/5, then the constant function protocol will no longer be better than the dictator protocol; both succeed with probability 4/5. And just as in Theorem 7.2, though with different numbers, this sufficient for making the dictator protocol optimal.

By using Fact 7.1 and Theorem 7.2 together with Corollary 4.19, we obtain the Max-Cut case Theorem 2.5; in other words, NP-hardness of $(\frac{17}{21}, \frac{16}{21} + \epsilon)$-deciding Max-Cut.

7.2 2Sat hardness

The next two tests we present are quite different from the $2\mathsf{Lin}(Z_2)$ and Max-Cut NICD tests. Even then, our analysis suggests that there is still an underlying similarity. Let ν be the following distribution:

$$(\boldsymbol{a}, \widetilde{\boldsymbol{b}}) \sim \nu \text{ means } (\boldsymbol{a}, \widetilde{\boldsymbol{b}}) = \begin{cases} \text{uniformly random from } \{1\} \times \{-1,1\}^d, \text{w/prob } \frac{1}{2}; \\ \text{uniformly random from } \{-1\} \times *^d, \text{w/prob } \frac{1}{2}. \end{cases} \quad (14)$$

Note that we have written $\boldsymbol{a}$ rather than $\widetilde{\boldsymbol{a}}$. This is because $\boldsymbol{a}$ is never $*$. The following is our 2Sat test:

2Sat-TEST

- Given functions $f : \{-1,1\}^K \to \{-1,1\}$, $g : \{-1,1\}^{dK} \to \{-1,1\}$, and $h : \{-1,1\}^K \times \{-1,1,*\}^{dK} \to \{-1,1\}$:
- Sample $(\boldsymbol{x}, \widetilde{\boldsymbol{y}}) \sim \nu^{\otimes K}$.
- Form $\boldsymbol{y} \in \{-1,1\}^{dK}$ by replacing each $*$ of $\widetilde{\boldsymbol{y}}$ with a uniformly random element of $\{-1,1\}$.
- With probability 1/3, test $f(\boldsymbol{x}) \vee \neg h(\boldsymbol{x}, \widetilde{\boldsymbol{y}})$.
- With probability 2/3, test $g(\boldsymbol{y}) \vee h(\boldsymbol{x}, \widetilde{\boldsymbol{y}})$.

We will be concerned with folded protocols. Note that h is given the entire string $\boldsymbol{x}$; using the notation established earlier for 2-party correlation tests, we achieve this by setting $\widetilde{\boldsymbol{x}} = \boldsymbol{x}$.

Now, the following is an easy fact:

FACT 7.3. *Let f and g be matching dictators. Then* $\mathrm{Val}_{\text{2Sat-TEST}}(f, g) = 11/12$.

PROOF. When $f(\boldsymbol{x}) = -1$, $h(\boldsymbol{x}, \widetilde{\boldsymbol{y}})$ can always output -1, satisfying all the constraints and passing the test with probability 1. Now, condition on $f(\boldsymbol{x}) = 1$. In this case, because f and g are matching dictators, h is given the value of $g(\boldsymbol{y})$. So if $g(\boldsymbol{y}) = -1$, setting $h(\boldsymbol{x}, \widetilde{\boldsymbol{y}}) = 1$ will satisfy all the constraints and pass the test with probability 1. Finally, when $g(\boldsymbol{y}) = 1$, setting $h(\boldsymbol{x}, \widetilde{\boldsymbol{y}}) = -1$ will satisfy the second constraint only, passing the test with probability 2/3. The result is a total success probability of $3/4 \cdot 1 + 1/4 \cdot 2/3 = 11/12$. □

Let (f, g, h) be a strategy in which f and g are folded. Consider the test 2Sat-TEST′, the uncorrelated version of 2Sat-TEST. In 2Sat-TEST′, $(\boldsymbol{x}, \widetilde{\boldsymbol{y}})$ is sampled so that $\boldsymbol{x}$ is an independent $\{-1,1\}^K$ string, and $\widetilde{\boldsymbol{y}}$ is drawn from $(\mu_d)^K$. If f and g are dictators, they pass the 2Sat-TEST′ with probability 7//8. Our next theorem shows that this is optimal:

THEOREM 7.4. $\mathrm{Opt}_{\text{folded}}(\text{2Sat-TEST}') = 7/8$.

PROOF. Conditioned on $f(\boldsymbol{x}) = -1$, an optimal h will always output -1, and will pass the test with probability 1. On the other hand, when $f(\boldsymbol{x}) = 1$ the test reduces to testing $\neg h(\boldsymbol{x}, \widetilde{\boldsymbol{y}})$ with probability 1/3 and $g(\boldsymbol{y}) \vee h(\boldsymbol{x}, \widetilde{\boldsymbol{y}})$ with probability 2/3. The probability of success is therefore

$$\begin{aligned}
&\frac{1}{3}\mathbf{Pr}[h(\boldsymbol{x}, \widetilde{\boldsymbol{y}}) = 1] + \frac{2}{3}\mathbf{Pr}[g(\boldsymbol{y}) \vee h(\boldsymbol{x}, \widetilde{\boldsymbol{y}})] \\
=&\frac{1}{3}\mathbf{E}\left[\frac{1 + h(\boldsymbol{x}, \widetilde{\boldsymbol{y}})}{2}\right] + \frac{2}{3}\mathbf{E}\left[1 - \left(\frac{1 + g(\boldsymbol{y})}{2}\right)\left(\frac{1 + h(\boldsymbol{x}, \widetilde{\boldsymbol{y}})}{2}\right)\right] \\
=&\frac{1}{3}\mathbf{E}\left[\frac{1}{2} + \frac{h(\boldsymbol{x}, \widetilde{\boldsymbol{y}})}{2} + 2 - \frac{1}{2} - \frac{g(\boldsymbol{y})}{2} - \frac{h(\boldsymbol{x}, \widetilde{\boldsymbol{y}})}{2} - \frac{g(\boldsymbol{y})h(\boldsymbol{x}, \widetilde{\boldsymbol{y}})}{2}\right] \\
=&\frac{5}{6} - \frac{1}{3}\mathbf{E}\left[\frac{1}{2} + \frac{g(\boldsymbol{y})h(\boldsymbol{x}, \widetilde{\boldsymbol{y}})}{2}\right], \qquad (15)
\end{aligned}$$

where we are able to drop the $-g(\boldsymbol{y})/2$ term because g is balanced. The expectation is equal to the probability that $g(\boldsymbol{y}) = h(\boldsymbol{x}, \widetilde{\boldsymbol{y}})$, which Theorem 6.1 says is no less than 1/4 (it actually says it is no greater than 3/4, but we may negate h). So when $f(\boldsymbol{x}) = 1$, we can upper bound the success probability of the test by

$$(15) \leq \frac{5}{6} - \frac{1}{3} \cdot \frac{1}{4} = \frac{3}{4}.$$

Since f is balanced, both of these cases happens with the same probability. Thus, we can upper bound the success probability of the f, g, and h by $1 \cdot 1/2 + 3/4 \cdot 1/2 = 7/8$. □

By using Fact 7.3 and Theorem 7.4 together with Corollary 4.19, we obtain the 2Sat case Theorem 2.5; in other words, NP-hardness of $(\frac{11}{12}, \frac{7}{8} + \epsilon)$-deciding 2Sat.

7.3 2And hardness

Recall the definition of ν from Equation (14). The following is our 2And test:

2And-TEST

- Given functions $f : \{-1,1\}^K \to \{-1,1\}$, $g : \{-1,1\}^{dK} \to \{-1,1\}$, and $h : \{-1,1\}^K \times \{-1,1,*\}^{dK} \to \{-1,1\}$, in which f and g are folded:
- Sample $(\boldsymbol{x}, \widetilde{\boldsymbol{y}}) \sim \nu^{\otimes K}$.
- Form $\boldsymbol{y} \in \{-1,1\}^{dK}$ by replacing each $*$ of z with a uniformly random element of $\{-1,1\}$.
- With probability 1/3, test $f(\boldsymbol{x}) \wedge h(\boldsymbol{x}, \widetilde{\boldsymbol{y}})$.
- With probability 1/3, test $g(\boldsymbol{y}) \wedge h(\boldsymbol{x}, \widetilde{\boldsymbol{y}})$.
- With probability 1/3, test $\neg g(\boldsymbol{y}) \wedge \neg h(\boldsymbol{x}, \widetilde{\boldsymbol{y}})$.

We will be concerned with folded protocols. Note that h is again given the entire string $\boldsymbol{x}$. Now, the following is an easy fact:

FACT 7.5. *Let f and g be matching dictators. Then* $\mathrm{Val}_{\text{2And-TEST}}(f, g) = 10/24$.

PROOF. When $f(\boldsymbol{x}) = -1$, setting $h(\boldsymbol{x}, \widetilde{\boldsymbol{y}}) = -1$ will pass the test with probability $1/3 + \mathbf{Pr}[g(\boldsymbol{y}) = -1]/3 = 1/2$ (it can be checked that this is the best of the two settings for $h(\boldsymbol{x}, \widetilde{\boldsymbol{y}})$ in this case). Otherwise, when $f(\boldsymbol{x}) = 1$, because f and g are matching dictators, h is given the value of $g(\boldsymbol{y})$. No matter what $g(\boldsymbol{y})$ is, $h(\boldsymbol{x}, \widetilde{\boldsymbol{y}})$ can always be set to satisfy exactly one of the three constraints. This is an overall success probability of $1/2 \cdot 1/2 + 1/2 \cdot 1/3 = 5/12$. □

Consider 2And-TEST$'$, which is the uncorrelated version of the 2And-TEST. In 2And-TEST$'$, $(\boldsymbol{x}, \widetilde{\boldsymbol{y}})$ is sampled so that $\boldsymbol{x}$ is an independent $\{-1,1\}^K$ string, and $\widetilde{\boldsymbol{y}}$ is drawn from $(\mu_d)^K$. If f and g are dictators, they pass the 2And-TEST with probability 9/24. Our next theorem shows that this is optimal:

THEOREM 7.6. $\mathrm{Opt}_{\mathrm{folded}}(\text{2And-TEST}') = 9/24$.

PROOF. Conditioned on $f(\boldsymbol{x}) = -1$, an optimal h will always output -1. The probability that doing so passes the test is $1/3 + 1/3 \cdot \mathbf{Pr}[g(\boldsymbol{y}) = -1]$. Because g is balanced, this is 1/2. On the other hand, when $f(\boldsymbol{x}) = 1$ the test reduces to testing $g(\boldsymbol{y}) \wedge h(\boldsymbol{x}, \widetilde{\boldsymbol{y}})$ with probability 1/3, $\neg g(\boldsymbol{y}) \wedge \neg h(\boldsymbol{x}, \widetilde{\boldsymbol{y}})$ with probability 1/3, and rejecting outright with the remaining 1/3 probability. This is

$$\begin{aligned}&\frac{1}{3}\mathbf{Pr}[g(\boldsymbol{y}) \wedge h(\boldsymbol{x}, \widetilde{\boldsymbol{y}})] + \frac{1}{3}\mathbf{Pr}[\neg g(\boldsymbol{y}) \wedge \neg h(\boldsymbol{x}, \widetilde{\boldsymbol{y}})]\\ =&\frac{1}{3}\mathbf{E}\left[\left(\frac{1-g(\boldsymbol{y})}{2}\right)\left(\frac{1-h(\boldsymbol{x}, \widetilde{\boldsymbol{y}})}{2}\right)\right]\\ &+\frac{1}{3}\mathbf{E}\left[\left(\frac{1+g(\boldsymbol{y})}{2}\right)\left(\frac{1+h(\boldsymbol{x}, \widetilde{\boldsymbol{y}})}{2}\right)\right]\\ =&\frac{1}{3}\mathbf{E}\left[\frac{1}{2} + \frac{g(\boldsymbol{y})h(\boldsymbol{x}, \widetilde{\boldsymbol{y}})}{2}\right]. \qquad (16)\end{aligned}$$

The expectation is equal to the probability that $g(\boldsymbol{y}) = h(\boldsymbol{x}, \widetilde{\boldsymbol{y}})$, which Theorem 6.1 says is no more than 3/4. So when $f(\boldsymbol{x}) = 1$, we can upper bound the success probability of the test by

$$(16) \le \frac{1}{3} \cdot \frac{3}{4} = \frac{1}{4}.$$

Since f is balanced, each of these cases happens with equal probability. Thus, we can upper bound the success probability of the test by $1/2 \cdot 1/2 + 1/4 \cdot 1/2 = 3/8$. □

By using Fact 7.5 and Theorem 7.6 together with Corollary 4.19, we obtain the 2And case Theorem 2.5; in other words, NP-hardness of $(\frac{5}{12}, \frac{3}{8} + \epsilon)$-deciding 2And.

8. FUTURE DIRECTIONS

It seems reasonable that our hardness reductions could be converted into $n^{1-o(1)}$-round Lasserre SDP integrality gaps, using the methods of Tulsiani [Tul09]; we have not yet investigated this. This would give a new barrier for strongly approximating Unique-Games using Lasserre relaxations, a topic which has seen recent progress [BHK+11]. Relatedly, we believe our work motivates the problem of making the constants in recent subexponential-time algorithms for Unique-Games [ABS10, BRS11, GS11] more explicit.

Our new methodology seems to hold promise for improving the best known NP-hardness results for other notable 2-CSPs. Natural problems to try it on include Max-k-Cut and Khot's "2-to-1 problem". An intriguing further possibility would be to use the framework to improve the best known NP-hardness result for Metric-TSP, Min-Steiner-Tree, or Max-Acyclic-Subgraph. For each of these problems, the current best result is by a somewhat intricate gadget reduction from 3Lin(Z_2) [PV06, CC02, New00]. Such was the case previously for Max-Cut, 2Sat, 2And, and 2Lin(Z_2); perhaps our new approach could lead to an improved direct reduction from Label-Cover.

9. REFERENCES

[ABS10] Sanjeev Arora, Boaz Barak, and David Steurer. Subexponential algorithms for Unique Games and related problems. In *Proceedings of the 51st Annual IEEE Symposium on Foundations of Computer Science*, pages 563–572, 2010. 1, 2.1, 8

[AEH01] Gunnar Andersson, Lars Engebretsen, and Johan Håstad. A new way of using semidefinite programming with applications to linear equations mod p. *Journal of Algorithms*, 39(2):162–204, 2001. 2.1

[BHK+11] Boaz Barak, Aram Harrow, Jonathan Kelner, David Steurer, and Yuan Zhou. Hypercontractive inequalities, sums of squares proofs, and their applications. Manuscript, 2011. 8

[BOL90] Michael Ben-Or and Nathan Linial. Collective coin flipping. In Silvio Micali, editor, *Randomness and Computation*. Academic Press, New York, 1990. 6.2

[BRS11] Boaz Barak, Prasad Raghavendra, and David Steurer. Rounding semidefinite programming hierarchies via global correlation. In *Proceedings of the 52nd Annual IEEE Symposium on Foundations of Computer Science*, 2011. 1, 2.1, 8

[CC02] Miroslav Chlebík and Janka Chlebíková. Approximation hardness of the Steiner tree problem on graphs. In *Proceedings of the 8th Annual Scandinavian Workshop on Algorithm Theory*, pages 95–99, 2002. 8

[CC04] Miroslav Chlebík and Janka Chlebíková. On approximation hardness of the minimum 2SAT-DELETION problem. In *Proceedings of the 29th Annual International Symposium on Mathematical Foundations of Computer Science*, pages 263–273, 2004. 2.1

[DH09] Irit Dinur and Prahladh Harsha. Composition of low-error 2-query PCPs using decodable PCPs. In *Proceedings of the 50th Annual IEEE Symposium on Foundations of Computer Science*, pages 472–481, 2009. 2

[DMR09] Irit Dinur, Elchanan Mossel, and Oded Regev. Conditional hardness for approximate coloring. *SIAM Journal on Computing*, 39(3):843–873, 2009. 2

[DS05] Irit Dinur and Samuel Safra. On the hardness of approximating minimum vertex cover. *Annals of Mathematics*, 162(1):439–485, 2005. 2.1

[Fei99] Uriel Feige. *Randomized rounding of semidefinite programs — variations on the Max-Cut example*, volume 1761 of *Lecture Notes in Computer Science*, pages 189–196. Springer, 1999. 1

[Fei02] Uriel Feige. Relations between average case complexity and approximation complexity. In *Proceedings of the 34th Annual ACM Symposium on Theory of Computing*, pages 543–543, 2002. 1

[FK94] Uriel Feige and Joe Kilian. Two prover

protocols: low error at affordable rates. In *Proceedings of the 26th Annual ACM Symposium on Theory of Computing*, pages 172–183, 1994. 2

[FR04] Uriel Feige and Daniel Reichman. On systems of linear equations with two variables per equation. In *Proceedings of the 7th Annual International Workshop on Approximation Algorithms for Combinatorial Optimization Problems*, pages 117–127, 2004. 1.1, 2.1, 2.1, 2.1

[GS11] Venkatesan Guruswami and Ali Sinop. Lasserre hierarchy, higher eigenvalues, and approximation schemes for quadratic integer programming with PSD objectives. In *Proceedings of the 52nd Annual IEEE Symposium on Foundations of Computer Science*, 2011. 1, 8

[GW95] Michel Goemans and David Williamson. Improved approximation algorithms for maximum cut and satisfiability problems using semidefinite programming. *Journal of the ACM*, 42:1115–1145, 1995. 1

[Hås97] Johan Håstad. Some optimal inapproximability results. In *Proceedings of the 29th Annual ACM Symposium on Theory of Computing*, pages 1–10, 1997. 1, 1.1, 1.2

[Hås99] Johan Håstad. Clique is hard to approximate within $n^{1-\epsilon}$. *Acta Mathematica*, 182(1):105–142, 1999. 1

[Hås01] Johan Håstad. Some optimal inapproximability results. *Journal of the ACM*, 48(4):798–859, 2001. 1, 2.1, 2.1, 3, 3, 1.1, 6

[IP01] Russell Impagliazzo and Ramamohan Paturi. On the complexity of k-SAT. *Journal of Computer and System Sciences*, 62(2):367–375, 2001. 1

[Kho02] Subhash Khot. On the power of unique 2-prover 1-round games. In *Proc. 34th ACM Symposium on Theory of Computing*, pages 767–775, 2002. 1, 2

[KKMO07] Subhash Khot, Guy Kindler, Elchanan Mossel, and Ryan O'Donnell. Optimal inapproximability results for Max-Cut and other 2-variable CSPs? *SIAM Journal on Computing*, 37(1):319–357, 2007. 1, 2

[KO09] Subhash Khot and Ryan O'Donnell. SDP gaps and UGC-hardness for Max-Cut-Gain. *Theory of Computing*, 5(1):83–117, 2009. 1

[Kol10] Alexandra Kolla. Spectral algorithms for Unique Games. In *Proceedings of the 25th Annual IEEE Conference on Computational Complexity*, pages 122–130, 2010. 1

[MOO10] Elchanan Mossel, Ryan O'Donnell, and Krzysztof Oleszkiewicz. Noise stability of functions with low influences: invariance and optimality. *Annals of Mathematics*, 171(1), 2010. 2

[Mos10] Elchanan Mossel. Gaussian bounds for noise correlation of functions. *Geometric and Functional Analysis*, 19(6):1713–1756, 2010. 2, 4.3, 6.1, 6.1

[MR10] Dana Moshkovitz and Ran Raz. Two-query PCP with subconstant error. *Journal of the ACM*, 57(5):29, 2010. 1, 2, 2.5, 2.1

[New00] Alantha Newman. Approximating the maximum acyclic subgraph. Master's thesis, Massachusetts Institute of Technology, 2000. 8

[OW08] Ryan O'Donnell and Yi Wu. An optimal SDP algorithm for Max-Cut, and equally optimal Long Code tests. In *Proceedings of the 40th Annual ACM Symposium on Theory of Computing*, pages 335–344, 2008. 1, 2.1

[OWZ11] Ryan O'Donnell, Yi Wu, and Yuan Zhou. Hardness of Max-2Lin and Max-3Lin over integers, reals, and large cyclic groups. In *Proceedings of the 26th Annual IEEE Conference on Computational Complexity*, pages 23–33, 2011. 2

[PV06] Christos Papadimitriou and Santosh Vempala. On the approximability of the traveling salesman problem. *Combinatorica*, 26(1):101–120, 2006. 8

[Rag09] Prasad Raghavendra. *Approximating NP-hard problems: efficient algorithms and their limits.* PhD thesis, University of Washington, 2009. 1, 2

[Raz95] Ran Raz. A parallel repetition theorem. In *Proceedings of the 27th Annual ACM Symposium on Theory of Computing*, pages 447–456, 1995. 2

[Ste10] David Steurer. Subexponential algorithms for d-to-1 two-prover games and for certifying almost perfect expansion. Available at the author's website, 2010. 1, 2.1

[Ste11] David Steurer. Personal communication, 2011. 1

[TSSW00] Luca Trevisan, Gregory Sorkin, Madhu Sudan, and David Williamson. Gadgets, approximation, and linear programming. *SIAM Journal on Computing*, 29(6):2074–2097, 2000. 1, 1.2, 1.2, 2.1, 3, 6

[Tul09] Madhur Tulsiani. CSP gaps and reductions in the Lasserre hierarchy. In *Proceedings of the 41st Annual ACM Symposium on Theory of Computing*, pages 303–312, 2009. 8

[WZ10] Yi Wu and Yuan Zhou. Personal communication, 2010. 2

[Yan04] Ke Yang. On the (im)possibility of non-interactive correlation distillation. In *Proceedings of the 6th Annual Latin American Informatics Symposium*, pages 222–231, 2004. 3, 1.1

[Yan07] Ke Yang. On the (im)possibility of non-interactive correlation distillation. *Theoretical Computer Science*, 382(2):157–166, 2007. 3, 6.1, 6.1

Hypercontractivity, Sum-of-Squares Proofs, and their Applications

Extended Abstract*

Boaz Barak
Microsoft Research New England
Cambridge, MA

Fernando G.S.L. Brandão
Department of Physics
Universidade Federal de Minas Gerais
Belo Horizonte, Brazil

Aram W. Harrow†
Department of Computer Science & Engineering
University of Washington

Jonathan Kelner
Department of Mathematics
Massachusetts Institute of Technology

David Steurer
Microsoft Research New England
Cambridge, MA

Yuan Zhou‡
Department of Computer Science
Carnegie Mellon University

ABSTRACT

We study the computational complexity of approximating the *2-to-q* norm of linear operators (defined as $\|A\|_{2\to q} = \max_{v\neq 0}\|Av\|_q/\|v\|_2$) for $q > 2$, as well as connections between this question and issues arising in quantum information theory and the study of Khot's Unique Games Conjecture (UGC). We show the following:

1. For any constant even integer $q \geqslant 4$, a graph G is a *small-set expander* if and only if the projector into the span of the top eigenvectors of G's adjacency matrix has bounded $2 \to q$ norm. As a corollary, a good approximation to the $2 \to q$ norm will refute the *Small-Set Expansion Conjecture* — a close variant of the UGC. We also show that such a good approximation can be obtained in $\exp(n^{2/q})$ time, thus obtaining a different proof of the known subexponential algorithm for SMALL-SET EXPANSION.
2. Constant rounds of the "Sum of Squares" semidefinite programing hierarchy certify an upper bound on the $2 \to 4$ norm of the projector to low degree polynomials over the Boolean cube, as well certify the unsatisfiability of the "noisy cube" and "short code" based instances of UNIQUE GAMES considered by prior works. This improves on the previous upper bound of $\exp(\log^{O(1)} n)$ rounds (for the "short code"), as well as separates the "Sum of Squares"/"Lasserre" hierarchy from weaker hierarchies that were known to require $\omega(1)$ rounds.
3. We show reductions between computing the $2 \to 4$ norm and computing the *injective tensor norm* of a tensor, a problem with connections to quantum information theory. Three corollaries are: **(i)** the $2 \to 4$ norm is NP-hard to approximate to precision inverse-polynomial in the dimension, **(ii)** the $2 \to 4$ norm does not have a good approximation (in the sense above) unless 3-SAT can be solved in time $\exp(\sqrt{n}\,\mathrm{poly}\log(n))$, and **(iii)** known algorithms for the quantum separability problem imply a non-trivial additive approximation for the $2 \to 4$ norm.

*A full version of this paper is available on the Arxiv.

†Much of the work done while visiting Microsoft Research New England.

‡Much of the work done while the author was an intern at Microsoft Research New England.

STOC'12, May 19–22, 2012, New York, New York, USA.

Categories and Subject Descriptors

F.2 [**Theory of Computation**]: Analysis of Algorithms and Problem Complexity

Keywords

Semidefinite programming, hypercontractive, injective tensor norm, unique games conjecture

1. INTRODUCTION

For a function $f\colon \Omega \to \mathbb{R}$ on a (finite) probability space Ω, the *p-norm* is defined as $\|f\|_p = (\mathbb{E}_\Omega f^p)^{1/p}$.[1] The *$p \to q$ norm* $\|A\|_{p\to q}$ of a linear operator A between vector spaces of such functions is the smallest number $c \geqslant 0$ such that $\|Af\|_q \leqslant c\|f\|_p$ for all functions f in the domain of A. We also define the *$p \to q$ norm* of a *subspace* V to be the maximum of $\|f\|_q/\|f\|_p$ for $f \in V$; note that for $q = 2$ this is the same as the norm of the projector operator into V.

In this work, we are interested in the case $p < q$ and we will call such $p \to q$ norms *hypercontractive*.[2] Roughly speaking, for $q > p$, a function f with large $\|f\|_q$ compared to $\|f\|_p$ can be thought of as "spiky" or somewhat sparse (i.e., much of the mass concentrated in small portion of the entries). Hence finding a function f in a linear subspace V maximizing $\|f\|_q/\|f\|_2$ for some $q > 2$ can be thought of as a geometric analogue of the problem finding the shortest word in a linear code. This problem is equivalent to computing the $2 \to q$ norm of the projector P into V (since $\|Pf\|_2 \leqslant \|f\|_2$). Also when A is a normalized adjacency matrix of a graph (or more generally a Markov operator), upper bounds on the $p \to q$ norm are known

[1] We follow the convention to use *expectation* norms for *functions* (on probability spaces) and *counting* norms, denoted as $\|v\|_p = (\sum_{i=1}^n |v_i|^p)^{1/p}$, for *vectors* $v \in \mathbb{R}^m$. All normed spaces here will be finite dimensional. We distinguish between expectation and counting norms to avoid recurrent normalization factors.

[2] We use this name because a bound of the form $\|A\|_{p\to q} \leqslant 1$ for $p < q$ is often called a *hypercontractive inequality*.

as *mixed-norm*, *Nash* or *hypercontractive inequalities* and can be used to show rapid mixing of the corresponding random walk (e.g., see the surveys [Gro75, SC97]). Such bounds also have many applications to theoretical computer science, which are described in the survey [Bis11].

However, very little is known about the complexity of computing these norms. This is in contrast to the case of $p \to q$ norms for $p \geqslant q$, where much more is known both in terms of algorithms and lower bounds, see [Ste05, KNS08, BV11].

2. OUR RESULTS

We initiate a study of the computational complexity of approximating the $2 \to 4$ (and more generally $2 \to q$ for $q > 2$) norm. While we there are still many more questions than answers on this topic, we are able to show some new algorithmic and hardness results, as well as connections to both Khot's unique games conjecture [Kho02] (UGC) and questions from quantum information theory. In particular our paper gives some conflicting evidence regarding the validity of the UGC and its close variant— the small set expansion hypothesis (SSEH) of [RS10]. (See also our conclusions section.)

First, we show in Theorem 2.5 that approximating the $2 \to q$ problem (for even $q \geqslant 4$) to within any constant factor cannot be done in polynomial time (unless SAT can be solved in $\exp(o(n))$ time) but yet this problem is seemingly related to the Unique Games and Small-Set Expansion problems. In particular, we show that approximating the $2 \to 4$ norm is Small-Set Expansion- hard but yet has a subexponential algorithm which closely related to the [ABS10] algorithm for Unique Games and Small-Set Expansion. Thus the computational difficulty of this problem can be considered as some indirect evidence *supporting* the validity of the UGC or (perhaps more likely) some weaker variants of it. To our knowledge, this is the first evidence of this kind for the UGC.

On the other hand, we show that a natural polynomial-time algorithm (based on an SDP hierarchy) that solves the previously proposed hard instances for Unique Games. The previous best algorithms for some of these instances took almost exponential ($\exp(\exp(\log^{\Omega(1)} n))$) time, and in fact they were shown to require super-polynomial time for some hierarchies. Thus this result suggests that this algorithm could potentially refute the UGC, and hence can be construed as evidence *opposing* the UGC's validity.

2.1 Algorithms

We show several algorithmic results for the $2 \to 4$ (and more generally $2 \to q$) norm.

2.1.1 *Subexponential algorithm for "good" approximation*

For $q \geqslant 2$, we say that an algorithm provides a (c, C)-*approximation* for the $2 \to q$ norm if on input an operator A, the algorithm can distinguish between the case that $\|A\|_{2\to q} \leqslant c\sigma$ and the case that $\|A\|_{2\to q} \geqslant C\sigma$, where $\sigma = \sigma_{\min}(A)$ is the minimum nonzero singular value of A. (Note that since we use the expectation norm, $\|Af\|_q \geqslant \|Af\|_2 \geqslant \sigma\|f\|_2$ for every function f such that $Af \neq 0$.) We say that an algorithm provides a *good approximation* for the $2 \to q$ norm if it provides a (c, C)-approximation for some (dimension independent) constants $c < C$. The motivation behind this definition is to capture the notion of a *dimension independent* approximation factor, and is also motivated by Theorem 2.4 below, that relates a good approximation for the $2 \to q$ norm to solving the Small-Set Expansion problem.

We show the following:

Theorem 2.1. *For every $1 < c < C$, there is a* $\mathrm{poly}(n)\exp(n^{2/q})$-*time algorithm that computes a (c, C)-approximation for the $2 \to q$ norm of any linear operator whose range is $\mathbb{R}^n$.*

Combining this with our results below, we get as a corollary a subexponential algorithm for the Small-Set Expansion problem matching the parameters of [ABS10]'s algorithm. We note that this algorithm can be achieved by the "Sum of Squares" SDP hierarchy described below (and probably weaker hierarchies as well, although we did not verify this).

2.1.2 *Polynomial algorithm for specific instances*

We study a natural semidefinite programming (SDP) relaxation for computing the $2 \to 4$ norm of a given linear operator which we call Tensor-SDP.[3] While Tensor-SDP is very unlikely to provide a poly-time constant-factor approximation for the $2 \to 4$ norm in general (see Theorem 2.5 below), we do show that it provides such approximation on two very different types of instances:

- We show that Tensor-SDP certifies a constant upper bound on the ratio $\|A\|_{2\to4}/\|A\|_{2\to2}$ where $A : \mathbb{R}^n \to \mathbb{R}^m$ is a *random linear operator* (e.g., obtained by a matrix with entries chosen as i.i.d Bernoulli variables) and $m \geqslant \Omega(n^2 \log n)$. In contrast, if $m = o(n^2)$ then this ratio is $\omega(1)$, and hence this result is almost tight in the sense of obtaining "good approximation" in the sense mentioned above. We find this interesting, since random matrices seem like natural instances; indeed for superficially similar problems such shortest codeword, shortest lattice vector (or even the $1 \to 2$ norm), it seems hard to efficiently certify bounds on random operators. (The proof of this result is omitted in this extended abstract.)

- We show that Tensor-SDP gives a good approximation of the $2 \to 4$ norm of the operator projecting a function $f : \{\pm1\}^n \to \mathbb{R}$ into its low-degree component:

  Theorem 2.2. *Let $\mathcal{P}_d$ be the liner operator that maps a function $f : \{\pm1\}^n \to \mathbb{R}$ of the form $f = \sum_{\alpha\subseteq[n]} \hat{f}_\alpha \chi_\alpha$ to its low-degree part $f' = \sum_{|\alpha|\leqslant d} \hat{f}_\alpha \chi_\alpha$ (where $\chi_\alpha(x) = \prod_{i\in\alpha} x_i$). Then* Tensor-SDP$(\mathcal{P}_d) \leqslant 9^d$.

  The fact that $\mathcal{P}_d$ has bounded $2 \to 4$ norm is widely used in the literature relating to the UGC. Previously, no general-purpose algorithm was known to efficiently certify this fact.

2.1.3 *Quasipolynomial algorithm for additive approximation*

We also consider the generalization of Tensor-SDP to a natural SDP *hierarchy*. This is a convex relaxation that starts from an initial SDP and tightens it by adding additional constraints. Such hierarchies are generally paramaterized by a number r (often called the *number of rounds*), where the 1st round corresponds to the initial SDP, and the nth round (for discrete problems where n is the instance size) corresponds to the exponential brute force algorithm that outputs an optimal answer. Generally, the rth-round of each such hierarchy can be evaluated in $n^{O(r)}$ time (though in some cases $n^{O(1)}2^{O(r)}$ time suffices [BRS11]). See Section 3, as well as the surveys [CT10, Lau03] and the papers [SA90, LS91, RS09, KPS10] for more information about these hierarchies.

[3]We use the name Tensor-SDP for this program since it will be a canonical relaxation of the polynomial program $\max_{\|x\|_2=1} \langle T, x^{\otimes 4}\rangle$ where T is the 4-tensor such that $\langle T, x^{\otimes 4}\rangle = \|Ax\|_4^4$. See Section 4.5 for more details.

We call the hierarchy we consider here the *Sum of Squares* (SoS) hierarchy. It is not novel but rather a variant of the hierarchies studied by several authors including Shor [Sho87], Parrilo [Par00, Par03], Nesterov [Nes00] and Lasserre [Las01]. (Generally in our context these hierarchies can be made equivalent in power, though there are some subtleties involved; see the full version of this paper and [Lau09] for more details.) We describe the SoS hierarchy formally in Section 3. We show that Tensor-SDP's extension to several rounds of the SoS hierarchy gives a non-trivial *additive* approximation:

THEOREM 2.3. *Let* Tensor-SDP$^{(d)}$ *denote the* $n^{O(d)}$*-time algorithm by extending* Tensor-SDP *to d rounds of the Sum-of-Squares hierarchy. Then for all* ε, *there is* $d = O(\log(n)/\varepsilon^2)$ *such that*

$$\|A\|_{2\to4}^4 \leqslant \text{Tensor-SDP}^{(d)}(A) \leqslant \|A\|_{2\to4}^4 + \varepsilon\|A\|_{2\to2}^2\|A\|_{2\to\infty}^2 .$$

The term $\|A\|_{2\to2}^2\|A\|_{2\to\infty}^2$ is a natural upper bound on $\|A\|_{2\to4}^4$ obtained using Hölder's inequality. Since $\|A\|_{2\to2}$ is the largest singular value of A, and $\|A\|_{2\to\infty}$ is the largest 2-norm of any row of A, they can be computed quickly. Theorem 2.3 shows that one can improve this upper bound by a factor of ε using run time $\exp(\log^2(n)/\varepsilon^2))$. Note however that in the special case (relevant to the UGC) that A is a projector to a subspace V, $\|A\|_{2\to2} = 1$ and $\|A\|_{2\to\infty} \geqslant \sqrt{\dim(V)}$ (see Lemma 9.1), which unfortunately means that Theorem 2.3 does not give any new algorithms in that setting.

Despite Theorem 2.3 being a non-quantum algorithm for for an ostensibly non-quantum problem, we actually achieve it using the results of Brandão, Christiandl and Yard [BaCY11] about the quantum separability problem. In fact, it turns out that the SoS hierarchy extension of Tensor-SDP is equivalent to techniques that have been used to approximate separable states [DPS04]. We find this interesting both because there are few positive general results about the convergence rate of SDP hierarchies, and because the techniques of [BaCY11], based on entanglement measures of quantum states, are different from typical ways of proving correctness of semidefinite programs, and in particular different techniques from the ones we use to analyze Tensor-SDP in other settings. This connection also means that integrality gaps for Tensor-SDP would imply new types of separable states that pass most of the known tests for entanglement.

2.2 Reductions

We relate the question of computing the hypercontractive norm with two other problems considered in the literature: the *small set expansion* problem [RS10, RST10a], and the *injective tensor norm* question studied in the context of quantum information theory [HM10, BaCY11].

2.2.1 Hypercontractivity and small set expansion

Khot's *Unique Games Conjecture* [Kho02] (UGC) has been the focus of intense research effort in the last few years. The conjecture posits the hardness of approximation for a certain constraint-satisfaction problem, and shows promise to settle many open questions in the theory of approximation algorithms. Many works have been devoted to studying the plausibility of the UGC, as well as exploring its implications and obtaining unconditional results inspired or motivated by this effort. Tantalizingly, at the moment we have very little insight on whether this conjecture is actually true, and thus producing evidence on the UGC's truth or falsity is a central effort in computational complexity. Raghavendra and Steurer [RS10] proposed a hypothesis closely related to the UGC called the *Small-Set Expansion* hypothesis (SSEH). Loosely speaking, the SSEH states that it is NP-hard to certify that a given graph $G = (V, E)$ is a *small-set expander* in the sense that subsets with size $o(|V|)$ vertices have almost all their neighbors outside the set. [RS10] showed that the UGC implies the SSEH. While a reduction in the other direction is not known, all currently known algorithmic and integrality gap results apply to both problems equally well (e.g., [ABS10, RST10b]), and thus the two conjectures are likely to be equivalent.

We show, loosely speaking, that a graph is a small-set expander if and only if the projection operator to the span of its top eigenvectors has bounded $2 \to 4$ norm. To make this precise, if $G = (V, E)$ is a regular graph, then let $P_{\geqslant\lambda}(G)$ be the projection operator into the span of the eigenvectors of G's normalized adjacency matrix with eigenvalue at least λ, and $\Phi_G(\delta)$ be $\min_{S\subseteq V, |S|\leqslant\delta|V|} \mathbb{P}_{(u,v)\in E}[v \notin S \mid u \in S]$.

Then we relate small-set expansion to the $2 \to 4$ norm (indeed the $2 \to q$ norm for even $q \geqslant 4$) as follows:

THEOREM 2.4. *For every regular graph* G, $\lambda > 0$ *and even* q,

1. (Norm bound implies expansion) *For all* $\delta > 0, \varepsilon > 0$, $\|P_{\geqslant\lambda}(G)\|_{2\to q} \leqslant \varepsilon/\delta^{(q-2)/2q}$ *implies that* $\Phi_G(\delta) \geqslant 1 - \lambda - \varepsilon^2$.

2. (Expansion implies norm bound) *There is a constant c such that for all* $\delta > 0$, $\Phi_G(\delta) > 1 - \lambda 2^{-cq}$ *implies* $\|P_{\geqslant\lambda}(G)\|_{2\to q} \leqslant 2/\sqrt{\delta}$.

While one direction (bounded hypercontractive norm implies small-set expansion) was already known,[4] to our knowledge the other direction is novel. As a corollary we show that the SSEH implies that there is no good approximation for the $2 \to 4$ norm.

2.2.2 Hypercontractivity and the injective tensor norm

We are able to make progress in understanding both the complexity of the $2 \to 4$ norm and the quality of our SDP relaxation by relating the $2 \to 4$ norm to several natural questions about tensors. An r-tensor can be thought of as an r-linear form on $\mathbb{R}^n$, and the *injective tensor norm* $\|\cdot\|_{\text{inj}}$ of a tensor is given by maximizing this form over all unit vector inputs. See Section 8 for a precise definition. When $r = 1$, this norm is the 2-norm of a vector and when $r = 2$, it is the operator norm (or $2 \to 2$-norm) of a matrix, but for $r = 3$ it becomes NP-hard to calculate. One motivation to study this norm comes from quantum mechanics, where computing it is equivalent to a number of long-studied problems concerning entanglement and many-body physics [HM10]. More generally, tensors arise in a vast range of practical problems involving multidimensional data [vL09] for which the injective tensor norm is both of direct interest and can be used as a subroutine for other tasks, such as tensor decomposition [dlVKKV05].

It is not hard to show that $\|A\|_{2\to4}^4$ is actually equal to $\|T\|_{\text{inj}}$ for some 4-tensor $T = T_A$. Not all 4-tensors can arise this way, but we show that the injective tensor norm problem for general tensors can be reduced to those of the form T_A. Combined with known results about the hardness of tensor computations, this reduction implies the following hardness result. To formulate the theorem, recall that the Exponential Time Hypothesis (ETH) [IPZ98] states that 3-SAT instances of length n require time $\exp(\Omega(n))$ to solve.

[4]While we do not know who was the first to point out this fact explicitly, within theoretical CS it was implicitly used in several results relating the Bonami-Beckner-Gross hypercontractivity of the Boolean noise operator to isoperimetric properties, with one example being O'Donnell's proof of the soundness of [KV05]'s integrality gap (see Section 9.1 in [KV05]).

THEOREM 2.5 (INFORMAL VERSION). *Assuming ETH, then for any ε, δ satisfying $\varepsilon + \delta < 1$, the $2 \to 4$ norm of an $m \times m$ matrix A cannot be approximated to within a m^{ε} multiplicative factor in time less than $m^{\log^{\delta}(m)}$ time. This hardness result holds even with A is a projector.*

While we are primarily concerned with the case of $\Omega(1)$ approximation factor, we note that poly-time approximations to within multiplicative factor $1 + 1/n^{1.01}$ are not possible unless $\mathbf{P} = \mathbf{NP}$. This, along with Theorem 2.5, is restated more formally as Theorem 8.3 in Section 8.2 . We also whose there that Theorem 2.5 yields as a corollary that, assuming ETH, there is no polynomial-time algorithm obtaining a good approximation for the $2 \to 4$ norm. We note that these results hold under weaker assumptions than the ETH; see Section 8.2.

Previously no hardness results were known for the $2 \to 4$ norm, or any $p \to q$ norm with $p < q$, even for calculating the norms exactly. However, hardness of approximation results for $1+1/\operatorname{poly}(n)$ multiplicative error have been proved for other polynomial optimization problems [BTN98].

2.3 Relation to the Unique Games Conjecture

Our results and techniques have some relevance to the unique games conjecture. Theorem 2.4 shows that obtaining a good approximation for the $2 \to q$ norm is SMALL-SET EXPANSION hard, but Theorem 2.1 shows that this problem is not "that much harder" than UNIQUE GAMES and SMALL-SET EXPANSION since it too has a subexponential algorithm. Thus, the $2 \to q$ problem is in some informal sense "of similar flavor" to the UNIQUE GAMES/ SMALL-SET EXPANSION. On the other hand, we actually are able to show in Theorem 2.5 *hardness* (even if only quasipolynomial) to this problem, whereas a similar result for UNIQUE GAMES or SMALL-SET EXPANSION would be a major breakthrough. So there is a sense in which these results can be thought of as some "positive evidence" in favor of at least weak variants of the UGC. (We emphasize however that there are inherent difficulties in extending these results for UNIQUE GAMES, and it may very well be that obtaining a multiplicative approximation to the $2 \to 4$ of an operator is significantly harder problem than UNIQUE GAMES or SMALL-SET EXPANSION.) In contrast, our positive algorithmic results show that perhaps the $2 \to q$ norm can be thought of as a path to refuting the UGC. In particular we are able to extend our techniques to show a polynomial time algorithm can approximate the canonical hard instances for UNIQUE GAMES considered in prior works.

THEOREM 2.6. *(Informal) Eight rounds of the SoS relaxation certifies that it is possible to satisfy at most 1/100 fraction of the constraints of* UNIQUE GAMES *instances of the "quotient noisy cube" and "short code" types considered in [RS09, KS09, KPS10, BGH⁺11]*

These instances are the same ones for which previous works showed that weaker hierarchies such as "SDP+Sherali Adams" and "Approximate Lasserre" require $\omega(1)$ rounds to certify that one cannot satisfy almost all the constraints [KV05, RS10, KS09, BGH⁺11]. In fact, for the "short code" based instances of [BGH⁺11] there was no upper bound known better than $\exp(\log^{\Omega(1)} n)$ on the number of rounds required to certify that they are not almost satisfiable, regardless of the power of the hierarchy used.

This is significant since the current best known algorithms for UNIQUE GAMES utilize SDP hierarchies [BRS11, GS11],[5] and the instances above were the only known evidence that polynomial time versions of these algorithms do not refute the unique games conjecture. Our work also show that strong "basis independent" hierarchies such as Sum of Squares [Par00, Par03] and Lasserre [Las01] can in fact do better than the seemingly only slightly weaker variants.[6]

3. THE SOS HIERARCHY

For our algorithmic results in this paper we consider a semidefinite programming (SDP) hierarchy that we call the *Sum of Squares* (SoS) hierarchy. We call the hierarchy we consider here the *Sum of Squares* (SoS) hierarchy. This is not a novel algorithm and essentially the same hierarchies were considered by many other researchers (see the survey [Lau09]). Because different works sometimes used slightly different definitions, in this section we formally define the hierarchy we use as well as explain the intuition behind it. While there are some subtleties involved, one can think of this hierarchy as equivalent in power to the programs considered by Parrilo, Lasserre and others, while stronger than hierarchies such "SDP+Sherali-Adams" and "Approximate Lasserre" considered in [RS09, KPS10, BRS11].

The SoS SDP is a relaxation for polynomial equations. That is, we consider a system of the following form: maximize $P_0(x)$ over $x \in \mathbb{R}^n$ subject to $P_i^2(x) = 0$ for $i = 1 \ldots m$ and $P_0, \ldots, P_m$ polynomials of degree at most d.[7] For $r \geqslant 2d$, the *r-round SoS SDP* optimizes over $x_1, \ldots, x_n$ that can be thought of as formal variables rather than actual numbers. For these formal variables, expressions of the form $P(x)$ are well defined and correspond to a real number (which can be computed from the SDP solution) as long as P is a polynomial of degree at most r. These numbers obey the *linearity* property which is that $(P + Q)(x) = P(x) + Q(x)$, and, most importantly, the *positivity* property that $P^2(x) \geqslant 0$ for every polynomial P of degree at most $r/2$. These expressions satisfy all initial constraints (i.e., $P_i^2(x) = 0$ for $i = 1 \ldots m$) and the *value* of the SDP is set to be the expression $P_0(x)$. The above means that to show that the SoS relaxation has value at most v it is sufficient to give any proof that derives from the constraints $\{P_i^2(x) = 0\}_{i=1..m}$ the conclusion that $P_0(x) \leqslant v$ using only the linearity and positivity properties, without using any polynomials of degree larger than r in the intermediate steps. In fact, such a proof always has the form

$$v - P_0(x) = \sum_{i=1}^{k} R_i(x)^2 + \sum_{i=1}^{m} P_i(x)Q_i(x), \qquad (3.1)$$

where $R_1, \ldots, R_k, Q_1, \ldots, Q_m$ are arbitrary polynomials satisfying $\deg R_i \leqslant r/2, \deg P_iQ_i \leqslant r$. The polynomial $\sum_i R_i(x)^2$ is a SoS (sum of squares) and optimizing over such polynomials (along with the $Q_1, \ldots, Q_m$) can be achieved with a semi-definite program.

Pseudo-expectation view.

For more intuition about the SoS hierarchy, one can imagine that instead of being formal variables, $x_1, \ldots, x_n$ actually correspond to

[5]Both these works showed SDP-hierarchy-based algorithms matching the performance of the subexponential algorithm of [ABS10]. [GS11] used the Lasserre hierarchy, while [BRS11] used the weaker "SDP+Sherali-Adams" hierarchy.

[6]The only other result of this kind we are aware of is [KMN11], that show that Lasserre gives a better approximation ratio than the linear programming Sherali-Adams hierarchy for the knapsack problem. We do not know if weaker semidefinite hierarchies match this ratio, although knapsack of course has a simple dynamic programming based PTAS.

[7]This form is without loss of generality, as one can translate an inequality constraint of the form $P_i(x) \geqslant 0$ into the equality constraint $(P_i(x) - y^2)^2 = 0$ where y is some new auxiliary variable. The proof is omitted in this extended abstract.

correlated random variables $X_1, \ldots, X_n$ over $\mathbb{R}^n$, and the expression $P(x)$ is set to equal the expectation $\mathbb{E}[P(X)]$. In this case, the linearity and positivity properties are obviously satisfied by these expressions, although other properties that would be obtained if $x_1, \ldots, x_n$ were simply numbers might not hold. For example, the property that $R(x) = P(x)Q(x)$ if $R = P \cdot Q$ does not necessarily hold, since its not always the case that $E[XY] = E[X]E[Y]$ for every three random variables X, Y, Z. So, another way to describe the r-round SoS hierarchy is that the expressions $P(x)$ (for P of degree at most r) satisfy some of the constraints that would have been satisfied if these expressions corresponded to expectations over some correlated random variables $X_1, \ldots, X_N$. For this reason, we will use the notation $\tilde{\mathbb{E}}_x P(x)$ instead of $P(x)$ where we refer to the operator $\tilde{\mathbb{E}}$ as a level-r *pseudo-expectation operator* (or r-p.e.o. for short). Also, rather than describing $x_1, \ldots, x_n$ as formal variables, we will refer to them as level-r *fictitious random variables* (or r-f.r.v. for short) since in some sense they look like true correlated random variables up to their r^{th} moment.

We can now present our formal definition of pseudo-expectation and the SoS hierarchy:[8]

Definition 3.1. *Let $\tilde{\mathbb{E}}$ be an operator that maps polynomial P over $\mathbb{R}^n$ of degree at most r into a real number which we denote by $\tilde{\mathbb{E}}_x P(x)$ or $\tilde{\mathbb{E}} P$ for short. We say that $\tilde{\mathbb{E}}$ is a* level-r pseudo-expectation operator *(r-p.e.o. for short) if it satisfies:*

Linearity *For every polynomials P, Q of degree at most r and $\alpha, \beta \in \mathbb{R}$, $\tilde{\mathbb{E}}(\alpha P + \beta Q) = \alpha \tilde{\mathbb{E}} P + \beta \tilde{\mathbb{E}} Q$.*

Positivity *For every polynomial P of degree at most $r/2$, $\tilde{\mathbb{E}} P^2 \geqslant 0$.*

Normalization $\tilde{\mathbb{E}} 1 = 1$ *where on the RHS, 1 denotes the degree-0 polynomial that is the constant 1.*

Definition 3.2. *Let $P_0, \ldots, P_m$ be polynomials over $\mathbb{R}^n$ of degree at most d, and let $r \geqslant 2d$. The value of the r-round SoS SDP for the program "*max P_0 *subject to $P_i^2 = 0$ for $i = 1 \ldots m$", is equal to the maximum of $\tilde{\mathbb{E}} P_0$ where $\tilde{\mathbb{E}}$ ranges over all level r pseudo-expectation operators satisfying $\tilde{\mathbb{E}} P_i^2 = 0$ for $i = 1 \ldots m$.*

The operator $\tilde{\mathbb{E}}$ can be represented by a table of size $n^{O(r)}$ containing the pseudo-expectations of every monomial of degree at most r (or some other linear basis for polynomials of degree at most r). For a linear operator $\tilde{\mathbb{E}}$, the map $P \mapsto \tilde{\mathbb{E}} P^2$ is a quadratic form. Hence, $\tilde{\mathbb{E}}$ satisfies the positivity condition if and only if the corresponding quadratic form is positive semidefinite. It follows that the convex set of level-r pseudo-expectation operators over $\mathbb{R}^n$ admits an $n^{O(r)}$-time separation oracle, and hence the r-round SoS relaxation can be solved up to accuracy ε in time $(mn \cdot \log(1/\varepsilon))^{O(r)}$.

As noted above, for every random variable X over $\mathbb{R}^n$, the operator $\tilde{\mathbb{E}} P := \mathbb{E} P(X)$ is a level-r pseudo-expectation operator for every r. As $r \to \infty$, this hierarchy of pseudo-expectations will converge to the expectations of a true random variable [Las01], but the convergence is in general not guaranteed to happen in a finite number of steps [dKL11].

Whenever there can be ambiguity about what are the variables of the polynomial P inside an r-p.e.o. $\tilde{\mathbb{E}}$, we will use the notation $\tilde{\mathbb{E}}_x P(x)$ (e.g., $\tilde{\mathbb{E}}_x x_3^2$ is the same as $\tilde{\mathbb{E}} P$ where P is the polynomial $x \mapsto x_3^2$). As mentioned above, we call the inputs x to the polynomial *level-r fictitious random variables* or r-f.r.v. for short.

[8]We use the name "Sum of Squares" since the positivity condition below is the most important constraint of this program. However, some prior works used this name for the *dual* of the program we define here. We are able to show that in many cases of interest to us there is no duality gap, but the proof is omitted in this extended abstract.

Remark 3.3. *The main difference between the SoS hierarchy and weaker SDP hierarchies considered in the literature such as SDP+Sherali Adams and the Approximate Lasserre hierarchies [RS09, KPS10] is that the SoS hierarchy treats all polynomials equally and hence is agnostic to the choice of basis. For example, the approximate Lasserre hierarchy can also be described in terms of pseudo-expectations, but these pseudo-expectations are only defined for monomials, and are allowed some small error. While they can be extended linearly to other polynomials, for non-sparse polynomials that error can greatly accumulate.*

3.1 Basic properties of pseudo-expectation

For two polynomials P and Q, we write $P \preceq Q$ if $Q = P + \sum_{i=1}^{m} R_i^2$ for some polynomials $R_1, \ldots, R_m$.

If P and Q have degree at most r, then $P \preceq Q$ implies that $\tilde{\mathbb{E}} P \leqslant \tilde{\mathbb{E}} Q$ every r-p.e.o. $\tilde{\mathbb{E}}$. This follows using linearity and positivity, as well as the (not too hard to verify) observation that if $Q - P = \sum_i R_i^2$ then it must hold that $\deg(R_i) \leqslant \max\{\deg(P), \deg(Q)\}/2$ for every i.

We would like to understand how polynomials behave on linear subspaces of $\mathbb{R}^n$. A map $P\colon \mathbb{R}^n \to \mathbb{R}$ is *polynomial* over a linear subspace $V \subseteq \mathbb{R}^n$ if P restricted to V agrees with a polynomial in the coefficients for some basis of V. Concretely, if $g_1, \ldots, g_m$ is an (orthonormal) basis of V, then P is *polynomial* over V if $P(f)$ agrees with a polynomial in $\langle f, g_1 \rangle, \ldots, \langle f, g_m \rangle$. We say that $P \preceq Q$ holds over a subspace V if $P - Q$, as a polynomial over V, is a sum of squares.

Lemma 3.4. *Let P and Q be two polynomials over $\mathbb{R}^n$ of degree at most r, and let $B\colon \mathbb{R}^n \to \mathbb{R}^k$ be a linear operator. Suppose that $P \preceq Q$ holds over the kernel of B. Then, $\tilde{\mathbb{E}} P \leqslant \tilde{\mathbb{E}} Q$ holds for any r-p.e.o. $\tilde{\mathbb{E}}$ over $\mathbb{R}^n$ that satisfies $\tilde{\mathbb{E}}_f \|Bf\|^2 = 0$.*

Proof. Since $P \preceq Q$ over the kernel of B, we can write $Q(f) = P(f) + \sum_{i=1}^{m} R_i^2(f) + \sum_{j=1}^{k} (Bf)_j S_j(f)$ for polynomials $R_1, \ldots, R_m$ and $S_1, \ldots, S_k$ over $\mathbb{R}^n$. By positivity, $\tilde{\mathbb{E}}_f R_i^2(f) \geqslant 0$ for all $i \in [m]$. We claim that $\tilde{\mathbb{E}}_f (Bf)_j S_j(f) = 0$ for all $j \in [k]$ (which would finish the proof). This claim follows from the fact that $\tilde{\mathbb{E}}_f (Bf)_j^2 = 0$ for all $j \in [k]$ and Lemma 3.5 below. □

Lemma 3.5 (Pseudo Cauchy-Schwarz). *Let P and Q be two polynomials of degree at most r. Then, $\tilde{\mathbb{E}} PQ \leqslant \sqrt{\tilde{\mathbb{E}} P^2} \cdot \sqrt{\tilde{\mathbb{E}} Q^2}$ for any degree-$2r$ pseudo-expectation functional $\tilde{\mathbb{E}}$.*

Proof. We first consider the case $\tilde{\mathbb{E}} P^2, \tilde{\mathbb{E}} Q^2 > 0$. Then, by linearity of $\tilde{\mathbb{E}}$, we may assume that $\tilde{\mathbb{E}} P^2 = \tilde{\mathbb{E}} Q^2 = 1$. Since $2PQ \preceq P^2 + Q^2$ (by expanding the square $(P - Q)^2$), it follows that $\tilde{\mathbb{E}} PQ \leqslant \frac{1}{2} \tilde{\mathbb{E}} P^2 + \frac{1}{2} \tilde{\mathbb{E}} Q^2 = 1$ as desired. It remains to consider the case $\tilde{\mathbb{E}} P^2 = 0$. In this case, $2\alpha PQ \preceq P^2 + \alpha^2 Q^2$ implies that $\tilde{\mathbb{E}} PQ \leqslant \alpha \cdot \frac{1}{2} \tilde{\mathbb{E}} Q^2$ for all $\alpha > 0$. Thus $\tilde{\mathbb{E}} PQ = 0$, as desired. □

Lemma 3.5 also explains why our SDP in Definition 3.2 is dual to the one in (3.1). If $\tilde{\mathbb{E}}$ is a level-r pseudo-expectation operator satisfying $\tilde{\mathbb{E}}[P_i^2] = 0$, then Lemma 3.5 implies that $\tilde{\mathbb{E}}[P_i Q_i] = 0$ for all Q_i with $\deg P_i Q_i \leqslant r$.

The full version of this paper contains some additional useful facts about pseudo-expectation operators. In particular, we will make repeated use of the fact that they satisfy another Cauchy-Schwarz analogue: namely, for any level-2 f.r.v.'s f, g, we have $\tilde{\mathbb{E}}_{f,g} \langle f, g \rangle \leqslant \sqrt{\tilde{\mathbb{E}}_f \|f\|^2} \sqrt{\tilde{\mathbb{E}}_g \|g\|^2}$.

3.2 Why is this SoS hierarchy useful?

Consider the following example. It is known that if $f : \{\pm 1\}^\ell \to \mathbb{R}$ is a degree-d polynomial then

$$9^d \left(\mathop{\mathbb{E}}_{w \in \{\pm 1\}^\ell} f(w)^2 \right)^2 \geqslant \mathop{\mathbb{E}}_{w \in \{\pm 1\}^n} f(w)^4 , \qquad (3.2)$$

(see e.g. [O'D07]). Equivalently, the linear operator $\mathcal{P}_d$ on $\mathbb{R}^{\{\pm 1\}^\ell}$ that projects a function into the degree d polynomials satisfies $\|\mathcal{P}_d\|_{2\to4} \leqslant 9^{d/4}$. This fact is known as the hypercontractivity of low-degree polynomials, and was used in several integrality gaps results such as [KV05]. By following the proof of (3.2) we show in Lemma 5.1 that a stronger statement is true:

$$9^d \left(\mathop{\mathbb{E}}_{w \in \{\pm 1\}^\ell} f(w)^2 \right)^2 = \mathop{\mathbb{E}}_{w \in \{\pm 1\}^\ell} f(w)^4 + \sum_{i=1}^{m} Q_i(f)^2 , \qquad (3.3)$$

where the Q_i's are polynomials of degree $\leqslant 2$ in the $\binom{\ell}{d}$ variables $\{\hat{f}(\alpha)\}_{\alpha \in \binom{[\ell]}{d}}$ specifying the coefficients of the polynomial f. By using the positivity constraints, (3.3) implies that (3.2) holds even in the 4-round SoS relaxation where we consider the coefficients of f to be given by 4-f.r.v. This proves Theorem 2.2, showing that the SoS relaxation certifies that $\|\mathcal{P}_d\|_{2\to4} \leqslant 9^{d/4}$.

Remark 3.6. *Unfortunately to describe the result above, we needed to use the term "degree" in two different contexts. The SDP relaxation considers polynomial expressions of degree at most* 4 *in the coefficients of* f. *This is a different notion of degree than the degree* d *of* f *itself as a polynomial over* $\mathbb{R}^\ell$. *In particular the variables of this SoS program are the* $\binom{\ell}{d}$ *coefficients* $\{\hat{f}(\alpha)\}_{\alpha \in \binom{[\ell]}{d}}$. *Note that for every fixed* w, *the expression* $f(w)$ *is a linear polynomial over these variables, and hence the expressions* $\left(\mathbb{E}_{w \in \{\pm 1\}^\ell} f(w)^2\right)^2$ *and* $\mathbb{E}_{w \in \{\pm 1\}^\ell} f(w)^4$ *are degree* 4 *polynomials over the variables.*

While the proof of (3.3) is fairly simple, we find the result—that hypercontractivity of polynomials is efficiently certifiable—somewhat surprising. The reason is that hypercontractivity serves as the basis of the integrality gaps results which are exactly instances of maximization problems where the objective value is low but this is supposedly hard to certify. In particular, we consider integrality gaps for Unique Games considered before in the literature. All of these instances follow the framework initiated by Khot and Vishnoi [KV05]. Their idea was inspired by Unique Games hardness proofs, with the integrality gap obtained by composing an initial instance with a gadget. The proof that these instances have "cheating" SDP solutions is obtained by "lifting" the completeness proof of the gadget. On the other hand, the soundness property of the gadget, combined with some isoperimetric results, showed that the instances do not have real solutions. This approach of lifting completeness proofs of reductions was used to get other integrality gap results as well [Tul09]. We show that the SoS hierarchy allows us to lift a certain *soundness* proof for these instances, which includes a (variant of) the invariance principle of [MOO05], influence-decoding a la [KKMO04], and hypercontractivity of low degree polynomials. It turns out all these results can be proven via sum-of-squares type arguments and hence lifted to the SoS hierarchy.

4. OVERVIEW OF PROOFS

We now give a very high level overview of the tools we use to obtain our results, leaving details to the later sections and the full version.

4.1 Subexponential algorithm for the $2 \to q$ norm

Our subexponential algorithm for obtaining a good approximation for the $2 \to q$ norm is extremely simple. It is based on the observation that a subspace $V \subseteq \mathbb{R}^n$ of too large a dimension must contain a function f such that $\|f\|_q \gg \|f\|_2$. For example, if $\dim(V) \gg \sqrt{n}$, then there must be f such that $\|f\|_4 \gg \|f\|_2$. This means that if we want to distinguish between, say, the case that $\|V\|_{2\to4} \leqslant 2$ and $\|V\|_{2\to4} \geqslant 3$, then we can assume without loss of generality that $\dim(V) = O(\sqrt{n})$ in which case we can solve the problem in $\exp(O(\sqrt{n}))$ time. To get intuition, consider the case that V is spanned by an orthonormal basis $f^1, \dots, f^d$ of functions whose entries are all in ± 1. Then clearly we can find coefficients $a_1, \dots, a_d \in \{\pm 1\}$ such that the first coordinate of $g = \sum a_j f^j$ is equal to d, which means that its 4-norm is at least $(d^4/n)^{1/4} = d/n^{1/4}$. On the other hand, since the basis is orthonormal, the 2-norm of g equals $\sqrt{d}$ which is $\ll d/n^{1/4}$ for $d \gg \sqrt{n}$.

Note the similarity between this algorithm and [ABS10]'s algorithm for Small-Set Expansion, that also worked by showing that if the dimension of the top eigenspace of a graph is too large then it cannot be a small-set expander. Indeed, using our reduction of Small-Set Expansion to the $2 \to q$ norm, we can reproduce a similar result to [ABS10].

4.2 Bounding the value of SoS relaxations

We show that in several cases, the SoS SDP hierarchy gives strong bounds on various instances. At the heart of these results is a general approach of "lifting" proofs about one-dimensional objects into the SoS relaxation domain. Thus we transform the prior proofs that these instances have small objective value, into a proof that the SoS relaxation also has a small objective The crucial observation is that many proofs boil down to the simple fact that a sum of squares of numbers is always non-negative. It turns out that this "sum of squares" axiom is surprisingly powerful (e.g. implying a version of the Cauchy–Schwarz inequality), and many proofs boil down to essentially this principle.

4.3 The 2-to-4 norm and small-set expansion

Bounds on the $p \to q$ norm of operators for $p < q$ have been used to show fast convergence of Markov chains. In particular, it is known that if the projector to the top eigenspace of a graph G has bounded $2 \to 4$ norm, then that graph is a *small-set expander* in the sense that sets of $o(1)$ fraction of the vertices have most of their edges exit the set. In this work we show a converse to this statement, proving that if G is a small-set expander, then the corresponding projector has bounded $2 \to 4$ norm. As mentioned above, one corollary of this result is that a good (i.e., dimension-independent) approximation to the $2 \to 4$ norm will refute the Small-Set Expansion hypothesis of [RS10].

We give a rough sketch of the proof. Suppose that G is a sufficiently strong small-set expander, in the sense that every set S with $|S| \leqslant \delta|V(G)|$ has all but a tiny fraction of the edges (u, v) with $u \in S$ satisfying $v \notin S$. Let f be a function in the eigenspace of G corresponding to eigenvalues larger than, say 0.99. Since f is in the top eigenspace, for the purposes of this sketch let's imagine that it satisfies

$$\forall x \in V, \mathop{\mathbb{E}}_{y \sim x} f(y) \geqslant 0.9 f(x), \qquad (4.1)$$

where the expectation is over a random neighbor y of x. Now, suppose that $\mathbb{E} f(x)^2 = 1$ but $\mathbb{E} f(x)^4 = C$ for some $C \gg \mathrm{poly}(1/\delta)$. That means that most of the contribution to the 4-norm comes from the set S of vertices x such that $f(x) \geqslant (1/2)C^{1/4}$, but $|S| \ll \delta|V(G)|$. Moreover, suppose for simplicity that $f(x) \in ((1/2)C^{1/4}, 2C^{1/4})$, in which case the condition (*) together with the small-set expansion condition that for most vertices y in $\Gamma(S)$ (the neighborhood of S)

satisfy $f(y) \geqslant C^{1/4}/3$, but the small-set expansion condition, together with the regularity of the graph imply that $|\Gamma(S)| \geqslant 200|S|$ (say), which implies that $\mathbb{E} f(x)^4 \geqslant 2C$—a contradiction.

The actual proof is more complicated, since we can't assume the condition (4.1). Instead we will approximate it it by assuming that f is the function in the top eigenspace that *maximizes* the ratio $\|f\|_4/\|f\|_2$. See Section 7 for the details.

4.4 The 2-to-4 norm and the injective tensor norm

To relate the $2 \to 4$ norm to the injective tensor norm, we start by establishing equivalences between the $2 \to 4$ norm and a variety of different tensor problems. Some of these are straightforward exercises in linear algebra, analogous to proving that the largest eigenvalue of $M^T M$ equals the square of the operator norm of M.

One technically challenging reduction is between the problem of optimizing a general degree-4 polynomial $f(x)$ for $x \in \mathbb{R}^n$ and a polynomial that can be written as the sum of fourth powers of linear functions of x. Straightforward approaches will magnify errors by poly(n) factors, which would make it impossible to rule out a PTAS for the $2 \to 4$ norm. This would still be enough to prove that a $1/\text{poly}(n)$ additive approximation is **NP**-hard. However, to handle constant-factor approximations, we will instead use a variant of a reduction in [HM10]. This will allow us to map a general tensor optimization problem (corresponding to a general degree-4 polynomial) to a $2 \to 4$ norm calculation without losing very much precision.

To understand this reduction, we first introduce the $n^2 \times n^2$ matrix $A_{2,2}$ (defined in Section 8) with the property that $\|A\|_{2\to4}^4 = \max z^T A_{2,2} z$, where the maximum is taken over unit vectors z that can be written in the form $x \otimes y$. Without this last restriction, the maximum would simply be the operator norm of $A_{2,2}$. Operationally, we can think of $A_{2,2}$ as a quantum measurement operator, and vectors of the form $x \otimes y$ as unentangled product states. Thus the difference between $\|A\|_{2\to4}^4$ and $\|A_{2,2}\|_{2\to2}$ can be thought of as the extent to which the measurement $A_{2,2}$ can notice the difference between product states and (some) entangled state.

Next, we define a matrix A' whose rows are of the form $(x' \otimes y')^* \sqrt{A_{2,2}}$, where $x', y' \in \mathbb{R}^n$ range over a distribution that approximates the uniform distribution. If A' acts on a vector of the form $x \otimes y$, then the maximum output 4-norm (over L_2-unit vectors x, y) is precisely $\|A\|_{2\to4}$. Intuitively, if A' acts on a highly "entangled" vector z, meaning that $\langle z, x \otimes y\rangle$ is small for all unit vectors x, y, then $\|A'z\|_4$ should be small. This is because z will have small overlap with $x' \otimes y'$, and $A_{2,2}$ is positive semi-definite, so its off-diagonal entries can be upper-bounded in terms of its operator norm. These arguments (detailed in Section 8.2) lead to only modest bounds on A', but then we can use an amplification argument to make the $2 \to 4$ norm of A' depend more sensitively on that of A, at the cost of blowing up the dimension by a polynomial factor.

The reductions we achieve also permit us, in Section 8.3, to relate our Tensor-SDP algorithm with the sum-of-squares relaxation used by Doherty, Parrilo, and Spedalieri [DPS04] (henceforth DPS). We show the two relaxations are essentially equivalent, allowing us to import results proved, in some cases, with techniques from quantum information theory. One such result, from [BaCY11], requires relating $A_{2,2}$ to a quantum measurement of the 1-LOCC form. This means that there are two n-dimensional subsystems, combined via tensor products, and $A_{2,2}$ can be implemented as a measurement on the first subsystem followed by a measurement on the second subsystem that is chosen conditioned on the results of the first measurement. The main result of [BaCY11] proved that such LOCC measurements exhibit much better behavior under DPS, and they obtain nontrivial approximation guarantees with only $O(\log(n)/\varepsilon^2)$ rounds. Since this is achieved by DPS, it also implies an upper bound on the error of Tensor-SDP. This upper bound is εZ, where Z is the smallest number for which $A_{2,2} \leqslant ZM$ for some LOCC measurement M. While Z is not believed to be efficiently computable, it is at least $\|A_{2,2}\|_{2\to2}$, since any measurement M has $\|M\|_{2\to2} \leqslant 1$. To upper bound Z, we can explicitly construct $A_{2,2}$ as a quantum measurement. This is done by the following protocol. Let $a_1, \ldots, a_m$ be the rows of A. One party performs the quantum measurement with outcomes $\{\alpha a_i a_i^T\}_{i=1}^m$ (where α is a normalization factor) and transmits the outcome i to the other party. Upon receiving message i, the second party does the two outcome measurement $\{\beta a_i a_i^T, I - \beta a_i a_i^T\}$ and outputs 0 or 1 accordingly, where β is another normalization factor. The measurement $A_{2,2}$ corresponds to the "0" outcomes. For this to be a physically realizable measurement, we need $\alpha \leqslant \|A^T A\|_{2\to2}$ and $\beta \leqslant \|A\|_{2\to\infty}^2$. Combining these ingredients, we obtain the approximation guarantee in Theorem 2.3.

4.5 Definitions and Notation

Let $\mathcal{U}$ be some finite set. For concreteness, and without loss of generality, we can let $\mathcal{U}$ be the set $\{1, \ldots, n\}$, where n is some positive integer. We write $\mathbb{E}_{\mathcal{U}} f$ to denote the average value of a function $f\colon \mathcal{U} \to \mathbb{R}$ over a random point in $\mathcal{U}$ (omitting the subscript $\mathcal{U}$ when it is clear from the context). We let $L_2(\mathcal{U})$ denote the space of functions $f\colon \mathcal{U} \to \mathbb{R}$ endowed with the inner product $\langle f, g\rangle = \mathbb{E}_{\mathcal{U}} fg$ and its induced norm $\|f\| = \langle f, f\rangle^{1/2}$. For $p \geqslant 1$, the *p-norm* of a function $f \in L_2(\mathcal{U})$ is defined as $\|f\|_p := (\mathbb{E}|f|^p)^{1/p}$. A convexity argument shows $\|f\|_p \leqslant \|f\|_q$ for $p \leqslant q$. If A is a linear operator mapping functions from $L_2(\mathcal{U})$ to $L_2(\mathcal{V})$, and $p, q \geqslant 1$, then the p-to-q norm of A is defined as $\|A\|_{p\to q} = \max_{0 \neq f \in L_2(\mathcal{U})} \|Af\|_q / \|f\|_p$. If $V \subseteq L_2(\mathcal{U})$ is a linear subspace, then we denote $\|V\|_{p\to q} = \max_{f \in V} \|f\|_q / \|f\|_p$.

Counting norms.

In most of this paper we use *expectation norms* defined as above, but in some contexts the *counting norms* will be more convenient. We will stick to the convention that *functions* use expectation norms while *vectors* use the counting norms. For a vector $v \in \mathbb{C}^{\mathcal{U}}$ and $p \geqslant 1$, the *p counting norm* of v, denoted $\|v\|_p$, is defined to be $(\sum_{i \in \mathcal{U}} |v_i|^p)^{1/p}$. The *counting inner product* of two vectors $u, v \in \mathbb{R}^{\mathcal{U}}$, denoted as $\langle u, v\rangle$, is defined to be $\sum_{i \in \mathcal{U}} u_i v_i^*$.

5. THE Tensor-SDP ALGORITHM

There is a very natural SoS program for the $2 \to 4$ norm for a given linear operator $A\colon L_2(\mathcal{U}) \to L_2(\mathcal{V})$:

> ALGORITHM Tensor-SDP$^{(d)}(A)$:
>
> Maximize $\tilde{\mathbb{E}}_f \|Af\|_4^4$ subject to
>
> – f is a d-f.r.v. over $L_2(\mathcal{U})$,
>
> – $\tilde{\mathbb{E}}_f(\|f\|^2 - 1)^2 = 0$.

Note that $\|Af\|_4^4$ is indeed a degree 4 polynomial in the variables $\{f(u)\}_{u \in \mathcal{U}}$. The Tensor-SDP$^{(d)}$ algorithm makes sense for $d \geqslant 4$, and we denote by Tensor-SDP its most basic version where $d = 4$. The Tensor-SDP algorithm applies not just to the $2 \to 4$ norm, but to optimizing general polynomials over the unit ball of $L_2(\mathcal{U})$ by replacing $\|Af\|_4^4$ with an arbitrary polynomial P.

While we do not know the worst-case performance of the Tensor-SDP algorithm, we do know that it performs well on random instances, and (perhaps more relevant to the UGC) on the projector to low degree polynomials (see Theorem 2.2). The latter is a corollary of the following result:

Lemma 5.1. *Over the space of n-variate Fourier polynomials*[9] *f with degree at most d,*

$$\mathbb{E} f^4 \leq 9^d \left(\mathbb{E} f^2\right)^2 ,$$

where the expectations are over $\{\pm 1\}^n$.

Proof. The result is proven by a careful variant of the standard inductive proof of the hypercontractivity for low degree polynomials (see e.g. [O'D07]). We include it in this part of the paper since it is the simplest example of how to "lift" known proofs about functions over the reals into proofs about the fictitious random variables that arise in semidefinite programming hierarchies. To strengthen the inductive hypothesis, we will prove the more general statement that for f and g being n-variate Fourier polynomials with degrees at most d and e, it holds that $\mathbb{E} f^2 g^2 \leq 9^{\frac{d+e}{2}} \left(\mathbb{E} f^2\right)\left(\mathbb{E} g^2\right)$. (Formally, this polynomial relation is over the linear space of pairs of n-variate Fourier-polynomials (f, g), where f has degree at most d and g has degree at most e.) The proof is by induction on the number of variables.

If one of the functions is constant (so that $d = 0$ or $e = 0$), then $\mathbb{E} f^2 g^2 = (\mathbb{E} f^2)(\mathbb{E} g^2)$, as desired. Otherwise, let f_0, f_1, g_0, g_1 be Fourier-polynomials depending only on $x_1, \ldots, x_{n-1}$ such that $f(x) = f_0(x) + x_n f_1(x)$ and $g(x) = g_0(x) + x_n g_1(x)$. The Fourier-polynomials f_0, f_1, g_0, g_1 depend linearly on f and g (because $f_0(x) = \frac{1}{2} f(x_1, \ldots, x_{n-1}, 1) + \frac{1}{2} f(x_1, \ldots, x_{n-1}, -1)$ and $f_1(x) = \frac{1}{2} f(x_1, \ldots, x_{n-1}, 1) - \frac{1}{2} f(x_1, \ldots, x_{n-1}, -1)$). Furthermore, the degrees of f_0, f_1, g_0, and g_1 are at most d, $d-1$, e, and $e-1$, respectively.

Since $\mathbb{E} x_n = \mathbb{E} x_n^3 = 0$, if we expand $\mathbb{E} f^2 g^2 = \mathbb{E}(f_0 + x_n f_1)^2 (g_0 + x_n g_1)^2$ then the terms where x_n appears in an odd power vanish, and we obtain

$$\mathbb{E} f^2 g^2 = \mathbb{E} f_0^2 g_0^2 + f_1^2 g_1^2 + f_0^2 g_1^2 + f_1^2 g_0^2 + 4 f_0 f_1 g_0 g_1$$

By expanding the square expression $2\,\mathbb{E}(f_0 f_1 - g_0 g_1)^2$, we get $4\,\mathbb{E} f_0 f_1 g_0 g_1 \leq 2\,\mathbb{E} f_0^2 g_1^2 + f_1^2 g_0^2$ and thus

$$\mathbb{E} f^2 g^2 \leq \mathbb{E} f_0^2 g_0^2 + \mathbb{E} f_1^2 g_1^2 + 3\,\mathbb{E} f_0^2 g_1^2 + 3\,\mathbb{E} f_1^2 g_0^2 . \qquad (5.1)$$

Applying the induction hypothesis to all four terms on the right-hand side of (5.1) (using for the last two terms that the degree of f_1 and g_1 is at most $d-1$ and $e-1$),

$$\begin{aligned}\mathbb{E} f^2 g^2 &\leq 9^{\frac{d+e}{2}} \left(\mathbb{E} f_0^2\right)\left(\mathbb{E} g_0^2\right) + 9^{\frac{d+e}{2}} \left(\mathbb{E} f_1^2\right)\left(\mathbb{E} g_1^2\right) \\ &\quad + 3 \cdot 9^{\frac{d+e}{2}-1/2} \left(\mathbb{E} f_0^2\right)\left(\mathbb{E} g_1^2\right) + 3 \cdot 9^{\frac{d+e}{2}-1/2} \left(\mathbb{E} f_1^2\right)\left(\mathbb{E} g_0^2\right) \\ &= 9^{\frac{d+e}{2}} \left(\mathbb{E} f_0^2 + \mathbb{E} f_1^2\right)\left(\mathbb{E} g_0^2 + \mathbb{E} g_1^2\right) .\end{aligned}$$

Since $\mathbb{E} f_0^2 + \mathbb{E} f_1^2 = \mathbb{E}(f_0 + x_n f_1)^2 = \mathbb{E} f^2$ (using $\mathbb{E} x_n = 0$) and similarly $\mathbb{E} g_0^2 + \mathbb{E} g_1^2 = \mathbb{E} g^2$, we derive the desired relation $\mathbb{E} f^2 g^2 \leq 9^{\frac{d+e}{2}} \left(\mathbb{E} f^2\right)\left(\mathbb{E} g^2\right)$. □

6. SOS SUCCEEDS ON UNIQUE GAMES INTEGRALITY GAPS

In this section we prove Theorem 2.6, showing that 8 rounds of the SoS hierarchy can beat the Basic SDP program on the canonical integrality gaps considered in the literature.

Theorem 6.1 (Theorem 2.6, restated). *For sufficiently small ε and large k, and every $n \in \mathbb{N}$, let $\mathcal{W}$ be an n-variable k-alphabet* Unique Games *instance of the type considered in [RS09, KS09, KPS10] obtained by composing the "quotient noisy cube" instance of [KV05] with the long-code alphabet reduction of [KKMO04] so that the best assignment to $\mathcal{W}$'s variable satisfies at most an ε fraction of the constraints. Then, on input $\mathcal{W}$, eight rounds of the SoS relaxation outputs at most $1/100$.*

6.1 Proof sketch of Theorem 6.1

The proof is very technical, as it is obtained by taking the already rather technical proofs of soundness for these instances, and "lifting" each step into the SoS hierarchy, a procedure that causes additional difficulties. The high level structure of all integrality gap instances constructed in the literature was the following: Start with a basic integrality gap instance of Unique Games where the Basic SDP outputs $1 - o(1)$ but the true optimum is $o(1)$, the *alphabet size* of $\mathcal{U}$ is (necessarily) $R = \omega(1)$. Then, apply an *alphabet reduction gadget* (such as the long-code, or in the recent work [BGH+11] the so called "short code") to transform $\mathcal{U}$ into an instance $\mathcal{W}$ with some constant alphabet size k. The soundness proof of the gadget guarantees that the true optimum of $\mathcal{U}$ is small, while the analysis of previous works managed to "lift" the completeness proofs, and argue that the instance $\mathcal{U}$ survives a number of rounds that tends to infinity as ε tends to zero, where $(1-\varepsilon)$ is the completeness value in the gap constructions, and exact tradeoff between number of rounds and ε depends on the paper and hierarchy.

The fact that the basic instance $\mathcal{U}$ has small integral value can be shown by appealing to hypercontractivity of low degree polynomials, and hence can be "lifted" to the SoS world via Lemma 5.1. The bulk of the technical work is in lifting the soundness proof of the gadget. On a high level this proof involves the following components: **(1)** The *invariance principle* of [MOO05], saying that low influence functions cannot distinguish between the cube and the sphere; this allows us to argue that functions that perform well on the gadget must have an influential variable, and **(2)** the *influence decoding* procedure of [KKMO04] that maps these influential functions on each local gadget into a good global assignment for the original instance $\mathcal{U}$.

The invariance principle poses a special challenge, since the proof of [MOO05] uses so called "bump" functions which are not at all low degree polynomials.[10] We use a weaker invariance principle, only showing that the 4 norm of a low influence function remains the same between two probability spaces that agree on the first 2 moments. Unlike the usual invariance principle, we do not move between Bernoulli variables and Gaussian space, but rather between two different distributions on the discrete cube. It turns out that for the purposes of these Unique Games integrality gaps, the above suffices. The lifted invariance principle is proven via a "hybrid" argument similar to the argument of [MOO05], where hypercontractivity of low degree polynomials again plays an important role.

The soundness analysis of [KKMO04] is obtained by replacing each local function with an average over its neighbors, and then choosing a random influential coordinate from the new local function as an assignment for the original uniquegames instance. We follow the same approach, though even simple tasks such as independent randomized rounding turn out to be much subtler in the lifted setting. However, it turns out that by making appropriate

[9]An n-variate Fourier polynomial with degree at most d is a function $f\colon \{\pm 1\}^n \to \mathbb{R}$ of the form $f = \sum_{\alpha \subseteq [n], |\alpha| \leq d} \hat{f}_\alpha \chi_\alpha$ where $\chi_\alpha(x) = \prod_{i \in \alpha} x_i$.

[10]A similar, though not identical, challenge arises in [BGH+11] where they need to extend the invariance principle to the "short code" setting. However, their solution does not seem to apply in our case, and we use a different approach.

modification to the analysis, it can be lifted to complete the proof of Theorem 2.6.

In the following, we give a more technical description of the proof. Let $T_{1-\eta}$ be the η-noise graph on $\{\pm 1\}^R$. Khot and Vishnoi [KV05] constructed a unique game $\mathcal{U}$ with label-extended graph $T_{1-\eta}$. A solution to the level-4 SoS relaxation of $\mathcal{U}$ is 4-f.r.v. h over $L_2(\{\pm 1\}^R)$. This variable satisfies $h(x)^2 \equiv_h h(x)$ for all $x \in \{\pm 1\}^R$ and also $\tilde{\mathbb{E}}_h(\mathbb{E}\, h)^2 \leqslant 1/R^2$. (The variable h encodes a 0/1 assignment to the vertices of the label-extended graph. A proper assignment assigns 1 only to a $1/R$ fraction of these vertices.) Lemma 6.7 allows us to bound the objective value of the solution h in terms of the fourth moment $\tilde{\mathbb{E}}_h\, \mathbb{E}(P_{>\lambda}h)^4$, where $P_{>\lambda}$ is the projector into the span of the eigenfunctions of $T_{1-\eta}$ with eigenvalue larger than $\lambda \approx 1/R^\eta$. (Note that $\mathbb{E}(P_{>\lambda}h)^4$ is a degree-4 polynomial in h.) For the graph $T_{1-\eta}$, we can bound the degree of $P_{>\lambda}h$ as a Fourier-polynomial (by about $\log(R)$). Hence, the hypercontractivity bound (Lemma 5.1) allows us to bound the fourth moment $\tilde{\mathbb{E}}_h\, \mathbb{E}(P_{>\lambda}h)^4 \leqslant \tilde{\mathbb{E}}_h(\mathbb{E}\, h^2)^2$. By our assumptions on h, we have $\tilde{\mathbb{E}}_h(\mathbb{E}\, h^2)^2 = \tilde{\mathbb{E}}_h(\mathbb{E}\, h)^2 \leqslant 1/R^2$. Plugging these bounds into the bound of Lemma 6.7 demonstrates that the objective value of h is bounded by $1/R^{\Omega(\eta)}$ (see Theorem 6.11).

Next, we consider a unique game $\mathcal{W}$ obtained by composing the unique game $\mathcal{U}$ with the alphabet reduction of [KKMO04]. Suppose that $\mathcal{W}$ has alphabet $\Omega = \{0, \ldots, k-1\}$. The vertex set of $\mathcal{W}$ is $V \times \Omega^R$ (with V being the vertex set of $\mathcal{U}$). Let $f = \{f_u\}_{u \in V}$ be a solution to the level-8 SoS relaxation of $\mathcal{W}$. To bound the objective value of f, we derive from it a level-4 random variable h over $L_2(V \times [R])$. (Encoding a function on the label-extended graph of the unique game $\mathcal{U}$.) We define $h(u, r) = \mathrm{Inf}_r^{(\leqslant \ell)} \bar{f}_u$, where $\ell \approx \log k$ and $\bar{f}_u$ is a variable of $L_2(\Omega^R)$ obtained by averaging certain values of f_u ("folding"). It is easy to show that $h^2 \preceq h$ and $\tilde{\mathbb{E}}_h(\mathbb{E}\, h)^2 \leqslant \ell/R$ (bound on the total influence of low-degree Fourier-polynomials). Theorem 6.9 (influence decoding) allows us to bound the objective value of f in terms of the correlation of h with the label-extended graph of $\mathcal{U}$ (in our case, $T_{1-\eta}$). Here, we can use again Theorem 6.11 to show that the correlation of h with the graph $T_{1-\eta}$ is very small. (An additional challenge arises because h does not satisfy $h^2 \equiv_h h$, but only the weaker condition $h^2 \preceq h$. Corollary 6.5 fixes this issue by simulating independent rounding for fictitious random variables.) To prove Theorem 6.9 (influence decoding), we analyze the behavior of fictitious random variables on the alphabet reduction gadget of [KKMO04]. This alphabet reduction gadget essentially corresponds to the ε-noise graph $T_{1-\varepsilon}$ on Ω^R. Suppose g is a fictitious random variables over $L_2(\Omega^R)$ satisfying $g^2 \preceq g$. By Lemma 6.7, we can bound the correlation of h with the graph $T_{1-\varepsilon}$ in terms of the fourth moment of $P_{>\lambda}g$. At this point, the hypercontractivity bound (Lemma 5.1) is too weak to be helpful. Instead we show an "invariance principle" result (Lemma 6.2), which allows us to relate the fourth moment of $P_{>\lambda}g$ to the fourth moment of a nicer random variable and the influences of g.

Organization of the proof.

We now turn to the actual proof of Theorem 6.1. The proof consists of lifting to the SoS hierarchy all the steps used in the analysis of previous integrality gaps, which themselves arise from hardness reductions. We start in Section 6.2 by showing a sum-of-squares proof for a weaker version of [MOO05]'s invariance principle. Then in Section 6.3 we show how one can perform independent rounding in the SoS world (this is a trivial step in proofs involving true random variables, but becomes much more subtle when dealing with SoS solutions). In Sections 6.4 and 6.5 we lift variants of the [KKMO04] dictatorship test. The proof uses a SoS variant of influence decoding, which is covered in Section 6.6. Together all these sections establish SoS analogs of the soundness properties of the hardness reduction used in the previous results. Then, in Section 6.7 we show that analysis of the basic instance has a sum of squares proof (since it is based on hypercontractivity of low degree polynomials). Finally in Section 6.8 we combine all these tools to conclude the proof. In Section 6.9 we discuss why this proof applies (with some modifications) also to the "short-code" based instances of [BGH+11].

6.2 Invariance Principle for 4-Norm

In this section, we will give a sum-of-squares proof for a variant of the invariance principle of [MOO05]. Instead of for general smooth functionals (usually constructed from "bump functions"), we show invariance only for the fourth moment. It turns out that invariance of the fourth moment is enough for our applications.

Let $\Omega = \{0, \ldots, k-1\}$ and let f be a 4-f.r.v. over $L_2(\Omega^R)$ for some $R \in \mathbb{Z}^+$. We identify $\Omega = \mathbb{F}_2^t$ for $t = \log k$. let $\psi_0, \ldots, \psi_{k-1} \colon \Omega \to \{\pm 1\}$ be an orthonormal basis of $L_2(\Omega)$ such that ψ_0 is constant. For example, we choose the set characters of $\Omega = \mathbb{F}_2^t$ as this basis. Suppose that f has block-degree at most ℓ, i.e. each Ω-block contributes at most 1 to the degree, as opposed to up to t. More specifically, we suppose that there are 4-f.r.v. $\{\hat{f}_\alpha\}_{\alpha \in \Omega^R}$ such that

$$f(x) = \sum_{\alpha : |\alpha| \leqslant \ell} \hat{f}_\alpha \cdot \prod_{i \in [R]} \psi_{\alpha_i}(x_i),$$

where $|\alpha|$ is the number of non-zero entries in α. Note that the degree of f as a 4-f.r.v. over $L_2(\mathbb{F}_2^{tR})$ is at most $t \cdot \ell$.

We define a linear mapping Lift from $L_2(\Omega)$ to $L_2(\mathbb{F}_2^{k-1})$ by setting $\mathsf{Lift}\,\psi_j = \chi_{\{j\}}$ for $j \in \{1, \ldots, k-1\}$ and $\mathsf{Lift}\,\psi_0 = \chi_\emptyset$. Here, χ_S for $S \subseteq [k-1]$ are the characters of $\mathbb{F}_2^{k-1}$. Note that the operator Lift preserves L_2-norms. We extend the linear operator Lift so that it maps $L_2(\Omega^R)$ to $L_2(\mathbb{F}_2^{(k-1)R})$. The extended operator is the R-fold tensor power of the original operator. That is, for each $\psi = \otimes_{i \in [R]} \psi_{\alpha_i}$ (where $\alpha \in \Omega^R$), we map it to $\mathsf{Lift}\,\psi = \otimes_{i \in [R]} \mathsf{Lift}\,\psi_{\alpha_i}$. This leads to the following definition for every $f : \Omega^R \to \mathbb{R}$,

$$\mathsf{Lift}\, f(y) = \sum_{\alpha} \hat{f}_\alpha \cdot \prod_{i \in [R] : \alpha_i \neq 0} y_{i(k-1)+\alpha_i}.$$

Note that the degree of $\mathsf{Lift}\, f$ (as a Fourier polynomial in $(k-1) \cdot R$ variables) equals the (block-)degree of f.

Next we define a map H from Ω to $\mathbb{F}_2^{k-1}$. For $a \in \Omega$, let $H(a)$ be the point $y \in \mathbb{F}_2^{k-1}$ such that $\chi_{\{j\}}(y) = \psi_j(a)$ for every $j \in \{1, 2, \ldots, k-1\}$. (This map corresponds to the Hadamard code in case the functions ψ_j are the characters of $\mathbb{F}_2^t$.) We extend H block-wise so that it maps Ω^R to $\mathbb{F}_2^{(k-1)R}$. The map H is compatible with the previously defined map Lift in the sense that $\mathsf{Lift}\, f(H(x)) = f(x)$, which is because

$$\mathsf{Lift}\, f(H(x)) = \sum_{\alpha} \hat{f}_\alpha \cdot \prod_{i \in [R] : \alpha_i \neq 0} \chi_{\alpha_i}(H(x_i)) = \sum_{\alpha} \hat{f}_\alpha \cdot \prod_{i \in [R] : \alpha_i \neq 0} \psi_{\alpha_i}(x_i) = f(x).$$

The map H gives rise to a distribution $\mathcal{D}$ over $\mathbb{F}_2^{(k-1)R}$: Sample $x \in \Omega^R$ and output $H(x)$. Since H is compatible with Lift, the following polynomial identity holds

$$\mathop{\mathbb{E}}_{\Omega^R} f^4 = \mathop{\mathbb{E}}_{\mathcal{D}^R} (\mathsf{Lift}\, f)^4 .$$

We will also use that the distribution $\mathcal{D}$ is three-wise independent in the sense that $\mathbb{E}_{\mathcal{D}}\, \chi_\alpha = 0$ for all $1 \leqslant |\alpha| \leqslant 3$.

Lemma 6.2. *Let f be as above and let $g = \mathsf{Lift}\, f$. Then,*

$$\mathop{\tilde{\mathbb{E}}}_{g} \mathop{\mathbb{E}}_{\mathcal{D}^R} g^4 = \mathop{\tilde{\mathbb{E}}}_{g} \mathop{\mathbb{E}}_{\mathbb{F}_2^{(k-1)R}} g^4 \pm \tau \cdot k^{O(\ell)}$$

where $\tau = \tilde{\mathbb{E}}_g \sum_{r\in[R]}(\mathrm{Inf}_r f)^2$.

The following corollary shows that if f has low-degree and large fourth moment, then f has influential coordinates.

COROLLARY 6.3. *For f and τ as above,*

$$\tilde{\mathbb{E}}_f \mathbb{E} f^4 \leqslant 2^{O(\ell)} \tilde{\mathbb{E}}_f(\mathbb{E} f^2)^2 + \tau \cdot k^{O(\ell)}$$

PROOF. Using the lemma and properties of the distribution $\mathcal{D}$,

$$\tilde{\mathbb{E}}_f \mathbb{E} f^4 = \tilde{\mathbb{E}}_g \mathbb{E}_{\mathcal{D}^R} g^4 \leqslant \tilde{\mathbb{E}}_g \mathbb{E}_{\mathbb{F}_2^{(k-1)R}} g^4 + \tau \cdot k^{O(\ell)}.$$

Since g has degree at most ℓ, we can bound its 4-norm using Lemma 5.1 (Hypercontractivity),

$$\tilde{\mathbb{E}}_g \mathbb{E} g^4 \leqslant 2^{O(\ell)} \tilde{\mathbb{E}}_g \left(\mathbb{E} g^2\right)^2 = 2^{O(\ell)} \tilde{\mathbb{E}}_f \left(\mathbb{E} f^2\right)^2.$$

The last equality uses that Lift preserves L_2-norms. □

PROOF OF LEMMA 6.2. We construct a sequence of distributions $\mathcal{X}^{(0)}, \ldots, \mathcal{X}^{(R)}$ over $\mathbb{F}_2^{(k-1)R}$ with $\mathcal{X}^{(0)} = \mathcal{D}^R$ and $\mathcal{X}^{(R)}$ being the uniform distribution. Concretely, $\mathcal{X}^{(r)} = \mathcal{D}^{R-r} \times \mathbb{F}_2^{(k-1)r}$. To prove the lemma, it is enough to show that for all $r \in [R]$,

$$\tilde{\mathbb{E}}_g \mathbb{E}_{\mathcal{X}^{(r)}} g^4 = \tilde{\mathbb{E}}_g \mathbb{E}_{\mathcal{X}^{(r-1)}} g^4 \pm k^{O(\ell)}(\mathrm{Inf}_r f)^2.$$

We express $g = E_r g + D_r g$, where $E_r g$ is the part of g independent of the rth block of coordinates. Note that $\|D_r g\|^2 = \mathrm{Inf}_r f$. (Also note that $\|D_r g\|^2 = \mathbb{E}_{\mathcal{X}^{(r')}}(D_r g)^2$ for any $r' \in \{0, \ldots, R\}$. The reason is that the distribution $\mathcal{D}$ is pairwise-independent and unbiased.) Since $\mathbb{E}_r g$ is independent of the rth coordinate block and $D_r g$ is (block-)linear in the rth coordinate block, the three-wise independence of $\mathcal{D}$ implies the polynomial identity,

$$\tilde{\mathbb{E}}_g \mathbb{E}_{\mathcal{X}^{(r)}} g^4 = \tilde{\mathbb{E}}_g \mathbb{E}_{\mathcal{X}^{(r-1)}} g^4 + \mathbb{E}_{\mathcal{X}^{(r)}}(D_r g)^4 - \mathbb{E}_{\mathcal{X}^{(r-1)}}(D_r g)^4$$

We claim that for any $r' \in \{0, \ldots, R\}$,

$$\mathbb{E}_{\mathcal{X}^{(r')}}(D_r g)^4 \le k^{O(\ell)} \|D_r g\|^4 = k^{O(\ell)}(\mathrm{Inf}_r f)^2.$$

One way to see this bound is to "unlift" the first $R - r'$ coordinate blocks (corresponding to the distribution $\mathcal{D}$). In this way, we obtain a Fourier polynomial with the same moments as $D_r g$ (over the distribution $\mathcal{X}^{(r-1)}$). This Fourier polynomial has degree at most $\log k \cdot \ell$. Hence, by Lemma 5.1 (Hypercontractivity), its fourth moment is at most $k^{O(\ell)}$ times the square of the second moment. □

6.3 Interlude: Independent Rounding

In this section, we will show how to convert variables that satisfy $f^2 \preceq f$ to variables $\bar{f}$ satisfying $\bar{f}^2 = \bar{f}$. The derived variables $\bar{f}$ will inherit several properties of the original variables f (in particular, multilinear expectations). This construction corresponds to the standard independent rounding for variables with values between 0 and 1. The main challenge is that our random variables are fictitious.

Let f be a 4-f.r.v. over $\mathbb{R}^n$. Suppose $f_i^2 \preceq f_i$ (in terms of an unspecified jointly-distributed 4-f.r.v.). Note that for real numbers x, the condition $x^2 \leqslant x$ is equivalent to $x \in [0, 1]$.

LEMMA 6.4. *Let f be a 4-f.r.v. over $\mathbb{R}^n$ and let $i \in [n]$ such that $f_i^2 \preceq f_i$. Then, there exists an 4-f.r.v. $(f, \bar{f}_i)$ over $\mathbb{R}^{n+1}$ such that $\tilde{\mathbb{E}}_{f,\bar{f}_i}(\bar{f}_i^2 - \bar{f}_i)^2 = 0$ and for every polynomial P which is linear in $\bar{f}_i$ and has degree at most* 4,

$$\tilde{\mathbb{E}}_{f,\bar{f}_i} P(f, \bar{f}_i) = \tilde{\mathbb{E}}_f P(f, f_i).$$

PROOF. We define the pseudo-expectation operator $\tilde{\mathbb{E}}_{f,\bar{f}_i}$ as follows: For every polynomial P in $(f, \bar{f}_i)$ of degree at most 4, let P' be the polynomial obtained by replacing $\bar{f}_i^2$ by $\bar{f}_i$ until P' is (at most) linear in $\bar{f}_i$. (In other words, we reduce P modulo the relation $\bar{f}_i^2 = \bar{f}_i$.) We define $\tilde{\mathbb{E}}_{f,\bar{f}_i} P(f, \bar{f}_i) = \tilde{\mathbb{E}}_f P'(f, f_i)$. With this definition, $\tilde{\mathbb{E}}_{f,\bar{f}_i}(\bar{f}_i^2 - \bar{f}_i)^2 = 0$. The operator $\tilde{\mathbb{E}}_{f,\bar{f}_i}$ is clearly linear (since $(P + Q)' = P' + Q'$). It remains to verify positivity. Let P be a polynomial of degree at most 4. We will show $\tilde{\mathbb{E}}_{f,\bar{f}_i} P^2(f, \bar{f}_i) \geqslant 0$. Without loss of generality P is linear in $\bar{f}_i$. We express $P = Q + \bar{f}_i R$, where Q and R are polynomials in f. Then, $(P^2)' = Q^2 + 2\bar{f}_i QR + \bar{f}_i R^2$. Using our assumption $f_i^2 \preceq f_i$, we get $(P^2)'(f, f_i) = Q^2 + 2f_i QR + f_i R^2 \succeq Q^2 + 2f_i QR + f_i^2 R^2 = P^2(f, f_i)$. It follows as desired that

$$\tilde{\mathbb{E}}_{f,\bar{f}_i} P^2 = \tilde{\mathbb{E}}_f(P^2)'(f, f_i) \geqslant \tilde{\mathbb{E}}_f P^2(f, f_i) \geqslant 0.$$

□

COROLLARY 6.5. *Let f be a 4-f.r.v. over $\mathbb{R}^n$ and let $I \subseteq [n]$ such that $f_i^2 \preceq f_i$ for all $i \in I$. Then, there exists an 4-f.r.v. $(f, \bar{f}_I)$ over $\mathbb{R}^{n+|I|}$ such that $\tilde{\mathbb{E}}_{f,\bar{f}_I}(\bar{f}_i^2 - \bar{f}_i)^2 = 0$ for all $i \in I$ and for every polynomial P which is multilinear in the variables $\{\bar{f}_i\}_{i\in I}$ and has degree at most* 4,

$$\tilde{\mathbb{E}}_{f,\bar{f}_I} P(f, \bar{f}_I) = \tilde{\mathbb{E}}_f P(f, f_I).$$

6.4 Dictatorship Test for Small-Set Expansion

Let $\Omega = \{0, \ldots, k-1\}$ and let $T_{1-\varepsilon}$ be the noise graph on Ω^R with second largest eigenvalue $1-\varepsilon$. Let f be a 4-f.r.v. over $L_2(\Omega^R)$. Suppose $f^2 \preceq f$ (in terms of an unspecified jointly-distributed 4-f.r.v.). Note that for real numbers x, the condition $x^2 \leqslant x$ is equivalent to $x \in [0, 1]$.

The following theorem is an analog of the "Majority is Stablest" result [MOO05].

THEOREM 6.6. *Suppose $\tilde{\mathbb{E}}_f(\mathbb{E} f)^2 \leqslant \delta^2$. Let $\tau = \tilde{\mathbb{E}}_f \sum_r (\mathrm{Inf}_r^{(\leqslant \ell)} f)^2$ for $\ell = \Omega(\log(1/\delta))$. Then,*

$$\tilde{\mathbb{E}}_f\langle f, T_{1-\varepsilon} f\rangle \leqslant \delta^{1+\Omega(\varepsilon)} + k^{O(\log(1/\delta))} \cdot \tau^{1/4}.$$

(Here, we assume that ε, δ and τ are sufficiently small.)

The previous theorem is about graph expansion (measured by the quadratic form $\langle f, T_{1-\varepsilon} f\rangle$). The following lemma allows us to relate graph expansion to the 4-norm of the projection of f into the span of the eigenfunctions of $T_{1-\varepsilon}$ with significant eigenvalue. We will be able to bound this 4-norm in terms of the influences of f (using the invariance principle in the previous section).

LEMMA 6.7. *Let f be a 4-f.r.v. over $L_2(\Omega^R)$. Suppose $f^2 \preceq f$ (in terms of unspecified jointly-distributed 4-f.r.v. s). Then for all $\lambda > 0$,*

$$\tilde{\mathbb{E}}_f\langle f, T_{1-\varepsilon} f\rangle \leqslant (\tilde{\mathbb{E}}_f \mathbb{E} f)^{3/4} (\tilde{\mathbb{E}}_f \mathbb{E}(P_{>\lambda} f)^4)^{1/4} + \lambda \tilde{\mathbb{E}}_f \mathbb{E} f.$$

Here, $P_{>\lambda}$ is the projector into the span of the eigenfunctions of $T_{1-\varepsilon}$ with eigenvalue larger than λ.

PROOF. The following relation between polynomials holds

$$\langle f, T_{1-\varepsilon} f\rangle \preceq \mathbb{E} f \cdot (P_{>\lambda} f) + \lambda \mathbb{E} f^2.$$

By Corollary 6.5, there exists a 4-f.r.v. $(f, \bar{f})$ over $L_2(\Omega^R) \times L_2(\Omega^R)$ such that $\bar{f}^2 \equiv_{\bar{f}} \bar{f}$. Then,

$$\tilde{\mathbb{E}}_f \mathbb{E} f \cdot (P_{>\lambda} f)$$

$$= \tilde{\mathbb{E}}_{f,\bar{f}} \mathbb{E} \bar{f} \cdot (P_{>\lambda} f) \quad \text{(using linearity in } \bar{f}\text{)}$$
$$= \tilde{\mathbb{E}}_{f,\bar{f}} \mathbb{E} \bar{f}^3 \cdot (P_{>\lambda} f) \quad \text{(using } \bar{f}^2 \equiv_{\bar{f}} \bar{f}\text{)}$$
$$\leqslant \left(\tilde{\mathbb{E}}_{\bar{f}} \mathbb{E} \bar{f}^4\right)^{3/4} \cdot \left(\tilde{\mathbb{E}}_f \mathbb{E}(P_{>\lambda} f)^4\right)^{1/4} \quad \text{(using pseudoexpecation Hölder)}$$
$$= \left(\tilde{\mathbb{E}}_{\bar{f}} \mathbb{E} \bar{f}\right)^{3/4} \cdot \left(\tilde{\mathbb{E}}_f \mathbb{E}(P_{>\lambda} f)^4\right)^{1/4} \quad \text{(using } \bar{f}^2 \equiv_{\bar{f}} \bar{f}\text{)}$$
$$= \left(\tilde{\mathbb{E}}_f \mathbb{E} f\right)^{3/4} \cdot \left(\tilde{\mathbb{E}}_f \mathbb{E}(P_{>\lambda} f)^4\right)^{1/4} \quad \text{(using linearity in } \bar{f}\text{)}$$

□

Proof of Theorem 6.6. By Lemma 6.7,

$$\tilde{\mathbb{E}}_f \langle f, T_{1-\varepsilon} f\rangle \leqslant (\tilde{\mathbb{E}}_f \mathbb{E} f)^{3/4} (\tilde{\mathbb{E}}_f \mathbb{E}(P_{>\lambda} f)^4)^{1/4} + \lambda \tilde{\mathbb{E}}_f \mathbb{E} f^2 .$$

Using Corollary 6.3,

$$\tilde{\mathbb{E}}_f \langle f, T_{1-\varepsilon} f\rangle \leqslant 2^{O(\ell)} \cdot (\tilde{\mathbb{E}}_f \mathbb{E} f)^{3/4} (\tilde{\mathbb{E}}_f (\mathbb{E} f^2)^2 + \tau \cdot k^{O(\ell)})^{1/4} + \lambda \tilde{\mathbb{E}}_f \mathbb{E} f^2 .$$

Here, $\ell = \log(1/\lambda)/\varepsilon$. Using the relation $f^2 \preceq f$ and our assumption $\tilde{\mathbb{E}}_f (\mathbb{E} f)^2 \leqslant \delta^2$, we get $\tilde{\mathbb{E}}_f \mathbb{E} f^2 \leqslant \tilde{\mathbb{E}}_f \mathbb{E} f \leqslant (\tilde{\mathbb{E}}_f (\mathbb{E} f)^2)^{1/2} \leqslant \delta$ (by Cauchy–Schwarz). Hence,

$$\begin{aligned}\tilde{\mathbb{E}}_f \langle f, T_{1-\varepsilon} f\rangle &\leqslant (1/\lambda)^{O(1/\varepsilon)} \delta^{3/4} (\delta^2 + \tau \cdot (1/\lambda)^{O(\log k)/\varepsilon})^{1/4} + \lambda\delta \\ &\leqslant (1/\lambda)^{O(1/\varepsilon)} \delta^{5/4} + (1/\lambda)^{O(\log k)/\varepsilon} \delta^{3/4} \tau^{1/4} + \lambda \cdot \delta .\end{aligned}$$

To balance the terms $(1/\lambda)^{O(1/\varepsilon)} \delta^{5/4}$ and $\lambda\delta$, we choose $\lambda = \delta^{\Omega(\varepsilon)}$. We conclude the desired bound,

$$\tilde{\mathbb{E}}_f \langle f, T_{1-\varepsilon} f\rangle \leqslant \delta^{1+\Omega(\varepsilon)} + k^{O(\log(1/\delta))} \cdot \tau^{1/4} .$$

□

6.5 Dictatorship Test for Unique Games

Let $\Omega = \mathbb{Z}_k$ (cyclic group of order k) and let f be a 4-f.r.v. over $L_2(\Omega \times \Omega^R)$. Here, $f(a,x)$ is intended to be 0/1 variable indicating whether symbol a is assigned to the point x.

The following graph $T'_{1-\varepsilon}$ on $\Omega \times \Omega^R$ corresponds to the 2-query dictatorship test for Unique Games [KKMO04],

$$T'_{1-\varepsilon} f(a,x) = \mathop{\mathbb{E}}_{c\in\Omega} \mathop{\mathbb{E}}_{y\sim_{1-\varepsilon} x} f(a+c, y - c \cdot \mathbb{1}) .$$

Here, $y \sim_{1-\varepsilon} x$ means that y is a random neighbor of x in the graph $T_{1-\varepsilon}$ (the ε-noise graph on Ω^R).

We define $\bar{f}(x) := \mathbb{E}_{c\in\Omega} f(c, x - c \cdot \mathbb{1})$. (We think of $\bar{f}$ as a variable over $L_2(\Omega^R)$.) Then, the following polynomial identity (in f) holds

$$\langle f, T'_{1-\varepsilon} f\rangle = \langle \bar{f}, T_{1-\varepsilon} \bar{f}\rangle .$$

Theorem 6.8. *Suppose $f^2 \preceq f$ and $\tilde{\mathbb{E}}_f (\mathbb{E} f)^2 \leqslant \delta^2$. Let $\tau = \tilde{\mathbb{E}}_f \sum_r (\mathrm{Inf}_r^{(\leqslant \ell)} \bar{f})^2$ for $\ell = \Omega(\log(1/\delta))$. Then,*

$$\tilde{\mathbb{E}}_f \langle f, T'_{1-\varepsilon} f\rangle \leqslant \delta^{1+\Omega(\varepsilon)} + k^{O(\log(1/\delta))} \cdot \tau^{1/4} .$$

(Here, we assume that ε, δ and τ are sufficiently small.)

Proof. Apply Theorem 6.6 to bound $\tilde{\mathbb{E}}_f \langle \bar{f}, T_{1-\varepsilon} \bar{f}\rangle$. Use that fact that $\mathbb{E} f = \mathbb{E} \bar{f}$ (as polynomials in f). □

6.6 Influence Decoding

Let $\mathcal{U}$ be a unique game with vertex set V and alphabet $[R]$. Recall that we represent $\mathcal{U}$ as a distribution over triples (u, v, π) where $u, v \in V$ and π is a permutation of $[R]$. The triples encode the constraints of $\mathcal{U}$. We assume that the unique game $\mathcal{U}$ is regular in the same that every vertex participates in the same fraction of constraints.

Let $\Omega = \mathbb{Z}_k$ (cyclic group of order k). We reduce $\mathcal{U}$ to a unique game $\mathcal{W} = \mathcal{W}_{\varepsilon,k}(\mathcal{U})$ with vertex set $V \times \Omega^R$ and alphabet Ω. Let $f = \{f_u\}_{u\in V}$ be a variable over $L_2(\Omega \times \Omega^R)^V$. The unique game $\mathcal{W}$ corresponds to the following quadratic form in f,

$$\langle f, \mathcal{W} f\rangle := \mathop{\mathbb{E}}_{u\in V} \mathop{\mathbb{E}}_{\substack{(u,v,\pi)\sim\mathcal{U}|u \\ (u,v',\pi')\sim\mathcal{U}|u}} \langle f_v^{(\pi)}, T'_{1-\varepsilon} f_{v'}^{(\pi')}\rangle .$$

Here, $(u, v, \pi) \sim \mathcal{U} \mid u$ denotes a random constraint of $\mathcal{U}$ incident to vertex u, the graph $T'_{1-\varepsilon}$ corresponds to the dictatorship test of Unique Games defined in Section 6.5, and $f_v^{(\pi)}(a, x) = f_v(a, \pi.x)$ is the function obtained by permuting the last R coordinates according to π (where $\pi.x(i) = x_{\pi(i)}$).

We define $g_u = \mathbb{E}_{(u,v,\pi)\sim\mathcal{U}|u} f_v^{(\pi)}$. Then,

$$\langle f, \mathcal{W} f\rangle = \mathop{\mathbb{E}}_{u\in V} \langle g_u, T'_{1-\varepsilon} g_u\rangle . \tag{6.1}$$

Bounding the value of SoS solutions.

Let $f = \{f_u\}_{u\in V}$ be a solution to the level-d SoS relaxation for the unique game $\mathcal{W}$. In particular, f is a d-f.r.v. over $L_2(\Omega \times \Omega^R)^V$. Furthermore, $\tilde{\mathbb{E}}_f (\mathbb{E} f_u)^2 \leqslant 1/k^2$ for all vertices $u \in V$.

By applying Theorem 6.8 to (6.1), we can bound the objective value of f

$$\tilde{\mathbb{E}}_f \langle f, \mathcal{W} f\rangle \leqslant 1/k^{1+\Omega(\varepsilon)} + k^{O(\log k)} \left(\tilde{\mathbb{E}}_f \mathop{\mathbb{E}}_{u\in V} \tau_u\right)^{1/4} ,$$

where $\tau_u = \sum_r (\mathrm{Inf}_r^{(\leqslant \ell)} \bar{g}_u)^2$, $\bar{g}_u(x) = \mathbb{E}_{(u,v,\pi)\sim\mathcal{U}|u} \bar{f}_v^{(\pi)}$, and $\bar{f}_v(x) = \mathbb{E}_{c\in\Omega} f_v(c, x - c \cdot \mathbb{1})$.

Since $\mathrm{Inf}_r^{(\leqslant \ell)}$ is a positive semidefinite form,

$$\tau_u \preceq \sum_r \left(\mathop{\mathbb{E}}_{(u,v,\pi)\sim\mathcal{U}|u} \mathrm{Inf}_r^{(\leqslant \ell)} \bar{f}_v^{(\pi)}\right)^2 = \sum_r \left(\mathop{\mathbb{E}}_{(u,v,\pi)\sim\mathcal{U}|u} \mathrm{Inf}_{\pi(r)}^{(\leqslant \ell)} \bar{f}_v\right)^2 .$$

Let h be the level-$d/2$ fictitious random variable over $L_2(V \times [R])$ with $h(u,r) = \mathrm{Inf}_r^{(\leqslant \ell)} \bar{f}_u$. Let $G_{\mathcal{U}}$ be the label-extended graph of the unique game $\mathcal{U}$. Then, the previous bound on τ_u shows that $\mathbb{E}_{u\in V} \tau_u \preceq R \cdot \|G_{\mathcal{U}} h\|^2$. which by not too hard to show properties of pseudo-expectation implies that $h^2 \preceq h$. On the other hand, $\sum_r h(u,r) \preceq \ell \|\bar{f}_u\|^2 \preceq \ell \|f_u\|^2$ (bound on the total influence of low-degree Fourier polynomials). In particular, $\mathbb{E} h \preceq \ell\, \mathbb{E}_{u\in V} \|f_u\|^2/R$. Since f is a valid SoS solution for the unique game $\mathcal{W}$, we have $\tilde{\mathbb{E}}_f \|f_u\|^d \leqslant 1/k^{d/2}$ for all $u \in V$. (Here, we assume that d is even.) It follows that $\tilde{\mathbb{E}}_h (\mathbb{E} h)^{d/2} \leqslant (\frac{\ell}{k \cdot R})^{d/2}$.

The arguments in this subsection imply the following theorem.

Theorem 6.9. *The optimal value of the level-d SoS relaxation for the unique game $\mathcal{W} = \mathcal{W}_{\varepsilon,k}(\mathcal{U})$ is bounded from above by*

$$1/k^{\Omega(\varepsilon)} + k^{O(\log k)} \left(R \cdot \max_h \tilde{\mathbb{E}}_h \|G_{\mathcal{U}} h\|^2\right)^{1/4} ,$$

where the maximum is over all level-$d/2$ fictitious random variables h over $L_2(V \times [R])$ satisfying $h^2 \preceq h$ and $\tilde{\mathbb{E}}_h (\mathbb{E} h)^{d/2} \leqslant \ell/R^{d/2}$.

Remark 6.10. *Since the quadratic form $\|G_{\mathcal{U}} h\|^2$ has only non-negative coefficients (in the standard basis), we can use Corollary 6.5 to ensure that the level-$d/2$ random variable h satisfies in addition $h^2 \equiv_h h$.*

6.7 Certifying Small-Set Expansion

Let $T_{1-\varepsilon}$ be a the noise graph on $\{\pm 1\}^R$ with second largest eigenvalue $1 - \varepsilon$.

THEOREM 6.11. *Let f be level-4 fictitious random variables over* $L_2(\{\pm 1\}^R)$. *Suppose that* $f^2 \preceq f$ *(in terms of unspecified jointly-distributed level-4 fictitious random variables) and that* $\tilde{\mathbb{E}}_f(\mathbb{E} f)^2 \leqslant \delta^2$. *Then,*

$$\tilde{\mathbb{E}}_f \langle f, T_{1-\varepsilon} f \rangle \leqslant \delta^{1+\Omega(\varepsilon)} .$$

PROOF. By Lemma 6.7 (applying it for the case $\Omega = \{0, 1\}$), for every $\lambda > 0$,

$$\tilde{\mathbb{E}}_f \langle f, T_{1-\varepsilon} f \rangle \leqslant (\tilde{\mathbb{E}}_f \mathbb{E} f)^{3/4} (\tilde{\mathbb{E}}_f \mathbb{E}(P_{>\lambda} f)^4)^{1/4} + \lambda \tilde{\mathbb{E}}_f \mathbb{E} f .$$

For the graph $T_{1-\varepsilon}$, the eigenfunctions with eigenvalue larger than λ are characters with degree at most $\log(1/\lambda)/\varepsilon$. Hence, Lemma 5.1 implies $\mathbb{E}(P_{>\lambda} f)^4 \preceq (1/\lambda)^{O(1/\varepsilon)} \|f\|^4$. Since $f^2 \preceq f$, we have $\|f\|^4 \preceq (\mathbb{E} f)^2$. Hence, $\tilde{\mathbb{E}}_f \mathbb{E}(P_{>\lambda} f)^4 \leqslant (1/\lambda)^{O(1/\varepsilon)} \delta^2$. Plugging in, we get

$$\tilde{\mathbb{E}}_f \langle f, T_{1-\varepsilon} f \rangle \leqslant (1/\lambda)^{O(1/\varepsilon)} \delta^{5/4} + \lambda \cdot \delta .$$

To balance the terms, we choose $\lambda = \delta^{\Omega(\varepsilon)}$, which gives the desired bound. □

6.8 Putting Things Together

Let $T_{1-\eta}$ be a the noise graph on $\{\pm 1\}^R$ with second largest eigenvalue $1 - \eta$. Let $\mathcal{U} = \mathcal{U}_{\eta,R}$ be an instance of UNIQUE GAMES with label-extended graph $G_{\mathcal{U}} = T_{1-\eta}$ (e.g., the construction in [KV05]).

Combining Theorem 6.9 (with $d = 4$) and Theorem 6.11 gives the following result.

THEOREM 6.12. *The optimal value of the level-8 SoS relaxation for the unique game* $\mathcal{W} = \mathcal{W}_{\varepsilon,k}(\mathcal{U}_{\eta,R})$ *is bounded from above by*

$$1/k^{\Omega(\varepsilon)} + k^{O(\log k)} \cdot R^{-\Omega(\eta)} .$$

In particular, the optimal value of the relaxation is close to $1/k^{\Omega(\varepsilon)}$ *if* $\log R \gg (\log k)^2/\eta$.

6.9 Refuting Instances based on Short Code

Let $\mathcal{U}' = \mathcal{U}'_{\eta,R}$ be an instance of UNIQUE GAMES according to the basic construction in [BGH+11]. (The label-extended graph of $\mathcal{U}$ will be a subgraph of $T_{1-\varepsilon}$ induced by the subset of $\{\pm 1\}^R$ corresponding to a Reed–Muller code, that is, evaluations of low-degree $\mathbb{F}_2$-polynomials.)

Let $\mathcal{W}' = \mathcal{W}'_{\varepsilon,k}(\mathcal{U}'_{\eta,R})$ be the unique game obtained by applying the short-code alphabet reduction of [BGH+11].

The following analog of Theorem 6.12 holds.

THEOREM 6.13. *The optimal value of the level-8 SoS relaxation for the unique game* $\mathcal{W}' = \mathcal{W}'_{\varepsilon,k}(\mathcal{U}'_{\eta,R})$ *is bounded from above by*

$$1/k^{\Omega(\varepsilon)} + k^{O(\log k)} \cdot R^{-\Omega(\eta)} .$$

In particular, the optimal value of the relaxation is close to $1/k^{\Omega(\varepsilon)}$ *if* $\log R \gg (\log k)^2/\eta$.

The proof of Theorem 6.13 is almost literally the same as the proof of Theorem 6.12. In the following, we sketch the main arguments why the proof doesn't have to change. First, several of the results of the previous sections apply to general graphs and instances of UNIQUE GAMES. In particular, Lemma 6.7 applies to general graphs and Theorem 6.9 applies to general gadget-composed instances of unique games assuming a "Majority is Stablest" result for the gadget. In fact, the only parts that require further justification are the invariance principle (Lemma 6.2) and hypercontractivity bound (Lemma 5.1). Both the invariance principle and the hypercontractivity bound are about the fourth moment of a low-degree Fourier polynomial (whose coefficients are fictitious random variables). For the construction of [BGH+11], we need to argue about the fourth moment with respect to a different distribution over inputs. (Instead of the uniform distribution, [BGH+11] considers a distribution over inputs related to the Reed–Muller code.) However, this distribution happens to be k-wise independent for $k/4$ larger than the degree of our Fourier polynomial. Hence, as a degree-4 polynomial in Fourier coefficients, the fourth moment with respect to the [BGH+11]-input distribution is the same as with respect to the uniform distribution, which considered here.

7. THE 2-TO-Q NORM AND SMALL-SET EXPANSION

In this section we show that a graph is a *small-set expander* if and only if the projector to the subspace of its adjacency matrix's top eigenvalues has a bounded $2 \to q$ norm for even $q \geqslant 4$. While the "if" part was known before, the "only if" part is novel. This characterization of small-set expanders is of general interest, and also leads to a reduction from the SMALL-SET EXPANSION problem considered in [RS10] to the problem of obtaining a good approximation for the $2 \to q$ norms.

Notation.

For a regular graph $G = (V, E)$ and a subset $S \subseteq V$, we define the *measure* of S to be $\mu(S) = |S|/|V|$ and we define $G(S)$ to be the distribution obtained by picking a random $x \in S$ and then outputting a random neighbor y of x. We define the *expansion* of S, to be $\Phi_G(S) = \mathbb{P}_{y \in G(S)}[y \notin S]$, where y is a random neighbor of x. For $\delta \in (0, 1)$, we define $\Phi_G(\delta) = \min_{S \subseteq V: \mu(S) \leqslant \delta} \Phi_G(S)$. We often drop the subscript G from Φ_G when it is clear from context. We identify G with its normalized adjacency (i.e., random walk) matrix. For every $\lambda \in [-1, 1]$, we denote by $V_{\geqslant \lambda}(G)$ the subspace spanned by the eigenvectors of G with eigenvalue at least λ. The projector into this subspace is denoted $P_{\geqslant \lambda}(G)$. For a distribution D, we let $\mathsf{cp}(D)$ denote the collision probability of D (the probability that two independent samples from D are identical).

Our main theorem of this section is the following:

Theorem 2.4 (restated). *For every regular graph* G, $\lambda > 0$ *and even* q,

1. (Norm bound implies expansion) *For all* $\delta > 0, \varepsilon > 0$, $\|P_{\geqslant \lambda}(G)\|_{2 \to q} \leqslant \varepsilon / \delta^{(q-2)/2q}$ *implies that* $\Phi_G(\delta) \geqslant 1 - \lambda - \varepsilon^2$.
2. (Expansion implies norm bound) *There is a constant* c *such that for all* $\delta > 0$, $\Phi_G(\delta) > 1 - \lambda 2^{-cq}$ *implies* $\|P_{\geqslant \lambda}(G)\|_{2 \to q} \leqslant 2/\sqrt{\delta}$.

One corollary of Theorem 2.4 is that a good approximation to the $2 \to 4$ norm implies an approximation of $\Phi_\delta(G)$ [11].

COROLLARY 7.1. *If there is a polynomial-time computable relaxation* $\mathcal{R}$ *yielding good approximation for the* $2 \to q$, *then the* Small-Set Expansion Hypothesis *of [RS10] is false.*

PROOF. Using [RST10a], to refute the small-set expansion hypothesis it is enough to come up with an efficient algorithm that given an input graph G and sufficiently small $\delta > 0$, can distinguish between the *Yes* case: $\Phi_G(\delta) < 0.1$ and the *No* case $\Phi_G(\delta') > 1 - 2^{-c \log(1/\delta')}$ for any $\delta' \geqslant \delta$ and some constant c. In particular for all $\eta > 0$ and constant d, if δ is small enough then in

[11]Note that although we use the $2 \to 4$ norm for simplicity, a similar result holds for the $2 \to q$ norm for every constant even q.

the *No* case $\Phi_G(\delta^{0.4}) > 1 - \eta$. Using Theorem 2.4, in the *Yes* case we know $\|V_{1/2}(G)\|_{2\to 4} \geqslant 1/(10\delta^{1/4})$, while in the *No* case, if we choose η to be smaller then $\eta(1/2)$ in the Theorem, then we know that $\|V_{1/2}(G)\|_{2\to 4} \leqslant 2/\sqrt{\delta^{0.2}}$. Clearly, if we have a good approximation for the $2 \to 4$ norm then, for sufficiently small δ we can distinguish between these two cases. □

The first part of Theorem 2.4 follows from previous work (e.g., see [KV05]). The second part will follow from the following lemma:

LEMMA 7.2. *Set $e = e(\lambda, q) := 2^{cq}/\lambda$, with a constant $c \leqslant 100$. Then for every $\lambda > 0$ and $1 \geqslant \delta \geqslant 0$, if G is a graph that satisfies $\mathsf{cp}(G(S)) \leqslant 1/(e|S|)$ for all S with $\mu(S) \leqslant \delta$, then $\|f\|_q \leqslant 2\|f\|_2/\sqrt{\delta}$ for all $f \in V_{\geqslant\lambda}(G)$.*

Proving the second part of Theorem 2.4 from Lemma 7.2.

We use the variant of the local Cheeger bound obtained in Theorem 2.1 of [Ste10], stating that if $\Phi_G(\delta) \geqslant 1 - \eta$ then for every $f \in L_2(V)$ satisfying $\|f\|_1^2 \leqslant \delta\|f\|_2^2$, $\|Gf\|_2^2 \leqslant c\sqrt{\eta}\|f\|_2^2$. The proof follows by noting that for every set S, if f is the characteristic function of S then $\|f\|_1 = \|f\|_2^2 = \mu(S)$, and $\mathsf{cp}(G(S)) = \|Gf\|_2^2/(\mu(S)|S|)$. □

PROOF OF LEMMA 7.2. Fix $\lambda > 0$. We assume that the graph satisfies the condition of the Lemma with $e = 2^{cq}/\lambda$, for a constant c that we'll set later. Let $G = (V, E)$ be such a graph, and f be function in $V_{\geqslant\lambda}(G)$ with $\|f\|_2 = 1$ that maximizes $\|f\|_q$. We write $f = \sum_{i=1}^m \alpha_i\chi_i$ where $\chi_1, \dots, \chi_m$ denote the eigenfunctions of G with values $\lambda_1, \dots, \lambda_m$ that are at least λ. Assume towards a contradiction that $\|f\|_q > 2/\sqrt{\delta}$. We'll prove that $g = \sum_{i=1}^m(\alpha_i/\lambda_i)\chi_i$ satisfies $\|g\|_q \geqslant 10\|f\|_q/\lambda$. This is a contradiction since (using $\lambda_i \in [\lambda, 1]$) $\|g\|_2 \leqslant \|f\|_2/\lambda$, and we assumed f is a function in $V_{\geqslant\lambda}(G)$ with a maximal ratio of $\|f\|_q/\|f\|_2$.

Let $U \subseteq V$ be the set of vertices such that $|f(x)| \geqslant 1/\sqrt{\delta}$ for all $x \in U$. Using Markov and the fact that $\mathbb{E}_{x\in V}[f(x)^2] = 1$, we know that $\mu(U) = |U|/|V| \leqslant \delta$, meaning that under our assumptions any subset $S \subseteq U$ satisfies $\mathsf{cp}(G(S)) \leqslant 1/(e|S|)$. On the other hand, because $\|f\|_q^q \geqslant 2^q/\delta^{q/2}$, we know that U contributes at least half of the term $\|f\|_q^q = \mathbb{E}_{x\in V} f(x)^q$. That is, if we define α to be $\mu(U)\,\mathbb{E}_{x\in U} f(x)^q$ then $\alpha \geqslant \|f\|_q^q/2$. We'll prove the lemma by showing that $\|g\|_q^q \geqslant 10\alpha/\lambda$.

Let c be a sufficiently large constant ($c = 100$ will do). We define U_i to be the set $\{x \in U : f(x) \in [c^i/\sqrt{\delta}, c^{i+1}/\sqrt{\delta})\}$, and let I be the maximal i such that U_i is non-empty. Thus, the sets $U_0, \dots, U_I$ form a partition of U (where some of these sets may be empty). We let α_i be the contribution of U_i to α. That is, $\alpha_i = \mu_i\,\mathbb{E}_{x\in U_i} f(x)^q$, where $\mu_i = \mu(U_i)$. Note that $\alpha = \alpha_0 + \cdots + \alpha_I$. We'll show that there are some indices $i_1, \dots, i_J$ such that:

(i) $\alpha_{i_1} + \cdots + \alpha_{i_J} \geqslant \alpha/(2c^{10})$.

(ii) For all $j \in [J]$, there is a non-negative function $g_j : V \to \mathbb{R}$ such that $\mathbb{E}_{x\in V}\, g_j(x)^q \geqslant e\alpha_{i_j}/(10c^2)^{q/2}$.

(iii) For every $x \in V$, $g_1(x) + \cdots + g_J(x) \leqslant |g(x)|$.

Showing these will complete the proof, since it is easy to see that for two non-negative functions and even q, g', g'', $\mathbb{E}(g'(x) + g''(x))^q \geqslant \mathbb{E}\,g'(x)^q + \mathbb{E}\,g''(x)^q$, and hence **(ii)** and **(iii)** imply that

$$\|g\|_4^4 = \mathbb{E}\,g(x)^4 \geqslant (e/(10c^2)^{q/2}) \sum_j \alpha_{i_j}\,. \tag{7.1}$$

Using **(i)** we conclude that for $e \geqslant (10c)^q/\lambda$, the right-hand side of (7.1) will be larger than $10\alpha/\lambda$.

We find the indices $i_1, \dots, i_J$ iteratively. We let $\mathcal{I}$ be initially the set $\{0..I\}$ of all indices. For $j = 1, 2, \ldots$ we do the following as long as $\mathcal{I}$ is not empty:

1. Let i_j be the largest index in $\mathcal{I}$.

2. Remove from $\mathcal{I}$ every index i such that $\alpha_i \leqslant c^{10}\alpha_{i_j}/2^{i-i_j}$.

We let J denote the step when we stop. Note that our indices $i_1, \dots, i_J$ are sorted in descending order. For every step j, the total of the α_i's for all indices we removed is less than $c^{10}\alpha_{i_j}$ and hence we satisfy **(i)**. The crux of our argument will be to show **(ii)** and **(iii)**. They will follow from the following claim:

CLAIM 7.3. *Let $S \subseteq V$ and $\beta > 0$ be such that $|S| \leqslant \delta$ and $|f(x)| \geqslant \beta$ for all $x \in S$. Then there is a set T of size at least $e|S|$ such that $\mathbb{E}_{x\in T}\, g(x)^2 \geqslant \beta^2/4$.*

The claim will follow from the following lemma:

LEMMA 7.4. *Let D be a distribution with $\mathsf{cp}(D) \leqslant 1/N$ and g be some function. Then there is a set T of size N such that $\mathbb{E}_{x\in T}\, g(x)^2 \geqslant (\mathbb{E}\,g(D))^2/4$.*

PROOF. Identify the support of D with the set $[M]$ for some M, we let p_i denote the probability that D outputs i, and sort the p_i's such that $p_1 \geqslant p_2 \cdots p_M$. We let β' denote $\mathbb{E}\,g(D)$; that is, $\beta' = \sum_{i=1}^M p_i g(i)$. We separate to two cases. If $\sum_{i>N} p_i g(i) \geqslant \beta'/2$, we define the distribution D' as follows: we set $\mathbb{P}[D' = i]$ to be p_i for $i > N$, and we let all $i \leqslant N$ be equiprobable (that is be output with probability $(\sum_{i=1}^N p_i)/N$). Clearly, $\mathbb{E}\,|g(D')| \geqslant \sum_{i>N} p_i g(i) \geqslant \beta'/2$, but on the other hand, since the maximum probability of any element in D' is at most $1/N$, it can be expressed as a convex combination of flat distributions over sets of size N, implying that one of these sets T satisfies $\mathbb{E}_{x\in T}\,|g(x)| \geqslant \beta'/2$, and hence $\mathbb{E}_{x\in T}\, g(x)^2 \geqslant \beta'^2/4$.

The other case is that $\sum_{i=1}^N p_i g(i) \geqslant \beta'/2$. In this case we use Cauchy-Schwarz and argue that

$$\beta'^2/4 \leqslant \left(\sum_{i=1}^N p_i^2\right)\left(\sum_{i=1}^N g(i)^2\right)\,. \tag{7.2}$$

But using our bound on the collision probability, the right-hand side of (7.2) is upper bounded by $\frac{1}{N}\sum_{i=1}^N g(i)^2 = \mathbb{E}_{x\in[N]}\, g(x)^2$. □

PROOF OF CLAIM 7.3 FROM LEMMA 7.4. By construction $f = Gg$, and hence we know that for every x, $f(x) = \mathbb{E}_{y\sim x}\, g(y)$. This means that if we let D be the distribution $G(S)$ then

$$\mathbb{E}\,|g(D)| = \mathop{\mathbb{E}}_{x\in S}\mathop{\mathbb{E}}_{y\sim x}|g(y)| \geqslant \mathop{\mathbb{E}}_{x\in S}|\mathop{\mathbb{E}}_{y\sim x} g(y)| = \mathop{\mathbb{E}}_{x\in S}|f(x)| \geqslant \beta\,.$$

By the expansion property of G, $\mathsf{cp}(D) \leqslant 1/(e|S|)$ and thus by Lemma 7.4 there is a set T of size $e|S|$ satisfying $\mathbb{E}_{x\in T}\, g(x)^2 \geqslant \beta^2/4$. □

We will construct the functions $g_1, \dots, g_J$ by applying iteratively Claim 7.3. We do the following for $j = 1, \dots, J$:

1. Let T_j be the set of size $e|U_{i_j}|$ that is obtained by applying Claim 7.3 to the function f and the set U_{i_j}. Note that $\mathbb{E}_{x\in T_j}\, g(x)^2 \geqslant \beta_{i_j}^2/4$, where we let $\beta_i = c^i/\sqrt{\delta}$ (and hence for every $x \in U_i$, $\beta_i \leqslant |f(x)| \leqslant c\beta_i$).

2. Let g'_j be the function on input x that outputs $\gamma\cdot|g(x)|$ if $x \in T_j$ and 0 otherwise, where $\gamma \leqslant 1$ is a scaling factor that ensures that $\mathbb{E}_{x\in T_j}\, g'(x)^2$ equals exactly $\beta_{i_j}^2/4$.

3. We define $g_j(x) = \max\{0, g'_j(x) - \sum_{k<j} g_k(x)\}$.

Note that the second step ensures that $g'_j(x) \leqslant |g(x)|$, while the third step ensures that $g_1(x) + \cdots + g_j(x) \leqslant g'_j(x)$ for all j, and in particular $g_1(x) + \cdots + g_J(x) \leqslant |g(x)|$. Hence the only thing left to prove is the following:

CLAIM 7.5. $\mathbb{E}_{x\in V} g_j(x)^q \geqslant e\alpha_{i_j}/(10c)^{q/2}$

PROOF. Recall that for every i, $\alpha_i = \mu_i \mathbb{E}_{x\in U_i} f(x)^q$, and hence (using $f(x) \in [\beta_i, c\beta_i)$ for $x \in U_i$):

$$\mu_i\beta_i^q \leqslant \alpha_i \leqslant \mu_i c^q \beta_i^q \,. \tag{7.3}$$

Now fix $T = T_j$. Since $\mathbb{E}_{x\in V} g_j(x)^q$ is at least (in fact equal) $\mu(T)\,\mathbb{E}_{x\in T} g_j(x)^q$ and $\mu(T) = e\mu(U_{i_j})$, we can use (7.3) and $\mathbb{E}_{x\in T} g_j(x)^q \geqslant (E_{x\in T} g_j(x)^2)^{q/2}$, to reduce proving the claim to showing the following:

$$\mathop{\mathbb{E}}_{x\in T} g_j(x)^2 \geqslant (c\beta_{i_j})^2/(10c^2) = \beta_{i_j}^2/10 \,. \tag{7.4}$$

We know that $\mathbb{E}_{x\in T} g'_j(x)^2 = \beta_{i_j}^2/4$. We claim that (7.4) will follow by showing that for every $k < j$,

$$\mathop{\mathbb{E}}_{x\in T} g'_k(x)^2 \leqslant 100^{-i'} \cdot \beta_{i_j}^2/4 \,, \tag{7.5}$$

where $i' = i_k - i_j$. (Note that $i' > 0$ since in our construction the indices $i_1, \ldots, i_J$ are sorted in descending order.)

Indeed, (7.5) means that if we let momentarily $\|g_j\|$ denote $\sqrt{\mathbb{E}_{x\in T} g_j(x)^2}$ then

$$\|g_j\| \geqslant \|g'_j\| - \|\textstyle\sum_{k<j} g_k\| \geqslant \|g'_j\| - \displaystyle\sum_{k<j} \|g_k\| \geqslant \|g'_j\|(1 - \sum_{i'=1}^{\infty} 10^{-i'}) \geqslant 0.8\|g'_j\| \,. \tag{7.6}$$

The first inequality holds because we can write g_j as $g'_j - h_j$, where $h_j = \min\{g'_j, \sum_{k<j} g_k\}$. Then, on the one hand, $\|g_j\| \geqslant \|g'_j\| - \|h_j\|$, and on the other hand, $\|h_j\| \leqslant \|\sum_{k<j} g_k\|$ since $g'_j \geqslant 0$. The second inequality holds because $\|g_k\| \leqslant \|g'_k\|$. By squaring (7.6) and plugging in the value of $\|g'_j\|^2$ we get (7.4).

Proof of (7.5).

By our construction, it must hold that

$$c^{10}\alpha_{i_k}/2^{i'} \leqslant \alpha_{i_j} \,, \tag{7.7}$$

since otherwise the index i_j would have been removed from the $\mathcal{I}$ at the kth step. Since $\beta_{i_k} = \beta_{i_j}c^{i'}$, we can plug (7.3) in (7.7) to get $\mu_{i_k}c^{10+4i'}/2^{i'} \leqslant c^4\mu_{i_j}$ or $\mu_{i_k} \leqslant \mu_{i_j}(2/c)^{4i'}c^{-6}$.

Since $|T_i| = e|U_i|$ for all i, it follows that $|T_k|/|T| \leqslant (2/c)^{4i'}c^{-6}$. On the other hand, we know that $\mathbb{E}_{x\in T_k} g'_k(x)^2 = \beta_{i_k}^2/4 = c^{2i'}\beta_{i_j}^2/4$. Thus, $\mathbb{E}_{x\in T} g'_k(x)^2 \leqslant 2^{4i'}c^{2i'-4i'-6}\beta_{i_j}^2/4 \leqslant (2^4/c^2)^{i'}\beta_{i_j}^2/4$, and now we just choose c sufficiently large so that $c^2/2^4 > 100$. □

8. RELATING THE 2-TO-4 NORM AND THE INJECTIVE TENSOR NORM

In this section, we present several equivalent formulations of the 2-to-4 norm: 1) as the injective tensor norm of a 4-tensor, 2) as the injective tensor norm of a 3-tensor, and 3) as the maximum of a linear function over a convex set, albeit a set where the weak membership problem is hard. Additionally, we can consider maximizations over real or complex vectors. These equivalent formulations are discussed in Section 8.1.

We use this to show hardness of approximation (Theorem 2.5) for the 2-to-4 norm in Section 8.2, and then show positive algorithmic results (Theorem 2.3) in Section 8.3. Somewhat surprisingly, many of the key arguments in these sections are imported from the quantum information literature, even though no quantum algorithms are involved. It is an interesting question to find a more elementary proof of the result in Section 8.3.

We will generally work with the counting norms $\|.\|$, defined as $\|x\|_p := (\sum_i |x_i|^p)^{1/p}$, and the counting inner product, defined by $\langle x, y\rangle := x^* y$, where * denotes the conjugate transpose.

8.1 Equivalent maximizations

8.1.1 Injective tensor norm and separable states

Recall from the introduction the definition of the injective tensor norm: if $V_1, \ldots, V_r$ are vector spaces with $T \in V_1 \otimes \cdots \otimes V_r$, then $\|T\|_{\text{inj}} = \max\{|\langle T, (x_1 \otimes \cdots \otimes x_r)\rangle| : x_1 \in \mathbf{S}(V_1), \ldots, x_r \in \mathbf{S}(V_r)\}$, where $\mathbf{S}(V)$ denotes the L_2-unit vectors in a vector space V. In this paper we use the term "injective tensor norm" to mean the injective tensor norm of ℓ_2 spaces, and we caution the reader that in other contexts it has a more general meaning. These norms were introduced by Grothendieck, and they are further discussed in [Rya02].

We will also need the definition of separable states from quantum information. For a vector space V, define $L(V)$ to be the linear operators on V, and define $\mathcal{D}(V) := \{\rho \in L(V) : \rho \geq 0, \operatorname{Tr}\rho = 1\} = \operatorname{conv}\{vv^* : v \in \mathbf{S}(V)\}$ to be the *density operators* on V. The trace induces an inner product on operators: $\langle X, Y\rangle := \operatorname{Tr} X^* Y$. An important class of density operators are the *separable density operators*. For vector spaces $V_1, \ldots, V_r$, these are

$$\operatorname{Sep}(V_1, \ldots, V_r) := \operatorname{conv}\{v_1v_1^* \otimes \cdots \otimes v_rv_r^* : \forall i, v_i \in \mathbf{S}(V_i)\}\,.$$

If $V = V_1 = \cdots = V_r$, then let $\operatorname{Sep}^r(V)$ denote $\operatorname{Sep}(V_1, \ldots, V_r)$. Physically, density operators are the quantum analogues of probability distributions, and separable density operators describe unentangled quantum states; conversely, entangled states are defined to be the set of density operators that are not separable. For readers familiar with quantum information, we point out that our treatment differs principally in its use of the expectation for norms and inner products, rather than the sum.

For any bounded convex set K, define the *support function* of K to be

$$\mathbf{h}_K(x) := \max_{y\in K} |\langle x, y\rangle|.$$

Define $e_i \in \mathbb{F}^n$ to be the vector with 1 in the ith position. Now we can give a convex optimization formulation of the injective tensor norm.

LEMMA 8.1. *Let $V_1, \ldots, V_r$ be vector spaces with $n_i := \dim V_i$, and $T \in V_1 \otimes \cdots \otimes V_r$. Choose an orthonormal basis $e_1, \ldots, e_{n_r}$ for V_r. Define $T_1, \ldots, T_{n_r} \in V_1 \otimes \cdots \otimes V_{r-1}$ by $T = \sum_{i=1}^{n_r} T_i \otimes e_i$ and define $M \in L(V_1 \otimes \cdots \otimes V_{r-1})$ by $M = \sum_{i=1}^{n_r} T_i T_i^*$. Then*

$$\|T\|_{\text{inj}}^2 = \mathbf{h}_{\operatorname{Sep}(V_1,\ldots,V_{r-1})}(M). \tag{8.1}$$

Observe that any $M \geq 0$ can be expressed in this form, possibly by padding n_r to be at least rank M. Thus calculating $\|\cdot\|_{\text{inj}}$ for r-tensors is equivalent in difficulty to computing $\mathbf{h}_{\operatorname{Sep}^{r-1}}$ for p.s.d. arguments. This argument appeared before in [HM10], where it was explained using quantum information terminology.

It is instructive to consider the $r = 2$ case. In this case, T is equivalent to a matrix $\hat{T}$ and $\|T\|_{\text{inj}} = \|\hat{T}\|_{2\to 2}$. Moreover $\operatorname{Sep}^1(\mathbb{F}^{n_1}) = \mathcal{D}(\mathbb{F}^{n_1})$ is simply the convex hull of vv^* for unit vectors v. Thus $\mathbf{h}_{\operatorname{Sep}^1(\mathbb{F}^{n_1})}(M)$ is simply the maximum eigenvalue of $M = TT^*$. In this case, Lemma 8.1 merely states that the square of the largest singular value of $\hat{T}$ is the largest eigenvalue of $\hat{T}\hat{T}^*$. Due to space constraints, the general proof is omitted in this extended abstract.

In what follows, we will also need to make use of some properties of symmetric tensors. Define $\mathcal{S}_k$ to be the group of permutations of $[k]$ and define $P_n(\pi) \in L((\mathbb{F}^n)^{\otimes k})$ to be the operator that permutes k tensor copies of $\mathbb{F}^n$ according to π. Formally,

$$P_n(\pi) := \sum_{i_1,\ldots,i_r \in [d]} \bigotimes_{k=1}^{r} e_{i_k} e_{i_{\pi(k)}}^T. \tag{8.2}$$

Then define $\vee^k\mathbb{F}^n$ to be the subspace of vectors in $(\mathbb{F}^n)^{\otimes r}$ that are unchanged by each $P_n(\pi)$. This space is called the *symmetric subspace*. A classic result in symmetric polynomials states that $\vee^r\mathbb{F}^n$ is spanned by the vectors $\{v^{\otimes r} : v \in \mathbb{F}^n\}$.[12]

8.1.2 Connection to the 2-to-4 norm

Let $A = \sum_{i=1}^m e_i a_i^T$, so that $a_1, \ldots, a_m \in \mathbb{R}^n$ are the rows of A. Define

$$A_4 = \sum_{i=1}^m a_i^{\otimes 4} \qquad \in (\mathbb{R}^n)^{\otimes 4} \tag{8.3}$$

$$A_3 = \sum_{i=1}^m a_i \otimes a_i \otimes e_i \qquad \in \mathbb{R}^n \otimes \mathbb{R}^n \otimes \mathbb{R}^m \tag{8.4}$$

$$A_{2,2} = \sum_{i=1}^m a_i a_i^T \otimes a_i a_i^T \qquad \in L((\mathbb{R}^n)^{\otimes 2}) \tag{8.5}$$

The subscripts indicate that that A_r is an r-tensor, and $A_{r,s}$ is a map from r-tensors to s-tensors.

Further, for a real tensor $T \in (\mathbb{R}^n)^{\otimes r}$, define $\|T\|_{\mathrm{inj}[\mathbb{C}]}$ to be the injective tensor norm that results from treating T as a complex tensor; that is, $\max\{|\langle T, x_1 \otimes \cdots \otimes x_r\rangle| : x_1, \ldots, x_r \in \mathbf{S}(\mathbb{C}^n)\}$. For $r \geqslant 3$, $\|T\|_{\mathrm{inj}[\mathbb{C}]}$ can be larger than $\|T\|_{\mathrm{inj}}$ by as much as $\sqrt{2}$ [CKP00].

Our main result on equivalent forms of the $2 \to 4$ norm is the following.

Lemma 8.2.

$$\begin{aligned}\|A\|_{2\to4}^4 &= \|A_4\|_{\mathrm{inj}} = \|A_3\|_{\mathrm{inj}}^2 = \|A_4\|_{\mathrm{inj}[\mathbb{C}]} = \|A_3\|_{\mathrm{inj}[\mathbb{C}]}^2 \\ &= \mathbf{h}_{\mathrm{Sep}^2(\mathbb{R}^n)}(A_{2,2}) = \mathbf{h}_{\mathrm{Sep}^2(\mathbb{C}^n)}(A_{2,2})\end{aligned}$$

Due to space constraints, the proof is omitted.

8.2 Hardness of approximation for the 2-to-4 norm

This section is devoted to the proof of Theorem 2.5, establishing hardness of approximation for the 2-to-4 norm.

First, we restate Theorem 2.5 more precisely. We omit the reduction to when A is a projector, deferring this argument to Corollary 8.8, where we will further use a randomized reduction.

Theorem 8.3. *(restatement of Theorem 2.5) Let ϕ be a 3-SAT instance with n variables and $O(n)$ clauses. Determining whether ϕ is satisfiable can be reduced in polynomial time to determining whether $\|A\|_{2\to4} \geqslant C$ or $\|A\|_{2\to4} \leqslant c$ where $0 \leqslant c < C$ and A is an $m \times m$ matrix. This is possible for two choices of parameters:*

1. *$m = \mathrm{poly}(n)$, and $C/c > 1 + 1/n \,\mathrm{poly}\log(n)$; or,*
2. *$m = \exp(\sqrt{n}\,\mathrm{poly}\log(n)\log(C/c))$.*

The key challenge is establishing the following reduction.

[12]For the proof, observe that $v^{\otimes r} \in \vee^r\mathbb{F}^n$ for any $v \in \mathbb{F}^n$. To construct a basis for $\vee^r\mathbb{F}^n$ out of linear combinations of different $v^{\otimes r}$, let $z_1, \ldots, z_n$ be indeterminates and evaluate the r-fold derivatives of $(z_1e_1 + \cdots + z_ne_n)^{\otimes r}$ at $z_1 = \cdots = z_n = 0$.

Lemma 8.4. *Let $M \in L(\mathbb{C}^n \otimes \mathbb{C}^n)$ satisfy $0 \leqslant M \leqslant I$. Assume that either (case Y) $\mathbf{h}_{\mathrm{Sep}(n,n)}(M) = 1$ or (case N) $\mathbf{h}_{\mathrm{Sep}(n,n)}(M) \leqslant 1 - \delta$. Let k be a positive integer. Then there exists a matrix A of size $n^{4k} \times n^{2k}$ such that in case Y, $\|A\|_{2\to4} = 1$, and in case N, $\|A\|_{2\to4} = (1-\delta/2)^k$. Moreover, A can be constructed efficiently from M.*

Proof of Theorem 8.3. Once Lemma 8.4 is proved, Theorem 2.5 follows from previously known results about the hardness of approximating $\mathbf{h}_{\mathrm{Sep}}$. Let ϕ be a 3-SAT instance with n variables and $O(n)$ clauses. In Theorem 4 of [GNN] (improving on earlier work of [Gur03]), it was proved that ϕ can be reduced to determining whether $\mathbf{h}_{\mathrm{Sep}(n^c,n^c)}(M)$ is equal to 1 ("case Y") or $\leqslant 1 - 1/n\log^c(n)$ ("case N"), where $c > 0$ is a universal constant, and M is an efficiently constructible matrix with $0 \leqslant M \leqslant I$. Now we apply Lemma 8.4 with $k = 1$ to find that exists a matrix A of dimension $\mathrm{poly}(n)$ such that in case Y, $\|A\|_{2\to4} = 1$, and in case N, $\|A\|_{2\to4} \leqslant 1 - 1/2n\log^c(n)$. Thus, distinguishing these cases would determine whether ϕ is satisfiable. This establishes part (1) of Theorem 2.5.

For part (2), we start with Corollary 14 of [HM10], which gives a reduction from determining the satisfiability of ϕ to distinguishing between ("case Y") $\mathbf{h}_{\mathrm{Sep}(m,m)}(M) = 1$ and ("case N") $\mathbf{h}_{\mathrm{Sep}(m,m)}(M) \leqslant 1/2$. Again $0 \leqslant M \leqslant I$, and M can be constructed in time $\mathrm{poly}(m)$ from ϕ, but this time $m = \exp(\sqrt{n}\,\mathrm{poly}\log(n))$. Applying Lemma 8.4 in a similar fashion completes the proof. □

Proof of Lemma 8.4. The previous section shows that computing $\|A\|_{2\to4}$ is equivalent to computing $\mathbf{h}_{\mathrm{Sep}(n,n)}(A_{2,2})$, for $A_{2,2}$ defined as in (8.5). However, the hardness results of [Gur03, GNN, HM10] produce matrices M that are not in the form of $A_{2,2}$. The reduction of [HM10] comes closest, by producing a matrix that is a sum of terms of the form $xx^* \otimes yy^*$. However, we need a sum of terms of the form $xx^* \otimes xx^*$. This will be achieved by a variant of the protocol used in [HM10].

Let $M_0 \in L(\mathbb{C}^n \otimes \mathbb{C}^n)$ satisfy $0 \leqslant M \leqslant I$. Consider the promise problem of distinguishing the cases $\mathbf{h}_{\mathrm{Sep}(n,n)}(M_0) = 1$ (called "case Y") from $\mathbf{h}_{\mathrm{Sep}(n,n)}(M_0) \leqslant 1/2$ (called "case N"). We show that this reduces to finding a multiplicative approximation for $\|A\|_{2\to4}$ for some real A of dimension n^α for a constant $\alpha > 0$. Combined with known hardness-of-approximation results (Corollary 15 of [HM10]), this will imply Theorem 2.5.

Define P to be the projector onto the subspace of $(\mathbb{C}^n)^{\otimes 4}$ that is invariant under $P_n((1,3))$ and $P_n((2,4))$ (see Section 8.1 for definitions). This can be obtained by applying $P_n((2,3))$ to $\vee^2\mathbb{C}^n \otimes \vee^2\mathbb{C}^n$, where we recall that $\vee^2\mathbb{C}^n$ is the symmetric subspace of $(\mathbb{C}^n)^{\otimes 2}$. Since P projects onto the vectors invariant under the 4-element group generated by $P_n((1,3))$ and $P_n((2,4))$, we can write it as

$$P = \frac{I + P_n((1,3))}{2} \cdot \frac{I + P_n((2,4))}{2}. \tag{8.6}$$

An alternate definition of P (whose equivalence can be seen either by direct calculation or by applying Wick's theorem) is:

$$P = \mathop{\mathbb{E}}_{a,b}[aa^* \otimes bb^* \hat{\otimes}\, aa^* \otimes bb^*], \tag{8.7}$$

where the expectation is taken over complex-Gaussian-distributed vectors $a, b \in \mathbb{C}^n$ normalized so that $\mathbb{E}\|a\|_2^2 = \mathbb{E}\|b\|_2^2 = n/\sqrt{2}$. Here we use the notation $\hat{\otimes}$ to mark the separation between systems that we will use to define the separable states $\mathrm{Sep}(n^2, n^2)$. We could equivalently write $P = \mathbb{E}_{a,b}[(aa^* \otimes bb^*)^{\hat{\otimes}2}]$. We will find that (8.6) is more useful for doing calculations, while (8.7) is helpful for converting M_0 into a form that resembles $A_{2,2}$ for some matrix A.

Define $M_1 = (\sqrt{M_0} \hat{\otimes} \sqrt{M_0})P(\sqrt{M_0} \hat{\otimes} \sqrt{M_0})$, where $\sqrt{M_0}$ is taken to be the unique positive-semidefinite square root of M_0. Observe that

$$M_1 = \mathbb{E}_{a,b}[v_{a,b}v_{a,b}^* \hat{\otimes} v_{a,b}v_{a,b}^*] = \mathbb{E}_{a,b}[V_{a,b}^{\hat{\otimes}2}], \tag{8.8}$$

where we define $v_{a,b} := \sqrt{M_0}(a \otimes b)$ and $V_{a,b} := v_{a,b}v_{a,b}^*$. We claim that $\mathbf{h}_{\mathrm{Sep}}(M_1)$ gives a reasonable proxy for $\mathbf{h}_{\mathrm{Sep}}(M_0)$ in the following sense.

LEMMA 8.5.

$$\mathbf{h}_{\mathrm{Sep}(n^2,n^2)}(M_1) \begin{cases} = 1 & \textit{in case Y} \\ \leqslant 1 - \delta/2 & \textit{in case N.} \end{cases} \tag{8.9}$$

The proof of Lemma 8.5 is deferred to the end of this section. The analysis is very similar to Theorem 13 of [HM10], but the analysis here is much simpler because M_0 acts on only two systems. However, it is strictly speaking not a consequence of the results in [HM10], because that paper considered a slightly different choice of M_1.

The advantage of replacing M_0 with M_1 is that (thanks to (8.7)) we now have a matrix with the same form as $A_{2,2}$ in (8.5), allowing us to make use of Lemma 8.2. However, we first need to amplify the separation between cases Y and N. This is achieved by the matrix $M_2 := M_1^{\otimes k}$. This tensor product is *not* across the cut we use to define separable states; in other words:

$$M_2 = \mathbb{E}_{\substack{a_1,\dots,a_k \\ b_1,\dots,b_k}}[(V_{a_1,b_1} \otimes \cdots \otimes V_{a_k,b_k})^{\hat{\otimes}2}]. \tag{8.10}$$

Now Lemma 12 from [HM10] implies that $\mathbf{h}_{\mathrm{Sep}(n^{2k},n^{2k})}(M_2) = \mathbf{h}_{\mathrm{Sep}(n^2,n^2)}(M_1)^k$. This is either 1 or $\leqslant (3/4)^k$, depending on whether we have case Y or N.

Finally, we would like to relate this to the $2 \to 4$ norm of a matrix. It will be more convenient to work with M_1, and then take tensor powers of the corresponding matrix. Naively applying Lemma 8.2 would relate $\mathbf{h}_{\mathrm{Sep}}(M_1)$ to $\|A\|_{2\to4}$ for an infinite-dimensional A. Instead, we first replace the continuous distribution on a (resp. b) with a finitely-supported distribution in a way that does not change $\mathbb{E}_a aa^* \otimes aa^*$ (resp. $\mathbb{E}_b bb^* \otimes bb^*$). Such distributions are called complex-projective (2,2)-designs or quantum (state) 2-designs, and can be constructed from spherical 4-designs on $\mathbb{R}^{2n}$ [AE07]. Finding these designs is challenging when each vector needs to have the same weight , but for our purposes we can use Carathéodory's theorem to show that there exist vectors $z_1, \dots, z_m$ with $m = n^2$ such that

$$\mathbb{E}_a[aa^* \otimes aa^*] = \sum_{i \in [m]} z_i z_i^* \otimes z_i z_i^*. \tag{8.11}$$

In what follows, assume that the average over a, b used in the definitions of P, M_1, M_2 is replaced by the sum over $z_1, \dots, z_m$. By (8.11) this change does not affect the values of P, M_1, M_2.

For $i, j \in [m]$, define $w_{i,j} := \sqrt{M_0}(z_i \otimes z_j)$, and let $e_{i,j} := e_i \otimes e_j$. Now we can apply Lemma 8.2 to find that $\mathbf{h}_{\mathrm{Sep}}(M_1) = \|A_1\|_{2\to4}^4$, where $A_1 = \sum_{i,j \in [m]} e_{i,j} w_{i,j}^*$. The amplified matrix M_2 similarly satisfies $\mathbf{h}_{\mathrm{Sep}(n^{2k},n^{2k})}(M_2) = \|A_2\|_{2\to4}^4$, where

$$A_2 := A_1^{\otimes k} = \sum_{i_1,\dots,i_k,j_1,\dots,j_k \in [m]} (e_{i_1,j_1} \otimes e_{i_k,j_k})(w_{i_1,j_1} \otimes \cdots \otimes w_{i_k,j_k})^*.$$

The last step is to relate the complex matrix A_2 to a real matrix A_3 with the same $2 \to 4$ norm once we restrict to real inputs. This can be achieved by replacing a single complex entry $\alpha + i\beta$ with the 6×2 real matrix

$$\frac{1}{\sqrt{2}} \begin{pmatrix} 1 & 1 \\ 1 & -1 \\ 2^{1/4} & 0 \\ 2^{1/4} & 0 \\ 0 & 2^{1/4} \\ 0 & 2^{1/4} \end{pmatrix} \cdot \begin{pmatrix} \alpha & -\beta \\ \beta & \alpha \end{pmatrix}$$

A complex input $x + iy$ is represented by the column vector $\begin{pmatrix} x \\ y \end{pmatrix}$. The initial 2×2 matrix maps this to the real representation of $(\alpha + i\beta)(x + iy)$, and then the fixed 6×2 matrix maps this to a vector whose 4-norm equals $|(\alpha + i\beta)(x + iy)|^4$.

□

We conclude with the proof of Lemma 8.5, mostly following [HM10].

PROOF. Case Y is simplest, and it also provides intuition for the choices of the M_1 construction. Since the extreme points of $\mathrm{Sep}(n, n)$ are of the form $xx^* \otimes yy^*$ for $x, y \in \mathbf{S}(\mathbb{C}^n)$, it follows that there exists $x, y \in \mathbf{S}(\mathbb{C}^n)$ with $\langle x \otimes y, M(x \otimes y)\rangle = 1$. Since $M \leqslant I$, this implies that $M(x \otimes y) = (x \otimes y)$. Thus $\sqrt{M_0}(x \otimes y) = (x \otimes y)$. Let

$$z = x \otimes y \otimes x \otimes y.$$

Then z is an eigenvector of both $\sqrt{M_0} \otimes \sqrt{M_0}$ and P, with eigenvalue 1 in each case. To see this for P, we use the definition in (8.6). Thus $\langle z, M_1 z\rangle = 1$, and it follows that $\mathbf{h}_{\mathrm{Sep}(n^2,n^2)}(M_1) \geqslant 1$. On the other hand, $M_1 \leqslant I$, implying that $\mathbf{h}_{\mathrm{Sep}(n^2,n^2)}(M_1) \leqslant 1$. This establishes case Y.

For case N, we assume that $\mathbf{h}_{\mathrm{Sep}(n,n)}(M_0) \leqslant 1 - \delta$ for any $x, y \in \mathbf{S}(\mathbb{C}^n)$. The idea of the proof is that for any $x, y \in \mathbf{S}(\mathbb{C}^{n^2})$, we must either have x, y close to a product state, in which case the $\sqrt{M_0}$ step will shrink the vector, or if they are far from a product state and preserved by $\sqrt{M_0} \otimes \sqrt{M_0}$, then the P step will shrink the vector. In either case, the length will be reduced by a dimension-independent factor.

We now spell this argument out in detail. Choose $x, y \in \mathbf{S}(\mathbb{C}^{n^2})$ to achieve

$$s := \langle x \otimes y, M_1(x \otimes y)\rangle = \mathbf{h}_{\mathrm{Sep}(n^2,n^2)}(M_1). \tag{8.12}$$

Let $X, Y \in L(\mathbb{C}^n)$ be defined by

$$\sqrt{M_0}x =: \sum_{i,j \in [n]} X_{i,j} e_i \otimes e_j \qquad \text{and} \qquad \sqrt{M_0}y =: \sum_{i,j \in [n]} Y_{i,j} e_i \otimes e_j. \tag{8.13}$$

Note that $\langle X, X\rangle = \langle x, M_0 x\rangle \leqslant 1$ and similarly for $\langle Y, Y\rangle$. We wish to estimate

$$s = \sum_{i,j,k,l,i',j',k',l' \in [n]} \bar{X}_{i',j'} \bar{Y}_{k',l'} X_{i,j} Y_{k,l} \langle e_{i'} \otimes e_{j'} \otimes e_{k'} \otimes e_{l'}, P(e_i \otimes e_j \otimes e_k \otimes e_l)\rangle. \tag{8.14}$$

Using (8.6) we see that the expression inside the $\langle \cdot \rangle$ is

$$\frac{\delta_{i,i'}\delta_{j,j'}\delta_{k,k'}\delta_{l,l'} + \delta_{i,k'}\delta_{j,j'}\delta_{k,i'}\delta_{l,l'} + \delta_{i,i'}\delta_{j,l'}\delta_{k,k'}\delta_{l,j'} + \delta_{i,k'}\delta_{j,l'}\delta_{k,i'}\delta_{l,j'}}{4}. \tag{8.15}$$

Rearranging, we find

$$s = \frac{\langle X, X\rangle\langle Y, Y\rangle + \langle X, Y\rangle\langle X, Y\rangle + \langle YY^*, XX^*\rangle + \langle Y^*Y, X^*X\rangle}{4}. \tag{8.16}$$

Using the AM-GM inequality we see that the maximum of this expression is achieved when $X = Y$, in which case we have

$$s = \frac{\langle X, X\rangle^2 + \langle X^*X, X^*X\rangle}{2} \leqslant \frac{1 + \langle X^*X, X^*X\rangle}{2}. \tag{8.17}$$

Let the singular values of X be $\sigma_1 \geqslant \cdots \geqslant \sigma_n$. Observe that $\|\sigma\|_2^2 = \langle X, X\rangle \leqslant 1$, and thus $\|\sigma\|_4^4 = \langle X^*X, X^*X\rangle \leqslant \sigma_1^2$. On the other hand,

$$\sigma_1^2 = \max_{a,b \in \mathbf{S}(\mathbb{C}^n)} |\langle a, Xb\rangle|^2 \tag{8.18}$$

$$= \max_{a,b \in \mathbf{S}(\mathbb{C}^n)} |\langle a \otimes b, \sqrt{M_0}x\rangle|^2 \tag{8.19}$$

$$= \max_{a,b \in \mathbf{S}(\mathbb{C}^n)} |\langle \sqrt{M_0}(a \otimes b), x\rangle|^2 \tag{8.20}$$

$$= \max_{a,b \in \mathbf{S}(\mathbb{C}^n)} \langle \sqrt{M_0}(a \otimes b), \sqrt{M_0}(a \otimes b)\rangle \tag{8.21}$$

$$= \max_{a,b \in \mathbf{S}(\mathbb{C}^n)} \langle a \otimes b, M_0(a \otimes b)\rangle \tag{8.22}$$

$$= \mathbf{h}_{\mathrm{Sep}(n,n)}(M_0) \leqslant 1 - \delta. \tag{8.23}$$

□

Remark: It is possible to extend Lemma 8.4 to the situation when case Y has $\mathbf{h}_{Sep}(M) > 1 - \delta'$ for some constant $\delta' < \delta$. Since the details are somewhat tedious and repeat arguments in [HM10], we omit them here.

8.2.1 Hardness of approximation for projectors

Can Theorem 2.5 give any super-polynomial lower bound for the SSE problem if we assume the Exponential-Time Hypothesis for 3-SAT? To resolve this question using our techniques, we would like to reduce 3-SAT to estimating the $2 \to 4$ norm of the projector onto the eigenvectors of a graph that have large eigenvalue. We do not know how to do this. However, instead, we show that the matrix A constructed in Theorem 2.5 can be taken WLOG to be a projector.

Lemma 8.6. *Let A be a linear map from $\mathbb{R}^k$ to $\mathbb{R}^n$ and $1 < c < C$, $\varepsilon > 0$ some numbers. Then there is $m = \tilde{O}(n^2/\varepsilon^2)$ and a map A' from $\mathbb{R}^k$ to $\mathbb{R}^m$ such that $\sigma_{\min}(A') \geqslant 1 - \varepsilon$ and **(i)** if $\|A\|_{2\to4} \leqslant c$ then $\|A'\|_{2\to4} \leqslant 1 + \varepsilon$, **(ii)** $\|A\|_{2\to4} \geqslant C$ then $\|A'\|_{2\to4} \geqslant \Omega(\varepsilon C/c)$.*

Proof. We let B be a random map from $\mathbb{R}^k$ to $\mathbb{R}^{O(n^2/\delta^2)}$ such that for every $f \in \mathbb{R}^k$, $\|Bf\|_4 \in (1 \pm \delta)\|f\|_2$ (the proof is omitted in this extended abstract). Consider the operator $A' = A \circ B$ that maps f into the concatenation of Af and Bf. Moreover we take multiple copies of each coordinate so that the measure of output coordinates of A' corresponding to A is $\alpha = \delta/c^4$, while the measure of coordinates corresponding to B is $1 - \alpha$.

Now for every function f, we get that $\|A'f\|_4^4 = \alpha\|Af\|_4^4 + (1 - \alpha)\|Bf\|_4^4$. In particular, since $\|Bf\|_4^4 \in (1 \pm \delta)\|f\|_2^4$, we get that if f is a unit vector and $\|Af\|_4^4 \leqslant c^4$ then $\|A'f\|_4^4 \leqslant \delta + (1 + \delta)$, while if $\|Af\|_4^4 \geqslant C^4$, then $\|A'f\|_4^4 \geqslant \delta(C/c)^4$.

Also note that the random operator B will satisfy that for every function f, $\|Bf\|_2 \geqslant (1-\delta)\|f\|_2$, and hence $\|A'f\| \geqslant (1-\alpha)(1-\delta)\|f\|$. Choosing $\delta = \varepsilon/2$ concludes the proof. □

It turns out that for the purposes of hardness of good approximation, the case that A is a projector is without loss of generality.

Lemma 8.7. *Suppose that for some $\varepsilon > 0, C > 1 + \varepsilon$ there is a $\mathrm{poly}(n)$ algorithm that on input a subspace $V \subseteq \mathbb{R}^n$ can distinguish between the case **(Y)** $\|\Pi_V\|_{2\to4} \geqslant C$ and the case **(N)** $\|\Pi_V\|_{2\to4} \leqslant 1+\varepsilon$, where Π_V denotes the projector onto V. Then there is $\delta = \Omega(\varepsilon)$ and a $\mathrm{poly}(n)$ algorithm that on input an operator $A : \mathbb{R}^k \to \mathbb{R}^n$ with $\sigma_{\min}(A) \geqslant 1 - \delta$ can distinguish between the case **(Y)** $\|A\|_{2\to4} \geqslant C(1 + \delta)$ and **(N)** $\|A\|_{2\to4} \leqslant 1 + \delta$.*

Proof. First we can assume without loss of generality that $\|A\|_{2\to2} = \sigma_{\max}(A) \leqslant 1 + \delta$, since otherwise we could rule out case **(N)**. Now we let V be the image of A. In the case **(N)** we get that that for every $f \in \mathbb{R}^k$

$$\|Af\|_4 \leqslant (1 + \delta)\|f\|_2 \leqslant (1 + \delta)\|Af\|_2/\sigma_{\min}(A) \leqslant (1 + O(\delta))\|Af\|_2 ,$$

implying $\|\Pi_V\|_{2\to4} \leqslant 1 + O(\delta)$. In the case **(Y)** we get that there is some f such that $\|Af\|_4 \geqslant C(1 + \delta)\|f\|_2$, but since $\|Af\|_2 \leqslant \sigma_{\max}(A)\|f\|_2$, we get that $\|Af\|_4 \geqslant C$, implying $\|\Pi_V\|_{2\to4} \geqslant C$. □

Together these two lemmas effectively extend Theorem 2.5 to the case when A is a projector. We focus on the hardness of approximating to within a constant factor.

Corollary 8.8. *For any $\ell, \varepsilon > 0$, if ϕ is a 3-SAT instance with n variables and $O(n)$ clauses, then determining satisfiability of ϕ can be reduced to distinguishing between the cases $\|A\|_{2\to4} \leqslant 1 + \varepsilon$ and $\|A\|_{2\to4} \geqslant \ell$), where A is a projector acting on $m = \exp(\sqrt{n}\,\mathrm{poly}\log(n)\log(\ell/\varepsilon))$ dimensions.*

Proof. Start as in the proof of Theorem 2.5, but in the application of Lemma 8.4, take $k = O(\log(\ell/\varepsilon))$. This will allow us to take $C/c = \Omega(\ell/\varepsilon)$ in Lemma 8.6. Translating into a projector with Lemma 8.7, we obtain the desired result. □

8.3 Algorithmic applications of equivalent formulations

In this section we discuss the positive algorithmic results that come from the equivalences in Section 8.1. Since entanglement plays such a central role in quantum mechanics, the set $\mathrm{Sep}^2(\mathbb{C}^n)$ has been extensively studied. However, because its hardness has long been informally recognized (and more recently has been explicitly established [Gur03, Liu07, HM10, GNN]), various relaxations have been proposed for the set. These relaxations are generally efficiently computable, but also have limited accuracy; see [BS10] for a review.

Two of the most important relaxations are the PPT condition and k-extendability. For an operator $X \in L((\mathbb{C}^n)^{\otimes r})$ and a set $S \subseteq [r]$, define the *partial transpose* X^{T_S} to be the result of applying the transpose map to the systems S. Formally, we define

$$(X_1 \otimes \cdots \otimes X_r)^{T_S} := \bigotimes_{k=1}^{r} f_k(X_k), \qquad f_k(M) := \begin{cases} M & \text{if } k \notin S \\ M^T & \text{if } k \in S \end{cases}$$

and extend T_S linearly to all of $L((\mathbb{C}^n)^{\otimes r})$. One can verify that if $X \in \mathrm{Sep}^r(\mathbb{C}^n)$ then $X^{T_S} \geq 0$ for all $S \subseteq [r]$. In this case we say that X is PPT, meaning that it has Positive Partial Transposes. However, the converse is not always true. If $n > 2$ or $r > 2$, then there are states which are PPT but not in Sep [HHH96].

The second important relaxation of Sep is called r-extendability. To define this, we need to introduce the partial trace. For $S \subseteq [r]$, we define Tr_S to be the map from $L((\mathbb{C}^n)^{\otimes r})$ to $L((\mathbb{C}^n)^{\otimes r-|S|})$ that results from applying Tr to the systems in S. Formally $\mathrm{Tr}_S \bigotimes_{k=1}^r X_k = \prod_{k\in S} \mathrm{Tr}\, X_k \bigotimes_{k\notin S} X_k$, and Tr_S extends by linearity to all of $L((\mathbb{C}^n)^{\otimes r})$.

To obtain our relaxation of Sep, we say that $\rho \in \mathcal{D}(\mathbb{C}^n \otimes \mathbb{C}^n)$ is r-extendable if there exists a *symmetric extension* $\sigma \in \mathcal{D}(\mathbb{C}^n \otimes \vee^r\mathbb{C}^n)$ such that $\mathrm{Tr}_{\{3,\ldots,r+1\}}\sigma = \rho$. Observe that if $\rho \in \mathrm{Sep}^2(\mathbb{C}^n)$, then we can write $\rho = \sum_i x_i x_i^* \otimes y_i y_i^*$, and so $\sigma = \sum_i x_i x_i^* \otimes (y_i y_i^*)^{\otimes r}$ is a valid symmetric extension. Thus the set of k-extendable states contains the set of separable states, but again the inclusion is strict. Indeed, increasing k gives an infinite hierarchy of strictly tighter approximations of $\mathrm{Sep}^2(\mathbb{C}^n)$. This hierarchy ultimately converges [DPS04], although not always at a useful rate (see Example

IV.1 of [CKMR07]). Interestingly this relaxation is known to completely fail as a method of approximating $\mathrm{Sep}^2(\mathbb{R}^n)$ [CFS02], but our Lemma 8.2 is evidence that those difficulties do not arise in the $2\to4$-norm problem.

These two relaxations can be combined to optimize over symmetric extensions that have positive partial transposes [DPS04]. Call this the *level-r DPS relaxation*. It is known to converge in some cases more rapidly than r-extendability alone [NOP09], but also is never exact for any finite r [DPS04]. Like SoS, this relaxation is an SDP with size $n^{O(r)}$. In fact, for the case of the $2\to4$ norm, the relaxations are equivalent.

LEMMA 8.9. *When the level-r DPS relaxation is applied to $A_{2,2}$, the resulting approximation is equivalent to* Tensor-SDP$^{(2r+2)}$

Due to space constraints, the proof is omitted.

Approximation guarantees. Many approximation guarantees for the k-extendable relaxation (with or without the additional SDP constraints) required that k be $\mathrm{poly}(n)$, and thus do not lead to useful algorithms. Recently, [BaCY11] showed that in some cases it sufficed to take $k = O(\log n)$, leading to quasi-polynomial algorithms. It is far from obvious that their proof translates into our sum-of-squares framework, but nevertheless Lemma 8.9 implies that Tensor-SDP can take advantage of their analysis.

To apply the algorithm of [BaCY11], we need to upper-bound $A_{2,2}$ by an LOCC measurement operator. That is, a quantum measurement that can be implemented by Local Operations and Classical Communication (LOCC). A full definition of LOCC measurements is somewhat cumbersome[13], but for our purposes, it suffices to note that for complex vectors $v_1,\dots,v_m,w_1,\dots,w_m$ satisfying $\sum_i v_iv_i^* \preceq I_n$ and $\forall i,\ w_iw_i^* \preceq I_n$, the operator $\sum_i v_iv_i^*\otimes w_iw_i^*$ is a LOCC measurement.

To upper-bound $A_{2,2}$ by an LOCC measurement, we note that $a_ia_i^T \preceq \|a_i\|_2^2 I_n$. Thus, if we define $Z := \|\sum_i a_ia_i^T\|_{2\to2}\max_i\|a_i\|^2$, then $A_{2,2}/Z$ is an LOCC measurement. Note that this is a stricter requirement than merely requiring $A_{2,2}/Z \preceq I_{n^2}$. On the other hand, in some cases (e.g. a_i all orthogonal), it may be too pessimistic.

In terms of the original matrix $A = \sum_i e_ia_i^T$, we have $\max_i\|a_i\|_2 = \|A\|_{2\to\infty}$. Also $\|\sum_i a_ia_i^T\|_{2\to2} = \|A^TA\|_{2\to2} = \|A\|_{2\to2}^2$. Thus $Z = \|A\|_{2\to2}^2\|A\|_{2\to\infty}^2$. Recall from the introduction that Z is an upper bound on $\|A\|_{2\to4}^4$, based on the fact that $\|x\|_4 \leqslant \sqrt{\|x\|_2\|x\|_\infty}$ for any x. (This bound also arises from using interpolation of norms [Ste56].)

We can now apply the argument of [BaCY11] and show that optimizing over $O(r)$-extendable states will approximate $\|A\|_{2\to4}^4$ up to additive error $\sqrt{\frac{\log(n)}{r}}Z$. Equivalently, we can obtain additive error εZ using $O(\log(n)/\varepsilon^2)$-round Tensor-SDP. Whether the relaxation used is the DPS relaxation or our SoS-based Tensor-SDP algorithm, the resulting runtime is $\exp(O(\log^2(n)/\varepsilon^2))$.

Gap instances: Since Tensor-SDP is stronger than the DPS relaxation for separable states, any gap instance for Tensor-SDP would translate into a gap instance for the DPS relaxation. This would mean the existence of a state that passes the k-extendability and PPT test, but nevertheless is far from separable, with $A_{2,2}$ serving as the entanglement witness demonstrating this. While such states are already known [DPS04, BS10], it would be of interest to find new such families of states, possibly with different scaling of r and n.

[13]For convenience we describe it here. LOCC measurements on $\mathbb{C}^n\otimes\mathbb{C}^n$ are defined recursively as follows. First, $I_n\otimes I_n$ is an LOCC measurement. Second, for any LOCC measurements $M_1,\dots,M_k$ and operators $E_1,\dots,E_k$ such that $\sum_{i=1}^k E_i^*E_i \preceq I$, the measurements $\sum_{i=1}^k(E_i^*\otimes I_n)M_i(E_i\otimes I_n)$ and $\sum_{i=1}^k(I_n\otimes E_i^*)M_i(I_n\otimes E_i)$ are both LOCC

9. SUBEXPONENTIAL ALGORITHM FOR THE $2\to q$ NORM

In this section we prove Theorem 2.1:

Theorem 2.1 (restated). *For every $1 < c < C$, there is a $\mathrm{poly}(n)\exp(n^{2/q})$-time algorithm that computes a (c,C)-approximation for the $2\to q$ norm of any linear operator whose range is $\mathbb{R}^n$.*

and obtain as a corollary a subexponential algorithm for SMALL-SET EXPANSION. The algorithm roughly matches the performance of [ABS10]'s for the same problem, and in fact is a very close variant of it. The proof is obtained by simply noticing that a subspace V cannot have too large of a dimension without containing a vector v (that can be easily found) such that $\|v\|_q \gg \|v\|_2$, while of course it is always possible to find such a vector (if it exists) in time exponential in $\dim(V)$. The key observation is the following basic fact (whose proof we include here for completeness):

LEMMA 9.1. *For every subspace $V\subseteq\mathbb{R}^n$, $\|V\|_{2\to\infty}\geqslant\sqrt{\dim(V)}$.*

PROOF. Let $f^1,\dots,f^d$ be an orthonormal basis for V, where $d = \dim(V)$. For every $i\in[n]$, let g^i be the function $\sum_{j=1}^d f_i^j f^i$. Note that the ith coordinate of g^i is equal to $\sum_{j=1}^d (f_i^j)^2$ (*) which also equals $\|g^i\|_2^2$ since the f^j's are an orthonormal basis. Also the expectation of (*) over i is $\sum_{j=1}^d \mathbb{E}_{i\in[n]}(f_i^j)^2 = \sum_{j=1}^d\|f^j\|_2^2 = d$ since these are unit vectors. Thus we get that $\mathbb{E}_i\|g^i\|_\infty \geqslant \mathbb{E}_i\, g_i^i = d = \mathbb{E}_i\|g\|_2^2$. We claim that one of the g^i's must satisfy $\|g^i\|_\infty\geqslant\sqrt{d}\|g^i\|_2$. Indeed, suppose otherwise, then we'd get that

$$d = \mathop{\mathbb{E}}_i\|g^i\|_2^2 > E_i\|g^i\|_\infty^2/d$$

meaning $E_i\|g^i\|_\infty^2 < d^2$, but $E_i\|g^i\|_\infty^2 \geqslant \left(\mathbb{E}_i\|g^i\|_\infty\right)^2 = d^2$— a contradiction. □

COROLLARY 9.2. *For every subspace $V\subseteq\mathbb{R}^n$, $\|V\|_{2\to q}\geqslant\sqrt{\dim(V)}/n^{1/q}$*

PROOF. By looking at the contribution to the qth-norm of just one coordinate one can see that for every function f, $\|f\|_q \geqslant (\|f\|_\infty^q/n)^{1/q} = \|f\|_\infty/n^{1/q}$. □

Proof of Theorem 2.1 from Corollary 9.2.

Let $A:\mathbb{R}^m\to\mathbb{R}^n$ be an operator, and let $1<c<C$ be some constants and $\sigma = \sigma_{\min}(A)$ be such that $\|Af\|_2\geqslant\sigma\|f\|_2$ for every f such that Af is nonzero. We want to distinguish between the case that $\|A\|_{2\to q}\leqslant c$ and the case that $\|A\|_{2\to q}\geqslant C$. If $\sigma > c$ then clearly we are not in the first case, and so we're done. Let V be the image of A. If $\dim(V)\leqslant C^2n^{2/q}$ then we can use brute force enumeration to find out if such v exists in the space. Otherwise, by Corollary 9.2 we must be in the second case. □

Note that by applying Theorem 2.3 we can replace the brute force enumeration step by the SoS hierarchy, using the fact that unless $\|V\|_{2\to\infty}\leqslant$ and $\|V\|_{2\to2}$ are bounded appropriately, we'll be in the second case.

A corollary of Theorem 2.1 is a subexponential algorithm for SMALL-SET EXPANSION

COROLLARY 9.3. *For every $0.4 > \nu > 0$ there is an $\exp(n^{1/O(\log(1/\nu))})$ time algorithm that given a graph with the promise that either (i) $\Phi_G(\delta)\geqslant 1-\nu$ or (ii) $\Phi_G(\delta^2)\leqslant 0.5$ decides which is the case.*

Proof. For $q = O(\log(1/\nu))$ we find from Theorem 2.4 that in case (i), $\|V_{\geqslant 0.4}\|_{2\to q} \leqslant 2/\sqrt{\delta}$, while in case (ii) $\|V_{\geqslant 0.4}\|_{2\to q} \geqslant 0.1/\delta^{1-2/q}$. Thus it sufficies to obtain a $(2/\sqrt{\delta}, 0.1/\delta^{1-2/q})$-approximation for the $2 \to q$ norm to solve the problem, and by Theorem 2.1 this can be achieved in time $\exp(n^{O(\log(1/\nu))})$ for sufficiently small δ. □

Conclusions

This work motivates further study of the complexity of approximating hypercontractive norms such as the $2 \to 4$ norm. A particulary interesting question is what is the complexity of obtaining a good approximation for the $2 \to 4$ norm and what's the relation of this problem to the Small-Set Expansion problem. Our work leaves possible at least the following three scenarios: **(i)** both these problems can be solved in quasipolynomial time, but not faster, which would mean that the UGC as stated is essentially false but a weaker variant of it is true, **(ii)** both these problems are **NP**-hard to solve (via a reduction with polynomial blowup) meaning that the UGC is true, and **(iii)** the Small-Set Expansion and Unique Games problems are significantly easier than the $2 \to 4$ problem with the most extreme case being that the former two problems can be solved in polynomial time and the latter is **NP**-hard and hence cannot be done faster than subexponential time. This last scenario would mean that one can improve on the subexponential algorithm for the $2 \to 4$ norm for general instances by using the structure of instances arising from the Small-Set Expansion reduction of Theorem 2.4 (which indeed seem quite different from the instances arising from the hardness reduction of Theorem 2.5). In any case we hope that further study of the complexity of computing hypercontractive norms can lead to a better understanding of the boundary between hardness and easiness for Unique Games and related problems.

Acknowledgements.
We thank Pablo Parrilo for useful discussions, and the anonymous STOC referees for numerous comments that greatly improved the presentation of this paper. Aram Harrow was funded by NSF grants 0916400, 0829937, 0803478, DARPA QuEST contract FA9550-09-1-0044 and the IARPA QCS contract. Jonathan Kelner was partially supported by NSF awards 1111109 and 0843915.

10. REFERENCES

[ABS10] Sanjeev Arora, Boaz Barak, and David Steurer, *Subexponential algorithms for unique games and related problems*, FOCS, 2010, pp. 563–572.

[AE07] Andris Ambainis and Joseph Emerson, *Quantum t-designs: t-wise independence in the quantum world*, IEEE Conference on Computational Complexity 2007 (2007), 129–140, arXiv:quant-ph/0701126v2.

[BaCY11] Fernando G.S.L. Brandão, Matthias Christandl, and Jon Yard, *A quasipolynomial-time algorithm for the quantum separability problem*, Proceedings of the 43rd annual ACM symposium on Theory of computing, STOC '11, 2011, arXiv:1011.2751, pp. 343–352.

[BGH+11] Boaz Barak, Parikshit Gopalan, Johan Håstad, Raghu Meka, Prasad Raghavendra, and David Steurer, *Making the long code shorter, with applications to the unique games conjecture*, 2011, Manuscript.

[Bis11] Punyashloka Biswal, *Hypercontractivity and its applications*, Manuscript. Available as eprint arXiv:1101.2913v1, 2011.

[BRS11] Boaz Barak, Prasad Raghavendra, and David Steurer, *Rounding semidefinite programming hierarchies via global correlation*, FOCS, 2011, To appear. arXiv:1104.4680v1.

[BS10] Salman Beigi and Peter W. Shor, *Approximating the set of separable states using the positive partial transpose test*, J. Math. Phys. **51** (2010), no. 4, 042202, arXiv:0902.1806.

[BTN98] Aharon Ben-Tal and Arkadi Nemirovski, *Robust convex optimization*, Mathematics of Operations Research **23** (1998), no. 4, 769–805.

[BV11] Aditya Bhaskara and Aravindan Vijayaraghavan, *Approximating matrix p-norms*, SODA, 2011, pp. 497–511.

[CFS02] Carlton M. Caves, Christopher A. Fuchs, and Rüdiger Schack, *Unknown quantum states: The quantum de finetti representation*, J. Math. Phys. **43** (2002), no. 9, 4537–4559, arXiv:quant-ph/0104088.

[CKMR07] Matthias Christandl, Robert König, Graeme Mitchison, and Renato Renner, *One-and-a-half quantum de finetti theorems*, Commun. Math. Phys. **273** (2007), 473–498, arXiv:quant-ph/0602130.

[CKP00] Fernando Cobos, Thomas Kühn, and Jaak Peetre, *Remarks on symmetries of trilinear forms*, Rev. R. Acad. Cienc. Exact. Fis.Nat. (Esp) **94** (2000), no. 4, 441–449.

[CT10] Eden Chlamtac and Madhur Tulsiani, *Convex relaxations and integrality gaps*, 2010, Chapter in Handbook on Semidefinite, Cone and Polynomial Optimization.

[dKL11] Etienne de Klerk and Monique Laurent, *On the lasserre hierarchy of semidefinite programming relaxations of convex polynomial optimization problems*, SIAM J. on Optimization **21** (2011), no. 3, 824–832.

[dlVKKV05] Wenceslas Fernandez de la Vega, Marek Karpinski, Ravi Kannan, and Santosh Vempala, *Tensor decomposition and approximation schemes for constraint satisfaction problems*, Proceedings of the thirty-seventh annual ACM symposium on Theory of computing, STOC '05, 2005, pp. 747–754.

[DPS04] Andrew C. Doherty, Pablo A. Parrilo, and Federico M. Spedalieri, *Complete family of separability criteria*, Phys. Rev. A **69** (2004), 022308, arXiv:quant-ph/0308032.

[GNN] Francois Le Gall, Shota Nakagawa, and Harumichi Nishimura, *On qma protocols with two short quantum proofs*, arXiv:1108.4306.

[Gro75] Leonard Gross, *Logarithmic sobolev inequalities*, Amer. J. Math. **97** (1975), 1061–1083.

[GS11] Venkatesan Guruswami and Ali Kemal Sinop, *Lasserre hierarchy, higher eigenvalues, and approximation schemes for quadratic integer programming with psd objectives*, FOCS, 2011, To appear.

[Gur03] Leonid Gurvits, *Classical deterministic complexity of Edmonds' problem and quantum entanglement*, STOC, 2003, arXiv:quant-ph/0303055, pp. 10–19.

[HHH96] Michal Horodecki, Pawel Horodecki, and Ryszard Horodecki, *Separability of mixed states: necessary and sufficient conditions*, Phys. Lett. A **223** (1996), no. 1–2, 1–8, arXiv:quant-ph/9605038.

[HM10] Aram W. Harrow and Ashley Montanaro, *An efficient test for product states, with applications to quantum Merlin-Arthur games*, Proc. 51st Symp. on FOCS, 2010, arXiv:1001.0017.

[IPZ98] R. Impagliazzo, R. Paturi, and F. Zane, *Which problems have strongly exponential complexity?*, Foundations of Computer Science, 1998. Proceedings. 39th Annual Symposium on, IEEE, 1998, pp. 653–662.

[Kho02] Subhash Khot, *On the power of unique 2-prover 1-round games*, STOC, 2002, pp. 767–775.

[KKMO04] Subhash Khot, Guy Kindler, Elchanan Mossel, and Ryan O'Donnell, *Optimal inapproximability results for Max-Cut and other 2-variable CSPs?*, FOCS, 2004, pp. 146–154.

[KMN11] Anna R. Karlin, Claire Mathieu, and C. Thach Nguyen, *Integrality gaps of linear and semi-definite programming relaxations for knapsack*, IPCO, 2011, pp. 301–314.

[KNS08] Guy Kindler, Assaf Naor, and Gideon Schechtman, *The UGC hardness threshold of the ℓ_p Grothendieck problem*, SODA, 2008, pp. 64–73.

[KPS10] Subhash Khot, Preyas Popat, and Rishi Saket, *Approximate lasserre integrality gap for unique games*, APPROX-RANDOM, 2010, pp. 298–311.

[KS09] Subhash Khot and Rishi Saket, *SDP integrality gaps with local ℓ_1-embeddability*, FOCS, 2009, pp. 565–574.

[KV05] Subhash Khot and Nisheeth K. Vishnoi, *The unique games conjecture, integrality gap for cut problems and embeddability of negative type metrics into ℓ_1*, FOCS, 2005, pp. 53–62.

[Las01] Jean B. Lasserre, *Global optimization with polynomials and the problem of moments*, SIAM Journal on Optimization **11** (2001), no. 3, 796–817.

[Lau03] Monique Laurent, *A comparison of the sherali-adams, lovász-schrijver, and lasserre relaxations for 0-1 programming*, Math. Oper. Res. **28** (2003), no. 3, 470–496.

[Lau09] M. Laurent, *Sums of squares, moment matrices and optimization over polynomials*, Emerging applications of algebraic geometry **149** (2009), 157–270.

[Liu07] Yi-Kai. Liu, *The complexity of the consistency and N-representability problems for quantum states*, Ph.D. thesis, Univ. of California, San Diego, 2007, arXiv:0712.3041.

[LS91] L. Lovász and A. Schrijver, *Cones of matrices and set-functions and 0–1 optimization*, SIAM Journal on Optimization **1** (1991), 166–190.

[MOO05] Elchanan Mossel, Ryan O'Donnell, and Krzysztof Oleszkiewicz, *Noise stability of functions with low influences invariance and optimality*, FOCS, 2005, pp. 21–30.

[Nes00] Y. Nesterov, *Squared functional systems and optimization problems*, High performance optimization **13** (2000).

[NOP09] Miguel Navascues, Masaki Owari, and Martin B. Plenio, *The power of symmetric extensions for entanglement detection*, Phys. Rev. A **80** (2009), 052306, arXiv:0906.2731.

[O'D07] Ryan O'Donnell, *Analysis of boolean functions*, Lecture Notes. Available online at http://www.cs.cmu.edu/~odonnell/boolean-analysis/, 2007.

[Par00] Pablo A. Parrilo, *Structured semidefinite programs and semialgebraic geometry methods in robustness and optimization*, Tech. report, 2000.

[Par03] Pablo A. Parrilo, *Semidefinite programming relaxations for semialgebraic problems*, Mathematical Programming **96** (2003), 293–320.

[RS09] Prasad Raghavendra and David Steurer, *Integrality gaps for strong SDP relaxations of unique games*, FOCS, 2009, pp. 575–585.

[RS10] ———, *Graph expansion and the unique games conjecture*, STOC, 2010, pp. 755–764.

[RST10a] Prasad Raghavendra, David Steurer, and Prasad Tetali, *Approximations for the isoperimetric and spectral profile of graphs and related parameters*, STOC, 2010, pp. 631–640.

[RST10b] Prasad Raghavendra, David Steurer, and Madhur Tulsiani, *Reductions between expansion problems*, Manuscript. Available as eprint arXiv:1011.2586v1, 2010.

[Rya02] Raymond A. Ryan, *Introduction to tensor products of banach spaces*, Springer monographs in mathematics, Springer, 2002.

[SA90] Hanif D. Sherali and Warren P. Adams, *A hierarchy of relaxations between the continuous and convex hull representations for zero-one programming problems*, SIAM J. Discrete Math. **3** (1990), no. 3, 411–430. MR MR1061981 (91k:90116)

[SC97] Laurent Saloff-Coste, *Lectures on finite markov chains*, Lectures on probability theory and statistics **1665** (1997), 301–413.

[Sho87] NZ Shor, *An approach to obtaining global extremums in polynomial mathematical programming problems*, Cybernetics and Systems Analysis **23** (1987), no. 5, 695–700.

[Ste56] Elias M. Stein, *Interpolation of linear operators*, Trans. Amer. Math. Soc. **83** (1956), 482–492.

[Ste05] Daureen Steinberg, *Computation of matrix norms with applications to robust optimization*, Master's thesis, Technion, 2005, Available on A. Nemirovski's website `http://www2.isye.gatech.edu/~nemirovs/`.

[Ste10] David Steurer, *Subexponential algorithms for d-to-1 two-prover games and for certifying almost perfect expansion*, Manuscript, available from the author's website., 2010.

[Tul09] Madhur Tulsiani, *CSP gaps and reductions in the Lasserre hierarchy*, STOC, 2009, pp. 303–312.

[vL09] Charles van Loan, *Future directions in tensor-based computation and modeling*, 2009, Unpublished NSF Workshop Report.

From Irreducible Representations to Locally Decodable Codes

Klim Efremenko
The Blavatnik School of Computer Science, Tel-Aviv University
Tel-Aviv, Israel, 69978
klimefrem@gmail.com

ABSTRACT

A q-query *Locally Decodable Code* (LDC) is an error correcting code that allows to read any particular symbol of the message by reading only q symbols of the codeword even if the codeword is adversary corrupted.

In this paper we present a new approach for the construction of LDCs. We show that if there exists an irreducible representation (ρ, V) of G and q elements $g_1, g_2, \ldots, g_q$ in G such that there exists a linear combination of matrices $\rho(g_i)$ that is of rank one, then we can construct a q-query Locally Decodable Code $\mathcal{C} : V \rightarrow \mathbb{F}^G$.

We show the potential of this approach by constructing constant query LDCs of sub-exponential length matching the best known constructions.

Categories and Subject Descriptors

E.4 [**Coding and Information Theory**]: Error control codes

General Terms

Theory

Keywords

Locally Decodable Codes, Representation Theory

1. INTRODUCTION

A *Locally Decodable Codes (LDC)* is a code that allows the retrieval of any symbol of a message by reading only a constant number of symbols from its codeword, even if a large fraction of the codeword is adversarially corrupted. Formally, a code $\mathcal{C}$ is said to be locally decodable with parameters (q, δ, ϵ) if for all message x and for all indices i it is possible to recover any symbol x_i of a message x by making at most q queries to $\mathcal{C}(x)$, such that even if a δ fraction of $\mathcal{C}(x)$ is adversarially corrupted, the decoding algorithm returns the correct answer with probability at least $1 - \epsilon$.

STOC'12, May 19–22, 2012, New York, New York, USA.

Local decoding is an important concept in theoretical computer science and cryptography. Many important results in these fields use such codes in different variations. LDCs are closely related to such subjects as worst case – average case reductions, pseudo-random generators, hardness amplification, private information retrieval schemes and many others. See the surveys [11, 2] for more details.

Locally decodable codes were first formally defined by Katz and Trevisan [6], although this notion already appeared implicitly in previous works. When the number of queries is *poly* $\log k$, where k is the length of the message, Reed-Muller codes give polynomial length LDCs. When the number of queries is k^{ε}, a variant of Reed-Muller [8] gives LDCs of rate approaching one. For more details on recent results on LDCs see the survey by Yekhanin [14].

The main focus of this paper is LDCs with a constant number of queries. The Hadamard code is the best-known 2-query LDC and is of length 2^k. Tight lower bound of $2^{\Theta(k)}$ on the length of *linear* 2-query locally decodable codes were given in Goldreich et al. [3], and were extended to general codes by Kerenidis and de Wolf [7]. When the number of queries is constant and greater than two, much less is known. For an arbitrary constant number of queries q, only weak super-linear lower bounds are known, see [6, 7, 12]. For many years it was conjectured that LDCs should have an exponential dependence on k for any constant number of queries, until Yekhanin's breakthrough [13]. Yekhanin obtained 3-query LDCs with sub-exponential length under a highly believable conjecture. Later on in [1] this construction was generalized and the dependence on the conjecture was removed. We are still very far from understanding what are the best parameters of LDCs. For example, the best upper bound on three query LDCs is

$$\exp(\exp(\sqrt{\log k \log\log k})),$$

where k is message length in contrast to $\tilde{\Omega}(k^2)$ lower bound. No better lower bounds are known, even for some very restricted special cases of LDCs.

Today all known sub-exponential constructions of LDCs with constant number of queries could be described in the framework of *matching vector codes* (MVCs), which are based on two ingredients: a set of *matching vectors* (MV) and a *decoding polynomial.*(See [1], where this was made explicit.) Some progress was obtained recently in understanding the latter component [5, 9], but it seems that in order to make a significant improvement in MVCs, we need to improve also matching vectors, where there was almost no progress in the last ten years. We say that $\{u_i\}_{i=1}^{k} \subset \mathbb{Z}_m^h$

are S-Matching Vectors (MV), where S is a subset of $\mathbb{Z}_m$ if $\langle u_i, u_j\rangle \in S \Leftrightarrow i \neq j$. The history of Matching Vectors is similar to the history of LDCs. It was conjectured for many years that there must be a polynomial upper bound on the size of MV, until Grolmusz's [4] breakthrough. This construction is the basis for subexponential constructions of LDCs in [1]. For MVs as well, there is not even a conjecture today of what are their best possible parameters.

Although the framework of MVCs is pretty simple it still does not explain the real nature of LDCs. This leads us to seek a new approach to understanding LDCs. In this paper we start a systematic study of LDCs from the point of view of the representation theory. We present a new framework for the construction of LDCs and show that it captures two important classes of LDCs: Reed Muller codes and MVCs. We believe that this is the real algebraic nature behind LDCs.

1.1 Our Results

Let G be a finite group. A *representation* of the group G is a pair (ρ, V) of a vector space V and a mapping $\rho : G \to GL(V)$ from G to the group of invertible matrices over V which is a group homomorphism, i.e., for all $g_1, g_2 \in G$ it holds that $\rho(g_1 g_2) = \rho(g_1)\rho(g_2)$. A subspace $W \subset V$ is a *sub-representation* of (ρ, V) if for every $g \in G$ the matrix $\rho(g)$ maps W to W. A representation is called *irreducible* if it does not have any non-trivial sub-representations. (See Section 2.1.2 for formal definitions.)

In this paper we study the connection between the representations of finite groups and LDCs. We show that if (ρ, V) is an irreducible representation and there exists a small number of elements $g_1, \ldots, g_q$ in G such that some linear combination of $\rho(g_i)$ is a rank one matrix, then we can construct a q-query LDC of length $|G|$ and dimension $\dim V$.[1]

THEOREM 1.1. *(Informal) Let G be a finite group and let (ρ, V) be an irreducible representation of G with $g_1, \ldots, g_q$ in G and $c_1, \ldots c_q \in \mathbb{F}$ such that $\mathrm{Rank}(\sum c_i \rho(g_i)) = 1$. Then there exists a $(q, \delta, q\delta)$-locally decodable code $\mathcal{C} : V \to \mathbb{F}^G$.*

This gives a completely new approach to constructing LDCs. Now in order to construct an LDC it is enough to construct irreducible representations with a sparse element of the group algebra of rank one. This theorem gives what we believe is the real algebraic nature behind LDCs.

Given this, we ask a natural question: When can one construct such a representation? We show that in this framework we can achieve the parameters of the best known construction. The code that we get is the same as in [1].

On the connection between Matching Vectors and our approach:.

The question when do MV codes fall in the framework of irreducible representations is completely not obvious. We say that MV are *symmetric* if they are an orbit of some group acting on $\mathbb{Z}_m^h$. We show in Section 4 that MV Codes can be explained in the framework of irreducible representations for MV that are symmetric. Next we show that the construction given in [4] is symmetric.[2] This gives a way to interpret the construction in [Efr09] as a construction of an irreducible representation. The relationship between MV and LDCs is summarized in the following diagram:

$$\begin{array}{ccc} \text{Irreducible Representation} & \Rightarrow & \text{LDC} \\ \Uparrow & & \Uparrow \\ \text{Symmetric MV} & \Rightarrow & \text{MV} \end{array}$$

We want to mention that all MV codes can be constructed from very specific class of representations of a very specific class of groups. We do not see any reason why such representations will give best possible LDCs although today we do not know how to construct representations which will lead to a better codes

Modular Representations and Reed-Muller Codes:.

One might wonder if the requirement on the representation being irreducible is essential. Perhaps better locally decodable codes can be constructed with reducible representations? We deal with this question in Section 6. We distinguish two cases. The first is when the characteristic of the field does not divide the size of the group. In this case we show that irreducibility is essential for our construction to lead to locally decodable codes. The second case is when the characteristic of the field divides the size of the group; this brings us to a slightly less familiar territory of representation theory known as *modular representation theory*. We show that in this case, it *is* possible to construct locally decodable codes based on reducible representations. We still don't know, unfortunately, if this can lead to improvements over the best known constructions of LDCs, although this is definitely a promising direction. We illustrate this case by showing how one can view Reed-Muller codes as a special case of our result for reducible modular representations.

Future Research.

Our main open question is, of course, to construct a *sparse* element of the group algebra that acts as a *rank one* element on a large irreducible representation. Rank one elements arise naturally in representation theory and have been investigated extensively before. Unfortunately, the sparseness property is hard to capture with existing algebraic tools. We hope that this paper will provide motivation to the study of sparse elements in the group algebra.

1.2 Organization of the paper

In Section 2 we give basic definitions and facts about representations of finite groups and LDCs. Section 3 is the main section of this paper where we prove that irreducible representations with a sparse element of rank one imply LDCs. Next we show the connection between the MV Codes construction and the irreducible representations with a sparse element. In order to do so, we present the construction given in [1] in a different way. In Section 4 we show that a Symmetric MV imply irreducible representations with a sparse element of rank one. In Section 5 we show that a variant of Grolmusz [4] gives a Symmetric MV with essentially the same parameters. In Section 6 we generalize Theorem 1.1 to *reducible* representations and we show that this generalizations is useful only for modular representations. We show that Reed-Muller code is an example of an LDC from the such representations. A reader who is not familiar with representation theory may want read first Appendix A were

[1]In fact we prove a stronger statement. For details see Theorem 3.1.

[2]In fact, for sake of simplicity, we show it only for a slight modification of Grolmusz [4] construction. While it is true for the Grolmusz construction as well.

we explain the connection between G-invariant codes and representations of G.

2. NOTATION AND PRELIMINARIES

2.1 Representation Theory

In this section we give basic facts about representation theory. We do not give proofs here and the interested reader is referred to any standard textbook on the subject such as [10].

2.1.1 Group Action

First let us start with the definition of the action of a group on a set.

DEFINITION 2.1. *We say that a group G acts on a set X if there exists a mapping $T : G \times X \to X$ such that $T(g_2, T(g_1, x)) = T(g_2 g_1, x)$ and $T(1, x) = x$.*

Usually the action is obvious from the context and then we write $g \cdot x$ instead of $T(g, x)$. Note that each $g \in G$ defines a permutation on the set X.

DEFINITION 2.2. *We say that G acts transitively on the set X iff for every $x, y \in X$ there exists $g \in G$ such that $gx = y$. In this case we say that X is an orbit of G.*

Let us assume that G acts on the set X. Then using this action we can define a new action of the group G on Σ^X. It is more convenient to view Σ^X as the set of functions from X to Σ rather than a string of symbols, i.e., we view $f \in \Sigma^X$ as $f : X \to \Sigma$.

DEFINITION 2.3. *Suppose G acts on the set X. Define an action of G on Σ^X by $(gf)(x) = f(g^{-1}x)$. We call such an action a permutation action.*

Note that we need to prove that this is indeed an action. That is, we need to check that $(g_1 \cdot (g_2 \cdot f)) = (g_1 \cdot g_2) \cdot f$. Note also that if we view Σ^X as a set of strings, then G acts on it by permuting coordinates.

DEFINITION 2.4. *An* order *of the group G is a minimal number m such that for every $g \in G$ it holds that $g^m = 1$.*

DEFINITION 2.5. *We say that the group H* acts on the *group N if it acts on it as a set and for every $h \in H, n_1, n_2 \in N$ it holds that*

$$h \cdot (n_1 n_2) = (h \cdot n_1)(h \cdot n_2) \ . \tag{2.1}$$

Note that action on the group in particular is an action on the set but the converse is not true. Any group N has a natural action on itself as a set. Note that this action does not satisfy Equation 2.1. Therefore N acts on itself as a set by not as a group.

DEFINITION 2.6 (SEMI-DIRECT PRODUCT). *Let N be a group. Let H be a group acting on the group N. Then the semi-direct product of N by H denoted by $N \rtimes H$ is a sub-group of permutations of N. Generated by the permutations defined by the actions of N on H and the natural actions of N on itself.*

2.1.2 Group Representations

NOTATION 2.1. *We denote by* $\mathrm{Mat}(V)$ *the set of all matrices on the vector space V. $GL(V)$ denotes the group of invertible matrices on the vector space V.*

DEFINITION 2.7 (REPRESENTATION OF A GROUP). *A representation (ρ, V) of a group G in a vector space V is a group homomorphism $\rho : G \to GL(V)$, that is, for every $g_1, g_2 \in G$ it holds that $\rho(g_1) \cdot \rho(g_2) = \rho(g_1 \cdot g_2)$.*

We also can define a representation of group G as an action of G on the vector space as follows:

DEFINITION 2.8. *Let V be a vector space over the field $\mathbb{F}$. A representation of a group G in V is an action of the group G on the set V which satisfies the following conditions:*

- *For any $v_1, v_2 \in V$ it holds that $g \cdot (v_1 + v_2) = g \cdot v_1 + g \cdot v_2$.*
- *For any $\lambda \in \mathbb{F}$ it holds that $g \cdot (\lambda v) = \lambda g \cdot v$.*
- *For any $v \in V$ it holds that $1 \cdot v = v$.*

DEFINITION 2.9 (SUB-REPRESENTATION). *Let ρ be a representation of a group G in a vector space V. We say that $U \subset V$ is a sub-representation of ρ if U is a linear subspace of V and U is invariant under ρ, namely: for every $g \in G$ it holds that $\rho(g)U = U$.*

DEFINITION 2.10 (IRREDUCIBLE-REPRESENTATION). *Let ρ be a representation of a group G in a vector space V. We say that ρ is an irreducible representation if it does not have any non trivial sub-representations, else we say that ρ is reducible.*

We need the following decomposition theorem:

THEOREM 2.2 (COMPLETE REDUCIBILITY). *Let G be a group. Let V be a vector space over an algebraically closed field $\mathbb{F}$ of characteristic co-prime to the size of G. Let ρ be a representation of the G in the vector space V. Then $V = \oplus V_i$ where V_i are irreducible sub-representations of ρ.*

The following theorem says that any orbit of an irreducible representation spans the entire space.

LEMMA 2.3. *Let (ρ, V) be an irreducible representation of G. Let $v \in V$ be a non-zero vector. Then the set $\{\rho(g)v | g \in G\}$ spans V, and thus there exist $g_1, g_2, \ldots, g_k \in G$ such that $\{\rho(g_i)v\}_{i=1}^k$ is a basis for V.*

2.1.3 Homomorphisms between Representations

DEFINITION 2.11. *Let ρ_1 be a representation of the group G in a vector space V and ρ_2 be a representation of the group G in a vector space W. We say that a linear mapping $T : V \to W$ is a homomorphism from (ρ_1, V) to (ρ_2, W) iff $\forall g \in G \ \rho_2(g) \circ T = T \circ \rho_1(g)$. Sometimes we also say that T is a G-homomorphism.*

Schematically a linear mapping T is a homomorphism between (ρ_1, V) and (ρ_2, W) if the following diagram is commutative:

$$\begin{array}{ccc} V & \xrightarrow{T} & W \\ \rho_1(g) \downarrow & & \downarrow \rho_2(g) \\ V & \xrightarrow{T} & W \end{array}$$

We say that a homomorphism T from (ρ_1, V) to (ρ_2, W) is an embedding/isomorphism if T is an embedding/isomorphism of the vector spaces V and W. Note also that kernel of T is a sub-representation. Thus if (ρ_1, V) is irreducible then T is either embedding or zero homomorphism.

LEMMA 2.4. *Let (ρ, V) be a representation of G. Let $\{V_i\}_{i=1}^k$ be irreducible non-isomorphic sub-representations of V. Then vector spaces $\{V_i\}_{i=1}^k$ are linearly independent.*

2.1.4 Permutational Representation, Group Algebra

Assume that a group G acts on a set X. Consider the permutation action of G on $\mathbb{F}^X$. It is easy to see that this action admits the properties of Definition 2.8 . Thus we can define a representation τ of the group G in $\mathbb{F}^X$. We call τ the *permutational representation.* Specifically:

$$(\tau(g) \cdot f)(x) = f(g^{-1}x). \tag{2.2}$$

For any $f \in \mathbb{F}^X$ we define support of f by the number of non-zero entries of $f : X \to \mathbb{F}$ i.e.,

$$\text{supp}(f) = |\{x \in X | f(x) \neq 0\}| \ .$$

For linear subspace $U \subset F^X$, we define support as a union of supports of all vectors in U, i.e.,

$$\text{supp}(U) = |\cup_{f \in U}\{x \in X | f(x) \neq 0\}| \ .$$

LEMMA 2.5. *Let U be a vector subspace of $\mathbb{F}^X$ of the full support and let $|\mathbb{F}| \geq t$. Then there exist a vector $u \in U$ such that $supp(u) \geq (1 - \frac{1}{t})|X|$.*

Now let us define the group algebra $\mathbb{F}[G]$:

DEFINITION 2.12 (GROUP ALGEBRA). *The group algebra $\mathbb{F}[G]$ is the set of all functions from G to $\mathbb{F}$. Multiplication in this group algebra is given by*

$$(f * h)(x) = \sum_{g_1 \cdot g_2 = x} f(g_1)h(g_2) \ .$$

We write $f \in \mathbb{F}[G]$ as a formal sum: $f = \sum_{i=1}^n a_i g_i$ meaning that $f(g_i) = a_i$ for $g_1, g_2, \ldots, g_n$ and zero on the rest of G. We say that $f \in \mathbb{F}[G]$ is a q-sparse element if it has support of size at most q i.e., it can be written in the form $f = \sum_{i=1}^q a_i g_i$.

DEFINITION 2.13 (REGULAR REPRESENTATION). *The regular representation of the group G is the representation ρ in the group algebra $\mathbb{F}[G]$ given by: $\rho(g)f = g * f$.*

Note that an equivalent way to define the regular representation is as a permutational representation of $\mathbb{F}^G$, where the group G acts on G in a natural way.

The regular representation plays an important role since it contains all irreducible representations. It follows from the following basic theorem from representation theory.

THEOREM 2.6. *Let V be a vector space over the field $\mathbb{F}$. Then for every irreducible representation (ρ, V) there exists some G-embedding from V to $\mathbb{F}[G]$.*

NOTATION 2.7. *Let $\rho : G \to GL(V)$ be any representation of the group G. Then we can linearly extend ρ to the group algebra $\mathbb{F}[G]$ i.e., $\rho : \mathbb{F}[G] \to \text{Mat}(V)$ where $\rho(f)$ is defined as $\sum_{g \in G} f(g)\rho(g)$. Note that now $\rho(f)$ may be any matrix, not necessary invertible.*

Note that if $(\rho_1, V), (\rho_2, W)$ are two representations and $T : V \to W$ is a homomorphism between them, then for any $f \in \mathbb{F}[G]$ it holds that

$$T \circ \rho_1(f) = \rho_2(f) \circ T. \tag{2.3}$$

2.1.5 Dual Space, Dual Representation

DEFINITION 2.14. *Let V be a linear vector space over field $\mathbb{F}$. Then the* dual space *of V, denoted by V^* is the set of all linear functionals from V to $\mathbb{F}$.*

We want to mention here that $\dim V = \dim V^*$.

DEFINITION 2.15. *Let V be a vector space of dimension k. Let $u_1, u_2, \ldots, u_k$ be a basis of V and $v_1, \ldots, v_k$ be a basis of V^*. We say these bases are* dual *if $v_i(u_j) = \delta_{i,j}$, where δ_{ij} is Kronecker delta i.e., $\delta_{ij} = 1$ is iff $i = j$ and zero otherwise.*

THEOREM 2.8. *For every basis there exists a dual basis.*

Now let us define the dual representation:

DEFINITION 2.16 (DUAL REPRESENTATION). *Let V be a vector space over $\mathbb{F}$. Let (ρ, V) be a representation of the group G. Let V^* be the set of all linear functionals from V to $\mathbb{F}$. The dual representation $(\bar{\rho}, V^*)$ is given by $\bar{\rho}(g)(\ell) = \ell \circ \rho(g^{-1})$, i.e., $\bar{\rho}(g)(\ell)(v) = \ell(\rho(g^{-1})v)$.*

Note that $\dim V = \dim V^*$. Also it holds that $(V^*)^* = V$. We leave to the reader to check that this is indeed a representation. In many cases a representation is isomorphic to its dual representation, but not always. However, a representation is irreducible if and only if its dual is irreducible.

THEOREM 2.9. *The representation (ρ, V) is irreducible if and only if $(\bar{\rho}, V^*)$ is irreducible.*

The dual group for Abelian groups is very similar to dual representation.

DEFINITION 2.17. *Let A be an Abelian group. Let m be an order of A. A dual group A^* is a set of group homomorphisms $\theta : A \to \mathbb{Z}_m$.*

Note that if θ_1, θ_2 are group homomorphisms then $\theta_1 + \theta_2$ is also group homomorphism. Therefore, A^* is an Abelian group. Moreover A^* isomorphic to A. For example if $A = \mathbb{Z}_m^h$ then isomorphism is given by $a \mapsto \langle -, a \rangle$. If some group H acts on an Abelian group A then it also acts on its dual A^*. For $h \in H$ and $\theta \in A^*$ the action of is given by the rule $h \cdot \theta(x) = \theta(h^{-1} \cdot x)$.

2.2 Locally Decodable Codes

DEFINITION 2.18. *A code $\mathcal{C} : \mathbb{F}^k \to \mathbb{F}^n$ is said to be (q, δ, ε) locally decodable if there exists a randomized decoding algorithm D^w with an oracle access to the received word w such that the following holds:*

1. *For every message $m = (m_1, m_2, \ldots, m_k) \in \mathbb{F}^k$ and for every $w \in \mathbb{F}^n$ such that $\Delta(\mathcal{C}(m), w) \leq \delta n$ for every i, it holds that $\Pr(D^w(i) = m_i) \geq 1 - \varepsilon$, where probability is taken over internal randomness of D. This means that the decoding algorithm can recover the relevant symbol even if up to δ fraction of the codeword symbols are corrupted.*

2. *The algorithm $D^w(i)$ makes at most q queries to w.*

A code $\mathcal{C}$ is called linear if $\mathcal{C}$ is a linear transformation over $\mathbb{F}$. A locally decodable code is called non-adaptive if D makes all its queries simultaneously. Our constructions of locally decodable codes are linear and non-adaptive.

DEFINITION 2.19. *A code $\mathcal{C} : \mathbb{F}^k \to \mathbb{F}^n$ is said to have a c-smooth decoder if $D^{\mathcal{C}(m)}(i) = m_i$ for every $m \in \mathbb{F}^k$ and for every i. Each query of $D(i)$ is uniformly distributed over a domain of size cn.*

FACT 2.10 (FROM [11]). *Any code with a c-smooth decoder which makes q queries is also $(q, \delta, \frac{q\delta}{c})$ locally decodable.*

PROOF. Note that if the decoding algorithm D queries w in uncorrupted places then D outputs the correct answer. The probability that any specific query will be corrupted is at most $\frac{\delta}{c}$. By a union bound, the probability that some query will be corrupted is at most $\frac{q\delta}{c}$. Therefore, the decoder outputs the correct answer with probability at least $1 - \frac{q\delta}{c}$. □

3. LOCALLY DECODABLE CODES FROM IRREDUCIBLE REPRESENTATIONS

Let us start from the main theorem of this paper.

THEOREM 3.1. *Let G be a group acting on a set X. Let $(\tau, \mathbb{F}^X)$ be the permutational representation defined by this action. Let (ρ, V) be a representation of G. Let $\mathcal{C} : V \to \mathbb{F}^X$ be a G-homomorphism between representations (ρ, V) and $(\tau, \mathbb{F}^X)$. Assume that the following conditions hold:*

1. *(a) There exists a q-sparse element $D \in \mathbb{F}[G]$, $D = \sum_{i=1}^{q} c_i g_i$ such that $\mathrm{Rank}(\rho(D)) = 1$.*
   (b) (ρ, V) is an irreducible representation.
2. *Let $v \in \mathrm{Im}(\rho(D))$ be a non-zero vector.[3] Then $supp(\mathcal{C}(v)) \geq c|X|$.*

Let $k = \dim V$. Then there exists a basis $b_1, \ldots, b_k$ for V such that

$$(m_1, m_2, \ldots, m_k) \mapsto \mathcal{C}(\sum_{i=1}^{k}(m_i b_i))$$

is a $(q, \delta, \frac{q\delta}{c})$-Locally Decodable Code.

In Subsection 3.2 we show that if one constructs a representation ρ that satisfies Condition 1 of Theorem 3.1, then we can always embed it into the regular representation in a way that satisfies Condition 2 of the theorem. In Subsection 3.3 we show that if $\mathbb{F}$ is an algebraic extension of $\mathbb{F}_p$, we can reduce the alphabet to $\mathbb{F}_p$ almost at no cost. In Section 6 we show that when $|\mathbb{F}|$ and $|G|$ are co-prime then the irreducibility of (ρ, V) is essential for having a rank one element. Moreover, we show that (ρ, V) should be irreducible not only over $\mathbb{F}$ but also over the algebraic closure of $\mathbb{F}$.

PROOF. The proof is divided into two parts. The first part is Lemma 3.2 which constructs a basis for V. This basis defines the encoding algorithm. In the second part we construct a decoding algorithm with q queries and show that it is a c-smooth decoder.

[3]Note that since $\mathrm{Rank}(\rho(D)) = 1$, the vector v is unique up to scalar multiplication.

LEMMA 3.2. *There exists a basis $\{b_1, b_2, \ldots, b_k\}$ for V and $h_1, \ldots, h_k \in G$ such that $b_i \in \mathrm{Ker}(\rho(D * h_j))$ if and only if $i \neq j$.*

PROOF. Set $L = \mathrm{Ker}\,\rho(D)$. L is a linear subspace of V of dimension $k-1$. Therefore, there exists unique (up to scalar multiplication) non-zero linear functional $u \in V^*$ such that $u(L) = 0$. Since (ρ, V) is an irreducible representation, it follows by Theorem 2.9 that its dual $(\bar{\rho}, V^*)$ is also irreducible. Therefore, from Lemma 2.3[4] it follows that there exist $h_1^{-1}, h_2^{-1}, \ldots, h_k^{-1} \in G$ such that $\{\bar{\rho}(h_i^{-1})u\}_{i=1}^{k}$ is a basis for V^*. By Theorem 2.8 it follows that for this basis there exists a dual basis $\{b_1, b_2, \ldots, b_k\}$ for V. From the definition of the dual basis it holds that $(\bar{\rho}(h_i^{-1})u)(b_j) = \delta_{ij}$. Thus $b_i \in \mathrm{Ker}\,\bar{\rho}(h_i^{-1})u$ if and only if $i \neq j$. In order to complete the proof of the lemma we need to show that $\mathrm{Ker}(\bar{\rho}(h_i^{-1})u) = \mathrm{Ker}\,\rho(D * h_i)$. Let $v \in \mathrm{Ker}\,\rho(D * h_i)$ then $0 = \rho(D * h_i)v = \rho(D)\rho(h_i)v$. Thus $\rho(h_i)v \in \mathrm{Ker}\,\rho(D)$ by definition of u it also holds that $u(\rho(h_i)v) = 0$. Therefore $\bar{\rho}(h_i^{-1})u(v) = 0$. □

Let $b_1, \ldots, b_k$ and $h_1, \ldots, h_k$ be given by Lemma 3.2. The encoding $\mathcal{C}$ of our Locally Decodable Code encodes a message $m = (m_1, \ldots, m_k)$ by

$$m \mapsto \mathcal{C}(\sum_{i=1}^{k} m_i b_i)\ .$$

In order to prove Theorem 3.1 we show that the following algorithm is a c-smooth decoder (see Definition 2.19).

Input: An oracle access to $w \in \mathbb{F}^X$ and an index $i \in \{1, \ldots, k\}$. Let $D_i = D * h_i = \sum_{j=1}^{q} c_j \cdot g_j h_i$.

1. Set $y = \mathcal{C}(\rho(D_i)b_i) \in \mathbb{F}^X$. Pick $r \in X$ at random from the support of y.
2. For $j = 1, \ldots, q$ query w at location: $(g_j h_i)^{-1} \cdot r \in X$.
3. Calculate $n_i = \sum_{j=1}^{q} c_j w[(g_j h_i)^{-1} \cdot r]$.
4. Return $m_i = y[r]^{-1} n_i$.

In order to show that this algorithm is a c-smooth decoder we need to show that:

- Completeness, i.e., if $w = \mathcal{C}(\sum m_i b_i)$ then the algorithm returns m_i on input i.
- Smoothness, i.e., each query is uniformly distributed over a domain of size $c|X|$.

Completeness:.

Recall that by definition of the permutational representation it holds that $\tau(g)w[r] = w[g^{-1}r]$. Thus n_i (line 3 of the decoding algorithm) is equal to

$$n_i = \sum_{j=1}^{q} c_j w[(g_j h_i)^{-1} \cdot r] = (\tau(D_i)w)[r]\ .$$

[4]Note that this is the only place where we use the irreducibility of (ρ, V). We discuss it later in Section 6.

Let us substitute $w = \mathcal{C}(\sum_j m_j b_j)$ in this equation.

$$n_i = (\tau(D_i)w)[r] = (\tau(D_i)\mathcal{C}(\sum_{j=1}^{k} m_j b_j))[r] \quad (3.1)$$

$$\stackrel{1}{=} \mathcal{C}\left(\rho(D_i)\sum_{j=1}^{k} m_j b_j\right)[r]$$

$$= \sum_{j=1}^{k} m_j \mathcal{C}(\rho(D_i)b_j)[r] \stackrel{2}{=} m_i \mathcal{C}(\rho(D_i)b_i)[r] .$$

Here Equality 1 holds since $\mathcal{C}$ is a homomorphism of the representations ρ and τ and Equality 2 follows from Lemma 3.2. Thus from the definition of y it follows that $n_i = m_i y[r]$. Therefore, the algorithm returns a correct answer at line 4.

Smoothness:.
Note that if r is uniformly distributed over a domain of size $c|X|$, then so is $g_j h_i \cdot r$. Thus we need to prove that r is uniformly distributed over a domain of size $c|X|$, This is equivalent to say that the support of y is of size $c|X|$.

Since $\rho(D)$ is of rank one it holds that $\mathrm{Im}\,\mathcal{C} \cdot \rho(D)$ is one dimensional. Therefore, from Condition 2 if follows that for every non-zero vector in $\mathrm{Im}\,\mathcal{C} \cdot \rho(D)$ has support of size at least $c|X|$. Note that $y = \mathcal{C}(\rho(D * h_i)b_i) = \mathcal{C} \cdot \rho(D)(\rho(h_i)b_i)$. Thus $y \in \mathrm{Im}\,\mathcal{C} \cdot \rho(D)$ and from Lemma 3.2 it follows that $y \neq 0$.

3.1 Example: Two Query LDC from Representations of S_n

The goal of this subsection is to give a concrete example of irreducible representation which allows to construct two query LDC from Theorem 3.1. We want to mention that Hadamard Code can be captured by generalization of Theorem 3.1 see Section 6.2 for more details. The example given in this section has slightly worse parameters, but it is much simpler.

Let $\mathbb{F}$ be any algebraically closed field. The group S_n has a natural action on $[n]$. This action defines representation ρ on $\mathbb{F}^n$. This representation decomposes into a trivial representation which is spanned by vector of all ones and its complement which is the set of all vectors with sum zero. Let V be this representation, i.e., $V = \{v \in \mathbb{F}^n | \sum_{i=1}^{n} v[i] = 0\}$. One can show that this is indeed an irreducible representation. We denote it by ρ_1. Consider $f = id - (1,2) \in \mathbb{F}[S_n]$ then we claim that rank of $\rho_1(f)$ is one. Indeed let $\vec{x} = (x_1, x_2, \ldots, x_n) \in V$ then

$$\rho_1(f)(x_1, x_2, \ldots, x_n) = (x_1, x_2, \ldots, x_n) - (x_2, x_1, x_3, \ldots, x_n)$$
$$= (x_1 - x_2, x_2 - x_1, 0, \ldots, 0) \in V.$$

Thus $\mathrm{Im}\,\rho_1(f)$ is $\lambda(1, -1, 0, 0, \ldots, 0)$.
Therefore $\mathrm{Rank}(\rho_1(f)) = 1$. Theorem 1.1 gives us immediately a 2 query $[n-1, n!]$ LDC.

Now let us show that using different sets X on which group S_n acts we can achieve tradeoff rate/soundness. Now let X be the set of all subsets of $[n]$ of size k. Then there exist a natural action of S_n on X which gives us permutational representation $\mathbb{F}^X$ (we think of $\mathbb{F}^X$ as all functions from subsets of size k to $\mathbb{F}$). Let us define $\mathcal{C}(x_1, x_2, \ldots, x_n) = g$ where g is a function which takes subset of size k as input and outputs the sum of this subset, i.e., g defined by

$$g(S) = \sum_{j \in S}^{k} x_j.$$

We can see that the support of $\mathcal{C}(\rho_1(f)) = \mathcal{C}(1, -1, 0, \ldots, 0)$ is all subsets which contains exactly one of the elements: 1 or 2. The length of the code is $\binom{n}{k}$. The number of k-subsets that contain exactly one of the elements 1 or 2 is $2\binom{n-2}{k-1}$. Therefore, the relative support is $2\binom{n-2}{k-1}/\binom{n}{k} = \frac{2k(n-k)}{n(n-1)}$.

Using Theorem 3.1 we get two-query locally decodable codes $[n-1, \binom{n}{k}]$ with soundness $2\frac{k}{n}\frac{n-k}{n-1}$. This example shows that the parameters of the LDC depends not only on the representation it defines but also on the space in which we embed it into.

3.2 Embedding to the Regular Representation

Theorem 3.1 shows that in order to construct an LDC it is sufficient to do two things: First, construct an irreducible representation with a sparse rank one element. Second, embed it into a permutational representation such that the second condition of the theorem is satisfied. In this subsection we show that we can always embed any representation into the regular representation in a way that satisfies the second condition of the theorem.

LEMMA 3.3. *Let V be a vector space over a field $\mathbb{F}$. Then for every irreducible representation (ρ, V) and for every $v \in V$, $v \neq 0$ there exist a homomorphism $\mathcal{C} : V \to \mathbb{F}[G]$ of representations (ρ, V) and the regular representation in $\mathbb{F}[G]$ such that $supp(\mathcal{C}(v)) \geq |G|(1 - \frac{1}{|\mathbb{F}|})$.*

PROOF. We view $\mathbb{F}[G]$ as a left representation of G. That is, $\tau(g)(f) = g * f$. For any $u \in V^*$ let us define a mapping $T_u : V \to \mathbb{F}[G]$ by:

$$T_u(x) = \sum_{g \in G} (\bar{\rho}(g)u(x))g. \quad (3.2)$$

We claim that T_u is an homomorphism from the representation (ρ, V) to regular representation $\mathbb{F}[G]$. Indeed:

$$T_u(\rho(h)x) = \sum_{g \in G} \bar{\rho}(g)u(\rho(h)x)g = h * \sum_{g \in G} u(\rho(g^{-1}h)x)h^{-1}g.$$

Substituting $g = h^{-1}g$ we get

$$T_u(\rho(h)x) = h * \sum_{g \in G} u(\rho(g^{-1})x)g = \tau(h)T_u(x).$$

Now we want to show that for some $u \in V^*$ vector $T_u(v)$ has large support. Consider the set $U = \{T_u(v) : u \in V^*\}$. It is easy to see that it is a linear subspace of $\mathbb{F}[G]$ and that it have full support. From Lemma 2.5 it follows that there exists a vector with support at least $|G|(1 - \frac{1}{|\mathbb{F}|})$. Therefore, exist an u such that T_u is a G-homomorphism such that $T_u(v)$ has desired support. □

Note that when $\mathbb{F}$ is infinite field then we can get full support and all algebraically closed fields are infinite. As a corollary the last lemma we get Theorem 1.1.

COROLLARY 3.4 (THEOREM 1.1). *Let V be a vector space over an algebraically closed field $\mathbb{F}$. Let G be a finite group and let (ρ, V) be an irreducible representation of G. Let $D \in \mathbb{F}[G]$ be an element of group algebra of sparsity q such* *that* $\mathrm{Rank}(\rho(D)) = 1$. *Then there exist locally* $(q, \delta, q\delta)$ *decodable code* $\mathcal{C} : V \to \mathbb{F}^G$.

Assume that we have $(\rho, V), D \in \mathbb{F}[G]$ which satisfies the first condition of Theorem 3.1. Then from the corollary above it follows that we can embed (ρ, V) to the regular representation in a way that satisfies the second condition. A natural question to ask is can we embed it to a smaller permutational representation. The next lemma gives characterization of all such permutational representations.

LEMMA 3.5. *Let* $(\rho, V), D \in \mathbb{F}[G]$ *which satisfies the first condition of Theorem 3.1. Let* $v \in \mathrm{Im}\,\rho(D)$ *a non-zero vector and* $H < G$ *is any subgroup of* G. *Assume that exist* $u \in V^*$ *such that* $\rho(h)u = u$ *for every* $h \in H$ *and* $|\{g \in G/H : u(\rho(g)v) \neq 0\}| \geq c|G/H|$ *then there exist* G*-homomorphism* $C : V \to \mathbb{F}^X$, *where* $X = G/H$, *such that* $supp(C(v)) \geq c|X|$, *i.e., it satisfies the second condition of Theorem 3.1.*

PROOF. Consider a subspace L_H of the regular representation $\mathbb{F}^G$ of functions constant on cosets of H, i.e., $L_H = \{f \in \mathbb{F}^G : \forall g \in G, \forall h \in H, f(gh) = f(g)\}$. It is easy to see that L_H is a sub-representation of the regular representation isomorphic to the permutational representation $\mathbb{F}^X$, where $X = G/H$. Let T_u be an embedding as in proof of Lemma 3.3 defined by Equation 3.2. Note that since $Hu = u$ for every $x \in V, h \in H_u$ it holds that $T_u(x)[g] = T_u(x)[gh]$, i.e., $T_u(x) \in L_H$. Therefore T_u is an embedding to the permutational representation $\mathbb{F}^X$, where $X = G/H_u$. From the definition of T_u it follows that the support of $T_u(v)$ is exactly $|\{g \in G/H_u : u(\rho(g)v) \neq 0\}|$. $\square$

REMARK 3.6. *It could be shown that any embedding satisfying second condition of Theorem 3.1 could be decribed by Lemma 3.5.*

3.3 Alphabet Reduction

In this section we show that we can transform codes over any algebraic extension of $\mathbb{F}_p$ to codes over $\mathbb{F}_p$. The reduction which we give here adapts the reduction from [1] to our settings.

THEOREM 3.7. *Let* $\mathbb{F}$ *be a field of characteristic* p *and let* $\mathcal{C} : \mathbb{F}^k \to \mathbb{F}^X$ *be a* $(q, \delta, \frac{q\delta}{c})$*-LDC as in Theorem 3.1. Then there exist a code* $\tilde{\mathcal{C}} : \mathbb{F}_p \to \mathbb{F}_p^{X \times [q]}$ *which is* $(q, \delta, \frac{p}{p-1}\frac{q\delta}{c})$*-LDC.*

PROOF. First let us rescale the basis so that we will have the same decoding vector for every message symbol. Let v be any vector in $\mathrm{Im}(\rho(D))$. Set $y = \mathcal{C}(v)$. Recall that in the proof of Theorem 3.1 we have showed that $\mathcal{C}(\rho(D_i)b_i) = \lambda_i y$. We can replace b_i with $\lambda_i^{-1}b_i$ so that $\mathcal{C}(\rho(D_i)b_i) = y$. It follows from the assumption that y has support $c|X|$. For a linear functional $\ell : \mathbb{F} \to \mathbb{F}_p$, we denote by $\ell(y)$ vector achieved by applying ℓ on each coordinate of y. From standard random argument there exists a linear functional ℓ such that support of $\ell(y)$ is at least $\frac{p-1}{p}c|X|$. Let us fix such an ℓ. Let $D = \sum_{i=1}^{q} c_i g_i \in \mathbb{F}[G]$ be a rank one element. Let us define $\tilde{\mathcal{C}}$ by $\tilde{\mathcal{C}}(m)[x, i] = \ell(c_i\mathcal{C}(m)[x])$. We need to show that this is an LDC. Let us describe the decoding algorithm:

Input: An oracle access to $w \in \mathbb{F}^X$ and bit index i. Let $D_i = D * h_i = \sum_{j=1}^{q} c_j \cdot g_j h_i$ be where $h_i \in G$ is a group element as in Lemma 3.2.

1. Set $y = \mathcal{C}(\rho(D_i)b_i) \in \mathbb{F}^X$. Pick r at random from the support of $\ell(y)$.
2. For $j = 1, \ldots, q$ query w at location: $((g_j h_i)^{-1} \cdot r, j)$.
3. Calculate $\tilde{n}_i = \sum_{j=1}^{q} w[(g_j h_i)^{-1} \cdot r, j]$.
4. Return $m_i = \ell(y[r])^{-1}\tilde{n}_i$.

Now let us show that this decoding algorithm returns the correct answer when it receives an uncorrupted codeword. If $w = \tilde{\mathcal{C}}(m)$, then

$$\tilde{n}_i = \ell(\sum_{j=1}^{q} c_j \mathcal{C}((g_j h_i)^{-1} r)) = \ell(\tau(D_i)\mathcal{C}(m)[r]).$$

Recall that from Equation 3.1 it follows that $\tau(D_i)\mathcal{C}(m)[r] = m_i y[r]$. Thus we get that $\tilde{n}_i = m_i \ell(y[r])$. Thus, the decoding algorithm returns the correct answer on line 4 on an uncorrupted codeword.

Now let us prove that if $\tilde{\mathcal{C}}(m)$ is corrupted in at most δ coordinates, then the decoder reads a corrupted place with probability at most $\frac{p}{p-1}\frac{q\delta}{c}$. Let us call the coordinates of type (x, i) the ith block. Let δ_i proportion of coordinates i^{th} block which are corrupted, and notice that $\sum \delta_i = q\delta$. Note that i^{th} query is distributed uniformly over $\frac{p-1}{p}c$ fraction of coordinates of the ith block. Therefore, the probability that i^{th} coordinate is corrupted is $\frac{p}{p-1}\frac{\delta_i}{c}$. Thus by union bound we get that at least one of the coordinates is corrupted with probability at most $\sum \frac{p}{p-1}\frac{\delta_i}{c} = \frac{p}{p-1}\frac{q\delta}{c}$. $\square$

We have the following corollary from this theorem and Theorem 1.1.

COROLLARY 3.8. *Let* $\mathbb{F}$ *be a field of characteristic* p. *Let* G *be a finite group and let* (ρ, V) *be an irreducible representation of* G *and let* $k = \dim V$. *Let* $D \in \mathbb{F}[G]$ *be an element of group algebra of sparsity* q *such that* $\mathrm{Rank}(\rho(D)) = 1$. *Then there exist* $(q, \delta, \frac{p}{p-1}q\delta)$*-LDC* $\mathcal{C} : \mathbb{F}_p^k \to \mathbb{F}_p^{G \times [q]}$.

4. MATCHING VECTOR CODES AND ABELIAN INVARIANT CODES

In the next two sections we show that there exists irreducible representations such that Theorem 3.1 gives codes matching the parameters of [1]. We show that the codes constructed in [1] could be interpreted as a construction of an irreducible representation.

In this section we show that if MV is an orbit of a group H then one can construct from such MV an irreducible representation with a sparse element in the group algebra of rank one. In the next section, we show that the variant of the Grolmusz's [4] construction described in [1],[5] is MV that is an orbit of the symmetric group.

Let A be an Abelian group. Recall that *the dual group* A^* is the set of all group homomorphisms $v : A \to \mathbb{Z}_m$, where m is the order of the group. In this paper it will be more convenient for us to work with the following generalization of MV to any Abelian group:

DEFINITION 4.1. *Let* A *be an Abelian group. Let* m *be the order of* A. *For any set* $S \subset \mathbb{Z}_m - \{0\}$ *the families* $\mathcal{U} = \{u_i\}_{i=1}^{k} \subset A, \mathcal{V} = \{v_i\}_{i=1}^{k} \subset A^*$ *are* S-Matching Vectors(MV) *if the following conditions hold:*

1. $v_j(u_i) \in S$ *for every* $i \neq j$.

[5]Using the same ideas it is also possible to prove the statement for Grolmusz's construction.

2. $v_i(u_i) = 0$ *for every* $i \in [k]$.

Note that if $A = \mathbb{Z}_m^h$ using the isomorphism $\psi : A \to A^*$ given by $\psi(v)(x) = \langle v, x\rangle$ we get the standard definition of MV.

In this section we assume that the characteristics of $\mathbb{F}$ is co-prime to m and that there exists $\gamma \in \mathbb{F}^*$ an element of order m, i.e., $\gamma^m = 1$ and $\gamma^i \neq 1$ for $0 < i < m$. Then for any $v \in A^*$ we denote by γ^v the function from A to $\mathbb{F}$ defined by $\gamma^v(a) = \gamma^{v(a)}$. Let H be any *group that acts on the group* A. (Recall Definition 2.5 of an action of a group on a group.) In this case H also acts on A^*, where an action is given by the rule: $(h \cdot v)(x) = v(h^{-1} \cdot x)$. The group $G = A \rtimes H$ by Definition 2.6 acts on the set A. Let $(\tau, \mathbb{F}^A)$ be the corresponding permutational representation of G.

Definition 4.2. *A polynomial* $p(x) \in \mathbb{F}[x]$ *is* S*-decoding if* $p(\gamma^s) = 0$ *for all* $s \in S$ *and* $p(1) = 1$.

The goal of this section is to prove the following theorem:

Theorem 4.1. *Let* $\mathcal{U}, \mathcal{V}$ *be* S*-Matching Vectors such that* $\mathcal{V}$ *is an orbit of* H. *Let* $p(x)$ *be an* S*-decoding polynomial of sparsity* q. *Then there exists an irreducible representation* (ρ, L), *a permutational representation* $(\tau, \mathbb{F}^A)$ *of* $G = A \rtimes H$ *and* $D = \sum_{i=1}^{q} c_i g_i$ *which satisfy the conditions of Theorem 3.1 with* $c = 1, \dim L = |\mathcal{V}|$.

Proof. First we need to construct a representations (L, ρ). We do it in next two lemmas.

Lemma 4.2. *For any* $\mathcal{V} \subset A^*$, *the vector space* $L \subset \mathbb{F}^A$ *defined by*

$$L = \mathrm{Span}\{\gamma^v : v \in \mathcal{V}\} \subset \mathbb{F}^A \quad (4.1)$$

is a sub-representation of the regular representation of group A *of dimension* $|\mathcal{V}|$.

Proof. First let us show that L is closed under action of A. For any $v \in A^*$ it holds that:

$$\gamma^v(a+b) = \gamma^{v(a+b)} = \gamma^{v(a)+v(b)} = \gamma^v(a)\gamma^v(b).$$

Thus γ^v is a one-dimensional sub-representation of the regular representation of the group A. Therefore, L is a sub-representation. Note that for $v_1 \neq v_2$, the representations γ^{v_1} and γ^{v_2} are non isomorphic one-dimensional sub- representations. Therefore, from Lemma 2.4 it follows that $\{\gamma^v\}_{v\in\mathcal{V}}$ are linearly independent vectors. Thus the dimension of L is $|\mathcal{V}|$. $\square$

Lemma 4.3. *For any* $\mathcal{V} \subset A^*$ *closed under action of* H *it holds that the vector space* L *defined by Equation 4.1 is a sub-representation of the permutational representation* $(\tau, \mathbb{F}^A)$ *of the group* $G = A \rtimes H$.

Proof. Let $v \in A^*$ and consider the vector $\gamma^v \in \mathbb{F}^A$. Then for $h \in H$ it holds that

$$(\tau(h)\gamma^v)(x) = \gamma^{v(h^{-1}x)} = \gamma^{h\cdot v}(x) \ .$$

Thus if $\mathcal{V}$ is closed under the action of H then the vector space L is closed under the action of $\tau(h)$ for $h \in H$. Since L is a representation of A, it is also closed under the action of $\tau(a)$ for $a \in A$. Since H and A generate G, the space L is a sub-representation of $(\tau, \mathbb{F}^A)$. $\square$

Let us denote this sub-representation by (ρ, L) and by $\mathcal{C} : L \to \mathbb{F}^A$ its embedding into $\mathbb{F}^A$. Note that $\dim L = |\mathcal{V}|$.

Lemma 4.4. *If* H *acts transitively on* $\mathcal{V}$ *then the representation* (ρ, L) *of* G *is irreducible.*

Proof. Assume that $\tilde{L} \subset L$ is a non-zero sub- representation of L. In order to prove that (ρ, L) is an irreducible representation we need to prove that $\tilde{L} = L$. Now let us look on L and $\tilde{L}$ as a representations of the group A. Then $L = \oplus_{v\in\mathcal{V}}\gamma^v$ is a direct sum of non-isomorphic irreducible representations. Therefore there exists some subset $\tilde{\mathcal{V}} \subset \mathcal{V}$ such that $\tilde{L} = \oplus_{v\in\tilde{\mathcal{V}}}\gamma^v$. In particular for some $v \in \mathcal{V}$ it holds that $\gamma^v \in \tilde{L}$. Since H acts transitively on $\mathcal{V}$ for every $v' \in \mathcal{V}$ there exists $h \in H$ such that $h \cdot v = v'$. Thus it holds that

$$\tau(h)\gamma^v = \gamma^{h\cdot v} = \gamma^{v'} \ .$$

Therefore, we proved that:

$$L = \mathrm{Span}\{\gamma^v : v \in \mathcal{V}\} \subset \tilde{L} \subset L.$$

Thus $\tilde{L} = L$. $\square$

Let $p(x) = \sum_{i=1}^{q} c_i x^{t_i}$ be the given S-decoding polynomial. We define D as $D = \sum_{i=1}^{q} c_i(-t_i u_1)$, where we think of $-t_i u_1$ as an element of G. We claim that $\mathrm{Rank}\,\rho(D) = 1$.

Note that the set $\{\gamma^{v_i}\}_{i=1}^{k}$ forms a basis of L. Let us show that $\rho(D)\gamma^{v_i} = 0$ for $i \neq 1$ and $\rho(D)\gamma^{v_1} = \gamma^{v_1}$. Indeed:

$$\begin{aligned}\rho(D)\gamma^{v_i} &= \sum c_i\rho(-t_i u_1)\gamma^{v_i} = \gamma^{v_i}\sum c_i\gamma^{v_i(t_i u_1)} \\ &= \gamma^{v_i}\sum c_i(\gamma^{v_i(u_1)})^{t_i} = \gamma^{v_i}p(\gamma^{v_i(u_1)}).\end{aligned}$$

Since $v_i(u_1) \in S$ for all $i \neq 1$ it follows that $p(\gamma^{v_i(u_1)}) = p(\gamma^s)$ for some $s \in S$ and since p is an S-decoding polynomial it is equal to 0. Thus $\rho(D)\gamma^{v_i} = 0$ for $i \neq 1$ and for $i = 1$

Note that for natural embedding of $\mathcal{C} : L \to \mathbb{F}^A$ it holds that $\mathrm{Im}\,\mathcal{C}(\rho(D)) = \mathrm{Span}\{\gamma^{v_1}\}$ has full support. Therefore, smoothness constant c in Theorem 3.1 is 1.

Remark 4.5. *The representation of* (ρ, L) *defined in the proof is:* $\mathrm{Ind}_{A\rtimes F}^{G}\gamma^v$, *where* v *is any element in* $\mathcal{V}$ *and* $F = \{h \in H : h \cdot v = v\}$ *be a subgroup of* H.

Note that in the proof of the above theorem we used only one element u_1 of $\mathcal{U}$. The following lemma shows that if $\mathcal{V}$ is an orbit of some group and "matching" one element then we can construct $\mathcal{U}$ to be orbit of the same group such that $\mathcal{U}, \mathcal{V}$ are Matching Vectors.

Lemma 4.6. *Let* $\mathcal{V} = \{h_i \cdot v\}_{i=1}^{k} \subset A^*$ *be an orbit of* H *such that for some* $u \in A$ *it holds that* $h_1 v(u) = 0$ *and* $h_i v(u) \in S$ *for* $i \neq 1$. *Then the family* $\mathcal{U} = \{h_i u\}_{i=1}^{k}, \mathcal{V} = \{h_i \cdot v\}_{i=1}^{k}$ *is a family of* S*-Matching Vectors.*

Proof. First note that $h_i v(h_i u) = h_i^{-1}h_i v(u) = v(u) = 0$. Next for $i \neq j$ it holds that $h_i v(h_j u) = h_j^{-1}h_i v(u)$. Since $\mathcal{V}$ is an orbit there exist k such that $h_j^{-1}h_i v = h_k v$, $k \neq 1$ since $i \neq j$. Therefore $h_i v(h_j u) = h_k(u) \in S$. $\square$

5. SYMMETRY & MATCHING VECTORS

The goal of this section is to show that the variant of the Grolmusz's [4] construction described in [1] is *symmetric* MV that is an orbit of the symmetric group (let us call it H). The construction from [1] starts from the base construction with $S = \mathbb{Z}_m - \{0\}$ and next it reduces the size of S using the tensor power. In order to show that this construction is an orbit of H, we observe that the base construction is an orbit of H. Next we define an action of H on the tensor power of group such that the tensor power of orbit of H remains an orbit of H. For the sake of completeness, we review here the variant of the Grolmusz's [4] construction.

Let us define a tensor product and action of group on it.

Tensor Product.

DEFINITION 5.1. *Let A, B be Abelian groups. Then tensor product of A and B, denoted by $A \otimes B$, is an Abelian group generated by $\{a \otimes b : a \in A, b \in B\}$ with relations*

$$\begin{aligned}(a_1 + a_2) \otimes b_1 &= a_1 \otimes b_1 + a_2 \otimes b_1 \\ a_1 \otimes (b_1 + b_2) &= a_1 \otimes b_1 + a_1 \otimes b_2\end{aligned}$$

for every a_1, a_2, b_1, b_2.

For example, if $A = \mathbb{Z}_m^h$, then $A \otimes A = \mathbb{Z}_m^{h^2}$. There exist a canonical isomorphism between $A^* \otimes B^*$ and $(A \otimes B)^*$. For $v_1 \in A^*, v_2 \in B^*$ we define a mapping on the generators by: $v_1 \otimes v_2(u_1 \otimes u_2) = v_1(u_1)v_2(u_2)$ for every u_1, u_2 and extend it by linearity.

If some group H acts on the groups A and B, then we can define an action of H on generators of $A \otimes B$ by the rule $h \cdot (a \otimes b) = (h \cdot a) \otimes (h \cdot b)$ and extend it by linearity. The tensor power $A^{\otimes k}$ is just tensor product of A with itself k times. Consider the mapping $P^k : A \to A^{\otimes k}$ defined by:

$$P^k(u) = \underbrace{u \otimes u \otimes \ldots \otimes u}_{k \text{ times}} .$$

From the definition of action on tensor product it follows that

$$P^k(h \cdot u) = h \cdot P^k(u) . \tag{5.1}$$

Thus if $\mathcal{U}$ is an orbit of H then $P^k(\mathcal{U})$ is also an orbit of H. For $v \in A^*, u \in A$ it holds that

$$P^k(v)(P^k(u)) = v(u)^k . \tag{5.2}$$

THEOREM 5.1. *For every integer $k > 0$ there exists an integer $m = p_1p_2$ and a set $S = \{p_1, p_2, p_1 + p_2\} \subset \mathbb{Z}_m$ and families $\mathcal{U} \subset A, \mathcal{V} \subset A^*$ of S-Matching Vectors, where $\mathcal{U}, \mathcal{V}$ are orbits of the symmetric group, such that $|\mathcal{V}| \geq k$ and $|A| \leq \exp\exp(O(\sqrt{\log k \log\log k}))$.*

PROOF. We start from the base construction of MV and show that this construction is an orbit of a symmetric group. Next we make transformations on this construction and we show that such transformation maps orbit to orbit.

Base Construction.

In the base construction $B = \mathbb{Z}_m^h$ and each subset of size $m - 1$ of $[h]$ we set u_i to be its indicator. Set $v_i(x) = \langle x, u_i \rangle$. It is easy to see $v_i(u_i) = m - 1$ and $v_i(u_j) \neq m - 1$ for $j \neq i$. Let $H = S_h$ act on $\mathbb{Z}_m^h$ by permuting its coordinates. Then it is easy to see that $\mathcal{U}$ and $\mathcal{V}$ are orbits of S_h. For sake of simplicity let us add one additional coordinate to B so that $B = \mathbb{Z}_m^{h+1}$ and set all u_i, v_i to be one on this coordinate. Now we have that $v_i(u_i) = 0$ and $v_i(u_j) \neq 0$. Thus $\mathcal{U} = \{u_i\}, \mathcal{V} = \{v_i\}$ are S-MV, where $S = \mathbb{Z}_m - \{0\}$.

Reducing size of S:.

Let us assume that $m = p_1p_2$ where p_1, p_2 are primes. Now assume that $\mathcal{U}, \mathcal{V}$ be any S-MV with $S = \mathbb{Z}_m - \{0\}$. Let us show how to reduce size of S to 3. Let us set the Abelian group $A = B^{\otimes p_1 - 1} \oplus B^{\otimes p_2 - 1}$. Consider a mapping $R : B \to A$ defined by:

$$R(u) = \left(p_2 P^{p_1 - 1}(u), p_1 P^{p_2 - 1}(u)\right) .$$

In the same way let us define R on dual group by:

$$R^*(v) = \left(P^{p_1 - 1}(v), P^{p_2 - 1}(v)\right) .$$

Let us define action of H on the direct sum coordinate-wise i.e., $h \cdot (a, b) = (h \cdot a, h \cdot b)$. From Equation 5.1 it follows that $h \cdot R^*(v) = R^*(h \cdot v)$. Thus it holds that if $\mathcal{V}$ is the orbit of group H then $R^*(\mathcal{V})$ is also the orbit of H. Therefore we proved that:

LEMMA 5.2. *The mapping R, R^* maps orbits to orbits.*

From this lemma it follows that if we apply R, R^* on the base construction we get orbit of the symmetric group. The rest of the proof shows that for suitable choice of parameters this will give us parameters as in the theorem.

First let us show that $S = \{p_1, p_2, p_1 + p_2\}$. From the Equation 5.2 it follows that for any $u \in B, v \in B^*$ it holds that:

$$R^*(v)(R(u)) = p_2 v(u)^{p-1} + p_1 v(u)^{p_2 - 1} = f(v(u)) ,$$

where $f(x) = p_2 x^{p_1 - 1} + p_1 x^{p_2 - 1}$.

CLAIM 5.3. *$f(x) \in \{p_1, p_2, p_1 + p_2\}$ for $x \neq 0$ and $f(0) =$ 0.*

PROOF. For $x = 0$ the claim is trivial. Let $x \neq 0$. Then $f(x) \mod p_1 = p_2 x^{p_1 - 1}$. If $x = 0 \mod p_1$ then $f(x) = 0 \mod p_1$. From Fermat little theorem it follows that $f(x) = p_2 \mod p_1$ if $x \neq 0 \mod p_1$. Thus $f(x) \in \{0, p_2\} \mod p_1$. The same holds modulo p_2. Thus from Chines Reminder Theorem it follows that $f(x) \in \{0, p_1, p_2, p_1 + p_2\}$. Note that $f(x) = 0$ implies that $x = 0$. □

Therefore, $R(\mathcal{U}), R^*(\mathcal{V})$ (where $\mathcal{U}, \mathcal{V}$ is the base construction) are S-Matching Vectors with $S = \{p_1, p_2, p_1 + p_2\}$.

Setting Parameters.

Let us take $p_1 \approx p_2 = O(\sqrt{m})$ and $h = m^2$. Then $|\mathcal{V}| = \binom{h}{m-1} = \exp(O(m \log m))$ and $|A| = m^{h^{p_1 - 1}} + m^{h^{p_2 - 1}} = \exp\exp(\sqrt{m} \log m)$. Note that $\log |\mathcal{V}| = O(m \log m)$. Therefore

$$|A| = \exp\exp(O(\sqrt{\log |\mathcal{V}| \log\log |\mathcal{V}|}))$$

6. IS IRREDUCIBILITY ESSENTIAL?

Representation theory when characteristic of the field divides the size of the group called modular representation theory. Modular representation theory is very different from non-modular case. In this section we ask the question does irreducibility in Theorem 3.1 essential. We show that in non-modular case the answer is Yes[6]. We show that in modular case we can construct reducible representation which will

[6]In fact we show that the representation should be indecomposable. In non-modular case all indecomposable representations are irreducible.

lead to LDC. Thus we can see Theorem 6.1 as a generalization of the Theorem 3.1 to modular representation theory.

It may happen that some representation is irreducible over field $\mathbb{F}$, but reducible over algebraic closure of $\mathbb{F}$. Representations which are irreducible over algebraic closure of $\mathbb{F}$ called completely irreducible. Although for the proof of the Theorem 3.1 we do not need complete irreducibility we show that in order to have rank one element complete irreducibility is essential for non-modular representations.

In the proof of Theorem 3.1, the only reason why we need the fact that (ρ, V) is irreducible is to show that the orbit of u spans all the dual space. Therefore, we can make the following generalization of Theorem 3.1:

THEOREM 6.1. *Let G be a finite group. Let (ρ, V) be any representation of G ,$(\tau, \mathbb{F}^X)$ be a permutational representation of G. Let $\mathcal{C} : V \to \mathbb{F}^X$ be a G-embedding. Assume that the following conditions hold:*

1. (a) *There exists a q-sparse element $D \in \mathbb{F}[G]$, $D = \sum_{i=1}^{q} c_i g_i$ such that $\mathrm{Rank}(\rho(D)) = 1$.*
   (b) *Let $u \in V^*$ be a non-zero linear functional such that $\mathrm{Ker}\, u = \mathrm{Ker}\, \rho(D)$. Then the set $\{\bar{\rho}(g)u | g \in G\}$ spans V^*.*
2. *$\mathrm{Im}(\mathcal{C} \circ \rho(D))$ has a support $c|X|$.*

Then there exists a basis $b_1, \ldots, b_k$ for V such that $\mathcal{C}(\sum(m_i b_i))$ is $(q, \delta, \frac{q\delta}{c})$-LDC.

From Lemma 2.3 it follows that irreducibility of the representation (ρ, V) implies Condition 1b of this theorem. Here we show that if characteristics of the field $\mathbb{F}$ is does not divides $|G|$ then the converse is also true, i.e., if u spans dual space V^* then (ρ, V) is irreducible.

6.1 Yes!

THEOREM 6.2. *Let V be a vector space over an algebraically closed field $\mathbb{F}$ of characteristic which does not divides $|G|$. Let ρ be a representation of group G in the vector space V. Let $f \in \mathbb{F}[G]$ such that $\mathrm{Rank}\, \rho(f) = 1$. Let $u \in V^*$ such that $\mathrm{Ker}\, u = \mathrm{Ker}\, \rho(f)$. If $V^* = \mathrm{Span}\{\bar{\rho}(g)u | g \in G\}$, then V is an irreducible representation.*

PROOF. Let us assume by contradiction that V is reducible. Then from Theorem 2.2 it follows that $V = V_1 \oplus V_2$. This mean that in basis of V_1 and V_2 for every $g \in G$ the matrix $\rho(g)$ is of form

$$\rho(g) = \begin{pmatrix} \rho_1(g) & 0 \\ 0 & \rho_2(g) \end{pmatrix} ,$$

where ρ_1, ρ_2 restrictions of ρ to V_1, V_2. Therefore $\rho(f) = \sum a_i \rho(g_i)$ is of form

$$\rho(f) = \begin{pmatrix} A & 0 \\ 0 & B \end{pmatrix} .$$

But this matrix may be of rank one only if A or B is zero. Let us assume w.l.g. that B is zero. But then $V_2 \subset \mathrm{Ker}\, \rho(f)$. Therefore it holds that $u(V_2) = 0$. Since V_2 is invariant space, it also holds that $\bar{\rho}(g)u(V_2) = 0$. Since $\bar{\rho}(g)u$ span V^*, it must be that $V_2 = 0$. ☐

If V is a vector space over some field $\mathbb{F}$, then $\mathrm{Rank}\, \rho(f) = 1$ also over algebraic closure of $\mathbb{F}$ and thus (ρ, V) should be irreducible not just over $\mathbb{F}$, but also over the algebraic closure of $\mathbb{F}$.

6.2 No!

Let us now give an example of reducible representations (ρ, V) when vector u spans all the dual space. Of course in this example characteristics of $\mathbb{F}$ divides $|G|$. This example is a well know Reed-Muller Code. Let $\mathbb{F}$ be a field of characteristic $p \geq d$. Let us consider the group G of affine transformations over $\mathbb{F}_p^k$, i.e., $G = \{A\vec{x} + b : A \in \mathrm{GL}(p, k), b \in \mathbb{F}_p^k\}$. Let us set $X = \mathbb{F}_p^k$ and $(\tau, \mathbb{F}^X)$ be corresponding permutational representation of G. Let $\mathrm{RM}(d, k) \subset \mathbb{F}^X$ be a vector space of polynomials of total degree at most d with coefficients in $\mathbb{F}$. It is easy to verify that $\mathrm{RM}(d, k)$ is invariant under permutations of G. Thus $\mathrm{RM}(d, k)$ is a sub-representation of $\mathbb{F}^X$. Let us denote it by $(\rho, \mathrm{RM}(d, k))$. Let const $\subset \mathrm{RM}(d, k)$ be a subspace of constant functions. Note that const is a sub-representation of V. Thus $\mathrm{RM}(d, k)$ is reducible. Let us pick $\lambda \neq 1 \in \mathbb{F}_p$ be a generator of the $\mathbb{F}_p^*$. Let $m_\lambda \in G$ be a permutation $\vec{x} \mapsto \lambda\vec{x}$.

LEMMA 6.3. *There exists $c_0, c_2, \ldots, c_d$ such that the following holds: Let $D = \sum c_i m_\lambda^i \in \mathbb{F}[G]$ then the mapping $\rho(D)$ is of rank one and given a polynomial $p \in \mathbb{F}^X$ the mapping $\rho(D)$ returns a constant function $p(\vec{0})$.*

PROOF. Let us consider how $\rho(m_\lambda)$ acts on p. Let $p = \sum_{j=0}^{d} p_j$, where p_j is a homogeneous part of p of degree j. Then it holds that

$$\rho(m_\lambda)p(x) = p(\lambda^{-1}x) = \sum_{j=0}^{d} \lambda^{-j} p_j(x) .$$

In the same way it for every i it also holds that

$$\rho(m_\lambda^i)p(x) = p(\lambda^{-i}x) = \sum_{j=0}^{d} \lambda^{-ij} p_j(x) . \tag{6.1}$$

Let $V[i, j] = \lambda^{-ij}$ be a Vandermonde matrix. For vector $\vec{c} = (c_0, c_2, \ldots, c_d)$ let $a = (a_0, \ldots a_d) = V \cdot \vec{c}$. Then from Equation 6.1 it follows that:

$$\rho(\sum_{i=0}^{d} c_i m_\lambda^i)p = \sum_{i=0}^{d} a_i p_i . \tag{6.2}$$

Note that V is invertible matrix. Thus we can choose $\vec{c}$ such that $V \cdot \vec{c} = (1, 0, \ldots, 0)$. Substituting this $\vec{c}$ in Equation 6.2 we get:

$$\rho(\sum_{i=0}^{d} c_i m_\lambda^i) = p_0 .$$

But p_0 is a constant term of p which exactly equal to $p(\vec{0})$. ☐

Now consider a linear functional $u : \mathrm{RM}(d, k) \to \mathbb{F}$ given by $u(p) = p(\vec{0})$. Then definitely it holds that $\mathrm{Ker}\, u = \mathrm{Ker}\, \rho(D)$.

LEMMA 6.4. *Then the set $\{\bar{\rho}(g)u | g \in G\}$ spans the dual space of $\mathrm{RM}(d, k)$.*

PROOF. Note that linear functionals $u_1, u_2, \ldots, u_k$ span the dual space iff $\cap_{i=1}^{k} \mathrm{Ker}\, u_i = 0$. For $b \in \mathbb{F}_p^k$ let $g_b \in G$ be a permutation $x \mapsto x + b$. Let us show that:

$$\cap_{b \in \mathbb{F}_p^k} \mathrm{Ker}\, g_b u = 0 .$$

Indeed $g_b u(p) = p(b)$. Thus if $p \in \cap_{b \in \mathbb{F}_p^k} \mathrm{Ker}\, g_b u$ then $p(b) = 0$ for every $b \in \mathbb{F}_p^k$. Thus it must be that $p = 0$. ☐

Acknowledgements

I am grateful to Amnon Ta-Shma and Oded Regev for many helpful, in-depth discussions and for helpful comments on this paper. I want to thank to Dmitry Gourevitch, Venkatesan Guruswami, Alex Lubotzky, Zeev Rudnik , Avi Wigderson, and Chris Umans for very helpful conversions. I also want to thank to my wife Rivka for editing this paper for grammar mistakes.

7. REFERENCES

[1] K. Efremenko. 3-query locally decodable codes of subexponential length. In *STOC*, pages 39–44, 2009.

[2] W. I. Gasarch. A survey on private information retrieval (column: Computational complexity). *Bulletin of the EATCS*, 82:72–107, 2004.

[3] O. Goldreich, H. J. Karloff, L. J. Schulman, and L. Trevisan. Lower bounds for linear locally decodable codes and private information retrieval. In *IEEE Conference on Computational Complexity*, pages 175–183, 2002.

[4] V. Grolmusz. Superpolynomial size set-systems with restricted intersections mod 6 and explicit ramsey graphs. *Combinatorica*, 20(1):71–86, 2000.

[5] T. Itoh and Y. Suzuki. New constructions for query-efficient locally decodable codes of subexponential length. *CoRR*, abs/0810.4576, 2008.

[6] J. Katz and L. Trevisan. On the efficiency of local decoding procedures for error-correcting codes. In *STOC*, pages 80–86, 2000.

[7] I. Kerenidis and R. de Wolf. Exponential lower bound for 2-query locally decodable codes via a quantum argument. In *STOC*, pages 106–115, 2003.

[8] S. Kopparty, S. Saraf, and S. Yekhanin. High-rate codes with sublinear-time decoding. In *STOC*, pages 167–176, 2011.

[9] Y. Meng Chee, T. Feng, S. Ling, H. Wang, and L. F. Zhang. Query-Efficient Locally Decodable Codes of Subexponential Length. *ArXiv e-prints*, Aug. 2010.

[10] J. P. Serre. *Linear representations of finite groups / Jean-Pierre Serre ; translated from the French by Leonard L. Scott.* Springer-Verlag, New York :, 1977.

[11] L. Trevisan. Some applications of coding theory in computational complexity. Technical Report 043, Electronic Colloquium on Computational Complexity (ECCC), 2004.

[12] D. Woodruff. New lower bounds for general locally decodable codes. *Electronic Colloquium on Computational Complexity (ECCC)*, 2007.

[13] S. Yekhanin. Towards 3-query locally decodable codes of subexponential length. *J. ACM*, 55(1), 2008.

[14] S. Yekhanin. Locally decodable codes. *Foundations and trends in theoretical computer science*, 2010.

APPENDIX

A. G-INVARIANT CODES AND REPRESENTATIONS OF G

In this section we show tight connections between linear G-invariant codes and the representations of the group G. We show that there exists a one-to-one correspondence between sub-representations of the permutational representations and G-invariant codes. Furthermore we can define a representation in the message space so that the code becomes a G-homomorphism.

Let us first define G-invariant codes:

Definition A.1. *Let G be a group acting on a set $X = \{x_i\}_{i=1}^n$. Let $\mathcal{C} : \mathbb{F}^k \to \mathbb{F}^X$ be a code. We say $\mathcal{C}$ is G-invariant iff for every $c = (c_{x_1}, c_{x_2}, \dots, c_{x_n}) \in \mathrm{Im}(\mathcal{C})$, and for every $g \in G$ it holds that*

$$g \cdot c = (c_{g^{-1} \cdot x_1}, c_{g^{-1} \cdot x_2}, \dots, c_{g^{-1} \cdot x_n}) \in \mathrm{Im}(\mathcal{C}) .$$

The action of G on X defines a permutational representation $(\tau, \mathbb{F}^X)$ of G (see Equation 2.2). We claim that there is a one to one correspondence between linear G-invariant codes and sub-representations of $(\tau, \mathbb{F}^X)$.

Lemma A.1. *Let G be a group that acts on the set X. Let $(\tau, \mathbb{F}^X)$ be the permutational representation defined by this action. Let $\mathcal{C} : \mathbb{F}^k \to \mathbb{F}^X$ be a linear code. Then $\mathcal{C}$ is G-invariant if and only if $\mathrm{Im}\,\mathcal{C}$ is a sub-representation of $(\tau, \mathbb{F}^X)$.*

Proof. The proof almost follows from the definition. Let $c \in \mathrm{Im}\,\mathcal{C}$, where $c = (c_{x_1}, c_{x_2}, \dots, c_{x_n})$ and consider c as a function from X to $\mathbb{F}$. Then $(g \cdot c)(x) = c(g^{-1}x)$ and by the definition of τ we have that $(\tau(g)c)(x) = c(g^{-1}x)$. Thus the code $\mathcal{C}$ is G-invariant if and only if for every $c \in \mathrm{Im}(\mathcal{C})$ and for every $g \in G$ it holds that $\tau(g)c \in \mathcal{C}$ i.e., if and only if $\mathrm{Im}\,\mathcal{C}$ is a sub-representation of $(\tau, \mathbb{F}^X)$. □

As a corollary we get that G-homomorphisms into permutational representations are G-invariant codes.

Corollary A.2. *Let G be a group acting on X. Let $(\tau, \mathbb{F}^X)$ be the permutational representation defined by this action. Let $(\rho, \mathbb{F}^k)$ be any representation of G. Let $\mathcal{C} : \mathbb{F}^k \to \mathbb{F}^X$ be a homomorphism of the representations $(\rho, \mathbb{F}^k)$ and $(\tau, \mathbb{F}^X)$ then $\mathcal{C}$ is a G-invariant code.*

Proof. This follows from Lemma A.1 and the fact that image of a G-homomorphism is a sub-representation. □

Let $\mathcal{C} : \mathbb{F}^k \to \mathbb{F}^X$ be a linear one-to-one G-invariant code. We already know that $\mathrm{Im}(\mathcal{C})$ is a sub-representation of $(\tau, \mathbb{F}^X)$. Let us show that we can define a representation $(\rho, \mathbb{F}^k)$ such that $\mathcal{C}$ is a G-homomorphism.

Theorem A.3. *Let G be a group acting on X. Let $(\tau, \mathbb{F}^X)$ be the permutational representation defined by this action. Let $\mathcal{C} : \mathbb{F}^k \to \mathbb{F}^X$ be a linear one-to-one G-invariant code. Define a representation ρ of G in $\mathbb{F}^k$ by:*

$$\rho(g)(v) = \mathcal{C}^{-1}(\tau(g)\mathcal{C}(v)) . \qquad (A.1)$$

Then $\mathcal{C}$ is an embedding of the representations $(\rho, \mathbb{F}^k)$ in $(\tau, \mathbb{F}^X)$.

Proof. First we need to proof that $\rho(g)$ is well defined: Since $\mathcal{C}$ is one-to-one $\mathcal{C}^{-1}$ is defined on $\mathrm{Im}\,\mathcal{C}$. Since $\mathcal{C}$ is closed under G it holds that $\tau(g)\mathcal{C}(v) \in \mathcal{C}$ therefore $\mathcal{C}^{-1}$ is defined on $(\tau(g)\mathcal{C}(v))$.

Now let us show that $\mathcal{C}$ is a G homomorphism:

$$\mathcal{C}(\rho(g)v) = \mathcal{C}(\mathcal{C}^{-1}(\tau(g)\mathcal{C}(v))) = \tau(g)\mathcal{C}(v) .$$

□

Folded Codes from Function Field Towers and Improved Optimal Rate List Decoding

(Extended Abstract)

Venkatesan Guruswami[*]
Computer Science Department.
Carnegie Mellon University
Pittsburgh, PA, USA
guruswami@cmu.edu

Chaoping Xing[†]
Division of Mathematical Sciences
School of Physical & Mathematical Sciences
Nanyang Technological University, Singapore
xingcp@ntu.edu.sg

ABSTRACT

We give a new construction of algebraic codes which are efficiently list decodable from a fraction $1 - R - \varepsilon$ of adversarial errors where R is the rate of the code, for any desired positive constant ε. The worst-case list size output by the algorithm is $O(1/\varepsilon)$, matching the existential bound for random codes up to constant factors. Further, the alphabet size of the codes is a constant depending only on ε — it can be made $\exp(\tilde{O}(1/\varepsilon^2))$ which is not much worse than the non-constructive $\exp(1/\varepsilon)$ bound of random codes. The code construction is Monte Carlo and has the claimed list decoding property with high probability. Once the code is (efficiently) sampled, the encoding/decoding algorithms are deterministic with a running time $O_\varepsilon(N^c)$ for an absolute constant c, where N is the code's block length.

Our construction is based on a careful combination of a linear-algebraic approach to list decoding folded codes from towers of function fields, with a special form of subspace-evasive sets. Instantiating this with the explicit "asymptotically good" Garcia-Stichtenoth (GS for short) tower of function fields yields the above parameters. To illustrate the method in a simpler setting, we also present a construction based on Hermitian function fields, which offers similar guarantees with a list-size and alphabet size polylogarithmic in the block length N.

In comparison, algebraic codes achieving the optimal trade-off between list decodability and rate based on folded Reed-Solomon codes have a decoding complexity of $N^{\Omega(1/\varepsilon)}$, an alphabet size of $N^{\Omega(1/\varepsilon^2)}$, and a list size of $O(1/\varepsilon^2)$ (even after combination with subspace-evasive sets). Thus we get an improvement over the previous best bounds in all three aspects simultaneously, and are quite close to the existential random coding bounds. Along the way, we shed light on how to use automorphisms of certain function fields to enable list decoding of the folded version of the associated algebraic-geometric codes.

[*]Research supported in part by a Packard Fellowship and NSF CCF 0963975. Some of this work was done during a visit to Nanyang Technological University. Any opinions, findings, and conclusions or recommendations expressed in this material are those of the author(s) and do not necessarily reflect the views of the National Science Foundation.

[†]Research supported by the Singapore National Research Foundation under Research Grant NRF-CRP2-2007-03 and Singapore A*STAR SERC under Research Grant 1121720011.

STOC'12, May 19–22, 2012, New York, New York, USA.

Categories and Subject Descriptors

E.4 [**Data**]: Coding and Information Theory

General Terms

Theory

Keywords

List error-correction, Algebraic codes, Subspace-evasive sets, Pseudorandomness, List decoding capacity.

1. INTRODUCTION

An error-correcting code C of block length N over an alphabet Σ maps a set $\mathcal{M}$ of messages into codewords in Σ^N. The rate of the code C, denoted R, equals $\frac{1}{N}\log_{|\Sigma|}|\mathcal{M}|$. In this work, we will be interested in codes for adversarial noise, where the channel can arbitrarily corrupt up to a fraction τ of the N symbols. The goal will be to correct such errors and recover the original message/codeword. It is easy to see that information-theoretically, we need to receive at least RN symbols correctly in order to recover the message (since $|\mathcal{M}| = |\Sigma|^{RN}$), so we must have $\tau \leqslant 1 - R$.

Perhaps surprisingly, in a model called list decoding, recovery up to this information-theoretic limit becomes possible. Let us say that a code $C \subseteq \Sigma^N$ is (τ, ℓ)-list decodable if for every received word $\mathbf{y} \in \Sigma^N$, there are at most ℓ codewords $\mathbf{c} \in C$ such that $\mathbf{y}$ and $\mathbf{c}$ differ in at most τN positions. Such a code allows, in principle, the correction of a fraction τ of errors, outputting at most ℓ candidate codewords one of which is the originally transmitted codeword.

The probabilistic method shows that a random code of rate R over an alphabet of size $\exp(O(1/\varepsilon))$ is with high probability $(1-R-\varepsilon, O(1/\varepsilon))$-list decodable [2]. However, it is not known how to construct or even randomly sample such a code for which the associated algorithmic task of list decoding (i.e., given $\mathbf{y} \in \Sigma^N$, find the list of codewords within fractional radius $1-R-\varepsilon$) can be performed efficiently. This work takes a big step in that direction, giving a randomized construction of such efficiently list-decodable codes over a slightly worse alphabet size of $\exp(\tilde{O}(1/\varepsilon^2))$. We note that the alphabet size needs to be at least $\exp(\Omega(1/\varepsilon))$ in order to list decode from a fraction $1-R-\varepsilon$ of errors, so this is close to optimal. For the list-size needed as a function of ε for decoding a $1-R-\varepsilon$ fraction of errors, the best lower bound is only $\Omega(\log(1/\varepsilon))$ [7], but as mentioned above, even random coding arguments only achieve a list-size of $O(1/\varepsilon)$, which our construction matches up to constant factors.

We now review some of the key results on algebraic list decoding leading up to this work. A more technical comparison with related work appears in Section 1.1. The first construction of codes that achieved the optimal trade-off between rate and list-decoding radius, i.e., enabled list decoding up to a fraction $1-R-\varepsilon$ of worst-case errors with rate R, was due to Guruswami and Rudra [8]. They showed that a variant of Reed-Solomon (RS) codes called *folded* RS codes admit such a list decoder. For a decoding radius of $1-R-\varepsilon$, the code was based on bundling together disjoint windows of $m = \Theta(1/\varepsilon^2)$ consecutive symbols of the RS codeword into a single symbol over a larger alphabet. As a result, the alphabet size of the construction was $N^{\Omega(1/\varepsilon^2)}$. Ideas based on code concatenation and expander codes can be used to bring down the alphabet size to $\exp(\tilde{O}(1/\varepsilon^4))$, but this compromises some nice features such as list recovery and soft decoding of the folded RS code. Also, the decoding time complexity as well as proven bound on worst-case output list size for these constructions were $N^{\Omega(1/\varepsilon)}$ which is rather large.

Our main final result statement is the following. The codes we construct are a randomly sampled subcode of an analog of folded RS codes for an asymptotically optimal tower of function fields due to Garcia and Stichtenoth [3, 4].

THEOREM 1.1. *For any $R \in (0,1)$ and positive constant $\varepsilon \in (0,1)$, there is a Monte Carlo construction of a family of codes of rate at least R over an alphabet size $\exp(O(\log(1/\varepsilon)/\varepsilon^2))$ that are encodable and $(1-R-\varepsilon, O(1/(R\varepsilon))$-list decodable in $\mathrm{poly}(N)$ time, where N is the block length of the code.*

To illustrate our ideas in an algebraically simpler setting, we first give a construction based on a tower of Hermitian field extensions [12]. This gives a similar result, albeit with alphabet size and list-size upper bound polylogarithmic in N.

1.1 Prior and related work

Let us recap a bit more formally the construction of folded RS codes from [8]. One begins with the RS encoding of a polynomial $f \in \mathbb{F}_q[X]$ of degree $< k$ with the evaluation points ordered as $1, \gamma, \dots, \gamma^{n-1}$ for some primitive element $\gamma \in \mathbb{F}_q$ and $n < q$. For an integer "folding" parameter $m \geqslant 1$ that divides n, the folded RS codeword is defined over alphabet $\mathbb{F}_q^m$ and consists of n/m blocks, with the j'th block consisting of the m-tuple $(f(\gamma^{(j-1)m}), f(\gamma^{(j-1)m+1}), \dots, f(\gamma^{jm-1}))$. The algorithm in [8] for list decoding these codes was based on the algebraic identity $\overline{f(\gamma X)} = \overline{f(X)}^q$ in the residue field $\mathbb{F}_q[X]/(X^{q-1}-\gamma)$ where $\overline{f}$ denotes the residue f mod $(X^{q-1}-\gamma)$. This identity is used to solve for f from an equation of the form $Q(X, f(X), f(\gamma X), \dots, f(\gamma^{s-1}X)) = 0$ for some low-degree nonzero multivariate polynomial Q. The high degree $q > n$ of this identity, coupled with $s \approx 1/\varepsilon$, led to the large bounds on list-size and decoding complexity in [8].

One possible approach to reduce q (as a function of the code length) in this construction would be to work with algebraic-geometric codes based on function fields K over $\mathbb{F}_q$ with more rational points. However, an automorphism σ of K that can play the role of the automorphism $f(X) \mapsto f(\gamma X)$ of $\mathbb{F}_q(X)$ is only known (or even possible) for very special function fields. This approach was used in [5] to construct list-decodable codes based on cyclotomic function fields using as σ certain Frobenius automorphisms. These codes improved the alphabet size to polylogarithmic in N, but the bound on list-size and decoding complexity remained $N^{\Omega(1/\varepsilon)}$.

Recently, a linear-algebraic approach to list decoding folded RS codes has been discovered in [16, 6]. Here, in the interpolation stage, which is common to all list decoding algorithms for algebraic codes [15, 9, 11, 8], following the idea in [16] one finds a *linear* multivariate polynomial $Q(X, Y_1, \dots, Y_s)$ whose total degree in the Y_i's is 1. The simple but key observation driving [6] is that the equation $Q(X, f(X), \dots, f(\gamma^{s-1}X)) = 0$ now becomes a linear system in the coefficients of f. Further, it is shown that the solution space has dimension less than s, which again gives a list-size upper bound of q^{s-1}. Finally, since the list of candidate messages fall in an affine space, it was noted in [6] that one can bring down the list size by carefully "pre-coding" the message polynomials so that their k coefficients belong to a "subspace-evasive set" (which has small intersection with every s-dimensional subspace of $\mathbb{F}_q^k$). This idea was used in [6] to give a *randomized* construction of $(1-R-\varepsilon, O(1/\varepsilon^2))$-list decodable codes of rate R (in fact, the list size bound is worse — it is $\tilde{\Omega}(N)$ — if one requires efficient encoding of the code). However, the alphabet size and runtime of the decoding algorithm both remained $N^{\Omega(1/\varepsilon)}$. In [10], similar results were also shown for derivative codes, where the encoding of a polynomial f consists of the evaluations of f and its first $m-1$ derivates at distinct field elements.

In a concurrent independent work, Dvir and Lovett gave an elegant construction of explicit subspace evasive sets based on certain algebraic varieties [1]. This yields an explicit version of the codes from [6], albeit with a worse list size bound of $(1/\varepsilon)^{O(1/\varepsilon)}$. This work and [1] are incomparable in terms of results. The big advantage of [1] is the deterministic construction of the code. The benefits in our work are (i) our list-size of $O(1/\varepsilon)$ is much better and in fact optimal up to constant factors,[1] and (ii) we are able to construct codes over an alphabet size that is a constant independent of N, whereas in [1] the $N^{\Omega(1/\varepsilon^2)}$ alphabet size of folded RS codes is inherited. Both our work and [1] achieve a decoding complexity of $O_\varepsilon(N^c)$ with exponent independent of ε.

We should note that since we require sets that are evasive with respect to subspaces of large dimension, and which have

[1] As mentioned above, the bound in [1] is $(1/\varepsilon)^{O(1/\varepsilon)}$ and it seems very difficult to get a sub-exponential dependence on $1/\varepsilon$ with the algebraic approach relying on Bezout's theorem to construct subspace-evasive sets.

further structural properties needed in the decoding, we cannot use the construction in [1] to make the codes in this work explicit.

1.2 Our techniques

We describe some of the main new ingredients that go into our work. We need both new algebraic insights and constructions, as well as ideas in pseudorandomness relating to subspace-evasive sets with additional structure. We describe these in turn below.

Algebraic ideas. As mentioned above, effecting the original "non-linear" approach in [8, 5] with automorphisms of more general function fields seems intricate at best. The correct generalization of the linear-algebraic list decoding approach to the function field case is also not obvious. One of the main algebraic insights in this work is noting that the right way to generalize the linear-algebraic approach to codes based on algebraic function fields is to rely on the *local power series expansion* of functions from the message space at a suitable rational point. (The case for Reed-Solomon codes being the expansion around 0, which is a finite polynomial form.)

Working with a suitable automorphism which has a "diagonal" action on the local expansion lets us extend the linear-algebraic decoding method to AG codes. Implementing this for specific AG codes requires an explicit specification of a basis for an associated message (Riemann-Roch) space, and the efficient computation of the local expansion of the basis elements at a special rational point on the curve. We show how to do this for two towers of function fields: the Hermitian tower [12] and the asymptotically optimal Garcia-Stichtenoth tower [3, 4]. The former tower is quite simple to handle — it has an easily written down explicit basis, and we show how to compute the local expansion of functions around the point with all zero coordinates. However, the Hermitian tower does not have bounded ratio of the genus to number of rational points, and so does not give constant alphabet codes (we can get codes over an alphabet size that is polylogarithmic in the block length though). Explicit basis for Riemann-Roch spaces of the Garcia-Stichtenoth tower were constructed in [13]. Regarding local expansions, one major difference is that we work with local expansion of functions at the point at infinity, which is fully "ramified" in the tower. For both these towers, we find and work with a nice automorphism that acts diagonally on the local expansion, and use it for folding the codes and decoding them by solving a linear system.

Pseudorandomness. These algebraic ideas enable us to pin down the messages into a subspace of dimension linear in the message length. To prune this list, we need several additional ideas. The starting point is to follow [6] and only encode messages in a subspace-evasive set which has small intersection with low-dimensional subspaces. Implementing this in our case, however, leads to several problems. First, since the subspace we like to avoid intersecting much has large dimension, the list size bound will be linear in the code length and not a constant like in our final result. More severely, we cannot go over the elements of this subspace to prune the list as that would take exponential time. To solve the latter problem, we observe that the subspace has a special "periodic" structure, and exploit this to show the existence of large "hierarchically subspace evasive" (h.s.e) subsets which have small intersection with the projection of the subspace on certain prefixes. Isolating the periodic property of the subspaces, and formulating the right notion of evasiveness w.r.t to such subspaces, is an important aspect of this work.

We also give a pseudorandom construction of good h.s.e sets using limited wise independent sample spaces, in a manner enabling the efficient iterative computation of the final list of intersecting elements. With some additional ideas, we ensure that one can efficiently index into a large subset of our h.s.e set construction (this is needed to get an efficient encoding algorithm for our code). As a further ingredient, we note that the number of possible subspaces that arise in the decoding is much smaller than the total number of possibilities. Using this together with a trick to take the intersection of two subspace evasive set constructions, we are able to reduce the list size to a constant.

1.3 Organization

We begin by isolating the special notion of subspaces which our evasive sets should avoid intersecting too much (Section 2). We describe our construction of folded Hermitian codes and a linear-algebraic list decoding algorithm for these codes in Section 3. In Section 4, we define and construct the special "hierarchically" subspace-evasive (h.s.e) sets that we need (the proofs are omitted and appear in the full version). We show how to combine the h.s.e sets with folded Hermitian codes in Section 5; this gives a result similar to Theorem 1.1 with polylogarithmic alphabet and list size. We show how similar ideas can be used to construct folded codes based on the Garcia-Stichtenoth tower, and how to combine them with h.s.e sets to get our main result (Theorem 1.1) in Section 6.

2. PERIODIC SUBSPACES

The list decoding algorithm for our algebraic codes will first pin down the candidate messages to a subspace. The structure of the subspace will be important to us in order to be able to efficiently prune it to a much smaller list. In this section, we make some important definitions capturing this property. Let us begin with some notation.

NOTATION 1. **(Projection of vectors and sets)** *For a vector* $\mathbf{y} = (y_1, y_2, \ldots, y_m) \in \mathbb{F}_q^m$ *and positive integers* $t_1 \leqslant t_2 \leqslant m$, *we denote by* $\text{proj}_{[t_1,t_2]}(\mathbf{y}) \in \mathbb{F}_q^{t_2-t_1+1}$ *its projection onto coordinates* t_1 *through* t_2, *i.e.,* $\text{proj}_{[t_1,t_2]}(\mathbf{y}) = (y_{t_1}, y_{t_1+1}, \ldots, y_{t_2})$. *When* $t_1 = 1$, *we use* $\text{proj}_t(\mathbf{y})$ *to denote* $\text{proj}_{[1,t]}(\mathbf{y})$.

For a subset $S \subseteq \mathbb{F}_q^k$ *and positive integers* $t_1 \leqslant t_2 \leqslant k$, *we denote the projection of* S *onto the coordinates in the range* $[t_1, t_2]$ *by* $\text{proj}_{[t_1,t_2]}(S)$. *Formally,* $\text{proj}_{[t_1,t_2]}(S) = \{\text{proj}_{[t_1,t_2]}(\mathbf{y}) \mid \mathbf{y} \in S\}$. *Again, we use* $\text{proj}_t(S)$ *to denote* $\text{proj}_{[1,t]}(S)$.

The specific definition of periodic subspaces below (which might appear rather technical) is motivated by the structure of the subspaces arising in our list decoding application (for example, as guaranteed by Lemma 3.7). The special structure of these subspaces is important to guarantee the existence of "subspace evasive sets" (defined later) that are good enough for our purposes.

DEFINITION 1. (s, Δ)**-periodic subspaces**[2]) *For positive integers* s, Δ, b, *an affine subspace* W *of* $\mathbb{F}_q^k$ *where* $k =$

[2]According to the definition, an (s, Δ)-periodic subspace is

$b\Delta$ *is said to be* (s, Δ)-periodic *if there is a subspace* U *of* $\mathbb{F}_q^\Delta$ *of dimension less than* s *such that for all* $\mathbf{y} \in W$ *and* $1 \leqslant i \leqslant b$, $\mathrm{proj}_{[(i-1)\Delta+1, i\Delta]}(\mathbf{y})$ *belongs to the affine space* $U + \mathbf{b}_i$, *where* $\mathbf{b}_i$ *is a column vector whose coordinates are affine combinations (depending only on* i*) of the first* $(i-1)\Delta$ *coordinates of* $\mathbf{y}$*; formally,* $\mathbf{b_i} = C_i \cdot \mathrm{proj}_{(i-1)\Delta}(\mathbf{y}) + \mathbf{v}_i$ *for some matrix* $C_i \in \mathbb{F}_q^{\Delta \times (i-1)\Delta}$ *and* $\mathbf{v}_i \in \mathbb{F}_q^\Delta$. *We can represent such an affine subspace by* $U, \{C_i, \mathbf{v}_i\}_{i=1}^b$.

Note that if W is an (s, Δ)-periodic subspace of $\mathbb{F}_q^{b\Delta}$, for every i, $1 \leqslant i \leqslant b$, and every $\mathbf{a} \in \mathbb{F}_q^{(i-1)\Delta}$, the affine space $\{\mathrm{proj}_{[(i-1)\Delta+1, i\Delta]}(\mathbf{w}) \mid \mathbf{w} \in W \text{ and } \mathrm{proj}_{(i-1)\Delta}(\mathbf{w}) = \mathbf{a}\}$ has dimension at most s (and in particular it has at most q^s elements). Therefore, by an inductive argument, we have $|\mathrm{proj}_{i\Delta}(W)| \leqslant q^{is}$ for $1 \leqslant i \leqslant b$, which together with the fact that $\mathrm{proj}_{i\Delta}(W)$ is an affine subspace implies the following.

OBSERVATION 2.1. *If* W *is an* (s, Δ)*-periodic subspace of* $\mathbb{F}_q^{b\Delta}$, *then for* $i = 1, 2, \ldots, b$, $\mathrm{proj}_{i\Delta}(W)$ *is also* (s, Δ)*-periodic and has dimension at most* $s \cdot i$ *as an affine subspace of* $\mathbb{F}_q^{i\Delta}$.

3. FOLDED CODES FROM THE HERMITIAN TOWER

In this section, we will describe a family of folded codes based on the Hermitian function field (or rather a tower of such fields).

3.1 Background on Hermitian tower

In what follows, let r be a prime power and let $q = r^2$. We denote by $\mathbb{F}_q$ the finite field with q elements. The Hermitian function tower that we are going to use for our code construction was discussed in [12]. The reader may refer to [12] for the detailed background on the Hermitian function tower, and Stichtenoth's book [14] for general background on algebraic function fields and their use in constructing algebraic-geometric codes. The Hermitian tower is defined by the following recursive equations

$$x_{i+1}^r + x_{i+1} = x_i^{r+1}, \quad i = 1, 2, \ldots, e-1.$$

Put $F_e = \mathbb{F}_q(x_1, x_2, \ldots, x_e)$ for $e \geqslant 2$. We will assume that $r \geqslant 2e$.

Rational places. The function field F_e has $r^{e+1} + 1$ rational places. One of these is the "point at infinity" which is the unique pole P_∞ of x_1 (and is fully ramified). The other r^{e+1} come from the rational places lying over the unique zero P_α of $x_1 - \alpha$ for each $\alpha \in \mathbb{F}_q$. Note that for every $\alpha \in \mathbb{F}_q$, P_α splits completely in F_e, i.e., there are r^{e-1} rational places lying over P_α. Intuitively, one can think of the rational places of F_e (besides P_∞) as being given by e-tuples $(\alpha_1, \alpha_2, \ldots, \alpha_e) \in \mathbb{F}_q^e$ that satisfy $\alpha_{i+1}^r + \alpha_{i+1} = \alpha_i^{r+1}$ for $i = 1, 2, \ldots, e-1$. For each value of $\alpha \in \mathbb{F}_q$, there are precisely r solutions to $\beta \in \mathbb{F}_q$ satisfying $\beta^r + \beta = \alpha^{r+1}$, so the number of such e-tuples is r^{e+1} ($q = r^2$ choices for α_1, and then r choices for each successive α_i, $2 \leqslant i \leqslant e$).

Riemann-Roch spaces. For a place P of F_e, we denote by ν_P the discrete valuation of P: for a function $h \in F_e$, if h has a zero at P, then $\nu_P(h)$ gives the number (multiplicity) of zeroes, if h has a pole at P, then $-\nu_P(h)$ gives the pole order of h at P, and $\nu_P(h) = 0$ if h has neither a zero or a pole at P.

For an integer l, we consider the Riemann-Roch space defined by

$$\mathcal{L}(lP_\infty) := \{h \in F_e \setminus \{0\} : \nu_{P_\infty}(h) \geqslant -l\} \cup \{0\}.$$

Then the dimension $\ell(lP_\infty)$ is at least $l - g_e + 1$ and furthermore, $\ell(lP_\infty) = l - g_e + 1$ if $l \geqslant 2g_e - 1$. A basis over $\mathbb{F}_q$ of $\mathcal{L}(lP_\infty)$ can be explicitly constructed as follows

$$\left\{ x_1^{j_1} \cdots x_e^{j_e} : (j_1, \ldots, j_e) \in \mathbb{Z}_{\geqslant 0}^e, \sum_{i=1}^{e} j_i r^{e-i}(r+1)^{i-1} \leqslant l \right\}. \quad (1)$$

We stress that evaluating elements of $\mathcal{L}(lP_\infty)$ at the rational places of F_e (other then P_∞) is easy: we simply have to evaluate a linear combination of the monomials allowed in (1) at the tuples $(\alpha_1, \alpha_2, \ldots, \alpha_e) \in \mathbb{F}_q^e$ mentioned above. In other words, it is just evaluating an e-variate polynomial at a specific subset of r^{e+1} points of $\mathbb{F}_q^e$, and can be accomplished in polynomial time.

Genus. The genus g_e of the function field F_e is given by

$$\begin{aligned} g_e &= \tfrac{1}{2}\left(\textstyle\sum_{i=1}^{e-1} r^e \left(1 + \tfrac{1}{r}\right)^{i-1} - (r+1)^{e-1} + 1\right) \\ &\leqslant \tfrac{r^e}{2} \textstyle\sum_{i=1}^{e} \binom{e}{i} \tfrac{1}{r^{i-1}} \leqslant \tfrac{er^e}{2} \textstyle\sum_{i=1}^{e} \left(\tfrac{e}{r}\right)^{i-1} \leqslant er^e \end{aligned} \quad (2)$$

where the last step used $r \geqslant 2e$.

A useful automorphism. Let γ be a primitive element of $\mathbb{F}_q$ and consider the automorphism $\sigma \in \mathrm{Aut}(F_e/\mathbb{F}_q)$ defined by

$$\sigma : x_i \mapsto \gamma^{(r+1)^{i-1}} x_i \quad \text{for } i = 1, 2, \ldots, e.$$

The order of σ is $q-1$ and furthermore, we have the following facts:

(i) Let P_0 be the unique common zero of $x_1, x_2, \ldots, x_e$ (this corresponds to the e-tuple $(0, 0, \ldots, 0)$), and P_∞ the unique pole of x_1. The automorphism σ keeps P_0 and P_∞ unchanged, i.e., $P_0^\sigma = P_0$ and $P_\infty{}^\sigma = P_\infty$,

(ii) Let $\mathbb{P}$ be the set of all the rational places which are neither P_∞ nor zeros of x_1. Then $|\mathbb{P}| = (q-1)r^{e-1}$. Moreover, σ divides $\mathbb{P}$ into r^{e-1} orbits and each orbit has $q-1$ places. For an integer m with $1 \leqslant m \leqslant q-1$, we can label Nm distinct elements $P_1, P_1^\sigma, \ldots, P_1^{\sigma^{m-1}}, \ldots, P_N, P_N^\sigma, \ldots, P_N^{\sigma^{m-1}}$ in $\mathbb{P}$, as long as $N \leqslant r^{e-1} \lfloor \frac{q-1}{m} \rfloor$.

DEFINITION 2. **(Folded codes from the Hermitian tower)** *Assume that* m, l, N *are positive integers satisfying* $1 \leqslant m \leqslant q-1$ *and* $l/m \leqslant N \leqslant r^{e-1} \lfloor \frac{q-1}{m} \rfloor$. *The folded code from* F_e *with parameters* N, l, q, e, m, *denoted by* $\widetilde{\mathsf{FH}}(N, l, q, e, m)$, *encodes a message function* $f \in \mathcal{L}(lP_\infty)$ *as*

$$f \mapsto \left(\begin{bmatrix} f(P_1) \\ f(P_1^\sigma) \\ \vdots \\ f(P_1^{\sigma^{m-1}}) \end{bmatrix}, \ldots, \begin{bmatrix} f(P_N) \\ f(P_N^\sigma) \\ \vdots \\ f(P_N^{\sigma^{m-1}}) \end{bmatrix} \right) \in \left(\mathbb{F}_q^m\right)^N. \quad (3)$$

LEMMA 3.1. *The above code* $\widetilde{\mathsf{FH}}(N, l, q, e, m)$ *is an* $\mathbb{F}_q$*-linear code over alphabet size* q^m, *rate at least* $\frac{l - g_e + 1}{Nm}$, *and minimum distance at least* $N - \frac{l}{m}$.

in fact an affine space. For convenience, we blur this distinction, which is not too important for us, and use the terminology periodic subspace to refer to them.

PROOF. It is clear that the map (3) is an $\mathbb{F}_q$-linear map. The dimension over $\mathbb{F}_q$ of the message space $\mathcal{L}(lP_\infty)$ is at least $l - g_e + 1$ by the Riemann-Roch theorem, which gives the claimed lower bound on rate. For the distance property, observe that if the i-th column is zero, then f has m zeros. This implies that the encoding of a nonzero function f can have at most l/m zero columns since $f \in \mathcal{L}(lP_\infty)$. □

3.2 Redefining the code in terms of local expansion at P_0

For our decoding, we will actually recover the message $f \in \mathcal{L}(lP_\infty)$ in terms of the coefficients of its power series expansion around P_0

$$f = f_0 + f_1 x + f_2 x^2 + \cdots$$

where $x := x_1$ is the local parameter at P_0 (which means that x_1 has exactly one zero at P_0, i.e., $\nu_{P_0}(x_1) = 1$). In fact, realizing that one must work in this power series representation is one of the key insights in this work.

Let us first show that one can efficiently move back-and-forth between the representation of $f \in \mathcal{L}(lP_\infty)$ in terms of a basis for $\mathcal{L}(lP_\infty)$ and its power series representation $(f_0, f_1, \ldots)$ around P_0. Since the mapping $f \mapsto (f_0, f_1, \ldots)$ is $\mathbb{F}_q$-linear, it suffices to compute the local expansion at P_0 of a basis for $\mathcal{L}(lP_\infty)$. By the structure of the basis functions in (1), it is sufficient to find an algorithm of efficiently finding local expansions of x_i at P_0 for every $i = 1, 2, \ldots, e$. This can be done inductively leading to the following lemma (proof skipped and deferred to the full version).

LEMMA 3.2. *For any n, one can compute the first n terms of the local expansion of the basis elements* (1) *at P_0 using* poly(n) *operations over $\mathbb{F}_q$.*

To keep the list output by the algorithm at a controllable size, we will combine the code with certain special subspace evasive sets. For this purpose, we will actually need to index the messages of the code by the first k coefficients $(f_0, f_1, \ldots, f_{k-1})$ of the local expansion of the function f at P_0. This requires that for every $(f_0, f_1, \ldots, f_{k-1})$ there is a $f \in \mathcal{L}(lP_\infty)$ whose power series expansion has the f_i as the first k coefficients. This is easy to ensure by taking $l = k + 2g_e - 1$ as we argue below. Note that to ensure that $\mathcal{L}(lP_\infty)$ has dimension k, it suffices to pick $l = k + g_e - 1$ by the Riemann-Roch theorem. We pick l to be g_e more than this bound. Since the genus will be much smaller than the code length, we can afford this small loss in parameters.

Let us define the local expansion map $\mathsf{ev}_{P_0} : \mathcal{L}((k + 2g_e - 1)P_\infty) \to \mathbb{F}_q^k$ that maps f to $(f_0, f_1, \ldots, f_{k-1})$ where $f = f_0 + f_1 x + f_2 x^2 + \cdots$ is the local expansion of f at P_0.

CLAIM 3.3. *ev_{P_0} is an $\mathbb{F}_q$-linear surjective map. Further, we can compute ev_{P_0} using* poly(k, g_e) *operations over $\mathbb{F}_q$ given a representation of the input $f \in \mathcal{L}((k + 2g_e - 1)P_\infty)$ in terms of the basis* (1).

PROOF. The $\mathbb{F}_q$-linearity of ev_{P_0} is clear. The kernel of ev_{P_0} is $\mathcal{L}((k+2g_e-1)P_\infty - kP_0)$ which has dimension exactly g_e by the Riemann-Roch theorem. By the rank-nullity theorem, the image must have dimension k, and so the map is surjective. The claimed complexity of computation follows immediately from Lemma 3.2. □

For each $(f_0, f_1, \ldots, f_{k-1}) \in \mathbb{F}_q^k$, we can therefore pick a pre-image in $\mathcal{L}((k + 2g_e - 1)P_\infty)$. For convenience, we will denote an injective map making such a unique choice by $\kappa_{P_0} : \mathbb{F}_q^k \to \mathcal{L}((k + 2g_e - 1)P_\infty)$. By picking the pre-images of a basis of $\mathbb{F}_q^k$ and extending it by linearity, we can assume κ_{P_0} to be $\mathbb{F}_q$-linear, and thus specify it by a $(k + g_e) \times k$ matrix. We record this fact for easy reference below.

CLAIM 3.4. *The map $\kappa_{P_0} : \mathbb{F}_q^k \to \mathcal{L}((k + 2g_e - 1)P_\infty)$ is $\mathbb{F}_q$-linear and injective. We can compute a representation of this linear transformation using* poly(k, g_e) *operations over $\mathbb{F}_q$, and the map itself can be evaluated using* poly(k, g_e) *operations over $\mathbb{F}_q$.*

We will now redefine a version of the folded Hermitian code that maps $\mathbb{F}_q^k$ to $(\mathbb{F}_q^m)^N$ by composing the folded encoding (3) from the original Definition 2 with κ_{P_0}.

DEFINITION 3. **(Folded Hermitian code using local expansion)** *The folded Hermitian code* $\mathsf{FH}(N, k, q, e, m)$ *maps* $\mathbf{f} = (f_0, f_1, \ldots, f_{k-1}) \in \mathbb{F}_q^k$ *to* $\widetilde{\mathsf{FH}}(N, k+2g_e-1, q, e, m)(\kappa_{P_0}(\mathbf{f})) \in (\mathbb{F}_q^m)^N$.

The rate of the above code equals $k/(Nm)$ and its distance is at least $N - (k + 2g_e - 1)/m$.

3.3 List decoding folded codes from the Hermitian tower

We now present a list decoding algorithm for the above codes. The algorithm follows the linear-algebraic list decoding algorithm for folded Reed-Solomon codes. Suppose a codeword (3) encoding $f \in \mathrm{Im}(\kappa_{P_0}) \subseteq \mathcal{L}((k + 2g_e - 1)P_\infty)$ is transmitted and received as

$$\mathbf{y} = \begin{pmatrix} y_{1,1} & y_{2,1} & & y_{N,1} \\ y_{1,2} & y_{2,2} & & \vdots \\ & & \ddots & \\ y_{1,m} & \cdots & & y_{N,m} \end{pmatrix} \qquad (4)$$

where some columns are erroneous. Let $s \geqslant 1$ be an integer parameter associated with the decoder.

LEMMA 3.5. *Given a received word as in (4), using* poly(N) *operations over $\mathbb{F}_q$, we can find a nonzero linear polynomial in $F_e[Y_1, Y_2, \ldots, Y_s]$ of the form*

$$Q(Y_1, Y_2, \ldots, Y_s) = A_0 + A_1 Y_1 + A_2 Y_2 + \cdots + A_s Y_s \qquad (5)$$

satisfying

$$Q(y_{i,j}, y_{i,j+1}, \cdots, y_{i,j+s-1}) = A_0(P_i^{\sigma^j}) + A_s(P_i^{\sigma^j}) y_{i,j+1} + \cdots + A_s(P_i^{\sigma^j}) y_{i,j+s} = 0 \qquad (6)$$

for $i = 1, 2, \ldots, N$ and $j = 0, 1, \ldots, m-s$. The coefficients A_i of Q satisfy $A_i \in \mathcal{L}(DP_\infty)$ for $i = 1, 2, \ldots, s$ and $A_0 \in \mathcal{L}((D + k + 2g_e - 1)P_\infty)$ for a "degree" parameter D chosen as

$$D = \left\lfloor \frac{N(m - s + 1) - k + (s-1)g_e + 1}{s+1} \right\rfloor. \qquad (7)$$

PROOF. If we fix a basis of $\mathcal{L}(DP_\infty)$ (of the form (1)) and extend it to a basis of $\mathcal{L}((D + k + 2g_e - 1)P_\infty)$, then the number of freedoms of A_0 is at least $D + k + g_e$ and the number of freedoms of A_i is at least $D - g_e + 1$ for $i \geqslant 1$. Thus, the total number of freedoms in the polynomial Q equals

$$s(D - g_e + 1) + D + k + g_e = (s+1)(D+1) - (s-1)g_e - 1 + k > N(m - s + 1) \qquad (8)$$

for the above choice (7) of D. The interpolation requirements on $Q \in F_e[Y_1, \ldots, Y_s]$ are the following:

$$Q(y_{i,j}, y_{i,j+1}, \cdots, y_{i,j+s-1}) = A_0(P_i^{\sigma^j}) + A_s(P_i^{\sigma^j})y_{i,j+1} + \cdots + A_s(P_i^{\sigma^j})y_{i,j+s} = 0 \quad (9)$$

for $i = 1, 2, \ldots, N$ and $j = 0, 1, \ldots, m-s$. The interpolation requirements on Q give a total of $N(m-s+1)$ homogeneous linear equations that the coefficients of the A_i's w.r.t the chosen basis of $\mathcal{L}((D+k+2g_e-1)P_\infty)$ must satisfy. Since the number of such coefficients (degrees of freedom in Q) exceeds $N(m-s+1)$, we can conclude that such a linear polynomial Q as required by the lemma must exist, and can be found by solving a homogeneous linear system over $\mathbb{F}_q$ with about $N(m-s+1)$ variables and constraints. □

Similar to earlier interpolation based list decoding algorithms, the following lemma gives an algebraic condition that the message functions $f \in \mathcal{L}((k+2g_e-1)P_\infty)$ we are interested in list decoding must satisfy. The proof is a standard argument comparing the pole order to the number of zeroes.

Lemma 3.6. *If f is a function in $\mathcal{L}((k+2g_e-1)P_\infty)$ whose encoding (3) agrees with the received word $\mathbf{y}$ in at least t columns with $t > \frac{D+k+2g_e-1}{m-s+1}$, then*

$$Q(f, f^{\sigma^{-1}}, \ldots, f^{\sigma^{-(s-1)}}) = A_0 + A_1 f + A_2 f^{\sigma^{-1}} + \cdots + A_s f^{\sigma^{-(s-1)}} = 0. \quad (10)$$

Proof. The proof proceeds by comparing the number of zeros of the function $Q(f, f^{\sigma^{-1}}, \ldots, f^{\sigma^{-(s-1)}}) = A_0 + A_1 f + A_2 f^{\sigma^{-1}} + \cdots + A_s f^{\sigma^{-(s-1)}}$ with $D+k+2g_e-1$. Note that $Q(f, f^{\sigma^{-1}}, \ldots, f^{\sigma^{-(s-1)}})$ is a function in $\mathcal{L}((D+k+2g_e-1)P_\infty)$. If column i of the encoding (3) of f agrees with $\mathbf{y}$, then for all $j = 0, 1, \ldots, m-s$, we have

$$\begin{aligned} 0 &= A_0(P_i^{\sigma^j}) + A_1(P_i^{\sigma^j})y_{i,j+1} + A_2(P_i^{\sigma^j})y_{i,j+2} + \cdots + A_s(P_i^{\sigma^j})y_{i,j+s} \\ &= A_0(P_i^{\sigma^j}) + A_1(P_i^{\sigma^j})f(P_i^{\sigma^j}) + A_2(P_i^{\sigma^j})f(P_i^{\sigma^{j+1}}) + \cdots + A_s(P_i^{\sigma^j})f(P_i^{\sigma^{j+s-1}}) \\ &= A_0(P_i^{\sigma^j}) + A_1(P_i^{\sigma^j})f(P_i^{\sigma^j}) + A_2(P_i^{\sigma^j})f^{\sigma^{-1}}(P_i^{\sigma^j}) + \cdots + A_s(P_i^{\sigma^j})f^{\sigma^{-(s-1)}}(P_i^{\sigma^j}) \\ &= (A_0 + A_1 f + A_2 f^{\sigma^{-1}} + \cdots + A_s f^{\sigma^{-(s-1)}})(P_i^{\sigma^j}). \end{aligned}$$

Note that here we use the fact that $f^\sigma(P^\sigma) = f(P)^\sigma = f(P)$, or equivalently $f(P^\sigma) = f^{\sigma^{-1}}(P)$. In other words, $Q(f, f^{\sigma^{-1}}, \ldots, f^{\sigma^{-(s-1)}})$ has $(m-s+1)$ distinct zeros from this agreeing column. Thus, there are a total of at least $t(m-s+1)$ zeros for all the agreeing columns. Hence, $Q(f, f^{\sigma^{-1}}, \ldots, f^{\sigma^{-(s-1)}})$ must be the zero function when $t(m-s-1) > D+k+2g_e-1$. □

Solving the functional equation for f. Our goal next is to recover the list of solutions f to the functional equation (10). Recall that our message functions lie in $\mathrm{Im}(\kappa_{P_0})$, so we can recover f by recovering the top k coefficients $(f_0, f_1, \ldots, f_{k-1})$ of its local expansion $f = \sum_{j=0}^\infty f_j x^j$ at P_0. We now prove that $(f_0, f_1, \ldots, f_{k-1})$ for f satisfying Equation (10) belong to a "periodic" subspace (in the sense of Definition 1) of not too large dimension.

Lemma 3.7. *The set of solutions $(f_0, f_1, \ldots, f_{k-1}) \in \mathbb{F}_q^k$ such that $f = f_0 + f_1 x + f_2 x^2 + \cdots \in \mathcal{L}((k+2g_e-1)P_\infty)$ obeys equation*

$$A_0 + A_1 f + A_2 f^{\sigma^{-1}} + \cdots + A_s f^{\sigma^{-(s-1)}} = 0\,, \quad (11)$$

when the A_i's obey the pole order restrictions of Lemma 3.5 and at least one A_i is nonzero, is an affine subspace W of dimension at most $(s-1)\left\lceil \frac{k}{q-1} \right\rceil$.

Further, there are at most q^{Nm+s+1} possible choices of the subspace W (as a function of the A_i's), each of which is $(s, q-1)$-periodic. Given the representation of each A_i w.r.t the basis (1), we can find a representation of W in terms of the periodic subspace U of dimension less than s, and the affine shifts in each window of $q-1$ coordinates, in the sense of Definition 1.

Proof. Let $u = \min\{\nu_{P_0}(A_i) : i = 1, 2, \ldots, s\}$. Then it is clear that $u \geqslant 0$ and $\nu_{P_0}(A_0) \geqslant u$. Each A_i has a local expansion at P_0:

$$A_i = x^u \sum_{j=0}^\infty a_{i,j} x^j$$

for $i = 0, 1, \ldots, s-1$, which can be efficiently computed from the basis representation of the A_i's. From the definition of u, one knows that the polynomial

$$B_0(X) := a_{1,0} + a_{2,0}X + \cdots + a_{s,0}X^{s-1}$$

is nonzero. Assume that at P_0, the function f has a local expansion $\sum_{j=0}^\infty f_j x^j$. Then $f^{\sigma^{-i}}$ has a local expansion at P_0 as follows

$$f^{\sigma^{-i}} = \sum_{j=0}^\infty \xi^{ij} f_j x^j,$$

where $\xi = 1/\gamma$. The coefficient of x^{d+u} in the local expansion of $Q(f, f^{\sigma^{-1}}, \ldots, f^{\sigma^{-(s-1)}})$ is

$$0 = B_0(\xi^d) f_d + \sum_{i=0}^{d-1} b_i f_i + a_{0,d}, \quad (12)$$

where $b_i \in \mathbb{F}_q$ is a linear combination of $a_{i,j}$ which does not involve f_j. Hence, f_d is uniquely determined by $f_0, \ldots, f_{d-1}$ as long as $B_0(\xi^d) \neq 0$. Let $S := \{0 \leqslant d \leqslant q-2 : B_0(\xi^d) = 0\}$. Then it is clear that $|S| \leqslant s-1$ since the order of ξ is $q-1$ and $B_0(X)$ has degree at most $s-1$. Thus, $B_0(\xi^j) \neq 0$ if and only if $j \mod (q-1) \notin S$; and in this case f_j is a fixed affine linear combination of f_i for $0 \leqslant i < j$. Note that $B_0(X)$ has at most $(s-1)\left\lceil \frac{k}{q-1} \right\rceil$ roots among $\{\xi^i : i = 0, 1, \ldots, k-1\}$. It follows that the set of solutions $(f_0, f_1, \ldots, f_{k-1})$ is an affine space $W \subset \mathbb{F}_q^k$, and the dimension of W is at most $(s-1)\left\lceil \frac{k}{q-1} \right\rceil$.

The fact that W is $(s, q-1)$-smooth follows from (12) and noting that the coefficients b_{d-j} for $j \geqslant 1$ in that equation are given by $B_j(\xi^{d-j})$ where $B_j(X) := a_{1,j} + a_{2,j}X + \cdots + a_{s,j}X^{s-1}$. Therefore, once the values of f_i, $0 \leqslant i < (j-1)(q-1)$ are fixed, the possible choices for the next block of $(q-1)$ coordinates, $f_{(j-1)(q-1)}, \cdots, f_{j(q-1)-1}$, lie in an affine shift of a fixed subspace of dimension at most $(s-1)$. Further, this shift is an easily computed affine linear combination of the f_i's in the previous blocks. This implies the efficient computability of the claimed representation of W.

Finally, by the choice of D in (7), the total number of possible $(A_0, A_1, \ldots, A_s)$ and hence the number of possible functional equations (11), is at most $q^{N(m-s+1)+s+1} \leqslant q^{Nm+s+1}$. Therefore, the number of possible candidate subspaces W is also at most q^{Nm+s+1}. $\square$

Combining Lemmas 3.6 and 3.7, we conclude, after some simple calculations, that one can find a representation of the $(s, q-1)$-periodic subspace containing all candidate messages $(f_0, f_1, \ldots, f_{k-1})$ in polynomial time, when the fraction of errors $\tau = 1 - t/N$ satisfies

$$\tau \leqslant \frac{s}{s+1} - \frac{s}{s+1}\frac{k}{N(m-s+1)} - \frac{3m}{m-s+1}\frac{g_e}{mN}. \quad (13)$$

Pruning the subspace. Applying Lemma 3.7 directly we would get a list size bound of $\approx q^{sk/q}$ which would be superpolynomial in the code length unless $k = O(q)$. Thus this idea does not directly allow us to get good list decodable codes while keeping the base field size small or achieve a list size that grows polynomially in s. Instead what we show is that by only encoding $(f_0, f_1, \ldots, f_{k-1}) \in \mathbb{F}_q^k$ that are restricted to belong to a special *subspace-evasive set*, we can (i) bring down the list size, *and* (ii) find this list efficiently in polynomial time (and further the exponent of the polynomial is independent of ε, the gap to capacity). To this end, we develop the necessary machinery concerning subspace evasive sets next. Later, in Section 5, we combine these subspace evasive sets with our folded Hermitian codes to get good list-decodable codes.

4. SUBSPACE EVASIVE SETS WITH ADDITIONAL STRUCTURE

Let us first recall the notion of "ordinary" subspace-evasive sets from [6].

Definition 4. *A subset $S \subset \mathbb{F}_q^k$ is said to be (d, ℓ)-subspace-evasive if for all d-dimensional affine subspaces W of $\mathbb{F}_q^k$, we have $|S \cap W| \leqslant \ell$.*

We next define the notion of evasiveness w.r.t a collection of subspaces instead of all subspaces of a particular dimension.

Definition 5. *Let $\mathcal{F}$ be a family of (affine) subspaces of $\mathbb{F}_q^k$, each of dimension at most d. A subset $S \subset \mathbb{F}_q^k$ is said to be $(\mathcal{F}, d, \ell)$-evasive if for all $W \in \mathcal{F}$, we have $|S \cap W| \leqslant \ell$.*

The key to pruning the list to a small size is the notion of a *hierarchical subspace-evasive set*, which is defined as a subset of $\mathbb{F}_q^k$ with the property that some of its prefixes are subspace-evasive with respect to (s, Δ)-periodic subspaces. We will show how the special subspace-evasive sets help towards pruning the list in our list decoding context in Lemma 4.2.

Definition 6. *Let $\mathcal{F}$ be a family of (s, Δ)-periodic subspaces of $\mathbb{F}_q^k$. A subset $S \subset \mathbb{F}_q^k$ is said to be $(\mathcal{F}, s, \Delta, L)$-h.s.e (for hierarchically subspace evasive for block size Δ) if for every affine subspace $W \in \mathcal{F}$, the following bound holds for $j = 1, 2, \ldots, b$: $|\mathrm{proj}_{j\Delta}(S) \cap \mathrm{proj}_{j\Delta}(W)| \leqslant L$.*

Pseudorandom construction of large h.s.e subsets. Our goal is to give a randomized construction of large h.s.e sets that works with high probability, with the further properties that one can index into elements of this set efficiently (necessary for efficient encoding), and one can check membership in the set efficiently (which is important for efficient decoding).

Suppose, for some fixed subset $\mathcal{F}$ of (s, Δ)-periodic subspaces of $\mathbb{F}_q^k$, we are interested in an $(\mathcal{F}, s, \Delta, \ell)$-h.s.e subset of $\mathbb{F}_q^k$ of size $\approx q^{(1-\zeta)k}$ for a constant ζ, $1/\Delta < \zeta < 1$. For simplicity, let us assume that the block size Δ divides k, though arbitrary k can be easily handled. Define $b = \frac{k}{\Delta}$ to be the number of blocks. The parameters b, Δ, k and field size q will be considered fixed for the rest of the discussion in this section.

Our construction will use some *arbitrary fixed* subsets Λ_1, $\Lambda_2, \ldots, \Lambda_b$ where $\Lambda_i \subseteq \mathbb{F}_{q^{i\Delta}}$ with $|\Lambda_i| = q^{(i-\zeta)\Delta}$. The only requirement from the subsets Λ_i is that membership in them can be checked using at most poly$(i\Delta)$ operations over $\mathbb{F}_q$. In what follows we assume that, for $i = 1, 2, \ldots, b$, some fixed bases of the fields $\mathbb{F}_{q^{i\Delta}}$ have been chosen, giving us some canonical $\mathbb{F}_q$-linear injective maps $\rho_i : \mathbb{F}_q^{i\Delta} \to \mathbb{F}_{q^{i\Delta}}$.

The random part of the construction will consist of two sets of mutually independent, random polynomials P_1, P_2, $\ldots, P_b$ and $Q_1, Q_2, \ldots, Q_b$ where $P_i, Q_i \in \mathbb{F}_{q^{i\Delta}}[T]$ are random polynomials of degree λ for $1 \leqslant i \leqslant b$. [3] The degree parameter will be chosen to be $\lambda = \Theta(k)$.

Note that by virtue of the λ-wise independence of the values of a random degree λ polynomial, and the independent choices of P_i, Q_i, for a collection of subsets $T_i \subseteq \mathbb{F}_{q^{i\Delta}}$ with $|T_i| \leqslant \lambda$, the values $\{P_i(\alpha_i), Q_i(\alpha_i)\}_{\alpha_i \in T_i}$ are independent random values in $\mathbb{F}_{q^{i\Delta}}$, and moreover the values for different i's are independent.

With these ingredients in place, we now describe our construction of the h.s.e subset. Our construction is based on an encoding map from strings in $\mathbb{F}_q^{(1-3\zeta)k}$ to $\mathbb{F}_q^k$, and letting the image of this map be the set. (The full version of the paper gradually works its way to this construction, but here we directly give this construction.)

Definition 7 (Encoding into the h.s.e set). *Given the polynomials $P_1, P_2, \ldots, P_b$ and $Q_1, \ldots, Q_b$, and the subsets $\Lambda_i \subseteq \mathbb{F}_{q^{i\Delta}}$, the encoding of $\mathbf{x} = (x_1, x_2, \ldots, x_b)$ where $x_i \in \mathbb{F}_q^{(1-3\zeta)\Delta}$, proceeds as follows:*

For $i = 1, 2, \ldots, b$

- *Let $\beta_i \in \mathbb{F}_q^{3\zeta\Delta}$ be the lexicographically first string such that $P_i(\rho_i(x_1 \circ \beta_1 \circ \cdots \circ x_i \circ \beta_i)) \in \Lambda_i$ and $Q_i(\rho_i(x_1 \circ \beta_1 \circ \cdots \circ x_i \circ \beta_i)) \in \Lambda_i$. If no such β_i exists, fail.*

Output $x_1 \circ \beta_1 \circ x_2 \circ \beta_2 \circ \cdots \circ x_b \circ \beta_b \in \mathbb{F}_q^k$ as the encoding of $\mathbf{x}$.

We will denote the above encoding map by HSE *and refer to Δ as its period size (we suppress the dependence of the map on the P_i's and Q_i's for convenience).*

The following is the main theorem regarding this construction. The proof that HSE is well defined is based on the fact at each stage i, regardless of the choice of $\beta_1, \ldots, \beta_{i-1}$, there

[3] We will assume that representations of the necessary extension fields $\mathbb{F}_q^{i\Delta}$ are all available. For this purpose, we only need irreducible polynomials over $\mathbb{F}_q$ of degree $i\Delta$, which can be constructed by picking random polynomials and checking them for irreducibility. Our final construction is anyway randomized, so the randomized nature of this step does not affect the results.

are an expected $q^{\zeta\Delta}$ choices of β_i satisfying the required condition, and this random variable is well-concentrated due to λ-wise independence. The h.s.e property is proved by a careful inductive argument, showing that for $i = 1, 2, \ldots, b$, the projection of the image HSE onto the first $i\Delta$ coordinates intersects the corresponding projection of all subspaces in $\mathcal{F}$ in at most L points. By the definition of (s, Δ)-periodic subspaces, this means that at the next stage $i+1$, only $L \cdot q^s$ candidates are in play to belong to the intersection, which is small enough for us to afford a union bound and perform the inductive step (the λ-wise independence is again used in this step). The details appear in the full version of the paper.

THEOREM 4.1. **(Main construction of h.s.e. subsets)** *Suppose b, c, Δ, k, s are positive integers and $\zeta \in (0, 1)$ such that following requirements are met:*

$$k = b\Delta; \quad s < \zeta\Delta/10; \quad q^{\zeta\Delta} \geqslant (2cqk)^{10/9} . \tag{14}$$

Let $\mathcal{F}$ be a family of (s, Δ)-periodic subspaces of $\mathbb{F}_q^k$ with $|\mathcal{F}| \leqslant q^{ck}$. Then, for a random and independent choice of polynomials $P_i, Q_i \in \mathbb{F}_{q^{i\Delta}}[T]$ of degree $\lambda = \max\{6k, ck+1\}$ and any subsets Λ_i of size $q^{(i-\zeta)\Delta}$ for $i = 1, 2, \ldots, b$, the following conditions both hold with probability at least $1 - 2^{-\Omega(k)}$:

1. *$\mathsf{HSE} : \mathbb{F}_q^{(1-3\zeta)k} \to \mathbb{F}_q^k$ from Definition 7 is a well-defined injective map, and can be computed using $O(q^{3\zeta\Delta}k^3 \log^2 k)$ operations over $\mathbb{F}_q$.*
2. *The set $H = \Gamma(P_1, \ldots, P_b) \cap \Gamma(Q_1, \ldots, Q_b)$, and in particular the image of HSE, is a $(\mathcal{F}, s, \Delta, ck)$-h.s.e and a $(\mathcal{F}, sb, 20c/\zeta)$-evasive subset of $\mathbb{F}_q^k$.*

Efficient computation of intersection with h.s.e. subsets. The key aspect which makes h.s.e subsets useful in our context to prune the affine space of candidate messages, and indeed guided the exact specifics of the definition and construction, is the following claim which shows that intersection of a (s, Δ)-periodic subspace with our h.s.e set can found efficiently.

LEMMA 4.2. *Suppose polynomials P_i, Q_i, $i = 1, 2, \ldots, b$, of degree $\lambda = \max\{6k, ck+1\}$ have been picked so that the map HSE satisfies the conditions of Theorem 4.1 w.r.t some family $\mathcal{F}$ of at most q^{ck} affine subspaces of $\mathbb{F}_q^k$ each of which is (s, Δ)-periodic. Then given a representation of $W \in \mathcal{F}$ (as in Definition 1), we can find the list of at most $O(c/\zeta)$ values of $\mathbf{x} \in \mathbb{F}_q^{(1-3\zeta)k}$ such that $\mathsf{HSE}(\mathbf{x}) \in \mathcal{F}$ using $O\left(c^2(kq^s + q^{3\zeta\Delta})k^3 \log^2 k\right)$ operations over $\mathbb{F}_q$.*

PROOF. The fact that there are at most ℓ solutions $\mathbf{x}$ follows immediately from the fact that the image of HSE is $(\mathcal{F}, sb, \ell)$-evasive. So we only need to argue about the time complexity.

For $1 \leqslant i \leqslant b$, define $H_i = \mathrm{proj}_{i\Delta}(H)$ where $H = \Gamma(P_1, \ldots, P_b) \cap \Gamma(Q_1, \ldots, Q_b)$. Likewise, define $W_i = \mathrm{proj}_{i\Delta}(W)$. To compute the intersection $H \cap W$ list efficiently, we iteratively find $W_i \cap H_i$ for $i = 1, 2, \ldots, b$ as follows. Recall that we know that $|H_i \cap W_i| \leqslant L$ for each i as H is $(\mathcal{F}, s, \Delta, L)$-h.s.e. For each of the at most $L = ck$ candidates in $W_{i-1} \cap H_{i-1}$, as W is (s, Δ)-periodic, there are at most q^s possible extensions to the next block of $(q-1)$ coordinates which we can find and list using $O(q^s \cdot k\Delta)$ operations. (The $k\Delta$ term comes from computing the affine shift for the i'th block for that particular prefix of $(i-1)\Delta$ symbols.)

We then test each of $L \cdot q^s$ candidates for membership in Γ_i which can be done using $O(ck^2 \log^2 k)$ $\mathbb{F}_q$-operations time by evaluating the degree λ polynomial and checking that the resulting value belongs to Λ_i. By the $(\mathcal{F}, s, \Delta, L)$-h.s.e property of H there are at most L of these candidates that can belong to H_i, thus bringing our list size back to L. The runtime for each iterative step is $O(Lq^s k\Delta + Lq^s ck^2 \log^2 k) = O(cLq^s k^2 \log^2 k)$ $\mathbb{F}_q$-operations, leading to an overall runtime for all $b < k$ stages of $O(cLq^s k^3 \log^2 k)$ operations over $\mathbb{F}_q$ to recover the intersection $H \cap W$. Finally for each $\mathbf{y} \in H \cap W$, we can check if it is the range of HSE by writing $\mathbf{y} = x_1 \circ \beta_1 \circ \cdots \circ x_b \circ \beta_b$ and checking that $\mathsf{HSE}(x_1 \circ x_2 \circ \cdots \circ x_b) = \mathbf{y}$, which takes $O(q^{3\zeta\Delta}ck^3 \log^2 k)$ operations over $\mathbb{F}_q$. □

5. COMBINING FOLDED HERMITIAN CODES AND H.S.E SETS

Instead of encoding arbitrary $\mathbf{f} \in \mathbb{F}_q^k$ by the folded Hermitian code (Definition 3), we can restrict the messages $\mathbf{f}$ to belong to the range of our h.s.e set, so that the affine space of solutions guaranteed by Lemma 3.7 can be efficiently pruned to a small list. The formal claim is below.

THEOREM 5.1. *Let $e \geqslant 2$ be an integer, $r \geqslant 2e$ be a large enough prime power, $q = r^2$, and $\zeta \in (1/q, 1)$. Let $k \leqslant q^{\zeta q/2}$ be a positive integer. Let s, m be positive integers satisfying $1 \leqslant s \leqslant m \leqslant q-1$ and $s < \zeta q/12$. Finally let N be an integer satisfying $k + 2er^e \leqslant Nm \leqslant (q-1)r^e$.*

Consider the code C_1 with encoding $E_1 : \mathbb{F}_q^{(1-3\zeta)k} \to (\mathbb{F}_q^m)^N$ defined as

$$E_1(\mathbf{x}) = \mathsf{FH}(N, k, q, e, m)(\mathsf{HSE}(\mathbf{x})) ,$$

for $\mathsf{HSE} : \mathbb{F}_q^{(1-3\zeta)k} \to \mathbb{F}_q^k$ from Definition 7 for a period size $\Delta = q - 1$.

Then, with high probability over the choice of HSE, this code has rate $R = (1-3\zeta)k/(Nm)$, can be encoded in $\mathrm{poly}(Nmq^{\zeta q})$ time, and is (τ, ℓ)-list decodable in time $\mathrm{poly}(Nmq^{\zeta q})$ for $\ell \leqslant O(1/(R\zeta))$ and

$$\tau = \frac{s}{s+1}\left(1 - \frac{k}{N(m-s+1)}\right) - \frac{3m}{m-s+1}\frac{er^e}{mN} .$$

PROOF. This follows by just combining the ingredients we have developed so far. Since $g_e \leqslant er^e$ by (2), the condition on N, m meets the requirement for the construction of the folded Hermitian tower based code in Definition 2.

Whp, the map HSE is well-defined and injective, and so E_1 is an injective encoding. The rate of the code is therefore clearly as claimed. With $\Delta = q-1$, one can check that the conditions of Theorem 4.1 are met for our choice of ζ, s, q, k. By Theorem 4.1 , Part 1, HSE can be computed in time $\mathrm{poly}(Nmq^{\zeta q})$ and hence so can E_1 (as FH is efficiently encodable as well).

The claimed value of the error fraction τ satisfies (13) since the genus is at most er^e by (2). By Lemma 3.7, we know that the candidate messages found by the decoder lie in one of at most q^{2Nm} possible $(s, q-1)$-periodic subspaces. Appealing to Theorem 4.1 and Lemma 4.2 with the choice $c = 2Nm/k = O(1/R)$, we conclude that there is a decoding algorithm running in time $\mathrm{poly}(Nmq^{\zeta q})$ to list decode C_1 from a fraction τ of errors, outputting at most $O(1/(R\zeta))$ messages in the worst-case. □

Let $\varepsilon > 0$ be a small positive constant, and a family of codes of length N (assumed large enough) and rate $R \in (0,1)$ is sought. Pick n to be a growing parameter.

By picking $s = \Theta(1/\varepsilon)$, $m = \Theta(1/\varepsilon^2)$, $r = \lfloor \log n \rfloor$, $e = \lceil \frac{\log n}{\log\log n} \rceil$, $\zeta = (\log n \log\log n)^{-1}$, $N = \lfloor \frac{(r^2-1)r^e}{m} \rfloor$, and k proportional to Nm in Theorem 5.1, we can conclude the following.

COROLLARY 5.2. *For any $R \in (0,1)$ and positive constant $\varepsilon \in (0,1)$, there is a Monte Carlo construction of a family of codes of rate at least R over an alphabet size $(\log N)^{O(1/\varepsilon^2)}$ that are encodable and $(1-R-\varepsilon, O(R^{-1}\log N \log\log N))$-list decodable in $\mathrm{poly}(N, 1/\varepsilon)$ time, where N is the block length of the code.*

Our main result (Theorem 1.1) achieves better parameters than the above — an alphabet size of $\exp(\tilde{O}(1/\varepsilon^2))$ and list-size of $O(1/(R\varepsilon))$. This is based on the Garcia-Stichtenoth tower and is described next.

6. FOLDED CODES FROM THE GARCIA-STICHTENOTH TOWER

Compared with the Hermitian tower of function fields, the Garcia-Stichtenoth tower of function fields yields folded codes with better parameters due to the fact that it achieves the optimal ratio between number of rational places and the genus. The construction of folded codes from the Garcia-Stichtenoth tower is almost identical to the one from the Hermitian tower except for one major difference: the redefined code from the Garcia-Stichtenoth tower is constructed in terms of the local expansion at point P_∞, while in the Hermitian case local expansion at P_0 is considered. For convenience of the reader, we give a parallel description of folded codes from the Garcia-Stichtenoth tower, while only sketching the identical parts.

6.1 Background on Garcia-Stichtenoth tower

Again let r be a prime power and let $q = r^2$. We denote by $\mathbb{F}_q$ the finite field with q elements. The Garcia-Stichtenoth towers that we are going to use for our code construction were discussed in [3, 4]. The reader may refer to [3, 4] for the detailed background on the Garcia-Stichtenoth function tower. There are two optimal Garcia-Stichtenoth towers that are equivalent. For simplicity, we introduce the tower defined by the following recursive equations [4]

$$x_{i+1}^r + x_{i+1} = \frac{x_i^r}{x_i^{r-1}+1}, \quad i = 1, 2, \dots, e-1.$$

Put $K_e = \mathbb{F}_q(x_1, x_2, \dots, x_e)$ for $e \geqslant 2$.

Rational places. The function field K_e has at least $r^{e-1}(r^2 - r) + 1$ rational places. One of these is the "point at infinity" which is the unique pole P_∞ of x_1 (and is fully ramified). The other $r^{e-1}(r^2 - r)$ come from the rational places lying over the unique zero of $x_1 - \alpha$ for each $\alpha \in \mathbb{F}_q$ with $\alpha^r + \alpha \neq 0$. Note that for every $\alpha \in \mathbb{F}_q$ with $\alpha^r + \alpha \neq 0$, the unique zero of $x_1 - \alpha$ splits completely in K_e, i.e., there are r^{e-1} rational places lying over the zero of $x_1 - \alpha$. Let $\mathbb{P}$ be the set of all the rational places lying over the zero of $x_1 - \alpha$ for all $\alpha \in \mathbb{F}_q$ with $\alpha^r + \alpha \neq 0$. Then, intuitively, one can think of the $r^{e-1}(r^2-r)$ rational places in $\mathbb{P}$ as being given by e-tuples $(\alpha_1, \alpha_2, \dots, \alpha_e) \in \mathbb{F}_q^e$ that satisfy $\alpha_{i+1}^r + \alpha_{i+1} = \frac{\alpha_i^r}{\alpha_i^{r-1}+1}$ for $i = 1, 2, \dots, e-1$ and $\alpha_1^r + \alpha_1 \neq 0$. For each value of $\alpha \in \mathbb{F}_q$, there are precisely r solutions to $\beta \in \mathbb{F}_q$ satisfying $\beta^r + \beta = \frac{\alpha^r}{\alpha^{r-1}+1}$, so the number of such e-tuples is $r^{e-1}(r^2 - r)$ ($r^2 - r$ choices for α_1, and then r choices for each successive α_i, $2 \leqslant i \leqslant e$).

Riemann-Roch spaces. As shown in [13], every function of K_e with a pole only at P_∞ has an expression of the form

$$x_1^a \left(\sum_{i_1=0}^{(e-2)r+1} \sum_{i_2=0}^{r-1} \cdots \sum_{i_e=0}^{r-1} c_i h_1 \frac{x_1^{i_1} x_2^{i_2} \cdots x_e^{i_e}}{\pi_2 \dots \pi_{e-1}} \right), \tag{15}$$

where $a \geqslant 0, c_i \in \mathbb{F}_q$, and for $1 \leqslant j < e$, $h_j = x_j^{r-1} + 1$ and $\pi_j = h_1 h_2 \dots h_j$. Moreover, Shum et al. [13] present an algorithm running in time polynomial in l that outputs a basis of over $\mathbb{F}_q$ of $\mathcal{L}(lP_\infty)$ explicitly in the above form.

We stress that evaluating elements of $\mathcal{L}(lP_\infty)$ at the rational places of $\mathbb{P}$ is easy: we simply have to evaluate a linear combination of the monomials allowed in (15) at the tuples $(\alpha_1, \alpha_2, \dots, \alpha_e) \in \mathbb{F}_q^e$ mentioned above. In other words, it is just evaluating an e-variate polynomial at a specific subset of $r^{e-1}(r^2 - r)$ points of $\mathbb{F}_q^e$, and can be accomplished in polynomial time.

Genus. The genus g_e of the function field K_e is given by

$$g_e = \begin{cases} (r^{e/2} - 1)^2 & \text{if } e \text{ is even} \\ (r^{(e-1)/2} - 1)(r^{(e+1)/2} - 1) & \text{if } e \text{ is odd.} \end{cases}$$

Thus the genus g_e is at most r^e. (Compare this with the er^e bound for the Hermitian tower; this smaller genus is what allows to pick e as large as we want in the Garcia-Stichtenoth tower, while keeping the field size q fixed.)

A useful automorphism. Let γ be a primitive element of $\mathbb{F}_r$ and consider the automorphism $\sigma \in \mathrm{Aut}(K_e/\mathbb{F}_q)$ defined by

$$\sigma : x_i \mapsto \gamma^{(r+1)r^{i-1}} x_i \quad \text{for } i = 1, 2, \dots, e.$$

Then the order of σ is $r - 1$ and furthermore, we have the following facts:

(i) σ keeps P_∞ unchanged, i.e., $P_\infty{}^\sigma = P_\infty$;

(ii) Let $\mathbb{P}$ be the set of all the rational places lying over $x_1 - \alpha$ for all $\alpha \in \mathbb{F}_q$ with $\alpha^r + \alpha \neq 0$. Then $|\mathbb{P}| = (r-1)r^e$. Moreover, σ divides $\mathbb{P}$ into r^e orbits and each orbit has $r - 1$ places. For an integer m with $1 \leqslant m \leqslant r - 1$, we can label Nm distinct elements

$$P_1, P_1^\sigma, \dots, P_1^{\sigma^{m-1}}, \dots, P_N, P_N^\sigma, \dots, P_N^{\sigma^{m-1}}$$

in $\mathbb{P}$, as long as $N \leqslant r^e \lfloor \frac{r-1}{m} \rfloor$.

The folded codes from the Garcia-Stichtenoth tower are defined similarly to the Hermitian case.

DEFINITION 8. **(Folded codes from the GS tower)** *Assume that m, k, N are positive integers satisfying $1 \leqslant m \leqslant r - 1$ and $l/m < N \leqslant r^e \lfloor \frac{r-1}{m} \rfloor$. The folded code from K_e with parameters N, l, q, e, m, denoted by $\widetilde{\mathsf{FGS}}(N, l, q, e, m)$, encodes a message function $f \in \mathcal{L}(lP_\infty)$ as*

$$f \mapsto \left(\begin{bmatrix} f(P_1) \\ f(P_1^\sigma) \\ \vdots \\ f(P_1^{\sigma^{m-1}}) \end{bmatrix}, \dots, \begin{bmatrix} f(P_N) \\ f(P_N^\sigma) \\ \vdots \\ f(P_N^{\sigma^{m-1}}) \end{bmatrix} \right) \in \left(\mathbb{F}_q^m\right)^N. \tag{16}$$

Then we have a similar result on parameters of $\widetilde{\mathsf{FGS}}(N, l, q, e, m)$.

LEMMA 6.1. *The above code $\widetilde{\mathsf{FGS}}(N, l, q, e, m)$ is an $\mathbb{F}_q$-linear code over alphabet size q^m, rate at least $\frac{l-g_e+1}{Nm}$, and minimum distance at least $N - \frac{l}{m}$.*

6.2 Redefining the code in terms of local expansion at P_∞

In the Hermitain case, we use coefficients of its power series expansion around P_0. However, for the Garcia-Stictenoth tower we do not have such a nice point P_0. Fortunately, we can use point P_∞ to achieve our mission.

Again for our decoding, we will actually recover the message $f \in \mathcal{L}(lP_\infty)$ in terms of the coefficients of its power series expansion around P_∞

$$f = T^{-l}(f_0 + f_1T + f_2T^2 + \cdots)$$

where $T := \frac{1}{x_e}$ is the local parameter at P_∞ (which means that x_e has exactly one pole at P_∞, i.e., $\nu_{P_\infty}(x_e) = -1$).

In this case we can also show that one can efficiently move back-and-forth between the representation of $f \in \mathcal{L}(lP_\infty)$ in terms of a basis for $\mathcal{L}(lP_\infty)$ and its power series representation $(f_0, f_1, \dots)$ around P_∞. Since the mapping $f \mapsto (f_0, f_1, \dots)$ is $\mathbb{F}_q$-linear, it suffices to compute the local expansion at P_∞ of a basis for $\mathcal{L}(lP_\infty)$.

LEMMA 6.2. *For any n, one can compute the first n terms of the local expansion of the basis elements* (15) *at P_∞ using* poly(n) *operations over $\mathbb{F}_q$.*

PROOF. First let h be a nonzero function in $\mathbb{F}_q(x_1, x_2, \dots, x_e)$ with $\nu_{P_\infty}(h) = v \in \mathbb{Z}$. Assume that the local expansion $h = T^v \sum_{j=0}^{\infty} a_jT^j$ is known. To find the local expansion $\frac{1}{h} = T^{-v} \sum_{j=0}^{\infty} c_jT^j$. Consider the identity

$$1 = \left(\sum_{j=0}^{\infty} c_jT^j\right)\left(\sum_{j=0}^{\infty} a_jT^j\right).$$

Then by comparing the coefficients of T^i in the above identity, one has $c_0 = a_0^{-1}$ and $c_i = -a_0^{-1}(c_{i-1}a_1 + \cdots + c_0a_i)$ can be easily computed recursively for all $i \geqslant 1$.

Thus, by the structure of the basis functions in (15), it is sufficient to find an algorithm of efficiently finding local expansions of x_i at P_∞ for every $i = 1, 2, \dots, e$. We can inductively find the local expansions of x_i at P_∞ as follows. We note that $\nu_{P_\infty}(x_i) = -r^{e-i}$ for $i = 1, 2, \dots, e$.

For $i = e$, x_e has the local expansion $\frac{1}{T}$ at P_∞.

Now assume that we know the local expansion of x_i. Then we can easily compute the local expansion of $x_i^r + x_i$ and hence the local expansion of $1/(x_i^r + x_i)$. Let us assume that $1/(x_i^r + x_i)$ has local expansion

$$1/(x_i^r + x_i) = T^{r^{e-i+1}} \sum_{j=0}^{\infty} \alpha_jT^j$$

at P_∞ for some $\alpha_i \in \mathbb{F}_q$. Assume that $1/x_{i-1}$ has the local expansion $1/x_{i-1} = T^{r^{e-i+1}} \sum_{j=0}^{\infty} \beta_jT^j$. To find β_j, we consider the identity

$$\begin{aligned} T^{r^{e-i+1}} \sum_{j=0}^{\infty} \beta_jT^j + T^{r^{e-i+2}} \sum_{j=0}^{\infty} \beta_j^rT^{rj} &= \frac{1}{x_{i-1}} + \left(\frac{1}{x_{i-1}}\right)^r \\ &= \frac{1}{x_i^r + x_i} \\ &= T^{r^{e-i+1}} \sum_{j=0}^{\infty} \alpha_jT^j. \end{aligned}$$

By comparing the coefficients of $T^{j+r^{e-i+1}}$ in the above identity, we have that $\beta_0 = \alpha_0$ and β_j can be easily computed recursively by the following formula for all $i \geqslant 1$.

$$\beta_j = \begin{cases} \alpha_j & \text{if } r \not| j \\ \alpha_j - \beta_{j/r-1}^r & \text{if } r|j. \end{cases}$$

Therefore, the local expansion of x_{i-1} at P_∞ can be easily computed. □

As in the Hermitian case, we will actually need to index the messages of the code by the first k coefficients $(f_0, f_1, \dots, f_{k-1})$ of the local expansion of the function f at P_∞.

Let us define the local expansion map $\mathsf{ev}_{P_\infty} : \mathcal{L}((k+2g_e-1)P_\infty) \to \mathbb{F}_q^k$ that maps f to $(f_0, f_1, \dots, f_{k-1})$ where $f = T^{-(k+2g_e-1)}(f_0 + f_1T + f_2T^2 + \cdots)$ is the local expansion of f at P_∞.

CLAIM 6.3. *ev_{P_∞} is an $\mathbb{F}_q$-linear surjective map. Further, we can compute ev_{P_∞} using* poly(k, g_e) *operations over $\mathbb{F}_q$ given a representation of the input $f \in \mathcal{L}((k+2g_e-1)P_\infty)$ in terms of the basis* (15).

The proof of this claim is similar to Claim 3.3. Note that the kernel of ev_{P_∞} is $\mathcal{L}((2g_e-1)P_\infty)$ which has dimension exactly g_e by the Riemann-Roch theorem.

For each $(f_0, f_1, \dots, f_{k-1}) \in \mathbb{F}_q^k$, we can therefore pick a pre-image in $\mathcal{L}((k+2g_e-1)P_\infty)$. For convenience, we will denote an injective map making such a unique choice by $\kappa_{P_\infty} : \mathbb{F}_q^k \to \mathcal{L}((k+2g_e-1)P_\infty)$. By picking the pre-images of a basis of $\mathbb{F}_q^k$ and extending it by linearity, we can assume κ_{P_∞} to be $\mathbb{F}_q$-linear, and thus specify it by a $(k+g_e) \times k$ matrix. We record this fact for easy reference below.

CLAIM 6.4. *The map $\kappa_{P_\infty} : \mathbb{F}_q^k \to \mathcal{L}((k+2g_e-1)P_\infty)$ is $\mathbb{F}_q$-linear and injective. We can compute a representation of this linear transformation using* poly(k, g_e) *operations over $\mathbb{F}_q$, and the map itself can be evaluated using* poly(k, g_e) *operations over $\mathbb{F}_q$.*

Now we redefine a version of the folded Garcia-Stichtenoth code that maps $\mathbb{F}_q^k$ to $(\mathbb{F}_q^m)^N$ by composing the folded encoding (16) from the original Definition 8 with κ_{P_∞}.

DEFINITION 9. **(Folded Garcia-Stichtenoth code using local expansion)** *The folded Garcia-Stichtenoth code (FGS code for short) $\mathsf{FGS}(N, k, q, e, m)$ maps $\mathbf{f} = (f_0, f_1, \dots, f_{k-1}) \in \mathbb{F}_q^k$ to $\widetilde{\mathsf{FGS}}(N, k+2g_e-1, q, e, m)(\kappa_{P_\infty}(\mathbf{f})) \in (\mathbb{F}_q^m)^N$.*

The rate of the above code equals $k/(Nm)$ and its distance is at least $N - (k+2g_e-1)/m$.

6.3 List decoding FGS codes

The list decoding part for the codes from the Garcia-Stichtenoth tower is almost identical to the Hermitian tower. We only sketch this part briefly.

If f is a function in $\mathcal{L}((k+2g_e-1)P_\infty)$ whose encoding (16) agrees with the received word $\mathbf{y}$ in at least t columns with $t > \frac{D+k+2g_e-1}{m-s+1}$ and

$$D = \left\lfloor \frac{N(m-s+1)-k+(s-1)g_e+1}{s+1} \right\rfloor ,$$

then there exist $A_i \in \mathcal{L}(DP_\infty)$ for $i = 1, 2, \ldots, s$ and $A_0 \in \mathcal{L}((D+k+2g_e-1)P_\infty)$ such that they are not all zero and

$$Q(f, f^{\sigma^{-1}}, \ldots, f^{\sigma^{-(s-1)}}) = A_0 + A_1 f + A_2 f^{\sigma^{-1}} + \cdots + A_s f^{\sigma^{-(s-1)}} = 0. \quad (17)$$

Solving the functional equation for f. As in the Hermitian case, our goal next is to recover the list of solutions f to the functional equation (17). Recall that our message functions lie in $\mathrm{Im}(\kappa_{P_\infty})$, so we can recover f by recovering the top k coefficients $(f_0, f_1, \ldots, f_{k-1})$ of its local expansion.

$$f = T^{-(k+2g_e-1)} \sum_{j=0}^{\infty} f_j T^j \quad (18)$$

at P_∞. We now prove that $(f_0, f_1, \ldots, f_{k-1})$ for f satisfying Equation (17) belong to a "periodic" subspace (in the sense of Definition 1) of not too large dimension. The proof, which is similar to Lemma 3.7, is omitted here and can be found in the full version.

Lemma 6.5. *The set of solutions* $(f_0, f_1, \ldots, f_{k-1}) \in \mathbb{F}_q^k$ *such that* $f = T^{-(k+2g_e-1)} \sum_{j=0}^{\infty} f_j T^j \in \mathcal{L}((k+2g_e-1)P_\infty)$ *obeys equation*

$$A_0 + A_1 f + A_2 f^{\sigma^{-1}} + \cdots + A_s f^{\sigma^{-(s-1)}} = 0 \quad (19)$$

when at least one A_i *is nonzero is an affine subspace* W *of dimension at most* $(s-1)\left\lceil \frac{k}{r-1} \right\rceil$.

Further, there are at most q^{Nm+s+1} *possible choices of the subspace* W*, each of which is* $(s, r-1)$*-periodic.*

Given the representation of each A_i *w.r.t the basis (15), we can find a representation of* W *in terms of the periodic subspace* U *of dimension less than* s*, and the affine shifts in each window of* $r-1$ *coordinates, in the sense of Definition 1.*

Similar to the bound (13) for the Hermitian case, we conclude, after some simple calculations and using the upper bound on genus $g_e \leqslant r^e$, that one can find a representation of the $(s, r-1)$-periodic subspace containing all candidate messages $(f_0, f_1, \ldots, f_{k-1})$ in polynomial time, when the fraction of errors $\tau = 1 - t/N$ satisfies

$$\tau \leqslant \frac{s}{s+1}\left(1 - \frac{k}{N(m-s+1)}\right) - \frac{3m}{m-s+1}\frac{r^e}{mN}. \quad (20)$$

6.4 Combining FGS codes and h.s.e sets

Similarly to Section 5, we now show how to pre-code the messages of the FGS code with a h.s.e subset. The approach is similar, though we need one idea to ensure that we can pick parameters so that the base field $\mathbb{F}_q$ can be constant-sized and obtain a final list-size bound that is a constant independent of the code length. This idea is to work with a larger "period size" Δ for the periodic subspaces, based on the following observation.

Observation 6.6. *Let* W *be an* (s, Δ)*-periodic subspace of* $\mathbb{F}_q^k$ *for* $k = b\Delta$*. Then* W *is also* $(su, \Delta u)$*-periodic for every integer* u*,* $1 \leqslant u \leqslant b$*.*

As in the Hermitian case, instead of encoding arbitrary $\mathbf{f} \in \mathbb{F}_q^k$ by the folded Garcia-Stichtenoth code (Definition 3), we will restrict the messages $\mathbf{f}$ to belong to the range of our h.s.e set. This will ensure that the affine space of solutions guaranteed by Lemma 6.5 can be efficiently pruned to a small list.

Theorem 6.7. *Let* r *be a prime power,* $q = r^2$*, and* $e \geqslant 2$ *be an integer, and* $\zeta \in (0, 1)$*. Let* $k \leqslant q^{\zeta\Delta/2}$ *be a positive integer. Let* $\Delta \leqslant k$ *be a multiple of* $(r-1)$*, say* $\Delta = u(r-1)$ *for a positive integer* u*.*

Let s, m *be positive integers satisfying* $1 \leqslant s \leqslant m \leqslant r-1$ *and* $s < \zeta r/12$*. Finally let* N *be an integer satisfying* $k + 2r^e \leqslant Nm \leqslant (r-1)r^e$*.*

Consider the code C_2 *with encoding* $E_2 : \mathbb{F}_q^{(1-3\zeta)k} \to (\mathbb{F}_q^m)^N$ *defined as*

$$E_2(\mathbf{x}) = \mathsf{FGS}(N, k, q, e, m)(\mathsf{HSE}(\mathbf{x})) ,$$

for $\mathsf{HSE} : \mathbb{F}_q^{(1-3\zeta)k} \to \mathbb{F}_q^k$ *from Definition 7 for a period size* Δ*.*

Then, with high probability over the choice of HSE *with period size* Δ*, this code has rate* $R = (1-3\zeta)k/(Nm)$*, can be encoded in* $\mathrm{poly}(Nmq^{\zeta\Delta})$ *time, and is* (τ, ℓ)*-list decodable in time* $\mathrm{poly}(Nmq^{\zeta\Delta})$ *for* $\ell \leqslant O(1/(R\zeta))$ *and*

$$\tau = \frac{s}{s+1}\left(1 - \frac{k}{N(m-s+1)}\right) - \frac{3m}{m-s+1}\frac{r^e}{mN}. \quad (21)$$

The proof of the above theorem follows by just combining the ingredients we have developed so far and is similar to that of Theorem 5.1 with the use of Observation 6.6. The details can be found in the full version.

Finally, all that is left to be done is to pick parameters to show how the above can lead to optimal rate list-decodable codes over a constant-sized alphabet which further achieve very good lists-size.

Let $\varepsilon > 0$ be a small positive constant, and a family of codes of length N (assumed large enough) and rate $R \in (0, 1)$ is sought. Pick n to be a growing parameter.

Let us pick $s = \Theta(1/\varepsilon)$, $m = \Theta(1/\varepsilon^2)$, $\zeta = \varepsilon/6$, $r = \Theta(1/\varepsilon)$, $q = r^2$, and $e = \lceil \frac{\log n}{\log r} \rceil$, $N = \lfloor \frac{(r-1)r^e}{m} \rfloor$, and $k = RNm(1+\varepsilon)$. This ensures that (i) there are at least $n = Nm$ rational places and so we get a code of length at least $n/m = N$, (ii) the rate of the code C_2 is at least R, and (iii) the error fraction (21) is at least $1 - R - \varepsilon$.

The remaining part is to pick a multiple Δ of $(r-1)$ so that the $k \leqslant q^{\zeta\Delta/2}$ condition is met. This can be achieved by choosing $u = \lceil \frac{\log n}{\log(1/\varepsilon)} \rceil$ and $\Delta = (r-1)u$. With these choices, we can conclude the following, which is the main final result of this paper.

Theorem 6.8. **(Main; Corollary to Theorem 6.7 with above choice of parameters)** *For any* $R \in (0, 1)$ *and positive constant* $\varepsilon \in (0, 1)$*, there is a Monte Carlo construction of a family of codes of rate at least* R *over an alphabet* *size* $\exp(O(\log(1/\varepsilon)/\varepsilon^2))$ *that are encodable and* $(1 - R - \varepsilon, O(1/(R\varepsilon))$*-list decodable in* $\mathrm{poly}(N)$ *time, where* N *is the block length of the code.*

It may be instructive to recap why the Hermitian tower could not give a result like the above one. In the Hermitian case, the ratio g_e/n of the genus to the number of rational places was about $e/r = e/\sqrt{q}$, and thus we needed $q > e^2$. Since the period Δ was about q, the running time of the decoder was bigger than $q^{\Omega(\zeta q)}$, whereas the length of the code was at most $q^{O(\sqrt{q})}$. This dictated the choice of $q \approx \log^2 n$, and then to keep the running time polynomial, we had to take $\zeta \approx (\log n \log\log n)^{-1}$.

7. REFERENCES

[1] Z. Dvir and S. Lovett. Subspace-evasive sets. *Electronic Colloquium on Computational Complexity*, TR11-139, 2011.

[2] P. Elias. Error-correcting codes for list decoding. *IEEE Transactions on Information Theory*, 37:5–12, 1991.

[3] A. Garcia and H. Stichtenoth. A tower of Artin-Schreier extensions of function fields attaining the Drinfeld-Vlădut bound. *Inventiones Mathematicae*, 121:211–222, 1995.

[4] A. Garcia and H. Stichtenoth. On the asymptotic behavior of some towers of function fields over finite fields. *Journal of Number Theory*, 61(2):248–273, 1996.

[5] V. Guruswami. Cyclotomic function fields, Artin-Frobenius automorphisms, and list error-correction with optimal rate. *Algebra and Number Theory*, 4(4):433–463, 2010.

[6] V. Guruswami. Linear-algebraic list decoding of folded Reed-Solomon codes. In *Proceedings of the 26th IEEE Conference on Computational Complexity*, June 2011.

[7] V. Guruswami and S. Narayanan. Combinatorial limitations of a strong form of list decoding. *CoRR*, abs/1202.6086, 2012.

[8] V. Guruswami and A. Rudra. Explicit codes achieving list decoding capacity: Error-correction with optimal redundancy. *IEEE Transactions on Information Theory*, 54(1):135–150, 2008.

[9] V. Guruswami and M. Sudan. Improved decoding of Reed-Solomon and Algebraic-geometric codes. *IEEE Transactions on Information Theory*, 45(6):1757–1767, 1999.

[10] V. Guruswami and C. Wang. Optimal rate list decoding via derivative codes. In *Proceedings of APPROX/RANDOM 2011*, pages 593–604, August 2011.

[11] F. Parvaresh and A. Vardy. Correcting errors beyond the Guruswami-Sudan radius in polynomial time. In *Proceedings of the 46th Annual IEEE Symposium on Foundations of Computer Science*, pages 285–294, 2005.

[12] B. Z. Shen. A Justesen construction of binary concatanated codes that asymptotically meet the Zyablov bound for low rate. *IEEE Transactions on Information Theory*, 39:239–242, 1993.

[13] K. Shum, I. Aleshnikov, P. V. Kumar, H. Stichtenoth, and V. Deolalikar. A low-complexity algorithm for the construction of algebraic-geometric codes better than the Gilbert-Varshamov bound. *IEEE Transactions on Information Theory*, 47(6):2225–2241, 2001.

[14] H. Stichtenoth. *Algebraic Function Fields and Codes.* Universitext, Springer-Verlag, Berlin, 1993.

[15] M. Sudan. Decoding of Reed-Solomon codes beyond the error-correction bound. *Journal of Complexity*, 13(1):180–193, 1997.

[16] S. Vadhan. *Pseudorandomness.* Foundations and Trends in Theoretical Computer Science (FnT-TCS). NOW publishers, 2010. To appear. Draft available at `http://people.seas.harvard.edu/~salil/pseudorandomness/`.

Subspace Evasive Sets

Zeev Dvir
Princeton University
Computer Science department
35 Olden Street
Princeton, NJ 08540
zeev.dvir@gmail.com

Shachar Lovett
Institute for Advanced Study
School of Mathematics
Einstein drive
Princeton, NJ 08540
slovett@math.ias.edu

ABSTRACT

We construct explicit subspace-evasive sets. These are subsets of $\mathbb{F}^n$ of size $|\mathbb{F}|^{(1-\epsilon)n}$ whose intersection with any k-dimensional subspace is bounded by a constant $c(k, \epsilon)$. This problem was raised by Guruswami (CCC 2011) as it leads to optimal rate list-decodable codes of constant list size. The main technical ingredient is the construction of k low-degree polynomials whose common set of zeros has small intersection with any k-dimensional subspace.

Categories and Subject Descriptors

F.2 [**Theory of Computation**]: Analysis of algorithms and problem complexity

General Terms

Theory

Keywords

List-decodable codes, affine varieties, pseudo-randomness

1. INTRODUCTION

In this work we describe an explicit, simple, construction of large subsets of $\mathbb{F}^n$, where $\mathbb{F}$ is a finite field, that have small intersection with every k-dimensional affine subspace. Interest in the explicit construction of such sets, termed *subspace-evasive* sets, started in the work of Pudlák and Rödl [8] who showed how such constructions over the binary field can be used to construct explicit Ramsey graphs. More recently, Guruswami [4] showed that, over large finite fields, subspace evasive sets can be used to obtain explicit list-decodable codes with optimal rate and constant list-size. In this work we construct subspace evasive sets over large fields and use them to reduce the list size of certain families of list-decodable codes.

STOC'12, May 19–22, 2012, New York, New York, USA.

1.1 Subspace evasive sets

Defined formally, a (k, c)-subspace evasive set $S \subset \mathbb{F}^n$ has intersection of size at most c with every k-dimensional affine subspace $H \subset \mathbb{F}^n$. This definition makes sense over finite fields, as well as over infinite fields. Over finite fields, a simple probabilistic argument shows that a random set S of size $|\mathbb{F}|^{(1-\epsilon)n}$ will have intersection of size at most $c(k, \epsilon) = O(k/\epsilon)$ with any k-dimensional affine subspace H. In this work we give the first explicit construction of a subspace-evasive set S of size $|\mathbb{F}|^{(1-\epsilon)n}$ that has intersection size at most $c(k, \epsilon) = (k/\epsilon)^k$ with every k-dimensional affine subspace H. This is stated in the next theorem. We postpone the exact definition of the term *explicit* to the following sections (see Theorem 3.2 for the formal statement of this theorem and Section 4 for a discussion of explicitness).

THEOREM 1 (MAIN THEOREM). *For any finite field $\mathbb{F}$ and parameters $k \geq 1, \epsilon > 0$ there exists an explicit construction of a set $S \subset \mathbb{F}^n$ of size $|S| > |\mathbb{F}|^{(1-\epsilon)n}$ that is $(k, c(k, \epsilon))$-subspace evasive with $c(k, \epsilon) = (k/\epsilon)^k$.*

While being far from the optimal bound of $O(k/\epsilon)$ and despite being exponential in k the bound is still interesting when k is small and the field is sufficiently large. As we will see below, this is precisely the setting that was raised by Guruswami in connection to error correcting codes.

The main ingredient in our construction is an explicit family of degree d polynomials $f_1, \ldots, f_k \in \mathbb{F}[x_1, \ldots, x_n]$, for all $k \leq n \leq |\mathbb{F}|$, such that for every injective (i.e full rank) affine map $\ell : \mathbb{F}^k \mapsto \mathbb{F}^n$ the system of equations

$$f_1(\ell(t_1, \ldots, t_k)) = 0$$
$$\vdots$$
$$f_k(\ell(t_1, \ldots, t_k)) = 0.$$

has at most d^k solutions. The degree d can be any number between n and $|\mathbb{F}|$. Using algebraic-geometry terminology, the set of common zeros of $f_1, \ldots, f_k$ forms an $(n-k)$-dimensional variety which has finite intersection with any k dimensional affine sub-space. We call such varieties *everywhere-finite* varieties (see Section 2 for a longer discussion of this particular choice of name).

Constructing subspace evasive sets with parameters as described above is then obtained by partitioning the n coordinates of the space into blocks of size k/ϵ and applying the basic construction (of an everywhere-finite variety) on each block independently. The polynomials we use in the basic construction are extremely simple (weighted sums of powers of variables) which makes the final construction explicit enough to be useful for the list-decoding application described in [4] (allowing for both efficient encoding *and* list-decoding). Our proofs are elementary and do not use any sophisticated algebraic machinery (apart from Bezout's theorem).[1]

1.2 List-decodable codes

An error-correcting codes allows one to encode a message into a codeword so that two encodings of two distinct messages differ in many coordinates. This allows one to (theoretically) recover the original message from an encoding that is corrupted in a small number of coordinates. More formally, A code is a subset $C \subset \Sigma^m$, where Σ is some finite alphabet. The *rate* of the code is denoted $R = \frac{\log|C|}{m \log|\Sigma|}$ and the *distance* of the code, denoted ρ, is the minimal Hamming distance between two codewords divided by m. It is easy to show that $\rho < 1 - R$ and that *unique decoding* (i.e decoding a message uniquely from a corrupted codeword) is only possible from a fraction $(1 - R)/2$ of errors. When the number of errors goes beyond $(1 - R)/2$ one has to be satisfied with *list-decoding*, in which a possible (short) list of candidate messages is returned. Non explicitly, one can show the existence of a code that can be list-decoded from $1 - R - \epsilon$ errors with list-size bounded by $O(1/\epsilon)$. Obtaining an explicit construction of such a code (with efficient encoding/decoding) is a major open problem in coding theory. The first work to give explicit codes that can be list-decoded from $1 - R - \epsilon$ errors was the paper of Guruswami and Rudra [5]. Their work showed that a certain family of codes, called *folded Reed-Solomon (RS) codes* can be list-decoded from $1 - R - \epsilon$ errors with list size bounded by $m^{O(1/\epsilon)}$, where m is the number of coordinates (or block length) of the code.

In a recent work, Guruswami [4] gave a new list-decoding algorithm for folded RS codes which have some nice advantages over previous decoding algorithms. Among these advantages is the property that the list of possible messages, returned by the decoder, is contained in a low dimensional subspace. More precisely, the code represents messages as elements of $\mathbb{F}^n$, where $\mathbb{F}$ is a finite fields of size $q \sim n$, and the list returned by the decoder turns out to be a subspace of dimension $O(1/\epsilon)$. This immediately gives the size bound for the list of $q^{O(1/\epsilon)}$ mentioned above but also shows a way for improving further the list size. Guruswami observed that restricting the messages to come from a $((1/\epsilon), c(\epsilon))$-evasive set $S \subset \mathbb{F}^n$, instead of coming from the entire space $\mathbb{F}^n$, will reduce the list size to $c(\epsilon)$ and remove the dependency on the block length. In order for the rate to not degrade by much we need the size of S to be sufficiently large, say $|S| > |\mathbb{F}|^{(1-\epsilon)n}$.

For this application the evasive set S must satisfy two explicitness conditions. The first is that messages can be encoded and decoded efficiently into S. The second condition is that, given a subspace, one can efficiently compute the intersection of this subspace with S. Our construction of subspace evasive sets satisfies both of these conditions (see Section 4) and so we obtain the following theorem.

THEOREM 2. *For every R and ϵ, there exists an explicit family of codes $C \subset \Sigma^m$ with rate R that can be list-decoded from a fraction $1 - R - \epsilon$ of errors in time* $\mathsf{poly}\left(m, (1/\epsilon)^{O(1/\epsilon)}\right)$ *and with list size* $(1/\epsilon)^{O(1/\epsilon)}$.

The use of evasive sets to enhance list-decoding is completely black-box and only uses the property that the returned list is a subspace of a certain dimension in a sufficiently large field. Thus, Instead of re-stating the construction of folded RS codes and showing how to combine it with our evasive sets, we refer the reader to [4] for more details.

Following [4], Guruswami and Wang [6] showed another family of codes with optimal distance list decoding and with the additional property that the list returned by the decoder is a subspace. This family of codes, called derivative codes (also called multiplicity codes in [7]), obtains roughly the same parameters as folded RS codes and can be also combined with our construction of evasive sets in the same way to reduce the list size.

1.3 Affine and two-source extractors

The work of Pudlák and Rödl [8] showed that constructing $(n/2, c)$-subspace evasive sets $S \subset \mathbb{F}_2^n$ gives explicit constructions of bipartite Ramsey graphs. These are bipartite graphs that do not contain bipartite cliques or independent sets of certain size. A recent work of Ben-Sasson and Zewi [1] explored this connection further and showed (under some number theoretic conjectures) that such sets can also be used to construct two-source extractors which are strong variants of bipartite Ramsey graphs. Another application given in [1] was to the construction of affine extractors which are functions that have uniform output whenever the input chosen uniformly from a subspace of sufficiently high dimension. Both of these applications require that the construction be over a field of two elements. Our construction requires the field to be at least of size n and so is not useful for these applications. An important direction for progress is to generalize our construction for smaller fields.

1.4 Organization

The rest of the paper is organized as follows. Section 2 contains, after some preliminaries, the main construction of everywhere-finite varieties (Theorem 2.4). In Section 3, we show how to compose this basic construction to obtain our main theorem, Theorem 3.2, which gives explicit evasive sets. In Section 4 we prove two claims which show the explicitness of our construction, and use them to derive Theorem 2. Claim 4.1 shows that there is an efficient way to encode elements into the evasive set and Claim 4.2 shows that one can compute efficiently the intersection of the evasive set with a given subspace.

2. EVERYWHERE-FINITE VARIETIES

Let $\mathbb{F}$ be a field and $\overline{\mathbb{F}}$ its algebraic closure. A variety in $\overline{\mathbb{F}}^n$ is the set of common zeros of one or more polynomials. Given k polynomials $f_1, \ldots, f_k \in \overline{\mathbb{F}}[x_1, \ldots, x_n]$, we denote the variety they define as

$$\mathbf{V}(f_1, \ldots, f_k) := \{x \in \overline{\mathbb{F}}^n \mid f_1(x) = \ldots = f_k(x) = 0\}.$$

The dimension of a variety is, informally, the number of degrees of freedom it has. In particular, k polynomials $f_1, \ldots, f_k$ define, in general, a variety $\mathbf{V}(f_1, \ldots, f_k)$ with dimension $n - k$. It is well known that the intersection of

[1]We do use Weil's exponential sum estimates to analyze a certain variant of the construction but this part of the proof can be omitted by choosing the polynomials $f_1, \ldots, f_k$ more carefully.

an $(n-k)$-dimensional variety $V \subset \overline{\mathbb{F}}^n$ with a generic k dimensional affine subspace $H \subset \overline{\mathbb{F}}^n$ is finite. Our main result in this section is a variety V where this holds for *all* affine subspaces H of dimension k. Using Bezout theorem and the bound on the degrees of the polynomials defining V we also get an explicit bound on the size of the intersections $|\mathbf{V} \cap H|$.

We start with the formal definition.

DEFINITION 2.1 (EVERYWHERE-FINITE VARIETY). *Let $f_1, \ldots, f_k \in \overline{\mathbb{F}}[x_1, \ldots, x_n]$ be polynomials. The variety $\mathbf{V} = \mathbf{V}(f_1, \ldots, f_k)$ is* everywhere-finite *if for any affine subspace $H \subset \overline{\mathbb{F}}^n$ of dimension k, the intersection $\mathbf{V} \cap H$ is finite.*

The importance of showing that the intersection is finite comes from Bezout theorem. It allows one to give explicit bounds on the intersection size, given that it is finite. This result can be found in most elementary texts on Algebraic Geometry (for an elementary proof of this particular formulation see [9]).

THEOREM 2.2 (BEZOUT). *Let $g_1, \ldots, g_k \in \overline{\mathbb{F}}[t_1, \ldots, t_k]$ be polynomials. If $\mathbf{V}(g_1, \ldots, g_k)$ is finite then $|\mathbf{V}(g_1, \ldots, g_k)| \leq \prod_{i=1}^k \deg(g_i)$.*

In our setting, it gives the following immediate corollary.

COROLLARY 2.3. *Let $f_1, \ldots, f_k \in \overline{\mathbb{F}}[x_1, \ldots, x_n]$ be polynomials such that $\mathbf{V} = \mathbf{V}(f_1, \ldots, f_k)$ is everywhere-finite. Then for any k-dimensional affine subspace $H \subset \overline{\mathbb{F}}^n$ we have*

$$|\mathbf{V} \cap H| \leq \prod_{i=1}^{k} \deg(f_i).$$

PROOF. Let the k-dimensional affine subspace H be given as the image of an affine map $\ell = (\ell_1, \ldots, \ell_n) : \overline{\mathbb{F}}^k \to \overline{\mathbb{F}}^n$. Let $g_i \in \overline{\mathbb{F}}[t_1, \ldots, t_k]$ denote the restriction of f_i to H, i.e.

$$g_i(t_1, \ldots, t_k) := f_i(\ell_1(t_1, \ldots, t_k), \ldots, \ell_n(t_1, \ldots, t_k)).$$

Clearly $\mathbf{V} \cap H = \mathbf{V}(g_1, \ldots, g_k)$ and $\deg(g_i) = \deg(f_i)$. The corollary now follows from Theorem 2.2. $\square$

Our main result is an explicit construction of an everywhere-finite variety. We will need the following definition. A $k \times n$ matrix (where $k \leq n$) is *k-regular* if all its $k \times k$ minors are regular (i.e have non-zero determinant). For example, if $\mathbb{F}$ is a field with at least n distinct nonzero elements $\gamma_1, \ldots, \gamma_n$ then $A_{i,j} = \gamma_j^i$ is k-regular.

THEOREM 2.4. *Let $1 \leq k \leq n$ be parameters and $\mathbb{F}$ be a field. Let A be a $k \times n$ matrix with coefficients in $\mathbb{F}$ which is k-regular. Let $d_1 > d_2 > \ldots > d_n \geq 1$ be integers. Let the polynomials $f_1, \ldots, f_k \in \mathbb{F}[x_1, \ldots, x_n]$ be defined as follows:*

$$f_i(x_1, \ldots, x_n) := \sum_{j=1}^{n} A_{i,j} \cdot x_j^{d_j}.$$

Then $\mathbf{V} = \mathbf{V}(f_1, \ldots, f_k)$ is everywhere-finite. In particular, for any k-dimensional affine subspace $H \subset \overline{\mathbb{F}}^n$ we have $|\mathbf{V} \cap H| \leq (d_1)^k$.

We prove Theorem 2.4 in the remainder of this section. Let $H \subset \overline{\mathbb{F}}^n$ be a k-dimensional affine subspace. Our goal is to show that $\mathbf{V} \cap H$ is finite, and then the size bound follows from Corollary 2.3. The first step is to present H as the image of an affine map $\ell : \overline{\mathbb{F}}^k \mapsto \overline{\mathbb{F}}^n$ with a convenient choice of basis. In the following let $t = (t_1, \ldots, t_k) \in \overline{\mathbb{F}}^k$ and $x = (x_1, \ldots, x_n) \in \overline{\mathbb{F}}^n$.

CLAIM 2.5. *There exists an affine map $\ell = (\ell_1, \ldots, \ell_n) : \overline{\mathbb{F}}^k \to \overline{\mathbb{F}}^n$ whose image is H and such that the following holds. There exist k indices $1 \leq j_1 < j_2 < \ldots < j_k \leq n$ such that*

1. *For all $i \in [k]$, $\ell_{j_i}(t) = t_i$.*
2. *If $j < j_1$ then $\ell_j(t) \in \overline{\mathbb{F}}$ (i.e ℓ_j is constant).*
3. *If $j < j_i$ for $i > 1$ then $\ell_j(t)$ is an affine function just of the variables $t_1, t_2, \ldots, t_{i-1}$.*

PROOF. Let $\ell' : \overline{\mathbb{F}}^k \to \overline{\mathbb{F}}^n$ be an arbitrary affine map whose image is H. We construct ℓ by a basis change of ℓ' which puts it in an upper-echelon form. That is, let j_1 be the minimal index such that $\ell'_{j_1}(t)$ is not constant. We take $\ell_{j_1}(t) = t_1$. Let j_2 be the minimal index after j_1 such that $\ell'_{j_2}(t)$ is not an affine function of $\ell'_{j_1}(t)$. We take $\ell_{j_2}(t) = t_2$, and we have that $\ell_j(t)$ for $j_1 < j < j_2$ are affine functions of t_1. Generally, let j_i be the minimal index after j_{i-1} such that $\ell'_{j_i}(t)$ is not an affine function of $\ell'_{j_1}(t), \ldots, \ell'_{j_{i-1}}(t)$. We take $\ell_{j_i}(t) = t_i$ and have that $\ell_j(t)$ for $j_{i-1} < j < j_i$ are affine functions of $t_1, \ldots, t_{i-1}$. Obviously, for $j > j_k$ we have that $\ell_j(t)$ are affine functions of all $t_1, \ldots, t_k$. $\square$

Let $\ell = (\ell_1, \ldots, \ell_n) : \overline{\mathbb{F}}^k \to \overline{\mathbb{F}}^n$ be given by Claim 2.5 and let $1 \leq j_1 < j_2 < \ldots < j_k \leq n$ be the indices given by the claim. Let $J := \{j_1, \ldots, j_k\}$. Our goal is to show that the following system has a finite number of solutions:

$$f_i(\ell_1(t_1, \ldots, t_k), \ldots, \ell_n(t_1, \ldots, t_k)) = 0, \ i \in [k].$$

Clearly, applying an invertible linear transformation on the set $f_1, \ldots, f_k$ (replacing each f_i with a linear combination of $f_1, \ldots, f_k$) will not affect the number of solutions. Our next step is to find such a linear transformation that will put the f_i's in a more convenient form, eliminating some of their coefficients.

CLAIM 2.6. *Let $f(x) = (f_1(x), \ldots, f_k(x))$. There exist k linearly independent vectors $u_1, \ldots, u_k \in \overline{\mathbb{F}}^k$ such that, for all $i \in [k]$,*

$$\langle u_i, f(x) \rangle = x_{j_i}^{d_{j_i}} + \sum_{j \in [n] \setminus J} c_{ij} \cdot x_j^{d_j}, \qquad (1)$$

where the coefficients c_{ij} are elements of $\overline{\mathbb{F}}$.

PROOF. Recall that by definition $f_i(x) = \sum_{j=1}^n A_{i,j} \cdot x_j^{d_j}$ where A is a k-regular matrix. Let A' be the $k \times k$ minor of A given by restriction to columns $j_1, \ldots, j_k$. Since A is k-regular we have that A' is regular. Let $u_1, \ldots, u_k \in \mathbb{F}^k$ denote the rows of $(A')^{-1}$. We thus have that $u_i A' = e_i$ where e_i is the i-th unit vector. That is, $\langle u_i, f(x) \rangle = x_{j_i}^{d_{j_i}} + \sum_{j \notin J} c_{ij} \cdot x_j^{d_j}$ where c_{ij} is the inner product of u_i and the j-th column of A. $\square$

Let $u_1, \ldots, u_k$ be the vectors given by Claim 2.6 and denote

$$\tilde{f}_i(x) := \langle u_i, f(x) \rangle.$$

Let us also denote

$$g_i(t_1,\ldots,t_k) := \tilde{f}_i(\ell_1(t_1,\ldots,t_k),\ldots,\ell_n(t_1,\ldots,t_k)).$$

Recall that, from the above discussion, our goal is to show that the system $\{g_i(t) = 0 : i \in [k]\}$ has a finite number of solutions in $\overline{\mathbb{F}}^k$. By Claims 2.5 and 2.6 we have that

$$g_i(t) = t_i^{d_{j_i}} + \sum_{j \in [n]\setminus J} c_{ij} \cdot \ell_j(t)^{d_j}. \tag{2}$$

We now perform one final transformation on our system. Contrary to the previous transformations which were linear transformations, this will be a polynomial transformation. Let

$$D := \prod_{i=1}^{k} d_{j_i}$$

and let

$$D_i := \frac{D}{d_{j_i}}.$$

For $i \in [k]$ define

$$h_i(t_1,\ldots,t_k) := g_i\left(t_1^{D_1},\ldots,t_k^{D_k}\right).$$

We first note that in order to show that $\mathbf{V}(g_1,\ldots,g_k)$ is finite it suffices to show that $\mathbf{V}(h_1,\ldots,h_k)$ is finite.

CLAIM 2.7. $|\mathbf{V}(g_1,\ldots,g_k)| \le |\mathbf{V}(h_1,\ldots,h_k)|$.

PROOF. For each $w \in \mathbf{V}(g)$ we can define $w' \in \mathbf{V}(h)$ by letting w'_i be some D_i root of w_i (it exists since $\overline{\mathbb{F}}$ is algebraically closed). Clearly distinct elements in $\mathbf{V}(g)$ are mapped to distinct elements in $\mathbf{V}(h)$. □

The reason for these transformations is that the final polynomials h_i have a specifically nice form: they are the sum of t_i^D with a polynomial of lower degree.

CLAIM 2.8. *For all $i \in [k]$ we have that*

$$h_i(t_1,\ldots,t_k) = t_i^D + r_i(t_1,\ldots,t_k)$$

where $\deg(r_i) < D$.

PROOF. By definition

$$\begin{aligned} h_i(t) &= g_i(t_1^{D_1},\ldots,t_k^{D_k}) \\ &= t_i^D + \sum_{j\in[n]\setminus J} c_{ij}\cdot \ell_j(t_1^{D_1},\ldots,t_k^{D_k})^{d_j}. \end{aligned}$$

To prove the claim we need to show that $\deg(\ell_j(t_1^{D_1},\ldots,t_k^{D_k})) < D/d_j$ for all $j \notin J$. If $j < j_1$ then ℓ_j is constant. Otherwise let $i \in [k]$ be maximal such that $j > j_i$. By Claim 2.5 we have that $\ell_j(t)$ is an affine function of $t_1,\ldots,t_i$. Since $D_1 < \ldots < D_k$ we have that

$$\deg(\ell_j(t_1^{D_1},\ldots,t_k^{D_k})) \le D_i = \frac{D}{d_{j_i}} < \frac{D}{d_j}$$

since $d_1 > \ldots > d_n$. □

To complete the proof of Theorem 2.4 we need to show that $\mathbf{V}(h_1,\ldots,h_k)$ is finite. This follows from a general bound for polynomials of the form $h_i(t) = t_i^D + r_i(t)$ where $\deg(r_i) < D$.

LEMMA 2.9. *Let $h_1,\ldots,h_k \in \overline{\mathbb{F}}[t_1,\ldots,t_k]$ be polynomials such that $h_i(t) = t_i^D + r_i(t)$ where $\deg(r_i) < D$. Then $\mathbf{V}(h_1,\ldots,h_k) \le D^k$.*

Lemma 2.9 follows immediately from the following two claims. In the following, let $R := \overline{\mathbb{F}}[t_1,\ldots,t_k]$ be the ring of polynomials; $I := \langle h_1,\ldots,h_k\rangle$ be the ideal in R generated by $h_1,\ldots,h_k$; and $M := R/I$ be their quotient. Note that M is a vector space over $\overline{\mathbb{F}}$.

CLAIM 2.10. $|\mathbf{V}(h_1,\ldots,h_k)| \le \dim M$.

PROOF. Assume by contradiction there exist $w_1,\ldots,w_m \in \mathbf{V}(h_1,\ldots,h_k)$ where $m > \dim(M)$. Let $q_i \in \overline{\mathbb{F}}[t_1,\ldots,t_k]$ be polynomials such that $q_i(w_i) = 1$ and $q_i(w_j) = 0$ for all $j \ne i$. Let $\tilde{q}_i$ be the image of q_i in M. Since $m > \dim(M)$ there must exist a nonzero linear dependency among $\tilde{q}_1,\ldots,\tilde{q}_m$. That is, there exist $c_1,\ldots,c_m \in \overline{\mathbb{F}}$ not all zero such that

$$\sum_{i\in[m]} c_i \cdot \tilde{q}_i(t) = 0 \quad (\text{in } M).$$

Equivalently put,

$$\sum_{i\in[m]} c_i \cdot q_i(t) \in I.$$

The key observation is that for any polynomial $h(t) \in I$ we have that $h(w) = 0$ for all $w \in \{w_1,\ldots,w_m\}$. This is because $h_i(w) = 0$ for all $i \in [k]$ by assumption. Thus substituting $t = w_j$ we get that

$$0 = \sum_{i\in[m]} c_i \cdot q_i(w_j) = c_j,$$

which contradicts the assumption that not all $c_1,\ldots,c_m$ are nonzero. □

CLAIM 2.11. $\dim M \le D^k$.

PROOF. We will show that M is spanned by the image in I of the monomials $t_1^{e_1}\ldots t_k^{e_k}$ where $0 \le e_1,\ldots,e_k \le D-1$. Thus in particular $\dim M \le D^k$. In order to do so, we need to show that if $q(t)$ is a polynomial then there exists a polynomial $\tilde{q}(t)$ such that $q - \tilde{q} \in I$ and the degree of each variable in $\tilde{q}$ is at most $D-1$. It suffices to show that if $q(t)$ has some variable of degree at least D then we can find $\tilde{q}$ such that $q - \tilde{q} \in I$ and such that $\deg(\tilde{q}) < \deg(q)$. The claim then follows by iterating this process until all variables have degrees below D. Moreover, it suffices to prove this in the case where q is a monomial, as this process can be applied to each monomial individually.

Thus, let $q(t) = t_1^{e_1}\ldots t_k^{e_k}$ be a monomial where $e_i \ge D$ for some $i \in [k]$. Define

$$\tilde{q}(t) = t_i^{e_i - D}(t_i^D - h_i(t)) \cdot \prod_{j\ne i} t_j^{e_j}.$$

We have that $\deg(\tilde{q}) < \deg(q)$ since $\deg(h_i(t) - t_i^D) < D$ by assumption; and $q(t) - \tilde{q}(t) = h_i(t)t_i^{e_i-D}\prod_{j\ne i} t_j^{e_j} \in I$ as required. □

3. SUBSPACE EVASIVE SETS

In this section we construct subspace evasive sets, based on the construction of everywhere-finite varieties given in Theorem 2.4. We first recall the definition of subspace evasive sets.

DEFINITION 3.1 (SUBSPACE EVASIVE SETS). *Let $S \subset \mathbb{F}^n$. We say S is (k,c)-subspace evasive if for all k-dimensional affine subspaces $H \subset \mathbb{F}^n$ we have $|S \cap H| \leq c$.*

We next give some necessary definitions. For polynomials $f_1, \ldots, f_k \in \mathbb{F}[x_1, \ldots, x_m]$ we define their common solutions in $\mathbb{F}^m$ as

$$\begin{aligned} \mathbf{V}_{\mathbb{F}}(f_1, \ldots, f_k) &:= \mathbf{V}(f_1, \ldots, f_k) \cap \mathbb{F}^m \\ &= \{x \in \mathbb{F}^m : f_1(x) = \ldots = f_k(x) = 0\}. \end{aligned}$$

We say that a $k \times m$ matrix is *strongly-regular* if all its $r \times r$ minors are regular for all $1 \leq r \leq k$. For example, if $\mathbb{F}$ is a field with at least m distinct nonzero elements $\gamma_1, \ldots, \gamma_m$ then $A_{i,j} = \gamma_j^i$ is strongly-regular.

We are now ready to give our construction of sets $S \subset \mathbb{F}^n$ of size $|S| = |\mathbb{F}|^{(1-\epsilon)n}$ which are evasive for subspaces of dimension k.

THEOREM 3.2. *Let $k \geq 1, \epsilon > 0$ and $\mathbb{F}$ be a finite field. Let $m := k/\epsilon$ and assume m is integer and $m|n$. Let A be a $k \times m$ matrix with coefficients in $\mathbb{F}$ which is strongly-regular. Let $d_1 > \ldots > d_m$ be integers. Define*

$$f_i(x_1, \ldots, x_m) := \sum_{j=1}^{m} A_{i,j} \cdot x_j^{d_j},$$

and define $S \subset \mathbb{F}^n$ to be the (n/m)-times cartesian product of $\mathbf{V}_{\mathbb{F}}(f_1, \ldots, f_k) \subset \mathbb{F}^m$. That is

$$\begin{aligned} S &= \mathbf{V}_{\mathbb{F}}(f_1, \ldots, f_k) \times \ldots \times \mathbf{V}_{\mathbb{F}}(f_1, \ldots, f_k) \\ &= \{x \in \mathbb{F}^n : f_i(x_{tm+1}, \ldots, x_{tm+m}) = 0, \\ &\qquad \forall\, 0 \leq t < n/m,\ 1 \leq i \leq k\}. \end{aligned}$$

Then S is $(k, (d_1)^k)$ subspace evasive. Moreover,

1. *If $\epsilon \leq 1/10$, $d_1 \leq |\mathbb{F}|^{1/4}$ and $|\mathbb{F}|^m \geq n^8$ then $|S| \geq p^{(1-\epsilon)n}/3$.*

2. *If at least k of the degrees $d_1, \ldots, d_m$ are co-prime to $|\mathbb{F}| - 1$ then $|S| = p^{(1-\epsilon)n}$.*

We prove Theorem 3.2 in the remainder of this section. We first show that $\mathbf{V}_{\mathbb{F}}(f_1, \ldots, f_k)$ has small intersection with affine subspaces of dimension *at most* k (this is a stronger statement than the one we proved in Section 2 since the dimension of the subspace can be smaller than k).

CLAIM 3.3. *Let $H \subset \mathbb{F}^m$ be an r-dimensional affine subspace for $r \leq k$. Then $|\mathbf{V}_{\mathbb{F}}(f_1, \ldots, f_k) \cap H| \leq (d_1)^r$.*

PROOF. Note that $\mathbf{V}_{\mathbb{F}}(f_1, \ldots, f_k) \cap H = \mathbf{V}(f_1, \ldots, f_k) \cap H$ since $H \subset \mathbb{F}^m$. We will show that in fact $|\mathbf{V}(f_1, \ldots, f_r) \cap H| \leq (d_1)^r$, from which the claim will follow since $\mathbf{V}(f_1, \ldots, f_k) \subset \mathbf{V}(f_1, \ldots, f_r)$. Now, since the matrix A is strongly-regular, its restriction to the first r rows is r-regular; hence $\mathbf{V}(f_1, \ldots, f_r)$ is r-subspace evasive and by Bezout Theorem (Theorem 2.2) $|\mathbf{V}(f_1, \ldots, f_r) \cap H| \leq (d_1)^r$. □

We now prove that $S = \mathbf{V}_{\mathbb{F}}(f_1, \ldots, f_k)^{(n/m)}$ is subspace evasive for dimensions up to k.

CLAIM 3.4. *Let $H \subset \mathbb{F}^n$ be an r-dimensional affine subspace for $r \leq k$. Then $|S \cap H| \leq (d_1)^r$.*

PROOF. Let $\mathbf{V}_{\mathbb{F}} = \mathbf{V}_{\mathbb{F}}(f_1, \ldots, f_k)$. We prove the claim by induction of the number of blocks $b = n/m$. If $b = 1$ then $S = \mathbf{V}_{\mathbb{F}}$ and the claim follows from Claim 3.3. We thus assume that $b > 1$. Decompose H as a disjoint union of subspaces based on the restriction to the first m coordinates $x_1, \ldots, x_m$ (i.e. the first block). That is, let $T := \{(x_1, \ldots, x_m) : (x_1, \ldots, x_n) \in H\}$ and for each $t \in T$ let $H_t := \{(x_1, \ldots, x_n) \in H : (x_1, \ldots, x_m) = t\}$. Thus $H = \cup_{t \in T} H_t$ and we have that

$$|\mathbf{V}_{\mathbb{F}}^{n/m} \cap H| = \sum_{t \in \mathbf{V}_{\mathbb{F}} \cap T} |\mathbf{V}_{\mathbb{F}}^{(n/m)-1} \cap H_t|.$$

Now, since H is an affine subspace so is T. Let $r' = dim(T)$ where $0 \leq r' \leq r$. We also have that H_t is an $(r - r')$-dimensional affine subspace for all $t \in T$. Now by Claim 3.3 we have that $|\mathbf{V}_{\mathbb{F}} \cap T| \leq (d_1)^{r'}$; and by induction we have that $|\mathbf{V}_{\mathbb{F}}^{(n/m)-1} \cap H_t| \leq (d_1)^{r-r'}$ for all $t \in T$. Hence $|\mathbf{V}_{\mathbb{F}}^{n/m} \cap H| \leq (d_1)^r$ as claimed. □

3.1 Bounding the Size of S

To lower-bound the size of S we will need some preliminary definitions and results from Fourier Analysis. Let $\mathbb{F}$ be a finite field. An additive character (e.g. Fourier basis) of $\mathbb{F}$ is a function $\chi : \mathbb{F} \to \mathbb{C}$ such that $\chi(x + y) = \chi(x)\chi(y)$ for all $x, y \in \mathbb{F}$. The set of characters form an orthogonal basis of functions from $\mathbb{F}$ to $\mathbb{C}$. Let $\mathrm{e}_p(x) := e^{2\pi i x/p}$. The set of characters of $\mathbb{F} = \mathbb{F}_{p^\ell}$ for p prime and $\ell \geq 1$ is given by $\chi_a(x) = \mathrm{e}_p(\mathrm{Tr}(ax))$ for $a \in \mathbb{F}_{p^\ell}$, where the trace $\mathrm{Tr} : \mathbb{F}_{p^\ell} \to \mathbb{F}_p$ is defined as $\mathrm{Tr}(x) = \sum_{i=0}^{e-1} x^{p^i}$. The constant function 1 is a trivial character for any field; any other character is called non-trivial. More generally, the characters of the vector space $\mathbb{F}^m$ are given by $\chi_a(x) = \mathrm{e}_p(\mathrm{Tr}(\langle a, x\rangle))$ where $a = (a_1, \ldots, a_m) \in \mathbb{F}^m$, $x = (x_1, \ldots, x_m) \in \mathbb{F}^m$ and $\langle a, x\rangle = a_1x_1 + \ldots + a_mx_m$.

Let X be a random variable taking values in $\mathbb{F}^m$. Its Fourier coefficients $\widehat{X}(a)$ for $a \in \mathbb{F}^m$ are given by

$$\widehat{X}(a) := \sum_{x \in \mathbb{F}^m} \Pr[X = x]\chi_a(x);$$

and for any $x \in \mathbb{F}^m$, the Fourier inversion formula gives that

$$\Pr[X = x] = |\mathbb{F}|^{-m} \sum_{a \in \mathbb{F}^m} \widehat{X}(a)\overline{\chi_a(x)}.$$

The Weil bound [10] is a strong tool which gives a bound on the average of a nontrivial character evaluated over the output of a low degree polynomial.

THEOREM 3.5 (WEIL). *Let $f(x)$ be a non-constant degree d polynomial over a finite field $\mathbb{F}$. Let $\chi : \mathbb{F} \to \mathbb{C}$ be a nontrivial additive character. Then $|\mathbb{E}_{x \in \mathbb{F}}[\chi(x)]| \leq \frac{d-1}{\sqrt{|\mathbb{F}|}}$.*

We are now ready to lower bound the size of S. To do so, we bound the size of $\mathbf{V}_{\mathbb{F}}(f_1, \ldots, f_k)$.

CLAIM 3.6. *Assume that $\epsilon \leq 1/10$, $d_1 \leq |\mathbb{F}|^{1/4}$ and $|\mathbb{F}|^m \geq n^8$. Then $|\mathbf{V}_{\mathbb{F}}(f_1, \ldots, f_k)| \geq (1 - 1/n)|\mathbb{F}|^{m-k}$. In particular $|S| \geq |\mathbb{F}|^{(1-\epsilon)n}/3$.*

PROOF. Let $x = (x_1, \ldots, x_m) \in \mathbb{F}^m$ be chosen uniformly. Our goal is to estimate the probability that $\sum_{j=1}^{m} A_{i,j} \cdot x_j^{d_j} = 0$ for all $i \in [k]$. Equivalently, let $X^{(j)} \in \mathbb{F}^k$ be a random variable defined as $X_i^{(j)} := A_{i,j} \cdot x_j^{d_j}$ and let $X := X^{(1)} + \ldots + X^{(m)}$. We need to estimate the probability that $X = 0^k$.

To this end, we apply Fourier analysis. Assume $\mathbb{F} = \mathbb{F}_q$ where $q = p^\ell$. The characters of $\mathbb{F}^k$ are given by $\chi_a(x) = e_p(\mathrm{Tr}(\langle a, x \rangle))$ for $a \in \mathbb{F}^k$ where $\mathrm{Tr} : \mathbb{F}_q \to \mathbb{F}_p$ is the trace operator. Since $X^{(1)}, \ldots, X^{(m)}$ are independent we have that

$$\begin{aligned} \widehat{X}(a) &= \mathbb{E}[\chi_a(X)] = \mathbb{E}[\chi_a(\sum_{j=1}^{m} X^{(j)})] \\ &= \prod_{j=1}^{m} \mathbb{E}[\chi_a(X^{(j)})] = \prod_{j=1}^{m} \widehat{X^{(j)}}(a). \end{aligned}$$

We proceed to estimate the Fourier coefficients of $X^{(j)}$. Let $A^{(j)} \in \mathbb{F}^k$ denote the j-th column of A. We have that

$$\widehat{X^{(j)}}(a) = \mathbb{E}_{x_j \in \mathbb{F}}[e_p(\mathrm{Tr}(\langle a, A^{(j)} \rangle \cdot x_j^{d_j}))].$$

Thus, if the inner product of a and $A^{(j)}$ is nonzero, we have by the Weil bound (Theorem 3.5) that

$$\left|\widehat{X^{(j)}}(a)\right| \leq \frac{d_j - 1}{\sqrt{|\mathbb{F}|}} \leq |\mathbb{F}|^{-1/4}.$$

Since we assume A is strongly-regular, for any nonzero $a \in \mathbb{F}^m$ there could by at most $k-1$ columns of A which are orthogonal to a; hence we deduce that for any nonzero a,

$$\left|\widehat{X}(a)\right| \leq (|\mathbb{F}|^{-1/4})^{(m-k+1)} \leq |\mathbb{F}|^{-k-m/8} \leq (1/n) \cdot |\mathbb{F}|^{-k}$$

by our choice of parameters. We now apply these bounds to estimate the probability that $X = 0$. We have that $\Pr[X = 0] = |\mathbb{F}|^{-k} \sum_a \widehat{X}(a)$ and $\widehat{X}(0) = 1$; hence

$$\left|\Pr[X = 0] - \mathbb{F}^{-k}\right| \leq \mathbb{F}^{-k} \sum_{a \neq 0} |\widehat{X}(a)| \leq (1/n) \cdot |\mathbb{F}|^{-k}.$$

Thus $|\mathbf{V}_{\mathbb{F}}(f_1, \ldots, f_k)| \geq (1 - 1/n)\mathbb{F}^{m-k} = (1 - 1/n)\mathbb{F}^{(1-\epsilon)m}$ and $|S| = |\mathbf{V}_{\mathbb{F}}(f_1, \ldots, f_k)|^{n/m} \geq (1/e) \cdot |\mathbb{F}|^{(1-\epsilon)n}$. □

CLAIM 3.7. *If at least k for the degrees $d_1, \ldots, d_m$ are co-prime to $|\mathbb{F}^*| = |\mathbb{F}| - 1$ then $|\mathbf{V}_{\mathbb{F}}(f_1, \ldots, f_k)| = p^{(1-\epsilon)m}$.*

PROOF. Let $\mathbf{V}_{\mathbb{F}} = \mathbf{V}_{\mathbb{F}}(f_1, \ldots, f_k)$. Let $d_{j_1}, \ldots, d_{j_k}$ be degrees among $d_1, \ldots, d_m$ co-prime to $|\mathbb{F}| - 1$ and let $J = \{j_1, \ldots, j_k\}$. We will show that for any setting of $\{x_j : j \notin J\}$ there exists a unique setting of $\{x_j : j \in J\}$ which makes $x \in \mathbf{V}_{\mathbb{F}}$. This will clearly show that $|\mathbf{V}_{\mathbb{F}}| = |\mathbb{F}|^{m-k} = |\mathbb{F}|^{(1-\epsilon)m}$ as claimed.

Substitute $x_j = c_j \in \mathbb{F}$ for all $j \notin J$. We have that $x \in \mathbf{V}_{\mathbb{F}}$ if

$$\sum_{j \in J} A_{i,j} \cdot x_j^{d_j} = -\sum_{j \notin J} A_{i,j} \cdot c_j^{d_j} \qquad \forall i \in [k].$$

Let A' be the $k \times k$ minor of A given by restricting A to columns in J. Let $y = (x_{j_1}^{d_{j1}}, \ldots, x_{j_k}^{d_{jk}})$ and let $b \in \mathbb{F}^k$ be given by $b_i = -\sum_{j \notin J} A_{i,j} \cdot c_j^{d_j}$. Then $x \in \mathbf{V}_{\mathbb{F}}$ if

$$A'y = b.$$

We have that A' is regular since A is strongly regular; hence there exists a unique solution $y \in \mathbb{F}^k$ for the linear system $A'y = b$. We now apply our assumption that each degree d_{j_i} is co-prime to $|\mathbb{F}^*| = |\mathbb{F}| - 1$. This implies that raising to the d_{j_i} power in $\mathbb{F}$ is an automorphism of $\mathbb{F}^*$. That is, for each y_i there exists a unique solution to $x_{j_i}^{d_{j_i}} = y_i$ where $x_{j_i} \in \mathbb{F}$. □

4. EXPLICITNESS OF THE CONSTRUCTION

In this section we discuss the explicitness of our construction of subspace evasive sets. The construction of everywhere-finite varieties accomplished in Theorem 2.4 is given as the zero set of explicitly defined polynomials. One can use our construction over any finite field, including $\mathbb{F} = \mathbb{F}_{2^\ell}$ which is convenient for applications. The construction requires an explicit strongly regular $k \times n$ matrix A. Such a matrix can be easily obtained when $|\mathbb{F}| > n$ by taking $A_{i,j} = \gamma_j^i$ where $\gamma_1, \ldots, \gamma_n \in \mathbb{F}$ are n nonzero distinct elements in $\mathbb{F}$ (this is because each $k \times k$ sub-matrix is a Vandermonde matrix).

4.1 Efficient encoding of vectors as elements of S

The first non-trivial issue regarding explicitness is how to sample an element of the set uniformly. More precisely, for an evasive set $S \subset \mathbb{F}^n$ of size $|\mathbb{F}|^r$ we would like to have an efficiently computable bijection $\varphi : \mathbb{F}^r \mapsto S$. This is needed for the list-decoding application because we would like to encode messages as strings in S without losing much in the rate of the code and so that we can efficiently recover the original messages from their representation as elements of S. We now show how one can sample from the variety $\mathbf{V}_{\mathbb{F}}(f_1, \ldots, f_k)$ efficiently (this is enough since the construction of evasive sets is a direct product of such sets). We show this is simple when at least k of the degrees $d_1, \ldots, d_m$ are co-prime to $|\mathbb{F}| - 1$ (we will show below that this condition is easy to obtain). If the degrees are not co-prime to $|\mathbb{F}| - 1$ the situation is a bit more complicated but one can still find an encoding into a sufficiently large subset of S that is efficiently invertible (we omit the details).

CLAIM 4.1. *Assume that at least k of the degrees $d_1, \ldots, d_m$ are co-prime to $|\mathbb{F}| - 1$. Then there is an easy to compute bijection $\varphi : \mathbb{F}^{m-k} \to \mathbf{V}_{\mathbb{F}}(f_1, \ldots, f_k) \subset \mathbb{F}^m$. Moreover, there are $m - k$ coordinates in the output of φ that compute the identity mapping.*

PROOF. The proof is similar to the proof of Claim 3.7. Let $d_{j_1}, \ldots, d_{j_k}$ be degrees among $d_1, \ldots, d_m$ co-prime to $|\mathbb{F}| - 1$ and let $J = \{j_1, \ldots, j_k\}$. We showed in Claim 3.7 that for any setting for $\{x_j : j \notin J\}$ there exists a unique setting of $\{x_j : j \in J\}$ which makes $x \in \mathbf{V}_{\mathbb{F}}(f_1, \ldots, f_k)$. We now show that given this setting, the values of $\{x_j : j \in J\}$ can be found efficiently. Thus taking φ to be the identity map from $\mathbb{F}^{m-k}$ to $\mathbb{F}^{[m] \setminus J}$ and completing it uniquely to $\mathbb{F}^m$ will give the required map. As we showed in Claim 3.7 we have $x_{j_i}^{d_{j_i}} = y_j$ where $y = (y_1, \ldots, y_m)$ is a unique solution to a linear system $A'y = b$, where A', b are easy to compute and A' is regular. The value of y can be found by solving a linear system; and the value of x_{j_i} can be retrieved since $x_{j_i} = y_j^{e_j}$ where e_j is the inverse of d_{j_i} modulo $|\mathbb{F}| - 1$ (which exists by assumption). □

We now address the condition that at least k degrees are co-prime to $|\mathbb{F}| - 1$. If the field is fixed then it may be the case that $|\mathbb{F}| - 1$ has many small divisors, in which case one may be required to choose relatively large degrees for the polynomials. Note however that it always suffices to choose degrees bounded by $\approx \log |\mathbb{F}|$. However, if one is allowed to change the field size then the degrees can be chosen to be smaller (which in turn gives smaller intersection size with subspaces). Assume for simplicity that $\mathbb{F} = \mathbb{F}_{2^\ell}$ (similar arguments can be made for example for prime fields using Dirichlet theorem). Fix k, ϵ and let $m = k/\epsilon$. The following argument follows a similar unpublished argument of Bourgain.

Let K be the product of the first $\log k$ odd primes, so $K = O(\log k \cdot \log\log k)^{\log k}$. Let $d'_1, \ldots, d'_k \le K$ be the divisors of K given by products of all possible subsets of the prime factors of K. We will choose ℓ so that $2^\ell - 1$ is co-prime to K. Let $0 < \ell_0 \le K$ denote the order of 2 modulo K; that is $2^{\ell_0} \equiv 1 \pmod K$. Then setting $\ell = \ell_0 + 1$ has the property that $2^\ell - 1$ is co-prime to K, hence to all degrees $d'_1, \ldots, d'_k$. We will choose the m degrees $d_1, \ldots, d_m$ by completing $d'_1, \ldots, d'_k$ with $m - k$ distinct minimal degrees.

4.2 Computing the intersection with a given subspace

Another important explicitness issue is how to efficiently compute the intersection of a (k, c)-subspace evasive set $S \subset \mathbb{F}^n$ with a given affine subspace H of dimension k. This question comes up in the list-decoding application when we obtain a subspace (given in some basis) that is supposed to contain all possible decodings of a corrupted codeword and we wish to 'filter-out' this subspace to obtain the list of elements in it that are also in S. One way of doing this is to go over all elements in H and to check for each whether or not it is in S (in our case by evaluating the k polynomials and checking that they are all zero). Using the specific structure of our construction we can do much better and output the set $S \cap H$ in polynomial time in the size of the intersection.

CLAIM 4.2. *Let $S \subset \mathbb{F}^n$ be the (k, c)-subspace evasive set constructed in Theorem 3.2 (for some choice of the parameter m and degrees $d_1 > \ldots > d_m$). There exist an algorithm that, given a basis for any affine subspace H of dimension k, outputs $S \cap H$ in time polynomial in $|S \cap H| \le (d_1)^k$*

PROOF. This follows from powerful algorithms that can solve a system of polynomial equations (over finite fields) in time polynomial in the number of solutions, *provided that the number of solutions is finite in the algebraic closure* (i.e the 'zero-dimensional' case). See for example [2, 3]. In our basic construction of an everywhere finite variety, given as the common zero set of k polynomials $f_1, \ldots, f_k$ in n variables $x_1, \ldots, x_n$, the intersection with a k dimensional affine subspace reduces to solving a system of k equations in k variables – simply substitute $x_i = \ell_i(t_1, \ldots, t_k)$, where H is the image of the degree one map $\ell : \mathbb{F}^k \mapsto \mathbb{F}^n$. For the construction of the evasive set (which is the direct product of these simple varieties) we can use an iterative argument (similar to the proof of Theorem 3.2). Recall that in our construction we partitioned the set of coordinates into consecutive blocks of length m – each containing an independent copy of a the variety $\mathbf{V}(f_1, \ldots, f_k)$. In the first step we solve a system of equations for the projection of H on the first m coordinates. If the dimension of this projection is r_1 then this step will take time polynomial in $(d_1)^{r_1}$ which is the bound on the number of solutions. For every fixing of the first m coordinates to a solution obtained in this step, we reduce the dimension of H by r_1 and obtain a new subspace H' on the remaining coordinates. Continuing in the same fashion with H' on the second block we can compute all solutions in time $\mathsf{poly}((d_1)^{r_1}) \cdot \mathsf{poly}((d_1)^{r_2}) \cdot \cdots \cdot \mathsf{poly}((d_1)^{r_\ell})$, where $r_1 + r_2 + \ldots + r_\ell = k$. This will add up to a total of $\mathsf{poly}((d_1)^k)$ running time, which is polynomial in the number of solutions. □

4.3 Application for list-decodable codes

We give a proof sketch for Theorem 2. For full details see Section 4 in the paper of Guruswami [4]. For convenience of the user familiar with the work of Guruswami, we use the same notation he uses for message length, code length, etc.

Guruswami considers an explicit family of codes (folded Reed-Solomon codes) of the form

$$\mathcal{C} : \mathbb{F}^k \to (\mathbb{F}^m)^{n/m}$$

where $\mathbb{F} = \mathbb{F}_q$ is a finite field, $1 \le n \le q - 1$ is a multiple of m, $1 \le k \le n - 1$ is the message length, $\Sigma = \mathbb{F}^m$ is the alphabet, $N = n/m$ is the block length and $R = k/n$ is the rate. Let $\epsilon > 0$ be a small parameter and set $s \approx 1/\epsilon$ and $m \approx 1/\epsilon^2$. Guruswami [4] shows that for this choice of the parameters:

1. The encoding of $\mathcal{C}$ can be computed in polynomial time.
2. For every $y \in (\mathbb{F}^m)^{n/m}$, there exists a polynomial time algorithm which returns a subspace $H \subset \mathbb{F}^k$ of dimension s which contains all points $x \in \mathbb{F}^k$ whose encoding $\mathcal{C}(x)$ has hamming distance at most $1 - R - \epsilon$ from y.

Guruswami raised the problem of finding explicit subspace-evasive sets in order to decrease the list size of the code. That is, let $S \subset \mathbb{F}^k$ be a $(s, c = c(s, \epsilon))$ subspace-evasive set. Assume $|S| = \mathbb{F}^r$ and let $\varphi : \mathbb{F}^r \to \mathbb{F}^k$ be a bijection from $\mathbb{F}^r$ to S. Consider the composed code $\mathcal{C}' : \mathbb{F}^r \to (\mathbb{F}^m)^{n/m}$ defined as

$$\mathcal{C}'(x) = \mathcal{C}(\varphi(x)).$$

First, we claim that the composed code $\mathcal{C}'$ has list size at most c. This is since for every $y \in (\mathbb{F}^m)^{n/m}$, the subspace $H \subset \mathbb{F}^k$ returned by the list-decoding algorithm for $\mathcal{C}$ contains at most c messages who lie in S.

In order to maintain the efficiency of encoding and list-decoding of $\mathcal{C}'$, we need to guarantee three properties:

(i) Encoding: the map φ should be computable in polynomial time.

(ii) Decoding: the inverse map φ^{-1} should be computable in polynomial time.

(iii) List-decoding: for every subspace $H \subset \mathbb{F}^k$ of dimension s, we can find in polynomial time the intersection $S \cap H \subset \mathbb{F}^k$.

The first two items are guaranteed by Claim 4.1, and the third by Claim 4.2.

5. ACKNOWLEDGMENTS

We would like to thank Venkat Guruswami, Amir Yehudayoff and Avi Wigderson for helpful conversations. The first author was partially supported by NSF grant CCF-0832797 and by the Packard fellowship. The second author is supported by NSF grant DMS-0835373.

6. REFERENCES

[1] E. Ben-Sasson and N. Zewi. From affine to two-source extractors via approximate duality. In *Proceedings of the 43rd annual ACM symposium on Theory of computing*, STOC '11, pages 177–186, New York, NY, USA, 2011. ACM.

[2] D. and Lazard. Solving zero-dimensional algebraic systems. *Journal of Symbolic Computation*, 13(2):117 – 131, 1992.

[3] J. C. Faugère, P. Gianni, D. Lazard, and T. Mora. Efficient computation of zero-dimensional gröbner bases by change of ordering. *J. Symb. Comput.*, 16:329–344, October 1993.

[4] V. Guruswami. Linear-algebraic list decoding of folded reed-solomon codes. In *IEEE Conference on Computational Complexity*, pages 77–85, 2011.

[5] V. Guruswami and A. Rudra. Explicit codes achieving list decoding capacity: Error-correction with optimal redundancy. *Information Theory, IEEE Transactions on*, 54(1):135 –150, 2008.

[6] V. Guruswami and C. Wang. Optimal rate list decoding via derivative codes. In *APPROX-RANDOM*, pages 593–604, 2011.

[7] S. Kopparty, S. Saraf, and S. Yekhanin. High-rate codes with sublinear-time decoding. In *Proceedings of the 43rd annual ACM symposium on Theory of computing*, STOC '11, pages 167–176, New York, NY, USA, 2011. ACM.

[8] P. Pudlák and V. Rödl. Pseudorandom sets and explicit construction of Ramsey graphs. *Quaderni di Matematica*, 13:327–346, 2004.

[9] J. Schmid. On the affine bezout inequality. *Manuscripta Mathematica*, 88(1):225–232, 1995.

[10] A. Weil. Sur les courbes algebriques et les varietes qui s'en deduisent. *Actualities Sci. et Ind.*, (1041), 1948.

Edge Transitive Ramanujan Graphs and Symmetric LDPC Good Codes

Tali Kaufman *
Bar-Ilan University
ISRAEL
kaufmant@mit.edu

Alexander Lubotzky †
Hebrew University
ISRAEL
alexlub@math.huji.ac.il

ABSTRACT

We present the first explicit construction of a binary symmetric code with constant rate and constant distance (i.e., good code). Moreover, the code is LDPC and its constraint space is generated by the orbit of one constant weight constraint under the group action. In particular, it solves the main open problem raised by Kaufman and Wigderson in [8].

Categories and Subject Descriptors

F.0 [**Theory of Computation**]: GENERAL

General Terms

Theory

Keywords

Error correcting codes, LDPC codes, Ramanujan graphs

1. INTRODUCTION

An $[n,k,d]$-code is a linear subspace C of $\mathbb{F}_2^X$, where $|X| = n$, of dimension k such that the (Hamming) weight of every vector $0 \neq v \in C$ is at least d. A code (or rather a family of codes, when $n \to \infty$) is called *good* if there exists an $\epsilon > 0$ such that $r(C) = \frac{k}{n}$ (the rate) and $\delta(C) = \frac{d}{n}$ (normalized distance) are both at least ϵ. For a code $C \subseteq \mathbb{F}_2^X$ we denote by $C^\perp$ its dual (i.e., all vectors "orthogonal" to C) and we think of its vectors as the constraints defining the code (i.e., they define linear functionals on $\mathbb{F}_2^X$ whose common set of solutions is C). The code C is called *LDPC* if there exists a set of defining constraints (i.e., a spanning set for $C^\perp$) of bounded weight. This bound of the constraints weight is called the density of the code.

*Research supported in part by the Alon Fellowship.

†Research supported in part by the ERC and by the Israel Science Foundation.

STOC'12, May 19–22, 2012, New York, New York, USA.

The code C is said to be *symmetric* (w.r.t. H) if there exists a group H acting *transitively* on X such that the induced action on $\mathbb{F}_2^X$ preserves C. Symmetric codes have been always of great interest in coding theory for their "esthetic beauty" as well as practical reasons. Many of the classical codes are such. Note that if G is a finite group and $\mathbb{F}$ a field then any (left) ideal of the group algebra $\mathbb{F}[G]$ gives rise to a symmetric code. Many of the classical codes can be interpreted in this way (see e.g. [6]).

In [7] a stronger property was sought; The code C is called *single-orbit symmetric* if in addition there exists $v \in C^\perp$ such that $C^\perp$ is spanned by the orbit $H \cdot v$ (i.e. C is defined by the equation $x \cdot v = 0$ and its translations by H). In terms of the group algebra, this means that the ideal $C^\perp$ is generated by one element. One should note however, that many of the natural studied ideals in $\mathbb{F}[G]$ (e.g. powers of the augmentation ideal) do not tend to be one generated [16]. A *single-orbit symmetric* code is called *short single-orbit symmetric* if in addition the defining constraint is of bounded weight. Such codes are, in particular, LDPC. To simplify terms, let us call a *short single-orbit symmetric* code an *efficiently symmetric* code.

Kaufman and Sudan [7] studied the question of when symmetric k-LDPC code (i.e., LDPC codes with constraints of weight at most k) is k-efficiently symmetric (i.e., the constraint space is generated by a single k-weight constraint and its orbit under a group). They prove that codes which are k-efficiently symmetric over the affine group are k-locally testable. Their motivation in studying single-orbit codes is the relation (as they discovered) to the testability of codes (invariant under the affine group). We note here that [7] uses different terminology than ours. Namely, codes are called "properties", k-LDPCs are called "k-local characterizations" and k-efficiently symmetric property is called "k-formal characterization".

In [3] it was shown that there exists a symmetric k-LDPC which is single-orbit symmetric, but is *not* k-efficiently symmetric. For example, the dual code can generated by a single constraint and its orbit under a group, however, in order to generate the dual code by constraints of bounded weight, an *unbounded* number of constraints are needed.

It seems that all the known explicit constructions of symmetric codes give codes which are not good. E.g., all cyclic codes (see section 5 below) are symmetric and even single-orbit symmetric, but none of the known ones is good. Moreover, it is a long standing conjecture that there are no good cyclic codes. An old result of Berman from 1967 [4] proved it for infinitely many code lengths. In [1] Babai, Shpilka and Stefankovic show that cyclic good LDPC codes do not exist. The known good symmetric codes are the binary randomized ones in [2, 14] (by probabilistic methods), and the non-binary ones [18] (by function fields methods), but those lack any of the other desired properties like single orbit or LDPC.

This motivated Kaufman and Wigderson in [8] to raise the following basic question: **"To what extent can symmetric LDPC codes attain (or even come close to) the coding theory gold standards of linear distance and constant rate?"**

They consider the tradeoff between 1/rate and the density in symmetric codes. In the codes known prior to their work, if one was constant then the other was worst possible. They constructed a symmetric code with better tradeoff between 1/rate and the density, namely a symmetric code with constant rate, nearly constant distance, whose density is poly logarithmic in the code length. Thus, their code satisfy some of the gold standards but not all. Moreover, they show that if the group H is abelian or solvable (of bounded derived length) there are no codes satisfying all the desired properties and expressed some skepticism if such codes exist at all.

Our main result show that codes with all "coding theory gold standards" do exist!

THEOREM 1 (MAIN). *There exist explicit efficiently symmetric LDPC good codes.*

So, our codes meet all the "gold standards" of coding theory. Our code C has:

- Constant rate.
- Constant relative distance.
- Symmetric under a group action H.
- The dual code $C^{\perp}$ is generated by a single orbit $H \cdot v$.
- The above v can be chosen to have bounded weight. In particular, C is also LDPC.
- They are explicitly constructed.

Our constructions are of Cayley codes, in the framework of [8], but the "secret" is a very special choice of groups and generators. Cayley codes are defined in [8] as follows. Let G be a group of order m and S a symmetric (i.e., $S = S^{-1}$) set of generators of size t. Let $Cay(G, S)$ be the (right) Cayley graph of G w.r.t. S and E its set of edges. So $|E| = mt/2$. Assume $B \subseteq \mathbb{F}_2^S$ is a linear code. Let $C(G, S, B)$ be the linear subspace of $\mathbb{F}_2^E$ containing all the functions $f : E \to \mathbb{F}_2$ such that for every $g \in G$ the "local view" of f at the star of g is in B, i.e. the function $f_g : S \to \mathbb{F}_2$ given by $f_g(s) := f((g, gs))$ is in B.

In general, Cayley codes are *not* symmetric. The group G acts transitively on the vertices of $Cay(G, S)$ but not on its edges. The Cayley code is symmetric in the following situation. Let G be a group generated by a symmetric set S (i.e., $S = S^{-1}$) and T a group acting on G (i.e., there exists a homomorphism $\varphi : T \to Aut(G)$). Assume that S is an orbit of the action, namely, there exists $\gamma \in G$ such that

$$S = \{\varphi(\alpha)(\gamma) | \alpha \in T\}.$$

In this case one can show, see Section 3, that the semi-direct product group $H = G \rtimes T$ acts on $Cay(G, S)$ and this action is transitive on the edges.

Now, the group T acts on S and hence on $\mathbb{F}_2^S$. If the "small code" B is preserved by T (i.e. B is symmetric w.r.t T), then one can check that $H = G \rtimes T$ preserves $C(G, S, B)$. Moreover, if B is single-orbit symmetric (w.r.t. T), e.g., if T is a cyclic group and B is a cyclic code, then $C(G, S, B)$ is also single-orbit symmetric, and in this case it is also automatically efficiently symmetric when $|S|$ is bounded. (See Section 3 below).

The following theorem (proved in [8] inspired by [19] and [17]), estimates the parameters of $C = C(G, S, B)$ in terms of those of B and the eigenvalues of the graph $Cay(G, S)$.

THEOREM 2. *Let G, S, T, B as above, with B a code in $\mathbb{F}_2^S$ with rate $r(B)$ and normalized distance $\delta(B)$. Then $C = C(G, S, B)$ is a code with $r(C) \geq 2r(B) - 1$ and $\delta(C) \geq [(\delta(B) - \lambda)/(1 - \lambda)]^2$ where $\lambda = \lambda(Cay(G, S))$ is the second largest normalized eigenvalue of the Cayley graph $Cay(G, S)$.*

COROLLARY 1. *In the notations above; if $r(B) > \frac{1}{2}$ and $\delta(B) > \lambda(Cay(G, S))$ then $C(G, S, B)$ is a good code. If in addition B is single-orbit symmetric, then so is $C = C(G, S, B)$. Hence, if $|G| \to \infty$ and $|S|$ is bounded, C is efficiently symmetric.*

The last corollary gives the framework to prove Theorem 1, provided we can find G, S, T and B as above with the right parameters. To this end we will present first edge transitive Cayley graphs $Cay(G, S)$ (where S is the orbit of a cyclic group T of a fixed size $q + 1$ acting on G, when $|G| \to \infty$) with $\lambda = \lambda(Cay(G, S))$ sufficiently small. Secondly, we will find a cyclic code $B \subseteq \mathbb{F}_2^S$ with $r(B) > \frac{1}{2}$ and $\delta(B) > \lambda$. The resulting $C(G, S, B)$ will be efficiently symmetric and good by Corollary 1. In particular it is also LDPC as it is defined by local equations (in fact the orbit of one equation under the group $H = G \rtimes T$) which touches at most $q + 1$ variables. So, Theorem 1 will be proven once the two goals will be achieved.

For the first mission let us recall that a finite $q + 1$-regular connected graph is called Ramanujan if for every normalized eigenvalue λ either $|\lambda| = 1$ or $|\lambda| \leq \frac{2\sqrt{q}}{q+1}$. Such graphs were constructed in [11] for every prime p and for every prime power $q = p^{\ell}$ in [15]. We will make use of a more recent explicit construction of Ramanujan graphs by Lubotzky, Samuels and Vishne [13] which, as we show here, have some extra symmetry, and in particular are edge transitive.

THEOREM 3 (EDGE TRANSITIVE RAMANUJAN GRAPHS). *For a prime power q and for $\alpha \in \mathbb{N}$ such that $q^{\alpha} > 17$, let $G = PSL_2(q^{\alpha})$ or $G = PGL_2(q^{\alpha})$ and let T be the non split tori of order $q + 1$ in $PGL_2(q)$. There exists $\gamma \in G$ such that $Cay(G, S)$ is a $q + 1$-Ramanujan graph with $S = \{t\gamma t^{-1} | t \in T\}$, $|S| = q + 1$, in particular, the graph $Cay(G, S)$ is edge-transitive. The element γ will be explicitly defined in section 4. In the case that $G = PGL_2(q^{\alpha})$ the graph $Cay(G, S)$ is bi-partite.*

This theorem, to be proved in Section 4 will give us the desired Cayley graphs, including G,S and T as needed in Theorem 2.

For B we will make a very special choice. Assume now $m \geq 10$, $q = 2^{m+1} - 3$ and assume that q is a prime power.

For example, one can take $m = 11$, $q = 4093$ (so q is prime in this case).

THEOREM 4 (GOOD B THEOREM). *Let $q \in \mathbb{N}$ be a prime power such that $q + 1 = 2^{m+1} - 2 = 2(2^m - 1)$ for $m \geq 10$. Then there exists an explicit linear binary cyclic code $B \subseteq \mathbb{F}_2^{q+1}$ with $r(B) > \frac{1}{2}$ and $\delta(B) > \frac{2\sqrt{q}}{q+1}$.*

The proof of Theorem 4 will use classical methods of coding theory. The cyclic codes which are natural to be chosen to have the required rate and distance are BCH-codes. However, a little obstacle is caused by the fact that over $\mathbb{F}_2$, BCH codes are always of odd length, while for our construction we need them to be of even length. This is overcome using a trick from [20] (see Section 5 for details).
An interesting number theoretic problem is whether one can find infinitely many q's suitable for us. I.e., are there infinitely many m's for which $2^{m+1} - 3$ is a prime (power)? This is a question of the the same style of the famous *Mersanne Primes Problem*; Are there infinitely many primes of the form $2^m - 1$? It seems that with the current knowledge we also do not know the answer even if we replace "primes" with "prime powers". Luckily, we need only one such q and $2^{12} - 3 = 4093$ does the job for us!

2. NOTATIONS AND CONVENTIONS

We start with some basic definitions that are being used throughout this work.

2.1 Group theory definitions

DEFINITION 1 (ACTION OF A GROUP ON A SET). *An* action *of a group T on a set X is a group homomorphism $\phi : T \to Sym(X)$ that sends each element t to a permutation of the elements of X. Let x^t denotes the action of $t \in T$ on $x \in X$. That is, an action should satisfy for every $t, t' \in T, x \in X$*

$$x^{tt'} = (x^{t'})^t$$

The orbit *of an element $x \in X$ is*

$$x^T = \{x^t | t \in T\}.$$

The action is called transitive *if for some (and hence every) $x \in X$, $x^T = X$.*

DEFINITION 2 (ACTION OF A GROUP ON A GROUP). *An* action *of a group T on a group G is a group homomorphism $\phi : T \to Aut(G)$. Let $g^t = \phi_t(g)$ denotes the action of $t \in T$ on $g \in G$.*

DEFINITION 3 (SEMI-DIRECT PRODUCT GROUP). *Suppose a group T acts on a group G. The* semidirect product $G \rtimes T$ *is a group whose elements are pairs (g, t) where $g \in G$ and $t \in T$, and the product is given by:*

$$(g_1, t_1) \cdot (g_2, t_2) = (g_1 \cdot g_2^{t_1}, t_1 \cdot t_2).$$

Note that with the identification of G as a subgroup $\{(g, 1)\}$ of $G \rtimes T$, we have $g^t = tgt^{-1}$ which respects the equality $(g^{t'})^t = g^{tt'}$.

2.2 Graph definitions

DEFINITION 4 (CAYLEY GRAPH). *Given a group G and a set of generators $S \subset G$ $(S = S^{-1})$, the* Cayley graph *$Cay(G, S)$ is a graph, whose vertices are labeled by elements of G. The edges adjacent to $g \in G$ are (g, s), $s \in S$ and $(g, s) = (gs, s^{-1})$.*

DEFINITION 5 (EDGE-TRANSITIVE GRAPH). *A graph $Y = (V, E)$ is* edge-transitive *if $Aut(Y)$ acts transitively on the undirected edges.*

Here is a situation in which the Cayley graph is edge transitive.

DEFINITION 6 (SEMI-DIRECT PRODUCT GROUP ACTION). *Let G be a group and $S \subseteq G$ a generating subset with $S = S^{-1}$. Let T be a group acting on G (as group automorphisms) and assume S is invariant under T (i.e. $s^T \subseteq S$, for every $s \in S$). The semi-direct product group $G \rtimes T$ acts on the Cayley graph $Cay(G, S)$ as graph automorphism as follows. For $(g, t) \in G \rtimes T$, $(g', s) \in G \times S$.*

$$(g', s)^{(g,t)} = (gg'^t, s^t)$$

We have the following properties that can be easily verified by direct calculations.

- *This is a well defined action, i.e. for $(g_1, t_1), (g_2, t_2) \in G \rtimes T$, $(g', s) \in (G \times S)$,*

  $$((g', s)^{(g_2,t_2)})^{(g_1,t_1)} = (g', s)^{(g_1,t_1)\cdot(g_2,t_2)}.$$

  Note that the undirected edge (g', s) can be also presented as $(g's, s^{-1})$, and indeed:

  $$(g's, s^{-1})^{(g,t)} = (g(g's)^t, (s^{-1})^t) = (gg'^t s^t, (s^t)^{-1}).$$

  which represents the same edge as $(gg'^t, s^t) = (g', s)^{(g,t)}$.

- *This action is always transitive on the vertices, and if the action of T on S is transitive then the action of $G \rtimes T$ on $Cay(G, S)$ is edge transitive.*

- *This action when restricted to G (sitting as a subgroup $\{(g, 1) | g \in G\}$ in $G \rtimes T$) is the usual action of G on $Cay(G, S)$ by multiplication from the left.*

3. CAYLEY CODES

DEFINITION 7 (LINEAR CODE). *Let $\mathbb{F}$ be a field and X a finite set. A linear code $C \subseteq \mathbb{F}^X$ is a linear subspace. The orthogonal space to C is the* dual-code $C^\perp$. *The* length of the code C is $|X|$. *The* dimension of the code C *is its dimension as a subspace. The* rate *of C, denoted by $r(C)$, is the dimension of the code divided by its length. The* weight *of $c \in \mathbb{F}^X$, denoted $w(c)$, is the number of non-zero coordinates in c. The* normalized distance *of C, denoted $\delta(C)$, is the minimum weight of a non-zero codeword of C, divided by the length of C.*

DEFINITION 8 (SYMMETRIC CODES). *Continuing with the notations of Definition 7; We say that a code C is* symmetric *(or symmetric with respect to G) if there is a group G acting* transitively *on X such that C is invariant under the* *induced action of G on $\mathbb{F}^X$. In such a case $C^\perp$ is also invariant under G (since $v \cdot w^g = v^{g^{-1}} \cdot w$ for every $g \in G$ and $v, w \in \mathbb{F}^X$). We say that C is* single-orbit symmetric *if there exists $v \in C^\perp$ such that the G-orbit $v^G \subseteq \mathbb{F}^X$ of v spans $C^\perp$. A code C (or more precisely a family of codes C when $|X| \to \infty$) is said to be* efficiently-symmetric *if $C^\perp$ is spanned by an orbit of v^G where v is of bounded weight.*

So, symmetric C means that "all variables" look the same, and it is also single-orbit symmetric if one equation defines C as a symmetric code. Many of the codes studied classically in coding theory are single-orbit symmetric. For example, all cyclic codes are such (see below and in Section 5). Let us observe that the action of G on X, and hence on $\mathbb{F}^X$, makes $\mathbb{F}^X$ into an $\mathbb{F}[G]$-module, where $\mathbb{F}[G]$ denotes the group algebra of G over $\mathbb{F}$. If C is invariant under G, it simply means that C ia an $\mathbb{F}[G]$-submodule. So, given the transitive action of G on X, symmetric codes in $\mathbb{F}^X$ are the same as $\mathbb{F}[G]$-submodules. Now, if C is a submodule, so is $C^\perp$. The symmetric code/submodule C is single-orbit symmetric iff $C^\perp$ is 1-generated submodule (also called cyclic submodule). Note that an $\mathbb{F}[G]$-module M is 1-generated iff it is isomorphic to a quotient module of $\mathbb{F}[G]$ (as an $\mathbb{F}[G]$ module).
As G acts transitively on X, X can be identified with the coset space G/H of some subgroup H of G and $\mathbb{F}^X = \mathbb{F}^{G/H}$ is a quotient module of $\mathbb{F}^G = \mathbb{F}[G]$, i.e., $\mathbb{F}^X$ is a cyclic module (namely 1-generated). But here a word of warning is needed. In general an $\mathbb{F}[G]$-submodule of a cyclic $\mathbb{F}[G]$-module is not necessarily cyclic, which means that symmetric codes are not necessarily single-orbit symmetric.
Here is a well known example. Let $\mathbb{F}_p$ be the field of prime order p and G a finite p-group. Let Δ be the augmentation ideal of $\mathbb{F}_p[G]$, i.e., $\Delta = Ker(j)$ where $j : \mathbb{F}_p[G] \to \mathbb{F}_p$ is defined by $j(\sum a_g g) = \sum a_g$ (here $a_g \in \mathbb{F}_p$ and $g \in G$). Then Δ is a submodule (in fact, being the kernel of the homomorphism j, it is even a two sided ideal of the group algebra $\mathbb{F}_p[G]$), and it is well known that its minimal number of generators is equal to $d(G)$, the minimal number of generators of G as a group. Now, when G is not a cyclic group, $d(G) \geq 2$ which shows that if we take $X = G$, $\mathbb{F}_p^X$ has $C = \Delta^\perp$ as a symmetric code which is *not* single-orbit symmetric (since its dual $\Delta = (\Delta^\perp)^\perp$ is not cyclic). For more information about the number of generators of Δ, its powers and general (left) ideals of $\mathbb{F}_p[G]$ (which are exactly its submodules) see [16] - especially Section 5.
On the other hand, if G is a finite cyclic group acting transitively on a set X and $\mathbb{F}$ an arbitrary field, then every submodule of $\mathbb{F}^X$ is cyclic. Indeed $\mathbb{F}^X$ is a quotient of the group algebra $\mathbb{F}[G]$. The last is isomorphic to $\mathbb{F}[t]/(t^n - 1)$ with $n = |G|$, and hence it is a quotient of the polynomial ring $\mathbb{F}[t]$, which is a principle ideal domain and each of its ideals is 1-generated. So, when G is a cyclic group all the codes which are symmetric w.r.t G are automatically single-orbit symmetric. These are the classical so called "cyclic codes" (see more in Section 5).
There is another situation where symmetric codes are automatically single-orbit symmetric; This is when the characteristic of the field $\mathbb{F}$ is prime to the order of G. In this case every $\mathbb{F}[G]$ submodule M of $\mathbb{F}^X$ is also a quotient module (since every $\mathbb{F}[G]$-module is semi-simple) and as F^X is 1-generated so is M.

In [8], Kaufman and Wigderson initiated the study of Cayley codes as a method to construct symmetric and efficiently symmetric codes. We will use this framework in order to construct constant rate, constant distance LDPC codes whose constraint space is generated by one constraint of constant weight.

DEFINITION 9 (CAYLEY CODE). *Given a Cayley Graph $Cay(G, S)$ and a linear code $B \subseteq \mathbb{F}^S$ of length $|S| = t$ define the linear* Cayley code *$Cay(G, S, B) \subseteq \mathbb{F}^{|G|\cdot|S|/2}$ as follows. Its coordinates are the $|G|\cdot|S|/2$ undirected edges of the graph $Cay(G, S)$, namely the pairs $\{(g, s_i), (gs_i, s_i^{-1})\}$, $g \in G, s_i \in S = \{s_1, \cdots, s_t\}$. The defining linear constraints are the local constraints of B on the edges incident to every vertex, namely*
$c \in Cay(G, S, B)$ iff for every $g \in G$ the following holds:

- **Vertex consistency:**

$$(c_{\{(g,s_1),(gs_1,s_1^{-1})\}}, \cdots, c_{\{(g,s_t),(gs_t,s_t^{-1})\}}) \in B.$$

Assume T is a group acting on G and S is an orbit of T, i.e. there exists $\gamma \in G$ s.t. $S = \gamma^T$. Assume further that $S = S^{-1}$. Let $H = G \rtimes T$. As in Definition 6, H acts on $Cay(G, S)$ and this action is edge transitive. Let now $B \subseteq \mathbb{F}^S$ be a linear code, which is invariant under the action of T (which acts on S and hence on $\mathbb{F}^S$). It is straight forward now to check that $C = C(G, S, B)$ is invariant under H (see also [8]).
The following proposition now follows easily from the definition.

PROPOSITION 5. *If B is single-orbit symmetric w.r.t T then $C = C(G, S, B)$ is single-orbit symmetric w.r.t $H = G \rtimes T$. Moreover, $C^\perp$ is generated by the orbit of one vector of weight at most $|S|$.*

The second statement follows from the fact that each of the constraints defining C is "local" and touches only the variables associated with the edges around a single vertex.
Before bringing the main theorem of this section, let us recall that if Γ is an r-regular graph of size m, then the eigenvalues of its adjacency matrix are $r = \lambda_0 \geq \lambda_1 \geq \cdots \geq \lambda_{m-1} \geq -r$, and we denote $\lambda = \lambda(\Gamma) = \frac{\lambda_1}{r}$ the second normalized eigenvalue of Γ.
The following theorem is proved in [8], Theorem 7. It summarizes Theorem 2 and Corollary 1 from the introduction.

THEOREM 6 (DETAILED CAYLEY CODES THEOREM). *Let $\mathbb{F}$ be a field. Let G and T be groups, such that T acts on G, $S \subseteq G$ is an orbit for this action. Assume $S = S^{-1}$ and S generates G. The action of T on S induces an action on $\mathbb{F}^S$. Let $B \subseteq \mathbb{F}^S$ be a linear code invariant under T. Assume that:*

- *$Cay(G, S)$ is an expander with second normalized eigenvalue λ.*
- *Normalized distance of B is $\delta > \lambda$.*
- *Rate of B is greater than $\frac{1}{2}$ ($r_B > \frac{1}{2}$).*
- *B is T-single-orbit symmetric.*

Then the code $C(G,S,B) \subseteq \mathbb{F}^{|G||S|/2}$ has constant rate at least $2r(B)-1$ and normalized distance at least $[(\delta-\lambda)/(1-\lambda)]^2$. It is invariant under the action of the semi-direct product group $H = G \rtimes T$, and it is H-single-orbit symmetric. Moreover, $C(G,S,B)$ is LDPC defined by constraints of weight equal to the one constraint defining B (under the T-action).

4. EDGE TRANSITIVE RAMANUJAN GRAPHS

In this section we prove Theorem 3. This is just a special case of a much more general result in [13] but as the result there is so general, one may find it difficult to see the special case needed here, so we will review it here. In fact, the special case needed here has already been used in [10] for a different reason and was also explained there. We repeat the description for completeness and also in order to give the explicit description of the set of generators S, which amount to give an explicit description of γ in the notations of Theorem 3.

Let $\mathbb{F}_q$ and $\mathbb{F}_{q^2}$ be the fields of order q and q^2, say $\mathbb{F}_{q^2} = \mathbb{F}_q[\alpha]$ where $\alpha^2 \in \mathbb{F}_q$ is not a square in $\mathbb{F}_q$. Following the notations of [13], we denote by R the ring $R = \mathbb{F}_q[y, \frac{1}{y}, \frac{1}{1+y}]$, i.e. the subring of the field of rational functions $\mathbb{F}_q(y)$ generated by y , $\frac{1}{1+y}$ and $\frac{1}{y}$. Let $A(R)$ be the four-dimensional R-algebra with a basis $1, \alpha, z$ and αz (i.e. it contains the commutative R-subalgebra $R[\alpha] = \mathbb{F}_{q^2}[y, \frac{1}{y}, \frac{1}{1+y}]$ as a two-dimensional R-module). The multiplication in $A(R)$ is determined by the rules $z\alpha = -\alpha z$ and $z^2 = 1+y$. As $1+y$ is central and invertible, z is invertible, in fact, $z^{-1} = \frac{1}{1+y}z$. Denote $b = 1+z^{-1} \in A(R)$.

Now, $A(R)$ contains $\mathbb{F}_q[\alpha] = \mathbb{F}_{q^2}$. For every $u \in \mathbb{F}_{q^2}^*$, we denote $\tilde{b_u} = ubu^{-1}$. As $\mathbb{F}_q^*$ is in the center of $A(R)$, $\tilde{b_u}$ depends only on the coset of u in $\mathbb{F}_{q^2}^*/\mathbb{F}_q^*$. This gives $\frac{q^2-1}{q-1} = q+1$ elements $\tilde{S} = \{\tilde{b_u} \mid u \in \mathbb{F}_{q^2}^*/\mathbb{F}_q^*\}$ of $A(R)^*$, where for a ring D, we denote by D^* the group of invertible elements.

Let $\tilde{\Gamma}$ be the subgroup of $A(R)^*$ generated by the $\tilde{b_u}$'s and Γ will be its image in $A(R)^*/R^*$, generated by $S = \{\tilde{b_u}R^* \mid \tilde{b_u} \in \tilde{S}\}$. For every ideal $I \lhd R$, we get a map $\pi_I : A(R)^*/R^* \rightarrow A(R/I)^*/(R/I)^*$ and we denote the intersection $\Gamma \cap \mathrm{Ker}(\pi_I)$ by $\Gamma(I)$-the congruence subgroup. If $\{0\} \not\cong I \lhd R$ is a prime ideal and R/I is a finite field of order q^e, then $A(R/I)$ (a quaternion algebra) is isomorphic to the 2×2 matrix algebra over $\mathbb{F}_{q^e}$ (i.e. to $M_2(\mathbb{F}_{q^e})$) and so $A(R/I)^*/(R/I)^* \simeq PGL_2(q^e)$.

Theorem 6.2 of [13] says that for every $\{0\} \not\cong I \lhd R$, the Cayley graph of $\Gamma/\Gamma(I)$ w.r.t. the generators S (or more precisely the images of S in $\Gamma/\Gamma(I)$) is a $(q+1)$-regular Ramanujan graph. Along the way it is shown there that the set S is symmetric (i.e. $s \in S$ iff $s^{-1} \in S$).

Now if I is a prime ideal of R with $R/I = \mathbb{F}_{q^e}$, then $\Gamma/\Gamma(I)$ is isomorphic to a subgroup of $PGL_2(q^e)$, and Theorem 6.6 of [13] shows that it contains $PSL_2(q^e)$. As the latter is a subgroup of index 2 in the first, $\Gamma/\Gamma(I)$ can be either the first or the second. Moreover, we have enough choices: Theorem 7.1 of [13] ensures that for $q^e > 17$, one can choose I such that $G = PSL_2(q^e)$ or $G = PGL_2(q^e)$ will be obtained. This depends on the image of b : if its image is in $PSL_2(q^e)$ then, as the latter is a normal subgroup of $PGL_2(q^e)$, all its conjugates $\{b_u\}$ are also in $PSL_2(q^e)$ and vice versa. If the image of b is not in $PSL_2(q^e)$, then the resulting graph is bipartite since $PGL_2(q^e)/PSL_2(q^e)$ is a cyclic group of order 2, and as said before, all the generators are outside $PSL_2(q^e)$. As it is explained in Corollary 6.8 of [13], it all depends on the image of $\frac{y}{1+y}$ in $R/I = \mathbb{F}_{q^e}$. If this image is a quadratic residue there, we will get $PSL_2(q^e)$ and, if it is a non-quadratic residue, we get $PGL_2(q^e)$. The discussion in Section 7 of [13] shows that at least when $q^e > 17$, there are sufficiently many irreducible polynomials in $\mathbb{F}_q[y]$ of degree e to have both possibilities.

Finally, let us observe that since $\mathbb{F}_{q^2}^*$ normalizes S, the subgroup $\mathbb{F}_{q^2}^*$ of $A(R)^*$ normalizes $\tilde{\Gamma}$ and hence also $\Gamma(I)$, so $\mathbb{F}_{q^2}^*/\mathbb{F}_q^*$ also acts on $\Gamma/\Gamma(I)$ and the image of S is the orbit of (the image of) b there. Putting all this information together we see that $Cay(\Gamma/\Gamma(I), S) = Cay(G, S)$ is the promised edge transitive Ramanujan graph.

The above description of the results from [13] brings only what is needed for this paper. But let us say a few words about the bigger picture (see also Remark 3.6 of [10], but here we talk only on the case $d=2$, i.e. trees and not general buildings): The group $A(R)^*/R^*$ is a discrete cocompact lattice in $A(\mathbb{F}_q((y)))^*/\mathbb{F}_q((y))^*$. The latter is isomorphic to $K = PGL_2(\mathbb{F}_q((y)))$ and it acts on its Bruhat-Tits tree T, which is a $(q+1)$-regular tree. The element $b \in K$ takes the initial point of the tree (the vertex x_0 corresponding to the lattice $\mathbb{F}_q[[y]]^2$) to a vertex x_1 of distance one from it. The group $\mathbb{F}_{q^2}^*/\mathbb{F}_q^*$ fixes x_0 and acts transitively on the $q+1$ vertices adjacent to x_0 (which are in one to one correspondence with the projective line $\mathbf{P}^1(\mathbb{F}_q)$ on which indeed $\mathbb{F}_{q^2}^*/\mathbb{F}_q^*$ acts transitively!) The group Γ which is generated by the conjugates $\{b_u\}$ acts simply transitively on the vertices of T. This is a special one-dimensional case of a general result of Cartwright and Steger [5]. The Cayley graph of Γ with respect to $\{b_u\}$ can therefore be identified with T and hence the Cayley graph $Cay(\Gamma/\Gamma(I), \{b_u\})$ is isomorphic to $T/\Gamma(I)$. The fact that the last one is Ramanujan is a deep fact, which follows from the work of Drinfeld (see ([9], [15] and [12]). This is just as in the "old" Ramanujan graphs. The extra symmetry that we have in our case is due to the fact that Γ is normalized by $\mathbb{F}_{q^2}^*/\mathbb{F}_q^*$ which has order $q+1$ and acts transitively on the $q+1$ generators of Γ.

5. CONSTRUCTION OF CYCLIC CODES WITH PRESCRIBED PARAMETERS

To prove our main theorem, Theorem 1, we will use Theorems 6 and 3, i.e. Cayley codes based on the edge transitive Ramanujan graphs constructed in Theorem 3. What is left is to construct the "small code" B of Theorem 6. This is what we do now. Specifically, we restate and prove a slightly extended version of Theorem 4.

THEOREM 7 (DETAILED GOOD B THEOREM). *Let $q \in \mathbb{N}$ be a prime power such that $q+1 = 2^{m+1}-2 = 2(2^m-1)$ for $m \geq 10$. For any constant $a > 2$, there exists an explicit linear binary cyclic code $B \subseteq \mathbb{F}_2^{q+1}$ with $r(B) \geq \frac{1}{2} + \frac{1}{a} > \frac{1}{2}$ and $\delta(B) > \frac{1}{2\log(q+1)(a/(a-2))}$. In particular, a can be chosen such that $r(B) > \frac{1}{2}$ and $\delta(B) > \frac{2\sqrt{q}}{q+1}$ (e.g. $a \geq 8$).*

Theorem 7 can be deduced from known results in the literature but the requirement that the cyclic code is of even length (i.e. of length $q+1$ for q being a prime power), makes

it less routine. Thus, we provide a self contained proof for the existence of such codes.
In the proof we will also review some of the known properties of cyclic codes. Recall, that a linear code $C \subseteq \mathbb{F}_2^n$ is called *cyclic* if for every $(a_0, a_1, \cdots, a_{n-1}) \in C$ also $(a_{n-1}, a_0, a_1, \cdots, a_{n-2}) \in C$.
To every vector $(a_0, a_1, \cdots, a_{n-1}) \in \mathbb{F}_2^n$ we associate the polynomial $\sum_{i=0}^{n-1} a_i x^i \in \mathbb{F}_2[x]$ and so we can identify $\mathbb{F}_2^n$ with the subspace of polynomials of degree at most $n-1$ in $\mathbb{F}_2[x]$. The latter can be also thought as the elements of the ring $R = \mathbb{F}_2[x]/(x^n - 1)$, i.e., $\mathbb{F}_2[x]$ divided by the ideal generated by $x^n - 1$. Now, if C is a cyclic linear code in $\mathbb{F}_2^n$, it gives rise to a subspace of R which is invariant under multiplication by x, and hence also by its powers. As C is a subspace, it is invariant under multiplication by any element of R, i.e. C is an ideal in R. Conversely, every ideal of R gives a linear cyclic code in $\mathbb{F}_2^n$. Now, $\mathbb{F}_2[x]$ is a principle ideal domain and so is R. An ideal C in R is thus uniquely defined by its generator $h(x)$ which is a polynomial in $\mathbb{F}_2[x]$ which divides $x^n - 1$ (Since in $\mathbb{F}_2[x]$, $(h(x)) \supseteq (x^n - 1)$). Thus, we have a one to one correspondence between linear cyclic codes, ideals in R and divisors of $x^n - 1$ in $\mathbb{F}_2[x]$. We can also deduce the following proposition

PROPOSITION 8. *In the notation above, dim* $(C) = n -$ *deg* $h(x)$.

We now move to discuss properties of cyclic codes in $\mathbb{F}_2^n$ for $n = 2^m - 1$ for some $m \in \mathbb{N}$. These are the most studied cyclic codes. Let $E = \mathbb{F}_{2^m}$ be the field of order 2^m. Let $w \in E$ be a primitive element in E, i.e., an element of order exactly n. Every $\alpha \in E^* = E - \{0\}$ satisfies $\alpha^n = 1$. In fact, E^* is exactly the set of all the roots of $x^n - 1$. For $\alpha \in E^*$ denote $m_\alpha(x)$ the minimal polynomial of α over $\mathbb{F}_2$, i.e., it is the polynomial of minimal degree in $\mathbb{F}_2[x]$ satisfying $m_\alpha(x) = 0$. As $\alpha \in E$, which is extension of degree m, we know that $\deg(m_\alpha(x)) \leq m$. Also, we have $m_\alpha(x) | x^n - 1$ since α is a root of $x^n - 1$, and for every $\alpha \in E^*$, $m_\alpha(x) = m_{\alpha^2}(x)$.
In general, it is not so easy to estimate the distance of the cyclic code C from its generating polynomial $h(x)$. However, this is possible for the following special case that will be used for the proof of Theorem 7. For $1 \leq r \leq n$, denote

$$h_r(x) = l.c.m\{m_{w^i}(x) | 1 \leq i \leq r\}.$$

Since $m_\alpha(x) | x^n - 1$, also $h_r(x) | x^n - 1$. As $deg(m_\alpha(x)) \leq m$, $deg(h_r(x)) \leq rm$. In fact, for every $\alpha \in E^*$, $m_\alpha(x) = m_{\alpha^2}(x)$ and hence $deg(h_r(x)) \leq rm/2$ (for $r \geq 4$). The polynomial $h_r(x)$ gives rise to an ideal (i.e. to a linear cyclic code) C_r called the $BCH(m, r)$ code. The following proposition provides bounds on the dimension and distance of the $BCH(m, r)$ code.

PROPOSITION 9. *The dimension of the* $BCH(m, r)$ *code is at least* $n - mr/2$ *(for* $r \geq 4$*), and its distance is at least* $r + 1$.

PROOF. As the generating polynomial of $BCH(m, r)$ has degree at most $rm/2$ (for $r \geq 4$), we get the bound on the dimension of $BCH(m, r)$ from Proposition 8. For obtaining the bound on the distance of $BCH(m, r)$, note that if the code had a codeword c of weight at most r, the polynomial associated with this codeword $c(x)$ would be of the following form $c(x) = c_1 x^{k_1} + \cdots + c_r x^{k_r}$ with $k_1 < k_2 < \cdots < k_r$ (where $c_1, \cdots, c_k \in \{0, 1\}$ since the field is of order 2). As $h_r(x) | c(x)$ (since the generating polynomial divides every polynomial that is associated with a codeword of the code) we have that $c(w^i) = 0$ for every $i = 1, \cdots, r$. This means

$$\begin{pmatrix} w^{k_1} & w^{k_2} & . & . & . & w^{k_r} \\ w^{2k_1} & w^{2k_2} & . & . & . & w^{2k_r} \\ . & . & . & . & . & . \\ . & . & . & . & . & . \\ . & . & . & . & . & . \\ w^{rk_1} & w^{rk_2} & . & . & . & w^{rk_r} \end{pmatrix} \begin{pmatrix} c_1 \\ . \\ . \\ . \\ . \\ c_r \end{pmatrix} = \begin{pmatrix} 0 \\ . \\ . \\ . \\ . \\ 0 \end{pmatrix}$$

But the matrix of coefficients has determinant equal to $\prod_{i=1}^r w^{k_i}$ times the determinant of the Vandermonde matrix of $w^{k_1}, \cdots, w^{k_r}$. Thus, it is not zero. This implies that $c_1 = \cdots = c_r = 0$ □

We are now ready to prove Theorem 7. By Proposition 9 the $BCH(m, r)$ code for $r \geq 4$ is a linear cyclic code of (odd) length $n = 2^m - 1$, dimension at least $n - mr/2$ and distance at least $r + 1$. Thus, if we take $r = \lfloor \frac{n}{m}(1 - \frac{2}{a}) \rfloor$ for some constant $a > 2$, we get that $BCH(m, r)$ is a cyclic code of dimension at least $n(1/2 + 1/a)$, i.e with rate at least $1/2 + 1/a$. Moreover, this code has distance at least $\frac{n}{m}(1 - \frac{2}{a})$, i.e. normalized distance at least $\frac{a-2}{ma}$.
However, for our goal we need the final outcome B to be a cyclic linear code of (even) length $q + 1 = 2^{m+1} - 2 = 2(2^m - 1) = 2n$ over $\mathbb{F}_2$ (where q is a prime power). Using Lemma 10, we can transform the cyclic code $BCH(m, r)$ of length $n = 2^m - 1$, described above, to a cyclic code B of length $q + 1 = 2n$, with the same rate as in $BCH(m, r)$, that is, at least $1/2 + 1/a > 1/2$, and a normalized distance that is half the normalized distance of $BCH(m, r)$. Namely, a normalized distance which is at least $\frac{a-2}{2ma} > \frac{a-2}{2a \log q}$. Now if $m \geq 10$ and $a \geq 8$

$$\delta(B) \geq \frac{a-2}{2ma} > \frac{a-2}{2a \log q} > \frac{2\sqrt{q}}{q+1}.$$

So if we choose $m = 11$ and $q = 2^{m+1} - 3 = 4093$ all the requirements are satisfied and Theorem 1 is proved modulo the following a lemma.

LEMMA 10 (A CYCLIC CODE FROM ODD TO EVEN LENGTH) *If there exists a binary cyclic code* C *of (odd) length* $n = 2^m - 1$, *dimension* k *(i.e. rate* k/n*) and distance* d *(i.e. a normalized distance of* d/n*), then there exists a binary cyclic code* B *of (even) length* $2n = 2(2^m - 1)$, *dimension* $2k$ *(i.e. rate* k/n*) and distance* d *(i.e. a normalized distance of* $d/2n$*). Moreover,* B *is explicitly constructed from* C.

PROOF. The following proof is essentially from [20]. We include it here for completeness. Let $n = 2^m - 1$ and $N = 2n$. Define a map $\varphi : \mathbb{F}_2^n \times \mathbb{F}_2^n \to \mathbb{F}_2^N$ by:

$$(a_0, a_1, \cdots, a_{n-1}, b_0, b_1, \cdots, b_{n-1}) = (a_0, b_1, a_2, b_3, \cdots, b_{n-2}, a_{n-1}, b_0, a_1, b_2, \cdots, a_{n-2}, b_{n-1})$$

Clearly φ is one to one linear map. Denote $B = \varphi(C \times C)$. Thus, $dim(B) = 2k$, and so the rate of B, $r(B)$ satisfies $r(B) = 2k/2n = k/n = r(C)$. It is also easy to see that the distance of B is the same as the distance of C i.e. d. This mean that the relative distance of B, $\delta(B) = d/2n = \delta(C)/2$. We only need to show that B is a cyclic code, i.e. that B is an ideal when considered as a subspace of the ring $\mathbb{F}_2[x]/(x^N - 1)$. We claim that B is the ideal generated by $h^2(x)$ where $h(x)$ is the generator of C as an ideal of

$\mathbb{F}_2[x]/(x^n-1)$. Note first that $x^N-1=x^{2n}-1=(x^n-1)(x^n+1)=(x^n-1)^2$ and hence $h^2(x)|x^N-1$, since $h(x)|x^n-1$. Also, note that $dim(B)=2dim(C)=2(n-deg(h(x)))=N-deg(h^2(x))$. Thus, it suffices to show that every element of C is divided by $h^2(x)$. For $a(x),b(x)\in C$ write

$$\begin{aligned} a(x) &= a_0+a_1x+\cdots+a_{n-1}x^{n-1} \\ &= (a_0+a_2x^2+\cdots+a_{n-1}x^{n-1})+ \\ &\quad x(a_1+a_3x^2+\cdots+a_{n-2}x^{n-3}) \\ &= a_{even}(x^2)+xa_{odd}(x^2) \end{aligned}$$

Note that n is odd. Similarly $b(x)=b_{even}(x^2)+xb_{odd}(x^2)$. Then $w(x)=\varphi(a(x),b(x))$ can be written as

$$\begin{aligned} w(x) &= (a_{even}(x^2)+x^{n+1}a_{odd}(x^2))+(xb_{odd}(x^2)+x^nb_{even}(x^2)) \\ &= (a(x)+x(x^n+1)a_{odd}(x^2))+(b(x)+(x^n+1)b_{even}(x^2)) \end{aligned}$$

h Both terms $F(x)=(a(x)+x(x^n+1)a_{odd}(x^2))$ and $G(x)=(b(x)+(x^n+1)b_{even}(x^2))$ are divisible by $h(x)$, since $h(x)$ divides $a(x),b(x)$ and $x^n-1=x^n+1$. Also we have that $F(x)=(a(x)+x(x^n+1)a_{odd}(x^2))=(a_{even}(x^2)+x^{n+1}a_{odd}(x^2))$ contains only even powers of x, and $G(x)=(b(x)+(x^n+1)b_{even}(x^2))=(xb_{odd}(x^2)+x^nb_{even}(x^2))$ contains only odd powers of x. This implies that both terms are actually divisible by $h^2(x)$. Indeed, $F(x)=f^2(x)$ for some polynomial $f(x)\in\mathbb{F}_2[x]$ and $G(x)=xg^2(x)$ for some polynomial $g(x)\in\mathbb{F}_2[x]$. Now, $h(x)|F(x)$ and $h(x)|G(x)$, also, 0 is not a root of $h(x)$ and all the roots of $h(x)$ are of multiplicity one (here we use the fact that n is odd). Thus, we deduce that $h(x)$ divides $f(x)$ and $g(x)$, which implies that $h^2(x)$ divides $F(x)$ and $G(x)$ and hence $w(x)$.

□

In summary we have proved:

THEOREM 11 (EFFICIENTLY SYMMETRIC GOOD LDPC). *Let $q=4093$, $\alpha\in\mathbb{N}$, $G=PSL_2(q^\alpha)$ or $G=PGL_2(q^\alpha)$, T the group $T=\mathbb{F}_{q^2}^*/\mathbb{F}_q^*\leq PGL_2(q)$, $\gamma\in G$ as in Section 4, $S=\{t\gamma t^{-1}|t\in T\}$. Let $B\in\mathbb{F}^S$ be the code defined in Section 5, with $a\geq 8$. Then $C(G,S,B)$ is a linear code of rate at least $\frac{2}{a}$, normalized distance at least*

$$\left(\frac{\frac{a-2}{2a\log q}-\frac{2\sqrt{q}}{q+1}}{1-\frac{2\sqrt{q}}{q+1}}\right)^2.$$

The code is symmetric with respect to the action of the semi direct product group $G\rtimes T$, and $C^\perp$ is generated by the orbit of a single constraint of weight at most $q+1$. In particular, for $\alpha\to\infty$, this is a family of efficiently symmetric LDPC good codes.

6. ACKNOLEDGEMENTS

The authors are grateful to Boris Kunyavski, Madhu Sudan and Pascal Vontobel for providing some background, references and historical remarks.

7. REFERENCES

[1] L. Babai, A. Shpilka and D. Stefankovic, *Locally testable cyclic codes*,IEEE Transactions on Information Theory, Vol 51, No 8, 2849–2858. 2005.

[2] L.M.J. Bazzi and S.K. Mitter, *Some randomized code constructions from group actions*, IEEE Transactions on Information Theory, July 2006, 52(7), 3210 – 3219.

[3] E. Ben-Sasson, G. Maatouk, A. Shpilka, and M. Sudan. *Symmetric LDPC codes are not necessarily locally testable*, Electronic Colloquium on Computational Complexity, Technical Report TR-10-199, December 14, 2010

[4] S. D. Berman. *Semisimple Cyclic and Abelian Codes.* Cybernetics 3, 21Ű-30, 1967.

[5] D. I. Cartwright and T. Steger. *A family of $\tilde{A}_n$-groups*, Israel J. Math, Vol 103, 125–140, 1998.

[6] V. Drensky and P. Lakatos, *Monomial ideals, group algebras and error correcting codes*, Lecture Notes in Computer Science, 1989, Volume 357, Applied Algebra, Algebraic Algorithms and Error-Correcting Codes, 181–188.

[7] T. Kaufman and M. Sudan, *Algebraic Property Testing: The Role of Invariance*, Proceedings of the 40th ACM Symposium on Theory of Computing (STOC), 403–412, 2008.

[8] T. Kaufman and A. Wigderson *Symmetric LDPC and local Testing*, Innovations in Computer Science, 406–421, 2010.

[9] A. Lubotzky *Discrete groups, expanding graphs and invariant measures.* With an appendix by Jonathan D. Rogawski. Reprint of the 1994 edition, Modern Birkhauser Classics, Birkhauser Verlag, Basel, iii + 192, 2010.

[10] A. Lubotzky *Simple groups of Lie type as expanders*, J. of the European Math. Soc., Vol 13(5), 1331–1341, 2011.

[11] A. Lubotzky, R. Phillips and P. Sarnak, *Ramanujan graphs*, Combinatorica 8, no. 3, 261–277, 1988.

[12] A. Lubotzky, B. Samuels and U. Vishne, *Ramanujan complexes of type $\tilde{A}_d$* Israel J. Math. Vol 149, 267–299, 2005.

[13] A. Lubotzky, B. Samuels and U. Vishne, *Explicit constructions of Ramanujan complexes of type $\tilde{A}_d$*, European J. Combin. 26 , no. 6, 965–993, 2005.

[14] C. Martínez-Pérez and W. Willems, *Self-dual doubly even-quasi-cyclic transitive codes are asymptotically good*, Transactions on Information Theory, Vol 53, No 11, 4302–4308, 2007.

[15] M. Morgenstern, *Existence and explicit constructions of $q+1$ regular Ramanujan graphs for every prme power q*, Journal of Combinatorial Theory, Series B 62, 44–62, 1994.

[16] A. Shalev, *Subgroups, nilpotency indices, and the number of generators of ideals in p-group algebras*, J. Algebra 129, no. 2, 412–438, 1990.

[17] M. Sipser and D. A. Spielman, *Expander codes*, IEEE Transactions on Information Theory, Vol 42, No 6, 1710–1722, 1996.

[18] H. Stichtenoth, *Transitive and self-dual codes attaining the Tsfasman-Vladut-Zink bound* Transactions on Information Theory, Vol 52, No 5, 2218–2224, 2006.

[19] R. M. Tanner, *A recursive approach to low complexity codes*, IEEE Transactions on Information Theory, 27(5):533–547, 1981.

[20] J. H. van Lint *Repeated-Root Cyclic Codes* IEEE Transactions on Information Theory, Vol 37, No 2, 343–345, 1991.

Approximation Algorithms for Semi-random Partitioning Problems

Konstantin Makarychev
IBM Research

Yury Makarychev
Toyota Technological Institute at Chicago

Aravindan Vijayaraghavan
Princeton University

ABSTRACT

In this paper, we propose and study a new semi-random model for graph partitioning problems. We believe that it captures many properties of real–world instances. The model is more flexible than the semi-random model of Feige and Kilian and planted random model of Bui, Chaudhuri, Leighton and Sipser.

We develop a general framework for solving semi-random instances and apply it to several problems of interest. We present constant factor bi-criteria approximation algorithms for semi-random instances of the Balanced Cut, Multicut, Min Uncut, Sparsest Cut and Small Set Expansion problems. We also show how to almost recover the optimal solution if the instance satisfies an additional expanding condition. Our algorithms work in a wider range of parameters than most algorithms for previously studied random and semi-random models.

Additionally, we study a new planted algebraic expander model and develop constant factor bi-criteria approximation algorithms for graph partitioning problems in this model.

Categories and Subject Descriptors

F.2 [**Theory of Computation**]: Analysis of Algorithms

General Terms

Algorithms, Theory

Keywords

approximation algorithm, semi-random model, random planted model, average-case analysis, graph partitioning

1. INTRODUCTION

1.1 Overview

Graph partitioning problems are among the most fundamental problems in combinatorial optimization. They have numerous applications in science and engineering. They are also used as basic building blocks in many combinatorial algorithms. There has been extensive research on graph partitioning problems, which has been mostly focused on analyzing the worst case performance of optimization algorithms. Over the last two decades, poly-logarithmic approximation algorithms were developed for such fundamental graph partitioning problems as Minimum Bisection [34], Balanced Cut [30, 6], Multicut [21], Min Uncut [22, 1]. Yet, there has been little success in obtaining constant factor approximation algorithms for these problems, and some recent results [27, 28, 35, 36] suggest that this may even be hard, assuming the Unique Games conjecture [26] and its variants.

However, real-world instances of graph partitioning problems are very different from worst case instances. To take advantage of this, many attempts have been made [13, 17, 12, 25, 16, 19, 32, 10] to model average instances from practice and design algorithms that perform well in these models. The principal question now is — can we come up with a model, which on the one hand reasonably captures instances that often come up in practice, and on the other hand, leads to the development of new, interesting algorithms with good approximation guarantees in this model?

Moreover, if we were to believe that these basic graph partitioning problems were hard in worst-case it would be ideal to have a distribution of "hard" instances (as in random 3-SAT [18], planted clique [4], or densest k-subgraph [9]) that we can use as a test-bed for new algorithms. Further, in certain cases like the shortest vector problem on lattices [2, 3] and the densest k-subgraph problem [9], algorithms for an appropriate average-case distribution of instances have led to new insights for better algorithms in the worst case.

In this paper, we propose and study a new semi-random model for graph partitioning problems, which in our opinion captures many properties of real-world instances. We develop a general framework for analyzing semi-random instances of graph partitioning problems, and then present bi-criteria constant factor approximation algorithms for the "classical" problems of Balanced Cut, Sparsest Cut, Multicut and Min Uncut as well as for the Small Set Expansion problem (a problem which has recently attracted a lot of attention).

Before we proceed with the formal presentation of our model, let us discuss what we can reasonably assume about real-world instances. In a graph partitioning problem, the goal is to divide graph vertices into several parts, or clusters, so as to minimize the number of cut edges (subject to constraints that depend on a specific problem). When

STOC'12, May 19–22, 2012, New York, New York, USA.

a practitioner solves a graph partitioning problem, she usually expects that the problem has a good solution — she believes that there is some underlying reason why there should be very few edges between clusters. That is, a real-world process that "generates" the graph instance adds an edge between clusters only when some random unexpected event happens. Therefore, in our opinion, it is reasonable to assume that edges between clusters are added at random. However, we cannot in general assume anything about edges within clusters (since their absence or presence does not affect the size of the cut between clusters). Additionally, in our model we assume that some random edges between cluster might be removed by the adversary (this assumption makes the model more robust). One could also view these edges between the clusters as random noise in an otherwise perfect clustering (partitioning).

This discussion leads to the following informal definition of semi-random instances: consider a set of vertices V and some clustering of V. A semi-random graph G on V is a graph with *arbitrary (adversarial)* edges inside clusters and *random* edges between clusters (more generally, the set of edges between clusters might be a subset of a random set of edges).

Consider a toy example that illustrates why we believe that real-world instances are well described by our model. Suppose that we run a wiki website (or online store, online catalog etc). We track what pages our visitors read and construct a graph G on the set of all wiki pages V (see e.g., [33, 24]). If a visitor goes from page A to page B, we connect A and B with an edge. What is the structure of this graph? We expect that a visitor will read one article, then read an article that explains some term mentioned in the first one, then read another article related to the second one and so on. Sometimes, of course, the visitor will move to a completely unrelated article on a different subject. Consequently, there will be two types of edges in our graph — edges between pages on the same subject, and edges between pages on different subjects. Edges of the first type are not random and show real connections between related articles. However, edges of the second type are essentially random. Say, an edge between articles "Ravioli" and "Register Allocation" is likely to be completely random and does not show any connection between articles; it just happened that the visitor first read an article about ravioli and then decided to read an article on register allocation; in contrast, an edge between articles "Ravioli" and "Dumplings" is not random and shows a real connection between these food items. To summarize, in our example

- edges between pages on one subject are not random (i.e. edges within a cluster);
- edges between pages on different subjects are random (i.e. edges between clusters).

So G is a semi-random graph according to our model.

Our semi-random model and results. Now we are ready to give a formal definition. To be more specific, let us focus on the Balanced Cut problem.

Definition 1.1. (Semi-random Model for Balanced Cut) *We are given a set V of n vertices, and a parameter ε. In our model, a semi-random graph G is generated as follows.*

1. *The adversary chooses a subset $S \subset V$ of $n/2$ vertices.*
2. *The nature chooses a set of random edges E_R between S and $V \setminus S$ and adds edges from E_R to G. For every $u \in S$ and $v \in V \setminus S$, the edge (u, v) belongs to E_R with probability ε; choices for all edges (u, v) are independent.*
3. *The adversary arbitrarily adds edges within S and within $V \setminus S$.*
4. *The adversary deletes some edges between S and $V \setminus S$.*

Aim: *The performance of the algorithm is measured by comparing the cost of edges cut to the expected number of edges in E_R (the set of edges chosen at step 2).*

Note that the guarantees are not w.r.t the size of the cut $(S, V \setminus S)$ after step 4 or with the size of the optimal balanced cut. This is essential, since for example for $\varepsilon = 1$, $E_R = S \times (V \setminus S)$ the adversary can choose any graph G; so if we compared the cost of the cut with the cost of the optimal cut, our model would be the worst case model.

Informal Theorem. *Given a semi-random instance, our algorithm finds a balanced cut $(S', V \setminus S')$ with $|S'|, |V \setminus S'| = \Omega(n)$ of cost $O(|E_R|) = O(\varepsilon n^2)$ with high probability if*

$$\varepsilon > \sqrt{\log n}(\log \log n)^2/n.$$

Informal Theorem. *Given a semi-random instance, our algorithm finds a solution to the Small Set Expansion problem i.e., a subset $S \subset V$ of size ρn, of cost $O(|E_R|) = O(\varepsilon \rho n^2)$ with high probability if*

$$\varepsilon\rho > \sqrt{\log n \log(1/\rho)}(\log \log n)^2/n.$$

Such results also hold for other basic graph partitioning problems like the Minimum Multicut, Sparsest Cut and Min Uncut (the complementary problem to MaxCut). The algorithm for the Small Set Expansion is not only interesting on its own, but can also be used to almost recover the original balanced cut under certain conditions. See Section 3 for a formal statement of the results. We remark that as ε decreases, the problem becomes more challenging since the amount of randomness in the instances decreases.

Note that the algorithm does not necessarily find the planted cut $(S, V \setminus S)$ since in general this is impossible. Indeed the adversary can just delete all edges between S and $V \setminus S$ and obtain an empty graph, or she can add every edge within S and within $V \setminus S$ with probability ε and obtain a random $G(n, \varepsilon)$ graph. In either case, our algorithm has no information about the planted cut $(S, V \setminus S)$.

However, if we assume that graphs induced by S and by $V \setminus S$ are combinatorial expanders, we can almost recover sets S and $V \setminus S$. This assumption is reminiscent of the stability assumption of Balcan, Blum and Gupta [7] for clustering problems (we need the extra condition on semi-randomness though). This assumption for planted partitioning can be justified in the implicit belief that approximately optimal solutions are close to the planted partition.

Informal Theorem. *There is a constant $C > 1$, such that for every constant $\eta > 0$, given a semi-random instance G with combinatorial expansion $h(G[S]), h(G[V \setminus S]) \geq C\varepsilon n$ and $\varepsilon\eta > \sqrt{\log n \log(1/\eta)}(\log \log n)^2/n$, our algorithm finds with high probability the partition $(S, V \setminus S)$ up to an error of $\pm\eta n$ vertices.*

A similar result also holds for the Small Set Expansion problem.

Planted Spectral Expander Model. In this paper, we also develop bi-criteria approximation algorithms for graph partitioning problems on graphs with a planted spectral expander subgraph. Consider a graph G with a (planted) balanced cut $(S, V \setminus S)$. Assume that the normalized algebraic expansion of the induced graph $G[S]$ is greater than the combinatorial expansion $h_{(S,V\setminus S)}$ of the cut by some constant factor. Then our algorithm finds a balanced cut with expansion $O(h_{(S,V\setminus S)})$. (Note that we do not impose any restrictions on the graph $G[V \setminus S]$ and on edges in the cut $(S, V \setminus S)$; this result also applies to the case when $G[S]$ is a random graph with the appropriate parameters.) We obtain a similar result for the Small Set Expansion problem. See Section 7 for details.

1.2 Prior Research

Our work extends prior research on random and semi-random instances of graph partitioning problems. The first random model, the planted random model, was introduced in 1984 by Bui, Chaudhuri, Leighton and Sipser [13]. In this model, we generate a graph on a set V of size n as follows. First, we randomly choose a subset S of size $n/2$. Then we sample every edge between S and $V \setminus S$ with probability ε_1, and every edge within S and every edge within $V \setminus S$ with probability $\varepsilon_2 > \varepsilon_1$. Note that all choices in the planted random model are random (there are no adversarial choices), so the model describes a probability distribution on graphs. The model attracted a lot of attention and was studied in a series of papers by Dyer and Frieze [17], Boppana [12], Jerrum and Sorkin [25], Dimitriou and Impagliazzo [16], Condon and Karp [15] and Coja-Oghlan [14]. These papers explored several techniques for solving the problem — flow-based, combinatorial, spectral techniques, simulated annealing and go-with-the-leader technique. The algorithm of Boppana [12] finds the planted bisection $(S, V \setminus S)$ w.h.p. if $\varepsilon_2 - \varepsilon_1 > C\sqrt{\varepsilon_2 \log n/n}$. Later McSherry [32] obtained similar results for a more general class of graph partitioning problems.

Coja-Oghlan [14] extended the result of Boppana to the case when $\varepsilon_2 - \varepsilon_1 > C(\frac{1}{n} + \sqrt{\varepsilon_2 \log(n\varepsilon_2)/n})$. Note that if $\varepsilon_2 - \varepsilon_1 = o(\sqrt{\varepsilon_2 \log n/n})$ then the random graph has exponentially many minimum bisections and the planted bisection is not a minimum bisection w.h.p. [14]. The algorithm of Coja-Oghlan finds a minimum bisection rather than the planted bisection w.h.p.

In 2000, Feige and Kilian [19] proposed a more flexible *semi-random* model. The model adds an extra post-processing step to the random planted model: after a random graph is generated, the adversary may delete edges between S and $V \setminus S$ and add new edges within S and within $V \setminus S$. Semi-random instances of Feige and Kilian can have much more structure than random planted instances. Therefore, the model arguably captures real-world instances much better than the random model. From an algorithmic point of view, an important difference is that algorithms for the semi-random model of Feige and Kilian cannot overly exploit statistical properties of random graphs. In particular, spectral algorithms do not work for this model. Feige and Kilian [19] developed an SDP algorithm that finds the planted bisection if $\varepsilon_2 - \varepsilon_1 > C\sqrt{\varepsilon_2 \log n/n}$ (matching the bound of Boppana [12]).

In our semi-random model, the adversary has more power than in the model of Feige and Kilian. As in their model, the adversary can remove edges between S and $V \setminus S$ but additionally she has absolute control over induced graphs $G[S]$ and $G[V \setminus S]$ (whereas in the model of Feige and Kilian, she could only add extra edges to random $G(\frac{n}{2}, \varepsilon_2)$ subgraphs inside $G[S]$ and $G[V \setminus S]$).

Our algorithm for Balanced Cut, while designed for a more general model, also works in a wider range of parameters than the algorithms of Boppana, and Feige and Kilian (note that the objective of our algorithms is slightly different, particularly we do not aim to recover the original partition precisely). To compare the algorithms, let us assume that probabilities ε_1 and ε_2 are of the same order of magnitude, $\varepsilon_1 = \Theta(\varepsilon)$ and $\varepsilon_2 = \Theta(\varepsilon)$. While the algorithm of Bopanna[12] and Feige and Kilian [19] require that $\varepsilon > C \log n/n$, we require only that $\varepsilon > C\sqrt{\log n}(\log\log n)^2/n$. (The algorithm of Coja-Oghlan works in even wider range of parameters; in the planted random model, it finds an optimal bisection, different from the planted partition, when $\varepsilon > C/n$.)

Other Related Research. Previously semi-random models for other combinatorial problems were studied by Blum and Spencer [11], Feige and Kilian [19], Feige and Krauthgamer [20], and Kolla, Makarychev and Makarychev [29]. Recently, Balcan, Blum and Gupta [7] (for clustering) and Bilu and Linial [10] (for MaxCut) investigated another very interesting model for real-world instances. They suggested that real-world instances are stable — there is a unique optimal solution $\mathcal{S}$, and every solution that is far away from $\mathcal{S}$ is much more expensive then $\mathcal{S}$. Their results however are not comparable with results for the planted random model, semi-random model of Feige and Kilian, and our results.

Guruswami and Sinop [23] recently presented approximation algorithms for partitioning problems on graphs with good spectral expansion. Their results (as well as results based on Cheeger's inequality) are not applicable to semi-random instances of Balanced Cut. A semi-random adversary can choose k vertices in S and remove all (or almost all) edges incident to them from the graph, making the the first k eigenvalues of the Laplacian equal to zero (or close to zero). Moreover, even if the adversary does not modify a random planted graph, spectral algorithms based on Cheeger's inequality give only a trivial bound: the second eigenvalue of the normalized Laplacian of a random planted graph is $\lambda_2 \approx \varepsilon_1/\varepsilon_2$. Therefore, a $\Theta(\lambda_2)$-approximation algorithm finds a cut of cost $\Theta(\varepsilon_2 n^2)$, which is far from the cost of the optimal cut (it is actually within a constant factor of the cost of the worst/typical balanced cut in G).

Comparison of Techniques. Our approach was influenced by a recent paper of Kolla, Makarychev and Makarychev [29] on semi-random instances of Unique Games. In particular, we use Crude SDPs and the cut–long–edges method that were introduced in [29]. However, from the technical standpoint, this paper and [29] are very different and our algorithms require several new ideas . At high level, the algorithm of [29] (for the random edges adversarial constraints model) in one step finds a set of edges (constraints) E^- that contains almost all corrupted edges, and then processes E^-. This technique does not work with graph partitioning problems since we can find only a set E^- that contains a constant fraction of random edges (edges from E_R) in one step. In this paper, we have to iteratively solve an SDP or C-SDP program, and remove "long edges" at different scales in order to find almost all random edges. Moreover, we cannot just use the technique of [29] at each iteration by a number of reasons. Firstly, the argument of [29] inherently works only at one length scale (a constant scale); if we apply it at the same scale over and over, we will not make any progress. Secondly, the algorithm of [29] needs the set of edges between S and $V \setminus S$ to be random, but this set is no longer random after the first iteration (it depends on choices of the algorithm that in turn depend on E_R). Finally, in order to find almost all edges from E_R we have to cut "long edges" at smaller and smaller scales δ_t. Each time we have to charge the number of cut edges to the cost of the SDP solution. Then the cost OPT/δ_t incurred at iteration t will grow as δ_t goes to 0 and the total cost will significantly exceed OPT.

In this paper, we develop a technique of hidden solution sparsification that overcomes these difficulties. We design a procedure that at each iteration divides the graph into several pieces so that (i) the cost of the SDP solution in one of them is much smaller than OPT (the condition is more involved for the C-SDP solution), and roughly speaking (ii) all other pieces do not have to be further partitioned. Then we recursively apply the algorithm only to the first set. The hidden solution sparsification technique is the main technical and conceptual contribution of our paper. We briefly discuss it in Section 1.3 of the Introduction.

It seems that existing algorithms for random and semi-random instances of graph partitioning problems cannot be adapted to our semi-random model, since they make too strong assumptions about their input graphs, which are not true in our model. In particular, the algorithm of Feige and Kilian crucially uses that the cost of the optimal SDP solution for a semi-random instance of the Balanced Cut problem *exactly* equals the cost of the cut $(S, V \setminus S)$. In our model, this is not the case — the cost of the SDP solution can be two times smaller than the cost of the cut.

1.3 Our Techniques

In this paper, we develop a general framework for solving semi-random instances of graph partitioning problems.

Let us give a very brief and informal outline of our approach. The core of our algorithms is a *hidden solution sparsification* step (HSS). This step is the same in all our algorithms. Intuitively, the goal of this step is to find and remove almost all edges from E_R (edges between clusters) by removing at most $O(OPT)$ edges. More specifically, the HSS step finds a set of edges E^- and divides the graph $G - E^-$ into a set M and a number of sets Z_i such that:

1. The cost of the optimal solution for the sub-instance on $G[M] - E^-$ is at most $OPT/polylog(n)$.
2. Roughly speaking, each Z_i does not have to be further partitioned. Formally, we call this condition Φ-feasibility. Say, for the Balanced Cut problem, this condition means that each set Z_i contains at most cn vertices (for $c < 1$); for Multicut, it means that each Z_i contains at most one terminal from each source terminal pair.
3. All edges between M and Z_i and between sets Z_i lie in E^-.
4. There are "few" edges in E^-. For Balanced Cut and Multicut, we require that $|E^-| < O(OPT)$; for Small Set Expansion we have a more involved condition.

Then we run an existing $polylog(n)$-approximation algorithm for the sub-instance on the graph $G[M] - E^-$ (e.g. run the algorithm of Arora, Rao and Vazirani [6] for Balanced Cut). First condition guarantees, that the algorithm finds a partition $\{M_i\}$ of M of cost $O(OPT)$. We consider the combined partition $\{M_i, Z_j\}$ of V. When we solve Balanced Cut or Multicut, the total number of edges cut by this partition is $O(OPT)$. We join together some sets in $\{M_i, Z_j\}$ and obtain a feasible solution of cost $O(OPT)$ (this step depends on the problem at hand). When we solve Small Set Expansion, we get a weaker guarantee on the set E^-, so the cost of $\{M_i, Z_j\}$ might be very high. We use an extra post-processing step to find a subset of edges in E^- that we really need to cut.

Hidden Solution Sparsification. For simplicity, let us focus now on the Balanced Cut or Multicut problem. We find the partition $\{M, Z_i\}$ as follows. We start with the trivial partition $M = V$ and then iteratively cut sets Z_i from M. Once we cut a set Z_i, we do not further subdivide it. We ensure that after t rounds the cost of the optimal solution for the sub-instance on $G[M] - E^-$ is $O(OPT/2^t)$ and that properties (2)–(4) hold. Then after $O(\log\log n)$ iterations, we get the desired partitioning.

At iteration t, we solve the SDP relaxation for the problem on $G[M] - E^-$ and obtain an SDP solution $\varphi : M \to \mathbb{R}^n$ (the solution assigns vector $\varphi(u)$ to each vertex u). Since the cost of the optimal solution for $G[M] - E^-$ is $O(OPT/2^t)$, the cost of the SDP solution is also $O(OPT/2^t)$. The solution defines a metric $d(u, v) = \|\varphi(u) - \varphi(v)\|^2$ on the set M. We analyze the metric at scale $\delta_t = \delta_0/2^t$ (where $\delta_0 > 0$ is an absolute constant). For every vertex u, consider the set $B_u = \{v : d(u, v) \leq \delta_t\}$ of vertices at distance at most δ_t from u. Let us say that a vertex u is δ_t-*light* if $|B_u| < \delta_t^2 n$, and that u is δ_t-*heavy* if $|B_u| \geq \delta_t^2 n$. Denote the set of heavy vertices by H and light vertices by L. Broadly speaking, we first use a procedure to remove the heavy vertices H (and further process them to get Φ-feasible sets Z_i), while cutting only a few edges (these cut edges are added to E^-). In the remaining graph $G[M] - E^-$ all vertices are light. We show that in such a solution, at most an $O(\delta_t^2)$ fraction of edges from E_R are shorter than $\delta_t/2$. Here we crucially use that E_R is a random set of edges (and, thus, the graph $G = (V, E_R)$ is "geometrically expanding"). We cut all edges in $G[M] - E^-$ longer than $\delta_t/2$ and add them to E^-. In the obtained graph $G[M] - E^-$ all edges are shorter than $\delta_t/2$, hence it contains at most $O(\delta_t^2 OPT)$ edges from E_R. Thus in the next iteration, the cost of the optimal solution for the sub-instance on $G[M] - E^-$ is $O(\delta_{t+1}^2 OPT)$ (as we need).

The Heavy Vertex Removal procedure finds new sets Z_i that cover all heavy vertices H in several rounds. In each round, we define a few sets Z_i; each Z_i contains a subset of heavy vertices together with their r-neighborhoods (where $r \in (\delta_t, 2\delta_t)$). We cut sets Z_i away, add edges from Z_i to the rest of the graph to E^- and then process remaining heavy vertices. We ensure that all sets Z_i have a small diameter and this implies that sets Z_i are Φ-feasible. We cut sets Z_i so that sets Z_i cut in one round are far away from each other and the total number of rounds is small. This guarantees that the total number of cut edges by this procedure is small (here, we use that each set Z_i contains a ball B_u for some heavy vertex u, and hence Z_i is not very small).

To upper bound the number of edges cut by removing edges longer than $\delta_t/2$, we observe that the SDP value in iteration t is $O(\delta_t^2 OPT)$. The number of these cut edges is

$O(\delta_t^2 OPT/\delta_t) = O(\delta_t OPT)$. Thus, the number of edges cut in all iterations is $O(\sum_i \delta_i OPT) = O(OPT)$.

The algorithm for Small Set Expansion (SSE) requires several new ingredients. The main problem is that we cannot use the SDP relaxation of Bansal, Feige, Krauthgamer, Makarychev, Nagarajan, Naor and Schwartz [8] since it may assign zero vectors to all vertices in S. Instead we use a "Crude SDP" (C-SDP) for the problem. C-SDPs were recently introduced by [29]. The C-SDP for the Small Set Expansion is *not* a relaxation for the problem; its objective value may be much larger than the value of the optimal integral solution (in particular, the value of a C-SDP can be large even if the cost of the optimal solution is 0). To solve a semi-random instance of the Small Set Expansion problem, we first apply the HSS step. However, the number of edges in E^- is bounded in expectation by the cost of the C-SDP solution and may be much larger than the cost of the optimal solution. So our algorithm cannot afford to cut all these edges. Nevertheless, we prove that the number of edges in E^- incident to the set S (S is the optimal solution, which is not known to the algorithm) is bounded by $O(OPT)$ (the total number of edges in E^- can be much larger than OPT). Then we show how to find a good solution by combining the SDP based SSE algorithm [8] with a new LP algorithm.

Solution Purification. As mentioned earlier, we show that if we additionally assume that graphs $G[S]$ and $G[V \setminus S]$ are combinatorial expanders in the Balanced Cut or Small Set Expansion problem, then we can almost recover sets S and $G \setminus S$ (see Theorem 6.2). We do that by first finding a good approximate solution using our algorithm for Balanced Cut (or Small Set Expansion) and then improving the solution by repeatedly solving (semi-random) instances of the Sparsest Cut problem to obtain successively finer approximations to the planted partition.

Organization. In Section 2, we present our semi-random model and give definitions, which we use throughout the paper. In Section 3, we state the Hidden Solution Sparsification theorem. We describe our approximation algorithms for Balanced Cut, Multi Cut, Small Set Expansion and Sparsest Cut, which rely on the HSS theorem, in Sections 3.1, 3.2, 3.3 and 3.4. Then in Section 4, we prove the HSS theorem for graphs with the geometric expansion property. In Section 5, we show that semi-random graph satisfy the geometric expansion property and thus conclude the proof of our main result. In Section 6, we show that we can almost recover the original partitioning if all parts are combinatorial expanders. Finally, in Section 7, we study the planted algebraic expander model.

2. PRELIMINARIES

In this section, we define some notation that is convenient for working with partitioning problems. Throughout the paper, we let n to be the number of vertices $n = |V|$ and $\mathcal{H} = \mathbb{R}^n$. We denote by C a fixed constant, and this will usually correspond to the approximation ratio given by the algorithm. We do not make an attempt to optimize the constants in this version of the paper.

We use the following notation: the ℓ_2^2–diameter of a set $Z \subset \mathcal{H}$ equals $\mathrm{diam}(Z) = \max\{\|\bar{u} - \bar{v}\|^2 : \bar{u}, \bar{v} \in Z\}$; the ℓ_2^2–ball of radius r around a set $Z \subset \mathcal{H}$ is defined as $\mathrm{Ball}(Z, r) = \{\bar{u} \in \mathcal{H} : \exists \bar{v} \in Z \text{ s.t } \|\bar{u} - \bar{v}\|^2 \leq r\}$. We let $\mathrm{Ball}(v, r) = \mathrm{Ball}(\{v\}, r)$.

2.1 Partitions

DEFINITION 2.1. *Let V be a set of vertices. We say that $\mathcal{P}$ is a partition of V into disjoint sets or simply partition, if $V = \bigcup_{P \in \mathcal{P}} P$ and every two $P', P'' \in \mathcal{P}$ are disjoint. For every vertex $u \in V$, denote by $\mathcal{P}(u)$ the unique set $P \in \mathcal{P}$ containing u.*

Denote by $I_S : V \to \{0,1\}$ the indicator function of the set $S \subset V$:

$$I_S(u) = \begin{cases} 1, & \text{if } u \in S; \\ 0, & \text{otherwise.} \end{cases}$$

DEFINITION 2.2. *Let $G = (V, E)$ be a graph and $\mathcal{P}$ be a partition of V. Define the set of edges cut by the partition as follows*

$$\mathrm{cut}(\mathcal{P}, E) \equiv \{(u, v) \in E : \mathcal{P}(u) \neq \mathcal{P}(v)\}.$$

The cost of the cut equals the size of the set $\mathrm{cut}(\mathcal{P}, E)$*:*

$$\mathrm{cost}(\mathcal{P}, E) \equiv |\mathrm{cut}(\mathcal{P}, E)|.$$

The cost of the cut restricted to a subset $\mathcal{O} \subseteq V$ only considers those edges which are incident on $\mathcal{O}$:

$$\begin{aligned} \mathrm{cost}_{|\mathcal{O}}(\mathcal{P}, E) &\equiv |\{(u, v) \in \mathrm{cut}(\mathcal{P}, E) : u \in \mathcal{O} \text{ or } v \in \mathcal{O}\}| \\ &\equiv \sum_{(u,v) \in \mathrm{cut}(\mathcal{P}, E)} \max\{I_{\mathcal{O}}(u), I_{\mathcal{O}}(v)\}. \end{aligned}$$

2.2 Partitioning Problems

We now define three of the graph partitioning problems that we study in this paper.

DEFINITION 2.3. (BALANCED CUT) *Given a graph $G = (V, E)$, the aim is to find a partition $\mathcal{P}(P_1, P_2)$ of V with $|P_1| = |P_2| = n/2$ which minimizes* $\mathrm{cut}(\mathcal{P}, E)$.

A constant factor approximation algorithm finds a partition $\mathcal{P}'(P_1', P_2')$ with $|P_1'|, |P_2'| \leq \beta n/2$ for some fixed constant $1 \leq \beta < 2$, such that $\mathrm{cost}(\mathcal{P}', E) \leq O(1)\,\mathrm{cost}(\mathcal{P}^*, E)$, where $\mathcal{P}^*$ is an optimal balanced cut[1].

DEFINITION 2.4. (SMALL SET EXPANSION) *Given a graph $G = (V, E)$ and a parameter $\rho \in (0, 1/2]$, the aim is to find a partition $\mathcal{P}(P_1, P_2)$ of V with $|P_1| = \rho n$ that minimizes $\mathrm{cost}(\mathcal{P}, E)$. We will also be concerned with constant factor approximations (defined like in Balanced Cut).*

DEFINITION 2.5. (MULTICUT) *Given a graph $G = (V, E)$ and a set of terminal pairs $\{(s_i, t_i)\}_{1 \leq i \leq r}$, the aim is to find a partition $\mathcal{P}$ of V that separates all terminal pairs s_i,t_i (i.e., for all i, $\mathcal{P}(s_i) \neq \mathcal{P}(t_i)$) and minimizes* $\mathrm{cost}(\mathcal{P}, E)$.

2.3 Semi-random Models

We formally define the first semi-random model.

DEFINITION 2.6. *Consider a set of vertices V and a partition of vertices into disjoint sets $\mathcal{P}$. Let $E_K = \{(u, v) : \mathcal{P}(u) \neq \mathcal{P}(v)\}$ be the set containing all vertex-pairs crossing partition boundaries. Let $\widetilde{E_K} = \{(u, v) : \mathcal{P}(u) = \mathcal{P}(v)\}$ be the set containing all vertex-pairs not crossing partition boundaries. (Thus, $(V, E_K \cup \widetilde{E_K})$ is the complete graph on V.) Consider a random subset of edges E_R of the set E_K:*

[1]This is sometimes referred to as $O(1)$ pseudo-approximation [6].

each edge $(u,v) \in E_K$ belongs to E_R with probability ε and these choices are independent. We define a random set of graphs $SR(\mathcal{P},\varepsilon)$ as follows:

$$SR(\mathcal{P},\varepsilon) = \{G = (V,E) : E \subseteq E_R \cup \widetilde{E_K}\}.$$

The optimal cost of the semi-random partition is defined as

$$\text{sr-cost}(\mathcal{P},\varepsilon) = \mathbb{E}|E_R| = \varepsilon|E_K|.$$

2.4 Local SDP Relaxations, Heavy Vertices and Φ–Feasible Sets

DEFINITION 2.7. *Let V be a set of vertices. In this paper, we say that a map $\varphi : V \to \mathcal{H}$ is an SDP solution if vectors in $\varphi(V)$ satisfy ℓ_2^2-triangle inequalities: for every $u,v,w \in V$, $\|\varphi(u)-\varphi(v)\|^2 + \|\varphi(v)-\varphi(w)\|^2 \geq \|\varphi(u)-\varphi(w)\|^2$.*

For instance, solutions to the SDP relaxations in Appendix C satisfy the above definition. The SDP solution φ defines a metric on the vertices V (given by $\|\varphi(u)-\varphi(v)\|^2$ for $u,v \in V$). The cost of a solution φ corresponds to the total length of edges according to metric given by φ.

DEFINITION 2.8. *Let $G = (V,E)$ be a graph, $\mathcal{P}$ be a partition of V, and $\mathcal{O}$ be a subset of V. Define the cost of an SDP solution $\varphi : V \to \mathcal{H}$ to be*

$$\text{sdp-cost}(\varphi, E) \equiv \frac{1}{2}\sum_{(u,v)\in E} \|\varphi(u)-\varphi(v)\|^2,$$

and the cost of the SDP solution restricted to the set $\mathcal{O}$ to be

$$\text{sdp-cost}_{|\mathcal{O}}(\varphi, E) \equiv \frac{1}{2}\sum_{\substack{(u,v)\in E\\ u\in\mathcal{O} \text{ or } v\in\mathcal{O}}} \|\varphi(u)-\varphi(v)\|^2.$$

For any SDP relaxation, the cost of the optimum (minimum) SDP solution lower bounds the value of the best integral solution. However, this lower bound may not hold when restricted to a subset $\mathcal{O} \subseteq V$. This motivates the following definition:

DEFINITION 2.9. *Let V be a set of vertices, $\mathcal{P}$ be a partition of V and $\mathcal{O} \subseteq V$. We say that a non-empty set of SDP solutions Φ is a $\mathcal{O}$-local relaxation of $\mathcal{P}$ if there exists a constant $C \geq 1$ such that for every graph $G = (V,E)$ on V and for*

$$\varphi = \arg\min_{\varphi\in\Phi} \text{sdp-cost}(\varphi,E) \equiv \arg\min_{\varphi\in\Phi} \frac{1}{2}\sum_{(u,v)\in E} \|\varphi(u)-\varphi(v)\|^2,$$

the following inequality holds

$$\text{sdp-cost}_{|\mathcal{O}}(\varphi,E) \leq C \operatorname{cost}_{|\mathcal{O}}(\mathcal{P},E).$$

Note that an SDP relaxation of a problem is always a V-local SDP relaxation of the optimal integral solution.

DEFINITION 2.10. *Let V be a set of vertices and $\Phi \subset \{\varphi : V \to \mathcal{H}\}$ be a set of SDP solutions. We say that a subset $S \subset V$ is Φ-feasible if there exists $\varphi^* \in \Phi$ such that for every $u,v \in S$,*

$$\|\varphi^*(u)-\varphi^*(v)\|^2 \leq \frac{1}{4}.$$

Φ-feasibility captures sets that require no further processing, to belong to a solution. For example, Φ-feasible sets correspond to small enough sets for the Balanced Cut or Small Set Expansion problems, and to sets which do not contain any terminal pairs for the Multicut problem.

An SDP solution φ classifies the vertices into two types (heavy or light) depending on the number of vertices in their δ-neighborhoods.

DEFINITION 2.11. *Let V be a set of n vertices, and $M \subseteq V$. Consider an SDP solution $\varphi : V \to \mathcal{H}$. We say that a vertex $u \in M$ is δ-heavy in M if the ℓ_2^2-ball of radius δ around $\varphi(u)$ contains at least $\delta^2 n$ vectors from $\varphi(M)$ i.e., $|\{v \in M : \varphi(v) \in \text{Ball}(\varphi(u),\delta)\}| \geq \delta^2 n$. We denote the set of all heavy vertices by $H_{\delta,\varphi}(M)$.*

The following property of semi-random instances is crucially used in our algorithms.

DEFINITION 2.12. (GEOMETRIC EXPANSION) *A graph $G = (V,E)$ satisfies the geometric expansion property with cut value X at scale δ if for every SDP solution $\varphi : V \to \mathcal{H}$ and every subset of vertices $M \subseteq V$ satisfying $H_{\delta,\varphi}(M) = \varnothing$,*

$$|\{(u,v) \in E \cap (M\times M) : \|\varphi(u)-\varphi(v)\|^2 \leq \delta/2\}| \leq 2\delta^2 X.$$

A graph $G' = (V,E')$ satisfies the geometric expansion property with cut value X up to scale 2^{-T} ($T \in \mathbb{N}$) if it satisfies the geometric expansion property for every $\delta \in \{2^{-t} : 1 \leq t \leq T\}$.

We can slightly simplify the definition[2] above by requiring that φ satisfies the condition $H_{\delta,\varphi}(V) = \varnothing$ and $M = V$. See Section 5 for details.

In section 5, we will see that in semi-random instances $SR(\mathcal{P},\varepsilon)$, the graph consisting of the random edges (V,E_R) is geometrically expanding w.h.p. for sufficiently large ε.

3. HIDDEN SOLUTION SPARSIFICATION AND APPLICATIONS

In this section, we state the main technical result of the paper, and then show how it can be used to obtain constant factor approximation algorithms for the Balanced Cut, Multicut and Small Set Expansion problems in the semi-random model.

THEOREM 3.1. (HIDDEN SOLUTION SPARSIFICATION) *There exists a polynomial-time randomized algorithm that given a graph $G = (V,E)$, a separation oracle for an $\mathcal{O}$-local SDP relaxation Φ of a partition $\mathcal{P}$ (note: the set $\mathcal{O} \subset V$ and partition $\mathcal{P}$ are "hidden" and are not known to the algorithm), and a parameter $D = 2^T$ ($T \in \mathbb{N}$, $T > 1$), partitions the set of vertices V into a set M and a collection of disjoint sets $\mathcal{Z}$*

$$V = M \cup \bigcup_{Z\in\mathcal{Z}} Z,$$

and also partitions the set of edges into two disjoint sets E^+ and E^-

$$E = E^+ \cup E^-$$

such that

[2]We note that every Ramanujan expander is geometrically expanding with some parameters. However, we omit the details here.

- *all edges cut by the partition* $V = M \cup \bigcup_{Z\in\mathcal{Z}} Z$ *lie in* E^- *(i.e.,* $\mathrm{cut}(\{M\}\cup\mathcal{Z}, E) \subset E^-$*), or in other words,*

$$E^+ \subset M \times M \cup \bigcup_{Z\in\mathcal{Z}} Z \times Z;$$

- *if the graph* $(V, \mathrm{cut}(\mathcal{P}, E))$ *satisfies the geometric expansion property with cut value* X *up to scale* $1/\sqrt{D}$*, then (the expectation is taken over random bits of the algorithm)*

$$\mathbb{E}[\mathrm{cost}_{|\mathcal{O}\cap M}(\mathcal{P}, E^+)] \leq C\ X/D; \qquad (1)$$

and

$$|\{(u,v) \in E^- : u \in \mathcal{O} \text{ or } v \in \mathcal{O}\}| \leq C\ X; \qquad (2)$$

- *each* $Z \in \mathcal{Z}$ *is* Φ*–feasible.*

We first show how to construct constant factor approximation algorithms for Balanced Cut, Multicut and Small Set Expansion using the theorem. We prover the theorem in Section 4.

3.1 Balanced Cut

We show that there exists a constant factor bi-criteria approximation algorithm for the Balanced Cut problem in the semi-random model with $\varepsilon \geq \Omega(\sqrt{\log n}(\log\log n)^2/n)$.

THEOREM 3.2. *There exists a randomized polynomial-time algorithm, a function* $f : \mathbb{N} \to [0,1]$ *tending to 0 as* $n \to \infty$*, and absolute constants* C*,* C_{BC}*, such that for every set of vertices* V *of size* n *(for simplicity assume* n *is even), every partition* $\mathcal{P} = \{L, R\}$*,* $|L| = |R| = n/2$*, and every* $\varepsilon \in (0,1)$ *with probability* $1 - f(n) = 1 - o(1)$ *over random choice of* $SR(\mathcal{P}, \varepsilon)$ *the following statement holds: for every* $G = (V, E) \in SR(\mathcal{P}, \varepsilon)$ *the algorithm returns a balanced partition of* V *into sets* L' *and* R' *with* $|L'|, |R'| \geq n/C$ *and expected cost of the cut at most:*

$$\begin{aligned}&\mathbb{E}\big[\mathrm{cost}(\{L',R'\},E) \mid SR(\mathcal{P},\varepsilon)\big]\\ &\qquad\leq C_{BC}\max\{\text{sr-cost}(\mathcal{P},\varepsilon), n\sqrt{\log n}(\log\log n)^2\}.\end{aligned}$$

Particularly, if $\varepsilon \geq \sqrt{\log n}(\log\log n)^2/n$*, then*

$$\begin{aligned}\mathbb{E}\big[\mathrm{cost}(\{L',R'\},E) \mid SR(\mathcal{P},\varepsilon)\big] &\leq 4C_{BC}\,\text{sr-cost}(\mathcal{P},\varepsilon)\\ &= C_{BC}\varepsilon n^2.\end{aligned}$$

We use the standard SDP relaxation for the Balanced Cut problem. The SDP has a unit vector $\bar{u}$ for every vertex $u \in V$. All vectors satisfy ℓ_2^2 triangle inequalities: for all $u, v, w \in V$:

$$\|\bar{u} - \bar{v}\|^2 + \|\bar{v} - \bar{w}\|^2 \leq \|\bar{u} - \bar{w}\|^2.$$

Finally, all vectors satisfy the spreading constraint (below we count every pair as (u,v) and (v,u)):

$$\sum_{u,v\in V} \|\bar{u} - \bar{v}\|^2 \geq \frac{n^2}{2}.$$

The objective function of the SDP equals $1/2$ sdp-cost$(u \mapsto \bar{u}, E)$. (For clarity, we give the SDP in Appendix C.)

The SDP relaxation defines a set of feasible solutions Φ. This set is a V-local SDP relaxation for $\mathcal{P}$, since every SDP relaxation is always a V-local SDP relaxation. Indeed, $\text{sdp-cost}_{|V}(\varphi, E) = \text{sdp-cost}(\varphi, E)$ for every φ (just by definition), and particularly, for $\varphi^* = \arg\min_{\varphi\in\Phi} \text{sdp-cost}(\varphi, E)$,

$$\begin{aligned}\text{sdp-cost}_{|V}(\varphi^*, E) &\equiv \text{sdp-cost}(\varphi^*, E) = \min_{\varphi\in\Phi} \text{sdp-cost}(\varphi, E)\\ &\leq 2\,\mathrm{cost}(\mathcal{P}, E) \equiv 2\,\mathrm{cost}_{|V}(\mathcal{P}, E).\end{aligned}$$

(The factor of 2 appears because of a different normalization of the objective function.)

In the algorithm below, we use the ARV algorithm for finding a balanced cut (in the worst-case) of Arora, Rao, and Vazirani [6]. We denote the approximation factor of the algorithm by $D_{ARV} = O(\sqrt{\log n})$. For simplicity of exposition we assume that D_{ARV} is a power of 4.

Balanced Cut Algorithm in Semi-random Model

Input: a graph $G = (V, E) \in SR(\mathcal{P}, \varepsilon)$
Output: a cut (L', R'), with $|L'|, |R'| \geq n/C$

- Run the Hidden Solution Sparsification Algorithm with a separation oracle for Φ and obtain a set $M \subset V$, a partition $\mathcal{Z}$ of $V \setminus M$ in disjoint Φ–feasible sets and two disjoint sets of edges E^+ and E^- (with parameter $D = D_{ARV}$).
- Run the ARV algorithm on the graph $G = (V, E^+)$, and obtain a balanced partition (L', R');
- **return** (L', R').

Analysis. We show that every set Z in $\mathcal{Z}$ is balanced. Every set $Z \in \mathcal{Z}$ is Φ–feasible, that is, for some $\varphi \in \Phi$, $\varphi(Z)$ has ℓ_2^2 diameter at most $1/4$. Thus,

$$\begin{aligned}\frac{1}{2}\sum_{u,v\in V} \|\varphi(u) - \varphi(v)\|^2 &\leq \frac{1}{2}\sum_{u,v\in V} \max_{u,v\in V}(\|\varphi(u) - \varphi(v)\|^2) -\\ &- \frac{1}{2}\sum_{u,v\in Z}\big(\max_{u,v\in V}(\|\varphi(u)-\varphi(v)\|^2) - \max_{u,v\in Z}(\|\varphi(u)-\varphi(v)\|^2)\big)\\ &\leq n^2 - \frac{7}{8}|Z|^2.\end{aligned}$$

By the SDP spreading constraint, the left hand side is greater than or equal to $n^2/2$, thus $|Z| \leq \sqrt{4/7}\,n \leq 4/5\,n$.

By the Structural Theorem 5.1, with probability $1 - f(n) = 1 - o(1)$ for every graph $G = (V, E) \in SR(\mathcal{P}, \varepsilon)$, the graph $(V, \mathrm{cut}(\mathcal{P}, E))$ is geometrically expanding with cut cost

$$X = C\max\{\text{sr-cost}(\mathcal{P},\varepsilon), n\sqrt{\log n}(\log\log n)^2\}$$

up to scale $1/\sqrt{D_{ARV}}$. Thus, by Theorem 3.1,

$$\mathrm{cost}_{|M}(\{L, R\}, E^+) \leq C\ X/D_{ARV}.$$

Hence, there are at most $C\ X/D_{ARV}$ edges in E^+ going from $L \cap M$ to $R \cap M$. Observe, that $|L \cap M| \leq |L| = n/2$ and $|R \cap M| \leq |R| = n/2$. Therefore, there are at most $C\,X/D_{ARV}$ edges in E^+ cut by the the partition

$$V = (M \cap L) \cup (M \cap R) \cup \bigcup_{Z\in\mathcal{Z}} Z$$

(the only edges cut are the edges between $M \cap L$ and $M \cap R$) and each of the sets in the partition has size at most $4/5\,n$. These sets can be grouped into two balanced sets L^* and R^* with $|L^*|, |R^*| \geq 1/5\,n$. The ARV algorithm finds a possibly different balanced cut (L', R') (with slightly weaker bounds on $|L'|, |R'|$). The number of edges cut in E^+ is bounded (in expectation) by $D_{ARV} \times C\ X/D_{ARV} = C\ X$. The number of edges cut in E^- is bounded by $|E^-| \leq C\ X$.

3.2 Min Multicut and Min Uncut

The algorithm for the Multicut problem is similar to the algorithm for Balanced Cut. We use the standard SDP relaxation for Multicut: the SDP has a unit vector $\bar{u}$ for every vertex u; vectors $\bar{s}_i$, $\bar{t}_i$ corresponding to source–sink pairs s_i, t_i are orthogonal ($\langle \bar{s}_i, \bar{v}_i \rangle = 0$); all vectors satisfy the ℓ_2^2 triangle inequality constraints (please see Appendix C for details). The key observation is that every Φ–feasible set $Z \in \mathcal{Z}$ has a small diameter w.r.t. some SDP solution and thus may not contain a source–sink pair s_i, t_i. Finally, to find a solution in M we use the algorithm of Garg, Vazirani, and Yannakakis [21].

We get a constant factor approximation algorithm for the Multicut problem in the semi-random model with $\varepsilon \geq \log n (\log \log n)^2/n$.

THEOREM 3.3. *There exists a randomized polynomial-time algorithm, a function $f : \mathbb{N} \to [0, 1]$ tending to 0 as $n \to \infty$, and an absolute constant C, such that for every set of vertices V of size n, every partition $\mathcal{P}$, and every $\varepsilon \in (0, 1)$ with probability $1 - f(n) = 1 - o(1)$ over random choice of $SR(\mathcal{P}, \varepsilon)$ the following statement holds: for every $G = (V, E) \in SR(\mathcal{P}, \varepsilon)$ and every set of demands (s_i, t_i) (satisfying $\mathcal{P}(s_i) \neq \mathcal{P}(t_i)$), the algorithm returns a partition $\mathcal{P}'$ of V separating the demands $(\mathcal{P}'(s_i) \neq \mathcal{P}'(t_i))$ with expected cost of the cut at most:*

$$\mathbb{E}\big[\text{cost}(\mathcal{P}', E) \mid SR(\mathcal{P}, \varepsilon)\big] \leq C \max\{\text{sr-cost}(\mathcal{P},\ \varepsilon), n \log n (\log \log n)^2\}.$$

A similar statement holds for the Min Uncut problem if $\varepsilon \geq \sqrt{\log n}(\log \log n)^2/n$. A semi-random instance of Min Uncut is generated as follows: the adversary first chooses an arbitrary subset S of vertices, then the nature connects each pair of vertices $(u, v) \in S \times S \cup (V \setminus S) \times (V \setminus S)$ with an edge with probability ε, finally the adversary adds arbitrary edges between S and $V \setminus S$, and removes some random edges. The problem can be restated as a cut minimization problem that falls in our framework (see e.g. [1]). Our algorithm for Min Uncut first runs the Hidden Solution Sparsification algorithm and then uses the algorithm of Agarwal, Charikar, Makarychev, and Makarychev [1] for Min Uncut. We defer the details to the journal version of the paper.

3.3 Small Set Expansion

Our algorithm for the Small Set Expansion (SSE) problem is the most involved, and uses the full power of the Hidden Solution Sparsification theorem.

THEOREM 3.4. *There exists a randomized polynomial-time algorithm, a function $f : \mathbb{N} \to [0, 1]$ tending to 0 as $n \to \infty$, and an absolute constant C, such that for every set of vertices V of size n, every partition $\mathcal{P} = \{S, V \setminus S\}$, $|S| = \rho n$ (for $\rho \in (0, 1/2)$) and every $\varepsilon \in (0, 1)$ with probability $1 - f(n) = 1 - o(1)$ over random choice of $SR(\mathcal{P}, \varepsilon)$ the following statement holds: for every $G = (V, E) \in SR(\mathcal{P}, \varepsilon)$, the algorithm given G and ρ, returns a partition $\mathcal{P}' = (S', V \setminus S')$ of V such that $|S'| = \Theta(\rho n)$, $|S'| \leq |V|/2$ with expected cost of the cut at most:*

$$\mathbb{E}\big[\text{cost}(\mathcal{P}', E) \mid SR(\mathcal{P}, \varepsilon)\big] \leq C \max\{\text{sr-cost}(\mathcal{P},\ \varepsilon), n\sqrt{\log n \log(1/\rho)}(\log \log n)^2\}.$$

Particularly, if $\varepsilon\rho \geq \sqrt{\log n \log(1/\rho)}(\log \log n)^2/n$, then

$$\mathbb{E}\big[\text{cost}(\{L, R\}, E) \mid SR(\mathcal{P}, \varepsilon)\big] \leq C\,\text{sr-cost}(\mathcal{P}, \varepsilon) = C\varepsilon\rho(1 - \rho)n^2.$$

Moreover, instead of requiring that $G = (V, E) \in SR(\mathcal{P}, \varepsilon)$, it suffices that the graph $(V, \text{cut}(\mathcal{P}, E))$ is geometrically expanding with cut cost

$$X = C' \max\{\text{sr-cost}(\mathcal{P},\ \varepsilon), n\sqrt{\log n \log(1/\rho)}(\log \log n)^2\}$$

(for some absolute constant C') up to scale

$$s(n, \rho) = \Omega(\sqrt{\log n \log \frac{1}{\rho}}).$$

By Theorem 5.1, for every graph $G \in SR(\mathcal{P}, \varepsilon)$, the graph $(V, \text{cut}(\mathcal{P}, E))$ is geometrically expanding with cut cost

$$X = C' \max\{\text{sr-cost}(\mathcal{P},\ \varepsilon), n\sqrt{\log n \log(1/\rho)}(\log \log n)^2\}$$

up to scale $s(n, \rho) = \Omega(\sqrt{\log n \log \frac{1}{\rho}})$ with probability $1 - o(1)$ over random choice of $SR(\mathcal{P}, \varepsilon)$. We assume that the graph $(V, \text{cut}(\mathcal{P}, E))$ is geometrically expanding. Otherwise, the algorithm fails (this happens with probability $o(1)$).

We use an analog of the Crude SDP (C–SDP) introduced in the paper of Kolla, Makarychev and Makarychev [29]. For each vertex $u \in V$ the C–SDP has a unit vector $\bar{u} \in \mathcal{H}$. All vectors satisfy triangle inequality constraints and spreading constraints (similar to constraints introduced in Bansal et al. [8]; note that their SDP would not work in our case: loosely speaking, it may "find" a good fractional cut that assigns zero vectors to the real solution): for every $u \in V$,

$$\sum_{v \in V} \langle u, v \rangle \leq \rho n.$$

We give the C-SDP in its entirety in Section C. Note that this SDP is not a relaxation for SSE. However, it turns out that this is a S–local SDP relaxation of partition $(S, V \setminus S)$ (see Lemma A.1). We now use the Hidden Solution Sparsification algorithm to find the set M and a partition of $V \setminus M$ into Φ–feasible sets $Z \in \mathcal{Z}$. Here Φ is the set of feasible C–SDP solutions. We set the weight of every vertex $u \in M$ to be the number of edges in E^- incident on u: $w_u = |\{v : (u, v) \in E^-\}|$. w_u corresponds to the cost we would pay for cutting the w_u edges incident on u from E^-, if u were included in the solution (small set). Observe, that the weight of the "hidden" set S is at most $C_1 X$ (for some absolute constant C_1, see (2)). Then, we consider two cases: $|M \cap S| \geq |S|/2$ and $|(V \setminus M) \cap S| \geq |S|/2$, depending on whether most of the hidden set S vertices belong to M or the pieces $Z \in \mathcal{Z}$ of the partition (the algorithm does not know which of the inequalities holds and tries both options).

Case I: This case is handled similar to the proof in Sections 3.1. Since most of S (the hidden solution) belongs to M, we know that there is a good solution $M \cap S$ in $G(V, E^+)$ i.e. $S \cap M$ has size $\in [\rho n/2, \rho n]$ with weight $w(M \cap S) \leq C_1 X$, and there are at most CX/D_{SSE} from E^+ going out of $S \cap M$. Now, we use the following theorem of Bansal et al. [8] which finds small non-expanding sets.

THEOREM 3.5. (SPECIAL CASE OF THEOREM 2.1 [8], ARXIV VERSION) *There exists a polynomial-time algorithm ("SSE algorithm") that given as input a graph $G = (V, E)$, a set of positive weights w_u ($u \in V$), $\rho \in (0, 1/2]$ and $W \in \mathbb{R}^+$, finds a non-empty set $S \subset V$ satisfying $|S| \in [\Omega(\rho n), 3\rho n/2]$, and $w(S) \equiv \sum_{u \in S} w_u \leq CW$, such that*

$$E(S, V \backslash S) \leq D_{SSE} \cdot \min\{E(S, V \backslash S) : |S| = \rho n,\ w(S) \leq W\},$$

where $D_{SSE} = O(\sqrt{\log n \log(1/\rho)})$.

Remark: This theorem is stated in a slightly different form in Bansal et al. [8]. We discuss the differences in Appendix (Section B).

We use this SSE algorithm on $G(V, E^+)$ to find a set S' with $|S'| \in [\Omega(\rho n), 3\rho n/2]$, $w(S') \equiv \sum_{u \in S'} w_u \leq C \cdot C_1 X$, and

$$\text{cost}(\{S', V \setminus S'\}, E^+) \leq D_{SSE} \times CX/D_{SSE} \leq CX.$$

The total cost of the cut $E(S', V \setminus S')$ is bounded by the number of edges cut in E^+ and E^- which is at most CX and CC_1X respectively, which is $O(X)$ as needed.

If $\rho \in (1/3, 1/2)$, the set S' may contain more than $n/2$ vertices, but no more than $3\rho n/2 \leq 3/4\, n$. Then the algorithm returns $S'' = V \setminus S'$ satisfying $|S''| \in [n/4, n/2]$.

Case II: In this case, the hidden solution S could mostly be spread arbitrarily among the pieces $Z \in \mathcal{Z}$ in $V \backslash M$. Here, our algorithm uses an LP to extract the solution from the set $V \setminus M$. The key observation is that this set is already partitioned into pieces of small size. Indeed, every $Z \in \mathcal{Z}$ is Φ–feasible, and thus for some $\varphi \in \Phi$, $\text{diam}(\varphi(Z)) \leq 1/4$ and, consequently, for every $u, v \in Z$, $\langle \varphi(u), \varphi(v) \rangle = (\|\varphi(u)\|^2 + \|\varphi(v)\|^2 - \|\varphi(u) - \varphi(v)\|^2)/2 \geq 7/8$. Using the C-SDP spreading constraint (for an arbitrary $u \in Z$),

$$\sum_v \langle \varphi(u), \varphi(v) \rangle \leq \rho n,$$

we get $|Z| \leq 8/7\ \rho n$.

The LP has a variable $x_v \in [0, 1]$ for every vertex $v \in V \backslash M$; and the only constraint is that $\sum_{u \in V \backslash M} x_u \geq \rho n/2)$. The objective function is

$$\min \sum_{u \in V \backslash M} w_u x_u + \sum_{\substack{(u,v) \in E^+ \\ u,v \in V \backslash M}} |x_u - x_v|. \tag{3}$$

The canonical solution to this LP is as follows: $x_u = 1$, if $u \in S \cap (V \backslash M)$; $x_u = 0$, otherwise. The LP cost of this solution is at most CX, because the first term in the objective function is bounded by $C_1\ X$ (see (2)), the second term is bounded by the size of the cut$(\mathcal{P}, E)$, which is at most $C_2\ X$ (The expected size of the cut equals sr-cost$(\mathcal{P}, \varepsilon)$; by the Chernoff bound the size of the cut is less than $2\,$sr-cost$(\mathcal{P}, \varepsilon)$ with very high probability). Thus, the cost of the optimal solution $\{x_u^*\}$, which we denote by LP^*, is at most $C\ X = (C_1 + C_2)X$. For an integral solution $S' \subset V$, we define the cost

$$f(S') = \sum_{u \in S'} w_u + |E^+(S', V \setminus S')\}| \tag{4}$$

$$\equiv \sum_{u \in S'} w_u + |\{(u, v) \in E^+ : u \in S', v \notin S'\}|.$$

For every $r \in [0, 1]$ define $S_r = \{u : x_u^* \geq r\}$. The algorithm finds r^* that minimizes the ratio $f(S_r)/|S_r|$ subject to $|S_r| \geq \rho n/4$ (note: $|S_1| = |V \setminus M| \geq \rho n/2$). Then it sorts all sets $Z \in \mathcal{Z}$ in order of increasing ratio $f(S_{r^*} \cap Z)/|S_{r^*} \cap Z|$ (ignoring empty sets) and gets a list $Z_1, \dots Z_K$. It picks the first k pieces such that

$$|Z_1 \cap S_{r^*}| + |Z_2 \cap S_{r^*}| + \cdots + |Z_k \cap S_{r^*}| \in [\rho n/4, 2\rho n],$$

and returns

$$S' = \bigcup_{i=1}^{k} Z_i \cap S_{r^*}.$$

Note, that such k exists because each piece $Z_i \cap S_{r^*}$ has size at most $8/7\ \rho n$ (as $|Z_i| \leq 8/7\ \rho n$) and $\sum_{i=1}^{n} |Z_i \cap S_{r^*}| \equiv |S_{r^*}| \geq \rho n/4$.

Analysis of Case II. We first prove that

$$f(S_{r^*}) \leq 4LP^*/(\rho n) \cdot |S_{r^*}|.$$

Observe that

$$\int_0^1 f(S_r) dr = LP^* \qquad \int_0^1 |S_r| dr \geq \frac{\rho n}{2}.$$

The first equality easily follows from (3) and (4), the second equality follows from the LP constraint. Let $R = \{r : |S_r| \geq \rho n/4\}$. Then

$$\int_R |S_r| dr \geq \frac{\rho n}{2} - \int_{[0,1] \backslash R} |S_r| dr \geq \frac{\rho n}{4},$$

and, since $r^* = \min\{f(S_r)/|S_r| : r \in R\}$,

$$LP^* = \int_R f(S_r) dr \geq \int_R \frac{f(S_{r^*})}{|S_{r^*}|} |S_r| dr \geq \frac{f(S_{r^*})}{|S_{r^*}|} \cdot \frac{\rho n}{4}.$$

Thus, $f(S_{r^*}) \leq 4LP^*/(\rho n) \cdot |S_{r^*}|$. Using that edges in E^+ do not cross the boundaries of sets Z_i, we get

$$f(S_{r^*}) = \sum_{i=1}^{K} f(Z_i \cap S_{r^*}) \leq \frac{4LP^*}{\rho n} \sum_{i=1}^{K} |S_{r^*} \cap Z_i|.$$

Recall, that $\{f(Z_i \cap S_{r^*})/|S_{r^*} \cap Z_i|\}_i$ is an increasing sequence, thus

$$f(S') \equiv f(\bigcup_{i=1}^{k} Z_i \cap S_{r^*}) = \sum_{i=1}^{k} f(Z_i \cap S_{r^*})$$

$$\leq \frac{4LP^*}{\rho n} \sum_{i=1}^{k} |S_{r^*} \cap Z_i| = \frac{4LP^*}{\rho n} \cdot |S'| \leq 16LP^*.$$

3.4 Sparsest Cut

We now show how to find an approximate sparsest cut in a semi-random graph G using the algorithm for Small Set Expansion. Specifically, we give an algorithm that for every subset $U \subseteq V$ intersecting each of the pieces of the planted partition (S, T) (see below for details), returns a cut $(A, U \setminus A)$ of sparsity

$$\frac{E(A, U \setminus A)}{|A|} \leq O(\varepsilon n).$$

In Section 6, we show that the Sparsest Cut algorithm can be used to recover pieces S and T assuming that the graphs $G[S]$ and $G[T]$ have large expansion. We remark that while we are usually concerned with the case when $U = V$ for the sparsest cut problem, the following stronger statement is also useful for Section 6.

THEOREM 3.6. *There exists a randomized polynomial-time algorithm, a function $f : \mathbb{N} \to [0,1]$ tending to 0 as $n \to \infty$, and an absolute constant C, such that for every set of vertices V of size n, every partition $\mathcal{P} = \{S, V \setminus S\}$ and every $\varepsilon, \eta \in (0,1)$ satisfying $\varepsilon\eta \geq \sqrt{\log n}(\log\log n)^2/n$ with probability $1 - f(n) = 1 - o(1)$ over random choice of $SR(\mathcal{P}, \varepsilon)$ the following statement holds: for every $G = (V, E) \in SR(\mathcal{P}, \varepsilon)$, every $U \subseteq V$ such that $|U \cap S| \geq \eta n$ and $|U \cap T| \geq \eta n$, the algorithm given G, returns a partition $(A, U \setminus A)$ of $G[U]$ with $|A| \leq |U|/2$ such that with probability exponentially close to 1,*

$$\frac{|E(A, U \setminus A)|}{|A|} < C_{SC}\varepsilon n. \quad (5)$$

PROOF SKETCH. We first give a proof assuming $\varepsilon\eta \geq \sqrt{\log n \log(1/\eta)}(\log\log n)^2/n$.

Our algorithm guesses the size of $|S \cap U|$, computes the size of $|T \cap U| = |U| - |S \cap U|$. Then, it runs the Small Set Expansion algorithm on $G[U]$ with $\rho = \min(|S \cap U|, |T \cap U|)/|U|$, obtains a set A ($|A| \leq |U \setminus A|$) of size $\Theta(\rho|U|)$ and returns the cut $(A, U \setminus A)$. We need to show that the size of the cut $(A, U \setminus A)$ is at most $O(\varepsilon\rho|U|n)$, so that the sparsity of the cut is then $O(\varepsilon n)$.

Let us explain why we can use the Small Set Expansion algorithm for the graph $G[U]$ and why the algorithm finds a cut of cost at most $O(\varepsilon\rho|U|n)$. By the structural theorem (Theorem 5.1 part II), with probability $1 - o(1)$, for every $U \subset V$, the graph $(U, E \cap (U \times U) \cap (S \times T))$ (i.e., the bipartite graph between pieces $U \cap S$ and $U \cap T$) is geometrically expanding up to scale $\sqrt{\log n \log(1/\eta)}$ with cut value

$$\begin{aligned} X &= C \max\{\text{sr-cost}(\mathcal{P}_{|U}, \varepsilon),\ n\sqrt{\log n \log(1/\eta)}(\log\log n)^2\} \\ &= C \max\{\varepsilon|S \cap U| \cdot |T \cap U|,\ n\sqrt{\log n \log(1/\eta)}(\log\log n)^2\}. \end{aligned}$$

Below, we assume that the graph $(U, E \cap (U \times U) \cap (S \times T))$ is geometrically expanding; otherwise our algorithm fails (which happens with probability $o(1)$ over the choice of $SR(\mathcal{P}, \varepsilon)$). Write the lower bound on $\varepsilon\eta$ and a trivial inequality on $\varepsilon|S \cap U| \cdot |T \cap U|$:

$$\begin{aligned} \sqrt{\log n \log(1/\eta)}(\log\log n)^2 &\leq \varepsilon\eta n \leq \varepsilon \min(|S \cap U|, |T \cap U|)n; \\ \varepsilon|S \cap U| \cdot |T \cap U| &\leq \varepsilon \min(|S \cap U|, |T \cap U|)n. \end{aligned}$$

Together these inequalities give us an upper bound on X:

$$X \leq C\varepsilon \min(|S \cap U|, |T \cap U|)n \leq C\varepsilon\rho|U|n.$$

By Theorem 3.3, the Small Set Expansion algorithm returns a cut of size $O(X)$ (Here we use that the graph $(U, E \cap (U \times U) \cap (S \times T))$ is geometrically expanding up to scale $\sqrt{\log n \log(1/\eta)} \geq \sqrt{\log n \log(1/\rho)}$).

We showed that the algorithm finds a cut of sparsity $\alpha = O(\varepsilon n)$ in expectation. By Markov's inequality, it finds a cut of sparsity at most 2α with probability at least 1/2. So by repeating the algorithm many times and then picking the best solution, we can get a solution of cost at most 2α with probability exponentially close to 1.

Finally, let us briefly explain how to get rid of the $\sqrt{\log(1/\eta)}$ factor in the lower bound on $\varepsilon\eta$. Observe that it suffices for our algorithm to find a set A of size $|A| \in [\Theta(\rho|U|), |U|/2]$ i.e., we do not need a bound $|A| \leq O(\rho|U|)$. So we slightly modify the Small Set Expansion algorithm so that it works for smaller $\varepsilon\eta$, but possibly returns $|A| \gg \rho|U|$. In Case I of the algorithm (see Theorem 3.4), we use Theorem 2.1 (part I) instead of Theorem 2.1 (part II) of Bansal et al. [8] with $\rho = 1/2$. This algorithm returns a sparse cut of size at most $\rho|U| = |U|/2$ of sparsity $O(\sqrt{\log n})OPT$ (where OPT is the optimal sparsity of the cut). We repeatedly apply this algorithm and obtain disjoint sets $A_1, \dots, A_T$. After we get a set A_i, we remove it from U. We stop when $|\cup A_t| \geq \rho|U|/4$. We let $A = \cup A_t$. It is not hard to show that the sparsity of A is at most $O(\sqrt{\log n})OPT$ (where OPT is the value of the sparsest cut in (U, E^+)) and $|A| \in [\Theta(\rho|U|), 1/2|U|]$. The proof is similar to the proof of Theorem 2.1 (part II) in [8]. We omit it in this version of the paper. □

4. HIDDEN SOLUTION SPARSIFICATION ALGORITHM

We now present the Hidden Solution Sparsification Algorithm and prove Theorem 3.1. The algorithm runs in $O(\log\log n)$ phases. In each round, we first solve the SDP on the current instance. The heavy vertices w.r.t. to this vector solution are first processed and removed using the algorithm from Section 4.1. In the remaining graph, we remove (cut) long edges to further "sparsify" the hidden solution (E_R) and produce the instance for the next phase.

Hidden Solution Sparsification Algorithm

Input: a graph $G = (V, E)$ and a separation oracle for a set of SDP solutions $\Phi \subset \{V \to \mathcal{H}\}$.
Output: partitions $V = M \cup \bigcup_{Z \in \mathcal{Z}} Z$ and $E = E^+ \cup E^-$.

- Let $M_0 = V$, $\mathcal{Z}_0 = \varnothing$, $E_0^+ = E$, $E_0^- = \varnothing$, $T = \frac{1}{2}\log_2 D$, and $\delta_t = 2^{-t}$ for all $t = 1, \dots, T$.
- for $t = 1, \dots, T$ do

  A. *Solve the SDP for the remaining graph:* Find
  $$\varphi_t = \arg\min_{\varphi \in \Phi} \text{sdp-cost}(\varphi, E_{t-1}^+ \cap (M_{t-1} \times M_{t-1})).$$

  B. *Remove δ_t-heavy vertices:* run Heavy Vertices Removal Algorithm (described in Section 4.1) with parameters V, M_{t-1}, φ_t, and obtain a collection of Φ-feasible sets $\Delta\mathcal{Z}_t$. Add edges in E_{t-1}^+ cut by $\Delta\mathcal{Z}_t$ to the set ΔE_t^-. Let
  $$\mathcal{Z}_t = \mathcal{Z}_{t-1} \cup \Delta\mathcal{Z}_t; \quad M_t = M_{t-1} \setminus \bigcup_{Z \in \Delta\mathcal{Z}_t} Z.$$

  C. *Remove δ_t-long edges from E^+:* Find
  $$L_t = \{(u, v) \in E^+ : u, v \in M_t, \|\varphi_t(u) - \varphi_t(v)\|^2 \geq \delta_t\}.$$
  Let
  $$E_t^+ = E_{t-1}^+ \setminus (\Delta E_t^- \cup L_t); \quad E_t^- = E_{t-1}^- \cup (\Delta E_t^- \cup L_t).$$

- **return** $M = M_T$, $\mathcal{Z} = \mathcal{Z}_T$, $E^+ = E_T^+$, $E^- = E_T^-$.

PROOF OF THEOREM 3.1. We analyze the algorithm given above. We note that the step A of finding φ_k can be performed in polynomial-time using semidefinite programming; the step B is performed using the algorithm described in the next subsection.

At every iteration, the algorithm removes all edges crossing the partition $\Delta\mathcal{Z}_t$ from E_t^+ and adds them to E_t^-, hence the first item of Theorem 3.1 holds. The third item holds, because every set $Z \in \mathcal{Z}$ belongs to some $\Delta\mathcal{Z}_t$ and, thus by Lemma 4.1 (see below), $\operatorname{diam}(\varphi_t(Z)) \leq 1/4$.

We now show that the second item of Theorem 3.1 holds. We first prove that

$$\operatorname{cost}_{|M_t}(\mathcal{P}, E_t^+) \leq 2\, X \cdot \delta_t^2$$

for every $t \in \{0, \dots, T\}$. The Heavy Vertices Removal Procedure returns set M_t that does not contain any δ_t–heavy vertices w.r.t. φ_t i.e., $H_{\delta_t,\varphi_t}(M_t) = \varnothing$ (see Lemma 4.1). Using the geometric expansion property of the graph $(V, \operatorname{cut}(E,\mathcal{P}))$, we get $\left|\{(u,v) \in \operatorname{cut}(\mathcal{P},E) \cap (M_t \times M_t) : \|\varphi_t(u) - \varphi_t(v)\|^2 \leq \delta_t/2\}\right| \leq 2\delta_t^2 X$. The algorithm removes all $\delta_t/2$–long edges at step C, thus the set $E_t^+ \cap (M_t \times M_t)$ contains only edges (u,v) for which $\|\varphi_t(u) - \varphi_t(v)\|^2 \leq \delta_t/2$. Combining this observation with the previous inequality, and using that edges in E_t^+ do not cross the boundary of M_t, we get

$$\operatorname{cost}_{|M_t}(\mathcal{P}, E_t^+) = \left|\operatorname{cut}(E,\mathcal{P}) \cap E_t^+ \cap (M_t \times M_t)\right| \leq 2\delta_t^2 X. \quad (6)$$

For $t = T$, we get $\operatorname{cost}_{|M}(\mathcal{P}, E^+) \leq 2\, X/D$.

Finally, we estimate the size of the set $\{(u,v) \in E^- : u \in \mathcal{O} \text{ or } v \in \mathcal{O}\}$. To do so, we use that Φ is a $\mathcal{O}$–local relaxation of the partition $\mathcal{P}$. For graph $G = (V, E_{t-1}^+ \cap (M_{t-1} \times M_{t-1}))$, we obtain inequality

$$\begin{aligned}
&\text{sdp-cost}_{|\mathcal{O}}(\varphi_t, E_{t-1}^+ \cap (M_{t-1} \times M_{t-1})) \\
&\quad \leq C_1 \operatorname{cost}_{|\mathcal{O}}(\mathcal{P}, E_{t-1}^+ \cap (M_{t-1} \times M_{t-1})) \\
&\quad = C_1 \operatorname{cost}_{|\mathcal{O} \cap M_{t-1}}(\mathcal{P}, E_{t-1}^+) \leq 2CX \cdot \delta_{t-1}^2 \\
&\quad = 8C_1 \delta_t^2 X.
\end{aligned}$$

The third line of the inequality follows from (6).

Now, we bound the number of edges removed from $E_{t-1}^+ \cap \mathcal{O}$ and added to $E_t^- \cap \mathcal{O}$ in terms of "sdp-cost". At step t, we add two sets of edges to E^-: ΔE_t^- and L_t. Since all edges (u,v) in L_t are $\delta_t/2$–long (i.e., $\|\varphi(u) - \varphi(v)\|^2 \geq \delta_t/2$),

$$\begin{aligned}
&\text{sdp-cost}_{|\mathcal{O}}(\varphi_t, E_{t-1}^+ \cap (M_{t-1} \times M_{t-1})) \\
&\quad \equiv \sum_{\substack{(u,v) \in E_{t-1}^+ \cap (M_{t-1} \times M_{t-1}) \\ (u,v) \in \mathcal{O} \times V}} \frac{\|\varphi(u) - \varphi(v)\|^2}{2} \\
&\quad \geq \frac{|L_t \cap (\mathcal{O} \times V)| \cdot \delta_t/2}{2}.
\end{aligned}$$

Hence, $|L_t \cap (\mathcal{O} \times V)| \leq 32 C_1 \delta_t X$. The probability that the Heavy Vertices Removal Procedure separates two vertices u and v connected with an edges in E_{t-1}^+ is at most $C_2(\delta_t^{-1} + \delta_t^{-2}\mathbb{E}|M_{t-1} \setminus M_t|/n) \cdot \|\varphi(u) - \varphi(v)\|^2$ (see Lemma 4.1). Thus, the expected total number of edges in the set $\Delta E_t^- \cap (\mathcal{O} \times V)$ is at most

$$\begin{aligned}
&C_2\Big(\delta_t^{-1} + \delta_t^{-2} \frac{\mathbb{E}|M_{t-1} \setminus M_t|}{n}\Big) \\
&\qquad \cdot \text{sdp-cost}_{|\mathcal{O}}(\varphi_t, E_{t-1}^+ \cap (M_{t-1} \times M_{t-1})) \\
&\quad \leq 8C_1C_2\Big(\delta_t + \frac{\mathbb{E}|M_{t-1} \setminus M_t|}{n}\Big)X.
\end{aligned}$$

The total number of edges in $E^- \cap (\mathcal{O} \times V)$ is bounded by

$$\begin{aligned}
&\sum_{t=1}^{T} (32C_1\delta_t + 8C_1C_2\delta_t + 8C_1C_2 \cdot \frac{\mathbb{E}|M_{t-1} \setminus M_t|}{n})X \\
&\qquad \leq (32C_1 + 8C_1C_2 + 8C_1C_2)X.
\end{aligned}$$

□

4.1 Heavy Vertices Removal Procedure

In this section, we describe the algorithm which deals with the heavy vertices in a vector solution. Note that in the intended vector solution for all the above problems, all vertices are heavy (the intended solution for Balanced Cut has $n/2$ vectors at a fixed unit vector $\bar{v}_0$ and the rest $n/2$ of them at $-\bar{v}_0$). This algorithm also shows how we can take advantage of vector solutions which look like the intended solution (say, roughly low-dimensional solutions), with many heavy vertices.

LEMMA 4.1. *There exists a polynomial-time algorithm that given a set of vertices V, an SDP solution $\varphi : V \to \mathcal{H}$, a subset $M \subseteq V$, finds a set of vertices $M' \subset M$ and a partition of $M \setminus M'$ into disjoint sets $Z \in \Delta\mathcal{Z}$ such that*

- *the set M' does not contain any δ–heavy vertices w.r.t. φ (that is, $(H_{\delta,\varphi}(M') = \varnothing)$).*
- *$\operatorname{diam}(\varphi(Z)) \leq 1/4$ for every $Z \in \Delta\mathcal{Z}$;*
- *for every two vertices u^* and v^*, the probability that u^* and v^* are separated by the partition is bounded as follows:*

$$\begin{aligned}
&\Pr(\exists Z \in \Delta\mathcal{Z} \text{ s.t. } I_Z(u^*) \neq I_Z(v^*)) \\
&\qquad \leq C\Big(\delta^{-1} + \delta^{-2} \frac{\mathbb{E}[|M \setminus M'|]}{n}\Big)\|\varphi(u^*) - \varphi(v^*)\|^2.
\end{aligned}$$

We remark that some of the heavy vertices $H_{\delta,\varphi}(M)$ may belong to M', but they are not heavy anymore (w.r.t M').

PROOF. We use the following algorithm. If $\delta \geq 1/32$, we run the algorithm with $\delta' = 1/32$.

Heavy Vertices Removal Procedure

Input: a set of vertices V, a subset $M \subseteq V$, an SDP solution $\varphi : V \to \mathcal{H}$, a parameter $\delta \in (0, 1/32]$;
Output: a set $M \subseteq V$, partition $V \setminus M = \bigcup_{Z \in \Delta\mathcal{Z}} Z$;

- while $(H_{\delta,\varphi}(M) \neq \varnothing)$
  - Connect heavy vertices in M at ℓ_2^2 distance at most 4δ with an edge and denote the new set of edges by $A = \{(u,v) \in H_{\delta,\varphi}(M) \times H_{\delta,\varphi}(M) : \|\varphi(u) - \varphi(v)\|^2 \leq 4\delta\}$.
  - Break graph $(H_{\delta,\varphi}(M), A)$ into connected components.
  - Pick a random $r \in [\delta, 2\delta)$.
  - *Remove components of small diameter:* For each connected component U with $\operatorname{diam}(\varphi(U)) \leq 1/8$, let

    $$B_U = \{v \in M : \exists u \in U \text{ s.t. } \|\varphi(u) - \varphi(v)\|^2 \leq r\}.$$

    Denote the set of all connected components of diameter at most $1/8$ by $\mathcal{U}$.

– *Remove a maximal independent set:* In the remaining set $H_{\delta,\varphi}(M) \setminus \bigcup_{U\in\mathcal{U}} U$ find a maximal independent set[3] S. For each $u \in S$, let $B_u = \{v : \varphi(v) \in \text{Ball}(u, r)\}$.
– Remove sets B_U and B_u from M:

$$M = M \setminus \Big(\bigcup_{U\in\mathcal{U}} B_U \cup \bigcup_{u\in S} B_u \Big);$$

- **return** $M' = M$.

Analysis. It is clear that the algorithm always terminates in polynomial-time (since at every step at least one vertex is removed). When the algorithm terminates $H_{\delta,\varphi}(M) = \varnothing$ by the condition of the "while" loop. Every set $\varphi(B_u)$ removed from M and added to $\Delta\mathcal{Z}$ at one of the iterations is contained in a ball of radius at most 2δ; every set $\varphi(B_U)$ is contained in the 2δ–neighborhood of a set $\varphi(U)$ (for some $U \in \mathcal{U}$) whose diameter is at most $1/8$. Thus, the diameter of each $\varphi(B_u)$ and $\varphi(B_U)$ is at most $1/8 + 4\delta \leq 1/4$.

Verify the third item of Lemma 4.1. Fix two vertices u^* and v^*; and consider one iteration of the algorithm. We may assume that the algorithm first picks the independent set S and a collection of connected components $\mathcal{U}$, and only then chooses random $r \in [\delta, 2\delta)$. Observe, that the distance between (images of) any two vertices in S is at least 4δ (because S is an independent set), the distance between every two sets in $\mathcal{U}$ is at least 4δ (because every $U \in \mathcal{U}$ is a connected component), and the distance between every $U \in \mathcal{U}$ and $u \in S$ is at least 4δ (again because U is a connected component, and $u \notin U$). Thus, $\varphi(u^*)$ may belong to at most one $\text{Ball}(U, 2\delta)$ or $\text{Ball}(u, 2\delta)$. If $\varphi(u^*) \in \text{Ball}(u, 2\delta)$, then

$$\Pr(\varphi(u^*) \in \text{Ball}(u, r),\ \varphi(v^*) \notin \text{Ball}(u, r)) \leq \delta^{-1}\|\varphi(u) - \varphi(v)\|^2.$$

Of course, if $\varphi(u^*) \notin \text{Ball}(u, 2\delta)$, then

$$\Pr(\varphi(u^*) \in \text{Ball}(u, r), \varphi(v^*) \notin \text{Ball}(u, r)) \leq \Pr(\varphi(u^*) \in \text{Ball}(u, r)) = 0.$$

The same statements hold if we replace $u \in S$ with $U \in \mathcal{U}$. Thus, at one iteration, the probability that u^* belongs to a removed ball but v^* does not belong to the same ball is at most $\delta^{-1}\|\varphi(u) - \varphi(v)\|^2$. Denote by T the number of iterations of the algorithm. Then, the probability that u^* and v^* are separated at one of the iterations is at most $2\delta^{-1}\mathbb{E}[T]\|\varphi(u) - \varphi(v)\|^2$.

We now prove that at every iteration but possibly the last, the algorithm removes at least δn vertices from M. Thus, $\mathbb{E}[T] \leq 1 + \mathbb{E}|M' \setminus M|/(\delta n)$, and the third item of Lemma 4.1 follows. Observe, that if the independent set $S = \varnothing$, then the algorithm terminates. If $S \neq \varnothing$, there exists at least one connected component L with $\text{diam}(\varphi(L)) \geq 1/8$. The maximal independent set in L must contain at least $\Omega(\delta^{-1})$ vertices, since for every edge $(u, v) \in A$, $\|\varphi(u) - \varphi(v)\|^2 \leq 4\delta$. Thus, $|S| \geq \Omega(\delta^{-1})$. Since each $u \in S$ is δ–heavy and $r \geq \delta$, $|B_u| \geq \delta^2 n$. Hence (using the fact that sets B_u are disjoint),

$$\Big|\bigcup_{u\in S} B_u\Big| = \sum_{u\in S} |B_u| \geq \delta n.$$

[3]This is done independently of the random variable r, e.g., using a deterministic greedy algorithm.

□

5. STRUCTURAL THEOREM

We now prove that semi-random graphs are geometrically expanding, namely we prove that with high probability for every semi-random graph $G = (V, E) \in SR(\mathcal{P}, \varepsilon)$ the graph $(V, \text{cut}(\mathcal{P}, E))$ is geometrically expanding.

THEOREM 5.1. *I. There exists a function $f : \mathbb{N} \to [0, 1]$ satisfying $\lim_{n\to\infty} f(n) = 0$ such that for every set of vertices V of size n, every partition $\mathcal{P}$, and every $\varepsilon \in (0, 1)$, $D = 2^T$ ($T \in \mathbb{N}$, $T > 1$) with probability $1 - f(n) = 1 - o(1)$ the random set $SR(\mathcal{P}, \varepsilon)$ satisfies the following property: for every graph $G = (V, E) \in SR(\mathcal{P}, \varepsilon)$, the graph $(V, \text{cut}(\mathcal{P}, E))$ is geometrically expanding with cut cost*

$$X = C \max\{\text{sr-cost}(\mathcal{P}, \varepsilon),\ nD(\log^2 D)\}$$

up to scale $1/\sqrt{D}$.

II. Moreover, a slightly stronger statement holds. For every set of vertices V of size n, every partition $\mathcal{P}$, and every $\varepsilon \in (0, 1)$, $D = 2^T$ ($T \in \mathbb{N}$, $T > 1$) with probability $1 - f(n) = 1 - o(1)$ the random set $SR(\mathcal{P}, \varepsilon)$ satisfies the following property: for every graph $G = (V, E) \in SR(\mathcal{P}, \varepsilon)$ and every $U \subset V$, the graph $(U, \text{cut}(\mathcal{P}, E) \cap (U \times U))$ is geometrically expanding with cut cost

$$X = C \max\{\text{sr-cost}(\mathcal{P}_{|U}, \varepsilon),\ nD(\log^2 D)\}$$

up to scale $1/\sqrt{D}$. Here $\mathcal{P}_{|U} = \{P \cap U : P \in \mathcal{P}\}$ denotes the restriction of the partition $\mathcal{P}$ to the subset U.

We defined Geometric Expansion in Section 2. We now give a slightly different definition of Geometric Expansion which is equivalent to Definition 2.12, but is more convenient for proving Theorem 5.1.

DEFINITION 5.2. (GEOMETRIC EXPANSION; SEE DEFINITION 2.12) *A graph $G = (V, E)$ satisfies the geometric expansion property with cut value X at scale δ if for every SDP solution $\varphi : V \to \mathcal{H}$ satisfying $H_{\delta,\varphi}(V) = \varnothing$,*

$$|\{(u, v) \in E : \|\varphi(u) - \varphi(v)\|^2 \leq \delta/2\}| \leq 2\delta^2 X.$$

A graph $G = (V, E)$ satisfies the geometric expansion property with cut value X up to scale 2^{-T} ($T \in \mathbb{N}$) if it satisfies the geometric expansion property for every $\delta \in \{2^{-t} : 1 \leq t \leq T\}$.

CLAIM 5.3. *Definitions 2.12 and 5.2 are equivalent.*

PROOF SKETCH. It is easy to see that every graph satisfying Definition 2.12 satisfies Definition 5.2: we simply let $M = V$. Assume that $G = (V, E)$ satisfies Definition 5.2. Consider an SDP solution $\varphi : V \to \mathcal{H}$ and a set M such that $\varphi_{\delta,\varphi}(M) = \varnothing$. Replace φ with φ': $\varphi'(u) = \varphi(u)$ if $u \in M$, and $\varphi'(u) = e_u$ otherwise, where $\{e_u\}_u$ is a collection of orthogonal unit vectors, orthogonal to all vectors $\varphi(u)$. The ℓ_2^2–distance between every vector $\varphi'(u) = e_u$ ($u \in V \setminus M$) and any other vector $\varphi'(v)$ is at least 1. Thus, $H_{\delta,\varphi}(M) \subset H_{\delta,\varphi}(V) = \varnothing$. Hence,

$$\big|\{(u, v) \in E \cap (M \times M) : \|\varphi(u) - \varphi(v)\|^2 \leq \delta/2\}\big| = \\ = \big|\{(u, v) \in E : \|\varphi'(u) - \varphi'(v)\|^2 \leq \delta/2\}\big| \leq 2\delta^2 X.$$

□

PROOF OF THEOREM 5.1. We use Definition 5.2 in this proof. Let $E_K = \{(u,v) \in V \times V : \mathcal{P}(u) \neq \mathcal{P}(v)\}$ and $E_R \subset E_K$ be the set of random edges chosen for the set $SR(\mathcal{P}, \varepsilon)$ as in Definition 2.6. Since $\text{cut}(\mathcal{P}, E) \subset E_R$ it suffices to show that the graph (V, E_R) is geometrically expanding with high probability. We fix the parameter $\delta = 2^{-t}$ (where $1 \leq t \leq T$), and prove that the graph (V, E_R) is geometrically expanding with cut value X at scale δ. Then we apply the union bound for all $T = \log_2 D$ possible choices of δ.

We use the technique developed by Kolla, Makarychev and Makarychev [29]. Observe that the condition $H_{\delta,\varphi}(V) = \varnothing$ implies that

$$|\{v \in V : \|\varphi(u) - \varphi(v)\|^2 \leq \delta\}| \leq \delta^2 n,$$

and, consequently,

$$|\{(u,v) \in V \times V : \|\varphi(u) - \varphi(v)\|^2 \leq \delta\}| \leq \delta^2 n^2.$$

Thus we need to bound the probability of the bad event: *there exists an SDP solution $\varphi : V \to \mathcal{H}$ such that*

$$|\{(u,v) \in V \times V : \|\varphi(u) - \varphi(v)\|^2 \leq \delta\}| \leq \delta^2 n^2 \quad (7)$$

and

$$|\{(u,v) \in E_R : \|\varphi(u) - \varphi(v)\|^2 \leq \frac{\delta}{2}\} \geq 2\delta^2 X. \quad (8)$$

We now show that if such φ exists then there exists an embedding $\varphi' : V \to N_\delta$ to a relatively small set $N_\delta \subset \mathcal{H}$ satisfying slightly relaxed conditions:

$$|\{(u,v) \in V \times V : \|\varphi'(u) - \varphi'(v)\|^2 \leq \frac{3}{4}\,\delta\}| \leq \frac{5}{4}\,\delta^2 n^2, \quad (9)$$

and,

$$|\{(u,v) \in E_R : \|\varphi'(u) - \varphi'(v)\|^2 \leq \frac{3}{4}\,\delta\}| \geq \frac{3}{2}\delta^2 X. \quad (10)$$

Here $N_\delta \subset \mathcal{H}$ is a set of size $\exp(O(\log^2(1/\delta))$ depending only on δ. Then, we argue that such φ' exists with very small probability.

CLAIM 5.4. *If $|E_R| \leq 2X$ and there exists $\varphi : V \to \mathcal{H}$ satisfying (7) and (8), then there exists $\varphi' : V \to N_\delta$ satisfying (9) and (10).*

PROOF. We use the following simple lemma proved in [29].

LEMMA 5.5. (LEMMA 3.7 [29], ARXIV VERSION) *For every positive ζ, η and ν, there exists a set N_δ of unit vectors of size at most*

$$\exp\left(O(\zeta^{-2}\log(1/\eta)\log(1/\nu))\right)$$

such that for every set of unit vectors Z there exists a randomized mapping $\psi : Z \to N$ satisfying the following property: for every $u, v \in \mathcal{Z}$,

$$\Pr\Big((1+\zeta)^{-1}\|u-v\|^2 - \eta^2 \leq \|\psi(u) - \psi(v)\|^2 \quad (11)$$
$$\leq (1+\zeta)\|u-v\|^2 + \eta^2\Big) \geq 1 - \nu.$$

The proof of Lemma 5.5 is based on the Johnson–Lindenstrauss lemma: The set N is an "epsilon–net" in a low dimensional space. To construct ψ we first project Z in a low dimensional space using the Johnson–Lindenstrauss transform and then "round" each vector to the closest vector in N. See [29] for details.

We set parameters $\zeta = 1/7$, $\eta^2 = \delta/8$ and $\nu = \delta^2/8$ and pick N_δ as in Lemma 5.5. Then we choose a deterministic $\psi(u) : \varphi(V) \to N$ such that the condition

$$\frac{7}{8}\|\varphi(u) - \varphi(v)\|^2 - \frac{\delta}{8} \leq \|\psi(\varphi(u)) - \psi(\varphi(v))\|^2$$
$$\leq \frac{8}{7}\,\|\varphi(u) - \varphi(v)\|^2 + \frac{\delta}{8}$$

holds for at least a $(1 - \delta^2/4)$ fraction of all pairs $u, v \in V$ and at least a $(1-\delta^2/4)$ fraction of all edges $(u,v) \in E_R$ (the existence of such ψ follows from (11), by the probabilistic method). Define $\varphi'(u) = \psi(\varphi(u))$. We get:

- for all but at most $\delta^2/4\ n^2$ pairs $u, v \in V$, if $\|\varphi(u) - \varphi(v)\|^2 > \delta$, then $\|\varphi'(u) - \varphi'(v)\|^2 \geq 7/8\ \delta - \delta/8 = 3/4\ \delta$;
- for all but at most $\delta^2/4\ |E_R| \leq \delta^2/2\ X$ edges $(u,v) \in E_R$ if $\|\varphi(u) - \varphi(v)\|^2 \leq \delta/2$, then $\|\varphi'(u) - \varphi'(v)\|^2 \leq 8/7 \cdot \delta/2 + \delta/8 < 3/4\ \delta$.

Therefore, inequalities (9) and (10) hold. □

Observe, that $\mathbb{E}|E_R| = \text{sr-cost}(\mathcal{P}, \varepsilon) \leq X$. Hence, by the Chernoff bound (for some absolute constant C_1),

$$\Pr(|E_R| \geq 2X) \leq e^{-C_1 X}.$$

Similarly, by the Chernoff bound, inequalities (9) and (10) simultaneously hold with probability at most $e^{-C_2\delta^2 X}$. Thus, a fixed $\varphi' : V \to N$ satisfies (9) and (10) with probability (over random choice of E_R) at most $e^{-C_3\delta^2 X}$. The total number of different embeddings $\varphi' : V \to N$ equals $|N|^n \leq \exp(C_4 n \log^2 D)$. By the union bound the probability that at least one such φ' exists is at most $e^{-C_3\delta^2 X + C_4 n \log^2 D} \leq e^{-n}$ here we use that $\delta^2 X \geq Cn(\log^2 D)$ for sufficiently large C.

Part II follows from Part I by taking the union bound over all 2^n possible choices of the set U. We omit the details in this version of the paper.

6. RECOVERING THE PARTITIONS IN THE PLANTED MODEL

In the case of the Balanced Cut and Small Set Expansion problems, we can obtain better guarantees when the sets of the partition $\mathcal{P} = \{S, T\}$ have enough expansion within them. Note that to recover the planted partition, we need some conditions on the graph expansion inside $G[S]$ and $G[T]$: otherwise, there may exist a sparse cut in G cutting both S and T (for example, if the graphs $G[S]$ and $G[T]$ are random $G(n/2, \varepsilon)$ graphs, then the graph G is a $G(n, \varepsilon)$, and thus the sets S and T are indistinguishable from other sets of size $n/2$). This assumption is in the flavor of planted instances of Balanced Cut (or Small Set Expansion problem), where the cut given by the partition (S, T) is much sparser (sparser by a constant factor) than any cut inside the (adversarial) graph restricted to S or T. (This assumption is also similar to the stability assumption of Balcan, Blum, and Gupta [7] for clustering problems, where a c-factor approximation to the partitioning problem is $\eta(c)$-close to the target partition.) In this case, we can find the partition (S, T) up to $(1+\eta)$-accuracy for some sub-constant $\eta > 0$ i.e., a partition differing from (S, T) in at most ηn vertices. We obtain these guarantees by repeatedly defining instances of the Sparsest Cut problem, and using our algorithms for the semi-random model to obtain increasingly finer approximations to the planted partition.

DEFINITION 6.1. *Denote by $h(G)$ the expansion of the graph $G = (V_G, E_G)$:*

$$h(G) \equiv \min_{\substack{S \subset V_G \\ 0<|S|\leq 1/2\,|V_G|}} \frac{E(S, V_G \setminus S)}{|S|}.$$

THEOREM 6.2. *There exists a randomized polynomial-time algorithm, a function $f : \mathbb{N} \to [0,1]$ tending to 0 as $n \to \infty$, and positive absolute constants C, C_{exp}, such that for every set of vertices V of size n, every partition $\mathcal{P} = \{S, T\}$, $|S| = \rho n$ (for $\rho \in (0, 1/2]$) and every $\varepsilon \in (0,1)$, $\eta \in (0,1)$, satisfying*

$$\eta \geq \frac{C\sqrt{\log n}(\log\log n)^2}{\varepsilon n},$$

the following statement holds with probability $1 - f(n) = 1 - o(1)$ over a random choice of $SR(\mathcal{P}, \varepsilon)$: For every $G = (V, E) \in SR(\mathcal{P}, \varepsilon)$ satisfying $h(G[S]) \geq C_{exp}\varepsilon n$ and $h(G[T]) \geq C_{exp}\varepsilon n$, the algorithm given G and ε, returns a partition (X, Y) of V such that

$$|X \triangle S| = |Y \triangle T| \leq \eta n \quad \text{or} \quad |X \triangle T| = |Y \triangle S| \leq \eta n.$$

Remark 1: The conditions $h(G[S]) \geq C_{exp}\varepsilon n$ and $h(G[T]) \geq C_{exp}\varepsilon n$ can be slightly relaxed, by requiring that only sets of size at least ηn expand in $G[S]$ and $G[T]$.
Remark 2: We assume that $\eta \leq \rho/3$. Otherwise, if $\rho \leq \eta$, then the trivial solution $(\varnothing, V)$ satisfies the conditions of the theorem. If $\eta \in [\rho/3, \rho]$, we may replace η with $\eta' = \rho/3$ and slightly change the absolute constant C.

Our algorithm relies on the Sparsest Cut algorithm for the semi-random model presented in Section 3.4. We denote the approximation factor of the Sparsest Cut algorithm by C_{SC} (see 5). We let $C_{exp} = 4C_{SC}$. We will use this algorithm for finding approximate sparsest cuts in $G[X]$ for various $X \subset V$ satisfying $|X \cap S|, |X \cap T| \geq \eta n/2$ (sometimes these conditions on X may be violated, then we assume that the algorithm returns a solution A, but the cut $(A, X \setminus A)$ may be arbitrarily bad). By Theorem 3.6, the Balanced Cut algorithm finds a cut of sparsity at most $C_{SC}\varepsilon n$ with probability exponentially close to 1 unless the graph G does not satisfy the "strong geometric expansion" property described in Theorem 5.1, part II. This happens with probability $o(1)$; and in this case, the partition recovering algorithm described below fails as well.

We introduce a potential function f that measures the quality of a partition (X, Y):

$$f(X, Y) = C_{SC}\varepsilon n \min(|X|, |Y|) - |E(X, Y)|. \qquad (12)$$

The algorithm presented below tries to maximize f by finding non-expanding subsets A in X and moving them to Y and finding non-expanding subsets B in Y and moving them to X.

Algorithm. The algorithm first finds an approximate sparsest cut (X_0, Y_0) in G using the Sparsest Cut algorithm for semi-random graphs. Then, it repeats the following refinement procedure: find approximate sparsest cuts $(A, X_t \setminus A)$ in the graph $G[X_t]$ and $(B, Y_t \setminus B)$ in the graph $G[Y_t]$ using the Sparsest Cut algorithm for semi-random graphs and

- if $f(X_t \setminus A, Y_t \cup A) \geq f(X_t, Y_t) + 1/4$, move A from X_t to Y_t i.e., set $X_{t+1} = X_t \setminus A$ and $Y_{t+1} = Y_t \cup A$; otherwise,
- if $f(X_t \cup B, Y_t \setminus B) \geq f(X_t, Y_t) + 1/4$, move B from Y_t to X i.e., set $X_{t+1} = X_t \cup B$ and $Y_{t+1} = Y_t \setminus B$.

The order in which the algorithm considers the cases above does not matter. After each iteration the algorithm increases the counter t. The algorithm stops and outputs the cut (X_t, Y_t), when neither moving A from X to Y, nor moving B from Y to X increases $f(X, Y)$ by at least $1/4$.

Analysis. Notice that the number of iterations of the algorithm is polynomial, since $f(X, Y)$ is upper bounded by $C_{SC}\varepsilon n^2$, lower bounded by $-|E|$, and at every iteration (but last) f is increased by at least $1/4$. Thus, the algorithm runs in polynomial time. To prove that the algorithm works correctly, we need to show that the algorithm does not stop till (X_t, Y_t) is η-close to the planted solution (S, T) i.e., till $|X_t \triangle S| \leq \eta n$ or $|Y_t \triangle S| \leq \eta n$.

We first prove that $f(X_t, Y_t)$ is positive for every t. The Sparsest Cut algorithm finds a cut (X_0, Y_0) of sparsity at most $C_{SC}\varepsilon n$, hence $f(X_0, Y_0) \equiv C_{SC}\varepsilon n \min(|X_0|, |Y_0|) - |E(X_0, Y_0)| > 0$. Since the sequence $f(X_t, Y_t)$ is increasing, $f(X_t, Y_t)$ is positive for every t. Consequently, the sparsity of every cut (X_t, Y_t) is at most $C_{SC}\varepsilon n$.

We show that every relatively small set in G expands.

CLAIM 6.3. *For every set $U \subset V$ of size at most $2\rho n/3$, $E(U, V \setminus U) \geq C_{exp}\varepsilon n|U|/2$.*

PROOF. Since $h(G[S]) \geq C_{exp}\varepsilon n$, we have

$$\begin{aligned} E(U \cap S, S \setminus (U \cap S)) &\geq C_{exp}\varepsilon n \cdot \min(|U \cap S|, |S \setminus (U \cap S)|) \\ &\geq C_{exp}\varepsilon n|U \cap S|/2, \end{aligned}$$

where the second inequality follows from $|U \cap S| \leq 2\rho n/3 \leq 2(|S| - |U \cap S|) = 2|S \setminus (U \cap S)|$. Similarly,

$$E(U \cap T, T \setminus (U \cap T)) \geq C_{exp}\varepsilon n|U \cap T|/2.$$

Thus, $E(U, V \setminus U) \geq C_{exp}\varepsilon n|U|/2$. □

As a corollary, we get that $|X_t| \geq 2\rho n/3$ and $|Y_t| \geq 2\rho n/3$ for every t (otherwise, the sparsity of the cut (X_t, Y_t) would be large). To argue that the Sparsest Cut algorithm finds a $C_{SC}\varepsilon n$ sparse cut in $G[X_t]$ or $G[Y_t]$, we need to prove the following claim.

CLAIM 6.4. *Suppose that the partition (X_t, Y_t) is not ηn close to the planted partition (S, T) i.e., $|X_t \triangle S| = |Y_t \triangle T| > \eta n$ and $|X_t \triangle T| = |Y_t \triangle S| > \eta n$, then one of the following two statements holds:*

- *$|X_t \cap S| \geq \eta n/2$ and $|X_t \cap T| \geq \eta n/2$; or*
- *$|Y_t \cap S| \geq \eta n/2$ and $|Y_t \cap T| \geq \eta n/2$.*

PROOF. The set X_t is covered by S and T, and thus $|X_t \cap S| \geq |X_t|/2$ or $|X_t \cap T| \geq |X_t|/2$. Assume that $|X_t \cap S| \geq |X_t|/2$. Then $|X_t \cap S| \geq |X_t|/2 \geq \rho n/3 \geq \eta n$. If also $|X_t \cap T| \geq \eta n/2$, we are done. Otherwise, $|X_t \cap T| \leq \eta n/2$, and $|X_t \setminus S| = |X_t \cap T| \leq \eta n/2$. Consequently, $|Y_t \cap S| = |X_t \triangle S| - |X_t \setminus S| \geq \eta n - \eta n/2 = \eta n/2$. Also, $|Y_t \cap T| = |T| - |X_t \cap T| \geq \rho n - \eta n/2 \geq \eta n$.

The case $|T \cap X_t| \geq |X_t|/2$ is handled similarly. (Note that we have not used in the proof that $|S| \leq |T|$; we only used that $|T| \geq \rho n$.) □

Apply Claim 6.4 and suppose without loss of generality that $|X_t \cap S| \geq \eta n/2$ and $|X_t \cap T| \geq \eta n/2$. Then, the set X_t is partitioned in two pieces $X_t \cap S$ and $X_t \cap T$ each of size at least $\eta n/2$. Thus (as discussed in the beginning of the proof), the Balanced Cut algorithm finds a cut $(A, X_t \setminus A)$ (where $|A| \leq |X_t|/2$) of sparsity at most $C_{SC}\varepsilon n$. We now show that the cut $(A, V \setminus A)$ is large.

CLAIM 6.5. *Suppose that the graph G is partitioned into three non-empty sets U_1, U_2, U_3, then one of the sets U_i has large expansion: for some i,*

$$E(U_i, V \setminus U_i) \geq C_{exp}\varepsilon n|U_i|.$$

PROOF. Observe that for one of the sets U_i, $|U_i \cap S| \leq |S|/2$ and $|U_i \cap T| \leq |T|/2$. For this set, $E(U_i \cap S, S \setminus U_i) \geq C_{exp}\varepsilon n|U_i \cap S|$ and $E(U_i \cap T, T \setminus U_i) \geq C_{exp}\varepsilon n|U_i \cap T|$. Hence, $E(U_i, V \setminus U_i) \geq C_{exp}\varepsilon n|U_i|$. □

Consider the partition of G into three sets $X_t \cap A$, $X_t \setminus A$ and Y_t. One of them has expansion $C_{exp}\varepsilon n$. It cannot be the set Y_t, since the expansion of Y_t is at most $C_{SC}\varepsilon n$. Then,

$$\begin{aligned} E(X_t \setminus A, V \setminus (X_t \setminus A)) &\leq E(X_t, Y_t) + E(X_t \setminus A, A) \\ &\leq C_{SC}\varepsilon n|X_t| + C_{SC}\varepsilon n|A| \\ &\leq 3C_{SC}\varepsilon n|X_t \setminus A| < C_{exp}\varepsilon n|X_t \setminus A|. \end{aligned}$$

Thus the set with expansion at least $C_{exp}\varepsilon n$ is A, that is, $E(A, V \setminus A) \geq C_{exp}\varepsilon|A|\, n$.

Estimate the change in the potential function f after moving A from X_t to Y_t:

$$\begin{aligned} &f(X_t \setminus A, Y_t \cup A) - f(X_t, Y_t) \geq -C_{SC}|A|\varepsilon n - \big(E(A, X_t \setminus A) \\ &\quad - E(A, Y_t)\big) = -C_{SC}|A|\varepsilon n - E(A, X_t \setminus A) \\ &\quad + (E(A, V \setminus A) - E(A, X_t \setminus A)) = -C_{SC}|A|\varepsilon n \\ &\quad - 2E(A, X_t \setminus A) + E(A, V \setminus A) \geq -C_{SC}|A|\varepsilon n \\ &\quad - 2C_{SC}\varepsilon|A|\, n + {}^3\!/\!_4\, C_{exp}\varepsilon|A|\, n + {}^1\!/\!_4\, E(A, V \setminus A) \\ &\quad = {}^1\!/\!_4\, E(A, V \setminus A) \geq {}^1\!/\!_4. \end{aligned}$$

7. SECOND MODEL: ALGEBRAIC EXPANSION INSIDE PARTITIONS

In the previous sections, we have seen that we can get much better approximation algorithms for partitioning problems when the edges E_K crossing the boundaries of partition $\mathcal{P}$ satisfy some structural property (geometric expansion). In this section, we show that we can obtain good approximation algorithms for Balanced Cut and Small Set Expansion, when the edges $\widetilde{E_K}$ not crossing the partition boundaries satisfy some algebraic expansion condition. This is a much weaker condition than edges of $\widetilde{E_K}$ being chosen independently at random. More crucially, in this case, the edges E_K can be arbitrary. Our algorithms are inspired by the results of [5, 31], where they infer global correlations between the vectors from local correlations and algebraic expansion.

THEOREM 7.1. (BALANCED CUT) *There is a polynomial-time algorithm, that given a graph $G = (V, E)$ on n vertices with a "planted" bisection $\mathcal{P} = \{P_1, P_2\}$ (not known to the algorithm) of cut value εm, such that for some subset of edges $E_1 \subset E$ of size $|E_1| = m$, the graph $G_1 = (P_1, E_1)$ is a regular expander with a (normalized) algebraic expansion $\lambda(G_1) > 64\varepsilon$, finds a balanced cut of sparsity $O(\varepsilon)$.*

PROOF. Consider the Balanced Cut SDP used in Section 3.1. Since this is a relaxation, the SDP value $SDP \leq \varepsilon m$. In particular,

$$\frac{1}{2}\,\text{sdp-cost}(u \to \bar{u}, E_1) \equiv \frac{1}{4}\sum_{(u,v)\in E_1} \|\bar{u} - \bar{v}\|^2 \leq \varepsilon m,$$

and, since $|E_1| = m$,

$$\frac{1}{4}\mathbb{E}_{(u,v)\in E_1}\left[\|\bar{u} - \bar{v}\|^2\right] = \frac{1}{4|E_1|}\sum_{(u,v)\in E_1} \|\bar{u} - \bar{v}\|^2 \leq \varepsilon.$$

For the regular graph G_1, we have

$$\lambda(G_1) \equiv \min_{\{\bar{u}\}_{u\in V}} \frac{\mathbb{E}_{(u,v)\in E_1}\left[\|\bar{u} - \bar{v}\|^2\right]}{\mathbb{E}_{u,v\in P_1}\left[\|\bar{u} - \bar{v}\|^2\right]},$$

thus

$$\frac{1}{4}\mathbb{E}_{u,v\in P_1}\left[\|\bar{u} - \bar{v}\|^2\right] \leq \frac{\varepsilon}{\lambda(G_1)} < \frac{1}{64}.$$

Hence, there exists $u^* \in P_1$ such that $\mathbb{E}_{v\in P_1}\left[\|\bar{u}^* - \bar{v}\|^2\right] \leq 1/16$. Denote $d(u, v) = \|\bar{u} - \bar{v}\|^2$. By Markov's inequality,

$$|\operatorname{Ball}_d(u^*, \frac{1}{8}) \cap P_1| \geq \frac{|P_1|}{2} = \frac{n}{4}.$$

On the other hand, $|\operatorname{Ball}_d(u^*, 1/4)| < 4/5\ n$ (as shown in Section 3.1).

We are ready to describe the algorithm: The algorithm guesses the vertex u^* and picks a ball $S = \operatorname{Ball}_d(u^*, r)$ of radius $r \in [1/16, 1/4]$ around u^* with the smallest edge boundary. The cost of the cut $(S, V \setminus S)$ is at most $32 \cdot SDP$, and (since $\operatorname{Ball}(u^*, 1/16) \subset S \subset \operatorname{Ball}(u^*, 1/4)$),

$$\frac{n}{8} \leq |S| \leq \frac{4n}{5}.$$

□

THEOREM 7.2 (SMALL SET EXPANSION). *There is a randomized polynomial-time algorithm, that given a graph $G = (V, E)$ with a "planted" partition $\mathcal{P} = \{P_1, P_2\}$ ($|P_1| = \rho n$) (not known to the algorithm) with $E(P_1, P_2) \leq \varepsilon m$ such that for some subset of edges $E_1 \subset V$ of size $|E_1| = m$, the graph $G_1 = (P_1, E_1)$ is a regular expander with a (normalized) algebraic expansion $\lambda(G_1) > 16\varepsilon$, finds a set S of size $\rho n/4 \leq |S| \leq 2\rho n$ with expected cost of the cut $O(\varepsilon m)$.*

PROOF. Let $\{\bar{u}\}_{u\in V(G)}$ be the solution of the C-SDP for the Small Set Expansion considered in Section 3.3. Denote

$$SDP_{|P_1} = \text{sdp-cost}(u \to \bar{u}, E_1) \equiv \frac{1}{2}\sum_{(u,v)\in E_1} \|\bar{u} - \bar{v}\|^2.$$

Since SDP is P_1-local relaxation of $\mathcal{P}$, $SDP_{|P_1} \leq OPT \equiv \varepsilon m$ (see Lemma A.1). We first proceed similarly to the proof of Theorem 7.1. Write,

$$\lambda \equiv \min_{\{\bar{u}\}_{u\in V}} \frac{\mathbb{E}_{(u,v)\in E_1}\left[\|\bar{u} - \bar{v}\|^2\right]}{\mathbb{E}_{u,v\in P_1}\left[\|\bar{u} - \bar{v}\|^2\right]},$$

then

$$\mathbb{E}_{u,v\in P_1}\left[\|\bar{u} - \bar{v}\|^2\right] \leq \frac{SDP_{|P_1}}{\lambda(G_1)} \leq \frac{OPT}{\lambda(G_1)} \leq \frac{1}{16}.$$

Hence, there is a vertex $u^* \in P_1$, such that

$$\mathbb{E}_{v\in P_1}\left[\|\bar{u} - \bar{v}\|^2\right] \leq 1/16.$$

Let $d(u, v) = \|\bar{u} - \bar{v}\|^2$. By the SDP spreading constraint (as shown in Section 3.3), $\text{Ball}_d(u^*, \frac{1}{4}) \leq 8/7\ \rho n$.

Thus, for some radius $r \in [1/16, 1/4]$ (the algorithm can guess u^* and r by considering all possibilities), the set $S = \text{Ball}_d(u^*, r)$ contains at least $|P_1|/2$ vertices from P_1, but at most $8/7\ \rho n$ vertices in total. Furthermore, the cost of the cut $E(P_1 \cap S, V \setminus S)$ is at most $32OPT$.

The main difficulty and the main difference from the previous proof (Theorem 7.1) is that the set S may contain vertices from P_2 and, moreover, it may cut many edges in $E(P_2 \cap S, V \setminus S)$. However, we have already dealt with a similar problem in Section 3.3. We use the LP (from the proof of Theorem 3.4, Case 2) to extract solution of cost at most $O(OPT)$ from S. The LP is feasible with LP value at most $O(OPT)$, because one integral "canonical" solution exists: it is the set $S' = P_1 \cap S$. Indeed, $E(P_1 \cap S, P_2 \cap S) \leq E(P_1, P_2) \equiv OPT$, and thus $E(P_1 \cap S, V \setminus (P_1 \cap S)) \leq 33OPT$. □

8. REFERENCES

[1] A. Agarwal, M. Charikar, K. Makarychev, and Y. Makarychev. $O(\sqrt{\log n})$ approximation algorithms for Min UnCut, Min 2CNF Deletion, and directed cut problems. In *Proceedings of the thirty-seventh Annual ACM Symposium on Theory of Computing*, pages 573–581, 2005.

[2] M. Ajtai. Generating hard instances of lattice problems. In *Proceedings of the twenty-eighth Annual ACM Symposium on Theory of Computing*, pp. 99–108, 1996.

[3] M. Ajtai, R. Kumar, and D. Sivakumar. A sieve algorithm for the shortest lattice vector problem. In *Proceedings of the thirty-third Annual ACM Symposium on Theory of Computing*, pp. 601–610, 2001.

[4] N. Alon, M. Krivelevich, and B. Sudakov. Finding a large hidden clique in a random graph. *Random Structures & Algorithms*, 13(3-4):457–466, 1998.

[5] S. Arora, S. A. Khot, A. Kolla, D. Steurer, M. Tulsiani, and N. K. Vishnoi. Unique games on expanding constraint graphs are easy. In *Proceedings of the 40th Annual ACM Symposium on Theory of Computing*, pp. 21–28, 2008.

[6] S. Arora, S. Rao, and U. Vazirani. Expander flows, geometric embeddings and graph partitioning. In *Proceedings of the thirty-sixth Annual ACM Symposium on Theory of Computing*, pp. 222–231, 2004.

[7] M.-F. Balcan, A. Blum, and A. Gupta. Approximate clustering without the approximation. In *Proceedings of the twentieth Annual ACM-SIAM Symposium on Discrete Algorithms*, pp. 1068–1077, 2009.

[8] N. Bansal, U. Feige, R. Krauthgamer, K. Makarychev, V. Nagarajan, J. Naor, and R. Schwartz. Min-max graph partitioning and small set expansion. In *Proceedings of 52nd IEEE Symposium on Foundations of Computer Science*, pp. 17–26, 2011.

[9] A. Bhaskara, M. Charikar, E. Chlamtac, U. Feige, and A. Vijayaraghavan. Detecting high log-densities: an $O(n^{1/4})$ approximation for densest k-subgraph. In *Proceedings of the 42nd ACM Symposium on Theory of Computing*, pp. 201–210, 2010.

[10] Y. Bilu and N. Linial. Are stable instances easy? In *ICS'10*, pp. 332–341, 2010.

[11] A. Blum and J. Spencer. Coloring random and semi-random k-colorable graphs. *J. Algorithms*, 19:204–234, September 1995.

[12] R. B. Boppana. Eigenvalues and graph bisection: An average-case analysis. In *28th Annual Symposium on Foundations of Computer Science*, pp. 280–285, 1987.

[13] T. N. Bui, F. T. Leighton, S. Chaudhuri, and M. Sipser. Graph bisection algorithms with good average case behavior. *Combinatorica*, 7:171–191, June 1987.

[14] A. Coja-Oghlan. A spectral heuristic for bisecting random graphs. *Random Structures & Algorithms*, 29(3):351–398, 2006.

[15] A. Condon and R. Karp. Algorithms for graph partitioning on the planted partition model. In *Randomization, Approximation, and Combinatorial Optimization. Algorithms and Techniques*, volume 1671 of *Lecture Notes in Computer Science*, pp. 221–232. Springer Berlin / Heidelberg, 1999.

[16] T. Dimitriou and R. Impagliazzo. Go with the winners for graph bisection. In *Proceedings of the ninth Annual ACM-SIAM Symposium on Discrete Algorithms*, pp. 510–520, 1998.

[17] M. E. Dyer and A. M. Frieze. Fast solution of some random NP-hard problems. In *27th Annual Symposium on Foundations of Computer Science*, pp. 331–336, 1986.

[18] U. Feige. Relations between average case complexity and approximation complexity. In *Proceedings of the 34th Annual ACM Symposium on Theory of Computing*, pp. 534–543, 2002.

[19] U. Feige and J. Kilian. Heuristics for semirandom graph problems. *J. Comput. Syst. Sci.*, 63:639–673, December 2001.

[20] U. Feige and R. Krauthgamer. Finding and certifying a large hidden clique in a semirandom graph. *Random Struct. Algorithms*, 16:195–208, March 2000.

[21] N. Garg, V. V. Vazirani, and M. Yannakakis. Approximate max-flow min-(multi)cut theorems and their applications. In *Proceedings of the twenty-fifth Annual ACM Symposium on Theory of Computing*, pp. 698–707, 1993.

[22] M. X. Goemans and D. P. Williamson. Improved approximation algorithms for Maximum Cut and Satisfiability problems using semidefinite programming. *J. ACM*, 42(6):1115–1145, 1995.

[23] V. Guruswami and A. K. Sinop. Lasserre hierarchy, higher eigenvalues, and approximation schemes for quadratic integer programming with PSD objectives. In *Proceedings of 52nd IEEE Symposium on Foundations of Computer Science*, 2011.

[24] M. Jalali, N. Mustapha, A. Mamat, and M. Sulaiman. A new clustering approach based on graph partitioning for navigation patterns mining. In *19th International Conference on Pattern Recognition*, pp. 1–4, 2008.

[25] M. Jerrum and G. Sorkin. Simulated annealing for graph bisection. In *Proceedings of the 34th Annual IEEE Symposium on Foundations of Computer Science*, pp. 94–103, 1993.

[26] S. Khot. On the power of unique 2-prover 1-round games. In *Proceedings of the thiry-fourth Annual ACM Symposium on Theory of Computing*, pp. 767–775, 2002.

[27] S. Khot, G. Kindler, E. Mossel, and R. O'Donnell. Optimal inapproximability results for MAX-CUT and other 2-variable CSPs? *SIAM J. Comput.*, 37(1):319–357, 2007.

[28] S. Khot and N. K. Vishnoi. The unique games conjecture, integrality gap for cut problems and embeddability of negative type metrics into ℓ_1. In *46th Annual IEEE Symposium on Foundations of Computer Science*, pp. 53–62, 2005.

[29] A. Kolla, K. Makarychev, and Y. Makarychev. How to play unique games against a semi-random adversary. In *Proceedings of 52nd IEEE Symposium on Foundations of Computer Science*, 2011.

[30] T. Leighton and S. Rao. Multicommodity max-flow min-cut theorems and their use in designing approximation algorithms. *J. ACM*, 46:787–832, November 1999.

[31] K. Makarychev and Y. Makarychev. How to play unique games on expanders. In *Approximation and Online Algorithms*, volume 6534 of *Lecture Notes in Computer Science*, pp. 190–200. Springer Berlin / Heidelberg, 2011.

[32] F. McSherry. Spectral partitioning of random graphs. In *Proceedings of the 42nd IEEE Symposium on Foundations of Computer Science*, pp. 529–537, 2001.

[33] M. Perkowitz and O. Etzioni. Towards adaptive web sites: conceptual framework and case study. *Artif. Intell.*, 118:245–275, April 2000.

[34] H. Räcke. Optimal hierarchical decompositions for congestion minimization in networks. In *Proceedings of the 40th Annual ACM Symposium on Theory of Computing*, pp. 255–264, 2008.

[35] P. Raghavendra. Optimal algorithms and inapproximability results for every CSP? In *Proceedings of the 40th Annual ACM Symposium on Theory of Computing*, pp. 245–254, 2008.

[36] P. Raghavendra, D. Steurer, and M. Tulsiani. Reductions between expansion problems. *CoRR*, abs/1011.2586, 2010.

APPENDIX

A. LOCAL SDP RELAXATION FOR SSE

LEMMA A.1. *The set Φ of feasible solutions of the Crude SDP (C-SDP) given in Section 3.3 for the Small Set Expansion problem is a S-local relaxation of every partition $\mathcal{P} = \{S, V \setminus S\}$ (where $|S| = \rho n$).*

PROOF. Let $\varphi = \arg\min_{\varphi\in\Phi} \text{sdp-cost}(\varphi, E)$. Denote $\bar{u} = \varphi(u)$. Define a new SDP solution

$$\bar{u}' = \begin{cases} \bar{e}_\perp & \text{if } u \in S \\ \bar{u} & \text{otherwise.} \end{cases}$$

where $\bar{e}_\perp$ is a unit vector orthogonal to all the vectors $\{\bar{v}\}_{v\in V(G)}$. This solution also satisfies the ℓ_2^2-triangle inequalities, the spreading constraints (because $|S| \le \rho n$ and for all $u \in S$, $v \in V \setminus S$, $\langle \bar{u}', \bar{v}'\rangle = 0 \le \langle \bar{u}, \bar{v}\rangle$), and for all $u, v \in V$, $\langle \bar{u}', \bar{v}'\rangle \ge 0$. Thus, it lies in Φ.

Compute the cost of the new solution and compare it with the cost of the optimal solution:

$$\begin{aligned}\text{sdp-cost}(u \to \bar{u}', E) &= \frac{1}{2} \sum_{(u,v)\in E(G)} \|\bar{u}' - \bar{v}'\|^2 \\ &= \frac{1}{2} \sum_{\substack{(u,v)\in E(G)\\ u\in S \text{ or } v\in S}} \|\bar{u}' - \bar{v}'\|^2 + \frac{1}{2} \sum_{\substack{(u,v)\in E(G)\\ u,v\in V(G)\setminus S}} \|\bar{u}' - \bar{v}'\|^2 \\ &= \text{cost}_{|S}(\mathcal{P}, E) + \frac{1}{2} \sum_{\substack{(u,v)\in E(G)\\ u,v\in V(G)\setminus S}} \|\bar{u} - \bar{v}\|^2.\end{aligned}$$

The cost $\text{sdp-cost}(u \to \bar{u}, E)$ of the optimal solution $\bar{u}$ equals

$$\text{sdp-cost}_{|S}(u \to \bar{u}, E) + \frac{1}{2} \sum_{\substack{(u,v)\in E(G)\\ u,v\in V(G)\setminus S}} \|\bar{u} - \bar{v}\|^2.$$

Thus, $\text{sdp-cost}_{|S}(u \to \bar{u}, E) \le \text{cost}_{|S}(\mathcal{P}, E)$. □

B. REMARK ON THEOREM 3.5

Theorem 3.5 is stated in a slightly different form in Bansal et al. [8]. We use Theorem 2.1 (part II) [8, p. 6; arXiv, version 2] with $\mu(S) = \eta(S) = |S|/n$ and $H = \rho$. Theorem 2.1, as is, does not deal with weights w_u, so we need to very slightly change the algorithm and proof. We add an extra SDP constraint

$$\sum_{u\in V} \|\bar{u}\|^2 w_u \le W.$$

This constraint is clearly satisfied in the integral solution. We also change the function f' (see page 10 of [8]). We let (here w_u are the weights of vertices)

$$\begin{aligned} f''(S) &= f'(S) - \underbrace{\frac{w(S)}{32W} \times H}_{\text{new term}} \\ &\equiv \eta(S) - \frac{\delta(S)}{|E|} \times \frac{H}{4D \times SDP} \\ &\quad - \frac{\mu(S)}{4\rho} \times H - \frac{w(S)}{32W} \times H \\ &= \frac{3|S|}{4n} - \frac{E(S, V\setminus S)}{|E|} \times \frac{\rho}{4D \times SDP} - \frac{w(S)}{32W} \times \rho. \end{aligned}$$

Since,

$$\mathbb{E}\frac{w(S)}{32W} \times H \le \sum_{u\in V} \frac{w_u \alpha \|\bar{u}\|^2}{32W} \times H \le \sum_{u\in V} \frac{\alpha W}{32W} \times H = \frac{\alpha H}{32},$$

we get (compare with the third formula on page 10 [8]),

$$\mathbb{E}[f]''(S) \ge \mathbb{E}[f]'(S) - \frac{\alpha H}{32} \ge \frac{\alpha H}{32}.$$

This is sufficient for analysis in [8]. The SSE algorithm finds a set S with $f''(S) > 0$. This condition implies that

$$\frac{3|S|}{4n} > \frac{w(S)}{W} \times \rho$$

and, consequently (as $|S| = \Theta(\rho n)$), $w(S) \le O(W)$.

C. SDP RELAXATIONS

We provide SDP relaxations for the Minimum Balanced Cut, Small Set Expansion (SSE) and Minimum Multicut Problems in Figures 1, 2 and 3 (see the next page).

Figure 1 Minimum Balanced Cut: The input to the problem is a graph $G(V, E)$, and the objective is to find a set S of size $n/2$ with the minimum number of edges crossing it.

$$\min \quad \frac{1}{4} \sum_{(u,v)\in E(G)} \|\bar{u} - \bar{v}\|^2$$

subject to

$$\frac{1}{4} \sum_{u,v\in V} \|\bar{u} - \bar{v}\|^2 \geq \frac{n^2}{2} \qquad \text{(Spreading constraint)}$$

$$\text{for all } u, v, w \in V, \quad \|\bar{u} - \bar{v}\|^2 + \|\bar{v} - \bar{w}\|^2 \geq \|\bar{u} - \bar{w}\|^2 \qquad (\ell_2^2\text{–triangle inequalities})$$

$$\text{for all } u \in V, \quad \|\bar{u}\|^2 = 1$$

Figure 2 Crude SDP (C-SDP) for Small Set Expansion (SSE): The input to the problem is a graph $G(V, E)$ and a parameter ρ, and the objective is to find a set S of size ρn with the smallest number of edges crossing it.

$$\min \quad \frac{1}{2} \sum_{(u,v)\in E(G)} \|\bar{u} - \bar{v}\|^2$$

subject to

$$\text{for all } u \in V, \quad \sum_{v\in V} \langle \bar{u}, \bar{v} \rangle \leq \rho n \qquad \text{(Spreading constraints)}$$

$$\text{for all } u, v, w \in V, \quad \|\bar{u} - \bar{v}\|^2 + \|\bar{v} - \bar{w}\|^2 \geq \|\bar{u} - \bar{w}\|^2 \qquad (\ell_2^2\text{–triangle inequalities})$$

$$\text{for all } u, v \in V \quad \langle \bar{u}, \bar{v} \rangle \geq 0$$

$$\text{for all } u \in V, \quad \|\bar{u}\|^2 = 1$$

Figure 3 Minimum Multicut: The input to the problem is a graph $G(V, E)$ and a set of k source-sink pairs $\{(s_i, t_i)\}_{1\leq i\leq k}$, and the objective is to find a partition $\mathcal{P}'$ of the graph with minimum number of edges across partitions such that for all i, $\mathcal{P}'(s_i) \neq \mathcal{P}'(t_i)$.

$$\min \quad \frac{1}{2} \sum_{(u,v)\in E(G)} \|\bar{u} - \bar{v}\|^2$$

subject to

$$\text{for all } 1 \leq i \leq k, \quad \langle \bar{s}_i, \bar{t}_i \rangle = 0$$

$$\text{for all } u, v, w \in V, \quad \|\bar{u} - \bar{v}\|^2 + \|\bar{v} - \bar{w}\|^2 \geq \|\bar{u} - \bar{w}\|^2 \qquad (\ell_2^2\text{–triangle inequalities})$$

$$\text{for all } u \in V, \quad \|\bar{u}\|^2 = 1$$

A Near-Linear Time ε-Approximation Algorithm for Geometric Bipartite Matching*

R. Sharathkumar
Department of Computer Science
Duke University
sharath@cs.duke.edu

Pankaj K. Agarwal
Department of Computer Science
Duke University
pankaj@cs.duke.edu

ABSTRACT

For point sets $A, B \subset \mathbb{R}^d$, $|A| = |B| = n$, and for a parameter $\varepsilon > 0$, we present an algorithm that computes, in $O(n\text{poly}(\log n, 1/\varepsilon))$ time, an ε-approximate perfect matching of A and B with high probability; the previously best known algorithm takes $\Omega(n^{3/2})$ time. We approximate the L_p norm using a distance function, $\mathtt{d}(\cdot,\cdot)$ based on a randomly shifted quad-tree. The algorithm iteratively generates an approximate minimum-cost augmenting path under $\mathtt{d}(\cdot,\cdot)$ in time proportional to the length of the path. We show that the total length of the augmenting paths generated by the algorithm is $O((n/\varepsilon)\log n)$, implying that the running time of our algorithm is $O(n\text{poly}(\log n, 1/\varepsilon))$.

Categories and Subject Descriptors

G.2.2 [**Discrete Mathematics**]: Graph Theory—*graph algorithms*; F.2.2 [**Theory of Computation**]: Nonnumerical Algorithms and Problems—*geometrical problems and computations*

General Terms

Algorithms, Theory

Keywords

Matching, approximation algorithms

1. INTRODUCTION

Let $\mathcal{G} = (V, E)$, where $V = A \cup B$ and $E \subseteq A \times B$, be a weighted bipartite graph with $|A| = |B| = n$. Let $\mathtt{d}(a, b)$ be the cost of an edge $(a, b) \in E$. A *matching* M in $\mathcal{G}$ is a set of vertex-disjoint edges. The cost of M, $\mathtt{w}(M)$ is $\sum_{(a,b)\in M} \mathtt{d}(a, b)$. M is a *perfect matching* if $|M| = n$. An *optimal* matching is a perfect matching with minimum cost. An *ε-approximate* matching is a perfect matching whose cost is within $(1 + \varepsilon)$ times the cost of an optimal matching. In this paper, we consider geometric settings, namely, A and B are point sets in $\mathbb{R}^d$, $E = A \times B$, and the cost of an edge is the distance between a and b under some L_p-norm. We consider the problem of computing an ε-approximate matching in this setting.

Previous work. Optimal matching on weighted bipartite graphs with n vertices and m edges can be computed using the Hungarian algorithm in $O(mn)$ time [12].[1] If edge costs are positive integers bounded by $n^{O(1)}$, Gabow and Tarjan [5] show that an optimal matching can be computed in $O(m\sqrt{n}\log n)$ time. For unweighted regular bipartite graphs, Goel *et al.* present an $O(n \log n)$ algorithm for computing perfect matchings [7]. There is also extensive work on computing optimal matchings and maximum-cost matchings in non-bipartite graphs [4, 6, 11].

For the case where $A, B \subset \mathbb{R}^2$ and an L_p-norm, Vaidya [15] shows that an optimal matching can be computed in $O(n^{2.5})$ time. Agarwal *et al.* [1] improve the running time of the algorithm for computing optimal matching to $O(n^{2+\delta})$ where $\delta > 0$ is an arbitrarily small constant. For $A, B \subset \mathbb{R}^d$ and the L_1 and L_∞ norms, Vaidya [15] presents $O(n^2 \log^{O(d)} n)$ time algorithm for computing an optimal matching. If $A, B \subseteq [\Delta]^d$, i.e., points in A and B are from a bounded integer grid, Sharathkumar and Agarwal [14] show that an optimal matching can be computed in $O(n^{3/2} \log^{d+O(1)} n \log \Delta)$ time. It is an open question whether a subquadratic algorithm exists for computing an optimal Euclidean bipartite matching in $\mathbb{R}^2$, or even for L_1, L_∞-norms. In contrast, Varadarajan [16] presents an $O(n^{3/2} \text{ polylog } n)$ algorithm for the non-bipartite case — this is surprising because the non-bipartite case seems harder for graphs with arbitrary edge costs. See also [9, 10, 13].

For bipartite graphs on point sets $A, B \subset \mathbb{R}^2$ and for any L_p norm, Agarwal and Varadarajan [17] show that an ε-approximate matching can be computed in $O((n/\varepsilon)^{3/2} \log^5 n)$ time. In [14], Sharathkumar and Agarwal present an algorithm that computes an ε-approximate matching under L_p-norm in $O(n^{3/2}\Phi(n)\log(1/\varepsilon))$ time; here $\Phi(n)$ is the query and update time of a dynamic weighted nearest-neighbor data structure, thereby improving the dependency on ε by an exponential factor. In [2], Agarwal and Varadarajan present a Monte Carlo algorithm for computing an $O(\log(1/\delta))$-approximate matching in time $O(n^{1+\delta})$. Building on the ideas of Agarwal and Varadarajan, Indyk [8] presents an algorithm that estimates in $O(n \log^{O(1)} n)$ time, with probability at least $1/2$, the cost of an optimal matching within a constant factor. It, however, does not return such a matching. It is an open question whether an ε-approximate matching can be computed in near linear-time. Again, the non-bipartite case seems easier and an ε-approximate

*This work is supported by NSF under grants CNS-05-40347, IIS-07-13498, CCF-09-40671, and CCF-1012254, by ARO grants W911NF-07-1-0376 and W911NF-08-1-0452, by an NIH grant 1P50-GM-08183-01, and by a grant from the U.S.–Israel Binational Science Foundation.

[1]For arbitrary graphs, a perfect matching may not exist, so the goal is to compute a maximum cardinality minimum-cost matching.

Euclidean matching of a set of points can be computed in near-linear time [3, 17].

Our results. The following theorem states the main result of the paper.

THEOREM 1. *Let $A, B \subset \mathbb{R}^d$ be two point sets with $|A| = |B| = n$ and let $\varepsilon > 0$ be a parameter. For any L_p-norm, an ε-approximate matching of A and B can be computed with high probability in $O(n\text{poly}(\log n, 1/\varepsilon))$ time.*

A simple transformation, as the one discussed in [8], decomposes, with high probability, computing ε-approximate matching of A, B to computing ε-approximate matchings on several subsets

$$\{(A'_1, B'_1), \ldots, (A'_k, B'_k)\}.$$

Here $\bigcup_{i=1}^k A'_i = A$, $\bigcup_{i=1}^k B'_i = B$ and each pair of subsets $A'_i, B'_i \subseteq [\Delta]^d$, $|A'_i| = |B'_i|$, are point sets from an integer grid with $\Delta \leq n^{O(1)}$. We describe a Monte-Carlo algorithm for the case when $A, B \subseteq [\Delta]^d$, leading to the following result.

THEOREM 2. *Let $A, B \subseteq [\Delta]^d$ be two point sets with $|A| = |B| = n$, and let $\varepsilon > 0$ be a parameter. For any L_p-norm, an ε-approximate matching of A and B can be computed with high probability in $O(n\text{poly}(\log \Delta, 1/\varepsilon))$ time.*

There are three key ingredients of our algorithm.

- We use a randomly-shifted quad-tree Q based distance function $\mathtt{d}(\cdot,\cdot)$ that ε-approximates the L_p-norm. A similar distance function was used in [14]. It therefore suffices to compute an ε-approximate matching under $\mathtt{d}(\cdot,\cdot)$ (Section 2).
- For a matching M, we partition the edges in M into certain classes. The endpoints of all the edges in a class lie sufficiently close to each other and all of them have the same $\mathtt{d}(\cdot,\cdot)$ distance; see Figure 2. Based on these classes, we call certain edges special and set the cost of a special edge (a, b) to $\mathtt{d}(a, b) + \theta$ where $\theta = \varepsilon\mathtt{w}(M^*)/6n$ and $\mathtt{w}(M^*)$ is the cost of an optimal matching under $\mathtt{d}(\cdot,\cdot)$. Doing so allows us to show a bound of $O(n/\varepsilon \log n)$ on the total length of the augmenting paths computed by the algorithm while keeping the cost of the matching within $(1+\varepsilon)\mathtt{w}(M^*)$. Gabow and Tarjan [5] used a similar idea where they add to every non-matching edge a cost of 1. Their scheme introduces an additive error of n while the total length of all the augmenting paths produced by their algorithm is $O(n \log n)$ if $\mathtt{w}(M^*) = O(n)$. (Sections 3, 4).
- Unlike previous algorithms, our algorithm does not explicitly maintain dual variables. Instead we design a data structure that maintains the current matching, produces "shortest" augmenting paths in an output sensitive manner, and updates the current matching quickly. (Section 5).

2. APPROXIMATING L_P-NORM

In this section we describe a distance function $\mathtt{d}(\cdot,\cdot)$ that approximates the L_p-norm. For $A, B \subseteq [\Delta]^d$, we choose integers $i_1, \ldots, i_d \in [\Delta]$ uniformly at random and set $G = [0, 2\Delta]^d - (i_1, \ldots, i_d)$. G is a randomly-shifted hypercube that contains both A and B. We build a quad-tree Q of depth $\delta = \log_2(2\Delta) = 1 + \log_2 \Delta$ on G[2] — the root of Q is associated with G itself and the squares (cells) associated with the children of a node are obtained by splitting the hypercube associated with that node into 2^d equal hypercubes. The nodes at depth i induce a grid G_i in which each cell has a side length $2^{\delta - i}$. We view Q as the sequence of grids $G_0, G_1, \ldots, G_\delta$; G_0 is a single cell which is G itself and G_δ is the finest grid[3] associated with the leaves of Q. For any pair $(a, b) \in A \times B$ we define $\mathtt{d}(a, b)$ as follows: For a parameter $\varepsilon > 0$, we set $\omega = \lceil \log_2(8d^2 \log_2 \Delta/\varepsilon^2) \rceil$ and $\Omega = 2^\omega$ Let $\Box$ be the least common ancestor in Q of the leaves containing a and b. Suppose $\Box \in G_{\delta - i}$. Let

$$\mathbb{G}[\Box] = \Box \cap G_{\delta - i + \omega}$$

be a $\Omega \times \Omega$ grid that divides $\Box$ into *sub-cells* — sidelength of each sub-cell of $\Box$ is $2^{i-\omega} = 2^i/\Omega$. Let $a_\Box$ (resp. $b_\Box$) be the center of sub-cell of $\Box$ that contains a (resp. b). We set

$$\mathtt{d}(a, b) = ||a_\Box b_\Box||_p + d2^i/\Omega.$$

The following lemma proves that $\mathtt{d}(\cdot,\cdot)$ approximates the L_p-norm in the expected sense.

LEMMA 1. *For any pair $(a, b) \in A \times B$, $\mathtt{d}(a, b) \geq ||ab||_p$. Furthermore, $\mathbb{E}[\mathtt{d}(a, b)] \leq (1 + \varepsilon/2)||ab||_p$.*

PROOF. Let $\Box$ be the least common ancestor of a and b. Suppose $\Box \in G_{\delta - i}$. Let $\xi_1, \xi_2 \in \mathbb{G}[\Box]$ be the sub-cells that contain a and b, respectively. Since the length of both ξ_1 and ξ_2 is $2^i/\Omega$, by triangle inequality, $||ab||_p \leq ||a_\Box b_\Box||_p + d.2^i/\Omega$. Hence, $\mathtt{d}(a, b) \geq ||ab||_p$. Moreover, $||a_\Box b_\Box||_p \leq ||ab||_p + d2^i/\Omega$, there-

Figure 1. Randomly shifted quad-tree.

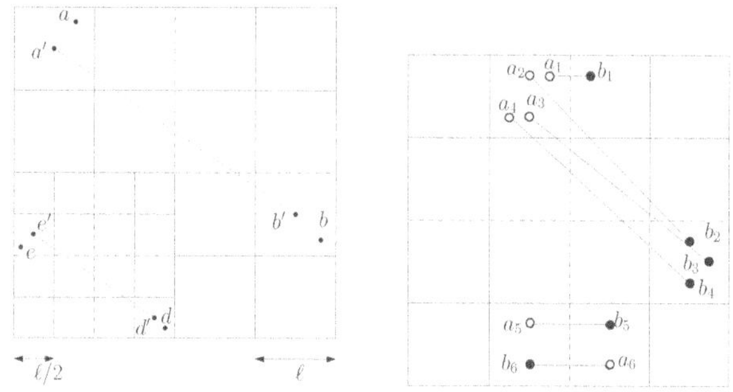

(i) (ii)

Figure 2. (i) Decomposition of a quad-tree cell and one of its children into sub-cells. a', b', d', e' are center points of sub-cells containing a, b, d, e respectively. $\mathtt{d}(a, b) = ||a'b'|| + 2\ell$, $\mathtt{d}(d, e) = ||d'e'|| + \ell$. (ii) $M = \{(a_1, b_1), (a_2, b_2), (a_3, b_3), (a_4, b_4), (a_5, b_5), (a_6, b_6)\}$, $\mathcal{K}_M = \{(\{a_1\}, \{b_1\}), (\{a_2, a_3, a_4\}, \{b_2, b_3, b_4\}), (\{a_5\}, \{b_5\}), (\{a_6\}, \{b_6\})\}$.

[2]We assume Δ is of the form 2^k for some positive integer k

[3]Although G_δ is the finest grid associated with the lowest level of Q, we can define G_i for $i > \delta$ in a straightforward manner

fore $\mathrm{d}(a,b) \le ||ab||_p + d2^{i+1}/\Omega$ which implies,

$$\begin{aligned}\mathbb{E}[\mathrm{d}(a,b)] &\le \sum_{i=1}^{\log\Delta+1} \Pr[\square \in G_{\delta-i}](||ab||_p + d2^{i+1}/\Omega) \\ &\le ||ab||_p + \frac{d}{\Omega}\sum_{i=1}^{\log\Delta+1} 2^{i+1}\Pr[\square \in G_{\delta-i}].\end{aligned}$$

Since $\square$ is the least common ancestor of a and b, they lie in two different children of $\square$. Recall that $G_{\delta-i+1}$ is shifted uniformly at random, as argued by Arora [3], $\Pr[\square \in G_{\delta-i}] \le ||ab||_1/2^{i-1} \le d||ab||_p/2^{i-1}$. Therefore,

$$\begin{aligned}\mathbb{E}[\mathrm{d}(a,b)] &\le ||ab||_p + \frac{4d^2}{\Omega}\sum_{i=0}^{\delta}||ab||_p \\ &= (1+4d^2\delta/\Omega)||ab||_p \\ &\le (1+\varepsilon/2)||ab||_p;\end{aligned}$$

the last inequality follows from the fact that $\Omega \ge 8d^2\delta/\varepsilon$. $\square$

COROLLARY 1. *Let $A, B \subseteq [\Delta]^d$ and let $\varepsilon > 0$ be a parameter. Let M^* be an optimal matching of A, B under $\mathrm{d}(\cdot,\cdot)$ and let $\mathtt{w}_{\mathrm{OPT}}$ be the cost of the optimal matching under any L_p-norm. Then $\mathtt{w}(M^*) \le (1+\varepsilon/2)\mathtt{w}_{\mathrm{OPT}}$.*

3. CLASSIFYING MATCHING EDGES

In this section, we describe how to cluster the edges of M into classes and prove a few useful properties of this classification. For a matching $M = \{(a_1,b_1),\ldots,(a_k,b_k)\}$ of A, B, a vertex is called *free* if it is not incident upon any edge of M, and *matched* otherwise. Let $A_F \subseteq A$ and $B_F \subseteq B$ be the set of free vertices. We classify the edges of M into equivalence classes as follows: Two edges in the matching $(a_l,b_l),(a_m,b_m) \in M$ belong to the same class if and only if: both (a_l,b_l) and (a_m,b_m) have the same least common ancestor $\square$ in Q, a_l, a_m are in the same sub-cell of $\mathbb{G}[\square]$, and b_l, b_m are in the same sub-cell of $\mathbb{G}[\square]$; see Figure 2. Let $\mathcal{K}_M = \{M_1,\ldots,M_r\}$ be the resulting partition of M into equivalence classes. For each M_i, let $A_i = \bigcup_{(a_j,b_j)\in M_i} a_j$ and $B_i = \bigcup_{(a_j,b_j)\in M_i} b_j$. $A \setminus A_F$ is partitioned into sets $A_1,\ldots,A_r$ and the set $B \setminus B_F$ is partitioned into sets $B_1,\ldots,B_r$ and $M_i \subseteq A_i \times B_i$. For an edge $(a,b) \in A \times B$, if there is an $i \le r$ such that $(a,b) \in A_i \times B_i$, then we call (a,b) a *local* edge. All other edges, including the edges incident on points in A_F and B_F, are *non-local* edges. Note that all edges of M are local edges. All pairs of $A_i \times B_i$ are referred to as edges of *class i*.

We fix a parameter θ. We describe how to choose θ in Section 4. Given a matching M, we define a modified cost function $\Phi_M : A \times B \to \mathbb{R}_{\ge 0}$ called the *adjusted cost* of an edge,

$$\Phi_M(a,b) = \begin{cases} \mathrm{d}(a,b) & \text{if } (a,b) \text{ is a local edge,} \\ \mathrm{d}(a,b)+\theta & \text{otherwise.}\end{cases}$$

For a set of edges $E \subseteq A \times B$, we define

$$\Phi_M(E) = \sum_{(a,b)\in E}\Phi_M(a,b).$$

Therefore, $\Phi_M(M) = \mathtt{w}(M)$.

Given a matching M, an *alternating path* (or cycle) Π is a simple path (resp. cycle) whose edges are alternately in and not in M. We define the *net cost* of Π, $\phi_M(\Pi)$, as

$$\phi_M(\Pi) = \Phi_M(\Pi \setminus M) - \Phi_M(\Pi \cap M).$$

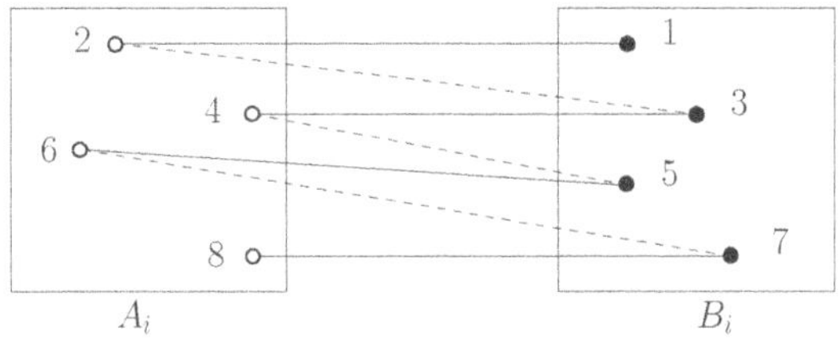

Figure 3. An alternating path consisting of local edges. Let $\pi_1 = \langle 1,2,3,4,5,6,7\rangle, \pi_2 = \langle 1,2,3,4,5\rangle, \pi_3 = \langle 1,2,3,4\rangle, \pi_4 = \langle 2,3,4,5\rangle$, then $\phi_M(\pi_1) = \phi_M(\pi_2) = 0$, $\phi_M(\pi_3) = -\mathrm{d}(1,2)$, $\phi_M(\pi_4) = \mathrm{d}(1,2)$.

An *augmenting path* Π is an alternating path between two free vertices. We *augment* M along Π, by updating M to $M \oplus \Pi$, i.e., remove the edges in $\Pi \cap M$ and add the edges in $\Pi \setminus M$. The following properties of local edges are relatively straightforward(See Figure 3):

(L1) For any $1 \le i \le r$, all local edges of class i have the same adjusted cost, say, φ_i.

(L2) Let Π be a path composed only of local edges, then all edges in Π belong to the same class.

(L3) Let $\Pi = \langle e_1, e_2, \ldots, e_k\rangle$ be an alternating path such that all edges in Π are local edges of class i. Then,

$$\phi_M(\Pi) = \begin{cases} \varphi_i & e_1, e_k \notin M, \\ -\varphi_i & e_1, e_k \in M, \\ 0 & \text{otherwise.}\end{cases}$$

(L4) Let $e = (a,b)$ be a local non-matching edge, say, of class i, then the matching edges incident on a and b also belong to the class i.

(L1) and (L2) follow from the definition of local edges, and (L3) follows from (L1) and the definition of net cost.

An alternating path Π is called *compact* if the total number of non-local edges of Π is at least $|\Pi|/4$, where $|\Pi|$ is the length, i.e., the number of edges in the alternating path.

LEMMA 2. *For a matching M and a compact augmenting path Π, let $M' = M \oplus \Pi$. Then*

$$\mathtt{w}(M') - \mathtt{w}(M) + \theta|\Pi| \ge \phi_M(\Pi) \ge \mathtt{w}(M') - \mathtt{w}(M) + \theta|\Pi|/4.$$

PROOF. Suppose Π has t non-local edges. Then,

$$\begin{aligned}\phi_M(\Pi) &= \Phi_M(\Pi\setminus M) - \Phi_M(\Pi\cap M) \\ &= \mathtt{w}(\Pi\setminus M) - \mathtt{w}(\Pi\cap M) + t\theta \\ &= \mathtt{w}(M') - \mathtt{w}(M) + t\theta. \qquad (1)\end{aligned}$$

Since Π is a compact path, $|\Pi| \ge t \ge |\Pi|/4$, the lemma follows from (1). $\square$

The following lemma shows that there is always an augmenting path of minimum net cost that is also a compact path.

LEMMA 3. *Given a matching M and an augmenting path Π, there is a compact augmenting path Π' with $\phi_M(\Pi) = \phi_M(\Pi')$.*

PROOF. Among all augmenting paths of the minimum net cost, let Π be an augmenting path with the fewest number of edges. Let $\pi = \langle e_1, \ldots e_k\rangle$ be the longest sub-path consisting only of local edges. Since π is maximal and all edges of M are local, $e_1, e_k \in$

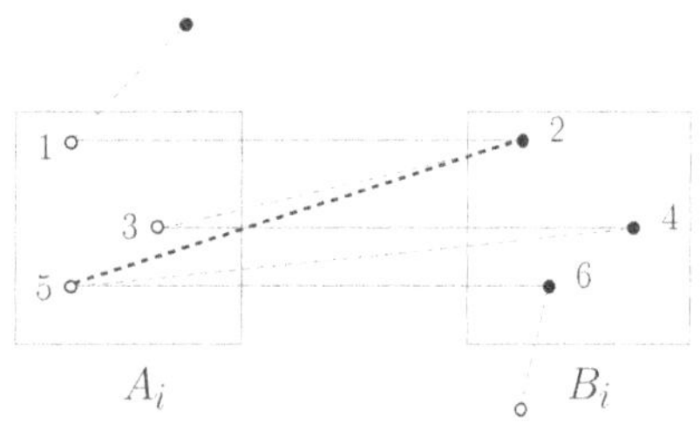

Figure 4. Shortcutting an alternating path — replace the path $\langle(2,3),(3,4),(4,5)\rangle$ with $(2,5)$.

M. If $|\pi| \leq 3$, then Π is obviously compact, so assume that $|\pi| > 3$. By (L2), all edges of π belong to the same class, say i. Let $b_1, a_1, b_2, a_2, \ldots, b_k, a_k$ be the sequence of vertices in π, i.e., $e_1 = (b_1, a_1)$ and $e_k = (b_k, a_k)$. Set $\tilde{\pi} = e_1 \circ (a_1, b_k) \circ e_k$. By (L3), $\phi_M(\pi) = \phi_M(\tilde{\pi})$ but $|\pi| > |\tilde{\pi}|$. If we replaces π with $\tilde{\pi}$ in Π (See Figure 4), we obtain another alternating path of the same net cost but with fewer edges, a contradiction. Hence $|\pi| \leq 3$ and Π is compact. $\square$

4. ALGORITHM

Let $A, B \subseteq [\Delta]^d$ be two point sets of n points each, and let $\mathtt{d}(\cdot,\cdot)$ be the quad-tree based distance function defined in Section 2. We present an algorithm for computing an ϵ-approximate matching of A and B under $\mathtt{d}(\cdot,\cdot)$. Let

$$\varepsilon \mathtt{w}(M^*)/6n \leq \theta \leq \varepsilon \mathtt{w}(M^*)/3n.$$

Given a θ that satisfies this inequality, our algorithm produces an ε-approximate matching in $O(n\mathrm{poly}(\log \Delta, 1/\varepsilon))$ time. There are various ways of obtaining θ. For a constant c that depends on the norm and the dimension of the problem, the cost of an optimal matching is $1 \leq \mathtt{w}(M^*) \leq cn\Delta$. For some sufficiently large constant c_2, we execute $c_2 n\mathrm{poly}(\log \Delta, 1/\varepsilon)$ steps of our algorithm by setting $\theta = \theta_i = \varepsilon 2^i/6n$ for $i \in [1, \ldots, \lceil \log_2 cn\Delta \rceil]$. Of all the perfect matchings produced by the $O(\log n\Delta)$ executions of our algorithm, we return the matching with the smallest cost. Since at least one of our guesses of θ is correct, we obtain an ε-approximate matching. In the rest of the paper, we work under the assumption that we have the desired θ.

Our algorithm relies on a data structure, described in Section 5, that stores A,B and a matching M and that supports the following two operations:

- FINDAP(): return a compact augmenting path Π of the smallest net cost.
- AUGMENT(Π): augment M along Π, i.e., update the matching to $M \oplus \Pi$.

Using the data structure we compute an ε-approximate matching $\mathbb{M}$ as follows: The algorithm maintains a matching M and iteratively repeats the following until $M = \mathbb{M}$ is perfect; initially $M = \emptyset$. The algorithm first finds an augmenting path Π using FINDAP(). Next, it augments M along Π using the AUGMENT(Π) procedure. The algorithm maintains the following invariant, which we call the *alternating cycle invariant*.

(ACI) For any alternating cycle C, $\phi_M(C) \geq 0$.

We first bound the cost of $\mathbb{M}$ assuming ACI, then analyze the running time, and finally prove ACI.

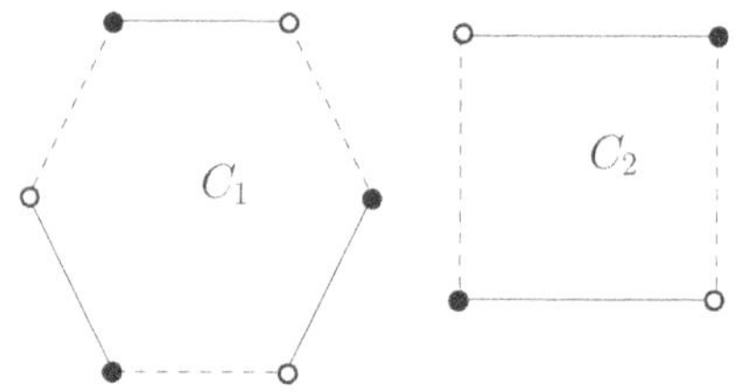

Figure 5. Proof of Lemma 4: Solid edges belong to $\mathbb{M}$ and dashed edges belong to M^*.

LEMMA 4. *Let M^* be an optimal matching of A, B under $\mathtt{d}(\cdot,\cdot)$. Then, $\mathtt{w}(\mathbb{M}) \leq (1+\varepsilon/3)\mathtt{w}(M^*)$.*

PROOF. $\mathbb{M} \cup M^*$ is a set of vertex disjoint alternating cycles $C_1, \ldots, C_k$(See Figure 5). For each i, $C_i \setminus \mathbb{M} = C_i \cap M^*$. Therefore,

$$\mathtt{w}(M^*) - \mathtt{w}(\mathbb{M}) = \sum_{i=1}^{k} (\mathtt{w}(C_i \setminus \mathbb{M}) - \mathtt{w}(C_i \cap \mathbb{M})). \quad (2)$$

On the other hand, by ACI, $\phi_{\mathbb{M}}(C_i) \geq 0$ for every $0 \leq i \leq k$, implying that

$$\sum_{i=1}^{k} \phi_{\mathbb{M}}(C_i) = \sum_{i=1}^{k} (\Phi_{\mathbb{M}}(C_i \setminus \mathbb{M}) - \Phi_{\mathbb{M}}(C_i \cap \mathbb{M})) \geq 0.$$

For every edge $(a,b) \in A \times B$, $\mathtt{d}(a,b) \leq \Phi_{\mathbb{M}}(a,b) \leq \mathtt{d}(a,b) + \theta$. Therefore,

$$\sum_{i=1}^{k} (\mathtt{w}(C_i \setminus \mathbb{M}) - \mathtt{w}(C_i \cap \mathbb{M})) + n\theta \geq 0. \quad (3)$$

Combining (2) and (3) and using the fact that $\theta \leq \varepsilon \mathtt{w}(M^*)/3n$, we obtain

$$\mathtt{w}(\mathbb{M}) \leq \mathtt{w}(M^*) + n\theta \leq (1+\varepsilon/3)\mathtt{w}(M^*). \quad \square$$

Next, we bound the running time of the algorithm. Let M_i be the matching after first i steps of the algorithm, and let Π_i be the augmenting path computed in the ith step of the algorithm. $M_0 = \emptyset$, $M_{i+1} = M_i \oplus \Pi_i$, and $M_n = \mathbb{M}$. We show in Section 5 that FINDAP and AUGMENT in step i take $O(|\Pi_i|\mathrm{poly}(\log \Delta, 1/\epsilon))$ time. We prove in the next lemma that $\sum_{i \geq 1} |\Pi_i| = O(n/\varepsilon \log n)$, which implies that the algorithm takes $O(n\mathrm{poly}(\log \Delta, 1/\varepsilon))$ time.

LEMMA 5. $\sum_{i=1}^{n} |\Pi_i| = O((n/\varepsilon)\log n)$.

PROOF. Fix a value of $i \leq n$. $M^* \cup M_i$ consists of a set of alternating cycles and $n-i+1$ augmenting paths $P_1, \ldots, P_{n-i+1}$. By definition of ϕ and Φ and the value of θ

$$\begin{aligned}
\sum_{j=1}^{n-i+1} \phi_{M_{i-1}}(P_j) &\leq \sum_{j=1}^{n-i+1} \Phi_{M_{i-1}}(P_j \setminus M_{i-1}) \\
&\leq \sum_{j=1}^{n-i+1} \mathtt{w}(P_j \setminus M_{i-1}) + n\theta \\
&= \sum_{j=1}^{n-i+1} \mathtt{w}(P_j \cap M^*) + n\theta \\
&\leq (1+\varepsilon/3)\mathtt{w}(M^*).
\end{aligned}$$

Since Π_i is an augmenting path of minimum net cost, $\phi_{M_{i-1}}(\Pi_i) \leq \phi_{M_{i-1}}(P_j)$ for each $j \leq n-i+1$. Therefore,

$$\phi_{M_{i-1}}(\Pi_i) \leq (1+\varepsilon/3)\mathtt{w}(M^*)/(n-i+1),$$

or

$$\sum_{i=1}^{n} \phi_{M_{i-1}}(\Pi_i) \leq (1+\varepsilon/3)\mathtt{w}(M^*)\ln n. \tag{4}$$

Since Π_i is a compact path, by Lemma 2, $\phi_{M_{i-1}}(\Pi_i) \geq \mathtt{w}(M_i) - \mathtt{w}(M_{i-1}) + \theta|\Pi_i|/4$, which implies that

$$\begin{aligned}\sum_{i=1}^{n} \phi_{M_{i-1}}(\Pi_i) &\geq \mathtt{w}(\mathbb{M}) - \mathtt{w}(M_0) + \theta\sum_{i=1}^{n}|\Pi_i|/4 \\ &\geq \mathtt{w}(M^*) + \frac{\varepsilon\mathtt{w}(M^*)}{24n}\cdot\sum_{i=1}^{n}|\Pi_i|. \end{aligned} \tag{5}$$

The lemma follows by combining (4) and (5). □

Proof of ACI. We prove ACI by induction on i. Since $M_0 = \emptyset$, ACI is true for $i = 0$. Suppose ACI holds for all $j < i$. Let us consider the ith step. Let $\Pi_i = \langle p_1, \ldots, p_u\rangle$ where $p_1 \in B$ and $p_u \in A$, be the augmenting path computed by the algorithm in step i. If there is a negative alternating cycle with respect to M_i, then let C be a negative alternating cycle with the *fewest number* of edges.

We call an edge *affected* by Π_i if at least one of its endpoints is a vertex of Π_i. Note that for any *unaffected* edge (p,q), $\Phi_{M_i}(p,q) = \Phi_{M_{i-1}}(p,q)$. Therefore, if C does not contain any affected edge, then C is an alternating cycle after step i and $\phi_{M_{i-1}}(C) = \phi_{M_i}(C)$. By induction hypothesis, C is non-negative. Hence, C must contain an affected edge. Since C is a cycle, i.e., $C \not\subseteq \Pi_i$, it contains an affected edge that does not lie in Π_i. Let (p,q) be such an affected edge, and suppose $p \in \Pi_i$. Since one of the edges of Π_i incident on p. say, (p,q') belongs to M_i, we can conclude $(p,q) \notin M_i$. C being an alternating cycle and (p,q') being the only matching edge incident on p imply that $(p,q') \in C$. Hence, C contains at least one edge of $\Pi_i \cap M_i$.

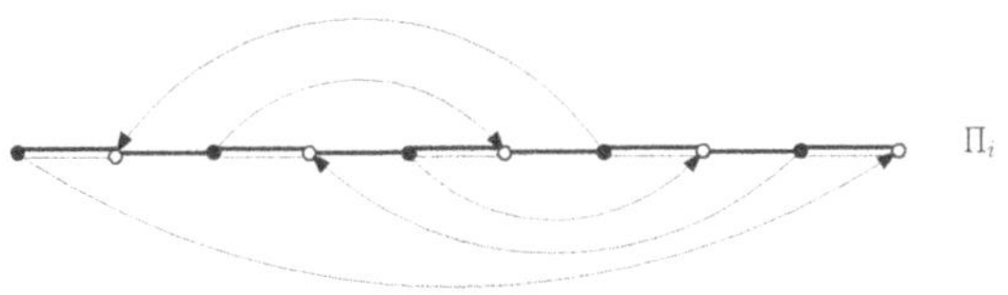

Figure 6. Illustration of forward and backward components in an alternating cycle C; circular arcs are components of $C \setminus \Pi_i$. Black (resp. white) circles are points of B (resp. A). Components oriented toward right (resp. left) are forward (resp. backward) components; double-line segments are components of $\Pi_i \cap C$.

Let $\mathcal{C}^0$ be the set of connected components of $\Pi_i \cap C$, each of which is an alternating path; the above discussion implies that the first edge and the last edge of each connected component are edges of M_i. Each connected component π of $C \setminus \Pi_i$ is an alternating path whose first and last edges do not belong to M_i. Let $p_r \in B$ and $p_s \in A$ be the endpoints of π. We use $\tilde{\pi}$ to denote the sub-path of Π_i between p_r and p_s. We call π a *forward* (resp. *backward*) component if $r < s$ (resp. $r > s$)(See Figure 6). Let $\mathcal{C}^+$ (resp. $\mathcal{C}^-$) denote the set of forward (resp. backward) components of $C \setminus \Pi_i$. We call an affected edge (p,q) of $C \setminus \Pi_i$ *reducing* if $\Phi_{M_i}(p,q) < \Phi_{M_{i-1}}(p,q)$. If (p,q) is a reducing edge, then it is a non-local edge with respect to M_{i-1} and local edge with respect to M_i. Let κ^+ (resp. κ^-) be the total number of reducing edges in forward (resp. backward) components and let κ be the number of edges in Π_i that were non-local edges with respect to M_{i-1}. We claim that

(C1) $\displaystyle\sum_{\pi\in\mathcal{C}^+} \phi_{M_i}(\pi) + \kappa^+\theta \geq \sum_{\pi\in\mathcal{C}^+} \phi_{M_{i-1}}(\tilde{\pi})$.

(C2) $\displaystyle\sum_{\pi\in\mathcal{C}^-} \phi_{M_i}(\pi) + \kappa^-\theta \geq -\sum_{\pi\in\mathcal{C}^-} \phi_{M_{i-1}}(\tilde{\pi})$.

(C3) $\displaystyle\sum_{\pi\in\mathcal{C}^0} \phi_{M_i}(\pi) \geq -\sum_{\pi\in\mathcal{C}^0} \phi_{M_{i-1}}(\pi) + \kappa\theta$.

(C4) $\kappa \geq \kappa^- + \kappa^+$.

Before proving (C1)–(C4), we show that they imply $\phi_{M_i}(C) \geq 0$, which contradicts the assumption that $\phi_{M_i}(C) \leq 0$. Indeed, C being a cycle implies if an edge of $(a,b) \in \Pi_i$ appears in $\tilde{\pi}$'s of j different forward components, then (a,b) has to appear j times in paths $\tilde{\pi}$ of backward components and $\mathcal{C}^0$ put together. Hence, adding equations (C1), (C2) and (C3), we get

$$\sum_{\pi\in\mathcal{C}^+} \phi_{M_i}(\pi) + \sum_{\pi\in\mathcal{C}^-} \phi_{M_i}(\pi) + \sum_{\pi\in\mathcal{C}^0} \phi_{M_i}(\pi) + (\kappa^- + \kappa^+ - \kappa)\theta \geq 0.$$

Since

$$\phi_{M_i}(C) = \sum_{\pi\in\mathcal{C}^+} \phi_{M_i}(\pi) + \sum_{\pi\in\mathcal{C}^-} \phi_{M_i}(\pi) + \sum_{\pi\in\mathcal{C}^0} \phi_{M_i}(\pi)$$

and $\kappa \geq \kappa^- + \kappa^+$, we get $\phi_{M_i}(C) \geq 0$. We now prove (C1)–(C4).

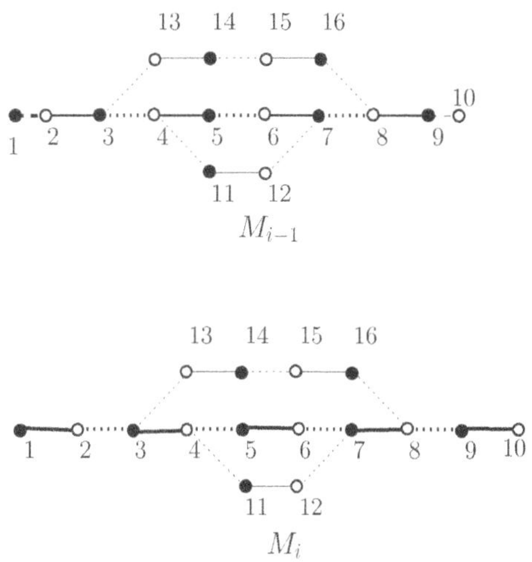

Figure 7. $\Pi_i = \langle 1,2,3,4,5,6,7,8,9,10\rangle$, $C = \langle 3,13,14,15,16,8,7,12,11,4,3\rangle$ is an alternating cycle with respect to M_i; C decomposes into $\pi_1 = \langle 3,13,14,15,16,8\rangle$, $\pi_2 = \langle 4,11,12,7\rangle$ and $\Pi_i \cap C = \langle 3,4\rangle, \langle 7,8\rangle$; the forward component consists of $\mathcal{C}^+ = \{\pi_1\}$ and the backward component consists of $\mathcal{C}^- = \{\pi_2\}$; $\tilde{\pi}_1 = \langle 3,4,5,6,7,8\rangle$, $\tilde{\pi}_2 = \langle 4,5,6,7\rangle$.

Proof of (C1): Let $\pi \in \mathcal{C}^+$ be a forward component. We note that $\overline{\Pi} = (\Pi_i \setminus \tilde{\pi}) \cup \pi$ is an augmenting path with respect to M_{i-1}; see Figure 7. Since Π_i is the smallest augmenting path (with respect to M_{i-1}) $\phi_{M_{i-1}}(\overline{\Pi}) \geq \phi_{M_{i-1}}(\Pi_i)$. This implies $\phi_{M_{i-1}}(\pi) \geq \phi_{M_{i-1}}(\tilde{\pi})$ or

$$\sum_{\pi\in\mathcal{C}^+} \phi_{M_{i-1}}(\pi) \geq \sum_{\pi\in\mathcal{C}^+} \phi_{M_{i-1}}(\tilde{\pi}). \tag{6}$$

Since the total number of reducing edges in forward components is κ^+ and since all other affected edges increase the adjusted cost, we have $\sum_{\pi \in \mathcal{C}^+} \phi_{M_i}(\pi) + \kappa^+\theta \geq \sum_{\pi \in \mathcal{C}^+} \phi_{M_{i-1}}(\pi)$. Combining this with (6), we obtain (C1).

Proof of (C2): For any backward component $\pi \in \mathcal{C}^-$, $\tilde{\pi} \cup \pi$ is an alternating cycle C w.r.t. M_{i-1}; see Figure 7. Since $\phi_{M_{i-1}}(C) \geq 0$, we have $\phi_{M_{i-1}}(\pi) + \phi_{M_{i-1}}(\tilde{\pi}) \geq 0$ or

$$\sum_{\pi \in \mathcal{C}^-} \phi_{M_{i-1}}(\pi) + \sum_{\pi \in \mathcal{C}^-} \phi_{M_{i-1}}(\tilde{\pi}) \geq 0. \quad (7)$$

There are κ^- reducing edges in $\mathcal{C}^-$, therefore

$$\sum_{\pi \in \mathcal{C}^-} \phi_{M_i}(\pi) + \kappa^-\theta \geq \sum_{\pi \in \mathcal{C}^-} \phi_{M_{i-1}}(\pi).$$

Plugging this into (7), we get (C2).

Proof of (C3): Let κ be the total number of non-local edges in paths of $\mathcal{C}^0$,

$$\begin{aligned}\sum_{\pi \in \mathcal{C}^0} \phi_{M_{i-1}}(\pi) &= \sum_{\pi \in \mathcal{C}^0} \Phi_{M_{i-1}}(\pi \setminus M_{i-1}) - \Phi_{M_{i-1}}(\pi \cap M_{i-1}) \\ &= \sum_{\pi \in \mathcal{C}^0} \mathtt{w}(\pi \setminus M_{i-1}) - \mathtt{w}(\pi \cap M_{i-1}) + \kappa\theta.\end{aligned}$$

Therefore

$$\begin{aligned}-\sum_{\pi \in \mathcal{P}} \phi_{M_{i-1}}(\pi) + \kappa\theta &= \sum_{\pi \in \mathcal{C}^0} \mathtt{w}(\pi \cap M_{i-1}) - \mathtt{w}(\pi \setminus M_{i-1}) \\ &= \sum_{\pi \in \mathcal{C}^0} \mathtt{w}(\pi \setminus M_i) - \mathtt{w}(\pi \cap M_i) \\ &\leq \sum_{\pi \in \mathcal{P}} \phi_{M_i}(\pi).\end{aligned}$$

Proof of (C4): Since C is a negative cycle with smallest length and since there are $\kappa^- + \kappa^+$ reducing edges of $\mathcal{C}^+$ and $\mathcal{C}^-$ that are incident on $C \cap \mathcal{C}^0$, from Lemma 6 below, it follows that there are at least $\kappa^- + \kappa^+$ non-local edges in $C \cap \mathcal{C}^0$. Hence, $\kappa \geq \kappa^+ + \kappa^-$.

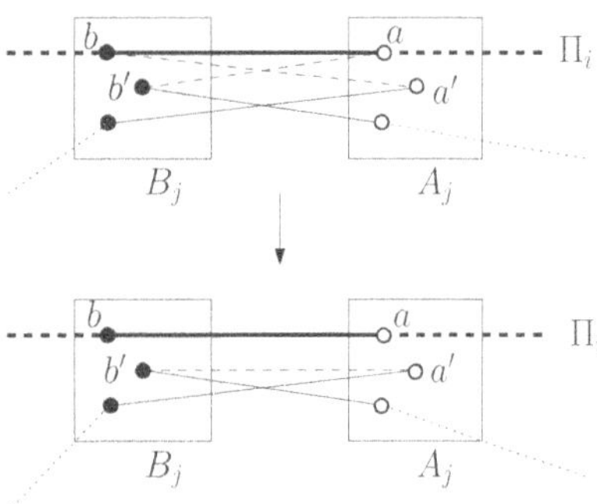

Figure 8. Shortcutting C: replacing $\langle b', a, b, a' \rangle$ with $\langle b', a' \rangle$.

LEMMA 6. *Each edge $e \in M_i \cap \Pi_i \cap C$ is adjacent to at most one reducing edge of C. Furthermore if e is adjacent to a reducing edge, then e was non-local w.r.t. M_{i-1}.*

PROOF. Suppose $e = (a, b)$ is adjacent to two reducing edges (b', a) and (b, a'); see Figure 8. The above discussion implies that both of them are local w.r.t. M_i and neither of them is in M_i or M_{i-1}. By (L2) and (L4), all three of them belong to the same class of $\mathcal{K}_{M_i}$, say, j, and the edge (a', b') also belongs to the class j. If $(a', b') \in M_i$, then $C = \langle a', b', a, b, a' \rangle$ and $\phi_{M_i} = 0$, contradicting the assumption that $\phi_{M_i}(C) < 0$. Hence $(a', b') \notin M_i$. Let $\pi = (b', a) \circ (a, b) \circ (b, a')$ and $\tilde{\pi} = (b', a')$. By (L3), $\phi_{M_i}(\pi) = \phi_{M_i}(\tilde{\pi})$. If we replace π with $\tilde{\pi}$ in C, we obtain another alternating cycle of the same net cost but with fewer edges, a contradiction; see Figure 8. Hence, at most one of (b', a) and (a', b) is reducing.

Next, suppose (b', a) is reducing. If a was not matched in M_{i-1}, then (a, b) was obviously non-local w.r.t. M_{i-1}, so assume that Π_i has another edge $(a, b'') \in M_{i-1}$; see Figure 9. Let (b', a'') be the other edge of C incident on b', then $(b', a'') \in (M_{i-1} \cap M_i) \setminus \Pi_i$. Since (b', a) is reducing, it is local edge w.r.t. M_i. By (L4), see Figure 9, (b', a'') and (b, a) belong to the same class as (b', a) (w.r.t. M_i). On the other hand, (b', a) being reducing also implies that it is non-local w.r.t. M_{i-1}. By (L4), we can conclude that $(b', a''), (a, b'') \in M_{i-1}$ do not belong to the same class of $\mathcal{K}_{M_{i-1}}$; see Figure 9. Using the condition of two matching edges lying in the same class, we can conclude that (a, b) and (a, b'') also do not belong to the same class w.r.t. M_{i-1}, implying that (a, b) is non-local w.r.t. M_{i-1}. □

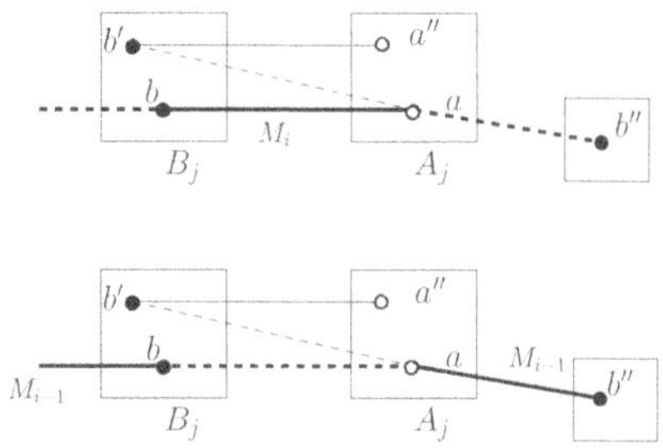

Figure 9. (b', a) is non-local w.r.t. M_{i-1}; b, b' lie in the same sub-cell and b'' lies in a different sub-cell.

5. DATA STRUCTURE

In this section we describe a data structure based on the quad-tree Q constructed in Section 2 that, given point sets A, B and a matching M for which ACI holds, supports FINDAP and AUGMENT operations. We describe a weighted directed graph $\vec{\mathbb{G}}_M(A, B)$ so that the problem of finding a compact augmenting path of minimum net cost (using FINDAP) corresponds to finding an "optimal" path between free vertices in this directed graph. Guided by the partition of the matching edges into classes (Section 3), we describe a hierarchical representation of $\vec{\mathbb{G}}_M$ that allows us to compute an optimal path in $\vec{\mathbb{G}}_M$ efficiently. We describe the information stored at each node of Q and two auxiliary procedures that compute optimal paths. Finally, we describe how FINDAP and AUGMENT are implemented using these auxiliary procedures.

Directed Graph and its properties. For A, B and a matching M, let $\vec{\mathbb{G}}_M(A, B)$ be the weighted graph with the vertex set $A \cup B$ and the edge set $A \times B$. For $(a, b) \in A \times B$, if (a, b) is a non-local edge then (a, b) is directed from b to a with a cost $\mu_M(a, b) = \Phi_M(a, b)$, otherwise, i.e., it is a local edge, there is an edge (a, b) directed from a to b with $\mu_M(a, b) = -\Phi_M(a, b)$. If M is obvious from the context we use $\vec{\mathbb{G}}$ to denote $\vec{\mathbb{G}}_M$ and $\mu(\cdot, \cdot)$ to denote $\mu_M(\cdot, \cdot)$. For any directed path $\vec{\Pi}$ in $\vec{\mathbb{G}}(A, B)$, let the cost of $\vec{\Pi}$, $\mu(\vec{\Pi})$, be the sum of cost of all the edges of $\vec{\Pi}$. Each free vertex of A is a *sink* in $\vec{\mathbb{G}}$, each free vertex of B is a *source* in $\vec{\mathbb{G}}$, and these are the only source and sink vertices in $\vec{\mathbb{G}}$. A path in $\vec{\mathbb{G}}$ alternates between local and non-local edges, but a local edge may not be a matching edge. The following two lemmas relate alternating paths Π with directed paths $\vec{\Pi}$ in $\vec{\mathrm{G}}$.

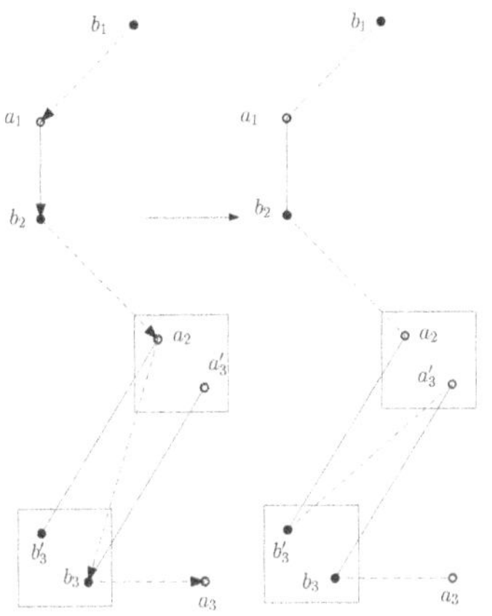

Figure 10. Transforming a directed path in $\vec{\mathrm{G}}$ to an alternating path.

LEMMA 7. *Let M be a matching that satisfies* ACI, *and let $b \in B$ and $a \in A$ be two free vertices w.r.t. M.*

(i) A (directed) path $\vec{\Pi}$ in $\vec{\mathrm{G}}_M(A, B)$ from b to a can be transformed into a compact augmenting path Π between a and b such that $\mu(\vec{\Pi}) = \phi_M(\Pi)$.

(ii) An augmenting path Π can be transformed into a (directed) path $\vec{\Pi}$ in $\vec{\mathrm{G}}(A, B)$ such that $\mu(\vec{\Pi}) \le \phi_M(\Pi)$.

PROOF. (i) Let $\vec{\Pi} = \langle b = b_1, a_1, \ldots, b_k, a_k = a\rangle$, which alternates between non-local and local edges — each (b_i, a_i) is a non-local edge and each (a_i, b_{i+1}) is a local edge. We transform $\vec{\Pi}$ into Π by processing each local edge (a_i, b_{i+1}) as follows (see Figure 10): if $(a_i, b_{i+1}) \in M$, we keep it in Π. Otherwise, by (L4), there are two matching edges (a_i, b'_i) and (a'_{i+1}, b_{i+1}) that belong to the same class as (a_i, b_{i+1}). Set $\pi_i = (a_i, b'_i) \circ (b'_i, a'_{i+1}) \circ (a'_{i+1}, b_{i+1})$. We replace the edge (a_i, b_{i+1}) with π_i. By construction, the resulting path Π is an augmenting path. By (L3), $\phi_M(\pi_i) = -\Phi_M(a_i, b_{i+1}) = \mu(a_i, b_{i+1})$. Hence, $\phi_M(\Pi) = \mu(\vec{\Pi})$. Finally, since $|\Pi| \le 4k$ and Π has k non-local edges, it is compact.

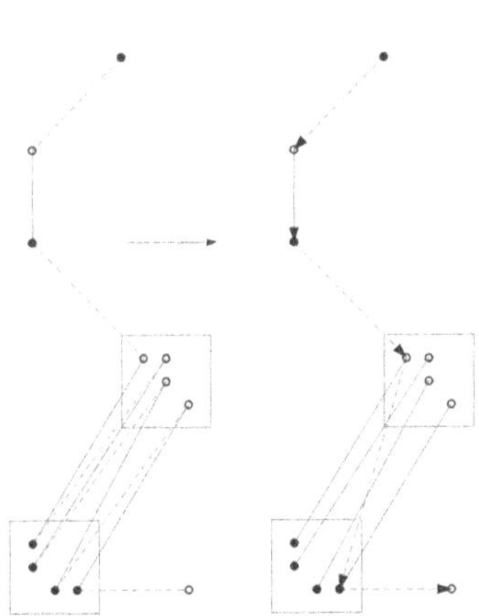

Figure 11. Transforming an alternating path to a directed path in $\vec{\mathrm{G}}$.

(ii) If the augmenting path $\Pi = \langle b = b_1, a_1, \ldots, b_k, a_k = a\rangle$ between b and a does not contain any non-matching local edge, then by the construction of $\vec{\mathrm{G}}$, Π is also a directed path in $\vec{\mathrm{G}}_M(A, B)$ and $\mu(\vec{\Pi}) = \phi_M(\Pi)$. So assume that Π has a non-matching local edge e. Suppose it belongs to class j. Let π be the maximally connected sub-path of Π composed of local edges that contains e. By (L2), all edges of π are in class j. Let $e_r = (a_r, b_r)$ and $e_l = (a_l, b_l), r < l$ be the first and last edges of π. We replace π by a single edge (a_r, b_l) in Π. Since π is maximal and all the edges of π are local, $e_r, e_l \in M$. Therefore (L3) implies that $\phi_M(\pi) = \mu(a_r, b_l)$. Repeating this for all the remaining non-matching local edges of Π, we obtain a path $\vec{\Pi}$ which alternates between non-local and local edges and whose cost $\mu(\vec{\Pi}) = \phi_M(\Pi)$ as desired. $\square$

An immediate corollary of the argument in the proof of Lemma 7 is the following:

COROLLARY 2. *Assuming M satisfies* ACI, *$\vec{\mathrm{G}}_M(A, B)$ does not contain any negative cycle.*

Lemma 7 implies that the problem of computing a compact augmenting path of minimum net cost reduces to finding a minimum-cost directed path from a source to a sink in $\vec{\mathrm{G}}$.

Hierarchical clustering of points. Next, we present a hierarchical clustering of the vertices of $\vec{\mathrm{G}}$ that allows us to compute such a minimum-cost directed path efficiently. For any cell $\square$ of Q, the quad-tree constructed in Section 2, we cluster the vertices of $\vec{\mathrm{G}}$ that lie in $\square$ into $O(\mathrm{poly}(\log\Delta, 1/\varepsilon))$ clusters. Rougly speaking, if two points p, q belong to the same cluster at $\square$, then for any point $r \in (A \cup B) \setminus \square$, $\mu(p, r) = \mu(q, r)$ and (p, r) and (q, r) have identical directions w.r.t.r, i.e., both edges are either directed toward r or away from r. Let $M = \{(a_1, b_1), \ldots, (a_k, b_k)\}$ be the matching, and let

$$\mathcal{K}_M = \{(A_1, B_1), \ldots, (A_u, B_u)\}$$

be the classification of points in A and B induced by M as described in Section 3. For any matched point a_i (resp. b_i), we refer to b_i (resp. a_i) as its *partner* point. Let $\square$ be a non-empty cell of Q, and let $A_\square = A \cap \square$, $B_\square = B \cap \square$. We partition $A_\square$ and $B_\square$ into three types of clusters. For any $\xi \in \mathbb{G}[\square]$, let $A_\xi = A \cap \xi$ and $B_\xi = B \cap \xi$.

- *Free clusters*: All free points of A_ξ and B_ξ belong to a single cluster
$$A^F_\xi = A_F \cap \xi, \quad B^F_\xi = B_F \cap \xi.$$
- *Internal clusters*: All points of A_ξ (B_ξ) whose partner point is also inside $\square$ belong to the same cluster
$$A^I_\xi = \{a_i \in A_\xi \mid (a_i, b_i) \in M, b_i \in B_\square\},$$
$$B^I_\xi = \{b_i \in B_\xi \mid (a_i, b_i) \in M, a_i \in A_\square\}.$$
- *Boundary clusters*: All points of A_ξ whose partner points lie outside $\square$ are partitioned into various clusters. Two such points belong to the same cluster if and only if they lie in the same class $(A_i, B_i) \in \mathcal{K}_M$. More precisely, let $N^*(\square) = \bigcup \mathbb{G}[\square']$ where the union is taken over all siblings $\square'$ of ancestors of $\square$. $|N^*(\square)| = \mathrm{poly}(\log\Delta, 1/\varepsilon)$, as there are $O(\log\Delta)$ ancestors of $\square$, each has three siblings, and each

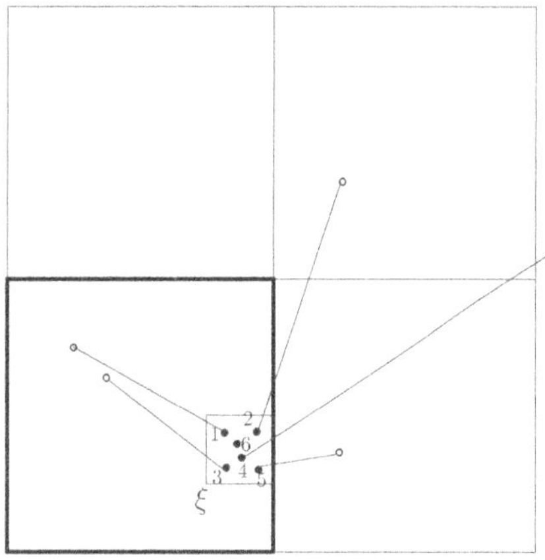

Figure 12. Partitioning of B_ξ into various clusters: $\{6\}$ is a free cluster, $\{1,3\}$ is an internal cluster, and $\{2\},\{4\},\{5\}$ are boundary clusters of the sub-cell ξ of the highlighted cell.

sibling has poly($\log\Delta, 1/\varepsilon$) sub-cells. For every sub-cell $\eta \in N^*(\Box)$, we have a cluster

$$A_\xi^\eta = \{a_i \in A_\xi \mid (a_i, b_i) \in M, b_i \in B_\eta\},$$

$$B_\xi^\eta = \{b_i \in B_\xi \mid (a_i, b_i) \in M, a_i \in A_\eta\}.$$

The points in each cluster at $\Box$ lie within a single sub-cell of $\mathbb{G}[\Box]$. Let $\mathbb{X}_\Box$ be the set of clusters at $\Box$; $|\mathbb{X}_\Box| = \text{poly}(\log\Delta, 1/\varepsilon)$. By definition, each free (resp. internal) cluster at $\Box$ is contained in a free (resp. internal) cluster at $\mathsf{p}(\Box)$, parent of $\Box$, and each boundary cluster at $\Box$ is contained in a boundary or an internal cluster at $\mathsf{p}(\Box)$.

The relationship between the clusters at $\Box$ and those at the children $\Box_1, \Box_2, \Box_3, \Box_4$ of $\Box$ can be summarized as follows. Each sub-cell $\xi \in \mathbb{G}[\Box]$ is contained in one of the four children of $\Box$, say $\Box_i$. Then ξ has four children $\xi_1, \xi_2, \xi_3, \xi_4$ in $\mathbb{G}[\Box_i]$ and we get the following relationship.

$$\begin{aligned}
A_\xi^F &= \bigcup_{i=1}^4 A_{\xi_i}^F, \qquad B_\xi^F = \bigcup_{i=1}^4 B_{\xi_i}^F,\\
A_\xi^\eta &= \bigcup_{i=1}^4 A_{\xi_i}^\eta, \qquad B_\xi^\eta = \bigcup_{i=1}^4 B_{\xi_i}^\eta.\\
A_\xi^I &= \bigcup_{i=1}^4 (A_{\xi_i}^I \cup (\bigcup_{\zeta \in N(\xi)} A_{\xi_i}^\zeta)),\\
B_\xi^I &= \bigcup_{i=1}^4 (B_{\xi_i}^I \cup (\bigcup_{\zeta \in N(\xi)} B_{\xi_i}^\zeta)).
\end{aligned} \tag{8}$$

For $z \in \Box_i$, $N(z) = \bigcup_{j \neq i} \mathbb{G}[\Box_j]$ is the set of sub-cells that lie inside the siblings of $\Box_i$. For a cluster X of $A_\Box$ (resp. $B_\Box$), we define $D(X)$ as the set of clusters of $A_{\Box_1}, A_{\Box_2}, A_{\Box_3}, A_{\Box_4}$ (resp. $B_{\Box_1}, B_{\Box_2}, B_{\Box_3}, B_{\Box_4}$) that are contained in X. The following lemma whose proof is straightforward states the property of the above hierarchical clustering scheme

LEMMA 8. *For any cell $\Box \in Q$, let $\Box_1, \Box_2$ be any two of its children. Let $X \in \mathbb{X}_{\Box_1}, Y \in \mathbb{X}_{\Box_2}$. Then the cost of all edges in $X \times Y$ is the same in $\vec{G}$ and all edges are oriented in the same direction — either all are oriented from B to A or all of them are oriented from A to B.*

Next, we partition the clusters in $\mathbb{X}_\Box$ into two subsets called the *entry* and *exit* clusters respectively,

$$\mathbb{X}_\Box^\downarrow = \{B_\xi^F, A_\xi^I, B_\xi^\eta \mid \xi \in \mathbb{G}[\Box], \eta \in N^*(\Box)\},$$

$$\mathbb{X}_\Box^\uparrow = \{A_\xi^F, B_\xi^I, A_\xi^\eta \mid \xi \in \mathbb{G}[\Box], \eta \in N^*(\Box)\}.$$

Let Π be a path in $\vec{G}$ from a source to a sink vertex and let $\overline{\pi}$ be a maximal connected sub-path of $\vec{\Pi}$ that lies inside $\Box$. Suppose $\overline{\pi}$ contains at least one edge. For the two endpoints p, q of $\overline{\pi}$, we refer to p as entry and q as exit point if $\overline{\pi}$ is directed from p to q. Then we claim that the entry point lies in an entry cluster and exit point lies in an exit cluster. Indeed, if $\overline{\pi}$ is an initial portion of $\vec{\Pi}$, then the entry point is a source vertex, belonging to some B_ξ^F – an entry cluster. Otherwise, if the first edge of $\overline{\pi}$ is a local edge, which lies inside $\Box$ by assumption, then, by construction, the entry point belongs to an internal cluster. Since all local edges are oriented from A to B, the entry point must belong to A_ξ^I – an entry cluster. Finally, if the first edge of $\overline{\pi}$ is a non-local edge then the preceding edge in $\vec{\Pi}$ is a local edge. By construction, the entry point belongs to a boundary cluster. Since all non-local edges are directed from B to A, the entry point must belong to B_ξ^η, for some $\xi \in \mathbb{G}[\Box], \eta \in N^*(\Box)$ – an entry cluster. A similar argument holds for the exit point.

Information stored at each node. For a cell $\Box \in Q$, let $\vec{G}_\Box = \vec{G}_M(A_\Box, B_\Box)$ be the subgraph of $\vec{G}(A, B)$ formed by the points $A_\Box$, $B_\Box$; $\vec{G}_\Box$ contains all directed paths of $\vec{G}$ that lie completely within $\Box$. We define the *mixed cost* of a path Π in $\vec{G}_\Box$, denoted by $\psi(\Pi)$, as $(\mu(\Pi), |\Pi|)$; $\mu(\Pi)$ is the cost of Π and $|\Pi|$ is the number of edges in Π. We order the mixed costs in lexicographic order, i.e., for two paths, Π_1 and Π_2 with $\psi(\Pi_1) = (\mu_1, \ell_1)$ and $\psi(\Pi_2) = (\mu_2, \ell_2)$, Π_1 has smaller mixed cost than Π_2 if $\mu_1 < \mu_2$ or $\mu_1 = \mu_2$ and $\ell_1 < \ell_2$. If $\Pi = \Pi_1 \circ \Pi_2$, then $\psi(\Pi) = (\mu_1 + \mu_2, \ell_1 + \ell_2)$. For a pair of points $a, b \in A_\Box \cup B_\Box$, let $\psi_\Box(a, b)$ be the smallest mixed cost path from a to b in $\vec{G}_\Box$, and we refer to such a path as an *optimal* path from a to b. The definition of mixed cost ensures that an optimal path is always simple.

For any pair of subsets $X \in A_\Box$, $Y \in B_\Box$, let

$$\psi_\Box(X, Y) = \min_{a \in X, b \in Y} \psi_\Box(a, b).$$

At each cell $\Box$ in Q, for all $X, Y \in \mathbb{X}_\Box^\downarrow \times \mathbb{X}_\Box^\uparrow$, we store

$$\psi_\Box(X, Y), \tag{9}$$

i.e., the mixed cost of the optimal path between every entry cluster to every exit clusters.

Compressed graph. We show that if we have (9) at the four children of a cell $\Box \in Q$, we can compute (9) for $\Box$ in poly($\log\Delta, 1/\varepsilon$) time, and that given $(X, Y) \in \mathbb{X}_\Box^\downarrow \times \mathbb{X}_\Box^\uparrow$, we can compute an optimal path from a vertex $a \in X$ to $b \in Y$ in $\vec{G}_\Box$, in time $O(k\text{poly}(\log\Delta, 1/\varepsilon))$ where k is the length of the optimal path, such that $\psi_\Box(a, b) = \psi_\Box(X, Y)$. We call these procedures ASCEND($\Box$) and EXTRACTPATH($X, Y, \Box$).

Let $\Box_1, \Box_2, \Box_3, \Box_4$ be the four children of the cell $\Box \in Q$. We construct a weighted directed graph $H_\Box = (V_\Box, E_\Box)$ where $V_\Box = \bigcup_{i=1}^4 (\mathbb{X}_{\Box_i})$. There are two sets of edges in $H_\Box$: (i) *interior edges* — between two clusters of the same $\Box_i$; (ii) *bridge edges* — between clusters of siblings. For each pair of entry and exit clusters, $(X, Y) \in \mathbb{X}_{\Box_i}^\downarrow \times \mathbb{X}_{\Box_i}^\uparrow$, we add an interior edge (X, Y) with $\psi_{\Box_i}(X, Y)$ as its mixed cost. Next, let $(X, Y) \in (\mathbb{X}_{\Box_i} \times \mathbb{X}_{\Box_j})$, for $i \neq j$. If there are edges between points of X and Y in $\vec{G}$, then from Lemma 8, the cost and direction of every edge in $X \times Y$ is identical. Let this cost be β. We add an edge between X and Y with the direction identical to edges in $X \times Y$ and set its mixed cost to be $(\beta, 1)$. For a pair of vertices $X, Y \in V_\Box$, let $\overline{\psi}_\Box(X, Y)$ be the smallest mixed cost of a path from X to Y in $H_\Box$.

Auxiliary procedures. Before describing the AUGMENT and EXTRACTPATH procedures, we describe a few properties of the compressed graph $H_\Box$.

LEMMA 9. *For any pair* $X, Y \in \mathbb{X}_\Box^{\downarrow} \times \mathbb{X}_\Box^{\uparrow}$,

$$\min_{\substack{X' \in D(X) \\ Y' \in D(Y)}} \overline{\psi}_\Box(X', Y') \leq \psi_\Box(X, Y).$$

PROOF. Let $a \in X, b \in Y$ be the points such that $\psi_\Box(a, b) = \psi_\Box(X, Y)$, and let Π be an optimal path in $\vec{G}_\Box$ from a to b. Suppose $a \in X' \in D(X)$ and $b \in Y' \in D(Y)$. We express Π as a sequence $\pi_1 \circ \pi_2 \circ \cdots \circ \pi_u$, where each π_i is either an edge of Π whose endpoints lie in different children of $\Box$ or a maximal sub-path of Π that lies inside a single child of $\Box$. If $\pi_i = (p_i, p_{i+1})$ is an edge of Π, then by construction, there is an edge (X_i, X_{i+1}) in $H_\Box$ such that $p_i \in X_i$ and $p_{i+1} \in X_{i+1}$ and the mixed cost of (X_i, X_{i+1}) is $(\mu(p_i, p_{i+1}), 1)$. If π_i is a maximal path lying in the child $\Box_j$ of $\Box$ then its initial and final endpoints lie in the entry and exit clusters, say, X_i and X_{i+1}, of $\mathbb{X}_{\Box_j}$. By construction, $H_\Box$ has an edge from X_i to X_{i+1} whose mixed cost is at most $\psi(\pi_i)$. In other words, $\Gamma = \langle X' = X_1, X_2, \ldots, X_{r+1} = Y' \rangle$ is a path in $H_\Box$ whose mixed cost is at most $\psi(\Pi)$. Hence, $\overline{\psi}_\Box(X', Y') \leq \psi_\Box(X, Y)$, which implies the lemma. $\Box$

Next, let Γ be an optimal path in $H_\Box$ from an entry cluster $X' \in \mathbb{X}_\Box^{\downarrow}$ to an exit cluster $Y' \in \mathbb{X}_\Box^{\uparrow}$. We show how to retrieve a path Π in $\vec{G}_\Box$ from a vertex $a \in X'$ to a vertex $b \in Y'$ such that $\psi_\Box(\Pi) = \overline{\psi}_\Box(X', Y')$.

Suppose $\Gamma = \langle X = X_0, X_1, \ldots, X_{u-1}, X_u = Y \rangle$. By construction, if (X_{i-1}, X_i) is an interior edge, then (X_i, X_{i+1}) has to be a bridge edge. If (X_{i-1}, X_i) is an interior edge, we recursively construct a path from X_{i-1} to X_i in the corresponding child of $\Box$. Suppose a path π_i with the endpoints $u_{i-1} \in X_{i-1}$ and $u_i \in X_i$ is returned. If (X_{i+1}, X_{i+2}) is also an interior edge and the path π_{i+2} with the endpoints $u_{i+1} \in X_{i+1}$, $u_{i+2} \in X_{i+2}$ is returned, we connect π_i and π_{i+1} by the edge (u_i, u_{i+1}). If (X_{i+1}, X_{i+2}) is also a bridge edge, we choose any point $u_{i+1} \in X_{i+1}$ and add the edge (u_i, u_{i+1}). Let $\vec{\Pi}$ be the path constructed by this procedure. Clearly, $\vec{\Pi}$ is a directed path in $\vec{G}(A_\Box, B_\Box)$. Using an inductive argument on the height of nodes, one can show that $\psi(\Pi) = \overline{\psi}_\Box(X', Y')$. Lemma 9 and this procedure imply the following:

LEMMA 10. *For every node* $\Box \in Q$ *and for any* $(X, Y) \in \mathbb{X}_\Box^{\downarrow} \times \mathbb{X}_\Box^{\uparrow}$,

$$\psi_\Box(X, Y) = \min_{\substack{X' \in D(X) \\ Y' \in D(Y)}} \overline{\psi}_\Box(X', Y').$$

The following is an immediate corollary of the above lemma

COROLLARY 3. *$H_\Box$ has no negative cycles.*

By Lemma 10 and Corollary 3, assuming we have computed $\psi_{\Box_i}$ at all children $\Box_i$ of $\Box$, we can compute $\psi_\Box(X, Y)$ for all $X, Y \in \mathbb{X}_\Box^{\downarrow} \times \mathbb{X}_\Box^{\uparrow}$ by constructing the graph $H_\Box$ and computing optimal paths between every pair of vertices. The total time taken by ASCEND procedure is poly$(\log \Delta, 1/\varepsilon)$.

EXTRACTPATH$(X, Y, \Box)$, where $X, Y \in \mathbb{X}_\Box^{\downarrow} \times \mathbb{X}_\Box^{\uparrow}$, is implemented by first constructing the graph $H_\Box$ and computing optimal paths for all pairs of vertices $X', Y' \in D(X) \times D(Y)$. Let Γ be the path with the smallest mixed cost among these paths. We now retrieve a path Π in $\vec{G}_\Box$ from a vertex $a \in X'$ to a vertex $b \in Y'$ such that $\psi(\Pi) = \overline{\psi}(X', Y') = \psi_\Box(X, Y)$. The total time spent is $O(k\text{poly}(\log \Delta, 1/\varepsilon))$ where k is the number of edges in Π. Since $H_\Box$ has no negative cycles and since minimizing mixed cost ensures that among minimum-cost paths we compute a path with fewest edges, Π is a simple path.

Implementing FINDAP and AUGMENT. Using EXTRACTPATH and ASCEND procedure, FINDAP and AUGMENT can be implemented in a straightforward manner. Let ∇ be the root of Q and let $S_\nabla \subseteq \mathbb{X}_\nabla^{\downarrow}$ (resp. $T_\nabla \subseteq \mathbb{X}_\nabla^{\uparrow}$) be the subset of free clusters at ∇. By definition, $B_F = \bigcup S_\nabla$ and $A_F = \bigcup T_\nabla$. Set

$$S, T = \arg\min_{X, Y \in S_\nabla \times T_\nabla} \psi_\nabla(X, Y).$$

Then, $\psi_\nabla(S, T)$ is the smallest mixed cost of a directed path in $\vec{G}_M(A, B)$ from a source to sink. We compute an optimal path $\vec{\Pi}$ from a vertex $b \in S$ to a vertex $a \in T$ in $\vec{G}_M(A, B) = \vec{G}_\nabla$, s.t., $\psi_\nabla(b, a) = \psi_\nabla(S, T)$, using EXTRACTPATH$(S, T, \nabla)$. As mentioned above, $\vec{\Pi}$ is a simple path. $\vec{\Pi}$ can be converted into a compact augmenting path Π, as described in Lemma 7, such that $\phi_M(\Pi) = \mu(\vec{\Pi})$. By Lemma 7, Π is a compact augmenting path of the smallest net cost. Hence, FINDAP takes $O(|\Pi|\text{poly}(\log \Delta, 1/\varepsilon))$ time.

Finally, the AUGMENT(Π) updates M to $M' = M \oplus \Pi$ and the information stored at Q, as follows. For a point $p \in A \cup B$, let $\mathbb{C}(p)$ be the set of ancestors of the leaf of Q that contains p. Set $\mathbb{C}(\Pi) = \bigcup_{p \in \Pi} \mathbb{C}(p)$. We observe that the only change in $\vec{G}_{M'}$ from $\vec{G}_M$ is that the direction and cost of the edges in Π change and the cost of edges incident on any vertex of Π may change. Hence, for a node $\Box \in Q$, $\vec{G}_\Box$ does not change if $\Box$ does not contain any vertex of Π, i.e., $\Box \notin \mathbb{C}(\Pi)$. For each point $p \in \Pi$, we update the information at nodes of $\mathbb{C}(p)$ in a bottom-up manner. More precisely, suppose we have already updated $\psi_\Box$ values for some cell $\Box \in \mathbb{C}(\Pi)$. Next, we call ASCEND$(\mathtt{p}(\Box))$ and update the information at $\mathtt{p}(\Box)$. Since $|\mathbb{C}(\Pi)| = O(|\Pi| \log \Delta)$, the total time spent by AUGMENT(Π) is $O(|\Pi|\text{poly}(\log \Delta, 1/\varepsilon))$. We thus obtain the following:

LEMMA 11. *A, B and a matching M that satisfies* ACI *can be maintained in a data structure so that* FINDAP *and* AUGMENT *take $O(k\text{poly}(\log \Delta, 1/\varepsilon))$ time where k is the length of the output and input path respectively.*

6. CONCLUSION

In this paper, we presented a near-linear time Monte-Carlo algorithm for computing ε-approximate bipartite matching of point sets in $\mathbb{R}^d$ under any L_p-metric. First, we presented a quad-tree based distance function $\mathtt{d}(\cdot, \cdot)$ that approximates the L_p-norm. Next, we presented an algorithm for computing an ε-approximate matching under $\mathtt{d}(\cdot, \cdot)$. By exploiting the quad-tree structure of the distance function, our algorithm iteratively generates minimum-cost augmenting paths in time proportional to its length. The total length of the augmenting paths generated by the algorithm is $O((n/\varepsilon) \log n)$ implying its near-linear running time. For simplicity of exposition, we did not minimize the exponent in poly$(\log n, 1/\varepsilon)$ factor. One way of reducing the exponent is by using an exponential grid instead of a uniform grid for $\mathbb{G}[\Box]$. This reduces the number of subcells to roughly $\log(n)/\varepsilon$, instead of $(\log(n)/\varepsilon)^2$. We conclude by stating two natural open questions:

- Is there a near-linear time ε-approximation algorithm for a generalization of bipartite matching called the *transportation problem* in geometric settings?

- Is there a sub-quadratic algorithm for computing an optimal Euclidean bipartite matching in $\mathbb{R}^2$?

7. REFERENCES

[1] P. K. Agarwal, A. Efrat, and M. Sharir, Vertical decomposition of shallow levels in 3-dimensional arrangements and its applications, *SIAM J. Comput.*, 29 (1999), 39–50.

[2] P. K. Agarwal and K. R. Varadarajan, A near-linear constant-factor approximation for euclidean bipartite matching?, *Proc. of 12th Annual Sympos. on Comput. Geom.*, 2004, pp. 247–252.

[3] S. Arora, Polynomial time approximation schemes for euclidean traveling salesman and other geometric problems, *J. ACM*, 45 (1998), 753–782.

[4] R. Duan and S. Pettie, Approximating maximum weight matching in near-linear time, *Proc. 51st Annual IEEE Sympos. on Foundations of Comp. Sc.*, 2010, pp. 673–682.

[5] H. N. Gabow and R. Tarjan, Faster scaling algorithms for network problems, *SIAM J. Comput.*, 18 (1989), 1013–1036.

[6] H. N. Gabow and R. E. Tarjan, Faster scaling algorithms for general graph-matching problems, *J. ACM*, 38 (1991), 815–853.

[7] A. Goel, M. Kapralov, and S. Khanna, Perfect matchings in o(n log n) time in regular bipartite graphs, *Proc. 42nd Annual Sympos. on Theory of Comput.*, 2010, pp. 39–46.

[8] P. Indyk, A near linear time constant factor approximation for euclidean bichromatic matching (cost), *Proc. 18th Annual Sympos. on Discrete Algorithms*, 2007, pp. 39–42.

[9] P. Indyk, R. Motwani, and S. Venkatasubramanian, Geometric matching under noise: Combinatorial bounds and algorithms, *Proc. 10th Annual Sympos. on Discrete Algorithms*, 1999, pp. 457–465.

[10] P. Indyk and S. Venkatasubramanian, Approximate congruence in nearly linear time, *Comput. Geom.*, 24 (2003), 115–128.

[11] S. Micali and V. V. Vazirani, An o(sqrt(v)e) algorithm for finding maximum matching in general graphs, *Proc. Annual 21st IEEE Sympos. on Foundations of Comp. Sc.*, 1980, pp. 17–27.

[12] C. H. Papadimitriou and K. Steiglitz, *Combinatorial optimization: algorithms and complexity*, Prentice-Hall, Inc., 1982.

[13] J. M. Phillips and P. K. Agarwal, On bipartite matching under the rms distance, *Proc. 18th Canadian Conf. on Comput. Geom.*, 2006.

[14] R.Sharathkumar and P. K. Agarwal, Algorithms for transportation problem in geometric settings, *Proc. of 23rd Annual Sympos. on Discrete Algorithms*, 2012, pp. 306–317.

[15] P. M. Vaidya, Geometry helps in matching, *SIAM J. Comput.*, 18 (1989), 1201–1225.

[16] K. R. Varadarajan, A divide-and-conquer algorithm for min-cost perfect matching in the plane, *Proc. 39th Annual IEEE Sympos. on Foundations of Comp. Sc.*, 1998, pp. 320–331.

[17] K. R. Varadarajan and P. K. Agarwal, Approximation algorithms for bipartite and non-bipartite matching in the plane, *Proc. 10th Annual ACM-SIAM Sympos. on Discrete Algorithms*, 1999, pp. 805–814.

Using Petal-Decompositions to Build a Low Stretch Spanning Tree

Ittai Abraham
Microsoft Research SVC
Mountain View, CA
ittaia@microsoft.com

Ofer Neiman*
Ben-Gurion University of the Negev
Beer-Sheva, Israel
neimano@cs.bgu.ac.il

ABSTRACT

We prove that any graph $G = (V, E)$ with n points and m edges has a spanning tree T such that $\sum_{(u,v)\in E(G)} d_T(u, v) = O(m \log n \log\log n)$. Moreover such a tree can be found in time $O(m \log n \log\log n)$. Our result is obtained using a new *petal-decomposition* approach which guarantees that the radius of each cluster in the tree is at most 4 times the radius of the induced subgraph of the cluster in the original graph.

Categories and Subject Descriptors

G.2.2 [**Graph Theory**]: [Graph Algorithms, Trees]

General Terms

Algorithms, Theory

Keywords

Stretch, Spanning Tree, Metric Embedding, distortion

1. INTRODUCTION

Let $G = (V, E, w)$ be a finite graph, where $w : E \to \mathbb{R}_+$ is a weight function on the edges. For any subgraph $H = (V', E', w')$ of G let d_H be the induced shortest path metric with respect to H, where w' is the restriction of w to E'. In particular, for any edge $(u, v) \in E$ and any spanning tree T of G, $d_T(u, v)$ denotes the (unique) shortest path distance between u and v in T.

Given a spanning tree T, let

$$\text{avg stretch}_T(G) = \frac{1}{|E|} \sum_{(u,v)\in E(G)} \frac{d_T(u, v)}{d_G(u, v)}. \quad (1)$$

avg stretch$(n) = \max_{G=(V,E,w):|V|=n} \inf_T\{\text{avg stretch}_T(G)\}$.

*Partially funded by the Lynne and William Frankel Center for Computer Sciences.

STOC'12, May 19–22, 2012, New York, New York, USA.

Figure 1 summarizes current progress on the bounds for avg stretch(n) and the time complexity of building such trees.

For the class of Series-Parallel graphs Emek and Peleg [14] obtained avg stretch$(n) = \Theta(\log n)$.

The main result of this paper is a new upper bound on avg stretch(n) that is tight up to a $O(\log\log n)$ factor and can be constructed in time $O(m \log n \log\log n)$.

THEOREM 1.

$$\text{avg stretch}(n) = O(\log n \log\log n)$$

Moreover such a tree can be found in time $O(m \log n \log\log n)$.

Our result may be applied to improve the running time of the Spielman and Teng [21] approach to solve sparse symmetric diagonally dominant linear systems, using the improved algorithms of Koutis, Miller and Peng [16, 17].

1.1 Related Work

Embedding metric spaces and graphs into tree metrics and spanning trees has received a lot of attention in the last two decades. The basic motivation is that problems on simple graphs such as trees are often much easier than on arbitrary graphs, and embedding the original graph into a tree (or a distribution over trees) is a basic step in approximation algorithms, network design, online algorithms and other settings. As mentioned above, the first results were obtained by [4] who showed a $\exp(O(\sqrt{\log n \log\log n}))$ bound on the average stretch. If we drop the requirement that the tree is spanning (that is, allow to add and not only delete edges, while maintaining that distances in the tree are larger than those in the graph), then [5, 6, 9, 15] in a sequence of works showed optimal average stretch of $\Theta(\log n)$. This line of work proved very fruitful, because in many settings we can suffer non-spanning trees. If we replace the right hand side of (1) by averaging over all pairs, then [2] showed a universal constant bound on that quantity, called the average distortion.

A related line of research studies a *relative guarantee* approximation: given a graph, can we approximate the best possible tree. For the question of maximum stretch over all pair distances, [8] obtained a $(c \log n)^{O(\sqrt{\log \Delta})}$ factor, where c is the optimal maximum stretch and Δ is the diameter. They also showed $O(1)$ approximation for the case where the graph is unweighted. The constant was recently improved by [10]. For embedding unweighted graphs into a *spanning* tree, [13] showed $O(\log n)$ approximation for maximum stretch. However, for the setting of average stretch,

	avg stretch(n)	time
[4]	$\Omega(\log n)$, $\exp(O(\sqrt{\log n \log\log n}))$	$O(m^2)$
[12]	$O((\log n)^2 \log\log n)$	$O(m \log^2 n)$
[3]	$O(\log n (\log\log n)^3)$	$O(m \log^2 n)$
[3]	$O(\log n \log\log n (\log\log\log n)^3)$	$O(m^2)$
[17]	$O(\log n (\log\log n)^3)$	$O(m \log n \log\log n)$
This paper	$O(\log n \log\log n)$	$O(m \log n \log\log n)$

Figure 1: Summary of Progress on Low Stretch Spanning Tree.

essentially nothing is known (except for the trivial $\tilde{O}(\log n)$[1] absolute bound shown here and in [3]).

1.2 Techniques

1.2.1 Petal Decomposition and Radius Increase

The star-decomposition technique of Elkin *et. al.*[12] is a method to iteratively build a spanning tree. In each iteration it partitions the vertices of the current graph into clusters that are connected in a star structure: a central cluster is connected to every other cluster by a single edge , and all other edges between clusters are dropped. In both previous manifestations of star-decompositions ([12] and [3]) the first step in each iteration is to define the central cluster as an appropriately chosen ball around some center point. After the central ball is defined then the remaining clusters (called cones) are defined sequentially.

The radius of a graph is the maximal distance from a designated center. One of the main difficulties in the spanning tree construction, is that the radius may increase by a small factor at every application of the star decomposition, which translates to increased stretch. If we drop the requirement that the tree is a *spanning tree* of the graph, and just require a tree metric, then this difficulty does not appear, and indeed optimal $\Theta(\log n)$ bound is known on the average stretch [15, 7]. In order to control the radius increase, [12] had to pay an additional factor of $O(\log n)$. This was improved by [3], in which a subtle change to the algorithm and a careful analysis of the radius increase allowed the factor to be reduced to $\tilde{O}(\log\log n)$. One of the main contributions of this work, is a new decomposition scheme which we call *petal-decomposition*, that allows essentially optimal control on the radius increase of the spanning tree; it increases by at most a factor of 4 over all the recursion levels.

Our new *petal-decomposition* technique is also a method to iteratively build a spanning tree. In each iteration it starts by sequentially building a series of clusters which we call *petals*. Once no more petals can be built, the remaining central cluster is called the *stigma*. Then the petals and the stigma are connected into a tree, using some of the inter cluster edges, and all other edges between clusters are dropped.

The petal-decomposition approach differs from the star-decompositions in three main aspects. First, it is not the case that all petals are necessarily connected to the stigma (as would be the case in the star-partition); petals are connected to each other in a tree structure whose root is the stigma. Second, the stigma is not necessarily a ball, it is the remaining subgraph once no more petals can be formed.

Third and most important, is the definition of a petal. In a star-decomposition each cone $C(x_0, x, r)$ is defined by three parameters: the center of the current cluster x_0, the center of the cone x and the radius r of the cone, then the cone consists of all the points v such that $d(x_0, x)+d(x, v)-d(x_0, v) \leq r$. The radius r of the cone determines the maximum increase in the radius of the graph. A petal $P(x_0, t, r)$ is also defined by three parameters: the center of the current cluster x_0, the *target* of the petal t and the radius r of the petal. The center of the petal (denoted by x) is the point on the shortest path from t to x_0 of distance r from t. Moreover, we call the path from the center of the petal x to the target of the petal t the *highway* of the petal. An important property of our construction is that this highway path is guaranteed to be a part of the final spanning tree. The petal is defined as a union of cones of varying radii. Specifically, let p_k be the point of distance k from the target t on the shortest path from t to x_0. Then the petal $P(x_0, t, r)$ is defined as the union of cones $C(x_0, p_k, (r-k)/2)$ for all $k \leq r$.

Informally, the crucial property of a petal and its highway is the following: Assume $z \in P(x_0, t, r)$, and $P_{x_0 z}$ is the shortest path from the center x_0 to z. By forming the petal, we remove all edges between $P(x_0, t, r)$ and $G \setminus P(x_0, t, r)$ except for the edge from the petal center x towards the center of the current cluster. Hence every path from x_0 to z will go through the petal center x. If the new shortest path $P'_{x_0 z}$ (after forming the petal) is (additively) α longer than the length of $P_{x_0 z}$, then $P'_{x_0 z}$ will contain part of the highway of length at least 2α, see Figure 2. Such a property could allow the following wishful thinking: Suppose that in each iteration we increase the distance of a point to the center by at most α, but also mark 2α of the path as edges that are guaranteed to appear in the final tree (part of a highway). In such a case it is easy to see that the final path will have stretch of at most $O(1)$ (intuitively, the highway part will quickly catch-up and the process stops when all the path is marked as highway). Unfortunately, the shortest path from x to z in the final tree may not use the prescribed highway of the parent cluster so the above "wishful thinking" argument does not work.

The key algorithmic idea to alleviate this problem is to decrease the weight of an edge by half when it becomes part of a highway (we ensure that this happens at most once for every edge). This re-weighting signals later iterations to either use the prescribed highway or to find an alternative path whose short length can compensate for the lack of using the prescribed highway.

Therefore, if we generate a *new* highway in the path from x_0 to some z when we form $P(x_0, t, r)$, then (after re-weighting the highway) *the length of the path does not increase at all* (it increased by at most α, but length of at least 2α was

[1]By $g(n) \leq \tilde{O}(f(n))$ we mean that there exists some constant k such that $g(n) \leq O(f(n)) \cdot \log^k(f(n))$

reduced by 1/2). The other case is that no new highway is generated, which can only happen for the first cluster created (some of the highway edges may have been re-weighted already). In this case we turn to the idea of [3], that one may choose a certain *target* point y_1 and have that the shortest path connecting x_0 to y_1 will appear in the tree. Here we choose y_1 as the point leading to the first cluster. This approach implies that even though we may increase the radius, a constant fraction of the path is guaranteed not to increase ever again. We use a subtle inductive argument to make this intuition precise, and in fact we lose a factor of 2 for each of these cases, so the maximal increase is by a factor of 4. Note that one must always lose a factor of at least 2 for any spanning tree.

Constructing Petals: An alternative way to define cones $C(x_0, x, r)$ and petals $P(x_0, t, r)$ as a ball growing procedure on a directed graph shows their similarities. This view is essential for a fast algorithm to construct the petals. We shall elaborate more on this in Section 7.

1.2.2 Sparse Graph Decompositions

A basic tool that is often used in constructing tree metrics and spanning trees with low stretch is sparse graph decomposition. The idea is to partition the graph into small diameter pieces, such that few edges are cut. Each cluster of the decomposition is partitioned recursively, which yields a hierarchical decomposition. Creating a tree recursively on each cluster of the decomposition, and connecting these in a tree structure, will yield a spanning tree of the graph. The edges cut by the decomposition are potentially stretched by a factor proportional to the diameter of the created tree. The construction has to balance between these two goals: cut a small number of edges while maintaining small diameter in the created tree.

For a spanning tree we require both *strong diameter* partitions and control of the diameter increase. [12] build a tree with average stretch $O(\log^2 n \log\log n)$. A factor of $O(\log n \log\log n)$ is due to the partitions based on the approach of [19, 6] and another $O(\log n)$ is required to control the diameter of the tree. [3] have a factor of $O(\log n)$ due to the partitions based on the approach of [7, 1] and another $\tilde{O}(\log\log n)$ is required to control the diameter of the tree.

In this work, we show a new petal decomposition that incurs only a constant cost to control the diameter of the tree. We hoped that the partition cost would be based on local growth ratio bounds (as in [15, 7, 1, 3]) and this would lead to optimal average stretch. Known strong diameter partitions ([3]) that obtain a local growth ratio bound require to carefully choose the center of each cluster. However, our current petal decomposition approach does not allow to choose the centers arbitrarily and hence we could not use directly the technique of [3]. Therefore, we turn to the partitions of [12] which is the only reason for the extra $O(\log\log n)$ factor. It remains an open question whether one can construct an optimal strong diameter partition whose centers can be chosen arbitrarily. Our results show that this open question is the only barrier for obtaining an optimal low stretch tree.

1.3 Applications

One of the most important problems in algorithm design is obtaining fast algorithms for solving linear systems. For many applications the matrix is sparse, and while little is known for general sparse matrices, the case of Symmetric Diagonally Dominant (SDD) matrices has received a lot of attention recently. In a seminal sequence of results, Spielman and Teng [21] showed a near linear time solver for this important case. This solver has proven a powerful algorithmic tool, and is used to calculate eigenvalues, obtain spectral graph sparsifiers [20], approximate maximum flow [11] and in many more applications. A basic step in solving these systems $Ax = b$ is combinatorial preconditioning. If one uses the Laplacian matrix corresponding to a spanning tree (and few extra edges) of the graph whose Laplacian matrix is A, then the condition number depends on the total stretch of the tree. This will improve the run-time of iterative methods, such as Conjugate Gradient or Chebyshev iterations. See [16, 17] for the latest progress on this direction. In this work we show that one can construct such a spanning tree with both run-time and total stretch bounded by $O(m \log n \log\log n)$.

There are more applications for low stretch spanning trees, such as minimum cost communication spanning tree, we refer the reader to [12, 3] for more details.

1.4 Structure of the Paper

In Section 3 we describe the new petal-decomposition and prove some of its basic properties. In Section 4 we bound the total radius increase by a factor of 4. In Section 5 we analyze the total stretch, and provide the improved bound of $O(\log n \log\log n)$ on the average stretch proving the first statement of Theorem 1. In Section 7 we show an alternative view of forming a petal, similar to region growing techniques that concludes the proof of Theorem 1. In Section 6 we discuss briefly how to extend the result to weighted graphs.

2. PRELIMINARIES

Let $G = (V, E)$ be an unweighted undirected graph. For any $X \subseteq V$, $G(X)$ is the subgraph induced on X with edges $E(X) = \{(u, v) \in E \mid u, v \in X\}$. Denote by $E^+(X) = \{(u, v) \in E : |X \cap \{u, v\}| \geq 1\}$ the set of edges with at least one edge point in X, and by $\partial(X) = \{(u, v) \in E : |X \cap \{u, v\}| = 1\}$ the set of edges with exactly one end point in X. Let $d_X : X^2 \to \mathbb{R}^+$ be the shortest path metric in $G(X)$. Let $\mathrm{diam}(X) = \max_{y,z \in X}\{d_X(y, z)\}$. For $x \in X$ let $\mathrm{rad}_x(X) = \max_{y \in X}\{d_X(x, y)\}$, we omit the subscript when clear from context (note that $\mathrm{diam}(X)/2 \leq \mathrm{rad}(X) \leq \mathrm{diam}(X)$). For any $x \in X$ and $r \geq 0$ let $B_{(X,d_X)}(x, r) = \{y \in X \mid d_X(x, y) \leq r\}$.

For a spanning tree $T = T[X]$ of a subgraph X define the total stretch of T by

$$\mathrm{TS}[X] = \sum_{(u,v) \in E(X)} d_T(u, v) \ .$$

For $X \subseteq V$ and vertices $u, v \in X$, let $P_{uv} = P_{uv}(G(X))$ be a fixed shortest path between u, v in X (assuming that $G(X)$ is connected). We shall assume that there is a unique such path; This can be achieved, for example, by adding an imaginary random tiny amount to every edge length. Adding a path of length k starting at vertex v means that we set $v = u_0$, add new vertices $u_1, \ldots, u_k$ and add edges (u_{i-1}, u_i) for all $i \in \{1, \ldots, k\}$. By $T = \mathrm{BFS}_x(G(X))$ we mean the Breadth First Search tree rooted at x (the subscript is dropped when the center x is clear from context). Observe that for such a tree $d_T(x, y) = d_X(x, y)$ for all $y \in X$.

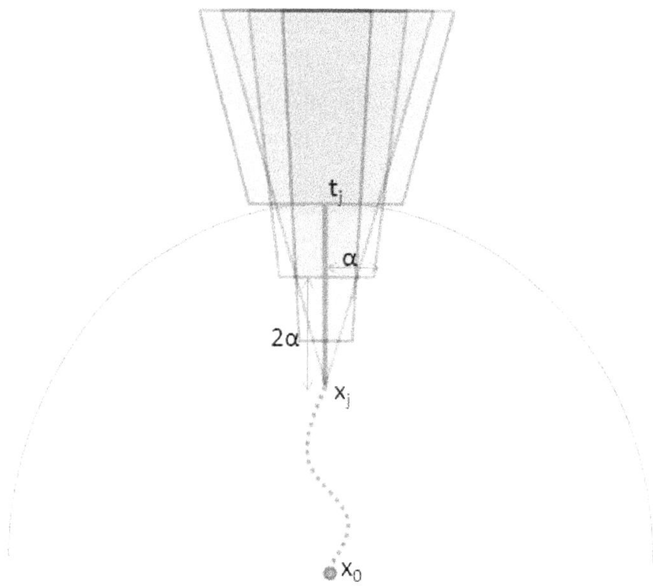

Figure 2: Definition of a petal with target t_j, center x_j and highway path $P_{x_j t_j}$. The side radius of each cone (that determines the maximum increase in the radius) is half of the highway path.

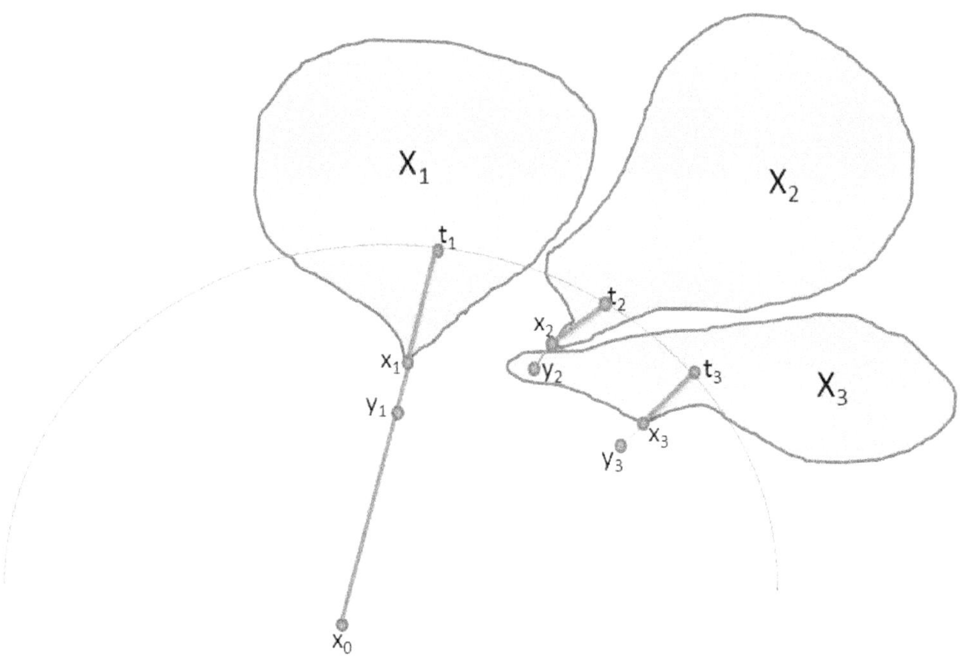

Figure 3: Creating the first three petals with their highways. The first portal is connected by a highway to x_0 (this means that the shortest path from x_0 to x_1 will be included in the final tree). Note that the portal edges do not necessarily connect the petal to the stigma, but may connect between petals. In this example, the portal node y_2 of X_2, is contained in the petal X_3. The algorithm guarantees that this cannot happen to the first portal node y_1 (thus y_1 will be a part of the stigma X_0).

DEFINITION 1 (CONE METRIC[2]). *For a graph $G=(V,E)$, subset $X\subseteq V$ and points $x,y\in X$, define the* cone-metric $\rho=\rho(X,x,y):X^2\to\mathbb{R}^+$ *as* $\rho(u,v)=|(d_X(x,u)-d_X(y,u))-(d_X(x,v)-d_X(y,v))|$.

Observe that this definition is slightly different from the definition given in [3] which is based on [12] (this one is less general). Note that a ball $B_{(X,\rho)}(y,r)$ in the cone-metric $\rho=\rho(X,x,y)$ is the set of all points $z\in X$ such that $d_X(x,y)+d_X(y,z)-d_X(x,z)\le r$.

3. PETAL-DECOMPOSITION

Hierarchical-petal-decomposition algorithm..
See Figure 4 for the algorithm. Let $G=(V,E)$ be an unweighted graph $G=(V,E)$. Here and in all that follows $n=|V|$ and $m=|E|$. Create a spanning tree $T=(V,E')$ by choosing some $x_0\in V$ and calling `hierarchical-petal-decomposition`(G,x_0,x_0).

3.1 Properties and Correctness

Fix some subset $X\subseteq V$, and consider running the `hierarchical-petal-decomposition` algorithm on $G(X)$, with some $x_0\in X$ and target $t\in X$. Denote by $\Delta=\mathrm{rad}_{x_0}(X)$. Let r_j be the radius chosen by the algorithm `create-petal` when it is invoked to create petal X_j. In order to show that the algorithm is correct, we need to show the following: that a tree is created, that every cluster is connected, and that for all integers $1\le j\le s$, $x_j,t_j\in X_j$. First we show that the shortest path from any $z\in Y_j$ to the center x_0 is fully contained in Y_j. This proof essentially appeared in [12, 3], and we give it for completeness.

CLAIM 1. *Let $1\le j\le s$ be an integer and let $z\in Y_j$, then $P_{x_0z}(X)\subseteq G(Y_j)$.*

PROOF. Seeking a contradiction, assume that $P_{x_0z}(X)\not\subseteq G(Y_j)$, and let $1\le h\le j$ be the minimal such that there exists $u\in P_{x_0z}(X)$ and $u\in X_h$. Let x_h and t_h be the center and target of the petal X_h, respectively. Let r_h be the radius that was chosen for creating X_h. Let p_k be the point on $P_{x_ht_h}$ of distance k from t_h such that $u\in B_{Y_{h-1},\rho(Y_{h-1},x_0,p_k)}(p_k,(r_h-k)/2)$. By Definition 1 this means that

$$d_{Y_{h-1}}(x_0,u)+(r_h-k)/2\ge d_{Y_{h-1}}(x_0,p_k)+d_{Y_{h-1}}(p_k,u)\ . \quad (2)$$

We claim that P_{x_0z} is fully contained in $G(Y_{h-1})$: if $h>1$ then it holds by the minimality of h, otherwise, this holds as $Y_0=X$. Since u lies on P_{x_0z}, it follows that $d_{Y_{h-1}}(x_0,z)=d_{Y_{h-1}}(x_0,u)+d_{Y_{h-1}}(u,z)$. Now

$$\begin{aligned}&d_{Y_{h-1}}(x_0,z)+(r_h-k)/2\\ &= d_{Y_{h-1}}(x_0,u)+(r_h-k)/2+d_{Y_{h-1}}(u,z)\\ &\overset{(2)}{\ge} d_{Y_{h-1}}(x_0,p_k)+d_{Y_{h-1}}(p_k,u)+d_{Y_{h-1}}(u,z)\\ &\ge d_{Y_{h-1}}(x_0,p_k)+d_{Y_{h-1}}(p_k,z)\ ,\end{aligned}$$

hence $z\in B_{Y_{h-1},\rho(Y_{h-1},x_0,p_k)}(p_k,(r_h-k)/2)$ and thus also in X_h, contradiction. □

COROLLARY 2. *The cluster X_0 is connected.*

PROOF. Applying Claim 1 to $Y_s=X_0$, we conclude that if $z\in X_0$ it is connected to x_0. □

OBSERVATION 3. *For each $j\ge 1$, $P_{x_jt_j}(X)\subseteq G(X_j)$.*

PROOF. As x_j was chosen on the shortest path connecting x_0 to t_j, and since by Claim 1 $P_{x_0t_j}(X)\subseteq Y_{j-1}$, we get that by definition of cone-metric $d_{(Y_{j-1},\rho(Y_{j-1},x_0,x_j))}(x_j,p)=0$ for all $p\in P_{x_jt_j}$. This suggests that $P_{x_jt_j}(X)\subseteq G(X_j)$. □

COROLLARY 4. *For each integer $j\ge 1$, X_j is connected.*

PROOF. By Observation 3, $P_{x_jt_j}$ is fully contained in $G(X_j)$, and since X_j is a union of balls (in a cone metric) centered at the points of $P_{x_jt_j}$, it is connected. □

OBSERVATION 5. *Algorithm* `create-petal`(X,Y,t,x_0,R) *chooses a radius $r\in[R/2,R]$.*

PROOF. This follows from Claim 14. □

The following two claims are similar to claims proven in [12, 3], we provide proofs for completeness.

CLAIM 6. $\Delta/4\le\mathrm{rad}_{x_0}(X_0)\le\Delta/2$.

PROOF. For the upper bound, note that for any $j\ge 1$, if there is a point in $Y_{j-1}\setminus B(x_0,\Delta/2)$ we continue creating petals, therefore $Y_s\setminus B(x_0,\Delta/2)=\emptyset$ and $X_0=Y_s\subseteq B(x_0,\Delta/2)$.

To see the lower bound, observe that Claim 1 implies that for any $j\ge 1$, $d_{Y_{j-1}}(x_0,t_j)=r_0=\Delta/2$, and also by Observation 5 we have that the radius r_j chosen for each of the petals, satisfies $r_j\le\Delta/4$. Consider some $z\in X$ with $d_X(x_0,z)<\Delta/4$, we will show that $z\in X_0$. For any $0\le k\le r_j$ and $p_k\in P_{x_jt_j}$ of distance k from t_j,

$$\begin{aligned}d_{Y_{j-1}}(z,p_k)+d_{Y_{j-1}}(p_k,x_0) &= d_{Y_{j-1}}(z,p_k)+d_X(p_k,x_0)\\ &\ge d_X(p_k,x_0)\\ &\ge \Delta/2-k\\ &\ge \Delta/4+(\Delta/4-k)/2\\ &> d_X(x_0,z)+(r_j-k)/2\ .\end{aligned}$$

By the definition of cone metric, this implies that $z\notin X_j$, for all $j\ge 1$. □

CLAIM 7. *For each $1\le j\le s$, $\mathrm{rad}_{x_j}(X_j)\le 7\Delta/8$.*

PROOF. Fix some integer $1\le j\le s$. We already know by Observation 3 that $P_{x_jt_j}(X)\subseteq G(X_j)$, recall that the petal X_j is created by union over balls (in a cone-metric) centered at the points of $P_{x_jt_j}(X)$. By Observation 5 the radius of each ball is bounded by $r_j\le\Delta/4$, and we also have by Claim 6 that

$$d_X(x_0,x_j)\ge\Delta/4\ . \quad (3)$$

Let $y\in X_j$, we will show that $d_{X_j}(x_j,y)\le 7\Delta/8$. Let $0\le k\le r_j$ and $p_k\in P_{x_jt_j}$ of distance k from t_j such that $y\in B_{(Y_{j-1},\rho(Y_{j-1},x_0,p_k))}(p_k,(r_j-k)/2)$. By definition of cone-metric and using Claim 1

$$\begin{aligned}d_X(x_0,p_k)+d_{Y_{j-1}}(p_k,y) &= d_{Y_{j-1}}(x_0,p_k)+d_{Y_{j-1}}(p_k,y)\\ &\le d_{Y_{j-1}}(x_0,y)+(r_j-k)/2\\ &= d_X(x_0,y)+(r_j-k)/2\\ &\le 9\Delta/8\ . \quad (4)\end{aligned}$$

Also note that $P_{x_0p_k}\subseteq Y_{j-1}$, so $d_{Y_{j-1}}(x_j,p_k)=d_X(x_j,p_k)$, thus we conclude that

$$\begin{aligned}d_{X_j}(x_j,y) &\le d_{Y_{j-1}}(x_j,p_k)+d_{Y_{j-1}}(p_k,y)\\ &\overset{(4)}{\le} d_X(x_j,p_k)+9\Delta/8-d_X(x_0,p_k)\\ &= 9\Delta/8-d_X(x_0,x_j)\overset{(3)}{\le} 9\Delta/8-\Delta/4=7\Delta/8\ .\end{aligned}$$

$T = $ `hierarchical-petal-decomposition`$(G(X), x_0, t)$:

1. If $\mathrm{rad}_{x_0}(X) \le 10 \log n \log\log n$ return BFS$(G(X))$.
2. $(X_0, \ldots, X_s, (y_1, x_1), \ldots, (y_s, x_s), t_0, \ldots, t_s) = $ `petal-decomposition`$(G(X), x_0, t)$;
3. For each $j \in [0, \ldots, s]$:
   (a) Set all the edges in $P_{x_j t_j}$ to be of weight $1/2$;
   (b) $T_j = $ `hierarchical-petal-decomposition`$(G(X_j), x_j, t_j)$;
4. Let T be the tree formed by connecting $T_0, \ldots, T_s$ using the edges $(y_1, x_1), \ldots, (y_s, x_s)$;

Figure 4: `hierarchical-petal-decomposition` **algorithm**

$(X_0, \ldots, X_s, (y_1, x_1), \ldots, (y_s, x_s), t_0, \ldots, t_s) = $ `petal-decomposition`$(G(X), x_0, t)$:

1. Let $\Delta = \mathrm{rad}_{x_0}(X)$; Let $r_0 = \Delta/2$; $Y_0 = X$; Set $j = 2$;
2. Creating the first petal X_1:
   (a) If $d_X(x_0, t) < r_0$, add to $G(X)$ a path $(u_0, u_1, \ldots, u_l)$ of length $l = r_0 - d_X(x_0, t)$ starting at $t = u_0$; Let $t'_1 = t_1 = u_l$; Otherwise, let $t_1 = t$ and let t'_1 be a vertex on $P_{x_0 t}$ such that $d_X(x_0, t'_1) = r_0$;
   (b) Let $(X_1, x_1) = $ `create-petal`$(X, X, t'_1, x_0, \Delta/4)$; $Y_1 = Y_0 \setminus X_1$;
   (c) Let y_1 be the neighbor of x_1 on $P_{x_0 t'_1}$ that is closer to x_0;
3. Creating the remaining petals $X_2, \ldots, X_s$:
   (a) While $Y_{j-1} \setminus B_X(x_0, r_0) \neq \emptyset$:
      i. Let $t_j \in Y_{j-1}$ be an arbitrary point satisfying $d_X(x_0, t_j) = r_0$;
      ii. Let $(X_j, x_j) = $ `create-petal`$(X, Y_{j-1}, t_j, x_0, \Delta/8)$; $Y_j = Y_{j-1} \setminus X_j$;
      iii. Let y_j be the neighbor of x_j on $P_{x_0 t_j}$ that is closer to x_0;
      iv. Let $j = j + 1$;
   (b) Let $s = j - 1$;
4. Creating the stigma X_0:
   (a) Let $X_0 = Y_s$; Let $t_0 = y_1$;

Figure 5: `petal-decomposition` **algorithm**

$(W, x) = $ `create-petal`(X, Y, t, x_0, R):

1. Let $W_r = \bigcup_{p \in P_{x_0 t} \,:\, d_Y(p,t) \le r} B_{(Y, \rho(Y, x_0, p))}(p, (r - d_Y(p,t))/2)$;
2. Let $L = \lceil \log\log n \rceil$; Let $1 \le p \le L$ be the minimal integer satisfying $|E(W_{(1+p/L)R/2})| \le \frac{2|E(X)|}{2^{\log^{1-p/L} m}}$; Set $a = (1 + (p-1)/L) \cdot R/2$;
3. Set $r = a$; Fix $\chi = \frac{|E(X)|}{|E(W_a)|}$;
4. Increase r as long as $|\partial(W_r)| \ge |E(W_r)| \cdot \frac{8L \ln \chi}{R}$.
5. Return (W_r, p_r).

Figure 6: `create-petal` **algorithm**

□

COROLLARY 8. $y_1 \in X_0$.

PROOF. Using Observation 5 we have that the radius of X_1 is at least $\Delta/8$, while the radius of any X_j with $j > 1$ is at most $\Delta/8$. Similarly to the proof of Claim 6 we have that all the t_j are of distance $\Delta/2$ from x_0. This suggests that $d_X(x_0, y_1) < 3\Delta/8$ and for $j > 1$ any point $u \in X_j$ satisfy $d_X(x_0, u) \geq 3\Delta/8$, so none of the X_j will contain y_1, thus $y_1 \in X_0$. □

CLAIM 9. $P_{x_0t}(X) \subseteq G(X_0 \cup X_1)$.

PROOF. If $t \in X_0$ then by Claim 1, $P_{x_0t}(G(X)) \subseteq G(X_0)$. Otherwise, the choice of t_1 guarantees that $P_{x_0t} \subseteq P_{x_0t_1}$. Observe that the edge (y_1, x_1) lies on this path, which is decomposed into $P_{x_0y_1}$ and $P_{x_1t_1}$. By Corollary 8 $y_1 \in X_0$, so by Claim 1, $P_{x_0y_1} \subseteq G(X_0)$, and also by Observation 3 $P_{x_1t_1} \subseteq G(X_1)$. □

CLAIM 10. *When invoking the algorithm* `hierarchical-petal-decomposition`$(G(X), x_0, t)$, *the only edges of* $G(X)$ *that are set to* $1/2$ *are those on* $P_{x_0t}(G(X))$.

PROOF. We will prove by induction on the depth of the recursion of `hierarchical-petal-decomposition`. The base case is trivial as V has x_0 as target. Assume by induction that X with center x_0 has a target t and only edges on P_{x_0t} are set to $1/2$. We partition X into $X_0, X_1, \ldots, X_s$, and we prove for these clusters.

For X_0 with x_0 as center and target y_1, which was chosen on $P_{x_0t_1}$. As $t \in P_{x_0t_1}$ as well, and all the edges after y_1 are no longer in X_0, it must be that the edges set by X to $1/2$ are all on $P_{x_0y_1}$.

For X_1 with center x_1 and target t_1, which was chosen either as t or on a new path $(t = u_0, \ldots, u_l = t_1)$. As x_1 is on $P_{x_0t_1}$ all the edges set by X to $1/2$ that are in X_1 are those on P_{x_1t}. These edge are a subset of the edges X_1 is setting to $1/2$.

For integer $j \geq 2$ and X_j, by Claim 9 all the edges set to $1/2$ by X lie in $G(X_0 \cup X_1)$, so X_j will contain only the edges that itself sets to $1/2$, which are on $P_{x_jt_j}$.

□

CLAIM 11. *The algorithm returns a tree.*

PROOF. Assume by induction on the size of $G(X)$ that running `hierarchical-petal-decomposition` on $G(X)$ returns a tree. The base case is trivial for $|X| = 1$. Let $X \subseteq V$ be a cluster that is partitioned by `petal-decomposition` algorithm into $X_0, X_1, \ldots, X_s$. By the induction hypothesis, running the algorithm on every subgraph $G(X_j)$ returns a tree T_j. Since every T_j contains $|X_j| - 1$ edges and we add s edges to create T, the total number of edges in the tree T created from X is $|X| - 1$. It remains to show that there are no cycles. Seeking a contradiction, assume that there is a cycle. Since the edges $(x_1, y_1), \ldots, (x_s, y_s)$ are not inside any cluster X_j, it must be that the cycle is not fully contained in a single X_j. Let $h \geq 1$ be the minimal integer such that the cycle contains vertices from X_h, thus there are at least 2 cycle edges leaving X_h. Observe that every edge (x_j, y_j) we added satisfies $y_j \in Y_j$, so $y_j \in X_k \cup X_0$ for some $k > j$. This means that only (x_h, y_h) can connect X_h to the other clusters in the cycle. All the other edges are either fully contained in some X_j, the (x_j, y_j) edges for $j > h$ cannot touch X_h, and for $j < h$, the minimality of h implies that there is no cycle edge touching X_j. □

4. RADIUS BOUND

Let T be the tree created by calling `hierarchical-petal-decomposition` on G with center and target x_0, and let d_T be the shortest path metric in T, with respect to the *original* edge weights. Denote by $G^{(0)} = \{V\}$, and for integer $i \geq 1$, $G^{(i)}$ is the collection of clusters created from $G^{(i-1)}$ by performing `petal-decomposition` on every cluster of $G^{(i-1)}$, and applying the new edge weight of $1/2$ on the appropriate edges as defined in `hierarchical-petal-decomposition`. For any cluster $X \in G^{(i)}$ let $d_i = d_i(X)$ be the shortest path metric induced on $G(X)$. Since the clusters in $G^{(i)}$ are pairwise disjoint, we abuse notation and write only d_i (the cluster is inferred from context). We begin by showing that the shortest path from a center to its target and to the first petal always exists in the tree T.

CLAIM 12. *Fix some integer* $i \geq 0$. *Let* $X \in G^{(i)}$ *be a cluster with center* x_0 *and target* t, *then the following holds*

$$d_T(x_0, y_1) \leq 2d_i(x_0, y_1) \ . \tag{5}$$

PROOF. We prove by induction on i that

- $d_T(x_0, y_1) \leq 2d_i(x_0, y_1)$,
- $d_T(x_0, t) = 2d_i(x_0, t)$.

First we prove the second bullet: by the induction hypothesis on $X_0 \in G^{(i+1)}$ with center x_0 and target which is by construction y_1, $d_T(x_0, y_1) = 2d_{i+1}(x_0, y_1) \leq 2d_i(x_0, y_1)$, where the last inequality holds because $P_{x_0y_1}(X) \subseteq G(X_0)$ (using Corollary 8 to see that $y_1 \in X_0$ then by Claim 1), and in d_{i+1} we may set additional edges on this path to $1/2$.

Next we prove the second bullet. If it is the case that $t \in X_0$, then by Claim 1 also $P_{x_0t}(X) \subseteq G(X_0)$. When forming X_1 we added a new path $P = (t = u_0, \ldots, u_l)$, and since $t \in X_0$ it must be that $(y_1, x_1) \in P$, so $t \in P_{x_0y_1}$. By induction on X_0 with center x_0 and target y_1, we get that $d_T(x_0, y_1) = 2d_{i+1}(x_0, y_1)$. Since t lies on this shortest path, also

$$d_T(x_0, t) = 2d_{i+1}(x_0, t) = 2d_i(x_0, t) \ ,$$

where the last equality holds because edges on P_{x_0t} are already set to $1/2$ in d_i. By Claim 9 the only other case is that $t \in X_1$, in which case we have as above that $P_{x_0y_1}(X) \subseteq G(X_0)$ and by Observation 3 also $P_{x_1t}(X) \subseteq G(X_1)$. By applying induction on X_0 (with center x_0 and target y_1) and on X_1 (with center x_1 and target t_1, where $t \in P_{x_1t_1}$), and noting that $(y_1, x_1) \in P_{x_0t}$ was added to T, we get that

$$\begin{aligned} d_T(x_0, t) &= d_T(x_0, y_1) + d_T(y_1, x_1) + d_T(x_1, t) \\ &= 2d_{i+1}(x_0, y_1) + 2d_i(y_1, x_1) + 2d_{i+1}(x_1, t) \\ &= 2d_i(x_0, t) \ . \end{aligned}$$

□

LEMMA 13. *For any* $i \geq 1$ *and any cluster* $X \in G^{(i)}$,

$$\mathrm{rad}(T[X]) \leq 4\mathrm{rad}(X) \ .$$

PROOF. It suffices to prove by induction on i that for any cluster $X \in G^{(i)}$ with center x_0 and target t, and for any $y \in X$

$$d_T(x_0, y) \leq 4d_i(x_0, y) \ . \tag{6}$$

Assume X is partitioned into clusters $X_0, X_1, \ldots, X_s$. There are three cases to consider: $y \in X_0$, $y \in X_1$ and $y \in X_j$ with

$j > 1$. Before showing the formal proof, the following is a high level description of these cases. Case 1 follows trivially by induction. Case 2 requires us to exploit the highway leading to the first portal, thus the path from x_0 to the first portal will surely appear in the tree Claim 12. The third case crucially uses the definition of petals and the re-weighting of the highways. For every point y in a petal, the re-weighting of the petal highway leading to y compensates for the increased distance incurred by its location in the petal.

Case 1.

$y \in X_0$. By Claim 1 $P_{x_0 y}(X) \subseteq X_0$. Applying the induction hypothesis on X_0 with the metric $d_{i+1} = d_{i+1}(X_0)$ we obtain that $d_T(x_0, y) \leq 4d_{i+1}(x_0, y) \leq 4d_i(x_0, y)$. The last inequality holds since the shortest path $P_{x_0 y}(X_0)$ can be the same as $P_{x_0 y}(X)$, and we might have made some edges even shorter. This concludes the first case.

In the other two cases $y \in X_j$ for some $j \geq 1$. We now introduce some notation and show properties that hold in these two cases. Let r_j be the radius chosen by `create-petal` for creating X_j. Fix some $j \geq 1$. For every $0 \leq \ell \leq r_j$ define $p_\ell = p_\ell^{(j)} \in P_{x_j t_j}$ be the point of distance ℓ from t_j. From here on fix any $0 \leq k \leq r_j$ such that $y \in B_{(Y_{j-1}, \rho(Y_{j-1}, x_0, p_k))}(p_k, (r_j - k)/2)$ (note that k is not unique). By definition of a ball in a cone-metric

$$d_i(x_0, p_k) + d_{Y_{j-1}}(p_k, y) \leq d_i(x_0, y) + (r_j - k)/2 \ , \quad (7)$$

we may write d_i instead of $d_{Y_{j-1}}$ because by Claim 1 we have that $d_i(x_0, z) = d_{Y_{j-1}}(x_0, z)$ for all $z \in Y_{j-1}$. We shall use the following observations:

$$d_{i+1}(p_k, y) \leq d_{Y_{j-1}}(p_k, y) \quad (8)$$
$$d_i(x_0, x_j) + d_i(x_j, p_k) = d_i(x_0, p_k) \ . \quad (9)$$

To see (8), note that when taking a cone in the metric Y_{j-1} centered at p_k that contains y, it must also contain the entire shortest path from p_k to y, $P_{p_k y}(Y_{j-1})$. The inequality follows because distances in X_j can only be made shorter due to re-weighting. For (9), this is simply because x_j is p_{r_j}, and all p_k are on the shortest path from t_j to x_0.

Case 2.

$y \in X_1$. In this case we have the following

$$d_{i+1}(x_1, p_k) \leq d_i(x_1, p_k) \ , \quad (10)$$

because $x_1 \in P_{x_0 p_k}(X)$, by Observation 3 we have that $P_{x_1 p_k}(X)$ is fully contained in X_1. The inequality follows because distances in X_1 can only be made shorter due to re-weighting.

By Claim 6 it follows that

$$2d_i(x_0, x_1) \geq \Delta/2 \quad (11)$$

By Observation 5 we have that

$$2(r_1 - k) \leq 2r_1 \leq \Delta/2 \ . \quad (12)$$

Recall that $Y_{j-1} = Y_0 = X$, hence $d_{Y_{j-1}} = d_i$. By the induction hypothesis on X_1,

$$\begin{aligned} d_T(x_0, y) & \\ &\leq d_T(x_0, y_1) + d_T(y_1, x_1) + d_T(x_1, y) \\ &\overset{(5)\wedge(6)}{\leq} 2d_i(x_0, y_1) + 2d_i(y_1, x_1) + 4d_{i+1}(x_1, y) \\ &\leq 2d_i(x_0, x_1) + 4d_{i+1}(x_1, p_k) + 4d_{i+1}(p_k, y) \\ &\overset{(8)\wedge(10)}{\leq} 4(d_i(x_0, x_1) + d_i(x_1, p_k) + d_i(p_k, y)) - 2d_i(x_0, x_1) \\ &\overset{(9)}{=} 4(d_i(x_0, p_k) + d_i(p_k, y)) - 2d_i(x_0, x_1) \\ &\overset{(7)}{\leq} 4(d_i(x_0, y) + (r_1 - k)/2) - 2d_i(x_0, x_1) \\ &\overset{(11)\wedge(12)}{\leq} 4d_i(x_0, y) \ . \end{aligned}$$

This concludes the proof for the second case.

Case 3.

Let us introduce some more notation. The *petal-tree* of a petal-decomposition on a subgraph $G(X)$ is a graph $H = (W, F)$, where $W = \{X_0, X_1, \ldots, X_s\}$ and $(X_h, X_{h'}) \in F$ iff $y_h \in X_{h'}$ or $y_{h'} \in X_h$ (that is, if the clusters are connected by one of the portal edges). Claim 11 suggests that W is a tree. Let X_0 be the root of the tree, and let $\text{rank}(X_h)$ denote the depth of X_h in W. Observe that in the case $j \geq 2$, we have the following

$$d_i(x_j, p_k) = 2d_{i+1}(x_j, p_k) \ , \quad (13)$$

this holds because when $j > 1$, Claim 9 and Claim 10 suggests that the edges along $P_{x_j t_j}$ were not set to $1/2$ in d_i, so by Observation 3 the shortest path $P_{x_j t_j} \subseteq X_j$, and when these edges are set to $1/2$ in d_{i+1}, we reduce the shortest path distance by a factor of 2.

We will prove (6) in the case $y \in X_j$, $j \geq 2$, by induction on $\text{rank}(X_j)$. The base case is when the rank is 1 and then it must be that $y_j \in X_0$. In this case by Claim 1 $P_{x_0 y_j} \subseteq G(X_0)$, so

$$d_{i+1}(x_0, y_j) \leq d_i(x_0, y_j) \ . \quad (14)$$

By the induction hypothesis of (6) on both X_0 and X_j,

$$\begin{aligned} d_T(x_0, y) & \\ &\leq d_T(x_0, y_j) + d_T(y_j, x_j) + d_T(x_j, y) \\ &\overset{(6)}{\leq} 4d_{i+1}(x_0, y_j) + 2d_i(y_j, x_j) + 4d_{i+1}(x_j, y) \\ &\overset{(14)}{\leq} 4(d_i(x_0, y_j) + d_i(y_j, x_j) + d_{i+1}(x_j, p_k) + d_{i+1}(p_k, y)) \\ &\overset{(13)\wedge(8)}{\leq} 4d_i(x_0, x_j) + 2d_i(x_j, p_k) + 4d_{Y_{j-1}}(p_k, y) \\ &\overset{(9)}{=} 4(d_i(x_0, p_k) + d_{Y_{j-1}}(p_k, y)) - 2d_i(x_j, p_k) \\ &\overset{(7)}{\leq} 4(d_i(x_0, y) + (r_j - k)/2) - 2(r_j - k) \\ &= 4d_i(x_0, y) \ . \end{aligned}$$

Now to prove for the case $\text{rank}(X_j) > 1$. Let $h \in [s]$ be such that $(X_j, X_h) \in F$ and $\text{rank}(X_h) = \text{rank}(X_j) - 1$. Observe that h is unique since H is a tree, and by definition of tank $y_j \in X_h$. By the induction on the rank,

$$d_T(x_0, y_j) \leq 4d_i(x_0, y_j) \ . \quad (15)$$

And finally

$$
\begin{aligned}
&d_T(x_0, y)\\
&\leq d_T(x_0, y_j) + d_T(y_j, x_j) + d_T(x_j, y)\\
&\overset{(6)\wedge(15)}{\leq} 4d_i(x_0, y_j) + 2d_i(y_j, x_j) + 4d_{i+1}(x_j, y)\\
&\leq 4(d_i(x_0, y_j) + d_i(y_j, x_j) + d_{i+1}(x_j, p_k) + d_{i+1}(p_k, y))\\
&\overset{(13)\wedge(8)}{\leq} 4d_i(x_0, x_j) + 2d_i(x_j, p_k) + 4d_{Y_{j-1}}(p_k, y)\\
&\overset{(9)}{=} 4(d_i(x_0, p_k) + d_{Y_{j-1}}(p_k, y)) - 2d_i(x_j, p_k)\\
&\overset{(7)}{\leq} 4(d_i(x_0, y) + (r_j - k)/2) - 2(r_j - k)\\
&= 4d_i(x_0, y) .
\end{aligned}
$$

This concludes the inductive proof.

□

5. ANALYSIS OF TOTAL STRETCH

Recall that we apply `hierarchical-petal-decomposition` on the graph $G = (V, E)$ with center and target x_0. We prove that the total stretch is bounded by $O(m \log n \log\log n)$. The proof is very similar to the proof of [12], and we give the details for completeness. Consider a single run of the algorithm `create-petal` on input (X, Y, t, x_0, R). Let $1 \leq p \leq L$ be as in the algorithm, and let $a = (1 + (p-1)/L) \cdot R/2$ and $b = (1 + p/L) \cdot R/2$.

Claim 14. *The algorithm `create-petal` finds $r \in [a, b]$ satisfying*

$$|\partial(W_r)| < |E(W_r)| \cdot \frac{8L \ln \chi}{R} . \quad (16)$$

Proof. Assume w.l.o.g that $R/2$ is even. First let us observe a basic property of our partition scheme, that if for some edge $(u, v) \in E$, $u \in W_r$, then $v \in W_{r+2}$. This holds simply because increasing r by 2 increases the radius of each cone in the petal by 1, and since cones are concentric system (see [12]), and u belongs to some cone, we have that v will be included in that cone as well. This property enables us to claim that $|E(W_{r+2})| \geq |E(W_r)| + |\partial(W_r)|$.

Assume by contradiction that there is no such $r \in [a, b]$, then for all $r \in [a, b-2]$,

$$|E(W_{r+2})| \geq |E(W_r)| + |\partial(W_r)| \geq |E(W_r)| \left(1 + \frac{8L \ln \chi}{R}\right),$$

Recall that $\chi = \frac{|E(X)|}{|E(W_a)|}$, and note that since $R \geq 10L \log n$, $(8L \ln \chi)/R \leq 1$ and thus $(1 + \frac{8L \ln \chi}{R}) \geq e^{(4L \ln \chi)/R} = \chi^{4L/R}$. Now

$$
\begin{aligned}
|E(W_b)| &\geq |E(W_{b-2})| \left(1 + \frac{8 \ln \chi}{R}\right)\\
&\geq |E(W_{b-4})| \left(1 + \frac{8 \ln \chi}{R}\right)^2\\
&\geq \cdots \geq |E(W_a)| \left(1 + \frac{8 \ln \chi}{R}\right)^{(b-a)/2}\\
&\geq |E(W_a)| \cdot \chi^{4L/R \cdot (b-a)/2}\\
&= |E(X)| ,
\end{aligned}
$$

but this is a contradiction. □

Consider now the algorithm `petal-decomposition` invoked on $G(X)$ with center x_0 and target t. It decomposes X into $X_0, X_1, \ldots, X_s$ (for some integer $s \geq 1$). For $j \in [s]$, let χ_j be the value defined at line 4. of `choose-radius` when creating the petal X_j, and denote by the index(X_j) the value of p chosen in line 3. By minimality of p, $|E(W_a)| \geq \frac{2|E(X)|}{2^{\log^{1-(p-1)/L} m}}$, so that

$$\ln \chi_j \leq 2 \log^{1-(p-1)/L} m \leq 5 \log^{1-p/L} m , \quad (17)$$

(the last inequality is because $\log^{1/L} m = 2^{\log\log m/\log\log n} \leq 5/2$). Also observe that if some edge $(u, v) \in E$ is separated while decomposing the cluster X with radius Δ, then by Lemma 13

$$d_T(u, v) \leq 2\text{rad}(T[X]) \leq 8\Delta . \quad (18)$$

Let avg stretch(BFS) denote the total stretch over all clusters whose radius was smaller than $10 \log n \log\log n$ and thus we created a BFS tree. Observe that avg stretch(BFS) $= O(m \log n \log\log n)$, so this will add at most an additive factor to the total stretch, and we may ignore it. We now start to calculate the total stretch:

$$
\begin{aligned}
&\text{TS}[X]\\
&\overset{(18)}{\leq} \sum_{j=1}^{s} (\text{TS}[X_j] + |\partial(X_j)| \cdot 8\Delta) \quad (19)\\
&\overset{(16)}{\leq} \sum_{j=1}^{s} (\text{TS}[X_j] + 8^3 L |E(X_j)| \cdot \ln \chi_j)\\
&\overset{(17)}{\leq} \sum_{j=1}^{s} \text{TS}[X_j] + O(L) \sum_{p=1}^{L} \sum_{j:\text{index}(X_j)=p} |E(X_j)| \cdot \log^{1-p/L} m
\end{aligned}
$$

Let us fix some edge $e \in E$, and analyze its contribution to (19). For every recursive level i in which $e \in E(X_j)$ with $p = \text{index}(X_j)$ it contributed $O(L) \cdot \log^{1-p/L} m$. However by the choice of p, and by Claim 14 the radius r chosen for creating X_j satisfies $r \leq b$, so $|E(X_j)| \leq |E(W_b)| \leq \frac{2|E(X)|}{2^{\log^{1-p/L} m}}$. Intuitively, if p is small and thus the contribution is rather large, the size of the next cluster that contains e becomes much smaller, so e will participate in few more levels. In particular, if the contribution to the total stretch of e in some level is $O(L \cdot i)$, then the number of edges in the cluster containing e is reduced by a factor of $\Omega(2^i)$. Since the number of times the number of edges can halve is at most $O(\log m)$, we get that the total contribution of each edge is at most $O(L \cdot \log m) = O(\log\log\log n)$.

Formally, let $\ell_p(e)$ denote the number of recursive levels i in which e was in a cluster of index p. Then the number of edges in the clusters containing e decreased by a factor of at least $2^{\log^{1-p/L} m - 1}$, for every one of the $\ell_p(e)$ levels, so the total decrease is

$$\prod_{p=1}^{L} 2^{\ell_p(e) \cdot (\log^{1-p/L} m - 1)} \leq m ,$$

because we started with m edges. This suggest that

$$\sum_{p=1}^{L} \ell_p(e)(\log^{1-p/L} m) \leq 2 \log m ,$$

where we used that $\sum_{p=1}^{L} \ell_p(e) \le \log n \le \log m$. Finally,

$$\begin{aligned} \mathrm{TS}[V] &\le O(L) \sum_{e \in E} \sum_{p=1}^{L} \ell_p(e) \log^{1-p/L} m \\ &= O(Lm \log m) \\ &= O(m \log n \log\log n) \ . \end{aligned}$$

6. EXTENSION TO WEIGHTED GRAPHS

Both papers [12, 3] already showed how to deal with arbitrary weights on the edges. There are two ideas: the first is to contract edges shorter than $\mathrm{rad}(X)/n^2$, so that each edge participates in a logarithmic number of scales. The second is to add imaginary portal points when constructing cones, so that the algorithm is well defined. In our algorithm, in line 3.a of `hierarchical-petal-decomposition` we simply set the weight of edges to be 1/2 of their original length, and observe that the analysis did not use the fact that edges have unit length.

For the analysis of stretch, the only real change is the proof of Claim 14, which still holds for weighted graphs, replacing $E(W_r)$ with $E^+(W_r)$ on the right hand side, see [12] for a proof. This does not affect the total stretch by more than a factor of 2 because by (16), $2|E(W_r)| \ge |E^+(W_r)|$.

7. FAST PETAL CONSTRUCTION

In order to bound the running time of our algorithm, we need to argue that the petal construction can be performed efficiently. It is shown in [17] how to construct a star-decomposition on $G(X) = (V, E)$ in time $O(|E| + |V| \log k)$, where k is the number of distinct edge weights. This factor essentially comes from running an improved version of Dijkstra's algorithm for computing shortest path from the center of the cluster, introduced by [18]. By rounding down weights to the nearest power of 2, we change distances by a factor of 2, and in every level there will be at most $O(\log n)$ different edge weights. As there are $O(\log n)$ scales in which any edge is active, we conclude that the total running time will be $O((m + n \log\log n) \cdot \log n)$. It remains to see that both cones and petals may be constructed efficiently, by a region growing scheme.

Given a weighted undirected graph $G = (V, E, w)$, let p_k be the point of distance k from t on the shortest path P_{tx} from t to x, and all distances d are with respect to G. Let $\tilde{G} = (V, A, w')$ be the weighted directed graph induced by adding the two edges $(u \to v), (v \to u) \in A$ for each $(u, v) \in E$, and setting $w'(u \to v) = d(u, v) - (d(v, x) - d(u, x))$. The cone $C(x, t, r)$ is simply the ball around t of radius r in $\tilde{G}$. The Petal $P(x, t, r)$ is the ball around t of radius $r/2$ in $\tilde{G}$ with one change: the weight of each edge $(p_i \to p_{i+1})$ is changed to $w(p_i, p_{i+1})/2$ for all $i < r$. Recall that the petal with center x, target t and radius r was defined in the algorithm as
$W_r = \bigcup_{p \in P_{xt} \,:\, d(p,t) \le r} B_{(V, \rho(V,x,p))}(p, (r - d(p, t))/2)$.

Claim 15. $P(x, t, r) = W_r$.

Proof. First we prove that for any $r \ge 0$, $W_r \subseteq P(x, t, r)$. Fix some $v \in W_r$, and let $0 \le k \le r$ be such that $v \in B_{(V, \rho(V,x,p_k))}(p_k, (r-k)/2)$. Observe that by the re-weighting of the edges from t to p_k we have that the length of the directed path P_{tp_k} in $\tilde{G}$ is $k/2$. It remains to show that there is a path in $\tilde{G}$ from p_k to v of length at most $(r - k)/2$. By definition of cone metric we have that $d(v, p_k) + d(p_k, x) \le d(v, x) + (r - k)/2$. Let $p_k = u_0, u_1, \ldots, u_l = v$ be the shortest path in G from p_k to v, then by definition of w' it follows that

$$\begin{aligned} \sum_{j=1}^{l} w'(u_{j-1} \to u_j) &= \sum_{j=1}^{l} d(u_{j-1}, u_j) - d(u_j, x) + d(u_{j-1}, x) \\ &= d(p_k, v) - d(v, x) + d(p_k, x) \\ &\le (r - k)/2 \ , \end{aligned}$$

as required.

Let $0 = r_1 < r_2 < \cdots < r_k$ be all the possible radii for which the size of $P(x, t, r)$ changes. We prove that $P(x, t, r) \subseteq W_r$ by induction on the radius. The base case for $r_1 = 0$, then $W_0 = \{y : d(y, x) = d(y, t) + d(t, x)\}$, and $P(x, t, 0)$ will contain all points reachable with 0 weight edges, by definition these edges $(u \to v)$ are the ones that satisfy $d(v, x) - d(u, x) = d(u, v)$, so any path leaving t using these edges will lead to a point y for which $d(y, x) = d(y, t) + d(t, x)$.

For the inductive step, assume $P(x, t, r_{i-1}) \subseteq W_{r_{i-1}}$, and prove for r_i. Let $\delta = r_i - r_{i-1}$. Let $v \in P(x, t, r_i) \setminus P(x, t, r_{i-1})$, and assume $u \in P(x, t, r_{i-1})$ is such that $(u \to v) \in A$ with $w'(u \to v) \le \delta/2$. Then by definition of w' we have that $d(u, v) \le \delta + d(v, x) - d(u, x)$. By the induction hypothesis we have that $u \in W_{r_{i-1}}$, so let k be such that $u \in B_{(V, \rho(V,x,p_k))}(p_k, (r_{i-1} - k)/2)$, by definition of cone metric $d(u, p_k) + d(p_k, x) \le d(u, x) + (r_{i-1} - k)/2$. It follows that

$$\begin{aligned} & d(v, p_k) + d(p_k, x) \\ &\le d(v, u) + d(u, p_k) + d(p_k, x) \\ &\le \delta + d(v, x) - d(u, x) + d(u, x) + (r_{i-1} - k)/2 \\ &= d(v, x) + (r_i - k)/2 \ , \end{aligned}$$

meaning that $v \in W_{r_i}$. □

Acknowledgments

We would like to thank Yair Bartal, Kunal Talwar and Michael Elkin for helpful discussions.

8. REFERENCES

[1] Ittai Abraham, Yair Bartal, and Ofer Neiman. Advances in metric embedding theory. In *Proceedings of the thirty-eighth annual ACM symposium on Theory of computing*, STOC '06, pages 271–286, New York, NY, USA, 2006. ACM.

[2] Ittai Abraham, Yair Bartal, and Ofer Neiman. Embedding metrics into ultrametrics and graphs into spanning trees with constant average distortion. In *Proceedings of the eighteenth annual ACM-SIAM symposium on Discrete algorithms*, SODA '07, pages 502–511, Philadelphia, PA, USA, 2007. Society for Industrial and Applied Mathematics.

[3] Ittai Abraham, Yair Bartal, and Ofer Neiman. Nearly tight low stretch spanning trees. In *FOCS '08: Proceedings of the 2008 49th Annual IEEE Symposium on Foundations of Computer Science*, pages 781–790, Washington, DC, USA, 2008. IEEE Computer Society.

[4] Noga Alon, Richard M. Karp, David Peleg, and Douglas West. A graph-theoretic game and its application to the k-server problem. *SIAM J. Comput.*, 24(1):78–100, 1995.

[5] Y. Bartal. Probabilistic approximation of metric spaces and its algorithmic applications. In *Proceedings of the 37th Annual Symposium on Foundations of Computer Science*, pages 184–, Washington, DC, USA, 1996. IEEE Computer Society.

[6] Yair Bartal. On approximating arbitrary metrices by tree metrics. In *Proceedings of the thirtieth annual ACM symposium on Theory of computing*, STOC '98, pages 161–168, New York, NY, USA, 1998. ACM.

[7] Yair Bartal. Graph decomposition lemmas and their role in metric embedding methods. In Susanne Albers and Tomasz Radzik, editors, *ESA*, volume 3221 of *Lecture Notes in Computer Science*, pages 89–97. Springer, 2004.

[8] Mihai Bădoiu, Piotr Indyk, and Anastasios Sidiropoulos. Approximation algorithms for embedding general metrics into trees. In *Proceedings of the eighteenth annual ACM-SIAM symposium on Discrete algorithms*, SODA '07, pages 512–521, Philadelphia, PA, USA, 2007. Society for Industrial and Applied Mathematics.

[9] Moses Charikar, Chandra Chekuri, Ashish Goel, and Sudipto Guha. Rounding via trees: deterministic approximation algorithms for group steiner trees and k-median. In *STOC '98: Proceedings of the thirtieth annual ACM symposium on Theory of computing*, pages 114–123, New York, NY, USA, 1998. ACM Press.

[10] Victor Chepoi, Feodor F. Dragan, Ilan Newman, Yuri Rabinovich, and Yann Vaxès. Constant approximation algorithms for embedding graph metrics into trees and outerplanar graphs. In *Proceedings of the 13th international conference on Approximation, and 14 the International conference on Randomization, and combinatorial optimization: algorithms and techniques*, APPROX/RANDOM'10, pages 95–109, Berlin, Heidelberg, 2010. Springer-Verlag.

[11] Paul Christiano, Jonathan A. Kelner, Aleksander Madry, Daniel A. Spielman, and Shang-Hua Teng. Electrical flows, laplacian systems, and faster approximation of maximum flow in undirected graphs. In *Proceedings of the 43rd annual ACM symposium on Theory of computing*, STOC '11, pages 273–282, New York, NY, USA, 2011. ACM.

[12] Michael Elkin, Yuval Emek, Daniel A. Spielman, and Shang-Hua Teng. Lower-stretch spanning trees. In *STOC '05: Proceedings of the thirty-seventh annual ACM symposium on Theory of computing*, pages 494–503, New York, NY, USA, 2005. ACM Press.

[13] Yuval Emek and David Peleg. Approximating minimum max-stretch spanning trees on unweighted graphs. In *Proceedings of the fifteenth annual ACM-SIAM symposium on Discrete algorithms*, SODA '04, pages 261–270, Philadelphia, PA, USA, 2004. Society for Industrial and Applied Mathematics.

[14] Yuval Emek and David Peleg. A tight upper bound on the probabilistic embedding of series-parallel graphs. In *Proceedings of the seventeenth annual ACM-SIAM symposium on Discrete algorithm*, SODA '06, pages 1045–1053, New York, NY, USA, 2006. ACM.

[15] Jittat Fakcharoenphol, Satish Rao, and Kunal Talwar. A tight bound on approximating arbitrary metrics by tree metrics. In *Proceedings of the thirty-fifth annual ACM symposium on Theory of computing*, STOC '03, pages 448–455, New York, NY, USA, 2003. ACM.

[16] Ioannis Koutis, Gary L. Miller, and Richard Peng. Approaching optimality for solving sdd linear systems. In *51th Annual IEEE Symposium on Foundations of Computer Science, October 23-26, 2010*, pages 235–244, Las Vegas, Nevada, USA.

[17] Ioannis Koutis, Gary L. Miller, and Richard Peng. A nearly $O(m \log n)$ time solver for SDD linear systems. In *52th Annual IEEE Symposium on Foundations of Computer Science, 2011.*

[18] James B. Orlin, Kamesh Madduri, K. Subramani, and M. Williamson. A faster algorithm for the single source shortest path problem with few distinct positive lengths. *J. of Discrete Algorithms*, 8:189–198, June 2010.

[19] P. D. Seymour. Packing directed circuits fractionally. *Combinatorica*, 15(2):281–288, June 1995.

[20] Daniel A. Spielman and Nikhil Srivastava. Graph sparsification by effective resistances. In *Proceedings of the 40th annual ACM symposium on Theory of computing*, STOC '08, pages 563–568, New York, NY, USA, 2008. ACM.

[21] Daniel A. Spielman and Shang-Hua Teng. Nearly-linear time algorithms for graph partitioning, graph sparsification, and solving linear systems. In *Proceedings of the thirty-sixth annual ACM symposium on Theory of computing*, STOC '04, pages 81–90, New York, NY, USA, 2004. ACM.

Improved Smoothed Analysis of Multiobjective Optimization*

Tobias Brunsch
Department of Computer Science
University of Bonn
Bonn, Germany
brunsch@cs.uni-bonn.de

Heiko Röglin
Department of Computer Science
University of Bonn
Bonn, Germany
heiko@roeglin.org

ABSTRACT

We present several new results about smoothed analysis of multiobjective optimization problems. Motivated by the discrepancy between worst-case analysis and practical experience, this line of research has gained a lot of attention in the last decade. We consider problems in which d linear and one arbitrary objective function are to be optimized over a set $\mathcal{S} \subseteq \{0,1\}^n$ of feasible solutions. We improve the previously best known bound for the smoothed number of Pareto-optimal solutions to $O(n^{2d}\phi^d)$, where ϕ denotes the perturbation parameter. Additionally, we show that for any constant c the c-th moment of the smoothed number of Pareto-optimal solutions is bounded by $O((n^{2d}\phi^d)^c)$. This improves the previously best known bounds significantly. Furthermore, we address the criticism that the perturbations in smoothed analysis destroy the zero-structure of problems by showing that the smoothed number of Pareto-optimal solutions remains polynomially bounded even for zero-preserving perturbations. This broadens the class of problems captured by smoothed analysis and it has consequences for non-linear objective functions. One corollary of our result is that the smoothed number of Pareto-optimal solutions is polynomially bounded for polynomial objective functions.

Categories and Subject Descriptors

G.2.1 [**Discrete Mathematics**]: Combinatorics—*combinatorial algorithms*; G.3 [**Probability and Statistics**]: Probabilistic Algorithms

Keywords

smoothed analysis, multi-objective optimization

General Terms

Theory

*A complete version of this paper is available online at `http://arxiv.org/abs/1111.1546`

STOC'12, May 19–22, 2012, New York, New York, USA.

1. INTRODUCTION

In most real-life decision-making problems there is more than one objective to be optimized. For example, when booking a train ticket, one wishes to minimize the travel time, the fare, and the number of train changes. As different objectives are often conflicting, usually no solution is simultaneously optimal in all criteria and one has to make a trade-off between different objectives. The most common way to filter out unreasonable trade-offs and to reduce the number of solutions the decision maker has to choose from is to determine the set of *Pareto-optimal solutions*, where a solution is called Pareto-optimal if no other solution is simultaneously better in all criteria.

Multiobjective optimization problems have been studied extensively in operations research and theoretical computer science (see, e.g., [9] for a comprehensive survey). In particular, many algorithms for generating the set of Pareto-optimal solutions for various optimization problems such as the (bounded) knapsack problem [16, 12], the multiobjective shortest path problem [7, 11, 19], and the multiobjective network flow problem [8, 15] have been proposed. Enumerating the set of Pareto-optimal solutions is not only used as a preprocessing step to eliminate unreasonable trade-offs, but often it is also used as an intermediate step in algorithms for solving optimization problems. For example, the Nemhauser–Ullmann algorithm [16] treats the single-criterion knapsack problem as a bicriteria optimization problem in which a solution with small weight and large profit is sought, and it generates the set of Pareto-optimal solutions, ignoring the given capacity of the knapsack. After this set has been generated, the algorithm returns the solution with the highest profit among all Pareto-optimal solutions with weight not exceeding the knapsack capacity. This solution is optimal for the given instance of the knapsack problem.

Generating the set of Pareto-optimal solutions (a.k.a. the *Pareto set*) only makes sense if few solutions are Pareto-optimal. Otherwise, it is too costly and it does not provide enough guidance to the decision maker. While, in many applications, it has been observed that the Pareto set is indeed usually small (see, e.g., [14] for an experimental study of the multiobjective shortest path problem), one can, for almost every problem with more than one objective function, easily find instances with an exponential number of Pareto-optimal solutions (see, e.g., [9]).

Motivated by the discrepancy between worst-case analysis and practical observations, *smoothed analysis* of multiobjective optimization problems has gained a lot of attention in the last decade. Smoothed analysis is a framework for judging the performance of algorithms that has been proposed in 2001 by Spielman and Teng [20] in order to explain why the simplex algorithm is efficient in practice even though it has an exponential worst-case running time. In this framework, inputs are generated in two steps: first, an adversary chooses an arbitrary instance, and then this instance is slightly perturbed at random. The smoothed performance of an algorithm is defined to be the worst expected performance the adversary can achieve. This model can be viewed as a less pessimistic worst-case analysis, in which the randomness rules out pathological worst-case instances that are rarely observed in practice but dominate the worst-case analysis. If the smoothed running time of an algorithm is low and inputs are subject to a small amount of random noise, then it is unlikely to encounter an instance on which the algorithm performs poorly. In practice, random noise can stem from measurement errors, numerical imprecision or rounding errors. It can also model arbitrary influences, which we cannot quantify exactly, but for which there is also no reason to believe that they are adversarial.

After its invention in 2001, smoothed analysis has been successfully applied in a variety of contexts, e.g., to explain the practical success of local search methods, heuristics for the knapsack problem, online algorithms, and clustering. A recent survey by Spielman and Teng [21] summarizes some of these results. One of the areas in which smoothed analysis has been applied extensively is multiobjective optimization. In 2003 Beier and Vöcking [3] initiated this line of research by showing that the smoothed number of Pareto-optimal solutions is polynomially bounded for any linear binary optimization problem with two objective functions. This was the first rigorous explanation why heuristics for generating the set of Pareto-optimal solutions are successful in practice despite their bad worst-case behavior. In the last years, Beier and Vöcking's original result has been improved and extended significantly in a series of papers. A discussion of this work follows in the next section after the formal description of the model.

1.1 Model and Previous Work

We consider a very general model of multiobjective optimization problems. An instance of such a problem consists of $d+1$ objective functions $V^1, \ldots, V^{d+1}$ that are to be optimized over a set $\mathcal{S} \subseteq \{0,1\}^n$ of feasible solutions. While the set $\mathcal{S}$ and the last objective function $V^{d+1}\colon \mathcal{S} \to \mathbb{R}$ can be arbitrary, the first d objective functions have to be linear of the form $V^t(x) = V_1^t x_1 + \ldots + V_n^t x_n$ for $x = (x_1, \ldots, x_n) \in \mathcal{S}$ and $t \in \{1, \ldots, d\}$. We assume without loss of generality that all objectives are to be minimized and we call a solution $x \in \mathcal{S}$ *Pareto-optimal* if there does not exist a solution $y \in \mathcal{S}$ with $V^t(y) \le V^t(x)$ for all $t \in \{1, \ldots, d+1\}$ and $V^t(y) < V^t(x)$ for at least one $t \in \{1, \ldots, d+1\}$.

If one is allowed to choose the set $\mathcal{S}$, the objective function V^{d+1}, and the coefficients of the linear objective functions arbitrarily, then, even for $d = 1$, one can easily construct instances with an exponential number of Pareto-optimal solutions. For this reason Beier and Vöcking introduced the model of *ϕ-smooth instances* [3], in which an adversary can choose the set $\mathcal{S}$ and the objective function V^{d+1} arbitrarily while he can only specify a probability density function $f_i^t\colon [-1,1] \to [0,\phi]$ for each coefficient V_i^t according to which it is chosen independently from the other coefficients. This model is more general than Spielman and Teng's original two-step model in which the adversary first chooses coefficients which are afterwards subject to Gaussian perturbations. In ϕ-smooth instances the adversary can additionally determine the type of noise. He could, for example, specify for each coefficient an interval of length $1/\phi$ from which it is chosen uniformly at random. The parameter $\phi \ge 1$ can be seen as a measure for the power of the adversary: the larger ϕ the more precisely he can specify the coefficients of the linear objective functions. The example of uniform distributions shows that for $\phi \to \infty$ smoothed analysis becomes a worst-case analysis.

The *smoothed number of Pareto-optimal solutions* depends on the number n of binary variables and the perturbation parameter ϕ. It is defined to be the largest expected number of Pareto-optimal solutions the adversary can achieve by any choice of $\mathcal{S} \subseteq \{0,1\}^n$, $V^{d+1}\colon \mathcal{S} \to \mathbb{R}$, and the densities $f_i^t\colon [-1,1] \to [0,\phi]$. In the following we assume that the adversary has made arbitrary fixed choices for these entities. Then we can associate with every matrix $V \in \mathbb{R}^{d \times n}$ the number $\mathrm{PO}(V)$ of Pareto-optimal solutions in $\mathcal{S}$ when the coefficients V_i^t of the d linear objective functions take the values given in V. Assuming that the adversary has made worst-case choices for $\mathcal{S}$, V^{d+1}, and the densities f_i^t, the *smoothed number of Pareto-optimal solutions* is the expected value $\mathbf{E}_V[\mathrm{PO}(V)]$, where the coefficients in V are chosen according to the densities f_i^t. For $c \ge 1$, we call $\mathbf{E}_V[\mathrm{PO}^c(V)]$ the *c-th moment of the smoothed number of Pareto-optimal solutions*.

Beier and Vöcking [3] showed that for the bicriteria case (i.e., $d = 1$) the smoothed number of Pareto-optimal solutions is $O(n^4\phi)$ and $\Omega(n^2)$. The upper bound was later simplified and improved by Beier et al. [2] to $O(n^2\phi)$. Beier [1] conjectured that the smoothed number of Pareto-optimal solutions is polynomially bounded in n and ϕ for every constant d. This was proven by Röglin and Teng [17], who showed that for any fixed $d \ge 1$, the smoothed number of Pareto-optimal solutions is $O((n^2\phi)^{f(d)})$, where the function f is roughly $f(d) = 2^d d!$. They also proved that for any constant c the cth moment of the smoothed number of Pareto-optimal solutions is bounded by $O((n^2\phi)^{c \cdot f(d)})$. Recently, Moitra and O'Donnell [13] improved the bound for the smoothed number of Pareto-optimal solutions significantly to $O(n^{2d}\phi^{d(d+1)/2})$. However, it remained unclear how to improve the bound for the moments by their methods. Very recently a combination of results by Goyal and Rademacher [10] and our results in [6] was observed to yield a lower bound of $\Omega(n^{d-1.5}\phi^d)$ [10].

1.2 Our Results

We present several new results about smoothed analysis of multiobjective binary optimization problems. Besides general ϕ-smooth instances, we consider for some results only the special case of *quasiconcave density functions*. This means that every coefficient V_i^t is chosen independently according to its own density function $f_i^t\colon [-1,1] \to [0,\phi]$ with the additional requirement that for every density f_i^t there is a value $x_i^t \in [-1,1]$ such that f_i^t is non-decreasing in the interval $[-1, x_i^t]$ and non-increasing in the interval $[x_i^t, 1]$. We do not think that this is a severe restriction because all natural perturbation models, like Gaussian or uniform perturbations, use quasiconcave density functions. Furthermore, quasiconcave densities capture the essence of a perturbation: each coefficient V_i^t has an unperturbed value x_i^t and the probability that the perturbed coefficient takes a value z becomes smaller with increasing distance $|z - x_i^t|$. We will call these instances *quasiconcave ϕ-smooth instances.*

Beier and Vöcking originally only considered ϕ-smooth instances for bicriteria optimization problems (i.e., for the case $d = 1$). The above described canonical generalization of this model to multiobjective optimization problems, on which Röglin and Teng's [17] and Moitra and O'Donnell's results [13] are based, appears to be very general and flexible on the first glance. However, one aspect limits its applicability severely and makes it impossible to formulate certain multiobjective linear optimization problems in this model. The weak point of the model is that it assumes that every binary variable x_i appears in every linear objective function as it is not possible to set some coefficients V_i^t deterministically to zero.

Already Spielman and Teng [20] and Beier and Vöcking [4] observed that the zeros often encode an essential part of the combinatorial structure of a problem and they suggested to analyze *zero-preserving perturbations* in which it is possible to either choose a density f_i^t according to which the coefficient V_i^t is chosen or to set it deterministically to zero. Zero-preserving perturbations have been studied in [18] and [4] for analyzing smoothed condition numbers of matrices and the smoothed complexity of binary optimization problems. For the smoothed number of Pareto-optimal solutions no upper bounds are known that are valid for zero-preserving perturbations (except trivial worst-case bounds), and in particular the bounds proven in [17] and [13] do not seem to generalize easily to zero-preserving perturbations. In this paper, we develop new techniques for analyzing the smoothed number of Pareto-optimal solutions that can also be used for analyzing zero-preserving perturbations.

THEOREM 1. *For any $d \geq 1$, the smoothed number of Pareto-optimal solutions is $O(n^{d^3+d^2+d}\phi^d)$ for quasiconcave ϕ-smooth instances with zero-preserving perturbations and $O((n\phi)^{d^3+d^2+d})$ for general ϕ-smooth instances with zero-preserving perturbations.*

In Section 1.3 we will present some applications of zero-preserving perturbations. We will see that they allow us not only to extend the smoothed analysis to linear multiobjective optimization problems that are not captured by the previous model without zero-preserving perturbations, but that they also enable us to bound the smoothed number of Pareto-optimal solutions in problems with *non-linear objective functions*. In particular, the number of Pareto-optimal solutions for polynomial objective functions can be bounded by Theorem 1. We say that a ϕ-smooth instance has polynomial objective functions if every objective function V^t, $t \in \{1, \dots, d\}$, is the weighted sum of at most m monomials, where the adversary can specify a ϕ-bounded density on $[0, 1]$ for every weight according to which it is chosen.

COROLLARY 2. *For any $d \geq 1$, the smoothed number of Pareto-optimal solutions is $O(m^{d^3+d^2+d}\phi^d)$ for quasiconcave ϕ-smooth instances with zero-preserving perturbations and polynomial objective functions. For general ϕ-smooth instances with zero-preserving perturbations and polynomial objective functions the smoothed number of Pareto-optimal solutions is $O((m\phi)^{d^3+d^2+d})$.*

In addition to zero-preserving perturbations we also study the standard model of ϕ-smooth instances. We present significantly improved bounds for the smoothed number of Pareto-optimal solutions and higher moments, answering two questions posed by Moitra and O'Donnell [13].

THEOREM 3. *For any $d \geq 1$, the smoothed number of Pareto-optimal solutions is $O(n^{2d}\phi^d)$ for quasiconcave ϕ-smooth instances.*

This improves upon the previously best known bound of $O(n^{2d}\phi^{d(d+1)/2})$ (which is, however, valid also for non-quasiconcave densities) and it answers a question posed by Moitra and O'Donnell whether it is possible to improve the factor of $\phi^{d(d+1)/2}$ in their bound [13]. Together with the recent lower bound of $\Omega(n^{d-1.5}\phi^d)$ [10], which is also valid for quasiconcave density functions, this shows that the exponents of both n and ϕ are linear in d.

THEOREM 4. *For any $d \geq 1$ and any constant $c \in \mathbb{N}$, the c-th moment of the smoothed number of Pareto-optimal solutions is $O((n^{2d}\phi^d)^c)$ for quasiconcave ϕ-smooth instances and $O((n^{2d}\phi^{d(d+1)})^c)$ for general ϕ-smooth instances.*

This answers a question in [13] whether it is possible to improve the bounds for the moments in [17] and it yields better concentration bounds for the smoothed number of Pareto-optimal solutions. Our results also have immediate consequences for the expected running times of various algorithms because most heuristics for generating the Pareto set of some problem (including the ones mentioned at the beginning of the introduction) have a running time that depends linearly or quadratically on the size of the Pareto set. The improved bounds on the smoothed number of Pareto-optimal solutions and the second moment of this number yield improved bounds on the smoothed running times of these algorithms.

Note that all of our results are significantly better for quasiconcave densities than for general densities. This is due to Theorem 35 which has already been stated in a similar way by Röglin and Teng [17] for general densities.

1.3 Zero-preserving Perturbations and their Applications

Let us first of all remark that in the bicriteria case, which was studied in [3], zero-preserving perturbations are not more powerful than other perturbations because they can be simulated by the right choice of $\mathcal{S} \subseteq \{0,1\}^n$ and the objective function $V^2 \colon \mathcal{S} \to \mathbb{R}$ (see paragraph "Non-linear Objective Functions" in this section). However, such a reduction of zero-preserving perturbations to other perturbations does not seem to be possible for $d \geq 2$ anymore.

Path Trading.

Berger et al. [5] study a model for routing in networks. In their model there is a graph $G = (V, E)$ whose vertex set V is partitioned into mutually disjoint sets $V_1, \dots, V_k$. We can think of G as the Internet graph whose vertices are owned and controlled by k different autonomous systems (ASes). We denote by $E_i \subseteq E$ the set of edges inside V_i. The graph G is undirected, and each edge $e \in E$ has a length $\ell_e \in \mathbb{R}_{\geq 0}$. The traffic is modeled by a set of requests, where each request is characterized by its source node $s \in V$ and its target node $t \in V$. We consider the case that a single request has to be routed from a source $s \in V_1$ to a target $t \in V_k$.

The Border Gateway Protocol (BGP) determines for this request the order in which it has to be routed through the ASes. We assume without loss of generality that the request has to be routed through $V_1, V_2, \dots, V_k$ in this order, and we say that a path P is valid if it connects s to t and visits the ASes in the order specified by the BGP protocol. This means that the first AS has to choose a path P_1 inside V_1 from s to some node in V_1 that is connected to some node $v_2 \in V_2$. Then the second AS has to choose a path P_2 inside V_2 from v_2 to some node in V_2 that is connected to some node $v_3 \in V_3$ and so on. For simplicity, the costs of routing a packet between two ASes are assumed to be zero, whereas AS i incurs costs of $\sum_{e \in P_i} \ell_e$ for routing the packet inside V_i along path P_i. In the common hot-potato routing, every AS is only interested in minimizing its own costs. To model this, there are k objective functions that map each valid path P to a cost vector $(C_1(P), \dots, C_k(P))$, where $C_i(P) = \sum_{e \in P \cap E_i} \ell_e$ for $i \in \{1, \dots, k\}$.

In [5] the problem of *path trading* is considered. This problem considers the question whether ASes can reduce their costs if they deviate from the hot-potato strategy and coordinate the chosen paths for multiple requests. A main ingredient in the algorithm proposed in [5] to solve this problem is to generate the set of Pareto-optimal valid paths with respect to the k objective functions defined above. As this Pareto set can be exponentially large in the worst case, Berger et al. proposed to study ϕ-smooth instances in which an adversary chooses the graph G and a density $f_e \colon [0,1] \to [0, \phi]$ for every edge length ℓ_e according to which it is chosen. It seems as if we could easily apply the results in [17] and [13] to bound the smoothed number of Pareto-optimal paths. If we set $S \subseteq \{0,1\}^{|E|}$ to be the set of incidence vectors of valid paths, then all objective functions C_i are linear in the binary variables x_e, $e \in E$. For $x \in S$, we have $C_i(x) = \sum_{e \in E_i} \ell_e x_e$.

Note, however, that different objective functions contain different variables x_e because the coefficients of all x_e with $e \notin E_i$ are set to zero in C_i. This is an important combinatorial property of the path trading problem that has to be obeyed. In the model in [17] and [13] it is not possible to set coefficients deterministically to zero. The best we can do is to replace each zero by a uniform density on the interval $[0, 1/\phi]$. Then, however, an AS would incur positive costs for any edge that is used and not only for its own edges, which does not resemble the structure of the problem. Theorem 1, which allows zero-preserving perturbations, yields immediately the following result.

COROLLARY 5. *The smoothed number of Pareto-optimal valid paths is polynomially bounded in $|E|$ and ϕ for any constant k.*

Non-linear Objective Functions.

Even though above we assumed that the objective functions $V^1, \dots, V^d$ are linear, we can also extend the smoothed analysis to non-linear objective functions. We consider first the bicriteria case $d = 1$. As above, we assume that the adversary has chosen a set $\mathcal{S} \subseteq \{0,1\}^n$ of feasible solutions and an arbitrary injective objective function $V^2 \colon \mathcal{S} \to \mathbb{R}$. In addition to that the adversary can choose m_1 arbitrary functions $I_i^1 \colon \mathcal{S} \to \{0,1\}$, $i \in \{1, \dots, m_1\}$. The objective function $V^1 \colon \mathcal{S} \to \mathbb{R}$ is defined to be a weighted sum of the functions I_i^1: $V^1(x) = \sum_{i=1}^{m_1} w_i^1 I_i^1(x)$, where each weight w_i^1 is randomly chosen according to a density $f_i^1 \colon [0,1] \to [0, \phi]$ chosen by the adversary. There is a wide variety of functions $V^1(x)$ that can be expressed in this way. We can, for example, express every polynomial if we let $I_1^1, \dots, I_{m_1}^1$ be its monomials.

We can linearize the problem by introducing a binary variable for every function I_i^1. Then the set of feasible solutions becomes $\mathcal{S}' = \{y \in \{0,1\}^{m_1} : \exists x \in \mathcal{S} \colon \forall i \in \{1, \dots, m_1\} \colon I_i^1(x) = y_i\}$. For this set of feasible solutions we define $W^1, W^2 \colon \mathcal{S}' \to \mathbb{R}$ as $W^1(y) = \sum_{j=1}^{m_1} w_j y_j$ and as

$$W^2(y) = \min\{V^2(x) : \forall i \in \{1, \dots, m_1\} \colon I_i^1(x) = y_i\}.$$

One can easily verify that the problem defined by $\mathcal{S}$, V^1, and V^2 and the problem defined by $\mathcal{S}'$, W^1, and W^2 are equivalent and have the same number of Pareto-optimal solutions. The latter problem is linear and hence we can apply the result by Beier et al. [2], which yields that the smoothed number of Pareto-optimal solutions is bounded by $O(m_1^2 \phi)$. This shows in particular that the smoothed number of Pareto-optimal solutions is polynomially bounded in the number of monomials and the density parameter for every polynomial objective function V^1.

We can extend this method to multiobjective problems with $d \geq 2$. For these problems the adversary chooses a set $\mathcal{S} \subseteq \{0,1\}^n$, numbers $m_1, \dots, m_d \in \mathbb{N}$, and an arbitrary injective objective function $V^{d+1} \colon \mathcal{S} \to \mathbb{R}$. In addition to that he chooses arbitrary functions $I_i^t \colon \mathcal{S} \to \{0,1\}$ for $t \in \{1, \dots, d\}$ and $i \in \{1, \dots, m_t\}$. Every objective function $V^t \colon \mathcal{S} \to \mathbb{R}$ is a weighted sum of the functions I_t^1: $V^t(x) = \sum_{i=1}^{m_t} w_i^t I_i^t(x)$, where each weight w_i^t is randomly chosen according to a density $f_i^t \colon [0,1] \to [0, \phi]$ chosen by the adversary. Similar as the bicriteria case, also this problem can be linearized. However, the previous results about the smoothed number of Pareto-optimal solutions can only be applied if every objective function V^t is composed of exactly the same functions I_i^t. Theorem 1 implies that the smoothed number of Pareto-optimal solutions is polynomially bounded in $\sum m_i$ and ϕ, for any choice of the I_i^t.

1.4 Notation

In this section, we introduce the necessary notation to follow the description of our approach in the following section. More notation for the proofs is introduced in Section 3.

For the sake of simplicity we write $V^t x$ instead of $V^t(x)$, even for the adversarial objective V^{d+1}. With $V^{k_1 \dots k_t} x$ we refer to the vector $(V^{k_1} x, \dots, V^{k_t} x)$. In the whole paper let $\varepsilon > 0$ be a small real for which $1/\varepsilon$ is integral. For $n \in \mathbb{N}$, let $[n] = \{1, \dots, n\}$. For a vector $x \in \{0,1\}^n$ and $I = \{i_1, \dots, i_k\} \subseteq [n]$, let x_I denote the vector $(x_{i_1}, \dots, x_{i_k})$. For an index set $I \subseteq [n]$ and a vector $y \in \{0,1\}^n$ let $\mathcal{S}_I(y)$ denote the set of all solutions $z \in \mathcal{S}$ such that $z_i = y_i$ for any index $i \in I$.

Outline

After introducing some notation in the next section, we present an outline of our approach in Section 2. The proofs of Theorems 3 and 4 is deferred to Appendix 4. The proof of Theorem 1 is deferred to Appendix 5.

2. OUTLINE OF OUR APPROACH

To prove our results we adapt and improve methods from the previous analyses by Röglin and Teng [17] and by Moitra and O'Donnell [13] and combine them in a novel way. Since all coefficients of the linear objective functions lie in the interval $[-1,1]$, for every solution $x \in \mathcal{S}$ the vector $V^{1\dots d}x$ lies in the hypercube $[-n,n]^d$. The first step is to partition this hypercube into hypercubes with side length ε which we call ε-boxes. If ε is sufficiently small, then it is unlikely that there are two different solutions $x \in \mathcal{S}$ and $y \in \mathcal{S}$ for which $V^{1\dots d}x$ and $V^{1\dots d}y$ lie in the same ε-box B unless x and y differ only in positions that are not perturbed in any of the objective functions, in which case we consider them as the same solution. In the remainder of this section we assume that no two solutions lie in the same ε-box. Then, in order to bound the number of Pareto-optima, it suffices to count the number of non-empty ε-boxes.

In order to prove Theorem 3 we show that for any fixed ε-box the probability that it contains a Pareto-optimal solution is bounded by $\kappa n^d \phi^d \varepsilon^d$ for a sufficiently large constant κ. This implies the theorem as the number of ε-boxes is $(2n/\varepsilon)^d$. Fix an arbitrary ε-box B. In the following we will call a solution $x \in \mathcal{S}$ a *candidate* if there is a realization of V such that x is Pareto-optimal and lies in B. If there was only a single candidate $x \in \mathcal{S}$, then we could bound the probability that there is a Pareto-optimal solution in B by the probability that this particular solution x lies in B. This probability can easily be bounded from above by $\varepsilon^d \phi^d$. However, in principle, every solution $x \in \mathcal{S}$ can be a candidate and a union bound over all of them leads to a factor of $|\mathcal{S}|$ in the bound, which we have to avoid.

Following ideas of Moitra and O'Donnell, we divide the draw of the random matrix V into two steps. In the first step some information about V is revealed that suffices to limit the set of candidates to a single solution $x \in \mathcal{S}$. The exact position $V^{1\dots d}x$ of this solution is determined in the second step. If the information that is revealed in the two steps is chosen carefully, then there is enough randomness left in the second step to bound the probability that x lies in the ε-box B. In Moitra and O'Donnell's analysis the coefficients in the matrix V are partitioned into two groups. In the first step the first group of coefficients is drawn, which suffices to determine the unique candidate x, and in the second step the remaining coefficients are drawn, which suffices to bound the probability that x lies in B. The second part consists essentially of $d(d+1)/2$ coefficients, which causes the factor of $\phi^{d(d+1)/2}$ in their bound.

We improve the analysis by a different choice of how to break the draw of V into two parts. As in the previous analysis, most coefficients are drawn in the first step. Only d^2 coefficients of V are drawn in the second step. However, these coefficients are not left completely random as in [13] because after the other coefficients have been drawn there can still be multiple candidates for Pareto-optimal solutions in B. Instead, the randomness is reduced further by drawing $d(d-1)$ linear combinations of these random variables in the first step. These linear combinations have the property that, after they have been drawn, there is a unique candidate x whose position can be described by d linear combinations that are linearly independent of the linear combinations already drawn in the first step. In [17] it was observed that linearly independent linear combinations of independent random variables behave in some respect similar to independent random variables. With this insight one can argue that in the second step there is still enough randomness to bound the probability that x lies in B. While the analysis in [17] yields only a bound proportional to $\phi^{d^2}\varepsilon^d$, we prove an improved result for quasiconcave densities that yields the desired bound proportional to $\phi^d \varepsilon^d$.

For analyzing higher moments, it does not suffice to bound the probability that a fixed ε-box contains a Pareto-optimal solution. Instead, in order to bound the cth moment, we sum over all c-tuples $(B_1,\dots,B_c)$ of ε-boxes the probability that all ε-boxes $B_1,\dots,B_c$ contain simultaneously a Pareto-optimal solution. We bound this probability from above by $\kappa n^{cd}\phi^{cd}\varepsilon^{cd}$ for a sufficiently large constant κ. Since there are $(2n/\varepsilon)^{cd}$ different c-tuples of ε-boxes, this implies the bound of $O((n^2\phi)^{cd})$ for the smoothed c^{th} moment of the number of Pareto-optimal solutions.

Let us fix a c-tuple $(B_1,\dots,B_c)$ of ε-boxes. The approach to bound the probability that all of these ε-boxes contain simultaneously a Pareto-optimal solution is similar to the approach for the first moment. We divide the draw of V into two steps. In the first step enough information is revealed to identify for each of the ε-boxes B_i a unique candidate $x_i \in \mathcal{S}$ for a Pareto-optimal solution in B_i. If we do this carefully, then there is enough randomness left in the second step to bound the probability that $V^{1\dots d}x_i \in B_i$ for every $i \in [c]$. Again most coefficients are drawn in the first step and some linear combinations of the other cd^2 coefficients are also drawn in the first step. However, we cannot simply repeat the construction for the first moment independently c times because then there might be dependencies between the events $V^{1\dots d}x_i \in B_i$ for different i. In order to bound the probability that in the second step all x_i lie in their corresponding ε-boxes B_i, we need to ensure that the events $V^{1\dots d}x_i \in B_i$ are (almost) independent after the information from the first step has been revealed.

The general approach to handle zero-preserving perturbations is closely related to the approach for bounding the first moment for non-zero-preserving perturbations. However, additional complications have to be handled. The main problem is that we cannot easily guarantee anymore that the linear combinations in the second step are linearly independent of the linear combinations revealed in the first step. Essentially, the revealed linear combinations describe the positions of some auxiliary solutions. For non-zero-preserving perturbations revealing this information is not critical as no solution has in any objective function exactly the same value as x. For zero-preserving solutions it can, however, happen that the auxiliary solutions take exactly the same value as x in one of the objective functions. Then there is not enough randomness left in the second step to bound the probability that x lies in this objective in the ε-interval described by the ε-box B.

In the remainder of this section we will present some more details on our analysis. We first present a simplified argument to bound the smoothed number of Pareto-optimal solutions. Afterwards we will briefly discuss which changes to this argument are necessary to bound higher moments and to analyze zero-preserving perturbations.

Smoothed Number of Pareto-optimal Solutions.

As an important building block in the proof of Theorem 3 we use an insight from [13] about how to test whether a given ε-box contains a Pareto-optimal solution. Let us fix an ε-box $B = (b_1, b_1+\varepsilon] \times \ldots \times (b_d, b_d+\varepsilon]$. The following algorithm takes as parameters the matrix V and the ε-box B and it returns a solution $x^{(0)}$.

```
Witness(V, B)
1: Set R_{d+1} = S.
2: for t = d, d-1, ..., 0 do
3:     Set C_t = {z ∈ R_{t+1} : V^{1...t} z ≤ b|_{1...t}}.
4:     Set x^(t) = arg min {V^{t+1} z : z ∈ C_t}.
5:     Set R_t = {z ∈ R_{t+1} : V^{t+1} z < V^{t+1} x^(t)}.
6: end for
7: return x^(0)
```

The actual Witness function that we use in the proof of Theorem 3 is more complex because it has to deal with some technicalities. In particular, the case that some set $\mathcal{C}_t$ is empty has to be handled. For the purpose of illustration we ignore these technicalities here and assume that $\mathcal{C}_t$ is never empty. The crucial oberservation that has been made by Moitra and O'Donnell is that if there is a Pareto-optimal solution $x \in \mathcal{S}$ that lies in B, then $x^{(0)} = x$ (assuming that no two solutions lie in the same ε-box). Hence, the solution $x^{(0)}$ returned by the Witness function is the only candidate for a Pareto-optimal solution in B. While this statement and the following reasoning are true for any $d \in \mathbb{N}$, we recommend the reader to think first only about the illustrative case $d = 2$, in which there are one adversarial and two linear objective functions.

Our goal is to execute the Witness function and to obtain the solution $x^{(0)}$ without revealing the entire matrix V. We will see that it is indeed possible to divide the draw of V into two steps such that in the first step enough information is revealed to execute the Witness function and such that in the second step there is still enough radnomness left to bound the probability that $x^{(0)}$ lies in B. For this let $I \subseteq [n]$ be a set of indices and assume that we know in advance which values the solutions $x^{(0)}, \ldots, x^{(d)}$ take at these indices, i.e., assume that we know $a^{(0)} = x^{(0)}|_I, \ldots, a^{(d)} = x^{(d)}|_I$ before executing the Witness function. Then we can reconstruct $x^{(0)}, \ldots, x^{(d)}$ without having to reveal the entire matrix V. This can be done by the following algorithm, which gets as additional parameters the set I and the matrix $A = (a^{(0)}, \ldots, a^{(d)})$.

```
Witness(V, I, A, B)
1: Set R_{d+1} = S ∩ ⋃_{t'=0}^{d} S_I(a^(t')).
2: for t = d, d-1, ..., 0 do
3:     Set C_t = {z ∈ R_{t+1} ∩ S_I(a^(t)) : V^{1...t} z ≤ b|_{1...t}}.
4:     Set x^(t) = arg min {V^{t+1} z : z ∈ C_t}.
5:     Set R_t = {z ∈ R_{t+1} ∩ ⋃_{t'=0}^{t-1} S_I(a^(t')) : V^{t+1} z <
       V^{t+1} x^(t)}.
6: end for
7: return (x^(0), ..., x^(d))
```

The additional restriction of the set $\mathcal{R}_{d+1}$ does not change the outcome of the Witness function as all solutions $x^{(t)}$ generated by the first Witness function are contained in the set $\mathcal{R}_{d+1}$ defined in line 1 of the second Witness function. Similarly one can argue that the additional restrictions in lines 3 and 5 do not change the outcome of the algorithm because all solutions $x^{(t)}$ generated by the first Witness function satisfy the restrictions that are made in the second Witness function. Hence, if $a^{(0)} = x^{(0)}|_I, \ldots, a^{(d)} = x^{(d)}|_I$, then both Witness functions generate the same $x^{(0)}$.

We will now discuss how much information about V needs to be revealed in order to execute the second Witness function, assuming that the additional parameters I and A are given. We assume that the coefficients V_i^t are revealed for every $t \in [d]$ and $i \notin I$. For the remaining coefficients only certain linear combinations need to be known in order to be able to execute the Witness function. By carefully looking at the Witness function, one can deduce that for $t \in [d]$ only the following linear combinations need to be known:

$$V^t|_I \cdot x^{(t)}|_I, \ldots, V^t|_I \cdot x^{(d)}|_I,$$
$$V^t|_I \cdot (x^{(t-1)} - x^{(0)})|_I, \ldots, V^t|_I \cdot (x^{(t-1)} - x^{(t-2)})|_I.$$

These terms can be viewed as linear combinations of the random variables V_i^t, $t \in [d]$, $i \in I$, with coefficients from $\{-1, 0, +1\}$. In addition to the already fixed random variables V_i^t, $t \in [d]$, $i \notin I$ the following d linear combinations determine the position $V^{1\ldots d}x$ of $x = x^{(0)}$:

$$V_I^1 \cdot x^{(0)}|_I, \ldots, V_I^d \cdot x^{(0)}|_I.$$

An important observation on which our analysis is based is that if the vectors $x^{(0)}|_I, \ldots, x^{(d)}|_I$ are linearly independent, then also all of the above mentioned linear combinations are linearly independent. In particular, the d linear combinations that determine the position of x cannot be expressed by the other linear combinations. Usually, however, it is not possible to find a subset $I \subseteq [n]$ of indices such that the vectors $x^{(0)}|_I, \ldots, x^{(d)}|_I$ are linearly independent. By certain technical modifications of the Witness function suggested by Moitra and O'Donnell we will ensure that there always exists such a set I with $|I| \le d+1$. Since we do not know the set I and the matrix A in advance, we apply a union bound over all valid choices for these parameters, which yields a factor of $O(n^d)$ in the bound for the probability that there exists a Pareto-optimal solution in B.

Röglin and Teng [17] observed that the linear independence of the linear combinations implies that even if the linear combinations needed to execute the Witness function are revealed in the first step, there is still enough randomness in the second step to prove an upper bound on the probability that $V^{1\ldots d}x$ lies in a fixed ε-box B that is proportional to ε^d. The bound proven in [17] is, however, not strong enough to improve Moitra and O'Donnell's result [13] because it is in the order of $\Theta(\varepsilon^d \phi^{d^2})$, which would yield a bound of $O(n^{2d}\phi^{d^2})$ for the smoothed number of Pareto-optimal solutions. We show that for quasiconcave density functions the bound in [17] can be significantly improved to $\Theta(\varepsilon^d \phi^d)$, which yields the improved bound of $O(n^{2d}\phi^d)$ in Theorem 3.

Higher Moments.

The analysis of higher moments is based on running the Witness function multiple times. As described above, we bound for a fixed c-tuple $(B_1, \ldots, B_c)$ of ε-boxes the probability that all of them contain a Pareto-optimal solution. For this, we run the Witness function c times. This way, we get for every $j \in [c]$ a sequence $x^{(j,0)}, \ldots, x^{(j,d)}$ of solutions such that $x^{(j,0)}$ is the unique candidate for a Pareto-optimal solution in B_j. As above, we would like to execute the c calls of the Witness function without having to reveal the entire matrix V. Again if we know for a subset $I \subseteq [n]$ the values that the solutions $x^{(j,t)}$, $j \in [c]$, $t \in [d]$, take at these positions, then we do not need to reveal the coefficients V_i^t with $i \in I$ to be able to execute the calls of the Witness function. As in the case of the first moment, it suffices to reveal some linear combinations of these coefficients.

In order to guarantee that these linear combinations are linearly independent of the linear combinations that determine the positions of the solutions $x^{(j,0)}$, $j \in [c]$, we need to coordinate the calls of the Witness function. Otherwise it might happen, for example, that the linear combinations revealed for executing the first call of the witness function already determine the position of $x^{(2,0)}$, the candidate for a Pareto-optimal solution in B_2. Assume that the first call of the Witness function returns a sequence $x^{(1,0)}, \ldots, x^{(1,d)}$ of solutions and that $I_1 \subseteq [n]$ is a set of indices that satisfies the desired property that $x^{(1,0)}|_{I_1}, \ldots, x^{(1,d)}|_{I_1}$ are linearly independent. In order to achieve that all solutions generated in the following calls of the Witness function are linearly independent of these linear combinations, we do not start a second independent call of the Witness function, but we restrict the set of feasible solutions first. Instead of choosing $x^{(2,0)}, \ldots, x^{(2,d)}$ among all solutions from $\mathcal{S}$, we restrict the set of feasible solutions for the second call to $\mathcal{S}' = \mathcal{S}_{I_1}(x)$. Essentially, all solutions generated in calls of the Witness function have to coincide with x in all positions that have been selected in one of the previous calls.

This and some additional tricks allow us to ensure that in the end there is a set $I \subseteq [n]$ with $|I| \leq (d+1)c$ such that all vectors $x^{(j,t)}|_I$, $j \in [c]$, $t \in [d]$ are linearly independent. Then we can again use the bound proven in [17] to bound the probability that $V^{1\ldots d}x^{(j,0)} \in B_j$ simultaneously for every $j \in [c]$ from above by a term proportional to $\varepsilon^{cd}\phi^{cd^2}$. With our improved bound for quasiconcave density functions, we obtain a bound proportional to $\varepsilon^{cd}\phi^{cd}$. Together with a union bound over all valid choices for I and the values $x^{(j,t)}|_I$, $j \in [c]$, $t \in [d]$, we obtain a bound of $\kappa n^{cd}\varepsilon^{cd}\phi^{cd}$ on the probability that all candidates $x^{(j,0)}$ lie in their corresponding ε-boxes for a sufficiently large constant κ. Together with the bound of $O(n^{cd}/\varepsilon^{cd})$ for the number of c-tuples $(B_1, \ldots, B_c)$ this implies Theorem 4.

Zero-preserving Perturbations.

If we use the same Witness function as above, then it can happen that there is a Pareto-optimal solution x in the ε-box B that does not coincide with the solution $x^{(0)}$ returned by the Witness function. This problem occurs, for example, if $V^d \cdot x^{(d-1)} = V^d \cdot x^{(0)}$, which we cannot exclude if we allow zero-preserving perturbations. We recommend to visualize this case for $d = 2$. On the other hand if we knew in advance that $V^d \cdot x^{(d-1)} = V^d \cdot x^{(0)}$, then we could bound the probability of $V^d x^{(0)} \in (b_d, d_d + \varepsilon]$ already after the solution $x^{(d-1)}$ has been generated. Hence, if we were only interested in bounding this probability, we could terminate the Witness function already after $x^{(d-1)}$ has been generated. Instead of terminating the Witness function at this point entirely, we keep in mind that $V^d x^{(0)}$ has already been determined and we restart the Witness function with the remaining objective functions only.

Let us make this a bit more precise. As long as the solutions $x^{(t)}$ generated by the Witness function differ in all objective functions from x, we execute the Witness function without any modification. Only if a solution $x^{(t)}$ is generated that agrees with x in some objective functions, we deviate from the original Witness function. Let $K \subseteq [d]$ denote the objective functions in which $x^{(t)}$ coincides with x. Then we can bound at this point the probability that $V^t \cdot x \in (b_t, b_t + \varepsilon]$ simultaneously for all $t \in K$. In order to also deal with the other objectives $t \notin K$, we restart the Witness function. In this restart, we ignore all objective functions in K and we execute the Witness function as if only objectives $t \notin K$ were present. Additionally we restrict in the restart the set of feasible solutions to those that coincide in the objectives $t \in K$ with x, i.e., to $\{y \in \mathcal{S} : \forall t \in K : V^t \cdot y = V^t \cdot x\}$. With similar techniques as in the analysis of higher moments we ensure that different restarts lead to linearly independent linear combinations.

This exploits that every Pareto-optimal solution x is also Pareto-optimal with respect to only the objective functions V^t with $t \notin K$ if the set $\mathcal{S}$ is restricted to solutions that agree with x in all objective functions V^t with $t \in K$. This guarantees that whenever the Witness function is restarted, x is still a Pareto-optimal solution with respect to the restricted solution set and the remaining objective functions.

It can happen that we have to restart the Witness function d times before a unique candidate for a Pareto-optimal solution in B is identified. As in each of these restarts at most d solutions are generated, the total number of solutions that is generated can increase from $d+1$, as in the case of non-zero-preserving perturbations, to roughly d^2. The set $I \subseteq [n]$ of indices restricted to which these solutions are linearly independent has a cardinality of at most d^3. The reason for this increase is that we have to choose more indices to obtain linear independence due to the fixed zeros. Taking a union bound over all valid choices of I, of the values that the generated solutions take at these positions, and the possibilities when and due to which objectives the restarts occur, yields Theorem 1. This theorem relies again on the result about linearly independent linear combinations of independent random variables from [17] and its improved version for quasiconcave densities that we show in this paper.

3. FURTHER NOTATION

In our analysis, we will shift the solutions $x \in \mathcal{S}$ by a certain vector $u \in \{0,1\}^n$ and consider the values $V^t \cdot (x - u)$. For the linear objectives we mean the value $V^t x - V^t u$, where $V^t u$ is well-defined even for a shift vector $u \in \{0,1\}^n \setminus \mathcal{S}$. For the adversarial objective, however, we define $V^{d+1} \cdot (x - u) := V^{d+1}x$. It should not be confused with $V^{d+1}y$ for $y = x - u$.

Let $b = (b_1, \ldots, b_d) \in \mathbb{R}^d$ be a vector such that b_k is an integral multiple of ε for any k. (Recall that $\varepsilon > 0$ is a small real for which $1/\varepsilon$ is integral.) We will call the set $B = \{(y_1, \ldots, y_d) \in \mathbb{R}^d : y_k \in (b_k, b_k + \varepsilon] \text{ for any } k\}$ an *ε-box* and b *the corner* of B. For a vector $x \in \{-1, 0, 1\}$ the expression $B_V(x)$ denotes the unique ε-box B for which $V^{1\ldots d}x \in B$. We call B the ε-box of x and say that x lies in B. With $\mathbb{B}_\varepsilon$ we denote the set of all ε-boxes having corners b for which $b \in \{-n/\varepsilon, \ldots, n/\varepsilon - 1\}^d$. Hence, $|\mathbb{B}_\varepsilon| = (2n/\varepsilon)^d$. If all coefficients V_i^k of V are from $[-1, 1]$, which is true for any of the models considered in this paper, and if for any $k = 1, \ldots, d$ there is an index i such that $|V_i^k| < 1$, which holds with probability 1 in any of our models, then the ε-box of any vector $x \in \{-1, 0, 1\}^n$ belongs to $\mathbb{B}_\varepsilon$. Note, that all vectors x constructed in this paper are from $\{-1, 0, 1\}^n$. Hence, without any further explanation we will use that $B_V(x) \in \mathbb{B}_\varepsilon$.

In this paper we extensively use tuples instead of sets. The reason for this is that we are not only interested in certain components of a vector or a matrix, but we also want to describe in which order they are considered. This will be clear after the introduction of the following notation. Note that some of the notation already appeared in Subsection 1.4, but we defined it slightly different there as we did not want the reader to be distracted by technical details. Let n, m be positive integers and let $a_1, \dots, a_n$, $b_1, \dots, b_m$ be arbitrary reals. We define $[n] = (1, \dots, n)$, $[n]_0 = (0, 1, \dots, n)$, $|(a_1, \dots, a_n)| = n$ and $(a_1, \dots, a_n) \cup (b_1, \dots, b_m) = (a_1, \dots, a_n, b_1, \dots, b_m)$. By the expressions $(a_1, \dots, a_n) \setminus (b_1, \dots, b_m)$ and $(a_1, \dots, a_n) \cap (b_1, \dots, b_m)$ we denote the tuples we obtain when we remove all elements from $(a_1, \dots, a_n)$ that (do not) belong to $(b_1, \dots, b_m)$. We write $(a_1, \dots, a_n) \subseteq (b_1, \dots, b_m)$ if $a_k \in (b_1, \dots, b_m)$ for any index $k \in [n]$. Let x be a vector and let A be a matrix. By $x|_{i_1 \dots i_n} = x|_{(i_1, \dots, i_n)}$ we denote the column vector $(x_{i_1}, \dots, x_{i_n})$, by $A|_{(i_1, \dots, i_n)}$ we denote the matrix consisting of the rows $i_1, \dots, i_n$ of matrix A in this order.

For an index set $I \subseteq [n]$ and a vector $y \in \{0,1\}^n$ let $\mathcal{S}_I(y)$ denote the set of all solutions $z \in \mathcal{S}$ such that $z_i = y_i$ for any index $i \in I$. For the sake of simplicity we also use the notation $\mathcal{S}_I(\hat{y})$ to describe the set $\{z \in \mathcal{S} : z_i = \hat{y}_i\}$ for a vector $\hat{y} \in \{0,1\}^{|I|}$ when the components of y are labeled by $y_{i_1}, \dots, y_{i_{|I|}}$ where $I = (i_1, \dots, i_{|I|})$.

With $\mathbb{I}_n$ we refer to the $n \times n$-identity matrix and with $\mathbb{O}_{m \times n}$ to the $m \times n$-zero matrix. If the number of rows and columns are clear, then we drop the indices.

4. NON-ZERO-PRESERVING PERTURBATIONS

4.1 Smoothed Number of Pareto-optimal Solutions

To prove Theorem 3 we assume without loss of generality that $n \geq d+1$ and consider the following function called the `Witness` function. It is very similar to the one suggested by Moitra and O'Donnell, but with an additional parameter I. This parameter is a tuple of forbidden indices: it restricts the set of indices we are allowed to choose from. For the analysis of the smoothed number of Pareto-optimal solutions we will set $I = ()$. The parameter becomes important in the next section when we analyze higher moments.

`Witness`(V, x, I)

1: Set $\mathcal{R}_{d+1} = \mathcal{S} \cap \mathcal{S}_I(x)$.
2: **for** $t = d, d-1, \dots, 0$ **do**
3: Set $\mathcal{C}_t = \{z \in \mathcal{R}_{t+1} : V^{1 \dots t} z < V^{1 \dots t} x\}$.
4: **if** $\mathcal{C}_t \neq \emptyset$ **then**
5: Set $x^{(t)} = \arg\min\{V^{t+1} z : z \in \mathcal{C}_t\}$.
6: **if** $t = 0$ **then return** $x^{(t)}$
7: Determine the first index $i_t \in [n]$ with $x^{(t)}_{i_t} \neq x_{i_t}$.
8: $I \hookleftarrow I \cup (i_t)$
9: Set $\mathcal{R}_t = \{z \in \mathcal{R}_{t+1} \cap \mathcal{S}_I(x) : V^{t+1} z < V^{t+1} x^{(t)}\}$.
10: **else**
11: Set $i_t = \min([n] \setminus I)$.
12: $I \hookleftarrow I \cup (i_t)$.
13: Set $x^{(t)}_i = \begin{cases} \overline{x_i} & \text{if } i = i_t\,, \\ x_i & \text{otherwise}\,. \end{cases}$
14: Set $\mathcal{R}_t = \mathcal{R}_{t+1} \cap \mathcal{S}_I(x)$.
15: **end if**
16: **end for**
17: **return** $(\bot, \dots, \bot)$.

Note, that $\mathcal{C}_0 = \mathcal{R}_1$ since $V^{1 \dots t} z < V^{1 \dots t} x$ is no restriction if $t = 0$. For $t \geq 1$ the index i_t in line 7 exists because $V^1 x^{(t)} < V^1 x$, which implies $x^{(t)} \neq x$. In the remainder of this section we only consider the case that x is Pareto-optimal, that I contains pairwise distinct indices and that the number $|I|$ of indices contained in I is at most $n - (d+1)$. This ensures that the indices $i_0, \dots, i_d$ exist. Unless stated otherwise, we assume that the OK-event occurs. That means that $|V^k \cdot (y - z)| \geq \varepsilon$ for every $k \in [d]$ and for any two distinct vectors $y \neq z \in \mathcal{S}$ and that for any $k \in [d]$ there is an index $i \in [n]$ such that $|V^k_i| < 1$. The first property ensures, amongst others, that there is a unique arg min in line 5. The latter property, which holds with probability 1, ensures that $B_V(x) \in \mathbb{B}_\varepsilon$ for any vector $x \in \{-1, 0, 1\}^n$.

LEMMA 6. *The call* `Witness`(V, x, I) *returns* $x^{(0)} = x$.

We will see that for the execution of `Witness`(V, x, I) we only need some information about x. This is one crucial property which will help us to bound the expected number of Pareto-optimal solutions.

DEFINITION 7. *Let $x^{(0)}, \dots, x^{(d)}$ be the vectors constructed during the call* `Witness`(V, x, I)*, let $\hat{I}$ be the tuple I at the moment when the* `Witness` *function terminates and let* $i^* = \min([n] \setminus \hat{I})$. *We call the pair (I^*, A^*) where $I^* = \hat{I} \cup (i^*)$ and $A^* = [x^{(d)}, \dots, x^{(0)}]$ the* (V, I)-certificate *of x. The pair $(I^*, A^*|_{I^*})$ is called the* restricted (V, I)-certificate *of x. We call a pair (I', A') a* (restricted) I-certificate, *if there exist a realization V such that* OK(V) *is true and a Pareto-optimal solution $x \in \mathcal{S}$ such that (I', A') is the (restricted) (V, I)-certificate of x. By $\mathcal{CS}(I)$ we denote the set of all restricted I-certificates.*

For the analysis of the first moment we only need restricted I-certificates. Our analysis of higher moments requires more knowledge about the vectors $x^{(t)}$ than just the values x_i for $i \in I^*$. The additional indices are, however, depending on further calls of the `Witness` function which we do not know a priori. This is why we have to define two types of certificates. For the sake of reusability we formulate some statements more general than necessary for this section.

LEMMA 8. *Let V be an arbitrary realization where* OK(V) *is true, let x be a Pareto-optimal solution with respect to V, and let (I^*, A) be the restricted (V, I)-certificate of x. Then, $I^* = (j_1, \dots, j_{|I|+d+1})$ consists of pairwise distinct indices and the $(|I| + d + 1) \times (d+1)$-matrix A is of the form*

$$A = \begin{bmatrix} x_{j_1} & \cdots & x_{j_{|I|}} & \overline{x_{j_{|I|+1}}} & * & \cdots & * \\ \vdots & & \vdots & x_{j_{|I|+1}} & \ddots & \ddots & \vdots \\ \vdots & & \vdots & \vdots & \ddots & \overline{x_{j_{|I|+d}}} & * \\ x_{j_1} & \cdots & x_{j_{|I|}} & x_{j_{|I|+1}} & \cdots & x_{j_{|I|+d}} & x_{j_{|I|+d+1}} \end{bmatrix}^{\mathrm{T}},$$

where each '$*$' can either be 0 or 1 independently of the other '$*$'-entries.

PROOF. Lemma 6 implies that the last column of A equals $x|_{I^*}$. Hence, we just have to consider the first d columns of A. Note, that $I = (j_1, \dots, j_{|I|})$ and $j_{|I|+1}, \dots, j_{|I|+d+1} = i_d, \dots, i_1, i^*$. Let $I_t = I \cup (i_d, \dots, i_t)$. The construction of the sets $\mathcal{R}_t$ yields $\mathcal{R}_t \subseteq \mathcal{S}_{I_t}(x)$ (see lines 1, 9, and 14). Index i_t

is always chosen such that $i_t \notin I_{t+1}$: If it is constructed in line 7, then $x^{(t)}_{i_t} \neq x_{i_t}$. Since in that case we have $x^{(t)} \in \mathcal{R}_{t+1} \subseteq \mathcal{S}_{I_{t+1}}(x)$ and, hence, index i_t cannot be an element of I_{t+1}. In line 11, index i_t is explicitely constructed such that $i_t \notin I_{t+1}$. The same argument holds for the index i^*. Hence, the indices of I^* are pairwise distinct.

Now, consider the column of A corresponding to vector $x^{(t)}$ for $t \in [d]$. If $\mathcal{C}_t = \emptyset$, then the form of the column follows directly from the construction of $x^{(t)}$ in line 13 and from the fact that the indices of I^* are pairwise distinct. If $\mathcal{C}_t \neq \emptyset$, then $x^{(t)} \in \mathcal{C}_t \subseteq \mathcal{R}_{t+1} \subseteq \mathcal{S}_{I_{t+1}}(x)$, i.e., $x^{(t)}$ agrees with x in all indices $i \in I_{t+1}$. By the choice of i_t in line 7 we get $x^{(t)}_{i_t} = \overline{x_{i_t}}$. This concludes the proof. □

Let (I^*, A^*) be the (V, I)-certificate of x and let $J \supseteq I^*$ be a tuple of pairwise distinct indices. We consider the following variant of the `Witness` function that uses information about x given by the index tuple J, the bit matrix $A = A^*|_J$ with columns $a^{(d)}, \dots, a^{(0)}$, a shift vector u and the ε-box $B = B_V(x-u)$ instead of vector x itself. The meaning of the shift vector will become clear when we analyze the probability of certain events. We will see that not all information about V needs to be revealed to execute the new `Witness` function, i.e., we have some randomness left which we can use later. With the choice of the shift vector we can control which information needs to be revealed for executing the `Witness` function.

`Witness`(V, J, A, B, u)

1: Let b be the corner of B.
2: Set $\mathcal{R}_{d+1} = \mathcal{S} \cap \bigcup_{t'=0}^{d} \mathcal{S}_J\big(a^{(t')}\big)$.
3: **for** $t = d, d-1, \dots, 0$ **do**
4: Set $\mathcal{C}_t = \big\{z \in \mathcal{R}_{t+1} \cap \mathcal{S}_J\big(a^{(t)}\big) : V^{1\dots t} \cdot (z-u) \leq b|_{1\dots t}\big\}$.
5: **if** $\mathcal{C}_t \neq \emptyset$ **then**
6: Set $x^{(t)} = \arg\min\big\{V^{t+1}z : z \in \mathcal{C}_t\big\}$.
7: **if** $t = 0$ **then return** $x^{(t)}$
8: Set $\mathcal{R}_t = \big\{z \in \mathcal{R}_{t+1} \cap \bigcup_{t'=0}^{t-1} \mathcal{S}_J\big(a^{(t')}\big) : V^{t+1}z < V^{t+1}x^{(t)}\big\}$.
9: **else**
10: Set $x^{(t)} = (\bot, \dots, \bot)$.
11: Set $\mathcal{R}_t = \mathcal{R}_{t+1} \cap \bigcup_{t'=0}^{t-1} \mathcal{S}_J\big(a^{(t')}\big)$.
12: **end if**
13: **end for**
14: **return** $(\bot, \dots, \bot)$

Lemma 9. *Let (I^*, A^*) be the (V, I)-certificate of x, let $J \supseteq I^*$ be an arbitrary tuple of pairwise distinct indices, let $A = A^*|_J$, let $u \in \{0,1\}^n$ be an arbitrary vector, and let $B = B_V(x-u)$. Then, the call* `Witness`(V, J, A, B, u) *returns vector x.*

Before we give a formal proof of Lemma 9 we try to give some intuition for it. Instead of considering the whole set $\mathcal{S}$ of solutions we restrict it to vectors that look like the vectors we want to reconstruct in the next rounds, i.e., we intersect the current set with the set $\bigcup_{t'=0}^{t-1} \mathcal{S}_J\big(a^{(t')}\big)$ in round t. That way we only deal with subsets of the original sets, but we do not lose the vectors we want to reconstruct since $J \supseteq I^*$.

Proof. Let $\mathcal{R}'_t$, $\mathcal{C}'_t$, and $x'^{(t)}$ denote the sets and vectors constructed in the call `Witness`(V, J, A, B, u) and let $\mathcal{R}_t$, $\mathcal{C}_t$, and $x^{(t)}$ denote the sets and vectors constructed in the call `Witness`(V, x, I). By induction we prove the following statements:

- $\mathcal{R}'_t \subseteq \mathcal{R}_t$ for any $t \in [d+1]$.
- $x'^{(t)} = x^{(t)}$ for any $t \in [d]_0$ for which $\mathcal{C}_t \neq \emptyset$.
- $x^{(t')} \in \mathcal{R}'_t$ for any $t \in [d+1]$ and any $t' \in [t-1]$ for which $\mathcal{C}_{t'} \neq \emptyset$.

With those claims Lemma 9 follows immediately: Since $x^{(0)} = x$ and $\mathcal{C}_0 \neq \emptyset$ due to Lemma 6 we obtain $x^{(0)} \in \mathcal{R}'_1 = \mathcal{C}'_0$ and, hence, we return $x'^{(0)} = x^{(0)} = x$.

Let us first focus on the shift vector u and compare line 3 of the first `Witness` function and line 4 of the second `Witness` function. The main difference is that in the first version we have the restriction $V^{1\dots t}z < V^{1\dots t}x$, whereas in the second version we seek for solutions z such that $V^{1\dots t} \cdot (z-u) \leq b|_{1\dots t}$. As b is the corner of the ε-box $B = B_V(x-u)$, those restrictions are equivalent for solutions $z \in \mathcal{S}$ since

$$V^{1\dots t} \cdot (z-u) \leq b|_{1\dots t} \iff V^{1\dots t} \cdot (z-u) < V^{1\dots t} \cdot (x-u) \iff V^{1\dots t}z < V^{1\dots t}x\,.$$

The first inequality is due to the occurrence of the OK-event. Now, we prove the statements by downward induction over t. Let $t = d+1$. Lemma 8 yields $a^{(t')}\big|_I = x|_I$ for any $t' \in [d]_0$, i.e., $\bigcup_{t'=0}^{d} \mathcal{S}_J\big(a^{(t')}\big) \subseteq \mathcal{S}_I(x)$. Consequently, $\mathcal{R}'_{d+1} \subseteq \mathcal{R}_{d+1}$. Consider an arbitrary index $t' \in [d]$ for which $\mathcal{C}_{t'} \neq \emptyset$. Then, $x^{(t')} \in \mathcal{R}_{t'} \subseteq \mathcal{S}$ and $x^{(t')} \in \mathcal{S}_J\big(a^{(t')}\big)$. Hence, $x^{(t')} \in \mathcal{R}'_{d+1}$.

Let $t \leq d$. By the observation above we have

$$\mathcal{C}'_t = \Big\{z \in \mathcal{R}'_{t+1} \cap \mathcal{S}_J\big(a^{(t)}\big) : V^{1\dots t}z < V^{1\dots t}x\Big\} \quad \text{and}$$
$$\mathcal{C}_t = \big\{z \in \mathcal{R}_{t+1} : V^{1\dots t}z < V^{1\dots t}x\big\}\,.$$

Since $\mathcal{R}'_{t+1} \subseteq \mathcal{R}_{t+1}$, we obtain $\mathcal{C}'_t \subseteq \mathcal{C}_t$. We first consider the case $\mathcal{C}_t = \emptyset$, which implies $\mathcal{C}'_t = \emptyset$. Then, $\mathcal{R}'_t = \mathcal{R}'_{t+1} \cap \bigcup_{t'=0}^{t-1} \mathcal{S}_J\big(a^{(t')}\big)$ and $\mathcal{R}_t = \mathcal{R}_{t+1} \cap \mathcal{S}_I(x)$ for the current index tuple I. According to Lemma 8, all vectors $x^{(0)}, \dots, x^{(t-1)}$ agree with x on the indices $i \in I$. Thus, $\bigcup_{t'=0}^{t-1} \mathcal{S}_J\big(a^{(t')}\big) \subseteq \mathcal{S}_I(x)$, and as $\mathcal{R}'_{t+1} \subseteq \mathcal{R}_{t+1}$ we obtain $\mathcal{R}'_t \subseteq \mathcal{R}_t$. Let $t' \in [t-1]$ be an index for which $\mathcal{C}_{t'} \neq \emptyset$. Then, $x^{(t')} \in \mathcal{R}'_{t+1}$ by the induction hypothesis, $x^{(t')} \in \mathcal{S}_J\big(a^{(t')}\big)$, and consequently $x^{(t')} \in \mathcal{R}'_t$.

Finally, let us consider the case $\mathcal{C}_t \neq \emptyset$. The induction hypothesis yields $x^{(t)} \in \mathcal{R}'_{t+1}$. Since $x^{(t)} \in \mathcal{S}_J\big(a^{(t)}\big)$ and $V^{1\dots t} \cdot x^{(t)} < V^{1\dots t}x$, also $x^{(t)} \in \mathcal{C}'_t$ and thus $\mathcal{C}'_t \neq \emptyset$. Hence, $x'^{(t)} = x^{(t)}$ as $\mathcal{C}'_t \subseteq \mathcal{C}_t$. The remaining claims have to be validated only if $t \geq 1$. Then, $\mathcal{R}'_t = \big\{z \in \mathcal{R}'_{t+1} \cap \bigcup_{t'=0}^{t-1} \mathcal{S}_J\big(a^{(t')}\big) : V^{t+1}z < V^{t+1}x^{(t)}\big\}$ and $\mathcal{R}_t = \big\{z \in \mathcal{R}_{t+1} \cap \mathcal{S}_I(x) : V^{t+1}z < V^{t+1}x^{(t)}\big\}$ for the current index tuple I. With the same argument used for the case $\mathcal{C}_t = \emptyset$ we obtain $\mathcal{R}'_{t+1} \cap \bigcup_{t'=0}^{t-1} \mathcal{S}_J\big(a^{(t')}\big) \subseteq \mathcal{R}_{t+1} \cap \mathcal{S}_I(x)$ and thus $\mathcal{R}'_t \subseteq \mathcal{R}_t$. Consider an arbitrary index $t' \in [t-1]$ for which $\mathcal{C}_{t'} \neq \emptyset$. Then, $x^{(t')} \in \mathcal{R}_{t'} \subseteq \mathcal{R}_t$. In particular, $V^{t+1}x^{(t')} < V^{t+1}x^{(t)}$. Furthermore, $x^{(t')} \in \mathcal{R}'_{t+1}$ due to the induction hypothesis, and $x^{(t')} \in \mathcal{S}_J\big(a^{(t')}\big)$. Consequently, $x^{(t')} \in \mathcal{R}'_t$. □

As mentioned earlier, with the shift vector u we control which information of V has to be revealed to execute the call `Witness`(V, J, A, B, u). While Lemma 9 holds for any vector u, we have to choose u carefully for our probabilistic analysis to work. We will see that the choice $u^* = u^*(J, A)$,

$$u_i^* = \begin{cases} \overline{x_i} & \text{if } i = i^*, \\ x_i & \text{if } i \in J \setminus (i^*), \\ 0 & \text{otherwise}, \end{cases} \quad (1)$$

is appropriate. Note, that i^* is the index that has been added to $\hat{I}$ in the definition of the (V, I)-certificate to obtain I^*. Moreover, the values x_i are encoded in the last column of A for any index $i \in J$ according to Lemma 8. Hence, if (I^*, A^*) is the (V, I)-certificate of x, then vector u^* can be defined when a tuple $J \supseteq I^*$ and the matrix $A = A^*|_J$ are known; we do not have to know the vector x itself.

For bounding the number of Pareto-optimal solutions consider the functions $\chi_{I^*,A,B}(V)$ parameterized by an arbitrary restricted I-certificate (I^*, A), and an arbitrary ε-box $B \in \mathbb{B}_\varepsilon$, defined as follows: $\chi_{I^*,A,B}(V) = 1$ if the call $\texttt{Witness}(V, I^*, A, B, u^*(J, A))$ returns a solution $x' \in \mathcal{S}$ such that $B_V(x' - u^*(I^*, A)) = B$, and $\chi_{I^*,A,B}(V) = 0$ otherwise.

Corollary 10. *Assume that* OK(V) *is true. Then, the number* PO(V) *of Pareto-optimal solutions is at most*

$$\sum_{(I^*,A)\in\mathcal{CS}(I)} \sum_{B\in\mathbb{B}_\varepsilon} \chi_{I^*,A,B}(V).$$

Proof. Let x be a Pareto-optimal solution, let (I^*, A) be the restricted (V, I)-certificate of x, and let $B = B_V(x - u^*(I^*, A)) \in \mathbb{B}_\varepsilon$ be the ε-box of $x - u^*(I^*, A)$. Due to Lemma 9, the call $\texttt{Witness}(V, I^*, A, B, u^*(I^*, A))$ returns vector x. Hence, $\chi_{I^*,A,B}(V) = 1$. It remains to show that the function $x \mapsto (I^*, A, B')$ is injective. Let x_1 and x_2 be distinct Pareto-optimal solutions and let (I_1^*, A_1) and (I_2^*, A_2) be the restricted (V, I)-certificates of x_1 and x_2, respectively. If $(I_1^*, A_1) \neq (I_2^*, A_2)$, then x_1 and x_2 are mapped to distinct triplets. Otherwise, $u^*(I_1^*, A_1) = u^*(I_2^*, A_2)$ and, hence, $B_V(x_1 - u^*(I_1^*, A_1)) \neq B_V(x_2 - u^*(I_2^*, A_2))$ because OK(V) is true. Consequently, also in this case x_1 and x_2 are mapped to distinct triplets. □

Corollary 10 immediately implies a bound on the expected number of Pareto-optimal solutions.

Corollary 11. *Let $E_{I^*,A,B}$ denote the event that the call* $\texttt{Witness}(V, I^*, A, B, u^*(I^*, A))$ *returns a vector x' such that $B_V(x' - u^*(I^*, A)) = B$. Then, the expected number of Pareto-optimal solutions is bounded by*

$$\sum_{(I^*,A)\in\mathcal{CS}(I)} \sum_{B\in\mathbb{B}_\varepsilon} \mathbf{Pr}_V[E_{I^*,A,B}] + 2^n \cdot \mathbf{Pr}_V\left[\overline{\text{OK}(V)}\right].$$

Proof. Let $p = \mathbf{Pr}_V[\text{OK}(V)]$, $\bar{p} = 1 - p$, and $X(V) = \sum_{(I^*,A)\in\mathcal{CS}(I)} \sum_{B\in\mathbb{B}_\varepsilon} \chi_{I^*,A,B}(V)$. Then

$$\begin{aligned} \mathbf{E}_V[\text{PO}(V)] &= \mathbf{E}_V[\text{PO}(V) \mid \text{OK}(V)] \cdot \mathbf{Pr}_V[\text{OK}(V)] \\ &\quad + \mathbf{E}_V\left[\text{PO}(V) \mid \overline{\text{OK}(V)}\right] \cdot \mathbf{Pr}_V\left[\overline{\text{OK}(V)}\right] \\ &\le \mathbf{E}_V[X(V) \mid \text{OK}(V)] \cdot p + 2^n \cdot \bar{p} \\ &\le \mathbf{E}_V[X(V)] + 2^n \cdot \bar{p} \\ &= \sum_{(I^*,A)\in\mathcal{CS}(I)} \sum_{B\in\mathbb{B}_\varepsilon} \mathbf{Pr}_V[E_{I^*,A,B}] + 2^n \cdot \bar{p}, \end{aligned}$$

where the first inequality is due to Corollary 10. □

We will see that the first term of the sum in Corollary 11 can be bounded independently of ε and that the limit of the second term is 0 for $\varepsilon \to 0$. First of all, we analyze the size of the restricted certificate space.

Lemma 12. *The size of the restricted certificate space for $I_0 = ()$ is bounded by $|\mathcal{CS}(I_0)| \le 2^{(d+1)^2} n^d = O(n^d)$ for fixed d.*

Proof. If OK(V) is true and if x is Pareto-optimal with respect to V, then given an index tuple I_0 exactly d indices $i_1, \ldots, i_d$ are created in $\texttt{Witness}(V, x, I_0)$. The index i^* is determined deterministicly depending on the indices $i_1, \ldots, i_d$. Matrix A of any restricted I_0-certificate (I^*, A) is a binary $(d+1) \times (d+1)$-matrix. Hence, the number of possible restricted I_0-certificates is bounded by $2^{(d+1)^2} \cdot n^d$. □

Let us now fix an arbitrary I-certificate (I^*, A^*), a tuple $J \supseteq I^*$, and an ε-box $B \in \mathbb{B}_\varepsilon$. We want to analyze the probability $\mathbf{Pr}_V[E_{J,A,B}]$ where $A = A^*|_J$. By V_J and $V_{\bar{J}}$ we denote the part of the matrix $V^{1\ldots d}$ that belongs to the indices $i \in J$ and to the indices $i \notin J$, respectively. For our analysis let us further assume that the $V_{\bar{J}}$ is fixed as well, i.e., we will only exploit the randomness of V_J.

As motivated above, the call $\texttt{Witness}(V, J, A, B, u)$ can be executed without the full knowledge of V_J. To formalize this, we introduce matrices Q_k that describe the linear combinations of V_J^k we have to know:

$$Q_k = \left[p^{(d)}, \ldots, p^{(k)}, p^{(k-2)} - p^{(k-1)}, \ldots, p^{(0)} - p^{(k-1)}\right] \quad (2)$$

for $p^{(t)} = p^{(t)}(J, A, u) = a^{(t)} - u|_J$ where $a^{(t)}$ are the columns of matrix A. Note, that the matrices $Q_k = Q_k(J, A, u)$ depend on the pair (J, A) and on the vector u.

Lemma 13. *Let $u \in \{0,1\}^n$ be an arbitrary shift vector and let U and W be two realizations of V such that $U_{\bar{J}} = W_{\bar{J}}$ and $U_J^k \cdot q = W_J^k \cdot q$ for any index $k \in [d]$ and any column q of the matrix $Q_k(J, A, u)$. Then the calls* $\texttt{Witness}(U, J, A, B, u)$ *and* $\texttt{Witness}(W, J, A, B, u)$ *return the same result.*

Proof. We fix $k \in [d]$ and analyze which information of V_J^k is required in the call $\texttt{Witness}(V, J, A, B, u)$. For the execution of line 4 we need to know $V^k \cdot (z - u)$ for solutions $z \in \mathcal{S}_J(a^{(t)})$ in all rounds $t \ge k$. Since we can assume $V_{\bar{J}}^k$ to be known, this means that $V_J^k \cdot (z|_J - u|_J) = V_J^k \cdot (a^{(t)} - u|_J) = V_J^k \cdot p^{(t)}$ must be revealed. For $t \ge k$ vector $p^{(t)}$ is a column of Q_k. The execution of line 6 does not require further information about V_J^k as all solutions in $\mathcal{C}_t$ agree on the indices $i \in J$. Hence, it remains to consider line 8. Only in round $t = k - 1$ we need information about V^k. In that round it suffices to know $V_J^k \cdot (z|_J - x^{(t)}|_J)$ for any solution $z \in \bigcup_{t'=0}^{t-1} \mathcal{S}_J(a^{(t')})$. Hence, for $z \in \mathcal{S}_J(a^{(t')})$, $t' \in [k-2]_0$, the linear combinations $V_J^k \cdot (z|_J - x^{(t)}|_J) = V_J^k \cdot ((a^{(t')} - u|_J) - (a^{(k-1)} - u|_J)) = V_J^k \cdot (p^{(t')} - p^{(k-1)})$ must be revealed. Since $t' \in [k-2]_0$, this is a column of Q_k. As U and W agree on all necessary information, both calls return the same result. □

We will now see why $u^* = u^*(J, A)$ defined in Equation (1) is a good shift vector.

Lemma 14. *Let $\hat{p}^{(t)} = p^{(t)}(J, A, u^*(J, A))\big|_{I^*}$ and $Q = [\hat{p}^{(d)}, \ldots, \hat{p}^{(0)}]$. Then, the $(|I| + d + 1) \times (d+1)$-matrix $|Q|$*

is of the form

$$|Q| = \begin{bmatrix} 0 & \dots & 0 & 1 & * & \dots & * \\ \vdots & & \vdots & 0 & \ddots & \ddots & \vdots \\ \vdots & & \vdots & \vdots & \ddots & \ddots & * \\ 0 & \dots & 0 & 0 & \dots & 0 & 1 \end{bmatrix}^{\mathrm{T}},$$

where $|Q|$ *denotes the matrix* Q' *for which* $q'_{ij} = |q_{ij}|$.

PROOF. Let $I^* = (j_1, \dots, j_{|I|+d+1})$, i.e., $i^* = j_{|I|+d+1}$. According to Lemma 8 and the construction of vector u^* in Equation (1) we obtain $Q = Q_1 - Q_2$ for $Q_2 = [\tilde{u}, \dots, \tilde{u}]$ and

$$Q_1 = \begin{bmatrix} x_{j_1} & \dots & \dots & x_{j_1} \\ \vdots & & & \vdots \\ x_{j_{|I|}} & \dots & \dots & x_{j_{|I|}} \\ \overline{x_{j_{|I|+1}}} & x_{j_{|I|+1}} & \dots & x_{j_{|I|+1}} \\ * & \ddots & \ddots & \vdots \\ \vdots & \ddots & \overline{x_{j_{|I|+d}}} & x_{j_{|I|+d}} \\ * & \dots & * & x_{j_{|I|+d+1}} \end{bmatrix},$$

where $\tilde{u} = u^*|_{I^*} = (x_{j_1}, \dots, x_{j_{|I|+d}}, \overline{x_{j_{|I|+d+1}}})^T$. The claim follows since $a - a = 0$ and $a - \overline{a} \in \{-1, 1\}$ for $a \in \{0, 1\}$. □

LEMMA 15. *For any* $k \in [d]$ *the columns of the matrix* $Q_k(J, A, u^*(J, A))$ *and the vector* $p^{(0)}$ *are linearly independent.*

PROOF. It suffices to show that the columns of the submatrix $\widehat{Q}_k = Q_k\big|_{I^*}$ and the vector $\hat{p}^{(0)} = p^{(0)}\big|_{I^*}$ are linearly independent. For this, we introduce the vectors $\hat{p}^{(t)} = p^{(t)}\big|_{I^*}$. Consider the matrix $Q = [\hat{p}^{(d)}, \dots, \hat{p}^{(0)}]$. Due to Lemma 14 the last $d+1$ rows of Q form a lower triangular matrix and the entries on the principal diagonal are from the set $\{-1, 1\}$. Consequently, the vectors $\hat{p}^{(t)}$ are linearly independent. As these vectors are the same as the columns of matrix $\widehat{Q}_1$ plus vector $\hat{p}^{(0)}$, the claim holds for $k = 1$. Now let $k \geq 2$. We consider an arbitrary linear combination of the columns of $\widehat{Q}_k$ and the vector $\hat{p}^{(0)}$ that computes to zero:

$$\begin{aligned} 0 &= \sum_{t=k}^{d} \lambda_t \cdot \hat{p}^{(t)} + \sum_{t=0}^{k-2} \lambda_t \cdot \left(\hat{p}^{(t)} - \hat{p}^{(k-1)}\right) + \mu \cdot \hat{p}^{(0)} \\ &= \sum_{t=k}^{d} \lambda_t \cdot \hat{p}^{(t)} + \sum_{t=1}^{k-2} \lambda_t \cdot \hat{p}^{(t)} - \left(\sum_{t=0}^{k-2} \lambda_t\right) \cdot \hat{p}^{(k-1)} \\ &\quad + (\lambda_0 + \mu) \cdot \hat{p}^{(0)}. \end{aligned}$$

As the vectors $\hat{p}^{(t)}$ are linearly independent, we first get $\lambda_t = 0$ for $t \in [d] \setminus \{k-1\}$, which yields $\lambda_0 = 0$ and, finally, $\mu = 0$. This concludes the proof. □

COROLLARY 16. *For an arbitrary restricted* I*-certificate* (I^*, A) *the probability of event* $E_{I^*,A,B}$ *is bounded by*

$$\mathbf{Pr}_V[E_{I^*,A,B}] \leq 2^d \gamma^{\gamma-d} \phi^d \varepsilon^d$$

if all densities are quasiconcave, where $\gamma = d \cdot (|I| + d + 1)$.

PROOF. Event $E_{I^*,A,B}$ occurs if the output is a vector x' such that $B_V(x' - u^*(I^*, A)) = B$. In accordance with Lemma 13 the output vector x' is determined when for any $k \in [d]$ the linear combinations of $V^k_{I^*}$ given by the columns of matrix Q_k are known. The equality $B_V(x' - u^*(I^*, A)) = B$ holds if and only if

$$\begin{aligned} V^k \cdot \left(x' - u^*(I^*, A)\right) &= V^k_{\overline{I^*}} \cdot \left(x' - u^*(I^*, A)\right)\big|_{\overline{I^*}} \\ &\quad + V^k_{I^*} \cdot \left(x' - u^*(I^*, A)\right)\big|_{I^*} \in B \end{aligned}$$

holds for any $k \in [d]$. Since x' is determined and as $\left(x' - u^*(I^*, A)\right)\big|_{I^*} = a^{(0)} - u^*(I^*, A)|_{I^*} = p^{(0)}$ for the vector $p^{(0)} = p^{(0)}(I^*, A, u^*(I^*, A))$, this is equivalent to the event that

$$V^k_{I^*} \cdot p^{(0)} \in B - V^k_{\overline{I^*}} \cdot \left(x' - u^*(I^*, A)\right)\big|_{\overline{I^*}} =: C_k,$$

where C_k is an interval of length ε depending on x' and hence on the linear combinations of V_{I^*} given by the matrices Q_k. We do not explicitly mention the dependence on $V_{\overline{I^*}}$ as we consider it to be fixed. By C we denote the d-dimensional hypercube $C = \prod_{k=1}^{d} C_k$ with side length ε defined by the intervals C_k.

For any $k \in [d]$ let Q'_k be the matrix consisting of the columns of Q_k and the vector $p^{(0)}$. This matrices form the diagonal blocks of the matrix

$$Q' = \begin{bmatrix} Q'_1 & \mathbb{O} & \dots & \mathbb{O} \\ \mathbb{O} & \ddots & \ddots & \vdots \\ \vdots & \ddots & \ddots & \mathbb{O} \\ \mathbb{O} & \dots & \mathbb{O} & Q'_d \end{bmatrix} \in \{-1, 0, 1\}^{d \cdot |I^*| \times d \cdot (d+1)}.$$

Lemma 15 implies that matrix Q' has full rank. We permute the columns of Q' to obtain a matrix Q where the last d columns belong to the last column of one of the matrices Q'_k. Let the rows of Q be labeled by $Q_{j_1,1}, \dots, Q_{j_m,1}, \dots, Q_{j_1,d}, \dots, Q_{j_m,d}$ assuming that $I^* = (j_1, \dots, j_m)$. We introduce random variables $X_{j,k} = V^k_j$, $j \in I^*$, $k \in [d]$, labeled in the same fashion as the rows of Q. Event $E_{I^*,A,B}$ holds if and only if the d linear combinations of the variables $X_{j,k}$ given by the last d columns of Q fall into the d-dimensional hypercube C depending on the linear combinations of the variables $X_{j,k}$ given by the remaining columns of Q. The claim follows by applying Theorem 35 for the matrix Q^{T} and due to the fact that the number of rows of Q is $d \cdot |I^*| = \gamma$. □

PROOF OF THEOREM 3. We begin the proof by showing that the OK-event is likely to happen. For any index $t \in [d]$ and any solutions $x \neq y \in \mathcal{S}$ the probability that $|V^t x - V^t y| \leq \varepsilon$ is bounded by $2\phi\varepsilon$. To see this, choose one index $i \in [n]$ such that $x_i \neq y_i$ and fix all coefficients V^t_j for $j \neq i$. Then, the value V^t_i must fall into an interval of length 2ε. A union bound over all indices $t \in [d]$ and over all pairs $(x, y) \in \mathcal{S} \times \mathcal{S}$ such that $x \neq y$ yields $\overline{p} := \mathbf{Pr}_V\left[\overline{\mathrm{OK}(V)}\right] \leq 2^{2n+1} d\phi\varepsilon$.

With $I_0 = ()$ and $\gamma = d \cdot (d+1)$ we obtain

$$\begin{aligned} \mathbf{E}_V[\mathrm{PO}(V)] &\leq \sum_{\substack{(I^*,A) \in \mathcal{CS}(I_0), \\ B \in \mathbb{B}_\varepsilon}} \mathbf{Pr}_V[E_{I^*,A,B}] + 2^n \overline{p} \\ &\leq \sum_{\substack{(I^*,A) \in \mathcal{CS}(I_0), \\ B \in \mathbb{B}_\varepsilon}} 2^d \gamma^{\gamma-d} \phi^d \varepsilon^d + 2^n \overline{p} \\ &\leq \sum_{\substack{(I^*,A) \in \mathcal{CS}(I_0), \\ B \in \mathbb{B}_\varepsilon}} 2^d (d+1)^{2d^2} \phi^d \varepsilon^d + 2^n \overline{p} \end{aligned}$$

$$\leq 2^{(d+1)^2} n^d \left(\frac{2n}{\varepsilon}\right)^d \cdot 2^d (d+1)^{2d^2} \phi^d \varepsilon^d + 2^n \overline{p}$$
$$\leq 2^{(d+2)^2} (d+1)^{2d^2} n^{2d} \phi^d + 2^{3n+1} d\phi\varepsilon .$$

The first inequality is due to Corollary 11. The second inequality is due to Corollary 16. The fourth inequality stems from Lemma 12. Since this bound is true for arbitrarily small $\varepsilon > 0$, the correctness of Theorem 3 follows. □

4.2 Higher Moments

The basic idea behind our analysis of higher moments is the following: If the OK-event occurs, then we can count the cth power of the number $\text{PO}(V)$ of Pareto-optimal solutions by counting all c-tuples $(B_1, \ldots, B_c)$ of ε-boxes where each ε-box B_i contains a Pareto-optimal solution x_i. We can bound this value as follows: First, call $\texttt{Witness}(V, x_1, ())$ to obtain a vector x_1' and consider an index tuple I_1 containing all indices created in this call and one additional index. In the second step, call $\texttt{Witness}(V, x_2, I_1)$ to obtain a vector x_2' and consider the tuple I_2 consisting of the indices of I_1, the indices created in this call, and one additional index. Now, call $\texttt{Witness}(V, x_3, I_2)$ and so on. If $(x_1, \ldots, x_c)$ is a tuple of Pareto-optimal solutions with $V^{1\ldots d} x_i \in B_i$ for $i \in [c]$, then $(x_1', \ldots, x_c') = (x_1, \ldots, x_c)$ due to Lemma 6. As in the analysis of the first moment, we use the variant of the $\texttt{Witness}$ function that uses certificates of the vectors x_ℓ instead of the vectors itself to simulate the calls. Hence we can reuse several statements of Subsection 4.1.

Unless stated otherwise, let V be a realization such that $\text{OK}(V)$ is true and fix arbitrary solutions $x_1, \ldots, x_c \in \mathcal{S}$ that are Pareto-optimal with respect to V.

Definition 17. *Let $I_0^* = ()$ and, for $\ell = 1, \ldots, c$, let (I_ℓ^*, A_ℓ^*) be the $(V, I_{\ell-1}^*)$-certificate of x_ℓ defined in Definition 7. The V-*certificate *of $(x_1, \ldots, x_c)$ is the pair $(I^*, \vec{A})$, where $I^* = I_c^*$ and $\vec{A} = (A_1, \ldots, A_c)$ for $A_\ell = A_\ell^*\big|_{I^*}$. We call a pair $(I', \vec{A}')$ a* c-certificate *if there is a realization V such that $\text{OK}(V)$ is true and if there are Pareto-optimal solutions $x_1, \ldots, x_c \in \mathcal{S}$ such that $(I', \vec{A}')$ is the V-certificate of $(x_1, \ldots, x_c)$. By $\mathcal{CS}_c$ we denote the set of all c-certificates.*

Note, that $I_0^* \subseteq \ldots \subseteq I_c^*$ and $|I_\ell^*| = |I_{\ell-1}^*| + d + 1$ for $\ell \in [c]$. We now consider the functions $\chi_{I^*, \vec{A}, \vec{B}}(V)$, parameterized by an arbitrary c-certificate $(I^*, \vec{A}) \in \mathcal{CS}_c$ and a vector $\vec{B} \in \mathbb{B}_\varepsilon^c$ of ε-boxes and defined as follows: $\chi_{I^*, \vec{A}, \vec{B}}(V) = 1$ if for any $\ell \in [c]$ the call $\texttt{Witness}(V, I^*, A_\ell, B_\ell, u^*(I^*, A_\ell))$ returns a solutions x_ℓ' such that $B_V(x_\ell' - u^*(I^*, A_\ell)) = B_\ell$, and $\chi_{I^*, \vec{A}, \vec{B}}(V) = 0$ otherwise. The vector $u^* = u^*(I^*, A_\ell)$ is the one defined in Equation 1.

Corollary 18. *Assume that $\text{OK}(V)$ is true. Then, the cth power of the number $\text{PO}(V)$ of Pareto-optimal solutions is at most $\sum_{(I^*, \vec{A}) \in \mathcal{CS}_c} \sum_{\vec{B} \in \mathbb{B}_\varepsilon^c} \chi_{I^*, \vec{A}, \vec{B}}(V)$.*

Proof. The cth power of the number $\text{PO}(V)$ of Pareto-optimal solutions equals the number of c-tuples $(x_1, \ldots, x_c)$ of Pareto-optimal solutions. Let $(x_1, \ldots, x_c)$ be such a c-tuple, let $(I^*, \vec{A})$ be the V-certificate of $(x_1, \ldots, x_c)$, an let $B_\ell = B_V(x_\ell - u^*(I^*, A_\ell)) \in \mathbb{B}_\varepsilon$. Due to Lemma 9, for any $\ell \in [c]$ the call $\texttt{Witness}(V, I^*, A_\ell, B_\ell, u^*(I^*, A_\ell))$ returns vector x_ℓ. Hence, $\chi_{I^*, \vec{A}, \vec{B}}(V) = 1$ for $\vec{B} = (B_1, \ldots, B_c)$. To conclude the proof we show that the function $(x_1, \ldots, x_c) \mapsto (I^*, \vec{A}, \vec{B})$ is injective. Let $(x_1, \ldots, x_c)$ and $(y_1, \ldots, y_c)$ be distinct c-tuples of Pareto-optimal solutions, i.e., there is an index $\ell \in [c]$ such that $x_\ell \neq y_\ell$, and let $(I_1^*, \vec{A}^{(1)})$ and $(I_2^*, \vec{A}^{(2)})$ be their V-certificates. If $(I_1^*, \vec{A}^{(1)}) \neq (I_2^*, \vec{A}^{(2)})$, then both tuples are maped to distinct triplets. Otherwise, $u^*(I_1^*, A_\ell^{(1)}) = u^*(I_2^*, A_\ell^{(2)})$ and thus $B_V(x_\ell - u^*(I_1^*, A_\ell^{(1)})) \neq B_V(y_\ell - u^*(I_2^*, A_\ell^{(2)}))$ since $\text{OK}(V)$ holds. Consequently, also in this case $(x_1, \ldots, x_c)$ and $(y_1, \ldots, y_c)$ are mapped to distinct triplets. □

Corollary 19. *The cth moment of the number of Pareto-optimal solutions is bounded by*

$$\sum_{(I^*, \vec{A}) \in \mathcal{CS}_c} \sum_{\vec{B} \in \mathbb{B}_\varepsilon^c} \mathbf{Pr}_V\left[E_{I^*, \vec{A}, \vec{B}}\right] + 2^n \cdot \mathbf{Pr}_V\left[\overline{\text{OK}(V)}\right]$$

where $E_{I^*, \vec{A}, \vec{B}}$ denotes the event that $\chi_{I^*, \vec{A}, \vec{B}}(V) = 1$.

Lemma 20. *The size of the restricted certificate space is bounded by $|\mathcal{CS}_c| \leq 2^{c^2(d+1)^2} n^{cd} = O(n^{cd})$ for fixed c and d.*

Proof. Let $(I^*, \vec{A})$ be an arbitrary c-certificate. Each matrix A_ℓ is a $|I^*| \times (d+1)$-matrix. The tuple I^* can be written as $I^* = (i_d^{(1)}, \ldots, i_1^{(1)}, i^{*(1)}, \ldots, i_d^{(c)}, \ldots, i_1^{(c)}, i^{*(c)})$, created by c successive calls of the $\texttt{Witness}$ function, where the indices $i^{*(\ell)}$ are chosen deterministicly in Definition 7. Since $|I^*| = c \cdot (d+1)$ the claim follows. □

Corollary 21. *For an arbitrary restricted c-certificate $(I^*, \vec{A})$ and an arbitrary vector $\vec{B} \in \mathbb{B}_\varepsilon^c$ of ε-boxes the probability of the event $E_{I^*, \vec{A}, \vec{B}}$ is bounded by*

$$\mathbf{Pr}_V\left[E_{I^*, \vec{A}, \vec{B}}\right] \leq (2\gamma)^{\gamma - cd} \phi^\gamma \varepsilon^{cd}, \quad \text{and by}$$
$$\mathbf{Pr}_V\left[E_{I^*, \vec{A}, \vec{B}}\right] \leq 2^{cd} \gamma^{\gamma - cd} \phi^{cd} \varepsilon^{cd}$$

if all densities are quasiconcave, where $\gamma = cd(d+1)$.

Proof. For $k \in [d]$ and $\ell \in [c]$ consider the matrices $Q_k(I^*, A_\ell, u_\ell^*)$ for $u_\ell^* = u^*(I^*, A_\ell)$ defined in Equation (2). By Lemma 13 the output of $\texttt{Witness}(V, I^*, A_\ell, B_\ell, u_\ell^*)$ is determined if $V_{\overline{I^*}}$ and the linear combinations $V_{I^*}^k \cdot q$ for any index $k \in [d]$ and any column q of the matrix $Q_k^{(\ell)} = Q_k(I^*, A_\ell, u_\ell^*)$ are given. With the same argument as in the proof of Corollary 21 event $E_{I^*, \vec{A}, \vec{B}}$ occurs if and only if $V_{I^*} \cdot \left[p^{(\ell,1)}, \ldots, p^{(\ell,d)}\right]$ falls into some d-dimensional hypercube C_ℓ with side length ε depending on the linear combinations $V_{I^*} \cdot Q_k^{(\ell)}$. Here, $p^{(\ell,t)}$ is short for $p^{(t)}(I^*, A_\ell, u_\ell^*)$.

Now, consider the matrix

$$Q_k' = \left[Q_k^{(1)}, p^{(1,k)}, \ldots, Q_k^{(c)}, p^{(c,k)}\right] .$$

Due to Lemma 14 this is a lower block triangular matrix, due to Lemma 15 the columns of $\left[Q_k^{(\ell)}, p^{(\ell,k)}\right]$ are linearly independent. Hence, matrix Q_k' is an invertible matrix and the same holds for the block diagonal matrix

$$Q' = \begin{bmatrix} Q_1' & \mathbb{O} & \ldots & \mathbb{O} \\ \mathbb{O} & \ddots & \ddots & \vdots \\ \vdots & \ddots & \ddots & \mathbb{O} \\ \mathbb{O} & \ldots & \mathbb{O} & Q_d' \end{bmatrix} \in \{-1, 0, 1\}^{(d \cdot |I^*|)^2} .$$

We permute the columns of Q' to obtain a matrix Q whose last $c \cdot d$ columns belong to the columns $p^{(1,1)}, \ldots, p^{(1,d)}, \ldots,$

$p^{(c,1)}, \dots, p^{(c,d)}$. We assume the rows of Q to be labeled by $Q_{j_1,1}, \dots, Q_{j_m,1}, \dots, Q_{j_1,d}, \dots, Q_{j_m,d}$ (recall that $I^* = (j_1, \dots, j_m)$) and introduce random variables $X_{j,k} = V_j^k$, $j \in I^*$, $k \in [d]$, indexed the same way as the rows of Q. Event $E_{I^*,\vec{A},\vec{B}}$ holds if and only if the cd linear combinations of the variables $X_{j,k}$ given by the last cd columns of Q fall into the cd-dimensional hypercube $C = \prod_{\ell=1}^{c} C_\ell$ with side length ε depending on the linear combinations of the variables $X_{j,k}$ given by the remaining columns of Q. The claim follows by applying Theorem 35 for the matrix Q^{T} and due to the fact that the number of rows of Q is $d \cdot |I^*| = cd \cdot (d+1) = \gamma$. □

PROOF OF THEOREM 4. In the proof of Theorem 3 we show that the probability $\overline{p}$ that the OK-event does not hold is bounded by $2^{2n+1} d\phi\varepsilon$. For $\gamma = cd(d+1)$, we set $s = (2\gamma)^{\gamma - cd}\phi^{\gamma}$ for general densities and $s = 2^{cd}\gamma^{\gamma-cd}\phi^{cd}$ in the case of quasiconcave density functions. Then, we obtain

$$\begin{aligned}
\mathbf{E}_V\left[\mathrm{PO}^c(V)\right] &\le \sum_{\substack{(I^*,\vec{A}) \in \mathcal{CS}_c, \\ \vec{B} \in \mathbb{B}_\varepsilon^c}} \mathbf{Pr}_V\left[E_{I^*,\vec{A},\vec{B}}\right] + 2^n \overline{p} \\
&\le \sum_{\substack{(I^*,\vec{A}) \in \mathcal{CS}_c, \\ \vec{B} \in \mathbb{B}_\varepsilon^c}} s\varepsilon^{cd} + 2^n \overline{p} \\
&\le 2^{c^2(d+1)^2} n^{cd} \left(\left(\frac{2n}{\varepsilon} \right)^d \right)^c s\varepsilon^{cd} + 2^n \overline{p} \\
&\le 2^{c^2(d+1)^2 + cd} n^{2cd} s + 2^{3n+1} d\phi\varepsilon \,.
\end{aligned}$$

The first inequality is due to Corollary 19. The second inequality is due to Corollary 21. The third inequality stems from Lemma 20. Since this bound is true for arbitrarily small $\varepsilon > 0$, the correctness of Theorem 4 follows. □

The proof of Theorem 4 yields that

$$\mathbf{E}_V\left[\mathrm{PO}^c(V)\right] \le s_c = 4^{c^2(d+1)^2} (cd(d+1))^{cd^2} n^{2cd} \phi^{c\beta}$$

where $\beta = d(d+1)$ in general and $\beta = d$ for quasiconcave densities. With the following Corollary we bound the probability that $\mathrm{PO}(V)$ exceeds a certain multiple of s_1. We obtain a significantly better concentration bound than we would by applying Markov's Inequality for the first moment.

COROLLARY 22. *The probability that the number of Pareto-optimal solutions is at least $k \cdot s_1$ is bounded by*

$$\mathbf{Pr}_V\left[\mathrm{PO}(V) \ge k \cdot s_1\right] \le \left(\frac{1}{k} \right)^{\frac{1}{2} \cdot \left\lfloor \frac{\log_8 k}{2(d+1)^2} \right\rfloor} .$$

5. ZERO-PRESERVING PERTURBATIONS

LEMMA 23. *W.l.o.g. in each objective function except for the adversarial one there are more than $f(d)$ perturbed coefficients, i.e., coefficients that are not deterministically set to zero, where f is an arbitrary fixed function.*

LEMMA 24. *W.l.o.g. for every $i \in [n]$ exactly one of the coefficients $V_i^1, \dots, V_i^d$ is perturbed, whereas the others are deterministically set to zero.*

In the remainder of this chapter we focus on instances having the structure described in Lemma 23 and Lemma 24. Then, $(P_1, \dots, P_d)$ is a partition of $[n]$, where P_t denotes the tuple of indices i for which V_i^t is perturbed. This structure also ensures that $B_V(x) \in \mathbb{B}_\varepsilon$ holds for any vector $x \in \{-1, 0, 1\}^n$.

We consider the following variant of the `Witness` function, which gets as parameters besides the usual V and x, a set $K \subseteq [d]$ of objective functions, a call number $r \in \mathbb{N}$, and a tuple $I \subseteq [n]$ of indices. In a call of the $\mathtt{Witness}_0$ function only the adversarial objective function V^{d+1} and the objective functions V^t with $t \in K$ are considered, and the solution set is restricted to solutions that coincide with x in all positions P_k with $k \notin K$. Additionally, as in the `Witness` function for higher moments, only solutions are considered that coincide with x in all positions $i \in I$. By the right choice of I, we can avoid choosing an index multiple times in different calls of the `Witness` function. The parameter r represents the number of the current call of $\mathtt{Witness}_0$. The $\mathtt{Witness}_0$ function always returns some subset of $\mathcal{S}$.

$\mathtt{Witness}_0(V, x, K, r, I)$

Let K be of the form $K = (k_1, \dots, k_{d'})$.
Set $k_{d'+1} = d+1$.
Set $\mathcal{R}_{d'+1}^{(r)} = \mathcal{S} \cap \mathcal{S}_I(x) \cap \bigcap_{k \in [d] \setminus K} \mathcal{S}_{P_k}(x)$.
if $d' = 0$ **then return** $\mathcal{R}_{d'+1}^{(r)}$
for $t = d', d'-1, \dots, 0$ **do**
  Set $\mathcal{C}_t^{(r)} = \left\{ z \in \mathcal{R}_{t+1}^{(r)} : V^{k_1 \dots k_t} z < V^{k_1 \dots k_t} x \right\}$.
  if $\mathcal{C}_t^{(r)} \neq \emptyset$ **then**
    Set $X_t^{(r)} = \arg\min \left\{ V^{k_{t+1}} z : z \in \mathcal{C}_t^{(r)} \right\}$.
    Let $x^{(r,t)}$ be the canonically first vector in $X_t^{(r)}$.
    Let $K_{\mathrm{EQ}} \subseteq K$ be the tuple of indices k such that $x^{(r,t)}|_{P_k} = x|_{P_k}$.
    Let $K_{\mathrm{NEQ}} \subseteq K$ be the tuple of the remaining indices.
    for $k \in K$ **do**
      if $k \in K_{\mathrm{EQ}}$ **then**
        Set $r_k = r$.
      else
        Determine the first index $i \in P_k$ for which $x_i^{(r,t)} \neq x_i$.
        $I \hookleftarrow I \cup (i)$
      end if
    end for
    if $K_{\mathrm{EQ}} = ()$ **then**
      Set $\mathcal{R}_t^{(r)} = \left\{ z : \begin{array}{l} z \in \mathcal{R}_{t+1}^{(r)} \cap \mathcal{S}_I(x) \text{ and} \\ V^{k_{t+1}} z < V^{k_{t+1}} x^{(r,t)} \end{array} \right\}$.
    else
      Set $t_r = t$.
      return $\mathtt{Witness}_0(V, x, K_{\mathrm{NEQ}}, r+1, I)$
    end if
  else
    for $k \in K$ **do**
      Set $i_k = \min(P_k \setminus I)$.
      $I \hookleftarrow I \cup (i_k)$.
    end for
    Set $x_i^{(r,t)} = \begin{cases} \overline{x_i} & \text{if } i \in \{i_{k_1}, \dots, i_{k_{d'}}\}, \\ x_i & \text{otherwise}. \end{cases}$
    Set $\mathcal{R}_t^{(r)} = \mathcal{R}_{t+1}^{(r)} \cap \mathcal{S}_I(x)$.
  end if
end for
return $\emptyset$

The index r_k defined in line 14 is the number of the last call in which the objective function V^k has been considered. In the following we use the term *round* to denote an iteration of the for-loop starting in line 5. The index t_r defined in line 23 is the number of the round in call number r of $\texttt{Witness}_0$ in which the recursive call of $\texttt{Witness}_0$ was made. In line 6 we define the winner set $\mathcal{C}_t^{(r)}$ using the functions $V^{k_1}, \ldots, V^{k_t}$. Note that in round $t = 0$ there is no restriction and this definition simplifies to $\mathcal{C}_0^{(r)} = \mathcal{R}_1^{(r)}$. In line 16 it is always possible to find an index from $i \in P_k$ on which the current vector $x^{(r,t)}$ and x disagree because this line is only reached for $k \in K_{\mathrm{NEQ}}$, i.e., only if $x^{(r,t)}|_{P_k} \neq x|_{P_k}$. In order for line 28 to be feasible, we have to guarantee that $P_k \setminus I \neq \emptyset$. This follows if we assume $|P_k| > d(d+1)$ (which is in accordance with Lemma 23 without loss if generality) because there are at most d calls of $\texttt{Witness}_0$ with non-empty K with at most $d+1$ rounds each and in each round at most one index from P_k is added to I.

One important property that we will exploit later is that every Pareto-optimal solution x is also Pareto-optimal with respect to the objective functions V^k with $k \in K_{\mathrm{NEQ}}$ if the set $\mathcal{S}$ is restricted to solutions that agree with x in all positions $i \in \bigcup_{k \in K_{\mathrm{EQ}}} P_k$, i.e., solutions z for which $V^k z = V^k x$ for every $k \in K_{\mathrm{EQ}}$. This property guarantees that whenever $\texttt{Witness}_0$ is called with a Pareto-optimal solution x as parameter, also in the recursive call in line 24 x is Pareto-optimal with respect to the restricted solution set and the remaining objective functions.

In the remainder of this section we only consider the case that x is Pareto-optimal. Unless stated otherwise, we consider the case that the OK_0-event occurs. That means that $|V^k \cdot (y - z)| \geq \varepsilon$ for every $k \in [d]$ and for any two vectors $y, z \in \mathcal{S}$ for which $y|_{P_k} \neq z|_{P_k}$.

LEMMA 25. *The call* $\texttt{Witness}_0(V, x, [d], 1, ())$ *returns the set* $\{x\}$. *Moreover,* $x^{(r^*, t_{r^*})} = x$ *for the last constructed vector* $x^{(r^*, t_{r^*})}$, *i.e., for* $r^* = \max\{r_1, \ldots, r_d\}$.

PROOF. We show that for all tuples $K \subseteq [d]$ and $I \subseteq [n]$ and any call number r the result of $\texttt{Witness}_0(V, x, K, r, I)$ is the set $\{x\}$ by induction over the size of K. If K is the empty tuple, then $\mathcal{R}_{d'+1}^{(r)} = \mathcal{S} \cap \mathcal{S}_I(x) \cap \bigcap_{k \in [d]} \mathcal{S}_{P_k}(x)$, i.e., the set $\mathcal{R}_{d'+1}^{(r)}$, which will be returned in line 4, consists of all solutions that are identical with x in every index. Consequently, $\mathcal{R}_{d'+1}^{(r)} = \{x\}$ in that case.

Now we consider non-empty tuples $K \subseteq [d]$. By the induction hypothesis it suffices to show that there is a call to the $\texttt{Witness}_0$ function before the end of the loop. Hence, let us assume that there is no such call during the rounds $t = d', d'-1, \ldots, 1$. As for the simple variant of the $\texttt{Witness}$ function we show two claims for that case:

CLAIM 1. *There is no* $t \in [d'+1]$ *such that there exists a solution* $z \in \mathcal{R}_t^{(r)}$ *that dominates* x *with respect to the objective functions* $V^{k_1}, \ldots, V^{k_t}$.

CLAIM 2. *For any* $t \in [d'+1]$ *solution* x *is an element of* $\mathcal{R}_t^{(r)}$.

As there is no call to the $\texttt{Witness}_0$ function during the first rounds we always get $K_{\mathrm{EQ}} = ()$ whenever $\mathcal{C}_t^{(r)} \neq \emptyset$. Hence, the rounds are basically the same as the rounds in the simple $\texttt{Witness}$ function and both claims hold due to the same arguments used to prove Lemma 6 and the fact that $x \in \mathcal{S}_J(x)$ for any index tuple $J \subseteq [n]$.

Using Claim 1 and Claim 2 we can prove the lemma: Solution x is an element of $\mathcal{C}_0^{(r)} = \mathcal{R}_1^{(r)}$ according to Claim 2. In particular, $\mathcal{C}_0^{(r)} \neq \emptyset$. Due to Claim 1 we get $x \in X_0^{(r)}$ and, hence, $V^{k_1} x^{(r,0)} = V^{k_1} x$. As the OK_0-event holds, this implies $x^{(r,0)}|_{P_{k_1}} = x|_{P_{k_1}}$, leading to $k_1 \in K_{\mathrm{EQ}}$. Consequently, the tuple K_{EQ} is not empty and we call the $\texttt{Witness}_0$ function again.

To conclude the proof of the lemma we have to show the equality $x^{(r^*, t_{r^*})} = x$. In the call of the $\texttt{Witness}_0$ function with number r^* the last recursive call in line 24 is made. We know that $x^{(r^*, t_{r^*})}\big|_{P_k} = x|_{P_k}$ for any $k \in [d] \setminus K$ where K is the parameter of call number r^* because $x^{(r^*, t_{r^*})} \in \mathcal{R}_{t_{r^*}+1}^{(r^*)} \subseteq \bigcap_{k \in [d] \setminus K} \mathcal{S}_{P_k}(x)$. Additionally, since the recursive call that is made in line 24 terminates immediately, all objective functions are removed from consideration in the call with number r^*, i.e., $K_{\mathrm{EQ}} = K$ in this call. Hence, the equation $x^{(r^*, t_{r^*})}\big|_{P_k} = x|_{P_k}$ holds also for any $k \in K$. Together this implies $x^{(r^*, t_{r^*})} = x$. □

Like for the simple $\texttt{Witness}$ function, we show that it is enough to know some information about one run of the $\texttt{Witness}_0$ function to reconstruct the vector x. As before, we call this data the certificate of x.

DEFINITION 26. *Let* $r_1, \ldots, r_d$ *and* $t_1, \ldots, t_{r^*}$, *where* $r^* = \max\{r_1, \ldots, r_d\}$, *be the indices and let* $x^{(r,t)}$ *be the vectors constructed during the execution of* $\texttt{Witness}_0(V, x, [d], 1, ())$ *and let* d'_r *be the value of* d' *in the* r^{th} *call of the* $\texttt{Witness}_0$ *function. Furthermore, consider the tuple* I *at the moment when the last call terminates. The pair* (I^*, A), *where* $I^* = I \cup (i_1^*, \ldots, i_d^*)$, $i_k^* = \min(P_K \setminus I)$, *and*

$$A = \left[x^{(1,d'_1)}, \ldots, x^{(1,t_1)}, \ldots, x^{(r^*,d'_{r^*})}, \ldots, x^{(r^*,t_{r^*})}\right]\Big|_{I^*},$$

is called the V-certificate *of* x. *We label the columns of* A *by* $a^{(r,t)}$. *Moreover, we call a pair* (I', A') *a* certificate *if there is some realization* V *such that* $\mathrm{OK}_0(V)$ *is true and if there exists a Pareto-optimal* $x \in \mathcal{S}$ *such that* (I', A') *is the* V*-certificate of* x. *By* $\mathcal{CS}$ *we denote the set of all certificates.*

We assume that the indices r_k and t_r (and hence also the indices d'_r) are implicitly encoded in a given certificate. Later we will take these indices into consideration again when we count the number of possible certificates.

LEMMA 27. *Let* V *be a realization for which* $\mathrm{OK}_0(V)$ *is true and let* (I^*, A) *be a* V*-certificate of some Pareto-optimal solution* x. *Let* A *be of the form*

$$A = \left[a^{(1,d'_1)}, \ldots, a^{(1,t_1)}, \ldots, a^{(r^*,d'_{r^*})}, \ldots, a^{(r^*,t_{r^*})}\right].$$

For fixed $k \in [d]$ *set*

$$M = \left[a^{(1,d'_1)}, \ldots, a^{(1,t_1)}, \ldots, a^{(r_k,d'_{r_k})}, \ldots, a^{(r_k,t_{r_k})}\right]\Big|_J,$$

where $J = I^* \cap P_k =: (j_1, \ldots, j_m)$, *and set* $y = x|_J$. *Then,* M *is of the form*

$$M = \begin{bmatrix} \overline{y_{j_1}} & y_{j_1} & \cdots & y_{j_1} \\ * & \ddots & \ddots & \vdots \\ \vdots & \ddots & \overline{y_{j_{m-1}}} & y_{j_{m-1}} \\ * & \cdots & * & y_{j_m} \end{bmatrix} \in \{0,1\}^{|J| \times |J|},$$

where each '$*$' can either be 0 or 1 independently of the other '$*$'-entries.

PROOF. Consider the call $\texttt{Witness}_0(V, x, [d], 1, ())$ and all subsequent calls $\texttt{Witness}_0(V, x, K, r, I)$. By definition of r_k we have $r \leq r_k \iff k \in K$. In each call where $r \leq r_k$ one vector $x^{(r,t)}$ is constructed each round. Also, in each round except for the last round of the r_k^{th} call one index $i \in P_k$ is chosen and added to I. Since J consists of the chosen indices $i \in P_k$ and the additional index i_k^*, matrix M is a square matrix.

We first consider the last column of M. As $x^{(r_k, t_{r_k})}$ is the last vector constructed before k is removed from K, index k must be an element of K_{EQ} at that time, i.e., $x^{(r_k, t_{r_k})}|_{P_k} = x|_{P_k}$. Hence, the last column of M has the claimed form.

Now consider the remaining columns of M. Due to the construction of the set $\mathcal{R}_t^{(r)}$ in line 21 or in line 32, all vectors z in a set $\mathcal{R}_t^{(r)}$ agree with x in the previously chosen indices i. As in the case $\mathcal{C}_t^{(r)} \neq \emptyset$ vector $x^{(r,t)}$ is an element of $\mathcal{R}_{t+1}^{(r)}$ and in the case $\mathcal{C}_t^{(r)} = \emptyset$ vector $x^{(r,t)}$ is constructed appropriately, the upper triangle of M, excluding the principal diagonal, has the claimed form. The form of the principal diagonal follows from the choice of index $i \in P_k$ such that $x_i^{(r,t)} \neq x_i$ in line 16 or from the construction of $x^{(r,t)}$ in line 31. $\square$

As in the simple case we now consider the following overloaded $\texttt{Witness}_0$ function that is based on the guess of the V-certificate of x, a shift vector $u \in \{0,1\}^n$ and the ε-box $B = B_V(x - u)$.

$\texttt{Witness}_0(V, K, r, I^*, A, \mathcal{S}', B, u)$

Let K be of the form $K = (k_1, \ldots, k_{d'})$.
Set $k_{d'+1} = d + 1$.
Let b be the corner of B.
Set $\mathcal{R}_{d'+1}^{(r)} = \mathcal{S}' \cap \bigcup_{t'=t_r}^{d'} \mathcal{S}_{I^*}(a^{(r,t')})$.
if $d' = 0$ **then return** $\mathcal{R}_{d'+1}^{(r)}$
for $t = d', d' - 1, \ldots, 0$ **do**
  Set $\mathcal{C}_t^{(r)} = \{z \in \mathcal{R}_{t+1}^{(r)} \cap \mathcal{S}_{I^*}(a^{(r,t)}) : V^{k_1 \ldots k_t} \cdot (z - u) \leq b|_{k_1 \ldots k_t}\}$.
  if $\mathcal{C}_t^{(r)} \neq \emptyset$ **then**
    Set $X_t^{(r)} = \arg\min\{V^{k_{t+1}} z : z \in \mathcal{C}_t^{(r)}\}$.
    Let $x^{(r,t)}$ be the canonically first vector in $X_t^{(r)}$.
    if $t = t_r$ **then**
      Let $K_{\text{EQ}} \subseteq K$ be the tuple of indices k such that $r_k = r$.
      Let $K_{\text{NEQ}} \subseteq K$ be the tuple of the remaining indices.
      Set $\mathcal{S}'' = \mathcal{S}' \cap \bigcap_{k \in K_{\text{EQ}}} \mathcal{S}_{P_k}(x^{(r,t)})$.
      return $\texttt{Witness}_0(V, K_{\text{NEQ}}, r+1, I^*, A, \mathcal{S}'', B, u)$
    else
      Set $\mathcal{R}_t^{(r)} = \left\{ z : \begin{array}{l} z \in \mathcal{R}_{t+1}^{(r)} \cap \bigcup_{t'=t_r}^{t-1} \mathcal{S}_{I^*}(a^{(r,t')}) \\ \text{and } V^{k_{t+1}} z < V^{k_{t+1}} x^{(r,t)} \end{array} \right\}$.
    end if
  else
    Set $x^{(r,t)} = (\perp, \ldots, \perp)$.
    Set $\mathcal{R}_t^{(r)} = \mathcal{R}_{t+1}^{(r)} \cap \bigcup_{t'=t_r}^{t-1} \mathcal{S}_{I^*}(a^{(r,t')})$.
  end if
end for
return $\emptyset$

LEMMA 28. *Let (I^*, A) be the V-certificate of x, let $u \in \{0,1\}^n$ be an arbitrary vector, and let $B = B_V(x-u)$. Then, the call $\texttt{Witness}_0(V, [d], 1, I^*, A, \mathcal{S}, B, u)$ returns $\{x\}$.*

Before we give a formal proof of Lemma 28 we try to give some intuition for it. As for the simple variant of the $\texttt{Witness}$ function we restrict the set of solutions to vectors that look like the vectors we want to reconstruct in the next rounds of the current call, i.e., we intersect the current set with the set $\bigcup_{t'=t_r}^{t-1} \mathcal{S}_{I^*}(a^{(r,t')})$ in round t. That way we only deal with subsets of the original sets, but we do not lose the vectors we want to reconstruct. In order to reconstruct the vectors, we need more information than in the simple variant: we need to know in which rounds the recursive calls of $\texttt{Witness}_0$ are made, in each call we need to know which objective functions V^k must not be considered anymore, and for each of these objective functions we need to know the vector $x|_{P_k}$. The information when the recursive calls are made and which objective functions must not be considered anymore is given in the certificate: The variable t_r contains the round number when the recursive call is made. The index r_k contains the number of the call where index k has to be removed from K. Hence, index k is removed in the $t_{r_k}^{\text{th}}$ round of call r_k. If we can reconstruct K_{EQ} and the vector $x^{(r,t)}$ in the round where we make the recursive call, then we can also reconstruct the bits of x at indices $i \in P_k$ for any index $k \in K_{\text{EQ}}$ since $x|_{P_k} = x^{(r,t)}|_{P_k}$ for these indices k.

PROOF OF LEMMA 28. To prove the lemma we show that in the execution of $\texttt{Witness}_0(V, [d], 1, I^*, A, \mathcal{S}, B, u)$ essentially the same sequence of vectors $x^{(r,t)}$ as in the execution of $\texttt{Witness}_0(V, x, [d], 1, ())$ is generated:

CLAIM 3. *Let $\texttt{Witness}_0(V, x, K, r, I)$ be the rth call to the $\texttt{Witness}_0$ function resulting from execution of the initial call $\texttt{Witness}_0(V, x, [d], 1, ())$, let $\mathcal{S}' = \mathcal{S} \cap \bigcap_{k \in [d] \setminus K} \mathcal{S}_{P_k}(x)$, and let $B = B_V(x-u)$ be the ε-box containing $x-u$. Consider the call $\texttt{Witness}_0(V, K, r, I^*, A, \mathcal{S}', B, u)$. If $K = ()$, then both calls return $\{x\}$. Otherwise, the following statements hold, where $\mathcal{R}_t'^{(r)}$, $\mathcal{C}_t'^{(r)}$, $X_t'^{(r)}$, $x'^{(r,t)}$, K'_{EQ}, and K'_{NEQ} denote the variables from the call $\texttt{Witness}_0(V, K, r, I^*, A, \mathcal{S}', B, u)$:*

- *$\mathcal{R}_t'^{(r)} \subseteq \mathcal{R}_t^{(r)}$ for any $t \in \{t_r + 1, \ldots, d' + 1\}$,*
- *$x'^{(r,t)} = x^{(r,t)}$ for any $t \in \{t_r, \ldots, d'\}$ where $\mathcal{C}_t^{(r)} \neq \emptyset$,*
- *$x^{(r,t')} \in \mathcal{R}_t'^{(r)}$ for any $t \in \{t_r + 1, \ldots, d' + 1\}$ and any $t' \in \{t_r, \ldots, t-1\}$ for which $\mathcal{C}_t^{(r)} \neq \emptyset$, and*
- *the next calls are both in round t_r and are of the form $\texttt{Witness}_0(V, x, K_1, r+1, I')$ and $\texttt{Witness}_0(V, K_2, r + 1, I^*, A, \mathcal{S}'', B, u)$ where $\mathcal{S}'' = \mathcal{S} \cap \bigcap_{k \in [d] \setminus K_2} \mathcal{S}_{P_k}(x)$ and $K_1 = K_2$.*

Using Claim 3, Lemma 28 follows immediately by an inductive argument. $\square$

By the choice of the vector u we can control which information about V has to be known in order to be able to execute the call $\texttt{Witness}_0(V, [d], 1, I^*, A, \mathcal{S}, B, u)$. While Lemma 28 is correct for any choice of $u \in \{0,1\}^n$, we have to choose u carefully in order for the following probabilistic analysis to work. Later we will see that $u^* = u^*(I^*, A)$,

$$u_i^* = \begin{cases} \overline{x_i} & \text{if } i \in (i_1^*, \ldots, i_d^*), \\ x_i & \text{if } i \in I^* \setminus (i_1^*, \ldots, i_d^*), \\ 0 & \text{otherwise}, \end{cases} \tag{3}$$

is well-suited for our purpose. Note, that $i_k^* \in P_k$ are the indices that have been added to I in the definition of the V-certificate to obtain I^*. Furthermore, x_i is encoded in the last column of A for any index $i \in I^*$. Hence, vector u^* can be defined with the help of the V-certificate of x; we do not have to know the vector x itself.

Next we bound the number of Pareto-optimal solutions. For this, consider the following functions $\chi_{I^*,A,B}(V)$ parameterized by an arbitrary certificate $(I^*, A) \in \mathcal{CS}$ and an arbitrary ε-box $B \in \mathbb{B}_\varepsilon$ and defined as follows: $\chi_{I^*,A,B}(V) = 1$ if $\texttt{Witness}_0(V, [d], 1, I^*, A, \mathcal{S}, B, u^*(I^*, A))$ returns a set $\{x'\}$ such that $B_V(x' - u^*(I^*, A)) = B$, and $\chi_{I^*,A,B}(V) = 0$ otherwise.

COROLLARY 29. *Assume that* $\mathrm{OK}_0(V)$ *is true. Then, the number* $\mathrm{PO}(V)$ *of Pareto-optimal solutions is at most*

$$\sum_{(I^*,A)\in\mathcal{CS}} \sum_{B\in\mathbb{B}_\varepsilon} \chi_{I^*,A,B}(V).$$

PROOF. Let x be a Pareto-optimal solution, let (I^*, A) be the V-certificate of x, and let $B = B_V(x - u^*(I^*, A)) \in \mathbb{B}_\varepsilon$. Due to Lemma 28, $\texttt{Witness}_0(V, [d], 1, I^*, A, \mathcal{S}, B, u^*(I^*, A))$ returns $\{x\}$. Hence, $\chi_{I^*,A,B}(V) = 1$. It remains to show that the function $x \mapsto (I^*, A, B')$ is injective. Let x_1 and x_2 be distinct Pareto-optimal solutions and let (I_1^*, A_1) and (I_2^*, A_2) be the V-certificates of x_1 and x_2, respectively. If $(I_1^*, A_1) \neq (I_2^*, A_2)$, then x_1 and x_2 are mapped to distinct triplets. Otherwise, $u^*(I_1^*, A_1) = u^*(I_2^*, A_2)$ and, hence, $B_V(x_1 - u^*(I_1^*, A_1)) \neq B_V(x_2 - u^*(I_2^*, A_2))$ because $\mathrm{OK}_0(V)$ is true. Consequently, also in this case x_1 and x_2 are mapped to distinct triplets. □

Corollary 29 immediately implies a bound on the expected number of Pareto-optimal solutions.

COROLLARY 30. *Let* $E_{I^*,A,B}$ *denote the event that the call* $\texttt{Witness}_0(V, [d], 1, I^*, A, \mathcal{S}, B, u^*(I^*, A))$ *returns a non-empty set* $\{x'\}$ *such that* $B_V(x' - u^*(I^*, A)) = B$. *Then the expected number of Pareto-optimal solutions is bounded by*

$$\sum_{(I^*,A)\in\mathcal{CS}} \sum_{B\in\mathbb{B}_\varepsilon} \mathbf{Pr}_V[E_{I^*,A,B}] + 2^n \cdot \mathbf{Pr}_V\left[\overline{\mathrm{OK}_0(V)}\right].$$

We will see that the first term of the sum in Corollary 30 can be bounded independently of ε and that the limit of the second term is 0 for $\varepsilon \to 0$. First of all, we analyze the size of the certificate space.

LEMMA 31. *The size of the certificate space* $\mathcal{CS}$ *is bounded by* $|\mathcal{CS}| \leq 2^{(d+1)^5} d^{2d+3} n^{d^2(d+1)} = O(n^{d^2(d+1)})$.

PROOF. Consider the execution of the $\texttt{Witness}_0$function, starting with the call $\texttt{Witness}_0(V, x, [d], 1, ())$. Including that call, there can be at most d calls to the $\texttt{Witness}_0$ function except for the call that terminates due to $d' = 0$ as in each of the other calls at least one index $k \in [d]$ is removed from the tuple K. Hence, $r_1, \ldots, r_d \in [d]$ and there are at most d^d possibilities to choose these numbers. In the rth call, the round number t_r is an element of $[d'_r]_0 \subseteq [d]_0$, and hence, there are at most $(d+1)^d$ possibilities to choose round numbers $t_1, \ldots, t_{r^*}$. In each round, at most d indices i are added to the tuple I. In total, tuple I contains at most $d^2 \cdot (d+1)$ indices, and hence, there are at most $d^2 \cdot (d+1) \cdot n^{d^2 \cdot (d+1)}$ choices for I. Once I is fixed also the indices in $I^* \setminus I$ are fixed because the indices added to I in Definition 26 are determined by I. The tuple I^* contains at most $d^3 + d^2 + d$ indices. In each call r, at most $d+1$ vectors $x^{(r,t)}$ are generated. Hence, matrix A has at most $d \cdot (d+1)$ columns and at most $d^3 + d^2 + d$ rows. This yields the desired bound

$$\begin{aligned} |\mathcal{CS}| &\leq d^d (d+1)^d d^2 (d+1) n^{d^2(d+1)} 2^{d(d+1)(d^3+d^2+d)} \\ &\leq 2^d d^{2d} 2 d^3 n^{d^2(d+1)} 2^{d^2(d^2+d+1)(d+1)} \\ &\leq 2^{(d+1)^5} d^{2d+3} n^{d^2(d+1)}. \end{aligned}$$ □

In the next step we analyze how much information of V is needed in order to execute $\texttt{Witness}_0(V, [d], 1, I^*, A, \mathcal{S}, B, u)$. We will see that V does not need to be revealed completely and that some randomness remains even after the necessary information to perform the call has been revealed. This is the key observation for analyzing the probability of event $E_{I^*,A,B}$ to happen. For this, let V be an arbitrary realization, i.e., we do not condition on the OK_0-event anymore, and fix an index $k \in [d]$. Only the indices $i \in P_k$ are relevant for function V^k. Hence, we set $I_k^* = I^* \cap P_k$ and we assume that the coefficients of V^k belonging to indices $i \notin I_k^*$ are known. We denote this part of V^k by $V^k_{\overline{I_k^*}}$ and concentrate on the remaining part of V^k which we denote by $V^k_{I_k^*}$. By the construction of index r_k we know that only in the calls $r = 1, \ldots, r_k$ information about the function V^k must be available as in all subsequent calls this function is not considered anymore.

Clearly, the outcome of $\texttt{Witness}_0(V, [d], 1, I^*, A, \mathcal{S}, B, u)$ would be determined if we would reveal all linear combinations $V^k_{I_k^*} \cdot (a^{(r,t)}_{I_k^*} - u|_{I_k^*})$. However, there would be no randomness left we could exploit. Therefore, we reveal these linear combinations for the calls $r = 1, \ldots, r_k - 1$, but for call r we do the same as we did in the case of non-zero-preserving perturbations:

Consider call $r = r_k$ and let $j_k \in [d'_r]$ be the index for which $k_{j_k} = k$ in call r, i.e., V^k is the j_k^{th} objective function in K in the rth call. For the last round t_r in call r the inequality $t_r \leq j_k - 1$ holds. This is due to the fact that $x^{(r,t_r)}|_{P_k} = x|_{P_k}$, i.e., $V^k x^{(r,t_r)} = V^k x$, since this is the round when k is removed from tuple K. On the other hand, $x^{(r,t_r)} \in \mathcal{C}_{t_r}^{(r)}$, which means that $V^{k_{t'}} x^{(r,t_r)} < V^{k_{t'}} x$ for all indices $t' = 1, \ldots, t_r$, where $k_1, \ldots, k_{d'_r}$ denote the indices tuple K consists of in the rth call. Hence, $t_r < j_k$ as $k = k_{j_k}$.

There are only three lines where information about V is required: line 7, line 9, and line 17. For line 7 the values $V^k_{I_k^*} \cdot (a^{(r,t)}|_{I_k^*} - u|_{I_k^*})$ from round $t = d'_r$ down to round j_k are needed. In line 9 no additional information about $V^k_{I^*}$ is needed since all considered vectors coincide on indices $i \in I_k^*$. For line 17 only in round $j_k - 1$ the values $V^k_{I_k^*} \cdot (a^{(r,t')}|_{I_k^*} - a^{(r,j_k-1)}|_{I_k^*})$ for $t' = t_r, \ldots, j_k - 2$ are required.

Using the notation $p_k^{(r,t)} = a^{(r,t)}|_{I_k^*} - u|_{I_k^*}$ we can write the linear combinations of $V^k_{I_k^*}$ that we need to know in the matrices $Q_k^{(r)}$ and obtain

$$Q_k^{(r)} = \left[p_k^{(r,d'_r)}, \ldots, p_k^{(r,t_r)}\right]$$

for $r = 1, \ldots, r_k - 1$ and $Q_k^{(r)} = \left[\widehat{Q}_k^{(r)}, \widetilde{Q}_k^{(r)}\right]$ where

$$\widehat{Q}_k^{(r)} = \left[p_k^{(r,d'_r)}, \ldots, p_k^{(r,j_k)}\right] \quad \text{and}$$

$$\widetilde{Q}_k^{(r)} = \left[p_k^{(r,j_k-2)} - p_k^{(r,j_k-1)}, \dots, p_k^{(r,t_r)} - p_k^{(r,j_k-1)}\right]$$

for $r = r_k$. Note that the matrices $Q_k^{(r)} = Q_k^{(r)}(I^*, A, u)$ depend on the choice of u.

COROLLARY 32. *Let $u \in \{0,1\}^n$ be an arbitrary shift vector, let $(I^*, A) \in \mathcal{CS}$ be an arbitrary certificate, and let V and W be two realizations such that $V_{\overline{I_k^*}}^k = W_{\overline{I_k^*}}^k$ and $V_{I_k^*}^k \cdot q = W_{I_k^*}^k \cdot q$ for any index $k \in [d]$ and any column q of the matrices $Q_k^{(r)}(I^*, A, u)$. Then, $\texttt{Witness}_0(V, [d], 1, I^*, A, \mathcal{S}, B, u)$ and $\texttt{Witness}_0(W, [d], 1, I^*, A, \mathcal{S}, B, u)$ return the same result for any ε-box $B \in \mathbb{B}_\varepsilon$.*

In the remainder of this section we assume that $V_{\overline{I_k^*}}^k$ and the ε-box B are fixed. In accordance with Corollary 32, the output of the call $\texttt{Witness}_0(V, [d], 1, I^*, A, \mathcal{S}, B, u)$ is determined if the linear combinations of $V_{I_k^*}^k$ given by the columns of the matrices $Q_k^{(r)}$ are known in addition. We are interested in the event $E_{I^*,A,B}$, i.e., in the event that the output is a set $\{x'\}$ such that $V^{1\dots d} \cdot (x' - u^*(I^*, A)) \in B$. Since (I^*, A) is a V-certificate of x for some V and x, the output is always of the form $\{x'\}$ due to Lemma 28. Hence, event $E_{I^*,A,B}$ occurs if and only if for all indices k the relation $V_{I_k^*}^k \cdot (x' - u^*(I^*, A))\big|_{I_k^*} \in C_k$ holds for some interval C_k of length ε that depends on the linear combinations of $V_{I_\ell^*}$ given by $Q_\ell^{(r)}$ for all indices $\ell \in [d]$.

LEMMA 33. *For any $k \in [d]$ the columns of all matrices $Q_k^{(r)}(I^*, A, u^*(I^*, A))$, $r \in [r_k]$, and the vector $p_k^{(r_k,t_{r_k})}$ are linearly independent.*

PROOF. Consider the square matrix Q_k consisting of the vectors $p_k^{(r,t)}$, for $r \in [r_k]$ and $t \in \{t_r, \dots, d'_r\}$. Due to Lemma 27 and due to the construction of $u^*(I^*, A)$ (see Equation 3) matrix Q_k is a lower triangular matrix and the elements of the principal diagonal are from the set $\{-1, 1\}$. Hence, $|\det Q_k| = 1$, i.e., the vectors $p_k^{(r,t)}$ are linearly independent. It remains to consider the columns of matrix $Q_k^{(r)}$ for $r = r_k$. The columns of matrix $Q_k^{(r)}$ and vector $p_k^{(r,t_r)}$ are linear combinations of the vectors $p_k^{(r,t_r)}, \dots, p_k^{(r,d'_r)}$. Thus, it suffices to show that the columns of matrix $Q_k^{(r)}$ and vector $p_k^{(r,t_r)}$ are linearly independent. Assume that the zero-vector can be expressed by the linear combination

$$\sum_{t=j_k}^{d'_r} \lambda_t \cdot p_k^{(r,t)} + \sum_{t=t_r}^{j_k-2} \lambda_t \cdot \left(p_k^{(r,t)} - p_k^{(r,j_k-1)}\right) + \mu \cdot p_k^{(r,t_r)}$$

of the columns of matrix $Q_k^{(r)}$ and vector $p_k^{(r,t_r)}$. If $t_r = j_k - 1$, then this is equivalent to

$$0 = \sum_{t=t_r+1}^{d'_r} \lambda_t \cdot p_k^{(r,t)} + \mu \cdot p_k^{(t_r)},$$

i.e., all coefficients are zero due to the linear independence of the vectors $p_k^{(r,t)}$. If $t_r < j_k - 1$, then this is equivalent to

$$0 = \sum_{t=j_k}^{d'_r} \lambda_t \cdot p_k^{(r,t)} + \sum_{t=t_r+1}^{j_k-2} \lambda_t \cdot p_k^{(r,t)} - \left(\sum_{t=t_r}^{j_k-2} \lambda_t\right) \cdot p_k^{(r,j_k-1)} + (\lambda_{t_r} + \mu) \cdot p_k^{(r,t_r)}.$$

Due to the linear independence of the vectors $p_k^{(r,t)}$ this implies $\lambda_t = 0$ for $t \in \{t_r + 1, \dots, j_k - 2\} \cup \{j_k, \dots, d'_r\}$, $\sum_{t=t_r}^{j_k-2} \lambda_t = 0$, and $\lambda_{t_r} + \mu = 0$, i.e., all coefficients are zero. In both cases, the linear independence of the columns of $Q_k^{(r)}$ and vector $p^{(r,t_r)}$ follows. □

COROLLARY 34. *Let $(I^*, A) \in \mathcal{CS}$ be an arbitrary certificate and let $B \in \mathbb{B}_\varepsilon$ be an arbitrary ε-box. Then,*

$$\mathbf{Pr}_V[E_{I^*,A,B}] \le (2\gamma)^{\gamma-d} \phi^\gamma \varepsilon^d,$$

and

$$\mathbf{Pr}_V[E_{I^*,A,B}] \le 2^d \gamma^{\gamma-d} \phi^d \varepsilon^d$$

in case of quasiconcave densities, where $\gamma = d^3 + d^2 + d$.

PROOF. For fixed index $k \in [d]$ we write the columns of the matrices $Q_k^{(r)}$ and the vector $p_k^{(r_k,t_{r_k})}$ into one matrix Q_k and consider the matrix

$$Q' = \begin{bmatrix} Q_1 & \mathbb{O} & \dots & \mathbb{O} \\ \mathbb{O} & \ddots & \ddots & \vdots \\ \vdots & \ddots & \ddots & \mathbb{O} \\ \mathbb{O} & \dots & \mathbb{O} & Q_d \end{bmatrix} \in \{-1, 0, 1\}^{|I^*| \times \ell}$$

for some integer $\ell \le |I^*|$. By Lemma 33 this matrix has (full) rank ℓ. Now, permute the columns of Q' to obtain a matrix Q where the last d columns belong to the d last columns of the matrices Q_k. For any index $i \in I^*$ let $X_i = V_i^k$ be the ith coefficient of V^k where k is the unique index such that $i \in P_k$. Event $E_{I^*,A,B}$ holds if and only if the d linear combinations of the variables X_i given by the last d columns of Q fall into a d-dimensional hypercube C depending on the linear combinations of the variables X_i given by the remaining columns. The claim follows by applying Theorem 35 for matrix $A = Q^{\mathrm{T}}$ and due to the fact that $|I^*| \le \gamma$ (see proof of Lemma 31). □

PROOF OF THEOREM 1. We begin the proof by showing that the OK_0-event is likely to happen. For any index $t \in [d]$ and any solutions $x, y \in \mathcal{S}$ such that $x|_{P_t} \ne y|_{P_t}$ the probability that $|V^t x - V^t y| \le \varepsilon$ is bounded by $2\phi\varepsilon$. To see this, choose one index $i \in P_t$ such that $x_i \ne y_i$ and fix all coefficients V_j^t for $j \ne i$. Then, the value V_i^t must fall into an interval of length 2ε. A union bound over all indices $t \in [d]$ and over all pairs $(x, y) \in \mathcal{S} \times \mathcal{S}$ such that $x|_{P_t} \ne y|_{P_t}$ yields $\overline{p} := \mathbf{Pr}_V\left[\overline{\mathrm{OK}_0(V)}\right] \le 2^{2n+1} d\phi\varepsilon$. For $\gamma = d^3 + d^2 + d$, we set $s = (2\gamma)^{\gamma-d}\phi^\gamma$ for general density functions and $s = 2^d \gamma^{\gamma-d} \phi^d$ in the case of quasiconcave density functions. Then, we obtain

$$\begin{aligned}
\mathbf{E}_V[\mathrm{PO}(V)] &\le \sum_{\substack{(I^*,A)\in\mathcal{CS},\\ B\in\mathbb{B}_\varepsilon}} \mathbf{Pr}_V[E_{I^*,A,B}] + 2^n \overline{p} \\
&\le \sum_{\substack{(I^*,A)\in\mathcal{CS},\\ B\in\mathbb{B}_\varepsilon}} s\varepsilon^d + 2^n \overline{p} \\
&\le 2^{(d+1)^5} d^{2d+3} n^{d^2(d+1)} \left(\frac{2n}{\varepsilon}\right)^d s\varepsilon^d + 2^n \overline{p} \\
&\le 2^{(d+1)^5+d} d^{2d+3} n^{d^3+d^2+d} s + 2^{3n+1} d\phi\varepsilon.
\end{aligned}$$

The first inequality is due to Corollary 30. The second inequality is due to Corollary 34. The third inequality stems from Lemma 31. Since this bound is true for arbitrarily small $\varepsilon > 0$, the correctness of Theorem 1 follows. □

6. SOME PROBABILITY THEORY

THEOREM 35. *Consider n independent random variables $X_1, \dots, X_n$, each with an own probability density function $f_i\colon [-1,1] \to [0,\phi]$. Let $m \in [n]$, let $A \in \{-1,0,1\}^{m\times n}$ be a matrix of full rank, let $k \in [m-1]$ be an integer, let $(Y_1,\dots,Y_{m-k},Z_1,\dots,Z_k)^{\mathrm{T}} = A\cdot(X_1,\dots,X_n)^{\mathrm{T}}$ be the linear combinations of $X_1,\dots,X_n$ given by A, and let C be a function mapping a tuple $(y_1,\dots,y_{m-k}) \in \mathbb{R}^{m-k}$ to a hypercube $C(y_1,\dots,y_{m-k}) \subseteq \mathbb{R}^k$ with side length ε. Then,*

$$\mathbf{Pr}\left[(Z_1,\dots,Z_k) \in C(Y_1,\dots,Y_{m-k})\right] \le (2n)^{n-k}\phi^n\varepsilon^k .$$

If all densities f_i are quasiconcave, then this bound can be improved to

$$\mathbf{Pr}\left[(Z_1,\dots,Z_k) \in C(Y_1,\dots,Y_{m-k})\right] \le 2^k n^{n-k}\phi^k\varepsilon^k .$$

PROOF. Without loss of generality let $m = n$, i.e., matrix A is a square matrix where $\det A \neq 0$. Otherwise, we could insert $m-n$ linearly independent rows from $\{0,1\}^n$ after row $m-k$ until matrix A is of that form. That way we get new random variables $Y_{m-k+1},\dots,Y_{n-k}$. Extending the domain of C to $\mathbb{R}^{n-k}$ by the definition $C(y_1,\dots,y_{n-k}) := C(y_1,\dots,y_{m-k})$ yields the claim.

As matrix A is a full-rank square matrix, its inverse A^{-1} exists and we can write

$$\begin{aligned}
&\mathbf{Pr}\left[(Z_1,\dots,Z_k) \in C(Y_1,\dots,Y_{n-k})\right]\\
&\quad= \int_{y\in\mathbb{R}^{n-k}}\int_{z\in C(y)} f_{Y,Z}(y,z)\,\mathrm{d}z\,\mathrm{d}y\\
&\quad= \int_{y\in\mathbb{R}^{n-k}}\int_{z\in C(y)} \left|\det\left(A^{-1}\right)\right|\cdot f_X\left(A^{-1}\cdot(y,z)\right)\mathrm{d}z\,\mathrm{d}y\\
&\quad\le \int_{y\in\mathbb{R}^{n-k}}\int_{z\in C(y)} f_X\left(A^{-1}\cdot(y,z)\right)\mathrm{d}z\,\mathrm{d}y\\
&\quad\le \varepsilon^k\cdot\int_{y\in\mathbb{R}^{n-k}}\max_{z\in\mathbb{R}^k} f_X\left(A^{-1}\cdot(y,z)\right)\mathrm{d}y\,, \qquad (4)
\end{aligned}$$

where $f_{Y,Z}$ denotes the common density of the variables $Y_1,\dots,Y_{n-k},Z_1,\dots,Z_k$ and $f_X = \prod_{i=1}^n f_i$ denotes the common density of the variables $X_1,\dots,X_n$. The second equality is due to a change of variables, the first inequality stems from the fact that $\left|\det\left(A^{-1}\right)\right| = |1/\det A| \in (0,1)$ since A is an integer matrix.

The integral in Formula (4) can be bounded by

$$\begin{aligned}
&\int_{y\in\mathbb{R}^{n-k}}\max_{z\in\mathbb{R}^k} f_X\left(A^{-1}\cdot(y,z)\right)\mathrm{d}y\\
&\quad\le \int_{y\in[-n,n]^{n-k}}\max_{z\in\mathbb{R}^k} f_X\left(A^{-1}\cdot(y,z)\right)\mathrm{d}y\\
&\quad\le \int_{y\in[-n,n]^{n-k}} \phi^n\,\mathrm{d}y = (2n)^{n-k}\phi^n\,,
\end{aligned}$$

where the first inequality is due to the fact that all variables Y_i can only take values in the interval $[-n,n]$ as all entries of matrix A are from $\{-1,0,1\}$.

To prove the statement about quasiconcave functions we first consider arbitrary rectangular functions, i.e., functions that are constant on a given interval, an zero otherwise. This will be the main part of our analysis. Afterwards, we analyze sums of rectangular functions and, finally, we show that quasiconcave functions can be approximated by such sums.

LEMMA 36. *For $i \in [n]$ let $\phi_i \ge 0$, let $I_i \subseteq \mathbb{R}$ be an interval of length ℓ_i, and let $f_i\colon \mathbb{R}\to\mathbb{R}$ be the function*

$$f_i(x) = \begin{cases}\phi_i & \text{if } x \in I_i,\\ 0 & \text{otherwise.}\end{cases}$$

Moreover, let $f\colon \mathbb{R}^n \to \mathbb{R}$ be the function $f(x_1,\dots,x_n) = \prod_{i=1}^n f_i(x_i)$ and let $A \in \{-1,0,1\}^{n\times n}$ be an invertible matrix. Then,

$$\int_{y\in\mathbb{R}^{n-k}}\max_{z\in\mathbb{R}^k} f\left(A^{-1}\cdot(y,z)\right)\mathrm{d}y \le 2^k(n-k)!\,\chi\cdot\sum_I\prod_{i\notin I}\ell_i\,,$$

where $\chi = \prod_{i=1}^n \phi_i$ and where the sum runs over all tuples $I = (i_1,\dots,i_k)$ where $1 \le i_1 < \ldots < i_k \le n$.

PROOF. Function f takes the value χ on the n-dimensional box $Q = \prod_{i=1}^n I_i$ and is zero otherwise. Hence,

$$\int_{y\in\mathbb{R}^{n-k}}\max_{z\in\mathbb{R}^k} f\left(A^{-1}\cdot(y,z)\right)\mathrm{d}y = \chi\cdot\mathrm{vol}(Q')$$

for

$$\begin{aligned}
Q' &= \left\{y\in\mathbb{R}^{n-k} : \exists z\in\mathbb{R}^k \text{ such that } A^{-1}\cdot(y,z)\in Q\right\}\\
&= \left\{y\in\mathbb{R}^{n-k} : \exists z\in\mathbb{R}^k\ \exists x\in Q \text{ such that } (y,z) = A\cdot x\right\}\\
&= M(Q)\,,
\end{aligned}$$

where $M = P\cdot A$ and $P = \left[\mathbb{I}_{n-k}, \mathbb{O}_{(n-k)\times k}\right]$ is the projection matrix that removes the last k entries from a vector of length n. In the remainder of this proof we bound the volume of $M(Q)$. Let $a_i =: c_i^0$ and $b_i =: c_i^1$ be the left and the right bound of interval I_i, respectively. For an index tuple $I = (i_1,\dots,i_k)$, $1 \le i_1 < \ldots < i_k \le n$, and a bit tuple $J = (j_1,\dots,j_k) \in \{0,1\}^k$, let

$$F_I^J = \prod_{i=1}^n \begin{cases}\{c_{i_t}^{j_t}\} & \text{if } i = i_t\,,\\ I_i & i \notin I\,,\end{cases}$$

be one of the $2^k\cdot\binom{n}{k}$ $(n-k)$-dimensional faces of Q. We show that $M(Q) \subseteq \bigcup_I\bigcup_J M\left(F_I^J\right)$. Let $y \in M(Q)$, i.e., there is a vector $x \in Q$ such that $y = M\cdot x$. Now, consider the polytope

$$R = \left\{(x',s')\in\mathbb{R}^n\times\mathbb{R}^n : \begin{array}{c} M\cdot x' = y',\ x'+s' = b',\\ \text{and } x', s' \ge 0\end{array}\right\},$$

where $y' = y - M\cdot a$ and $b' = b - a$ for $a = (a_1,\dots,a_n)$ and $b = (b_1,\dots,b_n)$. This polytope is bounded and nonempty since $(x',s') \in R$ for $x' = x - a$ and $s' = b - x$. Consequently, there exists a basic feasible solution (x^*,s^*). As there are $2n$ variables and $2n-k$ constraints, this solution has at least k zero-entries, i.e., there are indices $1 \le i_1 < \ldots < i_k \le n$ such that either $x_{i_t}^* = 0$ (in that case set $j_t = 0$) or $x_{i_t}^* = b_{i_t}'$ (in that case set $j_t = 1$) for any $t \in [k]$. Now, consider the vector $\hat{x} = x^* + a \in [0,b'] + a = Q$. We obtain $M\cdot\hat{x} = y$ and $\hat{x}_{i_t} = c_{i_t}^{j_t}$ for all $t\in[k]$. Hence, $x \in F_I^J$ for $I = (i_1,\dots,i_k)$ and $J = (j_1,\dots,j_k)$, and thus $y \in M\left(F_I^J\right)$.

Due to this observation we can bound the volume of $M(Q)$ by $\sum_I\sum_J \mathrm{vol}\left(M\left(F_I^J\right)\right)$. It remains to show how to bound the volume $\mathrm{vol}\left(M\left(F_I^J\right)\right)$. For the sake of simplicity we only consider $I = (n-k+1,\dots,n)$ in the following analysis. Other faces can be dealt with analogously but handling tuples of indices causes technicalities to obscure the essence of the proof. Let $\phi^J : \mathbb{R}^{n-k} \to F_I^J$ be the function $\phi^J(x) = T \cdot x + v^J$, where $T = \left[\mathbb{I}_{n-k}, \mathbb{O}_{(n-k)\times k}\right]^{\mathrm{T}}$ and $v^J = (0, \dots, 0, c_{n-k+1}^{j_1}, \dots, c_n^{j_k})$. Using function ϕ^J is the canonical way to describe the affine subspace defined by face F_I^J: it adds the fixed coordinates of F_I^J to a given vector of length $n-k$. Hence, function ϕ^J, restricted to the domain $F' = \prod_{i=1}^{n-k} I_i$, is bijective. With $\psi = M \circ \phi^J$ we obtain

$$\begin{aligned}\mathrm{vol}\big(M(F_I^J)\big) &= \int_{\psi(F')} 1 \,\mathrm{d}x = \int_{F'} |\det \mathrm{D}\psi(x)| \,\mathrm{d}x \\ &= \int_{F'} |\det(M \cdot T)| \,\mathrm{d}x = |\det(M \cdot T)| \cdot \mathrm{vol}(F') \\ &= |\det(M \cdot T)| \cdot \prod_{i=1}^{n-k} \ell_i \,.\end{aligned}$$

Matrix $M \cdot T = P \cdot A \cdot T$ is a $(n-k) \times (n-k)$-submatrix of A. Thus, $|\det(M \cdot T)| \leq (n-k)!$ and we obtain the bound

$$\begin{aligned}&\int_{y \in \mathbb{R}^{n-k}} \max_{z \in \mathbb{R}^k} f\big(A^{-1} \cdot (y, z)\big) \mathrm{d}y \\ &\quad = \chi \cdot \mathrm{vol}(M(Q)) \leq \chi \cdot \sum_I \sum_J \mathrm{vol}\big(M(F_I^J)\big) \\ &\quad \leq \chi \cdot \sum_I \sum_J (n-k)! \cdot \prod_{i \notin I} \ell_i \\ &\quad = 2^k (n-k)! \chi \cdot \sum_I \prod_{i \notin I} \ell_i \,.\end{aligned}$$

□

In the next step we generalize the statement of Lemma 36 to sums of rectangular functions.

COROLLARY 37. *Let $N_1, \dots, N_n$ be positive integers and, for $i \in [n]$ and $k \in [N_i]$, let $\phi_{i,k} \geq 0$ be a non-negative real, let $I_{i,k} \subseteq \mathbb{R}$ be an interval of length $\ell_{i,k}$, and let $f_{i,k} : \mathbb{R} \to \mathbb{R}$ be the function*

$$f_{i,k}(x) = \begin{cases} \phi_{i,k} & \text{if } x \in I_{i,k} \,, \\ 0 & \text{otherwise} \,. \end{cases}$$

Furthermore, let $f_i : \mathbb{R} \to \mathbb{R}$ be the function $f_i = \sum_{k=1}^{N_i} f_{i,k}$, let $f : \mathbb{R}^n \to \mathbb{R}$ be the function $f(x_1, \dots, x_n) = \prod_{i=1}^n f_i(x_i)$, and let $A \in \{-1, 0, 1\}^{n \times n}$ be an invertible matrix. Then,

$$\begin{aligned}&\int_{y \in \mathbb{R}^{n-k}} \max_{z \in \mathbb{R}^k} f\big(A^{-1} \cdot (y, z)\big) \mathrm{d}y \\ &\quad \leq 2^k (n-k)! \cdot \sum_I \left(\prod_{i \notin I} \sigma_i\right) \cdot \left(\prod_{i \in I} \chi_i\right)\end{aligned}$$

where $\sigma_i = \sum_{k=1}^{N_i} \phi_{i,k} \ell_{i,k}$ and $\chi_i = \sum_{k=1}^{N_i} \phi_{i,k}$ and where the first sum runs over all tuples $I = (i_1, \dots, i_k)$ for which $1 \leq i_1 < \dots < i_k \leq n$.

To finish the proof of Theorem 35 we round the probability densities f_i as follows: For an arbitrarily small positive real δ let $g_i := \lceil f_i / \delta \rceil \cdot \delta$, i.e., we round f_i up to the next integral multiple of δ. As the densities f_i are quasiconcave, there is a decomposition of g_i such that $g_i = \sum_{k=1}^{N_i} f_{i,k}$ where

$$f_{i,k} = \begin{cases} \phi_{i,k} & \text{if } x \in I_{i,k} \,, \\ 0 & \text{otherwise} \,, \end{cases} \quad \text{and}$$

$$\chi_i := \sum_{k=1}^{N_i} \phi_{i,k} = \max_{x \in [-1,1]} g_i(x) \,,$$

where $I_{i,k}$ are intervals of length $\ell_{i,k}$ and $\phi_{i,k}$ are positive reals. The second property is the interesting one and stems from the quasiconcaveness of f_i. Informally speaking the two-dimensional shape bounded by the horizontal axis and the graph of g_i is a stack of rectangles aligned with axes. Therefore, the sum χ_i of the rectangles' heights which appears in the formula of Corollary 37 is approximately ϕ. Without the quasiconcaveness χ_i might be unbounded.

Applying Corollary 37, we obtain

$$\begin{aligned}&\int_{y \in \mathbb{R}^{n-k}} \max_{z \in \mathbb{R}^k} f_X\big(A^{-1} \cdot (y, z)\big) \mathrm{d}y \\ &\quad = \int_{y \in \mathbb{R}^{n-k}} \max_{z \in \mathbb{R}^k} \prod_{i=1}^n f_i\big(\big(A^{-1} \cdot (y, z)\big)_i\big) \mathrm{d}y \\ &\quad \leq \int_{y \in \mathbb{R}^{n-k}} \max_{z \in \mathbb{R}^k} \prod_{i=1}^n g_i\big(\big(A^{-1} \cdot (y, z)\big)_i\big) \mathrm{d}y \\ &\quad \leq 2^k (n-k)! \cdot \sum_I \left(\prod_{i \notin I} \sum_{k_i=1}^{N_i} \phi_{i,k_i} \cdot \ell_{i,k_i}\right) \cdot \left(\prod_{i \in I} \chi_i\right) \\ &\quad = 2^k (n-k)! \cdot \sum_I \left(\prod_{i \notin I} \int_{[-1,1]} g_i \,\mathrm{d}x\right) \cdot \left(\prod_{i \in I} \chi_i\right) .\end{aligned}$$

Since $0 \leq \int_{[-1,1]} g_i \,\mathrm{d}x \leq \int_{[-1,1]} (f_i + \delta) \,\mathrm{d}x = 1 + 2\delta$ and $0 \leq \chi_i \leq \sup_{x \in [-1,1]} f_i(x) + \delta \leq \phi + \delta$, this implies

$$\begin{aligned}&\int_{y \in \mathbb{R}^{n-k}} \max_{z \in \mathbb{R}^k} f_X\big(A^{-1} \cdot (y, z)\big) \mathrm{d}y \\ &\quad \leq 2^k (n-k)! \cdot \sum_I \left(\prod_{i \notin I} (1 + 2\delta)\right) \cdot \left(\prod_{i \in I} (\phi + \delta)\right) \\ &\quad = 2^k (n-k)! \cdot \sum_I (1 + 2\delta)^{n-k} (\phi + \delta)^k \\ &\quad = 2^k (n-k)! \binom{n}{k} (1 + 2\delta)^{n-k} (\phi + \delta)^k \\ &\quad \leq 2^k n^{n-k} (1 + 2\delta)^{n-k} (\phi + \delta)^k \,.\end{aligned}$$

As this bound is true for arbitrarily small reals $\delta > 0$, we obtain the desired bound.

7. CONCLUSION AND OPEN PROBLEMS

With the techniques developed in this paper we settled two questions posed by Moitra and O'Donnell [13]: For quasiconcave densities we showed that the exponent of ϕ in the bound for the smoothed number of Pareto-optimal solutions is exactly d. Moreover, we significantly improved on the previously best known bound for higher moments of the smoothed number of Pareto-optima [17]. Maybe even more interesting are our results for the model of zero-preserving perturbations. For this model we proved the first non-trivial bound on the smoothed number of Pareto-optimal solutions. We showed that this result can be used to analyze multiobjective optimization problems with polynomial objective functions. Furthermore, our result implies that the smoothed running time of the algorithm proposed by Berger et al. [5] to compute a path trade in a routing network is polynomially bounded for any constant number of autonomous systems. We believe that there are many more applications of our result in the area of multi-objective optimization.

There are several interesting open questions. First of all it would be interesting to find asymptotically tight bounds for the smoothed number of Pareto-optimal solutions. There is still a gap between our upper bound of $O(n^{2d}\phi^d)$ for quasiconcave ϕ-smooth instances and the best lower bound of $\Omega(n^{d-1.5}\phi^d)$ [10]. Only for the case $d = 1$ we can show that the upper bound is tight [6]. Especially for zero-preserving perturbations there is still a lot of work to do. We conjecture that our techniques can be extended to also bound higher moments of the smoothed number of Pareto-optima for ϕ-smooth instances with zero-preserving perturbations. However, we feel that even our bound for the first moment is too pessimistic as we do not have a lower bound showing that setting coefficients to zero can lead to larger Pareto-sets. It would be very interesting to either prove a lower bound that shows that zero-preserving perturbations can lead to larger Pareto-sets than non-zero-preserving perturbations or to prove a better upper bound for zero-preserving perturbations.

It would also be interesting to know whether our results extend to sets $\mathcal{S} \subseteq \{-m, \dots, m\}^n$ of solutions for a constant $m > 1$. We conjecture that our results still hold with worse constants that depend on m.

8. REFERENCES

[1] René Beier. *Probabilistic Analysis of Discrete Optimization Problems.* PhD thesis, Universität des Saarlandes, 2004.

[2] René Beier, Heiko Röglin, and Berthold Vöcking. The smoothed number of Pareto optimal solutions in bicriteria integer optimization. In *Proceedings of the 12th International Conference on Integer Programming and Combinatorial Optimization (IPCO)*, pages 53–67, 2007.

[3] René Beier and Berthold Vöcking. Random knapsack in expected polynomial time. *Journal of Computer and System Sciences*, 69(3):306–329, 2004.

[4] René Beier and Berthold Vöcking. Typical properties of winners and losers in discrete optimization. *SIAM Journal on Computing*, 35(4):855–881, 2006.

[5] André Berger, Heiko Röglin, and Ruben van der Zwaan. Path trading: Fast algorithms, smoothed analysis, and hardness results. In *Proceedings of the 10th International Symposium on Experimental Algorithms (SEA)*, pages 43–53, 2011.

[6] Tobias Brunsch and Heiko Röglin. Lower bounds for the smoothed number of pareto optimal solutions. In *Proceedings of the 8th Annual Conference on Theory and Applications of Models of Computation (TAMC)*, pages 416–427, 2011.

[7] H. William Corley and I. Douglas Moon. Shortest paths in networks with vector weights. *Journal of Optimization Theory and Application*, 46(1):79–86, 1985.

[8] Matthias Ehrgott. Integer solutions of multicriteria network flow problems. *Investigacao Operacional*, 19:229–243, 1999.

[9] Matthias Ehrgott. *Multicriteria Optimization.* Springer, 2005.

[10] Navin Goyal and Luis Rademacher. Lower bounds for the average and smoothed number of pareto optima. *CoRR*, abs/1107.3876, 2011.

[11] Pierre Hansen. Bicriterion path problems. In *Multiple Criteria Decision Making: Theory and Applications*, volume 177 of *Lecture Notes in Economics and Mathematical Systems*, pages 109–127, 1980.

[12] Kathrin Klamroth and Margaret M. Wiecek. Dynamic programming approaches to the multiple criteria knapsack problem. *Naval Research Logistics*, 47(1):57–76, 2000.

[13] Ankur Moitra and Ryan O'Donnell. Pareto optimal solutions for smoothed analysts. In *Proceedings of the 43rd Annual ACM Symposium on Theory of Computing (STOC)*, pages 225–234, 2011.

[14] Matthias Müller-Hannemann and Karsten Weihe. Pareto shortest paths is often feasible in practice. In *Proceedings of the 5th International Workshop on Algorithm Engineering (WAE)*, pages 185–198, 2001.

[15] Adli Mustafa and Mark Goh. Finding integer efficient solutions for bicriteria and tricriteria network flow problems using dinas. *Computers & Operations Research*, 25(2):139–157, 1998.

[16] George L. Nemhauser and Zev Ullmann. Discrete dynamic programming and capital allocation. *Management Science*, 15(9):494–505, 1969.

[17] Heiko Röglin and Shang-Hua Teng. Smoothed analysis of multiobjective optimization. In *Proceedings of the 50th Annual IEEE Symposium on Foundations of Computer Science (FOCS)*, pages 681–690, 2009.

[18] Arvind Sankar, Daniel A. Spielman, and Shang-Hua Teng. Smoothed analysis of the condition numbers and growth factors of matrices. *SIAM Journal on Matrix Analysis Applications*, 28(2):446–476, 2006.

[19] Anders J. V. Skriver and Kim Allan Andersen. A label correcting approach for solving bicriterion shortest-path problems. *Computers & Operations Research*, 27(6):507–524, 2000.

[20] Daniel A. Spielman and Shang-Hua Teng. Smoothed analysis of algorithms: Why the simplex algorithm usually takes polynomial time. *Journal of the ACM*, 51(3):385–463, 2004.

[21] Daniel A. Spielman and Shang-Hua Teng. Smoothed analysis: an attempt to explain the behavior of algorithms in practice. *Communications of the ACM*, 52(10):76–84, 2009.

Prior-Free Auctions with Ordered Bidders

Stefano Leonardi*
Sapienza University of Rome
Via Ariosto 25
00185, Rome, Italy
leon@dis.uniroma1.it

Tim Roughgarden†
Stanford University
353 Serra Mall
Stanford, CA 94305
tim@cs.stanford.edu

ABSTRACT

Prior-free auctions are robust auctions that assume no distribution over bidders' valuations and provide worst-case (input-by-input) approximation guarantees. In contrast to previous work on this topic, we pursue good prior-free auctions with non-identical bidders.

Prior-free auctions can approximate meaningful benchmarks for non-identical bidders only when "sufficient qualitative information" about the bidder asymmetry is publicly known. We consider digital goods auctions where there is a *total ordering* of the bidders that is known to the seller, where earlier bidders are in some sense expected to have higher valuations. We use the framework of Hartline and Roughgarden (STOC '08) to define an appropriate revenue benchmark: the maximum revenue that can be obtained from a bid vector using prices that are nonincreasing in the bidder ordering and bounded above by the second-highest bid. This monotone-price benchmark is always as large as the well-known fixed-price benchmark $\mathcal{F}^{(2)}$, so designing prior-free auctions with good approximation guarantees is only harder. By design, an auction that approximates the monotone-price benchmark satisfies a very strong guarantee: it is, in particular, simultaneously near-optimal for essentially every Bayesian environment in which bidders' valuation distributions have nonincreasing monopoly prices, or in which the distribution of each bidder stochastically dominates that of the next. Of course, even if there is no distribution over bidders' valuations, such an auction still provides a quantifiable input-by-input performance guarantee.

In this paper, we design a simple prior-free auction for digital goods with ordered bidders, the RANDOM PRICE RESTRICTION (RPR) auction. We prove that its expected revenue on every bid profile $\mathbf{b}$ is $\Omega(\mathcal{M}^{(2)}(\mathbf{b})/\log^* n)$, where $\mathcal{M}^{(2)}$ denotes the monotone-price benchmark and $\log^* n$ denotes the number of times that the $\log_2$ operator can be applied to n before the result drops below a fixed constant.

*This work was partially supported from ERC Starting Grant 259515: Practical Approximation Algorithms.

†Supported in part by NSF grant CCF-1016885, an ONR PECASE Award, and an AFOSR MURI grant.

STOC'12, May 19–22, 2012, New York, New York, USA.

Categories and Subject Descriptors

F.0 [**Theory of Computation**]: General

General Terms

Algorithms, Economics, Theory

Keywords

Algorithmic Mechanism Design, Auction Theory

1. INTRODUCTION

Suppose you own a set of goods and want to make money by selling them. What is the best way to do it? This question is non-trivial even in *digital goods auctions*, where the seller has an unlimited supply of identical goods (like mp3s), and there are n bidders, each of whom wants only one good and has a private valuation (i.e., maximum willingness-to-pay) for it.

The question becomes easy if the seller has a prior product distribution on bidders' valuations. Since supply is unlimited and valuations are independent, the seller can optimize for each bidder separately. For a bidder i with valuation distribution F_i, the expected revenue is maximized by posting a monopoly price — that is, making a "take-it-or-leave-it" offer at a price in $\text{argmax}_p[p \cdot (1 - F_i(p))]$.

What if good prior information is expensive or impossible to acquire? What if a single auction is to be re-used several times, in settings with different or not-yet-known bidder valuations? Are there *prior-free* auctions that admit more robust, "worst-case" revenue guarantees? Particularly germane to this paper, do such auctions exist when none of the bidders are identical?

Revenue Benchmarks..

Goldberg et al. [10, 9] were the first to pursue prior-free auctions, and they proposed a competitive analysis framework based on *revenue benchmarks*. The idea is to define a real-valued function on inputs (i.e., bid vectors) that represents an upper bound on the maximum revenue achievable by any "reasonable" auction on each input. They proposed the *fixed-price benchmark* $\mathcal{F}^{(2)}$ for digital goods auctions, defined as the maximum revenue that can be obtained from a given bid vector by offering every bidder a common posted price that is at most the second-highest bid.

Comparing the revenue of an auction to $\mathcal{F}^{(2)}$ initially looks like an "apples vs. oranges" comparison — the auction does not know bidders' valuations but can employ arbitrary prices, while the benchmark is privy to all the private information but handicapped in the prices it can use. Nevertheless, Goldberg et al. [9] demonstrated the effectiveness of the fixed-price benchmark for meaningful competitive analysis: no auction achieves more than a $\approx .42$ fraction of $\mathcal{F}^{(2)}$ for every bid vector, and there are interesting auctions that obtain a constant fraction of this benchmark on every input. Subsequent attempts to extend this competitive analysis framework beyond digital goods auctions are surveyed by Hartline and Karlin [11].

The Bayesian Thought Experiment..

To extend the revenue benchmark approach to new objective functions and asymmetric outcome spaces, Hartline and Roughgarden [12] advocated a general framework based on a "Bayesian thought experiment". Roughly, this framework works as follows. The first step is to temporarily think of bidders' valuations as drawn i.i.d. from some valuation distribution. The second step is to characterize the collection $\mathcal{C}$ of all optimal auctions that can arise — those with maximum-possible expected objective function value with respect to some valuation distribution. For example, for revenue maximization in digital goods auctions, $\mathcal{C}$ is the set of common posted prices (bidders are i.i.d. and hence have a common monopoly price). Finally, given a bid vector $\mathbf{b}$, the benchmark is defined as the maximum objective function value obtained by an auction in $\mathcal{C}$ on the input $\mathbf{b}$. In digital goods auctions, this is the maximum revenue that can be obtained by offering every bidder a common posted price — modulo the restriction of being at most the second-highest bid, the Bayesian thought experiment automatically regenerates the $\mathcal{F}^{(2)}$ benchmark. (For technical reasons, the upper bound on prices still needs to be added to permit interesting results [9].) More importantly, all benchmarks generated by this framework are automatically well motivated: if the performance of an auction is within a constant factor of such a benchmark for every input, then in particular it is simultaneously near-optimal in every Bayesian i.i.d. environment.[1] In addition, if there is no distribution over inputs, then the auction still provides a quantifiable input-by-input guarantee.

Analogs elsewhere in theoretical computer science include worst-case regret guarantees in online decision-making (e.g., if cost vectors are drawn i.i.d. from a distribution, then the optimal action is time-invariant) and static optimality in data structure design (e.g., if searches are i.i.d., then there is some fixed optimal binary search tree). The framework in [12] and some variants of it have been successfully used to extend the reach of prior-free mechanism design to new objective functions [12] and more complex environments [5, 13, 14].

Beyond I.I.D. Bidders..

The primary goal of this paper is the following.

> *To design good prior-free auctions for benchmarks derived from non-identical bidders.*

Why is this non-trivial? Let's apply the Bayesian thought experiment to a digital goods auction, now assuming that bidder i's valuation is drawn (independently) from its own distribution F_i. For fixed distributions $F_1, \ldots, F_n$, the optimal auction offers each bidder its respective monopoly price. Ranging over all choices of $F_1, \ldots, F_n$, we find that the collection $\mathcal{C}$ corresponds to the set of *all posted price vectors.*[2] Thus, for every bid vector $\mathbf{b}$, there is an auction $A_{\mathbf{b}} \in \mathcal{C}$ that uses the price vector $\mathbf{b}$ and hence obtains the full welfare $\sum_{i=1}^{n} b_i$ as revenue. There is no digital goods auction that always obtains a constant fraction of the optimal welfare [9], so the Bayesian thought experiment with non-i.i.d. bidders generates a benchmark that is far too strong for meaningful competitive analysis.

The exercise above suggests the following principle for prior-free auction design with non-identical bidders.

> *Prior-free auctions can approximate benchmarks derived from non-identical bidders only if "sufficient qualitative information" about bidder asymmetry is publicly known.*

To give an easy example, suppose there is a publicly known partition of the bidders into groups of otherwise indistinguishable bidders. We then require the Bayesian thought experiment to conform to the public information, meaning that the valuations of bidders in the same group are i.i.d. draws from a distribution. Then, the optimal auctions $\mathcal{C}$ are the price vectors that offer a common posted price to each group of bidders. The induced prior-free benchmark is the maximum revenue that can be obtained from the given bid vector using such a price vector. This is essentially the same benchmark proposed in work on attribute auctions [3, 4] that predates the benchmark framework in [12]. There are prior-free digital goods auctions with expected revenue at least a constant fraction of this benchmark when every group has at least 2 bidders (by an easy reduction to the standard setup) and when there is a constant number of groups [3, 4].

Ordered Bidders and Stochastic Dominance..

What about the general case when all bidders are distinguishable? We consider digital goods auctions when there is a *total ordering* of the bidders that is known to the seller. Without loss of generality, we assume that bidders are ordered $1, 2, \ldots, n$.[3] Earlier bidders are in some sense expected to have higher valuations. This information could be derived from, for example, eBay bidding histories, credit history, previous transactions with the seller, and so on. We emphasize that the known information is only qualitative — and seems minimal subject to an interesting theory of prior-free auctions with non-identical bidders — and is not quantitative or statistical, as is standard in Bayesian auction design.

To generate a prior-free benchmark, we consider Bayesian thought experiments that conform to the known information. As a first step, call the distributions $F_1, \ldots, F_n$ *ordered* if the corresponding monopoly prices are nonincreasing. For example, the F_i's could be uniform distributions

[1]This weaker goal of good *prior-independent* auctions — where a distribution over inputs is assumed and used in the analysis of a mechanism, but not in its design — is now studied in its own right [6, 7].

[2]This fact holds even if we restrict the F_i's to be, say uniform distributions with support $[0, h_i]$ and hence monopoly price $h_i/2$.

[3]Ties between bidders can also be accommodated easily, either with cosmetic changes to the auction and analysis in this paper, or by handling groups of indistinguishable bidders separately using known techniques.

on intervals $[0, h_i]$ with nonincreasing h_i's; exponential distributions with nondecreasing rates; Gaussian distributions with nondecreasing means; and so on. Letting $(F_1, \ldots, F_n)$ range over all ordered distributions, the corresponding collection $\mathcal{C}$ of optimal auctions is the set of *monotone* price vectors $\mathbf{p}$, where $p_1 \geq \cdots \geq p_n$. We denote the induced revenue benchmark by $\mathcal{M}^{(1)}$, the maximum revenue that can be obtained from a given bid vector from a monotone price vector. For example, for a bid vector $\mathbf{b}$ that is itself monotone, with $b_1 \geq \cdots \geq b_n$, setting $\mathbf{p} = \mathbf{b}$ shows that $\mathcal{M}^{(1)}(\mathbf{b})$ is the full welfare $\sum_{i=1}^{n} b_i$. If $b_1 \leq \cdots \leq b_n$, however, then the revenue-maximizing monotone price vector is simply a constant price — equal to the bid b_i that maximizes $j \cdot b_j$. We emphasize that the benchmark $\mathcal{M}^{(1)}(\mathbf{b})$ is defined for *all* bid vectors $\mathbf{b}$, including those that defy the expectations of the bidder ordering. Similarly, auctions that strive to approximate such a benchmark on every input are allowed to use arbitrary prices, not merely monotone ones.

By definition, an auction with revenue at least a constant fraction of $\mathcal{M}^{(1)}$ on every input is simultaneously near-optimal in every Bayesian digital goods auction with independent and ordered distributions. Being prior-free, such an auction also has a well-defined worst-case performance guarantee even when no distribution over the inputs is assumed.

A similar simultaneous approximation result holds under the standard notion of stochastic dominance. Recall that a distribution F_i stochastically dominates another F_{i+1} if $F_i(x) \leq F_{i+1}(x)$ for every $x \geq 0$. Dhangwotnotai and Hartline (personal communication, November 2011) observed that, if F_i stochastically dominates F_{i+1} for every $i = 1, 2, \ldots, n-1$, then there is a monotone price vector with expected revenue at least 50% of that of an optimal price vector. It follows that an auction with revenue at least a constant fraction of $\mathcal{M}^{(1)}$ on every input is simultaneously near-optimal in every Bayesian digital goods auction in which the distribution each bidder stochastically dominates that of the next.

The Monotone Price Benchmark..

Given a digital goods environment with ordered bidders, we define the *monotone price benchmark* $\mathcal{M}^{(2)}(\mathbf{b})$ for every bid vector $\mathbf{b}$ as the maximum revenue obtainable via a monotone price vector in which every price is at most the second-highest bid. As in the conventional model with indistinguishable bidders [9], the upper bound on prices is necessary for the existence of prior-free auctions with non-trivial approximation guarantees.[4] Indeed, since a constant price vector is monotone, $\mathcal{M}^{(2)}(\mathbf{b}) \geq \mathcal{F}^{(2)}(\mathbf{b})$ for every $\mathbf{b}$ and so designing auctions competitive with the monotone-price benchmark is at least as difficult as with the fixed-price benchmark.

The monotone-price benchmark was previously considered, with a completely different motivation, by Aggarwal and Hartline [1]. In [1], which predates the benchmark framework in [12], $\mathcal{M}^{(2)}$ was one of three ad hoc benchmarks proposed for "knapsack auctions", where bidders have a public size and feasible solutions correspond to subsets of bidders with total size at most a publicly known budget. In particular, Aggarwal and Hartline [1] gave a digital goods auction that, for every bid vector $\mathbf{b}$, has expected revenue at least $\frac{1}{c}\mathcal{M}^{(2)}(\mathbf{b}) - O(h \log\log\log h)$, where $c > 0$ is a constant and h is the ratio between the maximum and minimum bids.

Our Results..

Our main result is a prior-free digital goods auction with ordered bidders that satisfies: there is a constant $c > 0$ such that, for every input $\mathbf{b}$, the auction's expected revenue is at least $\mathcal{M}^{(2)}(\mathbf{b})/c \log^* n$. Here $\log^* n$ denotes the number of times that the $\log_2$ operator can be applied to n before the result drops below a constant (2, say). Put differently, if n is roughly equal to a tower of t 2's, then $\log^* n$ is roughly t.

Our auction, which we call the RANDOM PRICE RESTRICTION (RPR) auction, is very simple. As is standard, the auction randomly partitions the bidders into two groups. It computes an optimal monotone price vector for the "training set" of bidders, subject to a randomly restricted set of permissible prices. Finally, it applies the computed price vector to the "test set" of bidders in the natural way. To obtain an approximation guarantee of $O(\log^* n)$, the random price restriction (and the analysis) has to be executed with some care.

Future Research..

Our model and results suggest several concrete open questions, the solutions to which would advance the theory of auctions with prior-free or prior-independent guarantees. There is the obvious open question of whether or not our approximation guarantee of $O(\log^* n)$ can be improved to a constant factor, presumably using a different auction. Another important next step is the study of limited-supply auctions with unit-demand and ordered bidders. Prior-free guarantees with limited supply are non-trivial even with indistinguishable bidders [5], and extending these results to ordered bidders poses an intriguing challenge. Finally, it would be interesting to pursue prior-independent guarantees in the spirit of [6, 7] in Bayesian environments with ordered or stochastically dominating distributions.

2. PRELIMINARIES

In a *digital goods auction*, there is one seller and n bidders. There is an unlimited supply of identical goods. Each bidder wants only one good, and has a private — i.e., unknown to the seller — *valuation* v_i. We study direct-revelation auctions, in which the bidders report bids $\mathbf{b}$ to the seller, and the seller then decides who wins a good and at what price.[5] For a fixed (randomized) auction, we use $X_i(\mathbf{b})$ and $P_i(\mathbf{b})$ to denote the winning probability and expected payment of bidder i when the bid profile is $\mathbf{b}$. As in previous works on prior-free auction design, we consider only auctions that are individually rational — meaning $P_i(\mathbf{b}) \leq v_i \cdot X_i(\mathbf{b})$ for every i and $\mathbf{b}$ — and truthful, meaning that for each bidder i and fixed bids $\mathbf{b}_{-i}$ by the other bidders, bidder i maximizes its quasi-linear utility $v_i \cdot X_i(b_i, \mathbf{b}_{-i}) - P_i(b_i, \mathbf{b}_{-i})$ by setting $b_i = v_i$. Since we consider only truthful auctions, from now on we use bids $\mathbf{b}$ and valuations $\mathbf{v}$ interchangeably.

Truthful and individually rational digital goods auctions have a nice canonical form: for every bidder i there is a

[4] Under mild extra conditions on the valuation distributions, an auctions that always has revenue at least a constant fraction of $\mathcal{M}^{(2)}$ is still simultaneously near-optimal in every Bayesian environment with ordered or stochastically dominating distributions (with somewhat worse constant factors).

[5] For the questions we ask, the "Revelation Principle" (see, e.g., Nisan [17]) ensures that there is no loss of generality by considering only direct-revelation auctions.

(possibly randomized) function $t_i(\mathbf{v}_{-i})$ that, given the valuations $\mathbf{v}_{-i}$ of the other bidders, gives bidder i a "take-it-or-leave-it offer" at the price $t_i(\mathbf{v}_{-i})$. This means that bidder i is given a good if and only if $v_i \geq t_i(\mathbf{v}_{-i})$, in which case it is charged the price $t_i(\mathbf{v}_{-i})$. It is clear that every choice $(t_1, \ldots, t_n)$ of such functions defines a truthful, individually rational digital goods auction; conversely, every such auction is equivalent to a choice of $(t_1, \ldots, t_n)$ [9]. A special case of such an auction is a *price vector* $\mathbf{p}$, in which each t_i is the constant function $t_i(\mathbf{v}_{-i}) = p_i$. As noted in Section 1, in Bayesian settings with independent valuations, price vectors maximize expected revenue over all truthful and individually rational auctions.

The *revenue* of an auction on the valuation profile $\mathbf{v}$ is the sum of the payments collected from the winners. Let $v^{(2)}$ denote the second-highest valuation of a profile $\mathbf{v}$. The *fixed-price benchmark* $\mathcal{F}^{(2)}$ is defined, for each valuation profile $\mathbf{v}$, as the maximum revenue that can be obtained from a constant price vector whose price is at most $v^{(2)}$:

$$\mathcal{F}^{(2)}(\mathbf{v}) = \max_{p \leq v^{(2)}} \left(\sum_{i : v_i \geq p} p \right).$$

Now suppose there is a known ordering on the bidders, say $1, 2, \ldots, n$. The *monotone-price benchmark* $\mathcal{M}^{(2)}$ is defined analogously to $\mathcal{F}^{(2)}$, except that non-constant monotone price vectors are also permitted:

$$\mathcal{M}^{(2)}(\mathbf{v}) = \max_{v^{(2)} \geq p_1 \geq p_2 \geq \cdots \geq p_n} \left(\sum_{i : v_i \geq p_i} p_i \right). \quad (1)$$

Clearly, $\mathcal{M}^{(2)}(\mathbf{v}) \geq \mathcal{F}^{(2)}(\mathbf{v})$ for every input $\mathbf{v}$.

We reiterate that the monotonicity and upper-bound constraints are enforced only in the computation of the benchmark $\mathcal{M}^{(2)}$; auctions, while obviously not privy to the private valuations, can employ whatever prices they see fit. This is natural for prior-free auctions and also necessary for non-trivial results [8].

Finally, when we say that an auction is *α-competitive* with or has *approximation factor* α for a benchmark, we mean that the auction's expected revenue is at least a $1/\alpha$ fraction of the benchmark for every input $\mathbf{v}$.

3. A PRIOR-FREE $O(\log^* n)$-APPROXIMATE DIGITAL GOODS AUCTION WITH ORDERED BIDDERS

3.1 The Random Price Restriction (RPR) Auction

We propose the Random Price Restriction (RPR) auction, displayed in Figure 1. We next elaborate on the steps of the auction. In the second step, in the case where $L = 0$, we run an arbitrary digital goods auction that is $O(1)$-competitive with respect to the fixed-price benchmark $\mathcal{F}^{(2)}$. The best-known approximation factor is 3.12 [15]; there are also very simple auctions with approximation factors 4 [9] and 4.68 [2]. Intuitively, this step is meant to extract good revenue from the set of bidders with valuations almost as high as the second-highest valuation.

The third step of the algorithm randomly partitions the bidders into a "training set" A and a "test set" B. Almost all prior-free auctions have this structure, with the bidders in the training set setting prices for those in the test set. For simplicity, we sell (in the sixth step) only to bidders in the test set B. An obvious optimization is sell simultaneously to bidders in A, using the bids of B; this would improve the hidden constant in our approximation guarantee by a factor of 2.

Input: a valuation profile $\mathbf{v}$ for a totally ordered set $N = \{1, 2, \ldots, n\}$ of bidders.

1. Choose a *level* $L \in \{0, 1, 2, \ldots, \log^* n\}$ uniformly at random.
2. If $L = 0$, run a digital goods auction on $\mathbf{v}$ that is $O(1)$-competitive with respect to the benchmark $\mathcal{F}^{(2)}$, and halt.
3. Choose a subset $A \subseteq N$ uniformly at random, and partition N into the two sets A and B.
4. Compute an optimal L-feasible price vector $\mathbf{p}^A$ for A (see details in the main text).
5. Extend $\mathbf{p}^A$ to a price vector $\mathbf{p}$ on all of N by, for each $i \in B$, setting p_i equal to p_j^A, where $j = \min\{h > i : h \in A\}$. If j is undefined, set $p_i = 0$.
6. Sell items to bidders in B only, using prices $\mathbf{p}$.

Figure 1: The auction Random Price Restriction (RPR).

To explain the fourth step, let $\mathbf{v}^A$ denote the valuations of the bidders in the sample A. Let $\log^{(\ell)} n$ denote the result of applying the $\log_2$ operator ℓ times to n. A price vector is *ℓ-feasible for* A if it is monotone and if every price is a power of two in the range

$$\left[\frac{\mathcal{M}^{(2)}(\mathbf{v}^A)}{(\log^{(\ell-1)} n)^3}, \frac{3\mathcal{M}^{(2)}(\mathbf{v}^A)}{(\log^{(\ell)} n)^3} \right]. \quad (2)$$

(Here and throughout the paper, $\log^{(0)} n$ is defined as n.) The optimal such price vector is the one that maximizes the revenue obtained from the bidders in A. Intuitively, the optimal ℓ-feasible price vector is meant to extract good revenue from the set of bidders with valuations in the range in (2).

The fifth step applies the prices computed in the fourth step to bidders in the test set B in the natural way, with each bidder inheriting the price computed for its "nearest neighbor" in the training set A.

The RPR auction is truthful, as each bidder faces a take-it-or-leave-it offer at a price (possibly $+\infty$) that is independent of its reported valuation. We also note that the RPR auction can be implemented in polynomial time, as both $\mathcal{M}^{(2)}(\mathbf{v}^A)$ and $\mathbf{p}^A$ can be computed efficiently using dynamic programming.

3.2 The Analysis

Our main result is a prior-free approximation guarantee for the RPR auction.

Theorem 3.1 *There is a constant $c > 0$ such that, for every valuation profile* $\mathbf{v}$*, the expected revenue of the* RPR *auction is at least* $\mathcal{M}^{(2)}(\mathbf{v})/(c \log^* n)$.

Recall that $\log^* n$ denotes the number of times that the $\log_2$ operator can be applied to n before the result drops below a fixed constant. (The choice of the constant doesn't matter, in that it changes the definition only by an additive term.)

When convenient, we assume that the number n of bidders is at least a sufficiently large constant — if not, the approximation ratio of the RPR auction is trivially constant.

To make our analysis as modular and transparent as possible, we factor it into three parts. In particular, we exert absolutely no effort to control the constant c of Theorem 3.1. In the first part, we define a collection of events and analyze their probabilities. The second part is more intricate, and it shows that if certain events occur, then certain portions of the monotone-price benchmark $\mathcal{M}^{(2)}(\mathbf{v})$ can be charged against analogous portions of the RPR auction's revenue. The third part stitches together our arguments into a proof of Theorem 3.1.

3.2.1 Some Events and Their Probabilities

Fix a valuation profile $\mathbf{v}$. Let $\mathcal{M}^*$ denote $\mathcal{M}^{(2)}(\mathbf{v})$. Let $\mathbf{v}^A$ denote the profile induced by a (random) training set A. Let $\mathcal{E}_A$ denote the event that

$$\mathcal{M}^{(2)}(\mathbf{v}^A) \geq \frac{1}{3} \cdot \mathcal{M}^*.$$

Lemma 3.2 *For every valuation profile* $\mathbf{v}$, $\Pr[\mathcal{E}_A] \geq \frac{1}{16}$.

PROOF. Let $\mathbf{p}$ achieve the maximum in (1) for $\mathbf{v}$, with revenue $\mathcal{M}^*$. With probability 1/4, the bidders with the highest and second-highest valuations lie in A. Given this event, the conditional expected revenue from bidders in A and B under the price vector $\mathbf{p}$ is at least $\mathcal{M}^*/2$ and at most $\mathcal{M}^*/2$, respectively. By Markov's inequality, the conditional expected revenue from bidders in A under $\mathbf{p}$ is at least $\frac{1}{3}\mathcal{M}^*$ with probability at least $\frac{1}{4}$. Since the bidders with highest and second-highest valuations lie in A, the projection of $\mathbf{p}$ on the bidders in A is a feasible price vector in the determination of the benchmark $\mathcal{M}^{(2)}(\mathbf{v}^A)$; the optimal price vector for A can only have higher revenue. Summarizing, with probability at least $\frac{1}{4} \cdot \frac{1}{4} = \frac{1}{16}$, $\mathcal{M}^{(2)}(\mathbf{v}^A) \geq \mathcal{M}^*/3$. □

With $\mathbf{v}$ still fixed, consider a choice of $\ell \in \{1, 2, \ldots, \log^* n\}$. A *level-$\ell$ price* is a power of 2 that lies in the range

$$\left[\frac{\mathcal{M}^*}{3(\log^{(\ell-1)} n)^3}, \frac{3\mathcal{M}^*}{(\log^{(\ell)} n)^3}\right]. \tag{3}$$

A *winning bidder* i for a price p satisfies $v_i \geq p$. A *level-ℓ triple* (i, j, p) meets the following criteria:

(i) p is a level-ℓ price

(ii) $i < j$

(iii) the number of winning bidders in $\{i, i+1, \ldots, j-1, j\}$ is at least

$$\frac{(\log^{(\ell)} n)^2}{432 \log^* n}, \tag{4}$$

and these include bidders i and j.

Observe that the set of level-ℓ triples depends only on $\mathbf{v}$ and ℓ, and not on the random choices of the RPR auction.

Lemma 3.3 *For every profile* $\mathbf{v}$ *and* $\ell \in \{1, 2, \ldots, \log^* n\}$*, there are* $O((\log^{(\ell-1)} n)^6 \log^{(\ell)} n)$ *level-ℓ triples.*

PROOF. Every level-ℓ price p is at least $\mathcal{M}^*/3(\log^{(\ell-1)} n)^3$; by the definition of $\mathcal{M}^*$, there are at most $3(\log^{(\ell-1)} n)^3$ winning bidders for such a price. Thus, there are at most $O((\log^{(\ell-1)} n)^3)$ choices for each of i and j. Since every level-ℓ price is a power of 2 between $\mathcal{M}^*$ and $\mathcal{M}^*/3(\log^{(\ell-1)} n)^3$, there are $O(\log^{(\ell)} n)$ choices for p. □

Call a level-ℓ triple (i, j, p) *balanced* if at least $\frac{1}{3}$ of the winning bidders in $\{i, i+1, \ldots, j-1, j\}$ for price p lie in A, and similarly in B. Let $\mathcal{E}_\ell$ denote the event that every level-ℓ triple is balanced.

Lemma 3.4 *For every valuation profile* $\mathbf{v}$ *with* n *sufficiently large, for every* $\ell \in \{1, 2, \ldots, \log^* n\}$, $\Pr[\mathcal{E}_\ell] \geq \frac{31}{32}$.

PROOF. Fix a level-ℓ triple (i, j, p) and a sufficiently large constant c. By definition (see (4)), the number of winning bidders in $\{i, i+1, \ldots, j-1, j\}$ for price p is at least $c \log^{(\ell)} n$, provided n is sufficiently large. We can choose c so that standard Chernoff bounds (e.g., [16]) imply that the probability that (i, j, p) is not balanced is at most $2^{-7 \log^{(\ell)} n} = (\log^{(\ell-1)} n)^{-7}$. Combining this fact with Lemma 3.3 and a Union Bound completes the proof. □

3.2.2 The Main Argument

Fix a valuation profile $\mathbf{v}$. As before, let $\mathcal{M}^*$ denote $\mathcal{M}^{(2)}(\mathbf{v})$. For $\ell \in \{1, 2, \ldots, \log^* n\}$, a *level-$\ell$ bidder* i is one satisfying

$$v_i \in \left[\frac{\mathcal{M}^*}{(\log^{(\ell-1)} n)^3}, \frac{\mathcal{M}^*}{(\log^{(\ell)} n)^3}\right]. \tag{5}$$

Also, recall that a price vector is *ℓ-feasible for the training set* A if it is monotone and if every price is a power of two in the range (2).

Lemma 3.5 *Fix an optimal price vector for* $\mathbf{v}$*, with revenue* $\mathcal{M}^*$*. For* $\ell \in \{1, 2, \ldots, \log^* n\}$*, let* C^*_ℓ *denote the revenue contributed by level-ℓ bidders. For every* $\ell \in \{1, 2, \ldots, \log^* n\}$*, if* $\mathcal{E}_A$ *holds, then there is an ℓ-feasible price vector for the full set* N *of bidders with revenue at least* $C^*_\ell/2$.

PROOF. Let $\mathbf{p}^*$ be an optimal price vector for $\mathbf{v}$ and fix $\ell \in \{1, 2, \ldots, \log^* n\}$. Let a and b denote the smallest and largest, respectively, powers of 2 that lie in the range (2). Derive $\mathbf{q}$ from $\mathbf{p}^*$ as follows: if $p^*_i > b$, set $q_i = b$; if $p^*_i < a$, set $q_i = a$; otherwise, set q_i to be the largest power of 2 less than or equal to p^*_i. Since $\mathbf{p}^*$ is monotone, so is $\mathbf{q}$. Hence, $\mathbf{q}$ is ℓ-feasible.

Since $\mathcal{E}_A$ holds, $\mathcal{M}^{(2)}(v^A) \in [\frac{1}{3}\mathcal{M}^*, \mathcal{M}^*]$. Comparing (2) with (5), we see that every level-ℓ bidder has valuation between a and b. Thus, $\mathbf{q}$ extracts at least half as much revenue as $\mathbf{p}^*$ from every such bidder. The lemma follows. □

Lemma 3.6 *Fix an optimal monotone price vector for* $\mathbf{v}$*, with revenue* $\mathcal{M}^*$*. For* $\ell \in \{1, 2, \ldots, \log^* n\}$*, let* C^*_ℓ *denote the revenue contributed by level-ℓ bidders, and suppose that*

$$C^*_\ell \geq \frac{\mathcal{M}^*}{2 \log^* n}. \tag{6}$$

If $\mathcal{E}_A$ *and* $\mathcal{E}_\ell$ *hold, then there is an ℓ-feasible price vector for the training set* A *of bidders with revenue at least* $C^*_\ell/12$.

PROOF. By Lemma 3.5, there is an ℓ-feasible price vector $\mathbf{q}$ for N that extracts revenue at least $C^*_\ell/2 \geq \mathcal{M}^*/4\log^* n$. We claim that the projection $\mathbf{q}^A$ of $\mathbf{q}$ onto the training set A satisfies the conditions of the lemma. It certainly inherits ℓ-feasibility from $\mathbf{q}$.

Going through the bidders of N from 1 to n, we greedily partition them into minimal intervals of bidders that contribute at least $\mathcal{M}^*/(24\log^* n \log^{(\ell)} n)$ revenue under the price vector $\mathbf{q}$. (For simplicity, we ignore the final leftover interval). First, since $\mathbf{q}$ is ℓ-feasible, all of its prices are at most $3\mathcal{M}^*/(\log^{(\ell)} n)^3$, and hence every interval has at least $(\log^{(\ell)} n)^2/(72\log^* n)$ winning bidders. Second, ignoring for simplicity the negligible discretization error, by minimality there are at least $6\log^{(\ell)} n$ intervals.

Call an interval *constant* if every winning bidder pays the same price under $\mathbf{q}$. Since $\mathbf{q}$ is ℓ-feasible, prices are monotone and are powers of 2 in the range in (2). It follows that prices change in $\mathbf{q}$ at most $3\log^{(\ell)} n$ times. Since there are at least $6\log^{(\ell)} n$ intervals, at least half of them are constant. Every price used by $\mathbf{q}$ lies in the range (2) and hence, since $\mathcal{E}_A$ holds by assumption, in the range (3). Since $\mathcal{E}_\ell$ holds by assumption and every interval has at least $(\log^{(\ell)} n)^2/72\log^* n$ winning bidders, A contains at least $\frac{1}{3}$ of the winning bidders (under $\mathbf{q}$) of every constant interval. Since half of the intervals are constant and every interval contributes (essentially) the same revenue under $\mathbf{q}$, the revenue from A under $\mathbf{q}^A$ is at least $\frac{1}{6}$ times that from N under $\mathbf{q}$. □

Lemma 3.7 *With the notation and assumptions of Lemma 3.6, and if also the auction* RPR *chooses $L = \ell$, then its revenue is at least $C^*_\ell/48$.*

PROOF. Let $\mathbf{q}^A$ denote the optimal ℓ-feasible prices for A computed by the RPR auction. By Lemma 3.6, the price vector $\mathbf{q}^A$ extracts revenue at least $C^*_\ell/12$ from A, which by (6) is at least $\mathcal{M}^*/(24\log^* n)$. Let $\mathbf{q}$ denote the extension of $\mathbf{q}^A$ to N defined in the fifth step of the RPR auction, and $\mathbf{q}^B$ the projection of $\mathbf{q}$ onto the test set B.

Analogously to the proof of Lemma 3.6, we greedily partition the bidders of A into minimal intervals that contribute at least $\mathcal{M}^*/(144\log^* n \log^{(\ell)} n)$ revenue under the price vector $\mathbf{q}^A$. There are at least $6\log^{(\ell)} n$ intervals, each with at least $(\log^{(\ell)} n)^2/(432\log^* n)$ winning bidders. Since $\mathbf{q}^A$ is ℓ-feasible, and least half of these intervals are constant, in the sense that all bidders are offered a common price by $\mathbf{q}^A$.

Consider a constant interval I of A, with common price q_I. Since $\mathcal{E}_A$ holds by assumption and $\mathbf{q}^A$ is ℓ-feasible, the common price q_I in an interval I of A lies in the range (3). Let i, j be the first and last winning bidders (of A) in I and consider the interval $\{i, i+1, \ldots, j-1, j\}$ of N. Then (i, j, q_I) is a level-ℓ triple. Since $\mathcal{E}_\ell$ holds by assumption, the test set B contains at least half as many bidders $h \in I$ with $v_h \geq q_I$ as does A. By its definition, $\mathbf{q}$ offers every bidder in $\{i, i+1, \ldots, j-i, j\}$ the price q_I. Thus $\mathbf{q}$ extracts at least half as much revenue from the bidders in $B \cap \{i, i+1, \ldots, j-i, j\}$ as in $A \cap \{i, i+1, \ldots, j-i, j\}$. Since half of the intervals of A are constant and every interval of A contributes (essentially) the same amount of revenue, the revenue from B under $\mathbf{q}^B$ is at least $\frac{1}{4}$ times that from A under $\mathbf{q}^A$. □

3.2.3 Putting It All Together

The gist of the final argument is: for the most important levels ℓ, the auction RPR extracts revenue $\Omega(C^*_\ell)$ when $L = \ell$. Since each value of ℓ is chosen with probability $\approx 1/\log^* n$, the approximation guarantee of $O(\log^* n)$ follows.

Proof of Theorem 3.1: Fix a valuation profile $\mathbf{v}$ and an optimal price vector $\mathbf{p}^*$ achieving revenue $\mathcal{M}^* := \mathcal{M}^{(2)}(\mathbf{v})$. For $\ell \in \{1, 2, \ldots, \log^* n\}$, recall that a level-$\ell$ bidder has valuation in the range (5), and let C^*_ℓ denote the revenue contributed by such bidders to $\mathcal{M}^*$ under $\mathbf{p}^*$. Let C^*_0 and $C^*_\perp$ denote the contributions of bidders with valuations more than $\mathcal{M}^*/(\log^{\log^* n} n)^3$ and less than $\mathcal{M}^*/n^3$, respectively. Define $S = \{\ell \in \{0, 1, 2, \ldots, \log^* n\} : C^*_\ell \geq \mathcal{M}^*/2\log^* n\}$ and the set of levels that contribute significant revenue. By averaging and the fact that $C^*_\perp \leq \mathcal{M}^*/n^2$,

$$\sum_{\ell \in S} C^*_\ell \geq \frac{\mathcal{M}^*}{3}.$$

Let R denote the revenue of the RPR auction on the profile $\mathbf{v}$. Conditioning on the choice of L and using that revenue is always nonnegative, we have

$$\begin{aligned} \mathbf{E}_{A,\ell}[R] &\geq \sum_{\ell \in S} \mathbf{E}_A[R \mid L = \ell] \cdot \mathbf{Pr}[L = \ell] \\ &= \frac{1}{\log^* n + 1} \sum_{\ell \in S} \mathbf{E}_A[R \mid L = \ell]. \end{aligned}$$

Thus, to complete the proof, we only need to show that $\mathbf{E}[R \mid L = \ell] = \Omega(C^*_\ell)$ for every $\ell \in S$.

For non-zero $\ell \in S$, since the random choices of A and ℓ are independent, and since the events $\mathcal{E}_A$ and $\mathcal{E}_\ell$ depend on the choice of A only, we can write

$$\mathbf{E}_A[R \mid L = \ell] = \mathbf{E}_A[R \mid L = \ell \wedge \mathcal{E}_A \wedge \mathcal{E}_\ell] \cdot \mathbf{Pr}[\mathcal{E}_A \wedge \mathcal{E}_\ell].$$

Combining Lemmas 3.2 and 3.4 with a Union Bound, $\mathbf{Pr}[\mathcal{E}_A \wedge \mathcal{E}_\ell] \geq \frac{1}{32}$. Since $\ell \in S$, Lemma 3.7 implies that $\mathbf{E}_A[R \mid L = \ell \wedge \mathcal{E}_A \wedge \mathcal{E}_\ell] \geq C^*_\ell/48$, and hence $\mathbf{E}[R \mid L = \ell] = \Omega(C^*_\ell)$.

Finally, recall that when $L = 0$, the RPR auction runs an auction that is $O(1)$-competitive with respect to the benchmark $\mathcal{F}^{(2)}$. Thus, to prove that $\mathbf{E}[R \mid L = 0] = \Omega(C^*_0)$, we only need to show that $\mathcal{F}^{(2)}(\mathbf{v}) = \Omega(C^*_0)$. Let N_0 denote the bidders with valuation more than $\mathcal{M}^*/(\log^{\log^* n} n)^3$, which is $\Omega(\mathcal{M}^*)$ by the definition of the $\log^*$ function. If there is only one bidder i in N_0, then offering all bidders the price p^*_i proves that $\mathcal{F}^{(2)}(\mathbf{v}) \geq C^*_0 = p^*_i$. (Since $\mathbf{p}^*$ determines $\mathcal{M}^{(2)}(\mathbf{v})$, p^*_i is at most the second-highest valuation of $\mathbf{v}$ and is a legitimate option for the fixed-price benchmark $\mathcal{F}^{(2)}(\mathbf{v})$.) If N_0 contains at least two bidders with q being the second-highest valuation, then offering all bidders the price q shows that $\mathcal{F}^{(2)}(\mathbf{v}) \geq 2v^{(2)} = \Omega(\mathcal{M}^*) = \Omega(C^*_0)$, which completes the proof. □

Acknowledgements

We thank Peerapong Dhangwotnotai, Amos Fiat, Jason Hartline, Elias Koutsoupias for several helpful discussions.

4. REFERENCES

[1] G. Aggarwal and J. D. Hartline. Knapsack auctions. In *Proceedings of the 17th Annual ACM-SIAM Symposium on Discrete Algorithms (SODA)*, pages 1083–1092, 2006.

[2] S. Alaei, A. Malekian, and A. Srinivasan. On random sampling auctions for digital goods. In *Proceedings of the 10th ACM Conference on Electronic Commerce (EC)*, pages 187–196, 2009.

[3] M.-F. Balcan, A. Blum, J. Hartline, and Y. Mansour. Mechanism Design via Machine Learning. *Journal of Computer and System Sciences*, 74(8):1245–1270, 2008.

[4] A. Blum and J. D. Hartline. Near-optimal online auctions. In *Proceedings of the 16th Annual ACM-SIAM Symposium on Discrete Algorithms (SODA)*, pages 1156–1163, 2005.

[5] N. Devanur and J. D. Hartline. Limited and online supply and the Bayesian foundations of prior-free mechanism design. In *Proceedings of the 10th ACM Conference on Electronic Commerce (EC)*, pages 41–50, 2009.

[6] N. Devanur, J. D. Hartline, A. R. Karlin, and T. Nguyen. A prior-independent mechanism for profit maximization in unit-demand combinatorial auctions. In *Proceedings of 7th Workshop on Internet & Network Economics*, 2011. To appear.

[7] Peerapong Dhangwatnotai, Tim Roughgarden, and Qiqi Yan. Revenue maximization with a single sample. In *Proceedings of the 11th ACM Conference on Electronic Commerce (EC)*, pages 129–138, 2010.

[8] A. Goldberg and J. Hartline. Envy-free auctions for digital goods. In *Proceedings of the 4th ACM Conference on Electronic Commerce (EC)*, pages 29–35, 2003.

[9] A. V. Goldberg, J. D. Hartline, A. Karlin, M. Saks, and A. Wright. Competitive auctions. *Games and Economic Behavior*, 55(2):242–269, 2006.

[10] A. V. Goldberg, J. D. Hartline, and A. Wright. Competitive auctions and digital goods. Technical Report STAR-TR-99.09.01, STAR Laboratory, InterTrust Tech. Corp., Santa Clara, CA, 1999.

[11] J. D. Hartline and A. Karlin. Profit maximization in mechanism design. In N. Nisan, T. Roughgarden, É. Tardos, and V. V. Vazirani, editors, *Algorithmic Game Theory*, chapter 13, pages 331–362. Cambridge University Press, 2007.

[12] J. D. Hartline and T. Roughgarden. Optimal mechanism design and money burning. In *Proceedings of the 40th Annual ACM Symposium on Theory of Computing (STOC)*, pages 75–84, 2008.

[13] J. D. Hartline and T. Roughgarden. Simple versus optimal mechanisms. In *Proceedings of the 10th ACM Conference on Electronic Commerce (EC)*, pages 225–234, 2009.

[14] J. D. Hartline and Q. Yan. Envy, truth, and optimality. In *Proceedings of the 12th ACM Conference on Electronic Commerce (EC)*, pages 243–252, 2011.

[15] T. Ichiba and K. Iwama. Averaging techniques for competitive auctions. In *Proceedings of the Workshop on Analytic Algorithmics and Combinatorics (ANALCO)*, pages 74–81, 2010.

[16] R. Motwani and P. Raghavan. *Randomized Algorithms*. Cambridge University Press, 1995.

[17] N. Nisan. Introduction to mechanism design (for computer scientists). In N. Nisan, T. Roughgarden, É. Tardos, and V. Vazirani, editors, *Algorithmic Game Theory*, chapter 9, pages 209–241. Cambridge University Press, 2007.

On the Limits of Black-Box Reductions in Mechanism Design

Shuchi Chawla*
University of Wisconsin - Madison
shuchi@cs.wisc.edu

Nicole Immorlica†
Northwestern University
nicimm@gmail.com

Brendan Lucier
MSR New England
brlucier@microsoft.com

ABSTRACT

We consider the problem of converting an arbitrary approximation algorithm for a single-parameter optimization problem into a computationally efficient truthful mechanism. We ask for reductions that are black-box, meaning that they require only oracle access to the given algorithm and in particular do not require explicit knowledge of the problem constraints. Such a reduction is known to be possible, for example, for the social welfare objective when the goal is to achieve Bayesian truthfulness and preserve social welfare in expectation. We show that a black-box reduction for the social welfare objective is not possible if the resulting mechanism is required to be truthful in expectation and to preserve the worst-case approximation ratio of the algorithm to within a subpolynomial factor. Further, we prove that for other objectives such as makespan, no black-box reduction is possible even if we only require Bayesian truthfulness and an average-case performance guarantee.

Categories and Subject Descriptors

J.4 [**Social And Behavioral Sciences**]: Economics

General Terms

Theory

Keywords

Mechanism design, algorithms, social welfare, makespan

1. INTRODUCTION

Mechanism design studies optimization in the presence of selfish agents, where the goal is to design a system in which agents' individual selfish behaviour leads to global optimization of a desired objective. A central theme in *algorithmic* mechanism design is to reconcile the incentive constraints of selfish agents with the requirement of computational tractability and to understand whether the combination of these two considerations limits algorithm design in a way that each one alone does not. In the best-case scenario, one might hope for a sort of equivalence between the requirements of algorithm design and mechanism design, manifested via reductions that convert arbitrary algorithms into incentive compatible mechanisms. One example is the seminal work of Vickrey, Clark, and Groves for converting *exact* algorithms into mechanisms for the social welfare objective. Much recent research has focused on generalizing such reductions to encompass approximation algorithms. Recently, striking positive results have been obtained for many important cases, especially single-parameter problems, in both Bayesian [12, 11, 4] and ex post (i.e. non-Bayesian) [15, 3, 8, 10, 14] settings. Given this progress and the notable lack of impossibility results for single-parameter problems, it is tempting to guess that a fully general reduction[1] is possible.

In this paper, we show that there is no such general black-box reduction, even for single-parameter problems. By *black-box reduction* we mean a mechanism that is given query access to an algorithm, and must return an allocation discovered by querying the algorithm. Our two main results address mechanisms in two different settings:

1. For the standard optimization objective of *social welfare*, or sum of agents' values, we prove that no general black-box reduction can guarantee ex post truthfulness while approximately preserving the worst-case approximation of the underlying algorithm.

2. In the Bayesian setting, we prove that there are monotone[2] optimization objectives (including makespan) for which no black-box reduction can guarantee truthfulness while approximately preserving the average-case approximation of the underlying algorithm.

Our results stand in contrast to existing constructions in Bayesian mechanism design [12, 11, 4]. In that prior work, it was shown that general black-box reductions for social welfare exist in a Bayesian setting, where the input is drawn from a commonly known distribution **F** and the optimization

*This author was supported in part by NSF awards CCF-0830494, CCF-0643763, and CCF-1101429.
†This author was supported in part by NSF CAREER grant AF-1055020, a Microsoft New Faculty Fellowship, and an Alfred P. Sloan Foundation Fellowship.

[1]That is, a reduction that applies to single-parameter optimization problems with arbitrary feasibility constraints.
[2]An objective is *monotone* if exact optimization leads to a truthful (i.e. monotone) allocation rule; see eq. (1).

and incentive compatibility requirements are with respect to **F**. Our first result demonstrates that no such reduction is possible when the solution concept is ex post incentive compatibility (i.e. truthfulness in dominant strategies) and the optimization goal is worst-case approximation. Specifically, we show that every black-box mechanism must degrade the worst-case performance of some algorithms (including constant approximations) by an unbounded amount. Our impossibility holds also for randomized transformations that aim to achieve truthfulness in expectation over their random bits[3].

In the Bayesian setting, we ask whether the known constructions for social welfare can be extended to other monotone objectives. In our second result, we prove that for the objective of makespan minimization, any black-box reduction from mechanism design to algorithm design must worsen the algorithm's performance by a factor that is polynomial in the problem size, even when we only desire Bayesian incentive compatibility with respect to a *known* distribution **F** and measure the algorithm's performance in expectation over **F**. Our construction serves to demonstrate that mechanisms like those known for social welfare cannot exist for arbitrary monotone objectives even under the weakest possible requirements on truthfulness and approximability.

Finally, we ask whether there are objectives that lie between the linear welfare objective and the highly non-linear makespan objective that admit reductions. Roughly speaking, known black-box mechanisms for Bayesian social welfare perform "ironing" operations for each agent independently, fixing non-monotonicities in the algorithm's output in a local fashion without hurting the overall social welfare. One property of social welfare that enables such an approach is that it is additive across agents. In our final result we show that, even restricting attention to objectives that are additive across agents, for almost any objective other than social welfare no per-agent ironing procedure can simultaneously ensure Bayesian incentive compatibility as well as a bounded loss in performance. The implication for mechanism design is that any successful reduction must take a holistic approach over agents and look very different from those known for social welfare.

Our results and techniques.

The existence of a black-box reduction from mechanism design to algorithm design can depend on the objective function to be optimized, the incentive requirements, and the performance metric. We distinguish between social welfare and arbitrary monotone objectives, and between the average performance of the algorithm (over a distribution of inputs) and its worst case performance. We further distinguish between two kinds of incentive requirements (defined formally in Section 2). Bayesian incentive compatibility (BIC) implies that truthtelling forms a Bayes-Nash equilibrium given the agents' value distributions. The stronger notion of truthfulness in expectation (TIE) implies that every agent maximizes her expected utility by truthtelling regardless of others' actions, with expectation taken over any randomness in the mechanism.

Table 1 below summarizes our findings as well as known results along these three dimensions. We find that there is a dichotomy of settings: some allow for essentially lossless transformations whereas others suffer an unbounded loss in performance.

Objective: social welfare

	Avg-case approx	Worst-case approx
BIC	Yes [12, 4, 11]	?
TIE	?	No (Section 3)

Objective: arbitrary monotone (e.g. makespan)

	Avg-case approx	Worst-case approx
BIC	No (Section 4)	No
TIE	No	No

Table 1: A summary of our results on the existence of black-box transformations. A "yes" indicates that a reduction exists and gives an arbitrarily small loss in performance; a "no" indicates that every reduction satisfying incentive constraints suffers a polynomially large loss in performance.

One way to establish our impossibility results would be to find single-parameter optimization problems for which there is a gap in the approximating power of arbitrary algorithms and incentive compatible algorithms. This is an important open problem that has resisted much effort by the algorithmic mechanism design community, and is beyond the scope of our work. Instead, we focus on the black-box nature of a reduction from mechanism design to algorithm design. In our model, a black-box mechanism has full knowledge of the problem instance including the distribution from which agents' values are drawn. In addition it is given oracle access to an algorithm that it can query at any input. Given an input value vector, the goal of the mechanism is to query the algorithm polynomially many times and return an outcome (allocation) that is nearly as good as the one that the original algorithm returns on the same input and is also consistent across inputs in that it satisfies the monotonicity conditions necessary for incentive compatibility.

Since the mechanism is meant to be "black-box," we will require that it can only output an allocation that it has observed while querying the algorithm at different vectors[4]. This last property is crucial in our constructions and allows us to "hide" good allocations from the transformation.

While the restriction to black-box mechanisms may appear strong at first glance, we note that many existing constructions for general mechanisms satisfy these requirements. For instance, the standard technique of maximal in range (MIR) mechanism design proceeds by restricting the range of outcomes to a subset of feasible allocations and then solving the optimization problem exactly over this range. An appropriate set of outcomes can be constructed by querying a given algorithm $\mathcal{A}$ at representative inputs [10, 14]. An alternative technique [12, 11, 4] proceeds by constructing a mapping π between input profiles: given input vector $\mathbf{v}$, the mechanism returns the original algorithm's allocation at vector $\pi(\mathbf{v})$. In both cases, the mechanism always satisfies any feasibility constraints of the problem, since it always returns an allocation in the range of the given algorithm.

[3]In this case, we use the usual definition of an algorithm's approximation ratio: in expectation over the random bits but in worst case over the input.

[4]We can think of this requirement as being necessitated by the presence of arbitrary feasibility constraints that are not known to the mechanism, but are satisfied by the algorithm.

To prove our impossibility result for social welfare, we describe a class of "public project" optimization problems and show that achieving ex post incentive compatibility essentially requires a MIR approach. Furthermore, an underlying algorithm can hide a "long-distance" non-monotonicity in such a way that, at some value vectors, the transformation must either query the algorithm at exponentially many inputs in order to detect the non-monotonicity, or return a default outcome that guarantees monotonicity but has a poor approximation ratio.

For our impossibility result in the Bayesian setting, we show that the per-agent mapping approach of [12] must fail for almost any objective other than social welfare. We consider the makespan objective, and construct a constant approximation algorithm for which any polytime BIC transformation must have large expected makespan. The key to our construction is that the algorithm will return good allocations only on typical (i.e. concentrated) inputs; this limits a mechanism's ability to explore the allocation space by quering at atypical inputs.

All of our constructions involve simple instances with symmetric value spaces: each agent has a high or a low value and gets a high or a low (or medium in one case) allocation. The complexity in our constructions lies in the feasibility constraints satisfied by the algorithm to be transformed. In particular, our constructions involve feasibility constraints that are asymmetric across agents. This is essential: when agents have few possible types, good mechanisms can always be constructed in the absence of a feasibility constraint, or when the constraint is symmetric across agents[5].

Related Work.

Reductions from mechanism design to algorithm design in the Bayesian setting were first studied by Hartline and Lucier [12], who showed that any approximation algorithm for a single-parameter social welfare problem can be converted into a Bayesian incentive compatible mechanism with arbitrarily small loss in expected performance. This was extended to multi-parameter settings by Hartline, Kleinberg and Malekian [11] and Bei and Huang [4].

Some reductions from mechanism design to algorithm design are known for prior-free settings, for certain restricted classes of algorithms. Lavi and Swamy [15] consider mechanisms for multi-parameter packing problems and show how to construct a (randomized) TIE β-approximation mechanism from any β-approximation that verifies an integrality gap. Dughmi, Roughgarden and Yan [9] extend this approach and obtain TIE mechanisms for a broad class of submodular combinatorial auctions. Dughmi and Roughgarden [8] give a construction that converts any FPTAS algorithm for a social welfare problem into a TIE mechanism.

Babaioff et al. [3] provide a technique for turning a β-algorithm for a single-valued combinatorial auction problem into a truthful $\beta(\log v_{max}/v_{min})$-approximation mechanism, when agent values are restricted to lie in $[v_{min}, v_{max}]$. Huang et al. [14] prove that any algorithm for a symmetric single-parameter social welfare problem can be converted into a truthful MIR mechanism with arbitrarily small loss in approximation, building upon a reduction with logarithmic loss due to Goel et al. [10].

Many papers have explored the limitations of truthful mechanisms for approximating social welfare in settings with multi-parameter types. Papadimitriou, Schapira and Singer [16] show a gap between the power of deterministic algorithms and truthful mechanisms, and a similar gap was established by Dobzinski [7] for randomized TIE mechanisms. However, prior to our work, it was not known whether a lossless black-box reduction could exist for the class of single-parameter problems.

For the makespan objective in multi-parameter settings (i.e. when the sizes of jobs on different machines are unrelated), Ashlagi et al. [2] proved a gap between the approximating power of algorithms and "anonymous" incentive compatible mechanisms. The situation for single-parameter (a.k.a. related machines) settings is quite different: a line of work on incentive compatible mechanisms [1, 6] recently culminated in the development of a deterministic truthful PTAS by Christodoulou and Kovács [5], matching the approximation of the best possible approximation algorithm [13]. Our negative result for makespan minimization differs in that we consider black-box mechanisms in a setting where the underlying algorithm may satisfy an additional feasibility constraint.

2. PRELIMINARIES

Optimization Problems. In a single-parameter optimization problem we are given as input a value vector $\mathbf{v} = (v_1, v_2, \ldots, v_n)$, where each v_i is drawn from a known set $V_i \subseteq \mathbb{R}$. Let $V = V_1 \times \cdots \times V_n$ denote the input space. The goal is to choose an allocation $\mathbf{x} \in \mathcal{F} \subseteq \mathbb{R}^n$ from a set of feasible allocations $\mathcal{F}$ such that a given objective function $\phi : \mathcal{F} \times V \to \mathbb{R}$ is optimized (i.e. either maximized or minimized, depending on the nature of the problem). We think of the feasibility set $\mathcal{F}$ and the objective function ϕ as defining an instance of the optimization problem. For example, the social welfare objective is $\phi(\mathbf{x}, \mathbf{v}) = \mathbf{x} \cdot \mathbf{v}$ and the makespan objective is $\phi(\mathbf{x}, \mathbf{v}) = \max_i x_i/v_i$.

An algorithm $\mathcal{A}$ defines a mapping from input vectors $\mathbf{v}$ to outcomes $\mathbf{x}$. We will write $\mathcal{A}(\mathbf{v})$ for the allocation returned by $\mathcal{A}$ as well as the value it obtains. In general $\mathcal{A}$ can be randomized, in which case $\mathcal{A}(\mathbf{v})$ is a random variable. Given an instance $(\mathcal{F}, \phi)$, we will write $OPT_{\mathcal{F}}(\mathbf{v})$ for the allocation in $\mathcal{F}$ that optimizes $\phi(\mathbf{x}, \mathbf{v})$. Let $approx_{\mathcal{F}}(\mathcal{A})$ denote the worst-case approximation ratio of $\mathcal{A}$ for problem $\mathcal{F}$. That is, $approx_{\mathcal{F}}(\mathcal{A}) = \min_{\mathbf{v} \in V} \frac{\mathbf{E}[\mathcal{A}(\mathbf{v})]}{OPT_{\mathcal{F}}(\mathbf{v})}$ for a maximization problem, where the expectation is over any randomness in $\mathcal{A}$. Note that $approx_{\mathcal{F}}(\mathcal{A}) \leq 1$ for all $\mathcal{F}$ and $\mathcal{A}$.

In the Bayesian version of our optimization problem, there is publicly-known product distribution $\mathbf{F} = F_1 \times \ldots \times F_n$ over input vectors. Given $\mathbf{F}$, the expected objective value of algorithm $\mathcal{A}$ is $\overline{\phi}(\mathcal{A}) = \mathbf{E}_{\mathbf{v} \sim \mathbf{F}}[\phi(\mathcal{A}(\mathbf{v}), \mathbf{v})]$. The goal in this setting is to optimize the expected objective value.

Mechanisms. We consider a mechanism design setting with n rational agents, where each agent possesses one value from the input vector as private information. An outcome $\mathbf{x}$ represents an *allocation* to the agents, where x_i is the allocation to agent i. A mechanism proceeds by eliciting declared values $\mathbf{b} \in \mathbb{R}^n$ from the agents, then applying an allocation algorithm $\mathcal{A} : \mathbb{R}^n \to \mathcal{F}$ that maps $\mathbf{b}$ to an allocation $\mathbf{x}$, and

[5]In particular, when agents have few possible types and the feasibility constraint is symmetric, an input profile is determined entirely by the number of agents of each type, of which there are only polynomially many such choices. One can therefore implement a MIR mechanism that queries the given algorithm on every type profile, up to permutation.

a payment rule that maps $\mathbf{b}$ to a payment vector $\mathbf{p}$. We will write $\mathbf{x}(\mathbf{b})$ and $\mathbf{p}(\mathbf{b})$ for the allocations and payments that result on input $\mathbf{b}$. The *utility* of agent i, given that the agents declare $\mathbf{b}$ and his true private value is v_i, is taken to be $v_i x_i(\mathbf{b}) - p_i(\mathbf{b})$.

A mechanism is *truthful in expectation* (TIE) if each agent maximizes its expected utility by reporting its value truthfully, regardless of the reports of the other agents, where expectation is taken over any randomness in the mechanism. We say that an algorithm is TIE if there exists a payment rule such that the resulting mechanism is TIE. It is known that an algorithm is TIE if and only if it is *monotone*: that is, for all i, all $\mathbf{v}_{-i}$, and all $v_i \le v_i'$,

$$\mathbf{E}[x_i(v_i, \mathbf{v}_{-i})] \le \mathbf{E}[x_i(v_i', \mathbf{v}_{-i})]. \quad (1)$$

We say that a mechanism is *Bayesian incentive compatible* (BIC) for distribution $\mathbf{F}$ if each agent maximizes its expected utility by reporting its value truthfully, given that the other agents' values are distributed according to $\mathbf{F}$ (and given any randomness in the mechanism). We say that an algorithm is BIC if there exists a payment rule such that the resulting mechanism is BIC. It is known that an algorithm is BIC if and only if, for all i and all $v_i \le v_i'$,

$$\mathbf{E}_{\mathbf{v}_{-i}}[x_i(v_i, \mathbf{v}_{-i})] \le \mathbf{E}_{\mathbf{v}_{-i}}[x_i(v_i', \mathbf{v}_{-i})]. \quad (2)$$

Transformations. A *transformation* $\mathcal{T}$ is an algorithm that has black-box access to some algorithm $\mathcal{A}$. Write $\mathcal{T}(\mathcal{A}, \mathbf{v})$ for the output of $\mathcal{T}$ on input $\mathbf{v}$, given that its black-box access is to $\mathcal{A}$. We write $\mathcal{T}(\mathcal{A})$ for the allocation rule[6] $\mathcal{T}(\mathcal{A}, \cdot)$. Note that $\mathcal{T}$ is not parameterized by $\mathcal{F}$; informally speaking, $\mathcal{T}$ has no knowledge of the feasibility constraint $\mathcal{F}$, so in particular we can assume that $\mathcal{T}(\mathcal{A}, \mathbf{v})$ is always an allocation observed by querying $\mathcal{A}$. We do assume that $\mathcal{T}$ is aware of the objective function ϕ, the input domain V, and (in Bayesian settings) the distribution $\mathbf{F}$.

Transformation $\mathcal{T}$ is truthful in expectation (TIE) if $\mathcal{T}(\mathcal{A})$ is TIE for all $\mathcal{A}$. Likewise, $\mathcal{T}$ is Bayesian incentive compatible (BIC) for distribution $\mathbf{F}$ if, for all $\mathcal{A}$, $\mathcal{T}(\mathcal{A})$ is BIC for $\mathbf{F}$. Note that whether or not $\mathcal{T}$ is TIE or BIC is independent of the objective ϕ and feasibility constraint $\mathcal{F}$.

3. A LOWER BOUND FOR TIE TRANSFORMATIONS

We will prove the following theorem, which states that *any* TIE transformation must convert some constant factor approximate algorithms into mechanisms with polynomial approximation factors.

THEOREM 3.1. *There are constants c_1, c_2 such that, for any polytime TIE transformation $\mathcal{T}$, there is an algorithm $\mathcal{A}$ and problem instance $\mathcal{F}$ with $approx_{\mathcal{F}}(\mathcal{A}) \ge c_1$ such that $approx_{\mathcal{F}}(\mathcal{T}(\mathcal{A})) \le 1/n^{c_2}$.*

Before describing our construction, let us build some intuition for the requirements of Theorem 3.1. Our goal is to construct an algorithm $\mathcal{A}$ that is difficult to monotonize (i.e. satisfy (1)). Since $\mathcal{T}$ is limited to making a polynomial number of queries on each input, a natural approach is to hide a non-monotonicity in the (exponentially large) input space. This idea is impeded by the locality of the monotonicity requirement: on input $\mathbf{v}$, transformation $\mathcal{T}$ can query $\mathcal{A}$ on each input that differs from $\mathbf{v}$ on a single coordinate, and hence find any pair $\mathbf{v}, \mathbf{v}'$ that violates (1).

Alternatively, one could embed a "high-dimensional" non-monotonicity into $\mathcal{A}$ by choosing input vectors $\mathbf{v}, \mathbf{v}'$ that differ on many coordinates and setting $\mathcal{A}_i(\mathbf{v}) > \mathcal{A}_i(\mathbf{v}')$ for each agent i with $v_i < v_i'$. Such a situation seems harder to detect, but does not directly imply non-truthfulness. For example, if $\mathcal{A}$ satisfies $\mathcal{A}(1,1) = (10,10)$ and $\mathcal{A}(2,2) = (5,5)$, then condition (1) is not necessarily violated: it may be that $\mathcal{A}(1,2) = (4,11)$ and $\mathcal{A}(2,1) = (11,4)$. However, if we additionally impose a feasibility constraint that the agents involved in the high-dimensional non-monotonicity *always receive the same allocation*, then we could infer that (1) must be violated somewhere. Thus, under certain feasibility constraints, $\mathcal{T}$ must find and correct high-dimensional non-monotonicities.

Motivated by this observation, our approach to proving Theorem 3.1 is as follows. We will construct an approximation algorithm $\mathcal{A}$ containing a high-dimensional non-monotonicity and a feasibility constraint that together imply that $\mathcal{A}$ is not TIE. Our algorithm will be such that $\mathcal{T}$ cannot detect the non-monotonicity (or even that one exists) with non-negligible probability. Thus, to guarantee incentive compatibility, $\mathcal{T}$ will be forced to modify the algorithm's output aggressively in order to address any possible non-monotonicity that could be present. However, our algorithm will be constructed so that such a modification must degrade its approximation factor significantly.

Various technical hurdles must be overcome to implement this plan. First, we must restrict the set of allocations that can be found by $\mathcal{T}$ (with non-negligible probability) when adaptively querying the algorithm, so that $\mathcal{T}$ cannot find a way to correct non-monotonicities without harming the algorithm's approximation factor. At the same time, we require that our algorithm obtain a constant approximation, which limits our ability to hide allocations from $\mathcal{T}$ via sub-optimality. The details of the construction involve carefully balancing the tension between these requirements.

3.1 Construction

In the instances we consider, each private value v_i is chosen from $\{v, 1\}$, where $v \in (0,1)$ is a parameter of our construction. We interpret an input vector as a subset $y \subseteq [n]$, corresponding to those agents with the "high" value 1. For $a \ge 0$ and $S \subseteq [n]$, we will write $\mathbf{x}_S^a$ for the allocation in which each agent $i \in S$ is allocated a, and each agent $i \notin S$ is allocated 0.

Feasible Allocations. We consider a family of feasibility constraints, which will be specified by parameters α, γ with $0 < \gamma < \alpha < 1$ and sets $S, T \subseteq [n]$ of agents. We think of S and T as being polynomially large sets, with a polynomially large intersection; see Figure 1(a). The feasible allocations will be $\mathbf{x}_{[n]}^\gamma$, $\mathbf{x}_S^1$, and $\mathbf{x}_T^\alpha$. That is, we can allocate γ to every agent, 1 to all agents in S, or α to all agents in T. We write $\mathcal{F}_{S,T,\alpha,\gamma}$ for this feasibility constraint.

The Algorithm. Fix feasibility constraint $\mathcal{F}_{S,T,\alpha,\gamma}$. Let $U = S \cap T$ and choose a set $V \subset U$. We will define an approximation algorithm $\mathcal{A} = \mathcal{A}_{V,S,T,\alpha,\gamma}$ for problem $\mathcal{F}_{S,T,\alpha,\gamma}$. This will be our candidate for the algorithm in the statement of Theorem 3.1.

[6]Note that a polynomial-time transformation can make only polynomially many queries to compute $\mathcal{T}(\mathcal{A}, \mathbf{v})$ for *each* $\mathbf{v}$, but $\mathcal{T}(\mathcal{A})$ may depend on the behaviour of $\mathcal{A}$ on a super-polynomially large subset of the input space.

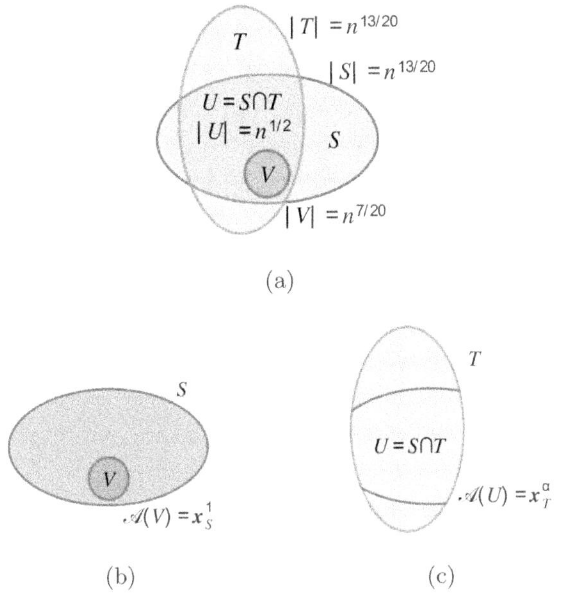

Figure 1: (a) Visualization of typical admissible sets of bidders V, S, and T, and the corresponding allocations of algorithm $\mathcal{A}$ on (b) input V and (c) input $U = S \cap T$.

We begin with an informal description of Algorithm $\mathcal{A}$ (formally listed as Algorithm 1 below). Recall that $\mathcal{A}$ accepts as input a vector $\mathbf{v} \in \{v, 1\}^n$. $\mathcal{A}$ will return $\mathbf{x}_T^\alpha$ if sufficiently many of the high-valued agents lie in set T, and will return $\mathbf{x}_S^1$ if sufficiently many of the high-valued agents lie in set S. When most high-valued agents lie in $S \cap T$, set V is used to determine the outcome: if sufficiently many high-valued agents lie in V then we return $\mathbf{x}_S^1$, otherwise we return $\mathbf{x}_T^\alpha$. If there are not enough high-valued agents, or if too many lie outside $S \cup T$, then we return $\mathbf{x}_{[n]}^\gamma$. See Figure 1.

Algorithm $\mathcal{A}$ has the following properties that will be important to our analysis. First, all outcomes of $\mathcal{A}$ are constant on U. Also, $\mathcal{A}(V) = \mathbf{x}_S^1$ and $\mathcal{A}(U) = \mathbf{x}_T^\alpha$, so if $\alpha < 1$ then $\mathcal{A}$ contains a high-dimensional non-monotonicity as described at the beginning of this section. Moreover, $\mathcal{A}$ will return $\mathbf{x}_S^1$ for any input y that is sufficiently close to V (i.e. small symmetric difference), and for a randomly chosen subset of S (with high probability). On the other hand, any input sufficiently close to U or chosen randomly as a subset of T will generate outcome $\mathbf{x}_T^\alpha$. These last properties will be important in arguing that a TIE transformation is unlikely to detect the non-monotonicity between inputs V and U. Finally, as we demonstrate in the next section, $\mathcal{A}$ obtains a constant approximation when parameters are chosen appropriately.

Before presenting the formal description of Algorithm $\mathcal{A}$ we require some definitions. Given $y \subset [n]$, we define

$$n_T(y) = |y \cap T| + |y \cap U|$$

and

$$n_S(y) = |y \cap S| + 2|y \cap V|.$$

That is, $n_T(y)$ is the number of elements of y that lie in T, with elements of U counted twice. Likewise, $n_S(y)$ is the number of elements of y that lie in S, with elements of V counted thrice.

The algorithm $\mathcal{A}_{V,S,T,\alpha}$ is then described as Algorithm 1.

Algorithm 1: Allocation Algorithm $\mathcal{A}_{V,S,T,\alpha}$

Input: Subset $y \in [n]$ of agents with value 1
Output: An allocation $\mathbf{x} \in \mathcal{F}_{V,S,T,\alpha}$

if $n_S(y) \geq t$, $n_S(y) \geq \gamma|y|$, *and* $n_S(y) \geq n_T(y)$ **then**
  | **return** $\mathbf{x}_S^1$
else if $n_T(y) \geq t$, $n_T(y) \geq \gamma|y|$, *and* $n_T(y) \geq n_S(y)$ **then**
  | **return** $\mathbf{x}_T^\alpha$
else
  | **return** $\mathbf{x}_{[n]}^\gamma$
end

3.2 Analysis

We now derive the key lemmas for the proof of Theorem 3.1.

Parameter Conditions. All of the results in this section will require that we impose certain technical constraints on the parameters α and γ and the sets V, S, and T. Roughly, parameter $1/\gamma$ and sets V, $S \cap T$, S, and T should be sufficiently large, and α should be sufficiently small (as functions of n and v).

Formally, we will choose parameters $t \geq r \geq 1$ (polynomially large in n) which will dictate the required sizes of sets V, S, and T. We will choose these parameters so that

$$t \gg r \gg \frac{1}{\gamma} \gg \frac{1}{\alpha}, \; r^5 t \leq n, \text{ and } \frac{t}{\gamma n} \ll 1.$$

Given this choice of r and t, we say that sets V, S, and T are *admissible* if the following conditions hold:

1. $|S| = |T| = r^3 t$,
2. $|S \cap T| = r^2 t$,
3. $V \subset S \cap T$, and
4. $|V| = rt$.

See Figure 1(a) for an illustration of the relationship between the sets in an admissible triple. For the remainder of this section we will assume that V, S, and T are feasible. We will set the values of parameters r, t, α, γ, and v in Section 3.3.

Algorithm Analysis. For our first lemma, we bound the approximation factor of $\mathcal{A}_{V,S,T,\alpha,\gamma}$ for problem $\mathcal{F}_{V,S,T,\alpha,\gamma}$. In particular, we note that if $\alpha = 1$ then $\mathcal{A}_{V,S,T,\alpha,\gamma}$ is a constant approximation.

LEMMA 3.2. *$approx_{\mathcal{F}_{S,T,\alpha,\gamma}}(\mathcal{A}_{V,S,T,\alpha,\gamma}) \geq \alpha/6$.*

PROOF. Choose $y \subseteq [n]$ and consider the three cases for the output of $\mathcal{A}_{V,S,T,\alpha}$.

Case 1: $n_S(y) \geq t$, $n_S(y) \geq \gamma|y|$, and $n_S(y) \geq n_T(y)$. Our algorithm returns allocation $\mathbf{x}_S^1$ and obtains welfare at least $|y \cap S|$. Note that

$$|y \cap S| \geq \frac{1}{3} n_S(y) \geq \frac{1}{3} t$$

and

$$|y \cap S| \geq \frac{1}{3} n_S(y) \geq \frac{1}{3} n_T(y) \geq \frac{1}{3} |y \cap T|.$$

The allocation $\mathbf{x}_T^\alpha$ obtains welfare at most $\alpha(|y \cap T| + |T \backslash y| v) \leq \alpha(|y \cap T| + nv\gamma) \leq |y \cap T| + t \leq 6|y \cap S|$. Note that here we used $|T| \leq n\gamma$, which follows since $r > \gamma^{-1}$.

The allocation $\mathbf{x}_{[n]}^\gamma$ obtains welfare at most $\gamma|y| + t \leq 2n_S(y) \leq 6|y \cap S|$. So we obtain at least a 1/6-approximation in this case.

Case 2: $n_T(y) \geq t$, $n_T(y) \geq \gamma|y|$, and $n_T(y) \geq n_S(y)$. Our algorithm returns allocation $\mathbf{x}_T^\alpha$ and obtains welfare at least $\alpha|y \cap T|$. The same argument as case 1 shows that our approximation factor is at least $\alpha/6$ in this case.

Case 3: $n_S(y) \leq t$ and $n_T(y) \leq t$. Our algorithm returns allocation $\mathbf{x}_{[n]}^\gamma$ for a welfare of at least $\gamma(|y| + v(n - |y|)) \geq t$. The allocation $\mathbf{x}_S^1$ obtains welfare at most $|y \cap S| + t \leq n_S(y) + t \leq 2t$, and allocation $\mathbf{x}_T^\alpha$ obtains welfare at most $2\alpha t \leq 2t$. So our approximation factor is at least 1/2 in this case.

Case 4: $n_S(y) \leq \gamma|y|$ and $n_T(y) \leq \gamma|y|$. Our algorithm returns allocation $\mathbf{x}_{[n]}^\gamma$ for a welfare of at least $\gamma(|y| + v(n - |y|)) \geq \gamma|y|$. The allocation $\mathbf{x}_S^1$ obtains welfare at most $|y \cap S| + t \leq 2n_S(y) \leq 2\gamma|y|$, and allocation $\mathbf{x}_T^\alpha$ obtains welfare at most $|y \cap T| + t \leq 2\alpha\gamma|y| \leq 2\gamma|y|$. So our approximation factor is at least 1/2 in this case. □

Our next claim restricts the behaviour of TIE algorithms for problem $\mathcal{F}_{S,T,\alpha,\gamma}$. The result uses the fact that all allocations in $\mathcal{F}_{S,T,\alpha,\gamma}$ are constant on U.

CLAIM 3.3. *Suppose $\mathcal{A}'$ is a truthful-in-expectation algorithm for problem $\mathcal{F}_{S,T,\alpha,\gamma}$. Then the expected allocation to each agent in U must be at least as large in $\mathcal{A}'(U)$ as in $\mathcal{A}'(V)$.*

PROOF. Take any set W with $V \subseteq W \subseteq U$, $|W| = |V| + 1$. Then, on input W, the expected allocation to the agent in $W \setminus V$ must not decrease relative to its allocation on input V. Since all allocations are constant on U, this means that the expected allocation to each agent in U on input W must not decrease relative to allocation on input V. By the same argument, $\mathcal{A}'$ returns an allocation to each agent in U at least this large for all W such that $V \subseteq W \subseteq U$, and in particular for $W = U$. □

Transformation Analysis. In light of Claim 3.3, our strategy for proving Theorem 3.1 will be to show that a polytime transformation $\mathcal{T}$ is unlikely to encounter the allocation $\mathbf{x}_T^\alpha$ during its sampling when the input is V, given that the sets V, S, and T are chosen uniformly at random over all admissible tuples. This means the transformation will be unable to learn the value of α. This is key since it prevents the transformation from satisfying the conditions of Claim 3.3 by giving an expected allocation of α to the agents in U on input V. Similarly, a transformation is unlikely to encounter the allocation $\mathbf{x}_S^1$ during its sampling on input U, and therefore cannot satisfy Claim 3.3 by allocating 1 to agents in U on input U.

Our next two lemmas demonstrate that if the sets V, S, and T were chosen at random, then it is exponentially unlikely that a transformation would observe allocation $\mathbf{x}_T^\alpha$ during its sampling when given input V (Lemma 3.4), or observe allocation $\mathbf{x}_S^1$ given input U (Lemma 3.5).

LEMMA 3.4. *Fix V and S satsifying the requirements of admissibility. Then for any $y \subseteq [n]$, $\Pr_T[\mathcal{A}_{V,S,T,\alpha}(y) = x_T^\alpha] \leq e^{-O(\frac{t}{r+1})}$, with probability taken over all choices of T that are admissible given V and S.*

PROOF. Fix any y. Write $n_V = |y \cap V|$, $n_S = |y \cap (S - V)|$, and $n_* = |y \cap ([n] - S)|$. Note that $|y| = n_V + n_S + n_*$. Define the random variables m_U and m_T by $m_U = |y \cap (U - V)|$ and $m_T = |y \cap (T \backslash S)|$.

The event $[\mathcal{A}_{V,S,T,\alpha}(y) = x_T^\alpha]$ occurs precisely if the following are true:

$$m_T + 2n_V + 2m_U \geq t, \tag{3}$$

$$m_T + 2n_V + 2m_U \geq \gamma(n_V + n_S + n_*), \tag{4}$$

$$m_T + 2n_V + 2m_U \geq n_S + 3n_V. \tag{5}$$

We will show that the probability of these three inequalities being true is exponentially small. To see this, note that (5) implies that $m_T + 2m_U \geq n_V$. Thus, (3) implies that $m_T + 2m_U \geq t/3$, and hence $m_T + m_U \geq t/6$. Now each element of y counted in n_S will count toward m_U with probability $\frac{1}{r+1}$, and each element of y counted in n_* will count toward m_T with probability $\frac{1}{r+1}$. Since $t \gg r$, Chernoff bounds imply that with probability at least $1 - e^{-O(t/r)}$, we will have $n_* + n_S \geq \frac{r}{2}(m_T + m_U)$. Then

$$\frac{m_T + 2n_V + 2m_U}{n_V + n_S + n_*} < \frac{3(m_T + 2m_U)}{n_S + n_*} < \frac{12}{r} \ll \gamma$$

contradicting (4). □

LEMMA 3.5. *Fix U and T satsifying the requirements of admissibility. Then for any $y \subseteq [n]$, $\Pr_S[\mathcal{A}_{V,S,T,\alpha}(y) = x_S^1] \leq e^{-O(\frac{t}{r+1})}$, with probability taken over all choices of V and S that are admissible given U and T.*

PROOF. Fix any y. Write $n_U = |y \cap U|$, $n_T = |y \cap (T - U)|$, and $n_* = |y \cap ([n] - T)|$. Note that $|y| = n_U + n_T + n_*$. Define the random variables m_V and m_S by $m_V = |y \cap V|$ and $m_S = |y \cap (S \backslash T)|$.

The event $[\mathcal{A}_{V,S,T,\alpha}(y) = x_S^1]$ occurs precisely if the following are true:

$$m_S + n_U + 2m_V \geq t, \tag{6}$$

$$m_S + n_U + 2m_V \geq \gamma(n_U + n_T + n_*), \tag{7}$$

$$m_S + n_U + 2m_V \geq n_T + 2n_U. \tag{8}$$

We will show that the probability of these three inequalities being true is exponentially small. To see this, first note that we can assume $n_T = 0$, as this only loosens the requirements of the inequalities. We then have that (8) implies $m_S + 2m_V \geq n_U$. Thus, (6) implies that $m_S + 2m_V \geq t/2$, and hence $m_S + m_V \geq t/4$. Now each element of y counted in n_U will count toward m_V with probability $\frac{1}{r}$, and each element of y counted in n_* will count toward m_S with probability $\frac{1}{r+1}$. Since $t \gg r$, Chernoff bounds imply that with probability at least $1 - e^{O(t/r)}$, we will have $n_* + n_T \geq \frac{r}{2}(m_S + m_V)$. Then

$$\frac{m_S + n_U + 2m_V}{n_U + n_*} < \frac{4(m_S + m_V)}{n_U + n_*} < \frac{8}{r} \ll \gamma$$

contradicting (7). □

We emphasize that the results of Lemma 3.4 and 3.5 hold for *every* possible input vector y. This is crucial, since we wish for these lemmas to apply even when inputs are chosen adaptively by transformation $\mathcal{T}$ to gain information about the given algorithm and feasibility constraint.

3.3 Proof of Main Theorem

We can now set our parameters t, r, α, and γ. We will choose $t = n^{1/5}$, $r = n^{3/20}$, and $\gamma = n^{-2/20}$. The values of α we will be considering are 1 and $n^{-1/20}$. Note that $t \gg r \gg \gamma^{-1} \gg \alpha^{-1}$ for each choice of α. Note also that $v = t\gamma^{-1}/n = n^{-14/20} \ll 1$.

Our idea now for proving Theorem 3.1 is that since the transformation cannot determine the value of α on input V (by Lemma 3.4), and since it cannot find the "good" allocation of $\mathbf{x}_S^1$ on input U (by Lemma 3.5), it must be pessimistic and allocate the minimum possible value of α to agents in V on input V in order to guarantee that the resulting allocation rule is TIE (by Claim 3.3). This implies a bad approximation on input V and hence a bad worst-case approximation.

Proof of Theorem 3.1 : For each admissible V, S, T and $\alpha \in \{1, n^{-1/20}\}$, write $\mathcal{A}'_{V,S,T,\alpha}$ for $\mathcal{T}(\mathcal{A}_{V,S,T,\alpha})$. Consider choosing V, S, and T uniformly at random over all admissible choices of these sets. Lemma 3.5 implies that, with all but exponentially small probability, $\mathcal{A}'_{V,S,T,\alpha}$ will not encounter allocation $\mathbf{x}_S^1$ on input U (where the probability is taken over the choice of sets and any randomness in the transformation). Furthermore, Lemma 3.4 implies that, with all but exponentially small probability, $\mathcal{A}'_{V,S,T,\alpha}$ will not encounter allocation $\mathbf{x}_T^\alpha$ on input V. We conclude that there exists an admissible choice of sets V, S, and T such that, with all but exponentially small probability, $\mathcal{A}'_{V,S,T,\alpha}$ will not encounter allocation $\mathbf{x}_S^1$ on input U nor allocation $\mathbf{x}_T^\alpha$ on input V.

Fix this choice of V, S, and T. In the exponentially unlikely event that $\mathcal{A}'_{V,S,T,\alpha}(U)$ encounters $\mathbf{x}_S^1$ or $\mathcal{A}'_{V,S,T,\alpha}(V)$ encounters $\mathbf{x}_T^\alpha$, algorithm $\mathcal{A}'_{V,S,T,\alpha}$ can obtain a welfare of at most $|V| = n^{7/20}$ on input V.

Suppose now that this exponentially unlikely event does not occur. We then have that, on input U, $\mathcal{A}'_{V,S,T,\alpha}$ can allocate at most α to each agent in U in expectation (using the fact that $\alpha > \gamma$). Then, since $\mathcal{A}'_{V,S,T,\alpha}$ is incentive compatible, Claim 3.3 implies that $\mathcal{A}'_{V,S,T,\alpha}$ must allocate at most α to each agent in U on input V.

On input V, $\mathcal{A}'_{V,S,T,\alpha}$ will not encounter allocation $\mathbf{x}_T^\alpha$ and thus is unaware of the value of α. Thus, to ensure incentive compatibility, $\mathcal{A}'_{V,S,T,1}(V)$ must allocate at most $n^{-1/20}$ to each agent in U. It therefore obtains a welfare of at most $|V|n^{-1/20} + t \leq n^{1/5} + n^{3/10}$.

We conclude that the expected welfare of $\mathcal{A}'_{V,S,T,1}$ on input V (over all events) is at most $n^{6/20}$, whereas a total of $|V| = n^{7/20}$ is possible with allocation $\mathbf{x}_S^1$. Thus $\mathcal{A}'_{V,S,T,1}$ has a worst-case approximation of $n^{-1/20}$, whereas $\mathcal{A}_{V,S,T,1}$ has an approximation factor of $1/6$. □

4. A LOWER BOUND FOR MAKESPAN

We now consider the makespan objective, which differs from the welfare objective in that it is not linear in agent values or allocations, and in that it is a minimization problem rather than a maximization. We will show that black-box reductions for approximation algorithms for makespan are not possible even if we relax the notion of truthfulness to Bayesian incentive compatibility and relax the performance measure to expected makespan with respect to the *known* prior distribution.

In a Bayesian setting, the makespan problem can be defined as follows. There are n selfish machines (i.e. agents) which must be allocated a set of m jobs. Each agent has a private parameter or value v_i representing its speed. If machine i is allocated jobs with a total length x_i, the finishing time of machine i is x_i/v_i. The selfish objective of a machine is to maximize its payment minus its finishing time. The makespan of allocation $\mathbf{x}$ given speeds $\mathbf{v}$ is the maximum finishing time of any machine: $\phi(\mathbf{x}, \mathbf{v}) = \max_i \frac{x_i}{v_i}$. The social objective is to output an allocation that *minimizes* the makespan. An instance of the (Bayesian) makespan problem is given by a feasibility constraint $\mathcal{F}$ specifying the set of permissable allocations and a value distribution $\mathbf{F}$ of machine speeds. Given an algorithm $\mathcal{A}$, we use $\overline{\phi}(\mathcal{A})$ to denote its expected makespan with respect to $\mathbf{F}$. Our main result is that any BIC transformation $\mathcal{T}$ must degrade the expected makespan of some algorithms by a polynomially large factor[7].

THEOREM 4.1. *There are constants c_1, c_2 such that, for any polytime black-box BIC transformation $\mathcal{T}$, there is an instance $(\mathcal{F}, \mathbf{F})$ of the makespan problem and an algorithm $\mathcal{A}$ with $\overline{\phi}(\mathcal{A}) \leq c_1$ and $\overline{\phi}(\mathcal{T}(\mathcal{A})) \geq c_2 n^{1/4}$ for n large enough.*

Our proof of this theorem is based on an instance in which machines have just two potential speeds, *fast* or *slow*, drawn uniformly at random, and jobs are of just two types, *long* or *short*. There are a small number of long jobs and a large number of short jobs. One of the many good algorithms for this instance simply assigns one job per machine, trying to give long jobs to fast machines and short jobs to slow ones. So long as the distributions of speeds is typical (i.e., concentrated around the expectation of half fast and half slow machines), there are enough machines of each type and so this algorithm has low expected makespan. On the other hand, the algorithm is highly non-monotone: since there are only a small number of long jobs, the expected allocation of the fast machines is very small, whereas the large number of short jobs means the expected makespan of slow machines is larger (for an appropriate setting of parameters). Any transformation that fixes this non-monotonicity must either increase the allocation to fast machines or decrease the allocation to slow machines. The crux of our argument is that any such fix necessarily increases expected makespan by a polynomially large factor. Intuitively, on a typical input vector of machine speeds, the transformation may either: 1) query the algorithm on a vector in which the speeds of some fast machines are swapped with the speeds of some slow machines, or 2) query the algorithm on a vector that is atypically unbalanced. In case 1), the transformation's hope is that the returned allocation will give short jobs to machines that appear slow but are truly fast while simultaneously not allocating long jobs to machines that appear fast but are truly slow. We show that in order to sufficiently increase the expected allocation of fast machines, the transformation would have to swap a very large number of machine speeds

[7]For simplicity of exposition, we prove a gap of $\Omega(n^{1/4})$, however, our construction can be tweaked to obtain a gap of $\Omega(n^{1/2-\delta})$ for any $\delta > 0$.

and so exposes itself to a high risk of giving a long job to a slow machine. Hence the expected makespan of each returned allocation is high. In case 2), our algorithm returns a uniformly random allocation which does significantly increase the allocation to fast machines. However, as before, there is a significant chance that some truly slow machines receive long jobs and drastically increase the makespan of the transformation.

We now provide the details of the proof suggested by this intuition.

Problem Instance: We will consider the following instance $(\mathcal{F}, \mathbf{F})$ of a makespan minimization problem. Let $\alpha < n^{1/2}$ be a parameter to be determined later. The value distribution $\mathbf{F}$ will be the uniform distribution over $\{1, \alpha\}^n$. That is, every value (i.e. speed) v_i is 1 or α with equal probability. There will be $n^{1/2}$ jobs of length α and $n/2 + n^{3/4}$ of length 1. Our feasibility constraint $\mathcal{F}$ will be that each machine can be assigned at most one job. That is, $\mathcal{F} \subseteq \{0, 1, \alpha\}^n$, and a vector in $\{0, 1, \alpha\}^n$ is feasible if and only if it contains $n^{1/2}$ entries with value α and $n/2 + n^{3/4}$ entries with value 1.

The Algorithm: Our algorithm $\mathcal{A}$ is described as Algorithm 2 below; we think of $\mathcal{A}$ as an approximation algorithm for problem instance described above. Roughly speaking, $\mathcal{A}$ behaves as follows. Recall that $\mathcal{A}$ takes as input a vector of speeds $\mathbf{v} \in \{1, \alpha\}^n$. Given input $\mathbf{v}$, write $H(\mathbf{v}) = \{i : v_i = \alpha\}$ for the set of machines that declare the high speed α. The behaviour of $\mathcal{A}$ will depend on the size of set $H(\mathbf{v})$. If $||H(\mathbf{v})| - \frac{1}{2}n| \leq n^{3/4}$ (i.e. if $|H(\mathbf{v})|$ is close to its expectation), then $\mathcal{A}$ will allocate a short job to each machine in $[n] \backslash H(\mathbf{v})$, and will allocate the $\sqrt{n}$ long jobs as well as any remaining short jobs (of which there are $t = \frac{1}{2}n + n^{3/4} - |H(\mathbf{v})| \leq 2n^{3/4}$) to the machines in $H(\mathbf{v})$, uniformly at random. Otherwise, if $|H(\mathbf{v})|$ is not close to its expectation, $\mathcal{A}$ will ignore the reported speeds and return an allocation chosen uniformly at random from all allocations that assign at most one job to each machine. Although we describe $\mathcal{A}$ as a randomized algorithm, we remark that Theorem 4.1 holds even when $\mathcal{A}$ is restricted to be a deterministic algorithm[8].

For any $\mathbf{v}$, let $H(\mathbf{v}) = \{i : v_i = \alpha\}$ be the set of high speed agents. Let C denote the event that $\frac{1}{2}n - n^{3/4} \leq |H(\mathbf{v})| \leq \frac{1}{2}n + n^{3/4}$, over randomness in $\mathbf{v}$. We think of C as the event that the number of high-speed agents is concentrated around its expectation. We note the following immediate consequence of Chernoff bounds.

Observation 4.2. $\Pr_{\mathbf{v}}[C] \geq 1 - 2e^{-n^{1/4}/4}$.

This allows us to bound the expected makespan of $\mathcal{A}$.

Lemma 4.3. $\overline{\phi}(\mathcal{A}) \leq 1 + 2\alpha e^{-n^{1/4}/4}$.

Proof. If event C occurs, then $\mathcal{A}$ returns an allocation in which each agent i with $v_i = 1$ receives allocation at most 1. Since each agent with $v_i = \alpha$ also receives allocation at most α, we conclude that if event C occurs then the makespan of $\mathcal{A}(\mathbf{v})$ is at most 1. Otherwise, the makespan of $\mathcal{A}(\mathbf{v})$ is trivially bounded by α. Since Observation 4.2 implies that this latter case occurs with probability at most $2e^{-n^{1/4}/4}$, the result follows. □

[8]In particular, if we consider the ensemble of deterministic algorithms defined by taking all possible settings of the random variables in Algorithm 2, then a straightforward extension of our results shows that, for every transformation, Theorem 4.1 holds for at least one algorithm in the ensemble.

Algorithm 2: Allocation Algorithm $\mathcal{A}$

Input: Vector $\mathbf{v} \in \{1, \alpha\}^n$
Output: An allocation $\mathbf{x} \in \mathcal{F}$

$H \leftarrow \{i : v_i = \alpha\}$;
if $\frac{1}{2}n - n^{3/4} \leq |H| \leq \frac{1}{2}n + n^{3/4}$ **then**
  $t \leftarrow \frac{1}{2}n + n^{3/4} - |H|$;
  Choose set $S \subset H$ with $|S| = n^{-1/2}$ uniformly at random;
  Choose set $T \subset H \setminus S$ with $|T| = t$ uniformly at random;
  for $i \notin H$ **do** $x_i \leftarrow 1$;
  for $i \in S$ **do** $x_i \leftarrow \alpha$;
  for $i \in T$ **do** $x_i \leftarrow 1$;
  for $i \in H \setminus (S \cup T)$ **do** $x_i \leftarrow 0$;
else
  Choose set $S \subset [n]$ with $|S| = n^{1/2}$ uniformly at random;
  Choose set $T \subset [n] \setminus S$ with $|T| = n/2 + n^{3/4}$ uniformly at random;
  for $i \in S$ **do** $x_i \leftarrow \alpha$;
  for $i \in T$ **do** $x_i \leftarrow 1$;
  for $i \notin S, i \notin T$ **do** $x_i \leftarrow 0$;
end
return $\mathbf{x}$

Transformation: Let $\mathcal{T}$ denote a BIC transformation that can make at most $e^{n^{1/4}/2}$ black-box queries to an algorithm for makespan. Write $\mathcal{T}(\mathcal{A})$ for the mechanism induced when $\mathcal{T}$ is given black-box access to an algorithm $\mathcal{A}$. Recall that we can assume $\mathcal{T}(\mathcal{A})$ can only return an allocation that it observed during black-box queries to algorithm $\mathcal{A}$.

Let p_{bad} denote the probability, over $\mathbf{v}$, $\mathcal{T}$, and $\mathcal{A}$, that $\mathcal{T}(\mathcal{A})$ returns an allocation with makespan α. We will show that if $\mathcal{T}(\mathcal{A})$ is BIC, then p_{bad} must be large; this will imply that the expected makespan of $\mathcal{T}(\mathcal{A})$ will be large as well.

Intuitively, the reason that $\mathcal{A}$ is not BIC is that low-speed agents are often allocated 1 while high-speed agents are often allocated 0. In order to fix such non-monotonicities, $\mathcal{T}$ must either increase the probability with which 1 is allocated to the high-speed agents, or increase the probability with which 0 is allocated to the low-speed agents. We will prove that a sufficiently large increase to these probabilities must imply that p_{bad} is large as well.

We first show that, if approximately half of the machines are fast, then $\mathcal{T}(\mathcal{A})$ is unlikely to find an allocation that allocates 0 to many slow machines but allocates long jobs only to fast machines.

Lemma 4.4. *Suppose* $\mathbf{v}$ *satisfies* $||H(\mathbf{v})| - \frac{1}{2}n| \leq n^{3/4}$, *and let random variable* $\mathbf{x}$ *denote the allocation returned by* $\mathcal{T}(\mathcal{A}, \mathbf{v})$. *Then the probability that* $\phi(\mathbf{x}, \mathbf{v}) < \alpha$ *and at least* $n^{3/4}$ *agents satisfy* $v_i = 1$ *and* $x_i = 0$ *is at most* $(\ln 4)e^{-n^{1/4}/2}$.

Proof. Let B denote the (bad) event, over randomness in $\mathbf{v}$, $\mathcal{T}$, and $\mathcal{A}$, that $\mathcal{T}(\mathcal{A})$ returns an allocation with makespan

α. Let $U(\mathbf{v})$ be the event that, on input $\mathbf{v}$, $\mathcal{T}(\mathcal{A})$ returns an allocation $\mathbf{x}$ in which at least $n^{3/4}$ agents satisfy $v_i = 1$ and $x_i = 0$. Recall that C denotes the event that $\frac{1}{2}n - n^{3/4} \leq |H(\mathbf{v})| \leq \frac{1}{2}n + n^{3/4}$, over randomness in $\mathbf{v}$.

Fix input $\mathbf{v}$ and suppose that event $C \wedge U(\mathbf{v}) \wedge \neg B$ occurs. Then $\mathbf{v}$ satisfies the event C, and moreover event $U(\mathbf{v}) \wedge \neg B$ occurs. Recall that $\mathcal{T}$ only returns an allocation that $\mathcal{A}$ outputs on a query $\mathbf{v}'$. We will refer to a query of $\mathcal{A}$ on input $\mathbf{v}'$ as a *successful* query if it returns an $\mathbf{x}$ that satisfies $U(\mathbf{v}) \wedge \neg B$. Let us bound the probability of a single query being successful. Let t_1 denote the number of agents with $v_i = 1$. Then C implies $t_1 \geq n/2 - n^{3/4}$.

First suppose that $\mathbf{v}'$ does not satisfy the event C. That is, the number of high speed agents in $\mathbf{v}'$ is far from its mean $n/2$. Then each of the t_1 agents has an $n^{-1/2}$ probability of being allocated α (from the definition of $\mathcal{A}$). The probability that none of the t_1 agents is allocated a load of α is at most $(1 - n^{-1/2})^{t_1} < e^{-n^{1/4}}$.

On the other hand, suppose that $\mathbf{v}'$ satisfies the event C. Then $U(\mathbf{v})$ implies that at least $t_2 \geq n^{3/4}$ agents satisfy $v_i = 1$ and $v_i{}' = \alpha$, since only agents for which $v_i{}' = \alpha$ can be allocated 0. In this case, each of these t_2 agents has probability at least $n^{-1/2}$ of being allocated α. The probability that none of them is allocated a load of α is at most $(1 - n^{-1/2})^{t_2} < e^{-n^{1/4}}$.

In either case, the probability that a single query is successful is at most $e^{-n^{1/4}}$. Transformation $\mathcal{T}$ can make at most $e^{n^{1/4}}/2$ queries on input $\mathbf{v}$. We will now bound the probability that any one of them is successful. Since the allocations returned by $\mathcal{A}$ on any two queries are independent, we can think of the $e^{n^{1/4}}/2$ queries as independent trials that are successful with probability at most $e^{-n^{1/4}}$. Thus, the probability that at least one of these queries is successful is at most

$$\begin{aligned} 1 - (1 - e^{-n^{1/4}})^{e^{n^{1/4}/2}} &= 1 - (1 - e^{-n^{1/4}})^{e^{n^{1/4}} e^{-n^{1/4}/2}} \\ &< 1 - (1/4)^{e^{-n^{1/4}/2}} \\ &= 1 - (1/e)^{(\ln 4) e^{-n^{1/4}/2}} \\ &< (\ln 4) e^{-n^{1/4}/2} \end{aligned}$$

as required. □

Now consider the probability with which $\mathcal{T}$ allocates a given job to an agent. For agent i, value v, and allocation x, write $p_i^x(v) = \Pr_{\mathbf{v}_{-i}, \mathcal{A}, \mathcal{T}}[x_i(v, \mathbf{v}_{-i}) = x]$. That is, $p_i^x(v)$ is the probability that, conditioned on agent i's value being v, $\mathcal{T}(\mathcal{A})$ allocates x to agent i.

We can express the fact that $\mathcal{T}$ satisfies BIC in terms of conditions on these probabilities (Lemma 4.5 below): either $p_i^0(1)$ should be large or one of $p_i^1(\alpha)$ and $p_i^\alpha(\alpha)$ should be large.

LEMMA 4.5. *Let* $\mathbf{x}$ *be the allocation rule of* $\mathcal{T}(\mathcal{A})$. *Then if* $x_i(1) \leq x_i(\alpha)$, $p_i^0(1) < 1/3$, *and* $p_i^1(\alpha) < 1/3$, *then* $p_i^\alpha(\alpha) > 3/\alpha$.

PROOF. Since $p_i^0(1) < \frac{1}{3}$, we have $x_i(1) > \frac{2}{3}$. Since $p_i^1(\alpha) < \frac{1}{3}$, we have $x_i(\alpha) < \frac{1}{3} + p_i^\alpha(\alpha)\alpha$. We conclude that $\frac{2}{3} < \frac{1}{3} + p_i^\alpha(\alpha)\alpha$ which implies the desired result. □

On the other hand, in Lemmas 4.6, 4.7, and 4.8, we will show that on average over all agents, each of these probabilities ($p_i^0(1)$, $p_i^1(\alpha)$, and $p_i^\alpha(\alpha)$) is small if p_{bad} is small. The proofs of these lemmas are deferred to the end of this section. In Lemma 4.9 we put these results together to argue that p_{bad} must be large.

LEMMA 4.6. $\frac{1}{2n}\sum_i p_i^\alpha(\alpha) \leq n^{-\frac{1}{2}}$.

LEMMA 4.7. $\frac{1}{2n}\sum_i p_i^0(1) \leq n^{-1/4} + p_{bad} + (\ln 4)e^{-n^{1/4}/2}$.

LEMMA 4.8. $\frac{1}{2n}\sum_i p_i^1(\alpha) \leq 3n^{-1/4} + p_{bad} + (\ln 4)e^{-n^{1/4}/2} + 2e^{-n^{1/4}/4}$.

We can now derive a lower bound on p_{bad}: since one of $p_i^0(1)$, $p_i^1(\alpha)$, or $p_i^\alpha(\alpha)$ must be large, the bad event of allocating a long job to a slow machine must occur with non-negligible probability.

LEMMA 4.9. *If* $\mathcal{T}$ *is a BIC transformation, then* $p_{bad} \geq n^{-1/4}(1 - o(1))$.

PROOF. We know that, for each i, either $p_i^0(1) \geq 1/3$, $p_i^1(\alpha) \geq 1/3$, or $p_i^\alpha(\alpha) > 3/\alpha$. So one of these inequalities must be true for at least one third of the agents, and hence one of the following must be true:

$$\frac{1}{2n}\sum_i p_i^0(1) \geq 1/18$$

$$\frac{1}{2n}\sum_i p_i^1(\alpha) \geq 1/18$$

$$\frac{1}{2n}\sum_i p_i^\alpha(\alpha) \geq 1/2\alpha.$$

Suppose first that the third inequality is true. Lemma 4.6 implies

$$n^{-\frac{1}{2}} \geq 1/2\alpha$$

which is a contradiction, since $\alpha = \frac{1}{4}n^{1/2}$.
Suppose the first inequality is true. Then by Lemma 4.7 we know

$$p_{bad} \geq 1/18 - n^{-1/4} - (\ln 4)e^{-n^{1/4}/2}$$

which implies the desired result for sufficiently large n (as the right hand side is at least a constant for large n, whereas $n^{-1/4} - 2e^{-n^{1/4}/4} - (\ln 4)e^{-n^{1/4}/2}$, from the statement of the lemma, vanishes as n grows).
Finally, suppose the second inequality is true. Then we know from Lemma 4.8

$$p_{bad} \geq 1/18 - 5n^{-1/4} - 2(\ln 4)e^{-n^{1/4}/2} - 2e^{-n^{1/4}/4}$$

which again implies the desired result. □

To complete the proof of Theorem 4.1, note Lemma 4.9 implies $\overline{\phi}(\mathcal{T}(\mathcal{A})) = 1 + \alpha p_{bad} = \Omega(n^{1/4})$. Since $\overline{\phi}(\mathcal{A}) = \theta(1)$ (Lemma 4.3), $\mathcal{T}$ degrades the expected makespan of $\mathcal{A}$ by a factor of $\Omega(n^{1/4})$.

Proofs of bounds on the allocation probabilities.

To conclude the analysis, we now present proofs of Lemmas 4.6, 4.7, and 4.8.

Proof of Lemma 4.6 : Note that, for any $\mathbf{v}$, exactly $n^{1/2}$ agents are allocated α by $\mathcal{A}$. Thus, keeping $\mathbf{v}$ fixed, we have

$$\frac{1}{n}\sum_i \Pr[(v_i = \alpha) \wedge (x_i(\alpha, \mathbf{v}_{-i}) = \alpha)] \leq \frac{1}{n}(n^{1/2}) = n^{-1/2}.$$

We conclude, taking probabilities over all $\mathbf{v}$, that

$$\frac{1}{2n}\sum_i p_i^{\alpha}(\alpha) \leq n^{-1/2}.$$

□

Proof of Lemma 4.7 : For each input vector $\mathbf{v}$, either event $\neg U(\mathbf{v})$ occurs, event B occurs, event $\neg C$ occurs, or event $C \wedge U(\mathbf{v}) \wedge \neg B$ occurs. Event $\neg U(\mathbf{v})$ by definition gives us a bound on the number of agents with value 1 that receive an allocation of 0. So conditioning on this event (and keeping $\mathbf{v}$ fixed) we have

$$\frac{1}{n}\sum_i \Pr[(v_i = 1) \wedge (x_i(1, \mathbf{v}_{-i}) = 0)] \leq \frac{1}{n}n^{3/4} = n^{-1/4}.$$

Thus, taking probabilities over all $\mathbf{v}$ and using Lemma 4.4, we have

$$\begin{aligned}\frac{1}{2n}\sum_i p_i^0(1) &\leq n^{-1/4} + \Pr[B] + \Pr[\neg C] \\ &\quad + \Pr[C \wedge U(\mathbf{v}) \wedge \neg B|\mathbf{v}] \\ &\leq n^{-1/4} + \Pr[B] + 2e^{-n^{1/4}/4} + (\ln 4)e^{-n^{1/4}/2}\end{aligned}$$

as required. □

Proof of Lemma 4.8 : Let us first fix $\mathbf{v}$ and condition on the event $\neg B \wedge \neg U(\mathbf{v}) \wedge C$. Suppose that $\mathcal{T}(\mathcal{A})$ returns an allocation $\mathbf{x}$ that is returned by $\mathcal{A}$ on input $\mathbf{v}'$. Let us consider whether $\mathbf{v}'$ satisfies event C. Note that, as in the proof of Lemma 4.4, the probability that $\mathcal{T}$ is able to find an allocation $\mathbf{v}'$ that does not satisfy event C and for which event B does not occur is at most $e^{-n^{1/4}/2}$. Thus the probability that $\neg B \wedge \neg U(\mathbf{v}) \wedge C$ occurs and moreover $\mathbf{v}'$ does not satisfy event C is at most $(\ln 4)e^{-n^{1/4}/2}$. Given that this (unlikely) event does occur, the number of agents satisfying $v_i = \alpha$ and $x_i = 1$ is at most $n/2 + n^{3/4} < n$.

Next suppose that $\mathbf{v}'$ does satisfy event C. Recall that we wish to bound the number of agents for which $v_i = \alpha$ and $x_i = 1$. Note, from the definition of $\mathcal{A}$, that at most $2n^{3/4}$ agents can have $v_i' \neq 1$ and $x_i = 1$. So what remains is to bound the number of agents for which $v_i = \alpha$ and $v_i' = 1$. Since $\mathbf{v}$ also satisfies event C, we have

$$-2n^{3/4} \leq |H(\mathbf{v})| - |H(\mathbf{v}')| \leq 2n^{3/4}.$$

Furthermore, $\neg U(\mathbf{v}) \wedge \neg B$ implies that $|H(\mathbf{v}') \backslash H(\mathbf{v})| \leq n^{3/4}$. Combining with the inequalities above, we conclude that $|H(\mathbf{v}) \backslash H(\mathbf{v}')| \leq 2n^{3/4} + n^{3/4} = 3n^{3/4}$. Note that this is a bound on the number of agents such that $v_i = \alpha$ and $v_i' = 1$. We conclude that the number of agents such that $v_i = \alpha$ and $x_i = 1$ is at most $3n^{3/4} + 2n^{3/4} = 5n^{3/4}$.

We conclude that, conditioning on event $\neg B \wedge \neg U(\mathbf{v}) \wedge C$ and keeping $\mathbf{v}$ fixed, we have

$$\begin{aligned}&\frac{1}{n}\sum_i \Pr[(v_i = \alpha) \wedge (x_i(\alpha, \mathbf{v}_{-i}) = 1)] \\ &\leq \frac{1}{n}(5n^{3/4} + n(\ln 4)e^{-n^{1/4}/2}).\end{aligned}$$

Thus, taking probabilities over all $\mathbf{v}$ and all events and using Lemma 4.4, we have

$$\begin{aligned}\frac{1}{2n}\sum_i p_i^0(1) &\leq 5n^{-1/4} + (\ln 4)e^{-n^{1/4}/2} + \Pr[B] \\ &\quad + \Pr[C \wedge U(\mathbf{v}) \wedge \neg B|\mathbf{v}] + \Pr[\neg C] \\ &\leq 5n^{-1/4} + \Pr[B] + 2(\ln 4)e^{-n^{1/4}/2} + 2e^{-n^{1/4}/4}\end{aligned}$$

as required. □

4.1 Symmetric Feasibility Constraints

Throughout this section, we have assumed that a transformation can only return allocations that it observes by querying the given algorithm on some input. While this captures the notion of a black box transformation, in some settings it may be reasonable to assume that the feasibility constraints exhibit some basic structure that could be exploited by a transformation. One such natural assumption is *symmetry*: if an allocation (x_i) is feasible, then for any permutation π of the agents, $(x_{\pi(i)})$ is also feasible. Symmetry occurs in any environment in which agents are treated anonymously, for example. In this section, we question whether one can circumvent the previous negative result in certain environments by allowing the transformation to leverage knowledge of the structure of the feasibility constraints. We will see that a negative result similar to Theorem 4.1 holds even when the transformation can exploit symmetry, if we consider environments in which agent values are not drawn from identical distributions. In other words, symmetry and identically-distributed priors are in some sense complementary. We leave as an open question whether there exist transformations with small loss in makespan for environments with identically distributed agent types and symmetric feasibility constraints.

We first note that if we allow our transformation to assume symmetry, then there is a trivial transformation for Algorithm 2 presented in the previous setting: given an input, the transformation queries the algorithm on that input, sorts the machines in the input by speed (breaking ties lexicographically), sorts the allocations returned by the algorithm by size, and then assigns each machine an allocation in this order (i.e. so that the fastest machines are assigned the greatest loads). This transformation is clearly monotone and preserves the makespan.

Our negative result for symmetric feasibility constraints is based on a construction very similar to the one in the previous section. Each machine will have a slow speed and a fast speed, as well as a small job and a large job. We use an environment with non-identically distributed values to vary the notions of slow and fast and small and large in order to create instances where allocations can not be permuted without significantly increasing the makespan.

Problem Instance.

There are $2n$ machines $m_1, \ldots, m_n$ and $m_1', \ldots, m_n'$. Machine m_i has speed v_i chosen uniformly from $\{\alpha^{3i}, \alpha^{3i+1}\}$, where we will choose $\alpha = \frac{1}{4}n^{1/2}$. Machine m_i' has speed α^{3i+2}. We refer to the machines m_i as the "type-1" machines and the machines m_i' as the "type-2" machines.

There are $3n$ jobs: one each of size $\alpha^{3i}, \alpha^{3i+1}$, and α^{3i+2} for $1 \leq i \leq n$. Our feasibility constraint allows each machine to be assigned at most three jobs. We will refer to the jobs of sizes α^{3i} and α^{3i+1} as "type-1" jobs, and the jobs of sizes α^{3i+2} as "type-2" jobs.

The Algorithm.

Our algorithm will be a slight modification of Algorithm 2 from the previous setting; we will only briefly describe the differences. The type-1 jobs and machines correspond to the jobs and machines used in the setting of Algorithm 2. We define the high speed machines to be the set $H = \{i : v_i = \alpha^{3i+1}\}$; note that H consists only of type-1 machines. Whenever Algorithm 2 assigns machine i a job of length α, our modified algorithm will instead assign machine m_i a job of length α^{3i+1}. Similarly, whenever Algorithm 2 assigns machine i a job of length 1, our modified algorithm will instead assign machine m_i a job of length α^{3i}. For each i, we will assign machine m_i' the unallocated jobs among those of size $\alpha^{3i}, \alpha^{3i+1}$, and α^{3i+2}.

The extra power granted to a transformation in the symmetric setting is that it can modify allocations returned by the original algorithm: given an observed allocation (x_i) and permutation π, the transformation can return allocation $(x_{\pi(i)})$. However, note that our algorithm is designed so that, for every input vector (v_i) and associated allocation (x_i), and every $i' > i$, it is the case that $x_{i'}/v_i \geq \alpha$. This implies that, for every observed allocation (x_i) and permutation π that is not the identity, the makespan of allocation $(x_{\pi(i)})$ is always at least α. (This uses the fact that, for every non-identity permutation π, there exists some i such that $\pi(i) > i$). We conclude that a transformation cannot make use of the symmetry assumption to reduce the probability with which it returns allocations with makespan α.

As in the analysis of Algorithm 2, the makespan of this algorithm is dominated by that of the "typical" case in which the number of high speed and low speed machines is approximately balanced. In this typical case, the makespan is constant. The atypical case, which occurs with exponentially small probability by the Chernoff bound, has makespan at most $\alpha = \theta(n^{1/2})$, and hence the expected makespan due to this atypical case is constant. On the other hand, any BIC black-box transformation that performs a sub-exponential number of queries has approximation factor at least α. This is because, as discussed above, the transformation cannot make use of the symmetry assumption without generating allocations with makespan α. Since the transformation cannot make use of symmetry, our previous analysis for the proof of Theorem 4.1 applies and we obtain the following similar impossibility result.

THEOREM 4.10. *There are constants c_1, c_2 such that, for any polytime black-box BIC transformation $\mathcal{T}$ for symmetric problem instances, there is a symmetric instance $(\mathcal{F}, \mathbf{F})$ of the makespan problem and an algorithm $\mathcal{A}$ with $\overline{\phi}(\mathcal{A}) \leq c_1$ and $\overline{\phi}(\mathcal{T}(\mathcal{A})) \geq c_2 n^{1/4}$ for n large enough.*

We note that our construction involves agent values that lie in the range $[1, n^{\theta(n)}]$, and that our approximability gap is polynomial in n. The multiplicative loss in expected makespan is therefore logarithmic in the range of values that can be assumed by the agents. We leave open the question of whether our construction can be modified so that the loss in approximation factor can be made independent of the input value space for symmetric settings.

5. THE LIMITATIONS OF IRONING

As mentioned earlier, BIC transformations can preserve social welfare in expectation through a technique known as ironing. One of the properties of the social welfare objective that allows such a transformation where one cannot exist for makespan is that the objective function is additive across agents. This allows a transformation to focus on each agent individually while taking an aggregate view over other agents and preserving the performance with respect to the respective component of the objective function alone. Can such a per-agent ironing approach be applied to other objectives, for example those that are additive across agents (but otherwise non-linear)? In this section we answer this question in the negative: informally, any kind of non-linearity in the objective leads to a loss in approximation that is related to the degree of non-linearity and can be made arbitrarily large.

The ironing approach of [12] and [11] can be described as follows: for each agent i they construct a mapping σ_i from the value space of i to itself, and on input $\mathbf{v}$ return the output of the algorithm on $\sigma(\mathbf{v}) = (\sigma_1(v_1), \sigma_2(v_2), \cdots)$. The mappings σ_i ensure the following three properties:

(P.1) the mapping preserves the distribution over values of i,

(P.2) the expected allocation of agent i upon applying the mapping, i.e. $x_i(\sigma_i(v_i))$, is monotone non-decreasing in v_i, and,

(P.3) the contribution of agent i to the overall social welfare is no worse than in the original algorithm.

(P.1) coupled with (P.2) implies that the transformation is BIC. (P.3) implies that the social welfare is preserved in expectation. Furthermore, the benefit of this approach is that if each agent's value space is single-dimensional or well structured in some other way, the computational problem of finding the mappings σ_i becomes easy. We call any mapping g that satisfies the properties (P.1) and (P.2) a per-agent ironing.

Our claim is that for any objective function that is nonlinear in the agents' allocations, there exists an instance such that for any per-agent ironing suffers a loss in performance that depends on the degree of non-linearity in the function. Our argument make use of randomness in the original (nontruthful) algorithm. This is essentially without loss of generality: from a single agent's point of view, the algorithm's outcome, dependent on others' a priori random values, appears random. Through most of this section we focus on a single agent setting.

We first deal with maximization problems, $\max \mathbf{E}_v[h(x, v)]$, where the function h is an increasing function of the allocations and values. (Note that maximizing a function that is either decreasing in allocations or in values leads to a non-monotone objective.) Our gap construction depends on whether the function displays convexity or concavity. We argue the convex case; The concave case, which is quite similar, is left as an exercise to the reader.

We begin by defining two definitions that the function h must satisfy in order for ironing to fail:

DEFINITION 5.1. *A function h is said to be α-**convex** with respect to a random variable X at v if $E[h(X, v)] \geq \alpha h(E[X], v)$.*

DEFINITION 5.2. *A function h is said to be α-**responsive** with respect to v at x if there exists a value v' such that $h(x,v) \geq \alpha h(x,v')$.*

The first definition is a quantitative version of Jensen's inequality and essentially quantifies the function's departure from convexity. The second asserts that the function is "responsive" to the agent's value. For example, consider the function $h(x,v) = vx^2$ defined over $x, v \in [0,1]$ and consider the random variable X that takes on values 0 and 1 with equal probability. Then, $E[h(X,v)] = 0.5v$ and $h(E[x],v) = 0.25v$. Therefore, the function is 2-convex with respect to X at any v. Moreover, it is α-responsive with respect for any $\alpha > 0$ to any v at any x. On the other hand, the function $h(x,v) = v(x+10)^2$ defined over $x, v \in [0,1]$ is not very convex with respect to the random variable X defined above: $E[h(X,v)] = 110.5v$ and $h(E[X],v) = 110.25v$. In fact this function admits a good linear approximation given by $v(21x+100)$; the ratio between the two functions is at most 1.002 within the range $x, v \in [0,1]$.

It should be immediately evident that both properties are necessary to show that ironing degrades the performance of an approximation algorithm. Indeed, an objective function that is not sensitive to the agents' values can be ironed because no permutation of allocations across values can affect the objective by too much. Likewise, a function that is nearly linear everywhere can be ironed because ironing maximizes a linear approximation to the function. We remark that for our argument it is sufficient for the function to satisfy the two properties over some appropriate interval rather than everywhere.

We are now ready to prove our claim.

THEOREM 5.3. *Let h be a continuous increasing function of x and an increasing function in v. Suppose that there exists a value v and a random variable X in the support of the function such that h is α-convex with respect to X at all values and α^2-responsive with respect to v at any allocation in the support of X. Then there exists a distribution over agent values and an algorithm $\mathcal{A}$ such that any transformation that performs a per-agent ironing of the allocation function of $\mathcal{A}$ obtains objective function value a factor of $\Omega(\alpha)$ worse than that of $\mathcal{A}$.*

PROOF. Let $\epsilon = 1/\alpha$. Let $\bar{x} = E[X]$ and $\bar{h}(v) = E[h(X,v)]$. Let $v' < v$ be a value such that $h(x,v) \geq 1/\epsilon^2 h(x,v')$ for all x in the support of X. Let $x' > \bar{x}$ be such that $h(x',v') \leq (1+\epsilon)h(\bar{x},v')$ and $h(x',v) \leq (1+\epsilon)h(\bar{x},v)$. The continuity of h implies that x' exists. The main idea behind the proof is the following. In terms of the objective function h, an allocation of x' is much worse than a randomized allocation of X. However, the expected allocation in the latter case is $\bar{x}$ which is smaller than x'. We will now define an instance where the ironing is forced to replace a randomized allocation of X by an allocation of x', thereby hurting the objective function value.

Consider an instance in which the agent's value is v' with probability $1-\epsilon$ and v otherwise. $\mathcal{A}$ is defined as follows. When the agent reports a value of v', the algorithm allocates x' to the agent. When the agent reports a value of v, the algorithm allocates according to X. Now the expected allocation at v is $\bar{x} < x'$, and therefore ironing is necessary. Suppose that the tranformation maps the value v' to v with probability $z/(1-\epsilon)$ for some z. Then, to preserve the distribution over values, we must have $z \leq \epsilon$ and v must get mapped to v' with probability z/ϵ.

How large does z have to be to fix the non-monotonicity? The new expected allocation at v' is $z/(1-\epsilon)\bar{x} + (1 - z/(1-\epsilon))x'$, while the new expected allocation at v is $(1-z/\epsilon)\bar{x} + x'z/\epsilon$. Setting the former to be no larger than the latter, and rearranging terms, we get

$$z/(1-\epsilon) + z/\epsilon \geq 1$$

implying $z \geq \epsilon(1-\epsilon)$.

Let us now compute the objective function value. The original objective function value is $(1-\epsilon)h(x',v') + \epsilon\bar{h}(v) > \epsilon\bar{h}(v)$. The new objective function value is given by

$$\begin{aligned}
&(1-\epsilon)\left(\frac{z}{1-\epsilon}\bar{h}(v') + \left(1 - \frac{z}{1-\epsilon}\right)h(x',v')\right) \\
&\quad + \epsilon\frac{z}{\epsilon}h(x',v) + \epsilon\left(1-\frac{z}{\epsilon}\right)\bar{h}(v) \\
&\leq (1-\epsilon^2)\bar{h}(v') + z(1+\epsilon)h(\bar{x},v) + \epsilon\left(1-\frac{z}{\epsilon}\right)\bar{h}(v) \\
&\leq \epsilon^2(1-\epsilon^2)\bar{h}(v) + \epsilon^2(1+\epsilon)\bar{h}(v) + \epsilon^2\bar{h}(v) \\
&< 4\epsilon^2\bar{h}(v)
\end{aligned}$$

Here the first inequality follows from the fact that $h(x',v') \leq (1+\epsilon)h(\bar{x},v') \leq (1+\epsilon)\bar{h}(v')$ and $h(x',v) \leq (1+\epsilon)h(\bar{x},v)$; The second follows from $\bar{h}(v') \leq \epsilon^2\bar{h}(v)$, $h(\bar{x},v) \leq \epsilon\bar{h}(v)$, $z \leq \epsilon$, and $z \geq \epsilon(1-\epsilon)$. This implies that any mapping σ that preserves the value distribution and achieves monotonicity must achieve an approximation fator of $\Omega(1/\epsilon)$. $\square$

We next consider algorithms for minimization problems of the form $\min \mathbf{E}_v[h(x,v)]$, where the function h is non-decreasing in x and non-increasing in v. Once again we focus on the case where h is convex in x; the concave case is similar and we skip it.

THEOREM 5.4. *Let h be a continuous increasing function of x and a decreasing function in v. Suppose that there exists a value v and a random variable X such that h is α-convex with respect to X at v and α-responsive with respect to v at any allocation in the support of X. Then there exists a distribution over agent values and an algorithm $\mathcal{A}$ such that any transformation that performs a per-agent ironing of the allocation function of $\mathcal{A}$ obtains objective function value a factor of $\Omega(\alpha)$ worse than that of $\mathcal{A}$.*

PROOF. Let $\epsilon = 1/\alpha$. Let $v' > v$ be a value such that $h(x,v) \geq 1/\epsilon h(x,v')$ for all x in the support of X. Consider an instance where the agent's distribution is uniform over $\{v, v'\}$. Let $\bar{x} = E[X]$. Let $x' > \bar{x}$ be such that $h(x',v) \leq (1+\epsilon)h(\bar{x},v)$. Let $\bar{h}(v) = E[h(X,v)]$.

The algorithm $\mathcal{A}$ is defined as follows. At v, the algorithm returns x'. At v', the algorithm returns X. The expected allocation at v_2 is $\bar{x}$, and therefore the allocation is non-monotone. Suppose that the tranformation maps v to v' with probability z and vice versa. Then it is easy to see that $z \geq 1/2$.

Now let us compute the objective function value. The objective function value of the original algorithm is $1/2h(x',v) + 1/2\bar{h}(v') \leq 1/2(1+\epsilon)\epsilon\bar{h}(v) + 1/2\epsilon\bar{h}(v) = (1+\epsilon/2)\epsilon\bar{h}(v)$.

On the other hand, we can bound from below the objective function value of the transformed mechanism by considering the term corresponding to value v when the allocation is randomized according to X (an event that happens with probability at least 1/4). The new objective function value is therefore at least $1/4\bar{h}(v)$. This proves the theorem. □

Finally, we remark that while our arguments above focused on settings consisting of a single agent, it is straightforward to extend the argument to settings that involve multiple agents—essentially, we can construct instances where a single agent makes a large contribution to the algorithm's (and transformation's) performance, and the allocations and therefore contributions of other agents to the objective function are fixed. We leave the details to the reader.

6. REFERENCES

[1] A. Archer and E. Tardos. Truthful mechanisms for one-parameter agents. In *Proc. 42nd IEEE Symp. on Foundations of Computer Science*, 2001.

[2] Itai Ashlagi, Shahar Dobzinski, and Ron Lavi. An optimal lower bound for anonymous scheduling mechanisms. In *Proceedings of the 10th ACM conference on Electronic commerce*, pages 169–176, 2009.

[3] M. Babaioff, R. Lavi, and E. Pavlov. Single-value combinatorial auctions and algorithmic implementation in undominated strategies. *Journal of the ACM*, 2009.

[4] X. Bei and Z. Huang. Bayesian incentive compatibility via fractional assignments. In *Proc. 22nd ACM Symp. on Discrete Algorithms*, 2011.

[5] George Christodoulou and Annamária Kovács. A deterministic truthful ptas for scheduling related machines. In *Proceedings of the Twenty-First Annual ACM-SIAM Symposium on Discrete Algorithms*, SODA '10, pages 1005–1016, Philadelphia, PA, USA, 2010. Society for Industrial and Applied Mathematics.

[6] P. Dhangwatnotai, S. Dobzinski, S. Dughmi, and T. Roughgarden. Truthful approximation schemes for single-parameter agents. In *Proc. 49th IEEE Symp. on Foundations of Computer Science*, 2008.

[7] S. Dobzinski. An impossibility result for truthful combinatorial auctions with submodular valuations. In *Proc. 42nd ACM Symp. on Theory of Computing*, 2011.

[8] S. Dughmi and T. Roughgarden. Black-box randomized reductions in algorithmic mechanism design. In *Proc. 51st IEEE Symp. on Foundations of Computer Science*, 2010.

[9] S. Dughmi, T. Roughgarden, and Q. Yan. From convex optimization to randomized mechanisms: Toward optimal combinatorial auctions. In *Proc. 42nd ACM Symp. on Theory of Computing*, 2011.

[10] G. Goel, C. Karande, and L. Wang. Single parameter combinatorial auctions with partially public valuations. In *Proc. 3rd Intl. Conf. on Algorithmic Game Theory*, 2010.

[11] J. Hartline, R. Kleinberg, and A. Malekian. Bayesian incentive compatibility via matchings. In *Proc. 22nd ACM Symp. on Discrete Algorithms*, 2011.

[12] J. Hartline and B. Lucier. Bayesian algorithmic mechanism design. In *Proc. 41st ACM Symp. on Theory of Computing*, 2010.

[13] Dorit s. Hochbaum and David B. Shmoys. A polynomial approximation scheme for scheduling on uniform processors: Using the dual approximation approach. *SIAM J. Comput.*, 17:539–551, June 1988.

[14] Z. Huang, L. Wang, and Y. Zhou. Black-box reductions in mechanism design. In *Proc. 14th Intl. Workshop on Approximation Algorithms for Combinatorial Optimization Problems*, 2011.

[15] R. Lavi and C. Swamy. Truthful and near-optimal mechanism design via linear programming. In *Proc. 46th IEEE Symp. on Foundations of Computer Science*, 2005.

[16] C. Papadimitriou, M. Schapira, and Y. Singer. On the hardness of being truthful. In *Proc. 49th IEEE Symp. on Foundations of Computer Science*, 2008.

Budget Feasible Mechanism Design: From Prior-Free to Bayesian

Xiaohui Bei*   Ning Chen†   Nick Gravin†   Pinyan Lu‡

ABSTRACT

Budget feasible mechanism design studies procurement combinatorial auctions in which the sellers have private costs to produce items, and the buyer (auctioneer) aims to maximize a social valuation function on subsets of items, under the budget constraint on the total payment. One of the most important questions in the field is "which valuation domains admit truthful budget feasible mechanisms with 'small' approximations (compared to the social optimum)?" Singer [35] showed that additive and submodular functions have a constant approximation mechanism. Recently, Dobzinski, Papadimitriou, and Singer [20] gave an $O(\log^2 n)$ approximation mechanism for subadditive functions; further, they remarked that: *"A fundamental question is whether, regardless of computational constraints, a constant-factor budget feasible mechanism exists for subadditive functions."*

In this paper, we address this question from two viewpoints: prior-free worst case analysis and Bayesian analysis, which are two standard approaches from computer science and economics, respectively.

- For the prior-free framework, we use a linear program (LP) that describes the fractional cover of the valuation function; the LP is also connected to the concept of approximate core in cooperative game theory. We provide a mechanism for subadditive functions whose approximation is $O(\mathcal{I})$, via the worst case integrality gap $\mathcal{I}$ of this LP. This implies an $O(\log n)$-approximation for subadditive valuations, $O(1)$-approximation for XOS valuations, as well as for valuations having a constant integrality gap. XOS valuations are an important class of functions and lie between the submodular and the subadditive classes of valuations. We further give another polynomial time $O(\frac{\log n}{\log \log n})$ sub-logarithmic approximation mechanism for subadditive functions. Both of our mechanisms improve the best known approximation ratio $O(\log^2 n)$.
- For the Bayesian framework, we provide a constant approximation mechanism for all subadditive functions, using the above prior-free mechanism for XOS valuations as a subroutine. Our mechanism allows correlations in the distribution of private information and is universally truthful.

Categories and Subject Descriptors

F.0 [**Theory of Computation**]: General; J.4 [**Social and Behavioral Sciences**]: Economics

General Terms

Theory, Economics

Keywords

Mechanism design, budget feasible, prior-free, Bayesian, submodular, subadditive, approximation

1. INTRODUCTION

Consider a procurement combinatorial auction problem where there is a buyer who wants to purchase resources from a set of agents A. Each $i \in A$ is able to supply a resource at an incurred cost $c(i)$. The buyer has a sharp budget B that gives an upper bound on the compensation that is distributed among agents, and a function $v(\cdot)$ describing the valuation that the buyer obtains for each subset of A. This defines a natural optimization problem: find a subset $S \subseteq A$ that maximizes $v(S)$ subject to $\sum_{i \in S} c(i) \le B$. The budgeted optimization problem has been considered in a variety of domains with respect to different valuation functions, e.g., additive (a.k.a. knapsack), and submodular [37].

Agents, as self-interested entities, may want to get as many subsidies as possible. In particular, an agent can hide his true incurred cost $c(i)$ (which is known only to himself) and claim 'any' amount $b(i)$ instead. We adopt the approach of mechanism design to manage self-interested, but strategic, behaviors of the agents: Given submitted bids $b(i)$ from all agents, a *mechanism* decides a winning set $S \subseteq A$ and a payment $p(i)$ to each winner $i \in S$. A mechanism is called

*Institute for Interdisciplinary Information Sciences, Tsinghua University, China. Email: beixiaohui@gmail.com.

†Division of Mathematical Sciences, School of Physical and Mathematical Sciences, Nanyang Technological University, Singapore.
Email: ningc@ntu.edu.sg, ngravin@pmail.ntu.edu.sg.

‡Microsoft Research Asia. Email: pinyanl@microsoft.com.

STOC'12, May 19–22, 2012, New York, New York, USA.

truthful (a.k.a. incentive compatible) if for every agent it is a dominant strategy to bid his true cost[1], i.e., $b(i) = c(i)$. Truthfulness is one of the central solution concepts in mechanism design. It ensures that every participant will behave truthfully to his best interest.

Our mechanism design problem has an important and practical ingredient: the budget, i.e., the total payment of a mechanism should be upper bounded by B. The budget constraint introduces a new dimension to mechanism design and restricts the space of truthful mechanisms. For example, in single-parameter domains where the private information of every individual is a single value (which is the case in our model), a monotone allocation rule with associated threshold payments provides a sufficient and necessary condition for truthfulness [31]. However, it may not necessarily generate a budget feasible solution. Thus, a number of well known truthful designs (e.g., the seminal VCG mechanism [38, 16, 24]) do not apply, and new ideas have to be developed.

Another significant challenge due to the budget constraint is that, unlike the VCG mechanism which always generates a socially optimal solution, we cannot hope to have a solution that is both socially optimal and budget feasible even if we are given unlimited computational power. Indeed, in a simple setting like path procurement with 0 or 1 valuation [35], any budget feasible mechanism may have an arbitrarily bad solution. Therefore, the question that one may ask is "under which valuation domains do there exist truthful budget feasible mechanisms that admit 'small' approximations (compared to the socially optimal solution)?"

The answer to this question crucially depends on the properties and classifications of the valuation function under consideration. In particular, given the following function hierarchy [29]:

$$\text{additive} \subset \text{gross substitutes} \subset \text{submodular} \subset \text{XOS} \subset \text{subadditive},$$

which one admits a positive answer? Singer [35] initiated the study of approximate budget feasible mechanism design and gave constant approximation mechanisms for additive and submodular functions. In subsequent work, Dobzinski, Papadimitriou, and Singer [20] considered subadditive functions and showed an $O(\log^2 n)$ approximation. Further, it was remarked in [20] that:

> *"A fundamental question is whether, regardless of computational constraints, a constant-factor budget feasible mechanism exists for subadditive functions."*
>
> — Dobzinski, Papadimitriou, Singer

In the present paper we attempt to answer this question.

1.1 Our Results and Techniques

We address this question from two viewpoints: prior-free worst case analysis and Bayesian analysis. The former is the standard framework used in computer science: in our model, the private cost $c(i)$ of every agent is assumed to be arbitrary without any prior knowledge. All previous research on budget feasible mechanism design, e.g. [35, 14, 20, 22] falls into this framework. The latter Bayesian analysis [31] is a classic economic approach that assumes the private information of the agents is drawn from a given prior-known distribution. Bayesian mechanism design has received a lot of attention in the computer science community in recent years, see, e.g., [27, 28, 26, 7, 11, 18, 13, 25, 5, 12, 17].

[1] The focus of our work is to consider strategic behaviors of the agents rather than the buyer. We thus assume that the information related to the buyer, i.e., budget B and valuation function $v(\cdot)$, is public knowledge.

Prior-free mechanism design.

Consider the following linear program (LP), where $\alpha(\cdot)$'s are variables.

$$\begin{aligned} \min \quad & \sum_{S \subseteq A} \alpha(S) \cdot v(S) \\ s.t. \quad & \alpha(S) \geq 0, \qquad \forall\, S \subseteq A \\ & \sum_{S:\, i \in S} \alpha(S) \geq 1, \quad \forall\, i \in A \end{aligned}$$

Constraints of this LP describe a fractional set cover of A, where each set S receives weight $\alpha(S)$ and we require that all agents in A are covered. An important observation about this LP is that for any monotone subadditive function $v(\cdot)$, the value of the optimal integral solution is precisely $v(A)$.

The above LP has a strong connection to the core of cost sharing games (considering $v(\cdot)$ instead as a cost function), which is a central notion in cooperative game theory [33]. Roughly speaking, the core of a game is a stable cooperation among all agents to share $v(A)$ where no subset of agents can benefit by breaking away from the grand coalition. It is well known that the cores of many cost sharing games are empty. This motivates the notion of α-approximate core, which requires all the agents to share only an α-fraction of $v(A)$. The classic Bondareva-Shapley Theorem [9, 34] says that for subadditive functions, the largest value α for which the α-approximate core is nonempty is equal to the integrality gap of the LP. Further, the integrality gap of the LP equals one (i.e., $v(A)$ is also an optimal fractional solution) if and only if the valuation function is XOS, which is also equivalent to the non-emptiness of the core.

Given an instance of our problem with an agent set A, we may consider the above LP and its integrality gap for every subinstance $A' \subseteq A$. We denote $\mathcal{I}$ as the largest integrality gap among all subinstances $A' \subseteq A$. In other words, the gap $\mathcal{I}$ characterizes the worst case scenario between the optimal integral and fractional solutions of the problem. We have the following result.

Theorem 1. *There is a budget feasible truthful mechanism for subadditive functions with approximation ratio $O(\mathcal{I})$. In particular, for XOS functions, the mechanism has a constant approximation ratio.*

Our results show an interesting connection between the budget feasible mechanism design and the integrality gap of the above linear program, as well as the existence of an α-approximate core. Note that the tight bound of the integrality gap is known to be $\Theta(\log n)$ [19, 8]; thus, our mechanism in the worst case has an approximation ratio of $O(\log n)$. (But for some special functions whose integrality gaps are bounded by constants, e.g., facility location [33], our mechanism gives a constant approximation.) Further, the mechanism may have exponential running time, though for some special XOS functions like matching it can be implemented in polynomial time. To remedy these issues, we further give a polynomial time sub-logarithmic approximation mechanism. Both of our mechanisms improve the best known approximation ratio $O(\log^2 n)$ of [20].

Theorem 2. *There is a polynomial time budget feasible truthful mechanism for subadditive functions with an approximation ratio $O(\frac{\log n}{\log \log n})$, where n is the number of agents.*

Bayesian mechanism design.

As a standard game theoretic model for incomplete information, Bayesian mechanism design assumes that agents' private information (i.e., $c(i)$ in our model) is drawn from a known distribution. In contrast to prior-free worst case analysis, if we have prior knowledge of the distribution, we can obtain more positive results in the form of constant approximation truthful mechanisms. In the Bayesian setting, we are able to answer the above question posed in [20] affirmatively.

Theorem 3. *There is a constant approximation budget feasible truthful mechanism for subadditive functions for any distribution under a mild assumption*[2].

It should be noted that our result does not completely rely on Bayesian analysis in the following aspects.

- Truthfulness. In most of the previous works in Bayesian mechanism design regarding social welfare maximization, e.g., [26, 5, 25, 12], the considered solution concept is Bayesian truthfulness, i.e., truth-telling is in expectation an equilibrium strategy when other agents' profiles are drawn from the known distribution. Our mechanism guarantees *universal truthfulness*, meaning that truth-telling is a dominant strategy of each agent for any coin flips of the mechanism and any instance of the costs. Thus universal truthfulness is a stronger solution concept than Bayesian truthfulness. Universal truthfulness in Bayesian mechanism design has also been used in, e.g. [11], but their focus was on profit maximization.

- Distribution. Regarding prior knowledge of the distribution, most of the previous related works consider independent distributions, e.g., [27, 26, 5, 25]. Our mechanism applies to general distributions that allow correlations on costs. Dependency on private information is a natural phenomenon arising in practice and it has been considered for, e.g., auctions [30]. In our model where costs are private information, correlations appear to be very common. For example, if the price of crude oil goes up, the costs of producing the items for *all* agents may go up as well.

Techniques.

In the design of budget feasible mechanisms, the major approach used in previous works [35, 14, 20] is based on a simple idea of adding agents one by one greedily and carefully ensuring that the budget constraint is not violated. Our mechanisms, from a high level structural point of view, use another simple, but powerful, approach: random sampling. We add agents into a test set T with probability half for each agent and compute an (approximately) optimal budget feasible solution on T. We use the agents in T only for the purpose of 'evaluation' and none of them will be a winner. The computed solution on T gives a close estimate of the optimal solution for the whole set with a high probability. We then compute a real winning set from the remaining agents using the evaluation from T as a threshold.

In the Bayesian setting, random sampling is often deemed to be unnecessary, because, when we have knowledge of the distribution, it is tempting to use a 'prior sampling' approach to generate random virtual instances and based on them to compute a threshold. While this works well when the private cost $c(i)$ of every agent is drawn independently, interestingly (and surprisingly), it fails when costs $c(i)$'s are correlated in the distribution. We therefore still use random sampling to compute a threshold based on the sampled test set; the collected information from random sampling correctly reflects the structure of the private costs (with a high probability) even for correlated distributions. To derive a constant approximation budget feasible mechanism for subadditive functions, we first generate a cost vector sampled from the known distribution and use it as a guidance for the payments to the winners. Then we adopt our (constant approximation) mechanism for prior-free XOS functions by feeding to this mechanism another valuation $\widetilde{v}(\cdot)$, which we define as the solution of the above LP computed for the various subsets of A.

Random sampling appears to be a powerful approach and has been used successfully in other domains of mechanism design, e.g., digital goods auctions [23], secretary problem [3, 2], social welfare maximization [19], and mechanism design without money [15]. It is intriguing to find applications of random sampling in other mechanism design problems.

1.2 Related Work

Our work falls into the field of algorithmic mechanism design, which is a fascinating area initiated by the seminal work of Nisan and Ronen [32]. There are many mechanism design models; see, e.g., [33], for a survey.

As mentioned earlier, the study of approximate mechanism design with a budget constraint was originated by Singer [35] and constant approximation mechanisms were given for additive and submodular functions. The approximation ratios were later improved in [14]. Dobzinski, Papadimitriou, and Singer [20] considered subadditive functions and showed an $O(\log^2 n)$ approximation mechanism. Ghosh and Roth [22] considered a budget feasible mechanism design model for selling privacy where there are externalities for each agent's cost. All these models considered prior-free worst case analysis.

For Bayesian mechanism design, Hartline and Lucier [26] first proposed a Bayesian reduction in single-parameter settings that converts any approximation algorithm to a Bayesian truthful mechanism that approximately preserves social welfare. The blackbox reduction results were later improved to multi-parameter settings in [5] and [25] independently. Chawla et al. [12] considered budget-constrained agents and gave Bayesian truthful mechanisms in various settings. A number of other Bayesian mechanism design works considered profit maximization, e.g., [27, 7, 13, 18, 11, 17]. Ours is the first to consider Bayesian analysis in budget feasible mechanisms with a focus on the valuation (social welfare) maximization.

[2]Technically, we require that the distribution has integrable marginal densities for any subset of variables (e.g., jointly independent distributions trivially satisfy this condition). The formal definition is referred to Section 4.

2. PRELIMINARIES

In a marketplace, there are n agents (or items), denoted by A. Each agent $i \in A$ has a privately known incurred *cost* $c(i) \geq 0$. We denote by $c = (c(i))_{i \in A}$ the cost vector of the agents. For any given subset $S \subseteq A$ of agents, there is a publicly known valuation $v(S)$, meaning the social welfare derived from S. We assume that $v(\emptyset) = 0$ and the valuation function is monotone, i.e., $v(S) \leq v(T)$ for any $S \subset T \subseteq A$. A centralized authority wants to pick a subset of agents with maximum possible valuation given a sharp budget B to cover their incurred costs, i.e., $\max_{S \subseteq A} v(S)$ given $c(S) = \sum_{i \in S} c(i) \leq B$. We denote the optimal solution of this optimization question by $\texttt{opt}(A)$ (or $\texttt{opt}(c)$) and its valuation by $v(\texttt{opt}(A))$.

We will consider XOS and subadditive functions in the paper; both are rather general classes and contain a number of well studied functions as special cases, e.g., additive, gross substitutes, and submodular.

- Subadditive (a.k.a. complement free): $v(S) + v(T) \geq v(S \cup T)$ for any $S, T \subseteq A$.
- XOS (a.k.a. fractionally subadditive): there is a set of linear functions $f_1, \ldots, f_m$ such that

  $$v(S) = \max\{f_1(S), f_2(S), \ldots, f_m(S)\}$$

  for any $S \subseteq A$. Note that the number of functions m can be exponential in $n = |A|$.

  An equivalent definition [21] is $v(S) \leq \sum_{T \subseteq A} x(T) \cdot v(T)$ whenever $\sum_{T \subseteq A:\, i \in T} x(T) \geq 1$ for any $i \in S$, where $0 \leq x(T) \leq 1$. That is, if every element in S is fractionally covered, then the sum of the values of all subsets weighted by the corresponding fractions is at least as large as $v(S)$.

Note that the representation of a valuation function usually requires exponential size in n. Thus, we assume that we are given an access to a *demand oracle*, which, for any given price vector $p(1), \ldots, p(n)$, returns us a subset $T \in \operatorname{argmax}_{S \subseteq A} \left(v(S) - \sum_{i \in S} p(i)\right)$; every such query is assumed to take unit time. The demand oracle is used in [20] as well, and it was shown that a weaker value query oracle is not sufficient [35].

Agents, as self-interested entities, have their own objective as well; each agent i may not tell his true privately known cost $c(i)$, but, instead, submit a *bid* $b(i)$ strategically. We use mechanism design and its solution concept truthfulness to manage strategic behaviors of the agents. Upon receiving $b(i)$ from each agent, a mechanism decides an *allocation* $S \subseteq A$ of the winners and a *payment* $p(i)$ to each $i \in A$. We assume that the mechanism has no positive transfer (i.e., $p(i) = 0$ if $i \notin S$) and is individually rational (i.e., $p(i) \geq b(i)$ if $i \in S$).

In a mechanism, agents bid strategically to maximize their utilities, which is $p(i) - c(i)$ if i is a winner and 0 otherwise. We say a mechanism is *truthful* if it is of the best interest for each agent to report his true cost, i.e., $b(i) = c(i)$. For randomized mechanisms, we consider universal truthfulness in this paper: a randomized mechanism is called *universally truthful* if it takes a distribution over deterministic truthful mechanisms.

Note that our model is in a single parameter domain, as each agent has only one private parameter which is his cost. Thus, by the well known characterization of single parameter truthful mechanisms [31], designing a monotone allocation, plus the corresponding threshold payment rule, is sufficient to derive a truthful mechanism. We therefore do not specify the payments to the winners in our mechanisms explicitly.

A mechanism is said to be *budget feasible* if its total payment is within the budget constraint, i.e., $\sum_i p(i) \leq B$. Our goal in the present paper is to design truthful and budget feasible mechanisms for XOS and subadditive functions in two frameworks: prior-free and Bayesian.

We first establish the following technical lemma, which is useful in the analysis of our mechanisms.

LEMMA 2.1. *Consider any subadditive function $v(\cdot)$. For any given subset $S \subseteq A$ and a positive integer k, we assume that $v(S) \geq k \cdot v(i)$ for any $i \in S$. Further, suppose that S is divided uniformly at random into two groups T_1 and T_2. Then, with probability of at least $\frac{1}{2}$, we have $v(T_1) \geq \frac{k-1}{4k} v(S)$ and $v(T_2) \geq \frac{k-1}{4k} v(S)$.*

3. PRIOR-FREE MECHANISM DESIGN

In this section we consider designing budget feasible mechanisms for XOS and subadditive functions in the prior-free setting. That is, the mechanism designer has no prior knowledge of the private information $c(i)$ of every agent, which can be an arbitrary cost, and the performance of a designed mechanism is analyzed in the worst case framework. That is, we evaluate a mechanism according to its *approximation ratio*, which is defined as $\max_c \frac{v(\texttt{opt}(c))}{\mathcal{M}(c)}$, where $\mathcal{M}(c)$ is the (expected) value of a mechanism $\mathcal{M}$ on instance $c = (c(i))_{i \in A}$ and $v(\texttt{opt}(c))$ is its optimal value. (We assume without loss of generality that $c(i) \leq B$ for any $i \in A$, since such an agent will never win in any budget feasible truthful mechanism.)

3.1 Constant Approximation for XOS

We will first consider XOS functions. Given an XOS function $v(\cdot)$, by its definition, we assume that

$$v(S) = \max\{f_1(S), f_2(S), \ldots, f_m(S)\}$$

for any $S \subseteq A$, where each $f_j(\cdot)$ is a nonnegative additive function, i.e., $f_j(S) = \sum_{i \in S} f_j(i)$.

In our mechanism, we use a random mechanism ADDITIVE-MECHANISM for additive valuation functions as an auxiliary procedure, where ADDITIVE-MECHANISM is a universally truthful mechanism and has an approximation factor of at most 3 (see, e.g., Theorem B.2, [14]).

<u>XOS-RANDOM-SAMPLE</u>

1. Pick each item independently at random with probability $\frac{1}{2}$ into group T.
2. Compute an optimal solution $\texttt{opt}(T)$ for items in T given budget B.
3. Set a threshold $t = \frac{v(\texttt{opt}(T))}{8B}$.
4. Consider items in $A \setminus T$ and find a set $S^* \in \operatorname{argmax}_{S \subseteq A \setminus T} \{v(S) - t \cdot c(S)\}$.
5. Find an additive function f with $f(S^*) = v(S^*)$ in the XOS representation of $v(\cdot)$.
6. Run ADDITIVE-MECHANISM for function $f(\cdot)$ with respect to set S^* and budget B.
7. Output the result of ADDITIVE-MECHANISM.

In the above mechanism, we first sample in expectation half items to form a testing group T, and compute an optimal solution for T given budget constraint B. By Lemma 2.1, we know that $v(\texttt{opt}(A)) \geq v(\texttt{opt}(T)) \geq \frac{k-1}{4k} v(\texttt{opt}(A))$ and $v(\texttt{opt}(A \setminus T)) \geq \frac{k-1}{4k} v(\texttt{opt}(A))$ with a probability of at least $\frac{1}{2}$. That is, we are able to learn the rough value of the optimal solution by random sampling, and still keep a nearly optimal solution formed with the remaining items. We then use the information from random sampling to compute a proper threshold t for the rest of items. Specifically, we find a subset $S^* \subseteq A \setminus T$ with the largest difference between its value and cost, multiplied by the threshold t (in the computation of S^*, if there are multiple choices, we break ties by any given fixed order). Finally, we use the property of XOS functions to find a linear representation of $v(S^*)$ and run a truthful mechanism for linear functions with respect to S^*.

The mechanism is designated for XOS functions; it is also used crucially as an auxiliary procedure for the more general subadditive functions in the subsequent sections. Note that the runtime of the mechanism for general XOS functions is exponential[3].

Note that in Step (4), the function $v(S) - t \cdot c(S)$ that we maximize is simply the Lagrangian function

$$v(S) - x \cdot c(S) + x \cdot B$$

(note that $x \cdot B$ is a fixed constant) of the original optimization problem $\max_S v(S)$ subject to $c(S) \leq B$. While we do not know the actual value of the variable x in the Lagrangian, a carefully chosen parameter t in the sampling step with a high probability ensures that $\max_S \big\{v(S) - t \cdot c(S) + t \cdot B\big\}$ gives a constant approximation of the optimum $\max_S \big\{v(S) - x \cdot c(S) + x \cdot B\big\}$ of the Lagrangian, which is precisely the targeted value $v(\texttt{opt}(A))$.

The linearity of the Lagrangian, together with the subadditivity of the valuations, is important in order to derive the following properties. (The threshold t, subset S^*, and additive function f are defined in the XOS-RANDOM-SAMPLE.)

Claim 3.1. *For any $S \subseteq S^*$, $f(S) - t \cdot c(S) \geq 0$.*

Proof. Suppose by a contradiction that there exists a subset $S \subseteq S^*$ such that $f(S) - t \cdot c(S) < 0$. Let $S' = S^* \setminus S$. Since f is an additive function, we have $c(S') + c(S) = c(S^*)$ and $f(S') + f(S) = f(S' \cup S) = f(S^*) = v(S^*)$. Thus,

$$\begin{aligned} v(S') - t \cdot c(S') &\geq f(S') - t \cdot c(S') \\ &= v(S^*) - t \cdot c(S^*) - \big(f(S) - t \cdot c(S)\big) \\ &> v(S^*) - t \cdot c(S^*), \end{aligned}$$

which contradicts the definition of S^*. □

The following claim says that any item in S^* cannot manipulate the selection of the set S^* if bidding a smaller cost. This fact is critical for the monotonicity, and thus, the truthfulness of the mechanism.

[3] In fact, in the second step of the mechanism, we can use any constant approximation solution (e.g., algorithm SA-ALG-MAX established in Section 3.3), which suffices for our purpose. Further, Step (4) can be done by simply asking a demand query. Hence, the mechanism can be implemented in polynomial time, if we have access to an oracle that, for any subset X of items, gives a linear function f with $f(X) = v(X)$ and $f(S) \leq v(S)$ for each $S \subseteq X$. For some classic XOS problems like matching (the value of a subset of edges is the size of the largest matching induced by them), our mechanism can be implemented in polynomial time.

Claim 3.2. *If any item $j \in S^*$ reports a smaller cost $b(j) < c(j)$, then set S^* remains the same.*

Proof. Let b be the bid vector where j reports $b(j)$ and others remain unchanged. First we notice that for any set S with $j \in S$, $\big(v(S) - t \cdot b(S)\big) - \big(v(S) - t \cdot c(S)\big) = t\big(c(j) - b(j)\big)$ is a fixed positive value. Hence,

$$\begin{aligned} v(S^*) - t \cdot b(S^*) &= v(S^*) - t \cdot c(S^*) + t\big(c(j) - b(j)\big) \\ &\geq v(S) - t \cdot c(S) + t\big(c(j) - b(j)\big) \\ &= v(S) - t \cdot b(S). \end{aligned}$$

Further, for any set S with $j \notin S$, we have

$$\begin{aligned} v(S^*) - t \cdot b(S^*) &> v(S^*) - t \cdot c(S^*) \\ &\geq v(S) - t \cdot c(S) \\ &= v(S) - t \cdot b(S). \end{aligned}$$

Therefore, we conclude that $S^* = \operatorname{argmax}_{S \subseteq A \setminus T} \big(v(S) - t \cdot b(S)\big)$; and by the fixed tie-breaking rule, S^* is selected as well. □

Our main mechanism for XOS functions is simply a uniform distribution of the mechanism XOS-RANDOM-SAMPLE and one that always picks an item from $\operatorname{argmax}_i v(i)$.

> XOS-MECHANISM-MAIN
>
> - With half probability, run XOS-RANDOM-SAMPLE.
> - With half probability, pick a most-valuable item as the only winner and pay him B.

Theorem 3.1. *The mechanism* XOS-MECHANISM-MAIN *is budget feasible and truthful, and provides a constant approximation ratio for XOS valuation functions.*

In the remaining of this section, we will prove the theorem. It follows from the following three lemmas.

Lemma 3.1. XOS-MECHANISM-MAIN *is universally truthful.*

Our mechanism, at a high level point of view, has a similar flavor to the mechanism composition introduced in [1]. In particular, we may consider Steps (1-4) as one mechanism of choosing candidate winners and Steps (5-7) as the other restricted on the survived agents; then the whole mechanism is a composition of the two. It was shown in [1] that if the first mechanism is composable (i.e., truthful plus the property that any winner cannot manipulate the winner set without losing) and the second one is truthful, then the composite mechanism is truthful. In our mechanism XOS-MECHANISM-MAIN, composability of Steps (1-4) follows from Claim 3.2 and truthfulness of Steps (5-7) is by the property of ADDITIVE-MECHANISM. Therefore, the mechanism is truthful.

Lemma 3.2. XOS-MECHANISM-MAIN *is budget feasible.*

In the mechanism XOS-RANDOM-SAMPLE, the payment to each winner is the maximum amount that the agent can bid and still win. This amount is the minimum of the threshold bids in each of the intermediate steps (e.g., Step (4) and (6)). In particular, the payment is upper bounded by the threshold of the mechanism ADDITIVE-MECHANISM in Step (6). As ADDITIVE-MECHANISM is budget feasible [14], our mechanism XOS-RANDOM-SAMPLE is budget feasible as well. Finally, picking the largest item and paying it the whole budget are clearly a budget feasible mechanism.

LEMMA 3.3. XOS-MECHANISM-MAIN *has a constant approximation ratio.*

PROOF. Let $\texttt{opt} = \texttt{opt}(A)$ denote the optimal winning set given budget B, and let $k = \min_{i \in \texttt{opt}} \frac{v(\texttt{opt})}{v(i)}$. Thus $v(\texttt{opt}) \geq k \cdot v(i)$ for each $i \in \texttt{opt}$. By Lemma 2.1, we have $v(\texttt{opt} \cap T) \geq \frac{k-1}{4k} v(\texttt{opt})$ with a probability of at least $\frac{1}{2}$. Thus, we have $v(\texttt{opt}(T)) \geq v(\texttt{opt} \cap T) \geq \frac{k-1}{4k} v(\texttt{opt})$ with a probability of at least $\frac{1}{2}$ (the first inequality is because $\texttt{opt} \cap T$ is a particular solution and $\texttt{opt}(T)$ is an optimal solution for set T with the budget constraint).

We let $\texttt{opt}^* = \texttt{opt}_f(S^*)$ be the optimal solution with respect to the item set S^*, additive value-function f and budget B. In the following we show that $f(\texttt{opt}^*)$ is a good approximation of the actual social optimum $v(\texttt{opt})$. Consider the following two cases:

- $c(S^*) > B$. With such assumption, we can always find a subset $S' \subseteq S^*$, such that $\frac{B}{2} \leq c(S') \leq B$. By Claim 3.1, we know $f(S') \geq t \cdot c(S') \geq \frac{v(\texttt{opt}(T))}{8B} \cdot \frac{B}{2} \geq \frac{v(\texttt{opt}(T))}{16}$. Then by the fact that $\texttt{opt}^*$ is an optimal solution and S' is a particular solution with budget constraint B, we have $f(\texttt{opt}^*) \geq f(S') \geq \frac{v(\texttt{opt}(T))}{16} \geq \frac{k-1}{64k} v(\texttt{opt})$ with a probability of at least $\frac{1}{2}$.

- $c(S^*) \leq B$. Then $\texttt{opt}^* = S^*$. Let $S' = \texttt{opt} \setminus T$; thus, $c(S') \leq c(\texttt{opt}) \leq B$. By Lemma 2.1, we have $v(S') \geq \frac{k-1}{4k} v(\texttt{opt})$ with a probability of at least $\frac{1}{2}$. Recall that $S^* = \text{argmax}_{S \subseteq A \setminus T}(v(S) - t \cdot c(S))$. Then with a probability of at least $\frac{1}{2}$, we have

$$\begin{aligned} f(\texttt{opt}^*) = f(S^*) &= v(S^*) \\ &\geq v(S^*) - t \cdot c(S^*) \\ &\geq v(S') - t \cdot c(S') \\ &\geq \frac{k-1}{4k} v(\texttt{opt}) - \frac{v(\texttt{opt}(T))}{8B} \cdot B \\ &\geq \frac{k-1}{4k} v(\texttt{opt}) - \frac{v(\texttt{opt})}{8} \\ &= \frac{k-2}{8k} v(\texttt{opt}). \end{aligned}$$

In either case, we get

$$f(\texttt{opt}^*) \geq \min\left\{\frac{k-1}{64k} v(\texttt{opt}), \frac{k-2}{8k} v(\texttt{opt})\right\} \geq \frac{k-2}{64k} v(\texttt{opt})$$

with a probability of at least $\frac{1}{2}$. At the end we output the result of ADDITIVE-MECHANISM(f, S^*, B) in the last step of XOS-RANDOM-SAMPLE. We recall that ADDITIVE-MECHANISM has an approximation factor of at most 3 with respect to the optimal solution $f(\texttt{opt}^*)$. Thus the solution given by XOS-RANDOM-SAMPLE is at least $\frac{1}{3} \cdot f(\texttt{opt}^*) \geq \frac{1}{3} \cdot \frac{1}{2} \cdot \frac{k-2}{64k} v(\texttt{opt}) = \frac{k-2}{384k} v(\texttt{opt})$.

On the other hand, since $k = \min_{i \in \texttt{opt}} \frac{v(\texttt{opt})}{v(i)}$, the solution given by picking the largest item satisfies $\max_i v(i) \geq \frac{1}{k} v(\texttt{opt})$. Combining the two mechanisms together, our main mechanism XOS-MECHANISM-MAIN has a performance of at least

$$\left(\frac{1}{2} \cdot \frac{k-2}{384k} + \frac{1}{2} \cdot \frac{1}{k}\right) v(\texttt{opt}) = \frac{k+382}{768k} v(\texttt{opt}) \geq \frac{1}{768} v(\texttt{opt}).$$

This completes the proof of the lemma. □

3.2 Integrality-Gap Approximations for Subadditive

Next we use our result for XOS functions to design a truthful mechanism for subadditive functions. Let $S_1, \ldots, S_N$ be a permutation of all possible subsets of A, where $N = |2^A|$ is the size of the power set 2^A. We consider the following linear program for each subset $S \subseteq A$, where each subset S_j is associated with a variable α_j.

$$\begin{aligned} LP(S): \quad & \min \sum_{j=1}^{N} \alpha_j \cdot v(S_j) & (\Diamond) \\ & s.t. \quad \alpha_j \geq 0, \quad 1 \leq j \leq N \\ & \sum_{j:\, i \in S_j} \alpha_j \geq 1, \quad \forall\, i \in S \end{aligned}$$

In the above linear program, the minimum is taken over all possible non-negative values of $\alpha = (\alpha_1, \ldots, \alpha_N)$. If we consider each α_j as the fraction of the cover by subset S_j, the last constraint implies that all items in S are fractionally covered. Hence, LP(S) describes a linear program for the set cover of S. For any subadditive function $v(\cdot)$, it can be seen that the value of the optimal integral solution to the above LP(S) is always $v(S)$. Indeed, one has $S \subseteq \bigcup_{j:\, \alpha_j \geq 1} S_j$ and $\sum_j \alpha_j \cdot v(S_j) \geq \sum_{j:\, \alpha_j \geq 1} v(S_j) \geq v\big(\bigcup_{j:\, \alpha_j \geq 1} S_j\big) \geq v(S)$.

Let $\widetilde{v}(S)$ be the value of the optimal fractional solution of LP(S), and $\mathcal{I}(S) = \frac{v(S)}{\widetilde{v}(S)}$ be the integrality gap of LP(S). Let $\mathcal{I} = \max_{S \subseteq A} \mathcal{I}(S)$; the integrality gap $\mathcal{I}$ gives a worst case upper bound on the integrality gap of all subsets. Hence, we have $\frac{v(S)}{\mathcal{I}} \leq \widetilde{v}(S) \leq v(S)$ for any $S \subseteq A$. The classic Bondareva-Shapley Theorem [9, 34] says that the integrality gap $\mathcal{I}(S)$ is one (i.e., $v(S)$ is also an optimal fractional solution to the LP) if and only if $v(\cdot)$ is an XOS function.

LEMMA 3.4. *$\widetilde{v}(\cdot)$ is an XOS function.*

We are now ready to present our mechanism for subadditive functions.

SA-MECHANISM-MAIN

1. For each subset $S \subseteq A$, compute $\widetilde{v}(S)$.
2. Run XOS-MECHANISM-MAIN for the instance with respect to the XOS function $\widetilde{v}(\cdot)$.
3. Output the result of XOS-MECHANISM-MAIN.

THEOREM 3.2. *The mechanism* SA-MECHANISM-MAIN *is budget feasible and truthful, and provides an approximation ratio of $O(\mathcal{I})$ for subadditive functions, where $\mathcal{I}$ is the largest integrality gap of $LP(S)$ for all $S \subseteq A$.*

PROOF. Note that the valuation $v(\cdot)$ is public knowledge and utilities of agents do not depend on $v(\cdot)$; thus computing $\widetilde{v}(\cdot)$ and running XOS-MECHANISM-MAIN with respect to $\widetilde{v}(\cdot)$ do not affect truthfulness. The claim then follows from Theorem 3.1 and the fact that $\frac{v(S)}{\mathcal{I}} \leq \widetilde{v}(S) \leq v(S)$ for any $S \subseteq A$ (i.e., by using $\widetilde{v}(\cdot)$ instead of $v(\cdot)$ we lose at most factor of $\mathcal{I}$ in the approximation ratio). □

In general, the approximation ratio of the mechanism can be as large as $\Theta(\log n)$ [19, 8]. But for those instances when the integrality gap of ($\Diamond$) is bounded by a constant (e.g., facility location [33]), our mechanism gives a constant approximation.

3.3 Sub-Logarithmic Approximations for Subadditive

In this section, we give another mechanism for subadditive functions based on the ideas of random sampling and cost sharing. In contrast to the previous section, the mechanism runs in polynomial time and has an $o(\log n)$ approximation ratio, improving the previously best known ratio $O(\log^2 n)$ [20]. Our mechanism relies on a constant factor approximation *algorithm* for subadditive function maximization under a knapsack constraint, which may have its own interest.

3.3.1 Subadditive Maximization with Budget

We first give an algorithm that approximates $\max_{S\subseteq A} v(S)$ given that $c(S) \le B$. That is, we ignore for a while strategic behaviors of the agents and consider a pure optimization problem. Dobzinski et al. [20] considered the same question and gave a 4-approximation algorithm for the unweighted case (i.e., the restriction is on the size of a selected subset). Our algorithm extends their result to the weighted case and runs in polynomial time if we are given a demand oracle[4].

SA-ALG-MAX

- Let $v^* = \max_{i\in A} v(i)$ and $\mathcal{V} = \{v^*, 2v^*, \dots, nv^*\}$
- For each $v \in \mathcal{V}$
  - Set $p(i) = \frac{v}{2B}\cdot c(i)$ for each $i \in A$, and find $T \in \text{argmax}_{S\subseteq A}\left(v(S) - \sum_{i\in S} p(i)\right)$.
  - Let $S_v = \emptyset$.
  - If $v(T) < \frac{v}{2}$, then continue to next v.
  - Else, in decreasing order of $c(i)$ put items from T into S_v while preserving the budget constraint.
- Output: S_v with the largest value $v(S_v)$ for all $v \in \mathcal{V}$.

LEMMA 3.5. SA-ALG-MAX *is an 8-approximation algorithm for subadditive maximization given a demand oracle.*

Note that we can actually modify the algorithm to get a $(4+\epsilon)$-approximation with running time polynomial in n and $\frac{1}{\epsilon}$. To do so one may simply replace $\mathcal{V}$ by a larger set $\{\epsilon v^*, 2\epsilon v^*, \dots, \lceil\frac{n}{\epsilon}\rceil \epsilon v^*\}$. Both algorithms suffice for our purpose; for the rest of the paper, for simplicity we will use the 8-approximation algorithm to avoid the extra parameter ϵ in the description.

We will use SA-ALG-MAX as a subroutine to build a mechanism SA-RANDOM-SAMPLE for subadditive functions in the next subsection. When there are different sets maximizing $v(S) - \sum_{i\in S} p(i)$, we require that the demand query oracle always returns a fixed set T. This property is important for the truthfulness of our mechanism. To implement this, we set a fixed order on all the items $i_1 \prec i_2 \prec \cdots \prec i_n$. We first compute

$$T_1 \in \underset{S\subseteq A}{\text{argmax}}\left(v(S) - \sum_{i\in S} p(i)\right)$$

and

$$T_2 \in \underset{S\subseteq A\setminus\{i_1\}}{\text{argmax}}\left(v(S) - \sum_{i\in S} p(i)\right).$$

[4]Independent to our work, Badanidiyuru et al. [4] gave a $2+\epsilon$ approximation algorithm to the same weighted problem.

If $v(T_1) - \sum_{i\in T_1} p(i) = v(T_2) - \sum_{i\in T_2} p(i)$, we know that there is a subset without i_1 that gives us the maximum; thus, we ignore i_1 for further consideration. If $v(T_1) - \sum_{i\in T_1} p(i) > v(T_2) - \sum_{i\in T_2} p(i)$, we know that i_1 should be in any optimal solution; hence, we keep i_1 and proceed with the process iteratively for $i_2, i_3, \dots, i_n$. This process clearly gives a fixed outcome that maximizes $v(S) - \sum_{i\in S} p(i)$.

3.3.2 Mechanism

Let us first consider the following mechanism based on random sampling and cost sharing.

SA-RANDOM-SAMPLE

1. Pick each item independently at random with a probability of $\frac{1}{2}$ into group T.
2. Run SA-ALG-MAX for items in group T, and let v be the value of the returned subset.
3. For $k = 1$ to $|A \setminus T|$
   - Run SA-ALG-MAX on the set $\left\{i \in A\setminus T \mid c(i) \le \frac{B}{k}\right\}$ where each item has cost $\frac{B}{k}$, denote the output by X.
   - If $v(X) \ge \frac{\log\log n}{80\log n}\cdot v$
     - Output X as the winning set and pay $\frac{B}{k}$ to each item in X.
     - Halt.
4. Output $\emptyset$.

In the above mechanism, we again first sample in expectation half of the items to form a testing group T, and then use SA-ALG-MAX to compute an approximate solution for the items in T given the budget constraint B. As can be seen in the analysis of the mechanism, the computed value v is in expectation within a constant factor of the optimal value of the whole set A. That is, we are able to learn the rough value of the optimal solution by random sampling. Next we consider the remaining items $A \setminus T$ and try to find a subset X with a relatively big value in which every item is willing to "share" the budget B at a fixed share $\frac{B}{k}$. (This part of our mechanism can be viewed as a reversion of the classic cost sharing mechanism.) Finally, we use the information v from random sampling as a benchmark to determine whether X should be a winning set or not.

The final mechanism for subadditive functions is described as follows.

SA-MECHANISM-MAIN-2

- With half probability, run SA-RANDOM-SAMPLE.
- With half probability, pick a most-valuable item as the only winner and pay him B.

THEOREM 3.3. SA-MECHANISM-MAIN-2 *runs in polynomial time given a demand oracle and is a truthful budget feasible mechanism for subadditive functions with an approximation ratio of* $O(\frac{\log n}{\log\log n})$.

4. BAYESIAN MECHANISM DESIGN

In this section, we study budget feasible mechanisms for subadditive functions from a standard economics viewpoint, where the costs of all agents $(c(i))_{i\in A}$ are drawn from a prior known distribution $\mathcal{D}$. More specifically, the mechanism designer and all participants know $\mathcal{D}$ in advance from which the real cost vector $(c(i))_{i\in A}$ is drawn. However, each $c(i)$ is the private information of agent i. Distribution $\mathcal{D}$ is given on the probability space Ω with the corresponding density function $\rho(\cdot)$ on $\mathbb{R}^{|A|}$. We allow dependencies on the agents' costs in $\mathcal{D}$ and consider the distributions that have integrable marginal densities for any subset of variables[5]; this includes, e.g., independent distributions as special cases.

Every agent submits a bid $b(i)$ as before and seeks to maximize his own utility. We again consider universally truthful mechanisms, i.e., for every coin flips of the mechanism and each cost vector, truth-telling is a dominant strategy for every agent. The performance of a mechanism $\mathcal{M}$ is measured by $\mathbf{E}[\mathcal{M}] = \mathbf{E}_{c\sim\mathcal{D}}[\mathcal{M}(c)]$. We compare a mechanism with the optimal expected value $\mathbf{E}[\texttt{opt}] = \mathbf{E}_{c\sim\mathcal{D}}\left[v(\texttt{opt}(c))\right]$; we say mechanism $\mathcal{M}$ is a (Bayesian) α-approximation if $\frac{\mathbf{E}[\texttt{opt}]}{\mathbf{E}[\mathcal{M}]} \le \alpha$.

In this section: Let $\texttt{opt}_v(c,S)$ denote the winning set in an optimal solution when the valuation function is $v(\cdot)$, the cost vector is c, and the agent set is S (the parameters are omitted if they are clear from the context); let $v(\texttt{opt}_v(c,S))$ denote the value of $\texttt{opt}_v(c,S)$.

Our mechanism is as follows.

SA-BAYESIAN-MECHANISM

- With a probability of $\frac{1}{2}$, let a most-valuable item be the only winner and pay him B.
- With a probability of $\frac{1}{2}$, run the following:
  1. Pick each item independently at random with a probability of $\frac{1}{2}$ into group T.
  2. Compute an optimal solution $\texttt{opt}(c,T)$ for items in T given budget B.
  3. Set a threshold $t = \frac{v(\texttt{opt}(c,T))}{8B}$.
  4. For items in $A\setminus T$ find a set $S^* \in \operatorname{argmax}_{S\subseteq A\setminus T}\{v(S) - t\cdot c(S)\}$.
  5. Sample a cost vector $d\sim\mathcal{D}$ conditioned on
     (a) $d(i)=c(i)$ for each $i\in T$, and
     (b) $S^* \in \operatorname{argmax}_{S\subseteq A\setminus T}\{v(S) - t\cdot d(S)\}$.
  6. If $d(S^*) < B$, let all $i\in S^*$ with $c(i)\le d(i)$ be the winners.
  7. If $d(S^*) \ge B$,
     - run XOS-MECHANISM-MAIN w.r.t. valuation $\widetilde{v}(\cdot)$, set S^*, cost $c(\cdot)$, and budget B.
     - Output the result of XOS-MECHANISM-MAIN.

In the mechanism, Steps (1-3) are the same as XOS-RANDOM-SAMPLE where we randomly sample a test group T and generate a threshold value t. In Steps (4-7), we consider a specific subset $S^*\subseteq A\setminus T$ and select winners only inside of it. Step (5) helps to give us a guidance on the threshold payments of the winners (see more discussions below). Step (7) runs XOS-MECHANISM-MAIN on the function $\widetilde{v}(\cdot)$ (defined as the optimal value of the LP $(\Diamond)$), which is XOS according to Lemma 3.4.

A few remarks about the mechanism are in order.

- It is tempting to remove the random sampling part, as given $\mathcal{D}$ one may consider a 'prior sampling' approach: Generate some virtual instances according to $\mathcal{D}$ and compute a threshold t based on them; then apply this threshold to all agents in A. Interestingly, the prior sampling approach works well in our mechanism when, e.g., all $c(i)$'s are independent, but it does not work for the case when variables are dependent.

  For instance, consider an additive valuation $v(\cdot)$ with $v(S)=|S|$, budget $B=2^k$ for a large k, and a set of $N=2^k$ agents with the following discrete distribution over costs ($c=\ell$ means that every $c(i)=\ell$):

  $$\mathbf{Pr}[c=1] = \frac{1}{2^{k+1}}, \mathbf{Pr}[c=2] = \frac{1}{2^k}, \ldots\ldots,$$
  $$\mathbf{Pr}\left[c=2^k\right] = \frac{1}{2}, \mathbf{Pr}\left[c=2^{k+1}\right] = \frac{1}{2^{k+1}}.$$

  Note that

  $$v(\texttt{opt}(c=1)) = 2^k, v(\texttt{opt}(c=2)) = 2^{k-1}, \ldots\ldots,$$
  $$v\big(\texttt{opt}\big(c=2^k\big)\big) = 1, v\big(\texttt{opt}\big(c=2^{k+1}\big)\big) = 0.$$

  Then the expected optimal value is $\mathbf{E}[\texttt{opt}] = \frac{k+1}{2}$ and it is equally spread over all possible costs except the last one $c=2^{k+1}$. Roughly speaking, on a given instance c, any prior estimate on $v(\texttt{opt}(c))$ that gives a constant approximation only applies to a constant number of distinct costs (the contribution of these cases to $\mathbf{E}[\texttt{opt}]$ is negligible). Hence for almost all other possible costs, we get a meaningless estimate for $\texttt{opt}(c)$. Therefore, the prior sampling will lead to a bad approximation ratio.

- Why do we generate another cost vector d in Step (5)? Recall that our target winner set is S^*, whose value $v(S^*)$ in expectation gives a constant approximation of $\mathbf{E}[\texttt{opt}]$. However, we are faced with the problems of selecting a winning set in S^* with a sufficiently large value and distributing the budget among the winners. These two problems together are closely related to cooperative game theory and the notion of approximate core. For subadditive functions, a constant approximate core may not exist [33] (e.g., set cover gives a logarithmic lower bound [8]). Thus we might not be able to pick a winning set with a constant approximation and set threshold payments in accordance with the valuation function. The question then is: Is there any other guidance we can take to bound budget feasible threshold payments and give a constant approximation?

  Our solution is to use another random vector d to serve as such a guidance. (Conditions in Steps (5a) and (5b), from a high level point of view, guarantee that the vector d is not too 'far' from c for the agents in S^*, in the sense that both vectors are derived from the same distribution. Thus, cost vectors c and d are distributed symmetrically and can be switched while preserving

[5]We need some mild technical restriction on $\mathcal{D}$ in order to sample a conditioned random variable. We assume that the density function $\rho(\cdot)$ of $\mathcal{D}$ is integrable over each subset $S\subseteq A$ of its variables for any choice of the rest parameters, i.e., $\rho(c_{A\setminus S}) = \int_\Omega \rho(c)\,dx_S$ is bounded. This condition is reminiscent of integrability of marginal density functions (see, e.g., page 331 of [36]), though in our case we require a slightly stronger condition.

some important parameters such as t and S^* in expectation.) If $d(S^*) \leq B$ (Step (6)), then we set $d(i)$ as an upper bound on the payment of each agent $i \in S^*$; this guarantees that we are always within the budget constraint. If $d(S^*) > B$, setting $d(i)$ as an upper bound is not sufficient to ensure budget feasibility; then we adopt our approach for XOS functions with inputs subset S^* and XOS valuation $\widetilde{v}(\cdot)$ defined by ($\Diamond$).

THEOREM 4.1. SA-BAYESIAN-MECHANISM *is a universally truthful budget feasible mechanism for subadditive functions and gives in expectation a constant approximation.*

Budget feasibility follows simply from the description of the mechanism and the fact that XOS-MECHANISM-MAIN is budget feasible.

For universal truthfulness, we note that in the mechanism, the sampled vector d comes from a distribution that depends on actual bid vector c. To see why our mechanism takes a distribution over deterministic truthful mechanisms, we can describe all possible samples d for (i) all possible cost vectors on T and (ii) all possible choices $S \subseteq A \backslash T$ of S^*; then we tell all flipped d's to the agents before looking at the costs of T. (Practically, we can provide all our randomness as a black box accessible by all agents.) Note that the selection rule of S^* is monotone, and, similarly to Claim 3.2, each agent in S^* cannot manipulate (i) the composition of S^* given c and T, and (ii) the choice of d, as long as he stays in S^*. Therefore, composing the first part choosing S^* (Step (4)) with the next monotone rule picking winners in S^* (Steps (6-7)), we again get a monotone winner selection rule. Hence, the mechanism is universally truthful.

Next we give a sketch of the idea of proving the constant approximation. Details of the proof are deferred to the full version of the paper.

Approximation analysis (sketch). We sketch the proof idea of the approximation ratio of the mechanism. First, similar to our analysis in Section 3.1, the optimal solution $v(\mathtt{opt}(c,T))$ obtained from random sampling in expectation gives a constant approximation to the optimal solution $\mathbf{E}[\mathtt{opt}]$. Further, we observe the following facts (which are reminiscent of Claim 3.1):

$$\widetilde{v}(S) - t \cdot c(S) \geq 0 \text{ and } \widetilde{v}(S) - t \cdot d(S) \geq 0, \quad \forall S \subseteq S^*$$

where the second inequality is based on the conditional distribution we choose for d.

If $c(S^*) \geq B$ and $d(S^*) \geq B$ (i.e., the mechanism runs Step (7)), we can pick a subset $S^0 \subseteq S^*$ with $B \geq c(S^0) \geq \frac{B}{2}$. By Theorem 3.1, XOS-MECHANISM-MAIN gives a constant approximation to the optimum of $\widetilde{v}(\cdot)$ on S^*. (This is the reason why in Step (7) of the mechanism, we run the whole XOS-MECHANISM-MAIN on the input instance $\widetilde{v}(\cdot)$ and S^*.) Hence,

$$\widetilde{v}(\mathtt{opt}_{\widetilde{v}}(c, S^*)) \geq \widetilde{v}(S^0) \geq t \cdot c(S^0) \geq t \cdot \frac{B}{2} \geq \frac{v(\mathtt{opt}(c,T))}{16},$$

where the first inequality follows from the fact that $S^0 \subseteq S^*$ is a budget feasible set. Thus, the optimum of $\widetilde{v}(\cdot)$ on S^* is within a constant factor of $v(\mathtt{opt}(c,T))$, as well as the benchmark $\mathbf{E}[\mathtt{opt}]$.

If $c(S^*) < B$ and $d(S^*) \geq B$, we have $\widetilde{v}(S^*) \geq t \cdot d(S^*) \geq \frac{v(\mathtt{opt}(c,T))}{8}$. Further, we notice that S^* is budget feasible with respect to cost vector c; thus, XOS-MECHANISM-MAIN gives a constant approximation to $\widetilde{v}(S^*)$, which in turn is within a constant factor of $v(\mathtt{opt}(c,T))$ and $\mathbf{E}[\mathtt{opt}]$.

We observe that the vectors d and c are restricted to the agents in S^* and conditioned on

$$S^* \in \underset{S \subseteq A \backslash T}{\operatorname{argmax}} \{v(S) - t \cdot d(S)\}$$

and

$$S^* \in \underset{S \subseteq A \backslash T}{\operatorname{argmax}} \{v(S) - t \cdot c(S)\}$$

have exactly the same distributions. Therefore, due to such a symmetry between d and c, in a run of our mechanism in expectation we will have the outcome T, t, S^* and a pair of vectors (c, d) as often as the outcome T, t, S^* and the pair (d, c). This implies that in the case when $d(S^*) < B$ and $c(S^*) < B$, we get on average a value of at least $\frac{1}{2}v(S^*)$, since (i) the winning sets on the two instances where c (resp., d) is the private cost and d (resp., c) is the sampled cost altogether cover S^*, and (ii) v is a subadditive function. By the choice of threshold t, we also know that

$$\begin{aligned} v(S^*) &\geq v(S^*) - t \cdot c(S^*) \\ &\geq v(\mathtt{opt}(c, A \setminus T)) - t \cdot c(\mathtt{opt}(c, A \setminus T)) \\ &\geq v(\mathtt{opt}(c, A \setminus T)) - t \cdot B. \end{aligned}$$

Thus, our mechanism gives a constant approximation to $v(\mathtt{opt}(c))$ with some constant probability.

The last case is when $c(S^*) \geq B$ and $d(S^*) < B$. Again due to the symmetry between c and d, intuitively, we can treat this case as the above one when c and d are switched; thus we also get a constant approximation of $\mathbf{E}[\mathtt{opt}]$. (The formal argument, however, due to multiple randomness used in the mechanism, is much more complicated.)

Therefore, the mechanism SA-BAYESIAN-MECHANISM on average has a constant approximation of the expected socially optimal value $\mathbf{E}[\mathtt{opt}]$. □

5. CONCLUSIONS

Our work considers budget feasible mechanism design in two analysis frameworks: prior-free and Bayesian. For XOS functions, we give a prior-free constant approximation mechanism. For subadditive functions, we present two prior-free mechanisms with integrality-gap and sub-logarithmic approximations, respectively, as well as a Bayesian constant approximation mechanism. All our mechanisms are universally truthful.

Our mechanisms continue to work for the extension when the valuation functions are non-monotone, i.e., $v(S)$ is not necessarily less than $v(T)$ for any $S \subset T \subseteq A$. For instance, the cut function studied in [20] is non-monotone. For such functions, we can define $\hat{v}(S) = \max_{T \subseteq S} v(T)$ for any $S \subseteq A$. It is easy to see that $\hat{v}(\cdot)$ can be computed easily given a demand oracle, is monotone, and inherits the classification of $v(\cdot)$. Further, any solution maximizing $v(\cdot)$ is also an optimal solution of $\hat{v}(\cdot)$. Hence, we can apply our mechanisms to $\hat{v}(\cdot)$ directly and obtain the same approximations.

We give a constant approximation mechanism for subadditive functions in the Bayesian framework where the costs are drawn from a given *known* distribution. Considering the gap between Bayesian and prior-free, a natural question is under which frameworks a constant approximation mechanism still exists. An interesting step along this direction is the prior-independent setting, where the costs are still drawn from an underlying distribution, but the mechanism designer does not have the prior knowledge of it. Our mechanism SA-BAYESIAN-MECHANISM can be adopted to the framework where all the costs are identically and independently distributed. (Specifically, by random sampling we are able to learn the underlying unknown distribution with sufficient precision.) However, we do not know how to handle independent but not necessarily identical distributions in the prior-independent framework, as well as the most general prior-free setting in the worst-case analysis.

Indeed, whether subadditive functions admit a prior-free constant approximation mechanism still remains an open problem. Our results show a separation between XOS and subadditive functions. Another angle to have such a distinction between the two classes is from exponential concentration: In the case of XOS the valuation of a randomly selected subset obeys an exponential concentration around its expected value[6], whereas in the case of general subadditive valuations it does not (see [39] for a counterexample). Such a difference on exponential concentration may suggest a possible distinction between XOS and subadditive functions in terms of their approximability in (budget feasible) mechanism design.

For those mechanisms with exponential runtime, it is natural to ask if there are truthful designs with the same approximations that can be implemented in polynomial time. Further, all of our mechanisms are randomized; it is intriguing to consider the approximability of deterministic mechanisms. We leave these questions as future work.

Acknowledgements

We thank the anonymous reviewers for their helpful comments. We are grateful to Jason Hartline for many valuable suggestions on exploiting intuitions of the mechanisms (in particular, the connection to Lagrangian).

6. REFERENCES

[1] G. Aggarwal, J. Hartline, *Knapsack Auctions*, SODA 2006, 1083-1092.

[2] M. Babaioff, M. Dinitz, A. Gupta, N. Immorlica, K. Talwar: *Secretary Problems: Weights and Discounts*, SODA 2009, 1245-1254.

[3] M. Babaioff, N. Immorlica, R. Kleinberg, *Matroids, Secretary Problems, and Online Mechanisms*, SODA 2007, 434-443.

[4] A. Badanidiyuru, S. Dobzinski, S. Oren, *Optimization with Demand Oracles*, arXiv.org/abs/1107.2869.

[5] X. Bei, Z. Huang, *Bayesian Incentive Compatibility via Fractional Assignments*, SODA 2011, 720-733.

[6] A. Berger, V. Bonifaci, F. Grandoni, G. Schafer, *Budgeted Matching and Budgeted Matroid Intersection via the Gasoline Puzzle*, Math. Program., V.128, 355-372, 2011.

[7] S. Bhattacharya, G. Goel, S. Gollapudi, K. Munagala, *Budget Constrained Auctions with Heterogeneous Items*, STOC 2010, 379-388.

[8] K. Bhawalkar, T. Roughgarden, *Welfare Guarantees for Combinatorial Auctions with Item Bidding*, SODA 2011, 700-709.

[9] O. Bondareva, *Some Applications of Linear Programming to Cooperative Games*, Problemy Kibernetiki, V.10, 119-139, 1963.

[6]Note that this fact can be used to improve the approximation ratios of the mechanisms of XOS functions substantially (but still up to a constant factor).

[10] S. Boucheron, G. Lugosi, P. Massart. *Concentration Inequalities Using the Entropy Method*, Annals of Probability, V.31, 1583-1614, 2003.

[11] S. Chawla, J. Hartline, D. Malec, and B. Sivan, *Multi-Parameter Mechanism Design and Sequential Posted Pricing*, STOC 2010, 311-320.

[12] S. Chawla, D. Malec, A. Malekian, *Bayesian Mechanism Design for Budget-Constrained Agents*, EC 2011, 253-262.

[13] S. Chawla, D. Malec, B. Sivan, *The Power of Randomness in Bayesian Optimal Mechanism Design*, EC 2010, 149-158.

[14] N. Chen, N. Gravin, P. Lu, *On the Approximability of Budget Feasible Mechanisms*, SODA 2011, 685-699.

[15] N. Chen, N. Gravin, P. Lu, *Mechanism Design without Money via Stable Matching*, arxiv.org/abs/1104.2872.

[16] E. Clarke, *Multipart Pricing of Public Goods*, Public Choice, V.11, 17-33, 1971.

[17] N. Devanur, J. Hartline, A. Karlin, T. Nguyen, *A Prior-Independent Mechanism for Profit Maximization in Unit-demand Combinatorial Auctions*, WINE 2011.

[18] P. Dhangwatnotai, T. Roughgarden, Q. Yan, *Revenue Maximization with a Single Sample*, EC 2010, 129-138.

[19] S. Dobzinski, *Two Randomized Mechanisms for Combinatorial Auctions*, APPROX 2007, 89-103.

[20] S. Dobzinski, C. Papadimitriou, Y. Singer, *Mechanisms for Complement Free Procurement*, EC 2011, 273-282.

[21] U. Feige, *On Maximizing Welfare When Utility Functions Are Subadditive*, SIAM J. Computing, V.39, 122-142, 2009.

[22] A. Ghosh, A. Roth, *Selling Privacy at Auction*, EC 2011, 199-208.

[23] A. Goldberg, J. Hartline, A. Karlin, M. Saks, A. Wright, *Competitive Auctions*, Games and Economic Behavior, V.55(2), 242-269, 2006.

[24] T. Groves, *Incentives in Teams*, Econometrica, V.41, 617-631, 1973.

[25] J. Hartline, R. Kleinberg, A. Malekian, *Bayesian Incentive Compatibility via Matchings*, SODA 2011, 734-747.

[26] J. Hartline, B. Lucier, *Bayesian Algorithmic Mechanism Design*, STOC 2010, 301-310.

[27] J. Hartline, T. Roughgarden, *Optimal Mechanism Design and Money Burning*, STOC 2008, 75-84.

[28] J. Hartline, T. Roughgarden, *Simple versus Optimal Mechanisms*, EC 2009, 225-234.

[29] B. Lehmann, D. Lehmann, N. Nisan, *Combinatorial Auctions with Decreasing Marginal Utilities*, EC 2001, 18-28.

[30] P. Milgrom, *Putting Auction Theory to Work*, Cambridge University Press, 2004.

[31] R. Myerson, *Optimal Auction Design*, Mathematics of Operations Research, V.6(1), 1981.

[32] N. Nisan, A. Ronen, *Algorithmic Mechanism Design*, STOC 1999, 129-140.

[33] N. Nisan, T. Roughgarden, E. Tardos, V. Vazirani, *Algorithmic Game Theory*, Cambridge University Press, 2007.

[34] L. Shapley, *On Balanced Sets and Cores*, Naval Research Logistics Quarterly, V.14, 453-460, 1967.

[35] Y. Singer, *Budget Feasible Mechanisms*, FOCS 2010, 765-774.

[36] C. Stone, *A Course in Probability and Statistics*, Duxbury Press, 1995.

[37] M. Sviridenko, *A Note on Maximizing a Submodular Set Function Subject to Knapsack Constraint*, Operations Research Letters, V.32, 41-43, 2004.

[38] W. Vickrey, *Counterspeculation, Auctions and Competitive Sealed Tenders*, Journal of Finance, V.16, 8-37, 1961.

[39] J. Vondrak, *A Note on Concentration of Submodular Functions*, arxiv.org/abs/1005.2791.

An Algorithmic Characterization of Multi-Dimensional Mechanisms

[Extended Abstract] *

Yang Cai†
EECS, MIT
Cambridge, MA
ycai@csail.mit.edu

Constantinos Daskalakis‡
EECS, MIT
Cambridge, MA
costis@mit.edu

S. Matthew Weinberg§
EECS, MIT
Cambridge, MA
smw79@mit.edu

ABSTRACT

We show that every feasible, Bayesian, multi-item multi-bidder mechanism for independent, additive bidders can be implemented as a mechanism that: (a) allocates every item independently of the other items; (b) for the allocation of each item it uses a strict ordering of all bidders' types; and allocates the item using a distribution over hierarchical mechanisms that iron this ordering into a non-strict ordering, and give the item uniformly at random to the bidders whose reported types dominate all other reported types according to the non-strict ordering. Combined with cyclic-monotonicity our results provide a characterization of feasible, Bayesian Incentive Compatible mechanisms in this setting.

Our characterization is enabled by a new, constructive proof of Border's theorem [Bor91], and a new generalization of this theorem to independent (but not necessarily identically distributed) bidders, improving upon the results of [Bor07, CKM11]. For a single item and independent bidders, we show that every feasible reduced form auction can be implemented as a distribution over hierarchical mechanisms that are consistent with the same strict ordering of all bidders' types, which every mechanism in the support of the distribution irons to a non-strict ordering. We also give a polynomial-time algorithm for determining feasibility of a reduced form auction, or providing a separation hyperplane from the set of feasible reduced forms. To complete the picture, we provide polynomial-time algorithms to find and exactly sample from a distribution over hierarchical mechanisms consistent with a given feasible reduced form. All these results generalize to multi-item reduced form auctions for independent, additive bidders. Finally, for multiple items, additive bidders with hard demand constraints, and arbitrary value correlation across items or bidders, we give a proper generalization of Border's Theorem, and characterize feasible reduced form auctions as multi-commodity flows in related multi-commodity flow instances. We also show that our generalization holds for a broader class of feasibility constraints, including the intersection of any two matroids.

As a corollary of our results we compute revenue-optimal, Bayesian Incentive Compatible (BIC) mechanisms in multi-item multi-bidder settings, when each bidder has arbitrarily correlated values over the items and additive valuations over bundles of items, and the bidders are independent. Our mechanisms run in time polynomial in the total number of bidder types (and not type profiles). This running time is polynomial in the number of bidders, but potentially exponential in the number of items. We improve the running time to polynomial in both the number of items and the number of bidders by using recent structural results on optimal BIC auctions in item-symmetric settings [DW11].

Categories and Subject Descriptors

J.4 [**Computer Applications**]: SOCIAL AND BEHAVIORAL SCIENCES—*Economics*; F.2.2 [**Analysis of Algorithms and Problem Complexity**]: ANALYSIS OF ALGORITHMS AND PROBLEM COMPLEXITY—*Nonnumerical Algorithms and Problems*

Keywords

Optimal Mechanism Design, Multidimensional Mechanisms, Border's Theorem

1. INTRODUCTION

In its most general form mechanism design is the task of selecting outcomes and charging prices in a way that maximizes some objective such as revenue or social-welfare. Accordingly, to specify a mechanism one needs to provide two, possibly randomized, functions: one that maps bids to outcomes, and another mapping bids to prices charged to the bidders. Consider, e.g., a setting where n items are (simultaneously) auctioned to m bidders. For every possible collection of bids the mechanism needs to specify (a) a possibly randomized allocation of items to bidders; and (b) a

†Supported by NSF Award CCF-0953960 (CAREER) and CCF-1101491.
‡Supported by a Sloan Foundation Fellowship and NSF Award CCF-0953960 (CAREER) and CCF-1101491.
§Supported by a NSF Graduate Research Fellowship and NSF Award CCF-0953960 (CAREER).
*Due to space constraints, the complete proofs of our claims can be found in the full version of our paper [CDW11] at `http://arxiv.org/abs/1112.4572`

STOC'12, May 19–22, 2012, New York, New York, USA.

possibly randomized collection of prices charged to them. The latter can be typically summarized by its expectation, which is just a vector of real numbers, recording the price charged to each bidder. But the former is a distribution over allocations and, in principle, would require $(m+1)^n$ probabilities to be specified, making such explicit specification completely impractical. It turns out that this calculation is too pessimistic, and the Birkhoff-von Neumann decomposition theorem allows one to summarize a randomized allocation by just providing its marginal allocation probabilities $\phi = \{\phi_{ij}\}_{ij}$, where ϕ_{ij} is the probability that item j is given to bidder i [DFK11]. All that these probabilities need to satisfy to be consistent with a joint allocation distribution is that no item is given out more than once in expectation, and no bidder gets more items than she wants (if she has any demand constraints).

Yet, the above description is still too demanding as, even when every bidder can place c possible bids to specify her preferences over the items, there are c^m possible bid vectors, and the mechanism needs to specify what to do for each. To decrease the specification complexity to linear in the number of bidders one can use the *reduced form of the mechanism*, which specifies a pair of possibly randomized allocation and price functions *per bidder*. In particular, if T_i denotes the possible bids that bidder i can submit,[1] the reduced form of the mechanism provides a collection $\mathcal{R} := \{(\pi_i : T_i \to [0,1]^n, p_i : T_i \to \mathbb{R})\}_i$ of functions such that, for all $t_i \in T_i$ and all j, $\pi_{ij}(t_i)$ is the marginal probability (over the randomness in the mechanism and the uncertainty about the bids submitted by the other bidders) that item j is allocated to bidder i when she reports t_i, and $p_i(t_i)$ is the expected price she pays. Indeed, the functions π_i and p_i provide sufficient information for the bidder to decide what bid in T_i optimizes her utility in expectation. The trouble is that, unless the uncertainty over the other bids can be modeled probabilistically, the notion of a marginal allocation probability π_{ij} is ill-defined.

Indeed, one can go around this obstacle by making average-case assumptions about the preferences of bidders [Mye81]. In particular, it is assumed that every bidder has a *type* $t_i \in T_i$ (forgive the temporary overload of notation), and that the joint type profile of the bidders is sampled from some known, joint distribution $\mathcal{D}$ over $\times_i T_i$. Now, the Revelation Principle implies that every auction is strategically equivalent to one where bidders submit not generic bids, but truthfully report their exact type. Hence w.l.o.g. we can restrict our attention to mechanisms where the bid space of bidder i is just T_i (`EndOf overload of notation`), and where the distribution of bids that bidders submit is exactly $\mathcal{D}$. For such auctions, the reduced form is perfectly well-defined. But a challenge remains: What conditions are necessary and sufficient for a reduced form $\{\pi_i\}_i$ to be feasible, i.e. correspond to a feasible auction (that never over-allocates items)? Can these conditions be verified in polynomial-time? And, given a feasible reduced form can we compute an auction implementing it in polynomial-time?

Before studying these questions, why do we even care? Even without answers, mechanism design has made great progress in designing auctions, which optimize various objectives in a wide-range of settings. When the objective is social-welfare, there is an optimal auction with a very clean allocation rule, namely the VCG auction [Vic61, Cla71, Gro73]. The auction always chooses the welfare-maximizing allocation, and just charges prices to ensure incentive compatibility. When the objective is revenue, things get more murky. Still, when we are auctioning a single item to bidders whose values are independently sampled from known distributions, we can employ Myerson's celebrated, revenue-optimal auction [Mye81]. Its allocation rule is still rather clean: it always chooses the allocation that maximizes virtual surplus, and just charges prices to ensure incentive compatibility.

While in the above cases we have clean allocation rules, these results remain quite exceptional. In particular, there is no known simple characterization of the set of all feasible single-item mechanisms, and (prior to this work) it is unclear if there is one. Additionally, it seems unlikely that there is a clean allocation rule implementing the revenue-optimal multi-item mechanism. Understanding the set of feasible multi-item mechanisms is therefore a crucial step along the path to understanding revenue-optimal mechanisms in this setting.

Indeed, in the past decades a large body of research in Economics has been devoted to finding revenue-optimal mechanisms (extending Myeson's result) to multi-item settings, but progress has been sporadic (see survey [MV07] and its references). More recently the problem has entered Theory of Computation, and there has been a number of results obtaining constant factor approximations in polynomial time [Ala11, BGGM10, CHMS10]. Our slow progress towards exactly optimal mechanisms is intimately related to the lack of a characterization result of feasible mechanisms. Loosely speaking, all known algorithms optimize using relaxed feasibility constraints for the reduced form of the mechanism, such as "every item can be awarded at most once in expectation" [Ala11, BGGM10] or "the expected number of items awarded from every subset must not exceed its rank" [CHMS10]. Using such relaxed feasibility constraints, the optimal (possibly infeasible) reduced form is found. To turn this into a feasible reduced form, some "rounding procedure" is applied; this procedure may be just scaling the allocation probabilities down by a constant so that no item is over-allocated [Ala11, BGGM10], or may invoke prophet inequalities [Ala11, CHMS10]. However, rounding comes with a loss in revenue. In view of this computational experience with the problem, it is crucial to try to characterize the feasible reduced forms exactly in a way that makes optimization tractable.

In this paper we carry out this program. We obtain characterization results for the set of all feasible single-item mechanisms (for independent bidders), as well as the set of all feasible multiple-item mechanisms when the bidders have arbitrarily correlated additive valuations over bundles of items (but there is no correlation across bidders). Our characterization results (explained in Section 3.2) are based on obtaining new, algorithmically constructive proofs of Border's theorem [Bor91] and recent extensions of this theorem [Bor07, CKM11], which are overviewed in Section 3.1. Using these constructive proofs and our characterization results, we compute revenue-optimal, Bayesian Incentive Compatible (BIC) mechanisms in multi-item multi-bidder settings, when each bidder has arbitrarily correlated values over the items and additive valuations over bundles of items, and the bidders are independent. Our mechanisms run in time polynomial

[1]We won't make any assumptions about T_i, except that it is measurable. In particular, it won't necessarily be a subset of $\mathbb{R}$, unless otherwise specified.

in the total number of bidder types, $\sum_i |T_i|$. This running time is polynomial in the number of bidders, but potentially exponential in the number of items. We improve the running time to polynomial in both the number of items and the number of bidders, by using recent structural results on optimal BIC auctions in symmetric settings [DW11]. These results are overviewed in Section 3.3. In Section 3.4 we present a generalization of Border's theorem to the multi-item setting where values are arbitrarily correlated across both items and bidders, and bidders have additive valuations with hard demand constraints, and provide a multi-commodity flow interpretation of this problem. In addition, we show that our generalization holds for a broader class of feasibility constraints. Simply put, our generalization holds in all instances where the feasibility constraints can be written as a system of inequalities that are linear in the marginal allocation probabilities (ϕ_{ij}'s). This includes feasibility constraints that are the intersection of any two matroids, as well as many other set systems [Sch03]. After a brief enumeration of our theorems and a couple of figures summarizing our results, we fix our notation and proceed to the technical sections.

Our main results are the following:

1. Theorems 2 and 6 state our main algorithmic results. We show that, if a reduced form auction for independent bidders and a single item is given to us as input, we can determine if the auction is feasible or not in polynomial-time. If it is feasible, we can compute a process that implements it in polynomial-time. If it is infeasible, then in polynomial-time we can provide a hyperplane separating it from the set of feasible reduced forms. These results extend to multi-item settings with additive, independent bidders and arbitrary correlation in the values of each bidder for the items.

2. Theorems 3 and 7 comprise the core of our characterization theorem. We show that every feasible reduced form auction for a single item and independent bidders can be implemented as a distribution over hierarchical mechanisms. The hierarchical mechanisms in the support of the distribution are consistent with the same strict ordering of all bidders' types; and every mechanism irons this ordering into a non-strict ordering, and always allocates the item uniformly at random among the bidders whose reported types dominate all other reported types according to the non-strict ordering. Using these theorems we obtain a clean characterization of the allocation rule of all multidimensional mechanisms in multi-item settings with independent, additive bidders and arbitrary correlation in the values of each bidder for the items. Our general characterization result is provided in Section 3.2.

3. Theorem 4 provides our analog of Myerson's virtual values. It states that we can transform the πs, i.e. the marginal probabilities of a reduced form, into *virtual* πs such that the total ordering of the types (across different bidders) induced by the virtual πs allows us to, in linear time, verify the feasibility of a reduced form auction or output a hyperplane separating it from the set of feasible reduced forms.

4. Theorems 8 through 11 provide algorithms for the computation of revenue-optimal mechanisms in multi-bidder multi-item settings for independent bidders with additive valuations. Figure 2 summarizes our results, placing them in context of what was known before. We note that it is folklore knowledge how to compute the revenue-optimal mechanisms in time $\prod_i |T_i|$ using linear programming (see, e.g., [DW11]). The interesting aspect of the algorithms recorded in the figure is that they overcome the exponentiality of the running time in the number of bidders.

5. Finally, Theorem 12 proves a generalization of Border's Theorem to a broad class of feasibility constraints that includes the case of many items, many additive bidders with hard demand constraints, and arbitrary value correlation across items or bidders.

Figures 1 and 2 summarize the current state of affairs on the two fronts studied in this paper. The first figure is on characterizing the allocation rule of feasible reduced forms and implementing it in polynomial-time, while the second is on solving the optimal multi-dimensional mechanism design problem in polynomial-time. The second figure only records mechanisms that achieve optimal or near-optimal revenue, i.e. come ϵ-close to optimal revenue for arbitrary accuracy ϵ. In particular, we do not quote constant factor approximations [Ala11, BGGM10, CHMS10], which are not the focus of this work. The "Item-Symmetric" column of the second figure refers to settings that are symmetric with respect to the items (see Section 3.3 for a formal definition of such settings and [DW11] for a formal definition and discussion), while the "Bidder-Symmetric" column to settings that are symmetric with respect to the bidders (see Section 3.3 and [DW11]). Moreover, the "Many items, Few bidders" row refers to settings where the number of bidders is an absolute constant but the number of items, n, is allowed to scale, and the "Few items, Many bidders" row refers to settings where the number of items is held constant but the number of bidders, m, is allowed to scale. In the cells of the same table we stress components of the running time/the setting that are the best we could hope for, and do not stress components that could be improved upon, leaving these improvements to future work. Finally, we use MHR to denote Monotone Hazard Rate (see Section 2 for a formal definition of MHR distributions) and we also use the concept of a polynomial-time approximation scheme, which is formally defined in Section 2.

Related Work.

A necessary and sufficient condition for the feasibility of a single-item bidder-symmetric reduced form was provided by Border [Bor91], building on prior work by Maskin and Riley [MR84] and Matthews [Mat84]. A simpler proof of Border's theorem and alternative criteria for feasibility were also provided by Hart and Reny [HR11]. Border's condition for the symmetric setting was generalized to the asymmetric setting by Border [Bor07] and Che et al. [CKM11]. Nevertheless, these results cannot be exploited algorithmically to compute optimal mechanisms, because either they do not lead to polynomial-time separation oracles for the feasibility of a reduced form, or they do not allow for implementing the computed reduced forms in polynomial-time, or both. The results of the present paper fill this gap, and at the same time provide a compelling characterization of the allocation rule of all feasible single-item mechanisms, as well as multi-item mechanisms for independent, additive bidders.

	Necessary &Sufficient Feasibility Conditions	Polynomial-time Implementation	Characterization of Feasible Mechanisms
Independent Bidders, No Demand Constraints	[Bor91], [Bor07] [CKM11]	**[this work]**	**[this work]**
Correlated Bidders, Demand Constraints, and Broader Settings†	**[this work]**	Open Question	Open Question

†: See Section 3.4.

Figure 1: Feasibility, Implementation and Characterization of Reduced Form Multi-Item Auctions. The bidders are assumed to be additive up to (if stated) some hard demand constraint. Both lines of the table allow correlation of values across different items, but the first row assumes that bidders have independent valuations while the second also allows correlation across bidders.

A manuscript with our results and all proofs that have been omitted from this extended abstract due to space constraints can be found on `arxiv.org` (submission date: December 20, 2011) [CDW11]. It has been communicated to us by [AFH$^+$11] that, independently from our work, they had also obtained polynomial-time algorithms for checking the feasibility of a given single-item reduced form, when the bidders are independent, as well algorithms for implementing the reduced form, if it is feasible (i.e. a result that would accompany our result in the top row and middle column of Figure 1 but only for single-item reduced forms). A manuscript with their results can be found on `arxiv.org` (submission date: March 22, 2012) [AFH$^+$12].

2. PRELIMINARIES AND NOTATION

Throughout the paper, we denote the number of bidders by m and the number of items by n. We also use T_i to denote the types of bidder i. We make no assumptions about T_i except that it is measurable. In particular, it is not assumed that T_i is a subset of $\mathbb{R}$, and it could well be multidimensional; e.g., when a bidder has additive valuations, the type of the bidder could be just a vector specifying how much she values each of the items. To obtain computationally meaningful results, we assume in Sections 3.1, 3.2 and 3.4 that the type sets $\{T_i\}_i$ are finite (as opposed to continuous/infinite, but not of constant size), and in this case use c as a shorthand for $\max_i |T_i|$. However, our results in Section 3.3 apply also to continuous type spaces, since when the type distributions are bounded or when they are unbounded but satisfy the *Monotone Hazard Rate* tail condition,[2] we can truncate and discretize the support of the distribution and still get nearly optimal ϵ-BIC mechanisms (Definition 1) using the techniques of [CD11] or [DW11]. We can then employ the ϵ-BIC to BIC reduction of [DW11] to get nearly optimal BIC mechanisms. See Section 3.3 for details.

To ease notation, we just use A (B, C, etc.) to denote the *type* of a bidder, without emphasizing whether it is a vector or a scalar. The elements of $\times_i T_i$ are called *type profiles*, and specify a type for every bidder. We assume type profiles are sampled from a distribution $\mathcal{D}$ over $\times_i T_i$. We denote by $\mathcal{D}_i$ the marginal of this distribution on bidder i's type, and use $\mathcal{D}_{-i}$ to denote the marginal of $\mathcal{D}$ over the types of all bidders, except bidder i. We use t_i for the random variable representing the type of bidder i. So when we write $\Pr[t_i = A]$, we mean the probability that bidder i's type is A. In the i.i.d. case, because $\Pr[t_i = A]$ is the same for all i, we will just write $\Pr[A]$.

The *reduced form* of a mechanism is a vector function $\pi(\cdot)$, specifying values $\pi_{ij}(A)$, for all items j, bidders i and types $A \in T_i$. $\pi_{ij}(A)$ is the probability that bidder i receives item j when reporting type A, where the probability is over the randomness of all other bidders' types and the internal randomness of the mechanism, assuming that the other bidders report their true types to the mechanism. When we only consider a single item (case $n = 1$), we drop the item subscript from the π_{ij}'s, writing $\pi_i(A)$ for the probability that the item is allocated to bidder i. In this case we may think of $\pi(\cdot)$ as a vector in $[0,1]^{\sum_i |T_i|}$. To emphasize the vector-view of the reduced form we may write $\vec{\pi}$ for the reduced form.

Sometimes we will be considering settings where the bidders are i.i.d., i.e. $T_i = T_{i'} = T$, for all i and i', and $\mathcal{D}$ is a product distribution over $\times_i T_i$ with the same marginal on every bidder. In such settings, we may be looking at *bidder-symmetric* reduced forms, satisfying $\pi_{ij}(A) = \pi_{i'j}(A)$, for all $j, i, i', A \in T$. In such cases, we will drop the bidder subscript from the π_{ij}'s, writing $\pi_j(A)$, for the probability that a bidder of type $A \in T$ receives item j, over the randomness of the mechanism and the types of the other bidders, assuming that the other bidders report their true types to the mechanism. If there is a single item and the reduced form is bidder-symmetric, we will drop both subscripts writing $\pi(A)$ for the same probability. In this case, we may think of the reduced form as a vector $\vec{\pi}$ in $[0,1]^{|T|}$.

Given a reduced form π of a mechanism we will be interested in whether the form can be "implemented". By this we mean designing a feasible mechanism M (i.e. one that never over-allocates items) such that the probability $M_{ij}(A)$ that bidder i receives item j when she reports type A to the mechanism is exactly $\pi_{ij}(A)$, where the probability is computed with respect to the randomness in the mechanism and the randomness in the types of the other bidders, assuming that the other bidders report their true types to the mechanism. In fact, we will relax this requirement and say that a mechanism M implements the reduced form π if $M_{ij}(A) \geq \pi_{ij}(A)$, for all i, j, A. This is because we can trivially modify such a mechanism so that all constraints are tight. Indeed, if $M_{ij}(A) = x \cdot \pi_{ij}(A)$ for some $i, j, A, x > 1$, we can rectify the mechanism as follows: whenever M wants to allocate item j to bidder i when he has reported type A, we instead throw the item away with probability $\frac{x-1}{x}$. It's easy to see that

[2] We say that a one-dimensional differentiable distribution F satisfies Monotone Hazard Rate, or succinctly MHR, if $\frac{f(x)}{1-F(x)}$ is monotonically non-decreasing in its domain, where $f = F'$ is the probability density function.

	Item-Symmetric	Bidder-Symmetric	**No Symmetries**
Many items, Few bidders	**poly(n)**†, **demand constraints allowed, item correlation allowed** [DW11]	Same as ⟶	**poly(n)**§, no demand constraints allowed, MHR independent items [CH12]
Few items, **Many bidders**	Same as below **[this work]**	**poly(m)**†, **demand constraints allowed, item correlation allowed** [DW11]	Same as below **[this work]**
Many items, Many bidders	**poly(n,m)**†, no demand constraints, **item correlation allowed** **[this work]**	Same as ⟶ **[this work]**	**poly**($\sum_i \lvert T_i\rvert$)‡, no demand constraints, **item correlation allowed** **[this work]**

§: For all $\epsilon > 0$, a $(1-\epsilon)$-fraction of the optimal revenue is achieved in the quoted running time. $1/\epsilon$ appears in the exponent of the running time.

†: Exactly optimal revenue is achieved in the quoted running time, when every marginal of the bidders' value distributions has constant size support. The size of the support appears in the exponent of the running time. When the size of the support is non-constant/infinite/unbounded, two types of polynomial-time approximation schemes are obtained:

- When every marginal is MHR, a $(1-\epsilon)$-fraction of the optimal revenue is achieved in the quoted running time, for all $\epsilon > 0$.
- When the value distributions are bounded and normalized to $[0,1]^n$, an additive approximation to the optimal revenue is achieved in the quoted running time, for all $\epsilon > 0$. The approximation error is $\epsilon \cdot \min\{n, \sum_i C_i\}$, where C_i is the demand constraint of bidder i (if any).

‡: Exactly optimal revenue is achieved in the quoted running time, where recall that T_i is the support of the value distribution of bidder i. When the supports are infinite/unbounded we can alternatively obtain two types of approximation schemes:

- When every marginal of the bidders' value distributions is MHR, a $(1-\epsilon)$-fraction of the optimal revenue is achieved in time polynomial in m and $(1/\epsilon)^n$, for all $\epsilon > 0$.
- When the value distributions are bounded and normalized to $[0,1]^n$, an additive approximation to the optimal revenue is achieved in time polynomial in m and $(1/\epsilon)^n$, for all $\epsilon > 0$. In this case, the approximation error is $\epsilon \cdot n$.

(Even though $(1/\epsilon)^n$ is exponential in the number of items, notice that to specify a general (i.e. non-product and non-symmetric) value-distribution over n items we need to pay description complexity exponential in the number of items n. I.e. the input size to our problem is already exponential in n in this case.)

Figure 2: Algorithmic Solutions to the Optimal Multi-Item Mechanism Design Problem with Independent Bidders. The bidders are assumed additive up to (if allowed/stated) some hard demand constraint. m denotes the number of bidders and n the number of items.

this results in $M_{ij}(A) = \pi_{ij}(A)$. When $M_{ij}(A) = \pi_{ij}(A)$ for all i, j, A, we will say that M *exactly* implements π. Finally, if a reduced form can be implemented by a mechanism, we say that the reduced form is *feasible*.

When a bidder is additive, we may write $\vec{v}_i$ to denote her type, with the convention that v_{ij} represents her value for item j and that her value for a bundle of items is just the sum of her values for the items in the bundle. Then, to fully specify a (direct-revelation) multi-item mechanism for additive bidders, we need to describe, potentially succinctly, for all type profiles $\vec{v} \in \times_i T_i$, and for every bidder i, the outcome $M_i(\vec{v}) = (\vec{\phi}_i(\vec{v}), p_i(\vec{v}))$ given by M to bidder i, when the reported bidder types are $\vec{v}$, where $\phi_{ij}(\vec{v})$ is the probability that item j is given to bidder i and $p_i(\vec{v})$ is the price that i pays. The *value* of bidder i for outcome $M_i(\vec{w})$ is just her expected value $\vec{v}_i \cdot \vec{\phi}_i(\vec{w})$ for the bundle allocated to her, while the *utility* of bidder i for the same outcome is $U(\vec{v}_i, M_i(\vec{w})) := \vec{v}_i \cdot \vec{\phi}_i(\vec{w}) - p_i(\vec{w})$. Such bidders subtracting price from expected value are called *quasi-linear*. The relation between ϕ's and π's is just the following: for all i, $\vec{v}_i \in T_i$: $\pi_{ij}(\vec{v}_i) = \mathbb{E}_{\vec{v}_{-i}\sim\mathcal{D}_{-i}}[\phi_{ij}(\vec{v}_i\ ;\ \vec{v}_{-i})]$, where the expectation is computed with respect to the values $\vec{v}_{-i}$ of all bidders except i as these are drawn from $\mathcal{D}_{-i}$. We conclude by formally defining Bayesian Incentive Compatibility:

Definition 1 ([DW11]). *(BIC/ϵ-BIC Mechanism) A mechanism M is called ϵ-BIC iff the following inequality holds for all $i, \vec{v}_i, \vec{w}_i$:*

$$\begin{aligned}&\mathbb{E}_{\vec{v}_{-i}\sim\mathcal{D}_{-i}}[U(\vec{v}_i, M_i(\vec{v}))]\\ \geq &\mathbb{E}_{\vec{v}_{-i}\sim\mathcal{D}_{-i}}[U(\vec{v}_i, M_i(\vec{w}_i\ ;\ \vec{v}_{-i}))] - \epsilon v_{\max}\cdot\sum_j \pi_{ij}(\vec{w}_i),\end{aligned}$$

where $v_{\max}$ is the maximum possible value of any bidder for any item in the support of the value distribution. In other words, M is ϵ-BIC iff when a bidder lies by reporting $\vec{w}_i$ instead of $\vec{v}_i$, they do not expect to gain more than $\epsilon v_{\max}$ times the expected number of items that $\vec{w}_i$ receives. A mechanism is called BIC iff it is 0-BIC.[3]

[3]This definition differs slightly from the more common definition of [BH11, HKM11, HL10]. We use the definition of [DW11] to be correct in applying their results.

We conclude our preliminaries section noting that the running times of the algorithms obtained in Sections 3.1.1 and 3.1.2 are quoted without accounting for the number of bits needed to represent a coordinate of $\vec{\pi}$. If ℓ bits are needed to describe a probability in $\vec{\pi}$, then it suffices to multiply all quoted running times by a poly(ℓ) factor. Moreover, in Sections 3.3 and 8 we use the concept of a *polynomial-time approximation scheme*, or PTAS for short. A PTAS for a family of computational problems, such as computing the revenue-optimal mechanism in multi-item multi-bidder settings, is a collection of algorithms $(\mathcal{A}_\epsilon)_\epsilon$, indexed by the approximation parameter ϵ, such that, for all $\epsilon > 0$ and for any given problem $\mathcal{P}$ in the family, Algorithm $\mathcal{A}_\epsilon$ computes an ϵ-optimal solution to $\mathcal{P}$ in time time $d(\mathcal{P})^{g(1/\epsilon)}$, where $d(\mathcal{P})$ is the number of bits required to describe problem $\mathcal{P}$ and g is some increasing function of $1/\epsilon$, which does not depend on $\mathcal{P}$ or its description complexity. The algorithms in the collection are called polynomial-time because for all fixed ϵ, e.g. $\epsilon = 1/10$, the running time of $\mathcal{A}_\epsilon$ is polynomial in the description of the problem.

3. OVERVIEW OF RESULTS AND TECHNIQUES

3.1 Feasible Reduced Forms

3.1.1 Single-item, Bidder-Symmetric Reduced Forms, i.i.d. Bidders

In the case of a single item and i.i.d. bidders, Border provided a necessary and sufficient condition for a bidder-symmetric reduced form to be feasible, generalizing prior partial results of Maskin-Riley [MR84] and Matthews [Mat84]. In [HR11] a simple proof and alternative criteria are also provided. Let us review Border's theorem.

THEOREM 1 ([BOR91]). *Suppose that the bidder's types are i.i.d. distributed according to some measure μ over T. Then a bidder-symmetric reduced form π is feasible if an only if*

$$\forall S \subseteq T: \quad m \cdot \int_S \pi(t) d\mu(t) \leq 1 - (1 - \mu(S))^m. \qquad (1)$$

Simply put, a reduced form is feasible if and only if the probability that the item is awarded to a type in some set S (as computed by the reduced form) is at most the probability that someone with type from S shows up to the auction (as computed by the type distribution), for all subsets of types $S \subseteq T$. We call a set that violates this condition a *constricting set*. Clearly, the existence of a constricting set bears witness that the reduced form is infeasible, as the auctioneer cannot possibly award the item to someone in S if no one in S shows up. Border's theorem states that this is in fact a sufficient condition.

Border's original paper considered continuous type spaces (hence the integral in (1)), and the proof was based on measure theory. The following extension of the theorem was also shown: If there exists a constricting set S, then there is also a constricting set of the form S_x, where $S_x = \{A | \pi(A) > x\}$, for some x. In the case of finite type spaces, we can determine the feasibility of a reduced form auction in time $O(c \log c + c \cdot m)$, where $c = |T|$, as after sorting the type space in decreasing π's there are only c different subsets of the form S_x, and a dynamic program can find us if any of them violates (1) in time $O(c \cdot m)$. In other words, determining the feasibility of a bidder-symmetric reduced form, for a single item, and many i.i.d. bidders is easy. However, the following important question was left unanswered: Given a feasible reduced form, can we obtain a mechanism implementing the reduced form in polynomial-time? Notice that answering this question in the affirmative is absolutely necessary to be able to run the auction specified by the given reduced form. Our first contribution is solving this problem.

THEOREM 2. *Under the same assumptions as Theorem 1, given a bidder-symmetric reduced form π we can determine if it is feasible, or find a hyperplane separating it from the set of feasible bidder-symmetric reduced forms, in time $O(c \cdot (\log c + m))$, where $c = |T|$. If the reduced form is feasible, we provide a succinct description of a mechanism implementing the reduced form, in time polynomial in $c \cdot m$. The description of the mechanism is (at most) $c + 1$ probabilities and an equal number of ironings of the ordering on T induced by π.*[4] *The mechanism itself runs as follows: given the reported type profile, the mechanism samples a random subset of bidders in time poly(m, c), and the item is allocated uniformly at random to some bidder in that subset, or the item is thrown away.*

We prove Theorem 2 in Section 6, as a corollary of Theorem 13 and Proposition 1 of Sections 5 and 6 respectively. In proving our result, we consider the following type of mechanisms:

DEFINITION 2. *A* ***hierarchical mechanism*** *consists of a function $H : T \rightarrow [|T|] \cup \{LOSE\}$; one should interpret LOSE as a value larger than $|T|$. On bid vector $(A_1, \ldots, A_m)$, the mechanism has the following behavior: If $H(A_i) = LOSE$ for all i, the mechanism throws the item away. Otherwise, the item is awarded uniformly at random to a bidder in* $\text{argmin}_i H(A_i)$.

In other words, a hierarchical mechanism breaks down the type space into a hierarchy. When the bidders arrive and submit their types, the mechanism finds the highest-priority level of the hierarchy that is populated by the submitted types, and gives the item uniformly at random to a bidder whose type falls in that level of the hierarchy (unless every bidder is a loser, in which case the mechanism throws the item away). We say that a hierarchical mechanism H is *well-ordered* w.r.t. π if: $\pi(A) \geq \pi(A') \Rightarrow H(A) \leq H(A')$. We prove the following characterization result about feasible bidder-symmetric reduced forms:

THEOREM 3. *When bidders are i.i.d., every feasible bidder-symmetric reduced form π can be exactly implemented as a distribution over at most $|T| + 1$ well-ordered with respect to π hierarchical mechanisms.*

REMARK 1. *We note that Border [Bor91] already showed a similar theorem to the one above, namely that every feasible bidder-symmetric reduced form can be implemented as*

[4] An *ordering* σ on T may have equalities, but must be total (i.e. compare every pair of elements in T). An *ironing* H of an ordering σ on T is an ordering on T such that σ is a refinement of H, i.e. for all $t, t' \in T$: $H(t) < H(t') \implies \sigma(t) < \sigma(t')$.

a distribution over hierarchical mechanisms. The subtle, albeit qualitatively important difference between Border's result and ours is this: we show that every hierarchical mechanism in the support of the distribution is consistent with the same ordering of the type-set T, which every hierarchical mechanism in the support of the distribution "irons" in some way. In particular, the types are ranked from more to less important according to π and the mechanisms in the support of the distribution iron various regions of this ranking, thereby treating the types falling in an ironed region equally. On the other hand, Border's result does not require the mechanisms in the support of the distribution to be consistent with a unique total ordering of the type-set T. So it is a less compelling characterization of the structure of the allocation rule.

Theorem 3 alone is not enough to allow us to implement a given bidder-symmetric reduced form. Indeed, if $\pi(\cdot)$ takes θ (can be as large as $|T|$) distinct values, there are 2^θ different well-ordered w.r.t. π hierarchical mechanisms. From here, we switch to our vector-view of reduced forms (as vectors $\vec{\pi}$ in $[0,1]^{|T|}$) and study the geometry of the space of feasible mechanisms respecting the order on the type-space induced by a given reduced form $\vec{\pi}$, which we will call P. We show that, in fact, P is a θ-dimensional polytope whose corners are *exactly* the 2^θ different well-ordered w.r.t. $\vec{\pi}$ hierarchical mechanisms. We provide a geometric algorithm in Section 5 that in polynomial time outputs a representation of $\vec{\pi}$ as a convex combination of at most $|T|+1$ corners of P. This convex combination is exactly a distribution over well-ordered w.r.t. $\vec{\pi}$ hierarchical mechanisms that implements $\vec{\pi}$. Our geometric algorithm runs in time poly$(m, |T|)$, and sampling from the distribution output by our algorithm also takes time poly$(m, |T|)$. We provide the details of our approach and proofs of the relevant claims in Sections 5 and 6.

3.1.2 Single-item, General Reduced Forms, Non-i.i.d. Bidders

Recently, an alternative proof of Border's theorem for distributions with finite support was discovered in [Bor07] and again in [CKM11], the latter using a clean network-flow interpretation. These proofs extend Theorem 1 to independent, but not necessarily identical, bidders and non-symmetric reduced forms. In this case, (1) is replaced by the following necessary and sufficient condition:

$$\forall S_1 \subseteq T_1, \ldots, S_m \subseteq T_m :$$

$$\sum_i \sum_{A\in S_i} \pi_i(A)\Pr[t_i = A] \leq 1 - \prod_i (1 - \Pr[t_i \in S_i]). \quad (2)$$

The interpretation of the LHS and RHS of the above inequality is the same as the one given above for (1) except generalized to the non-iid non-symmetric setting. In addition to the above condition, [CKM11] proves a generalization of Border's extended result: If there is a constricting $S = (S_1, \ldots, S_m)$, then there is also a constricting set of the form $S' = (S^{(1)}_{x_1}, \ldots, S^{(m)}_{x_m})$, where $S^{(i)}_{x_i} = \{A \in T_i | \pi_i(A) > x_i\}$. In other words, each bidder has a different threshold x_i, and $S^{(i)}_{x_i}$ contains all types of bidder i with π_i above x_i. Unfortunately, despite this simplification, there are still $\prod_i(|T_i|+1)$ possible constricting sets, and testing each of them would take time exponential in the number of bidders.

One might hope to obtain a stronger theorem that would only require testing a number of sets polynomial in $\sum_i |T_i|$ and m. We prove such a theorem by introducing a notion of a *virtual* π, defined next. We name it such not because the equation involves hazard rates or looks anything like that for virtual valuations [Mye81], but because the spirit of the transformation is the same. Myerson observed that he could make the most revenue not from the bidder with the highest valuation, but from the bidder with the highest virtual valuation. Likewise, in our setting, the most difficult types to satisfy are not the types with the highest π, but the types with the highest virtual π. The definition of virtual π, which we denote $\hat{\pi}$, is actually quite simple.

Definition 3. *If π is a reduced form, we define its corresponding* virtual reduced form $\hat{\pi}$ *as follows: for all i and type $A \in T_i$, $\hat{\pi}_i(A) := \Pr[\pi_i(t_i) \leq \pi_i(A)]\pi_i(A)$.*

It turns out that this definition exactly captures which types of different bidders are harder to satisfy. In the bidder-symmetric case of Section 3.1.1, we were able to compare a pair of types A and B submitted by bidders $i \neq k$ based only on their corresponding $\pi_i(A)$ and $\pi_k(B)$. This is no longer the case in the non-iid case, resulting in the more complicated constricting sets defined above. Nevertheless, we show that A and B can be compared at face value of $\hat{\pi}_i(A)$ and $\hat{\pi}_k(B)$:

Theorem 4. *Suppose that the bidders are independent and there is a single item for sale. A reduced form π is feasible if and only if: for all x, the sets $S^{(i)}_x = \{A \in T_i | \hat{\pi}_i(A) > x\}$ satisfy:*

$$\sum_i \sum_{A\in S^{(i)}_x} \pi_i(A)\Pr[t_i = A] \leq 1 - \prod_i (1 - \Pr[t_i \in S^{(i)}_x]). \quad (3)$$

In particular, we can test the feasibility of a reduced form, or obtain a hyperplane separating the reduced form from the set of feasible reduced forms, in time linear in $\sum_i |T_i| \cdot (\log(\sum_i |T_i|) + m)$.

The details of the proof can be found in Section 7.

We also provide two analogs of Theorem 3 in our setting: Theorem 5, which is handy for our algorithmic results of Theorem 6, and Theorem 7, which provides a more compelling characterization of feasible reduced forms. Both theorems are in terms of hierarchical mechanisms which in the present setting are defined as follows.

Definition 4. *A* ***hierarchical mechanism*** *consists of a function $H : \bigcup_i (T_i \times \{i\}) \to [\sum_i |T_i|] \cup \{LOSE\}$; one should interpret $LOSE$ as a value larger than $\sum_i |T_i|$. On bid vector $(A_1, \ldots, A_m)$, if $H(A_i, i) = LOSE$ for all i, the mechanism throws the item away. Otherwise, the item is awarded uniformly at random to a bidder in* $\text{argmin}_i H(A_i, i)$.

We say that a hierarchical mechanism H for non-identical bidders is *partially-ordered* w.r.t. π if for all i and $A, A' \in T_i$, $\pi_i(A) \geq \pi_i(A') \Rightarrow H(A,i) \leq H(A',i)$. We say that a hierarchical mechanism is *strict* if for all bidders i, j and types $A \in T_i$, $B \in T_j$: $i \neq j \Rightarrow (H(A,i) \neq H(B,j) \vee H(A,i) = H(B,j) = \text{LOSE})$ (i.e. there is always a unique winner in $\text{argmin}_i H(A_i, i)$ if one exists, because each level (except possibly for LOSE) contains types from only a single bidder). Our algorithmic extension of Theorem 3 is the following:

THEOREM 5. *When bidders are independent, but not necessarily identically distributed, every feasible reduced form π can be exactly implemented as a distribution over at most $\sum_i |T_i|+1$ strict, partially-ordered w.r.t. π hierarchical mechanisms.*

From here, we take the same geometric approach as in Section 3.1.1 and study the geometry of the set of feasible reduced forms that respect the partial-ordering of types induced by a given reduced-form π. Again we show that this is a $(\sum_i d_i)$-dimensional polytope, P, where d_i (could be as large as $|T_i|$) is the number of distinct values that $\pi_i(\cdot)$ takes on input from T_i, and that the corners of P are *exactly* the strict, partially-ordered w.r.t. π hierarchical mechanisms. Writing a point in P as a convex combination of $\sum_i |T_i|+1$ corners is no longer an easy procedure. Not only does P have an exponential number of corners, but there are also exponentially many hyperplanes defining the boundary of P (where there were only $2 \cdot |T|$ such hyperplanes in the i.i.d. case). Luckily, Theorem 4 provides a polynomial-time separation oracle for membership in P. By making use of this separation oracle instead of checking the exponentially-many boundary equations one by one, the geometric algorithm of Section 5 outputs a representation of a given π as a convex combination of at most $\sum_i |T_i|+1$ corners of P, which is exactly a distribution over the corresponding $\sum_i |T_i|+1$ strict, partially-ordered w.r.t. π hierarchical mechanisms. Putting this approach together with Theorems 4 and 5, we prove in Section 7 the algorithmic result of this section:

THEOREM 6. *When bidders are independent, given a reduced form we can determine if it is feasible, or find a hyperplane separating it from the set of feasible reduced forms, in time linear in $\sum_i |T_i| \cdot (\log(\sum_i |T_i|) + m)$. If the reduced form is feasible, we can compute a succinct description of a mechanism implementing the reduced form, in time polynomial in $\sum_i |T_i|$. The description of the mechanism is just (at most) $\sum_i |T_i| + 1$ probabilities and the same number of total orderings of $\bigcup_i (T_i \times \{i\})$. The mechanism itself runs as follows: given the reported type profile, the mechanism samples a random total ordering of all bidders' types in time polynomial in $\sum_i |T_i|$, and allocates the item to the bidder whose reported type is highest in that ordering, or throws the item away.*

While Theorem 5 does provide some structure to the otherwise unknown set of feasible mechanisms for independent bidders, the result is not as compelling as that of Theorem 3. One might have hoped that every feasible reduced form can be implemented as a distribution over *virtually-ordered* hierarchical mechanisms (that is, hierarchical mechanisms such that $\hat{\pi}_i(A) \geq \hat{\pi}_j(B) \Rightarrow H(A,i) \leq H(B,j)$). Unfortunately, this is not true, as is shown in Section 7. Despite this, we show that a strong generalization of Theorem 3 holds in this setting. Let σ be a total ordering on the elements of $\bigcup_i (T_i \times \{i\})$ (i.e. a mapping $\sigma : \bigcup_i (T_i \times \{i\}) \to [\sum_i |T_i|]$). We say that σ respects π if $\pi_i(A) > \pi_i(B) \Rightarrow \sigma(A,i) < \sigma(B,i)$. We also say that a hierachical mechanism H is σ-ordered if $\sigma(A,i) < \sigma(B,j) \Rightarrow H(A,i) \leq H(B,j)$. We prove the following theorem:

THEOREM 7. *If a reduced form π is feasible, there exists a total ordering σ on the elements of $\bigcup_i (T_i \times \{i\})$ that respects π such that π can be implemented as a distribution over σ-ordered hierarchical mechanisms.*

REMARK 2. *The analog of Remark 1 applies here too. It is not hard to extend Border's proof to show that every feasible reduced form can be implemented as a distribution over hierarchical mechanisms. The interesting aspect of Theorem 7 is that there exists a total ordering of the types of all bidders so that every hierarchical mechanism in the support of the distribution is consistent with this ordering. Indeed, Theorem 7 is qualitatively a stronger statement than its analog in symmetric settings (Theorem 3) as the geometric argument used for the proof of Theorem 3 falls short from giving Theorem 7, resulting in the partially ordered hierarchical mechanisms of Theorem 5.*

We provide the proof of Theorem 7 in the full version of our paper [CDW11].

3.2 A Simple Characterization of Feasible Multidimensional Mechanisms

The appeal of Myerson's single-item auction is not only its optimality, but its clean allocation rule. Let us revisit it. In a single-item setting the type-set of each bidder is a subset $T_i \subset \mathbb{R}$, as a bidder's type is how much she values the item. In brush strokes Myerson's allocation rule is then as follows. We present both the symmetric and the asymmetric case, as the symmetric one is even simpler.

- *The i.i.d. case:* Suppose that the bidders' values are independently and identically distributed in T. Myerson's auction in this setting maintains an ironing of the types $H : T \to [|T|] \cup \{\text{LOSE}\}$ (take LOSE $:= |T| + 1$) satisfying: $A \geq A' \implies H(A) \leq H(A')$; i.e. the ranking respects the order on T (as a subset of $\mathbb{R}$). If $|H^{-1}(k)| > 1$ for some k, we can think of the types in $H^{-1}(k)$ as having been *ironed* over by H. In fact, let us refer to H as an *ironing* of T. Given the ironing H, the allocation rule is simple: on bid vector $(A_1, \ldots, A_m)$, the item is allocated uniformly at random to a bidder in $\text{argmin}_i\{H(A_i)\}$ (other tie-breaking rules are fine too), or thrown away if $H(A_i) = \text{LOSE}, \forall i$.
- *The non-i.i.d. case:* Suppose that the bidders' values are independent but not necessarily identically distributed. In this case, Myerson's allocation rule is a bit more complicated. The auction maintains an ironing of all bidders' types $H : \cup_i (T_i \times \{i\}) \to [\sum_i |T_i|] \cup \{\text{LOSE}\}$ (take LOSE $:= \sum_i |T_i| + 1$) satisfying: for all bidders i, $A_i \geq A'_i \implies H(A_i, i) \leq H(A'_i, i)$; i.e. the ironing now only respects the order between types belonging to the same bidder. Given the ironing, the allocation rule is simple: on bid vector $(A_1, \ldots, A_m)$, the item is allocated uniformly at random to a bidder in $\text{argmin}_i\{H(A_i, i)\}$, or thrown away if $H(A_i, i) = \text{LOSE}$ for all i.

Simply put, Myerson's allocation rule maintains a strict ordering of all bidders' types together with an ironing of this ordering into a non-strict ordering, and a LOSE threshold. When the bidders submit their types, the auction gives the item uniformly at random to a bidder whose submitted type populates the highest level of the ironing, unless no type is above the LOSE threshold in which case the item remains unallocated.

In multi-item auctions, the type spaces of the bidders are subsets $T_i \subset \mathbb{R}^n$, i.e. are multidimensional, and it is a priori not clear how to order them for the purposes of allocating items. In fact, it is not clear whether feasible mechanisms/optimal mechanisms in these settings always have simple allocation rules. Indeed, it is not even clear that all feasible single-item auctions have a clean allocation rule, such as Myerson's allocation rule described above. In this work, we show a compelling characterization result of all feasible multi-item auctions when the bidders are independent, each bidder's type is sampled from an arbitrary distribution over her type space (i.e. we do not assume that the bidder's values for the items are necessarily independent), and the bidders have additive valuations over bundles of items. In particular, our results also characterize the set of all feasible single-item mechanisms.

As our characterization aims to characterize a broader set of mechanisms, the allocation rules it contains are necessarily more involved, albeit slightly. All we do is introduce randomization over ironings. Simply put, our characterization of multi-item multi bidder mechanisms with independent additive bidders is as follows. The reader should draw immediate connections between the allocation rule we are about to describe and Myerson's allocation rule described above.

Characterization of Multi-Bidder Multi-Item Auctions for Independent Additive Bidders (informal)

Every multi-bidder multi-item auction for independent, additive bidders takes the following form w.l.o.g.:

- Every item is allocated independently of the other items.
- The allocation rule of every item maintains:
    - a strict ordering of all bidders' types; and
    - a distribution over ironings of the strict ordering into non-strict orderings, and LOSE thresholds.
- Each item is then allocated as follows. First, a random ironing and LOSE threshold is sampled from the item's distribution. Then, the item is given uniformly at random to a bidder whose reported type populates the highest level of the sampled ironing, unless no type is above the sampled LOSE threshold in which case the item remains unallocated.

We proceed with a formal description of our characterization result. As in multi-item auctions the bidders' type-sets are multidimensional, it is helpful to view the reduced form of the auction as providing us with natural embeddings of the type-sets of bidders into $\mathbb{R}$. Indeed, for our discussion it will be useful to view $\pi_{ij}(\cdot)$ as an embedding of T_i into $\mathbb{R}$, for each bidder i and item j. As we did earlier with Myerson's allocation rule, we distinguish between the symmetric and the asymmetric cases.

Characterization of Multi-Bidder Multi-Item Auctions for Independent Additive Bidders (formal)

Every multi-bidder multi-item auction for independent, additive bidders is equivalent to one that allocates every item independently of the other items, and one in which the allocation of item j, for all j, takes the following form:

- *i.i.d. bidders* **and** *bidder-symmetric reduced forms:* Suppose that the bidders are i.i.d. and the reduced form π_j on item j is bidder-symmetric. In this case, the auction maintains a distribution $\mathcal{H}_j$ over rankings $H_j : T \to [|T|] \cup \{\text{LOSE}\}$ (take LOSE $:= |T| + 1$) satisfying: $\pi_j(A) \geq \pi_j(A') \implies H_j(A) \leq H_j(A')$, for all $A, A' \in T$; *i.e. each ranking in the support of $\mathcal{H}_j$ respects the order induced on T by its embedding into $\mathbb{R}$ by $\pi_j(\cdot)$.* If $|H_j^{-1}(k)| > 1$ for some k and some ranking H_j in the support of $\mathcal{H}_j$ we think of the types in $H_j^{-1}(k)$ as having been *ironed* over by H_j. Given $\mathcal{H}_j$, the allocation of item j is simple: on bid vector $(A_1, \ldots, A_m)$, a ranking H_j is sampled from $\mathcal{H}_j$, and the item is allocated uniformly at random to a bidder in $\text{argmin}_i\{H_j(A_i)\}$, or thrown away if $H_j(A_i) = \text{LOSE}$ for all i.
- *Non-i.i.d. bidders* **or** *different reduced forms:* When the bidders are independent but non-i.i.d. or the reduced form on item j is not bidder-symmetric, the auction maintains a distribution $\mathcal{H}_j$ over rankings $H_j : \cup_i(T_i \times \{i\}) \to [\sum_i |T_i|] \cup \{\text{LOSE}\}$ (take LOSE $:= \sum_i |T_i| + 1$) satisfying: for all bidders i, $\pi_{ij}(A) \geq \pi_{ij}(A') \implies H_j(A, i) \leq H_j(A', i)$; i.e. each ranking in the support respects the order between types belonging to the same bidder, for whatever order is induced on T_i by its embedding into $\mathbb{R}$ by $\pi_{ij}(\cdot)$. Additionally, if H_j and H_j' are two rankings in the support of $\mathcal{H}_j$ then, for all $i, i', A_i \in T_i, A_{i'} \in T_{i'}$: $H_j(A_i, i) < H_j(A_{i'}, i') \implies H_j'(A_i, i) \leq H_j'(A_{i'}, i')$, *i.e. all rankings in the support of $\mathcal{H}_j$ are consistent with a unique total ordering of $\cup_i(T_i \times \{i\})$.* Given $\mathcal{H}_j$, the allocation of item j is simple: on bid vector $(A_1, \ldots, A_m)$, a ranking H_j is sampled from $\mathcal{H}_j$, and the item is allocated uniformly at random to a bidder in $\text{argmin}_i\{H_j(A_i, i)\}$, or thrown away if $H_j(A_i, i) = \text{LOSE}$ for all i.

Our characterization result for single-item settings is an immediate corollary of Theorems 3 (for the i.i.d. case) and 7 (for the independent case). That the above characterization holds for multi-item settings and additive bidders follows by noting that, given the lack of demand constraints on the bidders, we can allocate items sequentially and the resulting allocation will be feasible given that the supply constraints on the items are met, i.e. every item is allocated exactly once.

3.3 Optimal Multi-Dimensional Mechanism Design

The additivity of the bidders notwithstanding, we know that optimal mechanisms in multi-item settings may be quite involved. For example, in [CMS10] it is shown that even when there are two items, and a single additive bidder whose values over the items are i.i.d. regular, a mechanism that sells lotteries over the items makes strictly more revenue than a mechanism that sells each item separately. This result implies that: we *should not* auction every item separately; and we *should* use the values of bidders on item j to decide how to allocate item j'. So if bidder i reports higher value on item j' than bidder i', we should not necessarily expect item j' to go to bidder i more often than bidder i', even if the bidders are i.i.d.. To rephrase, for allocating item j', we cannot just rank the bidders according to their bids on that particular item. We need to instead take into account their bids on all the other items.

Despite such complications, it is possible to use Theorems 2 and 6 to solve the following problem:

The BIC many-many problem. Given as input m arbitrarily correlated distributions $\mathcal{F}_1, \ldots, \mathcal{F}_m$ over valuation vectors for n items, output a BIC mechanism M whose expected revenue is optimal relative to any other, possibly randomized, BIC mechanism, when played by m additive bidders whose valuation vectors are sampled independently from $\mathcal{F}_1, \ldots, \mathcal{F}_m$.

Our approach to solving this problem is to use the separation oracle of Theorems 2 and 6 inside the LPs of [DW11]. Doing so we obtain the following:

THEOREM 8. *There is a solution to the BIC many-many problem with running time polynomial in n, m and in $\max_{i\in[m]} |supp(\mathcal{F}_i)|$.*

THEOREM 9. *If, for all i, $\mathcal{F}_i$ is item-symmetric (i.e. invariant under permutations of the item names), there exists a solution to the BIC many-many problem with runtime polynomial in m and n^c, where $c = \max_{i,j} |supp(\mathcal{F}_{ij})|$, where $\mathcal{F}_{ij}$ is the marginal of $\mathcal{F}_i$ on item j.*

THEOREM 10. *If, for all i, $\mathcal{F}_i$ is item-symmetric and supported on $[0,1]^n$ there is an additive PTAS for the BIC many-many problem whose running time is polynomial in m and n (and doesn't depend on the size of the support of $\mathcal{F}_1, \ldots, \mathcal{F}_m$). For all $\epsilon > 0$, the PTAS computes a BIC mechanism whose revenue is within an additive $\epsilon \cdot n$ of the optimal revenue achieved by any BIC mechanism.*

THEOREM 11. *If, for all i, $\mathcal{F}_i$ is item-symmetric and its n marginals satisfy the MHR condition, there is a multiplicative PTAS for the BIC many-many problem whose running time is polynomial in m and n (and doesn't depend on the size of the support of $\mathcal{F}_1, \ldots, \mathcal{F}_m$). For all $\epsilon > 0$, the PTAS computes a BIC mechanism whose revenue is at least a $(1-\epsilon)$-fraction of the optimal revenue achieved by any BIC mechanism.*

Further details are provided in Section 8.

3.4 Non-negative Linear Feasibility Constraints

Aside from the independent results of [AFH+11], it is unknown whether Border's theorem applies to other settings, or what the proper statement of Border's Theorem might even be as we depart from the single-item setting. On this front, we prove a generalization of Border's Theorem to settings with *Non-negative Linear Feasibility Constraints.* Throughout this section, P denotes a type profile, and $\vec{\phi}(P)$ denotes an *allocation* in terms of the marginal probability of giving bidder i item j, $\phi_{ij}(P)$, when the reported type profile is P. We are interested in the form of the region F where $\phi(P)$ needs to lie for there to exist a distribution over feasible allocations of items to bidders consistent with the marginal allocation probabilities specified by $\phi(P)$. In the following definition, we represent an inequality h as a vector of coefficients $\vec{c}(h)$, and a right-hand bound $d(h)$. We say that h is non-negative if every coefficient $c_{ij}(h)$ and $d(h)$ are non-negative.

DEFINITION 5. *A set of feasible allocations $F \subseteq [0,1]^{m\times n}$ has* ***Non-negative Linear Feasibility Constraints*** *if there exists a set H of non-negative inequalities such that $\vec{\phi}(P) \in F \Leftrightarrow \vec{c}(h) \cdot \vec{\phi}(P) \leq d(h)$, for all $h \in H$, and $\vec{\phi}(P) \geq \vec{0}$).* [5]

In a setting where no bidder i should be given more than C_i items and no item j should be given out more than once, an application of the Birkhoff-Von Neumann Theorem implies that F has non-negative linear feasibility constraints [DFK11, DW11].[6] In fact, it is shown in [Sch03] that a much broader range of settings have non-negative linear feasibility constraints, including settings where the constraint on the feasible allocations of items to bidders $\mathcal{S} \subseteq [m] \times [n]$ can be specified as the intersection of two arbitrary matroids.[7]

Below is our generalization of Border's Theorem to this setting, whose proof can be found in the full version of our paper [CDW11]. In the statement of the theorem, i ranges over all bidders, j ranges over all items, and P ranges over all possible type-profiles, with $\Pr[P]$ denoting the probability that profile P is sampled from $\mathcal{D}$ and P_i denoting the type of bidder i in P.

THEOREM 12. *Let F be any set of allocations with non-negative linear feasibility constraints, and $\mathcal{D}$ be any (possibly correlated) distribution over types. Then a reduced form $\vec{\pi}$ is feasible if and only if for all weights $\{W_{ij}(A)\}_{i,j,A} \in [0,1]^{n\times\sum_i |T_i|}$:*

$$\sum_i \sum_j \sum_{A\in T_i} W_{ij}(A) \cdot \pi_{ij}(A) \cdot \Pr[t_i = A]$$
$$\leq \sum_P \Pr[P] \max_{\vec{\phi}(P)\in F} \left\{ \sum_i \sum_j W_{ij}(P_i) \cdot \phi_{ij}(P) \right\}.$$

In other words, for fixed weights $\vec{W} = \{W_{ij}(A)\}_{i,j,A}$, consider the allocation rule $M(\vec{W})$ that on profile P picks the max-weight allocation (where the weight of giving item j to bidder i is $W_{ij}(P_i)$). Then a reduced form $\vec{\pi}$ is feasible if and only if for all weights $\vec{W}$, the LHS is at most the expected weight of items awarded by $M(\vec{W})$.

Like in the single-item setting, it is clear that this is a necessary condition. The expected weight of items awarded by any mechanism that implements $\vec{\pi}$ is exactly the LHS, and this value clearly must be less than the expected weight of items awarded by $M(\vec{W})$, as M maximizes this value over all feasible mechanisms. The content of the theorem is that these conditions are indeed sufficient.

[5]Here, we talk about feasible allocations, not feasible mechanisms (or allocation rules). A feasible mechanism for F maps every profile P to a feasible allocation $\vec{\phi}(P) \in F$.

[6]In particular, the constraints are: a) $\forall\, i$, $\sum_j \phi_{ij}(P) \leq C_i$, b) $\forall\, j$, $\sum_i \phi_{ij}(P) \leq 1$, and c) $\forall\, i,j$, $\phi_{ij}(P) \geq 0$.

[7]In this case, let $rk_i(S)$ denote the rank of set S in matroid $i = 1, 2$. Then the constraints are: a) $\forall S \subseteq [m] \times [n]$, $\sum_{(i,j)\in S} \phi_{ij}(P) \leq rk_1(S)$, b) $\forall S \subseteq [m] \times [n]$, $\sum_{(i,j)\in S} \phi_{ij}(P) \leq rk_2(S)$, and c) $\forall\, i,j$, $\phi_{ij}(P) \geq 0$.

In addition to a proof of Theorem 12, we provide in [CDW11] two false generalizations of Border's Theorem that fail even for unit-demand i.i.d. bidders in order to motivate the statement of Theorem 12.

3.4.1 Correlated Bidders, Demand Constraints

As mentioned previously, without demand constraints and without correlation among bidders' valuations, the multi-item allocation problem is no more difficult than the single-item allocation problem, as each item can just be allocated separately and independently from the other items. However, either demand constraints or correlation among bidders negates all known results (including those of Section 3.1) about feasible allocations. On this front, we give a multi-commodity flow interpretation of the problem for arbitrarily correlated bidders with demand constraints, which is similar to the network flow interpretation of [CKM11]. Simply put, the commodities/goods in our multi-commodity flow problem are denoted $G_{ij}(A)$, for all items j, bidders i, and types $A \in T_i$. We have a source node for every item, an intermediate node for every possible profile, and a sink node for every type. We put edges from every item node to every intermediate node and every intermediate node to every sink node. The capacities on the source-intermediate edges are chosen to ensure that each item is only given out once. The capacities on the intermediate-sink edges are chosen to ensure that no bidder violates his demand constraint. We then demand that a $\pi_{ij}(A)\cdot \Pr[t_i = A]$ amount of commodity $G_{ij}(A)$ is sent from source node j to sink node (i, A). We give the details of our flow network and the values of the capacities on its edges in [CDW11], and also explain how to view any solution to the multi-commodity flow problem as a mechanism that implements the reduced form and vice versa.

4. ROADMAP TO THE TECHNICAL SECTIONS

Sections 5–8 provide some of the technical details omitted from Section 3 for the sake of coherence. Section 5 is a preparatory section, providing a geometric algorithm for decomposing a point in a polytope as a convex combination of the polytope's corners, when the polytope is not given explicitly to us but indirectly via oracles certifying its facets and accessing its corners. Section 6 provides the technical details omitted from Section 3.1.1, while Section 7 contains the technical details omitted from Section 3.1.2, except for the proof of our main characterization result (Theorem 7) that we provide in the full version of our paper [CDW11]. Finally, Section 8 contains our results for the computation of revenue-optimal mechanisms outlined in Section 3.3. Our extension of Border's theorem beyond single-item settings with independent bidders stated in Section 3.4 is given in the full version of our paper [CDW11].

5. A GEOMETRIC ALGORITHM

Carathéodory's theorem states that every point $\vec{x}$ inside an n-dimensional polytope P can be written as a convex combination of at most $n + 1$ corners of P. In this section, we provide an algorithm for coming up with such a combination. We will consider polytopes that are described as an intersection of half-spaces. Each half-space is defined by a hyperplane h together with a choice of a side. We use $B(P)$ to denote the set of half-spaces defining polytope P, but overload notation using $B(P)$ to also denote the corresponding set of hyperplanes. We reserve the symbol h to denote hyperplanes. We consider cases where $|B(P)|$ may be exponentially large, and we only have an implicit description of $B(P)$. That is, we have access to a *boundary oracle* BO that outputs yes on input h if $h \in B(P)$, and no otherwise. We also have access to a separation oracle, SO, that outputs yes on input $\vec{x}$ if $\vec{x} \in P$, and outputs some $h \in B(P)$ if $\vec{x}$ is on the wrong side of h (and therefore not in P). We will talk about one more algorithm related to P:

DEFINITION 6. *CO is a **corner oracle** for P if it has the following behavior. Given as input a set of hyperplanes B, CO outputs no if $B \not\subseteq B(P)$, or $\left(\bigcap_{h\in B} h\right) \bigcap P = \emptyset$ (i.e. the hyperplanes are not boundary hyperplanes of P, or they are boundary hyperplanes, but do not intersect inside P). Otherwise, CO outputs a corner of P inside $\bigcap_{h\in B} h$.*

It is clear that CO has well-defined behavior on all inputs. If B contains only boundary hyperplanes of P, and the intersection of these hyperplanes with P is non-empty, this region must contain a corner of P. Now we describe our computational problem in terms of these oracles:

QUESTION 1. *Given as input a point $\vec{x} \in \mathbb{R}^n$, a separation oracle SO and a corner oracle CO for some n-dimensional polytope P, as well as an upper bound b on the number of bits required to describe a coefficient in the hyperplanes output by SO as well as any coordinate of $\vec{x}$, output no if $\vec{x} \notin P$. Otherwise, output $c_1, \ldots, c_{n+1}, \vec{a}_1, \ldots, \vec{a}_{n+1}$ such that $\vec{a}_i$ is a corner of P for all i, $\sum_i c_i = 1$, and $\sum_i c_i\vec{a}_i = \vec{x}$.*

It follows from Carathéodory's theorem that such $c_i, \vec{a}_i$ exist whenever $\vec{x} \in P$. We provide an computationally efficient algorithm to find such a solution whenever it exists. At a high level, we begin with the input $\vec{x}$ and maintain at all times two points $\vec{y} \in P$, $\vec{z} \in P$, such that $\vec{x} = c\vec{y} + (1 - c)\vec{z}$, for some $c \in [0, 1]$. After step t of the algorithm is completed, $\vec{y}$ is the convex combination of at most t corners of P, and $\vec{z}$ lies in the $(n - t)$-dimensional intersection of t hyperplanes of $B(P)$. Hence, after at most n steps, $\vec{z}$ will lie in a 0-dimensional space, and therefore must be a corner, so the algorithm will terminate after at most $n + 1$ steps.

To go from step t to step $t+1$, we pick an arbitrary corner, $\vec{a}_t$, that lies in the intersection of the t hyperplanes where $\vec{z}$ lies. Then, we let c_t be as large as possible without pushing the point $\frac{(1-\sum_{j<t} c_j)\vec{z} - c_t\cdot\vec{a}_t}{1-c_t-\sum_{j<t} c_j}$ outside of P. We update $\vec{z}$ to $\vec{z}_{\text{new}} = \frac{(1-\sum_{j<t} c_j)\vec{z}_{\text{old}} - c_t\cdot\vec{a}_t}{1-c_t-\sum_{j<t} c_j}$ and update $\vec{y}$ appropriately to include $\vec{a}_t$ in its convex combination of corners. The new $\vec{z}$ must lie at the intersection of the original t hyperplanes where the old $\vec{z}$ lied, as well as a new $h \in B(P)$ that stopped us from further increasing c_t.

Algorithm 1 provides the formal details. In its description E denotes the set of hyperplanes whose intersection contains $\vec{z}$ (the empty intersection is the entire space). The formal guarantees of the algorithm are given by Theorem 13, whose proof is presented in [CDW11].

THEOREM 13. *Algorithm 1 correctly answers Question 1. The running time of the algorithm is polynomial in n, b and the running times of SO and CO on inputs of bit-complexity polynomial in n and b.*

Algorithm 1 Algorithm for writing $\vec{x}$ as a convex combination of at most $n+1$ corners

Input: Point $\vec{x}$; separation oracle SO; corner oracle CO; bound b on the number of bits required to describe each coefficient in the hyperplanes output by SO, as well as the coordinates of $\vec{x}$.
Initialize: $i := 1$, $\vec{y} := \vec{0}$, $\vec{z} := \vec{x}$, $E := \emptyset$, $c_i := 0, \vec{a}_i := \vec{0}$ $\forall i \in [n+1]$.
Invariants: $c := \sum_i c_i$, $\vec{y} := \frac{1}{c}\sum_i c_i \vec{a}_i$, or $\vec{0}$ if $c = 0$, $c\vec{y} + (1-c)\vec{z} = \vec{x}$.
if $SO(\vec{x}) \neq$ yes **then**
  Output no.
end if
while $c < 1$ **do**
  Set $\vec{a}_i := CO(E)$.
  if $\vec{a}_i = \vec{z}$ **then**
    Set $c_i := 1 - c$.
    Output $c_1, \ldots, c_{n+1}, \vec{a}_1, \ldots, \vec{a}_{n+1}$.
  else
    Set $D := \max\{d \mid (1+d)\vec{z} - d\vec{a}_i \in P\}$.
    Set $E_i = SO((1 + D + \epsilon)\vec{z} - (D + \epsilon)\vec{a}_i)$ for sufficiently small $\epsilon > 0$. /* *the appropriate choice of* $\epsilon = \epsilon(n,b)$ *is explained in the proof of Theorem 13 in [CDW11]* */
    Update: $c_i := (1 - \frac{1}{1+D})(1-c)$, $\vec{z} := \frac{1-c}{1-c-c_i}\vec{z} - \frac{c_i}{1-c-c_i}\vec{a}_i$, $\vec{y} := \frac{c}{c+c_i}\vec{y} + \frac{c_i}{c+c_i}\vec{a}_i$, $c := c + c_i$, $E := E \cup E_i$, $i := i+1$.
  end if
end while

6. SINGLE ITEM, I.I.D. BIDDERS, BIDDER-SYMMETRIC REDUCED FORMS

We provide the details and proofs of the techniques discussed in Section 3.1.1, beginning with some technical lemmas.

LEMMA 1. *Every feasible bidder-symmetric reduced form auction π for i.i.d. bidders and a single item can be implemented (not necessarily exactly implemented) as a distribution over well-ordered w.r.t. π hierarchical mechanisms.*

PROOF. Our proof is by induction on the number of distinct non-zero values in $\{\pi(A)\}_{A \in T}$.

Base Case: There is a single non-zero value in this set, equal to some $x \leq 1$. The mechanism that gives the item uniformly at random to a bidder whose reported type A satisfies $\pi(A) = x$ (if such bidder shows up) implements this reduced form as long as it is feasible.

Inductive Hypothesis: For all $0 < k < \theta$, every feasible reduced form with k distinct non-zero values in $\{\pi(A)\}_{A \in T}$ can be implemented as a distribution over well-ordered w.r.t. π hierarchical mechanisms.

Inductive Step: We show that the inductive hypothesis extends to the case where there are exactly θ distinct non-zero values in $\{\pi(A)\}_{A \in T}$. Let X denote the set of all distributions over well-ordered w.r.t. π hierarchical mechanisms. Then X can be interpreted as a closed, bounded subset of $\mathbb{R}^{2^\theta}$, where each coordinate denotes the probability of using one of the 2^θ well-ordered w.r.t. π hierarchical mechanisms. Therefore, X is compact. For a distribution over hierarchical mechanisms $M \in X$, denote by $M(A)$ the probability that a bidder reporting type A receives the item under M. Define the function $F : X \to \mathbb{R}$ as:

$$F(M) = \max_A\{\pi(A) - M(A)\}.$$

Let us use the Euclidean distance in X as a subset of $\mathbb{R}^{2^\theta}$. As X is a compact space, and F is a continuous function, F attains its minimum in X. Let M denote one such minimizer of F. Then if $F(M) \leq 0$, M implements the reduced form. If $F(M) > 0$, we will show a contradiction. Let S denote the subset of types $\text{argmax}_A\{\pi(A) - M(A)\}$, i.e. the subset of types who are the most unsatisfied by M.

We show first that, if S contains every non-zero type, then the reduced form is infeasible. We may, w.l.o.g., assume that M always awards the item to a non-zero type if one shows up, as this will not decrease $M(A)$ for any non-zero A. Therefore, we know that

$$\sum_{A:\pi(A)\neq 0} \Pr[A]M(A) = \Pr[\text{see a non-zero type}].$$

However, if $\pi(A) - M(A) > 0$ for all non-zero types, then we must have $\sum_{A:\pi(A)\neq 0}\Pr[A]\pi(A) > \Pr[\text{see a non-zero type}]$ and the reduced form is infeasible. So if the reduced form is feasible, S must be missing at least one non-zero type.

Now let $s = |\{\pi(A)\}_{A \in S}|$ be the number of distinct non-zero values assigned by π to types in S. We argue that $s < \theta$. To see this, it suffices to observe the following: for all types B and B', $\pi(B) = \pi(B')$ implies that $M(B) = M(B')$ (this is because, by definition, all hierarchical mechanisms H in the support of M satisfy $H(B) = H(B')$). So in particular either $B, B' \in S$ or $B, B' \notin S$, but it cannot be that one of B, B' is in S and the other is not. And because S is missing at least one non-zero type, $s < \theta$.

To show a contradiction to $F(M) > 0$, let us define a new reduced form π' as follows. For all $A \in S$, set $\pi'(A) = \pi(A)$. For all $A \notin S$, set $\pi'(A) = \max_{B \in S|\pi(B)<\pi(A)}\{\pi(B)\}$, unless $\{B \mid B \in S \wedge \pi(B) < \pi(A)\}$ is empty in which case we set $\pi'(A) = 0$. Observe that the number of distinct non-zero values in $\{\pi'(A)\}_{A \in T}$ is exactly $s < \theta$. So it follows by our inductive hypothesis that π' can be implemented by a distribution over well-ordered (with respect to π') hierarchical mechanisms. In fact, as $\pi(A) \geq \pi(A') \Rightarrow \pi'(A) \geq \pi'(A')$, every hierarchical mechanism that is well-ordered with respect to π' is also well-ordered with respect to π. Call M' the distribution over well-ordered hierarchical mechanisms implementing π'. Now, set $\epsilon = (F(M) - \text{argmax}_{A \notin S}\{\pi(A) - M(A)\})/2$, and consider the distribution $M'' = (1-\epsilon)M + \epsilon M'$ (with probability $(1-\epsilon)$ sample from M, with probability ϵ sample from M').

What is $M''(A)$? If $A \in S$, then $M'(A) = \pi(A)$, so $M''(A) = (1-\epsilon)M(A) + \epsilon\pi(A)$. So for all $A \in S$, $M''(A) > M(A)$, hence $\pi(A) - M''(A) < F(M)$.

If $A \notin S$, then $M'(A) \geq 0$, so $M''(A) \geq (1-\epsilon)M(A) \geq M(A) - \epsilon$, so we get $\pi(A) - M''(A) \leq \pi(A) - M(A) + \epsilon < F(M)$. Putting both observations together, we see that $F(M'') < F(M)$, a contradiction.

So we must have $F(M) \leq 0$, meaning M implements the reduced form, completing the inductive step and the proof of the lemma. □

COROLLARY 1. *Every feasible bidder-symmetric reduced form π can be exactly implemented as a distribution over well-ordered w.r.t. π hierarchical mechanisms.*

PROOF. It follows from Lemma 1 that π can be implemented as a distribution over well-ordered w.r.t. π hierarchical mechanisms. Let then X denote the set of distributions over well-ordered w.r.t. π hierarchical mechanisms that implement π. As in Lemma 1 the set X, viewed as a subset of $\mathbb{R}^{2^\theta}$, where θ is the number of distinct non-zero values in π, is compact. We can also define the function $G : X \to \mathbb{R}$ as:

$$G(M) = \max_A \{M(A) - \pi(A)\}.$$

Equipping X with the Euclidean distance of $\mathbb{R}^{2^\theta}$, G is a continuous function on X. As X is compact and G continuous, G attains its minimum in X.

We show that the minimum of G is exactly 0 (i.e. that a minimizer of G exactly implements π), following an induction similar to the one used in Lemma 1 in terms of the number of distinct non-zero values in $\{\pi(A)\}_{A\in T}$. We sketch the steps involved for the inductive step. Take any minimizer M of G. If $G(M) \leq 0$, then because M has to implement π, M must exactly implement π. If $G(M) > 0$, then let $S = T - \text{argmax}_A\{M(A) - \pi(A)\}$. Then, for all $A \in S$, define $\pi'(A) = \pi(A)$. For all $A \notin S$, define $\pi'(A) = \max_{B\in S|\pi(B)\leq\pi(A)}\{\pi(B)\}$, unless $\{B : B \in S \wedge \pi(B) \leq \pi(A)\}$ is empty, in which case set $\pi'(A) = 0$. As $\text{argmax}\{M(A) - \pi(A)\}$ can't possibly be empty the number of distinct non-zero values in $\{\pi'(A)\}_{A\in T}$ is smaller than that in $\{\pi(A)\}_{A\in T}$. (We still use the observation that, for all types B and B', $\pi(B) = \pi(B')$ implies that $M(B) = M(B')$). The rest of the inductive step proceeds identically with that in the proof of Lemma 1, resulting in a contradiction. Hence, it can't be that the minimizer of G satisfies $G(M) > 0$. □

To proceed we need a definition. Let $>:= A_1 > A_2 > \ldots > A_k$ be a total ordering of a set $T_k := \{A_1, \ldots, A_k\}$ of k types, and consider a setting where we have m bidders whose types are distributed i.i.d. over T_k. We say that a bidder-symmetric reduced form $\pi : T_k \to [0, 1]$ respects $>$ iff $\pi(A_1) \geq \pi(A_2) \geq \ldots \geq \pi(A_k)$. We also say that an hierarchical mechanism H on T_k is well-ordered with respect to $>$ iff $H(A_1) \leq H(A_2) \leq \ldots \leq H(A_k)$.[8] With respect to these definitions we show the following proposition.

PROPOSITION 1. *Consider m bidders whose types are distributed i.i.d. over $T_k := \{A_1, \ldots, A_k\}$ and a total ordering $>:= A_1 > A_2 > \ldots > A_k$ of T_k. The set of feasible bidder-symmetric reduced forms that respect $>$ is a k-dimensional polytope whose corners are exactly the 2^k hierarchical mechanisms that are well-ordered with respect to $>$.*

PROOF. As a corollary of Theorem 1, a reduced form respects $>$ and is feasible if and only if

$$\pi(A_i) \geq \pi(A_{i+1}) \qquad \forall i \in [k]; \tag{4}$$

$$\sum_{j\leq i} m \cdot \Pr[A_j]\pi(A_j) \leq 1 - \left(1 - \sum_{j\leq i} \Pr[A_j]\right)^m \qquad \forall i \in [k]; \tag{5}$$

where for notational convenience we denote $\pi(A_{k+1}) = 0$. We have hence shown that the set of feasible bidder-symmetric reduced forms that respect $>$ is a k-dimensional polytope.

We proceed to show that each well-ordered w.r.t. $>$ hierarchical mechanism is a corner. Let H be such a mechanism and π be the reduced form that it induces. Then, for all i (including $i = k$, denoting $H(A_{k+1}) = \text{LOSE}$) we either have $H(A_i) = H(A_{i+1})$, in which case $\pi(A_i) = \pi(A_{i+1})$, or $H(A_i) < H(A_{i+1})$, in which case $\sum_{j\leq i} m \cdot \Pr[A_j]\pi(A_j) = 1 - (1 - \sum_{j\leq i} \Pr[A_j])^m$, because the item is always awarded to one of the top i types whenever one is present. Therefore, at least k of the inequalities defining the polytope are tight. And it is easy to see that there is a unique reduced form making these inequalities tight. It is also clear that every well-ordered w.r.t. $>$ hierarchical mechanism is inside the polytope. So every well-ordered w.r.t. $>$ hierarchical mechanism is a corner of the polytope.

Finally, we show that there are no other corners. Assume for contradiction that there was a corner π of the polytope that is not a well-ordered w.r.t. $>$ hierarchical mechanism. Then by Corollary 1, we know that π can be written as a convex combination of well-ordered w.r.t. π hierarchical mechanisms, and hence as a convex combination of well-ordered w.r.t. $>$ hierarchical mechanisms. (As π respects $>$ a hierarchical mechanism that is well-ordered w.r.t. π will also be well-ordered w.r.t. $>$). As every well-ordered w.r.t. $>$ hierarchical mechanism is a corner of the polytope, and π is not one of them, this means that π can be written as a convex combination of *other* corners of the polytope, which contradicts that π is itself a corner.

Therefore we have shown that every feasible bidder symmetric reduced form respecting $>$ lies inside the aforedescribed polytope, every well-ordered w.r.t. $>$ hierarchical mechanism is a corner of this polytope, and there are no other corners. This establishes the proposition. □

Now we can put everything together to prove Theorems 3 and 2.

Proof of Theorem 3: Suppose that the bidders' types are sampled i.i.d. from T according to $\mathcal{D}_1$, and let π be a feasible bidder-symmetric reduced form. We do the following preprocessing operation on the set of types T:

TYPEMERGE: Find a maximal set of types $A_1, \ldots, A_\ell \in T$ such that $\pi(A_1) = \ldots = \pi(A_\ell)$. Then remove types $A_1, \ldots, A_\ell$ from T and add super-type $\langle A_1, \ldots, A_\ell\rangle$ into T; change $\mathcal{D}_1$ to never sample any of $A_1, \ldots, A_\ell$ and sample the super-type $\langle A_1, \ldots, A_\ell\rangle$ with probability $\sum_i \Pr[A_i]$; and set $\pi(\langle A_1, \ldots, A_\ell\rangle) = \pi(A_1)$. Repeat this procedure until every type in T has different π value, i.e. until the set $\{\pi(A)\}_{A\in T}$ has cardinality $|T|$.

Let T', π', $\mathcal{D}'_1$ be the type-set, reduced-form, type distri-

[8]Notice that this definition of well-ordered hierarchical mechanism (with respect to $>$) is very similar to its counterpart in the main body (with respect to π), but different. Being well-ordered with respect to π certainly imposes the same constraints as being well ordered with respect to any $>$ that π respects. The difference is that being well-ordered with respect to π may also impose some equality constraints, if $\pi(A) = \pi(B)$ for types $A \neq B$.

bution resulting from the TYPEMERGE operation on input π. We claim that:

1. π' is a feasible bidder-symmetric reduced form for bidders sampled i.i.d. from $\mathcal{D}'_1$. This follows immediately from the feasibility of π. Indeed it follows from Theorem 1 and our discussion in Section 3.1.1 that a sufficient condition for the feasibility of π' is for it to satisfy Eq. (1) for all subsets of types of the form $\{A \mid A \in T' \wedge \pi'(A) \geq x\}$. On the other hand the feasibility of π implies that π satisfies Eq. (1) for all subsets of types of the form $\{A \mid A \in T \wedge \pi(A) \geq x\}$. This together with the nature of our TYPEMERGE operation implies that π' satisfies the afore-mentioned sufficient conditions for feasibility.

2. A mechanism that exactly implements π' immediately gives a mechanism exactly implementing π. Indeed, to implement π we just run the mechanism implementing π' after replacing in the reported type vector every type A that was removed from T by TYPEMERGE by its corresponding super-type.

3. A hierarchical mechanism H' that is well-ordered w.r.t. π' can be *expanded* into a hierarchical mechanism H that is well-ordered w.r.t. π. Indeed, if super-type $\langle A_1, \ldots, A_\ell \rangle$ replaced types $A_1, \ldots, A_\ell$ during the TYPEMERGE operation we set $H(A_i) := H'(\langle A_1, \ldots, A_\ell \rangle)$, for all $i = 1, \ldots, \ell$. On the other hand, if a type A belongs in both T and T', we set $H(A) := H'(A)$. Moreover, if $\pi_{H'}$, π_H are respectively the reduced forms induced by H' and H, the following property is satisfied. If super-type $\langle A_1, \ldots, A_\ell \rangle$ replaced types $A_1, \ldots, A_\ell$ during the TYPEMERGE operation, then $\pi_H(A_i) := \pi_{H'}(\langle A_1, \ldots, A_\ell \rangle)$, for all $i = 1, \ldots, \ell$. On the other hand, if a type A belongs in both T and T', then $\pi_H(A) := \pi_{H'}(A)$.

Now, suppose that the cardinality of T' is k. Given that π' assigns a distinct probability to every type in T', it induces a total ordering on T'. In particular, suppose that $T' := \{A_1, \ldots, A_k\}$, where $\pi'(A_1) > \pi'(A_2) > \ldots > \pi'(A_k)$. By Proposition 1, π' lies inside a k-dimensional polytope whose corners are exactly the 2^k hierarchical mechanisms that are well-ordered with respect to the order $> := A_1 > \ldots > A_k$. By Carathéodory's Theorem, every point in the polytope can be written as a convex combination of at most $k+1$ corners. As a convex combination of corners is exactly a distribution over well-ordered hierarchical mechanisms w.r.t. $>$, we get that π' can be written as a distribution over hierarchical mechanisms that are well-ordered w.r.t. $>$, and hence also w.r.t. π'. Now we can expand all hierarchical mechanisms in the support of the distribution, according to the procedure described in Step 3 above, to obtain that π can be written as a distribution over hierarchical mechanisms that are well-ordered w.r.t. π. □

Proof of Theorem 2: It follows from our discussion in Section 3.1.1 that a bidder-symmetric reduced form $\tilde{\pi}$ is infeasible if and only if it violates Eq. (1) for a subset of types of the form $\{A \mid A \in T \wedge \tilde{\pi}(A) \geq x\}$. Since there are at most $c \equiv |T|$ such sets we can efficiently determine feasibility of a given reduced from $\tilde{\pi}$ or provide a hyperplane separating it from the set of feasible reduced forms.

We now need to describe how to efficiently find a mechanism implementing a reduced form $\tilde{\pi}$ that is feasible. In view of the TYPEMERGE operation defined in the proof of Theorem 3, we can w.l.o.g. assume that $\tilde{\pi}$ assigns a distinct probability to every type in T. (Otherwise we can always run TYPEMERGE to merge types sharing the same $\tilde{\pi}$-probability to super-types and apply the procedure outlined below to the output of the TYPEMERGE operation, and then go back to the original $\tilde{\pi}$). Under the assumption that $\tilde{\pi}$ assigns distinct probabilities to all types in T, Proposition 1 implies that $\tilde{\pi}$ lies inside a c-dimensional polytope, P, whose corners are the well-ordered w.r.t. $\tilde{\pi}$ hierarchical mechanisms. Therefore we can directly apply Theorem 13 of Section 5 to write $\tilde{\pi}$ as a convex combination of such hierarchical mechanisms, as long as we can describe the boundary oracle BO, corner oracle CO and separation oracle SO that are needed for Theorem 13. BO is trivial to implement, as we just have to include in the set of halfspaces defining the boundary of P those inequalities described in the proof of Proposition 1. For CO, on input B, we first check that every hyperplane $h \in B$ satisfies $BO(h) =$ yes. If not, output no. Otherwise we need to check if $\bigcap_{h \in B} h$ contains a corner of P. We know that the corners of P are exactly the well-ordered w.r.t. $\tilde{\pi}$ hierarchical mechanisms. So none of the corners lies in the intersection of the hyperplanes $\pi(A_i) = \pi(A_{i+1})$ and $\sum_{j \leq i} m \cdot \Pr[A_j]\pi(A_j) = 1 - (1 - \sum_{j \leq i} \Pr[A_j])^m$, for any i. (Indeed, for a hierarchical mechanism H and its induced reduced form π, $\pi(A_i) = \pi(A_{i+1})$ implies that $H(A_i) = H(A_{i+1})$, yet $\sum_{j \leq i} m \cdot \Pr[A_j]\pi(A_j) = 1 - (1 - \sum_{j \leq i} \Pr[A_j])^m$ implies $H(A_i) > H(A_{i+1})$). So, if B contains any pair of hyperplanes of this form, output no. Otherwise, for all i such that $\pi(A_i) = \pi(A_{i+1}) \in B$, set $H(A_i) = H(A_{i+1})$, otherwise set $H(A_i) = H(A_{i+1}) - 1$. This defines a well-ordered w.r.t. $\tilde{\pi}$ hierarchical mechanism that is in $\bigcap_{h \in B} h$, so have CO output H. Finally, SO is easy to implement as we can just check each of the $2 \cdot c$ inequalities written in the proof of Proposition 1 one by one.

So because we can implement BO, CO, SO in polynomial time, we can apply Theorem 13 to write $\tilde{\pi}$ as a convex combination of at most $c+1$ corners, which is exactly a distribution over at most $c+1$ well-ordered w.r.t. $\tilde{\pi}$ hierarchical mechanisms in polynomial time. □

7. SINGLE ITEM, INDEPENDENT BIDDERS, GENERAL REDUCED FORMS

Here we provide the details of Section 3.1.2, and the proofs of Theorems 4, 5 and 6, postponing the proof of Theorem 7 to the full version [CDW11]. Before proving our theorems, we show that the concept of virtual πs is necessary. As in, Theorem 4 would be false if we tried to replace $\hat{\pi}$ with π.

PROPOSITION 2. *There exist reduced forms that are infeasible, yet for all S_x^i of the form $S_x^i = \{A \mid \pi_i(A) > x, \forall i\}$:*

$$\sum_i \sum_{A \in S_x^i} \pi_i(A) \Pr[t_i = A] \leq 1 - \prod_{i=1}^m (1 - \sum_{A \in S_x^i} \Pr[t_i = A]).$$

PROOF. Consider the case with two bidders. Bidder 1 has two types, with $\Pr[t_1 = A] = 1/8$, $\Pr[t_1 = B] = 7/8$, $\pi_1(A) = 5/8$, $\pi_1(B) = 0$. Bidder 2 has two types, with $\Pr[t_2 = C] = 1/2$, $\Pr[t_2 = D] = 1/2$, $\pi_2(C) = 1$, $\pi_2(D) = 3/4$.

Then this reduced form is infeasible. Indeed, observe that C must always receive the item whenever $t_2 = C$, which happens with probability 1/2. So if se have $\pi_2(C) = 1$, we cannot also have $\pi_1(A) > 1/2$. So the set $\{A, C\}$ forms a constricting set. However, the sets of the form S_x^i are $\{C\}, \{C, D\}, \{C, D, A\}, \{C, D, A, B\}$, and they all satisfy the above inequality. □

Proposition 2 shows us that ordering the types of all bidders by decreasing π doesn't allow us to correctly determine the feasibility of a reduced form. Similarly, a partial ordering of the types that only orders a single bidder's types by decreasing π doesn't give enough structure to efficiently determine the feasibility of the reduced form. What we need is a correct total ordering of the types of all bidders, and we can obtain it using virtual πs. Here is a quick observation about the virtual πs, followed by a proof of Theorem 4.

OBSERVATION 1. *For two types $A, B \in T_i$, $\hat{\pi}_i(A) \geq \hat{\pi}_i(B) \Leftrightarrow \pi_i(A) \geq \pi_i(B)$.*

PROOF. If $\pi_i(A) \geq \pi_i(B)$, then $\Pr[\pi_i(t_i) \leq \pi_i(A)] \geq \Pr[\pi_i(t_i) \leq \pi_i(B)]$. Therefore, $\hat{\pi}_i(A) \geq \hat{\pi}_i(B)$. The other direction is identical. □

Proof of Theorem 4: We know from [Bor07, CKM11], that if a reduced form mechanism is infeasible, then there is some constricting set of the form $S = \bigcup_{i=1}^m S_{x_i}$, where $S_{x_i} = \{A \mid \pi_i(A) \geq x_i, A \in T_i\}$. (Forgive the abuse of notation here. Formally, S is a collection of m sets of types, one for each bidder. To avoid cumbersome notation and take union casually in this proof, let us assume that a type $A \in T_i$ carries the name of bidder i, for all i.) Now consider any minimal constricting set of this form, i.e. a choice of $x_1, \ldots, x_m$ such that replacing S_{x_i} with $S_{x_i} - \{A\}$ ($A \in S_{x_i}$) results in S no longer being a constricting set. [9] Now let $(i, A) \in \operatorname{argmin}_{i,\, A \in S_{x_i}} \hat{\pi}_i(A)$. Then by Observation 1 and by our choice of S, $S - \{A\}$ is not a constricting set. Therefore, adding A to $S - \{A\}$ must increase the left-hand bound by more than it increases the right-hand bound:

$$\Pr[t_i = A]\pi_i(A) > \Pr[t_i = A] \prod_{j \neq i} \Pr[\pi_j(t_j) < x_j]$$

$$\Longrightarrow \frac{\pi_i(A)}{\prod_{j \neq i} \Pr[\pi_j(t_j) < x_j]} > 1.$$

Now consider any other $A' \in T_k$, $A' \notin S$ and $\hat{\pi}_k(A') \geq \hat{\pi}_i(A)$. Observe first that we must have A' from some bidder $k \neq i$, as every $A'' \in T_i$ with $\hat{\pi}_i(A'') \geq \hat{\pi}_i(A)$ has $\pi_i(A'') \geq \pi_i(A) \geq x_i$, so we would have $A'' \in S$. So for this A', we have:

$$\begin{aligned}
&\pi_k(A') \Pr[\pi_k(t_k) \leq \pi_k(A')] \geq \pi_i(A) \Pr[\pi_i(t_i) \leq \pi_i(A)] \\
\Longrightarrow &\pi_k(A') \Pr[\pi_k(t_k) < x_k] \geq \pi_i(A) \Pr[\pi_i(t_i) < \pi_i(A)] \\
\Longrightarrow &\pi_k(A') \Pr[\pi_k(t_k) < x_k] \geq \pi_i(A) \Pr[\pi_i(t_i) < x_i] \\
\Longrightarrow &\pi_k(A') \prod_{j \neq i} \Pr[\pi_j(t_j) < x_j] \geq \pi_i(A) \prod_{j \neq k} \Pr[\pi_j(t_j) < x_j] \\
\Longrightarrow &\frac{\pi_k(A')}{\prod_{j \neq k} \Pr[\pi_j(t_j) < x_j]} \geq \frac{\pi_i(A)}{\prod_{j \neq i} \Pr[\pi_j(t_j) < x_j]}.
\end{aligned}$$

[9]For a minimal set S, there could be many possible choices of $x_1, \ldots, x_m$. We simply use any of them.

And by our choice of A and the work above, we obtain:

$$\frac{\pi_k(A')}{\prod_{j \neq k} \Pr[\pi_j(t_j) < x_j]} > 1$$

$$\Longrightarrow \Pr[t_k = A']\pi_k(A') > \Pr[t_k = A'] \prod_{j \neq k} \Pr[\pi_j(t_j) < x_j].$$

This equation tells us directly that we could add A' to S and still get a constricting set. In fact, it tells us something stronger. If $S' = \bigcup_j S'_j$, where $S'_j \subseteq T_j$, is any constricting set containing S, then we could add A' to S' and still have a constricting set. This is because the change to the left-hand side of the inequality is the same, no matter what set we are adding A' to. It is always $\Pr[t_k = A']\pi_k(A')$. And the change to the right-hand side is exactly $\Pr[t_k = A']$ times the probability that none of the types in $\cup_{j \neq k} S'_j$ show up. As we add more types to S, the probability that none of the types in $\cup_{j \neq k} S'_j$ show up will never increase. So for any constricting set S' containing S, we can add A' to S'_k and still get a constricting set.

So starting from a constricting set S and a type $A \in T_i$ as above we can add every $B \in T_j$ with $\hat{\pi}_j(B) \geq \hat{\pi}_i(A)$ to S in order to obtain a constricting set of the form $S_x = \{B | B \in T_j \wedge \hat{\pi}_j(B) \geq x\}$, where $x = \hat{\pi}_i(A)$. So every infeasible reduced form has a constricting set of this form. Taking the contrapositive proves the theorem. □

We say that a hierarchical mechanism H is *virtually-ordered* if $\hat{\pi}_i(A) \geq \hat{\pi}_j(A') \Rightarrow H(A, i) \leq H(A', j)$. While the virtual πs give us a nice structural theorem about feasible reduced forms and a linear time separation oracle for determining feasibility (see proof of Theorem 6), the following observation shows that distributions over virtually-ordered hierarchical mechanisms are not sufficient to implement every feasible reduced form when the bidders are non-i.i.d.

OBSERVATION 2. *There exist feasible reduced forms that are not implementable as distributions over virtually-ordered hierarchical mechanisms.*

PROOF. Consider the following example with two bidders. Bidder one has a single type, A. Bidder two has two types, B and C and is each with probability 1/2. Then $\pi_1(A) = 1/3$, $\pi_2(B) = 2/3 + \epsilon$, $\pi_2(C) = 2/3 - \epsilon$ is a feasible reduced form. However, $\hat{\pi}_1(A) > \hat{\pi}_2(C)$, so no distribution over virtually-ordered hierarchical mechanisms can possibly have $\pi_2(C) > 1/2$. □

Now that we have motivated Theorems 5 and 6, we proceed to prove them, after providing the key steps as technical lemmas.

LEMMA 2. *Every feasible reduced form π for independent bidders and a single item can be implemented (not necessarily exactly implemented) as a distribution over strict, partially-ordered w.r.t. π hierarchical mechanisms.*

PROOF. The proof is almost identical to that of Lemma 1. Here are the main differences: We do induction on $\sum_i d_i$, where d_i is the number of distinct non-zero values in the set $\{\pi_i(A)\}_{A \in T_i}$. For the inductive step, X is now taken to be the set of distributions over strict, partially-ordered hierarchical mechanisms, and it is still compact, viewed as a subset of the Euclidean space. The function $F : X \to \mathbb{R}$ is now defined as

$$F(M) = \max_{i, A \in T_i} \{\pi_i(A) - M_i(A)\}.$$

Again, if we use the Euclidean distance on X, as a subset of the Euclidean space, F is continuous. Since F is continuous and X is compact, F achieves its minimum inside X. Let M be a minimizer. For all i, we define $S_i = \{A \in T_i | \pi_i(A) - M_i(A) = F(M)\}$. In terms of the sets $\{S_i\}_i$ we can define an alternative reduced form π' as follows. For all i, $A \in T_i$: if $A \in S_i$, then set $\pi'_i(A) = \pi_i(A)$; otherwise, set $\pi'_i(A) = \max_{B \in S_i | \pi_i(A) \geq \pi_i(B)} \{\pi(B)\}$, unless $\{B \in S_i | \pi_i(A) \geq \pi_i(B)\}$ is empty in which case set $\pi'_i(A)$ equal to 0. With these changes, the proof is truly identical to that of Lemma 1, and we avoid repeating the steps for brevity. □

COROLLARY 2. *Every feasible reduced form π for independent bidders and a single item can be exactly implemented as a distribution over strict, partially-ordered w.r.t. π hierarchical mechanisms.*

PROOF. The proof is identical to that of Corollary 1 after making the same modifications going from Lemma 1 to Lemma 2. □

We proceed to prove an analog of Proposition 1 in this setting. We need a definition. For all i, let $>^i := A_{i,1} >^i A_{i,2} >^i \ldots >^i A_{i,k_i}$ be a total ordering of the set $T_i := \{A_{i,1}, \ldots, A_{i,k_i}\}$ of bidder i's types. We say that a reduced form π respects $>^i$ iff $\pi_i(A_{i,1}) \geq \pi_i(A_{i,2}) \geq \ldots \geq \pi_i(A_{i,k_i})$. We also say that an hierarchical mechanism H is partially-ordered with respect to $>^i$ iff $H(A_{i,1}, i) \leq H(A_{i,2}, i) \leq \ldots \leq H(A_{i,k_i}, i)$.[10] With respect to these definitions we show the following proposition.

PROPOSITION 3. *For all i, let $>^i := A_{i,1} >^i A_{i,2} >^i \ldots >^i A_{i,k_i}$ be a total ordering of the set $T_i := \{A_{i,1}, \ldots, A_{i,k_i}\}$ of bidder i's types. The set of feasible reduced forms that respect $>^1, \ldots, >^m$ is a $(\sum_i k_i)$-dimensional polytope whose corners are exactly the strict, partially-ordered w.r.t. $>^1, \ldots, >^m$ hierarchical mechanisms.*

PROOF. We know from [Bor07, CKM11] that a reduced form π respects $>^1, \ldots, >^m$ and is feasible iff

$$\pi_i(A_{i,j}) \geq \pi_i(A_{i,j+1}) \qquad \forall i \in [m], j \in [k_i] \tag{6}$$

$$\forall x_1 \in [k_1], \ldots, x_m \in [k_m]$$

$$\sum_i \sum_{j \leq x_i} \Pr[t_i = A_{i,j}] \pi_i(A_{i,j}) \leq 1 - \prod_i \left(1 - \sum_{j \leq x_i} \Pr[t_i = A_{i,j}]\right) \tag{7}$$

where for notational convenience we denote $\pi_i(A_{i,k_i+1}) = 0$. In fact, to make our lives easier in a later proof, we will actually replace (7) with:

$$\forall x_1 \in [k_1 - 1], \ldots, x_m \in [k_m - 1]$$

$$\sum_i \sum_{j \leq x_i} \Pr[t_i = A_{i,j}] \pi_i(A_{i,j}) \leq 1 - \prod_i \left(1 - \sum_{j \leq x_i} \Pr[t_i = A_{i,j}]\right) \tag{8}$$

$$\sum_i \sum_{j \leq k_i} \Pr[t_i = A_{i,j}] \pi_i(A_{i,j}) \leq 1 \tag{9}$$

In the above above replacement, we are basically observing that if (9) holds, then so does (7) for any case where at least one i has $x_i = k_i$. In addition, (8) covers all other cases. We have hence shown that the set of feasible reduced forms that respect $>^1, \ldots, >^m$ is a $\sum_i k_i$-dimensional polytope.

We proceed to show that any strict, partially-ordered w.r.t. $>^1, \ldots, >^m$ hierarchical mechanism H whose reduced-form is π is a corner. For convenience in the proof assume that $T_i \cap T_k = \emptyset$, for all $i \neq k$. This is easy to achieve by having every type of bidder i carry the name of bidder i, for all i. Let now $y = \min_x \Pr[\exists i, H(t_i, i) \leq x] = 1$, i.e. the minimum y so that with probability 1 some bidder i will report a type $A_{i,j}$ such that $H(A_{i,j}, i) \leq y$. In terms of this y we define y^* as follows: $y^* := y$, if $y \neq$ LOSE (case 1), and $y^* := y - 1$, if $y =$ LOSE (case 2). We observe then that a type $A_{i,j} \in T_i$ with $H(A_{i,j}, i) > y^*$ cannot possibly win the item, as we are either guaranteed to see some bidder whose type lies on a higher level of the hierarchy (case 1) or the type is mapped to LOSE and is hence given no item (case 2). For all such $i, A_{i,j} \in T_i$, we therefore have $\pi_i(A_{i,j}) = \pi_i(A_{i,j+1}) = \cdots = \pi_i(A_{i,k_i+1}) = 0$.

We say that a set of types $S = \cup_i \{A_{i,1}, \ldots, A_{i,x_i}\}$ for some $x_1, \ldots, x_m$ is *near-constricting*, if the corresponding Inequality (7) is tight for $x_1, \ldots, x_m$. Then, for any $i, A_{i,j} \in T_i$ with $H(A_{i,j}, i) \leq y^*$, we know that $H^{-1}([H(A_{i,j}, i)])$ is a near-constricting set, because the item is always awarded to a type in $H^{-1}([H(A_{i,j}, i)])$ whenever at least one type from this set is reported. Moreover, if $H(A_{i,j_1}, i) = \ldots = H(A_{i,j_\ell}, i)$, for some types $A_{i,j_1}, \ldots, A_{i,j_\ell} \in T_i$, then $\pi_i(A_{i,j_1}) = \ldots = \pi_i(A_{i,j_\ell})$. Finally, because H is strict, if some $i, A_{i,j} \in T_i$ satisfy $H(A_{i,j}, i) \leq y^*$, then $H^{-1}(H(A_{i,j}, i)) \cap T_k = \emptyset$, for all $k \neq i$.

Let us now define the following mapping from types to tight inequalities:

- If a type $A_{i,j} \in T_i$ satisfies $H(A_{i,j}, i) > y^*$, then we map $A_{i,j}$ to the constraint $\pi_i(A_{i,j}) = \pi_i(A_{i,j+1})$, i.e. the tightness of inequality $\pi_i(A_{i,j}) \geq \pi_i(A_{i,j+1})$.
- If a type $A_{i,j} \in T_i$ satisfies $H(A_{i,j}, i) \leq y^*$, then:
  - if $H(A_{i,j}, i) = H(A_{i,j+1}, i)$, we map $A_{i,j}$ to the constraint $\pi_i(A_{i,j}) = \pi_i(A_{i,j+1})$, i.e. the tightness of inequality $\pi_i(A_{i,j}) \geq \pi_i(A_{i,j+1})$;
  - otherwise, we map $A_{i,j}$ to the tightness of Inequality (7) for the set of types $H^{-1}([H(A_{i,j}, i)])$.

The above discussion ensures that our mapping is injective. Hence π makes at least $\sum_i k_i$ of the inequalities defining our polytope tight. And it is not hard to see that there is a unique feasible reduced form making these inequalities tight. So π is a corner of the polytope. Thus, every strict, partially-ordered w.r.t. $>^1, \ldots, >^m$ hierarchical mechanism is a corner of the polytope.

We now make the same observation as in Proposition 1 to argue that there are no other corners. Corollary 2 implies

[10]Notice that this definition of partially-ordered hierarchical mechanism (with respect to $\{>^i\}_i$) is similar to its counterpart in the main body (with respect to π), but different. Being partially-ordered with respect to π certainly imposes the same constraints as being partially-ordered with respect to any $\{>^i\}_i$ that π respects. The difference is that being partially-ordered with respect to π may also impose some equality constraints, if $\pi_i(A) = \pi_i(B)$ for types $A \neq B$.

that every point in the polytope can be written as a convex combination of strict, partially-ordered w.r.t. $>^1, \ldots, >^m$ hierarchical mechanisms, all of which are corners of the polytope. As no corner of the polytope can be written as a convex combination of *other* corners of the polytope, there must not be any other corners. □

And now we are ready to prove Theorems 5 and 6.

Proof of Theorem 5: Using a similar argument as in the proof of Theorem 3 we can assume without loss of generality that, for all i, π assigns a distinct probability to every type in T_i. (Otherwise we can define a similar TYPEMERGE operation, like the one defined in the proof of Theorem 3, whereby types in T_i that receive the same π value are merged into super-types.) Under this assumption, Proposition 3 implies that π lies inside a $(\sum_i |T_i|)$-dimensional polytope, P, whose corners are the strict, partially-ordered w.r.t. π hierarchical mechanisms. By Carathéodory's Theorem, every point in the polytope can be written as a convex combination of at most $(\sum_i |T_i|) + 1$ corners. As a convex combination of corners is exactly a distribution over strict, partially-ordered w.r.t. π hierarchical mechanisms, this proves the theorem. □

Proof of Theorem 6: The first part of the theorem follows immediately as a corollary of Theorem 4.

We now need to describe how to efficiently find a mechanism implementing a reduced form $\tilde{\pi}$ that is feasible. Using a similar argument as in the proof of Theorem 2 we can assume without loss of generality that, for all i, $\tilde{\pi}$ assigns a distinct probability to every type in T_i. (Otherwise we can merge types in T_i that receive the same $\tilde{\pi}$ value into super-types, like we did in the proof of Theorem 2, then run the procedure outlined below, and finally un-merge types.) Under this assumption, Proposition 3 implies that $\tilde{\pi}$ lies inside a $(\sum_i |T_i|)$-dimensional polytope, P, whose corners are the strict, partially-ordered w.r.t. $\tilde{\pi}$ hierarchical mechanisms. Therefore we can directly apply Theorem 13 of Section 5 to write $\tilde{\pi}$ as a convex combination of such hierarchical mechanisms, as long as we can describe the boundary oracle BO, corner oracle CO and separation oracle SO that are needed for Theorem 13. BO is trivial to implement, as we just have to include in the set of halfspaces defining the boundary of P those inequalities described in the proof of Proposition 3. In particular, for convenience in the remaining of the proof, we include the inequalities of the form (6), (8) and (9). For CO, on input B, we first check that every hyperplane $h \in B$ satisfies $BO(h)$ = yes. If not, output no. Otherwise, we need to check if $\bigcap_{h\in B} h$ contains a corner of P. We know that the corners of P are exactly the strict, partially-ordered w.r.t. $\tilde{\pi}$ hierarchical mechanisms. To check if there is such a corner in $\bigcap_{h\in B} h$ we need to do some work.

First, let us use the same notation as in Proposition 3, denoting $T_i = \{A_{i,1}, \ldots, A_{i,k_i}\}$, where $k_i = |T_i|$ and $\tilde{\pi}_i(A_{i,1}) > \ldots > \tilde{\pi}_i(A_{i,k_i})$. Also, let us call a set of types S near-constricting if either $S = \cup_i\{A_{i,1}, \ldots, A_{i,x_i}\}$ for some $x_1 \leq k_1 - 1, \ldots, x_m \leq k_m - 1$ and Inequality (8) is tight for $x_1, \ldots, x_m$, or if $S = \cup_i T_i$ and Inequality (9) is tight.

Now given a set B of hyperplanes, if B contains a near-constricting set hyperplane for the sets of types $S_1, \ldots, S_k$, we check first whether these sets satisfy $S_1 \subset S_2 \ldots \subset S_k$ (possibly after renaming). If not, then there are some two near-constricting sets S_i, S_j with $A \in S_i - S_j$, $B \in S_j - S_i$ for some types $A \neq B$. Because S_i and S_j are different than $\cup_i T_i$ and they are near-constricting they must be of the form making Inequality (8) tight. Hence, both S_i and S_j miss at least one type of every bidder, so that the right-hand side of the inequality for S_i must be < 1 and similarly the right-hand side of the inequality for S_j must be < 1. In addition, we cannot have A and B be types of the same bidder, as we only consider near-constricting sets that respect the partial ordering within every bidder's type-set. Therefore, A and B belong to different bidders, and because the probability of seeing a type in S_i is < 1 (and the same holds for S_j), there is a non-zero probability that A and B are both present, but no other type of S_i or S_j is present. Then the near-constricting set equation for set S_i requires that we must give the item to A,[11] and the near-constricting set equation for S_j requires that we must give the item to B, which is impossible. So if we do not have $S_1 \subset S_2 \ldots \subset S_k$, the hyperplanes do not intersect in a feasible mechanism, and therefore CO should output no.

Otherwise, CO looks at the other hyperplanes (of the form $\pi_i(A_{i,j}) = \pi_i(A_{i,j+1})$) that belong to B, and chooses an arbitrary strict, partially-ordered w.r.t. $\tilde{\pi}$ hierarchical mechanism that satisfies the following constraints:

1. $H(A, i) < H(A', i')$ for all $(A, i) \in S_j, (A', i') \in S_{j+1} - S_j$, for all j.
2. $H(A, i) < H(A', i')$ for all $(A, i) \in S_k, (A', i') \notin S_k$.
3. For all $i, A_{i,j} \in T_i$:
   (a) if the hyperplanes $\pi_i(A_{i,j}) = \pi_i(A_{i,j+1})$, $\pi_i(A_{i,j+1}) = \pi_i(A_{i,j+2})$, ..., $\pi_i(A_{i,k_i}) = 0 (= \pi_i(A_{i,k_i+1}))$ are all in B, then $H(A_{i,j}, i) =$ LOSE;
   (b) otherwise, if $\pi_i(A_{i,j}) = \pi_i(A_{i,j+1})$ is in B, then either $H(A_{i,j}) = H(A_{i,j+1}) =$ LOSE or $H(A_{i,j}) \geq H(A_{i,j+1}) - 1$.

We claim that an H satisfying the above constraints exists if and only if $\bigcap_{h\in B} h \cap P \neq \emptyset$. By Proposition 3, we know that if there is a corner π in $\bigcap_{h\in B} h \cap P$, there is a strict, partially-ordered w.r.t. $\tilde{\pi}$ hierarchical mechanism H that implements it. Without loss of generality we can make two simplifying assumptions about H: (i) For all $t \neq$ LOSE, $|H^{-1}(t)| \leq 1$. Indeed, suppose that $|H^{-1}(t)| > 1$ for some $t \neq$ LOSE. Then because H is strict, location t of the hierarchy defined by H only contains types belonging to the same bidder i. And because H is partially ordered w.r.t. $\tilde{\pi}$ these types are consecutive in T_i. So we can change H to "expand" cell t of the hierarchy into consecutive cells containing a single type each in the right order. This has no effect in the mechanism defined by H. (ii) If H awards the item to bidder i of type $A_{i,j}$ with probability 0, we can assume that $H(A_{i,j}, i) =$ LOSE. Now given (i) and the nature of $S_1, \ldots, S_k$,[12] for H to have the sets $S_1, \ldots, S_k$ near-constricting it must satisfy the first two constraints above. Indeed for these constraints not to be satisfied there must exist ℓ, $i, A_{i,j}$, $i', A_{i',j'}$, $i \neq i'$ such that $H(A_{i,j}, i) <$

[11]Recall that a way to interpret a near-constricting set equation for set S is the following: whenever at least one bidder reports a type in S to the mechanism, the mechanism gives the item to a bidder who reported a type in S, with probability 1.

[12]in particular, the fact that the sets $S_1, \ldots, S_k$ respect the ordering of the type sets as follows: For all ℓ, $A_{i,j} \in S_\ell$ implies $A_{i,j'} \in S_\ell$, for all $j' \leq j$.

$H(A_{i',j'}, i')$ and $A_{i,j} \notin S_\ell$ while $A_{i',j'} \in S_\ell$. But then it must be $\pi(A_{i,j}) > 0$ (because of assumption (ii)), so there is a positive probability that bidder i of type $A_{i,j}$ is the highest in the hierarchy when every bidder except for i' has declared a type. Still, given that $H(A_{i,j}, i) < H(A_{i',j'}, i')$, even if i' declares $A_{i',j'}$, i will get the item, contradicting that S_ℓ is near-constricting. We argue next that H also needs to satisfy the third constraint above. That constraint 3(a) is satisfied follows immediately from assumption (ii). We argue next that 3(b) needs to be satisfied. Indeed, suppose there exist $A_{i,j}, A_{i,j+1} \in T_i$ and $A_{i',j'} \in T_{i'}$ such that $\pi_i(A_{i,j}) = \pi_i(A_{i,j+1}) > 0$ and $H(A_{i,j}, i) < H(A_{i',j'}, i') < H(A_{i,j+1}, i)$. As $\pi_i(A_{i,j+1}) > 0$, it follows that $H(A_{i,j+1}, i) <$ LOSE, so $H(A_{i',j'}, i') <$ LOSE, which implies that $\pi_{i'}(A_{i',j'}) > 0$ (otherwise it would be that $H(A_{i',j'}, i') =$ LOSE given (ii)). Now, because bidder i' wins the item with non-zero probability as type $A_{i',j'}$, there is a non-zero probability that $A_{i',j'}$ is on the highest level of the hierarchy after sampling from all bidders except for i. In this case, i will win the item by reporting $A_{i,j}$, and lose by reporting $A_{i,j+1}$. In all other cases, i is at least as likely to win the item by reporting $A_{i,j}$ as $A_{i,j+1}$, and therefore we see that bidder i gets the item strictly more often when reporting $A_{i,j}$ than $A_{i,j+1}$, violating the constraint $\pi_i(A_{i,j}) = \pi_i(A_{i,j+1})$. So if there is a corner π in $\bigcap_{h \in B} h \cap P$ it can be implemented by a strict, partially-ordered w.r.t. $\tilde{\pi}$ hierarchical mechanism H satisfying the above constraints. The other direction of our claim is even simpler. If a strict, partially-ordered w.r.t. $\tilde{\pi}$ hierarchical mechanism H satisfies all constraints above, then its induced reduced-form π will immediately satisfy all equalities in B.

Hence to implement CO one just needs to check if there is a strict, partially-ordered w.r.t. $\tilde{\pi}$ hierarchical mechanism H satisfying the four constraints above. This task is easy to do efficiently. If a mechanism is found it satisfies all equalities in B and it is a corner of the polytope by Proposition 3.

SO is also simple to implement. On input $\vec{\pi}$, we first check that Inequalities (6) are satisfied (i.e. that $\vec{\pi}$ respects the total orderings on the bidders' type-spaces induced by $\tilde{\pi}$). Then we use the separation oracle provided by Theorem 4 to verify that $\vec{\pi}$ is feasible. As all three oracles BO, CO, SO run in polynomial time, we can apply Theorem 13 to write $\tilde{\pi}$ as a convex combination of at most $\sum_i |T_i| + 1$ corners, which is exactly a distribution over at most $\sum_i |T_i| + 1$ strict, partially-ordered hierarchical mechanisms in polynomial time. □

8. OPTIMAL MULTI-DIMENSIONAL MECHANISMS

We sketch how to use our results from the previous sections and recent results of [DW11] to obtain the proofs of Theorems 8, 9, 10 and 11. Simply put, [DW11] provides a LP formulation for the problem of finding the optimal BIC mechanism for value distributions of finite support. In addition, [DW11] exploits any symmetry that may exist in the value distribution to reduce the size of the resulting LPs. However, without a separation oracle to determine the feasibility of the πs, these LP formulations will have size exponential in the number of bidders in the settings we consider, even when the bidders are i.i.d., because the LPs need to maintain variables for the ex-post allocation rule described by the ϕ's (See Section 2). Using the separation oracles of Theorems 2 and 6, we can eliminate the need for ϕ's in these LPs, turning the number of variables to polynomial in the number of bidders, and solving them in time polynomial in m, n and $\max_i |supp(\mathcal{F}_i)|$, thereby establishing Theorem 8. Theorem 9 follows immediately by combining our separation oracles with the symmetric LPs of Section 5 of [DW11]. Theorem 10 follows by discretizing the value distributions, applying the aforementioned symmetric LPs and the ϵ-BIC to BIC reduction of Section 6 of [DW11]. Finally, Theorem 11 is obtained by truncating and discretizing the value distributions, running the symmetric LP on the resulting distributions, and using the ϵ-BIC to BIC reduction of Section 6 of [DW11]. (This procedure is described in detail in Appendix J of [DW11].)

For completeness, in Figure 3 we describe how to modify the LP of [DW11] to exploit our separation oracles. We only describe the LP for the item-symmetric case to illustrate some extra work that is needed to handle symmetries. It is clear how to "un-symmetrize" the LP to treat the non-symmetric problem. The LP shown in Figure 3 is identical to the item-symmetric LP of [DW11] except that we have replaced the naïve feasibility constraints for the reduced form used in [DW11] (these were explicitly finding consistent $\vec{\phi}(P)$'s for every profile) with a separation oracle SO that takes as input a reduced form and decides whether it is feasible or not, in which case it also provides a separation hyperplane from the feasible set. The reader should refer to [DW11] for the correctness of the unmodified LP. So we only need to justify here that our separation oracle works properly. While this is obvious in the non-symmetric case (as it follows directly from Theorem 6), it is slightly trickier for the symmetric LP of Figure 3, as the LP does not explicitly maintain the whole reduced form. In particular, for every bidder i, we only maintain the reduced form for all types of bidder i in the set $E_i = \{\vec{v}_i \mid v_{i1} \geq \ldots \geq v_{in}\}$, and it is assumed that (because of symmetries) the reduced form of a type $\vec{w}_i \notin E_i$ is just $\{\pi_{ij}(\vec{w}_i) = \pi_{i\sigma^{-1}(j)}(\vec{v}_i)\}_j$ for whatever $\vec{v}_i \in E_i$ and $\sigma \in S$ satisfy $\sigma(\vec{v}_i) = \vec{w}_i$, where S is the set of all item permutations. (For why it is OK to assume that such symmetries are satisfied by the optimal reduced form, the reader is referred to [DW11].)

We proceed to describe how our separation oracle works in the item-symmetric case. The input to SO is the succinct description $\{\pi_{ij}(\vec{v}_i)\}_{i,j,\vec{v}_i \in E_i}$ of a reduced form and the value distribution $\mathcal{D}$. If we define $\Pi := \cup_{i,j,\vec{v}_i \in E_i}\{\hat{\pi}_{ij}(\vec{v}_i)\}$, where the $\hat{\pi}$'s are as in Definition 3, it follows from Theorem 4 and the symmetries satisfied by the complete reduced form (which is implied by the succinct one provided in the input to SO) that, for each item j, we only need to check $|\Pi|$ constricting sets for feasibility. (In fact, because the mechanism is item-symmetric, it suffices to only check these constraints for a single item.) Checking a particular set can be done in time polynomial in $|\Pi|$, i.e. without explicitly listing all types that belong to the set, due to the symmetries. If none of the sets is found constricting, output "yes." Otherwise, output the linear constraint violated by the constricting set. This is a hyperplane certifying that the $\pi_{ij}(\vec{v}_i)$'s are infeasible. If SO outputs "yes," this means that it is possible to allocate each item individually and satisfy the $\pi_{ij}(\vec{v}_i)$s. Because bidders have no demand constraints, this also means that we can simultaneously satisfy the $\pi_{ij}(\vec{v}_i)$'s of all items by simply allocating each item independently. It is now clear that SO acts correctly as a separation oracle determining whether or not the $\pi_{ij}(\vec{v}_i)$s are feasible. Moreover, notice that $|E_i| = \text{poly}(n^c)$, for all i, where $c = |supp(\mathcal{F}_{ij})|$. Hence, $|\Pi|$ is polynomial in m and n^c. So our SO runs in time polynomial in m and n^c.

Our LP has size polynomial in m, n^c and our separation oracle runs in time polynomial in m, n^c. So we can solve the LP to compute the optimal reduced form, $\{\pi_{ij}(\vec{v}_i)\}_{i,j,\vec{v}_i \in E_i}$. To execute the mechanism corresponding to the computed reduced form, we use Theorem 6, treating each item separately and allocating each item independently of the others.

Variables:

- $\pi_{ij}(\vec{v}_i)$, for all bidders i, items j, and $\vec{v}_i \in E_i$ ($mn|E_i|$), the ex-interim probability that bidder i gets item j when reporting type $\vec{v}_i$.
- $q_i(\vec{v}_i)$, for all bidders i, $\vec{v}_i \in E_i$ ($m|E_i|$), the ex-interim expected price that bidder i pays when reporting type $\vec{v}_i$.

Constraints:

- $0 \leq \pi_{ij}(\vec{v}_i) \leq 1$, for all $i, j, \vec{v}_i \in E_i$, guaranteeing that each $\pi_{ij}(\vec{v}_i)$ is a probability ($mn|E_i|$).
- $\sum_j v_{ij}\pi_{ij}(\vec{v}_i) - q_i(\vec{v}_i) \geq 0$, for all $i, \vec{v}_i \in E_i$, guaranteeing that the mechanism is ex-interim Individually Rational ($m|E_i|$).
- $\sum_j v_{ij}\pi_{ij}(\vec{v}_i) - q_i(\vec{v}_i) \geq \sum_j v_{ij}\pi_{ij}(\vec{v}_i') - q_i(\vec{v}_i')$, for all $i, \vec{v}_i \in E_i, \vec{v}_i' \in E_i$, guaranteeing that the mechanism is BIC ($m|E_i|^2$).
- $SO(\{\pi_{ij}(\vec{v}_i)\}_{i,j,\vec{v}_i}, \mathcal{D})$ = "yes", guaranteeing that there is a feasible mechanism implementing the $\pi_{ij}(\vec{v}_i)$s.

Maximizing:
$\sum_{i,\vec{v}_i \in E_i} q_i(\vec{v}_i) Pr[\vec{w}_i \leftarrow \mathcal{D}_i, \vec{w}_i \in \cup_{\sigma \in S}\{\sigma(\vec{v}_i)\}]$, the expected revenue.

Figure 3: LP of [DW11] for the item-symmetric setting, where we use a separation oracle to determine feasibility of the reduced form. In parentheses at the end of each line is the number of such variables/constraints .

9. REFERENCES

[AFH+11] Saeed Alaei, Hu Fu, Nima Haghpanah, Jason Hartline, and Azarakhsh Malekian. *Oral Communication*, 2011.

[AFH+12] Saeed Alaei, Hu Fu, Nima Haghpanah, Jason Hartline, and Azarakhsh Malekian. Bayesian Optimal Auctions via Multi- to Single-agent Reduction. *arxiv.org*, March 22, 2012. `http://arxiv.org/abs/1203.5099`.

[Ala11] Saeed Alaei. Bayesian Combinatorial Auctions: Expanding Single Buyer Mechanisms to Many Buyers. In *the 52nd Annual IEEE Symposium on Foundations of Computer Science (FOCS)*, 2011.

[BGGM10] Sayan Bhattacharya, Gagan Goel, Sreenivas Gollapudi, and Kamesh Munagala. Budget Constrained Auctions with Heterogeneous Items. In *the 42nd ACM Symposium on Theory of Computing (STOC)*, 2010.

[BH11] Xiaohui Bei and Zhiyi Huang. Bayesian Incentive Compatibility via Fractional Assignments. In *the Twenty-Second Annual ACM-SIAM Symposium on Discrete Algorithms (SODA)*, 2011.

[Bor91] Kim C. Border. Implementation of Reduced Form Auctions: A Geometric Approach. *Econometrica*, 59(4):1175–1187, 1991.

[Bor07] Kim C. Border. Reduced Form Auctions Revisited. *Economic Theory*, 31:167–181, 2007.

[CD11] Yang Cai and Constantinos Daskalakis. Extreme-Value Theorems for Optimal Multidimensional Pricing. In *the 52nd Annual IEEE Symposium on Foundations of Computer Science (FOCS)*, 2011.

[CDW11] Yang Cai, Constantinos Daskalakis, and S. Matthew Weinberg. An Algorithmic Characterization of Multi-Dimensional Mechanisms. *arxiv.org*, December 20, 2011. `http://arxiv.org/abs/1112.4572`.

[CH12] Yang Cai and Zhiyi Huang. Simple and Nearly Optimal Multi-Item Auction. *Manuscript*, 2012.

[CHMS10] Shuchi Chawla, Jason D. Hartline, David L. Malec, and Balasubramanian Sivan. Multi-Parameter Mechanism Design and Sequential Posted Pricing. In *the 42nd ACM Symposium on Theory of Computing (STOC)*, 2010.

[CKM11] Yeon-Koo Che, Jinwoo Kim, and Konrad Mierendorff. Generalized Reduced-Form Auctions: A Network-Flow Approach. *University of Zürich, ECON-Working Papers*, 2011.

[Cla71] Edward H. Clarke. Multipart Pricing of Public Goods. *Public Choice*, 11(1):17–33, 1971.

[CMS10] Shuchi Chawla, David L. Malec, and Balasubramanian Sivan. The Power of Randomness in Bayesian Optimal Mechanism Design. In *the 11th ACM Conference on Electronic Commerce (EC)*, 2010.

[DFK11] Shahar Dobzinski, Hu Fu, and Robert D. Kleinberg. Optimal Auctions with Correlated Bidders are Easy. In *the 43rd ACM Symposium on Theory of Computing (STOC)*, 2011.

[DW11] Constantinos Daskalakis and S. Matthew Weinberg. Symmetries and Optimal Multi-Dimensional Mechanism Design. *arXiv.org*, 2011. http://arxiv.org/abs/1112.4006.

[Gro73] Theodore Groves. Incentives in Teams. *Econometrica*, 41(4):617–631, 1973.

[HKM11] Jason D. Hartline, Robert Kleinberg, and Azarakhsh Malekian. Bayesian Incentive Compatibility via Matchings. In *the Twenty-Second Annual ACM-SIAM Symposium on Discrete Algorithms (SODA)*, 2011.

[HL10] Jason D. Hartline and Brendan Lucier.

Bayesian Algorithmic Mechanism Design. In *the 42nd ACM Symposium on Theory of Computing (STOC)*, 2010.

[HR11] Sergiu Hart and Philip J. Reny. Implementation of Reduced Form Mechanisms: A Simple Approach and a New Characterization. *Manuscript*, 2011.

[Mat84] Steven A. Matthews. Notes and Comments on the Implementability of Reduced Form Auctions. *Econometrica*, 52(6):1519–1522, 1984.

[MR84] Eric Maskin and John Riley. Optimal Auctions with Risk Averse Buyers. *Econometrica*, 52(6):1473–1518, 1984.

[MV07] A. M. Manelli and D. R. Vincent. Multidimensional Mechanism Design: Revenue Maximization and the Multiple-Good Monopoly. *Journal of Economic Theory*, 137(1):153–185, 2007.

[Mye81] Roger B. Myerson. Optimal Auction Design. *Mathematics of Operations Research*, 6(1):58–73, 1981.

[Sch03] Alexander Schrijver. *Combinatorial Optimization - Polyhedra and Efficiency*. Springer, 2003.

[Vic61] William Vickrey. Counterspeculations, Auctions, and Competitive Sealed Tenders. *Journal of Finance*, 16(1):8–37, 1961.

Tight Bounds on Computing Error-Correcting Codes by Bounded-Depth Circuits with Arbitrary Gates

Anna Gál*
University of Texas at Austin
panni@cs.utexas.edu

Kristoffer Arnsfelt Hansen†
Aarhus University
arnsfelt@cs.au.dk

Michal Koucký‡
Institute of Mathematics, Academy of Sciences, Prague
koucky@math.cas.cz

Pavel Pudlák§
Institute of Mathematics, Academy of Sciences, Prague
pudlak@math.cas.cz

Emanuele Viola¶
Northeastern University
viola@ccs.neu.edu

ABSTRACT

We bound the minimum number w of wires needed to compute any (asymptotically good) error-correcting code $C : \{0,1\}^{\Omega(n)} \to \{0,1\}^n$ with minimum distance $\Omega(n)$, using unbounded fan-in circuits of depth d with arbitrary gates. Our main results are:

(1) If $d = 2$ then $w = \Theta(n(\lg n/\lg\lg n)^2)$.

(2) If $d = 3$ then $w = \Theta(n \lg\lg n)$.

(3) If $d = 2k$ or $d = 2k + 1$ for some integer $k \geq 2$ then $w = \Theta(n\lambda_k(n))$, where $\lambda_1(n) = \lceil \lg n \rceil$, $\lambda_{i+1}(n) = \lambda_i^*(n)$, and the $*$ operation gives how many times one has to iterate the function λ_i to reach a value at most 1 from the argument n.

(4) If $d = \lg^* n$ then $w = O(n)$.

For depth $d = 2$, our $\Omega(n(\lg n/\lg\lg n)^2)$ lower bound gives the largest known lower bound for computing any linear map.

Using a result by Ishai, Kushilevitz, Ostrovsky, and Sahai [17], we also obtain similar bounds for computing pairwise-independent hash functions.

Our lower bounds are based on a superconcentrator-like condition that the graphs of circuits computing good codes must satisfy. This condition is provably intermediate between superconcentrators and their weakenings considered before.

Categories and Subject Descriptors

E.4 [**Coding and Information Theory**]: Error control codes; F.1.1 [**Computation by Abstract devices**]: Models of Computation—*Unbounded-action devices*

Keywords

Error-correcting codes, lower bounds, hashing, bounded-depth circuits, superconcentrators

1. INTRODUCTION

Error-correcting codes are fundamental objects with a myriad of applications, for example in information theory, cryptography, and combinatorial constructions. Of particular importance are codes over the binary alphabet $\{0,1\}$ that are *asymptotically good*: have constant rate (encode m bits into $n = O(m)$ bits) and can correct a constant fraction of errors. We refer to them simply as *good* codes.

In this paper we study the complexity of *encoding* good codes. Although the complexity of *de*coding is sometimes the bottleneck in applications, other times it is the complexity of encoding that matters the most. For example, jumping ahead, "efficient" encoding translates to efficient hashing thanks to a recent result by Ishai, Kushilevitz, Ostrovsky, and Sahai [17].

The complexity of encoding good codes has been studied before. It was shown that some popular encoding methods (e.g. concatenated convolutional codes, or repeat-convolute codes) cannot yield good codes under some assumptions on the complexity of the encoder [4, 5]. For example, Bazzi and Mitter [5] prove that if the encoder can be represented

*Supported in part by NSF Grant CCF-1018060.

†Supported by the Sino-Danish Center for the Theory of Interactive Computation, funded by the Danish National Research Foundation and the National Science Foundation of China (under the grant 61061130540).

‡Currently a visiting associate professor at Aarhus University, partially supported by the Sino-Danish Center CTIC (funded under the grant 61061130540). Part of the work was done while visiting the University of Toronto partially supported by NSERC. Partially supported by GA ČR P202/10/0854, grant IAA100190902 of GA AV ČR, project No. 1M0021620808 of MŠMT ČR and RVO: 67985840.

§Partially supported by the grant IAA100190902 of GA AV ČR, by the Center of Excellence CE-ITI under the grant P202/12/G061 of GA ČR and RVO: 67985840.

¶Supported by NSF grant CCF-0845003.

as a binary branching program (or equivalently a random access machine) that uses linear time and sublinear space, then the code computed cannot be good. This result should be contrasted with the existence of good codes that can be encoded in linear time [14]. Explicit constructions of good codes encodable (and decodable) in linear time and linear space were given by Spielman [29, 30]. It follows immediately from bounds on the noise-sensitivity of small AC^0 circuits [20, 6] that small AC^0 circuits cannot compute good codes. This result was generalized in [32, 21] (cf. [5]).

In this paper we consider unbounded fan-in circuits with *arbitrary* gates. In particular, we allow the use of parity gates. Giving lower bounds for arbitrary gates, that is, regardless of the operations computed by the individual gates, makes our lower bounds stronger. Our upper bounds hold for circuits that consist of parity gates only. Our focus is the tradeoffs between the number of wires and the depth of the circuits.

Previously, two main tradeoffs were known. Any code can be computed in depth 1 with $O(n^2)$ wires (since we allow arbitrary gates), and it is also easy to show that $\Omega(n^2)$ wires are necessary to compute any good code in depth 1. We can generalize the upper bound to $O(n^{1+1/d})$ wires and depth d, for any fixed d, by viewing the message as a d-dimensional cube and encoding one by one along each dimension. On the other hand, Spielman [30] gives explicit good codes that can be encoded by bounded fan-in circuits with $O(n)$ wires and depth $O(\lg n)$ (and also decoded in linear time). Thus, optimal number of wires for encoding good codes can be achieved using depth $O(\lg n)$. It is easy to see that with bounded fan-in circuits, linear number of wires for encoding good codes cannot be achieved in smaller than $\Omega(\lg n)$ depth. Can we achieve closer to optimal bounds on the number of wires in small depth with unbounded fan-in circuits?

1.1 Our results

We show that already depth 2 is sufficient to have a quasilinear $O(n(\lg n/\lg\lg n)^2)$ number of wires for computing asymptotically good codes. In fact, for any depth we obtain matching upper and lower bounds that reveal that the optimal number of wires is n times an inverse Ackermann-like function $\lambda(n)$ that is parameterized by the depth.

Notation.

Let $\lambda_1(n) = \lceil \lg n \rceil$ and $\lambda_{i+1}(n) = \lambda_i^*(n)$, where the $*$ operation gives how many times one has to iterate the function λ_i to reach a value at most 1 from the argument n.

We say that an injective function $C : \{0,1\}^m \to \{0,1\}^n$ is a (ρ, δ)-*good code* if $m \geq \rho n$ and any two distinct codewords have hamming distance at least δn. It is well known that there are constants $0 < \rho_0, \delta_0 < 1$ so that (ρ_0, δ_0)-good codes exist for all m. Indeed one may pick $1/32 \leq \rho_0$ and $1/8 \leq \delta_0$.

Let $w_d(C)$ be the wire complexity of encoding the code C by depth-d unbounded-fan-in circuits with arbitrary gates, that is the minimum number of wires over all circuits of depth d computing C. Let $w_{d,\rho,\delta}(n) = \min_C w_d(C)$, over all binary (ρ, δ)-good codes C with block-length n (and thus message length $m = \rho n$, and relative distance δn). An XOR circuit is a circuit consisting of input gates and XOR gates (i.e., gates that compute parity of their inputs).

Our results can be summarized in the following main theorem.

THEOREM 1 (COMPLEXITY OF ENCODING). *For any constants $0 < \rho \leq 1/32$ and $0 < \delta < 1/8$, we have*
$w_{2,\rho,\delta}(n) = \Theta(n(\lg n/\lg\lg n)^2)$,
$w_{3,\rho,\delta}(n) = \Theta(n \lg\lg n)$,
if $d = 2k$ or $d = 2k+1$ for some integer $k \geq 2$ then $w_{d,\rho,\delta}(n) = \Theta(n\lambda_k(n))$.
The upper bounds are witnessed by (non-explicit) circuits using only XOR gates (hence computing good codes that are linear). The lower bounds hold for any $\rho, \delta > 0$, for circuits with arbitrary gates, and computing arbitrary (possibly nonlinear) (ρ, δ)-good codes.

Each bound is obtained for the first time in this paper. For depth 2, our $\Omega(n(\lg n/\lg\lg n)^2)$ lower bound gives the largest known lower bound for computing any linear map, improving on the $\Omega(n \lg^{3/2} n)$ bound by Pudlák and Rödl in [27]. Moreover their lower bound only held against circuits consisting exclusively of XOR gates, as opposed to arbitrary gates in our result. For an excellent survey of lower bounds for circuits with arbitrary gates, see the recent book [18] by Jukna. As we discuss later, our lower bounds also apply to multiplication by an n-bit integer, by an n-bit field element, by an $n \times n$ Toeplitz matrix, and to computation of hash functions.

The lower bounds in Theorem 1 show that to compute good codes with a linear number of wires, the depth cannot be constant. However, the depth can grow very slowly as the following theorem indicates.

THEOREM 2. *For any constants $0 < \rho \leq 1/32$, $0 < \delta < 1/8$ and $d \geq 1$, we have $w_{\lambda_d(n),\rho,\delta}(n) = O(n)$.*

Spielman [29] achieves depth $O(\lg n)$ for linear-size circuits with *bounded fan-in* gates, and this is optimal for computing good codes with bounded fan-in circuits. Our theorem holds for circuits with unbounded fan-in gates.

Decomposing the generator matrix of good codes into sparse matrices.

Since the upper bounds in Theorem 1 hold for circuits with XOR gates only, they correspond to linear transformations. So those upper bounds can be interpreted as saying that there exist $n \times \Omega(n)$ matrices G generating good codes over GF(2), that can be decomposed as $G = G_1 \cdot G_2 \cdot \cdots \cdot G_d$, where the G_i are *sparse* (have quasilinear number of ones). By contrast, note it is easy to see that any generator matrix G itself must have $\Omega(n^2)$ ones, if it generates a good code. Our lower bounds show that no such decomposition exists with $d = O(1)$ and each matrix G_i having $O(n)$ ones.

Coding vs. hashing.

Our results on the complexity of encoding imply new upper and lower bounds on the complexity of computing pairwise independent hash functions. This follows from the close relationships between the complexity of encoding and that of hashing, the more surprising direction of which (i.e., codes imply hash functions) we extrapolate from an exciting result by Ishai, Kushilevitz, Ostrovsky, and Sahai [17]. The relationships show that depth-d circuits for codes imply depth-$2d$ circuits for hashing, while depth-d circuits for hashing imply depth-d circuits for codes; and the wire complexity only multiplies by a constant. Using this in conjunction with Theorem 1 immediately gives a superlinear lower bound on the wire-complexity of constant-depth hashing circuits, as well as upper bounds.

It is instructive to compare our results to those of the aforementioned paper [17]. [17] obtain circuits with $w = O(m)$ wires (and unspecified depth $d \geq \Omega(\lg m)$) for computing pairwise independent hash functions mapping m bits to m bits. This disproves a conjecture by Mansour, Nisan, and Tiwari [22] that $\Omega(m \lg m)$ wires were needed.

Our results show that one can go below $w = \Omega(m \lg m)$ wires (e.g. $w = O(m \lg^* m)$) even with constant-depth circuits. However, to get $w = O(m)$ super-constant depth is necessary.

1.2 Techniques

Lower bounds.

Slowly-growing bounds similar to those in our Theorem 1 are known to hold for the number of edges in *superconcentrator* graphs. Indeed, to establish our lower bounds we establish and exploit a relationship between superconcentrators and circuits computing good codes. However, despite this relationship, circuits computing good codes behave differently from superconcentrator graphs. In fact, jumping ahead, our bounds for depth 2 imply a gap between the wire complexity of circuits computing good codes and the wire complexity of superconcentrator graphs.

We now elaborate on the connection with superconcentrators. We state the following properties for circuits with m input nodes and n output nodes.

There are various connectivity requirements one could ask for in a circuit. Consider a circuit with m inputs and $n \geq m$ outputs. Let X be a subset of input bits and Y be a subset of output bits of the circuit. Denote by $f(X, Y)$ the maximum number of vertex disjoint paths from X to Y. For a fixed constant $0 < \delta \leq 1$ one can require:

1. For each $k \in \{1, \dots, m\}$, for each X and Y of size k, $f(X, Y) \geq \delta k$.

2. For each $k \in \{1, \dots, m\}$, for each X and a random Y of size k, $\mathrm{E}_Y[f(X, Y)] \geq \delta k$.

3. For each $k \in \{1, \dots, m\}$, for random X and Y of size k, $\mathrm{E}_{X,Y}[f(X, Y)] \geq \delta k$.

These are various versions of the *superconcentrator* property ordered by strength. The classical definition of superconcentrators [31] requires Property 1 to hold for $\delta = 1$ (and $n = m$). Property 3 corresponds to the so-called relaxed superconcentrators which were analyzed in [11, 26].

In this work we show that Property 2 is the property satisfied by circuits computing good codes. A connection between superconcentrators and circuits computing error-correcting codes was already observed by Spielman [30]. His construction of linear-size encoding circuits was inspired by known constructions of linear-size superconcetrators. Spielman also observed that some similarity to superconcentrators is necessary. He proved that circuits (with m inputs and n outputs) computing codes with minimum distance δn have δm vertex disjoint paths from any set of δm inputs to any set of $(1 - \delta)n$ outputs.

We prove the following, stronger connection between circuits encoding error-correcting codes and superconcentrators.

LEMMA 3. *Let $\delta > 0$ be a constant, $C : \{0, 1\}^m \to \{0, 1\}^n$ be a code with minimum distance δn and G be a circuit computing C. For any $0 < k \leq m$, and for any k-element subset X of inputs of G, if we take uniformly at random a k-element subset Y of outputs of G, then the expected number of vertex disjoint paths from X to Y in G is at least δk.*

We prove this lemma using a classical result in matroid theory. We give a self-contained proof of the necessary claim in the appendix.

Having established the above lemma, we proceed to prove lower bounds on the number of wires of circuits satisfying Property 2. The quality of the bounds we get depends on the rate $\rho = m/n$. For simplicity, we state our bounds for codes with constant rate ρ, that is our circuits have $m = \Omega(n)$ input nodes. The precise dependence of the bounds on $\rho = m/n$ is hidden in the Ω notation.

For the case of depth 2, we show that a depth-2 circuit satisfying Property 2 has at least $\Omega(n(\lg n/ \lg\lg n)^2)$ wires. Moreover, this is optimal due to our constructions.

We remark that the bounds for depth 2 circuits satisfying Property 1, 2 and 3 are different. Specifically, by results of Radhakrishnan and Ta-Shma [28], for any fixed $0 < \delta \leq 1$, a depth-2 circuit satisfying Property 1 has at least $\Omega(n \lg^2 n/ \lg\lg n)$ wires which is known to be optimal. ([28] state the claim only for $\delta = 1$ but their proof works for any constant $\delta > 0$.) For Property 3, [11, 26] show that a depth-2 circuit satisfying it has at least $\Omega(n \lg n)$ wires, which is again known to be optimal. An example of a circuit satisfying this property is a circuit computing the Prefix-XOR function [8, 9].

The lower bound for depth 2.

Our $\Omega(n(\lg n/ \lg\lg n)^2)$ lower bound for depth-2 is obtained by modifying the clever lower bound by Radhakrishnan and Ta-Shma [28], which was tailored for Property 1 and gives a stronger bound. As in [28], we classify the vertices in the intermediate level according to their degree. We consider $\Omega(\lg n/ \lg \lg n)$ disjoint classes and prove a lower bound $\Omega(n \lg n/ \lg \lg n)$ on the number of edges incident with these vertices for each of them, unless the number of edges non-incident with these vertices is already $\epsilon n(\lg n/ \lg \lg n)^2$ for some absolute constant $\epsilon > 0$.

Each of the classes on the intermediate level is associated with a number k and we use the condition of Lemma 3 for this k to prove the lower bound on the number of incident edges. The class associated with k is denoted by V_m^k. The assumption that the number of edges non-incident with the vertices of the given class V_m^k is less than $\epsilon n(\lg n/ \lg \lg n)^2$ implies that for every set of k input vertices and randomly chosen set of k output vertices, there are on average $\delta' k$ vertex-disjoint paths connecting them through V_m^k, for some positive constant δ'.

To prove the lower bound on the number of edges incident with V_m^k, we argue by contradiction. We assume that the number of these edges is small, and find a large subset of output vertices W^0 and a subset of input vertices U^0, $|U^0| \geq k$ such that there is no path going through V_m^k that connects U^0 with W^0. We show that with our setting of the parameters this is a contradiction.

To construct the sets U^0 and W^0 we use a technique based on the work of Hansel [16]. For every vertex $v \in V_m^k$, we randomly either delete all edges connecting v with output vertices or all edges connecting v with input vertices. We do the former with small probability, the latter with high. We put U^0 and W^0 to be the set of input (respectively, output) vertices that are not affected by this process. Since all paths through V_m^k have been disconnected, but no path has been removed between U^0 and W^0, the sets U^0 and W^0 are not connected through V_m^k in the original graph. This concludes the overview of the proof.

One novelty in our proof is that we use different probabilities for the two possible choices to obtain W^0 of linear size. In fact, this reflects a qualitative difference between superconcentrators and circuits computing good codes. Optimal depth-2 superconcentrators must have the same average degree for input and output nodes, while our optimal construction of circuits computing good codes has different average degrees. More detailed discussion of the difference between our proof and the proof of [28] is provided after the proof of Theorem 8, and Section 4.1 discusses the properties of depth-2 superconcentrators.

Lower bounds for depth > 2.

For depth > 2, our lower bounds follow from combining our Lemma 3 with off-the-shelf lower bounds on superconcentrators. Specifically, we use bounds by Pudlák [26] that improve on those by Dolev et al. [11]. We note that these lower bounds are for circuits satisfying (essentially) Property 3 above. Hence, for depth at least 3, Property 3 is sufficient to obtain a result tight up to constant factors.

Upper bounds.

Our constructions of circuits computing good codes are probabilistic, and we leave it as an open problem to obtain explicit constructions. (Jumping ahead, partial progress towards explicit constructions is discussed in Section 6.)

Basic building blocks of our constructions are circuits that we call *range detectors*. A (m, n, ℓ, k, r, s)-range detector is a circuit built from XOR gates that has m inputs, n outputs and on any input of Hamming weight between ℓ and k it outputs a string with Hamming weight between r and s. We will omit the last parameter if $s = n$. Clearly, an $(m, O(m), 1, m, \Omega(m))$-range detector is a circuit computing a good linear code as for linear codes one has to worry only about the number of ones produced on non-zero inputs. When $\ell \in \Theta(k)$ and $n \in \Theta\left(\lg \binom{m}{k}\right)$ then one can easily construct range detectors of depth one with $r \in \Theta(n)$ using $O(m \lg m)$ wires, by an application of the probabilistic method. If we take such range detectors for $\ell = m/2^i$ and $k = m/2^{i-1}$, for $i = 1, \ldots, \lg m$, in parallel then on any non-zero input at least one of them will output a constant fraction of ones (and say also a constant fraction of zeros). Hence, an XOR gate sampling one output from each of these range detectors will evaluate to one on non-zero input with constant probability. If we take $O(m)$ of such XOR gates chosen independently at random, then on any non-zero input a constant fraction of them will evaluate to one with overwhelming probability. Hence, a particular choice of these XOR gates will have such a property on any non-zero input. That in essence gives a depth-2 XOR circuit with $O(m \lg^2 m)$ wires computing good codes. By modifying the parameters slightly one can achieve $O(m \lg^2 m / \lg^2 \lg m)$-size depth-2 XOR circuits for good codes.

To obtain asymptotically better size in higher depth we use a similar recursive approach. We present the main idea of the construction here. First, one can *condense* the input using various depth-1 range detectors and then one can apply on the output of each of the range detectors a depth-d circuit computing a good code. Adding a layer of XOR gates that sample outputs of these depth-d range detectors concludes the construction of a depth-$d+2$ circuit for good codes. A careful choice of parameters leads to the overall reduction in size; the actual construction is slightly more involved.

This recursive approach is similar to the construction of superconcentrators [11]. However, there is a notable difference between the construction for codes and for superconcentrators. In known superconcentrator constructions, the bottom and top layers are symmetric so the whole circuit can be made symmetric with respect to the middle layer. In our construction, the bottom and top layers are different and although on intuitive level they fulfill symmetric functionality they cannot be interchanged with each other in general. Indeed, as observed before, for depth 2, the size bounds on codes are different than the size bounds on superconcentrators.

Bounds on hashing.

Our results on the complexity of encoding imply corresponding results on the complexity of computing pairwise independent hash functions $f : \{0,1\}^m \times \{0,1\}^r \to \{0,1\}^n$, i.e. functions such that $\forall x \neq y$, the joint distribution $(f(x,S), f(y,S))$ is uniform over $(\{0,1\}^n)^2$.

This implication relies on the fact that the complexity of hashing and coding are closely related. First, an application of the Chernoff bound shows that any pairwise independent hash function contains a good code, which was explicitly pointed out by Miltersen. This implication has no overhead. Hence our lower bounds for codes apply to hashing as well.

FACT 4 (PROPOSITION 7 IN [23]). *Let*

$$f : \{0,1\}^{\rho n} \times \{0,1\}^r \to \{0,1\}^n$$

be a pairwise independent hash function. For every $\delta < 1/2$ such that $2\rho < 1 - H(\delta)$, there is a fixed R such that the map $f(\cdot, R)$ is the encoding function of an error correcting code with relative distance $\geq \delta$ (and message length ρn and block length n).

For the reverse direction, we rely on a recent result by Ishai, Kushilevitz, Ostrovsky, and Sahai [17], who give a construction of pairwise independent hash functions using circuits with a linear number of wires. We observe that their construction can be seen as a reduction to encoding, and that the reduction blows up the wires and the depth by only a constant factor. So plugging our efficient encoding circuits we get correspondingly efficient hashing circuits.

THEOREM 5 (IMPLICIT IN [17]). *Suppose there are constants ρ, δ, d, and an increasing function $w(n) \geq n$ such that*

1. *for any n there is a $[n, \rho n, \delta n]_2$ code, that is a (ρ, δ)-good code, that can be computed by a depth-d XOR circuit with $w(n)$ wires.*

Then there is a constant c such that

2. *for every m we can compute a pairwise independent hash function $h : \{0,1\}^m \times \{0,1\}^r \to \{0,1\}^m$ with*

$r \leq cm$, by a depth-2d circuit with $\leq cw(cm)$ wires (using arbitrary gates).

Moreover, if the codes are explicit then the hash functions are too.

Organization.

In Section 2 we prove that circuits computing good codes must satisfy connectivity Property 2. In Section 3 we prove the lower bounds in Theorem 1. In Section 4 we prove the upper bounds in Theorem 1 and also Theorem 2. The constructions of hash functions are in Section 5. In this section we also deduce lower bounds for various types of multiplication. Finally, we make some remarks on making our upper bounds explicit in Section 6.

2. CONNECTIVITY OF CIRCUITS COMPUTING GOOD CODES

In this section we provide a proof of Lemma 3 which establishes that circuits computing good codes satisfy connectivity Property 2. We restate that lemma next.

LEMMA 3. *Let $\delta > 0$ be a constant, $C : \{0,1\}^m \to \{0,1\}^n$ be a code with minimum distance δn and G be a circuit computing C. For any $0 < k \leq m$, and for any k-element subset X of inputs of G, if we take uniformly at random a k-element subset Y of outputs of G, then the expected number of vertex disjoint paths from X to Y in G is at least δk.*

To prove the lemma we need the following definition and lemma. Let X be the set of inputs and let W be the set of outputs of a directed graph. Given a subset of outputs $Y \subseteq W$, we say that a vertex $v \in W \setminus Y$ is *bad* for Y if the largest number of vertex disjoint paths from X to $Y \cup \{v\}$ is not larger than the largest number of vertex disjoint paths from X to Y.

LEMMA 6. *Let $V \subseteq W \setminus Y$ be a set of bad vertices for Y. Then the largest number of vertex disjoint paths from X to $Y \cup V$ is not larger than the largest number of vertex disjoint paths from X to Y.*

First note that this statement would easily follow, if *any* collection of vertex disjoint paths could be extended to a collection of vertex disjoint paths with the largest possible cardinality in any graph. Such a property would be similar to having a matroid, where the sets of vertex disjoint paths form the independent sets. However this property does not hold, and one cannot define a matroid with vertex disjoint paths forming the independent sets. Consider the simple example of a graph that consists of a matching between vertices $x_1, \ldots x_k$ and $y_1, \ldots, y_k$, with edges from x_i to y_i, and an extra edge from x_1 to y_k. Then the largest number of vertex disjoint paths is k, but there is no collection of k vertex disjoint paths containing the path from x_1 to y_k. This example also illustrates why some seemingly simple approaches to prove Lemma 6 fail.

Despite the fact that the collections of vertex disjoint paths do not form a matroid, the collections of their endpoints do. The statement of Lemma 6 is equivalent to the following statement: the subsets of W formed by the sets of endpoints of vertex disjoint paths from X to W are independent sets of a matroid over W. This is a well known theorem of matroid theory, see e.g. Chapter 13 in [33], Chapter 2.4 in [24], or [25]. We include a self contained and direct proof of Lemma 6 in the Appendix.

In the special case of linear codes a version of Lemma 6 with a different definition of "bad" vertices would be substantially easier to prove. One could consider the rank of the submatrices $X \times Y$ of the generator matrix describing the code. The bad vertices are those outputs v that do not increase the rank, that is the rank of the submatrix $X \times Y \cup \{v\}$ is the same as the rank of the submatrix $X \times Y$. Then, adding the union of all bad vertices cannot increase the rank either: the bad vertices correspond to columns of the generator matrix that are in the linear span of the submatrix $X \times Y$. The rank of the submatrix $X \times Y$ of the generator matrix describing the code is at most the number of nodes in the smallest set S of vertices in the graph of the circuit such that every path from X to Y contains at least one vertex of the set S, since varying the inputs in X the number of different outputs over Y cannot be larger than $2^{|S|}$. The statement then follows by Menger's Theorem.

We use the following version of Menger's Theorem (see e.g. Theorem 4.2 in [13]).

THEOREM 7 (MENGER'S THEOREM). *Let G be a directed graph, X its set of input (indegree 0) nodes, and Y its set of output (outdegree 0) nodes. The largest number of pairwise vertex disjoint paths from X to Y equals the smallest number of vertices in a set S such that every path from X to Y contains a vertex from S.*

We refer to a set of vertices S such that every path from X to Y contains a vertex from S as a *(vertex) cut* separating X and Y.

We are ready to prove Lemma 3.

Proof of Lemma 3. For a fixed $k \in \{1, \ldots, m\}$ and given k-element set X of inputs, we prove that the expected number of vertex disjoint paths from X to a randomly chosen k-element subset Y of outputs is at least δk. We will pick Y one element at a time by choosing from the remaining outputs at random.

We claim that as long as $|Y| < k$ (so that there are less than k vertex disjoint paths from X to Y) with probability at least δ the next randomly chosen element of Y will increase the number of vertex disjoint paths from X to the current Y by one.

As above, call an output vertex v bad for Y, if adding it to Y does not increase the number of vertex disjoint paths from X to Y. We claim that for any Y with $|Y| < k$, at least δn output vertices are not bad. This suffices to prove the claim as with probability at least δ we will sample such a vertex at each step and then by linearity of expectation we get at least δk vertex disjoint paths on average.

Let $|Y| < k$. Denote the set of output vertices bad for Y by B. Let the number of vertex disjoint paths from X to the current Y be $\ell < k$. By Lemma 6, if we take the union of Y with all the bad vertices then there are still no more than ℓ vertex disjoint paths from X to the union $Y \cup B$. By Menger's theorem (Theorem 7), the smallest cut separating X and $Y \cup B$, is of size ℓ. If we set all input bits except for X to 0, then by varying inputs to X we have $2^{|X|} = 2^k$ different inputs. However, over these 2^k inputs, since the cut separating X and $Y \cup B$ is of size ℓ, outputs belonging to $Y \cup B$ will see at most 2^ℓ different settings as these output bits will be determined by the values at the gates of the cut.

Thus there exist two different inputs of the form $0x_1$ and $0x_2$ (they are both 0 outside X, but differ on X), such that the outputs of our circuit on these two inputs agree on the $Y \cup B$ part. So the Hamming distance between the outputs of the circuit on $0x_1$ and $0x_2$ is at most the number of output vertices outside of $Y \cup B$.

However, since G computes a code with minimum distance δn, the Hamming distance between the encodings of any two different inputs has to be at least δn. Thus, the number of output vertices outside of $Y \cup B$ is at least δn. □

3. LOWER BOUNDS ON COMPUTING GOOD CODES

In this section we prove lower bounds on the number of wires of circuits computing good codes. We start with the case of depth 2, then we discuss depth bigger than 2.

3.1 Lower bound for depth two

In this section we prove our lower bound for depth-2 circuits computing good codes:

THEOREM 8. $w_{\rho,\delta,2}(n) \in \Omega\left(n\left(\frac{\lg n}{\lg\lg n}\right)^2\right)$.

We need the following lemma, an easy corollary of Chebyshev's Inequality. Its proof is included in Appendix for completeness.

LEMMA 9. *Let $X_1, \ldots, X_k$ be 0-1 random variables and $C, \alpha > 0$ be reals. Suppose that for every $i \in \{1, \ldots, k\}$, there are at most C indices $j \in \{1, \ldots, k\}$ such that X_i and X_j are not independent. Let $\mu = \mathrm{E}\left(\sum_{i=1}^k X_i\right)$. Then*

$$\Pr\left[\left|\sum_{i=1}^{k} X_i - \mu\right| \geq \alpha\mu\right] \leq \frac{C}{\alpha^2\mu}.$$

Proof of Theorem 8. Fix a large enough n and consider the directed graph G that corresponds to a circuit computing a (ρ, δ)-good code on inputs of size $m = \rho n$. Let U be the set of vertices of G corresponding to the inputs of the circuit, V be the set of vertices of G that correspond to the middle layer of the circuit, and W be the vertices corresponding to the output gates of the circuit. Hence, $|U| = m$ and $|W| = n$. All the edges in G go either from U to V or from V to W.

Our goal is to show that for n sufficiently large, the number of edges of G is at least

$$\frac{\delta \cdot \min(\rho, \delta)}{1600} \cdot n \cdot \left(\frac{\lg n}{\lg\lg n}\right)^2. \tag{1}$$

We will prove this by contradiction so we will assume that G has fewer edges than (1).

By the degree $\deg(v)$ of a vertex v in G we understand the number of incident edges (incoming and outgoing) in G, and for a set of vertices A of G, $\deg_A(v)$ denotes the number of edges between A and v.

For every integer k such that $n^{1/4} \leq k \leq n^{1/2}$ we define

$$V_h^k = \{v \in V;\ \deg(v) \geq \frac{n}{k}\lg^2 n\} \quad \text{(high degree vertices)}$$

$$V_m^k = \{v \in V;\ \frac{n}{k}\lg^2 n > \deg(v) \geq \frac{n}{k\lg^2 n}\} \quad \text{(medium degree vertices)}$$

$$V_l^k = \{v \in V;\ \frac{n}{k\lg^2 n} > \deg(v)\} \quad \text{(low degree vertices)}$$

If for all k of the form $(\lg n)^{4i}$, where i is an integer between $\frac{1}{16} \cdot \frac{\lg n}{\lg\lg n}$ and $\frac{1}{8} \cdot \frac{\lg n}{\lg\lg n}$, V_m^k is incident with at least

$$\frac{\delta \cdot \min(\rho, \delta)}{100} \cdot n \cdot \frac{\lg n}{\lg\lg n} \tag{2}$$

edges, then we immediately obtain a contradiction with the number of edges in G. So for the rest of the proof we fix some k such that $n^{1/4} \leq k \leq n^{1/2}$ where the number of edges incident with V_m^k is less than (2). Since k is fixed, we will omit the upper index k in V_h^k, V_m^k and V_l^k.

Given the bound (2) on the number of edges incident with V_m, for at most $\frac{\delta}{10}n$ vertices w from W, $\deg_{V_m}(w) > \frac{\delta}{10} \cdot \frac{\lg n}{\lg\lg n}$. Call these vertices W_{bad}, and set

$$W_{\text{good}} = W \setminus W_{\text{bad}}.$$

Furthermore, for at most $\frac{\rho}{5}n = \frac{m}{5}$ vertices u from U,

$$\deg_{V_m}(u) > \frac{\delta}{10} \cdot \frac{\lg n}{\lg\lg n}, \text{ or } \deg(u) > \frac{\delta}{160} \cdot \left(\frac{\lg n}{\lg\lg n}\right)^2.$$

Call these vertices U_{bad}, and set $U_{\text{good}} = U \setminus U_{\text{bad}}$.

Let $p = 1/\lg n$. Consider the following random process: for each vertex $v \in V_m$, with probability p remove all the edges between v and W and with the remaining probability $1 - p$ remove all the edges between v and U. Let

$W^0 = \{w \in W_{\text{good}};$ no edge from w to V_m was removed by the random process$\}$,

$U^0 = \{u \in U_{\text{good}};$ no edge from u to V_m was removed by the random process$\}$.

Notice, the random process cuts all paths from U_{good} to W_{good} going through V_m. Since vertices U^0 and W^0 retain all their edges during the process, there is no path from U^0 to W^0 going through V_m in the original graph G.

CLAIM 10. *For large enough n, with probability at least 1/3, the following conditions are true simultaneously:*

$$|W^0| \geq (1 - \frac{\delta}{5})n,$$
$$|U^0| \geq \frac{2\rho}{5}m^{9/10}.$$

In particular, $|U^0| \geq k$ if n is sufficiently large.

Proof of the claim. First we show that the first condition is satisfied with probability at least 2/3. Each vertex $w \in W_{\text{good}}$ is originally connected to at most $\frac{\delta}{10} \cdot \frac{\lg n}{\lg\lg n}$ vertices in V_m so the probability of w being in W^0 is

$$\begin{aligned}(1-p)^{\deg_{V_m}(w)} &\geq (1-p\deg_{V_m}(w)) \\ &\geq \left(1-p\frac{\delta}{10}\cdot\frac{\lg n}{\lg\lg n}\right) \\ &\geq \left(1-\frac{\delta}{10\lg\lg n}\right).\end{aligned}$$

Consequently, the expected number of vertices $w \in W_{\text{good}}$ that are not in W^0 is at most $\frac{\delta}{10\lg\lg n}|W_{\text{good}}|$. Hence by the Markov Inequality, with probability at least $2/3$, $|W^0| \geq |W_{\text{good}}| - \frac{3\delta}{10\lg\lg n}|W_{\text{good}}|$. Since $|W_{\text{good}}| \geq (1-\frac{\delta}{10})n$, for n large enough, $|W^0| \geq (1-\frac{\delta}{5})n$.

Now it suffices to show that the second condition is satisfied with probability at least $2/3$. First, we estimate the expected size of U^0. Each vertex $u \in U_{\text{good}}$ will end up in U^0 with probability

$$p^{\deg_{V_m}(u)} \geq \left(\frac{1}{\lg n}\right)^{\frac{\delta}{10}\cdot\frac{\lg n}{\lg\lg n}} = \frac{1}{n^{\frac{\delta}{10}}}$$

Thus, the expected size of U^0 is at least $\frac{4}{5}\cdot m\cdot n^{-\frac{\delta}{10}} \geq \frac{4\rho}{5}\cdot m^{9/10}$. We want to use Lemma 9 to show that the size of U^0 is close to its expectation with high probability.

For two distinct $u, u' \in U_{\text{good}}$, the two events whether u and u' fall in U^0 are independent if u and u' do not share a neighbor in V_m. Hence for a given u, there are at most $\deg_{V_m}(u)\cdot\frac{n}{k}\lg^2 n \leq \frac{\delta}{10}\cdot\frac{\lg n}{\lg\lg n}\cdot\frac{n}{k}\lg^2 n \leq \frac{\delta}{10}\cdot\frac{\lg^3 n}{\lg\lg n}n^{3/4}$ distinct $u' \in U_{\text{good}}$ for which the events may be dependent. In Lemma 9, set $C = m^{4/5}$, $\alpha = 1/2$, and for $u \in U_{\text{good}}$, set X_u to be the indicator variable whether $u \in U^0$. Since $\mathrm{E}[|U^0|] \geq \frac{4\rho}{5}\cdot m^{9/10}$, by Lemma 9, the probability that $|U^0| \leq \frac{1}{2}\cdot\frac{4\rho}{5}\cdot m^{9/10}$ goes to zero as n grows. So for n large enough this event happens with probability less than $1/3$. □

For the rest of the proof we fix set U^0 and W^0 satisfying the bounds from the previous claim and we consider the original graph G. We know that there is no path from U^0 to W^0 going through V_m in G.

Our goal is to derive a contradiction from the fact that the number of edges incident with V_m is small, and that there is a small number of edges in the graph overall. We will consider the following quantities to derive the contradiction. Let $X \subseteq U^0$ and $Y \subseteq W$. Let $f^d(X,Y)$ denote the number of vertex disjoint paths connecting X and Y via vertices of V_l, and $f^a(X,Y)$ denote the number of all paths connecting X and Y via vertices of V_l. We will derive a contradiction by proving that $f^d(X,Y) > f^a(X,Y)$ for some X and Y.

CLAIM 11. *Let X be a random k-element subset of U^0 and let Y be a random k-element subset of W. Then the expected value of $f^d(X,Y)$ is at least $\frac{3}{4}\delta k$.*

Proof of the claim. Fix an arbitrary k-element subset X of U^0 and pick a random k-element subset of W. By Lemma 3, the expected number of vertex disjoint paths from X to Y is at least δk, so in expectation there are at least δk vertex disjoint paths connecting X and Y. Some of the paths may go via vertices in V_m or V_h. However, an $x \in X$ and a $y \in Y$ may be connected via V_m only if $y \notin W^0$, and at most $|V_h|$ vertex disjoint paths can go through V_h. The expected size of $Y \setminus W^0$ is at most $\delta k/5$, since $|W^0| \geq (1-\delta/5)|W|$. By the assumption on the number of edges in G and the degree of vertices in V_h

$$|V_h| \leq \frac{\delta\cdot\min(\rho,\delta)}{1600}\cdot n\cdot\left(\frac{\lg n}{\lg\lg n}\right)^2\cdot\frac{k}{n\lg^2 n} \leq \frac{\delta}{1600\cdot(\lg\lg n)^2}\cdot k.$$

Thus, by linearity of expectation there are at least

$$\delta k - \frac{\delta}{5}k - \frac{\delta}{1600\cdot(\lg\lg n)^2}k \geq \frac{3}{4}\delta k$$

vertex disjoint paths connecting X and Y via V_l. □

Finally, given our assumptions we derive an upper bound on the expected size of $f^a(X,Y)$ that will contradict the previous claim. Namely, we claim:

CLAIM 12. *Let X be a random k-element subset of U^0 and Y be a random k-element subset of W. Then the expected value of $f^a(X,Y)$ is at most $\frac{\delta}{160(\lg\lg n)^2}k$.*

Proof of the claim. By the bounds on the degree of vertices in U^0 and V_l, the number of distinct paths from U^0 to W via V_l is at most $|U^0|\cdot\frac{\delta}{160}\left(\frac{\lg n}{\lg\lg n}\right)^2\cdot\frac{n}{k\lg^2 n} = \frac{\delta}{160k(\lg\lg n)^2}\cdot|U^0|\cdot n$. A given path between U^0 and W will be connecting a randomly chosen X and Y with probability $\frac{k}{|U^0|}\cdot\frac{k}{|W|}$. Hence, the expected number of distinct paths between randomly chosen X and Y going through V_l is at most

$$\frac{\delta}{160k(\lg\lg n)^2}\cdot|U^0|\cdot n\cdot\frac{k^2}{|U^0|\cdot|W|} = \frac{\delta}{160(\lg\lg n)^2}k.$$

□

This proves our theorem. □

We make a few more remarks regarding the difference between the above proof and the one in [28]. We note that the sets U^0 of inputs and W^0 of outputs produced by the random process are both sub-linear in the case of [28]. This is not usable for purposes of the codes as there might be linear size sets of outputs that are completely disconnected from the inputs – some bits of the codeword can be constantly set to zero. So we modify the random process to be asymmetric to obtain linear size set W^0 of outputs; U^0 will still be of polynomial albeit sublinear size.

Another difference, that also comes from the difference of Properties 1 and 2 discussed in the introduction, is in the use of the connectivity. In [28] a part of the argument uses only the property that any two k elements subsets are connected by at least one path. In the case of codes this might not be true for all k-element subsets so we have to argue differently using the fact that on the average we have a fraction of k paths between the sets.

3.2 Lower bounds for depth three and more

To prove the lower bound on the size of circuits of depth more than two computing good codes we will use known bounds on the number of wires in circuits satisfying connectivity Property 3. We use the following definitions of Pudlák.

DEFINITION 13 (PUDLÁK [26]). *Let n be an integer and G be a directed acyclic graph with n inputs and n outputs. Let $0 < \epsilon, \delta$ and $0 \leq \mu \leq 1$. We say that G is ϵ, δ, μ-*densely regular *if for every k, where $\mu n \le k \le n$, there are probability distributions $\mathcal{X}$ and $\mathcal{Y}$ on k-element subsets of inputs and outputs, resp., such that for every $i, j \in \{1, \dots, n\}$,*

$$\Pr_{X \in \mathcal{X}}[i \in X] \le k/\delta n \qquad \Pr_{Y \in \mathcal{Y}}[j \in Y] \le k/\delta n$$

and the expected number of vertex disjoint paths from X to Y is at least ϵk for randomly chosen $X \in \mathcal{X}$ and $Y \in \mathcal{Y}$. We denote by $D(n, d, \epsilon, \delta, \mu)$ the minimum number of wires in any depth-d ϵ, δ, μ-densely regular graph with n inputs and n outputs.

Extending lower bounds on superconcentrator size of Dolev et al. [11], Pudlák [26] proves the following:

THEOREM 14 (PUDLÁK [26]). *Let $\epsilon, \delta > 0$ be constants. Then for every n, $1/n \le \mu \le 1$ and $d \ge 2$ the following holds:*

$$\begin{aligned} D(n, 3, \epsilon, \delta, \mu) &\in \Omega(n \cdot \lg\lg 1/\mu), \\ D(n, 2d, \epsilon, \delta, \mu) &\in \Omega(n \cdot \lambda_d(1/\mu)), \\ D(n, 2d+1, \epsilon, \delta, \mu) &\in \Omega(n \cdot \lambda_d(1/\mu)). \end{aligned}$$

Since Lemma 3 holds for any fixed k-element set X of inputs, it also holds in the case when the k-element set X of inputs is chosen at random. One gets the following corollary to Lemma 3.

COROLLARY 15. *Let $0 < \rho, \delta < 0$ be constants and C be a circuit computing a (ρ, δ)-good code. If we extend the circuit by $(1-\rho)n$ dummy inputs then its underlying graph is $\rho\delta, \rho, \frac{1}{n}$-densely regular.*

We add the dummy inputs only to have n inputs and n outputs. The parameters degrade because we apply the previous Lemma 3 which works only for k up-to ρn, over the ρn real inputs. So for $k \le \rho n$ we pick a random k-element subset X of the ρn real inputs, and for $k > \rho n$ we pick a random k-element subset X of inputs by taking all the real inputs and adding a random $k - \rho n$-element subset of the $(1-\rho)n$ dummy inputs.

THEOREM 16. *$w_{\rho,\delta,3}(n) \in \Omega(n \lg\lg n)$, and for any integer $d \ge 2$, $w_{\rho,\delta,2d}(n), w_{\rho,\delta,2d+1}(n) \in \Omega(n\lambda_d(n))$.*

PROOF. The proof directly follows from Corollary 15 and Theorem 14. □

4. CONSTRUCTION OF GOOD CODES WITH AN EFFICIENT ENCODING

In this section we construct bounded-depth circuits computing good codes. All our circuits will consist of only parity gates of arbitrary fan-in; hence, the codes computed by our circuits will be linear. Our constructions are probabilistic.

Recall that for $0 < \alpha < 1$ and integers $0 \le \ell \le k \le m$ and $0 < n$, a $(m, n, \ell, k, \alpha n)$-*range detector* is an XOR circuit with m inputs and n outputs such that on inputs of hamming weight at least ℓ and at most k, the circuit outputs at least αn ones.

The following proposition immediately follows from the existence of (ρ_0, δ_0)-good codes.

PROPOSITION 17. *For all $1 \le m$ there exists an $(m, m/\rho_0, 1, m, \delta_0 m)$-range detector of depth 1 and size m^2.*

We will use expander graphs to construct good range detectors. A bipartite graph $G = (V_1, V_2, E)$ is a (k, c) (vertex) expander if for all $S \subseteq V_1$ with $|S| \le k$ it holds that $|\Gamma(S)| \ge c|S|$. We are interested in expander graphs where $c = (1-\epsilon)d$, where d is the degree of the left side vertices V_1, for small $\epsilon > 0$. In this case G is known as a *lossless* expander. The reason we are interested in these is that when $\epsilon < 1/2$ at least $(1-2\epsilon)d|S|$ of the vertices in $\Gamma(S)$ must have a unique neighbor in S. In particular each of these vertices have an *odd* number of neighbors in S. For consistency with our application we will denote $m = |V_1|$ and $n = |V_2|$.

A (k, c) expander $G = (V_1, V_2, E)$ in particular is a $(k, 1 - ck/n)$ so-called disperser graph, and a lower bound for such graphs due to Radhakrishnan and Ta-Shma [28] states that $d = \Omega\left(\frac{\lg(m/k)}{\lg(n/(ck))}\right)$, when $k < m$, $2d \le n - ck$ and $ck < n/2$.

The common setting of parameters for lossless expanders have $n \ll m$ and $n = O(ck)$, and as a consequence of the lower bound above we get $d = \Omega(\lg m)$. We are interested in having $d = O(\lg m/\lg\lg m)$, and as a consequence we at least require $n = \Omega(ck \lg^\gamma m)$ for some $\gamma > 0$. We show below that this can indeed be achieved. Also, for our setting of parameters the usual probabilistic existence proof does not work – instead we proceed similarly to a proof due to Buhrman et al. [7, Lemma 3.10].

LEMMA 18. *Let $0 < \epsilon < 1$ and $\gamma > 0$ and let $k \le m$ be an integer. Then there exists a $(k, (1-\epsilon)d)$ expander graph $G = (V_1 = [m], V_2 = [n], E)$ with left side degree d, where $d = (2/\epsilon\gamma)\lg m/\lg\lg m$ and $n = (e/\epsilon)kd\lg^\gamma m = (2e/\epsilon^2\gamma)k\lg^{1+\gamma} m/\lg\lg m$.*

PROOF. We choose G by choosing (with replacement) d neighbors in V_2 for each left side vertex in V_1. We will show that G is a $(k, (1-\epsilon)d)$ expander with positive probability.

Let $S \subseteq V_1$ with $|S| = \ell \le k$. We consider the process of choosing the neighbors of S, by choosing a neighbor one at a time. Let for $i = 1, \dots, \ell d$ the random variable X_i indicate if the ith choice of neighbor was also chosen earlier, and let $X = \sum X_i$. We are interested in bounding the probability $\Pr[X > \epsilon\ell d]$. To this end, define for $i = 1, \dots, \ell d$ independent Bernoulli variables Y_i, by $\Pr[Y_i = 1] = \ell d/n$, and let $Y = \sum Y_i$. Conditioned on any values of $X_1, \dots, X_{i-1}$ we have $\Pr[X_i = 1] \le \ell d/n$ and thus we can bound $\Pr[X > \epsilon\ell d] \le \Pr[Y > \epsilon\ell d]$. We have $E[Y] = (\ell d)^2/n$ and by the Chernoff bound for the upper tail, letting $\alpha = \epsilon n/\ell d$ we have

$$\Pr[Y \ge \epsilon\ell d] = \Pr[Y \ge \alpha E[Y]]$$

$$\le \left(\frac{e^{\alpha-1}}{\alpha^\alpha}\right)^{E[Y]} \le \left(\frac{e}{\alpha}\right)^{\alpha E[Y]} = \left(\frac{e\ell d}{\epsilon n}\right)^{\epsilon\ell d}.$$

Using $n \ge (e/\epsilon)\ell d\lg^\gamma m$ we have

$$\Pr[X \ge \epsilon\ell d] \le (\lg^{-\gamma} m)^{\epsilon\ell d} = 2^{-\epsilon\gamma\ell d\lg\lg m} = 2^{-2\ell\lg m} = m^{-2\ell}.$$

Now, taking first a union bound over all $\binom{m}{\ell} \le m^\ell$ sets $S \subseteq V_1$ of size $|S| = \ell$ and then another union bound over all $\ell \le k$ we obtain the stated result. □

Setting $\epsilon = 1/4$, by the discussion and the lemma above we obtain the following.

COROLLARY 19. *Let $\gamma > 0$ be arbitrary. Then for any integers m and $\ell \le k \le m$ there exist a $(m, n, \ell, k, \alpha n, \beta n)$-range detector with m inputs, $n = (32ek\lg^{1+\gamma} m)/(\gamma\lg\lg m)$ outputs, $\beta = 1/(4e\lg^\gamma m)$, $\alpha = (\ell/2k)\beta$ that consists of at most $(8m\lg m)/(\gamma\lg\lg m)$ wires.*

We are now in position to present the construction of depth-2 circuits computing error correcting codes.

THEOREM 20. *Let $0 < \kappa < 1$ be arbitrary and let m be an integer. There exists a depth-2 XOR circuit with m inputs and $32m$ outputs, using $O(m(\lg m/\lg\lg m)^2)$ wires computing an error correcting code of minimum distance $1/8$. Furthermore, the fan-in of each output gate is $O(\lg^{1+\kappa} m)$.*

PROOF. Let $m \geq 1$ be an integer and let $\gamma, \lambda > 0$, be reals such that $\gamma + \lambda < \kappa$. Let k be an integer such that $k+1 = \lceil \frac{\lg m}{\lambda \lg\lg m} \rceil$. The middle layer of the circuit will consist of $k+1$ range detectors $W_0, \ldots, W_k$ where each W_i is a detector for the range of input weights $\lg^{\lambda i} m$ to $\lg^{\lambda(i+1)} m$. By Corollary 19 we can obtain this using a range detector of size $(8m \lg m)/(\gamma \lg\lg m)$ with parameters

$$\left(m, n, \lg^{\lambda i} m, \lg^{\lambda(i+1)} m, \frac{n}{8e \lg^{\gamma+\lambda} m}, \frac{n}{4e \lg^{\gamma} m}\right),$$

where

$$n = \frac{32e \lg^{1+\gamma+\lambda(i+1)} m}{\gamma \lg\lg m}.$$

Note that $k+1 = O(\lg m/\lg\lg m)$, and hence we have used $O(m(\lg m/\lg\lg m)^2)$ wires in total so far.

Define $\alpha = 1/(8e \lg^{\gamma+\lambda} m)$ and $\ell = 8e \lg^{\gamma+\lambda} m$. For the last layer, each node is an XOR of $(k+1)\ell$ nodes, where we chose ℓ nodes at random from each W_i. We will have a total of $32m$ such XOR's.

Consider now a fixed input x of weight $w > 0$, and let i be such that $\lg^{\lambda i} m \leq w \leq \lg^{\lambda(i+1)} m$. Our goal is to show that with high probability over the random choice of neighbors of the top XOR gates at least $4m$ of the top XOR gates will evaluate to 1 on x. On input x we have ensured that in W_i a fraction α of the XOR's of W_i are odd. Conditioned on the values of all the XOR's of the second layer outside W_i, by Proposition 37 the probability that a given XOR of the last layer is odd is at least $\alpha\ell/4 = 1/4$. Letting X be the random variable indicating the number of XOR's in the last layer that are odd, we then have $E[X] \geq 8m$, and using the Chernoff bound for the lower tail we have

$$\begin{aligned}\Pr[X < 4m] &\leq \Pr[X < E[X]/2] < \exp(-E[X]/8)\\ &\leq \exp(-m) < 2^{-m}\end{aligned}$$

Thus taking a union bound over all $2^m - 1$ inputs we have that the circuit can be constructed to compute an error correcting code of minimum distance $1/8$.

Between the second layer and the last layer we have used a total number of

$$32m(k+1)8e \lg^{\gamma+\lambda} m = O(m \lg^{1+\gamma+\lambda} m/\lg\lg m)$$

wires, and the fan-in of each gate of the last layer is $(k+1)8e \lg^{\gamma+\lambda} m = O(\lg^{1+\gamma+\lambda} m/\lg\lg m)$. Thus the total size of the circuit is $O(m(\lg m/\lg\lg m)^2)$ and the top fan-in is $O(\lg^{1+\kappa} m)$. □

4.1 Comparison with depth-2 superconcentrators

It is instructive to compare our construction to depth-2 superconcentrators. Radhakrishnan and Ta-Shma [28] show that depth-2 superconcentrators must be of size at least $\Omega(m \lg^2 m/\lg\lg m)$, while we show that error correcting codes can be computed by size $O(m(\lg m/\lg\lg m)^2)$ circuits. Furthermore we can have the fan-in of the output be $O(\lg^{1+\kappa} m)$ for arbitrary $\kappa > 0$, while maintaining the bound on the total size. Dutta and Radhakrishnan [12], show that if G is a depth-2 superconcentrator with m inputs and outputs, where the outputs have average fan-in a and inputs have average fanout b then $a \lg(2b/a) \lg b = \Omega(\lg^2 m)$ (by symmetry the reverse relation also holds). In particular if $a = \lg^{1+\kappa} m$ for $0 < \kappa < 1$ we have $b = 2^{\Omega(\lg^{(1-\kappa)/2} M)}$, hence the size is much bigger than in the case of circuits computing good codes.

4.2 Depth three and more

In this section we construct circuits of depth higher than two computing good codes. We will need several kinds of circuits—range detectors of depth 1 described in the following lemmas.

LEMMA 21. *There exists $c_0 > 1$ such that for all $1 \leq r \leq m/k^{1.5}$ and $c_0 \leq k \leq m$ there exists an $(m, m/k, r, m/k^{1.5}, r)$-range detector of depth 1 and size $3m$.*

PROOF. Let $n = m/k$. The edges of the range detector circuit form a bipartite graph where we denote by V_1 the input gates and by V_2 the output XOR gates. The bipartite graph could be a random graph where all vertices $x \in V_1$ have degree 3. However, to simplify the computation we will pick randomly 3 elements from V_2 for every $x \in V_1$ *allowing repetitions*. So some vertices in V_1 may have smaller degree.

Let $r \leq \ell \leq m/k^{1.5}$ and let $S \subseteq V_1$, $|S| = \ell$ be fixed. Let $y_1, \ldots, y_{3\ell}$ be the chosen neighbors, allowing repetitions. We want to show that S has at least r unique neighbors with high probability. That will suffice to prove the lower bound on the number of ones in the output.

For $i = 1, \ldots, 3\ell - 1$, let X_i be the random variable that is the indicator of the event $y_{i+1} \in \{y_1, \ldots, y_i\}$. Note that the number of unique neighbors is at least $3\ell - 2\sum X_i$. If $b_1, \ldots, b_j$ are fixed $\Pr[X_{j+1} = 1 | X_1 = b_1 \wedge \cdots \wedge X_j = b_j] \leq \frac{3\ell}{n}$. Hence we can apply the Chernoff bound, as in Lemma 18, to bound $\Pr[\sum_{i=1}^{3\ell-1} X_i \geq \ell]$. We have

$$E[\sum_{i=1}^{3\ell-1} X_i] \leq \frac{3\ell(3\ell-1)}{n} \leq \frac{9\ell^2 k}{m}.$$

Let $\alpha = \frac{m}{9\ell k}$. We have $\alpha > 1$ for $k > 81$ using $\ell \leq m/k^{1.5}$. By Lemma 35 we get

$$\begin{aligned}\Pr[\sum_{i=1}^{3\ell-1} X_i \geq \ell] &\leq \left(\frac{e^{\alpha-1}}{\alpha^{\alpha}}\right)^{\frac{9\ell^2 k}{m}} \leq \left(\tfrac{e}{\alpha}\right)^{\alpha\frac{9\ell^2 k}{m}}\\ &\leq \left(\tfrac{9e\ell k}{m}\right)^{\ell} \leq \left(\tfrac{9e}{\sqrt{k}}\right)^{\ell}.\end{aligned}$$

If k is sufficiently large, this is less than $2^{-\ell}$. Thus we have nonzero probability that for all ℓ, $r \leq \ell \leq m^{1.5}$, we have r unique neighbors. □

COROLLARY 22. *There exists $c_0 > 1$ such that for all $c_0^2 \leq m$ there is an $(m, \sqrt{m}/\rho_0, 1, m^{1/4}, \delta_0 m)$-range detector of depth 2 and size $4m$.*

PROOF. Lemma 21 gives a depth-1 $(m, \sqrt{m}, 1, m^{1/4}, 1)$-range detector with $3m$ wires. The result follows by applying Proposition 17 on the output of that range detector. □

We can amplify the quality of range detectors using the following lemma.

LEMMA 23. *For any $0 < \alpha$ and $1 \leq k \leq m \leq n \leq w$, if there is an $(m, n, m/k, m, \alpha n)$-range detector of depth d with w wires then there is an $(m, 32m, m/k, m, 4m)$-range detector of depth d with $65w/\alpha$ wires. Consequently, there is an $(m, 32m, m/k, m, 4m)$-range detector of depth 1 with $65mk$ wires.*

PROOF. First we construct a circuit of depth $d+1$. Each of the $32m$ output vertices will be an XOR of at most $\lceil 2/\alpha \rceil$ outputs of the depth-d range detector chosen by the following random process. In each of $\lceil 2/\alpha \rceil$ steps we with probability 1/2 do nothing and with probability 1/2 we pick a random gate of the range detector. We claim that on a fixed input of hamming weight at least m/k the XOR evaluates to 1 with probability at least 1/4. This follows immediately from Proposition 37. Hence, if we take $32m$ of such XOR gates independently at random, the probability that less than $4m$ of them are 1 is by the Chernoff bound at most e^{-m}.

Since we want to maintain the depth of the circuits we cannot add these XOR gates as another layer but instead we collapse them with the existing output gates and we remove the original output gates. This possibly leads to an increase in the number of wires. A single new XOR gate contributes by at most $w/\alpha n$ wires in expectation so the new XOR gates will contribute by at most $32wm/\alpha n \leq 32w/\alpha$ wires in expectation. As all the random choices are independent by the Chernoff bound, the probability that the new XOR gates contribute by more than $64w/\alpha$ wires is at most $(e/4)^{32w/\alpha} < (e/4)^{32m} < 2^{-2m}$. So there is a particular choice of the $32m$ output gates that will contribute by at most $64w/\alpha$ wires and on any input of hamming weight at least m/k at least $4m$ of the output gates will evaluate to 1. This proves the first part of the lemma.

The existence of the depth-1 range detector follows by noting that a circuit computing the identity function is an $(m, m, m/k, m, m/k)$-range detector. □

Combining the two lemmas we get:

COROLLARY 24. *There exists $c_0 > 1$ such that for all $c_0 \leq k \leq m$, there exists an $(m, 32m/k, m/k^2, m/k^{1.5}, 4m/k)$-range detector of depth 2 and size $68m$.*

We are ready to construct circuits of even depth bigger than two using the following lemma. The case of depth-three circuits is left to the end of this section.

LEMMA 25. *Let $d \geq 2$ and c_d be constants and $f(m) \leq \lg m$ be a non-decreasing unbounded function. There exists a constant c_{d+2} such that if for each $1 \leq r \leq m$, there is a depth-d $(m, 32m, m/r, m, 4m)$-range detector with at most $c_d m \cdot f^2(r)$ wires then for each $1 \leq r \leq m$ there is a depth-$d+2$ $(m, 32m, m/r, m, 4m)$-range detector with at most $c_{d+2} m \cdot f^*(r)$ wires.*

PROOF. Let $k_1 = \min\{r, m^{3/4}\}$, let $k_{i+1} = f(k_i)^3$ and let t be the least integer such that $k_t \leq c_0^{1.5}$. The first layer of the circuit contains an $(m, m/f(k_i)^2, m/k_i, m/f(k_i)^3, m/k_i)$-range detector provided by Lemma 21, for each $i = 1, \ldots, t-1$. We assume that the detectors are disjoint except for the same input vertices. The output of the i-th depth-1 range detector feeds into a depth-d $(m/f(k_i)^2, 32m/f(k_i)^2, m/k_i, m/f(k_i)^2, 4m/f(k_i)^2)$-range detector, called W_i, given by the assumptions of the lemma.

Furthermore, we add the depth-1 $(m, 32m, m/k_{t-1}, m, 4m)$-range detector, called W_t, given in Lemma 23. (Observe, that $k_{t-1} < \min\{a, f(a) > c_0^{1.5}\}$ so the size of this detector can be upper-bounded in terms of properties of f.) If $r > k_1$ then to capture the strings of weights $< m/k_1$ we add the depth-2 $(m, \sqrt{m}/\rho_0, 1, m^{1/4}, \delta_0 m)$-range detector, called W_0 from Corollary 22.

For the last layer, we take Cm XOR gates for a sufficiently large constant C and each of the gates will be fed by at most one randomly picked output gate of each $W_0, \ldots, W_t$ ($W_1, \ldots, W_t$ if $r \leq k_1$.) For each output XOR gate and each W_i we do not connect them with probability 1/2 and we connect them with probability 1/2 (via the random output gate of W_i.) Thus on any input of weight at least m/r, each output XOR gate is one with probability at least 1/16. An application of the Chernoff bound, as in the proof of Theorem 20 and amplification by Lemma 23 gives the required range detection property of the circuit.

To count the number of wires, notice that $f^3(f^3(a)) \leq \lceil 3 \lg f(a) \rceil^3 < f(a)$ for a sufficiently large, hence there is some constant c depending only on f such that $t \leq 2f^*(r) + c$. Furthermore, each W_i detector consists of at most $c_d \cdot \frac{m}{f(k_i)^2} \cdot f(k_i/f(k_i)^2)^2 \leq cm$ wires. Since all the other range detectors built into the construction also use only $O(m)$ wires, the total size of the resulting range detector is $O(tm) \in O(mf^*(r))$. □

We will use the above lemma recursively. As the base construction we will need also the following type of range detectors.

LEMMA 26. *There exists a constant c_2 such that for all $1 \leq r \leq m$, there is a depth-2 $(m, 32m, m/r, m, 4m)$-range detector with at most $c_2 m \cdot \lg^2(r)$ wires.*

PROOF. This construction is similar to our other constructions so we provide only a brief sketch. Let $k_1 = r$, let $k_{i+1} = k_i/2$ and let t be the least integer such that $k_t \leq 1$. Define $n_i = 2\lceil \lg \binom{m}{m/k_i} \rceil$. For $i = 1, \ldots, t-1$, one can construct $(m, 32n_i, m/k_i, m/k_{i+1}, 4n_i)$-range detectors of depth 1 and size $O(k_i n_i) = O(m \lg k_i)$ by a probabilistic argument. Hence, take these range detectors as the first layer of the circuit. The output layer is formed by taking random XOR's of outputs from these detectors similarly as in the proof of Lemma 25. Clearly, the size of the circuit is bounded by $O(tm \lg r) = O(m \lg^2 r)$. □

Recall that $(m, 32m, 1, m, 4m)$-range detector is a circuit computing a $(1/32, 1/8)$-good code. Thus, the previous two lemmas give the following corollary.

COROLLARY 27. *For any $d \geq 2$ there exists a constant c_d and a family of depth-2d circuits with $c_d m \lambda_d(m)$ wires that computes $(1/32, 1/8)$-good codes.*

It remains to construct a circuit of depth 3 that has size $O(m \lg \lg m)$ and computes a good code.

THEOREM 28. *There is a family of depth-3 circuits with $O(m \lg \lg m)$ wires that computes $(1/32, 1/8)$-good codes.*

PROOF. The proof is similar to the proof of Lemma 25. However, we let parameters $k_1 = \sqrt{m}$, $k_{i+1} = k_i^{3/4}$ and let t be the least integer such that $k_t \leq c_0$ (i.e., $t < \lg_{4/3} \lg_{k_1} \sqrt{m}$). The first two layers of the circuit consist of the depth-2

$(m, 32m/k_i, m/k_i^2, m/k_i^{1.5}, 4m/k_i)$-range detectors, for $i = 2, \dots, t-1$, given in Corollary 24, together with the $(m, 32m, m/k_t, m, 4m)$-range detector of depth 1 from Lemma 23 to capture the input strings of weight $> m/k_t$, and the depth-2 $(m, \sqrt{m}/\rho_0, 1, m^{1/4}, \delta_0 m)$-range detector from Corollary 22 to capture the strings of weights $\le m/k_1$. In total we use $O(m \lg\lg m)$ wires for the first two layers.

The output layer is formed by taking random XOR's of outputs from the above detectors as in previous proofs. □

4.3 Unbounded-depth circuits

In this section we prove Theorem 2: we obtain linear-size circuits computing good codes with slowly-growing depth. To obtain such circuits, consider the constant-depth constructions in Theorem 1. Then apply the following corollary to trade depth for size.

COROLLARY 29. *Let $d \ge 2$, c_d be a constant and $f(m) \le \lg m$ be a non-decreasing unbounded function. There exists a constant c such that if for each $1 \le m$, there is a depth-$2d$ $(m, 32m, 1, m, 4m)$-range detector with at most $c_d m \cdot f(m)$ wires then for any $m \ge 1$ there is depth-$2d + 2\lg_{c_0} f(m)$ $(m, 32m, 1, m, 4m)$-range detector with at most cm wires where c_0 is the constant from Lemma 21.*

Hence, for any fixed $d > 0$, there are linear size circuits of depth $O(\lg(\lambda_d(m)))$ computing good codes. The proof of the above corollary relies on a lemma which we state and prove next.

LEMMA 30. *For any $m \ge c_0$, any d and w if there is a depth-d $(m/c_0, 32m/c_0, 1, m/c_0, 4m/c_0)$-range detector of size w then there is also a depth-$d+2$ $(m, 32m, 1, m, 4m)$-range detector of size $w + (9 + (2c_0^{1.5} + 16)32)m$.*

PROOF. Take the $(m, m/c_0, 1, m/c_0^{1.5}, 1)$-range detector of depth 1 and size $9m$ provided by Lemma 21 and apply on its output the depth-d $(m/c_0, 32m/c_0, 1, m/c_0, 4m/c_0)$-range detector provided by the lemma. This gives a circuit with the property that on each non-zero input either the input has at least $1/c_0^{1.5}$ fraction of ones or the output of the depth-d detector has at least $1/8$ fraction of ones. Consider an XOR gate that takes at most $2c_0^{1.5}$ random bits of the input and at most 16 random outputs of the depth-d range detector and is obtained as follows: $2c_0^{1.5}$ times repeat: with probability 1/2 take a random input bit and with probability 1/2 take nothing; then repeat 16 times: with probability 1/2 take a random output bit of the detector and with probability 1/2 take nothing. Such an XOR gate will evaluate to one with probability at least 1/4 by Proposition 37. By the Chernoff bound, on any fixed input out of $32m$ such independently chosen XOR gates at least $4m$ will evaluate to one with probability at least $1 - e^{-m}$. Hence, there is a particular choice of the $32m$ XOR gates so that on any non-zero input at least $4m$ of them will evaluate to one. That forms our depth-$d+2$ $(m, 32m, 1, m, 4m)$-range detector of size at most $w + 9m + (2c_0^{1.5} + 16)32m$. □

PROOF OF COROLLARY 29. Let $t = \lceil \lg_{c_0} f(m) \rceil$ and for $i = 0, \dots, t$, define $m_i = m/c_0^{t-i}$. The depth-$2d$ range detector guaranteed by the assumption of the lemma on inputs of size m_0 uses $c_d m_0 f(m_0) \le c_d m$ wires. For $i = 1, \dots, t$, iteratively apply to this range detector the previous lemma to construct $(m_i, 32m_i, 1, m_i, 4m_i)$-range detector. The depth of the resulting range detector is $2d + 2t$ and its size is bounded by $c_d m + \sum_{i=1}^{t}(9 + (2c_0^{1.5} + 16)32)m_i \in O(m)$. □

5. HASH FUNCTIONS

In this section we first show how our constructions of efficient encoding circuits imply similarly efficient circuits for pairwise independent hash functions. At the end we also deduce lower bounds for various types of multiplication.

For the first result, we follow closely the results by Ishai, Kushilevitz, Ostrovsky, and Sahai [17]. Our main contribution is observing that their construction can be applied in our constant-depth setting. In fact, in our setting the proof is somewhat simpler (the presentation in [17] relies on several previous results in coding theory; it also uses an argument about obtaining a circuit for the transpose of the function computed by another circuit which is immediate in our setting).

A *pairwise independent hash function* is a map $h : \{0,1\}^m \times \{0,1\}^r \to \{0,1\}^m$ such that for fixed m-bit strings $x \ne y$, the values $f(x, R)$ and $f(y, R)$ are uniformly and independently distributed for uniform $R \in \{0,1\}^r$.

THEOREM 5 (IMPLICIT IN [17]). *Suppose there are constants ρ, δ, d, and an increasing function $w(n) \ge n$ such that*

1. *for any n there is a $[n, \rho n, \delta n]_2$ code, that is a (ρ, δ)-good code, that can be computed by a depth-d XOR circuit with $w(n)$ wires.*

Then there is a constant c such that

2. *for every m we can compute a pairwise independent hash function $h : \{0,1\}^m \times \{0,1\}^r \to \{0,1\}^m$ with $r \le cm$, by a depth-$2d$ circuit with $\le cw(cm)$ wires (using arbitrary gates).*

Moreover, if the codes are explicit then the hash functions are too.

We now turn to the proof of the reduction in Theorem 5. The explicitness of the reduction is immediate from the proof and we will not address it explicitly. The proof needs several ingredients. First, we need codes over large alphabet with relative distance close to 1. To achieve this with a linear number of wires, [17] cite [15] (presumably Theorem 11) which – inspired by [2] – uses expander graphs on top of the code in [29]. We observe that a similar approach works in our setting with no blow-up in the depth.

LEMMA 31. *Under the assumption of Theorem 5, for every $\epsilon > 0$ there is a constant $c \ge 2$ such that for every n we can compute, over an alphabet of size $\le c$, a $[cn, \rho n, (1-\epsilon)cn]$ code by a depth-d circuit with $\le cw(n)$ wires.*

PROOF. Consider an expander graph on n nodes with constant degree and normalized second largest eigenvalue $\le 1 - \Omega(1)$. Let $t = t(\epsilon)$ be a constant to be determined later. The indexes of codeword symbols of the new code are identified with walks of length t on the expander. Since a walk can be written with $\lg n + O(t)$ bits, the block length is $n2^{O(t)}$. For a message $x \in \{0,1\}^{\rho m}$, we encode x with the code in Theorem 5 with block-length n. Then we set the i-th symbol of the new code to be the concatenation of the t bits specified by the walk. Since to any $x \ne y$ there corresponds in C codewords at constant relative hamming distance, the encodings of x and y in the new code agree in at most $2^{-\Omega(t)}$ fraction of symbols. Here we use standard hitting properties of random walks on expanders [1, 19]. For large enough

$t = O(1)$, this gives the desired relative distance, with a block length $\leq cn$.

Regarding the complexity, note that the construction just amounts to repeating bits of the code according to the expander. This clearly does not affect depth. As for the number of wires, for example we can note that for any index bit i of C, a random walk hits i with probability $\leq t/n$, by the union bound. Since the number of walks is $n2^{O(t)}$, i participates in at most $2^{O(t)}$ walks. Therefore, the number of wires increases by a factor $\leq 2^{O(t)} = O(1)$. □

Another component of the construction is a *resilient function* [10]. A function $f : \{0,1\}^n \to \{0,1\}^m$ is *resilient to fixing t bits* if for every random variable $X \in \{0,1\}^n$ where at least $n - t$ bits are uniform and i.i.d. and the others are constants, we have that $f(X)$ is uniform over $\{0,1\}^m$. We denote by M^T the transpose of the matrix M.

FACT 32 ([10]). *Let G be the $n \times m$ generator matrix of a $[n, m, \delta n]_2$ code. Then $f : \{0,1\}^n \to \{0,1\}^m$ defined by $f(x) = G^T x$ is resilient to fixing $\delta n - 1$ bits.*

PROOF. Let $X \in \{0,1\}^n$ be a r.v. where at least $n - \delta n + 1$ bits are uniform and i.i.d. and the others are constants. By the XOR lemma in [10], it is enough to prove that for any vector $a \in \{0,1\}^m$ the value $aG^T X$ is a uniform bit. Note $aG^T X = (Ga)X$. Since G generates a linear code with distance δn, Ga is a vector of hamming weight $\geq \delta n$. Hence Ga has a 1 in a position corresponding to a uniform bit of X, and so $(Ga)X$ is unbiased. □

COROLLARY 33. *Under the assumption of Theorem 5, for every n there is a function $f : \{0,1\}^n \to \{0,1\}^{\rho n}$ that is resilient to fixing $\delta n - 1$ bits and is computable by a depth-d XOR circuit with w wires.*

PROOF. The generator matrix G of the code in Theorem 5 can be decomposed as $G = G_1 G_2 \cdots G_d$ where the sum of the number of 1's in the matrices is $\leq w$. Note $G^T = G_d^T G_{d-1}^T \cdots G_1^T$ and apply Fact 32. □

We can now prove Theorem 5.

PROOF OF THEOREM 5. The construction in [17] consists of the following 3 steps. On input $x \in \{0,1\}^m$ and r:

(1) Use Lemma 31 to encode $x \in \{0,1\}^m$ with a code over an alphabet of size $\leq c$ where to different messages there correspond codewords with at least $(1 - \epsilon)$ fraction of distinct symbols, for a sufficiently small ϵ and a c depending on ϵ only. For fixed ϵ, the block length is $n = cm/\rho$. Each codeword takes $n' := n \lg c = O(m)$ bits to specify.

(2) Use the randomness R to apply a pairwise-independent function to the bit-vector representation of every symbol of the codeword, using different seed for each symbol.

(3) Use Corollary 33 to apply a resilient function with input length $= n'$ and range $\rho n'$ bits that is resilient to fixing $\delta n' - 1$ bits.

For a small enough constant ϵ, for any $x \neq y$ the corresponding images after (1) have $n(1 - \epsilon)$ different symbols. After (2), we are in the following situation. There is a set of $S \subseteq [n']$ of size $\geq n'(1 - \epsilon)$ such that the projections over S of the encodings of x and y are jointly distributed, over the choice of R, uniformly over $\left(\{0,1\}^{|S|}\right)^2$.

Setting ϵ sufficiently small, the complement of S has size $\epsilon n' \leq \delta n' - 1$. (Recall δ is fixed.) Since the function in (3) is resilient to fixing $\delta n' - 1$, the images corresponding to x and y are uniformly and independently distributed over $\rho n' = cm \lg c \geq m$ bits.

Regarding the complexity, note that (2) can be collapsed with (1) with no increase in depth and only a constant-factor increase in the number of wires. Using Lemma 31 for (1) and Corollary 33 we get the desired complexity. □

We remark that in the previous proof if one were to settle for a hashing circuit of depth $2d + 1$ then one could build it from XOR gates and binary AND gates.

Finally, we mention three other natural functions to which our lower bounds in Theorem 1 apply as stated. The first is multiplication by some fixed (non-explicitly given) element a of the finite field with 2^n elements: $f_1 : \{0,1\}^n \to \{0,1\}^n$ defined as $f_1(x) := ax$. The second is multiplication by some fixed (non-explicitly given) $n \times n$ Toeplitz matrix M: $f_2 : \{0,1\}^n \to \{0,1\}^n$ defined as $f_2(x) := Mx$. The third is multiplication by some fixed (non-explicitly given) n-bit integer a: $f_3 : \{0,1\}^n \to \{0,1\}^{2n}$ defined as $f_3(x) := ax$.

We now give the details in the case of f_1. The reasoning for f_2 is identical. Recall that $h(x, (a, b)) := ax + b$ is a pairwise independent hash function. By Fact 4, there exist fixed a and b such that, for appropriate $m = \Omega(n)$, the map $f_1' : \{0,1\}^m \to \{0,1\}^n$ defined as $f_1'(x) = ax + b$ is the encoding map of a good error-correcting code. Hence, the lower bounds in Theorem 1 apply as stated to f_1'. Since addition by b does not affect complexity in our model, the same lower bounds apply to f_1.

Here is an alternative argument for f_1. One can directly argue that there are field elements a such that $x \to (x, ax)$ defines a good code. This is because if $x \neq 0$, then x and ax determine a. Since the number of pairs $(x, y) \in \{0,1\}^{2n}$ of hamming weight $< H^{-1}(1/2)2n$ is less than 2^n, we cannot have for every a an x such that both x and ax have hamming weight $< H^{-1}(1/2)n$.

This alternative argument also applies to f_3, except the relative distance is smaller. For depth $d \geq 3$, these lower bounds for f_2 and f_3 are not new; they follow from [11, 3, 26].

6. SOME REMARKS ON EXPLICIT CONSTRUCTIONS

In this section we make some remarks on explicit constructions. First, for every $d > 0$ the encoding circuit with depth d and size $O(n^{1+1/d})$ mentioned in the introduction is explicit: use $\Theta(n^{(d-1)/d})$ explicit depth-one circuits of size $O(n^{2/d})$ for computing good codes on input size $\Theta(n^{1/d})$. In the rest of this section we make some steps towards making our depth-2 construction with $n \cdot \text{poly} \lg n$ wires explicit. For simplicity, we refer to the depth-2 construction of size $O(n \lg^2 n)$ mentioned in the introduction. Recall in this construction the input length is m, the output length is $n = O(m)$, and the middle layer is made of the output gates of $\lg m$ range detectors. The i-th range detector has $\leq bm/c^i$ output gates for some constants $b > 1, c > 1$. Its property is that for every non-zero input, at least one range detector has a constant α fraction of its output gates that evaluate to 1. The output layer of the depth-2 construction then combines the outputs of the range detectors into the codeword. The next claim obtains this last layer explicitly.

It bounds the output degree by $O(\lg m)$ which obviously implies $\leq O(m \lg m)$ wires.

CLAIM 34. *Fix any $b > 1, c > 1, \alpha > 0$. For all sufficiently large m there is a depth-1 circuit, consisting of parity gates, with $O(m)$ output gates, $O(m)$ input gates divided in $\lg m$ groups of bm/c^i for $i = 1, 2, \ldots, \lg m$, and output degree $O(\lg m)$ such that: on any input where at least some group of input bits has $\geq \alpha$ relative hamming weight, the output has $\Omega(1)$ relative hamming weight.*

PROOF. We are going to construct a bipartite graph with the same input nodes as the input gates in the claim, $\ell := m/\lg m$ output nodes, and output degree $O(\lg m)$, with the property that on every input as in the statement of the claim a constant fraction of the output nodes are adjacent to at least one node set to 1. Then the claim follows by replacing each output node of the graph by a good error-correcting code on its $O(\lg m)$ neighbors. The code is implemented by a depth-1 circuit with $O(\lg m)$ output parity gates of output degree $O(\lg m)$. Thus the total number of output gates will be $O(\lg m)m/\lg m = O(m)$. The hamming weight guarantee follows from the fact that each node that is adjacent to at least one node set to 1 will give rise to $\Omega(\lg m)$ ones.

The graph is constructed by adding neighbors separately for each group.

If the group consists of $t \geq \ell$ nodes, we divide the t nodes in the group into ℓ blocks of size t/ℓ, and connect an output node to each node in the corresponding group. The output degree is $t/\ell \leq (bm/c^i)/(m/\lg m) = b \lg m/c^i$, if this is the i-th group. Since picking a random neighbor of a random output node yields a random node in the group, we see that if this group has a constant fraction of ones we also have a constant fraction of output nodes that are adjacent to some node set to one.

If the group consists of $t < \ell$ nodes, we divide the output nodes in t blocks of size ℓ/t; and we connect each node in the group to all the output nodes in the corresponding block. Here the output degree is 1. It is easy to see that if this group has a constant fraction of ones we also have a constant fraction of output nodes that are adjacent to some node set to one.

The i-th group contributes $\leq \max\{1, b \lg m/c^i\} \leq 1 + b \lg m/c^i$ to the output degree. Summing over all groups gives output degree $O(\lg m)$. □

It is an open problem to construct suitable range detectors. Specifically, we know of constructions when the hamming weight to be detected is close to 0 or close to m, but we do not know how to handle, say, hamming weight m^ϵ.

Acknowledgements.

We are grateful to Jaikumar Radhakrishnan for explaining us the proof of superconcentrator lower bound [28] during the workshop *Synergies in Lower Bounds* in Aarhus. We thank Mahdi Cheraghchi for pointing us to some references.

7. REFERENCES

[1] M. Ajtai, J. Komlós, and E. Szemerédi. Deterministic simulation in LOGSPACE. In *19th Annual ACM Symposium on Theory of Computing (STOC'87)*, pages 132–140. ACM Press, 1987.

[2] N. Alon, J. Bruck, J. Naor, M. Naor, and R. M. Roth. Construction of asymptotically good low-rate error-correcting codes through pseudo-random graphs. *IEEE Transactions on Information Theory*, 38(2):509–516, 1992.

[3] N. Alon and P. Pudlák. Superconcentrators of depth 2 and 3; odd levels help (rarely). *Journal of Computer and System Sciences*, 48(1):194–202, 1994.

[4] L. Bazzi, M. Mahdian, and D. A. Spielman. The minimum distance of turbo-like codes. *IEEE Transactions on Information Theory*, 55(1):6–15, 2009.

[5] L. Bazzi and S. K. Mitter. Encoding complexity versus minimum distance. *IEEE Transactions on Information Theory*, 51(6):2103–2112, 2005.

[6] R. Boppana. The average sensitivity of bounded-depth circuits. *Information Processing Letters*, 63(5):257–261, 1997.

[7] H. Buhrman, P. B. Miltersen, J. Radhakrishnan, and S. Venkatesh. Are bitvectors optimal? *SIAM Journal on Computing*, 31(6):1723–1744, 2002.

[8] A. K. Chandra, S. Fortune, and R. J. Lipton. Lower bounds for constant depth circuits for prefix problems. In *10th Colloquium on Automata, Languages and Programming (ICALP'83)*, volume 154 of *LNCS*, pages 109–117. Springer, 1983.

[9] A. K. Chandra, S. Fortune, and R. J. Lipton. Unbounded fan-in circuits and associative functions. *Journal of Computer and System Sciences*, 30(2):222–234, 1985.

[10] B. Chor, O. Goldreich, J. Håstad, J. Friedman, S. Rudich, and R. Smolensky. The bit extraction problem or t-resilient functions. In *26th Annual IEEE Symposium on Foundations of Computer Science (FOCS'85)*, pages 396–407. IEEE Computer Society Press, 1985.

[11] D. Dolev, C. Dwork, N. Pippenger, and A. Wigderson. Superconcentrators, generalizers and generalized connectors with limited depth. In *15th Annual ACM Symposium on Theory of Computing (STOC'83)*, pages 42–51. ACM Press, 1983.

[12] C. Dutta and J. Radhakrishnan. Tradeoffs in depth-two superconcentrators. In *23rd Annual Symposium on Theoretical Aspects of Computer Science (STACS'06)*, volume 3884 of *LNCS*, pages 372–383. Springer, 2006.

[13] L. R. Ford and D. R. Fulkerson. *Flows in networks.* Princeton University Press, 1962.

[14] S. Gelfand, R. Dobrushin, and M. Pinsker. On the complexity of coding. In *2nd International Symposium on Information Theory*, pages 177–184. Akademiai Kiado, 1973.

[15] V. Guruswami and P. Indyk. Expander-based constructions of efficiently decodable codes. In *42nd Annual IEEE Symposium on Foundations of Computer Science (FOCS'01)*, pages 658–667. IEEE Computer Society Press, 2001.

[16] G. Hansel. Nombre minimal de contacts de fermature nécessaires pour réaliser une fonction booléenne symétrique de n variables. *C. R. Acad. Sci. Paris*, 258:6037–6040, 1964.

[17] Y. Ishai, E. Kushilevitz, R. Ostrovsky, and A. Sahai. Cryptography with constant computational overhead. In *14th Annual ACM Symposium on Theory of*

Computing (STOC'08), pages 433–442. ACM Press, 2008.

[18] S. Jukna. *Boolean Function Complexity: Advances and Frontiers*, volume 27 of *Algorithms and Combinatorics*. Springer, 2012.

[19] N. Kahale. Eigenvalues and expansion of regular graphs. *Journal of the ACM*, 42(5):1091–1106, 1995.

[20] N. Linial, Y. Mansour, and N. Nisan. Constant depth circuits, Fourier transform, and learnability. *Journal of the ACM*, 40(3):607–620, 1993.

[21] S. Lovett and E. Viola. Bounded-depth circuits cannot sample good codes. In *25th Annual IEEE Conference on Computational Complexity (CCC'10)*, pages 243–251. IEEE Computer Society Press, 2010.

[22] Y. Mansour, N. Nisan, and P. Tiwari. The computational complexity of universal hashing. *Theoretical Computer Science*, 107(1):121–133, 1993.

[23] P. B. Miltersen. Error correcting codes, perfect hashing circuits, and deterministic dynamic dictionaries. In *9th Annual ACM-SIAM Symposium on Discrete Algorithms (SODA'98)*, pages 556–563. ACM Press, 1998.

[24] J. G. Oxley. *Matroid theory*. Oxford University Press, 1992.

[25] H. Perfect. Applications of Menger's graph theorem. *Journal of Mathematical Analysis and Applications*, 22:96–111, 1968.

[26] P. Pudlák. Communication in bounded depth circuits. *Combinatorica*, 14(2):203–216, 1994.

[27] P. Pudlák and V. Rödl. Some combinatorial-algebraic problems from complexity theory. *Discrete Mathematics*, 136(1-3):253–279, 1994.

[28] J. Radhakrishnan and A. Ta-Shma. Bounds for dispersers, extractors, and depth-two superconcentrators. *SIAM Journal on Discrete Mathematics*, 13(1):2–24, 2000.

[29] D. Spielman. *Computationally Efficient Error-Correcting Codes and Holographic Proofs*. PhD thesis, Massachusetts Institute of Technology, 1995.

[30] D. A. Spielman. Linear-time encodable and decodable error-correcting codes. *IEEE Transactions on Information Theory*, 42(6):1723–1731, 1996.

[31] L. Valiant. On non-linear lower bounds in computational complexity. In *7th Annual ACM Symposium on Theory of Computing (STOC'75)*, pages 45–53. ACM Press, 1975.

[32] E. Viola. The complexity of constructing pseudorandom generators from hard functions. *Computational Complexity*, 13(3-4):147–188, 2004.

[33] D. J. Welsh. *Matroid theory*. Academic Press, London, 1976.

8. APPENDIX

8.1 Some helpful facts

In this section we provide a few simple facts on probability.

LEMMA 35 (MULTIPLICATIVE CHERNOFF BOUND). *Let $X_1, \ldots, X_n$ be independent Bernoulli random variables, and $X = \sum X_i$. Then for any $\epsilon > 0$ we have the* upper tail *bound*

$$\Pr[X \geq (1+\epsilon)E[X]] \leq \left(\frac{e^{\epsilon}}{(1+\epsilon)^{(1+\epsilon)}}\right)^{E[X]} \leq \left(\frac{e}{1+\epsilon}\right)^{(1+\epsilon)E[X]}$$

and for any $0 < \epsilon < 1$ the lower tail *bound*

$$\Pr[X \leq (1-\epsilon)E[X]] \leq \left(\frac{e^{-\epsilon}}{(1-\epsilon)^{(1-\epsilon)}}\right)^{E[X]} \leq \exp\left(-\frac{\epsilon^2}{2}E[X]\right)$$

The following formula is well known.

LEMMA 36. *Let $X_1, \ldots, X_\ell$ be independent Bernoulli random variables, with $\Pr[X_i = 1] = \alpha$. Let $X = X_1 + \cdots + X_\ell$. Then $\Pr[X \equiv 1 \pmod 2] = \frac{1-(1-2\alpha)^\ell}{2}$.*

PROOF.

$$\begin{aligned}\Pr[X \equiv 1 \pmod 2] &= \mathrm{E}\left[(1-(-1)^X)/2\right] \\ &= \tfrac{1}{2} - \tfrac{1}{2}\mathrm{E}\left[\textstyle\prod_{i=1}^{\ell}(-1)^{X_i}\right] \\ &= \tfrac{1}{2} - \tfrac{1}{2}\textstyle\prod_{i=1}^{\ell}\mathrm{E}\left[(-1)^{X_i}\right] \\ &= \tfrac{1}{2} - \tfrac{1}{2}\textstyle\prod_{i=1}^{\ell}(1-2\alpha) \\ &= \tfrac{1-(1-2\alpha)^\ell}{2}\end{aligned}$$

□

PROPOSITION 37. *Let $n \geq 1$ be an integer and S be an arbitrary subset of $\{1, \ldots, n\}$ of size at most $n/2$. Let further $\ell \geq 1$ be an integer. Denote $\alpha = |S|/n$. Let $X \in \{1, \ldots, n\}^\ell$ be chosen uniformly at random.*

$$\frac{\min(1, \alpha\ell)}{4} < \Pr_X[|\{i;\ X_i \in S\}| \text{ is odd}] \leq \frac{1}{2} .$$

PROOF. By the lemma we have

$$\Pr_X[|\{i;\ X_i \in S\}| \text{ is odd}] = \frac{1-(1-2\alpha)^\ell}{2}$$

We can bound

$$0 \leq (1-2\alpha)^\ell < e^{-2\alpha\ell} ,$$

where we use the estimate $1 - x < e^{-x}$ valid for all $x \neq 0$. If $\alpha\ell \leq 1$ then

$$(1-2\alpha)^\ell < e^{-2\alpha\ell} < e^{-\alpha\ell} < 1 - \alpha\ell/2 .$$

using the estimate $e^{-x} < 1 - x/2$ valid for $0 < x \leq 1.59$. If $\alpha\ell > 1$ then

$$(1-2\alpha)^\ell < e^{-2\alpha\ell} < 1/4.$$

□

LEMMA 9. *Let $X_1, \ldots, X_k$ be 0-1 random variables and $C, \alpha > 0$ be reals. Suppose that for every $i \in \{1, \ldots, k\}$, there are at most C indices $j \in \{1, \ldots, k\}$ such that X_i and X_j are not independent. Let $\mu = \mathrm{E}\left(\sum_{i=1}^k X_i\right)$. Then*

$$\Pr\left[\left|\sum_{i=1}^{k} X_i - \mu\right| \geq \alpha\mu\right] \leq \frac{C}{\alpha^2\mu}.$$

PROOF. We need to estimate the variance.

$$\mathrm{Var}\left[\sum_i X_i\right] = \mathrm{E}\left[\left(\sum_i X_i\right)^2\right] - \mu^2$$
$$= \sum_{i,j} \mathrm{E}\left[X_i X_j\right] - \mu^2$$

Since any X_i and X_j are 0-1 random variables, $\mathrm{E}\left[X_i X_j\right] \leq \mathrm{E}\left[X_i\right]$. Furthermore, if X_i and X_j are independent then $\mathrm{E}\left[X_i X_j\right] = \mathrm{E}\left[X_i\right] \cdot \mathrm{E}\left[X_j\right]$. Since X_j's are non-negative, we get

$$\sum_{i,j} \mathrm{E}\left[X_i X_j\right] \leq \sum_i \mathrm{E}\left[X_i\right] \left(C + \sum_{j,\, j \text{ indep. of } i} \mathrm{E}\left[X_j\right]\right)$$
$$\leq \mu(C + \mu)$$

Thus, $\mathrm{Var}\left[\sum_i X_i\right] \leq C\mu$. The lemma now follows from Chebyshev's Inequality.

□

8.2 Proof of Lemma 6

We will use induction on the number of vertices in V, where $V \subseteq W \setminus Y$ is the set of bad vertices for Y.. The statement is trivial if $|V| = 1$. First we prove the statement for $|V| = 2$. We will see later, that this is sufficient to prove the induction step.

Let ℓ be the largest number of vertex disjoint paths from X to Y. Let v_1 and v_2 be bad vertices for Y, that is the largest number of vertex disjoint paths from X to $Y \cup \{v_1\}$ and from X to $Y \cup \{v_2\}$ is also ℓ.

Suppose for a contradiction, that there are $\ell + 1$ vertex disjoint paths from X to $Y \cup \{v_1, v_2\}$. Fix a collection of $\ell + 1$ vertex disjoint paths from X to $Y \cup \{v_1, v_2\}$. Note that both v_1 and v_2 must participate in this collection. Let us denote the paths in the collection by $Q_1, \ldots, Q_{\ell-1}, R_1, R_2$, where v_1 is the endpoint of R_1 and v_2 is the endpoint of R_2. Fix also a collection of ℓ vertex disjoint paths from X to Y, call them $P_1, \ldots, P_\ell$.

We refer to the paths P_i as "solid" paths, and the paths Q_i as "dotted" paths. The paths R_1 and R_2 are "curly". Note that while the solid paths form a vertex disjoint collection, they can intersect the dotted and curly paths in various ways. Some solid paths may even be identical to some dotted paths. It is also possible that the dotted collection of paths is a subcollection of the solid collection, but this does not have to be the case.

Next we note that since the largest number of vertex disjoint paths from X to $Y \cup \{v_1\}$ is ℓ, by Menger's theorem (Theorem 7), there exists a cut of size ℓ. That is, there are ℓ vertices, such that every path from X to $Y \cup \{v_1\}$ contains one of them. We will refer to this cut as the *blue cut*, and call the vertices in it *blue vertices*. Similarly, there are ℓ vertices, such that every path from X to $Y \cup \{v_2\}$ contains one of them. We will refer to this cut as the *red cut*, and call the vertices in it *red vertices*. Note that the blue cut and the red cut may intersect. We call the vertices that participate in both cuts *purple vertices*.

Next note that the solid paths $P_1, \ldots, P_\ell$ must be blocked by both cuts. Since the ℓ solid paths are vertex disjoint, this means that each solid path either contains one blue and one red vertex, or it contains one purple vertex. The collection $Q_1, \ldots, Q_{\ell-1}, R_1$ is blocked by the blue cut, thus each dotted path and the path R_1 contains exactly one vertex of the blue cut. Similarly, the collection $Q_1, \ldots, Q_{\ell-1}, R_2$ is blocked by the red cut, thus each dotted path and the path R_2 contains exactly one vertex of the red cut. Since $Q_1, \ldots, Q_{\ell-1}, R_1, R_2$ are vertex disjoint, the vertex of the blue cut on R_1 cannot participate in the red cut, so it cannot be purple. We call the vertex of the blue cut on R_1 the *blue star*. Similarly, the vertex of the red cut on R_2 cannot participate in the blue cut, so it cannot be purple. We call the vertex of the red cut on R_2 the *red star*. We also get that just like the solid paths, each dotted path either contains one blue and one red vertex, or it contains one purple vertex.

Since both the blue cut and the red cut consists of ℓ vertices, the above implies that the blue star must be at the intersection of R_1 with some solid path, and the red star must be at the intersection of R_2 with some solid path. All other vertices in the cuts (blue, red and purple) must be at the intersection of a solid path with a dotted path.

Recall that each solid path contains either a blue and a red vertex, or one purple vertex. Since the blue star cannot be purple, the solid path containing the blue star must also contain a red vertex. Similarly, the solid path containing the red star must also contain a blue vertex.

One of the consequences of the following two claims is that the blue star and the red star cannot be on the same solid path.

CLAIM 38. *Let P' from $x' \in X$ to $y' \in Y$ be the solid path that contains the blue star. Then the red vertex on P' must appear later in the path (that is closer to the output) than the blue star.*

PROOF. Suppose that the red vertex on P' appears before the blue star. Suppose that the path R_1 starts at the vertex x_1, that is R_1 is a path from x_1 to v_1. Consider the path P^* that consists of the first part of R_1 from x_1 to the blue star, and the second part of P' from the blue star to y_1. Then, we can show that the path P^* does not contain any vertex of the red cut. This is however a contradiction, since P^* is a path from X to Y and the red cut blocks every path from X to $Y \cup \{v_2\}$. Recall that the red star is on the path R_2, and all other vertices of the red cut are at the intersection of some solid path with a dotted path. However, R_1 is vertex disjoint from R_2 as well as from all dotted paths. Thus, the part of P^* from R_1 cannot contain any vertex of the red cut. On the other hand, the second part of P^* is part of the solid path P'. But P' contains only one vertex of the red cut, which appears before the blue star on the path P'. Thus, the common part of P' and P^* cannot contain any vertex from the red cut. Hence, P^* is not blocked by the red cut, which is a contradiction. □

We get the following analogous claim for the red star, by the same argument.

CLAIM 39. *Let P'' from $x'' \in X$ to $y'' \in Y$ be the solid path that contains the red star. Then the blue vertex on P'' must appear later in the path (that is closer to the output) than the red star.*

To continue the proof of the lemma, consider the following walk starting from the blue star. Recall that since the blue star cannot be purple, the solid path P' containing the blue star must also contain a red vertex, say r_1. We start the walk by following the segment of P' from the blue star to the red vertex r_1. By Claim 38, the red vertex r_1 appears after the blue star on the path P'. Thus, by Claim 39, the red vertex on P' cannot be the red star. Thus, r_1 is at the intersection of P' with some dotted path, say Q_1.

Note that while some solid paths may be identical to a dotted path, this is never the case for the solid paths containing the blue star and the red star, since R_1 and R_2 are vertex disjoint from all dotted paths. Thus, Q_1 is not identical to P'. Moreover, since Q_1 intersects P', and the solid paths are vertex disjoint, Q_1 cannot be identical to any solid path. By similar reasoning, the walk below never reaches a solid path that is identical to a dotted path.

Since r_1 is red (not purple), Q_1 must also contain a blue vertex, say b_1. We continue the walk by following the segment of Q_1 from r_1 to b_1. Note that b_1 may appear either before or after r_1 on the path Q_1, so we may be walking in the opposite direction (e.g. towards the inputs), in case b_1 appears before r_1 on the path Q_1. Note that since each dotted path is vertex disjoint from R_1, b_1 cannot be the blue star. On the other hand, b_1 is also at the intersection of Q_1 with some solid path P_1, that must be a different path than P' (since b_1 is not the blue star). P_1 must also contain a red vertex, say r_2 and we continue the walk by following the segment of P_1 from b_1 to r_2. Note that $r_2 \neq r_1$ since P' and P_1 are vertex disjoint. Unless we reached the red star, the red vertex r_2 is at the intersection of P_1 with a dotted path Q_2. Since $r_2 \neq r_1$, and each dotted path contains only one vertex from the red cut, we get that Q_2 is a different path than Q_1. Note that we can never run into a purple vertex, since we arrive to each new path at either a blue or a red vertex, and the paths that contain a blue or a red vertex never contain a purple vertex. Note also that along the walk, we always get to the next red vertex following a solid path. This guarantees that we do not revisit a previously visited red vertex, since the collection of solid paths is vertex disjoint. Similarly, we always get to the next blue vertex by following a dotted path. This guarantees that we do not revisit a previously visited blue vertex, since the collection of dotted paths is vertex disjoint. We never get back to the blue star, since the collection of dotted paths is vertex disjoint from R_1. Thus, we get a walk starting from the blue star, and passing through the vertices $r_1, b_1, r_2, b_2, \ldots$ until we reach the red star.

CLAIM 40. *In the walk constructed this way, we traverse each solid segment in the direction towards the outputs, and each dotted segment in the direction towards the inputs.*

PROOF. Recall that by Claim 38, the red vertex r_1 appears after the blue star on the path P'. Thus, we start the walk by following the segment of P' from the blue star to r_1 in the direction towards the outputs.

Suppose that the claim does not hold. This means that there must be two consecutive segments during the walk, where we do not switch direction: if we switched direction between each segment of the walk, we would have to traverse each solid segment of the walk in the direction towards the outputs, and each dotted segment in the direction towards the inputs.

We will show that having two consecutive segments of the walk where we do not switch direction gives a contradiction. Suppose without loss of generality, that the segments from b_{i-1} to r_i and from r_i to b_i are both going towards the outputs. That is on the solid path P_{i-1}, r_i appears after b_{i-1}, and on the dotted path Q_i, b_i appears after r_i. (Note that possibly P_{i-1} could be P', in which case b_{i-1} would be the blue star.)

Consider the path P^* that consists of the first part of Q_i from some input vertex to r_i, and the second part of P_{i-1} from r_i to some output vertex. Then, we can show that the path P^* does not contain any vertex of the blue cut. This is however a contradiction, since P^* is a path from X to Y and the blue cut blocks every path from X to $Y \cup \{v_1\}$. Recall that each dotted path contains exactly one vertex of the blue cut. The blue vertex b_i appears on the dotted path Q_i after the vertex r_i, thus the first part of P^* that consists of the first part of Q_i from some input to r_i does not contain any vertex of the blue cut. Similarly, each solid path contains exactly one vertex of the blue cut. The blue vertex b_{i-1} appears on the solid path P_{i-1} before the vertex r_i, thus the second part of P^* that consists of the second part of P_{i-1} from r_i to some output does not contain any vertex of the blue cut. Hence, P^* is not blocked by the blue cut, which is a contradiction. □

Let b_k be the last blue vertex visited during the walk, before we reach the red star. Recall that by Claim 39 the blue vertex b_k must appear after the red star on the path P''. Thus, we finish the walk by following the segment of P'' between the red star and the vertex b_k in the reverse direction, from b_k to the red star, that is in the direction towards the inputs. This however contradicts Claim 40. This concludes the proof of the statement of the Lemma when $|V| = 2$.

Next we show that this also implies the statement for any number of bad vertices. We use induction on the size of V. We have already seen that the statement holds when $|V| = 1$ and when $|V| = 2$. Suppose the statement of the lemma holds for $|V| = j$, we show that this implies the statement for $|V| = j + 1$.

Let $Y \subseteq W$ be a set of outputs. Let $V = \{v_1, \ldots, v_j, v_{j+1}\}$ be a set of bad vertices for Y. Let ℓ be the largest number of vertex disjoint paths from X to Y. Let $Y' = Y \cup \{v_1, \ldots, v_{j-1}\}$. Since the statement of the lemma holds for $|V| \leq j$, we have that the largest number of vertex disjoint paths from X to Y' is ℓ, and that v_j and v_{j+1} must be bad for Y'. Applying the statement with two bad vertices for Y' implies that the largest number of vertex disjoint paths from X to $Y' \cup \{v_j, v_{j+1}\} = Y \cup V$ is also ℓ. This concludes the proof of the lemma.

Tight Bounds for Monotone Switching Networks via Fourier Analysis

[Extended Abstract]

Siu Man Chan[*]
UC Berkeley
siuman@cs.berkeley.edu

Aaron Potechin[†]
MIT
aaron@potechin.org

ABSTRACT

We prove tight size bounds on monotone switching networks for the k-clique problem, and for an explicit monotone problem by analyzing the generation problem with a pyramid structure of height h. This gives alternative proofs of the separations of m-NC from m-P and of m-NC^i from m-NC^{i+1}, different from Raz–McKenzie (Combinatorica '99). The enumerative-combinatorial and Fourier analytic techniques in this work are very different from a large body of work on circuit depth lower bounds, and may be of independent interest.

Categories and Subject Descriptors

F.1.3 [**Computation by Abstract Devices**]: Complexity Measures and Classes—*complexity hierarchies, relations among complexity measures*

General Terms

Theory

Keywords

Lower bounds, space complexity, parallel complexity, monotone complexity, switching networks

1. INTRODUCTION

To study parallel time and memory usage complexity, lower bounds are sought in different models of computation. For example, parallel time is captured by the depth of boolean circuits of bounded fan-in, and memory usage (i.e. space complexity) is captured by the size of switching networks. It is therefore of interest to prove lower bounds for the depth of boolean circuits of bounded fan-in, and for the size of switching networks, for an explicit boolean function. Unfortunately, tight lower bounds which give interesting separations in complexity classes have not been proven without certain restrictions on computation.

To prove some lower bounds, researchers often restrict computation to be *monotone* (i.e. to disallow logical negations in computation) when computing monotone boolean functions. Improving on Razborov [48], the works of Alon and Boppana [4] and of Haken [25] implied that the clique problem requires polynomial ($n^{\Omega(1)}$) depth for monotone circuits.[1] In terms of complexity classes, it says m-NC $\subseteq$ m-P $\subset$ m-NP. This means the clique problem requires high parallel time when computed in a monotone fashion. As for the parallel time of efficiently computable functions, Karchmer and Wigderson [34] showed that the directed connectivity problem requires super-logarithmic ($\Omega(\log^2 n)$) depth for monotone circuits,[1] implying m-NC^1 $\subset$ m-NL $\subseteq$ m-NC^2. For more separations, Raz and McKenzie [44] extended the lower bound framework of Karchmer and Wigderson [34], proving that a monotone circuit[1] computing

(1) the complete problem for NL, directed connectivity, requires $\Omega(\log^2 n)$ depth, reproving the tight bound of Karchmer and Wigderson [34];

(2) the 'complete problem for NC^i', the Generation problem with a pyramid structure of height h, requires $\Omega(h \log n)$ depth when $h \leq n^{O(1)}$, giving m-NC $\subset$ m-P and m-NC^i $\subset$ m-NC^{i+1} for all i by setting $h = \log^i n$; and

(3) the complete problem for NP, the k-clique problem, requires $\Omega(k \log n)$ depth when $k \leq n^{O(1)}$, improving previous results on cliques for $\log n \ll k \ll n^{O(1)}$.

Much less work is done on switching networks. Most results are derived using the connection between circuits and switching networks. Namely, a circuit[1] of depth d can be simulated by a switching network of size 2^d, while a switching network of size s can be simulated by a circuit of depth $O(\log^2 s)$ [16]. As far as lower bounds go, a bound of $\Omega(s)$ for switching network size translates to a bound of $\Omega(\log s)$ for circuit depth, and a bound of $\Omega(d)$ for circuit depth

*This material is based upon work supported by the National Science Foundation under Grant No. CCF-1017403 and Grant No. CCF-0830797.
†This material is based on work supported by the National Science Foundation Graduate Research Fellowship under Grant No. 0645960.

STOC'12, May 19–22, 2012, New York, New York, USA.

[1]In this paper, we consider only *boolean* circuits of *bounded fan-in*, even when we do not spell it out.

translates to a bound of $2^{\Omega(\sqrt{d})}$ for switching network size. The simulations preserve monotonicity, therefore, so do the translations of lower bounds.

In particular, from the best lower bounds for the depth of monotone circuits by Raz and McKenzie [44], it follows that a monotone switching network computing

(1') directed connectivity requires $n^{\Omega(1)}$ size;

(2') the Generation problem with a pyramid structure of height h requires $n^{\Omega\left(\sqrt{h/\log n}\right)}$ size when $h \leq n^{O(1)}$; and

(3') the k-clique problem requires $n^{\Omega\left(\sqrt{k/\log n}\right)}$ size when $k \leq n^{O(1)}$.

Since a size bound of $s^{\Omega(1)}$ for switching networks is equivalent to a space bound of $\Omega(\log s)$ for Turing machines,[2] item (1') above is trivial and fails to separate m-L from m-NL for space complexity. Also, items (2') and (3') are not effective when, for example, h and k are $O(\log n)$. To match our intuition, we expect that monotone switching networks computing

(1") directed connectivity requires $n^{\Omega(\log n)}$ size,

(2") the Generation problem with a pyramid structure of height h requires $n^{\Omega(h)}$ size for $h \leq n^{O(1)}$; and

(3") k-clique requires $n^{\Omega(k)}$ for $k \leq n^{O(1)}$.

Note that the bound for monotone switching networks implies the corresponding bound for monotone circuits (e.g. (1") implies (1)) by the simulation argument.

Recently, Potechin [43] strengthened item (1) to item (1"), i.e. showed that any monotone switching network solving directed connectivity has quasi-polynomial size, thereby giving m-L $\subset$ m-NL. To avoid the loss in translation, it is necessary to depart from the circuit-depth lower bound framework of communication game by Karchmer and Wigderson [34],[3] which is the basis of most previous work for depth complexity of circuits [15, 19, 21, 24, 28, 33, 34, 44, 45]. Instead, Potechin [43] introduced a Fourier analytic framework for analyzing extremal instances (minterms and maxterms) of the monotone boolean function of directed connectivity.

This work extends the Fourier analytic framework to prove tight lower bounds, for (i) an explicit monotone problem by analyzing the Generation problem with a pyramid structure of height h, and for (ii) the k-clique problem, strengthening item (2) to item (2"), and item (3) to item (3").[4] For comparison, the previous bounds were (2') and (3'). As a result, presented are alternative proofs of the separations of monotone complexity classes like m-NC $\subset$ m-P and m-NC$^i \subset$ m-NC^{i+1}, using very different arguments from Raz–McKenzie [44]. These monotone separations are necessary for the corresponding non-monotone separations, because a non-monotone separation (e.g. NC $\subset$ P) implies the corresponding monotone separation (e.g. m-NC $\subset$ m-P).[5] For the lower bound for generation (item (2")), although in terms of techniques this work mainly reuses the existing Fourier analytic framework [43],[6] in terms of presentation this work highlights in a modular way the enumerative-combinatorial ideas and the 'universal networks' core to (but implicit in) the framework, which may be of independent interest.[7] However, the clique problem does not seem to fit into the existing framework. For the lower bound for cliques (item (3")), this work extends the Fourier analytic machinery, which turns out to be simpler for cliques both conceptually and technically, giving a shorter proof than Raz–McKenzie [44]. Perhaps, more previous results may be strengthened and other problems may be studied by extending this Fourier/combinatorial framework, as an alternative or complement to the Karchmer–Wigderson framework, after three separation results (1), (2) and (3) on monotone circuit-depth are strengthened to (1"), (2") and (3").

We did not discuss other work less relevant to the results presented here, but suggesting lower bounds to space and parallel complexity [2, 3, 8–10, 18, 20, 38, 39, 41, 46, 50, 57, 58], or implying lower bounds to monotone depth [5, 6, 11, 14, 22, 26, 31, 32, 40, 47, 49, 53–55, 60, 61] or applying monotone depth to study other complexity [12, 13, 27, 35, 37]. For more discussion on the complexity of monotone boolean circuits, the reader is referred to [44, §1], and [15, 23]. For more discussion on switching networks and other models of space bounded computation, the reader is referred to [51].

§2 collects notions, notations and conventions used in the introduction and common to §3 and §4. §3 treats the generation problem, whose lower bound (item (2")) is proved as Theorem 4. §4 treats the clique problem, whose lower bound (item (3")) is proved as Theorem 6. §3 and §4 can be read completely independently of each other. Many technical proofs are omitted in the extended abstract, see the full paper for details.

2. PRELIMINARIES

Recall the Iverson bracket notation: $[\![\textit{condition}]\!]$ to mean 1 if *condition* is TRUE, and 0 otherwise. Also, $[n] := \{1, 2, \ldots, n\}$ for $n \in \mathbb{N}$. For a boolean function $f\colon \{0,1\}^n \to \{0,1\}$, an instance $y \in \{0,1\}^n$ is a YES-instance if $f(y) = 1$, and a NO-instance if $f(y) = 0$. A boolean function is *monotone*

[2] Modulo uniformity, of course. The easy direction is folklore (e.g. see [43, §2]), and the hard direction is proved by Reingold [52].

[3] Indeed, the Karchmer–Wigderson framework is unlikely to separate m-L from m-NL, since it is able to prove the same bound of $\Omega(\log^2 n)$ for the depth of monotone circuits solving *undirected* connectivity (as a result of [34] or by slightly modifying [44]), which is in L [52] and computable by switching networks of size n^2. This shows that the quadratic relation between circuit-depth and (the logarithm of) switching-network-size in the simulation argument of Borodin [16] is tight. Also, this confirms that switching networks and their variants (e.g. those listed in [51]) are more natural models for studying space complexity than boolean circuits.

[4] There are monotone switching networks for (i) "the problem computed by the universal degree-h certain-knowledge switching network" of size $n^{O(h)}$; and (ii) the k-clique problem of size $k^{O(1)}n^{O(k)}$.

[5] And proving monotone lower bounds is in a sense sufficient, since non-monotone separations would follow from the monotone lower bounds of some variants of the problems, see e.g. [20, §4.1].

[6] The most notable difference with [43] is in pushing for a tight lower bound for an explicit problem, i.e. §3.3.3, where ideas from [43, §7] do not seem to work for the generation problem.

[7] For example, the Fourier analytic framework analyzes the distributive lattice of *filters* of structured NO-instances (e.g. see the full paper for details). Curiously, the use of filters *over* NO-instances appeared in the fusion method [32, 59], an abstract framework for proving monotone and non-monotone lower bounds.

if $f(x) \le f(y)$ whenever $x \preceq y$, i.e. whenever $x_i \le y_i$ for all $i \in [n]$. For a monotone boolean function f, a *minterm* y is a $\preceq$-minimal YES-instance, i.e. $f(y) = 1$ but $f(x) = 0$ for all $x \prec y$; a *maxterm* y is a $\preceq$-maximal NO-instance, i.e. $f(y) = 0$ but $f(x) = 1$ for all $x \succ y$. Often we write $V \setminus u$ to mean $V \setminus \{u\}$, not distinguishing an element u and its singleton-set $\{u\}$.

Definition 1. (Switching Networks) Consider a collection of boolean variables $x_1, x_2, \ldots, x_n \in \{0,1\}$. A *switching network* G' has data $(V', E', s', t', \lambda')$, where V' is nodes and E' is edges of an undirected (multi) graph with two distinguished nodes $s', t' \in V'$. Each edge $e' \in E'$ of G' is labeled with a literal x_i or $\bar{x}_i$ with $i \in [n]$, specified by $\lambda'(e')$. A switching network is *monotone* if all edges are labeled with positive literals (for all e', $\lambda'(e') = x_i$ for some i).

An instance $y \in \{0,1\}^n$ is *accepted* by G', if there is a path P' connecting s' and t' using edges labeled with literals in y; namely, $P' =: \langle e'_1, e'_2, \ldots, e'_\ell \rangle$, where $e'_j \in E'$ for $1 \le j \le \ell$ connects v'_{j-1} and v'_j, with $v'_0 = s'$ and $v'_\ell = t'$, satisfying (1) if $\lambda'(e'_j) = x_i$ then $y_i = 1$; or (2) $\lambda'(e'_j) = \bar{x}_i$ then $y_i = 0$. Otherwise, y is *rejected* by G'. The boolean function $f_{G'}$ *computed* by G' is identified with the collection of accepted instances, so $f_{G'}(y) = 1$ iff G' accepts y.

In general, say an instance $y \in \{0,1\}^n$ *reaches* a node $a' \in V'$ if there is a path P' connecting s' and a' using edges labeled with literals in y. The *size* of a switching network is the number of edges [51].[8]

Following Potechin [43], denote objects of instances (e.g. variable x_i, element u for GEN, vertex v for CLIQUE) using unprimed letters, and denote objects of switching networks (e.g. node $a' \in V'$, edge $e' \in E'$) with primed letters.

We need the following version of Nisan–Wigderson combinatorial design [42]. For a proof and further references, see [56, Appendix].

LEMMA 1. (COMBINATORIAL DESIGN) *For any positive integers q, m, k with $k \le m$, there exists q sets $Q_1, Q_2, \ldots, Q_q \subseteq [N]$ where $N := e^{\frac{\ln q}{k}+1} \cdot \frac{m^2}{k}$, such that $|Q_i| = m$ for $1 \le i \le q$ and $|Q_i \cap Q_j| \le k$ for $1 \le i < j \le q$.*

3. LOWER BOUND FOR GENERATION

This section proves the lower bound for (the promise problem of) generation as Theorem 4, and use it in a tight bound for a monotone problem as Theorem 5. After defining the problem and the model below (Definitions 2, 3), §3.1 introduces a semantic restriction, called certain-knowledge, and §3.2 proves an optimal lower bound for monotone switching networks with this restriction. §3.3 proves a lower bound without this restriction, by reducing the general case to the certain-knowledge case.

To compare with [43], most of the technical materials in §3 (not specific to the generation problem) before §3.3.3 can be found there with minor modifications. The differences lie in the presentation, and in the definition of knowledge sets in the semantic restriction. It turns out that the simpler Definition 4, where a knowledge is restricted to start from the source s, suffices to prove a tight lower bound in §3.3.3 for an explicit problem by analyzing the generation problem. Backporting this idea to the directed connectivity problem, §3.3.3 can serve as a slightly alternative proof for the main results in [43, §7], using simpler knowledge sets.

[8]All lower bounds in this work concern the number of *nodes*, which is polynomially-related to the number of edges. Also, constants are not optimized.

Definition 2. (Generation Problem) For a size parameter n, the *generation problem* (GEN) has input data $e\colon [n] \times [n] \times [n] \to \{0,1\}$ as n^3 boolean variables. Two elements of $[n]$ are distinguished: the source s (say 1) and the target t (say n). Say s *generates* $v \in [n]$ if (1) v is s; or (2) s generates both w and u, and $e(w, u, v) = 1$ (this positive literal is also denoted $w \wedge u \to v$ to suggest its meaning). GEN problem seeks to decide if s generates t.

GEN problem is a monotone variant of the first P-complete problem called PATH SYSTEMS [17]. Subproblems of GEN with additional restrictions on e are complete for smaller complexity classes like non-deterministic logspace (NL) and Nick's class (NC) [7, 30]. To specialize monotone switching networks (Definition 1) to GEN, we just need to specialize the labeling function λ'.

Definition 3. (Monotone Switching Networks for GEN) In a monotone switching network for GEN (mGEN network), each edge $e' \in E'$ is labeled with $\lambda'(e') = w \wedge u \to v$ for some $w, u, v \in [n]$. Given an instance for GEN with data e, the literal $\lambda'(e') = w \wedge u \to v$ is in the instance if $e(w, u, v) = 1$.

3.1 Certain-Knowledge for Generation

The following adapts notions of [43] from directed connectivity to GEN. An optimal size lower bound (Theorem 1) can be proved for a class of mGEN networks which are semantically restricted (Definition 5), where every node a' has a 'knowledge set' $K_{a'}$ specifying the elements that *must* be generated by all instances reaching a',[9] i.e. there is no ambiguity in what elements that *must* be generated by instances reaching every node.

Definition 4. (Knowledge Sets for GEN) For GEN, a *knowledge* is formally an element $v \in [n]$, suggesting the meaning that v *must* be generated from s, hence denoted $s \rightsquigarrow v$.[10] A *knowledge set* K is a collection of knowledge (formally a subset of $[n]$) satisfying (1) $s \rightsquigarrow s \in K$, and (2) if $s \rightsquigarrow t \in K$, then $K = [n]$.[11] For a knowledge set K and a triple $w \wedge u \to v$, define $K + w \wedge u \to v$ to be (1) the smallest knowledge set containing K and $s \rightsquigarrow v$ if both $s \rightsquigarrow w$ and $s \rightsquigarrow u$ are in K, or (2) K otherwise.

Definition 5. (Certain-Knowledge) Say an mGEN network G' is *certain-knowledge* if each node $a' \in V'$ can be associated with a knowledge set $K_{a'}$ satisfying the following conditions:

[9]Thus our knowledge set is similar to the *available sets* for branching programs in [20].

[10]Definition 4 should be read together with Definition 5 to make more sense. Also, the notation $s \rightsquigarrow v$ and the terminology of a knowledge set are inspired by their counterparts in directed connectivity [43].

[11]For technical reasons, as long as t must be generated, ignore whether other elements must be generated. This is because the lower bound framework focuses on whether certain NO-instances must not reach a node a', and uses $K_{a'}$ for that information. Once t must be generated in $K_{a'}$, all NO-instances must not reach a', regardless of whether other elements must be generated.

1. $K_{s'} = \{s \rightsquigarrow s\}$ and $K_{t'} \ni s \rightsquigarrow t$; and

2. If there is an edge with label $w \wedge u \to v$ between nodes a' and b', then $K_{b'} \subseteq K_{a'} + w \wedge u \to v$ and $K_{a'} \subseteq K_{b'} + w \wedge u \to v$.

3.2 Pyramid YES-Instances and Certain-Knowledge Lower Bound

Following Raz and McKenzie [44], consider those YES-instances of GEN having a structure of a pyramid graph.[12] Pyramid YES-instances to GEN are analogous to path YES-instances to directed connectivity in [43]. In particular, they are minterms of respective monotone boolean functions, hence 'hardest to accept'.

Definition 6. (Pyramid Graph and YES-Instance) For a parameter h, the *pyramid graph* of height h has $\binom{h+1}{2}$ vertices $V_h := \{v_{r,c}\}_{1\le c\le r\le h}$. The vertex $v_{r,c}$ is on the rth row, and V_h is laid out row by row with the first row on top and the hth row at the bottom. For $1 \le r \le h-1$, the vertex $v_{r,c}$ has left child $v_{r+1,c}$ and right child $v_{r+1,c+1}$. The pyramid graph is also viewed as a directed graph with arcs pointing from children to their parents (from $v_{r+1,c}$ to $v_{r,c}$ and from $v_{r+1,c+1}$ to $v_{r,c}$).[12]

An instance of GEN forms a *pyramid* YES-*instance* if there exists $Q \subseteq [n] \setminus \{s,t\}$ and a bijective identification $P\colon Q \to V_h$ to vertices V_h of a pyramid graph, and $e(w,u,v) = 1$ iff (w,u,v) is a triple in $[n]\times[n]\times[n]$ *consistent* with P, meaning that (1) $w = u = s$ and $v \in Q$ and $P(v)$ is on the bottom row of V_h; or (2) $w = u \in Q$ and $P(w)$ is on the top row of V_h, and $v = t$, or (3) $w,u,v \in Q$ and $P(w)$ and $P(u)$ are different children of $P(v)$. In this case, the YES-instance is simply called a *pyramid*, and is identified with P.

Note that the identification P specifies a structure of a pyramid graph over $V(P) := Q = P^{-1}(V_h) \subseteq [n] \setminus \{s,t\}$. Since a certain-knowledge switching network must 'learn vertices one at a time', on any computation path P' accepting a pyramid P, there must be a node $b' \in V(P')$ remembering lots of vertices of P exclusively, i.e. $K_{b'} \setminus s \subseteq V(P)$ and $|K_{b'} \setminus s| = h$ (Lemma 2).[13] Such b' is a *barrier node* for P. Note that if two pyramids share less than h vertices, then they must have different barrier nodes. With this idea, we are ready to prove size lower bounds for certain-knowledge mGEN networks (Theorems 1 and 2).

THEOREM 1. (CERTAIN-KNOWLEDGE LOWER BOUND FOR GEN) *Any certain-knowledge mGEN network G' having n' nodes and computing GEN of size n satisfies $n' \ge n^{\Theta(n^{1/10})}$.*

PROOF. Note that G' accepts all pyramid YES-instances, and it follows from Theorem 2. □

THEOREM 2. (CERTAIN-KNOWLEDGE LOWER BOUND FOR PYRAMIDS) *For any $4 \le h \le n^{1/10}$, any certain-knowledge mGEN network G' having n' nodes for GEN of size n, and accepting all pyramid YES-instances of height h, satisfies $n' \ge n^{h/10} = n^{\Theta(h)}$.*

[12]The pyramid graph is routinely used for studying space complexity, especially using pebbling games [17, 36]. We follow their convention that arcs point from the $(r+1)^{\text{st}}$ row to the rth row.

[13]To prove Theorems 1 and 2, it suffices for b' to have $|K_{b'} \setminus s| \ge h$, instead of an exact equality.

PROOF. Fix h, let $m := \binom{h+1}{2}$, $q := n^{h/10}$, $k := h-1$. Then Lemma 1 gives q sets $Q_1, Q_2, \ldots, Q_q \subseteq [N]$ with $|Q_i| = m$ and $|Q_i \cap Q_j| \le k$ for $1 \le i \ne j \le q$, where $N \le \exp(\frac{h \ln n}{10(h-1)} + 1)h^4 \le n^{1/3}h^4 \ll n$. For each Q_i, construct a pyramid YES-instance P_i by identifying Q_i arbitrarily with a pyramid graph of height h. Now P_i is accepted by G', via some path P_i' labeled with positive literals in P_i. Hence Lemma 2 gives a node b_i' whose knowledge set satisfies $K_{b_i'} \setminus s \subseteq Q_i$ and $|K_{b_i'} \setminus s| = h$. Since $|Q_i \cap Q_j| \le h-1$, we have $b_i' \ne b_j'$ for $1 \le i \ne j \le q$. Hence $n' \ge q = n^{h/10}$. □

LEMMA 2. (BARRIER SIZE LOWER BOUND) *Fix a pyramid P of height h. Consider a certain-knowledge walk $P' =: \langle e_1', e_2', \ldots, e_\ell' \rangle$, where e_j' connects v_{j-1}' and v_j' and is labeled a positive literal $\lambda'(e_j') \in P$, from $s' := v_0'$ to $t' := v_\ell'$. (Hence $K_{v_{j-1}'}$ can go to $K_{v_j'}$ with input triple $\lambda'(e_j')$ for $1 \le j \le \ell$.)*

If $K_{s'} = \{s \rightsquigarrow s\}$ and $K_{t'} \ni s \rightsquigarrow t$, then P' has a node $b' \in V(P')$ with $K_{b'} \setminus s \subseteq Q$ and $|K_{b'} \setminus s| = h$.

PROOF. The proof is modeled after the black pebbling lower bound of a pyramid graph [17]. □

3.3 Lower Bound beyond Certain-Knowledge

For the general lower bound for mGEN networks, we reuse the Fourier analysis framework of [43] (summarized below as Lemma 5). Fourier analysis will be done over structured NO-instances (Definition 7) which can be identified with the Fourier basis (Definition 9). It turns out that any mGEN network computing GEN must satisfy some non-trivial linear algebraic relations. The linear algebraic relations are that, for any pyramid P, any 'line integral' for P must evaluate to a constant when viewed at a certain 'Fourier angle', namely, there will be a $\mathcal{C}$-vector g specifying a Fourier spectrum exclusive to P, such that $\langle \int_{P'} dR, g \rangle$ is a constant independent of P' (Definition 14).

3.3.1 Fourier Analysis of Structured NO-Instances

Define $\tilde{V} := [n] \setminus \{s,t\}$ and $\mathcal{C} := \mathsf{PowerSet}(\tilde{V}) := \{C : C \subseteq \tilde{V}\}$. Any $C \in \mathcal{C}$ can be identified with a subset of $[n]$ containing s but excluding t by $C \mapsto C \cup s$. Through this identification, $\mathcal{C}$ is the sub-collection of the knowledge sets $\mathcal{K}$ not containing $s \rightsquigarrow t$.

Following Raz and McKenzie [44], consider structured NO-instances for GEN that can be identified with a $C \in \mathcal{C}$. Structured NO-instances to GEN are analogous to cut NO-instances to directed connectivity in [43]. In particular, they are maxterms of respective monotone boolean functions, hence 'hardest to reject'.

Definition 7. (Crossing and Structured NO-Instances) Say a triple $w \wedge u \to v$ *crosses* $C \in \mathcal{C}$ if $w \in C$ and $u \in C$ and $v \notin C$. Any $C \in \mathcal{C}$ is associated with the structured NO-instance where $e(w,u,v) = 1$ iff $w \wedge u \to v$ does not cross C. Then the NO-instance generates $v \in [n]$ iff $v \in C$.

A knowledge set K is *proper* if $K \not\ni s \rightsquigarrow t$. Hence $\mathcal{C}$ can be viewed as the collection of proper knowledge sets, or the collection of structured NO-instances.

Definition 8. (Inner Product Space of Structured NO-Instances) A $\mathcal{C}$-vector is a real vector indexed by $\mathcal{C}$, equivalently a function from $\mathcal{C}$ to $\mathbb{R}$. For two $\mathcal{C}$-vectors f and g, define an inner product $\langle f, g\rangle := \frac{1}{|\mathcal{C}|}\sum_{C\in\mathcal{C}} f(C)g(C)$, inducing a norm $\|f\| := \langle f, f\rangle^{1/2}$.

Definition 9. (Fourier Analysis) Given a structured No-instance $U \in \mathcal{C}$, define the $\mathcal{C}$-vector

$$\chi_U(C) := (-1)^{\sum_{v \in \tilde{V}} [\![v \in U]\!][\![v \in C]\!]} \ .$$

Then the collection $\{\chi_U\}_{U \in \mathcal{C}}$ forms an orthonormal basis for all $\mathcal{C}$-vectors, called the Fourier Basis. For a $\mathcal{C}$-vector g, its Fourier coefficient at $U \in \mathcal{C}$ is $\hat{g}(U) := \langle g, \chi_U \rangle$.

Definition 10. (Reachability) For $a' \in V'$, let $R_{a'}(C) :=$ TRUE if the structured No-instance C can reach a'.[14] Following Fourier analytic conventions, use $(-1)^{[\![condition]\!]} = 1 - 2[\![condition]\!]$ to arithmetize logical (boolean) conditions. The boolean vector $R_{a'}$ is identified with the $\mathcal{C}$-vector $R_{a'}(C) := (-1)^{[\![C \text{ can reach } a']\!]}$.

3.3.2 Invariants

Adapt to GEN the lower bound framework of [43, §5] as Lemma 5. Note that we distinguish between a *path* (nodes may not repeat) and a *walk* (nodes and edges may repeat) on switching networks.

Definition 11. (Standard Sign) Fix a pyramid P,[15] let

$$E_1 := \{w \wedge u \to v \colon v \text{ is on odd row}\}$$

and

$$E_0 := \{w \wedge u \to v \colon v \text{ is on even row}\} \cup \{v_{1,1} \wedge v_{1,1} \to t\} \ .$$

Note that E_0 and E_1 partition the positive literals in P. Define a function σ from positive literals in P, by (1) $\sigma(l) := -1$ if $l \in E_1$, or (2) $\sigma(l) := 1$ if $l \in E_0$.

Definition 12. (Line Integral) For a pyramid P, a *(combinatorial) sign* σ is a function from positive literals in P to $\{\pm 1\}$. A walk P' is a P-walk if $\lambda'(e') \in P$ for all $e' \in E(P')$. For such a walk P', it induces $\sigma \colon E(P') \to \mathbb{R}$ by $\sigma(e') := \sigma(\lambda'(e'))$. A walk P' is *oriented* from a' to b', if $P' = \langle e'_1, e'_2, \ldots, e'_\ell \rangle$, where e'_j is a *directed* arc from $e'_j(0) := v'_{j-1}$ to $e'_j(1) := v'_j$, with $v'_0 = a'$ and $v'_\ell = b'$. For an oriented P-walk P', define the *line integral* (with respect to P) as $\int_{P'} dR := \sum_{e' \in E(P')} \sigma(e')\big(R_{e'(1)} - R_{e'(0)}\big)$, where σ is the standard sign in Definition 11.[16]

Definition 13. (Exact g) Say a $\mathcal{C}$-vector g is *P-exact* if $\langle \int_{P'} dR, g \rangle = 0$ for any oriented P-cycle P', i.e. for any mGEN network G', for any oriented P-walk P' on G' whose first and last nodes are the same, we have $\langle \int_{P'} dR, g \rangle = 0$.

Definition 14. (Invariant g) Say a $\mathcal{C}$-vector g is *P-invariant* if $\langle \int_{P'} dR, g \rangle$ is 'path-independent': there is a constant z, so that for any sound mGEN network G', for any oriented P-walk P' from s' to t' on G', we have $\langle \int_{P'} dR, g \rangle = z$. If g is P-invariant, use z to denote $\langle \int_{P'} dR, g \rangle$ for any such P'.

[14] Hence $R_{a'}$ is the truth table at node a' restricted to the proper knowledge sets $\mathcal{C}$.

[15] Recall that P is identified with a minimal YES-instance, whose positive literals form a pyramid graph.

[16] The integral notation draws analogy from differential geometry: any $R \colon V' \to \mathbb{R}^{\mathcal{C}}$ with $R(v') := R_{v'}$ is regarded as a '0-form', and its derivative $dR \colon E' \to \mathbb{R}^{\mathcal{C}}$ with $dR(e') := R(e'(1)) - R(e'(0))$ is regarded as a '1-form'. The integral sign $\int_{P'}$ translates to $\sum_{e' \in E(P')} \sigma(e')$, automatically applying the sign σ of P to any chain P'.

LEMMA 3. (EXACT $\Rightarrow$ INVARIANT) *If g is P-exact, then g is P-invariant.*

PROPOSITION 4. (FOURIER SUPPORT) *For $C_1, C_2 \in \mathcal{C}$, say C_1* agrees with *C_2 over P if $v \in C_1$ iff $v \in C_2$ for all $v \in V(P)$. Say a $\mathcal{C}$-vector g is P*-supported *if (1) $g(C_1) = g(C_2)$ whenever C_1 agrees with C_2 over P; or equivalently (2) $\hat{g}$ is supported on subsets of $V(P)$, i.e. $\hat{g}(U) \neq 0$ implies $U \subseteq V(P)$.*

A size lower bound can be derived assuming a P-exact g supported on high Fourier frequencies, as an analogue to Potechin [43, Theorem 5.23] and Theorem 2.

LEMMA 5. (SIZE LOWER BOUND FROM INVARIANTS) *If for a pyramid P of height h, there is a P-exact g, such that (1) g is P-supported, (2) $z := \langle \int_{P'} dR, g \rangle \neq 0$, and (3) $\hat{g}(U) \neq 0$ implies $|U| \geq h$; then for any mGEN network G' with n' nodes computing GEN of size n, it satisfies $n' \geq \Theta(n^{h/10})$.*

THEOREM 3. ($n^{\omega(1)}$ LOWER BOUND FOR GEN) *Any mGEN network G' with n' nodes solving GEN of size n, satisfies $n' \geq n^{\omega(1)}$.*

PROOF. For any constant h, Lemma 5 and (1), (2), (3) of Lemma 6 gives $n' \geq \Theta(n^{h/10})$. □

Finally we construct invariants in Lemma 6, analogous to Potechin [43, §6]. Lots of technical proofs are omitted in the extended abstract, see the full paper for more details on the Fourier analytic and enumerative-combinatorial arguments.

LEMMA 6. (INVARIANT g) *For any pyramid $P \colon Q \to V_h$ of height h, there exists a P-exact $\mathcal{C}$-vector g, such that (1) g is P-supported, (2) $z := \langle \int_{P'}, g \rangle \geq 1$, (3) $\hat{g}(U) \neq 0$ implies $|U| \geq h$, (4) $g(C) \neq 0$ for any $C \subseteq Q$ implies $|C| \leq 3h$, and (5) $\langle g, g \rangle \leq 2^{|Q| + 10h \log |Q|}$.*

3.3.3 Tight Lower Bound

In the proof of Theorem 3, the hidden constant in $\Theta(n^{h/10})$ depends on h. Theorem 4 gets rid of this dependence (as long as $h \leq n^{\Theta(1)}$). To do so, exploit the relatively small support of invariants constructed in Lemma 6 (item (4)). Small support is translated to proximity to the bottom-half of P in (4) of Lemma 7, enabling rearrangement of multiple pyramids $\{P_1, P_2, \ldots, P_p\}$ over the same vertices Q_i for more invariants in Theorem 4.

Given a pyramid $P \colon Q \to V_h$ of height h, call $T \subseteq Q$ an *upper sub-pyramid* of P of height k if $P(T) \subseteq V_h$ are precisely the top k rows of V_h.

LEMMA 7. (INVARIANT $g_{S,T}$) *Consider a pyramid $P \colon Q \to V_h$ of height h, and an upper sub-pyramid T of P of height at least $h/2$, and $S := Q \backslash T$. There exists a P-exact $\mathcal{C}$-vector g, such that (1) g is P-supported, (2) $z := \langle \int_{P'}, g \rangle \geq 1$, (3) $\hat{g}(U) \neq 0$ implies $|U| \geq h/2$, (4) $g(C) \neq 0$ for $C \subseteq Q$ implies $|C \Delta S| \leq 3h$, and (5) $\langle g, g \rangle \leq 2^{|Q| + 10h \log |Q|}$.*

THEOREM 4. (SIZE LOWER BOUND FOR PYRAMIDS) *For any $4 \leq h \leq n^{1/500}$, any* sound *mGEN network G' having n' nodes and accepting all pyramid YES-instances of height h satisfies $n' \geq \frac{1}{2} n^{h/200} = n^{\Theta(h)}$.*

THEOREM 5. (TIGHT SIZE BOUND) *For any $12 \leq h \leq 3n^{\frac{1}{500}}$, any mGEN network G' having n' nodes and computing $f_{G''_{n,h}}$ satisfies $n' \geq \frac{1}{2} n^{h/600} = n^{\Theta(h)}$ (see the full paper for details).*

4. LOWER BOUND FOR CLIQUES

This section proves the lower bound for cliques as Theorem 6. After defining the problem and the model below (Definitions 15, 16), §4.1 introduces the Fourier analytic framework over structured NO-instances, and §4.2 proves the lower bound.

Definition 15. (Clique Problem) For a size parameter n, let $V := [n]$ be n vertices. For $2 \le k \le n$, the *k-clique problem* (k-CLIQUE) has input data $E \subseteq \binom{V}{2}$ as $\binom{n}{2}$ boolean variables. k-CLIQUE seeks to decide if the graph (V, E) has a k-clique, i.e. if there is $U \subseteq V$, $|U| = k$, and $\{u, v\} \in E$ for all $u \ne v \in U$.

Definition 16. (Monotone Switching Networks for CLIQUE) In a monotone switching network for CLIQUE (mCLIQUE network), each edge $e' \in E'$ is labeled with $\lambda'(e') = \{u, v\}$ for some $u \ne v \in V$. Given an instance for k-CLIQUE with data E, the literal $\lambda'(e') = \{u, v\}$ is in the instance if $\{u, v\} \in E$.

4.1 Fourier Analysis on Extremal Instances

The analysis focuses on the YES-instances of CLIQUE having a structure of a k-clique, and the NO-instances that are $(k-1)$-colorable.[17] In particular, those YES-instances are minterms and those NO-instances are *similar to* maxterms of CLIQUE as a monotone boolean function, and they are respectively 'hardest to accept' and 'hardest to reject'. Fourier analysis will be done on the truth tables restricted to the $(k-1)$-colorable instances (Definition 21).

Definition 17. (k-clique YES-Instances) An instance $P \in \{0,1\}^{\binom{n}{2}}$ of CLIQUE forms a *k-clique* YES-*instance* if there exists $Q \subseteq V$, $|Q| = k$ such that $\{u, v\} \in E$ iff $u \ne v$ and $u, v \in Q$. In this case, the YES-instance is simply called a k-clique, and $V(P) := Q \subseteq V$.

Definition 18. (Structured NO-Instances) Let $\mathcal{C} := \{C\colon V \to [k-1]\} \cong [k-1]^V$ be the collection of $k-1$ colorings of V. A coloring $C \in \mathcal{C}$ is associated with the structured NO-instance where an edge $\{u, v\}$ is in the instance iff $C(u) \ne C(v)$ for $u, v \in V$.

Definition 19. (Inner Product Space of Colorings) A $\mathcal{C}$-vector is a complex vector with index set $\mathcal{C}$, equivalently a function from $\mathcal{C}$ to $\mathbb{C}$. For two $\mathcal{C}$-vectors f and g, define $\langle f, g \rangle := \frac{1}{|\mathcal{C}|} \sum_{C \in \mathcal{C}} f(C)\overline{g(C)}$ as their inner product, inducing the norm $\|f\| := \langle f, f \rangle^{1/2}$. Then $\mathbb{C}^{\mathcal{C}}$ is an inner product space. Define $\mathbf{1}(C) := 1$ as the constant one vector.

Definition 20. (Fourier Analysis) For a coloring $U \in \mathcal{C}$, define the $\mathcal{C}$-vector $\chi_U(C) := \omega^{\sum_{v \in V} U(v)C(v)}$, where $\omega := \omega_{k-1} := e^{2\pi i/(k-1)}$ is the primitive $(k-1)^{\text{st}}$ root of unity. The collection $\{\chi_U\}_{U \in \mathcal{C}}$ forms an orthonormal basis for $\mathbb{C}^{\mathcal{C}}$, called the Fourier Basis. Denote $\hat{g}(U) := \langle g, \chi_U \rangle$ as the Fourier coefficient of g at 'frequency' U. Say the *support* of U is $supp(U) := \{v \in V : U(v) \ne 0\}$ for $U \in \mathcal{C}$.

Definition 21. (Reachability) For $a' \in V'$, let $R_{a'}(C) :=$ TRUE if the structured NO-instance C can reach a'.[18] Following Fourier analytic conventions, use $(-1)^{[\![condition]\!]} = 1 - 2[\![condition]\!]$ to arithmetize logical (boolean) conditions. The boolean vector $R_{a'}$ is identified with the $\mathcal{C}$-vector $R_{a'}(C) := (-1)^{[\![C \text{ can reach } a']\!]}$.

Note that $R_{s'} = -\mathbf{1}$; and if G' is sound, then $R_{t'} = \mathbf{1}$.

PROPOSITION 8. (ADJACENT REACHABILITY) *If a' and b' are connected by an edge labeled $\{u, v\}$, for any $C \in \mathcal{C}$ with $C(u) \ne C(v)$, then $R_{a'}(C) = R_{b'}(C)$.*

4.2 Generalized Invariants

It turns out that any mCLIQUE network computing k-CLIQUE must leak information about individual cliques in the Fourier spectrum. Namely, for any clique P and any computation path P' accepting P, there is a $\mathcal{C}$-vector g specifying a Fourier spectrum exclusive to P, and a node b' on $V(P')$ such that $R_{b'}$ has a non-negligible response with the signal g (as a result of Lemma 9). The idea is that along P', there are k players (one for each $v \in V(P)$) trying to make progress, from allowing NO-instances at s' to rejecting NO-instances at t'. However, on every edge $e' \in E(P')$ labeled $\lambda'(e') =: \{u, v\}$, there are at least two players u and v who cannot make progress. Since the k players cannot simultaneously make progress, there is a *barrier node* b' leaking information in the discrepancy in progress (Lemma 10).[19] Exploiting this 'Fourier leakage', the general lower bound framework is presented as Lemma 11, followed by the construction of generalized invariants in Lemma 12.

Definition 22. (Generalized Invariants $\{g_{P,v}\}_{v \in V(P)}$) Consider a k-clique P. A collection of $\mathcal{C}$-vectors $\{g_{P,v}\}_{v \in V(P)}$ forms *generalized invariants* if

1. $g_{P,v}$ depends only on coloring in P, i.e. $g_{P,v}(C_1) = g_{P,v}(C_2)$ if $C_1(v) = C_2(v)$ for all $v \in V(P)$;
2. If $g_{P,v}(C) \ne 0$ then C gives a unique color to v in P, i.e. $C(u) \ne C(v)$ for all $u \in V(P) \setminus v$;
3. $\langle \mathbf{1}, g_{P,v} \rangle = 1$; and
4. For all $U \in \mathcal{C}$ where $|supp(U)| \le k-2$, we have $\hat{g}_{P,u}(U) = \hat{g}_{P,v}(U)$ for any $u, v \in V(P)$.

Condition (1) is equivalent to $\hat{g}_{P,v}(U) \ne 0$ for $U \in \mathcal{C}$ implies $supp(U) \subseteq V(P)$. If a' and b' are connected by an edge labeled $e = \{u, v\}$, then Condition (2) gives $\langle R_{a'}, g_{P,v} \rangle = \langle R_{b'}, g_{P,v} \rangle$ and $\langle R_{a'}, g_{P,u} \rangle = \langle R_{b'}, g_{P,u} \rangle$ (Proposition 8). As $R_{t'} = -R_{s'} = \mathbf{1}$, Condition (3) implies $\langle R_{s'}, g_{P,v} \rangle = -1$ and $\langle R_{t'}, g_{P,v} \rangle = 1$ for all $v \in V(P)$. For any two $u, v \in V(P)$, consider $g_{P,u} - g_{P,v}$, then for any $U \in \mathcal{C}$ where $|supp(U)| \le k-2$, Condition (4) implies $\langle g_{P,u} - g_{P,v}, \chi_U \rangle = 0$.

LEMMA 9. (BARRIER) *Fix a k-clique P with generalized invariants $\{g_{P,v}\}_{v \in V(P)}$. Consider a path $P' =: \langle e'_1, e'_2, \dots, e'_\ell \rangle$ labeled with edges from P (that is, e'_j connects v'_{j-1} and v'_j and is labeled $\lambda'(e'_j) \in P$) from $s' := v'_0$ to $t' := v'_\ell$. If $R_{t'} = -R_{s'} = \mathbf{1}$, then there is a node b' on P', and distinct $u, v \in V(P)$, such that $|\langle R_{b'}, g_{P,u} - g_{P,v} \rangle| \ge \frac{2}{\ell+1}$.*

PROOF. Apply Lemma 10 with

$$d_{j,v} := \text{real part of } \langle R_{v'_j}, g_{P_v} \rangle \ . \quad \square$$

[17] This consideration is standard for studying the monotone complexity of k-CLIQUE, and similar ideas date back at least to Razborov [48].

[18] Hence $R_{a'}$ is the truth table at node a' restricted to the colorings $\mathcal{C}$.

[19] The lower bound framework for directed connectivity and generation is similar to the case $k = 2$, where at least one player cannot make progress.

LEMMA 10. (DISCREPANCY IN PROGRESS) *Consider real numbers $d_{j,v} \in \mathbb{R}$ for $0 \leq j \leq \ell$ and for $v \in V(P)$. If (1) for all $v \in V(P)$, $d_{0,v} \leq -1$ and $d_{\ell,v} \geq 1$, and (2) for any $0 < j \leq \ell$, there is $v_j \in V(P)$ such that $d_{j-1,v_j} = d_{j,v_j}$, then there exist j and distinct $u, v \in V(P)$, such that $|d_{j,u} - d_{j,v}| \geq \frac{c}{\ell+1}$ for $c := 1 - (-1) = 2$.*

PROOF. Clearly $\ell \geq 2$. The base case $\ell = 2$ is obvious, by taking $u := v_2$ and $v := v_1$, then $1 \leq d_{2,u} = d_{1,u}$ and $d_{1,v} = d_{0,v} \leq -1$, hence $|d_{1,u} - d_{1,v}| \geq 1 - (-1) = c$. For $\ell > 2$, either (i) there exists $u \in V(P)$ such that $d_{1,u} \geq -1 + \frac{c}{\ell+1}$, and for $v := v_1$ we have $|d_{1,u} - d_{1,v}| \geq \frac{c}{\ell+1}$; or (ii) for all $u \in V(P)$, $d_{1,u} \leq -1 + \frac{c}{\ell+1}$, then the inductive hypothesis (on the numbers $d_{j,v}$ for $1 \leq j \leq \ell$ and for $v \in V(P)$) gives a j and distinct $u, v \in P$ such that $|d_{j,u} - d_{j,v}| \geq \frac{1}{(\ell-1)+1}(c - \frac{c}{\ell+1}) = \frac{1}{\ell}\frac{c\ell}{\ell+1} = \frac{c}{\ell+1}$. □

LEMMA 11. (SIZE LOWER BOUND FROM INVARIANTS) *For $3 \leq k \leq n^{1/100}$, if there is generalized invariants $\{g_{P,v}\}_{v \in V(P)}$ such that $\|g_{P,v}\| \leq k^k$, then any mCLIQUE network G' having n' nodes and computing k-CLIQUE of size n, satisfies $n' \geq \frac{1}{2}n^{k/100} = n^{\Theta(k)}$.*

PROOF. Fix a k-clique P. As a YES-instance, it is accepted by G' via some path P' labeled with edges from P. Lemma 9 gives a node b'_P and a function $g_P := g_{P,u} - g_{P,v}$ such that $|\langle R_{b'_P}, g_P \rangle| \geq \frac{2}{n'+1} \geq \frac{1}{n'}$. Note that $\|g_P\| \leq \|g_{P,u}\| + \|g_{P,v}\| \leq 2k^k$. Also, for any $U \in \mathcal{C}$, if $\langle g_P, \chi_U \rangle \neq 0$ then $supp(U) \subseteq V(P)$ and $|supp(U)| > k - 2$ by (1) and (4) of Definition 22.

Let $q := n^{k/10}$, then Lemma 1 gives q sets $Q_1, Q_2, \ldots, Q_q \subseteq [N]$ satisfying $|Q_i| = k$ and $|Q_i \cap Q_j| \leq k-2$ for $1 \leq i \neq j \leq q$, where $N = \exp(\frac{k \ln n}{10(k-2)} + 1)\frac{k^2}{k-2} \leq n^{1/3}k^2 \ll n$. For each Q_i, construct the k-clique P_i with $V(P_i) = Q_i$, then the previous paragraph gives $b'_i := b'_{P_i}$ and $g_i := g_{P_i}$. Normalize $\tilde{g}_i := g_i/\|g_i\|$, then $\{\tilde{g}_i\}_{1 \leq i \leq q}$ is orthonormal (having disjoint Fourier support). Hence $1 = \|R_{b'}\|^2 \geq \sum_i |\langle R_{b'}, \tilde{g}_i \rangle|^2$. Now

$$n' = \sum_{a' \in V'} 1 \geq \sum_i \sum_{a' \in V'} |\langle R_{a'}, \tilde{g}_i \rangle|^2$$
$$\geq \sum_i |\langle R_{b'_i}, \tilde{g}_i \rangle|^2 \geq q\Big(\frac{1}{n'2k^k}\Big)^2,$$

since $|\langle R_{b'_i}, \tilde{g}_i \rangle| \geq \frac{1}{n'}\frac{1}{\|g_i\|} \geq \frac{1}{n'2k^k}$. It follows that $(n')^3 \geq q/4k^{2k} = n^{k/10}/4k^{2k} = \frac{1}{4}n^{k/20}$. □

Fix a collection of vertices $\mathfrak{D}$ (e.g. $Q \cong [k]$) and a color set $\mathfrak{R}$ (e.g. $[k-1]$). A coloring $C\colon \mathfrak{D} \to \mathfrak{R}$ has a *monopoly* if exactly one color class has more than one vertex, i.e. $\big|\{c \in \mathfrak{R}\colon |C^{-1}(c)| > 1\}\big| = 1$, in which case the monopoly refers to vertices in $\mathfrak{D}$ with the dominating color. Say C *proper* if $C(u) = C(v)$ implies $u = v$ for $u, v \in \mathfrak{D}$.

LEMMA 12. (GENERALIZED INVARIANTS) *Define the scaling factor $f(k) := (k-1)^{k-1}/(k-2)!(k-2)$. For any vertex v in a k-clique P, define a $\mathcal{C}$-vector*

$$g_{P,v}(C) := f(k)(-1)^{\mu}(\mu - 2)!$$

if C (restricted to P) has a monopoly with μ vertices and the monopoly does not contain v, and $g_{P,v}(C) := 0$ otherwise. Then $\{g_{P,v}\}_{v \in V(P)}$ forms generalized invariants with $\|g_{P,v}\| \leq k^{k/2}$.

THEOREM 6. (SIZE LOWER BOUND) *For $3 \leq k \leq n^{1/100}$, any mCLIQUE network G' having n' nodes and computing k-CLIQUE of size n, satisfies $n' \geq \frac{1}{2}n^{k/100} = n^{\Theta(k)}$.*

PROOF. Use Lemmas 11 and 12. □

Acknowledgements

The first-named author thanks Anand Bhaskar, Stephen Cook, Pierre McKenzie, Thomas Watson and Dustin Wehr for helpful discussions. We also thank anonymous reviewers for valuable comments.

5. REFERENCES

[1] *51th Annual IEEE Symposium on Foundations of Computer Science, FOCS 2010, October 23-26, 2010, Las Vegas, Nevada, USA* (2010), IEEE Computer Society.

[2] AJTAI, M. A non-linear time lower bound for boolean branching programs. *Theory of Computing 1*, 1 (2005), 149–176.

[3] AJTAI, M., BABAI, L., HAJNAL, P., KOMLÓS, J., PUDLÁK, P., RÖDL, V., SZEMERÉDI, E., AND TURÁN, G. Two lower bounds for branching programs. In *STOC* (1986), J. Hartmanis, Ed., ACM, pp. 30–38.

[4] ALON, N., AND BOPPANA, R. B. The monotone circuit complexity of boolean functions. *Combinatorica 7*, 1 (1987), 1–22.

[5] AMANO, K., AND MARUOKA, A. The potential of the approximation method. *SIAM Journal on Computing 33*, 2 (2004), 433–447.

[6] ANDREEV, A. E. On a method for obtaining lower bounds for the complexity of individual monotone functions. *Soviet Mathematics Doklady 31*, 3 (1985), 530–534.

[7] BARRINGTON, D. A. M., AND MCKENZIE, P. Oracle branching programs and Logspace versus P. *Information and Computation 95*, 1 (1991), 96–115.

[8] BARRINGTON, D. A. M., AND STRAUBING, H. Superlinear lower bounds for bounded-width branching programs. *Journal of Computer and System Sciences 50*, 3 (1995), 374–381.

[9] BEAME, P., JAYRAM, T. S., AND SAKS, M. TimeâĂŞspace tradeoffs for branching programs. *Journal of Computer and System Sciences 63*, 4 (2001), 542 – 572.

[10] BEAME, P., SAKS, M., SUN, X., AND VEE, E. Time-space trade-off lower bounds for randomized computation of decision problems. *Journal of the ACM 50* (March 2003), 154–195.

[11] BERG, C., AND ULFBERG, S. Symmetric approximation arguments for monotone lower bounds without sunflowers. *Computational Complexity 8*, 1 (1999), 1–20.

[12] BONET, M., PITASSI, T., AND RAZ, R. Lower bounds for cutting planes proofs with small coefficients. *The Journal of Symbolic Logic 62*, 3 (1997), pp. 708–728.

[13] BONET, M. L., ESTEBAN, J. L., GALESI, N., AND JOHANNSEN, J. Exponential separations between restricted resolution and cutting planes proof systems. *Electronic Colloquium on Computational Complexity (ECCC) 5*, 35 (1998).

[14] BOPPANA, R. B. Threshold functions and bounded depth monotone circuits. *Journal of Computer and System Sciences 32*, 2 (1986), 222 – 229.

[15] BOPPANA, R. B., AND SIPSER, M. The complexity of finite functions. In *Handbook of Theoretical Computer Science, Volume A: Algorithms and Complexity (A)*. Elsevier and MIT Press, 1990, pp. 757–804.

[16] BORODIN, A. On relating time and space to size and depth. *SIAM Journal on Computing 6*, 4 (1977), 733–744.

[17] COOK, S. A. An observation on time-storage trade off. *Journal of Computer and System Sciences 9* (December 1974), 308–316.

[18] COOK, S. A., MCKENZIE, P., WEHR, D., BRAVERMAN, M., AND SANTHANAM, R. Pebbles and branching programs for tree evaluation. *ACM Transactions on Computation Theory 3*, 2 (Jan. 2012), 4:1–4:43.

[19] EDMONDS, J., IMPAGLIAZZO, R., RUDICH, S., AND SGALL, J. Communication complexity towards lower bounds on circuit depth. *Computational Complexity 10* (2001), 210–246. 10.1007/s00037-001-8195-x.

[20] GÁL, A., KOUCKÝ, M., AND MCKENZIE, P. Incremental branching programs. *Theory of Computing Systems 43* (2008), 159–184. 10.1007/s00224-007-9049-y.

[21] GOLDMANN, M., AND HÅSTAD, J. A simple lower bound for monotone clique using a communication game. *Information Processing Letters 41*, 4 (1992), 221 – 226.

[22] GOLDMANN, M., AND HÅSTAD, J. Monotone circuits for connectivity have depth $(\log n)^{2-o(1)}$. *SIAM Journal on Computing 27*, 5 (1998), 1283–1294.

[23] GRIGNI, M. *Structure in Monotone Complexity*. PhD thesis, Massachusetts Institute of Technology, June 1991.

[24] GRIGNI, M., AND SIPSER, M. Monotone separation of logarithmic space from logarithmic depth. *Journal of Computer and System Sciences 50*, 3 (1995), 433–437.

[25] HAKEN, A. Counting bottlenecks to show monotone P $\neq$ NP. In *FOCS* (1995), IEEE Computer Society, pp. 36–40.

[26] HARNIK, D., AND RAZ, R. Higher lower bounds on monotone size. In *STOC* (2000), pp. 378–387.

[27] IMPAGLIAZZO, R., PITASSI, T., AND URQUHART, A. Upper and lower bounds for tree-like cutting planes proofs. In *LICS* (1994), IEEE Computer Society, pp. 220–228.

[28] JOHANNSEN, J. Depth lower bounds for monotone semi-unbounded fan-in circuits. *Theoretical Informatics and Applications 35*, 3 (2001), 277–286.

[29] JOHNSON, D. S., Ed. *Proceedings of the 21st Annual ACM Symposium on Theory of Computing, May 14-17, 1989, Seattle, Washigton, USA* (1989), ACM.

[30] JONES, N. D., AND LAASER, W. T. Complete problems for deterministic polynomial time. In *Proceedings of the Sixth Annual ACM Symposium on Theory of Computing* (New York, NY, USA, 1974), STOC '74, ACM, pp. 40–46.

[31] JUKNA, S. Finite limits and monotone computations: The lower bounds criterion. In *IEEE Conference on Computational Complexity* (1997), pp. 302–313.

[32] KARCHMER, M. On proving lower bounds for circuit size. In *Structure in Complexity Theory Conference* (1993), pp. 112–118.

[33] KARCHMER, M., RAZ, R., AND WIGDERSON, A. Super-logarithmic depth lower bounds via the direct sum in communication complexity. *Computational Complexity 5*, 3/4 (1995), 191–204.

[34] KARCHMER, M., AND WIGDERSON, A. Monotone circuits for connectivity require super-logarithmic depth. *SIAM Journal on Discrete Mathematics 3*, 2 (1990), 255–265.

[35] KARCHMER, M., AND WIGDERSON, A. On span programs. In *Structure in Complexity Theory Conference, 1993., Proceedings of the Eighth Annual* (May 1993), pp. 102 –111.

[36] KLAWE, M. M. A tight bound for black and white pebbles on the pyramid. *Journal of the ACM 32* (January 1985), 218–228.

[37] KRAJÍČEK, J. Interpolation theorems, lower bounds for proof systems, and independence results for bounded arithmetic. *The Journal of Symbolic Logic 62*, 2 (1997), pp. 457–486.

[38] KRAUSE, M. Lower bounds for depth-restricted branching programs. *Information and Computation 91*, 1 (1991), 1–14.

[39] MULMULEY, K. Lower bounds in a parallel model without bit operations. *SIAM Journal on Computing 28*, 4 (1999), 1460–1509.

[40] NAKAYAMA, K., AND MARUOKA, A. Loop circuits and their relation to Razborov's approximation model. *Information and Computation 119*, 2 (1995), 154–159.

[41] NEČIPORUK, È. I. On a boolean function. *Soviet Mathematics Doklady 7*, 4 (1966), 999–1000.

[42] NISAN, N., AND WIGDERSON, A. Hardness vs randomness. *Journal of Computer and System Sciences 49*, 2 (1994), 149–167.

[43] POTECHIN, A. Bounds on monotone switching networks for directed connectivity. In *FOCS* [1], pp. 553–562.

[44] RAZ, R., AND MCKENZIE, P. Separation of the monotone NC hierarchy. *Combinatorica 19*, 3 (1999), 403–435.

[45] RAZ, R., AND WIGDERSON, A. Monotone circuits for matching require linear depth. *Journal of the ACM 39*, 3 (1992), 736–744.

[46] RAZBOROV, A., WIGDERSON, A., AND YAO, A. Read-once branching programs, rectangular proofs of the pigeonhole principle and the transversal calculus. *Combinatorica 22* (2002), 555–574. 10.1007/s00493-002-0007-7.

[47] RAZBOROV, A. A. Lower bounds on monotone complexity of the logical permanent. *Mathematical Notes 37* (1985), 485–493. 10.1007/BF01157687.

[48] RAZBOROV, A. A. Lower bounds on the monotone complexity of some boolean functions. *Soviet Mathematics Doklady 31*, 2 (1985), 354–357.

[49] RAZBOROV, A. A. On the method of approximations. In Johnson [29], pp. 167–176.

[50] RAZBOROV, A. A. Lower bounds of the complexity of symmetric boolean functions of contact-rectifier circuits. *Mathematical Notes 48* (1990), 1226–1234. 10.1007/BF01240265.

[51] RAZBOROV, A. A. Lower bounds for deterministic and nondeterministic branching programs. In *FCT* (1991), L. Budach, Ed., vol. 529 of *Lecture Notes in Computer Science*, Springer, pp. 47–60.

[52] REINGOLD, O. Undirected connectivity in log-space. *Journal of the ACM 55* (September 2008), 17:1–17:24.

[53] ROSSMAN, B. The monotone complexity of k-clique on random graphs. In *FOCS* [1], pp. 193–201.

[54] SIMON, J., AND TSAI, S.-C. A note on the bottleneck counting argument. In *IEEE Conference on Computational Complexity* (1997), pp. 297–301.

[55] TARDOS, É. The gap between monotone and non-monotone circuit complexity is exponential. *Combinatorica 8*, 1 (1988), 141–142.

[56] TREVISAN, L. Extractors and pseudorandom generators. *Journal of the ACM 48*, 4 (2001), 860–879.

[57] WEHR, D. Pebbling and branching programs solving the tree evaluation problem. *CoRR abs/1002.4676* (2010).

[58] WEHR, D. Lower bound for deterministic semantic-incremental branching programs solving GEN. *CoRR abs/1101.2705* (2011).

[59] WIGDERSON, A. The fusion method for lower bounds in circuit complexity. In *Keszthely (Hungary)* (1993), pp. 453–467.

[60] YAO, A. C.-C. Circuits and local computation. In Johnson [29], pp. 186–196.

[61] YAO, A. C.-C. A lower bound for the monotone depth of connectivity. In *FOCS* (1994), IEEE Computer Society, pp. 302–308.

Interactive Information Complexity

Mark Braverman*

ABSTRACT

The primary goal of this paper is to define and study the interactive information complexity of functions. Let $f(x, y)$ be a function, and suppose Alice is given x and Bob is given y. Informally, the interactive information complexity $\mathsf{IC}(f)$ of f is the least amount of information Alice and Bob need to reveal to each other to compute f. Previously, information complexity has been defined with respect to a prior distribution on the input pairs (x, y). Our first goal is to give a definition that is independent of the prior distribution. We show that several possible definitions are essentially equivalent.

We establish some basic properties of the interactive information complexity $\mathsf{IC}(f)$. In particular, we show that $\mathsf{IC}(f)$ is equal to the amortized (randomized) communication complexity of f. We also show a direct sum theorem for $\mathsf{IC}(f)$ and give the first general connection between information complexity and (non-amortized) communication complexity. This connection implies that a non-trivial exchange of information is required when solving problems that have non-trivial communication complexity.

We explore the information complexity of two specific problems – Equality and Disjointness. We show that only a constant amount of information needs to be exchanged when solving Equality with no errors, while solving Disjointness with a constant error probability requires the parties to reveal a linear amount of information to each other.

Categories and Subject Descriptors

E.4 [**Coding and information theory**]: Formal models of communication; F.2.2 [**Analysis of algorithms and problem complexity**]: Nonnumerical Algorithms and Problems

*Princeton University and the University of Toronto, `mbraverm@cs.princeton.edu`. Partially supported by an NSERC Discovery Grant, a Sloan Research Fellowship and an NSF CAREER grant. The online version of this extended abstract can be found at `http://eccc.hpi-web.de/report/2011/123/`

STOC'12, May 19–22, 2012, New York, New York, USA.

General Terms

Theory

Keywords

Information theory; communication complexity; information complexity; privacy; interactive computation

1. INTRODUCTION

1.1 Information theory for one-way communication

Shannon [Sha48] originally developed his information theory in order to understand the *one way* data transmission problem over a channel. For a noiseless channel, an important early result in information theory is that the cost of transmitting a (random) message X over the channel is closely related to the entropy $H(X)$ of the message. Recall that $H(X)$ is defined as $H(X) := \mathbf{E}_{x\sim X}[-\log_2 P_X(x)]$. Shannon's noiseless coding theorem, also known as Shannon's source coding theorem states that the cost of sending a signal distributed according to X is essentially $H(X)$:

Theorem 1.1 (Shannon's noiseless coding theorem; Huffman coding). *Let $C(X)$ denote the expected number of bits that the optimal lossless scheme for sending a sample distributed according to X needs to send across the channel. Then for all X, $H(X) \le C(X) < H(X) + 1$.*

As a corollary, if we denote by $C_n := C(X^n)$ – the cost of sending n independent samples distributed according to X, then we see that

$$\lim_{n\to\infty} \frac{C_n}{n} = H(X). \quad (1)$$

Thus the entropy approximately measures the cost of sending a single message, and exactly measures the amortized cost of sending many independent messages from the distribution. The noiseless coding theorem connects the communication cost of sending a message from one player to another to the information content of the message.

An example of a more subtle one-way transmission scenario where the information-theoretic bound is asymptotically tight is given by the Slepian-Wolf Theorem [SW73]. We give one of the interpretations of the result here. Consider the following task: Alice is given an input A which she needs to transmit to Bob. Bob has an input B which is correlated with A, thus giving Bob partial information about A. Clearly this task is not harder than the task of transmitting A on its own, thus $H(A)$ is an upper bound on the amortized transmission cost of this task (i.e. the cost of this task when it is repeated many times). Can the players do better? For example, in the extreme case where A is a deterministic function $A = F(B)$, clearly the number of bits that need to be sent is 0. It turns out that information theory again gives the precise answer to this question:

Theorem 1.2 (Slepian-Wolf coding theorem [SW73]). *The amortized communication cost of transmitting the message A to a player that has prior information B is given by the conditional entropy $H(A|B) := H(AB) - H(B)$.*

Remark 1.3. Unlike Shannon's Theorem, Theorem 1.2 only gives the upper bound in the amortized sense – when one needs to solve multiple copies of the transmission problem, and the number of copies goes to infinity. In [BR11] a one-shot version of the theorem was proved – i.e. the transmission problem is solved in $\approx H(A|B) + o(H(A|B))$ bits of transmission – but the protocol solving it is interactive, rather than a transmission protocol.

These two examples – Shannon's Noiseless Coding Theorem and the Slepian-Wolf Theorem – demonstrate the tight connection between the communication cost of *one-way* transmission problems and their inherent information costs. Information-theoretic quantities are the "right" tools to study the transmission complexity of these problems. The goal of this paper is to develop the "right" information-theoretic notions for *two-way* interactive communication problems. Most importantly, we develop and study the *information complexity* of two-party problems.

Communication complexity studies the communication cost of functions. In the two player setting, the main question it tries to answer is: "How many bits do Alice and Bob need to transmit to each other in order to solve a given problem." Informally, information complexity tries to answer the question: "How much information do Alice and Bob need to reveal to each other in order to solve a give problem?". While – as discussed below – information theory has been used as a tool in the study of communication complexity, it is only recently that the information complexity of interactive problems has been considered in its full generality. The main goal of this paper is to work out the definition of the (two-party) interactive information complexity, and to initiate the study of its properties.

1.2 Information tools in communication complexity

Over the past decade, information theory has been an important tool in the study of communication complexity lower bounds, and their applications to lower bounds for data structures. Chakrabarti, Shi, Wirth and Yao [CSWY01] were the first to define the external information cost. In [CSWY01] information theory is used to prove a direct sum theorem for problems with one simultaneous round of communication. Direct sum theorems (and the related direct product theorems) are theorems giving lower bounds for the complexity of n copies of a certain problem in terms of the complexity of one copy. In the context of communication complexity, direct sum theorems in various contexts have been the focus of much work [FKNN95, CSWY01, Sha03, JRS03, HJMR07, BBCR10, Kla10, Jai11]. More recently, information-theoretic quantities have also been studied in the context of differential privacy [MMP+10].

Information theoretic tools have also been useful in contexts where the problem is not merely a repetition of multiple copies but some other aggregation function. A notable example is set disjointness $DISJ_n$, where the players are given two subsets of $\{1, \dots, n\}$ and need to determine whether the sets are disjoint or not. If we represent the sets by their indicator strings $(x_1, \dots, x_n)$ and $(y_1, \dots, y_n)$, then the disjointness function can be written as

$$DISJ_n((x_1, \dots, x_n), (y_1, \dots, y_n)) := \neg \bigvee_{i=1}^{n} (x_i \wedge y_i). \quad (2)$$

Here the basic function is the conjunction in $x_i \wedge y_i$, and n copies of the conjunction are combined by the big disjunction over all i. A linear communication lower bound for the problem is known [KS92, Raz92]. While $DISJ_n$ is not a direct sum over the $(x_i \wedge y_i)$'s, similar analysis can be adapted, and information-theoretic techniques yield a linear lower bound on this problem [BYJKS04] – we will see an extension of these techniques to information complexity in Section 7. Razborov's simplified proof can also be cast in this framework. The information-theoretic techniques have recently been applied to more complicated composition functions rather than just the AND function [JKR09, LS10, JKZ10]. Information-theoretic reasoning has also been successfully applied in the simpler deterministic setting [DW07].

The internal information cost for protocols over distributions of inputs was defined implicitly in [BYJKS04] and explicitly in [BBCR10]. As in our earlier works, we will refer to internal information cost as simply information cost in this paper. It is the tool that allows one to obtain the only known direct sum results for the general randomized communication complexity. If f is a function and $R(f)$ is its randomized communication complexity, it has been shown in [BBCR10] that the randomized communication complexity of n copies of f satisfies $R(f^n) = \tilde{\Omega}(\sqrt{n} \cdot R(f))$. In the follow-up work [BR11] a tight relationship between the amortized distributional communication complexity of a function and its internal information cost has been established. We further extend this relationship to the non-distributional randomized setting in Section 5.2.

1.3 Other related work

Information theory has played a prominent role in a number of works involving interactive scenarios. In [BKVV07, BKV08] the interactive complexity of an *individual* transmission problem with a prior is studied using Kolmogorov complexity. In [Kla04], Klauck introduces several notions of information complexity with the goal of understanding which computations can be performed *privately*, both in the classical and the quantum settings. One of the main definitions in the classical setting of [Kla04], accounting for the amount of information learned by the parties, coincides with the notion of the (distributional) information complexity.

Interactive information-theoretic quantities have also recently been a subject of study in the information theory community. In [MI11], Ma and Ishwar study the amortized communication complexity of intersection and other functions using information-theoretic tools.

1.4 Main contributions

Interactive information complexity

In [BYJKS04, BBCR10], the information cost $\mathsf{IC}_\mu(\pi)$ of executing a protocol π over an *a-priori* distribution μ of inputs is defined. This immediately yields a definition of the information cost of a function f with respect to a distribution μ: we simply look for a protocol π for f that minimizes $\mathsf{IC}_\mu(\pi)$. It turns out that there is a tight connection between the distributional information cost of f over μ and the amortized *distributional* communication complexity of f^n over μ^n [BR11].

Our first goal is to obtain a definition of the information cost of a function that does not depend on the *a-priori* distribution μ. Let f be a two-party function and $\rho < 1/3$ be an error parameter. Consider the following three quantities:

1. $I_1 = I_1(f, \rho)$ is such that for each $I > I_1$ there is a protocol π_I that on each input computes f except with error $\leq \rho$, and for each prior distribution μ reveals at most I bits of information about the inputs *to the players*. We later denote this quantity by $\mathsf{IC}(f, \rho)$.

2. $I_2 = I_2(f, \rho)$ is such that for each $I > I_2$ and for each prior distribution μ on inputs there is a protocol $\pi_{\mu,I}$ that computes f correctly except with probability $\leq \rho$ with respect to the distribution μ, and that reveals at most I bits of information about the inputs to the players. We later denote this quantity by $\mathsf{IC}_\mathsf{D}(f, \rho)$.

3. $I_3 = I_3(f, \rho)$ is the amortized randomized communication complexity of f as the number of copies goes to ∞: $I_3 = \lim_{n\to\infty} \frac{R^n_\rho(f^n)}{n}$. Here $R^n_\rho(f^n)$ denotes the communication complexity of computing n copies of f, where the protocol is allowed to err at most a ρ-fraction of the time on each input.

Note that the difference between I_1 and I_2 is in the order of quantifiers, and clearly $I_2 \leq I_1$. We prove that $I_1 = \Theta(I_2)$ (Theorem 3.5), more precisely, we show that

$$I_2(f, \rho) \leq I_1(f, \rho) \leq 2 \cdot I_2(f, \rho/2).$$

In the special case when $\rho = 0$ we show that $I_1(f, 0) = I_2(f, 0)$ (Theorem 3.6). We then establish the equality $I_3(f, \rho) = I_1(f, \rho)$ (Theorem 6.7), showing that the prior-free information complexity in the non-distributional case is equal to the amortized randomized communication complexity. These equivalences establish I_1 as the "right" notion of the interactive information complexity of f, which we denote by $\mathsf{IC}(f, \rho) := I_1$.

Properties of the interactive information complexity

We establish some properties of the interactive information complexity. The first one is that the interactive information complexity is *additive* (Theorem 4.2). The theorem holds for tasks. A task can be, for example, computing a function f with an error bounded by ρ. We show that if T_1 and T_2 are two tasks, and $T := T_1 \times T_2$ is the task comprised of performing one of copy of each of the two tasks, then the information complexity satisfies $\mathsf{IC}(T) = \mathsf{IC}(T_1) + \mathsf{IC}(T_2)$. Thus a direct sum statement holds *perfectly* for information complexity[1]

Next, we establish a lower bound for the information complexity of any problem in terms of the communication complexity of the problem. The bound is given by Theorem 5.3. For a constant ρ the bound is of the form $\mathsf{IC}(f) = \Omega(\log R(f))$. This is a fairly weak bound, as one may expect $\mathsf{IC}(f) = \Theta(R(f))$ to hold in many cases. Nonetheless, this is the first general bound on the information revealed by *any* protocol for a problem in terms of its communication complexity.

The interactive information complexity of specific functions

We consider two specific functions that have been studied extensively in the literature: the equality function $EQ(x, y) = \mathbf{1}_{x=y}$ and the disjointness function $DISJ_n$ that we discussed earlier. It turns out that the information complexity or EQ is constant, even when one does not allow the protocol to err at all: $\mathsf{IC}(EQ, 0) = O(1)$ (Proposition 3.21). This result is in sharp contrast with the fact that the zero-error randomized communication complexity of the equality function over n-bit strings is $\Omega(n)$.

On the other hand, the information complexity of $DISJ_n$ turns out to be linear (Theorem 7.2):

$$\mathsf{IC}(DISJ_n, 1/2 - \varepsilon) = \Omega(n) \text{ for all } 0 < \varepsilon < 1/2.$$

We give two proofs for this fact. One is through a reduction to the result about the communication complexity of disjointness, while the second one is a more direct information-theoretic proof.

Directions and open problems

The notion of interactive information complexity gives rise several research directions and many open problems, surrounding its properties (e.g. the relationship between information complexity, communication complexity and quantum communication complexity), as well as the information complexity of specific problems and generalizing information complexity to the multi-party setting. Unfortunately, due to space constraints, we defer the (lengthy) discussion of the open problems and directions to Section 8 in the Appendix.

Acknowledgments

I would like to thank Boaz Barak, Stephen Cook, Ankit Garg, Denis Pankratov, Toni Pitassi, Anup Rao, Alexander Razborov, Michael Saks, Omri Weinstein, Avi Wigderson, and the anonimous referees for the insightful conversations and comments on earlier drafts of this paper.

2. PRELIMINARIES

In an effort to make the paper as self-contained as possible, we provide some background on information theory and communication complexity here. Additional details may be found in [BR11]. A more thorough treatment of the subject may be found in the textbooks on the respective subjects [CT91, KN97]. We note that throughout the paper our protocols will make use of both public and private randomness.

Notation.

We reserve capital letters for random variables and distributions, calligraphic letters for sets, and small letters for elements of sets. Throughout this paper, we often use the notation $|b$ to denote conditioning on the event $B = b$. Thus $A|b$ is shorthand for $A|B = b$.

We use the standard notion of *statistical/total variation* distance between two distributions.

Definition 2.1. Let D and F be two random variables tak-

[1]In fact, we prove a slightly stronger statement in the case where the permissible set of prior distributions is restricted.

ing values in a set $\mathcal{S}$. Their *statistical distance* is

$$|D - F| \stackrel{def}{=} \max_{\mathcal{T} \subseteq \mathcal{S}}(|\Pr[D \in \mathcal{T}] - \Pr[F \in \mathcal{T}]|) = \frac{1}{2}\sum_{s \in \mathcal{S}} |\Pr[D = s] - \Pr[F = s]|$$

If $|D - F| \leq \varepsilon$ we shall say that D is *ε-close* to F. We shall also use the notation $D \stackrel{\varepsilon}{\approx} F$ to mean D is ε-close to F.

2.1 Information Theory

Definition 2.2 (Entropy). The *entropy* of a random variable X is

$$H(X) \stackrel{def}{=} \sum_x \Pr[X = x] \log(1/\Pr[X = x]).$$

The *conditional entropy* $H(X|Y)$ is defined to be $\mathbf{E}_{y \in_R Y}[H(X|Y = y)]$.

Fact 2.3. $H(AB) = H(A) + H(B|A)$.

Definition 2.4 (Mutual Information). The *mutual information* between two random variables A, B, denoted $I(A; B)$ is defined to be the quantity

$$H(A) - H(A|B) = H(B) - H(B|A).$$

The *conditional mutual information* $I(A; B|C)$ is $H(A|C) - H(A|BC)$.

In analogy with the fact that $H(AB) = H(A) + H(B|A)$,

Proposition 2.5 (Chain Rule). *Let C_1, C_2, D, B be random variables. Then*

$$I(C_1C_2; B|D) = I(C_1; B|D) + I(C_2; B|C_1D).$$

We also use the notion of *divergence* (also known as Kullback-Leibler distance or relative entropy), which is a different way to measure the distance between two distributions:

Definition 2.6 (Divergence). The informational divergence between two distributions is

$$\mathbf{D}(A||B) \stackrel{def}{=} \sum_x A(x) \log(A(x)/B(x)).$$

For example, if B is the uniform distribution on $\{0, 1\}^n$ then $\mathbf{D}(A||B) = n - H(A)$.

Proposition 2.7. *Let A, B, C be random variables in the same probability space. For every a in the support of A and c in the support of C, let B_a denote $B|A = a$ and B_{ac} denote $B|A = a, C = c$. Then $I(A; B|C) = \mathbf{E}_{a,c \in_R A,C}[\mathbf{D}(B_{ac}||B_c)]$*

Lemma 2.8.

$$\mathbf{D}(P_1 \times P_2||Q_1 \times Q_2) = \mathbf{D}(P_1||Q_1) + \mathbf{D}(P_2||Q_2).$$

We will use the following two simple corollaries of the Chain Rule many times throughout the paper:

Proposition 2.9. *Let A, B, C, D be four random variables such that $I(B; D|AC) = 0$. Then*

$$I(A; B|C) \geq I(A; B|CD).$$

PROOF. We apply the chain rule twice:

$$\begin{aligned} I(A; B|CD) &= I(AD; B|C) - I(D; B|C) = \\ &I(A; B|C) + I(D; B|AC) - I(D; B|C) = \\ &I(A; B|C) - I(D; B|C) \leq I(A; B|C). \end{aligned}$$

Proposition 2.10. *Let A, B, C, D be four random variables such that $I(B; D|C) = 0$. Then*

$$I(A; B|C) \leq I(A; B|CD).$$

PROOF. Once again, we apply the chain rule twice:

$$\begin{aligned} I(A; B|CD) &= I(AD; B|C) - I(D; B|C) = \\ I(AD; B|C) &= I(A; B|C) + I(D; B|AC) \geq I(A; B|C). \end{aligned}$$

2.2 Communication Complexity

Let $\mathcal{X}, \mathcal{Y}$ denote the set of possible inputs to the two players, who we name A and B. We view a *private coins protocol* for computing a function $f : \mathcal{X} \times \mathcal{Y} \to \mathbb{Z}_K$ as a rooted tree with the following structure:

- Each non-leaf node is *owned* by A or by B.
- Each non-leaf node owned by a particular player has a set of children that are owned by the other player. Each of these children is labeled by a binary string, in such a way that this coding is prefix free: no child has a label that is a prefix of another child.
- Every node is associated with a function mapping $\mathcal{X}$ to distributions on children of the node and a function mapping $\mathcal{Y}$ to distributions on children of the node.
- The leaves of the protocol are labeled by output values.

On input x, y, the protocol π is executed as in Figure 1.

A public coin protocol is a distribution on private coins protocols, run by first using shared randomness to sample an index r and then running the corresponding private coin protocol π_r. Every private coin protocol is thus a public coin protocol. The protocol is called deterministic if all distributions labeling the nodes have support size 1.

Definition 2.11. The *communication cost* (or communication complexity) of a public coin protocol π, denoted $\mathsf{CC}(\pi)$, is the maximum number of bits that can be transmitted in any run of the protocol.

Definition 2.12. The *number of rounds* of a public coin protocol is the maximum depth of the protocol tree π_r over all choices of the public randomness.

Given a protocol π, $\pi(x, y)$ denotes the concatenation of the public randomness with all the messages that are sent during the execution of π. We call this the *transcript* of the protocol. When referring to the random variable denoting the transcript, rather than a specific transcript, we will use the notation $\Pi(x, y)$, thus $\pi(x, y) \in_R \Pi(x, y)$. When x and y are random variables themselves, we will denote the transcript by $\Pi(X, Y)$, or just Π. We shall use the notation $\pi(x, y)_j$ or π_j to refer to the j'th transmitted message in the protocol. We write $\pi(x, y)_{\leq j}$ to denote the concatenation of the public randomness in the protocol with the first j message bits that were transmitted in the protocol. Given a transcript, or a prefix of the transcript, v, we write $\mathsf{CC}(v)$ to denote the number of message bits in v (i.e. the length of the communication).

Definition 2.13 (Communication Complexity notation). For a function $f : \mathcal{X} \times \mathcal{Y} \to \mathbb{Z}_K$, a distribution μ supported on $\mathcal{X} \times \mathcal{Y}$, and a parameter $\rho > 0$, $D^{\mu}_{\rho}(f)$ denotes the communication complexity of the cheapest deterministic

Generic Communication Protocol
1. Set v to be the root of the protocol tree. 2. If v is a leaf, the protocol ends and outputs the value in the label of v. Otherwise, the player owning v samples a child of v according to the distribution associated with her input for v and sends the label to indicate which child was sampled. 3. Set v to be the newly sampled node and return to the previous step.

Figure 1: A communication protocol.

protocol for computing f on inputs sampled according to μ with error ρ. $R_\rho(f)$ denotes the cost of the best randomized public coin protocol for computing f with error at most ρ on *every* input.

We should mention the following theorem due to Yao, which we will extend in this paper to information cost:

Theorem 2.14 (Yao's Min-Max). $R_\rho(f) = \max_\mu D^\mu_\rho(f)$.

2.3 Information + communication: the information cost of a protocol

In the sections that follow we will develop the information complexity theory for interactive communication. The most basic definition is that of the information cost of a protocol. This notion is implicit in [BYJKS04], and was explicitly defined in [BBCR10] (see also [BR11]).

Definition 2.15. The information cost of a protocol π over inputs from $\mathcal{X} \times \mathcal{Y}$ is given by:

$$\mathsf{IC}_\mu(\pi) := I(\Pi; X|Y) + I(\Pi; Y|X).$$

Intuitively, Definition 2.15 captures what the two parties learn about each other's inputs from the execution transcript of the protocol π. The first term captures what the second player learns about X from Π – the mutual information between the input X and the transcript Π given the input Y. Similarly, the second term captures what the first player learns about Y from Π.

Note that the information of a protocol π depends on the prior distribution μ, as the mutual information between the transcript Π and the inputs depends on the prior distribution on the inputs. To give an extreme example, if μ is a singleton distribution, i.e. one with $\mu(\{(x,y)\}) = 1$ for some $(x,y) \in \mathcal{X} \times \mathcal{Y}$, then $\mathsf{IC}_\mu(\pi) = 0$ for all possible π, as no protocol can reveal anything to the players about the inputs that the do not already know *a-priori*. Similarly, $\mathsf{IC}_\mu(\pi) = 0$ if $\mathcal{X} = \mathcal{Y}$ and μ is supported on the diagonal $\{(x,x) : x \in \mathcal{X}\}$.

As expected, one can show that the communication cost $\mathsf{CC}(\pi)$ of π is an upper bound on its information cost over *any* distribution μ:

Lemma 2.16. *[BR11] For any distribution μ, $\mathsf{IC}_\mu(\pi) \leq \mathsf{CC}(\pi)$.*

On the other hand, as demonstrated by the simple examples above, the converse need not hold. Moreover, while $\mathsf{CC}(\pi)$ is a combinatorial property that depends only on the protocol, $\mathsf{IC}_\mu(\pi)$ depends on μ. One of our first goals it to make the study of information cost independent of the prior distribution.

3. THE PRIOR-FREE INFORMATION COMPLEXITY OF A PROBLEM

Given a distribution μ on a two-player input space $\mathcal{X} \times \mathcal{Y}$, a function $f : \mathcal{X} \times \mathcal{Y} \to \{0,1\}$ and an error parameter ε, the *information complexity* $\mathsf{IC}_\mu(f,\varepsilon)$ is defined to be the *infimum* of the information cost over all (randomized) protocols π that achieve an error of $\leq \varepsilon$ with respect to μ.

Remark 3.1. We state all our results for boolean functions. In fact we do not need f to be binary or even a function. All our results hold if the goal is to implement a general relation F that accepts inputs in $\mathcal{X} \times \mathcal{Y}$ and for which a protocol is said to succeed if in the end the two players reach an acceptable pair of states. In the case of a boolean function f there is only one acceptable pair of states in which each player outputs "the answer is $f(x,y)$".

Definition 3.2.

$$\mathsf{IC}_\mu(f,\varepsilon) := \inf_{\pi:\ \mathbf{P}_{(x,y)\sim\mu}[\pi(x,y)\neq f(x,y)]\leq\varepsilon} \mathsf{IC}_\mu(\pi).$$

Clearly, $\mathsf{IC}_\mu(f,\varepsilon)$ is monotone non-decreasing in ε – i.e. a lower error ε requires higher information cost. We note that the definition of $\mathsf{IC}_\mu(f,0)$ – the zero-error information complexity also makes sense. By Lemma 2.16, it is easy to see that the information costs are smaller than the corresponding (distributional) communication costs.

Information-theoretic quantities, such as the mutual information between the parties' inputs and the protocol's transcript only make sense with respect to a prior distribution on inputs. Nonetheless, at least syntactically, we can factor out the distribution by taking the maximum over all possible distributions:

Definition 3.3. The max-distributional information complexity of a function f with error ε is

$$\mathsf{IC_D}(f,\varepsilon) \quad := \quad \max_{\mu \text{ a distribution on } \mathcal{X}\times\mathcal{Y}} \mathsf{IC}_\mu(f,\varepsilon).$$

Note that we are justified in using a max in place of sup since the set of all possible distributions over $X \times Y$ is compact and $\mathsf{IC}_\mu(f,\varepsilon)$ can be shown to be continuous in μ (and ε).

It is not immediately apparent that the definition of $\mathsf{IC_D}(f,\varepsilon)$ is an interesting one. While it gives an upper bound on the information cost for each distribution, this upper bound may be attained by a different protocol $\pi = \pi(\mu)$ for each distribution μ. We will show that the quantifiers may "almost" be reversed: there is a single (randomized) protocol π that achieves a low information cost *and* a low error with respect to *any* distribution μ. In fact, we define the *prior-free* information complexity of a problem in terms of such a protocol.

Definition 3.4. The information complexity of a function f with error ε is

$$\mathsf{IC}(f,\varepsilon) := \inf_{\pi \text{ is a protocol with } \mathbf{P}[\pi(x,y)\neq f(x,y)]\leq\varepsilon \text{ for all } (x,y)} \max_{\mu} \mathsf{IC}_{\mu}(\pi).$$

Clearly, $\mathsf{IC}(f,\varepsilon) \geq \mathsf{IC_D}(f,\varepsilon)$. The opposite direction is our main result connecting the prior-free information complexity with complexity with the distributional information complexity:

Theorem 3.5. *Let $f : \mathcal{X}\times\mathcal{Y}\to\{0,1\}$ be any function, and $\varepsilon \geq 0$ be an error parameter. For each value of the parameter $0<\alpha<1$ we have*

$$\mathsf{IC}\left(f,\frac{\varepsilon}{\alpha}\right) \leq \frac{\mathsf{IC_D}(f,\varepsilon)}{1-\alpha}$$

In other words, there is a protocol π such that:

1. *for each $(x,y)\in\mathcal{X}\times\mathcal{Y}$, $\mathbf{P}[\pi(x,y)\neq f(x,y)]\leq\frac{\varepsilon}{\alpha}$, i.e. the protocol π makes an error of at most ε/α on each input;*

2. *for each distribution μ on $\mathcal{X}\times\mathcal{Y}$, $\mathsf{IC}_{\mu}(\pi) \leq \frac{\mathsf{IC_D}(f,\varepsilon)}{1-\alpha}$, i.e. for* every *distribution the protocol π reveals not too much information to the participants.*

By selecting $\alpha=\frac{1}{2}$ we can ensure that both the error and the information cost increase by a factor of at most 2.

For the zero-error case, we similarly obtain the following zero-error version of Theorem 3.5:

Theorem 3.6. *Let $f : \mathcal{X}\times\mathcal{Y}\to\{0,1\}$ be any function. Then we have*

$$\mathsf{IC}(f,0) = \mathsf{IC_D}(f,0).$$

In other words, there is a protocol π such that:

1. *for each $(x,y)\in\mathcal{X}\times\mathcal{Y}$, $\pi(x,y)=f(x,y)$, i.e. the protocol π always works correctly;*

2. *for each distribution μ on $\mathcal{X}\times\mathcal{Y}$, $\mathsf{IC}_{\mu}(\pi)\leq\mathsf{IC}(f,0)$.*

3.1 Proof of Theorems 3.5 and 3.6

Proof Proof of Theorem 3.5. We prove the theorem using a minimax argument. For the remainder of the proof fix f and ε, and denote $I := \mathsf{IC_D}(f,\varepsilon)$. Define the following two-player zero-sum game. Player A will come up with a (randomized) two-party protocol $\pi(x,y)$ taking inputs in $\mathcal{X}\times\mathcal{Y}$. Player B will come up with a distribution μ on inputs (x,y). Player B's payoff is given by:

$$P_B(\pi,\mu) := (1-\alpha)\cdot\frac{\mathsf{IC}_{\mu}(\pi)}{I} + \alpha\cdot\frac{\mathbf{P}_{\mu}[\pi(x,y)\neq f(x,y)]}{\varepsilon}.$$

As the game is a zero-sum game, the payoff of player A is given by $P_A(\pi,\mu) := -P_B(\pi,\mu)$. Thus player A comes up with a protocol for f, and player B comes up with a distribution that tries to highlight the mistakes of π, and also make it reveal information about the inputs to the participants. We denote the game by $\mathcal{G}$. Our first goal is to show that the value of $\mathcal{G}$ to player B is bounded by 1.

Claim 3.7. *The value $V_B(\mathcal{G})\leq 1$.*

Proof. Let ν_B be a probability distribution representing a mixed strategy for player B. Thus ν_B is a distribution on probability distributions μ over $X\times Y$. We will actually show that $V_B(\mathcal{G}) < 1+\delta$ for each $\delta>0$. To show that $V_B(\mathcal{G})<1+\delta$ it suffices to show that there is a protocol π such that $\mathbf{E}_{\mu\sim\nu_B}[P_B(\pi,\mu)] < 1+\delta$. Let $\bar{\mu}$ be a distribution on $\mathcal{X}\times\mathcal{Y}$ that is obtained by taking the average of $\mu\sim\nu_B$. Formally,

$$\bar{\mu}(x,y) := \mathbf{E}_{\mu\sim\nu_B}\mu(x,y).$$

By the definition of $I=\mathsf{IC}(f,\varepsilon)$, we know that there is a protocol π such that $\mathbf{P}_{\bar{\mu}}[\pi(x,y)\neq f(x,y)]\leq\varepsilon$ and $\mathsf{IC}_{\bar{\mu}}(\pi) < I\cdot(1+\delta)$. We claim that

$$\mathbf{E}_{\mu\sim\nu_B}\left[I_{(X,Y)\sim\mu}(\pi(X,Y);X|Y)\right] \leq I_{(X,Y)\sim\bar{\mu}}(\pi(X,Y);X|Y). \tag{3}$$

In other words, the average amount of information revealed by π with respect to the different distributions $\mu\sim\nu_B$ is smaller or equal to the amount of information revealed with respect to $\bar{\mu}$ – the concavity works in the "right" direction.

To establish (3), consider the following four random variables. Let M be a random variable representing the distribution μ. Then M is distributed according to ν_B. Let X and Y be the inputs to the two parties in π such that (X,Y) is distributed according to μ. Finally, let $\Pi=\pi(X,Y)$ be the transcript of the protocol executed on X and Y. Π is randomized even conditioned on (X,Y) due to the public and private randomness used in the execution of the protocol. In this language, we have:

$$\mathbf{E}_{\mu\sim\nu_B}\left[I_{(X,Y)\sim\mu}(\pi(X,Y);X|Y)\right] = I(\Pi;X|YM),$$

and

$$I_{(X,Y)\sim\bar{\mu}}(\pi(X,Y);X|Y) = I(\Pi;X|Y).$$

Since the distribution of Π only depends on X and Y, we have $I(\Pi;M|XY)=0$. By substituting $A=X$, $B=\Pi$, $C=Y$, and $D=M$ into Proposition 2.9 we get

$$I(X;\Pi|Y)\geq I(X;\Pi|YM), \tag{4}$$

proving (3). Similarly to (3) the following symmetric inequality is established:

$$\mathbf{E}_{\mu\sim\nu_B}\left[I_{(X,Y)\sim\mu}(\pi(X,Y);Y|X)\right] \leq I_{(X,Y)\sim\bar{\mu}}(\pi(X,Y);Y|X). \tag{5}$$

Together, (3) and (5) imply

$$\mathbf{E}_{\mu\sim\nu_B}[\mathsf{IC}_{\mu}(\pi)] \leq \mathsf{IC}_{\bar{\mu}}(\pi). \tag{6}$$

Using (6) we obtain

$$\begin{aligned}
&\mathbf{E}_{\mu\sim\nu_B}[P_B(\pi,\mu)] = \\
&\mathbf{E}_{\mu\sim\nu_B}\left[(1-\alpha)\cdot\frac{\mathsf{IC}_{\mu}(\pi)}{I} + \alpha\cdot\frac{\mathbf{P}_{\mu}[\pi(x,y)\neq f(x,y)]}{\varepsilon}\right] \\
&= (1-\alpha)\cdot\mathbf{E}_{\mu\sim\nu_B}\left[\frac{\mathsf{IC}_{\mu}(\pi)}{I}\right] + \alpha\cdot\frac{\mathbf{P}_{\bar{\mu}}[\pi(x,y)\neq f(x,y)]}{\varepsilon} \\
&\leq (1-\alpha)\cdot\frac{\mathsf{IC}_{\bar{\mu}}(\pi)}{I} + \alpha\cdot\frac{\mathbf{P}_{\bar{\mu}}[\pi(x,y)\neq f(x,y)]}{\varepsilon} < \\
&\qquad (1-\alpha)\cdot(1+\delta)+\alpha\cdot 1 \leq 1+\delta.
\end{aligned}$$

This proves Claim 3.7.

By the Minimax Theorem, Claim 3.7 implies that there is a mixed strategy for player A such that for each response by player B, the value of the game for player B is at most

1. A mixed strategy for player A is a distribution ν_A on protocols. In other words,

$$\mathbf{E}_{\pi\sim\nu_A} P_B(\pi,\mu) \le 1, \text{ for all } \mu. \quad (7)$$

Let $\bar{\pi}$ be the randomized protocol obtained by publicly sampling $\pi \sim \nu_A$, and then applying π to the inputs. We claim that $\bar{\pi}$ is the protocol we are looking for. In other words, the randomized protocol $\bar{\pi}$ has the desired payoff properties that will translate into information cost/error properties.

Claim 3.8. *For each distribution μ, $P_B(\bar{\pi},\mu) \le 1$.*

PROOF. The proof proceeds similarly to the proof of Claim 3.7. We will prove first that

$$I_{(X,Y)\sim\mu}(\bar{\pi}(X,Y);X|Y) \le \mathbf{E}_{\pi\sim\nu_A}\left[I_{(X,Y)\sim\mu}(\pi(X,Y);X|Y)\right]. \quad (8)$$

In other words, the amount of information revealed by $\bar{\pi}$ is bounded by the average amount of information revealed by π that is drawn according to ν_A – once again, the concavity works in the "right" direction.

To establish (8), consider the following four random variables. Let S be a "selector" random variable, that picks the protocol π to run according to the distribution ν_A. Let X and Y be inputs distributed according to μ independently of S. Finally, let $\Pi = \pi(X,Y)$ be the transcript of the selected protocol executed on X and Y. We have:

$$\mathbf{E}_{\pi\sim\nu_A}\left[I_{(X,Y)\sim\mu}(\pi(X,Y);X|Y)\right] = I(\Pi;X|YS),$$

and

$$I_{(X,Y)\sim\mu}(\bar{\pi}(X,Y);X|Y) = I(\Pi;X|Y).$$

Since the protocol π is selected independently of the inputs, we have $I(X;S|Y) = 0$. By substituting $A = \Pi$, $B = X$, $C = Y$, and $D = S$ into Proposition 2.10 we get

$$I(\Pi;X|Y) \le I(\Pi;X|YS), \quad (9)$$

establishing (8). Similarly to (8) the following symmetric inequality is established:

$$I_{(X,Y)\sim\mu}(\bar{\pi}(X,Y);Y|X) \le \mathbf{E}_{\pi\sim\nu_A}\left[I_{(X,Y)\sim\mu}(\pi(X,Y);Y|X)\right]. \quad (10)$$

Together, (8) and (10) imply

$$\mathsf{IC}_\mu(\bar{\pi}) \le \mathbf{E}_{\pi\sim\nu_A}\left[\mathsf{IC}_\mu(\pi)\right]. \quad (11)$$

Finally, (11) implies that

$$\begin{aligned} P_B(\bar{\pi},\mu) &= (1-\alpha)\cdot\frac{\mathsf{IC}_\mu(\bar{\pi})}{I} + \alpha\cdot\frac{\mathbf{P}_\mu[\bar{\pi}(x,y)\ne f(x,y)]}{\varepsilon} \\ &= (1-\alpha)\cdot\frac{\mathsf{IC}_\mu(\bar{\pi})}{I} + \mathbf{E}_{\pi\sim\nu_A}\left[\alpha\cdot\frac{\mathbf{P}_\mu[\pi(x,y)\ne f(x,y)]}{\varepsilon}\right] \\ &\le (1-\alpha)\cdot\mathbf{E}_{\pi\sim\nu_A}\left[\frac{\mathsf{IC}_\mu(\pi)}{I}\right] + \\ \mathbf{E}_{\pi\sim\nu_A}&\left[\alpha\cdot\frac{\mathbf{P}_\mu[\pi(x,y)\ne f(x,y)]}{\varepsilon}\right] = \\ &\mathbf{E}_{\pi\sim\nu_A}\left[P_B(\pi,\mu)\right] \le 1, \end{aligned}$$

completing the proof of Claim 3.8.

To complete the proof of Theorem 3.5, we observe that the randomized protocol $\bar{\pi}$ satisfies the conclusions of the theorem. For each distribution μ we know that $P_B(\bar{\pi},\mu) \le 1$, and thus

$$\mathsf{IC}_\mu(\bar{\pi}) \le \frac{I}{1-\alpha} \quad \text{and} \quad \mathbf{P}_\mu[\bar{\pi}(x,y)\ne f(x,y)] \le \frac{\varepsilon}{\alpha}.$$

The first inequality is exactly the second requirement in Theorem 3.5. We obtain the second requirement by letting μ be the atomic distribution on $\{(x,y)\}$.

Remark 3.9. Note that the statement of Theorem 3.5 contains a gap in the following sense. We are unable to simultaneously achieve the goals of low information and low error with the same parameters as in the distributional setting. Instead we lose factors of $\frac{1}{1-\alpha}$ and $\frac{1}{\alpha}$. It is an interesting open problem whether this analysis is actually tight, i.e. whether $\mathsf{IC}(f,\varepsilon) = \mathsf{IC_D}(f,\varepsilon)$. It is quite possible that there is, in fact, a gap between the two quantities.

PROOF PROOF OF THEOREM 3.6. The proof is very similar to the proof of Theorem 3.5. The key difference is that now we only deal with zero-error protocols. Denote $I := \mathsf{IC_D}(f,0)$. We define the following zero-sum two player game $\mathcal{G}_0$. Player A will come up with a (randomized) two-party protocol $\pi(x,y)$ taking inputs in $\mathcal{X}\times\mathcal{Y}$. The protocol is required to always be correct: for any pair of inputs (x,y), $\pi(x,y) = f(x,y)$ with probability 1 with respect to the random coin tosses within π. Player B will come up with a distribution μ on inputs (x,y). Note that the protocol π has to be correct even on inputs outside of the support of μ. Player B's payoff is given by:

$$P_B(\pi,\mu) := \frac{\mathsf{IC}_\mu(\pi)}{I}.$$

Once again, we first need to establish that the value of the game for player B is bounded by 1.

Claim 3.10. *The value $V_B(\mathcal{G}_0) \le 1$.*

PROOF. The proof is quite similar to the proof of Claim 3.7 with one minor twist: by the assumption, for each distribution μ there is a zero-error protocol π_μ whose information cost with respect to μ is $< (1+\delta)\cdot I$. The problem is that π_μ only has to be zero-error *on the support of* μ. This problem is easily overcome by modifying μ very slightly to ensure that it has full support.

We will actually show that $V_B(\mathcal{G}) < 1+\delta$ for each $\delta > 0$. Let ν_B be a probability distribution representing a mixed strategy for player B. Thus ν_B is a distribution on probability distributions μ over $\mathcal{X}\times\mathcal{Y}$. We modify ν_B to select the distribution μ_u uniform on $\mathcal{X}\times\mathcal{Y}$ with probability $\delta/4$ to obtain ν'_B. Player B's payoff is always non-negative. Hence, if there is a strategy π for player A that guarantees that B's payoff with respect to ν'_B is $< 1+\delta/2$, then using the same strategy will guarantee that B's payoff with respect to ν_B is $< 1+\delta$. Otherwise, B's payoff with respect to ν'_B would be at least

$$(1+\delta)\cdot(1-\delta/4) = 1+3\delta/4-\delta^2/4 > 1+\delta/2.$$

Thus we need to show that there is a zero-error protocol π such that $\mathbf{E}_{\mu\sim\nu'_B}[\mathsf{IC}_\mu(\pi)] < 1+\delta/2$. Let $\bar{\mu}$ be a distribution on $\mathcal{X}\times\mathcal{Y}$ that is obtained by taking the average of $\mu\sim\nu'_B$. Formally,

$$\bar{\mu}(x,y) := \mathbf{E}_{\mu\sim\nu_B}\mu(x,y).$$

Note that since one of the distributions in ν'_B is the uniform distribution on $\mathcal{X}\times\mathcal{Y}$, $\bar{\mu}$ has full support.

By the definition of $I = \mathsf{IC}(f,0)$, we know that there is a protocol π that achieves zero-error with respect to $\bar{\mu}$ such that $\mathsf{IC}_{\bar{\mu}}(\pi) < I\cdot(1+\delta/2)$. Since $\bar{\mu}$ has full support, π is a feasible strategy for player A. Following the analysis in Claim 3.7 we obtain that (6) still holds here:

$$\mathbf{E}_{\mu\sim\nu'_B}[\mathsf{IC}_\mu(\pi)] \le \mathsf{IC}_{\bar\mu}(\pi).$$

Thus

$$\mathbf{E}_{\mu\sim\nu_B}[P_B(\pi,\mu)] = \mathbf{E}_{\mu\sim\nu'_B}[\mathsf{IC}_\mu(\pi)]/I \le \mathsf{IC}_{\bar\mu}(\pi)/I < 1+\delta/2,$$

completing the proof of Claim 3.10.

The rest of the proof of Theorem 3.6 is identical to the proof of Theorem 3.5. There is a distribution ν_A of strategies for player A such that each protocol in ν_A is a zero-error protocol, and for each distribution μ the expected payoff $\mathbf{E}_{\pi\sim\nu_A}[P_B(\pi,\mu)] \le 1$. If we let $\bar\pi$ be the randomized protocol obtained by sampling π according to ν_A and then running it, then exactly as in Claim 3.8 above we obtain

$$\mathsf{IC}_\mu(\bar\pi) \le \mathbf{E}_{\pi\sim\nu_A}[\mathsf{IC}_\mu(\bar\pi)] = I\cdot\mathbf{E}_{\pi\sim\nu_A}[P_B(\pi,\mu)] \le I.$$

3.2 External information complexity

We next turn our attention to the *external information complexity* of a problem. Recall that the regular (internal) information cost of a problem is the amount of information the participating parties have to learn about the inputs to solve the problem. By analogy, the external information cost is the amount of information an observer necessarily has to learn when the parties perform the computation.

We start by defining the external information cost of a protocol π.

Definition 3.11. Let π be a two-party communication protocol over inputs in $\mathcal{X}\times\mathcal{Y}$. Let μ be a distribution over $\mathcal{X}\times\mathcal{Y}$. We denote by (X,Y) the (random) pair of inputs given to the players that are distributed according to μ. Let $\Pi=\Pi(X,Y)$ denote the random variable that is the transcript of the protocol. Then the external information cost of π with respect to μ is given by:

$$\mathsf{IC}^{\mathsf{ext}}_\mu(\pi) := I(XY;\Pi).$$

We note that the external information cost is always greater or equal to the internal information cost of a protocol:

Proposition 3.12. *For each protocol π and distribution μ,*

$$\mathsf{IC}^{\mathsf{ext}}_\mu(\pi) \ge \mathsf{IC}_\mu(\pi).$$

Moreover, the two quantities are equal if $\mu=\mu_\mathcal{X}\times\mu_\mathcal{Y}$ is a product distribution on $\mathcal{X}\times\mathcal{Y}$.

Proof. The proposition is only true because π is a protocol: it is not hard to see that it would fail if Π was a general random variable that is correlated with the inputs X and Y. Denote by $\Pi_1,\Pi_2,\dots,\Pi_N$ the messages sent in the protocol π. We assume that Π_i is sent by Alice (who holds X) for odd i's and by Bob for even i's. N itself is also a random variable here.

By the chain rule, we have:

$$\mathsf{IC}_\mu(\pi) = I(X;\Pi|Y)+I(Y;\Pi|X) = \sum_{i=1}^N [I(X;\Pi_i|\Pi_1,\dots,\Pi_{i-1}Y)+I(Y;\Pi_i|\Pi_1,\dots,\Pi_{i-1}X)],$$

and

$$\mathsf{IC}^{\mathsf{ext}}_\mu(\pi) = I(XY;\Pi) = \sum_{i=1}^N I(XY;\Pi_i|\Pi_1,\dots,\Pi_{i-1}).$$

We will prove the inequality term-wise. Let i be an index. Without loss of generality assume that i is odd, so that Π_i is a message sent by Alice. This means that conditioned on prior communications and on X, Π_i is independent from Y:

$$I(\Pi_i;Y|\Pi_1,\dots,\Pi_{i-1}X)=0. \tag{12}$$

We can now write:

$$I(XY;\Pi_i|\Pi_1,\dots,\Pi_{i-1}) = I(X;\Pi_i|\Pi_1,\dots,\Pi_{i-1})+I(Y;\Pi_i|\Pi_1,\dots,\Pi_{i-1}X) \ge I(X;\Pi_i|\Pi_1,\dots,\Pi_{i-1}Y)+I(Y;\Pi_i|\Pi_1,\dots,\Pi_{i-1}X),$$

where the last inequality follows from (12) and Proposition 2.9 by taking $A=X$, $B=\Pi_i$, $C=\Pi_1,\dots,\Pi_{i-1}$ and $D=Y$.

It remains to prove the converse inequality in the case when μ is a product distribution. This direction actually holds when Π is any random variable. If μ is a product distribution, then X and Y are independent, and thus $I(X;Y)=0$. We have

$$\mathsf{IC}^{\mathsf{ext}}_\mu(\pi) = I(XY;\Pi) = I(X;\Pi)+I(Y;\Pi|X) \le I(X;\Pi|Y)+I(Y;\Pi|X) = \mathsf{IC}_\mu(\pi),$$

where the inequality holds by Proposition 2.10 with $A=\Pi$, $B=X$, $C=\emptyset$, and $D=Y$.

We can now define the natural analogues of Definitions 3.2, 3.3, and 3.4 for external information, starting with the distributional external information complexity.

Definition 3.13.

$$\mathsf{IC}^{\mathsf{ext}}_\mu(f,\varepsilon) := \inf_{\pi:\ \mathbf{P}_{(x,y)\sim\mu}[\pi(x,y)\ne f(x,y)]\le\varepsilon} \mathsf{IC}^{\mathsf{ext}}_\mu(\pi).$$

Definition 3.14. The max-distributional external information complexity of a function f with error ε is

$$\mathsf{IC}^{\mathsf{ext}}_{\mathsf{D}}(f,\varepsilon) := \max_{\mu \text{ a distribution on } \mathcal{X}\times\mathcal{Y}} \mathsf{IC}^{\mathsf{ext}}_\mu(f,\varepsilon).$$

Definition 3.15. The external information complexity of a function f with error ε is

$$\mathsf{IC}^{\mathsf{ext}}(f,\varepsilon) := \inf_{\pi \text{ is a protocol with } \mathbf{P}[\pi(x,y)\ne f(x,y)]\le\varepsilon \text{ for all } (x,y)} \max_\mu \mathsf{IC}^{\mathsf{ext}}_\mu(\pi).$$

Proposition 3.12 implies that for all μ, $\mathsf{IC}^{\mathsf{ext}}_\mu(f,\varepsilon)\ge\mathsf{IC}_\mu(f,\varepsilon)$, and also $\mathsf{IC}^{\mathsf{ext}}_{\mathsf{D}}(f,\varepsilon)\ge\mathsf{IC}_{\mathsf{D}}(f,\varepsilon)$ and $\mathsf{IC}^{\mathsf{ext}}(f,\varepsilon)\ge\mathsf{IC}(f,\varepsilon)$.

Finally, the analogues of Theorems 3.5 and 3.6 for external information cost are proved in the exact same way. We formulate the theorems here:

Theorem 3.16. *Let $f:\mathcal{X}\times\mathcal{Y}\to\mathbb{Z}_K$ be any function, and $\varepsilon\ge 0$ be an error parameter. For each value of the parameter $0<\alpha<1$ we have*

$$\mathsf{IC}^{\mathsf{ext}}\left(f,\frac{\varepsilon}{\alpha}\right) \le \frac{\mathsf{IC}^{\mathsf{ext}}_{\mathsf{D}}(f,\varepsilon)}{1-\alpha}$$

In other words, there is a protocol π such that:

1. *for each $(x,y)\in\mathcal{X}\times\mathcal{Y}$, $\mathbf{P}[\pi(x,y)\ne f(x,y)]\le\frac{\varepsilon}{\alpha}$, i.e. the protocol π makes an error of at most ε/α on each input;*
2. *for each distribution μ on $\mathcal{X}\times\mathcal{Y}$, $\mathsf{IC}^{\mathsf{ext}}_\mu(\pi)\le\frac{\mathsf{IC}^{\mathsf{ext}}_{\mathsf{D}}(f,\varepsilon)}{1-\alpha}$, i.e. for every distribution the protocol π reveals not too much information to the observer.*

Theorem 3.17. *Let $f : \mathcal{X}\times\mathcal{Y} \to \mathbb{Z}_K$ be any function. Then we have*

$$\mathsf{IC}^{\text{ext}}(f,0) = \mathsf{IC}_{\mathsf{D}}^{\text{ext}}(f,0).$$

In other words, there is a protocol π such that:

1. *for each $(x,y) \in \mathcal{X} \times \mathcal{Y}$, $\pi(x,y) = f(x,y)$, i.e. the protocol π always works correctly;*
2. *for each distribution μ on $\mathcal{X}\times\mathcal{Y}$, $\mathsf{IC}_{\mu}^{\text{ext}}(\pi) \leq \mathsf{IC}^{\text{ext}}(f,0)$.*

The only difference between the proofs of Theorem 3.5 and of its external version 3.16 is that equations (4) and (9) are slightly different. The external version of equation (4) is

$$I(XY;\Pi) \geq I(XY;\Pi|M), \qquad (13)$$

which still follows from Proposition 2.9 with $A = XY$, $B = \Pi$, $C = \emptyset$, and $D = M$, and the fact that $I(\Pi;M|XY) = 0$. The external version of equation (9) is

$$I(\Pi;XY) \leq I(\Pi;XY|S), \qquad (14)$$

which follows from Proposition 2.10 with $A = \Pi$, $B = XY$, $C = \emptyset$, and $D = S$, and the fact that $I(XY;S) = 0$.

3.3 The information complexity is convex in the error parameter

In this section we prove that the information complexity $\mathsf{IC}(f,\varepsilon)$ is convex in the error parameter ε. Note that this function is trivially non-increasing.

Theorem 3.18. *For any f, the function $I(\varepsilon) := \mathsf{IC}(f,\varepsilon)$ is convex on the interval $\varepsilon \in [0,1]$.*

Since a convex function on an interval must be continuous, the following is an immediate corollary of Theorem 3.18:

Corollary 3.19. *For any f, the function $I(\varepsilon) := \mathsf{IC}(f,\varepsilon)$ is continuous on the interval $\varepsilon \in (0,1)$.*

Remark 3.20. A statement analogous to Theorem 3.18, with a very similar proof, holds for the max-distributional information complexity $\mathsf{IC}_{\mathsf{D}}(f,\varepsilon)$.

Proof Proof of Theorem 3.18. Let $0 \leq \varepsilon_1 < \varepsilon_2 \leq 1$ be two values, and let $\alpha \in (0,1)$ be a parameter. Set $\varepsilon := \alpha \cdot \varepsilon_1 + (1-\alpha)\cdot\varepsilon_2$. Our goal is to show that

$$I(\varepsilon) \leq \alpha \cdot I(\varepsilon_1) + (1-\alpha)\cdot I(\varepsilon_2).$$

Let $\delta > 0$ be a parameter that tends to 0. By the definition of $\mathsf{IC}(f,\varepsilon)$, there is a pair of protocols π_1 and π_2 that attain an error of at most ε_1 and ε_2, respectively, on each input (x,y), and such that for each distribution μ,

$$\mathsf{IC}_{\mu}(\pi_1) < I(\varepsilon_1) + \delta, \text{ and } \mathsf{IC}_{\mu}(\pi_2) < I(\varepsilon_2) + \delta.$$

Let π be a protocol that publicly tosses a coin to select between π_1 and π_2 and then runs the selected protocol. π_1 is selected with probability α and π_2 is selected with probability $(1-\alpha)$. For each pair of inputs (x,y) we have

$$\mathbf{P}[\pi(x,y) \neq f(x,y)] = \alpha \cdot \mathbf{P}[\pi_1(x,y) \neq f(x,y)] + (1-\alpha)\cdot \mathbf{P}[\pi_2(x,y) \neq f(x,y)] \leq \varepsilon.$$

Following the same proof as the proof of (11) in Claim 3.8 we can obtain for each μ:

$$\mathsf{IC}_{\mu}(\pi) \leq \alpha \cdot \mathsf{IC}_{\mu}(\pi_1) + (1-\alpha)\cdot \mathsf{IC}_{\mu}(\pi_2) < \alpha \cdot I(\varepsilon_1) + (1-\alpha)\cdot I(\varepsilon_2) + \delta.$$

This implies that $I(\varepsilon) < \alpha \cdot I(\varepsilon_1) + (1-\alpha)\cdot I(\varepsilon_2) + \delta$ for each $\delta > 0$, and hence

$$I(\varepsilon) \leq \alpha \cdot I(\varepsilon_1) + (1-\alpha)\cdot I(\varepsilon_2).$$

3.4 Example: the information complexity of equality

As an instructive illustration let us consider the information complexity of the equality function. The equality function $EQ : \{0,1\}^n \times \{0,1\}^n \to \{0,1\}$ is given by $EQ(x,y) = 1$ if and only if $x = y$. It is well known that the deterministic communication complexity of EQ is $n+1$, while the randomized communication complexity if one allows error ε is bounded by $O(\log 1/\varepsilon)$ (assuming the parties have access to public randomness).

We will demonstrate a gap between the information complexity and the communication complexity of EQ. Specifically, we show that the information complexity of EQ is bounded by a constant that is independent of the error parameter ε. Moreover, we show that the zero-error information cost of equality is also constant. Thus there is a major gap between the deterministic communication complexity and the zero-error information cost (linear vs. constant).

Proposition 3.21. $\mathsf{IC}(EQ,0) = O(1)$.

Discussion: Proposition 3.21, together with our other results, sheds interesting light onto the results by Feder, Kushilevitz, Naor, and Nisan [FKNN95] on the (violation of) direct sum for randomized communication complexity. [FKNN95] (and related constructions) give EQ as an example that appears to violate direct sum for randomized communication complexity. It is not hard to see that the randomized communication complexity of EQ with error ε, $R_{\varepsilon}(EQ) = \Omega(\log 1/\varepsilon)$. On the other hand, the (non-trivial) algorithm from [FKNN95] shows that the amortized communication complexity of EQ, $R_{\varepsilon}(EQ^n)/n = O(1)$, even for relatively small $n = \log^2 1/\varepsilon$. This shows that there is no hope for a direct sum theorem to hold if one regards the error ε as a parameter. Combining Proposition 3.21 with the '$\geq$' direction of the general Theorem 6.7 gives an alternative proof of this fact for any $\varepsilon > 0$. Thus, intuitively, the gap between the randomized and the amortized communication complexity of equality for small values of ε is caused by the gap between the randomized communication complexity (which depends on ε) and the inherent information cost of the problem (which is constant, even in the extreme case when $\varepsilon = 0$). At the same time, in light of this explanation, it is not clear whether this gap sheds any light on the situation with constant ε. We will revisit these points in the discussion of Theorem 6.7.

Proof. We present a zero-error protocol π for equality that will have low information cost with respect to any prior distribution. Note that to prove the proposition it would have been sufficient to produce such a protocol π_{μ} for each given prior distribution μ, as Theorem 3.6 would guarantee the existence of a protocol π that simultaneously has low information cost with respect to all distributions μ. The protocol is presented on Figure 2.

Correctness. The protocol terminates on each input after at most n rounds. Both parties always output the same answer. If the protocol terminates and returns 0, then there is an a_i with $a_i \cdot x \neq a_i \cdot y$, and thus $x \neq y$. If the protocol terminates and outputs 1, then $Ax = Ay$. Since A is always chosen to be non-singular, this implies $x = y$.

A zero-error constant-information complexity protocol for EQ
1. The parties use public randomness to sample a uniformly random non-singular matrix $A \in \mathbb{F}_2^n$. Denote the rows of A by $a_1, a_2, \ldots, a_n$. 2. At step i, the first player sends $a_i \cdot x$ to the second player. If $a_i \cdot x \neq a_i \cdot y$, the second player responds "not equal" and the protocol terminates with $EQ(x, y) = 0$. 3. If the protocol hasn't terminated after n steps, the protocol terminates with $EQ(x, y) = 1$.

Figure 2: The protocol for Equality

Information cost. First of all, note that the protocol is essentially symmetric with respect to the two players: at each round the two players learn whether $a_i \cdot x = a_i \cdot y$, and only continue if this is the case. Let μ be any distributions on inputs (x, y). It suffices to show that $I_\mu(X; \pi(X, Y)|Y) = O(1)$ where $(X, Y) \sim \mu$. Let R be the public randomness used by the protocol to sample the matrix A, and let π_R be the deterministic protocol that uses this randomness. We know that (see e.g. [BR11]) $I_\mu(X; \pi|Y) = \mathbf{E}_R[I_\mu(X; \pi_R|Y)]$. In fact, we will show that

$$\mathbf{E}_R[H_\mu(\pi|Y)] = O(1),$$

which would suffice since $\mathbf{E}_R[I_\mu(X; \pi_R|Y)] \leq \mathbf{E}_R[H_\mu(\pi|Y)]$.

Given an input y to the second player, and given the matrix A that is publicly sampled, the possible protocol transcripts are of two kinds:

1. If $x \neq y$ then the protocol may last anywhere from 1 to n rounds, and the transcript will only depend on the number i of rounds. Let $p_i = p_i(R, y, \mu)$ denote the probability that the protocol lasts exactly i rounds and $x \neq y$.

2. if $x = y$ then the protocol lasts n rounds, and its transcript is completely determined by A and y. Let $p_0 = p_0(R, y, \mu)$ denote the probability that the protocol outputs $x = y$.

Denote by $\bar{p}_i(y, \mu) := \mathbf{E}_R p_i(R, y, \mu)$. We can now calculate $\mathbf{E}_R[H_\mu(\pi|Y)]$:

$$\mathbf{E}_R[H_\mu(\pi|Y)] = \mathbf{E}_R \mathbf{E}_{y \sim \mu_y} \sum_{i=0}^{n} p_i(R, y, \mu) \log \frac{1}{p_i(R, y, \mu)} =$$

$$\mathbf{E}_{y \sim \mu_y} \mathbf{E}_R \sum_{i=0}^{n} p_i(R, y, \mu) \log \frac{1}{p_i(R, y, \mu)} \leq$$

$$\mathbf{E}_{y \sim \mu_y} \sum_{i=0}^{n} \bar{p}_i(y, \mu) \log \frac{1}{\bar{p}_i(R, y, \mu)},$$

where the last inequality follows from the concavity of the $x \log(1/x)$ function. Next, note that for each $i \geq 2$, $\bar{p}_i(y, \mu) \leq 2^{-i+1}$, since the probability over R that the protocol will last for at least i rounds for each fixed pair $x \neq y$ is bounded by 2^{-i+1}. Thus for each y, and for each $i \geq 3$,

$$\bar{p}_i(y, \mu) \log \frac{1}{\bar{p}_i(R, y, \mu)} \leq 2^{-i+1} \cdot (i - 1).$$

In addition, it is always the case that $\bar{p}_i(y, \mu) \log \frac{1}{\bar{p}_i(R, y, \mu)} \leq 1$, and thus:

$$\mathbf{E}_R[H_\mu(\pi|Y)] \leq \mathbf{E}_{y \sim \mu_y} \sum_{i=0}^{n} \bar{p}_i(y, \mu) \log \frac{1}{\bar{p}_i(R, y, \mu)} <$$

$$3 + \sum_{i=3}^{\infty} 2^{-i+1} \cdot (i - 1) = 4.5 = O(1).$$

4. THE ADDITIVITY OF INFORMATION COMPLEXITY

In this section we will show that information complexity is additive. That is, the information complexity of performing two independent tasks is the sum of the information complexities of each individual task. This is a more general statement, though closely related, than a direct sum theorem that states that n copies of *the same* task cost n times as much as one copy [BR11]. In contrast with the information complexity, we do not know such a statement to be true for communication complexity, and it is known to be false in other settings. See [BBCR10] for a further discussion on direct sum problems.

We formulate the result in terms of tasks. A task is just a (possibly partial) relation $R(x, y, O_x, O_y)$, along with a required success criterion. Here O_x and O_y correspond to the outputs of the two players. For example, if the task is to compute a function f with probability $> 1 - \varepsilon$ then $R(x, y, O_x, O_y) = 1$ if and only if $O_x = O_y = f(x, y)$, and the success criterion is that $R(x, y, O_x, O_y) = 1$ with probability $> 1 - \varepsilon$. Another example of a task is computing n independent copies of a function f such that the probability of success on each copy is $> 1 - \varepsilon$. In this way, a task is essentially "anything that can be solved by a communication protocol".

The information cost of a task $T(x, y)$ is defined similarly to the information cost of a function. To be concrete and to avoid cumbersome notation, we assume that the inputs (x, y) belong to $\mathcal{U} := \{0, 1\}^n$. Let $\mathcal{M}$ be a set of distributions on $\mathcal{U} \times \mathcal{U}$. Then the information cost of T with respect to $\mathcal{M}$ is defined as:

Definition 4.1. $\mathsf{IC}(T, \mathcal{M}) := \inf_{\pi \text{ succeeds at } T} \sup_{\mu \in \mathcal{M}} \mathsf{IC}_\mu(\pi)$, where the infimum is taken over protocols that successfully perform the task T.

Let $T_1(x_1, y_1)$ and $T_2(x_2, y_2)$ be two tasks. Let

$$T(x_1, x_2, y_1, y_2) := T_1 \times T_2$$

be the task that consists of performing T_1 and T_2 in parallel on two pairs of inputs. A protocol is successful at T if it is successful at each of the two sub-tasks separately.

Next, we consider two products of sets of distributions. Let $\mathcal{M}_1$ be a set of distributions of pairs (x_1, y_1), and let $\mathcal{M}_2$ be a set of distributions of pairs (x_2, y_2). Denote

$$\mathcal{M}_1 \times \mathcal{M}_2 := \{\mu_1 \times \mu_2 : \ \mu_1 \in \mathcal{M}_1, \ \mu_2 \in \mathcal{M}_2\}.$$

We also define a bigger class of distributions which are not necessary product distributions, but whose projections fall into the sets $\mathcal{M}_1, \mathcal{M}_2$:

$$\mathcal{M}_1 \otimes \mathcal{M}_2 := \{\mu : \ \mu|_{(X_1,Y_1)} \in \mathcal{M}_1, \ \mu|_{(X_2,Y_2)} \in \mathcal{M}_2\} \supset \mathcal{M}_1 \times \mathcal{M}_2.$$

Theorem 4.2. *Let $T_1(x_1, y_1)$ and $T_2(x_2, y_2)$ be two tasks, let $\mathcal{M}_1$ and $\mathcal{M}_2$ be any sets of distributions over (x_1, y_1) and (x_2, y_2), respectively, and let $T := T_1 \times T_2$. Then:*

$$\mathsf{IC}(T, \mathcal{M}_1 \times \mathcal{M}_2) = \mathsf{IC}(T, \mathcal{M}_1 \otimes \mathcal{M}_2) = \mathsf{IC}(T_1, \mathcal{M}_1) + \mathsf{IC}(T_2, \mathcal{M}_2).$$

PROOF. We prove the theorem by establishing three non-strict inequalities.

$\underline{\mathsf{IC}(T, \mathcal{M}_1 \times \mathcal{M}_2) \le \mathsf{IC}(T, \mathcal{M}_1 \otimes \mathcal{M}_2)}$. This is obvious, since $\mathcal{M}_1 \otimes \mathcal{M}_2 \supset \mathcal{M}_1 \times \mathcal{M}_2$, and thus the sup in Definition 4.1 is taken over a larger set.

$\underline{\mathsf{IC}(T, \mathcal{M}_1 \otimes \mathcal{M}_2) \le \mathsf{IC}(T_1, \mathcal{M}_1) + \mathsf{IC}(T_2, \mathcal{M}_2)}$. Let $\varepsilon > 0$ be an arbitrarily small parameter. Let π_1 and π_2 be two protocols that succeed at tasks T_1 and T_2, respectively, such that

$$\mathsf{IC}_{\mu_1}(\pi_1) < \mathsf{IC}(T_1, \mathcal{M}_1) + \varepsilon \text{ and } \mathsf{IC}_{\mu_2}(\pi_2) < \mathsf{IC}(T_2, \mathcal{M}_2) + \varepsilon,$$

for all $\mu_1 \in \mathcal{M}_1$ and $\mu_2 \in \mathcal{M}_2$. Let π be the protocol that on (the random) inputs (X_1, X_2), (Y_1, Y_2) independently runs π_1 on the pair (X_1, Y_1) and π_2 on the pair (X_2, Y_2). Then clearly the protocol π succeeds at the task $T = T_1 \times T_2$. It remains to analyze π's information cost. Let μ be a distribution in $\mathcal{M}_1 \otimes \mathcal{M}_2$. We will show that

$$\mathsf{IC}_\mu(\pi) < \mathsf{IC}(T_1, \mathcal{M}_1) + \mathsf{IC}(T_2, \mathcal{M}_2) + 2\varepsilon,$$

since $\varepsilon > 0$ is arbitrary, this will complete the proof. Denote $\mu_1 := \mu|_{(X_1,Y_1)} \in \mathcal{M}_1$, and $\mu_2 := \mu|_{(X_2,Y_2)} \in \mathcal{M}_2$. Let Π_1 be the random variable denoting the transcript of π_1, and similarly let Π_2 denote the transcript of π_2. We know that

$$I(X_1; \Pi_1|Y_1) + I(Y_1; \Pi_1|X_1) = \mathsf{IC}_{\mu_1}(\pi_1) < \mathsf{IC}(T_1, \mathcal{M}_1) + \varepsilon,$$

and similarly

$$I(X_2; \Pi_2|Y_2) + I(Y_2; \Pi_2|X_2) = \mathsf{IC}_{\mu_2}(\pi_2) < \mathsf{IC}(T_2, \mathcal{M}_2) + \varepsilon.$$

Next we note that the execution of π_1 only depends on the inputs X_1, Y_1, and the public/private randomness pertaining to the execution of π_1. This implies

$$I(\Pi_1; X_2|X_1Y_1) = I(\Pi_1; Y_2|X_1Y_1) = I(\Pi_1; \Pi_2|X_1Y_1) = I(\Pi_1; X_2Y_2|X_1Y_1) = I(\Pi_1; Y_2\Pi_2|X_1Y_1) = I(\Pi_1; X_2\Pi_2|X_1Y_1) = I(\Pi_1; X_2Y_2\Pi_2|X_1Y_1) = 0, \quad (15)$$

and similar equalities hold for Π_2.

By Proposition 2.9 with $A = X_1$, $B = \Pi_1$, $C = Y_1$, $D = Y_2$, and the fact that $I(\Pi_1; Y_2|X_1Y_1) = 0$ we get

$$I(\Pi_1; X_1|Y_1Y_2) \le I(\Pi_1; X_1|Y_1). \quad (16)$$

Similarly, by Proposition 2.9 with $A = X_2$, $B = \Pi_2$, $C = Y_2$, $D = \Pi_1Y_1$, and the fact that $I(\Pi_2; \Pi_1Y_1|X_2Y_2) = 0$ we get

$$I(\Pi_2; X_2|\Pi_1Y_1Y_2) \le I(\Pi_2; X_2|Y_2). \quad (17)$$

Putting these and (15) together, we obtain

$$I(\Pi; X_1X_2|Y_1Y_2) = I(\Pi_1\Pi_2; X_1X_2|Y_1Y_2) = I(\Pi_1; X_1X_2|Y_1Y_2) + I(\Pi_2; X_1X_2|Y_1Y_2\Pi_1) = I(\Pi_1; X_1|Y_1Y_2) + I(\Pi_1; X_2|X_1Y_1Y_2) + I(\Pi_2; X_2|Y_1Y_2\Pi_1) + I(\Pi_2; X_1|X_2Y_1Y_2\Pi_1) \overbrace{=}^{\text{by (15)}} I(\Pi_1; X_1|Y_1Y_2) + I(\Pi_2; X_2|Y_1Y_2\Pi_1) \overbrace{\le}^{\text{by (16) and (17)}} I(\Pi_1; X_1|Y_1) + I(\Pi_2; X_2|Y_2).$$

Similarly, $I(\Pi; Y_1Y_2|X_1X_2) \le I(\Pi_1; Y_1|X_1) + I(\Pi_2; Y_2|X_2)$. Thus

$$\mathsf{IC}_\mu(\pi) = I(\Pi; X_1X_2|Y_1Y_2) + I(\Pi; Y_1Y_2|X_1X_2) \le I(\Pi_1; X_1|Y_1) + I(\Pi_2; X_2|Y_2) + I(\Pi_1; Y_1|X_1) + I(\Pi_2; Y_2|X_2) = \mathsf{IC}_{\mu_1}(\Pi_1) + \mathsf{IC}_{\mu_2}(\Pi_2) < \mathsf{IC}(T_1, \mathcal{M}_1) + \mathsf{IC}(T_2, \mathcal{M}_2) + 2\varepsilon.$$

$\underline{\mathsf{IC}(T_1, \mathcal{M}_1) + \mathsf{IC}(T_2, \mathcal{M}_2) \le \mathsf{IC}(T, \mathcal{M}_1 \times \mathcal{M}_2)}$. Let $\mu_1 \in \mathcal{M}_1$ and $\mu_2 \in \mathcal{M}_2$ be two distributions, and let $\varepsilon > 0$ be a parameter. We will show that there are protocols π_1 and π_2 that succeed at tasks T_1 and T_2 respectively such that

$$\mathsf{IC}_{\mu_1}(\pi_1) + \mathsf{IC}_{\mu_2}(\pi_2) < \mathsf{IC}(T, \mathcal{M}_1 \times \mathcal{M}_2) + \varepsilon.$$

By the definition of $\mathsf{IC}(T, \mathcal{M}_1 \times \mathcal{M}_2)$, there is a protocol π that succeed at the task $T_1 \times T_2$ such that

$$\mathsf{IC}_{\mu_1 \times \mu_2}(\pi) < \mathsf{IC}(T, \mathcal{M}_1 \times \mathcal{M}_2) + \varepsilon.$$

Define the protocols π_1 and π_2 as in Figure 3. From the definition of $T = T_1 \times T_2$ it follows that the protocols π_1 and π_2 succeed at T_1 and T_2 respectively. It remains to analyze their information complexity.

We have

$$\mathsf{IC}_{\mu_1}(\pi_1) = I(\pi_1; X_1|Y_1) + I(\pi_1; Y_1|X_1) = I(\pi; X_1|Y_1Y_2) + I(\pi; Y_1|X_1X_2Y_2) \quad (18)$$

and

$$\mathsf{IC}_{\mu_2}(\pi_2) = I(\pi_2; X_2|Y_2) + I(\pi_2; Y_2|X_2) = I(\pi; X_2|X_1Y_1Y_2) + I(\pi; Y_1|X_1X_2). \quad (19)$$

Putting the two equations together we get:

$$\mathsf{IC}_{\mu_1}(\pi_1) + \mathsf{IC}_{\mu_2}(\pi_2) = I(\pi; X_1|Y_1Y_2) + I(\pi; Y_1|X_1X_2Y_2) + I(\pi; X_2|X_1Y_1Y_2) + I(\pi; Y_1|X_1X_2) = I(\pi; X_1|Y_1Y_2) + I(\pi; X_2|X_1Y_1Y_2) + I(\pi; Y_1|X_1X_2) + I(\pi; Y_1|X_1X_2Y_2) = I(\pi; X_1X_2|Y_1Y_2) + I(\pi; Y_1Y_2|X_1X_2) = \mathsf{IC}_{\mu_1 \times \mu_2}(\pi) < \mathsf{IC}(T, \mathcal{M}_1 \times \mathcal{M}_2) + \varepsilon.$$

Theorem 4.2 can be now used in many different ways. Let us use it to show exact direct sum theorems for both the information cost and the distributional information cost.

Theorem 4.3. *Let $f(x, y)$ be any function, and $\rho \ge 0$ an error parameter. Let f^n be the problem of computing f on n pairs of inputs such that when one considers each coordinate separately, the error is bounded by ρ. Then*

1. $\mathsf{IC_D}(f^n, \rho) = n \cdot \mathsf{IC_D}(f, \rho)$.

Protocol $\pi_1(x_1, y_1)$

1. The parties jointly and publicly sample Y_2 according to $\mu_2|_{Y_2}$.
2. The first party privately samples $X_2 = X_2|Y_2$.
3. The parties run $\pi((x_1, X_2), (y_1, Y_2))$ and output the output of the task T_1.

Protocol $\pi_2(x_2, y_2)$

1. The parties jointly and publicly sample X_1 according to $\mu_1|_{X_1}$.
2. The second party privately samples $Y_1 = Y_1|X_1$.
3. The parties run $\pi((X_1, x_2), (Y_1, y_2))$ and output the output of the task T_2.

Figure 3: The protocols π_1 and π_2

2. $\mathsf{IC}(f^n, \rho) = n \cdot \mathsf{IC}(f, \rho)$.

PROOF. *We note that the proofs of the two parts are quite similar; the reader may want to only read the proof of the second part, which is more important (and also simpler).*

$\mathsf{IC_D}(f^n, \rho) \geq n \cdot \mathsf{IC_D}(f, \rho)$. *Let μ be the distribution that realizes $\mathsf{IC_D}(f, \rho)$. Let T^n be the task of computing n copies of f such that the error on each copy when measured against the distribution μ is $\leq \rho$. Further, let $\mathcal{M}^n = \{\mu^n\}$ be the set consisting of only one product distribution. Then by the definition of μ,*

$$\mathsf{IC_D}(f, \rho) = \mathsf{IC}(\mathcal{M}^1, T^1).$$

By Theorem 4.2 we have:

$$\mathsf{IC_D}(f^n, \rho) \geq \mathsf{IC}(\mathcal{M}^n, T^n) = \mathsf{IC}(\mathcal{M}^{n-1}, T^{n-1}) + \mathsf{IC}(\mathcal{M}^1, T^1) = \\ = \ldots = n \cdot \mathsf{IC}(\mathcal{M}^1, T^1) = n \cdot \mathsf{IC_D}(f, \rho).$$

$\mathsf{IC_D}(f^n, \rho) \leq n \cdot \mathsf{IC_D}(f, \rho)$. *Let μ be the distribution on n-tuples of inputs that realizes $\mathsf{IC_D}(f^n, \rho)$, and let μ_i be the restriction of μ to the i-th coordinate. In other words, any protocol that fails with probability $\leq \rho$ with respect to μ_i on the i-th coordinate must reveal at least $\mathsf{IC_D}(f^n, \rho)$ information with respect to μ. Let T_i be the task of computing f correctly with error $\leq \rho$ with respect to the distribution μ_i. Let $T := T_1 \times T_2 \times \ldots \times T_n$. By the definition of the task we have*

$$\mathsf{IC}(\{\mu\}, T) \geq \mathsf{IC_D}(f^n, \rho).$$

Let $\mathcal{M}_i := \{\mu_i\}$ and $\mathcal{M} := \mathcal{M}_1 \otimes \mathcal{M}_2 \otimes \ldots \otimes \mathcal{M}_n$. Then $\mu \in \mathcal{M}$. By Theorem 4.2 we have:

$$\mathsf{IC_D}(f^n, \rho) \leq \mathsf{IC}(\{\mu\}, T) \leq \mathsf{IC}(\mathcal{M}, T) = \\ \mathsf{IC}(\mathcal{M}_1, T_1) + \ldots + \mathsf{IC}(\mathcal{M}_n, T_n) \leq n \cdot \mathsf{IC_D}(f^n, \rho).$$

$\mathsf{IC}(f^n, \rho) = n \cdot \mathsf{IC}(f, \rho)$. *Let T^n be the task of computing n copies of f such that the (worst case) probability of error on each copy is $\leq \rho$. Let $\mathcal{M}^n$ be the set of all possible distributions over n-tuples of inputs. Then, by definition*

$$\mathsf{IC}(f, \rho) = \mathsf{IC}(\mathcal{M}^1, T^1),$$

and

$$\mathsf{IC}(f^n, \rho) = \mathsf{IC}(\mathcal{M}^n, T^n).$$

Note that $\mathcal{M}^n = \underbrace{\mathcal{M}^1 \otimes \ldots \otimes \mathcal{M}^1}_{n \text{ times}}$ *and* $T^n = \underbrace{T^1 \times \ldots \times T^1}_{n \text{ times}}$, *and thus by Theorem 4.2,*

$$\mathsf{IC}(f^n, \rho) = \mathsf{IC}(\mathcal{M}^n, T^n) = n \cdot \mathsf{IC}(\mathcal{M}^1, T^1) = n \cdot \mathsf{IC}(f, \rho).$$

5. INFORMATION COMPLEXITY VS. COMMUNICATION COMPLEXITY

5.1 A new sampling lemma

In this section we prove a new sampling lemma. The lemma is then used to establish a new connection between the information and the communication complexity of any problem. We start with the following claim about the information divergence of distributions:

Claim 5.1. *Supposed that $\mathbf{D}(\mu||\nu) \leq I$. Let ε be any parameter. Then*

$$\mu\left\{x :\ 2^{(I+1)/\varepsilon} \cdot \nu(x) < \mu(x)\right\} < \varepsilon.$$

PROOF. Recall that $\mathbf{D}(\mu||\nu) = \sum_{x \in \mathcal{U}} \mu(x) \log \frac{\mu(x)}{\nu(x)}$. Denote by $\mathcal{N} = \{x :\ \mu(x) < \nu(x)\}$ – the terms that contribute a negative amount to $\mathbf{D}(\mu||\nu)$. First we observe that for all $0 < x < 1$, $x \log x > -1$, and thus

$$\sum_{x \in \mathcal{N}} \mu(x) \log \frac{\mu(x)}{\nu(x)} \sum_{x \in \mathcal{N}} \nu(x) \cdot \frac{\mu(x)}{\nu(x)} \log \frac{\mu(x)}{\nu(x)} \geq \\ \sum_{x \in \mathcal{N}} \nu(x) \cdot (-1) > -1.$$

Denote by $\mathcal{L} = \left\{x :\ 2^{(I+1)/\varepsilon} \cdot \nu(x) < \mu(x)\right\}$; we need to show that $\mu(\mathcal{L}) < \varepsilon$. For each $x \in \mathcal{L}$ we have $\log \frac{\mu(x)}{\nu(x)} > (I+1)/\varepsilon$. Thus

$$I \geq \mathbf{D}(\mu||\nu) \geq \sum_{x \in \mathcal{L}} \mu(x) \log \frac{\mu(x)}{\nu(x)} + \sum_{x \in \mathcal{N}} \mu(x) \log \frac{\mu(x)}{\nu(x)} > \\ \mu(\mathcal{L}) \cdot (I+1)/\varepsilon - 1,$$

implying $\mu(\mathcal{L}) < \varepsilon$.

We are now ready to state and prove our main sampling lemma.

Lemma 5.2. *Let μ be any distribution over a universe $\mathcal{U}$ and let $I \geq 0$ be a parameter that is known to both A and B. Further, let ν_A and ν_B be two distributions over $\mathcal{U}$ such that $\mathbf{D}(\mu||\nu_A) \leq I$ and $\mathbf{D}(\mu||\nu_B) \leq I$. The players are each given a real function $p_A, q_A, p_B, q_B : \mathcal{U} \to [0,1]$ such that for all $x \in \mathcal{U}$, $\mu(x) = p_A(x) \cdot p_B(x)$, $\nu_A(x) = p_A(x) \cdot q_A(x)$, and $\nu_B(x) = p_B(x) \cdot q_B(x)$. Let $\varepsilon > 0$ be an error parameter. Then there is a sampling protocol $\Pi = \Pi(p_A, p_B, q_A, q_B, I, \varepsilon)$ that communicates $2^{O(1+I/\varepsilon)}$ bits such that the following hold:*

1. *at the end of the protocol, the players output $x_A \in \mathcal{U}$ and $x_B \in \mathcal{U}$, respectively;*
2. *there is an event $\mathcal{E}$ such that $\neg\mathcal{E} \Rightarrow x_A = x_B$ and $\mathbf{P}[\mathcal{E}] < \varepsilon$;*
3. *let μ' is the distribution of x_A conditioned on $\neg\mathcal{E}$, then $|\mu - \mu'| < \varepsilon$.*

Proof. Firstly, Alice and Bob interpret the shared random tape as a source of points (x_i, α_i, β_i) uniformly distributed in $\mathcal{U} \times [0,1] \times [0,1]$. Alice and Bob consider $T = 2|\mathcal{U}| \ln 1/\varepsilon$ such points. Their goal will be to discover the first index τ such that $\alpha_\tau \leq p_A(x_\tau)$ and $\beta_\tau \leq p_B(x_\tau)$. Note that the probability of each x to be such x_τ is proportional to $p_A(x_\tau) \cdot p_B(x_\tau) = \mu(x_\tau)$. Thus the distribution of x_τ is correct.

Denote $B_A := \{x : 2^{8(I+1)/\varepsilon} \cdot \nu_A(x) < \mu(x)\}$ and $B_B := \{x : 2^{8(I+1)/\varepsilon} \cdot \nu_B(x) < \mu(x)\}$. Then by Claim 5.1, $\mu(B_A), \mu(B_B) < \varepsilon/8$. Next, we note that the probability that an index t satisfies $\alpha_t \leq p_A(x_t)$ and $\beta_t \leq p_B(x_t)$ is exactly $1/|\mathcal{U}|$. Hence the probability that $\tau > T$ (i.e. that x_τ is not among the T points considered) is bounded by

$$(1 - 1/|\mathcal{U}|)^T < e^{-T/|\mathcal{U}|} = e^{-2\ln 1/\varepsilon} = \varepsilon^2 < \varepsilon/16.$$

Denote by $\mathcal{A}$ the set of indices

$$\mathcal{A} := \{i \leq T : \alpha_i \leq p_A(x_i) \text{ and } \beta_i \leq 2^{8(I+1)/\varepsilon} \cdot q_A(x_i)\}.$$

$\mathcal{A}$ is the set of indices that are candidates to be τ from A's viewpoint. Similarly,

$$\mathcal{B} := \{i \leq T : \alpha_i \leq 2^{8(I+1)/\varepsilon} \cdot q_B(x_i) \text{ and } \beta_i \leq p_B(x_i)\}.$$

Assuming $x_\tau \notin B_A \cup B_B$, we have that $\tau \in \mathcal{A} \cap \mathcal{B}$, because $x_\tau \notin B_A$ implies

$$\frac{p_B(x_\tau)}{q_A(x_\tau)} = \frac{\mu(x_\tau)}{\nu_A(x_\tau)} \leq 2^{8(I+1)/\varepsilon},$$

and thus $\beta_\tau < p_B(x_\tau) \leq 2^{8(I+1)/\varepsilon} \cdot q_A(x_\tau)$, and hence $\tau \in \mathcal{A}$. In fact, τ is the first element in $\mathcal{A} \cap \mathcal{B}$. Note that for each t, $\mathbf{P}[t \in \mathcal{A}] \leq 2^{8(I+1)/\varepsilon}/|\mathcal{U}|$. Thus $\mathbf{E}[|\mathcal{A}|] \leq 2^{8(I+1)/\varepsilon} \cdot 2\ln 1/\varepsilon < 2^{9I/\varepsilon}$. Thus, by Chernoff bound,

$$\mathbf{P}[|\mathcal{A}| > 2^{10I/\varepsilon}] \ll \varepsilon/16.$$

Let the event $\mathcal{E}_1 := [x_\tau \in B_A \cup B_B]$, and $\mathcal{E}_2 := [\tau > T$ or $|\mathcal{A}| > 2^{10I/\varepsilon}$ or $|\mathcal{B}| > 2^{10I/\varepsilon}]$. Then by union bound, setting $\mathcal{E} := \mathcal{E}_1 \cup \mathcal{E}_2$, $\mathbf{P}[\mathcal{E}] < 2 \cdot \varepsilon/8 + 3 \cdot \varepsilon/16 < \varepsilon/2$. The distribution μ' conditioned on on $\neg(\mathcal{E}_1 \cup \mathcal{E}_2)$ satisfies $|\mu' - \mu| < \varepsilon/2$, because it is the distribution μ restricted to the set $\mathcal{U} \setminus (B_A \cup B_B)$ (note that only the restriction by $\neg\mathcal{E}_1$ biases the distribution). We will show a protocol, such that assuming the event $\neg(\mathcal{E}_1 \cup \mathcal{E}_2)$ the parties succeed at outputting the same correct value of x_τ with probability $> 1 - \varepsilon/2$, thus completing the proof.

We have reduced the problem to the problem of finding and outputting the first element in $\mathcal{A} \cap \mathcal{B}$, where $|\mathcal{A}|, |\mathcal{B}| \leq 2^{10I/\varepsilon}$. The communication complexity of the protocol will be $2^{O(1+I/\varepsilon)}$. We note that the protocol can be organized in such a way that only Alice needs to communicate that many bits, while Bob communicates only $O(1 + I/\varepsilon)$ bits.

First note that the number of bits communicated by Alice is bounded by $2^{10I/\varepsilon} \cdot d = 2^{O(1+I/\varepsilon)}$. The number of bits communicated by Bob is bounded by $\log|\mathcal{A}| \leq 10I/\varepsilon$. To see that the protocol works, observe that for $a \in \mathcal{A}$ and $b \in \mathcal{B}$ such that $a \neq b$, the probability (over possible choices of the hash functions) that $h_j(a) = h_j(b)$ for $j = 1..d$ is bounded by $2^{-d} < \frac{\varepsilon}{4|\mathcal{A}|\cdot|\mathcal{B}|}$. Thus, by union bound, the probability that there is an $a \in c\mathcal{A}$, $b \in \mathcal{B}$ such that $a \neq b$ but the hashes match, is bounded by $\varepsilon/4$. Assuming there are no such a and b, and there is a $\tau \in \mathcal{A} \cap \mathcal{B}$, the protocol is guaranteed to find it, completing the proof.

5.2 Information vs. communication

In the language of communication complexity, Lemma 5.2 implies the following:

Theorem 5.3. *Let $f : \mathcal{X} \times \mathcal{Y} \to \mathbb{Z}_K$ be any function, and let $\rho, \varepsilon > 0$ be error parameters:*

1. *For any distribution μ, $D^{\mu}_{\rho+\varepsilon}(f) = 2^{O(1+\mathsf{IC}_\mu(f,\rho)/\varepsilon^2)}$.*
2. *$R_{\rho+\varepsilon}(f) = 2^{O(1+\mathsf{IC}(f,\rho)/\varepsilon^2)}$.*

Theorem 5.3 can be used as a generic (if weak) tool to obtain unconditional lower bounds on the information complexity of problems. For example, the fact that $R_{1/3}(DISJ_n) = \Omega(n)$ immediately implies that $\mathsf{IC}(DISJ_n, 1/6) = \Omega(\log n)$. In section 7 we will see that in fact $\mathsf{IC}(DISJ_n, 1/6) = \Omega(n)$.

Proof. We begin with the first part of the theorem. Let μ be any distribution. Let π be a protocol that realizes the value $I_\mu := \mathsf{IC}_\mu(f, \rho)$. In other words, π has an error rate of at most ρ and information cost of at most I_μ with respect to μ. Denote by π_{xy} the random variable that represents that transcript π given the inputs (x, y), and by π_x (resp. π_y) the protocol conditioned on only the input x (resp. y). We denote by π_{XY} the transcripts where (X, Y) are also a pair of random variables. We know that

$$I_\mu = I(X; \pi_{XY}|Y) + I(Y; \pi_{XY}|X) = \mathbf{E}_{(x,y)\sim\mu}[\mathbf{D}(\pi_{xy}||\pi_x) + \mathbf{D}(\pi_{xy}||\pi_y)].$$

Thus by Markov inequality, with probability at least $1 - \varepsilon/2$ (with respect to μ) we will have $\mathbf{D}(\pi_{xy}||\pi_x) \leq 2I_\mu/\varepsilon$ and $\mathbf{D}(\pi_{xy}||\pi_y) \leq 2I_\mu/\varepsilon$. Let us now run the sampling algorithm from Lemma 5.2. With the distribution μ in Lemma 5.2 taken to be π_{xy}, the distribution ν_A taken to be π_x, the distribution ν_B taken to be π_y, I taken to be $2I_\mu/\varepsilon$, and the error parameter is taken to be $\varepsilon/4$.

At each node v of the protocol tree that is owned by player X let $p_0(v)$ and $p_1(v) = 1 - p_0(v)$ denote the probabilities that the next bit sent by X is 0 and 1, respectively. For nodes owned by player Y, let $q_0(v)$ and $q_1(v) = 1 - q_0(v)$ denote the probabilities that the next bit sent by Y is 0 and

Information-cost only sampling protocol

1. Alice computes the set $\mathcal{A}$. If $|\mathcal{A}| > 2^{10I/\varepsilon}$ the protocol fails.
2. Bob computes the set $\mathcal{B}$. If $|\mathcal{B}| > 2^{10I/\varepsilon}$ the protocol fails.
3. For each $a \in \mathcal{A}$, Alice computes $d = \lceil 20I/\varepsilon + \log 1/\varepsilon + 2\rceil$ random hash values $h_1(a), \ldots, h_d(a)$, where the hash functions are evaluated using public randomness.
4. Alice sends the values $\{h_j(a_i)\}_{a_i \in \mathcal{A},\ 1\le j\le d}$ to Bob.
5. Bob finds the first index i such that there is a $b \in \mathcal{B}$ for which $h_j(b) = h_j(a_i)$ for $j = 1..d$ (if such an i exists). Bob outputs x_b and sends the index i to Alice.
6. Alice outputs x_{a_i}.

Figure 4: The main sampling protocol from Lemma 5.2

1, respectively, *as estimated by player X given the input x*. For each leaf ℓ let $p_X(\ell)$ be the product of all the values of $p_b(v)$ from the nodes that are owned by X along the path from the root to ℓ; let $q_X(\ell)$ be the product of all the values of $q_b(v)$ from the nodes that are owned by Y along the path from the root to ℓ. The values $p_Y(\ell)$ and $q_Y(\ell)$ are defined similarly. For each ℓ we have $\mathbf{P}[\pi_{xy} = \ell] = p_X(\ell) \cdot p_Y(\ell)$, $\mathbf{P}[\pi_x = \ell] = p_X(\ell) \cdot q_X(\ell)$, and $\mathbf{P}[\pi_y = \ell] = p_Y(\ell) \cdot q_Y(\ell)$. Thus we can apply Lemma 5.2, to successfully obtain a sample transcript T such that the statistical distance $|T - \pi_{xy}| < \varepsilon/2$. T is obtained using $2^{O(1+I_\mu/\varepsilon^2)}$ communication. Let T_{out} be the final output of the transcript T, and π_{out} be the final output of the original protocol. $|T - \pi_{xy}| < \varepsilon/2$ implies that $\mathbf{P}[T_{out} \neq \pi_{out}] < \varepsilon/2$.

It remains to bound the error probability of our new protocol. In other words, we need to show that

$$\mathbf{P}_{(x,y)\sim\mu,\text{protocol randomness}}[T_{out} \neq f(x,y)] < \rho + \varepsilon.$$

The protocol above only works for pairs (x, y) where $\mathbf{D}(\pi_{xy}||\pi_x) \le 2I_\mu/\varepsilon$ and $\mathbf{D}(\pi_{xy}||\pi_y) \le 2I_\mu/\varepsilon$. Call such pairs "good". We saw that $\mathbf{P}_{(x,y)\sim\mu}[(x, y) \text{ is good}] > 1-\varepsilon/2$. Thus we have:

$$\begin{aligned}&\mathbf{P}[T_{out} \neq f(x,y)] \le \\ &\quad \mathbf{P}[(x,y) \text{ not good}] + \mathbf{P}[T_{out} \neq \pi_{out}|(x,y) \text{ is good}] \\ &\qquad + \mathbf{P}[\pi_{out} \neq f(x,y)] < \varepsilon/2 + \varepsilon/2 + \rho = \rho + \varepsilon.\end{aligned}$$

To prove the second part of the theorem recall that by Yao's minimax theorem there is a distribution μ such that $D^\mu_{\rho+\varepsilon}(f) = R_{\rho+\varepsilon}(f)$. Since by definition $\mathsf{IC}_\mu(f,\rho) \le \mathsf{IC}(f,\rho)$, we obtain

$$R_{\rho+\varepsilon}(f) = D^\mu_{\rho+\varepsilon}(f) = 2^{O(1+\mathsf{IC}_\mu(f,\rho)/\varepsilon^2)} \le 2^{O(1+\mathsf{IC}(f,\rho)/\varepsilon^2)}.$$

6. INFORMATION COMPLEXITY AND AMORTIZED COMMUNICATION

6.1 Preliminaries: the distributional case

We next turn our attention to the relationship between the information cost of a problem and its amortized communication cost – the communication cost of solving n copies of the problem as n goes to ∞. In [BR11] such a connection has been established for the distributional setting. Here we extend the connection to the distribution-free setting. The extension is very similar to the original proof. In addition, we formulate a more careful statement of the result. This statement may be more useful in applications. For example, it will be useful in one of the proofs establishing the linear lower bound on the information cost of disjointness in Section 7. We will first repeat some definitions and theorems from prior works, before stating our main results.

Let $f : \mathcal{X} \times \mathcal{Y} \to \mathbb{Z}_K$ be any function[2]. The distributional communication cost of k copies of f has been defined in [BR11] as follows:

Definition 6.1. Let μ be a distribution on $\mathcal{X}\times\mathcal{Y}$ and let $0 < \rho < 1$. We denote by $D^{\mu,n}_\rho(f^n)$ the distributional complexity of computing f on each of n independent pairs of inputs drawn from μ, with probability of failure at most ρ on each of the inputs.

Note that trivially $D^{\mu,n}_\rho(f^n) \le n \cdot D^\mu_\rho(f)$ – this can be achieved by just running n copies of the protocol for f independently.

Remark 6.2. In Definition 6.1 we deliberately do not require the n-copy protocol to succeed with probability $1 - \rho$ on *all* n copies. This latter task may be qualitatively more difficult. Consider, for example, a scenario where f and μ are such that $D^\mu_{1/10}(f) \ll D^\mu_{1/100}(f)$. This may happen, for example, if 90% of the input pairs are "very easy", and thus $D^\mu_{1/10}(f)$ is very small, while the remaining 10% are "very hard", and thus $D^\mu_{1/100}(f)$ is very large. Then $D^{\mu,n}_{1/10}(f^n)$ as in Definition 6.1 will still be small. At the same time, computing f correctly on *all* n copies simultaneously (except with probability 10%) would require one so solve a lot of "very hard" instances, and would have a much higher communication complexity that cannot possibly be related to $D^\mu_{1/10}(f)$.

A version of the following theorem, giving a connection between (distributional) information cost and amortized communication complexity was proved in [BYJKS04]. The sharper statement presented below is from [BR11] (cf. also Theorem 4.3 above).

Theorem 6.3. *For every μ, f, ρ there exists a protocol τ computing f on inputs drawn from μ with probability of*

[2]As before, our results also hold for tasks and not just functions.

error at most ρ on each input and communication at most $D^{\mu,n}_\rho(f^n)$ such that $\mathsf{IC}_\mu(\tau) \le \frac{D^{\mu,n}_\rho(f^n)}{n}$, and thus $\mathsf{IC}_\mu(f,\rho) \le \frac{D^{\mu,n}_\rho(f^n)}{n}$.

Thus the amortized communication complexity gives an upper bound on the information cost of the problem. For each fixed n, we do not know whether the inequality in Theorem 6.3 is tight or not, and it probably isn't: for $n = 1$ this is equivalent to the question whether $\mathsf{IC}_\mu(f,\rho) = D^\mu_\rho(f)$ – which remains open. However, in [BR11] it has been shown that *in the limit* the inequality is tight:

Theorem 6.4. *The distributional information cost is equal to amortized communication:*

$$\mathsf{IC}_\mu(f,\rho) = \lim_{n\to\infty} \frac{D^{\mu,n}_\rho(f^n)}{n}.$$

To prove Theorem 6.4 one needs to use a low-information protocol for one copy of f to produce a low-amortized communication cost protocol for n copies, when n is large. The main technical ingredient in the proof is the following protocol compression lemma:

Lemma 6.5. *[BR11] Let (x,y) be inputs to an r-round communication protocol π whose (internal) information cost is $I := \mathsf{IC}_\mu(\pi)$. Then for every $\varepsilon > 0$ there exists a protocol τ such that at the end of the protocol, each party outputs a transcript for π. Furthermore, there is an event G with $\mathbf{P}[G] > 1 - r\varepsilon$ such that conditioned on G, the expected communication of τ is $I + O(\sqrt{rI} + 1) + 2r\log(1/\varepsilon)$, and both parties output the same transcript distributed according to $\pi(x,y)$.*

The lemma is proved in [BR11] using an iterated correlated sampling argument. We will return to some of the proof details in the next section. Our goal will be to establish the analogue of Theorem 6.4 for the randomized communication complexity.

6.2 The non-distributional case

Recall that $R_\rho(f)$ is the randomized communication complexity of f with error ρ. We know, by Yao's minimax theorem that $R_\rho(f) = \max_\mu D^\mu_\rho(f)$. We now give a definition of the randomized communication complexity of n copies of f. It is the distribution-free analogue of Definition 6.1.

Definition 6.6. Let $0 < \rho < 1$. We denote by $R^n_\rho(f^n)$ the randomized communication complexity of computing f so that on each set of n inputs the probability of failure on each of the inputs is at most ρ.

Our main result states that the prior-free information cost of f captures precisely f's amortized communication complexity:

Theorem 6.7. *For $\rho > 0$,*

$$\mathsf{IC}(f,\rho) = \lim_{n\to\infty} \frac{R^n_\rho(f^n)}{n}.$$

Remark 6.8. We note that Theorem 6.7 does not hold when $\rho = 0$, i.e. when the protocol is not allowed to err. Recall (Proposition 3.21) that $\mathsf{IC}(EQ, 0) = O(1)$. At the same time, it is not hard to see that if the function EQ is on the space $\{0,1\}^m \times \{0,1\}^m$ then $R^n_\rho(f^n) = \Omega(m \cdot n)$ and thus the right-hand-side in Theorem 6.7 is $\Omega(m)$. The '$\le$' direction of Theorem 6.7 holds even for $\rho = 0$. The other direction, however, requires the use of compression, such as Lemma 6.5. Such lemmas necessarily introduce a small amount of additional error. For each fixed $\rho > 0$, the additional error introduced can be made negligible, but this does not work for $\rho = 0$.

The proof of Theorem 6.7 will consist of proving inequalities in two directions. We will actually prove a slightly stronger statement in the '$\ge$' direction – showing that low information cost implies low amortized communication complexity. Here is the precise statement that we prove:

Theorem 6.9. *Let $f : X\times Y \to \{0,1\}$, and let $I := \mathsf{IC}(f,\rho)$ then for each $\delta_1, \delta_2 > 0$ there is an $N = N(f,\rho,\delta_1,\delta_2)$ such that for each $n \ge N$ there is a protocol*

$$\pi_n = \pi_n((x_1,\ldots,x_n),(y_1,\ldots,y_n))$$

for computing n instances of f. The protocol π_n will have communication complexity $< n \cdot I \cdot (1+\delta_1)$, and will have error $\lesssim \rho$ on each copy. Moreover, except with probability $< \delta_2$, the protocol errors will behave as if the n evaluations were independent.

More precisely, let $Q : \{0,1\}^n \to \{0,1\}$ be any monotone function. Fix the inputs $(x_1,\ldots,x_n)$, $(y_1,\ldots,y_n)$, let $(f_1,\ldots,f_n) := (f(x_1,y_1),\ldots,f(x_n,y_n))$ and let $(p_1,\ldots,p_n)$ be the random variable representing π_n's output. Let $\mathbf{e} = (e_1,\ldots,e_n)$ be the "errors vector" – $e_i = \chi_{p_i \ne f_i}$. Let $\mathbf{b} = (b_1,\ldots,b_n)$ be a vector of independent Bernoulli variables $b_i \sim B_\rho$. Then

$$\mathbf{P}[Q(\mathbf{e}) = 1] \le \mathbf{P}[Q(\mathbf{b}) = 1] + \delta_2.$$

Clearly, Theorem 6.9 (applied with Q being one coordinate indicator functions) implies that $R^n_{\rho+\delta_2}(f^n) \le n \cdot I \cdot (1+\delta_1)$. Taking $\delta_1 \to 0$ and $n \to \infty$, for each $\delta_2 > 0$ we get:

$$\mathsf{IC}(f,\rho) \ge \lim_{n\to\infty} \frac{R^n_{\rho+\delta_2}(f^n)}{n}.$$

Substituting $\rho - \delta_2$ for ρ we get:

$$\mathsf{IC}(f,\rho-\delta_2) \ge \lim_{n\to\infty} \frac{R^n_\rho(f^n)}{n}.$$

Finally, by the continuity of $\mathsf{IC}(f,\rho)$ in ρ (Corollary 3.19), we have $\mathsf{IC}(f,\rho) = \lim_{\delta_2\to 0} \mathsf{IC}(f,\rho-\delta_2)$, and thus

$$\mathsf{IC}(f,\rho) \ge \lim_{n\to\infty} \frac{R^n_\rho(f^n)}{n},$$

which proves the '$\ge$' direction of Theorem 6.7. It remains to prove the '$\le$' direction of Theorem 6.7 and Theorem 6.9.

Proof Proof of the '$\le$' direction of Theorem 6.7. It follows immediately from Part 2 of Theorem 4.3 that

$$\mathsf{IC}(f,\rho) = \frac{\mathsf{IC}(f^n,\rho)}{n} \le \frac{R^n_\rho(f^n)}{n}.$$

The second inequality holds because the amount of communication is always an upper bound on information cost.

The proof of the other direction of Theorem 6.7, i.e. Theorem 6.9, is unfortunately fairly complicated. It is easier to give a proof of the weaker statement that $\lim_{n\to\infty} \frac{R^n_\rho(f^n)}{n} = O(\mathsf{IC}(f,\rho))$ – if we didn't care to prove that the constant is 1. It would be interesting to see whether this proof can be simplified.

PROOF PROOF OF THEOREM 6.9.. Recall that f is a function on the space $X \times Y$. Let K be such that $|X|, |Y| \leq 2^K$. By the continuity of $\mathsf{IC}(f, \rho)$, there is a $\delta_3 > 0$ such that

$$\mathsf{IC}(f, \rho - \delta_3) < \mathsf{IC}(f, \rho) \cdot (1 + \delta_1/3).$$

By the definition of $\mathsf{IC}(f, \rho - \delta_3)$, there is a protocol π that on each pair of inputs succeeds except with probability $\leq \rho - \delta_3$, and such that for each distribution μ,

$$\mathsf{IC}_\mu(\pi) \leq \mathsf{IC}(f, \rho) \cdot (1 + \delta_1/3).$$

Our overall strategy will be to try and execute n copies of π in a communication-efficient way. We claim that it is possible. Set $\delta_4 := \min(\delta_2, \delta_3)/2$.

Claim 6.10. *For each sufficiently large n there is a protocol π_n that takes n instances of f as an input and has the following properties:*

1. *For each set of inputs, the statistical distance between the output of π_n and the output of π^n (i.e. an execution of n independent copies of π) is $< \delta_4/(2n^2)$.*
2. *The expected communication cost of π_n is $< n \cdot \mathsf{IC}(f, \rho) \cdot (1 + 2\delta_1/3)$.*
3. *The worst case communication cost of π_n is $< 100nK/\delta_1$.*

The bulk of the effort will go into proving Claim 6.10. Assuming Claim 6.10, note that the execution of π_n will be very similar to the execution of π^n. In turn, the errors in the execution of π^n are dominated by n independent Bernoulli random variables $B_{\rho-\delta_3} < B_\rho$, thus almost completing the proof of the theorem.

The reason the proof is not complete is the additional complication stemming from π^n using $< n \cdot \mathsf{IC}(f, \rho) \cdot (1 + 2\delta_1/3)$ communication *in expectation*, while we would like an upper bound on the worst-case communication complexity of f^n. We are able to prove the theorem with n replaced with n^3 by taking n^2 independent copies of π_n. The following claim thus completes the proof of the theorem.

Claim 6.11. *Let Π be the protocol that runs on n^3 pairs of inputs by dividing them into n^2 blocks of n pairs each and running π_n on each block. Further, the protocol Π is truncated (and fails) if it does not terminated after $< n^3 \cdot \mathsf{IC}(f, \rho) \cdot (1 + \delta_1)$ communication. Then for each set of inputs, the statistical distance between the output of Π and the output of π^{n^3} is $< \delta_4$.*

PROOF. Fix a set of n^3 inputs. There are two sources of statistical distance between the output of Π and the output of π^{n^3}: the first one is due to one of the n^2 blocks being different under π_n than under π^n; the second is from the probability that the protocol Π fails altogether by not terminating in the allotted time. The probability of the first event is bounded by $n^2 \cdot \delta_4/(2n^2) = \delta_4/2$. It remains to bound probability of the second event by $\delta_4/2$.

Let T_i for $i = 1, \ldots, n^2$ denote the random variable representing the amount of communication used by the i-th copy of π_n during the execution of Π. Denote $T := \sum_{i=1}^{n^2} T_i$. Our goal is to show that

$$\mathbf{P}\left[T \geq n^3 \cdot \mathsf{IC}(f, \rho) \cdot (1 + \delta_1)\right] < \delta_4/2.$$

We know that T_i are i.i.d., $\mathbf{E}[T_i] < n \cdot \mathsf{IC}(f, \rho) \cdot (1 + 2\delta_1/3)$ and

$$Var(T_i) < \mathbf{E}[T_i] \cdot 100nK/\delta_1 < 200n^2K \cdot \mathsf{IC}(f, \rho)/\delta_1.$$

Hence $\mathbf{E}[T] < n^3 \cdot \mathsf{IC}(f, \rho) \cdot (1 + 2\delta_1/3)$ and $Var(T) < 200n^4K \cdot \mathsf{IC}(f, \rho)/\delta_1$. Thus, by Chebyshev's inequality, we get

$$\begin{aligned}\mathbf{P}\left[T \geq n^3 \cdot \mathsf{IC}(f, \rho) \cdot (1 + \delta_1)\right] &< \\ \mathbf{P}\left[T > \mathbf{E}[T] + n^3 \cdot \mathsf{IC}(f, \rho) \cdot \delta_1/3\right] &< \\ \frac{200n^2K \cdot \mathsf{IC}(f, \rho)/\delta_1}{(n^3 \cdot \mathsf{IC}(f, \rho) \cdot \delta_1/3)^2} &< \delta_4/2,\end{aligned}$$

for a sufficiently large n.

Claim 6.11 implies that for each sufficiently large n,

$$\frac{R^n_\rho(f^{n^3})}{n^3} < \mathsf{IC}(f, \rho) \cdot (1 + \delta_1),$$

and, further, that the other conclusions of Theorem 6.9 hold.

It remains to prove Claim 6.10

PROOF PROOF OF CLAIM 6.10.. We first give a protocol π^n that satisfies the first condition and that has a slightly lower expected communication cost of $< n \cdot \mathsf{IC}(f, \rho) \cdot (1 + 3\delta_1/5)$. We then show how to modify it to satisfy the third condition without increasing the expected communication cost by too much.

Let r be the number of rounds in the protocols π, and let $\alpha > 0$ be a (small) parameter that we will set later. We let $\mathcal{G}$ be the following zero-sum game. The first player M produces a distribution μ on n-tuples of pairs of inputs. The second player T produces a (randomized) protocol τ. The payoff for the first player is the sum

$$P_M(\mu, \tau) := (1 - \alpha) \cdot \frac{\mathbf{E}_{\mathbf{x},\mathbf{y}\sim\mu}|\tau(\mathbf{x}, \mathbf{y})|}{n \cdot I \cdot (1 + \delta_1/2)} + \frac{\mathbf{E}_{\mathbf{x},\mathbf{y}\sim\mu}|\tau(\mathbf{x}, \mathbf{y}) - \pi^n(\mathbf{x}, \mathbf{y})|}{\delta_4/(2n^2)}. \quad (20)$$

Here $|\tau(\mathbf{x}, \mathbf{y})|$ denotes the expected communication cost of τ on inputs $(\mathbf{x}, \mathbf{y})$, and $|\tau(\mathbf{x}, \mathbf{y}) - \pi^n(\mathbf{x}, \mathbf{y})|$ denotes the statistical distance between the two protocols on a given input. We first establish that for any large enough n the value of the game is bounded by 1:

$Val_M(\mathcal{G}) < 1$: Let ν be any mixed strategy for player M. Denote by $\bar{\mu}$ the average distribution in ν: $\bar{\mu}(\mathbf{x}, \mathbf{y}) = \mathbf{E}_{\mu\sim\nu}\mu(\mathbf{x}, \mathbf{y}$ Since the payoff function is calculated in terms of expectations over $(\mathbf{x}, \mathbf{y}) \sim \mu$, for any τ we have:

$$\mathbf{E}_{\mu\sim\nu} P_M(\mu, \tau) = P_M(\bar{\mu}, \tau).$$

Thus it is enough to show that for each distribution μ there is a protocol τ such that $P_M(\mu, \tau) < 1$.

Fix a distribution μ. Let $\mu_1, \ldots, \mu_n$ be the projections of μ onto its n coordinates. As in the proof of the second part of Theorem 4.2, one can see that the information revealed by the protocol π^n that applies π to each copy independently has bounded information cost:

$$\mathsf{IC}_\mu(\pi^n) \leq \sum_{i=1}^n \mathsf{IC}_{\mu_i}(\pi) \leq n \cdot I \cdot (1 + \delta_1/3). \quad (21)$$

Furthermore, as π, the protocol π^n is still an r-round protocol, independently of n. Let

$$\varepsilon := \frac{\alpha \cdot \delta_4}{2n^2 r}.$$

By Lemma 6.5 the protocol π^n can be simulated by a protocol τ so that the expected communication $\mathbf{E}_{\mathbf{x},\mathbf{y}\sim\mu}|\tau(\mathbf{x},\mathbf{y})|$ is bounded by

$$n\cdot I\cdot(1+\delta_1/3)+O(\sqrt{r\cdot n\cdot I\cdot(1+\delta_1/3)}+1)+2r\log(1/\varepsilon) < n\cdot I\cdot(1+\delta_1/2),$$

so that the statistical distance between the execution of π^n and the execution of τ is $< r\cdot\varepsilon$. Putting the pieces together, we get

$$P_M(\mu,\tau) < (1-\alpha)\cdot\frac{n\cdot I\cdot(1+\delta_1/2)}{n\cdot I\cdot(1+\delta_1/2)}+\frac{r\cdot\varepsilon}{\delta_4/(2n^2)} = (1-\alpha)+\alpha = 1.$$

By the Minimax Theorem, there is a distribution ν on protocols τ, such that for each distribution μ, $\mathbf{E}_{\tau\sim\nu}[P_M(\mu,\tau)] < 1$. This implies that the randomized protocol π_n obtained by executing a protocol τ that is distributed according to ν also satisfies $P_M(\mu,\pi_n) < 1$ for all μ. This is in particular true for each singleton $\mu = 1_{(\mathbf{x},\mathbf{y})}$. Let

$$\alpha < 1 - \frac{1+\delta_1/2}{1+3\delta_1/5}.$$

Then for each $(\mathbf{x},\mathbf{y})$, $P_M(1_{(\mathbf{x},\mathbf{y})},\pi_n) < 1$ implies that the statistical distance between the output of π_n and the output of π^n is bounded by

$$P_M(1_{(\mathbf{x},\mathbf{y})},\pi_n)\cdot\frac{\delta_4}{2n^2} < \frac{\delta_4}{2n^2}.$$

At the same time, the expected running time of π_n on $(\mathbf{x},\mathbf{y})$ is bounded by

$$P_M(1_{(\mathbf{x},\mathbf{y})},\pi_n)\cdot\frac{n\cdot I\cdot(1+\delta_1/2)}{1-\alpha} < n\cdot I\cdot(1+3\delta_1/5).$$

To finish the proof, it remains to show how to modify π_n so that its worst-case communication cost is bounded by $100nK/\delta_1$. We modify π_n as follows. We let it run as usual for $80nK/\delta_1$ bits. If the protocol π_n does not terminate in this many steps, the players will use $2nK$ bits of communication to completely exchange their inputs $(\mathbf{x},\mathbf{y})$. They then finish the execution of the protocol π_n using private randomness but without communicating. They can do this since now they can simulate each other's internal state.

The bound on the worst-case communication cost clearly holds. To bound the expected communication, note that by Markov's inequality the probability of the protocol reaching $80nK/\delta_1$ bits of communication is bounded by

$$\frac{\textbf{Expected Communication}}{80nK/\delta_1} < \frac{2nI}{80nK/\delta_1} = \frac{\delta_1 I}{40K}.$$

Thus the additional contribution to the communication cost caused by the modification is bounded by

$$\frac{\delta_1 I}{40K}\cdot(2nK) = \frac{\delta_1 nI}{20}.$$

Overall, the modified protocol has expected communication complexity of less than

$$n\cdot I\cdot(1+3\delta_1/5)+\frac{\delta_1 nI}{20} < n\cdot I\cdot(1+2\delta_1/3),$$

thus still satisfying the second condition.

This concludes the proof of Theorem 6.9.

7. THE INFORMATION COMPLEXITY OF DISJOINTNESS

7.1 A linear lower bound, proof 1: using self-reducibility

Our goal in this section is to prove a linear lower bound on the information complexity of the disjointness function $DISJ_n : \{0,1\}^n \times \{0,1\}^n \to \{0,1\}$ given by

$$DISJ_n((x_1,\dots,x_n),(y_1,\dots,y_n)) := \neg\bigvee_{i=1}^{n}(x_i\wedge y_i).$$

In our first proof, we will rely on the following classical result on the *communication complexity* of $DISJ_n$:

Theorem 7.1. *[KS92, Raz92]* $R_{1/6}(DISJ_n) = \Omega(n)$.

We do not have a general bound that would show that $\mathsf{IC}(DISJ_n,\rho) = \Omega(R_{1/6}(DISJ_n)) = \Omega(n)$ for some constant ρ. However, we are able to exploit the self-similar structure of the disjointness function to prove the linear lower bound directly.

Theorem 7.2. $\mathsf{IC}(DISJ_n, 1/2-\varepsilon) = \Omega(n)$ *for all* $0<\varepsilon<1/2$.

PROOF. (Sketch, we omit a full proof due to space constraints) In the proof we combine theorems 6.9 and 7.1. By Theorem 7.1, we know that $R_{1/6}(DISJ_n) = \Omega(n)$. Let us say $R_{1/6}(DISJ_n) \geq n/50$ to be concrete. Suppose for contradiction that $DISJ_n$ had sublinear information cost. By repeating the protocol for disjointness a constant number of time, we obtain that $\mathsf{IC}(DISJ_n, 1/100) = o(n)$. Next we use the fact (Theorem 6.9) that information is equal to amortized communication to obtain a protocol π_N for N copies of disjointness on n bits each such that the probability of π_N to be wrong on each n-tuple is $< 1/100$. We use π_N to derive a protocol for $DISJ_{n\cdot N}$ by first running π_N (using communication $o(n\cdot N)$), and then only focus on the n-tuples where π_N returned 0 (i.e. which were determined to be non-disjoint). We expect there to be $\sim N/100$ mistakes, so we should expect to go over fewer than $N/75$ n-tuples that were incorrectly classified as non-disjoint before either terminating (and returning 1) or discovering an n-tuple that is not disjoint (and returning 0). Thus the total communication required to solve $DISJ_{n\cdot N}$ would be $< n\cdot N/75 + o(n\cdot N) < n\cdot N/50$, contradicting Theorem 7.1.

8. DIRECTIONS AND OPEN PROBLEMS

In this section we outline some open problems surrounding the interactive information complexity. We group these problems by topic. Some of the problems are very concrete, while others take the form of a potential research direction.

8.1 Properties of the interactive information complexity

The first set of problems has to do with the properties of $\mathsf{IC}(f,\varepsilon)$, and its relationship with other communication complexity measures. First and foremost, we would like to know whether interactive computation can be compressed. In other words, whether the interactive information complexity is equal to the communication complexity of any function:

Problem 1. *Is it true that for all* f, $\mathsf{IC}(f,\varepsilon) = \Omega(R(f,\varepsilon))$*?*

Note that we know that $\mathsf{IC}(f,\varepsilon) \leq R(f,\varepsilon)$. An affirmative answer to Problem 1 would prove a strong direct sum theorem for communication complexity. If would also mean that it is impossible to solve problems that have high communication complexity without violating the (information-theoretic) privacy of the participants' inputs. A negative answer to Problem 1 would give an example of a problem that violate the direct sum conjecture for randomized communication complexity [BR11]. The only general result in the direction of Problem 1 that we have is Theorem 5.3, and it only gives a lower bound of the form $\mathsf{IC}(f,\varepsilon/2) = \Omega(\log R(f,\varepsilon))$ for constant $\varepsilon > 0$.

A less ambitious problem is compressing communication to the *external* information cost of the problem:

Problem 2. *Is it true that for all f, $\mathsf{IC}^{\text{ext}}(f,\varepsilon) = \Omega(R(f,\varepsilon))$?*

As has been observed in [BBCR10], compressing a protocol to the external information cost can be much easier than compressing to the internal information cost. While an affirmative answer to Problem 2 would have no direct-sum implications, it would still mean that any protocol for a distribute function f that has high communication complexity must reveal a lot of information to an observer, and thus cannot be information-theoretically secure.

Also of interest is the relationship between $\mathsf{IC}(f,\varepsilon)$ and other quantities related to the communication complexity of f. One notable problem here is the relationship between the quantum communication complexity $Q(f,\varepsilon)$ and $\mathsf{IC}(f,\varepsilon)$. While we know that there is an exponential gap between $R(f,\varepsilon)$ and $Q(f,\varepsilon)$ [Raz99, KR11], it is not clear whether it carries over to the information complexity.

Problem 3. *What is the relationship between $Q(f,\varepsilon)$ and $\mathsf{IC}(f,\varepsilon)$? In particular are there problems for which $Q(f,\varepsilon) = O(\text{polylog}(\mathsf{IC}(f,\varepsilon)))$?*

Note that answering Problem 1 may provide an answer to Problem 3.

Another interesting problem is whether the log-rank conjecture holds for the interactive information complexity. Such a conjecture would be easier to prove than the regular log-rank conjecture since the information complexity is always bounded by the communication complexity:

Problem 4. *Let $f(x,y)$ be a binary function, and let M_f be the corresponding matrix. Is it true that*

$$\mathsf{IC}(f,0) = O(\text{polylog}\, rank(M_f))?$$

More generally, for any ε, is it the case that

$$\mathsf{IC}(f,\varepsilon) = O(\text{polylog} \min_{\|M-M_f\|_\infty \leq \varepsilon} rank(M))?$$

Finally, we turn our attention to the following surprising problem. Given a truth table of a function f and the error parameter ε, it is not clear how to compute $\mathsf{IC}(f,\varepsilon)$. Indeed, it is not even clear that when viewed as a function, $\mathsf{IC}(f,\varepsilon)$ is computable:

Problem 5. *What is the computational complexity of the problem of evaluating the information complexity of a function f? In other words, given a truth table of $f : \{0,1\}^n \times \{0,1\}^n \to \{0,1\}$, and a rational $\varepsilon \geq 0$, what is the complexity of evaluating $\mathsf{IC}(f,\varepsilon)$? Is this function computable?*

While it is clear that successive estimates of $\mathsf{IC}(f,\varepsilon)$ from above can be constructed by enumerating all two-party protocols, it is not clear how to estimate the rate of convergence of these estimates so as to compute $\mathsf{IC}(f,\varepsilon)$.

8.2 The information complexity of specific problems

To improve our understanding of the information complexity of problems we need to understand which communication complexity techniques can be adapted to the more challenging information setting. This may reveal additional insights about the functions in question, and also help us make progress towards Problem 1 above. Here we mention three specific such problems. The first one is the Gap Hamming Distance problem, that has received much attention recently, and has been shown to have linear communication complexity [CR11, Vid11, She11]. Given two vectors x, y in $\{-1,+1\}^n$, the GHD_n problem is distinguishing between the case when $\langle x,y\rangle > \sqrt{n}$ and the case when $\langle x,y\rangle < -\sqrt{n}$:

Problem 6. *Is it true that $\mathsf{IC}(GHD_n, 1/3) = \Omega(n)$?*

The second problem is closely related to Problem 3 above. The Vector in Subspace Problem (VSP) is the (promise) problem that yields an exponential separation between the one-way quantum and randomized communication complexity given by Klartag and Regev [KR11]. VSP_n is defined as follows. Alice is given a unit vector $u \in \mathbf{R}^n$, and Bob is given a subspace $H \subset \mathbf{R}^n$ of dimension $n/2$ with the promise that either $u \in H$ or $u \in H^\perp$. Their goal is to decide which is the case. [KR11] showed an $\Omega(n^{1/3})$ lower bound for this problem, we ask whether a polynomial lower bound on the information cost of the problem holds.

Problem 7. *Is it true that $\mathsf{IC}(VSP_n, 1/3) = n^{\Omega(1)}$?*

Finally, we turn our attention to the zero-error information cost of concrete functions. The simplest functions to consider are 2-bit functions $f : \{0,1\} \times \{0,1\} \to \{0,1\}$. It is not too difficult to see that the information complexity of the two-bit exclusive-OR function is $\mathsf{IC}(XOR_2, 0) = 2$. We do not know, however, the precise information complexity even for the two-bit AND function AND_2:

Problem 8. *What is the value of $\mathsf{IC}(AND_2, 0)$?*

We know that the value is in the interval $(1,2)$ – in fact, better estimates can be proved – but the precise value is unknown. Note that this value would also give the precise value of the amortized communication complexity of the two-bit AND. In addition, a solution to Problem 8 would probably shed some light on the computability of the information complexity (Problem 5).

8.3 Quantum information complexity

We next turn our attention to directions of interest. These are more open-ended than the problems above, and are less well-posed. The first one has to do with extending interactive information complexity into the quantum communication setting.

Problem 9. *What is the correct quantum analogue of $\mathsf{IC}(f,\varepsilon)$? What is its relationship with the quantum communication complexity? Is it an interesting quantity? In particular, is it always bounded by a constant?*

We note that it is quite possible that the quantum analogue of the interactive information complexity of boolean functions collapses to a constant due to the existence of reversible computing in the quantum world.

8.4 Multiparty information complexity

Perhaps the most natural extension to the present work one should consider is the extension to the communication setting with more than two players. There are several models for (randomized) multiparty communication complexity. They can be broadly split into the number-in-hand and the number-on-the-forehead models.

In the number-in-hand (NIH) model, each of the k players is given an input x_i, and the players need to compute a function $f(x_1, \ldots, x_k)$. The players may be communicating either through a blackboard that is visible to all players, or through private messages, depending on the model. Note that if k is constant, e.g. $k = 3$, then the two settings are equivalent up to a multiplicative constant. The NIH setting is usually very similar to the two-party setting. One communication complexity lower bound technique in this case is to partition the k players into two groups and show that a large number of bits must be exchanged between the two groups. This brings the natural question of extending the interactive information cost to the multiparty NIH setting:

Problem 10. *What is the "right" definition of the multiparty NIH information complexity, and what are its properties?*

It is quite plausible that a straight generalization of the information cost would work. One source of difficulty is that now there are potentially different kinds of "public" randomness – e.g. randomness that is accessible by some but not all players.

The number-on-the-forehead (NOF) model is notoriously more difficult. In this model there are still k players and k inputs $x_1, \ldots, x_k$, but each player i has access to *all* inputs but x_i – as if x_i was written on her forehead. Lower bounds in this model are notoriously more difficult. There is no straightforward reduction to the two-party case. Even the disjointness problem over $[n]$ with fewer than $\log n$ players proves to be a major challenge that has been resolved only recently [CA08, LS09]. Moreover, any explicit lower bound on the multiparty communication complexity in the NOF model with $(\log n)^{\omega(1)}$ players, would yield to superpolynomial circuit lower bounds for the class $\mathbf{ACC^0}$ of bounded-depth circuits with modulo gates [Yao90, BT91, HG90]. Thus proving lower bounds in the NOF model is a well-motivated problem.

Problem 11. *Is there a way to define information complexity in the multiparty NOF model, and what are its properties?*

Note that in this model one has to be particularly careful since, at least when there is randomness-on-the-forehead available, one can design protocols that reveal no information to the participants except for the output of the computation.

8.5 Continuous complexity measures

Finally, we take a higher level view on the relationship between the (two-party) information complexity of problems and their communication complexity. One way to look at $\mathsf{IC}(f,\varepsilon)$ is as a continuous relaxation of the communication complexity $R(f,\varepsilon)$: $\mathsf{IC}(f,\varepsilon) \leq R(f,\varepsilon)$, since communication is always an upper bound of information. On the other hand, as far as we know, $\mathsf{IC}(f,\varepsilon)$ may be smaller than $R(f,\varepsilon)$. The advantage comes from the fact that when considering *information*, each communication round may carry a non-integral amount of information – potentially much smaller than 1 bit. Thus if during the execution of a protocol a bit is sent that is not very "informative", $\mathsf{IC}(\cdot,\cdot)$ will measure the amount of information correctly, while the communication complexity of sending this bit is "rounded" to cost 1. One can argue that if $\mathsf{IC}(\cdot,\cdot)$ has nicer properties than $R(\cdot,\cdot)$ – such as an exact direct sum theorem – it is because $\mathsf{IC}(\cdot,\cdot)$ is non-integral and measures the interaction between the player more accurately.

This raises the open-ended question on whether there are reasonable (and useful) continuous "relaxations" of other classically integral complexity measures.

Problem 12. *Is there a good way to define continuous relaxations of the classically integral complexity measures such as circuit complexity and branching program size?*

Such continuous measures, may potentially lead to lower bounds that are currently obfuscated by the integrality of the complexity measures involved. More broadly, information-theoretic considerations may inspire lower bounds in these models. For example, the derandomization technique in [BRRY10] has been inspired by information-theoretic considerations.

9. REFERENCES

[BBCR10] Boaz Barak, Mark Braverman, Xi Chen, and Anup Rao. How to compress interactive communication. In *Proceedings of the 42nd Annual ACM Symposium on Theory of Computing*, 2010.

[BKV08] Harry Buhrman, Michal Koucký, and Nikolai K. Vereshchagin. Randomised individual communication complexity. In *IEEE Conference on Computational Complexity*, pages 321–331, 2008.

[BKVV07] Harry Buhrman, Hartmut Klauck, Nikolai K. Vereshchagin, and Paul M. B. Vitányi. Individual communication complexity. *J. Comput. Syst. Sci.*, 73(6):973–985, 2007.

[BR11] Mark Braverman and Anup Rao. Information equals amortized communication. *FOCS'11*, abs/1106.3595, 2011.

[BRRY10] Mark Braverman, Anup Rao, Ran Raz, and Amir Yehudayoff. Pseudorandom generators for regular branching programs. In *FOCS*, pages 40–47, 2010.

[BT91] Richard Beigel and Jun Tarui. On acc. In *FOCS*, pages 783–792, 1991.

[BYJKS04] Ziv Bar-Yossef, T. S. Jayram, Ravi Kumar, and D. Sivakumar. An information statistics approach to data stream and communication complexity. *Journal of Computer and System Sciences*, 68(4):702–732, 2004.

[CA08] Arkadev Chattopadhyay and Anil Ada. Multiparty communication complexity of disjointness. *Electronic Colloquium on Computational Complexity (ECCC)*, 15(002), 2008.

[CR11] Amit Chakrabarti and Oded Regev. An optimal lower bound on the communication complexity of gap-hamming-distance. In *STOC*, pages 51–60, 2011.

[CSWY01] Amit Chakrabarti, Yaoyun Shi, Anthony Wirth, and Andrew Yao. Informational complexity and the direct sum problem for simultaneous message complexity. In Bob Werner, editor, *Proceedings of the 42nd Annual IEEE Symposium on Foundations of Computer Science*, pages 270–278, Los Alamitos, CA, October 14–17 2001. IEEE Computer Society.

[CT91] Thomas M. Cover and Joy A. Thomas. *Elements of Information Theory*. Wiley series in telecommunications. J. Wiley and Sons, New York, 1991.

[DW07] M. Dietzfelbinger and H. Wunderlich. A characterization of average case communication complexity. *Information processing letters*, 101(6):245–249, 2007.

[FKNN95] Tomàs Feder, Eyal Kushilevitz, Moni Naor, and Noam Nisan. Amortized communication complexity. *SIAM Journal on Computing*, 24(4):736–750, 1995. Prelim version by Feder, Kushilevitz, Naor FOCS 1991.

[HG90] Johan Håstad and Mikael Goldmann. On the power of small-depth threshold circuits. In *FOCS*, pages 610–618, 1990.

[HJMR07] Prahladh Harsha, Rahul Jain, David A. McAllester, and Jaikumar Radhakrishnan. The communication complexity of correlation. In *IEEE Conference on Computational Complexity*, pages 10–23. IEEE Computer Society, 2007.

[Jai11] Rahul Jain. New strong direct product results in communication complexity. *Electronic Colloquium on Computational Complexity (ECCC)*, 18:24, 2011.

[JKR09] T. S. Jayram, Swastik Kopparty, and Prasad Raghavendra. On the communication complexity of read-once ac^0 formulae. In *IEEE Conference on Computational Complexity*, pages 329–340, 2009.

[JKZ10] Rahul Jain, Hartmut Klauck, and Shengyu Zhang. Depth-independent lower bounds on the communication complexity of read-once boolean formulas. In *COCOON*, pages 54–59, 2010.

[JRS03] Rahul Jain, Jaikumar Radhakrishnan, and Pranab Sen. A direct sum theorem in communication complexity via message compression. In Jos C. M. Baeten, Jan Karel Lenstra, Joachim Parrow, and Gerhard J. Woeginger, editors, *ICALP*, volume 2719 of *Lecture Notes in Computer Science*, pages 300–315. Springer, 2003.

[Kla04] H. Klauck. Quantum and approximate privacy. *Theory of Computing Systems*, 37(1):221–246, 2004.

[Kla10] Hartmut Klauck. A strong direct product theorem for disjointness. In Leonard J. Schulman, editor, *STOC*, pages 77–86. ACM, 2010.

[KN97] Eyal Kushilevitz and Noam Nisan. *Communication complexity*. Cambridge University Press, Cambridge, 1997.

[KR11] Bo'az Klartag and Oded Regev. Quantum one-way communication can be exponentially stronger than classical communication. In *STOC*, pages 31–40, 2011.

[KS92] Bala Kalyanasundaram and Georg Schnitger. The probabilistic communication complexity of set intersection. *SIAM Journal on Discrete Mathematics*, 5(4):545–557, November 1992.

[LS09] Troy Lee and Adi Shraibman. Disjointness is hard in the multiparty number-on-the-forehead model. *Computational Complexity*, 18(2):309–336, 2009.

[LS10] Nikos Leonardos and Michael Saks. Lower bounds on the randomized communication complexity of read-once functions. *Computational Complexity*, 19(2):153–181, 2010.

[MI11] N. Ma and P. Ishwar. Some results on distributed source coding for interactive function computation. *IEEE Transactions on Information Theory*, 57(9):6180, 2011.

[MMP+10] A. McGregor, I. Mironov, T. Pitassi, O. Reingold, K. Talwar, and S. Vadhan. The limits of two-party differential privacy. In *2010 IEEE 51st Annual Symposium on Foundations of Computer Science*, pages 81–90. IEEE, 2010.

[Raz92] Alexander Razborov. On the distributed complexity of disjointness. *TCS: Theoretical Computer Science*, 106, 1992.

[Raz99] Ran Raz. Exponential separation of quantum and classical communication complexity. In *STOC*, pages 358–367, 1999.

[Sha48] Claude E. Shannon. A mathematical theory of communication. *Bell System Technical Journal*, 27, 1948. Monograph B-1598.

[Sha03] Ronen Shaltiel. Towards proving strong direct product theorems. *Computational Complexity*, 12(1-2):1–22, 2003. Prelim version CCC 2001.

[She11] Alexander A. Sherstov. The communication complexity of gap hamming distance. *Electronic Colloquium on Computational Complexity (ECCC)*, 18:63, 2011.

[SW73] David Slepian and Jack K. Wolf. Noiseless coding of correlated information sources. *IEEE Transactions on Information Theory*, 19(4):471–480, July 1973.

[Vid11] Thomas Vidick. A concentration inequality for the overlap of a vector on a large set, with application to the communication complexity of the gap-hamming-distance problem. *Electronic Colloquium on Computational Complexity (ECCC)*, 18:51, 2011.

[Yao90] Andrew Chi-Chih Yao. On acc and threshold circuits. In *FOCS*, pages 619–627, 1990.

The Multiparty Communication Complexity of Set Disjointness

Alexander A. Sherstov*
Computer Science Department
University of California, Los Angeles
Los Angeles, CA 90095
sherstov@cs.ucla.edu

ABSTRACT

We study the set disjointness problem in the number-on-the-forehead model of multiparty communication.

(i) We prove that k-party set disjointness has communication complexity $\Omega(n/4^k)^{1/4}$ in the randomized and nondeterministic models and $\Omega(n/4^k)^{1/8}$ in the Merlin-Arthur model. These lower bounds are close to tight. Previous lower bounds (2007-2008) for $k \geqslant 3$ parties were weaker than $\Omega(n/2^{k^3})^{1/(k+1)}$ in all three models.

(ii) We prove that solving ℓ instances of set disjointness requires $\ell \cdot \Omega(n/4^k)^{1/4}$ bits of communication, even to achieve correctness probability exponentially close to $1/2$. This gives the first direct-product result for multiparty set disjointness, solving an open problem due to Beame, Pitassi, Segerlind, and Wigderson (2005).

(iii) We construct a read-once $\{\wedge, \vee\}$-circuit of depth 3 with exponentially small discrepancy for up to $k \approx \frac{1}{2}\log n$ parties. This result is optimal with respect to depth and solves an open problem due to Beame and Huynh-Ngoc (FOCS '09), who gave a depth-6 construction. Applications to circuit complexity are given.

Categories and Subject Descriptors

F.0 [**Theory of Computation**]: General; F.1.3 [**Computation by Abstract Devices**]: Complexity Measures and Classes.

General Terms

Theory

Keywords

Set disjointness problem, multiparty communication complexity, direct product theorems, circuit complexity

*Supported by NSF CAREER award CCF-1149018.

1. INTRODUCTION

In a seminal paper thirty years ago, Yao [50] introduced the two-party model of communication complexity. In this model, two parties seek to evaluate a function $f(x, y)$ with minimal communication, where the first party knows only x and the second party only y. To capture communication among three or more parties, one considers a function f with several arguments that are somehow distributed among the parties, possibly with overlap. For a model to be meaningful, no party should know *all* the arguments (making communication necessary to evaluate f), and every argument should be known to *some* party (making communication sufficient). The *number-on-the-forehead* model of multiparty communication, due to Chandra, Furst, and Lipton [16], is the most powerful model that obeys these two principles. This model features k parties and a function $f(x_1, x_2, \ldots, x_k)$ with k arguments. The ith party knows all the arguments except for x_i—one can think of x_i as written on the ith party's forehead, hence the name of the model. Communication occurs in broadcast, a bit sent by any given party instantly reaching everyone else. The main research question is whether f has low *communication complexity,* i.e., can be computed by a protocol in which the number of bits communicated is small on every input. We will primarily be interested in *randomized* protocols, which are allowed to err with a small constant probability, as well as *nondeterministic* and *Merlin-Arthur* protocols. The multiparty model is a natural computational model in its own right and has additionally found a variety of applications, including streaming algorithms, circuit complexity, pseudorandomness, and proof complexity [6, 51, 25, 41, 12].

The multiparty model draws its richness from the overlap in the parties' inputs, which makes it challenging to prove lower bounds. For this reason, several fundamental questions in this model remain open despite much research. One such unresolved question is the communication complexity of *set disjointness*, arguably the most studied problem in the area [3, 27, 4, 7, 40, 47, 31, 13, 49, 42, 46, 35, 19, 11, 14, 30]. In the k-party version of set disjointness, the inputs are sets $S_1, S_2, \ldots, S_k \subseteq \{1, 2, \ldots, n\}$, and the ith party knows all the inputs except for S_i. The goal is to determine whether $S_1 \cap S_2 \cap \cdots \cap S_k = \varnothing$. One also studies a promise version of this problem called *unique set disjointness*, in which the input sets $S_1, S_2, \ldots, S_k$ either have empty intersection or intersect in a unique element, i.e., either $|\bigcap S_i| = 0$ or $|\bigcap S_i| = 1$. It is common to represent set disjointness in function form as

$$\mathrm{DISJ}_{n,k}(x_1, x_2, \ldots, x_k) = \bigwedge_{j=1}^{n} \bigvee_{i=1}^{k} \overline{x_{ij}},$$

where the bit strings $x_1, x_2, \ldots, x_k \in \{0, 1\}^n$ are the characteristic vectors of the k sets. Unique set disjointness $\mathrm{UDISJ}_{n,k}$ is represented by an identical formula, with the understanding that the strings $x_1, x_2, \ldots, x_k$ are legal inputs if and only if their bitwise conjunction $x_1 \wedge x_2 \wedge \cdots \wedge x_k$ has at most one nonzero bit. In communication complexity, set disjointness plays a role closely similar to the role of satisfiability in computational complexity. Outside of communication complexity the study of set disjointness is motivated by a number of applications, which we will discuss shortly in the context of our results.

Previous work. In the model with two parties, the communication complexity of set disjointness is thoroughly understood. One of the earliest results in the area is a tight lower bound of $n+1$ bits for deterministic protocols solving set disjointness. For randomized protocols, a lower bound of $\Omega(\sqrt{n})$ was obtained by Babai, Frankl, and Simon [3] and strengthened to a tight $\Omega(n)$ by Kalyanasundaram and Schnitger [27]. Simpler proofs of the linear lower bound were discovered by Razborov [39] and Bar-Yossef et al. [7]. All three proofs [27, 39, 7] of the linear lower bound apply to unique set disjointness. Finally, Razborov [40] obtained a tight lower bound of $\Omega(\sqrt{n})$ on the bounded-error *quantum* communication complexity of set disjointness and unique set disjointness, with a simpler proof discovered several years later in [42]. Already in the two-party model, set disjointness has been a driving force for various technical innovations, including ideas from combinatorics, Kolmogorov complexity, information theory, matrix analysis, and Fourier analysis.

For $k \geqslant 3$ parties, progress on the communication complexity of set disjointness prior to this paper is summarized in Table A. In a surprising result, Grolmusz [24] proved an upper bound of $O(\log^2 n + k^2 n/2^k)$ on the deterministic communication complexity of this problem. Proving a strong lower bound, even for $k = 3$, turned out to be difficult. Tesson [47] and Beame et al. [13] obtained a lower bound of $\Omega\big(\frac{1}{k}\log n\big)$ for randomized protocols. Four years later, Lee and Shraibman [35] and Chattopadhyay and Ada [19] gave an improved result. These authors generalized the two-party method of [43, 42] to $k \geqslant 3$ parties and thereby obtained a lower bound of $\Omega(n/2^{2^k}k)^{1/(k+1)}$ on the randomized communication complexity of set disjointness. The only subsequent work of which we are aware is due to Beame and Huynh-Ngoc [11], who proved a lower bound of $\big(2^{\Omega(\sqrt{k\log n})}/2^{k^2}\big)^{1/(k+1)}$ on the randomized communication complexity. This improves on the previous bound for k sufficiently large. For more than three years now, set disjointness has seen no progress. In what follows, we state the new results of this paper on set disjointness and related questions.

Bound	Reference
$O\left(\frac{k^2 n}{2^k} + \log^2 n\right)$	[24]
$\Omega\left(\frac{\log n}{k}\right)$	[47, 13]
$\Omega\left(\frac{n}{2^{2^k}k}\right)^{1/(k+1)}$	[35, 19]
$\Omega\left(\frac{2^{\Omega(\sqrt{k\log n})}}{2^{k^2}}\right)^{1/(k+1)}$	[11]
$\Omega\left(\frac{n}{4^k}\right)^{1/4}$	This paper

Table A: Bounds for the randomized number-on-the-forehead communication complexity of set disjointness for $k \geqslant 3$ parties.

Randomized communication complexity of set disjointness. To summarize Table A, lower bounds on the k-party communication complexity of set disjointness prior to this paper, both deterministic and randomized, were weaker than $\Omega(n/2^{k^3})^{1/(k+1)}$. In particular, no polynomial lower bounds were known for $k = \omega(1)$ parties. Our first result is the following theorem, where R_ϵ denotes randomized communication complexity with error probability ϵ.

THEOREM 1.1. *Set disjointness and unique set disjointness have randomized communication complexity*

$$R_{1/3}(\mathrm{DISJ}_{n,k}) \geqslant R_{1/3}(\mathrm{UDISJ}_{n,k}) = \Omega\Big(\frac{n}{4^k}\Big)^{1/4}.$$

Theorem 1.1 comes close to matching Grolmusz's longstanding upper bound and shows in particular that the randomized communication complexity of set disjointness remains polynomial for up to $k \approx \frac{1}{2}\log n$ parties. This is representative of the state of the art in multiparty communication complexity in general: no explicit function $F\colon (\{0,1\}^n)^k \to \{0,1\}$ is currently known with nontrivial communication complexity for $k \geqslant \log n$ parties. Theorem 1.1 subsumes all previous multiparty lower bounds, with a strict improvement starting at $k = 4$. Finally, several restrictions of the number-on-the-forehead model have been considered [4, 47, 13, 49, 14, 30], including simultaneous message passing, one-way protocols, and certain intermediate models. The strongest communication lower bound [47, 13] in these restricted models was $\Omega(n/k^k)^{1/(k-1)}$, which is already weaker than Theorem 1.1 starting at $k = 6$.

XOR lemmas and direct product theorems. A natural question to ask of any computational model is how the resources needed to solve ℓ instances of a problem scale with ℓ. Suppose that solving a single instance of a given decision problem, with probability of correctness $2/3$, requires R units of a computational resource (such as time, memory, communication, or queries). How many units of the resource are needed to solve ℓ independent instances of the problem? Common sense suggests that the answer should be $\Omega(\ell R)$. After all, having less than $\epsilon\ell R$ units overall, for a small constant $\epsilon > 0$, leaves less than ϵR units per instance, intuitively forcing the algorithm to guess random answers for many of the instances and resulting in overall correctness probability $2^{-\Theta(\ell)}$. Such a statement is called a *strong direct product theorem*. A related notion is an *XOR lemma*, which asserts that computing the XOR of the answers to the ℓ problem instances requires $\Omega(\ell R)$ resources, even to achieve correctness probability $\frac{1}{2} + 2^{-\Theta(\ell)}$. While intuitively satisfying, XOR lemmas and strong direct product theorems are hard to prove and sometimes simply not true.

In communication complexity, the direct-product question has been studied for over twenty years. We refer the interested reader to [30, 45] for an up-to-date overview of the literature, focusing here exclusively on set disjointness. The direct-product question for *two-party* set disjointness has been resolved completely and definitively [31, 13, 14, 26, 30, 45], including classical one-way protocols [26], classical two-way protocols [13, 30], quantum one-way protocols [14], and quantum two-way protocols [31, 45]. Starting at $k = 3$, however, we are not aware of direct-product results of any kind for set disjointness. In fact, obtaining such a result was posed as an open problem by Beame et al. [13, p. 426]. We prove a direct-product result for up to $k \approx \frac{1}{2}\log n$ parties.

THEOREM 1.2. *The following tasks require $\ell \cdot \Omega(n/4^k)^{1/4}$ bits of communication each:*

(i) *computing the XOR of ℓ independent instances of unique set disjointness* $\text{UDISJ}_{n,k}$ *with probability of correctness $\frac{1}{2} + 2^{-\Theta(\ell)}$;*

(ii) *solving with probability $2^{-\epsilon\ell}$ at least $(1-\epsilon)\ell$ among ℓ instances of unique set disjointness* $\text{UDISJ}_{n,k}$, *where $\epsilon > 0$ is a small enough constant.*

Clearly, this result also holds for set disjointness, a communication problem harder than $\text{UDISJ}_{n,k}$. Theorem 1.2 generalizes Theorem 1.1, showing that $\Omega(n/4^k)^{1/4}$ is in fact a lower bound on the per-instance cost of set disjointness. Note that by (ii), this lower bound remains valid if the protocol only needs to solve a $1-\epsilon$ fraction of the given ℓ instances, rather than all ℓ. Results of this type are known as *threshold direct product theorems.*

Nondeterministic and Merlin-Arthur communication. Nondeterministic communication is a natural counterpart to determinism and randomization. Analogous to computational complexity, a nondeterministic protocol starts with a guess string, whose length counts toward the protocol's communication cost, and proceeds deterministically thenceforth. A nondeterministic protocol for a given communication problem F is required to output the correct answer for *all* guess strings when $F = 0$, and for *some* guess string when $F = 1$. Observe that the complement of set disjointness has a highly efficient nondeterministic protocol. Indeed, it suffices to guess an element $i \in \{1, 2, \ldots, n\}$ and verify with two bits of communication that $i \in S_1 \cap S_2 \cap \cdots \cap S_k$. We show that set disjointness, unlike its complement, has high nondeterministic complexity.

THEOREM 1.3. *Set disjointness has nondeterministic communication complexity*

$$N(\text{DISJ}_{n,k}) = \Omega\left(\frac{n}{4^k}\right)^{1/4}.$$

The best previous lower bound [23] on the nondeterministic complexity of set disjointness was $(n/2^{2^k}k)^{\Omega(1/k)}$.

We further consider *Merlin-Arthur* protocols [2, 5], a communication model that combines the power of randomization and nondeterminism. As before, a Merlin-Arthur protocol for a given problem F starts with a guess string, whose length counts toward the communication cost. From then on, the parties run an ordinary randomized protocol. The randomized phase in a Merlin-Arthur protocol must produce the correct answer with probability $2/3$ for *all* guess strings when $F = 0$ and for *some* guess string when $F = 1$. We prove that set disjointness has high Merlin-Arthur complexity, denoted *MA*:

THEOREM 1.4. *Set disjointness has Merlin-Arthur communication complexity*

$$MA(\text{DISJ}_{n,k}) = \Omega\left(\frac{n}{4^k}\right)^{1/8}.$$

Theorem 1.4 can be viewed as a generalization of Theorems 1.1 and 1.3 on randomized and nondeterministic communication, respectively. These lower bounds are close to optimal, in view of Grolmusz's deterministic upper bound. As with nondeterminism, the best previous lower bound [23] on the Merlin-Arthur complexity of set disjointness was $(n/2^{2^k}k)^{\Omega(1/k)}$.

Theorems 1.1, 1.3, and 1.4 shed new light on communication complexity classes, defined in the seminal work of Babai, Frankl, and Simon [3]. An infinite family of functions $\{F_n\}_{n=1}^{\infty}$, where each $F_n: (\{0,1\}^n)^k \to \{0,1\}$ is a k-party number-on-the-forehead communication problem, is considered to be efficiently solvable by a given class of protocols if F_n has communication complexity at most $\log^c n$, for a large enough constant $c > 1$ and all $n > c$. This convention allows one to define BPP_k, NP_k, coNP_k, and MA_k as the classes of families with efficient randomized, nondeterministic, co-nondeterministic, and Merlin-Arthur protocols, respectively. In recent years, the relationships among these classes have been almost fully determined [9, 35, 19, 22, 11, 10, 23]. It particular, for $k \leqslant \Theta(\log n)$, it is known [10, 23] that coNP_k is not contained in BPP_k, NP_k, or even MA_k. As a corollary to Theorem 1.4, we show that coNP_k can be separated from all these classes by a particularly simple function, set disjointness.

COROLLARY. *For $k \leqslant (\frac{1}{2}-\epsilon)\log n$, where $\epsilon > 0$ is any constant,*

$$\text{DISJ}_{n,k} \in \mathsf{coNP}_k \setminus \mathsf{BPP}_k,$$
$$\text{DISJ}_{n,k} \in \mathsf{coNP}_k \setminus \mathsf{NP}_k,$$
$$\text{DISJ}_{n,k} \in \mathsf{coNP}_k \setminus \mathsf{MA}_k.$$

Prior to this paper, the separation $\text{DISJ}_{n,k} \in \mathsf{coNP}_k \setminus \mathsf{BPP}_k$ was known to hold for up to $k \leqslant \Theta(\log^{1/3} n)$ parties [11], with a much weaker lower bound on randomized communication complexity (see Table A). The other two separations were known to hold for up to $k \leqslant \Theta(\log\log n)$ parties [23], again with a much weaker lower bound on nondeterministic and Merlin-Arthur communication complexity.

Discrepancy and circuit complexity. Theorem 1.1 rules out an efficient protocol that solves set disjointness with correctness probability $\frac{2}{3}$. However, for any number of parties k, set disjointness has a simple and efficient protocol with nonnegligible correctness probability, $\frac{1}{2} + n^{-\Theta(1)}$. In fact, such a protocol exists not just for set disjointness but any function computable by a polynomial-size $\{\wedge, \vee, \neg\}$-circuit of depth 2, regardless of how the bits are assigned to the parties. We show that this phenomenon is special to depth 2, by constructing a read-once $\{\wedge, \vee\}$-circuit of depth 3 whose communication complexity remains high even for correctness probability exponentially close to $\frac{1}{2}$.

THEOREM 1.5. *There is a k-party communication problem $H_{n,k}: (\{0,1\}^n)^k \to \{0,1\}$, given by an explicit read-once $\{\wedge, \vee\}$-formula of depth 3, such that solving $H_{n,k}$ with correctness probability $\frac{1}{2} + \exp(-\Omega(n/4^k)^{1/7})$ requires $\Omega(n/4^k)^{1/7}$ bits of communication.*

To use a technical term, Theorem 1.5 shows that depth-3 circuits have exponentially small *discrepancy* for up to $k \approx \frac{1}{2}\log n$ parties, i.e., exponentially small correlation with low-cost communication protocols. As we mentioned in the previous paragraph, Theorem 1.5 is optimal with respect to circuit depth. It is also qualitatively optimal with respect to the number of parties k: by the results in [1, 25], every polynomial-size $\{\wedge, \vee, \neg\}$-circuit of constant depth admits a $\log^c n$-party protocol with communication $\log^c n$ and correctness probability $\frac{1}{2} + 2^{-\log^c n}$, where $c > 1$ is a suitably large constant. Theorem 1.5 solves an open problem posed by Beame and Huynh-Ngoc [11], who constructed a similarly hard depth-6 formula and asked whether the depth can be reduced. The communication lower bound in Theorem 1.5 is stronger than in [11], where a lower bound of $\Omega(n/2^{31k})^{1/29}$ bits is derived for correctness probability $\frac{1}{2} + \exp(-\Omega(n/2^{31k})^{1/29})$.

Theorem 1.5 has applications to circuit complexity, which we now pause to explain. Circuits of majority gates are a biologically inspired computational model whose study spans several decades and several disciplines. Research has shown that majority circuits of depth 3 already are surprisingly powerful. In particular, Allender [1] proved that depth-3 majority circuits of quasipolynomial size can simulate all of AC^0, the class of $\{\wedge, \vee, \neg\}$-circuits of constant depth and polynomial size. Yao [51] further proved that depth-3 majority circuits of quasipolynomial size can simulate all of ACC, the class of $\{\wedge, \vee, \neg, \text{mod } m\}$-circuits of constant depth and polynomial size for an arbitrary but fixed modulus m. For several years, it was open whether these simulations are optimal. Håstad and Goldmann [25] showed that Yao's simulation of ACC is optimal with respect to *circuit depth*, by exhibiting a function in ACC whose simulation by a depth-2 majority circuit requires exponential size. The analogous question for AC^0 remained open [32]. It was solved several years ago in [42, 43], where an AC^0 function was constructed whose simulation by depth-2 majority circuits requires exponential size. The simulations of Allender [1] and Yao [51] were thus shown to be optimal with respect to circuit depth.

Another natural parameter to study is the *fan-in* of a circuit's bottom gates. The simulations of Allender [1] and Yao [51] had bottom fan-in $\log^{O(1)} n$. The paper of Håstad and Goldmann [25] showed that this fan-in is not far from optimal, in that simulating ACC by a depth-3 majority circuit with bottom fan-in $\approx \frac{1}{2}\log n$ requires exponentially many gates. The analogous question for AC^0 was considered by Chattopadhyay [17], who generalized the method of [42, 43] to show that depth-3 majority circuits with constant bottom fan-in require exponentially many gates to simulate AC^0. More recently, Beame and Huynh-Ngoc [11] proved an analogous result for bottom fan-in $\approx \frac{1}{31}\log n$. It was thus shown that the simulations of Allender [1] and Yao [51] are close to optimal in bottom fan-in.

Function	Circuit lower bound	Reference
$\bigoplus_{j=1}^{n} \bigwedge_{i=1}^{k+1} x_{ij}$	$\exp\left(\frac{1}{k} \cdot \Omega\left(\frac{n}{4^k}\right)\right)$	[25]
read-once depth-3 $\{\wedge, \vee\}$-formula	$\exp\left(\Omega\left(n^{1/3}\right)\right)$ for $k = 1$	[42, 43]
depth-3 $\{\wedge, \vee\}$-formula	$\exp\left(\Omega\left(n^{\frac{1}{6k2^k}}\right)\right)$	[17]
read-once depth-6 $\{\wedge, \vee\}$-formula	$\exp\left(\frac{1}{k} \cdot \Omega\left(\frac{n}{2^{31k}}\right)^{1/29}\right)$	[11]
read-once depth-3 $\{\wedge, \vee\}$-formula	$\exp\left(\frac{1}{k} \cdot \Omega\left(\frac{n}{4^k}\right)^{1/7}\right)$	This paper

Table B: Lower bounds for computing functions in ACC and AC^0 by circuits of type MAJ ∘ SYMM ∘ ANY with bottom fan-in k. All functions are on $n(k+1)$ bits.

The lower bounds surveyed in the previous paragraphs [25, 42, 43, 17, 11] apply not only to majority circuits but all circuits of type MAJ ∘ SYMM ∘ ANY (with a majority gate at the top, arbitrary symmetric gates at the middle level, and arbitrary gates at the bottom). This line of research is summarized in Table B, with quantitative detail. Theorem 1.5 in this paper implies the following new lower bound.

THEOREM 1.6. *Let* $H_{n,k} : (\{0,1\}^n)^k \to \{0,1\}$ *be the depth-3 read-once* $\{\wedge, \vee\}$*-formula constructed in Theorem* 1.5. *Then every circuit of type* MAJ ∘ SYMM ∘ ANY *with bottom fan-in at most k that computes* $H_{n,k+1}$ *has size*

$$\exp\left(\frac{1}{k} \cdot \Omega\left(\frac{n}{4^k}\right)^{1/7}\right).$$

As Table B shows, Theorem 1.6 improves on previous AC^0 constructions [17, 11] with respect to all parameters: the function is simpler than those considered previously, whereas the circuit lower bound is stronger and applies to MAJ ∘ SYMM ∘ ANY circuits with larger fan-in. In particular, the construction in Theorem 1.6 has optimal depth because $\{\wedge, \vee\}$-circuits of depth 2 are clearly computable by MAJ ∘ SYMM circuits of the same size.

Using the method of random restrictions, Razborov and Wigderson [41] discovered a way to convert lower bounds for MAJ ∘ SYMM ∘ ANY circuits with restricted fan-in into lower bounds for MAJ ∘ SYMM ∘ AND without any fan-in restrictions. Using that technique, we obtain the following consequence of Theorem 1.6.

THEOREM 1.7. *Every circuit of type* MAJ ∘ SYMM ∘ AND *that computes the function*

$$x \mapsto \bigvee_{i=1}^{n} \bigwedge_{j=1}^{n} \bigvee_{k=1}^{\log n} \bigoplus_{\ell=1}^{\log^2 n} x_{i,j,k,\ell}$$

has size $n^{\Omega(\log \log n)}$.

Again, Theorem 1.7 improves on previous work [11], where the same lower bound was derived for a more complicated, depth-8 AC^0 function.

Additional results and generalizations. Theorem 1.1 on the randomized communication complexity of set disjointness and Theorem 1.2 on the direct product phenomenon are proved here in greater generality. Specifically, our results apply to any k-party communication problem of the form $F = f(\text{UDISJ}_{r,k}, \text{UDISJ}_{r,k}, \ldots, \text{UDISJ}_{r,k})$, i.e., an arbitrary Boolean function f composed componentwise with independent instances of the k-party set disjointness problem on a small number of variables r. We bound the ϵ-error randomized complexity of F from below in terms of the ϵ-*approximate degree* of f, defined as the least degree of a real polynomial that approximates f within ϵ pointwise. The approximate degree is a thoroughly studied quantity, with tight estimates known for various ϵ and various functions of interest to us. By taking $\epsilon = 1/3$, we derive lower bounds for bounded-error communication, including the lower bound for set disjointness (f = AND). Letting $\epsilon \nearrow 1/2$, we obtain lower bounds for protocols with error exponentially close to random guessing, including the discrepancy result for constant-depth circuits.

In the setting of bounded-error communication, we are further able to give a near-optimal lower bound on the k-party communication complexity of every composition of the form $f(\text{OR}_k \vee \text{AND}_k, \ldots, \text{OR}_k \vee \text{AND}_k)$, where f is an arbitrary Boolean function. The same holds for XOR lemmas and direct-product theorems. Finally, in this introduction and throughout the paper, we focus on randomized communication in the context of *classical* multiparty protocols; however, by the results of [34, 15], our randomized lower bounds carry over in full to the quantum model. We defer formal statements of the quantum multiparty lower bounds and background on quantum multiparty protocols to the final version of this paper.

Previous analyses. In a precise technical sense, our approach to set disjointness is the opposite of previous multiparty analyses [17, 35, 19, 21, 22, 11]. In the overview that follows, we describe the limitations of previous analyses and how this paper overcomes them. Let $F: (\{0,1\}^n)^k \to \{0,1\}$ be a given k-party communication problem. A fundamental fact [6] in communication complexity is that a cost-c deterministic protocol for F gives a representation $F = \chi_1 + \chi_2 + \cdots + \chi_{2^c}$, where the χ_i are highly structured Boolean functions called *cylinder intersections*. This fact immediately generalizes to randomized communication since a cost-c randomized protocol is a probability distribution on cost-c deterministic protocols. Specifically, a cost-c randomized protocol for F gives a representation $F \approx \sum_\chi a_\chi \chi$, where the sum is over cylinder intersections and $\sum |a_\chi| \leqslant 2^c$. Accordingly, proofs of high communication complexity typically work by bounding the *correlations* of a relevant function with cylinder intersections. The simplest such technique is the *discrepancy method* [20, 6, 33], whereby one carefully chooses a probability distribution μ on the domain $(\{0,1\}^n)^k$ and argues that F has small correlation under μ with all cylinder intersections. This property of F is referred to as *small discrepancy* with respect to μ, hence the name of the technique. A more powerful technique is the *generalized discrepancy method* [28, 40], whereby one constructs a real function Ψ such that Ψ is highly correlated with F but almost uncorrelated with cylinder intersections.

Even in the two-party setting, it is difficult to construct the right μ or Ψ and analyze the associated correlations. To illustrate, it was an open problem until recently whether AC^0 circuits have small two-party discrepancy with respect to some distribution. This problem was solved in considerable generality four years ago in [43, 42]. The technique developed in that work, called the *pattern matrix method*, automates the choice of μ and Ψ as well as the subsequent analysis of correlations for a class of communication problems. The communication problems F to which the pattern matrix method applies are of the following form. Let $f: \{0,1\}^m \to \{0,1\}$ be a given function, fixed once and for all. In the two-party model, the first party receives a bit string $x \in \{0,1\}^n$ where $n \gg m$, the second party receives a subset $S \subset \{1, 2, \ldots, n\}$ of cardinality m, and their goal is to compute $F(x, S) = f(x|_S)$. For any f, the pattern matrix method uses the approximate degree of f to construct the desired μ and Ψ. This results in a lower bound of $\Omega(\deg_\epsilon(f))$ on the ϵ-error randomized communication complexity, where $\deg_\epsilon(f)$ denotes the ϵ-approximate degree of f.

Originally formulated in [43, 42] for the two-party model, the pattern matrix method has been adapted to three or more parties by several authors [17, 35, 19, 21, 22, 11], resulting among other things in improved multiparty lower bounds for set disjointness. Analogous to the two-party setting, one starts with a Boolean function $f: \{0,1\}^m \to \{0,1\}$. In the case of k parties, the inputs to the communication problem are Boolean strings $x, y_1, y_2, \ldots, y_{k-1}$ and the goal is to compute the function $F(x, y_1, y_2, \ldots, y_{k-1}) = f(x|_{S(y_1, y_2, \ldots, y_{k-1})})$, where the *selector* $S(y_1, y_2, \ldots, y_{k-1})$ is some mapping into cardinality-m subsets. In other words, in the multiparty setting, the bit strings $y_1, y_2, \ldots, y_{k-1}$ jointly determine to which bits f is to be applied. What fundamentally differentiates the various multiparty extensions of the pattern matrix method [17, 35, 19, 21, 22, 11] is the definition of the selector. The simpler the selector, the more widely applicable the communication lower bounds—and the harder they are to prove. Arguably the simplest meaningful selector is a small CNF or DNF formula. This is the selector used in the original two-party pattern matrix method [43, 42] as well as its first multiparty adaptations [17, 35, 19]. This selector is desirable in that it embeds nicely in the disjointness function and thus directly gives communication lower bounds for this problem. While the simple selector works well for $k = 2$ parties, the situation changes qualitatively at $k = 3$, and the multiparty lower bounds degrade rapidly with k. In the case of set disjointness, one obtains a lower bound of $\Omega(\sqrt{n})$ for $k = 2$ parties [42] and $\Omega(n/2^{2^k k})^{1/(k+1)}$ for $k \geqslant 3$ parties [35, 19]. At the other extreme, one can use the most complicated selector possible, namely, a random mapping. This is the approach taken in [21]. The communication lower bounds for the random selector remain very strong up to $k \approx \log n$ parties, which is excellent. The problem here is that the random selector cannot be computed by a small circuit, let alone a small CNF formula, and thus the communication lower bounds do not apply to set disjointness. Finally, selectors of intermediate complexity were considered in [22, 11], using bounded independence and XOR gates. These ideas were fruitful, giving an explicit separation of NP_k and BPP_k in communication [22] and strong multiparty lower bounds for constant-depth circuits [11]. However, a strong lower bound for set disjointness has remained off-limits—the above approaches have not yielded a bound better than $\Omega(n/2^{k^3})^{1/(k+1)}$ for the problem.

At a technical level, previous approaches to multiparty set disjointness face the following fundamental difficulty. Recall that the goal in multiparty lower bounds is to bound correlations of relevant functions with cylinder intersections. For the past twenty-two years [6], the maximum correlation of a given real function $\Psi(x, y_1, \ldots, y_{k-1})$ with a cylinder intersection is bounded in terms of the expected product of various subfunctions of Ψ. Concretely, one bounds the correlation in terms of the quantity

$$\Delta(\Psi) = \left(\mathop{\mathbf{E}}_{y_1', y_1''} \mathop{\mathbf{E}}_{y_2', y_2''} \cdots \mathop{\mathbf{E}}_{y_{k-1}', y_{k-1}''} \left| \mathop{\mathbf{E}}_{x} \left[\prod_{z \in \{\prime, \prime\prime\}^{k-1}} \Psi(x, y_1^{z_1}, y_2^{z_2}, \ldots, y_{k-1}^{z_{k-1}}) \right] \right| \right)^{1/2^{k-1}}.$$

In the pattern matrix method, the relevant function is of the form $\Psi(x, y_1, y_2, \ldots, y_{k-1}) = \psi(x|_{S(y_1, \ldots, y_{k-1})})$, where the Fourier coefficients of ψ of low order are zero. This Fourier-theoretic fact is what allows one to bound $\Delta(\Psi)$. Specifically, previous papers—starting with the original two-party work [43, 42]—argue that the 2^{k-1}-fold product will likely have 0 for the constant Fourier coefficient and thus zero expectation. To handle the unlikely complementary event, one needs to additionally control the growth of the 2^{k-1}-fold product. As the number of parties k grows, this argument requires an increasingly complex selector.

Our proof. Our proof *reverses* the steps in the above argument: we first apply the Fourier-theoretic property and then the correlation bound. In more detail, we first write ψ in terms of its Fourier expansion $\psi = \sum_A \hat{\psi}(A) \chi_A$, where χ_A denotes a character of the Fourier transform. We then observe that by linearity, the correlation of Ψ with a cylinder intersection is bounded by $\sum_A |\hat{\psi}(A)| \Delta(\chi_A)$.

From then on, we work with the quantities $\Delta(\chi_A)$, whereas previous multiparty papers work directly with $\Delta(\psi)$. Intuitively, the switch from an arbitrary real function ψ to χ_A is motivated by the convenient multiplicative structure of the characters and their global boundedness.

This leaves us with the challenge of proving a strong upper bound on $\Delta(\chi_A)$ with a selector as weak as a small CNF formula. Prior to this paper, it was unclear whether it could be done at all, let alone how to do it. Indeed, the "reverse" argument has been widely known to researchers since 2007; it was introduced as a refinement [42] of the two-party pattern matrix method and as part of another duality-based technique [46]. Previous attempts to use the reverse argument in multiparty communication were unsuccessful. In particular, it was shown in [18, p. 189] that its direct application gives a lower bound worse than $(n/k^k)^{1/(2+k2^k)}$ on the $(k+1)$-party communication complexity of set disjointness, which is substantially weaker than the lower bound obtained by following the steps of the pattern matrix method in the original order [35, 19].

We are nevertheless able to prove a strong, essentially exact upper bound on $\Delta(\chi_A)$ for a selector which is computable by a small CNF formula and thus efficiently embeds in the disjointness function. This part of the proof exploits *metric* properties of distributions induced by set disjointness on the Boolean cube (such as conditional independence), as opposed to the *Fourier-theoretic* content of previous work. Specifically, we use conditioning to make appropriate variables independent and thereby simulate XOR-like behavior with an OR gate. This simulation is of course only approximate, and the bounding of error terms is done via a different careful conditioning. The argument proceeds by induction on the number of parties, the base case admitting a first-principles solution.

Once $\Delta(\chi_A)$ has been bounded, we are in a strong position to prove Theorem 1.1 and its generalization to arbitrary compositions and arbitrary error rates. To be more precise, we give two alternate proofs of this result. One proof is based, like previous work [43, 42, 46, 17, 35, 19, 21, 22, 11], on the dual view of the problem. The other proof is quite different and works with the primal view, explicitly converting a low-cost protocol for a given communication problem into a low-degree approximant for the given Boolean function. In addition to being more intuitive, the primal approach allows us to prove the direct product theorems and XOR lemmas for set disjointness (Theorem 1.2), by reducing them to a corresponding direct product theorem and XOR lemma for polynomial approximation and appealing to known results in that setting [45].

Once Theorem 1.1 has been established, we are able to use it almost like a black box to obtain Theorems 1.3 and 1.4 on nondeterministic and Merlin-Arthur communication. Specifically, we are able to apply an earlier argument for these models, due to Gavinsky and the author [23], using the new randomized lower bound of Theorem 1.1 in place of earlier bounds.

2. PRELIMINARIES

In the remainder of this paper, we will view Boolean functions as mappings $f\colon X \to \{-1,+1\}$ for some finite set X, where -1 and $+1$ correspond to "true" and "false," respectively. A *partial function* f on a set X is a function whose domain of definition, denoted $\operatorname{dom} f$, is a proper subset of X. For emphasis, we will sometimes refer to functions with $\operatorname{dom} f = X$ as *total*. We use lowercase letters (x, y, u, v) for vectors and Boolean strings, and uppercase letters (A, B, X, Y) for real and Boolean matrices. The empty string is denoted ε. The complement of a set S is denoted $\overline{S}$.

For a bit string $x \in \{0,1\}^n$, we let $|x| = x_1 + x_2 + \cdots + x_n$. The componentwise conjunction of $x, y \in \{0,1\}^n$ is denoted $x \wedge y = (x_1 \wedge y_1, \ldots, x_n \wedge y_n)$. In particular, $|x \wedge y|$ refers to the number of components in which x and y both have a 1. The bitwise negation of a string $x \in \{0,1\}^n$ is denoted $\overline{x} = (1-x_1, \ldots, 1-x_n)$. For a string $x = (x_1, \ldots, x_n)$ and a set $S \subseteq \{1, 2, \ldots, n\}$, we adopt the shorthand $x|_S = (x_{i_1}, x_{i_2}, \ldots, x_{i_{|S|}})$, where $i_1 < i_2 < \cdots < i_{|S|}$ are the elements of S. For convenience, we adopt the convention that $0/0 = 0$. The symbol $\doteq$ means "equal by definition." The indicator function of an event E is given by

$$\mathbf{I}[E] = \begin{cases} 1 & \text{if } E \text{ holds}, \\ 0 & \text{otherwise}. \end{cases}$$

The set membership sign $\in$, when used in the subscript of an expectation operator, means that the expectation is taken over a uniformly random member of the indicated set. The uniform distribution on $\{0,1\}^n$ is denoted $\mathscr{U}_n$. The notation $\log x$ refers to the logarithm of x to base 2. For a real function ϕ on a finite set X, the *support* of ϕ is the subset $\operatorname{supp}\phi = \{x \in X : \phi(x) \neq 0\}$. For probability distributions μ and λ on finite sets X and Y, respectively, the symbol $\mu \times \lambda$ refers to the probability distribution on $X \times Y$ given by $(\mu \times \lambda)(x, y) = \mu(x)\lambda(y)$. The total degree of a multivariate real polynomial p is denoted $\deg p$. For (possibly partial) Boolean functions f and g on $\{-1,+1\}^n$ and X, respectively, the symbol $f \circ g$ refers to the (possibly partial) Boolean function on X^n given by $(f \circ g)(x_1, x_2, \ldots, x_n) = f(g(x_1), g(x_2), \ldots, g(x_n))$. Clearly, the domain of $f \circ g$ is the set of all $(x_1, x_2, \ldots, x_n) \in (\operatorname{dom} g)^n$ for which $(g(x_1), g(x_2), \ldots, g(x_n)) \in \operatorname{dom} f$.

The symbol $\{0,1\}^{n \times k}$ denotes the family of $n \times k$ matrices with entries 0, 1. The notation $(\{0,1\}^n)^k$ refers to the set of vector sequences $(x_1, x_2, \ldots, x_k)$, where each $x_i \in \{0,1\}^n$. Throughout this paper, we identify the sets $\{0,1\}^{n \times k}$ and $(\{0,1\}^n)^k$. This means that $(x_1, x_2, \ldots, x_k)$ can be viewed both as a sequence of vectors in $\{0,1\}^n$ and as a matrix of size $n \times k$ with columns $x_1, x_2, \ldots, x_k$. Taking this convention a step further, we view $(X_1, X_2, \ldots, X_r)$ as an element of $(\{0,1\}^n)^{k_1+\cdots+k_r} \equiv \{0,1\}^{n \times (k_1+\cdots+k_r)}$ whenever $X_i \in \{0,1\}^{n \times k_i}$ $(i = 1, 2, \ldots, r)$.

For $X \in \{0,1\}^{n \times k}$, the *disjointness predicate* $D(X) \in \{-1,+1\}$ is defined as $D(X) = -1$ if and only if each row of X has a 0 entry. By the convention of the previous paragraph, this also gives meaning to the symbols $D(X_1, X_2, \ldots, X_r)$ and $D(x_1, x_2, \ldots, x_k)$, where $X_i \in \{0,1\}^{n \times k_i}$ and $x_i \in \{0,1\}^n$. For example,

$$D(x_1, x_2, \ldots, x_k) = \begin{cases} -1 & \text{if } x_1 \wedge x_2 \wedge \cdots \wedge x_k = 0^n, \\ 1 & \text{otherwise}. \end{cases}$$

By convention, $D(\varepsilon) = -1$.

For a Boolean matrix $X = [X_{i,j}] \in \{0,1\}^{n \times k}$ and a string $y \in \{0,1\}^n$, we let $X|_y$ denote the submatrix of X obtained by keeping only those rows i for which $y_i = 1$. More formally,

$$X|_y = \begin{bmatrix} X_{i_1,1} & X_{i_1,2} & \cdots & X_{i_1,k} \\ X_{i_2,1} & X_{i_2,2} & \cdots & X_{i_2,k} \\ \vdots & \vdots & \ddots & \vdots \\ X_{i_{|y|},1} & X_{i_{|y|},2} & \cdots & X_{i_{|y|},k} \end{bmatrix},$$

where $i_1 < i_2 < \cdots < i_{|y|}$ are the indices with $y_{i_1} = y_{i_2} = \cdots = y_{i_{|y|}} = 1$. In particular, $X|_{0^n} = \varepsilon$. It is useful to keep in mind that $D(X, y) \equiv D(X|_y)$.

The familiar functions AND_n, OR_n, and PARITY_n on the hypercube $\{-1,+1\}^n$ are given as usual by $\mathrm{AND}_n(x) = \bigwedge_{i=1}^n x_i$, $\mathrm{OR}_n(x) = \bigvee_{i=1}^n x_i$, and $\mathrm{PARITY}_n(x) = \bigoplus_{i=1}^n x_i$. We also define a partial Boolean function $\widetilde{\mathrm{AND}}_n$ on $\{-1,+1\}^n$ as the restriction of AND_n to the set $\{x : |\{i : x_i = -1\}| \geqslant n-1\}$:

$$\widetilde{\text{AND}}_n(x) = \begin{cases} \text{AND}_n(x) & \text{if } |\{i : x_i = -1\}| \geqslant n-1, \\ \text{undefined} & \text{otherwise.} \end{cases}$$

Similarly, we define a partial Boolean function $\widetilde{\text{OR}}_n$ on $\{-1,+1\}^n$ as the restriction of OR_n to the set $\{x : |\{i : x_i = -1\}| \leqslant 1\}$.

Norms and products. For a finite set X, the linear space of real functions on X is denoted $\mathbb{R}^X$. This space is equipped with the usual norms and inner product: $\|\phi\|_\infty = \max_{x\in X} |\phi(x)|$, $\|\phi\|_1 = \sum_{x\in X} |\phi(x)|$, and $\langle \phi, \psi\rangle = \sum_{x\in X} \phi(x)\psi(x)$ for $\phi, \psi \in \mathbb{R}^X$. The tensor product of $\phi \in \mathbb{R}^X$ and $\psi \in \mathbb{R}^Y$ is the function $\phi\otimes\psi \in \mathbb{R}^{X\times Y}$ given by $(\phi\otimes\psi)(x,y) = \phi(x)\psi(y)$. The tensor product $\phi\otimes\phi\otimes\cdots\otimes\phi$ (n times) is abbreviated $\phi^{\otimes n}$. When specialized to real matrices, the tensor product is the usual Kronecker product. The *pointwise*, or *Hadamard*, product of $\phi, \psi \in \mathbb{R}^X$ is denoted $\phi\circ\psi \in \mathbb{R}^X$ and given by $(\phi\circ\psi)(x) = \phi(x)\psi(x)$. Note that as functions, $\phi\circ\psi$ is a restriction of $\phi\otimes\psi$. Tensor product notation generalizes to partial functions in the natural way: if ϕ and ψ are partial real functions on X and Y, respectively, then $\phi\otimes\psi$ is a partial function on $X\times Y$ with domain $\text{dom}\,\phi\times\text{dom}\,\psi$ and is given by $(\phi\otimes\psi)(x,y) = \phi(x)\psi(y)$ on that domain. Similarly, $\phi^{\otimes n} = \phi\otimes\phi\otimes\cdots\otimes\phi$ (n times) is a partial function on X^n with domain $(\text{dom}\,\phi)^n$.

The *spectral norm* of a real matrix A is given by the formula $\|A\| = \max_{x\neq 0} \|Ax\|_2/\|x\|_2$, where $\|\cdot\|_2$ stands for the Euclidean norm on vectors. The spectral norm is multiplicative with respect to tensor product: $\|A\otimes B\| = \|A\|\,\|B\|$.

Fourier transform. Consider the real vector space of functions $\{-1,+1\}^n \to \mathbb{R}$. For $S \subseteq \{1,2,\ldots,n\}$, define $\chi_S\colon\{-1,+1\}^n \to \{-1,+1\}$ by $\chi_S(x) = \prod_{i\in S} x_i$. Then every $\phi\colon\{-1,+1\}^n \to \mathbb{R}$ has a unique representation of the form $\phi = \sum_S \hat\phi(S)\,\chi_S$, where $\hat\phi(S) = 2^{-n}\sum_{x\in\{-1,+1\}^n} \phi(x)\chi_S(x)$. The reals $\hat\phi(S)$ are called the *Fourier coefficients of* ϕ. The following fact is immediate:

PROPOSITION 2.1. *For all* $\phi\colon\{-1,+1\}^n \to \mathbb{R}$,

$$\max_{S\subseteq\{1,2,\ldots,n\}} |\hat\phi(S)| \leqslant 2^{-n}\|\phi\|_1.$$

Approximation by polynomials. Let $\phi\colon X \to \mathbb{R}$ be given, for finite $X \subset \mathbb{R}^n$. The ϵ*-approximate degree* of ϕ, denoted $\deg_\epsilon(\phi)$, is the smallest degree of a real polynomial p such that $\|\phi - p\|_\infty \leqslant \epsilon$. We extend this definition to partial functions ϕ on X by letting $\deg_\epsilon(\phi)$ be the least degree of a real polynomial p with

$$\left.\begin{array}{ll} |\phi(x) - p(x)| \leqslant \epsilon, & x \in \text{dom}\,\phi, \\ |p(x)| \leqslant 1+\epsilon, & x \in X\setminus\text{dom}\,\phi. \end{array}\right\} \qquad (2.1)$$

For a (possibly partial) real function ϕ on a finite subset $X \subset \mathbb{R}^n$, we define $E(\phi, d)$ to be the least ϵ such that (2.1) holds for some polynomial of degree at most d. In this notation, $\deg_\epsilon(\phi) = \min\{d : E(\phi,d) \leqslant \epsilon\}$. We will need the following dual characterization of the approximate degree, which follows from linear programming duality [45, 42].

FACT 2.2. *Let* ϕ *be a (possibly partial) real function on* $\{-1,+1\}^n$. *Then* $\deg_\epsilon(\phi) > d$ *if and only if there exists* $\psi\colon\{-1,+1\}^n \to \mathbb{R}$ *with* $\hat\psi(S) = 0$ *for* $|S| \leqslant d$ *and*

$$\sum_{x\in\text{dom}\,\phi} \phi(x)\psi(x) - \sum_{x\notin\text{dom}\,\phi} |\psi(x)| - \epsilon\|\psi\|_1 > 0.$$

A related notion is the *threshold degree* $\deg_\pm(f)$, defined for a (possibly partial) Boolean function f as the limit $\deg_\pm(f) = \lim_{\epsilon\searrow 0} \deg_{1-\epsilon}(f)$. Equivalently, $\deg_\pm(f)$ is the least degree of a real polynomial p with $f(x) = \text{sgn}\,p(x)$ for $x \in \text{dom}\,f$. We recall two well-known results on the polynomial approximation of Boolean functions, the first due to Minsky and Papert [37] and the second due to Nisan and Szegedy [38].

THEOREM 2.3 (Minsky and Papert). $\text{MP}_n(x) = \bigvee_{i=1}^n \bigwedge_{j=1}^{4n^2} x_{ij}$ *satisfies* $\deg_\pm(\text{MP}_n) = n$.

THEOREM 2.4 (Nisan and Szegedy). *The functions* AND_n, $\widetilde{\text{AND}}_n$ *satisfy* $\deg_{1/3}(\text{AND}_n) \geqslant \deg_{1/3}(\widetilde{\text{AND}}_n) = \Theta(\sqrt{n})$.

Multiparty communication. An excellent reference on communication complexity is the monograph by Kushilevitz and Nisan [33]. In this overview, we will limit ourselves to key definitions and notation. The simplest model of communication in this work is the two-party randomized model. Consider a (possibly partial) Boolean function F on $X\times Y$, where X and Y are finite sets. Alice receives an input $x \in X$, Bob receives $y \in Y$, and their objective is to compute $F(x,y)$ with high accuracy whenever $(x,y) \in \text{dom}\,F$. To this end, Alice and Bob share a communication channel and have an unlimited supply of shared random bits. Alice and Bob's protocol is said to have *error* ϵ if on every input $(x,y) \in \text{dom}\,F$, the computed output differs from the correct answer $F(x,y)$ with probability no greater than ϵ. The *cost* of a given protocol is the maximum number of bits exchanged on any input. The ϵ*-error randomized communication complexity* of F, denoted $R_\epsilon(F)$, is the least cost of an ϵ-error protocol for F. The canonical quantity to study is $R_{1/3}(F)$, where the choice of $1/3$ is largely arbitrary since the error probability of a protocol can be decreased from $1/3$ to any other positive constant at the expense of increasing the communication cost by a constant factor.

A generalization of two-party communication is the *multiparty number-on-the-forehead* model, due to Chandra, Furst, and Lipton [16]. Here one considers a (possibly partial) Boolean function F on $X_1\times X_2\times\cdots\times X_k$, for some finite sets $X_1, X_2, \ldots, X_k$. There are k parties. A given input $(x_1, x_2, \ldots, x_k) \in X_1\times X_2\times\cdots\times X_k$ is distributed among the parties by placing x_i on the forehead of party i (for $i = 1, 2, \ldots, k$). In other words, party i knows $x_1, \ldots, x_{i-1}, x_{i+1}, \ldots, x_k$ but not x_i. The parties communicate by writing bits on a shared blackboard, visible to all. They additionally have access to a shared source of random bits. Their goal is to devise a communication protocol that will allow them to accurately predict the value of F everywhere on the domain of F. As before, an ϵ-error protocol for F is one which, on every input $(x_1, x_2, \ldots, x_k) \in \text{dom}\,F$, produces the correct answer $F(x_1, x_2, \ldots, x_k)$ with probability at least $1-\epsilon$. The *cost* of a communication protocol is the total number of bits written to the blackboard on the worst-case input. Analogous to the two-party case, the randomized communication complexity $R_\epsilon(F)$ is the least cost of an ϵ-error communication protocol for F in this model.

Let G be a (possibly partial) Boolean function on $X_1\times X_2\times\cdots\times X_k$, representing a k-party communication problem, and let f be a (possibly partial) Boolean function on $\{-1,+1\}^n$. We view the composition $f\circ G$ as a k-party communication problem on $X_1^n\times X_2^n\times\cdots\times X_k^n$. The primary problem of interest to us is *set disjointness* $\text{DISJ}_{n,k}\colon(\{0,1\}^n)^k \to \{-1,+1\}$, given by the formula $\text{DISJ}_{n,k}(x_1, x_2, \ldots, x_k) = D(x_1, x_2, \ldots, x_k)$. We will also consider the partial Boolean function $\text{UDISJ}_{n,k}$ on $(\{0,1\}^n)^k$

given by: $\text{UDISJ}_{n,k}(x_1, x_2, \dots, x_n) = D(x_1, x_2, \dots, x_n)$ when $|x_1 \wedge x_2 \wedge \cdots \wedge x_k| \leqslant 1$, and undefined otherwise. The k-party communication problem that corresponds to $\text{UDISJ}_{n,k}$ is known as *unique set disjointness*. In other words, unique set disjointness is a promise version of set disjointness, the promise being that the input matrix $(x_1, x_2, \dots, x_k) \in \{0,1\}^{n \times k}$ has at most one row consisting entirely of ones. It will be helpful to keep in mind that for all positive integers r, s, one has $\text{DISJ}_{rs,k} = \text{AND}_r \circ \text{DISJ}_{s,k}$ and analogously $\text{UDISJ}_{rs,k} = \widetilde{\text{AND}}_r \circ \text{UDISJ}_{s,k}$.

A k-dimensional *cylinder intersection* is a function $\chi: X_1 \times X_2 \times \cdots \times X_k \to \{0,1\}$ of the form

$$\chi(x_1, \dots, x_k) = \prod_{i=1}^{k} \chi_i(x_1, \dots, x_{i-1}, x_{i+1}, \dots, x_k),$$

where $\chi_i: X_1 \times \cdots \times X_{i-1} \times X_{i+1} \times \cdots \times X_k \to \{0,1\}$. In other words, a k-dimensional cylinder intersection is the product of k functions with range $\{0,1\}$, where the ith function does not depend on the ith coordinate but may depend in an arbitrary way on the other $k-1$ coordinates. Cylinder intersections were introduced by Babai, Nisan, and Szegedy [6] and play a fundamental role in the theory due to the following fact.

FACT 2.5. *Let $\Pi: X_1 \times X_2 \times \cdots \times X_k \to \{-1,+1\}$ be a deterministic k-party communication protocol with cost c. Then $\Pi = \sum_{i=1}^{2^c} a_i \chi_i$ for some cylinder intersections $\chi_1, \dots, \chi_{2^c}$ with pairwise disjoint support and some $a_1, \dots, a_{2^c} \in \{-1,+1\}$.*

Recall that a randomized protocol with cost c is a probability distribution on deterministic protocols of cost c. Therefore, Fact 2.5 immediately implies the following two results on randomized communication complexity.

COROLLARY 2.6. *Let F be a (possibly partial) Boolean function on $X_1 \times X_2 \times \cdots \times X_k$. If $R_\epsilon(F) = c$, then*

$$|F(x) - \Pi(x)| \leqslant \frac{\epsilon}{1-\epsilon}, \qquad x \in \operatorname{dom} F,$$

$$|\Pi(x)| \leqslant \frac{1}{1-\epsilon}, \qquad x \in X_1 \times \cdots \times X_k,$$

where $\Pi = \sum_\chi a_\chi \chi$ is a linear combination of cylinder intersections with $\sum_\chi |a_\chi| \leqslant 2^c/(1-\epsilon)$.

COROLLARY 2.7. *Let Π be a randomized k-party protocol with domain $X_1 \times X_2 \times \cdots \times X_k$. If Π has communication cost c bits, then*

$$\mathbf{P}[\Pi(x_1, x_2, \dots, x_k) = -1] \equiv \sum_\chi a_\chi \chi(x_1, x_2, \dots, x_k)$$

on $X_1 \times X_2 \times \cdots \times X_k$, where the sum is over cylinder intersections and $\sum_\chi |a_\chi| \leqslant 2^c$.

Discrepancy and generalized discrepancy. For a communication problem $F: X_1 \times X_2 \times \cdots \times X_k \to \{-1,+1\}$ and a probability distribution P on $X_1 \times X_2 \times \cdots \times X_k$, the *discrepancy* of F with respect to P is defined as $\operatorname{disc}_P(F) = \max_\chi |\langle F \circ P, \chi \rangle|$, where the maximum is over cylinder intersections. We generalize this definition to partial functions as follows: for a partial Boolean function F on $X_1 \times X_2 \times \cdots \times X_k$ and a probability distribution P on $X_1 \times X_2 \times \cdots \times X_k$,

$$\operatorname{disc}_P(F) = \sum_{x \notin \operatorname{dom} F} P(x) + \max_\chi \left| \sum_{x \in \operatorname{dom} F} F(x)P(x)\chi(x) \right|,$$

where the maximum is again over cylinder intersections; this agrees with the previous definition if $\operatorname{dom} F = X_1 \times X_2 \times \cdots \times X_k$. The least discrepancy over all distributions is denoted $\operatorname{disc}(F) = \min_P \operatorname{disc}_P(F)$. Estimating the discrepancy is difficult and represents a central obstacle in multiparty communication complexity. In two-party communication, the following method is frequently useful.

PROPOSITION 2.8 (see Kushilevitz and Nisan [33]). *Fix a function $F: X \times Y \to \{-1,+1\}$ and probability distribution P on $X \times Y$. Define $\Phi \doteq [F(x,y)P(x,y)]_{x \in X, y \in Y}$. Then*

$$\operatorname{disc}_P(F) \leqslant \|\Phi\| \sqrt{|X|\,|Y|}.$$

As Fact 2.5 suggests, upper bounds on the discrepancy give lower bounds on communication complexity. This technique is known as the *discrepancy method*. The original treatment of the discrepancy method [20, 6, 33] was specialized to total Boolean functions. In the theorem that follows, we extend the method to partial functions.

THEOREM 2.9 (Discrepancy method). *Let F be a (possibly partial) Boolean function on $X_1 \times X_2 \times \cdots \times X_k$. Then*

$$2^{R_\epsilon(F)} \geqslant \frac{1-2\epsilon}{\operatorname{disc}(F)}.$$

PROOF (based on [33, pp. 36–38]). Fix any probability distribution P such that $\operatorname{disc}(F) = \operatorname{disc}_P(F)$. The distribution P' induced by P on $\operatorname{dom} F$ satisfies $\operatorname{disc}_{P'}(F) \leqslant \operatorname{disc}_P(F)$. Thus, we may assume that $\operatorname{supp} P \subseteq \operatorname{dom} F$ to start with.

Now, suppose that F has a communication protocol with error ϵ and cost c. Approximate F uniformly by $\Pi = \sum_\chi a_\chi \chi$ as in Corollary 2.6. Then

$$\sum_{\operatorname{dom} F} (F(x) - \Pi(x))F(x)P(x) \leqslant \left(\max_{\operatorname{dom} F} |F(x) - \Pi(x)| \right) \sum_{\operatorname{dom} F} P(x) \leqslant \frac{\epsilon}{1-\epsilon}.$$

On the other hand,

$$\begin{aligned}\sum_{\operatorname{dom} F} (F(x) - \Pi(x))F(x)P(x) &= \sum_{\operatorname{dom} F} P(x) - \sum_{\operatorname{dom} F} \Pi(x)F(x)P(x) \\ &\geqslant 1 - \sum_\chi |a_\chi| \left| \sum_{\operatorname{dom} F} \chi(x)F(x)P(x) \right| \\ &\geqslant 1 - \frac{2^c}{1-\epsilon} \operatorname{disc}_P(F).\end{aligned}$$

The claimed lower bound on 2^c follows. ∎

A more general technique, originally applied by Klauck [28] in the two-party quantum model and subsequently adapted to many other settings [40, 36, 42, 35, 19], is the *generalized discrepancy method*. Again, previous treatments focused on total Boolean functions. In what follows, we derive a version of the method that applies to partial functions as well.

THEOREM 2.10 (Generalized discrepancy method). *Let F be a (possibly partial) Boolean function on $X_1 \times X_2 \times \cdots \times X_k$. Then for every nonzero $\Psi: X_1 \times X_2 \times \cdots \times X_k \to \mathbb{R}$,*

$$2^{R_\epsilon(F)} \geqslant \frac{1-\epsilon}{\max_\chi |\langle \chi, \Psi\rangle|} \times \times \left\{ \sum_{x\in \operatorname{dom} F} F(x)\Psi(x) - \sum_{x\notin \operatorname{dom} F} |\Psi(x)| - \frac{\epsilon}{1-\epsilon}\|\Psi\|_1 \right\},$$

where the maximum is over cylinder intersections χ.

PROOF. (Based on [40, 42, 35, 19]). Suppose that F has a communication protocol with error ϵ and cost c. Extend F to a total function $G: X_1 \times \cdots \times X_k \to \mathbb{R}$ by letting $G = 0$ outside dom F. By Corollary 2.6, there is a linear combination of cylinder intersections $\Pi = \sum_\chi a_\chi \chi$ such that $\sum_\chi |a_\chi| \leqslant 2^c/(1-\epsilon)$ and Π approximates F in the sense that $\|\Pi\|_\infty \leqslant 1/(1-\epsilon)$ and $|F - \Pi| \leqslant \epsilon/(1-\epsilon)$ on the domain of F. It follows that

$$\langle G - \Pi, \Psi\rangle \leqslant \frac{\epsilon}{1-\epsilon} \sum_{x\in \operatorname{dom} F} |\Psi(x)| + \frac{1}{1-\epsilon} \sum_{x\notin \operatorname{dom} F} |\Psi(x)|.$$

However,

$$\langle G - \Pi, \Psi\rangle \geqslant \sum_{x\in \operatorname{dom} F} F(x)\Psi(x) - \sum_\chi |a_\chi|\,|\langle \Psi, \chi\rangle|$$
$$\geqslant \sum_{x\in \operatorname{dom} F} F(x)\Psi(x) - \frac{2^c}{1-\epsilon} \max_\chi |\langle \Psi, \chi\rangle|.$$

Comparing these two estimates of $\langle G - \Pi, \Psi\rangle$ gives the claimed lower bound on 2^c. □

3. PREPARATORY WORK

For positive integers n, k, we let $\mu_{n,k}$ denote the uniform probability distribution on those matrices in $\{0,1\}^{n\times k}$ that have exactly one row composed of all ones. Thus $\mu_{n,k}$ is supported on $n(2^k-1)^{n-1}$ matrices, each occurring with the same probability. For a Boolean matrix $Y = (y_1, \ldots, y_{k-1}) \in \{0,1\}^{n\times(k-1)}$, we consider the marginal probability distribution

$$\mu_{n,k}(Y) \doteq \sum_{u\in\{0,1\}^n} \mu_{n,k}(Y,u)$$
$$= \frac{|y_1 \wedge \cdots \wedge y_{k-1}|\, 2^{n - |y_1\wedge\cdots\wedge y_{k-1}|}}{n(2^k-1)^{n-1}}, \qquad (3.1)$$

and the conditional probability

$$\mu_{n,k}(u \mid Y) \doteq \frac{\mu_{n,k}(Y,u)}{\mu_{n,k}(Y)}. \qquad (3.2)$$

Note that the argument to $\mu_{n,k}$ is a matrix of size either $n\times k$ or $n\times(k-1)$, depending on the meaning intended. Finally, we let $\lambda_{n,k}$ be the probability distribution on $\{0,1\}^{n\times(k-1)} \times \{0,1\}^n \times \{0,1\}^n$ given by $\lambda_{n,k}(Y,u,v) \doteq \mu_{n,k}(Y)\,\mu_{n,k}(u \mid Y)\,\mu_{n,k}(v \mid Y)$. In other words, $\lambda_{n,k}$ corresponds to an experiment whereby one first chooses Y according to the marginal distribution (3.1) and then, given Y, chooses u and v independently according to the conditional distribution (3.2). The remainder of this section is devoted to establishing various metric properties of $\lambda_{n,k}$. The four lemmas that follow, Lemmas 3.1–3.4, are independent and can be read in any order. We alert the reader that we will refer to the distributions $\mu_{n,k}$ and $\lambda_{n,k}$ in later sections as well, without restating the definitions just given.

LEMMA 3.1 (On decomposition). *For each (Y,u,v) in the support of $\lambda_{n,k}$ and each $x \in \{0,1\}^n$,*

$$D(x,Y,u)D(x,Y,v) = \begin{cases} D(x,Y,u\wedge\overline{v})D(x,Y,\overline{u}\wedge v) & \text{if } D(Y,u,v) = -1,\\ 1 & \text{otherwise.}\end{cases}$$

PROOF. By definition of $\lambda_{n,k}$, there is exactly one coordinate, call it i, where u and the columns of Y all have a 1. Analogously, there is exactly one coordinate, call it j, where v and the columns of Y all have a 1. If $D(Y,u,v) = 1$, it follows that $i = j$ and hence $D(x,Y,u)D(x,Y,v) = (-1)^{x_i + x_j} = 1$. If $D(Y,u,v) = -1$, we have

$$D(x,Y,u) = D(x,Y,u,v) \wedge D(x,Y,u,\overline{v}) = D(x,Y,u,\overline{v}),$$
$$D(x,Y,v) = D(x,Y,u,v) \wedge D(x,Y,\overline{u},v) = D(x,Y,\overline{u},v),$$

whence $D(x,Y,u)D(x,Y,v) = D(x,Y,u,\overline{v})D(x,Y,\overline{u},v)$. □

LEMMA 3.2 (On conditional independence). *Let $(Y,u,v) \sim \lambda_{n,k}$. Conditioned on fixed values of u, v, $Y|_{u\wedge v}$, and $Y|_{\overline{u}\wedge\overline{v}}$ such that $D(Y|_{u\wedge v}) = -1$, the remaining parts $Y|_{u\wedge\overline{v}}$ and $Y|_{\overline{u}\wedge v}$ are independent and distributed according to $\mu_{|u\wedge\overline{v}|,k-1}$ and $\mu_{|\overline{u}\wedge v|,k-1}$, respectively.*

PROOF. Put $Y = (y_1, \ldots, y_{k-1})$. By (3.1) and (3.2), the support of $\lambda_{n,k}$ consists of tuples (Y,u,v) with

$$|y_1 \wedge \cdots \wedge y_{k-1} \wedge u| = |y_1 \wedge \cdots \wedge y_{k-1} \wedge v| = 1, \qquad (3.3)$$

each such tuple with probability

$$\lambda_{n,k}(Y,u,v) = \frac{2^{|y_1\wedge\cdots\wedge y_{k-1}|}}{n(2^k-1)^{n-1}2^n\,|y_1 \wedge \cdots \wedge y_{k-1}|}. \qquad (3.4)$$

Now fix values of u, v, $Y|_{u\wedge v}$, and $Y|_{\overline{u}\wedge\overline{v}}$ such that $D(Y|_{u\wedge v}) = -1$. We are to determine the conditional distribution of the remaining variables $Y|_{u\wedge\overline{v}}$ and $Y|_{\overline{u}\wedge v}$. It follows from (3.3) that each of these two matrices will have exactly one row made up entirely of ones. But by (3.4), any such assignment to $Y|_{u\wedge\overline{v}}$ and $Y|_{\overline{u}\wedge v}$ carries the same probability. Hence, $Y|_{u\wedge\overline{v}}$ and $Y|_{\overline{u}\wedge v}$ are independent and have the claimed distributions. □

LEMMA 3.3 (On expected intersection size). *For $\lambda_{n,k}$ defined above,*

$$\mathop{\mathbf{E}}_{\lambda_{n,k}}\left[\frac{\mathbf{I}[D(Y,u,v) = -1]}{\sqrt{|u\wedge\overline{v}|\,|\overline{u}\wedge v|}}\right] \leqslant \frac{4}{n}\cdot\frac{2^k-1}{2^k-2}.$$

PROOF. By convexity,

$$\frac{1}{\sqrt{|u\wedge\overline{v}|\,|\overline{u}\wedge v|}} \leqslant \frac{1}{2|u\wedge\overline{v}|} + \frac{1}{2|\overline{u}\wedge v|}.$$

It is clear by symmetry that the strings $u\wedge\overline{v}$ and $\overline{u}\wedge v$ have identical distributions, leading to

$$\mathop{\mathbf{E}}_{\lambda_{n,k}}\left[\frac{\mathbf{I}[D(Y,u,v) = -1]}{\sqrt{|u\wedge\overline{v}|\,|\overline{u}\wedge v|}}\right] \leqslant \mathop{\mathbf{E}}_{\lambda_{n,k}}\left[\frac{\mathbf{I}[D(Y,u,v) = -1]}{|u\wedge\overline{v}|}\right]. \qquad (3.5)$$

Let $y_1, \ldots, y_{k-1}$ denote the columns of Y. Recall that $|y_1 \wedge \cdots \wedge y_{k-1} \wedge u| = 1$ on the support of $\lambda_{n,k}$, whence by symmetry the right member of (3.5) is unchanged after conditioning on $y_1 \wedge \cdots \wedge y_{k-1} \wedge u = 0^{n-1}1$. But then the first $n-1$ bits of $u\wedge\overline{v}$ are distributed independently, each taking on 1 with probability $p \doteq \frac{2^{k-1}-1}{2^k-1}\cdot\frac{1}{2}$, whereas the nth bit of $u\wedge\overline{v}$ takes on 1 whenever

$D(Y,u,v) = -1$. These facts bound the right member of (3.5) from above by

$$\sum_{i=0}^{n-1} \binom{n-1}{i} p^i (1-p)^{n-1-i} \frac{1}{i+1} = \frac{1-(1-p)^n}{pn} \leqslant \frac{4}{n} \cdot \frac{2^k-1}{2^k-2}. \qquad \square$$

LEMMA 3.4 (On the probability of disjointness). *For $\lambda_{n,k}$ defined above,*

$$\mathop{\mathbf{P}}_{\lambda_{n,k}} [D(Y,u,v) = 1] \leqslant \frac{2^k-1}{n}. \tag{3.6}$$

PROOF. Conditioned on $Y = (y_1, \ldots, y_{k-1})$, the probability that $y_1 \wedge \cdots \wedge y_{k-1} \wedge u \wedge v \neq 0^n$ is $1/|y_1 \wedge \cdots \wedge y_{k-1}|$. Thus, the left member of (3.6) equals

$$\begin{aligned}
&\sum_{y_1,\ldots,y_{k-1}} \frac{\mu_{n,k}(y_1,\ldots,y_{k-1})}{|y_1 \wedge \cdots \wedge y_{k-1}|} \\
&\leqslant \frac{2^{nk}}{n(2^k-1)^{n-1}} \mathop{\mathbf{E}}_{y_1,\ldots,y_{k-1} \in \{0,1\}^n} \left[\frac{1}{2^{|y_1 \wedge \cdots \wedge y_{k-1}|}}\right] \\
&= \frac{2^{nk}}{n(2^k-1)^{n-1}} \left(1 - \frac{1}{2^k}\right)^n \\
&= \frac{2^k-1}{n},
\end{aligned}$$

where the inequality holds by (3.1). $\square$

4. A DISCREPANCY RESULT

The goal of this section is to analyze the k-party discrepancy of $(\mathrm{UDISJ}_{n,k})^{\otimes m}$, the XOR of m independent copies of the unique disjointness problem. In actuality, we will derive a somewhat more general result. For positive integers $n_1, n_2, \ldots, n_m$, define

$$\Gamma_k(n_1, n_2, \ldots, n_m) \doteq \max_{\chi} \left| \mathop{\mathbf{E}}_{(x^1,W^1),\ldots,(x^m,W^m)} \left[\chi \cdot \prod_{i=1}^m D(x^i, W^i)\right]\right|,$$

where $(x^i, W^i) \sim \mathscr{U}_{n_i} \times \mu_{n_i,k}$ independently for each i, and the maximum is taken over all $(k+1)$-dimensional cylinder intersections $\chi: (\{0,1\}^{n_1+n_2+\cdots+n_m})^{k+1} \to \{0,1\}$. Our objective is to bound Γ_k from above. The proof will use induction on k, the base case corresponding to the following proposition.

PROPOSITION 4.1. *For all positive integers $n_1, n_2, \ldots, n_m$,*

$$\Gamma_1(n_1, n_2, \ldots, n_m) \leqslant \frac{1}{\sqrt{n_1 n_2 \cdots n_m}}.$$

PROOF. Define $M_i = [(-1)^{x_j}]_{j,x}$, where the indices range as follows: $j = 1, 2, \ldots, n_i$ and $x \in \{0,1\}^{n_i}$. Then $\|M_i\| = \sqrt{2^{n_i}}$, whence by Proposition 2.8

$$\Gamma_1(n_1, n_2, \ldots, n_m) \leqslant \left\|\bigotimes_{i=1}^m \frac{M_i}{n_i 2^{n_i}}\right\| \left(\prod_{i=1}^m n_i 2^{n_i}\right)^{1/2} = \frac{1}{\sqrt{n_1 n_2 \cdots n_m}}. \qquad \square$$

We now proceed to bound Γ_k for all k. We will use the general technique of Babai, Nisan, and Szegedy [6] to pass from $(k+1)$-party discrepancy to k-party discrepancy. Unlike the functions studied in [6], however, set disjointness does not have a multiplicative structure. This complicates the passage from $(k+1)$-party problems to k-party subproblems. To overcome this difficulty, we use the metric properties of the distribution $\lambda_{n,k}$ established in the previous section. More concretely, we use conditional independence among variables to *simulate* a multiplicative structure.

THEOREM 4.2. *For all positive integers $n_1, n_2, \ldots, n_m$, and k,*

$$\Gamma_k(n_1, n_2, \ldots, n_m) \leqslant \frac{(2^k-1)^m}{\sqrt{n_1 n_2 \cdots n_m}}.$$

PROOF. We adopt the following notational shorthand: if X, Y are random variables with some joint distribution and $\Phi(X,Y)$ is a real function, we let $\mathbf{E}_X \mathbf{E}_Y [\Phi(X,Y)] \doteq \mathbf{E}_X \mathbf{E}_Y [\Phi(X,Y) \mid X]$. In other words, the inner expectation is always with respect to the conditional probability distribution induced by the outer variable.

The proof will proceed by induction on k, the base case $k = 1$ having already been established in Proposition 4.1. For the inductive step, fix an integer $k \geqslant 2$ and consider a cylinder intersection $\chi: (\{0,1\}^{n_1+\cdots+n_m})^{k+1} \to \{0,1\}$ for which Γ_k is achieved:

$$\Gamma_k(n_1, n_2, \ldots, n_m) = \left| \mathop{\mathbf{E}}_{(x^1,Y^1,u^1),\ldots,(x^m,Y^m,u^m)} \left[\chi \cdot \prod_{i=1}^m D(x^i, Y^i, u^i)\right]\right|, \tag{4.1}$$

where $(x^i, (Y^i, u^i)) \sim \mathscr{U}_{n_i} \times \mu_{n_i,k}$ independently for each i, and χ is shorthand for $\chi(x^1, \ldots, x^m, Y^1, \ldots, Y^m, u^1, \ldots, u^m)$. Then

$$\begin{aligned}
\chi(x^1, \ldots, x^m, Y^1, \ldots, Y^m, u^1, \ldots, u^m) &= \chi_{u^1,\ldots,u^m}(x^1, \ldots, x^m, Y^1, \ldots, Y^m) \\
&\quad \times \xi(x^1, \ldots, x^m, Y^1, \ldots, Y^m),
\end{aligned}$$

where $\chi_{u^1,\ldots,u^m}: (\{0,1\}^{n_1+\cdots+n_m})^k \to \{0,1\}$ is a k-dimensional cylinder intersection for each $(u^1, \ldots, u^m)$, and ξ is some function into $\{0,1\}$. Rearranging the right member of (4.1) gives

$$\begin{aligned}
&\Gamma_k(n_1, \ldots, n_m) \\
&= \left| \mathop{\mathbf{E}}_{(x^1,Y^1),\ldots,(x^m,Y^m)} \mathop{\mathbf{E}}_{u^1,\ldots,u^m} \left[\chi \cdot \prod_{i=1}^m D(x^i, Y^i, u^i)\right]\right| \\
&\leqslant \mathop{\mathbf{E}}_{(x^1,Y^1),\ldots,(x^m,Y^m)} \left| \mathop{\mathbf{E}}_{u^1,\ldots,u^m} \left[\chi_{u^1,\ldots,u^m} \cdot \prod_{i=1}^m D(x^i, Y^i, u^i)\right]\right|.
\end{aligned}$$

We now apply the technique of Babai, Nisan, and Szegedy [6]. Squaring both sides and using the Cauchy-Schwarz inequality, one arrives at

$$\begin{aligned}
&\Gamma_k(n_1, \ldots, n_m)^2 \\
&\leqslant \mathop{\mathbf{E}}_{(x^1,Y^1),\ldots,(x^m,Y^m)} \left[\mathop{\mathbf{E}}_{u^1,\ldots,u^m} \left[\chi_{u^1,\ldots,u^m} \cdot \prod_{i=1}^m D(x^i, Y^i, u^i)\right]^2\right] \\
&= \mathbf{E}\left[\chi' \cdot \prod_{i=1}^m D(x^i, Y^i, u^i) D(x^i, Y^i, v^i)\right],
\end{aligned} \tag{4.2}$$

where $\chi' \doteq \chi_{u^1,\ldots,u^m} \cdot \chi_{v^1,\ldots,v^m}$ and the expectation in (4.2) is taken with respect to $(x^i, (Y^i, u^i, v^i)) \sim \mathscr{U}_{n_i} \times \lambda_{n_i,k}$, independently for each i. Note that with $u^1, \dots, u^m$ and $v^1, \dots, v^m$ fixed, χ' is a cylinder intersection on $(\{0,1\}^{n_1+\cdots+n_m})^k$.

We now need to analyze (4.2). It is here that similarities with Babai, Nisan, and Szegedy [6] end, and we must exploit properties specific to set disjointness. To restate Lemma 3.1,

$$\begin{aligned} & D(x^i, Y^i, u^i) D(x^i, Y^i, v^i) \qquad (4.3) \\ &= \mathbf{I}\left[D\left(Y^i|_{u^i \wedge v^i}\right) = 1\right] \\ &+ \mathbf{I}\left[D\left(Y^i|_{u^i \wedge v^i}\right) = -1\right] D\left((x^i, Y^i)|_{u^i \wedge \overline{v}^i}\right) D\left((x^i, Y^i)|_{\overline{u}^i \wedge v^i}\right) \end{aligned}$$

on the support of $\lambda_{n_i,k}$. To bound (4.2), we will take advantage of conditioning. Specifically, using (4.3) and conditioning on u_i, v_i, $Y^i|_{u^i \wedge v^i}$, and $Y^i|_{\overline{u}^i \wedge \overline{v}^i}$ for each i, we arrive at the following expectation over the remaining variables x^i, $Y^i|_{u^i \wedge \overline{v}^i}$, and $Y^i|_{\overline{u}^i \wedge v^i}$:

$$\begin{aligned} & \mathbf{E}\left[\chi' \cdot \prod_{i=1}^{m} D(x^i, Y^i, u^i) D(x^i, Y^i, v^i)\right] \qquad (4.4) \\ &= \sum_{z \in \{-1,+1\}^m} \mathbf{E}\left[\chi' \cdot \prod_{i: z_i = -1} D\left((x^i, Y^i)|_{u^i \wedge \overline{v}^i}\right) \times \right. \\ &\qquad \left. \times D\left((x^i, Y^i)|_{\overline{u}^i \wedge v^i}\right)\right] \prod_{i=1}^{m} \mathbf{I}\left[D\left(Y^i|_{u^i \wedge v^i}\right) = z_i\right]. \end{aligned}$$

The expectations in the right member of (4.4) admit direct analysis. By Lemma 3.2, conditioning on any fixed value of $u^i, v^i, Y^i|_{u^i \wedge v^i}$, $Y^i|_{\overline{u}^i \wedge \overline{v}^i}$ with $D(Y^i|_{u^i \wedge v^i}) = -1$ makes the remaining variables $Y^i|_{u^i \wedge \overline{v}^i}$ and $Y^i|_{\overline{u}^i \wedge v^i}$ independent and distributed according to $\mu_{|u^i \wedge \overline{v}^i|, k-1}$ and $\mu_{|\overline{u}^i \wedge v^i|, k-1}$, respectively. Since χ' is a cylinder intersection for fixed $u^1, \dots, u^m$ and $v^1, \dots, v^m$, the inductive hypothesis applies to the right member of (4.4), bounding it in absolute value by

$$\sum_{z \in \{-1,+1\}^m} \prod_{i: z_i = -1} \frac{(2^{k-1} - 1)^2\, \mathbf{I}\left[D\left(Y^i|_{u^i \wedge v^i}\right) = -1\right]}{\sqrt{|u^i \wedge \overline{v}^i|\,|\overline{u}^i \wedge v^i|}} \times \prod_{i: z_i = 1} \mathbf{I}\left[D\left(Y^i|_{u^i \wedge v^i}\right) = 1\right].$$

Passing to expectations, one concludes that $\Gamma_k(n_1, n_2, \dots, n_m)^2$ is bounded from above by

$$\begin{aligned} & \sum_{z \in \{-1,+1\}^m} \prod_{i: z_i = -1} \mathop{\mathbf{E}}_{\lambda_{n_i,k}}\left[\frac{(2^{k-1} - 1)^2\, \mathbf{I}\left[D\left(Y^i|_{u^i \wedge v^i}\right) = -1\right]}{\sqrt{|u^i \wedge \overline{v}^i|\,|\overline{u}^i \wedge v^i|}}\right] \\ &\qquad \times \prod_{i: z_i = 1} \mathop{\mathbf{P}}_{\lambda_{n_i,k}}\left[D\left(Y^i|_{u^i \wedge v^i}\right) = 1\right] \\ &= \prod_{i=1}^{m}\left((2^{k-1} - 1)^2 \mathop{\mathbf{E}}_{\lambda_{n_i,k}}\left[\frac{\mathbf{I}\left[D\left(Y^i|_{u^i \wedge v^i}\right) = -1\right]}{\sqrt{|u^i \wedge \overline{v}^i|\,|\overline{u}^i \wedge v^i|}}\right] \right. \\ &\qquad \left. + \mathop{\mathbf{P}}_{\lambda_{n_i,k}}\left[D\left(Y^i|_{u^i \wedge v^i}\right) = 1\right]\right). \end{aligned}$$

The probabilities and expectations in the final expression are given by Lemmas 3.3 and 3.4, forcing $\Gamma_k(n_1, n_2, \dots, n_m)^2 \leqslant (2^k - 1)^{2m}/(n_1 n_2 \cdots n_m)$. This completes the inductive proof. ◻

Notes. We are only interested in $\Gamma_k(n_1, n_2, \dots, n_m)$ for $n_1 = n_2 = \cdots = n_m$. However, the above inductive proof requires consideration of the more general quantity.

The base case, given by Proposition 4.1, could have been handled by a first-principles argument analogous to Theorem 4.2. However, we find the above treatment more concise and modular.

5. RANDOMIZED COMMUNICATION

Combining the technical work of the previous sections with additional ideas, we will now derive a general lower bound on randomized communication complexity for composed functions (Section 5.1). We will specifically be interested in compositions of the form $f \circ \mathrm{UDISJ}_{r,k}$. In Sections 5.2 and 5.3, we will apply our findings to the bounded-error and small-bias communication complexity of AC^0 circuits, including set disjointness itself.

5.1 Master Theorem

We start with the main technical result of the section. We present two different proofs for it, one based on the primal view of the problem and the other, on the dual view. The primal proof appears more intuitive to us, whereas the dual proof is more versatile. Each of the proofs will be used in later sections to obtain additional results.

THEOREM 5.1. *Let f be a (possibly partial) Boolean function on $\{-1,+1\}^n$. Then for $\epsilon, \delta \geqslant 0$, the k-party communication problem $F = f \circ \mathrm{UDISJ}_{r,k}$ obeys*

$$2^{R_\epsilon(F)} \geqslant (\delta - \epsilon(1+\delta))\left(\frac{\deg_\delta(f)\sqrt{r}}{2^k e n}\right)^{\deg_\delta(f)}. \qquad (5.1)$$

The idea of the primal proof is to convert a communication protocol for F into a low-degree polynomial approximating f in the infinity norm. The dual proof proceeds in the reverse direction and manipulates explicit witness objects, in the sense of Fact 2.2 and Theorem 2.10. More specifically, the dual proof converts a witness of f's inapproximability by polynomials to a witness of F's high communication complexity. The primal point of view is original to this paper, whereas the dual approach is due to [42, 46].

PRIMAL PROOF OF THEOREM 5.1. Define $\mu = \mathscr{U}_r \times \mu_{r,k-1}$, a probability distribution on the domain of $\mathrm{UDISJ}_{r,k}$. Let μ_{-1} and μ_{+1} stand for the probability distributions induced by μ on $\mathrm{UDISJ}_{r,k}^{-1}(-1)$ and $\mathrm{UDISJ}_{r,k}^{-1}(+1)$, respectively. Consider the following averaging operator M, which linearly sends real functions χ on $(\{0,1\}^{r \times k})^n$ to real functions on $\{-1,+1\}^n$:

$$(M\chi)(z) \doteq \mathop{\mathbf{E}}_{X_1 \sim \mu_{z_1}} \cdots \mathop{\mathbf{E}}_{X_n \sim \mu_{z_n}} [\chi(X_1, \dots, X_n)].$$

When χ is a k-dimensional cylinder intersection,

$$\begin{aligned} & |\widehat{M\chi}(S)| \\ &= \left|\mathop{\mathbf{E}}_{z \in \{-1,+1\}^n} \mathop{\mathbf{E}}_{X_1 \sim \mu_{z_1}} \cdots \mathop{\mathbf{E}}_{X_n \sim \mu_{z_n}}\left[\chi(X_1, \dots, X_n) \prod_{i \in S} z_i\right]\right| \\ &= \left|\mathop{\mathbf{E}}_{X_1, \dots, X_n \sim \mu}\left[\chi(X_1, \dots, X_n) \prod_{i \in S} \mathrm{UDISJ}_{r,k}(X_i)\right]\right| \\ &\leqslant \Gamma_{k-1}(\overbrace{r, r, \dots, r}^{|S|}) \\ &\leqslant \left(\frac{2^{k-1}}{\sqrt{r}}\right)^{|S|}, \qquad (5.2) \end{aligned}$$

where the second equality uses the fact that $\mu = (\mu_{-1} + \mu_{+1})/2$, and the final step follows by Theorem 4.2.

Fix a randomized protocol for F with error ϵ and cost $c \doteq R_\epsilon(F)$. Approximate F as in Corollary 2.6 by a linear combination of cylinder intersections $\Pi = \sum_\chi a_\chi \chi$, where $\sum_\chi |a_\chi| \leqslant 2^c/(1-\epsilon)$. We claim that $M\Pi$ is approximable by a low-degree polynomial. Indeed, let d be a positive integer to be chosen later. Discarding the Fourier coefficients of $M\Pi$ of order d and higher gives

$$\begin{aligned} E(M\Pi, d-1) &\leqslant \min\left\{\frac{1}{1-\epsilon}, \sum_\chi |a_\chi| \sum_{|S|\geqslant d} |\widehat{M\chi}(S)|\right\} \\ &\leqslant \min\left\{\frac{1}{1-\epsilon}, \frac{2^c}{1-\epsilon}\sum_{i=d}^{n}\binom{n}{i}\left(\frac{2^{k-1}}{\sqrt{r}}\right)^i\right\} \\ &\leqslant \frac{2^c}{1-\epsilon}\left(\frac{2^k \mathrm{e}n}{d\sqrt{r}}\right)^d, \end{aligned} \tag{5.3}$$

where the second step uses (5.2). On the other hand, recall from Corollary 2.6 that Π approximates F in the sense that $\|\Pi\|_\infty \leqslant 1/(1-\epsilon)$ and $|F - \Pi| \leqslant \epsilon/(1-\epsilon)$ on the domain of F. It follows that $\|M\Pi\|_\infty \leqslant 1/(1-\epsilon)$ and $|f - M\Pi| \leqslant \epsilon/(1-\epsilon)$ on the domain of f, whence

$$E(f, d-1) \leqslant \frac{\epsilon}{1-\epsilon} + E(M\Pi, d-1).$$

Substituting the estimate from (5.3),

$$E(f, d-1) \leqslant \frac{\epsilon}{1-\epsilon} + \frac{2^c}{1-\epsilon}\left(\frac{2^k \mathrm{e}n}{d\sqrt{r}}\right)^d. \tag{5.4}$$

For $d = \deg_\delta(f)$, the left member of (5.4) must exceed δ, forcing the claimed lower bound on 2^c. ∎

We now present an alternate proof, which combines the argument in [42, 46] with the discrepancy result in this paper.

DUAL PROOF OF THEOREM 5.1. As before, consider the distribution $\mu = \mathscr{U}_r \times \mu_{r,k-1}$ on the domain of $\mathrm{UDISJ}_{r,k}$. For $d \doteq \deg_\delta(f)$, Fact 2.2 provides $\psi\colon \{-1,+1\}^n \to \mathbb{R}$ with

$$\sum_{z\in \operatorname{dom} f} f(z)\psi(z) - \sum_{z\notin \operatorname{dom} f} |\psi(z)| > \delta, \tag{5.5}$$

$$\|\psi\|_1 = 1, \tag{5.6}$$

$$\hat\psi(S) = 0, \qquad |S| < d. \tag{5.7}$$

Define $\Psi\colon (\{0,1\}^{r\times k})^n \to \mathbb{R}$ by

$$\begin{aligned} &\Psi(X_1,\ldots,X_n) \\ &= 2^n \psi\left(\mathrm{DISJ}_{r,k}(X_1),\ldots,\mathrm{DISJ}_{r,k}(X_n)\right)\prod_{i=1}^n \mu(X_i). \end{aligned}$$

Since μ places equal weight on $\mathrm{UDISJ}_{r,k}^{-1}(-1)$ and $\mathrm{UDISJ}_{r,k}^{-1}(+1)$, we have

$$\|\Psi\|_1 = 2^n \mathop{\mathbf{E}}_{z\in\{-1,+1\}^n}[|\psi(z)|] = 1 \tag{5.8}$$

and analogously

$$\begin{aligned} &\sum_{\operatorname{dom} F} F(X_1,\ldots,X_n)\Psi(X_1,\ldots,X_n) - \sum_{\overline{\operatorname{dom} F}} |\Psi(X_1,\ldots,X_n)| \\ &\quad = \sum_{z\in\operatorname{dom} f} f(z)\psi(z) - \sum_{z\notin\operatorname{dom} f}|\psi(z)| \\ &\quad > \delta, \end{aligned} \tag{5.9}$$

where the final step in the two derivations uses (5.5) and (5.6). It remains to bound the inner product of Ψ with a k-dimensional cylinder intersection χ. By (5.7),

$$\begin{aligned} &|\langle\Psi,\chi\rangle| \\ &\leqslant 2^n \sum_{|S|\geqslant d} |\hat\psi(S)| \left| \mathop{\mathbf{E}}_{\substack{X_1\sim\mu \\ \cdots \\ X_n\sim\mu}}\left[\chi(X_1,\ldots,X_n)\prod_{i\in S}\mathrm{DISJ}_{r,k}(X_i)\right]\right| \\ &\leqslant 2^n \sum_{|S|\geqslant d}|\hat\psi(S)|\, \Gamma_{k-1}(\overbrace{r,r,\ldots,r}^{|S|}) \\ &\leqslant \sum_{|S|\geqslant d}\left(\frac{2^{k-1}}{\sqrt{r}}\right)^{|S|}, \end{aligned}$$

where the final step uses Proposition 2.1 and Theorem 4.2. Combining this with the trivial bound $|\langle\Psi,\chi\rangle| \leqslant \|\Psi\|_1\|\chi\|_\infty = 1$,

$$|\langle\Psi,\chi\rangle| \leqslant \min\left\{1, \sum_{i=d}^n \binom{n}{i}\left(\frac{2^{k-1}}{\sqrt{r}}\right)^i\right\} \leqslant \left(\frac{2^k\mathrm{e}n}{d\sqrt{r}}\right)^d. \tag{5.10}$$

By (5.8)–(5.10) and Theorem 2.10, the proof is complete. ∎

5.2 Bounded-Error Communication

The general theorem that we have just proved allows one to obtain lower bounds on bounded-error communication in terms of the $1/3$-approximate degree, as follows.

THEOREM 5.2. *Let f be a (possibly partial) Boolean function on $\{-1,+1\}^n$. Let $d = \deg_{1/3}(f)$. Then*

$$R_{1/3}\left(f \circ \mathrm{UDISJ}_{4^{k+2}\lceil \frac{n}{d}\rceil^2, k}\right) \geqslant \Omega(d).$$

PROOF. Let $\epsilon = 1/5$, $\delta = 1/3$, $r = 4^{k+2}\lceil n/d\rceil^2$ in Theorem 5.1. ∎

In particular, we obtain the following lower bound on the randomized communication complexity of set disjointness.

THEOREM 1.1 (restated). *The k-party set disjointness problem obeys*

$$R_{1/3}(\mathrm{DISJ}_{n,k}) \geqslant R_{1/3}(\mathrm{UDISJ}_{n,k}) = \Omega\left(\frac{n}{4^k}\right)^{1/4}.$$

PROOF. Recall that $\mathrm{UDISJ}_{nr,k} = \widetilde{\mathrm{AND}}_n \circ \mathrm{UDISJ}_{r,k}$ for all integers n, r. Theorem 2.4 shows that $\deg_{1/3}(\widetilde{\mathrm{AND}}_n) > \delta\sqrt{n}$ for some constant $\delta > 0$. Thus, taking $f = \widetilde{\mathrm{AND}}_n$ and $d = \delta\sqrt{n}$ in Theorem 5.2 gives $R_{1/3}(\mathrm{UDISJ}_{4^{k+2}n\lceil\sqrt{n}/\delta\rceil^2,k}) = \Omega(\sqrt{n})$, which is equivalent to the claimed bound. ∎

Theorem 5.2 gives a general lower bound on bounded-error communication complexity for compositions $f \circ G$, where G is a gadget on a relatively large number of variables. We will now derive an alternate lower bound, in which the gadget G is essentially as simple as possible and in particular depends on only $2k$ variables.

We recall some combinatorial complexity measures. Consider a Boolean function $f:\{-1,+1\}^n \to \{-1,+1\}$. For a string $x \in \{-1,+1\}^n$ and a subset $S \subseteq \{1,2,\ldots,n\}$, let x^S stand for the string obtained from x by negating the bit positions in S, i.e.,

$$(x^S)_i = \begin{cases} -x_i & \text{if } i \in S, \\ x_i & \text{otherwise.} \end{cases}$$

The *block sensitivity of f*, denoted $\mathrm{bs}(f)$, is the maximum number of nonempty, pairwise disjoint sets $S_1, S_2, S_3, \ldots \subseteq \{1,2,\ldots,n\}$ such that $f(x) \neq f(x^{S_1}) = f(x^{S_2}) = f(x^{S_3}) = \cdots$ for some string $x \in \{-1,+1\}^n$. The *sensitivity of f*, denoted $\mathrm{s}(f)$, is defined analogously with the additional requirement that $S_1, S_2, S_3, \ldots$ contain exactly one element each. Thus, the sensitivity of f is the maximum of $|\{i : f(x) \neq f(x_1,\ldots,x_{i-1},-x_i,x_{i+1},\ldots,x_n)\}|$ over all strings $x \in \{-1,+1\}^n$. The *decision tree complexity of f*, denoted $\mathrm{dt}(f)$, is the minimum depth of a decision tree for f. Surprisingly, the quantities $\mathrm{bs}(f)$, $\mathrm{dt}(f)$, $\deg_{1/3}(f)$ are polynomially related for every total Boolean function [38]. Finally, a *contraction* of a Boolean function $f:\{-1,+1\}^n \to \{-1,+1\}$ is any function $g:\{-1,+1\}^n \to \{-1,+1\}$ such that $g(x) \equiv f(x_{i_1}, x_{i_2}, \ldots, x_{i_n})$ for some indices $i_1, i_2, \ldots, i_n \in \{1,2,\ldots,n\}$. Informally, a contraction is the result of replacing groups of variables by a single variable (and possibly permuting the variables).

We are now in a position to prove the alternate lower bound on communication for composed functions. We will study compositions of the form $f \circ (\mathrm{OR}_k \vee \mathrm{AND}_k)$. Here $\mathrm{OR}_k \vee \mathrm{AND}_k$ refers to the k-party communication problem $(x_1,\ldots,x_{2k}) \mapsto x_1 \vee \cdots \vee x_k \vee (x_{k+1} \wedge \cdots \wedge x_{2k})$ in which the ith party sees all the bits except for x_i and x_{k+i}. It is clear that $f \circ (\mathrm{OR}_k \vee \mathrm{AND}_k)$ has a deterministic k-party communication protocol with cost $3\,\mathrm{dt}(f)$. In what follows, we prove that this trivial upper bound is close to tight, even for randomized protocols.

THEOREM 5.3. *Let $f:\{-1,+1\}^n \to \{-1,+1\}$ be given, with approximate degree $\deg_{1/3}(f) = d$. Then*

$$R_{1/3}(f \circ (\mathrm{OR}_k \vee \mathrm{AND}_k)) \geqslant \Omega\left(\frac{\mathrm{bs}(f)}{4^k}\right)^{1/4} \geqslant \Omega\left(\frac{\mathrm{dt}(f)^{1/3}}{4^k}\right)^{1/4} \geqslant \Omega\left(\frac{d^{1/3}}{4^k}\right)^{1/4}.$$

By symmetry, the theorem also holds with $\mathrm{OR}_k \wedge \mathrm{AND}_k$ in place of $\mathrm{OR}_k \vee \mathrm{AND}_k$. Finally, note that the above result implies a lower bound of $\Omega(n/4^k)^{1/4}$ on the randomized communication complexity of set disjointness. But Theorem 5.3 does not give a *new* proof of Theorem 1.1 because the latter is used to prove the former.

PROOF OF THEOREM 5.3. It is clear that $d \leqslant \mathrm{dt}(f)$, and it is known [8, p. 791] that $\mathrm{dt}(f) \leqslant \mathrm{bs}(f)^3$. Thus, it suffices to prove the lower bound in terms of $\mathrm{bs}(f)$. We will actually prove the following stronger result: for some fixed $z \in \{-1,+1\}^n$,

$$R_{1/3}(f_z \circ \mathrm{AND}_k) \geqslant \Omega\left(\frac{\mathrm{bs}(f)}{4^k}\right)^{1/4},$$

with $f_z:\{-1,+1\}^n \to \{-1,+1\}$ defined by $f_z(x) = f(z \oplus x)$.

Fix z such that $f(z) \neq f(z^{S_1}) = f(z^{S_2}) = \cdots = f(z^{S_{\mathrm{bs}(f)}})$ for some nonempty, pairwise disjoint subsets $S_1, S_2, \ldots, S_{\mathrm{bs}(f)} \subseteq \{1,2,\ldots,n\}$. This means that $f_z(\mathbf{1}) \neq f_z(\mathbf{1}^{S_1}) = f_z(\mathbf{1}^{S_2}) = \cdots = f_z(\mathbf{1}^{S_{\mathrm{bs}(f)}})$, where $\mathbf{1} = (1,1,\ldots,1)$. But then there is a contraction g of f_z such that

$$g(1,1,\ldots,1) \neq g(\underbrace{1,\ldots,1,-1}_{i},1,\ldots,1)$$

for $i = 1,2,\ldots,\mathrm{bs}(f)$. Indeed, such a contraction can be obtained from f_z by replacing the variables in each block S_i by a single variable, and suitably permuting the resulting variable set. In other words, $\widetilde{\mathrm{OR}}_{\mathrm{bs}(f)}$ is a subfunction of g. Therefore, $\widetilde{\mathrm{OR}}_{\mathrm{bs}(f)} \circ \mathrm{AND}_k = \neg\mathrm{UDISJ}_{\mathrm{bs}(f),k}$ is a subfunction of $g \circ \mathrm{AND}_k$, and $R_{1/3}(g \circ \mathrm{AND}_k) = \Omega(\mathrm{bs}(f)/4^k)^{1/4}$ by Theorem 1.1. The same lower bound holds for $f_z \circ \mathrm{AND}_k$ since passage to a contraction cannot increase communication complexity. □

It is tempting to go further and try to bound $R_{1/3}(f \circ \mathrm{AND}_k)$ from below in terms of the approximate degree of f. Unfortunately, the gap between $R_{1/3}(f \circ \mathrm{AND}_k)$ and $\deg_{1/3}(f)$ can be as large as $\Theta(1)$ versus $\Theta(\sqrt{n})$; simply take $f = \mathrm{AND}_n$. As it turns out, the right approach is to consider the *maximum* of the communication complexities of $f \circ \mathrm{AND}_k$ and $f \circ \mathrm{OR}_k$.

THEOREM 5.4. *Let $f:\{-1,+1\}^n \to \{-1,+1\}$ be given, with approximate degree $\deg_{1/3}(f) = d$. Then*

$$\max\{R_{1/3}(f \circ \mathrm{OR}_k),\ R_{1/3}(f \circ \mathrm{AND}_k)\} \geqslant \Omega\left(\frac{\mathrm{bs}(f)^{1/4}}{2^k}\right)^{1/2} \qquad (5.11)$$

$$\geqslant \Omega\left(\frac{\mathrm{dt}(f)^{1/12}}{2^k}\right)^{1/2} \geqslant \Omega\left(\frac{d^{1/12}}{2^k}\right)^{1/2}.$$

PROOF. As in the previous proof, it suffices to prove the first inequality, and moreover we may replace f in (5.11) by a contraction of f. The argument is closely analogous to the one in [44] for two-party communication. Specifically, by [44, Lem. 3.3], there is a contraction g of f such that $\mathrm{s}(g) \geqslant \alpha\sqrt{\mathrm{bs}(f)}$ for some absolute constant $\alpha > 0$. So, fix a subset $S \subseteq \{1,2,\ldots,n\}$ of size $|S| \geqslant \alpha\sqrt{\mathrm{bs}(f)}$ and a string $z \in \{-1,+1\}^n$ such that $g(z) \neq g(z_1,\ldots,z_{i-1},-z_i,z_{i+1},\ldots,z_n)$ for all $i \in S$. Consider two cases.

(i) If $z|_S$ has more "-1" entries than "$+1$" entries, then $\widetilde{\mathrm{AND}}_{|S|/2}$ is a subfunction of g. As a result, $\mathrm{UDISJ}_{|S|/2,k}$ is a subfunction of $g \circ \mathrm{OR}_k$ (up to negations of the input variables), and the proof is complete in view of Theorem 1.1.

(ii) If $z|_S$ has no more "-1" entries than "$+1$" entries, then $\widetilde{\mathrm{OR}}_{|S|/2}$ is a subfunction of g. As a result, $\neg\mathrm{UDISJ}_{|S|/2,k}$ is a subfunction of $g \circ \mathrm{AND}_k$, and the proof is again complete in view of Theorem 1.1. □

5.3 Small-Bias Communication and Discrepancy

The counterpart to bounded-error communication is small-bias communication, when the protocol is only required to produce the correct output with probability vanishingly close to $1/2$. We will now see that Theorem 5.1 gives communication lower bounds in this setting as well, in terms of the approximate degree with an appropriate error parameter.

THEOREM 5.5. *Let f be a (possibly partial) Boolean function on $\{-1,+1\}^n$. Then*

$$R_{\frac{1}{2}-\frac{\epsilon}{2}}\left(f\circ \mathrm{UDISJ}_{4^{k+3}\lceil n/\deg_{1-\gamma}(f)\rceil^2,k}\right) \geqslant \deg_{1-\gamma}(f)-\log\frac{1}{\epsilon-\gamma},$$

$$R_{\frac{1}{2}-\frac{\epsilon}{2}}\left(f\circ \mathrm{UDISJ}_{4^{k+3}\lceil n/\deg_{\pm}(f)\rceil^2,k}\right) \geqslant \deg_{\pm}(f)-\log\frac{1}{\epsilon}.$$

PROOF. The first lower bound follows by taking $\delta = 1-\gamma$ and $r = 4^{k+3}\lceil n/\deg_{1-\gamma}(f)\rceil^2$ in Theorem 5.1. The second lower bound follows from the first by letting $\gamma \searrow 0$. □

Finally, Theorem 5.1 allows one to directly prove upper bounds on discrepancy, a complexity measure of interest in its own right. We have:

THEOREM 5.6. *Let f be a (possibly partial) Boolean function on $\{-1,+1\}^n$. Then for every $\gamma>0$,*

$$\mathrm{disc}(f\circ \mathrm{UDISJ}_{r,k}) < \left(\frac{2^k en}{\deg_{1-\gamma}(f)\sqrt{r}}\right)^{\deg_{1-\gamma}(f)} + \gamma.$$

In particular,

$$\mathrm{disc}(f\circ \mathrm{UDISJ}_{r,k}) \leqslant \left(\frac{2^k en}{\deg_{\pm}(f)\sqrt{r}}\right)^{\deg_{\pm}(f)}.$$

PROOF. The second bound follows directly from the first by letting $\gamma\searrow 0$. To prove the first bound, take $\delta = 1-\gamma$, $d=\deg_\delta(f)$, and define $\Psi\colon (\{0,1\}^{r\times k})^n \to \mathbb{R}$ as in the dual proof of Theorem 5.1. Then (5.8) shows that $\Psi = H\circ P$, where H is a sign tensor and P a probability distribution. Letting $F = f\circ \mathrm{UDISJ}_{r,k}$, we can restate (5.9) as

$$\sum_{\mathrm{dom}\,F} F(x)H(x)P(x) - P(\overline{\mathrm{dom}\,F}) > 1-\gamma. \tag{5.12}$$

For every cylinder intersection χ,

$$\left|\sum_{\mathrm{dom}\,F} F(x)P(x)\chi(x)\right| \tag{5.13}$$

$$\begin{aligned}
&= \left|\langle H\circ P,\chi\rangle + \sum_{\mathrm{dom}\,F}(F(x)-H(x))P(x)\chi(x) - \sum_{\overline{\mathrm{dom}\,F}} H(x)P(x)\chi(x)\right| \\
&\leqslant \mathrm{disc}_P(H) + \sum_{\mathrm{dom}\,F}|F(x)-H(x)|P(x) + P(\overline{\mathrm{dom}\,F}) \\
&= \mathrm{disc}_P(H) + P(\mathrm{dom}\,F) - \sum_{\mathrm{dom}\,F} F(x)H(x)P(x) + P(\overline{\mathrm{dom}\,F}) \\
&< \mathrm{disc}_P(H) + P(\mathrm{dom}\,F) - 1 + \gamma,
\end{aligned}$$

where the last step uses (5.12). Maximizing over all cylinder intersections χ gives:

$$\begin{aligned}
\mathrm{disc}_P(F) &= \max_\chi \left|\sum_{\mathrm{dom}\,F} F(x)P(x)\chi(x)\right| + P(\overline{\mathrm{dom}\,F}) \\
&< \mathrm{disc}_P(H) + \gamma \\
&\leqslant \left(\frac{2^k en}{d\sqrt{r}}\right)^d + \gamma,
\end{aligned}$$

where the second step uses (5.13) and the third uses (5.10). □

As an application of the above results on small-bias computation, we exhibit a hard multiparty communication problem $F\in \mathsf{AC}^0$. This k-party communication problem is given by an $\{\wedge,\vee\}$-circuit of size kn and depth 3 and has exponentially small discrepancy: $\mathrm{disc}(F)\leqslant \exp(-\Omega(n/4^k)^{1/7})$. In particular, the communication complexity of F remains high even to achieve an exponentially small advantage over random guessing. A more detailed statement follows.

THEOREM 5.7. *Consider the k-party communication problem $F_{n,k}\colon (\{0,1\}^{4^k n^7})^k \to \{-1,+1\}$ given by*

$$F_{n,k}(x) = \bigvee_{i=1}^{n}\bigwedge_{j=1}^{4^k n^6}(x_{i,j,1}\vee x_{i,j,2}\vee\cdots\vee x_{i,j,k}).$$

Then

$$\mathrm{disc}(F_{4n,k}) \leqslant 2^{-n},$$

$$R_{\frac{1}{2}-\frac{\gamma}{2}}(F_{4n,k}) \geqslant n - \log\frac{1}{\gamma} \qquad (\gamma>0).$$

This construction achieves optimal circuit depth because AC^0 circuits of depth less than 3 have multiparty discrepancy $1/n^{O(1)}$, regardless of how the bits are assigned to the parties. The previous best construction, due to Beame and Huynh-Ngoc [11], was a depth-6 circuit of size kn with discrepancy $\exp(-\Omega(n/2^{31k})^{1/29})$.

PROOF OF THEOREM 5.7. Let MP_n be given by Theorem 2.3, so that $\deg_{\pm}(\mathrm{MP}_n) = n$. Since $\mathrm{MP}_n\circ \mathrm{DISJ}_{4^{k+5}n^4,k}$ is a subfunction of $F_{4n,k}$ (up to negations of the input variables), Theorem 5.6 yields the discrepancy bound. The communication lower bound follows by Theorem 2.9. □

Theorem 5.7 settles Theorem 1.5 from the introduction.

6. XOR LEMMAS AND DIRECT PRODUCT THEOREMS

In Section 5, we proved that $\Omega(n/4^k)^{1/4}$ bits of communication are required to solve the set disjointness problem with probability of correctness 2/3. In this section, we consider the task of simultaneously solving ℓ instances of set disjointness and prove that $\ell\cdot\Omega(n/4^k)^{1/4}$ bits of communication are necessary to even achieve advantage $2^{-\Omega(\ell)}$ over random guessing. We prove an analogous result for computing the XOR of ℓ instances. The theorems in this section hold in somewhat greater generality, applying to compositions $f\circ G$ where f is an arbitrary function and G is an instance of set disjointness on a small number of variables. Our proof works by reducing these communication statements to analogous statements about polynomial approximation. We then appeal to known direct product theorems and XOR lemmas for the latter setting, which were recently obtained in [45].

6.1 XOR Lemmas

We start by proving the XOR lemma for set disjointness, which happens to admit a more intuitive and direct analysis than the corresponding direct product theorem. We recall an analogous XOR lemma for polynomial approximation [45, Cor. 5.2].

THEOREM 6.1 (Sherstov). *Let f be a (possibly partial) Boolean function on $\{-1,+1\}^n$. Then for some absolute constant $c > 0$ and every ℓ,*

$$\deg_{1-2^{-\ell-1}}(\underbrace{f \otimes \cdots \otimes f}_{\ell}) \geqslant c\ell \deg_{1/3}(f).$$

Using the small-bias version of the master theorem (Theorem 5.5), we are able to immediately translate this result to communication.

THEOREM 6.2 (XOR lemma). *Let f be a (possibly partial) Boolean function on $\{-1,+1\}^n$. Define $d = \deg_{1/3}(f)$. Then for some absolute constant $C > 1$, the k-party communication problem*

$$F = f \circ \mathrm{UDISJ}_{4^k\left\lceil \frac{Cn}{d}\right\rceil^2, k}$$

obeys

$$R_{\frac{1}{2}-\left(\frac{1}{2}\right)^{\ell+1}}(\underbrace{F \otimes \cdots \otimes F}_{\ell}) \geqslant \ell \cdot \Omega(d).$$

PROOF. Define $g = f^{\otimes \ell}$. Theorem 6.1 provides an absolute constant $c > 0$ such that $\deg_{1-1/2^{\ell+1}}(g) \geqslant c\ell d$. Letting $C = 8/c$, Theorem 5.5 implies that $g \circ \mathrm{UDISJ}_{4^k\lceil\frac{Cn}{d}\rceil^2,k} = F^{\otimes\ell}$ obeys $R_{1/2-1/2^{\ell+1}}(F^{\otimes \ell}) = \ell \cdot \Omega(d)$. □

The desired XOR lemma for set disjointness, stated as Theorem 1.2(i) in the introduction, now falls out as a corollary.

COROLLARY 6.3. *For every ℓ,*

$$R_{\frac{1}{2}-\left(\frac{1}{2}\right)^{\ell+1}}(\underbrace{\mathrm{UDISJ}_{n,k} \otimes \cdots \otimes \mathrm{UDISJ}_{n,k}}_{\ell}) \geqslant \ell \cdot \Omega\left(\frac{n}{4^k}\right)^{1/4}.$$

PROOF. Theorem 2.4 shows that $\deg_{1/3}(\widetilde{\mathrm{AND}}_n) \geqslant \epsilon\sqrt{n}$ for a constant $\epsilon > 0$. Thus, letting $f = \widetilde{\mathrm{AND}}_n$ and $d = \epsilon\sqrt{n}$ in Theorem 6.2 leads to $R_{1/2-1/2^{\ell+1}}(\mathrm{UDISJ}_{4^k n\lceil C\sqrt{n}/\epsilon\rceil^2,k}{}^{\otimes\ell}) \geqslant \ell \cdot \Omega(\sqrt{n})$, which is equivalent to the claimed bound. □

Using the argument of Theorem 5.3, we will now give an XOR lemma for arbitrary compositions of the form $f \circ (\mathrm{OR}_k \vee \mathrm{AND}_k)$. For this, we will use the combinatorial complexity measures $\mathrm{bs}(f)$ and $\mathrm{dt}(f)$, defined in Section 5.

THEOREM 6.4. *Let $f\colon \{-1,+1\}^n \to \{-1,+1\}$ be given. Put $F = f \circ (\mathrm{OR}_k \vee \mathrm{AND}_k)$. Then for every ℓ,*

$$\begin{aligned} R_{\frac{1}{2}-\left(\frac{1}{2}\right)^{\ell+1}}(\overbrace{F \otimes F \otimes \cdots \otimes F}^{\ell}) &\geqslant \ell \cdot \Omega\left(\frac{\mathrm{bs}(f)}{4^k}\right)^{1/4} \\ &\geqslant \ell \cdot \Omega\left(\frac{\mathrm{dt}(f)^{1/3}}{4^k}\right)^{1/4} \\ &\geqslant \ell \cdot \Omega\left(\frac{\deg_{1/3}(f)^{1/3}}{4^k}\right)^{1/4}. \end{aligned}$$

Recall from Section 5 that F has a *deterministic* protocol with cost $3\,\mathrm{dt}(f)$, and thus $F^{\otimes\ell}$ has a deterministic protocol with cost $3\ell\,\mathrm{dt}(f)$. In other words, Theorem 6.4 is reasonably close to tight.

PROOF OF THEOREM 6.4. The argument is essentially identical to that of Theorem 5.3. As argued there, any communication protocol for $f \circ (\mathrm{OR}_k \vee \mathrm{AND}_k)$ also solves $\mathrm{UDISJ}_{\mathrm{bs}(f),k}$, so that the first inequality is immediate from Corollary 6.3. The other two inequalities follow from general relationships among $\mathrm{bs}(f)$, $\mathrm{dt}(f)$, and $\deg_{1/3}(f)$; see the proof of Theorem 5.3. □

6.2 Direct Product Theorems

Let $F\colon X_1 \times X_2 \times \cdots \times X_k \to \{-1,+1\}$ be a given k-party communication problem. We are interested here in the communication complexity of simultaneously solving ℓ instances of F. More formally, the communication protocol now receives ℓ inputs $x^1,\ldots,x^\ell \in X_1 \times X_2 \times \cdots \times X_k$ and outputs a string $\{-1,+1\}^\ell$, representing a guess at $(F(x^1),\ldots,F(x^\ell))$. As usual, an ϵ-error communication protocol is one whose output differs from the correct answer with probability no greater than ϵ, on any given input. The least cost of such a protocol for solving ℓ instances of F is denoted $R_\epsilon(F,F,\ldots,F)$, where the number of instances will always be specified with an underbrace.

It is also meaningful to consider communication protocols that solve all but m of the ℓ instances (m for "mistake"), where the ratio m/ℓ is a small constant. In other words, given ℓ input instances $x^1,\ldots,x^\ell$, the protocol is required to output, with probability at least $1-\epsilon$, a vector $z \in \{-1,+1\}^\ell$ such that $z_i = F(x^i)$ for at least $\ell - m$ indices i. We let

$$R_{\epsilon,m}(\underbrace{F,F,\ldots,F}_{\ell})$$

stand for the least cost of such a protocol. When referring to this formalism, we will write that a protocol "solves with probability $1-\epsilon$ at least $\ell-m$ of the ℓ instances." This setting corresponds to *threshold direct product theorems*, as opposed to the more restricted notion of *strong direct product theorems* for which $m = 0$. All of our results belong to the former category. The following definition from [45] analytically formalizes the simultaneous solution of ℓ instances.

DEFINITION 6.5 (Approximants). Let f be a (possibly partial) Boolean function on a finite set X. A *(σ,m,ℓ)-approximant* for f is any system $\{\phi_z\}$ of functions $\phi_z\colon X^\ell \to \mathbb{R}$, $z \in \{-1,+1\}^\ell$, such that

$$\sum_{z\in\{-1,+1\}^\ell} |\phi_z(x^1,\ldots,x^\ell)| \leqslant 1$$

for all $x^1,\ldots,x^\ell \in X$, and

$$\sum_{\substack{z\in\{-1,+1\}^\ell \\ |\{i: z_i=-1\}|\leqslant m}} \phi_{(z_1 f(x^1),\ldots,z_\ell f(x^\ell))}(x^1,\ldots,x^\ell) \geqslant \sigma$$

for all $x^1,\ldots,x^\ell \in \operatorname{dom} f$.

The following result [45, Cor. 5.7] on polynomial approximation is naturally regarded as a threshold direct product theorem in that model of computation.

THEOREM 6.6 (Sherstov). *Let f be a (possibly partial) Boolean function on $\{-1,+1\}^n$. Let $\beta > 0$ be a small enough absolute* *constant. Then every $(2^{-\beta\ell}, \beta\ell, \ell)$-approximant $\{\phi_z\}$ for f obeys*

$$\max_{z\in\{-1,+1\}^\ell} \{\deg \phi_z\} \geqslant \beta\ell \deg_{1/3}(f).$$

Using the technique of Theorem 5.1, we are able to translate this result to multiparty communication complexity.

THEOREM 6.7 (Direct product theorem). *Let $\alpha > 0$ be a sufficiently small absolute constant. Let f be a (possibly partial) Boolean function on $\{-1,+1\}^n$, with $d = \deg_{1/3}(f)$. Then the k-party communication problem*

$$F = f \circ \mathrm{UDISJ}_{4^k \lceil \frac{n}{\alpha d}\rceil^2, k}$$

obeys

$$R_{1-2^{-\alpha\ell},\alpha\ell}(\underbrace{F, F, \ldots, F}_{\ell}) \geqslant \alpha\ell d.$$

PROOF. Our strategy will be to convert a low-cost communication protocol for solving ℓ instances of F into a low-degree approximant for f, in the sense of Definition 6.5. Such an approximant would be in contradiction to Theorem 6.6, thus ruling out the assumed low-cost protocol. The critical part of the proof is the passage from communication protocols to polynomials, to which end we will mimic the primal proof of Theorem 5.1.

Abbreviate $r = 4^k \lceil \frac{n}{\alpha d}\rceil^2$ and let $\mu = \mathscr{U}_r \times \mu_{r,k-1}$, a probability distribution on the domain of $\mathrm{UDISJ}_{r,k}$. Let μ_{-1} and μ_{+1} stand for the probability distributions induced by μ on $\mathrm{UDISJ}_{r,k}^{-1}(-1)$ and $\mathrm{UDISJ}_{r,k}^{-1}(+1)$, respectively. Consider the following averaging operator M, which linearly sends real functions ϕ on $(\{0,1\}^{r\times k})^{\ell n}$ to real functions on $\{-1,+1\}^{\ell n}$:

$$(M\phi)(z) \doteq \mathop{\mathbf{E}}_{X_{1,1}\sim\mu_{z_{1,1}}} \cdots \mathop{\mathbf{E}}_{X_{\ell,n}\sim\mu_{z_{\ell,n}}} \left[\phi(X_{1,1}, \ldots, X_{\ell,n})\right].$$

Now fix a cost-c randomized protocol Π which solves, with probability $2^{-\alpha\ell}$, at least $(1-\alpha)\ell$ from among ℓ instances of F. We will take $\alpha = \alpha(\beta) > 0$ small enough, where $\beta > 0$ is the constant from Theorem 6.6. Starting with the assumption that $c < \alpha\ell d$, we will arrive at a contradiction.

For $z \in \{-1,+1\}^\ell$, consider the protocol Π_z with Boolean output which on input from $(\{0,1\}^{r\times k})^{\ell n}$ runs Π and outputs -1 if and only if Π outputs z. Let $\phi_z\colon (\{0,1\}^{r\times k})^{\ell n} \to [0,1]$ be the acceptance probability function for Π_z. Then $\phi_z = \sum a_\chi \chi$ by Corollary 2.7, where the sum is over k-dimensional cylinder intersections and $\sum |a_\chi| \leqslant 2^c$. By the argument in the primal proof of Theorem 5.1, for every positive integer D,

$$E(M\phi_z, D-1) \leqslant 2^c \left(\frac{2^k e\ell n}{D\sqrt{r}}\right)^D. \qquad (6.1)$$

Observe that $\{\phi_z\}$ is a $(2^{-\alpha\ell}, \alpha\ell, \ell)$-approximant for F, and analogously $\{M\phi_z\}$ is a $(2^{-\alpha\ell}, \alpha\ell, \ell)$-approximant for f. By (6.1), each $M\phi_z$ can in turn be approximated by a polynomial of degree less than $\beta\ell d$ to within $2^{\alpha\ell d}(\alpha e/\beta)^{\beta\ell d}$. Taking $\alpha = \alpha(\beta) > 0$ small enough, we arrive at a $(2^{-\beta\ell}, \beta\ell, \ell)$-approximant for f of degree less than $\beta\ell d$, in contradiction to Theorem 6.6. Hence, $c \geqslant \alpha\ell d$. ☐

As a corollary, we obtain a direct product result for set disjointness, originally stated as Theorem 1.2(ii) in the introduction.

COROLLARY 6.8. *For some absolute constant $\alpha > 0$ and every ℓ,*

$$R_{1-2^{-\alpha\ell},\alpha\ell}(\underbrace{\mathrm{UDISJ}_{n,k}, \ldots, \mathrm{UDISJ}_{n,k}}_{\ell}) \geqslant \ell \cdot \Omega\left(\frac{n}{4^k}\right)^{1/4}.$$

PROOF. Theorem 2.4 gives $\deg_{1/3}(\widetilde{\mathrm{AND}}_n) \geqslant \epsilon\sqrt{n}$ for a constant $\epsilon > 0$. Thus, taking $f = \widetilde{\mathrm{AND}}_n$ and $d = \epsilon\sqrt{n}$ in Theorem 6.7 leads to

$$R_{1-2^{-\alpha\ell},\alpha\ell}(\underbrace{\ldots, \mathrm{UDISJ}_{4^k n\lceil\sqrt{n}/\alpha\epsilon\rceil^2,k}, \ldots}_{\ell}) = \ell \cdot \Omega(\sqrt{n}),$$

which is equivalent to the claimed bound. ☐

Again, the above corollary readily generalizes to arbitrary compositions of the form $F = f \circ (\mathrm{OR}_k \vee \mathrm{AND}_k)$.

THEOREM 6.9. *Let $f\colon \{-1,+1\}^n \to \{-1,+1\}$ be given. Put $F = f \circ (\mathrm{OR}_k \vee \mathrm{AND}_k)$. Then for some absolute constant $\alpha > 0$ and every ℓ,*

$$R_{1-2^{-\alpha\ell},\alpha\ell}(\overbrace{F, F, \ldots, F}^{\ell}) \geqslant \ell \cdot \Omega\left(\frac{\mathrm{bs}(f)}{4^k}\right)^{1/4}$$
$$\geqslant \ell \cdot \Omega\left(\frac{\mathrm{dt}(f)^{1/3}}{4^k}\right)^{1/4}$$
$$\geqslant \ell \cdot \Omega\left(\frac{\deg_{1/3}(f)^{1/3}}{4^k}\right)^{1/4}.$$

PROOF. Identical to Theorem 6.4, with Corollary 6.8 invoked in place of Corollary 6.3. ☐

We have focused here on XOR lemmas and direct product theorems for ℓ instances of the *same* communication problem. The results and proofs above generalize easily to ℓ distinct communication problems, by invoking, in place of Theorems 6.1 and 6.6, correspondingly more general results from [45] on polynomial approximation.

7. NONDETERMINISTIC AND MERLIN-ARTHUR COMMUNICATION

In this section, we study the communication complexity of set disjointness in the nondeterministic and Merlin-Arthur multiparty models. We will see that the lower bound of Theorem 1.1 carries over. We will reinterpret our findings in terms of communication complexity classes.

7.1 Definitions

We start by describing the *nondeterministic* k-party model of communication, which is similar in some ways and different in others from the randomized model. As in the randomized model, one considers a function $F\colon X_1 \times X_2 \times \cdots \times X_k \to \{-1,+1\}$ for some finite sets $X_1, X_2, \ldots, X_k$. An input $(x_1, x_2, \ldots, x_k) \in X_1 \times X_2 \times \cdots \times X_k$ is distributed among the k parties as before, giving the ith party all the arguments except x_i. Beyond this setup, nondeterministic computation proceeds as follows. At the start of the protocol, c_1 bits appear on the shared blackboard. Given the values of those bits, the parties execute an agreed-upon deterministic protocol with communication cost at most c_2. A nondeterministic protocol for F is required to output the correct answer for *at least one* nondeterministic choice of the c_1 bits when $F(x_1, x_2, \ldots, x_k) = -1$

and for *all* possible choices when $F(x_1, x_2, \ldots, x_k) = +1$. The *cost* of a nondeterministic protocol is defined to be the sum $c_1 + c_2$. The *nondeterministic communication complexity* of F, denoted $N(F)$, is the least cost of a nondeterministic protocol for F. The *co-nondeterministic communication complexity* of F is the quantity $N(-F)$.

The *Merlin-Arthur* model [2, 5] combines the power of randomization and nondeterminism. Similar to the nondeterministic model, the protocol starts with a nondeterministic guess of c_1 bits, followed by c_2 bits of communication. However, the communication can be randomized, and the requirement is that the error probability be at most ϵ for *at least one* nondeterministic guess when $F(x_1, x_2, \ldots, x_k) = -1$ and for *all* possible nondeterministic guesses when $F(x_1, x_2, \ldots, x_k) = +1$. The *cost* of a Merlin-Arthur protocol is defined as $c_1 + c_2$. The *ϵ-error Merlin-Arthur communication complexity* of F, denoted $MA_\epsilon(F)$, is the least cost of an ϵ-error Merlin-Arthur protocol for F. Clearly, $MA_\epsilon(F) \leqslant \min\{N(F), R_\epsilon(F)\}$ for every F.

7.2 Communication Lower Bounds

To analyze the nondeterministic and Merlin-Arthur complexity of set disjointness, we start with a criterion for high communication complexity in these models. It was derived recently by Gavinsky and the author [23, Thm. 4.1] and builds on earlier work by Klauck [28, 29], including the generalized discrepancy method.

THEOREM 7.1 (Gavinsky and Sherstov). *Let $F: X \to \{-1, +1\}$ be a given k-party communication problem, where $X = X_1 \times X_2 \times \cdots \times X_k$. Fix a function $H: X \to \{-1, +1\}$ and a probability distribution P on X. Put*

$$\alpha = P(F^{-1}(-1) \cap H^{-1}(-1)),$$
$$\beta = P(F^{-1}(-1) \cap H^{-1}(+1)),$$
$$Q = \log \frac{\alpha}{\beta + \operatorname{disc}_P(H)}.$$

Then

$$N(F) \geqslant Q,$$
$$MA_{1/3}(F) \geqslant \min\left\{\Omega(\sqrt{Q}),\ \Omega\left(\frac{Q}{\log(2/\alpha)}\right)\right\}.$$

A key technical ingredient in [23] is the following property of the AND function, which we will use in a similar way in this paper.

THEOREM 7.2 (Gavinsky and Sherstov). *There exists a function $\psi: \{-1, +1\}^n \to \mathbb{R}$ with*

$$\langle \psi, \mathrm{AND}_n \rangle > \frac{1}{3},$$
$$\|\psi\|_1 = 1,$$
$$\hat{\psi}(S) = 0, \qquad |S| < \deg_{1/3}(\mathrm{AND}_n),$$
$$\psi(-1, \ldots, -1) < -\frac{1}{6}. \tag{7.1}$$

PROOF (Gavinsky and Sherstov). The first three properties of ψ are guaranteed by Fact 2.2. To establish the remaining property, note that $\langle \psi, 1 \rangle = 0$ because $\hat{\psi}(\varnothing) = 0$. Thus,

$$\begin{aligned} -2\psi(-1, \ldots, -1) &= \sum_{z \in \{-1,+1\}^n} \psi(z)\{\mathrm{AND}_n(z) - 1\} \\ &= \sum_{z \in \{-1,+1\}^n} \psi(z)\mathrm{AND}_n(z) \\ &> \frac{1}{3}. \end{aligned}$$ ☐

Two years ago, Gavinsky and the author [23] obtained a lower bound of $n^{\Omega(1/k)}/2^{2^k}$ on the nondeterministic and Merlin-Arthur communication complexity of set disjointness. The main result of this section, which we are about to establish, is an improved lower bound of $\Omega(n/4^k)^{1/4}$ for nondeterministic and $\Omega(n/4^k)^{1/8}$ for Merlin-Arthur protocols. Our proof closely follows the proof in [23], i.e., we use Theorem 7.2 to construct H and P for Theorem 7.1. The main difference resides in the discrepancy calculation, for which we turn to the master theorem in this paper on randomized communication complexity.

THEOREM 7.3 (restatement of Theorems 1.3 and 1.4). *The set disjointness problem obeys*

$$N(\mathrm{DISJ}_{n,k}) \geqslant \Omega\left(\frac{n}{4^k}\right)^{1/4},$$
$$MA_{1/3}(\mathrm{DISJ}_{n,k}) \geqslant \Omega\left(\frac{n}{4^k}\right)^{1/8}.$$

PROOF. Let r be a parameter to be set later. Put $f = \mathrm{AND}_n$, $d = \deg_{1/3}(\mathrm{AND}_n)$, and fix $\psi: \{-1, +1\}^n \to \mathbb{R}$ as in Theorem 7.2. Let $F = f \circ \mathrm{DISJ}_{r,k}$ and define $\Psi: (\{0, 1\}^{r \times k})^n \to \mathbb{R}$ as in the dual proof of Theorem 5.1, viz.,

$$\Psi(X_1, \ldots, X_n) = 2^n \psi\left(\mathrm{DISJ}_{r,k}(X_1), \ldots, \mathrm{DISJ}_{r,k}(X_n)\right) \prod_{i=1}^{n} \mu(X_i),$$

where $\mu = \mathscr{U}_r \times \mu_{r,k-1}$ as before. Then (5.8) shows that $\Psi = H \circ P$ for some sign tensor H and probability distribution P. In particular, (5.10) asserts that

$$\operatorname{disc}_P(H) \leqslant \left(\frac{2^k en}{d\sqrt{r}}\right)^d. \tag{7.2}$$

By (7.1), we have $\psi(z) < 0$ whenever $f(z) = -1$, so that

$$P(F^{-1}(-1) \cap H^{-1}(+1)) = 0. \tag{7.3}$$

Also,

$$\begin{aligned} P(F^{-1}(-1) \cap H^{-1}(-1)) &= P(F^{-1}(-1)) \\ &= |\psi(-1, \ldots, -1)| \\ &> \frac{1}{6}, \end{aligned} \tag{7.4}$$

where the first step uses (7.3), the second step uses the fact that μ places equal weight on the sets $\mathrm{DISJ}_{r,k}^{-1}(-1)$ and $\mathrm{DISJ}_{r,k}^{-1}(+1)$, and the final inequality uses (7.1). By (7.2)–(7.4) and Theorem 7.1,

$$N(F) = \Omega\left(d \log\left\{\frac{d\sqrt{r}}{2^k en}\right\}\right),$$

$$MA_{1/3}(F) = \Omega\left(d \log\left\{\frac{d\sqrt{r}}{2^k en}\right\}\right)^{1/2}.$$

Recall now from Theorem 2.4 that $d > c\sqrt{n}$ for some constant $c > 0$. As a result, setting $r = 4^{k+2}n\lceil 1/c\rceil^2$ gives $N(F) = \Omega(\sqrt{n})$ and $MA_{1/3}(F) = \Omega(n^{1/4})$. It remains to note that $F = \mathrm{DISJ}_{4^{k+2}n^2\lceil 1/c\rceil^2,k}$. ∎

7.3 Applications to Communication Classes

Babai, Frankl, and Simon [3] defined analogues of computational complexity classes in communication. We will only mention a few of them, namely, those corresponding to efficient randomized, nondeterministic, and Merlin-Arthur protocols. For a given number of parties $k = k(n)$, fix a family $\{F_n\}_{n=1}^{\infty}$ of k-party communication problems, where $F_n\colon (\{0,1\}^n)^k \to \{-1,+1\}$. The family $\{F_n\}$ is said to belong to the communication class BPP_k if and only if $R_{1/3}(F_n) \leqslant \log^c n$ for some constant $c > 1$ and all $n > c$. Analogously, the family $\{F_n\}$ is said to belong to NP_k and MA_k if and only if the communication complexity of F_n in the nondeterministic and Merlin-Arthur models, respectively, is at most $\log^c n$ for some constant $c > 1$ and all $n > c$. The derived classes coNP_k and coMA_k have the usual definition, e.g., $\{F_n\} \in \mathsf{coNP}_k$ if and only if $\{-F_n\} \in \mathsf{NP}_k$.

A corollary to Theorem 7.3 is that the set disjointness problem separates coNP_k from NP_k, BPP_k, and even MA_k for up to $k = (\frac{1}{2} - \epsilon)\log n$, where $\epsilon > 0$ is any constant.

THEOREM 7.4. *For $k \leqslant (\frac{1}{2} - \epsilon)\log n$, where $\epsilon > 0$ is any constant,*

$$\mathrm{DISJ}_{n,k} \in \mathsf{coNP}_k \setminus \mathsf{NP}_k,$$
$$\mathrm{DISJ}_{n,k} \in \mathsf{coNP}_k \setminus \mathsf{BPP}_k,$$
$$\mathrm{DISJ}_{n,k} \in \mathsf{coNP}_k \setminus \mathsf{MA}_k.$$

PROOF. It suffices to prove the final statement, since MA_k contains NP_k and BPP_k.

Theorem 7.3 shows that $\mathrm{DISJ}_{n,k} \notin \mathsf{MA}_k$. On the other hand, it is well-known that $N(-\mathrm{DISJ}_{n,k}) \leqslant \lceil \log n\rceil + 2$. Specifically, the parties choose $i \in \{1,2,\ldots,n\}$ nondeterministically and compute $x_{1,i} \wedge \cdots \wedge x_{k,i}$ with two bits of communication. As a result, $\mathrm{DISJ}_{n,k} \in \mathsf{coNP}_k$. ∎

8. APPLICATIONS TO CIRCUIT COMPLEXITY

We will now apply our results on small-bias communication to circuit complexity. We start with a well-known connection between multiparty communication and circuits, due to Håstad and Goldmann [25].

PROPOSITION 8.1 (Håstad and Goldmann). *Let f be a Boolean function computable by a* MAJ ∘ SYMM ∘ ANY *circuit, where the top gate has fan-in m, the middle gates have fan-in at most s, and the bottom gates have fan-in at most $k-1$. Then the k-party number-on-the-forehead communication complexity of f obeys*

$$R_{\frac{1}{2}-\frac{1}{2(m+1)}}(f) \leqslant k\lceil \log(s+1)\rceil,$$

regardless of how the bits are assigned to the parties.

PROOF (Håstad and Goldmann). The parties pick a uniformly random gate G at the middle level, evaluate it deterministically using $k\lceil\log(s+1)\rceil$ bits of communication, and output the answer. The deterministic computation is possible because every input to the gate G can be computed by some party without communication, which makes it possible to partition the bottom gates among the parties and have each party report the sum of those inputs to G assigned to him. Since G is symmetric, the sum of its inputs uniquely determines its output. ∎

We arrive at the first result of this section, a lower bound on the size of MAJ ∘ SYMM ∘ ANY circuits with small bottom fan-in computing a depth-3 formula.

THEOREM 8.2. *Let $F_{n,k}\colon \{0,1\}^{4^k n^7 k} \to \{-1,+1\}$ be the depth-3 read-once $\{\wedge,\vee\}$-formula defined in Theorem 5.7. Then any circuit of type* MAJ ∘ SYMM ∘ ANY *with bottom fan-in at most $k-1$ computing $F_{n,k}$ has size $2^{\Omega(n/k)}$.*

PROOF. We interpret $F_{n,k}$ as the k-party communication problem defined in Theorem 5.7. Let C be a circuit of type MAJ ∘ SYMM ∘ ANY that computes $F_{n,k}$, where the bottom fan-in of C is at most $k-1$. If C has size s, then the fan-in of the gates at the top and middle levels is bounded by s, which in view of Proposition 8.1 gives

$$R_{\frac{1}{2}-\frac{1}{2(s+1)}}(F_{n,k}) \leqslant k\lceil\log(s+1)\rceil.$$

By Theorem 5.7, this leads to $s \geqslant \exp(\Omega(n/k))$. ∎

Theorem 8.2 establishes Theorem 1.6 from the introduction.

Consider now a different computational model, that of MAJ ∘ SYMM ∘ AND circuits without any fan-in restrictions. We will prove a superpolynomial lower bound in this model as well. We will use an argument due to Razborov and Wigderson [41] which reduces the job to proving lower bounds for MAJ ∘ SYMM ∘ ANY circuits with small bottom fan-in. This argument has already been used by several authors [48, 11] in the context of proving lower bounds for computing AC^0 functions.

THEOREM 8.3 (Razborov and Wigderson). *Let $\delta > 0$ be a sufficiently small absolute constant, $f\colon\{0,1\}^N \to \{-1,+1\}$ a given function. For $\epsilon \in (0,\delta)$, define*

$$F_\epsilon = f \circ \mathrm{PARITY}_{\frac{1}{\epsilon}\ln^2 N}.$$

If F_ϵ is computable by a MAJ ∘ SYMM ∘ AND *circuit C of size at most $N^{\epsilon^2 \ln\ln N}$, then f is computable by a* MAJ ∘ SYMM ∘ AND *circuit of the same size with bottom fan-in at most $\epsilon \ln N$.*

For completeness, we include the short proof of this theorem. In what follows, we let G_ρ denote the result of applying a random restriction ρ to a gate or function G.

PROOF OF THEOREM 8.3 (adapted from [41, 48, 11]). Let ρ be a random restriction that leaves each variable unset independently with probability $p \doteq 2\epsilon/\ln N$, and otherwise sets it to 0 or 1 with equal probability. For a conjunction K, let $|K|$ denote the number of literals in K. We claim that for every conjunction K,

$$\mathbf{P}[|K_\rho| \geqslant \epsilon\ln N] \leqslant N^{-\Theta(\epsilon\ln\ln N)}. \qquad (8.1)$$

Indeed, for $|K| \leqslant \ln N \ln\ln N$,

$$\mathbf{P}[|K_\rho| \geqslant \epsilon\ln N] \leqslant \binom{|K|}{\epsilon\ln N} p^{\epsilon\ln N} \leqslant N^{-\Theta(\epsilon\ln\ln N)},$$

whereas for $|K| > \ln N\ln\ln N$

$$\mathbf{P}[|K_\rho| \geqslant \epsilon\ln N] \leqslant \mathbf{P}[K_\rho \not\equiv 1] = \left(\frac{1+p}{2}\right)^{|K|} \leqslant N^{-\Theta(\ln\ln N)}.$$

Applying (8.1) with a union bound across the bottom gates of C, we find that with probability $1 - o(1)$ the bottom fan-in of C_ρ is at most $\epsilon \ln N$. Furthermore, the probability that ρ does not turn any parity gate in F_ϵ into a constant is at least $1 - N(1-p)^{\frac{1}{\epsilon}\ln^2 N} = 1 - o(1)$. In particular, there is a random restriction ρ such that on the one hand, C_ρ has bottom fan-in at most $\epsilon \ln N$, and on the other hand f is a subfunction of C_ρ. ∎

We are now in a position to prove the promised lower bound.

THEOREM 1.7 (restated). *Every* MAJ ∘ SYMM ∘ AND *circuit that computes*

$$H_n(x) = \bigvee_{i=1}^{n} \bigwedge_{j=1}^{n} \bigvee_{k=1}^{\log n} \bigoplus_{\ell=1}^{\log^2 n} x_{i,j,k,\ell}$$

has size $n^{\Omega(\log \log n)}$.

PROOF. Without loss of generality, we may assume that n is a power of 2. Let $F_{n,k}$ be the depth-3 read-once $\{\wedge, \vee\}$-formula constructed in Theorem 5.7. By Theorem 8.2, every MAJ∘SYMM∘ANY circuit with bottom fan-in $\log n - 1$ that computes $F_{n,\log n}$ has size $2^{\Omega(n/\log n)}$. As a result, Theorem 8.3 gives a lower bound of $n^{\Omega(\log\log n)}$ on the size of any MAJ ∘ SYMM ∘ AND circuit computing the composition $H'_n = F_{n,\log n} \circ \text{PARITY}_{c\log^2 n}$, where $c > 1$ is a sufficiently large constant. It remains to note that H'_n is a subfunction of H_{n^C} for a sufficiently large absolute constant $C = C(c) > 1$. ∎

Acknowledgments

The author is thankful to Paul Beame, Amit Chakrabarti, Dmitry Gavinsky, Dang-Trinh Huynh-Ngoc, and the anonymous reviewers for their feedback on an earlier version of this manuscript.

9. REFERENCES

[1] E. Allender. A note on the power of threshold circuits. In *Proceedings of the Thirtieth Annual IEEE Symposium on Foundations of Computer Science* (FOCS), pages 580–584, 1989.

[2] L. Babai. Trading group theory for randomness. In *Proceedings of the Seventeenth Annual ACM Symposium on Theory of Computing* (STOC), pages 421–429, 1985.

[3] L. Babai, P. Frankl, and J. Simon. Complexity classes in communication complexity theory. In *Proceedings of the Twenty-Seventh Annual IEEE Symposium on Foundations of Computer Science* (FOCS), pages 337–347, 1986.

[4] L. Babai, T. P. Hayes, and P. G. Kimmel. The cost of the missing bit: Communication complexity with help. *Combinatorica*, 21(4):455–488, 2001.

[5] L. Babai and S. Moran. Arthur-Merlin games: A randomized proof system, and a hierarchy of complexity classes. *J. Comput. Syst. Sci.*, 36(2):254–276, 1988.

[6] L. Babai, N. Nisan, and M. Szegedy. Multiparty protocols, pseudorandom generators for logspace, and time-space trade-offs. *J. Comput. Syst. Sci.*, 45(2):204–232, 1992.

[7] Z. Bar-Yossef, T. S. Jayram, R. Kumar, and D. Sivakumar. An information statistics approach to data stream and communication complexity. *J. Comput. Syst. Sci.*, 68(4):702–732, 2004.

[8] R. Beals, H. Buhrman, R. Cleve, M. Mosca, and R. de Wolf. Quantum lower bounds by polynomials. *J. ACM*, 48(4):778–797, 2001.

[9] P. Beame, M. David, T. Pitassi, and P. Woelfel. Separating deterministic from nondeterministic NOF multiparty communication complexity. In *Proc. of the 34th International Colloquium on Automata, Languages, and Programming (ICALP)*, pages 134–145, 2007.

[10] P. Beame, M. David, T. Pitassi, and P. Woelfel. Separating deterministic from randomized multiparty communication complexity. *Theory of Computing*, 6(1):201–225, 2010.

[11] P. Beame and D.-T. Huynh-Ngoc. Multiparty communication complexity and threshold circuit complexity of AC^0. In *Proceedings of the Fiftieth Annual IEEE Symposium on Foundations of Computer Science* (FOCS), pages 53–62, 2009. Preliminary version in ECCC Report TR08-082, September 2008.

[12] P. Beame, T. Pitassi, and N. Segerlind. Lower bounds for Lovász-Schrijver systems and beyond follow from multiparty communication complexity. *SIAM J. Comput.*, 37(3):845–869, 2007.

[13] P. Beame, T. Pitassi, N. Segerlind, and A. Wigderson. A strong direct product theorem for corruption and the multiparty communication complexity of disjointness. *Computational Complexity*, 15(4):391–432, 2006.

[14] A. Ben-Aroya, O. Regev, and R. de Wolf. A hypercontractive inequality for matrix-valued functions with applications to quantum computing and LDCs. In *Proceedings of the Forty-Ninth Annual IEEE Symposium on Foundations of Computer Science* (FOCS), pages 477–486, 2008.

[15] J. Briet, H. Buhrman, T. Lee, and T. Vidick. Multiplayer XOR games and quantum communication complexity with clique-wise entanglement. Manuscript at `http://arxiv.org/abs/0911.4007`, 2009.

[16] A. K. Chandra, M. L. Furst, and R. J. Lipton. Multi-party protocols. In *Proceedings of the Fifteenth Annual ACM Symposium on Theory of Computing* (STOC), pages 94–99, 1983.

[17] A. Chattopadhyay. Discrepancy and the power of bottom fan-in in depth-three circuits. In *Proceedings of the Forty-Eighth Annual IEEE Symposium on Foundations of Computer Science* (FOCS), pages 449–458, 2007.

[18] A. Chattopadhyay. *Circuits, Communication, and Polynomials*. PhD thesis, McGill University, 2008.

[19] A. Chattopadhyay and A. Ada. Multiparty communication complexity of disjointness. In *Electronic Colloquium on Computational Complexity (ECCC)*, January 2008. Report TR08-002.

[20] B. Chor and O. Goldreich. Unbiased bits from sources of weak randomness and probabilistic communication complexity. *SIAM J. Comput.*, 17(2):230–261, 1988.

[21] M. David and T. Pitassi. Separating NOF communication complexity classes RP and NP. In *Electronic Colloquium on Computational Complexity (ECCC)*, February 2008. Report TR08-014.

[22] M. David, T. Pitassi, and E. Viola. Improved separations between nondeterministic and randomized multiparty communication. *ACM Transactions on Computation Theory (TOCT)*, 1(2), 2009.

[23] D. Gavinsky and A. A. Sherstov. A separation of NP and coNP in multiparty communication complexity. *Theory of Computing*, 6(10):227–245, 2010.

[24] V. Grolmusz. The BNS lower bound for multi-party

protocols in nearly optimal. *Inf. Comput.*, 112(1):51–54, 1994.

[25] J. Håstad and M. Goldmann. On the power of small-depth threshold circuits. *Computational Complexity*, 1:113–129, 1991.

[26] R. Jain, H. Klauck, and A. Nayak. Direct product theorems for classical communication complexity via subdistribution bounds. In *Proceedings of the Fortieth Annual ACM Symposium on Theory of Computing* (STOC), pages 599–608, 2008.

[27] B. Kalyanasundaram and G. Schnitger. The probabilistic communication complexity of set intersection. *SIAM J. Discrete Math.*, 5(4):545–557, 1992.

[28] H. Klauck. Lower bounds for quantum communication complexity. In *Proceedings of the Forty-Second Annual IEEE Symposium on Foundations of Computer Science* (FOCS), pages 288–297, 2001.

[29] H. Klauck. Rectangle size bounds and threshold covers in communication complexity. In *Proceedings of the Eighteenth Annual IEEE Conference on Computational Complexity* (CCC), pages 118–134, 2003.

[30] H. Klauck. A strong direct product theorem for disjointness. In *Proceedings of the Forty-Second Annual ACM Symposium on Theory of Computing* (STOC), pages 77–86, 2010.

[31] H. Klauck, R. Špalek, and R. de Wolf. Quantum and classical strong direct product theorems and optimal time-space tradeoffs. *SIAM J. Comput.*, 36(5):1472–1493, 2007.

[32] M. Krause and P. Pudlák. On the computational power of depth-2 circuits with threshold and modulo gates. *Theor. Comput. Sci.*, 174(1–2):137–156, 1997.

[33] E. Kushilevitz and N. Nisan. *Communication complexity*. Cambridge University Press, 1997.

[34] T. Lee, G. Schechtman, and A. Shraibman. Lower bounds on quantum multiparty communication complexity. In *Proceedings of the Twenty-Fourth Annual IEEE Conference on Computational Complexity* (CCC), pages 254–262, 2009.

[35] T. Lee and A. Shraibman. Disjointness is hard in the multiparty number-on-the-forehead model. *Computational Complexity*, 18(2):309–336, 2009. Preliminary version at `http://arxiv.org/abs/0712.4279v1`, December 2007.

[36] N. Linial and A. Shraibman. Lower bounds in communication complexity based on factorization norms. *Random Struct. Algorithms*, 34(3):368–394, 2009.

[37] M. L. Minsky and S. A. Papert. *Perceptrons: An Introduction to Computational Geometry*. MIT Press, Cambridge, Mass., 1969.

[38] N. Nisan and M. Szegedy. On the degree of Boolean functions as real polynomials. *Computational Complexity*, 4:301–313, 1994.

[39] A. A. Razborov. On the distributional complexity of disjointness. *Theor. Comput. Sci.*, 106(2):385–390, 1992.

[40] A. A. Razborov. Quantum communication complexity of symmetric predicates. *Izvestiya of the Russian Academy of Sciences, Mathematics*, 67:145–159, 2002.

[41] A. A. Razborov and A. Wigderson. $n^{\Omega(\log n)}$ lower bounds on the size of depth-3 threshold circuits with AND gates at the bottom. *Inf. Process. Lett.*, 45(6):303–307, 1993.

[42] A. A. Sherstov. The pattern matrix method for lower bounds on quantum communication. In *Proceedings of the Fortieth Annual ACM Symposium on Theory of Computing* (STOC), pages 85–94, 2008. Preliminary version in ECCC Report TR07-100, September 2007.

[43] A. A. Sherstov. Separating AC^0 from depth-2 majority circuits. *SIAM J. Comput.*, 38(6):2113–2129, 2009. Preliminary version in *Proceedings of the Thirty-Ninth Annual ACM Symposium on Theory of Computing* (STOC), 2007.

[44] A. A. Sherstov. On quantum-classical equivalence for composed communication problems. *Quantum Information & Computation*, 10(5-6):435–455, 2010.

[45] A. A. Sherstov. Strong direct product theorems for quantum communication and query complexity. In *Proceedings of the Forty-Third Annual ACM Symposium on Theory of Computing* (STOC), pages 41–50, 2011. Full version available as ECCC Report TR11-040.

[46] Y. Shi and Y. Zhu. Quantum communication complexity of block-composed functions. *Quantum Information & Computation*, 9(5–6):444–460, 2009.

[47] P. Tesson. *Computational complexity questions related to finite monoids and semigroups*. PhD thesis, McGill University, 2003.

[48] E. Viola. Pseudorandom bits for constant-depth circuits with few arbitrary symmetric gates. *SIAM J. Comput.*, 36(5):1387–1403, 2007.

[49] E. Viola and A. Wigderson. One-way multiparty communication lower bound for pointer jumping with applications. *Combinatorica*, 29(6):719–743, 2009.

[50] A. C.-C. Yao. Some complexity questions related to distributive computing. In *Proceedings of the Eleventh Annual ACM Symposium on Theory of Computing* (STOC), pages 209–213, 1979.

[51] A. C.-C. Yao. On ACC and threshold circuits. In *Proceedings of the Thirty-First Annual IEEE Symposium on Foundations of Computer Science* (FOCS), pages 619–627, 1990.

Author Index

www.ingramcontent.com/pod-product-compliance
Ingram Content Group UK Ltd.
Pitfield, Milton Keynes, MK11 3LW, UK
UKHW051455290926
15471UKWH00008B/1224

9 781450 319423